The Pocket Oxford–Hachette French Dictionary

The Pocket Oxford–Hachette French Dictionary

Edited by

Marie-Hélène Corréard

Oxford New York

OXFORD UNIVERSITY PRESS

Oxford University Press, Walton Street, Oxford OX2 6DP

Oxford New York
Athens Auckland Bangkok Bogota Bombay
Buenos Aires Calcutta Cape Town Dar es Salaam
Delhi Florence Hong Kong Istanbul Karachi
Kuala Lumpur Madras Madrid Melbourne
Mexico City Nairobi Paris Singapore
Taipei Tokyo Toronto

and associated companies in
Berlin Ibadan

Oxford is a trade mark of Oxford University Press

First published 1996

British Library Cataloguing in Publication Data
Data available

Library of Congress Cataloging in Publication Data
Data available

ISBN 0-19-864533-3 (Hardback)
ISBN 0-19-864534-1 (Paperback)

10 9 8 7 6 5 4 3

Typeset in Monotype Amasis, Arial, and Nimrod

Printed in Great Britain by
Mackays of Chatham

Contents

The Pocket Oxford–Hachette French Dictionary

Chief Editor
Marie-Hélène Corréard

Editors
Frances Illingworth
Natalie Pomier

Associate Editor
Mary O'Neill

Lexical usage notes and correspondence
Henri Béjoint
Richard Wakely

North American English
Kristin Clayton

Phonetics
Isabelle Vodoz

Data-capture
Diane Diffley

Administration
Alison Curr

Proofreading
Alison Curr
Diane Diffley
Genevieve Hawkins
Isabelle Lemoine

Design
Fran Holdsworth
Raynor Design
Jeffrey Tabberner

There are many people, not mentioned in the list of contributors, whose work is also represented in the present dictionary. We would like to thank the editorial team of the *Oxford–Hachette French Dictionary* on which the present publication is largely based and, in particular, Dr Valerie Grundy (Joint Chief Editor). We are also grateful to the numerous freelance translators and lexicographers who were involved in the parent project.

We are indebted to Sue Atkins who from the first has given us the benefit of her expertise in the field of lexicography and whose enthusiasm has been an inspiration.

Contents

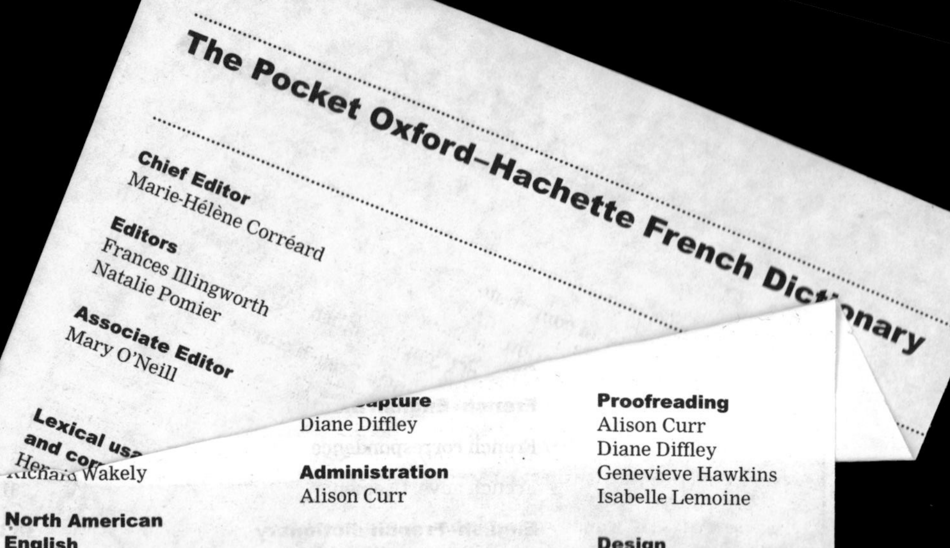

The Pocket Oxford–Hachette French Dictionary

Chief Editor
Marie-Hélène Corréard

Editors
Frances Illingworth
Natalie Pomier

Associate Editor
Mary O'Neill

Lexical usa
and cor
Richard Wakely

apture
Diane Diffley

Administration
Alison Curr

Proofreading
Alison Curr
Diane Diffley
Genevieve Hawkins
Isabelle Lemoine

North American English
Kristin Clayton

Phonetics
Isabelle Vodoz

Design
Fran Holdsworth
Raynor Design
Jeffrey Tabberner

There are many people, not mentioned in the list of contributors, whose work is also represented in the present dictionary. We would like to thank the editorial team of the *Oxford–Hachette French Dictionary* on which the present publication is largely based and, in particular, Dr Valerie Grundy (Joint Chief Editor). We are also grateful to the numerous freelance translators and lexicographers who were involved in the parent project.

We are indebted to Sue Atkins who from the first has given us the benefit of her expertise in the field of lexicography and whose enthusiasm has been an inspiration.

Introduction

The *Pocket Oxford-Hachette French Dictionary* represents a totally new concept in smaller format bilingual dictionaries. It marks the completion of the range of English/French dictionaries based on the highly acclaimed *Oxford-Hachette French Dictionary*. Designed as a language aid for the English-speaking general dictionary user, it pays particular attention to those beginning to learn French who may be less familiar with bilingual dictionaries. The dictionary is innovative in that it makes use of the native speaker's knowledge of English, thus removing the need for phonetics or excessive grammatical information. Emphasis is placed on those areas of the foreign language where the user is likely to need most help, providing a level of essential detail which is often lacking in smaller dictionaries for reasons of space. Entries are clearly laid out, with numbered categories for different senses and parts of speech, as well as detailed treatment of important structures and usages.

As it is derived in the main from the larger *Oxford-Hachette French Dictionary*, the material in the English and French wordlists is up to date and authentic because it is corpus-based. A corpus is a database containing extracts from the text of books, newspapers, magazine articles etc, as well as transcripts of a variety of recordings of spoken language. In seconds, the corpus finds and displays all the contexts in which a particular word occurs. Displaying the word in context allows editors to focus on important uses and structures of the word and is an excellent indicator of frequency.

A distinctive feature of the dictionary is the presentation of idiomatic phrases (*to put one's foot in it*) and English phrasal verbs (*to get away, to go up, to come out*) which appear as independent categories within an entry to facilitate consultation. Compounds (*black eye, black sheep, blackboard*), often grouped in 'nests' for reasons of space, are treated as independent headwords, making it easier for the user to locate them in the wordlist. Another new feature is the marking of all the feminine variants of regular adjectives in French (*fort/-e, lourd/-e*), reminding the user of this most basic aspect of French grammar. In addition to the generous coverage of proper nouns and abbreviations, users will find a unique feature in the form of helpful usage notes dealing with key topics such as *age, clocktime, illnesses, forms of address* etc, as well as detailed notes for important and often complex grammar words.

The French-English side is specially adapted for English speakers. The information concerning the scope of a translation is given in English where such information is deemed necessary. The reader will find a broad coverage of current French, including often difficult idiomatic usage, geared to the needs of a wide range of users, from GCSE students and adult learners of French to the enthusiastic tourist or business professional. The streamlined presentation of translations is designed to ensure that users are able to understand most of the language they are likely to encounter in a wide variety of contexts, both written and spoken.

Designed with the specific requirements of the English-speaking user in mind, the *Pocket Oxford-Hachette French Dictionary* is an efficient and practical linguistic resource for learners of French.

The structure of French-English entries

headword — **cocotte** /kɔkɔt/ *nf* **1**○ **(baby talk)** hen; **2 ma ~**○ honey; **3** (Culin) casserole (GB), pot. — level of language

feminine form of the headword — **délicieux, -ieuse** /delisjø, øz/ *adj* **1** delicious; **2** [*feeling, music*] delightful; [*joy*] exquisite. — IPA pronunciation for feminine form

pencher /pɑ̃ʃe/ [1] **I** *vtr* to tilt; to tip [sth] up; **~ la tête en avant** to bend one's head forward(s).
II *vi* **1** [*tower, tree*] to lean; [*boat*] to list; [*picture*] to slant; **2 ~ pour** to incline toward(s) [*theory*]; to be in favour[GB] of [*solution*]. — Arabic sense number
Roman grammatical category number — **III se pencher** *v refl* (+ *v être*) **1** to lean; **2** to bend down; **3 se ~ sur** to look into [*problem*].

trademark symbol — **photomaton®** /fɔtɔmatɔ̃/ ***nm*** photo booth. — part of speech plus gender

field label — **piston** /pistɔ̃/ *nm* **1** **(Tech)** piston; **2**○ contacts; **avoir du ~** to have connections in the right places.

IPA pronunciation — **pompe** /pɔ̃p/ *nf* **1** pump; **2**◑ shoe; **3** pomp; **4**○ (Sport) press-up (GB), push-up.
compounds in block at end of entry — ■ **~ à essence** petrol pump (GB), gas pump (US); **~s funèbres** undertaker's (GB), funeral director's.
IDIOMS **avoir un coup de ~**○ to be knackered◑ (GB) or pooped○.

register symbol
○ informal
◑ very informal
● vulgar or taboo

number of verb group, referring to the French verb tables at the end of the dictionary — **pomper** /pɔ̃pe/ [1] *vtr* **1** to pump [*liquid, air*]; **2**○ (students' slang) to copy.
IDIOMS **~ l'air**○ **à qn** to get on sb's nerves.

pomponner: se pomponner /pɔ̃pɔne/ [1] *v*
grammatical information — *refl* (+ *v être*) to get dolled up.

pont /pɔ̃/ **I** *nm* **1** bridge; **2** link, tie; **couper les ~s** to break off all contact; **3** extended weekend ***(including days between a public holiday and a weekend)***; **4** deck. — explanatory gloss where there is no direct translation equivalent
II ponts *nm pl* **~s (et chaussées)** highways department.
■ **~ aérien** airlift; **~ à péage** toll bridge.
idioms in block at end of entry — IDIOMS **coucher sous les ~s** to sleep rough, to be a tramp; **il coulera beaucoup d'eau sous les ~s avant que...** it will be a long time before...; **faire un ~ d'or à qn** to offer sb a large sum to accept a job.

pyjama /piʒama/ *nm* (pair of) pyjamas (GB), (pair of) pajamas **(US)**. — North American translation

abbreviation — **TGV** /teʒeve/ *nm* (*abbr* = **train à grande vitesse**) TGV, high-speed train.

torchon /tɔʀʃɔ̃/ *nm* **1** (gen) cloth; **~ (de cuisine)** tea towel (GB), dish towel (US); **2**
pejorative use — (newspaper) **(derogatory)** rag○; **3**○ messy piece of work.
IDIOMS **le ~ brûle**○ it's war. — swung dash as substitute for headword in example

trouvé, ~e /tʀuve/ **I** *pp* ▶ **trouver**. — cross-reference
example — **II** *pp adj* **réplique bien ~e** neat riposte; **tout ~** [*solution*] ready-made; [*culprit*] obvious.

The structure of English–French entries

headword — **aid** I *n* aide *f* (**from** de; **to, for** à); **in ~ of** au profit de [*charity*].
II *adj* [*organization*] d'entraide.
III *vtr* aider [*person*] (**to do** à faire); faciliter [*digestion, recovery*]. — structures, complementation giving information on how to use the translation

acronym — **Aids** *n* (*abbr* = **Acquired Immune Deficiency Syndrome**) sida *m*.

sense indicators — **bug** I *n* **1**○ (insect) (gen) bestiole *f*; (bedbug) punaise *f*; **2**○ (also **stomach ~**) ennuis *mpl* gastriques; **3** (germ) microbe *m*; **4** (fault) (gen) défaut *m*; (Comput) bogue *f*, bug *m*; **5** (hidden microphone) micro *m* caché. — field labels for specialist terms
II *vtr* **1** poser des micros dans [*room, building*]; **the room is ~ged** il y a un micro (caché) dans la pièce; **2**○ (annoy) embêter○ [*person*]. — example

champagne *n, adj* champagne (*m*) **inv**. — grammatical information

register symbol
○ informal
◑ very informal
● vulgar or taboo

— **chum**○ *n* copain/copine○ ***m/f***, pote○ ***m***. — gender of translation

churn I *n* **1** (for butter) baratte *f*; **2** (GB) (for milk) bidon *m*.
II *vtr* **to ~ butter** baratter.

phrasal verb — ■ **churn out** pondre [qch] en série [***novels***]; produire [qch] en série [***goods***]. — typical object collocates
■ **churn up** faire des remous dans [*water*].

page number cross-reference to a lexical usage note — **cinnamon** ▶ **438** *n* cannelle *f*.

circle I *n* **1** (gen) cercle *m*; **to go round in ~s** tourner en rond; **to have ~s under one's eyes** avoir les yeux cernés; **2** (in theatre) balcon *m*; **in the ~** au balcon. — Roman grammatical category number
II *vtr* **1** [***plane***] tourner autour de [*airport*]; [***person, animal, vehicle***] faire le tour de [*building*]; tourner autour de [*person, animal*]; **2** (surround) encercler. — typical subject collocates
III *vi* tourner en rond (**around** autour de).

citizen *n* **1** (of state) citoyen/-enne *m/f*; (when abroad) ressortissant/-e *m/f*; **2** (of town) habitant/-e *m/f*. — feminine ending in translation

North American variant spelling — **colour** (GB), **color** (US) ▶ **438** I *n* **1** couleur *f*; **what ~ is it?** de quelle couleur est-il/elle?; **to put ~ into sb's cheeks** redonner des couleurs à qn; **2** (dye) (for food) colorant *m*; (for hair) teinture *f*. — swung dash as substitute for headword in examples

Arabic sense number — II *vtr* **1** (with paints, crayons) colorier; (with food dye) colorer; **2** (prejudice) fausser [*judgment*].
III *vi* [*person*] rougir.

idioms in block at end of entry — IDIOMS **to be off ~** ne pas être en forme; **to show one's true ~s** se montrer sous son vrai jour.

colour blind *adj* daltonien/-ienne. — part of speech

separate entries for compounds — **colour film** *n* (for camera) pellicule *f* couleur.

colour scheme *n* couleurs *fpl*, coloris *m*. — translations

North American usage — **corn** *n* **1** (GB) (wheat) blé *m*; **2** (US) (maize) maïs *m*; **3** (on foot) cor *m*.

Using this dictionary

Task 1 You have just bought a postcard and you now want to buy a stamp

Goal Translate: **Where can I buy a stamp?**

1 Pick out the main words to be translated

can *buy* *stamp*

2 Now look up *can* and choose the appropriate headword

can¹ *modal aux* **1** (be able to) pouvoir; **~ you come?** est-ce que tu peux venir?, peux-tu venir?; **we will do all we ~** nous ferons tout

can¹ *modal aux* **1** (be able to) pouvoir; **~ y come?** est-ce que tu peux venir?, peu

can² **I** *n* (of food) boite *f*; (of drink) cannett (aerosol) bombe *f*; (for petrol) bidon *m*; (of pa pot *m*.
II *vtr* mettre [qch] en conserve.

3 Study the different senses of *can¹* to find the one you want

1 (be able to) pouvoir

can¹ *modal aux* **1** (be able to) pouvoir; **~ y**
2 (know how to) savoir; **she ~ swim** elle s
3 (permission, requests, offers, suggestions) pouv
4 (with verbs of perception) **~ they see us?** est
5 (in expressions) **you can't be hungry!** tu peux pas avoir faim!; **you can't be serious!** veux rire!; **this can't be right** il doit y avoir u

4 Within this sense category, see if there are examples similar to what you want to translate

Note the translation

est-ce que tu peux venir?

can¹ *modal aux* **1** (be able to) pouvoir; **~ y come?** est-ce que tu peux venir?, peux venir?; **we will do all we ~** nous ferons t ce que nous pouvons or tout notre possible

5 Now look up *buy*

Note the translation

acheter

buy **I** *n* **a good ~** une bonne affaire.
II *vtr* acheter (**from sb** à qn); **to ~ sth fr the supermarket/from the baker's** ache qch au supermarché/chez le boulanger; **to sb sth** acheter qch à qn; **to ~ some ti** gagner du temps.

6 Look up *stamp* and choose the part of speech or grammatical category

n

stamp **I** *n* **1** (for envelope) timbre *m*; **2** (on pa port, document) cachet *m*; **3** (marker) (rub tampon *m*; (metal) cachet *m*.
II *vtr* **1** apposer [qch] au tampon [*date*, *na* (**on** sur); tamponner [*ticket*, *book*]; viser [*do ment*, *passport*]; **2 to ~ one's foot** (in an taper du pied.
III *vi* [*horse*] piaffer; **to ~ on** écraser (pied) [*toy*, *foot*]; piétiner [*soil*, *ground*].

7 Study the different senses of *stamp* to find the one you want

Note the translation

timbre ***m***

The *m* tells you that the French word *timbre* is masculine in gender

stamp **I** *n* **1** (for envelope) timbre *m*; **2** (on pa port, document) cachet *m*; **3** (marker) (rub tampon *m*; (metal) cachet *m*.

Result You can now ask in French **Où est-ce que je peux acheter timbre?**

ask 2 On the telephone, you tell someone that you will contact him/her at a later date

oal Translate: **I'll call you back on Tuesday**

Call and *back* work together in English, so look up *call* and scan the entry until you find the block with this type of verb

■ call back: ¶ ~ back 1 (on phone) rappeler; **¶ ~ [sb] back** rappeler [*person*].

■ call back: ¶ ~ back (on phone) rappeler; **¶ ~ [sb] back** rappeler [*person*].
■ call for: ¶ ~ for [sth] 1 (shout) appeler [*ambulance, doctor*]; **to ~ for help** appeler à l'aide; **2** (demand) réclamer; **3** (require) exiger [*treatment, skill*]; nécessiter [*change*].
■ call in: ¶ ~ in (visit) passer; **¶ ~ [sb] in** faire entrer [*client, patient*]; faire appel à [*expert*].

Study the information to see what pattern your phrase matches

¶ ~ [sb] back

Note the translation

rappeler

■ call back: ¶ ~ back (on phone) rappeler; **¶ ~ [sb] back** rappeler [*person*].

To find out how to form the future tense of *rappeler*, you must consult the French entry

rappeler /ʀaple/ [19] **I** *vtr* **1 ~ qch à qn to**

rappeler /ʀaple/ [19] **I** *vtr* **1 ~ qch à qn** to remind sb of sth; **rappelons-le** let's not forget; **~ qn à l'ordre** to call sb to order; **2** to call [sb] back; **3** (on phone) to call or ring [sb] back. **II se rappeler** *v refl* (+ *v être*) to remember.

The number [19] tells you where to find the model for conjugating *rappeler* in the French verb tables

je rappellerai

INFINITIVE	Rules	INDICATIVE	
		Present	**Future**
19 appeler	ll *before mute e*	j'appelle, -es, -e, -ent	**j'appellerai ...**
	l	nous appelons, -ez	

Look up *Tuesday*. You will see a cross-reference page number

▶ 456 |

Tuesday ▶ 456 | *pr n* mardi *m*.

Consult the usage note on **Dates, Days, and Months** and scan the typical examples of use to find a model for your phrase

on Monday

Note the translation

lundi

lundi in the notes below stands for any day; they all work the same way.
Note the use of ***le*** for regular occurrences, and no article for single ones.
(*Remember*: do not translate ***on***.)

on Monday	**= lundi**
on Mondays	= le lundi
what day is it?	= quel jour sommes-nous? / on est quel jour?

---

esult You can now translate your sentence into French **je rappellerai mardi**

Task 3 You are writing to a hotel to book a room

Goal Translate: **I would like to book a double room**

1 Pick out the main words to be translated

like *book* *double room*

2 Look up *like* and choose the appropriate headword

like²

> **like¹ I** *prep* **1** (gen) comme; **to be ~ sb/s** être comme qn/qch; **to look ~** ressembler
>
> **like²** *vtr* **1** aimer bien [*person*]; aimer (bie [*artist, food, music, style*]; **to ~ doing** or **to** aimer (bien) faire; **to ~ A best** préférer

3 Choose the part of speech or grammatical category

> **like²** *vtr*

4 Study the different senses of *like²* to find the one you want

2 (wish)

> **like²** *vtr* **1 aimer bien** [*person*]; aimer (bie [*artist, food, music, style*]; **to ~ doing** or **to** aimer (bien) faire; **to ~ A best** préférer **how do you ~ living in London?** ça te pla de vivre à Londres?; **she doesn't ~ to b kept waiting** elle n'aime pas qu'on la fas attendre; **2** (wish) vouloir, aimer; **I would ~ ticket** je voudrais un billet; **I would ~ to d** je voudrais or j'aimerais faire; **would you to come to dinner?** voudriez-vous ven dîner?; **we'd ~ her to come** nous voudrio or aimerions qu'elle vienne; **if you ~** si

5 Within this sense category, see if there are examples similar to what you want to translate

I would ~ to do

Note the translation

je voudrais or j'aimerais faire

> **kept waiting** elle n'aime pas qu'on la fas attendre; **2** (wish) vouloir, aimer; **I would ~ ticket** je voudrais un billet; **I would ~ to d je voudrais or j'aimerais faire; would you to come to dinner?** voudriez-vous ven dîner?; **we'd ~ her to come** nous voudrio or aimerions qu'elle vienne; **if you ~** si veux; **you can do what you ~** tu peux fai

6 Now look up *book* and choose the appropriate grammatical and sense categories. For the translation, look for the context (in square brackets) closest to your own

[*table, room, taxi, ticket*]

Note the translation

réserver

> **book I** *n* **1** livre *m* (**about** sur; **of** de): **histor ~** livre d'histoire; **2** (exercise book) cahier *n* **3** (of cheques, tickets, stamps) carnet *m*; **~** **matches** pochette *f* d'allumettes.
> **II books** *n pl* (accounts) livres *mpl* de comptes.
> **III** *vtr* **1** réserver [***table, room, taxi, ticke*** faire les réservations pour [*holiday*]; **to be ful ~ed** être complet/-ète; **2** [*policeman*] dresse un procès-verbal or un P.V.© à [*motoris offender*]; (US) (arrest) arrêter [*suspect*]; **3** [*refe*

7 Look up *double room* which you will find listed in alphabetical order as a headword

Note the translation

chambre *f* pour deux personnes.

The *f* tells you that the French word *chambre* is feminine in gender

> **double room** *n* chambre *f* pour deu personnes.

Result You can now translate your sentence into French

Je voudrais réserver une chambre pou deux personnes

Task 4 You need to explain why you can't play tennis

Goal Translate: **I sprained my wrist**

1 Pick out the main words to be translated

sprain *wrist*

2 Look up *sprain* and choose the part of speech or grammatical category

II *vtr*

sprain I *n* entorse *f*.
II *vtr* **to ~ one's ankle** se faire une entorse à la cheville; (less severely) se fouler la cheville.

3 Within this category, see if there are examples similar to what you want to translate

to ~ one's ankle

Note the translation

se faire une entorse à la cheville; (less severely) se fouler la cheville

II *vtr* **to ~ one's ankle** se faire une entorse à la cheville; (less severely) se fouler la cheville.

4 To find out how to form the past tense of *se fouler*, you must consult the French entry

(+ v être)

fouler /fule/ [1] **I** *vtr* to tread [*grapes*].
II se fouler *v refl* **(+ *v être*) 1** (Med) **se ~ le**

5 Look up *wrist*. You will see a cross-reference page number

▶413|

wrist ▶413| *n* poignet *m*.

6 Consult the usage note on *The Human Body* and scan the typical examples of use to find a model for your phrase

she has broken her leg

Note the translation

elle s'est cassé la jambe

For expressions such as *he hurt his foot* or *she brushed her teeth*, where the action involves more than the simple movement of a body part, use a reflexive verb in French:

she has broken her leg	= **elle s'est cassé** la jambe
he was rubbing his hands	= **il se frottait** les mains
she was holding her head	= **elle se tenait** la tête

Result You should now be able to translate your sentence into French **Je me suis foulé le poignet**

Task 5 You are at the station about to board a train and you see a notice

Goal Work out what the notice says: **N'oubliez pas de composter votre billet**

1 Isolate the words which you need to translate

oubliez *composter*

2 *oubliez* is not in the dictionary but *oublier* is

Note the translation

to forget

oublier /ublije/ [2] **I** *vtr* **1** to forget [*name, date, fact*]; to forget about [*worries, incident*]; **se faire ~** to keep a low profile; **2** to leave out [*person, detail*]; **3** to neglect [*duty, friend*].
II s'oublier *v refl* (+ *v être*) **1** to be forgotten; **2** to leave oneself out.

3 Look up the conjugation tables and find out what this form corresponds to

It is an imperative which, combined with *n'* (standing for *ne* before a vowel) and *pas*, means *don't forget*

French verbs

2 plier

IMPERATIVE			**INFINITIVE**		
Present	plie		**Present**	plier	
	plions		**Past**	avoir	plié
	pliez				
Past	aie	plié			
	ayons	plié			
	ayez	plié			

4 Look up *composter*. Scan the entry for potential translations

You notice that there is a translation with a context similar to yours

to punch [*ticket*]

composter /kɔ̃pɔste/ [1] *vtr* to (date)stamp; to punch [*ticket*].

5 You now have the following information

don't forget punch ticket

If you do not know what *votre* means, look up the entry

Note the translation

your

votre, *pl* **vos** /vɔtʀ, vo/ det **your; c'est pour ~ bien** it's for your own good; **à ~ arrivée** when you arrive; when you arrived.

Result You should now be able to understand the notice in French

Don't forget to punch your (train) ticket

The pronunciation of French

Vowels

a	*as in*	patte	/pat/	œ	*as in*	leur	/lœʀ/
ɑ		pâte	/pɑt/	œ̃		brun	/bʀœ̃/
ɑ̃		clan	/klɑ̃/	ø		deux	/dø/
e		dé	/de/	u		fou	/fu/
ɛ		belle	/bɛl/	y		pur	/pyʀ/
ɛ̃		lin	/lɛ̃/				
ə		demain	/dəmɛ̃/				
i		gris	/gʀi/				
o		gros	/gʀo/				
ɔ		corps	/kɔʀ/				
ɔ̃		long	/lɔ̃/				

Semi-vowels

j	*as in*	fille	/fij/
ɥ		huit	/ɥit/
w		oui	/wi/

Consonants

b	*as in*	bal	/bal/	ŋ	*as in*	dancing	/dɑ̃siŋ/
d		dent	/dɑ̃/	p		porte	/pɔʀt/
f		foire	/fwaʀ/	ʀ		rire	/ʀiʀ/
g		gomme	/gɔm/	s		sang	/sɑ̃/
k		clé	/kle/	ʃ		chien	/ʃjɛ̃/
l		lien	/ljɛ̃/	t		train	/tʀɛ̃/
m		mer	/mɛʀ/	v		voile	/vwal/
n		nage	/naʒ/	z		zèbre	/zɛbʀ/
ɲ		gnon	/ɲɔ̃/	ʒ		jeune	/ʒœn/

The symbols used in this dictionary for the pronunciation of French are those of the IPA (International Phonetic Alphabet). Certain differences in pronunciation are shown in the phonetic transcription, although many speakers do not observe them—e.g. the long 'a' /ɑ/ in *pâte* and the short 'a' /a/ in *patte*, or the difference between the nasal vowels 'un' /œ̃/ as in *brun* and 'in' /ɛ̃/ as in *brin*.

Transcription

Each entry is followed by its phonetic transcription between slashes, with a few exceptions.

Morphological variations

The phonetic transcription of the plural and feminine forms of certain nouns and adjectives does not repeat the root, but shows only the change in ending. Therefore, in certain cases, the presentation of the entry does not correspond to that of the phonetic transcription e.g. *électricien, -ienne* /elɛktʀisjɛ̃, ɛn/.

Phrases

Full phonetic transcription is given for adverbial or prepositional phrases which are shown in alphabetical order within the main headword e.g. *emblée, d'emblée* /dɑ̃ble/, *plain-pied, de plain-pied* /d(ə)plɛ̃pje/.

Consonants

Aspiration of 'h'

Where it is impossible to make a liaison this is indicated by /ˈ/ immediately after the slash e.g. *haine* /ˈɛn/.

Assimilation

A voiced consonant can become unvoiced when it is followed by an unvoiced consonant within a word e.g. *absorber* /apsɔʀbe/.

Vowels

Open 'e' and closed 'e'

A clear distinction is made at the end of a word between a closed 'e' and an open 'e' e.g. *pré* /pʀe/ and *près* /pʀɛ/, *complet* /kɔ̃plɛ/ and *combler* /kɔ̃ble/.

Within a word the following rules apply:

- 'e' is always open in a syllable followed by a syllable containing a mute 'e' e.g. *règle* /ʀɛgl/, *réglementaire* /ʀɛgləmɑ̃tɛʀ/
- in careful speech 'e' is pronounced as a closed 'e' when it is followed by a syllable containing a closed vowel (*y, i, e*) e.g. *pressé* /pʀese/
- 'e' is pronounced as an open 'e' when it is followed by a syllable containing an open vowel e.g. *pressant* /pʀɛsɑ̃/.

Mute 'e'

The pronunciation of mute 'e' varies considerably depending on the level of language used and on the region from which the speaker originates. As a general rule it is only pronounced at the end of a word in the South of France or in poetry and it is, therefore, not shown. In an isolated word the mute 'e' preceded by a single consonant is dropped e.g. *parfaitement* /paʀfɛtmɑ̃/, but *probablement* /pʀɔbabləmɑ̃/.

In many cases the pronunciation of the mute 'e' depends on the surrounding context. Thus one would say *une reconnaissance de dette* /ynʀəkɔnɛsɑ̃sdədɛt/, but, *ma reconnaissance est éternelle* /maʀkɔnɛsɑ̃sɛteteʀnɛl/. The mute 'e' is shown in brackets in order to account for this phenomenon.

Stress

There is no real stress as such in French. In normal unemphasized speech a slight stress falls on the final syllable of a word or group of words, providing that it does not contain a mute 'e'. This is not shown in the phonetic transcription of individual entries.

I.V.

Abbreviations and symbols

abbr	abbreviation
adj	adjective
adv	adverb
Anat	anatomy
Aut	automobile
aux	auxiliary
Bot	botany
Comput	computing
conj	conjunction
Culin	culinary
dem pron	demonstrative pronoun
det	determiner
Econ	economy
excl	exclamation
f	feminine
Fr	French
GB	British English
gen	generally
indic	indicative
inv	invariable
m	masculine
Med	medicine
Mil	military
Mus	music
n	noun
nf	feminine noun
nm	masculine noun
nmf	masculine and feminine noun
nm,f	masculine and feminine noun
Naut	nautical
phr	phrase
pl	plural
Pol	politics
pp	past participle
pp adj	past participle adjective
pr n	proper noun
pref	prefix
prep	preposition
pres p adj	present participle adjective
pron	pronoun
qch	quelque chose (something)
qn	quelqu'un (somebody)
quantif	quantifier
rel pron	relative pronoun
sb	somebody
Sch	school
sg	singular
sth	something
subj	subjunctive
Tech	technology
Univ	university
US	American English
v	verb
v aux	auxiliary verb
vi	intransitive verb
v impers	impersonal verb
v refl	reflexive verb
vtr	transitive verb
Zool	zoology
†	dated
®	trademark
○	colloquial
◑	very colloquial
●	vulgar or taboo
~	swung dash used as a substitute for a headword
GB	British spelling only: US spelling varies
≈	indicates an approximate translation equivalent
▶	cross-reference

Note on proprietary status This dictionary includes some words which have, or are asserted to have, proprietary status as trademarks or otherwise. Their inclusion does not imply that they have acquired for legal purposes a non-proprietary or general significance, nor any other judgement concerning their legal status. In cases where the editorial staff have some evidence that a word has proprietary status this is indicated in the entry for that word by the symbol ®, but no judgement concerning the legal status of such words is made or implied thereby.

Aa

a, **A** /a, ɑ/ **I** *nm inv* a, A; **démontrer qch à qn par A plus B** to demonstrate sth conclusively to sb.
II A *nf* (*abbr* = **autoroute**) motorway (GB), freeway (US).

à /a/ *prep*

■ **Note** You will find translations for expressions such as *machine à écrire*, *aller à la pêche* etc, at the entries ***machine***, ***pêche*** etc.
– For the uses of *à* with the verbs *aller*, *être*, *avoir*, *penser* etc, see the entries for these verbs.

1 to; **aller ~ Paris** to go to Paris; **se rendre au travail** to go to work; **2** at; in; **~ la maison** at home; **être ~ Paris** to be in Paris; **au printemps** in (the) spring; **~ midi** at midday; **~ quatre kilomètres d'ici** four kilometres[GB] from here; **~ 100 kilomètres-heure** at 100 kilometres[GB] per or an hour; **un timbre ~ trois francs** a three-franc stamp; **(de) huit ~ dix heures par jour** between eight and ten hours a day; **3** with; **le garçon aux cheveux bruns** the boy with dark hair; **4 ~ qui est cette montre?** whose is this watch?; **elle est ~ elle** it's hers; **je suis ~ vous tout de suite** I'll be with you in a minute; **c'est ~ qui de jouer?** whose turn is it?; **5 il est ~ plaindre** he's to be pitied; **6 ~ nous tous on devrait y arriver** between all of us we should be able to manage; **~ trois on est serrés** with three people it's a squash; **7 ~ ce qu'il paraît** apparently; **~ ta santé, ~ la tienne!** cheers!; **~ tes souhaits!** bless you!

abaisser /abese/ [1] **I** *vtr* to pull down [*lever*]; to lower [*safety curtain, window*].
II s'abaisser *v refl* (+ *v être*) **1** [*stage curtain*] to fall; **2 s'~ à faire** to stoop to doing.

abandon /abɑ̃dɔ̃/ *nm* **1 être à l'~** [*house*] to be abandoned; [*garden*] to be neglected; **2** (of project, method) abandonment; (of right) relinquishment; **3** (from race, competition) withdrawal.

abandonner /abɑ̃dɔne/ [1] *vtr* **1** (gen) to give up; (in school) to drop [*subject*]; **2** (from game, tournament) to withdraw; to retire; **3** to leave [*person, place*]; to abandon [*car, object*]; **4** to abandon [*child, animal*]; to desert [*home, post, cause*]; **5** [*courage, chance*] to fail [*person*].

abat-jour /abaʒuʀ/ *nm inv* lampshade.

abats /aba/ *nm pl* offal; (of poultry) giblets.

abattement /abatmɑ̃/ *nm* **1** despondency; **2 ~ fiscal** tax allowance (GB) or deduction (US).

abattoir /abatwaʀ/ *nm* abattoir, slaughterhouse.

abattre /abatʀ/ [61] **I** *vtr* **1** to shoot [sb] down [*person*]; to shoot [*animal*]; to slaughter [*cattle, sheep*]; **2** to pull down [*building*]; to knock down [*wall*]; [*person*] to fell [*tree*]; [*storm*] to bring down [*tree*]; **3** to show [*card, hand*]; **4** to demoralize; **5 ~ de la besogne** to get through a lot of work.
II s'abattre *v refl* (+ *v être*) **s'~ sur** [*storm*] to break over; [*rain*] to beat down on; [*bird of prey*] to swoop down on.

abbaye /abei/ *nf* abbey.

abbé /abe/ *nm* **1** priest; **2** abbot.

abcès /apsɛ/ *nm inv* abscess; **crever l'~** to resolve a crisis.

abdiquer /abdike/ [1] *vi* [*sovereign*] to abdicate.

abdomen /abdɔmɛn/ *nm* abdomen, stomach.

abdominal, **~e**, *mpl* **-aux** /abdɔminal, o/ **I** *adj* abdominal.
II abdominaux *nm pl* abdominal muscles.

abeille /abɛj/ *nf* bee.

aberrant, **~e** /abɛʀɑ̃, ɑ̃t/ *adj* **1** absurd; **2** aberrant.

aberration /abɛʀasjɔ̃/ *nf* aberration.

abîme /abim/ *nm* **1** abyss; **2** (figurative) gulf.

abîmer /abime/ [1] **I** *vtr* to damage.
II s'abîmer *v refl* (+ *v être*) [*object*] to get damaged; [*fruit*] to spoil.

abject, **~e** /abʒɛkt/ *adj* despicable, abject.

ablation /ablasjɔ̃/ *nf* excision, removal.

abnégation /abnegasjɔ̃/ *nf* self-sacrifice.

aboiement /abwamɑ̃/ *nm* barking.

abolir /abɔliʀ/ [3] *vtr* to abolish.

abominable /abɔminabl/ *adj* abominable.

abondamment /abɔ̃damɑ̃/ *adv* [*drink*] a lot; [*illustrate*] amply; **rincer ~** rinse thoroughly.

abondance /abɔ̃dɑ̃s/ *nf* **1** (of information) wealth; (of resources) abundance; **2** affluence.

abondant, **~e** /abɔ̃dɑ̃, ɑ̃t/ *adj* [*food*] plentiful; [*illustrations*] numerous; [*vegetation*] lush.

abonder /abɔ̃de/ [1] *vi* to be plentiful; to abound.
IDIOMS **~ dans le sens de qn** to agree wholeheartedly with sb.

abonné, **~e** /abɔne/ **I** *pp* ▶ **abonner**.
II *nm,f* **1** subscriber; **2** season ticket holder.

abonnement /abɔnmɑ̃/ *nm* **1** subscription; **2 (carte d')~** season ticket.

abonner /abɔne/ [1] **I** *vtr* **~ qn à qch** (to magazine) to take out a subscription to sth for sb; (for theatre) to buy sb a season ticket for sth.
II s'abonner *v refl* (+ *v être*) to subscribe (**à** to); to buy a season ticket (**à** for).

abord /abɔʀ/ **I** *nm* **1 elle est d'un ~ difficile** she is rather unapproachable; **2 être d'un ~ aisé** [*subject, book*] to be accessible; **3 au premier ~** at first sight.
II d'abord *phr* first; **tout d'~** first of all.
III abords *nm pl* surrounding area, area around.

abordable /abɔʀdabl/ *adj* [*product, price*] affordable; [*text*] accessible.

abordage /abɔʀdaʒ/ *nm* (by pirates) boarding.
aborder /abɔʀde/ [1] **I** *vtr* **1** to tackle [*problem*]; **2** to approach [*person*]; **3** to reach [*place, shore*].
II *vi* [*traveller, ship*] to land.
aboutir /abutiʀ/ [3] **I aboutir à** *v+prep* to lead to.
II *vi* [*negotiations, project*] to succeed.
aboutissement /abutismɑ̃/ *nm* **1** culmination; **2** (successful) outcome.
aboyer /abwaje/ [23] *vi* [*dog*] to bark (**après** at).
abracadabrant, **~e** /abʀakadabʀɑ̃, ɑ̃t/ *adj* bizarre.
abrasif, **-ive** /abʀazif, iv/ *adj* abrasive.
abrégé /abʀeʒe/ *nm* (book) concise guide.
abréger /abʀeʒe/ [15] *vtr* **1** to shorten [*word, expression*]; **2** to cut short [*visit, career*].
abreuver: **s'abreuver** /abʀøve/ [1] *v refl* (+ *v être*) [*animal*] to drink.
abreuvoir /abʀøvwaʀ/ *nm* drinking trough.
abréviation /abʀevjasjɔ̃/ *nf* abbreviation.
abri /abʀi/ *nm* **1** shelter; **à l'~ de** sheltered from; (figurative) safe from; **2** shed.
abricot /abʀiko/ *nm* apricot.
abricotier /abʀikɔtje/ *nm* apricot tree.
abriter /abʀite/ [1] **I** *vtr* **1** [*building*] to shelter [*people, animals*]; **2** [*country, region*] to provide a habitat for [*animals, plant life*].
II s'abriter *v refl* (+ *v être*) to take shelter.
abroger /abʀɔʒe/ [13] *vtr* to repeal.
abrupt, **~e** /abʀypt/ *adj* **1** [*hill, road*] steep; [*cliff*] sheer; **2** [*person, tone*] abrupt.
abruti, **~e** /abʀyti/ *nm,f* (offensive) moron○.
abrutir /abʀytiʀ/ [3] **I** *vtr* [*noise*] to deafen; [*alcohol, medication, fatigue*] to have a numbing effect on; [*blow*] to stun.
II s'abrutir *v refl* (+ *v être*) **1** to become dull-witted; **2 s'~ de travail** to wear oneself out with work.
abrutissant, **~e** /abʀytisɑ̃, ɑ̃t/ *adj* [*music, noise*] deafening; [*job*] mind-numbing.
absence /apsɑ̃s/ *nf* **1** absence; **2** lack; **l'~ de pluie** the lack of rain.
absent, **~e** /apsɑ̃, ɑ̃t/ **I** *adj* **1 être ~** to be away; (for brief spell) to be out; **2** [*pupil, employee*] absent; **3** (missing) absent (**de** from); **4** absent-minded.
II *nm,f* absentee.
absenter: **s'absenter** /apsɑ̃te/ [1] *v refl* (+ *v être*) to go away; to go out.
absolu, **~e** /apsɔly/ *adj* absolute; [*rule*] hard and fast.
absolument /apsɔlymɑ̃/ *adv* absolutely.
absolution /apsɔlysjɔ̃/ *nf* absolution.
absolutisme /apsɔlytism/ *nm* absolutism.
absorbant, **~e** /apsɔʀbɑ̃, ɑ̃t/ *adj* **1** [*substance*] absorbent; **2** [*job, work*] absorbing.
absorber /apsɔʀbe/ [1] *vtr* **1** [*material, plant*] to absorb; **2** to take [*food, medicine*]; **3** to occupy [*mind*].
absorption /apsɔʀpsjɔ̃/ *nf* **1** (of liquid) absorption; **2** (of food, medicine) taking.
abstenir: **s'abstenir** /apstəniʀ/ [36] *v refl* (+ *v être*) **1** (from voting) to abstain; **2 s'~ de faire** to refrain from doing.
abstention /apstɑ̃sjɔ̃/ *nf* abstention.
abstinence /apstinɑ̃s/ *nf* abstinence.
abstraction /apstʀaksjɔ̃/ *nf* abstraction; **faire ~ de** to set aside.
abstrait, **~e** /apstʀɛ, ɛt/ **I** *adj* abstract.
II *nm* (gen) abstract; (art) abstract art.
absurde /apsyʀd/ *adj, nm* absurd.
absurdité /apsyʀdite/ *nf* absurdity.
abus /aby/ *nm inv* abuse.
abuser /abyze/ [1] **I** *vtr* to fool.
II abuser de *v+prep* **1 ~ de l'alcool** to drink to excess; **2 ~ de** to exploit [*situation, credibility*]; **3 ~ de qn** to sexually abuse sb.
III *vi* to go too far; **je ne voudrais pas ~** I don't want to impose.
IV s'abuser *v refl* (+ *v être*) **si je ne m'abuse** if I'm not mistaken.
abusif, **-ive** /abyzif, iv/ *adj* **1** excessive; **2** unfair; **3** improper; **4** over-possessive.
acabit /akabi/ *nm* **du même ~** of that sort.
acacia /akasja/ *nm* **1** (European) **(faux) ~** locust tree; **2** (tropical) acacia.
académicien, **-ienne** /akademisjɛ̃, ɛn/ *nm,f* academician.
académie /akademi/ *nf* (Sch) ≈ local education authority (GB), school district (US).
acajou /akaʒu/ *nm* mahogany.
acariâtre /akaʀjɑtʀ/ *adj* cantankerous.
accablant, **~e** /akablɑ̃, ɑ̃t/ *adj* **1** [*heat, silence*] oppressive; **2** [*evidence, testimony*] damning.
accabler /akable/ [1] *vtr* **1** [*bad news*] to devastate; **être accablé par** to be overcome by [*heat, grief*]; **2** [*testimony, person*] to condemn.
accalmie /akalmi/ *nf* **1** lull; **2** slack period.
accaparant, **~e** /akapaʀɑ̃, ɑ̃t/ *adj* very demanding.
accaparer /akapaʀe/ [1] *vtr* to corner [*market*]; to monopolize [*person, power*].
accéder /aksede/ [14] *v+prep* **1 ~ à** to reach [*place*]; **2 ~ à** to achieve [*fame, glory*]; to obtain [*job*]; to rise to [*high office*].
accélérateur /akseleʀatœʀ/ *nm* accelerator.
accélération /akseleʀasjɔ̃/ *nf* acceleration.
accélérer /akseleʀe/ [14] **I** *vtr* to speed up [*rhythm, process*]; **~ le pas** to quicken one's step.
II *vi* [*driver*] to accelerate.
III s'accélérer *v refl* (+ *v être*) [*pulse, movement*] to become faster; [*phenomenon*] to accelerate.
accent /aksɑ̃/ *nm* **1** (of person, region) accent; **2** (on a letter) accent; **3** (on a syllable) **~ tonique** stress; **mettre l'~ sur qch** to emphasize sth, to put the emphasis on sth; **4 ~ de sincérité** hint of sincerity.
accentuer /aksɑ̃tɥe/ [1] **I** *vtr* **1** (gen) to emphasize, to accentuate; **2** to heighten [*tension*]; to increase [*tendency*]; **3** (in pronouncing) to stress [*syllable*].

II s'accentuer *v refl* (+ *v être*) to become more marked.

acceptable /akseptabl/ *adj* **1** acceptable; **2** passable; satisfactory.

acceptation /akseptasjɔ̃/ *nf* acceptance.

accepter /aksepte/ [1] *vtr* to accept; to agree to.

accès /aksɛ/ *nm inv* **1** access; **d'un ~ facile** [*place*] easy to get to; **'~ aux quais'** 'to the trains'; **'~ interdit'** 'no entry'; **l'~ à** access to [*profession, course*]; admission to [*club, school*]; **2 ~ de colère** fit of anger; **~ de fièvre** bout of fever; **par ~** by fits and starts.

accessible /aksesibl/ *adj* **1** [*place, book, information*] accessible; **2 ~ à** [*job*] open to; **3** [*price, fare*] affordable.

accession /aksesjɔ̃/ *nf* **~ à** accession to [*throne, power*]; attainment of [*independence*].

accessoire /akseswaʀ/ **I** *adj* incidental.
II *nm* **1** accessory; attachment; **~s de toilette** toilet requisites; **2** (in the theatre) **~s** props.

accessoirement /akseswaʀmɑ̃/ *adv* **1** incidentally, as it happens; **2** if desired.

accident /aksidɑ̃/ *nm* **1** accident; **2** hitch; mishap; **~ de parcours**○ hitch.
■ **~ domestique** accident in the home.

accidenté, ~e /aksidɑ̃te/ **I** *adj* **1** [*person*] injured; [*car*] involved in an accident; **2** [*road, ground*] uneven.
II *nm,f* accident victim.

accidentel, -elle /aksidɑ̃tɛl/ *adj* accidental.

accidentellement /aksidɑ̃tɛlmɑ̃/ *adv* **1** in an accident; **2** by accident, accidentally.

acclamation /aklamasjɔ̃/ *nf* cheering.

acclamer /aklame/ [1] *vtr* to cheer, to acclaim.

acclimater /aklimate/ [1] **I** *vtr* to acclimatize.
II s'acclimater *v refl* (+ *v être*) to become acclimatized; to adapt.

accointances /akwɛ̃tɑ̃s/ *nf pl* contacts.

accolade /akɔlad/ *nf* embrace.

accommoder /akɔmɔde/ [1] **I** *vtr* to prepare.
II *vi* [*eyes*] to focus.
III s'accommoder *v refl* (+ *v être*) **s'~ de qch** to make the best of sth; to put up with sth.

accompagnateur, -trice /akɔ̃paɲatœʀ, tʀis/ *nm,f* **1** (Mus) accompanist; **2** (with children) accompanying adult; (with tourists) courier.

accompagnement /akɔ̃paɲmɑ̃/ *nm* accompaniment.

accompagner /akɔ̃paɲe/ [1] *vtr* **1** [*person*] to accompany, to go with, to come with; **2** to accompany [*phenomenon, event*]; **3** (Mus) to accompany; **4** [*wine*] to be served with.

accomplir /akɔ̃pliʀ/ [3] **I** *vtr* to accomplish [*task*]; to fulfil[GB] [*obligation*].
II s'accomplir *v refl* (+ *v être*) to be fulfilled.

accomplissement /akɔ̃plismɑ̃/ *nm* (of mission) accomplishment, fulfilment[GB]; (of ambition, aim) realization, achievement.

accord /akɔʀ/ *nm* **1** agreement; (tacit) understanding; **d'~** all right, OK○; **je suis d'~** I agree (**avec** with); **se mettre** or **tomber d'~** to come to an agreement; **2** harmony; **3** (in grammar) **~ en genre/en nombre** gender/number agreement; **4** (Mus) chord.

accordéon /akɔʀdeɔ̃/ *nm* accordion.

accorder /akɔʀde/ [1] **I** *vtr* **1 ~ qch à qn** to grant sb sth [*favour, loan, interview, permission, right*]; to give sb sth [*grant, reduction, chance*]; **il n'a pas entièrement tort, je te l'accorde** he's not entirely wrong, I'll give you that; **2** to attach [*importance, value*] (**à** to); to pay [*attention*]; **3** (Mus) to tune [*instrument*]; **4** to make [sth] agree [*word, adjective*].
II s'accorder *v refl* (+ *v être*) **1** to give oneself [*rest, time off*]; **2** to agree (**sur** about, on); **3** [*colours, clothes*] to go (together) well; **4** [*adjective, verb*] to agree (**avec** with).

accordeur /akɔʀdœʀ/ *nm* tuner.

accoster /akɔste/ [1] **I** *vtr* to accost [*person*].
II *vi* [*ship*] to dock.

accotement /akɔtmɑ̃/ *nm* verge.

accouchement /akuʃmɑ̃/ *nm* delivery.

accoucher /akuʃe/ [1] *vi* to give birth.

accoucheur /akuʃœʀ/ *nm* obstetrician.

accouder: **s'accouder** /akude/ [1] *v refl* (+ *v être*) to lean on one's elbows.

accoudoir /akudwaʀ/ *nm* arm-rest.

accouplement /akupləmɑ̃/ *nm* mating.

accourir /akuʀiʀ/ [26] *vi* to run up.

accoutrement /akutʀəmɑ̃/ *nm* get-up○.

accoutrer: **s'accoutrer** /akutʀe/ [1] *v refl* (+ *v être*) to get oneself up (**de** in).

accoutumance /akutymɑ̃s/ *nf* addiction.

accoutumer /akutyme/ [1] **I** *vtr* to accustom (**à** to).
II s'accoutumer *v refl* (+ *v être*) to grow accustomed (**à** to).

accrédité, ~e /akʀedite/ *adj* authorized; accredited.

accréditer /akʀedite/ [1] *vtr* **1** to give credence to [*rumour*]; **2** to accredit [*ambassador*].

accro○ /akʀo/ *adj* hooked○ (**à** on).

accroc /akʀo/ *nm* tear (**à** in).

accrochage /akʀɔʃaʒ/ *nm* (between people) clash; (between vehicles) collision.

accrocher /akʀɔʃe/ [1] **I** *vtr* **1** to hang (**à** from); **2** to hook [sth] on (**à** to); **3** to catch [*stocking, sweater*] (**à** on); **4** to catch [*eye, attention*].
II s'accrocher *v refl* (+ *v être*) **1** (to ledge) to hang on; (to post) to cling (on) (**à** to); **2** [*person*] **s'~ à qn** to cling to sb; **3 l'hameçon s'est accroché à ma veste** the hook got caught in my jacket; **4**○ **s'~ pour faire** to try hard to do.
IDIOMS **avoir le cœur** or **l'estomac bien accroché** to have a strong stomach.

accroissement /akʀwasmɑ̃/ *nm* growth.

accroître /akʀwɑtʀ/ [72] *vtr*, **s'accroître** *v refl* (+ *v être*) to increase.

accroupir: **s'accroupir** /akʀupiʀ/ [3] *v refl* (+ *v être*) to squat (down); to crouch (down).

accru, ~e /akʀy/ *pp* ▸ **accroître**.

accueil /akœj/ *nm* **1** welcome; **2** reception desk.

accueillant, **~e** /akœjɑ̃, ɑ̃t/ *adj* **1** hospitable, welcoming; **2** homely (GB), homey (US).
accueillir /akœjiʀ/ [27] *vtr* **1** to welcome; **2** to receive, to greet; **3** [*room, hotel*] to accommodate; **4** [*hospital, organization*] to cater for.
accumulation /akymylasjɔ̃/ *nf* **1** accumulation; **2** storage.
accumuler /akymyle/ [1] **I** *vtr* **1** to store (up) [*things*]; to accumulate [*capital*]; to make a succession of [*mistakes*]; **2** to store (up) [*energy*].
II s'accumuler *v refl* (+ *v être*) [*snow, rubbish*] to pile up; [*stocks, debts*] to accrue.
accusation /akyzasjɔ̃/ *nf* **1** accusation; (Law) charge; **2 l'~** the prosecution.
accusé, **~e** /akyze/ **I** *pp* ▶ **accuser**.
II *pp adj* [*wrinkles*] deep; [*relief*] marked.
III *nm,f* defendant; **les ~s** the accused.
■ **~ de réception** acknowledgement (of receipt).
accuser /akyze/ [1] **I** *vtr* **1** to accuse [*person*]; to blame [*fate*]; [*evidence*] to point to [*person*]; [*judge*] to charge [*defendant*] (**de** with); **2** to show, to register [*fall, deficit*].
II s'accuser *v refl* (+ *v être*) **1** [*person*] to take the blame; **2** to become more marked.
IDIOMS **~ le coup** to be visibly shaken.
acerbe /asɛʀb/ *adj* acerbic.
acéré, **~e** /aseʀe/ *adj* sharp.
acharné, **~e** /aʃaʀne/ *adj* [*supporter*] passionate; [*work*] unremitting; [*struggle*] fierce.
acharnement /aʃaʀnəmɑ̃/ *nm* furious energy.
acharner: **s'acharner** /aʃaʀne/ [1] *v refl* (+ *v être*) **1** to persevere; **s'~ contre** to fight against [*project*]; **2 s'~ sur** [*person, animal*] to keep going at [*victim, prey*]; (figurative) to hound [*person*]; **la malchance s'acharne contre lui** he is dogged by bad luck.
achat /aʃa/ *nm* purchase.
acheminement /aʃ(ə)minmɑ̃/ *nm* transportation.
acheminer /aʃ(ə)mine/ [1] **I** *vtr* to transport.
II s'acheminer *v refl* (+ *v être*) **s'~ vers** to make one's way toward(s); to move toward(s).
acheter /aʃte/ [18] **I** *vtr* to buy; **~ qch à qn** to buy sth from sb; to buy sth for sb.
II s'acheter *v refl* (+ *v être*) **1 s'~ qch** to buy oneself sth; **2 cela s'achète où?** where can you get it?
acheteur, **-euse** /aʃtœʀ, øz/ *nm,f* buyer.
achever /aʃve/ [16] **I** *vtr* **1** to finish [*work*]; to conclude [*discussions*]; to complete [*project, inquiry*]; to end [*life*]; **2** to destroy [*animal*]; to finish off [*person*].
II s'achever *v refl* (+ *v être*) to end.
acide /asid/ *adj, nm* acid.
acidité /asidite/ *nf* acidity, tartness, sharpness.
acidulé, **~e** /asidyle/ *adj* slightly acid; tangy.
acier /asje/ **I** *adj inv* steel(y).
II *nm* steel; **d'~** [*girder, column*] steel; [*nerves*] of steel.
aciérie /asjeʀi/ *nf* steelworks.
acné /akne/ *nf* acne; **~ juvénile** teenage acne.
acolyte /akɔlit/ *nmf* henchman, acolyte.
acompte /akɔ̃t/ *nm* **1** deposit; **2** part payment.
à-côté, *pl* **~s** /akote/ *nm* **1** perk; **2** extra expense; **3** extra profit.
à-coup, *pl* **~s** /aku/ *nm* jolt; **par ~s** by fits and starts.
acoustique /akustik/ **I** *adj* acoustic.
II *nf* acoustics.
acquéreur /akeʀœʀ/ *nm* buyer, purchaser.
acquérir /akeʀiʀ/ [35] *vtr* **1** to acquire; (by buying) to purchase; **2** to acquire [*reputation*].
acquiescer /akjese/ [12] *vi* to acquiesce.
acquis, **~e** /aki, iz/ **I** *pp* ▶ **acquérir**.
II *pp adj* **1** [*skills*] acquired; **2** [*principle, right*] accepted, established; **les avantages ~** the gains made; **tenir qch pour ~** to take sth for granted.
III *nm inv* **1** acquired knowledge; **2 ~ sociaux** social benefits.
IDIOMS **bien mal ~ ne profite jamais** (Proverb) ill-gotten gains never prosper.
acquisition /akizisjɔ̃/ *nf* **1** purchase; **2** acquisition.
acquit /aki/ *nm* **je le ferai par ~ de conscience** I'll do it to put my mind at rest.
acquittement /akitmɑ̃/ *nm* (Law) acquittal.
acquitter /akite/ [1] **I** *vtr* (Law) to acquit.
II s'acquitter *v refl* (+ *v être*) **s'~ de son devoir** to do one's duty; **s'~ d'une dette** to pay off a debt.
acre /akʀ/ *nf* acre.
âcre /ɑkʀ/ *adj* [*taste*] sharp; [*smell*] acrid.
acrobate /akʀɔbat/ *nmf* acrobat.
acrobatie /akʀɔbasi/ *nf* acrobatics.
acte /akt/ *nm* **1** act; **~ manqué** Freudian slip; **être libre de ses ~s** to do as one wishes; **faire ~ de candidature** to put oneself forward as a candidate; **2** (Law) deed; **~ de naissance** birth certificate; **3** (in play) act.
acteur, **-trice** /aktœʀ, tʀis/ *nm,f* **1** actor/actress; **2** protagonist.
actif, **-ive** /aktif, iv/ **I** *adj* (gen) active; [*market*] buoyant; **la vie active** working life.
II *nm* **1 l'~** the assets; **2 à l'~ de qn** in sb's favour[GB].
action /aksjɔ̃/ *nf* **1** action, act; **une bonne ~** a good deed; **2 l'~** action; **moyens d'~** courses of action; **en ~** in operation; **3** effect; **l'~ de qn sur** sb's influence on; **4 ~ en justice** legal action; **5** (in finance) share.
actionnaire /aksjɔnɛʀ/ *nmf* shareholder.
actionner /aksjɔne/ [1] *vtr* to activate.
activement /aktivmɑ̃/ *adv* actively.
activer /aktive/ [1] **I** *vtr* **1** to speed up [*work*]; to stimulate [*digestion*]; **2** [*wind*] to stir up [*flames*]; **3** to stoke [*fire*].
II s'activer○ *v refl* (+ *v être*) to hurry up.
activiste /aktivist/ *adj, nmf* activist.
activité /aktivite/ *nf* **1** activity; **~ professionnelle** occupation; **2 être en pleine ~** [*street*] to be bustling with activity; [*person*] to be very busy; **volcan en ~** active volcano.
actrice *nf* ▶ **acteur**.

actualiser /aktɥalize/ [1] *vtr* to update.

actualité /aktɥalite/ I *nf* **1** current affairs; **l'~ culturelle** cultural events; **2 d'~** topical; **toujours d'~** still relevant today.
II **actualités** *nfpl* **1** news; **2** newsreel.

actuel, **-elle** /aktɥɛl/ *adj* **1** present, current; **2** [*film, discussion*] topical.

actuellement /aktɥɛlmɑ̃/ *adv* **1** at the moment; **2** currently.

acuité /akɥite/ *nf* **1** acuity; **2** shrillness; **3** (of pain) intensity.

acupuncture /akypɔ̃ktyʀ/ *nf* acupuncture.

adage /adaʒ/ *nm* saying, adage.

adaptation /adaptasjɔ̃/ *nf* adaptation.

adapté, **~e** /adapte/ *adj* **1** suitable; **2 ~ à** [*solution*] suited to; **3** (for TV, stage) adapted.

adapter /adapte/ [1] I *vtr* **1** to fit (**à** to); **2** to adapt [*equipment*]; **3** to adapt [*novel*].
II **s'adapter** *v refl* (+ *v être*) **1** [*tool, part*] to fit; **2** to adapt, to adjust (**à** to).

addition /adisjɔ̃/ *nf* **1** addition; **2** bill, check (US).

additionner /adisjɔne/ [1] *vtr* to add up.

adepte /adɛpt/ *nmf* **1** (of theory) supporter; (of person) disciple; **2** enthusiast.

adéquat, **~e** /adekwa, at/ *adj* **1** appropriate, suitable; **2** adequate.

adhérence /adeʀɑ̃s/ *nf* (of tyre, sole) grip.

adhérent, **~e** /adeʀɑ̃, ɑ̃t/ *nm,f* member.

adhérer /adeʀe/ [14] *v+prep* **1 ~ à** [*glue*] to stick to; [*tyre*] to grip; **2 ~ à** to join.

adhésif, **-ive** /adezif, iv/ *adj* adhesive.

adhésion /adezjɔ̃/ *nf* **1** membership; **2** support.

adieu, *pl* **~x** /adjø/ *nm* goodbye, farewell.

adipeux, **-euse** /adipø, øz/ *adj* fatty.

adjectif /adʒɛktif/ *nm* adjective.

adjoint, **~e** /adʒwɛ̃, ɛ̃t/ *nm,f* assistant; deputy; **~ au maire** deputy mayor.

adjudant /adʒydɑ̃/ *nm* ≈ warrant officer.

adjuger /adʒyʒe/ [13] *vtr* to auction; **une fois, deux fois, adjugé!** going, going, gone!

admettre /admɛtʀ/ [60] *vtr* **1** to accept, to admit [*fact*]; **2** to admit [*person, student*]; **être admis à un examen** to pass an exam; **3 ~ que** to suppose (that).

administrateur, **-trice** /administʀatœʀ, tʀis/ *nm,f* **1** administrator; **2** director; **3** trustee.

administratif, **-ive** /administʀatif, iv/ *adj* **1** [*staff, building*] administrative; **2** [*report*] official.

administration /administʀasjɔ̃/ *nf* **1** administration; **2** civil service; **3 être placé sous ~ judiciaire** to go into receivership; **4** management; **5** (of drugs, sacrament) administration, giving.

administrer /administʀe/ [1] *vtr* **1** to administer [*funds*]; to run [*company, country*]; **2** to administer, to give [*drug, sacrament*].

admirable /admiʀabl/ *adj* admirable.

admirateur, **-trice** /admiʀatœʀ, tʀis/ *nm,f* admirer.

admiration /admiʀasjɔ̃/ *nf* admiration.

admirer /admiʀe/ [1] *vtr* to admire.

admis, **~e** /admi, iz/ I *pp* ▶ **admettre**.
II *pp adj* accepted; [*candidate*] successful.

admissible /admisibl/ *adj* **1** acceptable; **2** eligible.

admission /admisjɔ̃/ *nf* admission; **service des ~s** reception.

adolescence /adɔlesɑ̃s/ *nf* adolescence.

adolescent, **~e** /adɔlesɑ̃, ɑ̃t/ I *adj* teenage.
II *nm,f* teenager, adolescent.

adonner: **s'adonner** /adɔne/ [1] *v refl* (+ *v être*) **s'~ à** to devote all one's time to; **il s'adonne à la boisson** he drinks too much.

adopter /adɔpte/ [1] *vtr* to adopt [*child, method*]; to pass [*law*].

adoptif, **-ive** /adɔptif, iv/ *adj* **1** [*child, country*] adopted; **2** [*parent*] adoptive.

adoption /adɔpsjɔ̃/ *nf* **1** adoption; **2** passing.

adorable /adɔʀabl/ *adj* adorable.

adoration /adɔʀasjɔ̃/ *nf* worship, adoration.

adorer /adɔʀe/ [1] *vtr* to adore, to worship.

adosser: **s'adosser** /adose/ [1] *v refl* (+ *v être*) **s'~ à** to lean back on.

adoucir /adusiʀ/ [3] I *vtr* to soften [*skin, water*]; to moderate [*tone of voice*]; to soothe [*throat*]; to ease [*suffering*].
II **s'adoucir** *v refl* (+ *v être*) [*temperature*] to become milder; [*slope*] to become more gentle.

adoucissant, **~e** /adusisɑ̃, ɑ̃t/ I *adj* soothing.
II *nm* softener.

adrénaline /adʀenalin/ *nf* adrenalin.

adresse /adʀɛs/ *nf* **1** address; **se tromper d'~** to get the wrong address; to pick the wrong person; **remarque lancée à l'~ de qn** remark directed at sb; **2** dexterity; **3** skill.

adresser /adʀese/ [1] I *vtr* **1** to direct [*criticism*] (**à** at); to make [*request, declaration, appeal*]; to deliver [*ultimatum*]; to present [*petition*]; to aim [*blow*]; **~ la parole à qn** to speak to sb; **2** to send [*letter*]; **3** to refer [sb] (**à** to).
II **s'adresser** *v refl* (+ *v être*) **1 s'~ à qn** to speak to sb; **2 s'~ à** to contact [*embassy*]; **s'~ au guichet 8** to go to window 8; **3 s'~ à** [*measure*] to be aimed at.

adroit, **~e** /adʀwa, at/ *adj* skilful[GB]; clever.

adulte /adylt/ *adj, nmf* adult.

adultère /adyltɛʀ/ I *adj* adulterous.
II *nm* adultery.

advenir /advəniʀ/ [36] *v impers* **1** to happen; **advienne que pourra** come what may; **2 ~ de** to become of.

adverbe /advɛʀb/ *nm* adverb.

adversaire /advɛʀsɛʀ/ *nmf* (gen) opponent; (Mil) adversary.

adverse /advɛʀs/ *adj* **1** opposing; **2** opposite.

adversité /advɛʀsite/ *nf* adversity.

aérer /aeʀe/ [14] I *vtr* **1** to air; **2** to space out.
II **s'aérer** *v refl* (+ *v être*) to get some fresh air.

aérien, **-ienne** /aeʀjɛ̃, ɛn/ *adj* [*transport*] air; [*photography*] aerial; **métro ~** elevated section of the underground (GB), elevated railroad (US).

aéro-club, *pl* **~s** /aeʀoklœb/ *nm* flying club.

aérodrome /aeʀodʀom/ *nm* aerodrome (GB), (small) airfield.

aérodynamique /aeʀodinamik/ *adj* aerodynamic.

aérogare /aeʀogaʀ/ *nf* air terminal.

aéroglisseur /aeʀoglisœʀ/ *nm* hovercraft.

aéronautique /aeʀonotik/ *nf* aeronautics.

aérophagie /aeʀɔfaʒi/ *nf* aerophagia.

aéroport /aeʀɔpɔʀ/ *nm* airport.

aérosol /aeʀɔsɔl/ *nm* **1** aerosol; **2** spray.

aérospatiale /aeʀɔspasjal/ *nf* aerospace industry.

affabulation /afabylasjɔ̃/ *nf* fabrication.

affaiblir /afɛbliʀ/ [3] **I** *vtr* to weaken.
II s'affaiblir *v refl* (+ *v être*) to get weaker.

affaiblissement /afɛblismɑ̃/ *nm* **1** weakening; **2** weakened state.

affaire /afɛʀ/ **I** *nf* **1** affair; (political) crisis, affair; (moral) scandal; (legal) case; **2** affair, matter; **une ~ délicate** a delicate matter; **c'est l'~ de quelques jours** it'll only take a few days; **j'en fais mon ~** I'll deal with it; **c'est une autre ~** that's another matter; **c'est une ~ d'argent** there's money involved; **et voilà toute l'~** and that's that; **c'est toute une ~, ce n'est pas une petite ~** it's quite a business; **3** (skill, trade) **il connaît bien son ~** he knows his job; **la mécanique, c'est leur ~** mechanics is their thing; **4** deal; **faire ~ avec** to do a deal with; **avoir ~ à** to be dealing with; **5** bargain; **la belle ~**○! big deal○!; **ça fera l'~** that'll do; **6** business, concern; **7** (difficulty) **être tiré d'~** to be out of danger.
II affaires *nf pl* **1** business; **2** (personal) business affairs; **occupe-toi de tes ~s!** mind your own business!; **3** things, belongings.
■ **~s courantes** daily business.

affairer: **s'affairer** /afeʀe/ [1] *v refl* (+ *v être*) to bustle about (**à faire** doing).

affaisser: **s'affaisser** /afese/ [1] *v refl* (+ *v être*) **1** to subside; **2** [*shoulders, roof*] to sag; **3** [*person*] to collapse.

affaler: **s'affaler** /afale/ [1] *v refl* (+ *v être*) **1** to collapse; **2**○ to fall.

affamé, **~e** /afame/ **I** *pp* ▶ **affamer**.
II *pp adj* **1** starving; **2 ~ de** hungry for.

affamer /afame/ [1] *vtr* to starve.

affectation /afɛktasjɔ̃/ *nf* **1** allocation (**à** to); **2** appointment (**à** to); posting (**à** to); **3** affectation.

affecter /afɛkte/ [1] *vtr* **1** to feign, to affect [*interest*]; to affect [*behaviour*]; **~ de faire/d'être** to pretend to do/to be; **2** to allocate [*funds*] (**à** to); **3** to appoint (**à** to); to post (**à, en** to); **4** to affect [*market, person*].

affectif, **-ive** /afɛktif, iv/ *adj* **1** emotional; **2** affective.

affection /afɛksjɔ̃/ *nf* **1** affection; **prendre qn en ~** to become fond of sb; **2** (Med) disease.

affectionner /afɛksjɔne/ [1] *vtr* to be fond of.

affectivité /afɛktivite/ *nf* feelings.

affectueusement /afɛktɥøzmɑ̃/ *adv* affectionately, fondly.

affectueux, **-euse** /afɛktɥø, øz/ *adj* affectionate.

affermir /afɛʀmiʀ/ [3] **I** *vtr* to strengthen [*will*]; to consolidate [*power*]; to firm up [*muscles*].
II s'affermir *v refl* (+ *v être*) [*power*] to be consolidated; [*voice*] to become stronger; [*muscles*] to firm up; [*ground*] to become firmer.

affichage /afiʃaʒ/ *nm* **1** billsticking; **campagne d'~** poster campaign; **2** (Comput) display.
■ **~ à cristaux liquides** liquid crystal display, LCD.

affiche /afiʃ/ *nf* poster; (official) notice; **à l'~** [*film*] now showing; [*play*] on; **quitter l'~** to come off.
■ **~ de théâtre** playbill.

affiché, **~e** /afiʃe/ **I** *pp* ▶ **afficher**.
II *pp adj* **1** [*ad, picture*] (put) up; [*information*] posted (up); **2** [*result*] published; **3** [*optimism, opinion*] declared; **4** (Comput) [*data*] displayed.

afficher /afiʃe/ [1] **I** *vtr* **1** to put up [*poster, notice*]; **2** to display [*prices, result*]; **~ complet** [*film, play*] to be sold out; [*hotel*] to be fully booked; **3** [*market*] to show [*rise*]; **4** to declare [*ambitions*]; to display [*scorn*]; to flaunt [*opinions, liaison*].
II s'afficher *v refl* (+ *v être*) **1** to flaunt oneself; **2** [*smile*] to appear (**sur** on).

affilée: **d'affilée** /dafile/ *phr* in a row.

affiler /afile/ [1] *vtr* to sharpen.

affilier: **s'affilier** /afilje/ [2] *v refl* (+ *v être*) to become affiliated.

affiner /afine/ [1] **I** *vtr* **1** to hone [*style*]; **2** to slim down [*waistline*].
II s'affiner *v refl* (+ *v être*) **1** [*style, taste*] to become (more) refined; **2** [*waistline*] to slim down.

affinité /afinite/ *nf* affinity.

affirmatif, **-ive**[1] /afiʀmatif, iv/ *adj* affirmative; **faire un signe de tête ~** to nod agreement.

affirmation /afiʀmasjɔ̃/ *nf* assertion; **l'~ de soi** assertiveness.

affirmative[2] /afiʀmativ/ **I** *adj f* ▶ **affirmatif**.
II *nf* affirmative.

affirmer /afiʀme/ [1] **I** *vtr* **1** to maintain; **~ faire** to claim to do; **2** to assert [*talent, authority*]; **3** to declare, to affirm [*will*].
II s'affirmer *v refl* (+ *v être*) [*tendency*] to become apparent; [*personality*] to assert itself.

affleurer /aflœʀe/ [1] *vi* [*reef*] to show on the surface; [*rock*] to come through the soil.

affligeant, **~e** /afliʒɑ̃, ɑ̃t/ *adj* pathetic.

affliger /afliʒe/ [13] *vtr* **1** to afflict (**de** with); **2** to distress.

affluence /aflɥɑ̃s/ *nf* crowd(s).

affluent /aflɥɑ̃/ *nm* tributary.

affluer /aflɥe/ [1] *vi* [*people*] to flock (**à, vers** to); [*letters*] to pour in.

affolant○, **~e** /afɔlɑ̃, ɑ̃t/ *adj* frightening.

affolement /afɔlmɑ̃/ *nm* panic.

affoler /afɔle/ [1] **I** *vtr* to throw [sb] into a panic.
II s'affoler *v refl* (+ *v être*) to panic.

affranchir /afʀɑ̃ʃiʀ/ [3] **I** *vtr* **1** to stamp [*letter*]; **2** to free [*slave, country*].
II s'affranchir *v refl* (+ *v être*) to free oneself.

affranchissement /afʀɑ̃ʃismɑ̃/ *nm* **1** stamping; (cost) postage; **2** liberation; freeing.

affréter /afʀete/ [14] *vtr* to charter.

affreusement○ /afʀøzmɑ̃/ *adv* terribly.

affreux, **-euse** /afʀø, øz/ *adj* **1** hideous; **2** awful, dreadful.

affront /afʀɔ̃/ *nm* affront.

affrontement /afʀɔ̃tmɑ̃/ *nm* confrontation.

affronter /afʀɔ̃te/ [1] *vtr* to face [*situation*]; to brave [*weather*].

affubler /afyble/ [1] *vtr* **~ qn de** to deck sb out in [*clothes*]; to saddle sb with [*nickname*].

affût /afy/ *nm* **se tenir** or **être à l'~** to lie in wait; (figurative) to be on the lookout (**de** for).

affûter /afyte/ [1] *vtr* **1** to sharpen; **2** to grind.

afin /afɛ̃/ **I afin de** *phr* **~ de faire** in order to do.
II afin que *phr* so that.

AFP /aɛfpe/ *nf* (*abbr* = **Agence France-Presse**) AFP (*French news agency*).

africain, **~e** /afʀikɛ̃, ɛn/ *adj* African.

Afrique /afʀik/ *pr nf* Africa.

agaçant, **~e** /agasɑ̃, ɑ̃t/ *adj* annoying.

agacement /agasmɑ̃/ *nm* irritation.

agacer /agase/ [12] *vtr* to annoy, to irritate.

agate /agat/ *nf* **1** agate; **2** marble.

âge /ɑʒ/ *nm* **1** age; **faire son ~** to look one's age; **un homme d'un certain ~** a middle-aged man; **2** old age; **avec l'~** as one gets older; **prendre de l'~** to grow old; **3** age, era.
■ **l'~ bête** or **ingrat** the awkward or difficult age; **l'~ mûr** maturity.

âgé, **~e** /ɑʒe/ *adj* old.

agence /aʒɑ̃s/ *nf* **1** agency; **2** (of bank) branch.
■ **~ immobilière** estate agents (GB), real-estate agency (US).

agencer /aʒɑ̃se/ [12] *vtr* to lay out [*room*].

agenda /aʒɛ̃da/ *nm* diary.

agenouiller: **s'agenouiller** /aʒnuje/ [1] *v refl* (+ *v être*) to kneel (down).

agent /aʒɑ̃/ *nm* **1** officer, official; **2** agent; **3** employee.
■ **~ de change** stockbroker; **~ de la circulation** traffic policeman; **~ commercial** sales representative; **~ de police** policeman.

agglomération /aglɔmeʀasjɔ̃/ *nf* town; village; **l'~ lyonnaise** Lyons and its suburbs.

aggloméré /aglɔmeʀe/ *nm* chipboard.

agglutiner: **s'agglutiner** /aglytine/ [1] *v refl* (+ *v être*) [*onlookers*] to crowd together (**à** at); [*insects*] to cluster together.

aggravation /agʀavasjɔ̃/ *nf* (of situation) worsening; (in debt) increase.

aggraver /agʀave/ [1] **I** *vtr* to aggravate, to make [sth] worse.
II s'aggraver *v refl* (+ *v être*) to get worse.

agile /aʒil/ *adj* agile, nimble.

agilité /aʒilite/ *nf* agility.

agir /aʒiʀ/ [3] **I** *vi* **1** to act; **2** to behave; **~ en lâche** to act like a coward; **3** [*medicine*] to take effect, to work.
II s'agir de *v impers* (+ *v être*) **de quoi s'agit-il?** what is it about?; **il s'agit de votre mari** it's about your husband; **mais il ne s'agit pas de ça!** but that's not the point!; **il s'agit de faire vite** we must act quickly.

agissements /aʒismɑ̃/ *nm pl* activities.

agitateur, **-trice** /aʒitatœʀ, tʀis/ *nm,f* agitator.

agitation /aʒitasjɔ̃/ *nf* **1** restlessness; **2** bustle (**de** in); activity; **3** unrest.

agité, **~e** /aʒite/ *adj* **1** [*sea*] rough, choppy; [*sleep*] troubled; [*period*] turbulent; [*night*] restless; **2** [*street*] bustling; [*life*] hectic.

agiter /aʒite/ [1] **I** *vtr* to wave [*hand*]; to shake [*can*]; to shake up [*liquid*].
II s'agiter *v refl* (+ *v être*) **1** to fidget; (in bed) to toss and turn; **2** to sway (in the wind); **3** to bustle about; **4** to become restless.

agneau, *pl* **~x** /aɲo/ *nm* **1** lamb; **2** lambskin.

agonie /agɔni/ *nf* death throes.

agoniser /agɔnize/ [1] *vi* to be dying.

agrafe /agʀaf/ *nf* **1** (for paper) staple; **2** (on waistband, bra) hook; **3** (Med) skin clip.

agrafer /agʀafe/ [1] *vtr* **1** to staple [sth] (together); **2** to fasten.

agrafeuse /agʀaføz/ *nf* stapler.

agraire /agʀɛʀ/ *adj* agrarian; **réforme ~** land reform.

agrandir /agʀɑ̃diʀ/ [3] **I** *vtr* **1** to enlarge [*town, photo*]; to extend [*house*]; **2** to expand [*organization*].
II s'agrandir *v refl* (+ *v être*) [*hole*] to get bigger; [*town, family*] to expand; [*eyes*] to widen.

agrandissement /agʀɑ̃dismɑ̃/ *nm* enlargement.

agréable /agʀeabl/ *adj* nice, pleasant; **~ à vivre** [*person*] pleasant to be with.

agréer /agʀee/ [11] *vtr* **1** to agree to [*request*]; **veuillez ~ mes salutations distinguées** yours faithfully; yours sincerely; **2** to register [*taxi, doctor*]; **agent agréé** authorized dealer.

agrégation /agʀegasjɔ̃/ *nf*: *high-level competitive examination for recruitment of teachers.*

agrément /agʀemɑ̃/ *nm* **1** charm; **plein d'~** very pleasant; full of charm; **sans ~** dull; unattractive; cheerless; **voyage d'~** pleasure trip; **2** (by official body) approval.

agrémenter /agʀemɑ̃te/ [1] *vtr* to liven up [*story*]; to brighten up [*garden*].

agrès /agʀɛ/ *nm pl* (Sport) apparatus.

agresser /agʀese/ [1] *vtr* **1** to attack; **2** to mug; **3** to be aggressive with.

agresseur /agʀesœʀ/ *nm* **1** attacker; **2** (in war) aggressor.

agressif, **-ive** /agʀesif, iv/ *adj* **1** aggressive; **2** violent; ear-splitting; harsh.

agression /agʀesjɔ̃/ *nf* **1** attack; **2** mugging; **3** act of aggression.

agressivité /agʀesivite/ *nf* aggressiveness, aggression.

agricole /agʀikɔl/ *adj* **produit ~** farm produce; **coopérative ~** farming cooperative.

agriculteur, **-trice** /agʀikyltœʀ, tʀis/ *nm,f* farmer.

agriculture /agʀikyltyʀ/ *nf* farming.

agripper /agʀipe/ [1] **I** *vtr* to grab.
II s'agripper *v refl* (+ *v être*) to cling (**à** to).

agro-alimentaire, *pl* **~s** /agʀoalimɑ̃tɛʀ/ *adj* food-processing.

agronomie /agʀɔnɔmi/ *nf* agronomy.

agrume /agʀym/ *nm* citrus fruit.

aguerrir /ageʀiʀ/ [3] **I** *vtr* to harden [*person*].
II s'aguerrir *v refl* (+ *v être*) to become hardened.

aguets: **aux aguets** /ozagɛ/ *phr* **être aux ~** to be on one's guard.

aguicher /agiʃe/ [1] *vtr* to lead [sb] on.

aguicheur, **-euse** /agiʃœʀ, øz/ *adj* alluring.

ah /ɑ/ *excl* oh!; **~ oui?**, **~ bon?** really?

ahuri, **~e** /ayʀi/ *adj* **1** dazed; **2** stunned.

ahurissant, **~e** /ayʀisɑ̃, ɑ̃t/ *adj* [*news, strength*] incredible; [*figure*] staggering.

aide[1] /ɛd/ **I** *nmf* assistant.
II aide- (*combining form*) **~-soignant** nursing auxiliary (GB), nurse's aide (US).

aide[2] /ɛd/ *nf* **1** (from individual, group) help, assistance; (from state) assistance; **apporter son ~ à qn** to help sb; **2** (financial) aid; **~ au développement** foreign aid; **~ judiciaire** legal aid.

aider /ede/ [1] **I** *vtr* **1** to help (**à faire** to do); **2** to aid; to give aid to.
II aider à *v+prep* to help toward(s) [*understanding, funding*].
III s'aider *v refl* (+ *v être*) **1 s'~ de** to use [*dictionary, tool*]; **2** to help each other.

aïeul, **~e** /ɑjœl/ *nm,f* grandfather/grandmother.

aïeux /ɑjø/ *nm pl* ancestors.

aigle /ɛgl/ *nm, nf* eagle.

aiglefin /ɛgləfɛ̃/ *nm* haddock.

aigre /ɛgʀ/ *adj* [*smell, taste*] sour.

aigre-doux, **-douce**, *pl* **aigres-doux**, **aigres-douces** /ɛgʀədu, dus/ *adj* (Culin) [*fruit, taste*] bitter-sweet; [*sauce*] sweet and sour.

aigreur /ɛgʀœʀ/ *nf* **1** sourness; sharpness; **2 ~s d'estomac** heartburn; **3** (figurative) bitterness.

aigrir /egʀiʀ/ [3] *vtr* to embitter.

aigu, **aiguë** /egy/ **I** *adj* **1** [*sound, voice*] high-pitched; **2** [*pain, symptom*] acute; **3** [*sense*] keen.
II *nm* (Mus) treble; high notes.

aiguillage /egɥijaʒ/ *nm* (for trains) points (GB), switch (US); **une erreur d'~** a signalling[GB] error.

aiguille /egɥij/ *nf* **1** needle; **~ à coudre** sewing needle; **2** (of watch, chronometer) hand; (of gauge) needle; (of weighing scales) pointer; **dans le sens des ~s d'une montre** clockwise.

aiguiller /egɥije/ [1] *vtr* **1** to direct [*person*]; to send [*mail*]; **2** (towards career) to guide [*person*].

aiguilleur /egɥijœʀ/ *nm* **~ du ciel** air traffic controller.

aiguiser /egize/ [1] *vtr* **1** to sharpen [*knife*]; **2** to whet [*appetite*]; to arouse [*curiosity*].

ail, *pl* **~s** or **aulx** /aj, o/ *nm* garlic.

aile /ɛl/ *nf* (gen) wing; (of windmill) sail; (of car) wing (GB), fender (US); (of army) flank.
IDIOMS **battre de l'~** to be in a bad way; **se sentir pousser des ~s** to feel exhilarated; **prendre un coup dans l'~** to suffer a setback; **voler de ses propres ~s** to stand on one's own two feet.

aileron /ɛlʀɔ̃/ *nm* (of bird) wing tip; (of shark) fin; (of plane) aileron; (of ship) fin.

ailier /elje/ *nm* (in football) winger; (in rugby) wing three-quarter.

ailleurs /ajœʀ/ **I** *adv* elsewhere.
II d'ailleurs *phr* besides, moreover.
III par ailleurs *phr* **ils se sont par ~ engagés à faire** they have also undertaken to do.
IDIOMS **être ~** to be miles away.

aimable /ɛmabl/ *adj* **1** [*word*] kind; **2** [*remark*] polite.

aimant, **~e** /ɛmɑ̃, ɑ̃t/ **I** *adj* affectionate.
II *nm* magnet.

aimer /eme/ [1] **I** *vtr* **1** to love [*person*]; **~ qn à la folie** to adore sb; **2** to like, to be fond of [*person, activity, thing*]; **~ faire** to like doing; **il aime autant le vin que la bière** he likes wine as much as he likes beer; **j'aime autant te dire que** I may as well tell you that; **~ mieux** to prefer; **il n'a rien de cassé? j'aime mieux ça!** (in relief) nothing's broken? thank goodness!; **j'aime mieux ça!** (threateningly) that's more like it!
II s'aimer *v refl* (+ *v être*) **1** to love each other; **2** to like each other.

aine /ɛn/ *nf* groin.

aîné, **~e** /ene/ **I** *adj* elder; eldest.
II *nm,f* **1** elder son/daughter, elder child; **2** eldest son/daughter, eldest child; **3** elder brother/sister; **4** elder; oldest.

ainsi /ɛ̃si/ **I** *adv* **1** thus; **le mélange ~ obtenu** the mixture obtained in this way; **Charlotte, c'est ~ qu'on m'appelait** Charlotte, that's what they used to call me; **s'il en est ~** if that's the way it is; **le jury se compose ~** the panel is made up as follows; **~ soit-il** amen; **2** thus, so
II ainsi que *phr* **1** as well as; **2** as; **~ que nous en avions convenu** as we had agreed.

air /ɛʀ/ *nm* **1** air; **le bon ~** clean air; **concert en plein ~** open-air concert; **activités de plein ~** outdoor activities; **aller prendre l'~** to go and get some fresh air; **on manque d'~ ici** it's stuffy in here; **être dans l'~** [*reform, idea*] to be in the air; **regarder en l'~** to look up; **avoir le nez en l'~** to daydream; **en l'~** [*threat, words*] empty; [*plan, idea*] vague; **tout mettre en l'~**○ to make a dreadful mess; **de l'~**○! get lost○!; **2 il y a de l'~** (in room) there's a draught (GB) or draft (US); (outside) there's a breeze; **il n'y a pas d'~** there's no wind; **un courant d'~** a draught (GB) or draft (US); **3** manner; expression; **avoir un drôle**

d'~ to look odd; **d'un ~ fâché** angrily; **il y a un ~ de famille entre vous deux** you two share a family likeness; **cela m'en a tout l'~** it seems like it to me; **j'aurais l'~ de quoi?** I'd look a right idiot!; **cela a l'~ d'être une usine** it looks like a factory; **il a l'~ de vouloir faire beau** it looks as if it's going to be fine; **4** tune; **un ~ d'opéra** an aria.

IDIOMS **il ne manque pas d'~**○**!** he's got a nerve!; **se donner des grands ~s** to put on airs; **j'ai besoin de changer d'~** I need a change of scene.

aire /ɛʀ/ *nf* **1** (surface) area; **2** eyrie.
■ **~ d'atterrissage** (for plane) landing strip; (for helicopter) landing pad; **~ de jeu** playground; **~ de services** motorway (GB) or freeway (US) service station; **~ de stationnement** parking area.

airelle /ɛʀɛl/ *nf* **1** bilberry; **2** cranberry.

aisance /ɛzɑ̃s/ *nf* **1** ease; **2** affluence, comfort.

aise /ɛz/ **I aises** *nf pl* **aimer ses ~s** to like one's creature comforts; **il prenait ses ~s sur le canapé** he was stretched out on the sofa.
II à l'aise *phr* **être à l'~** or **à son ~** (physically) to be comfortable; (financially) to be comfortably off; (psychologically) to be at ease; **mal à l'~** ill at ease; **à votre ~!** as you wish or like!

aisé, **~e** /eze/ *adj* **1** easy; **2** wealthy.

aisément /ezemɑ̃/ *adv* easily.

aisselle /ɛsɛl/ *nf* armpit.

ajouré, **~e** /aʒuʀe/ *adj* [*tablecloth*] openwork; [*edge, border*] hemstitched.

ajournement /aʒuʀnəmɑ̃/ *nm* (of decision) postponement; (of trial) adjournment.

ajourner /aʒuʀne/ [1] *vtr* to postpone [*decision, plan*]; to adjourn [*debate, trial*].

ajout /aʒu/ *nm* addition.

ajouter /aʒute/ [1] **I** *vtr* to add (**à** to).
II s'ajouter *v refl* (+ *v être*) **s'~ à** to be added to.

ajuster /aʒyste/ [1] *vtr* **1** to adjust [*strap, price, timetable*]; to alter [*garment*] (**à** to); to calibrate [*weighing scales*]; **~ qch à** or **sur qch** to make sth fit sth; **corsage ajusté** close-fitting bodice; **2** to arrange [*hair*]; to straighten [*hat, tie*]; **3 ~ son tir** to adjust one's aim.

alaise = **alèse**.

alambic /alɑ̃bik/ *nm* still.

alangui, **~e** /alɑ̃gi/ *adj* **1** languid; **2** listless.

alarmant, **~e** /alaʀmɑ̃, ɑ̃t/ *adj* alarming.

alarme /alaʀm/ *nf* alarm.

alarmer /alaʀme/ [1] **I** *vtr* to alarm.
II s'alarmer *v refl* (+ *v être*) to become alarmed (**de qch** about sth).

Albanie /albani/ *pr nf* Albania.

albâtre /albɑtʀ/ *nm* alabaster.

albatros /albatʀos/ *nm inv* albatross.

albinos /albinos/ *adj inv, nmf inv* albino.

album /albɔm/ *nm* **1** illustrated book; **~ de bandes dessinées** comic strip book; **2** album.
■ **~ à colorier** colouring[GB] book.

albumine /albymin/ *nf* albumin.

alchimie /alʃimi/ *nf* alchemy.

alcool /alkɔl/ *nm* **1** alcohol; **~ de poire** pear brandy; **teneur en ~** alcohol content; **2** drink; **l'~ au volant** drink-driving; **3 un ~** a spirit.
■ **~ à brûler** methylated spirits; **~ à 90°** ≈ surgical spirit (GB), rubbing alcohol (US).

alcoolémie /alkɔlemi/ *nf* presence of alcohol in the blood.

alcoolique /alkɔlik/ *adj, nmf* alcoholic.

alcoolisé, **~e** /alkɔlize/ *adj* alcoholic.

alcoolisme /alkɔlism/ *nm* alcoholism.

alcootest /alkɔtɛst/ *nm* **1** Breathalyzer®; **2** breath test.

alcôve /alkov/ *nf* alcove.

aléas /alea/ *nm pl* vagaries; (financial) hazards.

aléatoire /aleatwaʀ/ *adj* **1** [*events*] unpredictable; [*profession*] insecure; **2** [*number*] random.

alentours /alɑ̃tuʀ/ *nm pl* surrounding area.

alerte /alɛʀt/ **I** *adj* alert; lively.
II *nf* alert; **donner l'~** to raise the alarm; **~ générale** full alert.
■ **~ à la bombe** bomb scare.

alerter /alɛʀte/ [1] *vtr* to alert (**sur** to).

alèse /alɛz/ *nf* undersheet, mattress protector.

algèbre /alʒɛbʀ/ *nf* algebra.

Algérie /alʒeʀi/ *pr nf* Algeria.

algérien, **-ienne** /alʒeʀjɛ̃, ɛn/ *adj* Algerian.

algue /alg/ *nf* **1 des ~s** algae; **2** seaweed.

alias /aljas/ *adv* alias.

alibi /alibi/ *nm* **1** (Law) alibi; **2** excuse.

aliénation /aljenasjɔ̃/ *nf* alienation.

aliéné, **~e** /aljene/ *nm,f* insane person.

alignement /aliɲ(ə)mɑ̃/ *nm* **1** row, line; **2** alignment; **3 ~ de qch sur qch** [*currency, salaries*] bringing into line of sth with sth.

aligner /aliɲe/ [1] **I** *vtr* **1** to line [sth] up; **2 ~ qch sur qch** to bring sth into line with sth; **3** to give a list of [*figures*]; **4** to line up [*players*].
II s'aligner *v refl* (+ *v être*) **1** [*houses, trees*] to be in a line; **2** [*people*] to line up; **3 s'~ sur** to align oneself with [*country, party, ideas*].

aliment /alimɑ̃/ *nm* (gen) food; (for farm animals) feed; (for plants) nutrient.

alimentaire /alimɑ̃tɛʀ/ *adj* [*needs, habits*] dietary; [*industry, shortage*] food; **régime ~** diet.

alimentation /alimɑ̃tasjɔ̃/ *nf* **1** diet; **2** feeding; **3** food; **magasin d'~** food shop; **4** food industry; **5** supply, feeding; **l'~ en eau** the water supply.

alimenter /alimɑ̃te/ [1] **I** *vtr* **1** to feed [*person, animal*]; **2** to feed, to supply [*engine, boiler*]; **3** to fuel [*conversation, hostility*].
II s'alimenter *v refl* (+ *v être*) **1** [*person*] to eat; [*animal*] to feed; **2** (with water, gas) **s'~ en** to be supplied with.

alinéa /alinea/ *nm* **1** indentation; **2** indented line; **3** paragraph.

alité, **~e** /alite/ *adj* **être ~** to be confined to bed.

allaitement /alɛtmɑ̃/ *nm* **1** breast-feeding; **2** suckling.

allaiter /alete/ [1] *vtr* **1** to breast-feed; **2** to suckle.

allant /alɑ̃/ *nm* drive, bounce.

allécher /aleʃe/ [14] *vtr* to tempt (**avec** with).

allée /ale/ **I** *nf* **1** (in garden, wood) path; (leading to house) drive; (in town) avenue; **2** aisle.

II allées *nf pl* **~s et venues** comings and goings.

allégé, **~e** /aleʒe/ **I** *pp* ▶ **alléger**.

II *pp adj* low-fat; [*chocolate*] diet.

allégement /alɛʒmɑ̃/ *nm* (of charges) reduction; (of restrictions, controls) relaxing; **~ fiscal** tax relief.

alléger /aleʒe/ [15] **I** *vtr* **1** to lighten [*load, weight*]; **2** to reduce [*debt*] (**de** by); to cut [*taxes*]; to relax [*control, restrictions*].

II s'alléger *v refl* (+ *v être*) **1** [*load*] to get lighter; **2** [*debt, taxation*] to be reduced; [*embargo*] to be relaxed.

allégorie /alegɔʀi/ *nf* allegory.

allègre /alɛgʀ/ *adj* [*style*] light; [*tone*] lighthearted; [*step, mood*] buoyant.

allégrement /alegʀəmɑ̃/ *adv* joyfully; (ironic) blithely.

allégresse /alegʀɛs/ *nf* joy.

allegro /alegʀo/ *adv* allegro.

alléguer /alege/ [14] *vtr* **1** to invoke; **2** to allege.

Allemagne /almaɲ/ *pr nf* Germany.

allemand, **~e** /almɑ̃, ɑ̃d/ **I** *adj* German.

II *nm* (language) German.

aller[1] /ale/ [9] **I** *v aux* **je vais apprendre l'italien** I'm going to learn Italian; **j'allais partir quand il est arrivé** I was about to leave when he arrived; **il est allé voir l'exposition** he went to see the exhibition; **va leur parler** go and speak to them.

II *vi* (+ *v être*) **1 comment vas-tu, comment ça va?** how are you?; **ça va (bien)** I'm fine; **~ beaucoup mieux** to be much better; **bois ça, ça ira mieux** drink this, you'll feel better; **les affaires vont bien** business is good; **qu'est-ce qui ne va pas?** what's the matter?; **ne pas ~ sans peine** or **mal** not to be easy; **ça devrait ~ de soi** it should be obvious; **ça va pas non**○, **ça va pas la tête**○**?** are you crazy○?; **2** to go; **où vas-tu?** where are you going?; **~ nager/au travail** to go swimming/to work; **vas-y, demande-leur!** go on, ask them!; **allons-y!** let's go!; **allons!**, **allez!** come on!; **~ et venir** to pace up and down; to run in and out; **les nouvelles vont vite** news travels fast; **j'y vais** (answering phone, door) I'll get it; (when leaving)○ I'm off○; **~ contre la loi** to break the law; to be against the law; **3 ça va, ça ira**○, **ça peut aller**○ that'll do; it'll do; **ça va comme ça** it's all right as it is; **ça ne va pas du tout** that's no good at all; **lundi ça (te) va?** would Monday suit you?; **4 ~ à qn** to fit sb; **5 ~ à qn** to suit sb; **ta cravate ne va pas avec ta chemise** your tie doesn't go with your shirt; **6 ~ jusqu'à tuer** to go as far as to kill; **la voiture peut ~ jusqu'à 200 km/h** the car can do up to 200 kph; **la période qui va de 1918 à 1939** the period between 1918 and 1939; **~ sur ses 17 ans** to be going on 17; **7 y ~ de sa petite larme** to shed a little tear.

III s'en aller *v refl* (+ *v être*) **1 s'en aller** to go, to leave, to be off; to go away; **2 la tache ne s'en va pas** the stain won't come out; **3** (formal) to pass away, to die.

IV *v impers* **1 il y va de ma réputation** my reputation is at stake; **2 il en va de même pour toi** that goes for you too.

aller[2] /ale/ *nm* **1 j'ai pris le bus à l'~** I took the bus there; I took the bus here; **il n'arrête pas de faire des ~s et retours entre chez lui et son bureau** he's always going to and fro between the house and the office; **2 ~ (simple)** single (ticket) (GB), one-way ticket (**pour** to); **~ retour** return ticket, round trip (US); **3** (Sport) **(match) ~** first leg.

allergie /alɛʀʒi/ *nf* (Med) allergy.

allergique /alɛʀʒik/ *adj* allergic (**à** to).

alliage /aljaʒ/ *nm* **1** alloy; **2** (figurative) combination.

alliance /aljɑ̃s/ *nf* **1** wedding ring; **2** alliance.

allié, **~e** /alje/ **I** *pp* ▶ **allier**.

II *pp adj* allied.

III *nm,f* **1** ally; **les ~s** the Allies; **2** relative.

allier /alje/ [2] **I** *vtr* **1** to combine (**et, à** with); **2** (Tech) to alloy [*metals*] (**à, avec** with).

II s'allier *v refl* (+ *v être*) to form an alliance.

alligator /aligatɔʀ/ *nm* alligator.

allô /alo/ *excl* hello!, hallo!

allocation /al(l)ɔkasjɔ̃/ *nf* **1** allocation, granting; **2** benefit (GB), benefits (US).

■ **~ chômage** unemployment benefit (GB) or benefits (US); **~s familiales** family allowance.

allocution /al(l)ɔkysjɔ̃/ *nf* address.

allongé, **~e** /alɔ̃ʒe/ *adj* **1 être ~** [*person*] to be lying down; to be reclining; **2** elongated.

allonger /alɔ̃ʒe/ [13] **I** *vtr* **1** to lay [sb] down; **2** to extend [*list, holiday*]; **cette coiffure t'allonge le visage** that hairstyle makes your face look longer; **3** to water [sth] down [*coffee*].

II s'allonger *v refl* (+ *v être*) **1** to lie down; **2** to get longer.

allouer /alwe/ [1] *vtr* to allocate [*sum, allowance, budget*]; to grant [*loan*]; to allot [*time*].

allumage /alymaʒ/ *nm* (Aut) ignition.

allumé○, **~e** /alyme/ *adj* **1** mad○; **2** tipsy○.

allumer /alyme/ [1] **I** *vtr* **1** to light [*candle, gas*]; to start [*fire*]; **2** to switch [sth] on, to turn [sth] on; **laisser ses phares allumés** to leave one's headlights on.

II s'allumer *v refl* (+ *v être*) **1** [*heating, radio, lighting*] to come on; **2 son regard s'alluma** his face lit up.

allumette /alymɛt/ *nf* match, matchstick.

allumeur○, **-euse** /alymœʀ, øz/ *nm,f* tease.

allure /alyʀ/ *nf* **1** (of walker) pace; (of vehicle) speed; **ralentir son ~** to slow down; **à toute ~** at top speed; **à cette ~** at this rate; **2** (of animal) gait; **3** (of person) appearance; **4** style; **avoir de l'~** to have style.

allusif, **-ive** /alyzif, iv/ *adj* [*remark*] allusive; [*person*] indirect.

allusion /alyzjɔ̃/ *nf* allusion (**à** to); **faire ~ à** to allude to.

alluvial, **~e**, *mpl* **-iaux** /alyvjal, o/ *adj* alluvial.

alluvion /alyvjɔ̃/ *nf* alluvium; **des ~s** alluvia.

almanach /almana(k)/ *nm* almanac.

alors /alɔʀ/ **I** *adv* **1** then; **il avait ~ 18 ans** he was 18 at the time; **la mode d'~** the fashion in those days; **jusqu'~** until then; **2** then; **(mais) ~ cela change tout!** but that changes everything!; **et (puis) ~?** so what?; **3** so; **il y avait une grève des trains, ~ j'ai pris l'autobus** there was a train strike, so I took the bus; **4 ou ~** or else; **5**○ so; **~ il me dit**... so he said to me...; **6 non mais ~!** honestly!
II alors que *phr* **1** while; **2** when.
III alors même que *phr* even though.

alouette /alwɛt/ *nf* lark.

alourdir /aluʀdiʀ/ [3] **I** *vtr* **1** to weigh [sb] down [*person*]; to make [sth] tense [*atmosphere*]; **2** to increase [*tax, charges*].
II s'alourdir *v refl* (+ *v être*) [*eyelids*] to begin to droop; [*air*] to grow heavy.

alphabet /alfabɛ/ *nm* alphabet.

alphabétique /alfabetik/ *adj* alphabetical.

alphabétiser /alfabetize/ [1] *vtr* to teach [sb] to read and write.

alpin, **~e** /alpɛ̃, in/ *adj* alpine.

alpinisme /alpinism/ *nm* mountaineering.

altération /alteʀasjɔ̃/ *nf* (of faculties) impairment (**de** of); (of foodstuff) spoiling (**de** of); (in environment) deterioration (**de** in).

altérer /alteʀe/ [14] *vtr* **1** to affect [*taste, health*]; **2** to spoil [*foodstuff*]; to fade [*colour*]; **3** to distort [*text*]; to adulterate [*substance*].

alternance /altɛʀnɑ̃s/ *nf* alternation; **en ~ avec** alternately with.

alternateur /altɛʀnatœʀ/ *nm* alternator.

alternatif, **-ive**[1] /altɛʀnatif, iv/ *adj* **1** (gen) alternate; **2** [*current*] alternating; **3** [*culture, theatre*] alternative.

alternative[2] /altɛʀnativ/ **I** *adj f* ▸ **alternatif**.
II *nf* alternative.

alterner /altɛʀne/ [1] **I** *vtr* to alternate.
II *vi* **1** to alternate; **2 ~ avec qn pour faire** to take turns with sb (at) doing.

altesse /altɛs/ *nf* **1** highness; **2** prince/princess.

altier, **-ière** /altje, ɛʀ/ *adj* haughty.

altitude /altityd/ *nf* altitude; **en ~** high up (in the mountains).

alto /alto/ **I** *adj* alto.
II *nm* **1** (instrument) viola; **2** viola player (GB), violin (US); **3** (voice) alto.

altruiste /altʀɥist/ *adj* altruistic.

alu○ /aly/, **aluminium** /alyminjɔm/ *nm* aluminium (GB), aluminum (US).

alvéole /alveɔl/ *nf* **1** (in honeycomb) cell; **2** (in rock) cavity.

alvéolé, **~e** /alveɔle/ *adj* honeycombed.

amabilité /amabilite/ *nf* **1** kindness; **2** courtesy.

amadouer /amadwe/ [1] *vtr* to coax, to cajole.

amaigrir /amegʀiʀ/ [3] *vtr* to make [sb] thinner.

amaigrissant, **~e** /amegʀisɑ̃, ɑ̃t/ *adj* slimming.

amalgame /amalgam/ *nm* **1** (gen) mixture; **2** (in dentistry, chemistry) amalgam.

amalgamer /amalgame/ [1] *vtr* **1** to lump together [*problems*]; to mix [*feelings, people*]; **2** to blend, to amalgamate [*ingredients*].

amande /amɑ̃d/ *nf* **1** almond; **2** kernel.

amant /amɑ̃/ *nm* lover.

amarre /amaʀ/ *nf* rope; **les ~s** moorings.

amarrer /amaʀe/ [1] *vtr* **1** to moor [*boat*]; **2** to tie (**à, sur** to).

amas /ama/ *nm inv* pile; heap.

amasser /amase/ [1] **I** *vtr* to amass, to accumulate [*fortune, books*]; to collect [*proof*].
II s'amasser *v refl* (+ *v être*) [*snow, objects*] to pile up; [*proof, evidence*] to build up.

amateur /amatœʀ/ **I** *adj inv* amateur.
II *nm* **1** (non-professional) amateur; **2** (of sport, photography) enthusiast; (of wine) connoisseur; **3 il vend sa voiture, vous êtes ~?** he's selling his car, are you interested?

amazone /amazon/ *nf* **en ~** sidesaddle.

ambassade /ɑ̃basad/ *nf* embassy.

ambassadeur /ɑ̃basadœʀ/ *nm* ambassador.

ambassadrice /ɑ̃basadʀis/ *nf* **1** ambassador; **2** ambassador's wife.

ambiance /ɑ̃bjɑ̃s/ *nf* atmosphere.

ambiant, **~e** /ɑ̃bjɑ̃, ɑ̃t/ *adj* **1** [*air*] surrounding; **à température ~e** at room temperature; **2** prevailing.

ambigu, **ambiguë** /ɑ̃bigy/ *adj* [*remark, situation*] ambiguous; [*feeling, attitude*] ambivalent.

ambiguïté /ɑ̃bigɥite/ *nf* ambiguity; enigmatic nature; ambivalence.

ambitieux, **-ieuse** /ɑ̃bisjø, øz/ *adj* ambitious.

ambition /ɑ̃bisjɔ̃/ *nf* ambition.

ambitionner /ɑ̃bisjɔne/ [1] *vtr* to aspire to.

ambivalent, **~e** /ɑ̃bivalɑ̃, ɑ̃t/ *adj* ambivalent.

ambre /ɑ̃bʀ/ *nm* **1 ~ (jaune)** amber; **2 ~ (gris)** ambergris.

ambulance /ɑ̃bylɑ̃s/ *nf* ambulance.

ambulancier, **-ière** /ɑ̃bylɑ̃sje, ɛʀ/ *nm,f* ambulance driver.

ambulant, **~e** /ɑ̃bylɑ̃, ɑ̃t/ *adj* [*circus*] travelling[GB]; **vendeur ~** (in station) snack trolley man; **un cadavre ~**○ a walking skeleton○.

âme /ɑm/ *nf* soul; **Dieu ait son ~** God rest his/her soul; **socialiste dans l'~** a socialist to the core; **en mon ~ et conscience** in all honesty; **pas ~ qui vive** not a (single) soul; **~ sœur** soul mate.

amélioration /ameljɔʀasjɔ̃/ *nf* improvement.

améliorer /ameljɔʀe/ [1] *vtr*, **s'améliorer** *v refl* (+ *v être*) to improve.

amen /amɛn/ *nm inv* amen.

aménagé, **~e** /amenaʒe/ **I** *pp* ▸ **aménager**.
II *pp adj* **1** converted; **2** equipped.

aménagement /amenaʒmɑ̃/ *nm* **1** (of r

town) development; **2** (of roads) construction; (of parks, green spaces) creation; **3** (of house, boat) fitting; **4** (of timetable) adjustment; **l'~ du temps de travail** flexible working hours.

aménager /amenaʒe/ [13] *vtr* **1** to convert; to do up [*house, attic*]; **2** to equip [*kitchen*]; to develop [*region*]; **3** to create [*parks, green spaces*]; to build [*road*]; to lay out [*garden*]; **4** to arrange [*timetable*]; to adjust [*regulations*].

amende /amɑ̃d/ *nf* fine.

amener /amne/ [16] *vtr* **1 ~ qn quelque part** to take sb somewhere; **2** (accompany) **~ qn (quelque part)** to bring sb (somewhere); **3** (controversial) **~ qch (à qn)** to bring (sb) sth; **4** to cause [*problems, illness*]; to bring [*rain, fame*]; **5** to bring up [*issue, subject*]; **être bien amené** [*conclusion*] to be well-presented; **6 ~ qn à qch/faire** to lead sb to sth/to do.

amenuiser: **s'amenuiser** /amənɥize/ [1] *v refl* (+ *v être*) [*supplies*] to dwindle; [*risk*] to lessen.

amer, **-ère** /amɛʀ/ *adj* bitter.

américain, **~e** /ameʀikɛ̃, ɛn/ **I** *adj* American; **à l'~e** (gen) in the American style; (Culin) à l'américaine.

II *nm* American English.

Amérique /ameʀik/ *pr nf* America.

amerrir /ameʀiʀ/ [3] *vi* [*hydroplane*] to land (on water); [*spacecraft*] to splash down.

amertume /amɛʀtym/ *nf* bitterness.

ameublement /amœbləmɑ̃/ *nm* **1** furniture; **2** furniture trade; **3** (of room, house) furnishing.

ameuter /amøte/ [1] *vtr* **1** [*person, noise*] to bring [sb] out; **2** to stir [sb] up.

ami, **~e** /ami/ **I** *adj* friendly.

II *nm,f* friend; **en ~** as a friend; **un ~ des bêtes** an animal lover; ▶ **faux**[1].

IDIOMS **les bons comptes font les bons ~s** (Proverb) a debt paid is a friend kept.

amiable: **à l'amiable** /alamjabl/ *phr* [*separate*] on friendly terms; [*separation*] amicable; [*divorce*] by mutual consent; ▶ **constat**.

amiante /amjɑ̃t/ *nm* asbestos.

amical, **~e**[1], *pl* **-aux** /amikal, o/ *adj* friendly.

amicale[2] /amikal/ *nf* association.

amicalement /amikalmɑ̃/ *adv* **1** [*greet, receive*] warmly; [*compete*] in a friendly way; **2** (at end of letter) (**bien**) **~** best wishes.

amidon /amidɔ̃/ *nm* starch.

amincir /amɛ̃siʀ/ [3] *vtr* to make [sb] look slimmer.

amiral, *mpl* **-aux** /amiʀal, o/ *nm* admiral.

amitié /amitje/ **I** *nf* friendship; **se lier d'~ avec qn** to strike up a friendship with sb.

II amitiés *nf pl* (at end of letter) kindest regards.

ammoniac /amɔnjak/ *nm* (gas) ammonia.

ammoniaque /amɔnjak/ *nf* ammonia.

amnésie /amnezi/ *nf* amnesia.

amnésique /amnezik/ *adj* amnesic.

amnistie /amnisti/ *nf* amnesty.

amoindrir /amwɛ̃dʀiʀ/ [3] *vtr* to reduce [*resistance*]; to weaken [*person*].

amonceler /amɔ̃sle/ [19] **I** *vtr* to pile up.

II s'amonceler *v refl* (+ *v être*) [*clouds, snow*] to build up; [*evidence, problems*] to pile up.

amoncellement /amɔ̃sɛlmɑ̃/ *nm* pile; mass.

amont /amɔ̃/ *nm* (of river) upper reaches; **en ~** upstream (**de** from); **naviguer d'~ en aval** to sail downstream.

amoral, **~e**, *mpl* **-aux** /amɔʀal, o/ *adj* amoral.

amorce /amɔʀs/ *nf* **1** (of discussion) initiation; **2** bait; **3** (of explosive) cap, primer; (of gun) cap.

amorcer /amɔʀse/ [12] *vtr* **1** to begin; **2** to prime.

amorphe /amɔʀf/ *adj* apathetic.

amortir /amɔʀtiʀ/ [3] *vtr* **1** to deaden [*noise*]; to absorb [*shock, impact*]; to break [*fall*]; **2** to pay off [*debt*]; **3 j'ai amorti mon ordinateur en quelques mois** my computer paid for itself in a few months.

amortissement /amɔʀtismɑ̃/ *nm* **1** (of noise) deadening; (of shock) absorption; (of fall) cushioning; **2** (of debt) paying off; **3** (of equipment) depreciation.

amortisseur /amɔʀtisœʀ/ *nm* shock absorber.

amour /amuʀ/ **I** *nm* love; **pour l'~ de** for the sake of; out of love for; **c'était un ~ de jeunesse** it was a youthful romance.

II amours *nm pl* or *nf pl* **1** (Zool) mating; **2** love affairs; **à tes ~s!** (to somebody sneezing) bless you!

amouracher: **s'amouracher** /amuʀaʃe/ [1] *v refl* (+ *v être*) **s'~ de** to become infatuated with.

amourette /amuʀɛt/ *nf* passing infatuation.

amoureux, **-euse** /amuʀø, øz/ *adj* in love.

amour-propre /amuʀpʀɔpʀ/ *nm* self-esteem; pride.

amovible /amɔvibl/ *adj* detachable; removable.

ampère /ɑ̃pɛʀ/ *nm* amp, ampère.

amphibie /ɑ̃fibi/ *adj* (Zool, Aut) amphibious.

amphithéâtre /ɑ̃fiteɑtʀ/ *nm* **1** (natural, ancient) amphitheatre[GB]; **2** (at university) lecture hall.

amphore /ɑ̃fɔʀ/ *nf* amphora.

ample /ɑ̃pl/ *adj* **1** [*coat, dress*] loose-fitting; [*skirt, sleeve*] full; [*gesture*] sweeping; **2** [*quantity*] ample; [*harvest*] abundant; [*details*] full.

amplement /ɑ̃pləmɑ̃/ *adv* fully; **c'est ~ suffisant** that's more than enough!

ampleur /ɑ̃plœʀ/ *nf* (of problem) size; (of project, subject, survey) scope; (of event, disaster, task) scale; (of damage, reaction) extent.

amplificateur /ɑ̃plifikatœʀ/ *nm* amplifier.

amplifier /ɑ̃plifje/ [2] **I** *vtr* to amplify [*sound, current*]; to magnify [*rumour*].

II s'amplifier *v refl* (+ *v être*) [*sound*] to grow louder; [*trade*] to increase; [*strike*] to intensify.

ampoule /ɑ̃pul/ *nf* **1 ~ (électrique)** (light) bulb; **2** (Med) (drinkable) phial; (injectable) ampoule; **3** blister.

amputation /ɑ̃pytasjɔ̃/ *nf* amputation.

amputer /ɑ̃pyte/ [1] *vtr* **1** (Med) to amputate [*limb*]; to perform an amputation on [*person*]; **2** to cut [sth] drastically [*budget*].

amusant, **~e** /amyzɑ̃, ɑ̃t/ *adj* **1** entertaining; **2** funny.

amuse-gueule /amyzgœl/ *nm inv* cocktail snack (GB), munchies (US).

amusement /amyzmɑ̃/ *nm* entertainment.

amuser /amyze/ [1] **I** *vtr* **1** to entertain; to amuse; **2** to distract.
II s'amuser *v refl* (+ *v être*) **1** to play; **pour s'~** for fun; **2 bien s'~** to have a good time.

amuseur, **-euse** /amyzœʀ, øz/ *nm,f* entertainer.

amygdale /amidal/ *nf* tonsil.

an /ɑ̃/ *nm* year; **avoir huit ~s** to be eight (years old); **en l'~ deux mille** in the year two thousand; **l'~ 55 avant J.-C./après J.-C.** 55 BC/AD.
IDIOMS **bon ~, mal ~** year in, year out.

anabolisant /anabolizɑ̃/ *nm* anabolic steroid.

anachronique /anakʀɔnik/ *adj* anachronistic.

anal, **~e**, *mpl* **-aux** /anal, o/ *adj* anal.

analogie /analɔʒi/ *nf* analogy.

analogue /analɔg/ *adj* similar (**à** to).

analphabète /analfabɛt/ *adj*, *nmf* illiterate.

analyse /analiz/ *nf* **1** analysis; **faire l'~ de qch** to analyse[GB] sth; **2** (Med) test; **3** psychoanalysis.

analyser /analize/ [1] *vtr* **1** (gen) to analyse[GB]; **2** (Med) to test [*blood, urine*].

ananas /anana(s)/ *nm inv* pineapple.

anarchie /anaʀʃi/ *nf* anarchy.

anarchiste /anaʀʃist/ **I** *adj* anarchistic.
II *nmf* anarchist.

anatomie /anatɔmi/ *nf* anatomy.

ancêtre /ɑ̃sɛtʀ/ *nmf* ancestor.

anchois /ɑ̃ʃwa/ *nm inv* anchovy.

ancien, **-ienne**[1] /ɑ̃sjɛ̃, ɛn/ **I** *adj* **1** [*champion, president, capital*] former; **2** [*history, language*] ancient; **3** [*style, book, building*] old; [*car*] vintage; [*piece of furniture*] antique; **4 c'est lui le plus ~** (in job) he's been here longest.
II *nm* **1** (in tribe, congregation) elder; (in company) senior member; **les ~s** the older people; **2** old member; former student; **3 l'~** older property; (furniture) antiques.
■ **~ combattant** veteran.

ancienne[2]: **à l'ancienne** /alɑ̃sjɛn/ *phr* [*jam, piece of furniture*] traditional-style.

anciennement /ɑ̃sjɛnmɑ̃/ *adv* formerly.

ancienneté /ɑ̃sjɛnte/ *nf* **1** (of person) seniority; **trois ans d'~** three years' service; **2** (of tradition, relic) antiquity; (of building) age.

ancre /ɑ̃kʀ/ *nf* (Naut) anchor.

ancrer /ɑ̃kʀe/ [1] **I** *vtr* **1** to anchor [*ship*]; **2** to fix [*idea*]; to establish [*custom*].
II s'ancrer *v refl* (+ *v être*) **1** to anchor; **2** [*idea*] to become fixed; [*custom*] to become established.

Andorre /ɑ̃dɔʀ/ *pr nf* Andorra.

andouille /ɑ̃duj/ *nf* **1** (Culin) andouille; **2**° fool.

âne /ɑn/ *nm* **1** (Zool) donkey, ass; **2**° dimwit°.
IDIOMS **faire l'~ pour avoir du son** to act dumb to find out more.

anéantir /aneɑ̃tiʀ/ [3] *vtr* **1** to ruin [*crops, harvest*]; to lay waste to [*town*]; to shatter [*hopes*]; **2** [*news*] to crush; [*strain*] to exhaust.

anéantissement /aneɑ̃tismɑ̃/ *nm* **1** destruction, devastation; **2** (of hope) shattering; **3** (of person) total collapse.

anecdote /anɛkdɔt/ *nf* anecdote.

anémie /anemi/ *nf* **1** anaemia; **2** weakness.

anémique /anemik/ *adj* **1** anaemic; **2** weak.

anémone /anemɔn/ *nf* anemone.

ânerie /anʀi/ *nf* **1** silly remark; **2** silly blunder.

ânesse /anɛs/ *nf* she-ass, female donkey.

anesthésie /anɛstezi/ *nf* anaesthesia.

aneth /anɛt/ *nm* dill.

ange /ɑ̃ʒ/ *nm* angel.
IDIOMS **être aux ~s** to be in (one's) seventh heaven.

angélique[1] /ɑ̃ʒelik/ *adj* angelic.

angélique[2] /ɑ̃ʒelik/ *nf* angelica.

angelot /ɑ̃ʒlo/ *nm* cherub.

angine /ɑ̃ʒin/ *nf* throat infection.

anglais, **~e**[1] /ɑ̃glɛ, ɛz/ **I** *adj* English.
II *nm* (language) English.

Anglais, **~e** /ɑ̃glɛ, ɛz/ *nm,f* Englishman/Englishwoman.

anglaise[2] /ɑ̃glɛz/ **I** *adj f* ▶ **anglais I**.
II *nf* ringlet.

angle /ɑ̃gl/ *nm* **1** angle; **2** corner.

Angleterre /ɑ̃glətɛʀ/ *pr nf* England.

anglo-américain, **~e**, *mpl* **~s** /ɑ̃glo ameʀikɛ̃, ɛn/ **I** *adj* **1** Anglo-American; **2** American English.
II *nm* (language) American English.

anglo-normand, **~e**, *mpl* **~s** /ɑ̃glonɔʀmɑ̃, ɑ̃d/ *adj* Anglo-Norman.

Anglo-Normande /ɑ̃glonɔʀmɑ̃d/ *adj f* **les îles ~s** the Channel Islands.

anglophone /ɑ̃glɔfɔn/ **I** *adj* English-speaking.
II *nmf* English speaker; Anglophone.

anglo-saxon, **-onne**, *mpl* **~s** /ɑ̃glosaksɔ̃, ɔn/ *adj* Anglo-Saxon.

angoissant, **~e** /ɑ̃gwasɑ̃, ɑ̃t/ *adj* [*prospect*] alarming; [*film, silence*] frightening.

angoisse /ɑ̃gwas/ *nf* anxiety.

angoissé, **~e** /ɑ̃gwase/ *adj* anxious.

angoisser /ɑ̃gwase/ [1] **I** *vtr* to worry.
II° *vi* to be anxious, to be nervous.

anguille /ɑ̃gij/ *nf* eel.

angulaire /ɑ̃gylɛʀ/ *adj* angular.

animal, **~e**, *mpl* **-aux** /animal, o/ **I** *adj* animal.
II *nm* animal; **~ familier** pet; **~ domestique** domestic animal; **~ nuisible** pest.

animateur, **-trice** /animatœʀ, tʀis/ *nm,f* **1** (of group of holidaymakers, club) coordinator; (of association) leader; (of festival) organizer; **2** presenter.

animation /animasjɔ̃/ *nf* **1** (of group, exhibition, festival) organization; (of sales) coordination; **2** life, liveliness; **ville qui manque d'~** dull town; **3** (of street, market) hustle and bustle; (of people) excitement.

animé, **~e** /anime/ *adj* **1** animated; lively; busy; **2 ~ de mauvaises intentions** spurred on by bad intentions.

animer /anime/ [1] **I** *vtr* **1** to lead [*discussion, group*]; to run [*course, show*]; to present [*programme*]; **2** to liven up [*town, story, meeting*].
II s'animer *v refl* (+ *v être*) **1** [*conversation*] to become lively; [*meeting*] to liven up; [*face*] to light up; **2** [*statue*] to come to life.

anis /ani/ *nm inv* **1** anise; **2** aniseed.

ankyloser: **s'ankyloser** /ɑ̃kiloze/ [1] *v refl* (+ *v être*) to get stiff.

annales /anal/ *nf pl* **1** annals; **2** (of exams) (book of) past papers.

anneau, *pl* **~x** /ano/ *nm* ring.

année /ane/ *nf* year; **l'~ en cours** this year, the current year; **avec les ~s** over the years; **d'~ en ~** year by year; **ces dix dernières ~s** over the last ten years; **souhaiter la bonne ~ à qn** to wish sb a happy new year; **(dans) les ~s 80** (in) the eighties; **location à l'~** annual rent.
■ **~ bissextile** leap year; **~ civile** calendar year; **~ universitaire** academic year.

année-lumière, *pl* **années-lumière** /anelymjɛʀ/ *nf* light-year.

annexe[1] /anɛks/ *adj* **1** [*room*] adjoining; **2** [*questions*] additional; [*file, document*] attached.

annexe[2] /anɛks/ *nf* **1** (building) annexe (GB), annex (US); **2** (document) appendix.

annexer /anɛkse/ [1] *vtr* to annex.

anniversaire /anivɛʀsɛʀ/ **I** *adj* **date** or **jour ~ de** anniversary of.
II *nm* **1** birthday; **2** anniversary.

annonce /anɔ̃s/ *nf* **1** announcement; **2** advertisement, ad°; **petite ~** classified advertisement; **3** declaration; **faire une ~** (in bridge) to bid; **4** sign.

annoncer /anɔ̃se/ [12] **I** *vtr* **1** to announce; **2** to forecast [*rain, event*]; **3** [*event, signal*] to herald.
II s'annoncer *v refl* (+ *v être*) **1** [*crisis, storm*] to be brewing; **2 la récolte 92 s'annonce excellente** the '92 harvest promises to be very good.

annonciateur, **-trice** /anɔ̃sjatœʀ, tʀis/ *adj* [*sign, signal*] warning.

annuaire /anɥɛʀ/ *nm* **1** directory; **2** yearbook.

annuel, **-elle** /anɥɛl/ *adj* (gen) annual, yearly; [*contract*] one-year.

annulaire /anylɛʀ/ *nm* ring finger.

annulation /anylasjɔ̃/ *nf* **1** (gen) cancellation; (of law) repeal; **2** (Law) (of verdict) quashing; (of elections) cancellation[GB]; (of marriage) annulment.

annuler /anyle/ [1] **I** *vtr* **1** to cancel [*appointment, trip*]; to write off [*debt*]; to discount [*result of match*]; **2** (Law) to declare [sth] void [*elections*]; to quash [*verdict*].
II s'annuler *v refl* (+ *v être*) to cancel each other out.

anodin, **~e** /anɔdɛ̃, in/ *adj* [*subject*] safe, neutral; [*question, joke*] innocent.

anomalie /anɔmali/ *nf* **1** anomaly; **2** fault.

anonymat /anɔnima/ *nm* **1** anonymity; **2** confidentiality.

anonyme /anɔnim/ *adj* anonymous.

anorexie /anɔʀɛksi/ *nf* anorexia.

anormal, **~e**, *mpl* **-aux** /anɔʀmal, o/ *adj* abnormal.

ANPE /aɛnpeœ/ *nf* (*abbr* = **Agence nationale pour l'emploi**) *French national employment agency*.

anse /ɑ̃s/ *nf* (of cup, basket) handle.

antagoniste /ɑ̃tagɔnist/ *adj* [*groups*] opposing; [*interests*] conflicting.

antarctique /ɑ̃taʀktik/ *adj* Antarctic.

Antarctique /ɑ̃taʀktik/ *pr nm* **1** Antarctic; **océan ~** Antarctic Ocean; **2** Antarctica.

antécédent, **~e** /ɑ̃tesedɑ̃, ɑ̃t/ **I** *adj* previous.
II *nm* **1** past history; **2** medical history; **3** (in grammar, mathematics) antecedent.

antenne /ɑ̃tɛn/*nf* **1** (of radio, television) aerial; (of radar, satellite) antenna; **passer à l'~** [*programme, person*] to go on the air; **2** (of organization, service) branch; **3** (of insect, shrimp) antenna; **avoir des ~s** (figurative) to have a sixth sense.

antérieur, **~e** /ɑ̃teʀjœʀ/ *adj* **1** [*situation, work*] previous; **2** [*limb, ligament*] anterior.

anthracite /ɑ̃tʀasit/ *adj inv* charcoal grey (GB), charcoal gray (US).

anthropologie /ɑ̃tʀɔpɔlɔʒi/ *nf* anthropology.

anthropophage /ɑ̃tʀɔpɔfaʒ/*nmf* cannibal.

antiaérien, **-ienne** /ɑ̃tiaeʀjɛ̃, ɛn/ *adj* anti-aircraft.

antiatomique /ɑ̃tiatɔmik/ *adj* (anti-)radiation; **abri ~** nuclear shelter.

antibiotique /ɑ̃tibjɔtik/ *adj, nm* antibiotic.

antibrouillard /ɑ̃tibʀujaʀ/ *adj inv* **phare ~** fog light.

antibruit /ɑ̃tibʀɥi/ *adj inv* soundproof.

antichambre /ɑ̃tiʃɑ̃bʀ/ *nf* anteroom.

antichoc /ɑ̃tiʃɔk/ *adj inv* **1 casque ~** crash helmet; **2** [*watch*] shockproof.

anticipation /ɑ̃tisipasjɔ̃/ *nf* anticipation; **roman d'~** science fiction novel.

anticipé, **~e** /ɑ̃tisipe/ *adj* early.

anticiper /ɑ̃tisipe/ [1] **I** *vtr* to anticipate [*reaction, change, movement*].
II *vi* **1** to get ahead of oneself; **2** to think ahead.

anticonformiste /ɑ̃tikɔ̃fɔʀmist/ *adj, nmf* nonconformist.

anticorps /ɑ̃tikɔʀ/ *nm inv* antibody.

antidater /ɑ̃tidate/ [1] *vtr* to backdate.

antidérapant, **~e** /ɑ̃tideʀapɑ̃, ɑ̃t/ *adj* [*tyre*] nonskid; [*sole*] nonslip.

antidopage /ɑ̃tidɔpaʒ/ *adj* [*measure*] anti-doping; **contrôle ~** dope test.

antidote /ɑ̃tidɔt/ *nm* antidote.

antigang /ɑ̃tigɑ̃g/ *adj inv* **brigade ~** crime squad.

antigel /ɑ̃tiʒɛl/ *adj inv, nm* antifreeze.

anti-inflammatoire, *pl* **~s** /ɑ̃tiɛ̃flamatwaʀ/ *adj, nm* anti-inflammatory.

antillais, **~e** /ɑ̃tijɛ, ɛz/ *adj* West Indian.

Antilles /ɑ̃tij/ *pr nf pl* **les ~** the West Indies; **les Petites/Grandes ~** the Lesser/Greater Antilles.
antilope /ɑ̃tilɔp/ *nf* antelope.
antimite /ɑ̃timit/ *adj, nm* moth-repellent.
antipathie /ɑ̃tipati/ *nf* antipathy.
antipathique /ɑ̃tipatik/ *adj* unpleasant.
antipelliculaire /ɑ̃tipelikylɛʀ/ *adj* antidandruff.
antipode /ɑ̃tipɔd/ *nm* antipodes.
antipoison /ɑ̃tipwazɔ̃/ *adj inv* **centre ~** poisons unit.
antiquaire /ɑ̃tikɛʀ/ *nmf* antique dealer.
antique /ɑ̃tik/ *adj* ancient.
antiquité /ɑ̃tikite/ **I** *nf* antique.
II antiquités *nf pl* antiquities.
Antiquité /ɑ̃tikite/ *nf* antiquity.
antireflet /ɑ̃tiʀəflɛ/ *adj inv* nonreflective; (in photography) antiglare.
antirouille /ɑ̃tiʀuj/ *adj inv* **1** rust-proofing; **2** rust-removing.
antisémite /ɑ̃tisemit/ **I** *adj* anti-Semitic.
II *nmf* anti-Semite.
antitabac /ɑ̃titaba/ *adj inv* antismoking.
antiterroriste /ɑ̃titɛʀɔʀist/ *adj* **lutte ~** fight against terrorism.
antithèse /ɑ̃titɛz/ *nf* antithesis.
antituberculeux, -euse /ɑ̃titybɛʀkylø, øz/ *adj* **vaccin ~** tuberculosis vaccine.
antivol /ɑ̃tivɔl/ *nm* (of bicycle, motorbike) lock; (of car) anti-theft device.
anus /anys/ *nm inv* anus.
Anvers /ɑ̃vɛʀ/ *pr n* Antwerp.
anxiété /ɑ̃ksjete/ *nf* anxiety.
anxieux, -ieuse /ɑ̃ksjø, øz/ *adj* [*person*] anxious; [*attitude*] concerned.
aorte /aɔʀt/ *nf* aorta.
août /u(t)/ *nm* August.
apaisant, ~e /apɛzɑ̃, ɑ̃t/ *adj* **1** soothing; **2** calming.
apaiser /apeze/ [1] **I** *vtr* **1** to pacify, to appease; **2** to ease [*conflict*]; **3** to calm [*rage*].
II s'apaiser *v refl* (+ *v être*) **1** to die down; **2** to calm down.
apathie /apati/ *nf* **1** apathy; **2** stagnation.
apatride /apatʀid/ *adj* stateless.
APEC /apɛk/ *nf* (*abbr* = **Agence pour l'emploi des cadres**) *executive employment agency*.
apercevoir /apɛʀsəvwaʀ/ [5] **I** *vtr* **1** to make out; **2** to catch sight of.
II s'apercevoir *v refl* (+ *v être*) **1 s'~ que** to realize that; **s'~ de** to notice [*mistake*]; **2** to catch sight of each other; **3** to meet briefly.
aperçu /apɛʀsy/ *nm* **1** glimpse; **2** outline; **3** insight.
apéritif /apeʀitif/ *nm* drink.
apesanteur /apəzɑ̃tœʀ/ *nf* weightlessness.
à-peu-près /apøpʀɛ/ *nm inv* vague approximation.
aphone /afɔn/ *adj* **être ~** to have lost one's voice.
aphte /aft/ *nm* mouth ulcer.
apiculture /apikyltyʀ/ *nf* beekeeping.
apitoiement /apitwamɑ̃/ *nm* pity (**sur** for).
apitoyer /apitwaje/ [23] **I** *vtr* to move [sb] to pity.
II s'apitoyer *v refl* (+ *v être*) **s'~ sur (le sort de) qn** to feel sorry for sb.
aplanir /aplaniʀ/ [3] *vtr* to level.
aplati, ~e /aplati/ **I** *pp* ▶ **aplatir**.
II *pp adj* **1** flattened; **2** [*nose*] flat.
aplatir /aplatiʀ/ [3] *vtr* **1** to flatten; **2** to smooth out [*cushion*]; to smooth down [*hair*]; **3** to press [*seams*].
aplomb /aplɔ̃/ **I** *nm* **1** confidence; **vous ne manquez pas d'~!** you've got a nerve!; **2** plumb, perpendicularity.
II d'aplomb *phr* **1 être d'~** to be straight, to be plumb vertical; **2**° **ça va te remettre d'~** it will put you back on your feet.
apocalypse /apɔkalips/ *nf* apocalypse.
apogée /apɔʒe/ *nm* **1** (of moon, satellite) apogee; **2** (of career, empire) peak.
apologie /apɔlɔʒi/ *nf* panegyric; apologia; **faire l'~ de** to justify; to praise.
a posteriori /apɔsteʀjɔʀi/ *phr* after the event.
apostolat /apɔstɔla/ *nm* **1** apostolate; **2** (figurative) apostolic mission.
apostrophe /apɔstʀɔf/ *nf* apostrophe.
apostropher /apɔstʀɔfe/ [1] *vtr* to heckle.
apothéose /apɔteoz/ *nf* **1** (of show) high point; **2** (of career, work) culmination.
apôtre /apotʀ/ *nm* apostle.
apparaître /apaʀɛtʀ/ [73] **I** *vi* (+ *v être*) **1** [*person, problem*] to appear; [*sun, moon*] to come out; **2 laisser** or **faire ~** to show; **3** to seem.
II *v impers* **il apparaît que** it appears that.
apparat /apaʀa/ *nm* grandeur; **d'~** ceremonial.
appareil /apaʀɛj/ *nm* **1** device; **2** appliance; **3** telephone; **qui est à l'~?** who's calling please?; **4** aircraft; **5** system; **l'~ digestif** the digestive system; **6** apparatus; **l'~ du parti** the party apparatus.
■ **~ auditif** hearing aid; **~ (dentaire)** brace (GB), braces (US); **~ à sous** slot machine; **~ photo** camera.
IDIOMS **être dans son plus simple ~** to be in one's birthday suit.
appareiller /apaʀeje/ [1] *vi* to cast off.
apparemment /apaʀamɑ̃/ *adv* **1** apparently; **2** seemingly.
apparence /apaʀɑ̃s/ *nf* appearance.
apparent, ~e /apaʀɑ̃, ɑ̃t/ *adj* **1** visible; **2** [*embarrassment*] apparent; **3** seeming, apparent.
apparenté, ~e /apaʀɑ̃te/ *adj* **1** [*person*] related (**à** to); **2** [*company*] allied.
apparenter: **s'apparenter** /apaʀɑ̃te/ [1] *v refl* (+ *v être*) **s'~ à** to resemble.
apparition /apaʀisjɔ̃/ *nf* **1** (of product) appearance; (of problem) emergence; **2** apparition.
appartement /apaʀtəmɑ̃/ *nm* flat (GB), apart-

ment; **~ témoin** show flat (GB), show apartment (US).

appartenance /apaʀtənɑ̃s/ *nf* membership (**à** of).

appartenir /apaʀtəniʀ/ [36] **I appartenir à** *v+prep* **1 ~ à** to belong to; **2 ~ à** to be a member of.

II *v impers* **il appartient à qn de faire** it is up to sb to do.

appât /apɑ/ *nm* **1** bait; **2** lure.

appâter /apɑte/ [1] *vtr* **1** to bait; **2** to lure.

appauvrir /apovʀiʀ/ [3] **I** *vtr* to impoverish.

II s'appauvrir *v refl* (+ *v être*) to become impoverished.

appel /apɛl/ *nm* **1** call; (urgent) appeal; **~ à** call for [*solidarity*]; appeal for [*calm*]; **~ au secours** call for help; cry for help; **faire ~ à** to appeal to [*person*]; to call [*fire brigade*]; [*task*] to call for [*skills*]; **2** roll call; (Sch) registration; **3** (Mil) call up (GB), draft (US); **4** (Law) appeal; **faire ~** to appeal; **5** (Sport) take off.

■ **~ d'air** draught (GB), draft (US); **~ de phares** flash of headlights (GB) or high beams (US).

appelé, **~e** /aple/ **I** *pp* ▶ **appeler**.

II *pp adj* **~ à qch/à faire** destined for sth/to do.

III *nm* (Mil) conscript, draftee (US).

appeler /aple/ [19] **I** *vtr* **1** to call; **~ (qn) à l'aide** to call (to sb) for help; **2** to phone (GB), to call; **3** to call [*doctor, taxi*]; to send for [*pupil*]; **~ qn sous les drapeaux** (Mil) to call sb up; **4 ~ qn à faire** to call on sb to do; **~ à la grève** to call for strike action; **5 mon travail m'appelle à beaucoup voyager** my work involves a lot of travel.

II en appeler à *v+prep* to appeal to.

III s'appeler *v refl* (+ *v être*) to be called; **comment t'appelles-tu?** what's your name?; **je m'appelle Vladimir** my name is Vladimir; **voilà ce qui s'appelle une belle voiture!** now, that's what you call a nice car!

IDIOMS **~ les choses par leur nom, ~ un chat un chat** to call a spade a spade.

appellation /apɛlɑsjɔ̃/ *nf* name, appellation.

appendice /apɛ̃dis/ *nm* (Anat) appendix.

appendicite /apɛ̃disit/ *nf* appendicitis.

appesantir: **s'appesantir** /apəzɑ̃tiʀ/ [3] *v refl* (+ *v être*) **s'~ sur** to dwell on.

appétissant, **~e** /apetisɑ̃, ɑ̃t/ *adj* appetizing.

appétit /apeti/ *nm* appetite.

applaudir /aplodiʀ/ [3] **I** *vtr* to applaud.

II *vi* **1** to applaud, to clap; **2** (figurative) to approve; **~ des deux mains** to approve heartily.

applaudissement /aplodismɑ̃/ *nm* **1** applause; **2** acclaim.

applicateur /aplikatœʀ/ *nm* applicator.

application /aplikasjɔ̃/ *nf* **1** care; **il manque d'~** he doesn't apply himself; **2** implementation, enforcement; **mettre en ~** to apply [*theory*]; to implement [*law*]; **3** (of device, program) **~s** applications; **4** (of ointment) application; **5** (Comput) application program.

applique /aplik/ *nf* wall light.

appliqué, **~e** /aplike/ *adj* **1** hardworking; **2** [*work*] careful; **3** [*science*] applied.

appliquer /aplike/ [1] **I** *vtr* **1** to apply [*ointment*] (**sur** to); to put [*stamp*] (**sur** on); **2** to implement [*policy, law*]; **3** to apply [*technique*] (**à** to).

II s'appliquer *v refl* (+ *v être*) **1** to take great care (**à faire** to do); **2 s'~ à qn/qch** [*law, remark*] to apply to sb/sth.

appoint /apwɛ̃/ *nm* **1** exact change; **faire l'~** to give the exact change; **2 d'~** [*salary*] supplementary; [*heating*] additional.

appointements /apwɛ̃tmɑ̃/ *nm pl* salary.

apport /apɔʀ/ *nm* **1** provision; **2** contribution.

apporter /apɔʀte/ [1] *vtr* **1** to bring [*improvement, news*]; to bring in [*revenue*]; to bring about [*change*]; **~ qch à qn** to bring sb sth, to take sb sth; **2** to give [*support, explanation*].

apposer /apoze/ [1] *vtr* to affix (**sur** on).

apposition /apozisjɔ̃/ *nf* apposition.

appréciable /apʀesjabl/ *adj* **1** substantial; **2 c'est ~** it's nice.

appréciatif, **-ive** /apʀesjatif, iv/ *adj* **1** appreciative; **2** appraising.

appréciation /apʀesjasjɔ̃/ *nf* **1** (of quantity) estimate; **2** (financial) evaluation; **3** (of quality) assessment; **être laissé à l'~ de qn** to be left to sb's discretion.

apprécier /apʀesje/ [2] *vtr* **1** to appreciate [*art*]; to like [*person*]; **2** (financially) to value; **3** to estimate [*distance*]; **4** to assess [*situation*].

appréhender /apʀeɑ̃de/ [1] *vtr* **1** to arrest; **2** to dread; **3** to comprehend, to understand.

appréhension /apʀeɑ̃sjɔ̃/ *nf* apprehension.

apprendre /apʀɑ̃dʀ/ [52] *vtr* **1** to learn (**à faire** to do); **2** to learn [*truth*]; to hear (about) [*news*]; **3** to teach; **4 ~ qch à qn** to tell sb sth.

apprenti, **~e** /apʀɑ̃ti/ *nm,f* **1** apprentice, trainee; **2** novice; **~ poète** novice poet.

apprentissage /apʀɑ̃tisaʒ/ *nm* **1** training, apprenticeship; **2** learning.

apprêté, **~e** /apʀɛte/ **I** *pp* ▶ **apprêter**.

II *pp adj* **1** affected; **2** [*hairstyle*] fussy.

apprêter: **s'apprêter** /apʀɛte/ [1] *v refl* (+ *v être*) **s'~ à faire** to get ready to do.

apprivoiser /apʀivwaze/ [1] *vtr* to tame.

approbateur, **-trice** /apʀɔbatœʀ, tʀis/ *adj* **sourire ~** smile of approval.

approbation /apʀɔbasjɔ̃/ *nf* approval.

approche /apʀɔʃ/ *nf* approach.

approcher /apʀɔʃe/ [1] **I** *vtr* **1 ~ qch de la fenêtre** to move sth near to the window; **2** to go up to; to come up to; **3** to come into contact with.

II approcher de *v+prep* to be (getting) close to.

III *vi* to approach.

IV s'approcher *v refl* (+ *v être*) **s'~ de** to go near; to come near.

approfondi, **~e** /apʀɔfɔ̃di/ **I** *pp* ▶ **approfondir**.

II *pp adj* detailed, in-depth.

approfondir /apʀɔfɔ̃diʀ/ [3] *vtr* **1** to go into [sth] in depth; **2 ~ ses connaissances en français** to improve one's knowledge of French; **3** to make [sth] deeper.

approprié, **~e** /apʀɔpʀije/ *adj* appropriate.

approprier: **s'approprier** /apʀɔpʀije/ [2] *v refl* (+ *v être*) **1** to take, to appropriate [*object, idea*]; **2** to seize [*power*].

approuver /apʀuve/ [1] *vtr* **1** to approve of; **je t'approuve d'avoir accepté** I think you were right to accept; **2** to approve [*budget*].

approvisionnement /apʀɔvizjɔnmɑ̃/ *nm* supply (**en** of).

approvisionner /apʀɔvizjɔne/ [1] **I** *vtr* **1** to supply (**en** with); **mal approvisionné** [*shop*] badly stocked; **2** to pay money into [*account*].
II s'approvisionner *v refl* (+ *v être*) **1 s'~ en** to get one's supplies of (**auprès de** from); **2** to stock up (**en** on, with).

approximatif, **-ive** /apʀɔksimatif, iv/ *adj* [*estimate, translation*] rough.

approximation /apʀɔksimasjɔ̃/ *nf* **1** rough estimate; **2** approximation.

appui /apɥi/ *nm* support; **à l'~ de** in support of [*theory*]; **prendre ~ sur** to lean on.

appui-tête, *pl* **appuis-tête** /apɥitɛt/ *nm* headrest.

appuyé, **~e** /apɥije/ **I** *pp* ▶ **appuyer**.
II *pp adj* **1** [*look*] intent; **2** [*joke*] laboured[GB].

appuyer /apɥije/ [22] **I** *vtr* **1** to rest (**sur** on); to lean (**sur** on); **2** to press (**contre** against); **3** to support, to back (up).
II *vi* **1 ~ sur** to press [*switch*]; to put one's foot on [*brake*]; **2 ~ sur** to stress [*word*].
III s'appuyer *v refl* (+ *v être*) **1** to lean (**sur** on; **contre** against); **2 s'~ sur** to rely on [*theory*]; to draw on [*report*].

âpre /ɑpʀ/ *adj* **1** [*taste, cold*] bitter; **2** [*voice*] harsh; **3** [*struggle*] fierce; [*argument*] bitter.

après /apʀɛ/ **I** *adv* afterward(s), after; later; **peu/bien ~** shortly/long afterward(s); **une heure ~** one hour later; **peu ~ il y a un lac** a bit further on there's a lake; **et ~?** and then what?; so what○?
II *prep* after; **~ mon départ** after I leave; after I left; **~ coup** afterward(s); **il est toujours ~ son fils**○ he's always on at his son.
III d'après *phr* **1 d'~ moi** in my opinion; **d'~ lui/la météo** according to him/the weather forecast; **d'~ ma montre** by my watch; **2** from; based on; **d'~ un dessin de Gauguin** from a drawing by Gauguin; **3 l'année d'~** the year after; **la fois d'~** the next time.
IV après que *phr* after; **~ qu'il a parlé** after he had spoken.
V après- (*combining form*) **l'~-guerre** the postwar years.

après-demain /apʀɛdmɛ̃/ *adv* the day after tomorrow.

après-midi /apʀɛmidi/ *nm inv* or *nf inv* afternoon.

après-rasage, *pl* **~s** /apʀɛʀazaʒ/ *adj inv*, *nm* after-shave.

après-ski /apʀɛski/ *nm inv* snowboot.

après-vente /apʀɛvɑ̃t/ *adj inv* after-sales.

a priori /apʀijɔʀi/ **I** *phr* a priori.
II *phr* **~, ça ne devrait pas poser de problèmes** on the face of it there shouldn't be any problems.

à-propos /apʀɔpo/ *nm inv* **intervenir avec ~** to make an apposite remark; **agir avec ~** to do the right thing.

apte /apt/ *adj* **~ à qch/à faire** capable of sth/of doing; fit for sth/to do.

aptitude /aptityd/ *nf* aptitude; fitness.

aquarelle /akwaʀɛl/ *nf* **1** watercolours[GB]; **2** watercolour[GB].

aquarium /akwaʀjɔm/ *nm* aquarium, fish tank.

aquatique /akwatik/ *adj* **1** aquatic; **2 sport ~** water sport.

aqueduc /akdyk/ *nm* aqueduct.

aquilin /akilɛ̃/ *adj m* aquiline.

arabe /aʀab/ **I** *adj* **1** Arab; **2** Arabic.
II *nm* (language) Arabic.

Arabe /aʀab/ *nmf* Arab.

arabesque /aʀabɛsk/ *nf* arabesque.

Arabie /aʀabi/ *pr nf* Arabia.
■ **~ Saoudite** Saudi Arabia.

arachide /aʀaʃid/ *nf* groundnut, peanut.

araignée /aʀeɲe/ *nf* spider.
■ **~ de mer** spider crab.
IDIOMS **avoir une ~ au plafond**○ to have a screw loose○.

arbalète /aʀbalɛt/ *nf* crossbow.

arbitraire /aʀbitʀɛʀ/ *adj* arbitrary.

arbitre /aʀbitʀ/ *nm* **1** referee, umpire; **2** arbitrator.

arbitrer /aʀbitʀe/ [1] **I** *vtr* **1** to referee, to umpire; **2** to arbitrate in.
II *vi* to arbitrate (**entre** between).

arborer /aʀbɔʀe/ [1] *vtr* **1** to wear [*smile*]; to sport [*badge*]; **2** to bear [*banner*]; to fly [*flag*].

arboriculture /aʀbɔʀikyltyʀ/ *nf* arboriculture.

arbre /aʀbʀ/ *nm* **1** tree; **2** (Tech) shaft.
■ **~ généalogique** family tree.

arbrisseau, *pl* **~x** /aʀbʀiso/ *nm* small tree.

arbuste /aʀbyst/ *nm* shrub.

arc /aʀk/ *nm* **1** (Sport) bow; **2** arc; **3** arch.

arcade /aʀkad/ *nf* arcade; **~s** archways.
■ **~ sourcilière** arch of the eyebrow.

arc-bouter: **s'arc-bouter** /aʀkbute/ [1] *v refl* (+ *v être*) to brace oneself.

arceau, *pl* **~x** /aʀso/ *nm* **1** arch; **2** (in croquet) hoop; **3** (in car) roll bar.

arc-en-ciel, *pl* **arcs-en-ciel** /aʀkɑ̃sjɛl/ *nm* rainbow.

archaïque /aʀkaik/ *adj* archaic.

archange /aʀkɑ̃ʒ/ *nm* archangel.

arche /aʀʃ/ *nf* arch; **~ de Noé** Noah's Ark.

archéologie /aʀkeɔlɔʒi/ *nf* archaeology.

archéologique /aʀkeɔlɔʒik/ *adj* archaeological.

archet /aʀʃɛ/ *nm* (Mus) bow.

archétype /aʀketip/ *nm* archetype.

archevêché /aʀʃəveʃe/ *nm* **1** archdiocese; **2** archbishop's palace.

archevêque /aʀʃəvɛk/ *nm* archbishop.

archi○ /aʀʃi/ *pref* **~connu** really well-known.

archipel /aʀʃipɛl/ *nm* archipelago.

architecte /aʀʃitɛkt/ *nmf* architect.

architecture /aʀʃitɛktyʀ/ *nf* **1** architecture; **2** structure.

archives /aʀʃiv/ *nf pl* archives, records.

Arctique /aʀktik/ *pr nm* Arctic.

ardemment /aʀdamɑ̃/ *adv* passionately.

ardent, **~e** /aʀdɑ̃, ɑ̃t/ *adj* **1** [*ember*] glowing; [*sun*] blazing; **2** [*faith*] burning; [*patriot*] fervent; [*speech*] impassioned; [*nature*] passionate.

ardeur /aʀdœʀ/ *nf* (of person) ardour^GB^; (of beliefs) fervour^GB^; (of beginner) enthusiasm.

ardoise /aʀdwaz/ *nf* **1** slate; **2**○ account.

ardu, **~e** /aʀdy/ *adj* **1** arduous; **2** taxing.

arène /aʀɛn/ *nf* **1** arena; **2** bullring; **3** **~s** amphitheatre^GB^.

arête /aʀɛt/ *nf* **1** fishbone; **2** (of roof, mountain) ridge; (of prism) edge; (of nose) bridge.

argent /aʀʒɑ̃/ *nm* **1** money; **2** silver.
■ **~ liquide** cash.
IDIOMS **prendre qch pour ~ comptant** to take sth at face value.

argenté, **~e** /aʀʒɑ̃te/ *adj* **1** silver-plated; **2** (in colour) silvery.

argenterie /aʀʒɑ̃tʀi/ *nf* silverware, silver.

Argentine /aʀʒɑ̃tin/ *pr nf* Argentina.

argile /aʀʒil/ *nf* clay.

argot /aʀgo/ *nm* slang.

arguer /aʀge/ [1] **I** *vtr* **~ que** to claim that.
II arguer de *v+prep* to give [sth] as a reason.

argument /aʀgymɑ̃/ *nm* argument.

argumentation /aʀgymɑ̃tasjɔ̃/ *nf* line of argument.

argumenter /aʀgymɑ̃te/ [1] *vi* to argue.

argus /aʀgys/ *nm inv*: *used car prices guide*.

aride /aʀid/ *adj* arid.

aridité /aʀidite/ *nf* aridity.

aristocratie /aʀistɔkʀasi/ *nf* aristocracy.

aristocratique /aʀistɔkʀatik/ *adj* aristocratic.

arithmétique /aʀitmetik/ **I** *adj* arithmetical.
II *nf* arithmetic.

armateur /aʀmatœʀ/ *nm* shipowner.

armature /aʀmatyʀ/ *nf* **1** (of tent) frame; **2** (in construction) framework.

arme /aʀm/ **I** *nf* **1** weapon; **charger une ~** to load a gun; **rendre les ~s** to surrender; **en ~s** armed; **à ~s égales** on equal terms; **faire ses premières ~s dans l'enseignement** to start out as a teacher; **2** branch of the armed services.
II armes *nf pl* coat of arms.
■ **~ blanche** *weapon with a blade*; **~ à feu** firearm.

armé, **~e**[1] /aʀme/ **I** *pp* ▶ **armer**.
II *pp adj* **1** armed; **vol à main ~e** armed robbery; **2** equipped (**de** with; **contre** against).

armée[2] /aʀme/ *nf* army.
■ **~ de l'air** air force; **l'~ de réserve** the reserves; **l'~ de terre** the army.

armement /aʀməmɑ̃/ *nm* **1** armament; arming; **2** arms, weapons; **3** (of rifle) cocking; (of camera) winding on; **4** (of ship) fitting out.

armer /aʀme/ [1] **I** *vtr* **1** to arm (**de** with; **contre** against); **2** to fit out [*ship*]; **3** to wind on [*camera*]; to cock [*rifle*].
II s'armer *v refl* (+ *v être*) to arm oneself.

armistice /aʀmistis/ *nm* armistice.

armoire /aʀmwaʀ/ *nf* **1** cupboard; **2** wardrobe.
■ **~ à glace** wardrobe with a full length mirror; **c'est une ~ à glace**○ he/she is built like a tank○; **~ métallique** metal locker; **~ à pharmacie** medicine cabinet; **~ de toilette** bathroom cabinet.

armoiries /aʀmwaʀi/ *nf pl* arms.

armure /aʀmyʀ/ *nf* armour^GB^.

armurier /aʀmyʀje/ *nm* **1** gunsmith; **2** armourer^GB^.

aromates /aʀɔmat/ *nm pl* herbs and spices.

aromatique /aʀɔmatik/ *adj* aromatic.

aromatiser /aʀɔmatize/ [1] *vtr* to flavour^GB^.

arôme /aʀom/ *nm* **1** aroma; **2** flavouring^GB^.

arpège /aʀpɛʒ/ *nm* arpeggio.

arpenter /aʀpɑ̃te/ [1] *vtr* **1** to stride along; **2** to pace up and down; **3** to survey [*piece of land*].

arqué, **~e** /aʀke/ *adj* [*brows*] arched; [*nose*] hooked; [*legs*] bandy.

arquebuse /aʀkəbyz/ *nf* arquebus.

arquer /aʀke/ [1] **I** *vtr* to bend [*bar*].
II s'arquer *v refl* (+ *v être*) to become bowed.

arraché /aʀaʃe/ *nm* snatch; **obtenir à l'~** to snatch [*victory*]; **vol à l'~** bag snatching.

arrache-pied: **d'arrache-pied** /daʀaʃpje/ *phr* [*work*] flat out.

arracher /aʀaʃe/ [1] **I** *vtr* **1** to pull up or dig up [*weeds*]; to pull out [*tooth*]; to tear down [*poster*]; to rip out [*page*]; to tear off [*mask*]; to uproot [*tree*]; to blow off [*tiles*]; **2 ~ à qn** to snatch [sth] from sb [*bag, victory*]; to extract [sth] from sb [*promise*]; to get [sth] from sb [*smile*]; **3 ~ qn à** to uproot sb from [*home*]; to drag sb away from [*work*]; to rouse sb from [*thoughts*]; to rescue sb from [*poverty*].
II s'arracher *v refl* (+ *v être*) **1 ~ qch** to fight over sth; **2 s'~ à** to rouse oneself from [*thoughts*]; to tear oneself away from [*work*].
IDIOMS **c'est à s'~ les cheveux**○! it's enough to make you tear your hair out!; **~ les yeux à** or **de qn** to scratch sb's eyes out.

arracheur /aʀaʃœʀ/ *nm* **mentir comme un ~ de dents** to be a born liar.

arraisonner /aʀɛzɔne/ [1] *vtr* to board and inspect.

arrangeant, **~e** /aʀɑ̃ʒɑ̃, ɑ̃t/ *adj* obliging.

arrangement /aʀɑ̃ʒmɑ̃/ *nm* arrangement.

arranger /aʀɑ̃ʒe/ [13] **I** *vtr* **1** to arrange, to organize; **2** to sort out; **pour ne rien ~, pour tout ~** to make matters worse; **3** to arrange [*flowers*]; **4** to tidy [*hair*]; to straighten [*skirt*]; **5** (Mus) to arrange; **6** [*events*] to suit [*person*].
II s'arranger *v refl* (+ *v être*) **1** to get better,

to improve; **2 s'~ avec qn** to arrange it with sb; **3** to manage; **4 on s'arrangera après** we'll sort it out later; **5**° **elle ne sait pas s'~** she doesn't know how to make the most of herself.

arrangeur, **-euse** /arɑ̃ʒœr, øz/ *nm,f* (Mus) arranger.

arrestation /arɛstasjɔ̃/ *nf* arrest.

arrêt /arɛ/ *nm* **1** (gen) stopping; (of conflict) cessation; (of delivery) cancellation; (in production) halt; **2** stop; **sans ~** [*travel*] nonstop; [*interrupt*] constantly; **à l'~** [*vehicle*] stationary; [*machine*] idle; [*electrical appliance*] off; **marquer un temps d'~** to pause; **être aux ~s** (Mil) to be under arrest; **3** stop; **un ~ de bus** a bus stop; **4** (Law) ruling.
■ **~ du cœur** heart failure; **~ sur image** freeze-frame, still; **~ de jeu** stoppage time; **~ de mort** death sentence; **~ de travail** stoppage of work; sick leave; sick note.

arrêté, **~e** /arete/ **I** *pp* ▸ **arrêter**.
II *pp adj* **1** [*matter*] settled; **2** [*ideas*] fixed.
III *nm* order, decree.

arrêter /arete/ [1] **I** *vtr* **1** to stop (**de faire** doing); **être arrêté pour trois semaines** to be given a sick note for three weeks; **2** to switch off [*machine*]; to halt [*process*]; **3** to give up (**de faire** doing); **4** to arrest; **5** to decide on [*plan*].
II *vi* to stop; **arrête!** stop it!
III s'arrêter *v refl* (+ *v être*) **1** to stop; **2** to give up (**de faire** doing); **3** to end; **4 s'~ sur** to dwell on; **s'~ à** to focus on.

arrhes /ar/ *nf pl* deposit.

arrière /arjɛr/ **I** *adj inv* back; rear.
II *nm* **1** rear; **à l'~** (in car) in the back; (on plane, train, ship) at the rear; **en ~** backward(s); (position) behind; **pencher la tête en ~** to tilt one's head back; **revenir en ~** [*person*] to turn back; (figurative) to take a backward step; (on tape) to rewind; **2** (Sport) fullback.

arriéré, **~e** /arjere/ **I** *adj* **1** outdated; **2** backward; **3** behind the times; **4** retarded.
II *nm* arrears.

arrière-cour, *pl* **~s** /arjɛrkur/ *nf* backyard.

arrière-goût, *pl* **~s** /arjɛrgu/ *nm* aftertaste.

arrière-grands-parents /arjɛrgrɑ̃parɑ̃/ *nm pl* great-grandparents.

arrière-pays /arjɛrpei/ *nm inv* hinterland.

arrière-pensée, *pl* **~s** /arjɛrpɑ̃se/ *nf* **1** ulterior motive; **2 sans ~** without reservation.

arrière-petits-enfants /arjɛrpətizɑ̃fɑ̃/ *nm pl* great-grandchildren.

arrière-plan, *pl* **~s** /arjɛrplɑ̃/ *nm* (of picture) background.

arrière-saison, *pl* **~s** /arjɛrsɛzɔ̃/ *nf* late autumn (GB), late fall (US).

arrière-train, *pl* **~s** /arjɛrtrɛ̃/ *nm* hindquarters.

arrimer /arime/ [1] *vtr* **1** to fasten; **2** (Naut) to stow.

arrivage /arivaʒ/ *nm* delivery, consignment.

arrivant, **~e** /arivɑ̃, ɑ̃t/ *nm,f* **un nouvel ~** a newcomer.

arrivé, **~e**[1] /arive/ **I** *pp* ▸ **arriver**.
II *pp adj* **1 le premier ~** the first person to arrive; **2 être ~** to have made it (socially).

arrivée[2] /arive/ *nf* **1** arrival; **trains à l'~** arrivals; **2** (in race) finish; **3** (Tech) inlet.

arriver /arive/ [1] (+ *v être*) **I** *vi* **1** (gen) to arrive; (Sport) to finish; **~ à/de Paris** to arrive in/from Paris; **2** to come; **~ en courant** to come running up; **3 ~ à** to reach [*level, agreement*]; to find [*solution*]; **~ (jusqu')à qn** to reach sb; **4 ~ à faire** to manage to do; **je n'y arrive pas** I can't do it; **~ à ses fins** to achieve one's ends; **5 en ~ à** to come to; **6** to happen.
II *v impers* **qu'est-il arrivé?** what happened? (**à** to); **il m'arrive d'y aller, il arrive que j'y aille** I sometimes go there.

arrivisme /arivism/ *nm* ruthless ambition.

arrogance /arɔgɑ̃s/ *nf* arrogance.

arrogant, **~e** /arɔgɑ̃, ɑ̃t/ *adj* arrogant.

arroger: **s'arroger** /arɔʒe/ [13] *v refl* (+ *v être*) to appropriate [*title*]; to assume [*right, role*].

arrondi, **~e** /arɔ̃di/ **I** *adj* rounded; round.
II *nm* (of face) roundness; (of shoulder) curve.

arrondir /arɔ̃dir/[3] **I** *vtr* **1** to round off [*edge*]; **coiffure qui arrondit le visage** hairstyle that makes one's face look round; **2** to open wide [*eyes*]; **3** to round off [*figure*] (**à** to).
II s'arrondir *v refl* (+ *v être*) **1** [*object*] to become round(ed); [*eyes*] to widen; **2** [*face*] to fill out; **3** [*fortune*] to be growing.
IDIOMS **~ les angles** to smooth the rough edges.

arrondissement /arɔ̃dismɑ̃/ *nm* **1** (in city) arrondissement; **2** (region) *administrative division in France*.

arrosage /arozaʒ/ *nm* watering.

arroser /aroze/ [1] **I** *vtr* **1** to water, to spray; **on va se faire ~**°**!** we're going to get soaked!; **2** to baste [*meat*]; to sprinkle [*cake*]; **3** to drink to; **4 repas arrosé au bourgogne** meal washed down with Burgundy.
II s'arroser° *v refl* (+ *v être*) **ça s'arrose** that calls for a drink.

arroseur /arozœr/ *nm* sprinkler.

arrosoir /arozwar/ *nm* watering can.

arsenal, *pl* **-aux** /arsənal, o/ *nm* **1** naval shipyard; **2** arsenal; **3**° gear.

art /ar/ *nm* **1** art; **2** art, skill; **avoir l'~ de faire** to have a knack of doing.
■ **~ dramatique** drama; **~ lyrique** opera; **~ de vivre** art of living; **~s ménagers** home economics; **~s plastiques** plastic arts.

artère /artɛr/ *nf* **1** (Anat) artery; **2** arterial road; **3** main street.

artériel, **-ielle** /arterjɛl/ *adj* arterial.

arthrite /artrit/ *nf* arthritis.

arthrose /artroz/ *nf* osteoarthritis.

artichaut /artiʃo/ *nm* (globe) artichoke.
IDIOMS **avoir un cœur d'~** to be fickle (*in love*).

article /artikl/ *nm* **1** (in paper, law) article; (in contract) clause; **2** (in grammar) article; **3** item; **~s de consommation courante** basic con-

sumer goods; **faire l'~ à qn** to give sb the sales pitch.
IDIOMS **être à l'~ de la mort** to be at death's door.

articulaire /aRtikylɛR/ *adj* articular.

articulation /aRtikylasjɔ̃/ *nf* **1** (Anat) joint; **2** (of lamp, sunshade) mobile joint; **3** (in phonetics) articulation; **4** (in sentence) link; **5** (of speech, essay) structure.

articuler /aRtikyle/ [1] **I** *vtr* **1** to articulate; **articule!** speak clearly!; **2** to utter; **3** to structure [*ideas*].
II s'articuler *v refl* (+ *v être*) **s'~ autour de** to be based on, to hinge on.

artifice /aRtifis/ *nm* **1** trick; **2** device; **les ~s du style** stylistic devices; **3 sans ~** unpretentious.

artificiel, **-ielle** /aRtifisjɛl/ *adj* **1** artificial; man-made; **2** superficial; forced.

artificier /aRtifisje/ *nm* **1** bomb disposal expert; **2** explosives manufacturer; **3** fireworks manufacturer.

artillerie /aRtijRi/ *nf* artillery.

artisan /aRtizɑ̃/ *nm* **1** artisan, craftsman; **2** architect, author.

artisanal, **~e**, *mpl* **-aux** /aRtizanal, o/ *adj* [*method*] traditional; **de fabrication ~e** handcrafted; home-made.

artisanat /aRtizana/ *nm* **1** craft industry, cottage industry; **2** artisans.
■ **~ d'art** arts and crafts.

artiste /aRtist/ **I** *adj* **1** artistic; **2 il est un peu ~** he's a bit of a dreamer.
II *nmf* **1** artist; **~ peintre** painter; **2** (on stage) performer; (in music hall) artiste; **~ lyrique** opera singer.

artistique /aRtistik/ *adj* artistic.

as /ɑs/ *nm inv* ace.
IDIOMS **être plein aux ~**○ to be loaded○; **passer à l'~**○ [*money*] to go down the drain; [*holidays*] to go by the board; **être fagoté comme l'~ de pique**○ to look a mess.

ascendance /asɑ̃dɑ̃s/ *nf* descent, ancestry.

ascendant, **~e** /asɑ̃dɑ̃, ɑ̃t/ **I** *adj* [*curve*] rising; [*movement*] upward; [*star*] ascending.
II *nm* **1** influence (**sur** over); **2** (Law) ascendant.

ascenseur /asɑ̃sœR/ *nm* lift (GB), elevator (US).
IDIOMS **renvoyer l'~** to return the favour[GB].

ascension /asɑ̃sjɔ̃/ *nf* **1** ascent; **faire l'~ de** to climb; **2** (figurative) rise.

ascensionnel, **-elle** /asɑ̃sjɔnɛl/ *adj* [*movement*] upward; **parachute ~** parascending.

ascète /asɛt/ *nmf* ascetic.

aseptique /asɛptik/ *adj* aseptic.

aseptisé, **~e** /asɛptize/ *adj* [*art*] sanitized; [*world*] sterile; [*decor*] impersonal.

aseptiser /asɛptize/ [1] *vtr* to disinfect [*wound*]; to sterilize [*instrument*].

asexué, **~e** /asɛksɥe/ *adj* asexual.

asiatique /azjatik/ *adj* Asian.

Asie /azi/ *pr nf* Asia; **~ Mineure** Asia Minor.

asile /azil/ *nm* **1** refuge; **chercher ~** to seek refuge; **2** (political) asylum; **3 ~ de vieillards** old people's home; **~ de nuit** night shelter.

asocial, **~e**, *mpl* **-iaux** /asɔsjal, o/ **I** *adj* antisocial.
II *nm,f* social misfit.

aspect /aspɛ/ *nm* **1** side; **voir qch sous son ~ positif** to see the good side of sth; **2** aspect; **par bien des ~s** in many respects; **3** appearance.

asperge /aspɛRʒ/ *nf* **1** asparagus; **2**○ beanpole○, string bean (US).

asperger /aspɛRʒe/ [13] *vtr* to spray; to splash.

aspérité /aspeRite/ *nf* (in terrain) bump.

asphalte /asfalt/ *nm* asphalt.

asphyxie /asfiksi/ *nf* asphyxiation.

asphyxier /asfiksje/ [2] **I** *vtr* **1** to asphyxiate [*person*]; **2** to paralyze [*network, company*].
II s'asphyxier *v refl* (+ *v être*) **1** to suffocate to death; **2** to gas oneself; **3** [*network, company*] to become paralyzed.

aspirateur /aspiRatœR/ *nm* vacuum cleaner, hoover® (GB).

aspiration /aspiRasjɔ̃/ *nf* **1** aspiration (**à** for); **2** sucking up, drawing up; **3** inhalation.

aspirer /aspiRe/ [1] **I** *vtr* **1** to breathe in, to inhale ; **2** to suck [sth] up; **3 consonne aspirée** aspirated consonant.
II aspirer à *v+prep* to yearn for; to aspire to.

assagir: **s'assagir** /asaʒiR/ [3] *v refl* (+ *v être*) to quieten down (GB), to quiet down (US).

assaillant, **~e** /asajɑ̃, ɑ̃t/ *nm,f* **1** attacker; **2** (Mil) **les ~s** the attacking forces.

assaillir /asajiR/ [28] *vtr* **1** to attack; **2** to plague; **~ qn de questions** to bombard sb with questions.

assainir /aseniR/ [3] *vtr* **1** to clean up; **2** to stabilize [*economy*]; to streamline [*company*].

assainissement /asenismɑ̃/ *nm* **1** cleaning up; **2** (of economy) stabilization; (of company) streamlining.

assaisonnement /asɛzɔnmɑ̃/ *nm* (Culin) seasoning; (on salad) dressing.

assaisonner /asɛzɔne/ [1] *vtr* to season [*dish*]; to dress [*salad*].

assassin, **~e** /asasɛ̃, in/ **I** *adj* **1** murderous; **2** [*campaign*] vicious.
II *nm* **1** murderer; **2** assassin.

assassinat /asasina/ *nm* **1** murder; **2** assassination.

assassiner /asasine/ [1] *vtr* **1** to murder; **2** to assassinate; **3**○ to slate○.

assaut /aso/ *nm* attack, assault; **se lancer** or **monter à l'~ de** to launch an attack on; **prendre d'~** to storm; **les ~s du froid** the onslaught of cold weather.

assécher /aseʃe/ [14] *vtr* **1** to drain; **2** [*heat*] to dry up.

ASSEDIC /asedik/ *nf* (*abbr* = **Association pour l'emploi dans l'industrie et le commerce**) *organization managing unemployment contributions and payments.*

assemblage /asɑ̃blaʒ/ *nm* **1** (of motor)

assembly (**de** of); **2** (of ideas) assemblage; (of objects) collection; (of colours) combination.

assemblée /asɑ̃ble/ *nf* **1** gathering; **2** meeting; **3** assembly.

■ **~ générale**, **AG** general meeting; **l'Assemblée nationale** the French National Assembly.

assembler /asɑ̃ble/ [1] **I** *vtr* to assemble, to put together.

II s'assembler *v refl* (+ *v être*) [*crowd*] to gather; [*ministers*] to assemble.

IDIOMS **qui se ressemble s'assemble** (Proverb) birds of a feather flock together.

asséner /asene/ [14] *vtr* **~ un coup à qn/qch** to deal sb/sth a blow.

assentiment /asɑ̃timɑ̃/ *nm* assent, consent.

asseoir /aswaʀ/ [41] **I** *vtr* **1** to sit [sb] down; (in bed) to sit [sb] up; **faire ~ qn** to make sb sit down; (politely) to offer a seat to sb; **2** to establish [*reputation*]; **3**° to stagger, to astound.

II s'asseoir *v refl* (+ *v être*) to sit (down); (in bed) to sit up.

assermenté, **~e** /asɛʀmɑ̃te/ *adj* sworn, on oath.

assertion /asɛʀsjɔ̃/ *nf* assertion.

asservir /asɛʀviʀ/ [3] *vtr* **1** to enslave [*person*]; **2** to subjugate [*country*].

asservissement /asɛʀvismɑ̃/ *nm* **1** (of country, people) subjugation; **2** subjection; **3** subservience.

assesseur /asesœʀ/ *nm* magistrate's assistant.

assez /ase/ *adv* **1** enough; **~ fort** strong enough; **j'en ai ~** I've got enough; I'm fed up°; **2** quite; **je suis ~ pressé** I'm in rather a hurry; **je suis ~ d'accord** I tend to agree.

assidu, **~e** /asidy/ *adj* **1** diligent; **2** [*care*] constant; **3** [*presence, visits*] regular; **4** devoted.

assiduité /asidɥite/ *nf* **1** diligence; **avec ~** [*work*] diligently; [*train*] assiduously; [*read*] regularly; **2** regular attendance; **3 ~s** assiduities.

assiéger /asjeʒe/ [15] *vtr* to besiege.

assiette /asjɛt/ *nf* **1** (for food) plate; **2 ~ (fiscale)** tax base.

■ **~ anglaise** assorted cold meats; **~ en carton** paper plate; **~ creuse** soup plate; **~ à dessert** dessert plate.

IDIOMS **ne pas être dans son ~** to be out of sorts.

assignation /asiɲasjɔ̃/ *nf* **1** allocation; **2** (Law) summons.

assigner /asiɲe/ [1] *vtr* **1** to assign [*task*]; **2** to set [*objective*]; **3** to ascribe [*value, role*] (**à** to); **4** (Law) **~ à comparaître** to summons; **~ qn à résidence** to put sb under house arrest.

assimilation /asimilasjɔ̃/ *nf* **1** comparison; **2** assimilation.

assimilé, **~e** /asimile/ *adj* similar.

assimiler /asimile/ [1] **I** *vtr* **1** to assimilate; **être assimilé cadre** to have executive status; **2 ~ qn/qch à** to liken sb/sth to.

II s'assimiler *v refl* (+ *v être*) **1 s'~ à** [*method*] to be comparable to; [*person*] to compare oneself to; **2** [*minority*] to become assimilated; [*substances*] to be assimilated.

assis, **~e** /asi, iz/ **I** *pp* ▶ **asseoir**.

II *pp adj* **1** seated; **être ~** to be sitting down; (in bed) to be sitting up; **reste ~** don't get up; (as reprimand) sit still; **2** [*reputation*] well-established; **3**° staggered.

assises /asiz/ *nf pl* **1** meeting; **2** (Law) assizes.

assistance /asistɑ̃s/ *nf* **1** assistance; aid; **2** audience; **3** attendance (**à** at).

■ **~ respiratoire** artificial respiration; **l'Assistance publique** ≈ welfare services.

assistant, **~e** /asistɑ̃, ɑ̃t/ *nm,f* assistant.

■ **~e sociale** social worker.

assisté, **~e** /asiste/ **I** *pp* ▶ **assister**.

II *pp adj* **1** assisted (**de** by); **2** receiving benefit (GB), on welfare (US); **3 ~ par ordinateur** computer-aided; **4 direction ~e** power steering.

III *nm,f*: *person receiving benefit* (GB) or *welfare* (US).

assister /asiste/ [1] **I** *vtr* to assist; to aid.

II assister à *v+prep* **1 ~ à** to be at, to attend; **2 ~ à** to witness.

associatif, **-ive** /asɔsjatif, iv/ *adj* **1** [*memory*] associative; **2 vie associative** community life.

association /asɔsjasjɔ̃/ *nf* **1** association; **2** combination.

associé, **~e** /asɔsje/ **I** *adj* [*member*] associate; [*companies*] associated.

II *nm,f* associate, partner.

associer /asɔsje/ [2] **I** *vtr* **1 ~ qn à** to include sb in [*success*]; to make sb a partner in [*business*]; to give sb a share of [*profits*]; **2 ~ qch à** to combine sth with; to associate sth with.

II s'associer *v refl* (+ *v être*) **1** to go into partnership, to link up; **s'~ pour faire** to join forces to do; **2 s'~ à** to join [*movement*]; to share in [*grief*]; **3** to combine.

assoiffé, **~e** /aswafe/ *adj* **1** thirsty; **2 ~ de** thirsting for.

assombrir /asɔ̃bʀiʀ/ [3] **I** *vtr* **1** to make [sth] dark, to darken; **2** to spoil; **la tristesse assombrit son visage** his/her face clouded.

II s'assombrir *v refl* (+ *v être*) **1** [*sky*] to darken; **2** [*face*] to become gloomy.

assommer /asɔme/ [1] *vtr* **1** to knock [sb] senseless; **2**° **~ qn** to get on sb's nerves; **3**° [*news*] to stagger; [*heat*] to overcome.

assorti, **~e** /asɔʀti/ *adj* **1** matching; **2** assorted.

assortiment /asɔʀtimɑ̃/ *nm* **1** set; **2** assortment, selection; **3** (in shop) stock.

assortir /asɔʀtiʀ/ [3] **I** *vtr* **1** to match (**à** to; **avec** with); **2 ~ qch de qch** to add sth to sth.

II s'assortir *v refl* (+ *v être*) **1 s'~ à** or **avec** to match; **2 s'~ de** to come with.

assoupir /asupiʀ/ [3] **I** *vtr* **1** to make [sb] drowsy; **2** to dull [*senses, passion*].

II s'assoupir *v refl* (+ *v être*) to doze off.

assouplir /asupliʀ/ [3] **I** *vtr* **1** to soften [*washing*]; **2** to make [sth] more supple [*body, leather*]; **3** to relax [*rule*].

II s'assouplir *v refl* (+ *v être*) **1** to get softer;

2 to become more supple; **3** [*person, rule*] to become more flexible.

assouplissant /asuplisɑ̃/ *nm* fabric softener.

assourdir /asuʀdiʀ/ [3] *vtr* **1** to deafen; **2** to muffle.

assouvir /asuviʀ/ [3] *vtr* to satisfy [*hunger*]; to assuage [*anger*].

assouvissement /asuvismɑ̃/ *nm* **1** (of hunger) satisfying; (of anger) assuaging; **2** satisfaction.

assujetti, **~e** /asyʒeti/ *adj* **~ à** liable for [*tax*]; subject to [*rule*].

assujettir /asyʒeti/ [3] **I** *vtr* **1** to subject (**à** to); **2** to subjugate, to subdue; **3** to secure.
II s'assujettir *v refl* (+ *v être*) [*person*] to submit (**à** to).

assumer /asyme/ [1] **I** *vtr* **1** to take [*responsibility*]; to hold [*post*]; to meet [*costs*]; **2** to come to terms with [*conditions, identity, past*]; to accept [*consequences*].
II s'assumer *v refl* (+ *v être*) **1** to take responsibility for oneself; **2** to come to terms with oneself.

assurable /asyʀabl/ *adj* insurable.

assurance /asyʀɑ̃s/ *nf* **1** (self-)confidence, assurance; **avec ~** confidently; **2** assurance; **donner à qn l'~ que** to assure sb that; **3** insurance (policy); **4** insurance company; **5** insurance (premium); **6** insurance (sector); **7** benefit (GB), benefits (US).
■ **~ au tiers** third-party insurance; **~ maladie** health insurance; sickness benefit (GB) or benefits (US); **~ tous risques** comprehensive insurance; **~s sociales** social insurance.

assurance-vie, *pl* **assurances-vie** /asyʀɑ̃svi/ *nf* life insurance.

assuré, **~e** /asyʀe/ **I** *pp* ▶ **assurer**.
II *pp adj* **1** sure, certain (**de faire** of doing); **soyez ~ de ma reconnaissance** I am very grateful to you; **2** insured.
III *adj* **1** [*step, air*] confident; [*hand*] steady; **mal ~** [*step, voice*] faltering; [*gesture*] nervous; **2** certain, assured.
IV *nm,f* insured party.
■ **~ social** social insurance contributor.

assurément /asyʀemɑ̃/ *adv* **1** definitely; **2** most certainly.

assurer /asyʀe/ [1] **I** *vtr* **1 ~ à qn que** to assure sb that; **ce n'est pas drôle, je t'assure** believe me, it's no joke; **2 ~ qn de** to assure sb of [*support*]; **3** to insure [*property, goods*]; **4** to carry out [*maintenance*]; to provide [*service*]; **~ la liaison entre** [*train, bus, ferry*] to operate between; **~ la gestion de** to manage; **5** to ensure [*victory*]; to secure [*right, post*] (**à qn** for sb); to assure [*future*]; **~ un revenu à qn** to give sb an income; **~ ses vieux jours** to provide for one's old age; **6** to secure [*rope*]; to belay [*climber*].
II s'assurer *v refl* (+ *v être*) **1 s'~ de qch** to make sure of sth; **2** to secure [*advantage, help*]; **3** to take out insurance; **4** (figurative) **s'~ contre** to insure against [*eventuality, risk*].

assureur /asyʀœʀ/ *nm* **1** insurance agent; **2** insurance company.

astérisque /asteʀisk/ *nm* asterisk.

asthmatique /asmatik/ *adj, nmf* asthmatic.

asthme /asm/ *nm* asthma.

asticot /astiko/ *nm* maggot.

astigmate /astigmat/ *adj* astigmatic.

astiquer /astike/ [1] *vtr* to polish.

astral, **~e**, *mpl* **-aux** /astʀal, o/ *adj* astral.

astre /astʀ/ *nm* star.

astreindre /astʀɛ̃dʀ/ [55] **I** *vtr* **~ qn à qch** [*person*] to force sth upon sb; [*rule*] to bind sb to sth; **~ qn à faire** to compel sb to do.
II s'astreindre *v refl* (+ *v être*) **s'~ à qch** to subject oneself to sth.

astringent, **~e** /astʀɛ̃ʒɑ̃, ɑ̃t/ *adj* astringent.

astrologie /astʀɔlɔʒi/ *nf* astrology.

astrologue /astʀɔlɔg/ *nmf* astrologer.

astronautique /astʀɔnotik/ *nf* astronautics.

astronomie /astʀɔnɔmi/ *nf* astronomy.

astronomique /astʀɔnɔmik/ *adj* astronomical.

astuce /astys/ *nf* **1** cleverness; **2** shrewdness, astuteness; **3** trick; **4** pun; joke.

astucieux, **-ieuse** /astysjø, øz/ *adj* **1** clever; **2** shrewd, sharp.

asymétrique /asimetʀik/ *adj* asymmetrical.

atelier /atəlje/ *nm* **1** (place) workshop; (artist's) studio; **2** working group; **3** (seminar) workshop.

athée /ate/ **I** *adj* atheistic.
II *nmf* atheist.

athénien, **-ienne** /atenjɛ̃, ɛn/ *adj* Athenian.

athlète /atlɛt/ *nmf* athlete.

athlétique /atletik/ *adj* athletic.

athlétisme /atletism/ *nm* athletics (GB), track and field events.

Atlantique /atlɑ̃tik/ *pr nm* **l'~** the Atlantic.

atlas /atlas/ *nm inv* atlas.

atmosphère /atmɔsfɛʀ/ *nf* atmosphere.

atoll /atɔl/ *nm* atoll.

atome /atom/ *nm* atom.
IDIOMS **avoir des ~s crochus avec qn**○ to get on well with sb.

atomique /atɔmik/ *adj* atomic.

atomiseur /atɔmizœʀ/ *nm* spray, atomizer.

atone /atɔn/ *adj* **1** lifeless, apathetic; **2** [*syllable*] unstressed.

atours† /atuʀ/ *nm pl* finery.

atout /atu/ *nm* **1** trump (card); trumps; **2** (figurative) asset; trump card; **mettre tous les ~s dans son jeu** to leave nothing to chance.

âtre /atʀ/ *nm* hearth.

atroce /atʀɔs/ *adj* atrocious, dreadful, terrible.

atrocité /atʀɔsite/ *nf* **1** atrocity; **2** monstrosity.

atrophier: **s'atrophier** /atʀɔfje/ [2] *v refl* (+ *v être*) to atrophy; **bras atrophié** wasted arm.

attabler: **s'attabler** /atable/ [1] *v refl* (+ *v être*) to sit down at (the) table.

attachant, **~e** /ataʃɑ̃, ɑ̃t/ *adj* engaging.

attache /ataʃ/ *nf* **1** tie; string; rope; strap; **~s familiales** family ties; **2 avoir des ~s fines** to have delicate ankles and wrists.

attaché, **~e** /ataʃe/ *nm,f* attaché.
■ **~ de presse** press attaché.

attachement /ataʃmɑ̃/ *nm* **1** (to person) attachment; **2** (to principle, cause) commitment.

attacher /ataʃe/ [1] **I** *vtr* **1** to tie [*person, hands, laces*] (**à** to); to tether [*horse, goat*]; to chain [*dog*] (**à** to); to lock [*bicycle*] (**à** to); to tie up [*person, parcel*]; **2** to fasten [*belt*]; **3** to attach [*importance*]; **4 les privilèges attachés à un poste** the privileges attached to a post.
II s'attacher *v refl* (+ *v être*) **1** to fasten; **2 s'~ à qn/qch** to become attached to sb/sth.

attaquant, **~e** /atakɑ̃, ɑ̃t/ *nm,f* attacker.

attaque /atak/ **I** *nf* **1** attack; (on bank) raid; **passer à l'~** to move into the attack; (figurative) to go on the attack; **~ à main armée** armed raid; **2** (Med) stroke; **~ cardiaque** heart attack.
II d'attaque○ *phr* on (GB) or in (US) form; **être d'~ pour faire** to feel up to doing.

attaquer /atake/ [1] **I** *vtr* **1** to attack; to raid [*bank*]; **2** (Law) to contest [*contract, will*]; **~ qn en justice** to bring a lawsuit against sb; **3** to tackle [*problem*].
II *vi* **1** (in tennis, golf) to drive; **2** [*speaker*] to begin (brusquely).
III s'attaquer *v refl* (+ *v être*) **s'~ à** to attack [*person, policy*]; to tackle [*problem*].

attardé, **~e** /ataʀde/ **I** *adj* retarded.
II *nm,f* mentally retarded person.

attarder: **s'attarder** /ataʀde/ [1] *v refl* (+ *v être*) **1** to stay until late; to linger; **2 s'~ sur** to dwell on [*point*].

atteindre /atɛ̃dʀ/ [55] **I** *vtr* **1** to reach [*place, age, level, target*]; to achieve [*aim*]; **2** [*projectile, marksman*] to hit [*target*]; **3** [*illness*] to affect.
II atteindre à *v+prep* to reach; to achieve.

atteint, **~e**[1] /atɛ̃, ɛ̃t/ **I** *pp* ▶ **atteindre**.
II *pp adj* **1** affected (**de, par** by); **être ~ de** to be suffering from [*illness*]; **2** hit (**de, par** by).

atteinte[2] /atɛ̃t/ **I** *nf* **~ à** attack on; **porter ~ à** to undermine [*prestige*]; to damage [*reputation*]; to endanger [*security*]; to infringe [*right*]; **~ à la vie privée** breach of privacy.
II hors d'atteinte *phr* **hors d'~** [*person*] beyond reach; [*target*] out of range.

attelage /atlaʒ/ *nm* **1** (of horse) harness; (of oxen) yoke; (of wagon) coupling; (of trailer) towing attachment; **2** (animals) team; (of oxen) yoke; **3** horse-drawn carriage.

atteler /atle/ [19] **I** *vtr* to harness [*horse*]; to yoke [*oxen*]; to couple [*wagon*].
II s'atteler *v refl* (+ *v être*) **s'~ à une tâche** to get down to a job.

attelle /atɛl/ *nf* (Med) splint.

attenant, **~e** /atnɑ̃, ɑ̃t/ *adj* adjacent.

attendre /atɑ̃dʀ/ [6] **I** *vtr* **1** to wait for [*person, event*]; **j'attends de voir pour le croire** I'll believe it when I see it; **se faire ~** to keep people waiting; **la réaction ne se fit pas ~** the reaction was instantaneous; **~ son jour** or **heure** to bide one's time; **en attendant mieux** until something better turns up; **on ne t'attendait plus!** we'd given up on you!; **2** to await, to be in store for [*person*]; **3** to expect; **~ qch de qn/qch** to expect sth from sb/sth; **elle attend un bébé** she's expecting a baby.
II *vi* to wait; (on phone) to hold; **faire ~ qn** to keep sb waiting; **en attendant** in the meantime; all the same, nonetheless; **tu ne perds rien pour ~**○! I'll get you○, just you wait!
III s'attendre *v refl* (+ *v être*) **s'~ à qch** to expect sth; **s'~ à ce que qn fasse** to expect sb to do.

attendrir /atɑ̃dʀiʀ/ [3] **I** *vtr* to touch, to move [*person*]; **se laisser ~** to soften.
II s'attendrir *v refl* (+ *v être*) to feel moved.

attendrissant, **~e** /atɑ̃dʀisɑ̃, ɑ̃t/ *adj* touching, moving; [*innocence*] endearing.

attendrissement /atɑ̃dʀismɑ̃/ *nm* emotion.

attendu[1]: **attendu que** /atɑ̃dy/ *phr* **1** given or considering that; **2** (Law) whereas.

attendu[2], **~e** /atɑ̃dy/ *adj* **1** expected; **2 le jour (tant) ~** the long-awaited day.

attentat /atɑ̃ta/ *nm* assassination attempt, attack; **~ à la bombe** bomb attack.
■ **~ à la pudeur** (Law) indecent assault.

attente /atɑ̃t/ *nf* **1** waiting; wait; **mon ~ a été vaine** I waited in vain; **dans l'~ de vous lire** looking forward to hearing from you; **en ~** [*passenger*] waiting; [*file*] pending; [*call*] on hold; **2** expectation; **répondre à l'~ de qn** to come up to sb's expectations.

attenter /atɑ̃te/ [1] *v+prep* **~ à ses jours** to attempt suicide; **~ à la vie de qn** to make an attempt on sb's life.

attentif, **-ive** /atɑ̃tif, iv/ *adj* attentive; **sous l'œil ~ de leur mère** under the watchful eye of their mother.

attention /atɑ̃sjɔ̃/ **I** *nf* **1** attention; **faire ~ à qch** to mind [*cars, step*]; to watch out for [*black ice*]; to take care of [*clothes, belongings*]; to watch [*diet, health*]; to pay attention to [*fashion, details*]; **faire ~ à qn** to pay attention to sb; to keep an eye on sb; to take notice of sb; **2** kind gesture; **être plein d'~s pour qn** to be very attentive to sb.
II *excl* **1** (cry) look out!, watch out!; (written) attention!; (in case of danger) warning!; (on road sign) caution!; **2 ~, je ne veux pas dire**... don't get me wrong, I don't mean...

attentionné, **~e** /atɑ̃sjɔne/ *adj* attentive, considerate.

attentivement /atɑ̃tivmɑ̃/ *adv* **1** attentively; **2** carefully.

atténuantes /atenɥɑ̃t/ *adj f pl* **circonstances ~** (Law) mitigating circumstances.

atténuer /atenɥe/ [1] **I** *vtr* to ease [*pain, distress*]; to lessen [*impact*]; to smooth over [*differences*]; to weaken [*effect*]; to soften [*blow*]; to reduce [*inequalities*]; to dim [*light*]; to make [sth] less strong [*smell, taste*].
II s'atténuer *v refl* (+ *v être*) [*pain*] to ease; [*anger, grief*] to subside; [*corruption, pessimism*] to lessen; [*gaps*] to be reduced; [*wrinkles, colour*] to fade; [*storm, noise*] to die down.

atterrant, **~e** /atɛʀɑ̃, ɑ̃t/ *adj* **1** appalling; **2** shattering.

atterré, **~e** /ateʀe/ *adj* **1** appalled; **2** shattered.

atterrir /ateʀiʀ/ [3] *vi* to land.

atterrissage /ateʀisaʒ/ *nm* landing.

attestation /atɛstasjɔ̃/ *nf* **1** attestation; **2** certificate.

attester /atɛste/ [1] *vtr* **1** to vouch for; to testify to; **2** to prove, to attest to.

attirail /atiʀɑj/ *nm* gear, equipment.

attirance /atiʀɑ̃s/ *nf* attraction.

attirant, **~e** /atiʀɑ̃, ɑ̃t/ *adj* attractive.

attirer /atiʀe/ [1] I *vtr* **1** to attract [*person, capital*]; to draw [*crowd, attention*]; **~ qn dans un coin** to take sb into a corner; **~ qn dans un piège** to lure sb into a trap; **2** [*country, profession*] to appeal to; **3** to bring [*shame, anger*]; **~ des ennuis à qn** to cause sb problems.

II **s'attirer** *v refl* (+ *v être*) **s'~ le soutien de qn** to win sb's support; **s'~ des ennuis** to get into trouble.

attiser /atize/ [1] *vtr* **1** to kindle [*feeling*]; to fuel [*discord*]; to stir up [*hatred*]; **2** to fan [*fire*].

attitré, **~e** /atitʀe/ *adj* **1** [*chauffeur*] official; **2** [*customer*] regular.

attitude /atityd/ *nf* **1** bearing; posture; **2** attitude.

attouchement /atuʃmɑ̃/ *nm* **1** molesting; **2** fondling; **3** (by healer) laying on of hands.

attractif, **-ive** /atʀaktif, iv/ *adj* attractive.

attraction /atʀaksjɔ̃/ *nf* attraction.

■ **~ terrestre** earth's gravity; **~ universelle** gravitation.

attrait /atʀɛ/ *nm* **1** appeal, attraction; lure; **2 l'~ de qn pour qn/qch** sb's liking for sb/sth.

attraper /atʀape/ [1] *vtr* **1** to catch; **se faire ~** to get caught; **attrapez-le!** stop him!; **2** to catch hold of [*rope, hand, leg*]; **3**○ to catch [*cold, illness*]; **4**○ to tell [sb] off.

attrayant, **~e** /atʀɛjɑ̃, ɑ̃t/ *adj* **1** attractive; **2** pleasant.

attribuer /atʀibɥe/ [1] I *vtr* **1** to allocate [*seat, task*]; to grant [*right*]; to award [*prize*]; to lend [*importance*]; **~ qch à la fatigue** to put sth down to tiredness; **2 ~ qch à qn** to credit sb with sth [*quality*]; to attribute sth to sb [*work*].

II **s'attribuer** *v refl* (+ *v être*) **s'~ la meilleure part** to give oneself the largest share; **s'~ tout le mérite** to take all the credit.

attribut /atʀiby/ *nm* **1** (quality, symbol) attribute; **2** (in grammar) complement; **adjectif ~** predicative adjective; **nom ~** complement.

attribution /atʀibysjɔ̃/ I *nf* **1** allocation; **2** awarding.

II **attributions** *nf pl* (of individual) remit; (of court) competence.

attrister /atʀiste/ [1] *vtr* to sadden; **j'ai été attristé d'apprendre** I was sorry to hear.

attroupement /atʀupmɑ̃/ *nm* gathering.

attrouper: **s'attrouper** /atʀupe/ [1] *v refl* (+ *v être*) to gather.

au /o/ *prep* (= **à le**) ▶ **à**.

aubaine /obɛn/ *nf* **1** godsend; **2** bargain.

aube /ob/ *nf* **1** dawn; **2** alb; cassock.

aubépine /obepin/ *nf* hawthorn.

auberge /obɛʀʒ/ *nf* inn; **~ de jeunesse** youth hostel.

IDIOMS **tu n'es pas sorti de l'~**○! you're not out of the woods yet!

aubergine /obɛʀʒin/ *nf* aubergine, eggplant.

aubergiste /obɛʀʒist/ *nmf* innkeeper.

aucun, **~e** /okœ̃, yn/ I *adj* no, not any; **en ~ cas** under no circumstances.

II *pron* none; **je n'ai lu ~ de vos livres** I haven't read any of your books; **~ de ses arguments n'est convaincant** none of his arguments are convincing.

aucunement /okynmɑ̃/ *adv* in no way.

audace /odas/ *nf* **1** boldness; **2** daring; **3** audacity, nerve○; impudence.

audacieux, **-ieuse** /odasjø, øz/ *adj* **1** bold; **2** audacious, daring.

au-delà /od(ə)la/ I *nm* **l'~** the hereafter.

II *adv* beyond; **jusqu'à 1000 francs mais pas ~** up to 1,000 francs but no more.

III **au-delà de** *phr* beyond; over.

au-dessous /odəsu/ I *adv* **1** below; **2** under; **les enfants de dix ans et ~** children of ten years and under.

II **au-dessous de** *phr* below; **être ~ de tout**○ to be absolutely useless.

au-dessus /odəsy/ I *adv* above; **les enfants de 10 ans et ~** children of 10 and over; **la taille ~** the next size up.

II **au-dessus de** *phr* above; **~ de chez moi** in the apartment above mine; **un pont ~ de la rivière** a bridge over the river; **se pencher ~ de la table** to lean across the table.

au-devant: **au-devant de** /odəvɑ̃də/ *phr* **aller ~ de qn** to go to meet sb; **aller ~ des ennuis** to let oneself in for trouble.

audible /odibl/ *adj* audible.

audience /odjɑ̃s/ *nf* **1** (Law) hearing; **salle d'~** courtroom; **2** (interview) audience; **3** (public) audience.

Audimat® /odimat/ *nm* audience ratings.

audiovisuel, **-elle** /odjɔvisɥel/ I *adj* **1** broadcasting; **2** audiovisual.

II *nm* **1** broadcasting; **2** audiovisual equipment; **3** audiovisual methods.

audit /odit/ *nm* audit.

auditeur, **-trice** /oditœʀ, tʀis/ *nm,f* listener.

auditif, **-ive** /oditif, iv/ *adj* [*nerve*] auditory; [*problems*] hearing; [*memory*] aural.

audition /odisjɔ̃/ *nf* **1** (sense) hearing; **2** audition; **3** (Law) hearing, examination.

auditionner /odisjɔne/ [1] *vtr*, *vi* to audition.

auditoire /oditwaʀ/ *nm* audience.

auge /oʒ/ *nf* (for animal feed) trough.

augmentation /ɔgmɑ̃tasjɔ̃/ *nf* increase; **une ~ (de salaire)** a pay rise (GB) or raise (US).

augmenter /ɔgmɑ̃te/ [1] I *vtr* to raise, to increase; to extend; **~ le loyer de qn** to put sb's rent up.

II *vi* to increase, to go up, to rise.

augure /ogyʀ/ *nm* **1** omen; **2** augury.

augurer /ogyʀe/ [1] *vtr* **que peut-on ~ de**

cette attitude? what should we expect from this attitude?

auguste /ogyst/ *adj* august, noble.

aujourd'hui /oʒuʀdɥi/ *adv* **1** today; **2** nowadays, today; **la France d'~** present-day France.

aulne /on/ *nm* alder.

aumône /omon/ *nf* hand-out, alms; **demander l'~** to ask for charity.

aumônerie /omonʀi/ *nf* chaplaincy.

aumônier /omonje/ *nm* chaplain.

aune /on/ *nm* = **aulne**.

auparavant /opaʀavɑ̃/ *adv* before; beforehand; previously; formerly.

auprès: **auprès de** /opʀɛdə/ *phr* **1** next to, beside; **il s'est rendu ~ de sa tante** he went to see his aunt; **2** compared with; **3 s'excuser ~ de qn** to apologize to sb; **renseigne-toi ~ de la mairie** ask for information at the town hall; **représentant ~ de l'ONU** representative to the UN.

auquel ▶ **lequel**.

auréole /ɔʀeɔl/ *nf* **1** (stain) ring; **2** halo.

auréolé, **~e** /ɔʀeɔle/ *adj* **~ de** basking in the glow of.

auriculaire /oʀikylɛʀ/ **I** *adj* auricular.

II *nm* little finger, pinkie.

aurifère /oʀifɛʀ/ *adj* **1** [*mineral*] auriferous; **2 valeurs ~s** gold stocks.

aurore /oʀɔʀ/ *nf* dawn; **~ boréale** Northern Lights, aurora borealis.

auscultation /ɔskyltasjɔ̃/ *nf* examination.

ausculter /ɔskylte/ [1] *vtr* (Med) to examine.

auspices /ospis/ *nm pl* auspices.

aussi /osi/ **I** *adv* **1** too, as well, also; **il sera absent et moi ~** he'll be away and so will I; **2 ~ bien que** as well as; **~ âgé que** as old as; **3** so; **je ne savais pas qu'il était ~ vieux** I didn't know he was so old; **dans une ~ belle maison** in such a nice house.

II *conj* so, consequently.

aussitôt /osito/ **I** *adv* **1** immediately, straight away; **2 ~ arrivé** as soon as he arrived; **~ dit ~ fait** no sooner said than done.

II aussitôt que *phr* as soon as.

austère /ɔstɛʀ, ostɛʀ/ *adj* austere; severe.

austérité /osteʀite/ *nf* austerity; severity.

austral, **~e**, *mpl* **~s** /ostʀal/ *adj* southern, south.

Australie /ostʀali/ *pr nf* Australia.

australien, **-ienne** /ostʀaljɛ̃, ɛn/ *adj* Australian.

autant /otɑ̃/ **I** *adv* **il n'a jamais ~ neigé** it has never snowed so much; **je t'aime toujours ~** I still love you as much; **essaie d'en faire ~** try and do the same; **je les hais tous ~ qu'ils sont** I hate every single one of them; **j'aime ~ partir tout de suite** I'd rather leave straight away; **~ dire que la réunion est annulée** in other words the meeting is cancelled[GB]; **~ parler à un mur** you might as well be talking to the wall; **~ que je sache** as far as I know; **~ que tu peux** as much as you can.

II autant de *quantif* **1 ~ de cadeaux** so many presents; **il y a ~ de femmes que d'hommes** there are as many women as (there are) men; **2 ~ de gentillesse** such kindness; **je n'ai pas eu ~ de chance que lui** I haven't had as much luck as he has.

III d'autant *phr* **cela va permettre de réduire d'~ les coûts de production** this will allow an equivalent reduction in production costs; **d'~ plus!** all the more reason!; **d'~ moins** even less, all the less; **d'~ que** all the more so as.

IV pour autant *phr* for all that; **sans pour ~ tout modifier** without necessarily changing everything; **pour ~ que je sache** as far as I know.

autarcie /otaʀsi/ *nf* autarky; **vivre en ~** to be self-sufficient.

autel /otɛl/ *nm* altar.

auteur /otœʀ/ *nm* **1** author; **2** creator; (of song) composer; (of crime) perpetrator.

■ **~ dramatique** playwright.

auteur-compositeur, *pl* **auteurs-compositeurs** /otœʀkɔ̃pozitœʀ/ *nm* songwriter.

authenticité /otɑ̃tisite/ *nf* authenticity.

authentifier /otɑ̃tifje/ [2] *vtr* to authenticate.

authentique /otɑ̃tik/ *adj* [*story*] true; [*painting, document*] authentic; [*feeling*] genuine.

autiste /otist/ *nm,f* autistic person.

auto /auto/ *nf* car, automobile (US).

■ **~ tamponneuse** bumper car, dodgem.

autobiographie /otobjogʀafi/ *nf* autobiography.

autobus /otɔbys/ *nm inv* bus.

autocar /otɔkaʀ/ *nm* coach (GB), bus (US).

autochtone /otɔkton/ *adj*, *nmf* native.

autocollant, **~e** /otɔkɔlɑ̃, ɑ̃t/ **I** *adj* self-adhesive.

II *nm* sticker.

autocuiseur /otokɥizœʀ/ *nm* pressure cooker.

autodéfense /otodefɑ̃s/ *nf* self-defence[GB].

autodestruction /otodɛstʀyksjɔ̃/ *nf* self-destruction.

autodétruire: **s'autodétruire** /otodetʀɥiʀ/ [69] *v refl* (+ *v être*) [*person*] to destroy oneself; [*tape*] to self-destruct; [*missile*] to autodestruct.

autodidacte /otodidakt/ *nmf* self-educated person.

auto-école, *pl* **~s** /otoekɔl/ *nf* driving school.

automate /otɔmat/ *nm* robot, automaton.

automatique /otɔmatik/ **I** *adj* **1** automatic; **2** inevitable.

II *nm* **1** automatic (revolver); **2** automatic camera.

automatiquement /otɔmatikmɑ̃/ *adv* **1** automatically; **2**○ inevitably.

automatiser /otɔmatize/ [1] *vtr* to automate.

automatisme /otɔmatism/ *nm* automatism;

automatic functioning; **acquérir des ~s** to acquire automatic reflexes.

automne /otɔn/ *nm* autumn (GB), fall (US).

automobile /otomɔbil/ **I** *adj* **1** car; **2** (Sport) [*racing*] motor; [*circuit*] motor racing.
II *nf* **1** (motor) car, automobile (US); **2** the motor (GB) or automobile (US) industry.

automobiliste /otomɔbilist/ *nmf* motorist.

autonome /otɔnɔm/ *adj* autonomous; independent; self-sufficient.

autonomie /otɔnɔmi/ *nf* **1** autonomy; **2** (of car, plane) range; **~ de vol** flight range.

autonomiste /otɔnɔmist/ *adj*, *nmf* separatist.

autoportrait /otopɔʀtʀɛ/ *nm* self-portrait.

autopsie /otɔpsi/ *nf* postmortem (examination).

autoradio /otoʀadjo/ *nm* car radio.

autorisation /otɔʀizasjɔ̃/ *nf* **1** permission; authorization; **2** permit.

autorisé, **~e** /otɔʀize/ *adj* authorized; legal; accredited; permitted.

autoriser /otɔʀize/ [1] *vtr* **1** to allow, to authorize; **2 ~ qn à faire** to entitle sb to do; **3** to make [sth] possible.

autoritaire /otɔʀitɛʀ/ *adj*, *nmf* authoritarian.

autorité /otɔʀite/ *nf* **1** authority; **faire qch d'~** to do sth without consultation; **il n'a aucune ~ sur ses enfants** he has no control over his children; **faire ~** [*person*] to be an authority; [*work*] to be authoritative; **2** (person) authority, expert.

autoroute /otoʀut/ *nf* motorway (GB), freeway (US); **~ à péage** toll motorway.

auto-stop /otostɔp/ *nm* hitchhiking.

auto-stoppeur, **-euse**, *mpl* **~s** /otostɔpœʀ, øz/ *nm,f* hitchhiker.

autour /otuʀ/ **I** *adv* **une parterre de fleurs avec des pierres ~** a flower bed with stones around it; **tout ~** all around.
II autour de *phr* **1** around, round (GB); **~ de la table** around the table; **2** around, about; **~ de 10 heures** around 10 o'clock; **3** about, on; **un débat ~ du thème du pouvoir** a debate on the theme of power.

autre /otʀ/ **I** *det* **1** other; **une ~ histoire** another story; **rien d'~** nothing else; **l'effet obtenu est tout ~** the effect produced is completely different; **2**○ **nous ~s professeurs/Français** we teachers/French.
II *pron* **1 où sont les ~s?** where are the other ones?; where are the others?; **je t'ai pris pour un ~** I mistook you for someone else; **ils se respectent les uns les ~s** they respect each other; **chez lui c'est tout l'un ou tout l'~** with him it's all or nothing; **à d'~s**○! pull the other one!; **2 prends-en un ~** have another one; **si je peux je t'en apporterai d'~s** if I can I'll bring you some more.
III autre part *phr* somewhere else.

autrefois /otʀəfwa/ *adv* in the past; before, formerly; in the old days; **~, quand Paris s'appelait Lutèce** long ago, when Paris was called Lutetia; **les légendes d'~** old legends.

autrement /otʀəmɑ̃/ *adv* **1** differently, in a different way; **c'est comme ça, et pas ~** that's just the way it is; **je n'ai pas pu faire ~ que de les inviter** I had no alternative but to invite them; **on ne peut y accéder ~ que par bateau** you can only get there by boat; **je ne l'ai jamais vue ~ qu'en jean** I've never seen her in anything but jeans; **~ dit** in other words; **2** otherwise; **3**○ **~ grave** (much) more serious; **il n'était pas ~ impressionné** he wasn't particularly impressed.

Autriche /otʀiʃ/ *pr nf* Austria.

autrichien, **-ienne** /otʀiʃjɛ̃, ɛn/ *adj* Austrian.

autruche /otʀyʃ/ *nf* ostrich.
IDIOMS **pratiquer la politique de l'~** to bury one's head in the sand.

autrui /otʀɥi/ *pron* others, other people.

auvent /ovɑ̃/ *nm* **1** canopy; **2** awning.

aux /o/ *prep* (= **à les**) ▶ **à**.

auxiliaire /oksiljɛʀ/ **I** *adj* **1** [*verb*] auxiliary; **2** [*equipment, service*] auxiliary; [*motor*] back-up; **3 maître ~** assistant teacher; **infirmier ~** nursing auxiliary (GB), nurse's aide (US).
II *nmf* assistant, helper.
III *nm* auxiliary (verb).

auxquels, **auxquelles** ▶ **lequel**.

avachir: **s'avachir** /avaʃiʀ/ [3] *v refl* (+ *v être*) **1** [*chair*] to sag; **2** [*person*] to let oneself go.

aval /aval/ *nm* **1** (of river) lower reaches; **en ~** downstream; **2** approval.

avalanche /avalɑ̃ʃ/ *nf* avalanche.

avaler /avale/ [1] *vtr* **1** to swallow; **'ne pas ~'** (Med) 'not to be taken internally'; **2** to inhale [*smoke, fumes*].

avance /avɑ̃s/ **I** *nf* **1** advance; **2** lead; **avoir/prendre de l'~ sur** to be/pull ahead of; **3 une ~ (sur salaire)** an advance (on one's salary).
II à l'avance *phr* in advance.
III d'avance *phr* in advance; **avoir cinq minutes d'~** to be five minutes early.
IV en avance *phr* **1** early; **2 être en ~ sur qn** to be ahead of sb; **3 il est en ~ pour son âge** he's advanced for his age.
V avances *nf pl* advances.

avancé, **~e**[1] /avɑ̃se/ **I** *pp* ▶ **avancer**.
II *pp adj* [*ideas*] progressive; **la saison est bien ~e** it's late in the season; **te voilà bien ~!** that's done you a lot of good!

avancée[2] /avɑ̃se/ *nf* (of roof, rock) overhang.

avancement /avɑ̃smɑ̃/ *nm* **1** promotion; **2** progress; **3 ~ de l'âge de la retraite** lowering of the retirement age.

avancer /avɑ̃se/ [12] **I** *vtr* **1** to move [sth] forward [*object*]; to push [sth] forward [*plate*]; **2** to bring forward [*trip, meeting*]; **3 ~ sa montre de cinq minutes** to put one's watch forward (by) five minutes; **4** to get ahead with [*work*]; **cela ne nous avance à rien** that doesn't get us anywhere; **5 ~ de l'argent à qn** [*bank*] to advance money to sb; **6** to put forward [*argument, theory*]; to propose [*figure*].
II *vi* **1** [*person, vehicle*] to move (forward); [*army*] to advance; **elle avança vers le guichet** she went up to the ticket office; **2** to make progress, to progress; **faire ~ la science** to further science; **3 ma montre avance de deux**

minutes my watch is two minutes fast; **4** [*teeth, chin*] to stick out; [*peninsula*] to jut out.

III **s'avancer** *v refl* (+ *v être*) **1 s'~ vers qch** to move toward(s) sth; **s'~ vers qn** to go toward(s) sb; to come up to sb; **2** to get ahead; **3** to jut out, to protrude; **4 je me suis un peu avancé en lui promettant le dossier pour demain** I shouldn't have committed myself by promising him/her I'd have the file ready for tomorrow.

avant[1] /avɑ̃/ I *adv* before; first; **bien ~** long before; **il l'a mentionné ~ dans l'introduction** he mentioned it earlier in the introduction.

II *prep* before; **~ mon retour** before I get back; before I got back; **~ le 1er juillet** by 1 July; **~ peu** shortly; **~ tout, ~ toute chose** above all; first and foremost.

III **d'avant** *phr* **la séance d'~** the previous performance; **la fois d'~ nous nous étions déjà perdus** we got lost the last time as well.

IV **avant de** *phr* **~ de faire** before doing.

V **avant que** *phr* before.

VI **en avant** *phr* forward(s); **en ~ toute!** full steam ahead!; **mettre en ~ le fait que** to point out the fact that; **se mettre en ~** to push oneself forward.

VII **en avant de** *phr* ahead of [*group*].

avant[2] /avɑ̃/ I *adj inv* [*wheel, seat, paw*] front.

II *nm* **1 l'~** the front; **aller de l'~** to forge ahead; **2** (Sport) forward.

III **avant-** (*combining form*) **l'~-Thatcher** the pre-Thatcher era.

avantage /avɑ̃taʒ/ *nm* **1** advantage; **tirer ~ de qch** to take advantage of sth; **paraître à son ~** to look one's best; **2** benefit; **~ fiscaux** tax benefits.

avantager /avɑ̃taʒe/ [13] *vtr* **1** [*person*] to favour[GB]; [*situation*] to be to the advantage of; **2** [*clothes*] to show [sb/sth] off to advantage.

avantageusement /avɑ̃taʒøzmɑ̃/ *adv* favourably[GB].

avantageux, -euse /avɑ̃taʒø, øz/ *adj* **1** [*conditions, offer*] favourable[GB], advantageous; [*rate, price*] attractive; **tirer un parti ~ de qch** to use sth to one's advantage; **2** [*description, outfit*] flattering.

avant-bras /avɑ̃bʀa/ *nm inv* forearm.

avant-coureur, *pl* **~s** /avɑ̃kuʀœʀ/ *adj* **signes ~s** early warning signs.

avant-dernier, -ière, *pl* **~s** /avɑ̃dɛʀnje, ɛʀ/ I *adj* penultimate; **l'~ jour** the last day but one.

II *nm,f* the last but one; **l'~ d'une famille de cinq** the second youngest of five children.

avant-garde, *pl* **~s** /avɑ̃gaʀd/ *nf* **1** avant-garde; **2** vanguard; **à l'~** in the vanguard.

avant-goût, *pl* **~s** /avɑ̃gu/ *nm* foretaste.

avant-hier /avɑ̃tjɛʀ/ *adv* the day before yesterday.

avant-première, *pl* **~s** /avɑ̃pʀəmjɛʀ/ *nf* preview.

avant-propos /avɑ̃pʀɔpo/ *nm inv* foreword.

avant-veille, *pl* **~s** /avɑ̃vɛj/ *nf* two days before.

avare /avaʀ/ I *adj* mean, miserly; **~ de** sparing with.

II *nmf* miser.

avarice /avaʀis/ *nf* meanness (GB), miserliness.

avarier: **s'avarier** /avaʀje/ [2] *v refl* (+ *v être*) [*meat, fish*] to go rotten.

avatar /avataʀ/ *nm* **1** mishap; **2** change.

avec /avɛk/ I° *adv* **elle est partie ~** she went off with it.

II *prep* with; **~ attention** carefully; **et ~ cela, que désirez-vous?** what else would you like?; **je fais tout son travail et ~ ça il n'est pas content!** I do all his work and he's still not happy!; **sa séparation d'~ sa femme** his separation from his wife.

avenant, ~e /avnɑ̃, ɑ̃t/ I *adj* pleasant.

II **à l'avenant** *phr* in keeping.

avenir /avniʀ/ *nm* future; **d'~** [*job*] with a future; [*technique, science*] of the future.

aventure /avɑ̃tyʀ/ *nf* **1** adventure; **2 il m'est arrivé une drôle d'~** something strange happened to me; **3** venture; **4** (love) affair.

IDIOMS **dire la bonne ~ à qn** to tell sb's fortune.

aventurer: **s'aventurer** /avɑ̃tyʀe/ [1] *v refl* (+ *v être*) to venture.

aventurier, -ière /avɑ̃tyʀje, ɛʀ/ *nm,f* adventurer/adventuress.

avenue /avny/ *nf* avenue.

avérer: **s'avérer** /aveʀe/ [14] *v refl* (+ *v être*) **s'~ utile** to prove useful; **il s'avère que** it turns out that.

averse /avɛʀs/ *nf* shower.

aversion /avɛʀsjɔ̃/ *nf* aversion; **avoir qn/qch en ~** to loathe sb/sth.

averti, ~e /avɛʀti/ I *pp* ▶ **avertir**.

II *pp adj* **1** [*reader*] informed; **2** experienced.

avertir /avɛʀtiʀ/ [3] *vtr* **1** to inform; **2** to warn.

avertissement /avɛʀtismɑ̃/ *nm* **1** warning; **2** (Sport) caution; **3** (in book) foreword.

avertisseur /avɛʀtisœʀ/ *nm* **1** alarm; **2** (of car) horn.

aveu, *pl* **~x** /avø/ *nm* confession; admission.

aveuglant, ~e /avœglɑ̃, ɑ̃t/ *adj* blinding.

aveugle /avœgl/ I *adj* **1** blind; **2** [*faith, love*] blind; [*violence*] indiscriminate.

II *nmf* blind person; **les ~s** the blind.

aveuglement /avœgləmɑ̃/ *nm* blindness.

aveuglément /avœglemɑ̃/ *adv* blindly.

aveugler /avœgle/ [1] *vtr* to blind.

aveuglette: **à l'aveuglette** /alavœglɛt/ *phr* **1** blindly; **2** at random.

aviateur /avjatœʀ/ *nm* airman.

aviation /avjasjɔ̃/ *nf* **1** aviation; **2** aircraft industry; **3 l'~** the air force.

aviatrice /avjatʀis/ *nf* woman pilot.

avide /avid/ *adj* **1** greedy; **2 ~ de** avid for, eager for.

avidité /avidite/ *nf* **1** greed; **2** eagerness.

avilir /aviliʀ/ [3] *vtr* to demean.

avilissant, **~e** /avilisɑ̃, ɑ̃t/ *adj* demeaning.

avilissement /avilismɑ̃/ *nm* degradation.

avion /avjɔ̃/ *nm* **1** (aero)plane (GB), airplane (US), aircraft; **aller à Rome en ~** to fly to Rome; **'par ~'** 'by air mail'; **2** flight.
■ **~ de chasse** fighter; **~ à réaction** jet; **~ de tourisme** light passenger aircraft.

aviron /aviʀɔ̃/ *nm* **1** rowing; **2** oar.

avis /avi/ *nm inv* **1** opinion; **je suis de ton ~** I agree with you; **changer d'~** to change one's mind; **2** advice; **sauf ~ contraire** unless otherwise informed; **3** (of jury, commission) recommendation; **4** notice; **lancer un ~ de recherche** to issue a description of a missing person/wanted person.
■ **~ au lecteur** foreword; **~ de passage** calling card (*left by postman etc*).

avisé, **~e** /avize/ *adj* sensible; **être bien/mal ~** to be well-/ill-advised.

aviser /avize/ [1] **I** *vtr* to notify.
II *vi* to decide.
III s'aviser *v refl* (+ *v être*) **ne t'avise pas de recommencer** don't dare do that again.

aviver /avive/ [1] **I** *vtr* **1** to intensify [*feeling*]; to stir up [*quarrel*]; to make [sth] more acute [*pain*]; **2** to liven up [*colour*]; **3** to kindle [*fire*].
II s'aviver *v refl* (+ *v être*) [*desire, anger*] to grow; [*pain, grief*] to become more acute.

avocat /avɔka/ *nm* **1** lawyer, solicitor (GB), attorney (at law) (US); **2** barrister (GB), (trial) lawyer (US); **~ de l'accusation** counsel for the prosecution; **3** (of idea) advocate; (of cause, person) champion; **4** avocado (pear).

avocate /avɔkat/ *nf* woman lawyer.

avoine /avwan/ *nf* oats.

avoir[1] /avwaʀ/ [8]

■ **Note** You will find translations for expressions such as *avoir raison, avoir beau, en avoir marre* etc, at the entries ***raison***, ***beau***, ***marre*** etc.

I *v aux* to have; **j'ai perdu mon briquet** I've lost my lighter; **il aurait aimé te parler** he would have liked to speak to you.
II *vtr* **1** to have (got) [*child, book, room, time*]; **elle avait les larmes aux yeux** there were tears in her eyes○; **2** to get [*object, job*]; to catch [*train, plane*]; (on the phone) **j'ai réussi à l'~** I managed to get through to him; **3** to wear, to have [sth] on; **4** to feel; **~ du chagrin** to feel sad; **qu'est-ce que tu as?** what's wrong with you?; **5 avoir faim/froid/20 ans** to be hungry/cold/20 years old; **6** to beat; to have○, to con○; **j'ai été eu** I've been had.
III avoir à *v+prep* to have to; **tu n'as pas à le critiquer** you shouldn't criticize him; **j'ai beaucoup à faire** I have a lot to do; **tu n'as qu'à leur écrire** all you have to do is write to them.
IV en avoir pour *v+prep* **1 vous en avez pour combien de temps?** how long will it take you?; how long are you going to be?; **2 j'en ai eu pour 500 francs** it cost me 500 francs.
V il y a *v impers* **1** there is/there are; **qu'est-ce qu'il y a?** what's wrong?; what's going on?; **il y a qu'elle m'énerve** she's getting on my nerves, that's what's wrong; **il y a à manger pour quatre** there's enough food for four; **il y en a toujours qui se plaignent** there's always someone who complains; **il n'y en a que pour leur chien** their dog comes first; **2 il y a longtemps** a long time ago; **il n'y a que cinq ans que j'habite ici** I have only been living here for five years; **3 combien y a-t-il jusqu'à la gare?** how far is it to the station?; **il y a au moins 15 kilomètres** it's at least 15 kilometres[GB] away.

avoir[2] /avwaʀ/ *nm* **1** credit; **2** credit note; **3** assets, holdings.

avoisinant, **~e** /avwazinɑ̃, ɑ̃t/ *adj* neighbouring[GB].

avoisiner /avwazine/ [1] *vtr* **1** [*costs, sum*] to be close to, to be about; **2** [*place*] to be near.

avortement /avɔʀtəmɑ̃/ *nm* (Med) abortion.

avorter /avɔʀte/ [1] *vi* **1** (Med) to have an abortion; **2** [*cow, ewe*] to abort, to miscarry; **3** [*plan*] to be aborted; [*uprising*] to fail.

avorton /avɔʀtɔ̃/ *nm* runt.

avouable /avwabl/ *adj* worthy; respectable.

avoué, **~e** /avwe/ **I** *pp* ▶ **avouer**.
II *pp adj* [*enemy*] declared; [*intention*] avowed.
III *nm* ≈ solicitor (GB), attorney(-at-law) (US).

avouer /avwe/ [1] **I** *vtr* to confess, to admit.
II *vi* to confess; to own up.
III s'avouer *v refl* (+ *v être*) **s'~ rassuré** to say one feels reassured; **s'~ vaincu** to admit defeat.

avril /avʀil/ *nm* April.

axe /aks/ *nm* **1** axis; **2** (Tech) axle; **3** major road; **4 dans l'~ du bâtiment** in a line with the building; **la cible est dans l'~ du viseur** the target is lined up in the sights.

axer /akse/ [1] *vtr* **1** to centre[GB] [*screw*]; to line up [*part*]; **2** to base, to centre[GB] (**sur** on).

axiome /aksjom/ *nm* axiom.

ayant droit, *pl* **ayants droit** /ɛyɑ̃dʀwa/ *nm* **1** legal claimant, beneficiary; **2** assignee.

azalée /azale/ *nf* azalea.

Azerbaïdjan /azɛʀbajdʒɑ̃/ *pr nm* Azerbaijan.

azimut /azimyt/ *nm* **1** (in astronomy) azimuth; **2** (figurative) **une offensive tous ~s** an all-out offensive; **dans tous les ~s** everywhere.

azote /azɔt/ *nm* nitrogen.

aztèque /astɛk/ *adj* Aztec.

azur /azyʀ/ *nm* azure.

azyme /azim/ *adj* unleavened.

Bb

b, **B** /be/ *nm inv* b, B; **le b a ba** the rudiments.

baba○ /baba/ *adj inv* **en être** or **rester ~** to be flabbergasted○.

babillage /babijaʒ/ *nm* babbling.

babines /babin/ *nf pl* lips; **retrousser les ~** [*dog*] to bare its teeth; **se lécher les ~** to lick one's chops.

babiole /babjɔl/ *nf* **1** trinket; **2** trifle.

bâbord /babɔʀ/ *nm* port (side).

babouin /babwɛ̃/ *nm* baboon.

baby-foot /babifut/ *nm inv* table football (GB), table soccer.

bac /bak/ *nm* **1**○ *abbr* = **baccalauréat**; **2** ferry; **3** tub; **évier à deux ~s** double sink.
■ **~ à sable** sandpit (GB), sandbox (US).

baccalauréat /bakalɔʀea/ *nm* baccalaureate (*school-leaving certificate taken at 17–18*); **~ professionnel** vocational baccalaureate (*vocationally-oriented school-leaving certificate*).

bâche /bɑʃ/ *nf* tarpaulin.

bachelier, **-ière** /baʃəlje, ɛʀ/ *nm,f*: *holder of the baccalaureate.*

bâcler /bakle/ [1] *vtr* to dash [sth] off [*piece of work*]; to rush through [*ceremony*].

bactérie /bakteʀi/ *nf* bacterium.

badaud, **~e** /bado, od/ *nm,f* **1** passerby; **2** onlooker.

badigeonner /badiʒɔne/ [1] *vtr* **1** to paint; **2** to daub (**de** with); **3** (Culin) to brush (**de** with).

badin, **~e** /badɛ̃, in/ *adj* [*tone*] bantering.

baffe○ /baf/ *nf* clout, slap.

baffle /bafl/ *nm* **1** speaker; **2** baffle.

bafouiller /bafuje/ [1] *vtr*, *vi* to mumble.

bagage /bagaʒ/ *nm* piece of luggage; **faire ses ~s** to pack.
IDIOMS **plier ~**○ to pack up and go.

bagarre /bagaʀ/ *nf* fight, scuffle.

bagarrer○: **se bagarrer** /bagaʀe/ [1] *v refl* (+ *v être*) to fight.

bagarreur○, **-euse** /bagaʀœʀ, øz/ *adj* aggressive.

bagatelle /bagatɛl/ *nf* **1** trifle, triviality; **2** **pour la ~ de** (ironic) for the trifling sum of.

bagne /baɲ/ *nm* penal colony.

bagou(t)○ /bagu/ *nm* **avoir du ~** to have the gift of the gab.

bague /bag/ *nf* **1** ring; **2** (around pipe) collar.

baguette /bagɛt/ *nf* **1** baguette, French stick; **2** stick; **mener qn à la ~** to rule sb with a rod of iron; **~ de chef d'orchestre** conductor's baton; **3** drumstick; **4** chopstick.
■ **~ magique** magic wand.

bahut /bay/ *nm* **1** sideboard; **2**○ (students' slang) school; **3**○ truck.

baie /bɛ/ *nf* **1** bay; **2** berry; **3** **~ (vitrée)** picture window.

baignade /bɛɲad/ *nf* swimming.

baigner /beɲe/ [1] **I** *vtr* **1** to give [sb] a bath; **2** to bathe [*wound*].
II *vi* **~ dans l'huile** to be swimming in grease.
III se baigner *v refl* (+ *v être*) to go swimming.
IDIOMS **ça baigne**○ things are going fine.

baigneur, **-euse** /bɛɲœʀ, øz/ *nm,f* swimmer.

baignoire /bɛɲwaʀ/ *nf* bathtub; **~ sabot** hip bath.

bail, *pl* **baux** /baj, bo/ *nm* lease; **ça fait un ~**○ it's ages (**que** since).

bâiller /bɑje/ [1] *vi* **1** to yawn; **2** to gape (open).

bâillon /bɑjɔ̃/ *nm* gag.

bain /bɛ̃/ *nm* **1** bath; **2** swim; **3** **grand/petit ~** deep/shallow pool.
■ **~ de bouche** mouthwash; **~ de foule** walkabout; **prendre un ~ de soleil** to sunbathe.
IDIOMS **se remettre dans le ~** to get back into the swing of things.

baïonnette /bajɔnɛt/ *nf* bayonet.

baiser /beze/ *nm* kiss.

baisse /bɛs/ *nf* **1** fall; **en ~** falling; **2** fading; **3** decline; **4** cut.

baisser /bese/ [1] **I** *vtr* **1** to lower [*blind*]; to wind [sth] down [*window*]; to turn down [*collar*]; **~ les bras** (figurative) to give up; **~ le nez** (figurative) to hang one's head; **2** to turn down [*volume*]; to dim [*light*]; to cut [*prices*].
II *vi* to go down, to fall, to drop (**à** to; **de** by); [*water*] to subside; [*sight*] to fail; [*hearing*] to deteriorate; **~ d'un ton**○ [*person*] to calm down.
III se baisser *v refl* (+ *v être*) **1** to bend down; **2** to duck; **3** to go down.

bajoue /baʒu/ *nf* cheek.

bal /bal/ *nm* **1** ball, dance; **2** dancehall.

balade /balad/ *nf* walk; ride.

balader○ /balade/ [1] **I** *vtr* **1** to take [sb] for a walk/drive; **2** to carry [sth] around.
II se balader *v refl* (+ *v être*) to go for a walk/ride/drive.
IDIOMS **envoyer qn ~**○ to send sb packing○.

baladeur /baladœʀ/ *nm* walkman®, personal stereo.

balafre /balafʀ/ *nf* **1** scar; **2** slash, gash.

balai /balɛ/ *nm* broom; **passer le ~** to sweep the floor; **du ~**○! go away!

balance /balɑ̃s/ *nf* **1** (weighing) scales; **faire pencher la ~** (figurative) to tip the scales; **2** balance.

Balance /balɑ̃s/ *pr nf* Libra.

balancelle /balɑ̃sɛl/ *nf* swing seat.

balancement /balɑ̃smɑ̃/ *nm* swaying; swinging.

balancer /balɑ̃se/ [12] **I** *vtr* **1** to sway; to swing; **2**○ to chuck○ (**sur** at); to chuck out○ [*old clothes, junk*]; **3**○ to squeal on○.
II *vi* **1** to sway; **2** to hesitate.
III se balancer *v refl* (+ *v être*) **1** [*person*] to sway; [*boat*] to rock; **2**○ **je m'en balance** I couldn't care less.

balancier /balɑ̃sje/ *nm* pendulum.

balançoire /balɑ̃swaʀ/ *nf* swing.

balayer /baleje/ [21] *vtr* **1** to sweep (up); **~ le sol** [*coat*] to brush the ground; **2** to brush [sth] aside [*objections*]; **3** [*radar*] to scan.

balayette /balɛjɛt/ *nf* (short-handled) brush.

balayeur, **-euse** /balɛjœʀ, øz/ *nm,f* road-sweeper.

balbutiement /balbysimɑ̃/ *nm* **les ~s du cinéma** the early days of the cinema.

balbutier /balbysje/ [2] *vtr*, *vi* to mumble.

balcon /balkɔ̃/ *nm* **1** balcony; **2** (in theatre, cinema) balcony, circle.

Bâle /bɑl/ *pr n* Basel.

baleine /balɛn/ *nf* **1** whale; **2** whalebone; stay; rib.

balise /baliz/ *nf* **1** beacon; **2** signpost, waymark; **3** (Comput) tag.

baliser /balize/ [1] *vtr* **1** to mark [sth] out with beacons; **2** to signpost, to waymark.

balistique /balistik/ *nf* ballistics.

baliverne /balivɛʀn/ *nf* nonsense.

ballade /balad/ *nf* ballad; ballade.

balle /bal/ *nf* **1** ball; **renvoyer la ~ (à qn)** (figurative) to retort (to sb); **se renvoyer la ~** to keep up an animated discussion; to keep passing the buck; **2** (in ball games) shot; **faire des ~s** to knock the ball around; **~ de jeu** game point; **3** bullet; **4**○ franc.

ballerine /balʀin/ *nf* **1** ballerina; **2** ballet pump.

ballet /balɛ/ *nm* ballet.

ballon /balɔ̃/ *nm* **1** ball; **2** balloon; **3** wine glass; **4 ~ (alcootest)** Breathalyzer®.
■ **~ dirigeable** airship (GB), blimp (US); **~ d'eau chaude** hot water tank; **~ ovale** rugby ball; **~ rond** soccer ball.

ballonnement /balɔnmɑ̃/ *nm* bloating.

ballot○ /balo/ *nm* nerd○, fool.

ballottage /balɔtaʒ/ *nm*: *absence of an absolute majority in the first round of an election.*

ballotter /balɔte/ [1] *vtr* **1** [*sea*] to toss [sb/sth] around; [*movement*] to jolt; **2 être ballotté entre sa famille et son travail** to be torn between one's family and one's job.

balluchon = **baluchon**.

balnéaire /balneɛʀ/ *adj* [*resort*] seaside.

balte /balt/ *adj* Baltic; **les pays ~s** the Baltic States.

baluchon /balyʃɔ̃/ *nm* bundle.

balustrade /balystʀad/ *nf* **1** parapet; **2** railing; **3** balustrade.

bambin, **~e** /bɑ̃bɛ̃, in/ *nm,f* kid○, child.

bambou /bɑ̃bu/ *nm* bamboo.

ban /bɑ̃/ **I** *nm* round of applause.
II bans *nm pl* banns.
IDIOMS **mettre qn au ~ de la société** to ostracize sb.

banal, **~e** /banal/ *adj* **1** commonplace, ordinary; **peu ~** unusual; **2** trivial, trite.

banaliser /banalize/ [1] *vtr* **1** to make [sth] commonplace; **2 voiture banalisée** unmarked car.

banalité /banalite/ *nf* **1** ordinariness; **2** triteness; **3** trite remark.

banane /banan/ *nf* **1** banana; **2** quiff; **3** bumbag (GB), fanny pack (US).

banc /bɑ̃/ *nm* **1** bench; **2** (of fish) shoal.
■ **~ des accusés** dock; **~ d'essai** test bench; testing ground; **~ de sable** sandbank.

bancaire /bɑ̃kɛʀ/ *adj* **1** [*business*] banking; **2** [*card*] bank.

bancal, **~e** /bɑ̃kal/ *adj* **1** [*chair*] rickety; **2** [*solution*] unsatisfactory.

bande /bɑ̃d/ *nf* **1** gang; group; **~ de crétins!** you bunch of idiots!; **ils font ~ à part** they don't join in; **2** (of animals) pack; **3** (of material, paper) strip; band; **4** bandage; **5** broad stripe; **6** (for recording) tape.
■ **~ d'arrêt d'urgence**, **BAU** hard shoulder; **~ dessinée**, **BD**○ comic strip; comic book; **~ de fréquences** waveband; **~ originale** (of film) original soundtrack.

bande-annonce, *pl* **bandes-annonces** /bɑ̃danɔ̃s/ *nf* trailer.

bandeau, *pl* **~x** /bɑ̃do/ *nm* **1** blindfold; **2** eye patch; **3** headband.

bandelette /bɑ̃dlɛt/ *nf* bandage.

bander /bɑ̃de/ [1] *vtr* **1** to bandage; **2 ~ les yeux à qn** to blindfold sb.

banderole /bɑ̃dʀɔl/ *nf* banner.

bande-son, *pl* **bandes-son** /bɑ̃dsɔ̃/ *nm* soundtrack.

bandit /bɑ̃di/ *nm* **1** bandit; **~ de grand chemin** highwayman; **2** crook; **3** rascal.

banditisme /bɑ̃ditism/ *nm* **le (grand) ~** (organized) crime.

bandoulière /bɑ̃duljɛʀ/ *nf* shoulder strap.

banlieue /bɑ̃ljø/ *nf* **1** suburbs; **de ~** suburban; **2** suburb.

banlieusard, **~e** /bɑ̃ljøzaʀ, aʀd/ *nm,f* suburbanite.

bannière /banjɛʀ/ *nf* banner; **la ~ étoilée** the star-spangled banner.
IDIOMS **c'est la croix et la ~** it's hell (**pour faire** doing).

bannir /baniʀ/ [3] *vtr* **1** to banish (**de** from); **2** to ban.

banque /bɑ̃k/ *nf* **1** bank; **2** banking.
■ **~ de données** data bank.

banqueroute /bɑ̃kʀut/ *nf* bankruptcy.

banquet /bɑ̃kɛ/ *nm* **1** banquet; **2** feast.

banquette /bɑ̃kɛt/ *nf* (in café) wall seat; (in car, train) seat.

banquier /bɑ̃kje/ *nm* banker.

banquise /bɑ̃kiz/ *nf* ice floe.

baptême /batɛm/ *nm* **1** baptism, christening; **2** (of ship) christening; (of bell) blessing.

■ **~ de l'air** first flight.

baptiser /batize/ [1] *vtr* **1** to baptize, to christen; **2** to call, to name; to nickname; **3** to christen [*ship*]; to bless [*bell*].

bar /baʀ/ *nm* **1** bar; **2** (Zool) sea bass.

baragouiner○ /baʀagwine/ [1] *vtr* to gabble [*sentence*]; to speak [sth] badly [*language*].

baraka○ /baʀaka/ *nf* luck.

baraque /baʀak/ *nf* **1** shack; **2**○ pad○, house.

baraqué○, **~e** /baʀake/ *adj* hefty.

baraquement /baʀakmɑ̃/ *nm* **1** group of huts; **2** hut; **3** army camp.

baratin○ /baʀatɛ̃/ *nm* **1** sales pitch; **2** sweet-talk; smooth talk○ (GB).

baratiner○ /baʀatine/ [1] *vtr* **1** to give [sb] the spiel; **2** to chat [sb] up; **3** to try to persuade.

barbant○, **~e** /baʀbɑ̃, ɑ̃t/ *adj* boring.

barbare /baʀbaʀ/ **I** *adj* barbaric; barbarian.
II *nmf* barbarian.

barbe /baʀb/ **I** *nf* beard; **~ naissante** stubble.
II○ *excl* **la ~!** I've had enough!; **la ~ avec leurs consignes!** to hell with their orders○!
■ **~ à papa** candyfloss (GB), cotton candy (US).
IDIOMS **à la ~ de qn** under sb's nose.

barbelé /baʀbəle/ *nm* barbed wire (GB), barbwire (US).

barbiche /baʀbiʃ/ *nf* **1** goatee (beard); **2** (on goat) (small) beard.

barbier /baʀbje/ *nm* barber.

barbiturique /baʀbityʀik/ *nm* barbiturate.

barbouiller /baʀbuje/ [1] **I** *vtr* **1** to smear (**de** with); **2** to daub (**de** with); **3 ~ des toiles** to do daubs; **~ du papier** to write drivel; **4 être barbouillé** to feel queasy.
II se barbouiller *v refl* (+ *v être*) **se ~ le visage de qch** to get one's face all covered in sth.

barbu, **~e** /baʀby/ *adj* bearded; **il est ~** he has a beard.

barde /baʀd/ *nf* thin slice of bacon, bard.

bardé, **~e** /baʀde/ *adj* covered (**de** in).

barème /baʀɛm/ *nm* scale; **~ des prix** price list.

baril /baʀil/ *nm* barrel, cask; keg; drum.

barillet /baʀijɛ/ *nm* cylinder.

bariolé, **~e** /baʀjɔle/ *adj* multicoloured[GB].

baromètre /baʀɔmɛtʀ/ *nm* barometer.

baron /baʀɔ̃/ *nm* baron.

baronne /baʀɔn/ *nf* baroness.

baroque /baʀɔk/ *adj* **1** baroque; **2** bizarre.

baroudeur /baʀudœʀ/ *nm* **1** fighter, warrior; **2** adventurer.

barque /baʀk/ *nf* (small) boat.

barquette /baʀkɛt/ *nf* punnet (GB), basket (US); tub; container.

barrage /baʀaʒ/ *nm* **1** dam; **2** roadblock; barricade; **faire ~ à** to block.

barre /baʀ/ *nf* **1** bar, rod; **2** (of chocolate) piece; **3** tiller, helm; **4** band, stripe; **5** stroke; **la ~ du t** the cross on the t; **6** (of goal) crossbar; (in high jump) bar; **7** (in ballet practice) barre; **8** (Law) bar; ≈ witness box (GB), witness stand (US); **9** mark; **franchir la ~ des 13%** to go over the 13% mark.
■ **~ fixe** horizontal bar; **~ oblique** slash.
IDIOMS **avoir un coup de ~**○ to feel drained all of a sudden.

barreau, *pl* **~x** /baʀo/ *nm* **1** (of cage) bar; **2** rung; **3** (Law) **le ~** the Bar.

barrer /baʀe/ [1] *vtr* **1** to block [*way*]; **'route barrée'** 'road closed'; **2** to cross out.

barrette /baʀɛt/ *nf* (hair) slide (GB), barrette (US).

barricade /baʀikad/ *nf* barricade.

barrière /baʀjɛʀ/ *nf* **1** fence; **2** gate; **3** barrier.

barrique /baʀik/ *nf* barrel.

barrir /baʀiʀ/ [3] *vi* [*elephant*] to trumpet.

bar-tabac, *pl* **bars-tabac** /baʀtaba/ *nm* café (*selling stamps and cigarettes*).

bas, **basse**[1] /bɑ, bɑs/ **I** *adj* low; [*room*] low-ceilinged; [*land*] low-lying; **le ciel est ~** the sky is overcast; **un enfant en ~ âge** a very young child; **être au plus ~** [*prices*] to have reached rock bottom.
II *adv* **1** low; **comment peut-on tomber si ~!** how can one sink so low!; **2 voir plus ~** see below; **3** quietly; **tout ~** [*speak*] in a whisper; [*sing*] softly; **4 être au plus ~** to be extremely weak; to be at one's lowest.
III *nm inv* **1** bottom; **le ~ du visage** the lower part of the face; **les pièces du ~** the downstairs rooms; **2** stocking.
IV en bas *phr* downstairs; down below; at the bottom.
■ **~ de gamme** *adj* low-quality; *nm* lower end of the market; **~ morceaux** (Culin) cheap cuts; **basse saison** low season.
IDIOMS **avoir des hauts et des ~** to have one's ups and downs; **à ~ les tyrans!** down with tyranny!

basané, **~e** /bazane/ *adj* swarthy.

bas-côté, *pl* **~s** /bɑkote/ *nm* **1** verge (GB), shoulder (US); **2** (side) aisle.

basculant, **~e** /baskylɑ̃, ɑ̃t/ *adj* **pont ~** bascule bridge; **camion à benne ~e** dump truck.

bascule /baskyl/ *nf* **fauteuil à ~** rocking chair.

basculer /baskyle/ [1] **I** *vtr* to transfer [*call*].
II *vi* **1** to topple over; **faire ~** to tip up [*skip*]; to tip out [*load*]; to knock [sb] off balance [*person*]; **2** (figurative) to change radically.

base /bɑz/ *nf* **1** base; **le riz forme la ~ de leur alimentation** rice is their staple diet; **2** basis; **reposer sur des ~s solides** to rest on a firm foundation; **à la ~ de qch** at the root or heart of sth; **salaire de ~** basic salary; **repartir sur de nouvelles ~s** to make a fresh start; **3** (in politics) **la ~** the rank and file.
■ **~ de données** database; **~ de lancement** launching site.

baser /bɑze/ [1] **I** *vtr* to base (**sur** on).
II se baser *v refl* (+ *v être*) **se ~ sur qch** to go by sth.

bas-fond, *pl* **~s** /bafɔ̃/ **I** *nm* **1** shallows; **2** dip.
II bas-fonds *nm pl* seedy areas.
basilic /bazilik/ *nm* basil.
basilique /bazilik/ *nf* basilica.
basket /baskɛt/ *nm* **1** basketball; **2** trainer (GB), sneaker (US).
basque /bask/ *adj, nm* Basque.
basse² /bɑs/ **I** *adj* ▶ **bas I**.
II *nf* (Mus) bass.
basse-cour, *pl* **basses-cours** /baskuʀ/ *nf* **1** poultry-yard; **2** poultry.
bassement /bɑsmɑ̃/ *adv* basely.
bassesse /bɑsɛs/ *nf* **1** baseness; **2** base act.
bassin /basɛ̃/ *nm* **1** pond; fountain; pool; **2** (in geography) basin; **3** pelvis; **4** bedpan.
▪ **~ houiller** coal field.
bassine /basin/ *nf* bowl; basin.
bassiste /bɑsist/ *nmf* bass player.
bas-ventre, *pl* **~s** /bɑvɑ̃tʀ/ *nm* lower abdomen.
bataille /batɑj/ **I** *nf* **1** battle; **2** fight.
II en bataille *phr* [*hair*] dishevelled[GB]; [*eyebrows*] bushy.
bataillon /batɑjɔ̃/ *nm* battalion; **Dupont?, inconnu au ~** Dupont?, never heard of him.
bâtard, **~e** /bɑtaʀ, aʀd/ **I** *adj* **1** [*dog*] mongrel; **2** [*work, style*] hybrid; **3** (offensive) [*child*] bastard.
II *nm,f* **1** mongrel; **2** (offensive) bastard.
bateau, *pl* **~x** /bato/ **I** *adj inv* hackneyed.
II *nm* **1** boat, ship; **faire du ~** to go boating; to go sailing; **2** dropped kerb (GB) or curb (US).
▪ **~ amiral** flagship; **~ pneumatique** rubber dinghy; **~ de sauvetage** lifeboat.
bateau-école, *pl* **bateaux-écoles** /bato ekɔl/ *nm* training ship.
bateau-mouche, *pl* **bateaux-mouches** /batomuʃ/ *nm*: *large river boat for sightseeing*.
batelier, **-ière** /batəlje, ɛʀ/ *nm,f* boatman/boatwoman.
bâti, **~e** /bɑti/ **I** *pp* ▶ **bâtir**.
II *pp adj* **1** built; **terrain ~** developed site; **2 un homme bien ~** a well-built man.
batifoler /batifɔle/ [1] *vi* **1** to romp about; **2** to flirt.
bâtiment /bɑtimɑ̃/ *nm* **1** building; **2** building trade; **3** ship.
bâtir /bɑtiʀ/ [3] *vtr* **1** to build; **2** to tack [*hem*].
bâton /bɑtɔ̃/ *nm* **1** stick; **2** vertical stroke; **3**○ ten thousand francs.
▪ **~ de rouge (à lèvres)** lipstick.
IDIOMS **discuter à ~s rompus** to talk about this and that; **mettre des ~s dans les roues de qn** to put a spoke in sb's wheel.
bâtonnet /bɑtɔnɛ/ *nm* stick.
▪ **~ de poisson** fish finger (GB), fish stick (US).
batracien /batʀasjɛ̃/ *nm* batrachian.
battage○ /bataʒ/ *nm* publicity, hype○.
battant, **~e** /batɑ̃, ɑ̃t/ **I** *adj* **le cœur ~** with a beating heart.
II *nm,f* fighter.
III *nm* **porte à deux ~s** double door.
batte /bat/ *nf* (Sport) bat (GB), paddle (US).
battement /batmɑ̃/ *nm* **1** beating; beat; fluttering; flutter; **2** break, gap; wait.
batterie /batʀi/ *nf* **1** percussion section; **2** drum kit; **3** battery.
▪ **~ de cuisine** pots and pans.
batteur /batœʀ/ *nm* **1** percussionist; **2** drummer; **3** whisk.
battre /batʀ/ [61] **I** *vtr* **1** (defeat) to beat [*opponent*]; to break [*record*]; **2** (hit) to beat [*person, animal, carpet*]; to thresh [*corn*]; **3** [*rain, sea*] to beat against; **4** to whisk [*eggs*]; to whip [*cream*]; **5** to shuffle [*cards*]; **6** (Mus) **~ la mesure** to beat time; **7** to scour [*countryside*].
II battre de *v+prep* **~ des ailes** to flap its wings; **~ des cils** to flutter one's eyelashes; **~ des mains** to clap (one's hands).
III *vi* **1** [*heart, pulse*] to beat; **2** [*door*] to bang.
IV se battre *v refl* (+ *v être*) to fight.
IDIOMS **~ en retraite devant qch** to retreat before sth; **~ son plein** to be in full swing.
battu, **~e** /baty/ **I** *pp* ▶ **battre**.
II *pp adj* [*child, wife*] battered.
BAU /beay/ *nf*: *abbr* ▶ **bande**.
baudet○ /bodɛ/ *nm* donkey, ass.
baume /bom/ *nm* balm, balsam.
baux /bo/ *nm pl* ▶ **bail**.
bavard, **~e** /bavaʀ, aʀd/ **I** *adj* **1** talkative; **2** indiscreet; **3** long-winded.
II *nm,f* **1** chatterbox; **2** blabbermouth○.
bavardage /bavaʀdaʒ/ *nm* **1** gossip; **2** idle chatter.
bavarder /bavaʀde/ [1] *vi* **1** to talk, to chatter; **2** to chat; **3** to gossip (**sur** about).
bave /bav/ *nf* dribble; spittle; slaver; slime.
baver /bave/ [1] *vi* **1** [*person*] to dribble; [*animal*] to slaver; **2** [*pen*] to leak; [*brush*] to drip; [*ink, paint*] to run.
IDIOMS **il leur en a fait ~**○ he gave them a hard time.
bavette /bavɛt/ *nf* **1** bib; **2** (Culin) flank.
bavoir /bavwaʀ/ *nm* bib.
bavure /bavyʀ/ *nf* **1** smudge; **2** blunder.
bazar /bazaʀ/ *nm* **1** general store; **2**○ mess; **3**○ clutter; **4** bazaar.
bazarder○ /bazaʀde/ [1] *vi* to throw out.
BCBG○ /besebeʒe/ *adj* (*abbr* = **bon chic bon genre**) chic and conservative, Sloaney (GB).
BCG /beseʒe/ *nm* (*abbr* = **bacille bilié de Calmette et Guérin**) BCG.
BD○ /bede/ *nf*: *abbr* ▶ **bande**.
béant, **~e** /beɑ̃, ɑ̃t/ *adj* gaping.
béat, **~e** /bea, at/ *adj* [*person*] blissfully happy; [*smile*] blissful, beatific.
beau (**bel** *before vowel or mute h*), **belle¹**, *mpl* **~x** /bo, bɛl/ **I** *adj* **1** beautiful; handsome; **se faire ~** to do oneself up; **ce n'est pas ~ à voir**○! it's not a pretty sight!; **2** good; fine; nice; lovely; **un ~ geste** a noble gesture; **fais de ~x rêves!** sweet dreams!; **au ~ milieu de** right in the middle of; **c'est bien ~ tout**

ça, mais○ that's all well and good, but; **3** [*sum*] tidy; [*salary*] very nice.
II *nm* **qu'est-ce que tu as fait de ~?** done anything interesting?
III **avoir beau** *phr* **j'ai ~ essayer, je n'y arrive pas** it's no good my trying, I can't do it.
IV **bel et bien** *phr* **1** well and truly; **2** definitely.
■ **~ fixe** fine weather; **~x jours** fine weather; palmy days, good days.
IDIOMS **faire le ~** [*dog*] to sit up and beg; **c'est du ~**○**!** (ironic) lovely!

beaucoup /boku/ I *adv* **1** a lot; much; **c'est ~ dire** that's going a bit far; **c'est déjà ~ qu'elle soit venue** it's already quite something that she came; **~ moins de livres** far fewer books; **c'est ~ trop** it's far too much; **~ trop longtemps** far too long, much too long; **2 ~ de** a lot of, a great deal of; much; many; **il ne reste plus ~ de pain** there isn't much bread left; **avec ~ de soin** very carefully; **~ d'entre eux** many of them.
II **de beaucoup** *phr* by far.
III **pour beaucoup** *phr* **être pour ~ dans** to have a lot to do with.

beau-fils, *pl* **beaux-fils** /bofis/ *nm* **1** son-in-law; **2** stepson.

beau-frère, *pl* **beaux-frères** /bofʀɛʀ/ *nm* brother-in-law.

beau-père, *pl* **beaux-pères** /bopɛʀ/ *nm* **1** father-in-law; **2** stepfather.

beauté /bote/ *nf* beauty; **se faire une ~** to do oneself up; **finir en ~** to end with a flourish.

beaux-arts /bozaʀ/ *nm pl* fine arts and architecture.

bébé /bebe/ *nm* baby.

bec /bɛk/ *nm* **1** beak; **donner des coups de ~** to peck; **il a toujours la cigarette au ~**○ he's always got a cigarette stuck in his mouth; **2** (of jug) lip; (of teapot) spout; (of wind instrument) mouthpiece; **~ verseur** pourer(-spout).
IDIOMS **clouer le ~ à qn**○ to shut sb up○; **tomber sur un ~**○ to come across a snag.

bécane○ /bekan/ *nf* bike, bicycle.

bécasse /bekas/ *nf* woodcock.

bec-de-lièvre, *pl* **becs-de-lièvre** /bɛkdəljɛvʀ/ *nm* harelip.

bêche /bɛʃ/ *nf* **1** spade; **2** garden fork.

bêcher /beʃe/ [1] *vtr* to dig (with a spade).

bedaine○ /bədɛn/ *nf* paunch.

bée /be/ *adj f* **être bouche ~** to stand open-mouthed or gaping.

beffroi /befʀwɑ/ *nm* belfry.

bégayer /begeje/ [21] *vtr, vi* to stammer.

bègue /bɛg/*adj* **être ~** to stammer.

béguin○ /begɛ̃/ *nm* **avoir le ~ pour qn** to have a crush on sb.

beige /bɛʒ/ *adj, nm* beige.

beignet /bɛɲɛ/ *nm* **1** fritter; **2** doughnut, donut○ (US).

bel *adj m* ▶ **beau I, IV.**

bêler /bɛle/ [1] *vi* to bleat.

belette /bəlɛt/ *nf* weasel.

belge /bɛlʒ/ *adj* Belgian.

Belgique /bɛlʒik/ *pr nf* Belgium.

bélier /belje/ *nm* **1** ram; **2** battering ram.

Bélier /belje/ *pr nm* Aries.

belle[2] /bɛl/ I *adj f* ▶ **beau** I.
II *nf* decider, deciding game.
III **de plus belle** *phr* with renewed vigour[GB].
IDIOMS **(se) faire la ~**○ to do a bunk○ (GB), to take a powder○ (US); **en faire voir de ~s**○ **à qn** to give sb a hard time.

belle-famille, *pl* **belles-familles** /bɛlfamij/ *nf* in-laws.

belle-fille, *pl* **belles-filles** /bɛlfij/ *nf* **1** daughter-in-law; **2** stepdaughter.

belle-mère, *pl* **belles-mères** /bɛlmɛʀ/ *nf* **1** mother-in-law; **2** stepmother.

belle-sœur, *pl* **belles-sœurs** /bɛlsœʀ/ *nf* sister-in-law.

belligérant /bɛliʒeʀɑ̃/ *nm* **1** belligerent, warring party; **2** combatant.

belliqueux, **-euse** /bɛlikø, øz/ *adj* aggressive.

bémol /bemɔl/ *nm* (Mus) flat; **mi ~** E flat.

bénédiction /benediksjɔ̃/ *nf* blessing.

bénéfice /benefis/ *nm* **1** profit; **2** benefit, beneficial effect; **3** advantage.

bénéficiaire /benefisjɛʀ/ *nmf* beneficiary.

bénéficier /benefisje/ [2] *v+prep* **~ de** to receive [*help*]; to enjoy [*immunity*]; to get [*special treatment*].

bénéfique /benefik/ *adj* beneficial.

benêt /bənɛ/ *nm* half-wit.

bénévole /benevɔl/ **I** *adj* voluntary.
II *nmf* voluntary worker.

bénin, **-igne** /benɛ̃, iɲ/ *adj* minor; benign.

bénir /beniʀ/ [3] *vtr* to bless.

bénit, **~e** /beni, it/ *adj* blessed; holy.

bénitier /benitje/ *nm* holy water font.

benjamin, **~e** /bɛ̃ʒamɛ̃, in/ *nm,f* youngest child.

benne /bɛn/ *nf* **1** skip (GB), dumpster® (US); **2** (colliery) wagon; **3** (cable) car.

béquille /bekij/ *nf* **1** crutch; **2** kickstand.

bercail○ /bɛʀkaj/ *nm* home.

berceau, *pl* **~x** /bɛʀso/ *nm* cradle.

bercer /bɛʀse/ [12] I *vtr* to rock [*baby*].
II **se bercer** *v refl* (+ *v être*) **se ~ d'illusions** to delude oneself.

berceuse /bɛʀsøz/ *nf* lullaby.

béret /beʀɛ/ *nm* beret.

bergamote /bɛʀgamɔt/ *nf* bergamot.

berge /bɛʀʒ/ *nf* (of river, canal) bank.

berger, **-ère** /bɛʀʒe, ɛʀ/ *nm,f* shepherd/shepherdess.
■ **~ allemand** Alsatian (GB), German shepherd.

bergerie /bɛʀʒəʀi/ *nf* sheepfold.

berlue○ /bɛʀly/ *nf* **avoir la ~** to be seeing things.

bermuda /bɛʀmyda/ *nm* bermudas.

Bermudes /bɛʀmyd/ *pr nf pl* **les ~s** Bermuda.

berner /bɛʀne/ [1] *vtr* to fool, to deceive.

besogne /bəzɔɲ/ *nf* job.

besoin /bəzwɛ̃/ **I** *nm* need (**de** for; **de faire** to do); **avoir ~ de** to need; **répondre à un ~** to meet a need; **au ~** if need be; **pour les ~s de la cause** for the good of the cause; **être dans le ~** to be in need.
II besoins *nm pl* needs; **subvenir aux ~s de qn** to provide for sb.
IDIOMS **faire ses ~s**○ [*person*] to relieve oneself; [*animal*] to do its business.

bestial, **~e**, *mpl* **-iaux** /bɛstjal, o/ *adj* brutish, bestial.

bestiaux /bɛstjo/ *nm pl* **1** livestock; **2** cattle.

bestiole○ /bɛstjɔl/ *nf* **1** creepy-crawly○, bug; **2** animal.

bétail /betaj/ *nm* livestock; cattle.

bête /bɛt/ **I** *adj* stupid, silly; **je suis restée toute ~** I was dumbfounded.
II *nf* creature; animal.
■ **~ à bon Dieu** ladybird (GB), ladybug (US); **~ noire** bête noire (GB), pet hate.
IDIOMS **il est ~ comme ses pieds**○ he's as dumb as can be; **chercher la petite ~**○ to nit-pick○; **reprendre du poil de la ~**○ to perk up; **travailler comme une ~**○ to work like crazy○.

bêtise /betiz/ *nf* **la ~** stupidity; **faire une ~** to do something stupid; **dire des ~s** to talk nonsense; **surtout pas de ~s!** be good now!

bêtisier /betizje/ *nm* collection of howlers○.

béton /betɔ̃/ *nm* concrete; (figurative) watertight.
■ **~ armé** reinforced concrete.

bétonnière /betɔnjɛʀ/ *nf* concrete mixer.

betterave /bɛtʀav/ *nf* beet; **~ rouge** beetroot; **~ sucrière** sugar beet.

beugler /bøgle/ [1] *vi* to moo; to bellow.

beur○ /bœʀ/ *nmf* second-generation North African (*living in France*).

beurre /bœʀ/ *nm* butter; **~ doux** unsalted butter.
■ **~ d'escargot** garlic and parsley butter; **~ noir** black butter; **œil au ~ noir**○ black eye.
IDIOMS **faire son ~**○ to make a packet○; **compter pour du ~**○ to count for nothing; **vouloir le ~ et l'argent du ~**○ to want to have one's cake and eat it.

beurré○, **~e** /bœʀe/ *adj* drunk, plastered○.

beurrer /bœʀe/ [1] *vtr* to butter.

beurrier /bœʀje/ *nm* butter dish.

beuverie /bœvʀi/ *nf* drinking session.

biais /bjɛ/ **I** *nm inv* **1** (of material) bias; **2** way; **par le ~ de qn** through sb; **par le ~ de qch** by means of sth.
II de biais, **en biais** *phr* **couper une étoffe en ~** to cut material on the cross.

bibelot /biblo/ *nm* ornament.

biberon /bibʀɔ̃/ *nm* (baby's) bottle (GB), (nursing) bottle (US).

bible /bibl/ *nf* bible; **la Bible** the Bible.

bibliographie /biblijɔgʀafi/ *nf* bibliography.

bibliothécaire /biblijɔtekɛʀ/ *nmf* librarian.

bibliothèque /biblijɔtɛk/ *nf* **1** library; **2** bookcase.

biblique /biblik/ *adj* biblical.

bic® /bik/ *nm* biro®.

bicarbonate /bikaʀbɔnat/ *nm* bicarbonate.

bicentenaire /bisɑ̃tnɛʀ/ *nm* bicentenary, bicentennial.

biceps /bisɛps/ *nm inv* biceps.

biche /biʃ/ *nf* doe.

bichonner○ /biʃɔne/ [1] *vtr* to pamper.

bicoque○ /bikɔk/ *nf* dump○, house.

bicyclette /bisiklɛt/ *nf* **1** bicycle; **2** cycling.

bidasse○ /bidas/ *nm* soldier.

bidet /bidɛ/ *nm* bidet.

bidon /bidɔ̃/ **I**○ *adj inv* bogus; phoney○.
II *nm* **1** can; drum; flask; **2**○ stomach, paunch; **3**○ **c'est du ~** it is a load of hogwash○.

bidonville /bidɔ̃vil/ *nm* shanty town.

bidule○ /bidyl/ *nm* thingy○ (GB), thingamajig○.

bielle /bjɛl/ *nf* connecting rod.

bien /bjɛ̃/ **I** *adj inv* **1 être ~ dans un rôle** to be good in a part; **être ~ de sa personne** to be good-looking; **ce n'est pas ~ de mentir** it's not nice to lie; **ça fait ~ d'aller à l'opéra**○ it's the done thing to go to the opera; **2** well; **ne pas se sentir ~** not to feel well; **t'es pas ~**○**!** you're out of your mind○!; **3 je suis ~ dans ces bottes** these boots are comfortable; **on est ~ au soleil!** isn't it nice in the sun!; **4**○ **un quartier ~** a nice district; **des gens ~** respectable people.
II *adv* **1** well; [*function*] properly; [*interpret*] correctly; **~ joué!** well done!; **aller ~** [*person*] to be well; [*business*] to go well; **ni ~ ni mal** so-so; **j'ai cru ~ faire** I thought I was doing the right thing; **c'est ~ fait pour elle!** it serves her right!; **tu ferais ~ d'y aller** it would be a good idea for you to go; **2** [*mix*] thoroughly; [*fill*] completely; [*listen*] carefully; **3** [*presented*] well; [*furnished*] tastefully; [*live*] comfortably; **femme ~ faite** shapely woman; **aller ~ ensemble** to go well together; **aller ~ à qn** to suit sb; **~ prendre une remarque** to take a remark in good part; **4** [*nice, sad*] very; [*fear, enjoy*] very much; [*simple, true*] quite; **il y a ~ longtemps** a very long time ago; **merci ~** thank you very much; **~ rire** to have a good laugh; **c'est ~ compris?** is that clear?; **~ au contraire** on the contrary; **~ mieux** much or far better; **~ sûr** of course; **~ entendu** or **évidemment** naturally; **il y a ~ des années** a good many years ago; **~ des fois** often, many a time; **5 je veux ~ t'aider** I don't mind helping you; **j'aimerais ~ essayer** I would love to try; **6 il faut ~ que ça finisse** it has just got to come to an end; **7 ça montre ~ que** it just goes to show that; **je sais ~ que** I know that; **insiste ~** make sure you insist; **on verra ~** well, we'll see; **il le fait ~ lui, pourquoi pas moi?** if he can do it, why can't I?; **tu peux très ~ le faire toi-même** you can easily do it yourself; **que peut-il ~ faire à Paris?** what on earth can he be doing in Paris?; **8** definitely; **c'est ~ ce qu'il a dit** that's exactly what he said; **tu as ~ pris**

les clés? are you sure you've got the keys?; **c'est ~ de lui!** it's just like him!; **c'est ~ le moment!** (ironic) great timing!; **c'est ~ le moment de partir!** (ironic) what a time to leave!; **9** at least; **elle a ~ 40 ans** she's at least 40.
III *nm* **1** good; **le ~ et le mal** good and evil; **ça fait du ~ aux enfants** it's good for the children; **vouloir le ~ de qn** to have sb's best interests at heart; **vouloir du ~ à qn** to wish sb well; **dire du ~/le plus grand ~ de qn** to speak well/very highly of sb; **2** possession; **des ~s considérables** substantial assets.
IV **bien que** *phr* although.
■ **~s de consommation** consumer goods; **~s immobiliers** real estate; **~s mobiliers** personal property; **~s personnels** private property.

bien-être /bjɛ̃nɛtʀ/ *nm* **1** well-being; **2** welfare; **3** comforts.

bienfaisance /bjɛ̃fəzɑ̃s/ *nf* charity.

bienfaisant, ~e /bjɛ̃fəzɑ̃, ɑ̃t/ *adj* beneficial, beneficent.

bienfait /bjɛ̃fɛ/ *nm* **1** kind deed; **~ du ciel** godsend; **2** beneficial effect.

bienfaiteur, -trice /bjɛ̃fɛtœʀ, tʀis/ *nm,f* benefactor/benefactress.

bien-fondé /bjɛ̃fɔ̃de/ *nm* (of idea) validity; (of claim) legitimacy.

bien-pensant, ~e, *mpl* **~s** /bjɛ̃pɑ̃sɑ̃, ɑ̃t/ *adj* **1** right-thinking; **2** self-righteous.

bientôt /bjɛ̃to/ *adv* soon; **à ~** see you soon.

bienveillant, ~e /bjɛ̃vɛjɑ̃, ɑ̃t/ *adj* benevolent.

bienvenu, ~e[1] /bjɛ̃vəny/ *adj* welcome.

bienvenue[2] /bjɛ̃vəny/ *nf* welcome.

bière /bjɛʀ/ *nf* **1** beer; **~ (à la) pression** draught (GB) or draft (US) beer; **2** coffin, casket (US).
■ **~ blonde** lager; **~ brune** ≈ stout; **~ rousse** brown ale.

bifteck /biftɛk/ *nm* steak.
IDIOMS **gagner son ~**○ to earn a living.

bifurcation /bifyʀkasjɔ̃/ *nf* (in road) fork.

bifurquer /bifyʀke/ [1] *vi* **1** [*road*] to fork; **2** [*driver*] to turn off; **3** (in career) to change tack.

bigame /bigam/ *adj* bigamous.

bigarré, ~e /bigaʀe/ *adj* **1** multicoloured[GB]; **2** [*crowd*] colourful[GB].

bigorneau, *pl* **~x** /bigɔʀno/ *nm* winkle.

bigot, ~e /bigo, ɔt/ *nm,f* religious zealot.

bigoudi /bigudi/ *nm* roller, curler.

bijou, *pl* **~x** /biʒu/ *nm* **1** piece of jewellery (GB) or jewelry (US); **2** jewel; (figurative) gem.

bijouterie /biʒutʀi/ *nf* (shop) jeweller's (GB), jewelry store (US).

bilan /bilɑ̃/ *nm* **1** balance sheet; **déposer son ~** to file a petition in bankruptcy; **2** outcome; **3** (after disaster) toll; **4** assessment; **~ de santé** check-up; **5** report.

bilatéral, ~e, *mpl* **-aux** /bilateʀal, o/ *adj* bilateral.

bile /bil/ *nf* bile.
IDIOMS **se faire de la ~**○ to worry.

bilingue /bilɛ̃g/ *adj* bilingual.

billard /bijaʀ/ *nm* **1** billiards; **2** billiard table.
■ **~ américain** pool; **~ anglais** snooker.
IDIOMS **passer sur le ~**○ to have an operation.

bille /bij/ *nf* **1** marble; **2** (billiard) ball.

billet /bijɛ/ *nm* **1** (bank)note, bill (US); **2** ticket.
■ **~ doux** love letter.

billion /biljɔ̃/ *nm* billion (GB), trillion (US).

bimensuel /bimɑ̃sɥɛl/ *nm* fortnightly magazine (GB), semimonthly (US).

bimoteur /bimɔtœʀ/ *nm* twin-engined plane.

binaire /binɛʀ/ *adj* binary.

biniou /binju/ *nm* Breton bagpipes.

binocles○ /binɔkl/ *nf pl* specs○, glasses.

biochimie /bjoʃimi/ *nf* biochemistry.

biographie /bjɔgʀafi/ *nf* biography.

biologie /bjɔlɔʒi/ *nf* biology.

biophysique /bjofisik/ *nf* biophysics.

bip /bip/ *nm* beep; **~ sonore** tone.

bipède /bipɛd/ *nm* biped.

biplace /biplas/ *adj, nm* two-seater.

bique○ /bik/ *nf* **une vieille ~** an old bag○.

biréacteur /biʀeaktœʀ/ *nm* twin-engined jet.

bis[1] /bis/ *adv* **1** (in address) bis; **33 ~ rue Juliette Lamber** 33 bis rue Juliette Lamber; **2** (at show, concert) encore.

bis[2]**, ~e**[1] /bi, biz/ *adj* greyish (GB) or grayish (US) brown.

bisannuel, -elle /bizanɥɛl/ *adj* biennial.

biscornu, ~e /biskɔʀny/ *adj* quirky.

biscotte /biskɔt/ *nf* continental toast.

biscuit /biskɥi/ *nm* biscuit (GB), cookie (US).
■ **~ à la cuillère** sponge finger (GB), ladyfinger (US); **~ salé** cracker.

bise[2] /biz/ I *adj f* ▶ **bis**[2].
II *nf* **1**○ kiss; **faire la ~ à qn** to kiss sb on the cheeks; **2** North wind.

biseau, *pl* **~x** /bizo/ *nm* **1** bevel (edge); **tailler en ~** to bevel; **2** (tool) bevel.

bison /bizɔ̃/ *nm* **1** bison; **2** buffalo.

bissextile /bisɛkstil/ *adj* **année ~** leap year.

bistouri /bistuʀi/ *nm* (Med) bistoury.

bistro(t)○ /bistʀo/ *nm* bistro, café.

bit /bit/ *nm* bit.

BIT /beite/ *nm* (*abbr* = **Bureau international du travail**) ILO.

bitume /bitym/ *nm* (on road) asphalt.

bivouac /bivwak/ *nm* bivouac.

bizarre /bizaʀ/ *adj* odd, strange.

blafard, ~e /blafaʀ, aʀd/ *adj* pale.

blague○ /blag/ *nf* **1** joke; **~ à part** seriously; **2** fib○; **3** trick; **faire une ~ à qn** to play a trick on sb.

blaguer○ /blage/ [1] *vi* to joke.

blagueur○**, -euse** /blagœʀ, øz/ *nm,f* joker.

blaireau, *pl* **~x** /blɛʀo/ *nm* **1** badger; **2** shaving brush.

blâmer /blɑme/ [1] *vtr* to criticize; to blame.

blanc, **blanche**[1] /blɑ̃, blɑ̃ʃ/ **I** *adj* (gen) white; [*page*] blank; **~ cassé** off-white.
II *nm* **1** white; **habillé/peint en ~** dressed in/painted white; **2** household linen; **3** white meat; **4** (egg) white; **5** blank; gap; **j'ai eu un ~** my mind went blank; **6**○ correction fluid; **7** **tirer à ~** to fire blanks.
III blancs *nm pl* (in chess, draughts) white.

Blanc, **Blanche** /blɑ̃, blɑ̃ʃ/ *nm,f* white man/woman.

blanc-bec, *pl* **blancs-becs** /blɑ̃bɛk/ *nm* greenhorn.

blanchâtre /blɑ̃ʃɑtʀ/ *adj* whitish.

blanche[2] /blɑ̃ʃ/ **I** *adj f* ▶ **blanc I**.
II *nf* (Mus) minim (GB), half note (US).

blanchir /blɑ̃ʃiʀ/ [3] **I** *vtr* **1** to whiten [*shoes*]; **2** to clear [*name*]; **3** to launder [*money*].
II *vi* **1** to turn grey (GB) or gray (US); **2 faire ~** to blanch [*vegetables*].
III se blanchir *v refl* (+ *v être*) to clear oneself.

blanchisserie /blɑ̃ʃisʀi/ *nf* laundry.

blanchisseur /blɑ̃ʃisœʀ/ *nm* (shop) laundry.

blanchisseuse /blɑ̃ʃisøz/ *nf* laundress.

blasé, **~e** /blaze/ *adj* blasé.

blason /blazɔ̃/ *nm* coat of arms.
IDIOMS **redorer son ~** to restore one's reputation.

blasphème /blasfɛm/ *nm* blasphemy.

blasphémer /blasfeme/ [1] *vi* to blaspheme.

blatte /blat/ *nf* cockroach.

blé /ble/ *nm* wheat; **~ noir** buckwheat.

bled○ /blɛd/ *nm* village.

blême /blɛm/ *adj* pale.

blessant, **~e** /blesɑ̃, ɑ̃t/ *adj* [*remark*] cutting.

blessé, **~e** /blese/ *nm,f* injured or wounded man/woman; casualty.

blesser /blese/ [1] **I** *vtr* **1** to injure, to hurt; to wound; **il a été blessé à la tête** he sustained head injuries; **2** to hurt [*person, feelings*]; to wound [*pride*].
II se blesser *v refl* (+ *v être*) to hurt oneself.

blessure /blesyʀ/ *nf* injury; wound.

blet, **blette** /blɛ, blɛt/ *adj* overripe.

bleu, **~e** /blø/ **I** *adj* **1** blue; **2** [*steak*] very rare.
II *nm* **1** blue; **2** bruise; **3 ~ de travail** overalls; **4** blue cheese.
IDIOMS **avoir une peur ~e de qch** to be scared stiff○ of sth.

bleuâtre /bløɑtʀ/ *adj* bluish.

bleuet /bløɛ/ *nm* (Bot) cornflower.

blindé, **~e** /blɛ̃de/ *adj* armoured[GB].

blinder /blɛ̃de/ [1] *vtr* to put security fittings on [*door*]; to armour-plate[GB] [*car*].

blizzard /blizaʀ/ *nm* blizzard.

bloc /blɔk/ **I** *nm* **1** block; **faire ~ avec/contre qn** to side with/unite against sb; **2** notepad; **~ de papier à lettres** writing pad.
II à bloc *phr* [*screw*] tightly; [*inflate*] fully.
III en bloc *phr* [*deny*] outright.
■ **~ opératoire** surgical unit.

blocage /blɔkaʒ/ *nm* blocking; **~ des salaires** wage freeze.

blockhaus /blɔkos/ *nm inv* blockhouse.

bloc-notes, *pl* **blocs-notes** /blɔknɔt/ *nm* notepad.

blocus /blɔkys/ *nm inv* blockade.

blond, **~e** /blɔ̃, ɔ̃d/ **I** *adj* **1** blonde (GB), blond (US); **2** [*wheat*] golden; [*tobacco*] light.
II *nm,f* (female) blonde (GB), blond (US); (male) blond.

bloqué, **~e** /blɔke/ **I** *pp* ▶ **bloquer**.
II *pp adj* **1** blocked; **2** [*mechanism, door*] jammed; **elle/la voiture est ~e** she/the car is stuck; **3 être ~** [*activity*] to be at a standstill; [*situation*] to be deadlocked.

bloquer /blɔke/ [1] **I** *vtr* **1** to block [*road*]; **2** to lock [*steering wheel*]; to wedge [*door*]; (accidentally) to jam [*mechanism, door*]; **3** to stop [*vehicle, traveller*]; **4** to freeze [*prices*]; **5** to stop [*project*]; **6** to lump [sth] together [*days*].
II se bloquer *v refl* (+ *v être*) **1** [*brakes, door*] to jam; [*wheel*] to lock; **2** to retreat.

blottir: **se blottir** /blɔtiʀ/ [3] *v refl* (+ *v être*) **se ~ contre** to huddle up against; to snuggle up against.

blouse /bluz/ *nf* **1** overall; **2** coat; **~ blanche** white coat; **3** blouse.

blouson /bluzɔ̃/ *nm* **1** blouson; **~ d'aviateur** bomber jacket; **2 ~ noir** ≈ rocker.

blue-jean, *pl* **~s** /bludʒin/ *nm* jeans.

bluffer○ /blœfe/ [1] *vtr, vi* to bluff.

boa /bɔa/ *nm* boa.

bobard○ /bɔbaʀ/ *nm* fib○, tall story.

bobine /bɔbin/ *nf* (of film, cable) reel.

bobo○ /bobo/ *nm* (baby talk) **1** pain; **2** scratch.

bocage /bɔkaʒ/ *nm* hedged farmland.

bocal, *pl* **-aux** /bɔkal, o/ *nm* jar; bowl.

bœuf /bœf, *pl* bø/ *nm* **1** bullock (GB), steer (US); **2** ox; **3** beef.
IDIOMS **faire un effet ~**○ to make a fantastic○ impression.

bohème /bɔɛm/ **I** *adj* bohemian.
II *nf* **la ~** bohemia.

bohémien, **-ienne** /bɔemjɛ̃, ɛn/ *nm,f* Romany, gypsy.

boire /bwaʀ/ [70] **I** *vtr* **1** to drink; **2** [*paper*] to soak up.
II se boire *v refl* (+ *v être*) **ce vin se boit frais** this wine should be drunk chilled.
IDIOMS **~ comme un trou**○ to drink like a fish○; **il y a à ~ et à manger dans leur théorie** there's both good and bad in their theory.

bois /bwa/ **I** *nm inv* wood; **en ~** [*chair*] wooden; [*cheque*] dud○; **~ mort** firewood.
II *nm pl* **1** antlers; **2** woodwind section.
IDIOMS **être de ~** to be insensitive; **il va voir de quel ~ je me chauffe**○ I'll show him.

boisé, **~e** /bwaze/ *adj* wooded.

boiserie /bwazʀi/ *nf* **~(s)** panelling[GB].

boisson /bwasɔ̃/ *nf* drink.

boîte /bwat/ *nf* **1** box; **2** tin (GB), can; **petits pois en ~** canned peas; **3 ~ (de nuit)** nightclub; **4**○ firm; office.

■ **~ crânienne** cranium; **~ à gants** glove compartment; **~ à** or **aux lettres** post box (GB), mailbox (US); **~ à musique** musical box (GB), music box (US); **~ à outils** toolbox; **~ postale**, **BP** PO Box; **~ de vitesses** gearbox.

IDIOMS **mettre qn en ~**○ to tease sb.

boiter /bwate/ [1] *vi* to limp.

boiteux, **-euse** /bwatø, øz/ **I** *adj* **1** lame; **2** [*chair*] wobbly; **3** [*argument, alliance*] shaky.

II *nm,f* lame person.

boîtier /bwatje/ *nm* (gen) case; (of camera) body.

boitiller /bwatije/ [1] *vi* to limp slightly.

bol /bɔl/ *nm* **1** bowl; **~ d'air** breath of fresh air; **2**○ luck; **coup de ~** stroke of luck.

bolide /bɔlid/ *nm* high-powered car.

bombardement /bɔ̃baʀdəmɑ̃/ *nm* (Mil) bombardment; bombing; shelling; **~ aérien** air raid.

bombarder /bɔ̃baʀde/ [1] *vtr* **1** to bombard; to bomb; to shell; **2 ~ qn de questions** to bombard sb with questions; **3**○ **~ qn à un poste** to catapult sb into a job.

bombardier /bɔ̃baʀdje/ *nm* **1** bomber; **2** bombardier.

bombe /bɔ̃b/ *nf* **1** bomb; **faire l'effet d'une ~** to come as a bombshell; **2 ~ (aérosol)** spray; **3** riding hat.

IDIOMS **partir à toute ~**○ to rush off.

bombé, **~e** /bɔ̃be/ *adj* **1** [*forehead*] domed; [*shape*] rounded; **2** [*road*] cambered.

bomber /bɔ̃be/ [1] **I** *vtr* **~ le torse** to thrust out one's chest; (figurative) to swell with pride.

II *vi* **1** [*plank*] to bulge out; **2**○ to belt along○.

bon, **bonne**[1] /bɔ̃, bɔn/ **I** *adj* **1** good; **prends un ~ pull** take a warm jumper; **elle est (bien) bonne**○! that's a good one!; (indignantly) I like that!; **voilà une bonne chose de faite!** that's that out of the way!; **nous sommes ~s derniers** we're well and truly last; **il n'est pas ~ à grand-chose** he's pretty useless; **il serait ~ qu'elle le sache** she ought to know; **à quoi ~?** what's the point?; **2** [*person, words*] kind; [*smile*] nice; **avoir ~ cœur** to be good-hearted; **3** [*time, answer*] right; **c'est ~, vous pouvez y aller** it's OK, you can go; **4** [*ticket*] valid; **tu es ~ pour la vaisselle, ce soir!** you're in line for the dishes tonight!; **5 bonne nuit/chance** good night/luck.

II *nm,f* **les ~s et les méchants** good people and bad people; (in films) the good guys and the bad guys○.

III *nm* **1** coupon; voucher; **2 il y a du ~ dans cet article** there are some good things in this article.

IV *adv* **ça sent ~!** that smells good!; **il fait ~** the weather's mild; **il fait ~ dans ta chambre** it's nice and warm in your room.

VI pour de bon *phr* **1** really; **tu dis ça pour de ~?** are you serious?; **2** for good.

■ **~ de commande** order form; **~ enfant** good-natured; **~ de garantie** guarantee slip; **~ marché** cheap; **~ mot** witticism; **~ à rien** good-for-nothing; **~ sens** common sense; **~ du Trésor** Treasury bond; **~ vivant** *nm* bon viveur; **bonne action** good deed; **bonne femme**○ (derogatory) woman, dame○ (US); wife, old lady○; **bonne pâte** good sort; **bonne sœur**○ nun.

bonbon /bɔ̃bɔ̃/ *nm* sweet (GB), candy (US).

bonbonne /bɔ̃bɔn/ *nf* **1** demijohn; (bigger) carboy; **2** (for gas) cylinder.

bond /bɔ̃/ *nm* **1** leap; **se lever d'un ~** to leap to one's feet; **2** (in time) jump; **3** (in profits, exports) leap; (in prices) jump (**de** in); **la médecine a fait un ~ en avant avec cette découverte** this discovery was a medical breakthrough.

IDIOMS **saisir la balle au ~** to seize the opportunity; **faire faux ~ à qn** to let sb down.

bonde /bɔ̃d/ *nf* **1** (of swimming pool) outlet; (of sink) plughole; **2** (stopper) (in pool) outlet cover; (in sink) plug.

bondé, **~e** /bɔ̃de/ *adj* packed (**de** with).

bondir /bɔ̃diʀ/ [3] *vi* **1** to leap; **~ de joie** to jump for joy; **2 ~ sur qn/qch** to pounce on sb/sth; **3** [*animal*] to leap about; **4 ça m'a fait ~** I was absolutely furious (about it).

bonheur /bɔnœʀ/ *nm* **1** happiness; **2** pleasure; **faire le ~ de qn** [*present*] to make sb happy; [*event, exhibition*] to delight sb; **3 par ~** fortunately; **au petit ~ (la chance)** at random; **tu ne connais pas ton ~!** you don't realize how lucky you are!

IDIOMS **alors, tu as trouvé ton ~**○**?** did you find what you wanted?

bonhomme, *pl* **~s**, **bonshommes** /bɔnɔm, bɔ̃zɔm/ **I** *adj* good-natured.

II○ *nm* **1** fellow, chap○; **2** husband, old man○.

■ **~ de neige** snowman.

IDIOMS **aller** or **suivre son petit ~ de chemin** to go peacefully along.

boniments /bɔnimɑ̃/ *nm pl* stories; **raconter des ~ à qn** to give sb some story○ (**à propos de** about); to smooth-talk sb.

bonjour /bɔ̃ʒuʀ/ *nm, excl* hello.

IDIOMS **être simple comme ~**○ to be very easy.

bonne[2] /bɔn/ **I** *adj f* ▶ **bon I**.

II *nf* **1** maid, servant; **2 tu en as de ~s, toi!** you must be joking!

■ **~ d'enfants** nanny.

bonnement /bɔnmɑ̃/ *adv* **tout ~** (quite) simply.

bonnet /bɔnɛ/ *nm* **1** hat; (for baby) bonnet; **2** (on bra) cup.

■ **~ de nuit** nightcap; (figurative) wet blanket○.

bonneterie /bɔnɛtʀi/ *nf* hosiery.

bonshommes ▶ **bonhomme**.

bonsoir /bɔ̃swaʀ/ *nm, excl* good evening, good night.

bonté /bɔ̃te/ *nf* **1** kindness; **2** (of God) goodness.

bonus /bɔnys/ *nm inv* no-claims bonus.

boom /bum/ *nm* boom; **en plein ~** booming.

bord /bɔʀ/ *nm* **1** (of plate, bed) edge; (of road) side; (of river) bank; **au ~ de** on or at the edge of [*lake, road*]; (figurative) on the verge of; **au ~ de la mer** at the seaside; by the sea; **~ à ~**

edge-to-edge; **2** (of cup) rim; (of hat) brim; **3 à ~** [*work*] on board; **de ~** [*instruments, staff*] on board; **on fera**○ **avec les moyens du ~** we'll make do with what we've got; **4** side; **être du même ~** to be on the same side.

bordeaux /bɔʀdo/ I *adj inv* burgundy.
II *nm* Bordeaux; **~ rouge** claret.

border /bɔʀde/ [1] *vtr* **1** to line (**de** with); **2** [*plants*] to border [*lake*]; **3** to tuck [sb] in; **4** to edge [*garment*] (**de** with).

bordereau, *pl* **~x** /bɔʀdəʀo/ *nm* form, slip.

bordure /bɔʀdyʀ/ I *nf* **1** (of sports ground, carpet) border; **2** (of road, platform) edge.
II **en bordure de** *phr* **1** next to [*park, canal, track*]; **2** on the edge of [*park*]; on the side of [*road*]; **3** just outside [*village*].

boréal, **~e**, *mpl* **-aux** /bɔʀeal, o/ *adj* boreal.

borgne /bɔʀɲ/ *adj* one-eyed.

borne /bɔʀn/ I *nf* **1 ~ (kilométrique)** kilometre[GB] marker; **2** bollard (GB), post (US); **3**○ kilometre[GB]; **4** (for electricity) terminal.
II **bornes** *nf pl* **leur ambition est sans ~s** their ambition knows no bounds.
■ **~ téléphonique** emergency telephone; taxi stand telephone.

borné, **~e** /bɔʀne/ *adj* narrow-minded.

borner: **se borner** /bɔʀne/ [1] *v refl* (+ *v être*) **1 se ~ à faire** to content oneself with doing; **2 se ~ à faire** to be limited to doing.

bosquet /bɔskɛ/ *nm* grove.

bosse /bɔs/ *nf* **1** hump; **2** bump; **3** dent.
IDIOMS **avoir la ~ de**○ to have a flair for; **rouler sa ~** to knock about.

bosser○ /bɔse/ [1] *vi* to work.

bossu, **~e** /bɔsy/ *adj* hunchbacked.

bot /bo/ *adj m* **pied ~** club foot.

botanique /bɔtanik/ I *adj* botanical.
II *nf* botany.

botte /bɔt/ *nf* **1** boot; **2** (of flowers) bunch; (of hay) bale.
■ **~s de caoutchouc** wellington boots.

botter /bɔte/ [1] *vtr* **1 ça le botte**○**!** he loves it!; **2** to kick.

bottin® /bɔtɛ̃/ *nm* telephone directory.

bottine /bɔtin/ *nf* ankle-boot.

bouc /buk/ *nm* **1** billy goat; **2** goatee.
■ **~ émissaire** scapegoat.

boucan○ /bukɑ̃/ *nm* din, racket○.

bouche /buʃ/ *nf* mouth; **faire la fine ~ devant qch** to turn one's nose up at sth.
■ **~ d'aération** air vent; **~ d'égout** manhole; **~ d'incendie** fire hydrant; **~ de métro** tube (GB) or subway (US) entrance.

bouché, **~e**[1] /buʃe/ I *pp* ▶ **boucher**[1].
II *pp adj* **1** blocked; **2** [*profession*] oversubscribed; **3**○ dim○, stupid; **4 cidre ~** bottled cider.

bouche-à-bouche /buʃabuʃ/ *nm inv* mouth-to-mouth resuscitation.

bouche-à-oreille /buʃaɔʀɛj/ *nm inv* **le ~** word of mouth.

bouchée[2] /buʃe/ *nf* mouthful; **pour une ~ de pain** for next to nothing; **mettre les ~s doubles** to double one's efforts.

boucher[1] /buʃe/ [1] I *vtr* **1** to cork; **2** to block; to clog (up); **3** to fill [*crack*].
II **se boucher** *v refl* (+ *v être*) **1 se ~ le nez** to hold one's nose; **se ~ les oreilles** to put one's fingers in one's ears; **2** to get blocked.
IDIOMS **en ~ un coin à qn**○ to amaze sb.

boucher[2], **-ère** /buʃe, ɛʀ/ *nm,f* butcher.

boucherie /buʃʀi/ *nf* **1** butcher's shop; **2** butcher's trade; **3** slaughter.

bouchon /buʃɔ̃/ *nm* **1** cork; **2** (screw)cap; **3** (of wax) plug; **4** traffic jam; **5** (in fishing) float.

boucle /bukl/ *nf* **1** buckle; **~ d'oreille** earring; **2** curl; **3** loop.

bouclé, **~e** /bukle/ *adj* curly.

boucler /bukle/ [1] *vtr* **1** to fasten [*belt*]; **2**○ to lock [*door*]; **3**○ to cordon off [*district*]; **4**○ to complete [*investigation*]; **5**○ to lock [sb] up.
IDIOMS **la ~**○ to shut up; **~ la boucle** to come full circle.

bouclier /buklije/ *nm* shield.

bouddhisme /budism/ *nm* Buddhism.

bouder /bude/ [1] *vi* to sulk.

boudin /budɛ̃/ *nm* ≈ blood sausage.

boudiné, **~e** /budine/ *adj* podgy.

boudiner /budine/ [1] *vtr* **être boudiné dans qch** to be squeezed into sth.

boue /bu/ *nf* **1** (gen, figurative) mud; **2** silt.

bouée /bwe/ *nf* **1** rubber ring; **2** buoy.
■ **~ de sauvetage** or **de secours** lifebelt (GB), life preserver (US).

boueux, **-euse** /buø, øz/ *adj* muddy.

bouffant, **~e** /bufɑ̃, ɑ̃t/ *adj* **1** baggy; **2** [*sleeves*] puffed; **3** [*hairstyle*] bouffant.

bouffe○ /buf/ *nf* **1** eating; **2** food; **3** meal.

bouffée /bufe/ *nf* (of tobacco, steam) puff; **une ~ d'air frais** a breath of fresh air.
■ **~ de chaleur** hot flush (GB), hot flash (US).

bouffer○ /bufe/ [1] I *vtr* to eat.
II *vi* to eat; (greedily) to stuff oneself○.

bouffi, **~e** /bufi/ *adj* puffy.

bouffon /bufɔ̃/ *nm* **1** clown; **2** jester; buffoon.

bougeoir /buʒwaʀ/ *nm* **1** candleholder; **2** candlestick.

bougeotte○ /buʒɔt/ *nf* **avoir la ~** to be restless.

bouger /buʒe/ [13] I *vtr* to move.
II *vi* **1** to move; **2**○ [*sector, company*] to be on the move; **3**○ **ville qui bouge** lively town.
III **se bouger**○ *v refl* (+ *v être*) **1** to get a move on○; **2** to put some effort in.

bougie /buʒi/ *nf* **1** candle; **2** (Tech) spark plug.

bougonner /bugɔne/ [1] *vi* to grumble.

bouillabaisse /bujabɛs/ *nf* fish soup.

bouillant, **~e** /bujɑ̃, ɑ̃t/ *adj* boiling (hot).

bouille○ /buj/ *nf* face.

bouillie /buji/ *nf* **1** gruel; **en ~** mushy; **mettre qn/qch en ~** to reduce sb/sth to a pulp; **2** baby cereal.

bouillir /bujiʀ/ [31] *vi* **1** to boil; **2** to be seething (**de** with).

bouilloire /bujwaʀ/ *nf* kettle.

bouillon /bujɔ̃/ *nm* **1** broth; **2** (Culin) stock; **3 bouillir à gros ~s** to boil fiercely.

bouillonner /bujɔne/ [1] *vi* **1** to bubble; **2 ~ d'activité** to be bustling with activity.

bouillotte /bujɔt/ *nf* hot-water bottle.

boulanger, **-ère** /bulɑ̃ʒe, ɛʀ/ *nm,f* baker.

boulangerie /bulɑ̃ʒʀi/ *nf* bakery.

boule /bul/ *nf* (gen) ball; (in bowling) bowl; **mettre qch en ~** to roll sth up into a ball.
■ **~ de neige** snowball; **~ Quiès®** earplug.
IDIOMS **il a perdu la ~**○ he's gone mad; **mettre qn en ~**○ to make sb furious.

bouleau, *pl* **~x** /bulo/ *nm* birch.

boulet /bulɛ/ *nm* **1 ~ (de canon)** cannonball; **2** ball and chain; **3** (figurative) millstone.

boulette /bulɛt/ *nf* **1** (of bread, paper) pellet; **2 ~ de viande** meatball; **3**○ blunder.

boulevard /bulvaʀ/ *nm* boulevard.
■ **~ périphérique** ring road (GB), beltway (US).

bouleversant, **~e** /bulvɛʀsɑ̃, ɑ̃t/ *adj* deeply moving.

bouleversement /bulvɛʀsəmɑ̃/ *nm* upheaval.

bouleverser /bulvɛʀse/ [1] *vtr* **1** to move [sb] deeply; **2** [*experience*] to shatter; **3** to turn [sth] upside down [*house, files*]; **4** to disrupt [*schedule*]; **5** to change [*sth*] dramatically [*lifestyle*].

boulier /bulje/ *nm* abacus.

boulimie /bulimi/ *nf* bulimia.

boulon /bulɔ̃/ *nm* bolt.

boulot, **-otte** /bulo, ɔt/ **I** *adj* tubby.
II○ *nm* **1** work; **2** job.

boulotter○ /bulɔte/ [1] *vtr, vi* to eat.

boum[1] /bum/ *nm* **1** bang; **2**○ **en plein ~** [*business*] booming; **faire un ~** [*birth rates*] to soar.

boum[2] /bum/ *nf* party.

bouquet /bukɛ/ *nm* **1 ~ (de fleurs)** bunch of flowers; bouquet; **2** (of firework display) final flourish; **c'est le ~**○**!** (figurative) that's the limit○!

bouquin○ /bukɛ̃/ *nm* book.

bouquiner○ /bukine/ [1] *vtr, vi* to read.

bourbier /buʀbje/ *nm* quagmire.

bourde /buʀd/ *nf* blunder.

bourdon /buʀdɔ̃/ *nm* bumblebee.

bourdonnement /buʀdɔnmɑ̃/ *nm* (of insect) buzzing; (of engine) hum; (of plane) drone.

bourdonner /buʀdɔne/ [1] *vi* to buzz; to hum.

bourg /buʀ/ *nm* market town.

bourgeois, **~e** /buʀʒwa, az/ **I** *adj* bourgeois.
II *nm,f* **1** middle-class person; **2** (in Ancien Regime) bourgeois; **3** burgher.

bourgeoisie /buʀʒwazi/ *nf* **1** middle classes; **2** bourgeoisie.

bourgeon /buʀʒɔ̃/ *nm* bud; **en ~s** in bud.

bourgeonner /buʀʒɔne/ [1] *vi* to bud.

bourrage /buʀaʒ/ *nm* **~ de crâne** brainwashing.

bourrasque /buʀask/ *nf* (of wind) gust.

bourratif, **-ive** /buʀatif, iv/ *adj* very filling, stodgy.

bourre○ /buʀ/ *nf* **être à la ~** to be pushed for time.

bourreau, *pl* **~x** /buʀo/ *nm* executioner.

bourrelet /buʀlɛ/ *nm* roll of fat.

bourrer /buʀe/ [1] *vtr* **1** to cram [sth] full; to fill [*pipe*]; **2**○ **~ qn de** to dose sb up with [*medicine*].

bourricot /buʀiko/ *nm* donkey.

bourrique /buʀik/ *nf* **1** donkey; **2**○ pig-headed person.

bourru, **~e** /buʀy/ *adj* gruff.

bourse /buʀs/ *nf* **1** grant (GB), scholarship (US); **2** purse.

Bourse /buʀs/ *nf* **1** stock exchange; **2** shares.

boursier, **-ière** /buʀsje, ɛʀ/ **I** *adj* **le marché ~** share prices.
II *nm,f* grant holder (GB), scholarship student (US).

boursouflé, **~e** /buʀsufle/ *adj* **1** blistered; **2** puffy; **3** [*body*] bloated.

bousculade /buskylad/ *nf* **1** jostling; (accidental) crush; **2** rush.

bousculer /buskyle/ [1] **I** *vtr* **1** to push, to jostle [*person*]; **2** to rush.
II se bousculer *v refl* (+ *v être*) to fall over each other (**pour faire** to do).

bouse /buz/ *nf* **une ~ (de vache)** a cowpat.

bousiller○ /buzije/ [1] *vtr* to wreck [*engine*]; to smash up [*car*].

boussole /busɔl/ *nf* compass.

bout /bu/ *nm* **1** end; tip; (of shoe) toe; **au ~ du jardin** at the bottom of the garden; **aller jusqu'au ~** to go all the way; **aller (jusqu') au ~ de** to follow through [*idea, demand*]; **elle est à ~** she can't take any more; **ne me pousse pas à ~** don't push me; **être à ~ d'arguments** to have run out of arguments; **venir à ~ de** to overcome [*difficulty*]; to get through [*task, meal*]; **au ~ du compte** in the end; **à ~ portant** at point-blank range; **2** (of bread, paper) piece; (of land) bit.
■ **~ de chou**○ sweet little thing○; **~ d'essai** screen test.
IDIOMS **tenir le bon ~**○ to be on the right track; **ne pas être au ~ de ses peines** not to be out of the woods yet.

boutade /butad/ *nf* witticism.

bouteille /butɛj/ *nf* (gen) bottle; (of gas) cylinder.
IDIOMS **prendre de la ~**○ to be getting on (a bit).

boutique /butik/ *nf* shop (GB), store (US).

bouton /butɔ̃/ *nm* **1** (on clothes) button; **2** knob; button; **3** (Med) spot (GB), pimple (US); **4** (flower) bud.
■ **~ de fièvre** cold sore; **~ de manchette** cuff link; **~ de porte** doorknob.

boutonner /butɔne/ [1] *vtr*, **se boutonner** *v refl* (+ *v être*) to button up.

boutonneux, **-euse** /butɔnø, øz/ *adj* spotty (GB), pimply (US).

boutonnière /butɔnjɛʀ/ *nf* buttonhole.

bouture /butyʀ/ *nf* cutting.

bovin, **~e** /bɔvɛ̃, in/ **I** *adj* bovine.
II *nm* bovine; **des ~s** cattle.

box, *pl* **boxes** /bɔks/ *nm* **1** lock-up garage; **2** (for horse) stall; **3** (in bar) alcove.
■ **~ des accusés** (Law) dock.

boxe /bɔks/ *nf* (Sport) boxing; **~ française** savate.

boxer /bɔkse/ [1] *vi* (Sport) to box.

boxeur /bɔksœʀ/ *nm* (Sport) boxer.

boyau, *pl* **~x** /bwajo/ *nm* **1** gut; **2** catgut; **3** (for sausage) casing; **4** tubeless tyre (GB) or tire (US).

boycotter /bɔjkɔte/ [1] *vtr* to boycott.

bracelet /bʀaslɛ/ *nm* **1** bracelet; bangle; **2** wristband; **~ de montre** watchstrap.

braconnier /bʀakɔnje/ *nm* poacher.

brader /bʀade/ [1] *vtr* **1** to sell cheaply; **2** to sell off.

braderie /bʀadʀi/ *nf* **1** street market; **2** discount store; **3** clearance sale.

braguette /bʀagɛt/ *nf* flies (GB), fly (US).

braille /bʀaj/ *nm* Braille.

brailler○ /bʀaje/ [1] *vi* **1** to yell; **2** [*child, singer*] to bawl.

braire /bʀɛʀ/ [58] *vi* to bray.

braise /bʀɛz/ *nf* live embers.

brancard /bʀɑ̃kaʀ/ *nm* stretcher.

branche /bʀɑ̃ʃ/ *nf* **1** (of tree) branch; **2 céleri en ~s** sticks of celery; **3** field, sector; **4** (of family) branch; **5** (of candelabra) branch; (of spectacles) arm; (of star) point.

branché○, **~e** /bʀɑ̃ʃe/ *adj* trendy○.

branchement /bʀɑ̃ʃmɑ̃/ *nm* **1** (electrical) connection; **2** (for water) branch pipe; (for electricity) lead (GB), cable (US).

brancher /bʀɑ̃ʃe/ [1] *vtr* **1** to plug in; **2** to connect (up) [*water, electricity*]; **3**○ **~ qn sur** to get sb onto [*topic*]; **4**○ **je vais au cinéma, ça te branche?** I'm going to the cinema, are you interested?

branchie /bʀɑ̃ʃi/ *nf* (of fish) gill.

brandir /bʀɑ̃diʀ/ [3] *vtr* to brandish.

branlant, **~e** /bʀɑ̃lɑ̃, ɑ̃t/ *adj* [*chair*] rickety; [*tooth*] loose; [*argument*] shaky.

branle /bʀɑ̃l/ *nm* **mettre qch en ~** to set [sth] in motion [*project, convoy*].

branler /bʀɑ̃le/ [1] *vi* [*wall*] to wobble; [*chair*] to be rickety; [*tooth*] to be loose.

braquage○ /bʀakaʒ/ *nm* robbery.

braquer /bʀake/ [1] **I** *vtr* **1** to point [*gun, camera*] (**sur, vers** at); to turn or fix [*eyes*] (**sur, vers** on); **2 ~ à gauche/droite** to turn hard left/right; **3**○ to point a gun at; **4**○ to rob [*bank*]; **5**○ **~ qn contre qn/qch** to turn sb against sb/sth.
II *vi* [*driver*] to turn the wheel full lock (GB) or all the way (US).
III se braquer *v refl* (+ *v être*) to dig one's heels in.

bras /bʀa/ *nm inv* **1** arm; **~ dessus ~ dessous** arm in arm; **porter qch à bout de ~** (figurative) to keep sth afloat; **en ~ de chemise** in one's shirtsleeves; **2** manpower, labour[GB]; **3** (of river) branch; **~ de mer** sound; **4** (of armchair) arm.
■ **~ droit** right hand man; **~ de fer** arm wrestling; (figurative) trial of strength.
IDIOMS **les ~ m'en tombent** I'm absolutely speechless; **avoir le ~ long** to have a lot of influence.

brasier /bʀazje/ *nm* inferno.

bras-le-corps: **à bras-le-corps** /abʀalkɔʀ/ *phr* [*lift*] bodily.

brassard /bʀasaʀ/ *nm* armband.

brasse /bʀas/ *nf* (Sport) breaststroke.

brasser /bʀase/ [1] *vtr* **1** to toss around [*ideas*]; to shuffle around [*papers*]; to intermingle [*population*]; **il brasse des millions** he handles big money; **2** to brew [*beer*].

brasserie /bʀasʀi/ *nf* **1** brasserie; **2** brewery.

brassière /bʀasjɛʀ/ *nf* **1** baby's top; **2** crop top.

brave /bʀav/ *adj* **1** nice; **un ~ homme** a nice man; **2** brave; **un homme ~** a brave man.

braver /bʀave/ [1] *vtr* to defy [*person*]; to brave [*storm*].

bravo /bʀavo/ *excl* bravo!; well done!

bravoure /bʀavuʀ/ *nf* bravery.

break /bʀɛk/ *nm* estate car (GB), station wagon (US).

brebis /bʀəbi/ *nf inv* ewe.

brèche /bʀɛʃ/ *nf* **1** hole, gap; **2** (Mil) breach.

bredouille /bʀəduj/ *adj* empty-handed.

bredouiller /bʀəduje/ [1] *vtr, vi* to mumble.

bref, **brève**[1] /bʀɛf, bʀɛv/ **I** *adj* brief; short.
II *adv* **(en) ~** in short.

breloque /bʀəlɔk/ *nf* (on bracelet) charm.

Brésil /bʀezil/ *pr nm* Brazil.

Bretagne /bʀətaɲ/ *pr nf* **la ~** Brittany.

bretelle /bʀətɛl/ **I** *nf* **1** (gen) strap; **2** slip road (GB), ramp (US).
II bretelles *nf pl* braces.

breton, **-onne** /bʀətɔ̃, ɔn/ **I** *adj* Breton.
II *nm* (language) Breton.

breuvage /bʀœvaʒ/ *nm* beverage.

brève[2] /bʀɛv/ **I** *adj f* ▶ **bref I**.
II *nf* news flash.

brevet /bʀəvɛ/ *nm* **1 ~ (d'invention)** patent; **2 ~ de secourisme** first aid certificate; **~ de pilote** pilot's licence[GB].

breveter /bʀəvte/ [20] *vtr* **(faire) ~** to patent.

bréviaire /bʀevjɛʀ/ *nm* breviary.

bribes /bʀib/ *nf pl* (of conversation) snatches.

bric: **de bric et de broc** /dəbʀiked(ə)bʀɔk/ *phr* [*furnished*] with bits and pieces.

bric-à-brac /bʀikabʀak/ *nm inv* bric-à-brac.

bricolage /bʀikɔlaʒ/ *nm* DIY (GB), do-it-yourself.

bricole /bʀikɔl/ *nf* **acheter une ~** to buy a little something; **des ~s** bits and pieces.

bricoler /bʀikɔle/ [1] **I**○ *vtr* **1** to tinker with; **2** to throw [*sth*] together.
II *vi* to do DIY (GB), to fix things (US).

bride /bʀid/ *nf* **1** bridle; **2** button loop.
IDIOMS **partir à ~ abattue** to dash off; **avoir la ~ sur le cou** to have free rein.

bridé, **~e** /bʀide/ *adj* **yeux ~s** slanting eyes.
brièvement /bʀijɛvmɑ̃/ *adv* briefly.
brigade /bʀigad/ *nf* **1** (Mil) brigade; **2** (in police) squad.
brigadier /bʀigadje/ *nm* **1** ≈ corporal; **2** fire chief.
brigand /bʀigɑ̃/ *nm* brigand, bandit.
brillamment /bʀijamɑ̃/ *adv* brilliantly.
brillant, **~e** /bʀijɑ̃, ɑ̃t/ **I** *adj* **1** bright; shiny; glistening; **2** brilliant.
II *nm* (cut) diamond, brilliant.
briller /bʀije/ [1] *vi* **1** [*sun*] to shine; [*flame*] to burn brightly; [*gem*] to sparkle; [*nose*] to be shiny; **2** **~ de** [*eyes*] to blaze with [*anger*]; **3** [*person*] to shine; **elle brille par son esprit** she's extremely witty.
brimade /bʀimad/ *nf* bullying.
brimer /bʀime/ [1] *vtr* **1** to bully; **2** **se sentir brimé** to feel picked on.
brin /bʀɛ̃/ *nm* **1** (of parsley) sprig; (of straw) wisp; (of grass) blade; **2** **un ~ de** a bit of.
brindille /bʀɛ̃dij/ *nf* twig.
bringue○ /bʀɛ̃g/ *nf* **1** drinking party; **2** rave-up○; **3** (girl) **(grande) ~** beanpole.
brinquebaler /bʀɛ̃kbale/ [1] *vi* [*load*] to rattle about; [*vehicle*] to jolt along.
brio /bʀijo/ *nm* brilliance; (Mus) brio.
brioche /bʀijɔʃ/ *nf* **1** brioche, (sweet) bun; **2**○ paunch.
brique /bʀik/ *nf* **1** brick; **2** (for milk, juice) carton.
briquer /bʀike/ [1] *vtr* to polish [sth] up.
briquet /bʀikɛ/ *nm* (cigarette) lighter.
brise /bʀiz/ *nf* breeze; **bonne ~** fresh breeze.
brise-glace /bʀizglas/ *nm inv* icebreaker.
briser /bʀize/ [1] **I** *vtr* **1** (gen) to break; to break down [*resistance*]; **2** to shatter [*dream*]; to destroy [*career, person*]; **3** to shatter [*person*].
II se briser *v refl* (+ *v être*) **1** to break; **2** [*dream*] to be shattered; **3** [*voice*] to break.
brisure /bʀizyʀ/ *nf* **1** crack; **2** fragment.
britannique /bʀitanik/ *adj* British.
Britannique /bʀitanik/ *nmf* **un/une ~** a British man/woman; **les ~s** the British (people).
broc /bʀo/ *nm* ewer.
brocante /bʀɔkɑ̃t/ *nf* **1** bric-à-brac trade; **2** flea market.
broche /bʀɔʃ/ *nf* **1** brooch; **2** (for roasting) spit; **3** (in surgery) pin.
brocher /bʀɔʃe/ [1] *vtr* to bind [sth] (with paper) [*book*]; **livre broché** paperback.
brochet /bʀɔʃɛ/ *nm* (Zool) pike.
brochette /bʀɔʃɛt/ *nf* **1** skewer; **2** kebab.
brochure /bʀɔʃyʀ/ *nf* **1** booklet; **2** (travel) brochure.
brocoli /bʀɔkɔli/ *nm* broccoli.
broder /bʀɔde/ [1] *vtr, vi* to embroider.
broderie /bʀɔdʀi/ *nf* embroidery.
bromure /bʀɔmyʀ/ *nm* bromide.
bronche /bʀɔ̃ʃ/ *nf* **les ~s** the bronchial tubes.
broncher /bʀɔ̃ʃe/ [1] *vi* **sans ~** without turning a hair.
bronchite /bʀɔ̃ʃit/ *nf* bronchitis.
bronzage /bʀɔ̃zaʒ/ *nm* (sun)tan.
bronze /bʀɔ̃z/ *nm* bronze.
bronzer /bʀɔ̃ze/ [1] *vi* to get a tan, to go brown.
brosse /bʀɔs/ *nf* brush; **donner un coup de ~ à qch** to give sth a brush; **avoir les cheveux (taillés) en ~** to have a crew cut.
brosser /bʀɔse/ [1] **I** *vtr* **1** to brush; to scrub; **2** to give a quick outline of.
II se brosser *v refl* (+ *v être*) to brush oneself down; **se ~ les dents** to brush one's teeth.
brouette /bʀuɛt/ *nf* wheelbarrow.
brouhaha /bʀuaa/ *nm* hubbub.
brouillard /bʀujaʀ/ *nm* fog.
brouille /bʀuj/ *nf* **1** quarrel; **2** rift.
brouiller /bʀuje/ [1] **I** *vtr* **1** to make [sth] cloudy [*liquid*]; to blur [*text, vision*]; **~ les cartes** to confuse or cloud the issue; **2** to jam [*signal*]; to interfere with [*reception*].
II se brouiller *v refl* (+ *v être*) **1** to fall out (**avec** with); **2** [*liquid*] to become cloudy; [*vision*] to become blurred; [*mind*] to become confused; **avoir le teint brouillé** to look ill.
brouillon, **-onne** /bʀujɔ̃, ɔn/ **I** *adj* **1** untidy; **2** disorganized; **3** muddled.
II *nm* **1** rough draft; **2** rough paper.
broussaille /bʀusaj/ *nf* **1** undergrowth; **2** scrub; **3** bushes.
brousse /bʀus/ *nf* bush; **en pleine ~**○ in the sticks○.
brouter /bʀute/ [1] *vtr* to nibble; to graze.
broyer /bʀwaje/ [23] *vtr* **1** to grind [*wheat*]; **2** to crush.
IDIOMS **~ du noir** to brood.
bru /bʀy/ *nf* daughter-in-law.
brugnon /bʀyɲɔ̃/ *nm* nectarine.
bruiner /bʀɥine/ [1] *v impers* to drizzle.
bruissement /bʀɥismɑ̃/ *nm* (of leaves) rustle; (of brook) babbling.
bruit /bʀɥi/ *nm* **1** noise; **~ étouffé** thud; **un ~ de ferraille** a clang; **2** noise, din; **~ infernal** or **d'enfer** awful racket; **sans ~** silently; **3 le film a fait beaucoup de ~** the film attracted a lot of attention; **4 ~ (de couloir)** rumour[GB].
bruitage /bʀɥitaʒ/ *nm* sound effects.
brûlant, **~e** /bʀylɑ̃, ɑ̃t/ *adj* **1** [*tea*] boiling hot; [*sand, radiator, person*] burning hot; [*sun*] blazing; **2** [*issue*] burning; **3** [*passion*] burning.
brûlé, **~e** /bʀyle/ **I** *nm,f* **un grand ~** a third degree burns victim; **service des grands ~s** burns unit.
II *nm* **ça sent le ~** there's a smell of burning.
brûle-pourpoint: **à brûle-pourpoint** /abʀylpuʀpwɛ̃/ *phr* point-blank.
brûler /bʀyle/ [1] **I** *vtr* **1** to burn [*papers*]; to set fire to [*house*]; **2** to burn [*fuel*]; to use [*electricity*]; **3** [*acid*] to burn; [*water*] to scald; **j'ai les yeux qui me brûlent** my eyes are stinging; **4**○ **~ un feu (rouge)** to jump○ the lights.
II *vi* **1** [*wood*] to burn; [*forest, town*] to be on fire; **2 ~ (d'envie) de faire** to be longing to do.

III se brûler *v refl* (+ *v être*) to burn oneself.

brûlure /bʀylyʀ/ *nf* **1** burn; **~s d'estomac** heartburn; **2** burn mark.

brume /bʀym/ *nf* mist; fog; haze.

brumeux, **-euse** /bʀymø, øz/ *adj* **1** hazy; misty; **2** [*idea*] hazy.

brun, **~e** /bʀœ̃, bʀyn/ **I** *adj* brown, dark; dark-haired.

II *nm,f* dark-haired man/woman.

III *nm* brown.

brunir /bʀyniʀ/ [3] *vi* **1** [*skin*] to tan; **2** (Culin) to brown.

brushing /bʀœʃiŋ/ *nm* blow-dry.

brusque /bʀysk/ *adj* **1** [*tone, person*] abrupt; **2** [*movement*] sudden; [*bend*] sharp.

brusquer /bʀyske/ [1] *vtr* **1** to be brusque with; **2** to rush.

brut, **~e**[1] /bʀyt/ *adj* **1** [*material*] raw; [*oil*] crude; [*stone*] rough; [*sugar*] unrefined; **2** [*cider, champagne*] dry; **3** [*salary*] gross.

brutal, **~e** *mpl* **-aux** /bʀytal, o/ *adj* **1** [*blow*] violent; [*pain, death*] sudden; **2** [*tone*] brutal; [*gesture, temper*] violent; **3** stark.

brutalement /bʀytalmɑ̃/ *adv* **1** [*repress*] brutally; [*close*] violently; **2** [*die, stop*] suddenly.

brutaliser /bʀytalize/ [1] *vtr* to ill-treat.

brutalité /bʀytalite/ *nf* **1** brutality; **2** suddenness.

brute[2] /bʀyt/ **I** *adj f* ▶ **brut**.

II *nf* brute; **comme une ~** [*hit*] savagely.

Bruxelles /bʀysɛl/ *pr n* Brussels.

bruyant, **~e** /bʀɥijɑ̃, ɑ̃t/ *adj* **1** noisy; loud; **2** resounding.

bu, **~e** /by/ *pp* ▶ **boire**.

buanderie /bɥɑ̃dʀi/ *nf* laundry room.

buccal, **~e**, *mpl* **-aux** /bykal, o/ *adj* oral.

bûche /byʃ/ *nf* **1** log (of wood); **2**○ tumble, fall; **3** (Culin) **~ de Noël** yule log.

bûcher[1]○ /byʃe/ [1] *vi* to slog away○.

bûcher[2] /byʃe/ *nm* **1 le ~** the stake; **2** (funeral) pyre.

bûcheron /byʃʀɔ̃/ *nm* lumberjack.

bûchette /byʃɛt/ *nf* (for fire) stick.

bucolique /bykɔlik/ *adj* bucolic, pastoral.

budget /bydʒɛ/ *nm* budget.

budgétaire /bydʒetɛʀ/ *adj* [*deficit*] budget; [*year*] financial (GB), fiscal (US).

buée /bɥe/ *nf* **1** condensation; **2** steam.

buffet /byfɛ/ *nm* **1** sideboard; **2** dresser; **3** (station) buffet; **4** (Culin) buffet.

buffle /byfl/ *nm* buffalo.

buis /bɥi/ *nm* **1** box tree; **2** boxwood.

buisson /bɥisɔ̃/ *nm* **1** bush; **2** shrub.

buissonnière /bɥisɔnjɛʀ/ *adj f* **faire l'école ~** to play truant (GB), to play hooky○ (US).

bulbe /bylb/ *nm* (Bot) bulb.

bulgare /bylgaʀ/ *adj*, *nm* Bulgarian.

Bulgarie /bylgaʀi/ *pr nf* Bulgaria.

bulldozer /byldozœʀ/ *nm* bulldozer.

bulle /byl/ *nf* **1** bubble; **2** speech bubble.

bulletin /byltɛ̃/ *nm* **1** bulletin, report; **~ de santé** medical bulletin; **2** certificate; **~ de naissance** birth certificate; **3** form; **~ de salaire** payslip; **~ de participation** entry form; **4** bulletin, official publication; **5** ballot or voting paper.

bulot /bylo/ *nm* whelk.

bureau, *pl* **~x** /byʀo/ *nm* **1** desk; **2** study; **3** office; **4** board.

■ **~ d'accueil** reception; **~ de poste** post office; **~ de tabac** tobacconist's; **~ de vote** polling station.

bureaucratie /byʀokʀasi/ *nf* bureaucracy.

bureautique /byʀotik/ *nf* office automation.

burin /byʀɛ̃/ *nm* chisel.

buriné, **~e** /byʀine/ *adj* [*face*] craggy.

burlesque /byʀlɛsk/ *adj* ludicrous; farcical.

bus /bys/ *nm inv* bus.

buse /byz/ *nf* **1** buzzard; **2**○ clot○ (GB), clod○.

busqué, **~e** /byske/ *adj* [*nose*] hooked.

buste /byst/ *nm* **1** (in sculpture) bust; **2** (Anat) chest; **3** bust, breasts.

bustier /bystje/ *nm* **1** long-line bra; **2** bustier.

but /by(t)/ *nm* **1** goal; aim, purpose; **aller droit au ~** to go straight to the point; **2** (in football) goal; **3** (in archery) target.

IDIOMS **déclarer de ~ en blanc** to declare point-blank.

buté, **~e** /byte/ *adj* stubborn, obstinate.

buter /byte/ [1] *vi* **~ contre qch** to trip over sth; to bump into sth; **~ sur** or **contre** to come up against [*obstacle*].

butin /bytɛ̃/ *nm* (from robbery) haul.

butiner /bytine/ [1] *vi* to gather pollen.

butte /byt/ *nf* mound.

IDIOMS **être en ~ à** to come up against [*difficulties*]; to be the butt of [*jokes*].

buvable /byvabl/ *adj* **1** [*medicine*] to be taken orally; **2** drinkable.

buvard /byvaʀ/ *nm* **(papier) ~** blotting paper.

buvette /byvɛt/ *nf* refreshment area.

Cc

c, **C** /se/ *nm inv* c, C; **c cédille** c cedilla.
c' ▶ **ce II**.
CA *written abbr* ▶ **chiffre**.
ça /sa/ *pron* **1** that; this; **c'est pour ~ qu'il est parti** that's why he left; **sans ~** otherwise; **~, c'est bizarre** that's strange; **la rue a ~ de bien qu'elle est calme** one good thing about the street is that it's quiet; **2** it; that; **~ fait mal** it hurts; that hurts; **~ criait de tous les côtés** there was shouting everywhere.
IDIOMS **~ alors!** well I never○!; **~, oui!** definitely!; **elle est bête et méchante avec ~** she's stupid and what's more she's nasty; **et avec ~?** anything else?; **rien que ~!** (ironic) is that all!; **c'est ~!** that's right!; **~ y est, ~ recommence!** here we go again!; **~ y est, j'ai fini!** that's it, I've finished!
caban /kabɑ̃/ *nm* sailor's jacket.
cabane /kaban/ *nf* **1** hut; **2** shed; **3**◑ prison.
cabaret /kabaʀɛ/ *nm* cabaret.
cabas /kaba/ *nm* shopping bag.
cabillaud /kabijo/ *nm* cod.
cabine /kabin/ *nf* cabin; cab; booth; cubicle.
■ **~ d'essayage** fitting room; **~ de pilotage** cockpit; **~ téléphonique** phone box (GB), phone booth.
cabinet /kabinɛ/ **I** *nm* **1** (gen) office; (of doctor, dentist) surgery (GB), office (US); (of judge) chambers; **2** practice; **~ de médecins** medical practice; **ouvrir un ~** to set up in practice; **3** agency; **4** (Pol) cabinet; **~ ministériel** minister's personal staff.
II cabinets *nm pl* toilet.
■ **~ de toilette** bathroom.
cabinet-conseil, *pl* **cabinets-conseil** /kabinɛkɔ̃sɛj/ *nm* firm of consultants.
câble /kɑbl/ *nm* **1** cable; rope; **2** cable television.
câbler /kɑble/ [1] *vtr* **1** to install cable television in [*house, town*]; **2** to cable [*message*].
cabosser /kabɔse/ [1] *vtr* to dent.
cabot○ /kabo/ *nm* dog, mutt○.
cabotin, **~e** /kabɔtɛ̃, in/ *adj* **être ~** to like playing to the gallery.
cabrer: **se cabrer** /kabʀe/ [1] *v refl* (+ *v être*) **1** [*horse*] to rear (**devant** at); **2** [*person*] to jib.
cabri /kabʀi/ *nm* (Zool) kid.
cabriole /kabʀijɔl/ *nf* (of clown, child) caper.
caca /kaka/ *nm* (baby talk) poo○ (GB), poop○ (US).
cacahuète /kakawɛt/ *nf* peanut.
cacao /kakao/ *nm* cocoa.
cachalot /kaʃalo/ *nm* sperm whale.
cache[1] /kaʃ/ *nm* **se servir d'un ~ pour apprendre une liste de vocabulaire** to cover up the answers while learning a list of vocabulary.
cache[2] /kaʃ/ *nf* **~ d'armes** arms cache.
cache-cache /kaʃkaʃ/ *nm inv* hide and seek (GB), hide-and-go-seek (US).
cache-col /kaʃkɔl/ *nm inv* scarf.
cachemire /kaʃmiʀ/ *nm* cashmere.
cache-nez /kaʃne/ *nm inv* scarf, muffler.
cache-pot /kaʃpo/ *nm inv* flowerpot holder.
cacher /kaʃe/ [1] **I** *vtr* to hide; **~ son jeu** (figurative) to keep one's cards close to one's chest; **~ qch à qn** to conceal sth from sb.
II se cacher *v refl* (+ *v être*) **1** to hide; (temporarily) to go into hiding; **il ne s'en cache pas** he makes no secret of it; **2** [*sun*] to disappear.
cache-sexe /kaʃsɛks/ *nm inv* G-string.
cachet /kaʃɛ/ *nm* **1** tablet; **2** (for letter) stamp; seal; **~ de la poste** postmark; **3** (of actor) fee.
cacheter /kaʃte/ [20] *vtr* to seal.
cachette /kaʃɛt/ *nf* hiding place; **en ~** on the sly.
cachot /kaʃo/ *nm* **1** prison cell; **2** dungeon.
cachotterie /kaʃɔtʀi/ *nf* little secret.
cachou /kaʃu/ *nm* cachou.
cacophonie /kakɔfɔni/ *nf* cacophony.
cactus /kaktys/ *nm inv* cactus.
c-à-d (*written abbr* = **c'est-à-dire**) ie.
cadastre /kadastʀ/ *nm* **1** land register; **2** land registry.
cadavre /kadavʀ/ *nm* corpse, body.
caddie® /kadi/ *nm* shopping trolley.
cadeau, *pl* **~x** /kado/ **I** *nm* present, gift; **faire un ~ à qn** to give sb a present; **il ne fait pas de ~x** (examiner, judge) he's very strict.
II (-)cadeau (*combining form*) gift; **papier(-)~** wrapping paper.
cadenas /kadna/ *nm* padlock.
cadence /kadɑ̃s/ *nf* **1** rhythm; **2** (of work) rate.
cadet, **-ette** /kadɛ, ɛt/ **I** *adj* **1** younger; **2** youngest.
II *nm,f* **1** younger son/daughter, younger child; **2** youngest child; **3** younger brother/sister; **4** (Sport) *athlete between the ages of 15 and 17.*
IDIOMS **c'est le ~ de mes soucis** it's the least of my worries.
cadran /kadʀɑ̃/ *nm* (of watch) face; (of meter) dial; **~ solaire** sundial.
cadre /kadʀ/ **I** *nm* **1** frame; **2** setting; surroundings; **3 cela sort du ~ de mes fonctions** that's not part of my duties; **4** framework; **5** executive; **~ supérieur** senior executive; **les ~s moyens** middle management; **6 faire partie des ~s** to be on the company's books; **7** (of bicycle) frame; **8** (on form) space, box.
II dans le cadre de *phr* **1** on the occasion of; **2** (of negotiations) within the framework of; (of campaign, plan) as part of.
cadrer /kadʀe/ [1] **I** *vtr* to centre[GB] [*picture*].
II *vi* to tally, to fit (**avec** with).

cadreur /kadʀœʀ/ *nm* cameraman.

caduc, caduque /kadyk/ *adj* **1** obsolete; **2** (Law) null and void; **3** [*leaf*] deciduous.

cætera ▶ et cætera.

cafard /kafaʀ/ *nm* **1**○ depression; **avoir le ~** to be down in the dumps○; **2** cockroach.

café /kafe/ *nm* **1** coffee; **~ en grains** coffee beans; **~ soluble** instant coffee; **2** café.
■ **~ crème** espresso with milk; **~ au lait** coffee with milk; **peau ~ au lait** coffee-coloured[GB] skin.

caféine /kafein/ *nf* caffeine.

cafétéria /kafeteʀja/ *nf* cafeteria.

cafetière /kaftjɛʀ/ *nf* coffee pot; coffee maker.

cafouillage○ /kafujaʒ/ *nm* bungling○.

cafouiller○ /kafuje/ [1] *vi* [*person*] to get flustered; [*machine*] to be on the blink○; [*organization*] to get in a muddle.

cage /kaʒ/ *nf* **1** cage; **2**○ (Sport) goal.
■ **~ d'ascenseur** lift (GB) or elevator (US) shaft; **~ d'escalier** stairwell; **~ à lapins** rabbit hutch; **~ thoracique** rib cage.

cageot /kaʒo/ *nm* crate.

cagette /kaʒɛt/ *nf* tray.

cagibi /kaʒibi/ *nm* store cupboard.

cagnotte /kaɲɔt/ *nf* **1** kitty; **2** jackpot.

cagoule /kagul/ *nf* balaclava; hood.

cahier /kaje/ *nm* **1** notebook; (Sch) exercise book; **2** (in printing) section.
■ **~ de brouillon** rough book; **~ de textes** homework notebook.

cahin-caha○ /kaɛ̃kaa/ *adv* with difficulty.

cahot /kao/ *nm* jolt.

cahoter /kaɔte/ [1] *vi* [*vehicle*] to bounce along.

cahoteux, ~euse /kaɔtø, -øz/ *adj* [*road*] rough, bumpy.

cahute /kayt/ *nf* hut, shack.

caïd /kaid/ *nm* (in criminal underworld) boss; **jouer les ~s** to act tough.

caillasse /kajas/ *nf* stones.

caille /kɑj/ *nf* (Zool) quail.

cailler /kɑje/ [1] **I se cailler** *v refl* (+ *v être*) **1** [*milk*] to curdle; **2**○ [*person*] to be freezing.
II○ *v impers* **ça caille** it's freezing.

caillot /kajo/ *nm* clot.

caillou, *pl* **~x** /kaju/ *nm* **1** pebble; **gros ~** stone; **2**○ nut○; **ne plus avoir un poil sur le ~** to be as bald as a coot○.

caïman /kaimɑ̃/ *nm* cayman.

Caire /kɛʀ/ *pr n* **le ~** Cairo.

caisse /kɛs/ *nf* **1** crate; **2** (of car) shell, body; **3**○ car; **4** (for money) till; cash register; cash box; **les ~s de l'État** the Treasury coffers; **voler la ~** to steal the takings; **5** cash desk; (in supermarket) checkout (counter); (in bank) cashier's desk; **6** fund.
■ **~ d'épargne** ≈ savings bank; **~ noire** slush fund; **~ à outils** toolbox.

caissette /kɛsɛt/ *nf* small box or case.

caissier, -ière /kesje, ɛʀ/ *nm,f* cashier.

cajoler /kaʒɔle/ [1] *vtr* to cuddle [*child*].

cajou /kaʒu/ *nm* **noix de ~** cashew nut.

cake /kɛk/ *nm* fruit cake.

cal /kal/ *nm* callus.

calamar /kalamaʀ/ *nm* squid.

calamité /kalamite/ *nf* disaster, calamity.

calandre /kalɑ̃dʀ/ *nf* (Aut) (radiator) grille[GB].

calcaire /kalkɛʀ/ **I** *adj* [*water*] hard; [*soil*] chalky; [*rock*] limestone.
II *nm* **1** limestone; **2** fur (GB), sediment (US).

calciner /kalsine/ [1] *vtr* **1** to char; (in oven) to burn [sth] to a crisp; **2** (in chemistry) to calcine.

calcium /kalsjɔm/ *nm* calcium.

calcul /kalkyl/ *nm* **1** calculation; **faire le ~ de qch** to calculate sth; **2** arithmetic; **~ mental** mental arithmetic; **3** (scheming) calculation; **agir par ~** to act out of self-interest; **4** (Med) stone.

calculateur, -trice[1] /kalkylatœʀ, tʀis/ *adj* calculating.

calculatrice[2] /kalkylatʀis/ *nf* (pocket) calculator.

calculer /kalkyle/ [1] **I** *vtr* **1** to calculate, to work out; **2** to weigh up [*advantages, chances*]; **tout bien calculé** all things considered; **3 ~ son coup** to plan one's move.
II *vi* to calculate.

calculette /kalkylɛt/ *nf* pocket calculator.

cale /kal/ *nf* **1** wedge; (for wheel) chock; (for raising vehicle) block; **2** (Naut) (ship's) hold.

calé○**, ~e** /kale/ *adj* bright; **~ en qch** brilliant at sth.

calèche /kalɛʃ/ *nf* barouche, carriage.

caleçon /kalsɔ̃/ *nm* **1** boxer shorts; **~ long** long johns○; **2** (for woman) leggings.

calédonien, -ienne /kaledɔnjɛ̃, ɛn/ *adj* **1** New Caledonian; **2** Caledonian.

calembour /kalɑ̃buʀ/ *nm* pun, play on words.

calendrier /kalɑ̃dʀije/ *nm* **1** calendar; **2** schedule; **3** dates.

cale-pied, *pl* **~s** /kalpje/ *nm* toe clip.

calepin /kalpɛ̃/ *nm* notebook.

caler /kale/ [1] **I** *vtr* **1** to wedge [*wheel*]; to steady [*piece of furniture*]; to support [*row of books*]; **bien calé dans mon fauteuil** ensconced in my armchair; **2**○ **ça cale** it fills you up.
II *vi* [*car*] to stall.
III se caler *v refl* (+ *v être*) to settle (**dans** in).

calfeutrer /kalføtʀe/ [1] **I** *vtr* to stop up [*crack*]; to draughtproof [*door*].
II se calfeutrer *v refl* (+ *v être*) to shut oneself away.

calibre /kalibʀ/ *nm* **1** (of gun) bore, calibre[GB]; (of pipe, cable) diameter; **arme de gros ~** large-bore weapon; **2** (of eggs, fruit) size, grade; **3** gauge.

calibrer /kalibʀe/ [1] *vtr* **1** (Tech) to calibrate; **2** to grade, to size [*eggs, fruit*].

calice /kalis/ *nm* chalice.

calife /kalif/ *nm* caliph.

califourchon: **à califourchon** /akalifuʀʃɔ̃/ *phr* astride.

câlin, ~e /kɑlɛ̃, in/ **I** *adj* affectionate.
II *nm* cuddle.

câliner /kaline/ [1] *vtr* to cuddle.

calleux, -euse /kalø, øz/ *adj* calloused.

callosité /kalozite/ *nf* callus.

calmant, ~e /kalmɑ̃, ɑ̃t/ **I** *adj* soothing.
II *nm* sedative.

calmar /kalmaʀ/ *nm* squid.

calme /kalm/ **I** *adj* **1** [*sea, situation*] calm; [*night*] still; [*place, life*] quiet; **2** [*person*] calm.
II *nm* **1** peace (and quiet); **2** calm; (of crowd) calmness; (of night) stillness; **dans le ~** peacefully; **3** composure; **conserver son ~** to keep calm; **du ~!** calm down!; quiet!

calmer /kalme/ [1] **I** *vtr* **1** to calm down [*person*]; to calm [*stock market*]; to defuse [*situation*]; to tone down [*discussion*]; **~ les esprits** to calm people down; **2** to ease [*pain*]; to take the edge off [*hunger*]; to quench [*thirst*].
II se calmer *v refl* (+ *v être*) **1** [*person, situation*] to calm down; [*agitation, storm*] to die down; [*debate*] to quieten (GB) or quiet (US) down; [*ardour*] to cool; **2** [*pain*] to ease.

calomnie /kalɔmni/ *nf* slander.

calomnier /kalɔmnje/ [2] *vtr* to slander.

calorie /kalɔʀi/ *nf* calorie.

calorifère /kalɔʀifɛʀ/ *adj* heat-conveying.

calorique /kalɔʀik/ *adj* calorie; **ration/valeur ~** calorie intake/content.

calotte /kalɔt/ *nf* **1** skull cap; **2**○ slap; **3 ~ glaciaire** icecap.

calque /kalk/ *nm* **1** tracing; **2** tracing paper; **3** replica.

calquer /kalke/ [1] *vtr* **1** to copy [*behaviour*]; **2** to trace [*pattern, design*] (**sur** from).

calumet /kalymɛ/ *nm* **~ de la paix** peace pipe.

calvaire /kalvɛʀ/ *nm* **1** ordeal; **2** (monument) wayside cross; **3** Calvary.

calvitie /kalvisi/ *nf* baldness.

camaïeu /kamajø/ *nm* monochrome.

camarade /kamaʀad/ *nmf* **1** friend; **~ d'atelier** workmate; **2** comrade.

Cambodge /kɑ̃bɔdʒ/ *pr nm* Cambodia.

cambouis /kɑ̃bwi/ *nm* dirty grease.

cambré, ~e /kɑ̃bʀe/ *adj* [*back*] arched; [*foot, shoe*] with a high instep.

cambrer /kɑ̃bʀe/ [1] **I** *vtr* to curve, to arch.
II se cambrer *v refl* (+ *v être*) to arch one's back.

cambriolage /kɑ̃bʀijɔlaʒ/ *nm* burglary.

cambrioler /kɑ̃bʀijɔle/ [1] *vtr* to burgle (GB), to burglarize (US).

cambrioleur, -euse /kɑ̃bʀijɔlœʀ, øz/ *nm,f* burglar.

cambrure /kɑ̃bʀyʀ/ *nf* curve; (of foot) arch.
■ **~ des pieds** instep; **~ des reins** small of the back.

camée /kame/ *nm* cameo.

caméléon /kameleɔ̃/ *nm* chameleon.

camelote○ /kamlɔt/ *nf* junk○.

camembert /kamɑ̃bɛʀ/ *nm* **1** (Culin) Camembert; **2**○ pie chart.

camer◑: **se camer** /kame/ [1] *v refl* (+ *v être*) to be on drugs.

caméra /kameʀa/ *nf* (cine-)camera (GB), movie camera (US).

caméscope® /kameskɔp/ *nm* camcorder.

camion /kamjɔ̃/ *nm* truck.

camion-citerne, *pl* **camions-citernes** /kamjɔ̃sitɛʀn/ *nm* tanker.

camionnette /kamjɔnɛt/ *nf* van.

camionneur /kamjɔnœʀ/ *nm* truck driver.

camisole /kamizɔl/ *nf* camisole; **~ de force** straitjacket.

camomille /kamɔmij/ *nf* camomile.

camouflage /kamuflaʒ/ *nm* **1** (Mil) camouflage; **2** (figurative) concealing; disguising (**en** as).

camoufler /kamufle/ [1] *vtr* **1** (Mil) to camouflage; **2** to cover up [*crime, mistake, truth*]; to conceal [*intention, feelings*]; **3** to hide [*money*].

camp /kɑ̃/ *nm* **1** (gen) camp; **2** (Sport, Pol) side.
IDIOMS **ficher**○ **le ~** to split○, to leave.

campagnard, ~e /kɑ̃paɲaʀ, aʀd/ **I** *adj* country, rustic.
II *nm,f* country person.

campagne /kɑ̃paɲ/ *nf* **1** country; (open) countryside; **2** campaign; **faire ~** to campaign.

campanule /kɑ̃panyl/ *nf* bellflower.

campement /kɑ̃pmɑ̃/ *nm* camp, encampment.

camper /kɑ̃pe/ [1] **I** *vtr* to portray [*character*]; to depict [*landscape, scene*].
II *vi* to camp.
III se camper *v refl* (+ *v être*) **se ~ devant qn/qch** to stand squarely in front of sb/sth.

campeur, -euse /kɑ̃pœʀ, øz/ *nm,f* camper.

camphre /kɑ̃fʀ/ *nm* camphor.

camping /kɑ̃piŋ/ *nm* **1** camping; **faire du ~ sauvage** to camp rough; **2** campsite (GB), campground (US).

camping-car, *pl* **~s** /kɑ̃piŋkaʀ/ *nm* (controversial) camper.

camping-gaz® /kɑ̃piŋgaz/ *nm inv* (gas) camping stove.

campus /kɑ̃pys/ *nm inv* campus.

Canada /kanada/ *pr nm* Canada.

Canadair® /kanadɛʀ/ *nm* water bomber.

canadienne /kanadjɛn/ *nf* **1** sheepskin-lined jacket; **2** ridge tent.

canal, *pl* **-aux** /kanal, o/ *nm* **1** canal; **2** channel; **3** (Anat) duct.

canalisation /kanalizasjɔ̃/ *nf* **1** pipe; **2** mains.

canaliser /kanalize/ [1] *vtr* **1** to canalize [*river*]; **2** (figurative) to channel.

canapé /kanape/ *nm* **1** sofa; **~ convertible** sofa bed; **2** (Culin) canapé.

canaque /kanak/ *adj* Kanak.

canard /kanaʀ/ *nm* **1** duck; **~ laqué** Peking duck; **2**○ rag○, newspaper; **3** (Mus) wrong note.
IDIOMS **ça ne casse pas trois pattes à un ~**○ it's nothing to write home about.

canarder○ /kanaʀde/ [1] *vtr* to snipe at.

canari /kanaʀi/ *nm* canary.

cancan /kɑ̃kɑ̃/ *nm* **1**○ gossip; **2** cancan.

cancer /kɑ̃sɛʀ/ *nm* cancer.
Cancer /kɑ̃sɛʀ/ *pr nm* Cancer.
cancéreux, **-euse** /kɑ̃seʀø, øz/ *adj* [*cell*] cancerous; [*person*] with cancer.
cancérigène /kɑ̃seʀiʒɛn/ *adj* carcinogenic.
cancérologie /kɑ̃seʀɔlɔʒi/ *nf* cancer research; **service de ~** cancer ward.
cancre /kɑ̃kʀ/ *nm* dunce.
cancrelat /kɑ̃kʀəla/ *nm* cockroach.
candeur /kɑ̃dœʀ/ *nf* ingenuousness.
candi /kɑ̃di/ *adj m* **sucre ~** sugar candy.
candidat, **~e** /kɑ̃dida, at/ *nm,f* (Pol) candidate; (for job) applicant; (in competition) contestant; **être ~ aux élections** to stand for election (GB), to run for office (US); **être ~ (à un poste)** to apply (for a post); **pour la vaisselle, il n'y a pas beaucoup de ~s!** (humorous) when it comes to doing the dishes, there aren't many takers.
candidature /kɑ̃didatyʀ/ *nf* **1** candidature, candidacy; **retirer sa ~** to stand down (GB), to drop out (US); **2** (for a post) application; **faire acte de ~** to apply.
candide /kɑ̃did/ *adj* ingenuous.
cane /kan/ *nf* (female) duck.
caneton /kantɔ̃/ *nm* duckling.
canette /kanɛt/ *nf* **1 ~ (de bière)** (small) bottle of beer; **2** can; **~ de bière** can of beer; **3** (of sewing machine) spool.
canevas /kanva/ *nm inv* **1** canvas; **2** tapestry work; **3** (figurative) framework.
caniche /kaniʃ/ *nm* poodle.
canicule /kanikyl/ *nf* **1** scorching heat; **2** heatwave.
canif /kanif/ *nm* penknife.
canin, **~e**[1] /kanɛ̃, in/ *adj* canine.
canine[2] /kanin/ *nf* canine (tooth).
caniveau, *pl* **~x** /kanivo/ *nm* gutter.
cannabis /kanabis/ *nm* cannabis.
canne /kan/ *nf* **1** (walking) stick; **2** (Bot) cane.
■ **~ à pêche** fishing rod.
canneberge /kanbɛʀʒ/ *nf* cranberry.
cannelle /kanɛl/ *nf* cinnamon.
cannette = **canette**.
cannibale /kanibal/ *adj*, *nmf* cannibal.
canoë /kanɔe/ *nm* **1** canoe; **2** canoeing.
canoë-kayak /kanɔekajak/ *nm* canoeing.
canon /kanɔ̃/ **I** *adj m inv* **droit ~** canon law.
II *nm* **1** (big) gun; cannon; **tirer un coup de ~** to fire a gun; **entendre des coups de ~** to hear cannon fire; **2** (of firearm) barrel; **3** (Mus) canon; **chanter en ~** to sing in a round; **4** (rule, principle) canon; **5** (in religion) canon.
cañon /kanjɔ̃, kanjɔn/ *nm* canyon.
canonique /kanɔnik/ *adj* **droit ~** canon law; **d'âge ~** (humorous) of a venerable age.
canoniser /kanɔnize/ [1] *vtr* to canonize.
canot /kano/ *nm* (small) boat, dinghy; **~ pneumatique** rubber dinghy; **~ de sauvetage** (on ship) lifeboat; (on plane) life raft.
canotier /kanɔtje/ *nm* boater.
canson® /kɑ̃sɔ̃/ *nm* drawing paper.
cantaloup /kɑ̃talu/ *nm* cantaloupe melon.
cantate /kɑ̃tat/ *nf* cantata.
cantatrice /kɑ̃tatʀis/ *nf* (opera) singer.
cantine /kɑ̃tin/ *nf* **1** canteen (GB), cafeteria; **manger à la ~** [*child*] to have school dinners; **2** tin trunk.
cantique /kɑ̃tik/ *nm* hymn, canticle.
canton /kɑ̃tɔ̃/ *nm* canton.
cantonais, **~e** /kɑ̃tɔnɛ, ɛz/ **I** *adj* Cantonese.
II *nm* (language) Cantonese.
cantonal, **~e**, *mpl* **-aux** /kɑ̃tɔnal, o/ *adj* cantonal.
cantonner /kɑ̃tɔne/ [1] *vtr* **~ qn dans un lieu** to confine sb to a place; **~ qn dans le rôle de** to reduce sb to the role of.
cantonnier /kɑ̃tɔnje/ *nm* road-mender.
cantonnière /kɑ̃tɔnjɛʀ/ *nf* pelmet.
canular /kanylaʀ/ *nm* hoax.
canule /kanyl/ *nf* cannula.
canyon = **cañon**.
caoutchouc /kautʃu/ *nm* **1** rubber; **2** rubber plant; **3** rubber band.
caoutchouteux, **-euse** /kautʃutø, øz/ *adj* rubbery.
cap /kap/ *nm* **1** (in geography) cape; **2** mark; **passer le ~ de la cinquantaine** to pass the fifty mark; **3** (direction) course; **maintenir le ~** to hold one's course; **mettre le ~ sur** to head for.
Cap /kap/ *pr n* **le ~** Cape Town.
CAP /seape/ *nm*: *abbr* ▶ **certificat**.
capable /kapabl/ *adj* capable (**de faire** of doing); **ils sont bien ~s de nous mentir** I wouldn't put it past them to lie to us.
capacité /kapasite/ **I** *nf* **1** ability; **2** capacity.
II capacités *nf pl* (talent) abilities.
cape /kap/ *nf* cape; cloak.
IDIOMS **rire sous ~** to laugh up one's sleeve.
capeline /kaplin/ *nf* wide-brimmed hat.
CAPES /kapɛs/ *nm* (*abbr* = **certificat d'aptitude professionnelle à l'enseignement secondaire**) *secondary school teaching qualification.*
capharnaüm /kafaʀnaɔm/ *nm* shambles○.
capillaire /kapilɛʀ/ **I** *adj* **1** capillary; **2 soins ~s** hair care.
II *nm* capillary.
capitaine /kapitɛn/ *nm* **1** (Mil) (in army, navy) ≈ captain; **2** (Sport) captain.
capitainerie /kapitɛnʀi/ *nf* port authority.
capital, **~e**[1], *mpl* **-aux** /kapital, o/ **I** *adj* **1** [*importance*] major; [*role, question*] key; **il est ~ de faire** it's essential to do; **2** [*letter*] capital; **3 peine ~e** capital punishment.
II *nm* **1** capital; **2 le ~ humain/industriel** human/industrial resources.
III capitaux *nm pl* capital, funds.
capitale[2] /kapital/ *nf* **1** capital (city); **2** capital (letter); **en ~s d'imprimerie** in block capitals.
capitalisme /kapitalism/ *nm* capitalism.
capitaliste /kapitalist/ *adj*, *nmf* capitalist.
capitonner /kapitɔne/ [1] *vtr* to pad.

capituler /kapityle/ [1] *vi* to capitulate.

caporal, *pl* **-aux** /kapɔʀal, o/ *nm* (Mil) (in army) ≈ corporal.

capot /kapo/ *nm* (Aut) bonnet (GB), hood (US).

capotage /kapɔtaʒ/ *nm* collapse.

capote /kapɔt/ *nf* **1** great-coat; **2** (of car, pram) hood (GB), top; **3**° **~ (anglaise)** condom .

capoter /kapɔte/ [1] *vi* **1** to collapse; **2** [*car*] to overturn.

câpre /kɑpʀ/ *nf* caper.

caprice /kapʀis/ *nm* **1** (of person) whim; **céder aux ~s de qn** to indulge sb's whims; **c'est un ~ de la nature** (of plant, animal) it's a freak of nature; **2 faire un ~** to throw a tantrum.

capricieusement /kapʀisjøzmɑ̃/ *adv* capriciously; whimsically.

capricieux, **-ieuse** /kapʀisjø, øz/ *adj* [*person*] capricious; [*machine*] temperamental; [*weather*] changeable; [*destiny*] fickle.

capricorne /kapʀikɔʀn/ *nm* capricorn beetle.

Capricorne /kapʀikɔʀn/ *pr nm* Capricorn.

capsule /kapsyl/ *nf* **1** (of bottle) cap; top; **2** (Med) capsule; **3 ~ spatiale** space capsule.

capter /kapte/ [1] *vtr* **1** to get [*channel, programme*]; to pick up [*signal*]; **2** to catch [*attention*]; **3** to soak up [*light*].

captif, **-ive** /kaptif, iv/ *adj, nm,f* captive.

captivant, **~e** /kaptivɑ̃, ɑ̃t/ *adj* enthralling; gripping; riveting; captivating.

captiver /kaptive/ [1] *vtr* [*beauty*] to captivate; [*music*] to enthrall; [*story, person*] to fascinate.

captivité /kaptivite/ *nf* captivity.

capture /kaptyʀ/ *nf* capture.

capturer /kaptyʀe/ [1] *vtr* to capture.

capuche /kapyʃ/ *nf* hood; **à ~** with a hood.

capuchon /kapyʃɔ̃/ *nm* **1** (of garment) hood; **2** (of pen) cap.

caquet /kakɛ/ *nm* prattle; **rabattre le ~ à qn**° to put sb in his/her place.

caqueter /kakte/ [20] *vi* [*hen*] to cackle.

car[1] /kaʀ/ *conj* because, for.

car[2] /kaʀ/ *nm* bus; **~ de police** police van; **~ (de ramassage) scolaire** school bus.

carabine /kaʀabin/ *nf* rifle.

caracoler /kaʀakɔle/ [1] *vi* **1** to be well ahead; **2** [*horse*] to prance; [*rider*] to parade.

caractère /kaʀaktɛʀ/ *nm* **1** (written) character; **~s d'imprimerie** block capitals; **en petits/ gros ~s** in small/large print; **2** nature, temperament; **avoir mauvais ~** to be bad-tempered; **3** (personality) character; **il n'a aucun ~** he's got no backbone; **4** (of house, place) character; **5** characteristic; **6** nature; **à ~ commercial** of a commercial nature.
IDIOMS **avoir un ~ de cochon**°, **avoir un sale ~** to have a vile temper.

caractériel, **-ielle** /kaʀakteʀjɛl/ *adj* [*problems*] emotional; [*person*] disturbed.

caractériser /kaʀakteʀize/ [1] **I** *vtr* to characterize.
II se caractériser *v refl* (+ *v être*) to be characterized.

caractéristique /kaʀakteʀistik/ **I** *adj* characteristic.
II *nf* characteristics.

carafe /kaʀaf/ *nf* carafe.

caraïbe /kaʀaib/ *adj* Caribbean.

Caraïbes /kaʀaib/ *pr nf pl* Caribbean (islands).

carambolage /kaʀɑ̃bɔlaʒ/ *nm* pile-up.

caramel /kaʀamɛl/ *nm* **1** caramel; **2** toffee (GB), toffy (US); **~ mou** ≈ fudge.

carapace /kaʀapas/ *nf* shell, carapace.

carat /kaʀa/ *nm* carat; **or 18 ~s** 18-carat gold.

caravane /kaʀavan/*nf* **1** caravan (GB), trailer (US); **2** (convoy) caravan.

caravelle /kaʀavɛl/ *nf* (boat) caravel.

carbone /kaʀbɔn/ *nm* **1** carbon; **2** carbon paper; **3** sheet of carbon paper.

carbonique /kaʀbɔnik/ *adj* carbonic; **neige ~** dry ice.

carbonisé, **~e** /kaʀbɔnize/ *adj* burned-out; charred; burned to a cinder.

carboniser /kaʀbɔnize/ [1] *vtr* **1** to carbonize; **2** to reduce [sth] to ashes.

carburant /kaʀbyʀɑ̃/ *nm* fuel.

carburateur /kaʀbyʀatœʀ/ *nm* carburettor (GB), carburetor (US).

carcan /kaʀkɑ̃/ *nm* **1** (device) iron collar; **2 ~ administratif** administrative constraints.

carcasse /kaʀkas/ *nf* carcass.

carcéral, **~e**, *mpl* **-aux** /kaʀseʀal, o/ *adj* prison.

cardan /kaʀdɑ̃/ *nm* universal joint.

cardiaque /kaʀdjak/ *adj* **être ~** to have a heart condition; **crise ~** heart attack.

cardinal, **~e**, *mpl* **-aux** /kaʀdinal, o/ **I** *adj* cardinal.
II *nm* **1** cardinal; **2** cardinal number.

cardiologie /kaʀdjɔlɔʒi/ *nf* cardiology.

cardiologue /kaʀdjɔlɔg/ *nmf* cardiologist.

carême /kaʀɛm/ *nm* **le ~** Lent.

carence /kaʀɑ̃s/ *nf* **1** (Med) deficiency; **2** lack; **3 les ~s de la loi** the shortcomings of the law.

carène /kaʀɛn/ *nf* hull (*below the waterline*).

caresse /kaʀɛs/ *nf* caress, stroke; **faire une ~** or **des ~s à** to stroke.

caresser /kaʀese/ [1] *vtr* **1** to stroke, to caress; **~ qn du regard** to look at sb lovingly; **2** to entertain [*hope, idea*]; to cherish [*dream*].
IDIOMS **~ qn dans le sens du poil** to stay on the right side of sb.

cargaison /kaʀgɛzɔ̃/ *nf* **1** cargo; **2**° load.

cargo /kaʀgo/ *nm* (Naut) freighter, cargo ship.

caricatural, **~e**, *mpl* **-aux** /kaʀikatyʀal, o/ *adj* **1** grotesque; **2** caricatural.

caricature /kaʀikatyʀ/ *nf* caricature; **c'est une ~ de procès** it's a mockery of a trial.

caricaturer /kaʀikatyʀe/ [1] *vtr* to caricature.

caricaturiste /kaʀikatyʀist/ *nmf* caricaturist.

carie /kaʀi/ *nf* **la ~ (dentaire)** (tooth) decay; **avoir une carie** to have a hole in one's tooth.

carié, **~e** /kaʀje/ *adj* decayed.

carier: **se carier** /kaʀje/ [2] *v refl* (+ *v être*) [*tooth*] to decay.

carillon /kaʀijɔ̃/ *nm* **1** (of church) (set of) bells; (tune) chimes; **2** (chiming) clock; (sound) chimes; **3** (door) chimes.

carillonner /kaʀijɔne/ [1] *vi* **1** [*bells*] to ring out, to peal out; **2** (at door) to ring (loudly).

caritatif, **-ive** /kaʀitatif, iv/ *adj* charitable; **une association caritative** a charity.

carlingue /kaʀlɛ̃g/ *nf* (of plane) cabin.

carmin /kaʀmɛ̃/*nm, adj inv* carmine.

carnage /kaʀnaʒ/ *nm* carnage, massacre.

carnassier, **-ière** /kaʀnasje, ɛʀ/ *adj* carnivorous.

carnaval, *pl* **~s** /kaʀnaval/ *nm* carnival.

carnet /kaʀnɛ/ *nm* **1** notebook; **2** (of tickets, vouchers, stamps) book.
■ **~ de chèques** chequebook (GB), checkbook (US); **~ de correspondance** (Sch) mark book; **~ de santé** health record.

carnivore /kaʀnivɔʀ/ **I** *adj* carnivorous.
II *nm* carnivore.

carotide /kaʀɔtid/ *adj, nf* carotid.

carotte /kaʀɔt/ *nf* carrot.
IDIOMS **manier la ~ et le bâton** to use stick-and-carrot tactics.

caroube /kaʀub/ *nf* carob.

carpe[1] /kaʀp/ *nm* (Anat) carpus.

carpe[2] /kaʀp/ *nf* (fish) carp.
IDIOMS **il est resté muet comme une ~** he never said a word.

carpette /kaʀpɛt/ *nf* **1** rug; **2**○ doormat○.

carré, **~e** /kaʀe/ **I** *adj* **1** [*shape*] square; **il est ~ d'épaules** he has broad shoulders; **2** [*metre, root*] square.
II *nm* **1** square; **2** (of sky, ground) patch; (of chocolate) piece; **avoir une coupe au ~** to have one's hair cut in a bob; **~ blanc** *'suitable for adults only' sign on French TV*; **3** (in mathematics) square; **4 ~ d'agneau** rack of lamb.

carreau, *pl* **~x** /kaʀo/ *nm* **1** (floor) tile; (wall) tile; **2** window-pane; **faire les ~x** to clean the windows; **3** (on paper) square; (on fabric) check; **4** (in cards) diamonds.
IDIOMS **rester sur le ~**○ to be left high and dry○; **se tenir à ~**○ to watch one's step.

carrefour /kaʀfuʀ/ *nm* **1** junction; crossroads; **2** (figurative) crossroads.

carrelage /kaʀlaʒ/ *nm* **1** tiled floor; **2** tiles.

carreler /kaʀle/ [19] *vtr* to tile.

carrelet /kaʀlɛ/ *nm* plaice.

carrément /kaʀemɑ̃/ *adv* **1 la situation devient ~ inquiétante** quite frankly the situation is becoming worrying; **il vaut ~ mieux les jeter** it would be better just to throw them out; **2** completely; **dans un cas pareil, appelle ~ la police** in such a case, don't hesitate to call the police; **3** [*ask, say*] straight out; [*express*] clearly; **4 allez-y ~!** go straight ahead!

carrière /kaʀjɛʀ/ *nf* **1** career; **faire ~ dans** to make a career in; **2** quarry; **~ de sable** sandpit.

carriole /kaʀjɔl/ *nf* **1** cart; **2**○ jalopy○, car.

carrosse /kaʀɔs/ *nm* (horse-drawn) coach.

carrosserie /kaʀɔsʀi/ *nf* **1** bodywork; **2** coachbuilding; **3** body repair work.

carrure /kaʀyʀ/ *nf* **1** shoulders; **2** calibre[GB].

cartable /kaʀtabl/ *nm* **1** schoolbag, satchel; **2** briefcase.

carte /kaʀt/ *nf* **1** card; **~ à jouer** playing card; **2** pass; **3** map; chart; **4 ~ génétique** genetic map; **5** menu; **repas à la ~** à la carte meal.
■ **~ d'abonnement** season ticket; **~ d'adhérent** membership card; **~ bleue®** credit card; **~ grise** logbook; **~ d'identité** ID card; **~ orange®** season ticket (*in the Paris region*); **~ postale** postcard; **~ à puce** smart card; **~ de réduction** discount card; **~ de séjour** resident's permit; **~ vermeil®** senior citizen's railcard; **~ des vins** wine list; **~ de visite** visiting card; business card; **~ de vœux** greetings card.

cartel /kaʀtɛl/ *nm* **1** cartel; **2** coalition.

carter /kaʀtɛʀ/ *nm* (of engine) crankcase; (of gearbox) casing.

cartilage /kaʀtilaʒ/ *nm* **1** (Anat, Zool) cartilage; **2** (Culin) gristle.

cartomancie /kaʀtɔmɑ̃si/ *nf* fortune-telling.

carton /kaʀtɔ̃/ *nm* **1** cardboard; **en ~** [*folder*] cardboard; [*cups*] paper; **2** (cardboard) box; **3** card.
■ **~ à dessin** portfolio.
IDIOMS **faire un ~**○ to do great○.

cartonné, **~e** /kaʀtɔne/ *adj* **couverture ~e** (of book) hard cover.

carton-pâte /kaʀtɔ̃pɑt/ *nm inv* pasteboard.

cartouche /kaʀtuʃ/ *nf* **1** cartridge; (of gas) refill; **2 ~ de cigarettes** carton of cigarettes.

cas /kɑ/ **I** *nm inv* case; **auquel ~** in which case; **au ~ où il viendrait** in case he comes; **prends ta voiture, au ~ où** take your car, just in case; **en ~ de besoin** if necessary; **en ~ de décès** in the event of death; **le ~ échéant** if need be; **dans le ~ contraire, vous devrez...** should the opposite occur, you will have to...; **dans le meilleur/pire des ~** at best/worst; **en aucun ~** under no circumstances; **c'est le ~ de le dire!** you can say that again!; **être dans le même ~ que qn** to be in the same position as sb; **n'aggrave pas ton ~** don't make things worse for yourself; **un ~ rare** a rare occurrence; **c'est un ~ de renvoi** it's grounds for dismissal.
II en tout cas, **en tous les cas** *phr* **1** in any case, at any rate; **2** at least.
■ **~ de conscience** moral dilemma; **~ social** socially disadvantaged person.
IDIOMS **il a fait grand ~ de son avancement** he made a big thing of his promotion.

casanier, **-ière** /kazanje, ɛʀ/ *adj* [*person*] stay-at-home; [*existence*] unadventurous.

casaque /kazak/ *nf* (of jockey) jersey, silk.

cascade /kaskad/ *nf* **1** waterfall; **2** stunt.

cascadeur, **-euse** /kaskadœʀ, øz/ *nm,f* stuntman/stuntwoman.

case /kɑz/ *nf* **1** hut, cabin; **2** (in board games) square; **3** (on form) box.
■ **~ départ** (in board game) start; **retour à la ~ départ** (figurative) back to square one.
IDIOMS **il lui manque une ~**○ he's got a screw loose○.

caser○ /kɑze/ [1] **I** *vtr* **1** to put, to stick○; **2** to marry off; **3** to find a place or job for.
II se caser *v refl* (+ *v être*) to get married.

caserne /kazɛʀn/ *nf* barracks.
■ **~ de sapeurs-pompiers** fire station.

casher /kaʃɛʀ/ *adj inv* kosher.

casier /kɑzje/ *nm* **1** (in gym) locker; **2** pigeon-hole; **3 ~ judiciaire** police record.

casino /kazino/ *nm* casino.

casque /kask/ *nm* **1** helmet; crash helmet; safety helmet; **2** headphones; **3** hairdryer.

casqué, **~e** /kaske/ *adj* helmeted.

casquette /kaskɛt/ *nf* cap; **porter plusieurs ~s** (figurative) to wear several hats.

cassant, **~e** /kasɑ̃, ɑ̃t/ *adj* **1** brittle; **2** curt, abrupt.

casse[1]○ /kɑs/ *nm* break-in, heist○ (US).

casse[2] /kɑs/ *nf* **1** breakage; **2** breaker's yard, scrap yard; **mettre à la ~** to scrap.

cassé, **~e** /kase/ *adj* [*voice*] hoarse.

casse-cou /kasku/ *nmf inv* daredevil.

casse-croûte /kaskʀut/ *nm inv* snack.

casse-noisettes /kasnwazɛt/, **casse-noix** /kasnwa/ *nm inv* nutcrackers.

casser /kase/ [1] **I** *vtr* to break [*object, bone*]; to crack [*nut*]; **~ les prix** to slash prices; **~ la figure**○ **à qn** to beat sb up○.
II *vi* **1** to break; **2**○ [*couple*] to split up.
III se casser *v refl* (+ *v être*) **1** to break; **2 se ~ une** or **la jambe** to break one's leg; **se ~ la figure**○ [*pedestrian*] to fall over (GB) or down; [*venture*] to fail; [*people*] to have a scrap○; **il ne s'est pas cassé la tête**○ he didn't exactly strain himself; **3**○ to go away.
IDIOMS **~ les pieds**○ **à qn** to annoy sb; **~ la croûte** to eat; **ça te prendra trois heures, à tout ~**○ it'll take you three hours at the very most.

casserole /kasʀɔl/ *nf* saucepan, pan.
IDIOMS **chanter comme une ~**○ to sing atrociously.

casse-tête /kastɛt/ *nm inv* **1** headache, problem; **2** puzzle.

cassette /kasɛt/ *nf* **1** tape, cassette; **2** casket.

casseur /kasœʀ/ *nm* **1** scrap dealer; **2** rioting demonstrator.

cassis /kasis/ *nm inv* **1** blackcurrant; **2** (in road) dip.

cassoulet /kasulɛ/ *nm*: *meat and bean stew*.

cassure /kasyʀ/ *nf* **1** break; **2** split.

castagnettes /kastaɲɛt/ *nf pl* castanets.

caste /kast/ *nf* **1** caste; **2** (derogatory) (social) class.

castor /kastɔʀ/ *nm* beaver.

castrer /kastʀe/ [1] *vtr* to castrate.

cataclysme /kataklism/ *nm* cataclysm.

catacombes /katakɔ̃b/ *nf pl* catacombs.

catadioptre /katadjɔptʀ/ *nm* reflector.

catalepsie /katalɛpsi/ *nf* catalepsy.

catalogue /katalɔg/ *nm* catalogue[GB]; **acheter sur ~** to buy by mail order.

cataloguer /katalɔge/ [1] *vtr* **1** to catalogue[GB] [*objects*]; **2** to label [*people*].

catalyse /kataliz/ *nf* catalysis.

catamaran /katamaʀɑ̃/ *nm* catamaran.

cataplasme /kataplasm/ *nm* poultice.

catapulter /katapylte/ [1] *vtr* to catapult.

cataracte /kataʀakt/ *nf* cataract.

catastrophe /katastʀɔf/ *nf* disaster; **en ~** in a panic; **atterrissage en ~** crash landing.

catastropher /katastʀɔfe/ [1] *vtr* to devastate.

catastrophique /katastʀɔfik/ *adj* disastrous.

catch /katʃ/ *nm* wrestling.

catcheur, **-euse** /katʃœʀ, øz/ *nm,f* wrestler.

catéchisme /kateʃism/ *nm* catechism.

catégorie /kategɔʀi/ *nf* **1** category; **de première/deuxième ~** top-/low-grade; **2** (of staff) grade; **3** (in sociology) group; **4** (Sport) class.

catégorique /kategɔʀik/ *adj* categorical.

cathédrale /katedʀal/ *nf* cathedral.

cathode /katɔd/ *nf* cathode.

catholicisme /katɔlisism/ *nm* (Roman) Catholicism.

catholique /katɔlik/ *adj*, *nmf* Catholic; **ce n'est pas très ~**○ (humorous) it's a bit unorthodox.

cauchemar /koʃmaʀ/ *nm* nightmare.

causant○, **~e** /kozɑ̃, ɑ̃t/ *adj* talkative.

cause /koz/ *nf* **1** cause; **pour la ~ de la liberté** in the cause of freedom; **2** reason; **pour ~ de maladie** because of illness; **avoir pour ~ qch** to be caused by sth; **à ~ de** because of; **3** case; **être en ~** [*system, fact*] to be at issue; [*person*] to be involved; **mettre hors de ~** (gen) to clear; **remettre en ~** to call [sth] into question [*policy, right*]; to cast doubt on [*project, efficiency*]; to undermine [*efforts*]; **remise en ~** (of system) reappraisal; **avoir gain de ~** to win one's case.
IDIOMS **en toute connaissance de ~** in full knowledge of the facts.

causer /koze/ [1] **I** *vtr* **1** to cause; **~ des soucis** to give cause for concern; **2**○ to talk about; **~ travail** to talk shop.
II causer de *v+prep* to talk about.
III *vi* to talk; to chat.

causette○ /kozɛt/ *nf* chat; **faire la ~** to have a little chat.

caustique /kostik/ *adj* caustic.

cautériser /koteʀize/ [1] *vtr* to cauterize.

caution /kosjɔ̃/ *nf* **1** (when renting) deposit; (in finance) guarantee, security; (Law) bail; **2** support.

cautionner /kosjɔne/ [1] *vtr* **1** to give one's support to; **2** to stand surety for.

cavalcade /kavalkad/ *nf* **1** stampede, rush; **2** cavalcade.

cavale○ /kaval/ *nf* escape; **en ~** on the run.

cavaler○ /kavale/ [1] *vi* to rush about.

cavalerie /kavalʀi/ *nf* cavalry.

cavaleur○, **-euse** /kavalœʀ, øz/ *adj* **être ~** to be a womanizer/man-chaser.

cavalier, **-ière** /kavalje, ɛʀ/ **I** *adj* cavalier.
II *nm,f* **1** (horse) rider; **être bon ~** to be a good rider; **2** (dancing) partner.
III *nm* **1** cavalryman; **2** (in chess) knight.
IDIOMS **faire ~ seul** to go it alone.

cave /kav/ *nf* cellar; **avoir une bonne ~** to have good wines.

caveau, *pl* **~x** /kavo/ *nm* vault.

caverne /kavɛʀn/ *nf* cavern.

caviar /kavjaʀ/ *nm* caviar.

cavité /kavite/ *nf* cavity.

CCP /sesepe/ *nm*: *abbr* ▶ **compte**.

CD /sede/ *nm* (*abbr* = **compact disc**) CD.

ce /sə/ **I** (**cet** /sɛt/ *before vowel or mute h*, **cette** /sɛt/, *pl* **ces** /se/) *adj* **1** this; that; **~ crayon(-ci)** this pencil; **~ livre(-là)** that book; **cette nuit** tonight; last night; **un de ces jours** one of these days; **2**○ **cet entretien, ça s'est bien passé?** how did the interview go?; **3 et pour ces dames?** what are the ladies having?; **4 elle a eu cette chance que la corde a tenu** she was lucky in that the rope held; **5 cette arrogance!** what arrogance!; **j'ai un de ces rhumes!** I've got an awful cold!
II (**c'** *before e*) *pron* **qui est-~?** who's that?; who is it?; **~ faisant** in so doing; **c'est tout dire** that says it all; **fais ~ que tu veux** do what you like; **c'est ~ à quoi il a fait allusion** that's what he was alluding to; **il a fait faillite, ~ qui n'est pas surprenant** he's gone bankrupt, which is hardly surprising; **il tient à ~ que vous veniez** he's very keen that you should come; **~ que c'est grand!** it's so big!

CE /seə/ *nm*: *abbr* ▶ **cours**.

ceci /səsi/ *pron* this; **à ~ près que** except that; **cet hôtel a ~ de bien que**... one good thing about this hotel is that...

cécité /sesite/ *nf* blindness.

céder /sede/ [14] **I** *vtr* **1** to give up [*seat, share*]; to yield [*right*]; to make over [*property*]; **~ le passage** to give way; **~ la place** (figurative) to give way; **2** to sell.
II céder à *v+prep* to give in to, to yield to.
III *vi* **1** to give in; **2** [*beam*] to give way; [*handle*] to break off; [*door*] to yield.

cédille /sedij/ *nf* cedilla.

cèdre /sɛdʀ/ *nm* cedar.

CEE /seəə/ *nf*: *abbr* ▶ **communauté**.

ceinture /sɛ̃tyʀ/ *nf* **1** belt; **2** waistband; **3** girdle; **4** waist; **avoir de l'eau jusqu'à la ~** to be waist-deep in water; **5** (Sport) waist hold; **~ noire** black belt; **6** ring.
■ **~ de sauvetage** lifebelt; **~ de sécurité** safety or seat belt.
IDIOMS **faire ~**○ to go without; **se serrer la ~** to tighten one's belt.

ceinturer /sɛ̃tyʀe/ [1] *vtr* to encircle.

ceinturon /sɛ̃tyʀɔ̃/ *nm* belt.

cela /səla/ *pron*

■ **Note** *Cela* and *ça* are equivalent in many cases. See the entry *ça* for more information.
– *Cela* is used in formal contexts and in the expressions shown below.

1 it; that; **quant à ~** as for that; **~ dit** having said that; **2 ~ va sans dire** it or that goes without saying; **voyez-vous ~!** did you ever hear of such a thing!

célébration /selebʀasjɔ̃/ *nf* celebration.

célèbre /selɛbʀ/ *adj* famous.

célébrer /selebʀe/ [14] *vtr* **1** to celebrate [*event, mass*]; to perform [*rite*]; **2** to praise [*person*].

célébrité /selebʀite/ *nf* **1** fame; **2** celebrity.

céleri /sɛlʀi/ *nm* **1** celery; **2** celeriac.

céleri-rave, *pl* **céleris-raves** /selʀiʀav/ *nm* celeriac.

céleste /selɛst/ *adj* celestial; heavenly; divine.

célibat /seliba/ *nm* **1** single status; **2** celibacy.

célibataire /selibatɛʀ/ **I** *adj* single.
II *nmf* bachelor/single woman.

celle ▶ **celui**.

celle-ci ▶ **celui-ci**.

celle-là ▶ **celui-là**.

celles-ci ▶ **celui-ci**.

celles-là ▶ **celui-là**.

cellophane® /selɔfan/ *nf* cellophane®.

cellule /selyl/ *nf* **1** cell; **2** unit; **~ familiale** family unit.

cellulite /selylit/ *nf* **1** cellulite; **2** cellulitis.

celte /sɛlt/ *adj, nm* Celtic.

Celte /sɛlt/ *nmf* Celt.

celui /səlɥi/, **celle** /sɛl/, *mpl* **ceux** /sø/, *fpl* **celles** /sɛl/ *pron* the one; **le train du matin ou ~ du soir?** the morning train or the evening one?; **ceux, celles** those; the ones; **ceux d'entre vous qui veulent partir** those of you who want to leave; **ceux qu'il a vendus** the ones he sold; **faire ~ qui n'entend pas** to pretend not to hear.

celui-ci /səlɥisi/, **celle-ci** /sɛlsi/, *mpl* **ceux-ci** /søsi/, *fpl* **celles-ci** /sɛlsi/ *pron* **1** this one; **ceux-ci, celles-ci** these; **2 je n'ai qu'une chose à dire et c'est celle-ci** I have only one thing to say and it's this; **3 elle essaya la fenêtre mais celle-ci était coincée** she tried the window but it was jammed; **il entra, suivi de son père et de son frère; ~ portait un paquet** he came in, followed by his father and his brother; the latter was carrying a parcel.

celui-là /səlɥila/, **celle-là** /sɛlla/, *mpl* **ceux-là** /søla/, *fpl* **celles-là** /sɛlla/ *pron* **1** that one; **ceux-là, celles-là** those (ones); **2 si je n'ai qu'un conseil à te donner, c'est ~** if I only have one piece of advice for you, it's this; **3** the former; **4 il fit une autre proposition, plus réaliste celle-là** he made another proposal, a more realistic one this time; **5**○ **il exagère, ~!** that guy's pushing it a bit○!; **6**○ **elle est bien bonne, celle-là!** that's a good one!; **je ne m'attendais pas à celle-là** I didn't expect that!; **~ même** the very one.

cendre /sɑ̃dʀ/ *nf* ash.

cendré, **~e** /sɑ̃dʀe/ *adj* **blond ~** ash blond.

cendrier /sɑ̃dʀije/ *nm* ashtray.

Cène /sɛn/ *nf* **la ~** the Last Supper.

censé, **~e** /sɑ̃se/ *adj* **être ~ faire** to be supposed to do.

censure /sɑ̃syʀ/ *nf* **1** censorship; **2** board of censors; **3** censure.

censurer /sɑ̃syʀe/ [1] *vtr* **1** to censor; **2** to ban.

cent /sɑ̃/ **I** *adj* a hundred, one hundred.

II *nm* hundred.

III pour cent *phr* per cent.

IDIOMS **faire les ~ pas** to pace up and down; **être aux ~ coups**○ to be worried sick○; **attendre ~ sept ans**○ to wait for ages.

centaine /sɑ̃tɛn/ *nf* **1** hundred; **2** about a hundred.

centenaire /sɑ̃tnɛʀ/ **I** *adj* hundred-year-old, centenarian.

II *nmf* **c'est une ~** she's a hundred years old.

III *nm* centenary, centennial.

centième /sɑ̃tjɛm/ *adj* hundredth.

centilitre /sɑ̃tilitʀ/ *nm* centilitre[GB].

centime /sɑ̃tim/ *nm* centime.

centimètre /sɑ̃timɛtʀ/ *nm* **1** centimetre[GB]; **2 ne pas avancer d'un ~** not to move an inch; **3** tape measure.

central, **~e**[1], *mpl* **-aux** /sɑ̃tʀal, o/ **I** *adj* **1** central; **court ~** (in tennis) centre[GB] court; **ordinateur ~** host computer; **2** main.

II *nm* **~ (téléphonique)** (telephone) exchange.

centrale[2] /sɑ̃tʀal/ *nf* **1** power station; **2** prison.

centraliser /sɑ̃tʀalize/ [1] *vtr* to centralize.

centre /sɑ̃tʀ/ *nm* centre[GB]; **il se prend pour le ~ du monde** he thinks the whole world revolves around him.

■ **~ commercial** shopping centre[GB]; **~ hospitalier** hospital complex.

centrer /sɑ̃tʀe/ [1] *vtr* to centre[GB].

centre-ville, *pl* **centres-villes** /sɑ̃tʀəvil/ *nm* town centre[GB], city centre[GB].

centrifuge /sɑ̃tʀifyʒ/ *adj* centrifugal.

centrifugeuse /sɑ̃tʀifyʒøz/ *nf* **1** juice extractor; **2** centrifuge.

centriste /sɑ̃tʀist/ *adj*, *nmf* centrist.

centuple /sɑ̃typl/ *nm* **dix mille est le ~ de cent** ten thousand is a hundred times one hundred; **au ~** a hundred times over.

cep /sɛp/ *nm* **~ (de vigne)** vine stock.

cèpe /sɛp/ *nm* cep.

cependant /səpɑ̃dɑ̃/ **I** *conj* yet, however.

II cependant que *phr* whereas, while.

céramique /seʀamik/ *nf* **1** ceramic; **2** ceramics.

cerceau, *pl* **~x** /sɛʀso/ *nm* hoop.

cercle /sɛʀkl/ *nm* **1** circle; **en ~** in a circle; **décrire des ~s** [*plane, bird*] to circle (overhead); **le ~ de famille** the family circle; **2** circle, society; club; **3** hoop.

cercler /sɛʀkle/ [1] *vtr* to hoop [*barrel*]; **les noms cerclés en rouge** the names circled in red.

cercueil /sɛʀkœj/ *nm* coffin.

céréale /seʀeal/ *nf* cereal, grain.

cérébral, **~e**, *mpl* **-aux** /seʀebʀal, o/ *adj* **1** cerebral; **2** intellectual.

cérémonial, *pl* **~s** /seʀemɔnjal/ *nm* ceremonial.

cérémonie /seʀemɔni/ **I** *nf* ceremony; **tenue** or **habit de ~** ceremonial dress.

II cérémonies *nf pl* ceremony; **faire des ~s** to stand on ceremony; **sans ~s** [*dinner, invitation*] informal; [*receive*] informally.

cerf /sɛʀ/ *nm* stag.

cerfeuil /sɛʀfœj/ *nm* chervil.

cerf-volant, *pl* **cerfs-volants** /sɛʀvɔlɑ̃/ *nm* **1** kite; **2** stag beetle.

cerise /s(ə)ʀiz/ *nf* cherry.

cerisier /s(ə)ʀizje/ *nm* cherry (tree).

cerne /sɛʀn/ *nm* ring.

cerné, **~e** /sɛʀne/ *adj* **avoir les yeux ~s** to have rings under one's eyes.

cerner /sɛʀne/ [1] *vtr* **1** to surround; **2** to define [*problem*]; to figure out [*person*]; to determine [*personality*]; **3** to outline [*drawing*].

certain, **~e** /sɛʀtɛ̃, ɛn/ **I** *adj* **1 être ~ de** to be certain or sure of; **2** [*fact*] certain, sure; [*date, price, influence*] definite; [*rate*] fixed.

II *det* **elle restera un ~ temps** she'll stay for some time; **un ~ nombre d'erreurs** a certain number of mistakes; **d'une ~e manière** in a way; **il avait déjà un ~ âge** he was already getting on in years.

III certains, **certaines** *det pl* some; **à ~s moments** sometimes, at times.

IV certains, **certaines** *pron pl* some people; **~s d'entre eux** some of them.

certainement /sɛʀtɛnmɑ̃/ *adv* **1** most probably; **2** certainly; **mais ~!** certainly!, of course!

certes /sɛʀt/ *adv* **ce ne sera ~ pas facile mais...** admittedly it won't be easy but...

certificat /sɛʀtifika/ *nm* **1** certificate; **2** testimonial.

■ **~ d'aptitude professionnelle**, **CAP** *vocational training qualification*; **~ de décès** death certificate; **~ médical** medical certificate; **~ de résidence** proof of residence; **~ de scolarité** proof of attendance (*at school or university*); **~ de travail** *document from a previous employer giving dates and nature of employment*.

certifié, **~e** /sɛʀtifje/ *adj* **professeur ~** fully qualified teacher.

certifier /sɛʀtifje/ [2] *vtr* **1** to certify; **copie certifiée conforme** certified copy; **2 elle m'a certifié que** she assured me that.

certitude /sɛʀtityd/ *nf* **1** certainty; **on sait avec ~ que** we know for certain that; **2 avoir la ~ que** to be certain that.

cérumen /seʀymɛn/ *nm* earwax.

cerveau, *pl* **~x** /sɛʀvo/ *nm* **1** brain; **2** mind; **3** (person) brain○; **exode** or **fuite des ~x** brain drain; **c'est un ~** he/she has an outstanding mind; **4** brains; nerve centre[GB].

IDIOMS **avoir le ~ dérangé** to be deranged.

cervelas /sɛʀvəla/ *nm* saveloy.
cervelet /sɛʀvəlɛ/ *nm* cerebellum.
cervelle /sɛʀvɛl/ *nf* **1** brains; **~ de veau** (Culin) calf's brains; **2**○ **il n'a rien dans la ~** he's brainless; **~ d'oiseau** birdbrain○.
cervical, **~e**, *mpl* **-aux** /sɛʀvikal, o/ *adj* cervical.
ces ▸ **ce I**.
CES /seəɛs/ *nm*: *abbr* ▸ **collège**.
césar /sezaʀ/ *nm* César (*film award*).
césarienne /sezaʀjɛn/ *nf* caesarian (section).
cessation /sesasjɔ̃/ *nf* suspension.
cesse /sɛs/ *nf* **sans ~** constantly.
cesser /sese/ [1] **I** *vtr* to stop, to cease; to end; **~ de faire** to stop doing; to give up doing.
II *vi* [*activity*] to cease; [*wind*] to drop; [*rain*] to stop; **faire ~** to put an end or a stop to, to end.
cessez-le-feu /seselfø/ *nm inv* ceasefire.
cession /sesjɔ̃/ *nf* transfer.
c'est-à-dire /setadiʀ/ *phr* **1** that is (to say); **2 ~ que** which means (that); **'le travail est trop dur'—'~?'** 'the work is too hard'—'what do you mean?'
cet ▸ **ce I**.
CET /seəte/ *nm*: *abbr* ▸ **collège**.
cette ▸ **ce**.
ceux ▸ **celui**.
ceux-ci ▸ **celui-ci**.
ceux-là ▸ **celui-là**.
chacal, *pl* **~s** /ʃakal/ *nm* jackal.
chacun, **~e** /ʃakœ̃, yn/ *pron* **1** each (one); **ils ont ~ sa** or **leur chambre** they each have their own room; **2** everyone; **~ pour soi** every man for himself.
chagrin, **~e** /ʃagʀɛ̃, in/ **I** *adj* despondent.
II *nm* grief; **faire du ~ à qn** to cause sb grief; **avoir du ~** to be sad; **avoir un gros ~** to be very upset; **~ d'amour** unhappy love affair.
chagriner /ʃagʀine/ [1] *vtr* **1** to pain, to grieve; **2** to worry.
chahut /ʃay/ *nm* racket○.
chahuter /ʃayte/ [1] **I** *vtr* to play up [*teacher*]; to heckle [*speaker*].
II *vi* to mess around.
chaîne /ʃɛn/ **I** *nf* **1** chain; **attacher qn avec des ~s** to chain sb up; **des catastrophes en ~** a series of disasters; **réaction en ~** chain reaction; **2** assembly line; **produire (qch) à la ~** to mass-produce (sth); **3** network; **~ de solidarité** support network; **4 ~ (de télévision)** (television) channel; **5 ~ hi-fi/stéréo** hi-fi/stereo system.
II chaînes *nf pl* snow chains.
■ **~ de fabrication** production line.
chaînette /ʃɛnɛt/ *nf* chain.
chaînon /ʃɛnɔ̃/ *nm* link; **~ manquant** missing link.
chair /ʃɛʀ/ **I** *adj inv* flesh-coloured^GB.
II *nf* flesh; meat; **bien en ~** plump.
■ **~ de poule** gooseflesh, goose pimples; **donner la ~ de poule à qn** [*cold*] to give sb gooseflesh; [*fear*] to make sb's flesh creep.

chaire /ʃɛʀ/ *nf* **1** pulpit; **2** (at university) chair **3** rostrum.
chaise /ʃɛz/ *nf* chair.
■ **~ haute** high-chair; **~ longue** deckchair; **~ roulante** wheelchair.
IDIOMS **être assis entre deux ~s** to be in an awkward position.
châle /ʃɑl/ *nm* shawl.
chalet /ʃalɛ/ *nm* chalet.
chaleur /ʃalœʀ/ **I** *nf* **1** heat; warmth; **coup de ~** heat stroke; **~ animale** body heat; **2** (of person, welcome, colour) warmth; **3** (Zool) **(être) en ~** (to be) on heat.
II chaleurs *nf pl* **les grandes ~s** the hot season.
chaleureux, **-euse** /ʃaløʀø, øz/ *adj* [*person, greeting*] warm; [*audience*] enthusiastic.
challenge /ʃalɑ̃ʒ/ *nm* **1** (Sport) tournament; **2** trophy.
challenge(u)r /ʃalɑ̃ʒœʀ/ *nm* challenger.
chaloupe /ʃalup/ *nf* **1** rowing boat (GB), rowboat (US); **2** (motor) launch.
chalumeau, *pl* **~x** /ʃalymo/ *nm* blowtorch.
chalut /ʃaly/ *nm* trawl.
chalutier /ʃalytje/ *nm* **1** trawler; **2** trawlerman.
chamailler○: **se chamailler** /ʃamaje/ [1] *v refl* (+ *v être*) to squabble.
chamarré, **~e** /ʃamaʀe/ *adj* **1** richly ornamented; **2** brightly coloured^GB.
chambard○ /ʃɑ̃baʀ/ *nm* din, racket○.
chambardement○ /ʃɑ̃baʀdəmɑ̃/ *nm* **1** shake-up○; **2** mess.
chambouler○ /ʃɑ̃bule/ [1] *vtr* **1** to upset [*plans, routine*]; **2** to turn [sth] upside down [*house*]; to mess [sth] up [*papers*].
chambranle /ʃɑ̃bʀɑ̃l/ *nm* frame.
chambre /ʃɑ̃bʀ/ *nf* **1** bedroom; room; **~ pour une personne** single room; **~ à deux lits** twin room; **faire ~ à part** to sleep in separate rooms; **2 musique de ~** chamber music; **3** (in parliament) house; **4** (in administration) chamber.
■ **~ à air** inner tube; **~ d'amis** guest room; **~ de commerce** chamber of commerce; **~ à coucher** bedroom; bedroom suite; **'~s d'hôte'** 'bed and breakfast'; **~ noire** camera obscura; darkroom.
chambrée /ʃɑ̃bʀe/ *nf* (Mil) soldiers occupying barrack room.
chameau, *pl* **~x** /ʃamo/ *nm* (Zool) camel.
chamelier /ʃaməlje/ *nm* camel driver.
chamelle /ʃamɛl/ *nf* she-camel.
chamois /ʃamwa/ *nm* (Zool) chamois.
champ /ʃɑ̃/ **I** *nm* field; (figurative) field, domain; **en pleins ~s** in open country; **avoir le ~ libre** to have a free hand.
II à tout bout de champ○ *phr* all the time.
■ **~ de courses** racetrack.
champagne /ʃɑ̃paɲ/ *nm* champagne.
champêtre /ʃɑ̃pɛtʀ/ *adj* [*scene*] rural; **bal ~** village dance; **déjeuner ~** country picnic.
champignon /ʃɑ̃piɲɔ̃/ *nm* **1** (Culin) mushroom; **~ vénéneux** toadstool; **2** (Bot, Med) fungus; **3**○ throttle, accelerator.

■ **~ atomique** mushroom cloud; **~ de Paris** button mushroom (GB), champignon (US).

champion, **-ionne** /ʃɑ̃pjɔ̃, ɔn/ *nm,f* champion; **le ~ en titre** the titleholder.

championnat /ʃɑ̃pjɔna/ *nm* championship.

chance /ʃɑ̃s/ *nf* **1** (good) luck; **coup de ~** stroke of luck; **avoir de la ~** to be lucky; **avoir la ~ de trouver une maison** to be lucky enough to find a house; **par ~** luckily, fortunately; **tenter** or **courir sa ~** to try one's luck; **2** chance (**de** of); **il y a de fortes ~s (pour) que** there's every chance that; **il a ses ~s** he stands a good chance; **mettre toutes les ~s de son côté** to take no chances; **'il va pleuvoir?'—'il y a des ~s'** 'is it going to rain?'—'probably'; **3** chance, opportunity.

chancelant, **~e** /ʃɑ̃slɑ̃, ɑ̃t/ *adj* **1** [*gait*] unsteady; [*object*] rickety, shaky; [*person*] staggering; **d'un pas ~** unsteadily; **2** [*courage, faith*] wavering; [*empire*] tottering.

chanceler /ʃɑ̃sle/ [19] *vi* **1** [*person*] to stagger; [*object*] to wobble; **2** [*courage*] to waver; **3** [*empire*] to totter; [*health*] to be precarious.

chancelier /ʃɑ̃səlje/ *nm* chancellor.

chanceux, **-euse** /ʃɑ̃sø, øz/ *adj* lucky.

chandail /ʃɑ̃daj/ *nm* sweater, jumper (GB).

chandelier /ʃɑ̃dəlje/ *nm* candelabra[GB].

chandelle /ʃɑ̃dɛl/ *nf* **1** candle; **un dîner aux ~s** a candlelit dinner; **2** (Sport) shoulder stand.

IDIOMS **devoir une fière ~ à** to be hugely indebted to; **faire des économies de bouts de ~s** to make cheeseparing economies.

change /ʃɑ̃ʒ/ *nm* **1** exchange rate; **2** (foreign) exchange; **perdre au ~** (figurative) to lose out.

changeant, **~e** /ʃɑ̃ʒɑ̃, ɑ̃t/ *adj* changeable.

changement /ʃɑ̃ʒmɑ̃/ *nm* change; **~ en mieux/pire** change for the better/worse.

changer /ʃɑ̃ʒe/ [13] **I** *vtr* **1** to exchange [*object*]; to change [*secretary, job*]; **2** to change [*money*]; to cash [*traveller's cheque*]; **3** to change [*purchased item*]; **4 ~ qch de place** to move sth; **5** to change [*situation, appearance*]; **cette coiffure te change** you look different with your hair like that; **qu'est-ce que ça change?** what difference does it make?; **cela ne change rien au fait que** that doesn't alter the fact that; **6 ~ qn/qch en** to turn sb/sth into; **7 cela nous change de la pluie** it makes a change from the rain; **pour ne pas ~** as usual; **8** to change [*baby*].

II changer de *v+prep* to change; **~ d'avis** to change one's mind; **~ de domicile** to move house; **~ de trottoir** to cross over to the other side of the road; **nous avons changé de route au retour** we came back by a different route.

III *vi* to change.

IV se changer *v refl* (+ *v être*) **1** to get changed; **2 se ~ en** to turn or change into.

chanoine /ʃanwan/ *nm* canon.

chanson /ʃɑ̃sɔ̃/ *nf* **1** song; **vedette de la ~** singing star; **2 c'est toujours la même ~**° it's always the same old story; **je connais la ~**° I've heard it all before.

chansonnier, **-ière** /ʃɑ̃sɔnje, ɛʀ/ *nm,f* cabaret artist.

chant /ʃɑ̃/ *nm* **1** singing; **2** (of bird, whale) song; (of cock) crow(ing); (of cricket) chirp(ing); (of cicada) shrilling; **3** song; **4** ode; canto.

■ **~ de Noël** Christmas carol.

chantage /ʃɑ̃taʒ/ *nm* blackmail.

chantant, **~e** /ʃɑ̃tɑ̃, ɑ̃t/ *adj* singsong.

chanter /ʃɑ̃te/ [1] **I** *vtr* **1** to sing; **2**° **qu'est-ce qu'il nous chante?** what's he talking about?

II chanter à° *v+prep* **ça te chante d'y aller?** do you fancy° going?

III *vi* **1** to sing; **~ juste/faux** to sing in tune/out of tune; **2** [*bird*] to sing; [*cock*] to crow; **3 faire ~ qn** to blackmail sb.

chanteur, **-euse** /ʃɑ̃tœʀ, øz/ *nm,f* singer.

chantier /ʃɑ̃tje/ *nm* **1** building site; **en ~** [*building*] under construction; **notre maison sera en ~ tout l'hiver** the work on our house will go on all winter; **mettre en ~** to undertake [*project*]; **2** builder's yard; **3**° mess.

chantonner /ʃɑ̃tɔne/ [1] *vtr, vi* to hum.

chanvre /ʃɑ̃vʀ/ *nm* hemp.

chaos /kao/ *nm inv* chaos.

chaotique /kaɔtik/ *adj* chaotic.

chapeau, *pl* **~x** /ʃapo/ **I** *nm* hat.

II° *excl* well done!

■ **~ haut de forme** top hat; **~ melon** bowler (hat) (GB), derby (hat) (US); **~ de roue** (Aut) hubcap; **démarrer sur les ~x de roues**° [*car, driver*] to shoot off at top speed.

IDIOMS **tirer son ~ à** to take one's hat off to.

chapelet /ʃaplɛ/ *nm* **1** rosary; **2** (of onions, insults, islands) string.

chapelle /ʃapɛl/ *nf* **1** chapel; **2** clique, coterie.

chapelure /ʃaplyʀ/ *nf* breadcrumbs.

chaperon /ʃapʀɔ̃/ *nm* chaperon(e).

chapiteau, *pl* **~x** /ʃapito/ *nm* **1** marquee (GB), tent; (of circus) big top; **2** (of pillar) capital.

chapitre /ʃapitʀ/ *nm* **1** (of book) chapter; **2** subject.

IDIOMS **avoir voix au ~** to have a say in the matter.

chaque /ʃak/ *det* each, every.

char /ʃaʀ/ *nm* **1** (Mil) tank; **2** chariot; **3** (in carnival) float.

■ **~ d'assaut** (Mil) tank; **~ à bœufs** oxcart; **~ à voile** (Sport) sand yacht; ice yacht.

charabia° /ʃaʀabja/ *nm* gobbledygook°.

charade /ʃaʀad/ *nf* riddle.

charbon /ʃaʀbɔ̃/ *nm* coal; **~ de bois** charcoal.

IDIOMS **être sur des ~s ardents** to be like a cat on a hot tin roof.

charcuterie /ʃaʀkytʀi/ *nf* **1** cooked pork meats; **2** pork butcher's.

charcutier, **-ière** /ʃaʀkytje, ɛʀ/ *nm,f* pork butcher.

chardon /ʃaʀdɔ̃/ *nm* thistle.

charge /ʃaʀʒ/ **I** *nf* **1** burden, load; (of vehicle) load; (of ship) cargo, freight; **prise en ~** (in taxi) minimum fare; **2 avoir la ~ de qn/qch**

to be responsible for sb/sth; **avoir trois enfants à ~** to have three children to support; **prendre en ~** [*guardian*] to take charge of [*child*]; [*social security system*] to accept financial responsibility for [*sick person*]; to take care of [*fees*]; **3 ~ de notaire** ≈ solicitor's office; **4** (legal) charge; **5** (Mil) charge.

II charges *nf pl* **1** expenses, costs; **2** (payable by tenant) **~s (locatives)** service charges.

■ **~s patronales** employer's social security contributions.

IDIOMS **revenir à la ~** to try again.

chargement /ʃaʀʒəmɑ̃/ *nm* **1** (goods) load; cargo; **2** (action) loading.

charger /ʃaʀʒe/ [13] **I** *vtr* **1** to load; **2** to charge [*battery*]; **3 ~ qn de faire** to give sb the responsibility of doing; **c'est lui qui est chargé de l'enquête** he is in charge of the investigation; **4** to bring evidence against [*accused*]; **5** [*police*] to charge at [*crowd*].

II se charger *v refl* (+ *v être*) **se ~ de** to take responsibility for; **je m'en charge** I'll see to it.

chargeur /ʃaʀʒœʀ/ *nm* **1** (Mil) magazine; **2** (of camera) cartridge; **3** (Comput) loader.

chariot /ʃaʀjo/ *nm* **1** trolley (GB), cart (US); **2** truck; **3** waggon[GB]; **4** (of typewriter) carriage.

charisme /kaʀism/ *nm* charisma.

charitable /ʃaʀitabl/ *adj* charitable.

charité /ʃaʀite/ *nf* **1** charity; **2 par (pure) ~** out of the kindness of one's heart.

charlatan /ʃaʀlatɑ̃/ *nm* **1** quack○; **2** con man; **3** (politician) fraud.

charlotte /ʃaʀlɔt/ *nf* **1** (Culin) charlotte; **2** mobcap.

charmant, **~e** /ʃaʀmɑ̃, ɑ̃t/ *adj* charming.

charme /ʃaʀm/ **I** *nm* **1** charm; **faire du ~ à qn** to make eyes at sb; **cela ne manque pas de ~** (lifestyle, novel) it's not without its charms; (proposition) it's not unattractive; **2** spell.

II charmes *nm pl* (euphemistic) physical attributes.

IDIOMS **se porter comme un ~** to be as fit as a fiddle.

charmer /ʃaʀme/ [1] *vtr* to charm.

charmeur, **-euse** /ʃaʀmœʀ, øz/ **I** *adj* winning, engaging.

II *nm,f* charmer.

charnel, **-elle** /ʃaʀnɛl/ *adj* carnal.

charnier /ʃaʀnje/ *nm* mass grave.

charnière /ʃaʀnjɛʀ/ *nf* **1** hinge; **2** (figurative) bridge; junction; **rôle(-)~** pivotal role.

charnu, **~e** /ʃaʀny/ *adj* [*lip*] fleshy, thick.

charogne /ʃaʀɔɲ/ *nf* rotting carcass.

charpente /ʃaʀpɑ̃t/ *nf* (of roof) roof structure; (of building) framework; (of person) build.

charpentier /ʃaʀpɑ̃tje/ *nm* carpenter.

charpie /ʃaʀpi/ *nf* **réduire** or **mettre qch en ~** to tear sth to shreds.

charrette /ʃaʀɛt/ *nf* cart; **~ à bras** handcart.

charrier /ʃaʀje/ [2] **I** *vtr* **1** to carry, to haul; **2** [*river*] to carry [sth] along; **3**○ to tease [sb] unmercifully.

II○ *vi* to go too far.

charrue /ʃaʀy/ *nf* plough (GB), plow (US).

IDIOMS **mettre la ~ avant les bœufs** to put the cart before the horse.

charte /ʃaʀt/ *nf* charter.

charter /ʃaʀtɛʀ/ *adj inv* [*plane, flight*] charter.

chasse /ʃas/ *nf* **1** hunting; shooting; **~ au trésor** treasure hunt; **la ~ est ouverte** it's the open season; **2 ~ gardée** private hunting (ground); (figurative) preserve; **3 donner la ~ à, prendre en ~** to chase.

■ **~ à courre** hunting; **~ d'eau** (toilet) flush; **tirer la ~** to pull the chain.

IDIOMS **qui va à la ~ perd sa place** (Proverb) leave your place and you lose it.

chassé-croisé, *pl* **chassés-croisés** /ʃase kʀwaze/ *nm* continual coming and going.

chasse-neige /ʃasnɛʒ/ *nm inv* snowplough (GB), snowplow (US).

chasser /ʃase/ [1] **I** *vtr* **1** [*animal*] to hunt [*prey*]; **2** [*hunter*] to shoot (GB), to hunt; **3** [*person*] to chase away [*animal, intruder*]; [*rain*] to drive away [*tourists*]; to fire [*domestic servant*]; **4** to dispel [*smoke, doubt*].

II *vi* to go hunting.

chasseur /ʃasœʀ/ *nm* **1** hunter **2** (Mil) fighter (aircraft); fighter pilot; **3** (in hotel) bellboy (GB), bellhop (US).

■ **~ alpin** *soldier trained for mountain warfare*; **~ de têtes** head-hunter.

châssis /ʃɑsi/ *nm inv* **1** (of window) frame; **2** (Aut) chassis.

chaste /ʃast/ *adj* (gen) chaste; [*person*] celibate.

chasteté /ʃastəte/ *nf* chastity.

chat /ʃa/ *nm* cat; tomcat.

■ **~ de gouttière** ordinary cat; alley cat; **~ perché** off-ground tag.

IDIOMS **donner sa langue au ~** to give in; **il n'y a pas un ~** the place is deserted; **avoir un ~ dans la gorge** to have a frog in one's throat; **il ne faut pas réveiller le ~ qui dort** (Proverb) let sleeping dogs lie; **s'entendre comme chien et ~** to fight like cat and dog.

châtaigne /ʃɑtɛɲ/ *nf* (sweet) chestnut.

châtain /ʃɑtɛ̃/ *adj m* [*hair*] brown.

château, *pl* **~x** /ʃato/ *nm* **1** castle; **2** palace; **3** mansion.

■ **~ de cartes** house of cards; **~ d'eau** water tower; **~ fort** fortified castle.

IDIOMS **mener la vie de ~** to live the life of Riley (GB), to live like a prince.

châtelain, **~e** /ʃɑtlɛ̃, ɛn/ *nm,f* **1** lord/lady of the manor; **2** owner of a manor.

châtier /ʃɑtje/ [2] *vtr* to punish.

chatière /ʃatjɛʀ/ *nf* catflap.

châtiment /ʃɑtimɑ̃/ *nm* punishment.

chaton /ʃatɔ̃/ *nm* **1** kitten; **2** catkin.

chatouille○ /ʃatuj/ *nf* tickle.

chatouiller /ʃatuje/ [1] *vtr* to tickle.

IDIOMS **~ les côtes à qn** (euphemistic) to tan sb's hide.

chatoyer /ʃatwaje/ [23] *vi* to shimmer.

châtrer /ʃɑtʀe/ [1] *vtr* to castrate.

chatte /ʃat/ *nf* (female) cat.

chaud, **~e** /ʃo, ʃod/ I *adj* **1** hot; warm; **2** [*colour, voice*] warm; **3 ils n'ont pas été très ~s pour faire** they were not very keen on doing; **4** [*region*] turbulent; [*discussion*] heated; **un des points ~s du globe** one of the flash points of the world; **5 quartier ~**○ red light district.
II *adv* **il fait ~** it's warm; it's hot; **ça ne me fait ni ~ ni froid** it doesn't matter one way or the other to me.
III *nm* heat; **avoir ~** to be warm; to be hot; **nous avons eu ~** (figurative) we had a narrow escape; **se tenir ~** to keep warm.
IV **à chaud** *phr* **à ~** [*analyse*] on the spot; [*reaction*] immediate.
■ **~ et froid** (Med) chill.

chaudement /ʃodmɑ̃/ *adv* (gen) warmly; [*recommend*] heartily.

chaudière /ʃodjɛʀ/ *nf* boiler.

chaudron /ʃodʀɔ̃/ *nm* cauldron.

chauffage /ʃofaʒ/ *nm* **1** heating; **2** heater.

chauffard○ /ʃofaʀ/ *nm* reckless driver.

chauffe-eau /ʃofo/ *nm inv* water-heater.

chauffer /ʃofe/ [1] I *vtr* **1** to heat [*house*]; to heat (up) [*object, meal*]; **2** [*sun*] to warm.
II *vi* **1** [*food, oven*] to heat up; [*engine*] to warm up; to overheat; **2** [*radiator*] to give out heat; **3**○ **ça va ~!** there's going to be big trouble!
III **se chauffer** *v refl* (+ *v être*) **1 se ~ au soleil** to bask in the sun; **2 se ~ au charbon** to have coal-fired heating.

chaufferie /ʃofʀi/ *nf* **1** boiler room; **2** (in boat) stokehold.

chauffeur /ʃofœʀ/ *nm* **1** driver; **2** chauffeur.

chauffeuse /ʃoføz/ *nf* low armless easy chair.

chaume /ʃom/ *nm* **1** (in field) stubble; **2** thatch.

chaumière /ʃomjɛʀ/ *nf* **1** thatched cottage; **2 faire jaser dans les ~s** to cause tongues to wag.

chaussée /ʃose/ *nf* **1** roadway, highway; (in town) street; **2** (road) surface; **3** causeway.

chausse-pied, *pl* **~s** /ʃospje/ *nm* shoehorn.

chausser /ʃose/ [1] I *vtr* to put [sth] on [*shoes, spectacles*].
II *vi* **je chausse du 41** I take a (size) 41.
III **se chausser** *v refl* (+ *v être*) **1** to put (one's) shoes on; **2** to buy (one's) shoes.

chaussette /ʃosɛt/ *nf* sock.
IDIOMS **laisser tomber qn comme une vieille ~**○ to cast sb off like an old rag.

chausson /ʃosɔ̃/ *nm* **1** slipper; **2** bootee; **3** ballet shoe.
■ **~ aux pommes** (Culin) apple turnover.

chaussure /ʃosyʀ/ *nf* shoe; **~ montante** ankle boot.
IDIOMS **trouver ~ à son pied** [*man, woman*] to find the right person.

chauve /ʃov/ *adj* bald.

chauve-souris, *pl* **chauves-souris** /ʃovsuʀi/ *nf* (Zool) bat.

chauvin, **~e** /ʃovɛ̃, in/ *adj* chauvinistic.

chaux /ʃo/ *nf* lime.

chavirer /ʃaviʀe/ [1] I *vtr* to overwhelm.
II *vi* **1** [*boat*] to capsize; **2 faire ~ les cœurs** to be a heartbreaker; **3** [*objects*] to tip over.

chef /ʃɛf/ *nm* **1** leader; **2** superior, boss○; **3** head; (of sales department) manager; **architecte en ~** chief architect; **4 ~ cuisinier** or **de cuisine** chef; **5**○ ace; **se débrouiller comme un ~** to manage splendidly; **6 de mon/leur (propre) ~** on my/their own initiative; **7 au premier ~** primarily, first and foremost.
■ **~ d'accusation** (Law) count of indictment; **~ d'atelier** (shop) foreman; **~ d'équipe** foreman; (Sport) team captain; **~ d'État** head of state; **~ de gare** stationmaster.

chef-d'œuvre, *pl* **chefs-d'œuvre** /ʃɛdœvʀ/ *nm* masterpiece.

chef-lieu, *pl* **chefs-lieux** /ʃɛfljø/ *nm* administrative centre.

chemin /ʃ(ə)mɛ̃/ *nm* **1** country road; lane; **~ (de terre)** dirt track; path; **2** way; **sur le ~ du retour** on the way back; **reprendre le ~ du bureau** to go back to work; **on a fait un bout de ~ ensemble** we walked along together for a while; **~ faisant**, **en ~** on or along the way; **l'idée fait son ~** the idea is gaining ground; **prendre le ~ de la faillite** to be heading for bankruptcy; **s'arrêter en ~** to stop off on the way; (figurative) to stop.
■ **~ de fer** railway, railroad (US); rail.

cheminée /ʃ(ə)mine/ *nf* **1** chimney; chimney stack; **2** fireplace; **3** mantelpiece; **4** (of ship) funnel.

cheminement /ʃ(ə)minmɑ̃/ *nm* **1** slow progression; **2 le ~ de sa pensée** his/her train of thought.

cheminer /ʃ(ə)mine/ [1] *vi* **1** to walk (along); **2** [*idea*] to progress, to develop.

cheminot /ʃ(ə)mino/ *nm* railway worker (GB), railroader (US).

chemise /ʃ(ə)miz/ *nf* **1** shirt; **2** folder.
■ **~ de nuit** nightgown; (for man) nightshirt.
IDIOMS **je m'en moque comme de ma première ~**○ I don't give two hoots○ (GB) or a hoot○ (US); **changer d'avis comme de ~**○ to change one's mind at the drop of a hat.

chemisier /ʃ(ə)mizje/ *nm* blouse.

chenal, *pl* **-aux** /ʃənal, o/ *nm* channel, fairway.

chêne /ʃɛn/ *nm* **1** oak (tree); **2** oak.

chenil /ʃənil/ *nm* **1** (dog) kennel; **2** kennels.

chenille /ʃənij/ *nf* (Aut, Zool) caterpillar.

cheptel /ʃɛptɛl/ *nm* **~ (vif)** livestock.

chèque /ʃɛk/ *nm* cheque (GB), check (US).
■ **~ en blanc** blank cheque (GB) or check (US); **~ en bois**○ rubber cheque○ (GB) or check (US); **~ sans provision** bad cheque (GB) or check (US); **~ de voyage** traveller's cheque (GB) or check (US).

chéquier /ʃekje/ *nm* chequebook (GB), checkbook (US).

cher, **chère**[1] /ʃɛʀ/ I *adj* **1** dear; beloved; **un être ~** a loved one; **2** (as term of address) dear; **3** expensive; **pas ~** cheap.
II *nm,f* **mon ~/ma chère** my dear.
III *adv* **1** a lot (of money); **coûter plus/moins**

~ to cost more/less; **acheter ~** to buy at a high price; **2** (figurative) [*pay, cost*] dearly.
IDIOMS **ne pas donner ~ de la peau de qn**○ not to rate sb's chances highly.

chercher /ʃɛʀʃe/ [1] **I** *vtr* **1** to look for [*person, object, trouble*]; to try to find [*answer, ideas*]; to try to remember [*name*]; **~ fortune** to seek one's fortune; **~ qn du regard** to look about for sb; **2 ~ à faire** to try to do; **3 aller ~ qn/qch** to go and get sb/sth; to pick sb/sth up; **4 où est-il allé ~ cela?** what made him think that?; **5 une maison dans ce quartier, ça va ~ dans les 800000 francs** a house in this area must fetch (GB) or get (US) about 800,000 francs.
II se chercher *v refl* (+ *v être*) **1** to try to find oneself; **2 se ~ des excuses** to try to find excuses for oneself; **3**○ to be out to get each other○.

chercheur, **-euse** /ʃɛʀʃœʀ, øz/ *nm,f* researcher.
■ **~ d'or** gold-digger.

chère² /ʃɛʀ/ **I** *adj f* ▶ **cher**.
II *nf* **faire bonne ~** to eat well.

chèrement /ʃɛʀmɑ̃/ *adv* **~ acquise** gained at great cost.

chéri, **~e** /ʃeʀi/ **I** *pp* ▶ **chérir**.
II *pp adj* beloved.
III *nm,f* **1** darling; **2**○ boyfriend/girlfriend.

chérir /ʃeʀiʀ/ [3] *vtr* to cherish [*person*]; to hold [sth] dear [*idea*].

chérubin /ʃeʀybɛ̃/ *nm* cherub.

chétif, **-ive** /ʃetif, iv/ *adj* [*child*] puny.

cheval, *pl* **-aux** /ʃ(ə)val, o/ **I** *nm* **1** horse; **monter à ~** to ride a horse; **remède de ~** strong medicine; **fièvre de ~** raging fever; **2** (Sport) horse-riding; **3** horsemeat.
II à cheval sur *phr* **1** astride; **2** spanning; **3** in between; **4 être à ~ sur qch** to be a stickler for sth.
■ **~ à bascule** rocking horse; **~ de bataille** hobbyhorse; **chevaux de bois** merry-go-round horses.

chevaleresque /ʃ(ə)valʀɛsk/ *adj* **1** [*literature*] courtly; **2** [*person*] chivalrous.

chevalerie /ʃ(ə)valʀi/ *nf* chivalry.

chevalet /ʃ(ə)valɛ/ *nm* easel.

chevalier /ʃ(ə)valje/ *nm* knight.

chevalière /ʃ(ə)valjɛʀ/ *nf* signet ring.

cheval-vapeur, *pl* **chevaux-vapeur** /ʃ(ə)valvapœʀ, ʃ(ə)vovapœʀ/ *nm* horsepower.

chevauchée /ʃ(ə)voʃe/ *nf* ride.

chevaucher /ʃ(ə)voʃe/ [1] **I** *vtr* **1** to sit astride [*animal, chair*]; **2** to overlap.
II se chevaucher *v refl* (+ *v être*) to overlap.

chevelu, **~e** /ʃəvly/ *adj* long-haired.

chevelure /ʃəvlyʀ/ *nf* hair.

chevet /ʃəvɛ/ *nm* bedhead; **être au ~ de qn** to be at sb's bedside.

cheveu, *pl* **~x** /ʃəvø/ **I** *nm* hair; **être à un ~ de** to be within a hair's breadth of; **ne tenir qu'à un ~** to hang by a thread.
II cheveux *nm pl* hair.
IDIOMS **avoir un ~ sur la langue** to have a lisp; **venir comme un ~ sur la soupe** to come at an awkward moment; **se faire des ~x**○ **(blancs)** to worry oneself to death; **couper les ~x en quatre** to split hairs; **être tiré par les ~x** to be far-fetched.

cheville /ʃ(ə)vij/ *nf* **1** (Anat) ankle; **2** Rawlplug®; peg; dowel.
IDIOMS **il n'arrive pas à la ~ de Paul** he can't hold a candle to Paul; **être en ~ avec qn**○ to be in cahoots with sb○.

chèvre¹ /ʃɛvʀ/ *nm* goat's cheese.

chèvre² /ʃɛvʀ/ *nf* goat; nanny-goat.
IDIOMS **devenir ~**○ to go nuts◑.

chevreau, *pl* **~x** /ʃəvʀo/ *nm* (Zool) kid.

chèvrefeuille /ʃɛvʀəfœj/ *nm* honeysuckle.

chevreuil /ʃəvʀœj/ *nm* **1** roe (deer); roebuck; **2** (Culin) venison.

chevronné /ʃəvʀɔne/ *adj* [*person*] experienced.

chevroter /ʃəvʀɔte/ [1] *vtr, vi* to quaver.

chevrotine /ʃəvʀɔtin/ *nf* buckshot.

chez /ʃe/ *prep* **1 ~ qn** at sb's place; **rentre ~ toi** go home; **de ~ qn** [*telephone*] from sb's place; **fais comme ~ toi** make yourself at home; **2** (referring to shop, office) **aller ~ le boucher** to go to the butcher's; **être convoqué ~ le patron** to be called in before the boss; **3** (referring to a region) **~ nous** where I come from; where I live; **4** among; **~ l'animal** in animals; **5 ce que j'aime ~ elle, c'est son humour** what I like about her is her sense of humour[GB]; **6** in; **~ Cocteau** in Cocteau.

chic /ʃik/ **I** *adj* **1** smart (GB), chic; **2**○ chic, fashionable; **3**○ [*person*] nice.
II *nm* chic; **avoir le ~ pour faire** to have a knack for doing; **avec ~** with style.

chicane /ʃikan/ *nf* chicane; (on road, ski slope) double bend; **en ~** on alternate sides.

chicaner /ʃikane/ [1] *vi* to squabble.

chiche /ʃiʃ/ **I** *adj* **1** mean (GB), stingy; **2 être ~**○ **de faire** to be quite capable of doing.
II *excl* **'je vais le faire'—'~**○**!'** 'I'll do it'—'I dare you!'

chichement /ʃiʃmɑ̃/ *adv* [*live*] frugally; [*give*] stingily; [*pay*] poorly.

chichi /ʃiʃi/ *nm* fuss.

chicorée /ʃikɔʀe/ *nf* **1** (plant) chicory; (salad vegetable) endive (GB), chicory (US); **2** (Culin) (powder) chicory; (drink) chicory coffee.

chien, **chienne**¹ /ʃjɛ̃, ʃjɛn/ **I**○ *adj* **ne pas être ~** not to be too hard.
II *nm* **1** dog; **2** (of rifle) hammer.
III de chien○ *phr* [*job, weather*] rotten; **ça me fait un mal de ~** it hurts like hell○.
■ **~ d'aveugle** guide dog; **~ de berger** sheepdog; **~ de garde** guard dog; (figurative) watchdog; **~ de race** pedigree dog.
IDIOMS **être couché en ~ de fusil** to be curled up; **ce n'est pas fait pour les ~s**○ it's there to be used.

chiendent /ʃjɛ̃dɑ̃/ *nm* couch grass; **brosse de ~** scrubbing brush.

chienne² /ʃjɛn/ **I** *adj f* ▶ **chien**.
II *nf* (animal) bitch.

chiffon /ʃifɔ̃/ *nm* **1** rag, (piece of) cloth; **parler ~s** to talk (about) clothes; **2** duster.

chiffonner /ʃifɔne/ [1] **I** *vtr* **1** to crease, to crumple; **2**○ to bother [*person*].
II se chiffonner *v refl* (+ *v être*) to crease.

chiffonnier /ʃifɔnje/ *nm* **se battre comme des ~s** to fight like cat and dog.

chiffre /ʃifʀ/ *nm* **1** figure; **2** monogram.
■ **~ d'affaires, CA** turnover (GB), sales (US); **~ arabe** Arabic numeral; **~ romain** Roman numeral; **~ de vente** sales (figures).

chiffrer /ʃifʀe/ [1] **I** *vtr* **1** to put a figure on [*cost, loss*]; to cost [*job*]; **~ à** to put the cost of [sth] at [*job*]; **2** to encode [*message*].
II○ *vi* to add up; **ça chiffre vite** it soon adds up.
III se chiffrer *v refl* (+ *v être*) **se ~ à** to amount to, to come to.

chignon /ʃiɲɔ̃/ *nm* bun; chignon.

Chili /ʃili/ *pr nm* Chile.

chimère /ʃimɛʀ/ *nf* **1** wild dream, pipe dream; **2** (in mythology) Chimaera.

chimie /ʃimi/ *nf* chemistry.

chimiothérapie /ʃimjoteʀapi/ *nf* chemotherapy.

chimique /ʃimik/ *adj* **1** chemical; [*fibre*] man-made; **2** [*food, taste*] synthetic.

chimiste /ʃimist/ *nmf* chemist.

chimpanzé /ʃɛ̃pɑ̃ze/ *nm* chimpanzee.

Chine /ʃin/ *pr nf* China.

chiné, ~e /ʃine/ *adj* chiné.

chiner○ /ʃine/ [1] *vi* to bargain-hunt, to antique (US).

chinois, ~e /ʃinwa, az/ **I** *adj* Chinese.
II *nm* (language) Chinese.
IDIOMS **pour moi c'est du ~** it's double-Dutch (GB) or Greek to me.

chiot /ʃjo/ *nm* puppy, pup.

chiper○ /ʃipe/ [1] *vtr* to pinch○.

chipie○ /ʃipi/ *nf* cow○.

chipoter○ /ʃipɔte/ [1] *vi* **1** to quibble (**sur** over); **2** to pick at one's food.

chips /ʃips/ *nf inv* crisp (GB), potato chip (US).

chique /ʃik/ *nf* plug (of tobacco).
IDIOMS **couper la ~ à qn** to shut sb up○.

chiqué○ /ʃike/ *nm* **1 c'est du ~** it's a put-on; **2 faire du ~** to put on or give oneself airs.

chiquenaude /ʃiknod/ *nf* flick.

chiquer /ʃike/ [1] *vtr* **tabac à ~** chewing tobacco.

chiromancie /kiʀomɑ̃si/ *nf* palmistry.

chirurgie /ʃiʀyʀʒi/ *nf* surgery.

chirurgien /ʃiʀyʀʒjɛ̃/ *nm* surgeon.

chlore /klɔʀ/ *nm* chlorine.

chlorhydrique /klɔʀidʀik/ *adj* hydrochloric.

chloroforme /klɔʀɔfɔʀm/ *nm* chloroform.

chlorophylle /klɔʀɔfil/ *nf* chlorophyll.

chlorure /klɔʀyʀ/ *nm* chloride.

choc /ʃɔk/ **I** *adj inv* **'prix ~!'** 'huge reductions'.
II *nm* **1** impact, shock; collision; **sous le ~** under the impact; **2** (noise) crash, smash; thud; clang; chink; **3** (confrontation) (gen, Mil) clash; (Sport) encounter; **de ~** [*journalist*] ace○; **4** (emotional, physical) shock.

chocolat /ʃɔkɔla/ *nm* chocolate; **~ noir** or **à croquer** plain (GB) or dark (US) chocolate.

chœur /kœʀ/ *nm* **1** choir; (in opera, play) chorus; (figurative) chorus (**de** of); **en ~** [*say*] in unison; [*laugh*] all together; **2** (in church) chancel, choir.

choir /ʃwaʀ/ [51] *vi* to fall; **laisser ~ qn** to drop sb.

choisir /ʃwaziʀ/ [3] *vtr* to choose.

choix /ʃwa/ *nm inv* **1** choice; **arrêter son ~ sur** to settle or decide on; **2 de ~** [*item*] choice; [*candidate*] first-rate; **les places de ~** the best seats; **un morceau de ~** (of meat) a prime cut; **de second ~** of inferior quality.

choléra /kɔleʀa/ *nm* cholera.

cholestérol /kɔlɛsteʀɔl/ *nm* cholesterol.

chômage /ʃomaʒ/ *nm* unemployment; **mettre qn au ~** to make sb redundant (GB), to lay sb off.
■ **~ technique** layoffs.

chômer /ʃome/ [1] *vi* **1** to be idle; **2** to be out of work.

chômeur, -euse /ʃomœʀ, øz/ *nm,f* unemployed person.

chope /ʃɔp/ *nf* beer mug, tankard.

choquer /ʃɔke/ [1] *vtr* **1** to shock [*person*]; to offend [*sight, sensibility*]; **2** [*news*] to shake [*person*]; [*accident*] to shake [sb] (up).

chorale /kɔʀal/ *nf* choir.

chorégraphie /kɔʀegʀafi/ *nf* choreography.

choriste /kɔʀist/ *nmf* chorister; member of the choir; member of the chorus.

chorus /kɔʀys/ *nm inv* chorus; **faire ~ avec qn** (figurative) to join in with sb.

chose /ʃoz/ *nf* **1** (object, abstract) thing; **de deux ~s l'une** it's got to be one thing or the other; **une ~ communément admise** a widely accepted fact; **en mettant les ~s au mieux** at best; **mettre les ~s au point** to clear things up; **avant toute ~** before anything else; above all else; **2** matter; **la ~ en question** the matter in hand; **3 être un peu porté sur la ~**○ to be keen on sex.

chou, *pl* **~x** /ʃu/ *nm* **1** cabbage; **2** choux bun (GB), pastry shell (US); **3** dear, darling.
■ **~ de Bruxelles** Brussels sprout; **~ à la crème** cream puff; **~ rave** kohlrabi.
IDIOMS **bête comme ~** really easy; **faire ~ blanc**○ to draw a blank; **faire ses ~x gras de qch**○ to use sth to one's advantage; **rentrer dans le ~**○ **de qn** to beat sb up; to give sb a piece of one's mind.

chouchou○ /ʃuʃu/ *nm* **1** (teacher's) pet; (of adoring public) darling; **2** (for hair) scrunchie.

choucroute /ʃukʀut/ *nf* sauerkraut.

chouette /ʃwɛt/ **I**○ *adj* great○, neat○ (US).
II *nf* **1** owl; **2 vieille ~** old harridan.

chou-fleur, *pl* **choux-fleurs** /ʃuflœʀ/ *nm* cauliflower.

choyer /ʃwaje/ [23] *vtr* to pamper.

chrétien, -ienne /kʀetjɛ̃, ɛn/ *adj*, *nm,f* Christian.

chrétienté /kʀetjɛ̃te/ *nf* **la ~** Christendom.
Christ /kʀist/ *pr n* **le ~** Christ.
christianisme /kʀistjanism/ *nm* Christianity.
chromatique /kʀɔmatik/ *adj* chromatic.
chrome /kʀom/ *nm* chromium.
chromosome /kʀɔmozom/ *nm* chromosome.
chronique /kʀɔnik/ **I** *adj* chronic.
II *nf* (in newspaper) column, page.
chronologie /kʀɔnɔlɔʒi/ *nf* chronology.
chronomètre /kʀɔnɔmɛtʀ/ *nm* stopwatch.
chronométrer /kʀɔnɔmetʀe/ [14] *vtr* to time.
chrysalide /kʀizalid/ *nf* chrysalis.
chu ▶ **choir**.
chuchotement /ʃyʃɔtmɑ̃/ *nm* whisper.
chuchoter /ʃyʃɔte/ [1] *vtr, vi* to whisper.
chuinter /ʃɥɛ̃te/ [1] *vi* [*steam*] to hiss gently; [*tyre*] to swish.
chute /ʃyt/ *nf* **1** (gen) fall; (of empire) collapse; (of hair) loss; (of pressure) drop; **2** (of film) ending; (of story) punch line; **3** (of cloth) offcut.
■ **~ d'eau** waterfall; **la ~ des reins** the small of the back.
Chypre /ʃipʀ/ *pr nf* Cyprus.
ci /si/ **I** *det* **cette page-~** this page; **ces jours-~** (past) these last few days; (future) in the next few days; (present) at the moment.
II *pron* this; **~ et ça** this and that.
ci-après /siapʀɛ/ *adv* below.
cible /sibl/ *nf* target.
cibler /sible/ [1] *vtr* to target.
ciboulette /sibulɛt/ *nf* (Bot) chive; (Culin) chives.
cicatrice /sikatʀis/ *nf* scar.
cicatriser /sikatʀize/ [1] *vtr*, **se cicatriser** *v refl* (+ *v être*) to heal.
ci-contre /sikɔ̃tʀ/ *adv* opposite.
ci-dessous /sidəsu/ *adv* below.
ci-dessus /sidəsy/ *adv* above.
cidre /sidʀ/ *nm* cider.
ciel /sjɛl/, *pl* **cieux** /sjø/ *nm* **1** sky; **carte du ~** star chart; **à ~ ouvert** [*pool*] open-air; [*sewer*] open; **2** heaven; **c'est le ~ qui t'envoie** you're a godsend.
cierge /sjɛʀʒ/ *nm* (church) candle.
cieux ▶ **ciel**.
cigale /sigal/ *nf* cicada.
cigare /sigaʀ/ *nm* cigar.
cigarette /sigaʀɛt/ *nf* cigarette.
ci-gît /siʒi/ *phr* here lies.
cigogne /sigɔɲ/ *nf* stork.
ci-joint, **~e** /siʒwɛ̃, ɛ̃t/ **I** *adj* enclosed.
II *adv* enclosed.
cil /sil/ *nm* eyelash.
cime /sim/ *nf* (tree)top.
ciment /simɑ̃/ *nm* cement.
cimetière /simtjɛʀ/ *nm* cemetery, graveyard.
cinéaste /sineast/ *nmf* film director.
ciné-club, *pl* **~s** /sineklœb/ *nm* film club.
cinéma /sinema/ *nm* **1** **(salle de) ~** cinema (GB), movie theater (US); **2** cinema; film industry; **faire du ~** to be in films; **3**○ (figurative) **arrête ton ~** cut out the play-acting; stop making such a fuss○.
■ **~ d'art et d'essai** cinema showing art films (GB), art house (US).
cinémathèque /sinematɛk/ *nf* film archive.
cinématographique /sinematɔgʀafik/ *adj* film (GB), movie (US).
cinglant, **~e** /sɛ̃glɑ̃, ɑ̃t/ *adj* **1** [*wind*] biting; [*rain*] driving; **2** [*remark, irony*] scathing.
cinglé○, **~e** /sɛ̃gle/ *adj* mad○, crazy○.
cingler /sɛ̃gle/ [1] *vtr* **1** [*rain, wind*] to sting [*face*]; **2** (with whip) to lash.
cinq /sɛ̃k/ *adj inv, pron, nm inv* five.
cinquantaine /sɛ̃kɑ̃tɛn/ *nf* about fifty.
cinquante /sɛ̃kɑ̃t/ *adj inv, pron, nm inv* fifty.
cinquantenaire /sɛ̃kɑ̃tnɛʀ/ *nm* fiftieth anniversary.
cinquantième /sɛ̃kɑ̃tjɛm/ *adj* fiftieth.
cinquième /sɛ̃kjɛm/ **I** *adj* fifth.
II *nf* **1** (Sch) *second year of secondary school, age 12–13*; **2** (Aut) fifth (gear).
cintre /sɛ̃tʀ/ *nm* **1** (clothes) hanger; **2** (in architecture) curve.
cintré, **~e** /sɛ̃tʀe/ *adj* [*coat*] waisted; [*shirt*] tailored.
cirage /siʀaʒ/ *nm* (shoe) polish.
IDIOMS **être dans le ~**○ to be half-conscious.
circoncire /siʀkɔ̃siʀ/ [64] *vtr* to circumcise.
circonférence /siʀkɔ̃feʀɑ̃s/ *nf* circumference.
circonflexe /siʀkɔ̃flɛks/ *adj* **accent ~** circumflex (accent).
circonscription /siʀkɔ̃skʀipsjɔ̃/ *nf* district.
circonscrire /siʀkɔ̃skʀiʀ/ [67] *vtr* **1** to contain [*fire, epidemic*]; to limit [*subject*]; **2** to define.
circonspection /siʀkɔ̃spɛksjɔ̃/ *nf* caution.
circonstance /siʀkɔ̃stɑ̃s/ **I** *nf* **1** circumstance; **2** situation; **en toute ~** in any event; **pour la ~** for the occasion.
II **de circonstance** *phr* [*poem*] for the occasion; **faire une tête de ~** to assume a suitable expression.
■ **~s atténuantes** (Law) extenuating or mitigating circumstances.
circuit /siʀkɥi/ *nm* **1** (Sport, Tech) circuit; **2** (in tourism) tour; **3** (figurative) **être mis hors ~** [*person*] to be put on the sidelines; **vivre en ~ fermé** to live in a closed world.
circulaire /siʀkylɛʀ/ *adj, nf* circular.
circulation /siʀkylasjɔ̃/ *nf* **1** traffic; **2** circulation; **la libre ~ des personnes** the free movement of people; **disparaître de la ~** to go out of circulation.
circulatoire /siʀkylatwaʀ/ *adj* circulatory.
circuler /siʀkyle/ [1] *vi* **1** [*train, bus*] to run; **2** [*person*] to get around; to move about; (by car) to travel; **3** [*banknotes, rumour, information*] to circulate; **faire ~** to circulate; to spread [*rumour*]; **4** [*blood, air*] to circulate.
cire /siʀ/ *nf* wax.
ciré /siʀe/ *nm* oilskin.
cirer /siʀe/ [1] *vtr* to polish [*shoes, floor*].
cirque /siʀk/ *nm* **1** circus; **2**○ (figurative) racket○; **arrête ton ~!** stop your nonsense!

cirrhose /siRoz/ *nf* cirrhosis.
cisaille /sizɑj/ *nf* pair of shears; **~s** shears.
ciseau, *pl* **~x** /sizo/ **I** *nm* **1** (Tech) chisel; **2** (Sport) scissors jump; scissors hold.
II ciseaux *nm pl* scissors.
ciseler /sizle/ [17] *vtr* to chisel.
citadelle /sitadɛl/ *nf* citadel.
citadin, **~e** /sitadɛ̃, in/ **I** *adj* city.
II *nm,f* city-dweller.
citation /sitasjɔ̃/ *nf* quotation.
cité /site/ *nf* **1** (gen) city; town; **2** housing estate.
■ **~ universitaire** student halls of residence (GB), dormitories (US).
citer /site/ [1] *vtr* **1** to quote [*author, passage*]; **2** to name [*title, book*]; to cite [*person, example, fact*]; **3** (Law) to summon [*witness*].
citerne /sitɛRn/ *nf* tank.
citoyen, **-enne** /sitwajɛ̃, ɛn/ *nm,f* citizen.
citrique /sitRik/ *adj* citric.
citron /sitRɔ̃/ *nm* **1** lemon; **2**○ head, nut○.
■ **~ givré** lemon sorbet; **~ vert** lime.
citronnade /sitRɔnad/ *nf* lemon squash (GB), lemonade (US).
citronnelle /sitRɔnɛl/ *nf* (Bot) citronella.
citronnier /sitRɔnje/ *nm* lemon tree.
citrouille /sitRuj/ *nf* pumpkin.
civet /sivɛ/ *nm* ≈ stew.
civière /sivjɛR/ *nf* stretcher.
civil, **~e** /sivil/ **I** *adj* (gen) civilian; [*marriage*] civil; [*funeral*] non religious.
II *nm* civilian; **en ~** in civilian clothes; in plain clothes; **dans le ~** in civilian life.
civilisation /sivilizasjɔ̃/ *nf* civilization.
civique /sivik/ *adj* civic.
claie /klɛ/ *nf* **1** wicker rack; **2** fence, hurdle.
clair, **~e** /klɛR/ **I** *adj* **1** [*colour*] light; [*complexion*] fair; **2** [*room*] bright; **3** [*weather, water*] clear; **4** [*text*] clear; **passer le plus ~ de son temps** to spend most of one's time.
II *adv* [*speak*] clearly; **il faisait ~** it was already light; **voir ~** to see well.
III *nm* **1** light; **mettre ses idées au ~** to get one's ideas straight; **tirer une affaire au ~** to get to the bottom of things; **2** light colours[GB].
■ **~ de lune** moonlight.
IDIOMS **c'est ~ comme de l'eau de roche** it's crystal clear.
clairière /klɛRjɛR/ *nf* clearing, glade.
clairon /klɛRɔ̃/ *nm* **1** bugle; **2** bugler.
claironner /klɛRɔne/ [1] *vtr* to shout [sth] from the rooftops.
clairsemé, **~e** /klɛRsəme/ *adj* [*houses*] scattered; [*hair*] thin; [*population*] sparse.
clairvoyance /klɛRvwajɑ̃s/ *nf* perceptiveness.
clamer /klame/ [1] *vtr* to proclaim.
clameur /klamœR/ *nf* roar.
clan /klɑ̃/ *nm* clan.
clandestin, **~e** /klɑ̃dɛstɛ̃, in/ *adj* [*organization*] underground; [*immigration*] illegal; **passager ~** stowaway.
clandestinité /klɑ̃dɛstinite/ *nf* secret or clandestine nature; **dans la ~** [*live*] in hiding; [*operate*] in secret.
clap /klap/ *nm* clapperboard.
clapet /klapɛ/ *nm* **1** valve; **2**○ mouth, trap○.
clapier /klapje/ *nm* rabbit hutch.
clapoter /klapɔte/ [1] *vi* to lap.
claque /klak/ *nf* **1** slap; **2**○ slap in the face; **3** (in theatre) claque.
IDIOMS **en avoir sa ~**○ to be fed up.
claquement /klakmɑ̃/ *nm* (of door) bang; (of whip) crack; (of tongue) click; (of flag) flapping.
claquer /klake/ [1] **I** *vtr* **1** to slam [*door*]; **2**○ to exhaust [*person*]; **3**○ to blow○ [*money*].
II *vi* [*door*] to bang; (closing) to slam shut; [*flag*] to flap; **elle claque des dents** her teeth are chattering.
III se claquer *v refl* (+ *v être*) **se ~ un muscle** to pull or strain a muscle.
claquettes /klakɛt/ *nf pl* tap dancing.
clarifier /klaRifje/ [2] *vtr* to clarify.
clarinette /klaRinɛt/ *nf* clarinet.
clarté /klaRte/ *nf* **1** light; **2** (of water) clarity; (of complexion) fairness; **3** (of style) clarity.
classe /klas/ *nf* **1** (Sch) (group) class, form (GB); (level) year, form (GB), grade (US); **après la ~** after school; **2** (Sch) classroom; **3** (in society, transport) class; **les ~s sociales** social classes; **4 avoir de la ~** to have class; **5** (Mil) **faire ses ~s** to do one's basic training.
■ **~ d'âge** age group; **~ verte** *educational schooltrip to the countryside*; **~s préparatoires (aux grandes écoles)** *preparatory classes for entrance to Grandes Écoles.*
classement /klasmɑ̃/ *nm* **1** classification; **2** filing; **faire du ~ dans ses papiers** to sort one's papers out; **3** grading; **~ trimestriel** (Sch) termly position (in class); **4** (Sport) ranking; **en tête du ~** in first place; **5** (of hotel) rating.
classer /klase/ [1] **I** *vtr* **1** to classify; **2** to file (away) [*documents*]; **3** (Law) to close [*case*]; **4** to list [*old building*]; **5** to class [*country, pupils*]; to rank [*song, player*]; **6**○ to size [sb] up.
II se classer *v refl* (+ *v être*) to rank.
classeur /klasœR/ *nm* **1** ring binder; **2** file.
classicisme /klasisism/ *nm* **1** (in art) classicism; **2** (in clothes, tastes) traditionalism.
classification /klasifikasjɔ̃/ *nf* classification.
classifier /klasifje/ [2] *vtr* to classify.
classique /klasik/ **I** *adj* **1** classical; **faire des études ~s** (Sch) to do classics; **2** classic; [*method*] classic, standard; [*consequence*] usual; **de coupe ~** of classic cut; **c'est ~**○**!** it's typical!; **c'est le coup ~**○**!** it's the same old story!
II *nm* classic.
clause /kloz/ *nf* clause.
claustrophobie /klostRɔfɔbi/ *nf* claustrophobia.
clavecin /klavsɛ̃/ *nm* harpsichord.
clavicule /klavikyl/ *nf* collarbone.
clavier /klavje/ *nm* keyboard; **~ numérique** numeric keypad.
clé /kle/ **I** *nf* **1** (of lock, tin) key; **sous ~** under

lock and key; **fermer à ~** to lock; **prix ~s en main** [*car*] on the road price (GB), sticker price (US); **usine ~s en main** turnkey factory; **2** (solution) key (**de** to); **3** spanner (GB), wrench; **4** (of flute) key; (of violin) peg; **~ de fa** bass clef.
II **(-)clé** (*combining form*) **poste/mot(-)~** key post/word.
III **à la clé** *phr* at stake; **avec, à la ~, une récompense** with a reward thrown in.
■ **~ anglaise**, **~ à molette** adjustable spanner (GB) or wrench (US).

clef = **clé**.

clément, **~e** /klemɑ̃, ɑ̃t/ *adj* **1** [*judge*] lenient; **2** [*temperature, winter*] mild.

clémentine /klemɑ̃tin/ *nf* clementine.

cleptomanie /klɛptɔmani/ *nf* kleptomania.

clerc /klɛʀ/ *nm* (Law) clerk.

clergé /klɛʀʒe/ *nm* clergy.

cliché /kliʃe/ *nm* **1** snapshot; **2** cliché.

client, **~e** /klijɑ̃, ɑ̃t/ *nm,f* (of shop) customer; (of solicitor) client; (of hotel) guest; (in taxi) fare.
IDIOMS **c'est à la tête du ~** it depends whether they like the look of you.

clientèle /klijɑ̃tɛl/ *nf* (of shop) customers; (of solicitor) clients; (of doctor) patients; **se faire une ~** to build up a clientele.

cligner /kliɲe/ [1] *v+prep* **~ des yeux** to blink; **~ de l'œil** to wink.

clignotant, **~e** /kliɲɔtɑ̃, ɑ̃t/ *nm* (Aut) indicator (GB), blinker (US).

clignoter /kliɲɔte/ [1] *vi* [*light*] to flash; to flash on and off; [*star*] to twinkle.

climat /klima/ *nm* climate.

climatique /klimatik/ *adj* climatic.

climatisation /klimatizasjɔ̃/ *nf* air-conditioning.

climatiser /klimatize/ [1] *vtr* to air-condition.

clin /klɛ̃/ *nm* **~ d'œil** wink; (figurative) allusion; **en un ~ d'œil** in a flash.

clinique /klinik/ I *adj* clinical.
II *nf* private hospital; **~ vétérinaire** veterinary clinic.

clinquant, **~e** /klɛ̃kɑ̃, ɑ̃t/ *adj* flashy○.

clip /klip/ *nm* **1** pop video; **2** clip-on (earring).

clique /klik/ *nf* clique; **prendre ses ~s et ses claques** to pack up and go.

cliquer /klike/ [1] *vi* (Comput) to click (**sur** on).

cliqueter /klikte/ [20] *vi* [*keys*] to jingle; [*chain, machine*] to rattle.

clitoris /klitɔʀis/ *nm* clitoris.

clivage /klivaʒ/ *nm* divide; **~ d'opinion** division of opinion.

clochard, **~e** /klɔʃaʀ, aʀd/ *nm,f* tramp.

cloche /klɔʃ/ *nf* **1** bell; **2**○ clod○, idiot; **3 ~ à fromage** cover of cheese dish.
IDIOMS **entendre plusieurs sons de ~** to hear several versions; **sonner les ~s à qn** to bawl sb out○.

cloche-pied: **à cloche-pied** /aklɔʃpje/ *phr* **sauter à ~** to hop.

clocher[1]○ /klɔʃe/ [1] *vi* **il y a quelque chose qui cloche** there's something wrong.

clocher[2] /klɔʃe/ *nm* steeple; church or bell tower; **querelle de ~** local quarrel.

clochette /klɔʃɛt/ *nf* (little) bell.

cloison /klwazɔ̃/ *nf* **1** partition; **2** screen; **~ extensible** folding room-divider.

cloisonner /klwazɔne/ [1] *vtr* **1** to partition [*room*]; to divide up [*space*]; **2** to divide up [*society*]; to compartmentalize [*administration*].

cloître /klwɑtʀ/ *nm* cloister.

cloîtrer /klwatʀe/ [1] I *vtr* to shut [sb] away.
II **se cloîtrer** *v refl* (+ *v être*) to shut oneself away.

clone /klon/ *nm* clone.

clope○ /klɔp/ *nm* or *f* fag○ (GB), ciggy○, cigarette.

clopin-clopant○ /klɔpɛ̃klɔpɑ̃/ *phr* **aller ~** to hobble along.

cloporte /klɔpɔʀt/ *nm* woodlouse.

cloque /klɔk/ *nf* blister.

clore /klɔʀ/ [79] I *vtr* **1** to close [*debate*]; **2** to end, to conclude [*programme*]; **3** to close [*eyes*].
II **se clore** *v refl* (+ *v être*) to end (**par** with).

clos, **~e** /klo, oz/ *adj* [*system*] closed; [*area*] enclosed; **monde ~** self-contained world.

clôture /klotyʀ/ *nf* **1** fence; wire fence; railings; **2** (of debate, session) close; (of subscription) closing; **discours de ~** closing speech.

clôturer /klotyʀe/ [1] *vtr* **1** to fence in [*land*]; **2** [*person*] to close [*list*]; [*speech*] to end [*debate*].

clou /klu/ I *nm* **1** nail; stud; **2** (of show) star attraction; (of evening) high point; **3** (Med) boil.
II **clous** *nm pl* **1** pedestrian crossing (GB), crosswalk (US); **2**○ **des ~s!** no way!
■ **~ de girofle** (Bot, Culin) clove.
IDIOMS **enfoncer le ~** to drive the point home.

clouer /klue/ [1] *vtr* to nail down [*lid*]; to nail together [*planks*]; **~ au sol** (figurative) to pin [sb] down; **être cloué au lit** to be confined to bed.

clown /klun/ *nm* clown.

club /klœb/ *nm* **1** club; **2 ~ de vacances** holiday camp.

CM /seɛm/ *nm*: *abbr* ▶ **cours**.

CNRS /seɛnɛʀɛs/ *nm* (*abbr* = **Centre national de la recherche scientifique**) *national centre for scientific research.*

coaguler /kɔagyle/ [1] *vi*, **se coaguler** *v refl* (+ *v être*) [*blood*] to coagulate.

coalition /kɔalisjɔ̃/ *nf* coalition.

coasser /kɔase/ [1] *vi* to croak.

cobaye /kɔbaj/ *nm* guinea pig.

cobra /kɔbʀa/ *nm* cobra.

cocaïne /kɔkain/ *nf* cocaine.

cocarde /kɔkaʀd/ *nf* **1** rosette; (on uniform) cockade; **2** (on vehicle) official badge.

cocasse /kɔkas/ *adj* comical.

coccinelle /kɔksinɛl/ *nf* ladybird, ladybug (US).

coccyx /kɔksis/ *nm* coccyx.

coche /kɔʃ/ *nm* (stage)coach.
IDIOMS **manquer le ~** to miss the boat.

cocher[1] /kɔʃe/ [1] *vtr* to tick (GB), to check (US).

cocher² /kɔʃe/ *nm* coachman; cabman.

cochère /kɔʃɛʀ/ *adj f* **porte ~** carriage entrance.

cochon, -onne /kɔʃɔ̃, ɔn/ **I**○ *adj* **1** [*film*] dirty; [*person*] dirty-minded; **2** [*person*] messy, dirty.
II○ *nm,f* **1** pig○, slob○; **de ~** [*job*] botched; [*weather*] lousy○; **2** sex maniac.
III *nm* **1** (Zool) pig, hog; **2** (Culin) pork.
■ **~ d'Inde** Guinea pig; **~ de lait** suckling pig.

cochonnerie○ /kɔʃɔnʀi/ *nf* **1** junk○; **il ne mange que des ~s** he only eats junk food; **2** mess; **faire des ~s** to make a mess.

cocktail /kɔktɛl/ *nm* **1** cocktail; **2** (figurative) mixture; **3** cocktail party.

coco /koko/ *nm* coconut.

cocon /kɔkɔ̃/ *nm* cocoon.

cocorico /kɔkɔʀiko/ *nm* cock-a-doodle-do.

cocotier /kɔkɔtje/ *nm* coconut palm.

cocotte /kɔkɔt/ *nf* **1**○ (baby talk) hen; **2 ma ~**○ honey; **3** (Culin) casserole (GB), pot.

code /kɔd/ **I** *nm* code.
II codes *nm pl* (of vehicle) dipped (GB) or dimmed (US) (head)lights, low beam.
■ **~ confidentiel** personal identification number, PIN; **~ postal** post code (GB), zip code (US); **~ de la route** (Aut) highway code (GB), rules of the road (US); **passer son ~**○ (Aut) to take the written part of a driving test.

coder /kɔde/ [1] *vtr* to code, to encode.

codifier /kɔdifje/ [2] *vtr* to codify [*laws*]; to standardize [*language, custom*].

codirecteur, -trice /kodiʀɛktœʀ, tʀis/ *nm,f* joint manager; joint director.

coefficient /kɔefisjɑ̃/ *nm* **1** ratio; **2** margin; **3** *weighting factor in an exam*; **la chimie est au ~ 4** chemistry results are multiplied by 4; **4** (in arithmetic, physics) coefficient.

coéquipier, -ière /koekipje, ɛʀ/ *nm,f* team mate.

cœur /kœʀ/ **I** *nm* **1** heart; **il a le ~ malade** he has a heart condition; **serrer qn sur** or **contre son ~** to hold sb close; **écouter son ~** to go with one's feelings; **aller droit au ~ de qn** to touch sb deeply; **avoir un coup de ~ pour qch** to fall in love with sth; **ça me fait mal au ~ de voir** it sickens me to see; **problème de ~** emotional proble; **parler à ~ ouvert** to speak openly; **avoir bon ~** to be kind-hearted; **je n'ai plus le ~ à rien** I don't feel like doing anything any more; **2** (Culin) heart; **3** (figurative) (of fruit, rock) core; (of problem, debate) heart; **au ~ de** (of region, town) in the middle of; (of building, problem, system) at the heart of; **au ~ de l'hiver** in the dead of winter; **4** (person) **mon (petit) ~** sweetheart; **5** courage; **le ~ m'a manqué** my courage failed me; **redonner du ~ à qn** to give sb new heart; **6** (Games) (card) heart; (suit) hearts.
II à cœur *phr* **avoir à ~ de faire** to be intent on doing; **prendre qch à ~** to take sth seriously.
III de bon cœur *phr* willingly; **rire de bon ~** to laugh heartily.
IV par cœur *phr* by heart; **connaître qn par ~** to know sb inside out.
IDIOMS **avoir mal au ~** to feel sick (GB) or nauseous (US); **avoir du ~ au ventre** to be brave; **avoir le ~ sur la main** to be open-handed; **il ne le porte pas dans son ~** he's not his favourite^GB person; **j'irai mais le ~ n'y est pas** I'll go but my heart isn't in it; **si le ~ t'en dit** if you feel like it; **avoir qch sur le ~** to be resentful about sth.

coexister /koegziste/ [1] *vi* to coexist.

coffre /kɔfʀ/ *nm* **1** chest; **~ à jouets** toy box; **2** (for valuables) safe; (individual) safety deposit box; **la salle des ~s** the strongroom; **3** (of car) boot (GB), trunk (US).
IDIOMS **avoir du ~**○ to have a powerful voice.

coffre-fort, *pl* **coffres-forts** /kɔfʀəfɔʀ/ *nm* safe.

coffret /kɔfʀɛ/ *nm* **1** casket; **~ à bijoux** jewellery (GB) or jewelry (US) box; **2** (of records, cassettes, books) boxed set.

cogiter /kɔʒite/ [1] *vi* to cogitate, to think.

cogner /kɔɲe/ [1] **I** *vtr* to knock.
II *vi* **1 ~ contre** [*shutter*] to bang against; [*branch*] to knock against; [*projectile*] to hit; **~ à la porte** to bang on the door; **2**○ [*boxer*] to hit out; **3** [*heart*] to pound.
III se cogner *v refl* (+ *v être*) to bump into something; **se ~ le pied contre une pierre** to stub one's toe on a stone.

cohabiter /koabite/ [1] *vi* [*people*] to live together; [*things*] to coexist.

cohérence /kɔeʀɑ̃s/ *nf* **1** coherence; consistency; **2** (in physics) cohesion.

cohérent, ~e /kɔeʀɑ̃, ɑ̃t/ *adj* coherent; consistent.

cohéritier, -ière /koeʀitje, ɛʀ/ *nm,f* joint heir.

cohésion /kɔezjɔ̃/ *nf* cohesion.

cohorte○ /koɔʀt/ *nf* crowd, group.

cohue /kɔy/ *nf* crowd; **c'est la ~** it's a crush.

coi, coite /kwa, kwat/ *adj* **se tenir ~** to remain quiet.

coiffe /kwaf/ *nf* (gen) headgear; (of nun) wimple.

coiffer /kwafe/ [1] **I** *vtr* **1 ~ qn** to do sb's hair; to comb sb's hair; **2 coiffé d'une casquette** wearing a cap.
II se coiffer *v refl* (+ *v être*) **1** to do or comb one's hair; **2 se ~ de qch** to put sth on.
IDIOMS **~ qn au poteau**○ or **sur le fil**○ to beat sb by a whisker.

coiffeur, -euse¹ /kwafœʀ, øz/ *nm,f* hairdresser.

coiffeuse² /kwaføz/ *nf* dressing table.

coiffure /kwafyʀ/ *nf* **1** hairstyle; **2** hairdressing; **3** headgear.

coin /kwɛ̃/ **I** *nm* **1** corner; **à tous les ~s de rue** everywhere; **aux quatre ~s de la ville** all over the town; **aller au ~** (as punishment) to go and stand in the corner; **j'ai dû poser mon sac dans un ~** I must have put my bag down somewhere; **au ~ du feu** by the fire; **2** (of eye, mouth) corner; **un sourire en ~** a half-smile; **un regard en ~** a sidelong glance; **3** (of ground) plot; (of lawn) patch; **un ~ de paradis**

an idyllic spot; **4** (in region) **un ~ de France** a part of France; **dans le ~** around here, in these parts; around there, in those parts; **le café du ~** the local café; **les gens du ~** the locals; **connaître les bons ~s pour manger** to know all the good places to eat; **5** (for photograph) corner; (for file) reinforcing corner; **6** (Tech) wedge.
II **coin(-)** (*combining form*) **~-repas/-salon** dining/living area.

coincé, **~e** /kwɛ̃se/ **I** *pp* ▶ **coincer**.
II *pp adj* **1** stuck; trapped; **~ entre** [*house*] wedged between; **2**○ **j'ai le dos ~, je suis ~** my back has gone○; **3**○ (figurative) stuck○; **4**○ ill at ease; **5**○ uptight○.

coincer /kwɛ̃se/ [12] **I** *vtr* **1** to wedge [*object*]; to wedge [sth] open/shut [*door*]; [*snow*] to trap [*person*]; **2** to jam [*drawer, zip*]; **3**○ to catch [*person*]; **se faire ~ par** to get caught by; **4**○ to catch [sb] out [*person*].
II *vi* **1** [*zip, drawer*] to stick; **2**○ **ça coince** there's a problem.
III **se coincer** *v refl* (+ *v être*) **1** [*object*] to get stuck or jammed; **2 se ~ les doigts** to get one's fingers caught.

coïncidence /kɔɛ̃sidɑ̃s/ *nf* coincidence.

coïncider /kɔɛ̃side/ [1] *vi* to coincide.

coing /kwɛ̃/ *nm* quince.

coite ▶ **coi**.

col /kɔl/ *nm* **1** collar; **2** (in mountains) pass; **3** (of bottle) neck; **4** (Anat) neck.
■ **~ blanc** white-collar worker.

colère /kɔlɛʀ/ *nf* **1** anger; **être en ~** to be angry; **passer sa ~ sur qn** to take out or vent one's anger on sb; **sous le coup de la ~** in a fit of anger; **2 faire** or **piquer**○ **une ~** to have a fit; to throw a tantrum.

coléreux, **-euse** /kɔleʀø, øz/ *adj* [*person*] quick-tempered.

colifichet /kɔlifiʃɛ/ *nm* trinket; knick-knack.

colimaçon /kɔlimasɔ̃/ *nm* snail; **escalier en ~** spiral staircase.

colin /kɔlɛ̃/ *nm* (fish) hake; coley.

colique /kɔlik/ *nf* **1** diarrhoea; **2** stomach pain; (in babies) colic.

colis /kɔli/ *nm* parcel.
■ **~ piégé** parcel bomb; **~ postal** parcel sent by mail.

colite /kɔlit/ *nf* colitis.

collaborateur, **-trice** /kɔlabɔʀatœʀ, tʀis/ *nm,f* **1** colleague; assistant; **2** employee; **3** (journalist) contributor; **4** (derogatory) collaborator.

collaboration /kɔlabɔʀasjɔ̃/ *nf* **1** (to newspaper) contribution; (work on project) collaboration; **2** (in Second World War) collaboration.

collaborer /kɔlabɔʀe/ [1] *vi* **1 ~ à** to contribute to [*newspaper*]; to collaborate on [*project*]; **2** (as working partner) to collaborate.

collage /kɔlaʒ/ *nm* collage; (in photography) montage.

collant, **~e** /kɔlɑ̃, ɑ̃t/ **I** *adj* **1** [*substance, object*] sticky; **2** [*dress*] skintight.
II *nm* tights (GB), panty hose (US).

collation /kɔlasjɔ̃/ *nf* light meal.

colle /kɔl/ *nf* **1** glue; (wallpaper) paste; **2**○ (hard question) poser○; test; **3**○ (students' slang) detention.

collecte /kɔlɛkt/ *nf* **1** collection; **faire une ~** to raise funds; **2** (prayer) collect.

collecter /kɔlɛkte/ [1] *vtr* to collect.

collectif, **-ive** /kɔlɛktif, iv/ **I** *adj* collective; [*dismissals*] mass; [*heating*] shared; [*ticket*] group.
II *nm* **1** collective; **2** action group.

collection /kɔlɛksjɔ̃/ *nf* **1** collection; **~ de timbres** stamp collection; **2** (of books) series; (by same author) set.

collectionner /kɔlɛksjɔne/ [1] *vtr* **1** to collect; **2** (figurative) **~ les erreurs** to make one mistake after another.

collectionneur, **-euse** /kɔlɛksjɔnœʀ, øz/ *nm,f* collector.

collectivement /kɔlɛktivmɑ̃/ *adv* (gen) collectively; [*resign*] en masse, as a body.

collectivité /kɔlɛktivite/ *nf* **1** group; **2** community.
■ **~ locale** local authority (GB), local government (US).

collège /kɔlɛʒ/ *nm* **1** secondary school (GB), junior high school (US) (*up to age 16*); **2** college; **~ électoral** (Pol) electoral college.
■ **~ d'enseignement secondaire**, **CES** secondary school (GB), junior high school (US); **~ d'enseignement technique**, **CET** *technical secondary school in France*.

collégial, **~e**, *mpl* **-iaux** /kɔleʒjal, o/ *adj* [*church*] collegiate; [*system*] collegial.

collégien, **-ienne** /kɔleʒjɛ̃, ɛn/ *nm,f* schoolboy/schoolgirl.

collègue /kɔlɛg/ *nmf* colleague.

coller /kɔle/ [1] **I** *vtr* **1** to stick, to glue [*wood, paper*]; to paste up [*poster*]; to hang [*wallpaper*]; to stick [sth] on [*label*]; to stick down [*envelope*]; **2 ~ qch contre** or **à qch** to press sth against sth; **il la colla contre le parapet** he pushed her up against the parapet; **3**○ to stick○; **je leur ai collé la facture sous le nez** I stuck the bill (right) under their noses; **~ une amende/une gifle à qn** to fine/slap sb; **4**○ (in exam) **se faire ~** to fail; **5**○ to give [sb] detention [*pupil*].
II *vi* **1** to stick; **2**○ **~ avec** to be consistent or fit with.
III **se coller** *v refl* (+ *v être*) **1 se ~ à** or **contre qn/qch** to press oneself against sb/sth; **2**○ **dès qu'il rentre, il se colle devant son ordinateur** as soon as he comes in he's glued○ to his computer.

collerette /kɔlʀɛt/ *nf* **1** ruff; **2** ruffle.

collet /kɔlɛ/ *nm* **être ~ monté** to be prim.

collier /kɔlje/ *nm* **1** necklace; **~ de perles** string of pearls; **2** (of animal) collar; **3** beard.
IDIOMS **donner un coup de ~** to get one's head down; to put one's back into it.

collimateur /kɔlimatœʀ/ *nm* **avoir qn dans le ~**○ to have it in for sb○.

colline /kɔlin/ *nf* hill.

collision /kɔlizjɔ̃/ *nf* collision.

colloque /kɔl(l)ɔk/ *nm* conference, symposium.

collyre /kɔliʀ/ *nm* eyedrops.

colmater /kɔlmate/ [1] *vtr* to plug, to seal off [*leak*]; to seal [*crack*].

colombe /kɔlɔ̃b/ *nf* dove.

colombier /kɔlɔ̃bje/ *nm* dovecote.

colon /kɔlɔ̃/ *nm* colonist.

côlon /kolɔ̃, kɔlɔ̃/ *nm* colon.

colonel /kɔlɔnɛl/ *nm* (Mil) (in army) ≈ colonel; (in air force) ≈ group captain (GB), ≈ colonel (US).

colonial, **~e**, *mpl* **-iaux** /kɔlɔnjal, o/ *adj*, *nm,f* colonial.

colonialisme /kɔlɔnjalism/ *nm* colonialism.

colonie /kɔlɔni/ *nf* (gen) colony; **~ (de vacances)** holiday camp (*for children*).

colonnade /kɔlɔnad/ *nf* colonnade.

colonne /kɔlɔn/ *nf* column.
■ **~ vertébrale** (Anat) spinal column.

colorant, **~e** /kɔlɔʀɑ̃, ɑ̃t/ **I** *adj* colouring[GB].
II *nm* **1** colouring[GB] agent; **2** dye; **3** (in chemistry) stain; **4** (Culin) colouring[GB].

coloration /kɔlɔʀasjɔ̃/ *nf* **1** colouring[GB]; dyeing; staining; tinting; **2** colour[GB].

coloré, **~e** /kɔlɔʀe/ *adj* **1** (gen) coloured[GB]; **2** [*life, crowd*] colourful[GB]; [*style*] lively.

colorer /kɔlɔʀe/ [1] *vtr* to colour[GB]; to tint; to stain; to dye.

colorier /kɔlɔʀje/ [2] *vtr* to colour in (GB), to color (US).

coloris /kɔlɔʀi/ *nm inv* colour[GB]; shade.

colossal, **~e**, *mpl* **-aux** /kɔlɔsal, o/ *adj* colossal, huge.

colosse /kɔlɔs/ *nm* giant.

colporter /kɔlpɔʀte/ [1] *vtr* **1** to spread [*news*]; **2** to peddle [*goods*].

coltiner○: **se coltiner** /kɔltine/ [1] *v refl* (+ *v être*) **1** to lug○ [*heavy object*]; **2** to get stuck with○ [*chore, person*].

colza /kɔlza/ *nm* rape.

coma /kɔma/ *nm* coma.

comateux, **-euse** /kɔmatø, øz/ *adj* comatose.

combat /kɔ̃ba/ *nm* **1** (Mil) fighting; **~s aériens** air battles; **mettre hors de ~** to disable; **2** (in politics) struggle; **livrer un ~** to campaign; **3** (Sport) bout; **hors de ~** out of action.
■ **~ de coqs** cock fight.

combatif, **-ive** /kɔ̃batif, iv/ *adj* **1** assertive; **2** aggressive.

combativité /kɔ̃bativite/ *nf* fighting spirit.

combattant, **~e** /kɔ̃batɑ̃, ɑ̃t/ *nm,f* combatant.

combattre /kɔ̃batʀ/ [61] *vtr*, *vi* to fight.

combien[1] /kɔ̃bjɛ̃/ **I** *adv* **1 ~ mesure le salon?** how big is the lounge?; **j'aimerais savoir ~ il a payé son costume** I'd like to know how much he paid for that suit; **~ êtes-vous?** how many of you are there?; **2** (to what extent) **je ne saurais te dire ~ il me manque** I can't tell you how much I miss him.
II combien de *det* **1** how many, how much; **2 ~ de temps faut-il?** how long does it take?

combien[2] /kɔ̃bjɛ̃/ *nmf inv* **1 tu es le/la ~?** (in queue) how many people are before you?; **2 le ~ sommes-nous?** what's the date today?; **3** (for measurements) **tu chausses du ~?** what size shoes do you take?; **4 tu le vois tous les ~?** how often do you see him?

combinaison /kɔ̃binɛzɔ̃/ *nf* **1** combining; combination; **2** (of safe) combination; **3** (full-length) slip; **4** jumpsuit; **5** overalls (GB), coveralls (US).
■ **~ de plongée** wetsuit.

combine○ /kɔ̃bin/ *nf* trick○; scheme.

combiné /kɔ̃bine/ *nm* handset, receiver.

combiner /kɔ̃bine/ [1] *vtr* **1** to combine; **2** to work out [*plan*].

comble /kɔ̃bl/ **I** *adj* [*room*] packed.
II *nm* **1 le ~ de l'injustice/du mauvais goût** the height of injustice/of bad taste; **pour ~ de malchance j'ai...** to crown it all, I...; **c'est un** or **le ~**○**!** that's the limit!; **2** roof space; **de fond en ~** from top to bottom; completely.
III combles *nm pl* attic.

combler /kɔ̃ble/ [1] *vtr* **1** to fill (in) [*ditch*]; **2** to fill in [*gaps*]; to make up [*deficit*]; **3** to fulfil[GB] [*need, desire*]; **la vie m'a comblé** I've had a wonderful life; **~ qn** to fill sb with joy.

combustible /kɔ̃bystibl/ **I** *adj* combustible.
II *nm* fuel; **~ nucléaire** nuclear fuel.

combustion /kɔ̃bystjɔ̃/ *nf* combustion.

comédie /kɔmedi/ *nf* **1** comedy; **2** play-acting; **jouer la ~** to put on an act; **3**○ scene; **faire une ~** to make a scene.
■ **~ musicale** musical.

comédien, **-ienne** /kɔmedjɛ̃, ɛn/ **I** *adj* **il est (un peu) ~** (figurative) he puts it on.
II *nm,f* actor/actress.

comestible /kɔmɛstibl/ **I** *adj* edible.
II comestibles *nm pl* food.

comète /kɔmɛt/ *nf* comet.

comique /kɔmik/ **I** *adj* **1** comic; **2** funny.
II *nmf* comic actor/actress; comedian.
III *nm* **1** clown; **2** comedy

comité /kɔmite/ *nm* **1** committee; **2** group.

commandant /kɔmɑ̃dɑ̃/ *nm* (in army) ≈ major; (in air force) ≈ squadron leader (GB), ≈ major (US).
■ **~ de bord** captain.

commande /kɔmɑ̃d/ *nf* **1** order; **2** commission; **passer ~ de qch à qn** to commission sb to do sth; **3** (Tech) control; **levier de ~** control lever; **être aux** or **tenir les ~s** to be at the controls; (figurative) to be in control; **4** (Comput) command.

commandement /kɔmɑ̃dmɑ̃/ *nm* **1** (Mil) command; **2** (in religion) commandment.

commander /kɔmɑ̃de/ [1] **I** *vtr* **1** to order [sth] (**à qn** from sb); **2** to commission [*book, survey*]; **3** (Mil) to command [*army*]; to order [*attack*]; **4 ~ qn** to order sb about; **5 les circonstances commandent la prudence** the circumstances call for caution; **6** [*machine*] to control [*mechanism*].

II commander à *v+prep* **1 ~ à** to be in command of; **2 ~ à** to order, to command.

III *vi* to give the orders, to be in charge.

IV se commander *v refl* (+ *v être*) **ça ne se commande pas** it's not something you can control.

commanditer /kɔmɑ̃dite/ [1] *vtr* **1** to finance [*company*]; **2** to sponsor [*project*]; **3** to be behind [*crime*].

commando /kɔmɑ̃do/ *nm* commando.

comme /kɔm/ **I** *adv* how.

II *conj* **1** as; **ici ~ en Italie** here as in Italy; **il est paresseux, ~ sa sœur d'ailleurs** he's lazy, just like his sister; **jolie ~ tout** really pretty; **2** (in comparisons) **il est grand ~ sa sœur** he's as tall as his sister; **c'est tout ~**○ it comes to the same thing; **elle me traite ~ un enfant** she treats me like a child; **3** like; **un manteau ~ le tien** a coat like yours; **~ ça** like that; **puisque c'est ~ ça** if that's the way it is; **4** as if, as though; **~ pour faire** as if to do; **5**○ **elle a eu ~ un évanouissement** she sort of fainted; **6 avare ~ il est, il ne te donnera rien** he's so mean, he won't give you anything; **7** as; **travailler ~ jardinier** to work as a gardener; **8** as, since; **~ elle était seule** as or since she was alone; **9** as; **~ il traversait la rue** as he was crossing the road.

IDIOMS **~ quoi!** which just shows!; **~ ci ~ ça**○ so-so○.

commémorer /kɔmemɔʀe/ [1] *vtr* to commemorate.

commencement /kɔmɑ̃smɑ̃/ *nm* beginning.

commencer /kɔmɑ̃se/ [12] **I** *vtr* **1** to start, to begin; **2 ~ à** or **de faire** to start or begin to do; **ça commence à bien faire**○**!** it's getting to be a bit much!

II *vi* to start, to begin; **pour ~** for a start; **vous êtes tous coupables à ~ par toi** you're all guilty starting with you.

III *v impers* **il commence à neiger** it's starting or beginning to snow.

comment /kɔmɑ̃/ *adv* **1** how; **~ faire?** how can it be done?; **~ t'appelles-tu?** what's your name?; **~ ça se fait**○**?** how come○?; **2 ~? qu'est-ce que tu dis?** pardon? what did you say?; **Paul ~?** Paul who?; **3 ~ est leur maison/fils?** what's their house/son like?; **~ trouvez-vous ma robe?** what do you think of my dress?; **4 ~ cela?** what do you mean?; **~ donc!** but of course!; **et ~ (donc)**○**!** and how○!; **'c'était bon?'—'et ~**○**!'** 'was it nice?'—'it certainly was!'

commentaire /kɔmmɑ̃tɛʀ/ *nm* **1** comment; **2** commentary.

commentateur, **-trice** /kɔmmɑ̃tatœʀ, tʀis/ *nm,f* commentator.

commenter /kɔmmɑ̃te/ [1] *vtr* **1** to comment on [*decision, event*]; **2** to give a commentary on [*film, visit*]; **3** to commentate on [*match*].

commérage /kɔmeʀaʒ/ *nm* gossip.

commerçant, **~e** /kɔmɛʀsɑ̃, ɑ̃t/ **I** *adj* [*street*] shopping; [*nation*] trading.

II *nm,f* shopkeeper, storekeeper (US); retailer.

commerce /kɔmɛʀs/ *nm* **1** shop, store (US); **dans le ~** in the shops or stores (US); **2** business; **3** trade; **faire le ~ de** to trade in; **faire ~ de** to sell; **faire du ~** to be in business.

commercial, **~e**, *mpl* **-iaux** /kɔmɛʀsjal, o/ **I** *adj* **1** commercial; **carrière ~e** career in sales and marketing; **2** trade.

II *nm,f* sales and marketing person.

commercialiser /kɔmɛʀsjalize/ [1] *vtr* to market.

commère /kɔmɛʀ/ *nf* gossip.

commettre /kɔmɛtʀ/ [60] *vtr* to make [*error*]; to commit [*crime*]; to carry out [*attack*].

commis /kɔmi/ *nm* **1** (in office) clerk; **2** shop assistant (GB), salesclerk (US).

commissaire /kɔmisɛʀ/ *nm* **1 ~ (de police)** ≈ police superintendent; **2** commissioner; **3** (of sports event) steward; (of exhibition) organizer.

commissaire-priseur, *pl* **commissaires-priseurs** /kɔmisɛʀpʀizœʀ/ *nm* auctioneer.

commissariat /kɔmisaʀja/ *nm* **~ (de police)** police station.

commission /kɔmisjɔ̃/ **I** *nf* **1** committee; **2** commission; **payé à la ~** paid on a commission basis; **3** errand; **4 faire la ~ à qn** to give sb the message.

II commissions○ *nf pl* shopping.

commissure /kɔmisyʀ/ *nf* corner.

commode /kɔmɔd/ **I** *adj* **1** (gen) convenient; [*tool*] handy; **2** easy; **3 ne pas être (très) ~** to be strict; to be difficult (to deal with).

II *nf* chest of drawers.

commodité /kɔmɔdite/ *nf* convenience.

commotion /kɔmosjɔ̃/ *nf* **1 ~ (cérébrale)** concussion (*of the brain*); **2** (figurative) shock.

commun, **~e**[1] /kɔmœ̃, yn/ **I** *adj* **1** common; [*policy, property*] joint; [*friend*] mutual; [*room, memories, experience*] shared; **d'un ~ accord** by mutual agreement; **après dix ans de vie ~e** after living together for ten years; **2** [*person, tastes*] common; [*face*] plain; **3 elle est d'une beauté peu ~e** she's uncommonly beautiful.

II *nm* ordinary; **le ~ des mortels** ordinary mortals; **hors du ~** exceptional.

III en commun *phr* [*work, write*] jointly, together; **avoir qch en ~** to have sth in common; **nous mettons tout en ~** we share everything.

communal, **~e**, *mpl* **-aux** /kɔmynal, o/ *adj* [*budget, resources*] local council (GB), local government (US); [*building*] local council (GB), community (US).

communautaire /kɔmynotɛʀ/ *adj* **1** (referring to the EC) [*budget, law*] Community; **2 la vie ~** life in a community.

communauté /kɔmynote/ *nf* **1** community; **2** commune; **vivre en ~** to live in a commune.

■ **Communauté économique européenne, CEE** European Economic Community, EEC.

commune[2] /kɔmyn/ **I** *nf* village; town.

II communes *nf pl* **la Chambre des ~s** the (House of) Commons.

communément /kɔmynemɑ̃/ *adv* generally.

communicatif, **-ive** /kɔmynikatif, iv/ *adj* **1** [*person*] talkative; **2** [*gaiety*] infectious.

communication /kɔmynikasjɔ̃/ *nf* **1 ~ (téléphonique)** (telephone) call; **mettre qn en ~ avec qn** to put sb through to sb; **2** report; (at conference) paper; **3 demander ~ d'un dossier à qn** to ask sb for a file; **4** (between people) communication, contact; **5** (media) communications; **6** (by phone, radio) **moyens de ~** communications.

communier /kɔmynje/ [2] *vi* to receive Communion.

communion /kɔmynjɔ̃/ *nf* **1** Communion; **2** (figurative) communion.
■ **~ (privée)** first communion.

communiqué /kɔmynike/ *nm* **1** communiqué, press release; **2** statement.

communiquer /kɔmynike/ [1] **I** *vtr* **1** to announce [*date, result*]; to give [*address*]; **2** [*person*] to pass on [*document*]; to convey [*idea*].
II *vi* **1** to communicate; **2** [*rooms*] to be adjoining.
III se communiquer *v refl* (+ *v être*) **1** [*people*] to pass [sth] on to each other; **2** [*fire, disease*] to spread.

communisme /kɔmynism/ *nm* communism.

commutateur /kɔmytatœʀ/ *nm* switch.

commuter /kɔmyte/ [1] *vtr* to commute.

compact, **~e** /kɔ̃pakt/ *adj* **1** [*fog, crowd*] dense; [*earth*] compact; **2** [*car*] compact.

compagne /kɔ̃paɲ/ *nf* **1** (female) companion; **2** (female animal) mate.

compagnie /kɔ̃paɲi/ *nf* **1** company; **en ~ de** together with; **2 salut la ~!** hello everybody!; **3** (commercial) company; **4** theatre company.
■ **~ aérienne** airline.

compagnon /kɔ̃paɲɔ̃/ *nm* **1** companion; **2** partner; **3** mate; **4** journeyman.
■ **~ de route** fellow traveller[GB].

comparable /kɔ̃paʀabl/ *adj* comparable.

comparaison /kɔ̃paʀɛzɔ̃/ *nf* **1** comparison; **c'est sans ~ le plus confortable** it's far and away the most comfortable; **2** simile; **3 adjectif de ~** comparative adjective.

comparaître /kɔ̃paʀɛtʀ/ [73] *vi* (Law) to appear.

comparatif, **-ive** /kɔ̃paʀatif, iv/ *adj* comparative.

comparé, **~e** /kɔ̃paʀe/ *adj* [*literature, law*] comparative.

comparer /kɔ̃paʀe/ [1] **I** *vtr* to compare.
II se comparer *v refl* (+ *v être*) **1 se ~ à qn/qch** to compare oneself with sb/sth; **2** to be comparable.

comparse /kɔ̃paʀs/ *nmf* **1** (in theatre) extra; **2** sidekick○.

compartiment /kɔ̃paʀtimɑ̃/ *nm* compartment.

compartimenter /kɔ̃paʀtimɑ̃te/ [1] *vtr* **1 ~ un grenier** to divide up a loft with partitions; **2** (figurative) to compartmentalize [*administration*].

compas /kɔ̃pa/ *nm* compass.

compassion /kɔ̃pasjɔ̃/ *nf* compassion.

compatible /kɔ̃patibl/ *adj* compatible.

compatir /kɔ̃patiʀ/ [3] *vi* to sympathize.

compatissant, **~e** /kɔ̃patisɑ̃, ɑ̃t/ *adj* compassionate.

compatriote /kɔ̃patʀiɔt/ *nmf* fellow-countryman/-countrywoman, compatriot.

compensation /kɔ̃pɑ̃sasjɔ̃/ *nf* compensation.

compensé, **~e** /kɔ̃pɑ̃se/ *adj* **1 semelle ~e** wedge heel; **2** (Med) compensated.

compenser /kɔ̃pɑ̃se/ [1] *vtr* to compensate for; to make up for; to offset.

compère /kɔ̃pɛʀ/ *nm* partner; accomplice.

compétence /kɔ̃petɑ̃s/ *nf* **1** ability; competence, skill; **2** (Law) competence; **relever de la ~ de qn** to fall within the competence of sb; **3** domain.

compétent, **~e** /kɔ̃petɑ̃, ɑ̃t/ *adj* competent.

compétitif, **-ive** /kɔ̃petitif, iv/ *adj* competitive.

compétition /kɔ̃petisjɔ̃/ *nf* competition; **en ~ pour** competing for; **faire de la ~** to compete; **sport de ~** competitive sport.

complaire: **se complaire** /kɔ̃plɛʀ/ [59] *v refl* (+ *v être*) **se ~ à faire** to take pleasure in doing.

complaisance /kɔ̃plɛzɑ̃s/ *nf* **1** kindness; **2** (derogatory) soft attitude; **décrire la situation sans ~** to give an objective assessment of the situation; **3** (derogatory) complacency.

complaisant, **~e** /kɔ̃plɛzɑ̃, ɑ̃t/ *adj* **1** obliging; **2** (derogatory) indulgent; **3** (derogatory) complacent, self-satisfied.

complément /kɔ̃plemɑ̃/ *nm* **1 ~ de salaire** extra payment; **2** (to funding, programme) supplement; **3 ~ de nom** possessive phrase; **~ d'objet direct/indirect** direct object/indirect.

complémentaire /kɔ̃plemɑ̃tɛʀ/ *adj* **1** [*training, information*] further; [*activity, amount*] supplementary; **2** complementary.

complet, **-ète** /kɔ̃plɛ, ɛt/ **I** *adj* **1** (gen) complete; [*failure*] total; [*inquiry, range*] full; [*survey*] comprehensive; **2** [*train, hotel*] full; **être (réuni) au (grand) ~** to be all present.
II *nm* suit; **~ veston** two-/three-piece suit.

complètement /kɔ̃plɛtmɑ̃/ *adv* completely; [*read*] right through; **~ réveillé** fully awake.

compléter /kɔ̃plete/ [14] **I** *vtr* **1** to complete [*collection*]; to top up [*sum*]; **2** [*person*] to complement [*person*]; **3** to complete [*sentence*].
II se compléter *v refl* (+ *v être*) [*elements, people*] to complement each other.

complexe /kɔ̃plɛks/ **I** *adj* complex.
II *nm* **1** (psychological) complex; **il n'a pas de ~** he has no inhibitions; **2** (place) complex; **un ~ sportif** a sports complex.

complexer○ /kɔ̃plekse/ [1] *vtr* to give [sb] a complex.

complexité /kɔ̃plɛksite/ *nf* complexity.

complication /kɔ̃plikasjɔ̃/ *nf* complication.

complice /kɔ̃plis/ **I** *adj* **1 être ~ de qch** to be a party to sth; **2** [*air*] of complicity.
II *nmf* accomplice.

complicité /kɔ̃plisite/ *nf* **1** complicity; **2** bond.

compliment /kɔ̃plimɑ̃/ **I** *nm* compliment.

II compliments *nm pl* (gen) compliments; **(tous) mes ~s!** congratulations!

complimenter /kɔ̃plimɑ̃te/ [1] *vtr* to compliment.

compliqué, ~e /kɔ̃plike/ *adj* complicated; [*mind*] tortuous.

compliquer /kɔ̃plike/ [1] **I** *vtr* to complicate.
II se compliquer *v refl* (+ *v être*) **1** to become more complicated; **2 se ~ la vie** or **l'existence** to make life difficult for oneself.

complot /kɔ̃plo/ *nm* plot.

comploter /kɔ̃plɔte/ [1] *vtr, vi* to plot.

comportement /kɔ̃pɔʀtəmɑ̃/ *nm* **1** (gen) behaviour[GB]; **2** (of sportsman, car) performance.

comporter /kɔ̃pɔʀte/ [1] **I** *vtr* **1** to include; **2** to comprise, to consist of; **3** to entail, to involve.
II se comporter *v refl* (+ *v être*) **1** to behave, to act; **2** [*sportsman, car*] to perform.

composant /kɔ̃pozɑ̃/ *nm* (Tech) component.

composante /kɔ̃pozɑ̃t/ *nf* element; component.

composé, ~e /kɔ̃poze/ **I** *adj* [*salad*] mixed.
II *nm* (in chemistry) compound.

composer /kɔ̃poze/ [1] **I** *vtr* **1** [*elements, people*] to make up; **2** [*person*] to put [sth] together [*programme, menu*]; to select [*team*]; to make up [*bouquet*]; **3** [*artist*] to compose [*piece of music*]; to paint [*picture*]; **4** to dial [*number*].
II se composer *v refl* (+ *v être*) **se ~ de** to be made up of.

compositeur, -trice /kɔ̃pozitœʀ, tʀis/ *nm,f* **1** (Mus) composer; **2** typesetter.

composition /kɔ̃pozisjɔ̃/ *nf* **1** (of government, delegation) make-up; (of team) line-up; (of product) ingredients; (of drug) composition; **2** (of government) formation; (of team) selection; (of list, menu) drawing up; **de ma ~** of my invention; **3** (of piece of music, picture) composition; (of letter) writing; **4** (Sch) end-of-term test; **5** typesetting.
IDIOMS **être de bonne ~** to be good-natured.

composter /kɔ̃pɔste/ [1] *vtr* to (date)stamp; to punch [*ticket*].

compote /kɔ̃pɔt/ *nf* (Culin) stewed fruit, compote.

compréhensif, -ive /kɔ̃pʀeɑ̃sif, iv/ *adj* understanding.

compréhension /kɔ̃pʀeɑ̃sjɔ̃/ *nf* understanding; comprehension.

comprendre /kɔ̃pʀɑ̃dʀ/ [52] **I** *vtr* **1** to understand; **c'est à n'y rien ~** it's completely baffling; **mal ~** to misunderstand; **être compris comme une menace** to be interpreted as a threat; **se faire ~** to make oneself understood; **2** to consist of, to comprise; **3** to include.
II se comprendre *v refl* (+ *v être*) **1** [*people*] to understand each other or one another; **2 je me comprends** I know what I'm trying to say; **3** [*attitude*] to be understandable.

compresse /kɔ̃pʀɛs/ *nf* compress.

compression /kɔ̃pʀɛsjɔ̃/ *nf* **1** (Tech) compression; **2** reduction; **3** cut.

comprimé /kɔ̃pʀime/ *nm* tablet.

comprimer /kɔ̃pʀime/ [1] *vtr* **1** to constrict; to squeeze [*tube*]; **2** (Med) to compress; **3** (Tech) **air comprimé** compressed air.

compris, ~e /kɔ̃pʀi, iz/ **I** *pp* ▶ **comprendre**.
II *pp adj* including; **service ~/non ~** service included/not included.
III tout compris *phr* in total, all in○ (GB).
IV y compris *phr* including.

compromettre /kɔ̃pʀɔmɛtʀ/ [60] **I** *vtr* **1** to endanger, to jeopardize; **2** to compromise [*person*]; to damage [*reputation*].
II se compromettre *v refl* (+ *v être*) to compromise oneself.

compromis /kɔ̃pʀɔmi/ *nm* compromise.

comptabiliser /kɔ̃tabilize/ [1] *vtr* to count.

comptabilité /kɔ̃tabilite/ *nf* **1** accountancy; **2** bookkeeping; **faire sa ~** to do one's accounts; **3** accounts department.

comptable /kɔ̃tabl/ **I** *adj* **1** [*year*] accounting; [*department*] accounts; **2** [*noun*] countable.
II *nmf* accountant; bookkeeper.

comptant /kɔ̃tɑ̃/ *adv* cash.

compte /kɔ̃t/ **I** *nm* **1** count; **faire le ~ de qch** to work out [*expenditure*]; to count (up) [*objects*]; **comment fais-tu ton ~ pour faire...?** (figurative) how do you manage to do...?; **tout ~ fait** all things considered; **en fin de ~** at the end of the day; **2** (of money) amount; (of objects, people) number; **il n'y a pas le ~** that's not the right amount; that's not the right number; **il a son ~**○ he's done for○; (drunk) he's had a drop too much; **nous avons eu notre ~ d'ennuis** (figurative) we've had more than our fair share of problems; **à ce ~-là** in that case; **3 prendre qch en ~, tenir ~ de qch** to take sth into account; **4 être** or **travailler à son ~** to be self-employed; **pour le ~ de qn** on behalf of sb; **y trouver son ~** to get something out of it; **5** account; **~ en banque** bank account; **mettre qch sur le ~ de qn** to charge sth to sb's account; (figurative) to put sth down to sb; **6 rendre ~ de qch à qn** to give an account of sth to sb; to account for sth to sb; **devoir rendre des ~s à qn** to be answerable to sb; **demander des ~s à qn** to ask for an explanation from sb; **7 se rendre ~ de** to realize; to notice; **8 dire qch sur le ~ de qn** to say sth about sb; **9** (Sport) (in boxing) count.
II à bon compte *phr* **s'en tirer à bon ~** to get off lightly.
■ **~ chèques** current account (GB), checking account (US); **~ chèque postal, CCP** post office account; **~ à rebours** countdown.

compte-gouttes /kɔ̃tgut/ *nm inv* dropper; **au ~** (figurative) sparingly.

compter /kɔ̃te/ [1] **I** *vtr* **1** to count; **on compte deux millions de chômeurs** there is a total of two million unemployed; **il a toujours compté ses sous** he has always watched the pennies; **sans ~** [*give, spend*] freely; **ses jours sont ~s** his/her days are numbered; **2 ~ une bouteille pour trois** to allow a bottle between three people; **3** (as fee, price) **~ qch à qn** to charge sb for sth; **4** to count, to include; **sans**

~ les soucis not to mention the worry; **5** to have; **notre club compte des gens célèbres** our club has some well-known people among its members; **6 ~ faire** to intend to do; **7 il comptait que je lui prête de l'argent** he expected me to lend him some money.

II *vi* **1** to count; **~ au nombre de**, **~ parmi** to be counted among; **2** to matter; **c'est l'intention qui compte** it's the thought that counts; **ça compte beaucoup pour moi** it means a lot to me; **3** to count; **ça ne compte pas, il a triché** it doesn't count, he cheated; **4 ~ avec** to reckon with; to take [sb/sth] into account; **~ sans** not to take [sb/sth] into account; **5 ~ sur** to count on [*person, help*]; (for support) to rely on [*person, resource*]; (in anticipation) to reckon on [*sum, income*].

III se compter *v refl* (+ *v être*) **leurs victoires se comptent par douzaines** they have had dozens of victories.

IV à compter de *phr* as from.

V sans compter que *phr* and what is more; especially as.

compte(-)rendu, *pl* **comptes(-)rendus** /kɔ̃tʀɑ̃dy/ *nm* (gen) report; (of book) review.

compteur /kɔ̃tœʀ/ *nm* meter; clock.

■ **~ kilométrique** ≈ milometer; **~ de vitesse** speedometer.

comptine /kɔ̃tin/ *nf* nursery rhyme.

comptoir /kɔ̃twaʀ/ *nm* **1** (of café) bar; **2** (of shop) counter.

comte /kɔ̃t/ *nm* (title) count; earl.

comtesse /kɔ̃tɛs/ *nf* countess.

con●, **conne** /kɔ̃, kɔn/ *nm,f* bloody◑ idiot (GB), stupid jerk○; **idée à la ~** lousy○ idea.

concasser /kɔ̃kase/ [1] *vtr* (Culin, Tech) to crush.

concave /kɔ̃kav/ *adj* concave.

concéder /kɔ̃sede/ [14] *vtr* to concede.

concentration /kɔ̃sɑ̃tʀasjɔ̃/ *nf* concentration.

concentré, **~e** /kɔ̃sɑ̃tʀe/ **I** *pp* ▶ **concentrer**.

II *pp adj* **1 un air ~** a look of concentration; **2** concentrated; [*lait*] condensed.

III *nm* (Culin) **~ de tomate** tomato purée (GB) or paste (US).

concentrer /kɔ̃sɑ̃tʀe/ [1] **I** *vtr* to concentrate.

II se concentrer *v refl* (+ *v être*) to concentrate; [*attention*] to be concentrated.

concept /kɔ̃sɛpt/ *nm* concept.

conception /kɔ̃sɛpsjɔ̃/ *nf* **1** conception; **2** design; **3** idea.

concernant /kɔ̃sɛʀnɑ̃/ *prep* **1** concerning; **2** as regards, with regard to.

concerner /kɔ̃sɛʀne/ [1] *vtr* **1** to concern; **2** to affect.

concert /kɔ̃sɛʀ/ **I** *nm* (Mus) concert.

II de concert *phr* **ils ont agi de ~** they worked together.

concertation /kɔ̃sɛʀtasjɔ̃/ *nf* **1** consultation; **2** cooperation.

concerter: **se concerter** /kɔ̃sɛʀte/ [1] *v refl* (+ *v être*) to consult each other.

concerto /kɔ̃sɛʀto/ *nm* concerto.

concession /kɔ̃sesjɔ̃/ *nf* **1** (compromise) concession; **film sans ~s** uncompromising film; **2** (awarding of right) concession (**de** of); **3** (right, contract) (of mine, site) concession; (Aut) dealership.

concessionnaire /kɔ̃sesjɔnɛʀ/ *nmf* (commercial) agent; (Aut) dealer.

concevoir /kɔ̃s(ə)vwaʀ/ [5] **I** *vtr* **1** to design [*product, system*]; **2** to conceive [*child*]; **3** to understand [*attitude*]; **4** to see [*phenomenon, activity*]; **5** (formal) to conceive [*hatred*].

II se concevoir *v refl* (+ *v être*) **1** to be conceivable; **2** to be understandable.

concierge /kɔ̃sjɛʀʒ/ *nmf* caretaker (GB), superintendant (US).

concile /kɔ̃sil/ *nm* council.

conciliation /kɔ̃siljasjɔ̃/ *nf* conciliation.

concilier /kɔ̃silje/ [2] *vtr* to reconcile.

concis, **~e** /kɔ̃si, iz/ *adj* concise.

concision /kɔ̃sizjɔ̃/ *nf* conciseness.

concitoyen, **-enne** /kɔ̃sitwajɛ̃, ɛn/ *nm,f* fellow-citizen.

conclave /kɔ̃klav/ *nm* conclave.

concluant, **~e** /kɔ̃klyɑ̃, ɑ̃t/ *adj* conclusive.

conclure /kɔ̃klyʀ/ [78] *vtr* **1** to conclude (**que** that); **2** to conclude [*deal, agreement*]; **'marché conclu!'** 'it's a deal!'; **3** [*person*] to conclude [*speech*]; **4** to bring [sth] to a close [*festival*].

conclusion /kɔ̃klyzjɔ̃/ **I** *nf* **1** conclusion; **tirer les ~s d'une expérience** to learn from an experience; **ne tire pas de ~s hâtives** don't jump to conclusions; **2** (of deal, treaty) conclusion; **3** (of speech, session) close.

II conclusions *nf pl* **1** (of analysis, autopsy) results; (of inquiry) findings; **2** (Law) (of expert) opinion; (of jury) verdict; (of plaintiff) pleadings.

concocter○ /kɔ̃kɔkte/ [1] *vtr* to concoct [*dish*]; to devise [*programme*].

concombre /kɔ̃kɔ̃bʀ/ *nm* cucumber.

concordance /kɔ̃kɔʀdɑ̃s/ *nf* concordance; compatibility.

■ **~ des temps** sequence of tenses.

concorder /kɔ̃kɔʀde/ [1] *vi* [*results, evidence*] to tally; [*estimates*] to agree.

concourir /kɔ̃kuʀiʀ/ [26] **I** *vi* to compete.

II concourir à *v+prep* **~ à qch/à faire** [*factors*] to combine to bring about sth/to do; [*factor, person*] to help bring about sth/do.

concours /kɔ̃kuʀ/ *nm inv* **1** (gen) competition; (agricultural) show; **~ de beauté** beauty contest; **2** competitive examination; **~ d'entrée** entrance examination; **3** help, assistance; support; cooperation.

■ **~ de circonstances** combination of circumstances.

concret, **-ète** /kɔ̃kʀɛ, ɛt/ *adj* **1** [*result*] concrete; **2** [*mind, person*] practical.

concrètement /kɔ̃kʀɛtmɑ̃/ *adv* **1** in concrete terms; **2** in practical terms.

concrétiser /kɔ̃kʀetize/ [1] **I** *vtr* to make [sth] a reality [*plan, project*].

II se concrétiser *v refl* (+ *v être*) [*dream*] to become a reality; [*offer*] to materialize.

concubinage /kɔ̃kybinaʒ/ *nm* cohabitation.

concurrence /kɔ̃kyʀɑ̃s/ *nf* competition; **prix défiant toute ~** unbeatable price; **jusqu'à ~ de** up to a limit of.

concurrencer /kɔ̃kyʀɑ̃se/ [12] *vtr* to compete with.

concurrent, **~e** /kɔ̃kyʀɑ̃, ɑ̃t/ **I** *adj* rival.
II *nm,f* (for a job) rival; (Sport) competitor; (in competitive examination) candidate.

condamnable /kɔ̃danabl/ *adj* reprehensible.

condamnation /kɔ̃danasjɔ̃/ *nf* **1** (Law) conviction; sentence; **2** condemnation.

condamné, **~e** /kɔ̃dane/ **I** *adj* **1** [*person*] terminally ill; **2** [*door*] sealed up.
II *nm,f* convicted prisoner.

condamner /kɔ̃dane/ [1] *vtr* **1** (Law) to sentence; **~ qn à une amende** to fine sb; **~ qn pour vol** to convict sb of theft; **2** [*law*] to punish [*thieving, smuggling*]; **3** [*person, country*] to condemn [*act, decision*]; **4 ~ qn à faire** to compel sb to do; **5** to seal up [*window*]; to shut up [*room*]; **6** (figurative) to spell death for [*society, industry*]; **7 les médecins l'ont condamné** the doctors have given up hope of saving him.

condensation /kɔ̃dɑ̃sasjɔ̃/ *nf* condensation.

condensé /kɔ̃dɑ̃se/ *nm* summary; digest.

condenser /kɔ̃dɑ̃se/ [1] *vtr*, **se condenser** *v refl* (+ *v être*) to condense.

condescendance /kɔ̃desɑ̃dɑ̃s/ *nf* condescension.

condescendant, **~e** /kɔ̃desɑ̃dɑ̃, ɑ̃t/ *adj* condescending.

condiment /kɔ̃dimɑ̃/ *nm* (Culin) seasoning; condiment.

condisciple /kɔ̃disipl/ *nmf* fellow student.

condition /kɔ̃disjɔ̃/ **I** *nf* **1** condition; **à ~ d'avoir le temps** provided (that) one has the time; **sous ~** [*freed*] conditionally; **sans ~(s)** [*acceptance*] unconditional; [*accept*] unconditionally; **imposer ses ~s** to impose one's own terms; **~ préalable** precondition; **2** (Law) (of contract, treaty) term; **3 la ~ ouvrière** (the conditions of) working-class life; **4 ~ (sociale)** social status.
II conditions *nf pl* **1** conditions; **dans ces ~s** in these conditions; in that case; **2** terms.

conditionnel, **-elle** /kɔ̃disjɔnɛl/ **I** *adj* conditional.
II *nm* conditional.

conditionner /kɔ̃disjɔne/ [1] *vtr* **1** to condition; **2** to package.

condoléances /kɔ̃dɔleɑ̃s/ *nf pl* condolences.

condom /kɔ̃dɔm/ *nm* condom.

condor /kɔ̃dɔʀ/ *nm* condor.

conducteur, **-trice** /kɔ̃dyktœʀ, tʀis/ **I** *adj* **1** conductive; **2** [*principle*] guiding.
II *nm,f* (of vehicle) driver.
III *nm* conductor.

conduire /kɔ̃dɥiʀ/ [69] **I** *vtr* **1** to take [*person*]; (in car) to drive; **2** [*leader, studies*] to lead; **la route qui conduit à Oxford** the road that goes to Oxford; **~ qn au désespoir** to drive sb to despair; **3** to drive [*car, train*]; to ride [*motorbike*]; **4** to conduct [*research*]; to carry out [*project*]; to run [*business*]; **5** to conduct [*electricity, heat*].
II se conduire *v refl* (+ *v être*) to behave.

conduit /kɔ̃dɥi/ *nm* **1** conduit; **2** (Anat) canal.
■ **~ de fumée** flue; **~ de ventilation** ventilation shaft.

conduite /kɔ̃dɥit/ *nf* **1** behaviour[GB]; (of pupil) conduct; **2** (of inquiry) conducting; (of building works) supervision; (of company) management; **3** (of vehicle) driving; (of motorbike) riding; **4** (Aut) **voiture avec ~ à gauche** left-hand drive car; **5** (exam) driving test; **6** pipe.

cône /kon/ *nm* cone.

confection /kɔ̃fɛksjɔ̃/ *nf* **1** clothing industry; **2** making.

confectionner /kɔ̃fɛksjɔne/ [1] *vtr* (gen) to make; to prepare [*meal*].

confédération /kɔ̃fedeʀasjɔ̃/ *nf* confederation.
■ **la Confédération helvétique** Switzerland.

confédéré, **~e** /kɔ̃fedeʀe/ *adj* confederate.

conférence /kɔ̃feʀɑ̃s/ *nf* **1** lecture; **2** conference; **3** debate.
■ **~ au sommet** summit meeting.

conférencier, **-ière** /kɔ̃feʀɑ̃sje, ɛʀ/ *nm,f* speaker; lecturer.

conférer /kɔ̃feʀe/ [14] *vtr* to give; to confer.

confesser /kɔ̃fese/ [1] **I** *vtr* **1** to confess [*sin*]; **2 ~ qn** to hear sb's confession.
II se confesser *v refl* (+ *v être*) **1** to go to confession; **2 se ~ à un ami** to confide in a friend.

confession /kɔ̃fesjɔ̃/ *nf* **1** confession; **2** faith.

confessionnal, *pl* **-aux** /kɔ̃fesjɔnal, o/ *nm* confessional.

confetti /kɔ̃feti/ *nm* confetti.

confiance /kɔ̃fjɑ̃s/ *nf* **1** trust; **de ~** [*person*] trustworthy; [*mission*] which requires trust; **avoir ~ en qn**, **faire ~ à qn** to trust sb; **mettre qn en ~** to win sb's trust; **2** (in ability, self) confidence; **~ en soi** (self-)confidence.

confiant, **~e** /kɔ̃fjɑ̃, ɑ̃t/ *adj* **1** confident; **2** (self-)confident; **3** trusting.

confidence /kɔ̃fidɑ̃s/ *nf* secret, confidence; **être dans la ~** to be in on the secret.

confident, **~e** /kɔ̃fidɑ̃, ɑ̃t/ *nm,f* confidant/confidante.

confidentiel, **-ielle** /kɔ̃fidɑ̃sjɛl/ *adj* confidential.

confier /kɔ̃fje/ [2] **I** *vtr* **1 ~ qch à qn** to entrust sb with sth [*mission*]; to entrust sth to sb [*money, letters*]; **2 ~ qch à qn** to confide sth to sb [*intentions*].
II se confier *v refl* (+ *v être*) to confide.

configuration /kɔ̃figyʀasjɔ̃/ *nf* **1** shape; **la ~ des lieux** the layout of the premises; **2** configuration; **3** set-up.

confiné, **~e** /kɔ̃fine/ *adj* **1** [*atmosphere*] stuffy; [*air*] stale; **2** [*space*] confined, restricted.

confiner /kɔ̃fine/ [1] **I** *vtr* to confine.
II confiner à *v+prep* to border on.
III se confiner *v refl* (+ *v être*) to shut oneself away or up.

confins /kɔ̃fɛ̃/ *nm pl* boundaries.

confirmation /kɔ̃fiʀmasjɔ̃/ *nf* confirmation.

confirmer /kɔ̃fiʀme/ [1] **I** *vtr* to confirm [*order, fact*]; to uphold [*decision*]; to be evidence of [*attitude, quality*]; to affirm [*intention*].
II se confirmer *v refl* (+ *v être*) [*news*] to be confirmed; [*testimony*] to be corroborated.

confiserie /kɔ̃fizʀi/ *nf* **1** confectioner's (shop); **2** confectionery.

confisquer /kɔ̃fiske/ [1] *vtr* to confiscate, to seize.

confit, **~e** /kɔ̃fi, it/ **I** *adj* [*fruits*] crystallized.
II *nm* confit; **~ de canard** confit of duck.

confiture /kɔ̃fityʀ/ *nf* (Culin) jam, preserve; marmalade.
IDIOMS **donner de la ~ aux cochons** to cast pearls before swine.

conflictuel, **-elle** /kɔ̃fliktɥɛl/ *adj* [*subject*] controversial; [*relationship*] confrontational.

conflit /kɔ̃fli/ *nm* conflict.
■ **~ de générations** generation gap; **~ social** industrial strife.

confluence /kɔ̃flyɑ̃s/ *nf* confluence; (figurative) convergence.

confluent /kɔ̃flyɑ̃/ *nm* confluence.

confondre /kɔ̃fɔ̃dʀ/ [53] **I** *vtr* **1** to mix up, to confuse; **tous secteurs confondus** all sectors taken together; **2** to merge; **3** (formal) to stagger, to amaze; **4** to expose [*traitor*].
II se confondre *v refl* (+ *v être*) **1** [*shapes, colours*] to merge; [*events, facts*] to become confused; **2** [*interests, hopes*] to coincide; **3** (formal) **se ~ en excuses** to apologize profusely.

conforme /kɔ̃fɔʀm/ *adj* **1 être ~ à** to comply with [*regulations*]; **2 être ~ à l'original** to conform to the original.

conformément /kɔ̃fɔʀmemɑ̃/ *adv* **~ à** in accordance with.

conformer: **se conformer** /kɔ̃fɔʀme/ [1] *v refl* (+ *v être*) to comply with [*regulations*].

conformisme /kɔ̃fɔʀmism/ *nm* conformity.

conformité /kɔ̃fɔʀmite/ *nf* **1 ~ à la loi** compliance with the law; **en ~ avec** [*act*] in accordance with; **2** similarity; **vérifier la ~ de la traduction à l'original** to check that the translation is faithful to the original; **3** (of tastes, points of view) correspondence.

confort /kɔ̃fɔʀ/ *nm* comfort; **maison tout ~** house with all mod cons○ (GB) or modern conveniences.

confortable /kɔ̃fɔʀtabl/ *adj* comfortable.

conforter /kɔ̃fɔʀte/ [1] *vtr* to consolidate [*position*]; to reinforce [*situation*].

confrère /kɔ̃fʀɛʀ/ *nm* (at work) colleague; (in association) fellow member.

confrérie /kɔ̃fʀeʀi/ *nf* brotherhood.

confrontation /kɔ̃fʀɔ̃tasjɔ̃/ *nf* **1** (of ideas, witnesses) confrontation; (of texts) comparison; **2** (between people) debate; clash.

confronter /kɔ̃fʀɔ̃te/ [1] *vtr* **1** to confront [*witnesses*]; **2** to compare [*texts*].

confus, **~e** /kɔ̃fy, yz/ *adj* **1** confused; **2** [*feeling, fear*] vague; **3** sorry; embarrassed.

confusément /kɔ̃fyzemɑ̃/ *adv* [*explain*] confusedly; [*feel*] vaguely.

confusion /kɔ̃fyzjɔ̃/ *nf* **1** confusion; **2** embarrassment; **3** mix-up.

congé /kɔ̃ʒe/ *nm* **1** leave; **prendre quatre jours de ~** to take four days off; **être en ~ de maladie** to be on sick leave; **2** notice; **donner (son) ~ à qn** to give sb notice; **3 prendre ~ de qn** to take leave of sb.

congédier /kɔ̃ʒedje/ [2] *vtr* to dismiss.

congélateur /kɔ̃ʒelatœʀ/ *nm* freezer; (in refrigerator) freezer compartment.

congeler /kɔ̃ʒle/ [17] **I** *vtr* to freeze; **produits congelés** frozen foods.
II se congeler *v refl* (+ *v être*) to freeze.

congénital, **~e**, *mpl* **-aux** /kɔ̃ʒenital, o/ *adj* congenital.

congère /kɔ̃ʒɛʀ/ *nf* snowdrift.

congestion /kɔ̃ʒɛstjɔ̃/ *nf* congestion.
■ **~ cérébrale** stroke.

congestionner /kɔ̃ʒɛstjɔne/ [1] *vtr* **1 il est tout congestionné** he's all flushed; **2** to congest [*street*].

congrégation /kɔ̃gʀegasjɔ̃/ *nf* congregation; (humorous) assembly.

congrès /kɔ̃gʀɛ/ *nm* conference; **le Congrès** (US) Congress.

conifère /kɔnifɛʀ/ *nm* conifer.

conique /kɔnik/ *adj* cone-shaped.

conjecture /kɔ̃ʒɛktyʀ/ *nf* conjecture; **vaines ~s** idle speculation.

conjoint, **~e** /kɔ̃ʒwɛ̃, ɛt/ **I** *adj* [*action*] joint; [*questions*] linked.
II *nm,f* spouse; **les ~s** the husband and wife.

conjonction /kɔ̃ʒɔ̃ksjɔ̃/ *nf* conjunction.

conjonctivite /kɔ̃ʒɔ̃ktivit/ *nf* conjunctivitis.

conjoncture /kɔ̃ʒɔ̃ktyʀ/ *nf* situation; circumstances.

conjoncturel, **-elle** /kɔ̃ʒɔ̃ktyʀɛl/ *adj* [*situation*] economic.

conjugaison /kɔ̃ʒygɛzɔ̃/ *nf* **1** (of verb) conjugation; **2** (figurative) combination.

conjugal, **~e**, *mpl* **-aux** /kɔ̃ʒygal, o/ *adj* [*love*] conjugal; [*life*] married.

conjugalement /kɔ̃ʒygalmɑ̃/ *adv* [*live*] as man and wife.

conjuguer /kɔ̃ʒyge/ [1] *vtr* **1** to conjugate [*verbe*]; **2** to combine [*efforts*].

conjuration /kɔ̃ʒyʀasjɔ̃/ *nf* **1** conspiracy; **2** (of evil spirits) conjuration.

conjurer /kɔ̃ʒyʀe/ [1] *vtr* **1** to avert [*crisis*]; to ward off [*danger*]; **2 je vous en conjure** I beg you.

connaissance /kɔnɛsɑ̃s/ *nf* **1** knowledge; **prendre ~ d'un texte** to acquaint oneself with a text; **en ~ de cause** with full knowledge of the facts; **2** consciousness; **sans ~** unconscious; **3** acquaintance; **faire (plus ample) ~ avec qn** to get to know sb (better); **en pays de ~** among familiar faces; on familiar ground.

connaisseur, **-euse** /kɔnɛsœʀ, øz/ *nm,f* connoisseur, expert.

connaître /kɔnɛtʀ/ [73] **I** *vtr* **1** to know; **faire ~ à qn** to make [sth] known to sb [*decision*]; to introduce sb to [*music*]; **je l'ai connu en Chine** I met him in China; **tu connais la nouvelle?** have you heard the news?; **2** to experience [*hunger, failure*]; to enjoy [*success*]; to have [*difficulties*]; **~ une forte croissance** to show a rapid growth.
II se connaître *v refl* (+ *v être*) **1** to know oneself; **2** to know each other; **ils se sont connus à Rome** they met in Rome; **3 s'y ~ en vin** to know all about wine.
IDIOMS **on connaît la chanson** or **musique!** we've heard it all before!; **~ qch comme sa poche** to know sth like the back of one's hand.

conne• ▸ **con**.

connecter /kɔnɛkte/ [1] *vtr* to connect.

connexion /kɔnɛksjɔ̃/ *nf* connection.

connivence /kɔnivɑ̃s/ *nf* connivance; **signe de ~** sign of complicity.

connotation /kɔnɔtasjɔ̃/ *nf* connotation.

conquérant, **~e** /kɔ̃keʀɑ̃, ɑ̃t/ *nm,f* conqueror.

conquérir /kɔ̃keʀiʀ/ [35] *vtr* to conquer; to capture [*market*]; to win over [*audience*].
IDIOMS **se croire en pays** or **terrain conquis** to lord it over everyone.

conquête /kɔ̃kɛt/ *nf* conquest.

conquis, **~e** ▸ **conquérir**.

consacré, **~e** /kɔ̃sakʀe/ *adj* **formule ~e** time-honoured[GB] expression; **artiste ~** recognized artist.

consacrer /kɔ̃sakʀe/ [1] **I** *vtr* **1** to devote; **pouvez-vous me ~ un instant?** can you spare me a moment?; **2** to sanction; **3** to consecrate.
II se consacrer *v refl* (+ *v être*) **se ~ à** to devote oneself to.

consanguin, **~e** /kɔ̃sɑ̃gɛ̃, in/ *adj* [*marriage*] between blood relations.

consciemment /kɔ̃sjamɑ̃/ *adv* consciously.

conscience /kɔ̃sjɑ̃s/ *nf* **1** conscience; **avoir bonne/mauvaise ~** to have a clear/a guilty conscience; **2** awareness; **prendre ~ de** to become aware of; **prise de ~** realization; **perdre ~** to lose consciousness.
■ **~ professionnelle** conscientiousness.

consciencieux, **-ieuse** /kɔ̃sjɑ̃sjø, øz/ *adj* conscientious.

conscient, **~e** /kɔ̃sjɑ̃, ɑ̃t/ *adj* **1** aware; **2** conscious.

conscrit /kɔ̃skʀi/ *nm* conscript (GB), draftee (US).

consécration /kɔ̃sekʀasjɔ̃/ *nf* **1** (of author) recognition; **2** consecration.

consécutif, **-ive** /kɔ̃sekytif, iv/ *adj* consecutive; **~ à** resulting from; following.

conseil /kɔ̃sɛj/ *nm* **1** advice; **quelques ~s de prudence** a few words of warning; **il est de bon ~** he always gives good advice; **~s d'entretien** cleaning or care instructions; **2** council; **3** consultant.
■ **~ d'administration** board of directors; **~ de classe** (Sch) staff meeting; **~ de discipline** disciplinary committee; **~ général** *council of a French department*.

conseiller[1], **-ère** /kɔ̃seje, ɛʀ/ **I** *nm,f* **1** adviser[GB]; **2** counsellor[GB].
II *nm* councillor[GB].
■ **~ d'État** member of the Council of State; **~ général** *councillor*[GB] *for a French department*; **~ municipal** town councillor[GB]; **~ d'orientation** careers adviser.

conseiller[2] /kɔ̃seje/ [1] *vtr* to recommend; to advise; **~ à qn de faire** to advise sb to do.

consentant, **~e** /kɔ̃sɑ̃tɑ̃, ɑ̃t/ *adj* willing; (Law) consenting.

consentement /kɔ̃sɑ̃tmɑ̃/ *nm* consent.

consentir /kɔ̃sɑ̃tiʀ/ [30] **I** *vtr* to grant; to allow.
II consentir à *v+prep* **~ à qch/à faire** to agree to sth/to do.

conséquence /kɔ̃sekɑ̃s/ *nf* consequence; **être lourd de ~s** to have serious consequences; **sans ~(s)** of no consequence; **ne pas tirer à ~** to be of no consequence; **avoir pour ~ le chômage** to result in unemployment; **agir en ~** to act accordingly; **avoir des qualifications et un salaire en ~** to have qualifications and a corresponding salary.

conséquent, **~e** /kɔ̃sekɑ̃, ɑ̃t/ **I** *adj* **1** substantial; **2** consistent.
II par conséquent *phr* therefore, as a result.

conservateur, **-trice** /kɔ̃sɛʀvatœʀ, tʀis/ **I** *adj* **1** conservative; **2 produit ~** preservative.
II *nm,f* **1** conservative; **2** (museum) curator.

conservation /kɔ̃sɛʀvasjɔ̃/ *nf* conservation; preservation; **lait longue ~** long-life milk (GB).

conservatoire /kɔ̃sɛʀvatwaʀ/ *nm* academy; **~ de musique** conservatoire.

conserve /kɔ̃sɛʀv/ **I** *nf* **1 la ~, les ~s** canned food; **boîte de ~** can; **2** preserve.
II de conserve *phr* [*act*] in concert.

conserver /kɔ̃sɛʀve/ [1] *vtr* **1** to keep; to retain; **~ l'anonymat** to remain anonymous; **2** (Culin) to preserve; (in vinegar) to pickle; **3** [*activity*] to keep [sb] young.

conserverie /kɔ̃sɛʀvəʀi/ *nf* **1** cannery, canning plant; **2** canning industry.

considérable /kɔ̃sideʀabl/ *adj* considerable, significant; **l'enjeu est ~** the stakes are high.

considération /kɔ̃sideʀasjɔ̃/ *nf* **1** consideration; **prendre qch en ~** to consider sth, to take sth into account; **en ~ de** in view of; **sans ~ de** irrespective of; **2** consideration, factor; **3** respect, esteem.

considérer /kɔ̃sideʀe/ [14] **I** *vtr* **1** to consider, to take into account; **2** to consider, to regard; **~ qn/qch comme (étant)** to consider sb/sth to be, to regard sb/sth as being; **être bien considéré** to be highly regarded.
II se considérer *v refl* (+ *v être*) **se ~ (comme) 1** to consider oneself (to be); **2** to regard one another as being.

consigne /kɔ̃siɲ/ *nf* **1** orders, instructions; **passer la ~ à qn** to pass the word on to sb;

'~s à suivre en cas d'incendie' 'fire regulations'; **2** left luggage office (GB), baggage checkroom (US); **3** (on bottle) deposit.
■ **~ automatique** left luggage lockers (GB), baggage lockers (US).

consigné, **~e** /kɔ̃siɲe/ *adj* [*bottle*] returnable.

consigner /kɔ̃siɲe/ [1] *vtr* **1** to record, to write down; **2** to confine [*soldier*]; to give [sb] detention [*pupil*].

consistance /kɔ̃sistɑ̃s/ *nf* **1** consistency; **avoir de la/manquer de ~** to be quite thick/to be too runny; **2** substance, weight; **sans ~** [*person*] spineless; [*rumour*] groundless.

consistant, **~e** /kɔ̃sistɑ̃, ɑ̃t/ *adj* [*meal, investment*] substantial; [*dish*] nourishing.

consister /kɔ̃siste/ [1] *vi* **1 ~ en** or **dans** to consist in; **~ à faire** to consist in doing; **2 ~ en** to consist of, to be made up of; **en quoi consiste cette aide?** what form does this aid take?

consolation /kɔ̃sɔlasjɔ̃/ *nf* consolation.

console /kɔ̃sɔl/ *nf* console.

consoler /kɔ̃sɔle/ [1] **I** *vtr* to console; **si ça peut te ~** if it is any comfort to you.
II se consoler *v refl* (+ *v être*) to find consolation; **se ~ de** to get over.

consolider /kɔ̃sɔlide/ [1] **I** *vtr* to consolidate, to strengthen.
II se consolider *v refl* (+ *v être*) **1** to grow stronger, to be strengthened; **2** to consolidate.

consommateur, **-trice** /kɔ̃sɔmatœʀ, tʀis/ *nm,f* **1** consumer; **2** (in bar) customer.

consommation /kɔ̃sɔmasjɔ̃/ *nf* **1** consumption; **faire une grande ~ de** to use a lot of; **de ~** [*goods, society*] consumer; **2** drink; **3** consummation.

consommé, **~e** /kɔ̃sɔme/ *nm* consommé.

consommer /kɔ̃sɔme/ [1] *vtr* **1** to consume; to use; **2** to eat [*food*]; to drink [*tea*]; to take [*drugs*].

consonance /kɔ̃sɔnɑ̃s/ *nf* consonance; **mot aux ~s étrangères** foreign-sounding word.

consonne /kɔ̃sɔn/ *nf* consonant.

conspirateur, **-trice** /kɔ̃spiʀatœʀ, tʀis/ *nm,f* conspirator.

conspiration /kɔ̃spiʀasjɔ̃/ *nf* conspiracy.

conspirer /kɔ̃spiʀe/ [1] **I** *vi* to conspire, to plot.
II conspirer à *v+prep* to conspire to bring about; **~ à faire** to conspire to do.

constamment /kɔ̃stamɑ̃/ *adv* constantly.

constance /kɔ̃stɑ̃s/ *nf* **1** consistency; constancy; **2** steadfastness.

constant, **~e**[1] /kɔ̃stɑ̃, ɑ̃t/ *adj* **1** constant; consistent; **2** continuous; continual.

constante[2] /kɔ̃stɑ̃t/ *nf* constant.

constat /kɔ̃sta/ *nm* (Law) certified or official report.
■ **~ (à l')amiable** *accident report drawn up by the parties involved.*

constatation /kɔ̃statasjɔ̃/ *nf* observation.

constater /kɔ̃state/ [1] *vtr* **1** to notice, to note; **~ (par) soi-même** to see for oneself; **2** to ascertain, to establish; **3** to record.

constellation /kɔ̃stɛlasjɔ̃/ *nf* constellation.

constellé, **~e** /kɔ̃stelle/ *adj* **~ de** spangled with; riddled with; spotted with.

consternant, **~e** /kɔ̃stɛʀnɑ̃, ɑ̃t/ *adj* **1** distressing; **2** appalling.

consternation /kɔ̃stɛʀnasjɔ̃/ *nf* consternation.

consterner /kɔ̃stɛʀne/ [1] *vtr* to fill [sb] with consternation, to dismay.

constipé, **~e** /kɔ̃stipe/ *adj* constipated.

constiper /kɔ̃stipe/ [1] *vtr* to make [sb] constipated.

constitué, **~e** /kɔ̃stitɥe/ *adj* **1 personne bien/mal ~e** person of sound/unsound constitution; **2** constituted.

constituer /kɔ̃stitɥe/ [1] **I** *vtr* **1** to be, to constitute [*crime, reason*]; **2** to form, to set up [*team, commission*]; **3** to make up [*whole*]; **4** (Law) to settle; **~ qn héritier** to appoint sb as heir.
II se constituer *v refl* (+ *v être*) **1** to build up [*network, reserve*]; **2 se ~ en** to form [*party*]; **3 se ~ prisonnier** to give oneself up.

constitution /kɔ̃stitysjɔ̃/ *nf* **1** (of company) setting up; (of capital) accumulation; (of application) preparing; **2** constitution.

constructeur, **-trice** /kɔ̃stʀyktœʀ, tʀis/ *nm,f* **1** (car) manufacturer; **2** builder.

constructif, **-ive** /kɔ̃stʀyktif, iv/ *adj* constructive.

construction /kɔ̃stʀyksjɔ̃/ *nf* **1** construction; building; **en ~** under construction; **de ~ japonaise** Japanese built; **2 la ~** the construction industry; **~ navale** shipbuilding.

construire /kɔ̃stʀɥiʀ/ [69] **I** *vtr* to build; to construct.
II se construire *v refl* (+ *v être*) **1 ça s'est beaucoup construit par ici** there's been a lot of building here; **2 se ~ avec le subjonctif** to take the subjunctive.

consul /kɔ̃syl/ *nm* consul.

consulat /kɔ̃syla/ *nm* consulate.

consultant, **~e** /kɔ̃syltɑ̃, ɑ̃t/ *nm,f* consultant.

consultation /kɔ̃syltasjɔ̃/ *nf* **1** consultation; consulting; **~ électorale** election; **2** surgery hours (GB), office hours (US).

consulter /kɔ̃sylte/ [1] **I** *vtr* to consult; **~ le peuple** to hold a general election.
II *vi* [*doctor*] to see patients.
III se consulter *v refl* (+ *v être*) to consult together; **se ~ du regard** to exchange glances.

consumer /kɔ̃syme/ [1] **I** *vtr* [*fire*] to consume.
II se consumer *v refl* (+ *v être*) to burn.

contact /kɔ̃takt/ *nm* **1** contact; **garder le ~** to keep in touch; **entrer en ~ avec** to get in touch with; **elle est devenue plus sociable à ton ~** she's become more sociable through spending time with you; **2 mettre/couper le ~** to switch on/switch off the ignition.

contacter /kɔ̃takte/ [1] *vtr* to contact, to get in touch with.

contagieux, **-ieuse** /kɔ̃taʒjø, øz/ *adj* **1** contagious; **2** [*laughter*] infectious.

contagion /kɔ̃taʒjɔ̃/ *nf* contagion.

contamination /kɔ̃taminasjɔ̃/ *nf* contamination.

contaminer /kɔ̃tamine/ [1] *vtr* to contaminate; to infect.

conte /kɔ̃t/ *nm* tale, story.

contemplatif, **-ive** /kɔ̃tɑ̃platif, iv/ *adj* contemplative.

contemplation /kɔ̃tɑ̃plasjɔ̃/ *nf* contemplation.

contempler /kɔ̃tɑ̃ple/ [1] *vtr* to survey; to contemplate; to look at.

contemporain, **~e** /kɔ̃tɑ̃pɔʀɛ̃, ɛn/ *adj, nm,f* contemporary.

contenance /kɔ̃t(ə)nɑ̃s/ *nf* **1** (of container) capacity; **2** bearing, attitude; **perdre ~** to lose one's composure.

conteneur /kɔ̃t(ə)nœʀ/ *nm* container.

contenir /kɔ̃t(ə)niʀ/ [36] **I** *vtr* **1** to contain [*substance, error*]; **2** [*container*] to hold; [*hall*] to accommodate [*spectators*]; **3** to contain [*crowd*].
II se contenir *v refl* (+ *v être*) to contain oneself.

content, **~e** /kɔ̃tɑ̃, ɑ̃t/ **I** *adj* happy, pleased, glad; **~ de soi** pleased with oneself.
II *nm* **avoir son ~ de** to have had one's fill of.

contentement /kɔ̃tɑ̃tmɑ̃/ *nm* contentment.

contenter /kɔ̃tɑ̃te/ [1] **I** *vtr* to satisfy [*customer, curiosity*]; **facile à ~** easy to please.
II se contenter *v refl* (+ *v être*) **se ~ de qch** to content oneself with sth.

contentieux /kɔ̃tɑ̃sjø/ *nm* **1** bone of contention; **2** legal department; **3** litigation.

contenu, **~e** /kɔ̃t(ə)ny/ **I** *pp* ▶ **contenir**.
II *pp adj* restrained; suppressed.
III *nm* contents; content.

conter /kɔ̃te/ [1] *vtr* to tell, to recount.

contestable /kɔ̃tɛstabl/ *adj* questionable.

contestataire /kɔ̃tɛstatɛʀ/ **I** *adj* anti-authority.
II *nmf* protester.

contestation /kɔ̃tɛstasjɔ̃/ *nf* **1** protest; **2** challenging; **être sujet à ~**, **prêter à ~** to be questionable; **sans ~ possible** beyond dispute; **2 la ~** dissent.

conteste: **sans conteste** /sɑ̃kɔ̃tɛst/ *phr* unquestionably.

contesté, **~e** /kɔ̃tɛste/ *adj* controversial.

contester /kɔ̃tɛste/ [1] **I** *vtr* to question; to contest; to dispute; to challenge.
II *vi* **1** to raise objections; **2** to protest.

contexte /kɔ̃tɛkst/ *nm* context.

contigu, **-uë** /kɔ̃tigy/ *adj* [*rooms*] adjoining.

continent, **~e** /kɔ̃tinɑ̃, ɑ̃t/ **I** *adj* continent.
II *nm* **1** continent; **2** mainland.

continental, **~e**, *mpl* **-aux** /kɔ̃tinɑ̃tal, o/ *adj* **1** continental; **2** mainland.

contingent /kɔ̃tɛ̃ʒɑ̃/ *nm* **1** contingent; (Mil) conscripts, draft (US); **2** quota; **3** (Law, figurative) share.

continu, **~e** /kɔ̃tiny/ *adj* continuous.

continuation /kɔ̃tinɥasjɔ̃/ *nf* continuation.

continuel, **-elle** /kɔ̃tinɥɛl/ *adj* continual.

continuer /kɔ̃tinɥe/ [1] **I** *vtr* to continue.
II *vi* to continue, to go on.

continuité /kɔ̃tinɥite/ *nf* continuity.

contondant, **~e** /kɔ̃tɔ̃dɑ̃, ɑ̃t/ *adj* blunt.

contorsion /kɔ̃tɔʀsjɔ̃/ *nf* contortion.

contorsionner: **se contorsionner** /kɔ̃tɔʀsjɔne/ [1] *v refl* (+ *v être*) to tie oneself in knots.

contour /kɔ̃tuʀ/ *nm* **1** outline, contour; **2 ~s** (of road, river) twists and turns.

contourner /kɔ̃tuʀne/ [1] *vtr* to go round; to by-pass [*town*]; to get round [*problem*].

contraceptif, **-ive** /kɔ̃tʀasɛptif, iv/ **I** *adj* contraceptive.
II *nm* contraceptive.

contraception /kɔ̃tʀasɛpsjɔ̃/ *nf* contraception.

contracter /kɔ̃tʀakte/ [1] **I** *vtr* **1** to tense [*muscle*]; **2** to incur [*debt*]; to take out [*loan*]; **3** to contract [*disease*].
II se contracter *v refl* (+ *v être*) [*muscle, word*] to contract; [*face, person*] to tense up.

contraction /kɔ̃tʀaksjɔ̃/ *nf* **1** tenseness; **2** contraction.

contractuel, **-elle** /kɔ̃tʀaktɥɛl/ **I** *adj* contractual; **personnel ~** contract staff.
II *nm,f* **1** contract employee; **2** traffic warden (GB), meter reader (US).

contradiction /kɔ̃tʀadiksjɔ̃/ *nf* contradiction.

contradictoire /kɔ̃tʀadiktwaʀ/ *adj* contradictory; **~ à** in contradiction to.

contraignant, **~e** /kɔ̃tʀɛɲɑ̃, ɑ̃t/ *adj* restrictive.

contraindre /kɔ̃tʀɛ̃dʀ/ [54] **I** *vtr* **1 ~ qn à faire** to force sb to do; **2** to restrain, to curb.
II se contraindre *v refl* (+ *v être*) **se ~ à** to force oneself to.

contraint, **~e**[1] /kɔ̃tʀɛ̃, ɛ̃t/ *adj* **1 ~ et forcé** (Law) under duress; **2** strained, forced.

contrainte[2] /kɔ̃tʀɛ̃t/ *nf* **1** pressure; coercion; **2** constraint; **3 sans ~** without restraint, freely.

contraire /kɔ̃tʀɛʀ/ **I** *adj* **1** opposite; contrary; [*interests*] conflicting; **être ~ aux usages** to be contrary to custom; **dans le cas ~** (should it be) otherwise; **2** adverse.
II *nm* **le ~** the opposite, the contrary; **ne dites pas le ~** don't deny it; **au ~!** on the contrary!

contrairement /kɔ̃tʀɛʀmɑ̃/ *adv* **~ à ce qu'on pourrait penser** contrary to what one might think; **~ à qn** unlike sb.

contrariant, **~e** /kɔ̃tʀaʀjɑ̃, ɑ̃t/ *adj* **1** [*person*] contrary; **2** [*event*] annoying.

contrarier /kɔ̃tʀaʀje/ [2] *vtr* **1** to upset; **2** to annoy; **3** to frustrate, to thwart.

contrariété /kɔ̃tʀaʀjete/ *nf* vexation.

contraste /kɔ̃tʀast/ *nm* contrast.

contrasté, **~e** /kɔ̃tʀaste/ *adj* **1** contrasting; **2** [*photo*] with good contrast; **3** [*results*] uneven.

contraster /kɔ̃tʀaste/ [1] **I** *vtr* to contrast [*colours*]; to give contrast to [*photo*].
II *vi* to contrast.

contrat /kɔ̃tʀa/ *nm* contract.
■ **~ emploi solidarité, CES** part-time low-paid work for the long-term unemployed.

contravention /kɔ̃tʀavɑ̃sjɔ̃/ *nf* **1** parking ticket; speeding ticket; fine; **2** minor offence[GB].

contre[1] /kɔ̃tʀ/ **I** *prep* **1** against; **22% ~ 18% hier** 22% as against 18% yesterday; **allongés l'un ~ l'autre** lying side by side; **2** versus; **3** (in exchange) for; **échange-la ~ une bleue** exchange it for a blue one.

II par contre *phr* on the other hand.

contre[2] /kɔ̃tʀ/ **I** *nm* **1 le pour et le ~** the pros and cons; **2** (Sport) counter-attack.

II *pref* counter; **~ attaque** counter-attack; **~-allée** service road; **~-courant** counter-current; **à ~-courant** against the current; against the tide; **~-expertise** second opinion; **~-indication** contraindication; **~-interrogatoire** cross examination; **~-jour** backlighting; **prendre le ~-pied de ce que dit qn** to say the opposite of what sb says.

contrebande /kɔ̃tʀəbɑ̃d/ *nf* **1** smuggling; **2** smuggled goods, contraband.

contrebandier, **-ière** /kɔ̃tʀəbɑ̃dje, ɛʀ/ *nm,f* smuggler.

contrebas: **en contrebas** /ɑ̃kɔ̃tʀəbɑ/ *phr* (down) below; **en ~ de** below.

contrebasse /kɔ̃tʀəbas/ *nf* double bass.

contrecœur: **à contrecœur** /akɔ̃tʀəkœʀ/ *phr* reluctantly.

contrecoup /kɔ̃tʀəku/ *nm* effects; after-effects; **par ~** as a result.

contredire /kɔ̃tʀədiʀ/ [65] **I** *vtr* to contradict.

II se contredire *v refl* (+ *v être*) **1** to contradict oneself; **2** to contradict each other.

contrée /kɔ̃tʀe/ *nf* **1** land; **2** region.

contrefaçon /kɔ̃tʀəfasɔ̃/ *nf* **1** forging, counterfeiting; **2** forgery, counterfeit.

contrefaire /kɔ̃tʀəfɛʀ/ [10] *vtr* **1** to forge, to counterfeit; **2** to imitate; **3** to disguise.

contrefort /kɔ̃tʀəfɔʀ/ *nm* **1** foothills; **2** buttress; **3** (of shoe) back.

contremaître, **-esse** /kɔ̃tʀəmɛtʀ, kɔ̃tʀə mɛtʀɛs/ *nm,f* foreman/forewoman.

contrepartie /kɔ̃tʀəpaʀti/ *nf* **1** equivalent; **2** compensation; **en ~** in compensation; in return; **mais la ~ est que le salaire est élevé** but this is offset by the high salary.

contreplaqué /kɔ̃tʀəplake/ *nm* plywood.

contrepoids /kɔ̃tʀəpwa/ *nm* counterweight.

contrer /kɔ̃tʀe/ [1] *vtr* to counter; to block.

contresens /kɔ̃tʀəsɑ̃s/ *nm* **1** misinterpretation; **2** mistranslation; **3 à ~** in the opposite direction; the wrong way; against the grain.

contretemps /kɔ̃tʀətɑ̃/ *nm inv* **1** setback, contretemps; **2 à ~** (Mus) on the off-beat; out of time; (figurative) at the wrong moment.

contrevenir /kɔ̃tʀəvəniʀ/ [36] *v+prep* **~ à** to contravene.

contribuable /kɔ̃tʀibɥabl/ *nmf* taxpayer.

contribuer /kɔ̃tʀibɥe/ [1] *v+prep* **~ à** to contribute to; to pay one's share of; **cela y a beaucoup contribué** it was a major factor.

contribution /kɔ̃tʀibysjɔ̃/ *nf* **1** contribution; **mettre qn à ~** to call upon sb's services; **2 ~s** taxes; tax office.

contrit, **~e** /kɔ̃tʀi, it/ *adj* contrite, apologetic.

contrôle /kɔ̃tʀol/ *nm* **1** control; **2** check; **~ de police** police check; **~ des billets** ticket inspection; **3** (Sch) test; **~ de géographie** geography test; **4** check-up; **5** monitoring; **sous ~ médical** under medical supervision.

■ **~ continu (des connaissances)** continuous assessment; **~ fiscal** tax investigation; **~ technique (des véhicules)** MOT (test).

contrôler /kɔ̃tʀole/ [1] **I** *vtr* **1** to control; **2** to monitor; **3** to check; to inspect; to test.

II se contrôler *v refl* (+ *v être*) to control oneself.

contrôleur, **-euse** /kɔ̃tʀolœʀ, øz/ *nm,f* inspector; **~ aérien** air-traffic controller.

contrordre /kɔ̃tʀɔʀdʀ/ *nm* **1 ordres et ~s** conflicting orders; **j'irai vendredi, sauf ~** I'll go on Friday, unless I hear to the contrary; **2** counter command.

controverse /kɔ̃tʀɔvɛʀs/ *nf* controversy.

contusion /kɔ̃tyzjɔ̃/ *nf* bruise.

convaincant, **~e** /kɔ̃vɛ̃kɑ̃, ɑ̃t/ *adj* **1** convincing; **2** persuasive.

convaincre /kɔ̃vɛ̃kʀ/ [57] **I** *vtr* to convince; to persuade.

II se convaincre *v refl* (+ *v être*) to convince oneself.

convaincu, **~e** /kɔ̃vɛ̃ky/ **I** *pp* ▶ **convaincre**.

II *pp adj* **1** convinced; **d'un ton ~** with conviction; **2** [*supporter*] staunch.

convalescence /kɔ̃valesɑ̃s/ *nf* convalescence.

convalescent, **~e** /kɔ̃valesɑ̃, ɑ̃t/ *adj, nm,f* convalescent.

convenable /kɔ̃vnabl/ *adj* **1** suitable; **2** reasonable; **3** decent; proper; respectable.

convenablement /kɔ̃vnabləmɑ̃/ *adv* properly; reasonably well; decently.

convenance /kɔ̃vnɑ̃s/ *nf* **1 pour ~ personnelle** for personal reasons; **à votre ~** at your convenience; **2 ~s** (social) conventions.

convenir /kɔ̃vniʀ/ [36] **I** *vtr* **1** to admit; **2** to agree.

II convenir à *v+prep* to suit; to be suitable for.

III convenir de *v+prep* **1 ~ de** to admit, to acknowledge; **2 ~ de** to agree on.

IV *v impers* **1 il convient de faire/que vous fassiez** one/you should do; **2 ce qu'il est convenu d'appeler le réalisme** what is commonly called realism; **comme convenu** as agreed.

convention /kɔ̃vɑ̃sjɔ̃/ *nf* **1** agreement; **2** convention; **de ~** conventional.

conventionné, **~e** /kɔ̃vɑ̃sjɔne/ *adj* [*doctor, costs*] national health service; [*clinic*] registered; **médecin non ~** private doctor.

conventionnel, **-elle** /kɔ̃vɑ̃sjɔnɛl/ *adj* **1** conventional; **2** contractual.

convenu, **~e** /kɔ̃v(ə)ny/ **I** *pp* ▶ **convenir**.

II *pp adj* **1** [*date, terms*] agreed; **2** [*phrase*] conventional; [*smile*] polite.

convergence /kɔ̃vɛʀʒɑ̃s/ *nf* convergence.

converger /kɔ̃vɛʀʒe/ [13] *vi* to converge.
conversation /kɔ̃vɛʀsasjɔ̃/ *nf* conversation; **avoir de la ~** to be a good conversationalist; **dans la ~ courante** in everyday speech.
converser /kɔ̃vɛʀse/ [1] *vi* to converse.
conversion /kɔ̃vɛʀsjɔ̃/ *nf* conversion.
converti, **~e** /kɔ̃vɛʀti/ I *pp* ▶ **convertir**.
II *nm,f* convert.
convertible /kɔ̃vɛʀtibl/ *adj* **1** convertible; **2 canapé ~** sofa-bed.
convertir /kɔ̃vɛʀtiʀ/ [3] I *vtr* to convert.
II **se convertir** *v refl* (+ *v être*) to convert.
convexe /kɔ̃vɛks/ *adj* convex.
conviction /kɔ̃viksjɔ̃/ *nf* conviction.
convier /kɔ̃vje/ [2] *vtr* to invite [*person*].
convive /kɔ̃viv/ *nmf* guest.
convivial, **~e**, *mpl* **-iaux** /kɔ̃vivjal, o/ *adj* **1** convivial; **2** user-friendly.
convivialité /kɔ̃vivjalite/ *nf* **1** friendliness; conviviality; **2** user-friendliness.
convocation /kɔ̃vɔkasjɔ̃/ *nf* **1** (of meeting) convening; (of person) summoning; (Mil) calling up; **2** notice to attend; (Law) summons; (Mil) call-up papers; **~ aux examens** notification of examination timetables.
convoi /kɔ̃vwa/ *nm* **1** convoy; **'~ exceptionnel'** (Aut) 'wide or dangerous load'; **2** train.
convoiter /kɔ̃vwate/ [1] *vtr* to covet.
convoitise /kɔ̃vwatiz/ *nf* **la ~** covetousness; **~ de** lust for.
convoquer /kɔ̃vɔke/ [1] *vtr* to call, to convene [*meeting*]; to send for [*pupil*]; to summon [*witness*]; to call up [*soldier*]; **être convoqué à un examen** to be asked to attend an exam.
convoyer /kɔ̃vwaje/ [23] *vtr* to escort.
convoyeur, **-euse** /kɔ̃vwajœʀ/ *nm,f* **1** prison escort; **2** courier; **~ de fonds** security guard.
convulsif, **-ive** /kɔ̃vylsif, iv/ *adj* **1** convulsive; **2** [*laughter*] nervous.
convulsion /kɔ̃vylsjɔ̃/ *nf* convulsion.
convulsionner /kɔ̃vylsjɔne/ [1] *vtr* to convulse.
coopératif, **-ive** /kɔɔpeʀatif, iv/ I *adj* cooperative.
II **coopérative** *nf* cooperative.
coopération /kɔɔpeʀasjɔ̃/ *nf* **1** cooperation; **2** cultural/technical aid.
coopérer /kɔɔpeʀe/ [14] *vi* to cooperate.
coordinateur, **-trice** /kɔɔʀdinatœʀ, tʀis/ I *adj* coordinating.
II *nm,f* coordinator.
coordination /kɔɔʀdinasjɔ̃/ *nf* **1** coordination; **2** joint committee.
coordonné, **~e** /kɔɔʀdɔne/ I *pp* ▶ **coordonner**.
II *pp adj* coordinated; coordinating.
III **coordonnés** *nm pl* (in fashion) coordinates.
coordonnées /kɔɔʀdɔne/ *nf pl* **1** (on graph, map) coordinates; **2** information; **3** address and telephone number.
coordonner /kɔɔʀdɔne/ [1] *vtr* to coordinate.
copain, **copine** /kɔpɛ̃, in/ I *adj* pally○ (GB), chummy○.
II *nm,f* **1** friend; **2** boyfriend/girlfriend.
copeau, *pl* **~x** /kɔpo/ *nm* shaving.
Copenhague /kopɛnag/ *pr n* Copenhagen.
copie /kɔpi/ *nf* **1** copying; copy; **2** (Sch) paper.
copier /kɔpje/ [2] *vtr* **1** to copy; **2** (Sch) **~ sur qn** to copy or crib from sb.
copieur, **-ieuse** /kɔpjœʀ, øz/ I *nm,f* (Sch) cheat.
II *nm* photocopier.
copieusement /kɔpjøzmɑ̃/ *adv* heartily; lavishly; copiously.
copieux, **-ieuse** /kɔpjø, øz/ *adj* [*meal*] hearty; [*portion*] generous; [*notes*] copious.
copilote /kopilɔt/ *nmf* co-pilot; co-driver.
copine ▶ **copain**.
coprésident, **~e** /kopʀezidɑ̃, ɑ̃t/ *nm,f* joint president; co-chair.
coproduction /kopʀɔdyksjɔ̃/ *nf* co-production.
copropriété /kopʀɔpʀijete/ *nf* joint ownership; co-ownership.
coq /kɔk/ *nm* cockerel, rooster; cock; **au chant du ~** at cockcrow; **le ~ du village** (figurative) the local Casanova.
■ **~ de bruyère** grouse.
IDIOMS **être comme un ~ en pâte** to be in clover; **sauter du ~ à l'âne** to hop from one subject to another.
coque /kɔk/ *nf* **1** (of boat) hull; (of hydroplane) fuselage; (of car) body; **2** cockle; **3** (of nut) shell.
coquelicot /kɔkliko/ *nm* poppy.
coqueluche /kɔklyʃ/ *nf* **1** whooping-cough; **2**○ idol.
coquet, **-ette** /kɔkɛ, ɛt/ *adj* **1 être ~** to be particular about one's appearance; **2** pretty; **3**○ [*sum*] tidy○.
coquetier /kɔktje/ *nm* eggcup.
coquetterie /kɔkɛtʀi/ *nf* interest in one's appearance; vanity; **par ~** out of vanity.
coquillage /kɔkijaʒ/ *nm* **1** shellfish; **2** shell.
coquille /kɔkij/ *nf* **1** shell; **2** scallop-shaped dish; **~ de saumon** salmon served in a shell; **3** misprint; **4** (Med) spinal jacket.
■ **~ Saint-Jacques** scallop; scallop shell.
coquillette /kɔkijɛt/ *nf* small macaroni.
coquin, **~e** /kɔkɛ̃, in/ I *adj* **1** mischievous; **2** naughty, saucy.
II *nm,f* rascal.
cor /kɔʀ/ *nm* **1** (Mus) horn; **2** (Med) corn.
IDIOMS **réclamer** or **demander qch à ~ et à cri** to clamour[GB] for sth.
corail, *pl* **-aux** /kɔʀaj, o/ *adj inv*, *nm* coral.
Coran /kɔʀɑ̃/ *pr nm* **le ~** the Koran.
corbeau, *pl* **~x** /kɔʀbo/ *nm* **1** crow; **grand ~** raven; **2**○ writer of a poison-pen letter.
corbeille /kɔʀbɛj/ *nf* **1** basket; **2** dress circle.
corbillard /kɔʀbijaʀ/ *nm* hearse.
corde /kɔʀd/ *nf* **1** rope; **2 ~ (à sauter)** skipping rope; **3** (of racket, instrument) string.
■ **~ à linge** clothes line; **~ raide** tightrope; **~s vocales** vocal chords.
IDIOMS **mériter la ~** to deserve to be hanged;

pleuvoir or **tomber des ~s** to be raining cats and dogs○; **tirer sur la ~** to push one's luck; **faire jouer la ~ sensible** to tug at the heartstrings; **usé jusqu'à la ~** threadbare.

cordée /kɔʀde/ *nf* roped party (of climbers).

cordelière /kɔʀdəljɛʀ/ *nf* cord.

cordial, **~e**, *mpl* **-iaux** /kɔʀdjal, o/ *adj* cordial; warm-hearted; warm.

cordialement /kɔʀdjalmɑ̃/ *adv* warmly; **~ (vôtre** or **à vous)** yours sincerely.

cordialité /kɔʀdjalite/ *nf* warmth; friendliness.

cordillère /kɔʀdijɛʀ/ *nf* cordillera.

cordon /kɔʀdɔ̃/ *nm* **1** cord; string; lace; **2** flex (GB), cord (US); **3** cordon; **4** row; **5** ribbon.
■ **~ ombilical** umbilical cord.

cordonnerie /kɔʀdɔnʀi/ *nf* **1** shoemaking; **2** shoe repairing; **3** cobbler's.

Corée /kɔʀe/ *pr nf* Korea.

coriace /kɔʀjas/ *adj* tough.

coriandre /kɔʀjɑ̃dʀ/ *nf* coriander.

Corinthe /kɔʀɛ̃t/ *pr n* **raisins de ~** currants.

corne /kɔʀn/ *nf* **1** horn; antler; **à ~s** horned; **blesser d'un coup de ~** to gore; **2** (Mus) horn; **3**○ **avoir de la ~ aux pieds** to have calluses on one's feet.
■ **~ d'abondance** horn of plenty, cornucopia; **~ de brume** foghorn.

cornée /kɔʀne/ *nf* cornea.

corneille /kɔʀnɛj/ *nf* crow.

cornemuse /kɔʀnəmyz/ *nf* bagpipes.

corner /kɔʀne/ [1] *vtr* to turn down the corner of [*page*]; **page cornée** dog-eared page.

cornet /kɔʀnɛ/ *nm* **1** (paper) cone; **2** (ice-cream) cone, cornet (GB).
■ **~ à dés** dice cup; **~ à pistons** cornet.

corniche /kɔʀniʃ/ *nf* **1** cornice; **2** moulding (GB), molding (US); **3** ledge (of rock); **4** cliff road.

cornichon /kɔʀniʃɔ̃/ *nm* gherkin.

Cornouailles /kɔʀnuɑj/ *pr nf* Cornwall.

corolle /kɔʀɔl/ *nf* **1** corolla; **2 en ~** [*skirt*] flared.

coron /kɔʀɔ̃/ *nm* miners' terraced houses.

corporatif, **-ive** /kɔʀpɔʀatif, iv/ *adj* corporate.

corporation /kɔʀpɔʀasjɔ̃/ *nf* corporation.

corporel, **-elle** /kɔʀpɔʀɛl/ *adj* [*needs*] bodily; [*punishment*] corporal.

corps /kɔʀ/ *nm inv* body; **(combat) ~ à ~** hand-to-hand combat; **se donner ~ et âme à** to give oneself body and soul to; **faire ~ avec** [*person*] to stand solidly behind; [*building*] to be joined to; **prendre ~** to take shape.
■ **~ enseignant** teaching profession; **~ et biens** (to sink) with all hands; **~ expéditionnaire** expeditionary force; **~ gras** fatty substance; **~ médical** medical profession.
IDIOMS **tenir au ~** to be nourishing.

corpulence /kɔʀpylɑ̃s/ *nf* stoutness.

corpulent, **~e** /kɔʀpylɑ̃, ɑ̃t/ *adj* stout, corpulent.

correct, **~e** /kɔʀɛkt/ *adj* **1** [*calculation*] correct; [*copy*] accurate; **2** [*outfit*] proper; [*conduct*] correct; **3**○ [*result, wine*] reasonable, decent; **4** [*person*] polite; fair, correct.

correcteur, **-trice** /kɔʀɛktœʀ, tʀis/ **I** *adj* corrective.
II *nm,f* **1** examiner (GB), grader (US); **2** proofreader.

correction /kɔʀɛksjɔ̃/ *nf* **1** correcting; proofreading; marking (GB), grading (US); **2** correction; **3** thrashing; **4** correctness; good manners.

correctionnel, **-elle**[1] /kɔʀɛksjɔnɛl/ *adj* **tribunal ~** magistrate's court.

correctionnelle[2] /kɔʀɛksjɔnɛl/ *nf* magistrate's court.

corrélation /kɔʀelasjɔ̃/ *nf* correlation; **être en ~ avec qn** to be related to sth.

correspondance /kɔʀɛspɔ̃dɑ̃s/ *nf* **1** letters; mail; correspondence; **faire sa ~** to write some letters; **vendu par ~** available by mail order; **2** correspondence; **3** connection; **trains/vols en ~** connecting trains/flights.

correspondant, **~e** /kɔʀɛspɔ̃dɑ̃, ɑ̃t/ **I** *adj* corresponding.
II *nm,f* correspondent; (Sch) pen pal.

correspondre /kɔʀɛspɔ̃dʀ/ [6] **I correspondre à** *v+prep* to correspond to; to match; to suit [*tastes*].
II *vi* to correspond, to write.
III se correspondre *v refl* (+ *v être*) to correspond.

corrida /kɔʀida/ *nf* bullfight.

corridor /kɔʀidɔʀ/ *nm* corridor.

corrigé /kɔʀiʒe/ *nm* (Sch) correct version.

corriger /kɔʀiʒe/ [13] **I** *vtr* **1** to correct; to proofread [*manuscript*]; to mark (GB), to grade (US) [*exam papers*]; to redress [*situation*]; **2** to adjust [*position*]; to modify [*theory*]; **~ le tir** (Mil) to alter one's aim; (figurative) to adjust one's tactics; **3** to give [sb] a hiding○; to spank [*child*].
II se corriger *v refl* (+ *v être*) **1** to correct oneself; **2 se ~ d'un défaut** to cure oneself of a fault.

corroborer /kɔʀɔbɔʀe/ [1] *vtr* to corroborate.

corroder /kɔʀɔde/ [1] *vtr* to corrode.

corrompre /kɔʀɔ̃pʀ/ [53] *vtr* **1** to bribe; **2** to corrupt.

corrompu, **~e** /kɔʀɔ̃py/ **I** *pp* ▶ **corrompre**.
II *pp adj* corrupt.

corrosif, **-ive** /kɔʀɔzif, iv/ *adj* **1** [*substance*] corrosive; **2** [*humour*] caustic.

corrosion /kɔʀɔzjɔ̃/ *nf* corrosion.

corruption /kɔʀypsjɔ̃/ *nf* **1** corruption; **2** bribery.

corsage /kɔʀsaʒ/ *nm* **1** blouse; **2** bodice.

corsaire /kɔʀsɛʀ/ *nm* **1** corsair; **2** pedal pushers.

corse /kɔʀs/ *adj, nm* Corsican.

Corse /kɔʀs/ *pr nf* Corsica.

corsé, **~e** /kɔʀse/ *adj* [*coffee*] strong; [*sauce, story*] spicy; [*problem*] tough; [*bill*] steep.

corser /kɔʀse/ [1] **I** *vtr* **1** to make [sth] more

difficult; **pour ~ l'affaire** (just) to complicate matters; **2** to make [sth] spicier [*sauce*].

II **se corser** *v refl* (+ *v être*) to get more complicated.

corset /kɔʀsɛ/ *nm* corset.

corso /kɔʀso/ *nm* **~ fleuri** procession of floral floats.

cortège /kɔʀtɛʒ/ *nm* procession.

corvée /kɔʀve/ *nf* chore; (Mil) fatigue (duty).

cosmétique /kɔsmetik/ *adj, nm* cosmetic.

cosmique /kɔsmik/ *adj* cosmic.

cosmonaute /kɔsmɔnot/ *nmf* cosmonaut.

cosmopolite /kɔsmɔpɔlit/ *adj* cosmopolitan.

cosse /kɔs/ *nf* (of pea) pod; (of grain) husk.

cossu, **~e** /kɔsy/ *adj* [*person*] well-to-do; [*interior*] plush; [*house*] smart.

costaud○ /kɔsto/ *adj* strong, sturdy; hefty○.

costume /kɔstym/ *nm* **1** suit; **2** costume; **répétition en ~** dress rehearsal.

costumer: **se costumer** /kɔstyme/ [1] *v refl* (+ *v être*) **se ~ en** to dress up as; **soirée costumée** fancy-dress party.

cotation /kɔtasjɔ̃/ *nf* quotation.

cote /kɔt/ *nf* **1** (of stocks, commodities) quotation; (stock exchange) list; **2** (of stamp) quoted value; **3** (at races) odds; **4** (of person, film) rating; **avoir la ~**○ **auprès de** to be popular with; to be well thought of by; **5** (on plan) dimension; **6** (on map) spot height.

■ **~ d'alerte** flood level; (figurative) danger level; **~ de popularité** popularity rating.

côte /kot/ I *nf* **1** coast; **2** hill; **dans une ~** on a hill; **3** rib; **4** chop; **~ de bœuf** rib roast.

II **côte à côte** *phr* side by side.

■ **Côte d'Azur** French riviera.

coté, **~e** /kɔte/ I *pp* ▶ **coter**.

II *pp adj* **être ~** to be well thought of.

côté /kote/ I *nm* **1** side; **du ~ droit/gauche** on the righthand/lefthand side; **chambre ~ rue** room overlooking the street; **par certains ~s** in some respects; **~ santé** healthwise; **de mon ~, je pense que**... for my part, I think that...; **d'un ~...d'un autre ~**... on the one hand...on the other hand...; **2** way, direction; **de tous ~s** [*come*] from all directions; [*run*] all over the place; **du ~ de Nice** [*live*] near Nice; **aller du ~ de Dijon** to head for Dijon.

II **à côté** *phr* **1** nearby; **les gens d'à ~** the people next door; **à ~ de** next to; **le ballon est passé à ~ (du but)** the ball went wide (of the goal); **répondre à ~** (by mistake) to miss the point; (on purpose) to sidestep the question; **2** by comparison; **3** on the side; **elle est étudiante et travaille à ~** she's a student and works on the side.

III **de côté** *phr* **1** sideways; **2** aside; **mettre qch de ~** to put sth aside [*money, object*].

IV **aux côtés de** *phr* **aux ~s de qn** [*to be*] at sb's side; [*to work*] alongside sb.

coteau, *pl* **~x** /kɔto/ *nm* **1** hillside; **2** hill; **3** (sloping) vineyard.

côtelette /kotlɛt/ *nf* (Culin) chop.

coter /kɔte/ [1] *vtr* **1** to quote, to list [*shares*]; to price [*car*]; **2** to rate [*film*].

côtier, **-ière** /kotje, ɛʀ/ *adj* coastal; inshore.

cotisation /kɔtizasjɔ̃/ *nf* **1** contribution; **2** subscription.

cotiser /kɔtize/ [1] I *vi* **1** to pay one's contributions; **2** to pay one's subscription (**à** to).

II **se cotiser** *v refl* (+ *v être*) to club together (GB), to go in together.

coton /kɔtɔ̃/ *nm* **1** cotton; **2** thread; **3** cotton wool (GB), cotton (US).

IDIOMS **filer un mauvais ~** to be in a bad way; **élever un enfant dans du ~** to give a child a very sheltered upbringing; **j'ai les jambes en ~** (after shock) my legs have turned to jelly.

cotonnade /kɔtɔnad/ *nf* cotton fabric.

cotonneux, **-euse** /kɔtɔnø, øz/ *adj* [*fog*] like cotton-wool; [*cloud*] fleecy.

côtoyer /kotwaje/ [23] I *vtr* to walk alongside [*river*]; to move in [*milieu*]; to mix with [*people*]; to be in close contact with [*death*].

II **se côtoyer** *v refl* (+ *v être*) [*people*] to mix.

cotte /kɔt/ *nf* overalls.

■ **~ de mailles** coat of mail.

cou /ku/ *nm* neck; **être endetté jusqu'au ~** to be up to one's eyes in debt.

couchage /kuʃaʒ/ *nm* bedding; **un studio avec ~ pour six** a studio that sleeps six.

couchant /kuʃɑ̃/ I *adj* **au soleil ~** at sunset.

II *nm* **1** sunset; **2** west.

couche /kuʃ/ *nf* **1** layer; (of paint) coat; **2** nappy (GB), diaper (US); **3** class, sector.

couché, **~e** /kuʃe/ I *pp* ▶ **coucher**.

II *pp adj* [*grass*] flattened; [*writing*] sloping.

couche-culotte, *pl* **couches-culottes** /kuʃkylɔt/ *nf* disposable nappy (GB) or diaper (US).

coucher /kuʃe/ [1] I *nm* bedtime.

II *vtr* **1** to put [sb] to bed; to lay out [*wounded person*]; **2** to lay [sth] on its side; to lay [sth] down; **3** to flatten [*grass*].

III *vi* to sleep; **~ sous les ponts** to sleep rough (GB) or outdoors.

IV **se coucher** *v refl* (+ *v être*) **1** to lie (down); **2** to go to bed; **3** [*stem*] to bend; [*boat*] to list; **se ~ sur** [*cyclist*] to lean forward over [*handlebars*]; **4** [*sun*] to set.

■ **~ de soleil** sunset.

couchette /kuʃɛt/ *nf* couchette, berth.

coucou /kuku/ I *nm* **1** cuckoo; **2** cowslip; **3**○ (old) crate○, plane; **4** cuckoo clock.

II○ *excl* **1** cooee!; **2** peekaboo!

coude /kud/ *nm* **1** elbow; **travailler ~ à ~** to work shoulder to shoulder; **2** (in river, pipe) bend.

IDIOMS **se serrer les ~s** to stick together.

coudé, **~e**[1] /kude/ *adj* bent at an angle.

coudée[2] /kude/ *nf* **avoir les ~s franches** to have elbow room.

cou-de-pied, *pl* **cous-de-pied** /kudpje/ *nm* instep.

couder /kude/ [1] *vtr* to bend.

coudre /kudʀ/ [76] *vtr* to sew; to sew [sth] on; to stitch [sth] on; to stitch (up).
IDIOMS **leur histoire est cousue de fil blanc** you can see right through their story.

couenne /kwan/ *nf* (bacon) rind.

couette /kwɛt/ *nf* duvet.

couffin /kufɛ̃/ *nm* Moses basket (GB), bassinet (US).

couiner /kwine/ [1] *vi* to squeak, to squeal.

coulée /kule/ *nf* (of lava) flow; (of paint) drip.

couler /kule/ [1] **I** *vtr* **1** to cast [*metal, statue*]; to pour [*concrete*]; **2** to sink [*ship*]; **3**○ to put [sth] out of business; to bring [sb] down.
II *vi* **1** [*blood*] to flow; [*paint, cheese*] to run; **faire ~ qch** to run [*bath*]; **2** [*tap, pen*] to leak; [*nose*] to run; **3** [*boat*] to sink; [*company*] to go under.
III se couler *v refl* (+ *v être*) **se ~ dans/entre** to slip into/between.

couleur /kulœʀ/ *nf* **1** colour[GB]; **de ~** [*person*] coloured[GB]; **sans ~** colourless[GB]; **plein de ~** colourful[GB]; **2** paint; **3 les ~s** (washing) coloureds[GB]; (flag) the colours[GB]; **4** (in cards) suit; **5 sous ~ de faire** while pretending to do.
IDIOMS **ne pas voir la ~ de qch**○ never to get a sniff of sth○; **il m'en a fait voir de toutes les ~s**○ he put me through the mill.

couleuvre /kulœvʀ/ *nf* grass snake.
IDIOMS **avaler des ~s**○ to believe anything one is told.

coulissant, **~e** /kulisɑ̃, ɑ̃t/ *adj* sliding.

coulisse /kulis/ *nf* **1 les ~s, la ~** the wings; **en ~** backstage; (figurative) behind the scenes; **2** runner.

coulisser /kulise/ [1] *vi* to slide.

couloir /kulwaʀ/ *nm* **1** corridor (GB), hallway; passage; **bruits de ~s** rumours[GB]; **2** lane; **~ aérien** air (traffic) lane.

coup /ku/ *nm* **1** knock; blow; **~ à la porte** knock at the door; **à ~s de bâton** with a stick; **donner un ~ de qch à qn** to hit sb with sth; **donner un ~ de poing à qn** to punch sb; **porter un ~ (sévère) à** (figurative) to deal [sb/sth] a (severe) blow; **sa fierté en a pris un ~** it was a blow to his/her pride; **sous le ~ de la colère** in (a fit of) anger; **être sous le ~ d'une forte émotion** to be in a highly emotional state; **2** (noise) knock; bang; thump, thud; **au douzième ~ de minuit** on the last stroke of midnight; **sur le ~ de dix heures**○ around ten; **~ de sifflet** whistle blast; **3 un (petit) ~ de chiffon** a (quick) wipe; **un ~ de peinture** a lick of paint; **4** (in tennis, golf, cricket) stroke; shot; (in chess) move; (with dice) throw; (in boxing) punch; **tous les ~s sont permis** no holds barred; **5 ~ de feu/fusil** (gun)shot/(rifle) shot; **6**○ job○, racket○; trick○; **monter un ~** to plan a job○; **il a raté son ~**○ he blew it○; **être dans le ~** to be in on it; to be up to date; **qui a fait le ~?** who did it?; **7** time; **du premier ~** first time; **à tous les ~s** every time; **ce ~-ci** this time; **du ~**○ as a result; **après ~** afterward(s); **~ sur ~** in succession; **tout d'un ~, tout à ~** suddenly, all of a sudden; **d'un ~, d'un seul ~** just like that; **en un seul ~** in one go○; **sur le ~** at the time; instantly, on the spot; **pleurer un bon ~** to have a good cry; **8 à ~s de subventions** by means of subsidies; **9**○ drink.
■ **~ bas** blow below the belt; **~s et blessures** assault and battery; **~ dur** blow; **~ franc** free kick; **~ monté** put-up job.

■ **Note** For translations of expressions such as *coup d'envoi*, *coup de fil* etc, look up the entries at *envoi*, *fil* etc.

IDIOMS **tenir le ~** [*shoes*] to last out; [*repair*] to hold; [*person*] to hold on; **être aux cent ~s**○ to be worried sick○; **faire les quatre cents ~s**○ to be a real tearaway; **attraper le ~ pour faire**○ to get the knack of doing.

coupable /kupabl/ **I** *adj* guilty; [*negligence*] culpable; [*indifference*] shameful.
II *nmf* culprit.

coupant, **~e** /kupɑ̃, ɑ̃t/ *adj* sharp.

coup-de-poing, *pl* **coups-de-poing** /kudpwɛ̃/ *nm* **~ américain** knuckle-duster (GB), brass knuckles (US).

coupe /kup/ *nf* **1** cutting; cutting out; cut; **2** haircut; **3** (Sport) cup; **la ~ du Monde** the World Cup; **4** (fruit) bowl; (champagne) glass; **5** section; **~ transversale** cross section.
■ **~ en brosse** crew cut.
IDIOMS **la ~ est pleine** enough is enough; **être sous la ~ de qn** to be under sb's control.

coupe-feu /kupfø/ *nm inv* firebreak.

coupe-gorge /kupgɔʀʒ/ *nm inv* rough place; rough area.

coupe-papier /kuppapje/ *nm inv* paper knife.

couper /kupe/ [1] **I** *vtr* **1** to cut; to cut down; to chop; to cut out; to cut off; **~ qch en tranches** to slice sth; **2** [*road*] to cut across; **~ la route à qn** to cut in on sb; **3** to cut off [*road, supplies*]; to spoil [*appetite*]; to take the edge off [*hunger*]; to turn off [*water*]; **~ le souffle à qn** to take sb's breath away; **~ la parole à qn** to interrupt sb; **4 ~ qn de qn/qch** to cut sb off from sb/sth; **5** to dilute [*wine*]; **6** (in cards) to cut [*pack*]; to trump [*card*].
II *vi* **attention ça coupe!** be careful, it's sharp; **~ à travers champs** to cut across country.
III se couper *v refl* (+ *v être*) to cut oneself.
IDIOMS **c'est ton tour de faire à manger, tu n'y couperas pas** it's your turn to cook, you won't get out of it.

couperet /kupʀɛ/ *nm* cleaver; (of guillotine) blade; **la nouvelle est tombée comme un ~** the news came as a bolt from the blue.

couperose /kupʀoz/ *nf* broken veins.

coupe-vent /kupvɑ̃/ *nm inv* **1** windcheater (GB), windbreaker (US); **2** windbreak.

couple /kupl/ *nm* **1** couple; pair; **2** relationship.

couplet /kuplɛ/ *nm* **1** verse; **2** couplet.

coupole /kupɔl/ *nf* cupola, dome.

coupon /kupɔ̃/ *nm* **1** remnant; **2** ticket voucher; **3** multiuse ticket (*in travel pass*).

coupure /kupyʀ/ *nf* **1** cut; **~ d'électricité** or **de courant** power cut; **2** break; **3** gap; **4** (bank)note (GB), bill (US).

■ **~ de journal** or **de presse** (newspaper) cutting.

cour /kuʀ/ *nf* **1** courtyard; (school) playground; (farm) yard; **2** (of sovereign) court; (of celebrity) entourage; **3** courtship; **4** (Law) court.
■ **~ d'arrivée** arrivals area; **~ de départ** departures area; **~ martiale** court-martial; **~ de récréation** playground.

courage /kuʀaʒ/ *nm* **1** courage, bravery; **avoir du ~** to be brave; **2** energy; **je n'ai même pas le ~ de me doucher** I don't even have the energy to have a shower; **bon ~!** good luck!; **perdre ~** to lose heart; **je n'ai pas eu le ~ de dire non** I didn't have the heart to say no.

courageux, **-euse** /kuʀaʒø, øz/ *adj* courageous, brave.

couramment /kuʀamɑ̃/ *adv* **1** fluently; **2** [*used*] widely; **cela se fait ~** it's very common.

courant[1] /kuʀɑ̃/ *prep* **~ janvier** (some time) in January.

courant[2], **~e** /kuʀɑ̃, ɑ̃t/ **I** *adj* **1** [*word, practice, mistake*] common; **2** [*language*] everyday; [*procedure*] usual, ordinary; [*size*] standard; **3** [*month, price*] current; **le 15 du mois ~** the 15th of this month.
II *nm* **1** current; **il n'y a plus de ~** the power has gone off; **2** trend; **un ~ politique** a political trend; **3 dans le ~ de** in the course of.
III au courant *phr* **être au ~ de** to know about [*news*]; to be up to date on [*technique*]; **mettre qn au ~** to put sb in the picture; **tenir qn au ~** to keep sb posted.
■ **~ d'air** draught (GB), draft (US).

courbature /kuʀbatyʀ/ *nf* ache; **avoir des ~s** to be stiff.

courbe /kuʀb/ **I** *adj* curved.
II *nf* **1** curve; **2** bend.
■ **~ de température** temperature chart.

courber /kuʀbe/ [1] *vtr* to bend; **~ le dos** (figurative) to bow down.

courbette /kuʀbɛt/ *nf* (low) bow; **faire des ~s** (figurative) to bow and scrape.

courbure /kuʀbyʀ/ *nf* curve.

coureur, **-euse** /kuʀœʀ, øz/ *nm,f* runner; **~ automobile** racing driver; **~ de jupons** philanderer.

courge /kuʀʒ/ *nf* gourd; (vegetable) marrow.

courgette /kuʀʒɛt/ *nf* courgette (GB), zucchini (US).

courir /kuʀiʀ/ [26] **I** *vtr* **1** to compete in [*trials*]; **2 ~ le monde** to roam the world; **3 ~ les cocktails** to do the round of the cocktail parties; **~ les boutiques** to go round the shops (GB) or stores (US); **4 ~ un (grand) danger** to be in (great) danger; **~ un (gros) risque** to run a (big) risk; **faire ~ un risque à qn** to put sb at risk; **5**○ **~ les filles** to chase after girls.
II *vi* **1** to run; to race; **~ après qn/qch** to run after sb/sth; to chase after sb/sth; **les voleurs courent toujours** the thieves are still at large; **~ à la catastrophe** to be heading for disaster; **2** [*rumour*] to go around.

IDIOMS **tu peux toujours ~**○**!** you can go whistle for it○!; **laisser ~**○ to let things ride.

couronne /kuʀɔn/ *nf* **1** crown; **2 ~ de fleurs** garland; wreath; **3** ring-shaped loaf; **4** (in Paris) **la petite/grande ~** *the inner/outer suburbs.*

couronnement /kuʀɔnmɑ̃/ *nm* coronation.

couronner /kuʀɔne/ [1] *vtr* to crown.

courre /kuʀ/ *vtr* **chasse à ~** hunting.

courrier /kuʀje/ *nm* **1** mail, post (GB); **faire son ~** to write letters; **2 ~ des lecteurs** letters to the editor; **~ du cœur** problem page; **~ électronique** electronic mail.

courroie /kuʀwɑ/ *nf* **1** strap; **2** (on machine) belt.

cours /kuʀ/ *nm inv* **1** lesson, class; **avoir ~** to have a class; **faire ~** to teach; **2** course book, textbook; **3** school; **~ de théâtre** drama school; **4** price; exchange rate; **5** (of river) course; **6** (of tale, events) course; (of ideas) flow; **la vie reprend son ~** life returns to normal; **donner libre ~ à** to give free rein to [*imagination*]; **au** or **dans le ~ de** in the course of, during; **en ~** [*month*] current; [*project*] under way; [*work*] in progress; **en ~ de journée** in the course of the day.
■ **~ d'eau** watercourse; **~ élémentaire première année**, **CE1** *second year of primary school, age 7–8*; **~ moyen première année**, **CM1** *fourth year of primary school, age 9–10*; **~ particulier(s)** private tuition (GB), private tutoring (US); **~ préparatoire**, **CP** *first year of primary school, age 6–7.*

course /kuʀs/ *nf* **1** running; run; racing; race; **faire la ~ avec qn** to race sb; **c'est la course tous les matins pour me préparer** I'm always in a rush in the morning to get ready; **2** (in taxi) journey; **c'est 50 francs la ~** the fare is 50 francs; **3 faire une ~** to run an errand; **faire les ~s** to do the shopping; **4** (of star, planet) path; (of clouds) passage.
■ **~ de haies** (in athletics) hurdles; (for horses) steeplechase; **~ d'obstacles** obstacle race; (figurative) obstacle course; **~ de vitesse** (in athletics) sprint; (on motorbikes) speedway race.
IDIOMS **ne plus être dans la ~** to be out of touch; **être à bout de ~** to be worn out.

coursier, **-ière** /kuʀsje, ɛʀ/ *nm,f* messenger.

court, **~e** /kuʀ, kuʀt/ **I** *adj* **1** short; **de ~e durée** short-lived; short-term; **avoir le souffle ~** to get out of breath easily; **2** [*defeat, victory, majority*] narrow.
II *adv* **couper ~ à qch** to put paid to sth; **s'arrêter ~** to stop short.
III *nm* **~ de tennis** tennis court.
■ **~ métrage** short (film); **~e échelle**: **faire la ~e échelle à qn** to give sb a leg up○.
IDIOMS **être à ~ de** to be short of [*money*]; **prendre qn de ~** to catch sb unprepared.

court-circuit, *pl* **~s** /kuʀsiʀkɥi/ *nm* short-circuit.

courtier, **-ière** /kuʀtje, ɛʀ/ *nm,f* broker.

courtiser /kuʀtize/ [1] *vtr* to woo.

courtoisie /kuʀtwazi/ *nf* courtesy.

couru, **~e** /kuʀy/ **I** *pp* ▶ **courir**.
II *pp adj* [*place*] popular.

IDIOMS **c'est ~ d'avance**○ it's a foregone conclusion.

cousin, **~e** /kuzɛ̃, in/ *nm,f* cousin.

coussin /kusɛ̃/ *nm* cushion.

cousu, **~e** ▶ **coudre**.

coût /ku/ *nm* cost; **~ de la vie** cost of living.

coûtant /kutɑ̃/ *adj m* **prix ~** cost price.

couteau, *pl* **~x** /kuto/ *nm* **1** knife; **donner un coup de ~ à qn** to stab sb; **2** razor shell (GB) or clam (US); **3** knife edge.

IDIOMS **être à ~x tirés avec qn** to be at daggers drawn with sb; **avoir le ~ sous la gorge** to have a pistol to one's head.

coûter /kute/ [1] **I** *vtr* to cost.

II *vi* to cost; **~ cher** to be expensive; **ça m'a coûté de m'excuser** it was hard for me to apologize.

III *v impers* **il t'en coûtera d'avoir fait cela** you will pay for doing this; **coûte que coûte, quoi qu'il en coûte** at all costs.

IDIOMS **~ les yeux de la tête** to cost an arm and a leg○.

coûteux, **-euse** /kutø, øz/ *adj* costly.

coutume /kutym/ *nf* custom; **avoir ~ de faire** to be in the habit of doing.

IDIOMS **une fois n'est pas ~** it does no harm just this once.

couture /kutyʀ/ *nf* **1** sewing; dressmaking; **faire de la ~** to sew; **2** seam.

IDIOMS **sous toutes les ~s** from every angle; **battre qn à plates ~s** to beat sb hollow.

couturier /kutyʀje/ *nm* dress designer.

couturière /kutyʀjɛʀ/ *nf* dressmaker.

couvent /kuvɑ̃/ *nm* convent.

couver /kuve/ [1] **I** *vtr* **1** to sit on [*eggs*]; **la poule couve** the hen is brooding; **2** to overprotect; **~ qn/qch du regard** to look fondly at sb/sth; to gaze longingly at sb/sth; **3** to be coming down with [*illness*].

II *vi* [*rebellion*] to brew; [*fire, anger*] to smoulder (GB), to smolder (US).

couvercle /kuvɛʀkl/ *nm* **1** lid; **2** screwtop.

couvert, **~e** /kuvɛʀ, ɛʀt/ **I** *pp* ▶ **couvrir**.

II *pp adj* **1** covered (**de** in, with); **être ~ de diplômes** to have a lot of qualifications; **2** [*pool*] indoor; [*market*] covered; **3** [*sky*] overcast.

III *nm* **1** place setting; **mettre le ~** to lay the table; **un ~ en argent** a silver knife, fork and spoon; **2** cover charge.

IV à couvert *phr* **se mettre à ~** to take cover.

V sous le couvert de *phr* under the pretence[GB] of; **sous ~ de la plaisanterie** under the guise of a joke.

couverture /kuvɛʀtyʀ/ *nf* **1** blanket; rug (GB), lap robe (US); **2** cover.

IDIOMS **tirer la ~ à soi** to turn a situation to one's own advantage.

couveuse /kuvøz/ *nf* incubator.

couvre-feu, *pl* **~x** /kuvʀəfø/ *nm* curfew.

couvre-lit, *pl* **~s** /kuvʀəli/ *nm* bedspread.

couvrir /kuvʀiʀ/ [32] **I** *vtr* **1** to cover [*furniture, wall, fire, card*]; to roof [*house*]; **~ qn de qch** (with blows, jewels, compliments) to shower sb with sth; **2** [*sound*] to drown out; **3** [*transmitter, inspector*] to cover [*region*]; **4** to wrap [sb] up; to cover [sb] up; **5** to cover up for [*mistake, person*]; **6** (with gun) to cover [*soldier*]; **7** to cover [*distance*]; **8** [*book, journalist*] to cover [*story, event*]; **9** [*sum*] to cover [*expenses*].

II se couvrir *v refl* (+ *v être*) **1** to wrap up; to put on a hat; **2** [*sky*] to become overcast; **3 se ~ de** to become covered with; **4** (against accusations) to cover oneself.

CP /sepe/ *nm*: *abbr* ▶ **cours**.

crabe /kʀab/ *nm* crab.

crachat /kʀaʃa/ *nm* spit.

cracher /kʀaʃe/ [1] **I** *vtr* **1** to spit out; **c'est le portrait de sa mère tout craché**○ she's the spitting image of her mother; **2** to belch (out) [*flames, smoke*].

II *vi* to spit; **je ne cracherais pas dessus**○ I wouldn't turn up my nose at it.

crachin /kʀaʃɛ̃/ *nm* drizzle.

crachoir /kʀaʃwaʀ/ *nm* spittoon.

craie /kʀɛ/ *nf* chalk.

craindre /kʀɛ̃dʀ/ [54] *vtr* **1** to fear, to be afraid of; **2** to be sensitive to [*cold*]; to dislike [*sun*].

crainte /kʀɛ̃t/ *nf* fear; **avoir des ~s au sujet de qn** to be worried about sb; **n'ayez ~, soyez sans ~** have no fear.

craintif, **-ive** /kʀɛ̃tif, iv/ *adj* timorous, timid.

cramoisi, **~e** /kʀamwazi/ *adj* crimson.

crampe /kʀɑ̃p/ *nf* cramp.

crampon /kʀɑ̃pɔ̃/ *nm* crampon; **chaussures à ~s** (for football) boots with studs (GB) or cleats (US); (for running) spiked shoes.

cramponner: **se cramponner** /kʀɑ̃pɔne/ [1] *v refl* (+ *v être*) to hold on tightly.

cran /kʀɑ̃/ **I** *nm* **1** notch; (in belt) hole; **monter d'un ~** to move up a notch; **2** nick; **3**○ **avoir du ~** to have guts○; **4** (in hair) wave.

II à cran *phr* **être à ~** to be on edge.

■ **~ d'arrêt** flick knife (GB), switchblade (US); **~ de sûreté** safety catch.

crâne /kʀɑn/ *nm* **1** skull; **2**○ head; **ne rien avoir dans le ~** to have no brains; **bourrer le ~ à qn**○ to brainwash sb.

crânien, **-ienne** /kʀɑnjɛ̃, ɛn/ *adj* cranial; **boîte crânienne** cranium.

crapaud /kʀapo/ *nm* toad.

crapule /kʀapyl/ *nf* crook.

craqueler: **se craqueler** /kʀakle/ [19] *v refl* (+ *v être*) to crack.

craquement /kʀakmɑ̃/ *nm* **1** creaking sound, creak; **2** cracking sound, crack.

craquer /kʀake/ [1] **I** *vtr* **1** to split [*trousers*]; **2** to strike [*match*].

II *vi* **1** [*seam*] to split; [*branch*] to crack; **2** [*floor*] to creak; **3**○ [*person*] to crack up○.

crasse /kʀas/ *nf* grime, filth.

crasseux, **-euse** /kʀasø, øz/ *adj* filthy, grimy.

cratère /kʀatɛʀ/ *nm* crater.

cravache /kʀavaʃ/ *nf* whip.

cravate /kʀavat/ *nf* tie.

crawl /kʀol/ *nm* crawl.

crayon /kʀɛjɔ̃/ *nm* pencil; **~ noir** lead pencil; **~ optique** light pen.

créance /kʀeɑ̃s/ *nf* **1** debt (*owed by a debtor*); **2** letter of credit.

créancier, **-ière** /kʀeɑ̃sje, ɛʀ/ *nm,f* creditor.

créateur, **-trice** /kʀeatœʀ, tʀis/ *nm,f* creator; designer.

créatif, **-ive** /kʀeatif, iv/ *adj* creative.

création /kʀeasjɔ̃/ *nf* **1** creation; **la ~ d'une entreprise** the setting up of a company; **la ~ d'un nouveau produit** the development of a new product; **tous les livres de la ~** all the books in the world; **2** (work of art) creation; (play) first production; (commercial) new product.

créativité /kʀeativite/ *nf* creativity.

créature /kʀeatyʀ/ *nf* creature.

crèche /kʀɛʃ/ *nf* **1** crèche (GB), day-nursery; **2** (at Christmas) crib (GB), crèche (US).

crédibilité /kʀedibilite/ *nf* credibility.

crédible /kʀedibl/ *adj* credible.

crédit /kʀedi/ *nm* **1** funds; **les ~s de la recherche** research funding; **2** credit; **accorder un ~** to grant credit terms; **faire ~ à qn** to give sb credit; **porter une somme au ~ d'un compte** to credit sb's account with a sum of money; **mettre** or **porter qch au ~ de qn** (figurative) to give sb credit for sth.

créditer /kʀedite/ [1] *vtr* to credit.

créditeur, **-trice** /kʀeditœʀ, tʀis/ *adj* **être ~** to be in credit.

credo /kʀedo/ *nm* creed.

crédule /kʀedyl/ *adj* gullible, credulous.

créer /kʀee/ [11] **I** *vtr* (gen) to create; to develop [*new product*]; to set up [*company*].

II se créer *v refl* (+ *v être*) **se ~ des problèmes** to bring trouble on oneself.

crémaillère /kʀemajɛʀ/ *nf* **pendre la ~** to have a house-warming (party).

crémation /kʀemasjɔ̃/ *nf* cremation.

crématoire /kʀematwaʀ/ *nm* crematorium.

crème[1] /kʀɛm/ *adj inv* cream.

crème[2] /kʀɛm/ *nf* **1** cream; **2** cream dessert; **3**○ **la ~ des linguistes** the very best linguists.

■ **~ Chantilly** whipped cream; **~ glacée** dairy ice cream; **~ de marrons** chestnut spread; **~ renversée** caramel custard.

crémerie /kʀɛmʀi/ *nf* cheese shop (GB) or store (US).

crémeux, **-euse** /kʀemø, øz/ *adj* creamy.

créneau, *pl* **~x** /kʀeno/ *nm* **1** parallel parking; **2** gap; **tu as un ~ demain?** do you have any free time tomorrow?; **3** (in fortifications) **les ~x** crenellations.

■ **~ horaire** time slot.

créole /kʀeɔl/ *adj*, *nm* Creole.

crêpe[1] /kʀɛp/ *nm* **1** crepe; **2** black veil.

crêpe[2] /kʀɛp/ *nf* pancake, crêpe.

crêper /kʀepe/ [1] *vtr* to backcomb (GB), to tease [*hair*].

crépi /kʀepi/ *nm* rendering.

crépitement /kʀepitmɑ̃/ *nm* crackling, crackle; sizzling.

crépiter /kʀepite/ [1] *vi* [*fire*] to crackle; [*oil*] to sizzle; [*rain*] to patter.

crépon /kʀepɔ̃/ *nm* crepe paper.

crépu, **~e** /kʀepy/ *adj* frizzy.

crépuscule /kʀepyskyl/ *nm* twilight, dusk.

crescendo /kʀeʃɛndo/ **I** *adv* **aller ~** [*noise*] to intensify.

II *nm* crescendo.

cresson /kʀesɔ̃, kʀəsɔ̃/ *nm* watercress.

crête /kʀɛt/ *nf* **1** (of cock) comb; (of bird) crest; **2** (of mountain, wave) crest; (of roof) ridge.

crétin, **~e** /kʀetɛ̃, in/ *nm,f* moron○.

creuser /kʀøze/ [1] **I** *vtr* **1** to dig a hole in [*ground*]; to drill a hole in [*tooth*]; to dig into [*rock*]; **2** to dig [*hole, canal, grave*]; to sink [*well*]; **3** [*wrinkles*] to furrow [*face*]; **~ les reins** to arch one's back; **4** to deepen, to increase [*deficit, inequalities*]; **5** to go into [sth] in depth [*question, subject*].

II se creuser *v refl* (+ *v être*) [*cheeks*] to become hollow; [*gap*] to widen.

IDIOMS **ça creuse**○ it really gives you an appetite; **se ~ (la tête** or **la cervelle)**○ to rack one's brains.

creux, **-euse** /kʀø, øz/ **I** *adj* **1** [*trunk, tooth, sound, cheeks*] hollow; [*stomach, speech*] empty; [*analysis*] shallow; **un plat ~** a shallow dish; **assiette creuse** soup dish; **2** [*day, period*] slack, off-peak.

II *adv* **sonner ~** to make a hollow sound.

III *nm* **1** hollow; **le ~ des reins** the small of the back; **le ~ de l'aisselle** the armpit; **le ~ de la vague** the trough of the wave; **être au ~ de la vague** (figurative) to be at rock bottom; **2**○ **avoir un petit ~** to have the munchies○.

crevaison /kʀəvɛzɔ̃/ *nf* puncture.

crevasse /kʀəvas/ *nf* **1** crevasse; **2** crack, fissure; **3** chapped skin.

crever /kʀəve/ [16] **I** *vtr* to puncture, to burst; **~ les yeux de qn** to blind sb; to poke sb's eyes out; **ça crève les yeux** it's blindingly obvious; **ça crève le cœur** it's heartbreaking.

II *vi* **1** to burst; to burst open; **2** to die; **~ de faim** to be starving; **3 ~ d'envie** to be eaten up with envy; **~ d'orgueil** to be terribly full of oneself.

III se crever *v refl* (+ *v être*) **il s'est crevé un œil** he put his eye out.

IDIOMS **marche ou crève** sink or swim.

crevette /kʀəvɛt/ *nf* **~ grise** shrimp; **~ rose** prawn.

cri /kʀi/ *nm* **1** cry; shout; scream; **un ~ aigu** a shriek; **à grands ~s** loudly; **pousser les hauts ~s** to protest loudly; **2** (of bird) call.

criant, **~e** /kʀijɑ̃, ɑ̃t/ *adj* clear, striking.

criard, **~e** /kʀiaʀ, aʀd/ *adj* [*voice*] shrill; [*colour*] garish.

crible /kʀibl/ *nm* (for minerals) screen; (for sand) riddle; **passer au ~** (figurative) to sift through.

cribler /kʀible/ [1] *vtr* **1 ~ qn/qch de balles** to riddle sb/sth with bullets; **2 ~ qn de reproches** to heap reproaches on sb.

cric /kʀik/ *nm* (for car) jack.

criée /kʀije/ *nf* **(vente à la) ~** auction.

crier /kʀije/ [2] **I** *vtr* **1** to shout; **2** to proclaim; to protest [*innocence*].
II crier à *v+prep* **on a crié au scandale quand**... there was an outcry when...
III *vi* **1** to shout; to cry; to scream; **2** [*animal*] to give a cry; [*monkey*] to chatter; [*gull*] to cry; [*pig*] to squeal.

crieur, -ieuse /kʀijœʀ, øz/ *nm,f* **~ de journaux** news vendor.

crime /kʀim/ *nm* **1** crime; **2** murder; **~ crapuleux** murder for money.

criminalité /kʀiminalite/ *nf* crime.

criminel, -elle /kʀiminɛl/ **I** *adj* criminal.
II *nm,f* **1** criminal; **2** murderer.

crin /kʀɛ̃/ *nm* horsehair; **à tout ~** (figurative) dyed-in-the-wool.

crinière /kʀinjɛʀ/ *nf* mane.

crique /kʀik/ *nf* cove.

criquet /kʀikɛ/ *nm* locust.

crise /kʀiz/ *nf* **1** crisis; **~ agricole** crisis in the agricultural industry; **la ~** the economic crisis, the slump; **2** shortage; **~ de l'emploi** job shortage; **3** (Med) attack; **~ d'appendicite** appendicitis; **~ de toux** coughing fit; **4** fit; **~ de colère** fit of rage; **faire une ~** to have a tantrum; to have a fit○.
■ **~ cardiaque** heart attack; **~ de foie** indigestion; **~ de nerfs** hysterics.

crisper /kʀispe/ [1] **I** *vtr* **l'angoisse crispait son visage** his/her face was tense with worry.
II se crisper *v refl* (+ *v être*) [*hands*] to clench; [*face, person*] to tense (up); [*smile*] to freeze.

crisser /kʀise/ [1] *vi* [*shoes, chalk*] to squeak; [*snow*] to crunch; [*tyres, brakes*] to screech.

cristal, *pl* **-aux** /kʀistal, o/ *nm* crystal.

cristallin, ~e /kʀistalɛ̃, in/ **I** *adj* **1** crystalline; **2** crystal clear.
II *nm* (of eye) (crystalline) lens.

cristalliser /kʀistalize/ [1] *vtr, vi, v refl* (+ *v être*) to crystallize.

critère /kʀitɛʀ/ *nm* **1** criterion; **~s de gestion/de confort** standards of management/comfort; **le ~ déterminant** the crucial factor; **2** specification; **remplir les ~s d'âge et de diplôme** to meet the requirements as far as age and qualifications are concerned.

critiquable /kʀitikabl/ *adj* questionable.

critique[1] /kʀitik/ **I** *adj* critical.
II *nmf* critic.

critique[2] /kʀitik/ *nf* **1** criticism; **faire une ~ à qn** to criticize sb; **2** review; **faire la ~ d'un film** to review a film; **3 la ~ littéraire** literary criticism.

critiquer /kʀitike/ [1] *vtr* to criticize.

croasser /kʀɔase/ [1] *vi* to caw.

croc /kʀo/ *nm* fang.

croche /kʀɔʃ/ *nf* quaver (GB), eighth note (US); **double ~** semiquaver (GB), sixteenth note (US).

croche-pied○, *pl* **~s** /kʀɔʃpje/ *nm* **faire un ~ à qn** to trip sb up.

crochet /kʀɔʃɛ/ *nm* **1** hook; **2** picklock; **3** crochet hook; **faire du ~** to crochet; **4** square bracket; **5 faire un ~** to make a detour; **6** (in boxing) hook; **7** fang.
IDIOMS **vivre aux ~s**○ **de qn** to sponge off sb○.

crocheter /kʀɔʃte/ [18] *vtr* to pick [*lock*].

crochu, ~e /kʀɔʃy/ *adj* [*nose*] hooked; [*hands*] clawed.

crocodile /kʀɔkɔdil/ *nm* crocodile.

croire /kʀwaʀ/ [71] **I** *vtr* **1** to believe; **faire ~ à qn** to make sb believe; **2** to think; **je crois savoir que** I happen to know that; **il est malin, faut pas**○ **~!** he's clever, believe me!; **tu ne crois pas si bien dire** you don't know how right you are; **on croirait de la soie** it looks like silk; **3 si l'on en croit l'auteur, à en ~ l'auteur** if we are to believe the author; **crois-en mon expérience** take my word for it.
II croire à *v+prep* to believe [*story*]; to believe in [*ghosts*].
III croire en *v+prep* to believe in.
IV se croire *v refl* (+ *v être*) **il se croit beau** he thinks he's handsome.

croisade /kʀwazad/ *nf* crusade.

croisé, ~e[1] /kʀwaze/ **I** *pp* ▶ **croiser**.
II *pp adj* **1** [*legs*] crossed; [*arms*] folded; **2** crossbred; **3** [*agreements*] reciprocal.

croisée[2] /kʀwaze/ *nf* **1** junction; **à la ~ des chemins** at the crossroads; **2** window.

croisement /kʀwazmɑ̃/ *nm* **1** crossroads; crossing, junction; **2** (of threads, straps) crossing; **3** crossbreeding; hybrid, cross(breed).

croiser /kʀwaze/ [1] **I** *vtr* **1** to cross; **~ les bras** to fold one's arms; **2 ~ qn/qch** to pass sb/sth (coming the other way); **3** to meet; **mon regard croisa le sien** our eyes met; **4** to cross(breed).
II se croiser *v refl* (+ *v être*) [*cars*] to pass each other; [*letters*] to cross in the post (GB) or mail (US); [*roads*] to intersect; [*lines*] to cross.

croisière /kʀwazjɛʀ/ *nf* cruise.

croissance /kʀwasɑ̃s/ *nf* growth.

croissant /kʀwasɑ̃/ *nm* **1** croissant; **2** crescent; **~ de lune** crescent moon.

croître /kʀwatʀ/ [72] *vi* **1** to grow; **faire ~** to grow; **2** [*noise*] to get or grow louder.

croix /kʀwa/ *nf* cross; **bras en ~** arms out on either side of the body.
IDIOMS **ton argent, tu peux faire une ~ dessus**○ you can kiss your money goodbye; **un jour à marquer d'une ~** a red-letter day.

croquant, ~e /kʀɔkɑ̃, ɑ̃t/ *adj* crunchy.

croque-madame /kʀɔkmadam/ *nm inv*: *toasted ham and cheese sandwich topped with a fried egg*.

croque-monsieur /kʀɔkməsjø/ *nm inv*: *toasted ham and cheese sandwich*.

croque-mort○, *pl* **~s** /kʀɔkmɔʀ/ *nm* undertaker.

croquer /kʀɔke/ [1] **I** *vtr* **1** to crunch; **2** to sketch; **belle à ~** as pretty as a picture.
II *vi* **1** to be crunchy; **2 ~ dans une pomme** to bite into an apple.

croquette /kʀɔkɛt/ *nf* croquette.

croquis /kʀɔki/ *nm* sketch.

crosse /kʀɔs/ *nf* **1** (of rifle) butt; **2** (of cane) crook; **3** (Sport) stick.
crotte /kʀɔt/ *nf* dropping; **c'est de la ~ de chien** it's dog mess.
crottin /kʀɔtɛ̃/ *nm* **1** dung; **2** (*small round*) goat's cheese.
crouler /kʀule/ [1] *vi* **1** to collapse; to crumble; **2 ~ sous** to be weighed down by [*parcels, debts, work*]; **~ sous le poids de** [*table*] to groan under the weight of [*books*].
croupe /kʀup/ *nf* (of horse) croup.
croupi, **~e** /kʀupi/ *adj* stagnant.
croupier /kʀupje/ *nm* croupier.
croupir /kʀupiʀ/ [3] *vi* **1** [*water*] to stagnate; **2 ~ en prison** to rot in jail.
croustillant, **~e** /kʀustijɑ̃, ɑ̃t/ *adj* **1** crispy; crunchy; **2** [*story, details*] spicy.
croustiller /kʀustije/ [1] *vi* [*bread*] to be crusty; [*chocolate*] to be crunchy.
croûte /kʀut/ *nf* **1** (of bread) crust; (of cheese) rind; **casser la ~**○ to have a bite to eat; **2** (Culin) **pâté en ~** pâté en croute or in pastry; **3** (Med) scab; **4**○ daub, bad painting.
croûton /kʀutɔ̃/ *nm* **1** crust; **2** (Culin) crouton.
croyance /kʀwajɑ̃s/ *nf* belief.
croyant, **~e** /kʀwajɑ̃, ɑ̃t/ *adj* **être ~** to be a believer.
CRS /seɛʀɛs/ *nm* (*abbr* = **compagnie républicaine de sécurité**) **un ~** *a member of the French riot police.*
cru, **~e**[1] /kʀy/ **I** *adj* **1** raw; uncooked; [*milk*] unpasteurized; **se faire manger tout ~**○ to be eaten alive○; **2** [*light, colour*] harsh; **3** [*language*] crude.
II *nm* vineyard; vintage; vintage year; **du meilleur ~** [*collection*] vintage; **du ~** [*wine, author*] local.
cruauté /kʀyote/ *nf* cruelty.
cruche /kʀyʃ/ *nf* jug (GB), pitcher (US).
crucial, **~e**, *mpl* **-iaux** /kʀysjal, o/ *adj* crucial.
crucifier /kʀysifje/ [2] *vtr* to crucify.
crucifix /kʀysifi/ *nm* crucifix.
crudité /kʀydite/ *nf* **~s** raw vegetables, crudités.
crue[2] /kʀy/ **I** *adj f* ▶ **cru I**.
II *nf* rise in water level; flood; **en ~** in spate.
cruel, **-elle** /kʀyɛl/ *adj* cruel.
cruellement /kʀyɛlmɑ̃/ *adv* **1** cruelly; **2 manquer ~ de qch** to be desperately short of sth; **3** terribly; **la pénurie de carburant se fait ~ sentir** the fuel shortage is being sorely felt.
crûment /kʀymɑ̃/ *adv* **1** bluntly; **2** crudely.
crustacé /kʀystase/ *nm* shellfish.
crypte /kʀipt(ə)/ *nf* crypt.
crypté, **~e** /kʀipte/ *adj* coded; encrypted.
cube /kyb/ **I** *adj* cubic.
II *nm* **1** cube; **2** building block.
cubique /kybik/ *adj* **1** cubic; **2** cube-shaped.
cucul○ /kyky/ *adj* corny○; silly.
cueillette /kœjɛt/ *nf* **1** (of fruits, flowers) picking; **2** crop.
cueillir /kœjiʀ/ [27] *vtr* **1** to pick [*fruit, flowers*]; **2**○ to arrest [*criminal*].
cuiller, **cuillère** /kɥijɛʀ/ *nf* spoon; spoonful; **~ à café** teaspoon; coffee spoon.
IDIOMS **il n'y va pas avec le dos de la ~**○ he doesn't do things by halves; **en deux coups de ~ à pot** in two shakes of a lamb's tail○.
cuillerée /kɥij(ə)ʀe/ *nf* spoonful.
cuir /kɥiʀ/ *nm* **1** leather; **2** rawhide; hide.
■ **~ chevelu** scalp.
cuirassé /kɥiʀase/ *nm* battleship.
cuire /kɥiʀ/ [69] **I** *vtr* **1** to cook; to bake; to roast; **~ à la vapeur** to steam; **à ~** [*apple*] cooking; **2** to fire [*porcelain*].
II *vi* **1** [*food*] to cook; to be cooking; **laissez ~ à petit feu** allow to simmer gently; **2**○ **on cuit sur la plage** it's baking (hot) on the beach; **3** [*graze*] to sting; **ça me cuit** it stings.
cuisant, **~e** /kɥizɑ̃, ɑ̃t/ *adj* **1** [*defeat, regret*] bitter; [*remark*] stinging; **2** [*pain*] burning.
cuisine /kɥizin/ *nf* **1** kitchen; **2** galley; **3** kitchen furniture; **4** cooking; **5**○ intrigues.
cuisiner /kɥizine/ [1] *vtr, vi* to cook.
cuisinier, **-ière**[1] /kɥizinje, ɛʀ/ *nm,f* cook; chef.
cuisinière[2] /kɥizinjɛʀ/ *nf* cooker.
cuissarde /kɥisaʀd/ *nf* wader; thighboot.
cuisse /kɥis/ *nf* thigh; **des ~s de grenouille** frogs' legs.
cuisson /kɥisɔ̃/ *nf* **1** cooking; baking; roasting; **2** (of pottery) firing.
cuit, **~e**[1] /kɥi, kɥit/ *pp* ▶ **cuire**.
IDIOMS **c'est ~**○ we've had it○; **c'est du tout ~**○ it's a piece of cake○; it's in the bag○; **elle attend que ça (lui) tombe tout ~**○ she expects things to fall straight into her lap.
cuite[2] /kɥit/ *nf* **tenir une ~** to be plastered○.
cuivre /kɥivʀ/ **I** *nm* **1 ~ (rouge)** copper; **2 ~ (jaune)** brass.
II cuivres *nm pl* **1** copperware; **2** brass; **3** (Mus) **les ~s** the brass.
cul /ky/ *nm* **1**◑ bottom, arse● (GB), ass◑ (US); **2** (of bottle) bottom; **~ sec**○**!** bottoms up○!
culasse /kylas/ *nf* **1** cylinder head; **2** breechblock.
culbute /kylbyt/ *nf* somersault.
culbuter /kylbyte/ [1] *vi* [*person*] to take a tumble; [*vehicle*] to overturn.
cul-de-jatte, *pl* **culs-de-jatte** /kydʒat/ *nmf* person who has had both legs amputated.
cul-de-sac, *pl* **culs-de-sac** /kydsak/ *nm* **1** cul-de-sac; **2** dead end.
culinaire /kylinɛʀ/ *adj* culinary.
culminant, **~e** /kylminɑ̃, ɑ̃t/ *adj* **point ~** (of mountain) highest point or peak; (of career) peak; (of crisis) height; (of holiday) high point.
culminer /kylmine/ [1] *vi* **1 ~ au-dessus de qch** to tower above sth; **2** [*inflation, unemployment*] to reach its peak.
culot○ /kylo/ *nm* cheek○; **y aller au ~** to bluff.
culotte /kylɔt/ *nf* **1** pants (GB), panties (US); **2 en ~(s) courte(s)** in short trousers (GB) or pants (US).

culpabiliser /kylpabilize/ [1] I *vtr* to make [sb] feel guilty.
II *vi* to feel guilty.
culpabilité /kylpabilite/ *nf* guilt.
culte /kylt/ *nm* **1** cult; **2** religion.
cultivateur, **-trice** /kyltivatœʀ, tʀis/ *nm,f* farmer.
cultiver /kyltive/ [1] I *vtr* to grow; to cultivate.
II **se cultiver** *v refl* (+ *v être*) to improve one's mind.
culture /kyltyʀ/ I *nf* **1** cultivation; **la ~ du blé** wheat growing; **2** crop; **~ d'hiver** winter crop; **3** (in biology) culture; **4** (of society) culture; **~ de masse** mass culture; **5** knowledge; **~ classique** classical education; **6** arts; **subventionner la ~** to subsidize the arts.
II **cultures** *nf pl* cultivated land.
■ **~ physique** physical exercise.
culturel, **-elle** /kyltyʀɛl/ *adj* cultural.
culturisme /kyltyʀism/ *nm* body-building.
cumin /kymɛ̃/ *nm* cumin.
cumul /kymyl/ *nm* **1** **~ de fonctions** holding of several posts concurrently; **2** (Law) **~ des peines** ≈ sentences to be served consecutively.
cumuler /kymyle/ [1] *vtr* **1** to hold [sth] concurrently [*offices*]; to draw [sth] concurrently [*salaries*]; **2** to accumulate [*handicaps, degrees*]; **3** to combine [*results*]; to add up [*amounts*].
cumulus /kymylys/ *nm inv* cumulus.
cupide /kypid/ *adj* grasping.
cupidité /kypidite/ *nf* avarice, greed, cupidity.
cure /kyʀ/ *nf* **faire une ~** to go for a course of treatment in a spa.
■ **~ d'amaigrissement** slimming course (GB), reducing treatment (US); **~ de sommeil** sleep therapy.
curé /kyʀe/ *nm* (parish) priest.
cure-dents /kyʀdɑ̃/ *nm inv* toothpick.
curer /kyʀe/ [1] I *vtr* to clean out [*pipe, pond*].
II **se curer** *v refl* (+ *v être*) **se ~ les ongles** to clean one's nails.
curieusement /kyʀjøzmɑ̃/ *adv* **1** oddly, strangely; **2** oddly enough.
curieux, **-ieuse** /kyʀjø, øz/ I *adj* **1** inquisitive, curious; **2** strange; **3** **esprit ~** person with an enquiring mind; **être ~ d'apprendre** to be keen to learn.
II *nm,f* onlooker.
curiosité /kyʀjozite/ *nf* curiosity.
curriculum vitae /kyʀikylɔmvite/ *nm inv* curriculum vitae, résumé (US).
curry /kyʀi/ *nm* **1** curry powder; **2** curry.
curseur /kyʀsœʀ/ *nm* cursor.
cursus /kyʀsys/ *nm inv* course
cutané, **~e** /kytane/ *adj* [*irritation*] skin.
cutter /kytœʀ/ *nm* Stanley knife®.
cuve /kyv/ *nf* vat; tank.
cuvée /kyve/ *nf* vatful; **la ~ 1959** the 1959 vintage; **~ du patron** house wine.
cuvette /kyvɛt/ *nf* **1** bowl; **~ des wc** lavatory bowl or pan; **2** (in land) basin.
CV /seve/ *nm* **1** (*abbr* = **curriculum vitae**) CV (GB), résumé (US); **2** (*written abbr* = **cheval-vapeur**) HP.
cyclable /siklabl/ *adj* **piste ~** cycle track.
cycle /sikl/ *nm* **1** cycle; **~ infernal** vicious cycle; **2** series; **3** (Sch) **premier ~** *first two years of a university degree course leading to a diploma*; **deuxième ~** *final two years of a university degree course*; **troisième ~** postgraduate (GB) or graduate (US) studies; **4** (bi)cycle.
cyclique /siklik/ *adj* cyclic.
cyclisme /siklism/ *nm* cycling; cycle racing.
cycliste /siklist/ I *adj* [*club*] cycling; [*race*] cycle; **coureur ~** racing cyclist.
II *nmf* cyclist; **short de ~** cycling shorts.
cyclone /siklon/ *nm* **1** cyclone; **2** (in weather) depression.
cygne /siɲ/ *nm* swan; **~ mâle** cob; **~ femelle** pen; **jeune ~** cygnet.
cylindre /silɛ̃dʀ/ *nm* **1** cylinder; **2** roller.
cylindrée /silɛ̃dʀe/ *nf* capacity, size; **~ de 1200 cm³** 1200 cc engine.
cymbale /sɛ̃bal/ *nm* cymbal.
cynique /sinik/ *adj* cynical.
cynisme /sinism/ *nm* cynicism.
cyprès /sipʀɛ/ *nm* cypress.
cystite /sistit/ *nf* cystitis.

Dd

d, **D** /de/ *nm inv* d, D.
d' ▶ **de**.
DAB /deabe/ *nm*: (*abbr* = **distributeur automatique de billets**) automatic teller machine, ATM.
dactylographie /daktilɔgʀafi/ *nf* typing.
dada○ /dada/ *nm* **1** (baby talk) horsie○; **2** hobby; **3** hobbyhorse.
daigner /deɲe/ [1] *vtr* to deign (**faire** to do).
daim /dɛ̃/ *nm* **1** (fallow) deer; **2** venison; **3** buckskin; **4** suede.
dalle /dal/ *nf* **1** slab; **2** flagstone; **3** concrete foundation slab.
IDIOMS **avoir la ~**○ to be ravenous; **que ~**◑ nothing at all, zilch○.
daller /dale/ [1] *vtr* to pave.
daltonien, **-ienne** /daltɔnjɛ̃, ɛn/ *adj* colour[GB]-blind.
dam /dɑ(m)/ *nm* **au grand ~ de** to the great displeasure of.
dame /dam/ **I** *nf* **1** lady; **2** (in cards, chess) queen; (in draughts) King.
II dames *nf pl* draughts (GB), checkers (US).
damier /damje/ *nm* draughtboard (GB), checkerboard (US).
damnation /danasjɔ̃/ *nf* damnation.
damner /dɑne/ [1] **I** *vtr* to damn.
II se damner *v refl* (+ *v être*) to damn oneself; **se ~ pour qch**○ to sell one's soul for sth.
dancing /dɑ̃siŋ/ *nm* dance hall.
dandiner: **se dandiner** /dɑ̃dine/ [1] *v refl* (+ *v être*) [*duck*] to waddle.
Danemark /danmaʀk/*pr nm* Denmark.
danger /dɑ̃ʒe/ *nm* danger.
■ **~ public** danger to the public; (figurative) menace.
dangereux, **-euse** /dɑ̃ʒʀø, øz/ *adj* dangerous.
danois, **~e** /danwa, az/ **I** *adj* Danish.
II *nm* **1** (language) Danish; **2** (dog) Great Dane.
dans /dɑ̃/ *prep* **1** in; **être ~ la cuisine** to be in the kitchen; **être ~ un avion/bateau** to be on a plane/boat; **2** into; **entrer ~ une pièce** to go into a room; **monter ~ un avion** to get on a plane; **3 boire ~ un verre** to drink out of a glass; **prendre qch ~ un placard** to take sth out of a cupboard; **4 ~ deux heures** in two hours; **fait ~ les deux heures** done within two hours; **je t'appellerai ~ la journée** I'll phone you during the day; **5 ~ les 30 francs** about 30 francs.
danse /dɑ̃s/ *nf* **1** dance; **2** dancing; **faire de la ~** to take dancing classes.
■ **~ classique** classical ballet.
danser /dɑ̃se/ [1] *vtr*, *vi* to dance.
IDIOMS **ne pas savoir sur quel pied ~** not to know what to do.

danseur, **-euse** /dɑ̃sœʀ, øz/ *nm,f* dancer; **~ étoile** principal dancer.
dard /daʀ/ *nm* **1** (Zool) sting; **2** spear.
dare-dare○ /daʀdaʀ/ *adv* double quick.
darne /daʀn/ *nf* (fish) steak.
date /dat/ *nf* **1** date; **~ limite** deadline; **~ limite de vente** sell-by date; **2** time; **depuis cette ~** from that time; **un ami de longue ~** a longstanding friend; **le dernier scandale en ~** the latest scandal.
dater /date/ [1] **I** *vtr* to date; **à ~ du 31 juillet** as from 31 July.
II *vi* **1 ~ de** to date from; **2** to be dated.
datte /dat/ *nf* (Bot, Culin) date.
dattier /datje/ *nm* date palm.
daube /dob/ *nf* **bœuf en ~** beef casserole.
dauphin /dofɛ̃/ *nm* **1** dolphin; **2** heir apparent; **3** dauphin.
daurade /dɔʀad/ *nf* (sea) bream.
davantage /davɑ̃taʒ/ *adv* **1** more; **2** longer; **rester ~** to stay longer.
de (**d'** *before vowel or mute h*) /də, d/

■ **Note** You will find translations for expressions such as *d'abord*, *de travers*, *pomme de terre*, *chemin de fer* etc, at the entries ***abord***, ***travers***, ***pomme*** and ***chemin*** etc.

I *prep* **1** from; **venir ~ Paris** to come from Paris; **il est ~ père italien** his father is Italian; **2** by; **un poème ~ Victor Hugo** a poem by Victor Hugo; **3** of; **les chapeaux ~ Paul** Paul's hats; **le 20 du mois** the 20th of the month; **deux heures d'attente** a two-hour wait; **deux heures ~ libres** two hours free; **4** than; **plus/moins ~ dix** more/less than ten; **5** in; **d'un ton monocorde** in a monotone; **6** with; **pousser qch du pied** to push sth aside with one's foot; **7 travailler ~ nuit** to work at night; **ne rien faire ~ la journée** to do nothing all day; **8 être content ~ faire** to be happy to do.
II *det* **de, de l', de la, du** some; any; **voulez-vous ~ la bière?** would you like some beer?; **je n'ai pas d'argent** I haven't got any money.
dé /de/ *nm* **1** dice; **les ~s sont jetés** the die is cast; **2 ~ (à coudre)** thimble.
déambuler /deɑ̃byle/ [1] *vi* to wander (about).
débâcle /debɑkl/ *nf* **1** (Mil) rout; **2** (figurative) collapse.
déballer /debale/ [1] *vtr* **1** to unpack; **2** to display.
débandade /debɑ̃dad/ *nf* **1** stampede; **2** disarray.
débarbouiller /debaʀbuje/ [1] **I** *vtr* to wash.
II se débarbouiller *v refl* (+ *v être*) to wash one's face.
débarcadère /debaʀkadɛʀ/ *nm* landing stage, jetty.

débardeur /debaʀdœʀ/ *nm* tank top.

débarquement /debaʀkəmɑ̃/ *nm* **1** (of goods) unloading; **2** (of passengers) disembarkation; **3** (Mil) landing.

débarquer /debaʀke/ [1] **I** *vtr* to unload [*goods*].
II *vi* **1** to disembark; **2** (Mil) to land; **3**° to turn up° (**chez qn** at sb's place).

débarras /debaʀa/ *nm inv* **1** junk room; **2 bon ~**°! good riddance!

débarrasser /debaʀase/ [1] **I** *vtr* **1** to clear (out); **2 ~ [qn] de** to free [sb] from [*complex*]; **~ qn (de son manteau)** to take sb's coat.
II se débarrasser *v refl* (+ *v être*) **se ~ de** to get rid of; to dispose of.
IDIOMS **~ le plancher**° to clear off°.

débat /deba/ *nm* debate.

débattre /debatʀ/ [61] **I** *vtr* to negotiate.
II débattre de or **sur** *v+prep* **1 ~ de** or **sur** to discuss; **2 ~ de** or **sur** to debate.
III se débattre *v refl* (+ *v être*) to struggle.

débauche /deboʃ/ *nf* **1** debauchery; **2** profusion.

débaucher /deboʃe/ [1] *vtr* **1** to corrupt; **2** to lay [sb] off; **3**° to tempt [sb] away.

débile /debil/ **I**° *adj* daft°.
II *nmf* **~ mental** (Med) retarded person.

débiner° /debine/ [1] **I** *vtr* to badmouth°.
II se débiner *v refl* (+ *v être*) to clear off°; to make oneself scarce°.

débit /debi/ *nm* **1** debit; **la somme est inscrite au ~** the sum has been debited; **2** (when speaking) delivery; **3** (of river) rate of flow; **4** (of liquid) flow; (of gas) output.
■ **~ de boissons** bar.

débiter /debite/ [1] *vtr* **1** to debit; **2** to reel [sth] off; **~ des bêtises** to talk a lot of nonsense; **3** to cut [sth] up.

débiteur, **-trice** /debitœʀ, tʀis/ **I** *adj* **compte ~** debit account; **pays ~** debtor nation.
II *nm,f* debtor.

déblayer /debleje/ [21] *vtr* **1** to clear away [*earth, snow*]; **2** to clear [*place*].

débloquer /deblɔke/ [1] **I** *vtr* **1** to unlock [*steering wheel*]; to unjam [*mechanism*]; **2** to unfreeze [*prices*]; to end the deadlock in [*situation*]; **3** to make [sth] available [*credit*].
II° *vi* to be off one's rocker°.

déboires /debwaʀ/ *nm pl* **1** disappointments; **2** trials, difficulties; **3** setbacks.

déboiser /debwaze/ [1] *vtr* to deforest.

déboîter /debwate/ [1] **I** *vtr* to disconnect [*tubes*].
II *vi* [*car*] to pull out.
III se déboîter *v refl* (+ *v être*) **se ~ le genou** to dislocate one's knee.

débordant, **~e** /debɔʀdɑ̃, ɑ̃t/ *adj* **1** [*imagination*] overactive; **2 ~ de** brimming with [*energy*]; bursting with [*health*].

débordé, **~e** /debɔʀde/ **I** *pp* ▸ **déborder**.
II *pp adj* **1** overwhelmed; **2** overloaded.

débordement /debɔʀdəmɑ̃/ *nm* (of protest) flood; (of enthusiasm) excess.

déborder /debɔʀde/ [1] **I** *vtr* **1** [*problem, feeling*] to go beyond; **2 se laisser ~** to let oneself be overwhelmed; **3** (Mil, Sport) to outflank.
II déborder de *v+prep* to be brimming over with; to be bursting with.
III *vi* **1** [*river*] to overflow; **2** [*liquid*] to overflow; to boil over; **3** to jut out.

débouché /debuʃe/ *nm* **1** market; **~s à l'exportation** export outlets; **2** job opportunity.

déboucher /debuʃe/ [1] **I** *vtr* **1** to unblock; **2** to open; to uncork.
II *vi* **~ sur** [*street*] to open onto; [*talks*] to lead to.
III se déboucher *v refl* (+ *v être*) **1** to come unblocked; **2** [*ears*] to pop; **3 se ~ les oreilles/le nez** to unblock one's ears/nose.

débouler /debule/ [1] **I** *vtr* to charge down.
II *vi* **1** to tumble down; **2**° to turn up.

déboulonner /debulɔne/ [1] *vtr* to unbolt.

débourser /debuʀse/ [1] *vtr* to pay out.

déboussoler° /debusɔle/ [1] *vtr* to confuse.

debout /dəbu/ **I** *adj inv, adv* **1** standing; [*object*] upright; **se mettre ~** to stand up; **je ne tiens plus ~** I'm falling asleep on my feet; **2 ton histoire tient ~**° your story seems likely; **3** (out of bed) **être ~** to be up.
II *excl* get up!

déboutonner /debutɔne/ [1] **I** *vtr* to unbutton.
II se déboutonner *v refl* (+ *v être*) to come undone.

débraillé, **~e** /debʀɑje/ *adj* [*person*] dishevelled[GB]; [*clothes, style*] sloppy.

débrancher /debʀɑ̃ʃe/ [1] *vtr* to unplug [*appliance*]; to disconnect [*alarm system*].

débrayer /debʀeje/ [21] *vi* (Aut) to declutch.

débridé, **~e** /debʀide/ *adj* unbridled.

débris /debʀi/ *nm inv* **1** fragment; **des ~ de verre** broken glass; **2** piece of wreckage.

débrouillard, **~e** /debʀujaʀ, aʀd/ *adj* resourceful.

débrouiller /debʀuje/ [1] **I** *vtr* **1** to disentangle [*threads*]; **2** to solve [*riddle*].
II se débrouiller *v refl* (+ *v être*) **1** to manage; **2** to get by; **il se débrouille bien en espagnol** he speaks good Spanish.

débusquer /debyske/ [1] *vtr* to flush [sb/sth] out.

début /deby/ **I** *nm* beginning; start.
II débuts *nm pl* **1** debut; **2** early stages.

débutant, **~e** /debytɑ̃, ɑ̃t/ **I** *adj* [*driver, skier*] novice; [*engineer*] recently qualified.
II *nm,f* beginner.

débuter /debyte/ [1] *vi* **1** [*day, novel*] to begin, to start; [*person*] to start off; **2** to start out (**comme** as); **3** [*performer*] to make one's debut.

deçà /dəsa/ **I** *adv* **~, delà** here and there.
II en deçà *phr* **1** on this side; **2** below.

décacheter /dekaʃte/ [20] *vtr* to unseal.

décade /dekad/ *nf* **1** 10-day period; **2** (controversial) decade.

décadent, **~e** /dekadɑ̃, ɑ̃t/ *adj* **1** decadent; **2** in decline.

décaféiné, **~e** /dekafeine/ *adj* decaffeinated.

décalage /dekalaʒ/ *nm* **1** gap; **2** discrepancy; **3** interval, time-lag; **4** shift.
■ **~ horaire** time difference.

décaler /dekale/ [1] **I** *vtr* **1** to bring forward [*date, departure time*]; **2** to put (GB) or move (US) back [*date, departure time*]; **3** to move [sth] forward [*object*]; **4** to move [sth] back [*object*].
II se décaler *v refl* (+ *v être*) **se ~ sur la droite** to move or shift to the right.

décalquer /dekalke/ [1] *vtr* **1** to trace (**sur** from); **2** to transfer (**sur** onto).

décamper○ /dekɑ̃pe/ [1] *vi* to run off.

décanter /dekɑ̃te/ [1] **I** *vtr* to allow [sth] to settle [*liquid*]; to clarify [*waste water*].
II se décanter *v refl* (+ *v être*) **1** [*liquid*] to settle; **2** [*situation, ideas*] to become clearer.

décapant, **~e** /dekapɑ̃, ɑ̃t/ *adj* **1** scouring; **2**○ [*humour*] abrasive, caustic.

décaper /dekape/ [1] *vtr* **1** to clean; **2** to strip [*furniture*]; **~ avec un abrasif** to scour; **3**○ [*alcohol, soap*] to be harsh.

décapiter /dekapite/ [1] *vtr* to behead; to decapitate.

décapotable /dekapɔtabl/ *adj* **une (voiture) ~** a convertible.

décapsuler /dekapsyle/ [1] *vtr* to take the top off.

décapsuleur /dekapsylœʀ/ *nm* bottle-opener.

décathlon /dekatlɔ̃/ *nm* decathlon.

décéder /desede/ [14] *vi* (+ *v être*) to die.

déceler /desle/ [17] *vtr* **1** to detect; **2** to reveal [*anomaly, feeling*]; **3** to indicate [*presence*].

décembre /desɑ̃bʀ/ *nm* December.

décemment /desamɑ̃/ *adv* decently.

décence /desɑ̃s/ *nf* decency.

décennie /deseni/ *nf* decade.

décent, **~e** /desɑ̃, ɑ̃t/ *adj* **1** decent; **2** proper.

décentraliser /desɑ̃tʀalize/ [1] *vtr* to decentralize.

décentrer /desɑ̃tʀe/ [1] *vtr* to move away from the centre[GB].

déception /desɛpsjɔ̃/ *nf* disappointment.

décerner /desɛʀne/ [1] *vtr* to award.

décès /desɛ/ *nm inv* death.

décevant, **~e** /desəvɑ̃, ɑ̃t/ *adj* disappointing.

décevoir /desəvwaʀ/ [5] *vtr* **1** to disappoint; **2** to fail to fulfil[GB] [*hope*].

déchaîné, **~e** /deʃene/ **I** *pp* ▶ **déchaîner**.
II *pp adj* stirred up; **~ contre** furious with.

déchaîner /deʃene/ [1] **I** *vtr* to rouse [*feelings*]; to excite [*people*].
II se déchaîner *v refl* (+ *v être*) **1** [*sea*] to rage; [*feelings*] to burst out; **2** to go wild.

déchanter /deʃɑ̃te/ [1] *vi* to become disenchanted.

décharge /deʃaʀʒ/ *nf* **1** (of firearm) discharge; **2 ~ municipale** (municipal) dump; **3 ~ électrique** electric shock; **4** (Law) acquittal.

décharger /deʃaʀʒe/ [13] **I** *vtr* **1** to unload [*vessel, goods*]; **2** to unload [*firearm*]; **3** to fire [*gun*]; **4 ~ qn de** to relieve sb of [*task*]; **5** to discharge [*battery*]; **6** to unburden [*conscience*].
II se décharger *v refl* (+ *v être*) **1 se ~ de qch** to off-load sth; **2** [*battery*] to run down.

décharné, **~e** /deʃaʀne/ *adj* [*body*] emaciated; [*finger*] bony.

déchausser: **se déchausser** /deʃose/ [1] *v refl* (+ *v être*) **1** to take off one's shoes; **2** [*teeth*] to work loose due to receding gums.

dèche○ /dɛʃ/ *nf* **être dans la ~** to be broke○.

déchéance /deʃeɑ̃s/ *nf* **1** decline; **2** degeneration.

déchet /deʃɛ/ **I** *nm* **1** scrap; **2** waste; **3** wreck.
II déchets *nm pl* waste material, waste.

déchiffrer /deʃifʀe/ [1] *vtr* **1** to decipher; **2** (Mus) to sight-read.

déchiqueté, **~e** /deʃikte/ **I** *pp* ▶ **déchiqueter**.
II *pp adj* jagged, ragged.

déchiqueter /deʃikte/ [20] *vtr* **1** to tear [sth] to shreds; **2** [*machine, animal*] to tear to pieces.

déchirant, **~e** /deʃiʀɑ̃, ɑ̃t/ *adj* **1** heart-rending; **2** agonizing.

déchirer /deʃiʀe/ [1] **I** *vtr* **1** to tear up [*paper, material*]; **2** to tear [*garment*]; **3** to split [*group*]; **déchiré entre X et Y** torn between X and Y.
II se déchirer *v refl* (+ *v être*) **1** to tear; **2 se ~ un muscle** to tear a muscle; **3** to tear each other apart.

déchirure /deʃiʀyʀ/ *nf* (gen, Med) tear.

déchu, **~e** /deʃy/ *adj* [*monarch*] deposed; [*angel*] fallen.

décibel /desibɛl/ *nm* decibel.

décidé, **~e** /deside/ **I** *pp* ▶ **décider**.
II *pp adj* determined; resolute.

décidément /desidemɑ̃/ *adv* really.

décider /deside/ [1] **I** *vtr* **1** to decide; **c'est décidé** it's settled; **2** to persuade (**à faire** to do).
II décider de *v+prep* to decide on; to fix.
III se décider *v refl* (+ *v être*) **1** to make up one's mind; **2 se ~ pour** to decide on.

décimal, **~e**[1], *mpl* **-aux** /desimal, o/ *adj* decimal.

décimale[2] /desimal/ *nf* decimal.

décimer /desime/ [1] *vtr* to decimate.

décisif, **-ive** /desizif, iv/ *adj* **1** decisive; **2** conclusive.

décision /desizjɔ̃/ *nf* **1** decision; **2** decisiveness.

déclamer /deklame/ [1] *vtr* to declaim.

déclaration /deklaʀasjɔ̃/ *nf* **1** statement; declaration; **2** notification; **3** (Law) statement; **~ de vol/perte** report of theft/loss.
■ **~ d'impôts** (income-)tax return.

déclaré, **~e** /deklaʀe/ *adj* [*enemy*] avowed; [*hatred*] professed.

déclarer /deklaʀe/ [1] **I** *vtr* **1** to declare; **il a été déclaré coupable** he was found guilty; **2** to declare [*goods, revenue*]; to report [*theft*]; to register [*birth*]; **non déclaré** undeclared; illegal.
II se déclarer *v refl* (+ *v être*) **1** [*fire, epi-*

demic] to break out; [*fever*] to start; **2 se ~ pour/contre** to come out for/against.

déclenchement /deklɑ̃ʃmɑ̃/ *nm* (of mechanism) release; (of illness) onset; (of reaction) start.

déclencher /deklɑ̃ʃe/ [1] **I** *vtr* **1** to spark (off) [*protest*]; to cause [*reaction, explosion*]; to start [*avalanche*]; **2** to launch [*offensive*]; to start [*strike, debate*]; **3** to set off [*mechanism*].
II se déclencher *v refl* (+ *v être*) **1** to go off; to be activated; **2** to break out; to begin.

déclic /deklik/ *nm* **1** trigger; **2** (of camera) click.

déclin /deklɛ̃/ *nm* decline.

déclinaison /deklinɛzɔ̃/ *nf* declension.

décliner /dekline/ [1] **I** *vtr* **1** to decline; to turn [sth] down; **2 ~ son identité** to give one's name; **3** to decline.
II *vi* [*light, talent*] to fade; [*health*] to deteriorate; [*enthusiasm*] to wane; [*sun*] to go down.
III se décliner *v refl* (+ *v être*) to decline.

décocher /dekɔʃe/ [1] *vtr* to shoot [*arrow*].

décoder /dekɔde/ [1] *vtr* to decode.

décodeur /dekɔdœʀ/ *nm* decoder.

décoiffer /dekwafe/ [1] *vtr* **~ qn** to ruffle sb's hair.

décoincer /dekwɛ̃se/ [12] *vtr* to unjam [*mechanism, door*]; to free [*key*].

décollage /dekɔlaʒ/ *nm* take-off.

décoller /dekɔle/ [1] **I** *vtr* to peel off [*sticker*].
II *vi* [*plane*] to take off.
III se décoller *v refl* (+ *v être*) to come off.

décolleté, **~e** /dekɔlte/ **I** *adj* low-cut.
II *nm* low neckline.

décolleuse /dekɔløz/ *nf* steam stripper.

décolonisation /dekɔlɔnizasjɔ̃/ *nf* decolonization.

décolorant, **~e** /dekɔlɔʀɑ̃, ɑ̃t/ *adj* bleaching.

décolorer /dekɔlɔʀe/ [1] *vtr* **1** to bleach; **2** to cause to fade.

décombres /dekɔ̃bʀ/ *nm pl* rubble.

décommander /dekɔmɑ̃de/ [1] **I** *vtr* to call [sth] off.
II se décommander *v refl* (+ *v être*) to cry off (GB), to beg off.

décomposer /dekɔ̃poze/ [1] **I** *vtr* **1** to break down [*argument, water*]; **2** to distort [*features*].
II se décomposer *v refl* (+ *v être*) **1** to decompose; **2** to fall apart.

décomposition /dekɔ̃pozisjɔ̃/ *nf* **1** decomposition; **2** disintegration.

décompte /dekɔ̃t/ *nm* **1** discount; **2** count; **faire le ~ de** to count [sth] up [*votes, points*].

décompter /dekɔ̃te/ [1] *vtr* **1** to deduct (**de** from); **2** to count [*votes, points*].

déconcentrer /dekɔ̃sɑ̃tʀe/ [1] *vtr* to distract.

déconcerter /dekɔ̃sɛʀte/ [1] *vtr* to disconcert.

déconfit, **~e** /dekɔ̃fi, it/ *adj* crestfallen.

décongeler /dekɔ̃ʒle/ [17] *vtr, vi* to defrost.

déconnecter /dekɔnɛkte/ [1] *vtr* **1** to disconnect [*appliance*]; **2** to dissociate.

déconner◑ /dekɔne/ [1] *vi* **1** to kid around○; **faut pas ~!** come off it○!; **2** to mess around○; to piss around◑ (GB); **3** to play up○.

déconseiller /dekɔ̃seje/ [1] *vtr* to advise against.

décontenancer /dekɔ̃tnɑ̃se/ [12] *vtr* to disconcert.

décontracté, **~e** /dekɔ̃tʀakte/ **I** *pp* ▶ **décontracter**.
II *pp adj* **1** relaxed; **2** casual; **3** laid-back○.

décontracter /dekɔ̃tʀakte/ [1] *vtr*, **se décontracter** *v refl* (+ *v être*) to relax.

décontraction /dekɔ̃tʀaksjɔ̃/ *nf* **1** relaxation; **2** ease; **3** casual attitude.

décor /dekɔʀ/ *nm* **1** decor; **2** setting; **j'ai besoin de changer de ~** I need a change of scene; **partir dans le ~**○ to drive off the road; **3** (of film) set; **tourné en ~ naturel** shot on location.

décorateur, **-trice** /dekɔʀatœʀ, tʀis/ *nm,f* **1** interior decorator; **2** set designer.

décoratif, **-ive** /dekɔʀatif, iv/ *adj* **1** ornamental; **2** decorative.

décoration /dekɔʀasjɔ̃/ *nf* **1** decorating; **2** (gen, Mil) decoration; **3** interior design.

décorer /dekɔʀe/ [1] *vtr* to decorate.

décortiquer /dekɔʀtike/ [1] *vtr* to shell [*nut*]; to peel [*prawn*].

découcher /dekuʃe/ [1] *vi* to spend the night away from home.

découdre /dekudʀ/ [76] **I** *vtr* to undo, to unpick (GB) [*hem, seam*].
II *vi* **en ~** to have a fight (**avec** with).

découler /dekule/ [1] *vi* **1** to follow (**de** from); **2** to result (**de** from).

découpage /dekupaʒ/ *nm* cut-out.

découper /dekupe/ [1] *vtr* to cut up [*tart*]; to carve [*roast*]; to divide up [*land*].

découragement /dekuʀaʒmɑ̃/ *nm* discouragement, despondency.

décourager /dekuʀaʒe/ [13] *vtr* **1** to dishearten; **2** to discourage; **3** to deter.

décousu, **~e** /dekuzy/ **I** *pp* ▶ **découdre**.
II *pp adj* [*hem*] which has come undone.
III *adj* [*story*] rambling; [*conversation*] casual.

découvert, **~e**[1] /dekuvɛʀ, ɛʀt/ **I** *pp* ▶ **découvrir**.
II *pp adj* **1** bare; **avoir la tête ~e** to be bareheaded; **2** [*truck*] open; [*car*] open-topped.
III *nm* overdraft; **être à ~** to be overdrawn.

découverte[2] /dekuvɛʀt/ *nf* discovery.

découvrir /dekuvʀiʀ/ [32] **I** *vtr* **1** to discover; **faire ~ qch à qn** to introduce sb to sth; **2** to show [*arm, back*]; **3** to leave [sth] exposed [*border*].
II se découvrir *v refl* (+ *v être*) **1** to remove one's hat; **2 elle s'est découvert un talent** she found she had a talent.

décrépit, **~e** /dekʀepi, it/ *adj* [*person*] decrepit; [*building*] dilapidated; [*wall*] crumbling.

décret /dekʀɛ/ *nm* decree.

décréter /dekʀete/ [14] *vtr* **1** to order; **2** to decree (**que** that); **3** to declare (**que** that).

décrire /dekʀiʀ/ [67] *vtr* **1** to describe; **2** to follow.

décrocher /dekʀɔʃe/ [1] **I** *vtr* **1** to take down

[*picture*]; **2** to uncouple [*wagon*]; **3 ~ son téléphone** to pick up the receiver; to take the phone off the hook; **4**○ to get [*contract*].
II *vi* to give up.
IDIOMS **~ le gros lot** to hit the jackpot.

décroître /dekʀwatʀ/ [72] *vi* [*level*] to fall; [*moon*] to wane; [*day*] to get shorter; [*light, noise*] to fade; [*inflation*] to go down.

décrypter /dekʀipte/ [1] *vtr* **1** to decipher [*signs*]; **2** to interpret [*statement*].

déçu, **~e** /desy/ *pp* ▶ **décevoir**.

décupler /dekyple/ [1] *vtr*, *vi* to increase tenfold.

dédaigner /dedeɲe/ [1] *vtr* to despise.

dédain /dedɛ̃/ *nm* contempt, disdain.

dédale /dedal/ *nm* **1** (of buildings) maze; **2** (of laws, formalities) labyrinth.

dedans /dədɑ̃/ **I** *adv* inside.
II en dedans *phr* inside.

dédicace /dedikas/ *nf* **1** dedication (**à qn** to sb); **2** inscription.

dédicacer /dedikase/ [12] *vtr* **1** to dedicate [*book*] (**à** to); **2** to sign [*book, photo*].

dédier /dedje/ [2] *vtr* **1** to dedicate [*novel*] (**à** to); **2** to devote [*life*] (**à** to).

dédire: **se dédire** /dediʀ/ [65] *v refl* (+ *v être*) to back out.

dédommagement /dedɔmaʒmɑ̃/ *nm* compensation.

dédommager /dedɔmaʒe/ [13] *vtr* **1** to compensate; **2 ~ qn de qch** to make it up to sb for sth.

dédouaner /dedwane/ [1] *vtr* to clear through customs.

dédoubler: **se dédoubler** /deduble/ [1] *v refl* (+ *v être*) [*nail*] to split; [*image*] to split in two; [*cable*] to come apart.

déduction /dedyksjɔ̃/ *nf* deduction.

déduire /dedɥiʀ/ [69] **I** *vtr* **1** to deduce; **2** to infer; **3** to deduct.
II se déduire *v refl* (+ *v être*) **1** to be inferred; **2** to be deduced; **3** to be deducted.

déesse /deɛs/ *nf* goddess.

défaillance /defajɑ̃s/ *nf* failure.

défaillant, **~e** /defajɑ̃, ɑ̃t/ *adj* **1** [*motor, system*] faulty; **2** [*organization*] inefficient; **3** [*health, memory*] failing; [*person*] fainting.

défaillir /defajiʀ/ [28] *vi* **1** to faint; **se sentir ~** to feel faint; **2** [*health, memory*] to fail; **soutenir qn sans ~** to show unflinching support for sb.

défaire /defɛʀ/ [10] **I** *vtr* to undo; to untie.
II se défaire *v refl* (+ *v être*) **1** to come undone; **2 se ~ de** to get rid of; to part with; to rid oneself of; **3** [*face*] to fall; **avoir la mine défaite** to look haggard.

défaite /defɛt/ *nf* defeat.

défaut /defo/ **I** *nm* **1** fault, failing; **prendre qn en ~** to catch sb out; **2** defect; flaw; **présenter des ~s** to be faulty; **~ de fabrication** manufacturing fault; **~ de prononciation** speech impediment; **3** shortage; **faire ~** [*money, resources*] to be lacking.
II à défaut de *phr* **à ~ de** (**quoi**) failing (which); **à ~ de pouvoir acheter, elle loue** since she can't buy, she has to rent.

défaveur /defavœʀ/ *nf* **il s'est trompé de 30 francs en ma ~** he overcharged me by 30 francs.

défavorable /defavɔʀabl/ *adj* [*situation*] unfavourable[GB] (**à** to); [*person*] opposed (**à** to).

défavorisé, **~e** /defavɔʀize/ *adj* **1** underprivileged; **2** disadvantaged.

défection /defɛksjɔ̃/ *nf* **1** defection; **2** nonappearance; **3** (of friends) desertion.

défectueux, **-euse** /defɛktɥø, øz/ *adj* [*material*] faulty, defective; [*reasoning*] flawed.

défendre /defɑ̃dʀ/ [6] **I** *vtr* **1 ~ à qn de faire** to forbid sb to do; **2** to defend [*person, country, interests*]; **3** to fight for [*right*]; to stand up for [*friend, principle*]; **~ une cause** to champion a cause; **4** (Law, Sport) to defend.
II se défendre *v refl* (+ *v être*) **1** to defend oneself; to stand up for oneself; **2** to be tenable; **3** to protect oneself; **4**○ to get by; **5 on ne peut se ~ de penser que**... one can't help thinking that...

défense /defɑ̃s/ *nf* **1 '~ de fumer'** 'no smoking'; **~ d'en parler devant lui** don't mention it in front of him; **2** (Med, Mil, Sport) defence[GB]; **3** protection; **sans ~** helpless; unprotected; **la ~ de l'environnement** the protection of the environment; **prendre la ~ de** to stand up for; **4** (Zool) tusk.

défenseur /defɑ̃sœʀ/ *nm* defender.

défensive /defɑ̃siv/ *nf* **sur la ~** on the defensive.

déférence /defeʀɑ̃s/ *nf* **marques de ~** marks of respect.

déferler /defɛʀle/ [1] *vi* **1** [*wave*] to break (**sur** on); **2** [*violence*] to erupt; **3 ~ sur** [*people*] to pour into [*country, town*].

défi /defi/ *nm* **1** challenge; **mettre qn au ~ de faire** to challenge sb to do; **2 air de ~** defiant look.

défiance /defjɑ̃s/ *nf* distrust, mistrust.

déficience /defisjɑ̃s/ *nf* deficiency.

déficit /defisit/ *nm* **1** deficit; **2** (Med) deficiency.

déficitaire /defisitɛʀ/ *adj* showing a deficit; showing a loss; showing a shortfall.

défier /defje/ [2] *vtr* **1** to challenge [*rival*]; **2** to defy [*danger, death*]; **prix défiant toute concurrence** unbeatable price.

défigurer /defigyʀe/ [1] *vtr* to disfigure.

défilé /defile/ *nm* **1** parade; **2** (protest) march; **3** (of visitors, candidates) stream; **4** gorge.
■ **~ aérien** flypast (GB), flyover (US); **~ militaire** march-past; **~ de mode** fashion show.

défiler /defile/ [1] **I** *vi* **1** to parade; [*protesters*] to march; **2** [*people*] to come and go; **3** [*images, landscape*] to unfold; **4** (Comput) to scroll.
II se défiler○ *v refl* (+ *v être*) to wriggle out of it.

définir /definiʀ/ [3] *vtr* to define.

définitif, **-ive** /definitif, iv/ **I** *adj* [*accounts, report*] final; [*edition*] definitive; [*refusal*] flat.

II **en définitive** *phr* at the end of the day.

définition /definisjɔ̃/ *nf* definition.

définitivement /definitivmɑ̃/ *adv* for good.

déflagration /deflagʀasjɔ̃/ *nf* detonation.

défoncer /defɔ̃se/ [12] *vtr* to break down [*door*]; to smash in [*back of a car*].

déformation /defɔʀmasjɔ̃/ *nf* **1** distortion; **2** deformity; **3 c'est de la ~ professionnelle** it's a habit that comes from the job.

déformé, **~e** /defɔʀme/ *adj* [*face, image, truth*] distorted; [*object, mind*] warped; **chaussée ~e** uneven (road) surface.

déformer /defɔʀme/ [1] **I** *vtr* **1** to bend [sth] (out of shape); **2** to distort; **3 on a déformé mes propos** my words have been twisted.

II se déformer *v refl* (+ *v être*) to lose its shape.

défoulement /defulmɑ̃/ *nm* letting off steam.

défouler /defule/ [1] **I** *vtr* **ça me défoule** it helps me (to) unwind.

II se défouler *v refl* (+ *v être*) **1** to let off steam; **2 se ~ sur qn** to take it out on sb.

défraîchi, **~e** /defʀeʃi/ *adj* [*garment, curtain*] worn; [*material, beauty*] faded.

défrayer /defʀeje/ [21] *vtr* **~ la chronique** to be the talk of the town.

défricher /defʀiʃe/ [1] *vtr* to clear, to reclaim.

défroisser /defʀwase/ [1] *vtr* to smooth out.

défunt, **~e** /defœ̃, œ̃t/ **I** *adj* **1** former; **2** late.

II *nm,f* **le ~** the deceased.

dégagé, **~e** /degaʒe/ *adj* **1** [*road, sky*] clear; [*forehead*] bare; **2** [*look*] casual.

dégagement /degaʒmɑ̃/ *nm* **1** clearing; **2** (in football) clearance.

dégager /degaʒe/ [13] **I** *vtr* **1** to free; **~ qn d'une responsabilité** to relieve sb of a responsibility; **~ des crédits** to make funds available; **2** to unblock [*nose*]; **2** to clear [*way*]; **'dégagez, s'il vous plaît'** 'move along please'; **dégage**○**!** get lost○!; **3** to find [*idea, sense*]; **4** to emit [*odour, gas*]; **~ de la chaleur** to give off heat.

II se dégager *v refl* (+ *v être*) **1** to free oneself/itself; **2** [*weather, sky*] to clear; **3 se ~ de** to come out of; **4** to become clear.

dégaine○ /degɛn/ *nf* odd appearance.

dégainer /degene/ [1] *vtr* to draw [*gun*].

dégarnir: **se dégarnir** /degaʀniʀ/ [3] *v refl* (+ *v être*) to be going bald.

dégât /degɑ/ *nm* damage.

dégel /deʒɛl/ *nm* thaw.

dégeler /deʒle/ [17] **I** *vtr* **1** to improve [*relations*]; **2** to unfreeze [*credit*].

II *vi* to thaw (out).

III se dégeler *v refl* (+ *v être*) **1** [*relations, situation*] to thaw; **2** [*audience*] to warm up.

dégénérer /deʒeneʀe/ [14] *vi* **1** [*incident*] to get out of hand; **~ en** to degenerate into; **2** [*plant, species*] to degenerate.

dégingandé, **~e** /deʒɛ̃gɑ̃de/ *adj* lanky.

dégivrer /deʒivʀe/ [1] *vtr* **1** to de-ice [*windscreen*]; **2** to defrost [*fridge*].

déglingué○, **~e** /deglɛ̃ge/ *adj* dilapidated.

déglutir /deglytiʀ/ [3] *vtr*, *vi* to swallow.

dégonfler /degɔ̃fle/ [1] **I** *vtr* to deflate [*tyre*].

II *vi* [*swelling, bump*] to go down.

III se dégonfler *v refl* (+ *v être*) **1** to deflate; to go down; **2**○ to chicken out○.

dégot(t)er○ /degɔte/ [1] *vtr* to find.

dégouliner /deguline/ [1] *vi* **1** to trickle; **2** to drip (**de** with).

dégoupiller /degupije/ [1] *vtr* **~ une grenade** to pull the pin out of a grenade.

dégourdi, **~e** /deguʀdi/ *adj* smart.

dégourdir: **se dégourdir** /deguʀdiʀ/ [3] *v refl* (+ *v être*) **se ~ les jambes** to stretch one's legs.

dégoût /degu/ *nm* disgust.

dégoûtant, **~e** /degutɑ̃, ɑ̃t/ *adj* **1** filthy; **2**○ disgusting; revolting.

dégoûté, **~e** /degute/ *adj* disgusted; **faire le ~** to turn one's nose up.

dégoûter /degute/ [1] *vtr* **1** to disgust; **2** to make [sb] feel sick; **3 ~ qn de qch/de faire** to put sb off sth/off doing.

dégradant, **~e** /degʀadɑ̃, ɑ̃t/ *adj* degrading.

dégradé, **~e** /degʀade/ **I** *adj* **tons ~s** shaded tones; **coupe ~e** layered cut.

II *nm* (in colours) gradation.

dégrader /degʀade/ [1] **I** *vtr* **1** to damage; **2** (Mil) to cashier [*officer*]; **3** to degrade [*person*].

II se dégrader *v refl* (+ *v être*) to deteriorate.

dégrafer /degʀafe/ [1] **I** *vtr* to undo.

II se dégrafer *v refl* (+ *v être*) to come undone.

dégraisser /degʀese/ [1] *vtr* to trim the fat off.

degré /dəgʀe/ *nm* **1** degree; **par ~s** gradually; **à un moindre ~** to a lesser extent; **susceptible au plus haut ~** extremely touchy; **brûlures du premier ~** first-degree burns; **~ de parenté** degree of kinship; **2** step; **enseignement du second ~** secondary education; **c'est à prendre au deuxième ~** it is not to be taken literally; **3 titrer 40° d'alcool** ≈ to be 70% proof.

■ **~ Celsius** degree Celsius; **~ Fahrenheit** degree Fahrenheit.

dégressif, **-ive** /degʀesif, iv/ *adj* [*tax*] graduated; **tarifs ~s** tapering charges.

dégringoler○ /degʀɛ̃gɔle/ [1] **I** *vtr* to race down [*stairs, hill*].

II *vi* **1** [*person*] to take a tumble; [*books*] to tumble down; **2** to drop sharply.

dégriser /degʀize/ [1] *vtr* **1** to sober [sb] up; **2** to bring [sb] to his/her senses.

déguerpir /degɛʀpiʀ/ [3] *vi* to leave.

déguisé, **~e** /degize/ *adj* **1** in fancy dress; in disguise; **2** [*party*] fancy-dress; **3** [*attempt*] concealed; [*compliment*] disguised.

déguisement /degizmɑ̃/ *nm* costume.

déguiser /degize/ [1] **I** *vtr* **1** to dress [sb] up (**en** as); **2** to disguise.

II se déguiser *v refl* (+ *v être*) **1** to dress up; **2** to disguise oneself.

dégustation /degystasjɔ̃/ *nf* tasting.

déguster /degyste/ [1] *vtr* to savour[GB] [*drink, victory*]; to enjoy [*performance*].

déhanchement /deɑ̃ʃmɑ̃/ *nm* **1** swaying hips; **2** lopsidedness.

déhancher: **se déhancher** /deɑ̃ʃe/ [1] *v refl* (+ *v être*) to wiggle one's hips.

dehors /dəɔʀ/ **I** *adv* outside; **mettre qn ~** to throw sb out; to fire sb; to expel sb.
II *excl* get out!
III en dehors de *phr* **1** outside; **2** apart from.

déjà /deʒa/ *adv* **1** already; **2** before, already; **je te l'ai ~ dit** I've told you before; **3**○ **il s'est excusé, c'est ~ quelque chose** he apologized, that's something at least; **elle est ~ assez riche!** she's rich enough as it is; **c'est combien, ~?** how much was it again?

déjeuner[1] /deʒœne/ [1] *vi* to have lunch.

déjeuner[2] /deʒœne/ *nm* lunch.

déjouer /deʒwe/ [1] *vtr* to frustrate [*precaution, manoeuvre*]; to foil [*plan*]; to evade [*inspection*].

delà /dəla/ *adv* **deçà** or **de-ci, ~** here and there.

délabré, **~e** /delabʀe/ *adj* [*house, equipment*] dilapidated; [*health*] damaged.

délabrement /delabʀəmɑ̃/ *nm* dilapidation.

délabrer /delabʀe/ [1] **I** *vtr* to ruin.
II se délabrer *v refl* (+ *v être*) [*house*] to become run-down; [*business, country*] to go to rack and ruin; [*health*] to deteriorate.

délacer /delase/ [12] *vtr* to undo; to unlace.

délai /delɛ/ *nm* **1 dans un ~ de 24 heures** within 24 hours; **respecter un ~** to meet a deadline; **dans les meilleurs ~s** as soon as possible; **2** extension; **demander un ~** to ask for extra time.
■ **~ de livraison** delivery or lead time.

délaisser /delese/ [1] *vtr* **1** to abandon [*activity*]; **2** to neglect [*friends*].

délassement /delɑsmɑ̃/ *nm* relaxation.

délasser /delɑse/ [1] *vtr, v refl* (+ *v être*) to relax; **ça délasse** it's relaxing.

délateur, **-trice** /delatœʀ, tʀis/ *nm,f* informer.

délation /delɑsjɔ̃/ *nf* informing.

délavé, **~e** /delave/ *adj* **1** [*colour, sky*] washed-out; [*jeans*] faded; **2** waterlogged.

délayer /deleje/ [21] *vtr* to thin [*paint*]; to mix [*flour*].

délectation /delɛktasjɔ̃/ *nf* delight.

délecter: **se délecter** /delɛkte/ [1] *v refl* (+ *v être*) **se ~ à faire/en faisant** to delight in doing.

délégation /delegasjɔ̃/ *nf* delegation.

délégué, **~e** /delege/ *nm,f* delegate.
■ **~ syndical** union representative.

déléguer /delege/ [14] *vtr* **1** to appoint [sb] as a delegate; **2** to delegate [*responsibility, power*].

délester /delɛste/ [1] *vtr* **1** to get rid of the ballast from; **2** to divert traffic away from.

délibération /delibeʀasjɔ̃/ *nf* deliberation; **mettre qch en ~** to debate sth.

délibéré, **~e** /delibeʀe/ *adj* [*act, violation*] deliberate; [*choice, policy*] conscious.

délibérément /delibeʀemɑ̃/ *adv* [*wound, provoke*] deliberately; [*accept, choose*] consciously.

délibérer /delibeʀe/ [14] **I délibérer de** or **sur** *v+prep* to discuss.
II *vi* to be in session.

délicat, **~e** /delika, at/ *adj* **1** [*dish*] subtle; [*person*] refined; **2** tactful; **3** thoughtful; **des procédés peu ~s** unscrupulous means; **4** [*balance, task*] delicate; [*business, moment*] sensitive; [*mission*] tricky; **5** [*skin*] delicate.

délicatement /delikatmɑ̃/ *adv* **1** delicately; **2** tactfully.

délicatesse /delikatɛs/ *nf* **1** delicacy; **la ~ de ses traits** his/her fine features; **2** sensitivity; **3** delicacy, trickiness.

délice /delis/ *nm* delight.

délicieusement /delisjøzmɑ̃/ *adv* **1** deliciously; **2** delightfully.

délicieux, **-ieuse** /delisjø, øz/ *adj* **1** delicious; **2** [*feeling, music*] delightful; [*joy*] exquisite.

délié, **~e** /delje/ *adj* **1** [*waist*] slender; **2** [*movement*] loose; **3** [*mind*] nimble.

délier /delje/ [2] *vtr* to untie; **~ qn de** to release sb from [*promise*].
IDIOMS **~ la langue à qn** to loosen sb's tongue.

délimiter /delimite/ [1] *vtr* **1** to mark the boundary of; **2** to form the boundary of; **3** to define [*role*]; to define the scope of [*subject*].

délinquance /delɛ̃kɑ̃s/ *nf* crime; **la ~ juvénile** juvenile delinquency.

délinquant, **~e** /delɛ̃kɑ̃, ɑ̃t/ **I** *adj* delinquent.
II *nm,f* offender.

déliquescence /delikesɑ̃s/ *nf* decline.

délirant, **~e** /deliʀɑ̃, ɑ̃t/ *adj* **1** [*welcome*] ecstatic; **2**○ [*scenario*] crazy○.

délire /deliʀ/ *nm* **1** (Med) delirium; **2**○ madness; **3** frenzy; **salle en ~** ecstatic audience.

délirer /deliʀe/ [1] *vi* **1** (Med) to be delirious; **2**○ to be mad.

délit /deli/ *nm* offence[GB].

délivrance /delivʀɑ̃s/ *nf* relief.

délivrer /delivʀe/ [1] *vtr* **1** to free, to liberate; **~ qn de** to relieve sb of; **2** to issue [*passport*].

déloger /delɔʒe/ [13] *vtr* **1** to evict [*tenant*]; **2** to flush out [*rebels, game*]; **3** to remove [*dust*].

déloyal, **~e**, *mpl* **-aux** /delwajal, o/ *adj* [*person*] disloyal; [*competition*] unfair.

deltaplane /dɛltaplan/ *nm* hang-glider.

déluge /delyʒ/ *nm* downpour; **~ de** flood of [*tears, complaints*]; **le Déluge** the Flood.
IDIOMS **après moi le ~** I don't care what happens after I'm gone.

déluré, **~e** /delyʀe/ *adj* **1** smart, resourceful; **2** forward.

démagogie /demagɔʒi/ *nf* demagoguery, demagogy; **faire de la ~** to try to gain popularity.

démagogique /demagɔʒik/ *adj* demagogic.

demain /dəmɛ̃/ *adv* tomorrow; **l'Europe de ~** the Europe of the future.
IDIOMS **~ il fera jour** tomorrow is another day; **ce n'est pas ~ la veille!** that's not going to happen in a hurry!

démancher: **se démancher** /demɑ̃ʃe/ [1] *v refl* (+ *v être*) [*tool*] to come off its handle.

demande /dəmɑ̃d/ *nf* **1** request, application, claim (**de** for); **~ de dommages et intérêts** claim for damages; **faire une ~ de mutation** to apply for a transfer; **2** (in economics) demand; **3** application form.
■ **~ d'emploi** job application; **'~s d'emploi'** 'situations wanted'; **~ en mariage** marriage proposal.

demandé, **~e** /dəmɑ̃de/ *adj* **très ~** [*destination*] very popular; [*product*] in great demand.

demander /dəmɑ̃de/ [1] **I** *vtr* **1** to ask for [*advice, money, help*]; to apply for [*nationality*]; to claim [*damages*]; **~ le divorce** to sue for divorce; **~ en mariage** to propose to; **'on demande un plombier'** 'plumber wanted'; **fais ce qu'on te demande!** do as you're told!; **je ne demande pas mieux** there's nothing I would like better; **2 ~ qch à qn** to ask sb sth; **il m'a demandé de tes nouvelles** he asked after you; **3** to send for [*priest*]; to dial [*number*]; **le patron vous demande** the boss wants to see you; **4** to call for [*reforms*]; to require [*effort, qualification*]; to need [*attention*].
II se demander *v refl* (+ *v être*) to wonder.

demandeur[1], **-euse** /dəmɑ̃dœʀ, øz/ *nm,f* applicant.
■ **~ d'asile** asylum-seeker; **~ d'emploi** job-seeker.

demandeur[2], **-eresse** /dəmɑ̃dœʀ, d(ə)ʀɛs/ *nm,f* (Law) plaintiff.

démangeaison /demɑ̃ʒɛzɔ̃/ *nf* itch.

démanger /demɑ̃ʒe/ [13] *vtr* **ça me démange** it itches, it's itching; **l'envie de le gifler me démangeait** I was itching to slap him.

démanteler /demɑ̃tle/ [17] *vtr* to dismantle; to break up.

démaquillage /demakijaʒ/ *nm* make-up removal.

démaquillant, **~e** /demakijɑ̃, ɑ̃t/ **I** *adj* [*milk*] cleansing.
II *nm* make-up remover.

démaquiller: **se démaquiller** /demakije/ [1] *v refl* (+ *v être*) to remove one's make-up.

démarcation /demaʀkasjɔ̃/ *nf* demarcation.

démarchage /demaʀʃaʒ/ *nm* door-to-door selling; **~ électoral** canvassing; **~ téléphonique** cold calling.

démarche /demaʀʃ/ *nf* **1** walk; **2** step; **faire une ~ auprès de qn** to approach sb; **faire des ~s pour obtenir qch** to take steps to obtain sth; **3** reasoning; **~ de la pensée** thought process.

démarcher /demaʀʃe/ [1] *vtr* **1** to sell door-to-door; **2** to canvass.

démarquer /demaʀke/ [1] **I** *vtr* to mark down [*goods*].
II se démarquer *v refl* (+ *v être*) **1 se ~ de** to distance oneself from; **2** (Sport) to get free of one's marker.

démarrage /demaʀaʒ/ *nm* **1** starting up; **2** spurt.
■ **~ en côte** hill start.

démarrer /demaʀe/ [1] **I** *vtr* to start (up).
II *vi* **1** [*vehicle*] to pull away; [*engine*] to start; [*driver*] to drive off; [*business*] to start up; [*campaign*] to get under way; [*person*] to start off; **2** (Sport) to put on a spurt.

démarreur /demaʀœʀ/ *nm* (in car) starter.

démasquer /demaske/ [1] *vtr* to unmask [*person*]; to uncover [*plot*].

démêlé /demele/ *nm* wrangle; **avoir des ~s avec la justice** to get into trouble with the law.

démêler /demele/ [1] *vtr* **1** to disentangle; to untangle; **2** to sort out [*situation*].

démembrement /demɑ̃bʀəmɑ̃/ *nm* **1** break-up, dismemberment; **2** (of estate) division.

démembrer /demɑ̃bʀe/ [1] *vtr* to divide up, to dismember.

déménagement /demenaʒmɑ̃/ *nm* **1** moving house; move; **2** removal; **entreprise de ~s** removals firm (GB), moving company (US).

déménager /demenaʒe/ [13] **I** *vtr* **1** to move [*furniture*]; to relocate [*offices*]; **2** to clear [*room*].
II *vi* **1** to move (house); **2**○ to push off○; **3**○ to be off one's rocker○.

déménageur /demenaʒœʀ/ *nm* removal (GB) or moving (US) man.

démence /demɑ̃s/ *nf* **1** insanity; **2** dementia.

démener: **se démener** /dem(ə)ne/ [16] *v refl* (+ *v être*) **1** to thrash about; **2** to put oneself out, to exert oneself.

dément, **~e** /demɑ̃, ɑ̃t/ *adj* **1** insane, mad; **2**○ terrific○.

démenti /demɑ̃ti/ *nm* denial.

démentiel, **-ielle** /demɑ̃sjɛl/ *adj* insane.

démentir /demɑ̃tiʀ/ [30] *vtr* **1** to deny; **2** [*person*] to refute [*statement*]; [*fact*] to give the lie to [*statement*]; to belie [*appearance*].

démesure /deməzyʀ/ *nf* **1** (of ambition) excesses; **2** excessive size.

démesuré, **~e** /deməzyʀe/ *adj* excessive, immoderate.

démettre /demɛtʀ/ [60] **I** *vtr* **1** to dislocate [*joint*]; **2** to dismiss [*employee*].
II se démettre *v refl* (+ *v être*) **se ~ l'épaule** to dislocate one's shoulder.

demeurant: **au demeurant** /odəmœʀɑ̃/ *phr* as it happens, for all that.

demeure /dəmœʀ/ **I** *nf* **1** residence; **2 mettre qn en ~ de faire** to require sb to do.
II à demeure *phr* permanently; permanent.
IDIOMS **il n'y a pas péril en la ~** there's no rush.

demeuré, **~e** /dəmœʀe/ *adj* retarded.

demeurer /dəmœʀe/ [1] **I** *vi* **1** (+ *v avoir*) to reside, to live; **2** (+ *v être*) to remain.
II *v impers* **il n'en demeure pas moins que** nonetheless, the fact remains that.

demi, **~e**[1] /d(ə)mi/ **I et demi**, **et demie** *phr* and a half; **il est trois heures et ~e** it's half past three.
II *nm,f* half.
III *nm* **1** glass of beer; **2** (Sport) **~ de mêlée/d'ouverture** scrum/stand-off half.

IV **à demi** *phr* half; **à ~ éveillé** half awake.
V **demi-** (*combining form*) **1** half; **une ~-pomme** half an apple; **2** partial; **une ~-victoire** a partial victory.

demi-cercle, *pl* **~s** /d(ə)misɛʀkl/ *nm* semicircle.

demie[2] /d(ə)mi/ I *adj* ▶ **demi I**.
II *nf* **il est déjà la ~** it's already half past.

demi-écrémé, **~e**, *mpl* **~s** /d(ə)miekʀeme/ *adj* semi-skimmed.

demi-finale, *pl* **~s** /d(ə)mifinal/ *nf* semifinal.

demi-heure, *pl* **~s** /d(ə)mijœʀ/ *nf* half an hour.

démilitariser /demilitaʀize/ [1] *vtr* to demilitarize.

demi-litre, *pl* **~s** /d(ə)militʀ/ *nm* half a litre[GB].

demi-mesure, *pl* **~s** /d(ə)mim(ə)zyʀ/ *nf* half-measure.

demi-mot: **à demi-mot** /ad(ə)mimo/ *phr* **j'ai compris à ~** I didn't need to have it spelt out.

déminer /demine/ [1] *vtr* to clear [sth] of mines.

demi-pension /d(ə)mipɑ̃sjɔ̃/ *nf* half board.

demi-pensionnaire, *pl* **~s** /d(ə)mipɑ̃sjɔnɛʀ/ *nmf* (Sch) pupil who has school lunches.

démis, **~e** /demi, iz/ I *pp* ▶ **démettre**.
II *pp adj* dislocated.

demi-sel /d(ə)misɛl/ *adj* [*butter*] slightly salted.

démission /demisjɔ̃/ *nf* **1** resignation (**de** from); **2** (figurative) failure to take responsibility.

démissionner /demisjɔne/ [1] *vi* **1** to resign (**de** from); **2** to abdicate one's responsibilities.

demi-tarif, *pl* **~s** /d(ə)mitaʀif/ I *adj* half-price.
II *adv* half-price.
III *nm* half-price ticket.

demi-tour, *pl* **~s** /d(ə)mituʀ/ *nm* half-turn; **faire ~** to turn back.

démobiliser /demɔbilize/ [1] *vtr* **1** to demobilize; **2** to demotivate.

démocrate /demɔkʀat/ I *adj* democratic.
II *nmf* democrat.

démocratie /demɔkʀasi/ *nf* democracy.

démocratique /demɔkʀatik/ *adj* democratic.

démocratiser: **se démocratiser** /demɔkʀatize/ [1] *v refl* (+ *v être*) **1** to become more democratic; **2** to become more accessible.

démodé, **~e** /demɔde/ *adj* old-fashioned.

démoder: **se démoder** /demɔde/ [1] *v refl* (+ *v être*) to go out of fashion.

démographie /demɔgʀafi/ *nf* demography.

démographique /demɔgʀafik/ *adj* demographic.

demoiselle /d(ə)mwazɛl/ *nf* **1** young lady; **2** single woman.
■ **~ d'honneur** bridesmaid.

démolir /demɔliʀ/ [3] *vtr* to demolish; to wreck; to destroy.

démolition /demɔlisjɔ̃/ *nf* demolition.

démon /demɔ̃/ *nm* demon, devil.
■ **~ de midi** ≈ middle-age lust.

démoniaque /demɔnjak/ *adj* demonic.

démonstrateur, **-trice** /demɔ̃stʀatœʀ, tʀis/ *nm,f* (for products) demonstrator.

démonstratif, **-ive** /demɔ̃stʀatif, iv/ *adj* demonstrative.

démonstration /demɔ̃stʀasjɔ̃/ *nf* **1** display; **~ de courage** display of courage; **~s d'amitié** a show of friendship; **2** demonstration; **3** (of theory) demonstration, proof.

démontable /demɔ̃tabl/ *adj* [*furniture*] that can be taken apart.

démonté, **~e** /demɔ̃te/ *adj* [*sea*] stormy.

démonte-pneu, *pl* **~s** /demɔ̃t(ə)pnø/ *nm* tyre-lever (GB), tire iron (US).

démonter /demɔ̃te/ [1] I *vtr* **1** to dismantle, to take [sth] to pieces [*machine*]; to remove [*wheel*]; **2**○ to fluster; **ne pas se laisser ~** to remain unruffled.
II **se démonter** *v refl* (+ *v être*) **1** [*furniture*] to come apart; **2**○ [*person*] to become flustered.

démontrer /demɔ̃tʀe/ [1] *vtr* to demonstrate, to prove.

démoralisant, **~e** /demɔʀalizɑ̃, ɑ̃t/ *adj* demoralizing.

démoraliser /demɔʀalize/ [1] *vtr* to demoralize.

démordre /demɔʀdʀ/ [6] *v+prep* **il n'en démord pas** he sticks by it, he's sticking to it.

démouler /demule/ [1] *vtr* to turn [sth] out of the tin (GB) or pan (US) [*cake*]; to remove [sth] from the mould (GB) or mold (US) [*statue*].

démultiplier /demyltiplije/ [2] *vtr* **1** to reduce [*speed*]; **2** to increase [*powers, capacity*].

démuni, **~e** /demyni/ *adj* destitute; penniless; **~ de** devoid of, without [*talent*].

démunir /demyniʀ/ [3] I *vtr* to divest (**de** of).
II **se démunir** *v refl* (+ *v être*) **se ~ de qch** to leave oneself without sth.

dénaturé, **~e** /denatyʀe/ *adj* **1** [*alcohol*] denatured; **2** [*tastes*] warped; [*parents*] unnatural.

dénaturer /denatyʀe/ [1] *vtr* **1** to denature; **2** to distort [*facts*]; **3** to spoil [*taste, sauce*].

dénicher /deniʃe/ [1] *vtr* **1**○ to dig out○ [*object*]; to track down [*person*]; to find [*right address*]; **2** to flush out [*thief, animal*].

dénier /denje/ [2] *vtr* to deny.

deniers /dənje/ *nm pl* money; **~s publics** or **de l'État** public funds.

dénigrement /denigʀəmɑ̃/ *nm* denigration.

dénigrer /denigʀe/ [1] *vtr* to denigrate.

dénivellation /denivɛlasjɔ̃/ *nf* **1** difference in level; **2** gradient.

dénombrable /denɔ̃bʀabl/ *adj* countable; **non ~** uncountable.

dénombrement /denɔ̃bʀəmɑ̃/ *nm* count.

dénombrer /denɔ̃bʀe/ [1] *vtr* to count.

dénomination /denɔminasjɔ̃/ *nf* name, designation.

dénommer /denɔme/ [1] *vtr* to name.

dénoncer /denɔ̃se/ [12] I *vtr* to denounce.
II **se dénoncer** *v refl* (+ *v être*) to give oneself up.

dénonciation /denɔ̃sjasjɔ̃/ *nf* denunciation.

dénoter /denɔte/ [1] *vtr* denote.

dénouement /denumɑ̃/ *nm* **1** denouement; **2** outcome.

dénouer /denwe/ [1] **I** *vtr* **1** to undo [*knot*]; **2** to unravel [*intrigue*]; to resolve [*crisis*].
II se dénouer *v refl* (+ *v être*) **1** [*laces*] to come undone; **2** [*crisis*] to resolve itself.

dénoyauter /denwajote/ [1] *vtr* to stone (GB), to pit (US).

denrée /dɑ̃ʀe/ *nf* **1** foodstuff; **~ de base** staple; **2** commodity.

dense /dɑ̃s/ *adj* dense; concentrated; heavy.

densité /dɑ̃site/ *nf* **1** density; **2** denseness.

dent /dɑ̃/ *nf* **1** tooth; **à pleines** or **belles ~s** with relish; **ne rien avoir à se mettre sous la ~** to have nothing to eat; **2** (of comb) tooth; (of fork) prong; **en ~s de scie** [*blade*] serrated; [*results*] which go up and down; **3** crag.
■ **~ de lait** milk tooth.
IDIOMS **avoir une ~ contre qn** to bear sb a grudge; **avoir les ~s longues** to be ambitious.

dentaire /dɑ̃tɛʀ/ *adj* dental.

denté, **~e** /dɑ̃te/ *adj* **1** toothed; **2** dentate.

dentelé, **~e** /dɑ̃t(ə)le/ *adj* [*coast*] indented; [*crest*] jagged; [*stamp*] perforated; [*leaf*] dentate.

dentelle /dɑ̃tɛl/ *nf* lace.
IDIOMS **il ne fait pas dans la ~** he's not one to bother with niceties.

dentelure /dɑ̃tlyʀ/ *nf* (of stamp) perforation; (of crest) jagged outline; (of leaf) serration.

dentier /dɑ̃tje/ *nm* dentures.

dentifrice /dɑ̃tifʀis/ *nm* toothpaste.

dentiste /dɑ̃tist/ *nmf* dentist.

dentition /dɑ̃tisjɔ̃/ *nf* dentition.

dénuder /denyde/ [1] **I** *vtr* to strip.
II se dénuder *v refl* (+ *v être*) **1** to strip (off); **2** to become bare.

dénué, **~e** /denɥe/ *adj* **~ de** lacking in; **~ de sens** senseless.

déodorant, **~e** /deɔdɔʀɑ̃, ɑ̃t/ **I** *adj* deodorant.
II *nm* deodorant.

déontologie /deɔ̃tɔlɔʒi/ *nf* (professional) ethics.

dépannage /depanaʒ/ *nm* repair.

dépanner /depane/ [1] *vtr* **1** to fix [*car, machine*]; **2** to tow away; **3**° to help [sb] out.

dépanneur, **-euse**[1] /depanœʀ, øz/ *nm,f* engineer.

dépanneuse[2] /depanøz/ *nf* breakdown truck (GB), tow truck (US).

dépareillé, **~e** /depaʀeje/ *adj* **1** odd; **articles ~s** oddments; **2** incomplete.

déparer /depaʀe/ [1] *vtr* to spoil, to mar.

départ /depaʀ/ *nm* **1** departure; **~ des grandes lignes** main line departures; **téléphone avant ton ~** phone before you leave; **être sur le ~** to be about to leave; **2** resignation; **le ~ en retraite** retirement; **3** (gen, Sport) start; **donner le (signal du) ~ aux coureurs** to start the race; **prendre un nouveau ~** (figurative) to make a fresh start; **au ~** at first; at the outset; **de ~** initial; [*language*] source; [*salary*] starting.

départager /depaʀtaʒe/ [13] *vtr* to decide between [*competitors*].

département /depaʀtəmɑ̃/ *nm* department.

départemental, **~e**, *mpl* **-aux** /depaʀtəmɑ̃tal, o/ *adj* [*election*] local; [*road*] secondary.

dépassé, **~e** /depɑse/ *adj* **1** outdated, outmoded; **2**° overwhelmed.

dépasser /depɑse/ [1] **I** *vtr* **1** to overtake (GB), to pass (US) [*car, pedestrian*]; to go past [*place*]; **2** to exceed [*figure, dose, limit*]; **elle le dépasse de cinq centimètres** she's five centimetres[GB] taller than him; **il a dépassé la cinquantaine** he's over or past fifty; **~ la mesure** or **les bornes** to go too far; **3** to be ahead of, to outstrip [*rival*]; **ça me dépasse!** it's beyond me!
II *vi* to jut or stick out; [*underskirt*] to show.

dépatouiller°: **se dépatouiller** /depatuje/ [1] *v refl* (+ *v être*) to get by.

dépaysement /depeizmɑ̃/ *nm* **1** change of scenery; **2** disorientation.

dépayser /depeize/ [1] *vtr* **1** to provide [sb] with a pleasant change of scenery; **2** to disorient.

dépecer /dep(ə)se/ [16] *vtr* to tear apart, to cut up.

dépêche /depɛʃ/ *nf* dispatch.

dépêcher /depeʃe/ [16] **I** *vtr* to dispatch (**à** to).
II se dépêcher *v refl* (+ *v être*) to hurry up.

dépeigné, **~e** /depeɲe/ *adj* dishevelled[GB].

dépeindre /depɛ̃dʀ/ [55] *vtr* to depict.

dépénaliser /depenalize/ [1] *vtr* to decriminalize.

dépendance /depɑ̃dɑ̃s/ *nf* **1** dependence, dependency; **2** outbuilding; **3** dependency, dependent territory.

dépendant, **~e** /depɑ̃dɑ̃, ɑ̃t/ *adj* dependent (**de** on); **~s l'un de l'autre** interdependent.

dépendre /depɑ̃dʀ/ [6] *v+prep* **1 ~ de** to depend on; **2 ~ de** to be dependent on; **3 ~ de** [*organization*] to come under the control of; [*employee*] to be responsible to; **4 ~ de** [*environment*] to be the responsibility of; **5 ~ de** [*territory*] to be a dependency of; **6 ~ de** [*building, land*] to belong to.

dépens /depɑ̃/ *nm pl* **aux ~ de** at the expense of; **vivre aux ~ des autres** to live off other people.

dépense /depɑ̃s/ *nf* **1** spending, expenditure; **~s publiques** public expenditure; **2** expense; **réduire ses ~s** to cut down on expenses; **3** outlay; **une ~ de 300 francs** an outlay of 300 francs; **4** consumption; **~ d'énergie physique** expenditure of physical energy.

dépenser /depɑ̃se/ [1] **I** *vtr* to spend [*money, time*]; to use up [*energy, fuel*].
II se dépenser *v refl* (+ *v être*) to get (enough) exercise.

dépensier, **-ière** /depɑ̃sje, ɛʀ/ *adj* extravagant.

dépérir /deperiʀ/ [3] *vi* [*person*] to waste away; [*plant*] to wilt; [*economy*] to be on the decline.

dépêtrer: **se dépêtrer** /depɛtʀe/ [1] *v refl* (+ *v être*) **se ~ de** to extricate oneself from.

dépeuplement /depœpləmɑ̃/ *nm* depopulation.

dépeupler /depœple/ [1] *vtr* to depopulate [*region*]; to reduce the wildlife in [*forest*].

déphasé, **~e** /defɑze/ *adj* **1**○ out of step; **2** out of phase.

dépilation /depilasjɔ̃/ *nf* hair removal.

dépilatoire /depilatwaʀ/ *adj* depilatory, hair-removing.

dépistable /depistabl/ *adj* detectable.

dépistage /depistaʒ/ *nm* screening (**de** for); **test de ~ du sida** Aids test.

dépister /depiste/ [1] *vtr* **1** to track down [*criminal, game*]; **2** to detect [*illness*].

dépit /depi/ **I** *nm* pique; **par ~** out of pique.

II en dépit de *phr* in spite of; **en ~ du bon sens** in a very illogical way.

déplacé, **~e** /deplase/ *adj* inappropriate; **c'est ~** it's out of place; it's uncalled for.

déplacement /deplasmɑ̃/ *nm* **1** trip; **ça vaut le ~!** it's worth the trip!; **frais de ~** travelling[GB] expenses; **2** moving; shifting; transfer (**vers** to); **3** displacement.

■ **~ de vertèbre** slipped disc.

déplacer /deplase/ [12] **I** *vtr* to move [*object, person*]; to displace [*population*]; to shift [*attention*]; to change [*issue*].

II se déplacer *v refl* (+ *v être*) **1** to move; **se ~ une vertèbre** to slip a disc; **2** to get about; to travel; **3** [*doctor*] to go out on call.

déplaire /deplɛʀ/ [59] **I** *vi* **le spectacle a déplu** the show was not well received.

II déplaire à *v+prep* **cela m'a déplu** I didn't like it; **la situation n'est pas pour me ~** the situation quite suits me.

III *v impers* **ne vous en déplaise** (ironic) whether you like it or not.

déplaisant, **~e** /deplɛzɑ̃, ɑ̃t/ *adj* unpleasant.

déplâtrer /deplɑtʀe/ [1] *vtr* to remove the cast from [*limb*].

dépliant /deplijɑ̃/ *nm* **1** leaflet; **2** fold-out page.

déplier /deplije/ [2] *vtr* to unfold [*newspaper*]; to open out [*map*].

déploiement /deplwamɑ̃/ *nm* **1** display; array; **2** deployment.

déplorable /deplɔʀabl/ *adj* **1** regrettable; **2** appalling, deplorable.

déplorer /deplɔʀe/ [1] *vtr* to deplore.

déployer /deplwaje/ [23] *vtr* **1** to display [*talent, wealth*]; to expend [*energy*]; **2** to deploy [*troops*]; **3** to spread [*wings*]; to unfurl [*sail*].

déplumer: **se déplumer** /deplyme/ [1] *v refl* (+ *v être*) [*bird*] to lose its feathers.

dépoli, **~e** /depɔli/ *adj* **verre ~** frosted glass.

dépolluer /depɔlɥe/ [1] *vtr* to rid [sth] of pollution, to clean up.

dépopulation /depɔpylasjɔ̃/ *nf* depopulation.

déportation /depɔʀtasjɔ̃/ *nf* **1** internment in a concentration camp; **2** deportation.

déporté, **~e** /depɔʀte/ *nm,f* **1** prisoner interned in a concentration camp; **2** transported convict.

déporter /depɔʀte/ [1] **I** *vtr* **1** to send [sb] to a concentration camp; **2** to deport.

II se déporter *v refl* (+ *v être*) to swerve.

déposer /depoze/ [1] **I** *vtr* **1** to dump [*rubbish*]; to lay [*wreath*]; to drop off, to leave [*parcel, passenger*]; to deposit [*money*]; **~ les armes** to lay down one's arms; **2** to register [*trademark*]; to submit [*file, offer*]; to lodge [*complaint*]; **~ son bilan** to file a bankruptcy petition; **3** [*river*] to deposit [*alluvium*].

II *vi* (Law) to make a statement, to testify.

III se déposer *v refl* (+ *v être*) [*dust*] to settle; [*deposit*] to collect.

dépositaire /depozitɛʀ/ *nmf* **1** agent; **~ agréé** authorized dealer; **2** trustee.

déposition /depozisjɔ̃/ *nf* (Law) statement; deposition; evidence.

déposséder /depɔsede/ [14] *vtr* to dispossess.

dépôt /depo/ *nm* **1** warehouse; depot; **2** outlet; **l'épicerie fait ~ de pain** the grocer's sells bread; **3** (of trademark) registration; (of bill) introduction; **4 date limite de ~ des déclarations d'impôt** deadline for income tax returns; **5** deposit; **6** police cells.

■ **~ de bilan** voluntary liquidation; **~ d'ordures** (rubbish) tip or dump (GB), garbage dump (US).

dépotoir /depɔtwaʀ/ *nm* **1** dump; **2**○ shambles○.

dépôt-vente, *pl* **dépôts-ventes** /depovɑ̃t/ *nm* secondhand shop (GB) or store (*where goods are sold on commission*).

dépouille /depuj/ *nf* **1** skin, hide; **2** body; **~ mortelle** mortal remains; **3 ~s** spoils.

dépouillé, **~e** /depuje/ *adj* **1** [*style*] spare; **2** [*tree*] bare.

dépouillement /depujmɑ̃/ *nm* **1** (of votes) counting, count; (of mail) going through; **2** asceticism; **3** (of style) sobriety.

dépouiller /depuje/ [1] *vtr* **1** to skin [*animal*]; **2** to lay [sth] bare [*region*]; **3** to rob [*person*]; **4** to count [*votes*]; to go through [*mail*].

dépourvu, **~e** /depuʀvy/ **I** *adj* **~ de** devoid of [*interest, charm*]; without [*heating*].

II *nm* **prendre qn au ~** to take sb by surprise.

dépoussiérer /depusjeʀe/ [14] *vtr* to dust; (figurative) to revamp.

dépraver /depʀave/ [1] *vtr* to deprave.

dépréciation /depʀesjasjɔ̃/ *nf* depreciation.

déprécier /depʀesje/ [2] *vtr* **1** to depreciate; **2** to disparage, to depreciate.

déprédations /depʀedasjɔ̃/ *nf pl* damage.

dépressif, **-ive** /depʀesif, iv/ *adj, nm,f* depressive.

dépression /depʀesjɔ̃/ *nf* depression; **~ nerveuse** nervous breakdown.

dépressurisation /depʀesyʀizasjɔ̃/ *nf* **1** depressurization; **2** loss of pressure.

déprimant, **~e** /depʀimɑ̃, ɑ̃t/ *adj* depressing.
déprime○ /depʀim/ *nf* depression.
déprimer /depʀime/ [1] **I** *vtr* to depress.
II○ *vi* to be depressed.
déprogrammer /depʀɔgʀame/ [1] *vtr* to cancel.
depuis /dəpɥi/ **I** *adv* since; **~ je n'ai plus de nouvelles** since then I haven't had any news.
II *prep* **1** since; **~ quand vis-tu là-bas?** how long have you been living there?; **~ le début jusqu'à la fin** from start to finish; **2** for; **il pleut ~ trois jours** it's been raining for three days; **~ quand?** how long?; **~ peu** recently; **~ toujours** always; **3** from; **~ ma fenêtre** from my window.
III depuis que *phr* since, ever since; **il pleut ~ que nous sommes arrivés** it's been raining ever since we arrived.
député /depyte/ *nm* **1** (in politics) deputy; (in GB) member of Parliament; **2** representative.
député-maire, *pl* **députés-maires** /depytemɛʀ/ *nm* deputy and mayor.
déracinement /deʀasinmɑ̃/ *nm* **1** uprooting; **2** rootlessness.
déraciner /deʀasine/ [1] *vtr* **1** to uproot; **2** to eradicate [*prejudice*].
déraillement /deʀɑjmɑ̃/ *nm* derailment.
dérailler /deʀɑje/ [1] *vi* **1** to be derailed; **faire ~ un train** to derail a train; **2**○ to lose one's marbles○; to talk through one's hat○.
dérailleur /deʀɑjœʀ/ *nm* derailleur.
déraisonner /deʀɛzɔne/ [1] *vi* to talk nonsense.
dérangé, **~e** /deʀɑ̃ʒe/ *adj* **1** upset; **2**○ deranged.
dérangeant, **~e** /deʀɑ̃ʒɑ̃, ɑ̃t/ *adj* disturbing.
dérangement /deʀɑ̃ʒmɑ̃/ *nm* **1** trouble, inconvenience; **2 ~ intestinal** stomach upset; **3 être en ~** [*lift, phone*] to be out of order.
déranger /deʀɑ̃ʒe/ [13] **I** *vtr* to disturb [*person*]; to upset [*routine, plans*]; to affect [*mind*]; **excusez-moi de vous ~** (I'm) sorry to bother you; **est-ce que la fumée vous dérange?** do you mind if I smoke?
II se déranger *v refl* (+ *v être*) **1** to go out, to come out; **je me suis dérangé pour rien, c'était fermé** I wasted my time going there, it was shut; **2** to get up; to move; **3** to put oneself out.
dérapage /deʀapaʒ/ *nm* **1** skid; **2** blunder; **3** loss of control.
déraper /deʀape/ [1] *vi* **1** [*prices, discussion*] to get out of control; **2** [*knife*] to slip; **3** to skid; **4** [*skier*] to sideslip.
dératisation /deʀatizasjɔ̃/ *nf* pest control (*for rats*).
déréglé, **~e** /deʀegle/ *adj* [*mind*] unbalanced; [*life*] irregular; [*mechanism*] out, disturbed.
dérèglement /deʀɛgləmɑ̃/ *nm* **1** (in machine) fault; **2** disorder.
déréglementer /deʀegləmɑ̃te/ [1] *vtr* to deregulate.
dérégler /deʀegle/ [14] *vtr* to affect [*weather, organ*]; to upset [*process, mechanism*]; **~ la radio** to lose the station on the radio; **~ le réveil** to set the alarm clock wrong.
dérider /deʀide/ [1] **I** *vtr* to cheer [sb] up.
II se dérider *v refl* (+ *v être*) to start smiling.
dérision /deʀizjɔ̃/ *nf* scorn, derision; **tourner qn/qch en ~** to ridicule sb/sth.
dérisoire /deʀizwaʀ/ *adj* pathetic; trivial.
dérivatif, **-ive** /deʀivatif, iv/ **I** *adj* derivative.
II *nm* **1** diversion (**à** from); **2** (Med) derivative.
dérivation /deʀivasjɔ̃/ *nf* diversion (GB), detour.
dérive /deʀiv/ *nf* drift; **à la ~** adrift.
dérivé, **~e** /deʀive/ *nm* by-product.
dériver /deʀive/ [1] **I dériver de** *v+prep* **1 ~ de** to stem from; **2 ~ de** to be derived from.
II *vi* to drift.
dermatologie /dɛʀmatɔlɔʒi/ *nf* dermatology.
derme /dɛʀm/ *nm* dermis.
dernier, **-ière**[1] /dɛʀnje, ɛʀ/ **I** *adj* **1** last; [*floor, shelf*] top; **je les veux jeudi ~ délai** I want them by Thursday at the latest; **2** latest; **les dernières nouvelles** the latest news; **ces ~ temps** recently; **3 du ~ ridicule** utterly ridiculous; **c'était la dernière chose à faire** it was the worst possible thing to do.
II *nmf* last; **arriver le ~** to arrive last; **c'est bien le ~ de mes soucis** that is the least of my worries; **être le ~ de la classe** to be bottom of the class; **le petit ~** the youngest child; **ce ~** the latter; **le ~ des ~s** the lowest of the low.
III en dernier *phr* last; **j'irai chez eux en ~** I'll go to them last.
■ **~ cri** latest fashion; **dernières volontés** last requests.
dernière[2] /dɛʀnjɛʀ/ *nf* **1 la ~** the latest; **2** last performance.
dernièrement /dɛʀnjɛʀmɑ̃/ *adv* recently.
dernier-né, **dernière-née**, *mpl* **derniers-nés** /dɛʀnjene, dɛʀnjɛʀne/ *nm,f* **1** youngest (child); **2** latest model.
dérobade /deʀɔbad/ *nf* evasion.
dérobé, **~e** /deʀɔbe/ **I** *adj* [*door, stairs*] concealed.
II à la dérobée *phr* furtively.
dérober /deʀɔbe/ [1] **I** *vtr* to steal.
II se dérober *v refl* (+ *v être*) **1** to be evasive; **2** to shirk responsibility; **3 se ~ à** to shirk [*duty*]; **4** [*ground, knees*] to give way.
dérogation /deʀɔgasjɔ̃/ *nf* **1** (special) dispensation; **2** infringement (**à** of).
déroger /deʀɔʒe/ [13] *v+prep* **~ à** to infringe [*law*]; to depart from [*principles*]; to ignore [*obligation*]; to break with [*tradition*].
déroulement /deʀulmɑ̃/ *nm* **1 le ~ des événements** the sequence of events; **veiller au bon ~ de** to make sure [sth] goes smoothly; **~ de carrière** career development; **2** uncoiling, unwinding.
dérouler /deʀule/ [1] **I** *vtr* to unroll [*carpet*]; to uncoil [*rope*]; to unwind [*wire, film*].
II se dérouler *v refl* (+ *v être*) **1** to take place; **2** [*negotiations*] to proceed; [*story*] to unfold.

déroutant, **~e** /deʀutɑ̃, ɑ̃t/ *adj* puzzling.

déroute /deʀut/ *nf* crushing defeat, rout; **mettre en ~** to rout; **en ~** in disarray.

dérouter /deʀute/ [1] *vtr* **1** to puzzle; **2** to divert.

derrière[1] /dɛʀjɛʀ/ I *prep* behind; **~ les apparences** beneath the surface; **il faut toujours être ~ son dos** you have to keep after him.
II *adv* behind; (of room) at the back; (in car) in the back.

derrière[2] /dɛʀjɛʀ/ *nm* **1** (of house, object) back; **de ~** [*bedroom*] back; **2**○ behind○, backside○.

des /de/ I *det* ▶ **un** I.
II *det* ▶ **de**.

dès /dɛ/ I *prep* from; **~ (l'âge de) huit ans** from the age of eight; **~ maintenant** straight away; **je vous téléphone ~ mon arrivée** I'll phone you as soon as I arrive; **~ Versailles il y a des embouteillages** there are traffic jams from Versailles onwards.
II **dès que** *phr* as soon as.
III **dès lors** *phr* **1** from then on, from that time on, henceforth; **2** therefore, consequently.
IV **dès lors que** *phr* **1** once, from the moment that; **2** since.

désabusé, **~e** /dezabyze/ *adj* disillusioned; cynical.

désaccord /dezakɔʀ/ *nm* disagreement; **être en ~** to disagree (**avec** with; **sur** over).

désaccordé, **~e** /dezakɔʀde/ *adj* out-of-tune.

désaffecté, **~e** /dezafɛkte/ *adj* disused.

désagréable /dezagʀeabl/ *adj* unpleasant.

désagrégation /dezagʀegasjɔ̃/ *nf* disintegration, break-up, collapse.

désagréger: **se désagréger** /dezagʀeʒe/ [15] *v refl* (+ *v être*) to disintegrate, to break up.

désagrément /dezagʀemɑ̃/ *nm* inconvenience.

désaltérant, **~e** /dezalteʀɑ̃, ɑ̃t/ *adj* thirst-quenching.

désaltérer /dezalteʀe/ [14] I *vtr* **~ qn** to quench sb's thirst.
II **se désaltérer** *v refl* (+ *v être*) to quench one's thirst.

désamorcer /dezamɔʀse/ [12] *vtr* to defuse [*explosive, crisis*]; to drain [*pump*].

désappointer /dezapwɛ̃te/ [1] *vtr* to disappoint.

désapprobateur, **-trice** /dezapʀɔbatœʀ, tʀis/ *adj* disapproving.

désapprobation /dezapʀɔbasjɔ̃/ *nf* disapproval.

désapprouver /dezapʀuve/ [1] *vtr* to disapprove of.

désarçonner /dezaʀsɔne/ [1] *vtr* **1** to throw [*rider*]; **2** to take [sb] aback.

désarmant, **~e** /dezaʀmɑ̃, ɑ̃t/ *adj* disarming.

désarmé, **~e** /dezaʀme/ I *pp* ▶ **désarmer**.
II *pp adj* **1** disarmed; **2** [*ship*] laid up.

désarmement /dezaʀməmɑ̃/ *nm* **1** disarmament; **2** (of ship) laying up.

désarmer /dezaʀme/ [1] I *vtr* **1** to disarm; **2** to lay up [*ship*].
II *vi* **1** to disarm; **2** [*person*] to give up the fight; [*anger*] to abate.

désarroi /dezaʀwa/ *nm* distress; confusion.

désarticulé, **~e** /dezaʀtikyle/ *adj* [*chair*] wrecked; [*puppet*] with broken joints.

désastre /dezastʀ/ *nm* disaster.

désastreux, **-euse** /dezastʀø, øz/ *adj* disastrous.

désavantage /dezavɑ̃taʒ/ *nm* **1** disadvantage **2** drawback, disadvantage.

désavantager /dezavɑ̃taʒe/ [13] *vtr* to put [sb, sth] at a disadvantage, to disadvantage.

désavantageux, **-euse** /dezavɑ̃taʒø, øz/ *adj* unfavourable[GB], disadvantageous.

désaveu /dezavø/ *nm* **1** denial; **2** rejection.

désavouer /dezavwe/ [1] *vtr* **1** to deny; **2** to disown.

désaxé, **~e** /dezakse/ I *pp* ▶ **désaxer**.
II *pp adj* deranged.
III *nm,f* deranged person.

désaxer /dezakse/ [1] *vtr* **1** to put [sth] out of true [*wheel*]; **2** to unbalance [*person*].

desceller /desele/ [1] I *vtr* to work [sth] free.
II **se desceller** *v refl* (+ *v être*) to work loose.

descendance /desɑ̃dɑ̃s/ *nf* descendants.

descendant, **~e** /desɑ̃dɑ̃, ɑ̃t/ *nm,f* descendant.

descendre /dɛsɑ̃dʀ/ [6] I *vtr* (+ *v avoir*) **1** to take [sb/sth] down (**à** to), to bring [sb/sth] down (**de** from); **2** to lower [*shelf, blind*]; to wind [sth] down [*window*]; **3** to go down, to come down [*road, steps, river*]; **~ la rivière à la nage** to swim down the river; **4**○ to bump off○ [*person*]; to shoot down [*plane*]; **5**○ to down [*bottle*].
II *vi* (+ *v être*) **1** to go down (**à** to), to come down (**de** from); [*night*] to fall; **tu es descendu à pied?** did you walk down?; **la route descend en pente douce** the road slopes down gently; **2 ~ de** to step off [*step*]; to get off [*train, bike, horse*]; to get out of [*car*]; **3** [*temperature, prices*] to drop, to go down; [*tide*] to go out; **4 ~ dans le Midi** to go down to the South (of France); **5 ~ dans un hôtel** to stay at a hotel; **6 ~ de** to be descended from.

descente /desɑ̃t/ *nf* **1** descent; **la ~ a pris une heure** it took an hour to come down; **2 à ma ~ du train** when I got off the train; **3 ~ de police** police raid; **la police a fait une ~ dans l'immeuble** the police raided the building; **4** (in skiing) downhill (event).
■ **~ de lit** (bedside) rug.

descriptif, **-ive** /deskʀiptif, iv/ *adj* descriptive.

description /deskʀipsjɔ̃/ *nf* description; **faire une ~ de qch** to describe sth.

désembuer /dezɑ̃bye/ [1] *vtr* to demist (GB), to defog (US).

désemparé, **~e** /dezɑ̃paʀe/ I *pp* ▶ **désemparer**.
II *pp adj* distraught, at a loss.

désemparer /dezɑ̃paʀe/ [1] *vtr* to throw [sb] into confusion.

désemplir /dezɑ̃pliʀ/ [3] *vi* **ne pas ~** to be always full.

désenchanté, **~e** /dezɑ̃ʃɑ̃te/ *adj* disillusioned, disenchanted (**de** with).

désenclaver /dezɑ̃klave/ [1] *vtr* to open up [*region*].

désenfler /dezɑ̃fle/ [1] *vi* to become less swollen, to go down.

désengager: **se désengager** /dezɑ̃gaʒe/ [13] *v refl* (+ *v être*) to withdraw (**de** from).

déséquilibre /dezekilibʀ/ *nm* **1** unsteadiness; **en ~** [*table*] unstable; [*person*] off balance; **2** imbalance; **3** derangement.

déséquilibré, **~e** /dezekilibʀe/ **I** *pp* ▶ **déséquilibrer**.
II *pp adj* (Med) unbalanced.
III *nm,f* lunatic.

déséquilibrer /dezekilibʀe/ [1] *vtr* **1** to make [sb] lose their balance; to make [sth] unstable; **2** to destabilize [*country*]; **3** (Med) to unbalance.

désert, **~e** /dezɛʀ, ɛʀt/ **I** *adj* **1** uninhabited; **île ~e** desert island; **2** deserted.
II *nm* desert.

déserter /dezɛʀte/ [1] *vtr*, *vi* to desert.

déserteur /dezɛʀtœʀ/ *nm* deserter.

désertion /dezɛʀsjɔ̃/ *nf* **1** desertion; **2** defection.

désertique /dezɛʀtik/ *adj* **1** [*climate, region*] desert; **2** barren.

désespérant, **~e** /dezɛspeʀɑ̃, ɑ̃t/ *adj* [*person, situation*] hopeless.

désespéré, **~e** /dezɛspeʀe/ **I** *pp* ▶ **désespérer**.
II *pp adj* [*person*] in despair; [*situation*] hopeless; [*attempt*] desperate; **cri ~** cry of despair.

désespérément /dezɛspeʀemɑ̃/ *adv* despairingly; desperately; hopelessly.

désespérer /dezɛspeʀe/ [14] **I** *vtr* to drive [sb] to despair.
II désespérer de *v+prep* **~ de qn** to despair of sb; **il ne désespère pas de le sauver** he hasn't given up hope of saving him.
III *vi* to despair, to lose hope.
IV se désespérer *v refl* (+ *v être*) to despair.

désespoir /dezɛspwaʀ/ *nm* despair; **mettre** or **réduire qn au ~** to drive sb to despair.

déshabillé /dezabije/ *nm* negligee.

déshabiller /dezabije/ [1] **I** *vtr* to undress.
II se déshabiller *v refl* (+ *v être*) **1** to undress; **2** to take one's coat off.

déshabituer /dezabitɥe/ [1] *vtr* **~ qn du tabac** to get sb out of the habit of smoking.

désherbant /dezɛʀbɑ̃/ *nm* weedkiller.

désherber /dezɛʀbe/ [1] *vtr* to weed.

déshérité /dezeʀite/ **I** *pp* ▶ **déshériter**.
II *pp adj* underprivileged; disadvantaged; deprived.
III *nm,f* **les ~s** the underprivileged.

déshériter /dezeʀite/ [1] *vtr* to disinherit.

déshonorant, **~e** /dezɔnɔʀɑ̃, ɑ̃t/ *adj* dishonourable[GB], degrading.

déshonorer /dezɔnɔʀe/ [1] **I** *vtr* to bring disgrace on [*family*]; to bring [sth] into disrepute [*profession*].
II se déshonorer *v refl* (+ *v être*) to disgrace oneself.

déshydratation /dezidʀatasjɔ̃/ *nf* **1** dehydration; **2** drying.

déshydrater /dezidʀate/ [1] *vtr* to dehydrate.

desiderata /dezideʀata/ *nm pl* wishes.

désignation /deziɲasjɔ̃/ *nf* designation.

désigner /deziɲe/ [1] *vtr* **1** [*word*] to designate; [*triangle*] to represent; **2** to point out; **3** to choose; **être tout désigné pour** to be just right for.

désinence /dezinɑ̃s/ *nf* ending.

désinfectant, **~e** /dezɛ̃fɛktɑ̃, ɑ̃t/ **I** *adj* disinfecting.
II *nm* disinfectant.

désinfecter /dezɛ̃fɛkte/ [1] *vtr* to disinfect.

désintégrer: **se désintégrer** /dezɛ̃tegʀe/ [14] *v refl* (+ *v être*) to disintegrate.

désintéressé, **~e** /dezɛ̃teʀese/ **I** *pp* ▶ **désintéresser**.
II *pp adj* [*person, act*] selfless, unselfish; [*advice*] disinterested.

désintéresser: **se désintéresser** /dezɛ̃teʀese/ [1] *v refl* (+ *v être*) **se ~ de** to lose interest in.

désintérêt /dezɛ̃teʀɛ/ *nm* lack of interest.

désintoxiquer /dezɛ̃tɔksike/ [1] *vtr* to detoxify; **se faire ~** to undergo detoxification.

désinvolte /dezɛ̃vɔlt/ *adj* casual, offhand.

désinvolture /dezɛ̃vɔltyʀ/ *nf* casual manner.

désir /deziʀ/ *nm* wish, desire; **prendre ses ~s pour des réalités** to delude oneself.

désirable /deziʀabl/ *adj* desirable.

désirer /deziʀe/ [1] *vtr* to want; **effets non désirés** unwanted effects; **que désirez-vous?** what would you like? **laisser à ~** to leave something to be desired.

désistement /dezistəmɑ̃/ *nm* withdrawal.

désister: **se désister** /deziste/ [1] *v refl* (+ *v être*) to stand down (GB), to withdraw.

désobéir /dezɔbeiʀ/ [3] *v+prep* to disobey; **~ à qn** to disobey sb.

désobéissance /dezɔbeisɑ̃s/ *nf* disobedience.

désobéissant, **~e** /dezɔbeisɑ̃, ɑ̃t/ *adj* disobedient.

désobligeant, **~e** /dezɔbliʒɑ̃, ɑ̃t/ *adj* discourteous.

désodorisant /dezɔdɔʀizɑ̃/ *nm* deodorant.

désodoriser /dezɔdɔʀize/ [1] *vtr* to freshen.

désœuvré, **~e** /dezœvʀe/ *adj* at a loose end○ (GB), at loose ends○ (US).

désœuvrement /dezœvʀəmɑ̃/ *nm* **par ~** for lack of anything better to do.

désolation /dezɔlasjɔ̃/ *nf* **1** grief; **2** desolation.

désolé, **~e** /dezɔle/ **I** *pp* ▶ **désoler**.
II *pp adj* **1** sorry; **2** desolate.

désoler /dezɔle/ [1] **I** *vtr* **1** to upset, to distress; **2** to depress; **tu me désoles!** I despair of you!
II se désoler *v refl* (+ *v être*) to be upset.

désopilant, **~e** /dezɔpilɑ̃, ɑ̃t/ *adj* hilarious.

désordonné, **~e** /dezɔʀdɔne/ *adj* [*person*]

untidy; [*meeting*] disorderly; [*movements*] uncoordinated; [*existence*] wild.

désordre /dezɔʀdʀ/ I○ *adj inv* **faire ~** to look untidy or messy.

II *nm* **1** untidiness; mess; **pièce en ~** untidy room; **il a tout mis en ~** he made such a mess; **2** chaos; **semer le ~** to cause chaos; **3 dans le ~** in any order; **gagner dans le ~** (at races) to win with a combination forecast; **4** disorder; **~s mentaux** mental disorders.

désorganisé, **~e** /dezɔʀganize/ *adj* disorganized.

désorienter /dezɔʀjɑ̃te/ [1] *vtr* **1** to disorientate[GB]; **2** to confuse, to bewilder.

désormais /dezɔʀmɛ/ *adv* **1** from now on; **2** from then on.

désosser /dezɔse/ [1] *vtr* (Culin) to bone.

despote /dɛspɔt/ *nm* despot.

desquelles ▶ **lequel**.

desquels ▶ **lequel**.

dessaisir /desɛziʀ/ [3] I *vtr* **1 ~ qn de** to relieve sb of [*responsibility*]; **2 ~ qn de** to divest sb of [*property*].

II **se dessaisir** *v refl* (+ *v être*) **se ~ de** to relinquish.

dessaler /desale/ [1] *vtr* **1** to desalinate; **2** (Culin) to desalt.

dessécher /deseʃe/ [14] I *vtr* to dry [sth] out; **arbre desséché** withered tree.

II **se dessécher** *v refl* (+ *v être*) [*hair*] to become dry; [*tree*] to wither; [*ground*] to dry out.

dessein /desɛ̃/ *nm* design, intention; **à ~** deliberately.

desserrer /deseʀe/ [1] I *vtr* **1** to loosen; to release; to undo; **2** to relax [*grip, credit*].

II **se desserrer** *v refl* (+ *v être*) [*screw*] to work loose; [*knot*] to come undone.

IDIOMS **il n'a pas desserré les dents** he never once opened his mouth.

dessert /desɛʀ/ *nm* dessert.

desserte /desɛʀt/ *nf* **1** (transport) service; **la ~ d'une ville par les transports en commun** public transport services to and from a city; **2** sideboard.

desservir /desɛʀviʀ/ [30] *vtr* **1** [*train*] to serve [*town*]; **2** to lead to [*room, floor*]; **3** [*hospital*] to serve.

dessin /desɛ̃/ *nm* **1** drawing; **tu veux que je te fasse un ~○?** do I have to spell it out for you?; **2** design; **3** pattern; **4** outline.

■ **~ animé** cartoon.

dessinateur, **-trice** /desinatœʀ, tʀis/ *nm,f* **1** draughtsman (GB), draftsman (US); **2** designer.

■ **~ de bande dessinée** (strip) cartoonist.

dessiner /desine/ [1] I *vtr* **1** to draw; **2** to design [*material, decor*]; to draw up [*plans*].

II *vi* to draw.

III **se dessiner** *v refl* (+ *v être*) **1** [*future*] to take shape; **2 se ~ à l'horizon** to appear on the horizon; **il se dessinait nettement dans la lumière** he was clearly outlined in the light.

dessoûler /desule/ [1] *vtr* to sober up.

dessous[1] /dəsu/ I *adv* underneath.

II **en dessous** *phr* **1** underneath; **il habite juste en ~** he lives on the floor below; **2 la taille en ~** the next size down.

III **en dessous de** *phr* below; **les enfants en ~ de 13 ans** children under 13.

dessous[2] /dəsu/ I *nm inv* (of plate, tongue) underside; (of arm) inside (part); **le ~ du pied** the sole of the foot; **l'étagère de** or **du ~** the shelf below; the bottom shelf.

II *nm pl* **1** underwear; **2** inside story.

dessous-de-plat /d(ə)sudpla/ *nm inv* **1** table mat; **2** plate stand; **3** trivet.

dessous-de-table /d(ə)sudtabl/ *nm inv* backhanders○ (GB), bribes.

dessus[1] /dəsy/ *adv* on top; **le prix est marqué ~** the price is on it; **passe ~** go over it; **compte ~** count on it; **'ton rapport est fini?'—'non, je travaille** or **suis ~'** 'is your report finished?'—'no, I'm working on it'.

dessus[2] /dəsy/ *nm inv* (of shoe) upper; (of table, head) top; (of hand) back; **les voisins du ~** the people who live on the floor above.

IDIOMS **reprendre le ~** to regain the upper hand; (after illness) to get back on one's feet.

dessus-de-lit /d(ə)sydli/ *nm inv* bedspread.

déstabiliser /destabilize/ [1] *vtr* to unsettle [*person*]; to destabilize [*country*].

destin /dɛstɛ̃/ *nm* **1** fate; **2** destiny.

destinataire /dɛstinatɛʀ/ *nmf* **1** addressee; **2** beneficiary; **3** payee.

destination /dɛstinasjɔ̃/ I *nf* destination.

II **à destination de** *phr* [*train*] bound for.

destinée /dɛstine/ *nf* destiny.

destiner /dɛstine/ [1] I *vtr* **1 ~ qch à qn** to design sth for sb; **être destiné à faire** to be designed or intended to do; to be destined to do; **2 la lettre ne leur était pas destinée** the letter wasn't for them.

II **se destiner** *v refl* (+ *v être*) **elle se destine à une carrière de juriste** she's decided on a legal career.

destituer /dɛstitɥe/ [1] *vtr* to discharge [*officer*]; to depose [*monarch*].

destructeur, **-trice** /dɛstʀyktœʀ, tʀis/ *adj* destructive.

destruction /dɛstʀyksjɔ̃/ *nf* destruction.

désuet, **-ète** /dezɥɛ, ɛt/ *adj* [*decor*] old-world; [*style*] old-fashioned; [*word*] obsolete.

désunion /dezynjɔ̃/ *nf* **1** division; **2** discord.

désunir /dezyniʀ/ [3] *vtr* to divide, to break up.

détachant /detaʃɑ̃/ *nm* stain remover.

détaché, **~e** /detaʃe/ I *pp* ▶ **détacher**.

II *pp adj* **1** detached, unconcerned; **2** [*teacher, diplomat*] on secondment (GB), transferred.

détachement /detaʃmɑ̃/ *nm* **1** detachment (**de** from); **2** (Mil) detachment; **3** secondment.

détacher /detaʃe/ [1] I *vtr* **1** to untie; to unfasten; to undo; **2** to take down [*poster*]; **3 ~ les yeux** or **le regard de qch** to take one's eyes off sth; **4** to second (GB), to transfer; **5** to remove the stain(s) from.

II **se détacher** *v refl* (+ *v être*) **1** [*prisoner, animal*] to break loose; [*boat*] to come untied; **2** to come undone; **3** [*coupon*] to come out;

[*wallpaper*] to come away; **4** to grow away from [*person*]; **5** [*pattern*] to stand out; **6 se ~ de** to detach oneself from; to pull away from.

détail /detaj/ *nm* **1** detail; **2** breakdown; **analyse de ~** detailed analysis; **3** retail; **acheter (qch) au ~** to buy (sth) retail.

détailler /detaje/ [1] *vtr* **1** to detail; to itemize; **2** to scrutinize.

détartrer /detaRtRe/ [1] *vtr* **1** to descale [*kettle*]; **2** to scale [*teeth*].

détaxe /detaks/ *nf* **1** tax removal; **2** tax refund; **3** export rebate.

détecter /detɛkte/ [1] *vtr* to detect.

détection /detɛksjɔ̃/ *nf* detection.

détective /detɛktiv/ *nm* detective.

déteindre /detɛ̃dR/ [55] *vi* **1** [*garment*] to fade; **2** [*colour*] to run; **3** (figurative) to rub off.

détendre /detɑ̃dR/ [6] **I** *vtr* **1** to release [*spring*]; **2** to slacken [*rope, spring*]; **3** to relax [*muscle*]; to calm [*atmosphere, mind*].
II *vi* **1** to be relaxing; **2** to be entertaining.
III se détendre *v refl* (+ *v être*) **1** [*rope, spring*] to slacken; **2** [*person, muscle*] to relax.

détendu, **~e** /detɑ̃dy/ **I** *pp* ▶ **détendre**.
II *pp adj* **1** relaxed; **2** slack.

détenir /det(ə)niR/ [36] *vtr* **1** to keep [*objects*]; to hold [*power, record*]; to possess [*arms*]; to have [*secret, evidence*]; **2** to detain [*suspect*].

détente /detɑ̃t/ *nf* **1** relaxation; **2** détente; **3** (on gun) trigger.
IDIOMS **être lent** or **dur à la ~**○ to be slow on the uptake.

détention /detɑ̃sjɔ̃/ *nf* **1** (of passport, drugs, record) holding; (of arms, secret) possession; **2** detention; **~ préventive** custody.

détenu, **~e** /detəny/ *nm,f* prisoner.

détergent /detɛRʒɑ̃/ *nm* detergent.

détériorer /deteRjɔRe/ [1] **I** *vtr* to damage.
II se détériorer *v refl* (+ *v être*) [*situation, weather*] to deteriorate; [*foodstuff*] to go bad.

déterminant, **~e** /detɛRminɑ̃, ɑ̃t/ *adj* [*role, factor*] decisive.

détermination /detɛRminasjɔ̃/ *nf* determination.

déterminé, **~e** /detɛRmine/ **I** *pp* ▶ **déterminer**.
II *pp adj* **1** determined; **2** given.

déterminer /detɛRmine/ [1] *vtr* **1** to determine [*reason, responsibility*]; **2** to work out [*policy, terms*]; **3** to determine [*attitude, decision*]; **4 ~ qn à faire** to make sb decide to do.

déterrer /deteRe/ [1] *vtr* to dig [sb/sth] up.

détestable /detɛstabl/ *adj* [*style, weather*] appalling; [*habits*] revolting; [*person*] hateful.

détester /detɛste/ [1] *vtr* **1** to detest, to loathe [*person*]; **2** to hate.

détonateur /detɔnatœR/ *nm* **1** detonator; **2** (figurative) catalyst.

détonation /detɔnasjɔ̃/ *nf* detonation.

détonner /detɔne/ [1] *vi* to be out of place.

détordre /detɔRdR/ [6] *vtr* to straighten [*iron bar*]; to unwind [*cable*].

détour /detuR/ *nm* **1** detour; **ça vaut le ~** it's worth the trip; **2** roundabout means; **3** circumlocution; **il me l'a dit sans ~s** he told me straight; **4** (in road, river) bend.

détourné, **~e** /detuRne/ **I** *pp* ▶ **détourner**.
II *pp adj* [*reference*] oblique; [*means*] indirect.

détournement /detuRnəmɑ̃/ *nm* **1** misappropriation; **2** hijacking; **3** (of traffic) diversion.
■ **~ de mineur** (Law) corruption of a minor.

détourner /detuRne/ [1] **I** *vtr* **1** to divert [*attention*]; **2 ~ les yeux** or **le regard** or **la tête** to look away; **3** to divert [*traffic, river, flight*]; **~ la conversation** to change the subject; **4** to hijack [*plane, ship*]; to misappropriate [*funds*].
II se détourner *v refl* (+ *v être*) **1 se ~ de** to turn away from [*friend*]; **2** to look away.

détraqué○, **~e** /detRake/ *nm,f* deranged person.

détraquer /detRake/ [1] **I** *vtr* **1** to bust○ [sth]; to make [sth] go wrong; **2**○ [*medicine*] to upset [*stomach*]; to damage [*health*].
II se détraquer *v refl* (+ *v être*) [*mechanism*] to break down; [*weather*] to break.

détremper /detRɑ̃pe/ [1] *vtr* to saturate [*ground*]; to soak [*garment*].

détresse /detRɛs/ *nf* distress.

détriment: **au détriment de** /odetRimɑ̃də/ *phr* to the detriment of.

détritus /detRity(s)/ *nm pl* refuse, rubbish (GB), garbage (US).

détroit /detRwɑ/ *nm* straits.

détromper /detRɔ̃pe/ [1] **I** *vtr* to set [sb] straight.
II se détromper *v refl* (+ *v être*) **détrompez-vous!** don't you believe it!

détrôner /detRone/ [1] *vtr* to dethrone.

détruire /detRɥiR/ [69] *vtr* to destroy.

dette /dɛt/ *nf* debt; **avoir une ~ envers qn** to be indebted to sb.

DEUG /dœg/ *nm* (*abbr* = **diplôme d'études universitaires générales**) *university diploma taken after two years' study*.

deuil /dœj/ *nm* **1** bereavement; **2** mourning, grief.
IDIOMS **faire son ~ de qch**○ to kiss sth goodbye○.

deux /dø/ **I** *adj inv* **1** two; **~ fois** twice; **des ~ côtés de la rue** on either side or both sides of the street; **tous les ~ jours** every other day; **à nous ~** I'm all yours; (to enemy) it's just you and me now; **2** a few, a couple of; **3** second; **le deux mai** the second of May (GB), May second (US).
II *pron* **elles sont venues toutes les ~** they both came.
III *nm inv* two.
IDIOMS **faire ~ poids, ~ mesures** to have double standards; **un tiens vaut mieux que ~ tu l'auras** (Proverb) a bird in the hand is worth two in the bush; **en ~ temps, trois mouvements** very quickly; **je n'ai fait ni une ni ~** I didn't have a second's hesitation.

deuxième /døzjɛm/ **I** *adj* second; **dans un ~ temps nous étudierons**... secondly, we will study...

II *nmf* second.
■ **~ classe** second class, standard class (GB).
deuxièmement /døzjɛmmɑ̃/ *adv* secondly.
deux-points /døpwɛ̃/ *nm inv* colon.
deux-roues /døʀu/ *nm inv* two-wheeled vehicle.
dévaler /devale/ [1] *vtr* to hurtle down; to tear down.
dévaliser /devalize/ [1] *vtr* **1** to rob [*person, bank, safe*]; **2** to clean out○ [*shop, larder*].
dévaloriser /devalɔʀize/ [1] **I** *vtr* **1** to depreciate; **2** to belittle.
II se dévaloriser *v refl* (+ *v être*) **1** to lose value; to lose prestige; **2** to put oneself down.
dévaluation /devalɥasjɔ̃/ *nf* devaluation.
dévaluer /devalɥe/ [1] *vtr* to devalue.
devancer /dəvɑ̃se/ [12] *vtr* **1** to be ahead of, to outstrip [*competitor*]; **2** to anticipate [*demand, desire*]; to forestall [*attack, criticisms*].
devant[1] /dəvɑ̃/ **I** *prep* **1** in front of; **tous les hommes sont égaux ~ la loi** all men are equal in the eyes of the law; **fuir ~ le danger** to run away from danger; **le bus est passé ~ moi sans s'arrêter** the bus went straight past me without stopping; **2** outside; **il attendait ~ la porte** he was waiting outside the door; he was waiting by the door; **3** ahead of; **la voiture ~ nous** the car ahead or in front of us; **laisser passer quelqu'un ~ (soi)** to let somebody go first; **avoir toute la vie ~ soi** to have one's whole life ahead of one.
II *adv* **1 'où est la poste?'—'tu es juste ~'** 'where's the post office?'—'you're right in front of it'; **2 pars ~, je te rejoins** go ahead, I'll catch up with you; **3** (of hall, theatre) at the front; (in car) in the front.
devant[2] /dəvɑ̃/ *nm* front.
IDIOMS **prendre les ~s** to take the initiative.
devanture /dəvɑ̃tyʀ/ *nf* **1** (shop)front; **2** shop or store (US) window.
dévastation /devastasjɔ̃/ *nf* devastation.
dévaster /devaste/ [1] *vtr* **1** [*army*] to lay waste to; [*storm, fire*] to destroy; **2** [*burglar*] to wreck.
développement /devlɔpmɑ̃/ *nm* **1** development; **pays en voie de ~** developing nation or country; **2** (in photography) developing.
développer /devlɔpe/ [1] **I** *vtr* to develop.
II se développer *v refl* (+ *v être*) [*body, ability*] to develop; [*plant, company, town*] to grow.
devenir[1] /dəvniʀ/ [36] *vi* (+ *v être*) to become; **et Paul, qu'est-ce qu'il devient?** and what is Paul up to these days?
devenir[2] /dəvniʀ/ *nm* future.
dévergonder: **se dévergonder** /devɛʀgɔ̃de/ [1] *v refl* (+ *v être*) to be going to the bad.
déverser /devɛʀse/ [1] **I** *vtr* to pour [*liquid*]; to drop [*bombs*]; to dump [*refuse, sand*]; to discharge [*waste*]; to disgorge [*crowd*]; **~ du pétrole** to dump oil; to spill oil.
II se déverser *v refl* (+ *v être*) [*river*] to flow; [*sewer, crowd*] to pour.
dévêtir /devɛtiʀ/ [33] **I** *vtr* to undress.
II se dévêtir *v refl* (+ *v être*) to get undressed.
déviation /devjasjɔ̃/ *nf* **1** diversion (GB), detour (US); **2** departure, deviation; **3** (of compass) deviation; **4** (of light) deflection.
dévider /devide/ [1] *vtr* to unwind [*cable*].
dévier /devje/ [2] **I** *vtr* to deflect [*ball, trajectory*]; to divert [*traffic*].
II *vi* **1** [*bullet, ball*] to deflect; [*vehicle*] to veer off course; **2 ~ de** to deviate from [*plan*]; **3** [*tool*] to slip; **4** [*conversation*] to drift.
devin /dəvɛ̃/ *nm* soothsayer, seer.
deviner /dəvine/ [1] *vtr* **1** to guess [*secret*]; to foresee, to tell [*future*]; **2** to sense [*danger*]; **3** to make out, to discern.
devinette /dəvinɛt/ *nf* riddle.
devis /d(ə)vi/ *nm inv* estimate, quote.
dévisager /devizaʒe/ [13] *vtr* to stare at.
devise /dəviz/ *nf* **1** currency; **2** (foreign) currency; **3** motto.
deviser /dəvize/ [1] *vi* to converse.
dévisser /devise/ [1] *vtr* to unscrew.
dévoiler /devwale/ [1] *vtr* **1** to unveil; **2** to reveal; to uncover.
devoir[1] /dəvwɑʀ/ [44] **I** *v aux* **1** to have to; **je dois aller au travail** I've got to or I must go to work; **il a dû accepter** he had to accept; **il aurait dû partir** he should have left; **2 il a dû accepter** he must have accepted; **elle doit avoir 13 ans** she must be about 13 years old; **3 cela devait arriver** it was bound to happen; **un incident qui devait avoir de graves conséquences** an incident which was to have serious consequences; **ils doivent arriver vers 10 heures** they're due to arrive around 10 o'clock.
II *vtr* to owe; **il me doit des excuses** he owes me an apology.
III se devoir *v refl* (+ *v être*) **1 je me dois de le faire** it's my duty to do it; **2 les époux se doivent fidélité** spouses owe it to each other to be faithful; **3 un homme de son rang se doit d'avoir un chauffeur** a man of his standing has to have a chauffeur.
IV comme il se doit *phr* **1 agir comme il se doit** to behave in the correct way; **2 comme il se doit, elle est en retard!** as you might expect, she's late!
devoir[2] /dəvwɑʀ/ *nm* **1** duty; **il est de mon ~ de** it's my duty to; **2** test; homework.
dévorant, ~e /devɔʀɑ̃, ɑ̃t/ *adj* [*hunger*] voracious; [*flames, passion*] all-consuming.
dévorer /devɔʀe/ [1] *vtr* **1** to devour [*food, book*]; **~ qn de baisers** to smother sb with kisses; **2** [*obsession*] to consume.
dévot, ~e /devo, ɔt/ *adj* devout.
dévotion /devosjɔ̃/ *nf* **1** devoutness; **2** (religious) devotion (**à** to); **2** passion (**pour** for).
dévouement /devumɑ̃/ *nm* devotion.
dévouer: **se dévouer** /devwe/ [1] *v refl* (+ *v être*) **1** to devote or dedicate oneself; **2** to put oneself out.
dévoyer /devwaje/ [23] **I** *vtr* to deprave [sb], to lead [sb] astray.
II se dévoyer *v refl* (+ *v être*) to go astray.
dextérité /dɛksteʀite/ *nf* dexterity, skill.
diabète /djabɛt/ *nm* diabetes.

diabétique /djabetik/ *adj, nmf* diabetic.

diable /djɑbl/ **I** *nm* **1** devil; **en ~** diabolically; fiendishly; **un (petit) ~** a little devil; **2** two-wheeled trolley (GB), hand truck (US).
II *excl* my God!; **pourquoi ~** why on earth.
IDIOMS **habiter au ~** to live miles from anywhere; **que le ~ t'emporte!** to hell with you!; **ce n'est pas le ~!** it's not that difficult!; **avoir le ~ au corps** to be like someone possessed; **tirer le ~ par la queue** to live from hand to mouth.

diablement /djɑbləmɑ̃/ *adv* terrifically.

diabolique /djabɔlik/ *adj* **1** diabolic; [*invention*] fiendish; **2** [*person*] demonic; [*scheme, smile*] devilish; **3** [*precision*] uncanny.

diabolo /djabɔlo/ *nm* **~ menthe** mint cordial and lemonade (GB) or soda (US).

diadème /djadɛm/ *nm* **1** tiara; **2** diadem.

diagnostic /djagnɔstik/ *nm* (gen, Med) diagnosis.

diagnostiquer /djagnɔstike/ [1] *vtr* to diagnose.

diagonal, **~e**[1], *mpl* **-aux** /djagɔnal, o/ *adj* diagonal.

diagonale[2] /djagɔnal/ *nf* diagonal; **lire qch en ~** to skim through sth.

diagramme /djagʀam/ *nm* graph.

dialecte /djalɛkt/ *nm* dialect.

dialogue /djalɔg/ *nm* dialogue[GB].

dialoguer /djalɔge/ [1] *vi* to have talks.

dialoguiste /djalɔgist/ *nmf* screenwriter.

dialyse /djaliz/ *nf* dialysis.

diamant /djamɑ̃/ *nm* diamond.

diamantaire /djamɑ̃tɛʀ/ *nm* **1** diamond cutter; **2** diamond merchant.

diamétralement /djametʀalmɑ̃/ *adv* diametrically.

diamètre /djamɛtʀ/ *nm* diameter.

diapason /djapazɔ̃/ *nm* **1** (note) diapason; **2** tuning fork.
IDIOMS **se mettre au ~** to fall in step.

diaphragme /djafʀagm/ *nm* diaphragm.

diapo○ /djapo/ *nf* slide.

diaporama /djapoʀama/ *nm* slide show.

diapositive /djapozitiv/ *nf* slide, transparency.

diarrhée /djaʀe/ *nf* diarrhoea.

dico○ /diko/ *nm* dictionary.

dictateur /diktatœʀ/ *nm* dictator.

dictature /diktatyʀ/ *nf* dictatorship.

dictée /dikte/ *nf* dictation.

dicter /dikte/ [1] *vtr* **1** to dictate; **2** to motivate.

diction /diksjɔ̃/ *nf* diction; elocution.

dictionnaire /diksjɔnɛʀ/ *nm* dictionary.

dicton /diktɔ̃/ *nm* saying.

didacticiel /didaktisjɛl/ *nm* educational software program.

didactique /didaktik/ *adj* **1** [*work, tone*] didactic; **2** [*term, language*] technical, specialist.

dièse /djɛz/ *adj, nm* sharp; **do ~** C sharp.

diesel /djezɛl/ *nm* diesel.

diète /djɛt/ *nf* (Med) light diet.

diététicien, **-ienne** /djetetisjɛ̃, ɛn/ *nm,f* dietitian.

diététique /djetetik/ **I** *adj* dietary; **produits ~s** health foods; **magasin ~** health-food shop.
II *nf* dietetics.

dieu, *pl* **~x** /djø/ *nm* **1** god; **2 sur le terrain c'est un ~** he's brilliant on the sports field.
IDIOMS **nager comme un ~** to be a superb swimmer; **être dans le secret des ~x** to be privy to the secrets of those on high.

Dieu /djø/ *nm* God.
IDIOMS **se prendre pour ~ le père** to think one is God Almighty; **chaque jour que ~ fait** day in, day out; **il vaut mieux s'adresser à ~ qu'à ses saints** (Proverb) always go straight to the top.

diffamation /difamasjɔ̃/ *nf* slander; (Law) libel.

diffamer /difame/ [1] *vtr* (gen) to slander, to defame; (Law) to libel.

différé, **~e** /difeʀe/ **I** *pp* ▶ **différer**.
II *pp adj* **1** postponed; **2** [*payment*] deferred; **3** [*programme*] pre-recorded.
III *nm* (of match, event) recording.

différemment /difeʀamɑ̃/ *adv* differently.

différence /difeʀɑ̃s/ *nf* difference; **à la ~ de** unlike; **le droit à la ~** the right to be different.

différencier /difeʀɑ̃sje/ [2] **I** *vtr* **1** to differentiate; **rien ne les différencie** there's no way of telling them apart; **2** to make [sb/sth] different.
II se différencier *v refl* (+ *v être*) **1** [*person, organization*] to differentiate oneself; **2** to differ; **3** to become different.

différend /difeʀɑ̃/ *nm* disagreement.

différent, **~e** /difeʀɑ̃, ɑ̃t/ *adj* different, various; **pour ~es raisons** for various reasons.

différentiel, **-ielle** /difeʀɑ̃sjɛl/ *adj* differential.

différer /difeʀe/ [14] **I** *vtr* to postpone [*departure, meeting*]; to defer [*payment*].
II *vi* to differ.

difficile /difisil/ *adj* **1** (gen) difficult; [*victory*] hard-won; **le plus ~ reste à faire** the worst is yet to come; **2** [*person, personality*] difficult; **3** fussy (**sur** about); **tu n'es pas ~!** you're easy to please!

difficilement /difisilmɑ̃/ *adv* with difficulty; **~ supportable** hard to bear.

difficulté /difikylte/ *nf* difficulty.

difforme /difɔʀm/ *adj* [*body, limb*] deformed; [*object*] strangely shaped; [*tree*] twisted.

difformité /difɔʀmite/ *nf* deformity.

diffus, **~e** /dify, yz/ *adj* [*light, heat*] diffuse; [*feeling*] vague.

diffuser /difyze/ [1] *vtr* **1** to broadcast; **2** to spread; **~ le signalement de qn** to send out a description of sb; **3** to distribute [*article, book*]; **4** to diffuse [*light, heat*].

diffusion /difyzjɔ̃/ *nf* **1** broadcasting; **la ~ du film** the showing of the film; **2** dissemination, diffusion; **3** (commercial) distribution; **4** (of newspaper) circulation.

digérer /diʒeʀe/ [14] *vtr* **1** to digest; **2**○ to swallow [*insult*]; to stomach [*defeat*].
digeste /diʒɛst/ *adj* easily digestible.
digestif, **-ive** /diʒɛstif, iv/ **I** *adj* digestive.
II *nm* liqueur (*taken after dinner*); brandy.
digestion /diʒɛstjɔ̃/ *nf* digestion.
digicode® /diʒikɔd/ *nm* digital (access) lock.
digital, **~e**, *mpl* **-aux** /diʒital, o/ *adj* digital.
digne /diɲ/ *adj* **1** dignified; **2** worthy; **~ de confiance** or **de foi** trustworthy.
dignement /diɲmɑ̃/ *adv* **1** with dignity; **2** fittingly.
dignité /diɲite/ *nf* **1** dignity; **avoir sa ~** to have one's pride; **2** (title) dignity.
digression /digʀesjɔ̃/ *nf* digression.
digue /dig/ *nf* **1** sea wall; **2** dyke (GB), dike (US); **3** harbour[GB] wall.
dilapider /dilapide/ [1] *vtr* to squander.
dilatation /dilatasjɔ̃/ *nf* **1** (of gas) expansion; **2** (Med) dilation.
dilater /dilate/ [1] *vtr* **1** to dilate [*pupil, cervix*]; to distend [*stomach*]; **2** to expand [*gas*].
dilemme /dilɛm/ *nm* dilemma.
dilettante /dilɛtɑ̃t/ *nmf* amateur.
diligence /diliʒɑ̃s/ *nf* **1** stagecoach; **2** haste.
diligent, **~e** /diliʒɑ̃, ɑ̃t/ *adj* diligent.
diluant /dilɥɑ̃/ *nm* thinner.
diluer /dilɥe/ [1] *vtr* **1** to dilute; **2** to thin [sth] down.
diluvien, **-ienne** /dilyvjɛ̃, ɛn/ *adj* **pluies diluviennes** torrential rain.
dimanche /dimɑ̃ʃ/ *nm* Sunday.
IDIOMS **ce n'est pas tous les jours ~** not every day is a holiday.
dimension /dimɑ̃sjɔ̃/ *nf* **1** dimension; **2** size; **3** dimension, aspect; **4** (of problem) dimensions.
diminuer /diminɥe/ [1] **I** *vtr* **1** to reduce; to lower; **2** to dampen [*enthusiasm, courage*]; **3** to belittle [*person, achievement*]; **4** to weaken [*person*]; to sap [*strength*].
II *vi* **1** to come or go down; to be reduced; to fall; to decrease; **les jours diminuent** the days are getting shorter; **2** [*activity, violence*] to fall off; [*tension*] to decrease; [*noise, flames, rumours*] to die down; [*strength*] to diminish.
diminutif /diminytif/ *nm* **1** diminutive; **2** pet name.
diminution /diminysjɔ̃/ *nf* decrease; reduction; (in production, trade) fall-off.
dinde /dɛ̃d/ *nf* turkey (hen).
dindon /dɛ̃dɔ̃/ *nm* turkey (cock).
IDIOMS **être le ~ de la farce** to be fooled or duped.
dindonneau, *pl* **~x** /dɛ̃dɔno/ *nm* turkey.
dîner[1] /dine/ [1] *vi* to have dinner.
IDIOMS **qui dort dîne** (Proverb) when you're asleep you don't feel hungry.
dîner[2] /dine/ *nm* dinner.
dînette /dinɛt/ *nf* doll's tea set.
dingo○ /dɛ̃go/ *adj inv* crazy○.
dingue○ /dɛ̃g/ **I** *adj* **1** [*person*] crazy○; **2** [*noise, success*] wild; [*price, speed*] ridiculous.
II *nmf* **1** nutcase○; **2 un ~ de musique** a music freak○.
dinosaure /dinozɔʀ/ *nm* dinosaur.
diocèse /djɔsɛz/ *nm* diocese.
dioxyde /dijɔksid/ *nm* dioxide.
diphtongue /diftɔ̃g/ *nf* diphthong.
diplomate /diplɔmat/ **I** *adj* diplomatic.
II *nmf* diplomat.
diplomatie /diplɔmasi/ *nf* diplomacy.
diplôme /diplom/ *nm* **1** certificate, diploma; **il n'a aucun ~** he hasn't got any qualifications; **2** (at university) degree; diploma; **3** (in army, police) staff exam.
diplômé, **~e** /diplome/ **I** *adj* **une infirmière ~e** a qualified nurse.
II *nm,f* graduate.
dire[1] /diʀ/ [65] **I** *vtr* **1** to say [*words, prayer*]; to read [*lesson*]; to tell [*story, joke*]; **~ qch entre ses dents** to mutter sth; **2** to tell; **c'est ce qu'on m'a dit** so I've been told; **faire ~ à qn que** to let sb know that...; **je me suis laissé ~ que...** I heard that...; **c'est pas pour ~, mais..**○ I don't want to make a big deal of it, but○...; **à qui le dites-vous**○! don't I know it!; **je ne vous le fais pas ~**○! you don't need to tell me!; **dis donc, où tu te crois**○? hey! where do you think you are?; **3** to say (**que** that); **on dit que...** it is said that...; **si l'on peut ~** if one might say so; **autant ~ que...** you might as well say that...; **si j'ose ~** if I may say so; **c'est (tout) ~!** need I say more?; **cela dit** having said that; **tu peux le ~**○! you can say that again○!; **à vrai ~** actually; **entre nous soit dit** between you and me; **soit dit en passant** incidentally; **c'est ~ si j'ai raison** it just goes to show I'm right; **c'est beaucoup ~** that's going a bit far; **c'est vite dit** that's easy for you to say; **ce n'est pas dit** I'm not that sure; **comment ~?** how shall I put it?; **pour ainsi ~** so to speak; **autrement dit** in other words; **comme dirait l'autre**○ as they say; **il n'y a pas à ~, elle est belle**○ you have to admit, she's beautiful; **4** [*law*] to state; [*measuring device*] to show; **vouloir ~** to mean; **5 ~ à qn de faire** to tell sb to do; **6** to think; **on dirait de l'estragon** it looks like tarragon; it tastes like tarragon; **ça ne me dit rien de faire** I don't feel like doing; **notre nouveau jardinier ne me dit rien (qui vaille)** I don't think much of our new gardener.
II se dire *v refl* (+ *v être*) **1** to tell oneself; **il faut (bien) se ~ que...** one must realize that...; **2** to exchange [*insults*]; **se ~ adieu** to say goodbye to each other; **3** to claim to be; **4 ça ne se dit pas** you can't say that.
III se dire *v impers* **il ne s'est rien dit d'intéressant à la réunion** nothing of interest was said during the meeting.
dire[2] /diʀ/ *nm* **au ~ de, selon les ~s de** according to.
direct /diʀɛkt/ **I** *adj* **1** [*contact, descendent, tax*] direct; [*superior*] immediate; **2** [*route, access*] direct; **ce train est ~ pour Lille** this train is nonstop to Lille; **3** direct, frank.
II *nm* **1** live broadcasting; **en ~ de** live from;

2 (in boxing) jab; **~ du gauche** left jab; **3** express (train).

directement /dirɛktəmɑ̃/ *adv* **1** [*travel, go*] straight; **2** directly.

directeur, **-trice**[1] /dirɛktœr, tris/ **I** *adj* **principe ~** guiding principle; **idée directrice d'un ouvrage** central theme of a book.

II *nm,f* **1** headmaster/headmistress (GB), principal (US); (of private school) principal; **2** (of hotel, cinema) manager/manageress; **3** director; head.

■ **~ de banque** bank manager; **~ général** managing director (GB), chief executive officer (US); **~ de prison** prison governor (GB), warden (US); **~ sportif** (team) manager.

direction /dirɛksjɔ̃/ *nf* **1** direction; **il a pris la ~ du nord** he headed north; **en ~ de** toward(s); **indiquer la ~ à qn** to tell sb the way; **prenez la ~ Nation** take the train going to 'Nation'; **2** (gen) management; supervision; (of newspaper) editorship; (of movement) leadership; **orchestre sous la ~ de** orchestra conducted by; **3** management; **la ~ et les ouvriers** management and workers; **4** manager's office; head office; **5** (Aut) steering.

directive /dirɛktiv/ *nf* directive.

directrice[2] ▶ **directeur**.

dirigeable /diriʒabl/ *adj*, *nm* dirigible.

dirigeant, **~e** /diriʒɑ̃, ɑ̃t/ **I** *adj* [*class*] ruling.

II *nm* leader.

diriger /diriʒe/ [13] **I** *vtr* **1** to be in charge of [*people*]; to run [*service, party*]; to manage [*company*]; to lead [*investigation*]; to direct [*operation*]; **2** to steer; to pilot; **il vous dirigera dans la ville** he'll guide you around the town; **3** to turn [*light, jet*] (**sur** on); to point [*gun, telescope*] (**sur** at); **4** to dispatch [*goods*]; to direct [*convoy*]; **5** (Mus) to conduct; **6** to direct [*actors*]; to manage [*theatre company*].

II se diriger *v refl* (+ *v être*) **se ~ vers** to make for; **avoir du mal à se ~ dans le noir** to have difficulty finding one's way in the dark.

discale /diskal/ *adj f* **hernie ~** slipped disc.

discernement /disɛrnəmɑ̃/ *nm* judgment.

discerner /disɛrne/ [1] *vtr* **1** to detect [*sign, smell, expression*]; to make out [*shape, noise*]; **2** to make out [*motives*]; **~ le vrai du faux** to discriminate between truth and untruth.

disciple /disipl/ *nmf* **1** follower; **2** disciple.

disciplinaire /disiplinɛr/ *adj* disciplinary.

discipline /disiplin/ *nf* **1** discipline; **2** discipline, specialism; **3** (Sch) subject; **4** sport.

discipliner /disipline/ [1] *vtr* **1** to discipline; **2** to control [*troops*]; to discipline [*thoughts, feelings*]; **3** to keep [sth] under control [*hair*].

disco /disko/ **I** *adj inv* disco.

II *nm* disco music.

discontinu, **~e** /diskɔ̃tiny/ *adj* [*movement*] intermittent; [*line*] broken.

discordance /diskɔrdɑ̃s/ *nf* **1** (of opinions) conflict; **2** (of colours) clash; **3** (of sounds) dissonance.

discordant, **~e** /diskɔrdɑ̃, ɑ̃t/ *adj* **1** [*sound, instrument*] discordant; [*voice*] strident; **2** [*colours*] clashing; **3** [*opinions*] conflicting.

discorde /diskɔrd/ *nf* discord, dissension.

discothèque /diskɔtɛk/ *nf* **1** music library; **2** record collection; **3** discotheque.

discours /diskur/ *nm inv* **1** speech (**sur** on); **2** talk; **assez de ~, des actes!** let's have less talk and more action!; **3** views; **il tient toujours le même ~** his views haven't changed; **4** (in linguistics) speech; discourse.

discréditer /diskredite/ [1] *vtr* to discredit.

discret, **-ète** /diskrɛ, ɛt/ *adj* **1** [*person*] unassuming; [*colour*] sober; [*charm*] subtle; [*lighting*] subdued; [*smile, perfume*] discreet; [*place*] quiet; **2** discreet (**sur** about); **3** not inquisitive.

discrétion /diskresjɔ̃/ **I** *nf* discretion; **dans la plus grande ~** in the greatest secrecy.

II à discrétion *phr* **il y avait à boire à ~** you could drink as much as you liked.

III à la discrétion de *phr* at the discretion of.

discrimination /diskriminasjɔ̃/ *nf* discrimination.

discriminatoire /diskriminatwar/ *adj* discriminatory (**à l'encontre de** against).

disculper /diskylpe/ [1] **I** *vtr* to exculpate.

II se disculper *v refl* (+ *v être*) to vindicate oneself (**auprès de qn** in the eyes of).

discussion /diskysjɔ̃/ *nf* **1** discussion; **relancer la ~** to revive the debate; **2** argument.

discuté, **~e** /diskyte/ **I** *pp* ▶ **discuter**.

II *pp adj* controversial.

discuter /diskyte/ [1] **I** *vtr* **1** to discuss, to debate; **2** to question.

II discuter de *v+prep* to discuss.

III *vi* **1** to talk (**avec qn** to sb); **2** to argue.

IV se discuter *v refl* (+ *v être*) **ça se discute, ça peut se ~** that's debatable.

diseur, **-euse** /dizœr, øz/ *nm,f* **~ de bonne aventure** fortune-teller.

disgrâce /disgrɑs/ *nf* disgrace.

disgracieux, **-ieuse** /disgrasjø, øz/ *adj* ugly; unsightly.

disjoncter /disʒɔ̃kte/ [1] *vi* **ça a disjoncté** the trip switch has gone.

dislocation /dislɔkasjɔ̃/ *nf* **1** dismemberment; **2 ~ (articulaire)** dislocation (of a joint).

disloquer /dislɔke/ [1] *vtr* **1** to dismember [*empire, state*]; **2** to dislocate [*shoulder, arm*].

disparaître /disparɛtr/ [73] *vi* **1** to disappear; to vanish; **disparaissez!** out of my sight!; **des centaines de personnes disparaissent chaque année** hundreds of people go missing every year; **2** [*pain, smell*] to go; [*stain*] to come out; [*fever*] to subside; **faire ~** to get rid of [*pain, dandruff*]; to remove [*stain*]; **3** (euphemistic) to die; to die out; to become extinct; **voir ~** to witness the end of [*civilisation*].

disparate /disparat/ *adj* ill-assorted; mixed.

disparition /disparisjɔ̃/ *nf* **1** disappearance; (of species) extinction; **une espèce en voie de ~** an endangered species; **2** (euphemistic) death.

disparu, **~e** /dispary/ **I** *pp* ▶ **disparaître**.

II *pp adj* **1** missing; **porté ~** (Mil) missing in

action; **2** [*civilisation, traditions*] lost; [*species*] extinct; **3** (euphemistic) dead.

III *nm,f* **1** missing person; **2 les ~s** the dead.

dispense /dispɑ̃s/ *nf* **1** exemption (**de** from); **2** certificate of exemption.

dispenser /dispɑ̃se/ [1] I *vtr* **1** to give [*lessons, advice*]; **2 ~ qn de (faire) qch** to exempt sb from (doing) sth; to excuse sb from (doing) sth; **je vous dispense de commentaire** I don't need any comment from you.

II **se dispenser** *v refl* (+ *v être*) **se ~ de (faire) qch** to spare oneself (the trouble of doing) sth.

disperser /dispɛʀse/ [1] I *vtr* to scatter [*objects, family*]; to disperse [*crowd, smoke*]; to break up [*gathering, collection*].

II **se disperser** *v refl* (+ *v être*) to disperse; to scatter; to break up.

disponibilité /dispɔnibilite/ I *nf* availability.

II **disponibilités** *nf pl* available funds.

disponible /dispɔnibl/ *adj* available.

dispos, **~e** /dispo, oz/ *adj* **frais et ~** fresh as a daisy.

disposé, **~e** /dispoze/ I *pp* ▶ **disposer**.

II *pp adj* **1** arranged; laid out; **2 ~ à faire** willing to do; **3 être bien ~** to be in a good mood; **être bien ~ à l'égard de** or **envers qn** to be well-disposed toward(s) sb.

disposer /dispoze/ [1] I *vtr* **1** to arrange; to position; **2 les machines dont nous disposons** the machines we have at our disposal.

II **se disposer** *v refl* (+ *v être*) **1 se ~ à faire** to be about to do; **2 se ~ en cercle autour de qn** to form a circle around sb.

dispositif /dispozitif/ *nm* **1** device; system; **2** operation; **~ policier** police operation.

disposition /dispozisjɔ̃/ I *nf* **1** arrangement; layout; position; **2** disposal; **à la ~ du public** for public use; **3** measure, step.

II **dispositions** *nf pl* aptitude.

disproportionné, **~e** /dispʀɔpɔʀsjɔne/ *adj* [*effort, demand*] disproportionate; [*head*] out of proportion with one's body.

dispute /dispyt/ *nf* argument.

disputer /dispyte/ [1] I *vtr* **1** to compete in [*competition*]; to compete for [*cup*]; to play [*match*]; to run [*race*]; **2**° to tell [sb] off.

II **se disputer** *v refl* (+ *v être*) **1** to argue (**sur** about; **pour** over); **nous nous sommes disputés** we had an argument; **2** to fight over [*inheritance, bone*]; **3** [*tournament*] to take place.

disquaire /diskɛʀ/ *nmf* record dealer.

disqualifier /diskalifje/ [2] I *vtr* to disqualify; **se faire ~ (par)** to be disqualified (by).

II **se disqualifier** *v refl* (+ *v être*) to discredit oneself (**en faisant** by doing).

disque /disk/ *nm* **1** record; **passer un ~** to play a record; **2** (gen, Tech) disc; (Comput) disk; **3** (Sport) discus.

■ **~ dur** hard disk; **~ souple** flexi-disc; floppy disk; **~ de stationnement** parking disc.

disquette /diskɛt/ *nf* diskette, floppy disk.

dissection /disɛksjɔ̃/ *nf* dissection.

disséminer /disemine/ [1] I *vtr* to spread [*germs, ideas*]; to disperse [*pollen*].

II **se disséminer** *v refl* (+ *v être*) [*people*] to scatter; [*germs, ideas*] to spread.

disséquer /diseke/ [14] *vtr* to dissect.

dissertation /disɛʀtasjɔ̃/ *nf* essay.

dissidence /disidɑ̃s/ *nf* **1** dissent; dissidence; rebellion; **2 la ~** the dissidents.

dissident, **~e** /disidɑ̃, ɑ̃t/ I *adj* dissident.

II *nm,f* **1** dissident; **2** dissenter.

dissimulation /disimylasjɔ̃/ *nf* concealment.

dissimuler /disimyle/ [1] *vtr* to conceal (**qch à qn** sth from sb).

dissipation /disipasjɔ̃/ *nf* **1** (of misunderstanding) clearing up; **2** (of fog, clouds) clearing; **3** (of attention) wandering; **4** restlessness.

dissipé, **~e** /disipe/ *adj* [*pupil*] badly-behaved; [*life*] dissipated.

dissiper /disipe/ [1] I *vtr* **1** to dispel [*doubt*]; to clear up [*misunderstanding*]; to disperse [*smoke*]; **2** to distract [*person*].

II **se dissiper** *v refl* (+ *v être*) **1** [*doubt*] to vanish; [*misunderstanding*] to be cleared up; [*mist*] to clear; **2** to behave badly.

dissocier /disɔsje/ [2] *vtr* to separate (**de** from).

dissolu, **~e** /disɔly/ *adj* [*life*] dissolute; [*morals*] loose.

dissolution /disɔlysjɔ̃/ *nf* dissolution.

dissolvant, **~e** /disɔlvɑ̃, ɑ̃t/ I *adj* solvent.

II *nm* **1** nail varnish; **2** solvent.

dissonance /disɔnɑ̃s/ *nf* dissonance.

dissonant, **~e** /disɔnɑ̃, ɑ̃t/ *adj* [*voice*] dissonant; [*colours*] clashing.

dissoudre /disudʀ/ [75] I *vtr* **1** to dissolve [*assembly*]; to disband [*movement*]; **2** to dissolve [*substance*].

II **se dissoudre** *v refl* (+ *v être*) **1** [*organization*] to disband; **2** [*substance*] to dissolve.

dissuader /disɥade/ [1] *vtr* to dissuade; to put [sb] off; to deter.

dissuasif, **-ive** /disɥazif, iv/ *adj* **1** dissuasive; deterrent; **2** prohibitive.

dissuasion /disɥazjɔ̃/ *nf* (Mil) deterrence.

dissymétrie /disimetʀi/ *nf* asymmetry.

distance /distɑ̃s/ *nf* **1** distance; **Paris est à quelle ~ de Londres?** how far is Paris from London?; **j'ai couru sur une ~ de deux kilomètres** I ran for two kilometres[GB]; **être à faible ~ de** not to be far (away) from; **prendre ses ~s avec** to distance oneself from; **tenir** or **garder ses ~s** to stand aloof; **tenir la ~** [*runner*] to stay the course; **à ~** from a distance; **commande à ~** remote control; **2** gap; **à une semaine de ~** one week apart.

distancer /distɑ̃se/ [12] *vtr* to outdistance; to outrun; **se laisser ~** to get left behind.

distant, **~e** /distɑ̃, ɑ̃t/ *adj* **1** [*place, noise*] distant; **~s de trois kilomètres** three kilometres[GB] apart; **2** [*person*] distant; [*attitude*] reserved; [*relations*] cool.

distiller /distile/ [1] *vtr* to distil[GB].

distillerie /distilʀi/ *nf* **1** distillery; **2** distilling.

distinct, **~e** /distɛ̃, ɛ̃kt/ *adj* **1** distinct (**de** from); **2** [*sound*] distinct; [*voice*] clear; **3** [*firm*] separate.

distinctif, **-ive** /distɛ̃ktif, iv/ *adj* [*mark*] distinguishing; [*feature*] distinctive.

distinction /distɛ̃ksjɔ̃/ *nf* **1** distinction; **sans ~** without discrimination; indiscriminately; **2** honour[GB]; **~ honorifique** award; **3** refinement.

distingué, **~e** /distɛ̃ge/ *adj* distinguished.

distinguer /distɛ̃ge/ [1] **I** *vtr* **1** to distinguish between; **il est difficile de les ~** it's difficult to tell them apart; **2** to distinguish, to make out; **3** to discern; **4** to set [sb] apart; to make [sth] different; **5** to single [sb] out for an honour[GB].

II se distinguer *v refl* (+ *v être*) **1 se ~ de** to differ from; to set oneself apart from; **2** to distinguish oneself; **3** to be distinguishable; **4** to draw attention to oneself.

distorsion /distɔrsjɔ̃/ *nf* distortion.

distraction /distraksjɔ̃/ *nf* **1** leisure, entertainment; **les ~s sont rares ici** there's not much to do around here; **2** recreation; **3** absent-mindedness.

distraire /distrɛr/ [58] **I** *vtr* **1** to amuse; to entertain; **2 ~ qn de qch** to take sb's mind off sth; **3** to distract (**de** from; **par** by).

II se distraire *v refl* (+ *v être*) **1** to amuse oneself; to enjoy oneself; **2 j'ai besoin de me ~** I need to take my mind off things.

distrait, **~e** /distrɛ, ɛt/ *adj* [*person*] absent-minded; inattentive; [*air*] distracted; [*look*] vague.

distraitement /distrɛtmɑ̃/ *adv* absent-mindedly; **regarder ~ qch** to look vaguely at sth; **écouter ~** to listen with half an ear.

distrayant, **~e** /distrɛjɑ̃, ɑ̃t/ *adj* entertaining.

distribuer /distribɥe/ [1] *vtr* **1** to distribute (**à** to); to allocate (**à** to); **~ les cartes** to deal; **~ le courrier** to deliver the mail; **2** to supply [*water, heat*].

distributeur, **-trice** /distribytœr, tris/ **I** *nm,f* distributor.

II *nm* **1** dispenser; vending machine; **~ de tickets** ticket machine; **~ de billets (de banque)** cash dispenser; **2** retailing group.

distribution /distribysjɔ̃/ *nf* **1** retailing; **2** (in commerce) distribution; **3** (of water, electricity) supply; **4** distribution, handing out; allocation; **5** distribution, layout; **6** (of actors) casting; cast.

diurétique /djyretik/ *adj*, *nm* diuretic.

divaguer /divage/ [1] *vi* **1** to rave; **la fièvre le fait ~** he's delirious with fever; **2** to ramble; to talk nonsense; **3** to stray.

divan /divɑ̃/ *nm* divan; couch.

divergence /divɛrʒɑ̃s/ *nf* divergence; difference.

divergent, **~e** /divɛrʒɑ̃, ɑ̃t/ *adj* divergent.

diverger /divɛrʒe/ [13] *vi* to diverge (**de** from); to differ (**de** from).

divers, **~e** /divɛr, ɛrs/ *adj* **1** various; **les gens les plus ~** all sorts of people; **2** miscellaneous.

diversifier /divɛrsifje/ [2] *vtr* to widen the range of; to diversify.

diversion /divɛrsjɔ̃/ *nf* (Mil) diversion.

diversité /divɛrsite/ *nf* diversity; variety.

divertir /divɛrtir/ [3] **I** *vtr* to entertain; to amuse.

II se divertir *v refl* (+ *v être*) to amuse oneself; **pour se ~** for fun.

divertissant, **~e** /divɛrtisɑ̃, ɑ̃t/ *adj* amusing; entertaining; enjoyable.

divertissement /divɛrtismɑ̃/ *nm* entertainment; recreation.

dividende /dividɑ̃d/ *nm* dividend.

divin, **~e** /divɛ̃, in/ *adj* divine.

divinité /divinite/ *nf* deity; divinity.

diviser /divize/ [1] **I** *vtr* to divide.

II se diviser *v refl* (+ *v être*) **1** to become divided (**sur** over); **2** to be divided; **3** to be divisible; **4** to divide; to fork.

divisible /divizibl/ *adj* divisible.

division /divizjɔ̃/ *nf* division.

divorce /divɔrs/ *nm* divorce (**d'avec** from); **prononcer le ~ entre deux époux** to grant a divorce to a couple.

divorcé, **~e** /divɔrse/ *nm,f* divorcee.

divorcer /divɔrse/ [12] *vi* to get divorced.

divulguer /divylge/ [1] *vtr* to disclose.

dix /dis, *but before consonant* di, *before vowel or mute h* diz/ *adj inv*, *pron*, *nm inv* ten.

IDIOMS **ne rien savoir faire de ses ~ doigts** to be useless; **un de perdu, ~ de retrouvés** (Proverb) there's plenty more fish in the sea.

dix-huit /dizɥit/ *adj inv*, *pron*, *nm inv* eighteen.

dix-huitième /dizɥitjɛm/ *adj* eighteenth.

dixième /dizjɛm/ *adj* tenth.

dix-neuf /diznœf/ *adj inv*, *pron*, *nm inv* nineteen.

dix-neuvième /diznœvjɛm/ *adj* nineteenth.

dix-sept /dis(s)ɛt/ *adj inv*, *pron*, *nm inv* seventeen.

dix-septième /dis(s)ɛtjɛm/ *adj* seventeenth.

dizaine /dizɛn/ *nf* **1** ten; **2** about ten; **des ~s de personnes** dozens of people.

do /do/ *nm inv* (Mus) (note) C; (in sol-fa) doh.

docile /dɔsil/ *adj* [*animal, person*] docile.

dock /dɔk/ *nm* **1** dock; **2** warehouse.

docteur /dɔktœr/ *nm* doctor; **jouer au ~** to play doctors and nurses.

doctorat /dɔktɔra/ *nm* PhD, doctorate.

doctrinaire /dɔktrinɛr/ *adj* [*attitude*] doctrinaire; [*tone*] sententious.

doctrine /dɔktrin/ *nf* doctrine.

document /dɔkymɑ̃/ *nm* **1** document; **~ sonore** audio material; **avec ~s à l'appui** with documentary evidence; **2** document, paper.

documentaire /dɔkymɑ̃tɛr/ **I** *adj* documentary; **à titre ~** for your information.

II *nm* documentary (**sur** on, about).

documentaliste /dɔkymɑ̃talist/ *nmf* information officer; (school) librarian.

documentation /dɔkymɑ̃tasjɔ̃/ *nf* **1** material (**sur** on); **2** research; **3** brochures; **4 centre de ~** resource centre[GB].

documenter: **se documenter** /dɔkymɑ̃te/ [1] *v refl* (+ *v être*) **se ~ sur qch** to research sth.

dodeliner /dɔdline/ [1] *vi* **il dodelinait de la tête** his head was nodding.

dodo /dodo/ *nm* (baby talk) **faire ~** to sleep.

dodu, **-e** /dɔdy/ *adj* plump.

dogmatique /dɔgmatik/ *adj* dogmatic.

dogme /dɔgm/ *nm* dogma.

doigt /dwa/ *nm* finger; **petit ~** little finger (GB), pinkie; **bout des ~s** fingertips; **du bout des ~s** (figurative) reluctantly; **connaître une ville sur le bout des ~s** to know a city like the back of one's hand; **montrer du ~** to point at; (figurative) to point the finger at.
■ **~ de pied** toe.
IDIOMS **se brûler les ~s** to get one's fingers burned; **être à deux ~s de** to be a whisker away from; **filer entre les ~s de qn** [*money, thief*] to slip through sb's fingers; **se faire taper sur les ~s** to get one's knuckles rapped; **lever le ~** to put one's hand up.

doigté /dwate/ *nm* **1** tact; **2** (of pianist) fingering.

dollar /dɔlaʀ/ *nm* dollar.

domaine /dɔmɛn/ *nm* **1** estate; **2** field, domain; **3** territory.

dôme /dom/ *nm* dome.

domestique /dɔmɛstik/ **I** *adj* **1** [*staff, animal*] domestic; **2** [*market*] domestic, home.
II *nmf* servant.

domestiquer /dɔmɛstike/ [1] *vtr* to domesticate [*animal*].

domicile /dɔmisil/ **I** *nm* place of residence; (of company) registered address.
II à domicile *phr* **travail à ~** working at or from home; **'livraisons à ~'** 'home deliveries'.

domicilié, **~e** /dɔmisilje/ *adj* **1 être ~ à Arras** to live in Arras; **2 j'habite à Paris, mais je suis ~e à Rennes** I live in Paris, but my official address is in Rennes.

dominance /dɔminɑ̃s/ *nf* dominance.

dominant, **~e** /dɔminɑ̃, ɑ̃t/ *adj* **1** [*colour, gene*] dominant; [*wind, tendency*] prevailing; [*feature, idea*] main; **2** [*class*] ruling

domination /dɔminasjɔ̃/ *nf* domination; **être sous la ~ de** to be dominated by.

dominer /dɔmine/ [1] **I** *vtr* **1** to dominate; to tower above; **de là, on domine toute la vallée** from there you get a view of the whole valley; **2** to dominate [*match, sector*]; **3** [*theme*] to dominate; **4** to master [*subject*]; to overcome [*fear*]; **~ la situation** to be in control of the situation.
II *vi* **1** to rule, to hold sway; **2** to be in the lead; **3** [*impression*] to prevail; [*taste*] to stand out.
III se dominer *v refl* (+ *v être*) to control oneself.

dominical, **~e**, *mpl* **-aux** /dɔminikal, o/ *adj* [*walk, mass*] Sunday.

domino /dɔmino/ *nm* domino.

dommage /dɔmaʒ/ *nm* **1 c'est ~** it's a shame or pity; **2** damage; **3** (Law) tort.
■ **~s corporels** personal injury; **~s et intérêts** damages.

dompter /dɔ̃te/ [1] *vtr* to tame [*wild animal*]; to bring [sb] to heel [*unruly person*]; to subdue [*insurgents*]; to overcome [*passion*].

dompteur, **-euse** /dɔ̃tœʀ, øz/ *nm,f* tamer.

DOM-TOM /dɔmtɔm/ *nm pl* (*abbr* = **départements et territoires d'outre-mer**) *French overseas departments and territories.*

don /dɔ̃/ *nm* **1** donation; **faire ~ de** to give (**à** to); **~ de soi** self-sacrifice; **2** gift; **avoir le ~ de faire** to have a talent for doing.
■ **~ du sang** blood donation.

donation /dɔnasjɔ̃/ *nf* **1** donation; **2** (Law) gift.

donc /dɔ̃k/ *conj* so, therefore; **j'étais ~ en train de lire, lorsque**... so I was reading, when...; **je disais ~ que**... as I was saying...; **entrez ~!** do come in!; **mais où est-il ~ passé?** where on earth has he gone?

donjon /dɔ̃ʒɔ̃/ *nm* (of castle) keep.

donne /dɔn/ *nf* (in cards) deal.

donné, **~e**[1] /dɔne/ **I** *pp* ▸ **donner**.
II *pp adj* **1 il n'est pas ~ à tout le monde de faire** not everyone can do; **2** given; **à un moment ~** at one point; all of a sudden; **3** cheap.
III étant donné (que) *phr* given (that).

donnée[2] /dɔne/ *nf* **1** fact, element; **2** data.

donner /dɔne/ [1] **I** *vtr* **1** to give [*present, headache, advice, dinner, lesson*]; **~ l'heure à qn** to tell sb the time; **je lui donne 40 ans** I'd say he/she was 40; **~ faim à qn** to make sb feel hungry; **elle donne sa fille à garder à mes parents** she has my parents look after her daughter; **j'ai donné ma voiture à réparer** I've taken my car in to be repaired; **les sondages le donnent en tête** the polls put him in the lead; **2** to show [*film*]; to put on [*play*]; to give [*performance*]; **3** to produce, to yield [*fruit, juice*]; to produce [*results*]; **4** to show [*signs*]; **5**° to inform on [*accomplice*].
II *vi* **1 le poirier va bien ~ cette année** the pear tree will yield a good crop this year; **2 ne plus savoir où ~ de la tête** (figurative) not to know which way to turn; **3 ~ sur** [*room, window*] to overlook; [*door*] to give onto; **~ au nord** to face north; **la cuisine donne dans le salon** the kitchen leads into the living-room; **4 ~ dans** to tend toward(s); **5 ~ de sa personne** to give of oneself.
III se donner *v refl* (+ *v être*) **1 se ~ à** to devote oneself to; **2 se ~ le temps de faire** to give oneself time to do; **3 se ~ pour but de faire** to make it one's aim to do; **4 se ~ de grands airs** to put on airs; **5 se ~ des coups** to exchange blows; **se ~ le mot** to pass the word on.
IDIOMS **donnant donnant**: **je fais la cuisine, tu fais la vaisselle** fair's fair: I cook, you do

the washing-up; **avec lui, c'est donnant donnant** he never does anything for nothing.

donneur, **-euse** /dɔnœʀ, øz/ *nm,f* (Med) donor.

dont /dɔ̃/ *rel pron* **1** whose, of which; **la jeune fille ~ on nous disait qu'elle avait 20 ans** the girl who they said was 20; **Sylvaine est quelqu'un ~ on se souvient** Sylvaine is somebody (that) you remember; **la maladie ~ il souffre** the illness which he's suffering from; **la façon ~ il a été traité** the way he has been treated; **2 il y a eu plusieurs victimes ~ mon père** there were several victims, one of whom was my father; **des boîtes ~ la plupart sont vides** boxes, most of which are empty.

dopage /dɔpaʒ/ *nm* **1** (of horses) doping; **2** illegal drug-taking.

doper /dɔpe/ [1] *vtr* to dope.

dorade /dɔʀad/ *nf* (sea) bream.

doré, **~e** /dɔʀe/ **I** *pp* ▶ **dorer**.

II *pp adj* **1** [*paint*] gold; [*frame*] gilt; [*dome*] gilded; [*hair*] golden; [*skin*] tanned; [*bread*] golden brown; **~ à l'or fin** gilded; **2** [*exile*] luxurious; **jeunesse ~e** gilded youth.

III *nm* gilt.

dorénavant /dɔʀenavɑ̃/ *adv* from now on.

dorer /dɔʀe/ [1] **I** *vtr* **1** to gild; **2** (Culin) to glaze.

II *vi* (Culin) to brown.

III se dorer *v refl* (+ *v être*) **se ~ au soleil** to sunbathe.

dorloter /dɔʀlɔte/ [1] *vtr* to pamper.

dormeur, **-euse** /dɔʀmœʀ, øz/ *nm,f* sleeper; **c'est un gros ~** he sleeps a lot.

dormir /dɔʀmiʀ/ [30] *vi* **1** to sleep; **~ debout** (figurative) to be dead on one's feet; **ça m'empêche de ~** it keeps me awake; **il n'en dort plus** he's losing sleep over it; **2** [*money*] to lie idle.

IDIOMS **ne ~ que d'un œil** to sleep with one eye open; **~ sur ses deux oreilles, ~ tranquille** to rest easy; **~ comme un loir** to sleep like a log; **~ à poings fermés** to be fast asleep.

dorsal, *mpl* **-aux** /dɔʀsal, o/ *adj* [*pain*] back; [*fin*] dorsal.

dortoir /dɔʀtwaʀ/ **I** *nm* dormitory.

II (-)dortoir (*combining form*) **ville-~** dormitory town.

dorure /dɔʀyʀ/ *nf* gilt.

dos /do/ *nm inv* **1** back; **avoir le ~ rond** or **voûté** to stoop; **mal de ~** backache; **voir qn de ~** to see sb from behind; **robe décolletée dans le ~** dress with a low back; **il n'a rien sur le ~**○ he's wearing hardly anything; **tourner le ~ à** to have one's back to; to turn one's back to; (figurative) to turn one's back on; **2** (of book) spine; (of blade) blunt edge.

IDIOMS **mettre qch sur le ~ de**○ to blame sth on; **il a bon ~ le réveil**○! it's easy to blame it on the alarm-clock!

dosage /dozaʒ/ *nm* **1** amount; measurement; **2** mix; mixing; **3** proportions.

dos-d'âne /dodɑn/ *nm inv* hump.

dose /doz/ *nf* **1** dose; **forcer la ~**○ to go a bit far○; **2** measure.

doser /doze/ [1] *vtr* **1** to measure; **2** to use [sth] in a controlled way.

dossard /dosaʀ/ *nm* number (*worn by an athlete*).

dossier /dosje/ *nm* **1** file, dossier; **~ médical** medical records; **~ d'inscription** (Sch) registration form; **sélection sur ~** selection by written application; **2** (Law) file; case; **3 le ~ brûlant de la pollution** the controversial problem of pollution; **4** file, folder; **5** (of chair) back.

dot /dɔt/ *nf* dowry.

dotation /dɔtasjɔ̃/ *nf* allocation; endowment.

doter /dɔte/ [1] *vtr* **1 ~ qn de qch** to allocate sth to sb; **2 ~ qn/qch de** to equip sb/sth with; **3 ~ qn/qch de** to endow sb/sth with.

douane /dwan/ *nf* **1** customs; **2** (on goods) duty.

douanier, **-ière** /dwanje, ɛʀ/ **I** *adj* customs.

II *nm* customs officer.

double /dubl/ **I** *adj* double; **l'avantage est ~** the advantage is twofold; **valise à ~ fond** suitcase with a false bottom; **~ nationalité** dual nationality; **avoir le don de ~ vue** to have second sight; **en ~ exemplaire** in duplicate.

II *adv* double.

III *nm* **1** double; **leur piscine fait le ~ de la nôtre** their swimming-pool is twice as big as ours; **2** copy; **un ~ des clés** a spare set of keys; **3** (in tennis) doubles.

doublé, **~e** /duble/ **I** *pp* ▶ **doubler**.

II *pp adj* **1** [*coat*] lined; **2** [*film*] dubbed.

doubler /duble/ [1] **I** *vtr* **1** to double; **2** to line (**de** with); **3** to dub [*film*]; to stand in for [*actor*]; **4** to overtake (GB), to pass (US); **'défense de ~'** 'no overtaking' (GB), 'no passing' (US).

II *vi* to double.

III se doubler *v refl* (+ *v être*) **se ~ de qch** to be coupled with sth.

doublure /dublyʀ/ *nf* **1** lining; **2** (for actor) double.

douce ▶ **doux**.

doucement /dusmɑ̃/ *adv* **1** gently; **~ avec le vin!** go easy on the wine!; **2** quietly; **3** slowly.

doucereux, **-euse** /dusʀø, øz/ *adj* [*person*] smooth; [*words*] sugary; [*smile*] unctuous.

douceur /dusœʀ/ **I** *nf* **1** softness; mildness; mellowness; smoothness; gentleness; **~ de vivre** relaxed rhythm of life; **avec ~** gently; **2** sweet (GB), candy (US).

II en douceur *phr* **1** smoothly; **atterrissage en ~** smooth landing; **2 shampooing qui lave en ~** mild shampoo.

douche /duʃ/ *nf* shower; **~ froide** cold shower; letdown○.

doucher /duʃe/ [1] **I** *vtr* **1** to give [sb] a shower; **2**○ to dampen [*enthusiasm*].

II se doucher *v refl* (+ *v être*) to take a shower.

doué, **~e** /dwe/ *adj* **1** gifted, talented; **être**

~ pour to have a gift for; **2 ~ de** endowed with, gifted with.

douille /duj/ *nf* **1** cartridge (case); **2** (light) socket.

douillet, **-ette** /dujɛ, ɛt/ *adj* **1** oversensitive to pain; **2** cosy (GB), cozy (US).

douleur /dulœʀ/ *nf* **1** pain; **médicament contre la ~** painkiller; **2** grief.

douloureuse[1] ▶ **douloureux**.

douloureusement /duluʀøzmɑ̃/ *adv* **1** grievously; terribly; **2** painfully.

douloureux, **-euse**[2] /duluʀø, øz/ *adj* **1** painful; **2** [*event*] distressing; [*question*] painful.

doute /dut/ **I** *nm* doubt; **laisser qn dans le ~** to leave sb in a state of uncertainty; **mettre qch en ~** to call sth into question; **dans le ~, j'ai préféré ne rien dire** not being sure I didn't say anything; **il fait peu de ~ que** there's little doubt that; **nul ~ que** there's no doubt that.

II sans doute *phr* probably; **sans aucun ~** without any doubt.

douter /dute/ [1] **I** *vtr* **1 ~ que** to doubt that or whether **2 ~ de qch** to have doubts about sth; **elle l'affirme mais j'en doute** she says it's true but I have my doubts; **elle ne doute de rien**○**!** (ironic) she's so sure of herself!

II *vi* to doubt.

III se douter *v refl* (+ *v être*) **se ~ de** to suspect; **je m'en doutais!** I thought so!; **je me doute (bien) qu'il devait être furieux** I can (well) imagine that he was furious; **nous étions loin de nous ~ que** we didn't have the least idea that.

douteux, **-euse** /dutø, øz/ *adj* **1** uncertain; **2** ambiguous; **3** dubious; **4** [*deal, character*] shady.

douve /duv/ *nf* moat.

doux, **douce** /du, dus/ *adj* [*light, voice, substance*] soft; [*cider*] sweet; [*cheese, shampoo, weather*] mild; [*person, slope*] gentle.

IDIOMS **filer ~**○ to keep a low profile; **se la couler douce**○ to take it easy; **en douce**○ on the sly.

douzaine /duzɛn/ *nf* **1** dozen; **à la ~** by the dozen; **2** about twelve, a dozen or so.

douze /duz/ *adj inv, pron, nm inv* twelve.

douzième /duzjɛm/ *adj* twelfth.

doyen, **-enne** /dwajɛ̃, ɛn/ *nm,f* **1** oldest person; **2** the (most) senior member; **3** dean.

draconien, **-ienne** /dʀakɔnjɛ̃, ɛn/ *adj* draconian; very strict.

dragée /dʀaʒe/ *nf* **1** sugared almond; **2** sugar-coated pill.

dragon /dʀagɔ̃/ *nm* **1** dragon; **2** (Mil) dragoon.

draguer /dʀage/ [1] *vtr* **1**○ to come on to○; **2** to dredge, to drag [*river, canal*].

dragueur○, **-euse** /dʀagœʀ, øz/ *nm,f* **c'est un drôle de ~**○ he's a terrible flirt.

drain /dʀɛ̃/ *nm* drain.

drainage /dʀɛnaʒ/ *nm* **1** drainage; **2** (Med) draining (off).

drainer /dʀɛne/ [1] *vtr* to drain.

dramatique /dʀamatik/ *adj* **1** tragic; **ce n'est pas ~** it's not the end of the world; **2** dramatic; **art ~** drama; **auteur ~** playwright.

dramatiser /dʀamatize/ [1] *vtr* to dramatize.

dramaturge /dʀamatyʀʒ/ *nmf* playwright.

drame /dʀam/ *nm* **1** tragedy; **tourner au ~** to take a tragic turn; **2** drama; play; **~ lyrique** opera.

drap /dʀa/ *nm* **1** sheet; **2** woollen[GB] cloth.

■ **~ de plage** beach towel.

IDIOMS **se mettre dans de beaux ~s** to land oneself in a fine mess.

drapeau, *pl* **~x** /dʀapo/ *nm* flag; **être sous les ~x** to be doing military service.

drap-housse, *pl* **draps-housses** /dʀaus/ *nm* fitted sheet.

dressage /dʀɛsaʒ/ *nm* **1** training; (of horse) breaking in; **2** dressage.

dresser /dʀese/ [1] **I** *vtr* **1** to train [*animal*]; to break in [*horse*]; to teach [sb] how to behave [*person*]; **2** to put up [*scaffolding*]; **3** to prick up [*ears*]; **4** to lay out [*buffet*]; **5** to draw up [*list*]; **~ un procès-verbal à qn** to give sb a ticket; **6 ~ qn contre** to set sb against.

II se dresser *v refl* (+ *v être*) **1** to stand up; **2 se ~ contre** to rebel against; **3** [*statue, obstacle*] to stand; to tower up.

dresseur, **-euse** /dʀɛsœʀ, øz/ *nm,f* trainer.

dribbler /dʀible/ [1] *vi* to dribble.

drogue /dʀɔg/ *nf* drug; **la ~** drugs; **c'est devenu une ~** it has become an addiction.

drogué, **~e** /dʀɔge/ *nm,f* drug-addict.

droguer /dʀɔge/ [1] **I** *vtr* **1** [*doctor*] to dope; **2** to dope [*animal, sportsman*]; to drug [*victim*]; to doctor [*drink*].

II se droguer *v refl* (+ *v être*) **1** to dope oneself (**à, de** with); **2** to take drugs.

droguerie /dʀɔgʀi/ *nf* hardware shop (GB) or store (US).

droit, **~e**[1] /dʀwɑ, ɑt/ **I** *adj* **1** [*line, road, nose*] straight; [*writing*] upright; **se tenir ~** to stand up straight; to sit up straight; **s'écarter du ~ chemin** to stray from the straight and narrow; **2** right; **du côté ~** on the right-hand side; **3** [*person*] straight(forward); **4** [*skirt*] straight; **5** [*angle*] right.

II *adv* straight; **continuez tout ~** carry straight on; **marcher ~** to toe the line.

III *nm* **1** right; **être dans son (bon) ~** to be within one's rights; **cela leur revient de ~** it's theirs by right; **avoir ~ à** to be entitled to; **il a eu ~ à une amende** (ironic) he got a fine; **avoir le ~ de faire** to be allowed to do; to have the right to do; **avoir le ~ de vie ou de mort sur qn** to have power of life and death over sb; **il s'imagine qu'il a tous les ~s** he thinks he can do whatever he likes; **être en ~ de** to be entitled to; **2 le ~** law; **faire son ~** to study law; **3** fee; **4** (in boxing) right.

■ **(prisonnier de) ~ commun** nonpolitical prisoner; **~ d'entrée** entrance fee; **~ de passage** right of way (GB), easement (US); **un ~ de regard sur** a say in; **~s d'auteur** royalties; **~s de douane** customs duties;

les ~s de l'homme human rights; **~s de succession** inheritance tax.

droite[2] /dRwat/ *nf* **1** right; **la porte de ~** the door on the right; **à ta ~** on your right; **demander à ~ et à gauche** to ask everywhere; to ask everybody; **2 voter à ~** to vote for the right; **de ~** right-wing; **3** straight line.

droitier, **-ière** /dRwatje, ɛR/ *nm,f* right-hander.

droiture /dRwatyR/ *nf* honesty, uprightness.

drôle /dRol/ *adj* **1** funny, odd; **faire (tout) ~ à qn** to give sb a funny feeling; **faire une ~ de tête** to make a bit of a face; **2** funny, amusing; **3**○ **un ~ de courage** a lot of courage.

IDIOMS **j'en ai entendu de ~s** I heard some funny things; **en faire voir de ~s à qn** to lead sb a merry dance.

drôlement /dRolmɑ̃/ *adv* **1**○ really; **2** oddly.

dromadaire /dRɔmadɛR/ *nm* dromedary.

dru, **~e** /dRy/ **I** *adj* [*hair*] thick.

II *adv* **1** [*grow*] thickly; **2 la pluie tombait ~** it was raining heavily.

druide /dRɥid/ *nm* druid.

DST /deɛste/ *nf* (*abbr* = **Direction de la surveillance du territoire**) French counter-intelligence agency.

du /dy/ *det* ▶ **de**.

dû, **due**, *mpl* **dus** /dy/ **I** *pp* ▶ **devoir**[1].

II *pp adj* **1** owed, owing, due (**à** to); **en bonne et due forme** in due form; **2 ~ à** due to.

III *nm* **réclamer son ~** to claim one's due.

dualité /dɥalite/ *nf* duality.

dubitatif, **-ive** /dybitatif, iv/ *adj* sceptical (GB), skeptical (US).

duc /dyk/ *nm* duke.

duchesse /dyʃɛs/ *nf* duchess.

duel /dɥɛl/*nm* duel (**à** with); (figurative) battle.

dune /dyn/ *nf* dune.

duo /dyo, dɥo/ *nm* **1** duet; **en ~** as a duo; **2** double act (GB), duo (US); **3**○ pair.

dupe /dyp/ **I** *adj* **être ~** to be taken in or fooled (**de** by).

II *nf* dupe; **un marché de ~s** a fool's bargain.

duper /dype/ [1] *vtr* to fool; **facile à ~** gullible.

duplex /dyplɛks/ *nm inv* maisonette (GB), duplex apartment (US).

duplicata /dyplikata/ *nm inv* duplicate.

duquel ▶ **lequel**.

dur, **~e** /dyR/ **I** *adj* **1** [*ground, toothbrush, bread*] hard; [*meat*] tough; [*brush, cardboard*] stiff; [*plastic*] rigid; **2** [*zip, handle, pedal*] stiff; [*steering*] heavy; **3** [*sound, light, colour*] harsh; **4** [*face, expression*] severe; **5** [*parents, boss*] hard; harsh; [*policy*] hardline; **6** [*living conditions*] harsh; **7** [*job, sport*] hard; tough; [*climate, necessity*] harsh; **8** [*exam*] hard, difficult; **9** [*water*] hard.

II *nm,f* **1** tough nut○; **jouer les ~s** to act tough; **2** hardliner.

III *adv* [*work, hit*] hard.

IV *nm* **construction en ~** permanent structure.

V à la dure *phr* **élevé à la ~e** brought up the hard way.

IDIOMS **~ d'oreille** hard of hearing; **avoir la tête ~e** to be stubborn; to be dense; **avoir la vie ~e** [*habit*] to die hard; **mener la vie ~e à qn** to give sb a hard time.

durable /dyRabl/ *adj* [*impression*] lasting; [*interest*] enduring; [*material*] durable.

durant /dyRɑ̃/ *prep* **1** for; **des heures ~** for hours and hours; **2** during.

durcir /dyRsiR/ [3] **I** *vtr* **1** to harden [*ground, features, position*]; **2** to step up [*strike action*]; **~ sa politique en matière de** to take a harder line on.

II *vi* [*clay, artery*] to harden; [*cement, glue*] to set; [*bread*] to go hard.

III se durcir *v refl* (+ *v être*) **1** to harden; **2** to become harsher; to intensify.

durée /dyRe/ *nf* **1** (of reign, studies) length; (of contract) term; (of cassette) playing time; **séjour d'une ~ de trois mois** three-month stay; **contrat à ~ déterminée** fixed-term contract; **de courte ~** [*peace*] short-lived; [*absence*] brief; [*loan*] short-term; **2 ~ (de vie)** life; **pile longue ~** long-life battery.

durement /dyRmɑ̃/ *adv* **1** badly; **2** harshly; **3** [*look*] severely; **4** [*hit*] hard.

durer /dyRe/ [1] *vi* **1** to last; **2** to go on; **ça ne peut plus ~** it can't go on any longer; **faire ~** to prolong [*meeting*]; **faire ~ le plaisir** (ironic) to prolong the agony; **3** [*festival*] to run.

dureté /dyRte/ *nf* **1** (of material, face) hardness; (of meat) toughness; (of brush) stiffness; **2** (of expression, tone, climate) harshness; (of look) severity; **avec ~** [*look*] severely; [*punish*] harshly.

durillon /dyRijɔ̃/ *nm* callus.

durite /dyRit/ *nf* radiator hose.

DUT /deyte/ *nm* (*abbr* = **diplôme universitaire de technologie**) *two-year diploma from a university institute of technology*.

duvet /dyvɛ/ *nm* **1** (of bird) down; **2** sleeping bag.

dynamique /dinamik/ **I** *adj* dynamic, lively.

II *nf* **1** dynamics; **2** process.

dynamisme /dinamism/ *nm* dynamism; **être plein de ~** to be very dynamic.

dynamite /dinamit/ *nf* dynamite.

dynastie /dinasti/ *nf* dynasty.

dysenterie /disɑ̃tRi/ *nf* dysentery.

dysfonctionnement /disfɔ̃ksjɔnmɑ̃/ *nm* **1** (Med) dysfunction; **2** malfunctioning.

dyslexie /dislɛksi/ *nf* dyslexia.

Ee

e, **E** /ə/ *nm inv* e, E; **e dans l'o** o and e joined together.

eau, *pl* **~x** /o/ **I** *nf* **1** water; **l'~ de source** spring water; **prendre l'~** [*shoe*] to let in water; **être en ~** to be dripping with sweat; **mettre à l'~** to launch [*ship*]; **se jeter à l'~** to throw oneself into the water; (figurative) to take the plunge; **tomber à l'~** (figurative) to fall through; **nettoyer le sol à grande ~** to sluice the floor down; **2** rain.
II eaux *nf pl* **1** water; waters; **2** (Med) waters.
■ **~ bénite** holy water; **~ de chaux** limewater; **~ douce** fresh water; **~ de Javel** ≈ (chloride) bleach; **~ de mer** seawater; **~ oxygénée** hydrogen peroxide; **~ plate** plain water; still mineral water; **~ de rose**: **à l'~ de rose** [*novel*] sentimental; **~x et forêts** forestry commission; **~x usées** waste water.
IDIOMS **mettre l'~ à la bouche de qn** to make sb's mouth water; **ou dans ces ~x-là**○ or thereabouts; **vivre d'amour et d'~ fraîche** to live on love alone.

EAU *written abbr* ▶ **Émirats**.

eau-de-vie, *pl* **eaux-de-vie** /odvi/ *nf* brandy, eau de vie; **à l'~** in brandy.

ébahir /ebaiʀ/ [3] **I** *vtr* to dumbfound.
II s'ébahir *v refl* (+ *v être*) to be dumbfounded.

ébattre: **s'ébattre** /ebatʀ/ [61] *v refl* (+ *v être*) to frolic (about); to frisk about; to splash about.

ébauche /eboʃ/ *nf* **1** (for sculpture) rough shape; (for picture) preliminary sketch; (of novel) preliminary draft; **être encore à l'état d'~** to be still at an early stage; **2 l'~ d'un sourire** a hint of a smile.

ébaucher /eboʃe/ [1] **I** *vtr* to sketch out [*picture, solution*]; to draft [*novel, plan*]; to rough-hew [*statue*]; to begin [*conversation*].
II s'ébaucher *v refl* (+ *v être*) [*solution, novel*] to begin to take shape; [*friendship*] to begin to develop; [*talks*] to start.

ébène /ebɛn/ *nf* ebony.

ébéniste /ebenist/ *nmf* cabinetmaker.

éblouir /ebluiʀ/ [3] *vtr* to dazzle.

éblouissement /ebluismɑ̃/ *nm* **1** dazzle; **2** dizzy spell.

éborgner /ebɔʀɲe/ [1] *vtr* **~ qn** to blind sb in one eye; (humorous) to poke sb's eye out.

éboueur /ebuœʀ/ *nm* dustman (GB), garbageman (US).

ébouillanter /ebujɑ̃te/ [1] *vtr* **1** to scald; **2** to blanch [*vegetables*].

éboulement /ebulmɑ̃/ *nm* (of wall, cliff) collapse; **~ (de rochers)** rockfall.

éboulis /ebuli/ *nm inv* mass of fallen rocks; heap of fallen earth.

ébouriffer /ebuʀife/ [1] *vtr* to tousle; to ruffle.

ébranler /ebʀɑ̃le/ [1] *vtr* **1** to rattle [*windowpane*]; to shake [*house*]; to weaken [*building*]; **2** to shake [*person, confidence*].

ébrécher /ebʀeʃe/ [14] *vtr* to chip [*cup*].

ébriété /ebʀijete/ *nf* intoxication.

ébrouer: **s'ébrouer** /ebʀue/ [1] *v refl* (+ *v être*) **1** [*horse*] to snort; **2** [*person, dog*] to shake oneself/itself; [*bird*] to flap its wings.

ébruiter /ebʀɥite/ [1] **I** *vtr* to divulge.
II s'ébruiter *v refl* (+ *v être*) [*news*] to get out.

ébullition /ebylisjɔ̃/ *nf* (Culin) boiling.
IDIOMS **être en ~** [*crowd*] to be in a fever of excitement; [*country, brain*] to be in a ferment.

écaille /ekaj/ *nf* **1** (on fish, reptile) scale; (on oyster) shell; **2** tortoiseshell; **lunettes en ~** horn-rimmed glasses; **3** flake.

écailler /ekaje/ [1] **I** *vtr* **1** (Culin) to scale [*fish*]; to open [*oyster*]; **2 ~ qch** to chip [sth] off.
II s'écailler *v refl* (+ *v être*) to flake away.

écarlate /ekaʀlat/ *adj* scarlet.

écart /ekaʀ/ **I** *nm* **1** (between objects) distance, gap; (between dates) interval; (between ideas) gap; **2** (between versions, in prices) difference; **~ des salaires** pay differential; **3 faire un ~** [*horse*] to shy; [*car*] to swerve; **4** lapse; **~s de langage** bad language.
II à l'écart *phr* **être à l'~** to be isolated; **se tenir à l'~** to stand apart; to keep oneself to oneself; not to join in; **mettre qn à l'~** to push sb aside; to ostracize sb; **entraîner qn à l'~** to take sb aside.
III à l'écart de *phr* away from; **tenir qn à l'~ de** to keep sb away from [*place*]; to keep sb out of [*activity, talks*].

écarté, **~e** /ekaʀte/ **I** *pp* ▶ **écarter**.
II *pp adj* **1** [*fingers*] spread; [*knees, legs*] apart; [*teeth*] widely spaced; **2** [*place*] isolated.

écarteler /ekaʀtəle/ [17] *vtr* (kill) to quarter [sb].

écartement /ekaʀtəmɑ̃/ *nm* distance, space.

écarter /ekaʀte/ [1] **I** *vtr* **1** to move [sth] further apart [*objects*]; to open [*curtains*]; to spread [*fingers, legs*]; **2** to move [sth] aside [*chair*]; to remove [*obstacle*]; to push [sb] aside; to move [sb] on; **3** to dispel [*suspicion*]; to eliminate [*risk, rival*]; **4** to reject [*idea*]; to rule out [*possibility*].
II s'écarter *v refl* (+ *v être*) **1** [*crowd, clouds*] to part; [*shutters*] to open; **2** to move away; **s'~ de** to move away from [*direction, standard*]; to stray from [*path, subject*].

ecchymose /ekimoz/ *nf* bruise.

ecclésiastique /eklezjastik/ *nm* cleric.

écervelé, **~e** /esɛʀvəle/ *nm,f* featherbrain.

échafaud /eʃafo/ *nm* **1** scaffold; **2** guillotine.

échafaudage /eʃafodaʒ/ *nm* scaffolding.

échafauder /eʃafode/ [1] *vtr* to put [sth] together [*plan*]; to develop [*theory*].

échalas /eʃala/ *nm inv* **1** cane, stake; **2**○ bean-pole○.

échalote /eʃalɔt/ *nf* shallot.

échancré, **~e** /eʃɑ̃kʀe/ *adj* **1** [*dress*] low-cut; [*briefs*] high-cut; **trop ~** [*sleeve*] cut too wide; **2** [*blouse*] open-necked; **3** [*coast*] indented.

échange /eʃɑ̃ʒ/ **I** *nm* **1** exchange; **elles ont fait l'~ de leurs manteaux** they've swapped coats; **2** trade; **~s commerciaux** trade; **3** (cultural, linguistic) exchange; **4** (Sport) rally.
II en échange *phr* in exchange, in return.
III en échange de *phr* in exchange for, in return for.
■ **~ de bons procédés** quid pro quo.

échanger /eʃɑ̃ʒe/ [13] *vtr* **1** to exchange; **~ des insultes** to trade insults; **2** (Sport) **~ des balles** to rally.

échangeur /eʃɑ̃ʒœʀ/ *nm* interchange (GB), grade separation (US).

échantillon /eʃɑ̃tijɔ̃/ *nm* sample.

échappement /eʃapmɑ̃/ *nm* (Aut) **(tuyau d')~** exhaust (pipe).

échapper /eʃape/ [1] **I échapper à** *v+prep* **1 ~ à** to get away from; (cleverly) to elude; **2 ~ à** to escape [*death, failure*]; (to manage) to avoid [*accident*]; **3 ~ à** to escape from [*social background*]; **je sens qu'il m'échappe** [*partner*] I feel he is drifting away from me; [*child*] I feel he's growing away from me; **4 ~ à qn** or **des mains de qn** to slip out of sb's hands; **5 un soupir m'a échappé** I let out a sigh; **6 le titre m'échappe** the title escapes me; **7 ~ à** to defy [*logic*]; **~ à la règle** to be an exception to the rule.
II s'échapper *v refl* (+ *v être*) **1** to run away; to fly away; to escape; to get away; **2** [*gas, smoke*] to escape; **3** to get away; **s'~ pour quelques jours** to get away for a few days.
IDIOMS **l'~ belle** to have a narrow escape.

écharde /eʃaʀd/ *nf* splinter.

écharpe /eʃaʀp/ *nf* **1** scarf; **2** sash.

échasse /eʃɑs/ *nf* stilt.

échauder /eʃode/ [1] *vtr* to put [sb] off.
IDIOMS **chat échaudé craint l'eau froide** (Proverb) once bitten, twice shy.

échauffement /eʃofmɑ̃/ *nm* (Sport) warm-up.

échauffer /eʃofe/ [1] *vtr* **1** (Sport) to warm up; **2** to stir [*imagination*]; to stir up [*person, debate*]; **3** to start [sth] fermenting.
IDIOMS **~ les oreilles de qn** to vex sb.

échéance /eʃeɑ̃s/ *nf* **1** (of debt) due date; (of share, policy) maturity date; (of loan) redemption date; **arriver à ~** [*payment*] to fall due; [*investment, policy*] to mature; **2** expiry date; **3 à longue/brève ~** [*forecast*] long-/short-term; [*strengthen, change*] in the long/short term; **4** payment; repayment; **5** date; deadline.

échéant: **le cas échéant** /ləkazeʃeɑ̃/ *phr* if need be, should the case arise.

échec /eʃɛk/ **I** *nm* **1** failure; setback; **faire ~ à qn** to thwart sb; **2** (gen, Mil) defeat; **3 faire ~ au roi** to put the king in check.
II échecs *nm pl* **les ~s** chess; chess set.

échelle /eʃɛl/ *nf* **1** ladder; **~ coulissante** extending ladder (GB), extension ladder (US); **faire la courte ~ à qn** to give sb a leg up; **2** (of map, model) scale; **plan à l'~** scale plan; **à l'~ mondiale** on a worldwide scale; **~ des salaires** pay scale; **3**○ (in stocking) ladder.

échelon /eʃlɔ̃/ *nm* **1** (of ladder) rung; **2** grade; **sauter les ~s** to get accelerated promotion; **3** level.

échelonner /eʃlɔne/ [1] **I** *vtr* **1** to space [sth] out [*objects*]; **2** to spread [*payments, work*]; to stagger [*holidays*]; **3** to grade [*exercises*].
II s'échelonner *v refl* (+ *v être*) **1** to be positioned at intervals; **2** [*payments*] to be spread; [*departures*] to be staggered.

écheveau, *pl* **~x** /eʃvo/ *nm* hank, skein.

échevelé, **~e** /eʃəvle/ *adj* **1** tousled; **2** [*rhythm*] frenzied; [*romanticism*] unbridled.

échine /eʃin/ *nf* **1** (Anat) spine; **2** (Culin) ≈ spare rib.
IDIOMS **courber l'~ devant** to submit to.

échiquier /eʃikje/ *nm* **1** chessboard; **2** chequered (GB) or checkered (US) pattern.

Échiquier /eʃikje/ *pr nm* **l'~** the Exchequer, the Treasury.

écho /eko/ *nm* **1** echo; **faire ~ à qch**, **se faire l'~ de qch** to echo sth; **2** response; **nous n'avons eu aucun ~ des pourparlers** we have heard nothing about the talks.

échographie /ekogʀafi/ *nf* (Med) scan.

échoir /eʃwaʀ/ [51] *vi* (+ *v être*) [*rent*] to fall due; [*draft*] to be payable.

échoppe /eʃɔp/ *nf* stall.

échouer /eʃwe/ [1] **I** *vtr* to beach [*boat*].
II échouer à *v+prep* to fail [*exam, test*].
III *vi* **1** [*person, attempt*] to fail; **2** to end up (**dans** in).
IV s'échouer *v refl* (+ *v être*) [*boat*] to run aground; [*whale*] to be beached.

échu, **~e** /eʃy/ **I** *pp* ▶ **échoir**.
II *adj* expired; **payer à terme ~** to pay in arrears.

éclabousser /eklabuse/ [1] *vtr* **1** to splash; **2 il a été éclaboussé par ces rumeurs** the rumours[GB] have damaged his reputation.

éclair /eklɛʀ/ **I** *adj inv* **rencontre ~** brief meeting; **attaque ~** lightning strike; **guerre ~** blitzkrieg.
II *nm* **1** flash of lightning; **passer comme un ~** to flash past; **2** (of explosion, diamonds) flash; (of eyes) glint; **3** (of lucidity, triumph) moment; **il a eu un ~ de génie** he had a brainwave (GB) or brainstorm (US); **4** (Culin) éclair.

éclairage /eklɛʀaʒ/ *nm* lighting; light; **~ au gaz** gaslight.

éclairagiste /eklɛʀaʒist/ *nm* (in theatre, films) electrician.

éclaircie /eklɛʀsi/ *nf* sunny spell.

éclaircir /eklɛʀsiʀ/ [3] **I** *vtr* **1** to lighten [*colour*]; to lighten the colour[GB] of [*paint, hair*]; **2** to shed light on [sth].
II s'éclaircir *v refl* (+ *v être*) **1** [*weather*] to clear; **l'horizon s'éclaircit** (figurative) the outlook is getting brighter; **2** [*colour*] to fade; [*hair*] to get lighter; **3** [*situation, mystery*] to

become clearer; **4** [*crowd, forest*] to thin out; **5 s'~ les cheveux** to lighten one's hair; **s'~ la voix** or **la gorge** to clear one's throat.

éclaircissement /eklɛʀsismɑ̃/ *nm* **1** explanation; **2** clarification.

éclairé, **~e** /ekleʀe/ *adj* [*person, advice*] enlightened; [*art lover*] well-informed.

éclairer /ekleʀe/ [1] **I** *vtr* **1** to light [*street, room*]; [*sun*] to light up [*place, object*]; **2** to give [sb] some light; **3** [*remark*] to throw light on [*text, situation*]; **4** to enlighten [sb].
II *vi* [*lamp, candle*] to give out light.
III s'éclairer *v refl* (+ *v être*) **1** [*screen, face*] to light up; **2 s'~ à l'électricité** to have electric lighting.

éclaireur /ekleʀœʀ/ *nm* **1** scout (GB), Boy Scout (US); **2** (Mil) scout.

éclaireuse /ekleʀøz/ *nf* guide (GB), Girl Guide (US).

éclat /ekla/ *nm* **1** splinter; **un ~ d'obus** a piece of shrapnel; **voler en ~s** to shatter; **2** (of light, star) brightness; (of spotlight) glare; (of snow) sparkle; **3** (of colour, material) brilliance; (of hair, plumage) shine; (of metal) lustre[GB]; **4** (of face, smile) radiance; (of eyes) sparkle; **sans ~** [*eyes*] dull; [*beauty*] lifeless; **5** splendour[GB]; **manquer d'~** [*ceremony*] to lack sparkle; **6** scene, fuss; **faire un ~** to make a scene .
■ **~ de colère** fit of anger; **~ de rire** roar of laughter; **des ~s de voix** raised voices.
IDIOMS **rire aux ~s** to roar with laughter.

éclatant, **~e** /eklatɑ̃, ɑ̃t/ *adj* **1** [*light*] dazzling; [*sun*] blazing; **2** [*colour, plumage*] bright; **d'une blancheur ~e** sparkling white; **3** [*beauty, smile*] radiant; [*victory*] brilliant; **4** [*proof*] striking; **5** [*laughter*] ringing.

éclaté, **~e** /eklate/ *adj* (gen) fragmented; [*family*] divided.

éclater /eklate/ [1] *vi* **1** [*tyre, bubble*] to burst; [*shell, firework*] to explode; [*bottle*] to shatter; **faire ~** to burst [*bubble*]; to detonate [*bomb*]; **2** [*pipe, boil*] to burst; **3** [*laughter, firing*] to break out; [*shot*] to ring out; **4** [*scandal, news*] to break; [*truth*] to come out; **5** [*war*] to break out; [*storm*] to break; **6 laisser ~ sa joie** to be wild with joy; **7** [*coalition*] to break up (**en** into); [*party*] to split; **8** to lose one's temper; **~ de rire** to burst out laughing.

éclectique /eklɛktik/ *adj* eclectic.

éclipse /eklips/ *nf* eclipse.

éclipser /eklipse/ [1] **I** *vtr* **1** to eclipse; **2** to obscure; **3** to outshine.
II s'éclipser○ *v refl* (+ *v être*) to slip away.

éclopé, **~e** /eklɔpe/ *adj* injured, lame.

éclore /eklɔʀ/ [79] *vi* **1** [*chick, egg*] to hatch; [*flower*] to bloom; **faire ~ un œuf** to incubate an egg; **2** [*idea*] to dawn; [*talent*] to bloom.

écluse /eklyz/ *nf* lock.

écœurant, **~e** /ekœʀɑ̃, ɑ̃t/ *adj* **1** [*food, smell*] sickly; **2** nauseating; **3** (humorous) sickening.

écœurement /ekœʀmɑ̃/ *nm* nausea.

écœurer /ekœʀe/ [1] *vtr* **1** to make [sb] feel sick; **2** (figurative) to sicken.

école /ekɔl/ *nf* **1** school; **2** education system; **3** (**grande**) **~** *higher education institution with competitive entrance examination*; **une ~ de commerce** a business school; **4** training (**de** in); **être à bonne ~** to be in good hands; **5** (of art) school; **faire ~** to gain a following.
■ **~ élémentaire** primary school; **~ d'infirmières** nursing college; **~ maternelle** nursery school; **~ normale** primary teacher training college; **~ primaire** primary school; **École nationale d'administration**, **ENA** *Grande École for top civil servants*; **École normale supérieure**, **ENS** *Grande École from which the educational élite is recruited.*

écolier, **-ière** /ekɔlje, ɛʀ/ *nm,f* schoolboy/schoolgirl.

écologie /ekɔlɔʒi/ *nf* ecology.

écologique /ekɔlɔʒik/ *adj* ecological; [*speech*] on the environment; [*interest*] environmental; [*product*] environment-friendly.

écologiste /ekɔlɔʒist/ **I** *adj* **1** [*candidate*] Green; **2** [*measure*] ecological.
II *nmf* **1** environmentalist; **2** Green (candidate); **3** ecologist.

écomusée /ekomyze/ *nm* ≈ open air museum.

éconduire /ekɔ̃dɥiʀ/ [69] *vtr* to turn [sb] away.

économat /ekɔnɔma/ *nm* bursar's office.

économe /ekɔnɔm/ **I** *adj* thrifty.
II *nm* (Culin) potato peeler.

économie /ekɔnɔmi/ **I** *nf* **1** (of country) economy; **2** economics; **3** saving; **faire l'~ de** to save the cost of [*trip*]; **4** economy, thrift; **par ~** in order to save money; **s'exprimer avec une grande ~ de paroles** to express oneself succinctly.
II économies *nf pl* savings; **faire des ~s** to save up; to save money.
■ **~ de marché** free market (economy).
IDIOMS **il n'y a pas de petites ~s** every little helps.

économique /ekɔnɔmik/ *adj* **1** [*policy, crisis*] economic; **2** economical.

économiser /ekɔnɔmize/ [1] *vtr* **1** to save (up) [*money*]; **~ ses forces** to pace oneself; **2** to save [*petrol, water, energy*]; **3** to economize.

économiste /ekɔnɔmist/ *nmf* economist.

écoper /ekɔpe/ [1] *vtr* to bail out.

écorce /ekɔʀs/ *nf* (of tree) bark; (of fruit) peel; (of chestnut) skin.
■ **~ terrestre** earth's crust.

écorché, **~e** /ekɔʀʃe/ *adj* **~ (vif)** hypersensitive.

écorcher /ekɔʀʃe/ [1] *vtr* **1** to skin [*animal*]; to flay [*person*]; **2** to graze [*face, leg*]; **3** to mispronounce [*word*].

écorchure /ekɔʀʃyʀ/ *nf* graze.

écossais, **~e** /ekɔsɛ, ɛz/ **I** *adj* Scottish; [*whisky*] Scotch; [*language*] Scots; [*skirt*] tartan.
II *nm* **1** (dialect) Scots; **2** (Scottish) Gaelic; **3** tartan (cloth).

Écossais, **~e** /ekɔsɛ, ɛz/ *nm,f* Scotsman/Scotswoman, Scot.

Écosse /ekɔs/ *pr nf* Scotland.

écosser /ekɔse/ [1] *vtr* to shell.

écoulement /ekulmɑ̃/ *nm* **1** (of water, traffic) flow; (of time) passing; **2** (Med) discharge; **3** (of banknotes, drugs) circulation.

écouler /ekule/ [1] **I** *vtr* **1** to sell [*product*]; **les stocks sont écoulés** stocks are exhausted; **2** to fence [*stolen goods*]; to pass [*banknote*].
II s'écouler *v refl* (+ *v être*) **1** [*time, life*] to pass; **2** [*river*] to flow; **3** [*oil, water*] to escape; **4** [*water*] to drain away; **5** [*product*] to move.

écourter /ekuʀte/ [1] *vtr* to cut short [*stay*].

écoute /ekut/ *nf* **1 être à l'~ de** to be listening to [*programme*]; to be (always) ready to listen to [*problems*]; **2** audience; **heure de grande ~** peak listening time; peak viewing time; **3 un centre d'~(s)** monitoring centre[GB]; **je suis sur ~(s)** my phone is being tapped.

écouter /ekute/ [1] **I** *vtr* **1** to listen to [sb/sth]; **~ qn chanter** to listen to sb singing; **~ aux portes** to eavesdrop; **2 ~ son cœur** to follow one's own inclination.
II s'écouter *v refl* (+ *v être*) **1 s'~ parler** to like the sound of one's own voice; **2** to cosset oneself; **3 si je m'écoutais** if it was up to me.

écouteur /ekutœʀ/ *nm* **1** (on phone) earpiece; **2** earphones; **3** headphones.

écoutille /ekutij/ *nf* (Naut) hatch.

écran /ekʀɑ̃/ *nm* **1** (gen) screen; **crever l'~** [*actor*] to have a great screen presence; **une vedette du petit ~** a TV star; **2** cinema (GB), movie theater (US); **3** (on machine) display; **4 crème ~ total** sun block.
■ **~ antibruit** soundproofing; **~ de contrôle** monitor; **~ solaire** sunscreen.

écrasant, **~e** /ekʀɑzɑ̃, ɑ̃t/ *adj* **1** [*weight*] enormous; **2** [*heat*] sweltering; [*victory*] resounding; [*responsibility*] heavy.

écraser /ekʀɑze/ [1] **I** *vtr* **1** to crush [*finger, person*]; to squash, to crush [*insect, hat, fruit, box*]; [*driver*] to run over [*person, animal*]; **se faire ~** to get run over; **2** to flatten [*vegetation*]; **3** (Culin) to mash [*fruit*]; **4 ~ sa cigarette** to stub out one's cigarette; **~ une larme** to wipe away a tear; **5** to press [*nose, face*] (**contre** against); **6** to crush [*rebellion*]; to thrash○ [*opponent*]; **7** to outshine; **8** to put [sb] down; **9** [*fatigue, heat*] to overcome.
II s'écraser *v refl* (+ *v être*) **1** [*car, train*] to crash; [*driver, motorcyclist*] to have a crash; [*insect*] to splatter (**contre** on); **2**○ to shut up○; **3**○ to keep one's head down.

écrémé, **~e** /ekʀeme/ *adj* skimmed.

écrevisse /ekʀəvis/ *nf* crayfish (GB), crawfish (US).

écrier: **s'écrier** /ekʀije/ [2] *v refl* (+ *v être*) to exclaim.

écrin /ekʀɛ̃/ *nm* (for jewellery) case.

écrire /ekʀiʀ/ [67] **I** *vtr* **1** to write; **2** to spell.
II *vi* to write.
III s'écrire *v refl* (+ *v être*) **1** to be written; **2** to be spelled.

écrit, **~e** /ekʀi, it/ **I** *adj* written; **c'était ~** it was bound to happen.
II *nm* **1** work, piece of writing; **2** document; **par ~** in writing; **3** written examination.
IDIOMS **les paroles s'envolent, les ~s restent** never put anything in writing; (as security) get it in writing.

écriteau, *pl* **~x** /ekʀito/ *nm* sign.

écritoire /ekʀitwaʀ/ *nf* writing case.

écriture /ekʀityʀ/ **I** *nf* **1** handwriting; **2** (in printing) hand; **3** (text, activity) writing; **4** script; **~ phonétique** phonetic script.
II écritures *nf pl* accounts; **tenir les ~s** to do the books.

Écriture /ekʀityʀ/ *nf* **les (saintes) ~s** the Scriptures; **l'~ sainte** Holy Writ.

écrivain /ekʀivɛ̃/ *nm* writer.

écrou /ekʀu/ *nm* (Tech) nut.

écrouer /ekʀue/ [1] *vtr* (Law) to commit [sb] to prison.

écroulé, **~e** /ekʀule/ *adj* overwhelmed; **~**○ **de rire** doubled up with laughter.

écrouler: **s'écrouler** /ekʀule/ [1] *v refl* (+ *v être*) to collapse; to fade; to crumble.

écru, **~e** /ekʀy/ *adj* **1** [*canvas*] unbleached; [*wool*] undyed; [*silk*] raw; **2** (colour) ecru.

ECU /eky/ *nm*: (*abbr* = **European currency unit**) ECU.

écu /eky/ *nm* **1** (in EU) ecu; **2** ≈ crown; **3** shield.

écueil /ekœj/ *nm* **1** reef; **2** (figurative) pitfall.

écuelle /ekɥɛl/ *nf* **1** bowl; **2** bowlful.

écume /ekym/ *nf* **1** (on water) foam; (on beer) froth; (on metal) dross; **2** (at mouth) foam, froth.

écumer /ekyme/ [1] **I** *vtr* **1** to skim; **2** to scour, to search.
II *vi* [*sea*] to foam; [*wine*] to froth.

écumoire /ekymwaʀ/ *nf* skimming ladle.

écureuil /ekyʀœj/ *nm* squirrel.

écurie /ekyʀi/ *nf* **1** stable; **2** (Sport) stable; **3** (figurative) pigsty.

écusson /ekysɔ̃/ *nm* **1** (Mil) flash (GB); **2** (of school) crest, badge; (of club, movement) badge; (of car) insignia; **3** (in heraldry) coat of arms.

écuyer, **-ère** /ekɥije, ɛʀ/ **I** *nm,f* **1** horseman/horsewoman; **2** riding instructor; **3** bareback rider.
II *nm* **1** squire; **2** equerry.

eczéma /egzema/ *nm* eczema.

éden /edɛn/ *nm* paradise.

Éden /edɛn/ *pr nm* Eden.

édenté, **~e** /edɑ̃te/ *adj* **1** toothless; **2** gap-toothed; **3** [*comb*] broken.

EDF /œdeɛf/ *nf* (*abbr* = **Électricité de France**) *French electricity board*.

édicter /edikte/ [1] *vtr* to enact [*law*].

édifice /edifis/ *nm* **1** building; **2** structure.

édifier /edifje/ [2] *vtr* **1** to build [sth]; **2** to build [*empire*]; **3** to edify; **4** to enlighten.

Édimbourg /edɛ̃buʀ/ *pr n* Edinburgh.

éditer /edite/ [1] *vtr* **1** to publish [*book, author*]; to release [*record*]; **2** (Comput) to edit.

éditeur, **-trice** /editœʀ, tʀis/ **I** *nm,f* editor.
II *nm* **1** publisher; **2** (Comput) editor.

édition /edisjɔ̃/ **I** *nf* **1** (of book) publication; (of record) release; **2** (book, print) edition; (record) release; **3** publishing; **société d'~** publishing

firm; **4** editing; **5** (paper) **~ du soir** evening edition.
II **éditions** *nf pl* **les ~s de la Roulotte** la Roulotte (Publishing Company).

éditorial, **~e**, *mpl* **-iaux** /editɔʀjal, o/ I *adj* [*policy, service*] editorial.
II *nm* editorial, leader.

édredon /edʀədɔ̃/ *nm* eiderdown.

éducateur, **-trice** /edykatœʀ, tʀis/ I *adj* educational.
II *nm,f* youth worker.

éducatif, **-ive** /edykatif, iv/ *adj* educational.

éducation /edykasjɔ̃/ *nf* **1** education; **faire l'~ de qn** to educate sb; **2** training; **3** manners.
■ **Éducation nationale**, **EN** Ministry of Education; (system) state education.

édulcorer /edylkɔʀe/ [1] *vtr* **1** to sweeten; **2** to tone down [*letter, remark*].

éduquer /edyke/ [1] *vtr* to educate; to train.

effacé, **~e** /efase/ *adj* retiring.

effacement /efasmɑ̃/ *nm* **1** deletion; **2** (of cassette) erasure; **3** self-effacement.

effacer /efase/ [12] I *vtr* **1** to rub out; to delete; to erase; **2** to wipe [*tape*]; to clear [*file*]; to clean [*blackboard*]; **3** [*rain*] to erase [*tracks*]; [*snow*] to cover (up) [*tracks*]; [*cream*] to remove [*wrinkles*]; **4** to blot out [*memory*]; to remove [*differences*]; **5** to write off [*debt*].
II **s'effacer** *v refl* (+ *v être*) **1 ça s'efface** you can rub it out; **2** [*inscription, drawing, memory*] to fade; [*impression*] to wear off; [*fear*] to disappear; **3** to step aside; **4** to stay in the background.

effaceur /efasœʀ/ *nm* correction pen.

effarant, **~e** /efaʀɑ̃, ɑ̃t/ *adj* astounding.

effarer /efaʀe/ [1] *vtr* to alarm.

effaroucher /efaʀuʃe/ [1] *vtr* **1** to frighten [sb/sth] away; **2** to alarm.

effectif, **-ive** /efɛktif, iv/ I *adj* real.
II *nm* (of school) number of pupils; (of university) number of students; (of company) workforce; (of army) strength.

effectivement /efɛktivmɑ̃/ *adv* **1** indeed; **2** actually, really.

effectuer /efɛktɥe/ [1] *vtr* to do [*work, repairs*]; to make [*payment, trip*]; to carry out [*transaction*]; to conduct [*survey*]; to serve [*sentence*].

efféminé, **~e** /efemine/ *adj* effeminate.

effervescence /efɛʀvesɑ̃s/ *nf* **1** effervescence; **2** turmoil.

effervescent, **~e** /efɛʀvesɑ̃, ɑ̃t/ *adj* **1** effervescent; **2** (figurative) [*crowd*] seething; [*personality*] effervescent.

effet /efɛ/ I *nm* **1** effect; **prendre ~** [*measure, law*] to take effect; **sous l'~ de l'alcool** under the influence of alcohol; **couper tous ses ~s à qn** to steal sb's thunder; **2** impression; **être du plus mauvais ~** to be in the worst possible taste; **faire un drôle d'~** to make one feel strange; **un ~ de surprise** an element of surpri; **3 à cet ~** for that purpose.
II **en effet** *phr* indeed.
III **effets** *nm pl* things, clothes.
■ **~ de serre** greenhouse effect; **~s secondaires** (Med) side effects.

efficace /efikas/ *adj* effective; efficient.

efficacité /efikasite/ *nf* (of action, remedy) effectiveness; (of person, device) efficiency.

effigie /efiʒi/ *nf* **1** effigy; **à l'~ de** [*medal, stamp*] with the head of; **2** logo.

effilé, **~e** /efile/ *adj* [*almonds*] flaked.

effiler /efile/ [1] I *vtr* **1** to sharpen; **2** to string [*green beans*].
II **s'effiler** *v refl* (+ *v être*) to fray.

effilocher /efilɔʃe/ [1] I *vtr* to shred.
II **s'effilocher** *v refl* (+ *v être*) to fray.

efflanqué, **~e** /eflɑ̃ke/ *adj* emaciated.

effleurer /eflœʀe/ [1] *vtr* to touch lightly, to brush (against); **l'idée ne m'a même pas effleuré** the idea didn't even cross my mind.

effluent /eflyɑ̃/ *nm* effluent.

effluve /eflyv/ *nm* **1** unpleasant smell; **2** fragrance.

effondrement /efɔ̃dʀəmɑ̃/ *nm* **1** collapse; **2** subsidence.

effondrer: **s'effondrer** /efɔ̃dʀe/ [1] *v refl* (+ *v être*) **1** [*roof, person*] to collapse; [*dream*] to crumble; [*hopes*] to fall; **2 être effondré par la nouvelle** to be distraught at the news.

efforcer: **s'efforcer** /efɔʀse/ [12] *v refl* (+ *v être*) to try hard (**de faire** to do).

effort /efɔʀ/ *nm* **1** effort; **fais un petit ~ d'imagination!** use a bit of imagination!; **avec mon dos, je ne peux pas faire d'~** with this back of mine, I can't do anything strenuous; **2** (in physics) stress; strain.

effraction /efʀaksjɔ̃/ *nf* (Law) breaking and entering.

effrayant, **~e** /efʀɛjɑ̃, ɑ̃t/ *adj* [*sight, ugliness*] frightening; [*thinness, paleness*] dreadful.

effrayer /efʀeje/ [21] *vtr* **1** to frighten; to alarm; **2** [*difficulty, price*] to put [sb] off.

effréné, **~e** /efʀene/ *adj* [*rhythm, competition*] frenzied; [*ambition*] wild.

effriter /efʀite/ [1] I *vtr* to crumble; to break up.
II **s'effriter** *v refl* (+ *v être*) to crumble (away).

effroi /efʀwɑ/ *nm* dread, terror.

effronté, **~e** /efʀɔ̃te/ *adj* cheeky; shameless.

effroyable /efʀwɑjabl/ *adj* dreadful.

effroyablement /efʀwɑjabləmɑ̃/ *adv* **1** horribly; **2**° terribly.

effusion /efyzjɔ̃/ *nf* effusion.
■ **~ de sang** bloodshed.

égal, **~e**, *mpl* **-aux** /egal, o/ I *adj* **1** equal (**à** to); **à prix ~, je préfère celui-là** if the price is the same, I'd rather have that one; **2** [*ground*] level; [*light*] even; [*colour*] uniform; [*weather*] settled; [*pulse, breathing*] steady; **d'un pas ~** at an even pace; **3 ça m'est ~** I don't mind (either way); I don't care.
II *nm,f* equal; **traiter d'~ à ~ avec qn** to deal with sb as an equal.
IDIOMS **rester ~ à soi-même** to be one's usual self; **combattre à armes ~es** to be on an equal footing.

également /egalmɑ̃/ *adv* **1** also, too; **2** equally.

égaler /egale/ [1] *vtr* **1** to equal [*record*]; to be as good as [*person*]; to be as high as [*price*]; **2** **trois plus trois égalent six** three plus three equals six or is six.

égalisation /egalizasjɔ̃/ *nf* **1** levelling[GB] out; **2** (Sport) **le penalty a permis l'~** the penalty evened (GB) or tied (US) the score.

égaliser /egalize/ [1] **I** *vtr* **1** to level [*ground*]; **2** to make [sth] the same size [*planks*].
II *vi* (Sport) to equalize (GB), to tie (US).

égalitaire /egalitɛʀ/ *adj*, *nmf* egalitarian.

égalité /egalite/ *nf* **1** equality; **2** (Sport) **être à ~** to be level (GB), to be tied (US); **~!** deuce!

égard /egaʀ/ **I** *nm* **1** consideration; **sans ~ pour** without regard for; **2** **à l'~ de qn** toward(s) sb; **à cet ~** in this respect.
II égards *nm pl* **avec des ~s** with respect; **être plein d'~s envers qn** to be attentive to sb's every need.

égaré, **~e** /egaʀe/ *adj* **1** stray; **2** [*look*] wild.

égarement /egaʀmɑ̃/ *nm* **1** distraction, madness; **2** confusion; **3** erratic behaviour[GB].

égarer /egaʀe/ [1] **I** *vtr* **1** to lead [sb] astray; **2** to mislay.
II s'égarer *v refl* (+ *v être*) **1** to get lost; **2** (figurative) [*mind*] to wander; [*person*] to ramble.

égayer /egeje/ [21] *vtr* to enliven; to lighten; to brighten; to cheer [sb] up.

égérie /eʒeʀi/ *nf* muse.

égide /eʒid/ *nf* aegis.

églantine /eglɑ̃tin/ *nf* wild rose, dog-rose.

églefin /egləfɛ̃/ *nm* haddock.

église /egliz/ *nf* church.

ego /ego/ *nm inv* ego.

égocentrique /egosɑ̃tʀik/ *adj*, *nmf* egocentric.

égoïsme /egɔism/ *nm* selfishness.

égoïste /egɔist/ *adj* selfish.

égorger /egɔʀʒe/ [13] *vtr* **~ qn** to cut sb's throat.

égosiller: **s'égosiller** /egozije/ [1] *v refl* (+ *v être*) **1** to shout oneself hoarse; **2** to sing at the top of one's voice; **3** to yell.

égout /egu/ *nm* sewer.

égoutter /egute/ [1] **I** *vtr* to drain.
II s'égoutter *v refl* (+ *v être*) [*dishes, rice, vegetables*] to drain; [*washing*] to drip dry.

égouttoir /egutwaʀ/ *nm* draining rack (GB), (dish) drainer (US).

égratigner /egʀatiɲe/ [1] **I** *vtr* to scratch, to graze.
II s'égratigner *v refl* (+ *v être*) to scratch oneself; to graze oneself.

égratignure /egʀatiɲyʀ/ *nf* scratch; graze.

Égypte /eʒipt/ *pr nf* Egypt.

égyptien, **-ienne** /eʒipsjɛ̃, ɛn/ **I** *adj* Egyptian.
II *nm* (language) Egyptian.

éhonté, **~e** /eɔ̃te/ *adj* [*liar, lie*] brazen.

Éire /ɛʀ/ *pr n* Éire, Republic of Ireland.

éjectable /eʒɛktabl/ *adj* **siège ~** ejector seat (GB), ejection seat (US).

éjecter /eʒɛkte/ [1] *vtr* **1** (in accident) to throw [sb/sth] out; **2** (Tech) to eject.

élaboration /elabɔʀasjɔ̃/ *nf* development; working out; drafting; putting together.

élaboré, **~e** /elabɔʀe/ *adj* sophisticated; elaborate.

élaborer /elabɔʀe/ [1] *vtr* to work [sth] out; to draw [sth] up; to put [sth] together.

élaguer /elage/ [1] *vtr* to prune.

élan /elɑ̃/ *nm* **1** (Sport) run up; **saut sans ~** standing jump; **2** momentum; **3** impetus; **4** enthusiasm; **~ patriotique** patriotic fervour[GB]; **5** impulse; **~ de tendresse** surge of tenderness; **6** (Zool) elk.

élancé, **~e** /elɑ̃se/ *adj* slender.

élancement /elɑ̃smɑ̃/ *nm* throbbing pain.

élancer: **s'élancer** /elɑ̃se/ [12] *v refl* (+ *v être*) **1** to dash forward; **2** **s'~ vers le ciel** [*tree, spire*] to soar up toward(s) the sky.

élargi, **~e** /elaʀʒi/ *adj* enlarged; expanded.

élargir /elaʀʒiʀ/ [3] **I** *vtr* **1** to widen [*road*]; to let out [*garment*]; **2** to stretch [*shoes, sweater*]; **3** to extend [*contacts, law*]; to broaden [*knowledge*]; to increase [*majority*].
II s'élargir *v refl* (+ *v être*) [*group*] to expand; [*gap*] to increase; [*road*] to widen; [*person*] to fill out; [*garment*] to stretch.

élastique /elastik/ **I** *adj* **1** [*waistband*] elasticated (GB), elasticized (US); **2** [*gas, fibre*] elastic; **3** [*rule, timetable*] flexible; [*budget*] elastic.
II *nm* **1** rubber band; **2** (in haberdashery) elastic; **3** (Sport) bungee cord.
IDIOMS **les lâcher avec un ~**° to be tight-fisted.

élastomère /elastɔmɛʀ/ *nm* elastomer.

électeur, **-trice** /elɛktœʀ, tʀis/ *nm,f* voter.

élection /elɛksjɔ̃/ *nf* **1** election; **2** choice; **mon pays d'~** my chosen country.

électoral, **~e**, *mpl* **-aux** /elɛktɔʀal, o/ *adj* electoral; election.

électorat /elɛktɔʀa/ *nm* electorate, voters.

électricien, **-ienne** /elɛktʀisjɛ̃, ɛn/ *nm,f* electrician.

électricité /elɛktʀisite/ *nf* electricity.

électrifier /elɛktʀifje/ [2] *vtr* to electrify [*railtracks*].

électrique /elɛktʀik/ *adj* **1** electrical; **2** (figurative) [*atmosphere*] electric.

électriser /elɛktʀize/ [1] *vtr* to electrify.

électro(-) /elɛktʀo/ *pref* electro; **~cardiogramme** electrocardiogram.

électrochoc /elɛktʀoʃɔk/ *nm* **~s** electroshock therapy, EST.

électrocuter: **s'électrocuter** /elɛktʀɔkyte/ [1] *v refl* (+ *v être*) to be electrocuted.

électrode /elɛktʀɔd/ *nf* electrode.

électrogène /elɛktʀɔʒɛn/ *adj* **groupe ~** (electricity) generator.

électroménager /elɛktʀomenaʒe/ **I** *adj m* **appareil ~** household appliance.
II *nm* **1** domestic electrical appliances; **2** electrical goods industry.

électron /elɛktʀɔ̃/ *nm* electron.

électronicien, **-ienne** /elɛktʀɔnisjɛ̃, ɛn/ *nm,f* electronics engineer.

électronique /elɛktʀɔnik/ **I** *adj* **1** [*circuit*] electronic; **2** [*microscope*] electron.
II *nf* electronics.

électrophone /elɛktʀɔfɔn/ *nm* record player.

élégamment /elegamɑ̃/ *adv* [*dress*] elegantly.

élégance /elegɑ̃s/ *nf* elegance; **avec ~** [*dress*] elegantly; [*lose*] gracefully; [*behave*] honourably[GB]; [*resolve problem*] neatly.

élégant, **~e** /elegɑ̃, ɑ̃t/ *adj* elegant; **ce n'est pas très ~ de ta part** it's not very decent of you.

élément /elemɑ̃/ **I** *nm* **1** (in structure, ensemble) element; (in device) component; **~ moteur** driving force; **2** factor, element; **l'~-clé de** the key element in; **3** (of furniture) unit; **4** fact; **disposer de tous les ~s** to have all the facts; **5** (person) **bon ~** good pupil; good player; **6** (chemical) element.
II éléments *nm pl* elements.

élémentaire /elemɑ̃tɛʀ/ *adj* **1** [*principle*] basic; **2** elementary.

éléphant /elefɑ̃/ *nm* elephant.

éléphanteau, *pl* **~x** /elefɑ̃to/ *nm* (elephant) calf.

élevage /elvaʒ/ *nm* **1** livestock farming; **faire de l'~ de porcs** to breed pigs; **d'~** [*oysters*] farmed; [*pheasant*] captive-bred; **2** farm; **un ~ de visons** a mink farm; **3** stock (**de** of).

élévateur /elevatœʀ/ *nm* elevator.

élévation /elevasjɔ̃/ *nf* **1** rise (**de** in); **2** (to rank) elevation; **3** (in architecture) elevation.

élève /elɛv/ *nmf* (gen) student; (Sch) pupil; **~ officier** trainee officer.

élevé, **~e** /elve/ *adj* **1** [*level, price, rank*] high; **2** [*plateau*] high; **3** [*sentiment*] fine; [*principles*] high; [*ideal*] lofty; [*language*] elevated.

élever /elve/ [16] **I** *vtr* **1** to put up, to erect; **2** to raise [*temperature, level*]; **3** to lift, to raise [*load*]; **4 la poésie élève l'âme** poetry is elevating or uplifting; **5** to raise [*objection*]; **6** to bring [sb] up; **c'est mal élevé** it's bad manners (**de faire** to do); **7** to rear [*cattle*]; to keep [*bees*].
II s'élever *v refl* (+ *v être*) **1** [*rate*] to rise; **2 s'~ à** [*expenses*] to come to; [*death toll*] to stand at; **3** to rise (up); **s'~ dans les airs** [*smoke*] to rise up into the air; [*bird*] to soar into the air; **4** [*voice, protests*] to be heard; **5 s'~ contre qch** to protest against sth; **6** [*statue*] to stand; **s'~ au-dessus de qch** to rise above sth.

éleveur, **-euse** /elvœʀ, øz/ *nm,f* breeder.

elfe /ɛlf/ *nm* elf.

élider /elide/ [1] *vtr* to elide.

éligible /eliʒibl/ *adj* eligible for office.

élimer /elime/ [1] **I** *vtr* to wear [sth] thin.
II s'élimer *v refl* (+ *v être*) to wear thin.

éliminatoire /eliminatwaʀ/ *adj* [*question, match*] qualifying; [*mark*] eliminatory.

éliminer /elimine/ [1] *vtr* to eliminate.

élire /eliʀ/ [66] *vtr* to elect **se faire ~** to be elected; **~ domicile** to take up residence.

élision /elizjɔ̃/ *nf* elision.

élite /elit/ *nf* **l'~** the elite; **d'~** [*troops*] elite, crack; [*student*] high-flying; [*athlete*] top.

élitisme /elitism/ *nm* elitism.

élixir /eliksiʀ/ *nm* elixir.

elle /ɛl/ *pron f* she; it; **~s** they; **je les vois plus souvent qu'~** I see them more often than she does; I see them more often than (I see) her; **le bol bleu est à ~** the blue bowl is hers.

elle-même, *pl* **elles-mêmes** /ɛlmɛm/ *pron* herself; itself; **elles-mêmes** themselves; **'Mme Roc?'—'~'** 'Mrs Roc?'—'speaking'.

elles *pron* ▶ **elle**.

ellipse /elips/ *nf* ellipsis.

elliptique /eliptik/ *adj* **1** elliptical; **2** elliptic.

élocution /elɔkysjɔ̃/ *nf* diction; **défaut d'~** speech impediment.

éloge /elɔʒ/ *nm* **1** praise; **être tout à l'~ de qn** to do sb great credit; **2** eulogy; **~ funèbre** funeral oration.

élogieux, **-ieuse** /elɔʒjø, øz/ *adj* full of praise; laudatory.

éloigné, **~e** /elwaɲe/ *adj* **1** distant; **~ de tout** remote; **deux usines ~es de cinq kilomètres** two factories five kilometres[GB] apart; **2** [*memories*] distant; [*event*] remote; **~ dans le temps** distant (in time); **3** [*cousin*] distant.

éloignement /elwaɲmɑ̃/ *nm* **1** distance; **2** remoteness.

éloigner /elwaɲe/ [1] **I** *vtr* **1** to move [sb/sth] away; **2 ils font tout pour l'~ de moi** they are doing everything to drive us apart.
II s'éloigner *v refl* (+ *v être*) **1** to move away; **ne t'éloigne pas trop** don't go too far away; **2 s'~ de** to move away from [*party line*]; to stray from [*subject*].

élongation /elɔ̃gasjɔ̃/ *nf* (Med) pulled muscle.

éloquence /elɔkɑ̃s/ *nf* eloquence.

éloquent, **~e** /elɔkɑ̃, ɑ̃t/ *adj* eloquent.

élu, **~e** /ely/ *nm,f* **1** elected representative; **2** beloved; **3** (in religion) **les ~s** the Chosen Ones.

élucider /elyside/ [1] *vtr* to solve [*crime, problem*]; to clarify [*circumstances*].

élucubrations /elykybʀasjɔ̃/ *nf pl* rantings.

éluder /elyde/ [1] *vtr* to evade.

Élysée /elize/ *pr nm* (**palais de**) **l'~** *the official residence of the French President*.

émacier: **s'émacier** /emasje/ [2] *v refl* (+ *v être*) to become emaciated.

émail, *pl* **-aux** /emaj, o/ *nm* enamel.

émaillé, **~e** /emaje/ *adj* [*utensil*] enamel; [*metal*] enamelled.

émanation /emanasjɔ̃/ *nf* emanation; **~s de gaz** gas fumes.

émancipation /emɑ̃sipasjɔ̃/ *nf* emancipation.

émanciper /emɑ̃sipe/ [1] **I** *vtr* to emancipate [*people*]; to liberate [*country*].
II s'émanciper *v refl* (+ *v être*) to become emancipated.

émaner /emane/ [1] **I** *vi* **~ de** to emanate from; to come from.

II *v impers* **il émane d'elle un charme fou** she exudes charm.

émaux ▶ **email**.

emballage /ɑ̃balaʒ/ *nm* packaging; wrapping; packing.

■ **~ sous vide** vacuum packing.

emballer /ɑ̃bale/ [1] I *vtr* **1** to pack, to wrap; **2**○ **être emballé par** to be taken with.

II **s'emballer** *v refl* (+ *v être*) **1** [*horse*] to bolt; **2**○ to get carried away; **3** to get all worked up○; **4**○ [*engine*] to race; **5** [*prices, inflation*] to shoot up; [*currency*] to shoot up in value.

embarcadère /ɑ̃baʀkadɛʀ/ *nm* pier; wharf.

embarcation /ɑ̃baʀkasjɔ̃/ *nf* boat.

embardée /ɑ̃baʀde/ *nf* (of car) swerve.

embargo /ɑ̃baʀgo/ *nm* embargo.

embarquement /ɑ̃baʀkəmɑ̃/ *nm* boarding.

embarquer /ɑ̃baʀke/ [1] I *vtr* **1** to load [*goods*]; to take [sb] on board; **2**○ to take [*object*]; [*police*] to pick up [*criminal*].

II *vi* **1** to board; **2** to sail (**pour** for).

III **s'embarquer** *v refl* (+ *v être*) **1** to board; **2**○ **s'~ dans** to launch into [*explanation*].

embarras /ɑ̃baʀa/ *nm inv* **1** embarrassment; **2** awkward position; difficult situation; **3 n'avoir que l'~ du choix** to have too much to choose from.

embarrassant, **~e** /ɑ̃baʀasɑ̃, ɑ̃t/ *adj* **1** awkward; embarrassing; **2** cumbersome.

embarrassé, **~e** /ɑ̃baʀase/ I *pp* ▶ **embarrasser**.

II *pp adj* **1** embarrassed; **être bien ~ pour répondre** to be at a loss for an answer; **2** [*room*] cluttered; **~ d'une grosse valise** weighed down with a large suitcase.

embarrasser /ɑ̃baʀase/ [1] I *vtr* **1** to embarrass; **2** to clutter [sth] (up); **cette armoire m'embarrasse plutôt qu'autre chose** this wardrobe is more of a nuisance than anything else.

II **s'embarrasser** *v refl* (+ *v être*) **s'~ de** to burden oneself with [*baggage, person*].

embauche /ɑ̃boʃ/ *nf* appointment (GB), hiring (US); **salaire d'~** starting salary.

embaucher /ɑ̃boʃe/ [1] *vtr* **1** to take on (GB), to hire; **2**○ to recruit.

embaumer /ɑ̃bome/ [1] I *vtr* **1** [*smell*] to fill [*place*]; [*place*] to smell of [*wax*]; **2** to embalm.

II *vi* to be fragrant.

embaumeur, **-euse** /ɑ̃bomœʀ, øz/ *nm,f* embalmer.

embellir /ɑ̃beliʀ/ [3] I *vtr* **1** to improve [sth]; to make [sb] more attractive; **2** to embellish [*story, truth*].

II *vi* to become more attractive.

embellissement /ɑ̃belismɑ̃/ *nm* (of house) improving; **travaux d'~** improvements.

emberlificoter○ /ɑ̃bɛʀlifikɔte/ [1] I *vtr* **1** to entangle; **2** to take [sb] in○.

II **s'emberlificoter** *v refl* (+ *v être*) to get entangled; to get tangled up (**dans** in).

embêtant, **~e** /ɑ̃betɑ̃, ɑ̃t/ *adj* **1** annoying; **2** boring.

embêtement /ɑ̃betmɑ̃/ *nm* problem.

embêter /ɑ̃bete/ [1] I *vtr* **1** to bother; **2** to pester; to annoy; **3** to bore.

II **s'embêter** *v refl* (+ *v être*) **1** to be bored; **2 s'~ à faire** to go to the bother of doing.

emblée: **d'emblée** /dɑ̃ble/ *phr* **1** straightaway; **2** at first sight.

emblématique /ɑ̃blematik/ *adj* emblematic; symbolic.

emblème /ɑ̃blɛm/ *nm* emblem.

embobiner○ /ɑ̃bɔbine/ [1] *vtr* to hoodwink.

emboîter /ɑ̃bwate/ [1] I *vtr* to fit [sth] together; **~ qch dans** to fit sth into.

II **s'emboîter** *v refl* (+ *v être*) [*part*] to fit (**dans** into); [*parts*] to fit together.

IDIOMS **~ le pas à qn** to fall in behind sb.

embonpoint /ɑ̃bɔ̃pwɛ̃/ *nm* stoutness; **avoir de l'~** to be stout.

embouchure /ɑ̃buʃyʀ/ *nf* (of river) mouth; (of instrument) mouthpiece; (of pipe) opening.

embourber: **s'embourber** /ɑ̃buʀbe/ [1] *v refl* (+ *v être*) **1** to get stuck in the mud; **2** to get bogged down.

embourgeoiser: **s'embourgeoiser** /ɑ̃buʀʒwaze/ [1] *v refl* (+ *v être*) [*person*] to become middle-class; [*area*] to become gentrified.

embout /ɑ̃bu/ *nm* (of cigar, cane) tip; (of hosepipe) nozzle; (of pipe) mouthpiece.

embouteillage /ɑ̃butɛjaʒ/ *nm* traffic jam.

emboutir /ɑ̃butiʀ/ [3] *vtr* **1** to stamp, to press [*part, metal*]; **2**○ to crash into [*vehicle*].

embranchement /ɑ̃bʀɑ̃ʃmɑ̃/ *nm* **1** junction; **2** side road; **3** (on railways) branch line.

embrasé, **~e** /ɑ̃bʀaze/ *adj* **1** burning; **2** glowing.

embraser /ɑ̃bʀaze/ [1] I *vtr* **1** to set [sth] ablaze; **2** to set [sth] alight [*country*].

II **s'embraser** *v refl* (+ *v être*) **1** to catch fire; **2** [*country*] to erupt into violence[; **3** [*sky*] to be set ablaze; **4** to burn with desire.

embrasser /ɑ̃bʀase/ [1] I *vtr* **1** to kiss; **je t'embrasse** lots of love; **2** to embrace; to hug; **3** to take up [*career, cause*].

II **s'embrasser** *v refl* (+ *v être*) **1** to kiss (each other); **2** to embrace; to hug.

IDIOMS **~ qn comme du bon pain** to hug sb warmly.

embrasure /ɑ̃bʀazyʀ/ *nf* **~ de fenêtre** window; **~ de porte** doorway.

embrayage /ɑ̃bʀɛjaʒ/ *nm* **1** clutch; **2** clutch pedal.

embrayer /ɑ̃bʀeje/ [21] *vi* [*driver*] to engage the clutch; (Tech) to engage.

embrigader /ɑ̃bʀigade/ [1] *vtr* **1** to recruit; **2** (Mil) to brigade.

embrouiller /ɑ̃bʀuje/ [1] I *vtr* **1** to tangle [*wires*]; **2** to confuse [*matter, person*].

II **s'embrouiller** *v refl* (+ *v être*) **1** to become tangled; **2** [*ideas, person*] to become confused.

embroussaillé, **~e** /ɑ̃bʀusaje/ *adj* [*path*] overgrown; [*hair*] bushy.

embrumé, **~e** /ɑ̃bʀyme/ *adj* **1** misty; **2** [*mind*] befuddled; [*look*] glazed.

embruns /ɑ̃bʀœ̃/ *nm pl* spray.

embryon /ɑ̃bʀijɔ̃/ *nm* embryo.

embûche /ɑ̃byʃ/ *nf* **1** trap; **dresser des ~s** to set traps; **2** hazard; pitfall; **semé d'~s** hazardous; (figurative) fraught with pitfalls.

embuer /ɑ̃bɥe/ [1] **I** *vtr* to mist up, to fog up.
II s'embuer *v refl* (+ *v être*) [*window*] to mist up, to fog up; [*eyes*] to mist over.

embuscade /ɑ̃byskad/ *nf* ambush.

éméché○, **~e** /emeʃe/ *adj* tipsy.

émeraude /emʀod/ *nf* emerald.

émergence /emɛʀʒɑ̃s/ *nf* emergence.

émerger /emɛʀʒe/ [13] *vi* to emerge.

émeri /emʀi/ *nm* emery.

émérite /emeʀit/ *adj* **1** outstanding; **2 professeur ~** emeritus professor.

émerveiller /emɛʀveje/ [1] **I** *vtr* **~ qn** to fill sb with wonder.
II s'émerveiller *v refl* (+ *v être*) **s'~ de** or **devant qch** to marvel at sth.

émetteur, **-trice** /emetœʀ, tʀis/ **I** *adj* **1** [*station*] broadcasting; **2** [*bank*] issuing.
II *nm* **1** transmitter; **2** (of loan, card) issuer.

émettre /emɛtʀ/ [60] *vtr* **1** to express [*opinion, wish*]; to put forward [*hypothesis*]; **2** to utter [*cry*]; to produce [*sound, heat*]; **3** to issue [*document*]; **4** to broadcast [*programme*]; **5** to send out [*signal*]; **6** to emit [*radiation*].

émeute /emøt/ *nf* riot.

émietter /emjete/ [1] **I** *vtr* to crumble [sth].
II s'émietter *v refl* (+ *v être*) to crumble.

émigrant, **~e** /emigʀɑ̃, ɑ̃t/ *nm,f* emigrant.

émigration /emigʀasjɔ̃/ *nf* emigration.

émigré, **~e** /emigʀe/ *nm,f* emigrant; émigré.

émigrer /emigʀe/ [1] *vi* **1** to emigrate; **2** [*bird*] to migrate.

émincer /emɛ̃se/ [12] *vtr* to slice [sth] thinly.

éminence /eminɑ̃s/ *nf* **1** hillock; **2** (Anat) protuberance.

Éminence /eminɑ̃s/ *nf* Eminence.

éminent, **~e** /eminɑ̃, ɑ̃t/ *adj* distinguished, eminent.

émirat /emiʀa/ *nm* emirate.

Émirats /emiʀa/ *pr nm pl* **~ arabes unis, EAU** United Arab Emirates.

émis, **~e** /emi, iz/ *pp* ▶ **émettre**.

émissaire /emisɛʀ/ *nm* emissary.

émission /emisjɔ̃/ *nf* **1** programme[GB]; **2** (of document) issue; **3** (of waves, signals) emission.

emmagasiner /ɑ̃magazine/ [1] *vtr* **1** to store; **2** to stockpile [*goods*]; to store up [*knowledge*].

emmanchure /ɑ̃mɑ̃ʃyʀ/ *nf* armhole.

emmêler /ɑ̃mɛle/ [1] **I** *vtr* **1** to tangle; **2** to confuse [*matter*].
II s'emmêler *v refl* (+ *v être*) to get tangled up; **s'~ les pieds dans** to get one's feet caught in.

emménagement /ɑ̃menaʒmɑ̃/ *nm* moving in.

emménager /ɑ̃menaʒe/ [13] *vi* to move in.

emmener /ɑ̃mne/ [16] *vtr* **1** to take [*person*] (**à, jusqu'à** to); **veux-tu que je t'emmène en voiture?** do you want a lift (GB) or a ride (US)?; **2**○ (controversial) to take [sth] with one [*object*]; **3** to take [sb] away.

emmerder◑ /ɑ̃mɛʀde/ [1] **I** *vtr* to annoy, to hassle○; **~ le monde** to be a pain○ in the arse● (GB) or ass◑ (US).
II s'emmerder *v refl* (+ *v être*) **1** to be bored stiff○; **2 s'~ à faire** to go to the trouble of doing; **tu t'emmerdes pas!** you're doing all right for yourself!; you've got a nerve!

emmitoufler /ɑ̃mitufle/ [1] **I** *vtr* to wrap [sb/sth] up warmly.
II s'emmitoufler *v refl* (+ *v être*) to wrap (oneself) up warmly.

émoi /emwa/ *nm* agitation, turmoil.

émonder /emɔ̃de/ [1] *vtr* to prune.

émotif, **-ive** /emɔtif, iv/ *adj* emotional.

émotion /emosjɔ̃/ *nf* emotion.

émotivité /emɔtivite/ *nf* **enfant d'une grande ~** highly emotional child.

émousser /emuse/ [1] **I** *vtr* **1** to blunt; **2** to dull [*curiosity, sensitivity*].
II s'émousser *v refl* (+ *v être*) **1** to become blunt; **2** [*curiosity*] to become dulled.

émoustiller /emustije/ [1] *vtr* **1** to exhilarate; **2** to titillate.

émouvant, **~e** /emuvɑ̃, ɑ̃t/ *adj* moving.

émouvoir /emuvwaʀ/ [43] **I** *vtr* to move, to touch; **~ l'opinion** to cause a stir.
II s'émouvoir *v refl* (+ *v être*) **1** to be touched or moved; **2 s'~ de** to become concerned about; to be bothered by.

empailler /ɑ̃pɑje/ [1] *vtr* to stuff.

empailleur, **-euse** /ɑ̃pɑjœʀ, øz/ *nm,f* taxidermist.

empaler /ɑ̃pale/ [1] **I** *vtr* to impale.
II s'empaler *v refl* (+ *v être*) to become impaled.

empaqueter /ɑ̃pakte/ [20] *vtr* to package; to wrap [sth] up.

emparer: **s'emparer** /ɑ̃paʀe/ [1] *v refl* (+ *v être*) **1 s'~ de** (gen) to get hold of, to seize; to take over [*town*]; to seize [*power*]; **2 s'~ de** [*feeling*] to take hold of [sb/sth].

empâter: **s'empâter** /ɑ̃pɑte/ [1] *v refl* (+ *v être*) to become puffy; to put on weight.

empêchement /ɑ̃pɛʃmɑ̃/ *nm* unforeseen difficulty; **j'ai un ~** something's cropped up.

empêcher /ɑ̃peʃe/ [1] **I** *vtr* to prevent, to stop; **~ qn de faire** to prevent sb (from) doing.
II s'empêcher *v refl* (+ *v être*) **je n'ai pas pu m'~ de rire** I couldn't help laughing.
III *v impers* **(il) n'empêche** all the same; **il n'empêche que** the fact remains that.

empereur /ɑ̃pʀœʀ/ *nm* emperor.

empesé, **~e** /ɑ̃pəze/ *adj* [*collar*] starched; [*person, manner*] starchy.

empester /ɑ̃pɛste/ [16] **I** *vtr* to stink [sth] out (GB), to stink up (US).
II *vi* to stink.

empêtrer: **s'empêtrer** /ɑ̃petʀe/ [1] *v refl* (+ *v*

être) **s'~ dans** to get entangled in [*briars*]; to get tangled up in [*lies*].

emphase /ɑ̃fɑz/ *nf* **1** grandiloquence; **2** emphasis.

emphatique /ɑ̃fatik/ *adj* **1** grandiloquent; **2** emphatic.

empiècement /ɑ̃pjɛsmɑ̃/ *nm* (of garment) yoke.

empiéter /ɑ̃pjete/ [14] *vi* to encroach.

empiffrer○: **s'empiffrer** /ɑ̃pifʀe/ [1] *v refl* (+ *v être*) to stuff oneself.

empiler /ɑ̃pile/ [1] **I** *vtr* to pile [sth] (up).
II s'empiler *v refl* (+ *v être*) to pile up.

empire /ɑ̃piʀ/ *nm* empire.

Empire /ɑ̃piʀ/ *nm* **l'~** the Empire.
■ **l'~ d'Orient** the Byzantine Empire; **l'~ d'Occident** the Western Empire.

empirer /ɑ̃piʀe/ [1] *vi* to get worse.

empirique /ɑ̃piʀik/ *adj* empirical.

emplacement /ɑ̃plasmɑ̃/ *nm* **1** site; **2** parking space.

emplette /ɑ̃plɛt/ *nf* purchase.

emplir /ɑ̃pliʀ/ [3] *vtr*, **s'emplir** *v refl* (+ *v être*) to fill (**de** with).

emploi /ɑ̃plwɑ/ *nm* **1** job; **2** employment; **3** use; **téléviseur couleur à vendre, cause double ~** colour[GB] TV for sale, surplus to requirements; **4** usage.
■ **~ du temps** timetable.
IDIOMS **avoir la tête de l'~** to look the part.

employé, **~e** /ɑ̃plwaje/ *nm,f* employee.
■ **~ de banque** bank clerk; **~ municipal** local authority employee.

employer /ɑ̃plwaje/ [23] **I** *vtr* to employ [*person*]; to use [*word, product*].
II s'employer *v refl* (+ *v être*) **1** to be used; **2 s'~ à faire** to apply oneself to doing.

employeur, **-euse** /ɑ̃plwajœʀ, øz/ *nm,f* employer.

empocher /ɑ̃pɔʃe/ [1] *vtr* to pocket.

empoigner /ɑ̃pwaɲe/ [1] *vtr* to grab (hold of).

empoisonné, **~e** /ɑ̃pwazɔne/ **I** *pp* ▶ **empoisonner**.
II *pp adj* [*foodstuff*] poisoned; [*atmosphere*] sour.

empoisonnement /ɑ̃pwazɔnmɑ̃/ *nm* **1** poisoning; **2**○ trouble.

empoisonner /ɑ̃pwazɔne/ [1] **I** *vtr* to poison; **~ la vie de qn** to make sb's life a misery.
II s'empoisonner *v refl* (+ *v être*) to poison oneself; **il s'est empoisonné avec une huître pas fraîche** he got food poisoning from eating a bad oyster.

empoisonneur, **-euse** /ɑ̃pwazɔnœʀ, øz/ *nm,f* **1** poisoner; **2**○ nuisance.

emportement /ɑ̃pɔʀtəmɑ̃/ *nm* fit of anger; **avec ~** angrily.

emporter /ɑ̃pɔʀte/ [1] **I** *vtr* **1** to take [*object*]; **pizzas à ~** takeaway pizzas (GB), pizzas to go (US); **2** [*ambulance*] to take [sb] away; [*plane*] to carry [sb] away; **3** [*wind, river*] to sweep [sb/sth] away; [*shell, bullet*] to take [sth] off [*ear, leg*]; **4 une leucémie l'a emporté** he died of leukaemia; **5** to take [*position*]; **6 l'~** to win; to prevail; **l'~ sur qch** to overcome sth.
II s'emporter *v refl* (+ *v être*) to lose one's temper.

empoté○, **~e** /ɑ̃pɔte/ *adj* clumsy, awkward.

empreindre: **s'empreindre** /ɑ̃pʀɛ̃dʀ/ [55] *v refl* (+ *v être*) to become marked (**de** with), to become imbued (**de** with).

empreinte /ɑ̃pʀɛ̃t/ *nf* **1** footprint; track; **2** stamp, mark.
■ **~s digitales** fingerprints.

empressement /ɑ̃pʀɛsmɑ̃/ *nm* **1** eagerness; **avec ~** eagerly; **2** attentiveness.

empresser: **s'empresser** /ɑ̃pʀese/ [1] *v refl* (+ *v être*) **s'~ de faire** to hasten to do; **s'~ autour** or **auprès de qn** to fuss over sb.

emprise /ɑ̃pʀiz/ *nf* hold, influence.

emprisonnement /ɑ̃pʀizɔnmɑ̃/ *nm* imprisonment; **peine d'~** prison sentence.

emprisonner /ɑ̃pʀizɔne/ [1] *vtr* **1** to imprison (**à, dans** in); **2** to keep [sb] prisoner.

emprunt /ɑ̃pʀœ̃/ *nm* **1** (money) loan; **faire un ~** to take out a loan; **2** borrowing; **d'~** [*car, name*] borrowed; **3** (object, book) loan; **c'est un ~ fait à un musée** it's on loan from a museum; **4** (of idea, word) borrowing.

emprunté, **~e** /ɑ̃pʀœ̃te/ *adj* awkward.

emprunter /ɑ̃pʀœ̃te/ [1] *vtr* **1** to borrow; **2** to take [*road*].

empuantir /ɑ̃pyɑ̃tiʀ/ [3] *vtr* to stink out (GB), to stink up (US).

ému, **~e** /emy/ **I** *pp* ▶ **émouvoir**.
II *pp adj* moved; touched; nervous; **trop ~ pour parler** too overcome to speak.
III *adj* [*words*] full of emotion; [*memory*] fond.

émulation /emylasjɔ̃/ *nf* competitiveness.

émule /emyl/ *nmf* imitator; **être l'~ de qn** to model oneself on sb.

émulsifiant /emylsifjɑ̃/ *nm* emulsifier.

émulsion /emylsjɔ̃/ *nf* emulsion.

en /ɑ̃/ **I** *prep* **1** in; into; to; **vivre ~ ville** to live in town; **aller ~ Allemagne** to go to Germany; **~ hiver/1991** in winter/1991; **~ semaine** during the week; **voyager ~ train** to travel by train; **2 il est toujours ~ manteau** he always wears a coat; **3** as; **je vous parle ~ ami** I'm speaking (to you) as a friend; **4** into; **traduire ~ anglais** to translate into English; **5 c'est ~ or** it's (made of) gold; **le même ~ bleu/plus grand** the same in blue/only bigger; **~ hauteur, le mur fait trois mètres** the wall is three metres[GB] high; **6** (used with gerund) **je l'ai croisé ~ sortant** I met him as I was leaving; **prends un café ~ attendant** have a cup of coffee while you're waiting; **l'enfant se réveilla ~ hurlant** the child woke up screaming; **ouvrez cette caisse ~ soulevant le couvercle** open this box by lifting the lid; **tu aurais moins chaud ~ enlevant ta veste** you'd be cooler if you took your jacket off.
II *pron* **1** (indicating means) **il sortit son épée et l'~ transperça** he took out his sword and ran him/her through; **2** (indicating cause) **ça l'a telle-**

ment bouleversé qu'il ~ est tombé malade it distressed him so much that he fell ill (GB) or became sick (US); **3** (representing person) **ils aiment leurs enfants et ils ~ sont aimés** they love their children and they are loved by them; **4** (representing thing) **'veux-tu du vin?'—'oui, j'~ veux'** 'would you like some wine?'—'yes, I'd like some'; **il n'~ reste pas beaucoup** there isn't much (of it) left; there aren't many left; **j'~ suis fier** I'm proud of it; **5**° **tu ~ as un beau chapeau!** what a nice hat you've got!

ENA /ena/ *nf*: *abbr* ▶ **école**.

énarque /enaʀk/ *nmf* graduate of the ENA.

encadré /ɑ̃kadʀe/ *nm* (in newspaper) box.

encadrement /ɑ̃kadʀəmɑ̃/ *nm* **1** supervision; **2** supervisory staff; managerial staff; (Mil) officers; **3** (of picture) frame.

encadrer /ɑ̃kadʀe/ [1] *vtr* **1** to supervise [*staff*]; to train [*soldier*]; **2** to flank [*person*]; to frame [*face, window*]; **~ de rouge** to outline [sth] in red; **3** to frame [*picture*].

encaisser /ɑ̃kese/ [1] *vtr* **1** to cash [*cheque, sum of money*]; **2**° to take [*blow, defeat*]; **je ne peux pas ~ ton frère** I can't stand your brother.
IDIOMS **~ le coup**° to take it all in one's stride.

encart /ɑ̃kaʀ/ *nm* insert; **~ publicitaire** promotional insert.

en-cas /ɑ̃ka/ *nm inv* snack.

encastrer /ɑ̃kastʀe/ [1] **I** *vtr* to build in [*oven, refrigerator*]; to fit [*sink, hotplate*]; **baignoire encastrée** sunken bath.
II s'encastrer *v refl* (+ *v être*) to fit (**dans** into).

encaustique /ɑ̃kɔstik/ *nf* wax polish.

enceinte /ɑ̃sɛ̃t/ **I** *adj f* [*woman*] pregnant.
II *nf* **1** **(mur d')~** surrounding wall; **2** (of prison, palace) compound; (of church) interior.

encens /ɑ̃sɑ̃/ *nm inv* incense.

encenser /ɑ̃sɑ̃se/ [1] *vtr* to sing the praises of [*person*]; to acclaim [*work of art*].

encercler /ɑ̃sɛʀkle/ [1] *vtr* **1** to surround, to encircle; **2** (with pen) to circle.

enchaînement /ɑ̃ʃɛnmɑ̃/ *nm* **1** (of events) chain; **2** sequence; **3** (in music, sport) transition.

enchaîner /ɑ̃ʃene/ [1] **I** *vtr* to chain up [*person, animal*]; **~ à** to chain to.
II *vi* to go on; **~ avec une nouvelle chanson** to move on to a new song.
III s'enchaîner *v refl* (+ *v être*) [*shots, sequences in film*] to follow on.

enchantement /ɑ̃ʃɑ̃tmɑ̃/ *nm* enchantment, spell; **comme par ~** as if by magic.

enchanter /ɑ̃ʃɑ̃te/ [1] *vtr* **1** to delight; **ça ne m'enchante guère** it doesn't exactly thrill me; **enchanté (de faire votre connaissance)!** how do you do!; **2 forêt enchantée** enchanted forest.

enchère /ɑ̃ʃɛʀ/ **I** *nf* bid.
II enchères *nf pl* **vente aux ~s** auction.

enchevêtrement /ɑ̃ʃ(ə)vɛtʀəmɑ̃/ *nm* (of threads) tangle; (of corridors, streets) labyrinth.

enchevêtrer /ɑ̃ʃ(ə)vetʀe/ [1] **I** *vtr* **1** to tangle [sth] up [*threads*]; **2 être enchevêtré** [*sentence, plot*] to be muddled; [*case*] to be complicated.
II s'enchevêtrer *v refl* (+ *v être*) **1** [*branches, threads*] to get tangled; **2** [*phrases, ideas*] to become muddled.

enclave /ɑ̃klav/ *nf* enclave.

enclencher /ɑ̃klɑ̃ʃe/ [1] **I** *vtr* **1** to set [sth] in motion [*process*]; **2** to engage [*mechanism*].
II s'enclencher *v refl* (+ *v être*) **1** [*process*] to get under way; **2** [*mechanism*] to engage.

enclin, ~e /ɑ̃klɛ̃, in/ *adj* inclined (**à** to).

enclos /ɑ̃klo/ *nm inv* (gen) enclosure; (for animals) pen.

enclume /ɑ̃klym/ *nf* (Tech, Anat) anvil.

encoche /ɑ̃kɔʃ/ *nf* notch.

encolure /ɑ̃kɔlyʀ/ *nf* **1** (of garment) neckline; **2** collar size; **3** (of animal) neck.

encombrant, ~e /ɑ̃kɔ̃bʀɑ̃, ɑ̃t/ *adj* **1** bulky; cumbersome; **2** [*person, matter*] troublesome.

encombre: **sans encombre** /sɑ̃zɑ̃kɔ̃bʀ/ *phr* without a hitch.

encombré, ~e /ɑ̃kɔ̃bʀe/ *adj* [*road, sky*] congested (**de** with); [*room*] cluttered.

encombrement /ɑ̃kɔ̃bʀəmɑ̃/ *nm* **1** traffic congestion; **2** (of switchboard) jamming; **3** (of room) cluttering; **4** (of furniture) bulk.

encombrer /ɑ̃kɔ̃bʀe/ [1] **I** *vtr* **1** [*object, people*] to clutter up [*room*]; to obstruct [*road, path*]; **2** to jam [*switchboard*]; to clutter up [*mind*].
II s'encombrer *v refl* (+ *v être*) **s'~ de** to burden oneself with; **s'~ l'esprit** to clutter up one's mind (**de** with).

encontre: **à l'encontre de** /alɑ̃kɔ̃tʀədə/ *phr* **1** counter to; **2** against; **3** toward(s).

encorder: **s'encorder** /ɑ̃kɔʀde/ [1] *v refl* (+ *v être*) to rope up.

encore /ɑ̃kɔʀ/ **I** *adv* **1** still; **il n'est ~ que midi** it's only midday; **tu en es ~ là?** haven't you got (GB) or gotten (US) beyond that by now?; **qu'il soit impoli passe ~, mais**... the fact that he's rude is one thing, but...; **2 pas ~** not yet; **il n'est pas ~ rentré** he hasn't come home yet; he still hasn't come home; **cela ne s'est ~ jamais vu** it has never been seen before; **3** again; **~ toi!** you again!; **~!** encore!, more!; **~ une fois** once more, once again; **qu'est-ce que j'ai ~ fait?** what have I done now?; **4** more; **mange ~ un peu** have some more to eat; **c'est ~ mieux** it's even better; **5 ~ un gâteau?** another cake?; **pendant ~ trois jours** for another three days; **qu'est-ce qu'il te faut ~?** what more do you need?; **6 ~ faut-il qu'elle accepte** but she still has to accept; **si ~ il était généreux!** if he were at least generous!; **7** only, just; **il y a ~ trois mois** only three months ago.
II et encore *phr* if that; **c'est tout au plus mangeable, et ~!** it's only just edible, if that!
III encore que *phr* even though.

encourageant, ~e /ɑ̃kuʀaʒɑ̃, ɑ̃t/ *adj* encouraging.

encouragement /ɑ̃kuʀaʒmɑ̃/ *nm* encouragement.

encourager /ɑ̃kuʀaʒe/ [13] *vtr* **1** to encourage (**à faire** to do); **2** to cheer [sb] on.

encourir /ɑ̃kuʀiʀ/ [26] *vtr* to incur.

encrasser /ɑ̃kʀase/ [1] *vtr* **1** to clog [sth] (up) [*filter, artery*]; to make [sth] sooty [*chimney*]; **2** to dirty; (Aut) to foul up [*spark plugs*].

encre /ɑ̃kʀ/ *nf* ink.
■ **~ de Chine** Indian (GB) or India (US) ink; **~ sympathique** invisible ink.
IDIOMS **cela a fait couler beaucoup d'~** a lot of ink has been spilled over this; **se faire un sang d'~** to be worried sick.

encrier /ɑ̃kʀije/ *nm* inkwell; ink pot.

encyclopédie /ɑ̃siklɔpedi/ *nf* encyclopedia.

endetté, **~e** /ɑ̃dete/ *adj* in debt.

endettement /ɑ̃dɛtmɑ̃/ *nm* debt.

endetter /ɑ̃dete/ [1] **I** *vtr* to put [sb] into debt.
II s'endetter *v refl* (+ *v être*) to get into debt.

endiablé, **~e** /ɑ̃djɑble/ *adj* [*rhythm*] furious.

endiguer /ɑ̃dige/ [1] *vtr* to confine [*river*]; to contain [*demonstrators*]; to curb [*speculation*].

endimanché, **~e** /ɑ̃dimɑ̃ʃe/ *adj* in one's Sunday best.

endive /ɑ̃div/ *nf* chicory (GB), endive (US).

endoctriner /ɑ̃dɔktʀine/ [1] *vtr* to indoctrinate.

endolori, **~e** /ɑ̃dɔlɔʀi/ *adj* aching.

endolorir /ɑ̃dɔlɔʀiʀ/ [3] *vtr* to make [sb/sth] ache.

endommager /ɑ̃dɔmaʒe/ [13] *vtr* to damage.

endormi, **~e** /ɑ̃dɔʀmi/ *adj* **1** [*person, animal*] sleeping, asleep; **2** [*village, mind*] sleepy.

endormir /ɑ̃dɔʀmiʀ/ [30] **I** *vtr* **1** to send [sb] to sleep [*child*]; [*person, substance*] to put [sb] to sleep [*patient*]; **2** (from boredom) [*person, lecture*] to send [sb] to sleep [*person*]; **3** to dupe [*person, opinion, enemy*]; **4** to allay [*suspicion*]; to numb [*faculties*].
II s'endormir *v refl* (+ *v être*) **1** to fall asleep; **2** to get to sleep; **3** (figurative) to sit back.

endossable /ɑ̃dosabl/ *adj* [*cheque*] endorsable.

endosser /ɑ̃dose/ [1] *vtr* **1** to take on [*role, responsibility*]; **2** to endorse [*cheque*].

endroit /ɑ̃dʀwɑ/ **I** *nm* **1** place; **par ~s** in places; **à quel ~?** where?; **2** (of fabric) right side; **à l'~** (of object) the right way up; (of garment) the right way round (GB) or around (US).
II à l'endroit de *phr* toward(s).

enduire /ɑ̃dɥiʀ/ [69] **I** *vtr* to coat (**de** with).
II s'enduire *v refl* (+ *v être*) **s'~ de** to put [sth] on.

enduit /ɑ̃dɥi/ *nm* **1** coating; **2** filler.

endurance /ɑ̃dyʀɑ̃s/ *nf* **1** (of person) stamina; **~ à** resistance to; **2** (of engine) endurance.

endurant, **~e** /ɑ̃dyʀɑ̃, ɑ̃t/ *adj* [*person, athlete*] tough; [*engine, vehicle*] hard-wearing.

endurcir /ɑ̃dyʀsiʀ/ [3] **I** *vtr* **1** [*sport, hard work*] to strengthen [*body, character*]; **2** [*ordeal*] to harden [*person*].
II s'endurcir *v refl* (+ *v être*) **1** to become stronger; **2** to become hardened.

endurer /ɑ̃dyʀe/ [1] *vtr* **1** to endure; **faire ~ qch à qn** to put sb through sth; **2** to put up with.

énergétique /enɛʀʒetik/ *adj* **1** [*needs, resources*] energy; **2** [*food*] high-calorie.

énergie /enɛʀʒi/ *nf* energy; **avec l'~ du désespoir** driven on by despair; **avec ~** [*work*] energetically; [*protest*] strongly.

énergique /enɛʀʒik/ *adj* **1** [*person, gesture*] energetic; [*handshake*] vigorous; [*face, expression*] resolute; **2** [*action*] tough; [*protest*] strong; [*refusal*] firm; [*intervention*] forceful.

énergumène /enɛʀgymɛn/ *nmf* oddball.

énervé, **~e** /enɛʀve/ *adj* **1** irritated; **2** nervous; [*child*] overexcited.

énervement /enɛʀvəmɑ̃/ *nm* **1** irritation; **2** agitation; **elle pleura d'~** she was so on edge that she cried.

énerver /enɛʀve/ [1] **I** *vtr* **1** to put [sb] on edge; **2 ~ qn** to get on sb's nerves, to irritate sb.
II s'énerver *v refl* (+ *v être*) to get worked up.

enfance /ɑ̃fɑ̃s/ *nf* childhood; **la petite ~** early childhood.
IDIOMS **c'est l'~ de l'art** it's child's play.

enfant /ɑ̃fɑ̃/ *nmf* child; infant; **être ~ unique** to be an only child.
■ **~ de chœur** altar boy; **ce n'est pas un ~ de chœur** (figurative) he's no angel.

enfanter /ɑ̃fɑ̃te/ [1] *vtr* to give birth to.

enfantillage /ɑ̃fɑ̃tijaʒ/ *nm* childishness.

enfantin, **~e** /ɑ̃fɑ̃tɛ̃, in/ *adj* **1** simple, easy; **2 mode ~e** children's fashion; **3** childish.

enfer /ɑ̃fɛʀ/ *nm* Hell; (figurative) hell; **aller à un train d'~**○ to go hell for leather○; **soirée d'~**○ hell of a○ party.

enfermer /ɑ̃fɛʀme/ [1] **I** *vtr* **1** to shut [sth] in [*animal*]; to lock [sth] up [*money, jewellery*]; to lock [sb] up [*person*]; **elle est bonne à ~**○ she's stark raving mad○; **2 ~ qn dans un rôle** to confine sb to a role; **~ qn dans une situation** to trap sb in a situation.
II s'enfermer *v refl* (+ *v être*) **1** (gen) to lock oneself in; (accidentally) to get locked in; (in order to be alone) to shut oneself away; **ne reste pas enfermé toute la journée!** don't stay cooped up indoors all day!; **2 s'~ dans** to retreat into; **s'~ dans le mutisme** to remain obstinately silent.

enfilade /ɑ̃filad/ *nf* (of traps) succession; (of houses, tables) row.

enfiler /ɑ̃file/ [1] **I** *vtr* **1** to slip on; **2** to thread [*piece of thread, needle*].
II s'enfiler *v refl* (+ *v être*) **1**○ to guzzle down; **2 s'~ dans** to take [*street*].

enfin /ɑ̃fɛ̃/ *adv* finally; lastly; **~ et surtout** last but not least; **~ seuls!** alone at last!; **mais ~, cessez de vous disputer!** for heaven's sake, stop arguing!; **il pleut tous les jours, ~ presque** it rains every day, well almost.

enflammé, **~e** /ɑ̃flame/ *adj* **1** burning, on fire; **2** [*person, declaration*] passionate; [*speech*] impassioned; **3** (Med) [*throat, wound*] inflamed; **4** [*sky*] ablaze.

enflammer /ɑ̃flame/ [1] **I** *vtr* **1** to set fire to

[sth]; **2** to inflame [*public opinion, mind*]; to fire [*imagination*]; to fuel [*anger*].

II s'enflammer *v refl* (+ *v être*) **1** [*house, paper*] to go up in flames; [*wood*] to catch fire; **2** [*eyes*] to blaze; [*imagination*] to be fired (**de** with; **à la vue de** by); [*country*] to explode; **s'~ pour qn** to become passionate about sb; **s'~ pour qch** to get carried away by sth.

enfler /ɑ̃fle/ [1] **I** *vtr* to exaggerate [*story, event*].

II *vi* **1** [*part of body*] to swell (up); [*river, sea*] to swell; **2** [*rumour, anger*] to spread.

III s'enfler *v refl* (+ *v être*) [*anger*] to mount; [*voice*] to rise; [*rumour*] to grow.

enfoncer /ɑ̃fɔ̃se/ [12] **I** *vtr* **1** to push in [*cork, stake*]; **~ ses mains dans ses poches** to dig one's hands into one's pockets; **~ son doigt dans** to stick one's finger into; **~ un clou dans qch** to knock a nail into sth; **2** to break down [*door*]; to break through [*enemy lines*]; **~ des portes ouvertes** to state the obvious; **3 ne m'enfonce pas davantage** don't rub it in.

II s'enfoncer *v refl* (+ *v être*) **1 s'~ dans la neige** to sink in the snow; **s'~ dans l'erreur** to make error after error; **les piquets s'enfoncent facilement** the posts go in easily; **s'~ une épine dans le doigt** to get a thorn in one's finger; **s'~ dans la forêt** to go into the forest; **2**○ to make things worse for oneself.

enfouir /ɑ̃fwiʀ/ [3] **I** *vtr* **1** to bury; **2 ~ qch dans un sac** to shove sth into a bag.

II s'enfouir *v refl* (+ *v être*) **s'~ sous les couvertures** to burrow under the blankets.

enfourcher /ɑ̃fuʀʃe/ [1] *vtr* to mount [*horse*]; to get on [*motorbike*].

enfourner /ɑ̃fuʀne/ [1] *vtr* **1** to put [sth] in the oven; **2**○ to stuff down [*food*].

enfreindre /ɑ̃fʀɛ̃dʀ/ [55] *vtr* to infringe.

enfuir: **s'enfuir** /ɑ̃fɥiʀ/ [9] *v refl* (+ *v être*) **1** to run away; [*bird*] to fly away; **2** to escape.

enfumer /ɑ̃fyme/ [1] *vtr* to fill [sth] with smoke; **tu nous enfumes avec tes cigares!** you're smoking us out with your cigars!

engagé, **~e** /ɑ̃gaʒe/ *nm,f* enlisted man/woman.

engageant, **~e** /ɑ̃gaʒɑ̃, ɑ̃t/ *adj* [*person, manner*] welcoming; [*dish, place*] inviting.

engagement /ɑ̃gaʒmɑ̃/ *nm* **1** commitment; **prendre l'~ de faire** to undertake to do; **2** involvement; **3** (Mil) enlistment.

engager /ɑ̃gaʒe/ [13] **I** *vtr* **1** to hire [*staff*]; to enlist [*soldier*]; to engage [*artist*]; **2** to begin [*process, reform policy*]; **nous avons engagé la conversation** we struck up a conversation; **3** to commit, to bind [*person*]; **4** to stake [*honour*]; **~ sa parole** to give one's word; **5 ~ qch dans** to put sth in; **6** to lay out [*capital*]; **7 ~ qn à faire** to urge sb to do; **8** (Sport) **~ qn dans une compétition** to enter sb for a competition; **9** to pawn [*valuables*].

II s'engager *v refl* (+ *v être*) **1** to promise (**à faire** to do); **s'~ vis-à-vis de qn** to make a commitment to sb; **2 s'~ dans un projet** to embark on a project; **3** to get involved; **4 s'~ sur une route** to go into a road; **5** [*lawsuit*] to begin; **6 s'~ dans l'armée** to join the army.

engelure /ɑ̃ʒlyʀ/ *nf* chilblain.

engendrer /ɑ̃ʒɑ̃dʀe/ [1] *vtr* **1** to engender; **2** [*woman*] to give birth to; [*man*] to father.

engin /ɑ̃ʒɛ̃/ *nm* **1** device; **2** vehicle; **3** piece of equipment.

englober /ɑ̃glɔbe/ [1] *vtr* to include.

engloutir /ɑ̃glutiʀ/ [3] *vtr* **1** [*sea, storm, fog*] to engulf, to swallow up; **2**○ to gulp [sth] down; **3** [*person*] to squander [*money*].

engoncé, **~e** /ɑ̃gɔ̃se/ *adj* **il était ~ dans une veste trop étroite** he was squeezed into a tight jacket.

engorger /ɑ̃gɔʀʒe/ [13] *vtr* **1** to block (up) [*pipes, drains*]; **2** to clog up [*roads*].

engouement /ɑ̃gumɑ̃/ *nm* (for thing, activity) passion; (for person) infatuation.

engouer: **s'engouer** /ɑ̃gwe/ [1] *v refl* (+ *v être*) **s'~ de** to develop a passion for.

engouffrer: **s'engouffrer** /ɑ̃gufʀe/ [1] *v refl* (+ *v être*) (into a room) to rush; (into a taxi) to dive.

engourdir: **s'engourdir** /ɑ̃guʀdiʀ/ [3] *v refl* (+ *v être*) [*limb*] to go numb; [*mind*] to grow dull.

engourdissement /ɑ̃guʀdismɑ̃/ *nm* **1** (physical) numbness; (mental) drowsiness; **2** (of body) numbing; (of mind) dulling.

engrais /ɑ̃gʀɛ/ *nm inv* manure; fertilizer.

engraisser /ɑ̃gʀese/ [1] **I** *vtr* **1** to fatten [*cattle*]; **2** to fertilize [*soil*].

II *vi* to get fat.

III s'engraisser○ *v refl* (+ *v être*) **s'~ (sur le dos de qn)** to grow fat○ (off sb's back).

engrenage /ɑ̃gʀənaʒ/ *nm* **1** gears; **2** (figurative) (of violence) spiral.

engueuler● /ɑ̃gœle/ [1] **I** *vtr* to tell [sb] off; to give [sb] an earful○.

II s'engueuler *v refl* (+ *v être*) to have a row.

enhardir: **s'enhardir** /ɑ̃aʀdiʀ/ [3] *v refl* (+ *v être*) to become bolder.

énième /ɛnjɛm/ *adj* umpteenth.

énigmatique /enigmatik/ *adj* enigmatic.

énigme /enigm/ *nf* **1** enigma, mystery; **2** riddle; **parler par ~s** to speak in riddles.

enivrant, **~e** /ɑ̃nivʀɑ̃, ɑ̃t/ *adj* intoxicating.

enivrer /ɑ̃nivʀe/ [1] **I** *vtr* **1** to make [sb] drunk; **2 ~ qn** [*success*] to go to sb's head.

II s'enivrer *v refl* (+ *v être*) to get drunk.

enjambée /ɑ̃ʒɑ̃be/ *nf* stride; **avancer/s'éloigner à grandes ~s** to stride forward/off.

enjamber /ɑ̃ʒɑ̃be/ [1] *vtr* to step over [*obstacle*].

enjeu, *pl* **~x** /ɑ̃ʒø/ *nm* (Games) stake; **analyser l'~ des élections** to analyse[GB] what is at stake in the elections.

enjoindre /ɑ̃ʒwɛ̃dʀ/ [56] *vtr* **~ à qn de faire** to enjoin sb to do.

enjôler /ɑ̃ʒole/ [1] *vtr* to beguile.

enjoliver /ɑ̃ʒɔlive/ [1] *vtr* to embellish.

enjoliveur /ɑ̃ʒɔlivœʀ/ *nm* hubcap.

enjoué, **~e** /ɑ̃ʒwe/ *adj* [*character*] cheerful; [*tone*] light-hearted.

enlacer /ɑ̃lase/ [12] **I** *vtr* to embrace; [*snake*] to wrap itself around [*prey*].

II s'enlacer *v refl* (+ *v être*) [*people*] to embrace; [*body*] to intertwine.

enlaidir /ɑ̃lediʀ/ [3] *vtr* to spoil [*landscape*]; to make [sb] look ugly [*person*].

enlevé, **~e** /ɑ̃lve/ *adj* lively.

enlèvement /ɑ̃lɛvmɑ̃/ *nm* kidnapping[GB], abduction.

enlever /ɑ̃lve/ [16] **I** *vtr* **1** to take [sth] away, to remove [*piece of furniture, book*]; to take [sth] down [*curtains, pictures*]; to take [sth] off [*garment*]; to move, to remove [*vehicle*]; **2** to remove [*stain, paint*]; **3** to take [sb/sth] away [*people, object*]; **~ à qn l'envie de partir** to put sb off going; **4** to kidnap; to carry [sb] off ; **5** to carry [sth] off [*trophy*]; to capture [*market*].
II s'enlever *v refl* (+ *v être*) **1** [*varnish*] to come off; [*stain*] to come out; **2** [*part, section*] to be detachable; **3**○ **enlève-toi de là** get off○.

enliser /ɑ̃lize/ [1] **I** *vtr* to get [sth] stuck.
II s'enliser *v refl* (+ *v être*) **1** [*boat, vehicle*] to get stuck; **2** [*inquiry, negotiations*] to drag on.

enluminure /ɑ̃lyminyʀ/ *nf* illumination.

enneigé, **~e** /ɑ̃neʒe/ *adj* [*summit*] snowy; [*road*] covered in snow.

ennemi, **~e** /ɛnmi/ **I** *adj* **1** (Mil) enemy; **2** (gen) hostile.
II *nm,f* enemy.
III *nm* (Mil) enemy; **passer à l'~** to go over to the enemy.

ennui /ɑ̃nɥi/ *nm* **1** boredom; **tromper l'~** to escape from boredom; **quel ~!** what a bore!; **2** problem; **avoir des ~s** to have problems; **j'ai des ~s avec la police** I'm in trouble with the police; **s'attirer des ~s** to get into trouble.

ennuyé, **~e** /ɑ̃nɥije/ *adj* **1** bored; **2** embarrassed; **j'étais très ~ de laisser les enfants seuls** I felt awful about leaving the children on their own; **3 j'aurais été très ~ si je n'avais pas eu la clé** I would have been in real trouble if I hadn't had the key.

ennuyer /ɑ̃nɥije/ [22] **I** *vtr* **1** to bore; **2** to bother; **si ça ne vous ennuie pas trop** if you don't mind; **3** to annoy; **4** to hassle○.
II s'ennuyer *v refl* (+ *v être*) **1** to be bored; to get bored; **2 s'~ de** to miss [*friend*].

ennuyeux, **-euse** /ɑ̃nɥijø, øz/ *adj* **1** boring; **2** tedious; **3** annoying.
IDIOMS **être ~ comme la pluie** to be as dull as ditchwater.

énoncé /enɔ̃se/ *nm* **1** (of exam subject) wording (**de** of); **l'~ d'une théorie** the exposition of a theory; **2** (of fact) statement (**de** of).

énoncer /enɔ̃se/ [12] *vtr* to pronounce [*verdict*]; to set out, to state [*facts*]; to expound [*theory*].

enorgueillir: **s'enorgueillir** /ɑ̃nɔʀgœjiʀ/ [3] *v refl* (+ *v être*) to pride oneself (**de** on).

énorme /enɔʀm/ *adj* **1** [*object, person*] huge, enormous; **2** [*success, effort*] tremendous; [*mistake*] terrible; [*lie*] outrageous.

énormité /enɔʀmite/ *nf* **1** (of figure, size) hugeness; (of lie) enormity; **2** outrageous remark.

enquérir: **s'enquérir** /ɑ̃keʀiʀ/ [35] *v refl* (+ *v être*) **s'~ de** to enquire about sth.

enquête /ɑ̃kɛt/ *nf* **1** (Law) inquiry, investigation; (into a death) inquest; **~ de police** police investigation; **2** (by journalist) investigation; **3** (by sociologist) survey.

enquêter /ɑ̃kete/ [1] *vi* [*policeman*] to carry out an investigation; [*expert*] to hold an inquiry.

enquêteur, **-trice** /ɑ̃ketœʀ, tʀis/ *nm,f* **1** investigating officer; **2** pollster; **3** interviewer.

enquiquiner○ /ɑ̃kikine/ [1] **I** *vtr* **~ qn** to get on sb's nerves; to pester sb.
II s'enquiquiner *v refl* (+ *v être*) **s'~ à faire** to go to the trouble of doing.

enraciner: **s'enraciner** /ɑ̃ʀasine/ [1] *v refl* (+ *v être*) **1** to take root; **2** (figurative) [*person*] to put down roots; [*custom, idea*] to take root.

enragé, **~e** /ɑ̃ʀaʒe/ *adj* **1** fanatical; **2** enraged; **3** (Med) rabid.
IDIOMS **manger de la vache ~e**○ to go through hard times.

enrager /ɑ̃ʀaʒe/ [13] *vi* to be furious; **faire ~ qn** to tease sb.

enrayer /ɑ̃ʀeje/ [21] **I** *vtr* **1** to check [*epidemic, development*]; to curb [*inflation*]; to stop [sth] escalating [*crisis*]; **2** to jam [*mechanism, gun*].
II s'enrayer *v refl* (+ *v être*) to get jammed.

enregistrement /ɑ̃ʀəʒistʀəmɑ̃/ *nm* **1** (of music) recording; **2** (of data) recording; (of order) taking down; **3** (of baggage) check-in.

enregistrer /ɑ̃ʀəʒistʀe/ [1] *vtr* **1** to record [*cassette, album*]; **2** to note [*progress, failure*]; to record [*rise, drop*]; **3** to make a record of [*expenses*]; to take [*order*]; to record [*data*]; to set [*record*]; **4** to register [*birth, claim*]; **5** to check in [*baggage*]; **6 c'est enregistré, j'enregistre**○ I've made a mental note of it.

enrhumer: **s'enrhumer** /ɑ̃ʀyme/ [1] *v refl* (+ *v être*) to catch a cold.

enrichir /ɑ̃ʀiʃiʀ/ [3] **I** *vtr* **1** to make [sb] rich [*person*]; to bring wealth to [*country*]; **2** to enrich, to enhance [*collection, book*].
II s'enrichir *v refl* (+ *v être*) **1** [*person*] to become or grow rich; **2** to be enriched.

enrichissant, **~e** /ɑ̃ʀiʃisɑ̃, ɑ̃t/ *adj* [*experience*] rewarding; [*relationship*] fulfilling.

enrober /ɑ̃ʀɔbe/ [1] *vtr* **1** to coat; **2** (figurative) to wrap up [*news*].

enrôlement /ɑ̃ʀolmɑ̃/ *nm* (in the army) enlistment; (in political party) enrolment[GB].

enrôler /ɑ̃ʀole/ [1] **I** *vtr* to recruit.
II s'enrôler *v refl* (+ *v être*) to enlist.

enrouer: **s'enrouer** /ɑ̃ʀwe/ [1] *v refl* (+ *v être*) [*voice*] to go hoarse; [*person*] to make oneself hoarse; **d'une voix enrouée** hoarsely.

enrouler /ɑ̃ʀule/ [1] **I** *vtr* **1** to wind; **2** to wrap.
II s'enrouler *v refl* (+ *v être*) **1** [*thread, tape*] to wind; **2** [*person, animal*] to curl up.

ENS /œɛnɛs/ *nf*: *abbr* ▶ **école**.

ensabler: **s'ensabler** /ɑ̃sable/ [1] *v refl* (+ *v être*) [*vehicle*] to get stuck in the sand; [*boat*] to get stranded (*on a sandbank*).

ensanglanter /ɑ̃sɑ̃glɑ̃te/ [1] *vtr* **1** to cover [sth] with blood; **2** to bring bloodshed to [*country*].

enseignant, **~e** /ɑ̃sɛɲɑ̃, ɑ̃t/ **I** *adj* **corps ~** teaching profession.

II *nm,f* (Sch) teacher; (at university) lecturer.

enseigne /ɑ̃sɛɲ/ *nf* **1** (shop) sign; **~ lumineuse** neon sign; **2** (Mil, Naut) ensign.
IDIOMS **nous sommes logés à la même ~** we are in the same boat.

enseignement /ɑ̃sɛɲmɑ̃/ *nm* **1** education; **l'~ supérieur** higher education; **2** teaching; **méthodes d'~** teaching methods; **3** lesson.
■ **~ par correspondance** distance learning; **~ professionnel** vocational training; **~ religieux** religious instruction.

enseigner /ɑ̃seɲe/ [1] *vtr* to teach.

ensemble /ɑ̃sɑ̃bl/ I *adv* **1** together; **2** at the same time.
II *nm* **1** group; **un ~ de personnes** a group of people; **une vue d'~** an overall view; **plan d'~ d'une ville** general plan of a town; **dans l'~** by and large; **dans l'~ de** throughout; **dans son** or **leur ~** as a whole; **2** (of luggage, measures) set; **3** unity, cohesion; **former un bel ~** to form a harmonious whole; **4** (of gestures) coordination; (of sounds) unison; **un mouvement d'~** a coordinated movement; **5** (in mathematics) set; **6** (Mus) ensemble; **7** (of offices) complex; **~ hôtelier** hotel complex; **~ industriel** industrial estate (GB) or park (US); **8** (set of clothes) outfit; suit.

ensevelir /ɑ̃səvəliʀ/ [3] *vtr* to bury.

ensoleillé, ~e /ɑ̃sɔleje/ *adj* sunny.

ensommeillé, ~e /ɑ̃sɔmeje/ *adj* sleepy.

ensorcelé, ~e /ɑ̃sɔʀsəle/ *adj* enchanted.

ensorceler /ɑ̃sɔʀsəle/ [19] *vtr* **1** to cast or to put a spell on; **2** to bewitch, to enchant.

ensuite /ɑ̃sɥit/ *adv* **1** then; after; next; **très bien, mais ~?** fine, but then what?; **il ne me l'a dit qu'~** he only told me later; **2** secondly.

ensuivre: **s'ensuivre** /ɑ̃sɥivʀ/ [19] *v refl* (+ *v être*) to follow, to ensue.

entacher /ɑ̃taʃe/ [1] *vtr* to mar [*relations*].

entaille /ɑ̃taj/ *nf* **1** cut; gash; **2** notch.

entailler /ɑ̃taje/ [1] I *vtr* to cut into; (deeply) to make a gash in.
II **s'entailler** *v refl* (+ *v être*) **s'~ le doigt** to cut one's finger, to gash one's finger.

entame /ɑ̃tam/ *nf* **1** (Culin) first slice; **2** (in cards) lead.

entamer /ɑ̃tame/ [1] *vtr* **1** to start [*day, activity*]; to initiate [*procedure*]; to open [*negotiations*]; **2** to undermine [*credibility*]; **3** to eat into [*savings*]; **4** to cut into [*loaf, roast*]; to open [*bottle, jar*]; to start eating [*desert*]; **5** to cut into [*skin, wood*]; **6** to eat into [*metal*].

entartrer /ɑ̃taʀtʀe/ [1] I *vtr* to fur up (GB), to scale up.
II **s'entartrer** *v refl* (+ *v être*) to scale; [*teeth*] to be covered in tartar.

entasser /ɑ̃tase/ [1] I *vtr* **1** to pile [*books, clothes*]; **2** to hoard [*money, old things*]; **3** to pack, to cram [*people, objects*] (**dans** into).
II **s'entasser** *v refl* (+ *v être*) [*objects*] to pile up; [*people*] to squeeze (**dans** into; **sur** onto).

entendement /ɑ̃tɑ̃dmɑ̃/ *nm* understanding; **cela dépasse l'~** it's beyond belief.

entendre /ɑ̃tɑ̃dʀ/ [6] I *vtr* **1** to hear [*noise, word*]; **faire ~ un cri** to give a cry; **je n'en ai jamais entendu parler** I've never heard of it; **on n'entend plus parler de lui** his name is not mentioned any more; **2** [*judge*] to hear [*witness*]; **à t'~, tout va bien** according to you, everything is fine; **elle ne veut rien ~** she won't listen; **3** to understand; **il agit comme il l'entend** he does as he likes; **elle a laissé ~ que** she intimated that; **ils ne l'entendent pas de cette oreille** they don't see it that way; **4** to mean; **qu'entends-tu par là?** what do you mean by that?; **5 ~ faire** to intend doing; **j'entends qu'on fasse ce que je dis** I expect people to do what I say.
II **s'entendre** *v refl* (+ *v être*) **1** to get on or along; **2** to agree (**sur** on); **3** [*noise*] to be heard; **4** to hear oneself; [*two or more people*] to hear each other; **5 phrase qui peut s'~ de plusieurs façons** sentence which can be understood in several ways.

entendu, ~e /ɑ̃tɑ̃dy/ I *pp* ▶ **entendre**.
II *pp adj* **1 'tu viens demain?'—'~!'** 'will you come tomorrow?'—'OK°!'; **2 d'un air ~** with a knowing look.
III **bien entendu** *phr* of course.

entente /ɑ̃tɑ̃t/ *nf* **1** harmony; **vivre en bonne ~ avec qn** to be on good terms with sb; **2** understanding; **3** arrangement.

entériner /ɑ̃teʀine/ [1] *vtr* **1** to ratify; **2** to confirm.

enterré, ~e /ɑ̃teʀe/ *adj* buried; **mort et ~** dead and buried.

enterrement /ɑ̃tɛʀmɑ̃/ *nm* **1** burial; **2** funeral; **faire une tête d'~°** to look gloomy.

enterrer /ɑ̃teʀe/ [1] *vtr* to bury.
IDIOMS **~ sa vie de garçon** to have a stag party.

entêtant, ~e /ɑ̃tetɑ̃, ɑ̃t/ *adj* [*aroma*] heady; [*music*] insistent.

en-tête, *pl* **~s** /ɑ̃tɛt/ *nm* heading.

entêtement /ɑ̃tɛtmɑ̃/ *nm* stubbornness.

entêter: **s'entêter** /ɑ̃tete/ [1] *v refl* (+ *v être*) **1** to be stubborn; **2** to persist.

enthousiasme /ɑ̃tuzjasm/ *nm* enthusiasm.

enthousiasmer /ɑ̃tuzjasme/ [1] *vtr* to fill [sb] with enthusiasm.

enthousiaste /ɑ̃tuzjast/ *adj* enthusiastic.

enticher: **s'enticher** /ɑ̃tiʃe/ [1] *v refl* (+ *v être*) **s'~ de** to become infatuated with [*person*].

entier, -ière /ɑ̃tje, ɛʀ/ I *adj* **1** whole; **manger un pain ~** to eat a whole loaf; **des heures entières** for hours on end; **lait ~** full-fat milk; **2** [*success, satisfaction*] complete; **avoir l'entière responsabilité de qch** to have full responsibility for sth; **3** [*object, reputation*] intact; **le mystère reste ~** the mystery remains unsolved; **4 avoir un caractère ~** to be thoroughgoing.
II *nm* (in mathematics) integer.

entièrement /ɑ̃tjɛʀmɑ̃/ *adv* entirely, completely; **~ équipé** fully equipped.

entonner /ɑ̃tɔne/ [1] *vtr* to start singing [*song*].

entonnoir /ɑ̃tɔnwaʀ/ *nm* **1** funnel; **2** crater.

entorse /ɑ̃tɔʀs/ *nf* **1** (Med) sprain; **2** (figurative) infringement (**à** of); **faire une ~ au règlement** to bend the rules.

entortiller /ɑ̃tɔʀtije/ [1] **I** *vtr* **1** to wind (**autour de qch** round[GB] sth); **2** to tangle up.
II s'entortiller *v refl* (+ *v être*) [*thread, wool*] to get entangled (**dans** in).

entourage /ɑ̃tuʀaʒ/ *nm* **1** family circle; **2** circle (of friends); **on dit dans son ~ que** people close to him/her say that.

entouré, ~e /ɑ̃tuʀe/ **I** *pp* ▶ **entourer**.
II *adj* **1** [*person*] popular; **2 nos patients sont très ~s** our patients are well looked after.

entourer /ɑ̃tuʀe/ [1] **I** *vtr* **1** to surround; **2 ~ qch de qch** to put sth around sth; **~ qch de mystère** to shroud sth in mystery; **3** to rally round (GB) or around (US) [*sick person*].
II s'entourer *v refl* (+ *v être*) **s'~ d'objets** to surround oneself with things; **s'~ de précautions** to take every possible precaution.

entracte /ɑ̃tʀakt/ *nm* intermission.

entraider: s'entraider /ɑ̃tʀede/ [1] *v refl* (+ *v être*) to help each other or one another.

entrailles /ɑ̃tʀɑj/ *nf pl* (of animal) innards.

entrain /ɑ̃tʀɛ̃/ *nm* **1** (of person) spirit, go○ (GB); **retrouver son ~** to cheer up; **2** (of party, discussion) liveliness; **sans ~** half-hearted.

entraînant, ~e /ɑ̃tʀɛnɑ̃, ɑ̃t/ *adj* lively.

entraînement /ɑ̃tʀɛnmɑ̃/ *nm* **1** training, coaching; **2** practice[GB]; **avoir de l'~** to be highly trained; **l'~ à la lecture** reading practice[GB]; **3** training session.

entraîner /ɑ̃tʀene/ [1] **I** *vtr* **1** to lead to; **une panne a entraîné l'arrêt de la production** a breakdown brought production to a standstill; **2** [*river, current*] to carry [sb/sth] away [*swimmer, boat*]; **il a entraîné qn/qch dans sa chute** he dragged sb/sth down with him; **3** to take, to lead [*person*]; **~ qn à faire** [*person*] to make sb do; [*circumstances*] to lead sb to do; **4** (figurative) to carry [sb] away [*person, group*]; **5** to train, to coach [*athlete, team*] (**à** for); to train [*horse, soldier*] (**à** for); **6** [*engine, piston*] to drive [*machine, wheel, turbine*].
II s'entraîner *v refl* (+ *v être*) **1** [*player, soldiers*] to train; **2** to prepare oneself.

entraîneur /ɑ̃tʀɛnœʀ/ *nm* (of athlete) coach.

entrave /ɑ̃tʀav/ *nf* hindrance; (on freedom) restriction.

entraver /ɑ̃tʀave/ [1] *vtr* to hinder, to impede.

entre /ɑ̃tʀ/ *prep*

■ **Note** You will find translations for expressions such as *entre parenthèses*, *entre nous* etc, at the entries ***parenthèse***, ***nous*** etc.

---

1 between; **~ midi et deux** at lunchtime; **'doux ou très épicé?'—'~ les deux'** 'mild or very spicy?'—'in between'; **~ son travail et l'informatique, il n'a pas le temps de sortir** what with work and his computer he doesn't have time to go out; **2** among; **organiser une soirée ~ amis** to organize a party among friends; **chacune d'~ elles** each of them; **~ hommes** as one man to another; **~ nous** between you and me; **nous sommes ~ nous** there's just the two of us; we're among friends; **les enfants sont souvent cruels ~ eux** children are often cruel to each other.

entrebâillement /ɑ̃tʀəbɑjmɑ̃/ *nm* (in door, shutter, window) gap (**de** in).

entrebâiller /ɑ̃tʀəbɑje/ [1] *vtr* to half-open.

entrechoquer /ɑ̃tʀəʃɔke/ [1] **I** *vtr* to clatter [*saucepans*]; to clink [*glasses*].
II s'entrechoquer *v refl* (+ *v être*) **1** [*glasses*] to clink; **2** [*ideas, interests*] to clash.

entrecôte /ɑ̃tʀəkot/ *nf* **1** entrecôte (steak); **2** rib steak.

entrecouper /ɑ̃tʀəkupe/ [1] **I** *vtr* to punctuate.
II s'entrecouper *v refl* (+ *v être*) to intersect.

entrecroiser /ɑ̃tʀəkʀwaze/ [1] *vtr* to intertwine.

entrée /ɑ̃tʀe/ *nf* **1** entrance (**de** to); **se retrouver à l'~ du bureau** to meet outside the office; **2** (on motorway) (entry) slip road (GB), on-ramp (US); **3** (in house) hall; (in hotel) lobby; (door) entry; **4 l'~ dans la récession** the beginning of the recession; **d'~ (de jeu)** from the very start; **5 l'~ d'un pays dans une organisation** the entry of a country into an organization; **'~ libre'** 'admission free'; **'~ interdite'** 'no entry'; **6** ticket; **deux ~s gratuites** two free tickets; **7** (of person) entrance; **réussir son ~** [*actor*] to enter on cue; **8** (Culin) starter; **9** (in bookkeeping) **~s** receipts.
■ **~ des artistes** stage door; **~ en matière** introduction.

entrefaites: sur ces entrefaites /syʀsezɑ̃tʀəfɛt/ *phr* at that moment, just then.

entrefilet /ɑ̃tʀəfilɛ/ *nm* brief article.

entrejambes /ɑ̃tʀəʒɑ̃b/ *nm inv* crotch.

entrelacer /ɑ̃tʀəlase/ [12] *vtr*, **s'entrelacer** *v refl* (+ *v être*) to intertwine, to interlace.

entremêler: s'entremêler /ɑ̃tʀəmele/ [1] *v refl* (+ *v être*) (gen) to be mixed; [*hair, branches*] to get tangled.

entremets /ɑ̃tʀəmɛ/ *nm* dessert.

entremetteur, -euse /ɑ̃tʀəmɛtœʀ, øz/ *nm,f* **1** matchmaker; **2** go-between.

entremise /ɑ̃tʀəmiz/ *nf* intervention; **il l'a su par mon ~** he heard of it through me.

entreposer /ɑ̃tʀəpoze/ [1] *vtr* to store.

entrepôt /ɑ̃tʀəpo/ *nm* **1** warehouse; **2** stockroom.

entreprenant, ~e /ɑ̃tʀəpʀənɑ̃, ɑ̃t/ *adj* enterprising.

entreprendre /ɑ̃tʀəpʀɑ̃dʀ/ [52] *vtr* **1** to start, to undertake; **~ de faire** to set about doing; to undertake to do; **2 ~ qn sur un sujet** to engage sb in conversation about sth.

entrepreneur, -euse /ɑ̃tʀəpʀənœʀ, øz/ *nm,f* **1** builder; **2** contractor; **3** owner-manager (*of a small firm*).

entreprise /ɑ̃tʀəpʀiz/ *nf* **1** firm, business; **petites et moyennes ~s** small and medium-sized businesses; **2** business, industry; **la libre ~** free enterprise; **3** undertaking; venture.

entrer /ɑ̃tʀe/ [1] **I** *vtr* (+ *v avoir*) **1** to bring [sth] in; to take [sth] in; **2** (in computing) to enter.

II *vi* (+ *v être*) **1** to get in, to enter; to go in; to come in; **fais-la ~** show her in; **'défense d'~'** (on door) 'no entry'; (on gate) 'no trespassing'; **je ne fais qu'~ et sortir** I can only stay a minute; **2** to fit (in); **je n'arrive pas à faire ~ la pièce dans la fente** I can't get the coin into the slot; **3 ~ dans** to enter [*period, debate*]; to join [*company, army, party*]; **~ à** to enter [*school, charts*]; to get into [*university*]; **~ en** to enter into [*negotiations*]; **~ dans la vie de qn** to come into sb's life; **~ dans la légende** [*person*] to become a legend; [*fact*] to become legendary; **cela n'entre pas dans mes attributions** it's not part of my duties; **~ dans une colère noire** to fly into a blind rage.

entresol /ɑ̃tʀəsɔl/ *nm* mezzanine.

entre-temps /ɑ̃tʀətɑ̃/ *adv* meanwhile.

entretenir /ɑ̃tʀətniʀ/ [36] **I** *vtr* **1** to look after [*garment, house*]; to maintain [*road*]; **~ sa forme** to keep in shape; **2** to support [*family*]; to keep [*mistress*]; **3** to keep [sth] going [*conversation, fire*]; to keep [sth] alive [*friendship*]; **4 ~ qn de qch** to speak to sb about sth.

II s'entretenir *v refl* (+ *v être*) **1 s'~ de qch** to discuss sth; **2 s'~ facilement** [*house, fabric*] to be easy to look after.

entretien /ɑ̃tʀətjɛ̃/ *nm* **1** (of house) upkeep; (of car, road) maintenance; (of plant, skin) care; **2** cleaning; **3** (gen) discussion; (for a job) interview; (in newspaper) interview.

entrevoir /ɑ̃tʀəvwaʀ/ [46] *vtr* **1** to catch a glimpse of; (indistinctly) to make out; **2** to glimpse [*truth, solution*]; **3** to foresee [*difficulty*]; **laisser ~ qch** [*result, sign*] to point to sth.

entrevue /ɑ̃tʀəvy/ *nf* meeting; (Pol) talks.

entrouvrir /ɑ̃tʀuvʀiʀ/ [32] **I** *vtr* to open [sth] a little.

II s'entrouvrir *v refl* (+ *v être*) (gen) [*door, country*] to half-open; [*lips*] to part.

énumération /enymeʀasjɔ̃/ *nf* **1** listing; **2** catalogue[GB].

énumérer /enymeʀe/ [14] *vtr* to enumerate.

envahir /ɑ̃vaiʀ/ [3] *vtr* **1** [*troops, crowd*] to invade; [*animal*] to overrun; **2** to flood [*market*].

envahisseur /ɑ̃vaisœʀ/ *nm* invader.

enveloppe /ɑ̃vlɔp/ *nf* **1** (for letter) envelope; **sous ~** in an envelope; **2** (for parcel) wrapping; (of grains) husk; (of peas, beans) pod.

■ **~ budgétaire** budget.

enveloppé, ~e /ɑ̃vlɔpe/ *adj* [*person*] plump.

envelopper /ɑ̃vlɔpe/ [1] **I** *vtr* **1** [*person*] to wrap [sb/sth] (up); [*sheet*] to cover; **2** [*fog, silence*] to envelop; [*mystery*] to surround.

II s'envelopper *v refl* (+ *v être*) to wrap oneself (up).

envenimer /ɑ̃vnime/ [1] **I** *vtr* to inflame [*debate*]; to aggravate [*situation*].

II s'envenimer *v refl* (+ *v être*) [*dispute*] to worsen; [*situation*] to turn ugly.

envergure /ɑ̃vɛʀgyʀ/ *nf* **1** (of plane) wingspan; **2** (figurative) (of person) stature; (of project) scale; **un projet d'~** a substantial project; **sans ~** [*project*] limited; [*person*] of no account.

envers[1] /ɑ̃vɛʀ/ *prep* toward(s), to.

IDIOMS **~ et contre tous/tout** in spite of everyone/everything.

envers[2] /ɑ̃vɛʀ/ **I** *nm inv* (of sheet of paper) back; (of piece of cloth) wrong side; (of garment) inside; (of coin) reverse.

II à l'envers *phr* **1** the wrong way; **2** upside down; **3** inside out; **4** back to front; **5** the wrong way round (GB) or around (US); **mettre ses chaussures à l'~** to put one's shoes on the wrong feet; **6 passer un film à l'~** to run a film backward(s).

envie /ɑ̃vi/ *nf* **1** (gen) urge (**de faire** to do); (for food) craving; **avoir ~ de qch** to feel like sth; **avoir ~ de dormir** to want to go to bed; **mourir d'~ de faire** to be dying° to do; **donner (l')~ à qn de faire** to make sb want to do; **2** envy; **il te fait ~ ce jouet?** would you like that toy?; **3** birthmark.

envier /ɑ̃vje/ [2] *vtr* to envy.

envieux, -ieuse /ɑ̃vjø, øz/ **I** *adj* envious.

II *nm,f* **faire des ~** to make people jealous.

environ /ɑ̃viʀɔ̃/ *adv* about.

environnant, ~e /ɑ̃viʀɔnɑ̃, ɑ̃t/ *adj* surrounding.

environnement /ɑ̃viʀɔnmɑ̃/ *nm* environment.

environner /ɑ̃viʀɔne/ [1] *vtr* to surround.

environs /ɑ̃viʀɔ̃/ *nm pl* **être des ~** to be from the area; **aux ~ de** (place) in the vicinity of; (time, moment) around; (amount) in the region of.

envisager /ɑ̃vizaʒe/ [13] *vtr* **1** to plan (**de faire** to do); **2** to envisage [*hypothesis, situation*]; to foresee [*problem, possibility*]; **~ le pire** to imagine the worst; **3** to consider.

envoi /ɑ̃vwa/ *nm* **1 tous les ~s de colis sont suspendus** parcel post is suspended; **faire un ~ de** to send [*flowers, books*]; **2 demander l'~ (immédiat) de troupes** to ask for troops to be dispatched (immediately); **3 l'~ de la fusée** the rocket launch; **donner le coup d'~ de** to kick off [*match*]; to open [*festival*].

■ **~ recommandé** registered post (GB) or mail (US); **~ contre remboursement** cash on delivery.

envol /ɑ̃vɔl/ *nm* (of bird) flight; (of plane) takeoff.

envolée /ɑ̃vɔle/ *nf* **1** flight of fancy; **2** (in prices) surge (**de** in); (of political party) rise.

envoler: **s'envoler** /ɑ̃vɔle/ [1] *v refl* (+ *v être*) **1** [*bird*] to fly off; [*plane, passenger*] to take off; [*paper, hat*] to be blown away; **2** [*prices*] to soar; **3** to vanish; **4**° to do a runner°.

envoûtement /ɑ̃vutmɑ̃/ *nm* **1** bewitchment; **2** spell.

envoûter /ɑ̃vute/ [1] *vtr* to bewitch.

envoyé, ~e /ɑ̃vwaje/ **I** *adj* **ça c'est (bien) ~**°! well said!

II *nm,f* envoy; **~ spécial** special correspondent.

envoyer /ɑ̃vwaje/ [24] **I** *vtr* **1** to send; **~ qn étudier à Genève** to send sb off to study in Geneva; **2** to throw [*pebble*]; to fire [*missile*];

~ qch dans l'œil de qn to hit sb in the eye with sth; **~ le ballon dans les buts** to put the ball in the net.
II **s'envoyer** *v refl* (+ *v être*) to exchange; **s'~ des baisers** to blow each other kisses.
IDIOMS **~ qn promener**○ to send sb packing○; **tout ~ promener**○ to drop the lot○; **il ne me l'a pas envoyé dire**○ and he told me in no uncertain terms.

enzyme /ɑ̃zim/ *nm* or *f* enzyme.

épais, **épaisse** /epɛ, ɛs/ I *adj* **1** thick; **il n'est pas bien ~ ce petit**○! he's a skinny little fellow!; **2** [*mind*] dull; **3** [*night*] deep.
II *adv* a lot, much.

épaisseur /epɛsœʀ/ *nf* **1** thickness; **couper qch dans (le sens de) l'~** to cut sth sideways; **2** layer.

épaissir /epesiʀ/ [3] I *vtr* **1** to thicken; **2** to deepen [*mystery*].
II *vi* **1** [*sauce*] to thicken; [*jelly*] to set; **2** to put on weight.
III **s'épaissir** *v refl* (+ *v être*) [*sauce, waist, mist*] to thicken; [*mystery*] to deepen.

épancher: **s'épancher** /epɑ̃ʃe/ [1] *v refl* (+ *v être*) to open one's heart (**auprès de** to).

épanoui, **~e** /epanwi/ *adj* [*flower*] in full bloom; [*smile*] beaming; [*person*] well-adjusted.

épanouir /epanwiʀ/ [3] I *vtr* **1** [*sun*] to open (out) [*flower*]; [*joy*] to light up [*face*]; **2** (figurative) to make [sb/sth] blossom.
II **s'épanouir** *v refl* (+ *v être*) [*flower*] to bloom; [*face*] to light up; [*person*] to blossom.

épanouissement /epanwismɑ̃/ *nm* **1** (of flower) blooming; **2** (of person) development; (of talent) flowering.

épargne /epaʀɲ/ *nf* savings.

épargner /epaʀɲe/ [1] I *vtr* **1** to save [*money*]; **2** to spare; **~ qch à qn** to spare sb sth.
II *vi* to save.
III **s'épargner** *v refl* (+ *v être*) to save oneself.

éparpiller /epaʀpije/ [1] *vtr*, **s'éparpiller** *v refl* (+ *v être*) to scatter.

épars, **~e** /epaʀ, aʀs/ *adj* scattered.

épatant○, **~e** /epatɑ̃, ɑ̃t/ *adj* marvellous[GB].

épate○ /epat/ *nf* **faire de l'~** to show off.

épaté, **~e** /epate/ *adj* **1 nez ~** pug nose, flat nose; **2**○ amazed (**de** by).

épater○ /epate/ [1] *vtr* **1** to impress; **ça t'épate, hein?** surprised, aren't you?; **2** to amaze.

épaule /epol/ *nf* shoulder.
IDIOMS **changer son fusil d'~** to change one's tactics; **avoir la tête sur les ~s** to have one's head screwed on○.

épauler /epole/ [1] I *vtr* **1** to help; **2** to take aim with [*rifle*].
II *vi* to take aim.

épaulette /epolɛt/ *nf* **1** shoulder-pad; **2** (shoulder-)strap; **3** (Mil) epaulette.

épave /epav/ *nf* **1** wreck; **2** (car) (gen) wreck; (after accident) write-off○; **3** (person) wreck.

épée /epe/ *nf* sword; **c'est un coup d'~ dans l'eau** it was a complete waste of effort.

épeler /eple/ [19] *vtr* to spell [*word*].

éperdu, **~e** /epɛʀdy/ *adj* [*need, desire*] overwhelming; [*glance*] desperate; [*love*] boundless.

éperdument /epɛʀdymɑ̃/ *adv* [*in love*] madly; **je me moque ~ de ce qu'il pense** I couldn't care less about what he thinks.

éperon /epʀɔ̃/ *nm* spur.

épervier /epɛʀvje/ *nm* (Zool) sparrowhawk.

éphémère /efemɛʀ/ *adj* ephemeral; fleeting; short-lived.

épi /epi/ *nm* **1** (of corn) ear; (of flower) spike; **~ de maïs** corn cob; **2** (unmanageable) tuft of hair (GB), cow-lick (US).

épice /epis/ *nf* spice.

épicé, **~e** /epise/ *adj* spicy; hot.

épicentre /episɑ̃tʀ/ *nm* epicentre[GB].

épicer /epise/ [12] *vtr* to spice; to add spice to.

épicerie /episʀi/ *nf* **1** grocer's (shop) (GB), grocery (store) (US); **~ fine** delicatessen; **2** grocery trade; **3** groceries.

épicier, **-ière** /episje, ɛʀ/ *nm,f* grocer.

épidémie /epidemi/ *nf* epidemic.

épiderme /epidɛʀm/ *nm* skin.

épidermique /epidɛʀmik/ *adj* skin; [*sensitivity*] extreme; **réaction ~** gut reaction.

épier /epje/ [2] *vtr* **1** to spy on [*person, behaviour*]; **2** to be on the lookout for.

épilation /epilasjɔ̃/ *nf* removal of unwanted hair.

épilepsie /epilɛpsi/ *nf* **crise d'~** epileptic fit.

épiler /epile/ [1] *vtr* to remove unwanted hair from; to wax [*leg*]; to pluck [*eyebrows*].

épilogue /epilɔg/ *nm* epilogue[GB].

épiloguer /epilɔge/ [1] *vi* to go on and on (**sur** about).

épinard /epinaʀ/ *nm* spinach.
IDIOMS **ça met du beurre dans les ~s**○ it brings in a nice bit of extra money.

épine /epin/ *nf* thorn; **~ dorsale** spine.
IDIOMS **ôter à qn une ~ du pied** to take a weight off sb's shoulders.

épineux, **-euse** /epinø, øz/ *adj* [*stem, character*] prickly; [*problem*] tricky; [*question*] vexed.

épingle /epɛ̃gl/ *nf* pin; **~ de** or **à nourrice**, **~ de sûreté** safety pin.
IDIOMS **monter qch en ~** to blow sth up out of proportion; **être tiré à quatre ~s**○ to be immaculately dressed; **tirer son ~ du jeu** to get out while the going is good.

épinière /epinjɛʀ/ *adj f* **moelle ~** spinal cord.

épique /epik/ *adj* epic; **c'était ~**○ (humorous) it was quite something○.

épisode /epizɔd/ *nm* episode; **roman à ~s** serialized novel.

épisodique /epizɔdik/ *adj* sporadic.

épitaphe /epitaf/ *nf* epitaph.

épithète /epitɛt/ *nf* attributive adjective.

éploré, **~e** /eplɔʀe/ *adj* **1** grief-stricken; **2** tearful.

éplucher /eplyʃe/ [1] *vtr* to peel; (figurative) to go through [sth] with a fine-tooth comb.

épluchure /eplyʃyʀ/ *nf* **~s** peelings.

éponge /epɔ̃ʒ/ *nf* **1** sponge; **2** terry-towelling[GB].
IDIOMS **passer l'~** to forget the past.

éponger /epɔ̃ʒe/ [13] *vtr* **1** to mop (up); **2** to absorb [*deficit*]; to pay off [*debts*].

épopée /epɔpe/ *nf* **1** epic; **2** saga.

époque /epɔk/ *nf* **1** time; **vivre avec son ~** to move with the times; **quelle ~!** what's the world coming to!; **à mon ~** in my day; **2** (historical) era; **3 en costume d'~** in period costume; **des meubles d'~** antique furniture.

épouse /epuz/ *nf* wife, spouse.

épouser /epuze/ [1] *vtr* **1** to marry [*person*]; **2** to adopt [*cause, idea*].

épousseter /epuste/ [20] *vtr* to dust.

épouvantable /epuvɑ̃tabl/ *adj* **1** (gen) dreadful; **2** appalling.

épouvantail /epuvɑ̃taj/ *nm* **1** scarecrow; **2**° (ugly person) fright; **3** spectre[GB].

épouvante /epuvɑ̃t/ *nf* **1** terror; **2** horror.

épouvanter /epuvɑ̃te/ [1] *vtr* **1** to terrify; **2** to horrify.

époux /epu/ **I** *nm inv* husband.
II *nm pl* **les ~** the (married) couple.

éprendre: **s'éprendre** /epʀɑ̃dʀ/ [52] *v refl* (+ *v être*) **s'~ de qn** to become enamoured of sb.

épreuve /epʀœv/ *nf* **1** ordeal; **2** test; **mettre à rude ~** to put [sb] to a severe test [*person*]; to be very hard on [*car, shoes*]; to tax [*patience, nerves*]; **à toute ~** unfailing; **l'~ du feu** ordeal by fire; **à l'~ du feu/des balles** fire-/bullet-proof; **3** (part of an) examination; **~ écrite** written examination; **4** (Sport) **~ d'athlétisme** athletics event; **5** (photograph, print) proof.

épris, **~e** /epʀi, iz/ *adj* in love (**de** with).

éprouvant, **~e** /epʀuvɑ̃, ɑ̃t/ *adj* gruelling[GB]; trying.

éprouver /epʀuve/ [1] *vtr* **1** to feel [*regret, love*]; to have [*sensation, difficulty*]; **~ de la jalousie** to be jealous; **2** to test; **3** [*death, event*] to distress [*person*]; [*storm*] to hit [*region*].

éprouvette /epʀuvɛt/ *nf* **1** test tube; **2** sample.

EPS /œpeɛs/ *nf* (*abbr* = **éducation physique et sportive**) PE.

épuisé, **~e** /epɥize/ **I** *pp* ▶ **épuiser**.
II *pp adj* **1** exhausted, worn out; **2** [*publication, livre*] out of print; [*item*] out of stock.

épuisement /epɥizmɑ̃/ *nm* **1** exhaustion; **2 jusqu'à ~ des stocks** while stocks last.

épuiser /epɥize/ [1] **I** *vtr* **1** to exhaust, to wear [sb] out; **2** to exhaust [*subject, mine*].
II s'épuiser *v refl* (+ *v être*) **1** to exhaust oneself; **2** [*stocks, provisions*] to be running out.

épuisette /epɥizɛt/ *nf* **1** landing net; **2** shrimp net.

épuration /epyʀasjɔ̃/ *nf* **1** (of gas, liquid) purification; (of sewage) treatment; **2** purge.

épurer /epyʀe/ [1] *vtr* **1** to purify [*water, gas*]; **2** to purge [*party*]; **3** to expurgate [*text*].

équateur /ekwatœʀ/ *nm* equator.

équation /ekwɑsjɔ̃/ *nf* equation.

équerre /ekɛʀ/ *nf* **1** set square; **en** or **d'~** at right angles; **2** flat angle bracket.

équestre /ekɛstʀ/ *adj* equestrian; **centre ~** riding school.

équilibre /ekilibʀ/ *nm* **1** balance; **être en ~ sur** [*object*] to be balanced on; [*person*] to balance on; **2** equilibrium; **manquer d'~** to be unstable; **retrouver son ~** to get back to normal.

équilibrer /ekilibʀe/ [1] *vtr* to balance.

équilibriste /ekilibʀist/ *nmf* acrobat.

équinoxe /ekinɔks/ *nm* equinox.

équipage /ekipaʒ/ *nm* crew.

équipe /ekip/ *nf* team; crew; shift; **travailler en ~** to work as a team; **~ de tournage** film crew; **l'~ de nuit** the night shift.

équipé, **~e**[1] /ekipe/ **I** *pp* ▶ **équiper**.
II *pp adj* **bien/mal ~** well-/ill-equipped; **cuisine ~e** fitted kitchen.

équipée[2] /ekipe/ *nf* escapade.

équipement /ekipmɑ̃/ *nm* **1** equipment; kit; **2 ~s** facilities.

équiper /ekipe/ [1] **I** *vtr* to equip [*hospital, vehicle*]; to provide [*town*]; to fit out [*person*].
II s'équiper *v refl* (+ *v être*) to equip oneself.

équipier, **-ière** /ekipje, ɛʀ/ *nm,f* **1** team member; **2** crew member.

équitable /ekitabl/ *adj* fair-minded; fair.

équitation /ekitasjɔ̃/ *nf* (horse-)riding.

équité /ekite/ *nf* equity.

équivalence /ekivalɑ̃s/ *nf* **1** equivalence; **2 titre admis en ~** recognized qualification.

équivalent, **~e** /ekivalɑ̃, ɑ̃t/ *adj* **1** equivalent; **2** identical.

équivaloir /ekivalwaʀ/ [45] *v+prep* **~ à** to be equivalent to [*quantity*]; to amount to [*effect*].

équivoque /ekivɔk/ **I** *adj* **1** ambiguous; **2** [*reputation*] dubious; [*behaviour*] questionable.
II *nf* ambiguity; **sans ~** [*reply*] unequivocal; [*condemn*] unequivocally.

érable /eʀabl/ *nm* maple (tree).

érafler /eʀafle/ [1] **I** *vtr* to scratch.
II s'érafler *v refl* (+ *v être*) to scratch oneself.

érailler /eʀɑje/ [1] **s'érailler** *v refl* (+ *v être*) to become hoarse.

ère /ɛʀ/ *nf* **1** era; **en l'an 10 de notre ~** in the year 10 AD; **2** age; **à l'~ atomique** in the nuclear age.

érection /eʀɛksjɔ̃/ *nf* erection.

éreinter° /eʀɛ̃te/ [1] *vtr* to exhaust.

ergot /ɛʀgo/ *nm* **1** (of cock) spur; (of dog) dewclaw; **2** ergot.

ergoter /ɛʀgɔte/ [1] *vi* to split hairs.

ériger /eʀiʒe/ [13] **I** *vtr* to erect [*statue*].
II s'ériger *v refl* (+ *v être*) **s'~ en** to set oneself up as.

ermite /ɛʀmit/ *nm* **1** hermit; **2** recluse.

éroder /eʀɔde/ [1] *vtr* to erode.

érosion /eʀozjɔ̃/ *nf* erosion.

érotique /eʀɔtik/ *adj* erotic.

errance /ɛʀɑ̃s/ *nf* restless wandering.

errant, **~e** /ɛʀɑ̃, ɑ̃t/ *adj* wandering; rootless; **chien ~** stray dog.

errer /ɛʀe/ [1] *vi* [*person, gaze*] to wander; [*animal*] to roam.
erreur /ɛʀœʀ/ *nf* **1** mistake; **~ de jugement** error of judgment; **induire qn en ~** to mislead sb; **sauf ~ de ma part** if I'm not mistaken; **2** (Law) error.
erroné, **~e** /ɛʀɔne/ *adj* incorrect, erroneous.
ersatz /ɛʀzats/ *nm* ersatz.
érudit, **~e** /eʀydi, it/ *nm,f* scholar.
érudition /eʀydisjɔ̃/ *nf* erudition, scholarship.
éruption /eʀypsjɔ̃/ *nf* eruption.
ès /ɛs/ *prep* **licence ~ lettres** ≈ arts degree, B.A. (degree).
escabeau, *pl* **~x** /ɛskabo/ *nm* stepladder.
escadrille /ɛskadʀij/ *nf* squadron.
escadron /ɛskadʀɔ̃/ *nm* (Mil) company; **~ de la mort** death squad.
escalade /ɛskalad/ *nf* **1** (Sport) climbing; ascent; **2** escalation.
escalader /ɛskalade/ [1] *vtr* to scale [*wall*]; to climb [*mountain*].
escale /ɛskal/ *nf* (gen) stopover; (for ship) port of call; **~ technique** (for plane) refuelling[GB] stop; (for ship) overhaul.
escalier /ɛskalje/ *nm* **1** staircase; **2** stairs.
■ **~ mécanique** or **roulant** escalator; **~ de service** backstairs.
escalope /ɛskalɔp/ *nf* escalope.
escamotable /ɛskamɔtabl/ *adj* [*landing gear*] retractable; [*ladder*] foldaway.
escamoter /ɛskamɔte/ [1] *vtr* **1** [*magician*] to make [sth] disappear; **2** to evade [*issue*].
escapade /ɛskapad/ *nf* escapade.
escargot /ɛskaʀgo/ *nm* snail.
escarpé, **~e** /ɛskaʀpe/ *adj* **1** steep; **2** craggy.
escarpement /ɛskaʀpəmɑ̃/ *nm* steep slope.
escarpin /ɛskaʀpɛ̃/ *nm* court shoe (GB), pump (US).
escarre /ɛskaʀ/ *nf* bedsore.
escient /ɛsjɑ̃/ *nm* **à bon ~** wittingly; **à mauvais ~** ill-advisedly.
esclaffer: **s'esclaffer** /ɛsklafe/ [1] *v refl* (+ *v être*) to guffaw.
esclandre /ɛsklɑ̃dʀ/ *nm* scene.
esclavage /ɛsklavaʒ/ *nm* slavery; (figurative) tyranny.
esclave /ɛsklav/ *nmf* slave.
escompte /ɛskɔ̃t/ *nm* discount.
escompter /ɛskɔ̃te/ [1] *vtr* to anticipate; **~ faire** to count on doing, to hope to do.
escorte /ɛskɔʀt/ *nf* escort.
escorter /ɛskɔʀte/ [1] *vtr* to escort.
escrime /ɛskʀim/ *nf* fencing.
escrimer○: **s'escrimer** /ɛskʀime/ [1] *v refl* (+ *v être*) **s'~ à faire** to knock○ oneself out trying to do.
escroc /ɛskʀo/ *nm* swindler, crook.
escroquer /ɛskʀɔke/ [1] *vtr* to swindle.
escroquerie /ɛskʀɔkʀi/ *nf* **1** fraud, swindling; **tentative d'~** attempted fraud; **2** swindle.
ésotérique /ezɔteʀik/ *adj* esoteric.
espace /ɛspas/ *nm* **1** space; **2 ~ de loisirs** leisure complex; **3** gap; **4 en l'~ de** in the space of; **l'~ d'un instant** for a moment.
■ **~ vert** open space; **~ vital** living space.
espacer /ɛspase/ [12] **I** *vtr* to space [sth] out.
II s'espacer *v refl* (+ *v être*) to become less frequent.
espadon /ɛspadɔ̃/ *nm* swordfish.
espadrille /ɛspadʀij/ *nf* espadrille.
Espagne /ɛspaɲ/ *pr nf* Spain.
IDIOMS **bâtir des châteaux en ~** to build castles in the air.
espagnol, **~e** /ɛspaɲɔl/ **I** *adj* Spanish.
II *nm* (language) Spanish.
espalier /ɛspalje/ *nm* **1** espalier; **2** fruit-wall.
espèce /ɛspɛs/ **I** *nf* **1** species; **l'~ humaine** mankind; **2** kind.
II espèces *nf pl* **en ~s** in cash.
espérance /ɛspeʀɑ̃s/ *nf* hope; **~ de vie** life expectancy.
espérer /ɛspeʀe/ [14] **I** *vtr* **1 ~ qch** to hope for sth; **2** to expect; **je n'en espérais pas tant** it's more than I expected.
II *vi* to hope.
espiègle /ɛspjɛgl/ *adj* mischievous.
espion, **-ionne** /ɛspjɔ̃, ɔn/ *nm,f* spy.
espionnage /ɛspjɔnaʒ/ *nm* espionage, spying.
espionner /ɛspjɔne/ [1] *vtr* to spy on.
esplanade /ɛsplanad/ *nf* esplanade.
espoir /ɛspwaʀ/ *nm* hope; **reprendre ~** to feel hopeful again; **avec ~** hopefully.
esprit /ɛspʀi/ *nm* **1** mind; **avoir l'~ mal placé** to have a dirty mind○; **avoir un ~ de synthèse** to be good at synthesizing information; **avoir l'~ de contradiction** to be contrary; **dans mon ~ c'était facile** the way I saw it, it was easy; **cela ne t'est jamais venu à l'~?** didn't it ever occur to you?; **avoir l'~ ailleurs** to be miles away; **les choses de l'~** spiritual matters; **2** wit; **faire de l'~** to try to be witty; **~ d'à-propos** ready wit; **3 dans un ~ de vengeance** in a spirit of revenge; **ils ont l'~ de famille** they're a very close family; **4 l'un des plus grands ~s de son temps** one of the greatest minds of his/her time; **calmer les ~s** to calm people down; **les ~s sont échauffés** feelings are running high; **5** spirit; **croire aux ~s** to believe in ghosts.
■ **~ de corps** solidarity; **~ d'équipe** team spirit.
IDIOMS **perdre ses ~s** to faint; **les grands ~s se rencontrent** great minds think alike.
esquimau, **-aude**, *mpl* **~x** /ɛskimo, od/ **I** *adj* Eskimo; **chien ~** husky.
II *nm* **1** Eskimo; **2** ®chocolate-covered ice lolly (GB), ice-cream bar (US).
esquinter○ /ɛskɛ̃te/ [1] *vtr* to damage.
esquisse /ɛskis/ *nf* **1** sketch; **2** outline.
esquisser /ɛskise/ [1] *vtr* to sketch [*portrait*]; to outline [*programme*].
esquiver /ɛskive/ [1] **I** *vtr* to dodge, to duck [*blow*]; to sidestep [*issue*].
II s'esquiver *v refl* (+ *v être*) to slip away.
essai /esɛ/ **I** *nm* **1** (Tech, Med) trial; test; **être à l'~** to undergo trials; to be tested; **~ sur**

route road test; **2** try, attempt; **un coup d'~** a try; **prendre qn à l'~** to give sb a try-out; **3** essay; **4** (in rugby) try.
II **essais** *nm pl* (Aut) (Sport) qualifying round.

essaim /esɛ̃/ *nm* swarm.

essayage /esɛjaʒ/ *nm* fitting.

essayer /eseje/ [21] I *vtr* **1** to try; **~ sa force** to test one's strength; **2** to test [*weapon, product*]; to run trials on [*car*]; **3** to try on [*clothes*]; to try [*size, colour*]; to try out [*car*].
II *vi* to try; **~ à la poste** to try the post office; **j'essaierai que tout se passe bien** I'll try to make sure everything goes all right.
III **s'essayer** *v refl* (+ *v être*) **s'~ à** to have a go at, to try one's hand at.

essence /esɑ̃s/ *nf* **1** petrol (GB), gasoline (US); **2** essential oil; **3** tree species.
■ **~ à briquet** lighter fuel (GB), lighter fluid (US); **~ ordinaire** ≈ 2-star petrol (GB), regular gasoline (US); **~ sans plomb** unleaded (petrol) (GB), unleaded gasoline (US); **~ super** ≈ 4-star petrol (GB), premium gasoline (US).

essentiel, **-ielle** /esɑ̃sjɛl/ I *adj* essential.
II *nm* **c'est l'~** that's the main thing; **aller à l'~** to get to the heart of the matter; **l'~ des voix** the bulk of the vote; **pour l'~** mainly; **en voyage je n'emporte que l'~** when I travel I only take the bare essentials.

essentiellement /esɑ̃sjɛlmɑ̃/ *adv* **1** mainly; **2** essentially.

essieu, *pl* **~x** /esjø/ *nm* axle.

essor /esɔʀ/ *nm* (of technology, area) development; **être en plein ~** to be booming.

essorer /esɔʀe/ [1] *vtr* **1** to wring; **2** to spin-dry [*washing*]; to spin [*lettuce*].

essoufflement /esufləmɑ̃/ *nm* breathlessness; (figurative) loss of impetus.

essouffler /esufle/ [1] I *vtr* to leave [sb] breathless; **être essoufflé** to be out of breath.
II **s'essouffler** *v refl* (+ *v être*) **1** to get breathless; **2** to run out of steam.

essuie-glace, *pl* **~s** /esɥiglas/ *nm* windscreen wiper (GB), windshield wiper (US).

essuie-mains /esɥimɛ̃/ *nm inv* hand towel.

essuyer /esɥije/ [22] I *vtr* **1** to dry [*glass, hands*]; to wipe [*table*]; **~ la vaisselle** to dry up; **~ ses larmes** to wipe away one's tears; **2** to suffer [*defeat, losses*]; to meet with [*failure*].
II **s'essuyer** *v refl* (+ *v être*) to dry oneself; **s'~ les mains** to dry one's hands.

est /ɛst/ I *adj inv* east; eastern.
II *nm* **1** east; **un vent d'~** an easterly wind; **2 l'Est** the East; **de l'Est** eastern.

estafette® /ɛstafɛt/ *nf* van.

estampe /ɛstɑ̃p/ *nf* **1** engraving; **2** print.

esthète /ɛstɛt/ *nmf* aesthete.

esthéticienne /ɛstetisjɛn/ *nf* beautician.

esthétique /ɛstetik/ I *adj* aesthetic; [*decor*] aesthetically pleasing; [*pose*] graceful.
II *nf* aesthetics.

estimation /ɛstimasjɔ̃/ *nf* estimate; valuation.

estime /ɛstim/ *nf* respect.

estimer /ɛstime/ [1] *vtr* **1** to feel; **~ nécessaire de faire** to consider it necessary to do; **2** to think highly of [*friend, artist*]; **3** to value [*painting*]; to assess [*damage*]; **une vitesse estimée à 150 km/h** an estimated speed of 150 kph; **4** to reckon.

estival, **~e**, *mpl* **-aux** /ɛstival, o/ *adj* **1** summer; **2** summery.

estivant, **~e** /ɛstivɑ̃, ɑ̃t/ *nm,f* summer visitor.

estomac /ɛstɔma/ *nm* stomach; **avoir l'~ bien accroché** to have a strong stomach.
IDIOMS **avoir l'~ dans les talons**○ to be famished.

estomper /ɛstɔ̃pe/ [1] I *vtr* to blur [*shape*]; to gloss over [*details*].
II **s'estomper** *v refl* (+ *v être*) [*landscape*] to become blurred; [*hatred, memories*] to fade.

estrade /ɛstʀad/ *nf* platform.

estragon /ɛstʀagɔ̃/ *nm* tarragon.

estropié, **~e** /ɛstʀɔpje/*nm,f* cripple.

estropier /ɛstʀɔpje/ [2] I *vtr* to maim.
II **s'estropier** *v refl* (+ *v être*) to maim oneself.

estuaire /ɛstɥɛʀ/ *nm* estuary.

esturgeon /ɛstyʀʒɔ̃/ *nm* sturgeon.

et /e/ *conj* and; **~ voilà qu'il sort un couteau de sa poche!** and next thing he whips a knife out of his pocket!; **~ alors?** so what?

étable /etabl/ *nf* cowshed.

établi, **~e** /etabli/ I *pp* ▶ **établir**.
II *pp adj* **1** [*reputation, use*] established; **2** [*power, regime*] ruling; [*order*] established.
III *nm* workbench.

établir /etabliʀ/ [3] I *vtr* **1** to set up [*home*]; **2** to establish [*rule, link, reputation, innocence, fact*]; to introduce [*tax, discipline*]; to set [*record, standard*]; **3** to draw up [*list, plan, budget, file*]; to make out [*cheque, bill*]; to prepare [*quote*]; to make [*diagnosis*]; to draw [*parallel*].
II **s'établir** *v refl* (+ *v être*) **1** [*person*] to settle (**à, en** in); **s'~ à son compte** to set up one's own business; **2** [*links*] to develop.

établissement /etablismɑ̃/ *nm* **1** organization; **~ bancaire** banking institution; **2** (of relations, regime) establishment; (of tax, sanctions) introduction; **3** premises.
■ **~ scolaire** school.

étage /etaʒ/ *nm* **1** floor; **le premier ~** the first floor (GB), the second floor (US); **à l'~** upstairs; **2** (of tower) level; (of aquaduct, cake) tier.

étagère /etaʒɛʀ/ *nf* shelf.

étain /etɛ̃/ *nm* **1** tin; **2** pewter.

étal /etal/ *nm* **1** (market) stall; **2** butcher's block.

étalage /etalaʒ/ *nm* **1** window display; **2** display; **faire ~ de ses connaissances** to flaunt one's knowledge.

étalagiste /etalaʒist/ *nmf* window dresser.

étalement /etalmɑ̃/ *nm* (of holidays) staggering; (of payments) spreading.

étaler /etale/ [1] I *vtr* **1** to spread out [*sheet*]; to roll [sth] out [*pastry*]; **2** to scatter; **3** to spread [*butter, glue*]; to apply [*paint, ointment*]; **4** to spread [*work, payments*]; to stagger [*departures*]; **5** to flaunt [*wealth, knowledge*]; to display [*merchandise*]; **~ qch au grand jour** to bring sth out into the open.

II **s'étaler** *v refl* (+ *v être*) **1** [*butter, paint*] to spread; **2** [*person*] to sprawl, to spread out; **3**○ **s'~ de tout son long** to fall flat on one's face; **se faire ~ à un examen** to fail an exam.

étalon /etalɔ̃/ *nm* **1** stallion; **2** standard.

étalon-or /etalɔ̃ɔʀ/ *nm inv* gold standard.

étamine /etamin/ *nf* stamen.

étanche /etɑ̃ʃ/ *adj* **~ (à l'eau)** waterproof; watertight; **~ (à l'air)** airtight.

étanchéité /etɑ̃ʃeite/ *nf* waterproofness; watertightness; airtightness.

étancher /etɑ̃ʃe/ [1] *vtr* to quench [*thirst*].

étang /etɑ̃/ *nm* pond.

étant ▶ **donné III.**

étape /etap/ *nf* **1** stop; **2** (in journey) stage; (in race) leg; **3** (figurative) stage, step; **brûler les ~s** to go too far too fast.

état /eta/ I *nm* **1** condition; **mettre qn hors d'~ de nuire** to put sb out of harm's way; **leur ~ de santé est excellent** they're in excellent health; **maintenir qch en ~ de marche** to keep sth in working order; **hors d'~ de marche** [*car*] off the road; [*machine*] out of order; **j'ai laissé les choses en l'~** I left everything as it was; **2** state; **être dans un drôle○ d'~** to be in a hell of a state○; **être dans un ~ second** to be in a trance; **ce n'est encore qu'à l'~ de projet** it's still only at the planning stage; **3** statement.

II **faire ~ de** *phr* **1** to cite [*document*]; **2** to mention [*conversation*]; **3** to state [*preferences*]; **4** to make a point of mentioning [*success*].

■ **~ d'âme** qualm; feeling; **~ civil** registry office (GB); civil status; **~ d'esprit** state of mind; **~ de fait** fact; **~ des lieux** inventory and report on state of repair; **~s de service** service record.

IDIOMS **être/se mettre dans tous ses ~s**○ to be in/to get into a state○.

État /eta/ *nm* **1** state, State; **2** state, government.

étatique /etatik/ *adj* state (GB), public (US).

état-major, *pl* **états-majors** /etamaʒɔʀ/ *nm* **1** (Mil) staff; **2** headquarters.

États-Unis /etazyni/ *pr nm pl* **~ (d'Amérique)** United States (of America).

étau, *pl* **~x** /eto/ *nm* vice (GB), vise (US); (figurative) **l'~ se resserre** the net is tightening.

étayer /eteje/ [21] *vtr* **1** to prop up; **2** (figurative) to support [*theory*].

été /ete/ *nm* summer.

éteindre /etɛ̃dʀ/ [55] I *vtr* **1** to put out [*fire, cigarette*]; to blow out [*candle*]; **2** to switch off [*light, TV, oven*]; to turn off [*gas*].

II **s'éteindre** *v refl* (+ *v être*) **1** [*cigarette, fire, light*] to go out; [*radio*] to go off; **2** (euphemistic) to pass away or on; **3** [*desire, passion*] to fade.

éteint, **~e** /etɛ̃, ɛ̃t/ I *pp* ▶ **éteindre**.

II *pp adj* **1** [*gaze*] dull; **2** [*volcano*] extinct; [*star*] extinct, dead.

étendard /etɑ̃daʀ/ *nm* standard, flag.

étendre /etɑ̃dʀ/ [6] I *vtr* **1** to stretch [*arms, legs*]; **2** to spread (out) [*cloth*]; **~ le linge** to hang out the washing; **3** to extend [*embargo*].

II **s'étendre** *v refl* (+ *v être*) **1** [*land, forest*] to stretch; **2** [*strike, epidemic*] to spread; [*town*] to expand, to grow; **3** [*law, measure*] **s'~ à** to apply to; **4** [*period, work*] to stretch, to last; **5** to lie down; **6 s'~ sur** to dwell on.

étendu, **~e**[1] /etɑ̃dy/ I *pp* ▶ **étendre**.

II *pp adj* [*city*] sprawling; [*region, plain*] vast; [*vocabulary, knowledge, damage*] extensive.

étendue[2] /etɑ̃dy/ *nf* **1** expanse; **2** size; **3** scale, extent; range.

éternel, **-elle** /etɛʀnɛl/ *adj* endless; eternal.

éternellement /etɛʀnɛlmɑ̃/ *adv* **1** forever; **2** permanently; **3** perpetually; **4** eternally.

éterniser: **s'éterniser** /etɛʀnize/ [1] *v refl* (+ *v être*) to drag on; [*visitor*] to stay for ages○.

éternité /etɛʀnite/ *nf* eternity.

éternuer /etɛʀnɥe/ [1] *vi* to sneeze.

éther /etɛʀ/ *nm* ether.

éthique /etik/ I *adj* ethical.

II *nf* **1** ethics; **2** code of ethics.

ethnie /ɛtni/ *nf* ethnic group.

ethnique /ɛtnik/ *adj* ethnic.

ethnologie /ɛtnɔlɔʒi/ *nf* ethnology.

éthylique /etilik/ *adj, nmf* alcoholic.

étincelant, **~e** /etɛ̃slɑ̃, ɑ̃t/ *adj* [*sun*] blazing; [*star*] twinkling; [*gemstone, glass*] sparkling; [*feathers, colour*] brilliant.

étinceler /etɛ̃sle/ [19] *vi* to twinkle; to sparkle.

étincelle /etɛ̃sɛl/ *nf* spark; **jeter des ~s** to glitter; **faire des ~s** to do brilliantly.

étioler: **s'étioler** /etjɔle/ [1] *v refl* (+ *v être*) to wilt.

étiqueter /etikte/ [20] *vtr* to label.

étiquette /etikɛt/ *nf* **1** label; **2** tag; **porter une ~** to be labelled[GB]; **candidat sans ~** independent candidate; **3** etiquette.

étirer /etiʀe/ [1] I *vtr* to stretch.

II **s'étirer** *v refl* (+ *v être*) **1** [*person*] to stretch; **2** [*procession, road*] to stretch out.

étoffe /etɔf/ *nf* **1** fabric; **2** (figurative) substance; **avoir l'~ d'un grand homme** to have the makings of a great man.

étoffer /etɔfe/ [1] I *vtr* to expand.

II **s'étoffer** *v refl* (+ *v être*) to put on weight.

étoile /etwal/ *nf* star.

■ **~ filante** shooting star; **~ de mer** starfish; **~ polaire** Pole Star.

IDIOMS **coucher** or **dormir à la belle ~** to sleep out in the open.

étoilé, **~e** /etwale/ *adj* **1** starry; **2** [*glass, windscreen*] crazed.

étole /etɔl/ *nf* stole.

étonnant, **~e** /etɔnɑ̃, ɑ̃t/ *adj* **1** surprising; **2** amazing.

étonnement /etɔnmɑ̃/ *nm* surprise.

étonner /etɔne/ [1] I *vtr* to surprise.

II **s'étonner** *v refl* (+ *v être*) to be surprised.

étouffant, **~e** /etufɑ̃, ɑ̃t/ *adj* **1** stifling; **2** oppressive.

étouffé, **~e** /etufe/ *adj* **1** [*sound, voice*] muffled; **2** [*sob*] choked; [*laughter*] suppressed.

étouffement /etufmɑ̃/ *nm* asphyxiation.

étouffer /etufe/ [1] **I** *vtr* **1** to suppress [*protest*]; **2** to hush up [*scandal*]; **3** to suffocate [*person*]; to choke [*plant*]; **la générosité ne les étouffe pas** generosity is not their middle name; **4** to smother [*fire*]; **5** to stifle [*yawn*]; to hold back [*sigh*]; **6** to deaden [*noise*].
II *vi* to feel stifled; **on étouffe ici**○! it's stifling in here!; **mourir étouffé** to die of suffocation.
III **s'étouffer** *v refl* (+ *v être*) to choke.

étourdi, **~e** /eturdi/ *adj* **1** absent-minded; **2** unthinking.

étourdir /eturdir/ [3] **I** *vtr* **1** to stun, to daze; **2 ~ qn** [*noise*] to make sb's head spin.
II **s'étourdir** *v refl* (+ *v être*) **s'~ de paroles** to become intoxicated with words.

étourdissant, **~e** /eturdisɑ̃, ɑ̃t/ *adj* [*noise*] deafening; [*speed*] dizzying.

étourdissement /eturdismɑ̃/ *nm* **avoir un ~** to feel dizzy.

étrange /etrɑ̃ʒ/ **I** *adj* strange; **chose ~ elle n'a pas répondu** strangely enough she didn't answer.
II *nm* **1** strangeness; **2 l'~** the bizarre.

étrangement /etrɑ̃ʒmɑ̃/ *adv* **1** curiously; **vous me rappelez ~ un ami** it's strange but you remind me of a friend; **2** surprisingly.

étranger, **-ère** /etrɑ̃ʒe, ɛr/ **I** *adj* **1** foreign; **2 ~ à** [*person*] not involved in [*case*]; outside [*group*]; [*fact*] with no bearing on [*problem*]; **se sentir ~** to feel like an outsider; **3** unfamiliar.
II *nm,f* **1** foreigner; **2** outsider; **3** stranger.
III *nm* **à l'~** abroad.

étranglé, **~e** /etrɑ̃gle/ *adj* **1** [*voice*] choked; [*sound*] muffled; **2** [*street*] narrow.

étranglement /etrɑ̃gləmɑ̃/ *nm* **1** strangulation; **2** (of road, valley) narrow section.

étrangler /etrɑ̃gle/ [1] **I** *vtr* **1** to strangle; **2** to choke.
II **s'étrangler** *v refl* (+ *v être*) **1** to strangle oneself; **2** to choke.

étrangleur, **-euse** /etrɑ̃glœr, øz/ *nm,f* strangler.

être[1] /ɛtr/ [7] *vi* (+ *v avoir*)

■ **Note** You will find translations for fixed phrases using *être* such as *être en train de*, *être sur le point de*, *quoi qu'il en soit*, *étant donné* etc, at the entries ***train***, ***point***, ***quoi***, ***donné*** etc.

1 to be; **nous sommes pauvres** we are poor; **2** (as auxiliary verb) **elles sont tombées** they have fallen; they fell; **elle s'était vengée** she took her revenge; she had taken her revenge; **3** (to go) **je n'ai jamais été en Chine** I've never been to China; **4** (with *ce*) **est-ce leur voiture?** is it their car?; **c'est grave?** is it serious?; **qui est-ce?** who is he/she?; who is that?; who is it?; **est-ce que tu parles russe?** do you speak Russian?; **qu'est-ce que c'est?** what is it?; **ce sont mes enfants** these are my children; they are my children; **c'est cela** that's right; **c'est à Pierre/lui de choisir** it's Pierre's/his turn to choose; it's up to Pierre/to him to choose; **il aurait pu s'excuser, ne serait-ce qu'en envoyant un mot** he could have apologized if only by sending a note; **5** (with *il*) **il est facile de critiquer** it is easy to criticize; **il n'est pas jusqu'à l'Antarctique qui ne soit pollué** even the Antarctic is polluted; **il n'en est rien** this isn't at all the case; **6** (with *en*) **où en étais-je?** where was I?; **je ne sais plus où j'en suis** I'm lost; **'où en es-tu de tes recherches?'—'j'en suis à mi-chemin'** 'how far have you got in your research?'—'I'm halfway through'; **j'en suis à me demander si...** I'm beginning to wonder whether...; **~ en uniforme** to be wearing a uniform; **7** (with *y*) **j'y suis** I'm with you, I get it○; **je n'y suis pas** I don't get it○; **nous partons, vous y êtes?** we're leaving, do you understand?; we're leaving, are you ready?; **8** (with *à* and *de*) **ce livre est à moi/à mon frère** this book is mine/my brother's; **à qui est ce chien?** whose dog is this?; **je suis à vous tout de suite** I'll be with you right away; **je suis à vous** I'm all yours; **~ à ce qu'on fait** to have one's mind on what one is doing; **elle est d'un ridicule!** she's so ridiculous!

être[2] /ɛtr/ *nm* **1 ~ humain** human being; **les ~s animés et inanimés** animate and inanimate things; **un ~ sans défense** a defenceless[GB] creature; **2** person; **un ~ cher** a loved one; **3 de tout son ~** with one's whole being; **blessé au plus profond de son ~** hurt to the core.

étreindre /etrɛ̃dr/ [55] *vtr* to embrace, to hug [*friend*]; to clasp [*opponent*].

étreinte /etrɛ̃t/ *nf* embrace; grip.

étrenner /etrene/ [1] *vtr* to use [sth] for the first time.

étrennes /etrɛn/ *nf pl* **1** gift; **2** money.

étrier /etrije/ *nm* stirrup.
IDIOMS **mettre à qn le pied à l'~** (figurative) to get sb started.

étriper○ /etripe/ [1] *vtr* (figurative) **~ qn** to skin sb alive.

étriqué, **~e** /etrike/ *adj* [*jacket*] skimpy; [*life*] restricted.

étroit, **~e** /etrwa, at/ **I** *adj* **1** narrow; **avoir l'esprit ~** to be narrow-minded; **2** [*links*] close; **en ~e collaboration** closely.
II **à l'étroit** *phr* **nous sommes un peu à l'~** we're a bit cramped; **je me sens un peu à l'~ dans cette jupe** this skirt feels a bit too tight.

étroitement /etrwatmɑ̃/ *adv* closely.

étroitesse /etrwatɛs/ *nf* narrowness.

étude /etyd/ **I** *nf* **1** study; **2** survey; **3 (mise à l')~** consideration; **à l'~** under consideration; **4** (of lawyer) office; **5** (Sch) study room (GB), study hall (US); **6** study period.
II **études** *nf pl* studies; **faire des ~s** to be a student; **je n'ai pas fait d'~s (supérieures)** I didn't go to university or college.
■ **~ de marché** market research.

étudiant, **~e** /etydjɑ̃, ɑ̃t/ *nm,f* student.

étudier /etydje/ [2] I *vtr* to study; to examine [*file, situation*]; to learn [*lesson*].
II *vi* **1** to be a student; **2** to be studying.

étui /etɥi/ *nm* case; **~ à revolver** holster.

étuve /etyv/ *nf* **1** steam room; **le grenier est une ~** (figurative) the attic is like an oven; **2** incubator.

étymologie /etimɔlɔʒi/ *nf* etymology.

eucalyptus /økaliptys/ *nm inv* eucalyptus.

eucharistie /økaʀisti/ *nf* **1** Eucharist; **2** Sacrament.

eunuque /ønyk/ *nm* eunuch.

euphémisme /øfemism/ *nm* euphemism.

euphorie /øfɔʀi/ *nf* euphoria.

euphorique /øfɔʀik/ *adj* euphoric.

euphorisant, **~e** /øfɔʀizɑ̃, ɑ̃t/ I *adj* stimulating; uplifting; euphoriant.
II *nm* (Med) stimulant.

eurasien, **-ienne** /øʀazjɛ̃, ɛn/ *adj* Eurasian.

euromarché /øʀomaʀʃe/ *nm* Euromarket.

Europe /øʀɔp/ *pr nf* Europe; **l'~ communautaire** the European community.

européen, **-éenne** /øʀɔpeɛ̃, ɛn/ *adj* European.

Eurotunnel /øʀotynɛl/ *nm* Eurotunnel.

euthanasie /øtanazi/ *nf* euthanasia.

eux /ø/ *pron* **1** they; **je sais que ce n'est pas ~ qui ont fait ça** I know they weren't the ones who did it; **2** them; **les inviter, ~, quelle idée!** invite THEM, what an idea!; **c'est à ~** it's theirs.

eux-mêmes /ømɛm/ *pron* themselves; **les experts ~ reconnaissent que...** even the experts admit that...

évacuation /evakɥasjɔ̃/ *nf* **1** evacuation; **2** discharge; **il y a un problème d'~ de l'eau** the water doesn't drain away.

évacuer /evakɥe/ [1] *vtr* **1** to evacuate; **2** to drain off; **3** (figurative) to shrug off [*problem*].

évader: **s'évader** /evade/ [1] *v refl* (+ *v être*) **1** to escape; **faire ~ qn** to help sb to escape; **2** (figurative) to get away (**de** from).

évaluation /evalɥasjɔ̃/ *nf* **1** (of collection, house) valuation; **faire l'~ de** to value; **2** (of costs, damages) assessment; estimate, appraisal (US); **3** (of staff) appraisal.

évaluer /evalɥe/ [1] *vtr* **1** to estimate [*size, length*]; to assess [*risks, costs*]; **2** to value [*inheritance*]; **3** to assess [*employee, student*].

Évangile /evɑ̃ʒil/ *nm* Gospel.

évanouir: **s'évanouir** /evanwiʀ/ [3] *v refl* (+ *v être*) **1** to faint; **2** [*feeling*] to fade.

évanouissement /evanwismɑ̃/ *nm* **1** blackout, fainting fit; **2** fading.

évaporation /evapɔʀasjɔ̃/ *nf* evaporation.

évaporer: **s'évaporer** /evapɔʀe/ [1] *v refl* (+ *v être*) **1** to evaporate; **2**° to vanish.

évaser /evaze/ [1] I *vtr* to flare.
II **s'évaser** *v refl* (+ *v être*) [*duct*] to open out; [*skirt*] to be flared.

évasif, **-ive** /evazif, iv/ *adj* evasive.

évasion /evazjɔ̃/ *nf* escape.

Ève /ɛv/ *pr nf* Eve; **en tenue d'~** in her birthday suit.
IDIOMS **elle ne le connaît ni d'~ ni d'Adam** she doesn't know him from Adam.

évêché /eveʃe/ *nm* **1** diocese; **2** bishop's palace.

éveil /evɛj/ *nm* awakening.

éveiller /eveje/ [1] I *vtr* **1** to arouse [*curiosity, suspicions*]; to stimulate [*intelligence*]; to awaken [*conscience*]; **un enfant éveillé** a bright child; **2** to wake (up) [*sleeper*]; **être éveillé** to be awake.
II **s'éveiller** *v refl* (+ *v être*) **1** to wake up; **2** [*imagination*] to start to develop.

événement /evenmɑ̃/ *nm* event.

éventail /evɑ̃taj/ *nm* **1** fan; **2** range.

éventaire /evɑ̃tɛʀ/ *nm* stall.

éventer: **s'éventer** /evɑ̃te/ [1] *v refl* (+ *v être*) [*perfume, coffee*] to go off; [*wine*] to pass its best; [*beer, lemonade*] to go flat.

éventrer /evɑ̃tʀe/ [1] *vtr* **1** [*person*] to disembowel; [*bull*] to gore; **2** to rip open.

éventualité /evɑ̃tɥalite/ *nf* **1** eventuality; **2** possibility; **dans l'~ de** in the event of.

éventuel, **-elle** /evɑ̃tɥɛl/ *adj* possible.

éventuellement /evɑ̃tɥɛlmɑ̃/ *adv* **1** possibly; **2** if necessary.

évêque /evɛk/ *nm* bishop (**de** of).

évertuer: **s'évertuer** /evɛʀtɥe/ [1] *v refl* (+ *v être*) to try one's best (**à faire** to do).

éviction /eviksjɔ̃/ *nf* **1** ousting (**de** from); **2** (Law) eviction.

évidemment /evidamɑ̃/ *adv* of course.

évidence /evidɑ̃s/ I *nf* **1** obviousness; **2** obvious fact; **se rendre à l'~** to face the facts; **de toute ~, à l'~** obviously.
II **en évidence** *phr* **laisser qch en ~** to leave sth in an obvious place; **mettre en ~** to highlight [*feature*].

évident, **~e** /evidɑ̃, ɑ̃t/ *adj* obvious; **ce n'est pas ~**° not necessarily; it's not so easy.

évier /evje/ *nm* sink.

évincer /evɛ̃se/ [12] *vtr* to oust [*rival*].

éviter /evite/ [1] *vtr* **1** to avoid; **~ à qn de faire** to save sb (from) doing; **2** to dodge [*bullet, blow*].

évocation /evɔkasjɔ̃/ *nf* **1** evocation; reminiscence; **2** mention (**de** of).

évolué, **~e** /evɔlɥe/ *adj* **1** civilized; **2** evolved.

évoluer /evɔlɥe/ [1] *vi* **1** to evolve, to change; **2** to develop; **3** to glide.

évolutif, **-ive** /evɔlytif, iv/ *adj* progressive.

évolution /evɔlysjɔ̃/ *nf* **1** evolution; **2** development; **3** progress; **4** progression; **5** change; **en pleine ~** undergoing rapid change.

évoquer /evɔke/ [1] *vtr* **1** to recall; **2** to mention, to bring up; **3** to bring back [*memory*]; to be reminiscent of [*childhood*]; **4** to evoke.

ex /ɛks/ *nm* **1** (*written abbr* = **exemple**) eg; **2** (*written abbr* = **exemplaire**) copy.

ex- /ɛks/ *pref* **~champion** former champion.

exacerber /ɛgzasɛʀbe/ [1] *vtr* to exacerbate.

exact, **~e** /ɛgza(kt), akt/ *adj* **1** correct; **2** accurate; **3** exact; **4** punctual.

exactement /ɛgzaktəmɑ̃/ *adv* exactly.

exactitude /ɛgzaktityd/ *nf* **1** correctness; **2** accuracy; **3** exactness; **4** punctuality.

ex æquo /ɛgzeko/ *adv* **ils sont premiers ~** they've tied for first place.

exagéré, **~e** /ɛgzaʒeʀe/ *adj* **1** exaggerated; **2** excessive; **d'une sensibilité ~e** oversensitive.

exagérément /ɛgzaʒeʀemɑ̃/ *adv* excessively.

exagérer /ɛgzaʒeʀe/ [14] **I** *vtr* to exaggerate.
II *vi* to go too far.

exaltant, **~e** /ɛgzaltɑ̃, ɑ̃t/ *adj* thrilling; inspiring.

exaltation /ɛgzaltasjɔ̃/ *nf* **1** elation; **2** stimulation; **3** glorification.

exalté, **~e** /ɛgzalte/ **I** *pp* ▶ **exalter**.
II *pp adj* impassioned.

exalter /ɛgzalte/ [1] *vtr* **1** to glorify; **2** to heighten; **3** to elate, to thrill.

examen /ɛgzamɛ̃/ *nm* **1** (Sch, Univ) examination, exam; **passer un ~** to take an exam; **~ de rattrapage** retake, resit (GB); **2** (Med) examination; **3** examination; consideration; review; **être en cours d'~** to be under review; to be under consideration; **4** inspection.
■ **~ blanc** mock (exam), practice exam; **~ de conscience** self-examination.

examinateur, **-trice** /ɛgzaminatœʀ, tʀis/ *nm,f* examiner.

examiner /ɛgzamine/ [1] *vtr* **1** to examine; to review; **~ qch de près** to have a close look at sth; **2** (Med) to examine [*patient, wound*].

exaspération /ɛgzaspeʀasjɔ̃/ *nf* **1** exasperation; **2** intensification.

exaspérer /ɛgzaspeʀe/ [14] *vtr* **1** to exasperate, to infuriate; **2** to exacerbate.

exaucer /ɛgzose/ [12] *vtr* to grant.

excavatrice /ɛkskavatʀis/ *nf* excavator.

excédent /ɛksedɑ̃/ *nm* surplus; **~ de bagages** excess baggage.

excéder /eksede/ [14] *vtr* **1** to exceed; **2** to infuriate.

excellence /ɛksɛlɑ̃s/ *nf* excellence.

Excellence /ɛksɛlɑ̃s/ *nf* **Son ~** His/Her Excellency.

excellent, **~e** /ɛksɛlɑ̃, ɑ̃t/ *adj* excellent.

exceller /ɛksele/ [1] *vi* to excel.

excentré, **~e** /ɛksɑ̃tʀe/ *adj* **1** [*area*] outlying; **2 être ~** [*axis*] to be off-centre[GB].

excentricité /ɛksɑ̃tʀisite/ *nf* eccentricity.

excentrique /ɛksɑ̃tʀik/ *adj*, *nmf* eccentric.

excepté, **~e** /ɛksɛpte/ **I** *pp* ▶ **excepter**.
II *prep* except.
III excepté que *phr* except that.

excepter /ɛksɛpte/ [1] *vtr* **si l'on excepte** except for, apart from.

exception /ɛksɛpsjɔ̃/ *nf* exception; **faire ~** to be an exception; **à l'~ de**, **~ faite de** except for; **sauf ~** with the occasional exception; **d'~** [*person*] exceptional; [*law*] emergency.

exceptionnel, **-elle** /ɛksɛpsjɔnɛl/ *adj* (gen) exceptional; [*price*] bargain; [*meeting*] extraordinary.

exceptionnellement /ɛksɛpsjɔnɛlmɑ̃/ *adv* exceptionally.

excès /ɛksɛ/ *nm inv* excess; **commettre des ~** to go too far; **des ~ de langage** bad language; **tomber dans l'~ inverse** to go to the opposite extreme; **~ de confiance/zèle** overconfidence/overzealousness.
■ **~ de vitesse** speeding.

excessif, **-ive** /ɛksesif, iv/ *adj* **1** excessive **2** extreme; **il est ~** he is a man of extremes.

excision /ɛksizjɔ̃/ *nf* **1** excision; **2** female circumcision.

excitant, **~e** /ɛksitɑ̃, ɑ̃t/ **I** *adj* **1** [*substance*] stimulating; **2** exciting; thrilling.
II *nm* stimulant.

excitation /ɛksitasjɔ̃/ *nf* **1** excitement; **2** arousal; **3** stimulation.

excité, **~e** /ɛksite/ **I** *adj* **1** [*crowd*] in a frenzy [*atmosphere*] frenzied; **2** [*person*] thrilled excited; **3** (sexually) aroused.
II *nm,f* **1** rowdy; **2** fanatic; **3** neurotic.
IDIOMS **être ~ comme une puce**○ to be like a cat on a hot tin roof.

exciter /ɛksite/ [1] **I** *vtr* **1** to arouse [*anger*]; to kindle [*desire*]; **2** to thrill; **3** to arouse; **4** to tease [*animal*]; to get [sb] excited [*child*]; [*coffee*] to get [sb] hyped up; **5** to stimulate [*palate*].
II s'exciter *v refl* (+ *v être*) to get excited.

exclamatif, **-ive** /ɛksklamatif, iv/ *adj* exclamatory.

exclamation /ɛksklamasjɔ̃/ *nf* exclamation.

exclamer: **s'exclamer** /ɛksklame/ [1] *v refl* (+ *v être*) to exclaim.

exclu, **~e** /ɛkskly/ **I** *pp* ▶ **exclure**.
II *pp adj* excluded; **c'est exclu!** it's out of the question!; **se sentir ~** to feel left out.

exclure /ɛksklyʀ/ [78] *vtr* **1** to exclude [*person*] to rule out [*possibility*]; **2** to expel [*member*].

exclusif, **-ive** /ɛksklyzif, iv/ *adj* exclusive; **concessionaire ~** sole agent.

exclusion /ɛksklyzjɔ̃/ **I** *nf* **1** exclusion; **2** expulsion; **3** suspension.
II à l'exclusion de *phr* with the exception of.

exclusivité /ɛksklyzivite/ *nf* exclusive rights; **en ~** [*publish*] exclusively; [*product*] exclusive.

excommunier /ɛkskɔmynje/ [2] *vtr* to excommunicate.

excrément /ɛkskʀemɑ̃/ *nm* excrement.

excrétion /ɛkskʀesjɔ̃/ *nf* excretion.

excroissance /ɛkskʀwasɑ̃s/ *nf* **1** (Med) growth, excrescence; **2** (in botany) outgrowth.

excursion /ɛkskyʀsjɔ̃/ *nf* excursion, trip.

excuse /ɛkskyz/ *nf* **1** excuse; **2** apology.

excuser /ɛkskyze/ [1] **I** *vtr* to forgive; to pardon; to excuse; **excusez-moi** I'm sorry; **vous êtes tout excusé** it's quite all right.
II s'excuser *v refl* (+ *v être*) to apologize.

exécrable /ɛgzekʀabl/ *adj* loathsome; dreadful; detestable.

exécrer /ɛgzekʀe/ [14] *vtr* to loathe.

exécuter /ɛgzekyte/ [1] **I** *vtr* **1** to carry out [*task, mission*]; to do [*exercise*]; **2** to carry out [*orders, threat*]; to fulfil[GB] [*contract*]; to enforce [*law, ruling*]; **3** to execute [*prisoner*]; to kill [*victim*]; **4** (Mus) to perform.
II s'exécuter *v refl* (+ *v être*) to comply.

exécutif, **-ive** /ɛgzekytif, iv/ *adj* executive.

exécution /ɛgzekysjɔ̃/ *nf* **1** execution, carrying out; enforcement; fulfilment[GB]; **mettre à ~** to carry out [*threat*]; **travaux en cours d'~** work in progress; **veiller à la bonne ~ d'une tâche** to see that a job is done well; **2** execution; **~ capitale** capital punishment.

exemplaire /ɛgzɑ̃plɛʀ/ **I** *adj* **1** exemplary; **élève ~** model pupil; **2** (Law) exemplary.
II *nm* **1** copy; print; **2** specimen.

exemple /ɛgzɑ̃pl/ **I** *nm* **1** example; **sans ~** unprecedented; **être l'~ de la gentillesse** to be a model of kindness; **donner qn en ~** to hold sb up as an example; **2** warning (**pour** to).
II par exemple *phr* for example; **ça par ~!** how amazing!; well, honestly!

exempt, **~e** /ɛgzɑ̃, ɑ̃t/ *adj* exempt; **~ d'impôt** tax-free.

exempter /ɛgzɑ̃te/ [1] *vtr* to exempt.

exercer /ɛgzɛʀse/ [12] **I** *vtr* **1** to exercise [*right*]; to exert [*authority*]; **2** to exercise [*profession*]; to practise[GB] [*art*]; **3** to exercise [*body*].
II s'exercer *v refl* (+ *v être*) **1** [*athlete*] to train; [*musician*] to practise[GB]; **2** [*influence, force*] to be exerted.

exercice /ɛgzɛʀsis/ *nm* exercise; **faire de l'~** to get some exercise; **dans l'~ de ses fonctions** in the course of one's duty; while at work; **en ~** [*minister, president*] incumbent; **entrer en ~** to take up one's duties.

exergue /ɛgzɛʀg/ *nm* **1** epigraph; **2** inscription.

exhaler /ɛgzale/ [1] *vtr* to exhale.

exhaustif, **-ive** /ɛgzostif, iv/ *adj* exhaustive.

exhiber /ɛgzibe/ [1] **I** *vtr* to flaunt [*wealth*]; to show [*animal*]; to expose [*body*].
II s'exhiber *v refl* (+ *v être*) **1** to expose oneself; **2** to flaunt oneself.

exhibition /ɛgzibisjɔ̃/ *nf* **1** (of animals) show; exhibition; **2** (Sport) demonstration, display; **3** (of wealth) parade; (of emotion) display.

exhibitionniste /ɛgzibisjɔnist/ *adj*, *nmf* exhibitionist.

exhortation /ɛgzɔʀtasjɔ̃/ *nf* exhortation; **~ au calme** call for calm.

exhorter /ɛgzɔʀte/ [1] *vtr* to motivate; **~ qn à faire** to urge or exhort sb to do.

exhumer /ɛgzyme/ [1] *vtr* **1** to exhume; **2** to excavate.

exigeant, **~e** /ɛgziʒɑ̃, ɑ̃t/ *adj* demanding.

exigence /ɛgziʒɑ̃s/ *nf* demand (**de qch** for sth).

exiger /ɛgziʒe/ [13] *vtr* **1** to demand [*answer, reforms*]; **2** to require.

exigu, **-uë** /ɛgzigy/ *adj* [*room*] cramped; [*entrance*] narrow; [*space*] confined.

exil /ɛgzil/ *nm* exile; **en ~** in exile.

exilé, **~e** /ɛgzile/ *nm,f* exile.

exiler /ɛgzile/ [1] **I** *vtr* to exile.
II s'exiler *v refl* (+ *v être*) to go into exile.

existence /ɛgzistɑ̃s/ *nf* **1** existence; **2**° life.

existentialisme /ɛgzistɑ̃sjalism/ *nm* existentialism.

exister /ɛgziste/ [1] *vi* to exist; **si le paradis existe** if there is a heaven; **la maison existe encore** the house is still standing.

exode /ɛgzɔd/ *nm* exodus; **~ rural** rural depopulation.

exonération /ɛgzɔneʀasjɔ̃/ *nf* exemption.

exonérer /ɛgzɔneʀe/ [14] *vtr* to exempt.

exorbitant, **~e** /ɛgzɔʀbitɑ̃, ɑ̃t/ *adj* [*price*] exorbitant; [*demands*] outrageous.

exorbité, **~e** /ɛgzɔʀbite/ *adj* bulging.

exorciser /ɛgzɔʀsize/ [1] *vtr* to exorcize.

exotique /ɛgzɔtik/ *adj* exotic.

exotisme /ɛgzɔtism/ *nm* exoticism.

expansif, **-ive** /ɛkspɑ̃sif, iv/ *adj* communicative, outgoing.

expansion /ɛkspɑ̃sjɔ̃/ *nf* **1** growth; **en (pleine) ~** (rapidly) growing; **2** expansion.

expatrié, **~e** /ɛkspatʀije/ *adj*, *nm,f* expatriate.

expatrier /ɛkspatʀije/ [2] **I** *vtr* to deport.
II s'expatrier *v refl* (+ *v être*) to emigrate.

expectative /ɛkspɛktativ/ *nf* **rester dans l'~** to wait and see.

expédient /ɛkspedjɑ̃/ *nm* expedient; **vivre d'~s** to live by one's wits.

expédier /ɛkspedje/ [2] *vtr* **1** to send; to post (GB), to mail (US); to dispatch; **~ qch à qn** to send sb sth; **2** to get rid of [*person*]; to polish off [*work, meal*]; **~ un procès en une heure** to get a trial over within one hour.

expéditeur, **-trice** /ɛkspeditœʀ, tʀis/ *nm,f* sender.

expéditif, **-ive** /ɛkspeditif, iv/ *adj* [*person*] brisk; [*method*] cursory; **une justice expéditive** summary justice.

expédition /ɛkspedisjɔ̃/ *nf* expedition.

expérience /ɛkspeʀjɑ̃s/ *nf* **1** experience; **avoir de l'~** to be experienced; **j'en ai fait l'~ à mes dépens** I learned that lesson at my own expense; **2** experiment.

expérimental, **~e**, *mpl* **-aux** /ɛkspeʀimɑ̃tal, o/ *adj* experimental.

expérimentation /ɛkspeʀimɑ̃tasjɔ̃/ *nf* experimentation.

expérimenté, **~e** /ɛkspeʀimɑ̃te/ *adj* experienced.

expérimenter /ɛkspeʀimɑ̃te/ [1] *vtr* to test.

expert /ɛkspɛʀ/ *nm* **1** expert (**en** on); **l'avis d'un ~** expert advice; **2** adjuster.

expert-comptable, *pl* **experts-comptables** /ɛkspɛʀkɔ̃tabl/ *nm* ≈ chartered accountant (GB), certified public accountant (US).

expertise /ɛkspɛʀtiz/ *nf* **1** valuation (GB), appraisal (US); assessment; **2** expertise.

expertiser /ɛkspɛʀtize/ [1] *vtr* to value (GB), to appraise (US) [*jewellery*]; to assess [*damages*].

expier /ɛkspje/ [2] *vtr* to atone for, to expiate.

expiration /ɛkspiʀasjɔ̃/ *nf* **1** exhalation; **2** expiry (GB), expiration (US).

expirer /ɛkspiʀe/ [1] **I** *vtr* to exhale.
II *vi* **1** [*contract*] to expire; **2** to breathe out.

explicatif, **-ive** /ɛksplikatif, iv/ *adj* explanatory.

explication /ɛksplikasjɔ̃/ *nf* explanation; **nous avons eu une bonne ~** we've talked things through.

explicite /ɛksplisit/ *adj* [*text, film*] explicit; [*answer*] definite.

expliciter /ɛksplisite/ [1] *vtr* to clarify.

expliquer /ɛksplike/ [1] **I** *vtr* **1** to explain; **2** (Sch) to analyse[GB] [*text*].
II s'expliquer *v refl* (+ *v être*) **s'~ qch** to understand sth; **tout finira par s'~** everything will become clear.

exploit /ɛksplwɑ/ *nm* exploit, feat.

exploitant, **~e** /ɛksplwatɑ̃, ɑ̃t/ *nm,f* **~ agricole** farmer.

exploitation /ɛksplwatasjɔ̃/ *nf* **1** exploitation; **2 ~ agricole** farm; **~ commerciale** business concern; **3** (of land, forest) exploitation; (of airline, shipping line) operation.

exploiter /ɛksplwate/ [1] *vtr* **1** to exploit [*person*]; **2** to work [*mine*]; to mine [*coal*]; to exploit [*forest*]; to run [*firm*]; to operate [*airline*]; **3** to make the most of [*gift, knowledge*].

exploration /ɛksplɔʀasjɔ̃/ *nf* exploration.

explorer /ɛksplɔʀe/ [1] *vtr* to explore.

exploser /ɛksploze/ [1] *vi* to explode; to blow up; **faire ~** to blow up; to explode; to cause [sth] to blow up.

explosif, **-ive** /ɛksplozif, iv/ **I** *adj* explosive.
II *nm* explosive; **un attentat à l'~** bomb attack.

explosion /ɛksplozjɔ̃/ *nf* **1** explosion; **2** outburst; **3** (in market) boom.

export /ɛkspɔʀ/ *nm* export.

exportateur, **-trice** /ɛkspɔʀtatœʀ, tʀis/ *nm,f* exporter.

exportation /ɛkspɔʀtasjɔ̃/ *nf* export.

exporter /ɛkspɔʀte/ [1] *vtr* to export.

exposé, **~e** /ɛkspoze/ **I** *pp* ▸ **exposer**.
II *pp adj* **1** exposed; **maison ~e au sud** south-facing house; **2** on show; on display.
III *nm* **1 ~ de** account of; **faire un** or **l'~ des faits** to give a statement of the facts; **2** (Sch) talk; **faire un ~** to give a talk.

exposer /ɛkspoze/ [1] **I** *vtr* **1** to exhibit [*art*]; to display, to put [sth] on display [*goods*]; **2** to state [*facts*]; to outline [*idea, plan*]; to explain [*situation*]; **3** to risk [*life, reputation*]; **4** to expose [*skin, body*]; **ne reste pas exposé au soleil** stay out of the sun.
II s'exposer *v refl* (+ *v être*) **1** to put oneself at risk; **s'~ à** to lay oneself open to [*criticsm*]; **2 s'~ au soleil** to go out in the sun.

exposition /ɛkspozisjɔ̃/ *nf* **1** (of art) exhibition; (of animals, plants) show; (for trade) fair; **2** (in shop) display; **3** (of situation, facts) exposition; **4** (of house) aspect; **5** (to light, radiation) exposure.

exprès[1] /ɛkspʀɛ/ *adv* **1** deliberately, on purpose; **comme par un fait ~** as ill-luck would have it; **2** specially.

exprès[2], **-esse** /ɛkspʀɛs/ **I** *adj* express.
II exprès *adj inv* **envoyer qch en** or **par ~** to send sth special delivery or express.

express /ɛkspʀɛs/ **I** *adj inv* express.
II *nm inv* **1** express (train); **2** espresso.

expressément /ɛkspʀɛsemɑ̃/ *adv* expressly.

expressif, **-ive** /ɛkspʀɛsif, iv/ *adj* expressive.

expression /ɛkspʀɛsjɔ̃/ *nf* expression; **réduire qch à sa plus simple ~** (figurative) to reduce sth to a minimum.
■ **~ corporelle** self-expression through movement.

exprimer /ɛkspʀime/ [1] **I** *vtr* to express.
II s'exprimer *v refl* (+ *v être*) **1** to express oneself; **si j'ose m'~ ainsi** if I may put it that way; **2** to be expressed.

exproprier /ɛkspʀɔpʀije/ [2] *vtr* **~ qn** to put a compulsory purchase order on sb's property.

expulser /ɛkspylse/ [1] *vtr* **1** to evict; **2** to deport; **3** to expel; **4** (Sport) to send [sb] off.

expulsion /ɛkspylsjɔ̃/ *nf* **1** eviction; **2** deportation; **3** expulsion.

expurger /ɛkspyʀʒe/ [13] *vtr* to purge.

exquis, **~e** /ɛkski, iz/ *adj* exquisite; delightful.

exsuder /ɛksyde/ [1] **I** *vtr* to exude.
II *vi* to ooze (**de** from).

extase /ɛkstɑz/ *nf* ecstasy.

extasier: **s'extasier** /ɛkstazje/ [2] *v refl* (+ *v être*) to go into ecstasy or raptures.

extatique /ɛkstatik/ *adj* ecstatic.

extensible /ɛkstɑ̃sibl/ *adj* **1** extensible; **2** extendable.

extensif, **-ive** /ɛkstɑ̃sif, iv/ *adj* **1** extensive; **2** extended.

extension /ɛkstɑ̃sjɔ̃/ *nf* extension; **prendre de l'~** [*industry*] to expand; [*strike*] to spread.

exténuer /ɛkstenɥe/ [1] *vtr* to exhaust.

extérieur, **~e** /ɛksteʀjœʀ/ **I** *adj* **1** outside; **2** outer; **3** foreign; **4** outward.
II *nm* **1** outside; **à l'~** outside, outdoors; **d'~** outdoor; **2** exterior, appearance; **3 en ~** [*filmed*] on location.

extérieurement /ɛksteʀjœʀmɑ̃/ *adv* **1** on the outside; **2** outwardly.

extérioriser /ɛksteʀjɔʀize/ [1] *vtr* to show.

extermination /ɛkstɛʀminasjɔ̃/ *nf* extermination.

exterminer /ɛkstɛʀmine/ [1] *vtr* to exterminate; to wipe out.

externe /ɛkstɛʀn/ **I** *adj* external; outside; exterior.
II *nmf* **1** (Sch) day pupil; **2** (Med) non-residential medical student (GB), extern (US).

extincteur /ɛkstɛ̃ktœʀ/ *nm* fire extinguisher.

extinction /ɛkstɛ̃ksjɔ̃/ *nf* **1** (Med) **avoir une ~ de voix** to have lost one's voice; **2** extinction; **espèce en voie d'~** endangered species; **3 après l'~ de l'incendie** after the fire was put out; **après l'~ des feux** after lights out.

extirper /ɛkstiʀpe/ [1] *vtr* **1** to eradicate; **2**○ to drag [*person*] (**de** out of, from).

extorquer /ɛkstɔʀke/ [1] *vtr* to extort.

extorsion /ɛkstɔʀsjɔ̃/ *nf* extortion.

extra /ɛkstʀa/ **I** *adj inv* **1**○ great○; **2** [*product*] of superior quality.
II *nm inv* **1** extra; **se payer un petit ~** to have a little treat; **2 faire des ~** to do a few extra jobs; **3** extra worker.

extraction /ɛkstʀaksjɔ̃/ *nf* **1** (of oil, gas) extraction; (of coal, diamonds) mining; (of marble, slate) quarrying; **2** (of bullet, tooth) extraction.

extrader /ɛkstʀade/ [1] *vtr* to extradite.

extraire /ɛkstʀɛʀ/ [58] *vtr* **1** to extract [*mineral*]; to mine [*gold, coal*]; to quarry [*slate, marble*]; **2** to extract; to pull out; to remove.

extrait /ɛkstʀɛ/ *nm* **1** (from book, film) extract, excerpt; (from speech) extract; **2** essence, extract; **~ de viande** meat extract.
■ **~ (d'acte) de naissance** birth certificate; **~ de casier judiciaire (de qn)** copy of (sb's) criminal record; **~ de compte** abstract of accounts.

extralucide /ɛkstʀalysid/ *adj* clairvoyant.

extraordinaire /ɛkstʀaɔʀdinɛʀ/ *adj* **1** extraordinary, amazing, remarkable; **c'est quand même ~!** it's incredible!; **2** [*expenses, measures*] extraordinary.

extrapoler /ɛkstʀapɔle/ [1] *vtr, vi* to extrapolate.

extraterrestre /ɛkstʀatɛʀɛstʀ/ *nmf* extraterrestrial, alien.

extravagance /ɛkstʀavagɑ̃s/ *nf* **1** eccentricity; **2** extravagance.

extravagant, **~e** /ɛkstʀavagɑ̃, ɑ̃t/ *adj* **1** eccentric; **2** extravagant; **3** exorbitant.

extraverti, **~e** /ɛkstʀavɛʀti/ *adj, nm,f* extrovert.

extrême /ɛkstʀɛm/ **I** *adj* **1** furthest; **dans l'~ nord/sud du pays** in the extreme North/South of the country; **2** extreme; **3** drastic.
II *nm* extreme; **c'est pousser la logique à l'~** that's taking logic to extremes; **à l'~ inverse** at the other extreme.

extrêmement /ɛkstʀɛmmɑ̃/ *adv* extremely.

Extrême-Orient /ɛkstʀɛmɔʀjɑ̃/ *pr nm* **l'~** the Far East.

extrémiste /ɛkstʀemist/ *adj, nmf* extremist.

extrémité /ɛkstʀemite/ *nf* **1** end; (of finger) tip; (of mast) top; (of town, field) edge; **aux deux ~s** at both ends; **2** extreme.

exubérance /egzybeʀɑ̃s/ *nf* exuberance.

exubérant, **~e** /egzybeʀɑ̃, ɑ̃t/ *adj* exuberant.

exutoire /egzytwaʀ/ *nm* outlet.

Ff

f, **F** /ɛf/ *nm inv* **1** (letter f, F; **2 F3** 2-bedroom flat (GB) or apartment; **3** (*written abbr* = **franc**) **50 F** 50 F.

fa /fa/ *nm inv* (Mus) (note) F; (in sol-fa) fa.

fable /fɑbl/ *nf* **1** tale; **2** fable; **3** tall story.

fabricant /fabʀikɑ̃/ *nm* manufacturer.

fabrication /fabʀikasjɔ̃/ *nf* making; manufacture; **~ en série** mass production.
■ **~ assistée par ordinateur**, **FAO** computer-aided manufacturing, CAM.

fabrique /fabʀik/ *nf* factory.

fabriquer /fabʀike/ [1] *vtr* **1** to make; to manufacture; **2** to invent [*alibi*]; **qu'est-ce que tu fabriques○?** what are you up to?

fabuleux, **-euse** /fabylø, øz/ *adj* [*beauty*] fabulous; [*sum*] fantastic; [*creature*] mythical.

fac○ /fak/ *nf* **1** faculty; **2** university.

façade /fasad/ *nf* **1** (of building) front; **~ nord** north side; **2** façade.

face /fas/ **I** *nf* **1** face; **2** side; **le côté ~ d'une pièce** the heads side of a coin; **3 faire ~** to face up to things; **se faire ~** to face each other; to be opposite one another; **faire ~ à** to face [*place*]; (figurative) to face [*adversary, challenge*]; to cope with [*spending*]; to meet [*demand*].
II de face *phr* [*photo*] fullface; [*lighting*] frontal.
III en face *phr* **il habite en ~** he lives opposite; **voir les choses en ~** to see things as they are; **l'équipe d'en ~** the opposing team.
IV en face de *phr* **1 en ~ de l'église** opposite the church (GB), across from the church; **2** compared with.
V face à *phr* **1 mon lit est ~ à la fenêtre** my bed faces the window; **2 ~ à cette situation** in view of this situation.
IDIOMS **se voiler la ~** not to face facts.

face-à-face /fasafas/ *nm inv* **1** one-to-one debate (GB), one-on-one debate (US); **2** encounter.

facétieux, **-ieuse** /fasesjø, øz/ *adj* mischievous.

facette /fasɛt/ *nf* facet.

fâché, **~e** /fɑʃe/ **I** *pp* ▶ **fâcher**.
II *pp adj* angry; **être ~ avec qn** to have fallen out with sb.

fâcher: **se fâcher** /fɑʃe/ [1] *v refl* (+ *v être*) **1** to get angry; **2** to fall out.

fâcheux, **-euse** /fɑʃø, øz/ *adj* [*influence*] detrimental; [*delay*] unfortunate; [*news*] distressing.

facial, **~e**, *mpl* **-iaux** /fasjal, o/ *adj* facial.

faciès /fasjɛs/ *nm inv* **1** facies; **2** face.

facile /fasil/ **I** *adj* **1** easy; **avoir la larme ~** to be quick to cry; **2** easy-going.
II○ *adv* easily.

facilement /fasilmɑ̃/ *adv* **1** easily; **2○ j'ai mis ~ deux heures pour venir** it took me a good two hours to get here.

facilité /fasilite/ **I** *nf* **1** (of work) easiness; (of use, maintenance) ease; **2** fluency.
II facilités *nf pl* **1 donner toutes ~s pour faire** to afford every opportunity to do; **2 ~s (de paiement)** easy terms.

faciliter /fasilite/ [1] *vtr* to make [sth] easier.

façon /fasɔ̃/ **I** *nf* **1** way; **de toute ~**, **de toutes les ~s** anyway; **de ~ à faire** in order to do; in such a way as to do; **de ~ (à ce) qu'elle fasse** so (that) she does; **elle nous a joué un tour à sa ~** she played a trick of her own on us; **~ de parler** so to speak; **2 un peigne ~ ivoire** an imitation ivory comb; **3** (of garment) making-up.
II façons *nf pl* **en voilà des ~s!** what a way to behave!; **sans ~s** [*meal*] informal; [*person*] unpretentious.

façonner /fasɔne/ [1] *vtr* **1** to manufacture; to make; **2** to hew [*wood*]; to fashion [*clay*]; **3** to shape, to mould (GB), to mold (US).

fac-similé, *pl* **~s** /faksimile/ *nm* facsimile.

facteur, **-trice** /faktœʀ, tʀis/ **I** *nm,f* postman/postwoman.
II *nm* factor.

factice /faktis/ *adj* [*smile*] forced; [*jewellery*] imitation; [*flower, beauty*] artificial.

faction /faksjɔ̃/ *nf* **1** faction; **2** (Mil) guard duty.

factrice ▶ **facteur I**.

facture /faktyʀ/ *nf* bill; invoice.

facturer /faktyʀe/ [1] *vtr* to invoice [*goods*].

facultatif, **-ive** /fakyltatif, iv/ *adj* optional.

faculté /fakylte/ *nf* **1** (mental) faculty; ability; **2** option; **3** (at university) faculty; **4** (Law) right.

fade /fad/ *adj* [*person, book*] dull; [*food, taste*] tasteless; [*colour*] drab.

fadeur /fadœʀ/ *nf* blandness; dreariness.

fagot /fago/ *nm* bundle of firewood.

faible /fɛbl/ **I** *adj* **1** (gen) weak; [*sight*] poor; [*constitution*] frail; **être ~ avec qn** to be too soft on sb; **2** [*proportion, increase*] small; [*income, speed*] low; [*means, impact*] limited; [*chance*] slim; **3** [*noise, glow*] faint; [*lighting*] dim; [*wind, rain*] light; **4** [*result*] poor; [*argument*] feeble; **5** [*pupil, class*] slow; **~ d'esprit** feeble-minded; **6 le mot est ~!** that's putting it mildly!
II *nmf* weak-willed person.
III *nm* weakness; **avoir un ~ pour qn** to have a soft spot for sb.

faiblement /fɛbləmɑ̃/ *adv* weakly; [*influence, increase*] slightly; [*lit*] dimly.

faiblesse /fɛblɛs/ *nf* **1** weakness; (of invalid) frailty; **2** inadequacy; **3** (of voice) faintness; (of lighting) dimness.

faiblir /fɛbliʀ/ [3] *vi* **1** [*person, pulse*] to get weaker; [*sight*] to be failing; **2** [*person, currency*] to weaken; **3** [*athlete*] to flag; [*plot*] to decline; [*interest*] to wane; [*speed*] to slacken; **4** [*storm*] to abate; [*noise*] to grow faint.

faïence /fajɑ̃s/ *nf* earthenware.
IDIOMS **se regarder en chiens de ~** to look daggers at each other.

faille /fɑj/ *nf* **1** (in geology) fault; **2** flaw; **sans ~** unfailing; **3** rift.

faillir /fajiʀ/ [28] *vi* **1 elle a failli le gifler** she almost or (very) nearly slapped him; **2 sans ~** unfailingly.

faillite /fajit/ *nf* **1** bankruptcy; **2** failure.

faim /fɛ̃/ *nf* hunger; **avoir ~** to be hungry; **mourir de ~** to die of starvation; (figurative) to be starving; **je suis resté sur ma ~** I was disappointed.

fainéant, **~e** /feneɑ̃, ɑ̃t/ *adj* lazy.

faire /fɛʀ/ [10]

■ **Note** You will find translations for expressions such as *faire peur, faire semblant* etc, at the entries ***peur***, ***semblant*** etc.

I *vtr* **1** to make; **~ son lit/une faute** to make one's bed/a mistake; **~ des jaloux** to make people jealous; **deux et deux font quatre** two and two is four; **2** to do; **~ de la recherche** to do research; **j'ai à ~** I have things to do; **que fait-il?** what does he do?; what is he doing?; **que veux-tu que j'y fasse?** what do you want me to do about it?; **~ médecine/du violon** to do or study medicine/to study or play the violin; **~ une école de commerce** to go to business school; **~ un numéro de téléphone/une lettre** to dial a number/to write a letter; **~ du tennis/de la couture** to play tennis/to sew; **~ un poulet** to do or cook a chicken; **3** to do [*distance, journey*]; to go round [*shops*]; to do○ [*region, museums*]; **j'ai fait tous les tiroirs mais je ne l'ai pas trouvé** I went through all the drawers but I couldn't find it; **4**○ to have [*diabetes, complex*]; **5 ~ le malade** to pretend to be ill; **6 leur départ ne m'a rien fait** their departure didn't affect me at all; **ça y fait**○ it has an effect; **pour ce que ça fait**○**!** for all the good it does!; **7** to say; **'bien sûr,' fit-elle** 'of course,' she said; **le canard fait 'coin-coin'** ducks go 'quack'; **8 ça m'a fait rire** it made me laugh; **~ manger un bébé** to feed a baby; **fais voir** show me; **fais-leur prendre un rendez-vous** get them to make an appointment; **~ traverser la rue à un vieillard** to help an old man across the road; **9 ~ réparer sa voiture** to have or get one's car repaired; **10 je n'en ai rien à ~**○ I couldn't care less; **ça ne fait rien!** it doesn't matter!; **qu'est-ce que ça peut bien te ~**○**?** what is it to you?; **il sait y ~** he's got the knack; **il ne fait que pleuvoir** it never stops raining; **je ne fais qu'obéir aux ordres** I'm only obeying orders.

II *vi* **1** to do, to act; **fais comme tu veux** do as you like; **2** to look; **~ jeune** to look young; **3 ça fait 15 ans que j'habite ici** I've been living here for 15 years; **ça fait 2 mètres de long** it's 2 metres[GB] long; **4** to go (to the toilet); **tu as fait?** have you been?; **5**○ **~ avec** to make do with; to put up with.

III se faire *v refl* (+ *v être*) **1 se ~ un café** to make oneself a coffee; **se ~ comprendre** to make oneself understood; **2** to get, to become; **il se fait tard** it's getting late; **3 s'en ~** to worry; **il ne s'en fait pas!** he's not the sort of person to worry about things!; (as criticism) he's got a nerve!; **4 se ~ à** to get used to; **5 ça se fait encore ici** it's still done here; **ça ne se fait pas** it's not the done thing; **6** [*colour, style*] to be in (fashion); **7 c'est ce qui se fait de mieux** it's the best there is; **8 comment se fait-il que...?** how is it that...?, how come...?

faire-part /fɛʀpaʀ/ *nm inv* announcement.

faire-valoir /fɛʀvalwaʀ/ *nm inv* **être le ~ de** [*actor*] to be a foil for.

faisan /fəzɑ̃/ *nm* (cock) pheasant.

faisane /fəzan/ *nf* **(poule) ~** hen pheasant.

faisceau, *pl* **~x** /fɛso/ *nm* **1** beam; **~ lumineux** beam of light; **2** bundle.

fait, **~e** /fɛ, fɛt/ **I** *pp* ▶ **faire**.

II *pp adj* **1** done; **c'en est ~ de** that's the end of; **c'est bien ~ (pour toi)**○! it serves you right!; **2 ~ de** or **en** made (up) of; **idée toute ~e** ready-made idea; **elle est bien ~e** she's got a great figure; **la vie est mal ~e** life is unfair; **3 ~ pour qch/pour faire** meant for sth/to do; **4** [*programme, device*] designed; **5**○ done for; **6 un fromage bien ~** a ripe cheese.

III *nm* **1** fact; **le ~ est là** or **les ~s sont là, il t'a trompé** the fact (of the matter) is that he cheated you; **les ~s et gestes de qn** sb's movements; **2 de ce ~** because of this or that; **être le ~ de qn** to be due to sb; **3** event; **4 aller droit au ~** to go straight to the point.

IV au fait /ofɛt/ *phr* by the way.

V de fait *phr* **1** [*situation*] de facto; **2** [*exist, result in*] effectively; **3** indeed.

VI en fait *phr* in fact, actually.

VII en fait de *phr* as regards.

■ **~ divers** (short) news item; **~ de société** fact of life.

IDIOMS **être au ~ de** to be informed about; **prendre qn sur le ~** to catch sb in the act.

faîte /fɛt/ *nm* (of mountain) summit; (of house) rooftop; (of tree) top.

falaise /falɛz/ *nf* cliff.

fallacieux, **-ieuse** /falasjø, øz/ *adj* [*argument*] fallacious; [*pretext*] false.

falloir /falwaʀ/ [50] **I** *v impers* **1 il faut qn/qch** we need sb/sth; sb/sth is needed; **il va ~ deux jours/du courage** it will take two days/courage; **il me/te/leur faut qch** I/you/they need sth; **il me faut ce livre!** I've got to have that book!; **2 il faut faire** we/you etc have (got) to do; we/you etc must do; we/you etc should do; **il ne faut pas la déranger** she mustn't be disturbed; **il fallait le faire** it had to be done; **faut le faire**○**!** (admiring) it takes a bit of doing!; (critical) would you believe it?; **comme il faut** [*behave*] properly; **3 il faut que tu fasses** you have (got) to do, you must do; you should do.

II s'en falloir *v refl* (+ *v être*) **peu s'en faut**

very nearly; **elle a perdu, mais il s'en est fallu de peu** she lost, but only just.

IDIOMS **il faut ce qu'il faut!** there's no point in skimping!; **en moins de temps qu'il ne faut pour le dire** before you could say Jack Robinson.

falsification /falsifikasjɔ̃/ *nf* **1** falsification; **2** forging.

falsifier /falsifje/ [2] *vtr* **1** to falsify, to tamper with [*document*]; to distort [*facts*]; **2** to forge.

famé, **~e** /fame/ *adj* **un quartier mal ~** a disreputable or seedy area.

famélique /famelik/ *adj* emaciated, scrawny.

fameux, **-euse** /famø, øz/ *adj* **1** much talked-about; **2** famous; **3** excellent.

familial, **~e**, *mpl* **-iaux** /familjal, o/ *adj* **1** [*meal, life, firm*] family; **2 voiture ~e** estate car (GB), station wagon (US).

familiariser /familjaʀize/ [1] *vtr* to familiarize.

familiarité /familjaʀite/ *nf* familiarity.

familier, **-ière** /familje, ɛʀ/ *adj* **1** [*face, landscape*] familiar; **2** [*word*] informal, colloquial; **3** [*attitude*] informal; [*person, gesture*] familiar; **4 animal ~** pet.

familièrement /familjɛʀmɑ̃/ *adv* **1** commonly; **2** informally; **3** with undue familiarity.

famille /famij/ *nf* family; **c'est de ~** it runs in the family.

famine /famin/ *nf* famine.

fanatique /fanatik/ **I** *adj* [*believer*] fanatical; [*admiration, love*] ardent.
II *nmf* **1** fanatic; **2**○ enthusiast, freak○.

fanatisme /fanatism/ *nm* fanaticism.

faner /fane/ [1] **I** *vi* **1** to wither; **2** to make hay.
II se faner *v refl* (+ *v être*) **1** [*plant*] to wither, to wilt; **2** [*beauty, colour*] to fade.

fanfare /fɑ̃faʀ/ *nf* brass band; **annoncer qch en ~** to trumpet sth.

fanfaron, **-onne** /fɑ̃faʀɔ̃, ɔn/ *nm,f* boaster, swaggerer; **faire le ~** to boast.

fantaisie /fɑ̃tɛzi/ *nf* **1** imaginativeness; **manquer de ~** [*person*] to be staid; [*life*] to be dull; **2** whim, fancy; **3 s'offrir une petite ~** to spoil oneself; **un bijou ~** a piece of costume jewellery (GB) or jewelry (US).

fantaisiste /fɑ̃tɛzist/ *adj* **1** [*person*] unreliable; [*figures*] doubtful; **2** [*idea*] far-fetched.

fantasme /fɑ̃tasm/ *nm* fantasy.

fantasque /fɑ̃task/ *adj* [*character*] unpredictable; [*tale*] fanciful.

fantassin /fɑ̃tasɛ̃/ *nm* infantryman, footsoldier.

fantastique /fɑ̃tastik/ **I** *adj* fantastic.
II *nm* **le ~** fantasy.

fantoche /fɑ̃tɔʃ/ *adj* puppet.

fantôme /fɑ̃tom/ **I** *nm* ghost.
II (-)fantôme (*combining form*) [*train, city*] ghost; **image(-)~** (on screen) ghost; **société(-)~** (Law) dummy company.

FAO /ɛfao/ *nf* (Comput) (*abbr* = **fabrication assistée par ordinateur**) CAM.

faon /fɑ̃/ *nm* (Zool) fawn.

farandole /faʀɑ̃dɔl/ *nf* (dance) farandole; ≈ conga.

farce /faʀs/ *nf* **1** practical joke; **magasin de ~s et attrapes** joke shop (GB), novelty store (US); **2** joke; **3** (in theatre) farce; **4** stuffing, forcemeat.

farceur, **-euse** /faʀsœʀ, øz/ *nm,f* practical joker.

farcir /faʀsiʀ/ [3] *vtr* (Culin) to stuff.

fard /faʀ/ *nm* make-up; **sans ~** [*beauty*] natural; [*truth*] simple.
■ **~ à joues** blusher; **~ à paupières** eyeshadow.
IDIOMS **piquer un ~**○ to go as red as a beetroot (GB), to turn as red as a beet (US).

fardeau, *pl* **~x** /faʀdo/ *nm* burden.

farder /faʀde/ [1] **I** *vtr* to disguise [*truth*].
II se farder *v refl* (+ *v être*) [*actor*] to make up; [*woman*] to use make-up.

farfelu○, **~e** /faʀfəly/ *adj* [*idea*] hare-brained○; [*person*] scatter-brained○; [*show*] bizarre.

farine /faʀin/ *nf* **1** flour; **2** baby cereal.
■ **~ d'avoine** oatmeal.
IDIOMS **se faire rouler dans la ~**○ to be had○.

farineux, **-euse** /faʀinø, øz/ *adj* [*food*] starchy; [*potato*] floury.

farouche /faʀuʃ/ *adj* **1** [*child, animal*] timid, shy; [*adult*] unsociable; **2** [*look, warrior*] fierce; **3** [*enemy, hatred*] bitter; [*adversary*] fierce; [*supporter*] staunch; [*will*] iron.

farouchement /faʀuʃmɑ̃/ *adv* [*opposed, independent*] fiercely; [*refuse*] doggedly.

fascicule /fasikyl/ *nm* **1** booklet; **2** fascicule.

fascinant, **~e** /fasinɑ̃, ɑ̃t/ *adj* [*person, film*] fascinating; [*charm, music*] spellbinding.

fascination /fasinasjɔ̃/ *nf* fascination.

fasciner /fasine/ [1] *vtr* [*speaker, music*] to hold [sb] spellbound; [*sea, person*] to fascinate.

fascisme /faʃism/ *nm* fascism.

faste /fast/ **I** *adj* auspicious.
II *nm* splendour[GB], pomp; **avec ~** with pomp.

fastidieux, **-ieuse** /fastidjø, øz/ *adj* tedious.

fatal, **~e** /fatal/ *adj* **1** inevitable; **2** fatal, disastrous; **3** [*moment, day*] fateful.

fatalisme /fatalism/ *nm* fatalism.

fatalité /fatalite/ *nf* **1 la ~** fate; **2** mischance; **3** inevitability.

fatidique /fatidik/ *adj* fateful.

fatigant, **~e** /fatigɑ̃, ɑ̃t/ *adj* **1** [*sport, journey*] tiring; [*climate*] wearing; **2** [*work*] arduous; **3** [*person*] tiresome; [*film, conversation*] tedious.

fatigue /fatig/ *nf* **1** tiredness; **être mort de ~, tomber de ~** to be dead tired; **2** (Med) fatigue; **~ visuelle** eyestrain.

fatigué, **~e** /fatige/ **I** *pp* ▸ **fatiguer**.
II *pp adj* [*voice*] strained; [*eyes, smile*] weary.

fatiguer /fatige/ [1] **I** *vtr* **1** to make [sb/sth] tired; to strain [*eyes*]; **2** to tire [sb] out; **3** to wear [sb] out; **4** to wear out [*engine*].
II *vi* **1**○ to get tired; **2** [*engine, car*] to be labouring[GB].

III se fatiguer *v refl* (+ *v être*) **1** to get tired; **2** to tire oneself out; **3 se ~ les yeux** to strain one's eyes; **4 se ~ à faire** to bother doing.

fatras /fatʀa/ *nm inv* jumble.

faubourg /fobuʀ/ *nm* working class area (*on the outskirts*).

fauché○, **~e** /foʃe/ *adj* broke○, penniless.

faucher /foʃe/ [1] *vtr* **1** to mow; to scythe; **2** [*car, bullet*] to mow [sb] down; **3**○ to steal.

faucheuse /foʃøz/ *nf* mowing machine.

faucille /fosij/ *nf* sickle.

faucon /fokɔ̃/ *nm* falcon, hawk (US).

faudra ▸ **falloir**.

faufiler /fofile/ [1] **I** *vtr* to baste.
II se faufiler *v refl* (+ *v être*) **1 se ~ à l'extérieur** to slip out; **2 se ~ dans** [*mistakes*] to creep into [*text*]; **3** [*route*] to snake in and out.

faune /fon/ *nf* **1** wildlife, fauna; **la ~ marine** marine life; **2** (derogatory) set, crowd.

faussaire /fosɛʀ/ *nmf* forger.

fausse ▸ **faux**[1] **I**.

faussement /fosmɑ̃/ *adv* **1** falsely, wrongfully; **2** deceptively.

fausser /fose/ [1] *vtr* to distort [*result, mechanism*]; to damage [*lock*]; to buckle [*blade*].
IDIOMS **~ compagnie à qn** to give sb the slip.

faut ▸ **falloir**.

faute /fot/ *nf* **1** mistake, error; **il a fait un (parcours) sans ~** he's never put a foot wrong; **2** (gen) misdemeanour[GB]; (LAW) civil wrong; **être en ~** to be at fault; **prendre qn en ~** to catch sb out; **3** fault; **c'est (de) ma ~** it's my fault; **par la ~ de qn** because of sb; **rejeter la ~ sur qn** to lay the blame on sb; **4 ~ de temps** through lack of time; **~ de mieux** for want of anything better; **~ de quoi** otherwise, failing which; **sans ~** without fail; **5** (Sport) foul; (in tennis) fault.

fauteuil /fotœj/ *nm* **1** chair, armchair; **2** (in theatre) seat.

fautif, **-ive** /fotif, iv/ **I** *adj* **1** at fault; **2** [*memory*] faulty; [*reference*] inaccurate.
II *nm,f* culprit.

fauve /fov/ **I** *adj* tawny.
II *nm* **1** wild animal; **2** big cat; **3** (colour) fawn.

faux[1], **fausse** /fo, fos/ **I** *adj* **1** [*result, number, idea*] wrong; [*impression, promise, accusation*] false; **2** [*beard, tooth, eyelashes*] false; **3** [*wood, marble, diamonds*] imitation; fake; [*door, drawer*] false; **4** [*passport, money*] forged; **5** [*policeman, bishop*] bogus; [*candour, humility*] feigned; **6** [*hope*] false; [*fear*] groundless; **7** deceitful.
II *adv* [*play, sing*] out of tune.
III *nm inv* **1 le ~** falsehood; **2** fake; forgery.
■ **fausse couche** (Med) miscarriage; **fausse facture** bogus invoice; **fausse fenêtre** blind window; **fausse joie** ill-founded joy; **faire une fausse joie à qn** to raise sb's hopes in vain; **fausse note** jarring note; **fausse piste** wrong track; **~ ami** *foreign word which looks deceptively like a word in one's own language*; **~ frais** extras, incidental expenses; **~ jeton**○ two-faced person; **~ pas** slip; mistake; faux pas; **~ pli** crease; **~ témoignage** perjury.

faux[2] /fo/ *nf inv* scythe.

faux-filet, *pl* **~s** /fofilɛ/ *nm* sirloin.

faux-monnayeur, *pl* **~s** /fomɔnɛjœʀ/ *nm* forger, counterfeiter.

faux-semblant, *pl* **~s** /fosɑ̃blɑ̃/ *nm* **les ~s** pretence[GB].

faveur /favœʀ/ **I** *nf* favour[GB]; **régime** or **traitement de ~** preferential treatment; **des mesures en ~ des handicapés** measures to help the disabled; **intervenir en ~ de qn** to intervene on sb's behalf.
II à la faveur de *phr* thanks to; **à la ~ de la nuit** under cover of darkness.

favorable /favɔʀabl/ *adj* favourable[GB]; **être ~ à qch** to be in favour[GB] of sth.

favori, **-ite** /favɔʀi, it/ **I** *adj, nm,f* favourite[GB].
II favoris *nm pl* sideburns.

favoriser /favɔʀize/ [1] *vtr* **1** to favour[GB]; **les milieux favorisés** the privileged classes; **2** to encourage, to promote.

favorite ▸ **favori I**.

favoritisme /favɔʀitism/ *nm* favouritism[GB].

fax /faks/ *nm inv* **1** fax; **2** fax machine.

fayot[1]○ /fajo/ *nm* bean.

fayot[2]○, **-otte** /fajo, ɔt/ *nm,f* creep○, crawler○.

FB (*written abbr* = **franc belge**) BFr.

fébrile /febʀil/ *adj* **1** [*emotion, gesture*] feverish; [*person*] nervous; **2** (Med) feverish.

fébrilité /febʀilite/ *nf* **1** agitation; **avec ~** agitatedly; **2** nervousness.

fécal, **~e**, *mpl* **-aux** /fekal, o/ *adj* faecal.

fécond, **~e** /fekɔ̃, ɔ̃d/ *adj* **1** fertile; **2** fruitful.

fécondation /fekɔ̃dasjɔ̃/ *nf* (of female) impregnation; (of plant) pollination; (of egg) fertilization.

féconder /fekɔ̃de/ [1] *vtr* to impregnate [*female*]; to inseminate [*animal*]; to pollinate [*plant*]; to fertilize [*egg, ovum*].

fécondité /fekɔ̃dite/ *nf* **1** fertility; **2** (of author) productivity.

fécule /fekyl/ *nf* starch.

féculent /fekylɑ̃/ *nm* starch; starchy food.

fédéral, **~e**, *mpl* **-aux** /fedeʀal, o/ *adj* federal.

fédération /fedeʀasjɔ̃/ *nf* federation.

fée /fe/ *nf* fairy; **~ du logis** perfect housewife.
IDIOMS **avoir des doigts de ~** to have nimble fingers.

féerique /fe(e)ʀik/ *adj* [*beauty*] enchanting; [*landscape, moment*] enchanted.

feindre /fɛ̃dʀ/ [55] *vtr* to feign; **~ de faire/d'être** to pretend to do/to be.

feinte /fɛ̃t/ *nf* **1** feint; **faire une ~** (in football, rugby) to dummy (GB), to fake (US); **2**○ trick, ruse.

fêlé○, **~e** /fɛle/ *adj* cracked○.

fêler /fɛle/ [1] *vtr*, **se fêler** *v refl* (+ *v être*) to crack.

félicitations /felisitasjɔ̃/ *nf pl* congratulations.

féliciter /felisite/ [1] I *vtr* to congratulate.
II **se féliciter** *v refl* (+ *v être*) **se ~ de qch** to be very pleased about sth.

félin, **~e** /felɛ̃, in/ I *adj* **1** feline; **exposition ~e** cat show; **2** [*grace*] feline; [*eyes*] catlike.
II *nm* feline; **les ~s** felines, the cat family.

fêlure /fɛlyʀ/ *nf* crack.

femelle /fəmɛl/ I *adj* female; **éléphant ~** cow elephant; **moineau ~** hen sparrow.
II *nf* female; (in pair) mate.

féminin, **~e** /feminɛ̃, in/ I *adj* [*sex, occupation*] female; [*magazine, record*] women's; [*team, club*] ladies'; [*appearance*] feminine.
II *nm* feminine; **au ~** in the feminine.

féminiser: **se féminiser** /feminize/ [1] *v refl* (+ *v être*) [*profession*] to become more open to women; to become predominantly female.

féministe /feminist/ *adj, nmf* feminist.

féminité /feminite/ *nf* femininity.

femme /fam/ *nf* **1** woman; **2** wife.
■ **~ de chambre** chambermaid; **~ au foyer** housewife; **~ d'intérieur** homemaker; ▶**bon, jeune**.
IDIOMS **souvent ~ varie** (Proverb) woman is fickle.

fémur /femyʀ/ *nm* thighbone; **se casser le col du ~** to break one's hip.

fendiller: **se fendiller** /fɑ̃dije/ [1] *v refl* (+ *v être*) [*lips*] to chap; [*earth*] to craze over; [*wood*] to crack.

fendre /fɑ̃dʀ/ [6] I *vtr* **1** to chop [*wood*]; to slit [*material*]; **2** to crack [*wall, stone*]; to split [*lip*]; **3 ~ le cœur à qn** to break sb's heart; **4 ~ l'air** to slice through the air; **~ la foule** to push one's way through the crowd.
II **se fendre** *v refl* (+ *v être*) **1** to crack; **2**○ to cough up○ [*money*]; **tu ne t'es pas fendu!** that didn't break the bank!
IDIOMS **se ~ la pêche**○ to split one's sides○; **avoir la bouche fendue jusqu'aux oreilles** to be grinning from ear to ear.

fenêtre /fənɛtʀ/ *nf* window.
■ **~ à guillotine** sash window.
IDIOMS **jeter l'argent par les ~s** to throw money away.

fenouil /fənuj/ *nm* fennel.

fente /fɑ̃t/ *nf* **1** slit; (for coin, card) slot; (of jacket) vent; **2** crack; (in wood) split; (in rock) crevice.

féodal, **~e**, *mpl* **-aux** /feɔdal, o/ *adj* feudal.

fer /fɛʀ/ *nm* **1** iron; **de ~** [*discipline, fist, will*] iron; **2** (on shoe) steel tip; **3** branding iron; **4 croiser le ~ avec** to cross swords with.
■ **~ à cheval** horseshoe; **~ forgé** wrought iron; **~ à repasser** iron.
IDIOMS **croire dur comme ~** to believe wholeheartedly; **tomber les quatre ~s en l'air**○ to fall flat on one's back.

fer-blanc, *pl* **fers-blancs** /fɛʀblɑ̃/ *nm* tinplate.

férié, **~e** /feʀje/ *adj* **jour ~** public holiday (GB), holiday (US).

ferme[1] /fɛʀm/ I *adj* **1** firm; **2** (Law) **peine de prison ~** custodial sentence.
II *adv* [*argue, campaign*] vigorously; [*believe*] firmly; **tenir ~** to stand one's ground.
IDIOMS **attendre de pied ~** to be ready and waiting.

ferme[2] /fɛʀm/ *nf* farm, farmhouse.

ferment /fɛʀmɑ̃/ *nm* ferment.

fermenter /fɛʀmɑ̃te/ [1] *vi* to ferment.

fermer /fɛʀme/ [1] I *vtr* **1** to close, to shut [*door, book, eyes*]; to clench [*fist*]; to draw [*curtain*]; to turn off [*tap, gas, radio*]; to do up [*jacket*]; **~ à clé** to lock (up); **2** to close [*shop, airport, road*]; (definitively) to close [sth] down.
II *vi* to close (down).
III **se fermer** *v refl* (+ *v être*) **1** [*door*] to shut; [*flower*] to close up; [*coat, bracelet*] to fasten; **2** [*person*] to clam up; [*face*] to harden.
IDIOMS **~ les yeux sur** to turn a blind eye to.

fermeté /fɛʀməte/ *nf* firmness.

fermeture /fɛʀmətyʀ/ *nf* **1** (of business, account) closing; (definitive) closure, closing down; **2** (on handbag) clasp; (on garment) fastening.
■ **~ éclair**®, **~ à glissière** zip (GB), zipper (US).

fermier, **-ière** /fɛʀmje, ɛʀ/ I *adj* free-range.
II *nm,f* farmer.

fermoir /fɛʀmwaʀ/ *nm* (on necklace, bag) clasp.

féroce /feʀɔs/ *adj* **1** fierce; ferocious; **2** [*appetite*] voracious.

férocité /feʀɔsite/ *nf* **1** (of animal) ferociousness; **2** (of remark) savagery; **3** (of person) fierceness.

ferraille /feʀɑj/ *nf* **1** scrap metal; **2** scrapheap; **3**○ small change.

ferrailleur /feʀɑjœʀ/ *nm* scrap (metal) dealer.

ferronnerie /feʀɔnʀi/ *nf* **1** ironworks; **2** wrought iron work; **3** iron work.

ferroviaire /feʀɔvjɛʀ/ *adj* [*transport, collision*] rail; [*station, tunnel*] railway (GB), railroad (US).

fertile /fɛʀtil/ *adj* fertile; [*year*] productive.

fertilité /fɛʀtilite/ *nf* fertility.

fervent, **~e** /fɛʀvɑ̃, ɑ̃t/ *adj* [*believer*] fervent; [*admirer*] ardent.

ferveur /fɛʀvœʀ/ *nf* (of prayer) fervour[GB]; (of love) ardour[GB].

fesse /fɛs/ *nf* buttock.
IDIOMS **coûter la peau des ~s**○ to cost an arm and a leg○.

fessée /fese/ *nf* smack on the bottom, spanking.

festin /fɛstɛ̃/ *nm* feast.

festival /fɛstival/ *nm* festival.

festivités /fɛstivite/ *nf pl* festivities.

festoyer /fɛstwaje/ [23] *vi* to feast.

fête /fɛt/ *nf* **1** public holiday (GB), holiday (US); **2** (saint's) name-day; **ça va être ma ~**○**!** I'm going to cop it○!; **3** festival; **4** (day of) celebration; **5** party; **faire la ~** to live it up○; **6** fête, fair, celebrations.
■ **~ foraine** funfair; **~ du travail** May Day, Labour Day (GB).
IDIOMS **faire sa ~ à qn**○ to give sb a working over○.

fêter /fete/ [1] *vtr* to celebrate [*event*].

fétiche /fetiʃ/ I *adj* lucky.
II *nm* **1** mascot; **2** fetish.

fétide /fetid/ *adj* foul; foul-smelling.

feu[1], **~e** /fø/ *adj* late; **~ la reine**, **la ~e reine** the late queen.

feu[2], *pl* **~x** /fø/ *nm* **1** fire; ▶**huile**; **2** light; **sous le ~ des projecteurs** under the glare of the spotlights; (figurative) in the spotlight; **3** traffic light; **j'ai le ~ vert de mon patron** my boss has given me the go-ahead; **4** (on cooker) ring (GB), burner (US); **faire cuire à petit ~** cook over a gentle heat; **5 avez-vous du ~?** have you got a light?; **6** passion; **dans le ~ de la discussion** in the heat of the discussion; **7 ~!** (Mil) fire!; **faire ~** to fire; **coup de ~** shot; **8** (Mil) action.

■ **~ d'artifice** fireworks display; firework; **~ de cheminée** chimney fire; open fire; **~ follet** will-o'-the-wisp; **~ de joie** bonfire; **~ de signalisation**, **~ tricolore** traffic light; **~x de croisement** dipped (GB) or dimmed (US) headlights; **~x de détresse** warning lights; **~x de route** headlights.

IDIOMS **il n'y a pas le ~**○**!** there's no rush!; **ne pas faire long ~**○ not to last long; **il n'y a vu que du ~**○ he fell for it; **mourir à petit ~** to die a slow death.

feuillage /fœjaʒ/ *nm* foliage, leaves.

feuille /fœj/ *nf* **1** (Bot) leaf; **2** (of paper, metal) sheet.

■ **~ de chou**○ rag○, newspaper; **~ d'impôts** tax return; **~ de maladie** *a form for reclaiming medical expenses from the social security office*; **~ de paie** payslip (GB), pay stub (US).

feuillet /fœjɛ/ *nm* **1** (in book) leaf; **2** page.

feuilleté, **~e** /fœjte/ *adj* **pâte ~e** puff pastry.

feuilleter /fœjte/ [20] *vtr* to leaf through [sth].

feuilleton /fœjtɔ̃/ *nm* serial; soap (opera).

feutre /føtʀ/ *nm* **1** felt; **2** felt-tip (pen).

feutré, **~e** /føtʀe/ *adj* [*atmosphere*] hushed; [*sound*] muffled.

fève /fɛv/ *nf* **1** broad bean; **2** lucky charm (*hidden in Twelfth Night cake*).

février /fevʀije/ *nm* February.

fiable /fjabl/ *adj* reliable.

fiançailles /fjɑ̃saj/ *nf pl* engagement.

fiancé, **~e** /fjɑ̃se/ *nm,f* fiancé/fiancée.

fiancer: **se fiancer** /fjɑ̃se/ [12] *v refl* (+ *v être*) to get engaged.

fibre /fibʀ/ *nf* fibre[GB].

ficeler /fisle/ [19] *vtr* to tie up [*parcel*].

ficelle /fisɛl/ *nf* **1** string; **2** trick; **la ~ est un peu grosse** it's a bit obvious; **3** thin baguette.

IDIOMS **tirer sur la ~** to push one's luck.

fiche /fiʃ/ *nf* **1** index card; slip; **2** form; **~ d'inscription** enrolment[GB] form; **3** plug; **prise à trois ~s** three-pin plug.

■ **~ d'état civil** *record of personal details for administrative purposes*; **~ de paie** payslip (GB), pay stub (US).

ficher /fiʃe/ [1] **I** *vtr* **1** to put [sth] on a file; to open a file on [sb]; **être fiché (par la police)** to be on police files; **2** to drive [*stake, nail*]; **3**○ to do; **qu'est-ce que tu fiches?** what the heck○ are you doing?; **n'en avoir rien à ~** not to give a damn○; **4**○ **~ un coup à qn** (figurative) to be a real blow to sb; **~ la paix à qn** to leave sb alone; **5**○ **~ qch quelque part** to chuck○ sth somewhere; **~ qn dehors** to kick sb out○.

II se ficher *v refl* (+ *v être*) **1** [*arrow, knife*] to stick; **2**○ **se ~ de qn** to make fun of sb; **se ~ du monde** to have a hell of a nerve○; **3**○ **se ~ de ce que qn fait** not to give a damn○ (about) what sb does.

fichier /fiʃje/ *nm* file; (in library) index.

fichu○ /fiʃy/ **I** *pp* ▶**ficher I 3**, **4**, **5**, **II**.

II *adj* **1** [*weather, job*] rotten○; [*rain*] dreadful; [*car, TV*] damned○; **2** [*person, car*] done for○; **s'il pleut c'est ~** if it rains that's the end of that; **3 être bien ~** to be well designed; [*book*] to be well laid out; **je suis mal ~** I feel lousy○; **4 être ~ de faire** to be quite capable of doing.

fictif, **-ive** /fiktif, iv/ *adj* imaginary; false.

fiction /fiksjɔ̃/ *nf* **1** fiction; **2** (on TV) drama.

fidèle /fidɛl/ **I** *adj* **1** [*person, dog*] faithful; **être ~ au poste** to be always there; **2** loyal; **3** true (**à** to); **4** [*translation*] faithful.

II *nmf* **1** loyal supporter; **2 les ~s** the faithful.

fidélité /fidelite/ *nf* **1** fidelity; **2** loyalty; **3** (of translation) accuracy.

fief /fjɛf/ *nm* **1** fief; **2** (figurative) territory; (of party) stronghold.

fier[1], **fière** /fjɛʀ/ *adj* proud; **avoir fière allure** to cut a fine figure.

fier[2]: **se fier** /fje/ [2] *v refl* (+ *v être*) **1 se ~ à** to trust [*person, promise*]; **2 se ~ à** to rely on [*person, instrument*]; to trust to [*chance*].

fierté /fjɛʀte/ *nf* pride.

fièvre /fjɛvʀ/ *nf* **1** (high) temperature; **avoir de la ~** to have a (high) temperature; **2** frenzy; **3** fervour[GB]; **~ électorale** election fever.

■ **~ de cheval**○ raging fever.

figer /fiʒe/ [13] **I** *vtr* to congeal [*grease*]; to thicken [*sauce*]; to clot [*blood*].

II se figer *v refl* (+ *v être*) **1** [*smile, person*] to freeze; **2** [*grease*] to congeal; [*blood*] to clot.

fignoler /fiɲɔle/ [1] **I** *vtr* **1** to put the finishing touches to; **2** to take great pains over.

II *vi* to fiddle about.

figue /fig/ *nf* fig; **~ de Barbarie** prickly pear.

figuier /figje/ *nm* fig tree.

figurant, **~e** /figyʀɑ̃, ɑ̃t/ *nm,f* (in films) extra; (in theatre) bit player.

figuration /figyʀasjɔ̃/ *nf* **faire de la ~** (in films) to be an extra; (figurative) to have a token role.

figure /figyʀ/ *nf* **1** face; **2 faire ~ d'amateur** to look like an amateur; **reprendre ~ humaine** to look half-human again; **3** (in history, politics) figure; **4** (in drawing) figure.

IDIOMS **prendre ~** to take shape; **faire bonne ~** to keep an air of composure; to make the right impression; to do well.

figurer /figyʀe/ [1] **I** *vtr* to represent.

II *vi* [*name, object*] to appear.

III se figurer *v refl* (+ *v être*) to imagine.

figurine /figyʀin/ *nf* figurine.

fil /fil/ I *nm* **1** thread; ▶ **coudre**; **2** yarn; **3** string; **~ de fer** wire; **4** wire; (on appliance) flex (GB), cord (US); (on phone) lead; **coup de ~**○ (phone) call; **au bout du ~**○ on the phone; **5** (of conversation, text) thread; **perdre le ~ des événements** to lose track of events; **6** (of razor) edge.
II **au fil de** *phr* in the course of; **au ~ des ans** over the years; **aller au ~ de l'eau** to go with the flow.
■ **~ conducteur** (of heat) conductor; (of novel) thread; (of inquiry) lead; **~ directeur** guiding principle.
IDIOMS **ne tenir qu'à un ~** to hang by a thread.

filament /filamɑ̃/ *nm* filament.

filature /filatyʀ/ *nf* **1** textile mill; **2** spinning; **3 prendre qn en ~** to tail sb○.

file /fil/ *nf* **1 ~ (d'attente)** queue (GB), line (US); **2** line; **~ indienne** single file; **3** lane; **se garer en double ~** to double-park.

filer /file/ [1] I *vtr* **1** to spin [*wool, cotton*]; **2** to spin [*web, cocoon*]; **3** to ladder (GB), to get a run in [*tights*]; **4** to tail○ [sb]; **5**○ to give [sth] **(à qn** to sb).
II○ *vi* **1** to go off, to leave; **2** to rush; **3** [*time*] to fly by; [*prisoner*] to get away; **~ entre les mains** to slip through one's fingers.

filet /filɛ/ *nm* **1** net; **~ à provisions** string bag; **coup de ~** (police) raid; **2** fillet; **3** (of water) trickle; (of smoke) wisp; **~ de citron** dash of lemon juice.

filial, **~e**[1], *mpl* **-iaux** /filjal, o/ *adj* filial.

filiale[2] /filjal/ *nf* subsidiary.

filiation /filjasjɔ̃/ *nf* filiation.

filière /filjɛʀ/ *nf* **1** (Sch) course of study; **2** (Econ) field; **3 suivre la ~ habituelle** to climb up the usual career ladder; **4** official channels; **5 ~ (clandestine) de la drogue** drugs ring.

filiforme /filifɔʀm/ *adj* spindly; threadlike.

filigrane /filigʀan/ *nm* filigree.

filin /filɛ̃/ *nm* rope.

fille /fij/ *nf* **1** daughter; **2** girl; **~ mère** unmarried mother.

fillette /fijɛt/ *nf* **1** little girl; **2**○ half bottle.

filleul /fijœl/ *nm* godson, godchild.

filleule /fijœl/ *nf* goddaughter, godchild.

film /film/ *nm* **1** film, movie (US); **2** (thin) film.
■ **~ d'animation** cartoon.

filmer /filme/ [1] *vtr* to film.

filon /filɔ̃/ *nm* vein, seam.

fils /fis/ *nm inv* son; **Dupont ~** Dupont Junior.

filtre /filtʀ/ *nm* filter.

filtrer /filtʀe/ [1] I *vtr* **1** to filter; **2** to screen [*visitors, calls*].
II *vi* [*information*] to leak out; [*idea, liquid*] to filter through.

fin[1], **fine** /fɛ̃, fin/ I *adj* **1** [*rain, sand, brush*] fine; [*slice, layer*] thin; **2** [*ankle, waist*] slender; [*features*] fine; [*dish*] delicate; **3** [*person*] perceptive; [*taste, humour*] subtle; **vraiment c'est ~!** that's really clever!; **jouer au plus ~ avec qn** to try to outsmart sb; **avoir l'air ~**○ to look a fool; **4 avoir l'ouïe ~e** to have a keen sense of hearing; **5 au ~ fond de** in the remotest part of [*country*]; **le ~ mot de l'histoire** the truth of the matter.
II *adv* **1 être ~ prêt** to be all set; **2** [*write, grind*] finely; [*slice*] thinly.
III *nm* **le ~ du ~** the ultimate.
■ **~e mouche** sly customer○; **~es herbes** mixed herbs.

fin[2] /fɛ̃/ *nf* **1** end, ending; **à la ~ des années 70** in the late '70s; **tu vas te taire à la ~**○**!** for God's sake, be quiet!; **chômeur en ~ de droits** unemployed person no longer entitled to benefit; **2** end, death; **3** end, aim, purpose.
■ **~ de série** oddment.

final, **~e**[1], *mpl* **-aux** /final, o/ *adj* final.

finale[2] /final/ *nf* (Sport) final.

finalement /finalmɑ̃/ *adv* **1** in the end, finally; **2** in fact, actually.

finance /finɑ̃s/ I *nf* **1 la ~** finance; **2** financiers.
II **finances** *nf pl* **les ~s** finances; **moyennant ~s** for a consideration.

financer /finɑ̃se/ [12] *vtr* to finance.

financier, **-ière** /finɑ̃sje, ɛʀ/ I *adj* financial.
II *nm* **1** financier; **2** small cake.

finesse /finɛs/ *nf* **1** (of thread, writing) fineness; (of layer, paper) thinness; **2** (of dish) delicacy; (of face) fineness; (of waist) slenderness; **3** (of remark, person) perceptiveness; (of actor) sensitivity; **4** (of senses) keenness; **5 les ~s d'une langue** the subtleties of a language.

fini, **~e** /fini/ I *pp* ▶ **finir**.
II *pp adj* **être ~** to be over, to be finished.
III *nm* finish.

finir /finiʀ/ [3] I *vtr* **1** to finish (off), to complete; to end [*day*]; **2** to use up [*supplies*].
II *vi* to finish, to end; [*contract, lease*] to run out; **le film finit bien** the film has a happy ending; **ça va mal ~!** it'll end in tears!; **~ par faire** to end up doing; **ils finiront bien par céder** they're bound to give in in the end; **en ~ avec qn/qch** to have done with sb/sth; **finissons-en!** let's get it over with!

finition /finisjɔ̃/ *nf* **1** finishing; **2** finish.

finlandais, **~e** /fɛ̃lɑ̃dɛ, ɛz/ *adj* Finnish.

Finlandais, **~e** /fɛ̃lɑ̃dɛ, ɛz/ *nm,f* Finn.

Finlande /fɛ̃lɑ̃d/ *pr nf* Finland.

finnois, **~e** /finwa, az/ I *adj* Finnish.
II *nm* (language) Finnish.

fioriture /fjɔʀityʀ/ *nf* embellishment.

fioul /fjul/ *nm* fuel oil.

firme /fiʀm/ *nf* firm.

fisc /fisk/ *nm* tax office.

fiscal, **~e**, *mpl* **-aux** /fiskal, o/ *adj* fiscal, tax.

fiscalité /fiskalite/ *nf* **1** taxation; **2** tax system.

fissure /fisyʀ/ *nf* **1** crack; **2** (Anat) fissure.

fissurer /fisyʀe/ [1] *vtr* to crack, to fissure.

fixation /fiksasjɔ̃/ *nf* **1** fixing; fastening; **2** (on ski) binding; **3** fixation.

fixe /fiks/ *adj* **1** fixed; **2** permanent.

fixé, **~e** /fikse/ I *pp* ▶ **fixer**.

II *pp adj* **1 tu es ~ maintenant!** you've got the picture now○!; **2 nous ne sommes pas encore très ~s** we haven't really decided yet.

fixer /fikse/ [1] **I** *vtr* **1** to fix (**à** to); **2** to set [*date, price*]; to establish [*boundaries*]; **~ son choix sur** to decide on; **3** to fix [*colour, emulsion*]; **4** to focus [*attention*]; to stare at [*person*].
II se fixer *v refl* (+ *v être*) **1** [*part*] to be attached; **2** to set oneself [*goal, limit*].

flacon /flakɔ̃/ *nm* **1** (small) bottle; **2** decanter; **3** (in laboratory) flask.

flagada○ /flagada/ *adj inv* weary.

flageller /flaʒɛle/ [1] *vtr* to flog; (as religious punishment) to flagellate.

flageoler /flaʒɔle/ [1] *vi* **avoir les jambes qui flageolent** to feel wobbly.

flageolet /flaʒɔlɛ/ *nm* flageolet.

flagrant, ~e /flagʀɑ̃, ɑ̃t/ *adj* [*difference*] obvious; [*injustice*] flagrant; [*lie*] blatant; **prendre qn en ~ délit** to catch sb red-handed.

flair /flɛʀ/ *nm* **1** sense of smell, nose; **2** intuition.

flairer /fleʀe/ [1] *vtr* **1** to sniff [*object*]; **le chien a flairé une piste** the dog has picked up a scent; **2** [*animal*] to scent; [*person*] to smell; **3** to sense [*danger*].

flamand, ~e /flamɑ̃, ɑ̃d/ **I** *adj* Flemish.
II *nm* (language) Flemish.

flamant /flamɑ̃/ *nm* flamingo.

flambant /flɑ̃bɑ̃/ *adv* **~ neuf** brand new.

flambeau, *pl* **~x** /flɑ̃bo/ *nm* torch.

flambée /flɑ̃be/ *nf* **1** fire; **faire une ~** to light a fire; **2** (of hatred) flare-up; (of prices) explosion.

flamber /flɑ̃be/ [1] **I** *vtr* to flambé [*pancake*].
II *vi* to burn.

flamboyant, ~e /flɑ̃bwajɑ̃, ɑ̃t/ *adj* [*fire, light*] blazing; [*colour*] flaming.

flamme /flɑm/ *nf* **1** flame; **en ~s** on fire; **2** love, passion.
IDIOMS **descendre en ~s** to shoot down; **être tout feu tout ~** to be wildly enthusiastic.

flan /flɑ̃/ *nm* (Culin) custard tart (GB) or flan (US).
IDIOMS **en rester comme deux ronds de ~**○ to be dumbfounded.

flanc /flɑ̃/ *nm* (of person, mountain) side; (of animal) flank; **être sur le ~**○ to be exhausted.

flancher○ /flɑ̃ʃe/ [1] *vi* **1** to lose one's nerve; **2** to crack up; **3** [*heart, engine*] to give out.

flanelle /flanɛl/ *nf* flannel.

flâner /flɑne/ [1] *vi* to stroll; to loaf○ around.

flanquer /flɑ̃ke/ [1] **I** *vtr* **1** to flank; **il est toujours flanqué de son adjoint** his assistant never leaves his side; **2**○ to give [*blow, fine*]; **~ qch par terre** to throw sth to the ground; to drop sth; to knock sth to the ground.
II se flanquer○ *v refl* (+ *v être*) **se ~ dans** to run into.

flapi○**, ~e** /flapi/ *adj* worn out.

flaque /flak/ *nf* **~ (d'eau)** puddle; **~ d'huile** pool of oil.

flash, *pl* **~es** /flaʃ/ *nm* **1** (on camera) flash; **2 ~ (d'information)** news headlines; **~ publicitaire** advert (GB), commercial (US).

flasque[1] /flask/ *adj* [*skin, flesh*] flabby.

flasque[2] /flask/ *nf* flask.

flatter /flate/ [1] **I** *vtr* to flatter.
II se flatter *v refl* (+ *v être*) to pride oneself.

flatterie /flatʀi/ *nf* flattery.

flatteur, -euse /flatœʀ, øz/ *adj* **1** [*portrait*] flattering; **2** [*person, remarks*] sycophantic.

flatulence /flatylɑ̃s/ *nf* wind, flatulence.

fléau, *pl* **~x** /fleo/ *nm* **1** scourge; **2** (figurative) curse, plague; **3** (person) pest.

flèche /flɛʃ/ *nf* **1** arrow; **partir en ~** to shoot off; **monter en ~** [*prices*] to soar; **2** barbed remark; **3** spire.

flécher /fleʃe/ [14] *vtr* to signpost.

fléchette /fleʃɛt/ *nf* **1** dart; **2** (game) darts.

fléchir /fleʃiʀ/ [3] **I** *vtr* **1** to bend; **2** to sway [*person, opinion*]; to weaken [*will*].
II *vi* **1** [*knees*] to bend; [*legs*] to give way; **2** [*attention*] to flag; [*courage*] to waver; [*will*] to weaken; [*demand*] to fall off.

flegme /flɛgm/ *nm* phlegm, composure.

flemmard○**, ~e** /flemaʀ, aʀd/ *nm,f* lazybones○, lazy devil○.

flemme○ /flɛm/ *nf* laziness.

flétan /fletɑ̃/ *nm* halibut.

flétrir /fletʀiʀ/ [3] **I** *vtr* to blacken [*reputation*].
II se flétrir *v refl* (+ *v être*) [*plant*] to wither; [*flower, beauty*] to fade; [*fruit*] to shrivel.

fleur /flœʀ/ *nf* **1** flower; **être en ~s** [*garden*] to be full of flowers; [*plant, shrub*] to be in bloom; [*tree, lilac*] to be in blossom; **à ~s** flowery; **2 à ~ d'eau** just above the water.
■ **~ des champs** wild flower; **~ de lys** fleur-de-lis.
IDIOMS **être ~ bleue** to be romantic; **avoir une sensibilité à ~ de peau** to be hypersensitive; **avoir les nerfs à ~ de peau** to be a bundle of nerves; **faire une ~ à qn**○ to do sb a favour[GB].

fleuret /flœʀɛ/ *nm* (sword) foil.

fleurette /flœʀɛt/ *nf* (Culin) **crème ~** whipping cream.

fleuri, ~e /flœʀi/ **I** *pp* ▶ **fleurir**.
II *pp adj* **1** [*garden*] full of flowers; [*tree*] in blossom; in bloom; **2** [*table*] decorated with flowers; **3** [*wallpaper*] flowery.

fleurir /flœʀiʀ/ [3] *vi* **1** [*rose bush*] to flower; [*cherry tree*] to blossom; **2** [*new buildings*] to spring up; [*posters*] to appear; **3** to thrive, to flourish.

fleuriste /flœʀist/ *nmf* **1** florist; **2** flower shop.

fleuve /flœv/ **I** *nm* river.
II (-)fleuve (*combining form*) interminable; ▶ **roman-fleuve**.

flexible /flɛksibl/ *adj* **1** [*blade, tube*] flexible; [*body*] supple; **2** [*person, timetable*] flexible.

flexion /flɛksjɔ̃/ *nf* (of object) bending; (of arm, leg) flexing.

flic○ /flik/ *nm* cop○, policeman.

flipper /flipœʀ/ *nm* (Games) **1** pinball machine; **2** (device in machine) flipper; **3** (game) pinball.

flirter /flœʀte/ [1] *vi* to flirt.

flocon /flɔkɔ̃/ *nm* (of snow) flake; (of dust) speck;

(of wool) bit; **~s d'avoine** oat flakes (GB), oatmeal (US).

flop° /flɔp/ *nm* flop.

flopée° /flɔpe/ *nf* **(toute) une ~ de gamins** masses of kids.

floraison /flɔʀɛzɔ̃/ *nf* flowering.

floral, ~e, *mpl* **-aux** /flɔʀal, o/ *adj* floral.

flore /flɔʀ/ *nf* flora.

florin /flɔʀɛ̃/ *nm* (Dutch currency) guilder.

florissant, ~e /flɔʀisɑ̃, ɑ̃t/ *adj* **1** [*activity*] thriving; **2** [*complexion*] ruddy.

flot /flo/ **I** *nm* **1** (of letters, refugees) flood; (of visitors) stream; **2 les ~s** the deep, the sea.
II à flot *phr* **couler à ~(s)** to flow.

flottant, ~e /flɔtɑ̃, ɑ̃t/ *adj* [*wood, line*] floating; [*clothes, hair*] flowing.

flotte /flɔt/ *nf* **1** fleet; **2**° rain; **3**° water.

flottement /flɔtmɑ̃/ *nm* **1** wavering; **2** (of currency) floating.

flotter /flɔte/ [1] **I** *vi* **1** to float; **~ à la dérive** to drift; **2** [*mist*] to drift; [*flag*] to fly; **~ au vent** to flutter in the wind; **elle flotte dans ses vêtements** her clothes are hanging off her; **3** [*currency*] to float.
II° *v impers* to rain.

flotteur /flɔtœʀ/ *nm* float.

flou, ~e /flu/ **I** *adj* **1** [*outline*] blurred; **2** (figurative) vague, hazy.
II *nm* **1** fuzziness; **2** (figurative) vagueness.
■ **~ artistique** soft focus; (figurative) artistry.

fluctuant, ~e /flyktɥɑ̃, ɑ̃t/ *adj* [*prices, opinions*] fluctuating; [*person*] fickle.

fluet, -ette /flyɛ, ɛt/ *adj* [*body, person*] slight; [*voice*] thin, reedy.

fluide /flɥid/ **I** *adj* **1** [*oil, paint*] fluid; **2** [*style*] fluent; [*traffic*] moving freely.
II *nm* **1** (in physics) fluid; **2** (of clairvoyant) (psychic) powers.

fluo° /flyo/ *adj inv* fluorescent.

fluor /flyɔʀ/ *nm* fluorine.

fluorescent, ~e /flyɔʀɛsɑ̃, ɑ̃t/ *adj* fluorescent.

flûte /flyt/ **I** *nf* **1** (Mus) flute; **petite ~** piccolo; **2** (champagne) flute; **3** French stick.
II° *excl* damn°!, darn it°!
■ **~ à bec** recorder; **~ de Pan** panpipes.

fluvial, ~e, *mpl* **-iaux** /flyvjal, o/ *adj* fluvial, river.

flux /fly/ *nm inv* **1** (gen, Econ) flow; **2** (in physics) flux; **3 le ~ et le reflux** flood tide and ebb tide; (figurative) the ebb and flow; **4** influx.

FMI /ɛfɛmi/ *nm*: *abbr* ▶ **fonds**.

foc /fɔk/ *nm* jib.

focal, ~e, *mpl* **-aux** /fɔkal, o/ *adj* focal.

focaliser /fɔkalize/ [1] *vtr* to focus [*rays*]; to focalize [*electron beam*].

fœtus /fetys/ *nm inv* foetus.

foi /fwa/ *nf* **1** faith; **avoir la ~** to be a believer; **2 ma ~ oui** well yes; **en toute bonne ~ je crois que** in all sincerity, I believe that; **il est de mauvaise ~** he doesn't mean a word of it; **3 sur la ~ de témoins** on the evidence of witnesses; **qui fait** or **faisant ~** [*text, signature*] authentic; **sous la ~ du serment** under oath.
IDIOMS **sans ~ ni loi** fearing neither God nor man.

foie /fwa/ *nm* liver; **crise de ~** indigestion.

foin /fwɛ̃/ *nm* hay; **tas de ~** haystack; **la saison des ~s** the haymaking season.

foire /fwaʀ/ *nf* **1** fair; **~ du livre** book fair; **2** fun fair; **3**° bedlam; **faire la ~**° to live it up°.

fois /fwa/ **I** *nf inv* time; **une ~** once; **deux ~** twice; **quatre ~ trois font douze** four times three is twelve; **l'autre ~** last time; **une (bonne) ~ pour toutes** once and for all; **une ~ sur deux** half the time; **une ~ sur trois** every third time; **deux ~ sur cinq** two times out of five; **toutes les ~ que** every time (that); **deux ~ plus petit** half as big; **c'est dix ~ trop lourd!** it's far too heavy!; **régler en trois ~** to pay in three instalments[GB]; **pour la énième ~** for the hundredth time; **(à) la première ~** the first time; **la première ~ que je vous ai parlé** when I first talked to you.
II à la fois *phr* **deux à la ~** two at a time; **elle est à la ~ intelligente et travailleuse** she's both clever and hardworking.
III des fois° *phr* sometimes; **tu n'as pas vu mon chien, des ~?** you wouldn't have seen my dog, by any chance?
IV des fois que° *phr* in case.
IDIOMS **il était une ~** once upon a time there was.

foisonner /fwazɔne/ [1] *vi* to abound.

fol ▶ **fou I**.

folie /fɔli/ *nf* **1** madness; **aimer qn/qch à la ~** to be mad (GB) or crazy about sb/sth; **2** act of folly; **elle a fait une ~ en acceptant** she was mad to accept; **3** extravagance.
■ **~ des grandeurs** delusions of grandeur.

folk /fɔlk/ *nm* folk music.

folklo° /fɔlklo/ *adj* eccentric, crazy°.

folklore /fɔlklɔʀ/ *nm* **1** folklore; **2**° razzmatazz°.

folklorique /fɔlklɔʀik/ *adj* **1** [*music*] folk; [*costume*] traditional; **2**° eccentric.

folle ▶ **fou I, II**.

follement /fɔlmɑ̃/ *adv* **s'amuser ~** to have a terrific time.

follet /fɔlɛ/ *adj m* **feu ~** will-o'-the-wisp.

fomenter /fɔmɑ̃te/ [1] *vtr* to instigate.

foncé, ~e /fɔ̃se/ *adj* [*colour*] dark; [*pink*] deep.

foncer /fɔ̃se/ [12] **I** *vtr* **1** to make [sth] darker or deeper [*colour*]; **2** (Culin) to line.
II *vi* **1**° [*person, vehicle*] to tear along°; **fonce!** get a move on°!; go for it°!; **~ vers/dans** to rush toward(s)/into; **~ sur qch/vers la sortie** to make a dash for sth/for the exit; **~ sur qn** to charge at sb; **~ à New York** to dash over to New York; **2** [*colour*] (gen) to darken; [*pink, mauve*] to deepen; [*fabric*] to go darker.

foncier, -ière /fɔ̃sje, ɛʀ/ *adj* [*income*] from land; **impôt ~** property tax.

foncièrement /fɔ̃sjɛʀmɑ̃/ *adv* fundamentally.

fonction /fɔ̃ksjɔ̃/ *nf* **1** (in administration, company)

post; duties; **dans l'exercice de leurs ~s** while carrying out their duties; **occuper la ~ de** to hold the position of; **voiture de ~** company car; **2 en ~ de** according to; **3** function; **avoir pour ~ de faire** to be designed to do; **faire ~ de** to serve as; **4** profession; **~ enseignante** teaching profession.
■ **~ publique** civil service.

fonctionnaire /fɔ̃ksjɔnɛʀ/ *nmf* civil servant; (higher ranking) government official.

fonctionnel, **-elle** /fɔ̃ksjɔnɛl/ *adj* functional.

fonctionnement /fɔ̃ksjɔnmɑ̃/ *nm* **1** (of institution) functioning; **2** (of machinery) working; **mauvais ~** malfunction; **en ~** in service.

fonctionner /fɔ̃ksjɔne/ [1] *vi* to work; **~ à l'essence** to run on petrol (GB) or gas (US).

fond /fɔ̃/ **I** *nm* **1** (of vessel, lake, valley) bottom; (of cupboard, wardrobe) back; **~ de la mer** seabed; **~ de l'océan** ocean floor; **toucher le ~** (in water) to touch the bottom; (figurative) to hit rock bottom; **2** (of shop, yard) back; (of corridor, room) far end; **la chambre du ~** the back bedroom; **au ~ des bois** deep in the woods; **de ~ en comble** from top to bottom; **3 les problèmes de ~** the basic problems; **un débat de ~** an in-depth debate; **au ~** or **dans le ~, le problème est simple** basically, the problem is simple; **4** (of text) content; **5 regarder qn au ~ des yeux** (suspiciously) to give sb a searching look; **elle a un bon ~** she's very good at heart; **6** background; **7 un ~ de porto** a drop of port; **8** (Naut) **il y a 20 mètres de ~** the water is 20 metres[GB] deep; **9** (Sport) **épreuve de ~** long-distance event.
II à fond *phr* **1 connaître qch à ~** to be an expert in sth; **être à ~ pour**○ to support wholeheartedly; **respirer à ~** to breathe deeply; **mettre la radio à ~** to turn the radio right up; **2**○ **rouler à ~** to drive at top speed.
■ **~ d'artichaut** artichoke bottom; **~ de teint** foundation (GB), make-up base (US).

fondamental, **~e**, *mpl* **-aux** /fɔ̃damɑ̃tal, o/ *adj* **1** basic, fundamental; **2** essential.

fondamentalement /fɔ̃damɑ̃talmɑ̃/ *adv* **1** fundamentally; **2** radically.

fondant, **~e** /fɔ̃dɑ̃, ɑ̃t/ *adj* **1** [*ice*] melting; **2** [*pear*] which melts in the mouth.

fondateur, **-trice** /fɔ̃datœʀ, tʀis/ *nm,f* founder; **groupe ~** founding group.

fondation /fɔ̃dasjɔ̃/ **I** *nf* foundation.
II fondations *nf pl* foundations.

fondé, **~e** /fɔ̃de/ **I** *pp* ▶ **fonder**.
II *pp adj* justifiable, well-founded, legitimate; **non ~**, **mal ~** [*accusation*] groundless.
■ **~ de pouvoir** (of company) authorized representative; (of bank) senior banking executive.

fondement /fɔ̃dmɑ̃/ *nm* foundation; **être sans** or **dénué de ~** to be unfounded.

fonder /fɔ̃de/ [1] **I** *vtr* **1** to found; **2** to base.
II se fonder *v refl* (+ *v être*) **se ~ sur** [*theory, method*] to be based on; [*person*] to go on.

fonderie /fɔ̃dʀi/ *nf* **1** foundry; **2** casting.

fondre /fɔ̃dʀ/ [6] **I** *vtr* **1** to melt down [*metal*]; to smelt [*mineral*]; **2** to cast [*statue*].
II *vi* **1** [*snow, butter*] to melt; **2** [*sugar*] to dissolve; **3** [*savings*] to melt away; **4** (emotionally) to soften; **~ en larmes** to dissolve into tears.
III se fondre *v refl* (+ *v être*) **se ~ dans** [*person, figure*] to blend in with.

fonds /fɔ̃/ **I** *nm inv* **1** (in gallery, museum) collection; **2** fund.
II *nm pl* funds.
■ **~ de commerce** business; **Fonds monétaire international**, **FMI** International Monetary Fund, IMF.

fondu, **~e**[1] /fɔ̃dy/ **I** *pp* ▶ **fondre**.
II *pp adj* [*butter*] melted; [*metal*] molten.

fondue[2] /fɔ̃dy/ *nf* (Culin) fondue; **~ savoyarde** cheese fondue; **~ bourguignonne** fondue bourguignonne (*meat dipped in hot oil*).

fontaine /fɔ̃tɛn/ *nf* **1** fountain; **2** spring.

fonte /fɔ̃t/ *nf* **1** cast iron; **2** melting down, smelting; **3** thawing; **~ des neiges** thaw.

fonts /fɔ̃/ *nm pl* **~ baptismaux** font.

foot○ /fut/ *nm* = **football**.

football /futbol/ *nm* football (GB), soccer.

footing /futiŋ/ *nm* jogging.

forage /fɔʀaʒ/ *nm* drilling.

forain, **-aine** /fɔʀɛ̃, ɛn/ **I** *adj* fairground.
II *nm* stallkeeper; **les ~s** fairground people.

forçat /fɔʀsa/ *nm* **1** convict; **2** galley slave.

force /fɔʀs/ **I** *nf* **1** strength; **~s** strength; **avoir de la ~** to be strong; **c'est au-dessus de mes ~s** it's too much for me; **de toutes ses ~s** with all one's might; **ils sont de ~ égale aux échecs** they are evenly matched at chess; **2** force; **de ~** by force; **faire manger de ~** to force [sb] to eat; **entrer de ~ dans un lieu** to force one's way into a place; **3 ~ de vente** sales force; **~s** (Mil) forces; **d'importantes ~s de police** large numbers of police.
II à force○ *phr* **à ~, elle l'a cassé** she ended up breaking it.
III à force de *phr* **réussir à ~ de travail** to succeed by dint of hard work; **il est aphone à ~ de crier** he's been shouting so much (that) he's lost his voice.
■ **~ de dissuasion** (Mil) deterrent force; **~ de frappe** nuclear weapons; **~s de l'ordre** forces of law and order.

forcé, **~e** /fɔʀse/ **I** *pp* ▶ **forcer**.
II *pp adj* **1** (gen) forced; **2** [*consequence*] inevitable; **c'est ~**○**!** there's no way around it○!

forcément /fɔʀsemɑ̃/ *adv* inevitably; **pas ~** not necessarily.

forcené, **~e** /fɔʀsəne/ **I** *adj* [*rhythm*] furious; [*activity*] frenzied.
II *nm,f* **1** maniac; **2** crazed gunman.

forcer /fɔʀse/ [12] **I** *vtr* **1** to force; **2** to break through [*fence, enclosure*]; **~ la porte de qn** to force one's way into sb's house; **~ le passage** to force one's way through.
II forcer sur *v+prep* to overdo [*salt, colour*].
III *vi* **1** to overdo it; **2 serrez sans ~** do not tighten too much; **ne force pas!** don't force it!
IV se forcer *v refl* (+ *v être*) to force oneself.

IDIOMS **~ la main à qn** to force sb's hand.

forer /fɔʀe/ [1] *vtr* to drill.

forestier, **-ière** /fɔʀɛstje, ɛʀ/ *adj* [*area*] forested; **chemin ~** forest path; **exploitation forestière** (place) forestry plantation.

foret /fɔʀɛ/ *nm* drill.

forêt /fɔʀɛ/ *nf* forest; **~ tropicale** rain forest.

IDIOMS **c'est l'arbre qui cache la ~** you can't see the wood for the trees.

forfait /fɔʀfɛ/ *nm* **1** fixed rate; **un ~ de 15 francs** a fixed price of 15 francs; **2** package; **~ avion-auto** fly-drive package; **3 ~ skieur** ski pass; **4** (of player) withdrawal; **déclarer ~** to give up; (Sport) to withdraw.

forfaitaire /fɔʀfɛtɛʀ/ *adj* **prix ~** contract or all-inclusive price; **indemnité ~** basic allowance.

forge /fɔʀʒ/ *nf* **1** forge; **2** ironworks.

forgé, **~e** /fɔʀʒe/ **I** *pp* ▶ **forger**.

II *pp adj* [*object, metal*] wrought.

forger /fɔʀʒe/ [13] *vtr* **1** to forge; **2** to form [*character*].

forgeron /fɔʀʒəʀɔ̃/ *nm* blacksmith.

IDIOMS **c'est en forgeant qu'on devient ~** (Proverb) practice makes perfect.

formaliser: **se formaliser** /fɔʀmalize/ [1] *v refl* (+ *v être*) to take offence[GB] (**de** to).

formalité /fɔʀmalite/ *nf* formality; **les ~s à accomplir pour obtenir un visa** the necessary procedure to obtain a visa; **par pure ~** as a matter of form.

format /fɔʀma/ *nm* format, size.

formateur, **-trice** /fɔʀmatœʀ, tʀis/ *adj* formative.

formation /fɔʀmasjɔ̃/ *nf* **1** education; training; **avoir une ~ littéraire** to have an arts background; **en ~** undergoing training; **2** training course; **3** (of government, team) forming; **4** group.

■ **~ continue**, **~ permanente** adult continuing education; **~ professionnelle** professional training.

forme /fɔʀm/ **I** *nf* **1** shape; form; **en ~ de** in the shape of; **sous ~ de** in the form of; **sans ~** shapeless; **pour la ~** as a matter of form; **2** (of payment) method; **3** (physical condition) form; **en pleine ~** in great shape.

II formes *nf pl* **1** (of person) figure; **2** (of object, building) lines; **3 faire qch dans les ~s** to do sth in the correct manner; **y mettre les ~s** to be tactful.

formé, **~e** /fɔʀme/ **I** *pp* ▶ **former**.

II *pp adj* **1** made up; formed; **2** educated; trained; **3** [*writing, sentence*] formed.

formel, **-elle** /fɔʀmɛl/ *adj* **1** [*refusal, denial, person*] categorical; [*order*] strict; **être ~ sur qch** [*person*] to be definite about sth; **2 c'est purement ~** it's just a formality.

formellement /fɔʀmɛlmɑ̃/ *adv* **1** categorically; strictly; **2** officially; **~ identifié** clearly identified.

former /fɔʀme/ [1] **I** *vtr* **1** to form [*circle, rectangle*]; **2** to form, to constitute; **3** to train [*staff*]; to educate [*person, tastes*]; to develop [*intelligence*]; **4** to form [*abscess, film*].

II se former *v refl* (+ *v être*) **1** to form; **2** to be formed; **3** to train, to be trained; **4** [*character, style*] to develop.

formidable /fɔʀmidabl/ *adj* **1** [*force*] tremendous; **2**○ great, marvellous[GB]; **3**○ incredible.

formol /fɔʀmɔl/ *nm* formalin.

formulaire /fɔʀmylɛʀ/ *nm* form.

formule /fɔʀmyl/ *nf* **1** expression; **~ toute faite** set phrase; **2** (in travel, tourism) option; **~ à 75F** (in restaurant) set menu at 75F; **3** method; **4** concept; **5** (in science) formula; **6** (of car) **~ un** Formula One; **7** (of magazine) format.

■ **~ magique** magic words.

formuler /fɔʀmyle/ [1] *vtr* (gen) to express; to put [sth] into words [*idea*].

fort, **~e** /fɔʀ, fɔʀt/ **I** *adj* **1** strong; **armée ~e de 10000 hommes** 10,000-strong army; **~ d'un chiffre d'affaires en hausse** boasting an increased turnover; **2** [*noise*] loud; [*light*] bright; [*heat, activity*] intense; [*temperature, fever, rate*] high; [*blow, jolt*] hard; [*rain*] heavy; [*spice*] hot; [*majority*] large; [*lack, shortage*] great; [*drop, increase*] sharp; **~e émigration** high level of emigration; **3** (at school subject) good; **4** [*person*] stout; [*hips*] broad; [*bust*] large; [*thighs*] big; **5**○ **c'est un peu ~!** that's a bit much○!

II *adv* **1** extremely, very; **2** [*doubt*] very much; **avoir ~ à faire**○ to have a lot to do; **3** [*hit*] hard; [*squeeze*] tight; [*breathe*] deeply; [*speak*] loudly; **y aller un peu ~**○ to go a bit too far; **4 il ne va pas très ~** he's not very well.

III *nm* **1** fort; **2** strong person.

IV au plus fort de *phr* **au plus ~ de l'été** at the height of summer.

■ **~e tête** rebel.

IDIOMS **c'est plus ~ que moi/qu'elle** I/she just can't help it.

fortement /fɔʀtəmɑ̃/ *adv* [*criticize*] strongly; [*rise*] sharply; [*industrialized*] highly; [*shaken*] deeply; [*damaged*] badly; [*displease, dislike*] greatly; [*armed*] heavily; **il est ~ question de**... it is highly likely that...

forteresse /fɔʀtəʀɛs/ *nf* stronghold.

fortifiant /fɔʀtifjɑ̃/ *nm* (Med) tonic.

fortification /fɔʀtifikasjɔ̃/ *nf* fortification.

fortifier /fɔʀtifje/ [2] *vtr* **1** to strengthen [*nails, hair*]; **2** [*meal*] to fortify; [*holiday, vitamins*] to do [sb] good; **3** to reinforce [*construction*].

fortuit, **~e** /fɔʀtɥi, it/ *adj* [*meeting*] accidental; [*incident, discovery*] fortuitous.

fortune /fɔʀtyn/ *nf* **1** fortune; **2 de ~** makeshift.

IDIOMS **faire contre mauvaise ~ bon cœur** to put on a brave face.

fosse /fos/ *nf* **1** pit; **2** grave; **3** sandpit.

■ **~ commune** communal grave; **~ septique** septic tank.

fossé /fose/ *nm* **1** (gen) ditch; (of castle) moat; **2** (figurative) gap; rift.

fossette /fosɛt/ *nf* dimple.

fossile /fosil/ *adj, nm* fossil.

fossoyeur /foswajœʀ/ *nm* gravedigger.

fou (**fol** *before vowel or mute h*), **folle** /fu, fɔl/ I *adj* **1** (insane) mad; **devenir ~** to go mad; **un tueur ~** a crazed killer; **2** [*person, idea*] mad (GB), crazy; [*look*] wild; [*story*] crazy; **être ~ furieux**○ to be raving mad; **être ~ à lier**○ to be stark raving mad○; **entre eux c'est l'amour ~** they're madly in love; **~ de qn** crazy about sb; **3** [*success*] huge; **un monde ~** a huge crowd; **avoir un mal ~ à faire** to find it incredibly difficult to do; **4** [*vehicle, horse*] runaway; [*lock of hair*] stray; **avoir le ~ rire** to have a fit of the giggles.
II *nm,f* madman/madwoman; **envoyer qn chez les ~s**○ to send sb to the nuthouse○; **courir comme un ~** to run like mad; **c'est un ~ d'art contemporain** he's mad about contemporary art.
III *nm* **1** fool, court jester; **2** (in chess) bishop.
IDIOMS **faire les ~s**○ to fool about; **plus on est de ~s plus on rit**○ the more the merrier.

foudre /fudʀ/ *nf* lightning; **coup de ~** love at first sight; **avoir le coup de ~ pour** to be really taken with.

foudroyant, **~e** /fudʀwajɑ̃, ɑ̃t/ *adj* [*attack*] lightning; [*look*] furious; [*death*] sudden.

foudroyer /fudʀwaje/ [23] *vtr* **1** to strike [*tree*]; **mort foudroyé** struck dead by lightning; **~ qn du regard** to look daggers at sb○; **2** [*bad news*] to devastate.

fouet /fwɛ/ *nm* **1** whip; **dix coups de ~** ten lashes of the whip; **le grand air m'a donné un coup de ~** the fresh air invigorated me; **se heurter de plein ~** to collide head-on; **2** (Culin) whisk; **~ mécanique** hand whisk.

fouetter /fwɛte/ [1] *vtr* **1** to whip, to flog [*person*]; to whip [*animal*]; **2 la pluie leur fouettait le visage** the rain lashed their faces.
IDIOMS **il n'y a pas de quoi ~ un chat**○ it's no big deal○; **avoir d'autres chats à ~**○ to have other fish to fry.

fougère /fuʒɛʀ/ *nf* **1** fern; **2** bracken.

fougue /fug/ *nf* enthusiasm.

fouille /fuj/ *nf* **1** (of place, person, baggage) search; **2** excavation.

fouillé, **~e** /fuje/ I *pp* ▶ **fouiller**.
II *pp adj* [*study, portrait, piece of work*] detailed; [*style*] elaborate.

fouiller /fuje/ [1] I *vtr* **1** to search; to frisk; **2** to dig [*site*].
II *vi* **~ dans** (gen) to rummage through; to search [*memory*]; to delve into [*past*].

fouillis /fuji/ *nm inv* mess; jumble.

fouine /fwin/ *nf* (Zool) stone marten.

fouiner /fwine/ [1] *vi* **1** to forage about; **2 ~ dans** to rummage through [*objects, papers*]; to poke one's nose into [*life, past*].

foulard /fulaʀ/ *nm* scarf, headscarf.

foule /ful/ *nf* **1** crowd; mob; **il y avait ~ à la réunion** there were masses of people at the meeting; **venir en ~ à** to flock to; **2** mass.

foulée /fule/ *nf* (of horse, athlete) stride; **courir dans la ~ de qn** (Sport) to tail sb; **dans la ~ il a...** while he was at it, he...

fouler /fule/ [1] I *vtr* to tread [*grapes*].
II **se fouler** *v refl* (+ *v être*) **1** (Med) **se ~ le poignet** to sprain one's wrist; **2**○ **tu ne t'es pas foulé** you didn't kill yourself○.

foulure /fulyʀ/ *nf* sprain.

four /fuʀ/ *nm* **1** oven; **cuire au ~** to roast, to bake; **2** furnace; kiln.
■ **~ crématoire** crematory (furnace); **~ à micro-ondes** microwave oven.

fourbu, **~e** /fuʀby/ *adj* exhausted.

fourche /fuʀʃ/ *nf* fork; **faire une ~** to fork.

fourcher /fuʀʃe/ [1] *vi* **ma langue a fourché** it was a slip of the tongue.

fourchette /fuʀʃɛt/ *nf* **1** fork; **2** (of prices, temperature) range; (of income) bracket; **~ horaire** period.

fourchu, **~e** /fuʀʃy/ *adj* [*branch*] forked; **cheveux ~s** split ends.

fourgon /fuʀgɔ̃/ *nm* **1** van; **2** (of train) goods wagon (GB), freight car (US).
■ **~ à bestiaux** cattle truck.

fourgonnette /fuʀgɔnɛt/ *nf* (small) van.

fourmi /fuʀmi/ *nf* (Zool) ant; **travail de ~** laborious task.
IDIOMS **avoir des ~s dans les jambes** to have pins and needles in one's legs.

fourmilier /fuʀmilje/ *nm* anteater.

fourmilière /fuʀmiljɛʀ/ *nf* ant hill.

fourmillement /fuʀmijmɑ̃/ *nm* **1 un ~ de gens** a mass of people; **2** tingling sensation.

fourmiller /fuʀmije/ [1] I **fourmiller de** *v+prep* to be chock-full of [*mistakes*]; to be swarming with [*visitors*].
II *vi* to abound.

fournaise /fuʀnɛz/ *nf* blaze; **la ville est une ~ en été** the town is baking hot in summer.

fourneau, *pl* **~x** /fuʀno/ *nm* **1** (Tech) furnace; **2** stove.

fournée /fuʀne/ *nf* batch.

fourni, **~e** /fuʀni/ I *pp* ▶ **fournir**.
II *pp adj* [*hair*] thick; [*grass*] lush.

fournir /fuʀniʀ/ [3] I *vtr* to supply [*document, equipment*]; to provide [*energy*]; to contribute [*effort*]; to produce [*proof*].
II **se fournir** *v refl* (+ *v être*) **se ~ chez** or **auprès de** to get [sth] from.

fournisseur, **-euse** /fuʀnisœʀ, øz/ I *adj* **pays ~** exporting country.
II *nm* supplier; **~ de drogue** drug dealer.

fourniture /fuʀnityʀ/ *nf* **1** supply, provision; **2 ~s scolaires/de bureau** school/office stationery; **~s de laboratoire** laboratory equipment.

fourrage /fuʀaʒ/ *nm* forage; **~ sec** fodder.

fourré, **~e** /fuʀe/ I *pp* ▶ **fourrer**.
II *pp adj* **1** (Culin) filled; **2** fur-lined; lined; **3**○ **toujours ~ au café** always hanging about at the café.
III *nm* thicket.

fourrer /fuʀe/ [1] I *vtr* **1**○ to stick○; **~ qch dans la tête de qn** to put sth into sb's head; **2** (Culin) to fill; **3** to line [*garment*].
II **se fourrer**○ *v refl* (+ *v être*) **1 se ~ dans un coin** to get into a corner; **2 se ~ une idée dans la tête** to get an idea into one's head.

fourre-tout /fuʀtu/ *adj inv* **sac ~** holdall (GB), carryall (US).

fourrière /fuʀjɛʀ/ *nf* pound; **mettre une voiture à la ~** to impound a car.

fourrure /fuʀyʀ/ *nf* fur, coat.

foutre◑ /futʀ/ [6] **I** *vtr* **1 n'en avoir rien à ~** not to give a damn○; **2 ~ qch quelque part** to stick○ sth somewhere.

II se foutre *v refl* (+ *v être*) **1 il ne s'est pas foutu de toi!** he's been very generous!; **se ~ du monde** to have a bloody (GB) or hell of a◑ (US) nerve; **2** not to give a damn○.

IDIOMS **~ le camp** to bugger off○ (GB), to split○ (US).

foutu◑, **~e** /futy/ **I** *pp* ▶ **foutre**.

II *pp adj* **1** (*before n*) bloody awful◑ (GB), damned (US); **2 être ~** [*person, garment*] to have had it○; **3 être mal ~** to be unattractive; to feel lousy○; **4 être ~ de faire** to be totally capable of doing.

foyer /fwaje/ *nm* **1** home; **fonder un ~** to get married; **2** household; **3** hostel; **4** club; **5** hearth; **6** (of resistance) pocket; **un ~ d'incendie** a fire; **7** (of rebellion) seat; (of epidemic) source; **8** (in optics) focus; **lunettes à double ~** bifocals.

fracas /fʀaka/ *nm inv* (of falling object) crash; (of waves) roar; (of town, battle) din.

fracassant, **~e** /fʀakasɑ̃, ɑ̃t/ *adj* [*noise*] deafening; [*news*] sensational; [*success*] stunning.

fracasser /fʀakase/ [1] **I** *vtr* to smash.

II se fracasser *v refl* (+ *v être*) to crash.

fraction /fʀaksjɔ̃/ *nf* **1** (in mathematics) fraction; **2** (of sum of money) part; (of company) section; **en une ~ de seconde** in a split second.

fractionner /fʀaksjɔne/ [1] *vtr* to divide up [*work, group*]; to split [*party*].

fracture /fʀaktyʀ/ *nf* fracture; **~ du poignet** fractured wrist.

fracturer /fʀaktyʀe/ [1] **I** *vtr* to break down [*door*]; to break [*window*]; to force [*safe*].

II se fracturer *v refl* (+ *v être*) **se ~ la cheville** to break one's ankle.

fragile /fʀaʒil/ *adj* **1** fragile; **2** [*person*] frail; [*eye*] sensitive; [*heart*] weak.

fragiliser /fʀaʒilize/ [1] *vtr* to weaken.

fragilité /fʀaʒilite/ *nf* **1** fragility; **2** frailty.

fragment /fʀagmɑ̃/ *nm* **1** (of cup, bone) fragment; **2** (of book, novel) passage.

fragmenter /fʀagmɑ̃te/ [1] *vtr* to break up [*substance*]; to divide up [*work*].

fraîche ▶ **frais I, V**.

fraîchement /fʀɛʃmɑ̃/ *adv* **1** freshly, newly; **2** coldly; **elle a été ~ accueillie** she was given a cool reception.

fraîcheur /fʀɛʃœʀ/ *nf* **1** coolness; coldness; **la ~ du soir** the cold evening air; **2** freshness.

frais, **fraîche** /fʀɛ, fʀɛʃ/ **I** *adj* **1** cool; cold; **'servir ~'** 'serve chilled'; **2** [*news, snow*] fresh; [*paint*] wet; **3** [*complexion*] fresh; **4** [*troops*] fresh; **de l'argent ~** more money.

II *adv* **il fait ~** it's cool.

III *nm* **prendre le ~** to get some fresh air; **mettre au ~** to put in a cool place; to put to cool.

IV *nm pl* **1** expenses; **aux ~ de l'entreprise** paid for by the company; **rentrer dans ses ~** to cover one's expenses; **faire les ~ de qch** to bear the brunt of sth; **2** fees; **3** costs.

V à la fraîche *phr* in the cool of the morning; in the cool of the evening.

■ **~ d'annulation** cancellation fees; **~ de déplacement** (of employee) travel expenses; (for repairman) call-out charge; **~ d'expédition** (for parcel) postage and packing; **~ d'inscription** (gen) registration fees; (for school) school fees (GB), tuition fees (US); (at university) tuition fees; **~ de port** postage.

fraise /fʀɛz/ *nf* **1** strawberry; **~ des bois** wild strawberry; **2** (tool, instrument) reamer; milling-cutter; (of dentist) drill.

IDIOMS **ramener sa ~**○ to stick one's nose in○.

fraisier /fʀɛzje/ *nm* **1** strawberry plant; **2** strawberry gateau.

framboise /fʀɑ̃bwaz/ *nf* **1** raspberry; **2** raspberry liqueur.

framboisier /fʀɑ̃bwazje/ *nm* raspberry cane; raspberry bush.

franc, **franche** /fʀɑ̃, fʀɑ̃ʃ/ **I** *adj* **1** [*person*] frank, straight; [*reply*] straight; [*laughter, expression*] open, honest; **jouer ~ jeu** to play fair; **2** duty-free; **~ de port** postage paid.

II *nm* (currency) franc; **~ lourd** new franc.

français, **~e** /fʀɑ̃sɛ, ɛz/ **I** *adj* French.

II *nm* (language) French.

Français, **~e** /fʀɑ̃sɛ, ɛz/ *nm,f* Frenchman/ Frenchwoman.

France /fʀɑ̃s/ *pr nf* France.

franche ▶ **franc I**.

franchement /fʀɑ̃ʃmɑ̃/ *adv* **1** frankly, candidly; **je lui ai demandé ~** I asked him straight out; **2** [*lean*] firmly; [*enter*] boldly; **3** really; **il m'a franchement agacé** he really annoyed me; **~!** (well) really!

franchir /fʀɑ̃ʃiʀ/ [3] *vtr* to cross [*line*]; to get over [*fence*]; to cover [*distance*].

franchise /fʀɑ̃ʃiz/ *nf* **1** frankness, sincerity; **2** exemption; **3** (in insurance) excess (GB), deductible (US); **4** (to sell goods) franchise.

■ **~ de bagages** baggage allowance.

franc-jeu /fʀɑ̃ʒø/ *nm* fair play.

franc-maçon, **-onne**, *pl* **francs-maçons**, **franc-maçonnes** /fʀɑ̃masɔ̃, ɔn/ *nm,f* Freemason.

franco /fʀɑ̃ko/ *adv* **1 ~ de port** postage paid, carriage paid; **2**○ **y aller ~** to go right ahead.

francophone /fʀɑ̃kɔfɔn/ **I** *adj* French-speaking; [*literature*] in the French language.

II *nmf* French speaker.

franc-parler /fʀɑ̃paʀle/ *nm* **avoir son ~** to speak one's mind.

frange /fʀɑ̃ʒ/ *nf* **1** (on rug, curtain, garment) fringe; **2** (hair) fringe (GB), bangs (US).

frangin○ /fʀɑ̃ʒɛ̃/ *nm* brother.

frangine○ /fʀɑ̃ʒin/ *nf* sister.

franglais /fʀɑ̃glɛ/ *nm* Franglais.

franquette○: **à la bonne franquette** /alabɔnfʀɑ̃kɛt/ *phr* **recevoir qn à la bonne ~** to have sb over for an informal meal.

frappé, **~e** /fʀape/ **I** *pp* ▶ **frapper**.
II *pp adj* [*cocktail*] frappé; [*coffee*] iced.

frapper /fʀape/ [1] **I** *vtr* **1** (gen) to hit, to strike; **~ à coups de pied** to kick; **~ à coups de poing** to punch; **~ un grand coup** (gen) to hit hard; (on door) to knock; **2** to strike [*coin*]; **3** [*unemployment, epidemic*] to hit [*region*]; **les taxes qui frappent les produits français** duties imposed on French goods; **4 ce qui m'a frappé c'est**... what struck me was...; **j'ai été frappé de voir que**... I was amazed to see that...
II *vi* **1** to hit, to strike; **~ dans ses mains** to clap one's hands; **2** to knock; **on a frappé** there was a knock at the door; **3** [*criminals*] to strike.

frasque /fʀask/ *nf* escapade.

fraternel, **-elle** /fʀatɛʀnɛl/ *adj* fraternal, brotherly.

fraterniser /fʀatɛʀnize/ [1] *vi* to fraternize.

fraternité /fʀatɛʀnite/ *nf* fraternity.

fraude /fʀod/ *nf* (Law) fraud; **~ fiscale** tax fraud; **~ électorale** vote or election rigging; **en ~** [*enter*] illegally.

frauder /fʀode/ [1] *vi* (on public transport) to travel without a ticket; (in cinema) to slip in without paying.

frauduleux, **-euse** /fʀodylø, øz/ *adj* fraudulent.

frayer /fʀɛje/ [21] **I** *vtr* **~ un passage à qn à travers la foule** to clear a path for sb through the crowd; **~ le chemin** or **la voie à qch** (figurative) to pave the way for sth.
II se frayer *v refl* (+ *v être*) **se ~ un chemin dans** or **à travers** to make one's way through.

frayeur /fʀɛjœʀ/ *nf* **1** fear; **2** fright.

fredonner /fʀədɔne/ [1] *vtr* to hum.

freezer /fʀizœʀ/ *nm* icebox.

frégate /fʀegat/ *nf* (Naut) frigate.

frein /fʀɛ̃/ *nm* brake; **donner un coup de ~** to slam on the brakes; **mettre un ~ à** to curb.
IDIOMS **ronger son ~** to champ at the bit.

freiner /fʀene/ [1] **I** *vtr* **1** to slow down [*vehicle*]; **2** to impede [*person*]; **3** to curb [*inflation*].
II *vi* **1** to brake; **~ à fond** to slam on the brakes; **2** (in skiing) to slow down.

frelaté, **~e** /fʀəlate/ *adj* [*alcohol*] adulterated; [*taste*] unnatural.

frêle /fʀɛl/ *adj* frail.

frelon /fʀəlɔ̃/ *nm* hornet.

frémir /fʀemiʀ/ [3] *vi* **1** [*leaf*] to quiver; [*water*] to ripple; **2** (with emotion) [*lip*] to tremble; [*person*] to quiver; to shudder; **3** (Culin) to start to come to the boil.

frémissement /fʀemismɑ̃/ *nm* **1** quiver, tremor; **2** (of person, hand) quiver, shudder.

frêne /fʀɛn/ *nm* ash (tree).

frénésie /fʀenezi/ *nf* frenzy.

frénétique /fʀenetik/ *adj* frenzied; frenetic.

fréquence /fʀekɑ̃s/ *nf* frequency.

fréquent, **~e** /fʀekɑ̃, ɑ̃t/ *adj* **1** frequent; **2** common.

fréquentation /fʀekɑ̃tasjɔ̃/ *nf* **1** company; **avoir de bonnes/mauvaises ~s** to keep good/bad company; **2 ~ des théâtres** theatregoing[GB].

fréquenté, **~e** /fʀekɑ̃te/ **I** *pp* ▶ **fréquenter**.
II *pp adj* popular, busy; **lieu bien ~** place that attracts the right sort of people.

fréquenter /fʀekɑ̃te/ [1] **I** *vtr* **1** to associate with [*person*]; to move in [*milieu*]; **2** to attend [*school*]; to go to [*restaurant*].
II se fréquenter *v refl* (+ *v être*) [*friends*] to see one another.

frère /fʀɛʀ/ *nm* brother.

fresque /fʀɛsk/ *nf* **1** fresco; **2** panorama.

fret /fʀɛt/ *nm* freight.

frétiller /fʀetije/ [1] *vi* [*fish*] to wriggle; **~ de la queue** [*dog*] to wag its tail.

friable /fʀijabl/ *adj* [*rock, biscuit*] crumbly.

friand, **~e** /fʀijɑ̃, ɑ̃d/ **I** *adj* **être ~ de qch** to be very fond of sth.
II *nm* (Culin) puff; **~ au fromage** cheese puff.

friandise /fʀijɑ̃diz/ *nf* sweet (GB), candy (US).

fric○ /fʀik/ *nm* dough○, money.

friche /fʀiʃ/ *nf* waste land.

friction /fʀiksjɔ̃/ *nf* **1** (Med) rub; **2** friction.

frictionner /fʀiksjɔne/ [1] **I** *vtr* to give [sb] a rub [*person*]; to rub [*head, feet*].
II se frictionner *v refl* (+ *v être*) to rub oneself down.

frigidaire® /fʀiʒidɛʀ/ *nm* refrigerator.

frigide /fʀiʒid/ *adj* frigid.

frigo○ /fʀigo/ *nm* fridge○.

frigorifique /fʀigɔʀifik/ *adj* refrigerated.

frileux, **-euse** /fʀilø, øz/ *adj* **1** sensitive to the cold; **2** [*attitude, policy*] cautious.

frime○ /fʀim/ *nf* **pour la ~** for show; **c'est de la ~** it's all an act.

frimousse○ /fʀimus/ *nf* little face.

fringuer○: **se fringuer** /fʀɛ̃ge/ [1] *v refl* (+ *v être*) to dress.

friper /fʀipe/ [1] *vtr*, **se friper** *v refl* (+ *v être*) to crease, to crumple.

fripouille○ /fʀipuj/ *nf* crook○.

frire /fʀiʀ/ [64] *vtr*, *vi* to fry.

frisé, **~e**[1] /fʀize/ **I** *pp* ▶ **friser**.
II *pp adj* [*hair*] curly; [*person*] curly-haired.

frisée[2] /fʀize/ *nf* curly endive.

friser /fʀize/ [1] **I** *vtr* **1** to curl; **se faire ~** to have one's hair curled; **2** to border on; **cela frise les 10%** it's approaching 10%.
II *vi* to curl; [*person*] to have curly hair.

frisson /fʀisɔ̃/ *nm* shiver, shudder; **j'ai des ~s** I keep shivering; **grand ~** great thrill.

frissonner /fʀisɔne/ [1] *vi* **1** (with cold) to shiver; (with fear) to shudder; **2** [*leaves*] to tremble; **3** [*water, milk*] to simmer.

frite /fʀit/ *nf* (Culin) chip (GB), French fry (US).

friteuse /fʀitøz/ *nf* chip pan (GB), deep fat fryer (US).

friture /fʀityʀ/ *nf* **1** frying; **2** (for frying) fat; oil;

3 fried food; **4** (fish) **petite ~** ≈ whitebait; **5** (on radio) crackling.

frivole /fRivɔl/ *adj* frivolous.

froid, **~e** /fRwɑ, fRwɑd/ **I** *adj* cold; (figurative) cold, cool.

II *adv* **il fait ~** it's cold.

III *nm* **1** cold; **coup de ~** chill; **prendre ~** to catch a cold; **2** coldness; **ils sont en ~ avec moi** relations between them and me are strained; **jeter un ~** to cast a chill.

IV à froid *phr* **démarrage à ~** cold start.

IDIOMS **il fait un ~ de canard**○ it is bitterly cold; **donner ~ dans le dos** to send a shiver down the spine; **ne pas avoir ~ aux yeux** to be fearless.

froidement /fRwɑdmɑ̃/ *adv* **1** coolly; **abattre ~** to shoot [sb] down in cold blood; **2 regarder les choses ~** to look at things with a cool head.

froideur /fRwɑdœR/ *nf* (gen) coldness; (of reception) coolness.

froisser /fRwɑse/ [1] **I** *vtr* **1** to crease [*fabric*]; to crumple [*paper*]; **2** to offend [*person*]; **3** (Med) to strain.

II se froisser *v refl* (+ *v être*) **1** to crease; **2** to be hurt or offended; **3** (Med) to strain.

frôler /fRole/ [1] **I** *vtr* **1** [*person*] to brush (against); **2** [*bullet, car*] to miss narrowly; **il a frôlé la mort** he came close to dying.

II se frôler *v refl* (+ *v être*) [*people*] to brush against each other.

fromage /fRɔmaʒ/ *nm* cheese; **~ maigre** low-fat cheese; **~ de tête** brawn (GB), head cheese (US).

fromager /fRɔmaʒe/ *nm* **1** cheesemaker; **2** cheese seller.

fromagerie /fRɔmaʒRi/ *nf* cheese shop.

froment /fRɔmɑ̃/ *nm* wheat.

froncement /fRɔ̃smɑ̃/ *nm* **avoir un léger ~ de sourcils** to frown slightly.

froncer /fRɔ̃se/ [12] *vtr* **1** to gather [*pleats*]; **2 ~ les sourcils** to frown.

fronde /fRɔ̃d/ *nf* **1** (weapon) sling; **2** (toy) catapult (GB), slingshot (US); **3** revolt.

frondeur, **-euse** /fRɔ̃dœR, øz/ *adj* rebellious.

front /fRɔ̃/ **I** *nm* **1** forehead; **2** (Mil) front; **3** façade.

II de front *phr* **ils marchaient à quatre de ~** they were walking four abreast; **mener plusieurs tâches de ~** to have several jobs on the go.

IDIOMS **avoir le ~ de faire** to have the face or effrontery to do.

frontal, **~e**, *mpl* **-aux** /fRɔ̃tal, o/ *adj* [*attack*] frontal; [*collision*] head-on.

frontalier, **-ière** /fRɔ̃talje, ɛR/ *adj* border.

frontière /fRɔ̃tjɛR/ *nf* **1** frontier, border; **~ naturelle** natural boundary; **2 ~s entre les disciplines** boundaries between disciplines.

fronton /fRɔ̃tɔ̃/ *nm* pediment.

frottement /fRɔtmɑ̃/ *nm* **1** rubbing; **2** friction.

frotter /fRɔte/ [1] **I** *vtr* **1** to rub; **2** to scrub.

II *vi* to rub.

III se frotter *v refl* (+ *v être*) **1 se ~ les yeux** to rub one's eyes; **2** to scrub oneself; **3 se ~ à** to take on [*person*].

IDIOMS **qui s'y frotte s'y pique** if you go looking for trouble, you'll find it.

frottis /fRɔti/ *nm inv* (Med) smear.

frousse○ /fRus/ *nf* fright.

fructifier /fRyktifje/ [2] *vi* [*capital*] to yield a profit; [*business*] to flourish.

fructueux, **-euse** /fRyktɥø, øz/ *adj* **1** [*relationship, meeting*] fruitful; [*attempt, career*] successful; **2** (financially) profitable.

frugal, **~e**, *mpl* **-aux** /fRygal, o/ *adj* frugal.

fruit /fRɥi/ *nm* fruit.

■ **~ de la passion** passion fruit; **~ sec** dried fruit; **~s de mer** seafood.

fruité, **~e** /fRɥite/ *adj* [*alcohol, aroma*] fruity.

fruste /fRyst/ *adj* unsophisticated.

frustrant, **~e** /fRystRɑ̃, ɑ̃t/ *adj* frustrating.

frustré, **~e** /fRystRe/ *adj* frustrated.

frustrer /fRystRe/ [1] *vtr* **1 ~ qn** to thwart sb; **2 ~ qn de qch** to deprive sb of sth; to cheat sb (out) of sth; **3** to frustrate.

fuel /fjul/ *nm* = **fioul**.

fugace /fygas/ *adj* fleeting; [*symptom*] elusive.

fugitif, **-ive** /fyʒitif, iv/ **I** *adj* **1** [*prisoner*] escaped; **2** fleeting, elusive.

II *nm,f* fugitive.

fugue /fyg/ *nf* **1 faire une ~** to run away; **2** (Mus) fugue.

fugueur, **-euse** /fygœR, øz/ *nm,f* runaway (child).

fuir /fɥiR/ [29] **I** *vtr* **1** to flee [*country, oppression*]; **2** to avoid [*discussion, person*]; to steer clear of [*crowd*]; to stay out of [*sun*].

II *vi* **1** [*person*] to flee; [*animal*] to run away; **faire ~** to scare [sb] off [*person*]; **2** [*tap, gas, pen*] to leak; **3 ~ devant ses responsabilités** not to face up to one's responsibilities.

fuite /fɥit/ *nf* **1** (gen) flight; (of prisoner) escape; **prendre la ~** to flee; to escape; **2** (of information) leak; **3** (of liquid, gas) leak.

fulgurant, **~e** /fylgyRɑ̃, ɑ̃t/ *adj* [*attack*] lightning; [*progression*] dazzling; [*imagination*] brilliant.

fulminer /fylmine/ [1] *vi* to fulminate.

fumé, **~e**[1] /fyme/ **I** *pp* ▶ **fumer**.

II *pp adj* **1** (Culin) smoked; **2** [*lenses*] tinted; [*glass*] smoked.

fumée[2] /fyme/ *nf* **1** smoke; **~s** (from factory) fumes; **partir en ~** (figurative) to go up in smoke; **2** steam.

fumer /fyme/ [1] **I** *vtr* to smoke.

II *vi* **1** [*person, chimney*] to smoke; **2** [*soup*] to steam; [*acid*] to give off fumes.

IDIOMS **~ comme un pompier** or **sapeur** to smoke like a chimney.

fumet /fymɛ/ *nm* (Culin) (of meat) aroma; (of wine) bouquet.

fumeur, **-euse**[1] /fymœR, øz/ *nm,f* smoker; **zone non ~s** non-smoking area.

fumeux, **-euse**[2] /fymø, øz/ *adj* [*theory, ideas*] woolly (GB), wooly (US).

fumier /fymje/ *nm* manure.

fumigène /fymiʒɛn/ *adj* **grenade ~** smoke grenade.

fumiste○ /fymist/ *nm,f* **1** shirker; **2** phoney○.

fumoir /fymwaʀ/ *nm* smoking-room.

funambule /fynɑ̃byl/ *nmf* tightrope walker.

funèbre /fynɛbʀ/ *adj* **1 cérémonie/service ~** funeral ceremony/service; **2** gloomy.

funérailles /fyneʀɑj/ *nf pl* funeral.

funéraire /fyneʀɛʀ/ *adj* [*ceremony*] funeral; [*monument*] funerary.

funeste /fynɛst/ *adj* fatal; fateful.

funiculaire /fynikylɛʀ/ *nm* funicular.

fur: **au fur et à mesure** /ofyʀeaməzyʀ/ *phr* as one goes along; **le chemin se rétrécissait au ~ et à mesure qu'on avançait** the path grew progressively narrower as we went along.

furet /fyʀɛ/ *nm* ferret.

fureter /fyʀte/ [18] *vi* to rummage.

fureur /fyʀœʀ/ *nf* **1** rage, fury; **2** frenzy; **avec ~** frenziedly; **ce sport fait ~ en ce moment** that sport is all the rage at the moment.

furibond, **~e** /fyʀibɔ̃, ɔ̃d/ *adj* furious.

furie /fyʀi/ *nf* rage, fury.

furieusement /fyʀjøzmɑ̃/ *adv* **1** furiously, violently; **2**○ **j'ai ~ envie de dormir** I'm dying to go to sleep.

furieux, **-ieuse** /fyʀjø, øz/ *adj* **1** furious, angry; **2**○ [*desire*] terrible; **3** [*battle*] intense.

furoncle /fyʀɔ̃kl/ *nm* boil.

furtif, **-ive** /fyʀtif, iv/ *adj* **1** furtive; **marcher d'un pas ~** to creep along; **2** fleeting.

fusain /fyzɛ̃/ *nm* charcoal crayon; charcoal drawing.

fuseau, *pl* **~x** /fyzo/ *nm* **1** spindle; **en ~** tapering; **2** ski pants; **3 ~ horaire** time zone.

fusée /fyze/ *nf* **1** rocket; **2** (Aut) stub axle.

fuselage /fyzlaʒ/ *nm* fuselage.

fuselé, **~e** /fyzle/ *adj* tapering, spindle-shaped.

fuser /fyze/ [1] *vi* to ring out; **les rires fusaient** laughter came from all sides.

fusible /fyzibl/ *nm* fuse.

fusil /fyzi/ *nm* **1** gun, shotgun; (Mil) rifle; **2** sharpening steel; **3** gas igniter.

fusillade /fyzijad/ *nf* **1** gunfire; **2** shoot-out.

fusiller /fyzije/ [1] *vtr* **1** to shoot; **2**○ to wreck. IDIOMS **~ qn du regard** to look daggers at sb.

fusil-mitrailleur, *pl* **fusils-mitrailleurs** /fyzimitʀajœʀ/ *nm* light machine gun.

fusion /fyzjɔ̃/ *nf* **1** (of metal, ice) melting; **roche en ~** molten rock; **2** (in biology, physics) fusion; **3** (of companies, parties) merger; (of systems, cultures) fusion; (of peoples) mixing.

fusionner /fyzjɔne/ [1] *vtr*, *vi* to merge.

fût /fy/ *nm* cask, barrel; drum.

futaie /fytɛ/ *nf* forest of tall trees.

futé, **~e** /fyte/ **I** *adj* wily, crafty; **ce n'est pas très ~** that isn't or wasn't very clever.
II *nm,f* **(petit) ~** cunning little devil.

futile /fytil/ *adj* trivial; superficial.

futilité /fytilite/ **I** *nf* superficiality.
II futilités *nf pl* **1** banalities; **2** trifles; trifling activities; **3** trivial details.

futur, **~e** /fytyʀ/ **I** *adj* future; **mon ~ mari** my husband-to-be.
II *nm* future.

fuyant, **~e** /fɥijɑ̃, ɑ̃t/ *adj* [*look*] shifty.

fuyard, **~e** /fɥijaʀ, aʀd/ *nm,f* runaway.

Gg

g, **G** /ʒe/ *nm inv* **1** (letter) g, G; **2** (*written abbr* = **gramme**) **250 g** 250 g.

gabarit /gabaʀi/ *nm* **1** (of vehicle) size; **2**○ (of person) calibre[GB]; (physical) build.

gâcher /gɑʃe/ [1] *vtr* **1** to waste [*food, talent*]; to throw away [*life*]; **2** to spoil [*party*].

gâchette /gɑʃɛt/ *nf* **1** (of gun) tumbler; **2** (controversial) trigger; **3** (on lock) tumbler.

gâchis /gɑʃi/ *nm inv* **1** waste; **2** mess.

gadget /gadʒɛt/ *nm* gadget.

gadoue○ /gadu/ *nf* mud.

gaélique /gaelik/ *adj, nm* Gaelic.

gaffe○ /gaf/ *nf* **1** blunder; **faire une ~** to make a blunder; **2 faire ~** to watch out.

gag /gag/ *nm* **1** (in film, show) gag; **2** joke.

gaga○ /gaga/ *adj inv* **1** gaga○; **2** silly.

gage /gaʒ/ **I** *nm* **1** security; **mettre qch en ~** to pawn sth; **être le ~ de qch** to be a guarantee of sth; **2** (Games) forfeit; **3** pledge.
II gages† *nm pl* wages; **tueur à ~s** hired killer.

gageure /gaʒyʀ/ *nf* challenge.

gagnant, **~e** /gaɲɑ̃, ɑ̃t/ **I** *adj* winning.
II *nm,f* winner; winning horse; winning ticket.

gagne-pain /gaɲpɛ̃/ *nm inv* livelihood.

gagne-petit /gaɲpəti/ *nmf inv* low-wage earner.

gagner /gaɲe/ [1] **I** *vtr* **1** to win; **~ d'une longueur** to win by a length; **c'est gagné!** we've done it!; **à tous les coups on gagne!** every one a winner!; **2** to earn; **il gagne bien sa vie** he makes a good living; **3** to gain [*reputation, advantage, time*]; **~ de la vitesse** to gather speed; **4** to save [*time*]; **~ de la place en faisant** to make more room by doing; **5** to win [sb] over; **6** to reach [*place*]; **7** [*blaze, disease*] to spread to [*place*]; **8** [*fear*] to overcome; **9** to beat [sb]; **~ qn de vitesse** to outstrip sb.
II *vi* **1** to win; **2 le film gagne à être vu en version originale** the film is best seen in the original version; **3** to gain; **4 y ~** to come off better; **y ~ en** to gain in [*comfort*]; **5** [*sea*] to encroach.

gai, **~e** /gɛ/ *adj* **1** [*person*] happy; [*smile, expression*] cheerful; [*conversation*] lighthearted; **2** (ironic) **c'est ~** great!; **3** merry, tipsy.

gaiement /gɛmɑ̃/ *adv* **1** cheerfully, merrily; gaily; **2** (ironic) happily.

gaieté /gete/ *nf* gaiety, cheerfulness.

gain /gɛ̃/ *nm* **1** earnings; **mes ~s au jeu** my winnings; **2** (on stock exchange) gain; **3** saving; **c'est un ~ de temps considérable** it saves a considerable amount of time.

gaine /gɛn/ *nf* **1** (for dagger) sheath; **2** girdle; **3** (Tech) sheathing; casing; **4** (Bot) sheath.

gala /gala/ *nm* gala.

galant, **~e** /galɑ̃, ɑ̃t/ *adj* **1** gallant, gentlemanly; **2** romantic.

galaxie /galaksi/ *nf* galaxy.

galbe /galb/ *nm* curve.

gale /gal/ *nf* **1** scabies; **2** (on dog, cat) mange; (on sheep) scab; **3** (Bot) scab.

galère /galɛʀ/ *nf* **1** galley; **2**○ hell○.
IDIOMS **être dans la même ~** to be in the same boat.

galérer○ /galeʀe/ [14] *vi* to have a hard time.

galerie /galʀi/ *nf* **1** gallery; **2** tunnel.
■ **~ marchande** shopping arcade; **~ de toit** roof rack; **Galerie des Glaces** hall of mirrors.
IDIOMS **amuser la ~**○ to play to the gallery; **pour épater la ~**○ to impress the crowd.

galet /galɛ/ *nm* **1** pebble; **2** (Tech) roller.

galette /galɛt/ *nf* **1** round flat biscuit, cookie (US); **2** pancake.
■ **~ des Rois** Twelfth Night cake.

Galles /gal/ *pr nf pl* **le pays de ~** Wales.

gallois, **~e** /galwɑ, ɑz/ **I** *adj* Welsh.
II *nm* (language) Welsh.

Gallois, **~e** /galwɑ, ɑz/ *nm,f* Welshman/Welshwoman; **les ~** the Welsh.

gallon /galɔ̃/ *nm* gallon.

galoche /galɔʃ/ *nf* clog; **menton en ~** protruding chin.

galon /galɔ̃/ *nm* **1** (for trimming) braid; **2** (Mil) stripe; **prendre du ~** to be promoted.

galop /galo/ *nm* **1** gallop; **petit ~** canter; **grand ~** full gallop; **au ~!** (figurative) hurry up!; **2** (Mus) galop.
IDIOMS **chassez le naturel il revient au ~** (Proverb) what's bred in the bone will come out in the flesh.

galoper /galɔpe/ [1] *vi* **1** to gallop; **2**○ [*child*] to charge (around).

gamba /gɑ̃ba, *pl* as/ *nf* large (Mediterranean) prawn.

gambader /gɑ̃bade/ [1] *vi* to gambol.

gamelle /gamɛl/ *nf* (of soldier) dixie (GB), mess kit; (of camper) billycan (GB), tin dish; (of worker) lunchbox; (for pet) dish.
IDIOMS **prendre une ~**○ to fall flat on one's face○; (figurative) to come a cropper.

gamin, **~e** /gamɛ̃, in/ **I** *adj* [*air, look*] youthful; [*attitude*] childish.
II *nm,f* kid○; **~ des rues** street urchin.

gamme /gam/ *nf* **1** (Mus) scale; **2** range; **produit (de) bas de ~** low quality product; cheap product.

gammée /game/ *adj f* **croix ~** swastika.

ganglion /gɑ̃glijɔ̃/ *nm* ganglion.

gangrène /gɑ̃gʀɛn/ *nf* **1** (Med) gangrene; **2** (figurative) canker.

gangrener /gɑ̃gʀəne/ [16] **I** *vtr* to corrupt.
II se gangrener *v refl* (+ *v être*) **1** (Med) to become gangrenous; **2** (figurative) to become corrupt.

gangster /gɑ̃gstɛʀ/ *nm* **1** gangster; **2** swindler.

gant /gɑ̃/ *nm* glove.
■ **~ de boxe** boxing glove; **~ de ménage** rubber glove; **~ de toilette** ≈ (face) flannel (GB), wash cloth (US).
IDIOMS **son tailleur lui va comme un ~** her suit fits her like a glove; **mettre** or **prendre des ~s avec qn** to handle sb with kid gloves.

garage /gaʀaʒ/ *nm* **1** garage; **2** garage, filling station.
■ **~ à vélos** bicycle shed.

garagiste /gaʀaʒist/ *nmf* **1** garage owner; **2** car mechanic.

garant, **~e** /gaʀɑ̃, ɑ̃t/ **I** *adj* **être** or **se porter ~ de qn/qch** to vouch for sb/sth.
II *nm,f* guarantor.

garanti, **~e**[1] /gaʀɑ̃ti/ **I** *pp* ▶ **garantir**.
II *adj* **1** with a guarantee; **2** guaranteed.

garantie[2] /gaʀɑ̃ti/ *nf* **1** (gen, Law) guarantee; **2** (in finance) security; guarantee; **3** (in insurance) cover; **montant des ~s** sum insured.

garantir /gaʀɑ̃tiʀ/ [3] *vtr* **1** to guarantee; **~ qch à qn** to guarantee sb sth; **2** to safeguard [*security*]; **3** to guarantee [*loan, product*].

garçon /gaʀsɔ̃/ *nm* **1** boy; **2** young man; **un brave** or **gentil ~** a nice chap (GB) or guy (US); **3** bachelor; **4 ~ (de café)** waiter.
■ **~ d'écurie** stableboy; **~ d'honneur** best man; **~ manqué** tomboy.

garçonnet /gaʀsɔnɛ/ *nm* little boy.

garçonnière /gaʀsɔnjɛʀ/ *nf* bachelor flat (GB) or apartment.

garde[1] /gaʀd/ *nm* **1** guard; **2** (for invalid, patient) carer; (in prison) warder.
■ **~ champêtre** ≈ local policeman (*appointed by the municipality*); **~ du corps** bodyguard; **~ forestier** forest warden; **Garde des Sceaux** French Minister of Justice.

garde[2] /gaʀd/ *nf* **1** nurse; **2** (gen, Mil, Sport) guard; **la vieille ~** the old guard; **monter la ~ auprès de qn** to keep watch over sb; to stand guard over sb; **être de ~** [*doctor*] to be on call; [*soldier*] to be on guard duty; **3 mettre qn en ~** to warn sb; **prendre ~** to watch out; to be careful; **4** (of sword) hilt; **5 (page de) ~** endpaper.
■ **~ à vue** (Law) ≈ police custody.

garde-à-vous /gaʀdavu/ *nm inv* **se mettre au ~** to stand to attention.

garde-chasse, *pl* **~s** /gaʀdəʃas/ *nm* game warden; gamekeeper.

garde-côte, *pl* **~s** /gaʀdəkot/ *nm* coastguard ship.

garde-fou, *pl* **~s** /gaʀdəfu/ *nm* **1** parapet; **2** safeguard.

garde-malade, *pl* **gardes-malades** /gaʀdmalad/ *nmf* home nurse.

garde-manger /gaʀdmɑ̃ʒe/ *nm inv* meat safe.

garder /gaʀde/ [1] **I** *vtr* **1** to keep [*object*]; to keep on [*hat, sweater*]; to keep on [*employee*]; **2** [*soldier*] to guard; [*person*] to look after.
II se garder *v refl* (+ *v être*) **1 se ~ de faire** to be careful not to do; **2** [*foodstuff*] to keep.

garderie /gaʀdəʀi/ *nf* **1** day nursery; **2** after-school child-minding facility.

garde-robe, *pl* **~s** /gaʀdəʀɔb/ *nf* wardrobe.

gardien, **-ienne**[1] /gaʀdjɛ̃, ɛn/ *nm,f* **1** (in premises) security guard; (in apartment block) caretaker (GB), janitor (US); (in park) keeper; (in prison) warder; (in museum) attendant; **2** (Sport) keeper.
■ **~ de but** goalkeeper; **~ de nuit** night watchman; **~ de la paix** police officer.

gardiennage /gaʀdjɛnaʒ/ *nm* (of premises) security; (of apartment block) caretaking.

gardienne[2] /gaʀdjɛn/ *nf* **1** ▶ **gardien**; **2 ~ (d'enfant)** childminder (GB), day-care lady (US).

gardon /gaʀdɔ̃/ *nm* roach.
IDIOMS **être frais comme un ~** to be as fresh as a daisy.

gare /gaʀ/ **I** *nf* (railway) station.
II *excl* **~ (à toi)!** (threat) careful!, watch it○!
■ **~ maritime** harbour[GB] station; **~ routière** coach station (GB), bus station (US).
IDIOMS **sans crier ~** without any warning.

garenne /gaʀɛn/ *nf* (rabbit) warren.

garer /gaʀe/ [1] **I** *vtr* to park.
II se garer *v refl* (+ *v être*) **1** to park; **2** [*vehicle*] to pull over.

gargariser: **se gargariser** /gaʀgaʀize/ [1] *v refl* (+ *v être*) to gargle.

gargarisme /gaʀgaʀism/ *nm* **1** gargling; **2** mouthwash.

gargouille /gaʀguj/ *nf* **1** gargoyle; **2** water-spout.

gargouiller /gaʀguje/ [1] *vi* [*water, fountain*] to gurgle; [*stomach*] to rumble.

garnement /gaʀnəmɑ̃/ *nm* brat○.

garni, **~e** /gaʀni/ **I** *pp* ▶ **garnir**.
II *adj* **bien ~** [*wallet*] full; [*fridge*] well-stocked; [*buffet*] copious.

garnir /gaʀniʀ/ [3] *vtr* **1** [*objects*] to fill [*room*]; [*person*] to stock [*shelves*]; **2** to stuff [*cushion*]; **3** (Culin) to decorate [*cake*]; to garnish [*meat*].

garnison /gaʀnizɔ̃/ *nf* garrison.

garniture /gaʀnityʀ/ *nf* **1** (Culin) side dish; (for dessert) decoration; (for meat, fish) garnish; **2** (on hat, garment) trimming.
■ **~ de cheminée** mantelpiece ornaments.

garrot /gaʀo/ *nm* **1** (Med) tourniquet; **2** (Zool) withers; **le cheval mesure 1,50 m au ~** ≈ the horse is 15 hands.

gars○ /ga/ *nm inv* **1** boy; **2** chap○ (GB), guy○ (US).

Gascogne /gaskɔɲ/ *pr nf* **la ~** Gascony.

Gascon, **-onne** /gaskɔ̃, ɔn/ *nm,f* Gascon.
IDIOMS **faire une offre de ~** to raise false hopes.

gas-oil /gazwal/ *nm* diesel (GB), fuel oil (US).

gaspillage /gaspijaʒ/ *nm* **1** wasting; waste; **2** squandering.

gaspiller /gaspije/ [1] *vtr* **1** to waste [*time, food*]; **2** to squander [*resources, talent*].

gastronomie /gastʀɔnɔmi/ *nf* gastronomy.

gâteau, *pl* **~x** /gɑto/ *nm* cake; gâteau.
■ **~ apéritif** cocktail biscuit; **~ de cire** honeycomb; **~ de riz** ≈ rice pudding; **~ sec** biscuit (GB), cookie (US).
IDIOMS **c'est du ~**○**!** it's a piece of cake○!; **c'est pas du ~**○**!** it's no picnic!

gâter /gɑte/ [1] **I** *vtr* to spoil; to ruin [*teeth*].
II se gâter *v refl* (+ *v être*) **1** to go bad; to rot; **2** to take a turn for the worse.

gâteux, **-euse** /gɑtø, øz/ *adj* **1** senile; **2 il est ~ avec sa fille**○ he's dotty about his daughter○.

gauche[1] /goʃ/ *adj* **1** left; **2** [*person, manner*] awkward; [*style*] clumsy.
IDIOMS **se lever du pied ~**○ to get out of bed on the wrong side (GB), to get up on the wrong side of the bed (US).

gauche[2] /goʃ/ *nf* **1** left; **à ~** [*drive*] on the left; [*go, look*] to the left; [*turn*] left; **de ~** [*page*] left-hand; **2** Left; **de ~** left-wing.
IDIOMS **passer l'arme à ~**○ to kick the bucket○; **jusqu'à la ~**○ completely; **mettre de l'argent à ~**○ to put money aside.

gaucher, **-ère** /goʃe, ɛʀ/ *adj* left-handed.

gauchiste /goʃist/ *adj, nmf* leftist.

gaufre /gofʀ/ *nf* **1** waffle; **2** honeycomb.

gaufrette /gofʀɛt/ *nf* wafer.

gaufrier /gofʀije/ *nm* waffle iron.

Gaule /gol/ *pr nf* Gaul.

Gaulois, **~e** /golwa, az/ *nm,f* Gaul.

gaver /gave/ [1] **I** *vtr* to force-feed [*geese*].
II se gaver *v refl* (+ *v être*) **1** to stuff oneself; **2 se ~ de** to devour [*novels*].

gay /gɛ/ *adj inv, nm* gay, homosexual.

gaz /gaz/ **I** *nm inv* gas.
II *nm pl* **1** (Aut) air-fuel mixture; **rouler à pleins ~**○ to go at full throttle; **2** (Med) wind.
■ **~ d'échappement** exhaust fumes; **~ de ville** mains gas.
IDIOMS **il y a de l'eau dans le ~**○ there's trouble brewing.

gaze /gɑz/ *nf* gauze.

gazelle /gazɛl/ *nf* gazelle.

gazer /gaze/ [1] **I** *vtr* to gas.
II○ *vi* **ça gaze** things are fine.

gazette /gazɛt/ *nf* newspaper.

gazeux, **-euse** /gazø, øz/ *adj* **1** [*drink*] fizzy; **2** gaseous.

gazinière /gazinjɛʀ/ *nf* gas cooker (GB), gas stove.

gazoduc /gazɔdyk/ *nm* gas pipeline.

gazole /gazɔl/ *nm* diesel (oil) (GB), fuel oil (US).

gazon /gazɔ̃/ *nm* **1** grass, turf; **2** lawn.

gazouiller /gazuje/ [1] *vi* to twitter; to babble.

GDF /ʒedeɛf/ (*abbr* = **Gaz de France**) *French gas board*.

géant, **~e** /ʒeɑ̃, ɑ̃t/ **I** *adj* **1** huge; **2** giant.
II *nm,f* giant/giantess.

geindre /ʒɛ̃dʀ/ [55] *vi* (in pain) to moan, to groan; to whimper; (complainingly) to whine.

gel /ʒɛl/ *nm* **1** frost; **résistant au ~** frost-resistant; **2 ~ des prix/salaires** price/wage freeze; **3 après le ~ du projet** after the project had been put on ice; **4** gel.

gélatine /ʒelatin/ *nf* gelatine (GB), gelatin (US).

gelé, **~e**[1] /ʒəle/ **I** *pp* ▶ **geler**.
II *adj* **1** [*water, ground*] frozen; [*toe*] frost-bitten; **j'ai les oreilles ~es** my ears are frozen; **2** [*prices, negotiations*] frozen.

gelée[2] /ʒəle/ *nf* **1** (from fruit) jelly; (from meat, fish) gelatinous stock; **œuf en ~** egg in aspic; **2** gel; **3** frost.
■ **~ blanche** hoarfrost.

geler /ʒəle/ [17] **I** *vtr* **1** to freeze; to nip [*plant*]; **2** to freeze [*salaries*]; to suspend [*plan*].
II *vi* [*water, ground, finger, foot*] to freeze; [*plant*] to be frosted.
III *v impers* **il gèle** it's freezing.

gélule /ʒelyl/ *nf* capsule.

Gémeaux /ʒemo/ *pr nm pl* Gemini.

gémir /ʒemiʀ/ [3] *vi* to moan; to whimper.

gémissement /ʒemismɑ̃/ *nm* moan.

gemme /ʒɛm/ *nf* **1** gem, gemstone; **2** resin.

gênant, **~e** /ʒɛnɑ̃, ɑ̃t/ *adj* **1** [*box*] cumbersome; [*problem*] annoying; **2** embarrassing.

gencive /ʒɑ̃siv/ *nf* gum.

gendarme /ʒɑ̃daʀm/ *nm* **1** (Mil) gendarme, French policeman; **2** dried sausage.
■ **~ couché** road hump.

gendarmerie /ʒɑ̃daʀm(ə)ʀi/ *nf* **1** ≈ police station; **2 ~ (nationale)** gendarmerie.

gendre /ʒɑ̃dʀ/ *nm* son-in-law.

gène /ʒɛn/ *nm* gene.

gêne /ʒɛn/ *nf* **1** embarrassment; **2** discomfort; **3** inconvenience; **4** poverty.

gêné, **~e** /ʒene/ **I** *pp* ▶ **gêner**.
II *adj* **1** embarrassed; **2** short of money.

généalogie /ʒenealɔʒi/ *nf* genealogy.

généalogique /ʒenealɔʒik/ *adj* genealogical; **arbre ~** family tree.

gêner /ʒene/ [1] **I** *vtr* **1** to disturb, to bother; **2** [*smoke, noise*] to bother; **3** to embarrass; **4** [*belt*] to restrict [*breathing*]; **5** [*person*] to get in the way of [*progress*].
II se gêner *v refl* (+ *v être*) **1** to get in each other's way; **2 je vais me ~**○ see if I don't; **ne vous gênez pas pour moi** don't mind me.

général, **~e**[1], *mpl* **-aux** /ʒeneʀal, o/ **I** *adj* general; **de l'avis ~** in most people's opinion; **en ~, de façon ~e** generally, in general; **en règle ~e** as a rule.
II *nm* general.

générale[2] /ʒeneʀal/ *nf* **1** dress rehearsal; **2** general's wife.

généralisé, **~e** /ʒeneʀalize/ *adj* [*conflict*] widespread; [*process*] general; [*cancer*] generalized.

généraliser /ʒeneʀalize/ [1] **I** *vtr* to bring [sth] into general use.
II *vi* to generalize.
III se généraliser *v refl* (+ *v être*) [*technique*] to become standard; [*tax*] to become widely applicable; [*strike, illness*] to spread.

généraliste /ʒeneʀalist/ *adj* non-specialized; (**médecin**) **~** GP, general practitioner.

généralité /ʒeneʀalite/ *nf* generality.

génération /ʒeneʀasjɔ̃/ *nf* generation.

générer /ʒeneʀe/ [14] *vtr* to generate.

généreux, **-euse** /ʒeneʀø, øz/ *adj* **1** [*person, nature*] generous; [*idea, gesture*] noble; **2** [*portion*] generous; **poitrine généreuse** large bust.

générique /ʒeneʀik/ **I** *adj* generic.
II *nm* credits; **le ~ de fin** closing credits.

générosité /ʒeneʀɔzite/ *nf* generosity.

genèse /ʒənɛz/ *nf* **1** (of plan) genesis; (of state) birth; **2 la Genèse** Genesis.

genêt /ʒənɛ/ *nm* (Bot) broom.

génétique /ʒenetik/ **I** *adj* genetic.
II *nf* genetics.

Genève /ʒənɛv/ *pr n* Geneva.

génial, **~e**, *mpl* **-iaux** /ʒenjal, o/ *adj* **1** brilliant; **2**○ great○.

génie /ʒeni/ *nm* **1** genius; **idée de ~** brainwave; **2** spirit; genie; **3** engineering.

genièvre /ʒənjɛvʀ/ *nm* juniper.

génisse /ʒenis/ *nf* heifer.

génital, **~e**, *mpl* **-aux** /ʒenital, o/ *adj* genital.

génocide /ʒenɔsid/ *nm* genocide.

genou, *pl* **~x** /ʒ(ə)nu/ **I** *nm* knee; **sur les ~x de qn** on sb's lap.
II à genoux *phr* **se mettre à ~x** to kneel down; to go down on one's knees.
IDIOMS **faire du ~ à qn**○ to play footsie○ with sb; **mettre qn sur les ~x**○ to wear sb out.

genouillère /ʒənujɛʀ/ *nf* (Sport) knee pad; (Med) knee support.

genre /ʒɑ̃ʀ/ *nm* **1** sort, kind, type; **un peu dans le ~ de ta robe** a bit like your dress; **2 pour se donner un ~** (in order) to make oneself look different; **3** (in grammar) gender; **4** genre; **5** (Bot, Zool) genus.
■ **le ~ humain** mankind.

gens /ʒɑ̃/ *nm pl* **1** people; **2** servants; retinue.
■ **~ d'église** clergymen; **~ de lettres** writers; **~ de maison** servants; **~ du voyage** travelling[GB] people.

gentil, **-ille** /ʒɑ̃ti, ij/ *adj* **1** kind, nice; **2** good; **sois ~** be a good boy; **3 c'est bien ~ tout ça, mais**... that's all very well, but...

gentillesse /ʒɑ̃tijɛs/ *nf* **1** kindness; **2** (ironic) **échanger des ~s** to exchange insults.

gentiment /ʒɑ̃timɑ̃/ *adv* **1** kindly; **2** quietly.

géographie /ʒeɔgʀafi/ *nf* geography.

geôlier, **-ière** /ʒolje, ɛʀ/ *nm,f* jailer.

géologie /ʒeɔlɔʒi/ *nf* geology.

géomètre /ʒeɔmɛtʀ/ *nmf* land surveyor.

géométrie /ʒeɔmetʀi/ *nf* geometry; **à ~ variable** [*doctrine*] flexible.

géométrique /ʒeɔmetʀik/ *adj* geometric.

Géorgie /ʒeɔʀʒi/ *pr nf* **1** (in US) Georgia; **2** (in Europe) Georgia.

gérance /ʒeʀɑ̃s/ *nf* management; **mettre en ~** to appoint a manager for [*shop, company*]; to appoint a managing agent for [*property*].

géranium /ʒeʀanjɔm/ *nm* geranium.

gérant, **~e** /ʒeʀɑ̃, ɑ̃t/ *nm,f* manager; (of property) (managing) agent.

gerbe /ʒɛʀb/ *nf* **1** bouquet; wreath; **2** (of water) spray; **3** (of wheat) sheaf.

gercer /ʒɛʀse/ [12] *vi* to become chapped.

gerçure /ʒɛʀsyʀ/ *nf* (in skin, lips) crack.

gérer /ʒeʀe/ [14] *vtr* **1** to manage [*production, time*]; to run [*business*]; **2** to handle [*situation*].

gériatrie /ʒeʀjatʀi/ *nf* geriatrics.

germain, **~e** /ʒɛʀmɛ̃, ɛn/ *adj* **1** (**cousin**) **~** first cousin; **2** Germanic.

germanique /ʒɛʀmanik/ *adj, nm* Germanic.

germanophone /ʒɛʀmanɔfɔn/ *nmf* German speaker.

germe /ʒɛʀm/ *nm* (of embryo, seed) germ; (of potato) sprout.

germer /ʒɛʀme/ [1] *vi* **1** [*wheat*] to germinate; **2** [*idea, suspicion*] to form.

gérondif /ʒeʀɔ̃dif/ *nm* gerund, gerundive.

gésier /ʒezje/ *nm* gizzard.

gésir /ʒeziʀ/ [37] *vi* (formal) **ci-gît Luc Pichon** here lies Luc Pichon.

geste /ʒɛst/ *nm* **1** movement; gesture; **joindre le ~ à la parole** to suit the action to the word; **2** gesture, act.

gesticuler /ʒɛstikyle/ [1] *vtr* **1** to gesticulate; **2** to fidget.

gestion /ʒɛstjɔ̃/ *nf* **1** management; **2** (of situation) handling; **3** (classroom) management.
■ **~ administrative** administration; **~ des stocks** stock (GB) or inventory (US) control.

gestionnaire /ʒɛstjɔnɛʀ/ *nmf* administrator.

gestuel, **-elle**[1] /ʒɛstɥɛl/ *adj* gestural.

gestuelle[2] /ʒɛstɥɛl/ *nf* body language.

geyser /ʒezɛʀ/ *nm* geyser.

ghetto /geto/ *nm* ghetto.

gibecière /ʒibsjɛʀ/ *nf* gamebag.

gibier /ʒibje/ *nm* game; **gros ~** big game; (figurative) big-time criminals.

giboulée /ʒibule/ *nf* shower.

giclée /ʒikle/ *nf* spurt; squirt.

gicler /ʒikle/ [1] *vi* to spurt; to squirt.

gifle /ʒifl/ *nf* slap in the face.

gifler /ʒifle/ [1] *vtr* to slap [sb] across the face.

gigantesque /ʒigɑ̃tɛsk/ *adj* huge, gigantic.

gigogne /ʒigɔɲ/ *adj* **tables ~s** nest of tables.

gigot /ʒigo/ *nm* leg of lamb.

gigoter /ʒigɔte/ [1] *vi* **1** to wriggle; **2** to fidget.

gilet /ʒilɛ/ *nm* **1** cardigan; **2** waistcoat (GB), vest (US).
■ **~ pare-balles** bulletproof vest; **~ de sauvetage** lifejacket.

gin /dʒin/ *nm* gin; **~ tonic** gin and tonic.

gingembre /ʒɛ̃ʒɑ̃bʀ/ *nm* ginger.

girafe /ʒiʀaf/ *nf* (Zool) giraffe.

giratoire /ʒiʀatwaʀ/ *adj* gyratory.
■ **sens ~** roundabout (GB), traffic circle (US).

girofle /ʒiʀɔfl/ *nm* **un clou de ~** a clove.

girolle /ʒiʀɔl/ *nf* chanterelle.

girouette /ʒiʀwɛt/ *nf* windvane.
gisement /ʒizmɑ̃/ *nm* (of oil, minerals) deposit.
gît ▶ **gésir**.
gitan, **~e** /ʒitɑ̃, an/ *nm,f* Gypsy[GB].
gîte /ʒit/ *nm* **1** shelter; **2** (of hare) form.
■ **~ rural** self-catering cottage.
givrant /ʒivʀɑ̃/ *adj m* **brouillard ~** freezing fog.
givre /ʒivʀ/ *nm* frost; ice.
givré, **~e** /ʒivʀe/ *adj* **1** frosty; frost-covered; frozen; **2**○ crazy; **3** (Culin) [*glass*] frosted.
givrer /ʒivʀe/ [1] *vi*, **se givrer** *v refl* (+ *v être*) to frost over.
glaçage /glasaʒ/ *nm* (Culin) (on dessert) icing.
glace /glas/ *nf* **1** ice; **de ~** [*face*] stony; **2** ice cream; **3** mirror; **4** sheet of glass; (of shop window) glass; (of car) window.
IDIOMS **rester de ~** to remain unmoved.
glacé, **~e** /glase/ *adj* **1** [*rain*] ice-cold; [*hands*] frozen; **thé ~** iced tea; **2** [*cake*] iced; **3** [*atmosphere*] frosty; [*smile*] chilly; **4** [*paper*] glossy.
glacer /glase/ [12] **I** *vtr* **1** to freeze [*body*]; to chill [sb] to the bone; **2** to intimidate; **~ le sang de qn** to make sb's blood run cold.
II se glacer *v refl* (+ *v être*) to freeze.
glaciaire /glasjɛʀ/ *adj* glacial.
glacial, **~e**, *mpl* **~s** or **-iaux** /glasjal, o/ *adj* **1** icy; **2** [*person, reception*] frosty; [*silence*] stony; [*look*] icy.
glacier /glasje/ *nm* **1** glacier; **2** ice-cream maker; **3** ice-cream parlour[GB].
glacière /glasjɛʀ/ *nf* coolbox (GB), ice chest (US).
glaçon /glasɔ̃/ *nm* ice cube.
glaire /glɛʀ/ *nf* **1** mucus; **2** albumen.
glaise /glɛz/ *nf* clay.
glaive /glɛv/ *nm* double-edged sword.
gland /glɑ̃/ *nm* **1** acorn; **2** (Anat) glans; **3** tassel.
glande /glɑ̃d/ *nf* (Anat) gland.
glapir /glapiʀ/ [3] *vi* **1** [*pup*] to yap; [*fox*] to bark; **2** [*person*] to shriek.
glas /glɑ/ *nm inv* toll, knell.
glauque /glok/ *adj* murky; [*street*] squalid.
glissade /glisad/ *nf* slide; skid.
glissant, **~e** /glisɑ̃, ɑ̃t/ *adj* slippery.
glissement /glismɑ̃/ *nm* **1** sliding; **2** (in sense) shift; (among voters) swing; (in prices) fall.
glisser /glise/ [1] **I** *vtr* to slip [*object*] (**dans** into); to slip in [*remark, criticism*].
II *vi* **1** to be slippery; **2** to slip; **3** to slide; to glide; **4 ~ sur** to have no effect on.
III se glisser *v refl* (+ *v être*) **se ~ dans** to slip into, to sneak into; to creep into.
glissière /glisjɛʀ/ *nf* slide; **fermeture à ~** zip (GB), zipper (US).
global, **~e**, *mpl* **-aux** /glɔbal, o/ *adj* [*sum*] total; [*result, cost*] overall; [*agreement, solution*] global; [*study*] comprehensive.
globalement /glɔbalmɑ̃/ *adv* on the whole.
globe /glɔb/ *nm* **1 ~ (terrestre)** earth, globe; **parcourir le ~** to globe-trot; **2** round glass lampshade; glass case; **3** (in architecture) dome.
■ **~ oculaire** eyeball.
globule /glɔbyl/ *nm* globule; blood cell.
■ **~ blanc** white cell; **~ rouge** red cell.
gloire /glwaʀ/ *nf* **1** glory, fame; **2** credit; **faire qch pour la ~** to do sth (just) for the sake of it; **3** glory, praise; **4 tirer ~ de** to pride oneself on; **5** celebrity; star.
glose /gloz/ *nf* gloss; note.
glossaire /glɔsɛʀ/ *nm* glossary.
glotte /glɔt/ *nf* glottis.
gloussement /glusmɑ̃/ *nm* (of hen) clucking; (of person) chuckle.
glousser /gluse/ [1] *vi* [*hen*] to cluck; [*person*] to chuckle.
glouton, **-onne** /glutɔ̃, ɔn/ *adj* [*person*] gluttonous; [*appetite*] voracious.
glu /gly/ *nf* **1** bird lime; **2** glue.
gluant, **~e** /glyɑ̃, ɑ̃t/ *adj* **1** sticky; **2** slimy.
glucide /glysid/ *nm* carbohydrate.
glycérine /gliseʀin/ *nf* glycerin.
gnome /gnom/ *nm* gnome.
gnon○ /ɲɔ̃/ *nm* dent; bruise; **prendre un ~** to get hit.
go: **tout de go** /go/ *phr* [*say*] straight out.
goal○ /gol/ *nm* goalkeeper, goalie○.
gobelet /gɔblɛ/ *nm* cup; tumbler; beaker; **~ en carton** paper cup.
gober /gɔbe/ [1] *vtr* **1** to suck [*egg*]; to swallow [sth] whole; **2**○ to fall for○ [*story*].
godasse○ /gɔdas/ *nf* shoe.
godet /gɔdɛ/ *nm* **1** goblet; **2** pot.
goéland /gɔelɑ̃/ *nm* gull.
goémon /gɔemɔ̃/ *nm* wrack.
gogo○: **à gogo** /gogo/ *phr* galore; **vin à ~** wine galore.
goguette○: **en goguette** /ɑ̃gɔgɛt/ *phr* **partir en ~** to go on a spree.
goinfre○ /gwɛ̃fʀ/ *nmf* greedy pig○.
goître /gwatʀ/ *nm* goitre[GB].
golden /gɔldɛn/ *nf inv* Golden Delicious (apple).
golf /gɔlf/ *nm* **1** golf; **2** golf course.
golfe /gɔlf/ *nm* gulf; bay.
gomme /gɔm/ **I** *nf* **1** eraser, rubber (GB); **2** (substance) gum.
II à la gomme○ *phr* [*idea*] pathetic, useless; [*machine*] useless; [*plan*] hopeless.
IDIOMS **mettre (toute) la ~**○ to step on it○; to give it full throttle○; to turn it up full blast.
gommer /gɔme/ [1] *vtr* **1** to rub [sth] out; **2** to smooth out [*wrinkle*]; to erase [*past, boundaries*]; to iron out [*differences*].
gond /gɔ̃/ *nm* hinge; **sortir de ses ~s** to come off its hinges; to fly off the handle○.
gondole /gɔ̃dɔl/ *nf* **1** gondola; **2** sales shelf.
gondoler: **se gondoler** /gɔ̃dɔle/ [1] *v refl* (+ *v être*) [*paper*] to crinkle; [*wood*] to warp.
gonflable /gɔ̃flabl/ *adj* inflatable.
gonflé, **~e** /gɔ̃fle/ **I** *pp* ▶ **gonfler**.
II *adj* **1** [*tyre, balloon*] inflated; [*cheeks*] puffed out; **2** swollen; bloated; puffy; **yeux ~s de sommeil** eyes puffy with sleep; **3**○ **être ~** to have guts○; (critical) to have a nerve○.

gonfler /gɔ̃fle/ [1] **I** *vtr* **1** to blow up, to inflate [*balloon, tyre*]; to fill [*lungs, sail*]; to puff out [*cheeks*]; **être gonflé à bloc** to be fully inflated; to be raring○ to go; **2** to flex [*muscle*]; to make [sth] bulge [*pocket, bag*]; to saturate [*sponge*]; to make [sth] swollen [*river*]; to swell [*bud*]; **3 il est gonflé d'orgueil** he's full of his own importance; **4** to increase [*profits*]; to push up [*prices*]; to inflate [*statistics*].
II *vi* (gen) to swell (up); (Culin) to rise.

gonfleur /gɔ̃flœʀ/ *nm* (air) pump.

gong /gɔ̃g/ *nm* **1** gong; **2** (in boxing) bell.

goret /gɔʀɛ/ *nm* **1** piglet; **2**○ (child) little pig○.

gorge /gɔʀʒ/ *nf* **1** throat; **avoir mal à la ~** to have a sore throat; **tenir qn à la ~** to have sb by the throat; (figurative) to have a stranglehold over sb; **avoir la ~ serrée** or **nouée** to have a lump in one's throat; to have one's heart in one's mouth; **à ~ déployée, à pleine ~** [*sing*] at the top of one's voice; [*laugh*] uproariously; **ta remarque m'est restée en travers de la ~** I found your comment hard to swallow; **2** bosom, breast; **3** gorge.
IDIOMS **faire des ~s chaudes de qn/qch** to laugh sb/sth to scorn.

gorgé, ~e[1] /gɔʀʒe/ *adj* **~ d'eau** [*land*] waterlogged; [*sponge*] saturated with water; **fruit ~ de soleil** fruit bursting with sunshine.

gorgée[2] /gɔʀʒe/ *nf* sip; gulp.

gorille /gɔʀij/ *nm* **1** gorilla; **2**○ bodyguard.

gosier /gozje/ *nm* throat, gullet.

gosse○ /gɔs/ *nmf* **1** kid○; **sale ~** brat○; **2 il est beau ~** he's a good-looking fellow.

gothique /gɔtik/ *adj, nm* Gothic.

gouache /gwaʃ/ *nf* gouache, poster paint.

gouaille /gwɑj/ *nf* cheek, cheekiness.

goudron /gudʀɔ̃/ *nm* tar.

goudronner /gudʀɔne/ [1] *vtr* to tarmac.

gouffre /gufʀ/ *nm* chasm, abyss; **le ~ de Padirac** the caves of Padirac.

goujat /guʒa/ *nm* boor.

goujon /guʒɔ̃/ *nm* (Zool) gudgeon.

goulet /gulɛ/ *nm* **1** narrows; **2** gully.
■ **~ d'étranglement** bottleneck.

goulot /gulo/ *nm* (of bottle) neck.

goulu, ~e /guly/ *adj* greedy.

goupillon /gupijɔ̃/ *nm* **1** bottle brush; **2** holy water sprinkler.

gourd, ~e[1] /guʀ, guʀd/ *adj* numb.

gourde[2] /guʀd/ **I**○ *adj* dumb○, gormless○ (GB).
II *nf* **1** flask; gourd; **2**○ dope○.

gourdin /guʀdɛ̃/ *nm* bludgeon, cudgel.

gourmand, ~e /guʀmɑ̃, ɑ̃d/ *adj* fond of good food; **il est ~ (de sucreries)** he has a sweet tooth.

gourmandise /guʀmɑ̃diz/ **I** *nf* weakness for sweet things; weakness for good food.
II gourmandises *nf pl* sweets (GB), candies (US).

gourmet /guʀmɛ/ *nm* gourmet.

gourmette /guʀmɛt/ *nf* chain bracelet.

gourou /guʀu/ *nm* guru.

gousse /gus/ *nf* pod; **~ d'ail** clove of garlic.

gousset /gusɛ/ *nm* **1** (pocket) fob; **2** gusset.

goût /gu/ *nm* **1** (gen) taste; palate; **donner du ~ à qch** to give sth flavour[GB]; **2 de bon ~** in good taste; **s'habiller sans ~** to have no dress sense; **avoir le mauvais ~ de faire** to be tactless enough to do; **3** liking; **ne pas être du ~ de tout le monde** not to be to everyone's liking; not to be everyone's cup of tea; **chacun ses ~s** each to his own; **être au ~ du jour** to be trendy; **faire qch par ~** to do sth for pleasure.
IDIOMS **tous les ~s sont dans la nature** (Proverb) it takes all sorts to make a world.

goûter[1] /gute/ [1] **I** *vtr* **1** to taste, to try; **2** to enjoy [*peace, solitude*].
II goûter à *v+prep* **1 ~ à** to try [*food, drink*]; **2 ~ à** to have a taste of [*freedom, power*].

goûter[2] /gute/ *nm* **1** snack; **2** children's party.

goutte /gut/ **I** *nf* **1** drop (**de** of); **~ de pluie** raindrop; **à grosses ~s** [*rain*] heavily; [*perspire*] profusely; **2** (Med) gout.
II gouttes *nf pl* (Med) drops.
IDIOMS **se ressembler comme deux ~s d'eau** to be as alike as two peas in a pod.

goutte-à-goutte /gutagut/ *nm inv* (Med) drip.

goutter /gute/ [1] *vi* to drip.

gouttière /gutjɛʀ/ *nf* gutter; drainpipe.

gouvernail /guvɛʀnaj/ *nm* **1** rudder; **2** helm.

gouvernant, ~e[1] /guvɛʀnɑ̃, ɑ̃t/ **I** *adj* ruling.
II gouvernants *nm pl* **les ~s** the government.

gouvernante[2] /guvɛʀnɑ̃t/ *nf* housekeeper.

gouverne /guvɛʀn/ *nf* **pour votre ~** for your information.

gouvernement /guvɛʀnəmɑ̃/ *nm* government.

gouvernemental, ~e, *mpl* **-aux** /guvɛʀnəmɑ̃tal, o/ *adj* government; governmental.

gouverner /guvɛʀne/ [1] *vtr* **1** to govern, to rule; **2** [*money*] to rule; **3** to steer [*ship*].

gouverneur /guvɛʀnœʀ/ *nm* governor.

grabataire /gʀabatɛʀ/ *adj* bedridden.

grâce /gʀɑs/ **I** *nf* **1** (of person, gesture) grace; (of landscape) charm; **2 de bonne ~** with (a) good grace; **3** favour[GB]; **faire à qn la ~ d'accepter** to do sb the honour[GB] of accepting; **4** mercy; **~ présidentielle** presidential pardon; **je vous fais ~ des détails** I'll spare you the details; **5 ~ à Dieu!** thank God!
II grâce à *phr* thanks to.

Grâce /gʀɑs/ *nf* Grace; **votre ~** your Grace.

gracier /gʀasje/ [2] *vtr* to pardon, to reprieve.

gracieusement /gʀasjøzmɑ̃/ *adv* **1** free of charge; **2** gracefully.

gracieux, -ieuse /gʀasjø, øz/ *adj* **1** graceful; **2** gracious.

grade /gʀad/ *nm* rank; **monter en ~** to be promoted.

gradé, ~e /gʀade/ *nm,f* noncommissioned officer.

gradin /gʀadɛ̃/ *nm* (in hall) tier; (in arena) terrace.

gradué, **~e** /gʀadɥe/ *adj* **règle ~e** ruler.

graduer /gʀadɥe/ [1] *vtr* **1** to increase [*difficulty*]; **2** to graduate [*instrument*].

graffiti /gʀafiti/ *nm pl* graffiti.

grain /gʀɛ̃/ *nm* **1** grain; **nourri au ~** corn-fed (GB) or grain-fed; **2** grain; **~ de poivre** peppercorn; **~ de café** coffee bean; **~ de moutarde** mustard seed; **~ de raisin** grape; **3** speck; **4 le ~** the grain; **à gros ~** coarse grained.

■ **~ de beauté** beauty spot, mole.

IDIOMS **avoir un ~**○ to be loony○; **mettre son ~ de sel**○ to put one's oar in○.

graine /gʀɛn/ *nf* seed; birdseed; **monter en ~** [*vegetable*] to run to seed; [*child*] to shoot up.

IDIOMS **prends-en de la ~**○ let that be an example to you.

graisse /gʀɛs/ *nf* **1** (gen) fat; (of seal, whale) blubber; **2** (Tech) grease.

graisser /gʀese/ [1] *vtr* to grease [*pan*]; to lubricate [*mechanism*].

graisseux, **-euse** /gʀɛsø, øz/ *adj* (gen) greasy; (Med) fatty.

grammaire /gʀamɛʀ/ *nf* grammar.

grammatical, **~e**, *mpl* **-aux** /gʀamatikal, o/ *adj* grammatical.

gramme /gʀam/ *nm* gram.

grand, **~e** /gʀɑ̃, gʀɑ̃d/ **I** *adj* **1** [*person, tree, tower*] tall; [*arm, stride, journey*] long; [*margin, angle*] wide; [*place, object, fire*] big; **2** [*crowd, family, fortune*] large, big; **pas ~ monde** not many people; **il fait ~ jour** it's broad daylight; **laver à ~e eau** to wash [sth] in plenty of running water; to wash [sth] down; **3** [*dreamer, collector, friend*] great; [*cheat, gambler*] big; [*drinker, smoker*] heavy; **c'est un ~ timide** he's very shy; **4** [*discovery, news, expedition*] great; [*date*] important; [*role*] major; [*problem, decision*] big; **5** main; **6** [*company, brand*] leading; **les ~es industries** the big industries; **7** [*painter, wine*] great; [*heart, spirit*] noble; **8** [*brother, sister*] elder; [*pupil*] senior (GB), older; **assez ~ pour faire** old enough to do; **9** [*height, length, value, distance*] great; [*size, quantity*] large; [*speed*] high; **10** [*kindness, friendship, danger, interest*] great; [*noise*] loud; [*cold*] severe; [*heat*] intense; [*wind*] strong, high; [*storm*] big, violent; **à ma ~e surprise** much to my surprise; **11** [*family, name*] great; **la ~e bourgeoisie** the upper middle class; **12** [*reception, plan*] grand; **13** [*word*] big; [*phrase*] high-sounding; **faire de ~s gestes** to wave one's arms about; **et voilà, tout de suite les ~s mots** there you go, straight off the deep end.

II *nm,f* big boy/girl; (Sch) senior (GB) or older pupil.

III *adv* wide; **ouvrir tout ~ les bras** to throw one's arms open; **ouvrir ~ ses oreilles** to prick up one's ears; **voir ~** to think big.

IV *nm* **les ~s de ce monde** the great and the good; the world's leaders.

V en grand *phr* [*open*] wide; **faire les choses en ~** to do things on the grand scale.

■ **~ banditisme** organized crime; **le ~ capital** big money; **~ duc** eagle owl; **~ écart** (Sport) splits; **le ~ écran** the big screen; **~ ensemble** high-density housing complex; **le ~ large** the high seas; **~ magasin** department store; **le ~ monde** high society; **le Grand Nord** the Far North; **Grand Pardon** Day of Atonement; **~ prêtre** high priest; **~ prix** grand prix; **le ~ public** the general public; **produit ~ public** consumer product; **la ~e banlieue** the outer suburbs; **la ~e cuisine** haute cuisine; **la Grande Guerre** the First World War; **la ~e muraille de Chine** the Great Wall of China; **~e personne** grown-up, adult; **~e puissance** superpower; **~e roue** big wheel (GB), Ferris wheel (US); **~e surface** supermarket; **~es eaux** fountains; **dès qu'on la gronde, ce sont les ~es eaux** the minute you tell her off, she turns on the waterworks; **~es lignes** main train routes; **~es marées** spring tides; **~es ondes** long wave; **les ~s blessés** the seriously injured; **~s fauves** big cats.

grand-chose /gʀɑ̃ʃoz/ *pron* **pas ~** not much, not a lot; **il n'y a plus ~ à faire** there isn't much left to do.

Grande-Bretagne /gʀɑ̃dbʀətaɲ/ *pr nf* Great Britain.

grandement /gʀɑ̃dmɑ̃/ *adv* greatly; a great deal; extremely.

grandeur /gʀɑ̃dœʀ/ *nf* **1** size; **~ nature** [*reproduction*] full-scale; [*portrait*] life-size; **2** scale; **3** greatness.

grandiloquent, **~e** /gʀɑ̃dilɔkɑ̃, ɑ̃t/ *adj* pompous, grandiloquent.

grandiose /gʀɑ̃djoz/ *adj* [*site, decor*] grandiose; [*party*] spectacular; [*gesture*] grand.

grandir /gʀɑ̃diʀ/ [3] **I** *vtr* **1** to magnify; **2** to make [sb] look taller; **3** to exaggerate.

II *vi* **1** to grow; to grow up; **2** [*company*] to expand; [*crowd, anxiety*] to grow.

III se grandir *v refl* (+ *v être*) to make oneself (look) taller.

grand-mère, *pl* **grands-mères** /gʀɑ̃mɛʀ/ *nf* grandmother.

grand-oncle, *pl* **grands-oncles** /gʀɑ̃tɔ̃kl, gʀɑ̃zɔ̃kl/ *nm* great-uncle.

grand-père, *pl* **grands-pères** /gʀɑ̃pɛʀ/ *nm* grandfather.

grands-parents /gʀɑ̃paʀɑ̃/ *nm pl* grandparents.

grand-tante, *pl* **grand(s)-tantes** /gʀɑ̃tɑ̃t/ *nf* great-aunt.

grange /gʀɑ̃ʒ/ *nf* barn.

granit(e) /gʀanit/ *nm* granite.

granité, **~e** /gʀanite/ *adj* grained.

granulé /gʀanyle/ *nm* granule.

graphie /gʀafi/ *nf* **1** written form; **2** spelling.

graphique /gʀafik/ **I** *adj* **1** [*work*] graphic; **2** [*screen*] graphic; [*software*] graphics.

II *nm* graph.

graphisme /gʀafism/ *nm* **1** style of drawing; **2** handwriting; **3** graphic design.

graphologie /gʀafɔlɔʒi/ *nf* graphology.

grappe /gʀap/ *nf* (of fruit) bunch; (of flowers) cluster.

grappiller /gʀapije/ [1] *vtr* to pick up [*fruit*]; to glean [*information*].

grappin /gʀapɛ̃/ *nm* **mettre le ~ sur qn**° to get sb in one's clutches.

gras, **grasse** /gʀɑ, gʀɑs/ **I** *adj* **1** [*substance*] fatty; [*fish*] oily; [*paper*] greasy; **2** coarse, vulgar; **3** (in printing) bold; **4** loose, phlegmy.
II *adv* **manger ~** to eat fatty foods.
III *nm* **1** (from meat) fat; **2** grease; **3** (of arm, calf) **le ~** the fleshy part.

grassement /gʀɑsmɑ̃/ *adv* [*pay*] handsomely; [*feed*] lavishly.

gratifiant, **~e** /gʀatifjɑ̃, ɑ̃t/ *adj* gratifying.

gratin /gʀatɛ̃/ *nm* **1** gratin (*breadcrumbs and cheese*); **2**° **le ~** the upper crust°.

gratiné, **~e** /gʀatine/ *adj* **1** (Culin) au gratin; **2**° [*person*] weird; [*problem*] mind-bending°.

gratis /gʀatis/ **I** *adj inv* free.
II *adv* free (GB), for free.

gratitude /gʀatityd/ *nf* gratitude; **avoir de la ~ pour qn** to be grateful to sb.

gratte-ciel /gʀatsjɛl/ *nm inv* skyscraper.

gratter /gʀate/ [1] **I** *vtr* **1** to scratch; to scrape (off); **2** to make [sb] itch; **ça me gratte partout** I'm itching all over.
II *vi* **~ à la porte** to scratch at the door.
III se gratter *v refl* (+ *v être*) to scratch; **se ~ la tête** to scratch one's head.

grattoir /gʀatwaʀ/ *nm* **1** (tool) scraper; **2** (on matchbox) striking strip.

gratuit, **~e** /gʀatɥi, it/ *adj* **1** [*place, service*] free; **2** [*violence*] gratuitous; [*accusation*] spurious; [*exercise*] pointless.

gratuité /gʀatɥite/ *nf* **la ~ de l'enseignement** free education.

gratuitement /gʀatɥitmɑ̃/ *adv* **1** free (GB), for free; **2** [*work*] for nothing; **3** gratuitously.

gravats /gʀava/ *nm pl* rubble.

grave /gʀav/ *adj* **1** [*problem, injury*] serious; **2** [*expression*] grave, solemn; **3** [*voice*] deep; [*note*] low; [*sound*] low-pitched.

graver /gʀave/ [1] *vtr* to engrave.

gravier /gʀavje/ *nm* **du ~** gravel.

gravillon /gʀavijɔ̃/ *nm* grit.

gravir /gʀaviʀ/ [3] *vtr* to climb up.

gravitation /gʀavitasjɔ̃/ *nf* gravitation; **~ universelle** Newton's law of gravitation.

gravité /gʀavite/ *nf* **1** seriousness; **2** solemnity; **3** (in physics) gravity.

graviter /gʀavite/ [1] *vi* to orbit.

gravure /gʀavyʀ/ *nf* **1 la ~** engraving; **2** engraving; **3** print, reproduction.

gré /gʀe/ *nm* **1 contre le ~ de qn** against sb's will; **de ~ ou de force** one way or another; **2** (formal) **savoir ~ à qn de qch** to be grateful to sb for sth; **3 j'ai flâné au ~ de mon humeur** I strolled where the mood took me.

grec, **grecque**[1] /gʀɛk/ **I** *adj* Greek; Grecian.
II *nm* (language) Greek.

Grec, **Grecque** /gʀɛk/ *nm,f* Greek.

Grèce /gʀɛs/ *pr nf* Greece; **~ antique** Ancient Greece.

grecque[2] /gʀɛk/ *adj f* ▶ **grec**.

greffe /gʀɛf/ *nf* **1** (of organ) transplant; (of skin) graft; **2** (in agriculture) grafting; graft.

greffer /gʀefe/ [1] **I** *vtr* **1** to transplant [*organ*]; to graft [*tissue*]; **2** to graft [*tree*].
II se greffer *v refl* (+ *v être*) **se ~ sur qch** [*problem, event*] to come along on top of sth.

greffier, **-ière** /gʀefje, ɛʀ/ *nm,f* clerk of the court (GB), court clerk (US).

grégaire /gʀegɛʀ/ *adj* gregarious.

grêle /gʀɛl/ **I** *adj* **1** skinny; spindly; **2** [*voice*] reedy; [*sound*] thin.
II *nf* hail.

grêlé, **~e** /gʀele/ *adj* pockmarked.

grêler /gʀele/ [1] *v impers* **il grêle** it's hailing.

grêlon /gʀɛlɔ̃/ *nm* hailstone.

grelot /gʀəlo/ *nm* small bell.

grelotter /gʀəlɔte/ [1] *vi* to shiver.

grenade /gʀənad/ *nf* **1** grenade; **2** pomegranate.

Grenade /gʀənad/ **I** *pr n* Granada.
II *pr nf* **la ~** Grenada.

grenadine /gʀənadin/ *nf* grenadine.

grenaille /gʀənaj/ *nf* **1** steel filings; **2** lead shot.

grenat /gʀəna/ *adj inv* dark red.

grenier /gʀənje/ *nm* attic, loft; **~ à grain** granary.

grenouille /gʀənuj/ *nf* frog.

grès /gʀɛ/ *nm inv* **1** sandstone; **2** (piece of) stoneware.

grésiller /gʀezije/ [1] *vi* **1** [*radio*] to crackle; **2** [*butter, oil*] to sizzle.

grève /gʀɛv/ *nf* **1** strike; **mouvement de ~** industrial action; **2** shore.
■ **~ de la faim** hunger strike; **~ sur le tas** sit-down strike; **~ du zèle** work-to-rule.

gréviste /gʀevist/ *nmf* striker.

gribouiller° /gʀibuje/ [1] *vtr* to scribble.

grief /gʀijɛf/ *nm* grievance.

grièvement /gʀijɛvmɑ̃/ *adv* [*injured*] seriously; [*burned*] badly; [*affected*] severely.

griffe /gʀif/ *nf* **1** claw; **tomber entre les ~s de qn** to fall into sb's clutches; **2** (on garment) label; **3** signature stamp; **4** (in jewellery) claw.

griffer /gʀife/ [1] **I** *vtr* to scratch.
II se griffer *v refl* (+ *v être*) to scratch oneself.

griffonner /gʀifɔne/ [1] *vtr* **1** to scrawl; **2** to sketch.

griffure /gʀifyʀ/ *nf* scratch.

grignoter /gʀiɲɔte/ [1] **I** *vtr* **1** to nibble; **2** to encroach on [*territory*]; to conquer [*corner of market*]; **3** to fritter away [*inheritance*].
II *vi* **1** [*rodent*] to gnaw; **2** [*person*] to nibble.

gri-gri, *pl* **gris-gris** /gʀigʀi/ *nm* lucky charm.

gril /gʀil/ *nm* grill (GB), broiler (US).

grillage /gʀijaʒ/ *nm* wire netting; chicken wire; wire mesh.

grille /gʀij/ *nf* **1** railings; (iron) gate; (of sink, sewer) drain; (of air vent) grille; (in oven, fridge) shelf; (in fireplace, stove) grate; **2** (of crossword) grid; **3** (on TV, radio) programme[GB]; **4** (for assessing results) model; **5** (in administration) scale.

grillé, **~e** /gʀije/ **I** *pp* ▶ **griller**.
II *pp adj* **1** [*meat*] grilled; [*bread*] toasted; [*almonds*] roasted; **2** crispy, well-browned; **3** burned out; **l'ampoule est ~e** the bulb has blown; **4**○ [*spy*] exposed.

grille-pain /gʀijpɛ̃/ *nm inv* toaster.

griller /gʀije/ [1] **I** *vtr* **1** to grill [*meat*]; to toast [*bread*]; to roast [*almonds*]; **2**○ to jump○ [*light*]; to ignore [*give way sign*]; **3**○ to give the game away about [sb]; **4**○ **~ un adversaire** to manage to get ahead of one's opponent.
II *vi* **1** to grill; **faire ~** to grill; to toast; to roast; **2** [*bulb*] to blow.

grillon /gʀijɔ̃/ *nm* cricket.

grimace /gʀimas/ *nf* grimace; funny face.

grimacer /gʀimase/ [12] *vi* to grimace.

grimer: **se grimer** /gʀime/ [1] *v refl* (+ *v être*) to make oneself up.

grimpant, **~e** /gʀɛ̃pɑ̃, ɑ̃t/ *adj* climbing.

grimper /gʀɛ̃pe/ [1] **I** *vtr* to climb [*stairs*].
II *vi* **1 ~ aux arbres** to climb (up) trees; **grimpe sur mon dos** get on my back; **2**○ [*road*] to be steep; **3**○ [*prices*] to climb.

grimpeur, **-euse** /gʀɛ̃pœʀ, øz/ *nm,f* rock climber.

grinçant, **~e** /gʀɛ̃sɑ̃, ɑ̃t/ *adj* [*tone*] scathing; [*joke*] caustic; [*laugh*] nasty.

grincement /gʀɛ̃smɑ̃/ *nm* creak(ing); squeak(-ing); screech(ing).

grincer /gʀɛ̃se/ [12] *vi* [*door*] to creak; [*violin*] to screech; [*chalk*] to squeak; **~ des dents** to grind one's teeth; (figurative) to gnash one's teeth.

gringalet /gʀɛ̃galɛ/ *nm* runt.

griotte /gʀijɔt/ *nf* morello cherry.

grippe /gʀip/ *nf* flu; **~ intestinale** gastric flu (GB), intestinal flu (US).
IDIOMS **prendre qn/qch en ~**○ to take a sudden dislike to sb/sth.

gris, **~e** /gʀi, iz/ **I** *adj* **1** grey (GB), gray (US); **2** dreary; dull; **3** tipsy.
II *nm inv* grey (GB), gray (US).

grisaille /gʀizaj/ *nf* **1** dullness; **2** (of weather) greyness (GB), grayness (US).

grisant, **~e** /gʀizɑ̃, ɑ̃t/ *adj* **1** [*speed*] exhilarating; [*success*] intoxicating; **2** [*perfume*] heady.

grisâtre /gʀizɑtʀ/ *adj* [*colour, sky*] greyish (GB), grayish (US); [*morning*] dull.

griser /gʀize/ [1] *vtr* [*speed*] to exhilarate; [*success*] to intoxicate; **se laisser ~ par le pouvoir** to let power go to one's head.

grisou /gʀizu/ *nm* firedamp.

grive /gʀiv/ *nf* thrush.

grivois, **~e** /gʀivwa, az/ *adj* bawdy; coarse.

grizzli, **grizzly** /gʀizli/ *nm* grizzly bear.

grognement /gʀɔɲəmɑ̃/ *nm* grunt; growl.

grogner /gʀɔɲe/ [1] *vi* **1** to groan; (figurative) to grumble; **2** [*pig*] to grunt; [*dog*] to growl.

grognon /gʀɔɲɔ̃/ *adj* grouchy○.

groin /gʀwɛ̃/ *nm* snout.

grommeler /gʀɔmle/ [19] *vi* to grumble.

grondement /gʀɔ̃dmɑ̃/ *nm* (of torrent, machine) roar; (of crowd) angry murmur.

gronder /gʀɔ̃de/ [1] **I** *vtr* to tell [sb] off.
II *vi* **1** [*thunder*] to rumble; [*machine, wind*] to roar; **2** [*rebellion*] to be brewing.

groom /gʀum/ *nm* bellboy (GB), bellhop (US).

gros, **grosse** /gʀo, gʀos/ **I** *adj* **1** big, large; **2** thick; **3** fat; **4** [*customer, market*] big; [*damage*] considerable; **5** [*problem*] serious, big; [*flaw*] big, major; **6** [*cold*] bad; [*sobs*] loud; [*voice*] deep; [*rain*] heavy; [*smoker*] heavy.
II *adv* **1** [*write*] big; **2** [*bet, lose*] a lot of money; (figurative) a lot.
III *nm inv* **1 le ~ de** the majority of [*spectators*]; the bulk of [*work*]; most of [*winter*]; **2** wholesale trade; **3 la pêche au ~** game fishing.
IV en ~ *phr* **1** roughly; **en ~ je suis d'accord avec toi** basically, I agree with you; **2** wholesale; **3** in big letters.
■ **~ bonnet**○ big shot○; **~ lot** first prize; **~ mot** swearword; **~ œuvre** shell (of a building); **~ plan** close-up; **~ sel** cooking salt; **~ titre** headline; **grosse caisse** bass drum; **grosse tête**○ brain○.
IDIOMS **en avoir ~ sur le cœur** or **la patate**○ to be very upset; **c'est un peu ~ comme histoire**! that's a bit of a tall story!

groseille /gʀozɛj/ *nf* redcurrant; **~ à maquereau** gooseberry.

grosse ▶ **gros**.

grossesse /gʀosɛs/ *nf* pregnancy.
■ **~ nerveuse** phantom pregnancy (GB), false pregnancy.

grosseur /gʀosœʀ/ *nf* **1** size; **2** (of thread) thickness; **3** (Med) lump.

grossier, **-ière** /gʀosje, ɛʀ/ *adj* **1** [*person, gesture*] rude; [*language*] bad; **2** [*laugh*] coarse; **3** [*imitation*] crude; **4** [*sketch, idea*] rough; [*work*] crude; **5** [*error*] glaring.

grossièrement /gʀosjɛʀmɑ̃/ *adv* **1** [*calculate*] roughly; **2** [*built*] crudely; **3** [*speak*] rudely.

grossièreté /gʀosjɛʀte/ *nf* **1** rudeness; **2** dirty word; **3** coarseness.

grossir /gʀosiʀ/ [3] **I** *vtr* **1** to enlarge [*image*]; **2** to increase [*numbers*]; to boost [*profits*]; **3** to exaggerate [*incident*]; **4** to make [sb] look fat.
II *vi* **1** to put on weight; **2** (gen) to grow; [*river*] to swell.

grossissant, **~e** /gʀosisɑ̃, ɑ̃t/ *adj* magnifying.

grossiste /gʀosist/ *nmf* wholesaler.

grosso modo /gʀosomodo/ *adv* roughly.

grotesque /gʀɔtɛsk/ *adj* ridiculous.

grotte /gʀɔt/ *nf* **1** cave; **2** grotto.

grouiller /gʀuje/ [1] **I** *vi* to swarm about; to mill about.
II se grouiller○ *v refl* (+ *v être*) to get a move on○.

groupe /gʀup/ *nm* **1** (gen, Econ) group; **par ~s de deux** in pairs, in twos; **2** (of objects) group; cluster.
■ **~ d'autodéfense** vigilante group; **~**

électrogène (electricity) generator; **~ sanguin** blood group; **~ scolaire** school; **~ des Sept**, **G7** Group of Seven, G7 countries.

groupement /grupmɑ̃/ *nm* **1** association, group; **2** grouping.

grouper /grupe/ [1] **I** *vtr* to put together.
II se grouper *v refl* (+ *v être*) to gather (**autour de** around); to form a group; **se ~ par trois** to form groups of three; **restez groupés** keep together.

groupuscule /grupyskyl/ *nm* small group.

gruau, *pl* **~x** /gryo/ *nm* **1** gruel; **2** fine wheat flour.

grue /gry/ *nf* (Tech, Zool) crane.
IDIOMS **faire le pied de ~**○ to hang around.

grumeau, *pl* **~x** /grymo/ *nm* lump.

gruyère /gryjɛr/ *nm* Gruyère, Swiss cheese.

Guadeloupe /gwadlup/ *pr nf* **la ~** Guadeloupe.

gué /ge/ *nm* ford; **passer un ruisseau à ~** to ford a stream.

guenille /gənij/ *nf* rag; **en ~s** in rags.

guenon /gənɔ̃/ *nf* female monkey.

guépard /gepar/ *nm* cheetah.

guêpe /gɛp/ *nf* wasp.

guêpier /gepje/ *nm* **1** wasps' nest; **2** tight corner; **dans quel ~ es-tu allé te fourrer**○**?** what kind of mess have you got (GB) or gotten (US) yourself into?

guêpière /gepjɛr/ *nf* basque, bodyshaper with suspenders (GB) or garters (US).

guère /gɛr/ *adv* hardly; **il n'avait ~ le choix** he didn't really have a choice.

guéridon /geridɔ̃/ *nm* pedestal table.

guérilla /gerija/ *nf* **1** guerilla warfare; **2** guerillas.

guérir /gerir/ [3] **I** *vtr* **1** to cure [*person, disease*]; **2 ~ qn de** to cure sb of [*habit*].
II *vi* to recover; to heal; to get better.
III se guérir *v refl* (+ *v être*) **se ~ de** to overcome [*shyness*].

guérison /gerizɔ̃/ *nf* recovery; healing.

guérite /gerit/ *nf* **1** sentry box; **2** (on toll road) booth.

guerre /gɛr/ *nf* war; warfare; **les pays en ~** the warring nations.
■ **~ chimique** chemical war; chemical warfare; **~ éclair** blitzkrieg, lightning war; **~ mondiale** world war; **Première/Deuxième Guerre mondiale** World War I/II; **~ nucléaire** nuclear war; nuclear warfare; **~ de 14** 1914–18 war; **~ de Sécession** American Civil War; **~ d'usure** war of attrition.
IDIOMS **à la ~ comme à la ~** in time of hardship you have to make the best of things; **c'est de bonne ~** it's only fair; **de ~ lasse, elle renonça** realizing that she was fighting a losing battle, she gave up.

guerrier, **-ière** /gerje, ɛr/ *nm,f* warrior.

guet /gɛ/ *nm* **1** lookout; **faire le ~** to be on the lookout; **2** (Mil) watch.

guet-apens, *pl* **guets-apens** /gɛtapɑ̃/ *nm* ambush; (figurative) trap.

guêtre /gɛtr/ *nf* **1** (Sport) leggings; **2** gaiter.

guetter /gete/ [1] *vtr* **1** to watch [*prey, criminal, reaction*]; to watch out for [*sign*]; to look out for [*postman*]; **2** to threaten.

gueule /gœl/ *nf* **1**◑ face; **il a la ~ de l'emploi** he really looks the part; **2**◑ mouth; **(ferme) ta ~!** shut your face○ (GB) or mouth○!; **3** (of animal) mouth.
■ **~ de bois**○ hangover.
IDIOMS **faire la ~**◑ to be sulking.

gueuler◑ /gœle/ [1] **I** *vtr* to yell; to bawl out.
II *vi* to yell, to bawl; to kick up a real fuss; **~ après qn** to have a go at sb○.

gui /gi/ *nm* mistletoe.

guichet /giʃɛ/ *nm* window; (in bank) counter; (in museum, station) ticket office; (in theatre, cinema) box office; **la pièce se jouera à ~s fermés** the play is sold out.
■ **~ automatique** automatic teller machine.

guichetier, **-ière** /giʃtje, ɛr/ *nm,f* ticket clerk.

guide /gid/ *nm* guide.

guider /gide/ [1] *vtr* **1** (gen) to guide; **2** to show [sb] the way.

guidon /gidɔ̃/ *nm* handlebars.

guigne○ /giɲ/ *nf* bad luck.

guignol /giɲɔl/ *nm* **1** puppet show, ≈ Punch and Judy show; **2** (derogatory) clown.

guillemets /gijmɛ/ *nm pl* inverted commas (GB), quotation marks.

guillotine /gijɔtin/ *nf* guillotine.

guimauve /gimov/ *nf* **1** (Bot) (marsh) mallow; **2** (confectionery) marshmallow.

guimbarde /gɛ̃bard/ *nf* Jew's harp.

guindé, **~e** /gɛ̃de/ *adj* formal.

guingois: **de guingois** /degɛ̃gwa/ *phr* **être de ~** to be lopsided.

guirlande /girlɑ̃d/ *nf* garland; tinsel.
■ **~ électrique** set or string of fairy lights.

guise /giz/ *nf* **1 'à votre ~'** 'just as you like or please'; **2 en ~ de** by way of.

guitare /gitar/ *nf* guitar.

gustatif, **-ive** /gystatif, iv/ *adj* [*organ*] taste.

guttural, **~e**, *mpl* **-aux** /gytyral, o/ *adj* guttural.

Guyana /gɥijana/ *pr nf* Guyana; **République de ~** Republic of Guyana.

Guyane /gɥijan/ *pr nf* **~ (française)** (French) Guyana; **~ hollandaise** Dutch Guiana.

gym○ /ʒim/ *nf* (Sch) physical education; (Sport) gymnastics.

gymnase /ʒimnɑz/ *nm* gymnasium.

gymnaste /ʒimnast/ *nmf* gymnast.

gymnastique /ʒimnastik/ *nf* gymnastics; exercises.
■ **~ corrective** ≈ physiotherapy exercises.

gynécologie /ʒinekɔlɔʒi/ *nf* gynaecology.

gyrophare /ʒirɔfar/ *nm* flashing light, emergency rotating light.

Hh

h, **H** /aʃ/ *nm inv* **1** (letter) h, H; **h muet** mute h; **2** (*written abbr* = **heure**) **9 h 10** 9.10.

ha /ˈa/ (*written abbr* = **hectare**) ha.

habile /abil/ *adj* clever, skilful[GB].

habileté /abilte/ *nf* skill; skilfulness[GB].

habiliter /abilite/ [1] *vtr* to authorize.

habillé, **~e** /abije/ *adj* [*dress*] smart; [*dinner*] formal.

habillement /abijmɑ̃/ *nm* clothing.

habiller /abije/ [1] **I** *vtr* **1** to dress; to dress [sb] up; **2** to clothe; to provide [sb] with clothing; **3** to make [sb's] clothes; **4 un rien l'habille** she looks good in anything.

II s'habiller *v refl* (+ *v être*) **1** to get dressed; to dress up; **s'~ long/court** to wear long/short skirts; **2 s'~ chez** to get one's clothes from.

habit /abi/ *nm* **1 ~s** clothes; **2** outfit, costume; **3** (of monk, nun) habit.

■ **~ de lumière** matador's costume; **~s du dimanche** Sunday best.

habitable /abitabl/ *adj* **1** habitable; **2 surface ~** living space.

habitacle /abitakl/ *nm* **1** (of plane) cockpit; (of rocket) cabin; **2** (Naut) binnacle.

habitant, **~e** /abitɑ̃, ɑ̃t/ *nm,f* inhabitant; resident; **loger chez l'~** to stay as a paying guest.

habitat /abita/ *nm* **1** (Bot, Zool) habitat; **2** housing.

habitation /abitasjɔ̃/ *nf* **1** house, dwelling; home; **2** living; **immeuble d'~** block of flats (GB), apartment building (US).

■ **~ à loyer modéré**, **HLM** ≈ (block of) council flats (GB), low-rent apartment (building) (US).

habité, **~e** /abite/ *adj* **1** inhabited; **2** [*rocket*] manned.

habiter /abite/ [1] **I** *vtr* to live in.

II *vi* to live.

habitude /abityd/ **I** *nf* **1** habit; **par ~** out of habit; **ils ont l'~ de se coucher tôt** they usually go to bed early; **avoir l'~ de** to be used to; **2** custom.

II d'habitude *phr* usually.

habitué, **~e** /abitɥe/ *nm,f* regular.

habituel, **-elle** /abitɥɛl/ *adj* usual.

habituellement /abitɥɛlmɑ̃/ *adv* usually.

habituer /abitɥe/ [1] **I** *vtr* **1 ~ qn à** to get sb used to; **2** to teach.

II s'habituer *v refl* (+ *v être*) **s'~ à** to get used to.

hache /ˈaʃ/ *nf* axe (GB), ax (US).

IDIOMS **enterrer la ~ de guerre** to bury the hatchet.

haché, **~e** /ˈaʃe/ *adj* **1** [*meat*] minced; **2** [*speech*] disjointed.

hache-légumes /ˈaʃlegym/ *nm inv* vegetable chopper.

hacher /ˈaʃe/ [1] *vtr* to mince; to chop.

hachette /ˈaʃɛt/ *nf* hatchet.

hachis /ˈaʃi/ *nm inv* mince; **~ de persil** chopped parsley.

■ **~ Parmentier** ≈ shepherd's pie.

hachisch /ˈaʃiʃ/ *nm* hashish.

hachoir /ˈaʃwaʀ/ *nm* **1** mincer; **2** chopper.

hachurer /ˈaʃyʀe/ [1] *vtr* to hatch.

haddock /ˈadɔk/ *nm* smoked haddock.

hagard, **~e** /ˈagaʀ, aʀd/ *adj* [*person*] dazed; [*eyes*] wild.

haie /ˈɛ/ *nf* **1** hedge; **2** (Sport) hurdle; fence; **course de ~s** hurdle race; steeple chase; **3** line, row; **faire une ~ d'honneur** to form a guard of honour[GB].

haillon /ˈɑjɔ̃/ *nm* rag; **en ~s** in rags.

haine /ˈɛn/ *nf* hatred; **s'attirer la ~ de qn** to earn sb's hatred.

haïr /ˈaiʀ/ [25] *vtr* to hate.

halage /ˈalaʒ/ *nm* **chemin de ~** towpath.

hâle /ˈɑl/ *nm* (sun)tan.

hâlé, **~e** /ˈɑle/ *adj* tanned.

haleine /alɛn/ *nf* breath; breathing; **hors d'~** out of breath; **un travail de longue ~** a long-drawn-out job.

haler /ˈale/ [1] *vtr* to tow [*boat*]; to haul in [*chain*].

haleter /ˈalte/ [18] *vi* **1** to gasp for breath; to pant; **2** [*machine*] to puff; [*chest*] to heave.

hall /ˈol/ *nm* entrance hall (GB), lobby (US); **~ (de gare)** concourse.

halle /ˈal/ *nf* covered market.

hallucination /alysinasjɔ̃/ *nf* hallucination; **avoir des ~s** to hallucinate; to be seeing things.

hallucinogène /alysinɔʒɛn/ *adj* hallucinogenic.

halo /ˈalo/ *nm* halo; **entouré d'un ~ de mystère** shrouded in mystery.

halogène /alɔʒɛn/ *adj* halogen.

halte /ˈalt/ **I** *nf* **1** stop; **2** stopping place.

II *excl* stop!; (Mil) halt!

halte-garderie, *pl* **haltes-garderies** /ˈaltəgaʀdəʀi/ *nf* ≈ playgroup.

haltère /altɛʀ/ *nm* dumbbell; barbell; **faire des ~s** to do weightlifting.

hamac /ˈamak/ *nm* hammock.

hameau, *pl* **~x** /ˈamo/ *nm* hamlet.

hameçon /amsɔ̃/ *nm* hook; **mordre à l'~** to take the bait.

hanche /ˈɑ̃ʃ/ *nf* (of person) hip.

handicap /ˈɑ̃dikap/ *nm* handicap.

handicapé, **~e** /ˈɑ̃dikape/ **I** *adj* **1** disabled; **2 être ~** to be at a disadvantage.

II *nm,f* disabled person.
handicaper /ˈɑ̃dikape/ [1] *vtr* to handicap.
hangar /ˈɑ̃gaʀ/ *nm* shed; warehouse; hangar.
hanneton /ˈantɔ̃/ *nm* cockchafer (GB), June bug (US).
hanter /ˈɑ̃te/ [1] *vtr* to haunt.
hantise /ˈɑ̃tiz/ *nf* dread.
happer /ˈape/ [1] *vtr* to catch [*insect*]; **happé par** [*arm*] caught up in [*machine*]; [*person*] hit by [*train*]; (figurative) swallowed up by [*crowd*].
haranguer /ˈaʀɑ̃ge/ [1] *vtr* to harangue.
haras /ˈaʀa/ *nm inv* stud farm.
harasser /ˈaʀase/ [1] *vtr* to exhaust.
harcèlement /ˈaʀsɛlmɑ̃/ *nm* harassment.
harceler /ˈaʀsəle/ [17] *vtr* **1** to pester; **2** to harass.
hardi, **~e** /ˈaʀdi/ *adj* bold, daring.
hareng /ˈaʀɑ̃/ *nm* herring.
hargne /ˈaʀɲ/ *nf* aggression.
hargneux, **-euse** /ˈaʀɲø, øz/ *adj* aggressive.
haricot /ˈaʀiko/ *nm* (Bot) bean; **~ blanc** haricot bean; **~ vert** French bean.
IDIOMS **c'est la fin des ~s**○ we've had it○.
harmonica /aʀmɔnika/ *nm* mouth organ, harmonica.
harmonie /aʀmɔni/ *nf* harmony.
harmonieux, **-ieuse** /aʀmɔnjø, øz/ *adj* harmonious; [*movements*] graceful.
harmoniser /aʀmɔnize/ [1] **I** *vtr* **1** to coordinate [*colours*]; **2** to harmonize; to make [sth] consistent; to bring into line; **3** (Mus) to harmonize.
II s'harmoniser *v refl* (+ *v être*) **bien s'~** [*colours*] to go together well.
harnacher /ˈaʀnaʃe/ [1] *vtr* **1** to harness [*horse*]; **2**○ to rig out○ [*person*].
harnais /ˈaʀnɛ/ *nm inv* harness.
harpe /ˈaʀp/ *nf* harp.
harpie /ˈaʀpi/ *nf* harpy.
harpon /ˈaʀpɔ̃/ *nm* harpoon.
harponner /ˈaʀpɔne/ [1] *vtr* to harpoon.
hasard /ˈazaʀ/ *nm* chance; **par ~** by chance; **par un curieux ~** by a curious coincidence; **par un heureux ~** by a stroke of luck; **ce n'est pas un ~ si**... it's no accident that...; **le ~ a voulu que**... as luck would have it,...; **au ~** [*choose*] at random; [*walk*] aimlessly; [*answer*] off the top of one's head; **comme par ~, il a oublié son argent** (ironic) surprise, surprise, he's forgotten his money; **à tout ~** just in case, on the off chance; **les ~s de la vie** the fortunes of life.
IDIOMS **le ~ fait bien les choses** fate is a great provider.
hasarder /ˈazaʀde/ [1] **I** *vtr* **1** to venture [*advice*]; **2** to risk [*life*].
II se hasarder *v refl* (+ *v être*) to venture.
hâte /ˈɑt/ *nf* **1** haste; **à la ~** hastily; **2 j'ai ~ de partir/qu'elle parte** I can't wait to leave/for her to leave.
hâter /ˈɑte/ [1] **I** *vtr* to hasten; **~ le pas** to quicken one's step.
II se hâter *v refl* (+ *v être*) to hurry, to rush.
hâtif, **-ive** /ˈɑtif, iv/ *adj* **1** [*judgment*] hasty, hurried; **2** [*plant*] early.
hausse /ˈos/ *nf* increase, rise; **être en ~** [*prices*] to be rising; [*goods*] to be going up in price; **en ~ de 10%** up 10%.
haussement /ˈosmɑ̃/ *nm* **~ d'épaules** shrug.
hausser /ˈose/ [1] **I** *vtr* to raise; **~ les épaules** to shrug one's shoulders.
II se hausser *v refl* (+ *v être*) **se ~ sur la pointe des pieds** to stand on tiptoe.
haut, **~e**[1] /ˈo, ˈot/ **I** *adj* **1** high; tall; **l'étagère la plus ~e** the top shelf; **à ~e voix** [*speak*] loudly; [*read*] aloud, out loud; **à ~ risque** very risky; **au plus ~ point** immensely; **2** [*rank, society*] high; [*person, post*] high-ranking; **~e surveillance** close supervision; **3** (in geography) upper; **la ~e Égypte** Upper Egypt; **4 le ~ Moyen Âge** the early Middle Ages.
II *adv* **1** high; **un personnage ~ placé** a high-ranking person; **plus ~ sur la page** higher up on the page; **'voir plus ~'** see above; **de ~** from above; **2** (in time) far back; **3** loud(ly); **dire qch tout ~** to say sth aloud; **n'avoir jamais un mot plus ~ que l'autre** never to raise one's voice.
III *nm* **1** top; **le ~ du corps** the top half of the body; **l'étagère du ~** the top shelf; **les pièces du ~** the upstairs rooms; **parler du ~ d'un balcon** to speak from a balcony; **2 faire 50 mètres de ~** to be 50 metres[GB] high.
IV en haut *phr* upstairs; on an upper floor; **en ~ de** at the top of.
■ **~ en couleur** [*character*] colourful[GB]; **~ fait** heroic deed; **~ lieu de** centre[GB] of or for; **en ~ lieu** in high places; **~e mer** open sea; **~es sphères** high social circles.
IDIOMS **voir les choses de ~** to have a detached view of things; **tomber de ~** to be dumbfounded; **connaître des ~s et des bas** to have one's ups and downs; **~ les mains!** hands up!; **gagner ~ la main** to win hands down; **prendre qch de ~** to react indignantly.
hautain, **~e** /ˈotɛ̃, ɛn/ *adj* haughty.
hautbois /ˈobwɑ/ *nm inv* **1** oboe; **2** oboist.
haut-de-forme, *pl* **hauts-de-formes** /ˈodfɔʀm/ *nm* top hat.
haute[2] /ˈot/ **I** *adj f* ▶ **haut I**.
II○ *nf* **les gens de la ~** the upper crust.
haute(-)fidélité, *pl* **hautes(-)fidélités** /ˈotfidelite/ *nf* hi-fi, high fidelity.
hauteur /ˈotœʀ/ **I** *nf* **1** height; **prendre de la ~** [*plane*] to climb; **dans le sens de la ~** upright; **à ~ d'homme** at head height; **2** hill; **gagner les ~s** to reach high ground; **3** haughtiness; **4** (of voice) pitch.
II à la hauteur de *phr* **1 arriver à la ~ de** to come up to; to draw level with; **raccourcir une jupe à la ~ des genoux** to shorten a dress to the knee; **2** (figurative) **être à la ~** to measure up; **être à la ~ de sa tâche** to be equal to one's job.
IDIOMS **tomber de toute sa ~** to fall headlong.
haut-fond, *pl* **hauts-fonds** /ˈofɔ̃/ *nm* shallows.

haut(-)fourneau, *pl* **hauts(-)fourneaux** /'ofurno/ *nm* blast furnace.
haut-le-cœur /'olkœr/ *nm inv* retching, heaving; **avoir un ~** to retch.
haut-parleur, *pl* **~s** /'oparlœr/ *nm* loudspeaker.
havane /'avan/ **I** *adj inv* tobacco-brown.
II *nm* **1** Havana tobacco; **2** Havana cigar.
havre /'ɑvr/ *nm* haven.
Haye /'ɛ/ *pr n* **la ~** the Hague.
hebdomadaire /ɛbdomadɛr/ *adj, nm* weekly.
hébergement /ebɛrʒəmɑ̃/ *nm* **1** accommodation; **2** housing.
héberger /ebɛrʒe/ [13] *vtr* to put [sb] up; to accommodate; to provide shelter for.
hébété, **~e** /ebete/ *adj* [*look*] stupid.
hébraïque /ebraik/ *adj* Hebrew.
hébreu, *pl* **~x** /ebrø/ **I** *adj m* Hebrew.
II *nm* (language) Hebrew.
IDIOMS **pour moi, c'est de l'~** it's all Greek to me.
HEC /aʃəse/ *nf* (*abbr* = **Hautes études commerciales**) *major business school.*
hécatombe /ekatɔ̃b/ *nf* massacre, slaughter.
hectare /ɛktar/ *nm* hectare.
hecto /ɛkto/ **I** *nm* (*abbr* = **hectogramme**) hectogram.
II hecto(-) (*combining form*) hecto.
hélas /'elas/ *excl* alas; **~ non!** unfortunately not!
héler /'ele/ [14] *vtr* to hail.
hélice /elis/ *nf* **1** (screw) propeller; **2** helix.
hélicoptère /elikɔptɛr/ *nm* helicopter.
héliporté, **~e** /elipɔrte/ *adj* helicopter-borne.
hellène /ellɛn/ *adj* Hellenic.
helvétique /ɛlvetik/ *adj* Helvetic, Swiss; **la Confédération ~** Switzerland.
hématologie /ematɔlɔʒi/ *nf* haematology.
hématome /ematom/ *nm* bruise.
hémicycle /emisikl/ *nm* semicircular auditorium.
hémisphère /emisfɛr/ *nm* hemisphere.
hémoglobine /emɔglɔbin/ *nf* haemoglobin.
hémophile /emɔfil/ **I** *adj* haemophilic.
II *nmf* haemophiliac.
hémorragie /emɔraʒi/ *nf* **1** haemorrhage, bleeding; **2** (of capital) outflow.
hémorroïdes /emɔrɔid/ *nf pl* piles, haemorrhoids.
henné /'ene/ *nm* henna.
hennir /'enir/ [3] *vi* to neigh, to whinny.
hépatique /epatik/ **I** *adj* hepatic.
II *nmf* person with a liver complaint.
hépatite /epatit/ *nf* hepatitis.
héraldique /eraldik/ *adj* heraldic.
herbacé, **~e** /ɛrbase/ *adj* herbaceous.
herbage /ɛrbaʒ/ *nm* pasture.
herbe /ɛrb/ **I** *nf* **1** grass; **mauvaise ~** weed; **2** (Culin) herb.
II en herbe *phr* **1** [*wheat*] in the blade; **2** [*musician*] budding.
IDIOMS **couper l'~ sous le pied de qn** to pull the rug from under sb's feet.
herbeux, **-euse** /ɛrbø, øz/ *adj* grassy.
herbier /ɛrbje/ *nm* herbarium.
herbivore /ɛrbivɔr/ **I** *adj* herbivorous.
II *nm* herbivore.
herboriste /ɛrbɔrist/ *nmf* herbalist.
herboristerie /ɛrbɔristəri/ *nf* **1** herb trade; **2** herbalist's shop (GB) or store (US).
héréditaire /ereditɛr/ *adj* hereditary; (figurative) [*enemy*] traditional.
hérédité /eredite/ *nf* **1** heredity; **2** (of title) hereditary nature.
hérésie /erezi/ *nf* **1** heresy; **2** (humorous) sacrilege.
hérétique /eretik/ **I** *adj* heretical.
II *nmf* heretic.
hérissé, **~e** /'erise/ *adj* [*hair*] bristling, standing up on end; **~ de** spiked with [*nails*].
hérisser /'erise/ [1] **I** *vtr* **1** [*bird*] to ruffle (up) [*feathers*]; **2 ~ qch de** to spike sth with; **3° ça me hérisse** it makes my hackles rise.
II se hérisser *v refl* (+ *v être*) [*hair*] to stand on end.
hérisson /'erisɔ̃/ *nm* hedgehog.
héritage /eritaʒ/ *nm* **1** inheritance; **laisser qch en ~** to bequeath sth; **recevoir qch en ~** to inherit sth; **2** heritage.
hériter /erite/ [1] **I** *vtr* to inherit.
II hériter de *v+prep* to inherit.
III *vi* to inherit; to come into an inheritance; **~ de qn** to receive an inheritance from sb.
héritier, **-ière** /eritje, ɛr/ *nm,f* heir/heiress.
hermétique /ɛrmetik/ *adj* **1** hermetic; airtight; watertight; **2** [*milieu*] impenetrable; [*poetry, author*] abstruse; [*face*] inscrutable.
hermine /ɛrmin/ *nf* **1** stoat; **2** ermine.
hernie /'ɛrni/ *nf* **1** hernia; **2** (in tyre) bulge.
héroïne /erɔin/ *nf* **1** heroine; **2** heroin.
héroïque /erɔik/ *adj* heroic; epic.
héroïsme /erɔism/ *nm* heroism.
héron /'erɔ̃/ *nm* heron.
héros /'ero/ *nm inv* hero.
herse /'ɛrs/ *nf* **1** harrow; **2** portcullis.
hertzien, **-ienne** /ɛrtzjɛ̃, ɛn/ *adj* [*wave*] Hertzian; [*station*] radio-relay.
hésitant, **~e** /ezitɑ̃, ɑ̃t/ *adj* **1** hesitant; **2** [*start*] shaky.
hésitation /ezitasjɔ̃/ *nf* **1** indecision, hesitancy; **2** hesitation.
hésiter /ezite/ [1] *vi* to hesitate; **elle hésite encore** she's still undecided; **il n'y a pas à ~** it's got to be done; **j'hésite sur le chemin à prendre** I'm not sure which path to take; **~ à faire** to be hesitant to do.
hétéroclite /eterɔklit/ *adj* [*population, work*] heterogeneous; [*objects*] miscellaneous.
hétérogène /eterɔʒɛn/ *adj* mixed, heterogeneous.
hétérosexuel, **-elle** /eterɔsɛksɥɛl/ *adj, nm,f* heterosexual.
hêtre /'ɛtr/ *nm* **1** beech (tree); **2** beechwood.

heure /œʀ/ *nf* **1** hour; **24 ~s sur 24** 24 hours a day; **dans l'~ qui a suivi** within the hour; **d'~ en ~** [*increase*] by the hour; **à trois ~s d'avion de Paris** three hours from Paris by plane; **à trois ~s de marche de Paris** a three-hour walk from Paris; **faire du 60 à l'~**○ to do 60 km per hour; **payé à l'~** paid by the hour; **une petite ~** an hour at the most; **2** time; **quelle ~ est-il?** what time is it?; **il est 10 ~s** it's 10 (o'clock); **il est 10 ~s 20** it's 20 past 10; **il est 10 ~s moins 20** it's 20 to 10; **mettre sa montre à l'~** to set one's watch; **l'~ tourne** time is passing; **~s d'ouverture** opening times; **être à l'~** to be on time; **à une ~ avancée (de la nuit)** late at night; **de bonne ~** early; **c'est son ~** it's his/her usual time; **à l'~ où je te parle** while I'm speaking to you; **de la première ~** from the very beginning; **à la première ~** at first light; **ta dernière ~ est arrivée** your time has come; **à l'~ actuelle, pour l'~** at the present time; **l'~ du déjeuner** lunchtime; **l'~ est grave** the situation is serious; **il est peintre à ses ~s** he paints in his spare time; **à la bonne ~!** well done!; **3** era, age; **vivre à l'~ des satellites** to live in the satellite era.

■ **~ d'affluence** peak hour; **~ d'été** summer time (GB), daylight saving(s) time; **~ H** (Mil, figurative) zero hour; **~ d'hiver** winter time (GB), standard time; **~ de pointe** rush hour; **~s supplémentaires** overtime.

heureusement /œʀøzmɑ̃/ *adv* fortunately.

heureux, **-euse** /œʀø, øz/ *adj* **1** happy; **~ en ménage** happily married; **très ~ de faire votre connaissance** (very) pleased to meet you; **2** [*ending*] happy; [*proportions*] pleasing; [*choice*] fortunate; [*surprise*] pleasant; **3** [*winner*] lucky; **'il a réussi!'—'encore ~!'** 'he succeeded!'—'just as well!'

IDIOMS **attendre un ~ événement** to be expecting a baby.

heurt /'œʀ/ *nm* **1** collision; **2** (figurative) (between people) clash; **sans ~s** [*do*] smoothly; [*relationship*] smooth.

heurter /'œʀte/ [1] **I** *vtr* **1** [*object*] to hit; [*person*] to collide with, to bump into; **2** (figurative) to go against [*convention*]; to hurt [*feelings*].

II *vi* **~ contre** to strike.

III se heurter *v refl* (+ *v être*) to collide; (figurative) to clash; **se ~ à** to bump into [*table*]; to come up against [*refusal, problem*].

hévéa /evea/ *nm* rubber tree.

hexagonal, **~e**, *mpl* **-aux** /ɛgzagɔnal, o/ *adj* **1** hexagonal; **2**○ [*policy*] inward-looking.

hexagone /ɛgzagɔn/ *nm* **1** hexagon; **2**○ **l'Hexagone** France.

hiberner /ibɛʀne/ [1] *vi* to hibernate.

hibou, *pl* **~x** /'ibu/ *nm* owl.

hic○ /'ik/ *nm* snag; **voilà le ~** there's the snag.

hideux, **-euse** /'idø, øz/ *adj* hideous.

hier /jɛʀ/ *adv* yesterday; **ça ne date pas d'~** it's nothing new.

hiérarchie /'jeʀaʀʃi/ *nf* hierarchy.

hiérarchique /'jeʀaʀʃik/ *adj* hierarchical; **mon supérieur ~** my immediate superior; **par la voie ~** through the correct channels.

hiérarchiser /'jeʀaʀʃize/ [1] *vtr* to organize [sth] into a hierarchy [*structure*].

hiératique /jeʀatik/ *adj* hieratic.

hiéroglyphe /'jeʀɔglif/ *nm* hieroglyph; **les ~s** hieroglyphics.

hi-fi /'ifi/ *adj inv*, *nf inv* hi-fi.

hilarant, **~e** /ilaʀɑ̃, ɑ̃t/ *adj* hilarious; **gaz ~** laughing gas.

hilare /ilaʀ/ *adj* **être ~** to be laughing.

hilarité /ilaʀite/ *nf* mirth, hilarity.

hindou, **~e** /ɛ̃du/ *adj*, *nm,f* Hindu.

hindouisme /ɛ̃duism/ *nm* Hinduism.

hippique /ipik/ *adj* equestrian; **concours ~** showjumping event (GB), horse show.

hippocampe /ipɔkɑ̃p/ *nm* sea horse.

hippodrome /ipɔdʀom/ *nm* racecourse (GB), racetrack (US).

hippopotame /ipɔpɔtam/ *nm* hippopotamus.

hirondelle /iʀɔ̃dɛl/ *nf* swallow.

hirsute /'iʀsyt/ *adj* dishevelled[GB], unkempt.

hispanique /ispanik/ *adj*, *nmf* Hispanic.

hisse /'is/ *excl* **oh ~!** heave-ho!

hisser /'ise/ [1] **I** *vtr* to hoist [*flag*].

II se hisser *v refl* (+ *v être*) to heave oneself up.

histoire /istwaʀ/ *nf* **1** history; **l'~ jugera** posterity will be the judge; **2** story; **tout ça, c'est des ~s**○**!** that's all fiction!; **une ~ à dormir debout** a tall story; **raconter des ~s** to tell fibs; **3** matter, business; **~ d'amour** love affair; **~ de famille** family matter; **il m'est arrivé une drôle d'~** a funny thing happened to me; **4** fuss; trouble; **elle fait toujours des ~s** she's always making a fuss; **ça va faire des ~s** it will cause trouble; **c'est une femme à ~s** she's a troublemaker; **une vie sans ~s** an uneventful life; **ça a été toute une ~ pour faire** it was a terrible job doing; **au travail, et pas d'~s**○**!** get on with it, no messing about○!; **5**○ **~ de rire** just for fun.

historien, **-ienne** /istɔʀjɛ̃, ɛn/ *nm,f* historian.

historique /istɔʀik/ *adj* **1** historical; **2** historic; **3 passé ~** past historic.

hit-parade, *pl* **~s** /'itpaʀad/ *nm* charts.

hiver /ivɛʀ/ *nm* winter.

hivernal, **~e**, *mpl* **-aux** /ivɛʀnal, o/ *adj* **1** winter; **2** wintry.

HLM /aʃɛlɛm/ *nm* or *f*: *abbr* ▶ **habitation**.

hocher /'ɔʃe/ [1] *vtr* **~ la tête** to nod; to shake one's head.

hochet /'ɔʃɛ/ *nm* rattle.

hockey /'ɔkɛ/ *nm* hockey.

holà /'ɔla/ *excl* hey (there)!

IDIOMS **mettre le ~ à qch** to put an end or a stop to sth.

hold-up, *pl* **~** or **~s** /'ɔldœp/ *nm* hold-up.

hollandais, **~e** /'ɔlɑ̃dɛ, ɛz/ **I** *adj* Dutch.

II *nm* (language) Dutch.

Hollandais, **~e** /ˈɔlɑ̃ dɛ, ɛz/ *nm,f* Dutchman/ Dutchwoman; **les ~** the Dutch.

Hollande /ˈɔlɑ̃d/ *pr nf* Holland.

holocauste /ɔlɔkost/ *nm* holocaust.

homard /ˈɔmaʀ/ *nm* lobster.

homéopathie /ɔmeɔpati/ *nf* homeopathy.

homéopathique /ɔmeɔpatik/ *adj* homeopathic; **à doses ~s** (figurative) in small doses.

homicide /ɔmisid/ *nm* homicide; manslaughter; murder.

hommage /ɔmaʒ/ *nm* homage, tribute; **présenter ses ~s** to pay one's respects.

hommasse /ɔmas/ *adj* mannish.

homme /ɔm/ *nm* man; **l'~** man; mankind; **un ~ à la mer!** man overboard!; **comme un seul ~** as one; **leur ~ de confiance** their right-hand man; **il n'est pas ~ à se venger** he's not the type to want revenge.

■ **~ d'affaires** businessman; **~ des cavernes** caveman; **~ d'esprit** wit; **~ d'État** statesman; **~ à femmes** womanizer; **~ au foyer** house-husband; **~ de main** hired hand; **~ de paille** front, straw man (US); **~ de terrain** man with practical experience; **~ à tout faire** handyman; **~ de troupe** private; **~s en blanc** surgeons.

IDIOMS **un ~ averti en vaut deux** (Proverb) forewarned is forearmed.

homme-grenouille, *pl* **hommes-grenouilles** /ɔmgʀənuj/ *nm* frogman.

homogène /ɔmɔʒɛn/ *adj* homogeneous.

homogénéité /ɔmɔʒeneite/ *nf* homogeneity.

homologue /ɔmɔlɔg/ **I** *adj* homologous.

II *nmf* counterpart, opposite number.

homologuer /ɔmɔlɔge/ [1] *vtr* **1** to approve [*product*]; **2** (Sport) to recognize officially.

homonyme /ɔmɔnim/ *nm* **1** homonym; **2** namesake.

homosexualité /omɔsɛksɥalite/ *nf* homosexuality.

homosexuel, **~elle** /omɔsɛksɥɛl/ *adj, nm,f* homosexual.

Hongrie /ˈɔ̃gʀi/ *pr nf* Hungary.

honnête /ɔnɛt/ *adj* **1** honest; **2** decent; respectable; **3** fair, reasonable.

honnêtement /ɔnɛtmɑ̃/ *adv* **1** [*say, manage*] honestly; [*reply*] frankly; [*behave*] properly; [*judge*] fairly; **2** fairly, reasonably; **s'acquitter ~ d'une tâche** to do a decent job.

honnêteté /ɔnɛtte/ *nf* honesty.

honneur /ɔnœʀ/ *nm* **1** honour[GB]; **à toi l'~!** you do the honours[GB]!; **j'ai l'~ de vous informer que** I beg to inform you that; **j'ai l'~ de solliciter** I would respectfully request; **d'~** [*stairs*] main; **2** credit; **c'est tout à leur ~** it's all credit to them; **3 mettre qn à l'~** to honour[GB] sb; **être à l'** or **en ~** to be in favour[GB]; **faire ~ à un repas** to do justice to a meal; **faire les ~s de la maison à qn** to show sb around the house; **avoir les ~s de la presse** to be mentioned in the press; **en quel ~**°**?** (ironic) any particular reason why?

IDIOMS **en tout bien tout ~** with no hidden motive.

honnir /ˈɔniʀ/ [3] *vtr* **honni soit qui mal y pense** evil unto him who evil thinks.

honorable /ɔnɔʀabl/ *adj* **1** honourable[GB]; **2** [*score*] creditable; [*salary*] decent.

honorablement /ɔnɔʀabləmɑ̃/ *adv* **1** honourably[GB]; **2** decently.

honoraire /ɔnɔʀɛʀ/ **I** *adj* [*member*] honorary.

II honoraires *nm pl* fee, fees.

honorer /ɔnɔʀe/ [1] *vtr* **1** to honour[GB] [*god, person, memory*]; **2** to honour[GB] [*promise, debt*]; **3** to be a credit to [*country, profession*].

honorifique /ɔnɔʀifik/ *adj* honorary.

honte /ˈɔ̃t/ *nf* **1** shame; **avoir ~ de** to be ashamed of; **sans fausse ~** quite openly; **2** disgrace; **faire la ~ de** to be a disgrace to; **quelle ~!** what a disgrace!

honteusement /ˈɔ̃tøzmɑ̃/ *adv* **1** shamefully; **2** shamelessly.

honteux, **-euse** /ˈɔ̃tø, øz/ *adj* **1** disgraceful; **2** ashamed.

hôpital, *pl* **-aux** /ɔpital, o/ *nm* hospital.

IDIOMS **c'est l'~ qui se moque de la charité** it's the pot calling the kettle black.

hoquet /ˈɔkɛ/ *nm* **avoir le ~** to have hiccups.

hoqueter /ˈɔkte/ [20] *vi* [*person*] to hiccup.

horaire /ɔʀɛʀ/ **I** *adj* per hour, hourly; **tranche** or **plage ~** time-slot.

II *nm* timetable, schedule; **les ~s libres** or **à la carte** flexitime.

horde /ˈɔʀd/ *nf* horde.

horizon /ɔʀizɔ̃/ *nm* horizon.

horizontal, **~e**[1], *mpl* **-aux** /ɔʀizɔ̃tal, o/ *adj* horizontal.

horizontale[2] /ɔʀizɔ̃tal/ *nf* horizontal.

horloge /ɔʀlɔʒ/ *nf* clock.

horloger, **-ère** /ɔʀlɔʒe, ɛʀ/ *nm,f* watchmaker.

horlogerie /ɔʀlɔʒʀi/ *nf* **1** watchmaking; **2** watchmaker's (shop).

hormis /ˈɔʀmi/ *prep* (formal) save, except (for).

hormone /ɔʀmon/ *nf* hormone.

horodateur /ɔʀɔdatœʀ/ *nm* parking ticket machine.

horoscope /ɔʀɔskɔp/ *nm* horoscope.

horreur /ɔʀœʀ/ *nf* **1** horror; **quelle ~!** how horrible!; **2 dire des ~s de** or **sur qn** to say awful things about sb; **3** loathing; **avoir ~ de qn/de faire** to loathe sb/doing.

horrible /ɔʀibl/ *adj* **1** horrible; **2** revolting; **3** hideous.

horriblement /ɔʀibləmɑ̃/ *adv* [*damaged*] horribly; [*cold*] terribly.

horrifier /ɔʀifje/ [2] *vtr* to horrify.

horripiler /ɔʀipile/ [1] *vtr* to exasperate.

hors /ˈɔʀ/

■ **Note** You will find translations for expressions such as *hors série*, *hors d'usage* etc, at the entries ***série***, ***usage*** etc.

I *prep* outside; **longueur ~ tout** overall length.

II hors de *phr* out of, outside; **~ d'ici!** get out of here!

IDIOMS **être ~ de soi** to be beside oneself.

hors-bord /ˈɔʀbɔʀ/ *nm inv* speedboat.
hors-d'œuvre /ˈɔʀdœvʀ/ *nm inv* starter, hors d'oeuvre.
hors-la-loi /ˈɔʀlalwa/ *nm inv* outlaw.
hors-piste /ˈɔʀpist/ *nm inv* off-piste skiing.
hortensia /ɔʀtɑ̃sja/ *nm* hydrangea.
horticulteur, **-trice** /ɔʀtikyltœʀ, tʀis/ *nm,f* horticulturist.
hospice /ɔspis/ *nm* home; **~ de vieillards** old people's home.
hospitalier, **-ière** /ɔspitalje, ɛʀ/ *adj* **1** hospital; **centre ~** hospital; **2** hospitable.
hospitalisation /ɔspitalizasjɔ̃/ *nf* hospitalization; **~ à domicile** home (medical) care.
hospitaliser /ɔspitalize/ [1] *vtr* to hospitalize.
hospitalité /ɔspitalite/ *nf* hospitality.
hostie /ɔsti/ *nf* Host.
hostile /ɔstil/ *adj* hostile.
hostilité /ɔstilite/ *nf* hostility.
hôte /ot/ **I** *nm* **1** host; **2** occupant.
II *nmf* guest.
hôtel /otɛl/ *nm* hotel.
■ **~ particulier** town house; **~ de passe** hotel used by prostitutes; **~ des ventes** saleroom; **~ de ville** ≈ town hall.
hôtelier, **-ière** /otəlje, ɛʀ/ **I** *adj* [*industry*] hotel; [*school*] hotel management.
II *nm,f* hotelier.
hôtellerie /otɛlʀi/ *nf* hotel business.
hôtesse /otɛs/ *nf* (at home, at exhibition) hostess; (in company) receptionist; (in boat) stewardess.
■ **~ d'accueil** receptionist; **~ de l'air** air hostess.
hotte /ˈɔt/ *nf* **1** basket; **2** hood.
■ **~ aspirante** extractor hood (GB), ventilator (US); **la ~ du Père Noël** Santa Claus's sack.
houblon /ˈublɔ̃/ *nm* hop, hops.
houille /ˈuj/ *nf* coal.
houiller, **-ère** /ˈuje, ɛʀ/ *adj* [*industry*] coal; [*area*] coalmining.
houle /ˈul/ *nf* swell.
houlette /ˈulɛt/ *nf* (of shepherd) crook; **sous la ~ de** (figurative) under the leadership of.
houleux, **-euse** /ˈulø, øz/ *adj* **1** [*sea*] rough; **2** [*meeting*] stormy.
houppe /ˈup/ *nf* **1** (of hair) tuft; (of threads) tassel; **2** powder puff.
houppette /ˈupɛt/ *nf* powder puff.
hourra /ˈuʀa/ *nm* cheer.
houspiller /ˈuspije/ [1] *vtr* to scold.
housse /ˈus/ *nf* cover, slipcover; dustcover; garment bag.
houx /ˈu/ *nm inv* holly.
HT (*written abbr* = **hors taxes**) exclusive of tax.
hublot /ˈyblo/ *nm* (in plane) window; (in boat) porthole.
huche /ˈyʃ/ *nf* **1** chest; **2 ~ à pain** bread bin.
huer /ˈɥe/ [1] *vtr* to boo.
huile /ɥil/ *nf* **1** oil; **2** oil painting.
■ **~ de coude** (humorous) elbow grease; **~ solaire** suntan oil.
IDIOMS **tout/ça baigne dans l'~**° everything/it is going smoothly; **jeter** or **verser de l'~ sur le feu** to add fuel to the fire.
huiler /ɥile/ [1] *vtr* to oil.
huileux, **-euse** /ɥilø, øz/ *adj* oily.
huis /ˈɥi/ *nm inv* **à ~ clos** (Law) in camera; (figurative) behind closed doors.
huissier /ɥisje/ *nm* **1 ~ (de justice)** bailiff; **2** porter; usher.
huit /ˈɥit, but before consonant ˈɥi/ **I** *adj inv* eight; **mardi en ~** a week on Tuesday.
II *pron* eight.
III *nm inv* **1** eight; **2** a figure of eight.
huitaine /ˈɥitɛn/ *nf* **1** about a week; **sous ~** within a week; **2** about eight.
huitième /ˈɥitjɛm/ **I** *adj* eighth.
II *nf* (Sch) *fourth year of primary school, age 9–10.*
huître /ɥitʀ/ *nf* oyster.
hululer /ˈylyle/ [1] *vi* to hoot.
humain, **~e** /ymɛ̃, ɛn/ **I** *adj* **1** human; **pertes ~es** loss of life; **2** [*regime*] humane; [*person*] human, understanding.
II *nm* human (being).
humainement /ymɛnmɑ̃/ *adv* **1** humanly; **2** humanely.
humaniser /ymanize/ [1] **I** *vtr* to humanize.
II s'humaniser *v refl* (+ *v être*) to become more human.
humanitaire /ymanitɛʀ/ *adj* humanitarian.
humanité /ymanite/ *nf* humanity.
humble /œ̃bl/ *adj* humble.
humecter /ymɛkte/ [1] *vtr* to moisten.
humer /ˈyme/ [1] *vtr* to sniff; to smell.
humeur /ymœʀ/ *nf* **1** mood; **être de bonne/mauvaise ~** to be in a good/bad mood; **2** temperament; **être d'~ égale** to be even-tempered; **être d'~ inégale** to be moody; **elle est connue pour sa bonne ~** she's known for her good humour; **3** bad temper; **geste d'~** bad-tempered gesture; **avec ~** bad-temperedly.
humide /ymid/ *adj* **1** damp; **2** [*climate*] humid; [*season*] rainy; **il fait froid et ~** it's cold and damp; **il fait une chaleur ~** it's muggy.
humidifier /ymidifje/ [2] *vtr* to humidify.
humidité /ymidite/ *nf* **1** dampness, damp; **2** humidity.
humiliant, **~e** /ymiljɑ̃, ɑ̃t/ *adj* humiliating.
humiliation /ymiljasjɔ̃/ *nf* humiliation.
humilier /ymilje/ [2] *vtr* to humiliate.
humilité /ymilite/ *nf* **1** humility; **2** (of task) humble nature.
humoriste /ymɔʀist/ *nmf* **1** humorist; **2** joker.
humoristique /ymɔʀistik/ *adj* humorous; **dessin ~** cartoon.
humour /ymuʀ/ *nm* humour[GB]; **avoir de l'~** to have a sense of humour[GB]; **faire de l'~** to make jokes.
huppé, **~e** /ˈype/ *adj* **1**° [*person*] upper-crust; **2** [*bird*] crested.

hurlement /'yʀləmɑ̃/ *nm* (of animal) howl, howling; (of person) yell, howl; (of siren) wail, wailing.

hurler /'yʀle/ [1] I *vtr* to yell.
II *vi* **1** to yell; (with pain, anger) to howl; **2** [*siren*] to wail; [*wind*] to roar; [*radio*] to blare.
IDIOMS **~ avec les loups** to follow the crowd; **~ à la mort** to bay at the moon.

hurluberlu, ~e /yʀlybɛʀly/ *nm,f* oddball°.

hutte /'yt/ *nf* hut.

hybride /ibʀid/ *adj, nm* hybrid.

hydratant, ~e /idʀatɑ̃, ɑ̃t/ *adj* moisturizing.

hydratation /idʀatasjɔ̃/ *nf* **1** hydration; **2** moisturizing.

hydrater /idʀate/ [1] I *vtr* **1** to hydrate; **2** to moisturize [*skin*].
II **s'hydrater** *v refl* (+ *v être*) **bien s'~** to take plenty of fluids.

hydraulique /idʀolik/ *adj* hydraulic.

hydravion /idʀavjɔ̃/ *nm* seaplane, hydroplane.

hydro /idʀo/ *pref* hydro; **~électrique** hydroelectric.

hydrocution /idʀɔkysjɔ̃/ *nf* immersion hypothermia.

hydrofuge /idʀɔfyʒ/ *adj* water-repellent.

hydrogène /idʀɔʒɛn/ *nm* hydrogen.

hydroglisseur /idʀɔglisœʀ/ *nm* hydroplane.

hydrophile /idʀɔfil/ *adj* absorbent.

hydroxyde /idʀɔksid/ *nm* hydroxide.

hyène /'jɛn/ *nf* hyena.

hygiaphone® /iʒjafɔn/ *nm* grill (*perforated communication panel*).

hygiène /iʒjɛn/ *nf* hygiene; **bonne ~ alimentaire** healthy diet.
■ **~ corporelle** personal hygiene.

hygiénique /iʒjenik/ *adj* **1** hygienic; **2** [*lifestyle*] healthy.

hymen /imɛn/ *nm* **1** hymen; **2** nuptial bond.

hymne /imn/ *nm* hymn; **~ national** national anthem.

hyperactif, -ive /ipɛʀaktif, iv/ *adj* hyperactive.

hyperclassique /ipɛʀklasik/ *adj* [*reaction*] absolutely classic; **roman ~** great classic.

hypermarché /ipɛʀmaʀʃe/ *nm* hypermarket (GB), large supermarket.

hypermétrope /ipɛʀmetʀɔp/ *adj* longsighted.

hypernerveux, -euse /ipɛʀnɛʀvø, øz/ *adj* highly strung.

hypersensible /ipɛʀsɑ̃sibl/ *adj* hypersensitive.

hypertension /ipɛʀtɑ̃sjɔ̃/ *nf* **~ (artérielle)** high blood pressure.

hypertrophie /ipɛʀtʀɔfi/ *nf* **1** (Med) enlargement; **2** (of town) overdevelopment.

hypertrophier: **s'hypertrophier** /ipɛʀtʀɔfje/ [2] *v refl* (+ *v être*) **1** (Med) to hypertrophy; **2** [*town*] to become overdeveloped.

hypnose /ipnoz/ *nf* hypnosis.

hypnotique /ipnɔtik/ *adj, nm* hypnotic.

hypnotiser /ipnɔtize/ [1] *vtr* to hypnotize; (figurative) to mesmerize.

hypnotiseur, -euse /ipnɔtizœʀ, øz/ *nm,f* hypnotist.

hypocondriaque /ipɔkɔ̃dʀijak/ *adj, nmf* hypochondriac.

hypocrisie /ipɔkʀizi/ *nf* hypocrisy.

hypocrite /ipɔkʀit/ I *adj* hypocritical.
II *nmf* hypocrite.

hypodermique /ipɔdɛʀmik/ *adj* hypodermic.

hypotension /ipɔtɑ̃sjɔ̃/ *nf* **~ (artérielle)** low blood pressure.

hypothèque /ipɔtɛk/ *nf* mortgage.

hypothéquer /ipɔteke/ [14] *vtr* to mortgage.

hypothèse /ipɔtɛz/ *nf* hypothesis.

hypothétique /ipɔtetik/ *adj* hypothetical.

hystérie /isteʀi/ *nf* hysteria.

hystérique /isteʀik/ *adj* hysterical.

Ii

i, **I** /i/ *nm inv* i, I.
IDIOMS **mettre les points sur les i** to make things crystal clear.

ibérique /ibeʀik/ *adj* Iberian.

iceberg /ajsbɛʀg, isbɛʀg/ *nm* iceberg.

ici /isi/ *adv* **1** here; **c'est ~ que**... this is where...; **par ~** this way; around here; **les gens d'~** the locals; **je vois ça d'~!** I can just picture it!; **2 jusqu'~** until now; until then; **d'~ peu** shortly; **d'~ deux jours** two days from now; **d'~ là** by then; **il l'aime bien, mais d'~ à ce qu'il l'épouse**... he likes her, but as for marrying her...

ici-bas /isibɑ/ *adv* here below.

icône /ikon/ *nf* icon.

id. *written abbr* = **idem**.

idéal, **~e**, *mpl* **-aux** /ideal, o/ **I** *adj* ideal.
II *nm* ideal; **dans l'~** ideally.

idéalisme /idealism/ *nm* idealism.

idée /ide/ *nf* idea; thought; **avoir de l'~** to be inventive; **avoir une ~ derrière la tête** to have something in mind; **se faire des ~s** to imagine things; **avoir les ~s larges** to be broad-minded; **changer d'~** to change one's mind; **avoir de la suite dans les ~s** to be single-minded; not to be easily deterred; **avoir dans l'~ de faire** to plan to do; **tu ne m'ôteras pas de l'~ que**... I still think that...; **ça ne m'est pas venu à l'~** it never occurred to me.
■ **~ fixe** obsession; **~ de génie** brainwave○; **~ noire** dark thought; **~ reçue** received idea.

idem /idɛm/ *adv* ditto.

identification /idɑ̃tifikasjɔ̃/ *nf* identification.

identifier /idɑ̃tifje/ [2] **I** *vtr* to identify.
II s'identifier *v refl* (+ *v être*) **1** to become identified; **2** to identify.

identique /idɑ̃tik/ *adj* **1** identical; **2** unchanged.

identité /idɑ̃tite/ *nf* **1** identity; **2** similarity.

idéologie /ideɔlɔʒi/ *nf* ideology.

idiomatique /idjɔmatik/ *adj* idiomatic.

idiome /idjom/ *nm* idiom.

idiot, **~e** /idjo, ɔt/ **I** *adj* stupid.
II *nm* idiot; **faire l'~** to behave like an idiot.

idiotie /idjɔsi/ *nf* **1** stupid thing; **2** stupidity.

idolâtrer /idɔlɑtʀe/ [1] *vtr* to idolize.

idole /idɔl/ *nf* idol.

idylle /idil/ *nf* **1** love affair; **2** (in literature) idyll.

idyllique /idilik/ *adj* idyllic.

if /if/ *nm* **1** yew (tree); **2** yew (wood).

ignare /iɲaʀ/ *adj* ignorant.

ignifuge /iɲifyʒ/ *adj* fireproofing.

ignifuger /iɲifyʒe/ [13] *vtr* to fireproof.

ignoble /iɲɔbl/ *adj* **1** [*person, conduct*] vile; **2** [*place*] squalid; [*food*] revolting.

ignominie /iɲɔmini/ *nf* **1** ignominy; **2** dreadful thing.

ignorance /iɲɔʀɑ̃s/ *nf* ignorance.

ignorant, **~e** /iɲɔʀɑ̃, ɑ̃t/ *adj* ignorant.

ignoré, **~e** /iɲɔʀe/ *adj* unknown; ignored.

ignorer /iɲɔʀe/ [1] *vtr* **1 j'ignore comment/si** I don't know how/whether; **~ tout de qch** to know nothing of or about sth; **~ l'existence de** to be unaware of the existence of; **2** to ignore [*person*].

iguane /igwan/ *nm* iguana.

il /il/ **I** *pron m* he; it; **~s** they.
II *pron* it; **~ pleut** it's raining.

île /il/ *nf* island.
■ **l'~ de Beauté** Corsica.

illégal, **~e**, *mpl* **-aux** /ilegal, o/ *adj* illegal.

illégitime /ileʒitim/ *adj* [*child*] illegitimate.

illettré, **~e** /iletʀe/ *adj*, *nm,f* illiterate.

illicite /ilisit/ *adj* illicit; unlawful.

illico○ /iliko/ *adv* straightaway.

illimité, **~e** /ilimite/ *adj* unlimited.

illisible /ilizibl/ *adj* **1** illegible; **2** unreadable.

illogique /ilɔʒik/ *adj* illogical.

illumination /ilyminasjɔ̃/ **I** *nf* **1** floodlighting; **2** flash of inspiration.
II illuminations *nf pl* (in town) illuminations.

illuminé, **~e** /ilymine/ **I** *adj* **1** [*monument*] floodlit; **2** [*face*] radiant.
II *nm,f* **1** visionary; **2** crank.

illuminer /ilymine/ [1] **I** *vtr* **1** to illuminate; to floodlight; **2** [*smile*] to light up [*face*].
II s'illuminer *v refl* (+ *v être*) to light up.

illusion /ilyzjɔ̃/ *nf* illusion; **se faire des ~s** to delude oneself; **il ne fait pas ~** he doesn't fool anyone.

illusionniste /ilyzjɔnist/ *nmf* conjurer.

illusoire /ilyzwaʀ/ *adj* illusory.

illustration /ilystʀasjɔ̃/ *nf* illustration.

illustre /ilystʀ/ *adj* illustrious.

illustrer /ilystʀe/ [1] **I** *vtr* to illustrate.
II s'illustrer *v refl* (+ *v être*) to distinguish oneself.

îlot /ilo/ *nm* **1** islet; **2 ~s de végétation** isolated patches of vegetation.

ils ▶ **il**.

image /imaʒ/ *nf* **1** picture; **2** (on film) frame; **3** reflection, image; **4 à l'~ de ses prédécesseurs**... just like his/her predecessors...; **5** image; **les ~s d'un poème** the imagery of a poem.
■ **~ d'Épinal** *simplistic print of traditional French life*; (figurative) clichéd image; **~ de marque** brand image; corporate image; (public) image.

imagé, **~e** /imaʒe/ *adj* [*style*] colourful[GB].
imagerie /imaʒʀi/ *nf* **1** imagery; **2** print trade; **3** imaging.
imaginaire /imaʒinɛʀ/ *adj* imaginary.
imaginatif, **-ive** /imaʒinatif, iv/ *adj* imaginative.
imagination /imaʒinasjɔ̃/ *nf* imagination.
imaginer /imaʒine/ [1] **I** *vtr* **1** to imagine, to picture; **2** to suppose; **3** to devise, to think up.
II s'imaginer *v refl* (+ *v être*) **1** to imagine, to picture; **2** to picture oneself; **s'~ à 60 ans** to picture oneself at 60; **3** to think.
imbécile /ɛ̃besil/ **I** *adj* idiotic.
II *nmf* fool; **faire l'~** to play the fool.
imberbe /ɛ̃bɛʀb/ *adj* beardless.
imbiber /ɛ̃bibe/ [1] **I** *vtr* to soak.
II s'imbiber *v refl* (+ *v être*) **s'~ de** to become soaked with.
imbriquer: **s'imbriquer** /ɛ̃bʀike/ [1] *v refl* (+ *v être*) **1** [*slates*] to overlap; **2** [*issues*] to be interlinked; [*parts*] to interlock.
imbu, **~e** /ɛ̃by/ *adj* full; **~ de sa personne** full of oneself.
imbuvable /ɛ̃byvabl/ *adj* **1** undrinkable; **2**○ unbearable.
imitateur, **-trice** /imitatœʀ, tʀis/ *nm,f* **1** impressionist; **2** (of painting) imitator.
imitation /imitasjɔ̃/ *nf* imitation; (of person) impression.
imiter /imite/ [1] *vtr* **1** to imitate; to forge [*signature*]; **2** to do an impression of [sb]; **3 il part, je vais l'~** he's leaving and I'm going to do the same.
immaculé, **~e** /imakyle/ *adj* immaculate.
immangeable /ɛ̃mɑ̃ʒabl/ *adj* inedible.
immanquablement /ɛ̃mɑ̃kabləmɑ̃/ *adv* inevitably.
immatriculation /imatʀikylasjɔ̃/ *nf* registration; **numéro d'~** registration (GB) or license (US) number.
immatriculer /imatʀikyle/ [1] *vtr* to register; to register (GB) or license (US) [*car*].
immédiat, **~e** /imedja, at/ **I** *adj* immediate.
II *nm* **dans l'~** for the time being.
immense /imɑ̃s/ *adj* (gen) huge; [*pain, regret*] immense; [*joy, courage*] great.
immensité /imɑ̃site/ *nf* (of place) immensity; (of knowledge) breadth.
immerger /imɛʀʒe/ [13] *vtr* to immerse [*object*]; to bury [sth] at sea.
immersion /imɛʀsjɔ̃/ *nf* **1** (of body, object) immersion; (of corpse) burial at sea; **2** flooding.
immeuble /imœbl/ *nm* **1** building; **2** real asset.
immigrant, **~e** /imigʀɑ̃, ɑ̃t/ *adj*, *nm,f* immigrant.
immigration /imigʀasjɔ̃/ *nf* immigration.
immigré, **~e** /imigʀe/ *adj*, *nm,f* immigrant.
immigrer /imigʀe/ [1] *vi* to immigrate.
imminent, **~e** /iminɑ̃, ɑ̃t/ *adj* imminent.
immiscer: **s'immiscer** /imise/ [12] *v refl* (+ *v être*) to interfere.
immobile /imɔbil/ *adj* (gen) motionless; [*vehicle*] stationary; [*stare*] fixed.
immobilier /imɔbilje/ *nm* **l'~** property (GB), real estate (US).
immobiliser /imɔbilize/ [1] **I** *vtr* **1** to bring [sth] to a standstill [*vehicle*]; to stop [*machine*]; **2** to immobilize [*person*]; **3** to tie up [*capital*].
II s'immobiliser *v refl* (+ *v être*) to come to a halt; to stop.
immobilisme /imɔbilism/ *nm* opposition to change.
immobilité /imɔbilite/ *nf* **1** immobility; **2** stillness.
immodéré, **~e** /imɔdeʀe/ *adj* **1** excessive; **2** immoderate.
immonde /imɔ̃d/ *adj* **1** filthy; **2** revolting.
immondices /imɔ̃dis/ *nf pl* refuse (GB), trash (US).
immoral, **~e**, *mpl* **-aux** /imɔʀal, o/ *adj* immoral.
immortaliser /imɔʀtalize/ [1] *vtr* to immortalize.
immortel, **-elle** /imɔʀtɛl/ *adj* immortal.
immuable /imɥabl/ *adj* **1** immutable; **2** unchanging; **3** perpetual.
immuniser /imynize/ [1] *vtr* to immunize.
immunitaire /imynitɛʀ/ *adj* (Med) immune.
immunité /imynite/ *nf* immunity.
impact /ɛ̃pakt/ *nm* impact; mark.
impair, **~e** /ɛ̃pɛʀ/ **I** *adj* [*number*] odd; [*day, year*] odd-numbered.
II *nm* indiscretion, faux pas.
imparable /ɛ̃paʀabl/ *adj* **1** unstoppable; **2** unanswerable; **3** irrefutable.
imparfait, **~e** /ɛ̃paʀfɛ, ɛt/ **I** *adj* imperfect.
II *nm* **l'~** the imperfect (tense).
impartial, **~e**, *mpl* **-iaux** /ɛ̃paʀsjal, o/ *adj* impartial.
impartir /ɛ̃paʀtiʀ/ [3] *vtr* to give; **dans les temps impartis** within the given time.
impasse /ɛ̃pas/ *nf* **1** dead end; **2** deadlock.
impassible /ɛ̃pasibl/ *adj* impassive.
impatience /ɛ̃pasjɑ̃s/ *nf* impatience.
impatient, **~e** /ɛ̃pasjɑ̃, ɑ̃t/ *adj* impatient.
impatienter /ɛ̃pasjɑ̃te/ [1] **I** *vtr* to irritate.
II s'impatienter *v refl* (+ *v être*) to get impatient.
impayé, **~e** /ɛ̃pɛje/ *adj* unpaid.
impeccable /ɛ̃pɛkabl/ *adj* perfect; impeccable; spotless.
impénétrable /ɛ̃penetʀabl/ *adj* **1** impenetrable; **2** inscrutable.
impénitent, **~e** /ɛ̃penitɑ̃, ɑ̃t/ *adj* [*drinker*] inveterate; [*bachelor*] confirmed.
impensable /ɛ̃pɑ̃sabl/ *adj* unthinkable.
imper○ /ɛ̃pɛʀ/ *nm* raincoat, mac○ (GB).
impératif, **-ive** /ɛ̃peʀatif, iv/ **I** *adj* imperative.
II *nm* **1** (of situation) imperative; (for quality) necessity; **2** (in grammar) imperative.
impératrice /ɛ̃peʀatʀis/ *nf* empress.
imperceptible /ɛ̃pɛʀsɛptibl/ *adj* imperceptible.

imperfection /ɛ̃pɛʀfɛksjɔ̃/ *nf* imperfection.

impérial, **~e**[1], *mpl* **-iaux** /ɛ̃peʀjal, o/ *adj* imperial.

impériale[2] /ɛ̃peʀjal/ *nf* **autobus à ~** double-decker bus.

impérialisme /ɛ̃peʀjalism/ *nm* imperialism.

impérieux, **-ieuse** /ɛ̃peʀjø, øz/ *adj* **1** imperious; **2** pressing.

impérissable /ɛ̃peʀisabl/ *adj* imperishable.

imperméable /ɛ̃pɛʀmeabl/ **I** *adj* **1** [*material*] waterproof; [*ground*] impermeable; **2** impervious.
II *nm* raincoat.

impertinence /ɛ̃pɛʀtinɑ̃s/ *nf* **1** impertinence; **2** impertinent remark.

impertinent, **~e** /ɛ̃pɛʀtinɑ̃, ɑ̃t/ *adj* impertinent.

imperturbable /ɛ̃pɛʀtyʀbabl/ *adj* imperturbable; unruffled.

imperturbablement /ɛ̃pɛʀtyʀbabləmɑ̃/ *adv* [*continue, listen*] unperturbed.

impétueux, **-euse** /ɛ̃petɥø, øz/ *adj* (gen) impetuous; [*torrent*] raging.

impie /ɛ̃pi/ *adj* impious.

impitoyable /ɛ̃pitwajabl/ *adj* merciless, pitiless; relentless; ruthless.

implacable /ɛ̃plakabl/ *adj* implacable; tough; harsh.

implacablement /ɛ̃plakabləmɑ̃/ *adv* relentlessly; ruthlessly.

implantation /ɛ̃plɑ̃tasjɔ̃/ *nf* establishment; setting up; installation; settlement.

implanté, **~e** /ɛ̃plɑ̃te/ *adj* **1** [*factory, party*] established; [*population*] settled; **2** [*roots*] established; **dents mal ~es** crooked teeth.

implanter /ɛ̃plɑ̃te/ [1] **I** *vtr* **1** to establish [*factory*]; to build [*supermarket*]; to open [*agency*]; to introduce [*product, fashion*]; to instil[GB] [*ideas*]; **2** (Med) to implant.
II s'implanter *v refl* (+ *v être*) [*company, product*] to establish itself; [*factory*] to be built; [*person*] to settle; [*party*] to gain a following.

implication /ɛ̃plikasjɔ̃/ *nf* **1** involvement; **2** implication; **3** commitment.

implicite /ɛ̃plisit/ *adj* implicit.

impliquer /ɛ̃plike/ [1] *vtr* **1** to implicate; **2** to involve [*staff*]; **3** to involve (**de faire** doing); **4** to mean.

implorer /ɛ̃plɔʀe/ [1] *vtr* **1** to beseech, to implore; **2** to beg for.

imploser /ɛ̃ploze/ [1] *vi* to implode.

impoli, **~e** /ɛ̃pɔli/ *adj* rude, impolite.

impolitesse /ɛ̃pɔlitɛs/ *nf* rudeness.

impondérable /ɛ̃pɔ̃deʀabl/ *nm* imponderable.

impopulaire /ɛ̃pɔpylɛʀ/ *adj* unpopular.

importance /ɛ̃pɔʀtɑ̃s/ *nf* **1** importance; **quelle ~?** what does it matter?; **2** size; (of damage) extent; **prendre de l'~** to increase in size; **3 prendre de l'~** [*person*] to become more important.

important, **~e** /ɛ̃pɔʀtɑ̃, ɑ̃t/ **I** *adj* **1** important; **2** significant; considerable; sizeable; large; lengthy; **3 prendre un air ~** to adopt a self-important manner.
II *nm,f* **jouer les ~s** to act important○.

importateur, **-trice** /ɛ̃pɔʀtatœʀ, tʀis/ **I** *adj* importing.
II *nm,f* importer.

importation /ɛ̃pɔʀtasjɔ̃/ *nf* **1** importation; **2** import.

importer /ɛ̃pɔʀte/ [1] **I** *vtr* to import.
II *v impers* **peu importe** or **qu'importe que...** it doesn't matter or what does it matter if...; **n'importe quel enfant** any child; **n'importe qui** anybody, anyone; **n'importe lequel** any; **n'importe où** anywhere; **prends n'importe quoi** take anything; **elle dit n'importe quoi** she talks nonsense.

importun, **~e** /ɛ̃pɔʀtœ̃, yn/ **I** *adj* **1** troublesome; tiresome; **visiteur ~** unwelcome visitor; **2** [*visit*] ill-timed; [*remark*] ill-chosen.
II *nm,f* unwelcome visitor; tiresome individual.

importuner /ɛ̃pɔʀtyne/ [1] *vtr* **1** to bother; **2** to disturb.

imposable /ɛ̃pozabl/ *adj* [*person*] liable to tax; [*income*] taxable.

imposant, **~e** /ɛ̃pozɑ̃, ɑ̃t/ *adj* imposing.

imposer /ɛ̃poze/ [1] **I** *vtr* **1** [*person*] to impose [*sanctions, deadline*]; to lay down [*rule*]; **elle nous a imposé le silence** she made us be quiet; **2** to impose [*idea, opinion*]; to set [*fashion*]; **3** to command [*respect*]; **4** to tax.
II en imposer *v+prep* **elle en impose à ses élèves** she inspires respect in her pupils.
III s'imposer *v refl* (+ *v être*) **1** [*choice, solution*] to be obvious; [*change*] to be called for; **une visite au Louvre s'impose** a visit to the Louvre is a must; **2** to impose [sth] on oneself; **s'~ de travailler le soir** to make it a rule to work in the evening; **3** to impose (**à qn** on sb); **4 s'~ comme leader** to establish oneself/itself as the leader; **s'~ sur un marché** to establish itself in a market; **5** [*person*] to make one's presence felt; [*will*] to impose itself.

imposition /ɛ̃pozisjɔ̃/ *nf* taxation.

impossibilité /ɛ̃pɔsibilite/ *nf* impossibility; **être dans l'~ de faire** to be unable to do.

impossible /ɛ̃pɔsibl/ **I** *adj* impossible.
II *nm* **l'~** the impossible; **faire** or **tenter l'~** to do everything one can.

imposteur /ɛ̃pɔstœʀ/ *nm* impostor.

imposture /ɛ̃pɔstyʀ/ *nf* **1** deception; **2** fraud.

impôt /ɛ̃po/ *nm* tax; **après ~** after tax.
■ **~ sur le revenu** income tax.

impotent, **~e** /ɛ̃pɔtɑ̃, ɑ̃t/ **I** *adj* infirm.
II *nm,f* person with impaired mobility.

impraticable /ɛ̃pʀatikabl/ *adj* impassable.

imprécis, **~e** /ɛ̃pʀesi, iz/ *adj* [*outline, memory*] vague; [*concept*] hazy; [*aim*] inaccurate; [*results*] imprecise; [*person*] vague.

imprécision /ɛ̃pʀesizjɔ̃/ *nf* imprecision; vagueness; inaccuracy.

imprégner /ɛ̃pʀeɲe/ [14] **I** *vtr* to impregnate.
II s'imprégner *v refl* (+ *v être*) **s'~ de** to become soaked with [*water*]; to immerse oneself in [*language*].

imprenable /ɛ̃pʀənabl/ *adj* **avec vue ~** with unobstructed view guaranteed.

imprésario /ɛ̃pʀesaʀjo/ *nm* agent, impresario.

impression /ɛ̃pʀesjɔ̃/ *nf* **1** impression; **faire bonne ~** to make a good impression; **j'ai l'~ d'être surveillé** I feel I am being watched; **2** printing; **faute d'~** misprint; **3** pattern.

impressionnant, **~e** /ɛ̃pʀesjɔnɑ̃, ɑ̃t/ *adj* **1** impressive; **2** disturbing.

impressionner /ɛ̃pʀesjɔne/ [1] *vtr* **1** to impress; **2** [*image*] to disturb; **3** to act on [*retina*].

impressionnisme /ɛ̃pʀesjɔnism/ *nm* Impressionism.

imprévisible /ɛ̃pʀevizibl/ *adj* unpredictable.

imprévu, **~e** /ɛ̃pʀevy/ **I** *adj* **1** unforeseen; **2** unexpected.
II *nm* **1** hitch; **2 l'~** the unexpected; **plein d'~** [*person, film*] quirky; [*trip*] with a few surprises; **3** unforeseen expense.

imprimante /ɛ̃pʀimɑ̃t/ *nf* printer.

imprimé, **~e** /ɛ̃pʀime/ **I** *pp* ▶ **imprimer**.
II *pp adj* printed (**de** with).
III *nm* **1** form; **2** printed matter; **3** print; **un ~ à fleurs** a floral print.

imprimer /ɛ̃pʀime/ [1] *vtr* **1** to print [*text*]; **2** to put [*stamp, seal*]; **3** to leave an imprint of [sth].

imprimerie /ɛ̃pʀimʀi/ *nf* **1** printing; **atelier d'~** printing shop; **2** printing works; **3** printers, print workers.

imprimeur /ɛ̃pʀimœʀ/ *nm* printer.

improbable /ɛ̃pʀɔbabl/ *adj* unlikely.

improductif, **-ive** /ɛ̃pʀɔdyktif, iv/ *adj* unproductive; **capitaux ~s** idle capital.

impromptu, **~e** /ɛ̃pʀɔ̃pty/ **I** *adj* impromptu.
II *adv* impromptu.

impropre /ɛ̃pʀɔpʀ/ *adj* [*term, usage*] incorrect; **~ à** unfit for [*human consumption*].

improvisation /ɛ̃pʀɔvizasjɔ̃/ *nf* improvisation.

improvisé, **~e** /ɛ̃pʀɔvize/ *adj* [*speech*] improvised; [*meal*] impromptu; [*means*] makeshift; [*solution*] ad hoc; [*cook*] stand-in.

improviser /ɛ̃pʀɔvize/ [1] **I** *vtr* to improvise [*meal, speech*]; to concoct [*excuse, alibi*].
II *vi* to improvise.
III s'improviser *v refl* (+ *v être*) **1 s'~ cuisinier** to act as a cook; **2 un camp pour réfugiés ne s'improvise pas** you can't create a refugee camp just like that.

improviste: **à l'improviste** /alɛ̃pʀɔvist/ *phr* unexpectedly.

imprudemment /ɛ̃pʀydamɑ̃/ *adv* [*speak*] carelessly; [*act*] unwisely.

imprudence /ɛ̃pʀydɑ̃s/ *nf* **1** carelessness; **2 commettre une ~** to do something foolish.

imprudent, **~e** /ɛ̃pʀydɑ̃, ɑ̃t/ *adj* [*person, words*] careless; [*action*] rash.

impudence /ɛ̃pydɑ̃s/ *nf* impudence.

impudent, **~e** /ɛ̃pydɑ̃, ɑ̃t/ *adj* impudent.

impuissance /ɛ̃pɥisɑ̃s/ *nf* (gen, Med) impotence; **~ à faire** inability to do.

impuissant, **~e** /ɛ̃pɥisɑ̃, ɑ̃t/ *adj* **1** powerless, helpless; **2** (Med) impotent.

impulsif, **-ive** /ɛ̃pylsif, iv/ *adj* impulsive.

impulsion /ɛ̃pylsjɔ̃/ *nf* **1** (gen) impulse; (Tech) pulse; **2** (figurative) impetus.

impuni, **~e** /ɛ̃pyni/ *adj* unpunished.

impunité /ɛ̃pynite/ *nf* impunity.

impur, **~e** /ɛ̃pyʀ/ *adj* **1** [*thoughts*] impure; **2** [*air*] dirty; [*blood*] tainted; **3** [*ore*] impure.

impureté /ɛ̃pyʀte/ *nf* impurity.

imputer /ɛ̃pyte/ [1] *vtr* to attribute, to impute.

inabordable /inabɔʀdabl/ *adj* **1** [*coast*] inaccessible; **2** [*prices*] prohibitive.

inacceptable /inaksɛptabl/ *adj* unacceptable.

inaccessible /inaksesibl/ *adj* **1** inaccessible; **2** [*person*] unapproachable.

inaccoutumé /inakutyme/ *adj* unusual.

inachevé, **~e** /inaʃve/ *adj* unfinished.

inactif, **-ive** /inaktif, iv/ *adj* idle; [*person*] inactive; [*population*] non-working.

inactivité /inaktivite/ *nf* inactivity.

inadapté, **~e** /inadapte/ *adj* **1** [*child*] maladjusted; **2** [*means*] inappropriate; [*tool*] unsuitable; [*law*] ill-adapted.

inadéquat, **~e** /inadekwa, at/ *adj* inadequate; unsuitable.

inadmissible /inadmisibl/ *adj* **1** intolerable; **2** unacceptable.

inadvertance: **par inadvertance** /paʀ inadvɛʀtɑ̃s/ *phr* inadvertently.

inaltérable /inalteʀabl/ *adj* **1** [*substance*] unalterable, non-corroding; [*colour*] fade-resistant; **2** [*character*] constant; [*principle*] immutable; [*hope*] steadfast.

inaltéré, **~e** /inalteʀe/ *adj* [*substance*] unaltered; [*sky, air*] pure.

inamovible /inamɔvibl/ *adj* irremovable.

inanimé, **~e** /inanime/ *adj* [*matter*] inanimate; [*person*] unconscious; lifeless.

inanition /inanisjɔ̃/ *nf* starvation.

inaperçu, **~e** /inapɛʀsy/ *adj* **passer ~** to go unnoticed.

inapte /inapt/ *adj* unfit.

inaptitude /inaptityd/ *nf* unfitness.

inarticulé, **~e** /inaʀtikyle/ *adj* inarticulate.

inassouvi, **~e** /inasuvi/ *adj* [*appetite*] insatiable; [*person, desire*] unsatisfied.

inattaquable /inatakabl/ *adj* **1** (Mil) unassailable; **2** irreproachable; **3** irrefutable.

inattendu, **~e** /inatɑ̃dy/ *adj* unexpected.

inattentif, **-ive** /inatɑ̃tif, iv/ *adj* **1** inattentive; distracted; **2** heedless.

inattention /inatɑ̃sjɔ̃/ *nf* inattention; **faute d'~** careless mistake.

inaudible /inodibl/ *adj* inaudible.

inaugural, **~e**, *mpl* **-aux** /inogyʀal, o/ *adj* **1** [*ceremony*] inauguration; **2** [*flight*] maiden.

inauguration /inogyʀasjɔ̃/ *nf* (of building) inauguration; (of exhibition) opening.

inaugurer /inogyʀe/ [1] *vtr* **1** to unveil [*statue, plaque*]; to open [*motorway, school*]; **2** to open [*conference*]; **3** to mark the start of [*period*].

inavouable /inavwabl/ *adj* shameful.

inavoué, **~e** /inavwe/ *adj* [*crime, vice*] unconfessed; [*aim*] undisclosed; [*fear*] hidden.

incandescent, **~e** /ɛ̃kɑ̃dɛsɑ̃, ɑ̃t/ *adj* incandescent; white-hot; glowing.

incapable /ɛ̃kapabl/ *adj* **1** **~ de faire** incapable of doing; unable to do; **2** incompetent.

incapacité /ɛ̃kapasite/ *nf* **1** inability; **être dans l'~ de faire** to be unable to do; **2** incompetence; **3** disability; **4** (Law) incapacity.

incarcération /ɛ̃kaʀseʀasjɔ̃/ *nf* imprisonment.

incarcérer /ɛ̃kaʀseʀe/ [14] *vtr* to imprison.

incarnation /ɛ̃kaʀnasjɔ̃/ *nf* incarnation.

incarné, **~e** /ɛ̃kaʀne/ *adj* **1** **c'est la bêtise ~e** he/she is stupidity itself; **2** [*nail*] ingrowing.

incarner /ɛ̃kaʀne/ [1] **I** *vtr* **1** to embody; **2** to play, to portray.
II s'incarner *v refl* (+ *v être*) to become incarnate.

incendiaire /ɛ̃sɑ̃djɛʀ/ **I** *adj* **1** [*bomb*] incendiary; **2** [*statement*] inflammatory.
II *nmf* arsonist.

incendie /ɛ̃sɑ̃di/ *nm* fire; **~ criminel** arson.

incendier /ɛ̃sɑ̃dje/ [2] *vtr* **1** to burn (down), to torch; **2**○ to haul [sb] over the coals.

incertain, **~e** /ɛ̃sɛʀtɛ̃, ɛn/ *adj* [*person, date, result*] uncertain; [*effect*] unknown; [*colour*] indeterminate; [*smile*] vague; [*weather*] unsettle; [*step*] hesitant.

incertitude /ɛ̃sɛʀtityd/ *nf* uncertainty.

incessamment /ɛ̃sesamɑ̃/ *adv* very shortly.

incessant, **~e** /ɛ̃sɛsɑ̃, ɑ̃t/ *adj* [*noise, rain*] incessant; [*activity*] unceasing.

inceste /ɛ̃sɛst/ *nm* incest.

incestueux, **-euse** /ɛ̃sɛstɥø, øz/ *adj* incestuous.

incidemment /ɛ̃sidamɑ̃/ *adv* **1** in passing; **2** by chance.

incidence /ɛ̃sidɑ̃s/ *nf* **1** impact; **2** incidence.

incident, **~e** /ɛ̃sidɑ̃, ɑ̃t/ *nm* incident; **~ de parcours** hitch; **l'~ est clos** the matter is closed.

incinérateur /ɛ̃sineʀatœʀ/ *nm* **1** incinerator; **2** crematorium (GB), crematory (US).

incinération /ɛ̃sineʀasjɔ̃/ *nf* **1** incineration; **2** cremation.

incinérer /ɛ̃sineʀe/ [14] *vtr* **1** to burn; to incinerate; **2** to cremate.

inciser /ɛ̃size/ [1] *vtr* to make an incision in.

incisif, **-ive**[1] /ɛ̃sizif, iv/ *adj* [*criticism*] incisive; [*portrait*] telling; [*look*] piercing.

incision /ɛ̃sizjɔ̃/ *nf* incision.

incisive[2] /ɛ̃siziv/ **I** *adj f* ▶ **incisif**.
II *nf* incisor.

incitation /ɛ̃sitasjɔ̃/ *nf* **1** incentive; **2** (Law) incitement.

inciter /ɛ̃site/ [1] *vtr* [*person, situation*] to encourage; [*event, decision*] to prompt; **~ qn à la prudence** to make sb cautious.

inclinable /ɛ̃klinabl/ *adj* adjustable.

inclinaison /ɛ̃klinɛzɔ̃/ *nf* (of hill) incline; (of wall, seat) angle; (of roof) slope; (of boat) list.

inclination /ɛ̃klinasjɔ̃/ *nf* inclination.

incliné, **~e** /ɛ̃kline/ *adj* **1** [*ground*] sloping; [*roof*] steep; **2** [*wall*] leaning.

incliner /ɛ̃kline/ [1] **I** *vtr* to tilt [*sunshade*]; to tip up [*bottle*]; **~ le buste** to lean forward.
II s'incliner *v refl* (+ *v être*) **1** to lean forward; (politely) to bow; **2** **s'~ devant qch** to bow to sth, to accept sth; **3** to give in○; **4** **s'~ devant le courage de qn** to admire sb's courage.

inclure /ɛ̃klyʀ/ [78] *vtr* **1** to include; **2** to enclose.

inclus, **~e** /ɛ̃kly, yz/ **I** *pp* ▶ **inclure**.
II *pp adj* **1** **jusqu'à jeudi ~** up to and including Thursday (GB), through Thursday (US); **2** enclosed.

inclusion /ɛ̃klyzjɔ̃/ *nf* inclusion.

incohérence /ɛ̃kɔeʀɑ̃s/ *nf* **1** incoherence; **2** discrepancy.

incohérent, **~e** /ɛ̃kɔeʀɑ̃, ɑ̃t/ *adj* [*talk, behaviour*] incoherent; [*attitude*] illogical.

incolore /ɛ̃kɔlɔʀ/ *adj* colourless[GB]; [*glass*] clear.

incomber /ɛ̃kɔ̃be/ [1] *v+prep* **~ à** [*task*] to fall to; [*responsibility*] to lie with.

incommode /ɛ̃kɔmɔd/ *adj* **1** inconvenient; awkward; **2** uncomfortable.

incommodé, **~e** /ɛ̃kɔmɔde/ **I** *pp* ▶ **incommoder**.
II *pp adj* unwell, indisposed.

incommoder /ɛ̃kɔmɔde/ [1] *vtr* to bother.

incomparable /ɛ̃kɔ̃paʀabl/ *adj* incomparable.

incompatible /ɛ̃kɔ̃patibl/ *adj* incompatible.

incompétence /ɛ̃kɔ̃petɑ̃s/ *nf* (gen) incompetence; (Law) incompetency.

incompétent, **~e** /ɛ̃kɔ̃petɑ̃, ɑ̃t/ *adj* incompetent.

incomplet, **-ète** /ɛ̃kɔ̃plɛ, ɛt/ *adj* incomplete.

incompréhensible /ɛ̃kɔ̃pʀeɑ̃sibl/ *adj* incomprehensible.

incompréhension /ɛ̃kɔ̃pʀeɑ̃sjɔ̃/ *nf* **1** incomprehension; **2** lack of understanding.

incompressible /ɛ̃kɔ̃pʀɛsibl/ *adj* **1** incompressible; **2** [*costs*] fixed.

incompris, **~e** /ɛ̃kɔ̃pʀi, iz/ *nm,f* misunderstood person.

inconcevable /ɛ̃kɔ̃svabl/ *adj* inconceivable.

inconditionnel, **-elle** /ɛ̃kɔ̃disjɔnɛl/ **I** *adj* unconditional.
II *nm,f* devoted admirer; fan.

inconfortable /ɛ̃kɔ̃fɔʀtabl/ *adj* **1** uncomfortable; **2** awkward.

incongru, **~e** /ɛ̃kɔ̃gʀy/ *adj* [*behaviour*] unseemly; [*remark*] incongruous.

incongruité /ɛ̃kɔ̃gʀɥite/ *nf* incongruity.

inconnu, **~e** /ɛ̃kɔny/ **I** *adj* unknown; [*territories*] unexplored.
II *nm,f* **1** unknown (person); **2** stranger.

inconsciemment /ɛ̃kɔ̃sjamɑ̃/ *adv* **1** subconsciously; **2** unintentionally, unconsciously.

inconscience /ɛ̃kɔ̃sjɑ̃s/ *nf* **1** recklessness; **2** (Med) unconsciousness.

inconscient, **~e** /ɛ̃kɔ̃sjɑ̃, ɑ̃t/ I *adj* **1** unthinking; foolhardy; **2** (Med) unconscious; **3** [*act, gesture*] unconscious, automatic.
II *nm,f* **c'est un ~** he's irresponsible.
III *nm* **l'~** the unconscious.

inconséquent, **~e** /ɛ̃kɔ̃sekɑ̃, ɑ̃t/ *adj* [*person, behaviour*] inconsistent.

inconsidéré, **~e** /ɛ̃kɔ̃sideʀe/ *adj* **1** [*remark, act*] ill-considered; **2** [*consumption*] excessive.

inconsistant, **~e** /ɛ̃kɔ̃sistɑ̃, ɑ̃t/ *adj* [*argument, plot*] flimsy; [*programme*] lacking in substance; [*person*] characterless.

inconstant, **~e** /ɛ̃kɔ̃stɑ̃, ɑ̃t/ *adj* fickle.

incontestable /ɛ̃kɔ̃tɛstabl/ *adj* unquestionable, indisputable.

incontesté, **~e** /ɛ̃kɔ̃tɛste/ *adj* [*victory*] undisputed; [*fact*] uncontested.

incontinent, **~e** /ɛ̃kɔ̃tinɑ̃, ɑ̃t/ *adj* incontinent.

incontournable /ɛ̃kɔ̃tuʀnabl/ *adj* [*facts*] that cannot be ignored.

incontrôlable /ɛ̃kɔ̃tʀolabl/ *adj* **1** unverifiable; **2** uncontrollable.

inconvenance /ɛ̃kɔ̃vnɑ̃s/ *nf* impropriety.

inconvenant, **~e** /ɛ̃kɔ̃vnɑ̃, ɑ̃t/ *adj* unsuitable; improper, unseemly.

inconvénient /ɛ̃kɔ̃venjɑ̃/ *nm* drawback, disadvantage; **si vous n'y voyez pas d'~** if you have no objection.

incorporer /ɛ̃kɔʀpɔʀe/ [1] *vtr* **1** (Culin) to blend; **2** to incorporate.

incorrect, **~e** /ɛ̃kɔʀɛkt/ *adj* **1** incorrect; faulty; inaccurate; **2** [*behaviour*] improper; [*term*] unsuitable; [*person*] impolite; **3** unfair.

incorrection /ɛ̃kɔʀɛksjɔ̃/ *nf* (of style, language) incorrectness; (of behaviour) impropriety.

incorrigible /ɛ̃kɔʀiʒibl/ *adj* incorrigible.

incrédule /ɛ̃kʀedyl/ *adj* incredulous.

incrédulité /ɛ̃kʀedylite/ *nf* incredulity.

incriminer /ɛ̃kʀimine/ [1] *vtr* [*person*] to accuse; [*evidence*] to incriminate; **l'article incriminé** the offending article.

incroyable /ɛ̃kʀwajabl/ *adj* incredible, unbelievable; **~ mais vrai** strange but true.

incrustation /ɛ̃kʀystasjɔ̃/ *nf* **1** inlaying; **2** inlay; **3** encrustation.

incruster /ɛ̃kʀyste/ [1] I *vtr* **1** to inlay; **2 incrusté de diamants** encrusted with diamonds.
II **s'incruster** *v refl* (+ *v être*) [*pebble, shell*] to become embedded.

incubation /ɛ̃kybasjɔ̃/ *nf* incubation.

incuber /ɛ̃kybe/ [1] *vtr* to incubate, to hatch.

inculpation /ɛ̃kylpasjɔ̃/ *nf* (Law) charge.

inculpé, **~e** /ɛ̃kylpe/ *nm,f* **l'~** ≈ the accused.

inculper /ɛ̃kylpe/ [1] *vtr* (Law) to charge.

inculquer /ɛ̃kylke/ [1] *vtr* to inculcate.

inculte /ɛ̃kylt/ *adj* uncultivated.

incurable /ɛ̃kyʀabl/ *adj*, *nmf* incurable.

incursion /ɛ̃kyʀsjɔ̃/ *nf* incursion, foray.

incurver /ɛ̃kyʀve/ [1] *vtr*, **s'incurver** *v refl* (+ *v être*) to curve, to bend.

Inde /ɛ̃d/ *pr nf* India.

indécence /ɛ̃desɑ̃s/ *nf* (gen) indecency; (of remark) impropriety.

indécent, **~e** /ɛ̃desɑ̃, ɑ̃t/ *adj* indecent; [*luxury*] obscene.

indéchiffrable /ɛ̃deʃifʀabl/ *adj* **1** indecipherable; **2** [*mystery*] incomprehensible.

indécis, **~e** /ɛ̃desi, iz/ I *adj* **1 il est encore ~** he hasn't decided yet; **2** indecisive.
II *nm,f* **1** indecisive person; **2** (in opinion poll) 'don't know'; (in election) floating voter.

indécision /ɛ̃desizjɔ̃/ *nf* **1** indecision, uncertainty; **2** indecisiveness.

indéfini, **~e** /ɛ̃defini/ *adj* **1** [*number*] indeterminate; **2** [*sadness*] undefined; [*duration*] indefinite; **3** (in grammar) indefinite.

indéfiniment /ɛ̃definimɑ̃/ *adv* indefinitely.

indéfinissable /ɛ̃definisabl/ *adj* undefinable.

indélébile /ɛ̃delebil/ *adj* indelible.

indélicatesse /ɛ̃delikatɛs/ *nf* **1** indelicacy, tactlessness; **2** dishonesty; **3** act of dishonesty.

indemne /ɛ̃dɛmn/ *adj* unscathed, unharmed.

indemnisation /ɛ̃dɛmnizasjɔ̃/ *nf* **1** indemnification; **2** indemnity, compensation.

indemniser /ɛ̃dɛmnize/ [1] *vtr* to indemnify.

indemnité /ɛ̃dɛmnite/ *nf* **1** (Law) indemnity, compensation; **2** allowance.
■ **~ de chômage** unemployment benefit; **~ journalière** sick pay; **~ de licenciement** severance pay.

indéniable /ɛ̃denjabl/ *adj* undeniable.

indentation /ɛ̃dɑ̃tasjɔ̃/ *nf* indentation.

indépendamment /ɛ̃depɑ̃damɑ̃/ I *adv* independently.
II **indépendamment de** *phr* **1** regardless of; **2** in addition to.

indépendance /ɛ̃depɑ̃dɑ̃s/ *nf* independence.

indépendant, **~e** /ɛ̃depɑ̃dɑ̃, ɑ̃t/ I *adj* **1** independent; **2** [*room*] separate; **maison ~e** detached house.
II *nm,f* freelance, self-employed person.

indépendantiste /ɛ̃depɑ̃dɑ̃tist/ I *adj* [*organization*] (pro-)independence.
II *nmf* **1** freedom fighter; **2** member of an independence movement.

indescriptible /ɛ̃dɛskʀiptibl/ *adj* indescribable.

indésirable /ɛ̃deziʀabl/ *adj* [*person*] undesirable; **effets ~s** (Med) adverse reactions.

indéterminé, **~e** /ɛ̃detɛʀmine/ *adj* [*form, quantity*] indeterminate; [*reason*] unspecified.

index /ɛ̃dɛks/ *nm inv* **1** index; **mettre qn/qch à l'~** to blacklist sb/sth; **2** forefinger.

indexer /ɛ̃dɛkse/ [1] *vtr* **1** to index-link; **~ qch sur qch** to index sth to sth; **2** to index.

indicateur, **-trice** /ɛ̃dikatœʀ, tʀis/ I *adj* **panneau** or **poteau ~** signpost.
II *nm* **1** informer; **2** indicator; **3** gauge, indicator.

indicatif, **-ive** /ɛ̃dikatif, iv/ I *adj* indicative.
II *nm* **1** (in grammar) indicative; **2 ~ (téléphonique)** dialling[GB] code; **3** theme tune.

indication /ɛ̃dikasjɔ̃/ *nf* **1** indication; **2** information; **sauf ~ contraire** unless otherwise indicated; **3** (for use) instruction; **4** indication, clue.

indice /ɛ̃dis/ *nm* **1** sign, indication; **2** (in inquiry) clue; **3** (Econ) index; **4 l'~ d'écoute** audience ratings.

indicible /ɛ̃disibl/ *adj* inexpressible.

indien, **-ienne** /ɛ̃djɛ̃, ɛn/ *adj* **1** Indian; **2** (North American) Indian.

indifféremment /ɛ̃difeʀamɑ̃/ *adv* **1** equally; **2 servir ~ de salon ou de bureau** to be used either as a living room or a study.

indifférence /ɛ̃difeʀɑ̃s/ *nf* indifference.

indifférent, **~e** /ɛ̃difeʀɑ̃, ɑ̃t/ *adj* **1** indifferent; **2** irrelevant.

indigène /ɛ̃diʒɛn/ **I** *adj* **1** [*fauna, flora*] indigenous; **2** [*population, custom*] local; native.
II *nmf* local; native.

indigeste /ɛ̃diʒɛst/ *adj* indigestible.

indigestion /ɛ̃diʒɛstjɔ̃/ *nf* **1** indigestion; **2 avoir une ~ de qch** to be fed up○ with sth.

indignation /ɛ̃diɲasjɔ̃/ *nf* indignation.

indigne /ɛ̃diɲ/ *adj* **1** [*conduct*] disgraceful; [*mother, son*] bad; **2 ~ de qn** unworthy of sb.

indigné, **~e** /ɛ̃diɲe/ *adj* indignant.

indigner /ɛ̃diɲe/ [1] **I** *vtr* to make [sb] indignant, to outrage [sb].
II s'indigner *v refl* (+ *v être*) to be indignant.

indigo /ɛ̃digo/ *adj inv, nm* indigo.

indiqué, **~e** /ɛ̃dike/ **I** *pp* ▶ **indiquer**.
II *pp adj* **1** [*treatment*] recommended; **2 à l'heure ~e** at the specified time; **le village est très mal ~** the village is very badly signposted.

indiquer /ɛ̃dike/ [1] *vtr* **1** [*person*] to point out, to point to; [*signpost*] to show the way to; **pouvez-vous m'~ la banque la plus proche?** can you tell me where the nearest bank is?; **2** to indicate (**que** that); **3 je peux t'~ un bon médecin** I can give you the name of a good doctor; **4** to give; **l'heure indiquée sur le programme est fausse** the time given on the programme[GB] is wrong; **5** [*meter, map*] to show; **le restaurant n'est pas indiqué** there are no signs to the restaurant.

indirect, **~e** /ɛ̃diʀɛkt/ *adj* indirect.

indiscret, **-ète** /ɛ̃diskʀɛ, ɛt/ *adj* **1** [*person*] inquisitive; **à l'abri des regards ~s** away from prying eyes; **2** *person, question* indiscreet; **il est ~** he can't keep a secret.

indiscrétion /ɛ̃diskʀesjɔ̃/ *nf* **1** inquisitiveness; **sans ~, combien gagnez-vous?** if you don't mind my asking, how much do you earn?; **2** lack of discretion; **3** indiscreet remark.

indiscutable /ɛ̃diskytabl/ *adj* indisputable, unquestionable.

indispensable /ɛ̃dispɑ̃sabl/ **I** *adj* essential; **être ~ à qn** to be indispensable to sb.
II *nm* **l'~** the essentials.

indisposé, **~e** /ɛ̃dispoze/ *adj* unwell, indisposed.

indisposer /ɛ̃dispoze/ [1] *vtr* **1** to annoy; **2** to upset [sb], to make [sb] feel ill.

indisposition /ɛ̃dispozisjɔ̃/ *nf* indisposition.

indissociable /ɛ̃disɔsjabl/ *adj* inseparable.

indistinct, **~e** /ɛ̃distɛ̃, ɛ̃kt/ *adj* indistinct.

individu /ɛ̃dividy/ *nm* **1** individual; **2** human being, person; **3 un sinistre ~** a sinister individual or character; **un ~ armé** an armed man; **4** (in scientific study) subject.

individualiser /ɛ̃dividɥalize/ [1] **I** *vtr* **1** to tailor [sth] to individual needs; **2** to individualize.
II s'individualiser *v refl* (+ *v être*) to become more individual.

individualiste /ɛ̃dividɥalist/ *adj* individualistic.

individuel, **-elle** /ɛ̃dividɥɛl/ *adj* (gen) individual; [*responsibility*] personal; [*room*] single; **maison individuelle** (detached) house.

indivisible /ɛ̃divizibl/ *adj* indivisible.

Indochine /ɛ̃dɔʃin/ *pr n f* Indochine.

indo-européen, **-éenne**, *mpl* **~s** /ɛ̃doøʀɔpeɛ̃, ɛn/ *adj* Indo-European.

indolence /ɛ̃dɔlɑ̃s/ *nf* laziness, indolence.

indolent, **~e** /ɛ̃dɔlɑ̃, ɑ̃t/ *adj* lazy, indolent.

indolore /ɛ̃dɔlɔʀ/ *adj* painless.

Indonésie /ɛ̃dɔnezi/ *pr n f* Indonesia.

indu, **~e** /ɛ̃dy/ *adj* [*hour*] ungodly○, unearthly; [*remark, reaction*] inappropriate.

indubitable /ɛ̃dybitabl/ *adj* indubitable.

induction /ɛ̃dyksjɔ̃/ *nf* induction.

induire /ɛ̃dɥiʀ/ [69] *vtr* **1** [*event, measures*] to lead to, to bring about; **2** to infer, to conclude; **3** to induce; **~ qn en erreur** to mislead sb; **4** to induce [*current*].

indulgence /ɛ̃dylʒɑ̃s/ *nf* **1** (of parent, audience) indulgence; **2** (of jury) leniency.

indulgent, **~e** /ɛ̃dylʒɑ̃, ɑ̃t/ *adj* **1** [*parent, audience*] indulgent; **2** [*jury*] lenient.

industrialiser /ɛ̃dystʀijalize/ [1] **I** *vtr* to industrialize.
II s'industrialiser *v refl* (+ *v être*) to become industrialized.

industrie /ɛ̃dystʀi/ *nf* **1** industry; **l'~ hôtelière** the hotel trade; **2** industrial concern.

industriel, **-ielle** /ɛ̃dystʀijɛl/ **I** *adj* industrial; **pain ~** factory-baked bread.
II *nm,f* industrialist, manufacturer.

inébranlable /inebʀɑ̃labl/ *adj* **1** unshakeable, unwavering; **2** immovable.

inédit, **~e** /inedi, it/ *adj* [*book*] (previously) unpublished; [*situation*] (totally) new.

inefficace /inefikas/ *adj* **1** ineffective; **2** inefficient.

inefficacité /inefikasite/ *nf* **1** ineffectiveness, inefficacy; **2** inefficiency.

inégal, **~e**, *mpl* **-aux** /inegal, o/ *adj* unequal; uneven; irregular; [*mood*] changeable, erratic.

inégalable /inegalabl/ *adj* incomparable.

inégalé, **~e** /inegale/ *adj* unequalled[GB], unrivalled[GB].

inégalement /inegalmɑ̃/ *adv* **1** unequally; **2** unevenly.

inégalité /inegalite/ *nf* **1** disparity; **2** inequality; **3** (of mood) changeability; (of surface) unevenness.

inéluctable /inelyktabl/ *adj, nm* inevitable.
inénarrable /inenaʀabl/ *adj* hilarious.
inepte /inɛpt/ *adj* [*person*] inept; [*judgment*] inane; [*remark*] idiotic.
ineptie /inɛpsi/ *nf* **1** inanity; **2** idiotic remark; **3** (action) stupid thing.
inépuisable /inepɥizabl/ *adj* inexhaustible.
inerte /inɛʀt/ *adj* **1** inert; **2** apathetic.
inertie /inɛʀsi/ *nf* **1** inertia; **2** apathy, inertia.
inespéré, **~e** /inɛspeʀe/ *adj* [*victory*] unhoped for; **c'est une occasion ~e de faire** this is a heaven-sent opportunity to do.
inestimable /inɛstimabl/ *adj* [*value*] inestimable; [*help*] invaluable.
inévitable /inevitabl/ *adj* inevitable; unavoidable.
inexact, **~e** /inegza, akt/ *adj* inaccurate.
inexactitude /inegzaktityd/ *nf* **1** inaccuracy; **2** unpunctuality.
inexcusable /inɛkskyzabl/ *adj* inexcusable.
inexistant, **~e** /inegzistɑ̃, ɑ̃t/ *adj* [*means, help*] nonexistent.
inexpérience /inɛkspeʀjɑ̃s/ *nf* inexperience.
inexpérimenté, **~e** /inɛkspeʀimɑ̃te/ *adj* inexperienced.
inexplicable /inɛksplikabl/ *adj* inexplicable.
inexpressif, **-ive** /inɛkspʀesif, iv/ *adj* inexpressive.
in extremis /inɛkstʀemis/ *phr* at the last minute.
infaillible /ɛ̃fajibl/ *adj* infallible.
infaisable /ɛ̃fəzabl/ *adj* unfeasible, impossible.
infamant, **~e** /ɛ̃famɑ̃, ɑ̃t/ *adj* **1** [*remark*] defamatory; **2** [*act*] infamous.
infâme /ɛ̃fɑm/ *adj* **1** [*food, smell*] revolting; **2** [*person*] despicable; [*crime*] odious.
infamie /ɛ̃fami/ *nf* **1** infamy; **2** infamous act; **3** slanderous remark.
infanterie /ɛ̃fɑ̃tʀi/ *nf* infantry.
infantile /ɛ̃fɑ̃til/ *adj* **1** [*illness*] childhood; [*mortality*] infant; [*psychology*] child; **2** [*person, behaviour*] infantile, childish.
infarctus /ɛ̃faʀktys/ *nm inv* heart attack.
infatigable /ɛ̃fatigabl/ *adj* tireless.
infect, **~e** /ɛ̃fɛkt/ *adj* foul; revolting.
infecter /ɛ̃fɛkte/ [1] **I** *vtr* **1** (Med) to infect; **2** (figurative) to poison.
II s'infecter *v refl* (+ *v être*) to become infected, to go septic.
infectieux, **-ieuse** /ɛ̃fɛksjø, øz/ *adj* infectious.
infection /ɛ̃fɛksjɔ̃/ *nf* **1** (Med) infection; **2** (figurative) **c'est une ~**! it stinks to high heaven○!
inférieur, **~e** /ɛ̃feʀjœʀ/ **I** *adj* **1** lower; [*size*] smaller; [*length*] shorter; **~ à la moyenne** below average; **être en nombre ~** to be fewer in number; **2** inferior; **3** (in mathematics) **si a est ~ à b** if a is less than b.
II *nm,f* inferior.
infériorité /ɛ̃feʀjɔʀite/ *nf* inferiority.
infernal, **~e**, *mpl* **-aux** /ɛ̃fɛʀnal, o/ *adj* **1** [*noise, heat*] infernal; **cycle ~** unstoppable chain of events; **2** [*situation*] diabolical; **ce gosse est ~**○ that child is a monster.
infertile /ɛ̃fɛʀtil/ *adj* barren, infertile.
infester /ɛ̃fɛste/ [1] *vtr* to infest, to overrun; **infesté de puces** flea-ridden.
infidèle /ɛ̃fidɛl/ **I** *adj* unfaithful; disloyal.
II *nmf* infidel.
infidélité /ɛ̃fidelite/ *nf* **1** infidelity; **faire des ~s à** to be unfaithful to; **2** disloyalty.
infiltration /ɛ̃filtʀasjɔ̃/ *nf* **1 ~s d'eau** water seepage; **2** (of spies) infiltration; **3** (Med) injection.
infiltrer /ɛ̃filtʀe/ [1] **I** *vtr* to infiltrate.
II s'infiltrer *v refl* (+ *v être*) **1** [*liquid*] to seep; [*light, cold*] to filter in; **2** [*person*] **s'~ dans** to infiltrate [*group, place*].
infime /ɛ̃fim/ *adj* tiny, minute.
infini, **~e** /ɛ̃fini/ **I** *adj* infinite.
II *nm* **l'~** infinity.
infinité /ɛ̃finite/ *nf* **l'~** infinity; **une ~ de** an endless number of.
infinitif, **-ive** /ɛ̃finitif, iv/ *nm* infinitive.
infirme /ɛ̃fiʀm/ **I** *adj* (gen) disabled; (because of age) infirm.
II *nmf* disabled person; **les ~s** the disabled.
infirmer /ɛ̃fiʀme/ [1] *vtr* (gen, Law) to invalidate.
infirmerie /ɛ̃fiʀməʀi/ *nf* (gen) infirmary; sick room; sick bay.
infirmier /ɛ̃fiʀmje/ *nm* male nurse.
infirmière /ɛ̃fiʀmjɛʀ/ *nf* nurse.
infirmité /ɛ̃fiʀmite/ *nf* (gen) disability; (through old age) infirmity.
inflammable /ɛ̃flamabl/ *adj* flammable.
inflammation /ɛ̃flamasjɔ̃/ *nf* (Med) inflammation.
inflammatoire /ɛ̃flamatwaʀ/ *adj* (Med) inflammatory.
inflation /ɛ̃flasjɔ̃/ *nf* inflation.
infléchir /ɛ̃fleʃiʀ/ [3] *vtr*, **s'infléchir** *v refl* (+ *v être*) to soften; to deflect.
inflexible /ɛ̃flɛksibl/ *adj* inflexible.
infliger /ɛ̃fliʒe/ [13] *vtr* to impose [*fine*].
influençable /ɛ̃flyɑ̃sabl/ *adj* impressionable.
influence /ɛ̃flyɑ̃s/ *nf* influence.
influencer /ɛ̃flyɑ̃se/ [12] *vtr* to influence [*person*]; to affect [*situation*].
influent, **~e** /ɛ̃flyɑ̃, ɑ̃t/ *adj* influential.
influer /ɛ̃flye/ [1] *v+prep* **~ sur** to have an influence on.
informateur, **-trice** /ɛ̃fɔʀmatœʀ, tʀis/ *nm,f* **1** (gen) informant; **2** (police) informer.
informaticien, **-ienne** /ɛ̃fɔʀmatisjɛ̃, ɛn/ *nm,f* computer scientist.
information /ɛ̃fɔʀmasjɔ̃/ *nf* **1** information; **une ~** a piece of information; **2** (in newspaper, on television) **une ~** a piece of news; **écouter les ~s** to listen to the news; **contrôler l'~** to control the media; **3** (Comput) data, information.
informatique /ɛ̃fɔʀmatik/ **I** *adj* computer.
II *nf* computer science, computing.

informatiser /ɛ̃fɔʀmatize/ [1] *vtr* to computerize.

informe /ɛ̃fɔʀm/ *adj* shapeless.

informer /ɛ̃fɔʀme/ [1] **I** *vtr* to inform.
II s'informer *v refl* (+ *v être*) **1** to keep oneself informed; **2 s'~ de qch** to enquire about sth; **3 s'~ sur qn** to make enquiries about sb.

infortune /ɛ̃fɔʀtyn/ *nf* misfortune.

infra /ɛ̃fʀa/ *adv* below; **voir ~** see below.

infraction /ɛ̃fʀaksjɔ̃/ *nf* offence[GB]; **être en ~** to be in breach of the law.

infranchissable /ɛ̃fʀɑ̃ʃisabl/ *adj* [*obstacle*] insurmountable; [*border*] impassable.

infrarouge /ɛ̃fʀaʀuʒ/ *adj, nm* infrared; **missile guidé par ~** heat-seeking missile.

infrastructure /ɛ̃fʀastʀyktyʀ/ *nf* **1** facilities; **2** (Econ) infrastructure.

infuser /ɛ̃fyze/ [1] *vi* [*tea*] to brew, to infuse.

infusion /ɛ̃fyzjɔ̃/ *nf* **1** herbal tea; **2** infusion.

ingénier: **s'ingénier** /ɛ̃ʒenje/ [2] *v refl* (+ *v être*) to do one's utmost (**à faire** to do).

ingénierie /ɛ̃ʒeniʀi/ *nf* engineering.

ingénieur /ɛ̃ʒenjœʀ/ *nm* engineer.

ingénieux, **-ieuse** /ɛ̃ʒenjø, øz/ *adj* ingenious.

ingéniosité /ɛ̃ʒenjozite/ *nf* ingenuity.

ingénu, **~e** /ɛ̃ʒeny/ *adj* ingenuous.

ingénuité /ɛ̃ʒenɥite/ *nf* ingenuousness; **en toute ~** in all innocence.

ingérer /ɛ̃ʒeʀe/ [14] **I** *vtr* to ingest.
II s'ingérer *v refl* (+ *v être*) to interfere.

ingestion /ɛ̃ʒɛstjɔ̃/ *nf* ingestion.

ingrat, **~e** /ɛ̃gʀa, at/ *adj* **1** ungrateful; **2** [*face, landscape*] unattractive; **3** [*task, role*] thankless; [*land, soil*] unproductive.

ingratitude /ɛ̃gʀatityd/ *nf* ingratitude.

ingrédient /ɛ̃gʀedjɑ̃/ *nm* ingredient.

inhabitable /inabitabl/ *adj* uninhabitable.

inhabité, **~e** /inabite/ *adj* uninhabited.

inhabituel, **-elle** /inabitɥɛl/ *adj* unusual.

inhalation /inalasjɔ̃/ *nf* inhalation.

inhaler /inale/ [1] *vtr* to inhale.

inhérent, **~e** /ineʀɑ̃, ɑ̃t/ *adj* inherent.

inhibition /inibisjɔ̃/ *nf* inhibition.

inhumain, **~e** /inymɛ̃, ɛn/ *adj* inhuman.

inhumation /inymasjɔ̃/ *nf* **1** burial; **2** funeral.

inhumer /inyme/ [1] *vtr* to bury.

inimaginable /inimaʒinabl/ *adj* **1** unimaginable; **2** unthinkable.

inimitable /inimitabl/ *adj* inimitable.

ininflammable /inɛ̃flamabl/ *adj* nonflammable.

inintéressant, **~e** /inɛ̃teʀesɑ̃, ɑ̃t/ *adj* uninteresting.

ininterrompu, **~e** /inɛ̃tɛʀɔ̃py/ *adj* **1** [*process*] uninterrupted; [*drop*] continuous; [*traffic*] endless; **2** [*procession*] unbroken.

initial, **~e**[1], *mpl* **-iaux** /inisjal, o/ *adj* initial.

initiale[2] /inisjal/ *nf* initial.

initiateur, **-trice** /inisjatœʀ, tʀis/ *nm,f* **1** originator; instigator; **2** instructor.

initiation /inisjasjɔ̃/ *nf* **1** introduction; **2** initiation.

initiative /inisjativ/ *nf* initiative; **avoir l'esprit d'~** to have initiative.

initié, **~e** /inisje/ *nm,f* **1** initiate; **2** insider trader.

initier /inisje/ [2] **I** *vtr* **1** to introduce; **2** to initiate.
II s'initier *v refl* (+ *v être*) **s'~ à qch** to learn sth.

injecter /ɛ̃ʒɛkte/ [2] *vtr* to inject.

injection /ɛ̃ʒɛksjɔ̃/ *nf* injection.

injonction /ɛ̃ʒɔ̃ksjɔ̃/ *nf* injunction, command.

injure /ɛ̃ʒyʀ/ *nf* insult, abuse.

injurier /ɛ̃ʒyʀje/ [1] *vtr* to insult, to swear at.

injurieux, **-ieuse** /ɛ̃ʒyʀjø, øz/ *adj* [*remark*] abusive; [*attitude*] insulting.

injuste /ɛ̃ʒyst/ *adj* unfair.

injustice /ɛ̃ʒystis/ *nf* injustice; unfairness; **réparer une ~** to right a wrong.

inlassable /ɛ̃lasabl/ *adj* [*person*] tireless; [*curiosity*] insatiable; [*efforts*] unremitting.

inné, **~e** /inne/ *adj* innate.

innocence /inɔsɑ̃s/ *nf* innocence.

innocent, **~e** /inɔsɑ̃, ɑ̃t/ *adj* innocent.

innocenter /inɔsɑ̃te/ [1] *vtr* to prove [sb] innocent.

innombrable /innɔ̃bʀabl/ *adj* **1** countless; **2** [*crowd*] vast.

innommable /innɔmabl/ *adj* unspeakable.

innovateur, **-trice** /inɔvatœʀ, tʀis/ *nm,f* innovator.

innover /inɔve/ [1] *vi* to innovate.

inoculer /inɔkyle/ [1] *vtr* to inoculate.

inodore /inɔdɔʀ/ *adj* [*substance*] odourless[GB].

inoffensif, **-ive** /inɔfɑ̃sif, iv/ *adj* harmless.

inondation /inɔ̃dasjɔ̃/ *nf* **1** flood; **2** flooding.

inonder /inɔ̃de/ [1] *vtr* to flood.

inopérant, **~e** /inɔpeʀɑ̃, ɑ̃t/ *adj* ineffective.

inopiné, **~e** /inɔpine/ *adj* unexpected.

inopportun, **~e** /inɔpɔʀtœ̃, yn/ *adj* **1** inappropriate; **2** ill-timed.

inoubliable /inublijabl/ *adj* unforgettable.

inouï, **~e** /inwi/ *adj* [*event*] unprecedented; [*success*] incredible; **c'est ~** that's unheard of.

inox /inɔks/ *nm inv* stainless steel.

inoxydable /inɔksidabl/ *adj* [*metal*] non-oxidizing; **acier ~** stainless steel.

inqualifiable /ɛ̃kalifjabl/ *adj* unspeakable.

inquiet, **-iète** /ɛ̃kjɛ, ɛt/ *adj* **1** anxious; **2** worried.

inquiétant, **~e** /ɛ̃kjetɑ̃, ɑ̃t/ *adj* **1** worrying; **2** frightening.

inquiéter /ɛ̃kjete/ [14] **I** *vtr* **1** to worry; **2 les douaniers ne l'ont pas inquiété** the customs officers didn't bother him.
II s'inquiéter *v refl* (+ *v être*) **1** to worry; **2 s'~ de qch** to enquire about sth.

inquiétude /ɛ̃kjetyd/ *nf* **1** anxiety, concern; **2** worry; **il n'y a pas d'~ à avoir** there's nothing to worry about.

inquisiteur, **-trice** /ɛ̃kizitœʀ, tʀis/ I *adj* inquisitive.
II *nm,f* inquisitor.

inquisition /ɛ̃kizisjɔ̃/ *nf* inquisition.

insaisissable /ɛ̃sɛzisabl/ *adj* [*person, character*] elusive; [*nuance*] imperceptible.

insalubre /ɛ̃salybʀ/ *adj* insanitary.

insanité /ɛ̃sanite/ *nf* **1** rubbish, nonsense; **2** insanity.

insatiable /ɛ̃sasjabl/ *adj* insatiable.

insatisfaction /ɛ̃satisfaksjɔ̃/ *nf* dissatisfaction.

inscription /ɛ̃skʀipsjɔ̃/ *nf* **1** (in school) enrolment[GB]; (at university) registration; **2 l'~ au club coûte 200 francs** the membership fee for the club is 200 francs; **~ électorale** registration as a voter; **3** inscription; graffiti.

inscrire /ɛ̃skʀiʀ/ [67] I *vtr* **1** to enrol[GB] [*pupil*]; to register [*student*]; **2** to write down [*name, date*].
II **s'inscrire** *v refl* (+ *v être*) **1** to enrol[GB]; to register; **s'~ au chômage** to register as unemployed; **s'~ à un parti** to join a party; **2 s'~ dans le cadre de** to be in line with; **3 s'~ en faux contre qch** to dispute the validity of sth.

inscrit, **~e** /ɛ̃skʀi, it/ I *pp* ▶ **inscrire**.
II *nm,f* registered student; registered voter.

insecte /ɛ̃sɛkt/ *nm* insect.

insecticide /ɛ̃sɛktisid/ *nm* insecticide.

insécurité /ɛ̃sekyʀite/ *nf* insecurity.

insémination /ɛ̃seminasjɔ̃/ *nf* insemination; **~ artificielle** artificial insemination.

insensé, **~e** /ɛ̃sɑ̃se/ *adj* **1** insane; **2**○ [*crowd, traffic jam*] phenomenal.

insensibiliser /ɛ̃sɑ̃sibilize/ [1] *vtr* (Med) to anaesthetize.

insensibilité /ɛ̃sɑ̃sibilite/ *nf* insensitivity.

insensible /ɛ̃sɑ̃sibl/ *adj* **1** impervious; **2** insensitive.

insensiblement /ɛ̃sɑ̃sibləmɑ̃/ *adv* imperceptibly.

inséparable /ɛ̃sepaʀabl/ *adj* inseparable.

insérer /ɛ̃seʀe/ [14] I *vtr* to insert.
II **s'insérer** *v refl* (+ *v être*) (gen) to be inserted.

insertion /ɛ̃sɛʀsjɔ̃/ *nf* **1** insertion; **2** integration.

insidieux, **-ieuse** /ɛ̃sidjø, øz/ *adj* insidious.

insigne /ɛ̃siɲ/ I *adj* [*honour, favour*] great.
II *nm* badge.

insignifiant, **~e** /ɛ̃siɲifjɑ̃, ɑ̃t/ *adj* insignificant.

insinuation /ɛ̃sinɥasjɔ̃/ *nf* insinuation.

insinuer /ɛ̃sinɥe/ [1] I *vtr* to insinuate.
II **s'insinuer** *v refl* (+ *v être*) **s'~ dans** [*person*] to worm one's way into; [*liquid*] to seep into.

insipide /ɛ̃sipid/ *adj* insipid.

insistance /ɛ̃sistɑ̃s/ *nf* insistence.

insistant, **~e** /ɛ̃sistɑ̃, ɑ̃t/ *adj* insistent.

insister /ɛ̃siste/ [1] *vi* **1** to insist; **'ça ne répond pas'—'insiste'** 'there's no reply!'—'keep trying'; **2 ~ sur** to stress [*danger, need*]; to put the emphasis on [*spelling*]; **3 ~ sur** to pay particular attention to [*stain*].

insolation /ɛ̃sɔlasjɔ̃/ *nf* sunstroke.

insolence /ɛ̃sɔlɑ̃s/ *nf* **1** insolence; **2** insolent remark.

insolent, **~e** /ɛ̃sɔlɑ̃, ɑ̃t/ *adj* **1** [*child, tone*] insolent; **2** [*rival, winner*] arrogant.

insolite /ɛ̃sɔlit/ *adj, nm* unusual.

insoluble /ɛ̃sɔlybl/ *adj* insoluble.

insolvable /ɛ̃sɔlvabl/ *adj* insolvent.

insomniaque /ɛ̃sɔmnjak/ *adj, nmf* insomniac.

insomnie /ɛ̃sɔmni/ *nf* insomnia.

insondable /ɛ̃sɔ̃dabl/ *adj* unfathomable.

insonorisation /ɛ̃sɔnɔʀizasjɔ̃/ *nf* soundproofing.

insonoriser /ɛ̃sɔnɔʀize/ [1] *vtr* to soundproof.

insouciance /ɛ̃susjɑ̃s/ *nf* carefreeness.

insouciant, **~e** /ɛ̃susjɑ̃, ɑ̃t/ *adj* carefree.

insoumission /ɛ̃sumisjɔ̃/ *nf* **1** insubordination; **2** (Mil) draft-dodging.

insoupçonné, **~e** /ɛ̃supsɔne/ *adj* unsuspected.

insoutenable /ɛ̃sutnabl/ *adj* **1** [*pain*] unbearable; **2** [*opinion*] untenable.

inspecter /ɛ̃spɛkte/ [1] *vtr* to inspect.

inspecteur, **-trice** /ɛ̃spɛktœʀ, tʀis/ *nm,f* inspector.
■ **~ de police** ≈ detective constable (GB); **~ du travail** health and safety inspector.

inspection /ɛ̃spɛksjɔ̃/ *nf* **1** inspection; **2** inspectorate.

inspiration /ɛ̃spiʀasjɔ̃/ *nf* inspiration.

inspirer /ɛ̃spiʀe/ [1] I *vtr* **1** to inspire [*person*]; **être bien/mal inspiré de faire** to be well-/ill-advised to do; **un roman inspiré des vieux contes populaires** a novel based on old folk tales; **2** to appeal to; **ça ne m'inspire pas** that doesn't appeal to me; **3 ~ la méfiance à qn** to inspire distrust in sb.
II *vi* to breathe in, to inhale.
III **s'inspirer** *v refl* (+ *v être*) **s'~ de** to draw one's inspiration from.

instabilité /ɛ̃stabilite/ *nf* (gen) instability.

instable /ɛ̃stabl/ *adj* (gen) unstable; [*weather*] unsettled.

installateur, **-trice** /ɛ̃stalatœʀ, tʀis/ *nm,f* fitter.

installation /ɛ̃stalasjɔ̃/ I *nf* **1** installation, putting in; **2** system; **~ électrique** (electric) wiring; **3** move; **depuis mon ~ à Paris** since I moved to Paris.
II **installations** *nf pl* facilities.

installé, **~e** /ɛ̃stale/ I *pp* ▶ **installer**.
II *pp adj* [*person*] living (**à** in); [*company*] based; **être bien ~ dans un fauteuil** to be ensconced in an armchair; **ils sont bien ~s dans leur nouvelle maison** they're very snug in their new home; **c'est un homme ~** (figurative) he's very nicely set up.

installer /ɛ̃stale/ [1] I *vtr* **1** to install, to put in [*central heating, sink*]; to put up [*shelves*]; to connect [*gas*]; **2** to put [*guest*] (**dans** in); **~ qn**

dans un fauteuil to sit sb in an armchair; **~ qn à un poste** to appoint sb to a post.
II **s'installer** *v refl* (+ *v être*) **1** [*recession*] to set in; [*illness*] to take hold; **le doute commence à s'~ dans leur esprit** they're beginning to have doubts; **2 s'~ à son compte** to set up one's own business; **3** to settle; **partir s'~ à l'étranger** to go and live abroad; **je viendrai te voir quand tu seras installé** I'll come and see you when you're settled in; **s'~ au soleil** to sit in the sun; **s'~ à son bureau** to settle down at one's desk; **installe-toi, j'arrive!** make yourself at home, I'm coming!

instamment /ɛ̃stamɑ̃/ *adv* insistently.

instance /ɛ̃stɑ̃s/ *nf* **1** authority; **les ~s d'un parti politique** the leaders of a political party; **2 être en ~ de divorce** to be engaged in divorce proceedings.

instant, **~e** /ɛ̃stɑ̃, ɑ̃t/ *nm* moment, instant; **à tout** or **chaque ~** all the time; **par ~s** at times; **pour l'~** for the moment; **il devrait arriver d'un ~ à l'autre** he should arrive any minute now; **à l'~ même où** just when.

instantané, **~e** /ɛ̃stɑ̃tane/ **I** *adj* instantaneous; [*drink, soup*] instant.
II *nm* snapshot.

instar: **à l'instar de** /alɛ̃staʀdə/ *phr* following the example of.

instaurer /ɛ̃stoʀe/ [1] *vtr* to establish [*regime, dialogue*]; to impose [*curfew*].

instigateur, **-trice** /ɛ̃stigatœʀ, tʀis/ *nm,f* **1** instigator; **2** originator.

instigation /ɛ̃stigasjɔ̃/ *nf* **à l'~ de qn** at sb's instigation.

instiller /ɛ̃stile/ [1] *vtr* to instil[GB].

instinct /ɛ̃stɛ̃/ *nm* instinct; **d'~** instinctively.

instinctif, -ive /ɛ̃stɛ̃ktif, iv/ *adj* instinctive.

instituer /ɛ̃stitɥe/ [1] *vtr* to institute.

institut /ɛ̃stity/ *nm* **1** institute; **2 ~ de beauté** beauty salon or parlour[GB].
■ **Institut universitaire de formation des maîtres, IUFM** *primary teacher training college*; **Institut universitaire de technologie, IUT** university institute of technology.

instituteur, **-trice** /ɛ̃stitytœʀ, tʀis/ *nm,f* (primary school) teacher.

institution /ɛ̃stitysjɔ̃/ *nf* **1** institution; **2** private school.

institutrice ▸ **instituteur**.

instructeur /ɛ̃stʀyktœʀ/ *nm* (gen, Mil) instructor.

instructif, **-ive** /ɛ̃stʀyktif, iv/ *adj* (gen) instructive; [*experience*] enlightening.

instruction /ɛ̃stʀyksjɔ̃/ **I** *nf* **1** (gen) education; (Mil) training; **2** (Law) *preparation of a case for trial.*
II **instructions** *nf pl* instructions.
■ **~ civique** civics; **~ religieuse** religious instruction.

instruire /ɛ̃stʀɥiʀ/ [69] **I** *vtr* **1** to teach [*child*]; to train [*soldiers*]; **2** (Law) **~ une affaire** to prepare a case for trial.
II **s'instruire** *v refl* (+ *v être*) to learn.

instruit, **~e** /ɛ̃stʀɥi, it/ *adj* educated.

instrument /ɛ̃stʀymɑ̃/ *nm* (gen, Mus) instrument; **être l'~ de qn** to be sb's tool.
■ **~s de bord** controls.

insu: **à l'insu de** /alɛ̃sydə/ *phr* **à l'~ de qn** without sb knowing.

insubordination /ɛ̃sybɔʀdinasjɔ̃/ *nf* insubordination.

insuffisance /ɛ̃syfizɑ̃s/ *nf* **1** insufficiency, shortage; **2** poor standard; **l'~ de la production** the shortfall in production; **3** (Med) insufficiency.

insuffisant, **~e** /ɛ̃syfizɑ̃, ɑ̃t/ *adj* **1** insufficient; **2** inadequate.

insuffler /ɛ̃syfle/ [1] *vtr* to instil[GB]; **~ la vie à qn** to breathe life into sb.

insulaire /ɛ̃sylɛʀ/ *adj* [*population*] island; [*mentality*] insular.

insultant, **~e** /ɛ̃syltɑ̃, ɑ̃t/ *adj* insulting.

insulte /ɛ̃sylt/ *nf* insult.

insulter /ɛ̃sylte/ [1] *vtr* to insult; to shout abuse at; [*attitude*] to be an insult to.

insupportable /ɛ̃sypɔʀtabl/ *adj* unbearable.

insurgé, **~e** /ɛ̃syʀʒe/ *nm,f* insurgent, rebel.

insurger: **s'insurger** /ɛ̃syʀʒe/ [13] *v refl* (+ *v être*) **1** to rise up; **2** to protest.

insurrection /ɛ̃syʀɛksjɔ̃/ *nf* insurrection.

intact, **~e** /ɛ̃takt/ *adj* intact.

intarissable /ɛ̃taʀisabl/ *adj* [*imagination*] inexhaustible; [*source*] never-ending.

intégral, **~e**, *mpl* **-aux** /ɛ̃tegʀal, o/ *adj* **1** [*payment*] full, in full; **2** [*tan*] all-over; **3** [*text*] unabridged; **version ~e** uncut version.

intégralement /ɛ̃tegʀalmɑ̃/ *adv* [*pay*] in full.

intégralité /ɛ̃tegʀalite/ *nf* **l'~ de leur salaire** their entire salary.

intégrante /ɛ̃tegʀɑ̃t/ *adj f* **faire partie ~ de qch** to be an integral part of sth.

intégration /ɛ̃tegʀasjɔ̃/ *nf* integration.

intègre /ɛ̃tɛgʀ/ *adj* [*person, life*] honest.

intégrer /ɛ̃tegʀe/ [14] **I** *vtr* **1** to insert; **2** to integrate [*population*]; **3**° **il vient d'~ Harvard** he has just got into Harvard.
II **s'intégrer** *v refl* (+ *v être*) **1** [*population*] to integrate; **2** [*building*] to fit in.

intégrisme /ɛ̃tegʀism/ *nm* fundamentalism.

intégrité /ɛ̃tegʀite/ *nf* integrity.

intellect /ɛ̃telɛkt/ *nm* intellect.

intellectuel, **-elle** /ɛ̃telɛktɥɛl/ **I** *adj* [*work*] intellectual; [*effort*] mental.
II *nm,f* intellectual.

intelligence /ɛ̃teliʒɑ̃s/ *nf* **1** intelligence; **2 agir d'~ avec qn** to act in agreement with sb.

intelligent, **~e** /ɛ̃teliʒɑ̃, ɑ̃t/ *adj* intelligent; clever.

intelligible /ɛ̃teliʒibl/ *adj* intelligible.

intempéries /ɛ̃tɑ̃peʀi/ *nf pl* bad weather.

intempestif, **-ive** /ɛ̃tɑ̃pɛstif, iv/ *adj* untimely; [*curiosity, zeal*] misplaced.

intemporel, **-elle** /ɛ̃tɑ̃pɔʀɛl/ *adj* timeless.

intenable /ɛ̃t(ə)nabl/ *adj* **1** [*situation*] unbearable; **2** [*child*] difficult.

intendance /ɛ̃tɑ̃dɑ̃s/ *nf* (Sch) administration.

intendant, **~e** /ɛ̃tɑ̃dɑ̃, ɑ̃t/ **I** *nm,f* (Sch) bursar.
II *nm* (Mil) quartermaster; paymaster.

intense /ɛ̃tɑ̃s/ *adj* (gen) intense; [*red, green*] vivid; [*traffic*] heavy.

intensif, **-ive** /ɛ̃tɑ̃sif, iv/ *adj* intensive.

intensifier /ɛ̃tɑ̃sifje/ [2] *vtr*, **s'intensifier** *v refl* (+ *v être*) to intensify.

intensité /ɛ̃tɑ̃site/ *nf* intensity.

intenter /ɛ̃tɑ̃te/ [1] *vtr* **~ un procès à qn** to sue sb.

intention /ɛ̃tɑ̃sjɔ̃/ *nf* intention; **c'est l'~ qui compte** it's the thought that counts; **à l'~ de qn** [*remark*] aimed at sb.

intentionné, **~e** /ɛ̃tɑ̃sjɔne/ *adj* **bien/mal ~** well-/ill-intentioned.

interaction /ɛ̃tɛʀaksjɔ̃/ *nf* interaction.

intercalaire /ɛ̃tɛʀkalɛʀ/ **I** *adj* **feuille** or **feuillet ~** insert.
II *nm* divider.

intercaler /ɛ̃tɛʀkale/ [1] *vtr* to insert.

intercéder /ɛ̃tɛʀsede/ [14] *vi* to intercede.

intercepter /ɛ̃tɛʀsɛpte/ [1] *vtr* to intercept.

interchangeable /ɛ̃tɛʀʃɑ̃ʒabl/ *adj* interchangeable.

interdiction /ɛ̃tɛʀdiksjɔ̃/ *nf* **1** banning; **'~ de dépasser'** 'no overtaking' (GB), 'no passing' (US); **2** ban; **lever une ~** to lift a ban.
■ **~ de séjour** prohibition on residence.

interdire /ɛ̃tɛʀdiʀ/ [65] *vtr* to ban; **~ à qn de faire**, **~ que qn fasse** to forbid sb to do.

interdisciplinaire /ɛ̃tɛʀdisiplinɛʀ/ *adj* (Sch) cross-curricular; (Univ) interdisciplinary.

interdit, **~e** /ɛ̃tɛʀdi, it/ **I** *pp* ▶ **interdire**.
II *pp adj* prohibited, forbidden; **entrée ~e** no entry or admittance; **film ~ aux moins de 13 ans** film unsuitable for children under 13.
III *adj* dumbfounded.
IV *nm* proscription; taboo.

intéressant, **~e** /ɛ̃teʀɛsɑ̃, ɑ̃t/ **I** *adj* **1** interesting; **2** [*prices, conditions*] attractive; **il est plus ~ de payer au comptant qu'à crédit** it's better to pay in cash rather than by credit.
II *nm,f* **faire l'~** or **son ~** to show off.

intéressé, **~e** /ɛ̃teʀese/ **I** *pp* ▶ **intéresser**.
II *pp adj* **1** interested; **2** attentive; **3 les parties ~es** those concerned; **les personnes ~es aux bénéfices** people with a share in the profits; **4** [*person*] self-interested; [*action*] motivated by self-interest; **ses conseils étaient ~s** he/she had a selfish motive for giving that advice.
III *nm,f* person concerned.

intéresser /ɛ̃teʀese/ [1] **I** *vtr* **1** to interest; **ça ne m'intéresse pas** I'm not interested; **2** [*problem, decision*] to concern; **3 ~ les salariés aux bénéfices** to offer a profit-sharing scheme to employees.
II s'intéresser *v refl* (+ *v être*) **s'~ à** (gen) to be interested in; to take an interest in.

intérêt /ɛ̃teʀɛ/ *nm* **1** interest; **recherche digne d'~** worthwhile research; **l'~ supérieur de la nation** the higher good of the country; **je ne vois pas l'~ de cette réforme** I can't see the point of this reform; **par ~** [*act*] out of self-interest; [*marry*] for money; **2** (financial) interest.

interférence /ɛ̃tɛʀfeʀɑ̃s/ *nf* interference.

interférer /ɛ̃tɛʀfeʀe/ [14] *vi* to interfere.

intérieur, **~e** /ɛ̃teʀjœʀ/ **I** *adj* **1** internal, interior; [*sea*] inland; [*pocket*] inside; **le côté ~** the inside; **2** domestic; **sur le plan ~** on the domestic front; **3** [*regulations*] internal.
II *nm* (of box, newspaper) inside; (of car, house) interior; **à l'~** inside; indoors; **à l'~ des terres** inland; **d'~** [*game*] indoor; **être fier de son ~** to be proud of one's home.

intérim /ɛ̃teʀim/ *nm* **1** interim (period); **président par ~** acting president; **assurer l'~ de** to stand in for; **2** temporary work; **travailler en ~** to temp○.

intérimaire /ɛ̃teʀimɛʀ/ *adj* [*committee*] interim; [*minister*] acting; [*job, staff*] temporary.

intérioriser /ɛ̃teʀjɔʀize/ [1] *vtr* to internalize.

interjection /ɛ̃tɛʀʒɛksjɔ̃/ *nf* interjection.

interligne /ɛ̃tɛʀliɲ/ *nm* line space.

interlocuteur, **-trice** /ɛ̃tɛʀlɔkytœʀ, tʀis/ *nm,f* **1 mon ~** the person I am/was talking to; **2** (in negotiations) representative; **3 Louis est notre seul ~** Louis is our only contact.

interloquer /ɛ̃tɛʀlɔke/ [1] *vtr* to take [sb] aback.

interlude /ɛ̃tɛʀlyd/ *nm* interlude.

intermède /ɛ̃tɛʀmɛd/ *nm* interlude.

intermédiaire /ɛ̃tɛʀmedjɛʀ/ **I** *adj* [*rate, stage*] intermediate.
II *nmf* (in negotiations) go-between; (in industry) middleman.
III *phr* **par l'~ de** through.

interminable /ɛ̃tɛʀminabl/ *adj* **1** interminable, never-ending; **2** endless.

intermittence /ɛ̃tɛʀmitɑ̃s/ *nf* **par ~** [*rain*] on and off; [*work*] intermittently.

intermittent, **~e** /ɛ̃tɛʀmitɑ̃, ɑ̃t/ *adj* [*rain, fever*] intermittent; [*noise, efforts*] sporadic.

internat /ɛ̃tɛʀna/ *nm* boarding school.

international, **~e**, *mpl* **-aux** /ɛ̃tɛʀnasjɔnal, o/ *adj* international.

interne /ɛ̃tɛʀn/ **I** *adj* (gen) internal; [*training*] in-house; [*ear*] inner.
II *nmf* **1** (Sch) boarder; **2 ~ (en médecine)** houseman (GB), intern (US).

internement /ɛ̃tɛʀnəmɑ̃/ *nm* (Med) committal (to a psychiatric institution).

interner /ɛ̃tɛʀne/ [1] *vtr* to commit [*mental patient*].

interpellation /ɛ̃tɛʀpelasjɔ̃/ *nf* **procéder à des ~s** to take people in for questioning.

interpeller /ɛ̃tɛʀpəle/ [1] *vtr* **1** to call out to; to shout at; **2** to question; (in police station) to take [sb] in for questioning.

interphone® /ɛ̃tɛʀfɔn/ *nm* **1** intercom; **2** entry phone.

interposer: **s'interposer** /ɛ̃tɛʀpoze/ [1] *v refl*

(+ *v être*) to intervene; **par personne interposée** through an intermediary.

interprétariat /ɛ̃tɛʀpʀetaʀja/ *nm* interpreting.

interprétation /ɛ̃tɛʀpʀetasjɔ̃/ *nf* **1** (gen, Mus) interpretation; **2** (profession) interpreting.

interprète /ɛ̃tɛʀpʀɛt/ *nmf* **1** interpreter; **2** performer; **3** spokesperson.

interpréter /ɛ̃tɛʀpʀete/ [14] *vtr* **1** to play [*role, sonata*]; to sing [*song*]; **2** to interpret.

interrogateur, **-trice** /ɛ̃tɛʀɔgatœʀ, tʀis/ *adj* enquiring; **d'un air ~** enquiringly.

interrogatif, **-ive** /ɛ̃tɛʀɔgatif, iv/ *adj* interrogative.

interrogation /ɛ̃tɛʀɔgasjɔ̃/ *nf* **1** (of witness) questioning; **2** (in grammar) question; **3** (Sch) test; **~ orale** oral test.

interrogatoire /ɛ̃tɛʀɔgatwaʀ/ *nm* (gen) interrogation; (by police) questioning.

interroger /ɛ̃tɛʀɔʒe/ [13] **I** *vtr* **1** (gen) to question; to ask; (figurative) to examine [*conscience*]; **être interrogé comme témoin** (Law) to be called as a witness; **2 ~ son répondeur** to check one's calls; **3** (Sch) to test.
II s'interroger *v refl* (+ *v être*) **s'~ sur** to wonder about.

interrompre /ɛ̃tɛʀɔ̃pʀ/ [53] **I** *vtr* **1** to interrupt; to break off [*dialogue*]; [*person*] to cease [*activity*]; **~ son repas pour faire** to stop eating to do; **2** to put an end to [*holiday*]; to stop [*treatment*]; to terminate [*pregnancy*].
II s'interrompre *v refl* (+ *v être*) **1** [*person, conversation*] to break off; **2** [*rain*] to stop.

interrupteur /ɛ̃teʀyptœʀ/ *nm* switch.

interruption /ɛ̃teʀypsjɔ̃/ *nf* **1** break; **sans ~** continuously; **2** ending; **l'~ du dialogue entre** the breaking off of the dialogue[GB] between.

intersection /ɛ̃tɛʀsɛksjɔ̃/ *nf* intersection.

interstice /ɛ̃tɛʀstis/ *nm* (in floor) crack; (in shutters, blinds) chink.

intervalle /ɛ̃tɛʀval/ *nm* **1** space; **à ~s réguliers** at regular intervals; **2** interval; **dans l'~** meanwhile, in the meantime.

intervenir /ɛ̃tɛʀvəniʀ/ [36] *vi* **1** [*changes*] to take place; [*agreement*] to be reached; **2** [*speaker*] to speak; **3** (in emergency) [*police*] to intervene; **4 ~ auprès de qn pour qn** to intercede with sb on sb's behalf.

intervention /ɛ̃tɛʀvɑ̃sjɔ̃/ *nf* **1** intervention; **2** speech; lecture; **3** (Med) **~ (chirurgicale)** operation.

intervertir /ɛ̃tɛʀvɛʀtiʀ/ [3] *vtr* to invert.

intestin /ɛ̃tɛstɛ̃/ *nm* bowel, intestine.

intestinal, **~e**, *mpl* **-aux** /ɛ̃tɛstinal, o/ *adj* intestinal.

intime /ɛ̃tim/ **I** *adj* **1** [*life, diary*] private; [*friend, relationship*] intimate; [*hygiene*] personal; **2** [*gathering*] intimate; [*conversation*] private; [*dinner*] quiet; **3** [*room*] cosy (GB), cozy (US); **4** [*knowledge*] intimate.
II *nmf* close friend.

intimement /ɛ̃timmɑ̃/ *adv* intimately; **je suis ~ convaincu que**... I'm absolutely convinced that...

intimidation /ɛ̃timidasjɔ̃/ *nf* intimidation; **d'~** [*measures, remarks*] intimidatory.

intimider /ɛ̃timide/ [1] *vtr* to intimidate.

intimité /ɛ̃timite/ *nf* **1** intimacy; **2** privacy; **dans la plus stricte ~** in the strictest privacy; **3** private life; **4** (of house, setting) cosiness.

intitulé /ɛ̃tityle/ *nm* title, heading.

intituler /ɛ̃tityle/ [1] **I** *vtr* to call.
II s'intituler *v refl* (+ *v être*) to be called, to be entitled.

intolérable /ɛ̃tɔleʀabl/ *adj* intolerable; deeply shocking.

intolérance /ɛ̃tɔleʀɑ̃s/ *nf* intolerance.

intolérant, **~e** /ɛ̃tɔleʀɑ̃, ɑ̃t/ *adj* intolerant.

intonation /ɛ̃tɔnasjɔ̃/ *nf* intonation.

intoxication /ɛ̃tɔksikasjɔ̃/ *nf* **1** (Med) poisoning; **2** (figurative) disinformation.

intoxiquer /ɛ̃tɔksike/ [1] **I** *vtr* to poison.
II s'intoxiquer *v refl* (+ *v être*) to poison oneself.

intraitable /ɛ̃tʀɛtabl/ *adj* inflexible.

intransigeance /ɛ̃tʀɑ̃ziʒɑ̃s/ *nf* intransigence.

intransigeant, **~e** /ɛ̃tʀɑ̃ziʒɑ̃, ɑ̃t/ *adj* [*attitude*] uncompromising; [*person*] intransigent.

intraveineuse /ɛ̃tʀavenøz/ *nf* intravenous injection.

intrépide /ɛ̃tʀepid/ *adj* intrepid, bold.

intrépidité /ɛ̃tʀepidite/ *nf* boldness.

intrigant, **~e** /ɛ̃tʀigɑ̃, ɑ̃t/ *nm,f* schemer.

intrigue /ɛ̃tʀig/ *nf* **1** intrigue; **2** plot; **une ~ policière** a detective story.

intriguer /ɛ̃tʀige/ [1] *vtr* to intrigue.

intrinsèque /ɛ̃tʀɛ̃sɛk/ *adj* intrinsic.

introduction /ɛ̃tʀɔdyksjɔ̃/ *nf* **1** (gen) introduction; **2** (of key, probe) insertion.

introduire /ɛ̃tʀɔdɥiʀ/ [69] **I** *vtr* **1** to insert [*object*]; **2** to usher [sb] in [*visitor*]; (surreptitiously) to smuggle [sb] in; **3** to introduce [*person*]; **4** to introduce [*product, idea*].
II s'introduire *v refl* (+ *v être*) **s'~ dans** to get into.

introduit, **~e** /ɛ̃tʀɔdɥi, it/ *pp* ▶ **introduire**.

introspection /ɛ̃tʀɔspɛksjɔ̃/ *nf* introspection.

introverti, **~e** /ɛ̃tʀɔvɛʀti/ *nm,f* introvert.

intrus, **~e** /ɛ̃tʀy, yz/ *nm,f* intruder.

intrusion /ɛ̃tʀyzjɔ̃/ *nf* **1** (gen) intrusion; **2** interference.

intuitif, **~ive** /ɛ̃tɥitif, iv/ *adj* intuitive.

intuition /ɛ̃tɥisjɔ̃/ *nf* intuition.

inusable /inyzabl/ *adj* hardwearing.

inusité, **~e** /inyzite/ *adj* uncommon.

inutile /inytil/ *adj* useless; pointless; needless; **(il est) ~ de faire** there's no point in doing; **~ de dire que** needless to say; **sans risques ~s** without unnecessary risks.

inutilement /inytilmɑ̃/ *adv* unnecessarily; needlessly; in vain.

inutilisable /inytilizabl/ *adj* unusable.

inutilité /inytilite/ *nf* (of expense, action) pointlessness.

invalide /ɛ̃valid/ **I** *adj* disabled.

II *nmf* disabled person.

invalidité /ɛ̃validite/ *nf* (Med) disability.

invariable /ɛ̃vaʀjabl/ *adj* invariable.

invasion /ɛ̃vazjɔ̃/ *nf* invasion.

invendu, **~e** /ɛ̃vɑ̃dy/ *adj* unsold.

inventaire /ɛ̃vɑ̃tɛʀ/ *nm* **1** stocktaking (GB), inventory (US); **2** stocklist (GB), inventory (US); **3** (of wardrobe, suitcase) list of contents.

inventer /ɛ̃vɑ̃te/ [1] **I** *vtr* to invent; to devise; **je n'invente rien** I'm not making it up.
II s'inventer *v refl* (+ *v être*) **ça ne s'invente pas** that has to be true.
IDIOMS **il n'a pas inventé la poudre**○ he is not very bright.

inventeur, **-trice** /ɛ̃vɑ̃tœʀ, tʀis/ *nm,f* inventor.

inventif, **-ive** /ɛ̃vɑ̃tif, iv/ *adj* **1** inventive; **2** resourceful.

invention /ɛ̃vɑ̃sjɔ̃/ *nf* **1** invention; **2** fabrication; **c'est de l'~ pure** it's a complete fabrication.

inverse /ɛ̃vɛʀs/ **I** *adj* (gen) opposite; **dans l'ordre ~** (referring to list) in reverse order.
II *nm* (gen) **l'~** the opposite; **à l'~** conversely; **à l'~ de ce qu'il croyait** contrary to what he thought.

inversement /ɛ̃vɛʀsəmɑ̃/ *adv* (gen) conversely.

inverser /ɛ̃vɛʀse/ [1] *vtr* **1** to invert [*position*]; to reverse [*roles*]; **image inversée** mirror image; **2** to reverse [*electric current*].

inversion /ɛ̃vɛʀsjɔ̃/ *nf* inversion; reversal.

invertébré, **~e** /ɛ̃vɛʀtebʀe/ *adj* invertebrate.

invertir /ɛ̃vɛʀtiʀ/ [3] *vtr* to reverse; to switch [sth] round [*words*].

investigation /ɛ̃vɛstigasjɔ̃/ *nf* investigation; **d'~** investigative.

investir /ɛ̃vɛstiʀ/ [3] **I** *vtr* **1** to invest [*capital*]; **2** to invest [*person, ambassador*]; **3** [*police*] to go into; [*tourists, demonstrators*] to take over; **4** [*army*] to besiege.
II s'investir *v refl* (+ *v être*) **s'~ dans** to put a lot of oneself into; to invest emotionally in.

investissement /ɛ̃vɛstismɑ̃/ *nm* (gen) investment; (Mil) investing.

investisseur /ɛ̃vɛstisœʀ/ *nm* investor.

investiture /ɛ̃vɛstityʀ/ *nf* investiture.

invétéré, **~e** /ɛ̃veteʀe/ *adj* [*drinker, thief*] inveterate; [*liar*] compulsive.

invincible /ɛ̃vɛ̃sibl/ *adj* [*people*] invincible.

inviolable /ɛ̃vjɔlabl/ *adj* (gen) inviolable; [*door, safe*] impregnable.

invisible /ɛ̃vizibl/ *adj* **1** invisible; **la route était ~ depuis la maison** the road could not be seen from the house; **2** [*danger*] unseen.

invitation /ɛ̃vitasjɔ̃/ *nf* invitation.

invité, **~e** /ɛ̃vite/ *nm,f* guest.

inviter /ɛ̃vite/ [1] *vtr* to invite; **ceci invite à penser que**... this suggests that...

invivable /ɛ̃vivabl/ *adj* unbearable.

invocation /ɛ̃vɔkasjɔ̃/ *nf* invocation.

involontaire /ɛ̃vɔlɔ̃tɛʀ/ *adj* [*reaction*] involuntary; [*mistake*] unintentional.

invoquer /ɛ̃vɔke/ [1] *vtr* to invoke.

invraisemblable /ɛ̃vʀɛsɑ̃blabl/ *adj* **1** [*story*] unlikely; [*explanation*] implausible; **2**○ fantastic, incredible.

invraisemblance /ɛ̃vʀɛsɑ̃blɑ̃s/ *nf* **1** unlikelihood; **2** improbability.

invulnérable /ɛ̃vylneʀabl/ *adj* invulnerable.

iode /jɔd/ *nm* iodine.

irascible /iʀasibl/ *adj* [*person*] quick-tempered.

iris /iʀis/ *nm inv* **1** (flower) iris; **2** (of eye) iris.

irisé, **~e** /iʀize/ *adj* iridescent.

irlandais, **~e** /iʀlɑ̃dɛ, ɛz/ **I** *adj* Irish.
II *nm* (language) Irish.

Irlandais, **~e** /iʀlɑ̃dɛ, ɛz/ *nm,f* Irishman/Irishwoman.

Irlande /iʀlɑ̃d/ *pr nf* Ireland; **la République d'~** the Republic of Ireland; **l'~ du Nord** Northern Ireland.

ironie /iʀɔni/ *nf* irony; **faire de l'~** to be ironic.

ironique /iʀɔnik/ *adj* ironic.

irradier /iʀadje/ [2] **I** *vtr* to irradiate.
II *vi* to radiate.

irrattrapable /iʀatʀapabl/ *adj* irretrievable.

irréalisable /iʀealizabl/ *adj* [*dream*] impossible; [*plan*] unworkable.

irrécupérable /iʀekypeʀabl/ *adj* **1** irrecoverable; **2** damaged beyond repair; **3** [*delinquent*] beyond help.

irréductible /iʀedyktibl/ *nmf* diehard.

irréel, **-elle** /iʀeɛl/ *adj* unreal.

irréfléchi, **~e** /iʀefleʃi/ *adj* ill-considered.

irrégularité /iʀegylaʀite/ *nf* irregularity.

irrégulier, **-ière** /iʀegylje, ɛʀ/ *adj* **1** irregular; uneven; **2** [*procedure*] irregular; **immigré en situation irrégulière** illegal immigrant; **3** [*athlete*] whose performance is uneven.

irrémédiable /iʀ(ʀ)emedjabl/ *adj* irreparable.

irréparable /iʀepaʀabl/ **I** *adj* [*car*] beyond repair; [*damage, crime*] irreparable.
II *nm* **commettre l'~** to go beyond the point of no return.

irrépressible /iʀepʀesibl/ *adj* (gen) irrepressible; [*tears*] uncontrollable.

irréprochable /iʀepʀɔʃabl/ *adj* [*life, employee*] beyond reproach; [*work*] perfect.

irrésistible /iʀezistibl/ *adj* irresistible; [*person, joke*] hilarious.

irrespirable /iʀɛspiʀabl/ *adj* [*air*] unbreathable; [*atmosphere*] stifling.

irresponsable /iʀɛspɔ̃sabl/ *adj* irresponsible.

irrévérencieux, **-ieuse** /iʀʀeveʀɑ̃sjø, øz/ *adj* irreverent.

irréversible /iʀevɛʀsibl/ *adj* irreversible.

irrévocable /iʀevɔkabl/ *adj* irrevocable.

irrigation /iʀigasjɔ̃/ *nf* **1** (of land) irrigation; **2** (Med) supply of blood.

irriguer /iʀige/ [1] *vtr* to irrigate.

irritation /iʀitasjɔ̃/ *nf* (gen, Med) irritation.

irriter /iʀite/ [1] **I** *vtr* **1** to irritate, to annoy; **2** (Med) to irritate.

II s'irriter *v refl* (+ *v être*) **1** to get angry; **2** (Med) to become irritated.

irruption /iʀypsjɔ̃/ *nf* **faire ~ dans** to burst into [*room*].

islam /islam/ *nm* **l'~** Islam.

islamique /islamik/ *adj* Islamic.

Islande /islɑ̃d/ *pr nf* Iceland.

isolation /izɔlasjɔ̃/ *nf* insulation.

isolement /izɔlmɑ̃/ *nm* **1** (of village) remoteness; (of house) isolated location; **2** (of patient, politician) isolation; (of prisoner) solitary confinement.

isoler /izɔle/ [1] **I** *vtr* **1** to isolate [*sick person, dissident*]; to put [sb] in solitary confinement [*prisoner*]; **2** to isolate [*gene, substance*]; **3** to soundproof; to insulate; **4** to insulate [*wire*].
II s'isoler *v refl* (+ *v être*) to isolate oneself.

isoloir /izɔlwaʀ/ *nm* voting or polling (GB) booth.

issu, ~e[1] /isy/ *adj* **être ~ de** to come from; to result from.

issue[2] /isy/ *nf* **1** exit; **'sans ~'** 'no exit'; **2** solution; **situation sans ~** situation with no solution; **3** outcome; **à l'~ de** at the end of; **à l'~ de trois jours de pourparlers** at the close of three days of talks.
■ **~ de secours** emergency exit.

Italie /itali/ *pr nf* Italy.

italien, -ienne /italjɛ̃, ɛn/ **I** *adj* Italian.
II *nm* (language) Italian.

italique /italik/ *nm* italics.

itinéraire /itineʀɛʀ/ *nm* **1** (gen) route; (detailed) itinerary; **2** (figurative) career.
■ **~ bis** alternative route; **~ de délestage** relief route.

itinérant, ~e /itineʀɑ̃, ɑ̃t/ *adj* [*exhibition*] touring; [*life*] peripatetic; [*circus*] travelling[GB].

IUFM /iyɛfɛm/ *nm*: *abbr* ▶ **institut**.

IUT /iyte/ *nm*: *abbr* ▶ **institut**.

ivoire /ivwaʀ/ *adj inv, nm* ivory.

ivre /ivʀ/ *adj* **1** drunk, intoxicated; **2 ~ de rage** wild with rage.

ivresse /ivʀɛs/ *nf* **1** intoxication; **2** exhilaration.

ivrogne /ivʀɔɲ/ *nmf* drunkard.

Jj

j, **J** /ʒi/ *nm inv* j, J; **le jour J** D-day.
j' ▶**je**.
jabot /ʒabo/ *nm* **1** (of bird) crop; **2** (of shirt) jabot.
jacasser /ʒakase/ [1] *vi* to chatter.
jachère /ʒaʃɛʀ/ *nf* **(terre en) ~** fallow land.
jacinthe /ʒasɛ̃t/ *nf* hyacinth.
jackpot /(d)ʒakpɔt/ *nm* **1** jackpot; **2** slot machine.
jacquet /ʒakɛ/ *nm* backgammon.
jacter○ /ʒakte/ [1] *vi* to jaw○, to talk.
jade /ʒad/ *nm* jade.
jadis /ʒadis/ *adv* formerly, in the past.
jaguar /ʒagwaʀ/ *nm* jaguar.
jaillir /ʒajiʀ/ [3] *vi* [*liquid*] to gush out; [*tears*] to flow; [*flame*] to shoot up; [*truth*] to emerge.
jais /ʒɛ/ *nm inv* **1** jet; **2 (noir) de ~** jet-black.
jalon /ʒalɔ̃/ *nm* **1** marker; **2** (figurative) **poser les ~s de** to prepare the ground for.
jalonner /ʒalɔne/ [1] *vtr* **1** [*trees*] to line [*road*]; [*incidents*] to punctuate [*career*]; **2** to mark out [*road*].
jalouser /ʒaluze/ [1] *vtr* to be jealous of.
jalousie /ʒaluzi/ *nf* **1** jealousy; **2** slatted blind.
jaloux, **-ouse** /ʒalu, uz/ **I** *adj* jealous.
II *nm,f* jealous man/woman.
jamais /ʒamɛ/ *adv* **1** never; **rien n'est ~ certain** nothing is ever certain; **sait-on ~?** you never know; **~ de la vie!** never!; **2** ever; **plus belle que ~** prettier than ever; **si ~** if; **3 à tout ~** forever; **4 ne... ~ que** only; **il ne fait ~ que son devoir** he is only doing his duty.
jambe /ʒɑ̃b/ *nf* leg; **avoir de bonnes ~s** to have strong legs; **courir à toutes ~s** to run as fast as one's legs can carry one; **j'ai les ~s comme du coton**○ I feel weak at the knees; **traîner la ~**○ to trudge along.
IDIOMS **cela me fait une belle ~**○ a fat lot of good○ that does me; **il ne tient plus sur ses ~s** he can hardly stand up; **prendre ses ~s à son cou** to take to one's heels; **tenir la ~ à qn** to keep talking to sb; **par-dessus** or **par-dessous la ~** in a slipshod manner.
jambon /ʒɑ̃bɔ̃/ *nm* ham.
■ **~ blanc** or **de Paris** cooked ham; **~ de pays** cured ham.
jambonneau, *pl* **~x** /ʒɑ̃bɔno/ *nm* knuckle of ham.
jante /ʒɑ̃t/ *nf* **1** rim; **2** wheel.
janvier /ʒɑ̃vje/ *nm* January.
Japon /ʒapɔ̃/ *pr nm* Japan.
japonais, **~e** /ʒapɔnɛ, ɛz/ **I** *adj* Japanese.
II *nm* (language) Japanese.
japper /ʒape/ [1] *vi* to yap.
jaquette /ʒakɛt/ *nf* **1** morning coat; **2** dust jacket; **3** (on tooth) crown.
jardin /ʒaʀdɛ̃/ *nm* garden (GB), yard (US); **chaise de ~** garden chair (GB), patio chair (US).
■ **~ d'acclimatation** = **~ zoologique**; **~ d'agrément** ornamental garden; **~ d'enfants** kindergarten; **~ potager** vegetable garden; **~ public** park; **~ zoologique** zoo.
jardinage /ʒaʀdinaʒ/ *nm* gardening.
jardiner /ʒaʀdine/ [1] *vi* to do some gardening.
jardinier, **-ière**[1] /ʒaʀdinje, ɛʀ/ **I** *adj* garden.
II *nm,f* gardener.
jardinière[2] /ʒaʀdinjɛʀ/ *nf* jardinière.
jargon /ʒaʀgɔ̃/ *nm* **1** jargon; **~ administratif** officialese; **2** gibberish.
jarre /ʒaʀ/ *nf* (earthenware) jar.
jarret /ʒaʀɛ/ *nm* **1** (of human) ham, hollow of the knee; **2** (of animal) hock; **3** (Culin) **~ de veau** knuckle of veal.
jarretelle /ʒaʀtɛl/ *nf* suspender (GB), garter (US).
jars /ʒaʀ/ *nm inv* gander.
jaser /ʒaze/ [1] *vi* to gossip.
jasmin /ʒasmɛ̃/ *nm* jasmine.
jatte /ʒat/ *nf* bowl, basin.
jauge /ʒoʒ/ *nf* gauge; **~ d'huile** dipstick.
jaunâtre /ʒonɑtʀ/ *adj* yellowish.
jaune /ʒon/ **I** *adj* yellow; **~ d'or** golden yellow; **~ paille** straw-coloured[GB]; **~ poussin** bright yellow; **teint ~** sallow complexion.
II *nm* **1** yellow; **2 ~ (d'œuf)** (egg) yolk; **3** blackleg (GB), scab.
IDIOMS **rire ~**○ to give a forced laugh.
jaunir /ʒoniʀ/ [3] **I** *vtr* to turn [sth] yellow, to make [sth] go yellow.
II *vi* to go yellow.
jaunisse /ʒonis/ *nf* jaundice; **il va en faire une ~**○! that'll put his nose out of joint!
java /ʒava/ *nf* **1** popular dance; **2**○ rave-up○.
Javel /ʒavɛl/ *nf* **(eau de) ~** ≈ bleach.
javelot /ʒavlo/ *nm* javelin.
J.-C. (*written abbr* = **Jésus-Christ**) **avant ~** BC; **après ~** AD.
je (**j'** *before vowel or mute h*) /ʒ(ə)/ *pron* I.
jean /dʒin/ *nm* **1** (pair of) jeans; **2** denim.
je-ne-sais-quoi /ʒənsɛkwa/ *nm inv* **avoir un ~** to have a certain something.
jérémiades /ʒeʀemjad/ *nf pl* moaning.
jerrican /ʒeʀikan/ *nm* jerrycan.
jersey /ʒɛʀzɛ/ *nm* **1** jersey; **2** stocking stitch.
jésuite /ʒezɥit/ *adj*, *nm* Jesuit.
Jésus /ʒezy/ *pr n* Jesus.
jet[1] /ʒɛ/ *nm* **1** throwing; throw; **2** jet; spurt;

burst; **passer au ~** to hose down; **premier ~** (figurative) first sketch; **d'un seul ~** [*write*] in one go.
■ **~ d'eau** fountain; hosepipe.

jet[2] /dʒɛt/ *nm* jet (plane).

jetable /ʒətabl/ *adj* disposable.

jetée /ʒəte/ *nf* pier; jetty.

jeter /ʒəte/ [20] **I** *vtr* **1** to throw; to hurl; to throw away or out; **~ qch à qn** to throw sth to sb [*ball*]; to throw sth at sb [*stone*]; **~ qn dehors** to throw sb out; **~ quelques idées sur le papier** (figurative) to jot down a few ideas; **bon à ~** fit for the bin (GB) or the garbage (US); **2** to give [*cry, light*]; to cast [*glance, shadow*]; **3** to create [*confusion, terror*]; **~ l'émoi dans la ville** to throw the town into turmoil.
II se jeter *v refl* (+ *v être*) **1 se ~ du haut d'un pont** to throw oneself off a bridge; **se ~ sur** to fall upon [*opponent*]; to pounce on [*prey, newspaper*]; **se ~ au cou de qn** to fling oneself around sb's neck; **se ~ à l'eau** to jump into the water; (figurative) to take the plunge; **(aller) se ~ contre un arbre** to crash into a tree; **2** [*river*] to flow.

jeton /ʒ(ə)tɔ̃/ *nm* (for machine) token; (in board games) counter; (at casino) chip.

jeu, *pl* **~x** /ʒø/ *nm* **1 le ~** play; **un ~** a game; **faire un ~** to play a game; **par ~** for fun; **entrer en ~** to come into the picture; **se prendre** or **se piquer au ~** to get hooked; **mettre en ~** to bring [sth] into play; to stake; **hors ~** offside; **ils ont beau ~ de me critiquer** it's easy for them to criticize me; **2 le ~** gambling; **ton avenir est en ~** your future is at stake; **3** (in cards) hand; **cacher bien son ~** (figurative) to keep it quiet; **4** (of cards) deck; **~ d'échecs** chess set; **5** (of actor) acting; (of musician) playing; (of sportsman) game; **6** (of keys, spanners) set.
■ **~ d'argent** game played for money; **~ de construction** construction set; **~ de massacre** ≈ coconut shy (GB); **~ de mots** pun; **~ de l'oie** ≈ snakes and ladders (GB); **~ de société** board game; party game; **~ télévisé** (TV) game show; **~x Olympiques, JO** Olympic Games.
IDIOMS **jouer le ~** to play the game; **c'est pas de** or **du ~**○**!** that's not fair!; **faire le ~ de qn** to play into sb's hands.

jeu-concours, *pl* **jeux-concours** /ʒøkɔ̃kuʀ/ *nm* competition.

jeudi /ʒødi/ *nm* Thursday.
IDIOMS **ça aura lieu la semaine des quatre ~s**○**!** it won't happen, not in a month of Sundays!

jeun: **à jeun** /aʒœ̃/ *phr* **1** on an empty stomach; **2**○ sober.

jeune /ʒœn/ **I** *adj* **1** (gen) young; [*industry*] new; [*face, hairstyle*] youthful; **nos ~s années** our youth; **le ~ âge** youth; **le ~ marié** the groom; **la ~ mariée** the bride; **2** younger; **mon ~ frère** my younger brother.
II *nmf* young person; **les ~s** young people.
III *adv* **s'habiller ~** to wear young styles; **faire ~** to look young.
■ **~ femme** young woman; **~ fille** girl; **~ homme** young man; **~ loup** up-and-coming executive; **~ premier** romantic lead.

jeûne /ʒøn/ *nm* **1** fasting; fast; **2** period of fasting.

jeûner /ʒøne/ [1] *vi* to fast.

jeunesse /ʒœnɛs/ *nf* **1** youth; **une seconde ~** a new lease of life; **une erreur de ~** a youthful indiscretion; **2** young people.
IDIOMS **il faut que ~ se passe** youth will have its course; **les voyages forment la ~** travel broadens the mind.

jf *written abbr* = **jeune femme** or **fille**; ▶**jeune**.

jh *written abbr* = **jeune homme**; ▶**jeune**.

joaillerie /ʒɔajʀi/ *nf* **1** jeweller's shop (GB), jewelry store (US); **2** jewellery (GB), jewelry (US).

joaillier, -ière /ʒɔalje, ɛʀ/ *nm,f* jeweller (GB), jeweler (US).

joggeur, -euse /dʒɔgœʀ, øz/ *nm,f* jogger.

joie /ʒwa/ *nf* joy; **au comble de la ~** overjoyed; **se faire une ~ de faire** to look forward to doing; to be delighted to do.
IDIOMS **s'en donner à cœur ~** to enjoy oneself to the full; (figurative) to have a field day.

joindre /ʒwɛ̃dʀ/ [56] **I** *vtr* **1** to get hold of [*person*]; **2** to enclose [*cheque*]; to attach [*card*]; **3** to link [*points*]; to put [sth] together [*planks, feet*]; **~ l'intelligence à la simplicité** to be intelligent without being pretentious.
II se joindre *v refl* (+ *v être*) **1 se ~ à** to join [*person, group*]; to join in [*conversation*]; **2** [*lips*] to meet; [*hands*] to join.
IDIOMS **~ les deux bouts**○ to make ends meet.

joint /ʒwɛ̃/ *nm* (in wood) joint; (on pipes) seal.

jointure /ʒwɛ̃tyʀ/ *nf* joint.

joli, ~e /ʒɔli/ **I** *adj* (gen) nice; [*face*] pretty; [*sum*] tidy; **faire ~** to look nice.
II *nm* **c'est du ~!** (ironic) very nice!
■ **~ cœur** smooth talker; **faire le ~ cœur** to play Romeo.
IDIOMS **être ~ à croquer** or **comme un cœur** to be as pretty as a picture.

joliment /ʒɔlimɑ̃/ *adv* **1** prettily, nicely; **2**○ [*happy, well*] really; [*handle*] nicely.

jonc /ʒɔ̃/ *nm* rush.

joncher /ʒɔ̃ʃe/ [1] *vtr* [*papers, leaves*] to be strewn over [*ground*].

jonction /ʒɔ̃ksjɔ̃/ *nf* **1** junction; **2** link-up.

jongler /ʒɔ̃gle/ [1] *vi* to juggle.

jonque /ʒɔ̃k/ *nf* junk.

jonquille /ʒɔ̃kij/ *nf* daffodil.

jouable /ʒwabl/ *adj* **1** feasible; **le pari est ~** the gamble might pay off; **2** [*piece of music*] playable; **une pièce qui n'est pas ~** a play that's impossible to stage.

joue /ʒu/ *nf* **1** cheek; **2** (Mil) **en ~!** aim!; **mettre qn en ~** to take aim at sb.

jouer /ʒwe/ [1] **I** *vtr* **1** [*children, musician*] to play; **2** to back [*horse*]; to stake [*money*]; to risk [*reputation, life*]; **c'est joué d'avance** it's a foregone conclusion; **tout n'est pas encore joué** the game isn't over yet; **~ le tout pour le tout** to go for broke○; **3 qu'est-ce qu'on joue au théâtre/cinéma?** what's on at the theatre/cinema?; **4 ~ les imbéciles** to play dumb.

II **jouer à** *v+prep* to play [*tennis, game*]; to play with [*doll*]; **~ à qui perd gagne** to play 'loser takes all'; **~ à la marchande** to play shops.

III **jouer de** *v+prep* **1 ~ de** to play [*instrument*]; **2 ~ de** to use [*influence*].

IV *vi* **1** to play; **arrête de ~ avec ta bague!** stop fiddling with your ring!; **à toi de ~!** your turn!; (figurative) the ball's in your court!; **bien joué!** well played!; (figurative) well done!; **2** to gamble; **~ avec** to gamble with [*life, health*]; **~ aux courses** to bet on the horses; **~ sur** to bank on [*credulity*]; **3** to act; **il joue bien** he's a good actor; **4** [*argument, clause*] to apply; [*age*] to matter; **faire ~ ses relations** to make use of one's connections.

V **se jouer** *v refl* (+ *v être*) **1** [*future, peace*] to be at stake; [*drama*] to be played out; **2 se ~ de** to make light work of [*obstacle*].

jouet /ʒwɛ/ *nm* **1** toy; **2** plaything.

joueur, **-euse** /ʒwœʀ, øz/ I *adj* **1** playful; **2 être ~/joueuse** to be a gambling man/woman.

II *nm,f* **1** player; **être beau/mauvais ~** to be a good/bad loser; **2** gambler.

joufflu, **~e** /ʒufly/ *adj* [*person*] chubby-cheeked; [*face*] chubby.

joug /ʒu/ *nm* yoke.

jouir /ʒwiʀ/ [3] *v+prep* **~ de** to enjoy; to enjoy the use of [*property*]; [*place*] to have [*view, climate*].

jouissance /ʒwisɑ̃s/ *nf* **1** (Law) use; **2** pleasure.

joujou, *pl* **~x** /ʒuʒu/ *nm* (baby talk) toy.

jour /ʒuʀ/ *nm* **1** day; **quel ~ sommes-nous?** what day is it today?; **un ~ ou l'autre** some day; **~ pour ~** to the day; **à ce ~** to date; **à ~** up to date; **mettre à ~** to bring up to date [*work*]; to revise [*edition*]; **mise à ~** updating; **de nos ~s** nowadays; **d'un ~ à l'autre** [*expected*] any day now; [*change*] from one day to the next; **du ~ au lendemain** overnight; **d'un ~** [*fashion*] passing; [*queen*] for a day; **vivre au ~ le ~** to live one day at a time; **le ~ se lève** it's getting light; **au lever du ~** at daybreak; **le petit ~** the early morning; **de ~** [*work*] days; [*travel*] in the daytime; **2** daylight; light; **en plein ~** in broad daylight; **se faire ~** [*truth*] to come to light; **éclairer qch d'un ~ nouveau** to shed new light on sth; **je t'ai vu sous ton vrai ~** I saw you in your true colours[GB]; **3** (figurative) **donner le ~ à qn** to bring sb into the world; **voir le ~** [*person*] to come into the world; [*work of art*] to see the light of day; **mes ~s sont comptés** my days are numbered; **des ~s difficiles** hard times; **les beaux ~s reviennent** spring will soon be here; **4** (in wall) gap; **~s** openwork (embroidery).

■ **~ de l'An** New Year's Day; **~ férié** bank holiday (GB), legal holiday (US); **~ de fermeture** closing day; **~ ouvrable** working day.

journal, *pl* **-aux** /ʒuʀnal, o/ *nm* **1** newspaper; **2** magazine; **3** news (bulletin); **4** journal.

■ **~ de bord** logbook; **~ intime** diary; **Journal officiel** *government publication listing new acts, laws etc.*

journalier, **-ière** /ʒuʀnalje, ɛʀ/ *adj* daily.

journalisme /ʒuʀnalism/ *nm* journalism.

journaliste /ʒuʀnalist/ *nmf* journalist.

journalistique /ʒuʀnalistik/ *adj* journalistic.

journée /ʒuʀne/ *nf* day; **~ de repos** day off; **dans la ~** during the day; **la ~ d'hier/de mardi** yesterday/Tuesday; **faire des ~s de huit heures** to work an eight-hour day.

joute /ʒut/ *nf* **1** (figurative) jousting, battle; **~ oratoire** or **verbale** sparring match; **2** joust.

jouvence /ʒuvɑ̃s/ *nf* **fontaine de ~** Fountain of Youth.

jouxter /ʒukste/ [1] *vtr* to adjoin.

jovial, **~e**, *mpl* **~s** or **-iaux** /ʒɔvjal, o/ *adj* jovial.

joyau, *pl* **~x** /ʒwajo/ *nm* jewel, gem.

joyeusement /ʒwajøzmɑ̃/ *adv* merrily, cheerfully.

joyeux, **-euse** /ʒwajø, øz/ *adj* merry, cheerful.

jubilation /ʒybilasjɔ̃/ *nf* joy, jubilation.

jubilé /ʒybile/ *nm* jubilee.

jubiler /ʒybile/ [1] *vi* to be jubilant.

jucher /ʒyʃe/ [1] *vtr*, **se jucher** *v refl* (+ *v être*) to perch.

judaïsme /ʒydaism/ *nm* Judaism.

judas /ʒyda/ *nm inv* peephole.

judiciaire /ʒydisjɛʀ/ *adj* judicial.

judicieux, **-ieuse** /ʒydisjø, øz/ *adj* judicious, sensible.

judo /ʒydo/ *nm* judo.

juge /ʒyʒ/ *nm* judge; **être à la fois ~ et partie** to be judge and jury.

■ **~ d'instruction** examining magistrate; **~ de touche** linesman.

jugé: **au jugé** /oʒyʒe/ *phr* [*value*] by guesswork; [*shoot*] blind.

jugement /ʒyʒmɑ̃/ *nm* judgment; **passer en ~** [*case*] to come to court.

jugeote○ /ʒyʒɔt/ *nf* common sense.

juger /ʒyʒe/ [13] **I** *vtr* **1** to judge [*person, competition*]; **mal ~ qn** to misjudge sb; **2** to consider; **~ utile de faire** to consider it useful to do; **3** (Law) to try [*case*]; to judge [*case*]; **le tribunal jugera** the court will decide.

II **juger de** *v+prep* to assess; **j'en jugerai par moi-même** I'll judge for myself; **à en ~ par** judging by.

juguler /ʒygyle/ [1] *vtr* to stamp out [*epidemic, uprising*]; to curb [*inflation*].

juif, **juive** /ʒɥif, ʒɥiv/ **I** *adj* Jewish.

II *nm,f* Jew.

juillet /ʒɥijɛ/ *nm* July; **le 14 ~** Bastille Day.

juin /ʒɥɛ̃/ *nm* June.

juive ▸ **juif**.

jumeau, **-elle**[1], *mpl* **~x** /ʒymo, ɛl/ *adj, nm,f* twin.

jumelage /ʒymlaʒ/ *nm* twinning.

jumeler /ʒymle/ [19] *vtr* to twin.

jumelle[2] /ʒymɛl/ *nf*, **jumelles** *nf pl* binoculars; **~s de théâtre** opera glasses.

jument /ʒymɑ̃/ *nf* mare.

jungle /ʒœ̃gl/ *nf* jungle.

jupe /ʒyp/ *nf* skirt.
IDIOMS **il est toujours dans les ~s de sa mère** he's tied to his mother's apron strings.

jupe-culotte, *pl* **jupes-culottes** /ʒypkylɔt/ *nf* culottes, divided skirt.

jupon /ʒypɔ̃/ *nm* petticoat.
IDIOMS **courir le ~** to womanize.

juré, **~e** /ʒyʀe/ **I** *pp* ▶**jurer**.
II *pp adj* **1** on oath; sworn-in; **2** [*enemy*] sworn.
III *nm* juror; **les ~s** the members of the jury.

jurer /ʒyʀe/ [1] **I** *vtr* to swear; **on leur a fait ~ le secret** they were sworn to secrecy; **~ de tuer qn** to vow to kill sb; **ah mais je te jure**○! honestly○!
II jurer de *v+prep* to swear to.
III *vi* **1** to swear; **2** [*colours*] to clash; **3 ne ~ que par** to swear by.
IV se jurer *v refl* (+ *v être*) **1** to swear [sth] to one another; **2** to vow.
IDIOMS **il ne faut ~ de rien** (Proverb) never say never.

juridiction /ʒyʀidiksjɔ̃/ *nf* **1** jurisdiction; **2** courts.

juridique /ʒyʀidik/ *adj* legal; **vide ~** gap in the law.

jurisprudence /ʒyʀispʀydɑ̃s/ *nf* case law.

juriste /ʒyʀist/ *nmf* **1** jurist; **2** lawyer.

juron /ʒyʀɔ̃/ *nm* swearword.

jury /ʒyʀi/ *nm* **1** jury; **2** panel of judges; **3** board of examiners.

jus /ʒy/ *nm inv* **1** juice; **2** (from meat) juices; gravy; **3** electricity; **prendre le ~** to get a shock.

jusque (**jusqu'** *before vowel*) /ʒysk/ **I** *prep* **1 aller jusqu'à Paris** to go as far as Paris; to go all the way to Paris; **courir jusqu'au bout du jardin** to run right down to the bottom of the garden (GB) or the end of the yard (US); **suivre qn ~ dans sa chambre** to follow sb right into his/her room; **la nouvelle est arrivée jusqu'à nous** the news has reached us; **jusqu'où comptez-vous aller?** how far do you intend to go?; **2 jusqu'à, jusqu'en** until, till; **jusqu'à présent, jusqu'ici** (up) until now; **3 monter jusqu'à 20°** to go up to 20°; **4** to the point of; **aller jusqu'à faire** to go so far as to do; **5** even; **des détritus ~ sous la table** rubbish everywhere, even under the table.
II jusqu'à ce que *phr* until.

jusque-là /ʒyskəla/ *adv* **1** until then, up to then; **2** up to here; up to there.
IDIOMS **en avoir ~ de qn/qch**○ to have had it up to here with sb/sth○; **s'en mettre ~**○ to stuff one's face○.

juste /ʒyst/ **I** *adj* **1** [*person*] just, fair; **2** [*cause*] just; [*anger*] righteous; [*word, answer*] right, correct; **3** [*balance, watch*] accurate; **~ milieu** happy medium; **à ~ titre** with good reason; **dire des choses ~s** to make some valid points; **apprécier qn à sa ~ valeur** to get a fair picture of sb; **4** (Mus) [*piano, voice*] in tune; [*note*] true; **5 c'est un peu ~** (in width, time) it's a bit tight; (in quantity) it's barely enough.
II *adv* **1** [*sing*] in tune; [*guess*] right; **elle a vu ~** she was right; **viser ~** to aim straight; **2** just; **~ à temps** just in time; **3** (**tout**) **~** only just; **j'arrive ~** I've only just arrived; **c'est tout ~ s'il sait lire** he can hardly read.
III au juste *phr* exactly.
IV *nm* righteous man; **les ~s** the righteous.

justement /ʒystəmɑ̃/ *adv* **1** precisely; **2** just; **3** correctly; **4** justifiably.

justesse /ʒystɛs/ **I** *nf* **1** correctness; **avec ~** correctly; **2** accuracy; **avec ~** accurately.
II de justesse *phr* [*succeed*] only just.

justice /ʒystis/ *nf* **1** justice; **rendre la ~** to dispense justice; **il faut leur rendre cette ~ qu'ils sont...** one has to acknowledge that they are...; **ce n'est que ~** it is only fair; **se faire ~** to take the law into one's own hands; to take one's own life; **2 la ~** the law; the legal system; the courts; **action en ~** legal action.

justicier, **-ière** /ʒystisje, ɛʀ/ *nm,f* righter of wrongs.

justificatif, **-ive** /ʒystifikatif, iv/ *nm* documentary evidence; **~ de domicile** proof of domicile; **~ de frais** receipt.

justification /ʒystifikasjɔ̃/ *nf* **1** justification; **2** explanation; documentary evidence.

justifier /ʒystifje/ [2] **I** *vtr* to justify [*method, absence*]; to vindicate [*guilty party*]; to explain [*ignorance*]; **les faits ont justifié nos craintes** events proved our fears to have been justified; **tu essaies toujours de la ~** you are always making excuses for her.
II justifier de *v+prep* to give proof of.
III se justifier *v refl* (+ *v être*) **1** to make excuses; (in court) to clear oneself; **2** [*decision*] to be justified (by).

jute /ʒyt/ *nm* jute; **(toile de) ~** hessian.

juteux, **-euse** /ʒytø, øz/ *adj* [*fruit*] juicy.

juvénile /ʒyvenil/ *adj* youthful; juvenile.

juxtaposer /ʒykstapoze/ [1] *vtr* to juxtapose.

Kk

k, K /ka/ *nm inv* k, K.

kaki /kaki/ **I** *adj inv* khaki.
II *nm* **1** persimmon; **2** khaki.

kaléidoscope /kaleidɔskɔp/ *nm* kaleidoscope.

kangourou /kɑ̃guʀu/ **I** *adj inv* **poche ~** front pocket; **slip ~** pouch-front briefs.
II *nm* **1** kangaroo; **2** ®baby carrier.

karaté /kaʀate/ *nm* karate.

kart /kaʀt/ *nm* go-kart.

karting /kaʀtiŋ/ *nm* go-karting; **faire du ~** to go karting.

kasher /kaʃɛʀ/ *adj inv* kosher.

kayak /kajak/ *nm* kayak; **faire du ~** to go kayaking.

képi /kepi/ *nm* kepi.

kermesse /kɛʀmɛs/ *nf* fete.

kF *written abbr* = **kilofranc**.

kibboutz, *pl* **-tzim** /kibuts, kibutsim/ *nm* kibbutz.

kick /kik/ *nm* kick-start.

kidnapper /kidnape/ [1] *vtr* to kidnap; **se faire ~** to be kidnapped.

kidnappeur, **-euse** /kidnapœʀ, øz/ *nm,f* kidnapper.

kif-kif○ /kifkif/ *adj inv* **c'est ~ (bourricot)** it's all the same.

kilo[1] /kilo/ *pref* kilo.

kilo[2] /kilo/ *nm* (*abbr* = **kilogramme**) kilo; **prendre des ~s** to put on weight.

kilofranc /kilɔfʀɑ̃/ *nm* 1,000 French francs.

kilogramme /kilɔgʀam/ *nm* kilogram.

kilométrage /kilɔmetʀaʒ/ *nm* ≈ mileage.

kilomètre /kilɔmɛtʀ/ *nm* kilometre[GB].

kilomètre-heure *pl* **kilomètres-heure** /kilɔmɛtʀœʀ/ *nm* kilometre[GB] per hour.

kilométrique /kilɔmetʀik/ *adj* [*distance*] in kilometres[GB]; [*price*] per kilometre[GB].

kilo-octet /kilɔɔktɛ/ *nm* kilobyte.

kilotonne /kilɔtɔn/ *nf* kiloton.

kilowattheure /kilɔwatœʀ/ *nm* kilowatt-hour.

kimono /kimɔno/ *nm* **1** kimono; **2** judo suit.

kinésithérapeute /kineziteʀapøt/ *nmf* physiotherapist (GB), physical therapist (US).

kinésithérapie /kineziteʀapi/ *nf* physiotherapy (GB), physical therapy (US).

kiosque /kjɔsk/ *nm* kiosk.
■ **~ à musique** bandstand.

kiwi /kiwi/ *nm* kiwi.

klaxon® /klaksɔn/ *nm* (car) horn.

klaxonner /klaksɔne/ [1] *vi* to sound one's horn (GB), to honk the horn.

kleptomane /klɛptɔman/ *adj, nmf* kleptomaniac.

knock-out /nɔkaut/ **I** *adj inv* knocked out.
II *nm* knockout.

Ko (*written abbr* = **kilo-octet**) KB.

KO /kao/ **I** *adj inv* (*abbr* = **knocked out**) **1** KO'd○; **mettre qn ~** to KO○ sb; **2**○ exhausted.
II *nm* (*abbr* = **knockout**) KO○.

koala /kɔala/ *nm* koala (bear).

krach /kʀak/ *nm* (on stock exchange) crash.

kraft /kʀaft/ *nm* **(papier) ~** brown paper.

K-way® /kawe/ *nm* windcheater (GB), windbreaker (US).

kyrielle /kiʀjɛl/ *nf* **une ~ de** a string of.

kyste /kist/ *nm* cyst.

l, **L** /ɛl/ *nm inv* **1** (letter) l, L; **2** (*written abbr* = **litre**) **20 l** 20 l.

l' ▶ **le**.

la[1] *det, pron* ▶ **le**.

la[2] /la/ *nm* (Mus) (note) A; (in sol-fa) lah; **donner le ~** to give an A; (figurative) to set the tone.

là /la/ *adv* **1** there; here; **viens ~** come here; **~ où je travaille** where I work; **pas par ici, par ~** not this way, that way; **de ~ au village** from there to the village; **2** then; **d'ici ~** between now and then; by then; **et ~, le téléphone a sonné** and then the phone rang; **en ce temps-~** in those days; **ce jour-~** that day; **3 s'il en est (arrivé) ~, c'est que...** if he's got to that point, it's because...; **alors ~ tu exagères!** now you're going too far!; **que vas-tu chercher ~?** what are you thinking of?; **il a fallu en passer par ~** there was no alternative; **qu'entendez-vous par ~?** what do you mean by that?; **si tu vas par ~** if you are saying that; **de ~** hence; from that.

là-bas /labɑ/ *adv* over there.

labo○ /labo/ *nm* lab○.

laboratoire /labɔʀatwaʀ/ *nm* laboratory.
■ **~ d'analyses médicales** medical laboratory; **~ de langues** language laboratory; **~ pharmaceutique** pharmaceutical company.

laborieux, **-ieuse** /labɔʀjø, øz/ *adj* **1** [*work, process*] arduous; [*style*] laboured[GB]; **2 les classes laborieuses** the working classes.

labour /labuʀ/ *nm* ploughing (GB), plowing (US); **cheval de ~** plough (GB) or plow (US) horse.

labourer /labuʀe/ [1] *vtr* to plough (GB), to plow (US).

labyrinthe /labiʀɛ̃t/ *nm* maze; labyrinth.

lac /lak/ *nm* **1** lake; **2** reservoir.

lacer /lase/ [12] *vtr* to lace up [*shoes, corset*].

lacérer /laseʀe/ [14] *vtr* to lacerate; to slash.

lacet /lasɛ/ *nm* **1** lace; **chaussures à ~s** lace-up shoes; **nouer ses ~s** to do up one's laces; **2** (in road) **une route en ~s** a twisting road.

lâche /lɑʃ/ **I** *adj* **1** [*person, crime*] cowardly; **2** [*belt*] loose; **3** [*regulation*] lax.
II *nmf* coward.

lâcher[1] /lɑʃe/ [1] **I** *vtr* **1** to drop [*object*]; to let go of [*rope*]; **lâche-moi** let go of me; (figurative)○ give me a break○; **~ prise** to lose one's grip; **2** to reveal [*information*]; to let out [*scream*]; **3** to let [sb/sth] go [*person, animal*]; **4** to drop [*friend, activity*]; **la peur ne la lâche plus depuis** she's been living in constant terror ever since.
II *vi* [*rope*] to give way; [*brakes*] to fail; **ses nerfs ont lâché** he/she went to pieces.

lâcher[2] /lɑʃe/ *nm* (of balloons, birds) release.

lâcheté /lɑʃte/ *nf* **1** cowardice; **par ~** out of cowardice; **2** cowardly act.

lacrymal, **~e**, *mpl* **-aux** /lakʀimal, o/ *adj* lachrymal.

lacrymogène /lakʀimɔʒɛn/ *adj* [*grenade, bomb*] teargas; **gaz ~** teargas.

lacté, **~e** /lakte/ *adj* **1** [*product*] milk; **2** [*liquid*] milky; **la voie ~e** the Milky Way.

lacune /lakyn/ *nf* (in knowledge, law) gap.

là-dedans /lad(ə)dɑ̃/ *adv* in here; in there; **et moi ~ qu'est-ce que je fais**○**?** and where do I come in?

là-dessous /lad(ə)su/ *adv* under here; under there; **il y a qch de louche ~**○ there's something fishy○ about all this.

là-dessus /lad(ə)sy/ *adv* **1** on here; on there; **2 qu'as-tu à dire ~?** what have you got to say about it?; **3 ~ il a raccroché** with that he hung up.

ladite ▶ **ledit**.

lagon /lagɔ̃/ *nm* lagoon.

lagune /lagyn/ *nf* lagoon.

là-haut /lao/ *adv* **1** up here; up there; **tout ~** (all the) way up there; **2** upstairs; **3** in heaven.

laïc /laik/ *nm* layman.

laïcité /laisite/ *nf* secularism; secularity.

laid, **~e** /lɛ, lɛd/ *adj* **1** ugly; **2** disgusting.

laideur /lɛdœʀ/ *nf* ugliness.

lainage /lɛnaʒ/ *nm* **1** woollen[GB] material; **2** woollen[GB] garment.

laine /lɛn/ *nf* wool; **de** or **en ~** woollen[GB], wool.
■ **~ peignée** worsted; **~ de verre** glass wool; **~ vierge** new wool (GB), virgin wool.

laïque /laik/ **I** *adj* [*school*] nondenominational (GB), public (US); [*state, mind*] secular.
II *nmf* layman/laywoman; **les ~s** lay people.

laisse /lɛs/ *nf* (for dog) lead (GB), leash (US).

laissé-pour-compte, **laissée-pour-compte**, *mpl* **laissés-pour-compte** /lesepuʀkɔ̃t/ *nm,f* **les laissés-pour-compte** (gen) the forgotten people; **les laissés-pour-compte de la révolution technologique** the casualties of the technological revolution.

laisser /lese/ [1] **I** *vtr* to leave; **~ la liberté à qn** to let sb go free; **je te laisse** I must go; **~ le choix à qn** to give sb the choice; **laisse ce jouet à ton frère** let your brother have the toy; **laisse-le, ça lui passera** ignore him, he'll get over it; **cela me laisse sceptique** I'm sceptical (GB) or skeptical (US).
II *v aux* **~ qn/qch faire** to let sb/sth do; **laisse-moi faire** let me do it; leave it to me; **laisse faire!** so what!
III se laisser *v refl* (+ *v être*) **se ~ bercer par les vagues** to be lulled by the waves; **il se laisse insulter** he puts up with insults; **elle n'est pas du genre à se ~ faire** she won't be pushed around; **il ne veut pas se ~ faire** he

won't let you touch him; **se ~ aller** to let oneself go.

laisser-aller /lesеale/ *nm inv* **1** scruffiness; **2** sloppiness.

laissez-passer /lesepase/ *nm inv* pass.

lait /lɛ/ *nm* milk.
■ **~ de chaux** whitewash; **~ concentré non sucré** evaporated milk; **~ demi-écrémé** low-fat milk; **~ écrémé** skimmed milk (GB), skim or nonfat milk (US); **~ maternel** breastmilk; **~ de poule** eggnog.

laitage /lɛtaʒ/ *nm* dairy product.

laitance /lɛtɑ̃s/ *nf* (Culin, Zool) soft roe.

laiterie /lɛtʀi/ *nf* **1** dairy; **2** dairy industry.

laiteux, -euse /lɛtø, øz/ *adj* [*liquid, white*] milky; [*complexion*] creamy.

laitier, -ière /lɛtje, ɛʀ/ **I** *adj* [*industry, product*] dairy; [*production, cow*] milk.
II *nm,f* milkman/milkwoman.

laiton /lɛtɔ̃/ *nm* brass.

laitue /lɛty/ *nf* lettuce.

laïus○ /lajys/ *nm inv* speech.

lama /lama/ *nm* **1** (animal) llama; **2** (religious leader) lama.

lambda○ /lɑ̃bda/ *adj inv* average.

lambeau, *pl* **~x** /lɑ̃bo/ *nm* (of cloth) rag; (of paper, hide) strip; (of flesh) bit.

lambris /lɑ̃bʀi/ *nm inv* panelling[GB]; marble walls; (on ceiling) mouldings (GB), moldings (US).

lambrisser /lɑ̃bʀise/ [1] *vtr* to panel.

lame /lam/ *nf* **1** (of knife, saw) blade; **2** knife; **3** sword; **une fine ~** an expert swordsman; **4** (of metal, wood) strip; (on blind) slat.
■ **~ de fond** ground swell; (figurative) upheaval; **~ de rasoir** razor blade.

lamé /lame/ *nm* lamé; **en ~** lamé.

lamelle /lamɛl/ *nf* **1** (of wood, metal) small strip; **2** (Culin) sliver; **découper en fines ~s** to slice thinly; **3** (Bot) (of mushroom) gill.

lamentable /lamɑ̃tabl/ *adj* pathetic, awful.

lamentablement /lamɑ̃tabləmɑ̃/ *adv* [*fail*] miserably; [*cry*] piteously.

lamentation /lamɑ̃tasjɔ̃/ *nf* wailing.

lamenter: **se lamenter** /lamɑ̃te/ [1] *v refl* (+ *v être*) to moan; **se ~ sur son propre sort** to feel sorry for oneself.

lampadaire /lɑ̃padɛʀ/ *nm* **1** standard (GB) or floor (US) lamp; **2** streetlight.

lampe /lɑ̃p/ *nf* **1** lamp, light; **2** (light) bulb.
■ **~ à bronzer** sun lamp; **~ de chevet** bedside light; **~ électrique** torch (GB), flashlight (US); **~ de poche** pocket torch (GB), flashlight (US); **~ témoin** indicator light; **~ tempête** hurricane lamp.

lampée○ /lɑ̃pe/ *nf* gulp.

lampion /lɑ̃pjɔ̃/ *nm* paper lantern.

lance /lɑ̃s/ *nf* (gen) spear; (in jousting) lance.
■ **~ d'incendie** fire hose nozzle.

lancée /lɑ̃se/ *nf* **sur ma ~** while I was at it; **continuer sur sa ~** to continue to forge ahead.

lancement /lɑ̃smɑ̃/ *nm* **1** (of ship, company) launching; (of process) setting up; **2** (of product, book) launch; (of loan) floating; (of actor) promotion; **3** (of missile) launching; launch.

lance-pierres /lɑ̃spjɛʀ/ *nm inv* catapult.
IDIOMS **payer qn avec un ~**○ to pay sb peanuts○.

lancer[1] /lɑ̃se/ [12] **I** *vtr* **1** to throw [*ball, pebble, javelin*]; **~ le poids** to put the shot; **2** to launch [*rocket, ship*]; to fire [*arrow*]; to drop [*bomb*]; to start up [*engine*]; **3** to throw out [*smoke, flames*]; to give [*look*]; to put about [*rumour*]; to issue [*ultimatum*]; to send out [*invitation*]; **4** to hurl [*insult*]; to make [*accusation*]; **lança-t-il** he said.
II○ *vi* to throb; **mon doigt me lance** my finger is throbbing.
III se lancer *v refl* (+ *v être*) **1 se ~ dans des dépenses** to get involved in expense; **se ~ dans les affaires** to go into business; **2 se ~ dans le vide** to jump; **3** to throw [sth] to each other [*ball*]; to exchange [*insults*].

lancer[2] /lɑ̃se/ *nm* **1** (Sport) **~ du disque** discus event; **~ du poids** shot put (event); **2 le ~, la pêche au ~** rod and reel fishing.

lance-roquettes /lɑ̃sʀɔkɛt/ *nm inv* rocket launcher.

lancinant, ~e /lɑ̃sinɑ̃, ɑ̃t/ *adj* [*pain*] shooting; [*music, rhythm*] insistent.

landau /lɑ̃do/ *nm* pram (GB), baby carriage (US).

lande /lɑ̃d/ *nf* moor.

langage /lɑ̃gaʒ/ *nm* language.
■ **~ administratif** official jargon; **~ des sourds-muets** sign language.

lange /lɑ̃ʒ/ *nm* **1** swaddling clothes; **2** nappy (GB), diaper (US).

langer /lɑ̃ʒe/ [13] *vtr* **1** to wrap [sb] in swaddling clothes [*baby*]; **2** to put a nappy (GB) or diaper (US) on [*baby*].

langoureux, -euse /lɑ̃guʀø, øz/ *adj* languorous.

langouste /lɑ̃gust/ *nf* spiny lobster.

langoustine /lɑ̃gustin/ *nf* langoustine.

langue /lɑ̃g/ *nf* **1** tongue; **tirer la ~** to stick out one's tongue; (for doctor) to put out one's tongue; (figurative) to be dying of thirst; to struggle financially; **2** language; speech; **3 mauvaise ~** malicious gossip; **4 ~ de terre** spit of land.
■ **~ de bois** political cant; **~ maternelle** mother tongue; **~ verte** slang.
IDIOMS **avoir la ~ bien pendue**○ to be very talkative; **avoir qch sur le bout de la ~** to have sth on the tip of one's tongue.

languette /lɑ̃gɛt/ *nf* (on shoe) tongue; (on satchel, bag) strap; (of ham) long narrow strip.

langueur /lɑ̃gœʀ/ *nf* languor.

languir /lɑ̃giʀ/ [3] **I** *vi* **1** [*conversation*] to languish; [*economy*] to be sluggish; **2 je languis de vous revoir** I'm longing to see you; **faire ~ qn** to keep sb in suspense.
II se languir *v refl* (+ *v être*) to pine.

lanière /lanjɛʀ/ *nf* (gen) strap; (of whip) lash.

lanterne /lɑ̃tɛʀn/ *nf* **1** lantern; **2** (Aut) sidelight (GB), parking light (US).

IDIOMS **éclairer la ~ de qn** to enlighten sb.

laper /lape/ [1] *vtr* to lap (up) [*soup, milk*].

lapider /lapide/ [1] *vtr* **1** to stone [sb] to death; **2** to throw stones at.

lapin /lapɛ̃/ *nm* **1** rabbit; **~ de garenne** wild rabbit; **coup du ~** rabbit punch; (in accident) whiplash injury; **cage** or **cabane à ~s** rabbit hutch; (figurative)○ tower block; **2** rabbit(skin).
IDIOMS **poser un ~ à qn**○ to stand sb up; **se faire tirer comme des ~s**○ to be picked off like flies; **c'est un chaud ~**○ he's a randy devil.

lapine /lapin/ *nf* doe rabbit.

laps /laps/ *nm inv* **~ de temps** period of time.

lapsus /lapsys/ *nm inv* slip.

laquais /lakɛ/ *nm inv* lackey.

laque /lak/ *nf* **1** hairspray; **2** lacquer; gloss paint (GB), enamel (US).

laqué, **~e** /lake/ *adj* [*paint*] gloss.

laquelle ▸ **lequel**.

laquer /lake/ [1] *vtr* to lacquer; to paint [sth] in gloss (GB) or enamel (US).

larbin○ /laʀbɛ̃/ *nm* (derogatory) servant.

lard /laʀ/ *nm* ≈ fat streaky bacon.

larder /laʀde/ [1] *vtr* (Culin) to lard; **~ qn de coups de couteau** (figurative) to stab sb repeatedly.

lardon /laʀdɔ̃/ *nm* (Culin) bacon cube.

large /laʀʒ/ **I** *adj* **1** [*shoulders, hips*] broad; [*avenue, bed*] wide; [*coat*] loose-fitting; [*trousers*] loose; [*skirt*] full; [*jumper*] big; [*smile*] broad; [*curve*] long; **~ de trois mètres** three metres^GB wide; **2** [*advance, profit*] substantial; [*choice, public*] wide; [*majority*] large; **au sens ~** in a broad sense; **3** [*person*] generous; **4** [*life*] comfortable; **5 avoir les idées ~s, être ~ d'esprit** to be broad-minded.
II *adv* **1** [*plan*] on a generous scale; [*calculate, measure*] on the generous side; **2 s'habiller ~** to wear loose-fitting clothes.
III *nm* **1 faire quatre mètres de ~** to be four metres^GB wide; **2** open sea; **au ~** offshore.
IDIOMS **ne pas en mener ~**○ to be worried stiff○.

largement /laʀʒəmɑ̃/ *adv* **1** widely; **2** largely, to a large extent; **être ~ responsable de qch** to be largely responsible for sth; **3 arriver ~ en tête** to be a clear winner; **~ en dessous de la limite** well under the limit; **4 tu as ~ le temps** you've got plenty of time; **5** easily; **une chaîne en or vaudrait ~ le double** a gold chain would easily be worth twice as much; **6** [*contribute*] generously.

largesse /laʀʒɛs/ *nf* generous gift.

largeur /laʀʒœʀ/ *nf* **1** width, breadth; **dans le sens de la ~** widthwise; **2 ~ d'esprit** broadmindedness.

largué○, **~e** /laʀge/ *adj* **1** lost, out of one's depth; **2** out of touch.

larguer /laʀge/ [1] *vtr* **1** (Mil) to drop [*bomb, missile*]; to drop [*parachutist*]; to release [*satellite*]; **2** to unfurl [*sail*]; **~ les amarres** to cast off; (figurative) to set off; **3**○ to give up [*studies*]; to chuck○ [*boyfriend, girlfriend*].

larme /laʀm/ *nf* **1** tear; **elle a ri aux ~s** she laughed till she cried; **avoir la ~ à l'œil** to be a bit weepy; **2**○ drop.

larmoyant, **~e** /laʀmwajɑ̃, ɑ̃t/ *adj* **1** [*eyes*] full of tears; **2** [*voice*] whining; [*speech*] maudlin.

larmoyer /laʀmwaje/ [23] *vi* **1** [*eyes*] to water; **2** [*person*] to whine.

larron /laʀɔ̃/ *nm* **1** (humorous) scoundrel; **2** thief.
IDIOMS **s'entendre comme ~s en foire** to be as thick as thieves.

larve /laʀv/ *nf* **1** (Zool) larva; **2** (person) wimp○.

laryngite /laʀɛ̃ʒit/ *nf* laryngitis.

larynx /laʀɛ̃ks/ *nm inv* larynx.

las, **lasse** /lɑ, lɑs/ *adj* weary.

lasagnes /lazaɲ/ *nf pl* lasagna.

lascar○ /laskaʀ/ *nm* fellow.

lascif, **-ive** /lasif, iv/ *adj* [*person, look*] lascivious; [*temperament*] lustful.

laser /lazɛʀ/ *nm* laser.

lassant, **~e** /lasɑ̃, ɑ̃t/ *adj* **1** [*speech*] tedious; [*reproaches*] tiresome; **2** tiring.

lasser /lɑse/ [1] **I** *vtr* **1** to bore [*person, audience*]; **2** to weary [*person, audience*].
II se lasser *v refl* (+ *v être*) [*person*] to grow tired; **sans se ~** without tiring; patiently.

lassitude /lasityd/ *nf* weariness.

lasso /laso/ *nm* lasso; **prendre au ~** to lasso.

latence /latɑ̃s/ *nf* latency.

latent, **~e** /latɑ̃, ɑ̃t/ *adj* [*danger, illness*] latent; [*anxiety, jealousy*] underlying.

latéral, **~e**, *mpl* **-aux** /lateʀal, o/ *adj* [*door, exit*] side; [*tunnel, aisle*] lateral.

latin, **~e** /latɛ̃, in/ **I** *adj* **1** [*texts*] Latin; **2** [*temperament*] Latin; [*culture*] Mediterranean; **3 langues ~es** Romance languages.
II *nm* (language) Latin.
IDIOMS **c'est à y perdre son ~** you can't make head or tail of it.

latino-américain, **~e**, *mpl* **~s** /latino ameʀikɛ̃, ɛn/ *adj* Latin-American.

latitude /latityd/ *nf* latitude.
IDIOMS **avoir toute ~ de faire** to be entirely free to do.

latte /lat/ *nf* **1** lath; (of floor) board; **2** (of bed base) slat.

lauréat, **~e** /lɔʀea, at/ *nm,f* **1** (of competition) winner; **2** (in exam) successful candidate.

laurier /lɔʀje/ **I** *nm* **1** (Bot) laurel; **~ commun** bay (tree); **2** (Culin) **feuille de ~** bay leaf.
II lauriers *nm pl* laurels; **s'endormir sur ses ~s** to rest on one's laurels.

lavable /lavabl/ *adj* washable.

lavabo /lavabo/ *nm* washbasin, washbowl.

lavage /lavaʒ/ *nm* **1** washing; cleaning; **2** (washing machine cycle) wash.
■ **~ de cerveau** brainwashing; **faire un ~ d'estomac à qn** to pump sb's stomach (out).

lavande /lavɑ̃d/ *adj inv, nf* lavender.

lave /lav/ *nf* lava; **coulée de ~** lava flow.

lave-glace, *pl* **~s** /lavglas/ *nm* windscreen (GB) or windshield (US) washer.

lave-linge /lavlɛ̃ʒ/ *nm inv* washing machine.
lavement /lavmɑ̃/ *nm* (Med) enema.
laver /lave/ [1] **I** *vtr* **1** to wash [*clothes, child, car*]; **~ son linge** to do one's washing; **~ la vaisselle** to do the dishes; **~ qch à grande eau** to wash sth down; **2** to clean [*wound*]; **3** to clear; **~ qn d'une accusation** to clear sb of an accusation.
II se laver *v refl* (+ *v être*) **1** to wash; **se ~ les mains** to wash one's hands; **se ~ les dents** to brush one's teeth; **2** to be washable; **3 se ~ d'un affront** to take revenge for an insult.
IDIOMS **je m'en lave les mains** I'm washing my hands of it.
laverie /lavʀi/ *nf* **~ (automatique)** launderette, laundromat® (US).
lave-vaisselle /lavvɛsɛl/ *nm inv* dishwasher.
lavis /lavi/ *nm inv* wash drawing.
lavoir /lavwaʀ/ *nm* wash house.
laxatif /laksatif/ *nm* laxative.
laxisme /laksism/ *nm* laxity.
laxiste /laksist/ *adj* lax.
layette /lɛjɛt/ *nf* baby clothes, layette.
le, la[1] (**l'** *before vowel or mute h*), *pl* **les** /lə, la, l, lɛ/ **I** *det* **1** the; **la table de la cuisine** the kitchen table; **les Dupont** the Duponts; **elle aime les chevaux** she likes horses; **arriver sur** or **vers les 11 heures** to arrive about 11 o'clock; **2 elle s'est cogné ~ bras** she banged her arm; **3** a, an; **50 francs ~ kilo** 50 francs a kilo; **4 (oh) la jolie robe!** what a pretty dress!
II *pron* him; her; it; them; **je ne les comprends pas** I don't understand them.
III *pron neutre* **je ~ savais** I knew; I knew it; **je ~ croyais aussi, mais...** I thought so too, but...; **espérons-~!** let's hope so!
lé /le/ *nm* (of cloth, wallpaper) width.
LEA /ɛləa/ *nf pl* (*abbr* = **langues étrangères appliquées**) *university language course with emphasis on business and management.*
leadership /lidœʀʃip/ *nm* **1** leading role; **2** supremacy.
lèche-bottes○ /lɛʃbɔt/ **I** *nmf inv* crawler○ (GB), bootlicker○.
II *nm* crawling○ (GB), bootlicking○.
lécher /leʃe/ [1] **I** *vtr* **1** to lick [*spoon, plate*]; **2** [*flames*] to lick; [*sea*] to lap against.
II se lécher *v refl* (+ *v être*) **se ~ les doigts** to lick one's fingers.
lèche-vitrines /lɛʃvitʀin/ *nm inv* window-shopping.
leçon /ləsɔ̃/ *nf* lesson; **~ particulière** private lesson; **cela lui servira de ~** that'll teach him a lesson.
lecteur, -trice /lɛktœʀ, tʀis/ **I** *nm,f* **1** reader; **2** teaching assistant.
II *nm* **1** (Comput) reader; **~ optique** optical scanner or reader; **~ de disquettes** disk drive; **2** player; **~ laser** CD player.
lecture /lɛktyʀ/ *nf* **1** (of book, newspaper) reading; **faire la ~ à qn** to read to sb; **2** reading, interpretation; **3** reading material; **tu as pris de la ~?** have you brought something to read?; **4** (of music, X-ray, disk) reading; **5** (of cassette, CD) play; playing.
ledit, ladite, *pl* **lesdits, lesdites** /lədi, ladit, ledi, ledit/ *adj* the aforementioned.
légal, ~e, *mpl* **-aux** /legal, o/ *adj* legal; lawful.
légaliser /legalize/ [1] *vtr* to legalize.
légalité /legalite/ *nf* **1** legality; **2** lawfulness.
légataire /legatɛʀ/ *nmf* legatee.
légendaire /leʒɑ̃dɛʀ/ *adj* legendary.
légende /leʒɑ̃d/ *nf* **1** legend; **2** (accompanying picture) caption; (on map) key; **3** tall story.
léger, -ère /leʒe, ɛʀ/ **I** *adj* **1** light; **se sentir plus ~** (figurative) to have a great weight off one's mind; **2** (Culin) [*meal*] light; **3** [*person*] nimble; [*step*] light; **4** [*laugh*] gentle; [*blow, knock*] soft; [*error, delay*] slight; [*taste, hope*] faint; [*wind, rain*] light; [*cloud*] thin; [*injury*] minor; **5** [*tea, drink*] weak; [*perfume, wine*] light; [*tobacco*] mild (GB), light (US); **6** [*action*] ill-considered; [*remark*] thoughtless; [*argument, proof*] weak; **7**○ **c'est un peu ~** it's a bit skimpy; **8** [*woman, way of life*] loose; [*husband, mood*] fickle; **9** (Mil) light.
II *adv* [*travel*] light; **cuisiner/manger ~** to cook/to eat light meals.
III à la légère *phr* (gen) without thinking; [*accuse*] rashly; **prendre qch à la légère** not to take sth seriously.
légèrement /leʒɛʀmɑ̃/ *adv* **1** [*move*] gently; [*perfume*] lightly; [*tremble, injured*] slightly; **2** (Culin) [*eat*] lightly; **3** [*walk, run*] lightly, nimbly; **4** [*act, speak*] without thinking.
légèreté /leʒɛʀte/ *nf* **1** lightness; nimbleness; **2** thoughtlessness; fickleness; **la ~ de ses mœurs** his/her loose morals.
légion /leʒjɔ̃/ *nf* **1** (Mil) legion; **2** army.
■ **la Légion (étrangère)** the Foreign Legion.
légionnaire /leʒjɔnɛʀ/ *nm* (Roman) legionary; (in Foreign Legion) legionnaire.
législatif, -ive /leʒislatif, iv/ *adj* legislative; **élections législatives** ≈ general election.
législation /leʒislasjɔ̃/ *nf* legislation.
législature /leʒislatyʀ/ *nf* **1** term of office; **2** legislature.
légiste /leʒist/ *nm* jurist.
légitime /leʒitim/ *adj* **1** [*child, right*] legitimate; [*union, heir*] lawful; **2** [*action*] legitimate; [*anger*] justifiable; **3** [*reward*] just.
■ **~ défense** self-defence[GB].
légitimité /leʒitimite/ *nf* **1** legitimacy; **2** (of an act) lawfulness.
legs /lɛg/ *nm inv* (Law, gen) legacy; (of personal belongings) bequest.
léguer /lege/ [14] *vtr* **1** (in one's will) to leave sth; **2** to hand down [*traditions*]; to pass on [*flaw*].
légume /legym/ *nm* vegetable; **~s secs** pulses.
leitmotiv /lajtmɔtiv/ *nm* leitmotiv.
lendemain /lɑ̃dəmɛ̃/ **I** *nm* **1 le ~, la journée du ~** the following day; **dès le ~** the (very) next day; **le ~ de l'accident** the day after the accident; **du jour au ~** overnight; **2 au ~ de** (in the period) after; **au ~ de la guerre**

just after the war; **3 le ~** tomorrow, the future; **sans ~** [*happiness, success*] short-lived.

II **lendemains** *nm pl* **1** outcome; consequences; **2** future; **des ~s difficiles** difficult days ahead.

lénifiant, **~e** /lenifjɑ̃, ɑ̃t/ *adj* soothing.

lent, **~e**[1] /lɑ̃, ɑ̃t/ *adj* slow; [*film, vehicle*] slow-moving; [*poison*] slow-acting.

lente[2] /lɑ̃t/ *nf* (Zool) nit.

lentement /lɑ̃t(ə)mɑ̃/ *adv* slowly.

lenteur /lɑ̃tœʀ/ *nf* slowness; **avec ~** slowly.

lentille /lɑ̃tij/ *nf* **1** (Bot, Culin) lentil; **2** lens; **~s de contact** contact lenses.

léopard /leɔpaʀ/ *nm* **1** leopard; **2** leopardskin.

lèpre /lɛpʀ/ *nf* leprosy.

lépreux, **-euse** /lepʀø, øz/ *nm,f* leper.

lequel /ləkɛl/, **laquelle** /lakɛl/, **lesquels** *mpl*, **lesquelles** *fpl* /lekɛl/, (with *à*) **auquel**, **auxquels** *mpl*, **auxquelles** *fpl* /okɛl/, (with *de*) **duquel** /dykɛl/, **desquels** *mpl*, **desquelles** *fpl* /dekɛl/ I **lequel**, **laquelle**, **lesquels**, **lesquelles** *adj* who; which; **il m'a présenté son cousin, ~ cousin vit en Grèce** he introduced me to his cousin, who lives in Greece; **auquel cas** in which case.

II *rel pron* who; which; **les gens contre lesquels ils luttaient** the people (who) they were fighting against.

III *pron* which; **lesquels sont les plus compétents?** which are the most competent?

les ▶ **le**.

lesbienne /lɛsbjɛn/ *nf* lesbian.

lesdites ▶ **ledit**.

lesdits ▶ **ledit**.

lèse-majesté /lɛzmaʒɛste/ *nf inv* lese-majesty.

léser /leze/ [14] *vtr* to wrong [*person*]; to prejudice [*interests*].

lésiner /lezine/ [1] *vi* **ne pas ~ sur** to be liberal with [*ingredients, money, compliments*].

lésion /lezjɔ̃/ *nf* (Med) lesion.

lesquels, **lesquelles** ▶ **lequel**.

lessive /lesiv/ *nf* **1** washing powder; washing liquid; **2** washing.

lessiver /lesive/ [1] *vtr* **1** to wash; **2**° **être lessivé** (humorous) to be washed out°.

lest /lɛst/ *nm* **1** ballast; **jeter** or **lâcher du ~** to jettison ballast; **2** (on fishing net) weight.

leste /lɛste/ *adj* **1** [*person, animal*] agile, nimble; **2** [*joke, remark*] risqué.

lester /lɛste/ [1] *vtr* **1** to ballast; **2**° to stuff sth.

létal, **~e**, *mpl* **-aux** /letal, o/ *adj* lethal.

léthargie /letaʀʒi/ *nf* lethargy.

léthargique /letaʀʒik/ *adj* **1** [*person*] lethargic; [*industry*] sluggish; **2** (Med) lethargic.

lettre /lɛtʀ/ I *nf* **1** (of alphabet) letter; **~ majuscule** or **capitale** capital letter; **~ d'imprimerie** block letter; **en toutes ~s** in full; **c'est écrit en toutes ~s dans le rapport** it's down in black and white in the report; **les Romains furent des urbanistes avant la ~** the Romans were city planners before the concept was invented; **à la ~, au pied de la ~** to the letter; **il prend tout ce qu'on lui dit à la ~** he takes everything you say literally; **2** (message) letter; **~ de rupture** letter ending a relationship.

II **lettres** *nf pl* **1** (university subject) French; (more general) arts (GB), humanities (US); **2** letters; **femme de ~s** woman of letters; **avoir des ~s** to be well read.

■ **~ recommandée** registered letter; **~s classiques** French and Latin; **~s modernes** French language and literature.

IDIOMS **passer comme une ~ à la poste**° [*reform*] to go through smoothly; [*excuse*] to be accepted without any questions.

lettré, **~e** /letʀe/ *nm,f* man/woman of letters.

leu: **à la queue leu leu** /alakøløl ø/ *phr* in single file.

leucémie /løsemi/ *nf* leukaemia.

leur, (*pl* **leurs**) /lœʀ/ I *pron* them; **il ~ a écrit** he wrote to them; **il ~ a fallu faire** they had to do.

II *det* their; **un de ~s amis** a friend of theirs; **pendant ~ absence** while they were away.

III **le leur**, **la leur**, **les leurs** *pron* theirs; **c'est le ~** it's theirs; **il est des ~s** he's one of them; **ils m'ont demandé d'être des ~s** they asked me to come along; **ils vivent loin des ~s** they live far away from their families.

leurre /lœʀ/ *nm* **1** illusion; **2** (in fishing, hunting) lure; **3** (Mil) decoy.

leurrer /lœʀe/ [1] I *vtr* to delude.

II **se leurrer** *v refl* (+ *v être*) to delude oneself.

levain /ləvɛ̃/ *nm* (fermenting agent) starter; (for bread) leaven (GB), sourdough (US).

levant /ləvɑ̃/ I *adj m* **soleil ~** rising sun.

II *nm* east; **au ~** in the east; **du ~ au couchant** from east to west.

levé, **~e**[1] /ləve/ I *pp* ▶ **lever**[1].

II *pp adj* **1 voter à main ~e** to vote by a show of hands; **2** up; **elle est toujours la première ~e** she's always the first up.

levée[2] /ləve/ *nf* **1** (of embargo, sentence, martial law) lifting; (of diplomatic immunity) removal; (of secrecy, taboo) ending; (of session) close; **2** (of mail) collection; **3** (embankment) levee.

■ **~ de boucliers** outcry.

lever[1] /ləve/ [16] I *vtr* **1** to raise; **~ la main** or **le doigt** (for permission to speak) to put up one's hand; **~ la main sur qn** to raise a hand to sb; **~ les bras au ciel** to throw up one's hands; **lève les pieds quand tu marches!** don't drag your feet!; **~ les yeux** or **la tête** to look up; **2** to lift [*object*]; to raise [*barrier*]; **~ son verre** to raise one's glass; **3** (out of bed) to get [sb] up [*child, sick person*]; **4** to lift [*embargo, restriction*]; to raise [*siege*]; to end [*taboo, secret*]; to remove [*obstacle*]; to close [*session*]; **5** to levy [*tax*]; **6** to flush out [*game, partridges*].

II *vi* **1** (Culin) [*dough*] to rise; **2** [*seedlings, corn*] to come up.

III **se lever** *v refl* (+ *v être*) **1** to get up; **2** to stand up; **se ~ de table** to leave the table; **3** [*person, people*] to rise up; **4** [*sun*] to rise; **le jour se lève** it's getting light; **5** [*wind*] to rise; **6** [*fog, mist*] to clear; [*weather*] to clear up.

lever[2] /ləve/ *nm* **1 être là au ~ des enfants**

to be there when the children get up; **2 au ~ du jour** at daybreak.

lève-tôt /lɛvto/ *nmf inv* early riser.

levier /ləvje/ *nm* lever; **soulever qch avec un ~** to lever sth up.
■ **~ de changement de vitesse** (Aut) gear lever (GB), gear stick (US); **~ de commande** control stick.

lévitation /levitasjɔ̃/ *nf* levitation.

lèvre /lɛvʀ/ *nf* lip; **avoir le sourire aux ~s** to be smiling; **du bout des ~s** [*eat*] half-heartedly; [*reply*] grudgingly.
IDIOMS **être suspendu aux ~s de qn** to hang on sb's every word.

lévrier /levʀije/ *nm* greyhound.

levure /ləvyʀ/ *nf* yeast; **~ chimique** baking powder.

lexical, **~e**, *mpl* **-aux** /lɛksikal, o/ *adj* lexical.

lexique /lɛksik/ *nm* **1** glossary; (bilingual) vocabulary (book); **2** lexicon, lexis.

lézard /lezaʀ/ *nm* **1** lizard; **2** lizardskin.

lézarde /lezaʀd/ *nf* crack.

lézarder /lezaʀde/ [1] **I** *vtr* to crack.
II° *vi* **~ au soleil** to bask in the sun.
III se lézarder *v refl* (+ *v être*) to crack.

liaison /ljɛzɔ̃/ *nf* **1** link; **la ~ Calais–Douvres** the Calais–Dover line; **2 ~ radio** radio contact; **~ satellite** satellite link; **3 assurer la ~ entre différents services** to liaise between different services; **4** (love) affair; **5** (between words) liaison.

liane /ljan/ *nf* creeper, liana.

liant, **~e** /ljɑ̃, ɑ̃t/ *adj* sociable.

liasse /ljas/ *nf* (of banknotes) wad; (of letters, papers, documents) bundle.

Liban /libɑ̃/ *pr nm* Lebanon.

libellé /libɛlle/ *nm* wording.

libeller /libɛlle/ [1] *vtr* **1** to draw up [*contract*]; **2** to word [*article*]; **3** to make out [*cheque*].

libellule /libɛllyl/ *nf* dragonfly.

libéral, **~e**, *mpl* **-aux** /libeʀal, o/ *adj* **1** liberal; **2** (in politics) Liberal; **3** free-market.

libéraliser /libeʀalize/ [1] **I** *vtr* to liberalize.
II se libéraliser *v refl* (+ *v être*) [*country, attitudes*] to become more liberal.

libéralisme /libeʀalism/ *nm* liberalism.

libérateur, **-trice** /libeʀatœʀ, tʀis/ *adj* liberating.

libération /libeʀasjɔ̃/ *nf* **1** (of prisoner, hostage) release; **2** (of country, population) liberation; **~ des femmes** women's liberation; **3** relief; **4** (of prices) deregulation.

Libération /libeʀasjɔ̃/ *nf* (of 1944) **la ~** the Liberation.

libéré, **~e** /libeʀe/ **I** *pp* ▶ **libérer**.
II *pp adj* **1** [*man, woman*] liberated; **2** [*country, area, town*] free; **3** [*post, premises*] vacant.

libérer /libeʀe/ [14] **I** *vtr* **1** to liberate [*country, town*]; to free [*companion, hostage*]; **2** to release [*prisoner, hostage*]; to free [*slave, animal*]; **3** to allow [sb] to go [*employee*]; **4** to liberate [*person, imagination*]; (of post, duties) to relieve [*minister*]; **~ qn de l'emprise de qn** to get sb away from sb's influence; **5** to release [*emotion*]; to give free rein to [*imagination*]; **6** to relieve [*mind, person*]; **~ sa conscience** to unburden oneself; **7** to vacate [*apartment, office*]; **~ la chambre avant midi** (in hotel) to check out before noon; **8** to free [*arm, hand*]; to release [*spring, catch*]; **9** to liberalize [*economy, trade*]; to deregulate [*prices*]; **~ les loyers** to lift rent controls; **10** to release [*gas, energy*].
II se libérer *v refl* (+ *v être*) **1** to free oneself/itself; **se ~ d'une dette** to pay a debt; **2 j'essaierai de me ~ mercredi** I'll try and be free on Wednesday.

libertaire /libɛʀtɛʀ/ *adj, nmf* libertarian.

liberté /libɛʀte/ *nf* **1** (gen) freedom; **être en ~** to be free; **élever des animaux en ~** to raise animals in a natural habitat; **espèce vivant en ~** species in the wild; **l'assassin est toujours en ~** the killer is still at large; **prendre la ~ de faire** to take the liberty of doing; **~ de pensée** freedom of thought; **2** (Law) **mettre qn en ~ conditionnelle** to release sb on parole; **mise en ~ surveillée** release on probation.

libertin, **~e** /libɛʀtɛ̃, in/ *adj, nm,f* libertine.

libido /libido/ *nf* libido.

libraire /libʀɛʀ/ *nmf* bookseller.

librairie /libʀɛʀi/ *nf* **1** bookshop (GB), bookstore; **2** bookselling business.

libre /libʀ/ *adj* **1** [*person, country*] free; **~ à elle de partir** it's up to her whether she goes or not; **être ~ de ses actes** to do as one wishes; **2** [*person*] free and easy; [*manner*] free; [*opinion*] candid; [*morality*] easygoing; **3** [*hand, thumb*] free; [*road, way*] clear; **4** [*person, room*] available; [*seat*] free; **5** [*WC*] vacant; **la ligne n'est pas ~** (on telephone) the number is engaged (GB) or busy (US).
■ **~ arbitre** free will.
IDIOMS **être ~ comme l'air** to be as free as a bird.

libre-échange /libʀeʃɑ̃ʒ/ *nm* free trade.

librement /libʀəmɑ̃/ *adv* freely.

libre-service, *pl* **libres-services** /libʀə sɛʀvis/ **I** *adj inv* self-service.
II *nm* **1 le ~** self-service; **2** self-service shop (GB) or store (US); self-service restaurant.
■ **~ bancaire** automatic teller.

lice /lis/ *nf* **être en ~** to have entered the lists.

licence /lisɑ̃s/ *nf* **1** (bachelor's) degree; **~ en droit** law degree; **2** (Law) licence[GB]; **produit sous ~** licensed product.

licencié, **~e** /lisɑ̃sje/ **I** *pp* ▶ **licencier**.
II *pp adj* [*student*] graduate.
III *nm,f* **1** graduate (GB), college graduate (US); **2 ~ (économique)** redundant employee (GB), laid-off worker.

licenciement /lisɑ̃simɑ̃/ *nm* dismissal; **~ (économique)** redundancy (GB), lay-off; **~ collectif** mass redundancy; **~ sec** compulsory redundancy (*without compensation*).

licencier /lisɑ̃sje/ [2] *vtr* **1** to make [sb] redundant (GB), to lay [sb] off; **2** to dismiss (GB), to let [sb] go.

licencieux, **-ieuse** /lisɑ̃sjø, øz/ *adj* licentious.

lichen /likɛn/ *nm* lichen.

licite /lisit/ *adj* lawful.

licorne /likɔʀn/ *nf* unicorn.

lie /li/ *nf* **1** dregs, lees; **2** (figurative) dregs.

lie-de-vin /lidvɛ̃/ *adj inv* wine-coloured[GB].

liège /ljɛʒ/ *nm* cork; **bouchon en ~** cork.

liégeois, ~e /ljeʒwa, az/ *adj* of Liège; **café ~** *iced coffee topped with whipped cream.*

lien /ljɛ̃/ *nm* **1** strap; string; **2** connection, link (**entre** between); **3** (gen) link, tie (**avec** with); (emotional) tie, bond; **~s économiques** economic links; **~s de parenté** family ties.

lier /lje/ [1] **I** *vtr* **1** to tie [sb/sth] up; **il avait les mains liées** his hands were tied; **2** to bind; **ils sont très liés** they are very close; **3** to link [*ideas, events*]; **4 ~ amitié avec qn** to strike up a friendship with sb; **5** (Mus) to slur [*notes*].

II se lier *v refl* (+ *v être*) to make friends.

lierre /ljɛʀ/ *nm* ivy.

liesse /ljɛs/ *nf* jubilation; **en ~** jubilant.

lieu /ljø/ **I** *nm* **1** (*pl* **~x**) place; **~ de passage** thoroughfare; **en tous ~x** everywhere; **en ~ et place de qn** [*sign, act*] on behalf of sb; **en dernier ~** lastly; **avoir ~** to take place; **tenir ~ de** to serve as [*bedroom, study*]; **il y a ~ de s'inquiéter** there is cause for anxiety; **s'il y a ~** if necessary; **donner ~ à** to cause [*scandal*]; **2** (*pl* **~s**) coley.

II au lieu de *phr* instead of.

III lieux *nm pl* **1 sur les ~x** at or on the scene; on the spot; **repérer les ~x** to have a scout around; **2** premises; **visiter les ~x** to visit the premises.

■ **~ commun** platitude; **~ public** public place.

lieue /ljø/ *nf* league; **~ marine** league.

IDIOMS **j'étais à cent** or **mille ~s d'imaginer** I never for a moment imagined.

lieutenant /ljøtnɑ̃/ *nm* **1** (Mil) (in army) ≈ lieutenant (GB), ≈ first lieutenant (US); (in air force) ≈ flying officer (GB), ≈ first lieutenant (US); **2** (on boat) first officer.

lièvre /ljɛvʀ/ *nm* (Zool) hare.

IDIOMS **courir plusieurs ~s à la fois** to try to do too many things at once.

lifting /liftiŋ/ *nm* face-lift.

ligament /ligamɑ̃/ *nm* ligament.

ligaturer /ligatyʀe/ [1] *vtr* (Med) to tie.

ligne /liɲ/ *nf* **1** (gen) line; **lire les ~s de la main de qn** to read sb's palm; **~ droite** straight line; (driving) straight piece of road; **la dernière ~ droite avant l'arrivée** the home straigh; **je vous écris ces quelques ~s pour vous dire**... this is just a quick note to tell you...; **à la ~!** new paragraph!; **2** (in public transport) service; route; (of train, underground) line; **~ de chemin de fer** railway line; **~s intérieures** domestic flights; **3** cable; **~ aérienne** overhead cable; **4** (telephone) line; **5** figure; **garder la ~** to stay slim; **6** (of body) contours; (of face) shape; (of hills) outline; **la ~ aérodynamique d'une voiture** the aerodynamic lines of a car; **7** (of clothes, furniture, style) look; **8** outline; **raconter un événement dans ses grandes ~s** to give an outline of events; **9** fishing line; **pêche à la ~** angling; **10** line; row; **les ~s ennemies** (Mil) the enemy lines; **11** (Comput) **en ~** on line.

■ **~ de conduite** line of conduct; **se donner comme ~ de conduite de faire** to make it a rule to do; **~ de démarcation** (Mil) demarcation line; **~ de mire** line of sight; **~ de tir** line of fire.

IDIOMS **être en première ~** to be in the front line; (figurative) to be in the firing line; **entrer en ~ de compte** to be taken into account.

lignée /liɲe/ *nf* **1** descendants; lineage; **de haute ~** of noble descent; **2** tradition.

ligoter /ligɔte/ [1] *vtr* to truss [sb] up [*person*].

ligue /lig/ *nf* league.

liguer: se liguer /lige/ [1] *v refl* (+ *v être*) [*people*] to join forces.

lilas /lila/ *adj inv, nm* lilac.

lilliputien, -ienne /lilipysjɛ̃, ɛn/ *adj, nm,f* Lilliputian.

limace /limas/ *nf* (Zool) slug.

limaille /limaj/ *nf* filings.

limande /limɑ̃d/ *nf* (Zool) dab.

limande-sole, *pl* **limandes-soles** /limɑ̃dsɔl/ *nf* (Zool) lemon sole.

lime /lim/ *nf* **1** (Tech) file; **~ à ongles** nail file; **2** (Bot) lime; **3** (Zool) lima.

limer /lime/ [1] **I** *vtr* **1** to file [*nail, metal*]; to file down [*key*]; **2** to file through [*bars of cage*].

II se limer *v refl* (+ *v être*) **se ~ les ongles** to file one's nails.

limier /limje/ *nm* **1** bloodhound; **2**○ sleuth.

limitation /limitasjɔ̃/ *nf* (of power, liberty) limitation, restriction; (of prices, interest rates) control; **~ de vitesse** (Aut) speed limit.

limite /limit/ **I** *nf* **1** border; **2** (of estate, piece of land) boundary; (of sea, forest, village) edge; **3** limit; **connaître ses ~s** to know one's (own) limitations; **vraiment, il dépasse les ~s!** he's really going too far!; **à la ~, je préférerais qu'il refuse** I'd almost prefer it if he refused; **4 à la ~ de** on the verge of; **activités à la ~ de la légalité** activities bordering on the illegal; **5 dans une certaine ~** up to a point, to a certain extent; **dans la ~ de, dans les ~s de** within the limits of.

II (-)limite (*combining form*) **date(-)~** deadline; **date(-)~ de vente** sell-by date; **vitesse(-)~** maximum speed.

■ **~ d'âge** age limit.

limiter /limite/ [1] **I** *vtr* to limit, to restrict [*power, duration, number*]; **cela limite nos possibilités** that rather limits our scope.

II se limiter *v refl* (+ *v être*) **1 se ~ à deux verres de bière par jour** to limit oneself to two glasses of beer a day; **je me limiterai à quelques observations** I'll confine myself to a few observations; **2 se ~ à** to be limited to; **la vie ne se limite pas au travail** there's more to life than work.

limitrophe /limitʀɔf/ *adj* [*country, region*] adjacent; [*city*] border.

limoger /limɔʒe/ [13] *vtr* to dismiss.

limon /limɔ̃/ *nm* **1** silt; **2** (on horse-drawn carriage) shaft.
limonade /limɔnad/ *nf* lemonade (GB), lemon soda (US).
limousine /limuzin/ *nf* (Aut) limousine.
limpide /lɛ̃pid/ *adj* **1** clear, limpid; **2** (figurative) [*explanation, style*] clear, lucid.
limpidité /lɛ̃pidite/ *nf* clarity.
lin /lɛ̃/ *nm* **1** flax; **2** linen.
linceul /lɛ̃sœl/ *nm* shroud.
linéaire /lineɛʀ/ *adj* linear.
linge /lɛ̃ʒ/ *nm* **1** linen; **~ sale** dirty linen; **2** washing; **corde** or **fil à ~** clothes line; **3 ~ (de corps)** underwear; **4** cloth.
■ **~ de maison** household linen; **~ de toilette** bathroom linen.
lingerie /lɛ̃ʒʀi/ *nf* **1** linen room; **2** lingerie.
lingot /lɛ̃go/ *nm* ingot.
linguiste /lɛ̃gɥist/ *nmf* linguist.
linguistique /lɛ̃gɥistik/ **I** *adj* linguistic.
II *nf* linguistics.
linteau, *pl* **~x** /lɛ̃to/ *nm* lintel.
lion /ljɔ̃/ *nm* lion; **~ de mer** sealion.
IDIOMS **avoir mangé du ~**° to be full of beans° (GB), to be full of pep° (US).
Lion /ljɔ̃/ *pr nm* Leo.
lionceau, *pl* **~x** /ljɔ̃so/ *nm* lion cub.
lionne /ljɔn/ *nf* lioness.
lipide /lipid/ *nm* lipid.
liquéfier /likefje/ [2] *vtr*, **se liquéfier** *v refl* (+ *v être*) to liquefy.
liqueur /likœʀ/ *nf* liqueur.
liquidation /likidasjɔ̃/ *nf* **1** (Law) (of property) liquidation; (of debts) settlement; **2** clearance; **~ totale (du stock)** total clearance.
liquide /likid/ **I** *adj* **1** liquid; **miel ~** clear honey; **2 argent ~** cash.
II *nm* **1** liquid; **2** cash.
■ **~ correcteur** correction fluid, white-out (fluid) (US); **~ de frein** brake fluid.
liquider /likide/ [1] *vtr* **1** to settle [*accounts*]; to liquidate [*company, business*]; **2** to clear [*goods, stock*]; **3**° to liquidate° [*enemy, witness*]; **4**° to demolish [*meal*]; to empty [*glass*].
liquidité /likidite/ *nf* **des ~s** liquid assets.
lire[1] /liʀ/ [66] *vtr* to read; **~ qch en diagonale** to skim through sth; **~ sur les lèvres de qn** to lip-read what sb is saying; **~ dans les pensées de qn** to read sb's mind.
lire[2] /liʀ/ *nf* lira.
lis /lis/ *nm inv* lily.
liseré /lizʀe/ *nm*, **liséré** /lizeʀe/ *nm* (on dress) edging; piping.
liseron /lizʀɔ̃/ *nm* bindweed, convolvulus.
liseuse /lizøz/ *nf* **1** bed jacket; **2** small reading lamp.
lisible /lizibl/ *adj* **1** legible; **2** readable.
lisière /lizjɛʀ/ *nf* **1** (of wood, field) edge; (of village) outskirts; **2** (on piece of fabric) selvage.
lisse /lis/ *adj* [*skin, surface*] smooth; [*tyre*] worn.
lisser /lise/ [1] *vtr* to smooth [*hair, garment*]; to stroke [*beard*].
liste /list/ *nf* (gen) list; (at election) list (of candidates) (GB), ticket (US).
■ **~ d'attente** waiting list; **~ électorale** electoral roll; **~ de mariage** wedding list.
IDIOMS **être sur ~ rouge** to be ex-directory (GB), to have an unlisted number (US).
lit /li/ *nm* **1** bed; **~ à une place** or **d'une personne** single bed; **~ à deux places** or **de deux personnes** double bed; **aller** or **se mettre au ~** to go to bed; **tirer qn du ~** to drag sb out of bed; **au ~!** bedtime!; **~ métallique** iron bedstead; **le ~ n'était pas défait** the bed had not been slept in; **2** (Law) marriage; **3** (of river) bed; **la rivière est sortie de son ~** the river has overflowed its banks.
■ **~ de camp** camp bed (GB), cot (US); **~ pliant** folding bed; **~s superposés** bunk beds.
litanie /litani/ *nf* litany.
literie /litʀi/ *nf* bedding.
lithographie /litɔgʀafi/ *nf* **1** lithography; **2** lithograph.
litière /litjɛʀ/ *nf* **1** (for cattle) litter; (for horses) bedding; (for cats) cat litter; **2** (mode of transport) litter.
litige /litiʒ/ *nm* dispute; **point de ~** bone of contention; point at issue; **les parties en ~** the litigants.
litigieux, **-ieuse** /litiʒjø, øz/ *adj* [*case, point, argument*] contentious.
litre /litʀ/ *nm* **1** (measure) litre[GB]; **2** litre[GB] bottle.
littéraire /liteʀɛʀ/ **I** *adj* [*work, criticism*] literary; **études ~s** arts studies.
II *nm,f* **1** literary person; **2** arts or liberal arts (US) student.
littéral, **~e**, *mpl* **-aux** /liteʀal, o/ *adj* literal.
littérature /liteʀatyʀ/ *nf* literature.
littoral, **~e**, *mpl* **-aux** /litɔʀal, o/ **I** *adj* coastal.
II *nm* coast.
liturgie /lityʀʒi/ *nf* liturgy.
livide /livid/ *adj* deathly pale.
livraison /livʀɛzɔ̃/ *nf* delivery; **'~s à domicile'** 'we deliver'; **il est venu prendre ~ de la commande** he came to pick up the order.
livre[1] /livʀ/ *nm* book; **c'est mon ~ de chevet** it's my bedside book; (figurative) it's my bible.
■ **~ blanc** blue book; **~ de bord** logbook; **~ d'or** visitors' book; **~ de poche**® paperback; **~ scolaire** schoolbook.
livre[2] /livʀ/ *nf* **1** pound; **~ sterling** pound sterling; **~ irlandaise** Irish pound, punt; **2** (unit of weight) half a kilo; (in UK) pound.
livrée /livʀe/ *nf* livery.
livrer /livʀe/ [1] **I** *vtr* **1** to deliver [*goods*]; **~ qn** to deliver sb's order; **2** to hand [sb] over [*criminal*]; to betray [*accomplice, secret*]; **3 être livré à soi-même** to be left to one's own devices; **4 il nous livre un peu de lui-même** he reveals something of himself.
II se livrer *v refl* (+ *v être*) **1 se ~ à un trafic de drogue** to engage in drug trafficking; **2 se ~ à** [*criminal*] to give oneself up to; **3 se ~ à un ami** to confide in a friend.

livret /livʀɛ/ *nm* **1** booklet; **2** libretto.
■ **~ de caisse d'épargne** ≈ savings book (GB), bankbook (*for a savings account*) (US); **~ de famille** family record book (*of births, marriages and deaths*).

livreur, **-euse** /livʀœʀ, øz/ *nm,f* delivery man/ woman.

lobe /lɔb/ *nm* lobe; **~ de l'oreille** ear lobe.

local, **~e**, *pl* **-aux** /lɔkal, o/ **I** *adj* [*newspaper, authorities*] local; [*pain, showers*] localized.
II *nm* **1** place; **les scouts ont besoin d'un ~** the scouts need a place to meet; **2 ~ commercial** commercial premises; **les locaux du journal** the newspaper offices.

localement /lɔkalmɑ̃/ *adv* on a local level; **appliquer la crème ~** apply the cream locally.

localiser /lɔkalize/ [1] *vtr* **1** to locate [*person, noise*]; **2** to confine, to localize [*fire*].

localité /lɔkalite/ *nf* locality.

locataire /lɔkatɛʀ/ *nmf* tenant.

location /lɔkasjɔ̃/ *nf* **1** (by owner) renting out; (by tenant) renting; **agence de ~** rental agency; **2** rented accommodation; **3** rent; **4** (of equipment) hire; **~ de voitures** car hire, car rental; **contrat de ~** rental agreement; **~ de vidéos** video rental; **5** (of theatre seats) reservation, booking (GB).

location-vente, *pl* **locations-ventes** /lɔkasjɔ̃vɑ̃t/ *nf* 100% mortgage scheme.

locomotion /lɔkɔmɔsjɔ̃/ *nf* locomotion.

locomotive /lɔkɔmɔtiv/ *nf* engine, locomotive; **~ à vapeur** steam engine.

locuteur, **-trice** /lɔkytœʀ, tʀis/ *nm,f* speaker.

locution /lɔkysjɔ̃/ *nf* phrase; idiom.

logarithme /lɔgaʀitm/ *nm* logarithm, log.

loge /lɔʒ/ *nf* **1** (caretaker's dwelling) lodge; **2** (of actor) dressing room; (in theatre) box; **3** (in freemasonry) Lodge; **4** loggia.

logé, **~e** /lɔʒe/ **I** *pp* ▶ **loger**.
II *pp adj* housed; **être ~, nourri, blanchi** to have bed, board and one's laundry done.

logement /lɔʒmɑ̃/ *nm* **1** accommodation; **~ individuel** flat (GB), apartment (US); house; **2** housing; **la crise du ~** the housing crisis.

loger /lɔʒe/ [13] **I** *vtr* **1** to house [*student*]; **2** to put [sb] up [*friend*]; to provide accommodation for [*refugees*]; **3** [*hotel*] to have accommodation for; **4** to put; **je n'ai pas pu ~ tous mes meubles dans le salon** I couldn't fit all my furniture in the living room; **5 ~ une balle dans la tête de qn** to shoot sb in the head.
II *vi* **1** to live; **2** to stay; **~ à l'hôtel** to stay at a hotel.
III se loger *v refl* (+ *v être*) **1** to find accommodation; **se nourrir et se ~** to pay for food and accommodation; **2 se ~ dans qch** to get stuck in sth; [*dust*] to collect in sth; **la balle est venue se ~ dans le genou** the bullet lodged in his/her knee.

loggia /lɔdʒja/ *nf* loggia.

logiciel, **-ielle** /lɔʒisjɛl/ *nm* **1** software; **~ de base** system(s) software; **2** program.

logique /lɔʒik/ **I** *adj* **1** logical; **il n'est pas ~ avec lui-même** he is not consistent; **2**° reasonable; **ce serait ~ qu'ils soient en colère** one could understand why they would be angry.
II *nf* logic; **manquer de ~** to be illogical; **c'est dans la ~ des choses** it's in the nature of things; **en toute ~** logically.

logis /lɔʒi/ *nm inv* home, dwelling.

logistique /lɔʒistik/ *nf* logistics.

logo /lɔgo/ *nm* logo.

loi /lwa/ *nf* **1** law; **voter une ~** to pass a law; **2 la ~** the law; **enfreindre la ~** to break the law; **tomber sous le coup de la ~** to be or constitute an offence[GB]; **faire la ~** (figurative) to lay down the law; **3** rule; law; **la ~ du milieu** the law of the underworld; **c'est la ~ des séries** things always happen in a row.
■ **~ d'amnistie** *act granting amnesty to some offenders*; **~ communautaire** community law; **~ de la jungle** law of the jungle.

loin /lwɛ̃/ **I** *adv* **1** a long way, far (away); **c'est ~** it's a long way; **c'est trop ~** it's too far; **il habite plus ~** he lives further or farther away; **du plus ~ qu'il m'aperçut** as soon as he saw me; **voir plus ~** (in text) see below; **2** (in time) **tout cela est bien ~** that was all a long time ago; **aussi ~ que je me souvienne** as far back as I can remember; **l'été n'est plus très ~ maintenant** summer isn't far off now; **3** (figurative) **de là à dire qu'il est incompétent, il n'y a pas ~** that comes close to saying he's incompetent; **il n'est pas bête, ~ s'en faut!** he's not stupid, far from it!; **ça va beaucoup plus ~** it goes much further.
II loin de *phr* **1** (in space) far from; **est-ce encore ~ d'ici?** is it much further or farther from here?; **2** (in time) far from; **cela ne fait pas ~ de quatre ans que je suis ici** I've been here for almost four years now; **3** (figurative) far from, a long way from; **~ de moi cette idée!** nothing could be further from my mind!; **avec l'imprimante, il faut compter pas ~ de 50000 francs** if you include the printer, you're talking about 50,000 francs or thereabouts.
III de loin *phr* from a distance; **je ne vois pas très bien de ~** I can't see very well at a distance; **c'est de ~ ton meilleur roman** it's by far your best novel.
IV au loin *phr* **au ~** in the distance.
V de loin en loin *phr* **1 on pouvait voir des maisons de ~ en ~** you could see houses scattered here and there; **2** every now and then.
IDIOMS **~ des yeux, ~ du cœur** (Proverb) out of sight, out of mind.

lointain, **~e** /lwɛ̃tɛ̃, ɛn/ **I** *adj* **1** [*country, past*] distant; **2** [*link*] remote; **3** [*person*] distant.
II *nm* background; **dans le ~** [*see, hear*] in the distance.

loir /lwaʀ/ *nm* (edible) dormouse.

loisir /lwaziʀ/ *nm* **1** spare time; **(tout) à ~** at (great) leisure; **2 avoir tout ~ de faire** to have plenty of time to do; **3** leisure activity.

lombaire /lɔ̃bɛʀ/ *nf* lumbar vertebra.

londonien, **-ienne** /lɔ̃dɔnjɛ̃, ɛn/ *adj* (of) London.

Londres /lɔ̃dʀ/ *pr n* London.

long, **longue** /lɔ̃, lɔ̃g/ **I** *adj* long; **plus/trop ~ de deux mètres** two metres^GB longer/too long; **être ~ (à faire)** [*person*] to be slow (to do); **être en longue maladie** to be on extended sick leave; **il guérira, mais ce sera ~** he will get better, but it's going to take a long time; **être ~ à la détente**○ to be slow on the uptake○.
II *adv* **1 en dire ~/trop ~/plus ~** to say a lot/too much/more (**sur qn/qch** about sb/sth); **2 s'habiller ~** to wear longer skirts.
III *nm* **1 un câble de six mètres de ~** a cable six metres^GB long, a six-metre^GB long cable; **en ~** lengthwise; **en ~ et en large** [*tell*] in great detail; **marcher de ~ en large** to pace up and down; **en ~, en large et en travers**○ [*tell*] at great length; **le ~ du mur** along the wall; up or down the wall; **tomber de tout son ~** to fall flat (on one's face).
IV à la longue *phr* in the end, eventually.
■ **~ métrage** feature-length film.

long-courrier, *pl* **~s** /lɔ̃kuʀje/ *nm* **1** ocean-going ship; **2** long-haul aircraft.

longer /lɔ̃ʒe/ [13] *vtr* **1** [*person, train*] to go along [*forest, coast*]; to follow [*river*]; **2** [*garden, road*] to run alongside [*lake, field*].

longévité /lɔ̃ʒevite/ *nf* longevity.

longiligne /lɔ̃ʒiliɲ/ *adj* lanky, rangy.

longitude /lɔ̃ʒityd/ *nf* longitude.

longitudinal, **~e**, *mpl* **-aux** /lɔ̃ʒitydinal, o/ *adj* longitudinal, lengthwise.

longtemps /lɔ̃tɑ̃/ *adv* [*wait, sleep*] (for) a long time; **il t'a fallu ~?** did it take you long?; **~ avant/après** long before/after; **je peux le garder plus ~?** can I keep it a bit longer?; **il n'y a pas ~ qu'il travaille ici** he hasn't worked here long; **il y a** or **ça fait ~ qu'il n'a pas téléphoné** he hasn't phoned for ages○; **il est mort depuis ~** he died a long time ago; **il n'y a pas si ~ c'était encore possible** it was still possible until quite recently.

longue ▸ **long I, IV**.

longuement /lɔ̃gmɑ̃/ *adv* [*hesitate, talk*] for a long time; [*explain, interview*] at length.

longueur /lɔ̃gœʀ/ **I** *nf* **1** (in space, time) length; **la maison est tout en ~** the house is long and narrow; **traîner en ~** [*film, book*] to go on forever; **2** (in race, swimming) length; **avoir une ~ d'avance sur qn** (Sport) to be one length ahead of sb; (figurative) to be ahead of sb; **le saut en ~** the long or broad (US) jump; **4** length.
II longueurs *nf pl* (in film, book, speech) over-long passages.
III à longueur de *phr* **à ~ de journée** all day long; **à ~ d'année** all year round; **à ~ d'émissions** programme^GB after programme^GB.
■ **~ d'onde** wavelength.

longue-vue, *pl* **longues-vues** /lɔ̃gvy/ *nf* telescope.

looping /lupiŋ/ *nm* loop.

lopin /lɔpɛ̃/ *nm* **~ (de terre)** patch of land.

loquace /lɔkas/ *adj* talkative, loquacious.

loque /lɔk/ **I** *nf* **~ (humaine)** (human) wreck.
II loques *nf pl* rags.

loquet /lɔkɛ/ *nm* latch.

lorgner○ /lɔʀɲe/ [1] *vtr* to give [sb] the eye○ [*person*]; to cast longing glances at [*jewel, cake*]; to have one's eye on [*inheritance, job*].

lorgnette /lɔʀɲɛt/ *nf* **1** opera-glasses; **2** spy-glass.

lorgnon /lɔʀɲɔ̃/ *nm* **1** lorgnette; **2** pince-nez.

lors: **lors de** /lɔʀ/ *phr* **1** during; **2** at the time of.

lorsque (**lorsqu'** *before vowel or mute h*) /lɔʀsk(ə)/ *conj* when.

losange /lɔzɑ̃ʒ/ *nm* (shape) lozenge; **en ~** diamond-shaped.

lot /lo/ *nm* **1** (of inheritance) share; (of land) plot; **2** (in lottery) prize; **gagner le gros ~** to hit the jackpot; **3** (of objects for sale) batch; (at auction) lot; **4** (of person) **être au-dessus du ~** to be above the average; **5** fate, lot.

loterie /lɔtʀi/ *nf* raffle; (in fair) tombola (GB), raffle (US); (large scale) lottery.

loti, **~e** /lɔti/ *adj* **bien/mal ~** well/badly off.

lotion /losjɔ̃/ *nf* lotion.

lotissement /lɔtismɑ̃/ *nm* housing estate (GB), subdivision (US).

loto /lɔto/ *nm* lotto; **le ~ national** national lottery.

lotte /lɔt/ *nf* monkfish; (freshwater) burbot.

lotus /lɔtys/ *nm inv* lotus.

louage /luaʒ/ *nm* **voiture de ~** rented car (GB), rental car (US).

louange /luɑ̃ʒ/ *nf* praise.

louche /luʃ/ **I** *adj* [*person, past, affair*] shady; [*place*] seedy.
II *nf* ladle; ladleful.

loucher /luʃe/ [1] *vi* to have a squint.

louer /lue/ [1] *vtr* **1** [*owner, landlord*] to let (GB), to rent out [*house*]; to hire out [*premises*]; to rent out [*equipment*]; **'à ~'** 'for rent', 'to let' (GB); **2** [*tenant*] to rent [*house*]; to hire [*room*]; to rent [*equipment, film*]; **3** to hire [*staff*]; **4** to praise; **Dieu soit loué** thank God.

loufoque○ /lufɔk/ *adj* crazy○.

louis /lwi/ *nm inv* **~ d'or** (gold) louis.

loukoum /lukum/ *nm* Turkish delight.

loup /lu/ *nm* **1** wolf; **le grand méchant ~** the big bad wolf; **à pas de ~** stealthily; **2 ~ (de mer)** (sea) bass; **3** domino, mask.
■ **(vieux) ~ de mer** old salt, old tar.
IDIOMS **avoir une faim de ~** to be ravenous; **être connu comme le ~ blanc** to be known to everybody; **hurler avec les ~s** to follow the herd or crowd; **se jeter dans la gueule du ~** to stick one's head in the lion's mouth; **les ~s ne se mangent pas entre eux** (Proverb) (there is) honour^GB among thieves; **quand on parle du ~ (on en voit la queue)** (Proverb) speak of the devil; **l'homme est un ~ pour l'homme** (Proverb) dog eat dog.

loupe /lup/ *nf* magnifying glass.

louper○ /lupe/ [1] **I** *vtr* **1** to miss [*train, opportunity, visitor*]; **il n'en loupe pas une** he's always opening his big mouth; **2** to flunk○ [*exam*]; to screw up○ [*sauce, piece of work*].

II *vi* **j'avais dit que ça se casserait, ça n'a pas loupé** I said it would break, and sure enough it did; **tu vas tout faire ~** you'll mess everything up.

loup-garou, *pl* **loups-garous** /lugaʀu/ *nm* werewolf.

lourd, **~e** /luʀ, luʀd/ **I** *adj* **1** [*person, object, metal*] heavy; **2** [*stomach, head, steps*] heavy; [*gesture*] clumsy; **3** [*meal, food*] heavy; [*wine*] heady; **~ à digérer** heavy on the stomach; **4** [*equipment, weapons*] heavy; **5** [*fine, taxation*] heavy; **6** [*defeat, responsibility*] heavy; [*mistake*] serious; **7** [*administration, structure*] unwieldy; [*staff numbers*] large; **8** [*person, animal*] ungainly; [*body, object, architecture*] heavy; [*building*] cumbersome, ponderous; **9** [*joke*] flat; [*style*] clumsy; **10** [*atmosphere, silence*] heavy; [*heat*] sultry; **11 être ~ de dangers** to be fraught with danger.

II *adv* **1 peser ~** to weigh heavy; **peser ~** (figurative) to carry a lot of weight; **2** (of weather) **il fait ~** it's close; **3**° **pas ~** not a lot, not much; **dix personnes, ça ne fait pas ~** ten people, that's not a lot.

IDIOMS **avoir la main ~e** to be heavy-handed; **avoir la main ~e avec le sel/le parfum** to overdo the salt/the perfume.

lourde *adj f* ▶ **lourd I**.

lourdement /luʀdəmɑ̃/ *adv* **1** heavily; **se tromper ~** to be gravely mistaken; **2 marcher ~** to walk clumsily; **insister ~ sur** to keep going on about.

lourdeur /luʀdœʀ/ *nf* **1** (of organization) complexity; **2** heaviness; **3** (of style) clumsiness; (in a text) clumsy expression; **4** weight; **5** (of person) oafishness; (of joke) poorness; (of architecture) ungainliness; **6** (of weather) closeness.

loutre /lutʀ/ *nf* **1** otter; **2** otterskin.

louve /luv/ *nf* she-wolf.

louveteau, *pl* **~x** /luvto/ *nm* (Zool) wolf cub.

louvoyer /luvwaje/ [23] *vi* **1** [*ship*] to tack; **2** (figurative) to manoeuvre (GB), to maneuver (US).

lover: **se lover** /lɔve/ [1] *v refl* (+ *v être*) [*snake*] to coil itself up; [*person*] to curl up.

loyal, **~e**, *mpl* **-aux** /lwajal, o/ *adj* **1** [*friend*] true; [*servant*] loyal, faithful; **2** [*procedure, conduct*] honest; [*competition, game*] fair.

loyaliste /lwajalist/ *adj*, *nmf* loyalist.

loyauté /lwajote/ *nf* **1** loyalty; **2** honesty.

loyer /lwaje/ *nm* rent.

lubie /lybi/ *nf* whim.

lubrifier /lybʀifje/ [2] *vtr* to lubricate.

lubrique /lybʀik/ *adj* [*person*] lecherous; [*look, dance*] lewd.

lucarne /lykaʀn/ *nf* (small) window; (in roof) skylight.

lucide /lysid/ *adj* clear-sighted; lucid.

lucidité /lysidite/ *nf* lucidity; clear-headedness; clarity; **juger en toute ~** to judge without any illusions.

luciole /lysjɔl/ *nf* firefly.

lucratif, **-ive** /lykʀatif, iv/ *adj* lucrative.

ludique /lydik/ *adj* [*activity*] play.

ludothèque /lydɔtɛk/ *nf* toy library.

luette /lyɛt/ *nf* uvula.

lueur /lɥœʀ/ *nf* (faint) light; **les ~s de la ville** the city lights; **à la ~ d'une bougie** by candlelight; **à la ~ des événements d'hier** in the light of yesterday's events; **les dernières ~s du soleil couchant** the dying glow of the sunset.

luge /lyʒ/ *nf* **1** toboggan (GB), sled (US); **2** (Sport) luge.

lugubre /lygybʀ/ *adj* gloomy; mournful.

lui /lɥi/ *pron* **I** *pron m* **1** he; **elle lit, ~ regarde la télévision** she's reading, he's watching TV; **~ seul a le droit de parler** he alone has the right to talk; **2** him; **à cause de ~** because of him; **je les vois plus souvent que ~** I see them more often than he does; I see them more often than I see him; **c'est à ~** it's his, it belongs to him; it's his turn; **c'est à ~ de choisir** it's up to him to choose.

II *pron mf* it; **le parti lance un appel, apportez-~ votre soutien** the party is launching an appeal—give it your support; **l'Espagne a signé, le Portugal, ~, n'a pas encore donné son accord** Spain has signed while Portugal hasn't yet agreed.

III *pron f* her; **je ~ ai annoncé la nouvelle** I told her the news.

lui-même /lɥimɛm/ *pron* **1** (referring to person) himself; **'M. Greiner?'—'~'** (on phone) 'Mr Greiner?'—'speaking'; **2** (referring to object, concept) itself.

luire /lɥiʀ/ [69] *vi* to shine; to glow; **leur regard luisait de colère** their eyes blazed with anger.

luisant, **~e** /lɥizɑ̃, ɑ̃t/ *adj* shining; glistening.

lumbago /lœ̃bago/ *nm* back pain.

lumière /lymjɛʀ/ **I** *nf* **1** light; **~ naturelle/électrique** natural/electric light; **la ~ du jour** daylight; **il y a une ~ très particulière dans cette région** there's a very special quality to the light in this region; **les ~s de la ville** the city lights; **à la ~ d'une chandelle** by candlelight; **à la ~ des récents événements** in the light of recent events; **2** (person) **ce n'est pas une ~** he'll never set the world on fire.

II lumières *nf pl* **1** (of vehicle) lights; **2**° **j'ai besoin de vos ~s** I need to pick your brains.

Lumières /lymjɛʀ/ *nf pl* **le siècle des ~** the Age of Enlightenment.

luminaire /luminɛʀ/ *nm* light (fitting).

lumineux, **-euse** /lyminø, øz/ *adj* **1** luminous; **panneau ~** electronic display (board); **enseigne lumineuse** neon sign; **rayon ~** ray of light; **2 idée lumineuse** brilliant idea; **3** [*smile, gaze*] radiant.

luminosité /lyminozite/ *nf* brightness, luminosity.

lump /lœ̃p/ *nm* **œufs de ~** lumpfish roe.

lunaire /lynɛʀ/ *adj* lunar.

lunatique /lynatik/ *nmf* moody person.

lunch /lœ̃ʃ/ *nm* buffet (lunch); buffet (supper).

lundi /lœ̃di/ *nm* Monday.

lune /lyn/ *nf* moon; **pleine ~** full moon.

■ **~ de miel** honeymoon; **~ rousse** ≈ April moon.

IDIOMS **être dans la ~**○ to have one's head in the clouds; **avoir l'air de tomber de la ~** to look blank; **demander la ~**○ to cry for the moon; **promettre la ~**○ to promise the earth; **décrocher la ~** to do the impossible.

luné○, **~e** /lyne/ *adj* **mal ~** grumpy.

lunette /lynɛt/ **I** *nf* lavatory seat.
II lunettes *nf pl* **1** glasses; **2** (protective) goggles; **~s de natation** swimming goggles.
■ **~ arrière** (Aut) rear window; **~s noires** dark glasses; **~s de soleil** sunglasses.

lunule /lynyl/ *nf* (on nail) half-moon.

luron /lyʀɔ̃/ *nm* fellow.

lustre /lystʀ/ **I** *nm* **1** (gen) (decorative) ceiling light; (made of glass) chandelier; **2** sheen; **3** (of place, institution) prestigious image; **donner un nouveau ~ à** to give fresh appeal to.
II lustres○ *nm pl* **depuis des ~s** for ages○.

lustré, **~e** /lystʀe/ *adj* **1** glossy; (through wear) shiny; **2** [*fabric*] glazed.

lustrer /lystʀe/ [1] *vtr* to polish [*shoes, mirror*].

luth /lyt/ *nm* **1** (Mus) lute; **2** (Zool) leatherback.

lutin /lytɛ̃/ *nm* goblin.

lutte /lyt/ *nf* **1** conflict; struggle; fight; **~ d'influence** power struggle; **la ~ contre le cancer** the fight against cancer; **2** (Sport) wrestling.
■ **~ armée** armed conflict; **~ de classes** class war; **~ d'intérêts** clash of interests.

lutter /lyte/ [1] *vi* to struggle; to fight; **~ contre qn** to fight against sb; **~ contre** to fight [*crime, unemployment, illness*]; to fight against [*violence*]; to contend with [*noise, bad weather*]; **Louis luttait contre le sommeil** Louis was struggling to stay awake.

lutteur, **-euse** /lytœʀ, øz/ *nm,f* (gen) fighter; (Sport) wrestler.

luxe /lyks/ *nm* luxury; **s'offrir le ~ de faire** t afford the luxury of doing; (figurative) to giv oneself the satisfaction of doing; **je l'ai nettoy et ce n'était pas du ~**○ I gave it a muc needed clean; **avoir des goûts de ~** to hav expensive tastes.

Luxembourg /lyksɑ̃buʀ/ *pr nm* Luxembourg.

Luxembourgeois, **~e** /lyksɑ̃buʀʒwa, az *nm,f* **1** native of Luxembourg; **2** inhabitant o Luxembourg.

luxer: **se luxer** /lykse/ [1] *v refl* (+ *v être*) **s ~ l'épaule** to dislocate one's shoulder.

luxueux, **-euse** /lyksɥø, øz/ *adj* luxurious.

luxure /lyksyʀ/ *nf* lust.

luzerne /lyzɛʀn/ *nf* alfalfa, lucerne (GB).

lycée /lise/ *nm* secondary school (*preparin students aged 15–18 for the baccalaureate*).

lycéen, **-éenne** /liseɛ̃, ɛn/ *nm,f* secondar school student.

lyncher /lɛ̃ʃe/ [1] *vtr* to lynch.

lynx /lɛ̃ks/ *nm inv* lynx.

IDIOMS **avoir un œil** or **des yeux de ~** t have very keen eyesight.

lyonnais, **~e**[1] /ljɔnɛ, ɛz/ *adj* of Lyons.

lyonnaise[2] /ljɔnɛz/ *nf* **1** (Culin) **à la ~** à l lyonnaise; **2** *regional game of boules*.

lyophiliser /ljɔfilize/ [1] *vtr* to freeze-dry.

lyre /liʀ/ *nf* lyre.

lyrique /liʀik/ *adj* **1** (Mus) [*song, composer*] operatic; [*singer, season*] opera; **2** [*poetry, poet*] lyric; [*content, tone*] lyrical.

lyrisme /liʀism/ *nm* lyricism.

lys /lis/ *nm inv* lily.

Mm

n, **M** /ɛm/ *nm inv* **1** (letter) m, M; **2** (*written abbr* = **mètre**) **30 m** 30 m.
n' ▸ **me**.
M. (*written abbr* = **Monsieur**) Mr.
na ▸ **mon**.
nacabre /makabʀ/ *adj* macabre.
nacadam /makadam/ *nm* tarmac®.
nacaque /makak/ *nm* macaque.
nacaron /makaʀɔ̃/ *nm* **1** macaroon; **2** lapel badge; sticker.
nacédoine /masedwan/ *nf* mixed diced vegetables.
nacérer /maseʀe/ [14] *vi* [*plant, fruit*] to soak, to steep; [*meat*] to marinate.
nâche /mɑʃ/ *nf* corn salad, lamb's lettuce.
nâcher /mɑʃe/ [1] *vtr* to chew.
IDIOMS **~ la besogne** or **le travail à qn** to break the back of the work for sb; **il ne mâche pas ses mots** he doesn't mince his words.
nachette /maʃɛt/ *nf* machete.
nachiavélique /makjavelik/ *adj* Machiavellian.
nachin○ /maʃɛ̃/ *nm* **1** thing, thingummy○, whatsit○; **2** old fogey.
Machin○, **~e** /maʃɛ̃, in/ *nm,f* what's-his-name○/what's-her-name○.
nachinal, **~e**, *mpl* **-aux** /maʃinal, o/ *adj* [*gesture, reaction*] mechanical.
nachination /maʃinasjɔ̃/ *nf* plot.
nachine /maʃin/ *nf* **1** machine; **taper à la ~** to type; **coudre à la ~** to machine-sew; **faire deux ~s**○ **(de linge)** to do two loads of washing; **2** (Naut) engine; **faire ~ arrière** to go astern; (figurative) to back-pedal.
▪ **~ à calculer** calculating machine; **~ à coudre** sewing machine; **~ à écrire** typewriter; **~ à laver** washing machine; **~ à laver la vaisselle** dishwasher; **~ à sous** slot machine, one-armed bandit.
nachinerie /maʃinʀi/ *nf* **1** machinery; **2** machine room; (Naut) engine room.
nachiste /ma(t)ʃist/ *adj, nm* male chauvinist.
nâchoire /mɑʃwaʀ/ *nf* jaw.
nâchouiller○ /mɑʃuje/ [1] *vtr* to chew (on).
naçon /masɔ̃/ *nm* bricklayer; builder; mason.
naçonnerie /masɔnʀi/ *nf* building; bricklaying; masonry-work.
naculer /makyle/ [1] *vtr* to smudge; **~ qch de sang** to spatter sth with blood.
nadame, *pl* **mesdames** /madam, medam/ *nf* **1** (addressing a woman whose name you do not know) **Madame** (in letter) Dear Madam; **bonsoir ~!** good evening!; **mesdames et messieurs bonsoir** good evening ladies and gentlemen; **2** (addressing a woman whose name you know, for example Bon) Mrs, Ms; (in a letter) **Madame** Dear Ms Bon; **bonjour, ~** good morning, Mrs Bon; **3** (polite form of address) madam; **'~ a sonné?'** 'you rang, Madam?'
Madeleine /madlɛn/ *pr n* **pleurer comme une ~** to cry one's eyes out.
mademoiselle, *pl* **mesdemoiselles** /madmwazɛl, medmwazɛl/ *nf* **1** (addressing a woman whose name you do not know) **Mademoiselle** (in letter) Dear Madam; **bonjour, ~!** good morning!; **mesdames, mesdemoiselles, messieurs** ladies and gentlemen; **2** (addressing a woman whose name you know, for example Bon) Miss, Ms; (in a letter) **Mademoiselle** Dear Miss Bon; **bonjour, ~** good morning, Miss Bon; **3** (polite form of address) madam; **'~ a sonné?'** 'you rang, Madam?'
madone /madɔn/ *nf* madonna.
madrier /madʀije/ *nm* beam.
maestria /maɛstʀija/ *nf* brilliance, panache.
maf(f)ia /mafja/ *nf* mafia; **la Mafia** the Mafia.
maf(f)ieux, **-ieuse** /mafjø, øz/ *adj* mafia.
magasin /magazɛ̃/ *nm* **1** shop, store; **grand ~** department store; **faire les ~s** to go shopping; **2 avoir en ~** to have in stock.
magasinier, **-ière** /magazinje, ɛʀ/ *nm,f* **1** stock controller; **2** warehouse keeper.
magazine /magazin/ *nm* magazine.
mage /maʒ/ *nm* magus; **les rois ~s** the (Three) Wise Men.
maghrébin, **~e** /magʀebɛ̃, in/ *adj* North African, Maghrebi.
magicien, **-ienne** /maʒisjɛ̃, ɛn/ *nm,f* **1** magician/enchantress; **2** conjuror; **3** (figurative) wizard.
magie /maʒi/ *nf* **1** magic; **2** conjuring.
magique /maʒik/ *adj* **1** magic; **formule ~** magic words; **2** (figurative) magical.
magistère /maʒistɛʀ/ *nm*: *high-level University degree*.
magistral, **~e**, *mpl* **-aux** /maʒistʀal, o/ *adj* **1** brilliant; **réussir un coup ~** to bring off a masterstroke; **2** magisterial.
magistrat /maʒistʀa/ *nm* magistrate.
magistrature /maʒistʀatyʀ/ *nf* **1** magistracy; **2** public office.
magma /magma/ *nm* **1** magma; **2** (figurative) jumble.
magnanime /maɲanim/ *adj* magnanimous.
magnat /maɲa/ *nm* magnate, tycoon.
magnésie /maɲezi/ *nf* magnesia.
magnétique /maɲetik/ *adj* magnetic.
magnétiseur, **-euse** /maɲetizœʀ, øz/ *nm,f* healer.
magnétisme /maɲetism/ *nm* magnetism.
magnéto(phone) /maɲetɔ(fɔn)/ *nm* tape recorder.

magnétophone /maɲetɔfɔn/ *nm* tape recorder.

magnétoscope /maɲetɔskɔp/ *nm* VCR, video recorder.

magnifique /maɲifik/ *adj* gorgeous, magnificent.

magot○ /mago/ *nm* pile○ (of money).

magouille○ /maguj/ *nf* **1** wangling○, fiddling○; **2** trick; **~s politiques** political skulduggery; **~s électorales** election rigging.

magret /magʀɛ/ *nm* **~ de canard** duck breast.

Mahomet /maɔmɛ/ *pr n* Mohammed.

mai /mɛ/ *nm* May; **le premier ~** May Day.

maigre /mɛgʀ/ **I** *adj* **1** [*person*] thin; **2** [*meat*] lean; [*cheese*] low-fat; **3** [*day*] without meat; **faire** or **manger ~** to abstain from meat; **4** [*talents, savings*] meagre[GB]; [*applause*] scant; **5** [*lawn, hair*] sparse.

II *nmf* thin man/woman; **c'est une fausse ~** she looks thinner than she is.

maigrement /mɛgʀəmɑ̃/ *adv* [*paid*] poorly.

maigreur /mɛgʀœʀ/ *nf* **1** thinness; **2** meagreness[GB].

maigrichon, -onne /mɛgʀiʃɔ̃, ɔn/ *adj* skinny.

maigrir /mɛgʀiʀ/ [3] *vi* to lose weight.

mail /maj/ *nm* **1** mall; **2** (game) pall-mall.

mailing /mɛliŋ/ *nm* (controversial) **1** direct mail advertising; **2** mail shot; **3** mailing pack.

maille /maj/ *nf* **1** stitch; **une ~ qui file** (in tights) a ladder; **2** mesh; **passer à travers les ~s** to slip through the net; **3** (in fence) link.

IDIOMS **avoir ~ à partir avec qn** to have a brush with sb.

maillet /majɛ/ *nm* mallet.

maillon /majɔ̃/ *nm* (in chain) link.

maillot /majo/ *nm* **1 ~ (de corps)** vest (GB), undershirt (US); **2** (of footballer) shirt; (of cyclist) jersey; **3** swimsuit.

■ **~ de bain** swimsuit; **le ~ jaune** the leader in the Tour de France.

main /mɛ̃/ *nf* **1** hand; **se donner** or **se tenir la ~** to hold hands; **saluer qn de la ~** to wave at sb; **haut les ~s!** hands up!; **demander la ~ de qn** to ask for sb's hand in marriage; **avoir qch bien en ~(s)** to hold sth firmly; (figurative) to have sth well in hand; **si tu lèves la ~ sur elle** if you lay a finger on her; **à la ~** [*sew*] by hand; [*adjust*] manually; **fait ~** handmade; **vol à ~ armée** armed robbery; **donner un coup de ~ à qn** to give sb a hand; **2 une ~ secourable** a helping hand; **une ~ criminelle** someone with criminal intentions; **3 avoir qch sous la ~** to have sth to hand; **cela m'est tombé sous la ~** I just happened to come across it; **mettre la ~ sur qch** to get one's hands on sth; **je n'arrive pas à mettre la ~ dessus** I can't lay my hands on it; **je l'ai eu entre les ~s mais** I did have it but; **être entre les ~s de qn** [*power*] to be in sb's hands; **prendre qn/qch en ~s** to take sb/sth in hand; **à ne pas mettre entre toutes les ~s** [*book*] not for general reading; **tomber entre les ~s de qn** to fall into sb's hands; **les ~s vides** empty-handed; **je le lui ai remis e ~s propres** I gave it to him/her in person; **d la ~ à la ~** [*sell*] privately; [*be paid*] cash (i hand); **4 écrit de la ~ du président** writte by the president himself; **de ma plus belle ~** in my best handwriting; **5 avoir le coup de ~** to have the knack; **se faire la ~** to practise[G] **6** (in cards) hand; deal; **7 à ~ droite/gauch** on the right/left.

■ **~ courante** handrail.

IDIOMS **j'en mettrais ma ~ au feu** or **couper** I'd swear to it; **d'une ~ de fer** wit an iron rod; **il n'y est pas allé de ~ morte**○ he didn't pull his punches!; **avoir la ~ leste** t be always ready with a slap; **faire ~ bass sur** to help oneself to [*goods*]; to take ove [*market, country*]; **en venir aux ~s** to come t blows; **avoir la ~ heureuse** to be lucky.

main-d'œuvre, *pl* **mains-d'œuvre** /m dœvʀ/ *nf* labour[GB].

main-forte /mɛ̃fɔʀt/ *nf inv* **prêter ~ à qn** t come to sb's aid.

mainmise /mɛ̃miz/ *nf* seizure.

maint, ~e /mɛ̃, mɛ̃t/ *det* many, many a; **~es reprises** many times.

maintenance /mɛ̃tnɑ̃s/ *nf* maintenance.

maintenant /mɛ̃t(ə)nɑ̃/ *adv* now; nowadays **commence dès ~** start straightaway.

maintenir /mɛ̃t(ə)niʀ/ [36] **I** *vtr* **1** to keep; t maintain; to keep up; **~ qch debout** to kee sth upright; **2** to support [*wall, ankle*]; **3** t stand by [*decision*]; **~ que** to maintain tha **~ sa candidature** [*politician*] not to withdra one's candidacy.

II se maintenir *v refl* (+ *v être*) [*trend*] t persist; [*price*] to remain stable; [*weather*] t remain fair; [*political system*] to remain i force; [*currency*] to hold steady.

maintien /mɛ̃tjɛ̃/ *nm* **1** maintaining; **assure le ~ de l'ordre** to maintain order; **2** suppor **3** deportment.

maire /mɛʀ/ *nm* mayor.

■ **~ adjoint** deputy mayor.

mairie /mɛʀi/ *nf* **1** town council (GB) or ha (US); **être élu à la ~ de** to be elected mayo of; **2** town hall.

mais /mɛ/ *conj* but; **incroyable ~ vrai** strang but true; **il est bête, ~ bête**○**!** he's so incre ibly stupid!; **~, vous pleurez!** good heaven you're crying!; **~ j'y pense** now that I come t think of it.

maïs /mais/ *nm inv* **1** maize (GB), corn (US **2** sweetcorn; **épi de ~** corn on the cob.

maison /mɛzɔ̃/ **I** *adj inv* [*product*] home-made. **II** *nf* **1** house; **2** home; **3** family, househol **gens de ~** domestic staff; **4** firm; **avoir 1 ans de ~** to have been with the firm for 1 years.

■ **~ d'arrêt** prison; **~ bourgeoise** *impo ing town house*; **~ de campagne** house i the country; **~ close** brothel; **~ de corre tion** institution for young offenders; **~ de l culture** ≈ community arts centre[GB]; **~ de jeunes et de la culture**, **MJC** ≈ youth club **~ de maître** manor; **~ mère** hea

quarters; main branch; **~ de passe** brothel; **~ de retraite** old people's or retirement home; **~ de santé** nursing home; **la Maison Blanche** the White House.
IDIOMS **c'est gros comme une ~**○ it sticks out a mile.

maisonnée /mɛzɔne/ *nf* household; family.

maître, **-esse**[1] /mɛtʀ, ɛs/ **I** *adj* **1 être ~ de soi** to have self-control; **être ~ chez soi** to be master in one's own house; **être ~ de son véhicule** to be in control of one's vehicle; **2** main; key; major.
II *nm,f* **1** teacher; **2** (of house) master/mistress; **3** (of animal) owner.
III *nm* **1** ruler; **être (le) seul ~ à bord** to be in sole command; **être son propre ~** to be one's own master/mistress; **régner en ~ absolu** to reign supreme; **2** master; **être passé ~ dans l'art de qch/de faire** to be a past master of sth/at doing; **en ~** masterfully; **3** (also **Me**) Maître (*form of address given to members of the legal profession*).
■ **~ d'hôtel** maître d'hôtel (GB), maître d' (US); **~ à penser** mentor; **maîtresse femme** strong-minded woman.
IDIOMS **trouver son ~** to meet one's match.

maître-assistant, **~e**, *mpl* **maîtres-assistants** /mɛtʀasistɑ̃, ɑ̃t/ *nm,f* ≈ senior lecturer (GB), senior instructor (US).

maître-chanteur, *pl* **maîtres-chanteurs** /mɛtʀəʃɑ̃tœʀ/ *nm* blackmailer.

maître-nageur, *pl* **maîtres-nageurs** /mɛtʀənaʒœʀ/ *nm* **1** swimming instructor; **2** pool attendant.

maîtresse[2] /mɛtʀɛs/ **I** *adj f* ▶ **maître I**.
II *nf* **1** ▶ **maître II**; **2** mistress.

maîtrise /mɛtʀiz/ *nf* **1** mastery; **2** perfect command; **3 ~ (de soi)** self-control; **4** master's degree.

maîtriser /mɛtʀize/ [1] **I** *vtr* **1** to control [*feelings*]; to bring [sth] under control [*fire*]; to overcome [*opponent*]; **2** to master [*language*].
II se maîtriser *v refl* (+ *v être*) to have self-control.

maïzena® /maizena/ *nf* cornflour.

majesté /maʒɛste/ *nf* majesty.

majestueux, **-euse** /maʒɛstɥø, øz/ *adj* majestic; stately.

majeur, **~e** /maʒœʀ/ **I** *adj* **1 être ~** to be over 18 or of age; **2** main, major; **en ~e partie** for the most part; **3** (Mus) major.
II *nm* middle finger.

majoration /maʒɔʀasjɔ̃/ *nf* increase.

majordome /maʒɔʀdɔm/ *nm* butler.

majorer /maʒɔʀe/ [1] *vtr* to increase.

majoritaire /maʒɔʀitɛʀ/ *adj* majority.

majoritairement /maʒɔʀitɛʀmɑ̃/ *adv* **1** by a majority (vote); **2 province ~ catholique** predominantly Catholic province.

majorité /maʒɔʀite/ *nf* **1** majority; **ils sont en ~** they are in the majority; **ce sont, en ~, des enfants** they are, for the most part, children; **2 la ~** the government, the party in power.

majuscule /maʒyskyl/ **I** *adj* capital.
II *nf* capital (letter).

mal, *mpl* **maux** /mal, mo/ **I** *adj inv* **1** wrong; **qu'a-t-elle fait de ~?** what has she done wrong?; **2** bad; **ce ne serait pas ~ de déménager** it wouldn't be a bad idea to move out; **3**○ **il n'est pas mal** [*film*] it's not bad; [*man*] he's not bad(-looking).
II *nm* **1** trouble, difficulty; **avoir du ~ à faire** to find it difficult to do; **se donner du ~** to go to a lot of trouble; **ne te donne pas ce ~!** don't bother!; **2** pain; **faire ~** to hurt, to be painful; **se faire ~** to hurt oneself; **j'ai ~** it hurts; **avoir ~ partout** to ache all over; **elle avait très ~** she was in pain; **avoir ~ à la tête** to have a headache; **avoir ~ à la gorge** to have a sore throat; **j'ai ~ au genou** my knee hurts; **j'ai ~ au cœur** I feel sick (GB) or nauseous; **3** illness, disease; **4 être en ~ de** to be short of [*inspiration*]; to be lacking in [*affection*]; **5** harm; **faire du ~ à** to harm, to hurt; **une douche ne te ferait pas de ~** (humorous) a shower wouldn't do you any harm; **6 le ~** evil; **qu'elle parte, est-ce vraiment un ~?** is it really a bad thing that she is leaving?; **sans penser à ~** without meaning any harm; **dire du ~ de qn/qch** to speak ill of sb/sth.
III *adv* **1** badly; not properly; **elle travaille ~** her work isn't good; **je t'entends ~** I can't hear you very well; **2** with difficulty; **on voit ~ comment** it's difficult to see how; **3** [*diagnosed, addressed*] wrongly; **j'avais ~ compris** I had misunderstood; **~ informé** ill-informed; **4 se trouver ~** to faint; **être ~ (assis** or **couché** or **installé)** not to be comfortable; **être au plus ~** to be critically ill.
IV pas mal *phr* **1** [*travel, read*] quite a lot; **2 il ne s'en est pas ~ tiré** (in exam) he coped quite well; (in dangerous situation) he got off lightly.
■ **~ de l'air** airsickness; **~ de mer** seasickness; **~ du pays** homesickness; **~ du siècle** world-weariness; **~ des transports** travel sickness.

malade /malad/ **I** *adj* [*person*] ill, sick; [*animal*] sick; [*organ, plant*] diseased; **tomber ~** to fall ill or sick, to get sick (US); **être ~ en voiture/en avion** to get carsick/airsick; **j'en suis ~**○ (figurative) it makes me sick; **~ d'inquiétude** worried sick.
II *nmf* **1** sick man/woman; **2** patient.
■ **~ imaginaire** hypochondriac; **~ mental** mentally ill person.

maladie /maladi/ *nf* illness, disease; **il va en faire une ~**○ (figurative) he'll have a fit○.
■ **~ sexuellement transmissible**, **MST** sexually transmitted disease, STD; **~ du sommeil** sleeping sickness.

maladif, **-ive** /maladif, iv/ *adj* [*child*] sickly; [*jealousy*] pathological.

maladresse /maladʀɛs/ *nf* **1** clumsiness, awkwardness; **2** tactlessness; **3** blunder.

maladroit, **~e** /maladʀwa, wat/ **I** *adj* **1** clumsy; **2** tactless.
II *nm,f* **1** clumsy person; **2** tactless person.

maladroitement /maladʀwatmɑ̃/ *adv* **1** clumsily, awkwardly; **2** tactlessly; ineptly.

malaise /malɛz/ *nm* **1** dizzy turn; **avoir un ~** to feel faint; **2** (figurative) uneasiness; unrest.
■ **~ cardiaque** mild heart attack.

malaxer /malakse/ [1] *vtr* **1** to cream [*butter*]; to knead [*dough*]; **2** to mix [*cement*].

malchance /malʃɑ̃s/ *nf* bad luck, misfortune; **par ~** as ill luck would have it.

malchanceux, **-euse** /malʃɑ̃sø, øz/ *adj* unlucky.

mâle /mɑl/ I *adj* **1** male; [*elephant*] bull; [*antelope, rabbit*] buck; [*sparrow*] cock; **cygne ~** cob; **canard ~** drake; **2** manly.
II *nm* **1** male; **2** (humorous) he-man○.

malédiction /malediksjɔ̃/ *nf* curse.

maléfice /malefis/ *nm* evil spell.

maléfique /malefik/ *adj* evil.

malencontreux, **-euse** /malɑ̃kɔ̃tʀø, øz/ *adj* unfortunate.

malentendant, **~e** /malɑ̃tɑ̃dɑ̃, ɑ̃t/ *nm,f* **les ~s** the hearing-impaired.

malentendu /malɑ̃tɑ̃dy/ *nm* misunderstanding.

malfaiteur /malfɛtœʀ/ *nm* criminal.

malformation /malfɔʀmasjɔ̃/ *nf* malformation.

malgache /malgaʃ/ *adj, nm* Malagasy.

malgré /malgʀe/ *prep* in spite of, despite; **~ cela**, **~ tout** nevertheless; **~ moi** against my wishes; reluctantly.

malheur /malœʀ/ *nm* **1 le ~** misfortune, adversity; **faire le ~ de qn** to bring sb nothing but unhappiness; **2** misfortune; accident; **un grand ~** a tragedy; **un ~ est si vite arrivé!** accidents can so easily happen!; **3** misfortune; **ceux qui ont le ~ de faire** those who are unfortunate enough to do; **j'ai eu le ~ de le leur dire** I made the mistake of telling them; **par ~** as bad luck would have it; **si par ~ la guerre éclatait** if, God forbid, war should break out; **porter ~** to be bad luck.
IDIOMS **faire un ~**○ to be a sensation; to go wild; **à quelque chose ~ est bon** (Proverb) every cloud has a silver lining.

malheureusement /maløʀøzmɑ̃/ *adv* unfortunately.

malheureux, **-euse** /maløʀø, øz/ I *adj* **1** [*person, life*] unhappy, miserable; [*victim, choice, word*] unfortunate; [*candidate*] unlucky; **c'est ~ que** it's a pity or shame that; **2**○ [*sum*] paltry, pathetic.
II *nm,f* **1** poor wretch; **le ~!** poor man!; **2** poor person; **les ~** the poor.
IDIOMS **être ~ comme les pierres** to be as miserable as sin.

malhonnête /malɔnɛt/ *adj* dishonest.

malhonnêteté /malɔnɛtte/ *nf* dishonesty.

malice /malis/ *nf* **1** mischief; **2**† malice; **être sans ~** to be harmless.

malicieux, **-ieuse** /malisjø, øz/ *adj* mischievous.

malin, **maligne** /malɛ̃, maliɲ/ I *adj* **1** clever; **j'ai eu l'air ~!** (ironic) I looked like a tota fool!; **2** malicious; **3** (Med) malignant.
II *nm,f* **c'est un ~** he's a crafty one.
IDIOMS **à ~, ~ et demi** (Proverb) there' always someone who will outwit you.

malingre /malɛ̃gʀ/ *adj* [*person, tree*] sickly.

malintentionné, **~e** /malɛ̃tɑ̃sjɔne/ *adj* mal cious.

malle /mal/ *nf* trunk.

malléabilité /maleabilite/ *nf* malleability.

mallette /malɛt/ *nf* briefcase.

malmener /malməne/ [16] *vtr* **1** to manhandl **2** to give [sb] a rough ride.

malnutrition /malnytʀisjɔ̃/ *nf* malnutrition.

malodorant, **~e** /malɔdɔʀɑ̃, ɑ̃t/ *adj* fou smelling.

malotru, **~e** /malɔtʀy/ *nm,f* boor.

Malouines /malwin/ *pr nf pl* **les (îles) ~** th Falklands.

malpoli, **~e** /malpɔli/ *adj* rude.

malsain, **~e** /malsɛ̃, ɛn/ *adj* unhealthy.

Malte /malt/ *pr nf* Malta.

maltraiter /maltʀete/ [1] *vtr* to mistreat.

malveillance /malvɛjɑ̃s/ *nf* malice.

malveillant, **~e** /malvɛjɑ̃, ɑ̃t/ *adj* malicious.

malvenu, **~e** /malvəny/ *adj* out of place.

malversation /malvɛʀsasjɔ̃/ *nf* **1** malpractic **2** embezzlement.

maman /mɑmɑ̃/ *nf* mum○ (GB), mom○ (US).

mamelle /mamɛl/ *nf* udder; teat.

mamelon /mamlɔ̃/ *nm* **1** nipple; **2** hillock.

mamie○ /mami/ *nf* granny○, grandma○.

mammifère /mamifɛʀ/ *nm* mammal.

mammouth /mamut/ *nm* mammoth.

mamy = **mamie**.

manager, **manageur** /manaʒœʀ/ *nm* ma ager.

manche[1] /mɑ̃ʃ/ *nm* **1** (of tool) handle; (of violi neck; **2**○ clumsy idiot.
■ **~ à balai** broomhandle; broomstic joystick.

manche[2] /mɑ̃ʃ/ *nf* **1** sleeve; **sans ~s** sleev less; **2** (Sport) round; (in cards) hand; (in bridg game; (in tennis) set.
IDIOMS **avoir qn dans la ~** to have sb i one's pocket; **c'est une autre paire de ~s** it's a different ball game○.

Manche /mɑ̃ʃ/ *pr nf* **la ~** the (Englis Channel.

manchette /mɑ̃ʃɛt/ *nf* **1** (double) cuff; **2** ove sleeve; **3** headline.

manchot, **-otte** /mɑ̃ʃo, ɔt/ I *adj* one-arme one-handed; **il est ~** he's only got one arm; **n pas être ~**○ to be pretty good with one hands○.
II *nm* penguin.

mandarine /mɑ̃daʀin/ *nf* mandarin orange.

mandat /mɑ̃da/ *nm* **1 ~ (postal)** mone order; **2** term of office; **exercer son ~** to b in office; **3** mandate.
■ **~ d'arrêt** (arrest) warrant; **~ d'expu**

sion expulsion order; eviction order; **~ de perquisition** search warrant.

mandataire /mɑ̃datɛʀ/ *nmf* **1** representative, agent; **2** proxy.

mandater /mɑ̃date/ [1] *vtr* to appoint [sb] as one's representative; to give a mandate to.

mandat-lettre, *pl* **mandats-lettres** /mɑ̃dalɛtʀ/ *nm* postal order.

mandibule /mɑ̃dibyl/ *nf* mandible.

mandoline /mɑ̃dɔlin/ *nf* mandolin.

manège /manɛʒ/ *nm* **1** merry-go-round; **2** riding school; **3** (little) trick, (little) game; **j'ai bien observé ton ~** I know what you are up to.

manette /manɛt/ *nf* **1** lever; joystick; **2** (figurative) **~s** controls.

mangeable /mɑ̃ʒabl/ *adj* edible.

mangeoire /mɑ̃ʒwaʀ/ *nf* manger; trough; feeding tray.

manger[1] /mɑ̃ʒe/ [13] **I** *vtr* **1** to eat; **il n'y a rien à ~ dans la maison** there's no food in the house; **2** to use up [*savings*]; to go through [*inheritance*]; to take up [*time*]; **3** [*rust, acid*] to eat away; **4 ~ ses mots** to mumble.
II *vi* to eat; **~ au restaurant** to eat out; **~ à sa faim** to eat one's fill; **donner à ~ à qn** to feed sb; to give [sb] something to eat; **faire à ~** to cook; **inviter qn à ~** to invite sb for a meal; **~ chinois** to have a Chinese meal; **on mange mal ici** the food is not good here.
III se manger *v refl* (+ *v être*) **ça se mange?** can you eat it?; **le gaspacho se mange froid** gazpacho is served cold.

manger[2] /mɑ̃ʒe/ *nm* food.

mangeur, **-euse** /mɑ̃ʒœʀ, øz/ *nm,f* **bon/gros ~** good/big eater.
■ **mangeuse d'hommes** man-eater.

mangouste /mɑ̃gust/ *nf* **1** mongoose; **2** mangosteen.

mangue /mɑ̃g/ *nf* mango.

maniable /manjabl/ *adj* [*object, car*] easy to handle; [*book*] manageable in size.

maniaque /manjak/ **I** *adj* particular, fussy.
II *nmf* **1** fusspot (GB), fussbudget (US); **2** fanatic; **c'est un ~ de l'ordre** he's obsessive about tidiness; **3** maniac; **4** (Med) manic.

manie /mani/ *nf* **1** habit; **c'est une vraie ~** it's an absolute obsession; **2** quirk, idiosyncrasy; **3** (Med) mania.

maniement /manimɑ̃/ *nm* handling; (of machine) operation; (of language) command.
■ **~ d'armes** arms drill.

manier /manje/ [2] **I** *vtr* to handle.
II se manier *v refl* (+ *v être*) **se ~ aisément** [*tool*] to be easy to handle; [*car*] to handle well.
IDIOMS **~ la fourchette avec entrain**○ (humorous) to have a hearty appetite.

manière /manjɛʀ/ *nf* **1** way; **d'une certaine ~** in a way; **leur ~ de vivre/penser** their way of life/thinking; **de toutes les ~s possibles** in every possible way; **de telle ~ que** in such a way that; **de ~ à faire** so as to do; **de ~ à ce que** so that; **à ma ~** my (own) way; **de quelle ~?** how?; **de toute ~, de toutes ~s** anyway, in any case; **la ~ forte** strong-arm tactics, force; **2** style; **à la ~ de qn/qch** in the style of sb/sth; **3** manners; **faire des ~s** to stand on ceremony.

maniéré, **~e** /manjeʀe/ *adj* affected.

manifestant, **~e** /manifɛstɑ̃, ɑ̃t/ *nm,f* demonstrator.

manifestation /manifɛstasjɔ̃/ *nf* **1** demonstration; **2** event; **~s sportives** sporting events; **3** (of phenomenon) appearance; **4** (of feeling) expression, manifestation.
■ **~ silencieuse** vigil; **~ de soutien** rally.

manifeste /manifɛst/ **I** *adj* obvious, manifest.
II *nm* manifesto.

manifester /manifɛste/ [1] **I** *vtr* to show [*courage*]; to express [*desire, fears*]; **~ sa présence** to make one's presence known.
II *vi* to demonstrate; **appeler à ~ le 5 juin** to call a demonstration for 5 June.
III se manifester *v refl* (+ *v être*) **1** [*symptom*] to manifest itself; [*phenomenon*] to appear; [*worry*] to show itself; **2** [*witness*] to come forward; [*person*] to appear; to get in touch.

manigance /manigɑ̃s/ *nf* little scheme.

manigancer /manigɑ̃se/ [12] *vtr* **~ quelque chose** to be up to something; **~ un mauvais coup** to hatch up a scheme.

manipulation /manipylasjɔ̃/ *nf* **1** (of object) handling; **2** manipulation; **3** (Sch) experiment.

manipuler /manipyle/ [1] *vtr* **1** to handle [*object*]; to use [*words*]; **2** to manipulate [*person*].

manivelle /manivɛl/ *nf* handle.
IDIOMS **donner le premier tour de ~** to start filming.

manne /man/ *nf* godsend.

mannequin /mankɛ̃/ *nm* **1** (fashion) model; **2** dummy.

manœuvre[1] /manœvʀ/ *nm* unskilled worker.

manœuvre[2] /manœvʀ/ *nf* manoeuvre (GB), maneuver (US); **champ de ~** military training area; **fausse ~** mistake.

manœuvrer /manœvʀe/ [1] **I** *vtr* **1** to manoeuvre (GB), to maneuver (US) [*vehicle*]; **2** to operate [*machine*]; **3** to manipulate [*person*].
II *vi* to manoeuvre (GB), to maneuver (US).

manoir /manwaʀ/ *nm* manor (house).

manomètre /manɔmɛtʀ/ *nm* pressure gauge.

manquant, **~e** /mɑ̃kɑ̃, ɑ̃t/ *adj* missing.

manque /mɑ̃k/ **I** *nm* **1 ~ de** lack of; shortage of; **~ de chance, il est tombé malade** just his luck, he fell ill; **2** gap; **en ~ d'affection** in need of affection; **être en ~** [*drug addict*] to be suffering from withdrawal symptoms.
II à la manque○ *phr* **une idée à la ~** a useless idea.

manqué, **~e** /mɑ̃ke/ **I** *pp* ▸ **manquer**.
II *pp adj* [*attempt*] failed; [*opportunity*] missed.

manquer /mɑ̃ke/ [1] **I** *vtr* **1** to miss; **un film à ne pas ~** a film not to be missed; **tu l'as manquée de cinq minutes** you missed her/it by five minutes; **2 ~ son coup**○ to fail; **3**○ **la**

prochaine fois je ne le manquerai pas next time I won't let him get away with it.
II **manquer à** *v+prep* **1 ~ à qn** to be missed by sb; **ma tante me manque** I miss my aunt; **2 ~ à sa parole** to break one's word.
III **manquer de** *v+prep* **1 ~ de** to lack; **on ne manque de rien** we don't want for anything; **elle ne manque pas de charme** she's not without charm; **on manque d'air ici** it's stuffy in here; **2 je ne manquerai pas de vous le faire savoir** I'll be sure to let you know; **et évidemment, ça n'a pas manqué**○! and sure enough that's what happened!; **3 il a manqué (de) casser un carreau** he almost broke a windowpane.
IV *vi* **1 les vivres vinrent à ~** the supplies ran out; **le courage leur manqua** their courage failed them; **ce n'est pas l'envie qui m'en manque** it's not that I don't want to; **2** [*person*] to be absent; to be missing.
V *v impers* **il lui manque un doigt** he's got a finger missing; **il nous manque deux joueurs pour former une équipe** we're two players short of a team; **il ne manquerait plus que ça**○! that would be the last straw!
VI **se manquer** *v refl* (+ *v être*) to miss each other.

mansarde /mɑ̃saʀd/ *nf* attic room.

mansardé, **~e** /mɑ̃saʀde/ *adj* [*room*] attic.

manteau, *pl* **~x** /mɑ̃to/ *nm* coat.
■ **~ de cheminée** mantelpiece.
IDIOMS **sous le ~** illicitly.

manucure /manykyʀ/ I *nmf* manicurist.
II *nf* manicure.

manuel, **-elle** /manɥɛl/ I *adj* manual.
II *nm* manual; (Sch) textbook.
■ **~ de conversation** phrase book.

manuellement /manɥɛlmɑ̃/ *adv* manually.

manufacture /manyfaktyʀ/ *nf* **1** factory; **2** manufacture.

manu militari /manymilitaʀi/ *adv* forcibly.

manuscrit, **~e** /manyskʀi, it/ I *adj* handwritten.
II *nm* manuscript.

manutention /manytɑ̃sjɔ̃/ *nf* handling.

manutentionnaire /manytɑ̃sjɔnɛʀ/ *nm* warehouseman.

mappemonde /mapmɔ̃d/ *nf* **1** map of the world (in two hemispheres); **2** globe.

maquereau, *pl* **~x** /makʀo/ *nm* mackerel.

maquette /makɛt/ *nf* scale model.

maquillage /makijaʒ/ *nm* **1** making-up; **2** make-up.

maquiller /makije/ [1] I *vtr* **1** to make [sb] up; **2** to doctor [*truth*]; **~ un crime en accident** to disguise a crime as an accident.
II **se maquiller** *v refl* (+ *v être*) **1** to put make-up on; **2** to wear make-up.

maquis /maki/ *nm inv* maquis; **prendre le ~** to go underground.

maquisard, **~e** /makizaʀ, aʀd/ *nm,f* member of the Resistance.

marabout /maʀabu/ *nm* **1** marabou; **2** marabout.

maraîcher, **-ère** /maʀɛʃe, ɛʀ/ I *adj* **produits ~s** market garden produce (GB), truck (US).
II *nm,f* market gardener (GB), truck farmer (US).

marais /maʀɛ/ *nm inv* marsh; swamp.
■ **~ salant** saltern.

marasme /maʀasm/ *nm* stagnation.

marathon /maʀatɔ̃/ *nm* marathon.

marâtre /maʀɑtʀ/ *nf* cruel mother.

maraudeur, **-euse** /maʀodœʀ, øz/ *nm,f* petty thief.

marbre /maʀbʀ/ *nm* **1** marble; **2** marble top; **3** marble statue.
IDIOMS **rester de ~** to remain stony-faced; **la nouvelle les laissa de ~** they were completely unmoved by the news.

marbrer /maʀbʀe/ [1] *vtr* to marble.

marbrure /maʀbʀyʀ/ *nf* marbling.

marc /maʀ/ *nm* marc.
■ **~ de café** coffee grounds.

marcassin /maʀkasɛ̃/ *nm* young wild boar.

marchand, **~e** /maʀʃɑ̃, ɑ̃d/ I *adj* [*quality*] marketable; [*sector*] trade; [*value*] market.
II *nm,f* shopkeeper; stallholder; **~ d'armes/de bestiaux** arms/cattle dealer; **~ de charbon/vins** coal/wine merchant.
■ **~ ambulant** hawker; **~ de couleurs** ironmonger (GB), hardware merchant; **~ de glaces** ice cream vendor; **~ en gros** wholesaler; **~ de journaux** newsagent; news vendor; **~ des quatre saisons** costermonger (GB), fruit and vegetable merchant; **~ de sable** sandman; **~ de tapis** carpet salesman.

marchandage /maʀʃɑ̃daʒ/ *nm* haggling.

marchander /maʀʃɑ̃de/ [1] *vtr* **1** to haggle over; **2** (figurative) **~ sa peine** not to put oneself out.

marchandise /maʀʃɑ̃diz/ *nf* goods, merchandise; **tromper qn sur la ~** to swindle sb.

marche /maʀʃ/ *nf* **1** walking; walk; pace, step; **faire de la ~** to go walking; **à 10 minutes de ~** 10 minutes' walk away; **2** march; **fermer la ~** to bring up the rear; **ouvrir la ~** to be at the head of the march; **3** (of vehicle) progress; (of events) course; (of time) march; **bus en ~** moving bus; **dans le sens contraire de la ~** facing backward(s); **4** (of mechanism) operation; (of organization) running; **en état de ~** in working order; **mettre en ~** to start (up) [*machine*]; to switch on [*TV*]; **5** step; **les ~s** the stairs.
■ **~ arrière** reverse; **faire ~ arrière** to reverse; (figurative) to backpedal; **~ avant** forward; **~ à suivre** procedure.
IDIOMS **prendre le train en ~** to join halfway through; to climb onto the bandwagon.

marché /maʀʃe/ *nm* **1** market; **faire son ~** to do one's shopping at the market; **2** deal; **conclure un ~ avec qn** to strike a deal with sb; **~ conclu!** it's a deal!; **bon/meilleur ~** cheap/cheaper; **par-dessus le ~**○ to top it all.
■ **~ de l'emploi** job market; **~ libre** free market; **~ noir** black market; **~ aux**

puces flea market; **~ du travail** labour[GB] market; **Marché commun** Common Market.

marchepied /marʃəpje/ *nm* **1** step; **2** steps.

marcher /marʃe/ [1] *vi* **1** to walk; [*demonstrators*] to march; **2** to tread; **se laisser ~ sur les pieds** (figurative) to let oneself be walked over; **3** [*mechanism, system*] to work; **ma radio marche mal** my radio doesn't work properly; **faire ~ qch** to get sth to work; **~ au gaz** to run on gas; **les bus ne marchent pas le soir** the buses don't run in the evenings; **4**○ **~ (bien)/~ mal** [*work, relationship*] to go well/not to go well; [*film, student*] to do well/not to do well; [*actor*] to go down well/not to go down well; **5**○ **c'est trop risqué, je ne marche pas** it's too risky, count me out; **ça marche!** it's a deal!; **6**○ to fall for it; **7 faire ~ qn** to pull sb's leg; **faire ~ son monde**○ to be good at giving orders.
IDIOMS **il ne marche pas, il court**○**!** he's as gullible as they come.

marcheur, **-euse** /marʃœr, øz/ *nm,f* walker.

mardi /mardi/ *nm* Tuesday.

mare /mar/ *nf* **1** pond; **2 ~ de** pool of [*blood*].

marécage /marekaʒ/ *nm* marsh, swamp.

marécageux, **-euse** /marekaʒø, øz/ *adj* [*ground*] marshy, swampy; [*plant*] marsh.

maréchal, *pl* **-aux** /mareʃal, o/ *nm* ≈ field marshal (GB), general of the army (US).

maréchal-ferrant, *pl* **maréchaux-ferrants** /mareʃalfɛrɑ̃, mareʃofɛrɑ̃/ *nm* farrier.

marée /mare/ *nf* tide; **la ~ monte/descend** the tide is coming in/is going out; **à ~ haute/basse** at high/low tide.
■ **~ noire** oil slick.
IDIOMS **contre vents et ~s** come hell or high water; against all odds.

marelle /marɛl/ *nf* hopscotch.

marémoteur, **-trice** /maremɔtœr, tris/ *adj* tidal; **usine marémotrice** tidal power station.

margarine /margarin/ *nf* margarine.

marge /marʒ/ **I** *nf* **1** margin; **2** leeway; **on a 10 minutes de ~** we've got 10 minutes to spare; **3** scope; **tu devrais me laisser plus de ~ de décision** you should allow me more scope for making decisions; **4** profit margin; mark-up.
II en marge de *phr* **vivre en ~ de la loi** to live outside the law; **se sentir en ~** to feel like an outsider.
■ **~ bénéficiaire** profit margin; **~ d'erreur** margin of error; **~ de sécurité** safety margin.

marginal, **~e**, *mpl* **-aux** /marʒinal, o/ **I** *adj* **1** marginal; **2** [*artist*] fringe; **3** on the margins of society.
II *nm,f* dropout; **les marginaux** the fringe elements of society.

marginaliser /marʒinalize/ [1] *vtr* to marginalize.

marguerite /margərit/ *nf* daisy.

mari /mari/ *nm* husband.

mariage /marjaʒ/ *nm* **1** marriage; **né d'un premier ~** from a previous marriage; **~ de raison** marriage of convenience; **faire un riche ~** to marry into money; **2** wedding; **3** (figurative) (of colours) marriage; (of companies) merger; (of parties) alliance; (of techniques) fusion.
■ **~ blanc** marriage in name only; **~ civil** civil wedding; **~ religieux** church wedding.

Marianne /marjan/ *pr n* Marianne (*female figure personifying the French Republic*).

marié, **~e** /marje/ **I** *pp* ▶ **marier**.
II *pp adj* married.
III *nm,f* **le (jeune) ~** the (bride)groom; **la (jeune) ~e** the bride; **les ~s** the newlyweds.

marier /marje/ [2] **I** *vtr* to marry.
II se marier *v refl* (+ *v être*) **1** to get married; **2** [*colours*] to blend.

marijuana /marirwana/ *nf* marijuana.

marin, **~e**[1] /marɛ̃, in/ **I** *adj* **1** [*life*] marine; [*salt*] sea; [*drilling*] offshore; **2 pull ~** seaman's jersey; **costume ~** sailor suit.
II *nm* sailor.
■ **~ d'eau douce** fair-weather sailor; **~ pêcheur** fisherman.
IDIOMS **avoir le pied ~** not to get seasick.

marine[2] /marin/ **I** *adj inv* navy (blue).
II *nm* marine.

marine[3] /marin/ *nf* navy; **de ~** nautical.

mariner /marine/ [1] *vtr, vi* to marinate.

marinière /marinjɛr/ *nf* smock.

marionnette /marjɔnɛt/ *nf* **1** puppet; **2 ~s** puppet show.
■ **~ à fils** marionette.

marionnettiste /marjɔnetist/ *nmf* puppeteer.

maritalement /maritalmɑ̃/ *adv* [*live*] as man and wife.

maritime /maritim/ *adj* [*climate, commerce*] maritime; [*area*] coastal; [*company*] shipping.

marjolaine /marʒɔlɛn/ *nf* marjoram.

marmelade /marməlad/ *nf* stewed fruit.

marmite /marmit/ *nf* **1** (cooking-)pot; **2** potful.
IDIOMS **faire bouillir la ~**○ to bring home the bacon.

marmiton /marmitɔ̃/ *nm* chef's assistant.

marmonner /marmɔne/ [1] *vtr* to mumble, to mutter.

marmot○ /marmo/ *nm* kid○, brat○.

marmotte /marmɔt/ *nf* **1** marmot; **2** (figurative) sleepyhead○.

maroquinerie /marɔkinri/ *nf* **1** leather shop; **2** leather industry; leather trade; **(articles de) ~** leather goods.

marotte /marɔt/ *nf* **1** pet subject, hobby horse; pet or favourite[GB] hobby; **2** puppet.

marquant, **~e** /markɑ̃, ɑ̃t/ *adj* [*fact*] memorable; [*memory*] lasting.

marque /mark/ *nf* **1** brand, make; **de ~** [*product*] branded; [*guest*] distinguished; [*person*] eminent; **2** mark; sign; **~ de doigts** fingermarks; **on voit encore les ~s (de coups)** you can still see the bruises; **~ du pluriel** plural marker; **laisser sa ~** to make one's mark; **3** (Sport) score; **à vos ~s, prêts, partez!** on your marks, get set, go!

■ **~ déposée** registered trademark; **~ de fabrication** manufacturer's brand name; **~ de fabrique** trademark.

marqué, **~e** /maʀke/ I *pp* ▶ **marquer**.
II *pp adj* **1 il a le corps ~ de traces de coups** he's bruised all over; **elle est restée ~e par la guerre** the war left its mark on her; **visage ~** worn face; **2** [*difference*] marked.

marquer /maʀke/ [1] I *vtr* **1** to mark [*goods*]; to brand [*cattle*]; **2** to mark, to signal [*beginning, end*]; **3** to mark [*body, object*]; **4** (figurative) [*event, work*] to leave its mark on [*person*]; **c'est quelqu'un qui m'a beaucoup marqué** he/she was a strong influence on me; **5** to write [sth] down [*information*]; to mark [*price*]; **qu'est-ce qu'il y a de marqué?** what does it say?; **6** to show; **~ la mesure** (Mus) to beat time; **il faut ~ le coup** let's celebrate; **7 ~ un temps (d'arrêt)** to pause; **8** (Sport) to score [*goal*]; to mark [*opponent*].
II *vi* **1** to leave a mark; **2** (Sport) to score.

marqueur /maʀkœʀ/ *nm* marker pen.

marquis, **~e** /maʀki, iz/ *nm,f* marquis/marchioness.

marraine /maʀɛn/ *nf* **1** godmother; **2** sponsor.
■ **~ de guerre** *soldier's wartime female penfriend*.

marrant○, **~e** /maʀɑ̃, ɑ̃t/ *adj* funny.

marre○ /maʀ/ *adv* **en avoir ~** to be fed up○.

marrer○: **se marrer** /maʀe/ [1] *v refl* (+ *v être*) **1** to have a great time; **2** to have a good laugh.

marron, -onne /maʀɔ̃, ɔn/ I *adj* crooked.
II *adj* brown; **~ clair/foncé** light/dark brown.
III *nm* **1** chestnut; **2** brown.
■ **~ glacé** marron glacé; **~s chauds** roast chestnuts.

marronnier /maʀɔnje/ *nm* chestnut (tree).

mars /maʀs/ *nm inv* March.
IDIOMS **arriver comme ~ en carême** to come as sure as night follows day.

Marseillaise /maʀsɛjɛz/ *nf* Marseillaise (*French national anthem*).

marsouin /maʀswɛ̃/ *nm* porpoise.

marteau, *pl* **~x** /maʀto/ *nm* hammer; (of judge) gavel; (on door) knocker.

marteler /maʀtəle/ [17] *vtr* **1** to hammer, to pound; **2** to rap out [*words*].

martial, **~e**, *mpl* **-iaux** /maʀsjal, o/ *adj* [*art, law*] martial; [*music, step*] military.

martinet /maʀtinɛ/ *nm* **1** (Zool) swift; **2** whip.

martingale /maʀtɛ̃gal/ *nf* **1** (on jacket) half belt; **2** (for horse) martingale.

martre /maʀtʀ/ *nf* **1** marten; **2** sable.

martyr, **~e**[1] /maʀtiʀ/ I *adj* martyred; **enfant ~** battered child.
II *nm,f* martyr.

martyre[2] /maʀtiʀ/ *nm* **1** martyrdom; **2** agony; **souffrir le ~** to suffer agony.

martyriser /maʀtiʀize/ [1] *vtr* **1** to torment [*victim, animal*]; to batter [*child*]; **2** to martyr.

marxisme /maʀksism/ *nm* Marxism.

mas /mɑ/ *nm inv* farmhouse (*in Provence*).

mascarade /maskaʀad/ *nf* **1** farce; **~ d[e] justice** travesty of justice; **2** masked ball.

mascotte /maskɔt/ *nf* mascot.

masculin, **~e** /maskylɛ̃, in/ I *adj* [*populatio[n], sex, part*] male; [*sport*] man's; [*magazine, tea[m]*] men's; [*face, noun*] masculine.
II *nm* masculine.

masochisme /mazɔʃism/ *nm* masochism.

masochiste /mazɔʃist/ *nmf* masochist.

masque /mask/ *nm* **1** mask; **2** face-pack **3** expression.
■ **~ à gaz** gas mask; **~ de plongée** divin[g] mask; **~ de soudeur** face shield.
IDIOMS **jeter le ~** to show one's tru[e] colours[GB].

masqué, **~e** /maske/ *adj* **1** [*bandit*] masked **2** (figurative) concealed.

masquer /maske/ [1] I *vtr* **1** to conceal [*defect*] to mask [*problem*]; **2** to block [*opening, light*].
II **se masquer** *v refl* (+ *v être*) to hide [sth] from oneself [*truth*].

massacrante /masakʀɑ̃t/ *adj f* **être d'humeu[r] ~** to be in a foul mood.

massacre /masakʀ/ *nm* massacre, slaughter.

massacrer /masakʀe/ [1] *vtr* **1** to massacre, t[o] slaughter; **2**○ (figurative) to slaughter○ [*oppon[ent]*]; to massacre [*piece of music*]; to botc[h] [*job*]; to criticize [*play, actor*].

massage /masaʒ/ *nm* massage.

masse /mas/ *nf* **1** mass; **~ rocheuse** rock mass; **une ~ humaine** a mass of humanity **2 une ~ de** a lot of; **des ~s de**○ masses o[f] **départs en ~** mass exodus; **3 la ~**, **le[s] ~s** the masses; **culture de ~** mass culture.
■ **~ d'armes** mace; **~ monétaire** mone[y] supply; **~ salariale** (total) wage bill.
IDIOMS **(se laisser) tomber comme une ~** t[o] collapse; **dormir comme une ~** to sleep lik[e] a log○.

massepain /maspɛ̃/ *nm* marzipan cake.

masser /mase/ [1] I *vtr* to massage.
II **se masser** *v refl* (+ *v être*) **1** to mass; **2 s[e] ~ les jambes** to massage one's legs.

masseur, **-euse** /masœʀ, øz/ *nm,f* masseu[r] masseuse.

massicot /masiko/ *nm* (for paper) guillotine.

massif, **-ive** /masif, iv/ I *adj* **1** [*feature[s]*] heavy; [*silhouette*] massive; **2** [*dose*] massive [*redundancies*] mass; **3** [*gold, oak*] solid.
II *nm* **1** massif; **2** (flower) bed.

massivement /masivmɑ̃/ *adv* [*demonstrate*] i[n] great numbers; [*inject*] in massive doses; [*ap[prove]*] overwhelmingly.

mass media /masmedja/ *nm pl* mass media.

massue /masy/ *nf* (gen, Sport) club, bludgeon.

mastic /mastik/ I *adj inv* putty-coloured[GB].
II *nm* (for windows) putty; (for holes) filler.

mastiquer /mastike/ [1] *vtr* to chew.

mastoc○ /mastɔk/ *adj inv* huge.

mastodonte /mastɔdɔ̃t/ *nm* **1** mastodon; **[2]** (figurative) (person) colossus, hulk○; (anima[l]) monster.

masturber /mastyʀbe/ [1] *vtr*, **se masturber** *v refl* (+ *v être*) to masturbate.

m'as-tu-vu○ /matyvy/ *nmf inv* show-off.

mat, **~e** /mat/ I *adj* **1** [*paint*] matt (GB), matte (US); **2** [*complexion*] olive; **3** [*sound*] dull.
II *nm* **(échec et) ~!** checkmate!

mât /mɑ/ *nm* **1** mast; **2** pole; climbing pole; **~ de drapeau** flagpole.

matador /matadɔʀ/ *nm* matador.

match /matʃ/ *nm* match; (in team sports) match (GB), game (US); **~ nul** draw (GB), tie (US); **faire ~ nul** to draw (GB), to tie (US).
■ **~ de classement** league match.

matelas /matla/ *nm inv* mattress; **~ pneumatique** air bed.

matelassé, **~e** /matlase/ *adj* [*material*] quilted; [*door*] padded.

matelot /matlo/ *nm* **1** sailor; **2** ≈ ordinary seaman (GB), ≈ seaman apprentice (US).

mater /mate/ [1] *vtr* to bring [sb/sth] into line [*rebels*]; to take [sb/sth] in hand [*child, horse*].

matérialiser /mateʀjalize/ [1] I *vtr* **1** to realize [*dream*]; to make [sth] happen [*plan*]; **2** to mark; **'chaussée non matérialisée sur 3 km'** 'no road markings for 3 km'.
II **se matérialiser** *v refl* (+ *v être*) to materialize.

matérialisme /mateʀjalism/ *nm* materialism.

matérialiste /mateʀjalist/ *adj* materialistic.

matériau, *pl* **~x** /mateʀjo/ *nm* material; **~x de construction** building materials.

matériel, **-ielle** /mateʀjɛl/ I *adj* [*cause, conditions*] material; [*means*] practical.
II *nm* **1** equipment; **~ agricole** farm machinery; **2** material.
■ **~ informatique** hardware.

matériellement /mateʀjɛlmɑ̃/ *adv* **1 c'est ~ possible** it can be done; **2** financially.

maternel, **-elle**[1] /matɛʀnɛl/ *adj* **1** [*instinct*] maternal; [*love*] motherly; **2** [*aunt*] maternal; **du côté ~** on the mother's side.

maternelle[2] /matɛʀnɛl/ *nf* nursery school.

maternellement /matɛʀnɛlmɑ̃/ *adv* in a motherly way.

materner /matɛʀne/ [1] *vtr* **1** to mother; **2** to mollycoddle.

maternité /matɛʀnite/ *nf* **1** motherhood; **2** pregnancy; **de ~** [*leave*] maternity; **3** maternity hospital.

mathématicien, **-ienne** /matematisjɛ̃, ɛn/ *nm,f* mathematician.

mathématiquement /matematikmɑ̃/ *adv* **1** mathematically; **2** logically.

mathématiques /matematik/ *nf pl* mathematics.

maths○ /mat/ *nf pl* maths○ (GB), math○ (US).

matière /matjɛʀ/ *nf* **1** material; **fournir la ~ d'un roman** to provide the material for a novel; **2** matter; **en ~ d'emploi** as far as employment is concerned; **~ à réflexion** food for thought; **3** (Sch) subject.
■ **~s fécales** faeces; **~s grasses** fat; **~ grise** grey (GB) or gray (US) matter; **~ première** raw material.

Matignon /matiɲɔ̃/ *pr n*: *offices of the French Prime Minister*.

matin /matɛ̃/ *nm* morning; **de bon ~** early in the morning.
IDIOMS **être du ~** to be a morning person.

matinal, **~e**, *mpl* **-aux** /matinal, o/ *adj* [*walk*] morning; [*hour*] early; **être ~** to be an early riser, to be up early.

mâtiné, **~e** /mɑtine/ *adj* **un anglais ~ de français** a mixture of English and French.

matinée /matine/ *nf* **1** morning; **2** matinée.
IDIOMS **faire la grasse ~** to sleep in.

matines /matin/ *nf pl* matins.

matraquage /matʀakaʒ/ *nm* **1** bludgeoning; **2** (figurative) **~ publicitaire** hype○.

matraque /matʀak/ *nf* club; truncheon (GB), billy (US); **c'est le coup de ~**○ (figurative) it costs a fortune.

matraquer /matʀake/ [1] *vtr* **1** to club; **2** [*media*] to bombard [*public*].

matriarcal, **~e**, *mpl* **-aux** /matʀijaʀkal, o/ *adj* matriarchal.

matrice /matʀis/ *nf* **1** matrix; **2** (Tech) die.

matricule /matʀikyl/ *nm* reference number; (Mil) service number.

matrimonial, **~e**, *mpl*, **-iaux** /matʀimɔnjal, o/ *adj* marriage, matrimonial.

maturation /matyʀasjɔ̃/ *nf* ripening; maturing.

maturité /matyʀite/ *nf* maturity.

maudire /modiʀ/ [80] *vtr* to curse.

maudit, **~e** /modi, it/ I *pp* ▶ **maudire**.
II○ *adj* blasted○.
III *nm,f* damned soul; **les ~s** the damned.

maussade /mosad/ *adj* [*mood*] sullen; [*weather*] dull; [*landscape*] bleak.

mauvais, **~e** /mɔvɛ, ɛz/ I *adj* **1** bad, poor; [*lawyer, doctor*] incompetent; [*wage*] low; **du ~ tabac** cheap tobacco; **2** [*address*] wrong; **3** [*day, moment*] bad; [*method*] wrong; **4** bad; [*surprise*] nasty; [*taste, smell*] unpleasant; **par ~ temps** in bad weather; **ça a ~ goût** it tastes horrible; **5** [*cold, wound*] nasty; [*sea*] rough; **6** [*person, smile*] nasty; [*intentions, thoughts*] evil; **préparer un ~ coup** to be up to mischief.
II *adv* **sentir ~** to smell; **sentir très ~** to stink; **il fait ~** the weather is bad.
III *nm* **il n'y a pas que du ~ dans le projet** the project isn't all bad.
■ **~ esprit** scoffing person; scoffing attitude; **~ garçon** tough guy; **~ traitements** ill-treatment; **~e herbe** weed; **~es rencontres** bad company.
IDIOMS **l'avoir ~e**○ to be furious.

mauve[1] /mov/ *adj, nm* mauve.

mauve[2] /mov/ *nf* mallow.

mauviette /movjɛt/ *nf* wimp○.

maux ▶ **mal**.

maxi- /maksi/ *pref* **~-jupe** maxi-skirt; **~-bouteille** one-and-a-half litre[GB] bottle.

maxillaire /maksilɛʀ/ *nm* jawbone.

maxima ▶ **maximum**.

maximal, **~e**, *mpl* **-aux** /maksimal, o/ *adj* maximum.

maxime /maksim/ *nf* maxim.

maximum, *pl* **~s** or **maxima** /maksimɔm, maksima/ I *adj* maximum.
II *nm* **1** maximum; **10 francs au grand ~** 10 francs at the very most; **au ~** [*work*] to the maximum; [*reduce*] as much as possible; **obtenir le ~ d'avantages** to get as many advantages as possible; **faire le ~** to do one's utmost; **2** (Law) maximum sentence.

mayonnaise /majɔnɛz/ *nf* mayonnaise.

mazagran /mazagʀɑ̃/ *nm*: *thick china goblet for coffee*.

mazout /mazut/ *nm* (fuel) oil.

me (**m'** *before vowel or mute h*) /m(ə)/ *pron* **1** me; **tu ne m'as pas fait mal** you didn't hurt me; **2** myself; **je ~ lave (les mains)** I wash (my hands).

Me *written abbr* = **maître III 3**.

mec○ /mɛk/ *nm* guy○; **mon ~** my man○.

mécanicien, **-ienne** /mekanisjɛ̃, ɛn/ **I** *adj* mechanical.
II *nm,f* mechanic.
III *nm* (of train) engine driver (GB), (locomotive) engineer (US); (of plane) flight engineer; (of boat) engineer.

mécanique /mekanik/ **I** *adj* mechanical; [*toy*] clockwork; [*razor*] hand.
II *nf* **1** mechanics; **une merveille de ~** a marvel of engineering; **2**○ machine.

mécaniquement /mekanikmɑ̃/ *adv* mechanically; **fabriqué ~** machine-made.

mécaniser /mekanize/ [1] *vtr*, **se mécaniser** *v refl* (+ *v être*) to mechanize.

mécanisme /mekanism/ *nm* mechanism.

mécano○ /mekano/ *nm* mechanic.

mécénat /mesena/ *nm* patronage.

mécène /mesɛn/ *nm* patron of the arts.

méchamment /meʃamɑ̃/ *adv* **1** spitefully, maliciously; viciously; **traiter qn ~** to treat sb badly; **2**○ [*damage*] badly; [*good*] terribly.

méchanceté /meʃɑ̃ste/ *nf* **1** nastiness; **par pure ~** out of pure spite; **2** maliciousness, viciousness; **3** malicious act; malicious remark.

méchant, **~e** /meʃɑ̃, ɑ̃t/ **I** *adj* **1** [*person*] nasty, malicious; [*animal*] vicious; [*flu, business*] nasty, bad; **2**○ fantastic○, terrific○.
II *nm,f* **1** villain, baddie○; **2** naughty boy/girl.

mèche /mɛʃ/ *nf* **1** (of hair) lock; **2** (in hair) streak; **3** (of candle) wick; **4** (Med) packing; **5** (of explosive) fuse; **6** (drill) bit.
IDIOMS **être de ~ avec qn**○ to be in cahoots○ with sb; **vendre la ~** to let the cat out of the bag.

méchoui /meʃwi/ *nm* North African style barbecue; spit-roast lamb.

méconnaissable /mekɔnɛsabl/ *adj* unrecognizable.

méconnu, **~e** /mekɔny/ *adj* [*artist, work*] neglected; [*value*] unrecognized.

mécontent, **~e** /mekɔ̃tɑ̃, ɑ̃t/ *adj* dissatisfied; [*voter*] discontented; **pas ~** rather pleased.

mécontentement /mekɔ̃tɑ̃tmɑ̃/ *nm* **1** dissatisfaction; **2** discontent; **3** annoyance.

Mecque /mɛk/ *pr n* **la ~** Mecca.

médaille /medaj/ *nf* **1** medal; **~ d'or** gold medal; **2** coin; **3** medallion.

médaillon /medajɔ̃/ *nm* **1** locket; **2** (in art, architecture) medallion.

médecin /mɛdsɛ̃/ *nm* doctor; **~ traitant** general practitioner, GP (GB).
■ **~ de garde** duty doctor, doctor on duty; **~ légiste** forensic surgeon.

médecine /mɛdsin/ *nf* medicine.
■ **~ scolaire** ≈ school health service; **~ du travail** ≈ occupational medicine; **~s douces** or **parallèles** alternative medicine.

média /medja/ **I** *nm* medium.
II **médias** *nm pl* **les ~s** the media.

médiathèque /medjatɛk/ *nf* multimedia library.

médiation /medjasjɔ̃/ *nf* mediation.

médiatique /medjatik/ *adj* [*exploitation*] by the media; [*success*] media.

médiatiser /medjatize/ [1] *vtr* to give [sth] publicity in the media.

médical, **~e**, *mpl* **-aux** /medikal, o/ *adj* medical.

médicament /medikamɑ̃/ *nm* medicine, drug.

médication /medikasjɔ̃/ *nf* medication.

médicinal, **~e**, *mpl* **-aux** /medisinal, o/ *adj* medicinal.

médico-légal, **~e**, *mpl* **-aux** /medikolegal, o/ *adj* forensic; **certificat ~** autopsy report.

médiéval, **~e**, *mpl* **-aux** /medjeval, o/ *adj* medieval.

médiocre /medjɔkʀ/ *adj* mediocre; [*pupil, intelligence*] below-average; [*soil, light, return, food*] poor; [*interest, success*] limited; [*income*] meagre[GB].

médiocrité /medjɔkʀite/ *nf* **1** mediocrity; **2** meagreness[GB].

médire /mediʀ/ [65] *v+prep* **~ de** to speak ill of.

médisance /medizɑ̃s/ *nf* malicious gossip.

médisant, **~e** /medizɑ̃, ɑ̃t/ *adj* malicious.

méditation /meditasjɔ̃/ *nf* meditation.

méditer /medite/ [1] **I** *vtr* to mull over; **longuement médité** [*plan*] carefully considered.
II *vi* to meditate; **~ sur** to meditate on [*existence*]; to ponder on or over [*problem*].

Méditerranée /mediteʀane/ *pr nf* **la (mer) ~** the Mediterranean (Sea).

médium /medjɔm/ *nm* medium.

méduse /medyz/ *nf* jellyfish.

méduser /medyze/ [1] *vtr* to dumbfound.

meeting /mitiŋ/ *nm* meeting.

méfait /mefɛ/ **I** *nm* misdemeanour[GB]; crime.
II **méfaits** *nm pl* detrimental effect.

méfiance /mefjɑ̃s/ *nf* mistrust, suspicion; **~ de qn envers qn/qch** sb's wariness of sb/sth.

méfiant, **~e** /mefjɑ̃, ɑ̃t/ *adj* suspicious; **elle est d'un naturel ~** she's always very wary.

méfier: **se méfier** /mefje/ [2] *v refl* (+ *v être*) **1 se ~ de qn/qch** not to trust sb/sth; **sans se ~** quite trustingly; **2 se ~ de qch** to be wary of sth; **méfie-toi!** be careful!; watch it!

méga /mega/ *pref* mega; **~hertz** megahertz.

mégalomane /megalɔman/ *adj*, *nmf* megalomaniac.

mégarde: **par mégarde** /paʀmegaʀd/ *phr* inadvertently.

mégère /meʒɛʀ/ *nf* shrew.

mégot /mego/ *nm* cigarette butt.

meilleur, **~e**[1] /mɛjœʀ/ **I** *adj* **1** better (**que** than); **2** best; **au ~ prix** [*buy*] at the lowest price; [*sell*] at the highest price.
II *nm,f* **le ~**, **la ~e** the best one.
III *adv* better; **il fait ~ qu'hier** the weather is better than it was yesterday.
IV *nm* **le ~** the best bit; **pour le ~ et pour le pire** for better or for worse.

meilleure[2] /mɛjœʀ/ *nf* **ça c'est la ~!** that's the best one yet!

mélancolie /melɑ̃kɔli/ *nf* (gen) melancholy; (Med) melancholia.

mélange /melɑ̃ʒ/ *nm* (of teas, tobaccos) blend; (of products, ideas) combination; (of colours) mixture; **c'est un ~ (coton et synthétique)** it's a mix (of cotton and synthetic fibres[GB]).

mélanger /melɑ̃ʒe/ [13] **I** *vtr* **1** to blend [*teas, oils, tobaccos*]; to mix [*colours, shades*]; **2** to put together [*styles, people, objects*]; **3** to mix up; **~ les cartes** to shuffle (the cards).
II se mélanger *v refl* (+ *v être*) **1** [*teas, oils, tobaccos*] to blend; [*colours, shades*] to mix, to blend together; **2** [*ideas*] to get muddled.

mélangeur /melɑ̃ʒœʀ/ *nm* mixer.

mélasse /melas/ *nf* black treacle (GB), molasses.

mêlée /mele/ *nf* **1** mêlée; **~ générale** free-for-all; **2** (Sport) scrum; **3** (figurative) fray.

mêler /mele/ [1] **I** *vtr* **1** to mix [*products, colours*]; to blend [*ingredients, cultures*]; to combine [*influences*]; **2 être mêlé à un scandale** to be involved in a scandal.
II se mêler *v refl* (+ *v être*) **1** [*cultures, religions*] to mix; [*smells, voices*] to mingle; **2 se ~ à** to mingle with [*crowd*]; to mix with [*people*]; to join in [*conversation*]; **3 se ~ de** to meddle in; **mêle-toi de tes affaires**○ mind your own business.

méli-mélo, *pl* **mélis-mélos** /melimelo/ *nm* jumble, mess.

mélo○ /melo/ *adj* slushy○, schmaltzy○.

mélodie /melɔdi/ *nf* **1** melody, tune; **2** melodiousness.

mélodrame /melɔdʀam/ *nm* melodrama.

mélomane /melɔman/ *nmf* music lover.

melon /məlɔ̃/ *nm* **1** melon; **2** bowler (hat) (GB), derby (hat) (US).

membrane /mɑ̃bʀan/ *nf* (Anat) membrane.

membre /mɑ̃bʀ/ *nm* **1** member; **les pays ~s** the member countries; **2** limb; **~ postérieur** hind limb.

même /mɛm/ **I** *adj* **1** same; **2 c'est l'intelligence ~** he's/she's intelligence itself; **3 le jour ~ où** the very same day that; **c'est cela ~** that's it exactly.
II *adv* **1** even; **je ne m'en souviens ~ plus** I can't even remember now; **2** very; **c'est ici ~ que je l'ai rencontré** I met him at this very place.
III de même *phr* **agir** or **faire de ~** to do the same; **il en va de ~ pour** the same is true of.
IV de même que *phr* **le prix du café, de ~ que celui du tabac, a augmenté de 10%** the price of coffee, as well as that of tobacco, has risen by 10%.
V même si *phr* even if.
VI *pron* **le ~**, **la ~**, **les ~s** the same; **ce sac est le ~ que celui de Pierre** this bag is the same as Pierre's.

mémé○ /meme/ *nf* gran○, granny○.

mémento /memɛ̃to/ *nm* guide.

mémo○ /memo/ *nm* note.

mémoire[1] /memwaʀ/ **I** *nm* **1** memo; **2** dissertation.
II mémoires *nm pl* memoirs.

mémoire[2] /memwaʀ/ *nf* **1** memory; **si j'ai bonne ~** if I remember rightly; **ne pas avoir de ~** to have a bad memory; **de ~ d'homme** in living memory; **en ~ de** to the memory of, in memory of; **pour ~** for the record; for reference; **2** (Comput) memory; storage; **mettre des données en ~** to input data.
■ **~ morte** read-only memory, ROM; **~ vive** random access memory, RAM.

mémorable /memɔʀabl/ *adj* memorable.

mémorial, **~e**, *mpl* **-iaux** /memɔʀjal, o/ *nm* memorial.

mémoriser /memɔʀize/ [1] *vtr* to memorize.

menaçant, **~e** /mənasɑ̃, ɑ̃t/ *adj* menacing.

menace /mənas/ *nf* threat; **sous la ~** under duress; **sous la ~ d'une arme** at gunpoint.

menacer /mənase/ [12] *vtr* **1** to threaten [*person*]; **2** to pose a threat to; **être menacé** [*stability, economy*] to be in jeopardy; [*life*] to be in danger; [*population*] to be at risk.

ménage /menaʒ/ *nm* **1** household; **se mettre en ~ avec qn** to set up home with sb; **scènes de ~** domestic rows; **monter son ~** to buy the household goods; **2** housework; **faire le ~** to do the cleaning; **faire des ~s** to do domestic cleaning work.
IDIOMS **faire bon ~** to be compatible.

ménagement /menaʒmɑ̃/ *nm* **avec ~s** gently; **sans ~s** [*say*] bluntly; [*push*] roughly.

ménager[1] /menaʒe/ [13] **I** *vtr* **1** to handle [sb] carefully; to deal carefully with [sb]; to be gentle with [sb]; to be careful with [sth]; **~ la susceptibilité de qn** to humour[GB] sb; **2** to be careful with [*clothes, savings*]; **il ne ménage pas sa peine** he spares no effort.
II se ménager *v refl* (+ *v être*) to take it easy.

ménager[2], **-ère**[1] /menaʒe, ɛʀ/ *adj* [*jobs*] domestic; [*equipment*] household; **appareils ~s** domestic appliances; **travaux ~s** housework.

ménagère² /menaʒɛʀ/ *nf* **1** housewife; **2** canteen of cutlery.

ménagerie /menaʒʀi/ *nf* menagerie.

mendiant, **~e** /mɑ̃djɑ̃, ɑ̃t/ *nm,f* beggar.

mendicité /mɑ̃disite/ *nf* begging.

mendier /mɑ̃dje/ [2] **I** *vtr* to beg for.
II *vi* to beg.

mener /məne/ [16] **I** *vtr* **1 ~ qn quelque part** to take sb somewhere; to drive sb somewhere; **2** to lead [*people, country*]; to run [*company*]; **il ne se laisse pas ~ par sa grande sœur** he won't be bossed about○ by his sister; **3 ~ au village** [*road*] to go or lead to the village; **4 ~ à** to lead to; **cette histoire peut te ~ loin** it could be a very nasty business; **~ à bien** to complete [sth] successfully; to bring [sth] to a successful conclusion; to handle [sth] successfully; **5** to carry out [*study, reform*]; to run [*campaign*]; **~ une enquête** to hold an investigation; **~ sa vie comme on l'entend** to live as one pleases.
II *vi* (Sport) to be in the lead.
IDIOMS **~ la danse** or **le jeu** to call the tune.

ménestrel /menɛstʀɛl/ *nm* minstrel.

meneur, **-euse** /mənœʀ, øz/ *nm,f* leader.

menhir /meniʀ/ *nm* menhir.

méninge /menɛ̃ʒ/ **I** *nf* (Anat) meninx.
II méninges○ *nf pl* brains○.

méningite /menɛ̃ʒit/ *nf* meningitis.

ménisque /menisk/ *nm* meniscus.

ménopause /menɔpoz/ *nf* menopause.

menotte /mənɔt/ **I** *nf* tiny hand.
II menottes *nf pl* handcuffs.

mensonge /mɑ̃sɔ̃ʒ/ *nm* **1** lie; **2 le ~** lying.

mensonger, **-ère** /mɑ̃sɔ̃ʒe, ɛʀ/ *adj* [*accusations*] false; [*advertising*] misleading.

mensualité /mɑ̃sɥalite/ *nf* monthly instalment^GB.

mensuel, **-elle** /mɑ̃sɥɛl/ **I** *adj* monthly.
II *nm* monthly magazine.

mensuellement /mɑ̃sɥɛlmɑ̃/ *adv* once a month, monthly.

mensurations /mɑ̃syʀasjɔ̃/ *nf pl* measurements.

mental, **~e**, *mpl* **-aux** /mɑ̃tal, o/ *adj* mental; **handicapé ~** mentally handicapped person.

mentalité /mɑ̃talite/ *nf* mentality.

menteur, **-euse** /mɑ̃tœʀ, øz/ **I** *adj* [*person*] untruthful; [*statement*] full of lies.
II *nm,f* liar.

menthe /mɑ̃t/ *nf* **1** mint; **~ poivrée** peppermint; **~ verte** spearmint; **2** mint tea; **3 ~ (à l'eau)** mint cordial.

menthol /mɛ̃tɔl/ *nm* menthol.

mention /mɑ̃sjɔ̃/ *nf* **1** mention; **faire ~ de qch** to mention sth; **2** (Sch) **~ passable** *pass with 50 to 60%*; **~ très bien** *pass with 80% upward(s)*; **3** note; **rayer la ~ inutile** or **les ~s inutiles** delete as appropriate.

mentionner /mɑ̃sjɔne/ [1] *vtr* to mention.

mentir /mɑ̃tiʀ/ [30] **I** *vi* **1** to lie, to tell lies; **2** [*figures*] to be misleading.
II se mentir *v refl* (+ *v être*) **1** to fool oneself; **2** to lie to one another.

menton /mɑ̃tɔ̃/ *nm* chin.

menu, **~e** /məny/ **I** *adj* **1** [*person*] slight; [*foot, piece*] tiny; [*writing*] small; **2** [*jobs*] small; [*details*] minute; **~ fretin** small fry.
II *adv* [*write*] small; [*chop*] finely.
III *nm* menu.
IV par le menu *phr* in (great) detail.

menuiserie /mənɥizʀi/ *nf* woodwork.

menuisier /mənɥizje/ *nm* joiner (GB), finish carpenter.

méprendre: **se méprendre** /mepʀɑ̃dʀ/ [52] *v refl* (+ *v être*) to be mistaken.

mépris /mepʀi/ *nm inv* contempt; **au ~ de la loi** regardless of the law.

méprisable /mepʀizabl/ *adj* contemptible.

méprisant, **~e** /mepʀizɑ̃, ɑ̃t/ *adj* [*gesture*] contemptuous; [*person*] disdainful.

méprise /mepʀiz/ *nf* mistake.

mépriser /mepʀize/ [1] *vtr* to despise [*person, wealth*]; to scorn [*danger, offer*].

mer /mɛʀ/ *nf* **1** sea; **une ~ d'huile** a glassy sea; **en pleine ~** out at sea; **la ~ monte** the tide is coming in; **2** seaside.
IDIOMS **ce n'est pas la ~ à boire** it's not all that difficult.

mercantile /mɛʀkɑ̃til/ *adj* mercenary.

mercenaire /mɛʀsənɛʀ/ *adj, nmf* mercenary.

mercerie /mɛʀsəʀi/ *nf* haberdasher's shop (GB), notions store (US).

merci¹ /mɛʀsi/ *nm, excl* thank you.

merci² /mɛʀsi/ *nf* mercy; **on est toujours à la ~ d'un accident** there's always the risk of an accident.

mercredi /mɛʀkʀədi/ *nm* Wednesday.

mercure /mɛʀkyʀ/ *nm* mercury.

merde● /mɛʀd/ *nf, excl* shit●.

mère /mɛʀ/ **I** *nf* **1** mother; **2 ~ supérieure** Mother Superior.
II (-)mère (*combining form*) **cellule/maison ~** parent cell/company.
■ **~ célibataire** single mother; **~ de famille** mother; housewife; **~ porteuse** surrogate mother; **~ poule** mother hen.

merguez /mɛʀgɛz/ *nf inv* spicy sausage.

méridien /meʀidjɛ̃/ *nm* meridian.

méridional, **~e**, *mpl* **-aux** /meʀidjɔnal, o/ **I** *adj* southern.
II *nm,f* Southerner.

meringue /məʀɛ̃g/ *nf* meringue.

mérite /meʀit/ *nm* merit; credit; **au ~** according to merit; **vanter les ~s de** to sing the praises of.

mériter /meʀite/ [1] **I** *vtr* to deserve; **~ réflexion** to be worth considering.
II se mériter *v refl* (+ *v être*) **ça se mérite** it's something that has to be earned.

merlan /mɛʀlɑ̃/ *nm* whiting.

merle /mɛʀl/ *nm* blackbird.

mérou /meʀu/ *nm* grouper.

merveille /mɛʀvɛj/ **I** *nf* marvel, wonder.

II à merveille *phr* wonderfully.
merveilleux, **-euse** /mɛʀvɛjø, øz/ *adj* marvellous[GB], wonderful.
mes ▶ **mon**.
mésaventure /mezavɑ̃tyʀ/ *nf* misadventure.
mesdames ▶ **madame**.
mesdemoiselles ▶ **mademoiselle**.
mesquin, **~e** /mɛskɛ̃, in/ *adj* **1** petty-minded; petty; **2** [*person*] mean (GB), cheap○ (US).
mesquinerie /mɛskinʀi/ *nf* **1** meanness; **2** stinginess; **3** mean trick; mean remark.
message /mesaʒ/ *nm* message; **~ publicitaire** commercial.
messager, **-ère** /mesaʒe, ɛʀ/ *nm,f* **1** messenger; **2** envoy.
messagerie /mesaʒʀi/ *nf* **1** freight forwarding; **2 ~ vocale** voice messaging.
messe /mɛs/ *nf* mass; **~s basses**○ whispering.
messie /mesi/ *nm* messiah.
messieurs ▶ **monsieur**.
mesure /məzyʀ/ *nf* **1** measure; **prendre des ~s** to take measures; to take steps; **2** measurement; **c'est du sur ~** it's made to measure; **tu as un emploi sur ~** the job is tailor-made for you; **c'est une adversaire à ta ~** she is a match for you; **3 unité de ~** unit of measurement; **instrument de ~** measuring device; **deux ~s de lait pour une ~ d'eau** two parts milk to one of water; **4** moderation; **dépasser la ~** to go too far; **5** (Mus) bar; **battre la ~** to beat time; **6 être en ~ de rembourser** to be in a position to reimburse; **dans la ~ du possible** as far as possible; **dans la ~ où** insofar as.
mesurer /məzyʀe/ [1] **I** *vtr* **1** to measure; **~ le tour de cou de qn** to take sb's neck measurement; **2** to measure [*productivity, gap*]; to assess [*difficulties, risks, effects*]; to consider [*consequences*]; **~ ses paroles** to weigh one's words.
II *vi* **~ 20 mètres carrés** to be 20 metres[GB] square; **elle mesure 1,60 m** she's 1.60 m tall.
III se mesurer *v refl* (+ *v être*) **1 se ~ en mètres** to be measured in metres[GB]; **2 se ~ à** or **avec qn** to pit one's strength against sb.
métal, *pl* **-aux** /metal, o/ *nm* metal; **pièce de** or **en ~** metal coin; **~ jaune** gold.
métallique /metalik/ *adj* **1** metal; **c'est ~** it's made of metal; **2** metallic.
métallisé, **~e** /metalize/ *adj* [*green, blue*] metallic.
métallurgie /metalyʀʒi/ *nf* **1** metalworking industry; **2** metallurgy.
métamorphose /metamɔʀfoz/ *nf* metamorphosis.
métamorphoser /metamɔʀfoze/ [1] **I** *vtr* to transform [sb/sth] completely.
II se métamorphoser *v refl* (+ *v être*) **se ~ en** to metamorphose into.
métaphore /metafɔʀ/ *nf* metaphor.
météo /meteo/ *nf* weather forecast.
météore /meteɔʀ/ *nm* meteor.
météorite /meteɔʀit/ *nm* or *nf* meteorite.
météorologie /meteɔʀɔlɔʒi/ *nf* meteorology.
météorologique /meteɔʀɔlɔʒik/ *adj* meteorological; **conditions ~s** weather conditions.
méthane /metan/ *nm* methane.
méthode /metɔd/ *nf* **1** method; **2** (for languages) course book (GB), textbook (US); **3** way; **j'ai ma ~ pour le convaincre** I've got a way of convincing him.
méthodique /metɔdik/ *adj* methodical.
méticuleux, **-euse** /metikylø, øz/ *adj* meticulous; painstaking.
métier /metje/ *nm* **1** job; profession; trade; craft; **avoir 20 ans de ~** to have 20 years' experience; **c'est le ~ qui rentre!** you learn by your mistakes!; **2 ~ à tisser** weaving loom.
métis, **-isse** /metis/ *nm,f* person of mixed race.
métissage /metisaʒ/ *nm* (of people) miscegenation; (of plants, animals) crossing.
métrage /metʀaʒ/ *nm* **1** (of material) length; **2 long ~** feature(-length) film.
mètre /mɛtʀ/ *nm* **1** metre[GB]; **le 60 ~s** the 60 metres[GB]; **piquer un cent ~s**○ to break into a run; **2** rule (GB), yardstick (US); **~ ruban** or **de couturière** tape measure.
métro /metʀo/ *nm* underground (GB), subway (US).
IDIOMS **~, boulot, dodo**○ the daily grind.
métronome /metʀɔnɔm/ *nm* metronome.
métropole /metʀɔpɔl/ *nf* **1** metropolis; **2** major city; **3** Metropolitan France.
métropolitain, **~e** /metʀɔpɔlitɛ̃, ɛn/ *adj* **1** [*network*] underground (GB), subway (US); **2** from Metropolitan France.
mets /mɛ/ *nm inv* dish, delicacy.
metteur /mɛtœʀ/ *nm* **~ en scène** director.
mettre /mɛtʀ/ [60] **I** *vtr* **1** to put; to put in [*heating, shower*]; to put up [*curtains, shelves*]; **je mets les enfants à la crèche** I send the children to a creche; **mets ton écharpe** put your scarf on; **~ le linge à sécher** to put the washing out to dry; **faire ~ le téléphone** to have a telephone put in; **2** to wear; **3 ~ qn en colère** to make sb angry; **4** to put on [*radio, TV, heating*]; **mets moins fort!** turn it down!; **~ le réveil** to set the alarm; **5** to put up [*sign*]; **qu'est-ce que je dois ~?** what shall I put?; **je t'ai mis un mot** I've left you a note; **~ en musique** to set to music; **~ en anglais** to put into English; **6 y ~ du sien** to put oneself into it; **combien pouvez-vous ~?** how much can you afford?; how much can you put in?; **elle a mis une heure** it took her an hour (**pour faire** to do); **7** (Sch) **je vous ai mis trois sur vingt** I've given you three out of twenty; **8**○ **mettons qu'il vienne, qu'est-ce que vous ferez?** supposing he comes, what will you do?
II *vi* **~ bas** [*animal*] to give birth; to calve.
III se mettre *v refl* (+ *v être*) **1 se ~ devant la fenêtre** to stand in front of the window; **se ~ au lit** to go to bed; **se ~ debout** to stand up; **où est-ce que ça se met?** where does this go?; **2** to spill [sth] on oneself; **3 je ne sais pas**

quoi me ~ I don't know what to put on; **4 se ~ à l'anglais** to take up English; **il va se ~ à pleuvoir** it's going to start raining; **5 je préfère me ~ bien avec lui** I prefer to get on the right side of him; **se ~ à l'aise** to make oneself comfortable.

meuble /mœbl/ **I** *adj* [*soil*] loose.
II *nm* **un ~** a piece of furniture.
IDIOMS **sauver les ~s** to salvage something.

meublé /mœble/ *nm* furnished apartment.

meubler /mœble/ [1] *vtr* to furnish; **la plante meuble bien la pièce** the plant makes the room look more cosy (GB) or cozy (US).

meugler /møgle/ [1] *vi* to moo.

meule /møl/ *nf* **1** millstone; **2** grindstone; **3 ~ de foin** haystack.

meunier, **-ière** /mønje, ɛʀ/ *nm,f* miller.

meurtre /mœʀtʀ/ *nm* murder.

meurtrier, **-ière** /mœʀtʀije, ɛʀ/ **I** *adj* [*fighting, repression*] bloody; [*explosion, accident*] fatal; [*epidemic*] deadly; [*arm*] lethal.
II *nm,f* murderer.

meurtrir /mœʀtʀiʀ/ [3] *vtr* **1** to hurt; **2** to bruise; **3** to wound [*self-esteem*].

meute /møt/ *nf* pack of hounds.

mexicain, **~e** /mɛksikɛ̃, ɛn/ *adj* Mexican.

Mexico /mɛksiko/ *pr n* Mexico City.

Mexique /mɛksik/ *pr nm* Mexico.

mezzanine /medzanin/ *nf* mezzanine.

MF /ɛmɛf/ *nf* (*abbr* = **modulation de fréquence**) frequency modulation, FM.

mi /mi/ *nm inv* (Mus) (note) E; (in sol-fa) mi, me.

mi- /mi/ *pref* **à la ~-mai/saison** in mid-May/ -season; **~-chinois, ~-français** half Chinese, half French.

miam-miam○ /mjammjam/ *excl* yum-yum○!

miauler /mjole/ [1] *vi* to miaow (GB), to meow.

mi-bas /mibɑ/ *nm inv* knee sock, long sock.

miche /miʃ/ *nf* round loaf.

mi-chemin: **à mi-chemin** /amiʃmɛ̃/ *phr* halfway; (figurative) halfway through.

micmac○ /mikmak/ *nm* shady○ goings-on.

micro[1] /mikʀo/ *pref* micro.

micro[2] /mikʀo/ *nm* microphone, mike○; **~ caché** bug.

microbe /mikʀɔb/ *nm* germ, microbe.

microclimat /mikʀoklima/ *nm* microclimate.

microcosme /mikʀɔkɔsm/ *nm* microcosm.

micro-cravate, *pl* **micros-cravates** /mikʀokʀavat/ *nm* lapel-microphone.

microfilm /mikʀɔfilm/ *nm* microfilm.

micro-ondes /mikʀoɔ̃d/ *nm inv* microwave○.

microphone /mikʀɔfɔn/ *nm* microphone.

microscope /mikʀɔskɔp/ *nm* microscope.

microscopique /mikʀɔskɔpik/ *adj* microscopic; (figurative) tiny.

microsillon /mikʀɔsijɔ̃/ *nm* **(disque) ~** microgroove record.

midi /midi/ *nm* **1** twelve o'clock, midday, noon; **je fais mes courses entre ~ et deux**○ I go shopping in my lunch hour; **2** lunchtime; **3 le Midi** the South of France.

midinette /midinɛt/ *nf* bimbo○.

mie /mi/ *nf* bread without the crusts.

miel /mjɛl/ *nm* honey.
IDIOMS **être tout sucre tout ~** to be as nice as pie○.

mielleux, **-euse** /mjɛlø, øz/ *adj* [*tone*] unctuous, honeyed; [*person*] fawning.

mien, **mienne** /mjɛ̃, mjɛn/ **I** *det* **ces idées, je les ai faites miennes** I adopted these ideas.
II le mien, **la mienne**, **les miens**, **les miennes** *pron* mine.

miette /mjɛt/ *nf* crumb; **réduire en ~s** to smash [sth] to bits [*vase*]; to shatter [*hopes*]; **elle n'en perd pas une ~**○ she's taking it all in.

mieux /mjø/ **I** *adj inv* better; **le ~, la ~, les ~** the best; the nicest; the most attractive; **ce qu'il y a de ~** the best.
II *adv* **1** better; **je ne peux pas te dire ~** that's all I can tell you; **qui dit ~?** any other offers?; any advance on that bid?; **de ~ en ~** better and better; **on la critiquait à qui ~ ~** each person criticized her more harshly than the last; **2 le ~, la ~, les ~** the best; (of two) the better.
III *nm inv* **le ~ est de refuser** the best thing is to refuse; **il y a un/du ~** there is an/some improvement; **je ne demande pas ~ que de rester ici** I'm perfectly happy staying here; **fais pour le ~, fais au ~** do whatever is best; **tout va pour le ~** everything's fine; **elle est au ~ avec sa voisine** she is on very good terms with her neighbour[GB].

mièvre /mjɛvʀ/ *adj* vapid; soppy.

mièvrerie /mjɛvʀəʀi/ *nf* vapidity; soppiness.

mi-figue /mifig/ *adj inv* **~ mi-raisin** [*smile*] half-hearted; [*compliment*] ambiguous.

mignon, **-onne** /miɲɔ̃, ɔn/ *adj* **1** cute; **2** sweet, kind.

migraine /migʀɛn/ *nf* splitting headache.

migration /migʀasjɔ̃/ *nf* migration.

migrer /migʀe/ [1] *vi* to migrate.

mijaurée /miʒɔʀe/ *nf* **ne fais pas ta ~** don't put on such airs.

mijoter /miʒɔte/ [1] **I** *vtr* (Culin) to prepare.
II *vi* (Culin) to simmer.

mil /mil/ *adj inv* = **mille I**.

milice /milis/ *nf* militia; **~ de quartier** local vigilante group.

milieu, *pl* **~x** /miljø/ **I** *nm* **1** middle; **au beau** or **en plein ~** right in the middle; **au ~ de la nuit** halfway through the night; **2** middle ground; **3** environment; **en ~ rural** in the country; **4** background, milieu; **le ~** the underworld.
II au milieu de *phr* **1** among; **être au ~ de ses amis** to be with one's friends; **2** surrounded by; **au ~ du désastre** in the midst of disaster.

militaire /militɛʀ/ **I** *adj* military; army.
II *nm* serviceman.

militant, **~e** /militɑ̃, ɑ̃t/ **I** *adj* militant.
II *nm,f* (of organization) active member, activist; (for cause) campaigner.

militantisme /militɑ̃tism/ *nm* political activism.

militariste /militaʀist/ *adj* militaristic.

militer /milite/ [1] *vi* **1** to campaign; **2** to be a political activist.

mille /mil/ **I** *adj inv* a thousand, one thousand; **deux/trois ~** two/three thousand.
II *nm inv* **1** a thousand, one thousand; **2** bull's eye; **taper dans le ~** to hit the bull's-eye; (figurative) to hit the nail on the head.
III *nm* **1 ~ (marin** or **nautique)** (nautical) mile; **2** (air) mile.
IV pour mille *phr* per thousand.
IDIOMS **je vous le donne en ~** you'll never guess (in a million years).

millénaire /milenɛʀ/ **I** *adj* **1 un arbre ~** a one thousand year old tree; **2** [*tradition*] age-old.
II *nm* **1 pendant des ~s** for thousands of years; **2** millennium, millenary.

mille-pattes /milpat/ *nm inv* centipede, millipede.

millésime /milezim/ *nm* vintage, year.

milli /mili/ *pref* milli; **~mètre** millimetre[GB].

milliard /miljaʀ/ *nm* billion.

milliardaire /miljaʀdɛʀ/ *nmf* multimillionaire, billionaire.

millième /miljɛm/ *adj* thousandth.

millier /milje/ *nm* **1** thousand; **2 un ~** about a thousand.

million /miljɔ̃/ *nm* million.

millionième /miljɔnjɛm/ *adj* millionth.

millionnaire /miljɔnɛʀ/ **I** *adj* **être ~** [*firm*] to be worth millions; [*person*] to be a millionaire.
II *nmf* millionaire.

mime /mim/ *nm* mime.

mimer /mime/ [1] *vtr* **1** to mime; **2** to mimic.

mimétisme /mimetism/ *nm* **1** (Zool) mimicry; **2 par ~** through unconscious imitation.

mimique /mimik/ *nf* funny face.

minable○ /minabl/ *adj* **1** [*salary, person*] pathetic; **2** [*place*] crummy○; [*existence*] miserable.

minaret /minaʀɛ/ *nm* minaret.

minauder /minode/ [1] *vi* **1** to mince about; **2** to simper.

mince /mɛ̃s/ *adj* **1** slim, slender; [*face, slice*] thin; **2** [*consolation*] small; [*chance*] slim.

minceur /mɛ̃sœʀ/ *nf* slimness; slenderness; thinness.

mincir /mɛ̃siʀ/ [3] *vi* to lose weight.

mine /min/ *nf* **1** expression; **faire ~ d'accepter** to pretend to accept; **elle nous a dit, ~ de rien, que**○ she told us, casually, that; **il est doué, ~ de rien**○ it may not be obvious, but he's very clever; **2 avoir bonne ~** [*person*] to look well; **3** (in pencil) lead; **4** mine; **~ d'or** gold mine; **5** (Mil) mine.
IDIOMS **ne pas payer de ~**○ not to look anything special○.

miner /mine/ [1] *vtr* **1** to sap [*morale, energy*]; to undermine [*health*]; **2** (Mil) to mine.

minerai /minʀɛ/ *nm* ore; **~ de fer** iron ore.

minéral, **~e**, *mpl* **-aux** /mineʀal, o/ **I** *adj* [*water*] mineral; [*chemistry*] inorganic.
II *nm* mineral.

minéralogique /mineʀalɔʒik/ *adj* **plaque ~** number plate (GB), license plate (US).

minerve /minɛʀv/ *nf* (Med) surgical collar (GB), neck brace (US).

minet /minɛ/ *nm* **1** pussycat; **2**○ pretty boy○.

minette /minɛt/ *nf* **1** pussycat; **2**○ cool chick○.

mineur, **~e** /minœʀ/ **I** *adj* **1** (Law) under 18; **2** [*detail*] minor; **3** (Mus) **en ré ~** in D minor.
II *nm,f* (Law) person under 18.
III *nm* miner; **~ de fond** pit worker.

mini- /mini/ *pref* mini.

miniature /minjatyʀ/ *adj, nf* miniature.

minier, **-ière** /minje, ɛʀ/ *adj* mining.

mini-jupe, *pl* **~s** /miniʒyp/ *nf* mini-skirt.

minimal, **~e**, *mpl* **-aux** /minimal, o/ *adj* minimal, minimum.

minime /minim/ **I** *adj* negligible.
II *nmf* (Sport) junior (*7 to 13 years old*).

minimiser /minimize/ [1] *vtr* to minimize.

minimum, *pl* **~s** or **minima** /minimɔm, minima/ **I** *adj* minimum.
II *nm* **1** minimum; **un ~ de bon sens** a certain amount of common sense; **il faut au ~ deux heures pour faire le trajet** the journey takes at least two hours; **2** (Law) minimum sentence.
■ **~ vital** subsistence level.

ministère /ministɛʀ/ *nm* ministry; (in UK, US) department.

ministériel, **-ielle** /ministeʀjɛl/ *adj* ministerial, cabinet.

ministre /ministʀ/ *nm* **1** minister; (in UK) Secretary of State; (in US) Secretary; **2** (of religion) minister.

Minitel® /minitɛl/ *nm* Minitel (*terminal linking phone users to a database*).

minois /minwɑ/ *nm inv* fresh young face.

minoritaire /minɔʀitɛʀ/ *adj* minority.

minorité /minɔʀite/ *nf* **1** minority; **être mis en ~** to be defeated; **2** (age) minority.

minou /minu/ *nm* pussycat.

minuit /minɥi/ *nm* midnight.

minuscule /minyskyl/ **I** *adj* [*person, thing*] tiny; [*quantity*] tiny, minute.
II *nf* small letter; (in printing) lower-case letter.

minutage /minytaʒ/ *nm* (precise) timing.

minute /minyt/ *nf* minute; **la ~ de vérité** the moment of truth.

minuter /minyte/ [1] *vtr* **1** to time; **2** to work out the timing of.

minuterie /minytʀi/ *nf* **1** time-switch; **2** automatic lighting.

minuteur /minytœʀ/ *nm* timer.

minutie /minysi/ *nf* meticulousness.

minutieux, **-ieuse** /minysjø, øz/ *adj* meticulous; [*description*] detailed.

mioche○ /mjɔʃ/ *nmf* kid○.

mirabelle /miʀabɛl/ *nf* **1** mirabelle (*small yellow plum*); **2** plum brandy.
miracle /miʀɑkl/ I *adj inv* **un médicament ~** a wonder drug; **une méthode ~** a magic formula.
II *nm* **1** miracle; **faire un ~** to work a miracle; (figurative) to work miracles; **comme par ~** as if by magic; **2** miracle play.
miraculeux, **-euse** /miʀakylø, øz/ *adj* miraculous; [*product, remedy*] which works wonders.
mirador /miʀadɔʀ/ *nm* watchtower.
mirage /miʀaʒ/ *nm* mirage.
mi-raisin /miʀɛzɛ̃/ *adj inv* ▶ **mi-figue**.
miraud○, **~e** /miʀo, od/ *adj* shortsighted.
miroir /miʀwaʀ/ *nm* mirror.
miroiter /miʀwate/ [1] *vi* to shimmer; **faire ~ qch à qn** to hold out the prospect of sth to sb.
mis, **~e**[1] /mi, miz/ *pp* ▶ **mettre**.
misanthrope /mizɑ̃tʀɔp/ I *adj* misanthropic.
II *nmf* misanthropist, misanthrope.
mise[2] /miz/ *nf* **une ~ de cinq francs** a five-franc bet.
■ **~ de fonds** investment; **~ en plis** set.
IDIOMS **être de ~** [*conduct*] to be proper.
miser /mize/ [1] I *vtr* to bet.
II *vi* **1 ~ sur** to bet on, to place a bet on; **2 ~ sur qn** to place all one's hopes in sb.
misérable /mizeʀabl/ I *adj* **1** [*person*] destitute, poor; [*life*] poor; **2** [*salary*] meagre[GB].
II *nmf* **1** pauper; **2** scoundrel.
misère /mizɛʀ/ *nf* **1** destitution; **réduire qn à la ~** to reduce sb to poverty; **2** misery, wretchedness; **3** trouble, woe; **on a tous nos petites ~s** we all have our troubles; **4 être payé une ~** to be paid a pittance.
miséreux, **-euse** /mizeʀø, øz/ *nm,f* destitute person; **les ~** the destitute.
miséricorde /mizeʀikɔʀd/ *nf, excl* mercy.
misogyne /mizɔʒin/ *adj* misogynous.
misogynie /mizɔʒini/ *nf* misogyny.
missel /misɛl/ *nm* missal.
missile /misil/ *nm* missile.
mission /misjɔ̃/ *nf* mission.
missionnaire /misjɔnɛʀ/ *adj, nmf* missionary.
missive /misiv/ *nf* missive.
mistral /mistʀal/ *nm* mistral.
mitaine /mitɛn/ *nf* fingerless mitten.
mite /mit/ *nf* (clothes) moth.
mi-temps[1] /mitɑ̃/ *nm inv* part-time job.
mi-temps[2] /mitɑ̃/ *nf inv* (Sport) half-time.
miteux, **-euse** /mitø, øz/ *adj* seedy; shabby.
mitigé, **~e** /mitiʒe/ *adj* [*reception*] lukewarm; [*success*] qualified.
mitonner /mitɔne/ [1] *vtr* to cook [sth] lovingly.
mitoyen, **-enne** /mitwajɛ̃, ɛn/ *adj* [*hedge*] dividing; **mur ~** party wall.
mitraille /mitʀaj/ *nf* hail of bullets.
mitrailler /mitʀaje/ [1] *vtr* **1** to machine-gun; **2 ~ qn de questions** to fire questions at sb; **3**○ to take photo after photo of [sb/sth].
mitraillette /mitʀajɛt/ *nf* submachine gun.
mitrailleuse /mitʀajøz/ *nf* machine gun.
mixage /miksaʒ/ *nm* sound mixing.
mixer[1] /mikse/ [1] *vtr* to mix.
mixer[2] /miksɛʀ/ = **mixeur**.
mixeur /miksœʀ/ *nm* **1** mixer; **2** blender.
mixité /miksite/ *nf* (gen) mixing of sexes; (Sch) coeducation.
mixte /mikst/ *adj* **1** [*school*] coeducational; [*class*] mixed; **2** [*couple, marriage*] mixed; [*economy*] mixed; **société ~** joint venture.
mixture /mikstyʀ/ *nf* **1** concoction; **2** (in pharmacy) mixture; **3** mishmash○.
MJC /ɛmʒise/ *nf* (*abbr* = **maison des jeunes et de la culture**) ≈ youth club.
MLF /ɛmɛlɛf/ *nm* (*abbr* = **mouvement de libération des femmes**) ≈ Women's Lib.
Mlle (*written abbr* = **Mademoiselle**) Ms, Miss.
mm (*written abbr* = **millimètre**) mm.
MM. (*written abbr* = **Messieurs**) Messrs.
Mme (*written abbr* = **Madame**) Ms, Mrs.
mnémotechnique /mnemɔtɛknik/ *adj* mnemonic.
Mo (*written abbr* = **mégaoctet**) Mb, MB.
mobile /mɔbil/ I *adj* (gen) mobile; [*leaf*] loose.
II *nm* **1** motive; **2** mobile.
mobilier, **-ière** /mɔbilje, ɛʀ/ I *adj* **biens ~s** movable property.
II *nm* furniture.
mobilisation /mɔbilizasjɔ̃/ *nf* mobilization.
mobiliser /mɔbilize/ [1] I *vtr* to mobilize [*soldier*]; to call up [*civilian*].
II **se mobiliser** *v refl* (+ *v être*) to rally.
mobilité /mɔbilite/ *nf* mobility.
mobylette® /mɔbilɛt/ *nf* moped.
mocassin /mɔkasɛ̃/ *nm* moccasin, loafer.
moche○ /mɔʃ/ *adj* **1** [*person*] ugly; [*garment*] ghastly; **2** [*incident*] dreadful; **3** [*act*] nasty.
modalité /mɔdalite/ I *nf* modality.
II **modalités** *nf pl* terms; practical details.
mode[1] /mɔd/ *nm* **1** way, mode; **~ de paiement** method of payment; **2** (in grammar) mood.
■ **~ d'emploi** instructions for use.
mode[2] /mɔd/ *nf* **1** fashion; **lancer une ~** to start a trend; **à la ~** [*garment, club*] fashionable; [*singer*] popular; **2** fashion industry.
modèle /mɔdɛl/ I *adj* (gen) model; [*conduct*] perfect, exemplary.
II *nm* **1** (gen) model; **prendre ~ sur qn** to do as sb does/did; **~ à suivre** somebody to look up to; **la tente grand ~** large-size tent; **le ~ au-dessus** the next size up; **~ de signature** specimen signature; **2** pattern; **~ déposé** registered pattern.
■ **~ réduit** scale model.
modeler /mɔdle/ [17] *vtr* to model [*clay*]; to mould (GB) or mold (US) [*character*].
modélisme /mɔdelism/ *nm* modelling.
modération /mɔdeʀasjɔ̃/ *nf* **1** moderation; **2** (in price, tax) reduction.
modéré, **~e** /mɔdeʀe/ *adj* [*party, speed,*

words] moderate; [*price*] reasonable; [*temperament*] even; [*enthusiasm*] mild.

modérément /mɔdeʀemɑ̃/ *adv* **1** relatively; **2** slightly.

modérer /mɔdeʀe/ [14] *vtr* to curb [*expenses*]; to moderate [*language*]; to reduce [*speed*].

moderne /mɔdɛʀn/ *adj* modern.

moderniser /mɔdɛʀnize/ [1] *vtr* to modernize; to update.

modernité /mɔdɛʀnite/ *nf* modernity.

modeste /mɔdɛst/ *adj* [*sum, apartment, person*] modest; [*cost*] moderate; [*background*] humble.

modestie /mɔdɛsti/ *nf* modesty.

modification /mɔdifikasjɔ̃/ *nf* modification.

modifier /mɔdifje/ [2] *vtr* to change; to alter, to modify.

modique /mɔdik/ *adj* [*sum, resources*] modest.

modiste /mɔdist/ *nf* milliner.

modulation /mɔdylasjɔ̃/ *nf* modulation.
■ **~ de fréquence**, **MF** frequency modulation, FM.

module /mɔdyl/ *nm* (gen, Sch) module.

moduler /mɔdyle/ [1] *vtr* **1** to modulate; **2** to adjust [*price*]; to adapt [*policy*].

moelle /mwal/ *nf* marrow.
■ **~ épinière** spinal cord.

moelleux, **-euse** /mwalø, øz/ *adj* **1** [*carpet*] thick; [*bed*] soft; **2** [*wine*] mellow.

mœurs /mœʀ(s)/ *nf pl* **1** customs; habits; lifestyle; **l'évolution des ~** the change in attitudes; **2** morals; **des ~ dissolues** loose morals; **la police des ~**, **les Mœurs**○ the vice squad; **3** (of animals) behaviour.
IDIOMS **autres temps, autres ~** other days, other ways.

mohair /mɔɛʀ/ *nm* mohair.

moi[1] /mwɑ/ *pron* **1** I, me; **c'est ~** it's me; **2** me; **pour ~** for me; **des amis à ~** friends of mine; **c'est à ~** it's mine; it's my turn.

moi[2] /mwɑ/ *nm* **le ~** the self.

moignon /mwaɲɔ̃/ *nm* stump.

moi-même /mwamɛm/ *pron* myself.

moindre /mwɛ̃dʀ/ *adj* **1** lesser; **à ~ prix** more cheaply; **2 le ~** the least; **je n'en ai pas la ~ idée** I haven't got the slightest idea.

moine /mwan/ *nm* monk.
IDIOMS **l'habit ne fait pas le ~** (Proverb) you can't judge a book by its cover.

moineau, *pl* **~x** /mwano/ *nm* sparrow.

moins[1] /mwɛ̃/ **I** *prep* **1** minus; **2 il est huit heures ~ dix** it's ten (minutes) to eight; **il était ~ une**○ it was a close shave○.
II *adv* (comparative) less; (superlative) **le ~** the least; **le ~ difficile** the less difficult; the least difficult; **de ~ en ~** less and less; **~ je sors, ~ j'ai envie de sortir** the less I go out, the less I feel like going out; **il n'en est pas ~ vrai que** it's nonetheless true that; **il ressemble à son frère en ~ gros** he looks like his brother, only thinner; **à tout le ~**, **pour le ~** to say the least; **il y avait deux fourchettes en ~ dans la boîte** there were two forks missing from the box.
III moins de *quantif* **~ de livres** fewer books; **~ de sucre** less sugar; **les ~ de 20 ans** people under 20.
IV à moins de *phr* unless.
V à moins que *phr* unless.
VI au moins *phr* at least.
VII du moins *phr* at least.

moins[2] /mwɛ̃/ *nm inv* minus.
■ **~ que rien** good-for-nothing, nobody.

moiré, **~e** /mwaʀe/ *adj* moiré; watered.

mois /mwa/ *nm inv* month.

moisi /mwazi/ *nm* mould (GB), mold (US).

moisir /mwaziʀ/ [3] *vi* [*foodstuff*] to go mouldy (GB) or moldy (US); [*object, plant*] to become mildewed.

moisissure /mwazisyʀ/ *nf* **1** mould (GB), mold (US); **2** mildew.

moisson /mwasɔ̃/ *nf* harvest.

moissonner /mwasɔne/ [1] *vtr* to harvest.

moissonneuse /mwasɔnøz/ *nf* reaper.

moite /mwat/ *adj* [*heat*] muggy; [*skin*] sweaty.

moiteur /mwatœʀ/ *nf* (of air) mugginess; (of skin) sweatiness.

moitié /mwatje/ *nf* half; **à ~ vide** half empty.

moitié-moitié /mwatjemwatje/ *adv* half-and-half.

moka /mɔka/ *nm* **1** mocha; **2** mocha cake.

molaire /mɔlɛʀ/ *nf* molar.

molécule /mɔlekyl/ *nf* molecule.

molester /mɔlɛste/ [1] *vtr* to manhandle [sb].

molette /mɔlɛt/ *nf* (of spanner) adjusting knob.

mollasson○, **-onne** /mɔlasɔ̃, ɔn/ *adj* sluggish.

molle ▶ **mou** I.

mollement /mɔlmɑ̃/ *adv* **1** idly; **2** [*work*] without much enthusiasm; [*protest*] half-heartedly.

mollet /mɔlɛ/ **I** *adj m* **œuf ~** soft-boiled egg.
II *nm* (Anat) calf.

molleton /mɔltɔ̃/ *nm* **1** flannel; flannelette; **2** (table) felt; **3** (ironing board) cover.

molletonner /mɔltɔne/ [1] *vtr* to line with fleece.

mollir /mɔliʀ/ [3] *vi* **1** [*courage*] to fail; [*resistance*] to grow weaker; [*person*] to soften; **2** [*knees*] to give way; [*arm*] to go weak.

mollusque /mɔlysk/ *nm* mollusc (GB), mollusk (US).

molosse /mɔlɔs/ *nm* huge dog.

môme○ /mom/ *nmf* kid○; brat○.

moment /mɔmɑ̃/ *nm* moment; **le ~ venu** when the time comes/came; **il devrait arriver d'un ~ à l'autre** he should arrive any minute now; **à un ~ donné** at some point; at a given moment; **à ce ~-là** at that time; just then; in that case; **au ~ où** at the time (when); **au ~ où il quittait son domicile** as he was leaving his home; **jusqu'au ~ où** until; **du ~ que** as long as, provided; **il arrive toujours au bon** or **mauvais ~!** he certainly picks his moment to call!; **un ~!** just a moment!; **ça va prendre un ~** it will take a while; **au bout d'un ~** after a while; **par ~s** at times; **les ~s forts du film** the film's highlights; **dans ses meilleurs ~s, il fait penser à Orson Welles** at his best, he reminds one of Orson Welles; **à mes ~s perdus** in my spare time.

momentané, **~e** /mɔmɑ̃tane/ *adj* momentary.

momentanément /mɔmɑ̃tanemɑ̃/ *adv* for a moment, momentarily.

momie /mɔmi/ *nf* mummy.

mon, **ma**, *pl* **mes** /mɔ̃, ma, mɛ/ *det* my; **j'ai ~ idée** I have my own ideas about that.

monacal, **~e**, *mpl* **-aux** /mɔnakal, o/ *adj* monastic.

monarchie /mɔnaʀʃi/ *nf* monarchy.

monarchiste /mɔnaʀʃist/ *adj*, *nmf* monarchist.

monarque /mɔnaʀk/ *nm* monarch.

monastère /mɔnastɛʀ/ *nm* monastery.

monceau, *pl* **~x** /mɔ̃so/ *nm* (of rubbish) pile.

mondain, **~e** /mɔ̃dɛ̃, ɛn/ **I** *adj* [*life, ball*] society; [*conversation*] polite.
II *nm,f* socialite.

monde /mɔ̃d/ *nm* **1** world; **pas le moins du ~** not in the least; **aller** or **voyager de par le ~** to travel the world; **c'est le bout du ~!** it's in the back of beyond!; **ce n'est pas le bout du ~!** it's not such a big deal!; **à la face du ~** for all the world to see; **en ce bas ~** here below; **elle n'est plus de ce ~** she's no longer with us; **je n'étais pas encore au ~** I wasn't yet born; **le ~ médical** the medical world; **le ~ animal** the animal kingdom; **un ~ nous sépare** we are worlds apart; **2** people; **tout le ~** everybody; **tout mon petit ~** my family and friends; **3** society; **le beau** or **grand ~** high society.
IDIOMS **se faire un ~ de qch** to get all worked up about sth; **depuis que le ~ est ~** since the beginning of time; **c'est un ~**○**!** that's a bit much!

mondial, **~e**, *mpl* **-iaux** /mɔ̃djal, o/ *adj* world; [*success*] worldwide; **seconde guerre ~e** Second World War.

mondialement /mɔ̃djalmɑ̃/ *adv* **être ~ connu** to be world famous.

mondialisation /mɔ̃djalizasjɔ̃/ *nf* globalization.

mondovision /mɔ̃dɔvizjɔ̃/ *nf* satellite broadcasting.

monétaire /mɔnetɛʀ/ *adj* [*system, stability*] monetary; [*market*] money.

monétique /mɔnetik/ *nf* electronic banking.

Mongolie /mɔ̃gɔli/ *pr nf* Mongolia.

mongolien, **-ienne** /mɔ̃gɔljɛ̃, ɛn/ (controversial) *nm,f* Down's syndrome child.

moniteur, **-trice** /mɔnitœʀ, tʀis/ **I** *nm,f* **1** (Aut, Sport) instructor; **2** (in holiday camp) group leader (GB), counselor (US).
II *nm* **1** (TV) monitor; **2** (Comput) monitor system.

monnaie /mɔnɛ/ *nf* **1** currency; **fausse ~** forged or counterfeit currency; **2** change; **faire de la ~** to get some change; **3** coin; **battre ~** to mint or strike coins; **l'hôtel de la Monnaie**, **la Monnaie** the Mint; **4** (Econ) money.
■ **~ d'échange** trading currency; bargaining chip; **~ de papier** paper money.
IDIOMS **rendre à qn la ~ de sa pièce** to pay sb back in his/her own coin; **c'est ~ courante** it's commonplace.

monnayer /mɔnɛje/ [21] *vtr* **1** to convert [sth] into cash; **2** to capitalize on [*talent, experience*]; **~ qch contre qch** to exchange sth for sth.

mono[1] /mono/ *pref* mono; **~chrome** monochrome; **~lingue** monolingual.

mono[2] /mono/ *nf* (in hi-fi) mono.

monocle /mɔnɔkl/ *nm* monocle.

monocorde /mɔnɔkɔʀd/ *adj* [*voice, speech*] monotonous; [*instrument*] single-string.

monogame /mɔnɔgam/ *adj* monogamous.

monogamie /mɔnɔgami/ *nf* monogamy.

monoï /mɔnɔj/ *nm inv* coconut oil (*used in cosmetics*).

monologue /mɔnɔlɔg/ *nm* monologue[GB].
■ **~ intérieur** stream of consciousness.

mononucléose /mɔnonykleoz/ *nf* mononucleosis; **~ infectieuse** glandular fever.

monoparental, **~e**, *mpl* **-aux** /mɔnopaʀɑ̃tal, o/ *adj* **famille ~e** single-parent family.

monopole /mɔnɔpɔl/ *nm* monopoly.

monopoliser /mɔnɔpɔlize/ [1] *vtr* to monopolize.

monoski /mɔnɔski/ *nm* **1** monoski; **2** monoskiing.

monothéiste /mɔnɔteist/ *adj* monotheistic.

monotone /mɔnɔtɔn/ *adj* monotonous.

monotonie /mɔnɔtɔni/ *nf* monotony.

monoxyde /mɔnɔksid/ *nm* monoxide.

Monseigneur, *pl* **Messeigneurs** /mɔ̃sɛɲœʀ, mesɛɲœʀ/ *nm* Your Highness; Your Eminence; **~ le duc de Parme** His Grace, the duke of Parma.

monsieur, *pl* **messieurs** /məsjø, mesjø/ *nm* **1** (addressing a man whose name you do not know) **Monsieur** (in a letter) Dear Sir; **bonjour ~!** good morning!; **2** (addressing a man whose name you know, for instance Hallé) **Monsieur** (in a letter) Dear Mr Hallé; **bonjour ~!** good morning, Mr Hallé; **3** (polite form of address) **'Monsieur a sonné?'** 'you rang, sir?'; **4** man; **le double messieurs** the men's doubles; **c'était un (grand) ~!** he was a (true) gentleman!
■ **~ Tout le Monde** the man in the street.

monstre /mɔ̃stʀ/ **I**○ *adj* [*task, success, publicity*] huge; [*nerve*] colossal.
II *nm* **1** monster; **2** freak (of nature).
■ **~ marin** sea monster.

monstrueux, **-euse** /mɔ̃stʀyø, øz/ *adj* **1** [*crime, cruelty*] monstrous; **2** hideous; **d'une laideur monstrueuse** hideously ugly; **3** [*error*] colossal.

monstruosité /mɔ̃stʀyozite/ *nf* **1** (of conduct) monstrousness; **2** atrocity; **3** monstrosity; **dire des ~s** to say preposterous things.

mont /mɔ̃/ *nm* mountain.
■ **le ~ Blanc** Mont Blanc.

montage /mɔ̃taʒ/ *nm* **1** set-up; **2** (of machine)

assembly; (of tent) putting up; **chaîne de ~** assembly line; **3** (of film) editing; **salle de ~** cutting room; **4** (of gem) setting.
■ **~ photo** photomontage; **~ sonore** sound montage.

montagnard, **~e** /mɔ̃taɲaʀ, aʀd/ I *adj* [*people, plant*] mountain; [*custom*] highland.
II *nm,f* mountain dweller.

montagne /mɔ̃taɲ/ *nf* **1** mountain; **2 la ~** the mountains; **de ~** [*road, animal*] mountain; **il neige en haute ~** it's snowing on the upper slopes.
■ **~s russes** big dipper, roller coaster.
IDIOMS **se faire une ~ de qch** to get really worked up about sth.

montagneux, **-euse** /mɔ̃taɲø, øz/ *adj* mountainous.

montant, **~e** /mɔ̃tɑ̃, ɑ̃t/ I *adj* **1** [*cabin, group*] going up; **2** [*road*] uphill; **3** [*neck*] high; [*socks*] long; **chaussures ~es** ankle boots.
II *nm* **1** sum; **le ~ des pertes** the total losses; **d'un ~ de** [*deficit, savings*] amounting to; [*cheque*] to the amount of; [*goods*] for a total of; **2** (of door, window) upright, jamb; transom; (of scaffolding) pole; (of ladder) upright.

mont-de-piété, *pl* **monts-de-piété** /mɔ̃dpjete/ *nm* pawnshop, pawnbroker's.

monte-charge /mɔ̃tʃaʀʒ/ *nm inv* goods lift (GB) or elevator (US).

montée /mɔ̃te/ *nf* **1** (up slope) climb; (of mountain) ascent; **2** (of plane) climb; **3** rising; rise; **la ~ des eaux** the rise in the water level; **une brusque ~ d'adrénaline** a rush of adrenaline; **4** (in prices) rise; (in danger) increase; **5** hill; **une légère ~** a slight slope.

monter /mɔ̃te/ [1] I *vtr* (+ *v avoir*) **1** to take [sb/sth] up; to take [sb/sth] upstairs; to bring [sb/sth] up; to bring [sb/sth] upstairs; **impossible de ~ le piano par l'escalier** it's impossible to get the piano up the stairs; **2** to put [sth] up; to raise [*shelf*]; **3** to go up [sth]; to come up [sth]; **~ la colline à bicyclette** to cycle up the hill; **4** to turn up [*volume, gas*]; **5 ~ les blancs en neige** beat or whisk the egg whites until stiff; **6 ~ qn contre qn** to set sb against sb; **7** to ride [*horse*]; **8** (Zool) to mount; **9** to assemble [*appliance, unit*]; to put up [*tent, scaffolding*]; **~ un film** to edit a film; **10** to hatch [*plot*]; to set up [*company*]; to stage [*play*]; **monté de toutes pièces** [*story*] fabricated from beginning to end.
II *vi* (+ *v être*) **1** to go up; to go upstairs; to come up; to come upstairs; [*plane*] to climb; [*bird*] to fly up; [*sun, mist*] to rise; **tu es monté à pied?** did you walk up?; did you come up on foot?; **~ sur** to get onto [*footpath*]; to climb onto [*stool*]; **~ à l'échelle** to climb (up) the ladder; **faites-les ~** send them up; **2 ~ dans une voiture/dans un train** to get in a car/on a train; **~ sur** to get on [*bike, horse*]; **3** [*road*] to go uphill, to climb; [*ground*] to rise; **~ jusqu'à** [*path, wall*] to go up to; **~ en lacets** to wind its way up; **4** [*garment, water*] to come up (**jusqu'a** to); **5** [*temperature, price*] to rise, to go up; [*tide*] to come in; **6 ~ à** or **sur Paris** to go up to Paris; **7 ~ (à cheval)** to ride; **8** (Mil) **~ à l'assaut** or **l'attaque** to mount an attack; **9** [*employee*] to rise, to move up; [*artist*] to rise; **10** [*anger, emotion*] to mount; [*tears*] to well up; **le ton monta** the discussion became heated; **11 ~ à la tête de qn** to go to sb's head; **12** (Aut, Tech) **~ à 250 km/h** to go up to 250 kph.
IDIOMS **se ~ la tête**○ to get worked up○.

monteur, **-euse** /mɔ̃tœʀ, øz/ *nm,f* **1** fitter; **2** (in film-making) editor; **3** paste-up artist.

montgolfière /mɔ̃gɔlfjɛʀ/ *nf* hot-air balloon.

monticule /mɔ̃tikyl/ *nm* **1** hillock; **2** mound.

montrable /mɔ̃tʀabl/ *adj* [*person*] presentable; [*images*] suitable for viewing.

montre /mɔ̃tʀ/ *nf* watch; **trois heures ~ en main** three hours exactly.

Montréal /mɔ̃ʀeal/ *pr n* Montreal.

montrer /mɔ̃tʀe/ [1] I *vtr* **1** to show; **~ qch à qn** to show sb sth; **2** to show [*feelings, knowledge*]; **3** [*person*] to point out [*track, place, object*]; [*survey, table*] to show [*trend, results*]; **~ qn du doigt** to point at sb; to point the finger at sb.
II **se montrer** *v refl* (+ *v être*) **1** to show oneself to be; to prove (to be); **il faut se ~ optimiste** we must try to be optimistic; **2** [*person*] to show oneself; [*sun*] to come out.
IDIOMS **~ les dents** to bare one's teeth; **~ le bout de son nez** to show one's face; to peep through.

monture /mɔ̃tyʀ/ *nf* **1** (for rider) mount; **2** (of glasses) frames; (of ring) setting.

monument /mɔnymɑ̃/ *nm* **1** monument; **2** (historic) building; **visiter les ~s de Paris** to see the sights of Paris; **3 un des ~s de la littérature européenne** a masterpiece of European literature.
■ **~ historique** ancient monument; **~ aux morts** war memorial.

monumental, **~e**, *mpl* **-aux** /mɔnymɑ̃tal, o/ *adj* monumental.

moquer: **se moquer** /mɔke/ [1] *v refl* (+ *v être*) **1 se ~ de** to make fun of; **2 se ~ de** not to care about; **3 se ~ du monde** to take people for fools.

moquerie /mɔkʀi/ *nf* **1** mocking remark; **2** mockery.

moquette /mɔkɛt/ *nf* wall-to-wall carpet.

moqueur, **-euse** /mɔkœʀ, øz/ *adj* mocking.

moral, **~e**[1], *mpl* **-aux** /mɔʀal, o/ I *adj* **1** moral; **n'avoir aucun sens ~** to have no sense of right and wrong; **2** [*torture*] mental; [*support*] moral; **3** [*person*] moral; [*conduct*] ethical.
II *nm* **1** morale; **avoir le ~** to be in good spirits; **avoir le ~ à zéro**○ to feel very down; **remonter le ~ de qn** to raise sb's spirits; **2** mind; **au ~ comme au physique** mentally and physically.

morale[2] /mɔʀal/ *nf* **1** morality; **leur ~** their moral code; **2** moral; **faire la ~ à qn** to give sb a lecture; **3 la ~** moral philosophy, ethics.

moralement /mɔʀalmɑ̃/ *adv* **1** morally, ethically; **2** psychologically.

moralisateur, **-trice** /mɔʀalizatœʀ, tʀis/ *adj* moralizing, moralistic.

moraliser /mɔʀalize/ [1] *vtr* to clean up; to reform.

moraliste /mɔʀalist/ *nmf* moralist.

moralité /mɔʀalite/ *nf* **1** morals; **2** (of action) morality; **3** moral; **~, ne faites confiance à personne** the moral is: don't trust anybody.

morbide /mɔʀbid/ *adj* morbid.

morceau, *pl* **~x** /mɔʀso/ *nm* **1** piece, bit; **~ de sucre** sugar lump; **manger un ~**○ to have a snack; **2** (of meat) cut; **bas ~** cheap cut; **3** (Mus) piece; **~ de piano** piano piece; **4** (from book) extract.

IDIOMS **recoller les ~x** to patch things up.

morceler /mɔʀsəle/ [19] *vtr* to divide [sth] up.

mordant, **~e** /mɔʀdɑ̃, ɑ̃t/ **I** *adj* **1** caustic, scathing; **2** [*cold*] biting.

II *nm* **1** sarcasm; **2**○ (of person, team) zip○.

mordiller /mɔʀdije/ [1] *vtr* to nibble at.

mordoré, **~e** /mɔʀdɔʀe/ *adj* golden brown.

mordre /mɔʀdʀ/ [6] **I** *vtr* to bite.

II mordre à *v+prep* **~ à l'appât** or **l'hameçon** to take the bait.

III *vi* **1 ~ dans une pomme** to bite into an apple; **2 ~ sur** to go over [*white line*]; to encroach on [*territory*]; **3**○ to fall for it○.

IV se mordre *v refl* (+ *v être*) **se ~ la langue** to bite one's tongue.

IDIOMS **je m'en suis mordu les doigts** I could have kicked myself.

mordu, **~e** /mɔʀdy/ **I**○ *adj* **1 être ~ de qch** to be mad○ about sth; **2** smitten.

II○ *nm,f* fan; **les ~s du ski** skiing fans.

morfondre: **se morfondre** /mɔʀfɔ̃dʀ/ [6] *v refl* (+ *v être*) **1 se ~ à attendre** or **en attendant** to wait dejectedly; **2** to pine.

morgue /mɔʀg/ *nf* **1** morgue; (hospital) mortuary; **2** arrogance.

moribond, **~e** /mɔʀibɔ̃, ɔ̃d/ **I** *adj* [*person*] dying; [*civilization*] moribund.

II *nm,f* dying man/woman.

morille /mɔʀij/ *nf* morel (mushroom).

morne /mɔʀn/ *adj* **1** gloomy; [*face*] glum; **2** [*landscape, life*] dreary.

morose /mɔʀoz/ *adj* morose; gloomy.

morphine /mɔʀfin/ *nf* morphine.

morphologie /mɔʀfɔlɔʒi/ *nf* morphology.

mors /mɔʀ/ *nm inv* bit; **prendre le ~ aux dents** to take the bit between its/one's teeth.

morse /mɔʀs/ *nm* **1** walrus; **2** (code) **~** Morse code.

morsure /mɔʀsyʀ/ *nf* **1** bite; **~ de chien** dogbite; **2 la ~ du froid** the biting cold.

mort[1] /mɔʀ/ *nf* death; **mourir de sa belle ~** to die peacefully in old age; **il n'y a pas eu ~ d'homme** there were no fatalities; **trouver la ~** to die; **mise à ~** (of condemned) killing; (of bull) dispatch; **à ~** [*fight*] to the death; [*war*] ruthless; [*brake, squeeze*] like mad○.

■ **~ cérébrale** brain death.

IDIOMS **la ~ dans l'âme** with a heavy heart.

mort[2], **~e** /mɔʀ, mɔʀt/ **I** *pp* ▶ **mourir**.

II *pp adj* **1** dead; **2 je suis ~ de froid** I'm freezing to death; **je suis ~**○ I'm dead tired; **3** [*district*] dead; [*season*] slack; **4** [*civilization*] dead; [*city*] lost.

III *nm,f* dead person, dead man/woman.

IV *nm* **1** fatality; **il y a eu 12 ~s** there were 12 dead; **2** body; **faire le ~** to play dead; to lie low.

IDIOMS **ne pas y aller de main ~e**○ not to pull any punches.

mortalité /mɔʀtalite/ *nf* mortality.

mort-aux-rats /mɔʀoʀa/ *nf inv* rat poison.

mortel, **-elle** /mɔʀtɛl/ **I** *adj* **1** [*blow, illness*] fatal; [*poison*] lethal; [*venom*] deadly; **2** [*cold*] deathly; **3** [*enemy*] mortal; **4** [*person, meeting*] deadly boring; **5** [*being*] mortal.

II *nm,f* mortal.

mortellement /mɔʀtɛlmɑ̃/ *adv* **1** [*injured*] fatally; **2** [*boring*] deadly.

mortier /mɔʀtje/ *nm* mortar.

mort-né, **~e**, *mpl* **~s** /mɔʀne/ *adj* **1** stillborn; **2** [*plan*] abortive.

mortuaire /mɔʀtɥɛʀ/ *adj* **cérémonie ~** funeral ceremony; **veillée ~** wake.

morue /mɔʀy/ *nf* cod.

morve /mɔʀv/ *nf* nasal mucus, snot◐.

mosaïque /mɔzaik/ *nf* mosaic.

Moscou /mɔsku/ *pr n* Moscow.

mosquée /mɔske/ *nf* mosque.

mot /mo/ *nm* **1** word; **à ~s couverts** in veiled terms; **au bas ~** at least; **il est bête et le ~ est faible!** he's stupid and that's putting it mildly!; **dire un ~ à qn** to have a word with sb; **il ne dit jamais un ~ plus haut que l'autre** he never raises his voice; **avoir son ~ à dire** to be entitled to one's say; **2** note; **je t'ai laissé un ~** I left you a note.

■ **~ d'esprit** witticism; **~ d'ordre** watchword; **~ d'ordre de grève** strike call; **~ de passe** password; **~s croisés** crossword; **~s doux** sweet nothings.

IDIOMS **ne pas avoir peur des ~s** to call a spade a spade; **manger ses ~s** to mumble; **se donner le ~** to pass the word around.

motard, **~e** /mɔtaʀ, aʀd/ **I**○ *nm,f* biker○.

II *nm* police motorcyclist.

mot-clé, *pl* **mots-clés** /mokle/ *nm* key word.

moteur, **-trice**[1] /mɔtœʀ, tʀis/ **I** *adj* **1** [*force, principle*] driving; **la voiture a quatre roues motrices** the car has four-wheel drive; **2** (Med) **troubles ~s** motor problems.

II *nm* **1** motor; **2** engine; **3 être le ~ de qch** to be the driving force behind sth.

motif /mɔtif/ *nm* **1** grounds; **des ~s d'espérer** grounds for hope; **2** reason; **3** motive; **4** pattern; **à ~ floral** with a floral pattern.

motion /mɔsjɔ̃/ *nf* motion.

motivant, **~e** /mɔtivɑ̃, ɑ̃t/ *adj* [*salary*] attractive; [*work*] rewarding.

motivation /mɔtivasjɔ̃/ *nf* **1** motivation; **2** motive; **~s profondes** deeper motives.

motivé, **~e** /mɔtive/ *adj* **1** motivated; **2** [*complaint*] justifiable.

motiver /mɔtive/ [1] *vtr* **1** to motivate; **2** to lead to [*decision, action*]; **motivé par** caused by.

moto /moto/ *nf* **1** (motor)bike; **2** motorcycling.

motocyclette /motosiklɛt/ *nf* motorcycle.

motocyclisme /motosiklism/ *nm* motorcycle racing.

motocycliste /motosiklist/ **I** *adj* motorcycle. **II** *nmf* motorcyclist.

motoneige /motonɛʒ/ *nf* snowmobile.

motoriser /mɔtɔʀize/ [1] *vtr* to motorize; **être motorisé**○ to have transport (GB) or transportation (US).

motrice[2] /mɔtʀis/ *adj f* ▶ **moteur I**.

motte /mɔt/ *nf* **~ (de terre)** clod (of earth); **~ de gazon** sod, piece of turf; **~ (de beurre)** slab of butter.

mou (mol *before vowel or mute h*), **molle** /mu, mɔl/ **I** *adj* **1** [*substance, cushion*] soft; [*blow*] dull; **2** [*stomach*] flabby; **3** [*person*] listless; [*growth*] sluggish; **4** [*parent*] soft; **5** [*speech*] feeble.
II *nm* **1** wimp○; **2** (in butchery) lights (GB), lungs (US); **3** (in rope) slack; **donner du ~ à qn**○ to give sb a bit of leeway.

mouchard, **~e** /muʃaʀ, aʀd/ **I**○ *nm,f* **1** grass○ (GB), informer; **2** sneak○.
II *nm* **1** tachograph; **2** spyhole.

moucharder○ /muʃaʀde/ [1] *vtr* **1 ~ qn** to inform on sb; to squeal○ on sb; **2** to sneak○.

mouche /muʃ/ *nf* **1** fly; **2** patch, beauty spot; **3** bull's eye; **faire ~** to hit the bull's eye; (figurative) to be right on target; **4** (Sport) (on foil) button.
■ **~ verte** greenbottle; **~ du vinaigre** fruit fly.
IDIOMS **quelle ~ les a piqués**○? what's got (GB) or gotten (US) into them?; **prendre la ~** to fly off the handle.

moucher /muʃe/ [1] **I** *vtr* **~ qn** to blow sb's nose; (figurative)○ to put sb in their place.
II se moucher *v refl* (+ *v être*) to blow one's nose.
IDIOMS **il ne se mouche pas du pied** or **du coude**○ he's full of airs and graces.

moucheron /muʃʀɔ̃/ *nm* midge.

moucheté, **~e** /muʃte/ *adj* **1** [*material*] flecked; [*plumage, fish*] speckled; [*coat*] spotted; [*horse*] dappled; **2** (Sport) [*foil*] buttoned.

mouchoir /muʃwaʀ/ *nm* handkerchief; tissue.

moudre /mudʀ/ [77] *vtr* to grind.

moue /mu/ *nf* pout; **faire la ~** to pout; (doubtfully) to pull a face.

mouette /mwɛt/ *nf* (sea) gull.

moufle /mufl/ *nf* mitten.

mouiller /muje/ [1] **I** *vtr* **1** to wet; to get [sth] wet; **2** to drop [*anchor*]; to lay [*mine*].
II *vi* to anchor, to drop anchor.
III se mouiller *v refl* (+ *v être*) to get wet.

moulage /mulaʒ/ *nm* **1** casting; **faire un ~ de qch** to take a cast of sth; **2** (of grain) milling.

moulant, **~e** /mulɑ̃, ɑ̃t/ *adj* tight-fitting.

moule[1] /mul/ *nm* **1** mould (GB), mold (US); **2** tin, pan (US); **~ à gaufre** waffle iron.

moule[2] /mul/ *nf* mussel.

mouler /mule/ [1] *vtr* **1** to mould (GB), to mold (US) [*substance*]; to cast [*bronze*]; to mint [*medal*]; **2** to take a cast of; **3** [*garment*] to hug.

moulin /mulɛ̃/ *nm* mill.
■ **~ à paroles**○ chatterbox; **~ à vent** windmill.
IDIOMS **apporter de l'eau au ~ de qn** to fuel sb's arguments; **on ne peut être à la fois au four et au ~** one can't be in two places at once; **on y entre comme dans un ~**○ one can just slip in.

mouliner /muline/ [1] *vtr* to grind, to mill.

moulinet /mulinɛ/ *nm* **faire des ~s avec les bras** to wave one's arms about.

moulu, **~e** /muly/ **I** *pp* ▶ **moudre**.
II *pp adj* [*coffee, pepper*] ground.
III○ *adj* **~ (de fatigue)** worn out.

moumoute○ /mumut/ *nf* **1** toupee; **2** sheepskin jacket.

mourant, **~e** /muʀɑ̃, ɑ̃t/ *adj* [*person, animal*] dying; [*light*] fading; [*voice*] faint.

mourir /muʀiʀ/ [34] *vi* (+ *v être*) to die; **~ de froid** to die of exposure; to die of cold; **je meurs de soif/de froid** I'm dying of thirst/freezing to death; **c'était à ~ (de rire)!** it was hilarious!; **~ debout** to be active to the end.
IDIOMS **partir c'est ~ un peu** to say goodbye is to die a little; **je ne veux pas ~ idiot**○ I want to know.

mouroir /muʀwaʀ/ *nm* (derogatory) old people's home, twilight home.

mousquetaire /muskətɛʀ/ *nm* musketeer.

mousqueton /muskətɔ̃/ *nm* snap clasp.

moussant, **~e** /musɑ̃, ɑ̃t/ *adj* [*gel*] foaming.

mousse[1] /mus/ *nm* ship's apprentice.

mousse[2] /mus/ *nf* **1** moss; **2** foam; (from soap) lather; (on milk) froth; (on beer) head; **3 ~ au chocolat** chocolate mousse; **4** foam rubber.
■ **~ carbonique** fire foam; **~ à raser** shaving foam.

mousseline /muslin/ *nf* **1** muslin; **2** chiffon.

mousser /muse/ [1] *vi* to foam; to lather.
IDIOMS **se faire ~**○ to blow one's own trumpet.

mousseux, **-euse** /musø, øz/ *adj* **1** [*wine*] sparkling; [*beer*] fizzy; **2** [*lace*] frothy.

mousson /musɔ̃/ *nf* monsoon.

moustache /mustaʃ/ **I** *nf* moustache (GB), mustache (US).
II moustaches *nf pl* (Zool) whiskers.

moustachu, **~e** /mustaʃy/ *adj* [*person*] with a moustache (GB) or mustache (US).

moustiquaire /mustikɛʀ/ *nf* mosquito net.

moustique /mustik/ *nm* mosquito.

moutarde /mutaʀd/ *adj inv*, *nf* mustard.
IDIOMS **la ~ me monte au nez**○! I'm beginning to see red!

mouton /mutɔ̃/ **I** *nm* **1** sheep; **2** mutton; **3** sheepskin; **4** (derogatory) sheep.
II moutons *nm pl* **1** small fleecy clouds; **2** whitecaps; **3** fluff.
■ **~ à cinq pattes** rare bird.

IDIOMS **revenons à nos ~s**○ let's get back to the point.

mouture /mutyʀ/ *nf* **1** (of coffee) grind; **2 première/nouvelle ~** first/new version.

mouvant, **~e** /muvɑ̃, ɑ̃t/ *adj* **1** [*ground*] unstable; **2** [*group*] shifting; **3** [*opinion*] changing.

mouvement /muvmɑ̃/ *nm* **1** (gen) movement; **faire un ~** to move; **~ perpétuel** perpetual motion; **accélérer le ~** to speed up; **2** bustle; **suivre le ~** (figurative) to follow the crowd; **3** impulse, reaction; **un ~ de colère** a surge of anger; **4 le ~ étudiant** the student protest movement; **~ de grève** strike, industrial action; **5 le ~ des idées** the evolution of ideas; **un milieu en ~** a changing environment; **6** (Econ) **le ~ du marché** market fluctuations; **~ de hausse** upward trend.

mouvementé, **~e** /muvmɑ̃te/ *adj* **1** [*life, week, trip*] eventful, hectic; **2** [*terrain*] rough.

mouvoir: **se mouvoir** /muvwaʀ/ [43] *v refl* (+ *v être*) to move.

moyen, **-enne**[1] /mwajɛ̃, ɛn/ **I** *adj* **1** medium; medium-sized; **2** [*income*] middle; [*level*] intermediate; **3** average, mean; **le Français ~** the average Frenchman.

II *nm* **1** means, way (**de faire** of doing); **employer les grands ~s** to resort to drastic measures; **(il n'y a) pas ~ de lui faire comprendre qu'il a tort** it's impossible to make him realize he's wrong; **2** (of expression, production) means; (of investigation, payment) method.

III au moyen de *phr* by means of.

IV par le moyen de *phr* by means of.

V moyens *nm pl* **1** means; **faute de ~s** through lack of money; **avoir de petits ~s** not to be very well off; **2** resources; **donner à qn les ~s de faire** to give sb the means to do; **3** ability; **perdre ses ~s** to go to pieces.

■ **~ de locomotion** or **transport** means of transport (GB) or transportation (US); **Moyen Âge** Middle Ages.

moyennant /mwajenɑ̃/ *prep* **~ finances** for a fee; **~ quoi** in view of which; in return for which.

moyenne[2] /mwajɛn/ **I** *adj f* ▶ **moyen**.

II *nf* **1** average; **la ~ d'âge** the average age; **en ~** on average; **2** half marks (GB), 50%; **3** (Aut) average speed.

moyennement /mwajɛnmɑ̃/ *adv* [*intelligent, wealthy*] moderately; [*like*] to a certain extent.

Moyen-Orient /mwajɛnɔʀjɑ̃/ *pr nm* Middle East.

moyeu, *pl* **~x** /mwajø/ *nm* hub.

MST /ɛmɛste/ *nf*: *abbr* ▶ **maladie**.

mu, **~e**[1] /my/ *pp* ▶ **mouvoir**.

mucoviscidose /mykovisidoz/ *nf* cystic fibrosis.

mucus /mykys/ *nm inv* mucus.

mue[2] /my/ *nf* **1** (of insect) metamorphosis; (of reptile) sloughing of the skin; (of bird, mammal) moulting (GB), molting (US); (of stag) casting; **2** (of snake, insect) slough, sloughed skin; **3** breaking (GB) or changing (US) of voice.

muer /mɥe/ [1] **I** *vi* **1** [*insect*] to metamorphose; [*snake*] to slough its skin; [*bird, mammal*] to moult (GB), to molt (US); **2 sa voix mue, il mue** his voice is breaking (GB) or changing (US).

II se muer *v refl* (+ *v être*) **1** to be transformed; **2** to transform oneself.

muet, **-ette** /mɥɛ, ɛt/ **I** *adj* **1** dumb; speechless; **2** [*witness*] silent; **3** [*vowel, consonant*] mute; **4** [*film*] silent; [*role*] non-speaking.

II *nm,f* mute.

mufle /myfl/ **I** *adj* boorish, loutish.

II *nm* **1** (Zool) muffle; muzzle; **2** boor, lout.

muflerie /myflǝʀi/ *nf* boorishness.

mugir /myʒiʀ/ [3] *vi* **1** to low; to bellow; **2** [*wind*] to howl; [*siren*] to wail; [*torrent*] to roar.

muguet /mygɛ/ *nm* lily of the valley.

mulâtre /mylɑtʀ/ *adj* mulatto.

mule /myl/ *nf* **1** female mule; **2** (slipper) mule.

mulet /mylɛ/ *nm* (male) mule.

mulot /mylo/ *nm* fieldmouse.

multi /mylti/ *pref* multi; **~colore** multicoloured[GB]; **~media** multimedia.

multipare /myltipaʀ/ *adj* multiparous.

multiple /myltipl/ **I** *adj* **1** [*reasons, occasions*] numerous, many; [*births*] multiple; **à choix ~** multiple-choice; **2** [*causes, facets*] many, various; **3** (in science) multiple.

II *nm* multiple.

multipliable /myltiplijabl/ *adj* multiplicable.

multiplication /myltiplikasjɔ̃/ *nf* **1 ~ de** increase in the number of; **2** (in mathematics, science) multiplication.

multiplicité /myltiplisite/ *nf* multiplicity.

multiplier /myltiplije/ [2] **I** *vtr* **1** to multiply; **2** to increase [*risks, fortune*]; to increase the number of [*trains, accidents*].

II se multiplier *v refl* (+ *v être*) **1** [*branches, villas*] to grow in number; [*incidents*] to be on the increase; [*difficulties*] to increase; **2** [*animals, germs*] to multiply.

multipropriété /myltipʀɔpʀijete/ *nf* timesharing.

multirisque /myltiʀisk/ *adj* **assurance ~** comprehensive insurance.

multitude /myltityd/ *nf* **1 une ~ de** a mass of [*tourists, objects*]; a lot of [*reasons, ideas*]; **2** multitude, throng.

municipal, **~e**, *mpl* **-aux** /mynisipal, o/ *adj* [*council*] local, town; city; [*park, pool*] municipal; **arrêté ~** bylaw.

municipales /mynisipal/ *nf pl* local elections.

municipalité /mynisipalite/ *nf* **1** municipality; **2** town council; city council.

munir /myniʀ/ [3] **I** *vtr* to provide; **~ un bâtiment d'un escalier de secours** to put a fire escape on a building; **muni de** fitted with.

II se munir *v refl* (+ *v être*) **se ~ de** to bring; to take.

munitions /mynisjɔ̃/ *nf pl* ammunition.

muqueuse /mykøz/ *nf* mucous membrane.

mur /myʀ/ **I** *nm* wall; **faire les pieds au ~** to

do a handstand against the wall; to tie oneself up in knots.

II **murs** *nm pl* (of business) premises; (of palace, embassy) confines; **être dans ses ~s** to own one's own house.

■ **~ portant** or **porteur** load-bearing wall; **~ du son** sound barrier; **Mur des lamentations** Wailing Wall.

IDIOMS **faire le ~** to go over the wall; **mettre qn au pied du ~** to call sb's bluff; **être au pied du ~** to be up against the wall.

mûr, **~e**[1] /myʀ/ *adj* **1** ripe; **2** mature; **l'âge ~** middle age; **après ~e réflexion** after careful consideration; **3** ready; **il est ~ pour des aveux** he's ready to confess; **4** [*situation*] at a decisive stage.

IDIOMS **en voir des vertes et des pas ~es**○ to go through a lot.

muraille /myʀɑj/ *nf* great wall.

mural, **~e**, *mpl* **-aux** /myʀal, o/ *adj* [*covering, map*] wall; [*plant*] climbing.

mûre[2] /myʀ/ I *adj f* ▸ **mûr**.

II *nf* blackberry.

mûrement /myʀmɑ̃/ *adv* **~ réfléchi** carefully thought through.

murer /myʀe/ [1] *vtr* to build a wall around [sth]; to brick [sth] up; to block [sth] off.

muret /myʀɛ/ *nm* low wall.

mûrier /myʀje/ *nm* mulberry tree.

mûrir /myʀiʀ/ [3] I *vtr* **1** to ripen [*fruit*]; **2** to mature [*person*]; to develop [*plan*].

II *vi* **1** [*fruit*] to ripen; **2** [*person, talent*] to mature; [*plan, idea*] to evolve; [*passion*] to develop; **3** [*abscess*] to come to a head.

murmure /myʀmyʀ/ *nm* **1** murmur; **2** **~s** mutterings; **3** (of wind) whisper.

murmurer /myʀmyʀe/ [1] I *vtr* **1** to murmur; **2** to say; **on murmure qu'il est riche** he is rumoured[GB] to be rich.

II *vi* **1** [*person*] to murmur; [*wind*] to whisper.

musaraigne /myzaʀɛɲ/ *nf* (Zool) shrew.

musc /mysk/ *nm* musk.

muscade /myskad/ *nf* nutmeg.

muscle /myskl/ *nm* muscle.

musclé, **~e** /myskle/ *adj* **1** muscular; **2** [*music, speech*] powerful; [*reaction*] strong; [*intervention*] tough; **3** (Econ) competitive.

muscler /myskle/ [1] I *vtr* **1** **~ les bras** to develop the arm muscles; **2** to strengthen.

II **se muscler** *v refl* (+ *v être*) to develop one's muscles.

musculaire /myskylɛʀ/ *adj* muscle; muscular.

musculation /myskylasjɔ̃/ *nf* (**exercices de**) **~** (gen) bodybuilding; (Med) exercises to strengthen the muscles; **salle de ~** weights room.

musculature /myskylatyʀ/ *nf* musculature.

muse /myz/ *nf* **1** Muse; **2** (figurative) muse.

museau, *pl* **~x** /myzo/ *nm* **1** muzzle; snout; nose; **2**○ face.

musée /myze/ *nm* museum; art gallery (GB), art museum (US); **une ville ~** a city of great historical and artistic importance.

museler /myzəle/ [19] *vtr* to muzzle.

muselière /myzəljɛʀ/ *nf* muzzle.

musette[1] /myzɛt/ *nm* accordion music.

musette[2] /myzɛt/ *nf* **1** haversack; **2** lunchbag.

musical, **~e**, *mpl* **-aux** /myzikal, o/ *adj* [*event*] musical; [*critic*] music; [*choice*] of music.

music-hall, *pl* **~s** *nm* /mysikol/ music hall.

musicien, **-ienne** /myzisjɛ̃, ɛn/ I *adj* musical.

II *nm,f* musician.

musique /myzik/ *nf* music; **travailler en ~** to work with music in the background; **mettre en ~** to set [sth] to music; **faire de la ~** to play an instrument; **une ~ de film** a film score.

IDIOMS **connaître la ~**○ to know the score○; **je ne peux pas aller plus vite que la ~**○ I can't go any faster than I'm already going; **être réglé comme du papier à ~**○ [*person*] to be as regular as clockwork; [*conference, project*] to go very smoothly.

musulman, **~e** /myzylmɑ̃, an/ *adj, nm,f* Muslim.

mutant, **~e** /mytɑ̃, ɑ̃t/ *adj, nm,f* mutant.

mutation /mytasjɔ̃/ *nf* **1** transfer; **2** transformation; **en pleine ~** undergoing radical transformation; **3** mutation.

muter /myte/ [1] *vtr* to transfer [*official*].

mutilation /mytilasjɔ̃/ *nf* mutilation.

mutilé, **~e** /mytile/ *nm,f* disabled person; **~ de guerre** disabled war veteran.

mutiler /mytile/ [1] *vtr* to mutilate.

mutin, **~e** /mytɛ̃, in/ I *adj* mischievous.

II *nm* mutineer; rioter.

mutiner: **se mutiner** /mytine/ [1] *v refl* (+ *v être*) to mutiny; to riot.

mutinerie /mytinʀi/ *nf* mutiny; riot.

mutisme /mytism/ *nm* silence.

mutuel, **-elle**[1] /mytɥɛl/ *adj* mutual.

mutuelle[2] /mytɥɛl/ *nf* mutual insurance company.

mutuellement /mytɥɛlmɑ̃/ *adv* mutually; **s'aider ~** to help each other.

myope /mjɔp/ *adj* short-sighted.

myopie /mjɔpi/ *nf* short-sightedness.

myosotis /mjɔzɔtis/ *nm inv* forget-me-not.

myrrhe /miʀ/ *nf* myrrh.

myrtille /miʀtij/ *nf* bilberry, blueberry.

mystère /mistɛʀ/ *nm* **1** mystery; **2** secrecy; **3** rite.

mystérieux, **-ieuse** /misteʀjø, øz/ *adj* mysterious.

mysticisme /mistisism/ *nm* mysticism.

mystification /mistifikasjɔ̃/ *nf* **1** hoax; **2** myth.

mystique /mistik/ I *adj* mystical.

II *nf* **1** mysticism; **2** mystique; **3** blind belief.

mythe /mit/ *nm* myth.

mythique /mitik/ *adj* mythical.

mythologie /mitɔlɔʒi/ *nf* mythology.

mythologique /mitɔlɔʒik/ *adj* mythological.

mythomane /mitɔman/ *adj, nmf* mythomaniac.

Nn

n, **N** /ɛn/ **I** *nm inv* **1** (letter) n, N; **2 n°** (*written abbr* = **numéro**) no.
II N *nf* (*abbr* = **nationale**) **la N7** the N7.

n' ▶ **ne**.

nabot, **~e** /nabo, ɔt/ *nm,f* (offensive) dwarf.

nacelle /nasɛl/ *nf* **1** (of hot-air balloon) gondola; **2** carrycot (GB), carrier (US); **3** (of worker) cradle.

nacre /nakʀ/ *nf* mother-of-pearl.

nage /naʒ/ *nf* **1** swimming; **200 mètres quatre ~s** 200 metres[GB] medley; **traverser à la ~** to swim across; **2 être en ~** to be in a sweat.
■ **~ indienne** sidestroke; **~ libre** freestyle.

nageoire /naʒwaʀ/ *nf* **1** (of fish) fin; **2** (of seal) flipper.

nager /naʒe/ [13] **I** *vtr* to swim.
II *vi* **1** to swim; **2** (figurative) **~ dans le bonheur** to bask in contentment; **elle nage dans sa robe** her dress is far too big for her; **3**○ to be absolutely lost.
IDIOMS **~ entre deux eaux** to run with the hare and hunt with the hounds.

nageur, **-euse** /naʒœʀ, øz/ *nm,f* swimmer.

naguère /nagɛʀ/ *adv* **1** quite recently; **2** formerly.

naïf, **naïve** /naif, iv/ *adj* naïve.

nain, **~e** /nɛ̃, nɛn/ **I** *adj* [*tree*] dwarf; [*dog*] miniature.
II *nm,f* dwarf.

naissance /nɛsɑ̃s/ *nf* **1** (gen) birth; (of rumour) start; **de ~** [*Italian, French*] by birth; [*deaf*] from birth; **à ma ~** when I was born; **2 à la ~ du cou** at the base of the neck.

naissant, **~e** /nɛsɑ̃, ɑ̃t/ *adj* new.

naître /nɛtʀ/ [74] *vi* (+ *v être*) **1** to be born; **elle est née le 5 juin** she was born on 5 June; **le bébé doit ~ à la fin du mois** the baby is due at the end of the month; **l'enfant à ~** the unborn baby or child; **je l'ai vu ~** (figurative) I have known him since he was a baby; **2** (figurative) [*idea*] to be born; [*company*] to come into existence; [*love*] to spring up; [*day*] to break; **faire ~** to give rise to [*hope*]; **voir ~** to see the birth of [*newspaper, century*].

naïve ▶ **naïf**.

naïveté /naivte/ *nf* naivety.

nanisme /nanism/ *nm* dwarfism.

nantis /nɑ̃ti/ *nm pl* **les ~** the well-off.

naphtaline /naftalin/ *nf* mothballs.

nappe /nap/ *nf* **1** tablecloth; **2** (of oil, gas) layer; (of water, fire) sheet; (of fog) blanket.

napper /nape/ [1] *vtr* (Culin) to coat; to glaze.

napperon /napʀɔ̃/ *nm* mat.

narcisse /naʀsis/ *nm* (flower) narcissus.

narcissisme /naʀsisism/ *nm* narcissism.

narco(-) /naʀko/ *pref* drug; **~-dollars/-trafiquant** drug money/trafficker.

narcotique /naʀkɔtik/ *adj, nm* narcotic.

narguer /naʀge/ [1] *vtr* to taunt [*person*].

narine /naʀin/ *nf* nostril.

narquois, **~e** /naʀkwa, az/ *adj* mocking.

narrateur, **-trice** /naʀatœʀ, tʀis/ *nm,f* narrator.

narratif, **-ive** /naʀatif, iv/ *adj* narrative.

narration /naʀasjɔ̃/ *nf* narration.

narrer /naʀe/ [1] *vtr* to relate.

nasal, **~e**, *mpl* **-aux** /nazal, o/ *adj* nasal; **hémorragie ~e** heavy nosebleed.

naseau, *pl* **~x** /nazo/ *nm* nostril.

nasillard, **~e** /nazijaʀ, aʀd/ *adj* [*voice*] nasal; [*instrument*] tinny.

nasiller /nazije/ [1] *vi* **1** to speak with a nasal voice; **2** [*duck*] to quack.

nasse /nas/ *nf* **1** keepnet; **2** (figurative) net.

natal, **~e**, *mpl* **~s** /natal/ *adj* native.

nataliste /natalist/ *adj* [*policy*] pro-birth.

natalité /natalite/ *nf* (**taux de**) **~** birthrate.

natation /natasjɔ̃/ *nf* swimming.

natif, **-ive** /natif, iv/ *adj* **~ de** native of.

nation /nasjɔ̃/ *nf* nation.
■ **les Nations unies** the United Nations.

national, **~e**[1], *mpl* **-aux** /nasjɔnal, o/ *adj* national.

nationale[2] /nasjɔnal/ *nf* ≈ A road (GB), highway (US).

nationaliser /nasjɔnalize/ [1] *vtr* to nationalize.

nationalisme /nasjɔnalism/ *nm* nationalism.

nationalité /nasjɔnalite/ *nf* nationality.

nativité /nativite/ *nf* nativity.

natte /nat/ *nf* **1** plait, braid (US); **2** mat.

naturalisation /natyʀalizasjɔ̃/ *nf* naturalization.

naturalisé, **~e** /natyʀalize/ *adj* naturalized.

naturaliser /natyʀalize/ [1] *vtr* to naturalize [*foreigner, species*]; to assimilate [*word, custom*].

naturalisme /natyʀalism/ *nm* naturalism.

nature /natyʀ/ **I** *adj inv* **1** [*yoghurt*] plain; [*tea*] black; **2**○ [*person*] natural.
II *nf* **1** nature; **protection de la ~** protection of the environment; **en pleine ~** in the heart of the countryside; **lâcher qn dans la ~** to leave sb in the middle of nowhere; (figurative) to let sb loose; **2 de ~ à faire** likely to do; **des offres de toute ~** offers of all kinds; **3 peindre d'après ~** to paint from life; **plus vrai que ~** larger than life; **4 en ~** [*pay*] in kind.
■ **~ humaine** human nature; **~ morte** still life; ▶ **petit**.

naturel, **-elle** /natyʀɛl/ **I** *adj* natural.

II *nm* **1** nature, disposition; **être d'un ~ craintif** to be timid by nature; **2 il manque de ~** he's not very natural; **3 au ~** [*rice*] plain; [*tuna*] in brine.

naturisme /natyʀism/ *nm* nudism.

naturiste /natyʀist/ *nmf* naturist (GB), nudist.

naufrage /nofʀaʒ/ *nm* shipwreck, sinking; **faire ~** [*ship*] to be wrecked; [*sailor*] to be shipwrecked; [*company*] to collapse.

naufragé, ~e /nofʀaʒe/ **I** *adj* shipwrecked.
II *nm,f* survivor (of a shipwreck); castaway.

nauséabond, ~e /nozeabɔ̃, ɔ̃d/ *adj* sickening, nauseating.

nausée /noze/ *nf* nausea.

nautique /notik/ *adj* [*science*] nautical; [*sports*] water.

nautisme /notism/ *nm* water sports.

naval, ~e, *mpl* **~s** /naval/ *adj* **1** [*industry*] shipbuilding; **2** (Mil) naval.

navet /navɛ/ *nm* **1** turnip; **2** rubbishy film (GB), turkey○ (US).

navette /navɛt/ *nf* shuttle; shuttle service; **faire la ~** (to work) to commute.
■ **~ spatiale** space shuttle.

navigable /navigabl/ *adj* navigable.

navigant, ~e /navigɑ̃, ɑ̃t/ *adj* **personnel ~** (on plane) flying personnel; (Naut) seagoing personnel; **mécanicien ~** flight engineer.

navigateur, -trice /navigatœʀ, tʀis/ *nm,f* **1** navigator; **2** sailor.

navigation /navigasjɔ̃/ *nf* navigation.
■ **~ de plaisance** boating; yachting.

naviguer /navige/ [1] *vi* **1** [*ship, sailor*] to sail; [*pilot, plane*] to fly; **en état de ~** [*ship*] seaworthy; **2** to navigate; **3** (Comput) to browse.

navire /naviʀ/ **I** *nm* ship.
II navire- (*combining form*) **~-école/-usine** training/factory ship; **~s-citernes** tankers.
■ **~ amiral** flagship; **~ de guerre** warship.

navrant, ~e /navʀɑ̃, ɑ̃t/ *adj* **1** depressing; **2** distressing.

navré, ~e /navʀe/ *adj* **je suis vraiment ~** I am terribly sorry; **avoir l'air ~** to look sad.

nazi, ~e /nazi/ *adj, nm,f* Nazi.

nazisme /nazism/ *nm* Nazism.

ne /nə/ (**n'** *before vowel or mute h*) *adv*

■ **Note** In cases where *ne* is used with *pas, jamais, guère, rien, plus, aucun, personne* etc, one should consult the corresponding entry.
– *ne + verb + que* is treated in the entry below.

je n'ai que 100 francs I've only got 100 francs; **il n'y a que lui pour être aussi désagréable** only he can be so unpleasant; **tu n'es qu'un raté** you're nothing but a loser○; **je n'ai que faire de tes conseils** you can keep your advice.

né, ~e /ne/ **I** *pp* ▶ **naître**.
II *pp adj* **bien ~** highborn; **Madame Masson ~e Roux** Mrs Masson née Roux.
III (-)né (*combining form*) **musicien(-)/écrivain(-)~** born musician/writer.

néanmoins /neɑ̃mwɛ̃/ *adv* nevertheless.

néant /neɑ̃/ *nm* **1 le ~** nothingness; **réduire à ~** to destroy [*argument, hopes*]; **2 'revenus: ~'** 'income: nil'.

nébuleux, -euse /nebylø, øz/ *adj* **1** [*sky*] cloudy; **2** [*idea*] vague, nebulous.

nécessaire /nesesɛʀ/ **I** *adj* necessary (**à** for); **plus qu'il n'est ~** more than is necessary; **les voix ~s pour renverser le gouvernement** the votes needed in order to overthrow the government.
II *nm* **1 faire le ~** to do what is necessary; **2** essentials; **le strict ~** the bare essentials.
■ **~ de couture** sewing kit; **~ à ongles** manicure set; **~ de toilette** toiletries .

nécessairement /nesesɛʀmɑ̃/ *adv* necessarily; **passe-t-on ~ par Oslo?** do you have to go via Oslo?

nécessité /nesesite/ *nf* **1** necessity; **~ urgente** urgent need; **~ de qch/de faire/d'être** need for sth/to do/to be; **de première ~** vital; **par ~** out of necessity; **être dans la ~ de faire** to have no choice but to do; **2** need; **être dans la ~** to be in need.
IDIOMS **~ fait loi** (Proverb) necessity knows no law.

nécessiter /nesesite/ [1] *vtr* to require.

nécrologie /nekʀɔlɔʒi/ *nf* **1** deaths column; **2** obituary.

nécrologique /nekʀɔlɔʒik/ *adj* obituary.

nectar /nɛktaʀ/ *nm* nectar.

néerlandais, ~e /neɛʀlɑ̃dɛ, ɛz/ **I** *adj* Dutch.
II *nm* (language) Dutch.

Néerlandais, ~e /neɛʀlɑ̃dɛ, ɛz/ *nm,f* Dutchman/Dutchwoman; **les ~** the Dutch.

nef /nɛf/ *nf* nave; **~ latérale** side aisle.

néfaste /nefast/ *adj* harmful.

négatif, -ive[1] /negatif, iv/ **I** *adj* negative.
II *nm* negative.

négation /negasjɔ̃/ *nf* **1** negation; **2** (in grammar) negative.

négative[2] /negativ/ **I** *adj f* ▶ **négatif I**.
II *nf* **répondre par la ~** to reply in the negative.

négativement /negativmɑ̃/ *adv* negatively.

négligé, ~e /negliʒe/ **I** *adj* [*person*] sloppy; [*house*] neglected; [*injury*] untreated.
II *nm* negligée.

négligeable /negliʒabl/ *adj* [*amount*] negligible; [*person*] insignificant.

négligemment /negliʒamɑ̃/ *adv* **1** nonchalantly; **2** carelessly.

négligence /negliʒɑ̃s/ *nf* **1** negligence; **2** oversight.

négligent, ~e /negliʒɑ̃, ɑ̃t/ *adj* [*employee*] negligent, careless; [*glance*] casual.

négliger /negliʒe/ [13] **I** *vtr* (gen) to neglect; to leave untreated [*cold*]; to ignore [*rule*]; **une offre qui n'est pas à ~** an offer that's worth considering; **~ de faire** to fail to do.
II se négliger *v refl* (+ *v être*) **1** not to take care over one's appearance; **2** not to look after oneself.

négociable /negɔsjabl/ *adj* negotiable.

négociant, **~e** /negɔsjɑ̃, ɑ̃t/ *nm,f* merchant; wholesaler.

négociateur, **-trice** /negɔsjatœʀ, tʀis/ *nm,f* negotiator.

négociation /negɔsjasjɔ̃/ *nf* negotiation.

négocier /negɔsje/ [2] *vtr*, *vi* to negotiate.

nègre /nɛgʀ/ *nm* **1** (offensive) Negro; **2** ghost-writer.

négresse /negʀɛs/ *nf* (offensive) Negress.

négroïde /negʀɔid/ *adj* Negroid.

neige /nɛʒ/ *nf* snow; **~ fondue** slush; sleet; **aller à la ~** to go skiing; **blancs battus en ~** stiffly beaten eggwhites.

IDIOMS **être blanc comme ~** to be completely innocent.

neiger /neʒe/ [13] *v impers* to snow.

nénuphar /nenyfaʀ/ *nm* waterlily.

néo /neo/ *pref* neo.

néologisme /neɔlɔʒism/ *nm* neologism.

néon /neɔ̃/ *nm* **1** neon; **2** neon light.

néo-zélandais, **~e** /neozelɑ̃dɛ, ɛz/ *adj* New Zealand.

Néo-Zélandais, **~e** /neozelɑ̃dɛ, ɛz/ *nm,f* New Zealander.

népotisme /nepɔtism/ *nm* nepotism.

nerf /nɛʀ/ **1** nerve; **être malade des ~s** to suffer from nerves; **2** spirit, go○; **redonner du ~ à qn** to put new heart into sb.

IDIOMS **jouer avec les ~s de qn** to be deliberately annoying; **ses ~s ont lâché** he/she went to pieces; **avoir les ~s à fleur de peau** to have frayed nerves; **avoir les ~s en pelote**○ or **en boule**○ or **à vif** to be really wound up; **être sur les ~s**, **avoir ses ~s**○ to be on edge; **taper**○ or **porter sur les ~s de qn** to get on sb's nerves; **être à bout de ~s** to be at the end of one's tether or rope (US); **passer ses ~s sur**○ **qn/qch** to take it out on sb/sth; **l'argent est le ~ de la guerre** money is the sinews of war.

nerveusement /nɛʀvøzmɑ̃/ *adv* **1** [*wait*] nervously; **2 être épuisé ~** to be suffering from nervous exhaustion.

nerveux, **-euse** /nɛʀvø, øz/ **I** *adj* **1** [*person*] tense; **2** [*engine*] responsive; [*horse*] vigorous; **3** (Anat) [*cell*] nerve; [*system*] nervous.

II *nm,f* nervous person.

nervosité /nɛʀvozite/ *nf* **1** nervousness; **2** excitability; **3** (of engine) responsiveness.

nervure /nɛʀvyʀ/ *nf* (of leaf) nervure.

n'est-ce pas /nɛspa/ *adv* **c'est joli, ~?** it's pretty, isn't it?; **~ qu'il est gentil?** isn't he nice?

net, **nette** /nɛt/ **I** *adj* **1** [*price, weight*] net; **2** [*change*] marked; [*tendency*] distinct; **3** [*victory, memory*] clear; [*situation*] clear-cut; [*handwriting*] neat; [*break*] clean; **en avoir le cœur ~** to be clear in one's mind about it; **4** [*house, hands*] clean; (figurative) [*conscience*] clear; **faire place nette** to clear everything away.

II *adv* [*stop*] dead; [*kill*] outright; [*refuse*] flatly; **la corde a cassé ~** the rope snapped.

nettement /nɛtmɑ̃/ *adv* **1** [*increase, deteriorate*] markedly; [*dominate*] clearly; [*prefer*] definitely; **2** [*see, say*] clearly; [*refuse*] flatly; [*remember*] distinctly.

netteté /nɛtte/ *nf* **1** (of image, features) sharpness; (of result, statement) definite nature; **2** (of place) cleanness; (of work) neatness.

nettoyage /netwajaʒ/ *nm* **1** clean(up); **~ de printemps** spring-cleaning; **2** cleaning; (of skin) cleansing; **~ à sec** dry-cleaning; **3 opération de ~**○ (by army, police) mopping-up operation.

nettoyant /nɛtwajɑ̃/ *nm* cleaning agent.

nettoyer /netwaje/ [23] *vtr* **1** (gen) to clean; to clean up [*garden*]; to clean out [*river*]; to clean off [*stain*]; **2** (figurative) [*police*] to clean up [*town*].

neuf[1] /nœf/ *adj inv*, *pron*, *nm inv* nine.

neuf[2], **neuve** /nœf, nœv/ **I** *adj* new; **tout ~** brand new; **'état ~'** 'as new'.

II *nm inv* new; **quoi de ~?** what's new?; **habillé de ~** dressed in new clothes; **faire du ~ avec du vieux** to revamp things.

IDIOMS **faire peau neuve** to undergo a transformation.

neurasthénie /nøʀasteni/ *nf* depression.

neuro /nøʀo/ *pref* neuro.

neutraliser /nøtʀalize/ [1] *vtr* to neutralize.

neutralité /nøtʀalite/ *nf* neutrality.

neutre /nøtʀ/ *adj* neutral; neuter.

neutron /nøtʀɔ̃/ *nm* neutron.

neuvième /nœvjɛm/ **I** *adj* ninth.

II *nf* (Sch) *third year of primary school, age 8–9.*

neveu, *pl* **~x** /n(ə)vø/ *nm* nephew.

névralgie /nevʀalʒi/ *nf* neuralgia.

névrose /nevʀoz/ *nf* neurosis.

névrosé, **~e** /nevʀoze/ *adj*, *nm,f* neurotic.

New York /njujɔʀk/ *pr n* **1** New York City; **2 l'État de ~** New York (State).

nez /ne/ *nm* nose; **~ en trompette** turned-up nose; **ça sent le parfum à plein ~**○ there's a strong smell of perfume; **je n'ai pas mis le ~ dehors**○ I didn't set foot outside; **mettre le ~ à la fenêtre**○ to show one's face at the window; **lever le ~** to look up; **tu as le ~ dessus**○ it's staring you in the face; **avoir du ~**, **avoir le ~ fin** (figurative) to be shrewd.

IDIOMS **mener qn par le bout du ~**○ to have sb under one's thumb; **avoir qn dans le ~**○ to have it in for sb; **avoir un coup** or **verre dans le ~**○ to have had one too many○; **au ~ (et à la barbe) de qn** right under sb's nose; **filer** or **passer sous le ~ de qn** to slip through sb's fingers; **se casser le ~**○ to fail.

NF /ɛnɛf/ *adj*, *nf* (*abbr* = **norme française**) French manufacturing standard.

ni /ni/ *conj* nor, or; **elle ne veut ~ ne peut changer** she doesn't want to change, nor can she; **elle ne veut pas le voir ~ lui parler** she doesn't want to see him or talk to him; **~...~** neither...nor; **~ l'un ~ l'autre** neither of them; **il ne m'a dit ~ oui ~ non** he didn't say yes or no.

IDIOMS **~ vu ~ connu**○ on the sly○; **c'est ~ fait ~ à faire**○ it's a botched○ job; **il n'a fait ~ une ~ deux**○ he didn't have a second's hesitation.

niais, **~e** /njɛ, njɛz/ *adj* stupid.

niaiserie /njɛzʀi/ *nf* **1** stupidity; **2** stupid or inane remark.

niche /niʃ/ *nf* **1** kennel, doghouse (US); **2** recess; (for statue) niche; **3**○ trick.

nichée /niʃe/ *nf* (of birds) brood; (of mice) litter.

nicher /niʃe/ [1] **I** *vi* **1** [*bird*] to nest; **2**○ [*person*] to live.
II se nicher *v refl* (+ *v être*) **1** [*bird*] to nest; **2** [*person, cottage*] to nestle.

nickel /nikɛl/ **I**○ *adj* spotless.
II *nm* nickel.

nicotine /nikɔtin/ *nf* nicotine.

nid /ni/ *nm* nest.
■ **~ d'aigle** eyrie; **~ d'ange** snuggle suit; **~ à poussière** dust trap; **~ de résistance** pocket of resistance.

nid-d'abeilles, *pl* **nids-d'abeilles** /nidabɛj/ *nm* honeycomb weave.

nid-de-poule, *pl* **nids-de-poule** /nidpul/ *nm* pothole.

nièce /njɛs/ *nf* niece.

nième /ɛnjɛm/ = **énième**.

nier /nje/ [2] *vtr* to deny [*fact, existence*].

nigaud, **~e** /nigo, od/ *adj* silly.

nigérian, **~e** /niʒeʀjɑ̃, an/ *adj* Nigerian.

nigérien, **-ienne** /niʒeʀjɛ̃, ɛn/ *adj* of Niger.

nihiliste /niilist/ *adj, nmf* nihilist.

nipper○: **se nipper** /nipe/ [1] *v refl* (+ *v être*) to get rigged out○ in one's Sunday best.

nippes○ /nip/ *nf pl* rags○, old clothes.

nippon, **-onne** /nipɔ̃, ɔn/ *adj* Japanese.

niveau, *pl* **~x** /nivo/ *nm* (gen) level; (of knowledge, education) standard; **au ~ du sol** at ground level; **être de ~** to be level; **arrivé au ~ du bus, il...** when he drew level with the bus he...; **bâtiment sur deux ~x** two-storey (GB) or two-story (US) building; **'~ bac + 3'** baccalaureate or equivalent plus 3 years' higher education; **de haut ~** [*athlete*] top; [*candidate*] high-calibre[GB]; **au plus haut ~** [*discussion*] top-level.
■ **~ de langue** register; **~ social** social status; **~ sonore** sound level; **~ de vie** standard of living.

niveler /nivle/ [19] *vtr* **1** to level [*ground*]; **2** to bring [sth] to the same level [*salaries*]; **~ par le bas/haut** to level down/up.

noble /nɔbl/ **I** *adj* (gen) noble; [*family*] aristocratic; [*person*] of noble birth.
II *nmf* nobleman/noblewoman.

noblement /nɔbləmɑ̃/ *adv* **1** nobly; **2** handsomely.

noblesse /nɔblɛs/ *nf* nobility; **la petite ~** the gentry.

noce /nɔs/ *nf* **1**○ party; **faire la ~**○ (figurative) to live it up○, to party○; **2** wedding party; **3 ~s** wedding

noceur○, **-euse** /nɔsœʀ, øz/ *nm,f* party animal○.

nocif, **-ive** /nɔsif, iv/ *adj* noxious, harmful.

noctambule /nɔktɑ̃byl/ *nmf* night owl.

nocturne[1] /nɔktyʀn/ *adj* [*attack*] night; [*animal*] nocturnal; **la vie ~** nightlife.

nocturne[2] /nɔktyʀn/ *nf* **1** (in sport) evening fixture; **2** (of shop) late-night opening.

Noël /nɔɛl/ *nm* Christmas; **'Joyeux ~'** 'Merry Christmas'; **de ~** [*tree, gift*] Christmas.

nœud /nø/ *nm* **1** (gen) knot; **faire un ~ de cravate** to tie a tie; **2** (of matter) crux; (of play) core.
■ **~ coulant** slipknot; **~ papillon** bow tie; **~ de vipères** nest of vipers.

noir, **~e**[1] /nwaʀ/ **I** *adj* **1** (gen) black; [*eyes*] dark; [*person, race*] black; **être ~ de coups** to be black and blue; **être ~ de monde** to be swarming with people; **2** [*street*] dark; **il fait ~** it's dark; **3** [*year*] bad, bleak; [*poverty*] dire; [*idea*] gloomy, dark; **4** [*look*] black; [*plot, design*] evil, dark; **se mettre dans une colère ~e** to fly into a towering rage.
II *nm* **1** (colour) black; **2 avoir du ~ sur le visage** to have a black mark on one's face; **3** darkness; **4 au ~** [*sell*] on the black market; **travailler au ~** to work without declaring one's earnings; to moonlight○; **5**○ **un (petit) ~** an espresso.
IDIOMS **voir tout en ~** to look on the black side (of things).

Noir, **~e** /nwaʀ/ *nm,f* black man/woman.

noirceur /nwaʀsœʀ/ *nf* (gen) blackness; (of hair, night, eyes) darkness.

noircir /nwaʀsiʀ/ [3] **I** *vtr* **1** [*coal*] to make [sth] dirty; [*smoke*] to blacken; **2** (figurative) **~ du papier** to scribble away; **~ la situation** to paint a black picture of the situation.
II *vi* [*banana*] to go black; [*wall*] to get dirty; [*metal*] to tarnish; [*person*] to get brown.
III se noircir *v refl* (+ *v être*) [*sky*] to darken; **se ~ le visage** to blacken one's face.

noire[2] /nwaʀ/ **I** *adj f* ▶ **noir I**.
II *nf* (Mus) crotchet (GB), quarter note (US).

noise /nwaz/ *nf* **chercher ~** or **des ~s à qn** to pick a quarrel with sb.

noisetier /nwaztje/ *nm* hazel (tree).

noisette /nwazɛt/ *nf* **1** hazelnut; **2 ~ de beurre** small knob of butter.

noix /nwa/ *nf inv* **1** walnut (GB), English walnut (US); **2 ~ de beurre** knob of butter.
■ **~ de cajou** cashew nut; **~ de coco** coconut; **~ (de) muscade** nutmeg.

nom /nɔ̃/ **I** *nm* **1** name; **petit ~** first name; **~ et prénom** full name; **donner un ~ à** to name; **sans ~** unspeakable; **George Sand, de son vrai ~ Aurore Dupin** George Sand, whose real name was Aurore Dupin; **parler en son propre ~** to speak for oneself; **2** noun.
II au nom de *phr* **1** in the name of; **2** on behalf of.
■ **~ de baptême** Christian name; **~ d'emprunt** pseudonym; **~ de famille** surname; **~ de jeune fille** maiden name.
IDIOMS **traiter qn de tous les ~s**○ to call sb all the names under the sun; **appeler les choses par leur ~** to call a spade a spade.

nomade /nɔmad/ *nmf* nomad.

nombre /nɔ̃bʀ/ *nm* number; **un ~ à deux**

chiffres a two-digit number; **un certain ~ de** some; **être en ~ inférieur** [*players*] to be fewer in number; [*group*] to be smaller; **ils étaient au ~ de 30** there were 30 of them; **écrasé sous le ~** (of people) overcome by sheer weight of numbers; (of letters) overwhelmed by the sheer volume; **bon ~ de** a good many; **~ de fois** many times.

nombreux, **-euse** /nɔ̃bʀø, øz/ *adj* [*population, collection*] large; [*people, objects*] numerous, many; **ils étaient peu ~** there weren't many of them; **ils ont répondu ~ à l'appel** a great many people responded to the appeal; **les touristes deviennent trop ~** the number of tourists is becoming excessive.

nombril /nɔ̃bʀil/ *nm* navel; **elle se prend pour le ~ du monde**○ she thinks she's God's gift to mankind.

nomenclature /nɔmɑ̃klatyʀ/ *nf* nomenclature; (in dictionary) word list.

nominal, **~e**, *mpl* **-aux** /nɔminal, o/ *adj* (gen) nominal; [*list*] of names.

nominatif, **-ive** /nɔminatif, iv/ **I** *adj* [*list*] of names; [*invitation*] personal; [*share*] registered.

II *nm* nominative.

nomination /nɔminasjɔ̃/ *nf* **1** appointment; **2** letter of appointment; **3** (controversial) nomination.

nommément /nɔmemɑ̃/ *adv* specifically, by name.

nommer /nɔme/ [1] **I** *vtr* **1** to appoint; **être nommé à Paris** to be posted to Paris; **2** to name [*person*]; to call [*thing*]; **pour ne ~ personne** to mention no names.

II se nommer *v refl* (+ *v être*) **1** to be called; **2** to give one's name.

non /nɔ̃/ **I** *adv* **1** no; **'tu y vas?'—'~'** 'are you going?'—'no, I'm not'; **ah, ça ~!** definitely not!; **faire ~ de la tête** to shake one's head; **je pense que ~** I don't think so; **je te dis que ~** no, I tell you; **il paraît que ~** apparently not; **tu trouves ça drôle? moi ~** do you think that's funny? I don't; **~ sans raison** not without reason; **~ moins difficile** just as difficult; **qu'il soit d'accord ou ~** whether he agrees or not; **tu viens, oui ou ~?** are you coming or not?; **sois un peu plus poli, ~ mais**○! be a bit more polite, for heaven's sake!; **2** non; **~ alcoolisé** nonalcoholic; **~ négligeable** considerable.

II *nm inv* **1** no; **2** 'no' vote.

III non plus *phr* **je ne suis pas d'accord ~ plus** I don't agree either; **il n'a pas aimé le film, moi ~ plus** he didn't like the film and neither did I.

IV non(-) (/nɔn/ *before vowel or mute h*) (*combining form*) **~-fumeur** nonsmoker; **~-syndiqué** non union member.

nonagénaire /nɔnaʒenɛʀ/ *adj* **être ~** to be in one's nineties.

non-aligné, **~e**, *mpl* **~s** /nɔnaliɲe/ *nm,f* nonaligned country.

nonante /nɔnɑ̃t/ *adj inv*, *pron* ninety.

non-assistance /nɔnasistɑ̃s/ *nf* **~ à personne en danger** failure to render assistance.

nonchalance /nɔ̃ʃalɑ̃s/ *nf* nonchalance.

nonchalant, **~e** /nɔ̃ʃalɑ̃, ɑ̃t/ *adj* nonchalant.

non-lieu, *pl* **~x** /nɔ̃ljø/ *nm* (Law) dismissal (of a charge); **il y a eu ~** the case was dismissed.

non-recevoir /nɔ̃ʀəsəvwaʀ/ *nm* **fin de ~** flat refusal.

non-reconduction, *pl* **~s** /nɔ̃ʀəkɔ̃dyksjɔ̃/ *nf* (of contract) nonrenewal.

non-respect /nɔ̃ʀɛspɛ/ *nm* **~ de** failure to comply with [*clause*]; failure to respect [*person*].

non-sens /nɔ̃sɑ̃s/ *nm inv* nonsense.

non-voyant, **~e**, *mpl* **~s** /nɔ̃vwajɑ̃, ɑ̃t/ *nm,f* visually handicapped person.

nord /nɔʀ/ **I** *adj inv* north; northern.

II *nm* **1** north; **le vent du ~** the north wind; **le ~ de l'Europe** northern Europe; **2 le Nord** the North; **la Corée du Nord** North Korea.

IDIOMS **il ne perd pas le ~**○**!** he' s got his head screwed on○!

nord-africain, **~e**, *mpl* **~s** /nɔʀafʀikɛ̃, ɛn/ *adj* North African.

nord-américain, **~e**, *mpl* **~s** /nɔʀameʀikɛ̃, ɛn/ *adj* North American.

nord-est /nɔʀ(d)ɛst/ **I** *adj inv* northeast; northeastern.

II *nm* northeast.

nordique /nɔʀdik/ *adj* Nordic.

nord-ouest /nɔʀ(d)wɛst/ **I** *adj inv* northwest; northwestern.

II *nm* northwest.

normal, **~e**[1], *mpl* **-aux** /nɔʀmal, o/ *adj* normal; **il est ~ que** it is natural that; **il n'est pas ~ que** it is not right that.

normale[2] /nɔʀmal/ *nf* **1** average; **2** norm; **retour à la ~** return to normal.

normalement /nɔʀmalmɑ̃/ *adv* normally.

normaliser /nɔʀmalize/ [1] *vtr* **1** to normalize [*relations*]; **2** to standardize [*sizes*].

normalité /nɔʀmalite/ *nf* normality.

normand, **~e** /nɔʀmɑ̃, ɑ̃d/ **I** *adj* **1** [*conquest*] Norman; **2** [*coast*] Normandy; [*team*] from Normandy.

II *nm* Norman (French).

Normand, **~e** /nɔʀmɑ̃, ɑ̃d/ *nm,f* Norman.

IDIOMS **une réponse de ~** a noncommittal reply.

norme /nɔʀm/ *nf* (gen) norm; (Tech) standard.

Norvège /nɔʀvɛʒ/ *pr nf* Norway.

norvégien, **-ienne** /nɔʀveʒjɛ̃, ɛn/ **I** *adj* Norwegian.

II *nm* (language) Norwegian.

nos ▶ **notre**.

nostalgie /nɔstalʒi/ *nf* nostalgia.

nostalgique /nɔstalʒik/ *adj* nostalgic.

notable /nɔtabl/ **I** *adj* [*fact*] notable; [*progress*] significant.

II *nm* notable.

notaire /nɔtɛʀ/ *nm* notary public.

notamment /nɔtamɑ̃/ *adv* **1** notably; **2** in particular.

notation /nɔtasjɔ̃/ *nf* **1** notation; **2** (of pupil) marking (GB), grading (US); (of staff) grading.

note /nɔt/ *nf* **1** bill (GB), check (US); **faire la ~ de qn** to write out sb's bill (GB) or check (US); **2** (Mus) note; (figurative) note, touch; **forcer la ~** to overdo it; **3** mark (GB), grade (US); **~ éliminatoire** fail mark (GB) or grade (US); **4** (written) note; **prendre qch en ~** to make a note of sth; **prendre (bonne) ~ de qch** (figurative) to take (due) note of sth.
■ **~ de frais** expense account; **~ d'honoraires** bill; **~ de service** memorandum.

noter /nɔte/ [1] *vtr* **1** to write down [*idea, address*]; **2** to notice [*change*]; **notez (bien) que je n'ai rien à lui reprocher** mind you I haven't got anything particular against him; **il faut quand même ~** it has to be said; **3** to mark (GB), to grade (US) [*exercise*]; to give a mark (GB) or grade (US) to [*pupil*]; to grade [*employee*].

notice /nɔtis/ *nf* **1** note; **2** instructions.

notifier /nɔtifje/ [2] *vtr* **~ qch à qn** (gen) to notify sb of sth; (Law) to give sb notice of sth.

notion /nɔsjɔ̃/ *nf* **1** notion; **perdre la ~ de** to lose all sense of; **2 ~s** basic knowledge.

notoire /nɔtwaʀ/ *adj* [*fact, position*] well-known; [*swindler, stupidity*] notorious.

notoriété /nɔtɔʀjete/ *nf* **1** fame; (of product) reputation; **il est de ~ (publique) que** it's common knowledge that; **2** (person) celebrity.

notre, *pl* **nos** /nɔtʀ, no/ *det* our; **à nos âges** at our age; **c'était ~ avis à tous** we all felt the same; **nos enfants à nous**○ our children.

nôtre /notʀ/ **I** *det* **nous avons fait ~s ces idées** we've adopted these ideas.
II le nôtre, la nôtre, les nôtres *pron* ours; **soyez des ~s!** won't you join us?; **les ~s** our own people; (team, group) our side.

nouer /nwe/ [1] **I** *vtr* **1** (gen) to tie; to knot [*tie*]; to tie up [*parcel*]; **avoir la gorge nouée** to have a lump in one's throat; **2** to establish [*relations*]; to engage in [*dialogue*].
II se nouer *v refl* (+ *v être*) **1** [*plot*] to take shape; **2** [*diplomatic relations*] to be established; [*dialogue, friendship*] to begin.

nougat /nuga/ *nm* nougat.

nouille /nuj/ *nf* **~s** noodles, pasta.

nounou○ /nunu/ *nf* nanny (GB), nurse.

nounours○ /nunuʀs/ *nm inv* teddy bear.

nourrice /nuʀis/ *nf* **1** childminder (GB), babysitter (US); **2** wet nurse.

nourrir /nuʀiʀ/ [3] **I** *vtr* **1** to feed [*person, animal*]; to nourish [*skin, leather*]; **bien nourri** well-fed; **~ au sein/au biberon** to breast-/to bottle-feed; **mon travail ne me nourrit pas** I don't make enough to live on; **2** (figurative) to harbour[GB] [*hopes*]; to feed [*fire*]; to fuel [*passion*].
II se nourrir *v refl* (+ *v être*) [*animal*] to feed; [*person*] to eat; **se ~ de** to live on [*vegetables*]; to feed on [*illusions*].

nourrissant, **~e** /nuʀisɑ̃, ɑ̃t/ *adj* nourishing.

nourrisson /nuʀisɔ̃/ *nm* infant.

nourriture /nuʀityʀ/ *nf* **1** food; **2** diet.

nous /nu/ *pron* **1** (subject) we; (object) us; **~ sommes en avance** we're early; **donne-~ l'adresse** give us the address; **entre ~, il n'est pas très intelligent** between you and me, he isn't very intelligent; **une maison à ~** a house of our own; **pensons à ~** let's think of ourselves; **2** (with reflexive verb) **~ ~ soignons** we look after ourselves; **~ ~ aimons** we love each other.

nous-même, *pl* **nous-mêmes** /numɛm/ *pron* ourselves.

nouveau (**nouvel** *before vowel or mute h*), **nouvelle**[1], *mpl* **~x** /nuvo, nuvɛl/ **I** *adj* (gen) new; [*attempt, attack*] fresh; **tout ~** brand-new; **se faire faire un ~ costume** to have a new suit made; to have another suit made; **une nouvelle fois** once again; **les ~x élus** the newly-elected members; **les ~x mariés** the newlyweds.
II *nm,f* (in school) new boy/girl; (in company) new employee; (in army) new recruit.
III *nm* **téléphone-moi s'il y a du ~** give me a call if there is anything new to report; **j'ai du ~ pour toi** I've got some news for you.
IV à nouveau, **de nouveau** *phr* (once) again.

nouveau-né, **~e**, *mpl* **~s** /nuvone/ *nm,f* newborn baby.

nouveauté /nuvote/ *nf* **1** novelty; **ce n'est pas une ~!** that's nothing new!; **2** (gen) new thing; (book) new publication; (record) new release; (car, machine) new model.

nouvel ▶ **nouveau I**.

nouvelle[2] /nuvɛl/ **I** *adj f* ▶ **nouveau I**.
II *nf* **1** ▶ **nouveau II**; **2** news; **une ~** a piece of news; **tu connais la ~?** have you heard the news?; **recevoir des ~s de qn** to hear from sb; (through somebody else) to hear news of sb; **il m'a demandé de tes ~s** he asked after you; **aux dernières ~s**○**, il se porte bien** the last I heard he was doing fine; **il aura de mes ~s**○**!** he'll be hearing from me!; **goûte ce petit vin, tu m'en diras des ~s**○ have a taste of this wine, it's really good!; **3** short story.

Nouvelle-Zélande /nuvɛlzelɑ̃d/ *pr nf* New Zealand.

novateur, **-trice** /nɔvatœʀ, tʀis/ **I** *adj* innovative.
II *nm,f* innovator, pioneer.

novembre /nɔvɑ̃bʀ/ *nm* November.

novice /nɔvis/ **I** *adj* inexperienced, green.
II *nmf* novice.

noyade /nwajad/ *nf* drowning.

noyau, *pl* **~x** /nwajo/ *nm* **1** stone (GB), pit (US); **2** small group; **~x de résistance** pockets of resistance; **3** nucleus.

noyauter /nwajote/ [1] *vtr* to infiltrate.

noyé, **~e** /nwaje/ *nm,f* drowned person.

noyer[1] /nwaje/ [23] **I** *vtr* (gen) to drown; to flood [*village, engine*]; **~ qn sous un flot de paroles** to talk sb's head off.
II se noyer *v refl* (+ *v être*) to drown; (suicide) to drown oneself; **mourir noyé** to drown.
IDIOMS **se ~ dans un verre d'eau** to make a mountain out of a molehill.

noyer[2] /nwaje/ *nm* walnut (tree).

nu, **~e** /ny/ **I** *adj* [*person*] naked; [*wall, tree, coastline*] bare; [*truth*] plain; **pieds ~s** barefoot; **torse ~** stripped to the waist.

II *nm* (in art) nude.

III à nu *phr* **être à ~** to be exposed; **mettre son cœur à ~** to open one's heart.

nuage /nyaʒ/ *nm* cloud; **sans ~s** [*sky*] cloudless; [*happiness*] unclouded; **~ de lait** dash of milk.

IDIOMS **descendre de son ~** to come back to earth.

nuageux, **-euse** /nyaʒø, øz/ *adj* [*sky*] cloudy.

nuance /nyɑ̃s/ *nf* **1** (of colour) shade; **2** (of meaning) nuance; **sans ~** [*commentary*] clearcut; [*personality*] straightforward; **3** slight difference; **à cette ~ près que** with the small reservation that; **4** (Mus) nuance.

nuancer /nyɑ̃se/ [12] *vtr* **1** to qualify [*opinion*]; to modify [*view of situation*]; **peu nuancé** unsubtle; **2** to moderate [*remarks, statements*].

nucléaire /nykleɛʀ/ **I** *adj* nuclear.

II *nm* **le ~** nuclear energy; nuclear technology.

nudité /nydite/ *nf* **1** nakedness, nudity; **2** (of place, wall) bareness.

nuée /nye/ *nf* (of insects) swarm; (of people) horde.

nues /ny/ *nf pl* **tomber des ~**○ to be flabbergasted○; **porter qn aux ~** to praise sb to the skies.

nuire /nɥiʀ/ [69] **I nuire à** *v+prep* to harm [*person*]; to be harmful to [*health, interests, reputation*]; to damage [*crops*].

II se nuire *v refl* (+ *v être*) **1** to do each other a lot of harm; **2** to do oneself a lot of harm.

nuisance /nɥizɑ̃s/ *nf* nuisance.

nuisible /nɥizibl/ *adj* [*substance, waste*] dangerous; [*influence*] harmful; **insecte ~** (insect) pest; **~ à** detrimental to.

nuit /nɥi/ *nf* night; **cette ~** last night; tonight; **voyager de ~** to travel by night; **avant la ~** before dark; **à la tombée de la ~** at nightfall; **il fait ~** it's dark; **il faisait ~ noire** it was pitch dark; **ça se perd dans la ~ des temps** it is lost in the mists of time.

■ **~ blanche** sleepless night; **~ bleue** *night of terrorist bomb attacks.*

IDIOMS **c'est le jour et la ~** they're as different as chalk and cheese; **attends demain pour donner ta réponse: la ~ porte conseil** wait till tomorrow to give your answer: sleep on it first.

nul, **nulle** /nyl/ **I** *adj* **1**○ [*person*] hopeless; [*piece of work*] worthless; [*film*] trashy○; **2** (Law) [*contract*] void; [*will*] invalid; [*elections*] null and void; [*vote*] spoiled; **3** (Sport) **match ~** tie, draw (GB); nil-all draw; **4** [*difference*] nil; **5 ~ homme/pays** no man/country; **~ autre que vous** no-one else but you.

II○ *nm,f* idiot○; **c'est un ~** he's a dead loss○.

III *pron* no-one.

IV nulle part *phr* nowhere.

nullement /nylmɑ̃/ *adv* not at all.

nullité /nylite/ *nf* **1** (Law) nullity; **frapper de ~** to render void; **2** (of argument) invalidity; (of book, film)○ worthlessness; **3**○ (person) idiot○.

numéraire /nymeʀɛʀ/ *nm* cash.

numéral, **~e**, *mpl* **-aux** /nymeʀal, o/ **I** *adj* numeral.

II *nm* numeral.

numérique /nymeʀik/ *adj* (gen) numerical; [*display*] digital; **clavier ~** keypad.

numéro /nymeʀo/ *nm* **1** number; **~ de téléphone** telephone number; **2** (magazine) issue; **suite au prochain ~** to be continued; **3** (in show) act; **4**○ **quel ~!** what a character!

■ **~ d'abonné** customer's number; **~ d'appel gratuit** freefone number (GB), toll-free number (US); **~ vert** = **~ d'appel gratuit**.

IDIOMS **tirer le bon ~** to be lucky.

numérotation /nymeʀɔtasjɔ̃/ *nf* numbering.

numéroter /nymeʀɔte/ [1] *vtr* to number.

nu-pied, *pl* **~s** /nypje/ *nm* sandal.

nuptial, **~e**, *mpl* **-iaux** /nypsjal, o/ *adj* [*mass*] nuptial; [*room*] bridal; **cérémonie ~e** wedding.

nuque /nyk/ *nf* nape (of the neck).

nurse /nœʀs/ *nf* nanny (GB), nurse.

nutritif, **-ive** /nytʀitif, iv/ *adj* [*skin cream*] nourishing; [*value*] nutritive.

nutrition /nytʀisjɔ̃/ *nf* nutrition.

nymphe /nɛ̃f/ *nf* nymph.

nymphomane /nɛ̃fɔman/ *adj, nf* nymphomaniac.

Oo

o, **O** /o/ *nm inv* o, O.

oasis /ɔazis/ *nf inv* oasis.

obéir /ɔbeiʀ/ [3] *v+prep* **1** to obey; **~ à** to obey [*order*]; **2** [*brakes, vehicle*] to respond.

obéissance /ɔbeisɑ̃s/ *nf* obedience.

obéissant, **~e** /ɔbeisɑ̃, ɑ̃t/ *adj* obedient.

obélisque /ɔbelisk/ *nm* obelisk.

obèse /ɔbɛz/ *adj* obese.

objecter /ɔbʒɛkte/ [1] *vtr* to object.

objectif, **-ive** /ɔbʒɛktif, iv/ **I** *adj* objective.
II *nm* **1** objective; **2** lens; **3** target.

objection /ɔbʒɛksjɔ̃/ *nf* objection.

objectivité /ɔbʒɛktivite/ *nf* objectivity.

objet /ɔbʒɛ/ **I** *nm* **1** object; **~ fragile** fragile item; **~s personnels** personal possessions; **2** (of debate, research) subject; (of hatred, desire) object; **faire l'~ de** to be the subject of [*inquiry, research*]; to be subjected to [*surveillance*]; to be the object of [*desire, hatred*]; **3** purpose, object; **'~: réponse à votre lettre du...'** 're: your letter of...'; **4** (Law) **~ d'un litige** matter at issue.
II -objet (*combining form*) as an object; **femme-~** woman as an object.
■ **~s trouvés** lost property; **~ volant non identifié**, **ovni** unidentified flying object, UFO.

obligation /ɔbligasjɔ̃/ *nf* **1** obligation, responsibility; duty; **2** necessity; **se voir** or **trouver dans l'~ de faire** to be forced to do; **3** (Econ) bond; **4** (Law) obligation.
■ **~s militaires**, **OM** military service.

obligatoire /ɔbligatwaʀ/ *adj* **1** compulsory; **2°** inevitable.

obligatoirement /ɔbligatwaʀmɑ̃/ *adv* inevitably, necessarily.

obligeamment /ɔbliʒamɑ̃/ *adv* obligingly.

obligeance /ɔbliʒɑ̃s/ *nf* **avoir l'~ de** to be kind enough to.

obliger /ɔbliʒe/ [13] **I** *vtr* **1 ~ qn à faire** to force sb to do; [*rules*] to make it compulsory for sb to; [*duty*] to compel sb to; **je suis obligé de partir** I have to go; **2 ~ qn** to oblige sb.
II s'obliger *v refl* (+ *v être*) **s'~ à faire** to force oneself to do.

oblique /ɔblik/ *adj* slanting; sidelong; oblique.

oblitération /ɔbliteʀasjɔ̃/ *nf* (of stamp) cancelling[GB]; **(cachet d')~** postmark.

oblong, **-ongue** /ɔblɔ̃, ɔ̃g/ *adj* oblong.

obnubiler /ɔbnybile/ [1] *vtr* to obsess.

obscène /ɔpsɛn/ *adj* obscene.

obscur, **~e** /ɔpskyʀ/ *adj* **1** dark; **2** obscure; **3** lowly; **4** vague.

obscurcir /ɔpskyʀsiʀ/ [3] **I** *vtr* **1** to make [sth] dark [*place*]; **2** to obscure [*view*].
II s'obscurcir *v refl* (+ *v être*) **1** [*sky, place*] to darken; **2** [*situation*] to become confused.

obscurément /ɔpskyʀemɑ̃/ *adv* **1** [*feel*] vaguely; **2** [*live*] in obscurity.

obscurité /ɔpskyʀite/ *nf* darkness.

obsédant, **~e** /ɔpsedɑ̃, ɑ̃t/ *adj* [*memory, dream, music*] haunting; [*rhythm*] insistent.

obsédé, **~e** /ɔpsede/ *nm,f* **~ (sexuel)** sex maniac.

obséder /ɔpsede/ [14] *vtr* [*memory, dream*] to haunt; [*idea, problem*] to obsess.

obsèques /ɔpsɛk/ *nf pl* funeral.

obséquieux, **-ieuse** /ɔpsekjø, øz/ *adj* obsequious.

observateur, **-trice** /ɔpsɛʀvatœʀ, tʀis/ **I** *adj* observant.
II *nm,f* observer.

observation /ɔpsɛʀvasjɔ̃/ *nf* **1** observation; **2** observation, remark; comment; **3** reproach.

observatoire /ɔpsɛʀvatwaʀ/ *nm* **1** observatory; **2** look-out post.

observer /ɔpsɛʀve/ [1] **I** *vtr* **1** to watch, to observe; **2** to notice, to observe [*phenomenon, reaction*]; **3** to observe [*rules, treaty*]; to keep to [*diet*]; to maintain [*strategy*]; **~ le silence** to keep quiet.
II s'observer *v refl* (+ *v être*) **1** to watch each other; **2** to keep a check on oneself.

obsession /ɔpsɛsjɔ̃/ *nf* obsession.

obsolète /ɔpsɔlɛt/ *adj* obsolete.

obstacle /ɔpstakl/ *nm* **1** obstacle; **2** (in horse-riding) fence.

obstétricien, **-ienne** /ɔpstetʀisjɛ̃, ɛn/ *nm,f* obstetrician.

obstétrique /ɔpstetʀik/ *nf* obstetrics.

obstination /ɔpstinasjɔ̃/ *nf* obstinacy.

obstiné, **~e** /ɔpstine/ **I** *pp* ▶ **obstiner**.
II *pp adj* **1** stubborn; **2** dogged.

obstinément /ɔpstinemɑ̃/ *adv* obstinately.

obstiner: **s'obstiner** /ɔpstine/ [1] *v refl* (+ *v être*) to persist.

obstruction /ɔpstʀyksjɔ̃/ *nf* obstruction.

obstruer /ɔpstʀye/ [1] **I** *vtr* to obstruct.
II s'obstruer *v refl* (+ *v être*) to get blocked.

obtempérer /ɔptɑ̃peʀe/ [14] *v+prep* to comply; **~ à** to comply with [*order*].

obtenir /ɔptəniʀ/ [36] *vtr* to get, to obtain.

obtention /ɔptɑ̃sjɔ̃/ *nf* getting, obtaining.

obturation /ɔptyʀasjɔ̃/ *nf* **1** blocking (up); **2 vitesse d'~** shutter speed.

obturer /ɔptyʀe/ [1] *vtr* to block up.

obtus, **~e** /ɔpty, yz/ *adj* obtuse.

obus /oby/ *nm inv* shell.

occasion /ɔkazjɔ̃/ *nf* **1** occasion; **à l'~** some time; **à** or **en plusieurs ~s** on several occasions; **les grandes ~s** special occasions; **2** opportunity, chance; **être l'~ de qch** to give rise to sth; **3** second-hand buy; **4** bargain.

occasionnel, **-elle** /ɔkazjɔnɛl/ *adj* occasional.
occasionner /ɔkazjɔne/ [1] *vtr* to cause.
occident /ɔksidɑ̃/ *nm* **1** west; **2 l'Occident** the West.
occidental, **~e**, *mpl* **-aux** /ɔksidɑ̃tal, o/ *adj* western.
Occidental, **~e**, *mpl* **-aux** /ɔksidɑ̃tal, o/ *nm,f* Westerner.
occitan /ɔksitɑ̃/ *nm* langue d'oc.
occulte /ɔkylt/ *adj* **1** occult; **2** secret.
occulter /ɔkylte/ [1] *vtr* **1** to eclipse; **2** to obscure [*issue*]; to conceal [*truth*].
occupant, **~e** /ɔkypɑ̃, ɑ̃t/ **I** *adj* occupying.
II *nm,f* (of house) occupier; (of vehicle) occupant.
occupation /ɔkypasjɔ̃/ *nf* **1** (pastime) occupation; **2** occupation, job; **3** occupancy; **4** (of country, factory) occupation.
occupé, **~e** /ɔkype/ **I** *pp* ▶ **occuper**.
II *pp adj* **1** [*person, life*] busy; **2** [*seat*] taken; [*phone*] engaged (GB), busy; [*toilet*] engaged; **3** (Mil) [*country*] occupied.
occuper /ɔkype/ [1] **I** *vtr* **1** to live in, to occupy [*flat, house*]; to be in [*shower, cell*]; to sit in [*seat*]; **2** to take up [*space, time*]; **3** to occupy [*person, mind*]; **ça m'occupe!** it keeps me busy!; **le sujet qui nous occupe** the matter which we are dealing with; **4** to have [*employment*]; to hold [*job, office*]; **5** [*strikers, army*] to occupy [*place*]; **~ les locaux** to stage a sit-in.
II s'occuper *v refl* (+ *v être*) **1** to keep oneself busy or occupied; **2 s'~ de** to see to, to take care of [*dinner, tickets*]; to be dealing with [*file, matter*]; to take care of [*child, animal, plant*]; to attend to [*customer*]; to be in charge of [*finance, library*]; **occupe-toi de tes affaires**○ or **de ce qui te regarde**○**!** mind your own business○!
occurrence /ɔkyRɑ̃s/ *nf* **1** case, instance; **en l'~** in this case; **2** occurrence.
océan /ɔseɑ̃/ *nm* ocean.
océanique /ɔseanik/ *adj* oceanic.
ocre /ɔkR/ *adj inv*, *nm* ochre[GB].
octave /ɔktav/ *nf* octave.
octobre /ɔktɔbR/ *nm* October.
octogénaire /ɔktɔʒenɛR/ *nmf* octogenarian.
octroyer /ɔktRwaje/ [23] *vtr* **~ à qn** to grant sb [*pardon, favour*]; to allocate sb sth [*budget*].
oculaire /ɔkylɛR/ *adj* **troubles ~s** eye trouble; **témoin ~** eyewitness.
oculiste /ɔkylist/ *nmf* oculist, ophthalmologist.
ode /ɔd/ *nf* ode.
odeur /ɔdœR/ *nf* smell.
odieux, **-ieuse** /ɔdjø, øz/ *adj* horrible.
odorant, **~e** /ɔdɔRɑ̃, ɑ̃t/ *adj* which has a smell.
odorat /ɔdɔRa/ *nm* sense of smell.
œdème /edɛm/ *nm* (Med) oedema.
œdipe /edip/ *nm* Oedipus complex.
œil, *pl* **yeux** /œj, jø/ *nm* eye; **ouvrir l'~** to keep one's eyes open; **fermer les yeux sur qch** to turn a blind eye to sth; **acheter qch les yeux fermés** to buy sth with complete confidence; **avoir l'~ à tout** to be vigilant; **jeter un ~ à** or **sur qch** to have a quick look at sth; **aux yeux de tous** openly; **jeter un coup d'~ à qch** to glance at sth; **avoir le coup d'~** to have a good eye; **regarder qch d'un ~ neuf** to see sth in a new light; **voir qch d'un mauvais ~** to take a dim view of sth; **à mes yeux** in my opinion.
■ **~ de verre** glass eye.
IDIOMS **mon ~**○**!** my eye○!, my foot○!; **à l'~**○ for nothing, for free○; **faire les gros yeux à qn** to glare at sb; **dévorer qn/qch des yeux** to gaze longingly at sb/sth; **faire les yeux doux à qn** to make eyes at sb; **tourner de l'~**○ to faint; **cela me sort par les yeux**○ I've had it up to here○; **avoir bon pied bon ~** to be as fit as a fiddle; **sauter aux yeux** to be obvious.
œillade /œjad/ *nf* **1** wink; **2** glance.
œillère /œjɛR/ *nf* blinker.
œillet /œjɛ/ *nm* **1** carnation; **2** (in shoe, tarpaulin) eyelet; (in belt) hole; (made of metal) grommet.
œsophage /ezɔfaʒ/ *nm* oesophagus.
œuf /œf, *pl* ø/ *nm* egg; **~s de cabillaud** cod's roe.
■ **~ à la coque** boiled egg; **~ dur** hard-boiled egg; **~ sur le plat** fried egg; **~s brouillés** scrambled eggs.
œuvre /œvR/ *nf* **1** (artistic, literary) work; **~s complètes** complete works; **2 être à l'~** to be at work; **voir qn à l'~** to see sb in action; **mettre en ~** to implement [*reform*]; to display [*ingenuity*]; **tout mettre en ~ pour faire** to make every effort to do.
■ **~ d'art** work of art; **~ de bienfaisance** or **de charité** charity.
off○ /ɔf/ *adj inv* **voix ~** voice-over.
offense /ɔfɑ̃s/ *nf* insult.
offenser /ɔfɑ̃se/ [1] **I** *vtr* to offend.
II s'offenser *v refl* (+ *v être*) to take offence[GB].
offensif, **-ive**[1] /ɔfɑ̃sif, iv/ *adj* (Mil) offensive.
offensive[2] /ɔfɑ̃siv/ *nf* (Mil, figurative) offensive.
office /ɔfis/ **I** *nm* **1 faire ~ de table** to serve as a table; **2 ~ religieux** service; **3** butlery.
II d'office *phr* **d'~** without consultation; **nos propositions ont été rejetées d'~** our proposals were dismissed out of hand; **commis d'~** [*lawyer*] appointed by the court.
■ **~ du tourisme** tourist information office.
officiel, **-ielle** /ɔfisjɛl/ **I** *adj* official; **être en visite officielle** to be on a state visit.
II *nm* official.
officier[1] /ɔfisje/ [2] *vi* to officiate.
officier[2] /ɔfisje/ *nm* officer.
officieux, **-ieuse** /ɔfisjø, øz/ *adj* unofficial.
offrande /ɔfRɑ̃d/ *nf* offering.
offrant /ɔfRɑ̃/ *nm* **vendre qch au plus ~** to sell sth to the highest bidder.
offre /ɔfR/ *nf* **1** offer; **répondre à une ~ d'emploi** to reply to a job advertisement; **2** (Econ) supply.
■ **~ d'achat** bid; **~ publique d'achat**, **OPA** takeover bid.
offrir /ɔfRiR/ [4] **I** *vtr* **1 ~ qch à qn** to give sth to sb; **2** to buy (**à qn** for sb); **3** to offer [*choice*]; to offer [*resignation*]; to present [*problems*].
II s'offrir *v refl* (+ *v être*) **1 s'~** to buy

oneself [*flowers*]; **ils ne peuvent pas s'~ le théâtre** they can't afford to go to the theatre[GB]; **s'~ un jour de vacances** to give oneself a day off; **2** [*solution*] to present itself; **s'~ en spectacle** to make an exhibition of oneself.

offusquer /ɔfyske/ [1] **I** *vtr* to offend.
II s'offusquer *v refl* (+ *v être*) to be offended.

ogive /ɔʒiv/ *nf* rib.

ogre /ɔgʀ/ *nm* ogre.

oie /wa/ *nf* goose; **~ blanche** naïve young girl.

oignon /ɔɲɔ̃/ *nm* **1** onion; **2** (of flower) bulb.
IDIOMS **occupe-toi de tes ~s**○ mind your own business○.

oiseau, *pl* **~x** /wazo/ *nm* bird; **un (drôle d')~** an oddball○.
IDIOMS **trouver l'~ rare**○ to find the one person in a million.

oisif, **-ive** /wazif, iv/ **I** *adj* idle.
II *nm,f* idler; **les ~s** the idle rich.

oisillon /wazijɔ̃/ *nm* fledgling.

oisiveté /wazivte/ *nf* idleness.
IDIOMS **l'~ est mère de tous les vices** (Proverb) the devil makes work for idle hands.

olé○: **olé olé** /ɔleɔle/ *phr* [*joke*] naughty.

olfactif, **-ive** /ɔlfaktif, iv/ *adj* olfactory.

oligo-élément, *pl* **~s** /ɔligoelemɑ̃/ *nm* trace element.

olive /ɔliv/ *nf* olive.

olivier /ɔlivje/ *nm* **1** olive tree; **2** olive wood.

olympique /ɔlɛ̃pik/ *adj* Olympic.

ombrager /ɔ̃bʀaʒe/ [13] *vtr* to shade.

ombrageux, **-euse** /ɔ̃bʀaʒø, øz/ *adj* tetchy.

ombre /ɔ̃bʀ/ *nf* **1** shade; **tu leur fais de l'~** you're (standing) in their light; (figurative) you put them in the shade; **rester dans l'~ de qn** to be in sb's shadow; **2** shadow; **3** darkness; **4 laisser certains détails dans l'~** to be deliberately vague about certain details; **5** hint; **une ~ de tristesse passa dans son regard** a look of sadness crossed his/her face.
■ **~ chinoise** shadow puppet; **~ à paupières** eye shadow.
IDIOMS **jeter une ~ au tableau** to spoil the picture.

ombrelle /ɔ̃bʀɛl/ *nf* parasol, sunshade.

omelette /ɔmlɛt/ *nf* omelette.

omettre /ɔmɛtʀ/ [60] *vtr* to leave out, to omit.

omission /ɔmisjɔ̃/ *nf* omission.

omnibus /ɔmnibys/ *nm inv* slow or local train.

omniprésent, **~e** /ɔmnipʀezɑ̃, ɑ̃t/ *adj* omnipresent.

omnisports /ɔmnispɔʀ/ *adj inv* **salle ~** sports hall; **club ~** (multi-)sports club.

omnivore /ɔmnivɔʀ/ *nmf* omnivore.

omoplate /ɔmɔplat/ *nf* shoulder blade.

OMS /oɛmɛs/ *nf* (*abbr* = **Organisation mondiale de la santé**) WHO.

on /ɔ̃/ *pron* **1 ~ a refait la route** the road was resurfaced; **~ a prétendu que** it was claimed that; **il pleut des cordes, comme ~ dit** it's raining cats and dogs, as they say; **2** we; **mon copain et moi, ~ va en Afrique** my boyfriend and I are going to Africa; **3** you; **alors, ~ se promène?** so you're taking a stroll then?; **4 ~ fait ce qu'~ peut!** one does what one can!; **toi, ~ ne t'a rien demandé** nobody asked you for your opinion; **~ ne m'a pas demandé mon avis** they didn't ask me for my opinion.

once /ɔ̃s/ *nf* ounce.

oncle /ɔ̃kl/ *nm* uncle.

onctueux, **-euse** /ɔ̃ktɥø, øz/ *adj* **1** smooth, creamy; **2** unctuous.

onde /ɔ̃d/ *nf* wave; **grandes ~s** long wave; **sur les ~s** on the air.

ondée /ɔ̃de/ *nf* shower.

on-dit /ɔ̃di/ *nm inv* **les ~** hearsay.

ondulé, **~e** /ɔ̃dyle/ *adj* [*hair, shape*] wavy; [*cardboard*] corrugated.

onéreux, **-euse** /ɔneʀø, øz/ *adj* expensive.

ongle /ɔ̃gl/ *nm* nail.
IDIOMS **jusqu'au bout des ~s** through and through.

onglet /ɔ̃glɛ/ *nm* **1** tab; **avec ~s** with thumb-index; **2** (Culin) *prime cut of beef*.

onirique /ɔniʀik/ *adj* dream-like.

onomatopée /ɔnɔmatɔpe/ *nf* onomatopoeia.

ONU /ɔny, oɛny/ *nf* (*abbr* = **Organisation des Nations unies**) UN, UNO.

onyx /ɔniks/ *nm inv* onyx.

onze /ɔ̃z/ *adj inv, pron, nm inv* eleven.

onzième /ɔ̃zjɛm/ **I** *adj* eleventh.
II *nf* (Sch) *first year of primary school, age 6–7.*

OPA /opea/ *nf* (*abbr* = **offre publique d'achat**) takeover bid.

opaque /ɔpak/ *adj* **1** opaque; **2** (figurative) [*text*] opaque; [*night*] dark; [*wood, fog*] impenetrable.

OPEP /ɔpɛp/ *nf* (*abbr* = **Organisation des pays producteurs de pétrole**) OPEC.

opéra /ɔpeʀa/ *nm* **1** opera; **2** opera house.

opérateur, **-trice** /ɔpeʀatœʀ, tʀis/ *nm,f* operator; **~ de saisie** keyboarder.

opération /ɔpeʀasjɔ̃/ *nf* **1 ~ (chirurgicale)** operation, surgery; **2** calculation; **3** (Tech) operation; **4** process; **5** transaction.

opératoire /ɔpeʀatwaʀ/ *adj* **1** [*technique*] surgical; [*risk*] in operating; **2** operative.

opérer /ɔpeʀe/ [14] **I** *vtr* **1** to operate on; **~ qn de l'appendicite** to remove sb's appendix; **se faire ~** to have an operation, to have surgery; **2** to bring about [*change*].
II *vi* **1** (Med) to operate; **2** [*cure, charm*] to work; **3** to proceed; **4** [*thief*] to operate.

opérette /ɔpeʀɛt/ *nf* operetta, light opera.

ophtalmologiste /ɔftalmɔlɔʒist/ *nmf* ophthalmologist.

opiner /ɔpine/ [1] *vi* **~ du bonnet** or **de la tête** to nod in agreement.

opiniâtre /ɔpinjɑtʀ/ *adj* [*resistance*] dogged; [*work*] relentless; [*person*] tenacious.

opinion /ɔpinjɔ̃/ *nf* **1** opinion; **mon ~ est faite** my mind is made up; **2 l'~ (publique)** public opinion.

opium /ɔpjɔm/ *nm* opium.

opportun, **~e** /ɔpɔʀtœ̃, yn/ *adj* appropriate.

opportuniste /ɔpɔʀtynist/ *nmf* opportunist.

opportunité /ɔpɔʀtynite/ *nf* **1** appropriateness; **2** opportunity.

opposant, ~e /ɔpozɑ̃, ɑ̃t/ *nm,f* opponent.

opposé, ~e /ɔpoze/ **I** *adj* **1** [*direction*] opposite; **2** [*opinion*] opposite; [*parties, sides*] opposing; [*interests*] conflicting; **3** opposed.
II **à l'opposé** *phr* **1 à l'~ de mes frères** in contrast to my brothers; **2 il est parti à l'~** he went off in the opposite direction.

opposer /ɔpoze/ [1] **I** *vtr* **1** to put up [*resistance, argument*]; **2 ~ à** to match or pit [sb] against [*person, team*]; **3** [*problem*] to divide [*people*]; **4** to compare.
II **s'opposer** *v refl* (+ *v être*) **1 s'~ à qch** to be opposed to sth; **2 s'~ à** to stand in the way of [*change*]; **3** to contrast; **4** [*ideas, opinions*] to conflict; [*people*] to disagree; **5** [*teams*] to confront each other.

opposition /ɔpozisjɔ̃/ *nf* **1** opposition; **par ~ à** in contrast with or to; **2 faire ~ à un chèque** to stop a cheque (GB) or check (US).

oppresser /ɔpʀɛse/ [1] *vtr* to oppress; **se sentir oppressé** to feel breathless.

oppression /ɔpʀɛsjɔ̃/ *nf* oppression.

opprimer /ɔpʀime/ [1] *vtr* to oppress [*people*].

opter /ɔpte/ [1] *vi* to opt.

opticien, -ienne /ɔptisjɛ̃, ɛn/ *nm,f* optician.

optimal, ~e, *mpl* **-aux** /ɔptimal, o/ *adj* optimum.

optimisme /ɔptimism/ *nm* optimism.

optimiste /ɔptimist/ *adj* optimistic.

option /ɔpsjɔ̃/ *nf* option; **en ~** optional.

optique /ɔptik/ **I** *adj* **1** (Anat) optic; **2** optical.
II *nf* **1** optics; **2** perspective.

opulence /ɔpylɑ̃s/ *nf* opulence.

or[1] /ɔʀ/ *conj* and yet; **~, ce jour-là, il**... now, on that particular day, he...

or[2] /ɔʀ/ **I** *adj inv* gold; [*hair*] golden.
II *nm* **1** gold; **en ~** gold; [*husband*] marvellous[GB]; [*opportunity*] golden; **2** gilding.

oracle /ɔʀakl/ *nm* oracle.

orage /ɔʀaʒ/ *nm* storm.

orageux, -euse /ɔʀaʒø, øz/ *adj* stormy.

oraison /ɔʀɛzɔ̃/ *nf* prayer; **~ funèbre** funeral oration.

oral, ~e, *mpl* **-aux** /ɔʀal, o/ **I** *adj* **1** oral; **2** (Med) **par voie ~e** orally.
II *nm* (Sch) oral (examination).

orange[1] /ɔʀɑ̃ʒ/ *adj inv* orange; [*light*] amber (GB), yellow (US).

orange[2] /ɔʀɑ̃ʒ/ *nf* orange.

oranger /ɔʀɑ̃ʒe/ *nm* orange tree.

orangerie /ɔʀɑ̃ʒʀi/ *nf* orangery.

orateur, -trice /ɔʀatœʀ, tʀis/ *nm,f* **1** speaker; **2** orator.

orbite /ɔʀbit/ *nf* **1** orbit; **2** eye-socket.

orchestral, ~e, *mpl* **-aux** /ɔʀkɛstʀal, o/ *adj* orchestral.

orchestration /ɔʀkɛstʀasjɔ̃/ *nf* orchestration.

orchestre /ɔʀkɛstʀ/ *nm* **1** orchestra; **2** band; **3** orchestra stalls (GB), orchestra (US).

orchidée /ɔʀkide/ *nf* orchid.

ordinaire /ɔʀdinɛʀ/ **I** *adj* **1** ordinary; [*quality*] standard; [*reader, tourist*] average; **journée peu ~** unusual day; **2 très ~** [*meal, wine*] very average; [*person*] very ordinary.
II *nm* **sortir de l'~** to be out of the ordinary.
III **à l'ordinaire, d'ordinaire** *phr* usually.

ordinateur /ɔʀdinatœʀ/ *nm* computer.

ordination /ɔʀdinasjɔ̃/ *nf* ordination.

ordonnance /ɔʀdɔnɑ̃s/ *nf* prescription.

ordonner /ɔʀdɔne/ [1] *vtr* **1** to order; **2** to put [sth] in order; **3** to ordain.

ordre /ɔʀdʀ/ *nm* **1** (command) order; **j'ai des ~s** I'm acting under orders; **à vos ~s!** (Mil) yes, sir!; **jusqu'à nouvel ~** until further notice; **2** (sequence) order; **par ~ alphabétique** in alphabetical order; **3** tidiness, orderliness; **4** (orderly state) order; **rappeler qn à l'~** to reprimand sb; **tout est rentré dans l'~** everything is back to normal; **rétablir l'~ (public)** to restore law and order; **5** nature; **c'est dans l'~ des choses** it's in the nature of things; **de l'~ de 30%** in the order of 30% (GB), on the order of 30% (US); **de premier ~** first-rate; **6** (in religion) order; **entrer dans les ~s** to take (holy) orders; **7 libellez le chèque à l'~ de X** make the cheque (GB) or check (US) payable to X.
■ **~ du jour** agenda.

ordure /ɔʀdyʀ/ **I** *nf* filth.
II **ordures** *nf pl* refuse (GB), garbage (US).

ordurier, -ière /ɔʀdyʀje, ɛʀ/ *adj* filthy.

orée /ɔʀe/ *nf* **1** edge; **2** (figurative) start.

oreille /ɔʀɛj/ *nf* **1** ear; **n'écouter que d'une ~** to half-listen; **ouvre-bien les ~s!** listen carefully; **2** hearing; **avoir l'~ fine** to have keen hearing; **3 à l'abri des ~s indiscrètes** where no-one can hear.
IDIOMS **tirer les ~s à qn** to tell sb off.

oreiller /ɔʀɛje/ *nm* pillow.

oreillons /ɔʀɛjɔ̃/ *nm pl* mumps.

ores: **d'ores et déjà** /dɔʀzedeʒa/ *phr* already.

orfèvre /ɔʀfɛvʀ/ *nmf* goldsmith; **être ~ en la matière** to be an expert in the field.

orfèvrerie /ɔʀfɛvʀəʀi/ *nf* **1** goldsmith's art; **2** goldsmith's and silversmith's.

organe /ɔʀgan/ *nm* organ.

organigramme /ɔʀganigʀam/ *nm* organization chart.

organique /ɔʀganik/ *adj* organic.

organisation /ɔʀganizasjɔ̃/ *nf* organization.

organiser /ɔʀganize/ [1] **I** *vtr* to organize.
II **s'organiser** *v refl* (+ *v être*) **1** [*opposition*] to get organized; **2** to organize oneself; **3** [*fight, help*] to be organized.

organisme /ɔʀganism/ *nm* **1** body; **2** organism; **3** organization, body.

orgasme /ɔʀgasm/ *nm* orgasm.

orge /ɔʀʒ/ *nf* barley.

orgie /ɔʀʒi/ *nf* orgy.

orgue /ɔʀg/ *nm* (Mus) organ.

orgueil /ɔʀgœj/ *nm* pride.

orgueilleux, **-euse** /ɔʀgœjø, øz/ *adj* overproud.

orient /ɔʀjɑ̃/ *nm* **1** east; **2 l'Orient** the East.

oriental, **~e**, *mpl* **-aux** /ɔʀjɑ̃tal, o/ *adj* eastern; oriental.

Oriental, **~e**, *mpl* **-aux** /ɔʀjɑ̃tal, o/ *nm,f* Asian; **les Orientaux** Asians.

orientation /ɔʀjɑ̃tasjɔ̃/ *nf* **1** (of house) aspect; (of aerial) angle; **2** (of inquiry) direction; **3** (Sch) **changer d'~** to change courses.

orienter /ɔʀjɑ̃te/ [1] **I** *vtr* **1** to adjust [*aerial, lamp*]; **2 ~ la conversation sur** to bring the conversation around to; **3** to direct [*person*]; **4** (Sch) to give [sb] career advice.
II s'orienter *v refl* (+ *v être*) **1** to get or find one's bearings; **2 s'~ vers** [*person*] to turn toward(s); **s'~ vers les carrières scientifiques** to go in for a career in science.

orifice /ɔʀifis/ *nm* **1** orifice; **2** (of pipe) mouth; (of tube) neck.

originaire /ɔʀiʒinɛʀ/ *adj* [*plant, animal*] native; **famille ~ d'Asie** Asian family.

original, **~e**, *mpl* **-aux** /ɔʀiʒinal, o/ **I** *adj* **1** original; **2** eccentric.
II *nm* original.

originalité /ɔʀiʒinalite/ *nf* originality.

origine /ɔʀiʒin/ *nf* origin; **être d'~ modeste** to come from a modest background; **dès l'~** right from the start; **à l'~** originally.

originel, **-elle** /ɔʀiʒinɛl/ *adj* original.

orme /ɔʀm/ *nm* **1** elm (tree); **2** elm (wood).

ornement /ɔʀnəmɑ̃/ *nm* **1** ornament; **2** decorative detail.

orner /ɔʀne/ [1] *vtr* to decorate.

ornière /ɔʀnjɛʀ/ *nf* rut.

ornithologie /ɔʀnitɔlɔʒi/ *nf* ornithology.

ornithorynque /ɔʀnitɔʀɛ̃k/ *nm* (duck-billed) platypus, duckbill (US).

orphelin, **~e** /ɔʀfəlɛ̃, in/ *nm,f* orphan.

orphelinat /ɔʀfəlina/ *nm* orphanage.

orque /ɔʀk/ *nm* or *f* killer whale.

orteil /ɔʀtɛj/ *nm* toe; **gros ~** big toe.

orthodoxe /ɔʀtɔdɔks/ *adj, nmf* Orthodox.

orthographe /ɔʀtɔgʀaf/ *nf* spelling.

orthographier /ɔʀtɔgʀafje/ [2] *vtr* to spell.

orthopédie /ɔʀtɔpedi/ *nf* orthopedics.

orthophoniste /ɔʀtɔfɔnist/ *nmf* speech therapist.

ortie /ɔʀti/ *nf* (stinging) nettle.

os /ɔs, *pl* o/ *nm inv* bone; **en chair et en ~** in the flesh.
IDIOMS **il y a un ~**° there's a hitch; **tomber sur un ~**° to come across a snag; **être trempé jusqu'aux ~**° to be soaked to the skin°.

osciller /ɔsile/ [1] *vi* **1** [*pendulum*] to swing; [*boat*] to rock; [*head*] to roll from side to side; **2** [*currency*] to fluctuate; **3** to vacillate.

osé, **~e** /oze/ *adj* **1** risqué; **2** [*behaviour*] daring; [*words*] outspoken.

oseille /ozɛj/ *nf* **1** sorrel; **2**° dough°, money.

oser /oze/ [1] *vtr* to dare; **si j'ose dire** if I may say so.

osier /ozje/ *nm* **1** (tree) osier; **2** wicker, osier.

osmose /ɔsmoz/ *nf* osmosis.

ossature /ɔsatyʀ/ *nf* skeleton; **~ du visage** bone structure.

ossements /ɔsmɑ̃/ *nm pl* remains.

osseux, **-euse** /ɔsø, øz/ *adj* **1** bony; **2** [*disease*] bone.

ostentatoire /ɔstɑ̃tatwaʀ/ *adj* ostentatious.

ostéopathe /ɔsteɔpat/ *nmf* osteopath.

ostracisme /ɔstʀasism/ *nm* ostracism.

ostréiculture /ɔstʀeikyltyʀ/ *nf* oyster farming.

otage /ɔtaʒ/ *nm* hostage.

OTAN /ɔtɑ̃/ *nf* (*abbr* = **Organisation du traité de l'Atlantique Nord**) NATO.

otarie /ɔtaʀi/ *nf* eared seal, otary.

ôter /ote/ [1] **I** *vtr* **1** to take off [*clothes, glasses*]; to remove [*bones, stain*]; **2 ~ qch à qn** to take sth away from sb; **3** (in mathematics) **4 ôté de 9, il reste 5** 9 minus or take away 4 leaves 5.
II s'ôter *v refl* (+ *v être*) **s'~ qch de l'esprit** to get sth out of one's mind or head.

otite /ɔtit/ *nf* inflammation of the ear.

oto-rhino-laryngologiste, *pl* **~s** /otoʀinolaʀɛ̃gɔlɔʒist/ *nmf* ENT specialist.

ou /u/ *conj* or; **~ (bien)... ~ (bien)...** either... or...

où /u/ **I** *adv* where; **je l'ai perdu je ne sais ~** I've lost it somewhere or other; **par ~ êtes-vous passés pour venir?** which way did you come?; **~ en êtes-vous?** where have you got to?; **~ allons-nous?** what are things coming to!
II *rel pron* **1** where; **le quartier ~ nous habitons** the area we live in; **d'~ s'élevait de la fumée** out of which smoke was rising; **~ qu'ils aillent** wherever they go; **2 la misère ~ elle se trouvait** the poverty in which she was living; **au train** or **à l'allure ~ vont les choses** (at) the rate things are going; **le travail s'est accumulé, d'~ ce retard** there is a backlog of work, hence the delay; **3** when; **le matin ~ je l'ai rencontré** the morning I met him.

ouate /wat/ *nf* **1** cotton wool (GB), cotton (US); **2** wadding.

oubli /ubli/ *nm* **1 l'~ de qch** forgetting sth; (of duty) neglect of sth; **2** omission; **3** oblivion; **tomber dans l'~** to be completely forgotten.

oublier /ublije/ [2] **I** *vtr* **1** to forget [*name, date, fact*]; to forget about [*worries, incident*]; **se faire ~** to keep a low profile; **2** to leave out [*person, detail*]; **3** to neglect [*duty, friend*].
II s'oublier *v refl* (+ *v être*) **1** to be forgotten; **2** to leave oneself out.

oubliettes /ublijɛt/ *nf pl* oubliette.

ouest /wɛst/ **I** *adj inv* west; western.
II *nm* **1** west; **2 l'Ouest** the West.

ouf /uf/ **I** *nm* **faire ~** to breathe a sigh of relief.
II *excl* phew!

oui /wi/ **I** *adv* yes; **alors c'est ~?** so the answer is yes?; **découvrir si ~ ou non** to discover whether or not; **dire ~ à qch** to welcome sth; to agree to sth; **faire ~ de la tête** to nod; **lui, prudent? un lâche, ~!** him, cautious? a coward, more like○!; **je crois que ~** I think so.

II *nm inv* **1** yes; **2** 'yes' vote; **le ~ l'a emporté** the ayes have it.

IDIOMS **pour un ~ (ou) pour un non** [*get angry*] for the slightest thing; [*change one's mind*] at the drop of a hat.

ouï-dire /widiʀ/ *nm inv* **par ~** by hearsay.

ouïe /wi/ *nf* **1** hearing; **être tout ~** to be all ears; **2** (of fish) gill.

ouïr† /wiʀ/ [38] *vtr* to hear; **j'ai ouï dire que** word has reached me that.

ouistiti /wistiti/ *nm* marmoset.

ouragan /uʀagɑ̃/ *nm* hurricane.

ourler /uʀle/ [1] *vtr* to hem.

ourlet /uʀlɛ/ *nm* hem.

ours /uʀs/ *nm inv* **1** bear; **2 il est un peu ~** he's a bit surly.

■ **~ blanc** polar bear; **~ en peluche** teddy bear; **~ polaire** = **~ blanc**.

IDIOMS **vendre la peau de l'~ avant de l'avoir tué** (Proverb) to count one's chickens before they're hatched.

ourse /uʀs/ *nf* she-bear.

oursin /uʀsɛ̃/ *nm* (sea) urchin.

ourson /uʀsɔ̃/ *nm* bear cub.

outil /uti/ *nm* tool; **~ de travail** work tool.

outrage /utʀaʒ/ *nm* insult.

■ **~ à agent** *verbal assault of a policeman.*

outrager /utʀaʒe/ [13] *vtr* to offend.

outrance /utʀɑ̃s/ *nf* **à ~** excessively.

outrancier, **-ière** /utʀɑ̃sje, ɛʀ/ *adj* extreme.

outre /utʀ/ **I** *prep* in addition to.

II *adv* **passer ~** to pay no heed.

III **outre mesure** *phr* unduly.

IV **en outre** *phr* in addition.

outre-Atlantique /utʀatlɑ̃tik/ *adv* across the Atlantic; **d'~** American.

outre-Manche /utʀəmɑ̃ʃ/ *adv* across the Channel; **d'~** British.

outremer /utʀəmɛʀ/ *adj inv*, *nm* ultramarine.

outre-mer /utʀəmɛʀ/ *adv* overseas.

outrer /utʀe/ [1] *vtr* **1** to outrage; **2** to exaggerate.

ouvert, **~e** /uvɛʀ, ɛʀt/ **I** *pp* ▶ **ouvrir**.

II *pp adj* **1** open; **grand ~** wide open; **être ~ aux idées nouvelles** to be open to new ideas; **2** [*gas*] on; [*tap*] running; **3** [*question*] open-ended.

ouvertement /uvɛʀtəmɑ̃/ *adv* openly; blatantly.

ouverture /uvɛʀtyʀ/ *nf* **1** opening; **heures d'~** opening hours; **2** openness; **~ d'esprit** open-mindedness; **~ à l'Ouest** opening-up to the West; **3** (Mus) overture.

ouvrable /uvʀabl/ *adj* [*day*] working; [*hours*] business.

ouvrage /uvʀaʒ/ *nm* **1** work; **2** book, work; **3** piece of work; **~ de broderie** piece of embroidery.

IDIOMS **avoir du cœur à l'~** to work with a will.

ouvre-boîtes /uvʀəbwat/ *nm inv* can-opener.

ouvreur, **-euse** /uvʀœʀ, øz/ *nm,f* usher/usherette.

ouvrier, **-ière** /uvʀije, ɛʀ/ **I** *adj* of the workers; **classe ouvrière** working class.

II *nm,f* worker; workman.

ouvrir /uvʀiʀ/ [32] **I** *vtr* (gen) to open; to undo [*collar, shirt, zip*]; to intitiate [*dialogue*]; to open up [*possibilities, market*]; **ne pas ~ la bouche** not to say a word; **~ les bras à qn** to welcome sb with open arms; **~ l'esprit à qn** to open sb's mind.

II *vi* **1** to open the door; **ouvre-moi!** let me in!; **2** to open; **3** to be opened.

III **s'ouvrir** *v refl* (+ *v être*) (gen) to open; [*shirt, dress*] to come undone; [*dialogue, process*] to be initiated; [*country, economy*] to open up; [*ground, scar*] to open up; [*person*] to cut open [*head*]; **s'~ les veines** to slash one's wrists; **s'~ à qn** to open one's heart to sb.

ovaire /ɔvɛʀ/ *nm* ovary.

ovale /ɔval/ *adj*, *nm* oval.

ovation /ɔvasjɔ̃/ *nf* **1** ovation; **2** accolade.

ovni /ɔvni/ *nm* (*abbr* = **objet volant non identifié**) unidentified flying object, UFO.

ovulation /ɔvylasjɔ̃/ *nf* ovulation.

ovule /ɔvyl/ *nm* **1** (Anat) ovum; **2** (Bot) ovule.

oxyde /ɔksid/ *nm* oxide; **~ de carbone** carbon monoxide.

oxyder /ɔkside/ [1] *vtr*, **s'oxyder** *v refl* (+ *v être*) to oxidize.

oxygène /ɔksiʒɛn/ *nm* **1** oxygen; **2** air.

oxygéner /ɔksiʒene/ [14] **I** *vtr* to oxygenate.

II **s'oxygéner** *v refl* (+ *v être*) [*person*] to get some fresh air.

ozone /ozon/ *nf* ozone; **la couche d'~** the ozone layer.

Pp

p, **P** /pe/ *nm inv* p, P.
pacha /paʃa/ *nm* pasha.
pacifier /pasifje/ [1] *vtr* to establish peace in.
pacifique /pasifik/ **I** *adj* peaceful.
II *nmf* peace-loving person.
Pacifique /pasifik/ *pr nm* **le ~** the Pacific.
pacifiste /pasifist/ *adj*, *nmf* pacifist.
pacotille /pakɔtij/ *nf* **de la ~** cheap rubbish.
pacte /pakt/ *nm* pact.
pagaie /pagɛ/ *nf* (Naut) paddle.
pagaille○ /pagɑj/ **I** *nf* mess; **semer la ~** to cause chaos.
II en pagaille *phr* in a mess.
page[1] /paʒ/ *nm* page (boy).
page[2] /paʒ/ *nf* page; **en première ~** on the front page; **tourner la ~** (figurative) to turn over a new leaf.
■ **~ de publicité** commercial break.
IDIOMS **être à la ~** to be up to date.
pagination /paʒinasjɔ̃/ *nf* pagination.
paginer /paʒine/ [1] *vtr* to paginate.
pagne /paɲ/ *nm* **1** loincloth; **2** grass skirt.
pagode /pagɔd/ *nf* pagoda.
paie /pɛ/ *nf* pay; **bulletin** or **fiche de ~** payslip.
IDIOMS **ça fait une ~ que je ne l'ai pas vu**○ it's ages○ since I've seen him.
paiement /pɛmɑ̃/ *nm* payment.
païen, **-ïenne** /pajɛ̃, ɛn/ *adj*, *nm,f* pagan.
paillard, **~e** /pajaʀ, aʀd/ *adj* bawdy.
paillasse /pajas/ *nf* **1** straw mattress; **2** lab bench; **3** draining board.
paillasson /pajasɔ̃/ *nm* doormat.
paille /pɑj/ **I** *adj inv* **jaune ~** straw yellow.
II *nf* straw; **~ de fer** steel wool.
IDIOMS **être sur la ~**○ to be penniless; **tirer à la courte ~** to draw lots.
paillette /pajɛt/ *nf* **1** sequin, spangle (US); **robe à ~s** sequined or spangled (US) dress; **2** glitter; **3 savon en ~s** soap flakes.
pain /pɛ̃/ *nm* **1** bread; **des miettes de ~** breadcrumbs; **2** loaf; **un petit ~** a (bread) roll; **3 ~ de viande** meat loaf; **4** (of soap) bar.
■ **~ blanc** white bread; **~ de campagne** farmhouse bread; **~ complet** wholemeal bread; **~ d'épices** gingerbread; **~ grillé** toast; **~ au lait** milk roll; **~ de mie** sandwich loaf; **~ de seigle** rye bread; **~ de son** bran loaf.
IDIOMS **se vendre comme des petits ~s** to sell like hot cakes; **ça ne mange pas de ~**○ it doesn't cost anything; **je ne mange pas de ce ~-là**○ I won't have anything to do with it.
pair, **~e**[1] /pɛʀ/ **I** *adj* [*number*] even.
II *nm* **1** peer; **c'est une cuisinière hors ~** she's an excellent cook; **2 aller** or **marcher de ~ avec qch** to go hand in hand with sth.
III au pair *phr* **travailler au ~** to work as an au pair.
paire[2] /pɛʀ/ *nf* pair; **donner une ~ de gifles à qn** to box sb's ears.
IDIOMS **les deux font la ~!** they're two of a kind!
paisible /pɛzibl/ *adj* peaceful, quiet, calm.
paisiblement /pɛzibləmɑ̃/ *adv* peacefully.
paître /pɛtʀ/ [74] *vi* to graze.
IDIOMS **envoyer ~ qn**○ to send sb packing○.
paix /pɛ/ *nf inv* peace; **avoir la ~** to get some peace; **laisser qn en ~** to leave sb alone; **la ~**○**!** be quiet!
palabrer /palabʀe/ [1] *vi* to discuss endlessly.
palace /palas/ *nm* luxury hotel.
palais /palɛ/ *nm inv* **1** palate; **2** palace; **3** (Law) **~ (de justice)** law courts .
■ **~ des sports** sports centre[GB].
pale /pal/ *nf* (of propeller, oar) blade.
pâle /pɑl/ *adj* pale; **vert ~** pale green.
IDIOMS **faire ~ figure à côté de** to pale into insignificance beside.
palefrenier, **-ière** /palfʀənje, ɛʀ/ *nm,f* groom.
paléontologie /paleɔ̃tɔlɔʒi/ *nf* paleontology.
palet /palɛ/ *nm* **1** (in ice hockey) puck; **2** quoit.
palette /palɛt/ *nf* **1** palette; **2** range; **une ~ d'activités** a range of activities; **3** (of pork, mutton) ≈ shoulder.
pâleur /pɑlœʀ/ *nf* paleness; pallor.
palier /palje/ *nm* **1** landing; **mon voisin de ~** my neighbour[GB] on the same floor; **2** level; plateau; **3** (in diving) **~ (de décompression)** (decompression) stage.
palière /paljɛʀ/ *adj f* **porte ~** entry door.
pâlir /pɑliʀ/ [3] *vi* **1** to fade; **2** to grow pale.
palissade /palisad/ *nf* fence.
palliatif /paljatif/ *nm* palliative.
pallier /palje/ [2] *vtr* to compensate for.
palmarès /palmaʀɛs/ *nm inv* **1** honours[GB] list; list of (award) winners; **2** record of achievements; **3** hit parade; **4** bestsellers list.
palme /palm/ *nf* **1** palm leaf; **2** palm (tree); **3** (for diver) flipper; **4** (Mil) ≈ bar; **5** prize.
palmé, **~e** /palme/ *adj* **1** [*feet*] webbed; **2** [*leaf*] palmate.
palmier /palmje/ *nm* palm (tree).
palombe /palɔ̃b/ *nf* wood pigeon.
palourde /paluʀd/ *nf* clam.
palper /palpe/ [1] *vtr* **1** (Med) to palpate; **2** to feel.
palpitant, **~e** /palpitɑ̃, ɑ̃t/ *adj* thrilling.
palpitation /palpitasjɔ̃/ *nf* **1** (Med) palpitation; **2** twitching.
palpiter /palpite/ [1] *vi* [*heart*] to beat; to flutter; [*vein*] to pulse.
paludisme /palydism/ *nm* malaria.

pâmer†: **se pâmer** /pɑme/ [1] *v refl* (+ *v être*) **se ~ devant qch** to swoon over sth.
pamphlet /pɑ̃flɛ/ *nm* satirical tract.
pamphlétaire /pɑ̃fletɛʀ/ *nmf* pamphleteer.
pamplemousse /pɑ̃pləmus/ *nm* grapefruit.
pan /pɑ̃/ **I** *nm* **1** (of cliff, house) section; (of life) part; **2** (of tower) side; **~s d'un manteau** coat-tails.
II *excl* (*also onomatopoeic*) bang!; thump!; whack!
pan- /pɑ̃, pan/ *pref* Pan; **~-russe** Pan-Russian; **~-européen** Pan-European.
panacée /panase/ *nf* panacea.
panache /panaʃ/ *nm* **1** panache; **2** plume.
panaché, **~e** /panaʃe/ **I** *adj* [*bouquet, salad*] mixed; [*tulip, ivy*] variegated.
II *nm* shandy (GB), shandygaff (US).
panacher /panaʃe/ [1] *vtr* to mix.
panaris /panaʀi/ *nm inv* whitlow.
pancarte /pɑ̃kaʀt/ *nf* **1** notice (GB), sign (US); **2** placard (GB), sign (US).
pancréas /pɑ̃kʀeas/ *nm inv* pancreas.
panda /pɑ̃da/ *nm* panda.
paner /pane/ [1] *vtr* to coat with breadcrumbs.
panier /panje/ *nm* **1** basket; **2** (in dishwasher) rack; **3** (Sport) basket.
■ **~ à linge** linen basket; **~ à salade** salad shaker; Black Maria (GB), paddy wagon (US).
IDIOMS **être un ~ percé**○ to spend money like water; **ils sont tous à mettre dans le même ~**○ they are all about the same; **le dessus du ~**○ the pick of the bunch; **mettre au ~** to throw [sth] out; to get rid of [sth].
panique /panik/ *nf* panic; **semer** or **jeter la ~** to spread panic; **être pris de ~** to be panic-stricken.
paniquer○ /panike/ [1] *vi* to panic.
panne /pan/ *nf* (of vehicle, machine) breakdown; (of engine) failure; **~ de courant** power failure; **tomber en ~ sèche** or **d'essence** to run out of petrol (GB) or gas (US); **être en ~ de**○ to be out of [*coffee*]; to have run out of [*ideas*].
panneau, *pl* **~x** /pano/ *nm* **1** sign; board; **2** notice board; **3** panel.
■ **~ indicateur** signpost; **~ publicitaire** hoarding (GB), billboard; **~ de signalisation routière** road sign; **~ solaire** solar panel.
IDIOMS **tomber dans le ~**○ to fall for it○.
panoplie /panɔpli/ *nf* **1** outfit; **2** display of weapons.
panorama /panɔʀama/ *nm* **1** panorama; **2** (of art, culture) survey.
panoramique /panɔʀamik/ *adj* **1** [*view, visit*] panoramic; **2** [*windscreen*] wrap-around; **3** [*screen*] wide.
panse /pɑ̃s/ *nf* **1** (of cow) paunch; **2**○ belly○; **3** (of jug) belly.
pansement /pɑ̃smɑ̃/ *nm* dressing; **~ (adhésif)** plaster (GB), Band-Aid®.
panser /pɑ̃se/ [1] *vtr* to dress [*wound*]; to put a dressing on [*arm, leg*].
pantalon /pɑ̃talɔ̃/ *nm* trousers (GB), pants (US); **~ de pyjama** pyjama (GB) or pajama (US) bottoms.
panthère /pɑ̃tɛʀ/ *nf* panther.
pantin /pɑ̃tɛ̃/ *nm* puppet.
pantois, **~e** /pɑ̃twa, az/ *adj* flabbergasted.
pantomime /pɑ̃tɔmim/ *nf* **1** mime; **2** mime show.
pantoufle /pɑ̃tufl/ *nf* slipper.
panure /panyʀ/ *nf* breadcrumbs.
paon /pɑ̃/ *nm* peacock.
paonne /pan/ *nf* peahen.
papa /papa/ *nm* dad○, daddy○, father; **fils** or **fille à ~** spoiled little rich kid○.
pape /pap/ *nm* **1** pope; **2** (figurative) high priest.
paperasse○ /papʀas/ *nf* **1** bumph○ (GB), documents; **2** paperwork.
papeterie /papɛtʀi/ *nf* **1** stationer's (shop), stationery shop (GB) or store (US); **2** stationery; **3** papermaking industry; **4** paper mill.
papi○ /papi/ *nm* granddad○, grandpa○.
papier /papje/ *nm* **1** paper; **2 ~s (d'identité)** (identity) papers or documents; **3**○ (newspaper) article, piece○.
■ **~ alu**○, **~ (d')aluminium** aluminium (GB) or aluminum (US) foil, kitchen foil; **~ brouillon** rough paper (GB), scrap paper; **~ cadeau** gift wrap; **~ d'emballage** wrapping paper; **~ hygiénique** toilet paper; **~ journal** newsprint; **~ à lettres** writing paper; **~ peint** wallpaper; **~ de verre** sandpaper; **~s gras** litter.
IDIOMS **être dans les petits ~s de qn**○ to be in sb's good books; ▶ **musique**.
papier-calque, *pl* **papiers-calque** /papjekalk/ *nm* tracing paper.
papillon /papijɔ̃/ *nm* **1** butterfly; **~ de nuit** moth; **2 (brasse) ~** butterfly (stroke).
papillonner /papijɔne/ [1] *vi* **1** to flit about; **2** to flirt incessantly.
papillote /papijɔt/ *nf* **1** (Culin) foil parcel; **2** (for hair) curlpaper.
papoter○ /papɔte/ [1] *vi* to chatter.
paprika /papʀika/ *nm* paprika.
papy = **papi**.
Pâque /pɑk/ *nf* **la ~ juive** Passover.
paquebot /pakbo/ *nm* liner.
pâquerette /pɑkʀɛt/ *nf* daisy.
IDIOMS **être au ras des ~s**○ to be very basic.
Pâques /pɑk/ *nm, nf pl* Easter.
paquet /pakɛ/ *nm* **1** packet (GB), package (US); (of cigarettes, coffee) packet (GB), pack (US); **2** parcel; **3** (of clothes) bundle; **4**○ masses; **5**○ packet○ (GB), bundle○ (US).
■ **~ de muscles**○ muscleman.
IDIOMS **mettre le ~**○ to pull out all the stops.
par /paʀ/ **I** *prep* **1 elle est arrivée ~ la droite** she came from the right; **le peintre a terminé** or **fini ~ la cuisine** the painter did the kitchen last; **2 ~ le passé** in the past; **~ une belle journée d'été** on a beautiful summer's day; **ils sortent même ~ moins 40°** they go outdoors even when it's minus 40°; **3** per; **~ jour/an** a

day/year; **~ personne** per person; **4** by; **payer ~ carte de crédit** to pay by credit card; **être pris ~ son travail** to be taken up with one's work; **deux ~ deux** [*work*] in twos; [*walk*] two by two; **5** in; **~ étapes** in stages; **~ endroits** in places; **6 l'accident est arrivé ~ sa faute** it was his/her fault that the accident happened; **~ jalousie** out of jealousy; **7** through; **tu peux me faire passer le livre ~ ta sœur** you can get the book to me via your sister; **entre ~ le garage** come in through the garage.

II de par *phr* (formal) **1 voyager de ~ le monde** to travel all over the world; **2 de ~ leurs origines** by virtue of their origins.

parabole /paʀabɔl/ *nf* **1** parable; **2** parabola.

parachever /paʀaʃve/ [16] *vtr* **1** to complete; **2** to put the finishing touches to.

parachute /paʀaʃyt/ *nm* parachute.

parachuter /paʀaʃyte/ [1] *vtr* to parachute.

parachutisme /paʀaʃytism/ *nm* parachuting.

parachutiste /paʀaʃytist/ *nmf* **1** parachutist; **2** paratrooper.

parade /paʀad/ *nf* **1** (Mil) parade; **2** (in fencing) parry; **3** (by animal) display.

parader /paʀade/ [1] *vi* to strut about.

paradis /paʀadi/ *nm inv* **1** heaven; **2** paradise.
■ **~ terrestre** Garden of Eden.
IDIOMS **tu ne l'emporteras pas au ~**° you'll live to regret it.

paradisiaque /paʀadizjak/ *adj* heavenly.

paradoxal, **~e**, *mpl* **-aux** /paʀadɔksal, o/ *adj* paradoxical.

paradoxe /paʀadɔks/ *nm* paradox.

paraffine /paʀafin/ *nf* **1** paraffin (GB), kerosene (US); **2** paraffin wax.

parages /paʀaʒ/ *nm pl* neighbourhood[GB]; **elle est dans les ~** she is around somewhere.

paragraphe /paʀagʀaf/ *nm* paragraph.

paraître /paʀɛtʀ/ [73] **I** *vi* **1** to come out, to be published; **'à ~'** 'forthcoming titles'; **2** to appear, to seem, to look; **3** to appear; to show; **elle ne laisse rien ~ de ses sentiments** she doesn't let her feelings show at all; **~ en public** to appear in public; **~ à son avantage** to look one's best.

II *v impers* **il paraît qu'il a menti** apparently he lied; **oui, il paraît** so I hear.

parallèle[1] /paʀalɛl/ **I** *adj* **1** parallel; **2** [*market*] unofficial; [*medicine*] alternative.

II *nm* parallel.

parallèle[2] /paʀalɛl/ *nf* parallel line.

parallèlement /paʀalɛlmɑ̃/ *adv* **1 ~ à** parallel to; **2** at the same time.

paralyser /paʀalize/ [1] *vtr* **1** (Med) to paralyse[GB]; **2** to paralyse[GB] [sth]; to bring [sth] to a halt.

paralysie /paʀalizi/ *nf* paralysis.

paralytique /paʀalitik/ *adj*, *nmf* paralytic.

paramédical, **~e**, *mpl* **-aux** /paʀamedikal, o/ *adj* paramedical.

paramètre /paʀamɛtʀ/ *nm* parameter.

paranoïaque /paʀanɔjak/ *adj*, *nmf* paranoiac.

paranormal, **~e**, *mpl* **-aux** /paʀanɔʀmal, o/ *adj* paranormal.

parapente /paʀapɑ̃t/ *nm* **1** paraglider; **2** paragliding.

paraphe /paʀaf/ *nm* **1** initials; **2** signature.

paraphrase /paʀafʀɑz/ *nf* paraphrase.

paraplégique /paʀapleʒik/ *adj*, *nmf* paraplegic.

parapluie /paʀaplɥi/ *nm* umbrella.

parascolaire /paʀaskɔlɛʀ/ *adj* extracurricular.

parasitaire /paʀazitɛʀ/ *adj* parasitic(al).

parasite /paʀazit/ **I** *adj* [*organism*] parasitic(al); [*idea*] intrusive.

II *nm* **1** parasite; **2** (on TV, radio) **~s** interference.

parasol /paʀasɔl/ *nm* beach umbrella; sun umbrella.

paratonnerre /paʀatɔnɛʀ/ *nm* lightning rod.

paravent /paʀavɑ̃/ *nm* screen.

parc /paʀk/ *nm* **1** park; **2** playpen; **3** (for animals) pen; **4** (of facilities) (total) number; (of capital goods) stock; **~ automobile** fleet of cars; (nationwide) number of cars (on the road); **~ immobilier** housing stock.
■ **~ d'attractions** amusement or theme park; **~ de loisirs** theme park; **~ national** national park; **~ naturel** nature park.

parce: **parce que** /paʀs(ə)k(ə)/ *phr* because.

parcelle /paʀsɛl/ *nf* **1** plot (of land); **2 une ~ de bonheur** a bit of happiness.

parchemin /paʀʃəmɛ̃/ *nm* parchment.

par-ci /paʀsi/ *adv* **~ par-là** here and there.

parcimonie /paʀsimɔni/ *nf* parsimony.

parcmètre /paʀkmɛtʀ/ *nm* parking meter.

parcourir /paʀkuʀiʀ/ [26] *vtr* **1** to travel all over [*country*]; **~ la ville** to go all over town; **2** to cover [*distance*]; **3** to glance through [*letter*]; to scan [*horizon*].

parcours /paʀkuʀ/ *nm inv* **1** (of bus, traveller) route; (of river) course; **~ fléché** waymarked trail; **2** (Sport) course; **~ de golf** round of golf; **3** career; **son ~** (of artist) the development of his/her art; **incident de ~** hitch.

par-delà /paʀdəla/ *prep* beyond.

par-derrière /paʀdɛʀjɛʀ/ *adv* **1 passer ~** to go round (GB) or to the back; **ils m'ont attaqué ~** they attacked me from behind; **2 critiquer qn ~** to criticize sb behind his/her back.

par-dessous /paʀdəsu/ *prep*, *adv* underneath.

pardessus /paʀdəsy/ *nm inv* overcoat.

par-dessus /paʀdəsy/ **I** *adv* **1 pose ton sac dans un coin et mets ton manteau ~** put your bag in a corner and put your coat on top of it; **2 le mur n'est pas haut, passe ~** the wall isn't high, climb over it.

II *prep* **1 saute ~ le ruisseau** jump over the stream; **2 ce que j'aime ~ tout** what I like best of all.

par-devant /paʀdəvɑ̃/ *adv* **1 passer ~** to come round by the front; **2 il te fait des sourires ~ mais dit du mal de toi dans ton dos** he's all smiles to your face but says nasty things about you behind your back.

pardon /paʀdɔ̃/ *nm* **1** forgiveness; pardon; **je te demande ~** I'm sorry; **2 ~!** sorry!; **~ madame/monsieur, je cherche**... excuse me please, I'm looking for...

pardonner /paʀdɔne/ [1] **I** *vtr* to forgive; **pardonnez-moi, mais**... excuse me, but...
II *vi* **ne pas ~** [*illness, error*] to be fatal.

pare-balles /paʀbal/ *adj inv* bulletproof.

pare-brise /paʀbʀiz/ *nm inv* windscreen (GB), windshield (US).

pare-chocs /paʀʃɔk/ *nm inv* bumper.

pareil, **-eille** /paʀɛj/ **I** *adj* **1** similar; **c'est toujours ~ avec toi** it's always the same with you; **à nul autre ~** without equal; **2** such; **je n'ai jamais dit une chose pareille** I never said any such thing.
II *nm,f* equal; **d'un dynamisme sans ~** incredibly dynamic; **pour moi c'est du ~ au même**○ it makes no difference to me.
III○ *adv* **faire ~** to do the same.

parent, **~e** /paʀɑ̃, ɑ̃t/ **I** *adj* [*languages*] similar; **~ avec** [*person*] related to.
II *nm,f* **1** relative, relation; **2** (Zool) parent.
III *nm* **1** parent; **2 ~s** forebears.
■ **~ pauvre** poor relation.

parental, **~e**, *mpl* **-aux** /paʀɑ̃tal, o/ *adj* parental.

parenté /paʀɑ̃te/ *nf* **1** (between people) blood relationship; **2** (between stories) connection.

parenthèse /paʀɑ̃tɛz/ *nf* **1** bracket; **ouvrir une ~** (figurative) to digress; **entre ~s** (figurative) incidentally; **2** interlude.

parer /paʀe/ [1] **I** *vtr* **1** to ward off; **2** to protect; **3** to adorn; **4 ~ qn/qch de qch** to attribute sth to sb/sth.
II parer à *v+prep* **~ à toute éventualité** to be prepared for all contingencies; **~ au plus pressé** to deal with the most urgent matters first.

paresse /paʀɛs/ *nf* laziness.

paresser /paʀɛse/ [1] *vi* to laze (around).

paresseux, **-euse** /paʀɛsø, øz/ **I** *adj* lazy.
II *nm,f* lazy person.
III *nm* (Zool) sloth.

parfaire /paʀfɛʀ/ [10] *vtr* to complete [*education, works*]; to perfect [*technique*].

parfait, **~e** /paʀfɛ, ɛt/ **I** *adj* **1** perfect; **2** [*likeness*] exact; [*discretion*] absolute; **3** [*tourist*] archetypal; [*example*] classic.
II *nm* (in grammar) perfect.

parfaitement /paʀfɛtmɑ̃/ *adv* [*happy, capable*] perfectly; [*tolerate, accept*] fully.

parfois /paʀfwa/ *adv* sometimes.

parfum /paʀfœ̃/ *nm* **1** perfume; **2** (of flower, fruit) scent; (of bath salts) fragrance; (of wine) bouquet; (of coffee) aroma; **3** flavour[GB].
IDIOMS **mettre qn au ~**○ to put sb in the picture.

parfumé, **~e** /paʀfyme/ **I** *pp* ▶ **parfumer**.
II *pp adj* **1** [*flower*] sweet-scented; [*fruit, air*] fragrant; **2** [*handkerchief*] scented; **3 glace ~e au café** coffee-flavoured[GB] ice cream.

parfumer /paʀfyme/ [1] **I** *vtr* **1 les fleurs parfument la pièce** the room is fragrant with flowers; **2** to put scent on [*handkerchief*]; to put scent in [*bath*]; **3** to flavour[GB].
II se parfumer *v refl* (+ *v être*) **1** to wear perfume; **2** to put perfume on.

parfumerie /paʀfymʀi/ *nf* perfumery.

pari /paʀi/ *nm* **1** bet; **2** betting; **3** gamble.

parier /paʀje/ [2] *vtr* to bet; **il y a fort** or **gros à ~ que** it's a safe bet that; **je l'aurais parié!** I knew it!

Paris /paʀi/ *pr n* Paris.

parisien, **-ienne** /paʀizjɛ̃, ɛn/ *adj* Parisian, Paris.

parité /paʀite/ *nf* parity; **à ~** at parity.

parjure /paʀʒyʀ/ *nm* perjury.

parking /paʀkiŋ/ *nm* car park (GB), parking lot (US).

par-là /paʀla/ *adv* **par-ci ~** here and there.

parlant, **~e** /paʀlɑ̃, ɑ̃t/ *adj* **1** [*gesture*] eloquent; [*evidence, figure*] which speaks for itself; **2 le cinéma ~** the talkies○; **un film ~** a talking picture.

Parlement /paʀləmɑ̃/ *nm* Parliament.

parlementaire /paʀləmɑ̃tɛʀ/ **I** *adj* parliamentary.
II *nmf* **1** Member of Parliament; **2** negotiator.

parlementer /paʀləmɑ̃te/ [1] *vi* to negotiate.

parler /paʀle/ [1] **I** *vtr* **1** to speak; **~ (l')italien** to speak Italian; **2 ~ affaires/politique** to talk (about) business/politics.
II parler à *v+prep* **~ à qn** to talk or speak to sb.
III parler de *v+prep* **1 ~ de qn/qch** to talk about sb/sth; to mention sb/sth; **~ de tout et de rien, ~ de choses et d'autres** to talk about this and that; **les journaux en ont parlé** it was in the papers; **faire ~ de soi** to get oneself talked about; to make the news; **qui parle de vous expulser?** who said anything about throwing you out?; **ta promesse, parlons-en!** some promise!; **n'en parlons plus!** let's drop it; that's the end of it; **on m'a beaucoup parlé de vous** I've heard a lot about you; **2 ~ de** [*book, film*] to be about.
IV *vi* to talk, to speak; **parle plus fort** speak up, speak louder; **~ en connaissance de cause** to know what one is talking about; **une prime? tu parles**○! a bonus? you must be joking○!; **il s'écoute ~** he loves the sound of his own voice.
V se parler *v refl* (+ *v être*) **1** to talk or speak (to each other); **2** to be on speaking terms; **3** [*language, dialect*] to be spoken.
IDIOMS **trouver à qui ~** to meet one's match.

parloir /paʀlwaʀ/ *nm* (in school) visitors' room; (in prison) visiting room; (in convent) parlour[GB].

parme /paʀm/ *adj inv, nm* mauve.

Parmentier /paʀmɑ̃tje/ *pr n* **hachis ~** cottage pie, shepherd's pie.

parmi /paʀmi/ *prep* **1** among, amongst; **2 demain il sera ~ nous** he'll be with us tomorrow; **3 choisir ~ huit destinations** to choose from eight destinations.

parodie /paʀɔdi/ *nf* **1** parody; **2** mockery.

parodier /paʀɔdje/ [2] *vtr* to parody.

paroi /paʀwa/ *nf* **1** (of tunnel) side; (of cave) wall; (of tube, pipe) inner surface; **2** (of house) wall; **3 ~ rocheuse** rock face; **4** (Anat) wall.

paroisse /paʀwas/ *nf* parish.

paroissial, ~e, *mpl* **-iaux** /paʀwasjal, o/ *adj* parish.

parole /paʀɔl/ *nf* **1** speech; **avoir la ~ facile** to have the gift of the gab○; **2 laisser la ~ à qn** to let sb speak; **temps de ~** speaking time; **3** word; **~s en l'air** empty words; **une ~ blessante** a hurtful remark; **4** (promise) word; **donner sa ~** to give one's word; **~ d'honneur!** cross my heart!, I promise!; **ma ~!** (upon) my word!; **5** words; **c'est ~ d'évangile** it's gospel truth; **~s** words, lyrics; **film sans ~s** silent film.

parolier, -ière /paʀɔlje, ɛʀ/ *nm,f* **1** lyric writer; **2** librettist.

paroxysme /paʀɔksism/ *nm* (of pleasure) paroxysm; (of battle) climax; (of ridiculousness) height.

parquer /paʀke/ [1] *vtr* **1** to pen [*cattle*]; **2** to coop up [*people*]; **3** to park [*car*].

parquet /paʀkɛ/ *nm* **1** parquet (floor); **2** (Law) **le ~** ≈ the prosecution.

parrain /paʀɛ̃/ *nm* **1** godfather; **2** (of candidate) sponsor; (of organization) patron.

parrainer /paʀene/ [1] *vtr* **1** to be patron of [*organization*]; **2** to sponsor [*programme, race*].

parricide /paʀisid/ *nm* parricide.

parsemer /paʀsəme/ [16] *vtr* **une pelouse parsemée de fleurs** a lawn dotted with flowers.

part /paʀ/ **I** *nf* **1** (of cake) slice; (of meat, rice) helping; (of market, legacy) share; **avoir sa ~ de misères** to have one's (fair) share of misfortunes; **2** proportion; **une grande ~ de** a high proportion or large part of; **pour une bonne ~** to a large or great extent; **à ~ entière** [*member*] full; [*science*] in its own right; **3** share; **faire sa ~ de travail** to do one's share of the work; **prendre ~ à** to take part in; **il m'a fait ~ de ses projets** he told me about his plans; **4 de toute(s) ~(s)** from all sides; **de ~ et d'autre** on both sides, on either side; **de ~ en ~** [*pierce*] right or straight through; **5 pour ma/notre ~** for my/our part; **d'une ~..., d'autre ~...** on (the) one hand... on the other hand...; **prendre qch en mauvaise ~** to take sth badly.

II à part *phr* **1** [*file*] separately; **mettre qch à ~** to put sth to one side; **prendre qn à ~** to take sb aside; **une salle à ~** a separate room; **blague à ~** joking aside; **2 être un peu à ~** [*person*] to be out of the ordinary; **un cas à ~** a special case; **3** apart from; **à ~ ça** apart from that.

III de la part de *phr* **1 de la ~ de** [*write, act*] on behalf of; **2 de la ~ de qn** from sb; **donne-leur le bonjour de ma ~** say hello to them for me; **de leur ~, rien ne m'étonne** nothing they do surprises me.

IDIOMS **faire la ~ des choses** to put things in perspective.

partage /paʀtaʒ/ *nm* **1** dividing, sharing; **recevoir qch en ~** to be left sth (in a will); **2** distribution; **3** sharing, division; **régner sans ~** to reign absolutely; **une victoire sans ~** a total victory; **4** division, partition.

partagé, ~e /paʀtaʒe/ **I** *pp* ▶ **partager.**

II *pp adj* **1** [*opinion, unions*] divided; **2** [*reactions, feelings*] mixed; **3 être ~** to be torn; **4** [*grief*] shared; **les torts sont ~s** they are both to blame; **5** [*affection*] mutual.

partager /paʀtaʒe/ [13] **I** *vtr* **1** to share; **faire ~ qch à qn** to let sb share in sth; **il sait nous faire ~ ses émotions** he knows how to get his feelings across; **2** to divide [*country, room*]; **3** to divide [sth] (up), to split [*inheritance, work*].

II se partager *v refl* (+ *v être*) **1** to share [*money, work, responsibility*]; **2** to be divided, to be split; **3** [*costs, responsibility*] to be shared; [*cake*] to be cut (up).

partance /paʀtɑ̃s/ *nf* **en ~** about to take off; about to sail; about to leave; **être en ~ pour** or **vers** to be bound for.

partenaire /paʀtənɛʀ/ *nmf* partner; **qui était le ~ d'Arletty?** who played opposite Arletty?

partenariat /paʀtənaʀja/ *nm* partnership.

parterre /paʀtɛʀ/ *nm* **1** (in garden) bed; **2** stalls (GB), orchestra (US).

parti, ~e[1] /paʀti/ **I**○ *adj* **être ~** to be tight○.

II *nm* **1** group; party; **les ~s de l'opposition** the opposition parties; **2** option; **prendre ~** to commit oneself; **prendre le ~ de qn** to side with sb; **3**† **bon ~** suitable match.

■ **~ pris** bias.

IDIOMS **prendre son ~ de qch** to come to terms with sth; **tirer ~ de** to take advantage of [sth]; to turn [sth] to good account.

partial, ~e, *mpl* **-iaux** /paʀsjal, o/ *adj* biased[GB].

partialité /paʀsjalite/ *nf* bias.

participant, ~e /paʀtisipɑ̃, ɑ̃t/ *nm,f* participant.

participation /paʀtisipasjɔ̃/ *nf* **1** participation; involvement; **2** contribution; **~ aux frais** (financial) contribution.

participe /paʀtisip/ *nm* participle; **~ passé** past participle.

participer /paʀtisipe/ [1] *v+prep* **1 ~ à** to participate in, to take part in; to be involved in; **2 ~ à** to contribute to.

particularité /paʀtikylaʀite/ *nf* **1** special feature; **2** (of disease, situation) particular nature.

particule /paʀtikyl/ *nf* particle; **nom à ~** aristocratic name.

particulier, -ière /paʀtikylje, ɛʀ/ **I** *adj* **1** particular; **2** [*rights, privileges, role*] special; [*example, objective*] specific; **3** [*car, secretary*] private; **4** [*case, situation*] unusual; [*talent, effort*] special; [*habits*] odd; [*accent, style*] distinctive, unusual; **c'est quelqu'un de très ~** he's/she's somebody out of the ordinary; he's/she's weird.

II en particulier *phr* **1** in private; **2** individually; **3** in particular, particularly.

III *nm* **(simple) ~** private individual.

particulièrement /paʀtikyljɛʀmɑ̃/ *adv* **1** particularly, exceptionally; **2** in particular.

partie[2] /paʀti/ **I** *adj f* ▶ **parti I**.

II *nf* **1** part; (of amount, salary) proportion, part; **la majeure ~ des gens** most people; **en ~** partly, in part; **faire ~ des premiers** to be among the first; **cela fait ~ de leurs avantages** that's one of their advantages; **2** line (of work); **il est de la ~** it's in his line (of work); **3** game; **faire une ~** to have a game; **gagner la ~** to win the game; (figurative) to win the day; **j'espère que tu seras de la ~** I hope you can come; **ce n'est que ~ remise** maybe next time; **4** (in contract, negotiations) party; **les ~s en présence** the parties involved; **être ~ prenante dans** to be actively involved in; **5** (Mus) part.

■ **~ civile** plaintiff; **~ de pêche** fishing trip; **~ de plaisir** fun.

IDIOMS **avoir affaire à forte ~** to have a tough opponent; **prendre qn à ~** to take sb to task.

partiel, -ielle /paʀsjɛl/ *adj* [*payment*] part; [*destruction, agreement*] partial.

partir /paʀtiʀ/ [30] **I** *vi* (+ *v être*) **1** to leave, to go; **~ à pied** to leave on foot; **~ en courant** to run off; **~ sans laisser d'adresse** to disappear without trace; **~ loin/à Paris** to go far away/to Paris; **~ en week-end** to go away for the weekend; **~ à la pêche** to go fishing; **~ en tournée** to set off on tour (GB) or on a tour; **~ en retraite** to retire; **2** [*vehicle, train*] to leave; [*plane*] to take off; [*motor*] to start; **les coureurs sont partis** the runners are off; **à vos marques, prêts, partez!** on your marks, get set, go!; **3** [*bullet*] to be fired; [*cork*] to shoot out; [*capsule*] to shoot off; [*retort*] to slip out; **le coup de feu est parti** the gun went off; **il était tellement énervé que la gifle est partie toute seule** he was so angry that he slapped him/her before he could stop himself; **4** [*path, road*] to start; **~ favori** to start favourite[GB]; **~ battu d'avance** to be doomed from the start; **~ de rien** to start from nothing; **c'est parti!** go!; **et voilà, c'est parti, il pleut**○**!** here we go, it's raining!; **être bien parti** to have got (GB) or gotten (US) off to a good start; **être bien parti pour gagner** to seem all set to win; **c'est mal parti**○ things don't look too good; **5 ~ de** to start from [*idea*]; **~ du principe que** to work on the assumption that; **~ d'une bonne intention** to be well-meant; **6** [*stain*] to come out; [*smell*] to go; [*enamel, button*] to come off; **7** [*parcel, application*] to be sent (off); **8 quand il est parti on ne l'arrête plus**○ once he starts or gets going there's no stopping him.

II à partir de *phr* from; **à ~ de 16 heures/de 2000 francs** from 4 o'clock onwards/2,000 francs; **à ~ du moment où** as soon as; as long as; **fabriqué à ~ d'un alliage** made from an alloy.

partisan, ~e /paʀtizɑ̃, an/ **I** *adj* **1** partisan; **2 ~ de qch/de faire** in favour[GB] of sth/of doing; **être ~ du moindre effort**○ to be lazy.

II *nm,f* (gen) supporter, partisan; (Mil) partisan.

partition /paʀtisjɔ̃/ *nf* (Mus) score.

partout /paʀtu/ *adv* **1** everywhere; **avoir mal ~** to ache all over; **un peu ~ dans le monde** more or less all over the world; **~ où je vais** wherever I go; **2** (Sport) **trois (points** or **buts) ~** three all.

IDIOMS **fourrer son nez ~**○ to stick one's nose into everything○.

parure /paʀyʀ/ *nf* **1** finery; **2** set of jewels.

parution /paʀysjɔ̃/ *nf* publication.

parvenir /paʀvəniʀ/ [36] *v+prep* (+ *v être*) **1 ~ à** to reach [*place, person*]; **faire ~ qch à qn** to send sth to sb; to get sth to sb; **2 ~ à** to reach [*agreement*]; to achieve [*balance*]; **3 ~ à faire** to manage to do.

parvenu, ~e /paʀvəny/ *nm,f* upstart.

parvis /paʀvi/ *nm inv* (of church) square.

pas[1] /pa/ *adv* **1 je ne prends ~ de sucre** I don't take sugar; **ils n'ont ~ le téléphone** they haven't got a phone; **je ne pense ~** I don't think so; **elle a aimé le film, mais lui ~** she liked the film but he didn't; **2** (in expressions, exclamations) **~ du tout** not at all; **~ le moins du monde** not in the least; **~ tant que ça, ~ plus que ça** not all that much; **~ d'histoires!** I don't want any arguments or fuss!; **~ de chance!** hard luck!; **~ possible!** I can't believe it!; **~ vrai**○**?** isn't that so?

pas[2] /pa/ *nm inv* **1** step; **marcher à ~ feutrés** to walk softly; **faire ses premiers ~** to take one's first steps; **faire le premier ~** to make the first move; **suivre qn ~ à ~** to follow sb everywhere; **de là à dire qu'il s'en fiche**○**, il n'y a qu'un ~** there's only a fine line between that and saying he doesn't care; **j'habite à deux ~ (d'ici)** I live very near here; **l'hiver arrive à grands ~** winter is fast approaching; **apprendre les ~ du tango** to learn how to tango; **2** pace; **marcher d'un bon ~** to walk at a brisk pace; **marcher au ~** to march; (on horseback) to walk; **'roulez au ~'** 'dead slow' (GB), '(very) slow' (US); **mettre qn au ~** to bring sb to heel; **partir au ~ de course** to rush off; **j'y vais de ce ~** I'm on my way now; **3** footstep; **4** footprint; **revenir sur ses ~** to retrace one's steps.

IDIOMS **se tirer d'un mauvais ~** to get out of a tight corner; **sauter le ~** to take the plunge; **prendre le ~ sur qch** to overtake sth.

pascal, ~e, *mpl* **~s** or **-aux** /paskal, o/ *adj* [*weekend*] Easter; [*candle, lamb*] paschal.

passable /pasabl/ *adj* **1** [*film*] fairly good; [*results*] reasonable; **2** (Sch) fair.

passablement /pasabləmɑ̃/ *adv* [*drunk, annoyed*] rather; [*drink, worry*] quite a lot.

passage /pasaʒ/ *nm* **1** traffic; **interdire le ~ des camions dans la ville** to ban trucks from (driving through) the town; **2** stay; **ton ~ dans la ville a été bref** your stay in the town was brief; **3 attendre le ~ du boulanger** to wait for the baker's van to come; **je peux te prendre au ~** I can pick you up on the way; **des hôtes de ~** short-stay guests; **se servir au ~** to help oneself; (figurative) to take a cut (of the profits); to pocket some of the profits; **4 '~ interdit, voie privée'** 'no entry, private

road'; **pour céder le ~ à l'ambulance** in order to let the ambulance go past; **5 chaque ~ de votre chanson à la radio** every time your song is played on the radio; **6** way, path; **prévoir le ~ de câbles** to plan the route of cables; **7 ~ (de qch) à qch** transition (from sth) to sth; **8** alley; passageway; **9** (in novel) passage; (in film) sequence.
■ **~ à l'acte** acting out; **~ à niveau** level crossing (GB), grade crossing (US); **~ pour piétons** pedestrian crossing; **~ à tabac** beating; **~ à vide** bad patch; unproductive period.

passager, -ère /pasaʒe, ɛʀ/ **I** *adj* [*situation, crisis*] temporary; [*feeling*] passing; [*shower*] brief; [*unease*] slight, short-lived.
II *nm,f* passenger; **~ clandestin** stowaway.

passant, ~e /pasɑ̃, ɑ̃t/ **I** *adj* [*street*] busy.
II *nm,f* passer-by.
III *nm* (on belt, watchstrap) loop.

passe[1]○ /pɑs/ *nm* **1** master key; **2** pass.

passe[2] /pɑs/ *nf* **1** (Sport) pass; **2 être dans une ~ difficile** to be going through a difficult patch; **être en ~ de faire** to be (well) on the way to doing.

passé, ~e /pɑse/ **I** *pp* ▶ **passer**.
II *pp adj* **1** [*years, experiences*] past; **~ de mode** dated; **2 l'année passée** last year; **3** [*colour, material*] faded.
III *nm* **1** past; **2** past (tense).
IV *prep* after; **~ 8 heures il s'endort dans son fauteuil** come eight o'clock he goes to sleep in his armchair.
■ **~ antérieur** past anterior; **~ composé** present perfect; **~ simple** past historic.

passe-montagne, *pl* **~s** /pasmɔ̃taɲ/ *nm* balaclava.

passe-partout /paspaʀtu/ *adj inv* [*expression*] catch-all; [*garment*] for all occasions.

passe-passe /paspas/ *nm inv* **tour de ~** conjuring trick; (figurative) sleight of hand.

passeport /paspɔʀ/ *nm* passport.

passer /pɑse/ [1] **I** *vtr* **1** to cross [*river, border*]; to go through [*door, customs*]; to get over [*hedge, obstacle*]; **il m'a fait ~ la frontière** he got me across the border; **~ qch à la douane** to get sth through customs; **2** to go past, to pass; **quand vous aurez passé le feu, tournez à droite** turn right after the lights; **le malade ne passera pas la nuit** the patient won't last the night; **3 ~ le doigt sur la table** to run one's finger over the table-top; **~ la tête à la fenêtre** to stick one's head out of the window; **4** to pass [*object*]; to pass [sth] on [*instructions, disease*]; **~ sa colère sur ses collègues** to take one's anger out on one's colleagues; **5** to lend; to give; **6** (on phone) **tu peux me ~ Chris?** can you put Chris on?; **je vous le passe** I'm putting you through; **7** to take, to sit [*examination*]; to have [*interview*]; **faire ~ un test à qn** to give sb a test; **8** to spend [*time*]; **dépêche-toi, on ne va pas y ~ la nuit**○! hurry up, or we'll be here all night!; **9 elle leur passe tout** she lets them get away with murder; **10** to skip [*page, paragraph*]; **je vous passe les détails** I'll spare you the details; **11 ~ l'aspirateur** to vacuum; **12** to filter [*coffee*]; to strain [*fruit juice, sauce*]; to purée [*vegetables*]; **13** to slip [sth] on [*garment, ring*]; to slip into [*dress*]; **14** to play [*record, cassette*]; to show [*film, slides*]; to place [*ad*]; **15** to enter into [*agreement*]; to place [*order*]; **16** (Aut) **~ la troisième** to go into third gear; **17** (Games) **~ son tour** to pass.
II *vi* (+ *v être*) **1** to go past or by, to pass; **~ sur un pont** to go over a bridge; **le facteur n'est pas encore passé** the postman hasn't come yet; **~ à côté de** [*person*] to pass; [*road*] to run alongside; **~ à pied/à bicyclette** to walk/cycle past; **2 je ne fais que ~** I've just popped in (GB) or dropped by for a minute; **~ dans la matinée** [*plumber*] to come by in the morning; **~ prendre qn/qch** to pick sb/sth up; **3** to go; **passons au salon** let's go into the lounge; **les contrebandiers sont passés en Espagne** the smugglers have crossed into Spain; **4** to get through; **tu ne passeras pas, c'est trop étroit** you'll never get through, it's too narrow; **il m'a fait signe de ~** he waved me on; **vas-y, ça passe!** go on, there's plenty of room!; **~ par-dessus bord** to fall overboard; **il est passé par la fenêtre** he fell out of the window; he got in through the window; **5 ~ par** to go through; **~ par l'opératrice** to go through the operator; **je ne sais jamais ce qui te passe par la tête** I never know what's going on in your head; **6**○ **il accuse le patron, ses collègues, bref, tout le monde y passe** he's accusing the boss, his colleagues—basically, everyone in sight; **que ça te plaise ou non, il va falloir y ~** whether you like it or not, there's no alternative; **on ne peut pas faire autrement que d'en ~ par là** there is no other way around it; **7 ~ sur** to pass over [*question, mistake*]; **~ à côté d'une question** to miss the point; **laisser ~ une occasion** to miss an opportunity; **8 soit dit en ~** incidentally; **9** [*comments, speech*] to go down well; [*law, measure, candidate*] to get through; [*attitude, doctrine*] to be accepted; **j'ai mangé quelque chose qui n'est pas passé** I ate something which didn't agree with me; **que je sois critiqué, passe encore, mais calomnié, non!** criticism is one thing, but I draw the line at slander; **~ au premier tour** to be elected in the first round; **~ dans la classe supérieure** to move up to the next year; **(ça) passe pour cette fois**○ I'll let it go this time; **10 ~ à l'ennemi** to go over to the enemy; **~ de main en main** to be passed around; **~ constamment d'un sujet à l'autre** to flit from one subject to another; **~ à un taux supérieur** to go up to a higher rate; **11 ~ pour un imbécile** to look a fool; **~ pour un génie** to pass as a genius; **il passe pour l'inventeur de l'ordinateur** he's supposed to have invented computers; **il se fait ~ pour mon frère** he passes himself off as my brother; **12** [*pain, crisis*] to pass; **quand l'orage sera** or **aura passé** when the storm is over; **ça passera** [*bad mood*] it'll pass; [*hurt*] you'll get over it; **~ de mode** to go out of fashion; **faire ~ à qn l'envie de faire** to

cure sb of the desire to do; **ce médicament fait ~ les maux d'estomac** this medicine relieves stomach ache; **13** [*performer, group*] (on stage) to be appearing; (on TV, radio) to be on; [*show, film*] to be on; [*music*] to be playing; **14 ~ avant/après** to come before/after; **il fait ~ sa famille avant ses amis** he puts his family before his friends; **15**○ **où étais-tu passé?** where did you get to?; **où est passé mon livre?** where has my book got to?; **16** [*time*] to pass, to go by; **je ne vois pas le temps ~** I don't know where the time goes; **17** to turn to; **~ à l'étape suivante** to move on to the next stage; **nous allons ~ au vote** let's vote now; **18 ~ de père en fils** to be handed down from father to son; **l'expression est passée dans la langue** the expression has become part of the language; **19** to be promoted to; **elle est passée maître dans l'art de mentir** she's an accomplished liar; **20** [*money, amount*] to go on or into; [*product, material*] to go into; **21**○ **y ~** to die; **22** [*colour, material*] to fade; **23** [*coffee*] to filter; **24 ~ en marche arrière** to go into reverse; **la troisième passe mal** third gear is a bit stiff; **25** (in bridge, poker) to pass.

III se passer *v refl* (+ *v être*) **1** to happen; **tout s'est passé très vite** it all happened very fast; **tout se passe comme si le yen avait été dévalué** it's as if the yen had been devalued; **2** to take place; **la scène se passe au Viêt Nam** the scene is set in Vietnam; **3** [*examination, negotiations*] to go; **ça ne se passera pas comme ça!** I won't leave it at that!; **4** [*period*] to go by, to pass; **deux ans se sont passés depuis** that was two years ago; **5 se~ de** to do without [*object, activity, person*]; to go without [*meal, sleep*]; **se ~ de commentaires** to speak for itself; **6 se ~ la langue sur les lèvres** to run one's tongue over one's lips; **se ~ la main sur le front** to put a hand to one's forehead; **7 ils se sont passé des documents** they exchanged some documents.

IDIOMS **qu'est-ce qu'elle nous a passé**○**!** she really went for us○!

passerelle /pasʀɛl/ *nf* **1** footbridge; **2** link; **3** (to boat) gangway; (to plane) steps.

passe-temps /pastɑ̃/ *nm inv* pastime, hobby.

passeur, **-euse** /pasœʀ, øz/ *nm,f* **1** ferryman/ferrywoman; **2** smuggler; (for drugs) courier.

passible /pasibl/ *adj* (Law) **~ de** [*crime*] punishable by; [*person*] liable to.

passif, **-ive** /pasif, iv/ **I** *adj* passive.

II *nm* **1** passive (voice); **2** debit; **mettre qch au ~ de qn** to count sth amongst sb's failures.

passion /pasjɔ̃/ *nf* passion.

passionnant, **~e** /pasjɔnɑ̃, ɑ̃t/ *adj* exciting, fascinating, riveting.

passionné, **~e** /pasjɔne/ **I** *adj* [*love*] passionate; [*debate, argument*] impassioned; **être ~ de** or **pour qch** to have a passion for sth.

II *nm,f* enthusiast.

passionnel, **-elle** /pasjɔnɛl/ *adj* [*debate*] passionate; [*crime*] of passion.

passionner /pasjɔne/ [1] **I** *vtr* **1** to fascinate; **la botanique le passionne** he has a passion for botany; **2** to inflame [*debate*].

II se passionner *v refl* (+ *v être*) to have a passion (**pour** for).

passivité /pasivite/ *nf* passivity.

passoire /paswaʀ/ *nf* **1** colander; **2** strainer.

pastel /pastɛl/ **I** *adj inv* [*shade*] pastel.

II *nm* pastel.

pastèque /pastɛk/ *nf* watermelon.

pasteur /pastœʀ/ *nm* **1** minister, pastor; **2** priest; **3** shepherd.

pasteuriser /pastœʀize/ [1] *vtr* to pasteurize.

pastiche /pastiʃ/ *nm* pastiche.

pastille /pastij/ *nf* **1** pastille, lozenge; **~ contre la toux** cough drop; **2 ~ de menthe** peppermint; **3** spot; **4** (of cloth, rubber) patch; (of plastic) disc.

pastoral, **~e**[1], *mpl* **-aux** /pastɔʀal, o/ *adj* pastoral.

pastorale[2] /pastɔʀal/ *nf* (Mus) pastoral.

patate○ /patat/ *nf* **1** spud○; **~ douce** sweet potato; **2** blockhead○, idiot.

patati○ /patati/ *excl* **~, patata** and so on and so forth.

pataud, **~e** /pato, od/ *adj* clumsy.

patauger /patoʒe/ [13] *vi* **1** to splash about; to paddle; **2** to flounder.

pâte /pɑt/ **I** *nf* **1** pastry; dough; batter; **2** paste.

II pâtes *nf pl* **~s (alimentaires)** pasta.

■ **~ d'amandes** marzipan; **~s de fruit(s)** fruit jellies; **~ à modeler** Plasticine®; **~ à tartiner** spread.

IDIOMS **mettre la main à la ~** to pitch in.

pâté /pɑte/ *nm* **1** pâté; **2** pie; **~ en croûte** ≈ pie; **3 ~ de maisons** block (of houses); **4** (ink)blot; **5** sandcastle.

pâtée /pɑte/ *nf* dog food; cat food; swill.

patelin○ /patlɛ̃/ *nm* small village.

patente /patɑ̃t/ *nf*: *licence*[GB] *to exercise a trade or profession*.

patère /patɛʀ/ *nf* peg, hook.

paternel, **-elle** /patɛʀnɛl/ *adj* **1** paternal; **2** fatherly.

paternité /patɛʀnite/ *nf* **1** fatherhood; (Law) paternity; **2** authorship.

pâteux, **-euse** /pɑtø, øz/ *adj* **1** [*substance*] doughy; [*gruel*] mushy; **2** [*voice*] thick.

pathétique /patetik/ *adj* moving.

pathologique /patɔlɔʒik/ *adj* pathological.

patiemment /pasjamɑ̃/ *adv* patiently.

patience /pasjɑ̃s/ *nf* patience.

IDIOMS **prendre son mal en ~** to resign oneself to one's fate.

patient, **~e** /pasjɑ̃, ɑ̃t/ *adj, nm,f* patient.

patienter /pasjɑ̃te/ [1] *vi* to wait.

patin /patɛ̃/ *nm* **1** skate; **2** (Tech) (on helicopter) skid; (on sledge) runner.

■ **~ à glace** ice skate; ice-skating; **~ à roulettes** roller skate; roller-skating.

patinage /patinaʒ/ *nm* skating.

patine /patin/ *nf* patina; finish, sheen.

patiner /patine/ [1] **I** *vtr* to apply a finish to.

II *vi* **1** to skate; **2** (Aut) [*wheel*] to spin; [*clutch*] to slip; **faire ~ l'embrayage** to slip the clutch.
III se patiner *v refl* (+ *v être*) to acquire a patina.

patineur, **-euse** /patinœʀ, øz/ *nm,f* skater.

patinoire /patinwaʀ/ *nf* ice rink.

pâtir /pɑtiʀ/ [3] *vi* **~ de** to suffer as a result of.

pâtisserie /pɑtisʀi/ *nf* **1** cake shop, pâtisserie; **2** pastry, cake.

pâtissier, **-ière** /pɑtisje, ɛʀ/ *nm,f* confectioner, pastry cook.

patois /patwa/ *nm inv* patois, dialect.

patraque○ /patʀak/ *adj* **être ~** to be under the weather○.

patriarche /patʀijaʀʃ/ *nm* patriarch.

patrie /patʀi/ *nf* homeland, country.

patrimoine /patʀimwan/ *nm* **1** (of person, family) patrimony; (of firm) capital; **2** heritage.
■ **~ génétique** gene pool.

patriote /patʀijɔt/ **I** *adj* patriotic.
II *nmf* patriot; **en ~** patriotically.

patriotisme /patʀijɔtism/ *nm* patriotism.

patron, **-onne** /patʀɔ̃, ɔn/ **I** *nm,f* boss○.
II *nm* (sewing) pattern.
■ **~ de pêche** skipper, master.

patronal, **~e**, *mpl* **-aux** /patʀɔnal, o/ *adj* [*organization*] employers'.

patronat /patʀɔna/ *nm* employers.

patronne ▸ **patron I**.

patronyme /patʀɔnim/ *nm* patronymic.

patrouille /patʀuj/ *nf* patrol.

patrouiller /patʀuje/ [1] *vi* to be on patrol.

patte /pat/ *nf* **1** leg; paw; foot; **donner la ~** to give its paw; **retomber sur ses ~s** to fall on its feet; **2**○ leg, foot; **tu es toujours dans mes ~s** you are always getting under my feet; **marcher à quatre ~s** to walk on all fours; to crawl; **traîner la ~** to limp; **3**○ hand; **bas les ~s**○! keep your hands to yourself!; hands off○!; **4** tab; (on shelving unit) lug; (on garment) flap; **5** sideburn.
■ **~s d'éléphant** flares; **~ folle**○ gammy leg (GB), game leg (US); **~s de mouche** spidery scrawl.
IDIOMS **faire ~ de velours** [*cat*] to draw in its claws; [person] to switch on the charm; **montrer ~ blanche** to prove one is acceptable; **se tirer dans les ~s** to pull dirty tricks on each other.

patte-d'oie, *pl* **pattes-d'oie** /patdwɑ/ *nf* **1** crow's-foot; **2** junction.

pâturage /pɑtyʀaʒ/ *nm* pasture.

pâture /pɑtyʀ/ *nf* **1** feed; **être jeté en ~** (figurative) to be thrown to the lions; **2** pasture.

paume /pom/ *nf* palm (of the hand).

paumé○, **~e** /pome/ *adj* **1** [*person*] mixed up (GB), out of it○ (US); **2** [*place*] godforsaken.

paumer○ /pome/ [1] **I** *vtr, vi* to lose.
II se paumer *v refl* (+ *v être*) to get lost.

paupière /popjɛʀ/ *nf* eyelid.

paupiette /popjɛt/ *nf* **~ de veau** stuffed escalope of veal.

pause /poz/ *nf* **1** break; **faire une ~** to take a break; **2** (in process) pause; **3** (Mus) rest.

pauvre /povʀ/ **I** *adj* **1** poor; **2** sparse; **~ en sucre** low in sugar; lacking sugar; **3 un ~ type**○ a poor guy○; a dead loss○.
II○ *nmf* **le/la ~!** poor man/woman!; poor thing!
III *nm* **un ~** a poor man; **~ d'esprit** half-wit.

pauvrement /povʀəmɑ̃/ *adv* poorly.

pauvreté /povʀəte/ *nf* **1** poverty; **2** shabbiness.

pavaner: **se pavaner** /pavane/ [1] *v refl* (+ *v être*) to strut (about).

pavé /pave/ *nm* cobblestone; **se retrouver sur le ~** to find oneself out on the street.
IDIOMS **lancer un ~ dans la mare** to set the cat among the pigeons; **tenir le haut du ~** to head the field.

paver /pave/ [1] *vtr* to lay [sth] with cobblestones.

pavillon /pavijɔ̃/ *nm* **1** (detached) house; **2** (for exhibition) pavilion; (of hospital) wing; **3** (of ear) auricle; **4** (of loudspeaker) horn; **5** (Naut) flag.

pavoiser○ /pavwaze/ [1] *vi* to crow.

pavot /pavo/ *nm* poppy.

payant, **~e** /pɛjɑ̃, ɑ̃t/ *adj* **1** [*person*] paying; **2** [*show*] not free; **3**○ lucrative, profitable.

paye /pɛj/ = **paie**.

payement /pɛjmɑ̃/ = **paiement**.

payer /peje/ [21] **I** *vtr* **1** to pay; to pay for; **il est payé pour le savoir!** he knows that to his cost!; **faire ~ qch à qn** to charge sb for sth; **~ qch à qn**○ to buy sb sth; **2** to pay for [*mistake, carelessness*].
II *vi* **1** [*efforts, sacrifice*] to pay off; [*profession, activity*] to pay; **2**○ to be funny.
III se payer *v refl* (+ *v être*) **1** [*service, goods*] to have to be paid for; **2**○ to treat oneself to [*holiday*]; to get [*cold, bad mark*]; to get landed with [*job*]; **se ~ un arbre** to crash into a tree.
IDIOMS **se ~ du bon temps**○ to have a good time; **se ~ la tête**○ **de qn** to take the mickey○ out of sb (GB), to razz○ sb (US).

pays /pei/ *nm* **1** country; **2 la Bourgogne est le ~ du bon vin** Burgundy is the home of good wine; **gens du ~** local people.
IDIOMS **voir du ~** to do some travelling[GB].

paysage /peizaʒ/ *nm* landscape, scenery.

paysager, **-ère** /peizaʒe, ɛʀ/ *adj* **1** environmental; **2** [*garden*] landscaped.

paysagiste /peizaʒist/ *nmf* **(jardinier) ~** landscape gardener.

paysan, **-anne** /peizɑ̃, an/ **I** *adj* [*life*] rural; [*ways*] peasant; [*soup, bread*] country.
II *nm,f* **1** ≈ small farmer; **2** (derogatory) peasant.

Pays-Bas /peibɑ/ *pr nm pl* **les ~** The Netherlands.

PC /pese/ *nm* **1** (Pol) (*abbr* = **parti communiste**) CP, Communist Party; **2** (*abbr* = **personal computer**) PC.

PCV /peseve/ *nm* (*abbr* = **paiement contre vérification**) reverse charge call (GB), collect call (US).

PDG /pedeʒe/ *nm* (*abbr* = **président-directeur général**) chief executive officer.

péage /peaʒ/ *nm* **1** toll; **2** tollbooth.

peau, *pl* **~x** /po/ *nf* **1** skin; **n'avoir que la ~ sur les os** to be all skin and bone; **2** leather; **gants de ~** leather gloves; **3** peel; **4**○ life; **risquer sa ~** to risk one's life; **faire la ~ à qn** to kill sb; **vouloir la ~ de qn** to want sb dead.

IDIOMS **être bien dans sa ~**○ to feel good about oneself; **avoir qn dans la ~**○ to be crazy about sb; **prendre une balle dans la ~**○ to be shot.

peaufiner /pofine/ [1] *vtr* to put the finishing touches to [*work, text*].

pêche /pɛʃ/ *nf* **1** peach; **2** fishing; **aller à la ~** to go fishing; **3**○ clout○; **4**○ **avoir la ~** to be feeling great.

■ **~ à la ligne** angling.

péché /peʃe/ *nm* sin; **ce serait un ~ de rater ça**○ it would be a crime to miss that; **le chocolat, c'est mon ~ mignon** I've got a weakness for chocolate.

pécher /peʃe/ [14] *vi* to sin; **~ par excès de confiance** to be overconfident; **le roman pèche sur un point** the novel has one shortcoming.

pêcher[1] /pɛʃe/ [1] **I** *vtr* to go fishing for.

II *vi* to fish; **~ à la mouche** to fly-fish; **~ à la ligne** to angle.

pêcher[2] /pɛʃe/ *nm* peach tree.

pécheresse /peʃʀɛs/ *nf* sinner.

pécheur /peʃœʀ/ *nm* sinner.

pêcheur /pɛʃœʀ/ *nm* fisherman.

pectoral, *pl* **-aux** /pɛktɔʀal, o/ *nm* pectoral muscle.

pécule /pekyl/ *nm* savings, nest egg○.

pécuniaire /pekynjɛʀ/ *adj* financial.

pédagogie /pedagɔʒi/ *nf* **1** education, pedagogy; **2** teaching skills; **3** teaching method.

pédagogique /pedagɔʒik/ *adj* [*activity*] educational; [*system*] education; [*method*] teaching.

pédagogue /pedagɔg/ *nmf* educationalist.

pédale /pedal/ *nf* pedal.

IDIOMS **perdre les ~s**○ to lose one's grip.

pédaler /pedale/ [1] *vi* to pedal.

pédalier /pedalje/ *nm* (of bicycle) chain transmission; (of piano) pedals.

pédalo® /pedalo/ *nm* pedalo (GB), pedal boat.

pédant, **~e** /pedɑ̃, ɑ̃t/ *adj* pedantic.

pédérastie /pedeʀasti/ *nf* **1** pederasty; **2** homosexuality.

pédestre /pedɛstʀ/ *adj* **randonnée ~** ramble.

pédiatre /pedjatʀ/ *nmf* paediatrician.

pédiatrie /pedjatʀi/ *nf* paediatrics.

pédicure /pedikyʀ/ *nmf* chiropodist (GB), podiatrist (US).

pedigree /pedigʀe/ *nm* pedigree.

pègre /pɛgʀ/ *nf* underworld.

peigne /pɛɲ/ *nm* comb.

peigner /peɲe/ [1] **I** *vtr* to comb [*hair, wool*].

II se peigner *v refl* (+ *v être*) to comb one's hair.

peignoir /pɛɲwaʀ/ *nm* dressing gown (GB), robe (US); **~ de bain** bathrobe.

peinard○, **~e** /penaʀ, aʀd/ *adj* [*job*] cushy○; [*place*] snug.

peindre /pɛ̃dʀ/ [55] **I** *vtr* **1** to paint; **2** to depict.

II *vi* to paint.

peine /pɛn/ **I** *nf* **1** sorrow, grief; **avoir de la ~** to feel sad; **faire de la ~ à qn** [*person*] to hurt sb; [*event, remark*] to upset sb; **2** effort, trouble; **c'est ~ perdue** it's a waste of effort; **il n'est pas au bout de ses ~s** his troubles are far from over; he's still got a long way to go; **ce n'est pas la ~ de crier** there's no need to shout; **pour ta ~** for your trouble; **3** difficulty; **sans ~** easily; **avec ~** with difficulty; **4** (Law) penalty, sentence; **~ de prison** prison sentence; **'défense de fumer sous ~ d'amende'** 'no smoking, offenders will be fined'.

II à peine *phr* hardly; **il était à ~ arrivé qu'il pensait déjà à repartir** no sooner had he arrived than he was thinking of leaving again.

■ **~ capitale** capital punishment; **~ de cœur** heartache; **~ de mort** death penalty.

peiner /pene/ [1] **I** *vtr* to sadden, to upset.

II *vi* [*person*] to struggle; [*car*] to labour[GB].

peintre /pɛ̃tʀ/ *nm* painter.

peinture /pɛ̃tyʀ/ *nf* **1** paint; **2** paintwork; **3** painting; **je ne peux pas le voir en ~**○ I can't stand the sight of him; **4** portrayal.

peinturlurer /pɛ̃tyʀlyʀe/ [1] *vtr* to daub.

péjoratif, **-ive** /peʒɔʀatif, iv/ *adj* pejorative.

Pékin /pekɛ̃/ *pr n* Beijing, Peking.

pelage /pəlaʒ/ *nm* coat, fur.

pêle-mêle /pɛlmɛl/ *adv* higgledy-piggledy.

peler /pəle/ [17] **I** *vtr* to peel.

II *vi* **1** [*skin, nose*] to peel; **2**○ **~ (de froid)** to freeze.

pèlerin /pɛlʀɛ̃/ *nm* pilgrim.

pèlerinage /pɛlʀinaʒ/ *nm* pilgrimage.

pélican /pelikɑ̃/ *nm* pelican.

pelle /pɛl/ *nf* shovel; spade; **à la ~**○ by the dozen.

■ **~ à tarte** cake slice.

pelleteuse /pɛltøz/ *nf* mechanical digger.

pellicule /pelikyl/ **I** *nf* film.

II pellicules *nf pl* dandruff.

pelote /p(ə)lɔt/ *nf* (of wool) ball.

peloton /p(ə)lɔtɔ̃/ *nm* **1** platoon; **~ d'exécution** firing squad; **2** (in cycling) pack; **dans le ~ de tête** in the leading pack.

pelotonner: **se pelotonner** /p(ə)lɔtɔne/ [1] *v refl* (+ *v être*) **1** to snuggle up; **2** to huddle up.

pelouse /p(ə)luz/ *nf* lawn; **'~ interdite'** 'keep off the grass'.

peluche /p(ə)lyʃ/ *nf* **1** plush; **jouet en ~** cuddly toy (GB), stuffed animal (US); **2** fluff.

pelure /p(ə)lyʀ/ *nf* (of vegetable, fruit) peel; (of onion) skin.

pelvis /pɛlvis/ *nm inv* pelvis.

pénal, **~e**, *mpl* **-aux** /penal, o/ *adj* criminal.

pénaliser /penalize/ [1] *vtr* to penalize.

pénalité /penalite/ *nf* penalty.

penaud, **~e** /pəno, od/ *adj* sheepish.

penchant /pɑ̃ʃɑ̃/ *nm* **1** fondness; **2** weakness; **3** tendency.

penché, **~e** /pɑ̃ʃe/ **I** *pp* ▶ **pencher**.
II *pp adj* [*tree*] leaning; [*writing*] slanting.

pencher /pɑ̃ʃe/ [1] **I** *vtr* to tilt; to tip [sth] up; **~ la tête en avant** to bend one's head forward(s).
II *vi* **1** [*tower, tree*] to lean; [*boat*] to list; [*picture*] to slant; **2 ~ pour** to incline toward(s) [*theory*]; to be in favour[GB] of [*solution*].
III se pencher *v refl* (+ *v être*) **1** to lean; **2** to bend down; **3 se ~ sur** to look into [*problem*].

pendable /pɑ̃dabl/ *adj* **jouer un tour ~ à qn** to play a rotten trick on sb.

pendaison /pɑ̃dɛzɔ̃/ *nf* hanging.

pendant /pɑ̃dɑ̃/ **I** *prep* for; **je t'ai attendu ~ des heures** I waited for you for hours; **~ combien de temps avez-vous vécu à Versailles?** how long did you live in Versailles?; **il a été malade ~ tout le trajet** he was sick throughout the journey; **~ ce temps(-là)** meanwhile.
II pendant que *phr* while.

pendentif /pɑ̃dɑ̃tif/ *nm* pendant.

penderie /pɑ̃dʀi/ *nf* **1** wardrobe; **2** walk-in cupboard (GB) or closet.

pendre /pɑ̃dʀ/ [6] **I** *vtr* **1** to hang [*person*]; **2** to hang [*picture, curtains*]; to hang up [*clothes*].
II *vi* **1** [*object, clothes*] to hang; [*arms, legs*] to dangle; **2** [*strips, lock of hair*] to hang down; [*cheek, breasts*] to sag.
III se pendre *v refl* (+ *v être*) **1** to hang oneself; **2 se ~ à** to hang from [*branch*]; **se ~ au cou de qn** to throw one's arms around sb's neck.
IDIOMS **ça te pend au nez**○ you've got it coming to you.

pendu, **~e** /pɑ̃dy/ **I** *pp* ▶ **pendre**.
II *pp adj* **1** [*person*] hanged; **2** [*object*] hung, hanging; **être ~ aux lèvres de qn** to hang on sb's every word; **être toujours ~ au téléphone** to spend all one's time on the telephone.
III *nm,f* hanged man/woman.

pendule[1] /pɑ̃dyl/ *nm* pendulum.

pendule[2] /pɑ̃dyl/ *nf* clock.
IDIOMS **remettre les ~s à l'heure** to set the record straight.

pénétration /penetʀasjɔ̃/ *nf* penetration.

pénétré, **~e** /penetʀe/ **I** *pp* ▶ **pénétrer**.
II *pp adj* earnest, intense; **être ~ de** to be imbued with [*feeling*].

pénétrer /penetʀe/ [14] **I** *vtr* **1** [*rain*] to soak or seep into [*ground*]; [*sun*] to penetrate [*foliage*]; **2** to fathom [*secret, thoughts*]; **3** to penetrate; **4** [*idea, fashion*] to reach [*group*].
II *vi* **~ dans** to enter, to get into; to penetrate; **faire ~ la pommade en massant doucement** rub the ointment into your skin.

pénible /penibl/ *adj* [*effort*] painful; [*work*] hard; [*journey*] difficult; [*person*] tiresome.

péniblement /peniblәmɑ̃/ *adv* [*walk*] with difficulty; [*reach*] barely.

péniche /peniʃ/ *nf* barge.

pénicilline /penisilin/ *nf* penicillin.

péninsule /penɛ̃syl/ *nf* peninsula.

pénis /penis/ *nm inv* penis.

pénitence /penitɑ̃s/ *nf* **1** penance; **2** punishment.

pénitencier /penitɑ̃sje/ *nm* prison.

pénitentiaire /penitɑ̃sjɛʀ/ *adj* [*institution*] penal; [*regime*] prison.

pénombre /penɔ̃bʀ/ *nf* half-light.

pense-bête, *pl* **pense-bêtes** /pɑ̃sbɛt/ *nm* reminder.

pensée /pɑ̃se/ *nf* **1** thought; **être perdu dans ses ~s** to be lost in thought; **2** mind; **nous serons avec vous par la ~** we'll be with you in spirit; **3** thinking; **4** (Bot) pansy.

penser /pɑ̃se/ [1] **I** *vtr* **1** to think; **~ du bien de qn** to think well of sb; **je n'en pense rien** I have no opinion about it; **c'est bien ce que je pensais!** I thought as much!; **tu penses vraiment ce que tu dis?** do you really mean what you're saying?; **tout porte à ~ que** there's every indication that; **vous pensez si j'étais content!** you can imagine how pleased I was!; **'il s'est excusé?'—'penses-tu!'** 'did he apologize?'—'you must be joking!'; **2 ça me fait ~ qu'il faut que je leur écrive** that reminds me that I must write to them; **3 ~ faire** to be thinking of doing, to intend to do; **4** to think [sth] up [*plan, device*].
II penser à *v+prep* **1 ~ à** to think of, to think about; **ne pensez plus à rien** empty your mind; **sans ~ à mal** without meaning any harm; **tu n'y penses pas!** you can't be serious!; **n'y pensons plus!** let's forget about it!; **2 ~ à** to remember; **il me fait ~ à mon père** he reminds me of my father; **3 ~ à faire** to be thinking of doing.
III *vi* to think; **je lui ai dit ma façon de ~!** I gave him/her a piece of my mind!; **~ tout haut** to think out loud.

penseur /pɑ̃sœʀ/ *nm* thinker.

pensif, **-ive** /pɑ̃sif, iv/ *adj* pensive, thoughtful.

pension /pɑ̃sjɔ̃/ *nf* **1** pension; **2** boarding house; **3** boarding school.
■ **~ alimentaire** alimony; **~ complète** full board; **~ de famille** family hotel.

pensionnaire /pɑ̃sjɔnɛʀ/ *nmf* **1** (in hotel) resident; **2** (in prison) inmate; **3** (Sch) boarder.

pensionnat /pɑ̃sjɔna/ *nm* boarding school.

pentagone /pɛ̃tagɔn/ *nm* pentagon.

pente /pɑ̃t/ *nf* slope; **toit en ~** sloping roof.
IDIOMS **être sur la mauvaise ~** [*person*] to be going astray; [*company*] to be going downhill; **remonter la ~** to get back on one's feet.

Pentecôte /pɑ̃tkot/ *nf* Pentecost; **à la ~** at Whitsun.

pénurie /penyʀi/ *nf* shortage.

pépé○ /pepe/ *nm* **1** grandpa○; **2** old man.

pépère○ /pepɛʀ/ *adj* [*life*] cushy○; [*place*] nice.

pépin /pepɛ̃/ *nm* **1** pip; **sans ~s** seedless; **2**○ slight problem; **3**○ umbrella.

pépinière /pepinjɛʀ/ *nf* (for trees, plants) nursery.
pépite /pepit/ *nf* nugget.
perçant, **~e** /pɛʀsɑ̃, ɑ̃t/ *adj* **1** [*cry, voice*] shrill; [*gaze*] piercing; **2** [*vision*] sharp.
percée /pɛʀse/ *nf* **1** opening; **2** breakthrough.
perce-neige /pɛʀsənɛʒ/ *nm inv* or *nf inv* snowdrop.
perce-oreille, *pl* **~s** /pɛʀsɔʀɛj/ *nm* earwig.
percepteur /pɛʀsɛptœʀ/ *nm* tax inspector.
perceptible /pɛʀsɛptibl/ *adj* **1** [*sound*] perceptible; **2** [*tax*] payable.
perception /pɛʀsɛpsjɔ̃/ *nf* **1** tax office; **2** perception.
percer /pɛʀse/ [12] **I** *vtr* **1** to pierce [*body, surface*]; to burst [*abscess, eardrum*]; **2** to make [*door*]; to bore [*tunnel*]; to build [*road*]; **~ un trou dans** to make a hole in; **3** to pierce [*silence, air*]; to break through [*clouds*]; **4** to penetrate [*secret*]; **~ qn à jour** to see through sb; **5 ~ ses dents** to be teething.
II *vi* **1** [*sun*] to break through; [*plant*] to come up; [*tooth*] to come through; **2** (Mil, Sport) to break through; **3** [*actor*] to become known.
perceuse /pɛʀsøz/ *nf* drill.
percevoir /pɛʀsəvwaʀ/ [5] *vtr* **1** to collect [*tax*]; to receive [*rent*]; **2** to perceive [*change*]; to feel [*vibration*]; **être perçu comme** to be seen as.
perche /pɛʀʃ/ *nf* **1** (gen) pole; (of ski tow) T-bar; (for microphone) boom; **2**○ **(grande) ~** beanpole○; **3** (Zool) perch.
IDIOMS **tendre la ~ à qn** to throw sb a line.
percher /pɛʀʃe/ [1] **I** *vtr* **~ qch sur une étagère** to stick sth up on a shelf.
II *vi* to perch; to roost
III se percher *v refl* (+ *v être*) **1** to perch; **2 voix haut perchée** high-pitched voice.
perchoir /pɛʀʃwaʀ/ *nm* **1** perch; **2**○ (Pol) Speaker's Chair.
percolateur /pɛʀkɔlatœʀ/ *nm* (espresso) coffee machine.
percussions /pɛʀkysjɔ̃/ *nf pl* **les ~** percussion instruments; percussion section; drums.
percutant, **~e** /pɛʀkytɑ̃, ɑ̃t/ *adj* [*criticism*] hard-hitting; [*slogan*] punchy○.
percuter /pɛʀkyte/ [1] **I** *vtr* [*car, driver*] to hit.
II *vi* **~ contre** [*vehicle*] to crash into; [*shell*] to explode against.
III se percuter *v refl* (+ *v être*) to collide.
perdant, **~e** /pɛʀdɑ̃, ɑ̃t/ **I** *adj* losing; **être ~** to have lost out.
II *nm,f* loser.
perdition /pɛʀdisjɔ̃/ *nf* **1 lieu de ~** den of iniquity; **2 en ~** [*ship*] in distress.
perdre /pɛʀdʀ/ [6] **I** *vtr* **1** to lose; **~ de vue** to lose sight of; **leurs actions ont perdu 9%** their shares have dropped 9%; **2** to shed [*leaves, flowers*]; **3** to miss [*chance*]; **4** to waste [*day, years*]; **perdre son temps** to waste one's time; **5 je perds mes chaussures** my shoes are too big; **je perds mon pantalon** my trousers are falling down; **6** to bring [sb] down; **cet homme te perdra** that man will be your undoing.
II *vi* to lose; **j'y perds** I lose out.
III se perdre *v refl* (+ *v être*) **1** to get lost; **se ~ dans ses pensées** to be lost in thought; **2** [*tradition*] to die out.
IDIOMS **~ la raison** or **l'esprit** to go out of one's mind.
perdrix /pɛʀdʀi/ *nf inv* partridge.
perdu, **~e** /pɛʀdy/ **I** *pp* ▶ **perdre**.
II *pp adj* **1** lost; **chien ~** stray dog; **balle ~e** stray bullet; **c'est ~ d'avance** it's hopeless; **2** [*day, opportunity*] wasted; **c'est du temps ~** it's a waste of time; **3** [*harvest*] ruined; **il est ~** there's no hope for him; **4** [*person*] lost.
III *adj* remote, isolated.
IDIOMS **se lancer à corps ~ dans** to throw oneself headlong into; **ce n'est pas ~ pour tout le monde** somebody will do all right out of it.
père /pɛʀ/ *nm* father; **Dupont ~** Dupont senior; **le ~**○ **Dupont** old○ Dupont.
■ **le ~ Noël** Santa Claus.
péremption /peʀɑ̃psjɔ̃/ *nf* **date de ~** use-by date.
perfection /pɛʀfɛksjɔ̃/ *nf* perfection.
perfectionnement /pɛʀfɛksjɔnmɑ̃/ *nm* improvement.
perfectionner /pɛʀfɛksjɔne/ [1] **I** *vtr* to perfect [*technique*]; to refine [*art*].
II se perfectionner *v refl* (+ *v être*) to improve.
perfectionniste /pɛʀfɛksjɔnist/ *adj, nmf* perfectionist.
perfide /pɛʀfid/ *adj* perfidious, treacherous.
perfidie /pɛʀfidi/ *nf* perfidy, treachery.
perforation /pɛʀfɔʀasjɔ̃/ *nf* perforation.
perforer /pɛʀfɔʀe/ [1] *vtr* **1** to pierce; to perforate; **2** to punch; **carte perforée** punch card.
performance /pɛʀfɔʀmɑ̃s/ *nf* **1** result, performance; **2** achievement.
performant, **~e** /pɛʀfɔʀmɑ̃, ɑ̃t/ *adj* [*car, equipment*] high-performance; [*person, techniques*] efficient; [*company*] competitive.
perfusion /pɛʀfyzjɔ̃/ *nm* (Med) drip (GB), IV (US).
péricliter /peʀiklite/ [1] *vi* to be going downhill.
péridurale /peʀidyʀal/ *nf* epidural.
péril /peʀil/ *nm* peril, danger; **à ses risques et ~s** at his/her own risk; **il n'y a pas ~ en la demeure** what's the hurry?
périlleux, **-euse** /peʀijø, øz/ *adj* perilous.
périmé, **~e** /peʀime/ *adj* **1** out-of-date; **son passeport est ~** his/her passport has expired; **2** [*idea, custom*] outdated.
périmètre /peʀimɛtʀ/ *nm* **1** perimeter; **2** area.
périnée /peʀine/ *nm* perineum.
période /peʀjɔd/ *nf* period; era.
périodique /peʀjɔdik/ **I** *adj* **1** [*fever*] recurring; **2 serviette ~** sanitary towel (GB), sanitary napkin (US).
II *nm* periodical.
péripétie /peʀipesi/ *nf* **1** incident; **2** event; **3** adventure; **4 les ~s d'une intrigue** the twists and turns of a plot.

périphérie /peʀifeʀi/ *nf* periphery.

périphérique /peʀifeʀik/ **I** *adj* (gen) peripheral; [*area*] outlying; **radio ~** *broadcasting station situated outside the territory to which it transmits*.
II *nm* ring road (GB), beltway (US).

périphrase /peʀifʀɑz/ *nf* circumlocution.

périple /peʀipl/ *nm* journey; voyage.

périr /peʀiʀ/ [3] *vi* to die, to perish.

périscope /peʀiskɔp/ *nm* periscope.

périssable /peʀisabl/ *adj* perishable.

Péritel® /peʀitɛl/ *nf* **prise ~** scart socket; scart plug.

perle /pɛʀl/ *nf* **1** pearl; **~ fine** real pearl; **2** (figurative) gem; **~ rare** real treasure; **3**° howler°.

perler /pɛʀle/ [1] *vi* [*drop, tear*] to appear.

permanence /pɛʀmanɑ̃s/ **I** *nf* **1** permanence; **2** persistence; **3 ~ téléphonique** manned line; **assurer** or **tenir une ~** to be on duty; to hold a surgery (GB), to have office hours (US); **4** permanently manned office; **5** (Sch) (private) study room (GB), study hall (US).
II en permanence *phr* **1** permanently; **2** constantly.

permanent, ~e[1] /pɛʀmanɑ̃, ɑ̃t/ *adj* **1** [*staff, exhibition*] permanent; [*committee*] standing; **2** [*tension, danger*] constant; [*show*] continuous.

permanente[2] /pɛʀmanɑ̃t/ *nf* perm.

perméable /pɛʀmeabl/ *adj* permeable.

permettre /pɛʀmɛtʀ/ [60] **I** *vtr* **1 ~ à qn de faire** to allow sb to do, to give sb permission to do; **(vous) permettez! j'étais là avant!** excuse me! I was here first!; **il est menteur comme c'est pas permis**° he's an incredible liar; **2 ~ à qn de faire** to allow or enable sb to do, to give sb the opportunity to do; **leurs moyens ne le leur permettent pas** they can't afford it; **autant qu'il est permis d'en juger** as far as one can tell.
II se permettre *v refl* (+ *v être*) **1 je peux me ~ ce genre de plaisanterie avec lui** I can get away with telling him that kind of joke; **se ~ de faire** to take the liberty of doing; **2 je ne peux pas me ~ d'acheter une nouvelle voiture** I can't afford to buy a new car.

permis, ~e /pɛʀmi, iz/ **I** *pp* ▶ **permettre**.
II *pp adj* permitted.
III *nm inv* permit, licence[GB].
■ **~ de conduire** driver's licence[GB]; driving test; **~ de séjour** residence permit; **~ de travail** work permit.

permission /pɛʀmisjɔ̃/ *nf* **1** permission; **2** (Mil) leave; **partir en ~** to go on leave.

permuter /pɛʀmyte/ [1] *vtr* to switch [sth] around [*letters, labels*].

pernicieux, -ieuse /pɛʀnisjø, øz/ *adj* pernicious.

Pérou /peʀu/ *pr nm* Peru.
IDIOMS **ce n'est pas le ~** it's not a fortune.

perpendiculaire /pɛʀpɑ̃dikylɛʀ/ *adj*, *nf* perpendicular.

perpétrer /pɛʀpetʀe/ [14] *vtr* to perpetrate.

perpétuel, -elle /pɛʀpetɥɛl/ *adj* perpetual.

perpétuer /pɛʀpetɥe/ [1] *vtr* to perpetuate.

perpétuité /pɛʀpetɥite/ *nf* perpetuity; **à ~** (Law) [*imprisonment*] life.

perplexe /pɛʀplɛks/ *adj* perplexed, baffled.

perplexité /pɛʀplɛksite/ *nf* perplexity.

perquisition /pɛʀkizisjɔ̃/ *nf* search.

perquisitionner /pɛʀkizisjɔne/ [1] *vtr* to search [*house*].

perron /peʀɔ̃/ *nm* flight of steps.

perroquet /peʀɔkɛ/ *nm* parrot.

perruche /peʀyʃ/ *nf* budgerigar (GB), parakeet (US).

perruque /peʀyk/ *nf* wig.

persan, ~e /pɛʀsɑ̃, an/ *adj* Persian.

perse /pɛʀs/ *adj* Persian.

persécuter /pɛʀsekyte/ [1] *vtr* to persecute.

persécution /pɛʀsekysjɔ̃/ *nf* persecution.

persévérance /pɛʀseveʀɑ̃s/ *nf* perseverance.

persévérer /pɛʀseveʀe/ [14] *vi* **1** to persevere; **2** to persist.

persienne /pɛʀsjɛn/ *nf* (louvred[GB]) shutter.

persiflage /pɛʀsiflaʒ/ *nm* mockery.

persil /pɛʀsi(l)/ *nm* parsley.

persistance /pɛʀsistɑ̃s/ *nf* persistence.

persistant, ~e /pɛʀsistɑ̃, ɑ̃t/ *adj* [*heat, problem*] continuing; [*smell, snow*] lingering; [*cough, symptom*] persistent.

persister /pɛʀsiste/ [1] *vi* [*symptom, pain*] to persist; [*inflation*] to continue; **je persiste à croire que** I still think that.

personnage /pɛʀsɔnaʒ/ *nm* **1** character; **2** figure; **un ~ public** a public figure.

personnaliser /pɛʀsɔnalize/ [1] *vtr* to add a personal touch to.

personnalité /pɛʀsɔnalite/ *nf* **1** personality; **2** important person.

personne[1] /pɛʀsɔn/ *pron* anyone, anybody; no-one, nobody; **~ n'est parfait** nobody's perfect.

personne[2] /pɛʀsɔn/ *nf* person; **dix ~s** ten people; **les ~s âgées** the elderly; **bien fait de sa ~** good-looking; **le respect de la ~** respect for the individual; **il s'en occupe en ~** he's dealing with it personally; **c'est la cupidité en ~** he/she is greed personified.
■ **~ à charge** dependant; **~ civile** or **morale** artificial person, legal entity.

personnel, -elle /pɛʀsɔnɛl/ **I** *adj* **1** [*friend, effects*] personal; [*papers*] private; **2** individual; **3** selfish; **4** [*pronoun*] personal.
II *nm* staff; workforce; employees, personnel.

personnellement /pɛʀsɔnɛlmɑ̃/ *adv* personally.

personnifier /pɛʀsɔnifje/ [2] *vtr* to personify.

perspective /pɛʀspɛktiv/ *nf* **1** (in art) perspective; **2** view; **3** perspective, angle; **4** prospect.

perspicace /pɛʀspikas/ *adj* perceptive.

perspicacité /pɛʀspikasite/ *nf* insight, perspicacity.

persuader /pɛʀsɥade/ [1] *vtr* to persuade.

persuasif, -ive /pɛʀsɥazif, iv/ *adj* persuasive.

perte /pɛʀt/ *nf* **1** loss; **à ~ de vue** as far as

the eye can see; **2** waste; **3** ruin; **courir** or **aller à sa ~** to be heading for a fall.

pertinemment /pɛʀtinamɑ̃/ *adv* **1** perfectly well; **2** pertinently.

pertinence /pɛʀtinɑ̃s/ *nf* pertinence.

pertinent, **~e** /pɛʀtinɑ̃, ɑ̃t/ *adj* pertinent.

perturbant, **~e** /pɛʀtyʀbɑ̃, ɑ̃t/ *adj* disturbing.

perturbation /pɛʀtyʀbasjɔ̃/ *nf* **1** disruption; **2** disturbance; **3** upheaval.

perturber /pɛʀtyʀbe/ [1] *vtr* to disrupt [*traffic, market, meeting*]; to interfere with [*development*]; to disturb [*sleep*].

pervenche /pɛʀvɑ̃ʃ/ *nf* **1** periwinkle; **2**○ (female) traffic warden (GB), meter maid○ (US).

pervers, **~e** /pɛʀvɛʀ, ɛʀs/ **I** *adj* **1** wicked; **2** perverted; **3** [*effect*] pernicious.
II *nm,f* pervert.

perversion /pɛʀvɛʀsjɔ̃/ *nf* perversion.

perversité /pɛʀvɛʀsite/ *nf* perversity.

pervertir /pɛʀvɛʀtiʀ/ [3] *vtr* to corrupt.

pesant, **~e** /pəzɑ̃, ɑ̃t/ *adj* **1** heavy; **2** cumbersome; **3** [*atmosphere, silence*] oppressive.
IDIOMS **valoir son ~ d'or** to be worth its weight in gold.

pesanteur /pəzɑ̃tœʀ/ *nf* **1** (of style) heaviness; (of bureaucracy) inertia; **2** gravity.

pèse-personne, *pl* **~s** /pɛzpɛʀsɔn/ *nm* bathroom scales.

peser /pəze/ [16] **I** *vtr* **1** to weigh; **2** to weigh up; **~ ses mots** to choose one's words carefully; **tout bien pesé** all things considered.
II *vi* **1** to weigh; **je pèse 70 kg** I weigh 70 kg; **~ lourd** to weigh a lot; **2** to carry weight; **~ dans/sur une décision** to have a decisive influence in/on a decision; **3 ~ sur** [*suspicion*] to hang over [*person*]; **4** [*tax, debts*] to weigh [sb/sth] down [*person, country*]; **5** [*person, decision*] to influence (greatly) [*policy*].

pessimisme /pesimism/ *nm* pessimism.

pessimiste /pesimist/ **I** *adj* pessimistic.
II *nmf* pessimist.

peste /pɛst/ *nf* **1** plague; **2**○ pest○.
IDIOMS **je me méfie de lui comme de la ~**○ I don't trust him an inch.

pester /pɛste/ [1] *vi* **~ contre qn/qch** to curse sb/sth.

pesticide /pɛstisid/ *nm* pesticide.

pet○ /pɛ/ *nm* fart○.

pétale /petal/ *nm* petal.

pétanque /petɑ̃k/ *nf* petanque.

pétarader /petaʀade/ [1] *vi* to backfire.

pétard /petaʀ/ *nm* banger (GB), firecracker (US); **être en ~**○ to be hopping mad○ (GB), to be real mad○ (US).

péter /pete/ [14] *vi* **1**● to fart○; **2**○ [*balloon*] to burst; [*situation*] to blow up; [*thread*] to snap.

pétillant, **~e** /petijɑ̃, ɑ̃t/ *adj* sparkling.

pétiller /petije/ [1] *vi* [*drink*] to fizz; [*firewood*] to crackle; [*eyes*] to sparkle.

petit, **~e** /p(ə)ti, it/ **I** *adj* **1** small, little; short; **une toute ~e pièce** a tiny room; **se faire tout ~** (figurative) to try to make oneself inconspicuous; **2** [*walk, distance*] short; **3** young, little; **c'est notre ~ dernier** he's our youngest; **4** [*eater*] light; [*wage*] low; [*cry, worry*] little; [*hope*] slight; [*detail, defect*] minor; [*job*] modest; **5 une ~e trentaine de personnes** under thirty people.
II *adv* **tailler ~** to be small-fitting; **~ à ~** little by little.
■ **~ ami** boyfriend; **~ bois** kindling; **~ coin**○ (euphemistic) loo○ (GB), bathroom (US); **~ déjeuner** breakfast; **~ noir**○ coffee; **~ nom**○ first name; **~ pois** (garden) pea, petit pois; **~ pot** jar of baby food; **~ rat (de l'Opéra)** *pupil at Paris Opéra's ballet school*; **~ salé** streaky salted pork; **~e amie** girlfriend; **~e annonce** classified advertisement; **~e nature** weakling; **~e reine** cycling; **~e voiture** toy car; **~s chevaux** ≈ ludo.

petit-cousin, **petite-cousine**, *mpl* **petits-cousins** /p(ə)tikuzɛ̃n, p(ə)titkuzin/ *nm,f* second cousin.

petite-fille, *pl* **petites-filles** /p(ə)titfij/ *nf* granddaughter.

petitesse /p(ə)titɛs/ *nf* **1** pettiness; **2** small size.

petit-fils, *pl* **petits-fils** /p(ə)tifis/ *nm* grandson.

pétition /petisjɔ̃/ *nf* petition.

petit-lait /p(ə)tilɛ/ *nm* **ça se boit comme du ~**○! it slips down nicely!

petits-enfants /p(ə)tizɑ̃fɑ̃/ *nm pl* grandchildren.

pétrifier /petʀifje/ [2] *vtr* **1** to petrify; **2** (figurative) to transfix.

pétrin /petʀɛ̃/ *nm* dough trough.
IDIOMS **être dans le ~** to be in a fix○.

pétrir /petʀiʀ/ [3] *vtr* **1** to knead [*dough*]; **2** to mould (GB), to mold (US) [*personality*].

pétrole /petʀɔl/ *nm* oil, petroleum.

pétrolier, **-ière** /petʀɔlje, ɛʀ/ **I** *adj* oil.
II *nm* oil tanker.

pétulant, **~e** /petylɑ̃, ɑ̃t/ *adj* exuberant.

peu /pø/

■ **Note** See the entries *avant*, *depuis*, *d'ici* and *sous* for the use of *peu* with these words.

I *adv* **1** not much; **il parle ~** he doesn't talk much; **elle gagne très ~** she earns very little; **deux semaines c'est trop ~** two weeks isn't long enough; **si ~ que ce soit** however little; **très ~ pour moi**○! thanks, but no thanks!; **2** not very; **assez ~ connu** little-known; **elle n'est pas ~ fière** she's more than a little proud.
II *pron* few, not many.
III de peu *phr* only just.
IV peu de *quantif* **~ de mots** few words; **~ de temps** little time.
V *nm* **le ~ de** the little [*trust, freedom*]; the few [*books, friends*]; the lack of [*interest*].
VI un peu *phr* **1** a little, a bit; **reste encore un ~** stay a little longer; **parle un ~ plus fort** speak a little louder; **un ~ plus de** a few more [*books*]; a little more [*time*]; **un ~ beau-**

coup more than a bit; **2** just; **répète un ~ pour voir**○! you just try saying that again!; **pour un ~ ils se seraient battus** they very nearly had a fight.
VII peu à peu *phr* gradually, little by little.
VIII pour peu que *phr* if; **pour ~ qu'il ait bu, il va nous raconter sa vie** if he's had anything at all to drink, he'll tell us his life story.

peuplade /pœplad/ *nf* small tribe.
peuple /pœpl/ *nm* people.
peupler /pœple/ [1] **I** *vtr* **1** to populate [*country*]; to stock [*forest, pond*]; **2** [*animals, plants*] to colonize [*region*]; [*students*] to fill [*street*].
II se peupler *v refl* (+ *v être*) to fill up.
peuplier /pøplije/ *nm* poplar.
peur /pœʀ/ *nf* fear; fright, scare; **être mort** or **vert**○ **de ~** to be scared to death; **une ~ panique s'empara de lui** he was panic-stricken; **avoir ~** to be afraid; **j'en ai bien ~** I'm afraid so; **faire ~ à qn** to frighten sb; **maigre à faire ~** terribly thin.
peureux, -euse /pœʀø, øz/ *adj* fearful.
peut-être /pøtɛtʀ/ *adv* perhaps, maybe.
phalange /falɑ̃ʒ/ *nf* phalanx.
phallocrate /falɔkʀat/ *nm* male chauvinist.
phallus /falys/ *nm inv* phallus.
pharaon /faʀaɔ̃/ *nm* pharaoh.
phare /faʀ/ *nm* **1** headlight; **2** lighthouse.
pharmacie /faʀmasi/ *nf* **1** chemist's (shop) (GB), drugstore (US), pharmacy; **2** medicine cabinet; **3** (science) pharmacy.
pharmacien, -ienne /faʀmasjɛ̃, ɛn/ *nm,f* (dispensing) chemist (GB), pharmacist.
pharynx /faʀɛ̃ks/ *nm inv* pharynx.
phase /fɑz/ *nf* **1** stage; **2** phase.
phénoménal, ~e, *mpl* **-aux** /fenɔmenal, o/ *adj* phenomenal.
phénomène /fenɔmɛn/ *nm* **1** phenomenon; **2**○ **c'est un ~** he/she's quite a character.
philanthropie /filɑ̃tʀɔpi/ *nf* philanthropy.
philatéliste /filatelist/ *nmf* philatelist.
philosophe /filɔzɔf/ *nmf* philosopher.
philosophie /filɔzɔfi/ *nf* philosophy.
philosophique /filɔzɔfik/ *adj* philosophical.
phobie /fɔbi/ *nf* phobia.
phonétique /fɔnetik/ **I** *adj* phonetic.
II *nf* phonetics.
phonographe /fɔnɔgʀaf/ *nm* gramophone (GB), phonograph (US).
phoque /fɔk/ *nm* **1** seal; **2** sealskin.
phosphate /fɔsfat/ *nm* phosphate.
phosphore /fɔsfɔʀ/ *nm* phosphorus.
phosphorescent, ~e /fɔsfɔʀesɑ̃, ɑ̃t/ *adj* phosphorescent.
photo /fɔto/ *nf* **1** photography; **2** photo.
■ **~ d'identité** passport photo
photocomposition /fɔtokɔ̃pozisjɔ̃/ *nf* filmsetting (GB), photocomposition (US).
photocopie /fɔtokɔpi/ *nf* photocopy.
photocopier /fɔtokɔpje/ [2] *vtr* to photocopy.
photocopieuse /fɔtokɔpjøz/ *nf* photocopier.
photogénique /fɔtoʒenik/ *adj* photogenic.
photographe /fɔtogʀaf/ *nmf* photographer.
photographie /fɔtogʀafi/ *nf* **1** photography; **2** photograph, picture.
photographier /fɔtogʀafje/ [2] *vtr* to photograph, to take a photo of.
photographique /fɔtogʀafik/ *adj* photographic.
photomaton® /fɔtomatɔ̃/ *nm* photo booth.
photosynthèse /fɔtosɛ̃tɛz/ *nf* photosynthesis.
phrase /fʀɑz/ *nf* **1** sentence; **2** phrase; **avoir une ~ malheureuse** to say the wrong thing; **~ toute faite** stock phrase; **3** (Mus) phrase.
phréatique /fʀeatik/ *adj* **nappe ~** ground water.
physicien, -ienne /fizisjɛ̃, ɛn/ *nm,f* physicist.
physiologie /fizjɔlɔʒi/ *nf* physiology.
physiologique /fizjɔlɔʒik/ *adj* physiological.
physionomie /fizjɔnɔmi/ *nf* **1** face; **2** (figurative) (of country) face; (of area) appearance, look.
physiothérapie /fizjɔteʀapi/ *nf* physiotherapy (GB), physical therapy (US).
physique[1] /fizik/ **I** *adj* physical.
II *nm* **1** physical appearance; **2** physique; **avoir un ~ séduisant** to look attractive.
IDIOMS **avoir le ~ de l'emploi** to look the part.
physique[2] /fizik/ *nf* physics.
piaffer /pjafe/ [1] *vi* **1** [*horse*] to paw the ground; **2** [*person*] to be impatient; **~ d'impatience** to be champing at the bit.
piailler /pjɑje/ [1] *vi* [*bird*] to chirp.
pianiste /pjanist/ *nmf* pianist.
piano /pjano/ **I** *nm* piano; **jouer qch au ~** to play sth on the piano.
II *adv* (Mus) piano.
■ **~ à queue** grand piano.
pianoter /pjanɔte/ [1] *vi* to tinkle on the piano.
pic /pik/ **I** *nm* **1** peak; **2** pick; **3** woodpecker.
II à pic *phr* [*cliff*] sheer; [*ravine*] very steep.
IDIOMS **tomber à ~** to come just at the right time.
pichenette /piʃnɛt/ *nf* flick.
pichet /piʃɛ/ *nm* jug (GB), pitcher.
picorer /pikɔʀe/ [1] *vi* [*bird*] to peck about.
picotement /pikɔtmɑ̃/ *nm* tingling; tickling.
picoter /pikɔte/ [1] **I** *vtr* to sting [*eyes, nose, skin*]; to tickle [*throat*].
II *vi* [*throat*] to tickle; [*eyes*] to sting.
pie /pi/ *nf* **1** magpie; **2**○ chatterbox○.
pièce /pjɛs/ **I** *nf* **1** room; **2** coin; **~ de monnaie** coin; **3** play; **~ de théâtre** play; **4** bit, piece; **en ~s** in bits; **mettre qn/qch en ~s** to pull sb/sth to pieces; **5** part; **~ de rechange** spare part; **6** patch; **7** document; **juger sur ~s** to judge on the actual evidence; **c'est inventé de toutes ~s** (figurative) it's a complete fabrication; **8** piece, item; (in chess set, puzzle) piece; **~ de collection** collector's item; **on n'est pas aux ~s**○ we're not in a sweatshop.
II -pièces (*combining form*) **1 un trois-~s**

cuisine a three-roomed apartment with kitchen; **2 un deux-~s** a two-piece swimsuit.
■ **~ à conviction** exhibit; **~ détachée** spare part; **en ~s détachées** in kit form; dismantled; **~ d'identité** identity papers; **~ maîtresse** showpiece; key element; **~ montée** layer cake.

pied /pje/ *nm* **1** foot; **être ~s nus** to be barefoot(ed); **sauter à ~s joints** to jump with one's feet together; (figurative) to jump in with both feet; **coup de ~** kick; **à ~** on foot; **promenade à ~** walk; **taper du ~** to stamp one's foot; to tap one's foot; **de la tête aux ~s** from head to foot; **portrait en ~** full-length portrait; **avoir conscience de là où on met les ~s**○ to know what one is letting oneself in for; **sur un ~ d'égalité** on an equal footing; **2** (of hill, stairs) foot, bottom; (of glass) stem; (of lamp) base; (of camera) stand; **3** (of celery, lettuce) head; **~ de vigne** vine; **4** (measurement) foot.
■ **~ à coulisse** calliper rule.
IDIOMS **être sur ~** [*person*] to be up and about; [*business*] to be up and running; **mettre sur ~** to set up; **j'ai ~** I can touch the bottom; **perdre ~** to go out of one's depth; to lose ground; **être à ~ d'œuvre** to be ready to get down to work; **elle joue au tennis comme un ~**○ she's hopeless at tennis; **faire un ~ de nez à qn** to thumb one's nose at sb; **faire du ~ à qn** to play footsy with sb○; **faire des ~s et des mains**○ **pour obtenir** to work really hard at getting; **ça lui fera les ~s**○ that will teach him a lesson; **c'est le ~**○ that's terrific○; **mettre à ~** to suspend; **lever le ~**○ to slow down.

pied-à-terre /pjetatɛʀ/ *nm inv* pied-à-terre.

pied-bot, *pl* **pieds-bots** /pjebo/ *nm* person with a club foot.

piédestal, *pl* **-aux** /pjedɛstal, o/ *nm* pedestal.

pied-noir○, *pl* **pieds-noirs** /pjenwaʀ/ *nmf*: *French colonial born in Algeria.*

piège /pjɛʒ/ *nm* **1** trap; **il s'est laissé prendre au ~** he walked into the trap; **2** pitfall.

piéger /pjeʒe/ [15] *vtr* **1** to trap [*animal, criminal*]; **2** to trick, to trap [*person*]; **3** to booby-trap [*letter, parcel, car*].

pierre /pjɛʀ/ *nf* stone; rock; **poser la première ~** to lay the foundation stone.
IDIOMS **jeter la ~ à qn** to accuse sb; **faire d'une ~ deux coups** to kill two birds with one stone.

piété /pjete/ *nf* piety; **de ~** devotional.

piétiner /pjetine/ [1] **I** *vtr* **1** to trample [sth] underfoot; **2** to trample on.
II *vi* **1 ~ d'impatience** to hop up and down with impatience; **2** to shuffle along; to trudge along; **3** to make no headway.

piéton, **-onne** /pjetɔ̃, ɔn/ **I** *adj* pedestrianized.
II *nm,f* pedestrian.

piétonnier, **-ière** /pjetɔnje, ɛʀ/ *adj* pedestrianized.

piètre /pjɛtʀ/ *adj* [*actor, writer*] very mediocre; [*health, results*] very poor; **c'est une ~ consolation** that's small comfort.

pieu, *pl* **~x**[1] /pjø/ *nm* stake.

pieuvre /pjœvʀ/ *nf* octopus.

pieux[2], **pieuse** /pjø, øz/ *adj* **1** pious, religious; **2** [*affection, silence*] reverent.
■ **~ mensonge** white lie.

pif○ /pif/ *nm* **1** nose, conk○ (GB), schnozzle○ (US); **2** intuition; **j'ai eu du ~** I had a hunch○; **au ~** [*measure*] roughly; [*decide*] just like that.

pige /piʒ/ *nf* **travailler à la ~**, **faire des ~s** to do freelance work.

pigeon /piʒɔ̃/ *nm* **1** pigeon; **2**○ sucker○.
■ **~ voyageur** carrier pigeon.

piger○ /piʒe/ [13] *vtr* to understand.

pigment /pigmɑ̃/ *nm* pigment.

pignon /piɲɔ̃/ *nm* **1** gable; **2** gearwheel; **3** pine kernel.
IDIOMS **avoir ~ sur rue** to be well-established.

pilaf /pilaf/ *nm* pilau; **riz ~** pilau rice.

pile[1]○ /pil/ *adv* **1 s'arrêter ~** to stop dead; **2** exactly; **à 10 heures et demie ~** at ten-thirty sharp; **~ à l'heure** right on time; **tu tombes ~** you're just the person I wanted to see.

pile[2] /pil/ *nf* **1** pile; stack; **2 ~ (électrique)** battery; **à ~s** battery-operated; **3** pier; **4** (of coin) **le côté ~** the reverse side; **jouer à ~ ou face** to play heads or tails.
■ **~ bouton** button battery; **~ solaire** solar cell.

piler /pile/ [1] **I** *vtr* to grind; to crush.
II○ *vi* [*car*] to pull up short; [*driver*] to slam on the brakes.

pileux, **-euse** /pilø, øz/ *adj* **système ~** hair.

pilier /pilje/ *nm* **1** pillar; **2** (figurative) mainstay; **3** (in rugby) prop forward.

pillage /pijaʒ/ *nm* pillage, plundering; looting.

pillard, **~e** /pijaʀ, aʀd/ *nm,f* looter; pillager.

piller /pije/ [1] *vtr* to pillage [*town*]; to loot [*shop*]; to plunder [*temple*].

pilon /pilɔ̃/ *nm* **1** pestle; **2** (of poultry) drumstick.

pilotage /pilɔtaʒ/ *nm* piloting.

pilote /pilɔt/ **I** *nm* pilot.
II (-)pilote (*combining form*) **projet(-)~** pilot project; **hôpital(-)~** experimental hospital.
■ **~ automobile** racing driver.

piloter /pilɔte/ [1] *vtr* to pilot [*plane, ship*]; to drive [*car*].

pilotis /pilɔti/ *nm inv* stilts.

pilule /pilyl/ *nf* pill.
IDIOMS **avaler la ~**○ to grin and bear it; **faire passer la ~**○ to sweeten the pill.

pimbêche /pɛ̃bɛʃ/ *nf* stuck-up madam○.

piment /pimɑ̃/ *nm* **1** hot pepper; **2** spice.
■ **~ rouge** hot red pepper, chilli; **~ vert** green chilli pepper.

pimpant, **~e** /pɛ̃pɑ̃, ɑ̃t/ *adj* spruce, smart.

pin /pɛ̃/ *nm* pine (tree); **pomme de ~** pine cone.

pinailler○ /pinɑje/ [1] *vi* to split hairs.

pince /pɛ̃s/ *nf* **1** (pair of) pliers; (pair of) tongs; **2** (in garment) dart; **un pantalon à ~s** pleat front trousers (GB) or pants (US); **3** (of crab) pincer, claw.

■ **~ à cheveux** hair grip; **~ coupante** wire cutters; **~ à dessin** bulldog clip; **~ à épiler** tweezers; **~ à linge** clothes peg; **~ à sucre** sugar tongs; **~ à vélo** bicycle clip.

pincé, **~e**[1] /pɛ̃se/ *adj* [*smile*] tight-lipped; **prendre un air ~** to become stiff or starchy.

pinceau, *pl* **~x** /pɛ̃so/ *nm* (paint) brush.

pincée[2] /pɛ̃se/ **I** *adj f* ▶ **pincé**.

II *nf* (of pepper, salt) pinch.

pincement /pɛ̃smɑ̃/ *nm* pinch; **avoir un ~ de cœur** to feel a twinge of sadness.

pince-nez /pɛ̃sne/ *nm inv* pince-nez.

pincer /pɛ̃se/ [12] **I** *vtr* **1** [*person*] to pinch; [*crab*] to nip; **2**○ to nab○, to catch [*thief*]; **3 ~ les lèvres** to purse one's lips; **4** to pluck [*string*]; **5** [*wind, cold*] to sting [*face*].

II se pincer *v refl* (+ *v être*) to pinch oneself; **se ~ le nez** to hold one's nose; **elle s'est pincée en refermant le tiroir** she caught her fingers closing the drawer.

IDIOMS **en ~**○ **pour qn** to be stuck○ on sb.

pince-sans-rire /pɛ̃ssɑ̃ʀiʀ/ *nmf inv* **c'est un ~** he has a deadpan sense of humour[GB].

pincettes /pɛ̃sɛt/ *nf pl* **il n'est pas à prendre avec des ~**○ he's like a bear with a sore head.

pinède /pinɛd/ *nf* pine forest.

pingouin /pɛ̃gwɛ̃/ *nm* **1** auk; **2** penguin.

ping-pong®, *pl* **~s** /piŋpɔ̃ŋ/ *nm* table tennis, ping-pong®.

pingre /pɛ̃gʀ/ *adj* stingy, niggardly.

pin-pon /pɛ̃pɔ̃/ *nm: sound of a two-tone siren.*

pin's /pins/ *nm inv* lapel badge.

pintade /pɛ̃tad/ *nf* guinea fowl.

pinte /pɛ̃t/ *nf* **1** pint (GB) (= 0,57 litre); **2** ≈ quart (US) (= 0,94 litre); **3** pot, tankard.

pinter○: **se pinter** /pɛ̃te/ [1] *v refl* (+ *v être*) to get plastered○ or drunk.

pin-up○ /pinœp/ *nf inv* glamour[GB] girl.

pioche /pjɔʃ/ *nf* **1** mattock; pickaxe (GB), pickax (US); **2** (Games) stack.

piocher /pjɔʃe/ [1] *vtr* **1** to dig [sth] over [*soil*]; **2** (Games) to take [sth] from the stack [*card*].

piolet /pjɔlɛ/ *nm* ice axe (GB), ice pick (US).

pion, **pionne** /pjɔ̃, pjɔn/ **I**○ *nm,f* (Sch) *student paid to supervise pupils.*

II *nm* **1** (in games) counter; (in chess) pawn; (in draughts) draught (GB), checker (US); **2** (figurative) pawn.

pionnier, **-ière** /pjɔnje, ɛʀ/ *adj, nm,f* pioneer.

pipe /pip/ *nf* pipe.

IDIOMS **casser sa ~**○ to kick the bucket○.

pipeau, *pl* **~x** /pipo/ *nm* (reed-)pipe.

IDIOMS **c'est du ~**○ it's no great shakes○; **c'est pas du ~**○ it's for real○.

pipelette○ /piplɛt/ *nf* gossip(monger).

piper /pipe/ [1] *vtr* **1**○ **ne pas ~ (mot)** not to say a word; **2** to load [*dice*].

pipi○ /pipi/ *nm* pee○; wee-wee○.

piquant, **~e** /pikɑ̃, ɑ̃t/ **I** *adj* **1** [*stem, thistle*] prickly; [*nail*] sharp; **2** [*mustard, sauce*] hot; [*cheese*] sharp.

II *nm* **1** (of stem, thistle) prickle; (of hedgehog, cactus) spine; (of barbed wire) spike, barb; **2** (of story) spiciness; (of situation) piquancy.

pique[1] /pik/ *nm* (Games) spades.

pique[2] /pik/ *nf* **1** cutting remark; **2** pike; (of picador) lance.

piqué, **~e** /pike/ *adj* [*wood*] worm-eaten; [*linen, mirror, fruit*] spotted; [*paper*] foxed.

pique-assiette○ /pikasjɛt/ *nmf inv* sponger○.

pique-nique, *pl* **~s** /piknik/ *nm* picnic.

piquer /pike/ [1] **I** *vtr* **1** to sting; to bite; to prick; **2**○ to give [sb] an injection; **faire ~ un animal** to have an animal put down; **3** [*mildew, rust*] to spot [*linen, mirror*]; to fox [*paper, book*]; **4 ses yeux la piquaient** her eyes were stinging; **ça me pique partout** I'm itchy all over; **5**○ to pinch○ (GB), to steal [*book, idea*]; to borrow [*pencil, pullover*]; **6** to catch; **ils se sont fait ~ à tricher pendant l'examen** they got caught cheating in the exam; **7 ~ qn au vif** to cut sb to the quick; **8** to arouse [*curiosity*]; **9**○ **~ un fou rire** to have a fit of the giggles; **~ une crise de nerfs** to throw a fit○; **~ un cent mètres** to break into a run; **10 ~ une tête** to dive.

II *vi* **1** [*beard*] to be bristly; [*wool*] to be scratchy; [*throat, eyes*] to sting; **2** [*bird*] to swoop down; [*plane*] to dive; **~ du nez** [*person*] to nod off; [*plane*] to go into a nose-dive; **3**○ **arrête de ~ dans le plat** stop picking (things out of the dish).

III se piquer *v refl* (+ *v être*) **1** to prick oneself; **se ~ aux orties** to get stung by nettles; **2** to inject oneself; **3 se ~ de pouvoir réussir seul** to claim that one can manage on one's own.

IDIOMS **quelle mouche t'a piqué**○**?** what's eating○ you?; **son article n'était pas piqué des hannetons**○ his/her article didn't pull any punches.

piquet /pikɛ/ *nm* **1** stake; **2** peg; **3** (in skiing) gate pole; **4** (of sunshade) pole; **5** picket; **~ de grève** (strike) picket, picket line.

piquette○ /pikɛt/ *nf* plonk○ (GB), cheap wine.

piqûre /pikyʀ/ *nf* **1** injection, shot; **2** (of thorn, pin) prick; (of nettle, bee) sting; (of mosquito) bite; **3** stitch; stitching.

pirate /piʀat/ *nm* pirate.

■ **~ de l'air** hijacker, skyjacker.

pirater /piʀate/ [1] *vtr* to pirate.

piraterie /piʀatʀi/ *nf* piracy.

■ **~ aérienne** hijacking, skyjacking; **~ informatique** computer hacking.

pire /piʀ/ **I** *adj* **1** worse (**que** than); **2** worst; **les ~s mensonges** the most wicked lies.

II *nm* **le ~** the worst; **au ~** at the very worst.

pirogue /piʀɔg/ *nf* dugout canoe.

pirouette /piʀwɛt/ *nf* pirouette; **s'en tirer par une ~** to dodge the question skilfully[GB].

pis /pi/ **I** *adj inv* worse.

II *adv* worse; **tant ~** too bad.

III *nm inv* (of cow) udder.

pis-aller /pizale/ *nm inv* makeshift solution.

piscine /pisin/ *nf* swimming pool.

pisse◑ /pis/ *nf* piss◑.

pissenlit /pisɑ̃li/ *nm* dandelion.
IDIOMS **manger les ~s par la racine**◑ to be pushing up the daisies○.

pisser◑ /pise/ [1] **I** *vtr* **~ le sang** [*person, nose, injury*] to pour with blood.
II *vi* to pee○, to piss◑.
IDIOMS **il pleut comme vache qui pisse** it's pissing down◑; **laisse ~!** forget it!

pissotière○ /pisɔtjɛʀ/ *nf* street urinal.

pistache /pistaʃ/ *nf* pistachio.

piste /pist/ *nf* **1** trail; **être sur une fausse ~** to be on the wrong track; **2** (in police investigation) lead; **3** (in stadium) track; (in horseracing) racecourse (GB), racetrack (US); (in motor racing) racetrack; (in circus) ring; (in skiing) slope; (in cross-country skiing) trail; **~ de danse** dance floor; **entrer en ~** (at circus) to come into the ring; (figurative) to enter the fray; **4** track, path; (in desert) trail; **5** (in airport) runway; **6** (on record, cassette) track.
■ **~ cyclable** cycle lane; cycle path.

pistil /pistil/ *nm* pistil.

pistolet /pistɔlɛ/ *nm* **1** pistol, gun; **tirer au ~** to fire a pistol; **2** (Tech) gun; **~ à peinture** spray gun.

piston /pistɔ̃/ *nm* **1** (Tech) piston; **2**○ contacts; **avoir du ~** to have connections in the right places.

pistonner○ /pistɔne/ [1] *vtr* to pull strings for.

piteux, -euse /pitø, øz/ *adj* **1** [*results*] poor, pitiful; **2** [*air*] crestfallen.

pitié /pitje/ *nf* pity; mercy; **prendre qn en ~** to take pity on sb; **il fait ~** he's a pitiful sight; **par ~, tais-toi!** for pity's sake, be quiet!

piton /pitɔ̃/ *nm* **1** hook; **2** (in climbing) piton; **3** (of mountain) peak.

pitoyable /pitwajabl/ *adv* **1** pitiful; **2** pathetic.

pitre /pitʀ/ *nm* clown, buffoon.

pitrerie /pitʀəʀi/ *nf* clowning.

pittoresque /pitɔʀɛsk/ *adj* picturesque; colourful[GB].

pivert /pivɛʀ/ *nm* green woodpecker.

pivoine /pivwan/ *nf* peony.

pivot /pivo/ *nm* **1** (Tech) pivot; **2** (of economy, strategy, group) linchpin; (of plot) kingpin; **3** (Sport) (player) pivot, post; **4** (of tooth) post and core.

pivoter /pivɔte/ [1] *vi* [*person, animal, panel*] to pivot; [*door*] to revolve; [*chair*] to swivel.

PJ /peʒi/ *nf* **1** (*abbr* = **police judiciaire**) *detective division of the French police force*; **2** (*abbr* = **pièce(s) jointe(s)**) enc.

PL (*written abbr* = **poids lourd**) HGV (GB), heavy truck (US).

placard /plakaʀ/ *nm* **1** cupboard; **mettre au ~** (figurative) to put [sth] on ice [*plan*]; to shunt [sb] aside [*person*]; **2** poster, bill.

place /plas/ *nf* **1** room, space; **2** (in theatre, cinema, bus) seat; **payer sa ~** (in cinema, theatre) to pay for one's ticket; (on train) to pay one's fare; **3** place; **remettre qch à sa ~** to put sth back in its place; **être en bonne ~ pour gagner** to be well-placed or in a good position to win; **la ~ d'un mot dans une phrase** the position of a word in a sentence; **sur ~** to/on the scene; on the spot; **il faut savoir rester à sa ~** you must know your place; **tenir une grande ~ dans la vie de qn** to play a large part in sb's life; **4 à la ~ de** instead of, in place of; **(si j'étais) à ta ~** if I were in your position; **5 en ~** [*system, structure*] in place; [*troops*] in position; [*leader, party, regime*] ruling; **ne plus tenir en ~** to be restless; **mettre en ~** to put [sth] in place [*programme*]; to put [sth] in position [*team*]; to establish, to set up [*network, institution*]; **6** (in town) square; **la ~ du village** the village square; **7** (Econ) market; **~ financière** financial market; **8** job; **perdre sa ~** to lose one's job; **9 être dans la ~** to be on the inside; **avoir un pied dans la ~** to have a foot in the door.

placebo /plasebo/ *nm* placebo.

placement /plasmɑ̃/ *nm* **1** investment; **2 assurer le ~ des diplômés** to ensure that graduates find employment; **3** (of child) fostering.

placenta /plasɛ̃ta/ *nm* placenta.

placer /plase/ [12] **I** *vtr* **1** to put, to place [*object*]; to seat [*person*]; **~ sa confiance en qn** to put one's trust in sb; **~ ses espoirs en qn** to pin one's hopes on sb; **mal placé** [*pride*] misplaced; **2** to place, to find a job for [*person*]; **3** to invest [*money*]; **4** to slip in [*remark, anecdote*]; **je n'arrive pas à en ~ une**○ **avec elle!** I can't get a word in edgeways (GB) or edgewise (US) with her!; **5** to place [sb] in care [*child*].
II se placer *v refl* (+ *v être*) **1 se ~ près de** to sit next to; **2 se ~ premier** to come first; **des amis haut placés** friends in high places.

placide /plasid/ *adj* placid, calm.

plafond /plafɔ̃/ *nm* **1** ceiling; (of tent, vehicle, tunnel) roof; **2** ceiling, limit.

plafonnier /plafɔnje/ *nm* (gen) flush-fitting ceiling light; (in car) interior light.

plage /plaʒ/ *nf* beach.
■ **~ arrière** rear window shelf; **~ horaire** time slot.

plagiaire /plaʒjɛʀ/ *nmf* plagiarist.

plagiat /plaʒja/ *nm* plagiarism.

plagier /plaʒje/ [2] *vtr* to plagiarize.

plaid /plɛd/ *nm* tartan rug (GB), plaid blanket (US).

plaider /plede/ [1] **I** *vtr* to plead [*case*].
II *vi* **1** to plead; **2 ~ en faveur de qn** [*circumstances*] to speak in favour[GB] of sb.

plaidoirie /plɛdwaʀi/ *nf* plea.

plaidoyer /plɛdwaje/ *nm* **1** speech for the defence[GB]; **2** plea.

plaie /plɛ/ *nf* **1** wound; sore; cut; **2**○ **cet enfant, quelle ~**○**!** that child is such a pain○!

plaignant, ~e /plɛɲɑ̃, ɑ̃t/ *nm,f* plaintiff.

plaindre /plɛ̃dʀ/ [54] **I** *vtr* to pity.

II se plaindre *v refl* (+ *v être*) **1** to complain; **2** [*injured person*] to moan.

plaine /plɛn/ *nf* plain.

plain-pied: **de plain-pied** /dəplɛ̃pje/ *phr* **une maison de ~** a single-storey (GB) or single-story (US) house.

plainte /plɛ̃t/ *nf* **1** (gen, Law) complaint; **2** moan, groan.

plaintif, -ive /plɛ̃tif, iv/ *adj* plaintive.

plaire /plɛʀ/ [59] **I plaire à** *v+prep* **1 elle plaît aux hommes** men find her attractive; **elle m'a plu tout de suite** I liked her straight away; **2 mon travail me plaît** I like my job; **un modèle qui plaît beaucoup** a very popular model.
II se plaire *v refl* (+ *v être*) **1** [*people, couple*] to like each other; **2 ils se plaisent ici** they like it here; **3 il se plaît à dire qu'il est issu du peuple** he likes to say that he's a son of the people.
III *v impers* **s'il te plaît, s'il vous plaît** please.

plaisance /plɛzɑ̃s/ *nf* **la navigation de ~** boating; **bateau de ~** pleasure boat.

plaisant, ~e /plɛzɑ̃, ɑ̃t/ *adj* **1** pleasant; **2** amusing, funny.

plaisanter /plɛzɑ̃te/ [1] *vi* to joke.

plaisanterie /plɛzɑ̃tʀi/ *nf* joke.

plaisir /plɛziʀ/ *nm* pleasure; **prendre un malin ~ à faire** to take a wicked delight in doing; **faire ~ à qn** to please sb; **faites-moi le ~ de vous taire!** would you please shut up○!; **faire durer le ~** to make the pleasure last; (ironic) to prolong the agony.

plan /plɑ̃/ *nm* **1** (of town, underground) map; (in building) plan, map; **2** (for building) plan; **tirer des ~s** to draw up plans; **3** (of machine) blueprint; **4** (of essay, book) outline, framework; **5** (in cinematography) shot; **premier ~** foreground; **6** level; **au premier ~ de l'actualité** at the forefront of the news; **sur le ~ politique** from a political point of view; **7** plan; **c'est le bon ~**○ it's a good idea.
■ **~ d'eau** artificial lake; **~ d'épargne** savings plan.
IDIOMS **laisser qn en ~**○ to leave sb in the lurch; **laisser qch en ~**○ to leave sth unfinished.

planche /plɑ̃ʃ/ *nf* **1** (gen) plank; (for kneading dough) board; **faire la ~** to float on one's back; **2** plate.
■ **~ à roulettes** (Sport) skateboard; **~ de salut** lifeline; **~ à voile** windsurfing board.
IDIOMS **monter sur les ~s** to go on the stage; **avoir du pain sur la ~**○ to have one's work cut out.

plancher[1]○ /plɑ̃ʃe/ [1] *vi* (students' slang) to work.

plancher[2] /plɑ̃ʃe/ *nm* **1** floor; **2** (Econ) floor; **atteindre un ~** to bottom out.

plancton /plɑ̃ktɔ̃/ *nm* plankton.

planer /plane/ [1] *vi* **1** [*plane, bird*] to glide; **2 laisser ~ le doute** to allow uncertainty to persist; **3**○ to have one's head in the clouds.

planète /planɛt/ *nf* planet.

planeur /planœʀ/ *nm* **1** glider; **2** gliding.

planifier /planifje/ [2] *vtr* to plan.

planning○ /planiŋ/ *nm* (controversial) schedule.
■ **~ familial** family planning service.

planque○ /plɑ̃k/ *nf* (for person) hideout.

planquer○ /plɑ̃ke/ [1] **I** *vtr* to hide [*person*]; to hide [sth] away [*object*].
II se planquer *v refl* (+ *v être*) to hide.

plant /plɑ̃/ *nm* young plant.

plantaire /plɑ̃tɛʀ/ *adj* (Anat) plantar; **voûte ~** arch of the foot.

plantation /plɑ̃tasjɔ̃/ *nf* **1** plantation; **2** (of flowers) bed; (of vegetables) patch.

plante /plɑ̃t/ *nf* **1** plant; **~ verte** houseplant; **~ grasse** succulent; **2 ~ (des pieds)** sole (of the foot).

planter /plɑ̃te/ [1] **I** *vtr* **1** to plant [*flowers, shrub*]; **2** to drive in [*stake*]; to knock in [*nail*]; **~ un couteau dans** to stick a knife into; **3** to pitch [*tent*]; **~ le décor** to set the scene; **4 ~ (là)** to drop [*tool*]; to abandon [*car*].
II se planter *v refl* (+ *v être*) **1**○ **aller se ~ devant qch** to go and stand in front of sth; **2**○ to crash; **3**○ to get it wrong; **il s'est planté en histoire** he made a mess of the history exam.

plantureux, -euse /plɑ̃tyʀø, øz/ *adj* [*bosom*] ample; [*woman*] buxom.

plaque /plak/ *nf* (of ice) patch; (on skin) blotch; (of glass) plate; (of marble) slab; (on door of surgery) brass plate; (of policeman) badge.
■ **~ d'égout** manhole cover; **~ d'immatriculation** number plate (GB), license plate (US).
IDIOMS **être à côté de la ~**○ to be completely mistaken.

plaqué, ~e /plake/ *adj* **~ or** gold-plated.

plaquer /plake/ [1] **I** *vtr* **1 ~ qn contre qch** to pin sb against sth; **2**○ to leave [*job, spouse*].
II se plaquer *v refl* (+ *v être*) **se ~ contre un mur** to flatten oneself against a wall.

plaquette /plakɛt/ *nf* **1** (of butter) packet; **2** (of pills) ≈ blister strip.
■ **~ de frein** brake shoe.

plastic /plastik/ *nm* plastic explosive.

plastifier /plastifje/ [2] *vtr* to coat [sth] with plastic.

plastique[1] /plastik/ *nm* plastic.

plastique[2] /plastik/ *nf* (of object, statue) formal beauty; (of person) physique.

plastiquer /plastike/ [1] *vtr* to carry out a bomb attack on.

plastron /plastʀɔ̃/ *nm* shirt front.

plat, ~e /pla, plat/ **I** *adj* **1** flat; **2** [*boat*] flat-bottomed; [*watch, lighter*] slimline; [*hair*] limp; **3** [*style, description*] lifeless.
II *nm* **1** dish; **2** course.
III à plat *phr* **1 poser qch à ~** to lay sth down flat; **à ~ ventre** flat on one's stomach; **tomber à ~** [*joke*] to fall flat; **2** [*tyre*] flat; [*battery*] flat (GB), dead; **3**○ **être à ~** [*person*] to be run down.
■ **~ de résistance** main course.
IDIOMS **mettre les pieds dans le ~**○ to put one's foot in it; **faire tout un ~ de qch**○ to make a big deal about sth.

platane /platan/ *nm* plane tree.

plateau, *pl* **~x** /plato/ *nm* **1** tray; **2 ~ de tournage** film set; **3** (in geography) plateau; **4** (of weighing scales) pan.

plate-bande, *pl* **plates-bandes** /platbɑ̃d/ *nf* border, flower bed.

plate-forme, *pl* **plates-formes** /platfɔʀm/ *nf* platform; **~ pétrolière** oil rig.

platine[1] /platin/ *adj inv*, *nm* platinum.

platine[2] /platin/ *nf* (record player) turntable.

platitude /platityd/ *nf* platitude.

platonique /platɔnik/ *adj* platonic.

plâtre /plɑtʀ/ *nm* **1** plaster; **2** (Med) plaster cast.

IDIOMS **essuyer les ~s** to put up with the initial problems.

plâtrer /plɑtʀe/ [1] *vtr* **1** to plaster [*wall*]; **2** (Med) **~ le bras de qn** to put sb's arm in plaster.

plausible /plozibl/ *adj* plausible.

playback /plɛbak/ *nm inv* miming, lip syncing; **chanter en ~** to lip-sync (a song).

plébiscite /plebisit/ *nm* plebiscite.

plein, **~e** /plɛ̃, plɛn/ **I** *adj* **1** full; **2 un ~ panier** a basketful; **prendre à ~es mains** to pick up a handful of [*earth, sand, coins*]; **3** [*brick, wall*] solid; [*cheeks, face*] plump; [*shape*] rounded; **4** [*power, effect*] full; [*satisfaction, confidence*] complete; **5** [*day, month*] whole, full; [*moon*] full; **6 en ~e poitrine/réunion/forêt** (right) in the middle of the chest/meeting/forest; **en ~ jour** in broad daylight; **en ~ été** at the height of summer; **7** (Zool) **~e** [*animal*] pregnant; [*cow*] in calf; **8**○ sloshed○, drunk; **9 veste ~e peau** jacket made out of full skins.

II *adv* **1 avoir des billes ~ les poches** to have one's pockets full of marbles; **il a des idées ~ la tête** he's full of ideas; **2 être orienté ~ sud** to face due south.

III *nm* **faire le ~ de** to fill up with [*water, petrol*]; **le ~ s'il vous plaît** fill it up please.

IV plein de○ *quantif* **~ de** lots of, loads○ of.

V à plein *phr* fully.

VI tout plein○ *phr* really.

IDIOMS **en avoir ~ le dos**○ to be fed up.

plein-air /plɛnɛʀ/ *nm inv* (Sch) (outdoor) games.

plein-temps, *pl* **pleins-temps** /plɛ̃tɑ̃/ *nm* full-time job.

pléonasme /pleɔnasm/ *nm* pleonasm.

pleurer /plœʀe/ [1] **I** *vtr* to mourn [*friend*].

II *vi* **1** to cry, to weep; **2** [*eyes*] to water; **3 ~ sur qn/qch** to shed tears over sb/sth; **arrête de ~ sur ton sort!** stop feeling sorry for yourself!; **4**○ [*person*] to whine.

IDIOMS **elle n'a plus que ses yeux pour ~** all she can do is cry.

pleureur /plœʀœʀ/ *adj m* **saule ~** weeping willow.

pleurnicher○ /plœʀniʃe/ [1] *vi* to snivel.

pleurs /plœʀ/ *nm pl* tears; **en ~** in tears.

pleuvoir /pløvwaʀ/ [39] **I** *v impers* to rain; **il pleut** it's raining; **il pleut à torrents** it's pouring with rain.

II *vi* [*blows, bombs*] to rain down.

pli /pli/ *nm* **1** (gen) fold; (in trousers) crease; (in skirt) pleat; **2** (Games) trick; **3** letter; **sous ~ cacheté** in a sealed envelope.

IDIOMS **ça ne fait pas un ~**○ there's no doubt about it; **c'est un ~ à prendre** it's something you've got to get used to.

plier /plije/ [2] **I** *vtr* **1** to fold; to fold up; **2** to bend [*stem, arm*]; **3** to submit.

II *vi* **1** [*tree, branch, joint*] to bend; [*plank, floor*] to sag; **2** to give in.

III se plier *v refl* (+ *v être*) **1** to fold; **2 se ~ à** to submit to.

IDIOMS **être plié (en deux**○ or **quatre**○**)** to be doubled up with laughter.

plinthe /plɛ̃t/ *nf* skirting board (GB), baseboard (US).

plisser /plise/ [1] **I** *vtr* **1** to pleat [*cloth*]; **2** to crease [*garment*]; **3 ~ le front** to knit one's brows; **~ les yeux** to screw up one's eyes.

II *vi* [*stocking*] to wrinkle; [*skirt*] to be creased.

pliure /plijyʀ/ *nf* fold; **la ~ du genou** the back of the knee.

plomb /plɔ̃/ *nm* **1** lead; **sans ~** [*petrol*] unleaded; **soleil de ~** burning sun; **ciel de ~** leaden sky; **2** (in hunting) **un ~** a lead pellet; **du ~** lead shot; **3** fuse.

IDIOMS **avoir du ~ dans l'aile**○ to be in a bad way○; **cela va leur mettre du ~ dans la cervelle**○ that will knock some sense into them.

plombage /plɔ̃baʒ/ *nm* (in dentistry) filling.

plomber /plɔ̃be/ [1] *vtr* to fill [*tooth*].

plombier /plɔ̃bje/ *nm* plumber.

plonge○ /plɔ̃ʒ/ *nf* washing up, dishwashing (US).

plongée /plɔ̃ʒe/ *nf* **1** (skin) diving; **2** scuba diving; **3** snorkelling[GB]; **~ sous-marine** deep-sea diving; **faire de la ~** to go diving.

plongeoir /plɔ̃ʒwaʀ/ *nm* **1** diving-board; **2** springboard.

plongeon /plɔ̃ʒɔ̃/ *nm* **1** dive; **2** fall.

plonger /plɔ̃ʒe/ [13] **I** *vtr* to plunge.

II *vi* **1** to dive; **2** [*bird*] to swoop down.

III se plonger *v refl* (+ *v être*) **1** to plunge; **2** to bury oneself.

plongeur, **-euse** /plɔ̃ʒœʀ, øz/ *nm,f* **1** diver; **2** dishwasher.

plot /plo/ *nm* **1** (electrical) contact; **2** (of wood) block.

ployer /plwaje/ [23] *vi* [*branch, person*] to bend; **~ sous un fardeau** to be weighed down by a burden.

pluie /plɥi/ *nf* **1** rain; **sous une ~ battante** in driving rain; **2** (of missiles, insults) hail; (of sparks, compliments) shower.

■ **~s acides** acid rain.

IDIOMS **il n'est pas né de la dernière ~**○ he wasn't born yesterday○; **faire la ~ et le beau temps** to call the shots○.

plume /plym/ *nf* **1** (Zool) feather; **2** (pen) nib; **écrire au fil de la ~** to write as the thoughts come into one's head.

IDIOMS **voler dans les ~s de qn**○ to fly at sb.

plumeau, *pl* **~x** /plymo/ *nm* **1** feather duster; **2** tuft.

plumer /plyme/ [1] *vtr* to pluck [*bird*].

plumier /plymje/ *nm* pencil box.

plupart: **la plupart** /laplypaʀ/ *nf inv* **la ~ des gens** most people; **la ~ du temps** most of the time, mostly.

pluriel, **-elle** /plyʀjɛl/ I *adj* plural.
II *nm* plural.

plus[1] /ply, plys, plyz/ I *prep* plus.
II *adv* **1** (comparative) more; (superlative) **le ~** the most; **il travaille ~ (que moi)** he works more (than I do); **~ j'y pense, moins je comprends** the more I think about it, the less I understand; **~ ça va** as time goes on; **qui ~ est** furthermore; **de ~ en ~** more and more; **~ petit** smaller; **le ~ petit** the smallest; **trois heures ~ tôt** three hours earlier; **deux fois ~ cher** twice as expensive; **il est on ne peut ~ désagréable** he's as unpleasant as can be; **il est ~ ou moins artiste** he's an artist of sorts; **il a été ~ ou moins poli** he wasn't particularly polite; **2** (in negative constructions) **elle ne fume ~** she doesn't smoke any more; **il n'y a ~ d'œufs** there are no more eggs; **~ jamais ça!** never again!; **~ que trois jours avant Noël!** only three days to go until Christmas!
III **plus de** *quantif* **deux fois ~ de livres que** twice as many books as; **il a gagné le ~ d'argent** he won the most money; **les gens de ~ de 60 ans** people over 60.
IV **au plus** *phr* at the most.
V **de plus** *phr* **1** furthermore, what's more; **2 donnez-moi deux pommes de ~** give me two more apples; **une fois de ~** once more.
VI **en plus** *phr* **en ~ (de cela)** on top of that; **les taxes en ~** plus tax.

plus[2] /plys/ *nm inv* **1 le signe ~** the plus sign; **2**○ plus○.

plusieurs /plyzjœʀ/ I *adj* several; **une ou ~ personnes** one or more people.
II *pron* **~ ont déjà signé** several people have already signed.

plus-value, *pl* **~s** /plyvaly/ *nf* **1** (of property) increase in value; (sales profit) capital gain; **2** surcharge; **3** (Econ) surplus value.

plutôt /plyto/ *adv* rather; instead; **passe ~ le matin** call round (GB) or come by (US) in the morning preferably; **~ mourir!** I'd rather die!; **demande ~ à Corinne** ask Corinne instead; **dis ~ que tu n'as pas envie de le faire** why don't you just say that you don't want to do it?; **la nouvelle a été ~ bien accueillie** the news went down rather well.

pluvieux, **-ieuse** /plyvjø, øz/ *adj* wet, rainy.

PME /peɛmə/ *nf pl* (*abbr* = **petites et moyennes entreprises**) small and medium-sized enterprises, SMEs.

PMI /peɛmi/ *nf pl* (*abbr* = **petites et moyennes industries**) small and medium-sized industries.

PMU /peɛmy/ *nm* (*abbr* = **Pari mutuel urbain**) *French state-controlled betting system.*

PNB /peɛnbe/ *nm* (*abbr* = **produit national brut**) gross national product, GNP.

pneu /pnø/ *nm* tyre (GB), tire (US).

pneumatique /pnømatik/ *adj* inflatable.

pneumonie /pnømɔni/ *nf* pneumonia.

poche[1] /pɔʃ/ *nm* **(livre de) ~** paperback.

poche[2] /pɔʃ/ *nf* **1** (in garment, bag) pocket; **en ~** in one's pocket; **il avait 1000 francs en ~** he had 1,000 francs on him; **s'en mettre plein** or **se remplir les ~s**○ to line one's pockets; **faire les ~s de qn** to pick sb's pocket; **2 ~ de gaz/d'air** gas/air pocket; **3 avoir des ~s sous les yeux** to have bags under one's eyes; **4** (Zool) (of kangaroo) pouch.
■ **~ revolver** hip pocket.
IDIOMS **c'est dans la ~**○ it's in the bag○; **en être de sa ~**○ to be out of pocket; **ne pas avoir les yeux dans sa ~**○ not to miss a thing○; **connaître un endroit comme sa ~**○ to know a place like the back of one's hand.

pocher /pɔʃe/ [1] *vtr* (Culin) to poach.

pochette /pɔʃɛt/ *nf* **1** (for pencils) case; (for credit cards) wallet; (for make-up, glasses) pouch; (for document) folder; (for record) sleeve; **2** (of matches) book; **3** clutch bag.

pochoir /pɔʃwaʀ/ *nm* stencil.

podium /pɔdjɔm/ *nm* podium.

poêle[1] /pwal/ *nm* **1** stove; **2** (on coffin) pall.

poêle[2] /pwal/ *nf* frying pan.

poème /pɔɛm/ *nm* poem; **c'est tout un ~**○ it's quite something.

poésie /pɔezi/ *nf* **1** poetry; **2** poem.

poète /pɔɛt/ *nm* **1** poet; **2** dreamer.

poétique /pɔetik/ *adj* poetic.

poids /pwɑ/ *nm inv* **1** weight; **peser son ~** to be very heavy; **adversaire de ~** opponent to be reckoned with; **2** burden; **être un ~ pour qn** to be a burden on sb; **avoir un ~ sur la conscience** to have a guilty conscience; **3** influence; **4 des ~ en laiton** brass weights; **5** (in athletics) shot; **lancer le ~** to put the shot.
■ **~ et haltères** weightlifting; **~ lourd** (Sport) heavyweight; heavy truck.
IDIOMS **avoir** or **faire deux ~ deux mesures** to have double standards.

poignant, **~e** /pwaɲɑ̃, ɑ̃t/ *adj* **1** poignant; **2** heart-rending, harrowing.

poignard /pwaɲaʀ/ *nm* dagger; **coup de ~** stab.

poignarder /pwaɲaʀde/ [1] *vtr* to stab.

poigne /pwaɲ/ *nf* **avoir de la ~** to have a strong grip; **homme à ~** strong man.

poignée /pwaɲe/ *nf* **1** handful; **2** (of door, drawer, bag) handle; (of sword) hilt.
■ **~ de main** handshake.

poignet /pwaɲɛ/ *nm* **1** wrist; **2** (of shirt) cuff.

poil /pwal/ *nm* **1** (on body, animal) hair; **à ~**○ stark naked; **caresser dans le sens du ~** to stroke [sth] the way the fur lies; to butter [sb] up○; **ça marche au ~**○ it works like a dream; **2**○ (of irony) touch; (of commonsense) shred; **à un ~ près** by a whisker; **3** (of cloth) nap; (of brush) bristle.
■ **~ à gratter** itching powder.

IDIOMS **être de bon/mauvais ~**○ to be in a good/bad mood; **hérisser le ~**○ **de qn** to put sb's back up○; **avoir un ~ dans la main**○ to be bone idle.

poilu, **~e** /pwaly/ *adj* hairy.

poinçon /pwɛ̃sɔ̃/ *nm* **1** (tool) punch; **2** (on gold) die, stamp; hallmark.

poinçonner /pwɛ̃sɔne/ [1] *vtr* **1** to punch, to clip; **2** to hallmark.

poindre /pwɛ̃dʀ/ [56] *vi* [*day*] to break.

poing /pwɛ̃/ *nm* fist; **coup de ~** punch; **montrer le ~** to shake one's fist; **être pieds et ~s liés** (figurative) to have one's hands tied.

IDIOMS **dormir à ~s fermés** to sleep like a log.

point /pwɛ̃/ **I** *nm* **1** point; **un ~ de rencontre** a meeting point; **~ de vente** (sales) outlet; **2** (at sea) position; **faire le ~** to take bearings; (figurative) to take stock of the situation; **3 être sur le ~ de faire** to be just about to do; **au ~ où j'en suis, ça n'a pas d'importance!** I'm past caring!; **4 il m'agace au plus haut ~** he annoys me intensely; **je ne le pensais pas bête à ce ~** I didn't think he was that stupid; **à tel ~ que** to such an extent that; **douloureux au ~ que** so painful that; **5** (on agenda) item, point; **un ~ de détail** a minor point; **en tout ~, en tous ~s** in every respect or way; **6** dot; **un ~ de colle** a spot of glue; **un ~ de rouille** a speck of rust; **~ d'intersection** point of intersection; **7** (Games, Sport) point; **compter les ~s** to keep (the) score; **8** (Sch) mark (GB), point (US); **être un bon ~ pour** to be a plus point for; **9** full stop (GB), period (US); **mettre un ~ final à qch** (figurative) to put a stop to sth; **tu vas te coucher un ~ c'est tout**○**!** you're going to bed and that's final!; **10** (Med) pain; **avoir un ~ à la poitrine** to have a pain in one's chest; **11** (in sewing, knitting) stitch.

II à point *phr* **1 à ~ nommé** just at the right moment; **2 à ~** [*meat*] medium rare.

III au point *phr* **être au ~** [*system, machine*] to be well designed; [*show*] to be well put together; **mettre au ~** to perfect [*system, method*]; to develop [*vaccine, machine*]; **faire la mise au ~** (in photography) to focus; **faire une mise au ~** (figurative) to set the record straight.

■ **~ chaud** trouble or hot spot; **~ de côté** (pain) stitch; **~ de départ** starting point; **nous revoilà à notre ~ de départ** (figurative) we're back to square one; **~ d'eau** water tap (GB) or faucet (US); **~ d'exclamation** exclamation mark; **~ faible** weak point; **~ fort** strong point; **~ d'interrogation** question mark; **~ de mire** (Mil) target; (figurative) focal point; **~ mort** neutral; **être au ~ mort** (in car) to be in neutral; [*business, trade*] to be at a standstill; **~ noir** (Med) blackhead; (of situation) problem; **~ de repère** landmark; point of reference; **~ de suture** (Med) stitch; **~ de vue** point of view; viewpoint; **du ~ de vue du sens** as far as meaning is concerned; **~s de suspension** suspension points.

IDIOMS **être mal en ~** to be in a bad way.

pointage /pwɛ̃taʒ/ *nm* **1** (on list) ticking off (GB), checking off (US); **2** (of employee) clocking in.

pointe /pwɛ̃t/ **I** *nf* **1** (of knife) point; (of shoe) toe; (of hair) end; (of railing) spike; (of spear) tip; **en ~** pointed; **2 de ~** [*technology*] advanced, state-of-the-art; [*sector, industry*] high-tech; **à la ~ du progrès** state-of-the-art; **3** high; **une vitesse de ~ de 200 km/h** a maximum or top speed of 200 kph; **heure de ~** rush hour; **aux heures de ~** at peak time; **4** (of garlic) touch; (of accent) hint; **5** blocked shoe.

II pointes *nf pl* **faire des ~s** to dance on points.

■ **~ du pied** tiptoe.

pointer /pwɛ̃te/ [1] **I** *vtr* **1** to tick off (GB), to check off (US) [*names, figures*]; to check [*list*]; **2** to point [*weapon*]; **~ le doigt vers** to point at; **~ son nez**○ to show one's face.

II *vi* **1** [*employee*] to clock in; **~ à l'agence pour l'emploi** to sign on at the unemployment office; **2** [*sun, plant*] to come up; [*day*] to break.

III se pointer○ *v refl* (+ *v être*) to turn up.

pointillé, **~e** /pwɛ̃tije/ **I** *adj* dotted.

II *nm* dotted line.

pointilleux, **-euse** /pwɛ̃tijø, øz/ *adj* [*person*] fussy, pernickety.

pointu, **~e** /pwɛ̃ty/ *adj* **1** (gen) pointed; [*scissors*] with a sharp point; **2** [*check*] close, thorough; **3** [*question, approach*] precise.

pointure /pwɛ̃tyʀ/ *nf* (of glove, shoe) size.

point-virgule, *pl* **points-virgules** /pwɛ̃ viʀgyl/ *nm* semicolon.

poire /pwaʀ/ *nf* **1** pear; **2**○ sucker○.

IDIOMS **couper la ~ en deux** to split the difference; **garder une ~ pour la soif** to save something for a rainy day.

poireau, *pl* **~x** /pwaʀo/ *nm* leek.

poirier /pwaʀje/ *nm* **1** pear (tree); **2 faire le ~** to do a headstand.

pois /pwa/ *nm inv* **1** (Bot, Culin) pea; **petit ~** (garden) pea; **2** dot; **à ~** polka dot, spotted.

■ **~ cassé** split pea; **~ chiche** chickpea.

poison /pwazɔ̃/ *nm* poison.

poisse○ /pwas/ *nf* **1** rotten luck○; **2** drag○.

poisseux, **-euse** /pwasø, øz/ *adj* [*hands, table*] sticky; [*atmosphere*] muggy; [*restaurant*] greasy.

poisson /pwasɔ̃/ *nm* fish; **les ~s d'eau douce/de mer** freshwater/saltwater fish.

■ **~ rouge** goldfish.

IDIOMS **être comme un ~ dans l'eau** to be in one's element.

poissonnerie /pwasɔnʀi/ *nf* fishmonger's (shop) (GB), fish shop (US).

poissonnier, **-ière** /pwasɔnje, ɛʀ/ *nm,f* fishmonger (GB), fish vendor (US).

Poissons /pwasɔ̃/ *pr nm pl* Pisces.

poitrail /pwatʀaj/ *nm* breast.

poitrine /pwatʀin/ *nf* **1** chest; **tour de ~** chest size; **2** breasts; **tour de ~** bust size.

■ **~ fumée** ≈ smoked streaky bacon.

poivre /pwavʀ/ *nm* pepper.

poivré, **~e** /pwavʀe/ *adj* [*sauce*] peppery.

poivrer /pwavʀe/ [1] *vtr* to add pepper to.

poivron /pwavʀɔ̃/ *nm* sweet pepper, capsicum.

poivrot○, **~e** /pwavʀo, ɔt/ *nm,f* drunk.

poker /pɔkɛʀ/ *nm* poker; **coup de ~** gamble.

polaire /pɔlɛʀ/ *adj* polar; arctic.

polar○ /pɔlaʀ/ *nm* detective novel.

polariser /pɔlaʀize/ [1] *vtr*, **se polariser** *v refl* (+ *v être*) **1** to polarize; **2** to focus.

pôle /pol/ *nm* **1** pole; **2** centre[GB].

polémique /pɔlemik/ *nf* debate.

poli, **~e** /pɔli/ **I** *pp* ▶ **polir**.
II *pp adj* [*metal, style*] polished.
III *adj* polite.
IV *nm* shine.

police /pɔlis/ *nf* **1** police; police force; **2** security service; **3 faire la ~** to keep order; **4** (in insurance) policy.
■ **~ judiciaire**, **PJ** *detective division of the French police force*; **~ des mœurs** or **mondaine** vice squad; **~ secours** ≈ emergency services.

policier, **-ière** /pɔlisje, ɛʀ/ **I** *adj* (gen) police; [*novel*] detective.
II *nm* policeman; **femme ~** policewoman.

poliment /pɔlimɑ̃/ *adv* politely.

polir /pɔliʀ/ [3] *vtr* to polish [*stone, metal*].

polisson, **-onne** /pɔlisɔ̃, ɔn/ *nm,f* naughty child.

politesse /pɔlitɛs/ *nf* politeness; **rendre la ~ à qn** to return the compliment.

politicien, **-ienne** /pɔlitisjɛ̃, ɛn/ *nm,f* politician.

politique[1] /pɔlitik/ *adj* (gen) political; [*behaviour, act*] calculating.

politique[2] /pɔlitik/ *nf* **1** politics; **faire de la ~** [*militant*] to be involved in politics; **2** policy; **notre ~ des prix** our pricing policy.
IDIOMS **pratiquer la ~ de l'autruche** to stick one's head in the sand; **pratiquer la ~ du pire** to envisage the worst-case scenario.

politiser /pɔlitize/ [1] *vtr* to politicize.

pollen /pɔl(l)ɛn/ *nm* pollen.

polluer /pɔl(l)ɥe/ [1] *vtr* to pollute.

pollution /pɔl(l)ysjɔ̃/ *nf* pollution.

polo /pɔlo/ *nm* **1** polo shirt; **2** (Sport) polo.

polochon○ /pɔlɔʃɔ̃/ *nm* bolster; **bataille de ~s** pillow fight.

Pologne /pɔlɔɲ/ *pr nf* Poland.

polycopier /pɔlikɔpje/ [2] *vtr* to duplicate.

polygame /pɔligam/ *adj* polygamous.

polyglotte /pɔliglɔt/ *adj, nmf* polyglot.

Polytechnique /pɔlitɛknik/ *nf*: *Grande École of Science and Technology.*

polyvalence /pɔlivalɑ̃s/ *nf* **1** versatility; **2** (of employee) flexibility.

pommade /pɔmad/ *nf* (Med) ointment.
IDIOMS **passer de la ~**○ **à qn** to butter sb up○.

pomme /pɔm/ *nf* **1** apple; **2** (of watering can) rose; (of shower) shower-head; (of walking stick) pommel, knob; **3**○ mug○ (GB), sucker○; **ça va encore être pour ma ~** I'm in for it again○.
■ **~ d'Adam** Adam's apple; **~ de pin** pine cone; **~ de terre** potato; **~s frites** chips (GB), (French) fries.
IDIOMS **tomber dans les ~s**○ to faint.

pommeau, *pl* **~x** /pɔmo/ *nm* knob; pommel.

pommette /pɔmɛt/ *nf* cheekbone.

pommier /pɔmje/ *nm* apple tree.

pompe /pɔ̃p/ *nf* **1** pump; **2**◑ shoe; **3** pomp; **4**○ (Sport) press-up (GB), push-up.
■ **~ à essence** petrol pump (GB), gas pump (US); **~s funèbres** undertaker's (GB), funeral director's.
IDIOMS **avoir un coup de ~**○ to be knackered◑ (GB) or pooped○.

pomper /pɔ̃pe/ [1] *vtr* **1** to pump [*liquid, air*]; **2**○ (students' slang) to copy.
IDIOMS **~ l'air**○ **à qn** to get on sb's nerves.

pompette○ /pɔ̃pɛt/ *adj* tipsy○, drunk.

pompeux, **-euse** /pɔ̃pø, øz/ *adj* pompous.

pompier, **-ière** /pɔ̃pje, ɛʀ/ **I** *adj* pompous.
II *nm* fireman, firefighter; **appeler les ~s** to call the fire brigade (GB) or department (US).

pompiste /pɔ̃pist/ *nmf* petrol (GB) or gas (US) pump attendant.

pompon /pɔ̃pɔ̃/ *nm* (on hat) pompom, bobble; (on slipper) pompom.
IDIOMS **décrocher le ~**○ to win first prize.

pomponner: **se pomponner** /pɔ̃pɔne/ [1] *v refl* (+ *v être*) to get dolled up.

ponce /pɔ̃s/ *nf* **pierre ~** pumice stone.

poncer /pɔ̃se/ [12] *vtr* **1** (Tech) to sand; **2** to pumice.

ponceuse /pɔ̃søz/ *nf* sander.

ponction /pɔ̃ksjɔ̃/ *nf* **1** (Med) puncture; **2** levy.

ponctualité /pɔ̃ktɥalite/ *nf* punctuality.

ponctuation /pɔ̃ktɥasjɔ̃/ *nf* punctuation.

ponctuel, **-elle** /pɔ̃ktɥɛl/ *adj* **1** [*person*] punctual; **2** [*action*] limited; [*problem*] isolated.

ponctuer /pɔ̃ktɥe/ [1] *vtr* to punctuate.

pondéré, **~e** /pɔ̃deʀe/ *adj* **1** [*person*] level-headed; **2** [*factor*] weighted.

pondre /pɔ̃dʀ/ [6] *vtr* **1** to lay [*egg*]; **2**○ to churn out○ [*poetry, articles*].

poney /pɔnɛ/ *nm* pony.

pont /pɔ̃/ **I** *nm* **1** bridge; **2** link, tie; **couper les ~s** to break off all contact; **3** extended weekend (*including days between a public holiday and a weekend*); **4** deck.
II ponts *nm pl* **~s (et chaussées)** highways department.
■ **~ aérien** airlift; **~ à péage** toll bridge.
IDIOMS **coucher sous les ~s** to sleep rough, to be a tramp; **il coulera beaucoup d'eau sous les ~s avant que**... it will be a long time before...; **faire un ~ d'or à qn** to offer sb a large sum to accept a job.

pontife /pɔ̃tif/ *nm* **1** pontiff; **le souverain ~** the pope; **2**○ pundit○.

pontificat /pɔ̃tifika/ *nm* pontificate.

pontifier /pɔ̃tifje/ [2] *vi* to pontificate.

pont-levis, *pl* **ponts-levis** /pɔ̃ləvi/ *nm* drawbridge.

ponton /pɔ̃tɔ̃/ *nm* **1** landing stage; **2** pontoon.

pope /pɔp/ *nm* pope, orthodox priest.

popote° /pɔpɔt/ *nf* cooking.

populace /pɔpylas/ *nf* **la ~** the masses.

populaire /pɔpylɛʀ/ *adj* **1** [*suburb*] working-class; [*art, novel*] popular; [*edition*] cheap; [*restaurant*] basic; **classe ~** working class; **2** [*tradition*] folk; **culture ~** folklore; **3** popular; **4** [*revolt*] popular; [*will*] of the people; **5** [*expression, term*] vulgar; **6 République ~** People's Republic.

popularité /pɔpylaʀite/ *nf* popularity.

population /pɔpylasjɔ̃/ *nf* population.

porc /pɔʀ/ *nm* **1** pig, hog (US); **2** pork; **3** pigskin.

porcelaine /pɔʀsəlɛn/ *nf* porcelain, china.

porcelet /pɔʀsəlɛ/ *nm* piglet.

porc-épic, *pl* **~s** /pɔʀkepik/ *nm* porcupine.

porche /pɔʀʃ/ *nm* porch.

porcherie /pɔʀʃəʀi/ *nf* pigsty.

porcin, **~e** /pɔʀsɛ̃, in/ *adj* porcine.

pore /pɔʀ/ *nm* pore.

poreux, **-euse** /pɔʀø, øz/ *adj* porous.

porno° /pɔʀno/ *adj, nm* porn°.

pornographique /pɔʀnɔgʀafik/ *adj* pornographic.

port /pɔʀ/ *nm* **1** harbour[GB]; port; **2** haven; **3** wearing; carrying; **4** bearing; **5** (transport) carriage; postage.

■ **~ d'attache** port of registry; home base; **~ de pêche** fishing harbour[GB]; fishing port; **~ de plaisance** marina.

IDIOMS **arriver à bon ~** to arrive safe and sound.

portable /pɔʀtabl/ *adj* portable; **ordinateur ~** laptop computer.

portail /pɔʀtaj/ *nm* (of park) gate; (of church) great door.

portant, **~e** /pɔʀtɑ̃, ɑ̃t/ *adj* **1** [*wall*] load-bearing; **2 bien ~** in good health.

IDIOMS **à bout ~** at point-blank range.

portatif, **-ive** /pɔʀtatif, iv/ *adj* portable.

porte /pɔʀt/ *nf* **1** door; gate; **devant la ~ de l'hôpital** outside the hospital; **aux ~s du désert** at the edge of the desert; **ouvrir sa ~ à qn** to let sb in; **c'est la ~ ouverte à la criminalité** it's an open invitation to crime; **mettre à la ~** to expel; to fire; **ce n'est pas la ~ à côté**° it's quite far; **2** gateway; **la victoire leur ouvre la ~ de la finale** the victory clears the way to the final for them; **3** (in airport) gate; **4** (car) door.

■ **~ battante** swing door; **~ d'écluse** lock gate; **~ d'entrée** front door; main entrance; **~ de service** service entrance; **~ de sortie** exit; escape route.

IDIOMS **prendre la ~** to leave; **entrer par la petite/grande ~** to start at the bottom/top.

porté, **~e**[1] /pɔʀte/ *adj* **être ~ sur qch** to be keen on sth.

porte-à-faux /pɔʀtafo/ *nm inv* **être en ~** [*wall*] to be out of plumb; [*construction*] to be cantilevered; [*person*] to be in an awkward position.

porte-à-porte /pɔʀtapɔʀt/ *nm inv* **1** door-to-door selling; **2** door-to-door canvassing.

porte-avions /pɔʀtavjɔ̃/ *nm inv* aircraft carrier.

porte-bagages /pɔʀt(ə)bagaʒ/ *nm inv* carrier; luggage rack; roof rack.

porte-bébé /pɔʀt(ə)bebe/ *nm inv* baby carrier.

porte-bonheur /pɔʀt(ə)bɔnœʀ/ *nm inv* lucky charm.

porte-clés, **porte-clefs** /pɔʀt(ə)kle/ *nm inv* key ring.

porte-documents /pɔʀt(ə)dɔkymɑ̃/ *nm inv* briefcase, attaché case.

portée[2] /pɔʀte/ **I** *adj f* ▶ **porté**.

II *nf* **1** range; **être à ~ de main** or **à la ~ de la main** to be within reach; to be to hand; **2 c'est à la ~ de n'importe qui** anybody can do it; anybody can understand it; **se mettre à la ~ de qn** to come down to sb's level; **3** impact; **4** (of kittens) litter; **5** (Mus) staff, stave (GB).

porte-fenêtre, *pl* **portes-fenêtres** /pɔʀt(ə)fənɛtʀ/ *nf* French window.

portefeuille /pɔʀt(ə)fœj/ **I** *adj* **jupe ~** wrap-over skirt.

II *nm* **1** wallet, billfold (US); **2** portfolio.

porte-jarretelles /pɔʀt(ə)ʒaʀtɛl/ *nm inv* suspender belt (GB), garter belt (US).

portemanteau, *pl* **~x** /pɔʀt(ə)mɑ̃to/ *nm* **1** coat rack; **2** coat stand; **3** coat hanger.

portemine /pɔʀt(ə)min/ *nm* propelling (GB) or mechanical (US) pencil.

porte-monnaie /pɔʀt(ə)mɔnɛ/ *nm inv* purse (GB), coin purse (US).

porte-parapluies /pɔʀt(ə)paʀaplɥi/ *nm inv* umbrella stand.

porte-parole /pɔʀt(ə)paʀɔl/ *nm inv* spokesperson, spokesman/spokeswoman.

porter /pɔʀte/ [1] **I** *vtr* **1** to carry; **2 ~ qch quelque part** to take sth somewhere; **~ qch à qn** to take sb sth; **3** [*wall, chair*] to carry, to bear [*weight*]; **4** to wear [*dress, contact lenses*]; to have [*moustache*]; **5** to have [*initials, date, name*]; to bear [*seal*]; **il porte bien son nom** the name suits him; **6** to bear [*flowers*]; **7 ~ qch à** to bring sth up to, to put sth up to [*rate, number*]; **~ la température de l'eau à 80°C** to heat the water to 80°C; **8 ~ son regard vers** to look at; **si tu portes la main sur elle** if you lay a finger on her; **~ un jugement sur qch** to pass judgment on sth; **9 ~ qch sur un registre** to enter sth on a register; **se faire ~ malade** to report sick; **~ plainte** to lodge a complaint; **10 tout nous porte à croire que** everything leads us to believe that; **11 ~ bonheur** or **chance** to be lucky.

II porter sur *v+prep* [*debate*] to be about; [*measure*] to concern; [*ban*] to apply to.

III *vi* **une voix qui porte** a voice that carries; **le coup a porté** the blow hit home.

IV se porter *v refl* (+ *v être*) **1 se ~ bien/mal** [*person*] to be well/ill; [*business*] to be going well/badly; **2 se ~ sur** [*suspicion*] to fall on; [*infection*] to spread to.

porte-savon /pɔʀt(ə)savɔ̃/ *nm inv* soapdish.

porte-serviettes /pɔʀt(ə)sɛʀvjɛt/ *nm inv* towel rail.

porteur, **-euse** /pɔRtœR, øz/ **I** *adj* **1 être ~ d'un virus** to carry a virus; **2 mur ~** load-bearing wall; **3** [*market, sector*] expanding; **4** [*current, wave, frequency*] carrier.
II *nm,f* holder, bearer.
III *nm* **1** porter; messenger; **2** (of cheque) bearer; **~ d'actions** shareholder.
■ **~ sain** (Med) symptom-free carrier.

porte-voix /pɔRt(ə)vwɑ/ *nm inv* megaphone.

portier /pɔRtje/ *nm* porter.

portière /pɔRtjɛR/ *nf* (of car) door.

portillon /pɔRtijɔ̃/ *nm* gate.

portion /pɔRsjɔ̃/ *nf* **1** (Culin) portion; helping; **2** part, portion; (of road) stretch.
IDIOMS **réduire qn à la ~ congrue** to give sb the strict minimum.

portique /pɔRtik/ *nm* **1** portico; **2** (in gym) frame; **3** swing frame.

porto /pɔRto/ *nm* port.

portoricain, **~e** /pɔRtoRikɛ̃, ɛn/ *adj* Puerto Rican.

portrait /pɔRtRɛ/ *nm* **1** portrait; **2** description, picture; **3 tu es tout le ~ de ton père** you're the spitting image of your father; **4**○ face; **se faire tirer le ~** to have one's photo taken.

portrait-robot, *pl* **portraits-robots** /pɔRtRɛRɔbo/ *nm* photofit®, identikit®.

portuaire /pɔRtɥɛR/ *adj* port.

portugais, **~e** /pɔRtygɛ, ɛz/ **I** *adj* Portuguese.
II *nm* (language) Portuguese.

Portugal /pɔRtygal/ *pr nm* Portugal.

pose /poz/ *nf* **1** (of window) putting in; (of cupboard) fitting; (of carpet) laying; **2** pose; **prendre une ~** to strike a pose; **3** (in photography) exposure.

posé, **~e** /poze/ *adj* [*air, person*] composed; [*gesture, voice*] controlled.

posément /pozemɑ̃/ *adv* calmly, carefully.

poser /poze/ [1] **I** *vtr* **1** to put down [*book, glass*]; **2** to put in [*window*]; to install [*radiator*]; to fit [*lock*]; to lay [*tiling, cable*]; to plant [*bomb*]; to put up [*wallpaper, curtains*]; **3** to assert [*theory*]; **~ sa candidature à un poste** to apply for a job; **~ une addition** to write a sum down; **4** to ask [*question*]; to set [*riddle*]; **ça ne pose aucun problème** that's no problem at all; **5** (Mus) to place [*voice*].
II *vi* **1** to pose; **2** to put on airs.
III se poser *v refl* (+ *v être*) **1** [*bird, insect*] to settle; **2** [*plane*] to land; **3** [*eyes*] to fall; **4 se ~ en** to claim to be; to present oneself as; **5 se ~ des questions** to ask oneself questions; **6** [*problem, case*] to arise; **la question ne se pose pas** there's no question of it; it goes without saying.

poseur, **-euse** /pozœR, øz/ *nm,f* poser○.
■ **~ de bombes** bomber; **~ de moquette** carpet fitter.

positif, **-ive** /pozitif, iv/ *adj* **1** [*reply*] affirmative; **2** [*interview*] constructive; [*outcome*] positive; **3** [*reaction*] favourable[GB]; **4** [*person, attitude*] positive; **5** [*number*] positive.

position /pozisjɔ̃/ *nf* **1** position; **en ~ horizontale** horizontally; **placer qn dans une ~ difficile** to put sb in a difficult or an awkward position; **2** (in ranking) place, position; **3** position, stance; **prendre ~ sur un problème** to take a stand on an issue; **camper sur ses ~s** to stand one's ground; **4** (bank) balance.

positivement /pozitivmɑ̃/ *adv* [*answer*] positively; [*react, judge*] favourably[GB].

posologie /pɔzɔlɔʒi/ *nf* dosage.

possédé, **~e** /pɔsede/ *nm,f* **les ~s** the possessed.

posséder /pɔsede/ [14] *vtr* **1** to own, to possess [*property, army*]; to hold [*responsibility*]; **2** to have [*skill, quality*]; **3** to speak [sth] fluently; to have a thorough knowledge of [sth]; **4** [*anger, pain*] to overwhelm; **5**○ **il nous a bien possédés** he really had○ us there.

possesseur /pɔsɛsœR/ *nm* (of property) owner; (of diploma) holder; (of passport) bearer.

possessif, **-ive** /pɔsesif, iv/ *adj* possessive.

possession /pɔsesjɔ̃/ *nf* possession.

possibilité /pɔsibilite/ **I** *nf* **1** possibility; **2** opportunity; **~ d'embauche** job opportunity.
II possibilités *nf pl* **1** (of person) abilities; (of device) potential uses; **2** resources.

possible /pɔsibl/ **I** *adj* **1** possible; **dès que ~** as soon as possible; **tout le courage ~** the utmost courage; **tous les cas ~s et imaginables** every conceivable case; **le plus cher ~** [*sell*] at the highest possible price; **autant que ~** as much as possible; **il n'y a pas d'erreur ~, c'est lui** it's him, without a shadow of a doubt; **tout est ~** anything is possible; **pas ~**○! I don't believe it!; you're joking!; **'tu vas acheter une voiture?'—'~'** 'are you going to buy a car?'—'maybe'; **2**○ **il a une chance pas ~** he's incredibly lucky.
II *nm* **faire (tout) son ~** to do one's best.

post(-) /pɔst/ *pref* post(-).

postal, **~e**, *mpl* **-aux** /pɔstal, o/ *adj* [*van*] post office (GB), mail (US); [*services*] postal.

poste[1] /pɔst/ *nm* **1** position, job; post; **~s vacants** or **à pourvoir** vacancies; **2** (Sport) position; **3** post; **~ (de travail)** work station; **il est toujours fidèle au ~** you can always rely on him; **4 ~ de police** police station; **5 ~ de radio** radio set; **6** (tele)phone; extension; **7** shift; **8** (in accountancy) item.
■ **~ d'aiguillage** signal box; **~ de douane** customs post; **~ de pilotage** flight deck; **~ de secours** first-aid station.

poste[2] /pɔst/ *nf* post office; **envoyer par la ~** to send [sth] by post (GB), to mail (US).
■ **~ aérienne** airmail; **~ restante** poste restante (GB), general delivery (US).

poster[1] /pɔste/ [1] **I** *vtr* **1** to post (GB), to mail (US); **2** to post [*guard*]; to put [sb] in place [*spy*].
II se poster *v refl* (+ *v être*) **se ~ devant** to station oneself in front of.

poster[2] /pɔstɛR/ *nm* poster.

postérieur, **~e** /pɔsteRjœR/ *adj* **1** [*date*] later; [*event*] subsequent; **un écrivain ~ à Flaubert** a writer who came after Flaubert; **2** [*part, section*] posterior; [*legs*] hind.

postérité /pɔsteRite/ *nf* posterity; **passer à la**

~ [*person*] to go down in history; [*work*] to become part of the cultural heritage.

posthume /pɔstym/ *adj* posthumous.

postiche /pɔstiʃ/ **I** *adj* [*beard*] false.
II *nm* **1** hairpiece; toupee; wig; **2** false moustache (GB) or mustache (US); **3** false beard.

postier, -ière /pɔstje, ɛʀ/ *nm,f* postal worker.

postillon○ /pɔstijɔ̃/ *nm* drop of saliva.

postillonner○ /pɔstijɔne/ [1] *vi* to spit (saliva).

post-scriptum /pɔstskʀiptɔm/ *nm inv* postscript.

postsynchroniser /pɔstsɛ̃kʀɔnize/ [1] *vtr* to dub, to add the soundtrack to.

postulat /pɔstyla/ *nm* premise; postulate.

postuler /pɔstyle/ [1] *vi* to apply.

posture /pɔstyʀ/ *nf* **1** posture; **2** position.

pot /po/ *nm* **1** container; jar; carton, tub; (earthenware) pot; jug; **un ~ de peinture** a tin of paint; **2** (chamber) pot; **3**○ drink; **4**○ do○ (GB), drinks party; **5**○ **avoir du ~** to be lucky.
■ **~ catalytique** catalytic converter; **~ d'échappement** (Aut) silencer (GB), muffler (US); exhaust.
IDIOMS **payer les ~s cassés** to pick up the pieces; **tourner autour du ~**○ to beat about the bush.

potable /pɔtabl/ *adj* **1 eau ~** drinking water; **2**○ decent.

potage /pɔtaʒ/ *nm* soup.

potager, /pɔtaʒe/ *nm* kitchen garden.

pot-au-feu /pɔtofø/ *nm inv* **1** boiled beef (*with vegetables*); **2** boiling beef.

pot-de-vin, *pl* **pots-de-vin** /podvɛ̃/ *nm* bribe, backhander○ (GB).

pote○ /pɔt/ *nm* mate○ (GB), pal○ (US).

poteau, *pl* **~x** /pɔto/ *nm* post; goalpost.
■ **~ électrique** electricity pole (*supplying domestic power lines*).

potelé, ~e /pɔtle/ *adj* chubby.

potence /pɔtɑ̃s/ *nf* gallows.

potentiel, -ielle /pɔtɑ̃sjɛl/ **I** *adj* potential.
II *nm* potential.

poterie /pɔtʀi/ *nf* **1** pottery; **2** piece of pottery.

potiche /pɔtiʃ/ *nf* vase.

potier, -ière /pɔtje, ɛʀ/ *nm,f* potter.

potin○ /pɔtɛ̃/ *nm* **1** gossip; **2** din○.

potion /posjɔ̃/ *nf* potion.

potiron /pɔtiʀɔ̃/ *nm* pumpkin (GB), winter squash (US).

pot-pourri, *pl* **pots-pourris** /popuʀi/ *nm* **1** (Mus) medley; **2** potpourri.

pou, *pl* **~x** /pu/ *nm* louse.
IDIOMS **chercher des ~x**○ to nitpick○; **être laid comme un ~**○ to be as ugly as sin.

poubelle /pubɛl/ *nf* bin (GB), trash can (US); dustbin (GB), garbage can (US).

pouce /pus/ *nm* **1** thumb; **2** big toe; **3** inch; **ne pas bouger d'un ~** not to budge an inch.
IDIOMS **se tourner** or **rouler les ~s**○ to twiddle one's thumbs; **manger sur le ~** to have a quick bite to eat; **donner un coup de ~ à qn** to help sb get started.

poudre /pudʀ/ *nf* (gen) powder; **~ (à canon)** gunpowder; **~ à récurer** scouring powder.
IDIOMS **mettre le feu aux ~s** to bring things to a head; **jeter de la ~ aux yeux** to try to impress.

poudrer /pudʀe/ [1] *vtr* to powder.

poudreux, -euse /pudʀø, øz/ *adj* powdery.

poudrier /pudʀije/ *nm* powder compact.

poudrière /pudʀijɛʀ/ *nf* **1** powder magazine; **2** (figurative) time bomb.

pouf /puf/ *nm* **1** pouffe; **2 faire ~** to fall with a soft thud.

pouffer /pufe/ [1] *vi* **~ (de rire)** to burst out laughing.

pouilleux, -euse /pujø, øz/ *adj* **1**○ seedy; **2** flea-ridden.

poulailler /pulɑje/ *nm* **1** henhouse; hen run; **2** hens; **3**○ (in theatre) **le ~** the Gods (GB), the gallery.

poulain /pulɛ̃/ *nm* **1** colt; foal; **2** protégé.

poularde /pulaʀd/ *nf* fattened chicken.

poule /pul/ *nf* **1** hen; **2** boiling fowl; **3**○ **ma ~** my pet○, honey○ (US).
■ **~ d'eau** moorhen; **~ faisane** hen pheasant; **~ mouillée**○ wimp○; **~ naine** bantam; **~ au pot** boiled chicken.
IDIOMS **quand les ~s auront des dents**○ pigs might fly; **tuer la ~ aux œufs d'or** to kill the goose that lays the golden egg.

poulet /pulɛ/ *nm* chicken.
■ **~ d'élevage** ≈ battery chicken; **~ fermier** ≈ free-range chicken.

pouliche /puliʃ/ *nf* filly.

poulie /puli/ *nf* pulley.

poulpe /pulp/ *nm* octopus.

pouls /pu/ *nm inv* pulse.

poumon /pumɔ̃/ *nm* lung; **~ d'acier** or **artificiel** iron lung; **à pleins ~s** [*shout*] at the top of one's voice; [*breathe*] deeply.

poupe /pup/ *nf* stern; **avoir le vent en ~** to have the wind in one's sails.

poupée /pupe/ *nf* doll.

poupon /pupɔ̃/ *nm* **1** tiny baby; **2** baby doll.

pouponner○ /pupɔne/ [1] *vi* to play the doting father/mother.

pour[1] /puʀ/ *prep* **1** (in order) to; **~ faire** to do; in order to do; **pour ne pas faire** so as not to do; **c'était ~ rire** or **plaisanter** it was a joke; **~ que** so that; **~ ainsi dire** so to speak; **2** for; **le train ~ Paris** the train for Paris or to Paris; **ce sera prêt ~ vendredi?** will it be ready by Friday?; **~ toujours** forever; **le bébé c'est ~ quand?** when is the baby due?; **se battre ~ une femme** to fight over a woman; **c'est fait** or **étudié ~**○**!** that's what it's for; **je suis ~**○ I'm in favour[GB]; **3** about; as regards; **se renseigner ~** to find out about; **~ l'argent** as regards the money, as for the money; **~ moi, il a tort** as far as I am concerned, he's wrong; **4 elle a ~ ambition d'être pilote** her ambition is to be a pilot; **5 elle avait ~ elle de savoir écouter** she had the merit of being a good listener; **6 ~ autant que je sache** as far as I know; **~ être intelli-**

gente, ça elle l'est! she really is intelligent!; **7 j'ai mis ~ 200 francs d'essence** I've put in 200 francs' worth of petrol (GB) or gas (US); **merci ~ tout** thank you for everything; **je n'y suis ~ rien** I had nothing to do with it; **je n'en ai pas ~ longtemps** it won't take long; **8 dix ~ cent** ten per cent; **une cuillère de vinaigre ~ quatre d'huile** one spoonful of vinegar to four of oil; **~ une large part** to a large extent.

pour[2] /puʀ/ *nm* **le ~ et le contre** the pros and the cons.

pourboire /puʀbwaʀ/ *nm* tip.

pourcentage /puʀsɑ̃taʒ/ *nm* **1** percentage; **2** commission; **3** cut○.

pourchasser /puʀʃase/ [1] *vtr* **1** to hunt [*animal, criminal*]; **2** to pursue [*person*].

pourparlers /puʀparle/ *nm pl* talks; **être en ~** [*people*] to be engaged in talks.

pourpre /puʀpʀ/ *adj, nm* crimson.

pourquoi /puʀkwa/ **I** *adv, conj* why; **~ donc?** but why?; **~ pas** or **non?** why not?; **~ pas un week-end à Paris?** what or how about a weekend in Paris?; **va donc savoir ~!** God knows why!

II *nm inv* **le ~ et le comment** the why and the wherefore.

pourri, **~e** /puʀi/ **I** *pp* ▶ **pourrir**.

II *pp adj* **1** (gen) rotten; [*vegetation*] rotting; **2**○ [*weather, car*] rotten○; [*person*] crooked○.

III *nm* rotten part; **ça sent le ~** it smells rotten.

pourrir /puʀiʀ/ [3] **I** *vtr* **1** to rot [*wood*]; **2** to spoil [*person*]; **3**○ to spoil [sb] rotten○.

II *vi* **1** [*food*] to go bad; **2** [*wood*] to rot; **3** [*person*] to rot; [*situation*] to deteriorate.

pourriture /puʀityʀ/ *nf* **1** rot, decay; **2** corruption, rottenness.

poursuite /puʀsɥit/ *nf* **1** pursuit; **être à la ~ de** to be in pursuit of; **2** chase; **3** continuation; **4 ~ (judiciaire)** (judicial) proceedings.

poursuivre /puʀsɥivʀ/ [62] **I** *vtr* **1** to chase; **2** [*person*] to hound; [*nightmare*] to haunt; **~ qn de ses assiduités** to force one's attentions on sb; **3** to seek (after) [*honours, truth*]; to pursue [*goal*]; **4** to continue [*journey, studies*]; to pursue [*talks*]; **5** (Law) **~ qn (en justice** or **devant les tribunaux)** to sue sb.

II *vi* to continue; **~ sur un sujet** to continue talking on a subject.

III se poursuivre *v refl* (+ *v être*) [*talks, conflict, journey*] to continue.

pourtant /puʀtɑ̃/ *adv* though; **et ~** and yet; **techniquement ~, le film est parfait** technically, however, the film is perfect.

pourtour /puʀtuʀ/ *nm* **1** perimeter; circumference; **2** surrounding area.

pourvoir /puʀvwaʀ/ [40] **I** *vtr* **1** to fill [*post*]; **2 ~ qn de** to endow sb with.

II pourvoir à *v+prep* to provide for.

III se pourvoir *v refl* (+ *v être*) **se ~ de** to provide oneself with [*currency*]; to equip oneself with [*boots*].

pourvoyeur, **-euse** /puʀvwajœʀ, øz/ *nm,f* **~ de** source of [*jobs, funding*].

pourvu: **pourvu que** /puʀvyk(ə)/ *phr* **1** provided (that), as long as; **2** let's hope; **~ que ça dure!** let's hope it lasts!

pousse /pus/ *nf* **1** (Bot) shoot; **2** growth.

poussé, **~e**[1] /puse/ **I** *pp* ▶ **pousser**.

II *pp adj* [*inquiry*] thorough; [*studies*] advanced.

poussée[2] /puse/ *nf* **1** (of water, crowd) pressure; (of wind) force; **2** thrust; **3** (Med) attack; **~ de fièvre** sudden high temperature; **4** (in price) (sharp) rise; (in racism, violence) upsurge.

pousser /puse/ [1] **I** *vtr* **1** to push [*wheelbarrow, person*]; to move or shift [sth] (out of the way), to push [sth] aside; **~ une porte** to push a door to; to push a door open; **~ qn du coude** to give sb a dig or to nudge sb with one's elbow; **2 ~ qn à faire** to encourage sb to do; to urge sb to do; [*hunger, despair*] to drive sb to do; **~ à la consommation** to encourage people to buy more; to encourage people to drink more; **3** to push [*pupil*]; to keep [sb] at it [*employee*]; to drive [sth] hard [*car*]; **4** to push [*product, protégé*]; **5** to pursue [*studies, research*]; **c'est ~ un peu loin la plaisanterie** that's taking the joke a bit far; **6** to let out [*cry*]; to heave [*sigh*].

II *vi* **1** [*child*] to grow; [*plant*] to grow; to sprout; [*tooth*] to come through; [*buildings*] to spring up; **je fais ~ des légumes** I grow vegetables; **se laisser ~ les cheveux** to grow one's hair; **2 ~ plus loin** to go on further; **3**○ to overdo it, to go too far.

III se pousser *v refl* (+ *v être*) to move over.

IDIOMS **à la va comme je te pousse**○ any old how.

poussette /pusɛt/ *nf* pushchair (GB), stroller (US).

poussière /pusjɛʀ/ *nf* **1** dust; **tomber en ~** to crumble away; to fall to bits; **2** speck of dust.

IDIOMS **10 francs/20 ans et des ~s**○ just over 10 francs/20 years.

poussiéreux, **-euse** /pusjeʀø, øz/ *adj* **1** dusty; **2** outdated, fossilized.

poussin /pusɛ̃/ *nm* chick.

poussoir /puswaʀ/ *nm* (push) button.

poutre /putʀ/ *nf* **1** beam; **2** girder.

pouvoir[1] /puvwaʀ/ [49] **I** *v aux* **1** to be able to; **peux-tu soulever cette boîte?** can you lift this box?; **dès que je pourrai** as soon as I can; **je n'en peux plus** I've had it○; I'm full○; **tout peut arriver** anything could happen; **il ne peut pas ne pas gagner** he's bound to win; **on peut toujours espérer** there's no harm in wishing; **qu'est-ce que cela peut (bien) te faire○?** what business is it of yours?; **2** to be allowed to; **est-ce que je peux me servir de ta voiture?** can I use your car?; **on peut dire que** it can be said that; **on peut ne pas faire l'accord** the agreement is optional; **3 pouvez-vous/pourriez-vous me tenir la porte s'il vous plaît?** can you/could you hold the door (open) for me please?; **4 puisse cette nouvelle année exaucer vos vœux les plus chers** may the new year bring you everything you could wish for; **s'il**

croit que je vais payer il peut toujours attendre if he thinks I'm going to pay he's got another think coming; **ce qu'il peut être grand!** how tall he is!
II *vtr* **que puis-je pour vous?** what can I do for you?; **je fais ce que je peux** I'm doing my best.
III *v impers* **il peut faire très froid en janvier** it can get very cold in January; **ce qu'il a pu pleuvoir!** you wouldn't believe how much it rained!
IV **il se peut** *v impers* **il se peut que les prix augmentent en juin** prices may or might rise in June; **cela se pourrait qu'il soit fâché** he might be angry.
V **on ne peut plus** *phr* **il est on ne peut plus timide** he is as shy as can be.
VI **on ne peut mieux** *phr* **ils s'entendent on ne peut mieux** they get on extremely well.
IDIOMS **autant que faire se peut** as far as possible.

pouvoir² /puvwaʀ/ *nm* **1** (gen) power; **~ d'achat** purchasing power; **avoir le ~ de faire** to be able to do, to have the power to do; **je n'ai pas le ~ de décider** it's not up to me to decide; **2** (Pol) power; **avoir tous ~s** to have or exercise full powers; **le ~ en place** the government in power.
■ **le ~ judiciaire** the judiciary; **~ législatif** legislative power; **~s publics** authorities.

pragmatisme /pʀagmatism/ *nm* pragmatism.

praire /pʀɛʀ/ *nf* clam.

prairie /pʀɛʀi/ *nf* meadow.

praline /pʀalin/ *nf* sugared (GB) or sugar-coated (US) almond.

praliné, **~e** /pʀaline/ I *adj* praline.
II *nm* praline.

praticable /pʀatikabl/ *adj* [*road*] passable.

praticien, **-ienne** /pʀatisjɛ̃, ɛn/ *nm,f* **1** general practitioner, GP; **2** practitioner.

pratiquant, **~e** /pʀatikɑ̃, ɑ̃t/ *adj* practising[GB]; **être très ~** to be very devout.

pratique /pʀatik/ I *adj* practical; [*device*] handy; [*place, route*] convenient.
II *nf* **1 la ~ des arts martiaux est très répandue** many people practise[GB] martial arts; **cela nécessite de longues heures de ~** it takes hours of practice; **avoir une bonne ~ de l'anglais** to have a good working knowledge of English; **2** practical experience; **3** practice; **mettre qch en ~** to put sth into practice; **4 les ~s religieuses** religious practices.

pratiquement /pʀatikmɑ̃/ *adv* **1** in practice; **2** practically, virtually; **~ jamais** hardly ever.

pratiquer /pʀatike/ [1] I *vtr* **1** to play [*tennis*]; to do [*yoga*]; to take part in [*activity*]; to practise[GB] [*language*]; **il est croyant mais ne pratique pas** he believes in God but doesn't practise[GB] his religion; **2** to use [*method, blackmail*]; to pursue [*policy*]; to charge [*rate of interest*]; **3** to carry out [*examination, graft*].
II **se pratiquer** *v refl* (+ *v être*) [*sport*] to be played; [*technique, policy, strategy*] to be used; [*price, tariff*] to be charged.

pré /pʀe/ *nm* meadow.

pré- /pʀe/ *pref* pre(-); **~-accord** preliminary agreement.

préalable /pʀealabl/ I *adj* [*notice*] prior; [*study*] preliminary.
II *nm* precondition; preliminary.
III **au préalable** *phr* first, beforehand.

préalablement /pʀealabləmɑ̃/ *adv* beforehand.

préambule /pʀeɑ̃byl/ *nm* **1** preamble; **2** forewarning.

préau, *pl* **~x** /pʀeo/ *nm* (of school) covered playground; (of prison) exercise yard.

préavis /pʀeavi/ *nm inv* notice.

précaire /pʀekɛʀ/ *adj* [*existence*] precarious; [*job*] insecure; [*construction*] flimsy.

précariser /prekaʀize/ [1] *vtr* **~ l'emploi** to casualize labour[GB].

précarité /pʀekaʀite/ *nf* precariousness; **la ~ de l'emploi** job insecurity.

précaution /pʀekosjɔ̃/ *nf* precaution; caution; **par ~** as a precaution.

précédemment /pʀesedamɑ̃/ *adv* previously.

précédent, **~e** /pʀesedɑ̃, ɑ̃t/ I *adj* previous.
II *nm,f* **le ~**, **la ~e** the previous one.
III *nm* precedent; **sans ~** unprecedented.

précéder /pʀesede/ [14] *vtr* **1** [*person*] to go in front of, to precede; [*vehicle*] to be in front of; **2 il m'avait précédé de cinq minutes** he'd got there five minutes ahead of me; **3** [*paragraph, crisis*] to precede; **la semaine qui a précédé votre départ** the week before you left.

précepte /pʀesɛpt/ *nm* precept.

précepteur, **-trice** /pʀesɛptœʀ, tʀis/ *nm,f* (private) tutor.

prêcher /pʀeʃe/ [1] I *vtr* **1** to preach; **2** to advocate.
II *vi* to preach.
IDIOMS **~ le faux pour savoir le vrai** to tell a lie in order to get at the truth.

précieusement /pʀesjøzmɑ̃/ *adv* carefully.

précieux, **-ieuse** /pʀesjø, øz/ *adj* **1** [*stone, book*] precious; [*piece of furniture*] valuable; **2** [*information*] very useful; [*collaborator*] valued; **3** [*friendship, right*] precious; [*friend*] very dear; **4** [*style, language*] precious.

précipice /pʀesipis/ *nm* precipice.

précipitamment /pʀesipitamɑ̃/ *adv* hurriedly.

précipitation /pʀesipitasjɔ̃/ I *nf* haste.
II **précipitations** *nf pl* rainfall, precipitation.

précipité, **~e** /pʀesipite/ *adj* **1** rapid; **2** hasty, precipitate.

précipiter /pʀesipite/ [1] I *vtr* **1 ~ qn dans le vide** (from roof) to push sb off; (out of window) to push sb out; **2** to hasten [*departure, decision*]; to precipitate [*event*]; **~ les choses** to rush things.
II **se précipiter** *v refl* (+ *v être*) **1 il s'est précipité dans le vide** he jumped off; **2** to rush; **se ~ au secours de qn** to rush to sb's aid; **se ~ sur** to rush at [*person*]; to rush for [*object*]; **3** to rush; **4** [*action*] to move faster.

précis, **~e** /pʀesi, iz/ I *adj* **1** [*programme,*

criterion] specific; [*idea, date*] definite; [*moment*] particular; **2** [*person, gesture*] precise; [*figure, data*] accurate; [*place*] exact.
II *nm inv* handbook.

précisément /pʀesizemɑ̃/ *adv* precisely.

préciser /pʀesize/ [1] I *vtr* **1** to add; **faut-il le** or **est-il besoin de ~** needless to say; **2** to state; **~ ses intentions** to state one's intentions; **3** to specify; **pouvez-vous ~?** could you be more specific?; **4** to clarify [*ideas*].
II **se préciser** *v refl* (+ *v être*) **1** [*danger, future*] to become clearer; [*plan, trip*] to take shape; **2** [*shape, reality*] to become clear.

précision /pʀesizjɔ̃/ *nf* **1** precision; **2** accuracy; **localiser avec ~** to pinpoint; **instrument de ~** precision instrument; **3** detail.

précité, **~e** /pʀesite/ *adj* aforementioned.

précoce /pʀekɔs/ *adj* **1** precocious; **2** [*season*] early; **3** [*senility*] premature.

préconçu, **~e** /pʀekɔ̃sy/ *adj* preconceived.

préconiser /pʀekɔnize/ [1] *vtr* to recommend.

précuit, **~e** /pʀekɥi, it/ *adj* precooked.

précurseur /pʀekyʀsœʀ/ I *adj m* precursory; **signes ~s de l'orage** signs that herald a storm.
II *nm* pioneer; **~ de** precursor of.

prédateur /pʀedatœʀ/ *nm* **1** predator; **2** hunter-gatherer.

prédécesseur /pʀedesesœʀ/ *nm* predecessor.

prédestiner /pʀedɛstine/ [1] *vtr* to predestine.

prédicateur, **-trice** /pʀedikatœʀ, tʀis/ *nm,f* preacher.

prédiction /pʀediksjɔ̃/ *nf* prediction.

prédilection /pʀedilɛksjɔ̃/ *nf* predilection, liking; **de ~** favourite[GB].

prédire /pʀediʀ/ [65] *vtr* to predict.

prédisposer /pʀedispoze/ [1] *vtr* to predispose.

prédominant, **~e** /pʀedɔminɑ̃, ɑ̃t/ *adj* predominant.

prédominer /pʀedɔmine/ [1] *vi* to predominate.

préexister /pʀeɛgziste/ [1] *vi* to pre-exist.

préfabriqué /pʀefabʀike/ *nm* **1** prefabricated material; **2** prefab○.

préface /pʀefas/ *nf* preface.

préfectoral, **~e**, *mpl* **-aux** /pʀefɛktɔʀal, o/ *adj* [*level, authorization*] prefectorial; [*administration, building*] prefectural.

préfecture /pʀefɛktyʀ/ *nf* **1** prefecture; **2** *main city of a French department.*
■ **~ de police** police headquarters (*in some large French cities*).

préférable /pʀefeʀabl/ *adj* preferable.

préféré, **~e** /pʀefeʀe/ *adj, nm,f* favourite[GB].

préférence /pʀefeʀɑ̃s/ *nf* preference; **achète cette marque de ~** if you can, buy this brand.

préférer /pʀefeʀe/ [14] *vtr* to prefer; **j'aurais préféré ne jamais l'apprendre** I wish I'd never found out.

préfet /pʀefɛ/ *nm* prefect.

préfigurer /pʀefigyʀe/ [1] *vtr* to prefigure.

préfixe /pʀefiks/ *nm* prefix.

préhistoire /pʀeistwaʀ/ *nf* prehistory.

préjudice /pʀeʒydis/ *nm* harm, damage; **~ moral** moral wrong; **porter ~ à qn** to harm sb; **au ~ de qn** to the detriment of sb.

préjugé /pʀeʒyʒe/ *nm* prejudice; **~(s) en faveur de qn** bias in favour[GB] of sb.

préjuger /pʀeʒyʒe/ [13] *vtr*, **préjuger de** *v+prep* to prejudge.

prélasser: **se prélasser** /pʀelase/ [1] *v refl* (+ *v être*) to lounge.

prélat /pʀela/ *nm* prelate.

prélavage /pʀelavaʒ/ *nm* prewash.

prêle /pʀɛl/ *nf* (Bot) horsetail.

prélèvement /pʀelɛvmɑ̃/ *nm* **1** sampling; sample; **faire un ~ de sang** to take a blood sample; **2 faire un ~ bancaire de 100 francs** to make a debit of 100 francs.
■ **~ automatique** direct debit; **~ à la source** deduction at source.

prélever /pʀelve/ [16] *vtr* **1** to take a sample of [*blood, water*]; to remove [*organ*]; **2** to debit; **3** to deduct [*tax*]; **4** to take [*percentage*].

préliminaire /pʀeliminɛʀ/ I *adj* preliminary.
II **préliminaires** *nm pl* preliminaries.

prélude /pʀelyd/ *nm* prelude.

préluder /pʀelyde/ [1] *v+prep* **~ à** to be a prelude to.

prématuré, **~e** /pʀematyʀe/ I *adj* premature.
II *nm,f* premature baby.

préméditation /pʀemeditasjɔ̃/ *nf* premeditation.

préméditer /pʀemedite/ [1] *vtr* to premeditate.

premier, **-ière**[1] /pʀəmje, ɛʀ/ I *adj* **1** first; **(dans) les ~s temps** at first; **2** [*artist, power*] leading; [*student*] top; **être ~** to be top; to be first; **c'est le ~ prix** it's the cheapest; **3** [*impression*] first, initial; **4** [*quality*] prime; [*objective*] primary.
II *nm,f* first; **je préfère le ~** I prefer the first one; **arriver le ~** to come first; **être le ~ de la classe** to be top of the class.
III *nm* **1** first floor (GB), second floor (US); **2** first; **le ~ de l'an** New Year's Day; **3** first arrondissement.
IV **en premier** *phr* first.
V **de première**○ *phr* first-rate.
■ **~ âge** [*clothes*] for babies up to six months; **~ de cordée** (Sport) leader; **~ ministre** prime minister; **le ~ venu** just anybody; the first person to come along; **~s secours** first aid.

première[2] /pʀəmjɛʀ/ I ▶ **premier** I, II.
II *nf* **1** first; **~ mondiale** world first; **2** première; **3** (Sch) *sixth year of secondary school, age 16–17*; **4** (Aut) first (gear); **5**○ first class.

premièrement /pʀəmjɛʀmɑ̃/ *adv* **1** firstly, first; **2** for a start, for one thing.

prémisse /pʀemis/ *nf* premise, premiss (GB).

prémonition /pʀemɔnisjɔ̃/ *nf* premonition.

prémonitoire /pʀemɔnitwaʀ/ *adj* premonitory.

prémunir /pʀemyniʀ/ [3] **I** *vtr* to protect.
II se prémunir *v refl* (+ *v être*) to protect oneself.

prenant, **~e** /pʀənɑ̃, ɑ̃t/ *adj* [*film*] fascinating; [*voice*] captivating; [*work*] absorbing.

prendre /pʀɑ̃dʀ/ [52]

■ **Note** *Prendre* is very often translated by *to take* but see the entry below for a wide variety of usages.
– For translations of certain fixed phrases such as *prendre froid*, *prendre soin de*, *prendre parti* etc, refer to the entries ***froid***, ***soin***, ***parti***.

I *vtr* **1** to take; **~ un vase dans le placard** to take a vase out of the cupboard; **prenez donc une chaise** take a seat; **~ un congé** to take time off; **~ le train/l'avion** to take the train/plane; **on m'a pris tous mes bijoux** I had all my jewellery (GB) or jewelry (US) stolen; **la guerre leur a pris deux fils** they lost two sons in the war; **~ les mensurations de qn** to take sb's measurements; **~ les choses comme elles sont** to take things as they come; **ne le prends pas mal** don't take it the wrong way; **je vous ai pris pour quelqu'un d'autre** I thought you were someone else; **2 ~ un accent** to pick up an accent; to put on an accent; **3** to bring; **n'oublie pas de ~ des bottes** don't forget to bring a pair of boots; **4** to get [*food, petrol*]; **~ de l'argent au distributeur** to get some money out of the cash dispenser; **5** to have [*drink, meal*]; to take [*medicine*]; **aller ~ une bière** to go for a beer; **6** to choose [*topic, question*]; **7** to charge; **il prend 15% au passage**○ he takes a cut of 15%; **8** to take up [*space, time*]; **9** to take [sb] on; to engage [sb]; **10** to pick [sb/sth] up; **~ les enfants à l'école** to collect the children from school; **11** to catch; **elle s'est fait ~ en train de voler** she got caught stealing; **12**○ **qu'est-ce qui te prend?** what's the matter with you?; **ça te/leur prend souvent?** are you/they often like this?; **13** to involve [*spectator, reader*]; **être pris par un livre/film** to get involved in a book/film; **14** to get [*slap, sunburn*]; to catch [*cold*]; **15 il est très gentil quand on sait le ~** he's very nice when you know how to handle him; **16** to take [sth] down [*address*]; **17 où a-t-il pris qu'ils allaient divorcer?** where did he get the idea they were going to get divorced?; **18** to take over [*management, power*]; to assume [*control*]; **je prends ça sur moi** I'll see to it; **elle a pris sur elle de leur parler** she took it upon herself to talk to them; **19** to put on [*weight*]; to gain [*lead*]; **20** to take on [*lease*]; to take [*job*]; **21** to take on [*rival*]; **22** to take, to seize [*town*]; to capture [*ship, tank*]; to take [*chesspiece, card*].
II *vi* **1 ~ à gauche/vers le nord** to go left/north; **2** [*wood*] to catch; [*fire*] to break out; **3** [*jelly, glue*] to set; [*mayonnaise*] to thicken; **4** [*strike, innovation*] to be a success; [*idea, fashion*] to catch on; [*dye, cutting*] to take; **5 ~ sur son temps libre pour traduire un roman** to translate a novel in one's spare time; **6 ~ sur soi** to take a hold on oneself, to get a grip on oneself; **7**○ **ça ne prend pas!** it won't work!; **8**○ **c'est toujours moi qui prends!** I'm always the one who gets it in the neck○!; **il en a pris pour 20 ans** he got 20 years.
III se prendre *v refl* (+ *v être*) **1 en Chine le thé se prend sans sucre** in China they don't put sugar in their tea; **2 les mauvaises habitudes se prennent vite** bad habits are easily picked up; **3 se ~ par la taille** to hold each other around the waist; **4 se ~ les doigts dans la porte** to catch one's fingers in the door; **5**○ **il s'est pris une gifle** he got a slap in the face; **6 se ~ à faire** to find oneself doing; **se ~ de sympathie pour qn** to take to sb; **7 pour qui est-ce que tu te prends?** who do you think you are?; **8 s'en ~ à** to attack [*person, press*]; to take it out on [sb]; to go for [sb]; **9 savoir s'y ~ avec** to have a way with [*children*]; **10 il faut s'y ~ à l'avance pour avoir des places** you have to book ahead to get seats; **tu t'y es pris trop tard** you left it too late; **il s'y est pris à plusieurs fois** he tried several times; **elle s'y prend mal** she goes about it the wrong way.
IDIOMS **c'est à ~ ou à laisser** take it or leave it.

preneur, **-euse** /pʀənœʀ, øz/ *nm,f* **il n'y a pas ~** there are no takers; **trouver ~** to attract a buyer; to find a buyer.

prénom /pʀenɔ̃/ *nm* first name, forename.

prénommer /pʀenɔme/ [1] **I** *vtr* to name, to call.
II se prénommer *v refl* (+ *v être*) to be called.

prénuptial, **~e**, *pl* **-iaux** /pʀenypsjal, o/ *adj* prenuptial; prior to marriage.

préoccupant, **~e** /pʀeɔkypɑ̃, ɑ̃t/ *adj* worrying.

préoccupation /pʀeɔkypasjɔ̃/ *nf* worry.

préoccuper /pʀeɔkype/ [1] **I** *vtr* **1** to worry; **avoir l'air préoccupé** to look worried; **2** to preoccupy; **3** to concern.
II se préoccuper *v refl* (+ *v être*) **se ~ de** to be concerned about [*situation*]; to think about [*future*].

préparatifs /pʀepaʀatif/ *nm pl* preparations.

préparation /pʀepaʀasjɔ̃/ *nf* **1** preparation; **2** training.

préparatoire /pʀepaʀatwaʀ/ *adj* preliminary.

préparer /pʀepaʀe/ [1] **I** *vtr* **1** (gen) to prepare; to make [*meal*]; to get [sth] ready [*clothes, file*]; to plan [*holidays, future*]; to draw up [*plan*]; to hatch [*plot*]; **il est en train de ~ le dîner** he's getting dinner ready; **des plats préparés** ready-to-eat meals; **2 ~ qn à qch** (gen) to prepare sb for sth; to coach sb for sth [*race, examination*]; **essaie de la ~ avant de lui annoncer la nouvelle** try and break the news to her gently.
II se préparer *v refl* (+ *v être*) **1** to get ready; **2** to prepare; **3** [*storm, trouble*] to be brewing; [*changes*] to be in the offing; **un coup d'État se prépare dans le pays** a coup d'état is imminent in the country; **4 se ~ une tasse de thé** to make or fix (US) oneself a cup of tea.

prépondérant, **~e** /pʀepɔ̃deʀɑ̃, ɑ̃t/ *adj* predominant.

préposé, **~e** /pʀepoze/ *nm,f* **1** official; **~**

des douanes customs official; **~ au vestiaire** cloakroom attendant; **2** postman/postwoman.

préposition /pRepozisjɔ̃/ *nf* preposition.

prépuce /pRepys/ *nm* foreskin.

préretraite /pReRətRɛt/ *nf* early retirement.

prérogative /pReRɔgativ/ *nf* prerogative; **~ de qn/qch sur** primacy of sb/sth over.

près /pRɛ/ **I** *adv* **1** close; **ce n'est pas tout ~** it's quite a way; **se raser de ~** to have a close shave; **2 ça pèse 10 kg, à quelques grammes ~** it weighs 10 kg, give or take a few grams; **à ceci** or **cela ~ que** except that; **il m'a remboursé au centime ~** he paid me back to the very last penny; **gagner à deux voix ~** to win by two votes; **à une exception ~** with only one exception.

II près de *phr* **1** near; **être ~ du but** to be close to achieving one's goal; **j'aimerais être ~ de toi** I'd like to be with you; **2** near, nearly; **je ne suis pas ~ de recommencer** I'm not about to do that again; **le problème n'est pas ~ d'être résolu** the problem is nowhere near solved; **3** close; **ils sont très ~ l'un de l'autre** they are very close; **4** nearly, almost; **cela coûte ~ de 1000 francs** it costs nearly 1,000 francs.

III de près *phr* closely; **se suivre de ~** [*competitors*] to be close together; [*siblings*] to be close in age.

IV à peu près *phr* **~ vide** practically empty; **~ 200 francs** about 200 francs; **à peu ~ de la même façon** in much the same way.

présage /pRezaʒ/ *nm* **1** omen; **2** harbinger; **3** prediction.

présager /pRezaʒe/ [13] *vtr* [*event*] to presage; [*person*] to predict; **laisser ~** to suggest.

presbyte /pRɛsbit/ *adj* longsighted (GB), farsighted (US).

presbytère /pRɛsbitɛR/ *nm* presbytery.

prescription /pRɛskRipsjɔ̃/ *nf* prescription; **'se conformer aux ~s du médecin'** 'to be taken in accordance with doctor's instructions'.

prescrire /pRɛskRiR/ [67] *vtr* **1** (Med) to prescribe; **2** to stipulate.

présélectionner /pReselɛksjɔne/ [1] *vtr* **1** to shortlist; **2** to preselect; to preset.

présence /pRezɑ̃s/ *nf* (gen) presence; (at work) attendance; **il fait de la ~, c'est tout** he's present and not much else; **les forces en ~ dans le conflit** the forces involved in the conflict; **il a besoin d'une ~** he needs company; **avoir beaucoup de ~ (sur scène)** to have great stage presence.

■ **~ d'esprit** presence of mind.

présent, **~e**[1] /pRezɑ̃, ɑ̃t/ **I** *adj* **1** present; **M. Maquanne, ici ~** Mr Maquanne, who is here with us; **avoir qch ~ à l'esprit** to have [sth] in mind [*advice*]; to have [sth] fresh in one's mind [*memory*]; **2** actively involved; **un chanteur très ~ sur scène** a singer with a strong stage presence.

II *nm,f* **la liste des ~s** the list of those present.

III *nm* **1 le ~** the present; **2** present (tense); **3** gift, present.

IV à présent *phr* at present; now.

présentable /pRezɑ̃tabl/ *adj* presentable.

présentateur, **-trice** /pRezɑ̃tatœR, tRis/ *nm,f* presenter; newsreader (GB), newscaster (US).

présentation /pRezɑ̃tasjɔ̃/ *nf* **1** introduction; **faire les ~s** to make the introductions; **2** appearance; **3** (of dish, letter) presentation; (of products) display; **4** show, showing; **~ de mode** fashion show; **5** (of programme) presentation; **6** (of card, ticket) production; (of cheque) presentation; **7** presentation, exposé.

présente[2] /pRezɑ̃t/ **I** *adj f* ▶ **présent I**.

II *nf* **1 par la ~** hereby; **2** ▶ **présent II**.

présenter /pRezɑ̃te/ [1] **I** *vtr* **1** to introduce; to present; **2** to show [*ticket, card, menu*]; **3** to present [*programme, show, collection*]; to display [*goods*]; **4** to present [*receipt, bill*]; to submit [*estimate, report*]; to introduce [*proposal, bill*]; **~ une liste pour les élections** to put forward a list (of candidates) for the elections; **5** to present [*situation, budget, theory*]; to set out [*objections, point of view*]; **~ qn comme (étant) un monstre** to portray sb as a monster; **6** to offer [*condolences*]; **~ des excuses** to apologize; **7** to involve [*risk, difficulty*]; to show [*differences*]; to offer [*advantage*]; to have [*aspect, feature*].

II *vi* **~ bien** to have a smart appearance.

III se présenter *v refl* (+ *v être*) **1 il faut se ~ à la réception** you must go to reception; **présentez-vous à 10 heures** come at 10 o'clock; **2** to introduce oneself; **3 se ~ à** to take [*examination*]; to stand for [*election*]; **4** [*opportunity*] to arise; [*solution*] to emerge; **5 se ~ en, se ~ sous forme de** [*product*] to come in the form of; **6 l'affaire se présente bien** things are looking good.

présentoir /pRezɑ̃twaR/ *nm* **1** display stand or unit; **2** display shelf.

préservatif /pRezɛRvatif/ *nm* condom.

préservation /pRezɛRvasjɔ̃/ *nf* protection; preservation.

préserver /pRezɛRve/ [1] *vtr* **1** to preserve; **2** to protect.

présidence /pRezidɑ̃s/ *nf* **1** presidency; chairmanship; **2** presidential palace.

président /pRezidɑ̃/ *nm* president; chairman.

■ **~ de la République** President of the Republic.

présidente /pRezidɑ̃t/ *nf* **1** president; chairwoman, chairperson; chairman; **2** First Lady.

présidentiel, **-ielle** /pRezidɑ̃sjɛl/ *adj* presidential.

présidentielles /pRezidɑ̃sjɛl/ *nf pl* presidential election.

présider /pRezide/ [1] *vtr* **1** to chair; **2** to be the president of; to be the chairman/chairwoman of; to preside over.

présomption /pRezɔ̃psjɔ̃/ *nf* **1** (Law) presumption; **2** assumption; **3 plein de ~** presumptuous.

présomptueux, **-euse** /pRezɔ̃ptɥø, øz/ *adj* arrogant; presumptuous.

presque /pRɛsk/ *adv* almost, nearly; **il y a trois**

ans ~ jour pour jour it's nearly three years to the day; **c'était le bonheur ou ~** it was as close to happiness as one can get; **il ne reste ~ rien** there's hardly anything left.

presqu'île /pʀɛskil/ *nf* peninsula.

pressant, **~e** /pʀɛsɑ̃, ɑ̃t/ *adj* [*need*] pressing; [*appeal*] urgent; [*salesman*] insistent.

presse /pʀɛs/ *nf* **1** press; newspapers; **avoir bonne ~** to be well thought of; **2** (gen) press; (printing) press; **mettre sous ~** to send [sth] to press; **'sous ~'** 'in preparation'.

pressé, **~e** /pʀese/ *adj* **1** [*person*] in a hurry; [*steps*] hurried; **2 ~ de faire** keen to do; **3** [*business*] urgent; **parer au plus ~** to do the most urgent thing(s) first.

presse-ail /pʀɛsaj/ *nm inv* garlic press.

presse-citron /pʀɛssitʀɔ̃/ *nm inv* lemon squeezer.

pressentiment /pʀɛsɑ̃timɑ̃/ *nm* premonition.

pressentir /pʀɛsɑ̃tiʀ/ [30] *vtr* to have a premonition about.

presse-papiers /pʀɛspapje/ *nm inv* paperweight.

presser /pʀese/ [1] **I** *vtr* **1 ~ qn de faire** to urge sb to do; **2** to press [*debtor*]; to harry [*enemy*]; **3** [*hunger, necessity*] to drive [sb] on; **4** to increase [*rhythm*]; **~ le pas** or **mouvement** to hurry; **5** to press [*button*]; **6** to squeeze [*hand, object*]; **7** to squeeze [*orange, sponge*]; to press [*grapes*]; **8** to press [*record*].

II *vi* [*matter*] to be pressing; [*work*] to be urgent; **le temps presse** time is running out.

III se presser *v refl* (+ *v être*) **1 se ~ autour de qn/qch** to press around sb/sth; **2** to hurry up; **3** to flock.

pressing /pʀesiŋ/ *nm* dry-cleaner's.

pression /pʀɛsjɔ̃/ *nf* **1** (gen) pressure; **~ artérielle** blood pressure; **sous ~** under pressure; pressurized; **faire ~ sur** to press on [*surface*]; to put pressure on [*person*]; **2** snap (fastener).

pressoir /pʀɛswaʀ/ *nm* **1** pressing shed; **2** press; **~ à pommes** cider press.

pressuriser /pʀɛsyʀize/ [1] *vtr* to pressurize.

prestance /pʀɛstɑ̃s/ *nf* **avoir de la ~** to have great presence.

prestataire /pʀɛstatɛʀ/ *nm* **1 ~ de service** (service) contractor, service provider; **2** recipient (*of a state benefit*).

prestation /pʀɛstasjɔ̃/ *nf* **1** benefit; **2** provision; **~ de service** (provision of a) service; **3** service; **4** performance; **~ télévisée** televised appearance.

prestidigitation /pʀɛstidiʒitasjɔ̃/ *nf* conjuring.

prestige /pʀɛstiʒ/ *nm* prestige; **le ~ de l'uniforme** the glamour[GB] of a uniform.

prestigieux, **-ieuse** /pʀɛstiʒjø, øz/ *adj* prestigious.

présumer /pʀezyme/ [1] **I** *vtr* to presume; **le présumé terroriste** the alleged terrorist.

II présumer de *v+prep* **(trop) ~ de ses forces** to overestimate one's strength.

présupposer /pʀesypoze/ [1] *vtr* to presuppose.

prêt, **~e** /pʀɛ, pʀɛt/ **I** *adj* ready; **être fin ~** to be all set; **il est ~ à tout** he will stop at nothing.

II *nm* **1 le service de ~ de la bibliothèque** the library loans service; **2** loan.

prêt-à-porter /pʀɛtapɔʀte/ *nm* ready-to-wear.

prétendant, **~e** /pʀetɑ̃dɑ̃, ɑ̃t/ **I** *nm,f* **1** candidate; **2** pretender.

II *nm* suitor.

prétendre /pʀetɑ̃dʀ/ [6] **I** *vtr* to claim; **à ce qu'il prétend** according to him; **on le prétend très spirituel** he is said to be very witty.

II prétendre à *v+prep* to claim [*damages*]; to aspire to [*job*].

III se prétendre *v refl* (+ *v être*) **il se prétend artiste** he makes out or claims he is an artist.

prétendu, **~e** /pʀetɑ̃dy/ *adj* [*culprit*] alleged; [*doctor*] would-be.

prétendument /pʀetɑ̃dymɑ̃/ *adv* supposedly.

prête-nom, *pl* **~s** /pʀɛtnɔ̃/ *nm* frontman, man of straw; **société ~** dummy (US) company.

prétentieux, **-ieuse** /pʀetɑ̃sjø, øz/ **I** *adj* pretentious.

II *nm,f* pretentious person.

prétention /pʀetɑ̃sjɔ̃/ **I** *nf* **1** pretentiousness; **être sans ~** to be unpretentious; **2 avoir la ~ de faire** to claim to do.

II prétentions *nf pl* **quelles sont vos ~s?** what salary are you asking for?

prêter /pʀete/ [1] **I** *vtr* **1** to lend [*money, object*]; **~ sur gages** to loan against security; **2 ~ attention à** to pay attention to; **~ la main à qn** to lend sb a hand; **~ l'oreille** to listen; **~ serment** to take an oath; **3 ~ à qn** to attribute [sth] to sb.

II prêter à *v+prep* to give rise to [*confusion*]; **son attitude prête à rire** his/her attitude is ridiculous; **tout prête à croire** or **penser que** all the indications would suggest that.

III se prêter *v refl* (+ *v être*) **1 se ~ à** to take part in; **2 roman qui se prête à une adaptation cinématographique** novel which lends itself to a film adaptation.

prétérit /pʀeteʀit/ *nm* preterite.

prêteur, **-euse** /pʀɛtœʀ, øz/ **I** *adj* **il n'est pas ~** he's very possessive about his belongings.

II *nm,f* **~ sur gages** pawnbroker.

prétexte /pʀetɛkst/ *nm* excuse, pretext; **donner qch comme ~**, **prendre ~ de qch** to use sth as an excuse; **sous aucun ~** on no account.

prétexter /pʀetɛkste/ [1] **I** *vtr* to use [sth] as an excuse, to plead.

II prétexter de *v+prep* **~ de qch pour faire** to use sth as an excuse for doing.

prêtre /pʀɛtʀ/ *nm* priest.

prêtresse /pʀɛtʀɛs/ *nf* priestess.

preuve /pʀœv/ *nf* **1** proof; **une ~** a piece of evidence; **apporter la ~ de/que** to offer proof of/that; **la ~ est faite de/que** now there is proof of/that; **~ en main** with concrete proof; **faire ses ~s** to prove oneself; **2** demonstration; **faire ~ de** to show; **~ de bonne volonté** gesture of goodwill.

prévaloir /pʀevalwaʀ/ [45] I *vi* to prevail.
II **se prévaloir** *v refl* (+ *v être*) **se ~ de son ancienneté** to claim seniority.

prévenance /pʀevnɑ̃s/ *nf* consideration.

prévenant, **~e** /pʀevnɑ̃, ɑ̃t/ *adj* considerate.

prévenir /pʀevniʀ/ [36] *vtr* **1** to tell; **2** to call [*doctor, police*]; **3** to warn; **4** to prevent [*disaster*]; **5** to anticipate [*wishes*].
IDIOMS **mieux vaut ~ que guérir** (Proverb) prevention is better than cure.

préventif, **-ive** /pʀevɑ̃tif, iv/ *adj* preventive.

prévention /pʀevɑ̃sjɔ̃/ *nf* prevention; **faire de la ~** to take preventive action.

prévenu, **~e** /pʀevny/ *nm,f* (Law) defendant.

prévisible /pʀevizibl/ *adj* predictable.

prévision /pʀevizjɔ̃/ *nf* **1** forecasting; **en ~ de** in anticipation of; **2** prediction; forecast; **~s météorologiques** weather forecast.

prévisionnel, **-elle** /pʀevizjɔnɛl/ *adj* projected.

prévoir /pʀevwaʀ/ [42] *vtr* **1** to predict [*change*]; to foresee [*event, victory*]; to anticipate [*reaction*]; to forecast [*result, weather*]; **c'était à ~!** that was predictable!; **2** to plan [*meeting, journey, building*]; to set the date for [*return, move*]; (Law) to make provision for [*case, eventuality*]; **ce n'était pas prévu!** that wasn't meant to happen!; **remplissez le formulaire prévu à cet effet** fill in the appropriate form; **tout a été prévu** all the arrangements have been made; **3** to make sure one takes [*coat, umbrella*]; **4** to expect [*visitor, shortage, strike*]; **5** to allow [*sum of money, time*].

prévoyance /pʀevwajɑ̃s/ *nf* foresight.

prévoyant, **~e** /pʀevwajɑ̃, ɑ̃t/ *adj* far-sighted.

prier /pʀije/ [2] I *vtr* **1 ~ qn de faire** to ask sb to do; **je vous prie d'excuser mon retard** I'm so sorry I'm late; **je vous prie de vous taire** will you kindly be quiet; **elle ne s'est pas fait ~** she didn't have to be asked twice; **2** to pray to [*god*]; **~ que** to pray that.
II *vi* to pray.

prière /pʀijɛʀ/ *nf* **1** prayer; **faire sa ~** to say one's prayers; **2** request; plea, entreaty; **~ de ne pas fumer** no smoking please.

prieuré /pʀijœʀe/ *nm* **1** priory; **2** priory church.

primaire /pʀimɛʀ/ I *adj* **1** primary; **2** [*person*] limited; [*reasoning*] simplistic.
II *nm* **1** (Sch) **le ~** primary education; **2** (Econ) **le ~** the primary sector; **3 le ~** the palaeozoic era.

primate /pʀimat/ *nm* primate.

primauté /pʀimote/ *nf* primacy.

prime /pʀim/ I *adj* **1 de ~ abord** at first, initially; **2 A ~** A prime.
II *nf* **1** bonus; free gift; **2** allowance; **3** subsidy; **4** (in insurance) premium.
■ **~ d'ancienneté** seniority bonus; **~ de risque** danger money.

primer /pʀime/ [1] I *vtr* **1** to take precedence over, to prevail over; **2** to award a prize to.
II **primer sur** *v+prep* (controversial) = **primer** I 1.
III *vi* **pour moi, c'est la qualité qui prime** what counts for me is quality.

primeur /pʀimœʀ/ I *nf* **avoir la ~ de l'information** to be the first to hear sth.
II **primeurs** *nf pl* early fruit and vegetables.

primevère /pʀimvɛʀ/ *nf* primrose.

primitif, **-ive** /pʀimitif, iv/ *adj* (gen) primitive; [*budget*] initial; [*project, state*] original.

primordial, **~e**, *mpl* **-iaux** /pʀimɔʀdjal, o/ *adj* essential, vital.

prince /pʀɛ̃s/ *nm* prince.
IDIOMS **être bon ~** to be magnanimous.

princesse /pʀɛ̃sɛs/ *nf* princess.
IDIOMS **aux frais de la ~**° at the company's expense; at sb's expense.

princier, **-ière** /pʀɛ̃sje, ɛʀ/ *adj* [*title, tastes, sum*] princely; [*luxury*] dazzling.

principal, **~e**, *mpl* **-aux** /pʀɛ̃sipal, o/ I *adj* **1** [*factor*] main; [*task*] principal; **2** [*country, role*] leading; **3** [*inspector*] chief.
II *nm* **1 le ~** the main thing; **2** (Sch) principal.

principauté /pʀɛ̃sipote/ *nf* principality.

principe /pʀɛ̃sip/ I *nm* **1** principle; **par ~** on principle; **2** assumption; **3** (concept) principle; **quel est le ~ de la machine à vapeur?** how does a steam engine work?
II **en principe** *phr* **1** as a rule; **2** in theory.

printanier, **-ière** /pʀɛ̃tanje, ɛʀ/ *adj* [*sun*] spring; [*weather*] spring-like.

printemps /pʀɛ̃tɑ̃/ *nm inv* **1** spring; **2**° **mes 60 ~** my 60 summers.

priori ▸ **a priori**.

prioritaire /pʀijɔʀitɛʀ/ *adj* [*file, project*] priority; **être ~** to have priority.

priorité /pʀijɔʀite/ *nf* priority; **avoir la ~** to have right (GB) or the right (US) of way.

pris, **~e**[1] /pʀi, pʀiz/ I *pp* ▸ **prendre**.
II *pp adj* **1** busy; **j'ai les mains ~es** I've got my hands full; **les places sont toutes ~es** all the seats are taken; **2** [*nose*] stuffed up; [*lungs*] congested; **3 ~ de** overcome with; **~ de panique** panic-stricken.

prise[2] /priz/ *nf* **1** storming; **la ~ de la Bastille** the storming of the Bastille; **2** catching; **une belle ~** a fine catch; **3** (in judo, wrestling) hold; **4 n'offrir aucune ~** to have no handholds; to have no footholds; **avoir ~ sur qn** to have a hold over sb; **donner ~ à** to lay oneself open to; **5** socket (GB), outlet (US); plug; jack; **~ multiple** (multiplug) adaptor; trailing socket.
■ **~ de bec**° row, argument; **~ en charge** (of expenses) payment; **~ de conscience** realization; **~ de contact** initial contact; **~ de courant** socket (GB), outlet (US); **~ d'eau** water supply point; **~ de sang** blood test; **~ de vue** shooting; shot.
IDIOMS **être aux ~s avec des difficultés** to be grappling with difficulties.

priser /pʀize/ [1] *vtr* **1** to hold [sth] in esteem; **2 ~ (du tabac)** to take snuff.

prisme /pʀism/ *nm* prism.

prison /pʀizɔ̃/ *nf* prison; **condamné à trois ans de ~** sentenced to three years' imprisonment.

prisonnier, **-ière** /pʀizɔnje, ɛʀ/ **I** *adj* **il est ~** he is a prisoner.
II *nm,f* prisoner.

privation /pʀivasjɔ̃/ *nf* **1** (of rights) deprivation; **2** want; **s'imposer des ~s** to make sacrifices.

privatiser /pʀivatize/ [1] *vtr* to privatize.

privé, **~e** /pʀive/ **I** *pp* ▶ **priver**.
II *pp adj* **~ de** deprived of; **tu seras ~ de dessert!** you'll go without dessert!
III *adj* (gen) private; [*interview*] unofficial.
IV *nm* **1** (Econ) private sector; **2** (Sch) **le ~** private schools; **3 en ~** in private.

priver /pʀive/ [1] **I** *vtr* **~ qn/qch de** to deprive sb/sth of; **~ qn de sorties** to forbid sb to go out.
II se priver *v refl* (+ *v être*) **pourquoi se ~?** why deprive ourselves?; **se ~ de qch/de faire** to go or do without sth/doing.

privilège /pʀivilɛʒ/ *nm* privilege.

privilégié, **~e** /pʀivileʒje/ **I** *pp* ▶ **privilégier**.
II *pp adj* **1** privileged; **2** fortunate; **3** [*moment, links*] special; [*treatment*] preferential.

privilégier /pʀivileʒje/ [2] *vtr* **1** to favour[GB]; **2** to give priority to.

prix /pʀi/ *nm inv* **1** price; **à** or **au ~ coûtant** at cost price; **acheter qch à ~ d'or** to pay a small fortune for sth; **il faut être prêt à y mettre le ~** you have to be prepared to pay for it; **mettre qch à ~ à 50 francs** to start the bidding for sth at 50 francs; **2** (figurative) price; **à tout ~** at all costs; **attacher beaucoup de ~ à** to value [sth] highly [*friendship*]; **3** prize.

pro(-) /pʀo/ *pref* pro(-).

probabilité /pʀɔbabilite/ *nf* **1** probability, likelihood; **2 les ~s** probability theory.

probable /pʀɔbabl/ *adj* probable, likely.

probablement /pʀɔbabləmɑ̃/ *adv* probably.

probatoire /pʀɔbatwaʀ/ *adj* **examen ~** assessment test; **épreuve ~** aptitude test.

probité /pʀɔbite/ *nf* integrity, probity.

problématique /pʀɔblematik/ *adj* [*situation*] problematic; [*outcome*] uncertain.

problème /pʀɔblɛm/ *nm* problem.

procédé /pʀɔsede/ *nm* **1** process; **2** practice[GB]; **échange de bons ~s** exchange of courtesies.

procéder /pʀɔsede/ [14] **I procéder à** *v+prep* to carry out [*check, survey*]; to undertake [*reform*]; **~ à un tirage au sort/un vote** to hold a draw/a vote.
II procéder de *v+prep* to be a product of.
III *vi* to go about things; **~ par élimination** to use a process of elimination.

procédure /pʀɔsedyʀ/ *nf* **1** proceedings; **2** procedure.

procès /pʀɔsɛ/ *nm inv* **1** trial; **2** lawsuit, case; **intenter un ~ à qn** to sue sb; **3** indictment; **faire le ~ de qn/qch** to put sb/sth in the dock.
IDIOMS **sans autre forme de ~** without further ado.

processeur /pʀɔsesœʀ/ *nm* processor.

procession /pʀɔsesjɔ̃/ *nf* procession.

processus /pʀɔsesys/ *nm inv* **1** process; **2** (Med) evolution.

procès-verbal, *pl* **-aux** /pʀɔsɛvɛʀbal, o/ *nm* **1** (of meeting) minutes; **2** statement of offence[GB].

prochain, **~e** /pʀɔʃɛ̃, ɛn/ **I** *adj* **1** next; **en juin ~** next June; **à la ~e**○**!** see you○!; **2** [*meeting*] coming, forthcoming; [*departure, war*] imminent; **un jour ~** one day soon.
II *nm* fellow man; **aime ton ~** love thy neighbour[GB].

prochainement /pʀɔʃɛnmɑ̃/ *adv* soon.

proche /pʀɔʃ/ **I** *adj* **1** nearby; **~ de** close to, near; **2** [*departure*] imminent; **la victoire est ~** victory is at hand; **la fin est ~** the end is (drawing) near; **3** [*event*] recent; [*memory*] real, vivid; **4** similar; **~ de** [*figure, language*] close to; [*attitude*] verging on; **5** [*people*] close; (on form) **(plus) ~ parent** next of kin.
II *nm* **1** close relative; **2** close friend.

Proche-Orient /pʀɔʃɔʀjɑ̃/ *pr nm* **le ~** the Near East.

proclamation /pʀɔklamasjɔ̃/ *nf* proclamation.

proclamer /pʀɔklame/ [1] *vtr* **1** to proclaim; **2** to declare.

procréer /pʀɔkʀee/ [11] *vi* to procreate.

procuration /pʀɔkyʀasjɔ̃/ *nf* **1** power of attorney; **2** proxy; proxy form.

procurer /pʀɔkyʀe/ [1] **I** *vtr* to bring; to give.
II se procurer *v refl* (+ *v être*) **1** to obtain; **2** to buy.

procureur /pʀɔkyʀœʀ/ *nm* prosecutor.

prodige /pʀɔdiʒ/ *nm* **1** prodigy; **2** feat; **faire des ~s** to work wonders; **~ technique** technical miracle.

prodigieux, **-ieuse** /pʀɔdiʒjø, øz/ *adj* [*quantity*] prodigious; [*person*] wonderful.

prodigue /pʀɔdig/ *adj* **1** extravagant; **2 être ~ de** to be lavish with.

prodiguer /pʀɔdige/ [1] *vtr* **1** to give lots of [*advice*]; **2** to give [*treatment, first aid*].

producteur, **-trice** /pʀɔdyktœʀ, tʀis/ **I** *adj* **pays ~ de pétrole** oil-producing country.
II *nm,f* producer.

productif, **-ive** /pʀɔdyktif, iv/ *adj* [*work*] productive; [*investment*] profitable.

production /pʀɔdyksjɔ̃/ *nf* **1** (gen) production; (of energy) generation; **2** (gen) products, goods.

productivité /pʀɔdyktivite/ *nf* productivity.

produire /pʀɔdɥiʀ/ [69] **I** *vtr* **1** (gen) to produce; **cette usine produit peu** this factory has a low output; **un artiste/écrivain qui produit beaucoup** a prolific artist/writer; **2** to bring in [*money, wealth*]; to yield [*interest*]; **3** to produce, to have [*effect, result*]; to create, to make [*impression*]; to cause [*sensation, emotion*].
II se produire *v refl* (+ *v être*) **1** [*event*] to occur, to happen; **2** [*singer*] to perform.

produit /pʀɔdɥi/ *nm* **1** product; **des ~s** goods, products; **~s alimentaires** foodstuffs; **~s agricoles** agricultural produce; **2** income; yield, return; profit; **vivre du ~ de sa terre** to live off the land; **le ~ de la vente** the proceeds of the sale; **3** (of research) result; (of activity) product.

■ **~ chimique** chemical; **~ d'entretien** cleaning product, household product.

proéminent, **~e** /pRɔeminɑ̃, ɑ̃t/ *adj* prominent.

profanateur, **-trice** /pRɔfanatœR, tRis/ *nm,f* profaner.

profanation /pRɔfanasjɔ̃/ *nf* desecration; defilement; debasement.

profane /pRɔfan/ **I** *adj* secular.

II *nmf* **1** layman/laywoman; **2** nonbeliever.

III *nm* **le ~ et le sacré** the sacred and the profane.

profaner /pRɔfane/ [1] *vtr* to desecrate [*temple*]; to defile [*memory*]; to debase [*institution*].

proférer /pRɔfeRe/ [14] *vtr* to hurl [*insults*]; to make [*threats*]; to utter [*words*].

professer /pRɔfese/ [1] *vtr* to profess.

professeur /pRɔfesœR/ *nm* (in school) teacher; (in higher education) lecturer (GB), professor (US); (holding university chair) professor.

profession /pRɔfesjɔ̃/ *nf* **1** occupation; profession; **exercer la ~ d'infirmière** to be a nurse by profession; **être sans ~** to have no occupation; **2** declaration, profession.

■ **~ libérale** profession.

professionnel, **-elle** /pRɔfesjɔnɛl/ **I** *adj* **1** [*qualifications*] professional; [*life, environment*] working; [*disease*] occupational; [*training*] vocational; **2** [*player*] professional.

II *nm,f* professional; **le salon est réservé aux ~s** the fair is restricted to people in the trade.

professionnellement /pRɔfesjɔnɛlmɑ̃/ *adv* professionally.

professoral, **~e**, *mpl* **-aux** /pRɔfesɔRal, o/ *adj* professorial.

profil /pRɔfil/ *nm* profile; **être de ~** to be in profile; **se mettre de ~** to turn sideways.

profiler /pRɔfile/ [1] **I** *vtr* **la tour profile sa silhouette dans le ciel** the tower is silhouetted or outlined against the sky.

II se profiler *v refl* (+ *v être*) [*shape*] to stand out; [*problem*] to emerge; [*events*] to approach.

profit /pRɔfi/ *nm* **1** benefit, advantage; **au ~ des handicapés** in aid of the handicapped; **mettre à ~** to make the most of [*free time, course*]; to turn [sth] to good account [*situation*]; to make good use of [*idea*]; **2** profit; **être une source de ~ pour** to be a source of wealth for.

profitable /pRɔfitabl/ *adj* **1** beneficial; **2** profitable.

profiter /pRɔfite/ [1] **I profiter à** *v+prep* **~ à qn** to benefit sb.

II profiter de *v+prep* to use [*advantage*]; to make the most of [*holiday, situation*]; to take advantage of [*visit, weakness, person*].

III○ *vi* [*person*] to grow; [*plant*] to thrive.

profiteur, **-euse** /pRɔfitœR, øz/ *nm,f* profiteer.

profond, **~e** /pRɔfɔ̃, ɔ̃d/ **I** *adj* **1** deep; **peu ~** shallow; **2** [*boredom*] acute; [*sigh*] heavy; [*feeling, sleep, colour*] deep; **3** [*change, ignorance*] profound; **4** [*mind, remark*] profound; [*gaze*] penetrating; **5 la France ~e** provincial France; **l'Amérique ~e** small-town America.

II *adv* deeply, deep down.

profondément /pRɔfɔ̃demɑ̃/ *adv* **1** [*dig*] deep; **2** deeply; greatly; profoundly; **détester ~** to loathe.

profondeur /pRɔfɔ̃dœR/ *nf* **1** depth; **avoir une ~ de 3 mètres** to be 3 metres[GB] deep; **2** (of feeling) depth; (of remark, work) profundity; **en ~** [*analysis*] in-depth; [*work*] thorough.

profusion /pRɔfyzjɔ̃/ *nf* profusion; abundance.

progéniture /pRɔʒenityR/ *nf* progeny.

programmateur, **-trice** /pRɔgRamatœR, tRis/ **I** *nm,f* programme[GB] planner.

II *nm* timer.

programmation /pRɔgRamasjɔ̃/ *nf* programming.

programme /pRɔgRam/ *nm* **1** programme[GB]; **2** (of action) plan; (of work) programme[GB]; **c'est tout un ~!** (humorous) that'll take some doing!; **3** (Sch) syllabus; **4** (Comput) program.

programmer /pRɔgRame/ [1] *vtr* **1** to schedule [*broadcast*]; to plan [*work*]; **2** (Comput) to program.

programmeur, **-euse** /pRɔgRamœR, øz/ *nm,f* (computer) programmer.

progrès /pRɔgRɛ/ *nm inv* **1** progress; **les ~ de la médecine** advances in medicine; **être en ~** [*person*] to be making progress; [*results*] to be improving; **2** increase; **être en ~ de 10%** to be up by 10%; **3** (of illness) progression.

progresser /pRɔgRese/ [1] *vi* **1** to rise; to increase; **~ de 3%** [*rate*] to rise by 3%; [*party*] to gain 3%; **2** [*politician*] to make gains; [*illness*] to spread; [*crime*] to be on the increase; **3** [*pupil, inquiry, country*] to make progress; [*relations*] to improve; [*technology*] to progress; **4** [*climber*] to make progress; [*army*] to advance.

progressif, **-ive** /pRɔgResif, iv/ *adj* progressive.

progression /pRɔgRɛsjɔ̃/ *nf* **1** progress; advance; spread; increase; **2** (in mathematics, music) progression.

progressiste /pRɔgResist/ *adj* progressive.

prohiber /pRɔibe/ [1] *vtr* to prohibit.

prohibitif, **-ive** /pRɔibitif, iv/ *adj* **1** [*price*] prohibitive; **2** [*law*] prohibition.

prohibition /pRɔibisjɔ̃/ *nf* prohibition.

proie /pRwɑ/ *nf* prey; **être en ~ à l'angoisse** to be racked by anguish; **pays en ~ à la guerre civile** country in the grip of civil war.

projecteur /pRɔʒɛktœR/ *nm* **1** searchlight; floodlight; **être sous les ~s** to be in the spotlight; **2** projector.

projectile /pRɔʒɛktil/ *nm* missile; projectile.

projection /pRɔʒɛksjɔ̃/ *nf* **1 l'éruption commença par une ~ de cendres** the eruption began with a discharge of ashes; **2 le cuisinier a reçu des ~s d'huile bouillante** the cook got spattered with scalding oil; **3** projection; showing; **salle de ~** screening room.

projectionniste /pRɔʒɛksjɔnist/ *nmf* projectionist.

projet /pʀɔʒɛ/ *nm* **1** plan; **en ~, à l'état de ~** at the planning stage; **2** project; **3** (rough) draft; **4** (in architecture) execution plan.
■ **~ de loi** (government) bill.

projeter /pʀɔʒte/ [20] *vtr* **1** to throw; **le choc l'a projeté par terre** the shock sent him hurtling to the ground; **2** to cast [*shadow*]; **3** to show [*film*]; **4** to plan (**de faire** to do).

prolétaire /pʀɔletɛʀ/ *adj, nmf* proletarian.

prolétariat /pʀɔletaʀja/ *nm* proletariat.

proliférer /pʀɔlifeʀe/ [14] *vi* to proliferate.

prolifique /pʀɔlifik/ *adj* prolific.

prolixe /pʀɔliks/ *adj* verbose, prolix.

prologue /pʀɔlɔg/ *nm* prologue.

prolongation /pʀɔlɔ̃gasjɔ̃/ *nf* continuation; extension; (Sport) extra time.

prolongé, **~e** /pʀɔlɔ̃ʒe/ *adj* [*effort*] sustained; [*stay*] extended; [*exhibition*] prolonged.

prolongement /pʀɔlɔ̃ʒmɑ̃/ *nm* **1** (of road, stay) extension; **2 la rue Berthollet se trouve dans le ~ de la rue de la Glacière** Rue de la Glacière becomes Rue Berthollet.

prolonger /pʀɔlɔ̃ʒe/ [13] **I** *vtr* to extend [*stay*]; to prolong [*meeting, life*].
II se prolonger *v refl* (+ *v être*) **1** to persist; to go on; **2** [*street*] **se ~ jusqu'à** to go as far as.

promenade /pʀɔmnad/ *nf* **1** walk; ride; drive; **2** walkway; promenade.

promener /pʀɔmne/ [16] **I** *vtr* **1** to take [sb] out [*person*]; to take [sth] out for a walk [*animal*]; **ça te promènera**○ it'll get you out; **2** to carry [*object*]; **3** to show [sb] around.
II se promener *v refl* (+ *v être*) to go for a walk/drive/ride.

promeneur, **-euse** /pʀɔmnœʀ, øz/ *nm,f* walker.

promesse /pʀɔmɛs/ *nf* **1** promise; **avoir la ~ de qn** to have sb's word; **tenir ses ~s** to keep one's promises; **2 ~ de vente** agreement to sell.
■ **~ en l'air** or **de Gascon** or **d'ivrogne** empty or idle promise.

prometteur, **-euse** /pʀɔmɛtœʀ, øz/ *adj* promising.

promettre /pʀɔmɛtʀ/ [60] **I** *vtr* **1 ~ qch à qn** to promise sb sth; **je te promets qu'il le regrettera** he'll regret it, I guarantee you; **2 une soirée qui promet bien des surprises** an evening that holds a few surprises in store.
II *vi* [*pupil*] **1** to show promise; **un film qui promet** a film which sounds interesting; **2**○ **cet enfant promet!** that child is going to be a handful!; **ça promet!** that promises to be fun!
III se promettre *v refl* (+ *v être*) **1** to promise oneself; **2 se ~ de faire** to resolve to do.

promiscuité /pʀɔmiskɥite/ *nf* lack of privacy.

promontoire /pʀɔmɔ̃twaʀ/ *nm* promontory.

promoteur, **-trice** /pʀɔmɔtœʀ, tʀis/ *nm,f* **~ (immobilier)** property developer.

promotion /pʀɔmɔsjɔ̃/ *nf* **1** promotion; **2** (special) offer; **en ~** on (special) offer.

promotionnel, **-elle** /pʀɔmɔsjɔnɛl/ *adj* promotional.

promouvoir /pʀɔmuvwaʀ/ [43] *vtr* to promote.

prompt, **~e** /pʀɔ̃, pʀɔ̃t/ *adj* [*reaction*] prompt; [*gesture, glance*] swift; [*return*] sudden.

promulguer /pʀɔmylge/ [1] *vtr* to promulgate.

prôner /pʀone/ [1] *vtr* to advocate.

pronom /pʀɔnɔ̃/ *nm* pronoun.

pronominal, **~e**, *mpl* **-aux** /pʀɔnɔminal, o/ *adj* pronominal.

prononcé, **~e** /pʀɔnɔ̃se/ *adj* [*accent, taste*] strong; [*wrinkles*] deep; **avoir un goût ~ pour** to be particularly fond of.

prononcer /pʀɔnɔ̃se/ [12] **I** *vtr* **1** to pronounce [*word*]; **2** to mention [*name*]; to say [*phrase*]; **3** to deliver [*speech*]; **4** to pronounce [*death penalty*]; **~ le divorce** to grant a divorce.
II se prononcer *v refl* (+ *v être*) **1** to be pronounced; **2 se ~ contre/en faveur de qch** to declare oneself against/in favour[GB] of sth; **se ~ sur qch** to give one's opinion on sth.

prononciation /pʀɔnɔ̃sjasjɔ̃/ *nf* pronunciation.

pronostic /pʀɔnɔstik/ *nm* **1** forecast; **2** prediction; **3** (medical) prognosis.

propagande /pʀɔpagɑ̃d/ *nf* propaganda.

propagation /pʀɔpagasjɔ̃/ *nf* spread; propagation.

propager /pʀɔpaʒe/ [13] **I** *vtr* to spread [*rumour, disease*]; to propagate [*species, sound*].
II se propager *v refl* (+ *v être*) to spread; to propagate.

propension /pʀɔpɑ̃sjɔ̃/ *nf* propensity.

prophète /pʀɔfɛt/ *nm* prophet.

prophétie /pʀɔfesi/ *nf* prophecy.

propice /pʀɔpis/ *adj* favourable[GB]; **trouver le moment ~** to find the right moment.

proportion /pʀɔpɔʀsjɔ̃/ *nf* proportion; **en ~, ils sont mieux payés** they are proportionately better paid; **être sans ~ avec** to be out of (all) proportion to; **toutes ~s gardées** relatively speaking.

proportionnel, **-elle**[1] /pʀɔpɔʀsjɔnɛl/ *adj* proportional.

proportionnelle[2] /pʀɔpɔʀsjɔnɛl/ *nf* proportional representation.

proportionner /pʀɔpɔʀsjɔne/ [1] *vtr* **~ qch à qch** to make sth proportional to sth; **proportionné à** proportional to.

propos /pʀɔpo/ **I** *nm inv* **1 à ~, je...** by the way, I...; **à ~ de** about; **à ~ de qui?** about who?; **à ce ~, je voudrais...** in this connection, I would like...; **2 à ~** at the right moment; **mal à ~** at (just) the wrong moment.
II *nm pl* comments; **'~ recueillis par J. Brun'** 'interview by J. Brun'.

proposer /pʀɔpoze/ [1] **I** *vtr* **1** to suggest; **2** to offer [*drink, dish*]; **3** to put forward [*solution*]; to propose [*strategy*].
II se proposer *v refl* (+ *v être*) **1 se ~ pour faire** to offer to do; **2 se ~ de faire** to intend to do.

proposition /pʀɔpozisjɔ̃/ *nf* **1** suggestion; **2** proposal; **3** clause.
■ **~ de loi** ≈ bill.

propre /pʀɔpʀ/ **I** *adj* **1** clean; **nous voilà ~s!**

(figurative) we're in a fine mess now!; **2** tidy, neat; **3** [*person, life*] decent; **des affaires pas très ~s** unsavoury[GB] business; **4** own; **ma ~ voiture** my own car; **ce sont tes ~s paroles** you said so yourself; those were your very words; **5** of one's own; **chaque pays a des lois qui lui sont ~s** each country has its own particular laws; **6** [*baby*] toilet-trained; [*animal*] housetrained (GB), housebroken (US).
II **propre à** *phr* **1 ~ à** peculiar to; **2 ~ à faire** likely to do; liable to do; **3 ~ à** appropriate for; **produit déclaré ~ à la consommation** product fit for consumption.
III *nm* **1 mettre qch au ~** to make a fair copy of sth; **2 c'est du ~!** (ironic) that's very nice!; **3 le ~ de cette nouvelle technologie est de faire** what is peculiar to this new technology is that it does; **~ à rien** good-for-nothing.

proprement /pʀɔpʀəmɑ̃/ *adv* **1** purely; **à ~ parler** strictly speaking; **2** absolutely; **3** really; **4** literally; **l'air est devenu ~ irrespirable** the air has become literally unbreathable; **5** specifically; **6** well and truly; **le professeur l'a ~ remis à sa place** he was well and truly put in his place by the teacher; **7** neatly; **8** [*earn living*] honestly; [*live*] decently.

propreté /pʀɔpʀəte/ *nf* **1** cleanliness; **d'une ~ douteuse** not very clean; **2** honesty.

propriétaire /pʀɔpʀijetɛʀ/ *nmf* **1** owner; **un petit ~** a small-scale property owner; **ils sont ~s de leur maison** they own their own house; **faire le tour du ~** to look round (GB) or around the house; **2** landlord/landlady.

propriété /pʀɔpʀijete/ *nf* **1** ownership; **2** property; **~ privée** private property; **3** (of substance) property; **4** (of term) aptness.
■ **~ artistique et littéraire** copyright.

propulser /pʀɔpylse/ [1] *vtr* to propel.

propulseur /pʀɔpylsœʀ/ **I** *adj m* propellent.
II *nm* engine; **~ (de fusée)** (rocket) engine.
■ **~ à hélice** propeller.

propulsion /pʀɔpylsjɔ̃/ *nf* propulsion; **à ~ nucléaire** nuclear-powered.

prorata /pʀɔʀata/ *nm inv* proportion.

proroger /pʀɔʀɔʒe/ [13] *vtr* **1** to defer [*date*]; to renew [*passport*]; **2** to adjourn [*meeting*].

prosaïque /pʀɔzaik/ *adj* prosaic.

proscrire /pʀɔskʀiʀ/ [67] *vtr* to ban; to banish.

proscrit, **~e** /pʀɔskʀi, it/ *nm,f* outcast.

prose /pʀoz/ *nf* **1** prose; **poème en ~** prose poem; **2** (humorous) distinctive prose.

prosélytisme /pʀɔzelitism/ *nm* proselytizing.

prospecter /pʀɔspɛkte/ [1] *vtr* **1** to canvass; **2** to prospect.

prospecteur, **-trice** /pʀɔspɛktœʀ, tʀis/ *nm,f* **1** canvasser; **2** prospector.

prospection /pʀɔspɛksjɔ̃/ *nf* **1** canvassing; **2** prospecting.

prospectus /pʀɔspɛktys/ *nm inv* leaflet.

prospère /pʀɔspɛʀ/ *adj* thriving; prosperous.

prospérer /pʀɔspeʀe/ [14] *vi* to thrive; to prosper.

prospérité /pʀɔspeʀite/ *nf* prosperity.

prostate /pʀɔstat/ *nf* prostate (gland).

prosternation /pʀɔstɛʀnasjɔ̃/ *nf* **1** prostration; **2** (figurative) self-abasement.

prosternement /pʀɔstɛʀnəmɑ̃/ *nm* **1** prostrate position; **2** prostration.

prosterner: **se prosterner** /pʀɔstɛʀne/ [1] *v refl* (+ *v être*) **1** to prostrate oneself; **2** (figurative) to grovel.

prostitué /pʀɔstitɥe/ *nm* (male) prostitute.

prostituée /pʀɔstitɥe/ *nf* prostitute.

prostituer: **se prostituer** /pʀɔstitɥe/ [1] *v refl* (+ *v être*) to prostitute oneself.

prostration /pʀɔstʀasjɔ̃/ *nf* prostration.

protagoniste /pʀɔtagɔnist/ *nmf* protagonist.

protecteur, **-trice** /pʀɔtɛktœʀ, tʀis/ **I** *adj* **1** protective; **2** patronizing.
II *nm,f* protector.

protection /pʀɔtɛksjɔ̃/ *nf* **1** protection; **être sous haute ~** to be under tight security; **de ~** [*screen, measures*] protective; [*zone, system*] protection; **2** protective device.
■ **~ sociale** social welfare system.

protectionnisme /pʀɔtɛksjɔnism/ *nm* protectionism.

protégé, **~e** /pʀɔteʒe/ *nm,f* protégé.

protéger /pʀɔteʒe/ [15] **I** *vtr* to protect.
II **se protéger** *v refl* (+ *v être*) to protect oneself.

protéine /pʀɔtein/ *nf* protein.

protestant, **~e** /pʀɔtɛstɑ̃, ɑ̃t/ *adj, nm,f* Protestant.

protestantisme /pʀɔtɛstɑ̃tism/ *nm* Protestantism.

protestataire /pʀɔtɛstatɛʀ/ *nmf* protester.

protestation /pʀɔtɛstasjɔ̃/ *nf* protest.

protester /pʀɔtɛste/ [1] **I protester de** *v+prep* **~ de son innocence** to protest one's innocence.
II *vi* to protest.

prothèse /pʀɔtɛz/ *nf* prosthesis; artificial limb; dentures; **~ auditive** hearing aid.

prothésiste /pʀɔtezist/ *nmf* prosthetist.

protocolaire /pʀɔtɔkɔlɛʀ/ *adj* formal; official; **question ~** question of protocol.

protocole /pʀɔtɔkɔl/ *nm* **1** formalities; protocol; **2 ~ d'accord** draft agreement.

prototype /pʀɔtɔtip/ *nm* prototype.

protubérance /pʀɔtybeʀɑ̃s/ *nf* protuberance.

protubérant, **~e** /pʀɔtybeʀɑ̃, ɑ̃t/ *adj* protruding.

prou /pʀu/ *adv* **peu ou ~** more or less.

proue /pʀu/ *nf* prow, bow(s).

prouesse /pʀuɛs/ *nf* feat; (ironic) exploit.

prouver /pʀuve/ [1] **I** *vtr* **1** to prove; **2** to show; **3** to demonstrate.
II **se prouver** *v refl* (+ *v être*) **1** to prove to oneself; **2 ils se sont prouvé qu'ils s'aimaient** they proved their love for each other.
IDIOMS **n'avoir plus rien à ~** to have proved oneself.

provenance /pʀɔvnɑ̃s/ *nf* origin; **en ~ de** from.

provençal, **~e**, *mpl* **-aux** /pʀɔvɑ̃sal, o/ *adj* Provençal; **à la ~e** (Culin) (à la) provençale.
provenir /pʀɔvniʀ/ [36] *vi* **1** to come (**de** from); **provenant de** from; **2** to stem (**de** from).
proverbe /pʀɔvɛʀb/ *nm* proverb.
proverbial, **~e**, *mpl* **-iaux** /pʀɔvɛʀbjal, o/ *adj* proverbial.
providence /pʀɔvidɑ̃s/ **I** *nf* **1** salvation; **2** providence.
II (**-**)**providence** (*combining form*) **État**(**-**)**~** welfare state.
providentiel, **-ielle** /pʀɔvidɑ̃sjɛl/ *adj* providential.
province /pʀɔvɛ̃s/ *nf* **1** province; **2 la ~** the provinces; **ville de ~** provincial town.
provincial, **~e**, *mpl* **-iaux** /pʀɔvɛ̃sjal, o/ *adj, nm,f* provincial.
proviseur /pʀɔvizœʀ/ *nm* headteacher (GB) or principal (US) (*of a lycée*).
provision /pʀɔvizjɔ̃/ **I** *nf* **1** stock; supply; **2** deposit; credit (balance).
II provisions *nf pl* food shopping.
provisoire /pʀɔvizwaʀ/ *adj* provisional; temporary.
provisoirement /pʀɔvizwaʀmɑ̃/ *adv* provisionally.
provocant, **~e** /pʀɔvɔkɑ̃, ɑ̃t/ *adj* provocative.
provocateur, **-trice** /pʀɔvɔkatœʀ, tʀis/ *nm,f* agitator.
provocation /pʀɔvɔkasjɔ̃/ *nf* provocation.
provoquer /pʀɔvɔke/ [1] *vtr* **1** to cause [*accident*]; to provoke [*reaction, anger*]; **~ l'accouchement** to induce labour[GB]; **2** to provoke; **~ qn en duel** to challenge sb to a duel; **3** (sexually) to arouse.
proxénète /pʀɔksenɛt/ *nm* procurer, pimp.
proxénétisme /pʀɔksenetism/ *nm* procuring.
proximité /pʀɔksimite/ *nf* **1** nearness, proximity; **à ~** nearby; **à ~ de** near; **2** imminence; **à cause de la ~ de Noël** because it is/was so close to Christmas.
prude /pʀyd/ *adj* prudish.
prudemment /pʀydamɑ̃/ *adv* **1** carefully; **2** cautiously.
prudence /pʀydɑ̃s/ *nf* caution; **avec ~** cautiously; with caution; **par ~** as a precaution; **redoubler de ~** to be doubly careful.
prudent, **~e** /pʀydɑ̃, ɑ̃t/ *adj* **1** careful; **ce n'est pas ~ de faire** it isn't safe to do; **2** cautious; **3** wise.
prune /pʀyn/ *nf* **1** plum; **2** plum brandy.
IDIOMS **pour des ~s**° for nothing.
pruneau, *pl* **~x** /pʀyno/ *nm* prune.
prunelle /pʀynɛl/ *nf* **1** sloe; ≈ sloe gin; **2** (of eye) pupil.
prunier /pʀynje/ *nm* plum tree.
Prusse /pʀys/ *pr nf* Prussia.
PS /peɛs/ *nm* (*abbr* = **post-scriptum**) PS.
psaume /psom/ *nm* psalm.
pseudo- /psødo/ *pref* pseudo; **~-équilibre** so-called balance; **~-savant** self-styled scientist.
pseudonyme /psødɔnim/ *nm* pseudonym.
psychanalyse /psikanaliz/ *nf* psychoanalysis.
psychanalyser /psikanalize/ [1] *vtr* to psychoanalyse[GB].
psyché /psiʃe/ *nf* **1** cheval glass; **2** psyche.
psychiatrie /psikjatʀi/ *nf* psychiatry.
psychiatrique /psikjatʀik/ *adj* psychiatric.
psychique /psiʃik/ *adj* mental.
psychisme /psiʃism/ *nm* psyche.
psychologie /psikɔlɔʒi/ *nf* **1** psychology; **2** (psychological) insight.
psychologique /psikɔlɔʒik/ *adj* psychological.
psychologue /psikɔlɔg/ **I** *adj* **être ~** to understand people very well.
II *nmf* psychologist.
psychopathe /psikɔpat/ *nmf* psychopath.
psychose /psikoz/ *nf* **1** psychosis; **2 ~ de la guerre** obsessive fear of war.
psychosomatique /psikosɔmatik/ *adj* psychosomatic.
psychothérapie /psikoteʀapi/ *nf* psychotherapy.
PTT /petete/ *nf pl* (*abbr* = **Administration des postes et télécommunications et de la télédiffusion**) *former French postal and telecommunications service.*
puant, **~e** /pɥɑ̃, ɑ̃t/ *adj* **1** stinking; smelly; **2**° **un type ~** an incredibly arrogant guy°.
puanteur /pɥɑ̃tœʀ/ *nf* stench.
pub° /pyb/ *nf*: *abbr* ▶ **publicité**.
pubère /pybɛʀ/ *adj* pubescent.
puberté /pybɛʀte/ *nf* puberty.
pubis /pybis/ *nm inv* pubes; pubis.
public, **-ique** /pyblik/ **I** *adj* public; [*education*] state (GB), public (US); [*company*] state-owned; **la dette publique** the national debt.
II *nm* **1** public; **'interdit au ~'** 'no admittance'; **'avis au ~'** 'public notice'; **2** audience; spectators; **tous ~s** for all ages; **3** readership; **4 avoir un ~** to have a following; **5 le ~** the public sector.
publication /pyblikasjɔ̃/ *nf* publication.
■ **~ assistée par ordinateur**, **PAO** desktop publishing, DTP.
publicitaire /pyblisitɛʀ/ **I** *adj* [*campaign*] advertising; [*gift*] promotional.
II *nmf* **il/elle est ~** he/she's in advertising.
III *nm* advertising agency.
publicité /pyblisite/ *nf* **1** advertising; **faire de la ~ pour** to advertise; **2** (also **pub**°) advertisement, advert (GB), ad°; **3** publicity; **faire une mauvaise ~ à qn/qch** to give sb/sth a bad press.
■ **~ comparative** knocking copy°; **~ mensongère** misleading advertising.
publier /pyblije/ [2] *vtr* to publish.
publiquement /pyblikmɑ̃/ *adv* publicly.
puce /pys/ *nf* **1** flea; **2** (silicon) chip.
IDIOMS **ça m'a mis la ~ à l'oreille** that set me thinking; **secouer les ~**° **à qn** to bawl sb out°.
puceau°, *pl* **~x** /pyso/ *adj m* **il est encore ~** he's still a virgin.
pucelle° /pysɛl/ *adj f* **être ~** to be a virgin.

puceron /pysʀɔ̃/ *nm* aphid.
pudeur /pydœʀ/ *nf* **1** sense of modesty; **sans ~** shamelessly; **2** decency; sense of propriety.
pudibond, ~e /pydibɔ̃, ɔ̃d/ *adj* prudish.
pudique /pydik/ *adj* **1** modest; **2** discreet.
puer /pɥe/ [1] **I** *vtr* to stink of.
II *vi* to stink; **il puait des pieds** his feet stank.
puéricultrice /pɥeʀikyltʀis/ *nf* pediatric nurse.
puériculture /pɥeʀikyltyʀ/ *nf* childcare.
puéril, ~e /pɥeʀil/ *adj* childish; puerile.
puis /pɥi/ *adv* **1** then; **des poires et ~ des pêches** pears and peaches; **et ~ quoi encore**○! what next?; **2 il va être en colère? et ~ (après**○**)?** so what if he's angry!
puisard /pɥizaʀ/ *nm* soakaway (GB), sink hole (US).
puiser /pɥize/ [1] *vtr* **~ qch dans qch** to draw sth from sth.
puisque (**puisqu'** *before vowel or mute h*) /pɥisk(ə)/ *conj* since; **~ c'est comme ça, je m'en vais** if that's how it is, I'm off.
puissance /pɥisɑ̃s/ *nf* **1** power; **la ~ militaire** military strength or might; **2** (country) power; **une grande ~** a superpower; **3** (of light) intensity; (of sound) volume; **4** (in algebra) power; **dix ~ trois** ten to the power (of) three.
puissant, ~e /pɥisɑ̃, ɑ̃t/ **I** *adj* powerful; strong.
II puissants *nm pl* **les ~s** the powerful.
puits /pɥi/ *nm* **1** well; **~ de pétrole** oil well; **2** shaft.
■ **~ de science** fount of knowledge.
pull○ /pyl/ *nm* sweater.
pull-over, *pl* **~s** /pylɔvɛʀ/ *nm* sweater.
pulluler /pylyle/ [1] *vi* **1** to proliferate; **2 les touristes pullulent dans la région** the area is swarming with tourists.
pulmonaire /pylmɔnɛʀ/ *adj* [*disease*] lung; [*artery*] pulmonary.
pulpe /pylp/ *nf* (of fruit) pulp; (of potato) flesh.
pulpeux, -euse /pylpø, øz/ *adj* [*body, lips*] luscious; [*fruit*] fleshy.
pulsation /pylsasjɔ̃/ *nf* beat; **~s cardiaques** heartbeat; heartbeats.
pulsion /pylsjɔ̃/ *nf* impulse, urge.
pulvériser /pylveʀize/ [1] *vtr* **1** to spray; **2** to pulverize; **3** to shatter○ [*record*].
puma /pyma/ *nm* puma.
punaise /pynɛz/ *nf* **1** drawing pin (GB), thumbtack (US); **2** (Zool) bug.
punch[1] /pɔ̃ʃ/ *nm* (drink) punch.
punch[2] /pœnʃ/ *nm* **1** punch; **2** energy; **avoir du ~** [*slogan*] to be punchy○; [*person*] to have drive.
punching-ball, *pl* **~s** /pœnʃiŋbol/ *nm* punchball (GB), punching bag (US).
punir /pyniʀ/ [3] *vtr* to punish.
punitif, -ive /pynitif, iv/ *adj* punitive.
punition /pynisjɔ̃/ *nf* **1** punishment; **2 il n'a pas fait sa ~** he hasn't done the task he was given as punishment.
pupille[1] /pypij/ *nmf* ward; **~ de l'État** child in care; **~ de la Nation** war orphan.
pupille[2] /pypij/ *nf* (of eye) pupil.
pupitre /pypitʀ/ *nm* **1** control panel; console; **2** music stand; music rest; **3** desk; **4** lectern.
pur, ~e /pyʀ/ **I** *adj* **1** (gen) pure; [*diamond*] flawless; [*voice, sky*] clear; **2** [*truth*] pure; [*coincidence, madness*] sheer; **en ~e perte** to no avail; **c'est de la paresse ~e et simple** it's laziness, pure and simple; **~ et dur** hardline; **3** [*tradition*] true; **un ~ produit de** a typical product of; **à l'état ~** [*genius*] sheer.
II *nm,f* virtuous person.
purée /pyʀe/ *nf* purée; **~ (de pommes de terre)** mashed potatoes.
■ **~ de pois** pea souper (GB), fog.
purement /pyʀmɑ̃/ *adv* purely.
pureté /pyʀte/ *nf* purity.
purgatif, -ive /pyʀgatif, iv/ *adj* purgative.
purgatoire /pyʀgatwaʀ/ *nm* **le ~** purgatory.
purge /pyʀʒ/ *nf* **1** purgative; **2** purge.
purger /pyʀʒe/ [13] *vtr* **1** (Med) to purge; **2** to bleed [*radiator*]; to drain [*pipe*]; to purify [*metal*]; **3** (Law) to serve [*sentence*].
purifier /pyʀifje/ [2] *vtr* to purify; to cleanse.
purin /pyʀɛ̃/ *nm* slurry.
puriste /pyʀist/ *nmf* purist.
puritain, ~e /pyʀitɛ̃, ɛn/ **I** *adj* puritanical; Puritan.
II *nm,f* puritan; Puritan.
pur-sang /pyʀsɑ̃/ *nm inv* thoroughbred.
pus /py/ *nm inv* pus.
pustule /pystyl/ *nf* pustule.
putois /pytwa/ *nm inv* **1** polecat; **2** skunk (fur).
putréfaction /pytʀefaksjɔ̃/ *nf* putrefaction; **en état de ~** decomposing.
putsch /putʃ/ *nm* putsch.
puzzle /pœzl, pyzl/ *nm* jigsaw puzzle.
PV○ /peve/ *nm* (*abbr* = **procès-verbal**) fine; parking ticket; speeding ticket.
PVC /pevese/ *nm* (*abbr* = **chlorure de polyvinyle**) PVC.
pygmée /pigme/ *nmf* pygmy.
pyjama /piʒama/ *nm* (pair of) pyjamas (GB), (pair of) pajamas (US).
pylône /pilon/ *nm* pylon; (for radio, TV transmitter) mast; (of bridge) tower.
pyramide /piʀamid/ *nf* pyramid.
pyrénéen, -éenne /piʀeneɛ̃, ɛn/ *adj* Pyrenean.
pyrex® /piʀɛks/ *nm inv* Pyrex®.
pyrogravure /piʀogʀavyʀ/ *nf* pokerwork.
pyromane /piʀɔman/ *nmf* pyromaniac; (Law) arsonist.
python /pitɔ̃/ *nm* python.

Qq

q, Q /ky/ *nm inv* q, Q.

qcm /kyseɛm/ *nm* (*abbr* = **questionnaire à choix multiple**) multiple-choice questionnaire, mcq.

QG /kyʒe/ *nm*: *abbr* ▶ **quartier**.

QI /kyi/ *nm*: *abbr* ▶ **quotient**.

qu' ▶ **que**.

quadragénaire /kwadʀaʒenɛʀ/ *nmf* forty-year old.

quadriennal, ~e, *mpl* **-aux** /kwadʀijɛnal, o/ *adj* **1** [*plan*] four-year; **2** quadrennial.

quadrillage /kadʀijaʒ/ *nm* cross-ruling.

quadrillé, ~e /kadʀije/ *adj* [*paper*] squared.

quadriller /kadʀije/ [1] *vtr* **1** [*police*] to spread one's net over; **2** to cross-rule [*paper*].

quadrimoteur /k(w)adʀimɔtœʀ/ *nm* four-engined plane.

quadrupède /k(w)adʀypɛd/ *adj, nm* quadruped.

quadruple /k(w)adʀypl/ *nm* **le ~ de cette quantité** four times this amount.

quadruplé, ~e /k(w)adʀyple/ *nm,f* quadruplet, quad.

quai /kɛ/ *nm* **1** quay; **le navire est à ~** the ship has docked; **2** (of river) bank; **3** (station) platform.

■ **~ d'embarquement** loading dock; **Quai des Orfèvres** *criminal investigation department of the French police force*; **Quai d'Orsay** French Foreign Office.

qualificatif, -ive /kalifikatif, iv/ **I** *adj* qualifying.

II *nm* **1** (in grammar) qualifier; **2** term, word.

qualification /kalifikasjɔ̃/ *nf* **1** qualification; **2** skills; **sans ~** unskilled.

qualifié, ~e /kalifje/ *adj* [*staff, labour*] skilled; qualified.

qualifier /kalifje/ [2] **I** *vtr* **1** to describe; **2** to qualify.

II se qualifier *v refl* (+ *v être*) (Sport) to qualify.

qualitatif, -ive /kalitatif, iv/ *adj* qualitative.

qualité /kalite/ *nf* **1** quality; **de première ~** of the highest quality; **avoir beaucoup de ~s** to have many qualities; **2 en (sa) ~ de représentant** in his/her capacity as a representative; **nom, prénom et ~** surname, first name and occupation.

quand /kɑ̃, kɑ̃t/ **I** *conj* **1** when; **~ il arrivera, vous lui annoncerez la nouvelle** when he gets here, you can tell him the news; **~ je pense que ma fille va avoir dix ans!** to think that my daughter's almost ten!; **~ je vous le disais!** I told you so!; **2** whenever; **~ il pleut plus de trois jours la cave est inondée** whenever it rains for more than three days, the cellar floods; **3** even if; **~ (bien même) la terre s'écroulerait, il continuerait à dormir** he'd sleep through an earthquake.

II *adv* when; **de ~ date votre dernière réunion?** when was your last meeting?; **depuis ~ habitez-vous ici?** how long have you been living here?; **à ~ la semaine de 30 heures**○**?** when will we get a 30-hour working week?

III quand même *phr* still; **ils ne veulent pas de moi, mais j'irai ~ même!** they don't want me, but I'm still going!; **~ même, tu exagères**○**!** come on, that's going too far!

quant: **quant à** /kɑ̃ta/ *phr* **1** as for; **la France, ~ à elle,...** as for France, it...; **2** about, concerning.

quantifier /kɑ̃tifje/ [2] *vtr* to quantify.

quantitatif, -ive /kɑ̃titatif, iv/ *adj* quantitative.

quantité /kɑ̃tite/ *nf* **1** quantity, amount; **2 des ~s de** scores of [*people*]; a lot of [*things*]; **du pain/vin en ~** plenty of bread/wine.

quarantaine /kaʀɑ̃tɛn/ *nf* **1** about forty; **2 être en ~** to be in quarantine; to be ostracized.

quarante /kaʀɑ̃t/ *adj inv, pron, nm inv* forty.

quarante-cinq /kaʀɑ̃tsɛ̃k/ *adj inv, pron, nm inv* forty-five.

■ **~ tours** single.

quarantième /kaʀɑ̃tjɛm/ *adj* fortieth.

quart /kaʀ/ *nm* **1** quarter; **un ~ d'heure** a quarter of an hour; **les trois ~s du temps**○ most of the time; **2** a quarter-litre[GB] bottle; a quarter-litre[GB] pitcher; **3** (Naut) **être de ~** to be on watch.

■ **~ de cercle** quadrant; **~ de tour** 90° turn; **faire qch au ~ de tour**○ to do sth immediately.

quartier /kaʀtje/ *nm* **1** area, district; **de ~** [*cinema, grocer*] local; **2** quarter; **un ~ de pommes** a slice of apple; **un ~ d'orange** an orange segment; **3** (of moon) quarter; **4** (Mil) **~s** quarters; **avoir ~ libre** to be off duty; to have time off.

■ **~ général, QG** headquarters, HQ.

IDIOMS **ne pas faire de ~** to show no mercy.

quart-monde /kaʀmɔ̃d/ *nm inv* underclass.

quartz /kwaʀts/ *nm* quartz.

quasi /kazi/ **I** *adv* almost.

II quasi- (*combining form*) **~-indifférence** virtual indifference; **la ~-totalité de** almost all of; **à la ~-unanimité** almost unanimously.

quasiment○ /kazimɑ̃/ *adv* practically.

quaternaire /kwatɛʀnɛʀ/ *adj, nm* Quaternary.

quatorze /katɔʀz/ *adj inv, pron, nm inv* fourteen.

IDIOMS **chercher midi à ~ heures**○ to complicate matters.

quatorzième /katɔʀzjɛm/ *adj* fourteenth.

quatrain /katʀɛ̃/ *nm* quatrain.

quatre /katʀ/ *adj inv, pron, nm inv* four.
IDIOMS **faire les ~ volontés de qn** to give in to sb's every whim; **être tiré à ~ épingles** to be dressed up to the nines○; **ne pas y aller par ~ chemins** not to beat about the bush; **je vais leur parler entre ~ yeux** I'm going to talk to them face to face; **monter un escalier ~ à ~** to go up the stairs four at a time; **être entre ~ planches**○ to be six feet under.

quatre-heures /katʀœʀ/ *nm inv* afternoon snack (*for children*).

quatre-quarts /kat(ʀə)kaʀ/ *nm inv* pound cake.

quatre-vingt(s) /katʀəvɛ̃/ *adj, pron, nm* eighty.

quatre-vingt-dix /katʀəvɛ̃dis/ *adj inv, pron, nm inv* ninety.

quatre-vingt-dixième /katʀəvɛ̃dizjɛm/ *adj* ninetieth.

quatre-vingtième /katʀəvɛ̃tjɛm/ *adj* eightieth.

quatrième /katʀijɛm/ **I** *adj* fourth.
II *nf* **1** (Sch) *third year of secondary school, age 13–14*; **2** (Aut) fourth (gear).
■ **le ~ âge** very old people.
IDIOMS **en ~ vitesse**○ in double quick time○.

quatuor /kwatɥɔʀ/ *nm* quartet.

que (**qu'** *before vowel or mute h*) /kə/ **I** *conj* **1** that; **je pense qu'il a raison** I think he's right; **je veux ~ tu m'accompagne** I want you to come with me; **2** so (that); **approche, ~ je te regarde** come closer so I can look at you; **3** whether; **~ cela vous plaise ou non** whether you like it or not; **4 si vous venez et ~ vous ayez le temps** if you come and (if you) have the time; **5 il n'était pas sitôt parti qu'elle appela la police** no sooner had he left than she called the police; **6 ~ tout le monde sorte!** everyone must leave!; **~ ceux qui n'ont pas compris le disent** let anyone who hasn't understood say so; **qu'il crève**◐**!** let him rot○!; **7** than; as; **plus gros ~ moi** fatter than me; **aussi grand ~ mon frère** as tall as my brother.
II *pron* what; **~ dire?** what can you say?; **je ne sais pas ce qu'il a dit** I don't know what he said; **qu'est-ce que c'est que ça?** what's that?
III *rel pron* that; who(m); which; **je n'aime pas la voiture ~ tu as achetée** I don't like the car (that) you've bought.
IV *adv* **~ c'est joli** it's so pretty; **~ de monde** what a lot of people.

Québec /kebɛk/ **I** *pr nm* **le ~** Quebec.
II *pr n* Quebec.

québécois, **~e** /kebekwa, az/ *adj* of Quebec.

Québécois, **~e** /kebekwa, az/ *nm,f* Quebecois, Quebecker.

quel, **quelle** /kɛl/ **I** *det* who; what; which; **je me demande quelle est la meilleure solution** I wonder what the best solution is; **de ces deux médicaments, ~ est le plus efficace?** which of these two medicines is more effective?
II *adj* **1** what; which; **quelle heure est-il?** what time is it?; **dans ~ tiroir l'as-tu mis?** which drawer did you put it in?; **~ âge as-tu?** how old are you?; **2** what; how; **quelle coïncidence!** what a coincidence!; **3 quelle que soit la route que l'on prenne** whatever or whichever road we take; **~ que soit le vainqueur** whoever the winner may be.

quelconque /kɛlkɔ̃k/ **I** *adj* [*person*] ordinary; ordinary-looking; [*novel, actor*] poor; [*restaurant*] second-rate; [*place*] characterless.
II *adj* any; **si pour une raison ~** if for some reason or other; **si le livre avait un intérêt ~** if the book was in any way interesting.

quelle ▸ **quel**.

quelque /kɛlk/ **I** *quantif* some; a few; any; **depuis ~ temps** for some time; **je voudrais ajouter ~s mots** I'd like to add a few words; **ça dure trois heures et ~s** it lasts over three hours; **si pour ~ raison que ce soit** if for whatever reason.
II *adv* **1 les ~ deux mille spectateurs** the two thousand odd spectators; **2** however; **~ admirable que soit son attitude** however admirable his/her attitude may be.
III quelque chose *pron* something; anything; **il y a ~ chose qui ne va pas** something's wrong; **si ~ chose leur arrive** if anything should happen to them; **il a ~ chose de son grand-père** he's got a look of his grandfather about him; **ça me dit ~ chose** it rings a bell.
IV quelque part *phr* somewhere; anywhere.
V quelque peu *phr* somewhat.

quelquefois /kɛlkəfwɑ/ *adv* sometimes.

quelques-uns, **quelques-unes** /kɛlkəzœ̃, yn/ *pron* some, a few.

quelqu'un /kɛlkœ̃/ *pron* someone, somebody; anyone, anybody; **~ d'autre** someone else; **c'est ~ de compétent** he/she is competent.

quémander /kemɑ̃de/ [1] *vtr* to beg.

qu'en-dira-t-on /kɑ̃diʀatɔ̃/ *nm inv* gossip.

quenelle /kənɛl/ *nf*: *dumpling made of flour and egg, flavoured*[GB] *with meat or fish*.

quenouille /kənuj/ *nf* distaff.

querelle /kəʀɛl/ *nf* **1** quarrel; **chercher ~ à qn** to pick a quarrel with sb; **2** dispute.

quereller: **se quereller** /kəʀele/ [1] *v refl* (+ *v être*) to quarrel.

question /kɛstjɔ̃/ *nf* **1** question; **je ne me suis jamais posé la ~** I've never really thought about it; **pose-leur la ~** ask them; **2** matter, question; issue; **~ d'habitude!** it's a matter of habit; **en ~** in question; at issue; **(re)mettre en ~** to reappraise; to reassess; **se remettre en ~** to take a new look at oneself; **la ~ n'est pas là** that's not the point; **il est ~ d'elle dans l'article** she's mentioned in the article; **il n'est pas ~ que tu partes** you can't possibly leave; **pas ~!** no way○!; **3**○ **~ santé, ça va** where health is concerned, things are OK.

questionnaire /kɛstjɔnɛʀ/ *nm* questionnaire.

questionner /kɛstjɔne/ [1] *vtr* to question.

quête /kɛt/ *nf* **1** collection; **faire la ~** to take the collection; to pass the hat round; to collect for charity; **2** search; **la ~ du Graal** the quest for the Holy Grail.

quêter /kete/ [1] *vi* to take the collection; **~ pour une œuvre** to collect for a charity.

quetsche /kwɛtʃ/ *nf* (sweet purple) plum.

queue /kø/ *nf* **1** tail; **2** (of flower) stem; (of apple) stalk (GB), stem (US); **3** (of pot) handle; **4** (Sport) cue; **5** (of procession) tail(-end); (of train) rear, back; **ils arrivent en ~ (de peloton) des grandes entreprises** they come at the bottom of the league table of companies; **6 faire la ~** to stand in a queue (GB), to stand in line (US).
IDIOMS **une histoire sans ~ ni tête**○ a cock and bull story; **la ~ basse** with one's tail between one's legs; **il n'y en avait pas la ~ d'un(e)**○ there were none to be seen; **faire une ~ de poisson à qn** to cut in front of sb; **finir en ~ de poisson** to fizzle out.

queue-de-cheval, *pl* **queues-de-cheval** /kødʃəval/ *nf* ponytail.

queue-de-pie○, *pl* **queues-de-pie** /kødpi/ *nf* tails, tailcoat.

queux† /kø/ *nm inv* **maître ~** chef.

qui /ki/ **I** *pron* who; whom; **~ veut-elle voir?** who does she want to speak to?
II *rel pron* **1** who; that; which; **est-ce vous ~ venez d'appeler?** was it you who called just now?; **ce ~ me plaît chez lui** what I like about him; **2 ~ que vous soyez** whoever you are; **je n'ai jamais frappé ~ que ce soit** I've never hit anybody.

quiche /kiʃ/ *nf* quiche, flan.

quiconque /kikɔ̃k/ **I** *rel pron* whoever, anyone who.
II *pron* anyone, anybody.

quiétude /kjetyd/ *nf* tranquillity.

quignon /kiɲɔ̃/ *nm* crusty end (of a loaf).

quille /kij/ *nf* **1** skittle; **2** (Naut) keel.
IDIOMS **être reçu comme un chien dans un jeu de ~s**○ to be given a very unfriendly welcome.

quincaillerie /kɛ̃kajʀi/ *nf* **1** hardware shop (GB) or store (US); **2** hardware; **3** hardware business.

quinconce /kɛ̃kɔ̃s/ *nm* **en ~** in staggered rows.

quinquagénaire /kɛ̃kaʒenɛʀ/ *nmf* fifty-year old.

quinquennal, **~e**, *mpl* **-aux** /kɛ̃kenal, o/ *adj* **1** [*plan*] five-year; **2** five-yearly.

quintal, *pl* **-aux** /kɛ̃tal, o/ *nm* quintal.

quinte /kɛ̃t/ *nf* **1** (Mus) fifth; **2 une ~ (de toux)** a coughing fit.

quintette /kɛ̃tɛt/ *nm* quintet.

quintuple /kɛ̃typl/ *nm* **le ~ de cette quantité** five times the amount.

quintuplé, **~e** /kɛ̃typle/ *nm,f* quintuplet, quin (GB), quint (US).

quinzaine /kɛ̃zɛn/ *nf* **1** fortnight (GB), two weeks; **sous ~** within 2 weeks; **2** about fifteen.

quinze /kɛ̃z/ *adj inv*, *pron*, *nm inv* fifteen.

quinzième /kɛ̃zjɛm/ *adj* fifteenth.

quiproquo /kipʀɔko/ *nm* misunderstanding.

quittance /kitɑ̃s/ *nf* **1** receipt; **2** bill.

quitte /kit/ **I** *adj* **1 nous sommes ~s, je suis ~ avec lui** we're quits; **2 en être ~ pour la peur/un rhume** to get off with a fright/a cold.
II quitte à *phr* **~ à aller à Londres, autant que ce soit pour quelques jours** if you're going to London anyway, you might as well go for a few days.
■ **~ ou double** double or quits.

quitter /kite/ [1] **I** *vtr* **1** to leave [*place, person, road*]; **2** to leave [*job, organization*]; **~ la scène** to give up acting; **il ne l'a pas quittée des yeux de tout le repas** he didn't take his eyes off her throughout the meal; **ne quittez pas** hold the line; **3** [*company*] to move from [*street*]; to move out of [*building*]; **4 un grand homme nous a quittés** a great man has passed away; **5** to take off [*garment, hat*].
II se quitter *v refl* (+ *v être*) to part; **ils ne se quittent plus** they're inseparable now.

qui-vive /kiviv/ *nm inv* **être sur le ~** to be on the alert.

quoi /kwɑ/ **I** *pron* **1** what; **à ~ penses-tu?** what are you thinking about?; **à ~ bon recommencer?** what's the point of starting again?; **2 ~ qu'elle puisse en dire** whatever she may say; **~ qu'il en soit** be that as it may.
II *rel pron* **il n'y a rien sur ~ vous puissiez fonder vos accusations** there's nothing on which to base your accusations; **à ~ il a répondu** to which he replied; **après ~ ils sont partis** after which they left; **(il n'y a) pas de ~!** my pleasure; **il n'y a pas de ~ se fâcher** there's no reason to get angry; **il n'a (même) pas de ~ s'acheter un livre** he hasn't (even) got enough money to buy a book.

quoique (**quoiqu'** *before vowel or mute h*) /kwak(ə)/ *conj* although, though; **nous sommes mieux ici qu'à Paris, ~** we're better off here than in Paris, but then (again).

quota /kɔta/ *nm* quota (**sur** on).

quote-part, *pl* **quotes-parts** /kɔtpaʀ/ *nf* share.

quotidien, **-ienne** /kɔtidjɛ̃, ɛn/ **I** *adj* **1** daily; **2** everyday.
II *nm* **1** daily (paper); **2** everyday life.

quotidiennement /kɔtidjɛnmɑ̃/ *adv* every day, daily.

quotient /kɔsjɑ̃/ *nm* quotient.
■ **~ intellectuel**, **QI** intelligence quotient, IQ.

r, **R** /ɛʀ/ *nm inv* r, R.

rab○ /ʀab/ *nm* **1** extra; **faire du ~** to do extra hours; **2 demander du ~** to ask for seconds.

rabâcher /ʀabɑʃe/ [1] **I** *vtr* to keep repeating.
II *vi* to keep harping on.

rabais /ʀabɛ/ *nm inv* discount.

rabaisser /ʀabese/ [1] **I** *vtr* to belittle.
II se rabaisser *v refl* (+ *v être*) to demean oneself.

rabat /ʀaba/ *nm* (of bag, table, pocket) flap.

rabat-joie /ʀabajwɑ/ *adj inv* **être ~** to be a killjoy.

rabattre /ʀabatʀ/ [61] **I** *vtr* **1** [*person*] to shut [*lid*]; to put or fold up [*foldaway seat, tray*]; **2** to turn [sth] down [*collar, sheet*]; **3** [*player*] to smash [*ball*]; **4 ~ le gibier** to beat the undergrowth for game.
II se rabattre *v refl* (+ *v être*) **1** [*lid*] to shut; [*leaf of table*] to fold up; **2** [*driver, vehicle*] to pull back in; **3 se ~ sur** to make do with.

rabbin /ʀabɛ̃/ *nm* rabbi; **grand ~** chief rabbi.

rabot /ʀabo/ *nm* (tool) plane.

rabougri, **~e** /ʀabugʀi/ *adj* [*tree*] stunted.

rabrouer /ʀabʀue/ [1] *vtr* to snub.

racaille /ʀakaj/ *nf* scum.

raccommoder /ʀakɔmɔde/ [1] *vtr* **1** to darn [*socks*]; **2**○ to reconcile [*people*].

raccompagner /ʀakɔ̃paɲe/ [1] *vtr* **~ qn chez lui** to walk/to drive sb (back) home.

raccord /ʀakɔʀ/ *nm* **1** (in wallpaper) join; **2** (in painting) touch-up; **3** (in film) link shot.

raccordement /ʀakɔʀdəmɑ̃/ *nm* link road.

raccorder /ʀakɔʀde/ [1] *vtr* to connect.

raccourci /ʀakuʀsi/ *nm* (road) shortcut.

raccourcir /ʀakuʀsiʀ/ [3] **I** *vtr* **1** (gen) to shorten; **2** to cut [*text, speech*].
II *vi* [*days*] to get shorter, to draw in.
IDIOMS **tomber sur qn à bras raccourcis**○ to lay into sb.

raccrocher /ʀakʀɔʃe/ [1] **I** *vtr* to hang [sth] back up.
II *vi* to hang up.
III se raccrocher *v refl* (+ *v être*) **se ~ à** to grab hold of [*rail*]; (figurative) to cling to [*person, excuse*].

race /ʀas/ *nf* **1** race; **2** (Zool) breed; **chien de ~** pedigree (dog).

racheter /ʀaʃte/ [18] **I** *vtr* **1** to buy [sth] back; **2** to buy some more [*wine*]; **3** to buy new [*sheets*]; **4** to buy out [*company, factory*]; **je rachète votre voiture 5000 francs** I'll buy your car off you for 5,000 francs; **5** to redeem [*sinner*].
II se racheter *v refl* (+ *v être*) to redeem oneself.

rachitisme /ʀaʃitism/ *nm* rickets.

racial, **~e**, *mpl* **-iaux** /ʀasjal, o/ *adj* racial; **émeutes ~es** race riots.

racine /ʀasin/ *nf* root.

racisme /ʀasism/ *nm* racism.

raciste /ʀasist/ *adj*, *nmf* racist.

racket /ʀakɛt/ *nm* extortion racket; racketeering.

raclée○ /ʀɑkle/ *nf* hiding○.

racler /ʀɑkle/ [1] **I** *vtr* **1** to scrape [sth] clean [*plate*]; **2** to scrape off [*rust*]; **3** to scrape against.
II se racler *v refl* (+ *v être*) **se ~ la gorge** to clear one's throat.

raclette /ʀɑklɛt/ *nf* **1** raclette (*Swiss cheese dish*); **2** scraper.

racoler /ʀakɔle/ [1] *vtr* [*prostitute*] to solicit.

racontar○ /ʀakɔ̃taʀ/ *nm* **des ~s** idle gossip.

raconter /ʀakɔ̃te/ [1] *vtr* to tell [*story*]; to describe [*incident*]; **~ qch à qn** to tell sb sth; **qu'est-ce que tu racontes?** what are you talking about?

racornir /ʀakɔʀniʀ/ [3] *vtr*, **se racornir** *v refl* (+ *v être*) **1** to harden; **2** to shrivel (up).

radar /ʀadaʀ/ *nm* radar.

rade /ʀad/ *nf* harbour[GB]; **rester en ~**○ [*person*] to be left stranded.

radeau, *pl* **~x** /ʀado/ *nm* raft.

radiateur /ʀadjatœʀ/ *nm* radiator; **~ électrique** electric heater.

radiation /ʀadjasjɔ̃/ *nf* radiation.

radical, **~e**, *mpl* **-aux** /ʀadikal, o/ *adj*, *nm,f* radical.

radier /ʀadje/ [2] *vtr* **~ un médecin** to strike off a doctor (GB), to take away a doctor's license (US); **~ un avocat** to disbar a lawyer.

radieux, **-ieuse** /ʀadjø, øz/ *adj* **1** [*sun*] dazzling; **2** [*weather*] glorious; **3** [*face, smile*] radiant; [*person*] radiant with joy.

radin○, **~e** /ʀadɛ̃, in/ *adj* stingy○.

radio[1] /ʀadjo/ **I** *adj inv* [*contact, signal*] radio.
II *nm* radio operator.

radio[2] /ʀadjo/ *nf* **1** radio; **2** X-ray.

radioactivité /ʀadjoaktivite/ *nf* radioactivity.

radiocassette /ʀadjokasɛt/ *nm* radio cassette player.

radiographie /ʀadjɔgʀafi/ *nf* **1** radiography; **2** X-ray (photograph).

radiologue /ʀadjɔlɔg/ *nmf* radiologist.

radiophonique /ʀadjofɔnik/ *adj* radio.

radio-réveil, *pl* **radios-réveils** /ʀadjo ʀevɛj/ *nm* clock radio.

radioscopie /ʀadjɔskɔpi/ *nf* fluoroscopy.

radiothérapie /ʀadjoteʀapi/ *nf* radiotherapy.

radis /ʀadi/ *nm inv* radish; **je n'ai plus un ~**○ I haven't got a penny.

radoter /ʀadɔte/ [1] *vi* **1** to talk nonsense; **2** to repeat oneself.
radoucir: **se radoucir** /ʀadusiʀ/ [3] *v refl* (+ *v être*) [*person*] to soften up; [*weather*] to turn milder.
rafale /ʀafal/ *nf* **1** (of wind, rain) gust; (of snow) flurry; **2** (of gunfire) burst.
raffermir /ʀafɛʀmiʀ/ [3] *vtr* **1** to tone [*skin*]; to tone up [*muscles*]; **2** to strengthen [*position*]; to steady [*market*].
raffinage /ʀafinaʒ/ *nm* refining.
raffiné, **~e** /ʀafine/ *adj* refined; [*food*] sophisticated.
raffinement /ʀafinmɑ̃/ *nm* **1** refinement; **2** elegance.
raffiner /ʀafine/ [1] *vtr* to refine.
raffinerie /ʀafinʀi/ *nf* refinery; **~ de pétrole** oil refinery.
raffoler /ʀafɔle/ [1] *v+prep* **~ de** to be crazy○ about.
raffut○ /ʀafy/ *nm* **1** racket○; **2** stink○, row.
rafiot○ /ʀafjo/ *nm* boat, (old) tub○.
rafistoler○ /ʀafistɔle/ [1] *vtr* to patch up.
rafle /ʀɑfl/ *nf* **1** raid; **2** roundup.
rafler○ /ʀɑfle/ [1] *vtr* **1** to make off with, to swipe○; **2** to walk off with [*medal, reward*].
rafraîchir /ʀafʀɛʃiʀ/ [3] **I** *vtr* [*rain*] to cool [*atmosphere*]; **le thé glacé te rafraîchira** the iced tea will cool you down.
II se rafraîchir *v refl* (+ *v être*) [*weather*] to get cooler; [*person*] to refresh oneself.
IDIOMS **~ la mémoire**○ **de qn** to refresh sb's memory.
rafraîchissement /ʀafʀɛʃismɑ̃/ *nm* refreshment.
ragaillardir /ʀagajaʀdiʀ/ [3] *vtr* to cheer [sb] up.
rage /ʀaʒ/ *nf* **1** rabies; **2** rage; **être fou de ~** to be in a mad rage; **faire ~** [*disease*] to be rife; [*epidemic, fire*] to rage.
■ **~ de dents** raging toothache.
rageant○, **~e** /ʀaʒɑ̃, ɑ̃t/ *adj* infuriating.
ragot○ /ʀago/ *nm* malicious gossip.
ragoût /ʀagu/ *nm* stew, ragout.
rai /ʀɛ/ *nm* **~ de lumière** ray of light.
raid /ʀɛd/ *nm* **1** (Mil) raid; **2** (Sport) trek.
raide /ʀɛd/ *adj* **1** (gen) stiff; [*hair*] straight; [*rope*] taut; **2** steep; **3**○ **je trouve ça un peu ~** that's a bit steep.
IDIOMS **être ~ comme un piquet** to be stiff as a ramrod; **tomber ~** to be flabbergasted.
raideur /ʀɛdœʀ/ *nf* **1** stiffness; **2** steepness.
raidir /ʀɛdiʀ/ [3] **I** *vtr* to tense [*arm, body*].
II se raidir *v refl* (+ *v être*) [*body*] to tense up; **se ~ contre la douleur** to brace oneself against pain.
raie /ʀɛ/ *nf* **1** (in hair) parting (GB), part (US); **2** scratch; **3** (Zool) skate.
rail /ʀɑj/ *nm* rail, track.
■ **~ de sécurité** crash barrier.
raillerie /ʀɑjʀi/ *nf* mockery.
rainette /ʀɛnɛt/ *nf* tree frog.
rainure /ʀenyʀ/ *nf* groove.
raisin /ʀɛzɛ̃/ *nm* grapes; **~s secs** raisins.
raison /ʀɛzɔ̃/ *nf* **1** reason; **~ d'agir** reason for action; **en ~ d'une panne** owing to a breakdown; **à plus forte ~** even more so, especially; **avec ~** justifiably; **comme de ~** as one might expect; **2 avoir ~** to be right; **donner ~ à qn** to agree with sb; **3** reason; **se rendre à la ~** to see reason; **ramener qn à la ~** to bring sb to his/her senses; **se faire une ~ de qch** to resign oneself to sth; **plus que de ~** more than is sensible; **avoir ~ de qn/qch** to get the better of sb/sth; **à ~ de** at the rate of.
raisonnable /ʀɛzɔnabl/ *adj* reasonable; moderate; sensible.
raisonné, **~e** /ʀɛzɔne/ **I** *pp* ▶ **raisonner**.
II *pp adj* **1** [*attitude*] cautious; [*decision*] carefully thought out; **2** [*enthusiasm*] measured.
raisonnement /ʀɛzɔnmɑ̃/ *nm* reasoning; **selon le même ~** by the same token; **il tient le ~ suivant** his argument is as follows; **je ne tiens pas le même ~** I look at it differently.
raisonner /ʀɛzɔne/ [1] **I** *vtr* to reason with.
II *vi* to think.
III se raisonner *v refl* (+ *v être*) [*person*] to be more sensible, to pull oneself together.
rajeunir /ʀaʒœniʀ/ [3] **I** *vtr* **1** to make [sb] look/feel younger; **2 ~ qn** to make sb out to be younger; **3** to bring or inject new blood into.
II *vi* to look/to feel younger.
rajeunissement /ʀaʒœnismɑ̃/ *nm* **1 nous avons enregistré un ~ de la population** we see that the population is getting younger; **2** modernization; **3** updating; **4** rejuvenation.
rajouter /ʀaʒute/ [1] *vtr* to add; **en ~**○ to exaggerate.
râle /ʀɑl/ *nm* **1** rale; **2** groan; **3** death rattle.
ralenti, **~e** /ʀalɑ̃ti/ **I** *pp* ▶ **ralentir**.
II *pp adj* [*gesture, rhythm, growth*] slower.
III *nm* slow motion.
ralentir /ʀalɑ̃tiʀ/ [3] *vtr*, *vi*, **se ralentir** *v refl* (+ *v être*) to slow down.
ralentissement /ʀalɑ̃tismɑ̃/ *nm* **1** slowing down; **2** tailback.
ralentisseur /ʀalɑ̃tisœʀ/ *nm* speed ramp.
râler /ʀɑle/ [1] *vi* **1**○ to moan○; **ça me fait ~** it annoys me; **2** to groan.
râleur○, **-euse** /ʀɑlœʀ, øz/ *nm,f* moaner○.
ralliement /ʀalimɑ̃/ *nm* rallying.
rallier /ʀalje/ [2] **I** *vtr* **~ qn à sa cause** to win sb over.
II se rallier *v refl* (+ *v être*) **se ~ à** to rally to [*republicans*]; to come round to [*opinion*].
rallonge /ʀalɔ̃ʒ/ *nf* **1** extension cord, extension lead (GB); **2** (of table) leaf.
rallonger /ʀalɔ̃ʒe/ [13] **I** *vtr* to extend; to lengthen.
II *vi* **les jours rallongent** the days are drawing out.
rallye /ʀali/ *nm* (car) rally.
ramage /ʀamaʒ/ **I** *nm* (of bird) song.
II ramages *nm pl* foliage pattern.
ramassé, **~e** /ʀamase/ **I** *pp* ▶ **ramasser**.

II *pp adj* **1** stocky, squat; **2 être ~ sur soi-même** to be hunched up.

ramasser /ʀamase/ [1] **I** *vtr* to collect; to pick up; to dig up [*potatoes*]; **se faire ~ dans une rafle**○ to get picked up in a (police) raid.

II se ramasser *v refl* (+ *v être*) **1** to huddle up; **2**○ to come a cropper○; **se faire ~ à un examen** to fail an exam.

ramassis /ʀamasi/ *nm inv* (derogatory) (of people) bunch; (of ideas, objects) jumble.

rambarde /ʀɑ̃baʀd/ *nf* guardrail.

rame /ʀam/ *nf* **1** oar; **2** (of paper) ream; **3 une ~ de métro** a metro train.

rameau, *pl* **~x** /ʀamo/ *nm* (Bot) branch.

ramener /ʀamne/ [16] **I** *vtr* **1 ~ l'inflation à 5%** to reduce inflation to 5 per cent; **2** to restore [*order*]; **~ qn à la réalité** to bring sb back to reality; **~ qn à la vie** to bring sb round; **~ toujours tout à soi** always to relate everything to oneself; **3** to take [sb/sth] back; **4** to bring back; to return.

II se ramener *v refl* (+ *v être*) **se ~ à** to come down to, to boil down to.

ramer /ʀame/ [1] *vi* to row.

rameur, **-euse** /ʀamœʀ, øz/ *nm,f* rower.

rameuter /ʀamøte/ [1] *vtr* to round up.

ramification /ʀamifikasjɔ̃/ *nf* **1** network; **2** ramification.

ramifier: **se ramifier** /ʀamifje/ [2] *v refl* (+ *v être*) [*stem, nerve*] to branch; [*branch*] to divide.

ramollir /ʀamɔliʀ/ [3] **I** *vtr* to soften.

II se ramollir *v refl* (+ *v être*) **1** to become soft; **2**○ [*person*] to get soft.

ramoner /ʀamɔne/ [1] *vtr* to sweep [*chimney*].

ramoneur /ʀamɔnœʀ/ *nm* chimney sweep.

rampe /ʀɑ̃p/ *nf* **1** banister; hand-rail; **2** (in theatre) **la ~** the footlights.

■ **~ d'accès** (for motorway) sliproad (GB), entrance ramp (US); (of building) ramp.

ramper /ʀɑ̃pe/ [1] *vi* **1** to crawl; **2** to creep.

ramure /ʀamyʀ/ *nf* **1** (of tree) branches; **2** antlers.

rance /ʀɑ̃s/ *adj* rancid.

rancœur /ʀɑ̃kœʀ/ *nf* resentment.

rançon /ʀɑ̃sɔ̃/ *nf* **1** ransom; **2 la ~ de la gloire** the price of fame.

rancune /ʀɑ̃kyn/ *nf* **1** resentment; **2** grudge; **sans ~!** no hard feelings.

rancunier, **-ière** /ʀɑ̃kynje, ɛʀ/ *adj* **être ~** to be a person who holds grudges.

randonnée /ʀɑ̃dɔne/ *nf* hiking.

rang /ʀɑ̃/ *nm* **1** row; (in necklace) strand; **se mettre en ~s** [*children*] to get into (a) line; **2** (Mil, figurative) rank; **sortir du ~** to rise or come up through the ranks; **serrer les ~s** to close ranks; **3** (in a hierarchy) rank; **être au 5e ~ mondial des exportateurs** to be the 5th largest exporter in the world; **acteur de second ~** second-rate actor; **des personnes de son ~** people of one's own station.

rangé, **~e**[1] /ʀɑ̃ʒe/ **I** *pp* ▶ **ranger**[1].

II *pp adj* [*life*] orderly; [*person*] well-behaved.

rangée[2] /ʀɑ̃ʒe/ *nf* row.

rangement /ʀɑ̃ʒmɑ̃/ *nm* **1 c'est un maniaque du ~** he's obsessively tidy; **2** storage space.

ranger[1] /ʀɑ̃ʒe/ [13] **I** *vtr* **1** to put away; **où ranges-tu tes verres?** where do you keep the glasses?; **2** to arrange, to put into order; **~ un animal dans les mammifères** to class an animal as a mammal; **3** to tidy.

II se ranger *v refl* (+ *v être*) **1** to line up; **2** [*vehicle, driver*] to pull over; **3 se ~ à l'avis de qn** to go along with sb; **4** to settle down.

ranger[2] /ʀɑ̃dʒɛʀ/ *nm* **1** ranger; **2** heavy-duty boot.

ranimer /ʀanime/ [1] *vtr* **1** to revive [*person*]; **2** to rekindle [*fire, hope*]; to stir up [*quarrel*].

rapace /ʀapas/ **I** *adj* [*person*] rapacious.

II *nm* bird of prey.

rapatrier /ʀapatʀije/ [2] *vtr* to repatriate.

râpe /ʀɑp/ *nf* (Culin) grater.

râper /ʀɑpe/ [1] *vtr* to grate [*cheese, carrot*]; **c'est râpé**○ (figurative) it's off○.

rapetisser /ʀap(ə)tise/ [1] *vi* to shrink.

râpeux, **-euse** /ʀɑpø, øz/ *adj* rough.

raphia /ʀafja/ *nm* raffia.

rapide /ʀapid/ **I** *adj* quick, rapid; fast.

II *nm* **1** rapids; **descendre un ~** to shoot the rapids; **2** (train) express.

rapidement /ʀapidmɑ̃/ *adv* quickly; fast.

rapidité /ʀapidite/ *nf* speed.

rapiécer /ʀapjese/ [14] *vtr* to patch.

rappel /ʀapɛl/ *nm* **1** reminder; **~ à l'ordre** call to order; **2 (lettre de) ~** reminder; **3** back pay; **4** (of ambassador) recall; (of actors) curtain call; **5** (Med) booster.

rappeler /ʀaple/ [19] **I** *vtr* **1 ~ qch à qn** to remind sb of sth; **rappelons-le** let's not forget; **~ qn à l'ordre** to call sb to order; **2** to call [sb] back; **3** (on phone) to call or ring [sb] back.

II se rappeler *v refl* (+ *v être*) to remember.

rappliquer○ /ʀaplike/ [1] *vi* **1** to turn up○; **2** to come back.

rapport /ʀapɔʀ/ **I** *nm* **1** connection, link; **être sans ~ avec, n'avoir aucun ~ avec** to have nothing to do with; **2 ~s** relations; **avoir** or **entretenir de bons ~s avec qn** to be on good terms with sb; **3 être en ~ avec qn** to be in touch with sb; **4 sous tous les ~s** in every respect; **5** report; **6** return, yield; **immeuble de ~** block of flats (GB) or apartment block (US) that is rented out; **7** ratio; **bon ~ qualité prix** good value for money.

II par rapport à *phr* **1** compared with; **par ~ au dollar** against the dollar; **2 le nombre de voitures par ~ au nombre d'habitants** the number of cars per head of the population; **3** with regard to, toward(s); **l'attitude de la population par ~ à l'immigration** people's attitudes to immigration.

■ **~ de force** power struggle; **~s sexuels** sexual relations.

rapporter /ʀapɔʀte/ [1] **I** *vtr* **1** to bring back; to take back; **2** to bring in [*income*]; **~ 10%** to yield or return 10%; **3** to report; **on m'a rapporté que** I was told that.

II *vi* **1** to bring in money; **2**○ to tell tales.

III se rapporter *v refl* (+ *v être*) **se ~ à** to relate to, to bear a relation to.

rapproché, ~e /ʀapʀɔʃe/ **I** *pp* ▶**rapprocher**.
II *pp adj* close together.

rapprochement /ʀapʀɔʃmɑ̃/ *nm* **1** rapprochement; **2** connection.

rapprocher /ʀapʀɔʃe/ [1] **I** *vtr* **1** to move [sth] closer; **2** to bring [sth] forward(s) [*date*]; **3** to bring [sb] (closer) together [*people*]; **4** to compare.
II se rapprocher *v refl* (+ *v être*) to get closer, to get nearer; **leurs peintures se rapprochent des fresques antiques** their paintings are similar to classical frescoes.

rapt /ʀapt/ *nm* kidnapping[GB], abduction.

raquette /ʀakɛt/ *nf* **1** (for tennis) racket; (for table-tennis) bat (GB), paddle (US); **2** snowshoe.

rare /ʀɑʀ/ *adj* **1** (not common) (gen) rare; [*job*] unusual; [*intelligence*] exceptional; **il est ~ qu'il vienne en train** it's unusual for him to come by train; **2** (not numerous) few, rare; [*visits*] infrequent; (not abundant) (gen) scarce; [*hair*] thin; [*vegetation*] sparse; **se faire ~** [*product*] to become scarce; **vous vous faites ~ ces temps-ci** you are not around much these days.

raréfier /ʀɑʀefje/ [2] **I** *vtr* **1** to rarefy [*air, gas*]; **2** to make [sth] rare.
II se raréfier *v refl* (+ *v être*) [*air*] to become thinner; [*gas*] to rarefy; [*food, money*] to become scarce; [*species*] to become rare.

rarement /ʀɑʀmɑ̃/ *adv* rarely, seldom.

rareté /ʀɑʀte/ *nf* shortage, scarcity; rarity.

rarissime /ʀɑʀisim/ *adj* extremely rare.

ras, ~e /ʀɑ, ʀɑz/ **I** *adj* [*hair*] close-cropped; [*fur*] short; **à poil ~** [*animal*] short-haired; [*carpet*] short-piled; **en ~e campagne** in (the) open country; **une cuillère à café ~e** a level teaspoonful; **à ~ bord** to the brim.
II *adv* short; **couper (à) ~** to cut [sth] very short [*hair, lawn*].
III au ras de *phr* **au ~ du sol** at ground level.
IDIOMS **faire table ~e de** to make a clean sweep of.

rasade /ʀɑzad/ *nf* **1** glassful; **2** swig○.

ras-de-cou /ʀɑdku/ *nm inv* **1** crew-neck sweater; **2** choker.

rase-mottes /ʀɑzmɔt/ *nm inv* **faire du ~, voler en ~** to fly low.

raser /ʀɑze/ [1] **I** *vtr* **1** to shave; to shave off; **~ de près** to give [sb] a close shave; **2** to demolish; to raze [sth] to the ground; **3** [*bullet*] to graze; [*plane, bird*] to skim.
II se raser *v refl* (+ *v être*) to shave.
IDIOMS **~ les murs** to hug the walls.

ras-le-bol○ /ʀɑlbɔl/ *nm inv* discontent.

rasoir /ʀɑzwaʀ/ **I**○ *adj inv* boring.
II *nm* **~ mécanique** razor; **~ électrique** electric shaver.

rassasier /ʀasazje/ [2] **I** *vtr* [*food*] to fill [sb] up.
II se rassasier *v refl* (+ *v être*) to eat one's fill.

rassemblement /ʀasɑ̃bləmɑ̃/ *nm* **1** rally; **2** gathering; **3** meeting.

rassembler /ʀasɑ̃ble/ [1] **I** *vtr* to gather [sb/sth] together [*people*]; to round up [*sheep, herd*]; to unite [*citizens, nation*]; to gather [*information, proof*]; **~ ses forces** to summon up one's strength.
II se rassembler *v refl* (+ *v être*) **1** to gather; **2** to assemble.

rasseoir: **se rasseoir** /ʀaswaʀ/ [41] *v refl* (+ *v être*) to sit down (again).

rasséréner /ʀaseʀene/ [14] *vtr* to calm [sb] down [*person*].

rassis, ~e /ʀasi, iz/ *adj* [*bread*] stale.

rassurant, ~e /ʀasyʀɑ̃, ɑ̃t/ *adj* reassuring.

rassurer /ʀasyʀe/ [1] **I** *vtr* to reassure.
II se rassurer *v refl* (+ *v être*) to reassure oneself; **rassure-toi** don't worry; **je suis rassuré** I'm relieved.

rat /ʀa/ *nm* **1** rat; **2** skinflint, cheapskate○.

ratatouille /ʀatatuj/ *nf* ratatouille.

rate /ʀat/ *nf* **1** (Zool) female rat; **2** (Anat) spleen.

râteau, *pl* **~x** /ʀɑto/ *nm* rake.

râtelier /ʀɑtəlje/ *nm* hayrack.
IDIOMS **manger à tous les ~s** to run with the hare and hunt with the hounds.

rater /ʀate/ [1] **I** *vtr* **1** to fail [*exam*]; to spoil [*sauce*]; **elle a raté son coup**○ she has failed; **2** to miss [*train, target*].
II *vi* [*plan*] to fail; **il dit toujours des bêtises, ça ne rate jamais**○ he can always be relied upon to say something stupid.

ratifier /ʀatifje/ [2] *vtr* **1** to ratify [*treaty, contract*]; **2** to confirm [*plan, proposal*].

ration /ʀasjɔ̃/ *nf* **1** ration; **2** share.

rationaliser /ʀasjɔnalize/ [1] *vtr* to rationalize.

rationnel, -elle /ʀasjɔnɛl/ *adj* rational.

rationnement /ʀasjɔnmɑ̃/ *nm* rationing.

rationner /ʀasjɔne/ [1] **I** *vtr* to ration [*petrol*]; to impose rationing on [*population*].
II se rationner *v refl* (+ *v être*) to cut down.

ratisser /ʀatise/ [1] *vtr* **1** to rake over; to rake up; **2** to comb [*area*].

raton /ʀatɔ̃/ *nm* young rat.
■ **~ laveur** racoon.

rattachement /ʀataʃmɑ̃/ *nm* **1** (of country) unification; **2** (of person) **demander son ~ à** to ask to be posted to.

rattacher /ʀataʃe/ [1] *vtr* **1** to attach [*region*]; to post [*employee*]; **2** to retie; to fasten [sth] again; **3 plus rien ne la rattache à Lyon** she no longer has any ties with Lyons.

rattrapage /ʀatʀapaʒ/ *nm* **1** (Econ) adjustment; **2** catching up; **cours de ~** remedial lesson.

rattraper /ʀatʀape/ [1] **I** *vtr* **1** to catch up with [*competitor*]; **2** to catch [*fugitive*]; **3** to make up for [*lost time, deficit*]; to make up [*points, distance*]; **~ son retard** to catch up; **4** to put right [*error*]; to smooth over [*blunder*]; to save [*situation*]; **5** to catch [*object*].
II se rattraper *v refl* (+ *v être*) **1** to redeem oneself; **2** to make up for it; **3** (Sch) to catch up;

4 to make up one's losses; **5 se ~ de justesse** to stop oneself just in time; **se ~ à une branche** to save oneself by catching hold of a branch.

rature /RatyR/ *nf* crossing-out; deletion.

rauque /Rok/ *adj* **1** husky; **2** hoarse.

ravage /Ravaʒ/ *nm* **les ~s de la guerre** the ravages of war; **faire des ~s** to wreak havoc; [*epidemic*] to take a terrible toll; **tu vas faire des ~s avec ta mini-jupe** (humorous) you'll knock them dead in that mini-skirt.

ravagé○, **~e** /Ravaʒe/ *adj* crazy.

ravager /Ravaʒe/ [13] *vtr* **1** [*fire, war*] to devastate, to ravage; **2** [*disease*] to ravage [*face*]; [*grief*] to tear [sb] apart.

ravalement /Ravalmɑ̃/ *nm* **1** cleaning; **2** refacing; **3** (figurative) facelift.

ravaler /Ravale/ [1] *vtr* **1** to clean; to reface; to renovate [*building*]; **2** to revamp [*image*]; **3** to suppress [*anger*]; **~ ses larmes** to hold back one's tears.

ravier /Ravje/ *nm* small dish (*for hors-d'œuvre*).

ravin /Ravɛ̃/ *nm* ravine.

ravir /RaviR/ [3] *vtr* **1** to delight; **ça te va à ~** it really suits you; **2** to steal.

raviser: **se raviser** /Ravize/ [1] *v refl* (+ *v être*) to change one's mind.

ravissant, **~e** /Ravisɑ̃, ɑ̃t/ *adj* beautiful.

ravisseur, **-euse** /RavisœR, øz/ *nm,f* kidnapper[GB], abductor.

ravitaillement /Ravitajmɑ̃/ *nm* supplies.

ravitailler /Ravitaje/ [1] **I** *vtr* **1** to provide [sb] with fresh supplies [*town*]; **2** to refuel.
II se ravitailler *v refl* (+ *v être*) to obtain fresh supplies.

raviver /Ravive/ [1] *vtr* to rekindle; to revive.

rayé, **~e** /Reje/ **I** *pp* ▶ **rayer**.
II *pp adj* **1** [*fabric*] striped; **2** [*record*] scratched.

rayer /Reje/ [21] *vtr* **1** to cross [sth] out; **'~ la mention inutile'** 'delete whichever does not apply'; **2 la ville a été rayée de la carte** the town was wiped off the map; **3** to scratch.

rayon /Rɛjɔ̃/ *nm* **1** radius; **dans un ~ de 10 km** within a 10 km radius; **~ d'action** range; (figurative) sphere of activity; **2** ray; beam; **les ~s X** X-rays; **être soigné aux ~s** to undergo radiation treatment; **3** (of wheel) spoke; **4** shelf; **~ de bibliothèque** (book)shelf; **5** (in big store) department; (in small shop) section; **tous nos modèles sont en ~** all our styles are on display; **6**○ **c'est mon ~** that's my department○; **il en connaît un ~ à ce sujet** he knows a lot about it.

rayonnage /Rɛjɔnaʒ/ *nm* shelves.

rayonnant, **~e** /Rɛjɔnɑ̃, ɑ̃t/ *adj* radiant.

rayonne /Rɛjɔn/ *nf* rayon.

rayonnement /Rɛjɔnmɑ̃/ *nm* **1** radiation; **2** radiance; **3** (of country) influence.

rayonner /Rɛjɔne/ [1] *vi* **1** [*light, heat*] to radiate; **2** [*star*] to shine; **3** [*person*] to glow; **4** [*city*] to exert its influence; **5** [*soldiers*] to patrol; [*tourists*] to tour around; **6** [*streets*] to radiate.

rayure /RɛjyR/ *nf* **1** stripe; **2** scratch.

raz-de-marée /RadmaRe/ *nm inv* tidal wave.

razzia /Razja/ *nf* raid.

ré /Re/ *nm inv* (note) D; (in sol-fa) re.

réacteur /ReaktœR/ *nm* **1 ~ (nucléaire)** (nuclear) reactor; **2** jet engine.

réaction /Reaksjɔ̃/ *nf* **1** reaction; response; **2 avion à ~** jet aircraft.

réactionnaire /ReaksjɔnɛR/ *adj, nmf* reactionary.

réagir /ReaʒiR/ [3] *vi* to react; to respond.

réalisable /Realizabl/ *adj* feasible; workable.

réalisateur, **-trice** /RealizatœR, tRis/ *nm,f* director.

réalisation /Realizasjɔ̃/ *nf* **1** (of dream) fulfilment[GB]; **2** (of study) carrying out; **3** achievement; **4** (of film) production.

réaliser /Realize/ [1] **I** *vtr* **1** to fulfil[GB] [*ambition*]; to achieve [*ideal, feat*]; **2** to make [*model*]; to carry out [*survey, study*]; **3** to direct [*film*]; **4** to realize.
II se réaliser *v refl* (+ *v être*) **1** [*dream*] to come true; [*predictions*] to be fulfilled; **2 se ~ (dans qch)** to find fulfilment[GB] (in sth).

réalisme /Realism/ *nm* realism.

réaliste /Realist/ *adj* (gen) realistic; (in art) realist.

réalité /Realite/ *nf* **la ~** reality; **en ~** in reality; **tenir compte des ~s** to take the facts into consideration.

réanimation /Reanimasjɔ̃/ *nf* **1 (service de) ~** intensive care (unit); **2** resuscitation.

réapparaître /ReapaRɛtR/ [73] *vi* [*sun*] to come out again; [*illness*] to recur.

réapprovisionner /ReapRɔvizjɔne/ [1] *vtr* to restock [*shop*].

réassortir /ReasɔRtiR/ [3] *vtr* to replenish.

rébarbatif, **-ive** /RebaRbatif, iv/ *adj* off-putting; forbidding.

rebâtir /R(ə)batiR/ [3] *vtr* to rebuild.

rebattre /R(ə)batR/ [61] *vtr* **~ les oreilles de qn avec une histoire** to go on (and on) about something.

rebattu, **~e** /R(ə)baty/ **I** *pp* ▶ **rebattre**.
II *pp adj* [*joke, story*] hackneyed.

rebelle /Rəbɛl/ **I** *adj* **1** rebel; **2** rebellious; **3** [*curl, lock of hair*] stray; [*stain*] stubborn.
II *nmf* rebel.

rebeller: **se rebeller** /Rəbɛle/ [1] *v refl* (+ *v être*) to rebel.

rébellion /Rebɛljɔ̃/ *nf* rebellion.

reboiser /R(ə)bwaze/ [1] *vtr* to reafforest.

rebond /R(ə)bɔ̃/ *nm* **1** bounce; **2** recovery.

rebondi, **~e** /R(ə)bɔ̃di/ *adj* **1** [*shape*] round, rounded; [*cheek*] chubby; [*stomach*] fat; [*buttocks*] rounded; **2** (figurative) [*wallet*] bulging.

rebondir /R(ə)bɔ̃diR/ [3] *vi* **1** to bounce; **2** to start up again; to take a new turn.

rebondissement /R(ə)bɔ̃dismɑ̃/ *nm* (of controversy) sudden revival; (in trial) new development.

rebord /R(ə)bɔR/ *nm* **1** ledge; **~ de fenêtre** windowsill; **2** rim; **3** edge.

rebours: **à rebours** /aʀ(ə)buʀ/ *phr* [*count, walk*] backward(s).

rebouteux○, **-euse** /ʀ(ə)butø, øz/ *nm,f* bonesetter.

rebrousse-poil: **à rebrousse-poil** /aʀ(ə) bʀuspwal/ *phr* the wrong way.

rebrousser /ʀ(ə)bʀuse/ [1] *vtr* **~ chemin** to turn back.

rébus /ʀebys/ *nm inv* rebus.

rebut /ʀ(ə)by/ *nm* rubbish; **mettre qch au ~** to throw sth on the scrapheap.

rebuter /ʀ(ə)byte/ [1] *vtr* **1** to disgust; to repel; **2** to put [sb] off.

récalcitrant, **~e** /ʀekalsitʀɑ̃, ɑ̃t/ *adj* recalcitrant.

recaler○ /ʀ(ə)kale/ [1] *vtr* to fail [*candidate*].

récapituler /ʀekapityle/ [1] *vtr* to sum up.

receler /ʀəs(ə)le, ʀsəle/ [17] *vtr* **1 ~ des marchandises** to possess stolen goods; **2** to contain.

receleur, **-euse** /ʀ(ə)s(ə)lœʀ, ʀsəlœʀ, øz/ *nm,f* possessor of stolen goods.

récemment /ʀesamɑ̃/ *adv* recently.

recensement /ʀ(ə)sɑ̃smɑ̃/ *nm* **1** census; **2** inventory.

recenser /ʀ(ə)sɑ̃se/ [1] *vtr* **1** to take a census of [*population*]; **2** to list [*objects*].

récent, **~e** /ʀesɑ̃, ɑ̃t/ *adj* recent; [*house*] new.

récépissé /ʀesepise/ *nm* receipt.

réceptacle /ʀesɛptakl/ *nm* container; **~ à verre** bottle bank.

récepteur /ʀesɛptœʀ/ *nm* receiver.

réceptif, **-ive** /ʀesɛptif, iv/ *adj* receptive.

réception /ʀesɛpsjɔ̃/ *nf* **1** reception; **2** welcome; **3 s'occuper de la ~ des marchandises** to take delivery of the goods.

réceptionner /ʀesɛpsjɔne/ [1] *vtr* **1** to take delivery of [*goods*]; **2** to catch [*ball*].

réceptionniste /ʀesɛpsjɔnist/ *nmf* receptionist.

récession /ʀesesjɔ̃/ *nf* recession.

recette /ʀ(ə)sɛt/ *nf* **1 ~ (de cuisine)** recipe; **2** formula, recipe; **3** takings; **faire ~** to bring in money; (figurative) to be a success; **les ~s et (les) dépenses** receipts and expenses.

receveur, **-euse** /ʀəs(ə)vœʀ, øz/ *nm,f* (on bus) conductor.

■ **~ des postes** postmaster.

recevoir /ʀəsvwaʀ, ʀ(ə)səvwaʀ/ [5] *vtr* **1** to receive, to get; **il a reçu une tuile sur la tête** he got hit on the head by a tile; **je n'ai d'ordre à ~ de personne** I don't take orders from anyone; **2** to welcome [*guests*]; **être bien reçu** to be well received; to get a good reception; **ils reçoivent beaucoup** they do a lot of entertaining; **Laval reçoit Caen** (Sport) Laval is playing host to Caen; **3** to see [*patients*]; **4** to receive [*radio signal*]; **5** (Sch) to pass [*candidate*]; **être reçu à un examen** to pass an exam.

rechange: **de rechange** /dəʀ(ə)ʃɑ̃ʒ/ *phr* [*part*] spare; [*solution*] alternative.

réchapper /ʀeʃape/ [1] *v+prep* **~ de** to come through [*illness, accident*].

recharge /ʀ(ə)ʃaʀʒ/ *nf* refill; reload.

recharger /ʀ(ə)ʃaʀʒe/ [13] *vtr* to reload; to refill; to recharge [*battery*].

réchaud /ʀeʃo/ *nm* stove; **~ électrique** electric ring (GB), hotplate.

réchauffé, **~e** /ʀeʃofe/ **I** *pp* ▶ **réchauffer**.

II *pp adj* [*joke, story*] hackneyed.

III *nm* **c'est du ~** there's nothing new about it.

réchauffer /ʀeʃofe/ [1] **I** *vtr* **1** (Culin) to reheat, to heat [sth] up; **2** to warm up [*person, hands, room*].

II se réchauffer *v refl* (+ *v être*) to warm up.

rêche /ʀɛʃ/ *adj* [*hands, fabric*] rough.

recherche /ʀ(ə)ʃɛʀʃ/ *nf* **1** research; **2** search; **être à la ~ de** to be looking for; **3 ~ de** pursuit of [*happiness*]; **4 sans ~** without affectation.

■ **~ d'emploi** job-hunting.

recherché, **~e** /ʀ(ə)ʃɛʀʃe/ **I** *pp* ▶ **rechercher**.

II *pp adj* **1** sought-after; **2** in demand; **3** [*dress*] meticulous; [*style*] original; **4** [*aim*] intended.

rechercher /ʀ(ə)ʃɛʀʃe/ [1] *vtr* **1** to look for; **il est recherché par la police** he's wanted by the police; **'recherchons vendeuse qualifiée'** 'qualified sales assistant (GB) or clerk (US) required'; **2** to seek [*security*]; to fish for [*compliments*].

rechigner /ʀ(ə)ʃiɲe/ [1] **I** *v+prep* **~ à faire** to balk at doing.

II *vi* to grumble.

rechute /ʀəʃyt/ *nf* relapse.

récidive /ʀesidiv/ *nf* **1** (Law) second offence[GB]; **2** (figurative) repetition; **3** (Med) recurrence.

récidiver /ʀesidive/ [1] *vi* (Law) to reoffend.

récif /ʀesif/ *nm* reef.

récipient /ʀesipjɑ̃/ *nm* container.

réciproque /ʀesipʀɔk/ **I** *adj* reciprocal.

II *nf* reverse; **la ~ est vraie** the reverse is true.

récit /ʀesi/ *nm* **1** story; **2** narrative.

récital /ʀesital/ *nm* recital.

récitation /ʀesitasjɔ̃/ *nf* **apprendre une ~** to learn a text (off) by heart.

réciter /ʀesite/ [1] *vtr* to recite.

réclamation /ʀeklamasjɔ̃/ *nf* **1** complaint; **2** claim; **sur ~** on request.

réclame /ʀeklam/ *nf* **1** publicity; **2** advertisement; **3 'en ~'** 'on offer' (GB), 'on sale'.

réclamer /ʀeklame/ [1] **I** *vtr* to ask for [*person, thing, money*]; to call for [*reform, inquiry*]; to claim [*compensation*]; **travail qui réclame de l'attention** work that requires attention.

II se réclamer *v refl* (+ *v être*) **se ~ de** [*person, group*] to claim to be representative of.

reclasser /ʀəklase/ [1] *vtr* **1** to reclassify [*documents*]; **2** to redeploy.

reclus, **~e** /ʀəkly, yz/ *adj* reclusive; **vivre ~** to live as a recluse.

réclusion /ʀeklyzjɔ̃/ *nf* **1** (Law) imprisonment; **2** reclusion.

recoin /ʀəkwɛ̃/ *nm* corner; (figurative) recess.

récolte /ʀekɔlt/ *nf* harvest; crop.

récolter /ʀekɔlte/ [1] *vtr* **1** to harvest [*corn*]; to dig up [*potatoes*]; **2** [*bee*] to collect [*pollen*]; [*person*] to win [*points*]; to collect [*information*].

recommandation /ʀəkɔmɑ̃dasjɔ̃/ *nf* recommendation.

recommandé, **~e** /ʀəkɔmɑ̃de/ **I** *pp* ▶ **recommander**.
II *pp adj* [*letter*] registered.

recommander /ʀəkɔmɑ̃de/ [1] **I** *vtr* **1** to advise; **2** to recommend.
II se recommander *v refl* (+ *v être*) **se ~ de qn** to give sb's name as a reference.

recommencement /ʀəkɔmɑ̃smɑ̃/ *nm* **l'histoire est un éternel ~** history is constantly repeating itself.

recommencer /ʀəkɔmɑ̃se/ [12] *vtr* **1** to start [sth] again; **2** to do [sth] again.

récompense /ʀekɔ̃pɑ̃s/ *nf* **1** reward; **2** award.

récompenser /ʀekɔ̃pɑ̃se/ [1] *vtr* to reward.

réconciliation /ʀekɔ̃siljasjɔ̃/ *nf* reconciliation.

réconcilier /ʀekɔ̃silje/ [2] **I** *vtr* **~ Pierre avec Paul** to bring Pierre and Paul back together; **~ morale et politique** to reconcile morality with politics.
II se réconcilier *v refl* (+ *v être*) [*friends*] to make up; [*nations*] to be reconciled.

reconduction /ʀ(ə)kɔ̃dyksjɔ̃/ *nf* renewal.

reconduire /ʀ(ə)kɔ̃dɥiʀ/ [69] *vtr* **1** to see [sb] out; **~ qn chez lui** to take sb home; **2** to extend [*strike, ceasefire*]; to renew [*mandate*].

réconfort /ʀekɔ̃fɔʀ/ *nm* comfort.

réconfortant, **~e** /ʀekɔ̃fɔʀtɑ̃, ɑ̃t/ *adj* **1** comforting; **2** cheering; **3** fortifying.

réconforter /ʀekɔ̃fɔʀte/ [1] *vtr* **1** to comfort; to console; **2 ~ qn** to cheer sb up; **3** to fortify.

reconnaissance /ʀ(ə)kɔnɛsɑ̃s/ *nf* **1** gratitude; **en ~ de** in appreciation of; **2** recognition; **3** (of wrongs) admission, admitting; (of qualities) recognition, recognizing; **4** (Mil) reconnaissance.

reconnaissant, **~e** /ʀ(ə)kɔnɛsɑ̃, ɑ̃t/ *adj* grateful.

reconnaître /ʀ(ə)kɔnɛtʀ/ [73] **I** *vtr* **1** to recognize [*person*]; **2** to identify; **je reconnais bien là leur générosité** it's just like them to be so generous; **3** to admit [*facts, errors*]; **4** to recognize [*trade union, regime*]; **~ un enfant** to recognize a child legally; **5** to acknowledge.
II se reconnaître *v refl* (+ *v être*) **se ~ à qch** to be recognizable by sth.

reconnu, **~e** /ʀ(ə)kɔny/ **I** *pp* ▶ **reconnaître**.
II *pp adj* [*fact*] recognized.

reconquérir /ʀ(ə)kɔ̃keʀiʀ/ [35] *vtr* to reconquer, to recover [*territory*]; (figurative) to regain [*esteem*]; to win back [*person, right*].

reconstituer /ʀ(ə)kɔ̃stitɥe/ [1] *vtr* to re-form [*association*]; to reconstruct [*crime*]; to recreate [*era, decor*]; to piece [sth] together again [*broken object*]; to build up again [*reserves*].

reconstruire /ʀ(ə)kɔ̃stʀɥiʀ/ [69] *vtr* **1** to reconstruct; **2** to rebuild.

reconversion /ʀ(ə)kɔ̃vɛʀsjɔ̃/ *nf* (of worker) redeployment; (of region) redevelopment; (of economy) restructuring; (of factory) conversion.

reconvertir /ʀ(ə)kɔ̃vɛʀtiʀ/ [3] **I** *vtr* to redeploy [*staff*]; to convert [*factory*]; to adapt [*equipment*].
II se reconvertir *v refl* (+ *v être*) [*staff*] to switch to a new type of employment; [*company*] to switch to a new type of production.

recopier /ʀ(ə)kɔpje/ [2] *vtr* **1** to copy out; **2** to write up [*notes*].

record /ʀ(ə)kɔʀ/ **I** *adj inv* record.
II *nm* (Sport, figurative) record.

recoudre /ʀ(ə)kudʀ/ [76] *vtr* **1** to sew [sth] back on [*button*]; **2** (Med) to stitch up [*wound*].

recoupement /ʀ(ə)kupmɑ̃/ *nm* cross-check.

recouper /ʀ(ə)kupe/ [1] **I** *vtr* to cut [sth] again [*hair, hedge*]; to recut [*garment*].
II se recouper *v refl* (+ *v être*) **1** [*versions*] to tally; [*results*] to add up; **2** [*lines*] to intersect.

recourbé, **~e** /ʀ(ə)kuʀbe/ *adj* (gen) curved; [*nose, beak*] hooked.

recourir /ʀ(ə)kuʀiʀ/ [26] *v+prep* **~ à** to use [*remedy*]; to resort to [*strategy*].

recours /ʀ(ə)kuʀ/ *nm inv* **1** recourse; resort; **sans autre ~ que** with no other way out but; **avoir ~ à** to have recourse to [*remedy*]; to resort to [*strategy*]; to go to [*expert*]; **2** (Law) appeal.

recouvrer /ʀ(ə)kuvʀe/ [1] *vtr* to recover; to collect [*tax*].

recouvrir /ʀ(ə)kuvʀiʀ/ [32] *vtr* **1** to cover; **2** to re-cover; **3** to hide, to conceal.

recracher /ʀ(ə)kʀaʃe/ [1] *vtr* to spit out.

récréation /ʀekʀeasjɔ̃/ *nf* **1** playtime (GB), break (GB), recess (US); **2** recreation.

recréer /ʀ(ə)kʀee/ [11] *vtr* to recreate.

récrier: **se récrier** /ʀekʀije/ [2] *v refl* (+ *v être*) to exclaim.

récrimination /ʀekʀiminasjɔ̃/ *nf* recrimination.

récriminer /ʀekʀimine/ [1] *vi* to rail.

recroqueviller: **se recroqueviller** /ʀ(ə)kʀɔkvije/ [1] *v refl* (+ *v être*) **1** [*person*] to huddle up; **2** [*leaf, petal*] to shrivel up.

recrudescence /ʀ(ə)kʀydesɑ̃s/ *nf* (of violence, interest) fresh upsurge; (of bombing, demands) new wave; (of fire) renewed outbreak.

recrue /ʀəkʀy/ *nf* recruit.

recrutement /ʀ(ə)kʀytmɑ̃/ *nm* recruitment.

recruter /ʀ(ə)kʀyte/ [1] *vtr* to recruit.

rectangle /ʀɛktɑ̃gl/ *nm* rectangle.

rectangulaire /ʀɛktɑ̃gylɛʀ/ *adj* rectangular.

rectificatif, **-ive** /ʀɛktifikatif, iv/ *nm* **1** (in newspaper) correction; **2** (to law) amendment.

rectification /ʀɛktifikasjɔ̃/ *nf* correction; rectification; adjustment.

rectifier /ʀɛktifje/ [2] *vtr* to correct, to rectify; to adjust.

rectiligne /ʀɛktiliɲ/ *adj* straight.

recto /ʀɛkto/ *nm* front; **~ verso** on both sides.

rectorat /ʀɛktɔʀa/ *nm* ≈ local education authority (GB), ≈ board of education (US).

rectum /ʀɛktɔm/ *nm* rectum.

reçu, **~e** /ʀ(ə)sy/ **I** *pp* ▶ **recevoir**.

II *pp adj* [*candidate*] successful.
III *nm* receipt.
recueil /ʀ(ə)kœj/ *nm* collection; anthology.
recueillement /ʀəkœjmɑ̃/ *nm* **1** contemplation; **2** reverence.
recueilli, ~e /ʀəkœji/ I *pp* ▶ **recueillir**.
II *pp adj* [*air*] rapt; [*person*] rapt in prayer; [*crowd, silence*] reverential.
recueillir /ʀəkœjiʀ/ [27] I *vtr* **1** to collect [*donations, anecdotes*]; to gather [*evidence, testimonies*]; **2** to get [*votes, news*]; to gain [*consensus*]; to win [*praise*]; **3** to collect [*water, resin*]; to gather [*honey*]; **4** to take in [*orphan*]; **5** to record [*impressions, opinions*].
II **se recueillir** *v refl* (+ *v être*) to engage in private prayer.
recul /ʀ(ə)kyl/ *nm* **1** detachment; **avec le ~** with hindsight, in retrospect; **prendre du ~** to stand back; **2** (in production) drop, fall; (of doctrine) decline; **3** (of army) pulling back; (of tide, floodwaters) recession; **avoir un mouvement de ~** to recoil; **feu de ~** reversing light.
reculé, ~e /ʀəkyle/ *adj* remote.
reculer /ʀ(ə)kyle/ [1] I *vtr* **1** to move back [*object*]; **2** (in car) to reverse (GB), to back up; **3** to put off [*event, decision*]; to put back [*date*].
II *vi* **1** [*person*] to move back; to stand back; [*driver, car*] to reverse; **2** [*army*] to pull or draw back; **3** [*forest*] to be gradually disappearing; [*river*] to go down; [*sea*] to recede; **4** [*currency, exports*] to fall; [*doctrine*] to decline; **faire ~ le chômage** to reduce unemployment; **5** to back down; **ne ~ devant rien** to stop at nothing.
III **se reculer** *v refl* (+ *v être*) (gen) to move back; to stand back.
reculons: **à reculons** /aʀ(ə)kylɔ̃/ *phr* **aller à ~** to go backward(s).
récupération /ʀekypeʀasjɔ̃/ *nf* **1** salvage; recycling; **2** recovery; **3** appropriation.
récupérer /ʀekypeʀe/ [14] I *vtr* **1** to get back [*money, strength*]; **2** to retrieve; **3** to salvage [*scrap iron*]; to reclaim [*rags*]; **4** to save [*boxes*]; **5** to make up [*days*]; **6** to appropriate [*ideas*].
II *vi* to recover.
récurer /ʀekyʀe/ [1] *vtr* to scour; to scrub.
récurrent, ~e /ʀekyʀɑ̃, ɑ̃t/ *adj* recurrent.
récuser /ʀekyze/ [1] I *vtr* to challenge [*jury*].
II **se récuser** *v refl* (+ *v être*) [*judge*] to decline to act in a case.
recyclage /ʀ(ə)siklaʒ/ *nm* recycling.
recycler /ʀ(ə)sikle/ [1] I *vtr* **1** to recycle [*material*]; **2 ~ le personnel** to retrain the staff.
II **se recycler** *v refl* (+ *v être*) **1** to retrain; **2** to change jobs.
rédacteur, -trice /ʀedaktœʀ, tʀis/ *nm,f* **1** author, writer; **2** editor.
rédaction /ʀedaksjɔ̃/ *nf* **1** writing; **2** editing; **3** editorial offices; **4** editorial staff; **5** (Sch) essay (GB), theme (US).
reddition /ʀɛdisjɔ̃/ *nf* surrender.
rédemption /ʀedɑ̃psjɔ̃/ *nf* redemption.
redescendre /ʀədɛsɑ̃dʀ/ [6] I *vtr* (gen) to take [sb/sth] back down; [*person*] to go/come back down [*stairs*].
II *vi* (+ *v être*) to go (back) down; to go down again.
redevable /ʀədvabl, ʀ(ə)dəvabl/ *adj* **être ~ de qch à qn** to owe sth to sb; **être ~ de l'impôt** to be liable for tax.
redevance /ʀədvɑ̃s, ʀ(ə)dəvɑ̃s/ *nf* **1** (gen) charge; (for television) licence (GB) or license (US) fee; (for telephone) rental charge; **2** royalty.
rédhibitoire /ʀedibitwaʀ/ *adj* [*cost*] prohibitive; [*obstacle*] insurmountable.
rédiger /ʀediʒe/ [13] *vtr* to write [*article*]; to write up [*notes*]; to draft [*contract*].
redingote /ʀ(ə)dɛ̃gɔt/ *nf* (for man) frock coat; (for woman) fitted coat.
redire /ʀədiʀ/ [65] *vtr* to repeat; **trouver quelque chose à ~ à qch** to find fault with sth.
redondance /ʀ(ə)dɔ̃dɑ̃s/ *nf* redundancy.
redondant, ~e /ʀ(ə)dɔ̃dɑ̃, ɑ̃t/ *adj* **1** superfluous; **2** redundant.
redonner /ʀ(ə)dɔne/ [1] *vtr* **~ qch à qn** to give sb sth again.
redorer /ʀ(ə)dɔʀe/ [1] *vtr* to regild; **~ son blason** [*person*] to restore one's image.
redoublant, ~e /ʀ(ə)dublɑ̃, ɑ̃t/ *nm,f* student repeating a year.
redoublement /ʀ(ə)dubləmɑ̃/ *nm* intensification.
redoubler /ʀ(ə)duble/ [1] I *vtr* (Sch) **~ une classe** to repeat a year.
II **redoubler de** *v+prep* **~ de prudence** to be twice as careful; **la tempête a redoublé de violence** the storm has become even fiercer.
III *vi* **1** to repeat a year; **2** to intensify.
redoutable /ʀ(ə)dutabl/ *adj* [*weapon, exam*] formidable; [*disease*] dreadful.
redouter /ʀ(ə)dute/ [1] *vtr* to fear.
redressement /ʀədʀɛsmɑ̃/ *nm* **maison de ~** reformatory.
redresser /ʀ(ə)dʀese/ [1] I *vtr* **1** to straighten (up); to put [sth] up again; **~ la tête** to lift one's head up; **2** to put [sth] back on its feet [*economy*]; to turn [sth] around [*company*]; to aid the recovery of [*currency*]; **3** to straighten up [*glider, steering wheel*]; **~ la barre** to right the helm; (figurative) to put things back on an even keel; **4** to rectify [*error*].
II **se redresser** *v refl* (+ *v être*) **1** to stand up; to sit up; to stand up straight; to sit up straight; **2** [*economy, plant*] to recover; [*country*] to get back on its feet.
redresseur /ʀədʀɛsœʀ/ *nm* **~ de torts** righter of wrongs.
réduction /ʀedyksjɔ̃/ *nf* **1** discount, reduction; **~ étudiants** concession for students; **2** cutting, reducing; **3** reduction, cut; **~s d'effectifs** staff cuts; **4** (of statue) small replica.
réduire /ʀedɥiʀ/ [68] I *vtr* **1** to reduce; to cut [*tax*]; to cut down on [*staff, spending*]; **2** to reduce [*photograph*]; to scale down [*drawing*]; to cut [*text*]; **3 ~ qch en poudre** to crush sth to powder; **être réduit en cendres** [*city*] to be

reduced to ashes; [*dreams*] to turn to ashes; **4 ~ à** to reduce to; **voilà à quoi j'en suis réduit!** this is what I've been reduced to!; **5** to reduce [*sauce*].
II *vi* [*sauce*] to reduce; [*spinach*] to shrink.
III se réduire *v refl* (+ *v être*) **1** [*costs*] to be reduced; [*imports*] to be cut; **2 cela se réduit à bien peu de chose** it doesn't amount to very much.

réduit, **~e** /ʀedɥi, it/ **I** *pp* ▶ **réduire**.
II *pp adj* **1** [*rate, speed*] reduced, lower; [*time*] shorter; [*activity*] reduced; [*group*] smaller; **visibilité ~e** restricted visibility; **2** [*means, choice*] limited; [*group*] small; **3** [*size*] small.
III *nm* cubbyhole.

rééditer /ʀeedite/ [1] *vtr* to reprint [*book*].

rééducation /ʀeedykasjɔ̃/ *nf* **1** physiotherapy; **~ de la parole** speech therapy; **2** rehabilitation.

rééduquer /ʀeedyke/ [1] *vtr* to restore normal functioning to [*limb*]; to rehabilitate.

réel, **réelle** /ʀeɛl/ **I** *adj* (gen) real; [*fact*] true.
II *nm* **le ~** the real.

réellement /ʀeɛlmɑ̃/ *adv* really.

rééquilibrer /ʀeekilibʀe/ [1] *vtr* **1** (Aut) to balance [*wheels*]; **2** to balance [*budget*].

réévaluer /ʀeevalɥe/ [1] *vtr* **1** to revalue [*currency*]; to revise [*tax*]; **2** to reappraise.

réexpédier /ʀeɛkspedje/ [2] *vtr* **1** to forward, to redirect; **2** to send [sth] back.

réf (*written abbr* = **référence**) ref.

refaire /ʀəfɛʀ/ [10] **I** *vtr* **1** to do [sth] again [*exercise*]; to make [sth] again [*journey, mistake*]; **~ le même chemin** to go back the same way; **~ un numéro de téléphone** to redial a number; **2 je vais ~ de la soupe** I'll make some more soup; **3 vouloir ~ le monde** to want to change the world; **se faire ~ le nez** to have one's nose re-modelled[GB]; **~ sa vie** to start all over again; **4** to redo [*roof*]; to redecorate [*room*]; to resurface [*road*].
II se refaire *v refl* (+ *v être*) **1 se ~ une santé** to recuperate; **se ~ une beauté** to redo one's make-up; **2 se ~ à** to get used to [sth] again; **3 on ne se refait pas** a person can't change.

réfection /ʀefɛksjɔ̃/ *nf* repairing.

réfectoire /ʀefɛktwaʀ/ *nm* refectory; (Mil) mess.

référence /ʀefeʀɑ̃s/ **I** *nf* **1** reference; **en** or **par ~ à** in reference to; **faire ~ à** to refer to; **lui? ce n'est pas une ~!** who, him? well, he's not much of an example!; **2** reference number.
II références *nf pl* references.

référendum /ʀefeʀɛ̃dɔm/ *nm* referendum.

référer /ʀefeʀe/ [14] **I référer à** *v+prep* **en ~ à** to consult.
II se référer *v refl* (+ *v être*) **1 se ~ à** to refer to; **2 se ~ à** to consult.

refermer /ʀ(ə)fɛʀme/ [1] **I** *vtr* **1** to close; **2** to close [sth] again.
II se refermer *v refl* (+ *v être*) [*door*] to close; [*wound*] to close up.

réfléchi, **~e** /ʀefleʃi/ *adj* **1** [*person*] reflective, thoughtful; **2** [*decision*] considered; [*action*] well-considered; **c'est tout ~** my mind is made up; **3** [*image*] reflected; **4** [*verb*] reflexive.

réfléchir /ʀefleʃiʀ/ [3] **I** *vtr* to reflect [*heat*].
II réfléchir à *v+prep* to think about.
III *vi* to think; **mais réfléchis donc un peu!** use your brain!
IV se réfléchir *v refl* (+ *v être*) to be reflected.

réflecteur /ʀeflɛktœʀ/ *nm* reflector.

reflet /ʀ(ə)flɛ/ *nm* **1** reflection; **2** glint; shimmer; sheen; **cheveux châtains aux ~s roux** brown hair with auburn highlights.

refléter /ʀ(ə)flete/ [14] **I** *vtr* to reflect; **son visage reflétait son émotion** his/her emotion showed in his/her face.
II se refléter *v refl* (+ *v être*) to be reflected.

réflexe /ʀeflɛks/ **I** *adj* reflex.
II *nm* **1** reflex; **2** reaction; **manquer de ~** to be slow to react; **par ~** automatically.
■ **~ conditionné** conditioned reflex.

réflexion /ʀeflɛksjɔ̃/ *nf* **1** thought, reflection; **2** thinking, reflection; **~ faite** or **à la ~, je n'irai pas** on second thoughts, I won't go; **donner matière à ~** to be food for thought; **3** remark, comment; **s'attirer des ~s** to attract criticism; **4** study; **document de ~** discussion paper; **5** (of image) reflection.

refluer /ʀ(ə)flɥe/ [1] *vi* [*liquid*] to flow back.

reflux /ʀ(ə)fly/ *nm inv* ebb tide.

refonte /ʀ(ə)fɔ̃t/ *nf* **1** overhaul; **2** (of contract) rewriting.

reforestation /ʀ(ə)fɔʀɛstasjɔ̃/ *nf* reafforestation.

réformateur, **-trice** /ʀefɔʀmatœʀ, tʀis/ *nm,f* reformer.

réforme /ʀefɔʀm/ *nf* **1** reform; **2** (Mil) discharge; **3 la Réforme** the Reformation.

réformé, **~e** /ʀefɔʀme/ *nm,f* Calvinist.

reformer /ʀ(ə)fɔʀme/ [1] *vtr* to re-form.

réformer /ʀefɔʀme/ [1] *vtr* **1** to reform; **2** (Mil) to declare [sb] unfit for service [*conscript*]; to discharge [*soldier*].

refoulé, **~e** /ʀ(ə)fule/ *nm,f* repressed or inhibited person.

refoulement /ʀ(ə)fulmɑ̃/ *nm* **1** (of impulse) repression; **2** pushing back; turning back; driving back; forcing back.

refouler /ʀ(ə)fule/ [1] *vtr* **1** to suppress [*memory*]; to repress [*tendency*]; to hold back [*tears*]; **2** to force [sth] back [*liquid*]; to push back [*enemy*]; to turn back [*immigrant*].

réfractaire /ʀefʀaktɛʀ/ *adj* **1 ~ à** resistant to [*influence*]; impervious to [*music*]; **2** refractory.

réfracter /ʀefʀakte/ [1] *vtr* to refract.

réfraction /ʀefʀaksjɔ̃/ *nf* refraction.

refrain /ʀ(ə)fʀɛ̃/ *nm* **1** chorus; **2** (old) refrain.

refréner /ʀ(ə)fʀene/, **réfréner** /ʀefʀene/ [14] *vtr* to curb.

réfrigérant, **~e** /ʀefʀiʒeʀɑ̃, ɑ̃t/ *adj* cooling.

réfrigérateur /ʀefʀiʒeʀatœʀ/ *nm* refrigerator.

réfrigérer /ʀefʀiʒeʀe/ [14] *vtr* to refrigerate [*food*]; to cool [*place*].

refroidir /ʀəfʀwadiʀ/ [3] **I** *vtr* **1** to cool down; to cool; **2 ~ qn** to dampen sb's spirits.

II *vi* **1** to cool down; **2** to get cold.

III se refroidir *v refl* (+ *v être*) [*weather*] to get colder; [*joint*] to stiffen up; [*person*] to get cold.

refroidissement /ʀəfʀwadismɑ̃/ *nm* **1** drop in temperature; **2** cooling; **3** (Med) chill.

refuge /ʀ(ə)fyʒ/ *nm* **1** refuge; **2** (mountain) refuge; **3** (for animals) sanctuary; **4** traffic island.

réfugié, **~e** /ʀefyʒje/ *nm,f* refugee.

réfugier: **se réfugier** /ʀefyʒje/ [2] *v refl* (+ *v être*) to take refuge.

refus /ʀ(ə)fy/ *nm inv* refusal; **ce n'est pas de ~**° I wouldn't say no°.

■ **~ de priorité** failure to give way.

refuser /ʀ(ə)fyze/ [1] **I** *vtr* **1** (gen) to refuse; to turn down [*offer*]; **~ de faire** to refuse to do; **2** to reject [*budget, manuscript, racism*]; to refuse to accept [*fact*]; to turn away [*spectator*].

II se refuser *v refl* (+ *v être*) **1 ça ne se refuse pas** it's too good to pass up°; I wouldn't say no°; **2** to deny oneself [*pleasure*]; **on ne se refuse rien**°! you're certainly not stinting yourself!; **3 se ~ à** to refuse to accept [*evidence*]; to refuse to adopt [*solution*].

réfuter /ʀefyte/ [1] *vtr* to refute.

regagner /ʀ(ə)gaɲe/ [1] *vtr* **1** to get back to [*place*]; **2** to regain [*esteem*].

regain /ʀ(ə)gɛ̃/ *nm* **~ de** rise in [*inflation*]; revival of [*interest*]; resurgence of [*violence*].

régal /ʀegal/ *nm* **1** culinary delight; **c'est un ~**! it's delicious!; **2** (figurative) delight; **un ~ pour les yeux** a feast for the eyes.

régaler: **se régaler** /ʀegale/ [1] *v refl* (+ *v être*) **1 je me régale** it's delicious; **les enfants se sont régalés avec ton dessert** the children really enjoyed your dessert; **2** (figurative) **se ~ avec** to enjoy [sth] thoroughly [*film*]; **se ~ de** to love [*anecdote*].

regard /ʀ(ə)gaʀ/ **I** *nm* **1** look; **porter son ~ sur qch** to look at sth; **détourner le ~** to look away; **j'ai croisé son ~** our eyes met; **à l'abri des ~s indiscrets** far from prying eyes; **2** expression; **son ~ triste** his/her sad expression; **sous le ~ amusé de qn** under the amused eye of sb; **jeter un ~ noir à qn** to give sb a black look; **3 le ~ des autres** other people's opinion; **porter un ~ nouveau sur qch** to take a fresh look at sth.

II au regard de *phr* (formal) **au ~ de la loi** in the eyes of the law.

III en regard *phr* **avec une carte en ~** with a map on the opposite page.

regardant, **~e** /ʀəgaʀdɑ̃, ɑ̃t/ *adj* **ne pas être très ~** not to be very particular or fussy.

regarder /ʀ(ə)gaʀde/ [1] **I** *vtr* **1** to look at [*person, scene, landscape*]; **~ qch méchamment/fixement/longuement** to glare/stare/gaze at sth; **~ qn en face** to look sb in the face; **~ la réalité** or **les choses en face** to face facts; **~ qn de haut** to look down one's nose at sb; **2** to watch [*film, TV*]; **regarde bien comment je fais** watch what I do carefully; **3** to look at [*watch, map*]; to have a look at [*tyres, oil*]; **~ qch dans** to look sth up in [*dictionary*]; **~ si** to have a look and see if; **4** to look at [*situation*]; **~ pourquoi/si/qui** to see why/if/who; **5**° to concern [*person*]; **ça ne vous regarde pas** it's none of your business; **6 elle ne regarde que ses intérêts** she thinks only of her own interests.

II regarder à *v+prep* to think about; **ne pas ~ à la dépense** to spare no expense; **à y ~ de plus près** on closer examination.

III *vi* to look; **~ en l'air/par terre** to look up/down; **regarde où tu mets les pieds** watch where you put your feet.

IV se regarder *v refl* (+ *v être*) **1** to look at oneself; **2** to look at one another.

régate /ʀegat/ *nf* regatta.

régence /ʀeʒɑ̃s/ *nf* **1** regency; **2 la Régence** the Regency.

régénérer /ʀeʒeneʀe/ [14] **I** *vtr* **1** to regenerate; **2** to reactivate.

II se régénérer *v refl* (+ *v être*) **1** [*cells*] to regenerate; **2** (figurative) to regain one's strength.

régent, **~e** /ʀeʒɑ̃, ɑ̃t/ *nm,f* regent.

régenter /ʀeʒɑ̃te/ [1] *vtr* **1** to rule; **2** to regulate.

régie /ʀeʒi/ *nf* **1** state control; local government control; **2 ~ d'État** state-owned company; **3** stage management; production department; **4** central control room.

régime /ʀeʒim/ *nm* **1** diet; **être au ~** to be on a diet; **2** (Pol) system (of government); government; regime; **3** (in administration) system, regime; **~ de faveur** preferential treatment; **4** (Law) **~ matrimonial** marriage settlement; **5** (of engine) (running) speed; **tourner à plein ~** [*engine*] to run at top speed; [*factory*] to work at full capacity; **6** (of bananas) bunch.

régiment /ʀeʒimɑ̃/ *nm* regiment.

région /ʀeʒjɔ̃/ *nf* region; area.

régional, **~e**, *mpl* **-aux** /ʀeʒjɔnal, o/ *adj* regional.

régionalisme /ʀeʒjɔnalism/ *nm* regionalism.

régir /ʀeʒiʀ/ [3] *vtr* to govern.

régisseur /ʀeʒisœʀ/ *nm* **1** (of estate) steward, manager; **2** stage manager.

registre /ʀ(ə)ʒistʀ/ *nm* **1** register; **les ~s de la police** police records; **2** (of novel) style; **3** (of language, voice) register; **cet acteur a un ~ limité** this actor has a limited range.

réglable /ʀeglabl/ *adj* **1** adjustable; **2** payable.

réglage /ʀeglaʒ/ *nm* regulating; setting; adjustment.

règle /ʀɛgl/ **I** *nf* **1** ruler; **2** rule; **~s de sécurité** safety regulations; **respecter les ~s du jeu** to play by the rules; **dans les ~s de l'art** by the rule book; **en ~ générale** as a rule.

II règles *nf pl* period.

III en règle *phr* [*request*] formal; [*papers, accounts*] in order; **subir un interrogatoire en ~** to be given a grilling; **pour passer la frontière, il faut être en ~** to cross the border, your papers must be in order.

réglé, **~e** /regle/ *adj* **1** ruled, lined; **2** [*life*] well-ordered; **3 l'affaire est ~e** the matter is settled.

règlement /rɛgləmɑ̃/ *nm* **1** regulations, rules; **2** payment; **3** settlement.
■ **~ de comptes** settling of scores.

réglementaire /rɛgləmɑ̃tɛr/ *adj* [*uniform*] regulation; [*format*] prescribed; [*procedure*] statutory.

réglementation /rɛgləmɑ̃tasjɔ̃/ *nf* **1** rules, regulations; **2** regulation, control.

réglementer /rɛgləmɑ̃te/ [1] *vtr* to regulate.

régler /regle/ [14] *vtr* **1** to settle [*debt*]; to pay [*bill*]; to pay for [*purchase, work*]; **avoir des comptes à ~ avec qn** (figurative) to have a score to settle with sb; **~ son compte à qn**○ to sort sb out; **2** to settle, to sort out [*problem*]; **3** to settle [*details, terms*]; **4** to adjust [*height*]; to regulate [*speed*]; to tune [*engine*]; to set [*pressure*]; **5 ~ sa conduite sur celle de qn** to model one's behaviour[GB] on sb's; **6** to rule (lines on) [*paper*].

réglisse /reglis/ *nf* liquorice (GB), licorice (US).

régnant, **~e** /reɲɑ̃, ɑ̃t/ *adj* [*dynasty*] reigning; [*ideology*] prevailing.

règne /rɛɲ/ *nm* **1** reign; rule; **2** (figurative) reign; **3** (in biology) kingdom.

régner /reɲe/ [14] *vi* **1** [*sovereign*] to reign, to rule; **2** [*boss*] to be in control; **~ en maître sur** to reign supreme over; **3** [*confusion, fear*] to reign; [*smell*] to prevail; **la confiance règne!** (ironic) there's trust for you!; **faire ~** to give rise to [*insecurity*]; to impose [*order*].

regorger /r(ə)gɔrʒe/ [13] *vi* **~ de** [*shop*] to be packed with; [*region*] to have an abundance of.

régresser /regrese/ [1] *vi* **1** [*waters*] to recede; [*unemployment*] to go down; **2** [*industry*] to be in decline; **3** [*epidemic*] to die out.

régressif, **-ive** /regresif, iv/ *adj* regressive.

régression /regresjɔ̃/ *nf* **1** decline; **2** regression.

regret /rəgrɛ/ *nm* regret; **j'apprends avec ~ que** I'm sorry to hear that; **j'ai le ~ de vous annoncer** I regret to inform you.

regrettable /rəgrɛtabl/ *adj* regrettable.

regretter /rəgrete/ [1] *vtr* **1** to be sorry about, to regret [*situation, action*]; **je regrette de ne pas pouvoir t'aider** I'm sorry I can't help you; **2** to regret [*decision*]; **~ d'avoir fait** to regret doing; **je ne regrette rien** I have no regrets; **3** to miss [*person, place*]; **notre regretté collègue** (formal) our late colleague.

regroupement /r(ə)grupmɑ̃/ *nm* **1** grouping; pooling; bringing together; **2** merger; **3** getting [sb/sth] back together; rounding up.

regrouper /r(ə)grupe/ [1] **I** *vtr* **1** to group [sth] together; to bring [sth] together; to pool [*interests*]; **~ deux chapitres en un seul** to merge two chapters into one; **2** to reassemble [*pupils*]; to round up [*animals*].
II se regrouper *v refl* (+ *v être*) **1** [*companies*] to group together; [*malcontents*] to gather; **2** [*runners*] to bunch together again.

régulariser /regylarize/ [1] *vtr* **1** to sort out, to regularize [*position, situation*]; **2** to regulate [*flow*]; to stabilize [*price, market*].

régularité /regylarite/ *nf* **1** regularity; **2** (of rhythm, production, progress) steadiness; (of features) regularity; (of writing) neatness; (of surface) evenness; (of quantity) consistency; **3** legality.

régulation /regylasjɔ̃/ *nf* regulation, control.

régulier, **-ière** /regylje, ɛr/ *adj* **1** (gen) regular; [*flow, rise, effort*] steady; [*quality*] consistent; [*thickness*] even; [*writing*] neat; [*life*] (well-)ordered; **vol ~** scheduled flight; **2** [*person*] honest; [*papers, ballot*] in order; [*government*] legitimate; **3** [*verb*] regular.

régulièrement /regyljɛrmɑ̃/ *adv* **1** regularly; **2** steadily; **3** evenly; **4** normally.

régurgiter /regyrʒite/ [1] *vtr* to regurgitate.

réhabiliter /reabilite/ [1] **I** *vtr* **1** to rehabilitate; **2** to renovate.
II se réhabiliter *v refl* (+ *v être*) to redeem oneself.

rehausser /rəose/ [1] *vtr* **1** to raise; **2** to enhance [*prestige*]; **3** to set off [*pattern*].

réimprimer /reɛ̃prime/ [1] *vtr* to reprint.

rein /rɛ̃/ (Anat) **I** *nm* kidney; **~ artificiel** kidney machine.
II reins *nm pl* **les ~s** the small of the back; **une serviette autour des ~s** a towel around one's waist.

réincarner: **se réincarner** /reɛ̃karne/ [1] *v refl* (+ *v être*) to be reincarnated.

reine /rɛn/ *nf* **1** queen; **2** (figurative) **être la ~ des imbéciles**○ to be a prize idiot.

reine-claude, *pl* **reines-claudes** /rɛnklod/ *nf* greengage.

reinette /rɛnɛt/ *nf* rennet apple.

réinscrire: **se réinscrire** /reɛ̃skrir/ [67] *v refl* (+ *v être*) to re-enrol.

réinsérer /reɛ̃sere/ [14] *vtr* **1** to reintegrate; **2** to reinsert.

réinstaller /reɛ̃stale/ [1] **I** *vtr* to put [sth] back.
II se réinstaller *v refl* (+ *v être*) **se ~ dans un fauteuil** to settle (oneself) back into an armchair.

réintégrer /reɛ̃tegre/ [14] *vtr* **1** to return to [*place, group, system*]; **2 ~ qn (dans ses fonctions)** to reinstate sb.

réitérer /reitere/ [14] *vtr* to repeat.

rejaillir /r(ə)ʒajir/ [3] *vi* **1** [*liquid*] to splash back; to spurt back; **2 ~ sur qn** [*success*] to reflect on sb; [*scandal*] to affect sb adversely.

rejet /r(ə)ʒɛ/ *nm* **1** (gen) rejection; (of complaint) dismissal; (of motion) defeat; (of request) denial; **2** (of waste) discharge; disposal; **~s** waste.

rejeter /rəʒte, rʒəte/ [20] **I** *vtr* **1** to reject [*advice, candidacy, outsider*]; to turn down [*offer*]; to deny [*request*]; to set aside [*decision*]; **2 ~ qch sur qn** to shift sth onto sb [*blame*]; **3** [*factory*] to discharge [*waste*]; to eject [*smoke*]; **4** [*person, company*] to dispose of [*waste*]; [*sea*] to wash up [*body, debris*]; **5 ~ [qch] en arrière** to throw back [*head, hair*].
II se rejeter *v refl* (+ *v être*) **se ~ la faute** to blame each other.

rejeton /Rəʒ(ə)tɔ̃, Rʒətɔ̃/ *nm* **1** offshoot; **2**○ offspring.

rejoindre /R(ə)ʒwɛ̃dR/ [56] **I** *vtr* **1** to meet up with; **2** to catch up with; **3** to join; to rejoin; **4** to get to; to get back to, to return to; **5 ~ qn sur qch** to concur with sb on sth.
II se rejoindre *v refl* (+ *v être*) [*people*] to meet up; [*roads*] to meet.

rejouer /R(ə)ʒwe/ [1] *vtr* (gen) to play [sth] again; to replay [*match, point*].

réjoui, **~e** /Reʒwi/ *adj* cheerful.

réjouir /Reʒwir/ [3] **I** *vtr* **1** to delight [*person*]; to gladden [*heart*]; **2** to amuse.
II se réjouir *v refl* (+ *v être*) to rejoice; **se ~ de qch** to be delighted at [*news*]; to be delighted with [*success*].

réjouissance /Reʒwisɑ̃s/ **I** *nf* rejoicing.
II réjouissances *nf pl* celebrations; **quel est le programme des ~s**○**?** what delights are in store for us?

réjouissant, **~e** /Reʒwisɑ̃, ɑ̃t/ *adj* **1** heartening, delightful; **2** amusing.

relâche /R(ə)lɑʃ/ *nf* **1** (of theatre, cinema) closure; **faire ~** to be closed; **2** break, rest; **sans ~** relentlessly.

relâchement /R(ə)lɑʃmɑ̃/ *nm* **1** (of discipline, effort) slackening; (of morals) loosening; **2** (of muscle) slackening.

relâcher /R(ə)lɑʃe/ [1] **I** *vtr* **1** to loosen [*hold*]; **2** to release [*captive*]; **3** to relax [*discipline*]; **~ son attention** to let one's attention wander; **~ ses efforts** to let up.
II se relâcher *v refl* (+ *v être*) **1** [*hold, tie*] to loosen; [*muscle*] to relax; **2** [*effort*] to slacken; [*zeal*] to flag; [*pupil*] to grow slack.

relais /R(ə)lɛ/ *nm inv* **1** intermediary; **prendre le ~ (de qn/qch)** to take over (from sb/sth); **2** (Sport) relay; **3** restaurant; hotel; **4** (Tech) relay; **~ hertzien** radio relay station.

relance /R(ə)lɑ̃s/ *nf* (of industry, idea) revival; (of economy) reflation; (in inflation) rise; **mesures de ~** reflationary measures.

relancer /R(ə)lɑ̃se/ [12] *vtr* **1** to throw [sth] again [*ball*]; to throw [sth] back (again) [*ball*]; **2** to restart [*engine*]; to relaunch [*company*]; to revive [*idea*]; to reopen [*debate*]; to boost [*investment*]; to reflate [*economy*]; **3** [*creditor*] to chase [sb] up; [*person*] to pester.

relater /R(ə)late/ [1] *vtr* (formal) to recount.

relatif, **-ive**[1] /R(ə)latif, iv/ **I** *adj* relative; **le risque est très ~** there is relatively little risk.
II *nm* relative (pronoun).

relation /R(ə)lasjɔ̃/ **I** *nf* **1** connection; **2** acquaintance; **~s d'affaires** business acquaintances; **3** relationship; **avoir de bonnes ~s avec qn** to have a good relationship with sb; **entrer en ~ avec qn** to get in touch with sb.
II relations *nf pl* relations.
■ **~s extérieures** foreign affairs; **~s publiques** public relations.

relative[2] /R(ə)lativ/ **I** *adj f* ▶ **relatif I**.
II *nf* relative (clause).

relativement /R(ə)lativmɑ̃/ **I** *adv* relatively.
II relativement à *phr* in relation to.

relativiser /R(ə)lativize/ [1] *vtr* to put [sth] into perspective.

relativité /R(ə)lativite/ *nf* relativity.

relax○ /Rəlaks/ *adj inv* [*person*] laid-back○; [*clothes*] casual; [*party*] informal.

relaxant, **~e** /Rəlaksɑ̃, ɑ̃t/ *adj* relaxing.

relaxation /Rəlaksasjɔ̃/ *nf* relaxation.

relaxer /Rəlakse/ [1] **I** *vtr* **1** to discharge [*defendant*]; **2** to relax [*muscle, person*].
II se relaxer *v refl* (+ *v être*) to relax.

relayer /R(ə)leje/ [21] **I** *vtr* **1** to take over from, to relieve; **2** to relay [*broadcast*].
II se relayer *v refl* (+ *v être*) **1** to take turns; **2** to take over from each other.

reléguer /R(ə)lege/ [14] *vtr* (gen) to relegate; to consign [*object*]; **~ qn/qch au second plan** to push sb/sth into the background.

relent /R(ə)lɑ̃/ *nm* **1** lingering odour[GB]; **2** (figurative) whiff.

relève /R(ə)lɛv/ *nf* **1 la ~ s'effectue à 20 heures** the changeover takes place at 8 pm; **la ~ de la garde** the changing of the guard; **prendre la ~** to take over; **2** relief; relief team.

relevé, **~e** /Rəlve, Rləve/ **I** *adj* spicy.
II *nm* **1** noting down; **faire le ~ de** to list [*mistakes*]; to make a note of [*expenses*]; to read [*meter*]; **2 ~ bancaire** bank statement.

relever /Rəlve, Rləve/ [16] **I** *vtr* **1** to pick up [*person, stool*]; to put [sth] back up (again); **2** to raise [*lever*]; **3 ~ la tête** to raise one's head; to look up; (figurative) to refuse to accept defeat; **4** to turn up [*collar*]; to lift [*skirt*]; to wind up [*car window*]; to raise [*sail, blind*]; **~ ses cheveux** to put one's hair up; **5** to note, to notice; to point out; **~ la moindre inexactitude** to seize on the slightest inaccuracy; **6** to take down [*date, name*]; to take [*prints*]; **~ le compteur** to read the meter; **7** to take in [*exam papers*]; **8** to react to [*remark*]; **~ le défi/un pari** to take up the challenge/a bet; **9** to rebuild [*wall*]; to put [sth] back on its feet [*country, economy*]; **10** to raise [*standard, price*]; to increase [*productivity*]; **11** to relieve [*team*]; **~ la garde** to change the guard; **12** to spice up [*dish, story*]; **13 ~ qn de ses fonctions** to relieve sb of their duties.
II relever de *v+prep* **1 ~ de** [*department*] to come under [*Ministry*]; **cela ne relève pas de mes fonctions** that's not part of my duties; **2 cela relève de la gageure** this comes close to being impossible.
III se relever *v refl* (+ *v être*) **1** to pick oneself up; to get up again; **2 se ~ automatiquement** to be raised automatically; **3** [*blind*] to be raised; **4 se ~ de** to recover from.

relief /Rəljɛf/ *nm* **1** relief; (on medal, coin) raised pattern; **en ~** [*globe of the world*] in relief; [*letters*] raised; **cinéma en ~** three-dimensional cinema; **mettre qch en ~** to accentuate sth; **un ~ accidenté** a hilly landscape; **2** depth; **l'effet de ~** the effect of depth.

relier /Rəlje/ [2] *vtr* **1** to link; to link up; to link together; to join up; to connect; **2** to bind [*book*]; **relié cuir** leather-bound.

religieuse[1] /Rəliʒjøz/ **I** *adj f* ▶ **religieux I**.
II *nf* **1** nun; **2** (Culin) religieuse.

religieusement /Rəliʒjøzmɑ̃/ *adv* **1** religiously; **2** [*listen*] with rapt attention; **3** [*get married*] in church.

religieux, **-ieuse**[2] /Rəliʒjø, øz/ **I** *adj* **1** religious; [*school, wedding*] church; [*music*] sacred; **2** (figurative) [*silence*] reverent.
II *nm* monk.

religion /R(ə)liʒjɔ̃/ *nf* **1** religion; **2** faith; **3 entrer en ~** to enter the Church.

reliquaire /R(ə)likɛR/ *nm* reliquary.

reliquat /R(ə)lika/ *nm* (of sum) remainder; (of account) balance.

relique /R(ə)lik/ *nf* relic.

relire /R(ə)liR/ [66] *vtr* to reread; to read [sth] over.

reliure /RəljyR/ *nf* **1** binding; **2** bookbinding.

reloger /R(ə)lɔʒe/ [13] *vtr* to rehouse.

reluire /R(ə)lɥiR/ [69] *vi* to shine; to glisten.
IDIOMS **il sait passer la brosse à ~** he's a real flatterer.

reluisant, **~e** /R(ə)lɥizɑ̃, ɑ̃t/ *adj* shiny; glistening; **peu ~** (figurative) far from brilliant.

remâcher /R(ə)mɑʃe/ [1] *vtr* **1** to chew [sth] again; **2**○ to ruminate over [*problem, past*].

remaniement /R(ə)manimɑ̃/ *nm* modification; revision; reorganization.

remanier /R(ə)manje/ [2] *vtr* to modify; to redraft; to reorganize; to reshuffle.

remarier: **se remarier** /R(ə)maRje/ [2] *v refl* (+ *v être*) to remarry.

remarquable /R(ə)maRkabl/ *adj* **1** remarkable; **2** striking; **3** noteworthy.

remarque /R(ə)maRk/ *nf* **1** remark; **faire des ~s** to comment; **2** (written) comment; **3** critical remark, criticism.

remarqué, **~e** /R(ə)maRke/ *adj* [*initiative*] noteworthy; [*increase*] noticeable.

remarquer /R(ə)maRke/ [1] **I** *vtr* **1** to point out; **2** to observe; **3** to notice; **remarque, ce n'est pas très important** mind you, it's not very important; **se faire ~** to draw attention to oneself; **4 ~ un visage dans la foule** to spot a face in the crowd.
II se remarquer *v refl* (+ *v être*) **1** to attract attention; **2** to show.

remballer /Rɑ̃bale/ [1] *vtr* to pack [sth] up again.

remblai /Rɑ̃blɛ/ *nm* **1** embankment; **route en ~** raised road; **2** filling in; banking up; **3** (**terre de**) **~** (for railway, road) ballast; (for ditch) fill; (for excavation) backfill.

rembobiner /Rɑ̃bɔbine/ [1] *vtr* to rewind.

rembourrer /Rɑ̃buRe/ [1] *vtr* to stuff [*chair*]; to pad [*shoulders*].

remboursement /Rɑ̃buRsəmɑ̃/ *nm* **1** repayment; **2** refund; **3** reimbursement.

rembourser /Rɑ̃buRse/ [1] *vtr* **1** to pay off, to repay [*loan, debt*]; **2** to give a refund to [*customer*]; to refund the price of [*item*]; **3** to reimburse [*expenses, employee*]; **~ un ami** to pay a friend back.

remède /R(ə)mɛd/ *nm* medicine; remedy, cure.
■ **~ de bonne femme** folk remedy; **~ de cheval** strong medicine.
IDIOMS **aux grands maux les grands ~s** desperate times call for desperate measures.

remédier /R(ə)medje/ [2] *v+prep* **~ à** to remedy.

remémorer: **se remémorer** /R(ə)memɔRe/ [1] *v refl* (+ *v être*) to recall, to recollect.

remerciement /R(ə)mɛRsimɑ̃/ *nm* thanks; **je n'ai pas eu un seul ~** I didn't get a word of thanks; **lettre de ~** thank-you letter.

remercier /R(ə)mɛRsje/ [2] *vtr* **1** to thank; **je vous remercie** thank you; **2** (ironic) to dismiss.

remettre /R(ə)mɛtR/ [60] **I** *vtr* **1 ~ qch dans/sur** to put sth back in/on; **~ qch en mémoire à qn** to remind sb of sth; **2 ~ à qn** to hand [sth] over to sb [*keys*]; to hand [sth] in to sb [*letter*]; to present [sth] to sb [*reward*]; **3 ~ qch droit** or **d'aplomb** to put sth straight again; **4** to postpone [*visit*]; **5** to put [sth] on again [*heating*]; to play [sth] again [*record*]; **6 ~ une vis** to put a new screw in; **7** to add some more [*salt*]; to add another [*nail*]; **8** to put [sth] back on [*coat*]; **9** (Med) to put [sth] back in place [*joint*]; **10** [*medicine*] to make [sb] feel better; **11 ~ qn/le visage de qn** to remember sb/sb's face; **12**○ **~ ça** to start again; **on s'est bien amusé, quand est-ce qu'on remet ça?** that was fun, when are we going to do it again?
II se remettre *v refl* (+ *v être*) **1 se ~ à un endroit** to go or get back to a place; **2 se ~ au travail** to go back to work; **se ~ au dessin** to start drawing again; **3 se ~ en jean** to wear jeans again; **4 se ~ de** to recover from [*illness*]; to get over [*shock*]; **5 s'en ~ à qn** to leave it to sb; **s'en ~ à la décision de qn** to accept sb's decision; **6 se ~ avec qn** to get back together with sb.

réminiscence /Reminisɑ̃s/ *nf* **1** reminiscence; **2** recollection.

remise /R(ə)miz/ *nf* **1 attendre la ~ des clés** to wait for the keys to be handed over; **~ des prix** prizegiving; **~ des médailles** medals ceremony; **2** discount; **3 une ~ de peine** a remission; **4 ~ de fonds** remittance of funds; **5** shed.

rémission /Remisjɔ̃/ *nf* remission; **sans ~** [*punish*] mercilessly; [*rain*] without stopping.

remodeler /Rəmɔdle/ [17] *vtr* to restructure; to reshape; to replan.

remontant /R(ə)mɔ̃tɑ̃/ *nm* pick-me-up○, tonic.

remontée /R(ə)mɔ̃te/ *nf* **1** climb up; **la ~ de la Saône en péniche** going up the Saône by barge; **2** (in price) rise; (in violence) increase.
■ **~ mécanique** (Sport) ski lift.

remonte-pente, *pl* **~s** /R(ə)mɔ̃tpɑ̃t/ *nm* ski-tow.

remonter /Rəmɔ̃te/ [1] **I** *vtr* (+ *v avoir*) **1 ~ qch** to take sth back up/upstairs; to bring sth back up/upstairs; **2** to put [sth] back up; **~ un**

seau d'un puits to pull a bucket up from a well; **3** to raise [*shelf, blind*]; to wind [sth] back up [*car window*]; to roll up [*sleeves*]; to turn up [*collar*]; to pull up [*socks*]; **4** to go/to come back up; to climb back up; to drive back up; **5** to sail up [*river*]; to go up [*road*]; **~ une filière** or **piste** to follow a trail; **6 ~ qn** or **le moral de qn** to cheer sb up; **7** to put [sth] back together again; to put [sth] back [*wheel*]; **8** to wind [sth] up; **être remonté à bloc**○ to be full of energy; **9** to revive [*play, show*].

II *vi* (+ *v être*) **1** [*person*] to go/to come back up; [*tide*] to come in again; [*price, temperature*] to rise again; **~ sur** to step back onto [*pavement*]; to climb back onto [*wall*]; **~ à la surface** [*diver*] to surface; [*oil, object*] to rise to the surface; **~ dans les sondages** to move up in the opinion polls; **2 ~ dans le temps** to go back in time; **~ à** [*historian*] to go back to; [*event*] to date back to; **faire ~** to trace (back) [*origins*]; **3** [*skirt*] to ride up; **4 les odeurs d'égout remontent dans la maison** the smell from the drains reaches our house.

III se remonter *v refl* (+ *v être*) **se ~ le moral** to cheer oneself up; to cheer each other up.

remords /Rəmɔr/ *nm inv* remorse.

remorquage /Rəmɔrkaʒ/ *nm* towing.

remorque /Rəmɔrk/ *nf* **1** towrope; **prendre en ~** to tow [*car*]; **2** trailer.

remorquer /Rəmɔrke/ [1] *vtr* to tow [*vehicle*].

remorqueur /Rəmɔrkœr/ *nm* tug.

remous /R(ə)mu/ *nm inv* **1** eddy; **2** backwash; wash; **3** (of ideas) turmoil; (in crowd) stir.

rempailler /Rɑ̃pɑje/ [1] *vtr* to reseat [*chair*].

rempart /Rɑ̃par/ *nm* **1** rampart; battlements; **les ~s de la ville** the city walls; **2** defence[GB].

remplaçable /Rɑ̃plasabl/ *adj* replaceable.

remplaçant, ~e /Rɑ̃plasɑ̃, ɑ̃t/ *nm,f* **1** (gen) substitute; (at school) supply (GB) or substitute (US) teacher; (actor) stand-in; **2** successor.

remplacement /Rɑ̃plasmɑ̃/ *nm* replacement; **faire des ~s** [*teacher*] to do supply (GB) or substitute (US) teaching; [*temp*] to do temporary work; **produit de ~** substitute.

remplacer /Rɑ̃plase/ [12] *vtr* **1** to stand in for, to cover for [*colleague*]; **2** to replace; **on peut ~ le vinaigre par du jus de citron** you can use lemon juice instead of vinegar.

remplir /Rɑ̃plir/ [3] *vtr* **1** to fill (up) [*container*]; to fill in [*form*]; **~ qch à moitié** to half fill sth; **~ qn de joie** to fill sb with joy; **une vie bien remplie** a full life; **2** to carry out [*role, mission*]; to fulfil[GB] [*duty, role*].

remplissage /Rɑ̃plisaʒ/ *nm* **1** filling; **2** (derogatory) **faire du ~** to pad out one's work.

remporter /Rɑ̃pɔrte/ [1] *vtr* to win [*seat, title, victory*]; **~ un vif succès** to be a great success.

rempoter /Rɑ̃pɔte/ [1] *vtr* to repot.

remuant, ~e /R(ə)mɥɑ̃, ɑ̃t/ *adj* **1** rowdy; **2** boisterous; energetic.

remue-ménage /R(ə)mymenaʒ/ *nm inv* **1** commotion; **2** bustle.

remuer /R(ə)mɥe/ [1] **I** *vtr* **1** to move [*hand, head*]; to wiggle [*toe, hips*]; to wag [*tail*]; **2** to shake [*object*]; **3** to move [*object*]; **4** to stir [*soup*]; to toss [*salad*]; **5** to turn over [*earth*]; to poke [*ashes*]; **6** (figurative) to rake up [*past*]; to stir up [*memories*]; **7** to upset [*person*].

II *vi* [*person*] to move; [*leaves*] to flutter; [*boat*] to bob up and down.

III se remuer○ *v refl* (+ *v être*) **1** to get a move on○; **2 se ~ pour obtenir** to make an effort to get.

rémunération /Remynerasjɔ̃/ *nf* pay; payment.

rémunérer /Remynere/ [14] *vtr* to pay [*person*]; to pay for [*work*].

renâcler /R(ə)nɑkle/ [1] *vi* **1** [*person*] to show reluctance; **2** [*animal*] to snort.

renaissance /R(ə)nɛsɑ̃s/ *nf* rebirth; revival.

Renaissance /R(ə)nɛsɑ̃s/ *nf* Renaissance.

renaître /R(ə)nɛtr/ [74] *vi* (+ *v être*) **1** to come back to life; **2** [*hope, desire*] to return; **faire ~ l'espoir** to bring new hope.

rénal, ~e, *mpl* **-aux** /Renal, o/ *adj* [*artery*] renal; [*infection*] kidney.

renard /R(ə)nar/ *nm* **1** fox; **2** wily old fox.

renarde /R(ə)nard/ *nf* vixen.

renardeau, *pl* **~x** /R(ə)nardo/ *nm* fox cub.

renchérir /Rɑ̃ʃerir/ [3] *vi* **1** to add; **~ sur ce que dit qn** to add something to what sb says; **2** to go one step further; **3** to raise the bidding.

rencontre /Rɑ̃kɔ̃tr/ *nf* **1** meeting; encounter; **faire la ~ de qn** to meet sb; **2** (Sport) match (GB), game (US); **~ d'athlétisme** athletics meeting (GB), track meet (US).

■ **~ au sommet** summit meeting.

rencontrer /Rɑ̃kɔ̃tre/ [1] **I** *vtr* **1** to meet [*person*]; **~ qn sur son chemin** to come across sb; **2** to encounter, to meet with [*problem, opposition*]; **3** to come across [*object, word*]; **4** to meet [*player, team*].

II se rencontrer *v refl* (+ *v être*) **1** to meet; **2** [*quality, object, person*] to be found.

rendement /Rɑ̃dmɑ̃/ *nm* **1** (from land, investment) yield; (of machine, worker) output; **2** (of factory) productivity; (of machine, worker) efficiency; **3** (of sportsman, pupil) performance.

rendez-vous /Rɑ̃devu/ *nm inv* **1** appointment; date; **sur ~** by appointment; **j'ai ~ avec un ami** I'm meeting a friend; **le soleil n'était pas au ~** the sun didn't shine; **2** meeting; **3** gathering; meeting place.

rendormir: **se rendormir** /Rɑ̃dɔrmir/ [30] *v refl* (+ *v être*) to go back to sleep.

rendre /Rɑ̃dr/ [6] **I** *vtr* **1** (gen) to give back, to return; to repay, to pay back [*loan*]; to return [*greeting, invitation, goods*]; **~ la pareille à qn** to pay sb back; **il la déteste mais elle le lui rend bien** he hates her and she feels the same about him; **2 ~ la santé/vue à qn** to restore sb's health/sight; **3 ~ qch possible** to make sth possible; **~ qn fou** to drive sb mad; **4** to hand in [*homework*]; **5** [*land*] to yield [*crop, quantity*]; **6** to convey [*atmosphere, nuance*]; **ça ne rendra rien en couleurs** it won't come out in colour[GB]; **7**○ to bring up [*food, bile*]; **8** to

pronounce [*sentence*]; to return [*verdict*]; **9 les tomates rendent de l'eau (à la cuisson)** tomatoes give out water during cooking.
II *vi* **1** [*land*] to be productive; [*plant*] to produce a good crop; **2**○ to throw up○.
III se rendre *v refl* (+ *v être*) **1 se ~ à Rome/en ville** to go to Rome/to town; **2 se ~ indispensable/malade** to make oneself indispensable/ill; **3** to give oneself up; to surrender; **4 se ~ à qch** to bow to [*argument*].
IDIOMS **~ l'âme** or **l'esprit** to pass away.

rêne /ʀɛn/ *nf* rein.

renfermé, **~e** /ʀɑ̃fɛʀme/ **I** *pp* ▶ **renfermer**.
II *pp adj* [*person*] withdrawn; [*feeling*] hidden.
III *nm* **odeur de ~** musty smell.

renfermer /ʀɑ̃fɛʀme/ [1] **I** *vtr* to contain.
II se renfermer *v refl* (+ *v être*) to become withdrawn.

renflé, **~e** /ʀɑ̃fle/ *adj* [*vase*] rounded; [*dome*] bulbous; [*stomach*] bulging.

renflement /ʀɑ̃fləmɑ̃/ *nm* bulge.

renflouer /ʀɑ̃flue/ [1] *vtr* **1** to raise [*ship*]; **2** to bail out [*person, company*].

renfoncement /ʀɑ̃fɔ̃smɑ̃/ *nm* recess; **~ de porte** doorway.

renforcer /ʀɑ̃fɔʀse/ [12] **I** *vtr* to reinforce; to strengthen.
II se renforcer *v refl* (+ *v être*) [*power*] to increase; [*control*] to become tighter; [*team, numbers*] to grow; [*sector*] to grow stronger.

renfort /ʀɑ̃fɔʀ/ *nm* **1** (Mil) reinforcement; **2** support; **annoncé à grand ~ de publicité** well-publicized; **3** (Sport) substitute.

renfrogner: **se renfrogner** /ʀɑ̃fʀɔɲe/ [1] *v refl* (+ *v être*) to become sullen.

rengaine /ʀɑ̃gɛn/ *nf* **c'est toujours la même ~** (figurative) it's the same old thing every time.

rengainer /ʀɑ̃gɛne/ [1] *vtr* to sheathe [*sword*]; to put [sth] back in its holster [*pistol*].

rengorger: **se rengorger** /ʀɑ̃gɔʀʒe/ [13] *v refl* (+ *v être*) [*bird*] to puff out its breast; [*person*] to swell with conceit.

reniement /ʀ(ə)nimɑ̃/ *nm* disavowal.

renier /ʀənje/ [2] **I** *vtr* to renounce [*religion, opinion*]; to disown [*child, work, friend*].
II se renier *v refl* (+ *v être*) to go back on what one has said or promised.

reniflement /ʀ(ə)nifləmɑ̃/ *nm* **1** sniffing; **2** sniff.

renifler /ʀ(ə)nifle/ [1] *vtr*, *vi* to sniff.

renne /ʀɛn/ *nm* reindeer.

renom /ʀənɔ̃/ *nm* **1** fame; **2** reputation.

renommé, **~e**[1] /ʀənɔme/ *adj* famous.

renommée[2] /ʀənɔme/ *nf* **1** reputation; **2** fame.

renoncement /ʀ(ə)nɔ̃smɑ̃/ *nm* renunciation.

renoncer /ʀ(ə)nɔ̃se/ [12] *v+prep* to give up; **~ à** to give up; to abandon; to renounce; **~ à faire** to abandon the idea of doing.

renouer /ʀənwe/ [1] **I** *vtr* **1** to retie [*laces*]; **2** to pick up the thread of [*conversation*].
II ~ avec *v+prep* to get back in touch with [*person*]; to revive [*tradition*]; to go back to [*past*].

renouveau, *pl* **~x** /ʀənuvo/ *nm* revival.

renouveler /ʀənuvle/ [19] **I** *vtr* **1** (gen) to renew; to repeat [*suggestion, experience*]; to replace [*equipment, team*]; to change [*water*]; **2** to revitalize [*genre, style*].
II se renouveler *v refl* (+ *v être*) **1 une pièce où l'air ne se renouvelle pas** a room which isn't aired; **2** [*artist*] to try out new ideas; **3** [*experience*] to be repeated.

renouvellement /ʀənuvɛlmɑ̃/ *nm* **1** renewal; **2** replacement; **3** revitalization.

rénovateur, **-trice** /ʀenɔvatœʀ, tʀis/ *nm,f* reformer.

rénovation /ʀenɔvasjɔ̃/ *nf* renovation.

rénover /ʀenɔve/ [1] *vtr* **1** to renovate [*area, house*]; to restore [*furniture*]; **2** to reform [*institution, policy*]; to revamp [*project*].

renseignement /ʀɑ̃sɛɲmɑ̃/ **I** *nm* **1** information; **est-ce que je peux vous demander un ~?** can I ask you something?; **~s pris** upon investigation; **'pour tous ~s, s'adresser à...'** 'all enquiries to...'; **2** (Mil) intelligence.
II renseignements *nm pl* **1** information; **2** directory enquiries (GB) or assistance (US).

renseigner /ʀɑ̃seɲe/ [1] **I** *vtr* **~ qn** to give information to sb.
II se renseigner *v refl* (+ *v être*) to find out, to enquire; to make enquiries.

rentabiliser /ʀɑ̃tabilize/ [1] *vtr* to secure a return on [*investment*]; to make a profit on [*product*]; to make [sth] profitable [*business*].

rentable /ʀɑ̃tabl/ *adj* profitable.

rente /ʀɑ̃t/ *nf* **1** private income; **2** annuity; **~ viagère** life annuity; **3** government stock.

rentrée /ʀɑ̃tʀe/ *nf* **1** (general) return to work (*after the slack period of the summer break in France*); **~ (des classes** or **scolaire)** start of the (new) school year; **mon livre sera publié à la ~** my book will be published in the autumn (GB) or fall (US); **2** return (to work); **3** comeback; **~ politique** political comeback; **4** receipts; **~ (d'argent)** income; takings.
■ **~ parlementaire** reassembly of Parliament.

rentrer /ʀɑ̃tʀe/ [1] **I** *vtr* **1** to bring [sth] in; to take [sth] in; **2** to raise [*landing gear*]; to draw in [*claws*]; **rentrez le ventre!** hold your stomach in!; **3** to tuck [*shirt*] (**dans** into).
II *vi* (+ *v être*) **1** to go in; to get in; to fit; **~ dans un arbre**○ to hit a tree; **2 ~ dans** to go back into; to come back into; **3 ~ (chez soi)** to get (or go or come) back (home); to return (home); **4 ~ dans ses frais** to recoup one's money; **5** [*money*] to come in; **6 faire ~ qch dans la tête de qn** to get sth into sb's head.
IDIOMS **il m'est rentré dedans**○ he bumped or ran into me; he crashed into me.

renversant, **~e** /ʀɑ̃vɛʀsɑ̃, ɑ̃t/ *adj* astounding, astonishing.

renverse /ʀɑ̃vɛʀs/ *nf* **tomber à la ~** to fall flat on one's back.

renversement /ʀɑ̃vɛʀsəmɑ̃/ *nm* **1** reversal; **2** overthrow; removal from office.

renverser /ʀɑ̃vɛʀse/ [1] **I** *vtr* **1** to knock over; to knock down; **2** to spill; **3** to turn [sth] upside down; **4** to reverse; **5** to overthrow; to vote [sb/ sth] out of office.

II se renverser *v refl* (+ *v être*) [*boat*] to capsize; [*bottle*] to fall over; [*liquid*] to spill.

renvoi /ʀɑ̃vwa/ *nm* **1** expulsion; dismissal; **2** return; **~ d'un colis** return of a parcel; **3** postponement; **4** cross-reference; **5** belch, burp°.

renvoyer /ʀɑ̃vwaje/ [24] *vtr* **1** to throw [sth] back [*ball*]; to reflect [*light, heat*]; to echo [*sound*]; **2** to return [*mail*]; **3** to send [sb] back; **~ qn chez lui** to send sb home; **4** to expel; to dismiss; **5** to postpone [*debate*]; to adjourn [*case*]; **6 ~ à** to refer to.

réorganisation /ʀeɔʀganizasjɔ̃/ *nf* reorganization.

réouverture /ʀeuvɛʀtyʀ/ *nf* reopening.

repaire /ʀ(ə)pɛʀ/ *nm* den; hideout.

répandre /ʀepɑ̃dʀ/ [6] **I** *vtr* **1** to spread [*substance*]; to pour [*liquid*]; to spill [*liquid*]; **2** to scatter [*seeds, rubbish*]; **3** to spread [*news, religion*]; to give off [*heat, smoke, smell*].

II se répandre *v refl* (+ *v être*) to spread.

répandu, ~e /ʀepɑ̃dy/ *adj* widespread.

reparaître /ʀ(ə)paʀɛtʀ/ [73] *vi* **1** = **réapparaître**; **2** [*magazine*] to be back in print.

réparateur, -trice /ʀepaʀatœʀ, tʀis/ **I** *adj* refreshing.

II *nm,f* engineer (GB), fixer (US).

réparation /ʀepaʀasjɔ̃/ *nf* **1** repairing, mending; repair; **2** compensation; **3** redress.

réparer /ʀepaʀe/ [1] *vtr* **1** to repair, to mend, to fix; **2** to put [sth] right [*error*]; to make up for [*oversight*]; **3** to compensate for [*damage*].

repartie /ʀepaʀti/ *nf* rejoinder; **elle a de la ~** she always has a ready reply.

repartir /ʀ(ə)paʀtiʀ/ [30] *vi* (+ *v être*) **1** to leave (again); to go back; **2** [*person*] to set off again; [*machine*] to start again; [*sector*] to pick up again; **3 ~ à zéro** to start again from scratch.

répartir /ʀepaʀtiʀ/ [3] **I** *vtr* **1** to share [sth] out; to split [*profits, expenses*]; to distribute [*weight*]; **2** to spread [*payments*].

II se répartir *v refl* (+ *v être*) **1** to share out, to split; **2** [*work, votes*] to be split; **se ~ en** [*people, objects*] to divide (up) into.

répartition /ʀepaʀtisjɔ̃/ *nf* **1** sharing out; dividing up; **2** distribution.

repas /ʀ(ə)pɑ/ *nm inv* meal.

repassage /ʀ(ə)pasaʒ/ *nm* ironing.

repasser /ʀəpase/ [1] **I** *vtr* **1** to iron; **2** to cross [sth] again [*river, border*]; **3** to take [sth] again [*exam*]; **4** to pass [sth] again [*tool, salt*]; **je te repasse Jean** (on phone) I'll put you back on to Jean; **5**° **~ qch à qn** to give sb sth [*cold*].

II *vi* (+ *v être*) **1** to go past again; **si tu repasses à Lyon, viens me voir** if you're ever back in Lyons, come and see me; **2** [*film*] to be showing again; **3 quand elle fait la vaisselle, je dois ~ derrière elle** I always have to do the dishes again after she's done them.

repêchage /ʀ(ə)pɛʃaʒ/ *nm* **1** recovery (*from water*); **2 épreuve de ~** resit (GB), retest (US).

repêcher /ʀ(ə)peʃe/ [1] *vtr* to recover; to fish out.

repeindre /ʀ(ə)pɛ̃dʀ/ [55] *vtr* to repaint.

repenser /ʀ(ə)pɑ̃se/ [1] **I** *vtr* to rethink.

II repenser à *v+prep* to think back to [*childhood*]; to think again about [*anecdote*].

repenti, ~e /ʀ(ə)pɑ̃ti/ *adj* repentant.

repentir[1]: **se repentir** /ʀ(ə)pɑ̃tiʀ/ [30] *v refl* (+ *v être*) **1** to regret; **2** to repent.

repentir[2] /ʀ(ə)pɑ̃tiʀ/ *nm* repentance.

répercussion /ʀepɛʀkysjɔ̃/ *nf* repercussion.

répercuter /ʀepɛʀkyte/ [1] **I** *vtr* **1** to pass [sth] on [*increase*]; **2** to send back [*sound*].

II se répercuter *v refl* (+ *v être*) [*sound*] to echo; [*increase*] to be reflected (**sur** in).

repère /ʀ(ə)pɛʀ/ *nm* **1** marker; (reference) mark; **2** (event) landmark; (date) reference point.

repérer /ʀ(ə)peʀe/ [14] **I** *vtr* **1**° to spot; **~ les lieux** to check out a place; **2** to locate [*target*].

II se repérer *v refl* (+ *v être*) to get one's bearings.

répertoire /ʀepɛʀtwaʀ/ *nm* **1** notebook with thumb index; **2 ~ téléphonique** telephone book; **3** repertoire.

répertorier /ʀepɛʀtɔʀje/ [2] *vtr* **1** to list; to index; **2** to identify.

répéter /ʀepete/ [14] **I** *vtr* **1** to repeat; **~ qch à qn** to say sth to sb again; **je te répète que tu as tort** I'm telling you, you're wrong; **2** to rehearse [*play*]; to rehearse for [*concert*].

II se répéter *v refl* (+ *v être*) **1** to repeat oneself; **2 j'ai beau me ~ que** no matter how often I tell myself that; **3** [*incident*] to be repeated.

répétitif, -ive /ʀepetitif, iv/ *adj* repetitive.

répétition /ʀepetisjɔ̃/ *nf* **1** repetition; **2** rehearsal; **~ générale** dress rehearsal.

repeupler /ʀ(ə)pœple/ [1] *vtr* **1** to repopulate; **2** to restock; **3** to reforest.

repiquer /ʀ(ə)pike/ [1] *vtr* to transplant [*rice*]; to prick out [*seedlings*].

répit /ʀepi/ *nm* respite.

replanter /ʀ(ə)plɑ̃te/ [1] *vtr* **1** to transplant; **2** to replant.

replâtrer /ʀ(ə)plɑtʀe/ [1] *vtr* **1** to replaster; **2** to patch up [*group*].

replet, -ète /ʀəplɛ, ɛt/ *adj* plump, chubby.

repli /ʀ(ə)pli/ *nm* **1** double fold; **2** fold; **3** (Mil) withdrawal; **4 ~ sur soi(-même)** withdrawal.

replier /ʀ(ə)plije/ [2] **I** *vtr* **1** to fold up [*map*]; **2** to fold [sth] back [*sheet*]; **3** to fold up [*deckchair, fan*]; to close [*umbrella, penknife*]; **4 elle replia ses jambes** she tucked her legs under her; **~ ses ailes** [*bird*] to fold its wings.

II se replier *v refl* (+ *v être*) **1** [*blade*] to fold up; **2** [*army*] to withdraw; **3 se ~ sur soi-même** [*person*] to become withdrawn.

réplique /ʀeplik/ *nf* **1** retort, rejoinder; **il a la ~ facile** he's always ready with an answer; **2** line; **donner la ~ à qn** to play opposite sb; **3** replica; **elle est la ~ de sa mère** she is the image of her mother.

répliquer /ʀeplike/ [1] **I** *vtr* to retort.

II répliquer à *v+prep* to argue with [*person*]; to respond to [*criticism*].

III *vi* **1** to answer back; **2** to retaliate, to respond.

répondant, **~e** /ʀepɔ̃dɑ̃, ɑ̃t/ *nm,f* referee; (Law) surety, guarantor.

répondeur /ʀepɔ̃dœʀ/ *nm* **~ (téléphonique)** (telephone) answering machine.

répondre /ʀepɔ̃dʀ/ [6] **I** *vtr* to answer, to reply; **il m'a été répondu que** I was told that; **qu'as-tu à ~?** what's your answer?

II répondre à *v+prep* **1 ~ à** to reply to, to answer [*person, question, letter*]; to answer [*phone*]; **2 ~ à** to talk back to; **3 ~ à** to answer, to meet [*needs*]; to fulfil[GB] [*wishes*]; to fit [*description*]; to come up to [*expectations*]; **4 ~ à** to respond to [*appeal, criticism*]; to return [*greeting*]; **~ à un sourire** to smile back; **les freins ne répondent plus** the brakes have failed.

III répondre de *v+prep* **~ de qn** to vouch for sb; **~ de ses actes** to answer for one's actions.

réponse /ʀepɔ̃s/ *nf* **1** answer, reply; **2** response.

report /ʀəpɔʀ/ *nm* **1** adjournment; postponement; deferment; **2** transfer.

reportage /ʀ(ə)pɔʀtaʒ/ *nm* **1** report; **2** reporting.

reporter[1] /ʀ(ə)pɔʀte/ [1] **I** *vtr* **1** to put back [*date*]; to postpone [*event*]; to defer [*judgment*]; **2** to carry forward [*result*]; to copy out [*name*]; **3** to take [sth] back [*goods*]; **4** to transfer [*affection*]; **~ son agressivité sur qn** to take one's aggression out on sb.

II se reporter *v refl* (+ *v être*) **se ~ à** to refer to; to think back to.

reporter[2] /ʀəpɔʀtɛʀ/ *nm* reporter.

repos /ʀəpo/ *nm inv* rest; **mon jour de ~** my day off.

reposant, **~e** /ʀəpozɑ̃, ɑ̃t/ *adj* peaceful, restful; soothing; relaxing.

reposer /ʀəpoze/ [1] **I** *vtr* **1** to rest; **avoir le visage reposé** to look rested; **lire qch à tête reposée** to read sth at one's leisure; **2** to put [sth] down [*phone*]; to put [sth] down again; **3** to ask [sth] again [*question*].

II *vi* **1** to rest; **'ici repose le Dr Grunard'** 'here lies Dr Grunard'; **laisser ~ la terre** to rest the land; **'laisser ~ la pâte'** 'let the dough stand'; **2 ~ sur** to be based on; **la poutre repose sur**... the beam is supported by...

III se reposer *v refl* (+ *v être*) **1** to have a rest, to rest; **2 se ~ sur qn** to rely on sb.

repoussant, **~e** /ʀəpusɑ̃, ɑ̃t/ *adj* hideous.

repousser /ʀ(ə)puse/ [1] **I** *vtr* **1** to push [sth] to [*door*]; to push back [*object*]; **2** to push away [*objects*]; to push back [*lock of hair*]; **3** to push or drive back [*crowd, animal*]; (Mil) to repel [*attack*]; **4** to dismiss [*objection*]; to decline [*help*]; to turn down [*request*]; **5** to revolt; **6** to postpone [*event*]; to move [sth] back [*date*].

II *vi* to grow again; to grow back.

répréhensible /ʀepʀeɑ̃sibl/ *adj* reprehensible.

reprendre /ʀ(ə)pʀɑ̃dʀ/ [52] **I** *vtr* **1 ~ du pain/vin** to have some more bread/wine; **j'en ai repris deux fois** I had three helpings; **2** to pick [sth] up again [*object, tool*]; to take [sth] back [*present*]; to collect [*person, car*]; **3** to take [sb] on again [*employee*]; [*shop*] to take [sth] back [*item*]; **si on me reprend ma vieille voiture** if I can trade in my old car; **4** to resume [*walk, story*]; to take up [sth] again [*studies*]; to revive [*play, tradition*]; **~ le travail** to go back to work; **tu reprends le train à quelle heure?** what time is your train back?; **~ une histoire au début** to go back to the beginning of a story; **5** to take over [*business, shop*]; **6 on ne me reprendra plus à lui rendre service!** you won't catch me doing him/her any favours[GB] again!; **7 ~ confiance** to regain one's confidence; **8** to alter [*clothes*]; **~ le travail de qn** to correct sb's work; **9** to take up [*idea, thesis, policy*]; **10** to repeat [*argument*]; to take up [*slogan, news*]; **11** to correct [*pupil*]; **12 mon mal de dents m'a repris** my toothache has come back.

II *vi* **1** [*business*] to pick up again; [*plant*] to recover; **2** to start again; **3 'c'est étrange,' reprit-il** 'it's strange,' he continued.

III se reprendre *v refl* (+ *v être*) **1** to correct oneself; **2** to pull oneself together; **3 s'y ~ à trois fois pour faire** to make three attempts to do or at doing.

représailles /ʀ(ə)pʀezɑj/ *nf pl* reprisals; retaliation.

représentant, **~e** /ʀ(ə)pʀezɑ̃tɑ̃, ɑ̃t/ *nm,f* **1** representative; **2 ~ (de commerce)** sales representative.

représentatif, **-ive** /ʀəpʀezɑ̃tatif, iv/ *adj* representative.

représentation /ʀəpʀezɑ̃tasjɔ̃/ *nf* **1** representation; **2** performance; **3** commercial travelling[GB]; **~ exclusive** sole agency.

représenter /ʀəpʀezɑ̃te/ [1] **I** *vtr* **1** (in painting) to depict; to portray; **2** to represent; to mean; **les enfants représentent les deux tiers de la population** children make up two thirds of the population; **3** to represent [*person, company*]; **4** to perform [*play*].

II se représenter *v refl* (+ *v être*) **1** to imagine [*scene*]; **2** [*opportunity*] to arise again; **3 se ~ à un examen** to retake an examination.

répressif, **-ive** /ʀepʀesif, iv/ *adj* repressive.

répression /ʀepʀesjɔ̃/ *nf* suppression.

réprimande /ʀepʀimɑ̃d/ *nf* reprimand.

réprimander /ʀepʀimɑ̃de/ [1] *vtr* to reprimand.

réprimer /ʀepʀime/ [1] *vtr* to suppress; to repress [*desire*].

repris /ʀ(ə)pʀi/ *nm inv* **~ de justice** ex-convict.

reprise /ʀəpʀiz/ *nf* **1** (of work, negotiations) resumption; (of play, film) rerun; **à plusieurs** or **maintes ~s** on several occasions, repeatedly; **2** (of demand, production) increase; (of business) revival; (of economy) upturn; **3** (of goods) return, taking back; trade-in; (of company) takeover; **4** key money; **5** (Aut) acceleration; **6** mend; darn; **7** (in boxing) round; (in football) start of second half.

repriser /ʀəpʀize/ [1] *vtr* to mend; to darn.

réprobation /ʀepʀɔbasjɔ̃/ *nf* disapproval.

reproche /ʀ(ə)pʀɔʃ/ *nm* reproach; **j'ai un ou deux ~s à vous faire** I've one or two criticisms to make; **sans ~** beyond reproach.

reprocher /ʀəpʀɔʃe/ [1] **I** *vtr* **1 ~ qch à qn** to criticize or reproach sb for sth; **on ne peut rien lui ~** he's/she's beyond reproach; **elle me reproche de ne jamais lui écrire** she complains that I never write to her; **2 les faits qui lui sont reprochés** the charges against him/her.
II se reprocher *v refl* (+ *v être*) **se ~ qch** to blame or reproach oneself for sth.

reproducteur, **-trice** /ʀəpʀɔdyktœʀ, tʀis/ *adj* **1** reproductive; **2** [*animal*] breeding.

reproduction /ʀ(ə)pʀɔdyksjɔ̃/ *nf* **1** reproduction; **2** reproduction, copy; **droit de ~** copyright.

reproduire /ʀ(ə)pʀɔdɥiʀ/ [69] **I** *vtr* (gen) to reproduce; to recreate [*conditions*].
II se reproduire *v refl* (+ *v être*) **1** [*man, plants*] to reproduce; **2** [*situation*] to recur.

réprouver /ʀepʀuve/ [1] *vtr* to condemn.

reptile /ʀɛptil/ *nm* reptile.

républicain, **~e** /ʀepyblikɛ̃, ɛn/ *adj, nm,f* republican.

république /ʀepyblik/ *nf* republic; **on est en ~** it's a free country.

répudier /ʀepydje/ [2] *vtr* **1** to repudiate [*spouse*]; **2** to renounce [*right, faith*].

répugnance /ʀepyɲɑ̃s/ *nf* **1** revulsion; **2** reluctance; **avec ~** reluctantly.

répugnant, **~e** /ʀepyɲɑ̃, ɑ̃t/ *adj* **1** revolting; **2** disgusting; **3** loathsome.

répugner /ʀepyɲe/ [1] *v+prep* **1 ~ à** [*food*] to disgust [*person*]; **2 ~ à** [*person*] to be averse to [*work*]; **~ à faire** to be reluctant to do.

répulsion /ʀepylsjɔ̃/ *nf* repulsion.

réputation /ʀepytasjɔ̃/ *nf* reputation; **se faire une ~** to make a name for oneself.

réputé, **~e** /ʀepyte/ *adj* **1** [*company*] reputable; [*writer*] of repute; [*product*] well-known; **~ pour qch** renowned for sth; **l'avocat le plus ~ de Paris** the best lawyer in Paris; **2 ~ cher** reputed to be expensive.

requérir /ʀəkeʀiʀ/ [35] *vtr* **1** to request; **2** to require.

requête /ʀəkɛt/ *nf* **1** request; **2** (Law) petition.

requiem /ʀekwijɛm/ *nm inv* requiem.

requin /ʀ(ə)kɛ̃/ *nm* (Zool, figurative) shark.

requis, **~e** /ʀəki, iz/ **I** *pp* ▶ **requérir**.
II *pp adj* [*patience*] necessary; [*age*] required.

réquisition /ʀekizisjɔ̃/ *nf* requisitioning.

réquisitionner /ʀekizisjɔne/ [1] *vtr* **1** to requisition; **2** to commandeer [*premises*]; to conscript [*workers*].

réquisitoire /ʀekizitwaʀ/ *nm* closing speech for the prosecution.

RER /ɛʀəɛʀ/ *nm* (*abbr* = **réseau express régional**) *rapid-transit rail system in the Paris region.*

rescapé, **~e** /ʀɛskape/ **I** *adj* surviving.
II *nm,f* survivor.

rescousse: **à la rescousse** /alaʀɛskus/ *phr* **aller à la ~ de qn** to go to sb's rescue.

réseau, *pl* **~x** /ʀezo/ *nm* network.

réservation /ʀezɛʀvasjɔ̃/ *nf* reservation, booking (GB).

réserve /ʀezɛʀv/ *nf* **1** reservation; **sous ~ de changement** subject to alteration; **'sous (toute) ~'** (in a programme) 'to be confirmed'; **2** stock; **des ~s de sucre** a stock of sugar; **~(s) d'argent** money in reserve; **3** (Econ) **~s de charbon** coal reserves; **~s d'eau** water supply; **4** (of person, manner) reserve; **5** stockroom; **6** (in museum) storeroom; **7 ~ naturelle** nature reserve; **8 ~ indienne** Indian reservation; **9** (Mil) **officier de ~** reserve officer.

réservé, **~e** /ʀezɛʀve/ **I** *pp* ▶ **réserver**.
II *pp adj* **1** [*fishing*] private; **2 ~ à la clientèle** for patrons only; **voie ~e aux autobus** bus lane; **'tous droits ~s'** 'all rights reserved'; **3** [*person*] reserved.

réserver /ʀezɛʀve/ [1] **I** *vtr* **1** to reserve, to book [*seat, ticket*]; **2** to put aside [*goods*]; **3** to set aside [*money, time*]; **4 ~ un bon accueil à qn** to give sb a warm welcome; **sans savoir ce que l'avenir nous réserve** without knowing what the future has in store for us; **5 ~ son jugement** to reserve judgment.
II se réserver *v refl* (+ *v être*) **se ~ les meilleurs morceaux** to save the best bits for oneself; **se ~ le droit de faire** to reserve the right to do; **il se réserve pour la candidature à la présidence** he's saving himself for the presidential race.

réserviste /ʀezɛʀvist/ *nmf* reservist.

réservoir /ʀezɛʀvwaʀ/ *nm* **1** tank; **2** reservoir.

résidant, **~e** /ʀezidɑ̃, ɑ̃t/ *adj* resident.

résidence /ʀezidɑ̃s/ *nf* **1** residence; **2** place of residence; **assigné à ~** under house arrest.
■ **~ principale/secondaire** main/second home; **~ universitaire** (university) hall of residence (GB), residence hall (US).

résident, **~e** /ʀezidɑ̃, ɑ̃t/ *nm,f* resident.

résidentiel, **-ielle** /ʀezidɑ̃sjɛl/ *adj* residential.

résider /ʀezide/ [1] *vi* **1** to live; **2 ~ dans qch** to lie in sth.

résidu /ʀezidy/ *nm* **1** residue; **2** remnant; **3** waste.

résignation /ʀeziɲasjɔ̃/ *nf* resignation (**à** to).

résigner: **se résigner** /ʀeziɲe/ [1] *v refl* (+ *v être*) to resign oneself.

résilier /ʀezilje/ [2] *vtr* to terminate [*contract*].

résine /ʀezin/ *nf* resin.

résistance /ʀezistɑ̃s/ *nf* **1** resistance; **manquer de ~** [*person*] to lack stamina; **2** (in electricity) (gen) resistance; (of household appliance) element.

résistant, **~e** /ʀezistɑ̃, ɑ̃t/ **I** *adj* **1** [*person*] tough, resilient; [*plant*] hardy; **2** [*metal*] resistant; [*fabric, garment*] hard-wearing.
II *nm,f* Resistance fighter.

résister /ʀeziste/ [1] *v+prep* (gen) to resist; **~ à** to resist [*offer*]; to stand [*strain*]; to withstand [*pressure*]; to get through [*ordeal*]; **le mur n'a**

pas résisté the wall collapsed; **~ à l'épreuve du temps** to stand the test of time; **il ne supporte pas qu'on lui résiste** he doesn't like it when people stand up to him.

résolu, **~e** /ʀezɔly/ I *pp* ▶ **résoudre**.
II *pp adj* resolute, determined.

résolument /ʀezɔlymɑ̃/ *adv* resolutely.

résolution /ʀezɔlysjɔ̃/ *nf* **1** (gen, Pol) resolution; **2** resolve; **3** solution.

résonance /ʀezɔnɑ̃s/ *nf* (gen) resonance.

résonner /ʀezɔne/ [1] *vi* **1** [*step, laughter*] to ring out; [*alarm*] to resound; [*cymbals*] to clash; **2** [*room*] to echo; **~ de** to resound with.

résorber /ʀezɔʀbe/ [1] I *vtr* to absorb [*deficit, surplus*]; to reduce [*inflation*].
II **se résorber** *v refl* (+ *v être*) **1** [*deficit*] to be reduced; **2** (Med) to be resorbed.

résoudre /ʀezudʀ/ [75] I *vtr* to solve [*equation, problem*]; to resolve [*crisis*].
II **se résoudre** *v refl* (+ *v être*) **se ~ à faire** to resolve or make up one's mind to do; **être résolu à faire** to be determined to do.

respect /ʀɛspɛ/ *nm* (gen) respect; **manquer de ~ à qn** to be disrespectful to sb; **le ~ de soi** self-respect.
IDIOMS **sauf votre ~** with all due respect; **tenir qn en ~** to keep sb at bay.

respectable /ʀɛspɛktabl/ *adj* respectable.

respecter /ʀɛspɛkte/ [1] I *vtr* (gen) to respect; to treat [sth] with respect; to honour[GB] [*commitment*]; **faire ~ l'ordre/la loi** to enforce order/the law.
II **se respecter** *v refl* (+ *v être*) to respect oneself; **tout homme qui se respecte** any self-respecting man.

respectif, **-ive** /ʀɛspɛktif, iv/ *adj* respective.

respectueux, **-euse** /ʀɛspɛktɥø, øz/ *adj* respectful; **~ de la loi** law-abiding; **salutations respectueuses** yours faithfully.

respiration /ʀɛspiʀasjɔ̃/ *nf* **1** breathing; **avoir une ~ difficile** to have breathing difficulties; **2** breath; **retenir sa ~** to hold one's breath.

respiratoire /ʀɛspiʀatwaʀ/ *adj* respiratory.

respirer /ʀɛspiʀe/ [1] I *vtr* **1** to breathe in [*air, dust*]; **2** to smell [*perfume*]; **3** [*person, place*] to exude.
II *vi* **1** to breathe; **2** (figurative) to catch one's breath; **laisse-moi ~** let me get my breath back.

resplendir /ʀɛsplɑ̃diʀ/ [3] *vi* **1** [*light*] to shine brightly; [*snow*] to sparkle; **2 ~ de santé** to be glowing with health.

resplendissant, **~e** /ʀɛsplɑ̃disɑ̃, ɑ̃t/ *adj* **1** [*light*] brilliant; **2** [*beauty*] radiant.

responsabiliser /ʀɛspɔ̃sabilize/ [1] *vtr* to give [sb] a sense of responsibility.

responsabilité /ʀɛspɔ̃sabilite/ *nf* (gen) responsibility; (Law) liability; **avoir la ~ de** to be responsible for; **engageant la ~ de la société** for which the company is liable.
■ **~ civile** (in insurance) personal liability.

responsable /ʀɛspɔ̃sabl/ I *adj* **1** [*person, error*] responsible; **2** accountable; (Law) liable; **3 être ~ de qn/qch** to be in charge of sb/sth; **4** [*person, attitude, act*] responsible.
II *nmf* **1** (gen) person in charge; (of shop, project) manager; (of party) leader; (of department) head; **2 les ~s de la catastrophe** the people responsible for the catastrophe; **3 le grand ~ c'est le tabac** smoking is the main cause.

resquiller○ /ʀɛskije/ [1] *vi* (on train) not to pay the fare; (at show) to sneak in○.

resquilleur○, **-euse** /ʀɛskijœʀ, øz/ *nm,f* fare dodger.

ressac /ʀəsak/ *nm* backwash.

ressaisir: **se ressaisir** /ʀ(ə)seziʀ/ [3] *v refl* (+ *v être*) to pull oneself together.

ressasser /ʀ(ə)sase/ [1] *vtr* to brood over [*failure*]; to dwell on [*misfortunes*].

ressemblance /ʀ(ə)sɑ̃blɑ̃s/ *nf* **1** resemblance, likeness; **2** (between things) similarity.

ressembler /ʀ(ə)sɑ̃ble/ [1] **I ressembler à** *v+prep* to look like, to resemble; to be like.
II **se ressembler** *v refl* (+ *v être*) **1** to look alike; **2** to be alike.

ressemeler /ʀ(ə)səmle/ [19] *vtr* to resole.

ressentiment /ʀ(ə)sɑ̃timɑ̃/ *nm* resentment.

ressentir /ʀ(ə)sɑ̃tiʀ/ [30] I *vtr* to feel.
II **se ressentir** *v refl* (+ *v être*) **se ~ de** to feel the effects of; to suffer from.

resserrer /ʀ(ə)seʀe/ [1] I *vtr* **1** to tighten [*knot, screw, grip*]; **2 resserrez les rangs!** close up a bit!; **3** to tighten up on [*discipline, supervision*].
II **se resserrer** *v refl* (+ *v être*) **1** [*road*] to narrow; **2** [*friendship*] to become stronger; **3** [*link, knot, grip*] to tighten; **4** [*gap*] to close; **5** [*group of people*] to draw closer together; **6** [*discipline*] to become stricter.

resservir /ʀ(ə)sɛʀviʀ/ [30] I *vtr* **1** to serve [sth] (up) again; **2** to give [sb] another helping.
II **se resservir** *v refl* (+ *v être*) to take another helping.

ressort /ʀ(ə)sɔʀ/ *nm* **1** (Tech) spring; **2 avoir du ~** to have resilience; **3 être du ~ de qn** to be within sb's province; (Law) to fall within the jurisdiction of [*court*]; **en premier ~** in the first resort.

ressortir /ʀ(ə)sɔʀtiʀ/ [30] I *vtr* **1** to take [sth] out again; **2** to bring [sth] out again; to dig out○ [*affair, scandal*].
II *vi* (+ *v être*) **1** [*person*] to go out again; **2** [*bullet*] to come out; **3** to stand out; **voici ce qui ressort de l'étude** the results of the study are as follows; **faire ~** to bring to light [*contradiction*]; [*make-up*] to accentuate [*eyes*]; **4** [*film, record*] to be re-released.
III *v impers* (+ *v être*) **il ressort que** it emerges that.

ressortissant, **~e** /ʀ(ə)sɔʀtisɑ̃, ɑ̃t/ *nm,f* national.

ressouder /ʀ(ə)sude/ [1] *vtr* to solder [sth] again.

ressource /ʀ(ə)suʀs/ *nf* **1** resource; **les ~s énergétiques** energy resources; **2** option; **en dernière ~** as a last resort; **3 avoir de la ~**○ to be resourceful; **4 ~s** means; **être sans ~s** to have no means of support.

ressusciter /ʀesysite/ [1] I *vtr* **1** to revive [*tradition*]; to resurrect [*past*]; **2** to raise [sb] from the dead; (figurative) to bring [sb] back to life.
II *vi* [*dead person*] to rise from the dead.

restant, **~e** /ʀɛstɑ̃, ɑ̃t/ I *adj* remaining.
II *nm* **1** **le ~** the remainder; the rest; **2** **un ~ de poulet** some left-over chicken.

restaurant /ʀɛstɔʀɑ̃/ *nm* restaurant.
■ **~ universitaire**, **RU** university canteen (GB), cafeteria.

restaurateur, **-trice** /ʀɛstɔʀatœʀ, tʀis/ *nm,f* **1** restaurant owner; **2** restorer.

restauration /ʀɛstɔʀasjɔ̃/ *nf* **1** catering; **~ rapide** fast-food industry; **2** restoration.

restaurer /ʀɛstɔʀe/ [1] I *vtr* **1** to feed; **2** to restore.
II **se restaurer** *v refl* (+ *v être*) to have something to eat.

reste /ʀɛst/ I *nm* **le ~** the rest; the remainder; **un ~ de tissu** some left-over material; **au ~**, **du ~** besides.
II **restes** *nm pl* **1** remains; **2** leftovers.
IDIOMS **sans demander son ~** without further ado; **être en ~ avec qn** to feel indebted to sb; **pour ne pas être en ~** so as not to be outdone.

rester /ʀɛste/ [1] (+ *v être*) I *vi* **1** to stay, to remain; **que ça reste entre nous!** this is strictly between you and me!; **2** to remain; **restez assis!** remain seated!; don't get up!; **~ sans manger** to go without food; **~ paralysé** to be left paralyzed; **~ les bras croisés** (figurative) to stand idly by; **3** to be left, to remain; **4** [*memory, work of art*] to live on; **5** **~ sur une bonne impression** to be left with a good impression; **6** **en ~ à** to go no further than; **je compte bien ne pas en ~ là** I won't let the matter rest there; **restons-en là pour le moment** let's leave it at that for now.
II *v impers* **il reste une minute** there is one minute left; **il ne me reste plus que lui** he's all I've got left; **il reste que**, **il n'en reste pas moins que** the fact remains that.

restituer /ʀɛstitɥe/ [1] *vtr* **1** to restore; **2** to reconstruct [*text*]; to reproduce [*sound*].

restitution /ʀɛstitysjɔ̃/ *nf* **1** return; restoration; **2** reproduction.

restreindre /ʀɛstʀɛ̃dʀ/ [55] I *vtr* to curb, to cut back on; to limit; to restrict.
II **se restreindre** *v refl* (+ *v être*) **1** [*possibilities*] to become restricted; [*influence*] to wane; **2** **se ~ (dans ses dépenses)** to cut back (on one's expenses).

restreint, **~e** /ʀɛstʀɛ̃, ɛ̃t/ *adj* [*public, vocabulary*] limited; [*team*] small.

restrictif, **-ive** /ʀɛstʀiktif, iv/ *adj* restrictive.

restriction /ʀɛstʀiksjɔ̃/ *nf* **1** restriction; **~s salariales** wage restraints; **sans ~** freely; **2** **sans ~** [*approve*] without reservations; [*support*] unreservedly.

restructurer /ʀəstʀyktyʀe/ [1] *vtr* to restructure; to redevelop [*area*].

résultat /ʀezylta/ *nm* (gen) result; (of research) results, findings; (of negotiations, inquiry) result, outcome; **sans ~** without success.

résulter /ʀezylte/ [1] I **résulter de** *v+prep* to be the result of, to result from.
II *v impers* **il résulte de ce que vous venez de dire que** it follows from what you have just said that; **il en résulte que** as a result.

résumé /ʀezyme/ *nm* summary, résumé; **en ~** to sum up; **faire un ~ de qch (à qn)** to give (sb) a rundown of or on sth.

résumer /ʀezyme/ [1] I *vtr* **1** to summarize [*text*]; **2** to sum up [*news*].
II **se résumer** *v refl* (+ *v être*) **1** to sum up; **2** **se ~ à** to come down to.

resurgir /ʀ(ə)syʀʒiʀ/ [3] *vi* to reappear.

résurrection /ʀezyʀɛksjɔ̃/ *nf* **1** resurrection; **2** revival; **3** rebirth.

rétablir /ʀetabliʀ/ [3] I *vtr* **1** to restore; **~ la circulation** to get the traffic moving again; **2** to re-establish [*truth, facts*]; **3** **~ qn dans ses fonctions** to reinstate sb in his/her job.
II **se rétablir** *v refl* (+ *v être*) **1** to recover; **2** [*calm*] to return; [*situation*] to return to normal.

rétablissement /ʀetablismɑ̃/ *nm* **1** restoration; **2** re-establishment; **3** recovery.

retaper○ /ʀ(ə)tape/ [1] *vtr* **1** to do up [*house*]; **2** to put [sb] on his/her feet again.

retard /ʀ(ə)taʀ/ *nm* **1** lateness; **2** delay; **avoir du ~** to be late; **nous sommes en ~ sur l'emploi du temps** we're behind schedule; **prendre du ~** to fall or get behind; **avoir du courrier en ~** to have a backlog of mail; **sans ~** without delay; **3** backwardness; **il a deux ans de ~** (Sch) he's two years behind at school.

retardataire /ʀ(ə)taʀdatɛʀ/ *nmf* latecomer.

retardé, **~e** /ʀətaʀde/ *adj* [*person*] backward.

retardement: **à retardement** /aʀ(ə)taʀdəmɑ̃/ *phr* [*mechanism, device*] delayed-action; **bombe à ~** time-bomb; [*act, get angry*] after the event.

retarder /ʀ(ə)taʀde/ [1] I *vtr* **1** to make [sb] late; **être retardé** [*train*] to be delayed; **2** to hold [sb] up; **3** to put off, to postpone [*departure, operation*]; **4** to put back [*clock*].
II *vi* [*clock*] to be slow.

retenir /ʀət(ə)niʀ, ʀtəniʀ/ [36] I *vtr* **1** to keep [*person*]; **~ qn prisonnier** to hold sb captive; **~ qn à dîner** to ask sb to stay for dinner; **2** to hold [sb] up, to detain [*person*]; **3** to hold [*object, attention*]; to hold back [*hair, dog, crowd*]; to stop [*person*]; **~ sa langue** to hold one's tongue; **~ qn par la manche** to catch hold of sb's sleeve; **votre réclamation a retenu toute notre attention** your complaint is receiving our full attention; **4** to hold back [*tears*]; to hold [*breath*]; to stifle [*scream, yawn*]; to contain, to suppress [*anger*]; **5** to retain [*heat, water, odour*]; **6** to reserve, to book [*table, room*]; to set [*date*]; **7** to deduct [*sum*]; **8** to remember; **toi, je te retiens**○! I won't forget this!; **9** to accept [*argument, plan*]; (Law) to uphold [*charge*]; **10** (in mathematics) **je pose 5 et je retiens 2** I put down 5 and carry 2.
II **se retenir** *v refl* (+ *v être*) **1** to stop oneself; **se ~ à qch** to hang on to sth; **2** **se ~ de**

pleurer to hold back the tears; **3**° to control oneself.

rétention /Retɑ̃sjɔ̃/ *nf* **1** (Med) retention; **2** withholding.

retentir /R(ə)tɑ̃tiR/ [3] *vi* to ring out; to resound.

retentissant, **~e** /R(ə)tɑ̃tisɑ̃, ɑ̃t/ *adj* **1** [*failure*] resounding; [*trial, film*] sensational; **2** [*cry, noise*] ringing; resounding.

retentissement /R(ə)tɑ̃tismɑ̃/ *nm* (gen) effect; (of book, artist) impact.

retenue /Rət(ə)ny/ *nf* **1** restraint; **perdre toute ~** to lose one's inhibitions; **boire sans ~** to drink to excess; **2** deduction; **3** (Sch) detention; **4 tu as oublié la ~ des dizaines** you forgot to carry over from the tens column.

réticence /Retisɑ̃s/ *nf* **1** reluctance; **2 ses ~s en ce qui concerne le passé** his/her reticence about the past.

réticent, **~e** /Retisɑ̃, ɑ̃t/ *adj* **1** hesitant; **2** reluctant.

rétine /Retin/ *nf* retina.

retiré, **~e** /RətiRe/ *adj* **1** [*life*] secluded; **2** [*place*] remote.

retirer /RətiRe/ [1] **I** *vtr* **1** to take off [*garment, piece of jewellery*]; **2** to take out, to remove; **~ ses troupes d'un pays** to withdraw one's troops from a country; **3** to withdraw [*foot, hand*]; **retire ta main** move your hand away; **4** to withdraw [*permission, privilege*]; to take away [*right, property*]; **~ un produit de la vente** to recall a product; **~ une pièce de l'affiche** to close a play; **5** to withdraw [*complaint, offer, support*]; **je retire ce que j'ai dit** I take back what I said; **6** to collect, to pick up [*ticket, luggage*]; to withdraw [*money*]; **7** to get, to derive [*profits*]; **il en retire 10000 francs par an** he gets 10,000 francs a year out of it.
II se retirer *v refl* (+ *v être*) **1** to withdraw, to leave; **un homme retiré de la politique** a man retired from political life; **2 la mer se retire** the tide is going out.

retombées /Rətɔ̃be/ *nf pl* **1 ~ radioactives** radioactive fallout; **2** effects, consequences; **3** (of invention) spin-offs.

retomber /Rətɔ̃be/ [1] *vi* (+ *v être*) **1** to fall again; **~ en enfance** to regress to childhood; **2** [*person, cat, projectile*] to land; [*ball, curtain*] to come down; [*fog*] to set in again; **ça va te ~ sur le nez**° (figurative) it'll come down on your head; **3** [*anger*] to subside; [*interest*] to wane; **4** [*currency, temperature*] to fall; **5 ~ sur qn** [*responsibility*] to fall on sb; **faire ~ la responsabilité sur qn** to pass the buck° to sb.

retordre /R(ə)tɔRdR/ [6] *vtr* **donner du fil à ~ à qn** to give sb a hard time.

rétorquer /RetɔRke/ [1] *vtr* to retort.

retors, **~e** /RətɔR, ɔRs/ *adj* [*person*] crafty; [*argument*] devious.

rétorsion /RetɔRsjɔ̃/ *nf* retaliation.

retouche /R(ə)tuʃ/ *nf* alteration; (of photograph, picture) retouching.

retoucher /R(ə)tuʃe/ [1] *vtr* to make alterations to; to touch up.

retour /R(ə)tuR/ *nm* return; (**billet de**) **~** return ticket (GB), round trip (ticket) (US); **au ~** on the way back; **être de ~** (**à la maison**) to be back (home); **on attend le ~ au calme** people are waiting for things to calm down; **il connaît maintenant le succès et c'est un juste ~ des choses** he's successful now, and deservedly so; **elle s'engage, en ~, à payer la facture** she undertakes for her part to pay the bill; **'sans ~ ni consigne'** 'no deposit or return'; **par ~ du courrier** by return of post (GB), by the next mail (US).
■ **~ d'âge** change of life; **~ en arrière** flashback; **~ de bâton**° backlash.
IDIOMS **être sur le ~**° to be over the hill°.

retournement /R(ə)tuRnəmɑ̃/ *nm* reversal; **un ~ de l'opinion publique** a turn around in public opinion.

retourner /R(ə)tuRne/ [1] **I** *vtr* (+ *v avoir*) **1** to turn [sth] over; to turn [*mattress*]; **2** to turn [sth] inside out; **3** to turn over [*earth*]; to toss [*salad*]; **4** to return [*compliment, criticism*]; **~ la situation** to reverse the situation; **5** to turn [sth] upside down [*room*]; [*news, film*] to shake [*person*]; **6** to send [sth] back, to return.
II *vi* (+ *v être*) to go back, to return.
III se retourner *v refl* (+ *v être*) **1** to turn around; **2** to turn over; **il n'a pas arrêté de se ~** (**dans son lit**) he kept tossing and turning; **3**° to get organized; **4 se ~ contre qn** [*person*] to turn against sb; [*arguments*] to backfire on sb; **5 elle s'est retourné le doigt** she bent back her finger; **6 s'en ~** (**chez soi**) to go back (home).
IV *v impers* **j'aime savoir de quoi il retourne** I like to know what's going on.
IDIOMS **~ qn comme une crêpe**° to make sb change their mind completely.

retracer /RətRase/ [12] *vtr* **1** to redraw [*line*]; **2** to recount [*event*].

rétractable /RetRaktabl/ *adj* retractable.

rétracter /RetRakte/ [1] *vtr*, **se rétracter** *v refl* (+ *v être*) to retract.

retrait /R(ə)tRɛ/ **I** *nm* (gen) withdrawal; (of suitcase, packet) collection; **~ du permis** (**de conduire**) disqualification from driving.
II en retrait *phr* **maison en ~ de** house set back from [*road*]; **se tenir en ~** to stand back; **rester en ~** to stay in the background.

retraite /R(ə)tRɛt/ *nf* **1** retirement; **prendre sa ~** to retire; **2** pension; **3** (Mil) retreat; **4** (place) retreat; (of bandits) hiding place.

retraité, **~e** /RətRete/ *nm,f* retired person.

retrancher /R(ə)tRɑ̃ʃe/ [1] **I** *vtr* **1** to cut out [*word*]; **2** to subtract [*amount*]; to deduct [*costs*].
II se retrancher *v refl* (+ *v être*) (Mil, gen) to take up position; to entrench oneself.

retransmettre /RətRɑ̃smɛtR/ [60] *vtr* **1** to broadcast; **retransmis par satellite** relayed by satellite; **2** to retransmit.

retransmission /RətRɑ̃smisjɔ̃/ *nf* **1** broadcast; **2** relay; **3** retransmission.

rétrécir /ʀetʀesiʀ/ [3] *vi*, **se rétrécir** *v refl* (+ *v être*) **1** to narrow; **2** to shrink.

rétrécissement /ʀetʀesismɑ̃/ *nm* **1** shrinkage; **2** narrowing; **3** contraction.

rétribuer /ʀetʀibɥe/ [1] *vtr* to remunerate.

rétribution /ʀetʀibysjɔ̃/ *nf* remuneration.

rétro /ʀetʀo/ *nm* **1** nostalgic style; **2** retro fashions.

rétroactif, **-ive** /ʀetʀoaktif, iv/ *adj* (Law, gen) retroactive.

rétrograde /ʀetʀogʀad/ *adj* [*person*] reactionary; [*policy, measure*] retrograde.

rétrograder /ʀetʀogʀade/ [1] **I** *vtr* **1** to demote; **2** (Sport) to relegate.

II *vi* (Aut) to change down (GB), to downshift (US).

rétrospectif, **-ive**[1] /ʀetʀɔspɛktif, iv/ *adj* retrospective.

rétrospective[2] /ʀetʀɔspɛktiv/ *nf* (gen) retrospective; (of films) festival.

rétrospectivement /ʀetʀɔspɛktivmɑ̃/ *adv* in retrospect; looking back.

retroussé, **~e** /ʀ(ə)tʀuse/ *adj* [*nose*] turned up; [*lip*] curling.

retrousser /ʀ(ə)tʀuse/ [1] *vtr* to hitch up (GB), to hike up (US) [*skirt*]; to roll up [*sleeves*].

retrouvailles /ʀətʀuvɑj/ *nf pl* **1** reunion; **2** reconciliation.

retrouver /ʀətʀuve/ [1] **I** *vtr* **1** to find [*lost object*]; **2** to find [sth] again [*work, object*]; **3** to regain [*strength, health*]; **4** to remember [*name, tune*]; **5** to be back in [*place*]; **6** to recognize [*person, style*]; **je retrouve sa mère en elle** I can see her mother in her; **7** to join, to meet [*person*].

II se retrouver *v refl* (+ *v être*) **1** to meet (again); **on s'est retrouvé en famille** the family got together; **comme on se retrouve!** fancy seeing you here!; **2 se ~ enceinte** to find oneself pregnant; **se ~ sans argent** to be left penniless; **3 se** or **s'y ~ dans** to find one's way around in [*place, mess*]; to follow, to understand [*explanation*]; **il y a trop de changements, on ne s'y retrouve plus** there are too many changes, we don't know if we're coming or going; **4**○ **s'y ~** to break even; (making profit) to do well; **5** [*quality*] to be found; [*problem*] to occur; **6 se ~ dans qn/qch** to see or recognize oneself in sb/sth.

rétroviseur /ʀetʀovizœʀ/ *nm* **1** rear-view mirror; **2** wing mirror (GB), outside rear-view mirror (US).

réunification /ʀeynifikasjɔ̃/ *nf* reunification.

réunifier /ʀeynifje/ [2] **I** *vtr* to reunify.

II se réunifier *v refl* (+ *v être*) to be reunified.

réunion /ʀeynjɔ̃/ *nf* **1** meeting; **être en ~** [*person*] to be at a meeting; **2** gathering; **3** reunion; **4** (of different talents) combination; (of poems) collection; **5** union.

réunir /ʀeyniʀ/ [3] **I** *vtr* **1** [*conference*] to bring together [*participants*]; [*organizer*] to get [sb] together [*participants*]; **2** to call [sb] together [*delegates*]; to convene [*assembly*]; **3** to have [sb] round (GB) or over [*friends*]; **4** to join [*edges*]; **5** to unite [*provinces*]; **6 ~ les conditions nécessaires** to fulfil[GB] all the necessary conditions; **7** to raise [*funds*]; **8** to assemble [*elements, evidence*]; to gather [sth] together [*documents*]; **9** [*road, canal*] to connect.

II se réunir *v refl* (+ *v être*) to meet; to get together.

réussir /ʀeysiʀ/ [3] **I** *vtr* to achieve [*unification*]; to carry out [sth] successfully [*operation*]; to make a success of [*life*].

II réussir à *v+prep* **1 ~ à faire** to succeed in doing; **~ à un examen** to pass an exam; **2 ~ à qn** [*life, method*] to turn out well for sb; [*rest*] to do sb good.

III *vi* **1** to succeed; **2** [*attempt*] to be successful; **3** [*person*] to do well.

réussite /ʀeysit/ *nf* (gen) success.

revaloir /ʀ(ə)valwaʀ/ [45] *vtr* **je te revaudrai ça** (vengefully) I'll get even with you for that; (in gratitude) I'll return the favour[GB].

revaloriser /ʀ(ə)valɔʀize/ [1] *vtr* **1** to increase [*salary*]; to revalue [*currency*]; **2** to reassert the value of [*traditions*]; **3** to renovate [*area*].

revanche /ʀ(ə)vɑ̃ʃ/ **I** *nf* **1** revenge; **2** (Sport) return match (GB) or game (US).

II en revanche *phr* on the other hand.

rêvasser /ʀɛvase/ [1] *vi* to daydream.

rêve /ʀɛv/ *nm* **1** dreaming; **2** dream; **fais de beaux ~s!** sweet dreams!; **3 une maison de ~** a dream house; **3 c'est le ~** this is just perfect.

rêvé, **~e** /ʀeve/ *adj* ideal, perfect.

revêche /ʀəvɛʃ/ *adj* [*manner, tone*] sour; [*person*] crabby.

réveil /ʀevɛj/ *nm* **1** waking (up); **2** (after anaesthetic) **j'ai eu des nausées au ~** I felt nauseous when I regained consciousness; **3** (of movement) resurgence; (of pain) return; (of volcano) return to activity; **4** (Mil) reveille; **5** alarm clock.

réveille-matin /ʀevɛjmatɛ̃/ *nm inv* alarm clock.

réveiller /ʀeveje/ [1] **I** *vtr* **1** to wake [sb] up, to wake; **2** to revive [*person*]; to awaken [*feeling*]; to arouse [*curiosity*]; to stir up [*memory*].

II se réveiller *v refl* (+ *v être*) **1** to wake up; to awaken; **2** to regain consciousness; **3** [*volcano*] to become active again; **4** [*pain, appetite*] to come back; [*memory*] to be reawakened.

réveillon /ʀevɛjɔ̃/ *nm* **~ du Nouvel An** New Year's Eve party.

réveillonner /ʀevɛjɔne/ [1] *vi* to celebrate Christmas Eve; to see the New Year in.

révélateur, **-trice** /ʀevelatœʀ, tʀis/ **I** *adj* [*detail, fact*] revealing, telling.

II *nm* (in photography) developer.

révélation /ʀevelasjɔ̃/ *nf* revelation.

révéler /ʀevele/ [14] **I** *vtr* **1** to reveal; to give away [*secret*]; **2** to show; **3** to discover [*artist*]; **4** (in photography) to develop.

II se révéler *v refl* (+ *v être*) **se ~ faux** to turn out to be wrong.

revenant, **~e** /ʀəv(ə)nɑ̃, ɑ̃t/ *nm,f* ghost.

revendeur, **-euse** /ʀ(ə)vɑ̃dœʀ, øz/ *nm,f* **1**

stockist; **2 un ~ de drogue** a drug dealer; **3** seller (of stolen goods).

revendication /R(ə)vɑ̃dikasjɔ̃/ *nf* (of workers) demand; (of country) claim.

revendiquer /R(ə)vɑ̃dike/ [1] *vtr* **1** to demand [*pay rise*]; to claim [*territory*]; **2** to claim responsibility for [*attack*]; **3** to proclaim [*origins*].

revendre /R(ə)vɑ̃dR/ [6] *vtr* **1** to sell [sth] retail, to retail; **2** to resell [*car, house*]; to sell on [*stolen object*]; **avoir de l'énergie à ~** to have energy to spare.

revenir /Rəvnir, Rvənir/ [36] (+ *v être*) **I** *vi* **1** to come back; to come again; **2** [*person, animal, vehicle*] to come back, to return; **~ de loin** (figurative) to have had a close shave; **mon chèque m'est revenu** my cheque (GB) or check (US) was returned; **3 ~ à** to return to, to come back to [*method, story*]; **4** [*appetite, memory*] to come back; [*sun*] to come out again; [*season*] to return; [*idea, theme*] to recur; **~ à la mémoire** or **l'esprit de qn** to come back to sb; **ça me revient!** now I remember!; **5 ~ à 100 francs** to come to 100 francs; **ça revient cher** it works out expensive; **6 ~ sur** to go back over [*question, past*]; to go back on [*decision, promise*]; to retract [*confession*]; **7 ~ de** to get over [*illness, surprise*]; to lose [*illusion*]; **la vie à la campagne, j'en suis revenu** as for life in the country, I've seen it for what it is; **je n'en reviens pas**○ **des progrès que tu as faits** I'm amazed at the progress you've made; **8 ~ aux oreilles de qn** [*remark*] to reach sb's ears; **9 ~ à qn** [*property*] to go to sb; [*honour*] to fall to sb; **ça leur revient de droit** it's theirs by right; **la décision revient au rédacteur** it is the editor's decision; **10** (Culin) **faire ~** to brown.

II *v impers* **c'est à vous qu'il revient de trancher** it is for you to decide.

IDIOMS **il a une tête qui ne me revient pas** I don't like the look of him.

revenu /Rəv(ə)ny, Rvəny/ *nm* income; (of state) revenue.

■ **~ minimum d'insertion, RMI** *minimum benefit paid to those with no other source of income.*

rêver /Reve/ [1] **I** *vtr* **1** to dream; **2** to dream of [*success, revenge*].

II *vi* to dream.

réverbération /RevɛRbeRasjɔ̃/ *nf* **1** glare; **2** reflection; **3** reverberation.

réverbère /RevɛRbɛR/ *nm* street lamp or light.

réverbérer /RevɛRbeRe/ [14] **I** *vtr* to reflect.

II se réverbérer *v refl* (+ *v être*) [*light, heat*] to be reflected; [*sound*] to reverberate.

révérence /RevеRɑ̃s/ *nf* **1** curtsey; bow; **2** reverence.

IDIOMS **tirer sa ~**○ to take one's leave.

révérend, ~e /RevеRɑ̃, ɑ̃d/ *nm,f* **1** Father/Mother Superior; **2** reverend.

révérer /RevеRe/ [14] *vtr* to revere.

rêverie /RɛvRi/ *nf* **1** daydreaming; **2** daydream.

revers /R(ə)vɛR/ *nm inv* **1** (of hand) back; (of cloth) wrong side; (of coin) reverse; **le ~ de la médaille** (figurative) the downside○; **2** (on jacket) lapel; (of trousers) turn-up (GB), cuff (US); **3** (in tennis) backhand (stroke); **4** setback.

réversible /RevɛRsibl/ *adj* (gen) reversible.

revêtement /R(ə)vɛtmɑ̃/ *nm* **1** (of road) surface; **2** coating; covering.

revêtir /R(ə)vetiR/ [33] **I** *vtr* **1** to assume [*gravity, solemnity*]; to have [*disadvantage*]; to take on [*significance*]; **~ la forme de** to take the form of; **2** to put on [*garment*]; **3 ~ qch de** to cover sth with [*carpet, tiles*].

II se revêtir *v refl* (+ *v être*) **se ~ de** to put on [*cloak*]; to become covered with [*snow*].

rêveur, -euse /Rɛvœr, øz/ **I** *adj* dreamy.

II *nm,f* dreamer.

revient /R(ə)vjɛ̃/ *nm* **prix de ~** cost price.

revigorer /R(ə)vigɔRe/ [1] *vtr* to revive.

revirement /R(ə)viRmɑ̃/ *nm* turnaround.

réviser /Revize/ [1] *vtr* **1** to revise [*position, prices*]; to review [*constitution*]; **2** to overhaul [*car, boiler*]; to revise [*manuscript*]; **3** (Sch) to revise (GB), to review (US).

révision /Revizjɔ̃/ *nm* **1** revision; review; **2** (of car) service; (of manuscript) revision; (of accounts) audit; **3** (Sch) revision (GB), review (US).

revitaliser /R(ə)vitalize/ [1] *vtr* to revitalize.

revivre /R(ə)vivR/ [63] **I** *vtr* **1** to go over, to relive [*event, past*]; **faire ~ qch à qn** to bring back memories of sth to sb; **2** to live through [sth] again [*war*].

II *vi* **1** to come alive again; **2** to be able to breathe again; **3 faire ~** to revive [*tradition*].

revoici○ /R(ə)vwasi/ *prep* **~ Marianne!** here's Marianne again!

revoilà /R(ə)vwala/ = **revoici**.

revoir[1] /R(ə)vwaR/ [46] *vtr* **1** to see [sb/sth] again; **2** to go over [*exercise, lesson*]; to review [*method*]; to check through [*accounts*].

revoir[2]: **au revoir** /ɔR(ə)vwaR/ *phr* goodbye.

révoltant, ~e /Revɔltɑ̃, ɑ̃t/ *adj* appalling.

révolte /Revɔlt/ *nf* **1** revolt; **2** rebellion.

révolter /Revɔlte/ [1] **I** *vtr* to appal[GB].

II se révolter *v refl* (+ *v être*) **1** to rebel; **2** to be appalled.

révolu, ~e /Revɔly/ *adj* **1 ce temps est ~** those days are over or past; **2 avoir 12 ans ~s** to be over 12 years of age.

révolution /Revɔlysjɔ̃/ *nf* **1** revolution; **2** turmoil; **3** (of planet) revolution.

révolutionnaire /RevɔlysjɔnɛR/ *adj, nmf* revolutionary.

révolutionner /Revɔlysjɔne/ [1] *vtr* to revolutionize.

revolver /RevɔlvɛR/ *nm* **1** revolver; **2** handgun; **coup de ~** gunshot.

révoquer /Revɔke/ [1] *vtr* **1** to revoke [*will*]; **2** to dismiss [*person*].

revue /R(ə)vy/ *nf* **1** (gen) magazine; (academic) journal; **2** (Mil) parade; **passer en ~** to review [*troops*]; to inspect [*equipment*]; **3** revue; **4** examination; **passer qch en ~** to go over sth.

■ **~ de presse** review of the papers.

révulser /Revylse/ [1] **I** *vtr* to appal[GB].

II **se révulser** *v refl* (+ *v être*) [*eyes*] to roll (upward(s)); [*face*] to contort.

révulsion /ʀevylsjɔ̃/ *nf* (Med, gen) revulsion.

rez-de-chaussée /ʀɛdʃose/ *nm inv* ground floor (GB), first floor (US).

RF (*written abbr* = **République française**) French Republic.

rhapsodie /ʀapsɔdi/ *nf* rhapsody.

rhésus /ʀezys/ *nm inv* **1 facteur ~** rhesus factor; **2** rhesus monkey.

rhétorique /ʀetɔʀik/ I *adj* rhetorical.
II *nf* rhetoric.

Rhin /ʀɛ̃/ *pr nm* **le ~** the Rhine.

rhinocéros /ʀinɔseʀɔs/ *nm inv* rhinoceros.

rhubarbe /ʀybaʀb/ *nf* rhubarb.

rhum /ʀɔm/ *nm* rum.

rhumatisme /ʀymatism/ *nm* rheumatism.

rhume /ʀym/ *nm* cold; **~ des foins** hay fever.

ribambelle○ /ʀibɑ̃bɛl/ *nf* (of children) flock; (of friends) host; (of names) whole string.

ricaner /ʀikane/ [1] *vi* **1** to snigger; **2** to giggle.

riche /ʀiʃ/ I *adj* (gen) rich; [*person*] rich, wealthy; [*library*] well-stocked; [*decor*] elaborate; **une ~ idée** an excellent idea.
II *nmf* rich man/woman; **les ~s** the rich.

richesse /ʀiʃɛs/ I *nf* **1** wealth; **c'est toute notre ~** it's all we have; **2** (of jewellery) magnificence; (of garment) richness; **3** (of foodstuff) richness; **4** (of fauna, vocabulary) richness; (of documentation) wealth.
II **richesses** *nf pl* wealth; **~s naturelles** natural resources.

ricin /ʀisɛ̃/ *nf* **huile de ~** castor oil.

ricochet /ʀikɔʃɛ/ *nm* (of bullet) ricochet; (of stone) bounce; **faire des ~s** to skim stones.

rictus /ʀiktys/ *nm inv* (fixed) grin, rictus.

ride /ʀid/ *nf* (on face, fruit) wrinkle; (on lake) ripple.

rideau, *pl* **~x** /ʀido/ *nm* **1** curtain; **2** (of shop) roller shutter; **3** (of flames) wall.
■ **~ de fumée** blanket of smoke.

rider /ʀide/ [1] I *vtr* **1** to wrinkle [*face, skin*]; **2** to ripple [*surface, lake*].
II **se rider** *v refl* (+ *v être*) **1** [*skin*] to wrinkle; **2** [*lake*] to ripple.

ridicule /ʀidikyl/ I *adj* **1** ridiculous; **2** [*wage*] ridiculously low, pathetic.
II *nm* **1** ridicule; **2** (of situation) absurdity.

ridiculiser /ʀidikylize/ [1] I *vtr* to ridicule; to wipe the floor with [*competitor*].
II **se ridiculiser** *v refl* (+ *v être*) [*person*] to make a fool of oneself.

ridule /ʀidyl/ *nf* fine wrinkle.

rien[1] /ʀjɛ̃/ I *pron* **1** nothing; **il n'y a plus ~** there's nothing left; **~ n'y fait!** nothing's any good!; **~ d'autre** nothing else; **'pourquoi?'—'pour ~'** 'why?'—'no reason'; **'merci'—'de ~'** 'thank you'—'you're welcome' or 'not at all'; **en moins de ~** in no time at all; **ça ou ~, c'est pareil** it makes no odds; **c'est trois fois ~**○ it's next to nothing; **2 ~ que la bouteille pèse deux kilos** the bottle alone weighs two kilos; **elle voudrait un bureau ~ qu'à elle**○ she would like an office all to herself; **~ que ça**○**?** is that all?; **ils habitent un château, ~ que ça!** (ironic) they live in a castle, no less! or if you please!; **3** anything; **sans que j'en sache ~** without my knowing anything about it; **4** (Sport, gen) nil; (in tennis) love.
II **de rien (du tout)** *phr* **un petit bleu de ~ (du tout)** a tiny bruise.
III **un rien**○ *phr* a (tiny) bit.
IV **en rien** *phr* at all, in any way.
IDIOMS **~ à faire!** it's no good or use!; **ce n'est pas ~!** (exploit) it's quite something!; (task) it's no joke!; (sum of money) it's not exactly peanuts○!

rien[2] /ʀjɛ̃/ *nm* **un ~ le fâche** the slightest thing annoys him; **se disputer pour un ~** to quarrel over nothing; **les petits ~s qui rendent la vie agréable** the little things which make life pleasant; **un/une ~ du tout** a worthless person.

rieur, **rieuse** /ʀijœʀ, øz/ *adj* [*person, tone*] cheerful; [*face, eyes*] laughing.

rigide /ʀiʒid/ *adj* **1** rigid; **2** stiff.

rigidité /ʀiʒidite/ *nf* rigidity.

rigolade○ /ʀigɔlad/ *nf* **1 quelle ~!** what a laugh○!; **2** joke; **3 réparer ça, c'est de la ~!** repairing this is a piece of cake○.

rigole /ʀigɔl/ *nf* **1** channel; **2** rivulet.

rigoler○ /ʀigɔle/ [1] *vi* **1** to laugh; **2** to have fun; **3** to joke, to kid○.

rigolo○, **-ote** /ʀigɔlo, ɔt/ I *adj* **1** funny; **2** odd.
II *nm,f* **1** joker; **2 c'est un petit ~** he's quite a little comedian.

rigoriste /ʀigɔʀist/ *adj* [*attitude*] unbending, rigoristic; [*morals*] strict.

rigoureux, **-euse** /ʀiguʀø, øz/ *adj* **1** [*discipline, person*] strict; **2** [*climate, working conditions*] harsh, severe; **3** [*research, demonstration*] meticulous; [*analysis*] rigorous.

rigueur /ʀigœʀ/ I *nf* **1** strictness; **2** harshness; **3** rigour^GB; **4** (Econ) austerity.
II **de rigueur** *phr* obligatory.
III **à la rigueur** *phr* **à la ~ je peux te prêter 100 francs** at a pinch (GB) or in a pinch (US) I can lend you 100 francs.
IDIOMS **tenir ~ à qn de qch** to bear sb a grudge for sth.

rime /ʀim/ *nf* rhyme.

rimer /ʀime/ [1] *vi* **1** to rhyme; **2 cela ne rime à rien** it makes no sense.

rimmel® /ʀimɛl/ *nm* mascara.

rinçage /ʀɛ̃saʒ/ *nm* **1** rinsing; **2** rinse.

rince-doigts /ʀɛ̃sdwa/ *nm inv* **1** finger bowl; **2** finger wipe.

rincer /ʀɛ̃se/ [12] I *vtr* **1** to rinse; **2** to rinse [sth] out.
II **se rincer** *v refl* (+ *v être*) **se ~ les mains/les cheveux** to rinse one's hands/hair.

ring /ʀiŋ/ *nm* (boxing) ring.

ringard○, **~e** /ʀɛ̃gaʀ, aʀd/ *adj* out of date.

riper /ʀipe/ [1] *vi* [*foot*] to slip; [*bicycle*] to skid.

riposte /ʀipɔst/ *nf* **1** reply, riposte; **2** response; **3** (Sport) (in fencing) riposte; (in boxing) counter.

riposter /ʀipɔste/ [1] **I** *vtr* to retort.
II *vi* **1** to retort; **~ à qn/qch par** to counter sb/sth with; **2** to respond; **3** (Mil) to return fire, to shoot back; **4** (in sport) to ripost.

ripou○, *pl* **~x** /ʀipu/ *adj* crooked○, bent○.

riquiqui○ /ʀikiki/ *adj inv* [*room, car*] poky○; [*portion*] measly○.

rire[1] /ʀiʀ/ [68] **I** *vi* **1** to laugh; **tu nous feras toujours ~!** you're a real scream○!; **2** to have fun; **il faut bien ~ un peu** you need a bit of fun now and again; **fini de ~** the fun's over; **c'était pour ~** it was a joke; **sans ~**○ seriously; **laisse-moi ~**○, **ne me fais pas ~**○ don't make me laugh; **3 ~ de qn/qch** to laugh at sb/sth.
II se rire *v refl* (+ *v être*) **se ~ de qn** (formal) to laugh at sb; **se ~ des difficultés** (formal) to make light of difficulties.
IDIOMS **rira bien qui rira le dernier** (Proverb) he who laughs last laughs longest; **être mort de ~**○ to be doubled up (with laughter).

rire[2] /ʀiʀ/ *nm* laughter; **un ~** a laugh; **il a eu un petit ~** he chuckled.
■ **~s préenregistrés** canned laughter.

ris /ʀi/ *nm inv* **1** (Culin) **~ (de veau)** calf's sweetbread; **2** (Naut) reef.

risée /ʀize/ *nf* **être la ~ de** to be the laughing stock of.

risette○ /ʀizɛt/ *nf* smile.

risible /ʀizibl/ *adj* ridiculous, laughable.

risque /ʀisk/ *nm* risk; **c'est sans ~** it's safe; **à ~s** [*group, loan*] high-risk.
■ **les ~s du métier** occupational hazards.

risqué, **~e** /ʀiske/ *adj* **1** risky; [*investment*] high-risk; **2** [*joke*] risqué; [*hypothesis*] daring.

risquer /ʀiske/ [1] **I** *vtr* **1** to face [*accusation, condemnation*]; **2** to risk [*death, criticism*]; **vas-y, tu ne risques rien** go ahead, you're safe; (figurative) go ahead, you've got nothing to lose; **~ gros** to take a major risk; **3** to risk [*life, reputation, job*]; **4** to venture [*look, question*]; to attempt [*operation*]; **~ un œil** to venture a glance; **~ le coup**○ to risk it.
II risquer de *v+prep* **1 tu risques de te brûler** you might burn yourself; **2 il ne veut pas ~ de perdre son travail** he doesn't want to risk losing his job.
III se risquer *v refl* (+ *v être*) **1** to venture; **je ne m'y risquerais pas!** I wouldn't risk it; **2 se ~ à dire** to dare to say.
IV *v impers* **il risque de pleuvoir** it might rain; **il risque d'y avoir du monde** there may well be a lot of people there.
IDIOMS **~ le tout pour le tout** to stake or risk one's all.

rissoler /ʀisɔle/ [1] *vtr, vi* (Culin) to brown.

ristourne /ʀistuʀn/ *nf* discount, rebate.

rite /ʀit/ *nm* rite.

rituel, **-elle** /ʀitɥɛl/ *adj, nm* ritual.

rivage /ʀivaʒ/ *nm* shore.

rival, **~e**, *mpl* **-aux** /ʀival, o/ *adj, nm,f* rival.

rivaliser /ʀivalize/ [1] *vi* to compete with; **~ avec qch** to rival sth.

rivalité /ʀivalite/ *nf* rivalry.

rive /ʀiv/ *nf* **1** (of river) bank; **2** (of sea, lake) shore.

river /ʀive/ [1] *vtr* to clinch [*nail, rivet*]; **être rivé à qch** (figurative) to be tied to [*one's work*]; **avoir les yeux rivés sur** to have one's eyes riveted on.

riverain, **~e** /ʀivʀɛ̃, ɛn/ *nm,f* (of street) resident; (beside river) riverside resident.

rivet /ʀivɛ/ *nm* rivet.

rivière /ʀivjɛʀ/ *nf* river.
■ **~ de diamants** diamond necklace.

rixe /ʀiks/ *nf* brawl.

riz /ʀi/ *nm* rice.

rizière /ʀizjɛʀ/ *nf* paddy field.

RMI /ɛʀɛmi/ *nm* (*abbr* = **revenu minimum d'insertion**) *minimum benefit paid to those with no other source of income.*

RN /ɛʀɛn/ *nf* (*abbr* = **route nationale**) ≈ A road (GB), highway (US).

robe /ʀɔb/ *nf* **1** (gen) dress; **2** (of lawyer) gown; **3** (of horse) coat; (of wine) colour[GB].
■ **~ de chambre** dressing gown, robe (US).

robinet /ʀɔbinɛ/ *nm* (for water) tap (GB), faucet (US); (for gas) tap (GB), valve (US).

robot /ʀɔbo/ *nm* robot; **~ ménager** food processor.

robotique /ʀɔbɔtik/ *nf* robotics.

robotiser /ʀɔbɔtize/ [1] *vtr* to automate.

robuste /ʀɔbyst/ *adj* robust, sturdy; [*appetite*] healthy; [*faith*] strong.

robustesse /ʀɔbystɛs/ *nf* **1** robustness, sturdiness; **2** soundness.

roc /ʀɔk/ *nm* rock.

rocaille /ʀɔkaj/ *nf* **1** loose stones; **2** rock garden.

roche /ʀɔʃ/ *nf* rock.

rocher /ʀɔʃe/ *nm* rock.

rocheux, **-euse** /ʀɔʃø, øz/ *adj* rocky.

rock /ʀɔk/ *nm* **1** rock (music); **2** jive.

rockeur, **-euse** /ʀɔkœʀ, øz/ *nm,f* **1** rock musician; **2** rock fan.

rococo /ʀɔkoko/ *adj inv* [*art, style*] rococo.

rodage /ʀɔdaʒ/ *nm* (of vehicle, engine) running in (GB), breaking in (US).

rodéo /ʀɔdeo/ *nm* rodeo.

roder /ʀɔde/ [1] *vtr* **1** to run in (GB), to break in (US) [*engine*]; **2** to polish up [*show*]; **être (bien) rodé** [*department*] to be running smoothly.

rôder /ʀode/ [1] *vi* to prowl; **~ autour de qn** to hang around sb.

rôdeur, **-euse** /ʀodœʀ, øz/ *nm,f* prowler.

rogne○ /ʀɔɲ/ *nf* **se mettre en ~** to get mad○.

rogner /ʀɔɲe/ [1] *vtr* **1** to trim [*angle*]; to clip [*nails*]; **2 ~ sur** to cut down on [*budget*].

rognon /ʀɔɲɔ̃/ *nm* (Culin) kidney.

roi /ʀwa/ *nm* king.
■ **les ~s mages** the (three) wise men.
IDIOMS **tirer les Rois** to eat Twelfth Night cake.

roitelet /ʀwatlɛ/ *nm* **1** goldcrest; **2** kinglet.
rôle /ʀol/ *nm* **1** (for actor) part, role; **premier ~** lead, leading role; **2** (gen) role; (of heart, part of body) function, role; **à tour de ~** in turn.
IDIOMS **avoir le beau ~**○ to have the easy job.
romain, **~e**[1] /ʀɔmɛ̃, ɛn/ *adj* **1** Roman; **2 l'Église ~e** the Roman Catholic Church; **3 caractères ~s** Roman typeface.
romaine[2] /ʀɔmɛn/ *nf* cos lettuce.
roman, **~e** /ʀɔmɑ̃, an/ **I** *adj* **1** [*church, style*] Romanesque; (in England) Norman; **2** [*language*] Romance.
II *nm* **1** novel; **~ courtois** courtly romance; **2** (style) **le ~** the Romanesque.
■ **~ policier** detective story.
romance /ʀɔmɑ̃s/ *nf* **1** love song; **2** romance.
romancer /ʀɔmɑ̃se/ [12] *vtr* **1** to romanticize; **2** to fictionalize.
romanche /ʀɔmɑ̃ʃ/ *nm, adj* Romans(c)h.
romancier, **-ière** /ʀɔmɑ̃sje, ɛʀ/ *nm,f* novelist.
romand, **~e** /ʀɔmɑ̃, ɑ̃d/ *adj* [*Swiss person*] French-speaking.
romanesque /ʀɔmanɛsk/ **I** *adj* **1** [*person*] romantic; **2** [*narrative, story*] fictional.
II *nm* **1 le ~** fiction; **2 le ~ d'une situation** the fantastical aspect of a situation.
roman-feuilleton, *pl* **romans-feuilletons** /ʀɔmɑ̃fœjtɔ̃/ *nm* serial.
roman-fleuve, *pl* **romans-fleuves** /ʀɔmɑ̃ flœv/ *nm* roman-fleuve, saga.
roman-photo, *pl* **romans-photos** /ʀɔmɑ̃ foto/ *nm* photo-story.
romantique /ʀɔmɑ̃tik/ *adj, nmf* romantic.
romantisme /ʀɔmɑ̃tism/ *nm* romanticism.
romarin /ʀɔmaʀɛ̃/ *nm* rosemary.
rompre /ʀɔ̃pʀ/ [53] **I** *vtr* (gen) to break, to break off [*relationship*]; to upset [*equilibrium*]; to disrupt [*harmony*]; to end [*isolation*].
II *vi* **~ avec** to break with [*habit, tradition*]; to make a break from [*past*]; to break away from [*background*]; to break up with [*fiancé*].
III se rompre *v refl* (+ *v être*) to break.
rompu, **~e** /ʀɔ̃py/ **I** *pp* ▸ **rompre**.
II *pp adj* **~ (de fatigue)** worn-out.
romsteck /ʀɔmstɛk/ *nm* rump steak.
ronce /ʀɔ̃s/ *nf* bramble.
ronchon○, **-onne** /ʀɔ̃ʃɔ̃, ɔn/ *adj* grumpy○.
ronchonner○ /ʀɔ̃ʃɔne/ [1] *vi* to grumble.
rond, **~e**[1] /ʀɔ̃, ʀɔ̃d/ **I** *adj* **1** [*object, hole*] round; **2** [*writing*] rounded; [*face*] round; [*person*] plump; **3** [*number*] round; **4**○ drunk.
II *nm* circle; **faire des ~s dans l'eau** to make ripples in the water.
■ **~ de serviette** napkin ring.
IDIOMS **ouvrir des yeux ~s** to be wide-eyed with astonishment.
ronde[2] /ʀɔ̃d/ **I** *adj f* ▸ **rond I**.
II *nf* **1** round dance; **entrer dans la ~** to join the dance; **2** (of policeman) patrol; (of soldiers) watch; **3** (Mus) semibreve (GB), whole note (US).
III à la ronde *phr* around.
rondelle /ʀɔ̃dɛl/ *nf* **1** slice; **2** (Tech) washer.
rondement /ʀɔ̃dmɑ̃/ *adv* promptly.
rondeur /ʀɔ̃dœʀ/ *nf* **1** roundness; **2** curve.
rondin /ʀɔ̃dɛ̃/ *nm* log.
rond-point, *pl* **ronds-points** /ʀɔ̃pwɛ̃/ *nm* roundabout (GB), traffic circle (US).
ronflant, **~e** /ʀɔ̃flɑ̃, ɑ̃t/ *adj* **1** [*stove*] roaring; **2** [*style*] high-flown.
ronflement /ʀɔ̃fləmɑ̃/ *nm* **1** snore; **2** (of engine) purr.
ronfler /ʀɔ̃fle/ [1] *vi* **1** [*sleeper*] to snore; [*engine*] to purr; **2**○ to be fast asleep.
ronger /ʀɔ̃ʒe/ [13] **I** *vtr* **1** [*mouse, dog*] to gnaw; [*worms*] to eat into; [*caterpillar*] to eat away; **2** [*acid, rust*] to erode; **3** [*disease*] to wear down.
II se ronger *v refl* (+ *v être*) **se ~ les ongles** to bite one's nails.
IDIOMS **se ~ les sangs**○ to worry oneself sick.
rongeur /ʀɔ̃ʒœʀ/ *nm* rodent.
ronronnement /ʀɔ̃ʀɔnmɑ̃/ *nm* (of cat, engine) purring.
ronronner /ʀɔ̃ʀɔne/ [1] *vi* to purr.
roquet /ʀɔkɛ/ *nm* **1** yappy little dog; **2**○ bad-tempered little runt○.
roquette /ʀɔkɛt/ *nf* (Mil) rocket.
rosace /ʀozas/ *nf* **1** rosette; **2** rose window; **3** (decorative motif) rose.
rosaire /ʀozɛʀ/ *nm* rosary.
rosbif /ʀɔsbif/ *nm* joint of beef (GB), roast of beef (US); (meal) roast beef.
rose[1] /ʀoz/ *adj* (gen) pink; [*cheeks*] rosy.
IDIOMS **la vie n'est pas ~** life isn't a bed of roses.
rose[2] /ʀoz/ *nf* (Bot) rose.
■ **~ des sables** gypsum flower; **~ trémière** hollyhock.
IDIOMS **envoyer qn sur les ~s**○ to send sb packing○; **découvrir le pot aux ~s**○ to find out what is going on.
rosé /ʀoze/ *nm* rosé.
roseau, *pl* **~x** /ʀozo/ *nm* (Bot) reed.
rosée /ʀoze/ *nf* dew.
roseraie /ʀozʀɛ/ *nf* rose garden.
rosier /ʀozje/ *nm* (Bot) rosebush, rose.
rosse /ʀɔs/ **I**○ *adj* nasty, mean.
II *nf* **1** nag○; **2** meanie○, nasty person.
rosser○ /ʀɔse/ [1] *vtr* to give [sb] a good thrashing [*person*]; to beat [*animal*].
rossignol /ʀɔsiɲɔl/ *nm* nightingale.
rot○ /ʀo/ *nm* burp○; **faire un ~** to burp○.
rotation /ʀɔtasjɔ̃/ *nf* **1** (movement) rotation; **2** (Mil) turnaround; **3** (of crops, staff, shift) rotation.
roter○ /ʀɔte/ [1] *vtr* to burp○, to belch.
rôti /ʀɔti/ *nm* **1** joint; **2** roast.
rotin /ʀɔtɛ̃/ *nm* rattan.
rôtir /ʀɔtiʀ/ [3] *vtr* to roast [*meat*]; to toast, to grill [*bread*].
rôtissoire /ʀɔtiswaʀ/ *nf* rotisserie, roasting spit.
rotonde /ʀɔtɔ̃d/ *nf* (building) rotunda.
rotule /ʀɔtyl/ *nf* (Anat) kneecap.

IDIOMS **être sur les ~s**○ to be on one's last legs.

roturier, **-ière** /ʀɔtyʀje, ɛʀ/ *nm,f* commoner.

rouage /ʀwaʒ/ *nm* **1** (of machine) (cog)wheel; **les ~s** the parts or works; **2** (of administration) machinery; **les ~s bureaucratiques** the wheels of bureaucracy.

roucouler /ʀukule/ [1] *vi* **1** [*bird*] to coo; **2** [*lovers*] to bill and coo.

roue /ʀu/ *nf* wheel; **~ dentée** cogwheel.
■ **~ motrice** driving wheel; **~ de secours** spare wheel or tyre (GB), spare tire (US).
IDIOMS **être la cinquième ~ du carrosse** to feel unwanted; **pousser qn à la ~** to be behind sb; **faire la ~** [*peacock*] to spread its tail, to display; [*person*] to strut around; (in gymnastics) to do a cartwheel.

rouer /ʀwe/ [1] *vtr* **~ qn de coups** to beat sb up.

rouet /ʀwɛ/ *nm* spinning wheel.

rouge /ʀuʒ/ **I** *adj* **1** (gen) red; [*person, face*] flushed; **2** [*beard, hair, fur*] ginger; **3** red-hot.
II *nmf* (communist) Red.
III *nm* **1** red; **le ~ lui monta au visage** he/she went red in the face; **2 ~ à joues** blusher, rouge; **~ à lèvres** lipstick; **3 le feu est au ~** the (traffic) lights are red; **passer au ~** to jump the lights (GB) or a red light; **4**○ red (wine); **gros ~**○ cheap red wine; **un coup de ~**○ a glass of red wine.
IDIOMS **être ~ comme une tomate** or **une écrevisse** (from embarrassment) to be as red as a beetroot (GB) or a beet (US); (from running) to be red in the face.

rougeaud, **~e** /ʀuʒo, od/ *adj* [*person*] ruddy-faced; [*face, complexion*] ruddy.

rouge-gorge, *pl* **rouges-gorges** /ʀuʒgɔʀʒ/ *nm* robin (redbreast).

rougeoiement /ʀuʒwamɑ̃/ *nm* red glow.

rougeole /ʀuʒɔl/ *nf* measles.

rougeoyer /ʀuʒwaje/ [23] *vi* [*sun*] to glow fiery red; [*fire*] to glow red.

rouget /ʀuʒɛ/ *nm* red mullet, goatfish (US).

rougeur /ʀuʒœʀ/ *nf* **1** redness; **2** redness; flushing; **3** red blotch.

rougir /ʀuʒiʀ/ [3] **I** *vtr* to redden.
II *vi* **1** to blush; to flush; to go red; **ne ~ de rien** to have no shame; **2** [*fruit, sky*] to turn red; **3** [*metal*] to become red hot.

rouille /ʀuj/ **I** *adj inv* red-brown.
II *nf* rust.

rouiller /ʀuje/ [1] **I** *vtr* to rust.
II *vi* to rust, to go rusty.
III se rouiller *v refl* (+ *v être*) to get rusty.

roulade /ʀulad/ *nf* (Sport) roll.

roulé /ʀule/ *nm* (Culin) roll.

rouleau, *pl* **~x** /ʀulo/ *nm* **1** roll; **2** breaker, roller; **3** (Tech) roller; **4** roller, curler.
■ **~ compresseur** steamroller; **~ à pâtisserie** rolling pin.

roulement /ʀulmɑ̃/ *nm* **1** (of thunder) rumble; (of drum) roll; **2** (of capital) circulation; **3** rotation; **travailler par ~** to work (in) shifts; **4** (Tech) **~ à billes** ball bearing.

rouler /ʀule/ [1] **I** *vtr* **1** to roll [*barrel, tyre*]; to wheel [*cart*]; **2** to roll up [*carpet, sleeve, paper*]; to roll [*cigarette*]; **3 ~ les épaules** to roll one's shoulders; **4**○ **~ qn** to cheat sb.
II *vi* **1** [*ball, person*] to roll; **2** [*vehicle*] to go; **~ à gauche** to drive on the left; **les bus ne roulent pas le dimanche** the buses don't run on Sundays.
III se rouler *v refl* (+ *v être*) **se ~ dans** to roll in [*grass, mud*].

roulette /ʀulɛt/ *nf* **1** caster; **2** roulette; **3** (dentist's) drill.
IDIOMS **marcher comme sur des ~s**○ to go smoothly or like a dream.

roulis /ʀuli/ *nm* (of boat) rolling; (of car, train) swaying.

roulotte /ʀulɔt/ *nf* (horse-drawn) caravan (GB), trailer (US).

Roumanie /ʀumani/ *pr nf* Romania.

roupie /ʀupi/ *nf* rupee.

roupiller○ /ʀupije/ [1] *vtr* to sleep.

rouquin○, **~e** /ʀukɛ̃, in/ *nm,f* redhead.

rouspéter○ /ʀuspete/ [14] *vi* to grumble.

rousse /ʀus/ *adj f* ▶ **roux**.

rousseur /ʀusœʀ/ *nf* (of hair, foliage) redness; (of shade) russet colour[GB].

roussi /ʀusi/ *nm* **ça sent le ~** there's a smell of burning; there's trouble brewing.

roussir /ʀusiʀ/ [3] **I** *vtr* to turn [sth] brown.
II *vi* **1** to go brown; **2** (Culin) **faire ~** to brown.

routage /ʀutaʒ/ *nm* sorting and mailing.

route /ʀut/ *nf* **1** road, highway (US); **tenir la ~** [*car*] to hold the road; (figurative)○ [*argument*] to hold water; [*equipment*] to be well-made; **2** road; **il y a six heures de ~** it's a six-hour drive; **faire de la ~**○ to do a lot of mileage; **3** route; **~s maritimes** sea routes; **4** way; **la ~ sera longue** it will be a long journey; **j'ai changé d'avis en cours de ~** I changed my mind along the way; **être en ~** [*person*] to be on one's way; [*dish*] to be cooking; **être en ~ pour** to be en route to; **faire fausse ~** to go off course; to be mistaken; **se mettre en ~** to set off; **en ~!** let's go!; **mettre en ~** to start [*machine, car*]; to get [sth] going [*project*].
■ **~ départementale** secondary road; **~ nationale** trunk road (GB), ≈ A road (GB), national highway (US).

routier, **-ière** /ʀutje, ɛʀ/ **I** *adj* road.
II *nm* **1** lorry driver (GB), truck driver; **2** transport café (GB), truck stop (US).

routine /ʀutin/ *nf* routine.

rouvrir: **se rouvrir** /ʀuvʀiʀ/ [32] *v refl* (+ *v être*) [*door*] to open (again); [*wound*] to open up (again).

roux, **rousse** /ʀu, ʀus/ **I** *adj* [*leaves*] russet; [*hair*] red; [*person*] red-haired; [*fur*] ginger.
II *nm,f* red-haired person, redhead.

royal, **~e**, *mpl* **-aux** /ʀwajal, o/ *adj* **1** royal; **2** [*present*] fit for a king; [*tip, salary*] princely; **3** [*indifference*] supreme; [*peace*] blissful.

royalement /ʀwajalmɑ̃/ *adv* **1** royally; **être payé ~** to be paid handsomely; **2**○ **il se moque ~ de son travail** he really couldn't care less about his work.

royaliste /ʀwajalist/ *adj, nmf* royalist.
IDIOMS **être plus ~ que le roi** to be more Catholic than the pope.

royaume /ʀwajom/ *nm* kingdom.

Royaume-Uni /ʀwajomyni/ *pr nm* **le ~** the United Kingdom.

royauté /ʀwajote/ *nf* **1** kingship; **2** monarchy.

RSVP (*written abbr* = **répondez s'il vous plaît**) RSVP.

ruade /ʀyad/ *nf* **1** (by horse) buck; **2** (by person, party) attack.

ruban /ʀybɑ̃/ *nm* ribbon; **~ adhésif** adhesive tape, sticky tape (GB).

rubéole /ʀybeɔl/ *nf* German measles.

rubis /ʀybi/ *nm inv* **1** ruby; **2** ruby (red).

rubrique /ʀybʀik/ *nf* **1** (of newspaper) section; **~ mondaine** social column; **2** category.

ruche /ʀyʃ/ *nf* **1** beehive; **2** hive of activity.

rude /ʀyd/ *adj* **1** [*job, day*] hard, tough; [*winter*] harsh; [*ordeal*] severe; **2** [*material, beard*] rough; **3** [*features*] coarse; **4 c'est un ~ gaillard** he's a strapping fellow; **5** [*opponent*] tough.

rudement /ʀydmɑ̃/ *adv* **1** roughly; **2**○ really.

rudesse /ʀydɛs/ *nf* **1** harshness, severity; **2** coarseness.

rudimentaire /ʀydimɑ̃tɛʀ/ *adj* **1** basic; **2** (Anat) rudimentary.

rudiments /ʀydimɑ̃/ *nm pl* **avoir quelques ~ de** to have a rudimentary knowledge of.

rudoyer /ʀydwaje/ [23] *vtr* to bully.

rue /ʀy/ *nf* street.
IDIOMS **ça ne court pas les ~s**○ it's pretty thin on the ground; **descendre dans la ~** to take to the street.

ruée /ʀɥe/ *nf* rush; **~ vers l'or** gold rush.

ruelle /ʀɥɛl/ *nf* alleyway, back street.

ruer /ʀɥe/ [1] **I** *vi* [*horse*] to kick.
II se ruer *v refl* (+ *v être*) to rush.
IDIOMS **~ dans les brancards** to rebel.

rugby /ʀygbi/ *nm* rugby; **~ à treize** rugby league; **~ à quinze** rugby union.

rugbyman, *pl* **rugbymen** /ʀygbiman, mɛn/ *nm* rugby player.

rugir /ʀyʒiʀ/ [3] **I** *vtr* to bellow (out), to growl.
II *vi* [*animal, engine*] to roar; [*wind*] to howl.

rugissement /ʀyʒismɑ̃/ *nm* (of animal, person) roar; (of wind) howling.

rugosité /ʀygozite/ *nf* roughness.

rugueux, **-euse** /ʀygø, øz/ *adj* rough.

ruine /ʀɥin/ *nf* **1** (of building, person, reputation, company) ruin; (of civilization) collapse; (of hope) death; **en ~(s)** ruined; **ce n'est pas la ~**○ it's not that expensive; **2** ruin; **3** wreck.

ruiner /ʀɥine/ [1] **I** *vtr* **1** to ruin [*person, economy*]; **~ qn** to be a drain on sb's resources; **2** to destroy [*health, happiness*]; **3** to ruin [*life*]; to shatter [*hopes*].
II se ruiner *v refl* (+ *v être*) to be ruined, to lose everything; to ruin oneself.

ruisseau, *pl* **~x** /ʀɥiso/ *nm* **1** stream, brook; **2 ~ de larmes** stream of tears.

ruisseler /ʀɥisle/ [19] *vi* **1** [*water*] to stream; [*grease*] to drip; **2** to be streaming; **~ de sueur** to be dripping with sweat.

ruissellement /ʀɥisɛlmɑ̃/ *nm* (of rain) streaming; (of grease) dripping.

rumeur /ʀymœʀ/ *nf* **1** rumour^GB; **2** (of voices, wind) murmur.

ruminant /ʀyminɑ̃/ *nm* ruminant.

ruminer /ʀymine/ [1] **I** *vtr* **1** to ruminate; **2** to brood on [*misery*]; to chew over○ [*idea, plan*].
II *vi* **1** to ruminate; **2** [*person*] to brood.

rumsteck /ʀɔmstɛk/ *nm* rump steak.

rupestre /ʀypɛstʀ/ *adj* **1** [*plants*] rock; **2** [*paintings*] cave, rock.

rupture /ʀyptyʀ/ *nf* **1** (of relations) breaking-off; **2** breakdown; **3** break-up; **lettre de ~** letter ending a relationship; **4** (of dam, dyke) breaking; (of pipe) fracture.

rural, **~e**, *mpl* **-aux** /ʀyʀal, o/ *adj* [*exodus, environment*] rural; [*road, life*] country.

ruse /ʀyz/ *nf* **1** trick, ruse; **~ de guerre** (humorous) cunning stratagem; **2** cunning, craftiness.

rusé, **~e** /ʀyze/ *adj* cunning, crafty.

ruser /ʀyze/ [1] *vi* **1** to be crafty; **2 ~ avec** to trick [*enemy, police*].

rush, *pl* **rushes** /ʀœʃ/ **I** *nm* (in race) final burst.
II rushes *nm pl* (of film) rushes.

russe /ʀys/ *adj, nm* Russian.

Russie /ʀysi/ *pr nf* Russia.

rustaud, **~e** /ʀysto, od/ *adj* rustic.

rusticité /ʀystisite/ *nf* rustic character.

rustine® /ʀystin/ *nf* (puncture-repair) patch.

rustique /ʀystik/ *adj* rustic, country.

rustre /ʀystʀ/ **I** *adj* uncouth.
II *nm* lout.

rut /ʀyt/ *nm* rutting season.

rutilant, **~e** /ʀytilɑ̃, ɑ̃t/ *adj* sparkling; gleaming.

rythme /ʀitm/ *nm* **1** rhythm; **marquer le ~** to beat time; **2** (of growth) rate; (of life) pace.
■ **~ cardiaque** heart rate.

rythmer /ʀitme/ [1] *vtr* **1** to give rhythm to; **2** to regulate [*life, work*].

rythmique /ʀitmik/ *adj* rhythmic.

Ss

s, **S** /ɛs/ *nm inv* s, S.
s' 1 ▶ **se**; **2** ▶ **si**[1] **II**.
sa ▶ **son**[1].
sabbat /saba/ *nm* **1** Sabbath; **2** witches' Sabbath.
sabbatique /sabatik/ *adj* **1** Sabbatical; **2 congé ~** sabbatical (leave).
sable /sɑbl/ *nm* sand; **~s mouvants** quicksands.
sablé, **~e** /sable/ **I** *adj* **pâte ~e** shortcrust pastry.
II *nm* shortbread biscuit (GB) or cookie (US).
sabler /sable/ [1] *vtr* to grit [*roadway*].
IDIOMS **~ le champagne** to crack open some champagne.
sablier /sablije/ *nm* hourglass; egg timer.
sablonneux, **-euse** /sablɔnø, øz/ *adj* sandy.
sabot /sabo/ *nm* **1** clog; **2** (Zool) hoof.
sabotage /sabɔtaʒ/ *nm* sabotage.
saboter /sabɔte/ [1] *vtr* to sabotage.
saboteur, **-euse** /sabɔtœʀ, øz/ *nm,f* (of equipment) saboteur.
sabre /sɑbʀ/ *nm* **1** sword; **2** sabre[GB].
sabrer○ /sɑbʀe/ [1] *vtr* to cut chunks out of [*article*].
sac /sak/ *nm* **1** (gen) bag; **2** sack; **3** bag(ful), sack(ful); **4 mettre à ~** to sack [*city, region*]; to ransack [*shop, house*].
■ **~ de couchage** sleeping bag; **~ à dos** rucksack, backpack; **~ à main** handbag, purse (US); **~ postal** mail sack; **~ à provisions** shopping bag, carry-all (US).
IDIOMS **l'affaire est dans le ~**○ it's in the bag○; **avoir plus d'un tour dans son ~** to have more than one trick up one's sleeve; **vider son ~**○ to get it off one's chest; **se faire prendre la main dans le ~** to be caught red-handed; **mettre dans le même ~**○ to lump [sth] together.
saccade /sakad/ *nf* jerk.
saccadé, **~e** /sakade/ *adj* [*movement*] jerky; [*rhythm*] staccato; [*voice*] clipped.
saccager /sakaʒe/ [13] *vtr* **1** to wreck, to devastate [*region*]; to vandalize [*building*]; **2** to sack.
saccharine /sakaʀin/ *nf* saccharin.
sacerdoce /sasɛʀdɔs/ *nm* priesthood.
sachet /saʃɛ/ *nm* (of powder) packet; (of herbs, spices) sachet; **~ de thé** tea bag.
sacoche /sakɔʃ/ *nf* **1** bag; **2** (on bicycle) pannier (GB), saddlebag (US).
sacquer○ /sake/ [1] *vtr* **1** to sack○, to fire○; **2** [*teacher*] to mark [sb] strictly; **3 je ne peux pas le ~** I can't stand the sight of him.
sacre /sakʀ/ *nm* (of king) coronation; (of bishop) consecration.
sacré, **~e** /sakʀe/ *adj* **1** [*art, object, place*] sacred; [*cause*] holy; **2** [*rule, right*] sacred; **3**○ **être un ~ menteur** to be a hell of○ a liar; **4**○ **~ Paul, va!** Paul, you old devil!
IDIOMS **avoir le feu ~** to be full of zeal.
sacrement /sakʀəmɑ̃/ *nm* sacrament; **les derniers ~s** the last rites.
sacrément○ /sakʀemɑ̃/ *adv* incredibly○.
sacrer /sakʀe/ [1] *vtr* to crown [*king*]; to consecrate [*bishop*].
sacrifice /sakʀifis/ *nm* sacrifice.
sacrifier /sakʀifje/ [1] **I** *vtr* to sacrifice.
II sacrifier à *v+prep* to conform to [*fashion*].
III se sacrifier *v refl* (+ *v être*) **1** to sacrifice oneself; **2**○ to make sacrifices.
sacrilège /sakʀilɛʒ/ *nm* sacrilege.
sacristie /sakʀisti/ *nf* (of catholic church) sacristy; (of protestant church) vestry.
sacro-saint, **~e**, *mpl* **~s** /sakʀosɛ̃, ɛ̃t/ *adj* sacrosanct.
sadique /sadik/ **I** *adj* sadistic.
II *nmf* sadist.
sadisme /sadism/ *nm* sadism.
sadomasochisme /sadomazɔʃism/ *nm* sadomasochism.
safari /safaʀi/ *nm* safari.
safran /safʀɑ̃/ *adj inv, nm* saffron.
saga /saga/ *nf* saga.
sagacité /sagasite/ *nf* sagacity, shrewdness.
sage /saʒ/ **I** *adj* **1** wise, sensible; **2** good, well-behaved; **3** [*tastes, fashion*] sober.
II *nm* **1** wise man, sage; **2** expert.
sage-femme, *pl* **sages-femmes** /saʒfam/ *nf* midwife.
sagement /saʒmɑ̃/ *adv* **1** wisely; **2** [*sit, listen*] quietly; **3** [*dress*] soberly.
sagesse /saʒɛs/ *nf* **1** wisdom, common sense; (of advice) soundness; **la voix de la ~** the voice of reason; **2** good behaviour[GB].
Sagittaire /saʒitɛʀ/ *pr nm* Sagittarius.
Sahara /saaʀa/ *pr nm* Sahara.
saignant, **~e** /sɛɲɑ̃, ɑ̃t/ *adj* **1** [*meat*] rare; **2**○ (figurative) [*criticism*] savage.
saignée /sɛɲe/ *nf* **1** (Med) bloodletting, bleeding; **2** (in budget) hole; **3** (in tree) cut.
saignement /sɛɲ(ə)mɑ̃/ *nm* bleeding.
saigner /sɛɲe/ [1] **I** *vtr* **1** (Med) to bleed; **2** to kill [*animal*] (*by slitting its throat*); **~ un cochon** to stick a pig.
II *vi* to bleed; **~ du nez** to have a nosebleed.
IDIOMS **~ qn à blanc** to bleed sb dry; **se ~ (aux quatre veines) pour qn** to make big sacrifices for sb.
saillant, **~e** /sajɑ̃, ɑ̃t/ *adj* **1** [*jaw*] prominent; [*muscle, eyes*] bulging; [*angle*] salient; **2** [*fact, episode*] salient.
saillie /saji/ *nf* **1** projection; **le balcon est en ~** the balcony juts out; **2** (Zool) covering.

saillir /sajiʀ/ [28] *vi* **1** to jut out; **2** [*ribs, muscles*] to bulge.

sain, **~e** /sɛ̃, sɛn/ *adj* (gen) healthy, sound; [*wound*] clean; **~ d'esprit** sane; **~ de corps et d'esprit** sound in body and mind; **~ et sauf** [*return*] safe and sound.

saindoux /sɛ̃du/ *nm inv* lard.

sainement /sɛnmɑ̃/ *adv* **1** [*live*] healthily; **2** [*reason*] soundly.

saint, **~e** /sɛ̃, sɛ̃t/ **I** *adj* **1** holy; **vendredi ~** Good Friday; **2 ~ Paul** Saint Paul.

II *nm,f* saint.

■ **~e nitouche** goody-goody○; **la Sainte Vierge** the Virgin Mary.

Saint-Esprit /sɛ̃tɛspʀi/ *pr nm* Holy Spirit.

sainteté /sɛ̃tte/ *nf* saintliness.

saint-honoré /sɛ̃tɔnɔʀe/ *nm inv*: *cream-filled tart topped with choux and caramel.*

Saint-Jacques /sɛ̃ʒak/ *pr n* **coquille ~** scallop.

Saint-Jean /sɛ̃ʒɑ̃/ *nf* **la ~** Midsummer Day.

Saint-Sylvestre /sɛ̃silvɛstʀ/ *nf* **la ~** New Year's Eve.

saisie /sezi/ *nf* **1** (gen, Law) seizure; **2** keyboarding; **~ de données** data capture.

saisir /seziʀ/ [3] **I** *vtr* **1** to grab; to seize; **~ au vol** to catch [*ball*]; **'affaire à ~'** 'amazing bargain'; **2** to understand; **3** to catch [*name, bits of conversation*]; **4** [*emotion, cold*] to grip [*person*]; **5** to strike, to impress [*person*]; **6** (Law) to seize [*property*]; **~ la justice d'une affaire** to refer a matter to a court; **7** (Comput) to capture [*data*]; to key [*text*].

II se saisir *v refl* (+ *v être*) **se ~ de** to catch or grab hold of [*object*].

saisissant, **~e** /sezisɑ̃, ɑ̃t/ *adj* **1** [*cold*] piercing; **2** [*effect, resemblance*] striking.

saison /sɛzɔ̃/ *nf* (gen) season; **en cette ~** at this time of year; **en toute ~** all (the) year round; **la haute/morte ~** the high/slack season; **prix hors ~** off-season prices.

saisonnier, **-ière** /sɛzɔnje, ɛʀ/ **I** *adj* seasonal.

II *nm,f* (worker) seasonal worker.

salace /salas/ *adj* salacious.

salade /salad/ *nf* **1** lettuce; **2** salad; **3○** muddle; **raconter des ~s** to spin yarns○.

saladier /saladje/ *nm* salad bowl.

salaire /salɛʀ/ *nm* salary; wages.

salaison /salɛzɔ̃/ *nf* salt meat.

salamandre /salamɑ̃dʀ/ *nf* salamander.

salant /salɑ̃/ *adj m* **marais ~** saltern.

salarial, **~e**, *mpl* **-iaux** /salaʀjal, o/ *adj* **1** [*policy, rise*] wage; **2 cotisation ~e** employee's contribution.

salarié, **~e** /salaʀje/ **I** *adj* [*worker*] wage-earning; [*job*] salaried.

II *nm,f* **1** wage earner; **2** salaried employee.

salaud◑ /salo/ *nm* (offensive) bastard◑.

sale /sal/ **I** *adj* **1** (*after n*) dirty; **2○** (*before n*) [*person*] horrible; [*animal, illness, habit*] nasty; [*weather*] foul, horrible; [*work, place*] rotten; **~ menteur!** you dirty liar!; **il a une ~ tête** he looks dreadful; **faire une ~ tête** to look annoyed; **un ~ coup** a very nasty blow; **un ~ caractère** a foul temper.

II *nm* **mettre qch au ~** to put sth in the wash.

salé, **~e** /sale/ *adj* **1** salt, salty; **2** salted; [*snack*] savoury[GB]; **3○** [*bill*] steep.

salement /salmɑ̃/ *adv* **1 manger ~** to be a messy eater; **2○** badly, seriously.

saler /sale/ [1] *vtr* **1** to salt [*food*]; **~ et poivrer** to add salt and pepper; **2** to grit (GB), to salt (US) [*road*].

saleté /salte/ *nf* **1** dirtiness; dirt; filth; **ramasser les ~s** to pick up the rubbish (GB) or trash (US); **faire des ~s** to make a mess; **2○ c'est de la ~** (gadget, goods) it's rubbish; **c'est une vraie ~ ce virus!** it's a rotten bug!

salière /saljɛʀ/ *nf* saltcellar, saltshaker (US).

salir /saliʀ/ [3] **I** *vtr* **1** to dirty; to soil; **2** to sully [*reputation*].

II *vi* [*industry, coal*] to pollute.

III se salir *v refl* (+ *v être*) to get dirty, to dirty oneself.

salissant, **~e** /salisɑ̃, ɑ̃t/ *adj* **1** [*colour*] which shows the dirt; **2** [*work*] dirty.

salive /saliv/ *nf* saliva.

saliver /salive/ [1] *vi* to salivate; **~ devant qch** to drool over sth.

salle /sal/ *nf* **1** (gen) room; hall; (in restaurant) (dining) room; (in hospital) ward; (in theatre) auditorium; **faire ~ comble** [*show*] to be packed; **en ~** [*sport*] indoor; **2** audience.

■ **~ d'attente** waiting room; **~ de bains** bathroom; **~ de cinéma** cinema (GB), movie theater (US); **~ de classe** classroom; **~ de concert** concert hall; **~ d'eau** shower room; **~ d'embarquement** departure lounge; **~ des fêtes** village hall; community centre[GB]; **~ de garde** (in hospital) staff room; **~ de gymnastique** gymnasium; **~ de jeu(x)** (in casino) gaming room; (for children) playroom; **~ à manger** dining room; dining-room suite; **~ de séjour** living room; **~ des ventes** auction room.

salon /salɔ̃/ *nm* **1** (gen) lounge; drawing room; **2** sitting-room suite; **~ de jardin** garden furniture; **3** (trade) show; fair; exhibition; **~ du livre** book fair; **4** (of intellectuals) salon.

■ **~ de beauté** beauty salon; **~ de coiffure** hairdressing salon; **~ d'essayage** fitting room; **~ de thé** tearoom.

salopette /salɔpɛt/ *nf* overalls.

salpêtre /salpɛtʀ/ *nm* saltpetre[GB].

salsifis /salsifi/ *nm inv* salsify.

saltimbanque /saltɛ̃bɑ̃k/ *nmf* **1** street acrobat; **2** entertainer.

salubre /salybʀ/ *adj* [*lodgings*] salubrious.

saluer /salɥe/ [1] *vtr* **1** to greet [*person*]; **~ qn de la tête** to nod to sb; **2** to say goodbye to [*person*]; **3** (Mil) to salute; **4** to welcome [*decision, news*]; **5** to pay tribute to [*memory*].

salut /saly/ *nm* **1** greeting; **~!** hello!, hi!; bye!; **~ de la tête** nod; **2** salute; **3** salvation.

salutaire /salytɛʀ/ *adj* [*experience*] salutary; [*effect*] beneficial; [*air*] healthy.

salutation /salytasjɔ̃/ *nf* greeting.
salvateur, **-trice** /salvatœʀ, tʀis/ *adj* saving.
salve /salv/ *nf* **1** salvo; **tirer une ~ d'honneur** to fire a salute; **2 ~ d'applaudissements** burst of applause.
samedi /samdi/ *nm* Saturday.
SAMU /samy/ *nm* (*abbr* = **Service d'assistance médicale d'urgence**) ≈ mobile accident unit (GB), emergency medical service, EMS (US).
sanatorium /sanatɔʀjɔm/ *nm* sanatorium (GB), sanitarium (US).
sanctifier /sɑ̃ktifje/ [1] *vtr* to sanctify.
sanction /sɑ̃ksjɔ̃/ *nf* (Law) penalty, sanction; disciplinary measure; (Sch) punishment.
sanctionner /sɑ̃ksjɔne/ [1] *vtr* **1** to punish; **2** to give official recognition to [*training*].
sanctuaire /sɑ̃ktɥɛʀ/ *nm* **1** shrine; **2** sanctuary.
sandale /sɑ̃dal/ *nf* sandal.
sandwich, *pl* **~s** or **~es** /sɑ̃dwitʃ/ *nm* sandwich; (**pris**) **en ~** sandwiched.
sang /sɑ̃/ *nm* **1** blood; **être en ~** to be covered with blood; **se terminer dans le ~** to end in bloodshed; **2 de ~** [*brother, ties*] blood; **être du même ~** to be kin.
IDIOMS **il a ça dans le ~** it's in his blood; **mettre qch à feu et à ~** to put sth to fire and sword; **mon ~ n'a fait qu'un tour** my heart missed a beat; I saw red; **se faire du mauvais ~**○ to worry; **bon ~!** for God's sake○!
sang-froid /sɑ̃fʀwɑ/ *nm inv* composure; **garde ton ~!** keep calm!; **de ~** in cold blood.
sanglant, **~e** /sɑ̃glɑ̃, ɑ̃t/ *adj* bloody.
sangle /sɑ̃gl/ *nf* **1** (gen) strap; **2** (of saddle) girth; **3** (of seat, bed) webbing.
sangler /sɑ̃gle/ [1] *vtr* to girth [*horse*].
sanglier /sɑ̃glije/ *nm* wild boar.
sanglot /sɑ̃glo/ *nm* sob.
sangloter /sɑ̃glɔte/ [1] *vi* to sob.
sangsue /sɑ̃sy/ *nf* leech.
sanguin, **~e**[1] /sɑ̃gɛ̃, in/ *adj* blood.
sanguinaire /sɑ̃ginɛʀ/ *adj* [*crime*] bloody; [*person*] bloodthirsty.
sanguine[2] /sɑ̃gin/ **I** *adj f* ▶ **sanguin**.
II *nf* **1** blood orange; **2** red chalk drawing.
sanisette® /sanizɛt/ *nf* automatic public toilet.
sanitaire /sanitɛʀ/ **I** *adj* [*regulations*] health; [*conditions*] sanitary.
II sanitaires *nm pl* **les ~s** (in house) the bathroom; (in campsite) the toilet block.
sans /sɑ̃/ **I** *adv* without.
II *prep* **1** without; **un couple ~ enfant** a childless couple; **~ cela** otherwise; **2 il est resté trois mois ~ téléphoner** he didn't call for three months; **il est poli, ~ plus** he's polite, but that's as far as it goes; **3 on sera dix ~ les enfants** there'll be ten of us not counting the children; **3500 francs ~ l'hôtel** 3,500 francs not including accommodation.
III sans que *phr* without; **pars ~ qu'on te voie** leave without anyone seeing you.
■ **~ domicile fixe**, **SDF** of no fixed abode, NFA.
sans-abri /sɑ̃zabʀi/ *nmf inv* **un ~** a homeless person; **les ~** the homeless.
sans-emploi /sɑ̃zɑ̃plwɑ/ *nmf inv* unemployed person.
sans-faute /sɑ̃fot/ *nm inv* faultless performance.
sans-gêne /sɑ̃ʒɛn/ *adj inv* bad-mannered.
santal /sɑ̃tal/ *nm* sandalwood.
santé /sɑ̃te/ *nf* health; **avoir la ~** to enjoy good health; **se refaire une ~** to build up one's strength; **avoir une petite ~** to be frail; **à votre ~!** cheers!; **à la ~ de Janet!** here's to Janet!
santon /sɑ̃tɔ̃/ *nm* Christmas crib figure.
saoul, **~e** = **soûl**.
saper /sape/ [1] **I** *vtr* to undermine.
II se saper○ *v refl* (+ *v être*) to dress.
sapeur /sapœʀ/ *nm* sapper.
IDIOMS **fumer comme un ~** to smoke like a chimney.
sapeur-pompier, *pl* **sapeurs-pompiers** /sapœʀpɔ̃pje/ *nm* fireman.
saphir /safiʀ/ *nm* **1** sapphire; **2** (on record player) stylus.
sapin /sapɛ̃/ *nm* **1** fir tree; **~ de Noël** Christmas tree; **2** deal.
saquer○ /sake/ [1] *vtr* = **sacquer**.
sarbacane /saʀbakan/ *nf* blowpipe.
sarcasme /saʀkasm/ *nm* **1** sarcasm; **2** sarcastic remark.
sarcastique /saʀkastik/ *adj* sarcastic.
sarcophage /saʀkɔfaʒ/ *nm* sarcophagus.
sardine /saʀdin/ *nf* **1** (Zool) sardine; **2**○ tent peg.
sarment /saʀmɑ̃/ *nm* vine shoot.
sarrasin /saʀazɛ̃/ *nm* buckwheat.
sarrau /saʀo/ *nm* smock.
sas /sɑs/ *nm inv* **1** airlock; **2** (on canal) lock; **3** (in bank) security double door system.
satanique /satanik/ *adj* **1** [*smile, ruse*] fiendish; **2** [*cult*] Satanic.
satellite /satɛlit/ *nm* satellite.
satiété /sasjete/ **I** *nf* satiation, satiety.
II à satiété *phr* **1 manger à ~** to eat one's fill; **2** [*say, repeat*] ad nauseam.
satin /satɛ̃/ *nm* satin.
satiné, **~e** /satine/ *adj* [*fabric, cloth*] satiny; [*paint*] satin-finish.
satire /satiʀ/ *nf* satire.
satirique /satiʀik/ *adj* satirical.
satisfaction /satisfaksjɔ̃/ *nf* satisfaction; **la ~ de nos besoins** the fulfilment[GB] of our needs.
satisfaire /satisfɛʀ/ [10] **I** *vtr* (gen) to satisfy; to fulfil[GB] [*aspiration, requirement*].
II satisfaire à *v+prep* to fulfil[GB] [*obligation*]; to meet [*norm, standard*].
III se satisfaire *v refl* (+ *v être*) **se ~ de** to be satisfied with [*explanation*]; to be content with [*low salary*].

satisfaisant, **~e** /satisfəzɑ̃, ɑ̃t/ *adj* **1** satisfactory; **2** satisfying.

satisfait, **~e** /satisfɛ, ɛt/ *adj* [*customer, need, smile*] satisfied; [*desire*] gratified; [*person*] happy.

saturation /satyʀasjɔ̃/ *nf* (of market) saturation; (in trains, hotels) overcrowding; (of network) overloading; **arriver à ~** [*market, network*] to reach saturation point; [*person*] to have had as much as one can take.

saturé, **~e** /satyʀe/ *adj* [*market*] saturated; [*profession*] overcrowded.

saturer /satyʀe/ [1] *vtr* to saturate.

satyre /satiʀ/ *nm* **1** satyr; **2** lecher.

sauce /sos/ *nf* (Culin) sauce; **(r)allonger la ~**○ (figurative) to spin things out.
IDIOMS **mettre qch à toutes les ~s** to adapt sth to any purpose.

saucière /sosjɛʀ/ *nf* sauceboat.

saucisse /sosis/ *nf* sausage; **chair à ~** sausage meat.
■ **~ de Francfort** frankfurter.

saucisson /sosisɔ̃/ *nm* (slicing) sausage; **~ à l'ail** garlic sausage; **~ sec** ≈ salami.

sauf[1] /sof/ **I** *prep* **1** except, but; **2 ~ contrordre** failing an order to the contrary; **~ avis contraire** unless otherwise stated; **~ erreur de ma part** if I'm not mistaken.
II sauf si *phr* unless.
III sauf que *phr* except that.

sauf[2], **sauve** /sof, sov/ *adj* **1** safe; **laisser la vie sauve à qn** to spare sb's life; **2** [*honour, reputation*] intact.

sauf-conduit, *pl* **~s** /sofkɔ̃dɥi/ *nm* safe-conduct.

sauge /soʒ/ *nf* sage.

saugrenu, **~e** /sogʀəny/ *adj* crazy, potty○ (GB).

saule /sol/ *nm* willow.

saumâtre /somɑtʀ/ *adj* [*water*] brackish; [*taste*] bitter and salty.

saumon /somɔ̃/ *nm* salmon.

saumure /somyʀ/ *nf* brine.

sauna /sona/ *nm* sauna.

saupoudrer /sopudʀe/ [1] *vtr* **1** to sprinkle; **2** (figurative) to give [sth] sparingly.

saur /sɔʀ/ *adj m* **hareng ~** kippered herring.

saut /so/ *nm* **1** jump; **faire un petit ~** to skip; **au ~ du lit** first thing in the morning; **2** (Sport) **le ~** jumping; **3**○ **faire un ~ chez qn** to pop in and see sb.
■ **~ à la corde** skipping; **~ à l'élastique** bungee jumping; **~ en hauteur** high jump; **~ à la perche** pole vault; **~ périlleux** mid-air somersault.

saute /sot/ *nf* **~ de température** sudden change in temperature; **~ d'humeur** mood swing.

sauté, **~e** /sote/ **I** *adj* (Culin) sautéed.
II *nm* (Culin) **~ d'agneau** sautéed lamb.

saute-mouton /sotmutɔ̃/ *nm inv* leapfrog.

sauter /sote/ [1] **I** *vtr* **1** to jump [*distance, height*]; to jump over [*stream*]; **2** to skip [*meal, paragraph*]; to leave out [*details*]; (Sch) **~ une classe** to skip a year; **3** to miss [*word, turn*].
II *vi* **1** to jump; **~ à pieds joints** to jump with one's feet together; **~ à la corde** to skip; **faire ~ un enfant sur ses genoux** to dandle a child on one's knee; **~ sur qn** to pounce on sb; **~ à la gorge de qn** to go for sb's throat; **~ au cou de qn** to greet sb with a kiss; **2 ~ dans un taxi** to jump or hop into a taxi; **3 ~ d'un sujet à l'autre** to skip from one subject to another; **4**○ **faire ~ une réunion** to cancel a meeting; **faire ~ une contravention** to get out of paying a parking ticket; **5** [*bicycle chain, fan belt*] to come off; **6 faire ~ une serrure** to force a lock; **faire ~ les boutons** to burst one's buttons; **7** [*bridge, building*] to be blown up, to go up; **faire ~ les plombs** to blow the fuses; **8** (Culin) **faire ~** to sauté [*onions*].
IDIOMS **~ aux yeux** to be blindingly obvious; **et que ça saute**○**!** make it snappy○!; **~ au plafond**○ to jump for joy; to hit the roof○; to be staggered.

sauterelle /sotʀɛl/ *nf* grasshopper.

sauterie /sotʀi/ *nf* party.

sautillant, **~e** /sotijɑ̃, ɑ̃t/ *adj* [*rhythm, gait*] bouncy; [*bird*] hopping.

sautiller /sotije/ [1] *vi* **1** [*bird*] to hop; **2** [*child*] to skip along; to jump up and down.

sauvage /sovaʒ/ **I** *adj* **1** [*animal, plant*] wild; [*tribe*] primitive; **2** [*behaviour*] savage, wild; [*struggle*] fierce; **3** unsociable; **4** illegal.
II *nmf* **1** savage; **2** unsociable person, loner.

sauvagement /sovaʒmɑ̃/ *adv* savagely.

sauvageon, **-onne** /sovaʒɔ̃, ɔn/ *nm,f* wild child.

sauvagerie /sovaʒʀi/ *nf* savagery.

sauve ▶ **sauf**[2].

sauvegarde /sovgaʀd/ *nf* (of heritage, peace, values) maintenance; (of rights) protection.

sauvegarder /sovgaʀde/ [1] *vtr* **1** to safeguard; **2** (Comput) to save; to back [sth] up [*file*].

sauver /sove/ [1] **I** *vtr* **1** (gen) to save; **~ la vie à qn** to save sb's life; **elle est sauvée** [*ill person*] she has pulled through○; **2** to salvage [*goods*]; **3 ce qui le sauve à mes yeux, c'est sa générosité** his redeeming feature for me is his generosity.
II se sauver *v refl* (+ *v être*) **1** to escape; to run away; (from danger) to run; **2**○ **il faut que je me sauve** I've got to rush off now.
IDIOMS **~ la situation** to save the day; **sauve qui peut!** run for your life!

sauvetage /sovtaʒ/ *nm* rescue; **cours de ~** life-saving training.

sauveteur /sovtœʀ/ *nm* rescuer.

sauvette: **à la sauvette** /alasovɛt/ *phr* **1** [*prepare, sign*] in a rush; **2** [*film, record*] on the sly.

sauveur /sovœʀ/ *nm* saviour[GB].

savamment /savamɑ̃/ *adv* **1** learnedly, eruditely; **2** skilfully[GB].

savane /savan/ *nf* savannah.

savant, **~e** /savɑ̃, ɑ̃t/ **I** *adj* **1** [*person*] learned, erudite; **2** [*study*] scholarly; [*calcula-*

tion] complicated; **3** [*manoeuvre*] clever; [*direction*] skilful[GB]; **4** [*animal*] performing.
II *nm,f* scholar.
III *nm* scientist.

savate○ /savat/ *nf* **1** old slipper; **2** old shoe.

saveur /savœʀ/ *nf* flavour[GB]; **sans ~** tasteless.

savoir[1] /savwaʀ/ [47] I *vtr* **1** to know [*truth, answer*]; **vous n'êtes pas sans ~ que** you are no doubt aware that; **va** or **allez ~!** who knows!; **est-ce que je sais, moi!** how should I know!; **pour autant que je sache** as far as I know; **comment l'as-tu su?** how did you find out?; **je l'ai su par elle** she told me about it; **ne ~ que faire pour**... to be at a loss as to how to...; **sachant que** knowing that; given that; **qui vous savez** you-know-who; **je ne sais qui** somebody or other; **tu en sais des choses!** you really know a thing or two!; **2 ~ faire** to know how to do; **je sais conduire** I can drive; **~ écouter** to be a good listener; **elle sait y faire avec les hommes** she knows how to handle men.
II **se savoir** *v refl* (+ *v être*) **ça se saurait** people would know about that.
III **à savoir** *phr* that is to say.
IDIOMS **ne pas ~ où donner de la tête** not to know whether one is coming or going.

savoir[2] /savwaʀ/ *nm* **1** learning; **2** knowledge; **3** body of knowledge.

savoir-faire /savwaʀfɛʀ/ *nm inv* know-how.

savoir-vivre /savwaʀvivʀ/ *nm inv* manners.

savon /savɔ̃/ *nm* **1** soap; **~ de Marseille** household soap; **2** (bar of) soap.
IDIOMS **passer un ~**○ **à qn** to give sb a telling-off.

savonner /savɔne/ [1] *vtr* to soap.

savonnette /savɔnɛt/ *nf* small cake of soap.

savourer /savuʀe/ [1] *vtr* to savour[GB].

savoureux, -euse /savuʀø, øz/ *adj* [*dish*] tasty; [*anecdote*] juicy.

saxophone /saksɔfɔn/ *nm* saxophone.

saxophoniste /saksɔfɔnist/ *nmf* saxophonist.

scabreux, -euse /skabʀø, øz/ *adj* obscene.

scalp /skalp/ *nm* **1** scalp; **2** scalping.

scalpel /skalpɛl/ *nm* scalpel.

scalper /skalpe/ [1] *vtr* to scalp.

scandale /skɑ̃dal/ *nm* scandal; **faire (un** or **du) ~** (gen) to cause a scandal; [*person*] to cause a fuss; **la presse à ~** the gutter press; **c'est un ~!** it's scandalous!

scandaleux, -euse /skɑ̃dalø, øz/ *adj* scandalous, outrageous.

scandaliser /skɑ̃dalize/ [1] I *vtr* to outrage.
II **se scandaliser** *v refl* (+ *v être*) to be shocked.

scander /skɑ̃de/ [1] *vtr* **1** to scan; **2** to chant [*slogan, name*].

scandinave /skɑ̃dinav/ *adj* Scandinavian.

scanneur /skanœʀ/ *nm* scanner.

scaphandre /skafɑ̃dʀ/ *nm* **1** deep-sea diving suit; **2** spacesuit.

scarabée /skaʀabe/ *nm* **1** beetle; **2** scarab.

scarlatine /skaʀlatin/ *nf* scarlet fever.

scatologie /skatɔlɔʒi/ *nf* scatology.

sceau, *pl* **~x** /so/ *nm* **1** seal; **sous le ~ du secret** in strictest secrecy; **2** stamp, hallmark.

scélérat, ~e /seleʀa, at/ *nm,f* villain.

scellé /sele/ *nm* seal; **apposer les ~s** to affix seals.

sceller /sele/ [1] *vtr* **1** to seal; **2** to fix [sth] securely [*shelf, bar*].

scénario /senaʀjo/ *nm* **1** screenplay, script; **2** scenario; **~ catastrophe** nightmare scenario.

scénariste /senaʀist/ *nmf* scriptwriter.

scène /sɛn/ *nf* **1** (in theatre) stage; **entrer en ~** to come on; **2** scene; **la ~ se passe à Paris** the scene is set in Paris; **3 quitter la ~** to give up the stage; **mettre en ~** to stage [*play*]; to direct [*film*]; **4** scene; **occuper le devant de la ~** (figurative) to be in the news; **5 faire une ~** to throw a fit○; **6** scene; **~s de panique** scenes of panic.
■ **~ de ménage** domestic dispute.

scepticisme /sɛptisism/ *nm* scepticism (GB), skepticism (US).

sceptique /sɛptik/ I *adj* sceptical (GB), skeptical (US); **laisser qn ~** to leave sb unconvinced.
II *nmf* sceptic (GB), skeptic (US).

sceptre /sɛptʀ/ *nm* sceptre[GB].

schéma /ʃema/ *nm* **1** diagram; **2** outline; **3** pattern.

schématique /ʃematik/ *adj* **1** [*vision, argument*] simplistic; **2** schematic.

schématiser /ʃematize/ [1] *vtr* to simplify.

schizophrénie /skizɔfʀeni/ *nf* schizophrenia.

sciatique /sjatik/ I *adj* **nerf ~** sciatic nerve.
II *nf* **avoir une ~** to have sciatica.

scie /si/ *nf* saw; **~ sauteuse** jigsaw.

sciemment /sjamɑ̃/ *adv* knowingly.

science /sjɑ̃s/ *nf* **1** science; **2** knowledge.
■ **~s naturelles** ≈ biology (*sg*); **~s occultes** black arts; **Sciences Po**○ *Institute of Political Science.*

science-fiction /sjɑ̃sfiksjɔ̃/ *nf* science fiction.

scientifique /sjɑ̃tifik/ I *adj* scientific.
II *nmf* scientist.

scier /sje/ [2] *vtr* **1** to saw; **2**○ to stun.

scierie /siʀi/ *nf* sawmill.

scinder /sɛ̃de/ [1] I *vtr* to split [*group*].
II **se scinder** *v refl* (+ *v être*) to split up.

scintillant, ~e /sɛ̃tijɑ̃, ɑ̃t/ *adj* twinkling.

scintiller /sɛ̃tije/ [1] *vi* [*diamond*] to sparkle; [*star*] to twinkle; [*water*] to glisten.

scission /sisjɔ̃/ *nf* **1** split, schism; **2** fission.

sciure /sjyʀ/ *nf* **~ (de bois)** sawdust.

sclérose /skleʀoz/ *nf* **1** (Med) sclerosis; **2** fossilization, ossification.
■ **~ en plaques** multiple sclerosis, MS.

scléroser /skleʀoze/ [1] I *vtr* (Med) to sclerose.
II **se scléroser** *v refl* (+ *v être*) **1** [*institution, person*] to become fossilized; **2** (Med) [*tissue*] to become hardened.

scolaire /skɔlɛʀ/ *adj* [*holidays, book*] school;

[*reform, publication*] educational; [*failure*] academic; **établissement ~** school.

scolarisation /skɔlaʀizasjɔ̃/ *nf* schooling.

scolariser /skɔlaʀize/ [1] *vtr* to send [sb] to school.

scolarité /skɔlaʀite/ *nf* **1** schooling; **durant ma ~** when I was at school; **la ~ obligatoire** compulsory education; **2** (in university) registrar's office.

scoliose /skɔljoz/ *nf* scoliosis.

scooter /skutœʀ/ *nm* (motor) scooter.

score /skɔʀ/ *nm* **1** (Sch, Sport) score; **~ nul** draw (GB), tie (US); **2** results.

scorie /skɔʀi/ *nf* **1** scoria; **2** slag.

scorpion /skɔʀpjɔ̃/ *nm* (Zool) scorpion.

Scorpion /skɔʀpjɔ̃/ *pr nm* Scorpio.

scotch, *pl* **~es** /skɔtʃ/ *nm* **1** Scotch (whisky); **2** ®Sellotape® (GB), Scotch® tape (US).

scotcher /skɔtʃe/ [1] *vtr* to Sellotape® (GB), to Scotch-tape® (US).

scout, **~e** /skut/ **I** *adj* scout.

II *nm,f* boy scout/girl scout.

scribe /skʀib/ *nm* scribe.

scribouillard°, **~e** /skʀibujaʀ, aʀd/ *nm,f* pen pusher° (GB), pencil pusher (US).

script /skʀipt/ *nm* **1 écrire en ~** to print; **2** script.

scripte /skʀipt/ *nmf* continuity man/girl.

scrupule /skʀypyl/ *nm* scruple.

scrupuleusement /skʀypyløzmɑ̃/ *adv* scrupulously.

scrupuleux, **-euse** /skʀypylø, øz/ *adj* scrupulous; **peu ~** unscrupulous.

scruter /skʀyte/ [1] *vtr* to scan [*horizon*]; to scrutinize [*object*]; to examine [*ground, person*].

scrutin /skʀytɛ̃/ *nm* **1** ballot; **dépouiller le ~** to count the votes; **2** polls; **jour du ~** polling day; **mode de ~** electoral system.

■ **~ majoritaire** election by majority vote.

sculpter /skylte/ [1] *vtr* to sculpt, to carve.

sculpteur /skyltœʀ/ *nm* sculptor.

sculptural, **~e**, *mpl* **-aux** /skyltyʀal, o/ *adj* [*art*] sculptural; [*shape, beauty*] statuesque.

sculpture /skyltyʀ/ *nf* sculpture; **la ~ sur bois** woodcarving.

SDF /ɛsdeɛf/ ▶ **sans**.

se (**s'** *before vowel or mute h*) /sə, s/ *pron* **1** oneself; himself; herself; itself; **il ~ regarde** he's looking at himself; **2** each other; **ils ~ regardaient** they were looking at each other; **3 ~ ronger les ongles** to bite one's nails; **il ~ lave les pieds** he's washing his feet; **4 elle ~ comporte honorablement** she behaves honourably[GB]; **l'écart ~ creuse** the gap is widening; **5 les exemples ~ comptent sur les doigts de la main** the examples can be counted on the fingers of your hand; **6 comment ~ fait-il que**...? how come...?, how is it that...?

séance /seɑ̃s/ *nf* **1** (of court, parliament) session; (of committee) meeting; **~ tenante** immediately; **2** (in cinema) show.

■ **~ de spiritisme** séance.

seau, *pl* **~x** /so/ *nm* bucket, pail.

sébile /sebil/ *nf* begging bowl.

sec, **sèche** /sɛk, sɛʃ/ **I** *adj* **1** [*weather, hair*] dry; [*fruit*] dried; **2** [*wine, cider*] dry; **boire son gin ~** to like one's gin straight; **3** [*person, statement*] terse; [*letter*] curt; **4** [*noise*] sharp.

II *nm* **être à ~** [*river*] to have dried up; (figurative) [*person*] to have no money.

III *adv* **1 se briser ~** to snap; **2**° [*rain, drink*] a lot.

IDIOMS **aussi ~**° immediately.

sécateur /sekatœʀ/ *nm* clippers.

sécession /sesesjɔ̃/ *nf* secession.

sèche /sɛʃ/ *adj f* ▶ **sec I**.

sèche-cheveux /sɛʃʃəvø/ *nm inv* hairdrier (GB), blow-dryer.

sèche-linge /sɛʃlɛ̃ʒ/ *nm inv* tumble-drier (GB), tumble-dryer.

sèchement /sɛʃmɑ̃/ *adv* drily, coldly.

sécher /seʃe/ [1] **I** *vtr* **1** (gen) to dry; **2**° to skip [*class*].

II *vi* [*hair, clothes*] to dry; [*mud*] to dry up; **fleur séchée** dried flower; **mettre des vêtements à ~** to hang clothes up to dry.

sécheresse /seʃʀɛs/ *nf* **1** drought; **2** dryness; **3** curt manner.

séchoir /seʃwaʀ/ *nm* **1** clothes airer, clothes horse; **2** tumble-drier (GB), tumble-dryer.

second, **~e**[1] /səgɔ̃, ɔ̃d/ **I** *adj* **1** (in sequence, series) second; **chapitre ~** chapter two; **en ~ lieu** secondly; **dans un ~ temps**... subsequently...; **c'est à prendre au ~ degré** it is not to be taken literally; **2** (in hierarchy) second; **de ~ ordre** second-rate; **politicien de ~ plan** minor politician; **jouer un ~ rôle** (in theatre) to play a supporting role; **jouer les ~s rôles** (figurative) to play second fiddle.

II *nm,f* second one.

III *nm* **1** second-in-command; **2** second floor (GB), third floor (US).

IV en second *phr* [*arrive, leave*] second.

secondaire /səgɔ̃dɛʀ/ **I** *adj* **1** secondary; **2** minor; **3** (Sch) **école ~** secondary school (GB), high school (US); **4 effets ~s** side effects.

II *nm* (Sch) secondary school (GB) or high school (US) education.

seconde[2] /səgɔ̃d/ **I** ▶ **second I, II**.

II *nf* **1** ▶ **second II**; **2** second; **en une fraction de ~** in a split second; **3** (Sch) *fifth year of secondary school, age 15–16*; **4 billet de ~** second-class ticket; **5** (Aut) second (gear).

seconder /səgɔ̃de/ [1] *vtr* [*person*] to assist.

secouer /səkwe/ [1] **I** *vtr* **1** to shake [*bottle, branch, person*]; to shake out [*rug, umbrella*]; **~ la tête** to shake one's head; **être un peu secoué** (in car, plane) to have rather a bumpy ride; **2** to shake off [*dust, snow, yoke*]; **3** [*crisis*] to shake [*person, country*]; **4**° to get [sb] going°.

II se secouer *v refl* (+ *v être*) **1** to give oneself a shake; **2**° to pull oneself together; **3**° to wake up, to get moving°.

secourable /səkuʀabl/ *adj* [*person*] helpful.

secourir /səkuʀiʀ/ [26] *vtr* **1** to help; **2** to rescue; **3** to give first aid to.

secourisme /səkuʀism/ *nm* first aid.

secouriste /səkuʀist/ *nmf* first-aid worker.

secours /səkuʀ/ I *nm inv* help; **au ~!** help!; **appeler** or **crier au ~** to shout for help; **porter ~ à qn** to help sb; **le ~ en mer** sea rescue operations; **de ~** [*wheel*] spare; [*exit*] emergency; [*kit*] first-aid; [*team*] rescue; [*battery*] back-up.
II *nm pl* **1** rescuers; reinforcements; **2** relief supplies; supplies; **premiers ~** first aid.

secousse /səkus/ *nf* jolt; **~ (sismique)** (earth) tremor.

secret, **-ète** /səkʀɛ, ɛt/ I *adj* **1** secret; **2** [*person*] secretive.
II *nm* **1** secret; **ne pas avoir de ~s pour qn** to have no secrets from sb; **il n'en fait pas un ~** he makes no secret of it; **2** secrecy; **mettre qn dans le ~** to let sb in on the secret; **en ~** in secret; **encore une de ces gaffes dont il a le ~** another of those blunders that only he knows how to make; **3** solitary confinement.
■ **~ de Polichinelle** open secret; **~ professionnel** professional confidentiality.

secrétaire /s(ə)kʀetɛʀ/ I *nmf* secretary.
II *nm* (piece of furniture) secretaire (GB), secretary (US).
■ **~ de direction** personal assistant; **~ d'État** (in France) minister; (in Great Britain, America) Secretary of State; **~ de rédaction** subeditor (GB), copy-editor.

secrétariat /s(ə)kʀetaʀja/ *nm* **1** secretarial work; **2** secretariat.

secrète ▸ **secret** I.

sécréter /sekʀete/ [1] *vtr* **1** to secrete [*sap, bile*]; **2** to exude [*liquid*].

sécrétion /sekʀesjɔ̃/ *nf* secretion.

sectaire /sɛktɛʀ/ *adj*, *nmf* sectarian.

secte /sɛkt/ *nf* sect; faction.

secteur /sɛktœʀ/ *nm* **1** (Econ) sector; **~ tertiaire** service sector; **~ d'activité** sector; **2** area, territory; (Mil) sector; **3** (electrical) **le ~** the mains; **appareil fonctionnant sur ~** mains-operated appliance; **panne de ~** power failure.

section /sɛksjɔ̃/ *nf* **1** section; (of party, trade union) branch; (of book) part; **2** (Sch) stream (GB), track (US).
■ **~ d'autobus** fare stage.

sectionner /sɛksjɔne/ [1] *vtr* **1** to sever; **2** to divide up [*organization*].

séculaire /sekylɛʀ/ *adj* **1** [*tradition*] ancient; **2** [*house, tree*] hundred-year-old.

séculier, **-ière** /sekylje, ɛʀ/ *adj* secular.

sécuriser /sekyʀize/ [1] *vtr* **1** to reassure; **2** to make [sb] feel secure.

sécurité /sekyʀite/ *nf* **1** security; **~ de l'emploi** job security; **de ~** [*system*] security; [*reasons*] of security; **2** safety; **se sentir en ~** to feel secure or safe.
■ **~ routière** road safety; **~ sociale** *French national health and pensions organization.*

sédatif /sedatif/ *nm* sedative.

sédentaire /sedɑ̃tɛʀ/ *adj* sedentary.

sédentarité /sedɑ̃taʀite/ *nf* (of population) settled way of life; (of job) sedentary nature.

sédiment /sedimɑ̃/ *nm* sediment.

sédimentation /sedimɑ̃tasjɔ̃/ *nf* sedimentation.

séducteur, **-trice** /sedyktœʀ, tʀis/ I *adj* seductive, attractive.
II *nm,f* **1** charmer; **2** seducer/seductress.

séduction /sedyksjɔ̃/ *nf* **1** charm; **2** seduction; **pouvoir de ~** (of person) power of seduction; (of money) lure; (of words) seductive power.

séduire /sedɥiʀ/ [1] *vtr* **1** [*person*] to captivate; **il aime ~** he likes to charm people; **2** to appeal to [*person*]; **3** [*person*] to win over; **4** to seduce.

séduisant, **~e** /sedɥizɑ̃, ɑ̃t/ *adj* [*person*] attractive; [*idea*] appealing.

segment /sɛgmɑ̃/ *nm* segment.

segmenter /sɛgmɑ̃te/ [1] *vtr*, **se segmenter** *v refl* (+ *v être*) to segment.

ségrégation /segʀegasjɔ̃/ *nf* segregation.

seiche /sɛʃ/ *nf* cuttlefish.

seigle /sɛgl/ *nm* rye; **pain de ~** rye bread.

seigneur /sɛɲœʀ/ *nm* lord; **être grand ~** to be full of largesse.
■ **~ de la guerre** warlord.
IDIOMS **à tout ~ tout honneur** (Proverb) credit where credit is due.

Seigneur /sɛɲœʀ/ *nm* Lord; **~!** Good Lord!

seigneurial, **~e**, *mpl* **-iaux** /sɛɲœʀjal, o/ *adj* [*home*] stately; [*manner*] lordly.

sein /sɛ̃/ *nm* **1** (Anat) breast; **les ~s nus** topless; **nourrir (son enfant) au ~** to breast-feed (one's baby); **2 au ~ de** within.

séisme /seism/ *nm* earthquake, seism.

seize /sɛz/ *adj inv*, *pron*, *nm inv* sixteen.

seizième /sɛzjɛm/ *adj* sixteenth.

séjour /seʒuʀ/ *nm* **1** stay; **~s à l'étranger** (on CV) time spent abroad; **2 (salle de) ~** living room; **3 un ~ champêtre** a rural retreat.
■ **~ linguistique** language study vacation.

séjourner /seʒuʀne/ [1] *vi* **1** [*person*] to stay; **2** [*liquid*] to remain; [*snow*] to lie.

sel /sɛl/ *nm* **1** salt; **gros ~** coarse salt; **2** (figurative) **la situation ne manque pas de ~** the situation has a certain piquancy.
■ **~s de bain** bath salts.

sélect○, **~e** /selɛkt/ *adj* [*club, bar*] exclusive; [*clientele*] select.

sélectif, **-ive** /selɛktif, iv/ *adj* selective.

sélection /selɛksjɔ̃/ *nf* (gen) selection; (for a job) selection process; **~ à l'entrée** selective entry.

sélectionner /selɛksjɔne/ [1] *vtr* to select.

self-service, *pl* **~s** /sɛlfsɛʀvis/ *nm* self-service restaurant.

selle /sɛl/ I *nf* saddle; **remis en ~** [*player, regime*] firmly (re)established.
II **selles** *nf pl* (Med) stools.

seller /sele/ [1] *vtr* to saddle.

sellette /selɛt/ *nf* **être sur la ~** to be in the hot seat.

selon /səlɔ̃/ *prep* **1** according to; **~ moi, il va pleuvoir** in my opinion, it's going to rain; **~ les termes du président** in the President's words; **l'idée ~ laquelle** the idea that; **2** depending on [*time, circumstances*]; **la situation varie ~ les régions** the situation varies from region to region; **c'est ~**° it all depends.

semailles /səmɑj/ *nf pl* **1** sowing season; **2** seeds; **3 faire les ~** to sow.

semaine /s(ə)mɛn/ *nf* **1** week; **2** week's wages.
IDIOMS **vivre à la petite ~** to live from day to day.

sémantique /semɑ̃tik/ **I** *adj* semantic.
II *nf* semantics.

semblable /sɑ̃blabl/ **I** *adj* **1** similar; **2** identical.
II *nmf* fellow creature; **eux et leurs ~s** they and their kind.

semblant /sɑ̃blɑ̃/ *nm* **un ~ de légalité** a semblance of legality; **faire ~ d'être triste** to pretend to be sad.

sembler /sɑ̃ble/ [1] **I** *vi* to seem.
II *v impers* **il semble bon de faire** it seems appropriate to do; **le problème est réglé à ce qu'il me semble** the problem has been solved, or so it seems to me; **faites comme bon vous semble** do whatever you think best; **elle a, semble-t-il, refusé** apparently, she has refused.

semelle /s(ə)mɛl/ *nf* sole.
■ **~ compensée** wedge heel; **~ intérieure** insole.
IDIOMS **être dur comme de la ~**° to be as tough as old boots° (GB) or leather (US).

semence /s(ə)mɑ̃s/ *nf* seed.

semer /s(ə)me/ [1] *vtr* **1** to sow [*seeds*]; **2** to sow [*discord, doubt*]; to spread [*confusion, panic*]; **3** to scatter [*objects*]; **semé de difficultés** plagued with difficulties; **ciel semé d'étoiles** star-spangled sky; **on récolte ce qu'on a semé** as you sow so shall you reap; **4**° to drop [*purse, keys*]; **5**° to shake off [*pursuer*].

semestre /s(ə)mɛstʀ/ *nm* (Sch) semester.

semestriel, -ielle /səmɛstʀijɛl/ *adj* **1** twice-yearly; half-yearly; **2** (at university) [*exam*] end-of-semester (GB), final (US); [*class*] one-semester.

semeur, -euse /səmœʀ, øz/ *nm,f* sower; **~ de troubles** troublemaker.

semi /səmi/ *pref* **~-automatic** semiautomatic; **~-liberté** relative freedom; **~-remorque** articulated lorry (GB), tractor-trailer (US).

sémillant, ~e /semijɑ̃, ɑ̃t/ *adj* spirited.

séminaire /seminɛʀ/ *nm* **1** seminar; **2** seminary.

séminariste /seminaʀist/ *nm* seminarist.

semis /s(ə)mi/ *nm inv* **1** sowing; **2** seedling; **3** seedbed.

semonce /səmɔ̃s/ *nf* reprimand; **coup de ~** warning shot.

semoule /səmul/ *nf* semolina; **sucre ~** caster sugar.

sempiternel, -elle /sɑ̃pitɛʀnɛl/ *adj* perpetual.

sénat /sena/ *nm* senate.

sénateur /senatœʀ/ *nm* senator.

sénile /senil/ *adj* senile.

sénilité /senilite/ *nf* senility.

sens /sɑ̃s/ **I** *nm inv* **1** direction, way; **dans le ~ de la largeur** widthways, across; **être dans le bon ~** to be the right way up; **retourner un problème dans tous les ~** to consider a problem from every angle; **courir dans tous les ~** to run all over the place; **~ dessus dessous** /sɑ̃d(ə)sydəsu/ upside down; (figurative) very upset; **aller dans le bon ~** [*reforms*] to be a step in the right direction; **le ~ de l'histoire** the tide of history; **nous travaillons dans ce ~** that's what we are working toward(s); **2** meaning; **le ~ figuré d'un mot** the figurative sense of a word; **employer un mot au ~ propre** to use a word literally; **cela n'a pas de ~** it doesn't make sense; it's absurd; **3** sense; **retrouver l'usage de ses ~** to regain consciousness; **avoir le ~ pratique** to be practical; **ne pas avoir le ~ du ridicule** not to realize when one looks silly; **avoir le ~ des affaires** to have a flair for business; **n'avoir aucun ~ des réalités** to live in a dream world.
II *nm pl* senses; **plaisirs des ~** sensual pleasures.
■ **~ giratoire** roundabout (GB), traffic circle (US); **~ interdit** no-entry sign; one-way street; **~ obligatoire** one-way sign; **~ unique** one-way sign; one-way street.

sensation /sɑ̃sasjɔ̃/ *nf* feeling, sensation; **aimer les ~s fortes** to like one's thrills; **la décision a fait ~** the decision caused a sensation; **un journal à ~** a tabloid.

sensationnel, -elle /sɑ̃sasjɔnɛl/ *adj* **1**° fantastic°; **2** sensational, astonishing.

sensé, ~e /sɑ̃se/ *adj* sensible.

sensément /sɑ̃semɑ̃/ *adv* sensibly.

sensibilisation /sɑ̃sibilizasjɔ̃/ *nf* **1 campagne de ~** awareness campaign; **2** (Med) sensitizing.

sensibiliser /sɑ̃sibilize/ [1] *vtr* **1 ~ le public à un problème** to increase public awareness of an issue; **2** (Med) to sensitize.

sensibilité /sɑ̃sibilite/ *nf* **1** sensibility; **2** (in photography) sensitivity.

sensible /sɑ̃sibl/ *adj* **1** (gen) sensitive; **être ~ aux compliments** to like compliments; **je suis ~ au fait que** I am aware that; **un être ~** a sentient being; **je suis très ~ au froid** I really feel the cold; **2** [*skin*] sensitive; (because of injury) tender; [*limb*] sore; **j'ai la gorge ~** I often get a sore throat; **3** [*rise, difference*] appreciable; [*effort*] real; **la différence est à peine ~** the difference is hardly noticeable.

sensiblement /sɑ̃sibləmɑ̃/ *adv* **1** [*reduce, increase*] appreciably, noticeably; [*different*] perceptibly; **2** [*alike*] roughly.

sensiblerie /sɑ̃sibləʀi/ *nf* sentimentality.

sensitif, -ive /sɑ̃sitif, iv/ *adj* sensory.

sensoriel, -ielle /sɑ̃sɔʀjɛl/ *adj* sensory; **organe ~** sense organ.

sensualité /sɑ̃sɥalite/ *nf* sensuality.

sensuel, -elle /sɑ̃sɥɛl/ *adj* sensual.

sentence /sɑ̃tɑ̃s/ *nf* **1** sentence; **2** maxim.

sentencieux, **-ieuse** /sɑ̃tɑ̃sjø, øz/ *adj* sententious.

senteur /sɑ̃tœʀ/ *nf* scent.

senti, **~e** /sɑ̃ti/ *adj* **bien ~** [*words*] well-chosen; [*answer*] blunt; [*speech*] forthright.

sentier /sɑ̃tje/ *nm* path, track; **hors des ~s battus** off the beaten track.

sentiment /sɑ̃timɑ̃/ *nm* feeling; **il est incapable de ~** he's incapable of emotion; **faire du ~** to sentimentalize; **prendre qn par les ~s** to appeal to sb's better nature; **les beaux** or **bons ~s** fine sentiments; **être animé de mauvais ~s** to have bad intentions; **~s affectueux** or **amicaux** best wishes.

sentimental, **~e**, *mpl* **-aux** /sɑ̃timɑ̃tal, o/ *adj* sentimental; romantic; **vie ~e** lovelife.

sentinelle /sɑ̃tinɛl/ *nf* sentry.

sentir /sɑ̃tiʀ/ [30] **I** *vtr* **1** to smell; **2** to feel; **je ne sens rien** I can't feel anything; **je ne sens plus mes pieds** my feet are numb; **3** to be conscious of [*importance*]; to feel [*beauty, force*]; to appreciate [*difficulties*]; to sense [*danger, disapproval*]; **je sens qu'il est sincère** I feel that he's sincere; **je te sens inquiet** I can tell you're worried; **se faire ~** [*need*] to be felt.
II *vi* **1** to smell; **ça sent l'ail** it smells of garlic; **2 le poisson commence à ~** the fish is beginning to smell; **3** to smack of; **ciel nuageux qui sent l'orage** cloudy sky that heralds a storm.
III se sentir *v refl* (+ *v être*) **1** to feel; **se ~ mieux** to feel better; **2** [*effect*] to be felt.
IDIOMS **je ne peux pas le ~** I can't stand him.

seoir† /swaʀ/ [41] **I seoir à** *vtr* [*dress*] to suit.
II *v impers* **il sied de faire** it is appropriate to do.

sépale /sepal/ *nm* sepal.

séparable /sepaʀabl/ *adj* separable.

séparation /sepaʀasjɔ̃/ *nf* **1** (gen, Law) separation; **2** (between gardens) boundary; (figurative) boundary, dividing line.
■ **~ de biens** (Law) matrimonial division of property; **~ de corps** (Law) judicial separation.

séparatisme /sepaʀatism/ *nm* separatism.

séparé, **~e** /sepaʀe/ *adj* **1 vivre ~** to live apart; **2** separate.

séparément /sepaʀemɑ̃/ *adv* separately.

séparer /sepaʀe/ [1] **I** *vtr* **1** (gen) to separate; to pull [sb] apart [*fighters*]; **c'est un malentendu qui les a séparés** they parted because of a misunderstanding; **2** to distinguish between [*concepts, areas*]; **3** to divide; **tout les sépare** they are worlds apart.
II se séparer *v refl* (+ *v être*) **1** [*guests*] to part; [*partners, lovers*] to split up; **2 se ~ de** to leave [*friend, group*]; to split up with; (Law) to separate from [*husband, wife*]; **3 se ~ de** to let [sb] go [*employee*]; to part with [*personal possession*]; **4** to divide; **la route se sépare (en deux)** the road forks.

sépia /sepja/ *adj inv* sepia.

sept /sɛt/ *adj inv, pron, nm inv* seven.
■ **les ~ Familles** (Games) Happy Families.
IDIOMS **tourne ~ fois ta langue dans ta bouche avant de parler** think before you speak.

septante /sɛptɑ̃t/ *adj inv, pron* seventy.

septembre /sɛptɑ̃bʀ/ *nm* September.

septennat /sɛptena/ *nm* seven-year term (of office).

septentrional, **~e**, *mpl* **-aux** /sɛptɑ̃tʀijɔnal, o/ *adj* northern.

septicémie /sɛptisemi/ *nf* blood-poisoning.

septième /sɛtjɛm/ **I** *adj* seventh.
II *nf* (Sch) *fifth year of primary school, age 10–11.*
■ **le ~ art** cinematography.

septuagénaire /sɛptɥaʒenɛʀ/ *adj* **être ~** to be in one's seventies.

septuor /sɛptɥɔʀ/ *nm* septet.

sépulture /sepyltyʀ/ *nf* **1** grave; **2** burial.

séquelle /sekɛl/ *nf* **1** after-effect; **2** repercussion; **3** consequence.

séquence /sekɑ̃s/ *nf* sequence.

séquestrer /sekɛstʀe/ [1] *vtr* (gen) to hold [*hostage*]; (Law) to confine [sb] illegally.

sérail /seʀaj/ *nm* **1** seraglio; **2** innermost circle.

serein, **~e** /səʀɛ̃, ɛn/ *adj* [*sky*] clear; [*person, face*] serene; [*criticism*] objective.

sereinement /səʀɛnmɑ̃/ *adv* [*look*] serenely; [*speak*] calmly; [*judge*] dispassionately.

sérénade /seʀenad/ *nf* **1** serenade; **2**○ racket○, din.

sérénité /seʀenite/ *nf* **1** (of face, mind) serenity; (of person) equanimity; **2** (of judge, verdict) impartiality; **3** (of sky, weather) calmness.

serf, **serve** /sɛʀ, sɛʀv/ *nm,f* serf.

sergent /sɛʀʒɑ̃/ *nm* (Mil) (in army) ≈ sergeant.

série /seʀi/ *nf* **1** series; **catastrophes en ~** a series of catastrophes; **2 numéro de ~** serial number; **~ limitée** limited edition; **modèle de ~** (gen) mass-produced model; (car) production model; **numéro hors ~** special issue; **3** set, collection; **4** (on television) series; **5** (Sport) division.
■ **~ noire** series of disasters.

sérieusement /seʀjøzmɑ̃/ *adv* seriously; considerably.

sérieux, **-ieuse** /seʀjø, øz/ **I** *adj* **1** serious; **être ~ dans son travail** to be serious about one's work; **avoir des lectures sérieuses** to read serious books; **2** [*situation, threat*] serious; [*clue, lead*] important; [*offer*] genuine; **'pas ~ s'abstenir'** 'genuine enquiries only'; **3** reliable; **4** responsible; **cela ne fait pas très ~** that doesn't make a very good impression; **5** [*effort, need*] real; [*progress*] considerable; [*handicap*] serious.
II *nm* seriousness; **garder son ~** to keep a straight face; **perdre son ~** to start to laugh; **se prendre au ~** to take oneself seriously.

sérigraphie /seʀigʀafi/ *nf* **1** silkscreen printing; **2** silkscreen print.

serin /səʀɛ̃/ *nm* (Zool) canary.

seriner○ /səʀine/ [1] *vtr* **~ qch à qn** to drum sth into sb.

seringue /sərɛ̃g/ *nf* syringe.

serment /sɛrmɑ̃/ *nm* **1** oath; **prêter ~** to take the oath; **2** vow.
■ **un ~ d'ivrogne** an empty promise.

sermon /sɛrmɔ̃/ *nm* **1** sermon; **2** lecture.

sermonner /sɛrmɔne/ [1] *vtr* to lecture, to give [sb] a talking-to.

séronégatif, **-ive** /seronegatif, iv/ *adj* HIV negative.

séropositif, **-ive** /seropozitif, iv/ *adj* **1** (gen) seropositive; **2** HIV positive.

serpe /sɛrp/ *nf* billhook.

serpent /sɛrpɑ̃/ *nm* (Zool) snake; **~ à sonnette** rattlesnake.

serpenter /sɛrpɑ̃te/ [1] *vi* [*road, river*] to wind.

serpentin /sɛrpɑ̃tɛ̃/ *nm* streamer.

serpillière /sɛrpijɛr/ *nf* floorcloth.

serre /sɛr/ *nf* **1** greenhouse; **2** talon, claw.

serré, **~e** /sere/ **I** *adj* **1** [*screw, nut*] tight; [*skirt, trousers*] tight; **2** [*grass*] thick; [*writing*] cramped; **3** [*deadlines, budget*] tight; [*bend*] sharp; [*control*] strict; [*struggle*] hard; [*debate*] heated; [*match*] close; **4** [*coffee*] very strong.
II *adv* [*write*] in a cramped hand; [*knit*] tightly; **il va falloir jouer ~ si...** we can't take any chances if...

serre-livres /sɛrlivr/ *nm inv* book end.

serrer /sere/ [1] **I** *vtr* **1** to grip [*steering wheel, rope*]; **~ qn/qch dans ses bras** to hug sb/sth; **~ la main de qn** to shake hands with sb; **~ les poings** to clench one's fists; **ça me serre le cœur de voir ça** it wrings my heart to see that; **2** to tighten [*knot, screw*]; to turn [sth] off tightly [*tap*]; **sans ~** [*attach, screw*] loosely; **trop serré** too tight; **3** [*shoes, clothes*] to be too tight; **4 ~ à droite** to get or stay in the right-hand lane; **~ qn de près** to be hot on sb's tail; **5** to push [sth] closer together [*objects, tables*]; to squeeze [*person*]; **être serrés** to be packed together; **6** to cut [*expenses, prices*].
II se serrer *v refl* (+ *v être*) **1** to squeeze up; **ils se sont serrés les uns contre les autres** they huddled together; **2 se ~ dans une jupe** to squeeze oneself into a skirt; **nous nous sommes serré la main** we shook hands; **3 avoir la gorge qui se serre** to have a lump in one's throat.

serrure /seryr/ *nf* lock; **trou de ~** keyhole.

serrurerie /seryrri/ *nf* locksmith's.

serrurier /seryrje/ *nm* locksmith.

sertir /sɛrtir/ [3] *vtr* to set [*stone*].

sérum /serɔm/ *nm* serum; **~ de vérité** truth drug.

servante /sɛrvɑ̃t/ *nf* maidservant.

serve ▸ **serf**.

serveur, **-euse** /sɛrvœr, øz/ *nm,f* waiter/waitress.

servi, **~e** /sɛrvi/ **I** *pp* ▸ **servir**.
II *pp adj* **1 'prends de la viande'—'merci je suis déjà ~'** 'have some meat'—'I already have some, thank you'; **2**° **nous voulions du soleil, nous sommes ~s** we wanted some sunshine and we've certainly got it.

serviable /sɛrvjabl/ *adj* obliging, helpful.

service /sɛrvis/ **I** *nm* **1** favour[GB]; **rendre un ~ à qn** to do sb a favour[GB]; **2** (in transport) service; **~ de bus** bus service; **3 être en ~** [*lift*] to be in working order; [*motorway*] to be open; [*bus*] to be running; **4 rendre ~ à qn** [*machine*] to be a help to sb; [*shop*] to be convenient (for sb); **5** service; **être au ~ de son pays** to serve one's country; **travailler au ~ de la paix** to work for peace; **'à votre ~!'** 'don't mention it!', 'not at all!'; **avoir 20 ans de ~ dans une entreprise** to have been with a firm 20 years; **être de** or **en ~** to be on duty; **état de ~(s)** record of service; **pharmacie de ~** duty chemist; **6** (at table) service; **faire le ~** to serve; to act as waiter; **7** (domestic) service; **entrer au ~ de qn** to go to work for sb; **prendre qn à son ~** to take sb on; **escalier de ~** backstairs; **8** department; **~ des urgences** casualty department (GB), emergency room (US); **les ~s de sécurité** the security services; **chef de ~** (in administration) section head; (in hospital) senior consultant; **9** (Mil) **~ (militaire)** military or national service; **10** set; **un ~ à thé** a tea set; **~ de table** dinner service; **11** (in church) service; **12** (Sport) service, serve; **être au ~** to serve.
II services *nm pl* services; **se passer des ~s de qn** to dispense with sb's services.
■ **~ après-vente** after-sales service; **~ d'ordre** stewards; **~ de presse** press office; press and publicity department; **~ public** public service.

serviette /sɛrvjɛt/ *nf* **1 ~ (de toilette)** towel; **~ (de table)** (table) napkin; **2** briefcase.
■ **~ de bain** bath towel; **~ hygiénique** sanitary towel (GB), sanitary napkin (US).

serviette-éponge, *pl* **serviettes-éponges** /sɛrvjɛtepɔ̃ʒ/ *nf* terry towel.

servile /sɛrvil/ *adj* servile; slavish.

servilement /sɛrvilmɑ̃/ *adv* [*obey, imitate*] slavishly; [*flatter*] obsequiously.

servilité /sɛrvilite/ *nf* servility.

servir /sɛrvir/ [30] **I** *vtr* **1** to serve; **qu'est-ce que je vous sers (à boire)?** what would you like to drink?; **tu es mal servi** you haven't got much; **'Madame est servie'** 'dinner is served, Madam'; **au moment de ~** before serving; **2** [*situation*] to help [*person, cause*]; to serve [*interests*]; [*person*] to further [*ambition*]; **3** to deal [*cards*].
II servir à *v+prep* **1 ~ à qn** to be used by sb; **~ à qch** to be used for sth; **les exercices m'ont servi à comprendre la règle** the exercises helped me to understand the rule; **2** to come in useful; **cela ne sert à rien de faire** there's no point in doing.
III servir de *v+prep* **~ d'intermédiaire à qn** to act as an intermediary for sb; **~ d'arme** to be used as a weapon.
IV *vi* **1** (Mil) **~ dans** to serve in; **2** (Sport) to serve; **3 il a servi dix ans chez nous** he was in our service for ten years; **4** [*object*] to be used.
V se servir *v refl* (+ *v être*) **1** (at table) to help oneself; **se ~ un verre de vin** to pour oneself a glass of wine; **2** (in shop) to serve oneself;

3 se ~ de qn/qch to use sb/sth; **se ~ d'une situation** to make use of a situation; **4** (Culin) to be served.

serviteur /sɛʀvitœʀ/ *nm* servant.

servitude /sɛʀvityd/ *nf* **1** servitude; **2** (figurative) constraint.

ses ▶ son[1].

sésame /sezam/ *nm* sesame.

session /sɛsjɔ̃/ *nf* **1** session; **2** examination session; **~ de rattrapage** retakes; **3** course.

set /sɛt/ *nm* (Sport) set.
■ **~ de table** place mat.

seuil /sœj/ *nm* **~ (de la porte)** doorstep; doorway, threshold.

seul, **~e** /sœl/ **I** *adj* **1** alone, on one's own; **vous êtes ~ dans la vie?** are you single?; **elle veut vous parler ~ à ~** or **~e à ~(e)** she wants to speak to you in private; **parler tout ~** to talk to oneself; **2** by oneself, on one's own; **il a mangé un poulet à lui tout ~** he ate a whole chicken all by himself; **ça va tout ~** it's really easy; things are running smoothly; **3** only; **la ~e et unique personne** the one and only person; **pas un ~ client** not a single customer; **l'espion et l'ambassadeur sont une ~e et même personne** the spy and the ambassador are one and the same person; **d'une ~e pièce** in one piece; **à la ~e idée de faire** at the very idea of doing; **ils ont parlé d'une ~e voix** they were unanimous; **elle ~e pourrait vous le dire** only she could tell you; **4** lonely; **c'est un homme ~** he's a lonely man.
II *nm,f* **le ~, la ~e** the only one; **les ~s, les ~es** the only ones; **ils sont les ~s à croire que** they're alone in thinking that.

seulement /sœlmɑ̃/ *adv* **1** only; **nous étions ~ deux** there were only the two of us; **'nous étions dix'—'~?'** 'there were ten of us'—'is that all?'; **elle revient ~ demain** she's not coming back until tomorrow; **2 c'est possible, ~ je veux y réfléchir** it's possible, only or but I'd like to think about it; **3 si ~** if only.

sève /sɛv/ *nf* **1** sap; **2** (figurative) vigour[GB].

sévère /sevɛʀ/ *adj* [*look, tone, punishment*] severe; [*person, upbringing*] strict; [*selection*] rigorous; [*judgment*] harsh; [*losses*] heavy.

sévèrement /sevɛʀmɑ̃/ *adv* severely; harshly; strictly.

sévérité /seveʀite/ *nf* **1** strictness, harshness; **2** sternness, severity.

sévices /sevis/ *nm pl* physical abuse.

sévir /seviʀ/ [3] *vi* **1** to clamp down; **2** [*storm, war*] to rage; [*poverty*] to be rife; **3** (figurative) [*doctrine*] to hold sway; [*phenomenom*] to be rife.

sevrage /səvʀaʒ/ *nm* weaning.

sevrer /səvʀe/ [16] *vtr* to wean.

sexagénaire /sɛksaʒenɛʀ/ *nmf* sixty-year old.

sexe /sɛks/ *nm* **1** sex; **indépendamment du ~, de l'ethnie, de l'âge** irrespective of gender, race or age; **un bébé de ~ féminin** a female baby; **2** genitals.

sexiste /sɛksist/ *adj, nmf* sexist.

sexologue /sɛksɔlɔg/ *nmf* sex therapist.

sextuor /sɛkstɥɔʀ/ *nm* sextet.

sextuplé, **~e** /sɛkstyple/ *nm,f* sextuplet.

sexualité /sɛksɥalite/ *nf* sexuality.

sexué, **~e** /sɛksɥe/ *adj* sexed; sexual.

sexuel, **-elle** /sɛksɥɛl/ *adj* (gen) sexual; [*education, gland*] sex.

seyant, **~e** /sɛjɑ̃, ɑ̃t/ *adj* becoming.

SFP /ɛsɛfpe/ *nf* (*abbr* = **Société française de production et de création audiovisuelles**) *TV and video production company*.

shaker /ʃekœʀ/ *nm* cocktail shaker.

shampooing /ʃɑ̃pwɛ̃/ *nm* shampoo.

shampouiner /ʃɑ̃pwine/ [1] *vtr* to shampoo.

shérif /ʃeʀif/ *nm* sheriff.

shetland /ʃɛtlɑ̃d/ *nm* **1** Shetland wool; **2** Shetland pony.

shoot /ʃut/ *nm* **1** (Sport) shot; **2**○ (of drug) fix○.

shooter /ʃute/ [1] *vi* (Sport) to shoot.

short /ʃɔʀt/ *nm* shorts.

si[1] /si/ **I** *adv* **1** yes; **'tu ne le veux pas?'—'~!'** 'don't you want it?'—'yes I do!'; **il n'ira pas, moi ~** he won't go, but I will; **2** so; **c'est un homme ~ agréable** he's such a pleasant man; **~ bien que** so; so much so that; **rien n'est ~ beau qu'un coucher de soleil** there's nothing so beautiful as a sunset; **est-elle ~ bête qu'on le dit?** is she as stupid as people say (she is)?
II *conj* (**s'** *before* il *or* ils) **1** if; **~ j'étais riche** if I were rich; **~ j'avais su!** if only I'd known!; **vous pensez ~ j'étais content!** you can imagine how happy I was!; **~ ce n'est (pas) toi, qui est-ce?** if it wasn't you, who was it?; **il n'a rien pris avec lui ~ ce n'est un livre** he didn't take anything with him apart from a book; **à quoi servent ces réunions ~ ce n'est à nous faire perdre notre temps?** what purpose do these meetings serve other than to waste our time?; **~ tant est qu'une telle distinction ait un sens** if such a distinction makes any sense; **2 ~ tu venais avec moi?** how about coming with me? **3** whereas.

si[2] /si/ *nm inv* (note) B; (in sol-fa) ti.

siamois, **~e** /sjamwa, az/ **I** *adj* **1** [*cat*] Siamese; **2 des frères ~** male Siamese twins.
II *nm inv* **1** (language) Siamese; **2** Siamese cat.

sibylle /sibil/ *nf* sibyl.

sida /sida/ *nm* (*abbr* = **syndrome immunodéficitaire acquis**) Aids.

side-car, *pl* **~s** /sidkaʀ/ *nm* **1** sidecar; **2** motorcycle combination.

sidéral, **~e**, *mpl* **-aux** /sideʀal, o/ *adj* sidereal.

sidérer○ /sideʀe/ [14] *vtr* to stagger○.

sidérurgie /sideʀyʀʒi/ *nf* steel industry.

sidérurgique /sideʀyʀʒik/ *adj* steel.

siècle /sjɛkl/ *nm* **1** century; **au Ve ~ après J.-C.** in the 5th century AD; **d'ici la fin du ~** by the turn of the century; **il y a des ~s○ que je ne suis venu ici** I haven't been here for ages; **2** age; **le ~ de Louis XIV** the age of Louis XIV.

sied ▶ seoir.

siège /sjɛʒ/ *nm* **1** seat; **2 ~ (social)** (of company) head office; (of organization) headquarters; **3** (of MP) seat; **4** (Mil) siege; **5** (Anat) seat.

siéger /sjeʒe/ [15] *vi* **1** to sit; **2** to be in session; **3** to have its headquarters.

sien, **sienne** /sjɛ̃, sjɛn/ **I** *det* **cette maison est sienne à présent** the house is now his/hers.

II le sien, **la sienne**, **les siens**, **les siennes** *pron* his/hers/its; **être de retour parmi les ~s** to be back with one's family; to be back among one's own friends; **faire des siennes** [*person*] to be up to mischief; [*computer*] to act up.

sieste /sjɛst/ *nf* nap, siesta.

sifflement /sifləmɑ̃/ *nm* (of person, train) whistle; (of kettle, wind) whistling; (of bird, insect) chirping; (of snake) hissing.

siffler /sifle/ [1] **I** *vtr* **1** to whistle [*tune*]; to whistle for [*dog*]; to whistle at [*person*]; **2** [*referee*] to blow one's whistle for [*foul*]; **3** to hiss, to boo.

II *vi* **1** (gen) to whistle; [*projectile*] to whistle through the air; [*bird*] to chirp; [*snake*] to hiss; **2** to blow one's whistle.

sifflet /siflɛ/ *nm* **1** whistle; **coup de ~** whistle; **2** (of train) whistle; (of kettle) whistling; **3** hiss, boo.

IDIOMS **couper le ~ à qn**○ to shut sb up○.

sifflotement /siflɔtmɑ̃/ *nm* whistling.

siffloter /siflɔte/ [1] *vi* to whistle away to oneself.

sigle /sigl/ *nm* acronym.

signal, *pl* **-aux** /siɲal, o/ *nm* signal.

■ **~ d'alarme** alarm signal; **~ sonore** (on answerphone) tone.

signalement /siɲalmɑ̃/ *nm* description.

signaler /siɲale/ [1] **I** *vtr* **1 ~ qch à qn** to point sth out to sb; to inform sb of sth; **2 ~ à qn que** to remind sb that; **3** to indicate [*roadworks, danger*]; **4** to report [*fact*].

II se signaler *v refl* (+ *v être*) **se ~ par qch** to distinguish oneself by sth.

signalétique /siɲaletik/ *adj* descriptive; **fiche ~** specification sheet.

signalisation /siɲalizasjɔ̃/ *nf* **1** signalling[GB]; **2** signals.

■ **~ routière** roadsigns and markings.

signaliser /siɲalize/ [1] *vtr* to signpost [*road*]; to mark out and light [*runway*].

signataire /siɲatɛʀ/ *nmf* signatory.

signature /siɲatyʀ/ *nf* **1** signature; **2** signing.

signe /siɲ/ *nm* sign; **~ astral** star sign; **~ précurseur** omen; **~ distinctif** or **particulier** distinguishing feature; **c'était un ~ du destin** it was fate; **~s de ponctuation** punctuation marks; **faire ~ à qn** to wave to sb; (figurative) to get in touch with sb; **d'un ~ de la main/tête, elle m'a montré la cuisine** she pointed to/nodded her head in the direction of the kitchen; **faire ~ que oui** to indicate agreement.

IDIOMS **il n'a pas donné ~ de vie depuis six mois** there's been no sign of him for six months.

signer /siɲe/ [1] **I** *vtr* to sign; **il signe son troisième roman** he's written his third novel.

II se signer *v refl* (+ *v être*) to cross oneself.

signet /siɲɛ/ *nm* bookmark.

signifiant, **~e** /siɲifjɑ̃, ɑ̃t/ *adj* significant.

significatif, **-ive** /siɲifikatif, iv/ *adj* significant.

signification /siɲifikasjɔ̃/ *nf* **1** meaning; **2** importance.

signifier /siɲifje/ [1] *vtr* **1** to mean; **2 ~ qch à qn** to inform sb of sth.

silence /silɑ̃s/ *nm* **1** silence; **'un peu de ~ s'il vous plaît'** 'quiet please'; **passer qch sous ~** to say nothing about sth; **2** (Mus) rest.

silencieux, **-ieuse** /silɑ̃sjø, øz/ **I** *adj* silent; quiet.

II *nm* **1** (on gun) silencer; **2** (on exhaust) silencer (GB), muffler (US).

silex /silɛks/ *nm inv* flint; **en** or **de ~** flint.

silhouette /silwɛt/ *nf* **1** silhouette; outline; **2** figure; shape.

silice /silis/ *nf* silica.

silicium /silisjɔm/ *nm* silicon.

silicone /silikon/ *nf* silicone.

sillage /sijaʒ/ *nm* **1** (of ship) wake; (of plane) vapour[GB] trail; slipstream; **2** (of person) wake.

sillon /sijɔ̃/ *nm* **1** furrow; **2** line; **3** fissure; **4** groove.

sillonner /sijɔne/ [1] *vtr* **1** [*roads*] to criss-cross; [*police*] to patrol; **~ la France en voiture** to drive all over France; **2** to furrow.

silo /silo/ *nm* silo.

simagrée /simagʀe/ *nf* play-acting.

simiesque /simjɛsk/ *adj* ape-like.

similaire /similɛʀ/ *adj* similar.

similarité /similaʀite/ *nf* similarity.

similicuir /similikɥiʀ/ *nm* imitation leather.

similitude /similityd/ *nf* similarity.

simple /sɛ̃pl/ **I** *adj* **1** (gen) simple; **c'est (bien) ~, il ne fait plus rien** he simply doesn't do anything any more; **2** [*decor*] plain; [*person, air*] unaffected; **3** [*origins*] modest; **4** [*worker*] ordinary; **c'est un ~ avertissement** it's just a warning; **le ~ fait de poser la question** the mere fact of asking the question; **par ~ curiosité** out of pure curiosity; **sur ~ présentation du passeport** on presentation of one's passport; **5** [*ice-cream cone, knot*] single.

II *nm* **1 le prix varie du ~ au double** the price can turn out to be twice as high; **2** (Sport) **~ dames/messieurs** ladies'/men's singles.

■ **~ d'esprit** simple-minded.

simplement /sɛ̃pləmɑ̃/ *adv* **1** simply, merely, just; **vas-y, ~ fais attention** you can go, only be careful; **2** [*dress, live*] simply; **3** easily.

simplet, **-ette** /sɛ̃plɛ, ɛt/ *adj* simple.

simplicité /sɛ̃plisite/ *nf* **1** simplicity; **c'est d'une ~ enfantine** it's so easy a child could do it; **2** (of person) unpretentiousness; (of thing) simplicity; **avec ~** simply.

simplification /sɛ̃plifikasjɔ̃/ *nf* simplification.

simplifier /sɛ̃plifje/ [2] **I** *vtr* to simplify.

II **se simplifier** *v refl* (+ *v être*) **se ~ la vie** to make life easier for oneself.

simpliste /sɛ̃plist/ *adj* simplistic.

simulacre /simylakʀ/ *nm* **1** pretence[GB]; **~ de procès** mock trial; **2** sham; **~ de justice** travesty of justice.

simulateur, -trice /simylatœʀ, tʀis/ I *nm,f* **1** shammer, faker; **2** malingerer.
II *nm* (Tech) simulator.

simulation /simylasjɔ̃/ *nf* **1** simulation; **2** malingering.

simuler /simyle/ [1] *vtr* to feign; to simulate.

simultané, ~e /simyltane/ *adj* simultaneous.

sincère /sɛ̃sɛʀ/ *adj* (gen) sincere; [*friend*] true; [*emotion, offer*] genuine; [*opinion*] honest.

sincèrement /sɛ̃sɛʀmɑ̃/ *adv* **1** [*think*] really; [*regret, thank, speak*] sincerely; **2** frankly.

sincérité /sɛ̃seʀite/ *nf* sincerity; honesty; genuineness.

sinécure /sinekyʀ/ *nf* sinecure.

sine qua non /sinekwanɔn/ *phr* **condition ~** sine qua non.

singe /sɛ̃ʒ/ *nm* **1** monkey; ape; **les grands ~s** the apes; **2** mimic; **faire le ~** to clown around.

singer /sɛ̃ʒe/ [13] *vtr* to ape; to feign.

singeries /sɛ̃ʒʀi/ *nf pl* antics; **faire des ~** to monkey around; to pull funny faces.

singulariser: **se singulariser** /sɛ̃gylaʀize/ [1] *v refl* (+ *v être*) to draw attention to oneself.

singularité /sɛ̃gylaʀite/ *nf* **1** peculiarity, singularity; **2** uniqueness.

singulier, -ière /sɛ̃gylje, ɛʀ/ I *adj* **1** peculiar, unusual; **2 combat ~** single combat.
II *nm* **1** singular; **2** singularity.

singulièrement /sɛ̃gyljɛʀmɑ̃/ *adv* **1** oddly; **2** radically.

sinistre /sinistʀ/ I *adj* sinister; [*place, future*] bleak; [*evening*] dreary.
II *nm* disaster; accident; blaze.

sinistré, ~e /sinistʀe/ I *adj* stricken; **région ~e** disaster area.
II *nm,f* disaster victim.

sinon /sinɔ̃/ I *conj* **1** otherwise, or else; **2** except, apart from; **3** not to say; **c'est devenu difficile ~ impossible** it has become difficult if not impossible.
II **sinon que** *phr* except that, other than that.

sinueux, -euse /sinɥø, øz/ *adj* sinuous; winding; tortuous.

sinus /sinys/ *nm inv* sinus.

sinusite /sinyzit/ *nf* sinusitis.

siphon /sifɔ̃/ *nm* **1** (gen) siphon; **2** U-bend.

sire /siʀ/ *nm* Sire.

sirène /siʀɛn/ *nf* **1** (gen) siren; (of boat) foghorn; **2** mermaid, siren.
■ **~ d'alarme** fire alarm.

sirop /siʀo/ *nm* **1** syrup (GB), sirup (US); cordial; **2** (medicine) syrup (GB), sirup (US), mixture; **~ pectoral** cough mixture.

siroter○ /siʀɔte/ [1] *vtr* to sip.

sirupeux, -euse /siʀypø, øz/ *adj* syrupy (GB), sirupy (US).

sismique /sismik/ *adj* seismic.

sismographie /sismɔgʀafi/ *nf* seismography.

site /sit/ *nm* **1** area; **~ touristique** place of interest; **~ archéologique** archaeological site; **2** site.

sitôt /sito/ I *adv* **~ rentré** as soon as he gets back; as soon as he got back; **je n'y retournerai pas de ~** I won't go back there in a hurry○.
II *conj* **~ que** as soon as.
IDIOMS **~ dit, ~ fait** no sooner said than done.

situation /sitɥasjɔ̃/ *nf* **1** situation; **2** job, position; **3** location.
■ **~ de famille** marital status.

situer /sitɥe/ [1] I *vtr* **1** (in space and time) to place; **l'hôtel est bien situé** the hotel is in a good location; **2 ~ une histoire en 2001/à Palerme** to set a story in 2001/in Palermo.
II **se situer** *v refl* (+ *v être*) **1 se ~ à Paris en 1900** to be set in Paris in 1900; **2 politiquement, je me situe plutôt à gauche** politically, I'm more to the left.

six /sis, *but before consonant* si, *and before vowel or mute h* siz/ *adj inv, pron, nm inv* six.

sixième /sizjɛm/ I *adj* sixth.
II *nf* (Sch) *first year of secondary school, age 11–12.*

skaï® /skaj/ *nm* imitation leather.

skate-board, *pl* **~s** /skɛtbɔʀd/ *nm* **1** skateboard; **2** skateboarding.

sketch, *pl* **~es** /skɛtʃ/ *nm* sketch.

ski /ski/ *nm* **1** ski; **2 le ~** skiing.
■ **~ de fond** cross-country skiing; **~ nautique** water skiing; **~ de piste** downhill skiing.

skier /skje/ [2] *vi* to ski.

skieur, -ieuse /skjœʀ, øz/ *nm,f* skier.

slalom /slalɔm/ *nm* slalom.

slalomer /slalɔme/ [1] *vi* **1** (Sport) to slalom; **2** (figurative) to zigzag.

slave /slav/ *adj* Slavonic.

Slave /slav/ *nmf* Slav.

slip /slip/ *nm* **1** underpants; **2** slipway.

slogan /slɔgɑ̃/ *nm* slogan.

slow /slo/ *nm* slow dance.

smala○ /smala/ *nf* tribe○.

SMIC /smik/ *nm* (*abbr* = **salaire minimum interprofessionel de croissance**) guaranteed minimum wage.

smoking /smɔkiŋ/ *nm* dinner jacket (GB), tuxedo.

SNCF /ɛsɛnseɛf/ *nf* (*abbr* = **Société nationale des chemins de fer français**) *French national railway company.*

snob /snɔb/ I *adj* [*person*] stuck-up○; [*restaurant*] posh.
II *nmf* snob; **c'est un ~** he's a snob.

snobisme /snɔbism/ *nm* snobbery.

sobre /sɔbʀ/ *adj* **1** [*person*] abstemious; sober; temperate; [*life*] simple; **2** [*style*] plain, sober.

sobrement /sɔbʀəmɑ̃/ *adv* soberly; in moderation; [*live*] frugally.

sobriété /sɔbʀijete/ *nf* sobriety, temperance; restraint; moderation.

soc /sɔk/ *nm* ploughshare (GB), plowshare (US).

sociable /sɔsjabl/ *adj* **1** sociable; **2** social.

social, **~e**, *mpl* **-iaux** /sɔsjal, o/ **I** *adj* **1** social; **le milieu ~ de qn** sb's social background; **2 conflit ~** industrial dispute.
II *nm* **le ~** social issues.

socialisme /sɔsjalism/ *nm* socialism.

socialiste /sɔsjalist/ *adj*, *nmf* socialist.

sociétaire /sɔsjetɛʀ/ *nmf* member.

société /sɔsjete/ *nf* **1** society; **la haute ~** high society; **2** company; **~ de nettoyage** cleaning company; **3** (formal) **rechercher la ~ de qn** to seek sb's company.

socioculturel, **-elle** /sɔsjokyltyʀɛl/ *adj* sociocultural; **centre ~** recreation centre[GB].

sociologie /sɔsjɔlɔʒi/ *nf* sociology.

sociologue /sɔsjɔlɔg/ *nmf* sociologist.

socioprofessionnel, **-elle** /sɔsjopʀɔfɛsjɔnɛl/ *adj* social and occupational.

socle /sɔkl/ *nm* pedestal, plinth; base; stand.

socque /sɔk/ *nm* clog.

socquette /sɔkɛt/ *nf* ankle sock, anklet (US).

soda /sɔda/ *nm* fizzy drink (GB), soda (US).

sodium /sɔdjɔm/ *nm* sodium.

sodomiser /sɔdɔmize/ [1] *vtr* to sodomizer.

sœur /sœʀ/ *nf* sister; **~ jumelle** twin sister.

sofa /sɔfa/ *nm* sofa.

soi /swa/ *pron* **1 autour de ~** around one; **laisser la porte se refermer derrière ~** to let the door shut behind one; **trouver en ~ les ressources nécessaires** to find the necessary inner resources; **garder qch pour ~** to keep sth to oneself; **2 la logique n'est pas un objectif en ~** logic is not an end in itself; **cela va de ~** it goes without saying.

soi-disant /swadizɑ̃/ **I** *adj inv* **1** self-styled; **2** (controversial) so-called.
II *adv* supposedly; **elle a ~ la migraine** she has a migraine, or so she says.

soie /swɑ/ *nf* **1** silk; **2** bristle.

soierie /swaʀi/ *nf* **1** silk; **2** silk industry.

soif /swaf/ *nf* **1** thirst; **avoir ~** to be thirsty; **2 ~ de** thirst for; hunger for; lust for; **avoir ~ d'affection** to crave affection.

soigné, **~e** /swaɲe/ **I** *pp* ▶ **soigner**.
II *pp adj* **1** [*nails*] well-manicured; [*hair, clothes*] immaculate; **2** [*publication*] carefully produced; [*work*] meticulous; **peu ~** [*work*] careless.

soigner /swaɲe/ [1] **I** *vtr* **1** [*doctor*] to treat; **2** to look after [*person, customer*]; **3** to take care over [*appearance*]; to look after [*hands*].
II se soigner *v refl* (+ *v être*) **1** to treat oneself; to look after oneself; **2** [*illness*] to be treatable; **3** to take care over one's appearance.

soigneusement /swaɲøzmɑ̃/ *adv* carefully; meticulously; neatly.

soigneux, **-euse** /swaɲø, øz/ *adj* **1** [*work*] conscientious; [*examination*] careful; **2** [*person*] neat, tidy.

soi-même /swamɛm/ *pron* oneself.

soin /swɛ̃/ **I** *nm* **1** care; **prendre ~ de qch** to take care of sth; **prendre ~ de qn/sa santé** to look after sb/one's health; **prendre ~ de sa petite personne** to coddle oneself; **laisser à qn le ~ de faire** to leave it to sb to do; **2** product; **~ antipelliculaire** dandruff treatment.
II soins *nm pl* **1** (Med) treatment; care; **recevoir des ~s** to receive treatment; **~s dentaires** dental care; **les premiers ~s à donner aux brûlés** first-aid treatment for burns; **~s à domicile** homecare; **2** care; **~s corporels** or **du corps** body care; **3 'aux bons ~s de'** 'care of', 'c/o'.
IDIOMS **être aux petits ~s pour qn** to attend to sb's every need.

soir /swaʀ/ *nm* evening; night; **le ~ du 3**, **le 3 au ~** on the evening of the 3rd; **il sort tous les samedis ~** he goes out every Saturday night; **6 heures du ~** 6 pm; **à ce ~!** see you tonight!

soirée /swaʀe/ *nf* **1** evening; **dans** or **pendant la ~**, **en ~** in the evening; **2** party; **aller dans une ~** to go to a party; **3** evening performance or show.

soit[1] /swa/ **I** ▶ **être**[1].
II *conj* **1 ~, ~** either, or; **~ du fromage, ~ un gâteau** either cheese, or a cake; **2** that is, ie; **toutes mes économies, ~ 200 francs** all my savings, ie or that is, 200 francs; **3** (in mathematics) **~ un triangle ABC** let ABC be a triangle.

soit[2] /swat/ *adv* very well; **je me suis trompé, ~, mais là n'est pas la question** all right, so I was wrong, but that's not the point.

soixantaine /swasɑ̃tɛn/ *nf* **1** about sixty; **2 avoir la ~** to be about sixty.

soixante /swasɑ̃t/ *adj inv*, *pron*, *nm inv* sixty.

soixante-dix /swasɑ̃tdis/ *adj inv*, *pron*, *nm inv* seventy.

soixante-dixième /swasɑ̃tdizjɛm/ *adj* seventieth.

soixantième /swasɑ̃tjɛm/ *adj* sixtieth.

soja /sɔʒa/ *nm* soya bean (GB), soybean (US); **sauce de ~** soy sauce.

sol /sɔl/ *nm* **1** ground; floor; **2** soil; **3** (Mus) (note) G; (in sol-fa) soh.

solaire /sɔlɛʀ/ *adj* [*energy*] solar; [*engine*] solar-powered; [*cream*] sun.

soldat /sɔlda/ *nm* soldier, serviceman.

solde[1] /sɔld/ **I** *nm* balance; **faire le ~ d'un compte** to settle an account.
II en solde *phr* **acheter une veste en ~** to buy a jacket in a sale.
III soldes *nm pl* sales; sale.

solde[2] /sɔld/ *nf* (Mil) pay; **avoir qn à sa ~** (figurative) to have sb in one's pay.

solder /sɔlde/ [1] **I** *vtr* **1** to sell off [*merchandise*]; **2** to settle the balance of [*account*].
II se solder *v refl* (+ *v être*) **se ~ par qch** to end in sth.

sole /sɔl/ *nf* (Zool) sole.

soleil /sɔlɛj/ *nm* sun; **~ de minuit** midnight sun; **en plein ~** [*sit*] in (the) hot sun; [*leave something*] in direct sunlight; **quand il y a du ~** when it's sunny; **attraper un coup** or **des coups de ~** to get sunburned.

solennel, **-elle** /sɔlanɛl/ *adj* (gen) solemn; [*appeal, declaration*] formal.

solennité /sɔlanite/ *nf* solemnity.

solfège /sɔlfɛʒ/ *nm* **1** music theory; **~ chanté** sol-fa; **2** music theory book.

solidaire /sɔlidɛʀ/ *adj* **1** [*team, group*] united; **2** (Tech) [*parts*] interdependent.

solidariser: **se solidariser** /sɔlidaʀize/ [1] *v refl* (+ *v être*) **se ~ avec qn/qch** to stand by sb/sth.

solidarité /sɔlidaʀite/ *nf* solidarity.

solide /sɔlid/ **I** *adj* **1** [*food, matter*] solid; **2** [*house, friendship*] solid; [*shoes, bag*] sturdy; [*link, fastening, blade*] strong; [*position, base*] firm; **3** [*person, constitution, heart*] strong; **avoir la tête ~** (figurative) to have one's head screwed on (right); **4** [*business, experience, reasons*] sound; [*guarantees*] firm.

II *nm* **1** solid; **manger du ~** to eat solids; **2 ce qu'il te dit, c'est du ~** what he says is sound; **3 les meubles anciens, c'est du ~** antique furniture is solidly built.

solidement /sɔlidmɑ̃/ *adv* [*attach, establish*] firmly; [*barricaded*] securely; **un rapport ~ documenté** a well-documented report.

solidifier /sɔlidifje/ [2] *vtr*, **se solidifier** *v refl* (+ *v être*) to solidify.

solidité /sɔlidite/ *nf* **1** (of construction) solidity; (of machine) strength; (of link) firmness; (of clothes) hard-wearing quality; **d'une grande ~** well-built; sturdy; strong; hard-wearing; **2** (of argument) soundness.

soliloque /sɔlilɔk/ *nm* soliloquy.

soliste /sɔlist/ *nmf* soloist.

solitaire /sɔlitɛʀ/ **I** *adj* **1** [*person, life*] solitary; [*old age, childhood*] lonely; **navigateur ~** single-handed yachtsman; **2** [*house*] isolated.

II *nmf* solitary person, loner; **en ~** [*live*] alone; [*sail*] single-handed.

III *nm* **1** (diamond) solitaire; **2** rogue boar; **3** (Games) solitaire.

solitude /sɔlityd/ *nf* **1** solitude; **2** loneliness.

solliciter /sɔlisite/ [1] *vtr* **1** (formal) to seek [*interview, post, advice*]; **2** to approach [*person, organization*]; to canvass [*customer, voter*]; **être très sollicité** to be assailed by requests; to be very much in demand.

sollicitude /sɔlisityd/ *nf* concern, solicitude.

solstice /sɔlstis/ *nm* solstice.

soluble /sɔlybl/ *adj* soluble.

solution /sɔlysjɔ̃/ *nf* **1** solution, solving; resolution; **2** solution; **une ~ de facilité** an easy way out; **3** (in chemistry) solution.

solvabilité /sɔlvabilite/ *nf* **1** solvency; **2** creditworthiness.

solvant /sɔlvɑ̃/ *nm* solvent.

sombre /sɔ̃bʀ/ *adj* **1** dark; **il fait ~** it's dark; **2** [*thought, future*] dark, black; [*conclusion*] depressing; [*air, person*] solemn; **3**○ (*before n*) [*idiot*] absolute; [*affair*] murky.

sombrer /sɔ̃bʀe/ [1] *vi* **1** [*ship*] to sink; **2 ~ dans** [*person*] to sink into [*despair, alcoholism*].

sommaire /sɔmmɛʀ/ **I** *adj* [*explanation*] cursory; [*description*] rough; [*installation, meal*] rough and ready; [*execution*] summary.

II *nm* **1** contents; **au ~ de notre numéro de juillet** featured in our July issue; **2**○ **au ~: un débat sur le chômage** a debate on unemployment is on the programme[GB].

sommairement /sɔmmɛʀmɑ̃/ *adv* summarily.

sommation /sɔmmasjɔ̃/ *nf* (from police) warning; (from guard) challenge.

somme[1] /sɔm/ *nm* nap, snooze○.

somme[2] /sɔm/ *nf* **1** sum, amount; **2** sum total; **la ~ de nos connaissances** the sum total of our knowledge; **il a fourni une grosse ~ de travail** he did a great deal of work; **en ~, ~ toute** all in all.

sommeil /sɔmɛj/ *nm* sleep; **avoir le ~ agité** to sleep fitfully; **avoir le ~ léger** to be a light sleeper.

sommeiller /sɔmeje/ [1] *vi* **1** to doze; **2** to lie dormant.

sommelier, **-ière** /sɔməlje, ɛʀ/ *nm,f* wine waiter, sommelier.

sommer /sɔmme/ [1] *vtr* **~ qn de faire** to command sb to do.

sommet /sɔmmɛ/ *nm* **1** (of mountain) peak; summit; **2** (gen) top; (of wave) crest; (of curve, career) peak; **3** (of glory, stupidity) height; **atteindre des ~s** [*prices, sales*] to peak; **4** summit; **conférence au ~** summit meeting; **5** (of triangle, angle) apex; (of cone) vertex.

sommier /sɔmje/ *nm* (bed) base.

somnambule /sɔmnɑ̃byl/ **I** *adj* **être ~** to sleepwalk.

II *nmf* sleepwalker.

somnifère /sɔmnifɛʀ/ **I** *adj* soporific.

II *nm* **1** soporific; **2** sleeping pill.

somnolence /sɔmnɔlɑ̃s/ *nf* drowsiness.

somnolent, **~e** /sɔmnɔlɑ̃, ɑ̃t/ *adj* **1** drowsy; **2** [*town*] sleepy; [*industry, country*] lethargic.

somnoler /sɔmnɔle/ [1] *vi* **1** to drowse; **2** [*town*] to be sleepy; [*industry, country*] to be lethargic.

somptueux, **-euse** /sɔ̃ptɥø, øz/ *adj* sumptuous.

son[1], **sa**, *pl* **ses** /sɔ̃, sa, sɛ/ *det* his/her/its; **ses enfants** his/her children; **ses pattes** its paws; **elle a ~ lundi** she's off on Monday; she gets Mondays off; **~ étourdie de sœur**○ his/her absent-minded sister.

son[2] /sɔ̃/ *nm* **1** sound; **ingénieur du ~** engineer; **2** volume; **baisser le ~** to turn the volume down; **3** bran; **pain au ~** bran loaf.

■ **~ et lumière** son et lumière.

sonar /sɔnaʀ/ *nm* sonar.

sonate /sɔnat/ *nf* sonata.

sondage /sɔ̃daʒ/ *nm* **1** poll; survey; **2** (Med) catheterization; probe; **3** (Naut) sounding.

sonde /sɔ̃d/ *nf* **1** (Med) catheter; probe; **2** sounding lead; sounding line; **3** drill; **4** taster.

sonder /sɔ̃de/ [1] *vtr* **1** to poll; to survey; to sound out; **2** to probe; **3** (Med) to catheterize; to probe; **4** (Naut) to sound.

songe /sɔ̃ʒ/ *nm* dream.

songer /sɔ̃ʒe/ [13] *v+prep* **~ à qch/à faire** to think of sth/of doing; **tu n'y songes pas!** you can't be serious!

songeur, **-euse** /sɔ̃ʒœʀ, øz/ *adj* pensive.

sonnant, **~e** /sɔnɑ̃, ɑ̃t/ *adj* **à trois heures ~es** on the stroke of three.

sonné, **~e** /sɔne/ **I** *pp* ▶ **sonner**.
II *pp adj* **1** groggy; shattered; **2 elle a quarante ans bien ~s**○ she's well into her forties.

sonner /sɔne/ [1] **I** *vtr* **1** to ring [*bell*]; **2** [*clock*] to strike [*hour*]; [*person*] to sound [*retreat, alarm*]; to ring out [*vespers*]; **3** to ring for; **on ne t'a pas sonné**○! did anyone ask you?; **4**○ [*blow*] to make [sb] dizzy; [*news*] to stagger.
II sonner de *v+prep* to sound [*horn*]; to play [*bagpipes*].
III *vi* **1** [*bell, phone*] to ring; [*hour*] to strike; [*alarm clock*] to go off; [*alarm, trumpet*] to sound; **leur dernière heure a sonné** their hour has come; **2** [*word, expression*] to sound.

sonnerie /sɔnʀi/ *nf* **1** ringing; chimes; **système qui déclenche une ~** system that sets off an alarm; **2** (of horn) sounding.

sonnet /sɔnɛ/ *nm* sonnet.

sonnette /sɔnɛt/ *nf* bell; doorbell; **tirer la ~ d'alarme** to pull the emergency cord; (figurative) to sound the alarm.

sonore /sɔnɔʀ/ *adj* **1** [*laugh, kiss, slap*] resounding; **2** resonant; echoing; hollow-sounding; **3** [*vibrations*] sound; **le volume ~ est tel que...** the noise level is so high that...; **effets ~s** sound effects; **un document ~** a recording; **4** [*consonant*] voiced.

sonorisation /sɔnɔʀizasjɔ̃/ *nf* public address system, PA system.

sonorité /sɔnɔʀite/ *nf* **1** (of instrument, voice) tone; **les ~s de l'italien** the sound of Italian; **2** (of hi-fi) sound quality; **3** resonance.

sophistication /sɔfistikasjɔ̃/ *nf* sophistication.

sophistiqué, **~e** /sɔfistike/ *adj* **1** sophisticated; **2** artificial, mannered.

soporifique /sɔpɔʀifik/ *adj, nm* soporific.

soprano /sɔpʀano/ *nmf* soprano.

sorbet /sɔʀbɛ/ *nm* sorbet.

sorcellerie /sɔʀsɛlʀi/ *nf* witchcraft; sorcery.

sorcier /sɔʀsje/ **I**○ *adj m* **ce n'est (pourtant) pas ~!** (but) it's dead○ easy!
II *nm* **1** wizard; sorcerer; **2** witch doctor.

sorcière /sɔʀsjɛʀ/ *nf* witch; sorceress.

sordide /sɔʀdid/ *adj* squalid; sordid.

sornettes /sɔʀnɛt/ *nf pl* tall stories.

sort /sɔʀ/ *nm* **1** lot; **être satisfait de son ~** to be satisfied with one's lot; **2** fate; **le ~ est contre moi** I'm ill-fated; **tirer qch au ~** to draw lots for sth; **3** curse, spell; **jeter un ~ à qn** to put a curse on sb; **le ~ en est jeté** the die is cast.

sortable /sɔʀtabl/ *adj* **mon mari n'est pas ~** I can't take my husband anywhere.

sorte /sɔʀt/ **I** *nf* sort, kind.
II de la sorte *phr* in this way.
III de sorte que *phr* **1** so that; **2 la toile est peinte de ~ que** the canvas is painted in such a way that; **3 de ~ que je n'ai pas pu venir** with the result that I couldn't come.
IV en quelque sorte *phr* in a way.
V en sorte de *phr* **fais en ~ d'être à l'heure** try to be on time.
VI en sorte que *phr* **fais en ~ que tout soit en ordre** make sure everything is tidy.

sortie /sɔʀti/ *nf* **1** exit; **je t'attendrai à la ~** I'll wait for you outside (the building); **à la ~ de la ville** on the outskirts of the town; on the edge of the town; **2 à ma ~ du tribunal** when I left the court; **se retrouver à la ~ de l'école** to meet after school; **à la ~ de l'hiver** at the end of winter; **3 faire une ~ fracassante** to make a dramatic exit; **la ~ de la récession/crise** the end of the recession/crisis; **4** outing; **faire une ~ avec l'école** to go on a school outing; **ce soir, c'est mon soir de ~** tonight is my night out; **priver qn de ~** to keep sb in; **5** (of new product) launching; (of film) release; (of book) publication; (of fashion collection) showing; **6** (Tech) output; **faire une ~ sur imprimante** to print.
■ **~ des artistes** stage-door; **~ d'autoroute** exit; **~ de bain** bathrobe.

sortilège /sɔʀtilɛʒ/ *nm* spell.

sortir[1] /sɔʀtiʀ/ [30] **I** *vtr* **1** to take [sb/sth] out [*person, dog*]; **2** to get [sb/sth] out; **~ les mains de ses poches** to take one's hands out of one's pockets; **~ la poubelle** to put the bin out; **~ sa langue** to stick one's tongue out; **3**○ to chuck○ [sb] out [*person*]; to send [sb] out [*pupil*]; **4 ~ qn de** to get sb out of [*situation*]; **5** to bring out [*book*]; to release [*film*]; to show [*collection*]; **6** to turn out [*book, record, film, product*]; **7** to bring [sth] out [*newspaper*]; **8**○ to come out with○ [*remarks*]; **~ une blague** to crack a joke.
II *vi* (+ *v être*) **1** to go out; to come out; **~ déjeuner** to go out for lunch; **être sorti** to be out; **~ en courant** to run out; **faire ~ qn** to get sb outside; **laisser ~ qn** to allow sb out; **2** to go out; **~ avec qn** to go out with sb; **inviter qn à sortir** to ask sb out; **3 ~ de** to leave; **~ de chez qn** to leave sb's house; **sortez d'ici!** get out of here!; **~ de son lit** to get out of bed; **~ tout chaud du four** to be hot from the oven; **~ de chez le médecin** to come out of the doctor's; **4 ~ d'un rêve** to wake up from a dream; **~ de la récession** to pull out of the recession; **~ de l'hiver** to reach the end of winter; **5 ~ à peine de l'enfance** to be just emerging from childhood; **~ d'une guerre** to emerge from a war; **6** [*water, smoke, cork*] to come out; **faire ~** to squeeze [sth] out [*juice*]; to eject [*cassette*]; **7** [*bud, insect*] to come out; [*tooth*] to come through; **8** to stick out; **9** [*film, book, new model*] to come out; **~ tous les**

jours/tous les mois [*paper*] to be published daily/monthly; **10 ~ de** [*person, product*] to come from; **~ de Berkeley** to have graduated from Berkeley; **d'où sors-tu à cette heure**○**?** where have you been?; **11 ~ du sujet** [*remark*] to be beside the point; **cela sort de mes fonctions** that's not within my authority; **12** [*number*] to come up; **13** (Comput) to exit.

III se sortir *v refl* (+ *v être*) **1 se ~ de la pauvreté** to escape from poverty; **s'en ~** to get out of it; to get over it; **s'en ~ vivant** to escape with one's life; **2 s'en ~** to pull through; to cope; to manage; **s'en ~ à peine** to scrape a living.

sortir[2] /sɔʀtiʀ/ *nm* **au ~ de** at the end of.

SOS /ɛsoɛs/ *nm* **1** SOS; **2** emergency service; **~ médecins** emergency medical service; **3** helpline; **~ enfants battus** child abuse helpline.

sosie /sɔzi/ *nm* double; **c'est ton ~!** he/she's the spitting image of you!

sot, **sotte** /so, sɔt/ **I** *adj* silly.

II *nm,f* silly thing; **petit ~!** you silly thing!

sottement /sɔtmɑ̃/ *adv* foolishly, stupidly.

sottise /sɔtiz/ *nf* **1** silliness, foolishness; **2** silly remark; **dire des ~s** to talk rubbish; **3 faire des ~s** [*children*] to be naughty.

sou /su/ *nm* **1**○ penny (GB), cent (US); **il est près de ses ~s** he's a penny-pincher; **c'est une affaire de gros ~s** there's big money involved; **2**○ **il n'a pas un ~ de bon sens** he hasn't got a scrap of common sense; **3** (former unit of French currency) sou.

soubassement /subɑsmɑ̃/ *nm* **1** (of building, pillar) base; **2** bedrock.

soubresaut /subʀəso/ *nm* start; jolt.

soubrette /subʀɛt/ *nf* maid.

souche /suʃ/ *nf* **1** (tree) stump; (vine) stock; **2** stock; **de ~ paysanne** of peasant stock; **3** (of chequebook) stub.

IDIOMS **dormir comme une ~** to sleep like a log.

souci /susi/ *nm* **1 se faire du ~** to worry; **2** problem; **j'ai d'autres ~s (en tête)** I've got other things to worry about; **3** (formal) **avoir le ~ de qch** to care about sth; **avoir le ~ de faire** to be anxious to do; **dans le seul ~ de faire plaisir** with the sole intention of pleasing; **4** marigold.

soucier: **se soucier** /susje/ [2] *v refl* (+ *v être*) to care (**de** about); **sans se ~ de qch/faire** without concerning oneself with sth/doing.

soucieux, **-ieuse** /susjø, øz/ *adj* worried.

soucoupe /sukup/ *nf* saucer.

■ **~ volante** flying saucer.

soudain, **~e** /sudɛ̃, ɛn/ **I** *adj* sudden.

II *adv* suddenly, all of a sudden.

soudainement /sudɛnmɑ̃/ *adv* suddenly.

soude /sud/ *nf* **~ caustique** caustic soda.

souder /sude/ [1] **I** *vtr* **1** to weld; **2** to join [*edges*]; to bind [sb] together [*people*].

II se souder *v refl* (+ *v être*) [*vertebrae*] to fuse; [*bone*] to knit together.

soudoyer /sudwaje/ [23] *vtr* to bribe.

souffle /sufl/ *nm* **1** breath; **couper le ~ à qn** to wind sb; (figurative) to take sb's breath away; **(en) avoir le ~ coupé** to be winded; (figurative) to be speechless; **être à bout de ~** [*person*] to be out of breath; [*country, economy*] to be running out of steam; **donner un second** or **nouveau ~ à qn/qch** to put new life into sb/sth; **avoir du ~** [*saxophonist*] to have good lungs; [*singer*] to have a powerful voice; [*sportsman*] to be fit; (figurative) [*person*] to have staying power; **2** breathing; **3** breeze; **pas un ~ d'air** not a breath of air; **4** spirit; **~ révolutionnaire** revolutionary spirit; **5** inspiration; **6** (from fan, explosion) blast; **7** (Med) **~ au cœur** heart murmur.

soufflé, **~e** /sufle/ **I**○ *adj* flabbergasted.

II *nm* (Culin) soufflé.

souffler /sufle/ [1] **I** *vtr* **1** to blow out [*candle*]; **2** to blow [*air, smoke, dust*]; **3** to whisper [*words*]; **~ qch à l'oreille de qn** to whisper sth in sb's ear; **~ la réplique à un acteur** to prompt an actor; **4** to suggest [*idea*]; **5** to blow [*glass*]; to blast [*metal*]; **6** [*explosion*] to blow out [*window*]; to blow up [*building*]; **7**○ to flabbergast.

II *vi* **1** [*wind*] to blow; **le vent souffle fort** there's a strong wind; **2** [*person*] to get one's breath back; [*horse*] to get its wind back; **3** to puff; **suant et soufflant** huffing and puffing; **4** [*person, animal*] to blow; **~ dans une trompette** to blow into a trumpet; **5** to tell sb the answer; **on ne souffle pas!** no prompting!

IDIOMS **~ comme un bœuf** or **un phoque** or **une locomotive** to puff and pant.

soufflerie /sufləʀi/ *nf* **1** blower; blower house; **2** glassblower; glassblowing company.

soufflet /suflɛ/ *nm* **1** bellows; **2** gusset.

souffleur, **-euse** /suflœʀ, øz/ *nm,f* **1** prompter; **2 ~ (de verre)** glassblower.

souffrance /sufʀɑ̃s/ *nf* suffering.

souffrant, **~e** /sufʀɑ̃, ɑ̃t/ *adj* unwell.

souffre-douleur /sufʀədulœʀ/ *nm inv* punchbag (GB), punching-bag (US).

souffrir /sufʀiʀ/ [4] **I** *vtr* **1 ~ tout de qn** to put up with anything from sb; **il ne souffre pas la critique** he can't take criticism; **2 cette affaire ne peut ~ aucun retard** this matter brooks no delay.

II *vi* **1** [*person*] to suffer; **~ de** to suffer from; **ma cheville me fait ~** my ankle hurts; **est-ce qu'il souffre?** is he in pain?; **faire ~** [*person*] to make [sb] suffer; [*situation*] to upset; **~ du racisme** to be a victim of racism; **2** [*crops, economy*] to be badly affected; [*country, city*] to suffer.

soufre /sufʀ/ *nm* sulphur[GB].

souhait /swɛ/ *nm* wish.

IDIOMS **à vos ~s!** bless you!

souhaitable /swɛtabl/ *adj* desirable.

souhaiter /swete/ [1] *vtr* **1** to hope for; **2 ~ qch à qn** to wish sb sth; **~ la bienvenue à qn** to welcome sb; **je vous souhaite d'obtenir très bientôt votre diplôme** I hope you get your degree very soon; **3 il souhaite se rendre là-bas en voiture** he would like to go by car.

souiller /suje/ [1] *vtr* **1** to soil, to make [sth] dirty; **être souillé de** to be stained with; **2** to defile [*place, person*]; to sully [*memory*].

souillon /sujɔ̃/ *nf* slattern†.

souillure /sujyʀ/ *nf* stain.

souk /suk/ *nm* **1** souk; **2**○ mess; racket○.

soûl, **~e** /su, sul/ **I** *adj* drunk.
II tout son soûl *phr* [*drink, eat*] one's fill.

soulagement /sulaʒmɑ̃/ *nm* relief.

soulager /sulaʒe/ [13] *vtr* (gen) to relieve; to ease [*conscience*]; **le comprimé m'a soulagé** the tablet made me feel better; **tu m'as soulagé d'un grand poids** you've taken a great weight off my shoulders.

soûler /sule/ [1] **I** *vtr* **1** [*person*] to get [sb] drunk; [*alcohol*] to make [sb] drunk; **2** [*perfume*] to intoxicate; **3**○ **tu me soûles avec tes histoires** you're making my head spin!
II se soûler *v refl* (+ *v être*) to get drunk.

soulèvement /sulɛvmɑ̃/ *nm* uprising.

soulever /sulve/ [16] **I** *vtr* **1** to lift [*object*]; to raise [*dust*]; **~ qn/qch de terre** to pick sb/sth up; **2** to arouse [*enthusiasm, anger*]; to stir up [*crowd*]; to raise [*problems*].
II se soulever *v refl* (+ *v être*) **1** to raise oneself up; **2** to rise up.
IDIOMS **ça me soulève le cœur** it turns my stomach; it makes me sick.

soulier /sulje/ *nm* shoe.
IDIOMS **être dans ses petits ~s** to feel uncomfortable.

souligner /suliɲe/ [1] *vtr* **1** to underline [*word*]; to outline [*eyes*]; **2** to emphasize.

soumettre /sumɛtʀ/ [60] **I** *vtr* **1** to bring [sb/sth] to heel [*person, group, region*]; to subdue [*rebels*]; **2 ~ qn/qch à** to subject sb/sth to; **3** to submit; **4 ~ un produit à une température élevée** to subject a product to a high temperature.
II se soumettre *v refl* (+ *v être*) **1** to submit; **2 se ~ à** to accept [*rule*].

soumis, **~e** /sumi, iz/ *adj* submissive.

soumission /sumisjɔ̃/ *nf* submission.

soupape /supap/ *nf* valve.

soupçon /supsɔ̃/ *nm* **1** suspicion; **2**○ (of milk, wine) drop; (of salt) pinch; (of flavour) hint.

soupçonner /supsɔne/ [1] *vtr* to suspect.

soupçonneux, **-euse** /supsɔnø, øz/ *adj* suspicious, mistrustful.

soupe /sup/ *nf* **1** soup; **à la ~**○**!** (humorous) grub's up○!; **2**○ slush.
■ **~ populaire** soup kitchen.
IDIOMS **être ~ au lait**○ to be quick-tempered; **cracher dans la ~**○ to look a gift horse in the mouth.

souper[1] /supe/ [1] *vi* to have late dinner.

souper[2] /supe/ *nm* late dinner, supper.

soupeser /supəze/ [16] *vtr* **1** to feel the weight of; **2** to weigh up [*arguments*].

soupière /supjɛʀ/ *nf* soup tureen.

soupir /supiʀ/ *nm* sigh.

soupirail, *pl* **-aux** /supiʀaj, o/ *nm* cellar window.

soupirer /supiʀe/ [1] *vi* to sigh.

souple /supl/ *adj* **1** [*body*] supple; [*stalk*] flexible; [*hair*] soft; **2** [*step, style*] flowing; [*shape*] smooth; **3** [*rule*] flexible.

souplesse /suplɛs/ *nf* **1** (of stalk) flexibility; (of hair) softness; (of body) suppleness; **2** (of step) litheness; (of gesture) grace; (of car) smoothness; (of style) fluidity; **3** (of rule) flexibility.

source /suʀs/ *nf* **1** spring; **2** source; **prendre sa ~ dans** or **à** [*river*] to rise in or at; **citer ses ~s** to give one's sources.
IDIOMS **ça coule de ~** it's obvious; **retour aux ~s** return to basics.

sourcil /suʀsi/ *nm* eyebrow.

sourciller /suʀsije/ [1] *vi* to raise one's eyebrows; **sans ~** without batting an eyelid.

sourd, **~e** /suʀ, suʀd/ **I** *adj* **1** deaf; **~ à** deaf to [*pleas*]; **2** [*noise*] dull; [*voice*] muffled; **3** [*pain*] dull; **4** [*consonant*] voiceless, surd.
II *nm,f* deaf person; **les ~s** the deaf.
IDIOMS **faire la ~e oreille** to turn a deaf ear; **comme un ~** [*shout*] at the top of one's voice; **comme un ~** like one possessed; **ce n'est pas tombé dans l'oreille d'un ~** it didn't go unheard.

sourdine /suʀdin/ *nf* (Mus) mute; (on piano) soft pedal; **écouter la radio en ~** to have the radio on quietly.

sourd-muet, **sourde-muette**, *pl* **sourds-muets**, **sourdes-muettes** /suʀmɥɛ, suʀdmɥɛt/ **I** *adj* deaf and dumb.
II *nm,f* deaf-mute.

souriant, **~e**, /suʀjɑ̃, ɑ̃t/ *adj* smiling.

souricière /suʀisjɛʀ/ *nf* **1** mousetrap; **2** trap.

sourire[1] /suʀiʀ/ [68]*vi* **1** to smile; **~ jusqu'aux oreilles** to grin from ear to ear; **2 ~ à qn** [*fate, fortune*] to smile on sb.

sourire[2] /suʀiʀ/ *nm* smile; **le ~ aux lèvres** with a smile on one's face.

souris /suʀi/ *nf inv* mouse.

sournois, **~e** /suʀnwa, az/ *adj* [*person, look*] sly; [*behaviour*] underhand; [*pain*] insidious.

sous /su/ *prep* **1** under, underneath; **un journal ~ le bras** a newspaper under one's arm; **~ la pluie** in the rain; **2** under; **~ le numéro 4757** under number 4757; **3** during; **~ la présidence de Mitterrand** during Mitterrand's presidency; **4** within; **~ peu** before long; **5 ~ traitement** undergoing treatment; **~ antibiotiques** on antibiotics.

sous-alimenté, **~e**, *mpl* **~s** /suzalimɑ̃te/ *adj* undernourished.

sous-bois /subwɑ/ *nm inv* undergrowth.

sous-catégorie, *pl* **~s** /sukategɔʀi/ *nf* subcategory.

souscription /suskʀipsjɔ̃/ *nf* **1** subscription; **2 ~ d'un contrat d'assurances** taking out an insurance policy.

souscrire /suskʀiʀ/ [67] **I** *vtr* to take out [*insurance*]; to sign [*contract*]; to subscribe [*sum of money*].
II souscrire à *v+prep* to subscribe to.

sous-cutané, **~e**, *mpl* **~s** /sukytane/ *adj* subcutaneous.

sous-développé, **~e**, *mpl* **~s** /sudevlɔpe/ *adj* underdeveloped.

sous-directeur, **-trice**, *mpl* **~s** /sudiʀɛktœʀ, tʀis/ *nm,f* assistant manager.

sous-entendre /suzɑ̃tɑ̃dʀ/ [6] *vtr* to imply.

sous-entendu, **~e**, *mpl* **~s** /suzɑ̃tɑ̃dy/ **I** *pp* ▶ **sous-entendre**.
II *pp adj* understood.
III *nm* innuendo.

sous-évaluer /suzevalɥe/ [1] *vtr* to underestimate; to undervalue.

sous-fifre°, *pl* **~s** /sufifʀ/ *nm* underling.

sous-jacent, **~e**, *mpl* **~s** /suʒasɑ̃, ɑ̃t/ *adj* **1** [*idea, problem, tension*] underlying; **2** subjacent.

sous-louer /sulwe/ [1] *vtr* to sublet; to sublease.

sous-main /sumɛ̃/ **I** *nm inv* desk blotter.
II en sous-main *phr* secretly.

sous-marin, **~e**, *mpl* **~s** /sumaʀɛ̃, in/ **I** *adj* submarine, underwater; deep-sea.
II *nm* **1** submarine; **2**° spy.

sous-officier, *pl* **~s** /suzɔfisje/ *nm* noncommissioned officer.

sous-payer /supeje/ [21] *vtr* to underpay.

sous-préfecture, *pl* **~s** /supʀefɛktyʀ/ *nf*: *administrative subdivision of a department in France.*

sous-produit, *pl* **~s** /supʀɔdɥi/ *nm* **1** by-product; **2** second-rate product.

sous-prolétariat, *pl* **~s** /supʀɔletaʀja/ *nm* underclass.

soussigné, **~e** /susiɲe/ *adj, nm,f* undersigned.

sous-sol, *pl* **~s** /susɔl/ *nm* **1** basement; **2** subsoil.

sous-tasse, *pl* **~s** /sutas/ *nf* saucer.

sous-titre, *pl* **~s** /sutitʀ/ *nm* subtitle.

sous-titrer /sutitʀe/ [1] *vtr* to subtitle.

soustraction /sustʀaksjɔ̃/ *nf* subtraction.

soustraire /sustʀɛʀ/ [58] **I** *vtr* **1** to subtract; **2** to steal; **3** to take away [*person*]; **~ qn/qch à la vue de qn** to hide sb/sth from sb; **4** to shield [*person*]; **~ qn à la mort** to save sb's life.
II se soustraire *v refl* (+ *v être*) **1 se ~ à** to escape from; **2 se ~ à la justice** to escape justice.

sous-traitance, *pl* **~s** /sutʀɛtɑ̃s/ *nf* subcontracting.

sous-verre /suvɛʀ/ *nm inv* **1** clip-frame; **2** coaster.

sous-vêtement, *pl* **~s** /suvɛtmɑ̃/ *nm* underwear.

soutane /sutan/ *nf* cassock.

soute /sut/ *nf* hold; **~ à bagages** baggage hold.

soutenable /sutnabl/ *adj* **1** bearable; **pas ~** unbearable; **2** tenable.

soutenance /sutnɑ̃s/ *nf* viva voce (GB), orals (US).

soutènement /sutɛnmɑ̃/ *nm* retaining structure; (in mine) props.

souteneur /sutnœʀ/ *nm* pimp°, procurer.

soutenir /sutniʀ/ [36] **I** *vtr* **1** (gen) to support [*person, team, currency*]; **~ à bout de bras** to keep [sb/sth] afloat [*person, project*]; **~ qn contre qn** to side with sb against sb; **~ le moral de qn** to keep sb's spirits up; **2** to maintain [*contrary*]; to defend [*paradox*]; to uphold [*opinion*]; **3** to keep [sb] going; **4** to keep [sth] going [*conversation*]; to keep up [*effort, pace*]; **5** to withstand [*shock, attack, stares*]; to bear [*comparison*]; **6 ~ sa thèse** to have one's viva voce (GB) or defense (US).
II se soutenir *v refl* (+ *v être*) to support each other.

soutenu, **~e** /sutny/ **I** *pp* ▶ **soutenir**.
II *pp adj* [*effort, activity*] sustained; [*attention*] close; [*rhythm*] steady.
III *adj* **1** [*market*] firm; [*colour*] deep; [*language*] formal; **2** (Mus) [*note*] sustained.

souterrain, **~e** /suteʀɛ̃, ɛn/ **I** *adj* **1** underground; **2 économie ~e** black economy.
II *nm* underground passage, tunnel.

soutien /sutjɛ̃/ *nm* support.

soutien-gorge, *pl* **soutiens-gorge** /sutjɛ̃gɔʀʒ/ *nm* bra.

soutirer /sutiʀe/ [1] *vtr* **~ qch à qn** to squeeze [sth] out of sb [*money*]; to extract [sth] from sb [*confession*].

souvenir[1] /suvniʀ/ [36] **se souvenir** *v refl* (+ *v être*) **se ~ de qn/qch** to remember sb/sth.

souvenir[2] /suvniʀ/ *nm* **1** memory; **garder un bon ~ de qch** to have happy memories of sth; **ne pas avoir ~ de** to have no recollection of; **2** memory; **s'effacer du ~ de qn** to fade from sb's memory; **3** souvenir; memento; **en ~** as a souvenir; as a memento; as a keepsake; **boutique de ~s** souvenir shop (GB) or store (US); **4 mon bon ~ à** remember me to.

souvent /suvɑ̃/ *adv* often.

souverain, **~e** /suvʀɛ̃, ɛn/ **I** *adj* **1** [*state*] sovereign; [*authority*] supreme; **2** [*happiness, scorn*] supreme; **3** [*remedy*] sovereign; [*advice, virtue*] sterling; **4** [*person*] haughty.
II *nm,f* sovereign, monarch.

souverainement /suvʀɛnmɑ̃/ *adv* **votre attitude me déplaît ~** I dislike your attitude intensely.

souveraineté /suvʀɛnte/ *nf* sovereignty.

soviet /sɔvjɛt/ *nm* soviet; **Soviet suprême** Supreme Soviet.

soviétique /sɔvjetik/ *adj* Soviet.

soyeux, **-euse** /swajø, øz/ *adj* silky.

SPA /ɛspea/ *nf* (*abbr* = **Société protectrice des animaux**) society for the prevention of cruelty to animals.

spacieux, **-ieuse** /spasjø, øz/ *adj* spacious.

spaghetti /spageti/ *nm inv* **des ~** spaghetti.

sparadrap /spaʀadʀa/ *nm* **1** surgical or adhesive tape; **2** (sticking) plaster (GB), Band-aid®.

spasme /spasm/ *nm* spasm.

spatial, **~e**, *mpl* **-iaux** /spasjal, o/ *adj* **1** spatial; **2** space; **vaisseau ~** spaceship.

spatule /spatyl/ *nf* **1** spatula; **2** filling-knife.

speaker, **speakerine** /spikœʀ, spikʀin/ *nm,f* announcer.

spécial, **~e**, *mpl* **-iaux** /spesjal, o/ *adj* **1** special; **2** odd.
spécialement /spesjalmɑ̃/ *adv* **1** specially; **2** especially; **pas ~** not especially.
spécialiser: **se spécialiser** /spesjalize/ [1] *v refl* (+ *v être*) to specialize.
spécialiste /spesjalist/ *nmf* specialist.
spécialité /spesjalite/ *nf* speciality (GB), specialty (US).
spécificité /spesifisite/ *nf* **1** specificity; **2** characteristic; **3** uniqueness.
spécifier /spesifje/ [2] *vtr* to specify.
spécifique /spesifik/ *adj* specific.
spécimen /spesimɛn/ *nm* **1** specimen; **2** (free) sample; **3**○ odd specimen○.
spectacle /spɛktakl/ *nm* **1** sight; **se donner** or **s'offrir en ~** to make an exhibition of oneself; **2** show; **~ de danse** dance show; **'~s'** 'entertainment'; **film à grand ~** spectacular; **3** show business.
spectaculaire /spɛktakylɛʀ/ *adj* spectacular.
spectateur, **-trice** /spɛktatœʀ, tʀis/ *nm,f* **1** member of the audience; **2** spectator.
spectre /spɛktʀ/ *nm* **1** ghost; **2** spectre[GB]; **3 ~ lumineux** spectrum of light.
spéculer /spekyle/ [1] *vi* to speculate; **~ à la hausse/baisse** to bull/bear.
spéléologie /speleɔlɔʒi/ *nf* **1** caving, potholing (GB), spelunking (US); **2** speleology.
spermatozoïde /spɛʀmatɔzɔid/ *nm* **des ~s** spermatozoa.
sperme /spɛʀm/ *nm* sperm.
sphère /sfɛʀ/ *nf* sphere.
sphincter /sfɛ̃ktɛʀ/ *nm* sphincter.
sphinx /sfɛ̃ks/ *nm inv* **1** Sphinx; **2** hawkmoth.
spirale /spiʀal/ *nf* spiral.
spiritisme /spiʀitism/ *nm* spiritualism.
spiritualité /spiʀitɥalite/ *nf* spirituality.
spirituel, **-elle** /spiʀitɥɛl/ *adj* **1** spiritual; **2** witty.
spiritueux, **-euse** /spiʀitɥø, øz/ *nm inv* spirit.
splendeur /splɑ̃dœʀ/ *nf* (of scenery, site) splendour[GB]; (of era, reign) glory.
splendide /splɑ̃did/ *adj* splendid; stunning.
spongieux, **-ieuse** /spɔ̃ʒjø, øz/ *adj* spongy.
sponsoriser /spɔ̃sɔʀize/ [1] *vtr* to sponsor.
spontané, **~e** /spɔ̃tane/ *adj* spontaneous.
spontanéité /spɔ̃taneite/ *nf* spontaneity.
sporadique /spɔʀadik/ *adj* sporadic.
spore /spɔʀ/ *nf* spore.
sport /spɔʀ/ *nm* sport; sports; **aller aux ~s d'hiver** to go on a winter sports holiday (GB) or vacation (US).
sportif, **-ive** /spɔʀtif, iv/ **I** *adj* **1** [*event*] sports; **je ne suis pas ~** I'm not the sporty type; **2** [*appearance*] athletic, sporty○.
II *nm,f* sportsman/sportswoman; **c'est un ~** he's athletic.
spot /spɔt/ *nm* **1** spotlight; **2 ~ (publicitaire)** commercial.
square /skwaʀ/ *nm* small public garden.
squash /skwaʃ/ *nm* squash.
squatter[1] /skwate/ [1] *vtr* to squat in.
squatter[2] /skwatœʀ/ *nm* squatter.
squelette /skəlɛt/ *nm* **1** skeleton; **2**○ bag of bones○; **3** framework.
squelettique /skəlɛtik/ *adj* [*person, legs*] scrawny; [*tree*] skeletal; [*report*] sketchy.
stabiliser /stabilize/ [1] **I** *vtr* to stabilize; to consolidate.
II se stabiliser *v refl* (+ *v être*) [*unemployment*] to stabilize; [*person*] to become stable.
stabilité /stabilite/ *nf* stability.
stable /stabl/ *adj* stable.
stade /stad/ *nm* **1** (Sport) stadium; **2** stage; **à ce ~** at this stage.
stage /staʒ/ *nm* **1** professional training; **2** work experience; **~ pratique** period of work experience; **3** course; **suivre un ~ de formation** to go on a training course.
stagiaire /staʒjɛʀ/ *nmf* **1** trainee; **2** student teacher.
stagner /stagne/ [1] *vi* to stagnate.
stalactite /stalaktit/ *nf* stalactite.
stalagmite /stalagmit/ *nf* stalagmite.
stalle /stal/ *nf* stall.
stand /stɑ̃d/ *nm* stand; stall.
■ **~ de tir** shooting range; shooting gallery.
standard /stɑ̃daʀ/ **I** *adj inv* standard.
II *nm* switchboard.
standardisation /stɑ̃daʀdizasjɔ̃/ *nf* standardization.
standardiste /stɑ̃daʀdist/ *nmf* switchboard operator.
standing /stɑ̃diŋ/ *nm* **1 de ~** [*apartment*] luxury; **2** standard of living.
star /staʀ/ *nf* star.
starter /staʀtɛʀ/ *nm* (Aut) choke.
station /stasjɔ̃/ *nf* **1** station; taxi-rank (GB), taxi stand; **c'est à deux ~s d'ici** it's two stops from here; **2 ~ (de radio)** (radio) station; **3 ~ balnéaire** seaside resort; **~ thermale** spa; **4 ~ debout** or **verticale** upright posture or position; **6** stop, pause.
stationnaire /stasjɔnɛʀ/ *adj* **1** stationary; **2** stable.
stationnement /stasjɔnmɑ̃/ *nm* parking.
stationner /stasjɔne/ [1] *vi* to park.
station-service, *pl* **stations-service** /stasjɔ̃sɛʀvis/ *nf* service or filling station.
statique /statik/ *adj* static.
statistique /statistik/ *nf* **1** statistics; **2** statistic.
statue /staty/ *nf* statue.
statuer /statɥe/ [1] *vi* to give a ruling.
statuette /statɥɛt/ *nf* statuette.
statu quo /statykwo/ *nm inv* status quo.
stature /statyʀ/ *nf* **1** stature; **2** height.
statut /staty/ *nm* **1** statute; **2** status.
statutaire /statytɛʀ/ *adj* statutory.
steak /stɛk/ *nm* steak; **un ~ haché** a hamburger.
sténodactylo /stenodaktilo/ **I** *nmf* shorthand typist (GB), stenographer (US).

II *nf* shorthand typing (GB), stenography (US).

sténographier /stenɔgʀafje/ [2] *vtr* to take [sth] down in shorthand.

steppe /stɛp/ *nf* steppe.

stéréo /steʀeo/ *adj inv*, *nf* stereo.

stéréophonique /steʀeɔfɔnik/ *adj* stereophonic.

stéréotype /steʀeɔtip/ *nm* **1** stereotype; **2** cliché.

stérile /steʀil/ *adj* (gen) sterile; [*land*] barren; [*discussion*] fruitless.

stérilet /steʀilɛ/ *nm* coil, IUD.

stériliser /steʀilize/ [1] *vtr* to sterilize.

stérilité /steʀilite/ *nf* **1** sterility; barrenness; **2** fruitlessness.

sterling /stɛʀliŋ/ *adj inv* sterling; **livre ~** pound sterling.

sternum /stɛʀnɔm/ *nm* breastbone, sternum.

stéthoscope /stetɔskɔp/ *nm* stethoscope.

stigmate /stigmat/ *nm* **1** scar; **2** mark.

stimulant, **~e** /stimylɑ̃, ɑ̃t/ *adj* invigorating; bracing; stimulating.

stimuler /stimyle/ [1] **I** *vtr* **1** to stimulate [*organ, function*]; **2** to spur [sb] on.
II *vi* **1** to be bracing; **2**○ to act as a spur.

stimulus, *pl* **stimuli** /stimylys, stimyli/ *nm* stimulus.

stipuler /stipyle/ [1] *vtr* to stipulate.

stock /stɔk/ *nm* stock; **avoir qch en ~** to have sth in stock.

stocker /stɔke/ [1] *vtr* **1** to stock; **2** to stockpile; **3** to store [*data*].

stoïque /stɔik/ *adj* stoical.

stop /stɔp/ *nm* **1** stop sign; **2**○ hitch-hiking○; **prendre qn en ~** to give sb a lift (GB) or ride (US).

stopper /stɔpe/ [1] **I** *vtr* **1** to stop; to halt [*development*]; **2** to mend.
II *vi* to stop.

store /stɔʀ/ *nm* **1** blind; **2** awning.

strabisme /stʀabism/ *nm* squint.

strapontin /stʀapɔ̃tɛ̃/ *nm* foldaway seat.

stratagème /stʀataʒɛm/ *nm* stratagem.

strate /stʀat/ *nf* stratum.

stratégie /stʀateʒi/ *nf* strategy.

stratégique /stʀateʒik/ *adj* strategic.

stratifié, **~e** /stʀatifje/ *adj* **1** stratified; **2** laminated.

stratosphère /stʀatɔsfɛʀ/ *nf* stratosphere.

stress /stʀɛs/ *nm inv* stress.

stressant, **~e** /stʀɛsɑ̃, ɑ̃t/ *adj* stressful.

stresser /stʀese/ [1] *vtr* to put [sb] on edge; to put [sb] under stress.

strict, **~e** /stʀikt/ *adj* **1** (gen) strict; **au sens ~** in the strict sense of the word; **2** [*hairstyle, outfit*] severe.

strident, **~e** /stʀidɑ̃, ɑ̃t/ *adj* [*noise*] piercing; [*voice*] strident.

strie /stʀi/ *nf* **1** streak; **2** groove; **3** (in geology) **des ~s** striation.

strip-tease /stʀiptiz/ *nm* striptease.

strophe /stʀɔf/ *nf* stanza, verse.

structure /stʀyktyʀ/ *nf* **1** structure; **2** organization; **~ d'accueil** shelter, refuge.

structurer /stʀyktyʀe/ [1] *vtr* to structure.

stuc /styk/ *nm* stucco.

studieux, **-ieuse** /stydjø, øz/ *adj* [*pupil*] studious; [*holiday*] study.

studio /stydjo/ *nm* **1** studio flat (GB), studio apartment (US); **2** studio.

stupéfaction /stypefaksjɔ̃/ *nf* stupefaction.

stupéfait, **~e** /stypefɛ, ɛt/ *adj* astounded.

stupéfiant, **~e** /stypefjɑ̃, ɑ̃t/ **I** *adj* stunning.
II *nm* drug, narcotic.

stupéfier /stypefje/ [2] *vtr* to astound.

stupeur /stypœʀ/ *nf* **1** astonishment; **2** (Med) stupor.

stupide /stypid/ *adj* stupid.

stupidité /stypidite/ *nf* stupidity.

style /stil/ *nm* **1** style; **~ de vie** lifestyle; **c'est bien ton ~ de faire** it's just like you to do; **2 meubles de ~** (reproduction) period furniture; **3** speech form; **~ indirect** indirect or reported speech.

stylé, **~e** /stile/ *adj* well-trained.

styliser /stilize/ [1] *vtr* to stylize.

styliste /stilist/ *nmf* fashion designer.

stylo /stilo/ *nm* (fountain) pen; **~ bille** ballpoint pen; **~ feutre** felt-tip pen.

su /sy/ *nm* **au vu et au ~ de tous** openly.

suaire /sɥɛʀ/ *nm* shroud.

suave /sɥav/ *adj* [*perfume, music, smile*] sweet; [*voice*] mellifluous; [*person, manner*] suave.

subalterne /sybaltɛʀn/ *nmf* subordinate; (Mil) low-ranking officer, subaltern.

subconscient /sybkɔ̃sjɑ̃/ *nm* subconscious.

subdiviser /sybdivize/ [1] *vtr* to subdivide.

subir /sybiʀ/ [3] *vtr* **1** to be subjected to [*violence, pressure*]; to suffer [*defeat, damage*]; **2** to take [*examination*]; to have [*operation, test*]; **~ l'influence de qn** to be under sb's influence; **3** to put up with; **4** to undergo.

subit, **~e** /sybi, it/ *adj* sudden.

subitement /sybitmɑ̃/ *adv* suddenly.

subjectif, **-ive** /sybʒɛktif, iv/ *adj* subjective.

subjonctif /sybʒɔ̃ktif/ *nm* subjunctive.

subjuguer /sybʒyge/ [1] *vtr* **1** to captivate, to enthral[GB]; **2** to subjugate.

sublime /syblim/ *adj* sublime.

sublimer /syblime/ [1] *vtr*, *vi* to sublimate.

submerger /sybmɛʀʒe/ [13] *vtr* **1** to submerge; **2** to flood [*market, switchboard*]; **3** [*crowd, emotion*] to overwhelm; **4 ~ qn de travail** to inundate sb with work.

subordination /sybɔʀdinasjɔ̃/ *nf* subordination.

subordonné, **~e**[1] /sybɔʀdɔne/ *nm,f* subordinate.

subordonnée[2] /sybɔʀdɔne/ *nf* subordinate clause; **~ relative** relative clause.

subordonner /sybɔʀdɔne/ [1] *vtr* **1 être subordonné à qn** to be subordinate to sb; **2 être subordonné à qch** to be subject to sth.

suborner /sybɔʀne/ [1] *vtr* to bribe [*witness*].
subreptice /sybʀɛptis/ *adj* surreptitious.
subside /sybsid/ *nm* **1** grant; **2** allowance.
subsidiaire /sybzidjɛʀ/ *adj* subsidiary; **question ~** tiebreaker.
subsistance /sybzistɑ̃s/ *nf* subsistence; **(moyens de) ~** means of support.
subsister /sybziste/ [1] *vi* **1** to remain; **2** [*custom*] to survive; **3 ça leur suffit à peine pour ~** it's barely enough for them to live on.
substance /sypstɑ̃s/ *nf* substance.
substantif /sypstɑ̃tif/ *nm* noun, substantive.
substituer /sypstitɥe/ [1] **I** *vtr* to substitute.
II se substituer *v refl* (+ *v être*) **se ~ à** to take the place of.
substitut /sypstity/ *nm* substitute.
substitution /sypstitysjɔ̃/ *nf* substitution; **produit de ~ du sucre** sugar substitute.
subterfuge /sypteʀfyʒ/ *nm* ploy, subterfuge.
subtil, ~e /syptil/ *adj* subtle; skilful[GB].
subtiliser /syptilize/ [1] *vtr* **~ qch à qn** to steal sth from sb.
subtilité /syptilite/ *nf* subtlety.
subvenir /sybvəniʀ/ [36] *v+prep* **~ à** to meet [*expenses, needs*]; **~ aux besoins de sa famille** to provide for one's family.
subvention /sybvɑ̃sjɔ̃/ *nf* **1** grant; **2** subsidy.
subventionner /sybvɑ̃sjɔne/ [1] *vtr* to subsidize.
subversif, -ive /sybvɛʀsif, iv/ *adj* subversive.
subversion /sybvɛʀsjɔ̃/ *nf* subversion.
suc /syk/ *nm* (of fruit) juice; (of plant) sap; **~s digestifs** or **gastriques** gastric juices.
succédané /syksedane/ *nm* substitute, ersatz.
succéder /syksede/ [14] **I succéder à** *v+prep* **1 ~ à** to succeed [*person*]; **2 ~ à** to follow.
II se succéder *v refl* (+ *v être*) to succeed or follow one another.
succès /syksɛ/ *nm inv* success; **avoir du ~, être un ~** to be a success; [*record*] to be a hit; **à ~** [*actor, film*] successful.
successeur /syksesœʀ/ *nm* successor.
successif, -ive /syksesif, iv/ *adj* successive.
succession /syksesjɔ̃/ *nf* **1** series, succession; **2** (Law) succession; **prendre la ~ de** to succeed; **3** inheritance, estate.
succinct, ~e /syksɛ̃, ɛ̃t/ *adj* [*essay*] succinct; [*speech*] brief; [*meal*] frugal.
succomber /sykɔ̃be/ [1] *vi* **1** to die; **2** to give way, to yield; **~ sous le poids** to collapse under the weight; **3 ~ à** to succumb to [*charm, despair*]; to give in to [*temptation*].
succulent, ~e /sykylɑ̃, ɑ̃t/ *adj* delicious.
succursale /sykyʀsal/ *nf* branch, outlet.
sucer /syse/ [12] *vtr* to suck.
sucette /sysɛt/ *nf* lollipop, lolly○.
suçoter /sysɔte/ [1] *vtr* to suck.
sucre /sykʀ/ *nm* **1** sugar; **2** sugar lump
■ **~ cristallisé** granulated sugar; **~ glace** icing sugar (GB), powdered sugar (US); **~ en poudre** caster sugar (GB), superfine sugar (US); **~ roux** brown sugar.
IDIOMS **casser du ~ sur le dos de qn** to run sb down, to badmouth sb○.
sucré, ~e /sykʀe/ *adj* sweet; sweetened.
sucrer /sykʀe/ [1] *vtr* to put sugar in; to sweeten.
sucrerie /sykʀəʀi/ *nf* **1** sugar refinery; **2 ~s** sweets (GB).
sucrier /sykʀije/ *nm* sugar bowl.
sud /syd/ **I** *adj inv* south; southern.
II *nm* **1** south; **exposé au ~** south-facing; **2 le Sud** the South.
sud-est /sydɛst/ **I** *adj inv* southeast; southeastern.
II *nm* southeast; **le Sud-Est asiatique** South East Asia.
sud-ouest /sydwɛst/ **I** *adj inv* southwest; southwestern.
II *nm* southwest.
Suède /sɥɛd/ *pr nf* Sweden.
suédois, ~e /sɥedwa, az/ **I** *adj* Swedish.
II *nm* (language) Swedish.
Suédois, ~e /sɥedwa, az/ *nm,f* Swede.
suer /sɥe/ [1] **I** *vtr* to sweat; **~ sang et eau** to sweat blood and tears.
II *vi* to sweat; **faire ~ qn**○ to bore sb stiff○.
sueur /sɥœʀ/ *nf* sweat; **j'en avais des ~s froides** I was in a cold sweat about it.
suffire /syfiʀ/ [64] **I** *vi* to be enough; **un rien suffit à le mettre en colère** it only takes the slightest thing to make him lose his temper.
II se suffire *v refl* (+ *v être*) **se ~ (à soi-même)** to be self-sufficient.
III *v impers* **il suffit de me téléphoner** all you have to do is phone me; **il suffit d'une lampe pour éclairer la pièce** one lamp is enough to light the room; **il suffit que je sorte sans parapluie pour qu'il pleuve!** every time I go out without my umbrella, it's guaranteed to rain; **ça suffit (comme ça)!** that's enough!
suffisamment /syfizamɑ̃/ *adv* enough.
suffisance /syfizɑ̃s/ *nf* self-importance.
suffisant, ~e /syfizɑ̃, ɑ̃t/ *adj* **1** sufficient; **2** self-important.
suffixe /syfiks/ *nm* suffix.
suffocation /syfɔkasjɔ̃/ *nf* suffocation; choking.
suffoquer /syfɔke/ [1] **I** *vtr* to suffocate.
II *vi* **1** to suffocate; **2** to choke.
suffrage /syfʀaʒ/ *nm* suffrage; **~s exprimés** recorded votes.
suggérer /sygʒeʀe/ [14] *vtr* to suggest.
suggestif, -ive /sygʒɛstif, iv/ *adj* [*music*] evocative; [*pose*] suggestive; [*dress*] provocative.
suggestion /sygʒɛstjɔ̃/ *nf* suggestion.
suicide /sɥisid/ *nm* suicide.
suicider: se suicider /sɥiside/ [1] *v refl* (+ *v être*) to commit suicide.
suie /sɥi/ *nf* soot.
suinter /sɥɛ̃te/ [1] *vi* **1** [*liquid*] to seep; to ooze; **2** [*walls*] to sweat; [*wound*] to weep.
suisse /sɥis/ **I** *adj* Swiss.
II *nm* **1** Swiss Guard; **2** verger.

Suisse /sɥis/ *pr nf* Switzerland.

suite /sɥit/ **I** *nf* **1** rest; **la ~ des événements** what happens next; **2** (of story) continuation; (of series) next instalment[GB]; (of meal) next course; **3** sequel; **4** result; **les ~s** (of action) the consequences; (of incident) the repercussions; (of illness) the after-effects; **5 donner ~ à** to follow up [*complaint*]; to deal with [*order*]; **rester sans ~** [*plan*] to be dropped; **6 faire ~ à** to follow upon [*incident*]; **prendre la ~ de qn** to take over from sb; **7 avoir de la ~ dans les idées** to be single-minded; **8** (of incidents) series; (of successes) run; **9** (hotel) suite; **10** (of monarch) suite; **11** (Mus) suite.
II de suite *phr* in succession, in a row; **et ainsi de ~** and so on.
III par la suite *phr* **1** afterward(s); **2** later.
IV par suite de *phr* due to.
V à la suite de *phr* **1** following; **2** behind.

suivant[1] /sɥivɑ̃/ *prep* **1** in accordance with [*tradition*]; **~ leur habitude** as they usually do; **2** depending on; **3** according to.

suivant[2], **~e** /sɥivɑ̃, ɑ̃t/ **I** *adj* **1** following; **2** next.
II *nm,f* **le ~** the following one; the next one.
III le suivant, la suivante *phr* as follows.

suivi, **~e** /sɥivi/ **I** *pp* ▶ **suivre**.
II *pp adj* **1** [*work*] steady; [*effort*] sustained; [*correspondence*] regular; **2** [*policy*] coherent.
III *nm* **1** monitoring; **2** follow-up; **~ des malades** follow-up care for patients.

suivre /sɥivʀ/ [62] **I** *vtr* **1** to follow [*person, car*]; **suivez le guide!** this way, please!; **2** to follow, to come after [*period, incident*]; **'à ~'** 'to be continued'; **3** to follow [*route, coast*]; [*road*] to run alongside [*railway line*]; **~ le droit chemin** to keep to the straight and narrow; **4** to follow [*example*]; to obey [*impulse*]; **5** to follow [*lesson, match*]; to follow the progress of [*pupil, patient*]; **~ l'actualité** to keep up with the news; **6** to do [*course*]; **7** to follow [*explanation, logic*]; **je vous suis** I'm with you; **8** to keep pace with [sb/sth].
II *vi* **faire ~ son courrier** to have one's mail forwarded; **faire ~** please forward.
III se suivre *v refl* (+ *v être*) **1** [*numbers, pages*] to be in order; [*cards*] to be consecutive; **2** to happen one after the other.
IV *v impers* **comme suit** as follows.

sujet, **-ette** /syʒɛ, ɛt/ **I** *adj* **être ~ à** to be prone to [*migraine*].
II *nm* **1** subject; **un ~ d'actualité** a topical issue; **c'est à quel ~?** what is it about?; **au ~ de** about; **2** (Sch) question; **~ libre** topic of one's own choice; **hors ~** off the subject; **3** cause; **c'est un ~ d'étonnement** it is amazing; **4 c'est un brillant ~** he's a brilliant student; **5** (of kingdom) subject.

sulfate /sylfat/ *nm* sulphate[GB].

sulfureux, **-euse** /sylfyʀø, øz/ *adj* [*vapour*] sulphurous[GB]; [*bath*] sulphur[GB].

sultan /syltɑ̃/ *nm* sultan.

sultane /syltan/ *nf* sultana.

summum /sɔm(m)ɔm/ *nm* height.

sumo /sumo, symo/ *nm inv* sumo wrestling.

super[1] /sypɛʀ/ *pref* super.

super[2] /sypɛʀ/ **I**○ *adj inv* great○.
II *nm* four-star (petrol) (GB), super.

superbe /sypɛʀb/ *adj* superb, magnificent.

superbement /sypɛʀbəmɑ̃/ *adv* **1** superbly; **2** haughtily.

supercherie /sypɛʀʃəʀi/ *nf* **1** deception; **2** hoax.

superficie /sypɛʀfisi/ *nf* area.

superficiel, **-ielle** /sypɛʀfisjɛl/ *adj* (gen) superficial; [*layer*] surface.

superflu, **~e** /sypɛʀfly/ *adj* **1** superfluous; **2** unnecessary.

supérieur, **~e** /sypeʀjœʀ/ **I** *adj* **1** [*jaw, lip, floor*] upper; **2** [*ranks, classes*] upper; **3** higher (**à** than); [*size*] bigger (**à** than); [*length*] longer (**à** than); **4** [*work, quality*] superior (**à** to); **5** [*air, tone*] superior.
II *nm,f* **1** superior; **~ hiérarchique** immediate superior; **2** (in monastery, convent) Superior.
III *nm* higher education.

supériorité /sypeʀjɔʀite/ *nf* superiority.

superlatif, **-ive** /sypɛʀlatif, iv/ **I** *adj* superlative.
II *nm* superlative.

supermarché /sypɛʀmaʀʃe/ *nm* supermarket.

superposer /sypɛʀpoze/ [1] *vtr* **1** to stack [sth] (up); **lits superposés** bunk beds; **2** to superimpose [*drawings*].

superposition /sypɛʀpozisjɔ̃/ *nf* superposition.

superproduction /sypɛʀpʀɔdyksjɔ̃/ *nf* blockbuster○.

superstitieux, **-ieuse** /sypɛʀstisjø, øz/ *adj* superstitious.

superstition /sypɛʀstisjɔ̃/ *nf* superstition.

superviser /sypɛʀvize/ [1] *vtr* to supervise.

supplanter /syplɑ̃te/ [1] *vtr* to supplant.

suppléant, **~e** /sypleɑ̃, ɑ̃t/ *nm,f* replacement; (for judge) deputy; (for teacher) supply (GB) or substitute (US) teacher; (for doctor) locum.

suppléer /syplee/ [11] *v+prep* **~ à** to make up for, to compensate for.

supplément /syplemɑ̃/ *nm* **1** extra charge; supplement; **le vin est en ~** the wine is extra; **2 ~ d'informations** additional information; **3** (newspaper) supplement.

supplémentaire /syplemɑ̃tɛʀ/ *adj* additional, extra; **train ~** relief train.

suppliant, **~e** /syplijɑ̃, ɑ̃t/ *adj* [*voice*] pleading; [*look*] imploring.

supplice /syplis/ *nm* torture.

supplicier /syplisje/ [2] *vtr* **1** to torture; **2** to execute.

supplier /syplije/ [2] *vtr* to beg, to beseech.

support /sypɔʀ/ *nm* **1** support; **servir de ~ à qch** to serve as a support for sth; **2** (for ornaments) stand; **3** back-up; **~ audiovisuel** audiovisual aid.

supportable /sypɔʀtabl/ *adj* bearable.

supporter[1] /sypɔʀte/ [1] **I** *vtr* **1** to support, to bear the weight of [*structure*]; **2** to bear [*costs*]; **3** to put up with [*misery, behaviour, person*]; to

bear [*suffering*]; [*plant*] to withstand [*cold*]; **elle ne supporte pas d'attendre** she can't stand waiting.
II se supporter *v refl* (+ *v être*) **ils ne peuvent plus se ~** they can't stand each other any more.

supporter² /sypɔʀtœʀ/ *nmf* supporter.

supposer /sypoze/ [1] *vtr* **1** to suppose; **2** to assume; **3** to presuppose.

supposition /sypozisjɔ̃/ *nf* supposition.

suppositoire /sypozitwaʀ/ *nm* suppository.

suppôt /sypo/ *nm* **~ de Satan** fiend.

suppression /sypʀesjɔ̃/ *nf* removal; abolition; withdrawal; suppression; elimination; breaking, ending; deletion; **~s d'emplois** job cuts.

supprimer /sypʀime/ [1] *vtr* **1** to cut [*job*]; to stop [*aid, vibration*]; to abolish [*tax, law*]; to remove [*effect, obstacle*]; to do away with [*class*]; to withdraw [*licence*]; to break [*monopoly*]; to suppress [*evidence*]; to cut out [*sugar, salt*]; to delete [*word*]; **~ un train** to cancel a train; **2** to eliminate [*person*].

suppurer /sypyʀe/ [1] *vi* to suppurate.

supputer /sypyte/ [1] *vtr* to calculate, to work out.

suprématie /sypʀemasi/ *nf* supremacy.

suprême /sypʀɛm/ *adj* supreme.

sur¹ /syʀ/ *prep* **1** on; **~ la table** on the table; **prends un verre ~ la table** take a glass from the table; **appliquer la lotion ~ vos cheveux** apply the lotion to your hair; **la clé est ~ la porte** the key is in the door; **écrire ~ du papier** to write on paper; **elle est ~ la photo** she's in the photograph; **2** over; **un pont ~ la rivière** a bridge across or over the river; **3 une table d'un mètre ~ deux** a table that measures one metre[GB] by two; **~ 150 hectares** over an area of 150 hectares; **4 se diriger ~ Valence** to head for Valence; **5** [*debate, essay, thesis*] on; [*poem*] about; **6 être ~ une affaire** to be involved in a business deal; **7 une personne ~ dix** one person out of or in ten; **un mardi ~ deux** every other Tuesday; **8 faire proposition ~ proposition** to make one offer after another; **9 ils se sont quittés ~ ces mots** with these words, they parted; **~ le moment** at the time; **~ ce, je vous laisse** with that, I must leave you.

sur², **~e** /syʀ/ *adj* (slightly) sour.

sûr, **~e** /syʀ/ **I** *adj* **1** [*information, service, person*] reliable; [*opinion, investment*] sound; **d'une main ~e** with a steady hand; **2** safe; **3** certain; **c'est ~ et certain** it's definite; **à coup ~** definitely; **4** sure; **j'en suis ~ et certain** I'm positive; **il est ~ de lui** he's self-confident; **j'en étais ~!** I knew it!
II *adv* **bien ~ (que oui)** of course.
IDIOMS **être ~ de son coup**○ to be confident of success.

surabonder /syʀabɔ̃de/ [1] *vi* to abound.

suranné, **~e** /syʀane/ *adj* [*ideas*] outmoded; [*style*] outdated.

surcharge /syʀʃaʀʒ/ *nf* excess load, overload; **une ~ de travail** extra work.

surcharger /syʀʃaʀʒe/ [13] *vtr* to overload; **~ qn de travail** to overburden sb with work.

surchauffer /syʀʃofe/ [1] *vtr* to overheat.

surclasser /syʀklase/ [1] *vtr* to outclass.

surcroît /syʀkʀwa/ *nm* increase; **un ~ de travail** extra work; **de ~** moreover.

surdité /syʀdite/ *nf* deafness.

surdoué, **~e** /syʀdwe/ *adj* (exceptionally) gifted.

sureau, *pl* **~x** /syʀo/ *nm* elder (tree).

sureffectif /syʀefɛktif/ *nm* excess staff.

surélever /syʀelve/ [16] *vtr* to raise the height of [*house, road*].

sûrement /syʀmɑ̃/ *adv* **1** most probably; **2 ~ pas** certainly not; **3** safely.

surenchère /syʀɑ̃ʃɛʀ/ *nf* **1** higher bid; **2 faire de la ~** to try to go one better.

surenchérir /syʀɑ̃ʃeʀiʀ/ [3] *vi* **1** to make a higher bid; **2** to add; to chime in.

surestimer /syʀɛstime/ [1] **I** *vtr* to overvalue [*property*]; to overrate [*qualities*].
II se surestimer *v refl* (+ *v être*) to rate oneself too highly.

sûreté /syʀte/ *nf* **1** (of place, person) safety; (of country) security; **2** (of judgment) soundness; (of gesture) steadiness; **3** (on gun) safety catch; (on door) safety lock.

surexciter /syʀɛksite/ [1] *vtr* to overexcite.

surf /sœʀf/ *nm* surfing.

surface /syʀfas/ *nf* **1** surface; **de ~** [*installations*] above ground; [*friendliness*] superficial; **faire ~** to surface; **2** surface area; **en ~** in area.

surfait, **~e** /syʀfɛ, ɛt/ *adj* overrated.

surfer /sœʀfe/ [1] *vi* to go surfing.

surfiler /syʀfile/ [1] *vtr* to oversew.

surgelé, **~e** /syʀʒəle/ *adj* deep-frozen; **les produits ~s** frozen food.

surgeler /syʀʒəle/ [17] *vtr* to deep-freeze.

surgénérateur /syʀʒeneʀatœʀ/ *nm* fast-breeder reactor.

surgir /syʀʒiʀ/ [3] *vi* [*person*] to appear suddenly; [*difficulty*] to crop up; **faire ~ la vérité** to bring the truth to light.

surhomme /syʀɔm/ *nm* superman.

surhumain, **~e** /syʀymɛ̃, ɛn/ *adj* superhuman.

surimpression /syʀɛ̃pʀesjɔ̃/ *nf* double exposure; **en ~** superimposed.

sur-le-champ /syʀləʃɑ̃/ *adv* right away.

surlendemain /syʀlɑ̃d(ə)mɛ̃/ *nm* **le ~** two days later.

surligner /syʀliɲe/ [1] *vtr* to highlight.

surmenage /syʀmənaʒ/ *nm* overwork.

surmener /syʀmene/ [16] **I** *vtr* to overwork.
II se surmener *v refl* (+ *v être*) to push oneself too hard.

surmontable /syʀmɔ̃tabl/ *adj* surmountable.

surmonter /syʀmɔ̃te/ [1] *vtr* to overcome.

surnaturel, **-elle** /syʀnatyʀɛl/ *adj* **1** supernatural; **2** eerie.

surnom /syʀnɔ̃/ *nm* nickname.

surnombre /syʀnɔ̃bʀ/ *nm* **en ~** [*objects*] surplus; [*staff*] excess; [*passenger*] extra.
surnommer /syʀnɔme/ [1] *vtr* to nickname.
surpasser /syʀpase/ [1] **I** *vtr* to surpass.
II se surpasser *v refl* (+ *v être*) to surpass oneself, to excel oneself.
surpeuplé, **~e** /syʀpœple/ *adj* **1** overpopulated; **2** overcrowded.
surplace /syʀplas/ *nm inv* **faire du ~** (in traffic jam) to be stuck; (in work, inquiry) to be getting nowhere; (in cycling) to do a track stand.
surplomb /syʀplɔ̃/ *nm* **en ~** overhanging.
surplomber /syʀplɔ̃be/ [1] *vtr* to overhang.
surplus /syʀply/ *nm inv* (of goods) surplus.
surpopulation /syʀpɔpylasjɔ̃/ *nf* overpopulation.
surprenant, **~e** /syʀpʀənɑ̃, ɑ̃t/ *adj* surprising; amazing.
surprendre /syʀpʀɑ̃dʀ/ [52] **I** *vtr* **1** to surprise; **2** to take [sb] by surprise; **se laisser ~ par la pluie** to get caught in the rain; **3** to catch [*thief*]; **4** to overhear [*conversation*]; to intercept [*smile*].
II *vi* [*behaviour*] to be surprising; [*show*] to surprise; [*person*] to surprise people.
surprise /syʀpʀiz/ *nf* surprise; **créer la ~** to cause a stir; **il m'a fait la ~ de venir me voir** he came to see me as a surprise; **avoir la bonne ~ d'apprendre que** to be pleasantly surprised to hear that; **voyage sans ~** uneventful trip; **gagner sans ~** to win as expected.
surproduction /syʀpʀɔdyksjɔ̃/ *nf* overproduction.
surréalisme /suʀ(ʀ)ealism/ *nm* surrealism.
surréaliste /suʀ(ʀ)ealist/ **I** *adj* **1** surrealist; **2** [*landscape, vision*] surreal.
II *nmf* surrealist.
sursaut /syʀso/ *nm* **1** start; **en ~** with a start; **2** (of energy, enthusiasm) sudden burst; (of pride, indignation) flash; **dans un dernier ~** in a final spurt of effort.
sursauter /syʀsote/ [1] *vi* to jump, to start.
sursis /syʀsi/ *nm inv* **1** respite; **2** (Law) suspended sentence; **3** (Mil) deferment of military service.
surtaxe /syʀtaks/ *nf* surcharge.
surtout /syʀtu/ *adv* above all; **~ quand/que** especially when/as; **~ pas!** certainly not!
surveillance /syʀvɛjɑ̃s/ *nf* **1** watch; (police) surveillance; **déjouer la ~ de qn** to escape detection by sb; **2** supervision; **sous ~ médicale** under medical supervision.
surveillant, **~e** /syʀvɛjɑ̃, ɑ̃t/ *nm,f* **1** (Sch) supervisor; **2 ~ de prison** prison warder (GB) or guard; **3** store detective.
surveiller /syʀveje/ [1] **I** *vtr* **1** (gen) to watch; to keep watch on [*building*]; **2** to supervise [*work, pupils*]; to monitor [*progress*]; **3 ~ sa santé** to take care of one's health.
II se surveiller *v refl* (+ *v être*) to watch oneself.
survenir /syʀvəniʀ/ [36] *vi* (+ *v être*) [*death, storm*] to occur; [*difficulty, conflict*] to arise.
survêtement /syʀvɛtmɑ̃/ *nm* tracksuit.
survie /syʀvi/ *nf* survival.
survivant, **~e** /syʀvivɑ̃, ɑ̃t/ *nm,f* survivor.
survivre /syʀvivʀ/ [63] **I survivre à** *v+prep* [*person*] to survive [*event, injuries*]; to outlive [*person*]; [*work, influence*] to outlast [*person*].
II *vi* to survive.
survol /syʀvɔl/ *nm* **1** flying over; **2** synopsis.
survoler /syʀvɔle/ [1] *vtr* **1** to fly over [*place*]; **2** to do a quick review of [*problem*].
survolté○, **~e** /syʀvɔlte/ *adj* overexcited.
sus: **en sus** /ɑ̃sys/ *phr* **être en ~** to be extra; **en ~ de** on top of; in addition to.
susceptibilité /sysɛptibilite/ *nf* touchiness.
susceptible /sysɛptibl/ *adj* **1** touchy; **2 ~ de faire** likely to do.
susciter /sysite/ [1] *vtr* **1** to spark off [*reaction, debate*]; to create [*problem*]; **2** to arouse [*enthusiasm, interest*]; to give rise to [*fear*].
susmentionné, **~e** *adj* aforementioned.
suspect, **~e** /syspɛ, ɛkt/ **I** *adj* suspicious; [*information, logic*] dubious; [*foodstuff, honesty*] suspect; [*person*] suspicious-looking.
II *nm,f* suspect.
suspecter /syspɛkte/ [1] *vtr* to suspect.
suspendre /syspɑ̃dʀ/ [6] **I** *vtr* **1** to hang up; **être suspendu aux lèvres de qn** to be hanging on sb's every word; **2** to suspend [*programme, payment*]; to end [*strike*]; to adjourn [*session, inquiry*]; **3** to suspend [*official, athlete*].
II se suspendre *v refl* (+ *v être*) to hang; **se ~ à une corde** to hang from a rope.
suspens: **en suspens** /ɑ̃syspɑ̃/ *phr* **1 laisser qch en ~** to leave sth unresolved [*question*]; to leave sth unfinished [*work*]; **2 tenir qn en ~** to keep sb in suspense.
suspense /syspɛns/ *nm* suspense; **film** or **roman à ~** thriller.
suspension /syspɑ̃sjɔ̃/ *nf* **1** (gen, Tech) suspension; **2** (of aid, work) suspension; (of session, trial) adjournment; **3 en ~** [*particles*] in suspension; **4** pendant, ceiling light.
suspicion /syspisjɔ̃/ *nf* suspicion.
sustenter: **se sustenter** /systɑ̃te/ [1] *v refl* (+ *v être*) to have a little snack.
susurrer /sysyʀe/ [1] *vtr, vi* to whisper.
suture /sytyʀ/ *nf* suture; **point de ~** stitch.
suzerain, **~e** /syzʀɛ̃, ɛn/ *nm,f* suzerain.
svelte /svɛlt/ *adj* slender.
sveltesse /svɛltɛs/ *nf* slenderness.
SVP (*written abbr* = **s'il vous plaît**) please.
syllabe /sil(l)ab/ *nf* syllable.
sylviculture /silvikyltyʀ/ *nf* forestry.
symbiose /sɛ̃bjoz/ *nf* symbiosis.
symbole /sɛ̃bɔl/ *nm* **1** symbol; **2** creed.
symbolique /sɛ̃bɔlik/ *adj* **1** symbolic; **2** [*gesture*] token; [*price*] nominal.
symboliser /sɛ̃bɔlize/ [1] *vtr* to symbolize.
symétrie /simetʀi/ *nf* symmetry.
symétrique /simetʀik/ *adj* **1** [*design, face*] symmetrical; **2** [*relation*] symmetric.
sympa○ /sɛ̃pa/ *adj inv* nice.

sympathie /sɛ̃pati/ *nf* **1 avoir de la ~ pour qn** to like sb; **2** sympathy; **croyez à toute ma ~** you have my deepest sympathy.

sympathique /sɛ̃patik/ *adj* nice; pleasant.

sympathisant, **~e** /sɛ̃patizɑ̃, ɑ̃t/ *nm,f* sympathizer.

sympathiser /sɛ̃patize/ [1] *vi* to get on well.

symphonie /sɛ̃fɔni/ *nf* symphony.

symphonique /sɛ̃fɔnik/ *adj* symphonic.

symptomatique /sɛ̃ptɔmatik/ *adj* symptomatic.

symptôme /sɛ̃ptom/ *nm* symptom.

synagogue /sinagɔg/ *nf* synagogue.

synchroniser /sɛ̃kʀɔnize/ [1] *vtr* to synchronize.

syncope /sɛ̃kɔp/ *nf* **1** fainting fit; **tomber en ~** to faint; **2** (Mus) syncopation.

syndic /sɛ̃dik/ *nm* property manager.

syndical, **~e**, *mpl* **-aux** /sɛ̃dikal, o/ *adj* (trade) union.

syndicalisme /sɛ̃dikalism/ *nm* **1** trade unionism; **2** union activities.

syndicaliste /sɛ̃dikalist/ *nmf* union activist.

syndicat /sɛ̃dika/ *nm* **1** trade union; **2** (employers') association.
■ **~ d'initiative** tourist information office.

syndiqué, **~e** /sɛ̃dike/ *adj* **être ~** to be a union member.

syndrome /sɛ̃dʀom/ *nm* syndrome.
■ **~ immunodéficitaire acquis** acquired immunodeficiency syndrome.

synonyme /sinɔnim/ **I** *adj* synonymous.
II *nm* synonym; **dictionnaire de ~s** ≈ thesaurus.

syntaxe /sɛ̃taks/ *nf* syntax.

synthèse /sɛ̃tɛz/ *nf* **1** synthesis; **2 produit de ~** synthetic product; **3 images de ~** computer-generated images.

synthétique /sɛ̃tetik/ *adj* **1** synthetic; **2** [*vision*] global.

synthétiseur /sɛ̃tetizœʀ/ *nm* synthesizer.

syphilis /sifilis/ *nf inv* syphilis.

systématique /sistematik/ *adj* systematic.

système /sistɛm/ *nm* **1** system; **~ de canaux** canal system or network; **2 ~ pileux** hair.
■ **le ~ D**○ resourcefulness; **~ monétaire européen**, **SME** European Monetary System, EMS.

IDIOMS **taper sur le ~ de qn**○ to get on sb's nerves.

Tt

t, T /te/ *nm inv* t, T; **en (forme de) T** T-shaped.
t' ▶ **te.**
ta ▶ **ton**[1].
tabac /taba/ *nm* **1** tobacco; **2** tobacconist's (GB), smoke shop (US); **3**○ big hit.
■ **~ blond** Virginia tobacco; **~ brun** dark tobacco; **~ à priser** snuff.
IDIOMS **passer qn à ~**○ to beat sb up.
tabagisme /tabaʒism/ *nm* tobacco addiction.
tabernacle /tabɛʀnakl/ *nm* tabernacle.
table /tabl/ *nf* **1** table; **mettre** or **dresser la ~** to set or lay the table; **nous étions toujours à ~ quand...** we were still eating when...; **passer** or **se mettre à ~** to sit down at the table; (figurative)○ to spill the beans○; **2 ~ des négociations** negotiating table; **3 ~ de logarithmes** log table.
■ **~ basse** coffee table; **~ de chevet** bedside table (GB), night stand (US); **~ d'écoute** wiretapping set; **être mis sur ~ d'écoute** to have one's phone tapped; **~ des matières** (table of) contents; **~ de mixage** mixing desk; **~ de nuit** = **~ de chevet**; **~ ronde** round table.
IDIOMS **mettre les pieds sous la ~** to let others wait on you.
tableau, *pl* **~x** /tablo/ *nm* **1** picture; painting; **2** (description) picture; **en plus, il était ivre, tu vois un peu le ~**○**!** on top of that he was drunk, you can just imagine!; **3** table, chart; **4** (Sch) blackboard; **5** (displaying information) (gen) board; (for trains) indicator board; **~ horaire** timetable; **6** (in play) short scene.
■ **~ d'affichage** notice board; **~ de bord** (in car) dashboard; (on plane, train) instrument panel; **~ de chasse** (in hunting) total number of kills; (figurative) list of conquests.
IDIOMS **jouer sur les deux ~x** to hedge one's bets.
tabler /table/ [1] *vi* **~ sur** to bank○ on.
tablette /tablɛt/ *nf* **1** (of chocolate) bar; (of chewing-gum) stick; **2** shelf.
tablier /tablije/ *nm* **1** apron; **2** roadway.
IDIOMS **rendre son ~** to give in (GB) or give (US) one's notice.
tabloïd /tablɔid/ *adj*, *nm* tabloid.
tabou /tabu/ **I** *adj* **1** taboo; **2** sacred.
II *nm* taboo.
tabouret /tabuʀɛ/ *nm* stool.
tac /tak/ *nm* **répondre du ~ au ~** to answer as quick as a flash.
tache /taʃ/ *nf* **1** stain; **~ d'humidité** damp patch; **2** (figurative) stain, blot; **sans ~** [*reputation*] spotless; **3** (on fruit) mark; (on skin) blotch, mark; **4** (of colour) spot; patch.
■ **~s de rousseur** freckles.
IDIOMS **faire ~ d'huile** to spread like wildfire.
tâche /tɑʃ/ *nf* task, job; **tu ne me facilites pas la ~!** you're not making my job any easier!; **les ~s ménagères** household chores.
tacher /taʃe/ [1] **I** *vtr* **1** [*substance*] to stain; [*person*] to get a stain on [*garment*]; **2** to tarnish, to stain [*reputation*].
II *vi* to stain; **ça ne tache pas** it doesn't stain.
tâcher /tɑʃe/ [1] *v+prep* **~ de faire** to try to do.
tacheté /taʃte/ *adj* [*fur*] speckled.
tacite /tasit/ *adj* tacit.
taciturne /tasityʀn/ *adj* taciturn.
tact /takt/ *nm* tact; **avec ~** tactfully.
tactile /taktil/ *adj* [*sense*] tactile.
tactique /taktik/ **I** *adj* (gen, Mil) tactical.
II *nf* tactic; **la ~** tactics.
taie /tɛ/ *nf* **~ (d'oreiller)** pillowcase; **~ (de traversin)** bolstercase.
taillader /tajade/ [1] *vtr* to slash.
taille /taj/ *nf* **1** waist, waistline; **2** size; **de grande/petite ~** large/small; **de ~** [*problem, ambition*] considerable; [*event, question*] very important; **être de ~ à faire** to be up to or capable of doing; **3** (of garment) size; **'~ unique'** 'one size'; **essaie la ~ au-dessus** try the next size up; **4** height; **être de grande/petite ~** to be tall/short; **5** (of tree, shrub) pruning; (of hedge) clipping, trimming; (of diamond, glass) cutting.
taille-crayons /tajkʀɛjɔ̃/ *nm inv* pencil sharpener.
tailler /taje/ [1] **I** *vtr* **1** to cut [*glass, marble*]; to sharpen [*pencil*]; to prune [*tree, shrub*]; to trim [*hair, beard*]; **2** to cut [*steak*]; to carve [*sculpture*]; to cut out [*garment*]; **taillé sur mesure** [*garment*] custom-made; (figurative) [*role*] tailor-made.
II *vi* **~ grand/petit** [*garment*] to be cut on the large/small side.
III se tailler *v refl* (+ *v être*) **1** to carve out [sth] for oneself [*career, empire*]; to make [sth] for oneself [*reputation*]; **2**○ to beat it○.
tailleur /tajœʀ/ *nm* **1** (woman's) suit; **2** tailor; **s'asseoir en ~** to sit down cross-legged.
■ **~ de pierre** stone-cutter.
taillis /taji/ *nm inv* **1** undergrowth; **2** coppice.
tain /tɛ̃/ *nm* **miroir sans ~** two-way mirror.
taire /tɛʀ/ [59] **I** *vtr* **1** not to reveal [*name, secret*]; to hush up [*truth*]; **2** to keep [sth] to oneself [*sadness, resentment*].
II se taire *v refl* (+ *v être*) **1** [*person*] to be silent; **2** [*person*] to stop talking; [*bird, journalist*] to fall silent; **faire ~** to make [sb] be quiet [*pupils*]; to silence [*opponent, media*]; to put a stop to [*rumours*]; **tais-toi!** be quiet!; **3** [*noise*] to stop; [*orchestra*] to fall silent.
talc /talk/ *nm* talc, talcum powder.
talent /talɑ̃/ *nm* talent; **de ~** talented.

talentueux, -euse /talɑ̃tɥø, øz/ *adj* talented.

talisman /talismɑ̃/ *nm* talisman.

talkie-walkie, *pl* **talkies-walkies** /toki woki/ *nm* walkie-talkie.

talon /talɔ̃/ *nm* **1** (of foot, shoe) heel; **2** (of cheque, ticket) stub; **3** (in cards) pile.
■ **~ aiguille** stiletto heel.
IDIOMS **être sur les ~s de qn** to be hard or hot on sb's heels.

talonner /talɔne/ [1] *vtr* **1 ~ qn** to be hot on sb's heels; **2** [*person*] to badger [*person*]; [*hunger, anxiety*] to torment [*person*].

talonnette /talɔnɛt/ *nf* lift (in a shoe).

talus /taly/ *nm inv* **1** embankment; **2** bank, slope.

tamanoir /tamanwaʀ/ *nm* anteater.

tambour /tɑ̃buʀ/ *nm* drum; **mener qch ~ battant** to deal with sth briskly.

tambourin /tɑ̃buʀɛ̃/ *nm* tambourine.

tambouriner /tɑ̃buʀine/ [1] *vi* **~ à la porte de qn** to hammer on sb's door.

tamis /tami/ *nm inv* sieve.

Tamise /tamiz/ *pr nf* **la ~** the Thames.

tamiser /tamize/ [1] *vtr* to sieve, to sift [*sand, flour*]; to filter [*light, colours*].

tampon /tɑ̃pɔ̃/ *nm* **1** (in office) stamp; **~ (encreur)** (ink) pad; **2** (for sponging) (gen) pad; (Med) swab; **~ à récurer** scouring pad; **3 ~ hygiénique** tampon.

tamponner /tɑ̃pɔne/ [1] *vtr* **1** to swab [*wound, cut*]; to mop [*forehead*]; **2** to stamp [*document*]; **3** to crash into [*vehicle*].

tam-tam, *pl* **~s** /tamtam/ *nm* tomtom.

tandem /tɑ̃dɛm/ *nm* **1** tandem; **2** (figurative) duo.

tandis: **tandis que** /tɑ̃di(s)k(ə)/ *phr* while.

tangent, ~e[1] /tɑ̃ʒɑ̃, ɑ̃t/ *adj* **1** tangent, tangential; **2**○ **elle a été reçue, mais c'était ~** she got through, but only by the skin of her teeth○.

tangente[2] /tɑ̃ʒɑ̃t/ *nf* tangent.

tangible /tɑ̃ʒibl/ *adj* tangible.

tanguer /tɑ̃ge/ [1] *vi* [*ship, plane*] to pitch.

tanière /tanjɛʀ/ *nf* **1** den; **2** lair.

tank /tɑ̃k/ *nm* tank.

tanner /tane/ [1] *vtr* **1** to tan [*leather, hides*]; **2** [*sun*] to make [sth] leathery [*face, skin*].

tannerie /tanʀi/ *nf* **1** tannery; **2** tanning.

tant /tɑ̃/ **I** *adv* **1** (so) much; **il a ~ insisté que** he was so insistent that; **vous m'en direz ~**○! you don't say!; **le moment ~ attendu** the long-awaited moment; **2 n'aimer rien ~ que**... to like nothing so much as...; **~ bien que mal** [*repair, lead*] after a fashion; [*manage*] more or less; **essayer ~ bien que mal de s'adapter** to be struggling to adapt; **3 ~ que** as long as; **je ne partirai pas ~ qu'il ne m'aura pas accordé un rendez-vous** I won't leave until he's given me an appointment; **traite-moi de menteur ~ que tu y es**○! go ahead and call me a liar!; **4** (replacing number) **gagner ~ par mois** to earn so much a month.
II tant de *quantif* **Loulou, Pivachon et ~ d'autres** Loulou, Pivachon and so many others; **~ de travail** so much work.
III (in phrases) **~ pis** too bad; **~ mieux** so much the better; **~ mieux pour toi** good for you; **~ et plus** a great deal; a great many; **~ et si bien que** so much so that; **s'il avait un ~ soit peu de bon sens** if he had the slightest bit of common sense; **~ qu'à faire, autant repeindre toute la pièce** we may as well repaint the whole room while we're at it; **en ~ que** as; **en ~ que tel** as such; **si ~ est qu'il puisse y aller** that is if he can go at all; **je ne l'aime pas ~ que ça** I don't like him/her all that much.

tante /tɑ̃t/ *nf* aunt.

tantôt /tɑ̃to/ *adv* sometimes.

taon /tɑ̃/ *nm* horsefly.

tapage /tapaʒ/ *nm* **1** din, racket○; **2** furore (GB), furor (US); **3** hype; **~ médiatique** media hype.
■ **~ nocturne** disturbance of the peace at night.

tapageur, -euse /tapaʒœʀ, øz/ *adj* **1** [*person*] rowdy; **2** [*luxury*] showy; [*campaign*] hyped-up.

tapant, ~e /tapɑ̃, ɑ̃t/ *adj* **à trois heures ~es** at three o'clock sharp or on the dot.

tape /tap/ *nf* pat; slap.

tape-à-l'œil○ /tapalœj/ *adj inv* [*coulour*] loud; [*jewellery, decor*] garish.

taper /tape/ [1] **I** *vtr* **1** to hit [*person, dog*]; **2** to type [*letter*].
II taper sur *v+prep* to hit; **~ sur l'épaule de qn** to tap sb on the shoulder.
III *vi* **1 ~ des mains** to clap one's hands; **~ à la porte** to knock at the door; **le soleil tape**○ **aujourd'hui** the sun is beating down today; **2 ~ (à la machine)** to type.
IV se taper *v refl* (+ *v être*) **1**○ **se ~ dessus** to knock each other about; **2 c'est à se ~ la tête contre les murs** (figurative) it's enough to drive you up the wall; **3**○ to get stuck○ with [*chore, person*].
IDIOMS **elle m'a tapé dans l'œil**○ I thought she was striking.

tapette /tapɛt/ *nf* **1** carpet beater; **2** fly swatter; **3** mousetrap.

tapioca /tapjɔka/ *nm* tapioca.

tapir[1]: **se tapir** /tapiʀ/ [3] *v refl* (+ *v être*) **1** [*person, animal*] to hide; **2** to crouch.

tapir[2] /tapiʀ/ *nm* (Zool) tapir.

tapis /tapi/ *nm inv* rug; carpet; mat; **mettre qch sur le ~** (figurative) to bring sth up; **mettre** or **envoyer qn au ~** to throw sb.
■ **~ de bain(s)** bathmat; **~ roulant** moving walkway; (for luggage) carousel; (in factory, supermarket) conveyor belt.

tapisser /tapise/ [1] *vtr* **1** to wallpaper; to decorate [*room*]; to cover [*armchair*]; **2** [*snow*] to carpet [*ground*]; [*residue*] to line [*bottom of container*].

tapisserie /tapisʀi/ *nf* **1** tapestry; **2** wallpaper; **3** tapestry work.
IDIOMS **faire ~** to be a wallflower.

tapissier, -ière /tapisje, ɛʀ/ *nm,f* **1** upholsterer; **2** tapestry-maker.

tapoter /tapɔte/ [1] *vtr* to tap [*table, object*]; to pat [*cheeks, back*].

taquin, ~e /takɛ̃, in/ *adj* [*person*] teasing.

taquiner /takine/ [1] *vtr* [*person*] to tease.

tarabiscoté, ~e /taʀabiskɔte/ *adj* [*design*] over-ornate; [*reasoning*] convoluted.

tarama /taʀama/ *nm* taramasalata.

tard /taʀ/ **I** *adv* late; **plus ~** later; **bien plus ~** much later (on); **au plus ~** at the latest; **pas plus ~ qu'hier** only yesterday.
II sur le tard *phr* [*marry*] late in life.

tarder /taʀde/ [1] **I** *vi* **1 ~ à faire** to take a long time doing; to put off or delay doing; **2** [*reaction*] to be a long time coming; **les enfants ne vont pas ~** the children won't be long.
II *v impers* **il me tarde de la revoir** I'm longing to see her again.

tardif, -ive /taʀdif, iv/ *adj* late; belated.

tardivement /taʀdivmɑ̃/ *adv* [*arrive*] late; [*react*] rather belatedly.

tare /taʀ/ *nf* **1** tare; **2** defect.

taré○**, ~e** /taʀe/ *adj* crazy○.

targette /taʀʒɛt/ *nf* bolt.

targuer: **se targuer** /taʀge/ [1] *v refl* (+ *v être*) to claim, to boast.

tarif /taʀif/ *nm* **1** (gen) rate; (on bus, train) fare; (for consultation) fee; **payer plein ~** to pay full price; to pay full fare; **~ de nuit** night-time rate; **2** price list.
■ **~ douanier** customs tariff.

tarir /taʀiʀ/ [23] **I** *vtr* to dry up [*source, well*]; to sap [*strength*].
II *vi* **ne pas ~ d'éloges sur qn/qch** to be full of praise for sb/sth.
III se tarir *v refl* (+ *v être*) to dry up.

tarot /taʀo/ *nm* tarot (*card game*).

tartare /taʀtaʀ/ *adj* **1** Tartar; **2** (Culin) **sauce ~** tartare sauce.

tarte /taʀt/ *nf* **1** (Culin) tart; **2**● wallop○.
IDIOMS **c'est pas de la ~**○ it's no picnic○.

tartelette /taʀtəlɛt/ *nf* (small) tart.

tartine /taʀtin/ *nf* **1** slice of bread and butter; **2**○ **il en a écrit une ~** he wrote reams about it.

tartiner /taʀtine/ [1] *vtr* to spread.

tartre /taʀtʀ/ *nm* (in kettle) scale; (on teeth) tartar.

tas /tɑ/ **I** *nm inv* **1** heap, pile; **en ~** [*put, place*] in a heap or pile; **~ de ferraille** scrap heap; (figurative)○ wreck; **2**○ **un ~, des ~** loads○.
II dans le tas○ *phr* **tirer dans le ~** to fire into the crowd.
III sur le tas *phr* **apprendre sur le ~** to learn on the job; **grève sur le ~** sit-down strike.

tasse /tɑs/ *nf* cup; **~ à thé** teacup.
IDIOMS **boire la ~**○ to swallow a mouthful of water (when swimming).

tasser /tɑse/ [1] **I** *vtr* to press down [*earth*]; to pack down [*hay*]; to pack [*clothes, people*] **(dans** into); **il a la cinquantaine bien tassée**○ he's well over fifty.
II se tasser *v refl* (+ *v être*) **1** (with age) to shrink; **2** (in train, car) [*people*] to squash up; **3**○ [*rumour, conflict*] to die down.

tâter /tɑte/ [1] **I** *vtr* to feel; **~ le sol du pied** to test the ground.
II se tâter○ *v refl* (+ *v être*) **je me tâte** I'm thinking about it.
IDIOMS **~ le terrain** to put out feelers.

tatillon, -onne /tɑtijɔ̃, ɔn/ *adj* nit-picking.

tâtonner /tɑtɔne/ [1] *vi* to grope about or around.

tâtons: **à tâtons** /atɑtɔ̃/ *phr* **avancer à ~** to feel one's way along.

tatouage /tatwaʒ/ *nm* tattoo.

tatouer /tatwe/ [1] *vtr* to tattoo.

taudis /todi/ *nm inv* **1** hovel; **2** pigsty.

taule● /tol/ *nf* prison.

taupe /top/ *nf* **1** (Zool) mole; **2** moleskin.

taupinière /topinjɛʀ/ *nf* **1** molehill; **2** (mole) tunnels.

taureau, *pl* **~x** /tɔʀo/ *nm* (Zool) bull.
IDIOMS **prendre le ~ par les cornes** to take the bull by the horns.

Taureau /tɔʀo/ *pr nm* Taurus.

tauromachie /tɔʀɔmaʃi/ *nf* bullfighting.

taux /to/ *nm inv* **1** (gen) rate; **~ de chômage** unemployment rate; **2** (Med) (of alcohol, albumen, sugar) level; (of bacteria, sperm) count.

taxation /taksasjɔ̃/ *nf* **1** taxation; **2** assessment.

taxe /taks/ *nf* tax; **boutique hors ~s** duty-free shop (GB) or store (US); **1000 francs toutes ~s comprises** 1,000 francs inclusive of tax.
■ **~ d'habitation** ≈ council tax (*paid by residents to cover local services*).

taxer /takse/ [1] *vtr* **1** (Econ) to tax; **2 ~ qn de laxisme** to accuse sb of being lax.

taxi /taksi/ *nm* taxi, cab (US).

taxidermiste /taksidɛʀmist/ *nmf* taxidermist.

Tchad /tʃad/ *pr nm* Chad.

tchao○ /tʃao/ *excl* bye○!, see you○!

tchèque /tʃɛk/ **I** *adj* Czech; **République ~** Czech Republic.
II *nm* (Ling) Czech.

tchin(-tchin)○ /tʃin(tʃin)/ *excl* cheers!

TD○ /tede/ *nm pl* (*abbr* = **travaux dirigés**) (Sch) practical.

te (**t'** *before vowel or mute h*) /t(ə)/ *pron* **1** (direct or indirect object) you; **2** (reflexive pronoun) yourself; **va ~ laver les mains** go and wash your hands.

té /te/ *nm* T-square; **en ~** T-shaped.

technicien, -ienne /tɛknisjɛ̃, ɛn/ *nm,f* **1** technician; **2** technical expert; **3** engineer.
■ **~ de surface** cleaner.

technique[1] /tɛknik/ **I** *adj* technical.
II *nm* technical subjects.

technique[2] /tɛknik/ *nf* **1** technique; **2** technology.

technocrate /tɛknɔkʀat/ *nmf* technocrat.

technologie /tɛknɔlɔʒi/ *nf* technology.
teck /tɛk/ *nm* teak; **en ~** teak.
teckel /tekɛl/ *nm* dachshund.
tee-shirt, *pl* **~s** /tiʃœʀt/ *nm* T-shirt.
teigne /tɛɲ/ *nf* **1** (Med) ringworm; **2** moth; **3**○ **être méchant comme une ~** to be a nasty (GB) or real (US) piece of work○.
teigneux○, **-euse** /tɛɲø, øz/ *adj* cantankerous.
teindre /tɛ̃dʀ/ [73] **I** *vtr* to dye; to stain.
II se teindre *v refl* (+ *v être*) to dye one's hair.
teint, **~e**[1] /tɛ̃, tɛ̃t/ **I** *pp* ▶ **teindre**.
II *pp adj* dyed; stained.
III *nm* complexion; **avoir le ~ rose** or **frais** to have a healthy glow to one's cheeks.
teinte[2] /tɛ̃t/ *nf* **1** shade; **2** colour[GB].
teinter /tɛ̃te/ [1] **I** *vtr* **1** to tint; to stain; to dye; **2 ~ qch de** to tinge sth with.
II se teinter *v refl* (+ *v être*) **se ~ de** to become tinged with.
teinture /tɛ̃tyʀ/ *nf* dye; (for wood) stain.
teinturerie /tɛ̃tyʀʀi/ *nf* (dry-)cleaner's.
teinturier, **-ière** /tɛ̃tyʀje, ɛʀ/ *nm,f* **1** dry-cleaner; **2** dyer.
tel, **telle** /tɛl/ *adj* **1** such; **une telle conduite** such behaviour[GB]; **2** like; **~ père, ~ fils** like father like son; **3 telle est la vérité** that is the truth; **comme ~**, **en tant que ~** as such; **ses affaires étaient restées telles quelles** his/her things were left as they were; **4 avec un ~ enthousiasme** with such enthusiasm; **de telle sorte** or **façon** or **manière que** in such a way that; so that; **5 admettons qu'il arrive ~ jour, à telle heure** suppose that he arrives on such and such a day, at such and such a time.
télé○ /tele/ *adj inv*, *nf* TV.
télécommande /telekɔmɑ̃d/ *nf* remote control.
télécommunication /telekɔmynikasjɔ̃/ *nf* telecommunications.
téléconférence /telekɔ̃feʀɑ̃s/ *nf* **1** conference call; **2** teleconference.
télécopieur /telekɔpjœʀ/ *nm* fax machine, fax.
télé-enseignement, *pl* **~s** /teleɑ̃sɛɲəmɑ̃/ *nm* distance learning.
téléfilm /telefilm/ *nm* TV film, TV movie.
télégramme /telegʀam/ *nm* telegram.
télégraphier /telegʀafje/ [1] *vtr* to telegraph.
télégraphique /telegʀafik/ *adj* [*pole, message*] telegraph; [*style*] telegraphic.
téléguider /telegide/ [1] *vtr* **1** to control [sth] by radio; **2** (figurative) to mastermind.
télématique /telematik/ **I** *adj* [*service, network*] viewdata (GB), videotex®.
II *nf* telematics.
téléobjectif /teleɔbʒɛktif/ *nm* telephoto lens.
télépathie /telepati/ *nf* telepathy.
téléphérique /telefeʀik/ *nm* cable car.
téléphone /telefɔn/ *nm* phone.
■ **~ arabe**○ grapevine, bush telegraph; **~ portable** portable phone; **~ portatif** pocket car phone; **le ~ rouge** the hotline.
téléphoner /telefɔne/ [1] *vi* to phone; to make a phone call; **~ à qn** to phone sb.
téléphonique /telefɔnik/ *adj* (tele)phone.
télescope /telɛskɔp/ *nm* telescope.
télescoper /telɛskɔpe/ [1] **I** *vtr* [*truck, juggernaut*] to crush [*car*].
II se télescoper *v refl* (+ *v être*) **1** [*vehicles*] to collide; **2** [*notions, tendencies*] to overlap.
télescopique /telɛskɔpik/ *adj* telescopic.
télésiège /telesjɛʒ/ *nm* chair lift.
téléski /teleski/ *nm* ski tow.
téléspectateur, **-trice** /telespɛktatœʀ, tʀis/ *nm,f* viewer.
téléviseur /televizœʀ/ *nm* television (set).
télévision /televizjɔ̃/ *nf* television, TV.
télex /telɛks/ *nm inv* telex; **par ~** by telex.
tellement /tɛlmɑ̃/ **I** *adv* (modifying an adjective or adverb) so; (modifying a verb or comparative) so much; **pas ~** not much; **il n'aime pas ~ lire** he doesn't like reading much; **j'ai de la peine à suivre ~ c'est compliqué** it's so complicated that I find it hard to follow.
II tellement de○ *quantif* **il y a ~ de choses à voir** there's so much to see; **il a eu ~ de chance** he was so lucky; **il y en a ~ qui aimeraient le faire** so many people would like to do it.
téméraire /temeʀɛʀ/ *adj* [*person, plan*] reckless; [*judgment*] rash; **courageux mais pas ~** brave but not foolhardy.
témoignage /temwaɲaʒ/ *nm* **1** story; **2** account; **~s recueillis auprès de** accounts given by; **3** evidence; testimony; **des ~s contradictoires/qui concordent** conflicting/corroborating evidence; **4 ~ d'amitié** (gift) token of friendship; **les ~s de sympathie** expressions of sympathy.
témoigner /temwaɲe/ [1] **I** *vtr* **1** (Law) to testify; **2 ~ de l'affection** to show affection.
II témoigner de *v+prep* **1 ~ de** to show; **2 ~ du courage de qn** to vouch for sb's courage.
III *vi* **1** (Law) to give evidence; **2 'il était toujours poli', témoignent les voisins** neighbours[GB] say he was always polite.
témoin /temwɛ̃/ *nm* **1** (gen, Law) witness; **~ oculaire** eyewitness; **2** (at duel) second; **3** (Tech) indicator or warning light.
tempe /tɑ̃p/ *nf* temple.
tempérament /tɑ̃peʀamɑ̃/ *nm* disposition; **avoir du ~** to have a strong character.
tempérance /tɑ̃peʀɑ̃s/ *nf* temperance.
température /tɑ̃peʀatyʀ/ *nf* temperature.
tempéré, **~e** /tɑ̃peʀe/ *adj* temperate.
tempérer /tɑ̃peʀe/ [14] *vtr* to temper; to moderate [*argument*].
tempête /tɑ̃pɛt/ *nf* **1** gale; storm; **2** uproar; **déclencher une ~ de protestations** to trigger a wave of protest.
tempêter /tɑ̃pete/ [1] *vi* to rage.
temple /tɑ̃pl/ *nm* **1** (gen) temple; (protestant) church; **2** (figurative) temple.
tempo /tɛmpo/ *nm* (Mus) tempo.

temporaire /tɑ̃pɔʀɛʀ/ *adj* temporary.

temporel, **-elle** /tɑ̃pɔʀɛl/ *adj* (gen) temporal.

temporiser /tɑ̃pɔʀize/ [1] *vi* to stall.

temps /tɑ̃/ *nm inv* **1** weather; **un beau ~** fine weather; **le ~ est à la pluie** it looks like rain; **quel ~ fait-il?** what's the weather like?; **par tous les ~** in all weathers; **2** time; **le ~ arrangera les choses** time will take care of everything; **peu de ~ avant** shortly before; **en peu de ~** in a short time; **dans peu de ~** shortly; **dans quelque ~** before long; **pendant ce ~(-là)** meanwhile; **qu'as-tu fait tout ce ~(-là)?** what have you been doing all this time?; **en un rien de ~** in no time at all; **les trois quarts du ~** most of the time; **le ~ de ranger mes affaires et j'arrive** just let me put my things away and I'll be with you; **on a (tout) le ~** we've got (plenty of) time; **avoir dix** or **cent fois le ~** to have all the time in the world; **laisser à qn le ~ de faire** to give sb time to do; **mettre** or **prendre du ~** to take time; **beaucoup de ~** a long time; **tu y as mis le ~!**, **tu en as mis du ~!** you (certainly) took your time!; **le ~ passe vite** time flies; **faire passer le ~** to while away the time; **avoir du ~ à perdre** to have time on one's hands; **c'est du ~ perdu**, **c'est une perte de ~** it's a waste of time; **le ~ presse!** time is short!; **j'ai trouvé le ~ long** (the) time seemed to drag; **finir dans les ~** to finish in time; **à ~** [*leave, finish*] in time; **juste à ~** just in time; **de ~ en ~**, **de ~ à autre** from time to time; **il était ~!** (impatiently) (and) about time too!; (with relief) just in the nick of time!; **en ~ utile** in time; **en ~ voulu** in due course; at the right time; **ne durer qu'un ~** to be short-lived; **3 au** or **du ~ des Grecs** in the time of the Greeks; **au** or **du ~ où** in the days when; **le bon vieux ~** the good old days; **ces derniers ~** recently; **ces ~-ci** lately; **de mon ~** in my day; **dans le ~** in those days; **en ~ normal** usually; **en d'autres ~** at any other time; **4** stage; **en deux ~** in two stages; **dans un premier ~** first; **dans un deuxième ~** subsequently; **dans un dernier ~** finally; **5** (of verb) tense; **6 avoir un travail à ~ partiel/plein** to have a part-/full-time job; **7** (Sport) time; **il a réalisé le meilleur ~** he got the best time; **améliorer son ~ d'une seconde** to knock a second off one's time; **8** (of engine) stroke; **9** (Mus) time; **mesure à deux ~** two-four time.

■ **~ d'antenne** airtime; **~ fort** (Mus) forte; (figurative) high point; **~ mort** slack period; **~ universel** Greenwich Mean Time, GMT.

IDIOMS **au ~ pour moi!** my mistake!; **par les ~ qui courent** with things as they are; **se payer**○ **du bon ~** to have a whale of a time.

tenace /tənas/ *adj* **1** [*stain, headache*] stubborn; [*perfume*] long-lasting; [*fog, cough, memory*] persistent; **2** [*person*] tenacious; persistent; [*will*] tenacious.

tenaille /tənɑj/ *nf* pincers.

tenailler /tənɑje/ [1] *vtr* **il était tenaillé par le remords** he was racked with remorse.

tenancier, **-ière** /tənɑ̃sje, ɛʀ/ *nm,f* (of café) landlord/landlady; (of hotel, casino) manager/manageress.

tenant, **~e** /tənɑ̃, ɑ̃t/ **I** *nm,f* (Sport) **~ du titre** titleholder.

II *nm* **d'un seul ~** all in one piece.

IDIOMS **les ~s et les aboutissants de qch** the ins and outs of sth.

tendance /tɑ̃dɑ̃s/ *nf* **1** tendency; **2** (in politics) tendency; **toutes ~s politiques confondues** across party lines; **3** trend.

tendancieux, **-ieuse** /tɑ̃dɑ̃sjø, øz/ *adj* biased[GB], tendentious.

tendeur /tɑ̃dœʀ/ *nm* **1** (of tent) guy rope; **2** (for roof rack) elastic strap.

tendon /tɑ̃dɔ̃/ *nm* tendon.

tendre[1] /tɑ̃dʀ/ [6] **I** *vtr* **1** to tighten [*rope, cable*]; to stretch [*elastic, skin*]; to extend [*spring*]; **~ le bras** to reach out; **~ les bras à qn** to greet sb with open arms; **~ la main** to reach out; to hold out one's hand; **~ la main à qn** to hold one's hand out to sb; (figurative) to lend sb a helping hand; **2** to spread [*cloth, sheet*]; **3** to set [*trap*]; to put up [*clothes line*]; **4 ~ qch à qn** to hold sth out to sb.

II tendre à *v+prep* **~ à faire** to tend to do.

III *vi* **1 ~ vers** to strive for; **2 ~ vers** to approach [*value*]; to tend to [*zero*].

IV se tendre *v refl* (+ *v être*) **1** to tighten; **2** to become strained.

tendre[2] /tɑ̃dʀ/ **I** *adj* **1** [*wood, fibre*] soft; [*skin, vegetables*] tender; **2** [*shoot, grass*] new; **~ enfance** earliest childhood; **3** [*pink, green*] soft; **4** [*person*] loving; [*love, smile, words*] tender; [*temperament*] gentle; **ne pas être ~ avec qn/qch** to be hard on sb/sth; **5** [*husband, wife*] dear.

II *nmf* soft-hearted person.

tendresse /tɑ̃dʀɛs/ *nf* **1** tenderness; **2** affection.

tendu, **~e** /tɑ̃dy/ **I** *pp* ▶ **tendre**[1].

II *pp adj* [*rope*] tight.

III *adj* [*person, meeting*] tense.

ténèbres /tenɛbʀ/ *nf pl* **les ~** darkness.

ténébreux, **-euse** /tenebʀø, øz/ *adj* **1** dark; **2** obscure.

teneur /tənœʀ/ *nf* **1** (of solid) content; (of gas, liquid) level; **2** (of report) import.

ténia /tenja/ *nm* tapeworm.

tenir /təniʀ/ [36] **I** *vtr* **1** to hold; **~ qn par la main** to hold sb's hand; **tiens!** (giving sth to sb) here you are!; **tiens, regarde!** hey, look!; **si je le tenais!** if I could get my hands on him!; **2** to keep [sb] under control; **il nous tient** he's got a hold on us; **3** (Mil) to hold [*hill, bridge, city*]; **4** to hold [*captive, animal*]; **je te tiens!** I've caught you!; **5** to have [*information*]; **6** to hold [*job*]; to run [*shop, house, business*]; to be in charge of [*switchboard, reception*]; **7** to keep; **'~ hors de portée des enfants'** 'keep out of reach of children'; **8 ~ sa tête droite** to hold one's head upright; **~ les yeux baissés** to keep one's eyes lowered; **9** to hold down [*load, cargo*]; to hold up [*trousers, socks*]; **10** to keep to [*itinerary*]; **11 ~ la mer** [*ship*] to be seaworthy; **~ le coup** to hold out; **~ le choc**

[*person*] to stand the strain; **12** [*object*] to take up [*room*]; [*person*] to hold [*role, position*]; **13 ~ qn/qch pour responsable** to hold sb/sth responsible; **~ qn pour mort** to give sb up for dead.

II tenir à *v+prep* **1 ~ à** to be fond of, to like; **~ à la vie** to value one's life; **2 j'y tiens** I insist; **~ à ce que qn fasse** to insist that sb should do.

III tenir de *v+prep* **~ de qn** to take after sb.

IV *vi* **1** [*rope, shelf, dam*] to hold; [*stamp, glue*] to stick; [*bandage, structure*] to stay in place; [*hairstyle*] to stay tidy; **2 ~ (bon)** (gen) to hang on; (Mil) to hold out; **3 la neige tient** the snow is settling; **les fleurs n'ont pas tenu** the flowers didn't last long; **4** [*theory*] to hold good; [*alibi*] to stand up; **5** [*people, objects*] to fit; **~ à six dans une voiture** to fit six into a car; **mon article tient en trois pages** my article takes up only three pages.

V se tenir *v refl* (+ *v être*) **1 se ~ la tête à deux mains** to hold one's head in one's hands; **2 se ~ par le bras** to be arm in arm; **se ~ par la main** to hold hands; **3 se ~ à qch** to hold onto sth; **tiens-toi** or **tenez-vous bien**○ (figurative) prepare yourself for a shock; **4 se ~ accroupi** to be squatting; **se ~ au milieu** to be standing in the middle; **se ~ prêt** to be ready; **5** to behave; **se ~ bien/mal** to behave well/badly; **6 se ~ bien/mal** to have (a) good posture/(a) bad posture; **tiens-toi droit!** stand up straight!; **7** [*demonstration, exhibition*] to be held; **8** [*argument, book*] to hold together; **ça se tient** it makes sense; **9 tenez-vous le pour dit**○**!** I don't want to have to tell you again!; **10 s'en ~ à** to keep to; **s'en ~ aux ordres** to stick to orders; **ne pas savoir à quoi s'en ~** not to know what to make of it.

VI *v impers* **il ne tient qu'à toi de partir** it's up to you to decide whether to leave; **qu'à cela ne tienne!** never mind!

tennis /tenis/ **I** *nm inv* tennis; **~ de table** table tennis.

II *nm inv* or *nf inv* tennis shoe.

tennisman, *pl* **tennismen** /tenisman, mɛn/ *nm* (male) tennis player.

ténor /tenɔʀ/ *nm* tenor.

tension /tɑ̃sjɔ̃/ *nf* **1** (of cable, muscle) tension; **2** (Med) **~ (artérielle)** blood pressure; **être sous ~** to be under stress; **3** (in electricity) tension; **basse ~** low voltage; **sous ~** [*wire*] live; [*machine*] switched on; **4** (between people) tension.

tentacule /tɑ̃takyl/ *nm* tentacle.

tentation /tɑ̃tasjɔ̃/ *nf* temptation.

tentative /tɑ̃tativ/ *nf* attempt; **~ de meurtre** (gen) murder attempt; (Law) attempted murder.

tente /tɑ̃t/ *nf* tent.

tenter /tɑ̃te/ [1] *vtr* **1** to attempt; **~ sa chance** to try one's luck; **~ le tout pour le tout** to risk one's all; **2** to tempt; **cela ne la tente guère** that doesn't appeal to her very much; **laisse-toi ~!** be a devil!; **~ le diable** to court disaster.

tenture /tɑ̃tyʀ/ *nf* **1** curtain; **~s** draperies; **2** fabric wall covering.

tenu, **~e**[1] /təny/ **I** *pp* ▶ **tenir**.

II *pp adj* **1 bien/mal ~** [*child*] well/badly cared for; [*house*] well/badly kept; **2 ~ de faire** required to do; **~ à** bound by.

tenue[2] /təny/ *nf* **1 ~ (vestimentaire)** dress, clothes; **être en ~ légère** to be scantily dressed; **en ~** (Mil) uniformed; **2 avoir de la ~** to have good manners; **un peu de ~!** mind your manners!; **3** posture.

ter /tɛʀ/ *adv* **1** (in address) ter; **15 ~ rue du Rocher** 15 ter rue du Rocher; **2** three times.

térébenthine /teʀebɑ̃tin/ *nf* turpentine.

tergal® /tɛʀgal/ *nm* Terylene®.

tergiverser /tɛʀʒivɛʀse/ [1] *vi* **1** to dither; **2** to shilly-shally.

terme /tɛʀm/ **I** *nm* **1** term, word; **2** end; **mettre un ~ à qch** to put an end to sth; **toucher à son ~** to come to an end; **arriver à ~** [*period, contract*] to expire; **accoucher avant ~** to give birth prematurely; **3 passé ce ~ vous paierez des intérêts** after this date, you will pay interest; **à moyen ~** [*loan*] medium-term; **4 trouver un moyen ~** to find a compromise.

II termes *nm pl* terms; **~s de l'échange** terms of trade; **en bons ~s** on good terms.

terminaison /tɛʀminɛzɔ̃/ *nf* ending.

terminal, **~e**[1], *mpl* **-aux** /tɛʀminal, o/ **I** *adj* [*year*] final; **phase ~e** (of operation) concluding phase; (of illness) terminal phase.

II *nm* terminal.

terminale[2] /tɛʀminal/ *nf* (Sch) final year (*of secondary school*).

terminer /tɛʀmine/ [1] **I** *vtr* to finish; to end.

II *vi* to finish; **en ~ avec** to be through with; **pour ~** in conclusion.

III se terminer *v refl* (+ *v être*) **1** to end; **être terminé** to be over; **2 se ~ par** [*word, number, object*] to end in.

terminologie /tɛʀminɔlɔʒi/ *nf* terminology.

terminus /tɛʀminys/ *nm inv* (of train) end of the line; (of bus) terminus.

termite /tɛʀmit/ *nm* termite.

terne /tɛʀn/ *adj* [*hair, life*] dull; [*colour*] drab; [*eyes, expression*] lifeless.

ternir /tɛʀniʀ/ [3] **I** *vtr* **1** to tarnish [*metal*]; to fade [*fabric*]; **2** to tarnish [*image, reputation*].

II se ternir *v refl* (+ *v être*) to tarnish.

terrain /tɛʀɛ̃/ *nm* **1** (gen) ground; (Mil) field; **2** plot of land; **3** land; **4** (for football, rugby, cricket) pitch, field; ground; (for volley-ball, handball, tennis) court; (in golf) course; **5** (figurative) **nous ne vous suivrons pas sur ce ~** we won't go along with you there; **un ~ d'entente** common ground; **travailler sur le ~** to do fieldwork; **~ favorable** (Med) predisposing factors; (in sociology) favourable[GB] environment; **déblayer le ~** to clear the ground; **préparer le ~** to pave the way; **tâter le ~** to put out feelers.

■ **~ d'atterrissage** landing strip; **~ d'aviation** airfield; **~ de camping** campsite; **~ de jeu(x)** playground; **~ de sport(s)** sports ground; **~ vague** wasteland.

terrasse /tɛʀas/ *nf* **1** terrace; **s'installer à la ~ d'un café** to sit at a table outside a café; **2** flat roof; **3** large balcony.

terrasser /tɛʀase/ [1] *vtr* [*illness*] to strike down; **terrassé par** (by heat, grief) prostrated by.

terre /tɛʀ/ **I** *nf* **1** ground; **sous ~** underground; **2** earth; soil; **sortir de ~** [*plant*] to come up; **3** land; **le retour à la ~** the movement back to the land; **aller à ~** to go ashore; **s'enfoncer à l'intérieur des ~s** to go deep inland; **4** earth; **il croit que la ~ entière est contre lui** he thinks the whole world is against him; **redescends sur ~!** come back to earth!; **5 de la ~ (glaise)** clay; **un pot en ~** an earthenware pot; **6** (in electricity) earth (GB), ground (US).

II terre à terre *phr* [*question*] basic; [*conversation, person*] pedestrian.

III par terre *phr* on the ground; on the floor; **c'est à se rouler par ~**○ it's hilarious; **ça a fichu tous nos projets par ~**○ it messed up all our plans○.

■ **~ d'asile** country of refuge; **~ battue** trodden earth; **sur ~ battue** on a clay court.

IDIOMS **avoir les pieds sur ~**○ to have one's feet firmly planted on the ground.

Terre /tɛʀ/ *nf* Earth; **sur la ~** on Earth.

terreau, *pl* **~x** /tɛʀo/ *nm* compost; **~ de feuilles** leaf mould (GB), leaf mold (US).

terre-plein, *pl* **terres-pleins** /tɛʀplɛ̃/ *nm* (of road) central reservation (GB), median strip (US).

terrer: **se terrer** /tɛʀe/ [1] *v refl* (+ *v être*) **1** [*rabbit*] to disappear into its burrow; [*fox*] to go to earth; **2** [*fugitive*] to hide.

terrestre /tɛʀɛstʀ/ *adj* **1** [*surface, diameter*] of the Earth; **2** [*animals*] land; **3** [*war, transport*] land; **la vie/le paradis ~** life/heaven on earth.

terreur /tɛʀœʀ/ *nf* terror; **c'est ma grande ~** it's my greatest fear.

terrible /tɛʀibl/ *adj* **1** (gen) terrible; [*thirst, desire*] tremendous; **il est ~**○**, il ne veut jamais avoir tort** it's terrible the way he never wants to admit that he's wrong; **2**○ terrific○.

terrien, -ienne /tɛʀjɛ̃, ɛn/ *adj* **propriétaire ~** landowner.

terrier /tɛʀje/ *nm* **1** (gen) hole; **un ~ de renard** a fox's earth; **2** (Zool) terrier.

terrifiant, ~e /tɛʀifjɑ̃, ɑ̃t/ *adj* terrifying.

terrifier /tɛʀifje/ [2] *vtr* to terrify.

terrine /tɛʀin/ *nf* (gen) terrine; (round) earthenware bowl.

territoire /tɛʀitwaʀ/ *nm* territory.

■ **~ d'outre-mer, TOM** French overseas (administrative) territory.

territorial, ~e, *mpl* **-iaux** /tɛʀitɔʀjal, o/ *adj* **1** [*waters, integrity*] territorial; **2** [*administration*] divisional; regional.

terroir /tɛʀwaʀ/ *nm* land; **vin du ~** local wine.

terroriser /tɛʀɔʀize/ [1] *vtr* **1** to terrorize; **2** to terrify.

terrorisme /tɛʀɔʀism/ *nm* terrorism.

terroriste /tɛʀɔʀist/ *adj, nmf* terrorist.

tertiaire /tɛʀsjɛʀ/ *adj* **1** (Econ) [*sector, industry*] service; **2** (in geology) Tertiary.

tes ▶ **ton**[1].

tesson /tesɔ̃/ *nm* shard, fragment.

test /tɛst/ *nm* test; **~ (de dépistage) du sida** Aids test; **faire passer des ~s à qn** (gen) to give sb tests; (Med) to carry out tests on sb.

testament /tɛstamɑ̃/ *nm* (Law) will; (figurative) legacy.

tester /tɛste/ [1] *vtr* to test.

testicule /tɛstikyl/ *nm* testicle.

tétanos /tetanos/ *nm inv* tetanus.

têtard /tɛtaʀ/ *nm* (Zool) tadpole.

tête /tɛt/ *nf* **1** head; **en pleine ~** (right) in the head; **~ baissée** [*rush*] headlong; **la ~ en bas** [*hang*] upside down; **se laver la ~** to wash one's hair; **au-dessus de nos ~s** overhead; **être tombé sur la ~**○ (figurative) to have gone off one's rocker○; **ma ~ est mise à prix** there's a price on my head; **vouloir la ~ de qn** to want sb's head; to be after sb's head; **risquer sa ~** to risk one's neck○; **des ~s vont tomber** (figurative) heads will roll; **2** face; **une bonne/sale ~** a nice/nasty face; **tu en fais une ~!** what a face!; **quelle ~ va-t-il faire?** how's he going to react?; **il (me) fait la ~** he's sulking; **il a une ~ à tricher** he looks like a cheat; **tu as une ~ à faire peur, aujourd'hui!** you look dreadful today!; **3 de ~** [*quote, recite*] from memory; [*calculate*] in one's head; **tu n'as pas de ~!** you have a mind like a sieve!; **avoir qch en ~** to have sth in mind; **où avais-je la ~?** whatever was I thinking of?; **ça (ne) va pas, la ~**○**?** are you out of your mind or what?; **mets-lui ça dans la ~** drum it into him/her; **passer par la ~ de qn** [*idea*] to cross sb's mind; **monter la ~ à Pierre contre Paul** to turn Pierre against Paul; **j'ai la ~ qui tourne** my head's spinning; **monter à la ~ de qn** [*alcohol, success*] to go to sb's head; **il a encore toute sa ~ (à lui)** he's still got all his faculties; **n'en faire qu'à sa ~** to go one's own way; **tenir ~ à qn** to stand up to sb; **4** (person) **avoir ses ~s** to have one's favourites[GB]; **un dîner en ~ à ~** an intimate dinner for two **par ~** (gen) a head, each; (in statistics) per capita; **5** (measurement) head; **avoir une ~ d'avance sur qn** to be a short length in front of sb; **6 il a été nommé à la ~ du groupe** he was appointed head of the group; **prendre la ~ des opérations** to take charge of operations; **être à la ~ d'une immense fortune** to be the possessor of a huge fortune; **7** top; **être en ~** (of list, category) to be at the top; (in election, race, survey) to be in the lead; **en ~ de phrase** at the beginning of a sentence; **8** (of train) front; (of convoy) head; (of tree, mast) top; (of screw, nail) head; **en ~ de file** first in line; **9** (Sport) (in football) **faire une ~** to head the ball; **10** (Mil) (of missile) warhead; **11 ~ de lecture** (in tape recorder, video recorder) head.

■ **~ en l'air** scatterbrain; **~ brûlée** daredevil; **~ à claques**○ pain○; **~ de linotte** = **~ en l'air**; **~ de mort** skull; death's head; skull and crossbones; **~ de mule**○ mule;

être une vraie ~ de mule○ to be as stubborn as a mule; **~ de Turc**○ whipping boy.
IDIOMS **j'en mettrais ma ~ à couper** I'd swear to it; **en avoir par-dessus la ~**○ to be fed up to the back teeth○; **ça me prend la ~**○ it's a real drag○.

tête-à-tête /tɛtatɛt/ *nm inv* **1** tête-à-tête; **2** private meeting.

tête-bêche /tɛtbɛʃ/ *adv* **1** top-to-tail; **2** head-to-tail.

tétée /tete/ *nf* **1** feeding; **2** feed.

téter /tete/ [14] **I** *vtr* to suck at [*breast*]; to feed from [*bottle*]; to suck [*milk*].
II *vi* to suckle; **donner à ~ à** to feed [*baby*].

tétine /tetin/ *nf* **1** teat (GB), nipple (US); **2** dummy (GB), pacifier (US); **3** (of animal) teat.

têtu, **~e** /tety/ *adj* stubborn.

texte /tɛkst/ *nm* **1** text; **'~ intégral'** 'unabridged'; **2** (Law) **~ de loi** bill; law.

textile /tɛkstil/ **I** *adj* textile.
II *nm* **1** textile industry; **2 ~s synthétiques** synthetic fibres[GB].

textuellement /tɛkstɥɛlmɑ̃/ *adv* [*recount*] word for word.

texture /tɛkstyʀ/ *nf* **1** (of fabric, material) texture; **2** (of novel) structure.

TGV /teʒeve/ *nm* (*abbr* = **train à grande vitesse**) TGV, high-speed train.

thé /te/ *nm* **1** tea; **2** tea party.

théâtral, **~e**, *mpl* **-aux** /teɑtʀal, o/ *adj* **1** [*performance*] stage; [*season, company*] theatre[GB]; [*production, technique*] theatrical; **l'œuvre ~e de Racine** the plays of Racine; **2** [*gesture*] histrionic; [*tone*] melodramatic.

théâtre /teɑtʀ/ *nm* theatre[GB]; **le ~ antique** Greek classical drama; **de ~** [*actor, director, ticket*] theatre[GB]; [*decor, costume*] stage; **coup de ~** coup de théâtre; (figurative) dramatic turn of events; **faire du ~** (as profession) to be an actor; (at school) to do drama; **être le ~ d'affrontements** (figurative) to be the scene of fighting.
■ **~ de Boulevard** farce.

théière /tejɛʀ/ *nf* teapot.

théine /tein/ *nf* theine.

thème /tɛm/ *nm* **1** topic, subject; (of film) theme; **2** (translation) prose; **3** (Mus) theme.
■ **~ astral** birth chart.

théologie /teɔlɔʒi/ *nf* theology.

théorème /teɔʀɛm/ *nm* theorem.

théorie /teɔʀi/ *nf* theory; **en ~** in theory.

théorique /teɔʀik/ *adj* theoretical.

thérapeute /teʀapøt/ *nmf* therapist.

thérapeutique /teʀapøtik/ *adj* [*effect*] therapeutic; **choix ~** choice of treatment.

thérapie /teʀapi/ *nf* **1** (Med) treatment; **2** (in psychology) therapy.

thermal, **~e**, *mpl* **-aux** /tɛʀmal, o/ *adj* [*spring*] thermal; **station ~e** spa.

thermes /tɛʀm/ *nm pl* **1** (Roman) thermae; **2** thermal baths.

thermique /tɛʀmik/ *adj* thermal.

thermo /tɛʀmo/ *pref* thermo.

thermomètre /tɛʀmɔmɛtʀ/ *nm* thermometer.

thermostat /tɛʀmɔsta/ *nm* thermostat.

thèse /tɛz/ *nf* **1** (for doctorate) thesis (GB), dissertation (US); **2** thesis, argument; **3 avancer la ~ de l'accident** to put forward the theory that it was an accident.

thon /tɔ̃/ *nm* tuna.

thoracique /tɔʀasik/ *adj* **cage ~** ribcage.

thorax /tɔʀaks/ *nm inv* thorax.

thym /tɛ̃/ *nm* thyme.

thyroïde /tiʀɔid/ *adj, nf* thyroid.

tibia /tibja/ *nm* shinbone, tibia.

tic /tik/ *nm* **1** tic; **être plein de ~s** to be constantly twitching; **2 ~ de langage** verbal tic.

ticket /tikɛ/ *nm* (for train, platform) ticket; **~ de caisse** till receipt (GB), sales slip (US).

tic-tac /tiktak/ *nm inv* **faire ~** to tick.

tiède /tjɛd/ *adj* **1** lukewarm; warm; mild; **2** (figurative) lukewarm.

tièdement /tjɛdmɑ̃/ *adv* half-heartedly.

tien, **tienne** /tjɛ̃, tjɛn/ **le tien, la tienne, les tiens, les tiennes** *pron* yours; **un métier comme le ~** a job like yours; **à la tienne!** cheers!; (ironic) good luck to you!

tiens ▶ **tenir**.

tierce[1] /tjɛʀs/ *adj f* ▶ **tiers I**.

tiercé /tjɛʀse/ *nm* (Games) **jouer au ~** to bet on the horses.

tiers, **tierce**[2] /tjɛʀ, tjɛʀs/ **I** *adj* third; **un pays ~** (gen) another country; a non-member country; **une tierce personne** a third party.
II *nm inv* **1** third; **le ~/les deux ~ du travail** one third/two thirds of the work; **2** (person) outsider; (Law) third party.
■ **le Tiers État** the Third Estate.

tiers-monde /tjɛʀmɔ̃d/ *nm* Third World.

tige /tiʒ/ *nf* (of plant) (gen) stem, stalk.

tigre /tigʀ/ *nm* (Zool) tiger.

tigré, **~e** /tigʀe/ *adj* **1** striped; **2** spotted.

tigresse /tigʀɛs/ *nf* (Zool, figurative) tigress.

tilleul /tijœl/ *nm* **1** limetree; **2** limewood; **3** lime-blossom tea.

tilt○ /tilt/ *nm* **ça a fait ~**○ **(dans mon esprit)** the penny dropped○.

timbale /tɛ̃bal/ *nf* **1** (metal) tumbler; **2** (Mus) kettledrum; **~s** timpani; **3** (Culin) timbale.

timbre /tɛ̃bʀ/ *nm* **1** stamp; **2** postmark; **3** (of voice) tone, timbre; **4** (Med) patch.

timbre-poste, *pl* **timbres-poste** /tɛ̃bʀəpɔst/ *nm* postage stamp.

timbrer /tɛ̃bʀe/ [1] *vtr* to stamp.

timide /timid/ *adj* [*person*] shy, timid; [*criticism*] timid; [*success*] limited.

timidité /timidite/ *nf* shyness.

timoré, **~e** /timɔʀe/ *adj* timorous.

tintement /tɛ̃tmɑ̃/ *nm* chiming; tinkling.

tinter /tɛ̃te/ [1] *vi* [*bells*] to chime; [*doorbell*] to ring; [*small bell*] to tinkle; [*glass, coins*] to clink; [*keys*] to jingle; (Mus) [*triangle*] to ring.

tipi /tipi/ *nm* te(e)pee.

tique /tik/ *nf* (Zool) tick.

tiquer° /tike/ [1] *vi* to wince; **sans ~** without batting an eyelid (GB) or eyelash (US).

tir /tiʀ/ *nm* **1** (Mil) fire; **déclencher le ~** to open fire; **2** (Sport) shooting; **3 ~ de grenades** grenade firing; **4** (in games, sports) (with ball) shot; **5** shooting.

tirade /tiʀad/ *nf* **1** declamation; **2** tirade.

tirage /tiʀaʒ/ *nm* **1 ~ (au sort)** draw; **désigner par ~ (au sort)** to draw [*name, winner*]; **2** impression; **3** edition; **~ limité** limited edition; **4** (of book) run; (of newspaper) circulation.

tirailler /tiʀaje/ [1] *vtr* to tug (at), to pull (at) [*rope, sleeve*]; **être tiraillé entre son travail et sa famille** to be torn between one's work and one's family.

tire-bouchon, *pl* **~s** /tiʀbuʃɔ̃/ *nm* corkscrew; **en ~** [*tail*] curly.

tire-d'aile: **à tire-d'aile** /atiʀdɛl/ *phr* in a flurry of wings; (figurative) hurriedly.

tirelire /tiʀliʀ/ *nf* piggy bank.

tirer /tiʀe/ [1] **I** *vtr* **1** to pull [*vehicle*]; to pull up [*chair, armchair*]; to pull away [*rug*]; **2** to pull [*hair*]; to pull on [*rope*]; to tug at [*sleeve*]; **~ qn par le bras** to pull sb's arm; **3 ~ ses cheveux en arrière** to pull back one's hair; **avoir les traits tirés** to look drawn; **4** to draw [*bolt, curtain*]; to pull down [*blind*]; to close [*door, shutter*]; **5** to fire off [*bullet, grenade*]; to fire [*missile*]; to shoot [*arrow*]; **6** (Sport) **~ un penalty** to take a penalty; **7 ~ (au sort)** to draw [*card, name, winner*]; to draw for [*partner*]; **8** (in astrology) **~ les cartes à qn** to tell the cards for sb; **9** to draw [*wine*]; to withdraw [*money*]; **~ qch de sa poche** to pull sth out of one's pocket; **10 ~ le pays de la récession** to get the country out of recession; **tire-moi de là!** get me out of this!; **11 ~ [qch] de qn** to get [sth] from sb [*information, confession*]; **~ [qch] de qch** to draw [sth] from sth [*strength, resources*]; to derive [sth] from sth [*pride, satisfaction*]; to make [sth] out of sth [*money*]; **12 ~ de qch** to base [sth] on sth [*story, film*]; to get [sth] from sth [*name*]; **13** to print [*book, negative*]; to run off [*proofs, copies*]; **14** to draw [*line*]; **15**° **plus qu'une semaine à ~** only one more week to go; **16 ~ un chèque** to draw a cheque (GB) or check (US).

II *vi* **1** to pull; **~ sur qch** to pull on sth; to tug at sth; **2** (with firearm) to shoot; to fire; **3** (in football) to shoot; (in handball, basketball) to take a shot; **4 ~ (au sort)** to draw lots; **5 la cheminée tire bien** the chimney draws well; **6 ~ à mille exemplaires** [*periodical*] to have a circulation of one thousand; **7 ~ sur le jaune/l'orangé** [*colour*] to be yellowish/orangy.

III se tirer *v refl* (+ *v être*) **1 se ~ de** to come through [*situation, difficulties*]; **2 se ~ une balle** to shoot oneself; **se ~ dessus** to shoot at one another; **3**° **s'en ~** to cope; (from accident) to escape; (from illness) to pull through; **s'en ~ à bon prix** to get off lightly.

tiret /tiʀɛ/ *nm* dash.

tirette /tiʀɛt/ *nf* pull tab; cord.

tireur, **-euse** /tiʀœʀ, øz/ *nm, f* **1** (Mil, Sport) marksman/markswoman; **2** gunman.

tiroir /tiʀwaʀ/ *nm* (in piece of furniture) drawer; **à ~s** (figurative) [*novel, play*] episodic.

IDIOMS **racler les fonds de ~** to scrape some money together.

tiroir-caisse, *pl* **tiroirs-caisses** /tiʀwaʀ kɛs/ *nm* cash register.

tisane /tizan/ *nf* herbal tea, tisane.

tison /tizɔ̃/ *nm* (fire) brand.

tisonnier /tizɔnje/ *nm* poker.

tissage /tisaʒ/ *nm* **1** weaving; **2** weave.

tisser /tise/ [1] *vtr* **1** [*person, machine*] to weave; **2** [*spider*] to spin [*web*].

tisserand, **~e** /tisʀɑ̃, ɑ̃d/ *nm,f* weaver.

tissu /tisy/ *nm* **1** material, fabric; **2** (Anat) **le ~ osseux** bone tissue; **3** (of intrigue) web; (of lies) pack; (of insults) string; **~ social** social fabric.

titan /titɑ̃/ *nm* titan; **de ~** titanic.

titiller /titije/ [1] *vtr* to titillate.

titre /titʀ/ *nm* **1** (of book, film, chapter) title; (in newspaper) headline; **avoir pour ~** to be entitled; **les ~s de l'actualité** the headlines; **2** (rank) title; **~ mondial** world title; **~ nobiliaire** or **de noblesse** title; **le ~ d'ingénieur** the status of qualified engineer; **en ~** [*professor, director*] titular; [*supplier*] appointed; [*mistress, rival*] official; **~s universitaires** university qualifications; **3 à juste ~** quite rightly; **à ~ d'exemple** as an example; **à ~ définitif** on a permanent basis; **à ~ privé** in a private capacity; **à ~ gracieux** free; **à ~ indicatif** as a rough guide; **à quel ~ a-t-il été invité?** why was he invited?; **4** (Law) deed; **~ de propriété** title deed; **5** (on stock exchange) security; **6** (Econ) item; **~ budgétaire** budgetary item; **7** (of solution) titre[GB]; (of wines, spirits) strength; (of precious metal) fineness.

■ **~ de gloire** claim to fame; **~ de transport** ticket.

titré, **~e** /titʀe/ *adj* titled; **être ~** to be titled.

tituber /titybe/ [1] *vi* to stagger.

titulaire /titylɛʀ/ **I** *adj* (gen) permanent; [*lecturer*] tenured.

II *nmf* **1** (gen) permanent staff member; tenured lecturer (GB) or professor (US); **2** holder; **être ~ de** to hold [*degree, post*]; to have [*bank account*].

titulariser /titylaʀize/ [1] *vtr* to give permanent status to [*staff*]; to grant tenure to [*professor*].

toast /tost/ *nm* toast.

toboggan /tɔbɔgɑ̃/ *nm* **1** slide; **2** ®flyover (GB), overpass (US); **3** (Tech) (for rubble) chute.

toc /tɔk/ **I**° *nm* **c'est du ~** it's fake.

II *excl* **~! ~!** knock! knock!

tocsin /tɔksɛ̃/ *nm* alarm (bell), tocsin.

toge /tɔʒ/ *nf* **1** (of academic) gown; (of judge) robe; **2** toga.

toi /twa/ *pron* **1** you; **~, ne dis rien** don't say anything; **elle est plus âgée que ~** she's older than you; **à ~** (in game) your turn; **c'est à ~** it's yours; **c'est à ~ de choisir** it's your turn to choose; it's up to you to choose; **2** yourself; **reprends-~** pull yourself together.

toile /twal/ *nf* **1** cloth; **~ de lin** linen (cloth); **de la grosse ~** canvas; **2** (in art) canvas; painting; **~ de maître** master painting; **3** (Naut) canvas.
■ **~ d'araignée** spider's web; cobweb; **~ cirée** oilcloth; **~ de jute** hessian; **~ de tente** canvas; tent.

toilettage /twalɛtaʒ/ *nm* (of animal) grooming.

toilette /twalɛt/ **I** *nf* **1 faire sa ~** [*person*] to have a wash; [*animal*] to wash itself; **faire la ~ d'un mort** to lay out a corpse; **2** outfit; **en grande ~** all dressed up.
II toilettes *nf pl* toilet (GB), bathroom (US).

toiletter /twalete/ [1] *vtr* to groom [*dog*].

toi-même /twamɛm/ *pron* yourself.

toise /twaz/ *nf* height gauge.

toiser /twaze/ [1] *vtr* to look [sb] up and down.

toit /twɑ/ *nm* roof.
■ **le ~ du Monde** the roof of the world; **~ ouvrant** sunroof.
IDIOMS **crier qch sur (tous) les ~s** to shout sth from the rooftops.

toiture /twatyʀ/ *nf* **1** roof; **2** roofing.

tôle /tol/ *nf* **1** sheet metal; **2** metal sheet or plate; **3**◐ = **taule**.

tolérable /tɔleʀabl/ *adj* bearable; tolerable.

tolérance /tɔleʀɑ̃s/ *nf* **1** tolerance; indulgence; **2 ce n'est pas un droit, c'est une ~** it isn't legal but it is tolerated; **3** (of medicine, noise) tolerance.

tolérant, **~e** /tɔleʀɑ̃, ɑ̃t/ *adj* tolerant.

tolérer /tɔleʀe/ [14] *vtr* to tolerate.

tôlerie /tolʀi/ *nf* sheet-metal working; sheet-metal trade; sheet-metal works.

tollé /tɔle/ *nm* outcry, hue and cry.

TOM /tɔm/ *nm*: *abbr* ▶ **territoire**.

tomate /tɔmat/ *nf* **1** tomato; **2** tomato plant; **3** *pastis with a dash of grenadine*.

tombal, **~e**, *mpl* **-aux** /tɔ̃bal, o/ *adj* **inscription ~e** gravestone inscription.

tombant, **~e** /tɔ̃bɑ̃, ɑ̃t/ *adj* [*shoulders*] sloping; [*moustache, eyelids*] drooping; [*ears*] floppy.

tombe /tɔ̃b/ *nf* **1** grave; **2** gravestone.

tombeau, *pl* **~x** /tɔ̃bo/ *nm* **1** tomb; **mettre qn au ~** to lay sb in their grave; **2 c'est un ~** [*person*] he/she will keep quiet.

tombée /tɔ̃be/ *nf* **à la ~ du jour** at close of day; **la ~ de la nuit** nightfall.

tomber[1] /tɔ̃be/ [1] *vi* (+ *v être*) **1** (gen) to fall; [*person, chair*] to fall over; [*tree, wall*] to fall down; (from height) [*person, vase*] to fall off; [*hair, teeth*] to fall out; [*plaster, covering*] to come off; **~ du lit/de ma poche** to fall out of bed/out of my pocket; **le vent a fait ~ une tuile du toit** the wind blew a tile off the roof; **se laisser ~ dans un fauteuil** to flop into an armchair; **laisser ~ un gâteau sur le tapis** to drop a cake on the carpet; **2** [*rain, snow, theatre curtain*] to fall; [*fog*] to come down; **qu'est-ce que ça tombe**○! it's pouring down!; **la foudre est tombée sur un arbre** the lightning struck a tree; **3** [*price, temperature*] to fall; [*anger*] to subside; [*fever*] to come down; [*wind*] to drop; [*day*] to draw to a close; [*conversation*] to die down; **faire ~** to bring down [*price, temperature*]; to dampen [*enthusiasm*]; **je tombe de sommeil** I can't keep my eyes open; **4** [*dictator, regime, city*] to fall; [*obstacle*] to vanish; **faire ~** to bring down [*regime, dictator*]; (figurative) to break down [*barriers*]; **5** [*belly*] to sag; [*shoulders*] to slope; **6** [*lock of hair*] to fall; **~ bien/mal** [*garment, curtain*] to hang well/badly; **7 ~ dans un piège** (figurative) to fall into a trap; **~ sous le coup d'une loi** to fall within the provisions of a law; **~ aux mains** or **entre les mains de qn** [*document, power*] to fall into sb's hand; **~ malade/amoureux** to fall ill/in love; **8** [*decision, verdict*] to be announced; [*news*] to break; [*reply*] to be given; **9 ~ sur** to come across [*stranger, object*]; to run into [*friend*]; **~ sur la bonne page** to hit on the right page; **si tu prends cette rue, tu tomberas sur la place** if you follow that street, you'll come to the square; **10 c'est tombé juste au bon moment** it came just at the right time; **tu ne pouvais pas mieux ~!** you couldn't have come at a better time!; you couldn't have done better!; **tu tombes mal, j'allais partir** you're unlucky, I was just about to leave; **il faut toujours que ça tombe sur moi**○! (decision, choice) why does it always have to be me?; (misfortune) why does it always have to happen to me?; **11** [*birthday*] to fall on [*day*]; **12 laisser ~** to give up [*job, activity*]; to drop [*plan, habit*]; **laisse ~!** forget it!; **laisser ~ qn** to drop sb; to let sb down; **13 ~ sur qn** [*soldiers, thugs*] to fall on sb; [*raiders, police*] to descend on sb.

tomber[2] /tɔ̃be/ *nm* hang; **ce velours a un beau ~** this velvet hangs well.

tombeur○ /tɔ̃bœʀ/ *nm* lady-killer.

tombola /tɔ̃bɔla/ *nf* tombola (GB), lottery.

tome[1] /tom/ *nm* **1** volume; **2** part, book.

tome[2] /tɔm/ *nf* = **tomme**.

tomme /tɔm/ *nf* tomme or tome (cheese).

tommette /tɔmɛt/ *nf* hexagonal floor tile.

ton[1], **ta**, *pl* **tes** /tɔ̃, ta, te/ *det* your; **un de tes amis** a friend of yours.

ton[2] /tɔ̃/ *nm* **1** pitch; tone; **~ grave/aigu** low/high pitch; **d'un ~ dédaigneux** scornfully; **baisser le ~** to lower one's voice; (figurative) to moderate one's tone; **eh bien, si tu le prends sur ce ~** well, if you're going to take it like that; **2** (in linguistics) tone; **langue à ~s** tone language; **3 donner le ~** to set the tone; to set the fashion; **de bon ~** in good taste; **4** (Mus) pitch; key; tone; (instrument) pitch pipe; **5** (of colour) shade; **~ sur ~** in matching tones.

tonalité /tɔnalite/ *nf* **1** (Mus) key; tonality; **2** (of vowel) tone; **3** (of voice) tone; **4** (of colours) tonality; **5** dialling tone (GB), dial tone (US).

tondeuse /tɔ̃døz/ *nf* **1** (for sheep) shears; **2** (for cutting hair) clippers; **3 ~ (à gazon)** lawnmower.

tondre /tɔ̃dʀ/ [6] *vtr* to shear [*sheep*]; to clip [*dog*]; to mow [*lawn*]; **~ qn** to shave sb's head.

tongs /tɔ̃g/ *nf pl* flip-flops, thongs (US).

tonifiant, **~e** /tɔnifjɑ̃, ɑ̃t/ *adj* **1** [*climate, air*] bracing; **2** [*exercise, lotion*] toning.

tonifier /tɔnifje/ [2] *vtr* to tone up.

tonique[1] /tɔnik/ *adj* **1** [*drink*] tonic; (figurative) [*air*] bracing; [*book*] stimulating; **2 lotion ~** toning lotion; **3** [*accent*] tonic.

tonique[2] /tɔnik/ *nf* (Mus) tonic.

tonitruant, **~e** /tɔnitʀyɑ̃, ɑ̃t/ *adj* booming.

tonnage /tɔnaʒ/ *nm* tonnage.

tonne /tɔn/ *nf* (1,000 kg) tonne, metric ton; **des ~s de choses à faire**○ loads○ of things to do.

tonneau, *pl* **~x** /tɔno/ *nm* **1** barrel; **2** (of car) somersault; **3** (of plane) barrel roll; **4** (Naut) ton.
IDIOMS **du même ~**○ of the same kind.

tonnelle /tɔnɛl/ *nf* arbour[GB].

tonner /tɔne/ [1] *vi, v impers* to thunder.

tonnerre /tɔnɛʀ/ *nm* **1** thunder; **un coup de ~** a clap of thunder; (figurative) a thunderbolt; **2** (of cannons, artillery) thundering; **un ~ d'applaudissements** thunderous applause; **3**○ **ça marche du ~** it's going fantastically well.

tonsure /tɔ̃syʀ/ *nf* (of monk) tonsure.

tonte /tɔ̃t/ *nf* **1 ~ (des moutons)** shearing; **2** fleece.

tonus /tɔnys/ *nm inv* **1** (of person) energy, dynamism; **2** (of muscle) tone, tonus.

top /tɔp/ *nm* pip, beep; **donner le ~ de départ** to give the starting signal.

topaze /tɔpaz/ *nf* topaz.

toper /tɔpe/ [1] *vi* **topons là!** let's shake on it!

topographie /tɔpɔgʀafi/ *nf* topography.

toquade○ /tɔkad/ *nf* **1** (for thing) passion; **2** (on person) crush○.

toque /tɔk/ *nf* **1** (of woman) toque; (of chef) chef's hat; (of judge) hat; **~ en fourrure** fur cap; **2** (of jockey) cap.

toqué○, **~e** /tɔke/ *adj* crazy○.

torche /tɔʀʃ/ *nf* torch.
■ **~ électrique** torch (GB), flashlight.

torcher○ /tɔʀʃe/ [1] *vtr* **1** to wipe; **2** to dash off○ [*article, report*]; to cobble [sth] together.

torchis /tɔʀʃi/ *nm inv* cob (*for walls*).

torchon /tɔʀʃɔ̃/ *nm* **1** (gen) cloth; **~ (de cuisine)** tea towel (GB), dish towel (US); **2** (newspaper) (derogatory) rag○; **3**○ messy piece of work.
IDIOMS **le ~ brûle**○ it's war.

tordant○, **~e** /tɔʀdɑ̃, ɑ̃t/ *adj* hilarious.

tordre /tɔʀdʀ/ [6] **I** *vtr* **1** to twist [*arm, wrist*]; to wring [*neck*]; **2** to bend [*nail, bar, bumper*]; **3** to wring out [*washing*].
II se tordre *v refl* (+ *v être*) **1** [*person*] **se ~ la cheville** to twist one's ankle; **se ~ de douleur** to writhe in pain; **2** [*bumper*] to bend.

tordu, **~e** /tɔʀdy/ *adj* **1** [*nose, legs*] crooked; [*branches, trunk, iron bar*] twisted; **2** (figurative) [*idea*] weird, strange; [*logic, reasoning*] twisted.

tornade /tɔʀnad/ *nf* tornado.

torpeur /tɔʀpœʀ/ *nf* torpor.

torpille /tɔʀpij/ *nf* torpedo.

torpiller /tɔʀpije/ [1] *vtr* to torpedo.

torréfier /tɔʀefje/ [2] *vtr* to roast.

torrent /tɔʀɑ̃/ *nm* torrent; **pleuvoir à ~s** to rain very heavily.

torrentiel, **-ielle** /tɔʀɑ̃sjɛl/ *adj* torrential.

torride /tɔʀid/ *adj* torrid; [*sun*] scorching.

tors, **torse**[1] /tɔʀ, tɔʀs/ *adj* (gen) twisted.

torsade /tɔʀsad/ *nf* **1** twist, coil; **2** cable stitch; **3** (in architecture) cable moulding (GB), cable molding (US).

torsader /tɔʀsade/ [1] *vtr* to twist; **une colonne torsadée** a cable column.

torse[2] /tɔʀs/ *nm* **1** (gen) chest; **se mettre ~ nu** to strip to the waist; **2** (Anat) torso.

torsion /tɔʀsjɔ̃/ *nf* **1** twisting; **2** torsion.

tort /tɔʀ/ **I** *nm* **1 avoir ~** to be wrong; **j'aurais bien ~ de m'inquiéter!** it would be silly of me to worry!; **être en ~** to be in the wrong; **donner ~ à qn** [*referee, judge*] to blame sb; [*facts*] to prove sb wrong; **2** fault; **les ~s sont partagés** there are faults on both sides; **avoir des ~s envers qn** to have wronged sb; **3** mistake; **j'ai eu le ~ de le croire** I made the mistake of believing him; **4 faire du ~ à qn/qch** to harm sb/sth.
II à tort *phr* [*accuse*] wrongly; **à ~ et à travers** [*spend*] wildly; **parler à ~ et à travers** to talk a lot of nonsense.

torticolis /tɔʀtikɔli/ *nm inv* stiff neck.

tortiller /tɔʀtije/ [1] **I** *vtr* to twist [*fibres, strands*]; to twiddle [*handkerchief*].
II se tortiller *v refl* (+ *v être*) to wriggle.

tortionnaire /tɔʀsjɔnɛʀ/ *nmf* torturer.

tortue /tɔʀty/ *nf* **1** (sea) turtle; **2** tortoise, turtle (US); **3** (butterfly) tortoiseshell.

tortueux, **-euse** /tɔʀtɥø, øz/ *adj* **1** [*road, staircase*] winding; **2** (figurative) [*behaviour*] devious; [*mind, reasoning*] tortuous.

torture /tɔʀtyʀ/ *nf* torture.

torturer /tɔʀtyʀe/ [1] **I** *vtr* **1** to torture [*person*]; **2** [*thought, feeling*] to torment; **3** to distort [*text*]; **style torturé** tortured style.
II se torturer *v refl* (+ *v être*) to torment oneself; **se ~ l'esprit** to rack one's brains.

torve /tɔʀv/ *adj* [*look*] menacing, baleful.

tôt /to/ *adv* **1** [*start*] early; **~ le matin** early in the morning; **2** soon, early; **le plus ~ serait le mieux** the sooner the better; **~ ou tard** sooner or later; **on ne m'y reprendra pas de si ~** I won't do that again in a hurry.

total, **~e**, *mpl* **-aux** /tɔtal, o/ **I** *adj* complete, total.
II *nm* total.
III au total *phr* **au ~ cela fait 350 francs** altogether that comes to 350 francs.

totaliser /tɔtalize/ [1] *vtr* **1** to total [*profits*]; **2** to have a total of [*points, votes*].

totalitaire /tɔtalitɛʀ/ *adj* **1** [*regime, state*] totalitarian; **2** [*doctrine*] all-embracing.

totalitarisme /tɔtalitaʀism/ *nm* totalitarianism.

totalité /tɔtalite/ *nf* **la ~ du personnel** all the staff; **la ~ des dépenses** the total expenditure; **nous vous rembourserons en ~** we will refund you in full.

totem /tɔtɛm/ *nm* **1** totem; **2** totem pole.

toucan /tukɑ̃/ *nm* toucan.

touchant, **~e** /tuʃɑ̃, ɑ̃t/ *adj* moving; touching.

touche /tuʃ/ *nf* **1** (gen) button; (on keyboard) key; (on stringed instrument) fret; **2** (of paintbrush) stroke; (of paint) dash; (of artist) touch; **3** (Sport) sideline, touchline; **mettre qn sur la ~** (figurative) to push sb aside; **4** (in fencing) hit; **5** (in fishing) bite.

toucher[1] /tuʃe/ [1] **I** *vtr* **1 ~ (de la main)** to touch [*object, surface, person*]; **~ du bois** (superstitiously) to touch wood; **~ le front de qn** to feel sb's forehead; **2** to be touching [*wall, ceiling, bottom of sth*]; **~ le sol** to land; **3** to hit [*opponent, car, kerb*]; **4** to touch, to move [*person*]; **ça me touche beaucoup** I am very touched; **5** [*event, crisis*] to affect [*person, country*]; [*storm*] to hit [*region, city*]; **6** [*country, house*] to be next to; **7** [*person*] to get [*money*]; to cash [*cheque*].

II toucher à *v+prep* **1 ~ à** to touch [*object*]; **~ à tout** to be into everything; (figurative) to be a jack of all trades; **avec son air de ne pas y ~, c'est un malin**○ he looks as if butter wouldn't melt in his mouth, but he's a sly one; **2 ~ à** to concern [*activity, issue*]; **3 ~ à** to infringe on [*right, freedom*]; **4 ~ à** to get on to [*problem*].

III se toucher *v refl* (+ *v être*) [*houses, gardens*] to be next to each other.

toucher[2] /tuʃe/ *nm* **1 le ~** touch, the sense of touch; **2** (of pianist) touch.

touche-touche○: **à touche-touche** /atuʃtuʃ/ *phr* **être à ~** [*cars*] to be bumper to bumper; [*people*] to be on top of each other○.

touffe /tuf/ *nf* (of hair, grass) tuft.

touffu, **~e** /tufy/ *adj* **1** [*eyebrows, beard*] bushy; [*vegetation*] dense; [*bush*] thick; **au poil ~** with thick fur; **2** [*text*] dense.

touiller○ /tuje/ [1] *vtr* to stir [*sauce*].

toujours /tuʒuʀ/ *adv* **1** always; **comme ~** as always; **de ~** [*friend*] very old; [*friendship*] long-standing; **~ plus vite** faster and faster; **2** still; **il n'est ~ pas levé?** is he still not up?; **3** anyway; **on peut ~ essayer** we can always try; **c'est ~ ça de pris** or **de gagné** that's something at least; **~ est-il que** the fact remains that.

toupet /tupɛ/ *nm* **1**○ cheek○, nerve○; **2** (of hair) tuft; quiff (GB), forelock (US).

toupie /tupi/ *nf* top; **faire tourner une ~** to spin a top.

tour[1] /tuʀ/ *nm* **1** (gen) turn; (around axis) revolution; **donner un ~ de clé** to turn the key; **faire un ~ de manège** to have a go on the merry-go-round; **faire un ~ sur soi-même** [*dancer*] to spin around; [*planet*] to rotate; **fermer qch à double ~** to double-lock sth; **à ~ de bras**○ [*invest, buy up*] left, right and centre[GB]○; **2 faire le ~ de qch** (gen) to go around sth; to drive around sth; **la nouvelle a vite fait le ~ du village** the news spread rapidly through the village; **3** (of pond) edges; (of pipe, tree trunk) circumference; (of head, hips) measurement; (standard measurement) size; **4** walk, stroll; (on bicycle) ride; (in car) drive, spin; **je suis allé faire un ~ à Paris** I went to Paris; **5** look; **faire le ~ d'un problème** to have a look at a problem; **faire le ~ de ses relations** to go through one's acquaintances; **ce roman, on en a vite fait le ~**○ there's not much to this novel; **6** (gen) turn; (in competition) round; **à qui le ~?** whose turn is it?; **chacun son ~** each one in his turn; **il perd plus souvent qu'à son ~** he loses more often than he would like; he loses more often than he should; **~ à ~** by turns; in turn; **7 ~ de scrutin** ballot, round of voting; **8** trick; **jouer un ~ à qn** to play a trick on sb; **ça te jouera des ~s** it's going to get you into trouble one of these days; **9** trick; **~ de cartes** card trick; **~ d'adresse** feat of skill; **10** (in situation) turn; **donner un ~ nouveau à qch** to give a new twist to sth; **11** (Tech) lathe.

■ **~ de chant** song recital; **~ de garde** turn of duty; **~ de potier** potter's wheel; **~ de rein(s)** back strain.

tour[2] /tuʀ/ *nf* **1** tower; **2** tower block (GB), high rise (US); **3** (in chess) rook, castle; **4** siege-tower.

tourbe /tuʀb/ *nf* peat.

tourbillon /tuʀbijɔ̃/ *nm* **1** whirlwind; whirlpool; **~ de poussière** whirl of dust; **2** (of memories) swirl; (of reforms) whirlwind.

tourbillonner /tuʀbijɔne/ [1] *vi* [*snow, leaves*] to swirl, to whirl; [*dancers*] to twirl.

tourelle /tuʀɛl/ *nf* (of building, tank) turret; (of submarine) conning tower.

tourisme /tuʀism/ *nm* tourism.

touriste /tuʀist/ *nmf* tourist.

touristique /tuʀistik/ *adj* [*brochure, menu, season*] tourist; [*influx*] of tourists; [*town, area*] which attracts tourists.

tourment /tuʀmɑ̃/ *nm* torment.

tourmenté, **~e** /tuʀmɑ̃te/ *adj* **1** [*person, face*] tormented; [*soul*] tortured; **2** [*era, life*] turbulent; **3** [*landscape*] rugged.

tourmenter /tuʀmɑ̃te/ [1] **I** *vtr* **1** to worry; **2** to torment; **3** [*creditors*] to harass.

II se tourmenter *v refl* (+ *v être*) to worry.

tournage /tuʀnaʒ/ *nm* **1** shooting, filming; **2** film set.

tournant, **~e** /tuʀnɑ̃, ɑ̃t/ **I** *adj* **1** [*seat*] swivel; [*sprinkler*] rotating; [*door*] revolving; **2** [*presidency*] rotating; [*strike*] staggered.

II *nm* **1** (in road) bend; **2** turning point; **3** turn; **au ~ du siècle** at the turn of the century; **4** change of direction.

tourné, **~e**[1] /tuʀne/ *adj* **1 ~ vers** [*eyes, look, person*] turned toward(s); [*activity, policy*] oriented toward(s); **~ vers le passé/l'avenir** backward-/forward-looking; **porte ~e vers la mer** gate facing the sea; **2 bien ~** [*compliment, letter*] nicely phrased; **3** [*milk*] off.

tourne-disque, *pl* **~s** /tuʀnədisk/ *nm* record player.

tournée[2] /tuʀne/ *nf* **1** (of postman) round; **2** (of team, singer) tour; **3**○ (of drinks) round.

tournemain: **en un tournemain** /ɑ̃nɛ̃ tuʀnəmɛ̃/ *phr* in no time.

tourner /tuʀne/ [1] **I** *vtr* **1** to turn; **~ la tête**

vers to turn to look at; **~ les yeux vers** to look at; **2** to shoot [*film*]; **3** to get around [*difficulty, law*]; **4** to phrase [*letter, criticism*]; **5 ~ qn/qch en dérision** to deride sb/sth; **6 ~ et retourner qch dans son esprit** to mull sth over; **7** to stir [*sauce*]; to toss [*salad*].

II *vi* **1** (gen) to turn; [*planet*] to rotate; [*rotating door*] to revolve; [*dancer*] to spin; **faire ~** to turn; to spin; **faire ~ les tables** (in spiritualism) to do table-turning; **2 ~ autour de** (gen) to turn around; [*planet*] to revolve around; [*plane*] to circle; **3 ~ (en rond)** [*person*] to go around and around; [*driver*] to drive around and around; **~ en rond** (figurative) [*discussion*] to go around in circles; **4 ~ autour de** [*sum of money*] to be (somewhere) in the region of; **5** [*engine, factory*] to run; **~ rond** [*engine*] to run smoothly; [*business*] to be doing well; **faire ~** to run [*business, company*]; **mon frère ne tourne pas rond**° **depuis quelque temps** my brother has been acting strangely for some time; **6 les choses ont bien/mal tourné pour lui** things turned out well/badly for him; **7** [*director*] to shoot; **~ (dans un film)** [*actor*] to make a film (GB) or movie (US); **8** [*milk, meat*] to go off; **9 ~ autour de qn** to hang around sb.

III **se tourner** *v refl* (+ *v être*) **1 se ~ vers qn/qch** to turn to sb/sth; **2 se ~ vers qn/qch** to turn toward(s) sb/sth; **3** to turn around.

tournesol /tuʀnəsɔl/ *nm* sunflower.

tournevis /tuʀnəvis/ *nm inv* screwdriver.

tourniquet /tuʀnikɛ/ *nm* **1** turnstile; **2** revolving stand; **3** sprinkler.

tournoi /tuʀnwɑ/ *nm* tournament.

tournoyer /tuʀnwaje/ [23] *vi* **1** [*leaves, papers*] to swirl around; [*vultures*] to wheel; [*flies*] to fly around in circles; **2** [*dancers*] to whirl; **faire ~** to twirl [*stick, skirt*].

tournure /tuʀnyʀ/ *nf* **1** turn; **prendre ~** [*plan*] to take shape; **2 ~ (de phrase)** turn of phrase.

■ **~ d'esprit** frame of mind.

tourte /tuʀt/ *nf* pie; **~ à la viande** meat pie.

tourteau, *pl* **~x** /tuʀto/ *nm* (Culin, Zool) crab.

tourtereau, *pl* **~x** /tuʀtəʀo/ I *nm* (Zool) young turtle dove.

II **tourtereaux** *nm pl* (humorous) lovebirds.

tourterelle /tuʀtəʀɛl/ *nf* turtle dove.

tous ▶ **tout**.

Toussaint /tusɛ̃/ *nf* **la ~** All Saints' Day.

tousser /tuse/ [1] *vi* [*person*] to cough.

toussoter /tusɔte/ [1] *vi* [*person*] to have a slight cough; [*engine*] to splutter.

tout /tu/, **~e** /tut/, *mpl* **tous** /tu *adj*, tus *pron*/, *fpl* **toutes** /tut/

■ **Note** You will find translations for expressions such as *à tout hasard*, *tout compte fait*, *tout neuf* etc, at the entries ***hasard***, ***compte***, ***neuf*** etc.

I *pron* **1 tout** everything; all; anything; **~ est prétexte à querelle(s)** any pretext will do to start a quarrel; **~ n'est pas perdu** all is not lost; **en ~** in all; in every respect; **en ~ et pour ~** all told; **~ bien compté** or **pesé** or **considéré** all in all; **2 tous** /tus/, **toutes** all; all of them/us/you; **tous ensemble** all together; **est-ce que ça conviendra à tous?** will it suit everybody?

II *adj* **1 bois ~ ton lait** drink all your milk; **~ le reste** everything else; **~ le monde** everybody; **manger ~ un pain** to eat a whole loaf; **il a plu ~e la journée** it rained all day (long); **2 c'est ~ un travail** it's quite a job; **3** all; everything; anything; **~ ce qui compte** all that matters; **~ ce qu'il dit n'est pas vrai** not all of what he says is true; **être ~ ce qu'il y a de plus serviable** to be most obliging; **4** any; **à ~ moment** at any time; constantly; **~ autre que lui/toi aurait abandonné** anybody else would have given up; **5 en ~e franchise** in all honesty; **il aurait ~ intérêt à placer cet argent** it would be in his best interests to invest this money; **6 il a souri pour ~e réponse** his only reply was a smile; **7 tous, toutes** all, every; **j'ai ~es les raisons de me plaindre** I have every reason to complain; **nous irons tous les deux** we'll both go; **je les prends tous les trois** I'm taking all three; **8 tous/toutes les** every; **tous les deux jours** every other day; **tous les combien?** how often?

III *adv* **1** very, quite; all; **être ~ étonné** to be very surprised; **~ seul** all by oneself; **~ en haut** right at the top; **la colline est ~ en fleurs** the hill is a mass of flowers; **veste ~ cuir** all leather jacket; **2 ~ prêt** ready-made; **3** while; although; **il lisait ~ en marchant** he was reading as he walked; **elle le défendait ~ en le sachant coupable** she defended him although she knew he was guilty; **4 ~ malin/roi qu'il est, il...** he may be clever/a king, but he...

IV **du tout** *phr* **(pas) du ~** not at all.

V *nm* (*pl* **~s**) whole; **le ~** the (whole) lot; the main thing; **former un ~** to make up or form a whole.

VI **Tout-** (*combining form*) **le Tout-Paris/-Londres** the Paris/London smart set.

■ **~ à coup** suddenly; **~ d'un coup** suddenly; all at once; **~ à fait** quite, absolutely; **~ à l'heure** in a moment; a little while ago, just now; **à ~ à l'heure!** see you later!; **~ de même** all the same, even so; **~ de même!** really!; **~ de suite** at once.

IDIOMS **être ~ yeux ~ oreilles** to be very attentive.

tout-à-l'égout /tutalegu/ *nm inv* main drainage, main sewer.

toutefois /tutfwɑ/ *adv* however.

toute-puissance /tutpɥisɑ̃s/ *nf* omnipotence; supremacy.

tout-petit, *pl* **~s** /tup(ə)ti/ *nm* **1** baby; **2** toddler.

Tout-Puissant /tupɥisɑ̃/ *nm* **le ~** the Almighty, God Almighty.

tout-venant /tuv(ə)nɑ̃/ *nm inv* all and sundry.

toux /tu/ *nf inv* cough.

toxicité /tɔksisite/ *nf* toxicity.

toxicodépendance /tɔksikodepɑ̃dɑ̃s/ *nf* drug dependency.

toxicologie /tɔksikɔlɔʒi/ *nf* toxicology.

toxicomane /tɔksikɔman/ *nmf* drug addict.

toxicomanie /tɔksikɔmani/ *nf* drug addiction.

toxine /tɔksin/ *nf* toxin.

toxique /tɔksik/ *adj* toxic, poisonous.

TP /tepe/ *nm pl*: *abbr* ▶ **travail**.

trac○ /tʀak/ *nm* (of actor) stage fright; (before exam, conference) nerves; **avoir le ~** (gen) to feel nervous; [*actor, performer*] to have stage fright.

tracas /tʀaka/ *nm inv* **1** trouble; **2** problems; **~ quotidiens** everyday problems; **3** worries; **se faire du ~ pour qn/qch** to worry about sb/sth.

tracasser /tʀakase/ [1] **I** *vtr* to bother [*person*].
II se tracasser *v refl* (+ *v être*) to worry.

trace /tʀas/ *nf* **1** trail; **suivre qn à la ~** to track sb; (figurative) to follow sb's trail; **2 ~s** tracks; **~s d'ours/de ski** bear's/ski tracks; **~s de pas** footprints; **sur les ~s de Van Gogh** in the footsteps of Van Gogh; **3** (of burn) mark; (of wound) scar; (of paint) mark; (of blood, dampness) trace; **~s de doigts** fingermarks; **~s de coups** bruises; **4** (of activity) sign; (of presence) trace; **des ~s d'effraction** signs of a break-in.

tracé /tʀase/ *nm* **1** (of town) layout; (of road) plan; **2** (of road, railway) route; (of river) course; (of border, coast) line; **3** (on graph, in sketch) line.

tracer /tʀase/ [12] *vtr* **1** to draw [*line, map, portrait*]; (on graph) to plot [*curve*]; to write [*word, letters*]; **2 à 15 ans son avenir était déjà tout tracé** at 15, his/her future was already mapped out; **3 ~ le chemin à qn** (figurative) to show sb the way.

trachée /tʀaʃe/ *nf* windpipe.

trachéite /tʀakeit/ *nf* tracheitis.

tract /tʀakt/ *nm* pamphlet, tract.

tractation /tʀaktasjɔ̃/ *nf* negotiation.

tracter /tʀakte/ [1] *vtr* [*vehicle*] to tow [*trailer*]; [*cable*] to pull up [*cable car*].

tracteur /tʀaktœʀ/ *nm* tractor.

traction /tʀaksjɔ̃/ *nf* **1** traction; **à ~ mécanique** mechanically drawn; **2** (Tech) tension.
■ **~ arrière** (Aut) rear-wheel drive; **~ avant** (Aut) front-wheel drive.

tradition /tʀadisjɔ̃/ *nf* **1** tradition; **2** legend; **la ~ veut que**... legend has it that...

traditionaliste /tʀadisjɔnalist/ *adj*, *nmf* traditionalist.

traditionnel, **-elle** /tʀadisjɔnɛl/ *adj* traditional.

traducteur, **-trice** /tʀadyktœʀ, tʀis/ *nm,f* translator.

traduction /tʀadyksjɔ̃/ *nf* translation; **faire des ~s** to do translation work.

traduire /tʀadɥiʀ/ [69] **I** *vtr* **1** to translate; **2** [*word, artist, book*] to convey; [*rebellion, violence*] to be the expression of; [*price rise*] to be the result of; **3** (Law) **~ qn en justice** to bring sb to justice.
II se traduire *v refl* (+ *v être*) **1** [*joy, fear*] to show; **2** [*crisis, instability*] to result; **se ~ par un échec** to result in failure.

trafic /tʀafik/ *nm* **1** traffic; **~ d'armes** arms dealing; **~ de drogue** drug trafficking; **2 ~ (routier)** (road) traffic; **~ aérien** air traffic.

trafiquant, **~e** /tʀafikɑ̃, ɑ̃t/ *nm,f* trafficker, dealer; **~ de drogue** drugs dealer.

trafiquer /tʀafike/ [1] *vtr* **1** to fiddle with [*car, meter*]; **2**○ **je me demande ce qu'il trafique** I wonder what he's up to.

tragédie /tʀaʒedi/ *nf* tragedy.

tragique /tʀaʒik/ **I** *adj* tragic.
II *nm* tragedy.

trahir /tʀaiʀ/ [3] **I** *vtr* **1** to betray; to break [*promise*]; **2** [*writing, words*] to betray [*thoughts*]; **3** [*translator, words*] to misrepresent; **4** [*strength, legs*] to fail [*person*].
II se trahir *v refl* (+ *v être*) to give oneself away, to betray oneself.

trahison /tʀaizɔ̃/ *nf* **1** treachery; **~ de qn/qch** betrayal of sb/sth; **2** treason.

train /tʀɛ̃/ **I** *nm* **1** train; **par le** or **en ~** [*travel*] by train; **2** (convoy) train; **~ de péniches** train of barges; **3** series (**de** of); **4** pace; **aller bon ~** to walk briskly; **aller bon ~** [*rumours*] to be flying around; [*sales*] to be going well; [*conversation*] to flow easily; **au ~ où vont les choses** (at) the rate things are going; **à fond de ~**○ at top speed; **5** (Zool) **~ de derrière** hindquarters; **~ de devant** forequarter.
II en train *phr* **1 être en ~** to be full of energy; **2 mettre en ~** to get [sth] started [*process*]; **3 être en ~ de faire** to be (busy) doing; **j'étais en ~ de dormir** I was sleeping.
■ **~ d'atterrissage** undercarriage; **~ électrique** (toy) train set; **~ de vie** lifestyle.

traînant, **~e** /tʀɛnɑ̃, ɑ̃t/ *adj* shuffling; **voix ~e** drawl.

traîne /tʀɛn/ *nf* **1** (of dress) train; **2** seine (net).
IDIOMS **être à la ~** to lag behind.

traîneau, *pl* **~x** /tʀɛno/ *nm* **1** sleigh; **2** (of vacuum cleaner) cylinder.

traînée /tʀɛne/ *nf* **1** streak; **~ de sang** streak of blood; **2** trail.

traîner /tʀɛne/ [1] **I** *vtr* **1** to drag [sb/sth] (along) [*person, suitcase*]; to drag [sth] across the floor [*chair*]; **2**○ to lug○ [sth] around [*object*]; to drag [sth] around [*object*]; **3 ~ qn chez le médecin** to drag sb off to the doctor's; **4 il traîne un rhume depuis deux semaines** for two weeks now he's had a cold that he can't shake off; **~ les pieds** to drag one's feet.
II *vi* **1 ~ dans les rues** to hang around on the streets; **j'ai traîné au lit** I slept in; **2** to take forever; **ne traîne pas, on doit terminer à 4 heures** get a move on○, we've got to finish at four; **3** to dawdle; **4** [*building work, illness*] to drag on; **5 ~ par terre** [*skirt*] to trail on the ground; [*curtains*] to trail on the floor; **6 ~ derrière qch** to be trailing behind sth; **7** [*clothes, toys*] to be lying about or around; **laisser ~ qch** to leave sth lying about or around [*chequebook*].

III **se traîner** *v refl* (+ *v être*) **1** [*injured person*] **se ~ par terre** to drag oneself along the ground; **2 se ~ jusqu'à la cuisine** to drag oneself through to the kitchen; **3** [*train*] to crawl along; [*negotiations*] to drag on.
IDIOMS **~ la jambe** or **la patte**○ to limp; **~ ses guêtres**○ or **ses bottes**○ to knock around○.

train(-)train○ /tʀɛ̃tʀɛ̃/ *nm inv* (derogatory) daily routine.

traire /tʀɛʀ/ [58] *vtr* to milk [*cow, goat*].

trait /tʀɛ/ I *nm* **1** line; stroke; **souligner un mot d'un ~ rouge** to underline a word in red; **~ pour ~** [*replica*] line for line; [*reproduce*] line by line; **2** (of style, book) feature; (of person) trait; **~ caractéristique** characteristic; **~ de caractère** trait, characteristic; **3 ~ d'humour** or **d'esprit** witticism; **~ de génie** stroke of genius; **4 avoir ~ à** to relate to; **5 d'un (seul) ~** (gen) at one go; **6 de ~** [*animal*] draught (GB) or draft (US).
II **traits** *nm pl* features.
■ **~ d'union** hyphen; (figurative) link.
IDIOMS **tirer un ~ sur qch** to put sth firmly behind one.

traitant /tʀɛtɑ̃/ *adj m* **médecin ~** doctor, GP.

traite /tʀɛt/ I *nf* **1** (Econ) draft, bill; **2 la ~ des Blanches** the white slave trade; **3** milking; **la ~ des vaches** milking cows.
II **d'une traite** *phr* **d'une (seule) ~** [*recite*] in one breath; [*drink*] in one go.

traité /tʀete/ *nm* **1** (Law) treaty; **~ commercial** trade agreement; **2** treatise.

traitement /tʀɛtmɑ̃/ *nm* **1** (Med) treatment; **2** salary; **3** handling; **il faut accélérer le ~ des demandes** applications must be dealt with more quickly; **4** (of data) processing; **5** (Tech) (of water, waste) processing; (of wood) treatment.
■ **~ de faveur** preferential treatment; **~ de texte** word-processing (package).

traiter /tʀete/ [1] I *vtr* **1** to treat [*person, animal, object*]; **2** (Med) to treat [*sick person, infection*]; **3** to deal with [*question, problem*]; **4** to treat [*wood, textile*]; to process [*waste*]; **5** to process [*data*]; **6 ~ qn de qch** to call sb sth.
II **traiter de** *v+prep* to deal with.
III *vi* to negotiate, to do (GB) or make a deal.
IV **se traiter** *v refl* (+ *v être*) **ils se sont traités de tous les noms** they called each other all sorts of names.

traiteur /tʀɛtœʀ/ *nm* caterer.

traître, traîtresse /tʀɛtʀ, tʀɛtʀɛs/ *nm,f* traitor; **en ~** by surprise.

traîtrise /tʀɛtʀiz/ *nf* **1** act of treachery; **2** (of person) treachery.

trajectoire /tʀaʒɛktwaʀ/ *nf* **1** (of bullet, missile) trajectory; **2** (of planet, satellite) path; **3** career.

trajet /tʀaʒɛ/ *nm* **1** journey, trip; (by sea) crossing; **2** route.

trame /tʀam/ *nf* **1** (of fabric) weft; **2** (of story) framework.

tramer: **se tramer** /tʀame/ [1] *v refl* (+ *v être*) [*plot*] to be hatched.

trampoline /tʀɑ̃pɔlin/ *nm* trampoline.

tramway /tʀamwɛ/ *nm* **1** tram (GB), streetcar (US); **2** tramway (GB), streetcar line (US).

tranchant, ~e /tʀɑ̃ʃɑ̃, ɑ̃t/ I *adj* **1** sharp; **2** [*person*] forthright; [*tone*] curt.
II *nm* (of blade) sharp edge, cutting edge.

tranche /tʀɑ̃ʃ/ *nf* **1** (of bread, meat, cheese) slice; (of lard, bacon) rasher; **2** (of operation) phase; (in timetable) period, time slot; **3** (of book, coin) edge.
■ **~ d'âge** age bracket.

tranché, ~e[1] /tʀɑ̃ʃe/ I *pp* ▶ **trancher**.
II *pp adj* [*salmon*] pre-sliced.
III *adj* **1** [*opinion, position, reply*] cut-and-dried; [*inequalities*] marked; **2** [*colours*] bold.

tranchée[2] /tʀɑ̃ʃe/ *nf* **1** (Mil) trench; **2** (of road) cutting.

trancher /tʀɑ̃ʃe/ [1] I *vtr* to slice, to cut [*bread, meat*]; to cut through [*rope*]; to cut [sth] off [*head*]; to slit [*throat*].
II *vi* **1** [*colour, outline*] to stand out; **2** to come to a decision

tranquille /tʀɑ̃kil/ *adj* **1** quiet; calm; peaceful; **tiens-toi ~!** keep still!; be quiet!; **il s'est tenu ~ pendant quelques mois** he behaved himself for a few months; **2 être ~** to be or feel easy in one's mind; **sa mère n'est pas ~ quand il sort** his mother worries when he goes out; **3 avoir la conscience ~** to have a clear conscience.

tranquillement /tʀɑ̃kilmɑ̃/ *adv* **1 elle dort ~** she's sleeping peacefully; **j'aimerais pouvoir travailler ~** I wish I could work in peace; **2** quietly; **3 nous avons marché ~** we walked along at a leisurely pace; **4 nous étions ~ en train de discuter** we were chatting away happily.

tranquillisant, ~e /tʀɑ̃kilizɑ̃, ɑ̃t/ I *adj* reassuring, comforting.
II *nm* tranquillizer[GB].

tranquilliser /tʀɑ̃kilize/ [1] *vtr* to reassure.

tranquillité /tʀɑ̃kilite/ *nf* **1** calmness; calm; **2 ~ (d'esprit)** peace of mind.

transaction /tʀɑ̃zaksjɔ̃/ *nf* transaction.

transalpin, ~e /tʀɑ̃zalpɛ̃, in/ *adj* **1** transalpine; **2** Italian.

transat[1]○ /tʀɑ̃zat/ *nm* **1** deckchair; **2** baby chair.

transat[2] /tʀɑ̃zat/ *nf* (Sport) transatlantic race.

transatlantique /tʀɑ̃zatlɑ̃tik/ *adj* transatlantic.

transcendant, ~e /tʀɑ̃sɑ̃dɑ̃, ɑ̃t/ *adj* **1** (in philosophy) transcendent; **2**○ wonderful.

transcender /tʀɑ̃sɑ̃de/ [1] *vtr* to transcend.

transcription /tʀɑ̃skʀipsjɔ̃/ *nf* transcription.

transcrire /tʀɑ̃skʀiʀ/ [67] *vtr* to transcribe.

transe /tʀɑ̃s/ *nf* trance.

transférer /tʀɑ̃sfeʀe/ [14] *vtr* **1** (gen) to transfer; to relocate [*offices*]; **2** (Law) to transfer, to convey [*property*].

transfert /tʀɑ̃sfɛʀ/ *nm* **1** (of person, data, money, property) transfer; (of offices) relocation; **2** (psychological) transference.

transfigurer /tʀɑ̃sfigyʀe/ [1] *vtr* to transform.

transformable /tʀɑ̃sfɔʀmabl/ *adj* convertible.

transformateur /tʀɑ̃sfɔʀmatœʀ/ *nm* transformer.

transformation /tʀɑ̃sfɔʀmasjɔ̃/ *nf* transformation; (of mineral, energy) conversion.

transformer /tʀɑ̃sfɔʀme/ [1] **I** *vtr* **1** to alter [*garment, façade*]; to change [*person, landscape*]; **2 ~ qn/qch en** (gen) to turn sb/sth into; to transform sb/sth into; **~ un garage en bureau** to convert a garage into an office.
II se transformer *v refl* (+ *v être*) **1** [*person*] to transform oneself; to be transformed; **2** [*embryo, larva, bud*] to turn into.

transfuge /tʀɑ̃sfyʒ/ **I** *nmf* defector.
II *nm* (Mil) deserter.

transfusé, **~e** /tʀɑ̃sfyze/ **I** *pp* ▸ **transfuser**.
II *pp adj* [*blood*] transfused; [*person*] who has been given a blood transfusion.

transfuser /tʀɑ̃sfyze/ [1] *vtr* to give a blood transfusion to.

transfusion /tʀɑ̃sfyzjɔ̃/ *nf* transfusion.

transgresser /tʀɑ̃sgʀɛse/ [1] *vtr* to break [*law, rule, taboo*]; to defy [*ban*].

transi, **~e** /tʀɑ̃zi/ **I** *pp* ▸ **transir**.
II *pp adj* chilled; **~ de peur** paralysed[GB] with fear; **un amoureux ~** a bashful lover.

transiger /tʀɑ̃ziʒe/ [13] *vi* to compromise.

transir /tʀɑ̃ziʀ/ [3] *vtr* to chill; to paralyze.

transistor /tʀɑ̃zistɔʀ/ *nm* transistor.

transit /tʀɑ̃zit/ *nm* transit; **en ~** in transit.

transiter /tʀɑ̃zite/ [1] *vi* **~ par** [*goods, passengers*] to pass through, to go via.

transitif, **-ive** /tʀɑ̃zitif, iv/ *adj* transitive.

transition /tʀɑ̃zisjɔ̃/ *nf* transition.

transitoire /tʀɑ̃zitwaʀ/ *adj* transitional.

translucide /tʀɑ̃slysid/ *adj* translucent.

transmettre /tʀɑ̃smɛtʀ/ [60] **I** *vtr* **1** to pass [sth] on, to convey [*information, order, news*]; to pass [sth] on [*story, knowledge*]; to pass [sth] down [*culture, fortune*]; **transmets-leur mes félicitations** give them my congratulations; **2** to transmit [*image, signal, data*]; **3** to broadcast [*news, programme*]; **4** to hand [sth] on [*property, land*]; to hand over [*power*]; **5** (Med) to transmit [*virus, illness*].
II se transmettre *v refl* (+ *v être*) **1** to pass [sth] on to each other [*message, data*]; **2** [*signals, data*] to be transmitted; **3** [*tradition, culture*] to be handed down; [*story*] to be passed on; **4** [*virus, illness*] to be transmitted.

transmission /tʀɑ̃smisjɔ̃/ *nf* **1** transmission, passing on; **la ~ des connaissances** the communication of knowledge; **2** (of data, signals) transmission; **3** (of programme) broadcasting; **4** (of tradition, secret, culture) handing down; (of fortune, property) transfer; **5** (Aut, Med) transmission.
■ **~ de pensées** thought transference.

transparaître /tʀɑ̃spaʀɛtʀ/ [73] *vi* to show through; **laisser ~** [*face, words*] to betray; [*person*] to let [sth] show [*emotions*].

transparence /tʀɑ̃spaʀɑ̃s/ *nf* **1** (of glass, fabric) transparency; (of water) clearness; **on voyait ses jambes en ~ (à travers sa jupe)** you could see her legs through her skirt; **2** (of skin) translucency; (of colour) limpidity; **3** (of person) transparency; (of policy) openness.

transparent, **~e** /tʀɑ̃spaʀɑ̃, ɑ̃t/ **I** *adj* **1** transparent; [*water*] clear; **2** [*complexion*] translucent; **3** [*person*] transparent.
II *nm* (for overhead projector) transparency.

transpercer /tʀɑ̃spɛʀse/ [12] *vtr* **1** [*sword, arrow*] to pierce [*body*]; [*bullet*] to go through; **2** [*rain*] to go through; **3** [*pain*] to shoot through.

transpiration /tʀɑ̃spiʀasjɔ̃/ *nf* **1** sweating, perspiration; **2** sweat; **3** (Bot) transpiration.

transpirer /tʀɑ̃spiʀe/ [1] *vi* **1** to sweat, to perspire; **2** [*secret*] to leak out.

transplanter /tʀɑ̃splɑ̃te/ [1] *vtr* to transplant.

transport /tʀɑ̃spɔʀ/ **I** *nm* transport, transportation (US).
II transports *nm pl* **~s en commun** public transport or transportation (US).

transportable /tʀɑ̃spɔʀtabl/ *adj* transportable; **il n'est pas ~** (injured person) he cannot be moved.

transporter /tʀɑ̃spɔʀte/ [1] *vtr* **1** to carry [*person, object*]; to transport [*passengers, goods*]; **être transporté à l'hôpital** to be taken to hospital; **2** to carry [*pollen, virus, disease*]; **3 être transporté dans un monde féerique** to be transported to a magical world.

transporteur /tʀɑ̃spɔʀtœʀ/ *nm* carrier; **~ aérien** air carrier; **~ routier** road haulier (GB), road haulage contractor (GB), trucking company (US).

transposer /tʀɑ̃spoze/ [1] *vtr* to transpose.

transsexuel, **-elle** /tʀɑ̃ssɛksɥɛl/ *adj, nm,f* transsexual.

transvaser /tʀɑ̃svaze/ [1] *vtr* to decant [*liquid*].

transversal, **~e**, *mpl* **-aux** /tʀɑ̃svɛʀsal, o/ *adj* transverse; **rue ~e** side street.

trapèze /tʀapɛz/ *nm* **1** (Sport) trapeze; **2** (in geometry) trapezium (GB), trapezoid (US).

trapéziste /tʀapezist/ *nmf* trapeze artist.

trappe /tʀap/ *nf* (gen) trap door.

trappeur /tʀapœʀ/ *nm* trapper.

trapu, **~e** /tʀapy/ *adj* [*man, outline*] stocky.

traquenard /tʀaknaʀ/ *nm* trap.

traquer /tʀake/ [1] *vtr* (gen) to track down; [*photograph*] to hound [*film star*].

traumatisant, **~e** /tʀomatizɑ̃, ɑ̃t/ *adj* traumatic.

traumatiser /tʀomatize/ [1] *vtr* to traumatize.

traumatisme /tʀomatism/ *nm* **1** (Med) traumatism; **2** (psychological) trauma.

travail, *pl* **-aux** /tʀavaj, o/ **I** *nm* **1** (gen) work; job; **se mettre au ~** to get down to work; **avoir du ~** to have work to do; **les gros travaux** the heavy work; **(félicitations) c'est du beau ~!** you've done a great job on that!; **qu'est-ce que c'est que ce ~?** what do you call this; **ne me téléphone pas à mon ~** don't call me at work; **chercher du/un ~** to look for work/a job; **être sans ~** to be out of work; **le ~ temporaire** temporary work; **le ~ de nuit** nightwork; **2** (Econ) labour[GB]; **entrer dans le monde du ~** to enter the world of work; **3 le ~ musculaire** muscular effort; **4 le ~ de** working with or in [*metal, wood, stone*]; **5** workmanship; **un ~ superbe** a superb piece of workmanship; **6** (of water, erosion) action; **7** (of wine) fermentation; (of wood) warping; **8** (of woman in childbirth) labour[GB].

II **travaux** *nm pl* **1** (gen) work; (on road) roadworks (GB), roadwork (US); **faire faire des travaux dans sa maison** to have work done in one's house; **2** (of researcher) work; **3** (of commission) deliberations; **4 les travaux agricoles** agricultural work; **travaux de couture** needlework.

■ **~ à la chaîne** assembly-line work; **~ à domicile** working at or from home; **~ au noir** (gen) *work for which no earnings are declared*; (holding two jobs) moonlighting; **travaux manuels** handicrafts; **travaux pratiques**, **TP** practical work; lab work; **travaux publics**, **TP** civil engineering.

travaillé, **~e** /tʀavaje/ I *pp* ▶ **travailler**.
II *pp adj* [*jewel*] finely-worked; [*carving*] elaborate; [*gold, silver*] wrought; [*style*] polished.

travailler /tʀavaje/ [1] I *vtr* **1** to work on [*style, school subject, voice, muscles*]; to practise[GB] [*sport, instrument*]; **2** to work [*wood, metal*]; (Culin) to knead [*dough*]; to cultivate [*land*]; **3 ~ qn** [*idea, affair*] to be on sb's mind; [*jealousy, pain*] to plague sb; **un doute me travaillait** I had a nagging doubt.
II **travailler à** *v+prep* to work on [*project, essay*]; to work toward(s) [*objective*].
III *vi* **1** [*person, machine, muscles*] to work; **faire ~ son cerveau** to apply one's mind; **~ en équipes** to work shifts; **2** [*shop, hotel, shopkeeper*] to do business; **~ à perte** [*company, business*] to run at a loss; **3 nous voulons la paix et c'est dans ce sens que nous travaillons** we want peace and we are working toward(s) it; **4** [*athlete*] to train; [*musician*] to practise[GB]; **5** [*wood*] to warp.

travailleur, **-euse** /tʀavajœʀ, øz/ I *adj* **1** [*pupil*] hardworking; **2** [*classes*] working.
II *nm,f* worker.

travailliste /tʀavajist/ I *adj* Labour.
II *nmf* Labour MP.

travée /tʀave/ *nf* **1** row; **2** (Tech) span.

travelling /tʀavliŋ/ *nm* (in cinema) tracking; tracking shot.

travers /tʀavɛʀ/ I *nm inv* **1** foible, quirk; **2** (Naut) beam; **3** (Culin) **~ de porc** sparerib.
II **à travers** *phr* **1** [*see, look*] through; **2** [*walk*] across; **voyager à ~ le monde** to travel all over the world; **3 voyager à ~ le temps** to travel through time; **4** through; **à ~ ces informations** through this information.
III **au travers** *phr* through; **passer au ~ de** (figurative) to escape [*inspection*].
IV **de travers** *phr* **1** askew; **ta veste est boutonnée de ~** your jacket is buttoned up wrongly; **il a le nez de ~** he has a twisted nose; **j'ai avalé de ~** it went down the wrong way; **regarder qn de ~** to give sb filthy looks; **2** wrong; **comprendre de ~** to misunderstand.
V **en travers** *phr* across; **un bus était en ~ de la route** a bus was stuck across the road; **se mettre en ~ de la route** [*people*] to stand in the middle of the road; **rester en ~ de la gorge de qn**○ to be hard to swallow.

traverse /tʀavɛʀs/ *nf* (on railway line) sleeper (GB), tie (US).

traversée /tʀavɛʀse/ *nf* **1** crossing; **la ~ du désert** crossing the desert; (figurative) (of company) a difficult period; **2** (of city) **évitez la ~ de Paris** avoid going through Paris.

traverser /tʀavɛʀse/ [1] *vtr* **1** to cross [*road, bridge, border, town, ocean, room*]; to go through [*town, forest, tunnel*]; to make one's way through [*group, crowd*]; **il traversa le jardin en courant** he ran across the garden (GB) or yard (US); **2** [*river*] to run through [*region*]; [*road*] to go through [*region*]; [*bridge, river*] to cross [*railway line, town*]; **3** [*rain*] to soak through [*clothes*]; **la balle lui a traversé le bras** the bullet went right through his/her arm; **4** to go through [*crisis*]; to live through [*war*]; **5 ~ l'esprit de qn** to cross sb's mind.

traversin /tʀavɛʀsɛ̃/ *nm* bolster.

travesti, **~e** /tʀavɛsti/ I *pp* ▶ **travestir**.
II *pp adj* in disguise; **rôle ~** role played by a member of the opposite sex.
III *nm* **1** transvestite; **2** (actor) actor playing a female role; (in cabaret) drag artist○.

travestir /tʀavɛstiʀ/ [3] I *vtr* **1** to dress [sb] up [*person*]; **2** to distort [*truth*].
II **se travestir** *v refl* (+ *v être*) **1** to dress up; **2** to cross-dress.

trébucher /tʀebyʃe/ [1] *vi* to stumble.

trèfle /tʀɛfl/ *nm* **1** clover; **2** (Games) (card) club; (suit) clubs; **3** shamrock.

treillage /tʀɛjaʒ/ *nm* **1** trellis; **2** lattice fence.

treille /tʀɛj/ *nf* **1** (vine) arbour[GB]; **2** climbing vine.

treillis /tʀɛji/ *nm inv* **1** (Mil) fatigues; **2** canvas; **3** trellis; **~ métallique** wire grille.

treize /tʀɛz/ *adj inv, pron, nm inv* thirteen.

treizième /tʀɛzjɛm/ *adj* thirteenth.

tréma /tʀema/ *nm* diaeresis; **i ~** i diaeresis.

tremblant, **~e** /tʀɑ̃blɑ̃, ɑ̃t/ *adj* **1** [*person, hands*] shaking; **2** [*voice*] trembling; **3** [*image, light*] flickering; [*sound*] tremulous.

tremblement /tʀɑ̃bləmɑ̃/ *nm* **1** (of person, hands) shaking, trembling; (of lips) trembling; **2** (of voice) trembling; **3** (of leaves) quivering.
■ **~ de terre** earthquake.

trembler /tʀɑ̃ble/ [1] *vi* **1** [*person, legs*] to shake, to tremble; **2** [*voice*] to tremble; [*sound, note*] to waver; **3** [*building, floor*] to shake; **4** (be afraid) to tremble; **~ pour qn** to fear for sb; **5** [*light, image*] to flicker; **6** [*leaves*] to quiver.

trembloter /tʀɑ̃blɔte/ [1] *vi* **1** [*person, hands*] to tremble slightly; **2** [*voice*] to tremble.

trémolo /tʀemɔlo/ *nm* **1** (of voice) quaver; **2** (of instrument) tremolo.

trémousser: **se trémousser** /tʀemuse/ [1] *v refl* (+ *v être*) **1** to fidget; **2** to wiggle around.

trempe /tʀɑ̃p/ *nf* **avoir la ~ d'un dirigeant** to have the makings of a leader.

trempé, **~e** /tʀɑ̃pe/ **I** *pp* ▶ **tremper**.
II *pp adj* **1** [*person, garments*] soaked (through); [*grass*] sodden; **2** (Tech) [*steel*] tempered; [*glass*] toughened.

tremper /tʀɑ̃pe/ [1] **I** *vtr* **1** [*rain, person*] to soak [*person, garment*]; **2** to dip; **j'ai juste trempé mes lèvres** I just had a sip; **3** to soak [*hands*]; **4** (Tech) to temper.
II *vi* **1** [*clothes, vegetables*] to soak; **faire ~ qch** to soak sth; **2**○ **~ dans qch** to be mixed up in sth.

tremplin /tʀɑ̃plɛ̃/ *nm* **1** springboard; **2** ski jump; water-ski jump.

trentaine /tʀɑ̃tɛn/ *nf* **1** about thirty; **2 avoir la ~** to be about thirty.

trente /tʀɑ̃t/ *adj inv, pron, nm inv* thirty.

trente-et-un /tʀɑ̃teœ̃/ *nm* **être sur son ~**○ to be dressed up to the nines.

trentenaire /tʀɑ̃tənɛʀ/ *adj* [*person*] in his/her thirties; [*tree, building*] around thirty years old.

trente-six /tʀɑ̃tsis/ *adj inv, pron, nm inv* thirty-six.
IDIOMS **voir ~ chandelles**○ to see stars.

trente-trois /tʀɑ̃ttʀwa/ *adj inv, pron, nm inv* thirty-three.
■ **~ tours** LP.

trentième /tʀɑ̃tjɛm/ *adj* thirtieth.

trépas† /tʀepɑ/ *nm* demise.

trépidant, **~e** /tʀepidɑ̃, ɑ̃t/ *adj* [*rhythm, speed*] pulsating; [*life*] hectic; [*story*] exciting.

trépied /tʀepje/ *nm* (gen) tripod.

trépigner /tʀepiɲe/ [1] *vi* (with anger, impatience) to stamp one's feet.

très /tʀɛ/ *adv* very; **~ connu** very well-known; **être ~ amoureux** to be very much in love; **~ en avance** very early; **~ volontiers** gladly; **'tu vas bien?'—'non, pas ~'** 'are you well?'—'no, not terribly'; **elle a ~ envie de partir** she's dying○ to leave.

trésor /tʀezɔʀ/ *nm* **1** treasure; **2 déployer des ~s d'inventivité** to show infinite inventiveness; **3** (person) **mon ~** precious.

trésorerie /tʀezɔʀʀi/ *nf* **1** funds; cash; **2** (of company) accounts; **3** government finance.

trésorier, **-ière** /tʀezɔʀje, ɛʀ/ *nm,f* treasurer.

tressaillement /tʀɛsajmɑ̃/ *nm* **1** (from surprise, fear) start; (of hope, pleasure) quiver; (from pain) wince; **2** (of person, muscle, animal) twitch; (of machine, ground) vibration.

tressaillir /tʀɛsajiʀ/ [28] *vi* **1** (with surprise) to start; (with pleasure) to quiver; **2** [*person, muscle*] to twitch.

tresse /tʀɛs/ *nf* **1** plait; **2** (of thread) braid.

tresser /tʀɛse/ [1] *vtr* to plait [*hair, threads*]; to weave [*straw, string*].

tréteau, *pl* **~x** /tʀeto/ *nm* trestle.

treuil /tʀœj/ *nm* winch.

trêve /tʀɛv/ *nf* **1** (Mil) truce; **2** respite; **~ de plaisanteries!** that's enough joking!

tri /tʀi/ *nm* sorting; sorting out; **centre de ~ (postal)** sorting office; **faire le ~ de** to sort [*mail*]; to sort out [*documents, clothes*]; **faire un ~ parmi des choses** to select among things.

triage /tʀijaʒ/ *nm* **gare de ~** marshalling[GB] yard.

triangle /tʀijɑ̃gl/ *nm* triangle.
■ **~ des Bermudes** Bermuda Triangle.

triangulaire /tʀijɑ̃gylɛʀ/ *adj* **1** triangular; **2** [*agreement, partnership*] three-way.

triathlon /tʀiatlɔ̃/ *nm* triathlon.

tribal, **~e**, *mpl* **-aux** /tʀibal, o/ *adj* tribal.

tribord /tʀibɔʀ/ *nm* starboard.

tribu /tʀiby/ *nf* tribe.

tribulations /tʀibylasjɔ̃/ *nf pl* tribulations.

tribunal, *pl* **-aux** /tʀibynal, o/ *nm* (Law) court; **traîner qn devant les tribunaux** to take sb to court.

tribune /tʀibyn/ *nf* **1** (in stadium) stand; (in court) gallery; **2** (of speaker) platform, rostrum; **3** (in newspaper) comments column.

tribut /tʀiby/ *nm* tribute.

tributaire /tʀibytɛʀ/ *adj* **être ~ de** [*country, person*] to depend on.

tricentenaire /tʀisɑ̃tnɛʀ/ *adj* three-hundred-year-old.

triche○ /tʀiʃ/ *nf* **c'est de la ~** that's cheating.

tricher /tʀiʃe/ [1] *vi* to cheat; **~ sur son âge** to lie about one's age.

tricherie /tʀiʃʀi/ *nf* cheating.

tricheur, **-euse** /tʀiʃœʀ, øz/ *nm,f* cheat.

tricolore /tʀikɔlɔʀ/ *adj* **1** three-coloured[GB]; **feux ~s** traffic lights; **2**○ French; **l'équipe ~** the French team.

tricot /tʀiko/ *nm* **1** knitting; **faire du ~** to knit; **2** knitwear; **en ~** knitted.

tricoter /tʀikɔte/ [1] *vtr* to knit; **tricoté (à la) main** handknitted.

tricycle /tʀisikl/ *nm* tricycle.

trident /tʀidɑ̃/ *nm* trident.

triennal, **~e**, *mpl* **-aux** /tʀijenal, o/ *adj* **1** [*mandate*] three-year; **2** [*vote*] three-yearly.

trier /tʀije/ [2] *vtr* **1** to sort [*mail*]; **2** to sort [sth] out [*information*]; to select [*clients*].
IDIOMS **~ sur le volet** to handpick.

trilingue /tʀilɛ̃g/ *adj* trilingual.

trilogie /tʀilɔʒi/ *nf* trilogy.

trimbal(l)er○ /tʀɛ̃bale/ [1] *vtr* to lug [sth] around; to drag [sb] around.

trimer○ /tʀime/ [1] *vi* to slave away.

trimestre /tʀimɛstʀ/ *nm* **1** (period) quarter; (Sch) term; **2** quarterly income; quarterly payment.

trimestriel, **-ielle** /tʀimɛstʀijɛl/ *adj* (gen) quarterly; [*exam*] end-of-term.

trimoteur /tʀimɔtœʀ/ *nm* three-engined plane.

tringle /tʀɛ̃gl/ *nf* **1** (gen) rail; **2** (Tech) rod.

trinité /tʀinite/ *nf* trinity.

trinquer /tʀɛ̃ke/ [1] *vi* to clink glasses; **~ à qch** to drink to sth.

trio /tʀi(j)o/ *nm* trio.

triomphal, **~e**, *mpl* **-aux** /tʀijɔ̃fal, o/ *adj* triumphant.

triomphant, **~e** /tʀijɔ̃fɑ̃, ɑ̃t/ *adj* triumphant.

triomphateur, **-trice** /tʀijɔ̃fatœʀ, tʀis/ *adj* triumphant.
triomphe /tʀijɔ̃f/ *nm* triumph; **faire un ~ à qn** to give sb a triumphal reception.
triompher /tʀijɔ̃fe/ [1] **I triompher de** *v+prep* to triumph over [*enemy*]; to overcome [*resistance*].
II *vi* **1** [*fighter*] to triumph; [*truth*] to prevail; **2** to be triumphant.
tripatouiller○ /tʀipatuje/ [1] *vtr* to fiddle with○ [*object*]; to paw○ [*person*].
triperie /tʀipʀi/ *nf* **1** tripe shop; **2** tripe trade.
tripes /tʀip/ *nf pl* **1** (Culin) tripe; **2**○ guts, innards.
triplace /tʀiplas/ *adj* three-seater.
triple /tʀipl/ **I** *adj* triple; **l'avantage est ~** the advantages are threefold; **en ~ exemplaire** in triplicate; **~ idiot**○! prize idiot○!
II *nm* **coûter le ~** to cost three times as much.
triplé, **~e** /tʀiple/ *nm,f* triplet.
triplement /tʀipləmɑ̃/ *adv* **1** in three respects; **2** trebly.
tripler /tʀiple/ [1] **I** *vtr* to treble [*quantity, price*].
II *vi* to treble (**de** in).
triporteur /tʀipɔʀtœʀ/ *nm* delivery tricycle.
tripot /tʀipo/ *nm* **1** gambling joint○; **2** dive○.
tripotée○ /tʀipɔte/ *nf* **1** (good) hiding○; **2 une ~ de** hordes of.
tripoter○ /tʀipɔte/ [1] *vtr* to fiddle with [*object*].
trique /tʀik/ *nf* cudgel; **battre à coups de ~** to cudgel.
IDIOMS **être maigre** or **sec comme un coup de ~** to be as thin as a rake.
trisaïeul, **~e** /tʀizajœl/ *nm,f* great-great-grandfather/grandmother.
trisannuel, **-elle** /tʀizanɥɛl/ *adj* triennial.
trisomie /tʀizɔmi/ *nf* trisomy; **~ 21** Down's Syndrome.
trisomique /tʀizɔmik/ *adj* **enfant ~** Down's syndrome child.
triste /tʀist/ *adj* **1** (gen) sad; [*town, existence*] dreary; [*weather, day*] gloomy; [*colour*] drab; **2** [*end, business, reputation*] dreadful; [*show, state*] sorry; [*character*] unsavoury[GB]; **c'est la ~ vérité** unfortunately, that's the truth of the matter; **faire la ~ expérience de qch** to learn about sth to one's cost.
tristement /tʀistəmɑ̃/ *adv* sadly.
tristesse /tʀistɛs/ *nf* (gen) sadness; (of place, evening) dreariness; (of weather, day) gloominess.
triton /tʀitɔ̃/ *nm* (Zool) **1** (mollusc) triton; **2** newt.
triturer /tʀityʀe/ [1] *vtr* to fiddle with [*button*]; to knead [*dough*].
IDIOMS **se ~ la cervelle**○ or **les méninges**○ to rack one's brains○.
trivial, **~e**, *mpl* **-iaux** /tʀivjal, o/ *adj* **1** coarse; **2** ordinary, everyday; [*style*] mundane.
trivialité /tʀivjalite/ *nf* **1** coarseness; **2** triteness, triviality; **3** platitude.
troc /tʀɔk/ *nm* barter; **faire du ~** to barter.
troène /tʀɔɛn/ *nm* privet.
troglodyte /tʀɔglɔdit/ *nm* cave-dweller.
trognon /tʀɔɲɔ̃/ *nm* (of apple) core.
trois /tʀwa/ *adj inv, pron, nm inv* three.
IDIOMS **être haut comme ~ pommes** to be kneehigh to a grasshopper; **jamais deux sans ~** bad luck comes in threes.
trois-huit /tʀwaɥit/ *nm pl* system of three eight-hour shifts.
troisième /tʀwazjɛm/ **I** *adj* third.
II *nf* **1** (Sch) *fourth year of secondary school, age 14–15*; **2** (Aut) third (gear).
■ **le ~ âge** the elderly.
trois-mâts /tʀwamɑ/ *nm inv* three-master.
trois-quarts /tʀwakaʀ/ **I** *nm inv* **1** three-quarter length coat; **2** (rugby player) three-quarter.
II **de trois-quarts** *phr* [*portrait*] three-quarter length.
trombe /tʀɔ̃b/ *nf* **1** (caused by whirlwind) waterspout; **partir en ~** to go hurtling off; **2 ~s d'eau** masses of water; torrential rain.
trombone /tʀɔ̃bɔn/ *nm* **1** trombone; **2** trombonist; **3** paperclip.
trompe /tʀɔ̃p/ *nf* **1** (Zool) (of elephant) trunk; (of insect) proboscis; **2** (Mus) horn.
trompe-l'œil /tʀɔ̃plœj/ *nm inv* **1** (painting) trompe l'oeil; **2** (figurative) smokescreen.
tromper /tʀɔ̃pe/ [1] **I** *vtr* **1** (gen) to deceive; to be unfaithful to [*husband, wife*]; **~ les électeurs** to mislead the voters; **2 ~ la vigilance de qn** to slip past sb's guard; **3 pour ~ l'attente** to while away the time.
II **se tromper** *v refl* (+ *v être*) **1** to be mistaken; **se ~ sur qn** to be wrong about sb; **il ne faut pas s'y ~, qu'on ne s'y trompe pas** make no mistake about it; **2** to make a mistake; **se ~ de bus** to take the wrong bus.
tromperie /tʀɔ̃pʀi/ *nf* deceit.
trompette[1] /tʀɔ̃pɛt/ *nm* (in army) bugler.
trompette[2] /tʀɔ̃pɛt/ *nf* trumpet.
trompettiste /tʀɔ̃petist/ *nmf* trumpet (player).
trompeur, **-euse** /tʀɔ̃pœʀ, øz/ *adj* [*promise*] misleading; [*appearance*] deceptive.
tronc /tʀɔ̃/ *nm* **1** (of tree, body) trunk; (of column) shaft; **2** collection box.
■ **~ commun** (of species) common origin; (of disciplines) (common) core curriculum.
tronçon /tʀɔ̃sɔ̃/ *nm* section.
tronçonneuse /tʀɔ̃sɔnøz/ *nf* chain saw.
trône /tʀon/ *nm* throne.
trôner /tʀone/ [1] *vi* **le professeur trônait au milieu de ses étudiants** the professor was holding court among his students; **~ sur** [*photograph*] to have pride of place on.
tronquer /tʀɔ̃ke/ [1] *vtr* to truncate.
trop /tʀo/ **I** *adv* too; too much; **beaucoup** or **bien ~ lourd** far or much too heavy; **j'ai ~ mangé** I've had too much to eat; **j'ai ~ dormi** I've slept too long; **nous sommes ~ peu nombreux** there are too few of us; **12 francs c'est ~ peu** 12 francs is too little; **ce serait ~ beau!** one should be so lucky!; **c'est ~**

bête! how stupid!; **~ enthousiaste** overenthusiastic; **~ c'est ~!** enough is enough!; **c'était ~ drôle** it was so funny.
II trop de *quantif* **~ de pression/meubles** too much pressure/furniture; **~ de livres/monde** too many books/people.
III de trop, **en trop** *phr* **il y a une assiette en ~** there's one plate too many; **il y a 12 francs de ~** there's 12 francs too much; **ta remarque était de ~** your remark was uncalled for; **se sentir de ~** to feel one is in the way.

trophée /tʀɔfe/ *nm* trophy.

tropical, **~e**, *mpl* **-aux** /tʀɔpikal, o/ *adj* tropical.

tropique /tʀɔpik/ *nm* tropic.

trop-plein, *pl* **~s** /tʀoplɛ̃/ *nm* **1** (of energy) excess; **2** (Tech) (from bath) overflow.

troquer /tʀɔke/ [1] *vtr* (gen) **~ qch contre qch** to swap sth for sth; to barter sth for sth.

trot /tʀo/ *nm* trot.

trotte○ /tʀɔt/ *nf* **ça fait une ~** it's a fair walk.

trotter /tʀɔte/ [1] *vi* **1** [*horse, rider*] to trot; **2** [*person, mouse*] to scurry (about); **3** (figurative) **~ dans la tête** [*thought*] to go through one's mind; [*music*] to go through one's head.

trotteuse /tʀɔtøz/ *nf* (on watch) second hand.

trottiner /tʀɔtine/ [1] *vi* **1** [*horse*] to jog; **2** [*person, mouse*] to scurry along.

trottinette /tʀɔtinɛt/ *nf* scooter.

trottoir /tʀɔtwaʀ/ *nm* pavement (GB), sidewalk (US); **le bord du ~** the kerb (GB) or curb (US).

trou /tʀu/ *nm* **1** hole; **2** (in timetable) (gen) gap; (in budget) deficit; (in savings) hole; **3**○ **~ (perdu)** dump○.
■ **~ d'aération** airhole; **~ d'air** air pocket; **~ de mémoire** memory lapse; **~ normand** *glass of spirits between courses to aid digestion*; **~ de serrure** keyhole.

troublant, **~e** /tʀublɑ̃, ɑ̃t/ *adj* **1** disturbing; disconcerting; **2** (sexually) unsettling.

trouble /tʀubl/ **I** *adj* **1** [*liquid*] cloudy; [*glasses*] smudgy; **2** [*picture, outline*] blurred; **3** [*feeling*] confused; [*business, milieu*] shady.
II *adv* **je vois ~** my eyes are blurred.
III *nm* **1** unrest; **~s ethniques** ethnic unrest; **2** trouble; **jeter le ~** to stir up trouble; **3** confusion; embarrassment; **4** emotion; **ressentir un ~** to feel a thrill of emotion; **5** (Med) **~s** disorders.

trouble-fête /tʀubləfɛt/ *nmf inv* spoilsport.

troubler /tʀuble/ [1] **I** *vtr* **1** to make [sth] cloudy [*liquid*]; to blur [*sight, picture*]; **2** to disturb [*sleep, person*]; to disrupt [*plans*]; **en ces temps troublés** in these troubled times; **3** to disconcert [*person*].
II se troubler *v refl* (+ *v être*) **1** [*person*] to become flustered; **2** [*liquid*] to become cloudy; **ma vue se troubla** my eyes became blurred.

trouée /tʀue/ *nf* **1** gap; **2** (Mil) breach.

trouer /tʀue/ [1] *vtr* to make a hole (or holes) in; to wear a hole (or holes) in; **semelle trouée** sole with a hole (or holes) in it.

trouille○ /tʀuj/ *nf* **avoir la ~** to be scared.

troupe /tʀup/ *nf* **1** (Mil) troops; **2** (of actors) company; (on tour) troupe; **3** (of deer) herd; (of birds) flock; (of tourists) troop; (of children) band.

troupeau, *pl* **~x** /tʀupo/ *nm* (of buffalo, cattle) herd; (of sheep) flock; (of geese) gaggle.

trousse /tʀus/ *nf* **1** (little) case; **2** kit.
■ **~ d'écolier** pencil case; **~ de médecin** doctor's bag; **~ de secours** first-aid kit; **~ de toilette** toilet bag.
IDIOMS **être aux ~s de qn** to be hot on sb's heels.

trousseau, *pl* **~x** /tʀuso/ *nm* **1** (of keys) bunch; **2** (of bride) trousseau; (of baby) clothes.

trouvaille /tʀuvɑj/ *nf* **1** (object) find; **2** bright idea, brainwave.

trouvé, **~e** /tʀuve/ **I** *pp* ▶ **trouver**.
II *pp adj* **réplique bien ~e** neat riposte; **tout ~** [*solution*] ready-made; [*culprit*] obvious.

trouver /tʀuve/ [1] **I** *vtr* **1** (gen) to find; **~ qch par hasard** to come across sth; **~ un intérêt à qch** to find sth interesting; **~ à redire** to find fault; **~ le moyen de faire** to manage to do; **j'ai trouvé!** I've got it!; **tu as trouvé ça tout seul?** (ironic) did you work that out all by yourself?; **si tu continues tu vas me ~**○**!** don't push your luck○!; **~ du plaisir à faire** to get pleasure out of doing; **aller ~ qn** to go and see sb; **2 je trouve ça drôle** I think it's funny; **j'ai trouvé bon de vous prévenir** I thought it right to warn you; **je me demande ce qu'elle te trouve!** I wonder what she sees in you!; **je te trouve bien calme, qu'est-ce que tu as?** you're very quiet, what's the matter?
II se trouver *v refl* (+ *v être*) **1** to be; **se ~ à Rome** to be in Rome; **se ~ dans l'impossibilité de faire** to be unable to do; **2** to feel; **j'ai failli me ~ mal** I nearly passed out; **3 il se ~ beau** he thinks he's good-looking; **4** to find [*excuse*].
III *v impers* **il se trouve qu'elle ne leur avait rien dit** as it happened, she hadn't told them anything; **si ça se trouve**○ **ça te plaira** you might like it.

truand /tʀyɑ̃/ *nm* **1** gangster; **2** crook.

truc /tʀyk/ *nm* **1**○ knack; trick; **avoir un ~ pour gagner de l'argent** to know a good way of making money; **un ~ du métier** a trick of the trade; **2** thing; **il y a un tas de ~s à faire dans la maison** there are loads○ of things to do in the house; **il y a un ~ qui ne va pas** there's something wrong; **3**○ thingummy○, whatsit○; **4** (person) what's-his-name/what's-her-name, thingy○.

trucage /tʀykaʒ/ *nm* (in cinema) special effect.

truelle /tʀyɛl/ *nf* trowel.

truffe /tʀyf/ *nf* **1** (Culin) truffle; **2** (of dog) nose.

truffer /tʀyfe/ [1] *vtr* **ta lettre est truffée de fautes** your letter is riddled with mistakes.

truie /tʀɥi/ *nf* sow.

truite /tʀɥit/ *nf* trout.

truquage = **trucage**.

truquer /tʀyke/ [1] *vtr* **1** to fiddle○ [*accounts*]; **2** to mark [*cards*]; **3** to fix [*elections, match*].

trust /tʀœst/ *nm* trust.

tsar /tsaʀ/ *nm* tsar.
tsé-tsé /tsetse/ *nf inv* (**mouche**) **~** tsetse (fly).
tsigane = **tzigane**.
TTC (*abbr* = **toutes taxes comprises**) inclusive of tax.
tu /ty/ *pron* you.
IDIOMS **être à ~ et à toi avec qn** to be on familiar terms with sb.
tuant○, **~e** /tɥɑ̃, ɑ̃t/ *adj* exhausting.
tuba /tyba/ *nm* **1** (Mus) tuba; **2** (of swimmer) snorkel.
tube /tyb/ **I** *nm* **1** tube; pipe; **2**○ (song) hit.
II à pleins tubes○ *phr* **mettre le son à pleins ~s** to turn the sound right up○.
■ **~ cathodique** cathode ray tube; **~ digestif** digestive tract; **~ à essai** test tube.
tubercule /tybɛʀkyl/ *nm* **1** (Bot) tuber; **2** (Anat) tuberosity.
tuberculeux, **-euse** /tybɛʀkylø, øz/ *adj* tubercular; **être ~** to have TB.
tuberculose /tybɛʀkyloz/ *nf* tuberculosis, TB.
tubulaire /tybylɛʀ/ *adj* tubular.
TUC /tyk/ *nm pl* (*abbr* = **travaux d'utilité collective**) paid community service (*for the young unemployed*).
tuer /tɥe/ [1] **I** *vtr* **1** (gen) to kill; **2**○ to wear [sb] out.
II se tuer *v refl* (+ *v être*) **1** (accidentally) to be killed; **2** to kill oneself; **3 se ~ au travail** to work oneself to death.
tuerie /tyʀi/ *nf* killings.
tue-tête: **à tue-tête** /atytɛt/ *phr* at the top of one's voice.
tueur, **-euse** /tɥœʀ, øz/ *nm,f* **1** killer; **2** slaughterman/slaughterwoman.
■ **~ à gages** hired or professional killer.
tuile /tɥil/ *nf* **1** tile; **2**○ blow; **quelle ~!** what a blow!; **3** (Culin) *thin almond biscuit*.
tulipe /tylip/ *nf* tulip.
tuméfier /tymefje/ [2] *vtr* to make [sth] swell up.
tumeur /tymœʀ/ *nf* tumour[GB].
tumulte /tymylt/ *nm* **1** uproar; **2** turmoil.
tumultueux, **-euse** /tymyltɥø, øz/ *adj* turbulent; tempestuous; stormy.
tungstène /tœ̃gstɛn/ *nm* tungsten.
tunique /tynik/ *nf* tunic.
tunisien, **-ienne** /tynizjɛ̃, ɛn/ *adj* Tunisian.
tunnel /tynɛl/ *nm* tunnel; **le ~ sous la Manche** the Channel Tunnel.
IDIOMS **voir le bout du ~** to see light at the end of the tunnel.
turban /tyʀbɑ̃/ *nm* turban.
turbin○ /tyʀbɛ̃/ *nm* daily grind○, work.
turbine /tyʀbin/ *nf* turbine.
turbulence /tyʀbylɑ̃s/ *nf* **1** turbulence; **2** unruliness; **3** unrest.
turbulent, **~e** /tyʀbylɑ̃, ɑ̃t/ *adj* [*child*] unruly; [*class*] rowdy; [*teenager*] rebellious; **être ~ en classe** to be disruptive in class.
turc, **turque** /tyʀk/ **I** *adj* Turkish.
II *nm* (language) Turkish.
Turc, **Turque** /tyʀk/ *nm,f* Turk.
turlupiner○ /tyʀlypine/ [1] *vtr* to bother.
turque ▶ **turc I**.
Turquie /tyʀki/ *pr nf* Turkey.
turquoise /tyʀkwaz/ *adj inv*, *nf* turquoise.
tutelle /tytɛl/ *nf* guardianship.
tuteur, **-trice** /tytœʀ, tʀis/ **I** *nm,f* **1** (Law) guardian; **2** tutor.
II *nm* (Bot) stake.
tutoiement /tytwamɑ̃/ *nm* using the *'tu'* form.
tutoyer /tytwaje/ [23] *vtr* to address [sb] using the 'tu' form.
tutu /tyty/ *nm* tutu.
tuyau, *pl* **~x** /tɥijo/ *nm* **1** (Tech) pipe; **2**○ tip○.
■ **~ d'arrosage** hose; **~ d'échappement** exhaust.
tuyauterie /tɥijotʀi/ *nf* (Tech) piping.
TVA /tevea/ *nf* (*abbr* = **taxe à la valeur ajoutée**) VAT.
tympan /tɛ̃pɑ̃/ *nm* eardrum.
type /tip/ **I** *nm* **1** type, kind; **plusieurs accidents de ce ~** several accidents of this kind; **2** (classic) example; **elle est le ~ même de la femme d'affaires** she's the classic example of a business woman; **3** (physical) type; **4**○ guy○; **sale ~!** swine○!; **brave ~** nice chap○.
II (-)type (*combining form*) typical, classic.
typhoïde /tifɔid/ *adj*, *nf* typhoid.
typhon /tifɔ̃/ *nm* typhoon.
typique /tipik/ *adj* typical.
typographie /tipɔgʀafi/ *nf* typography.
typographique /tipɔgʀafik/ *adj* typographical.
tyran /tiʀɑ̃/ *nm* tyrant.
tyrannie /tiʀani/ *nf* tyranny.
tyranniser /tiʀanize/ [1] *vtr* to tyrannize.
tzigane /dzigan, tsigan/ **I** *adj*, *nmf* gypsy.
II *nm* (language) Romany.

Uu

u, **U** /y/ *nm inv* u, U; **en (forme de) U** U-shaped.
ubac /ybak/ *nm* north-facing side.
ubiquité /ybikɥite/ *nf* ubiquity; **je n'ai pas le don d'~**! I can't be everywhere at once!
ubuesque /ybyɛsk/ *adj* grotesque.
ulcère /ylsɛʀ/ *nm* ulcer.
ulcérer /ylseʀe/ [14] *vtr* **1** to sicken, to revolt; **2** (Med) to ulcerate.
ulcéreux, **-euse** /ylseʀø, øz/ *adj* [*wound*] ulcerated.
ULM /yɛlɛm/ *nm inv* (*abbr* = **ultraléger motorisé**) microlight; microlighting; **faire de l'~** to go microlighting.
ultérieur, **~e** /ylteʀjœʀ/ *adj* subsequent; **une date ~e** a later date.
ultérieurement /ylteʀjœʀmɑ̃/ *adv* **1** subsequently; **2** later.
ultimatum /yltimatɔm/ *nm* ultimatum.
ultime /yltim/ *adj* **1** final; **2** ultimate.
ultra /yltʀa/ *adj*, *nmf* extremist.
ultraconfidentiel, **-ielle** /yltʀakɔ̃fidɑ̃sjɛl/ *adj* top secret.
ultrafin, **~e** /yltʀafɛ̃, in/ *adj* [*slice*] wafer-thin; [*stocking*] sheer; [*fibre*] ultra-fine.
ultraléger, **-ère** /yltʀaleʒe, ɛʀ/ *adj* [*material, cigarette*] ultra light; [*clothing, fabric, equipment*] very light.
ultramoderne /yltʀamɔdɛʀn/ *adj* (gen) ultramodern; [*system, technology*] state-of-the-art.
ultrarapide /yltʀaʀapid/ *adj* high-speed.
ultrasecret, **-ète** /yltʀasɔkʀɛ, ɛt/ *adj* top secret.
ultrasensible /yltʀasɑ̃sibl/ *adj* [*person*] hypersensitive; [*film*] ultrasensitive; [*issue*] highly sensitive.
ultrason /yltʀasɔ̃/ *nm* ultrasound.
ultraviolet, **-ette** /yltʀavjɔlɛ, ɛt/ **I** *adj* ultraviolet.
II *nm* ultraviolet ray; **séance d'~s** session on a sunbed.
ululer /ylyle/ [1] *vi* to hoot.
un, **une**[1] /œ̃(n), yn/ **I** *det* (*pl* **des**) **1** a, an; one; **un homme** a man; **une femme** a woman; **avec ~ sang-froid remarquable** with remarkable self-control; **il n'y avait pas ~ arbre** there wasn't a single tree; **~ accident est vite arrivé** accidents soon happen; **2 il y avait des roses et des lis** there were roses and lilies; **il y a des gens qui trichent** there are some people who cheat; **3 il fait ~ froid** or **~ de ces froids**! it's so cold!; **elle m'a donné une de ces gifles**! she gave me such a slap!; **il y a ~ monde aujourd'hui**! there are so many people today!
II *pron* (*pl* **uns**, **unes**) one; **(l')~ de** or **d'entre nous** one of us; **les ~s pensent que**... some think that...
III *adj* one, a, an; **trente et une personnes** thirty-one people; **~ jour sur deux** every other day.
IV *nm,f* one; **~ par personne** one each; **les deux villes n'en font plus qu'une** the two cities have merged into one; **~ à** or **par ~** one by one.
V *nm* one; **page ~** page one.
IDIOMS **fière comme pas une** extremely proud; **il est menteur comme pas ~** he's the biggest liar; **~ pour tous et tous pour ~** all for one and one for all; ▶ **dix**.
unanime /ynanim/ *adj* unanimous.
unanimement /ynanimmɑ̃/ *adv* **1** [*adopted, elected*] unanimously; **2** (figurative) [*admired*] universally.
unanimité /ynanimite/ *nf* unanimity; **à l'~** [*elected*] unanimously; **à l'~ moins deux voix** with only two votes against; **faire l'~** to have unanimous support or backing.
une[2] /yn/ **I** *det, pron, adj* ▶ **un I**, **II**, **III**, **IV**.
II *nf* **la ~** the front page; **être à la ~** to be in the headlines.
uni, **~e** /yni/ **I** *pp* ▶ **unir**.
II *pp adj* **1** [*family*] close-knit; [*couple*] close; [*people, rebels*] united; **2** [*fabric, colour*] plain; **3** [*surface*] smooth, even.
unicité /ynisite/ *nf* uniqueness.
unième /ynjɛm/ *adj* first; **vingt et ~** twenty-first.
unification /ynifikasjɔ̃/ *nf* unification.
unifier /ynifje/ [2] **I** *vtr* **1** to unify [*country, market*]; **2** to standardize [*procedure, system*].
II s'unifier *v refl* (+ *v être*) [*countries, groups*] to unite.
uniforme /ynifɔʀm/ **I** *adj* (gen) uniform; [*buildings, streets, existence*] monotonous; [*regulation*] across-the-board.
II *nm* uniform; **en ~** uniformed.
uniformément /ynifɔʀmemɑ̃/ *adv* uniformly.
uniformiser /ynifɔʀmize/ [1] *vtr* to standardize [*rate*]; to make [sth] uniform [*colour*].
uniformité /ynifɔʀmite/ *nf* (of tastes) uniformity; (of life, buildings) monotony.
unijambiste /yniʒɑ̃bist/ **I** *adj* **être ~** to have only one leg.
II *nmf* one-legged person.
unilatéral, **~e**, *mpl* **-aux** /ynilateʀal, o/ *adj* unilateral; [*parking*] on one side only.
union /ynjɔ̃/ *nf* **1** union; **2** association; **~ de consommateurs** consumers' association; **3** marriage.
■ **~ libre** cohabitation; **~ sportive**, **US** sports club; **Union européenne** European Union.
IDIOMS **l'~ fait la force** (Proverb) united we stand, divided we fall.

unique /ynik/ *adj* **1** only; **il est l'~ témoin** he's the only witness; **être fille** or **fils ~** to be an only child; **2** single; **parti ~** single party; **système à parti ~** one-party system; **'prix ~'** 'all at one price'; **3** unique; **une occasion ~** a unique opportunity; **~ en son genre** [*person, object*] one of a kind; [*event*] one-off (GB), one-shot (US); **4**○ **ce type est ~!** that guy's priceless○!

uniquement /ynikmɑ̃/ *adv* (gen) only; **en vente ~ par correspondance** available by mail order only; **c'était ~ pour te taquiner** it was only to tease you; **il pense ~ à s'amuser** all he thinks about is having fun; **~ dans un but commercial** purely for commercial ends.

unir /yniʀ/ [3] **I** *vtr* **1** to unite [*people, country*]; **des hommes unis par les mêmes idées** men brought together by the same ideas; **2** to combine [*qualities, resources*]; **3** to join [sb] in matrimony .
II s'unir *v refl* (+ *v être*) **1** to unite; **2** to marry.

unisexe /ynisɛks/ *adj* unisex.

unisson /ynisɔ̃/ *nm* unison; **à l'~** (Mus) in unison; (figurative) in accord.

unitaire /ynitɛʀ/ *adj* [*cost*] unit.

unité /ynite/ *nf* **1** unity; **film qui manque d'~** film lacking in cohesion; **il y a ~ de vues entre eux** they share the same viewpoint; **2** unit; **~ monétaire** unit of currency; **20 francs l'~** 20 francs each; **vendre qch à l'~** to sell sth singly.
■ **~ centrale (de traitement)** (Comput) central processing unit, CPU; **~ de disque** (Comput) disk drive.

univers /ynivɛʀ/ *nm inv* **1** universe; **2** whole world; **3** world; **l'~ de Kafka** Kafka's world.

universalité /ynivɛʀsalite/ *nf* universality.

universel, **-elle** /ynivɛʀsɛl/ *adj* [*language, theme*] universal; [*history*] world; [*remedy*] all-purpose.

universitaire /ynivɛʀsitɛʀ/ **I** *adj* [*town*] university; [*work*] academic.
II *nmf* academic.

université /ynivɛʀsite/ *nf* university (GB), college (US).
■ **~ d'été** summer school.

uns *pron* ▶ **un II**.

Untel, **Unetelle** /œ̃tɛl, yntɛl/ *nm,f* **Monsieur ~** Mr so-and-so; **Madame Unetelle** Mrs so-and-so.

urbain, **~e** /yʀbɛ̃, ɛn/ *adj* **1** urban; **vie ~e** city life; **2** (formal) urbane.

urbanisation /yʀbanizasjɔ̃/ *nf* urbanization.

urbaniser /yʀbanize/ [1] *vtr* to urbanize [*region*]; **zone urbanisée** built-up area.

urbanisme /yʀbanism/ *nm* town planning (GB), city planning (US).

urbaniste /yʀbanist/ *nmf* town planner (GB), city planner (US).

urée /yʀe/ *nf* urea.

urgence /yʀʒɑ̃s/ *nf* **1** urgency; **il y a ~** it's urgent, it's a matter of urgency; **d'~** [*act*] immediately; [*summon*] urgently; [*measures, treatment*] emergency; **de toute** or **d'extrême ~** as a matter of great urgency; **transporter qn d'~ à l'hôpital** to rush sb to hospital; **en ~** as a matter of urgency; **2** (Med) **une ~** an emergency; **le service des ~s**, **les ~s** the casualty department.

urgent, **~e** /yʀʒɑ̃, ɑ̃t/ *adj* urgent.

urinaire /yʀinɛʀ/ *adj* urinary; **appareil ~** urinary tract.

urinal, *pl* **-aux** /yʀinal, o/ *nm* urinal.

urine /yʀin/ *nf* urine.

uriner /yʀine/ [1] *vi* to urinate.

urinoir /yʀinwaʀ/ *nm* urinal.

urne /yʀn/ *nf* **1 ~ (électorale)** ballot box; **se rendre aux ~s** to go to the polls; **2** urn.

urologie /yʀɔlɔʒi/ *nf* urology.

urologue /yʀɔlɔg/ *nmf* urologist.

URSS /yɛʀɛsɛs, yʀs/ *pr nf* (*abbr* = **Union des Républiques socialistes soviétiques**) USSR.

urticaire /yʀtikɛʀ/ *nf* hives.

uruguayen, **-enne** /yʀygwejɛ̃, ɛn/ *adj* Uruguayan.

us /ys/ *nm pl* **les ~ et coutumes** the ways and customs.

US /yɛs/ *nf* (*abbr* = **union sportive**) sports club.

USA /yɛsa/ *nm pl* (*abbr* = **United States of America**) USA.

usage /yzaʒ/ *nm* **1** use; **à l'~**, **par l'~** with use; **en ~** in use; **faire ~ de** to use [*product*]; to exercise [*authority*]; **faire bon/mauvais ~ de qch** to put sth to good/bad use; **faire de l'~** [*garment*] to last; **à ~ privé** for private use; **à ~s multiples** [*appliance*] multipurpose; **il a perdu l'~ d'un œil/l'~ de la parole** he's lost the use of one eye/the power of speech; **hors d'~** [*garment*] unwearable; [*machine*] out of order; **2** (in a language) usage; **en ~** in usage; **3** custom; **l'~ est de faire** the custom is to do; it's usual practice to do; **entrer dans l'~** [*word*] to come into common use; [*behaviour*] to become common practice; [*politeness*] customary; [*precautions*] usual.
■ **~ de faux** (Law) use of false documents; **faux et ~ de faux** forgery and use of false documents.

usagé, **~e** /yzaʒe/ *adj* **1** [*garment*] well-worn; [*tyre*] worn; **2** [*syringe*] used.

usager /yzaʒe/ *nm* (of service) user; (of language) speaker; **~ de la route** road-user.

usant, **~e** /yzɑ̃, ɑ̃t/ *adj* exhausting, wearing.

usé, **~e** /yze/ **I** *pp* ▶ **user**.
II *pp adj* [*object*] worn; [*person*] worn-down; [*heart, eyes*] worn-out; [*joke*] hackneyed; **~ jusqu'à la corde** [*carpet*] threadbare; [*tyre*] worn down to the tread; (figurative) [*joke*] hackneyed.

user /yze/ [1] **I** *vtr* to wear out [*shoes*]; to wear down [*person*]; **les piles sont usées** the batteries have run down or out; **~ ses vêtements jusqu'à la corde** to wear one's clothes out; **~ sa santé** to ruin one's health.
II user de *v+prep* (gen) to use; to exercise

[*right*]; to take [*precautions*]; **~ de diplomatie** to be diplomatic.
III s'user *v refl* (+ *v être*) **1** [*shoes*] to wear out; **2** [*person*] **s'~ à la tâche** or **au travail** to wear oneself out with overwork; **s'~ la santé** to ruin one's health.

usine /yzin/ *nf* factory, plant.
■ **~ métallurgique** ironworks; **~ sidérurgique** steelworks.

usiner /yzine/ [1] *vtr* **1** to machine; **2** to manufacture.

usité, **~e** /yzite/ *adj* commonly used.

ustensile /ystɑ̃sil/ *nm* utensil.

usuel, **-elle** /yzɥɛl/ *adj* [*object*] everyday; [*word*] common.

usufruit /yzyfʀɥi/ *nm* (Law) usufruct.

usufruitier, **-ière** /yzyfʀɥitje, ɛʀ/ *nm,f* tenant for life.

usure /yzyʀ/ *nf* **1** (of clothes) wear and tear; (of tyre, machine) wear; **résister à l'~** to wear well; **2** (of energy, enemy) wearing down; **3 ~ du temps** wearing effect of time; **4** usury.

usurier, **-ière** /yzyʀje, ɛʀ/ *nm,f* usurer.

usurpateur, **-trice** /yzyʀpatœʀ, tʀis/ *nm,f* usurper.

usurper /yzyʀpe/ [1] *vtr* to usurp.

ut /yt/ *nm* (Mus) C.

utérus /yteʀys/ *nm inv* womb.

utile /ytil/ **I** *adj* (gen) useful; **être ~** [*person, book*] to be helpful; [*umbrella*] to come in handy; **il est ~ de signaler** it's worth pointing out; **il n'a pas jugé ~ de me prévenir** he didn't think it necessary to let me know; **en quoi puis-je vous être ~?** how can I help you?
II *nm* **joindre l'~ à l'agréable** to mix business with pleasure.

utilement /ytilmɑ̃/ *adv* [*intervene*] effectively; [*occupy oneself*] usefully.

utilisable /ytilizabl/ *adj* usable.

utilisateur, **-trice** /ytilizatœʀ, tʀis/ *nm,f* user.

utilisation /ytilizasjɔ̃/ *nf* use.

utiliser /ytilize/ [1] *vtr* (gen) to use; to make use of [*resources*].

utilitaire /ytilitɛʀ/ *adj* [*role*] practical; [*object*] functional, utilitarian; [*vehicle*] commercial.

utilité /ytilite/ *nf* **1** usefulness; **d'une grande ~** [*book, machine*] very useful; [*person*] very helpful; **d'aucune ~** of no use; **2** use; **je n'en ai pas l'~** I have no use for it.

utopie /ytɔpi/ *nf* **1** Utopia; **2** wishful thinking.

utopique /ytɔpik/ *adj* utopian.

UV /yve/ *nm pl* (*abbr* = **ultraviolets**) ultraviolet rays; **séance d'~** session on a sunbed.

uvule /yvyl/ *nf* uvula.

Vv

v, **V** /ve/ *nm inv* v, V; **en (forme de) V** V-shaped; **pull en V** V-necked sweater.

va ▶ **aller**[1].

vacance /vakɑ̃s/ **I** *nf* vacancy.

II vacances *nf pl* holiday (GB), vacation (US); **être en ~s** to be on holiday (GB) or vacation (US).

■ **~s scolaires** (Sch) school holiday (GB) or vacation (US).

vacancier, **-ière** /vakɑ̃sje, ɛʀ/ *nm,f* holidaymaker (GB), vacationer (US).

vacant, **~e** /vakɑ̃, ɑ̃t/ *adj* vacant.

vacarme /vakaʀm/ *nm* din, racket○.

vacataire /vakatɛʀ/ *nmf* **1** temporary employee; **2** supply teacher (GB), substitute teacher (US).

vaccin /vaksɛ̃/ *nm* (Med) vaccine.

vaccination /vaksinasjɔ̃/ *nf* vaccination.

vacciner /vaksine/ [1] *vtr* **1** to vaccinate; **2** (humorous) **je suis vacciné○!** I've learned my lesson!

vache /vaʃ/ **I**○ *adj* mean, nasty.

II *nf* **1** cow; **2** cowhide.

■ **~ à eau** water bottle; **~ à lait** (figurative) money-spinner○; **années de ~s maigres** lean years.

IDIOMS **parler français comme une ~ espagnole**○ to speak very bad French.

vachement○ /vaʃmɑ̃/ *adv* really.

vacherie○ /vaʃʀi/ *nf* **1** meanness; **2** bitchy○ remark; **3** dirty trick; **4 c'est une vraie ~ ce virus** this virus is a damned○ nuisance.

vachette /vaʃɛt/ *nf* **1** young cow; **2** calfskin.

vaciller /vasije/ [1] *vi* **1** [*person*] to be unsteady on one's legs; [*legs*] to be unsteady; **2** [*person, object*] to sway; [*light, flame*] to flicker; **3** [*health*] to fail; [*majority*] to weaken.

vadrouille○ /vadʀuj/ *nf* stroll; **être en ~** to be wandering about.

va-et-vient /vaevjɛ̃/ *nm inv* **1** comings and goings; **faire le ~** to go to and fro; to go back and forth; **2** two-way switch.

vagabond, **~e** /vagabɔ̃, ɔ̃d/ **I** *adj* [*dog*] stray; [*mood*] ever-changing.

II *nm,f* vagrant.

vagabondage /vagabɔ̃daʒ/ *nm* **1** wandering; **2** (Law) vagrancy.

vagabonder /vagabɔ̃de/ [1] *vi* to wander.

vagin /vaʒɛ̃/ *nm* vagina.

vagissement /vaʒismɑ̃/ *nm* wail.

vague[1] /vag/ **I** *adj* vague; **ce sont de ~s parents** they're distant relatives.

II *nm* **1 il regardait dans le ~** he was staring into space; **2 avoir du ~ à l'âme** to feel melancholic.

vague[2] /vag/ *nf* wave; **faire des ~s** [*wind*] to make ripples; (figurative) [*scandal*] to cause a stir.

■ **~ de chaleur** heatwave; **~ de froid** cold spell.

IDIOMS **être au creux de la ~** to be at a low ebb.

vaguement /vagmɑ̃/ *adv* vaguely.

vaillant, **~e** /vajɑ̃, ɑ̃t/ *adj* **1** courageous; **2** strong.

vain, **~e** /vɛ̃, vɛn/ **I** *adj* **1** futile; **mes efforts ont été ~s** my efforts were in vain; **2** [*promises*] empty; [*hopes*] vain; **3** [*person*] vain.

II en vain *phr* in vain.

vaincre /vɛ̃kʀ/ [57] **I** *vtr* **1** to defeat [*opponent*]; **2** to overcome [*prejudices, complex*]; to beat [*unemployment, illness*].

II *vi* to win.

vainqueur /vɛ̃kœʀ/ **I** *adj m* victorious.

II *nm* victor; winner; prizewinner; conqueror.

vaisseau, *pl* **~x** /vɛso/ *nm* **1** (Anat, Bot) vessel; **2** (Naut) vessel; warship.

■ **~ spatial** spaceship.

vaisselle /vɛsɛl/ *nf* **1** crockery, dishes; **2** dishes; **faire la ~** to do the dishes.

val, *pl* **~s** or **vaux** /val, vo/ *nm* valley.

IDIOMS **être toujours par monts et par vaux** to be always on the move.

valable /valabl/ *adj* **1** [*explanation*] valid; [*solution*] viable; **2** [*document*] valid; **3**○ [*work, project*] worthwhile.

valdinguer○ /valdɛ̃ge/ [1] *vi* to go flying○.

valet /valɛ/ *nm* **1** manservant; **2** (in cards) jack.

■ **~ de chambre** valet; **~ de ferme** farm hand; **~ de nuit** rack, valet (US).

valeur /valœʀ/ *nf* **1** value; **prendre de la ~** to go up in value; **les objets de ~** valuables; **2** (of person, artist) worth; (of work) value, merit; (of method, discovery) value; **attacher de la ~ à qch** to value sth; **mettre qch en ~** to emphasize [*fact, talent*]; to set off [*eyes, painting*]; **se mettre en ~** to make the best of oneself; to show oneself to best advantage; **3** validity; **4** value; **nous n'avons pas les mêmes ~s** we don't share the same values; **5** (on stock exchange) security; **~s** securities, stock, stocks and shares.

■ **~ sûre** gilt-edged security (GB), blue chip; (figurative) safe bet; **~s mobilières** securities.

validation /validasjɔ̃/ *nf* **1** validation; **2** stamping.

valide /valid/ *adj* **1** valid; **2** able-bodied; fit.

valider /valide/ [1] *vtr* to stamp [*ticket*]; **faire ~** to have [sth] recognized [*diploma*].

validité /validite/ *nf* validity.

valise /valiz/ *nf* suitcase; **faire ses ~s** to pack.

IDIOMS **avoir des ~s sous les yeux**○ to have bags under one's eyes.

vallée /vale/ *nf* valley.
vallon /valɔ̃/ *nm* dale, small valley.
vallonné, **~e** /valɔne/ *adj* [*landscape*] undulating; [*country*] hilly.
valoir /valwaʀ/ [45] **I** *vtr* **~ qch à qn** to earn sb sth [*praise, criticism*]; to win sb sth [*friendship*]; to bring sb sth [*problems*].
II *vi* **1 ~ une fortune/cher** to be worth a fortune/a lot; **ça vaut combien?** how much is it worth?; **~ de l'or** (figurative) to be very valuable; **2 que vaut ce film/vin?** what's that film/wine like?; **il ne vaut pas mieux que son frère** he's no better than his brother; **ne rien ~** to be rubbish; to be useless; to be worthless; **la chaleur ne me vaut rien** the heat doesn't suit me; **ça ne me dit rien qui vaille** I don't like the sound of it; **3** to be as good as; **ton travail vaut bien/largement le leur** your work is just as good/every bit as good as theirs; **rien ne vaut la soie** nothing beats silk; **4** to be worth; **le musée vaut le détour** the museum is worth a detour; **ça vaut la peine** or **le coup**○ it's worth it; **5** [*rule, criticism*] to apply; **6 faire ~** to put [sth] to work [*money*]; to point out [*necessity*]; to emphasize [*quality*]; to assert [*right*]; **faire ~ que** to point out that; **se faire ~** to push oneself forward.
III se valoir *v refl* (+ *v être*) to be the same.
IV *v impers* **il vaut mieux faire, mieux vaut faire** it's better to do; **il vaut mieux que tu y ailles** you'd better go.
valorisation /valɔʀizasjɔ̃/ *nf* **1** (of product) promotion; **2** (of region, resources) development.
valoriser /valɔʀize/ [1] *vtr* **1** to promote [*product*]; to make [sth] attractive [*profession, course*]; **2** to develop [*region, resources*].
valse /vals/ *nf* waltz.
valser /valse/ [1] *vi* to waltz.
valve /valv/ *nf* valve.
vamp○ /vɑ̃p/ *nf* vamp.
vampire /vɑ̃piʀ/ *nm* **1** vampire; **2** (figurative) bloodsucker; **3** (Zool) vampire bat.
van /vɑ̃/ *nm* **1** horsebox (GB), horse-car (US); **2** van.
vandale /vɑ̃dal/ *nmf* vandal.
vandalisme /vɑ̃dalism/ *nm* vandalism.
vanille /vanij/ *nf* vanilla; **une gousse de ~** a vanilla pod.
vanité /vanite/ *nf* **1** vanity; **tirer ~ de qch** to pride oneself on sth; **2** (of efforts) futility; (of promise) emptiness; (of undertaking) uselessness.
vaniteux, **-euse** /vanitø, øz/ *adj* vain.
vanne /van/ *nf* **1** gate; sluice gate; floodgate; **2**○ dig○.
IDIOMS **fermer les ~s**○ to cut funding.
vanner○ /vane/ [1] *vtr* to tire [sb] out.
vannerie /vanʀi/ *nf* basket-making; **objets en ~** wickerwork.
vantardise /vɑ̃taʀdiz/ *nf* **1** boastfulness; **2** boast.
vanter /vɑ̃te/ [1] **I** *vtr* to praise, to extol.
II se vanter *v refl* (+ *v être*) **1** to boast; **2 se ~ de faire** to pride oneself on doing.
va-nu-pieds /vanypje/ *nmf inv* tramp, bum○ (US).

vapeur /vapœʀ/ **I** *nf* steam; **bateau à ~** steamboat; **renverser la ~** (figurative) to backpedal; **faire cuire qch à la ~** to steam sth.
II vapeurs *nf pl* fumes.
vaporeux, **-euse** /vapɔʀø, øz/ *adj* diaphanous.
vaporisateur /vapɔʀizatœʀ/ *nm* spray.
vaporiser /vapɔʀize/ [1] *vtr* to spray.
vaquer /vake/ [1] *v+prep* **~ à ses occupations** to attend to one's business.
varappe /vaʀap/ *nf* rock-climbing.
varech /vaʀɛk/ *nm* kelp.
vareuse /vaʀøz/ *nf* **1** jersey; **2** (Mil) uniform jacket.
variable /vaʀjabl/ **I** *adj* **1** variable; **2** [*weather*] changeable; [*mood*] unpredictable.
II *nf* variable.
variante /vaʀjɑ̃t/ *nf* variant.
variation /vaʀjasjɔ̃/ *nf* variation; **connaître de fortes ~s** to fluctuate considerably.
varice /vaʀis/ *nf* varicose vein.
varicelle /vaʀisɛl/ *nf* chicken pox.
varié, **~e** /vaʀje/ *adj* **1** varied; **2** various.
varier /vaʀje/ [2] **I** *vtr* to vary; **pour ~ les plaisirs** just for a (pleasant) change.
II *vi* to vary; **l'inflation varie de 4% à 6%** inflation fluctuates between 4% and 6%.
variété /vaʀjete/ **I** *nf* **1** variety; **une grande ~ d'articles** a wide range of items; **2** (Bot) variety; **3** sort.
II variétés *nf pl* **spectacle de ~s** variety show; **les ~s françaises** French popular music.
variole /vaʀjɔl/ *nf* smallpox.
vas ▸ **aller**[1].
vase[1] /vɑz/ *nm* vase.
IDIOMS **c'est la goutte d'eau qui fait déborder le ~** it's the last straw.
vase[2] /vɑz/ *nf* silt, sludge.
vasectomie /vazɛktɔmi/ *nf* vasectomy.
vaseux, **-euse** /vazø, øz/ *adj* **1** muddy; **2**○ **je me sens plutôt ~** I'm not really with it○; **3**○ [*speech, explanation*] woolly.
vasistas /vazistas/ *nm inv* louvre[GB] window.
vasque /vask/ *nf* **1** (of fountain) basin; **2** bowl.
vassal, **~e**, *mpl* **-aux** /vasal, o/ *nm,f* vassal.
vaste /vast/ *adj* **1** [*estate, sector*] vast; [*market*] huge; **2** [*audience, choice*] large; **3** [*fraud*] massive; [*campaign*] extensive; [*movement, attack*] large-scale; [*work*] wide-ranging.
va-tout /vatu/ *nm inv* **jouer/tenter son ~** to stake/to risk everything.
vaudeville /vodvil/ *nm* light comedy; **tourner au ~** to turn into a farce.
vaudou /vodu/ *adj inv, nm* voodoo.
vaurien, **-ienne** /voʀjɛ̃, ɛn/ *nm,f* **1** rascal; **2** lout, yobbo○ (GB), hoodlum○.
vautour /votuʀ/ *nm* vulture.
vautrer: **se vautrer** /votʀe/ [1] *v refl* (+ *v être*) **1 se ~ sur** to sprawl on; **2 se ~ dans un fauteuil** to loll in an armchair.
va-vite: **à la va-vite** /alavavit/ *phr* in a rush.

veau, *pl* **~x** /vo/ *nm* **1** calf; **2** (Culin) veal; **3** calfskin.

vecteur /vɛktœʀ/ *nm* **1** vector; **2** (figurative) vehicle; **3** (of disease) carrier.

vécu, **~e** /veky/ I *pp* ▶ **vivre**.
II *pp adj* [*drama, story*] real-life.
III *nm* personal experiences.

vedette /vədɛt/ *nf* **1** star; **avoir la ~** to have top billing; **2** (Naut) launch.

végétal, **~e**, *mpl* **-aux** /veʒetal, o/ I *adj* vegetable.
II *nm* vegetable.

végétalien, **-ienne** /veʒetaljɛ̃, ɛn/ *adj, nm,f* vegan.

végétarien, **-ienne** /veʒetaʀjɛ̃, ɛn/ *adj, nm,f* vegetarian.

végétatif, **-ive** /veʒetatif, iv/ *adj* vegetative.

végétation /veʒetasjɔ̃/ I *nf* vegetation.
II **végétations** *nf pl* (Med) adenoids.

végéter /veʒete/ [14] *vi* [*person*] to vegetate; [*project*] to stagnate.

véhémence /veemɑ̃s/ *nf* vehemence.

véhicule /veikyl/ *nm* vehicle.
■ **~ utilitaire** commercial vehicle.

véhiculer /veikyle/ [1] *vtr* to carry [*people, goods, substance*]; **~ une image** to promote an image.

veille /vɛj/ *nf* **1 la ~** the day before; **la ~ au soir** the night before; **à la ~ de** on the eve of; **2 être en état de ~** to be awake; **3** vigil.

veillée /veje/ *nf* **1** evening; **à la ~** in the evening; **2** vigil; **~ funèbre** wake.

veiller /veje/ [1] I *vtr* to watch over [*ill person*]; to keep watch over [*dead person*].
II **veiller à** *v+prep* to look after [*health*]; **~ à ce que** to see to it that, to make sure that.
III **veiller sur** *v+prep* to watch over [*child*].
IV *vi* **1** to stay up; **2** to be on watch; **3** to be watchful.
IDIOMS **~ au grain** to be on one's guard.

veilleur /vɛjœʀ/ *nm,f* **~ de nuit** night watchman.

veilleuse /vɛjøz/ *nf* **1** night light; **2** pilot light; **3** side light (GB), parking light (US).

veinard○, **~e** /venaʀ, aʀd/ *nm,f* lucky devil○.

veine /vɛn/ *nf* **1** vein; **2** (in wood) grain; **3** (of coal) seam; **4** inspiration; **dans la même ~** in the same vein; **en ~ de générosité** in a generous mood; **5**○ luck; **il a de la ~** he's lucky.

veinure /venyʀ/ *nf* (in wood) grain; (in marble) veining.

vêler /vɛle/ [1] *vi* [*cow*] to calve.

velléité /vɛlleite/ *nf* **1** vague desire; **2** vague attempt.

vélo○ /velo/ *nm* bike; **faire du ~** to cycle.
■ **~ d'appartement** exercise bike; **~ tout terrain**, **VTT** mountain bike.

vélo-cross /velokʀɔs/ *nm inv* **1** cyclo-cross; **2** cyclo-cross bike.

vélomoteur /velomɔtœʀ/ *nm* moped.

velours /vəluʀ/ *nm inv* **1** velvet; **2** corduroy.
IDIOMS **une main de fer dans un gant de ~** an iron fist in a velvet glove; **faire patte de ~** to switch on the charm.

velouté, **~e** /vəlute/ I *adj* [*skin, voice*] velvety; [*wine*] smooth.
II *nm* **1** (Culin) **~ de champignons** cream of mushroom soup; **2** softness; smoothness.

velu, **~e** /vəly/ *adj* **1** hairy; **2** (Bot) villous.

vénal, **~e**, *mpl* **-aux** /venal, o/ *adj* [*person*] venal; [*behaviour*] mercenary.

vendange /vɑ̃dɑ̃ʒ/ *nf* grape harvest.

vendanger /vɑ̃dɑ̃ʒe/ [13] I *vtr* to harvest [*grapes*]; to pick the grapes from [*vine*].
II *vi* to harvest the grapes.

vendeur, **-euse** /vɑ̃dœʀ, øz/ *nm,f* **1** shop assistant; **2** salesman/saleswoman.
■ **~ ambulant** pedlar (GB), peddler (US); **~ de journaux** news vendor.

vendre /vɑ̃dʀ/ [6] I *vtr* **1** to sell; **~ à crédit** to sell on credit; **~ en gros** to wholesale; **~ au détail** to retail; **'à ~'** 'for sale'; **2** to betray [*person*]; to sell [*secrets*].
II **se vendre** *v refl* (+ *v être*) **1** to be sold; **2 se ~ bien** to sell well; **3** to sell oneself; **se ~ à l'ennemi** to sell out to the enemy.

vendredi /vɑ̃dʀədi/ *nm* Friday; **~ saint** Good Friday.

vendu, **~e** /vɑ̃dy/ I *pp* ▶ **vendre**.
II *pp adj* bribed.
III *nm,f* traitor.

vénéneux, **-euse** /venenø, øz/ *adj* poisonous.

vénérable /veneʀabl/ *adj* [*person*] venerable; [*tree, object*] ancient.

vénération /veneʀasjɔ̃/ *nf* veneration.

vénérer /veneʀe/ [14] *vtr* to venerate; to revere.

vénérien, **-ienne** /veneʀjɛ̃, ɛn/ *adj* venereal.

vengeance /vɑ̃ʒɑ̃s/ *nf* revenge.

venger /vɑ̃ʒe/ [13] I *vtr* to avenge.
II **se venger** *v refl* (+ *v être*) to get one's revenge; **se ~ sur qn/qch** to take it out on sb/sth.

vengeur, **vengeresse** /vɑ̃ʒœʀ, vɑ̃ʒʀɛs/ *adj* vengeful; avenging; vindictive.

véniel, **-ielle** /venjɛl/ *adj* [*sin*] venial.

venimeux, **-euse** /vənimø, øz/ *adj* venomous.

venin /vənɛ̃/ *nm* venom.

venir /vəniʀ/ [36] I *v aux* **1 venir de faire** to have just done; **elle vient de partir** she's just left; **'vient de paraître'** (of book) 'new!'; **2 ~ aggraver la situation** to make the situation worse; **3 le ballon est venu rouler sous mes pieds** the ball rolled up to my feet; **4 s'il venait à pleuvoir** if it should rain.
II *vi* (+ *v être*) **1** to come; **~ de** to come from; **~ après/avant** to come after/before; **allez, viens!** come on!; **viens voir** come and see; **j'en viens** I've just been there; **je viens de sa part** he/she sent me to see you; **faire ~ qn** to send for sb; to get sb to come; **faire ~ le médecin** to call the doctor; **ça ne m'est jamais venu à l'idée** it never crossed my mind; **dans les jours à ~** in the next few days; **2 en ~ à** to come to; **en ~ aux mains** to come to blows.

vent /vɑ̃/ *nm* **1** wind; **~ d'est** east wind; **~**

du large seaward wind; **grand ~** gale, strong wind; **il fait** or **il y a du ~** it's windy; **en plein ~** exposed to the wind; in the open; **passer en coup de ~** (figurative) to rush through; **faire du ~** (with fan) to create a breeze; **~ favorable**, **bon ~** favourable[GB] wind; **avoir le ~ en poupe** to sail or run before the wind; (figurative) to have the wind in one's sails; **coup de ~** fresh gale; **2 un ~ de liberté** a wind of freedom; **un ~ de folie** a wave of madness; **3** (euphemistic) wind.

IDIOMS **c'est du ~!** it's just hot air!; **du ~**○**!** get lost○!; **quel bon ~ vous amène?** to what do I owe the pleasure (of your visit)?; **être dans le ~** to be trendy; **avoir ~ de qch** to get wind of sth; **contre ~s et marées** come hell or high water; against all odds.

vente /vɑ̃t/ *nf* sale; **en ~ libre** (gen) freely available; [*medicines*] available over the counter; **mettre qch en ~** to put [sth] up for sale.

■ **~ par correspondance** mail order selling; **~ au détail** retailing; **~ aux enchères** auction (sale); **~ en gros** wholesaling.

ventilateur /vɑ̃tilatœʀ/ *nm* fan; ventilator.

ventilation /vɑ̃tilasjɔ̃/ *nf* ventilation (system).

ventiler /vɑ̃tile/ [1] *vtr* **1** to ventilate; **2** to break down [*expenses, profits*]; **3** to assign [*staff*]; to allocate [*tasks, equipment*].

ventouse /vɑ̃tuz/ *nf* **1** suction pad (GB), suction cup (US); **faire ~** to stick; **2** plunger; **3** (Med) cupping glass.

ventral, **~e**, *mpl* **-aux** /vɑ̃tʀal, o/ *adj* ventral; **parachute ~** lap-pack parachute.

ventre /vɑ̃tʀ/ *nm* **1** stomach; **avoir mal au ~** to have stomach ache; **ça me donne mal au ~ de voir ça**○ (figurative) it makes me sick to see that sort of thing; **2** (of animal) (under)belly; **3 ne rien avoir dans le ~**○ to have no guts○; **avoir la peur au ~** to feel sick with fear; **4** (of pot, boat, plane) belly.

IDIOMS **courir ~ à terre** to run flat out.

ventricule /vɑ̃tʀikyl/ *nm* ventricle.

ventriloque /vɑ̃tʀilɔk/ *nmf* ventriloquist.

venu, **~e**[1] /vəny/ **I** *pp* ▶ **venir**.

II *pp adj* **bien ~** apt; **mal ~** badly timed; **il serait mal ~ de le leur dire** it wouldn't be a good idea to tell them.

III *nm,f* **nouveau ~** newcomer.

venue[2] /vəny/ *nf* visit; **~ au monde** birth.

vêpres /vɛpʀ/ *nf pl* vespers.

ver /vɛʀ/ *nm* worm; woodworm; maggot.

■ **~ à soie** silkworm; **~ solitaire** tapeworm; **~ de terre** earthworm.

IDIOMS **tirer les ~s du nez à qn**○ to worm information out of sb.

véranda /veʀɑ̃da/ *nf* veranda.

verbal, **~e**, *mpl* **-aux** /vɛʀbal, o/ *adj* verbal; verb.

verbaliser /vɛʀbalize/ [1] *vi* to record an offence[GB].

verbe /vɛʀb/ *nm* **1** verb; **2** language; **avoir le ~ haut** to be arrogant in one's speech.

verdâtre /vɛʀdɑtʀ/ *adj* greenish.

verdeur /vɛʀdœʀ/ *nf* sprightliness.

verdict /vɛʀdikt/ *nm* verdict.

verdir /vɛʀdiʀ/ [3] *vi* **1** (gen) to turn green; [*copper*] to tarnish; **2** to turn pale.

verdoyant, **~e** /vɛʀdwajɑ̃, ɑ̃t/ *adj* green.

verdure /vɛʀdyʀ/ *nf* **1** greenery; **2** green vegetables.

véreux, **-euse** /veʀø, øz/ *adj* **1** [*fruit*] worm-eaten; **2** [*politician, lawyer*] bent○, crooked.

verge /vɛʀʒ/ *nf* **1** penis; **2** switch, birch.

verger /vɛʀʒe/ *nm* orchard.

verglacé, **~e** /vɛʀglase/ *adj* icy.

verglas /vɛʀgla/ *nm inv* black ice.

vergogne: **sans vergogne** /sɑ̃vɛʀgɔɲ/ *phr* shamelessly.

véridique /veʀidik/ *adj* true.

vérification /veʀifikasjɔ̃/ *nf* (on equipment, identity) check; (of alibi, fact) verification.

vérifier /veʀifje/ [2] **I** *vtr* to check; to verify.

II se vérifier *v refl* (+ *v être*) [*hypothesis, theory*] to be borne out.

véritable /veʀitabl/ *adj* real; true; genuine.

véritablement /veʀitabləmɑ̃/ *adv* really.

vérité /veʀite/ *nf* **1** truth; **l'épreuve de ~** the acid test; **à la ~** to tell the truth; **2 énoncer des ~s premières** to state the obvious; **3** sincerity.

verlan /vɛʀlɑ̃/ *nm*: *French slang formed by inverting the syllables.*

vermeil, **-eille** /vɛʀmɛj/ **I** *adj* **1** bright red; **2** [*wine*] ruby.

II *nm* vermeil.

vermicelle /vɛʀmisɛl/ *nm* **du ~**, **des ~s** vermicelli.

vermifuge /vɛʀmifyʒ/ *nm* wormer.

vermillon /vɛʀmijɔ̃/ *adj inv* bright red.

vermine /vɛʀmin/ *nf* **1** vermin; **2** (figurative) scum.

vermoulu, **~e** /vɛʀmuly/ *adj* worm-eaten.

verni, **~e** /vɛʀni/ **I** *pp* ▶ **vernir**.

II *pp adj* varnished; patent-leather; glazed.

III○ *adj* lucky; **il n'est pas ~** he's unlucky.

vernir /vɛʀniʀ/ [3] **I** *vtr* to varnish; to glaze.

II se vernir *v refl* (+ *v être*) **se ~ les ongles** to paint one's nails.

vernis /vɛʀni/ *nm inv* **1** varnish; glaze; **2** (figurative) veneer; **si on gratte le ~, on voit que**... if you scratch the surface, you'll see that...

■ **~ à ongles** nail varnish (GB) or polish.

vernissage /vɛʀnisaʒ/ *nm* **1** (of art exhibition) preview, private view; **2** varnishing; glazing.

verre /vɛʀ/ *nm* **1** glass; **de** or **en ~** glass; **un ~ à eau/vin** a water/wine glass; **~s et couverts** glassware and cutlery; **lever son ~ à la santé de qn** to raise one's glass to sb; **2** glass, glassful; **un ~ d'eau/de vin** a glass of water/wine; **3** drink; **4** lens; **~ grossissant** magnifying glass.

■ **~ de contact** contact lens; **~ à pied** stemmed glass.

verrerie /vɛʀʀi/ *nf* **1** glassmaking; **2** glassworks, glass factory.

verrière /vɛʀjɛʀ/ *nf* **1** glass roof; **2** glass wall.
verroterie /vɛʀɔtʀi/ *nf* glass jewellery (GB) or jewelry (US).
verrou /vɛʀu/ *nm* bolt.
IDIOMS **être sous les ~s** to be behind bars.
verrouiller /vɛʀuje/ [1] *vtr* to bolt [*window, door*]; to lock [*car door, gun*].
verrue /vɛʀy/ *nf* wart; **~ plantaire** verruca.
vers[1] /vɛʀ/ *prep*

■ **Note** When *vers* is part of an expression such as *se tourner vers*, *tendre vers* etc, you will find the translation at the entries ***tourner***, ***tendre***[1] **III** etc.
– See below for other uses of *vers*.

1 toward(s); **se déplacer de la gauche ~ la droite** to move from left to right; **2** near, around; about; toward(s); **~ cinq heures** at about five o'clock; **~ le soir** toward(s) evening.
vers[2] /vɛʀ/ *nm inv* line (of verse).
versant /vɛʀsɑ̃/ *nm* side.
versatile /vɛʀsatil/ *adj* unpredictable, volatile.
verse: **à verse** /avɛʀs/ *phr* **il pleut à ~** it's pouring down.
Verseau /vɛʀso/ *pr nm* Aquarius.
versement /vɛʀsəmɑ̃/ *nm* **1** payment; **~ comptant** cash payment; **2** instalment[GB]; **3** deposit; **faire un ~ sur son compte** to pay money into one's account.
verser /vɛʀse/ [1] **I** *vtr* **1** to pour; **2** to pay [*sum, pension*]; **3** to shed [*tear, blood*]; **4 ~ une pièce à un dossier** to add a document to a file.
II *vi* **1** to overturn; **2** to lapse; **3** [*jug*] to pour.
verset /vɛʀsɛ/ *nm* (in Bible, Koran) verse.
version /vɛʀsjɔ̃/ *nf* **1** translation (*into one's own language*); **2** version.
■ **~ originale**, **vo** (of film) original version.
verso /vɛʀso/ *nm* back; **voir au ~** see over(-leaf).
vert, **~e** /vɛʀ, vɛʀt/ **I** *adj* **1** green; **être ~ de peur** to be white with fear; **2** [*fruit*] green, unripe; [*wine*] immature; **3** sprightly; **4** (*before n*) [*reprimand*] sharp, stiff.
II *nm* green.
III verts *nm pl* **les ~s** the Greens.
IDIOMS **avoir la main ~e** to have green fingers (GB) or a green thumb (US).
vert-de-gris /vɛʀdəgʀi/ **I** *adj inv* blue-green.
II *nm inv* verdigris.
vertébral, **~e**, *mpl* **-aux** /vɛʀtebʀal, o/ *adj* vertebral.
vertèbre /vɛʀtɛbʀ/ *nf* vertebra.
vertébré, /vɛʀtebʀe/ *nm* vertebrate.
vertement /vɛʀtəmɑ̃/ *adv* sharply.
vertical, **~e**[1], *mpl* **-aux** /vɛʀtikal, o/ *adj* vertical; upright.
verticale[2] /vɛʀtikal/ *nf* vertical.
verticalement /vɛʀtikalmɑ̃/ *adv* **1** vertically; **2** (in crossword) down.
vertige /vɛʀtiʒ/ *nm* **1** dizziness; vertigo; **avoir le ~** to suffer from vertigo; to feel dizzy; **2 avoir des ~s** to have dizzy or giddy spells.
vertigineux, **-euse** /vɛʀtiʒinø, øz/ *adj* dizzy, giddy; breathtaking; staggering.
vertu /vɛʀty/ **I** *nf* **1** virtue; **de petite ~** of easy virtue; **2** (of plant, remedy) property.
II en vertu de *phr* by virtue of [*law*]; in accordance with [*agreement*].
vertueux, **-euse** /vɛʀtɥø, øz/ *adj* virtuous.
verve /vɛʀv/ *nf* eloquence.
verveine /vɛʀvɛn/ *nf* verbena (tea).
vésicule /vezikyl/ *nf* vesicle; **~ biliaire** gall bladder.
vessie /vesi/ *nf* bladder.
IDIOMS **prendre des ~s pour des lanternes**○ to think the moon is made of green cheese.
veste /vɛst/ *nf* jacket; **~ de survêtement** tracksuit top.
IDIOMS **retourner sa ~**○ to change sides.
vestiaire /vɛstjɛʀ/ *nm* (in gym) changing room (GB), locker room; (in theatre) cloakroom; **laisser sa fierté au ~** to forget one's pride.
vestibule /vɛstibyl/ *nm* hall; foyer (GB), lobby.
vestige /vɛstiʒ/ *nm* **1** relic; **des ~s archéologiques** archaeological remains; **2** vestige.
vestimentaire /vɛstimɑ̃tɛʀ/ *adj* **tenue ~** way of dressing; **mode ~** fashion.
veston /vɛstɔ̃/ *nm* (man's) jacket.
vêtement /vɛtmɑ̃/ *nm* piece of clothing; **des ~s** clothes; **'~s pour hommes'** 'menswear'; **~s de sport** sportswear.
vétéran /veteʀɑ̃/ *nm* veteran.
vétérinaire /veteʀinɛʀ/ **I** *adj* veterinary.
II *nmf* veterinary surgeon (GB), veterinarian (US).
vétille /vetij/ *nf* trifle.
vêtir /vɛtiʀ/ [33] **I** *vtr* to dress [*person, doll*].
II se vêtir *v refl* (+ *v être*) to dress (oneself).
veto /veto/ *nm* veto; **mettre** or **opposer son ~ à qch** to veto sth.
vétuste /vetyst/ *adj* **1** dilapidated; **2** outdated.
veuf, **veuve** /vœf, vœv/ **I** *adj* widowed.
II *nm,f* widower/widow.
veule /vøl/ *adj* weak, spineless.
veuvage /vœvaʒ/ *nm* widowhood.
veuve *adj, nf* ▶ **veuf**.
vexant, **~e** /vɛksɑ̃, ɑ̃t/ *adj* **1** hurtful; **2** tiresome, vexing.
vexation /vɛksasjɔ̃/ *nf* humiliation.
vexer /vɛkse/ [1] **I** *vtr* **1** to offend; **2** to annoy.
II se vexer *v refl* (+ *v être*) to take offence[GB].
via /vja/ *prep* via; through.
viabilité /vjabilite/ *nf* **1** viability; **2** (of road) suitability for vehicles.
viable /vjabl/ *adj* **1** viable; **2** [*project*] feasible; [*situation*] bearable, tolerable.
viaduc /vjadyk/ *nm* viaduct.
viager /vjaʒe/ *nm* life annuity.
viande /vjɑ̃d/ *nf* meat; **~ de bœuf/mouton** beef/mutton.
■ **~ des Grisons** dried beef.
vibrant, **~e** /vibʀɑ̃, ɑ̃t/ *adj* **1** vibrating; **2**

[*voice*] resonant; [*speech*] vibrant; [*praise*] glowing; [*plea*] impassioned; [*crowd*] excited.

vibration /vibʀasjɔ̃/ *nf* vibration; **traitement par ~s** vibromassage.

vibrer /vibʀe/ [1] *vi* **1** to vibrate; **2** [*voice*] to quiver; [*heart*] to thrill.

vibromasseur /vibʀomasœʀ/ *nm* vibrator.

vicaire /vikɛʀ/ *nm* curate.

vice /vis/ *nm* **1** vice; **vivre dans le ~** to lead a dissolute life; **2** vice; **mon ~, c'est le tabac** my vice is smoking; **3** fault, defect; **~ de fabrication** manufacturing defect.

vice-président, **~e**, *mpl* **~s** /vispʀezidɑ̃, ɑ̃t/ *nm,f* (of state) vice-president; (of committee, company) vice-chair(man), vice-president (US).

vice-roi, *pl* **~s** /visʀwa/ *nm* viceroy.

vice(-)versa /visvɛʀsa/ *adv* vice versa.

vichy /viʃi/ *nm* **1** gingham; **2** vichy water.

vicier /visje/ [2] *vtr* to pollute [*air*]; to contaminate [*blood*].

vicieux, **-ieuse** /visjø, øz/ *adj* **1** lecherous; **il faut être ~ pour aimer ça** you've got to be perverted to like that; **2** [*person*] sly; [*attack*] well-disguised; [*question*] trick; [*argument*] deceitful; **3 un cercle ~** a vicious circle.

vicomte /vikɔ̃t/ *nm* viscount.

vicomtesse /vikɔ̃tɛs/ *nf* viscountess.

victime /viktim/ *nf* **1** victim, casualty; **être ~ d'un infarctus** to suffer a heart attack; **2** sacrificial victim.

victoire /viktwaʀ/ *nf* (gen) victory; (Sport) win.

victorien, **-ienne** /viktɔʀjɛ̃, ɛn/ *adj* Victorian.

victorieux, **-ieuse** /viktɔʀjø, øz/ *adj* [*army*] victorious; [*athlete*] winning; [*smile*] of victory.

victuailles /viktɥɑj/ *nf pl* provisions, victuals.

vidange /vidɑ̃ʒ/ *nf* **1** emptying; **2** oil change; **huile de ~** waste oil; **3** (of washing machine) waste pipe.

vidanger /vidɑ̃ʒe/ [13] **I** *vtr* **1** to empty, to drain [*tank, ditch*]; **2** to drain off [*liquid*].

II *vi* [*washing machine*] to empty.

vide /vid/ **I** *adj* **1** empty; [*tape, page*] blank; [*flat*] vacant; **tu l'as loué ~ ou meublé?** are you renting it unfurnished or furnished?; **2** [*mind, day*] empty; [*look*] vacant.

II *nm* **1** space; **sauter** or **se jeter dans le ~** to jump; (figurative) to leap into the unknown; **parler dans le ~** to talk to oneself; to talk at random; **2** vacuum; void; **emballé sous ~** vacuum-packed; **faire le ~ autour de soi** to drive everybody away; **j'ai besoin de faire le ~ dans ma tête** I need to forget about everything; **3** emptiness; **le ~ de l'existence** the emptiness of life; **4** gap; **combler un** or **le ~** to fill in a gap; (figurative) to fill a gap.

III à vide *phr* **1** empty; **2** with no result.

vidéo /video/ **I** *adj inv* video.

II *nf* video; **tourner un film en ~** to make a video.

vidéocassette /videokasɛt/ *nf* videotape.

vidéoclip /videoklip/ *nm* (music) video.

vidéoclub /videoklœb/ *nm* video store.

vide-ordures /vidɔʀdyʀ/ *nm inv* rubbish (GB) or garbage (US) chute.

vidéothèque /videɔtɛk/ *nf* **1** video library; **2** video collection.

vide-poches /vidpɔʃ/ *nm inv* tidy.

vider /vide/ [1] **I** *vtr* **1** to empty; to drain [*tank, pond*]; **2** to empty [sth] (out) [*water, rubbish*]; **3**° to throw [sb] out°; **4** (Culin) to gut [*fish*]; to draw [*game*]; **5**° to wear [sb] out; to drain.

II se vider *v refl* (+ *v être*) to empty; **en été, Paris se vide de ses habitants** in the summer all Parisians leave town.

videur°, **-euse** /vidœʀ, øz/ *nm,f* bouncer.

vie /vi/ *nf* (gen) life; **être en ~** to be alive; **il y a laissé sa ~** that was how he lost his life; **donner la ~ à qn** to bring sb into the world; **la ~ est chère** the cost of living is high; **mode de ~** lifestyle; **notre ~ de couple** our relationship; **donner de la ~ à une fête** to liven up a party; **sans ~** lifeless.

■ **~ active** working life.

IDIOMS **c'est la belle ~!** this is the life!; **avoir la ~ dure** [*prejudices*] to be ingrained; **mener la ~ dure à qn** to make life hard for sb; **faire la ~**° to have a wild time; to live it up°; **à la ~, à la mort!** till death us do part!

vieil ▶ **vieux**.

vieillard, **~e** /vjɛjaʀ, aʀd/ *nm,f* old man/woman; **les ~s** old people.

vieille ▶ **vieux**.

vieillesse /vjɛjɛs/ *nf* (of person) old age; (of building, tree) great age.

vieilli, **~e** /vjɛji/ **I** *pp* ▶ **vieillir**.

II *pp adj* **1** old-looking; **2** [*equipment*] outdated; [*expression*] dated; **3 vin ~ en fût** wine matured in the cask.

vieillir /vjɛjiʀ/ [3] **I** *vtr* **1** [*hairstyle*] to make [sb] look older; **2** [*illness*] to age [*person*].

II *vi* **1** to get older; **je vieillis** I'm getting old; **j'ai vieilli** I'm older; **notre population vieillit** we have an ageing population; **2** [*body, building*] to show signs of age; [*person*] to age; **il vieillit mal** he's losing his looks; **3** [*wine*] to mature; **4** [*work*] to become outdated.

III se vieillir *v refl* (+ *v être*) **1** to make oneself look older; **2** to make oneself out to be older.

vieillissement /vjɛjismɑ̃/ *nm* ageing.

viennois, **~e** /vjɛnwa, az/ *adj* **1** (in Austria) Viennese; (in France) of Vienne; **2** (Culin) [*chocolate, coffee*] Viennese.

viennoiserie /vjɛnwazʀi/ *nf* Viennese pastry.

vierge /vjɛʀʒ/ **I** *adj* **1** virgin; **2** blank; unused; clean; **3** [*wool*] new; [*olive oil*] virgin.

II *nf* virgin.

Vierge /vjɛʀʒ/ **I** *nf* **1 la (Sainte) ~** the (Blessed) Virgin; **2** madonna.

II *pr nf* Virgo.

vieux, (**vieil** *before vowel or mute h*), **vieille**, *mpl* **vieux** /vjø, vjɛj/ **I** *adj* old; **être ~ avant l'âge** to be old before one's time; **une institution vieille de 100 ans** a 100-year-old institution; **il est très vieille France** he's a gentleman of the old school.

II *nm,f* **1** old person; **un petit ~** a little old man; **les ~** old people; **mes ~**○ my parents; **2**○ **mon pauvre ~** you poor old thing.
III *adv* **vivre ~** to live to a ripe old age; **il s'habille ~** he dresses like an old man.
IV *nm* **prendre un coup de ~** to age; **faire du neuf avec du ~** to revamp things.
■ **vieille fille** old maid; **~ beau** ageing Romeo; **~ garçon** old bachelor; **~ jeu** old-fashioned; **~ rose** dusty pink.
IDIOMS **~ comme le monde**, **~ comme Hérode** as old as the hills.

vif, **vive**[1] /vif, viv/ I *adj* **1** [*colour, light*] bright; **2** [*person*] lively, vivacious; [*imagination*] vivid; **3** [*protests*] heated; [*opposition*] fierce; **sa réaction a été un peu vive** he/she reacted rather strongly; **4** [*contrast*] sharp; [*interest, desire*] keen; [*pain*] acute; [*success*] notable; **5** [*pace, movement*] brisk; **à vive allure** [*drive*] at high speed; **avoir l'esprit ~** to be very quick; **6** [*cold, wind*] biting; [*edge*] sharp; **air ~** fresh air; **cuire à feu ~** to cook over a high heat; **7 de vive voix** in person.
II *nm* **à ~** [*flesh*] bared; [*knee*] raw; [*wire*] exposed; **avoir les nerfs à ~** to be on edge; **la plaie est à ~** it's an open wound; **piquer qn au ~** to cut sb to the quick.

vigie /viʒi/ *nf* (Naut) **1** lookout; **2** crow's nest.

vigilance /viʒilɑ̃s/ *nf* vigilance; **échapper à la ~ de qn** to escape sb's attention.

vigilant, **~e** /viʒilɑ̃, ɑ̃t/ *adj* [*person*] vigilant; [*eye*] watchful.

vigile /viʒil/ *nm* **1** night watchman; **2** security guard.

vigne /viɲ/ *nf* **1** vine; **2** vineyard.
■ **~ vierge** Virginia creeper.

vigneron, **-onne** /viɲ(ə)ʀɔ̃, ɔn/ *nm,f* wine-grower.

vignette /viɲɛt/ *nf* **1** *detachable label on medicines for reimbursement by social security*; **2** tax disc (GB); **3** label; **4** vignette.

vignoble /viɲɔbl/ *nm* vineyard.

vigoureux, **-euse** /viguʀø, øz/ *adj* **1** [*person, handshake*] vigorous; [*athlete, body*] strong; [*plant*] sturdy; **2** [*resistance, style*] vigorous.

vigueur /vigœʀ/ I *nf* **1** vigour[GB]; **2** strength.
II **en vigueur** *phr* [*law, system*] in force; [*regime, conditions*] current; **entrer en ~** to come into force.

VIH /veiaʃ/ *nm* (*abbr* = **virus immunodéficitaire humain**) HIV.

viking /vikiŋ/ *adj* Viking.

vil, **~e** /vil/ *adj* [*person*] base; [*deed*] vile, base.

vilain, **~e** /vilɛ̃, ɛn/ I *adj* **1** ugly; **2**○ [*germ, creature*] nasty; [*child*] naughty; **3** [*fault*] bad; [*word*] dirty.
II *nm,f* naughty boy/girl.

villa /villa/ *nf* **1** ≈ detached house; **2** villa.

village /vilaʒ/ *nm* village.

villageois, **~e** /vilaʒwa, az/ *nm,f* villager.

ville /vil/ *nf* **1** town; city; **la vieille ~** the old town; **aller en ~** to go into town; **2** town or city council.
■ **~ d'eau(x)** spa town; **~ franche** free city; **~ nouvelle** new town.

villégiature /vileʒjatyʀ/ *nf* holiday (GB), vacation (US).

vin /vɛ̃/ *nm* wine; **~ blanc/rouge** white/red wine; **~ de pays** or **de terroir** *quality wine produced in a specific region*; **couper son ~** to add water to one's wine.
■ **~ d'appellation d'origine contrôlée** appellation contrôlée wine (*with a guarantee of origin*); **~ cuit** *wine which has undergone heating during maturation*; **~ d'honneur** reception.
IDIOMS **avoir le ~ gai/triste** to get happy/maudlin after one has had a few drinks; **mettre de l'eau dans son ~** to mellow; **quand le ~ est tiré, il faut le boire** (Proverb) once you have started something, you have to see it through.

vinaigre /vinɛgʀ/ *nm* vinegar.
IDIOMS **tourner au ~** to turn sour.

vinaigrette /vinɛgʀɛt/ *nf* French dressing.

vindicatif, **-ive** /vɛ̃dikatif, iv/ *adj* vindictive.

vingt /vɛ̃, vɛ̃t/ I *adj inv* twenty.
II *pron* twenty; (Sch) **j'ai eu ~ sur ~** ≈ I got full marks (GB) or full credit (US).
III *nm inv* twenty.

vingtaine /vɛ̃tɛn/ *nf* about twenty.

vingtième /vɛ̃tjɛm/ *adj* twentieth.

vinicole /vinikɔl/ *adj* [*sector, region*] wine-producing; [*cellar, trade*] wine.

vinyle /vinil/ *nm* vinyl.

viol /vjɔl/ *nm* **1** rape; **2** (of law, temple) violation.

violacé, **~e** /vjɔlase/ *adj* purplish.

violation /vjɔlasjɔ̃/ *nf* **1** (of law, territory) violation; **2** (of agreement, confidentiality) breach.
■ **~ de domicile** forcible entry (*into a person's home*).

violemment /vjɔlamɑ̃/ *adv* violently.

violence /vjɔlɑ̃s/ *nf* **1** violence; **~ verbale** verbal abuse; **par la ~** through violence; with violence; **se faire ~** to force oneself; **2** act of violence; **~s à l'enfant** child abuse.

violent, **~e** /vjɔlɑ̃, ɑ̃t/ *adj* violent; [*colour*] harsh.

violenter /vjɔlɑ̃te/ [1] *vtr* to assault sexually.

violer /vjɔle/ [1] *vtr* **1** to rape; **se faire ~** to be raped; **2** to desecrate [*tomb*]; **~ l'intimité de qn** to invade sb's privacy; **3** to infringe [*law*].

violet, **-ette**[1] /vjɔlɛ, ɛt/ I *adj* purple.
II *nm* purple.

violette[2] /vjɔlɛt/ *nf* violet.

violeur /vjɔlœʀ/ *nm* rapist.

violon /vjɔlɔ̃/ *nm* violin.
■ **~ d'Ingres** hobby.
IDIOMS **accorder ses ~s** to agree on which line to take.

violoncelle /vjɔlɔ̃sɛl/ *nm* cello.

violoncelliste /vjɔlɔ̃sɛlist/ *nmf* cellist.

violoniste /vjɔlɔnist/ *nmf* violinist.

vipère /vipɛʀ/ *nf* viper; **avoir une langue de ~** to have a wicked tongue.

virage /viʀaʒ/ *nm* **1** bend; **2** change of direction; **3** (in skiing) turn.

virago /viʀago/ *nf* virago.
viral, **~e**, *mpl* **-aux** /viʀal, o/ *adj* viral.
virement /viʀmɑ̃/ *nm* transfer; **faire un ~** to make a transfer.
■ **~ automatique** standing order.
virer /viʀe/ [1] **I** *vtr* **1** to transfer [*money*]; **2**○ to fire [*employee*]; **se faire ~** to get fired.
II virer à *v+prep* **~ au rouge** to turn red.
III *vi* **1** [*vehicle*] to turn; **~ de bord** (figurative) to do a U-turn, to do a flip-flop (US); **2** to change colour[GB]; [*colour*] to change.
virevolter /viʀvɔlte/ [1] *vi* to twirl.
virginité /viʀʒinite/ *nf* virginity.
virgule /viʀgyl/ *nf* **1** comma; **à la ~ près** down to the last comma; **2** (decimal) point.
viril, **~e** /viʀil/ *adj* manly, virile; masculine
virilité /viʀilite/ *nf* virility.
virtuel, **-elle** /viʀtɥɛl/ *adj* **1** potential; **2** (in science) virtual.
virtuose /viʀtɥoz/ **I** *adj* virtuoso.
II *nmf* **1** (Mus) virtuoso; **2** master.
virtuosité /viʀtɥozite/ *nf* **1** (Mus) virtuosity; **2** brilliance.
virulence /viʀylɑ̃s/ *nf* virulence.
virulent, **~e** /viʀylɑ̃, ɑ̃t/ *adj* virulent.
virus /viʀys/ *nm inv* **1** (Med, Comput) virus; **2** bug○, craze.
vis /vis/ *nf inv* screw.
IDIOMS **serrer la ~ à qn** to tighten the screws on sb.
visa /viza/ *nm* visa.
■ **~ de censure** (censor's) certificate.
visage /vizaʒ/ *nm* face; **à ~ découvert** openly.
vis-à-vis /vizavi/ **I** *nm inv* **1 maison sans ~** house with an open outlook; **2 assis en ~** sitting opposite each other; **3** (Sport) opponent; **4** meeting, encounter.
II vis-à-vis de *phr* **1 ~ de qch** in relation to sth; **~ de qn** toward(s) sb; **2** beside.
viscéral, **~e**, *mpl* **-aux** /viseʀal, o/ *adj* **1 réaction ~e** gut reaction; **2** visceral.
viscère /visɛʀ/ *nm* **1** internal organ; **2 les ~s** viscera.
viscosité /viskozite/ *nf* viscosity.
visée /vize/ *nf* **1** aim; **2** design; **3** sighting; aiming.
viser /vize/ [1] **I** *vtr* **1** to aim at [*target*]; to aim for [*heart, middle*]; **2** to aim for [*job, results*]; to aim at [*market*]; **3** [*law, campaign*] to be aimed at; [*remark, allusion*] to be meant for.
II viser à *v+prep* **~ à qch/à faire** to aim at sth/to do.
III *vi* to aim; **~ (trop) haut** (figurative) to set one's sights (too) high.
viseur /vizœʀ/ *nm* **1** viewfinder; **2** (of gun) sight.
visibilité /vizibilite/ *nf* visibility.
visible /vizibl/ *adj* **1** visible; **2** obvious.
visière /vizjɛʀ/ *nf* **1** (of cap) peak; **2** eyeshade.
vision /vizjɔ̃/ *nf* **1** eyesight, vision; **2** view; **~ globale** global view; **3** sight; **4 avoir des ~s** to see things, to have visions.
visionnaire /vizjɔnɛʀ/ *adj*, *nmf* visionary.
visionner /vizjɔne/ [1] *vtr* to view [*film, slides*].
visite /vizit/ *nf* visit; call; **rendre ~ à qn** to pay sb a call; **avoir de la ~** to have visitors.
■ **~ de contrôle** (Med) follow-up visit; **~ médicale** medical (examination).
visiter /vizite/ [1] *vtr* **1** to visit [*museum, town*]; **2** to view [*apartment*]; **3** to visit [*patient*].
visiteur, **-euse** /vizitœʀ, øz/ *nm,f* visitor.
vison /vizɔ̃/ *nm* **1** mink; **2** mink (coat).
visqueux, **-euse** /viskø, øz/ *adj* **1** viscous, viscid; **2** sticky, gooey○.
visser /vise/ [1] *vtr* **1** to screw [sth] on; **2 être vissé sur sa chaise** to be glued to one's chair.
visualiser /vizɥalize/ [1] *vtr* to visualize.
visuel, **-elle** /vizɥɛl/ *adj* visual.
vital, **~e**, *mpl* **-aux** /vital, o/ *adj* vital.
vitalité /vitalite/ *nf* vitality; energy.
vitamine /vitamin/ *nf* vitamin.
vitaminé, **~e** /vitamine/ *adj* with added vitamins.
vite /vit/ *adv* **1** quickly; **~!** quick!; **ça ira ~** it'll soon be over; it won't take long; **on a pris un verre ~ fait**○ we had a quick drink; **2 j'ai parlé trop ~** I spoke too hastily; I spoke too soon; **c'est ~ dit!** that's easy to say!
vitesse /vitɛs/ *nf* **1** speed; **partir à toute ~** to rush away; **à deux ~s** [*system*] two-tier; **faire de la ~** to drive fast; **prendre qn de ~** to outstrip sb; **en ~** quickly; in a rush; **2** gear.
IDIOMS **à la ~ grand V, en quatrième ~** at top speed.
viticole /vitikɔl/ *adj* wine; wine-producing.
viticulture /vitikyltyʀ/ *nf* wine-growing.
vitrage /vitʀaʒ/ *nm* windows; **double ~** double glazing.
vitrail, *pl* **-aux** /vitʀaj, o/ *nm* stained glass window.
vitre /vitʀ/ *nf* **1** windowpane; **2** pane of glass; **3** (of car, train) window.
vitrier /vitʀije/ *nm* glazier.
vitrifier /vitʀifje/ [2] *vtr* **1** to varnish [*floor*]; **2** (Tech) to vitrify.
vitrine /vitʀin/ *nf* **1** (shop or store) window; **faire les ~s** to go window-shopping; **2** display cabinet (GB), curio cabinet (US); **3** (show)case.
vitriol /vitʀijɔl/ *nm* vitriol.
vivable /vivabl/ *adj* bearable; **ce n'est pas ~ ici** it is impossible to live here.
vivace /vivas/ *adj* enduring.
vivacité /vivasite/ *nf* **1** (of person) vivacity; (of feeling) intensity; **2** (of intelligence) keenness; (of reaction, movement) swiftness; **avec ~** [*move, react*] swiftly; **3** (of memory, colour, impression) vividness; (in eyes) spark; (of light) brightness.
vivant, **~e** /vivɑ̃, ɑ̃t/ **I** *adj* **1** living; **il est ~** he is alive; **un homard ~** a live lobster; **2** [*person, style*] lively; [*description*] vivid; **3 être encore ~** [*custom*] to be still alive.
II *nm* **1** living being; **les ~s** the living; **2 du ~ de mon père** while my father was alive.
vive[2] /viv/ **I** *adj f* ▶ **vif I**.
II *nf* weever.

vivement /vivmɑ̃/ *adv* [*encourage, react*] strongly; [*contrast, speak*] sharply; [*move, feel, regret*] deeply; [*rise*] swiftly.

vivier /vivje/ *nm* **1** fishpond; **2** fish-tank.

vivifier /vivifje/ [2] *vtr* to invigorate.

vivisection /viviseksjɔ̃/ *nf* vivisection.

vivoter /vivɔte/ [1] *vi* to struggle along.

vivre /vivʀ/ [63] **I** *vtr* **1** to live through [*era*]; to go through [*difficult times*]; to experience [*love*]; **2** to cope with [*divorce, failure, change*].

II *vi* **1** to live; **~ vieux** to live to a great age; **vive la révolution!** long live the revolution!; **~ à la campagne** to live in the country; **être facile à ~** to be easy to live with; to be easy to get on with; **~ avec son temps** to move with the times; **se laisser ~** to take things easy; **apprendre à ~ à qn**○ to teach sb some manners○; **~ aux dépens de qn** to live off sb; **2** [*fashion*] to last; **avoir vécu** [*person*] to have seen a great deal of life; (humorous) [*object*] to have had its day; **3** [*town*] to be full of life.

IDIOMS **qui vivra verra** what will be will be.

vivres /vivʀ/ *nm pl* **1** food, supplies; **2 couper les ~ à qn** to cut off sb's allowance.

vizir /viziʀ/ *nm* vizier; **le Grand ~** the Grand Vizier.

vo /veo/ *nf*: *abbr* ▶ **version**.

vocabulaire /vɔkabylɛʀ/ *nm* vocabulary.

vocal, **~e**, *mpl* **-aux** /vɔkal, o/ *adj* vocal.

vocalise /vɔkaliz/ *nf* singing exercise.

vocation /vɔkasjɔ̃/ *nf* **1** vocation, calling; **2** purpose; **région à ~ agricole** farming area.

vociférer /vɔsifeʀe/ [14] *vtr, vi* to shout.

vodka /vɔdka/ *nf* vodka.

vœu, *pl* **~x** /vø/ *nm* **1** wish; **faire un ~** to make a wish; **2** New Year's greetings; **adresser ses ~x à qn** to wish sb a happy New Year; **3** vow; **~x de pauvreté** vows of poverty.

vogue /vɔg/ *nf* fashion, vogue.

voguer /vɔge/ [1] *vi* [*ship*] to sail.

IDIOMS **et vogue la galère!** come what may!

voici /vwasi/ **I** *prep* here is, this is; here are, these are; **~ mes clés** here are my keys; **~ un mois** a month ago; **~ bientôt deux mois qu'elle travaille chez nous** she's been working with us for nearly two months.

II voici que *phr* all of a sudden.

voie /vwa/ *nf* **1** way; **montrer la ~ à qn** to show sb the way; **ouvrir la ~ à** to pave the way for; **être sur la bonne ~** [*person*] to be on the right track; **les travaux sont en bonne ~** the work is progressing; **par ~ de conséquence** consequently; **espèce en ~ de disparition** endangered species; **2** channels; **par des ~ détournées** by roundabout means; **3** lane; **route à trois ~s** three-lane road; **4** (of railway) track; **le train entre en gare ~ 2** the train is arriving at platform 2; **5 par ~ buccale** or **orale** orally.

■ **~ aérienne** air route; **~ ferrée** railway track (GB), railroad track (US); **~ de garage** siding; **mettre qn sur une ~ de garage** (figurative) to shunt sb onto the sidelines; **Voie lactée** Milky Way; **~ privée** private road; **~ publique** public highway; **~ rapide** expressway; **~ sans issue** dead end; no through road; **~s respiratoires** respiratory tract.

voilà /vwala/ **I** *prep* here is, this is; here are, these are; **voici mon fils et ~ ma fille** this is my son and this is my daughter; **me ~!** I'm coming!; here I am!; **le ~ qui se remet à rire!** there he goes again laughing!; **~ tout** that's all; **~ un mois** a month ago.

II en voilà *phr* **tu veux des fraises? en ~** you'd like some strawberries? here you are.

III voilà que○ *phr* **et ~ qu'une voiture arrive** and the next thing you know, a car pulls up.

IV *excl* **~! j'arrive!** (I'm) coming!; **(et) ~! il remet ça!** there he goes again!

IDIOMS **il a de l'argent, en veux-tu en ~!** he has as much money as he could wish for!

voilage /vwalaʒ/ *nm* net curtain (GB), sheer curtain (US).

voile[1] /vwal/ *nm* **1** veil; **lever le ~ sur qch** to bring sth out in the open; **2** voile.

■ **~ islamique** yashmak; **~ du palais** soft palate, velum.

voile[2] /vwal/ *nf* (Naut) **1** sail; **faire ~ vers** to sail toward(s); **2** sailing.

voilé, **~e** /vwale/ *adj* **1** [*person, object*] veiled; **2** [*sun, sky*] hazy; [*eyes*] misty; [*voice*] with a catch in it; [*photo*] fogged; **3** [*threat, criticism*] veiled; **4** [*wheel*] buckled.

voiler /vwale/ [1] **I** *vtr* **1** to veil [*landscape, sun*]; [*person, fact*] to conceal [*event, fact*]; **2** to buckle [*wheel*]; **3** to mist [*eyes*]; **4** to cover [*face, nudity*]; to veil [*statue*].

II se voiler *v refl* (+ *v être*) **1** [*sky*] to cloud over; [*sun*] to become hazy; [*eyes*] to become misty; **2** [*person*] to wear a veil.

IDIOMS **se ~ la face** to look the other way.

voilette /vwalɛt/ *nf* veil.

voilier /vwalje/ *nm* **1** sailing boat (GB), sailboat (US); **2** yacht, sailing ship.

voir /vwaʀ/ [46] **I** *vtr* **1** to see; **faire ~ qch à qn** to show sb sth; **laisser ~ qch** to show sth; **~ si/pourquoi** to find out or to see if/why; **on l'a vue entrer** she was seen going in; **je le vois** or **verrais bien enseignant** I can just see him as a teacher; **aller ~ qn** to go to see sb; **le film est à ~** the film is worth seeing; **~ du pays** to see the world; **on voit bien qu'elle n'a jamais travaillé!** you can tell she's never worked!; **on n'a jamais vu ça!** it's unheard of!; **2 avoir quelque chose à ~ avec** to have something to do with.

II voir à *v+prep* to see to; **voyez à ce que tout soit prêt** see to it that everything is ready.

III *vi* **1 ~, y ~** to be able to see; **~ double** to see double; **2 ~ clair dans qch** to have a clear understanding of sth; **il faut ~** we'll have to see.

IV se voir *v refl* (+ *v être*) **1** to see oneself; **2** [*stain*] to show; **la tour se voit de loin** the tower can be seen from far away; **ça ne s'est jamais vu!** it's unheard of!; **3 se ~ obligé** or **dans l'obligation de faire** to find oneself forced to do; **4** to see each other; **ils ne peuvent pas se ~ (en peinture**○) they can't stand each other.

IDIOMS **ne pas ~ plus loin que le bout de son nez** to see no further than the end of one's nose; **j'en ai vu d'autres** I've seen worse; **en faire ~ à qn** to give sb a hard time.

voire /vwaʀ/ *adv* or even, not to say.

voirie /vwaʀi/ *nf* road, rail and waterways network.

voisin, **~e** /vwazɛ̃, in/ **I** *adj* **1** [*house, town*] neighbouring[GB]; [*lake, forest*] nearby; [*room*] next; **les régions ~es de la Manche** the regions bordering the English Channel; **2** [*date, result*] close (**de** to); **3** [*feelings, ideas*] similar; [*species*] (closely) related.

II *nm,f* neighbour[GB]; **ma ~e de palier** the woman across the landing; **mon ~ de table** the man next to me at table.

voisinage /vwazinaʒ/ *nm* **1** neighbourhood[GB]; **entretenir des rapports de bon ~** to maintain neighbourly[GB] relations; **2** proximity; **vivre dans le ~ d'une usine** to live close to a factory.

voiture /vwatyʀ/ *nf* **1** car, automobile (US); **2** carriage (GB), car (US); **en ~!** all aboard!

■ **~ à bras** hand-drawn cart; **~ de tourisme** saloon (car) (GB), sedan (US).

voiture-balai, *pl* **voitures-balais** /vwatyʀbalɛ/ *nf* support vehicle.

voix /vwa/ *nf inv* **1** (gen) voice; **élever la ~** to raise one's voice; **à ~ haute** out loud; **rester sans ~** to remain speechless; **à portée de ~** within earshot; **faire entendre sa ~** (figurative) to make oneself heard; **2** vote; **3 à la ~ active/passive** in the active/passive voice.

vol /vɔl/ **I** *nm* **1** (of bird, plane) flight; **prendre son ~** to fly off; **à ~ d'oiseau** as the crow flies; **il y a trois heures de ~** it's a three-hour flight; **de ~** [*conditions*] flying; [*plan*] flight; **2 un ~ de** a flock of [*birds*]; a cloud of [*insects*]; **de haut ~** (figurative) [*diplomat*] high-flying; [*burglar*] big-time; **3** theft, robbery.

II au vol *phr* **attraper une balle au ~** to catch a ball in mid-air; **saisir des bribes de conversation au ~** to catch snatches of conversation.

■ **~ à l'arraché** bag snatching; **~ avec effraction** burglary; **~ à l'étalage** shoplifting; **~ à la tire** pickpocketing.

volage /vɔlaʒ/ *adj* fickle.

volaille /vɔlɑj/ *nf* **1** poultry; **2** fowl.

volant, **~e** /vɔlɑ̃, ɑ̃t/ **I** *adj* flying.

II *nm* **1** steering wheel; **être au ~** to be at the wheel; **un brusque coup de ~** a sharp turn of the wheel; **un as du ~** an ace driver; **la sécurité au ~** safe driving; **2** flounce; **à ~s** flounced; **3** shuttlecock.

volatil, **~e**[1] /vɔlatil/ *adj* volatile.

volatile[2] /vɔlatil/ *nm* **1** fowl; **2** bird.

volatiliser: **se volatiliser** /vɔlatilize/ [1] *v refl* (+ *v être*) **1** to volatilize; **2** (humorous) to vanish into thin air.

volcan /vɔlkɑ̃/ *nm* volcano.

volcanique /vɔlkanik/ *adj* **1** [*region*] volcanic; **2** [*temperament*] explosive.

volée /vɔle/ **I** *nf* **1** (of birds) flock, flight; **2** (of blows, stones) volley; **donner une ~ à qn** to give sb a good thrashing; **3** flight (of stairs); **4** (Sport) volley.

II à toute volée *phr* **les cloches sonnaient à toute ~** the bells were pealing out.

voler /vɔle/ [1] **I** *vtr* **1 ~ qch à qn** to steal sth from sb; **tu ne l'as pas volé!** (figurative) it serves you right!; **2 ~ qn** to rob sb; **~ le client** to rip the customer off○.

II *vi* **1** to fly; **~ au secours de qn** to rush to sb's aid; **2 ~ en éclats** [*window*] to shatter.

volet /vɔlɛ/ *nm* **1** shutter; **2** (of leaflet, brochure) (folding) section; (of plan) part, component.

voleter /vɔlte/ [20] *vi* to flutter.

voleur, **-euse** /vɔlœʀ, øz/ **I** *adj* **être ~** [*cat*] to be a thief; [*shopkeeper*] to be dishonest.

II *nm,f* thief; swindler.

IDIOMS **se sauver comme un ~** to slip away like a thief in the night.

volière /vɔljɛʀ/ *nf* aviary.

volley(-ball) /vɔlɛ(bol)/ *nm* volleyball.

volontaire /vɔlɔ̃tɛʀ/ **I** *adj* **1** [*work*] voluntary; [*omission*] deliberate; **2** [*person, air*] determined; [*child*] self-willed.

II *nmf* volunteer; **se porter ~** to volunteer.

volonté /vɔlɔ̃te/ **I** *nf* **1** will; **bonne ~** goodwill; **aller contre la ~ de qn** to go against sb's wishes; **manifester la ~ de faire** to show one's willingness to do; **2** willpower; **avoir une ~ de fer** to have an iron will.

II à volonté *phr* **1 'vin/pain à ~'** 'unlimited wine/bread'; **2** [*modifiable*] as required.

volontiers /vɔlɔ̃tje/ *adv* **1** gladly; **j'irais ~ à Paris** I'd love to go to Paris; **'tu me le prêtes?'—'~'** 'will you lend it to me?'—'certainly'; **2** [*admit*] readily.

volt /vɔlt/ *nm* volt.

voltage /vɔltaʒ/ *nm* voltage.

volte-face /vɔlt(ə)fas/ *nf inv* **1 faire ~** to turn around; **2** (figurative) volte-face, U-turn.

voltige /vɔltiʒ/ *nf* **(haute) ~** acrobatics.

voltiger /vɔltiʒe/ [13] *vi* **1** to flutter; **2** to go flying.

volume /vɔlym/ *nm* (gen) volume; **donner du ~ à ses cheveux** to give one's hair body; **~ sonore** sound level.

volumineux, **-euse** /vɔlyminø, øz/ *adj* voluminous, bulky.

volupté /vɔlypte/ *nf* voluptuousness.

voluptueux, **-euse** /vɔlyptɥø, øz/ *adj* voluptuous.

volute /vɔlyt/ *nf* (on pillar, column) volute; (of violin) scroll; (of smoke) curl.

vomir /vɔmiʀ/ [3] **I** *vtr* to bring up [*meal*]; to vomit [*bile*].

II *vi* [*person*] to be sick.

vomissement /vɔmismɑ̃/ *nm* vomiting.

vorace /vɔʀas/ *adj* voracious.

voracité /vɔʀasite/ *nf* voracity, voraciousness.

vos ▶ **votre**.

votant, **~e** /vɔtɑ̃, ɑ̃t/ *nm,f* voter.

vote /vɔt/ *nm* **1** voting; (of law) passing; **2** vote.

voter /vɔte/ [1] **I** *vtr* to vote [*budget*]; to pass [*parliamentary bill*]; to vote for [*amnesty*].
II *vi* to vote; **~ blanc** to cast a blank vote.

votre, *pl* **vos** /vɔtʀ, vo/ *det* your; **c'est pour ~ bien** it's for your own good; **à ~ arrivée** when you arrive; when you arrived.

vôtre /votʀ/ **I** *det* **mes biens sont ~s** all I have is yours; **'amicalement ~'** 'best wishes'.
II le vôtre, **la vôtre**, **les vôtres** *pron* yours; **à la ~**○! cheers!

vouer /vwe/ [1] **I** *vtr* **1 ~ une reconnaissance éternelle à qn** to be eternally grateful to sb; **~ un véritable culte à qn** to worship sb; **2** to doom; **film voué à l'échec** film doomed to failure; **3 ~ sa vie à qch** to devote one's life to sth.
II se vouer *v refl* (+ *v être*) **1 se ~ à qch** to devote oneself to sth; **2 ils se vouent une haine féroce** they hate each other intensely.

vouloir[1] /vulwaʀ/ [48] **I** *vtr* **1** (gen) to want; **qu'est-ce qu'ils nous veulent**○ **encore?** what do they want now?; **il en veut 15000 francs** he wants 15,000 francs for it; **comme le veut la loi** as the law demands; **que veux-tu boire?** what do you want to drink?; what would you like to drink?; **je voudrais un kilo de poires** I'd like a kilo of pears; **je comprends très bien que tu ne veuilles pas répondre** I can quite understand that you may not wish to reply; **sans le ~** [*knock over, reveal*] by accident; [*annoy*] without meaning to; **que tu le veuilles ou non** whether you like it or not; **elle fait ce qu'elle veut de son mari** she twists her husband around her little finger; **je ne vous veux aucun mal** I don't wish you any harm; **tu ne voudrais pas me faire croire que** you're not trying to tell me that; **tu voudrais que je leur fasse confiance?** do you expect me to trust them?; **comment veux-tu que je le sache?** how should I know?; **j'aurais voulu t'y voir**○! I'd like to have seen you in the same position!; **tu l'auras voulu!** it'll be all your own fault!; **2 voulez-vous fermer la fenêtre?** would you mind closing the window?; **voudriez-vous avoir l'obligeance de faire** (formal) would you be so kind as to do; **veuillez patienter** (on phone) please hold the line; **si vous voulez bien me suivre** if you'd like to follow me; **veux-tu te taire!** will you be quiet!; **ils ont bien voulu nous prêter leur voiture** they were kind enough to lend us their car; **je veux bien te croire** I'm quite prepared to believe you; **je veux bien qu'il soit malade mais** I know he's ill, but; **'ce n'est pas cher'—'si on veut!'** 'it's not expensive'—'or so you say!'; **3 ~ dire** to mean; **qu'est-ce que ça veut dire?** what does that mean?; what's all this about?; **4 comme le veut la tradition** as tradition has it.
II en vouloir *v+prep* **1 en ~ à qn** to bear a grudge against sb; **je leur en veux de m'avoir trompé** I hold it against them for not being honest with me; **ne m'en veux pas** please forgive me; **2 en ~ à qch** to be after sth.
III se vouloir *v refl* (+ *v être*) **1** [*person*] to like to think of oneself as; [*book, method*] to be meant to be; **2 s'en ~** to be cross with oneself; **s'en ~ de** to regret; **je m'en serais voulu de ne pas vous avoir prévenu** I would never have forgiven myself if I hadn't warned you.
IDIOMS **~ c'est pouvoir** (Proverb) where there's a will there's a way.

vouloir[2] /vulwaʀ/ *nm* will.

voulu, **~e** /vuly/ *adj* **1** required; **on n'obtient jamais les renseignements ~s** you never get the information you want; **en temps ~** in time; **au moment ~** at the right time; **2** [*omission*] deliberate; [*meeting*] planned.

vous /vu/ *pron* **1** you; **je sais que ce n'est pas ~** I know it wasn't you; **c'est ~ qui avez gagné** you have won; **~ aussi, ~ avez l'air malade** you don't look very well either; **ce sont des amis à ~?** are they friends of yours?; **c'est à ~** it's yours, it belongs to you; it's your turn; **2** yourself; yourselves; **allez ~ laver les mains** go and wash your hands; **pensez à ~ deux** think of yourselves.

vous-même, *pl* **vous-mêmes** /vumɛm/ *pron* **1** yourself; **vous me l'avez dit ~** you told me yourself; **2 allez-y ~s** go yourselves; **vous verrez par ~s** you'll see for yourselves.

voûte /vut/ *nf* (gen) vault; (of porch) archway; (of tunnel) roof; (figurative) (of leaves, branches) arch.
■ **la ~ céleste** the sky; the heavens; **~ du palais** roof of the mouth; **~ plantaire** arch of the foot.

voûté, **~e** /vute/ *adj* **1** [*cellar*] vaulted; **2** [*back*] bent; **il est ~** he has a stoop.

voûter /vute/ [1] **I** *vtr* **1** (in architecture) to vault [*room*]; **2** to give [sb] a stoop.
II se voûter *v refl* (+ *v être*) [*person*] to develop a stoop; [*back*] to become bent.

vouvoiement /vuvwamɑ̃/ *nm* using the *'vous'* or polite form.

vouvoyer /vuvwaje/ [23] *vtr* to address [sb] using the 'vous' form.

voyage /vwajaʒ/ *nm* trip; journey; **partir en ~** to go on a trip; **le ~ aller** the outward journey; **aimer les ~s** to love travelling[GB].
■ **~ d'études** study trip; **~ de noces** honeymoon; **~ organisé** package tour.

voyager /vwajaʒe/ [13] *vi* to travel.

voyageur, **-euse** /vwajaʒœʀ, øz/ *nm,f* **1** passenger; **'réservé aux ~s munis de billets'** 'ticketholders only'; **2** traveller[GB].
■ **~ de commerce** travelling[GB] salesman.

voyance /vwajɑ̃s/ *nf* clairvoyance.

voyant, **~e** /vwajɑ̃, ɑ̃t/ **I** *adj* [*colour*] loud.
II *nm,f* **1** clairvoyant; **2** sighted person.
III *nm* light; **~ d'huile** (Aut) oil warning light.

voyelle /vwajɛl/ *nf* vowel.

voyeurisme /vwajœʀism/ *nm* voyeurism.

voyou /vwaju/ *nm* lout.

vrac: **en vrac** /ɑ̃vʀak/ *phr* **1** loose, unpackaged; **2** in bulk; **3 jeter ses idées en ~ sur le papier** to jot down one's ideas as they come.

vrai, **~e** /vʀɛ/ **I** *adj* true; real, genuine; **il n'y**

a rien de ~ dans ses déclarations there's no truth in his statements; **la ~e raison de mon départ** the real reason for my leaving; **des ~s jumeaux** identical twins; **plus ~ que nature** [*picture, scene*] larger than life.

II *nm* truth; **il y a du ~ dans ce que tu dis** there's some truth in what you say; **être dans le ~** to be in the right; **pour de ~** for real; **à ~ dire, à dire ~** to tell the truth.

III *adv* **faire ~** to look real; **son discours sonne ~** his speech has the ring of truth.

vraiment /vʀɛmɑ̃/ *adv* really.

vraisemblable /vʀɛsɑ̃blabl/ *adj* [*excuse*] convincing; [*scenario*] plausible; [*hypothesis*] likely; **il est ~ que** it is likely that.

vraisemblablement /vʀɛsɑ̃blabləmɑ̃/ *adv* probably.

vraisemblance /vʀɛsɑ̃blɑ̃s/ *nf* (of hypothesis) likelihood; (of situation, explanation) plausibility.

vrille /vʀij/ *nf* **1** spiral; (of airplane) tailspin; **descendre en ~** [*airplane*] to go into a spiral dive; **2** (Bot) tendril; **3** (Tech) gimlet.

vrombir /vʀɔ̃biʀ/ [3] *vi* [*engine*] to roar; **faire ~ un moteur** to rev up an engine.

VRP /veɛʀpe/ *nm* (*abbr* = **voyageur représentant placier**) representative, rep○.

VTT /vetete/ ▶ **vélo**.

vu, **~e**[1] /vy/ I *adj* **1 être bien/mal ~** [*person*] to be/not to be well thought of; **c'est bien ~ de faire cela** it's good form to do that; **ce serait plutôt mal ~** it wouldn't go down well; **2 bien ~!** good point!; **c'est tout ~** my mind is made up; **3 ~?** got it○?

II *prep* in view of.

III **vu que** *phr* in view of the fact that.

vue[2] /vy/ *nf* **1** sight; **avoir une bonne ~** to have good eyesight; **don de double ~** gift of second sight; **perdre qn de ~** (figurative) to lose touch with sb; **à ~** [*shoot*] on sight; [*fly plane*] without instruments; [*payable*] on demand; **2** view; **à ma ~, il s'enfuit** he took to his heels when he saw me; **avoir ~ sur le lac** to look out onto the lake; **3** (opinion) view; **~s** views; **~ optimiste des choses** optimistic view of things; **4 avoir des ~s sur qn/qch** to have designs on sb/sth; **5 en ~** in sight; [*person*] prominent; **mettre une photo bien en ~** to display a photo prominently; **c'est quelqu'un de très en ~** he's/she's very much in the public eye; **j'ai un terrain en ~** I have a plot of land in mind; I've got my eye on a piece of land; **en ~ de faire** with a view to doing.

■ **~ d'ensemble** overall view.

IDIOMS **à ~ d'œil** or **de nez**○ at a rough guess; **vouloir en mettre plein la ~ à qn** to try to dazzle sb.

vulgaire /vylgɛʀ/ *adj* **1** vulgar, coarse; **2** common, ordinary; **c'est un ~ employé** he's just a lowly employee.

vulgairement /vylgɛʀmɑ̃/ *adv* **1** [*speak*] coarsely; **2** commonly.

vulgarisation /vylgaʀizasjɔ̃/ *nf* popularization; **revue de ~ scientifique** scientific review for the general public.

vulgariser /vylgaʀize/ [1] I *vtr* to popularize; to bring [sth] into general use.

II **se vulgariser** *v refl* (+ *v être*) [*technology*] to become generally accessible; [*expression*] to come into general use.

vulgarité /vylgaʀite/ *nf* vulgarity, coarseness.

vulnérable /vylneʀabl/ *adj* vulnerable.

vulve /vylv/ *nf* vulva.

w, **W** /dubləve/ *nm inv* **1** (letter) w, W; **2 W** (*written abbr* = **watt**) **60 W** 60 W.

wagon /vagɔ̃/ *nm* **1** wagon (GB), car (US); (for passengers) carriage (GB), car (US); **2** wagonload (GB), carload (US).
■ **~ à bestiaux** cattle truck (GB), cattle car (US); **~ de marchandises** goods wagon (GB), freight car (US).

wagon-bar, *pl* **wagons-bars** /vagɔ̃baʀ/ *nm* buffet car.

wagon-citerne, *pl* **wagons-citernes** /vagɔ̃sitɛʀn/ *nm* tanker.

wagon-lit, *pl* **wagons-lits** /vagɔ̃li/ *nm* sleeper, sleeping car (US).

wagonnet /vagɔnɛ/ *nm* trolley (GB), cart (US).

wagon-restaurant, *pl* **wagons-restaurants** /vagɔ̃ʀɛstɔʀɑ̃/ *nm* restaurant car (GB), dining car (US).

wallon, **-onne** /walɔ̃, ɔn/ **I** *adj* Walloon.
II *nm* (language) Walloon.

waters○ /watɛʀ/ *nm pl* toilets.

WC /(dublə)vese/ *nm pl* toilet; **aller aux ~** to go to the toilet.

x, **X** /iks/ *nm inv* (letter) x, X; **il y a x temps que c'est fini** it's been over for ages; **porter plainte contre X** (Law) to take an action against person or persons unknown; **film classé X** X-rated movie.

xénophobe /gzenɔfɔb/ **I** *adj* xenophobic. **II** *nmf* xenophobe.

xénophobie /gzenɔfɔbi/ *nf* xenophobia.

xérès /kseʀɛs/ *nm inv* sherry.

xylophène® /ksilɔfɛn/ *nm* wood preservative.

y[1], **Y** /igʀɛk/ *nm inv* (letter) y, Y.

y[2] /i/ *pron* **1** it; **tu t'~ attendais?** were you expecting it?; **il n'~ connaît rien** he knows nothing about it; **j'~ pense parfois** I sometimes think about it; **elle n'~ peut rien** there's nothing she can do about it; **j'~ viens** I'm coming to that; **rien n'~ fait** it's no use; **je n'~ comprends rien** I don't understand a thing; **tu ~ as gagné** you got the best deal; **plus difficile qu'il n'~ paraît** harder than it seems; **2** there; **j'~ ai mangé une fois** I ate there once; **n'~ va pas** don't go; **3 il ~ a** there is/are; **du vin? il n'~ en a plus** wine? there's none left; **il n'~ a qu'à téléphoner** just phone.

IDIOMS **~ mettre du sien** to work at it.

ya(c)k /'jak/ *nm* yak.

yaourt /'jauʀ(t)/ *nm* yoghurt.

yaourtière /'jauʀtjɛʀ/ *nf* yoghurt-maker.

yéménite /'jemenit/ *adj* Yemeni.

yeux *nm pl* ▶ **œil**.

yoga /'jɔga/ *nm* yoga.

yole /'jɔl/ *nf* skiff.

yougoslave /'jugɔslav/ *adj* Yugoslavian.

youyou /'juju/ *nm* **1** ululation; **2** dinghy.

Zz

z, **Z** /zɛd/ *nm inv* z, Z.
zaïrois, **~e** /zairwa, az/ *adj* Zairean.
zambien, **-ienne** /zɑ̃bjɛ̃, ɛn/ *adj* Zambian.
zapper /zape/ [1] *vi* to flick through the TV channels.
zèbre /zɛbʀ/ *nm* **1** zebra; **2**○ (figurative) bloke○ (GB), guy○.
zébré, **~e** /zebʀe/ *adj* [*fabric*] zebra-striped; **~ de** streaked with.
zébrure /zebʀyʀ/ *nf* stripe.
zébu /zeby/ *nm* zebu.
zèle /zɛl/ *nm* zeal, enthusiasm; **faire du ~** or **de l'excès de ~** to be overzealous.
zélé, **~e** /zele/ *adj* enthusiastic, zealous.
zénith /zenit/ *nm* zenith; **à son ~** [*career*] at its height.
zéro /zeʀo/ **I** *adj* **~ heure** midnight, twenty-four hundred (hours); **il sera exactement ~ heure vingt minutes dix secondes** the time will be twelve twenty and ten seconds; **j'ai eu ~ faute dans ma dictée** I didn't make a single mistake in my dictation; **niveau/croissance ~** zero level/growth.
II *nm* **1** zero, nought (GB); **avoir un ~ en latin** to get zero or nought in Latin; **remettre un compteur à ~** to reset a counter to zero; **avoir le moral à ~** (figurative) to be down in the dumps○; **c'est beau à regarder mais question goût c'est ~**○ it's nice to look at, but no marks for flavour[GB]; **2** (in sport) (gen) nil; (in tennis) love; **trois (buts) à ~** three nil.
■ **~ de conduite** (Sch) bad mark for behaviour[GB].
IDIOMS **partir de ~** to start from scratch; **tout reprendre à ~** to start all over again.
zeste /zɛst/ *nm* **un ~ de citron** the zest of a lemon.
zézayer /zezeje/ [21] *vi* to lisp.
zibeline /ziblin/ *nf* sable.
zigoto○ /zigɔto/ *nm* guy○; **faire le ~** to clown around.
zigue○ /zig/ *nm* guy○.
zigzag /zigzag/ *nm* zigzag; **route en ~** winding road; **faire des ~s** to zigzag (**parmi** through); **partir en ~** to zigzag off.
zinc /zɛ̃g/ *nm* **1** zinc; **toiture de** or **en ~** tin roofing; **2**○ counter, bar.
zingueur /zɛ̃gœʀ/ *nm* roofer.
zinzin○ /zɛ̃zɛ̃/ **I** *adj inv* cracked○.
II *nm* thingamajig○.
zip /zip/ *nm* zip (GB), zipper (US).
zippé, **~e** /zipe/ *adj* zip-up.
zizanie /zizani/ *nf* ill-feeling, discord.
zizi○ /zizi, *nm* willy○ (GB), penis.
zodiac® /zɔdjak/ *nm* inflatable dinghy.
zodiaque /zɔdjak/ *nm* zodiac.
zona /zona/ *nm* shingles.
zonage /zonaʒ/ *nm* zoning.
zonard○, **~e** /zonaʀ, aʀd/ *nm,f* dropout○.
zone /zon/ *nf* **1** zone, area; **~ interdite** off-limits area; (on signpost) no entry; **2 la ~**○ the slum belt; **de seconde ~** second-rate.
■ **~ d'activités** business park; **~ artisanale** small industrial estate (GB) or park; **~ bleue** restricted parking zone; **~ industrielle** industrial estate (GB) or park.
zoner○ /zone/ [1] *vi* to hang about○.
zoo /zo/ *nm* zoo.
zoologie /zɔɔlɔʒi/ *nf* zoology.
zoom /zum/ *nm* **1** zoom lens; **2** zoom.
zouave /zwav/ *nm* **1**○ clown, comedian; **faire le ~** to clown around○; **2** (soldier) zouave.
zoulou, **~e** /zulu/ *adj* Zulu.
zozoter /zɔzɔte/ [1] *vi* to lisp.
zut○ /zyt/ *excl* damn○!

Windsor, le 19 septembre 1996

Cher Philippe,

Mon professeur de français, mademoiselle Jones, m'a donné ton adresse. Elle m'a dit que tu cherchais un correspondant anglais. Moi, j'aimerais bien avoir un copain français.

Je m'appelle Trevor. J'ai douze ans et j'habite à Windsor. Je fais beaucoup de sport. C'est le rugby que je préfère. Avec mes copains, on joue presque tous les samedis. A part ça, j'aime aller au cinéma et lire, surtout des romans de science-fiction.

J'espère que tu vas m'écrire bientôt pour me parler de toi et me dire ce que tu aimes faire. Voici mon adresse:

45 Kingston Road
Windsor SL4 5HU

A bientôt

Writing to a new penfriend

Nantucket, le 17 septembre 1995

Chers Monsieur et Madame Robin

Je voudrais vous remercier pour les vacances merveilleuses que j'ai passées dans votre propriété de Saint-Malo. Je n'oublierai jamais les repas où il y avait tant de bonnes choses, le bridge et les parties de pêche avec René. J'ai tant de bons souvenirs que je n'arrête pas de parler de la France à tous mes amis. J'espère que j'aurai très bientôt l'occasion de vous revoir tous.

Je vous embrasse affectueusement.

Doug

Thanking for hospitality

Enquiry to the tourist office

M. et Mme François Bolard
10, rue Eugène Delacroix
06200 Nice

Nice, le 24 mars 1995

Syndicat d'Initiative
de St-Gervais
74170 Saint-Gervais-les-Bains

Monsieur,

Mon mari et moi envisageons de passer nos vacances d'été à Saint-Gervais. Nous vous serions reconnaissants de bien vouloir nous faire parvenir toute la documentation dont vous disposez sur les hôtels, la station thermale ainsi que sur les activités proposées aux touristes en saison. Vous trouverez ci-joint une enveloppe timbrée pour la réponse.

Dans l'attente de vous lire, je vous prie d'agréer, Monsieur, l'expression de mes sentiments distingués.

E. Bolard

Booking a gîte

Claire Fauvel
36 avenue du Général de Gaulle
78400 Chatou
(1) 36 42 78 76

Madame Poterre
Route du Champ blanc
56630 Vernon

Le 4 février 1996

Madame,

J'ai eu votre adresse par l'intermédiaire du syndicat d'initiative de Vannes qui m'a envoyé une liste des gîtes de la région.

Mon mari et moi recherchons, pour les vacances de Pâques, une maison calme et avec un grand jardin. Nous avons trois enfants et nous souhaiterions prendre nos vacances du 1er au 8 avril. Auriez-vous l'amabilité de me faire savoir si votre gîte est disponible à ces dates? Pourriez-vous également me confirmer le tarif annoncé par le syndicat d'initiative, à savoir 1 800 francs la semaine?

Je vous remercie d'avance et vous prie d'agréer, Madame, mes salutations distinguées.

C. Fauvel

Booking a hotel room

Bourguignon, le 22 mars 1995

Madame Solange Vernon
125 bis, Route Nationale
18340 Levet

Maison de Famille Le Repos
Chemin des Lys
06100 Grasse

Monsieur le Directeur,

J'ai bien reçu le dépliant de votre maison, ainsi que les tarifs que je vous avais demandés, et je vous en remercie.

Je souhaite réserver une chambre calme avec bain et wc, en pension complète pour la période du 27 avril au 12 mai. Je vous adresse ci-joint un chèque de 600 francs d'arrhes.

Je vous en souhaite bonne réception, et vous remerciant par avance je vous prie de croire, Monsieur le Directeur, en mes sentiments les meilleurs.

S. Vernon

P.J.: un chèque postal de 600 francs

Cancelling a hotel booking

Bourg, le 15 décembre 1995

Fréderic Brunet
5, rue du Marché
73700 Bourg-Saint-Maurice

Hôtel des Voyageurs
9, cours Gambetta
91949 Les Ulis CEDEX

Monsieur,

Je suis au regret de devoir annuler ma réservation d'une chambre pour deux personnes pour la nuit du 24 au 25 décembre, que j'avais effectuée par téléphone le 18 novembre dernier, à mon nom.

Je vous remercie de votre compréhension et vous prie d'agréer, Monsieur, l'expression de mes sentiments distingués.

F. Brunet

Chers amis,
Juste un petit bonjour de Palma où nous passons de très agréables vacances. Il fait un temps splendide et les plages sont superbes. Merci encore d'avoir accepté de garder Félix pendant notre absence. Nous vous revaudrons cela à l'occasion.
A très bientôt!
Emmanuel et Pierline

Monsieur et Madame Pierret
78 rue du Chemin vert
54000 Nancy
FRANCE

Soleil, pistes enneigées et soirées raclette au coin du feu: on ne pouvait rêver mieux.
Notre séjour s'annonce très bien et nous espérons en profiter au maximum.
Bons baisers de Courchevel et à bientôt.

Frédéric et Josiane

Monsieur et Madame Gendre
56 rue Jean Jaurès
75018 Paris

le 17 mars 1995

Monsieur et Madame Yves Laplace
Villa Mon Rêve
56, rue du Bois
59600 Maubeuge
tél.: 27.09.66.46

Monsieur Berthin
Entreprise Mahieux et Cie
Zone Industrielle
Bloc Q7 T23
59600 Maubeuge

Monsieur,

Nous souhaiterions faire construire à l'adresse ci-dessus une piscine chauffée et éclairée qui puisse être utilisable dès l'été prochain. Pourrions-nous convenir d'un rendez-vous ici, afin que vous puissiez vous rendre compte sur place des caractéristiques de notre propriété?

Nous vous demanderons d'apporter une documentation variée afin que nous puissions faire notre choix. Nous souhaiterions avoir un devis précis au moment des vacances de Pâques.

Nous vous adressons, Monsieur, nos salutations distinguées.

Laplace

Y. Laplace

Asking for an estimate

Club des Sportifs
12, allée de la Plage
14800 Deauville
Tél.: 35 03 12 76

ENTREPRISE Roux
Route de Normandie
14001 Caen cedex

Deauville, le 15 mai 1995

Monsieur,

Nous avons le plaisir de vous faire savoir que le devis que vous nous avez adressé pour la construction d'un tennis "Clairdal" nous convient parfaitement.

Nous souhaitons que les travaux commencent le plus tôt possible afin que tout soit terminé, y compris l'aménagement floral, pour le 18 juin prochain, les tournois commençant la semaine suivante.

Nous vous prions de croire, Monsieur, en nos sentiments les meilleurs.

Lecarré

Monsieur Lecarré
Gérant

Asking for work to be undertaken

Applying for a job as an au pair

Sally Kendall
5, Tackley Place
Reading RG2 6RN
England

Reading, le 17 avril 1995

Madame, Monsieur,

Vos coordonnées m'ont été communiquées par l'agence "Au Pair International", qui m'a demandé de vous écrire directement. Je suis en effet intéressée par un emploi de jeune fille au pair pour une période de six mois au moins, à partir de l'automne prochain.

J'adore les enfants, quel que soit leur âge, et j'ai une grande expérience du baby-sitting, comme vous pourrez le constater au vu du CV ci-joint.

Dans l'espoir d'une réponse favorable, je vous prie d'agréer, Madame, Monsieur, l'expression de mes respectueuses salutations.

S. Kendall

P.J.: un CV

Replying to a job ad

Jean-Luc Morin
12, Avenue d'Angleterre
62107 Calais

Monsieur le Directeur
Arts et Design Gadgeteria
27, rue Victor Hugo
59001 Lille

Calais, le 14 février 1995

Monsieur,

L'annonce parue en page 2 de l'édition du 12 février du Courrier Picard concernant un poste de concepteur m'a vivement intéressé. Mon contrat à durée déterminée chez Solo and Co. touche à sa fin. Je pense posséder l'expérience et les qualifications requises pour vous donner toute satisfaction dans ce poste, comme vous pourrez le constater au vu de mon CV. Je me tiens à votre disposition pour un entretien éventuel, et vous prie d'agréer, Monsieur, l'expression de mes sentiments distingués.

J.L. Morin

P.J.: un CV avec photo

Immobilier

Locations

Part. à part. ag. s'abst., loue F3, 2ch., sdb, ds immeuble centre Villeurbanne, esp. verts, cave, t.b. état, 2 500F CC, 78 92 13 22 p. 249 hor. bur.

Loue ch. meublée, 18 m² dans tb villa, av. douche, poss. cuis., prise tél. et TV, entrée séparée, lib. imméd., loyer 1 800F cc, tél : 78 49 26 76

URG rech. appart. F3 à louer, env. Saverne, cuis. équip., balc., park., maxi. 3 500F/mois cc, tél. 85 34 37 29

Ventes

VDS mais. F4, tt cft, t. b. état, ch. c., ds résid. stand., px à déb., libre imméd. Tél.HR 72.88.63.29

Échanges vacances

Échange luxueux appt Paris Avenue Foch, 2ch, 2sdb, terrasse, a/c, parking, contre appt similaire centre Londres pour avril mai juin 1996. Tél. 16 (1) 45 27 98 12

Éch. bglw tt cft, 4/5 pers, PALAVAS LES FLOTS, contre logt équiv. Bret. sud, 14 juil/15 août. T. HR 98.72.41.68

House Sale
Apartment/Room Let
Holiday Exchanges

a/c (air conditionné) air conditioning
ag. s'abst. (agences s'abstenir) no agencies (i.e. only private individuals should apply)
appt (appartement) flat
av. (avec) with
balc. (balcon) balcony
bglw (bungalow) holiday chalet
Bret. sud (Bretagne sud) southern Brittany
cc, CC (charges comprises) service charges included (in the rent)
ch. (chambre) bedroom
ch. c. (chauffage central) central heating
cuis. équip. (cuisine équipée) fully fitted kitchen
ds (dans) in
éch. (échange) exchange (offered for)
env. (aux environs de) in the area of, close to
esp. verts (espaces verts) green space (e.g. gardens, parkland)
hor. bur. (horaires de bureau) office hours (between 8 and 12 or between 2 and 5)
HR (heures des repas) meal times (between 12 and 2 or between 7 and 9 p.m.)
imméd. (immédiatement) (available) immediately
lib. (libre) free (from a certain date)
logt équiv. (logement équivalent) equivalent accommodation
m² (mètres carrés) square metres
maxi (maximum) maximum
p. 249 (poste 249) extension 249
park. (parking) parking space
part. à part. (particulier à particulier) private let
pers. (personnes) people
poss. cuis. (possibilité de faire la cuisine) cooking facilities
px à déb. (prix à débattre) price to be discussed
rech. (recherche) is seeking
résid. (résidence) apartment complex
sdb (salle de bains) bathroom
stand. (de bon standing) desirable
T., tél. (téléphone, téléphoner) telephone
tb (très beau/belle) delightful
t.b. état (très bon état) (in) excellent condition
tt cft (tout confort) all mod cons
URG (urgent) urgent(ly)
vds/vd (vends) (I am) selling, for sale

Jobs

Emplois

Jne F., 23 a., diplômée Ec. Sup. Com., bil. fr/angl, tt txte, excel. présent. ch. empl. 1/2 tps, accept. déplcts. Ecr. jrnl Réf. OEZ98

Centre de vac. ch. H à tt faire pr petits trvx, surveill. enfts, sér. réf. exigées, logé, nourri, blanchi + 3 500F/ms. Ecr. jrnl réf. PLM258

Etud. donne crs anglais français ts niveaux tél: 27 42 31 86

Ch. f. de mén. 2x4h/sem., a.m. préfér., sér. réf. exig., Tél Mme PIERRAT 42 59 17 23

Entr. TP ch. VRP multic., départ. 42, 74, 01. Envoy. CV + photo + prétent. à BATIDUR 285 cours Lafayette 69100 Villeurbanne

1/2 tps (mi-temps) half-time
2x4h/sem. (deux fois quatre heures par semaine) 4 hours twice a week
a. (ans) years (old)
accept. déplcts (accepte les déplacements) will travel
angl (anglais) English
a.m. préfér. (l'après-midi de préférence) preferably afternoon
bil. fr/angl (bilingue français/anglais) bilingual French/English
ch. (cherche) seeks
crs (cours) lessons
départ. (départements) departments (French districts)
dispon. (disponible) available
Ec. Sup. Com. (École Supérieure de Commerce) Business School
ecr. (écrire à) (please) write to
empl. (emploi) job
enfts (enfants) children
entr. TP (entreprise de travaux publics) civil engineering firm
envoy. (envoyer) (please) send
étud. (étudiant(e)) student
excel. présent. (excellente présentation) very smart appearance
exig. (exigé) required, essential
f. de mén. (femme de ménage) cleaning lady
fam. (famille) family
F/ms (francs par mois) francs per month
Fr (français) French
H. à tt faire (homme à tout faire) odd-job man
h/sem. (heures par semaine) hours per week
J.F., Jne F (jeune fille/femme) young woman
jrnl (journal) newspaper
juil. (juillet) July
ms (mois) month
nat. (nationalité) nationality
petits trvx (petits travaux) light (manual) work
poss. (possible) possible
pr (pour) for
prétent. (prétentions) salary expectation
réf. (référence) reference (number)
sér. réf. (sérieuses références) excellent references
surveill. enfts (surveillance d'enfants) looking after children
tél. (téléphone) telephone
trav. scol. (travail scolaire) homework
ts (tous) all
tt txte (traitement de texte) word processing
vac. (vacances) holidays
voit. (voiture) car
VRP multic. (voyageur représentant placier multicartes) sales representative for several different companies

Aa

a[1], **A** *n* **1** (letter) a, A *m*; **2 A** (Mus) la *m*.
a[2], **an** *det* un/une.

■ **Note** The determiner or indefinite article *a* or *an* is translated by *un + masculine noun* and by *une + feminine noun*: *a tree* = un arbre; *a chair* = une chaise. There are, however, some cases where the article is not translated:
– with professions and trades: *her mother is a teacher* = sa mère est professeur;
– with other nouns used in apposition: *he's a widower* = il est veuf;
– with *what a*: *what a pretty house* = quelle jolie maison.
– When expressing prices in relation to weight, the definite article *le*/*la* is used in French: *ten francs a kilo* = dix francs le kilo. In other expressions where *a*/*an* means *per* the French translation is *par*: *twice a day* = deux fois par jour; but: *50 kilometres an hour* = 50 kilomètres/heure.

aback *adv* **to be taken ~** être déconcerté/-e.
abandon *vtr* abandonner [*person, hope*]; renoncer à [*activity, attempt*].
abbey *n* abbaye *f*.
abbreviation *n* abréviation *f*.
abdomen *n* abdomen *m*.
abide *vi* **to ~ by** respecter [*rule, decision*].
ability *n* **1** (capability) capacité *f*; **to the best of one's ~** de son mieux; **2** (talent) talent *m*.
able *adj*

■ **Note** *to be able to* meaning *can* is usually translated by the verb *pouvoir*: *I was not able to help him* = je ne pouvais pas l'aider.
– When *to be able to* implies the acquiring of a skill, *savoir* is used: *he's nine and he's still not able to read* = il a neuf ans et il ne sait toujours pas lire.

1 to be ~ to do pouvoir faire; **she was ~ to play the piano at the age of four** elle savait jouer du piano à quatre ans; **2** [*lawyer, teacher*] compétent/-e; [*child*] doué/-e.
abnormal *adj* anormal/-e.
abnormality *n* anomalie *f*.
aboard I *adv* à bord.
II *prep* à bord de [*plane*]; dans [*train*]; **~ ship** à bord.
abolish *vtr* abolir [*law, right*]; supprimer [*service, allowance*].
abominable *adj* abominable.
aborigine *n* aborigène *mf*.
abortion *n* avortement *m*; **to have an ~** se faire avorter.
about I *adj* **to be ~ to do** être sur le point de faire.
II *adv* **1** environ, à peu près; **~ an hour** environ une heure; **it's ~ the same** c'est à peu près pareil; **at ~ 6 pm** vers 18 h; **it's just ~ ready** c'est presque prêt; **2 there was no-one ~** il n'y avait personne; **there is a lot of flu ~** il y a beaucoup de grippes en ce moment; **he's somewhere ~** il est dans les parages.
III *prep* **1** (concerning) **a book ~ France** un livre sur la France; **what's it ~?** (of book, film) ça parle de quoi?; **may I ask what it's ~?** pourriez-vous me dire de quoi il s'agit?; **it's ~ my son** c'est au sujet de mon fils; **2 there's something odd ~ him** il a quelque chose de bizarre; **what I like ~ her is her honesty** ce que j'aime chez elle c'est sa franchise; **3** (around) **to wander ~ the streets** errer dans les rues; **4 how** or **what ~ some tea?** et si on prenait un thé?; **how ~ going into town?** et si on allait en ville?; **5 what ~ the legal costs?** et les frais de justice?; **what ~ you?** et toi?
IDIOMS **it's ~ time (that) somebody made an effort** il serait temps que quelqu'un fasse un effort; **~ time too!** ce n'est pas trop tôt○!
above I *prep* au-dessus de; **~ the painting** au-dessus du tableau; **~ it** au-dessus; **children ~ the age of 12** les enfants âgés de plus de 12 ans; **~ all else** par-dessus tout; **to hear sth ~ the shouting** entendre qch au milieu des cris.
II *adj* **the ~ items** les articles susmentionnés or figurant ci-dessus.
III *adv* **1** au-dessus; **a desk with a shelf ~** un bureau avec une étagère au-dessus; **the apartment ~** l'appartement du dessus; **2** (in text) **see ~** voir ci-dessus; **3** (more) plus; **children of 12 and ~** les enfants âgés de 12 ans et plus.
IV above all *phr* surtout.
above-mentioned *adj* susmentionné/-e.
abreast *adv* **to walk three ~** marcher à trois de front; **to keep ~ of** se tenir au courant de.
abroad *adv* à l'étranger; **from ~** de l'étranger.
abrupt *adj* brusque.
abscess *n* abcès *m*.
abseiling ▶504 *n* (GB) descente *f* en rappel.
absence *n* absence *f*.
absent *adj* absent/-e (**from** de).
absent-minded *adj* distrait/-e.
absolute *adj* absolu/-e.
absolutely *adv* absolument.
absorb *vtr* absorber; **~ed in one's work** plongé/-e dans son travail.
absorbent *adj* absorbant/-e.
abstain *vi* s'abstenir (**from** de).
abstract *adj* abstrait/-e.
absurd *adj* absurde, ridicule.
abundant *adj* abondant/-e.
abuse I *n* **1** (maltreatment) mauvais traitement *m*; (sexual) sévices *mpl* (sexuels); **2** (of alcohol,

power) abus *m*; **drug ~** usage *m* des stupéfiants; **3** (insults) injures *fpl*.
II *vtr* **1** (hurt) maltraiter; **2** abuser de [*position, power, trust*]; **3** (insult) injurier.

abusive *adj* [*person*] grossier/-ière; [*words*] injurieux/-ieuse.

abyss *n* abîme *m*.

academic I *n* universitaire *mf*.
II *adj* **1** [*career, book*] universitaire; [*year*] académique; **2** (theoretical) théorique.

academy *n* (school) école *f*; (learned society) académie *f*.

accelerate *vi* accélérer.

accelerator *n* accélérateur *m*.

accent *n* accent *m*.

accept *vtr* (gen) accepter; (tolerate) admettre.

acceptable *adj* acceptable.

acceptance *n* acceptation *f*.

access I *n* accès *m*; **to have ~ to** avoir accès à [*information, funds, place*].
II *vtr* accéder à [*database, information*].

accessible *adj* accessible (**to** à).

accessory *n* accessoire *m*; (on car) extra *m*.

accident *n* accident *m*; **car/road ~** accident de voiture/de la route; **by ~** accidentellement; (by chance) par hasard.

accidental *adj* **1** [*death*] accidentel/-elle; **2** [*mistake*] fortuit/-e.

accidentally *adv* **1** (by accident) accidentellement; **2** (by chance) par hasard.

accident-prone *adj* sujet/-ette aux accidents.

accommodate *vtr* **1** (put up) loger; **2** (hold, provide space for) contenir; **3** (adapt to) s'adapter à [*change, view*]; **4** (satisfy) satisfaire [*need*].

accommodating *adj* accommodant/-e (**to** envers).

accommodation *n* (also **~s** US) logement *m*.

accompany *vtr* accompagner.

accomplice *n* complice *mf*.

accomplish *vtr* accomplir [*task, mission*]; réaliser [*objective*].

accomplishment *n* réussite *f*.

accord *n* accord *m*; **of my own ~** de moi-même.

accordance: **in accordance with** *phr* [*act*] conformément à [*rules, instructions*]; [*be*] conforme à [*law, agreement*].

according: **according to** *phr* **1** [*act*] selon [*law, principles*]; **~ to plan** comme prévu; **2** d'après [*newspaper, person*].

accordion ▶586 *n* accordéon *m*.

accost *vtr* (approach) aborder; (sexually) accoster.

account I *n* **1** (in bank, post office, shop) compte *m* (**at, with** à); **in my ~** sur mon compte; **2 to take sth into ~, to take ~ of sth** tenir compte de qch; **3** (description) compte-rendu *m*; **4 on ~ of** à cause de; **on no ~** sous aucun prétexte; **on my ~** à cause de moi.
II **accounts** *n pl* **1** (records) comptabilité *f*, comptes *mpl*; **2** (department) (service *m*) comptabilité *f*.
■ **account for 1** (explain) expliquer [*fact, behaviour*]; justifier [*expense*]; **2** (represent) représenter [*proportion, percentage*].

accountable *adj* responsable (**to** devant; **for** de).

accountancy *n* comptabilité *f*.

accountant ▶626 *n* comptable *mf*.

account number *n* numéro *m* de compte.

accumulate I *vtr* accumuler.
II *vi* s'accumuler.

accuracy *n* (of figures, watch) justesse *f*; (of map, aim) précision *f*; (of forecast) exactitude *f*.

accurate *adj* [*figures, watch, information*] juste; [*report, map, forecast*] exact/-e.

accurately *adv* [*calculate*] exactement; [*report*] avec exactitude; [*assess*] précisément.

accusation *n* accusation *f*.

accuse *vtr* accuser (**of** de).

accused *n* **the ~** l'accusé/-e *m/f*.

accustomed *adj* **1 to be ~ to sth/to doing** avoir l'habitude de qch/de faire; **2** (usual) habituel/-elle.

ace *n* as *m*.

ache I *n* douleur *f* (**in** à).
II *vi* [*person*] avoir mal; **my back ~s** j'ai mal au dos.

achieve *vtr* atteindre [*aim*]; atteindre à [*perfection*]; obtenir [*result*]; réaliser [*ambition*].

achievement *n* réussite *f*.

aching *adj* [*body, limbs*] douloureux/-euse.

acid *n, adj* acide (*m*).

acid rain *n* pluies *fpl* acides.

acknowledge *vtr* admettre [*fact*]; reconnaître [*error, problem, authority*]; accuser réception de [*letter*].

acknowledgement I *n* **1** (of error, guilt) aveu *m*; **2** (confirmation of receipt) accusé *m* de réception.
II **acknowledgements** *n pl* (in book) remerciements *mpl*.

acne ▶533 *n* acné *f*.

acorn *n* gland *m*.

acoustic *adj* acoustique.

acoustic guitar ▶586 *n* guitare *f* sèche.

acoustics *n pl* **the ~ are good** l'acoustique *f* est bonne.

acquaintance *n* connaissance *f* (**with** de).

acquainted *adj* **to be ~** se connaître; **to get** or **become ~ with sb** faire la connaissance de qn; **to get** or **become ~ with sth** découvrir qch.

acquire *vtr* acquérir [*expertise*]; obtenir [*information*]; faire l'acquisition de [*possessions*]; acheter [*company*].

acquit *vtr* (Law) acquitter; **to be ~ted** être disculpé/-e (**of** de).

acre *n* acre *f*, ≈ demi-hectare *m*.

acrobat *n* acrobate *mf*.

acrobatics *n pl* acrobaties *fpl*.

across I *prep* **1 a journey ~ the desert** un voyage à travers le désert; **the bridge ~ the river** le pont qui traverse la rivière; **to go** or **travel ~ sth** traverser qch; **she leaned ~**

the table elle s'est penchée au-dessus de la table; **2** (on the other side of) de l'autre côté de; **~ the street (from me)** de l'autre côté de la rue.
II *adv* **to help sb ~** aider qn à traverser; **to go ~ to sb** aller vers qn; **to look ~ at sb** regarder dans la direction de qn.
III across from *phr* en face de.

acrylic *n* acrylique *m*.

act I *n* **1** acte *m*; **an ~ of kindness** un acte de bonté; **2** (Law) loi *f*; **Act of Parliament** loi votée par le Parlement; **3** (in show) numéro *m*; **4 to put on an ~** jouer la comédie.
II *vtr* jouer [*part, role*].
III *vi* **1** (take action) agir; **2** (behave) agir, se comporter; **3** [*actor*] jouer, faire du théâtre; **4** (pretend) jouer la comédie, faire semblant; **5** (take effect) [*drug*] agir; **6 to ~ as** [*person, object*] servir de.

acting I *n* (performance) jeu *m*, interprétation *f*; (occupation) métier *m* d'acteur; **I've done some ~** j'ai fait du théâtre.
II *adj* [*director, manager*] intérimaire.

action *n* **1** (gen) action *f*; (steps) mesures *fpl*; **to take ~** agir, prendre des mesures (**against** contre); **to put a plan into ~** mettre un projet à exécution; **~s speak louder than words** mieux vaut agir que parler; **2** (fighting) action *f*, combat *m*; **killed in ~** tué/-e au combat; **3** (in filming) action *f*; **~!** moteur!

activate *vtr* faire démarrer [*system*]; actionner [*switch*]; déclencher [*alarm*].

active *adj* [*person, life*] actif/-ive; [*volcano*] en activité.

activist *n* activiste *mf*.

activity *n* activité *f*.

actor *n* acteur *m*, comédien *m*.

actress *n* actrice *f*, comédienne *f*.

actual *adj* [*circumstances*] réel/réelle; [*words*] exact/-e; **in ~ fact** en fait; **the ~ problem** le problème lui-même.

actually *adv* **1** (in fact) en fait; **their profits have ~ risen** en fait, leurs bénéfices ont augmenté; **~, I don't feel like it** à vrai dire je n'en ai pas envie; **2** (really) vraiment; **yes, it ~ happened!** mais oui, c'est vraiment arrivé!

acupuncture *n* acupuncture *f*.

acute *adj* **1** [*anxiety, pain*] vif/vive; [*boredom*] profond/-e; **2** [*illness*] aigu/aiguë; **3** [*mind*] pénétrant/-e; **4** [*accent, angle*] aigu/aiguë.

ad *n* (*abbr* = **advertisement**) **1** (**small**) **~** (petite) annonce *f* (**for** pour); **2** (on radio, TV) pub° *f* (**for** pour).

AD (*abbr* = **Anno Domini**) ap J.-C.

adamant *adj* catégorique (**about** sur); **he is ~ that** il maintient que.

adapt I *vtr* adapter (**to** à; **for** pour; **from** de).
II *vi* [*person*] s'adapter (**to** à).

adaptable *adj* souple.

adapter, **adaptor** *n* adaptateur *m*.

add *vtr* **1** ajouter, rajouter (**onto, to** à); **2** (also **~ together**) additionner [*numbers*]; **to ~ sth to** ajouter qch à [*figure, total*].
■ **add up**: ¶ **~ up** [*facts, figures*] s'accorder; **to ~ up to** s'élever à [*total*]; ¶ **~ up [sth]** additionner [*cost, numbers*].

adder *n* (snake) vipère *f*.

addict *n* **1** (drug-user) toxicomane *mf*; **2** (of TV, coffee) accro° *mf* (**of** de).

addicted *adj* **to be ~** (to alcohol, drugs) avoir une dépendance (**to** à); (to TV, coffee) être accro° (**to** de).

addiction *n* dépendance *f* (**to** à).

addition I *n* **1** (to list, house) ajout *m*; **2** (in mathematics) addition *f*.
II in addition *phr* en plus.

additional *adj* supplémentaire.

additive *n* additif *m*.

address I *n* adresse *f*; **to change (one's) ~** changer d'adresse.
II *vtr* **1** mettre l'adresse sur [*parcel, letter*]; **to ~ sth to sb** adresser qch à qn; **2** (speak to) s'adresser à [*group*]; **3** (aim) adresser [*remark, complaint*] (**to** à).

address book *n* carnet *m* d'adresses.

adept *adj* expert/-e.

adequate *adj* **1** (sufficient) suffisant/-e; **2** (satisfactory) satisfaisant/-e.

adhere *vi* adhérer (**to** à).

adhesive I *n* colle *f*, adhésif *m*.
II *adj* collant/-e; **~ tape** papier *m* collant, Scotch® *m*.

adjacent *adj* contigu/contiguë; **~ to sth** attenant à qch.

adjective *n* adjectif *m*.

adjourn *vtr* ajourner [*trial*] (**for** pour; **until** à).

adjust I *vtr* régler [*component, level, position, speed*]; ajuster [*price, rate*]; rajuster [*clothing*]; modifier [*figures*].
II *vi* [*person*] s'adapter (**to** à).

adjustable *adj* réglable.

adjustment *n* **1** (of rates) rajustement *m* (**of** de); (of controls, machine) réglage *m* (**of** de); **2** (mental) adaptation *f* (**to** à); **3** (modification) modification *f*; **to make ~s to** apporter des modifications à [*system, machine*].

ad-lib *vtr, vi* improviser.

administer *vtr* (also **administrate**) gérer [*company, affairs, estate*]; gouverner [*territory*].

administration *n* (gen) administration *f*; (paperwork) travail *m* administratif.

administrative *adj* administratif/-ive.

admirable *adj* admirable.

admiral *n* amiral *m*.

admiration *n* admiration *f* (**for** pour).

admire *vtr* admirer.

admission *n* **1** (entry) entrée *f*, admission *f* (**to** dans); **'no ~'** 'entrée interdite'; **2** (fee) (droit *m* d')entrée *f*; **3** (confession) aveu *m*; **an ~ of guilt** un aveu de culpabilité.

admit *vtr* **1** reconnaître, admettre [*mistake, fact*]; **to ~ that...** reconnaître que...; **to ~ to** reconnaître, admettre [*mistake, fact*]; **2** (confess) reconnaître [*guilt*]; **to ~ to sth/doing** avouer qch/avoir fait; **3** (let in) laisser entrer [*person*] (**into** dans); **to be ~ted to hospital** être hospitalisé/-e.

admittance *n* accès *m*, entrée *f*; **'no ~'** 'accès interdit au public'.
admittedly *adv* il est vrai, il faut en convenir.
adolescent I *n* adolescent/-e *m/f*.
II *adj* **1** (gen) adolescent/-e; [*crisis, rebellion*] d'adolescent; [*problem*] des adolescents; **2** (childish) puéril/-e.
adopt *vtr* adopter.
adopted *adj* [*child*] adopté/-e; [*son, daughter*] adoptif/-ive.
adoption *n* adoption *f*.
adorable *adj* adorable.
adore *vtr* adorer (**doing** faire).
adrenalin(e) *n* adrénaline *f*.
Adriatic (Sea) *pr n* **the ~** la mer *f* Adriatique, l'Adriatique *f*.
adrift *adj*, *adv* [*person, boat*] à la dérive; **to come ~** se détacher (**of, from** de).
adult I *n* adulte *mf*.
II *adj* (gen) adulte; [*life*] d'adulte; [*film, magazine*] pour adultes.
adultery *n* adultère *m* (**with** avec).
advance I *n* **1** (forward movement) avance *f*; (progress) progrès *m*; **2** (sum of money) avance *f*, acompte *m* (**on** sur); **3 to make ~s to sb** (gen) faire des démarches auprès de qn; (sexually) faire des avances à qn.
II *vtr* **1** avancer [*sum of money*]; **2** faire avancer [*career, research*]; servir [*cause, interests*].
III *vi* **1** (move forward) [*person*] avancer, s'avancer (**on, towards** vers); (Mil) [*army*] avancer (**on** sur); **2** (progress) progresser, faire des progrès.
IV **in advance** *phr* à l'avance.
advanced *adj* [*course, class*] supérieur/-e; [*student, stage*] avancé/-e; [*equipment, technology*] de pointe, perfectionné/-e.
advance warning *n* préavis *m*.
advantage *n* **1** avantage *m*; **it is to our ~ to do** il est dans notre intérêt de faire; **2** (asset) atout *m*; **3 to take ~ of** utiliser, profiter de [*situation, offer, service*]; exploiter [*person*].
advantageous *adj* avantageux/-euse.
advent *n* (gen) apparition *f* (**of** de); **Advent** (prior to Christmas) l'Avent *m*.
adventure *n* aventure *f*.
adventurous *adj* aventureux/-euse.
adverb *n* adverbe *m*.
adverse *adj* [*reaction, conditions, publicity*] défavorable; [*effect, consequences*] négatif/-ive.
advert○ *n* (GB) (in paper) annonce *f*; (small ad) petite annonce *f*; (on TV, radio) pub○ *f*, spot *m* publicitaire.
advertise I *vtr* faire de la publicité pour [*product, event, service*]; mettre or passer une annonce pour [*car, house, job*].
II *vi* **1** (for publicity) faire de la publicité; **2** (in small ads) passer une annonce.
advertisement *n* **1** (for product, event) publicité *f* (**for** pour); **a good/bad ~ for** une bonne/mauvaise publicité pour; **2** (to sell house, get job) annonce *f*; (in small ads) petite annonce *f*.
advertising *n* publicité *f*.
advice *n* conseils *mpl* (**on** sur; **about** à propos de); **a piece of ~** un conseil; **it was good ~** c'était un bon conseil.
advisable *adj* **it is ~ to do** il est recommandé de faire.
advise *vtr* **1** conseiller, donner des conseils à (**about** sur); **to ~ sb to do** conseiller à qn de faire; **to ~ sb against doing** déconseiller à qn de faire; **2** recommander [*rest, course of action*]; **3** (inform) **to ~ sb** (**of**) aviser qn (de).
adviser, **advisor** *n* conseiller/-ère *m/f* (**to** auprès de).
Aegean (Sea) *pr n* **the ~** la mer Égée.
aerial I *n* antenne *f*.
II *adj* aérien/-ienne.
aerobics ▶ 504 *n* aérobic *m*.
aeroplane *n* (GB) avion *m*.
aerosol *n* bombe *f* aérosol.
aesthetic, **esthetic** (US) *adj* esthétique.
affair *n* **1** affaire *f*; **state of ~s** situation *f*; **2** (relationship) liaison *f* (**with** avec).
affect *vtr* **1** (have effect on) avoir une incidence sur [*price*]; affecter, avoir des conséquences pour [*career, environment*]; affecter, toucher [*region, population*]; influer sur [*decision, outcome*]; **2** (emotionally) émouvoir; **3** (Med) atteindre [*person*]; affecter [*health, heart*].
affection *n* affection *f* (**for sb** pour qn).
affectionate *adj* affectueux/-euse.
afford *vtr* **1** (financially) **to be able to ~ sth** avoir les moyens d'acheter qch; **if I can ~ it** si j'ai les moyens; **I can't ~ to pay the rent** je n'ai pas les moyens de payer le loyer; **2** (spare) **to be able to ~** disposer de [*time*]; **3** (risk) **to be able to ~ sth/to do** se permettre qch/de faire; **he can't ~ to wait** il ne peut pas se permettre d'attendre.
afield *adv* **far ~** loin; **further ~** plus loin.
afloat *adj*, *adv* **to stay ~** [*person, object*] rester à la surface (de l'eau); [*boat*] rester à flot.
afraid *adj* **1** (scared) **to be ~** avoir peur (**of** de; **to do, of doing** de faire); **2** (anxious) **she was ~ (that) there would be an accident** elle craignait un accident; **I'm ~ it might rain** je crains qu'il (ne) pleuve; **3 I'm ~ I can't come** je suis désolé mais je ne peux pas venir; **I'm ~ so/not** je crains que oui/non.
afresh *adv* à nouveau.
Africa ▶ 448 *pr n* Afrique *f*; **to ~** en Afrique.
African I *n* Africain/-e *m/f*.
II *adj* africain; [*elephant*] d'Afrique.
after I *adv* après; **soon** or **not long ~** peu après; **the year ~** l'année suivante or d'après; **the day ~** le lendemain.
II *prep* **1** après; **shortly ~ the strike** peu après la grève; **~ that** après (cela); **the day ~ tomorrow** après-demain; **to tidy up ~ sb** ranger derrière qn; **to ask ~ sb** demander des nouvelles de qn; **~ you!** après vous!; **2 that's the house they're ~** c'est la maison qu'ils veulent acheter; **the police are ~ him** il est recherché par la police; **3 year ~ year** tous les ans; **it was one disaster ~ another** on a

after

As a preposition or an adverb ⇨ I, II

When *after* is used as a preposition or an adverb, it is usually translated by *après:*

*three weeks **after***	= trois semaines **après**
***after** the meal*	= **après** le repas

As a conjunction ⇨ III

Referring to the past

- When the two verbs have the same subject, *after + verb* is usually translated by *après + past infinitive (past infinitive = auxiliary verb + past participle,* eg avoir mangé, être tombé etc).

  For more information on the auxiliary verbs, see the note for **have**.

***after** he had consulted Bill* *or **after** consulting Bill, he left*	= **après** avoir consulté Bill, il est parti
***after** he fell in love with her* *or **after** falling in love with her, he moved to London*	= **après** être tombé amoureux d'elle, il a déménagé à Londres
***after** she had showered* *or **after** showering, she went out again*	= **après** s'être douchée, elle est ressortie

- When the two verbs have different subjects, *after + verb* is usually translated by *après que + indicative (après qu'* before a vowel or mute 'h'):

***after** he phoned us, we went to pick him up*	= **après qu'**il nous eut téléphoné, nous sommes allés le chercher en voiture
*Jane went back to work **after** George had finished his studies*	= Jane a repris le travail **après que** George eut terminé ses études
***after** he had changed, she brought him to the office*	= **après qu'**il se fut changé, elle le conduisit au bureau

- When there is a corresponding noun for many of these verbs – *mourir/mort, partir/départ, se marier/mariage, se doucher/douche* etc – the construction *après + noun* is generally preferred by French native speakers, especially where the subjects differ:

*we went in **after** the film had started*	= nous sommes entrés **après** le début du film
***after** their son was born, they left Paris*	= ils ont quitté Paris **après** la naissance de leur fils
*they gave us the house **after** we married*	= ils nous ont donné la maison **après** notre mariage

Referring to the future

If the English refers to an event in the future, the translation is more likely to be *quand* or *une fois que + indicative (une fois qu'* before a vowel or mute 'h'):

***after** I've finished my book, I'll leave*	= je partirai **quand** j'aurai fini mon livre *or* je partirai **une fois que** j'aurai fini mon livre
*I'll lend it to you **after** Fred has read it*	= je te le prêterai **quand** Fred l'aura lu *or* je te le prêterai **une fois que** Fred l'aura lu

❑ See also the usage note on **The Clock**, ▶ 434

eu catastrophe sur catastrophe; **4 we called her Kate ~ my mother** nous l'avons appelée Kate comme ma mère; **5** (US) **it's twenty ~ eleven** il est onze heures vingt.
III *conj* **1** après avoir or être (+ *pp*), après que (+ *indicative*); **2 why did he do that ~ we'd warned him?** pourquoi a-t-il fait ça alors que nous l'avions prévenu?
IV after all *phr* après tout.

after-effect *n* (Med) contrecoup *m*; (figurative) répercussion *f*.

afternoon ▶434 *n* après-midi *m* or *f inv*; **in the ~** (dans) l'après-midi; **on Friday ~(s)** le vendredi après-midi; **good ~!** bonjour!

after-shave *n* après-rasage *m*.

after-sun *adj* après-soleil *inv*.

aftertaste *n* arrière-goût *m*.

afterthought *n* pensée *f* après coup.

afterwards, afterward (US) *adv* **1** (after) après; **straight ~** tout de suite après; **2** (later) plus tard.

again *adv* encore;

■ **Note** When used with a verb, *again* is often translated by adding the prefix *re* to the verb in French: *to start again* = recommencer; *to marry again* = se remarier; *I'd like to read that book again* = j'aimerais relire ce livre; *she never saw them again* = elle ne les a jamais revus. You can check *re+* verbs by consulting the French side of the dictionary.
– For other uses of *again*, see below.

sing it ~! chante-le encore!; **once ~** encore une fois; **yet ~ he refused** il a encore refusé; **when you are well ~** quand tu seras rétabli; **I'll never go there ~** je n'y retournerai jamais; **~ and ~** à plusieurs reprises.

against *prep* contre; **~ the wall** contre le mur; **I'm ~ it** je suis contre; **to be ~ doing** être contre l'idée de faire; **the pound fell ~ the dollar** la livre a baissé par rapport au dollar; **~ a background of** sur un fond de; **~ the light** à contre-jour.

age ▶389 **I** *n* **1** âge *m*; **to come of ~** atteindre la majorité; **to be under ~** (Law) être mineur/-e; **2** (era) ère *f*, époque *f* (**of** de); **the video ~** l'ère de la vidéo; **in this day and ~** à notre époque; **3**° **it's ~s since I've played golf** ça fait une éternité que je n'ai pas joué au golf; **I've been waiting for ~s** j'attends depuis des heures.
II *vtr, vi* vieillir.

aged *adj* **1 ~ between 20 and 25** âgé/-e de 20 à 25 ans; **a boy ~ 12** un garçon de 12 ans; **2** (old) âgé/-e.

age group *n* tranche *f* d'âge.

agency *n* agence *f*.

agenda *n* ordre *m* du jour.

agent *n* agent *m* (**for sb** de qn).

aggression *n* (gen) agression *f*; (of person) agressivité *f*.

aggressive *adj* agressif/-ive.

agile *adj* agile.

agitate *vi* faire campagne (**for** pour).

agitated *adj* agité/-e, inquiet/-iète.

AGM *n* (*abbr* = **annual general meeting**) assemblée *f* générale annuelle.

agnostic *n, adj* agnostique (*mf*).

ago *adv* **three weeks ~** il y a trois semaines; **long ~** il y a longtemps; **how long ~?** il y a combien de temps?; **not long ~** il y a peu de temps.

agonizing *adj* [*pain, death*] atroce; [*choice*] déchirant/-e.

agony *n* (physical) douleur *f* atroce; (mental) angoisse *f*.

agree I *vtr* **1** (concur) être d'accord (**that** sur le fait que); **2** (admit) convenir (**that** que); **3** (consent) **to ~ to do** accepter de faire; **she ~d to speak to me** elle a accepté de me parler; **4** (settle on, arrange) se mettre d'accord sur [*date, price*]; **to ~ to do** convenir de faire.
II *vi* **1** (hold same opinion) être d'accord (**with** avec; **about, on** sur; **about doing** pour faire); **'I ~!'** 'je suis bien d'accord!'; **2** (reach mutual understanding) se mettre d'accord (**about, on** sur); **3** (consent) accepter; **to ~ to** consentir à [*suggestion, terms*]; **4** (hold with, approve) **to ~ with** approuver [*belief, idea, practice*]; **5** (tally) [*stories, statements, figures*] concorder (**with** avec); **6** (suit) **to ~ with sb** [*climate*] être bon/bonne pour qn; [*food*] réussir à qn; **7** (in grammar) s'accorder (**with** avec; **in** en).
III agreed *pp adj* convenu/-e; **is that ~d?** c'est entendu?

agreeable *adj* agréable.

agreement *n* **1** accord *m* (**to do** pour faire); **to reach an ~** parvenir à un accord; **2** (undertaking) engagement *m*; **3** (contract) contrat *m*; **4** (in grammar) accord *m*.

agricultural *adj* agricole.

agriculture *n* agriculture *f*.

aground *adv* **to run ~** s'échouer.

ahead I *adv* **1** [*run*] en avant; **to send sb on ~** envoyer qn en éclaireur; **to send one's luggage on ~** faire envoyer ses bagages; **a few kilometres ~** à quelques kilomètres; **2** (in time) **in the months ~** pendant les mois à venir; **3** (in leading position) **to be ~ in the polls** être en tête des sondages; **to be 30 points ~** avoir 30 points d'avance.
II ahead of *phr* **1** (in front of) devant [*person, vehicle*]; **to be three metres ~ of sb** avoir trois mètres d'avance sur qn; **2 to be ~ of sb** (in polls, ratings) avoir un avantage sur qn; **to be ~ of the others** [*pupil*] être plus avancé/-e que les autres.

aid I *n* aide *f* (**from** de; **to, for** à); **in ~ of** au profit de [*charity*].
II *adj* [*organization*] d'entraide.
III *vtr* aider [*person*] (**to do** à faire); faciliter [*digestion, recovery*].

aide *n* aide *mf*, assistant/-e *m/f*.

Aids *n* (*abbr* = **Acquired Immune Deficiency Syndrome**) sida *m*.

aim I *n* **1** (purpose) but *m*; **2** (with weapon) **to take ~ at sb/sth** viser qn/qch.
II *vtr* **1 to be ~ed at sb** [*campaign, product, remark*] viser qn; **2** braquer [*gun, camera*] (**at** sur); lancer [*ball, stone*] (**at** sur).

Age

Note that where English says ***to be X years old***, French says ***avoir X ans*** (*to have X years*).

How old?

*how old **are you**?*	= quel âge **as-tu**?
*what age **is she**?*	= quel âge **a-t-elle**?

The word ***ans*** (*years*) is never dropped:

he is forty years old *he is forty* *he is forty years of age*	= il a quarante **ans**
the house is a hundred years old	= la maison a cent **ans**
a man of fifty	= un homme de cinquante **ans**
he looks sixteen	= on lui donnerait seize **ans**

Note the use of ***de*** after ***âgé*** and ***à l'âge***:

a woman aged thirty	= une femme âgée **de** trente ans
at the age of forty	= à l'âge **de** quarante ans

Do not confuse ***que*** and ***de*** used with ***plus*** and ***moins***:

*I'm older **than** you*	= je suis plus âgé **que** toi
*she's younger **than** him*	= elle est plus jeune **que** lui
*Anne's two years **younger***	= Anne a deux ans **de moins**
*Margot's five years **older than** Suzanne*	= Margot a cinq ans **de plus que** Suzanne

X-year-old

a forty-year-old	= quelqu'un de quarante ans
a sixty-year-old woman	= une femme de soixante ans

Approximate ages

Note the various ways of saying these in French:

*he is **about** fifty*	= il a **environ** cinquante ans = il **a une cinquantaine d'**années = (*less formally*) il **a dans les** cinquante ans

Other round numbers in ***-aine*** used to express age are ***dizaine*** (10), ***vingtaine*** (20), ***trentaine*** (30), ***quarantaine*** (40), ***soixantaine*** (60) and ***centaine*** (100).

she's just over sixty	= elle vient d'avoir soixante ans
she's just under seventy	= elle aura bientôt soixante-dix ans
she's in her sixties	= elle a entre soixante et soixante-dix ans
she's in her early sixties	= elle a entre soixante et soixante-cinq ans
she's in her late sixties	= elle va avoir soixante-dix ans = (*less formally*) elle va sur ses soixante-dix ans
he's in his mid-forties	= il a environ quarante-cinq ans = (*less formally*) il a dans les quarante-cinq ans
*he's **just** ten*	= il a **tout juste** dix ans
*games for **the under** twelves*	= jeux pour **les moins de** douze ans
*only for **the over** eighties*	= seulement pour **les plus de** quatre-vingts ans

III *vi* **to ~ for sth, to ~ at sth** viser qch; **to ~ at doing, to ~ to do** avoir l'intention de faire.

air I *n* **1** air *m*; **in the open ~** en plein air, au grand air; **to let the ~ out of sth** dégonfler qch; **he threw the ball up into the ~** il a jeté le ballon en l'air; **2 to travel by ~** voyager par avion; **3** (on radio, TV) **to be/go on the ~** être/passer à l'antenne.

II *vtr* **1** aérer [*garment, room, bed*]; **2** exprimer [*opinion, view*]; **to ~ one's grievances** exposer ses griefs.

IDIOMS **to put on ~s** se donner de grands airs; **to vanish into thin ~** se volatiliser.

air bed *n* (GB) matelas *m* pneumatique.

air-conditioned *adj* climatisé/-e.

air-conditioning *n* climatisation *f*, air *m* conditionné.

aircraft *n* avion *m*, aéronef *m*.

airfare *n* tarif *m* d'avion.

airfield *n* aérodrome *m*, terrain *m* d'aviation.

air force *n* armée *f* de l'air, forces *fpl* aériennes.

air-freshener *n* désodorisant *m* d'atmosphère.

air gun *n* fusil *m* à air comprimé.

air hostess ▶ 626 *n* hôtesse *f* de l'air.

airline *n* compagnie *f* aérienne.

airmail *n* poste *f* aérienne; **by ~** par avion.

airplane *n* (US) avion *m*.

airport *n* aéroport *m*.

air terminal *n* (at airport) aérogare *f*; (in town) terminal *m*.

air-traffic controller ▶ 626 *n* contrôleur/-euse *m/f* aérien/-ienne, aiguilleur *m* du ciel.

airy *adj* **1** [*room*] clair/-e et spacieux/-ieuse; **2** [*manner*] désinvolte, insouciant/-e.

aisle *n* **1** (in church) (side passage) bas-côté *m*; (centre passage) allée *f* centrale; **2** (in train, plane) couloir *m*; (in cinema, shop) allée *f*.

ajar *adj, adv* entrouvert/-e, entrebaillé/-e.

alarm I *n* **1** (warning) alarme *f*; **smoke ~** détecteur *m* de fumée; **2** (fear) frayeur *f*; (concern) inquiétude *f*.

II *vtr* inquiéter [*person*].

alarm clock *n* réveille-matin *m*, réveil *m*.

alarmed *adj* effrayé/-e.

album *n* album *m*.

alcohol *n* alcool *m*; **~-free** sans alcool.

alcoholic I *n* alcoolique *mf*.

II *adj* [*drink*] alcoolisé/-e; [*stupor*] alcoolique.

alcove *n* renfoncement *m*.

ale *n* bière *f*.

alert I *n* alerte *f*.

II *adj* **1** (lively) [*child*] éveillé/-e; [*adult*] alerte; **2** (attentive) vigilant/-e.

III *vtr* **1** alerter [*authorities*]; **2 to ~ sb to** mettre qn en garde contre [*danger*]; attirer l'attention de qn sur [*fact, situation*].

A-levels *n pl* (GB Sch) ≈ baccalauréat *m*.

algebra *n* algèbre *f*.

Algeria ▶ 448 *pr n* Algérie *f*.

alibi *n* **1** (Law) alibi *m*; **2** (excuse) excuse *f*.

alien *n* **1** (gen, Law) étranger/-ère *m/f* (**to** à); **2** (from space) extraterrestre *mf*.

alienate *vtr* éloigner [*supporters, colleagues*].

alight I *adj* **to set sth ~** mettre le feu à qch.

II *vi* [*passenger*] descendre (**from** de).

alike I *adj* (identical) pareil/-eille; (similar) semblable; **to look ~** se ressembler.

II *adv* [*dress, think*] de la même façon.

alimony *n* pension *f* alimentaire.

alive *adj* **1** vivant/-e, en vie; **to be burnt ~** être brûlé/-e vif/vive; **2 to come ~** [*party, place*] s'animer; [*history*] prendre vie; **3 to be ~** [*tradition*] être vivant/-e; [*interest*] être vif/vive; **4 ~ with** grouillant/-e de [*insects*].

alkaline *adj* alcalin/-e.

all

■ **Note** When *all* is used as a pronoun, it is generally translated by *tout*.

– When *all* is followed by a *that* clause, *all that* is translated by *tout ce que*: *after all (that) we've done* = après tout ce que nous avons fait.

– When referring to a specified group of people or objects, the translation of *all* reflects the number and gender of the people or objects referred to; *tous* is used for a group of people or objects of masculine or mixed or unspecified gender and *toutes* for a group of feminine gender: *we were all delighted* = nous étions tous ravis; *'where are the cups?'—'they're all in the kitchen'* = 'où sont les tasses?'—'elles sont toutes dans la cuisine'. ▶ I

– In French, determiners agree in gender and number with the noun that follows: *all the time* = tout le temps; *all the family* = toute la famille; *all men* = tous les hommes; *all the books* = tous les livres; *all women* = toutes les femmes; *all the chairs* = toutes les chaises. ▶ II

– As an adverb meaning *completely*, *all* is generally translated by *tout*: *he was all alone* = il était tout seul; *the girls were all excited* = les filles étaient tout excitées.

– However, when the adjective that follows is in the feminine and begins with a consonant the translation is *toute/toutes*: *she was all alone* = elle était toute seule; *the girls were all alone* = les filles étaient toutes seules. ▶ III 1

– For more examples and particular usages see the entry below.

I *pron* tout; **that's ~ I want** c'est tout ce que je veux; **I spent it ~, I spent ~ of it** j'ai tout dépensé; **~ of our things** toutes nos affaires.

II *det* tout/toute (+ *sg*); tous/toutes (+ *pl*); **~ those who came** (men, mixed group) tous ceux qui sont venus; (women) toutes celles qui sont venues; **~ his life** toute sa vie; **~ the time** tout le temps.

III *adv* **1** tout; **she's ~ wet** elle est toute mouillée; **~ in white** tout en blanc; **~ along the canal** tout le long du canal; **to be ~ for sth** être tout à fait pour qch; **tell me ~ about it!** raconte-moi tout!; **2** (Sport) **(they are) six ~** (il y a) six partout.

IV **all along** *phr* [*know*] depuis le début, toujours.

V **all the** *phr* **~ the more difficult** d'autant plus difficile; **~ the better!** tant mieux!

VI **all too** *phr* [*easy, often*] bien trop.
VII **at all** *phr* **not at ~!** (acknowledging thanks) de rien!; (answering query) pas du tout!; **it is not at ~ certain** ce n'est pas du tout certain; **nothing at ~** rien du tout.
VIII **of all** *phr* **the easiest of ~** le plus facile; **first of ~** pour commencer.

all clear *n* **to give sb the ~** donner le feu vert à qn (**to do** pour faire).

allegation *n* allégation *f*.

allege *vtr* **to ~ that** (claim) prétendre que (+ *conditional*); (publicly) déclarer que (+ *conditional*); **it was ~d that** il a été dit que.

allegedly *adv* prétendument.

allegiance *n* allégeance *f*.

allergic *adj* allergique (**to** à).

allergy *n* allergie *f* (**to** à).

alleviate *vtr* soulager [*boredom, pain*]; réduire [*overcrowding, stress*].

alley *n* (walkway) allée *f*; (for vehicles) ruelle *f*.

alliance *n* alliance *f*.

all-inclusive *adj* [*fee, price*] tout compris.

all-in-one *adj* [*garment*] d'une seule pièce.

all-night *adj* [*party, meeting*] qui dure toute la nuit; [*service*] ouvert/-e toute la nuit; [*radio station*] qui émet 24 heures sur 24.

allocate *vtr* affecter [*funds*] (**for, to** à); accorder [*time*] (**to** à); assigner [*tasks*] (**to** à).

allot *vtr* attribuer [*money*] (**to** à); **in the ~ted time** dans le temps imparti.

allotment *n* (GB) parcelle *f* de terre.

all-out *adj* [*strike*] total/-e; [*attack*] en règle; [*effort*] acharné/-e.

all over I *adj* fini/-e; **when it's ~** quand tout sera fini.
II *adv* (everywhere) partout; **to be trembling ~** trembler de partout.
III *prep* partout dans [*room, town*]; **~ China** partout en Chine.

allow *vtr* **1** (authorize) permettre à, autoriser [*person, organization*] (**to do** à faire); **it isn't ~ed** c'est interdit; **she isn't ~ed to go out** elle n'a pas le droit de sortir; **2** (let) laisser; **he ~ed the situation to get worse** il a laissé la situation s'aggraver; **3** (enable) **to ~ sb/sth to do** permettre à qn/qch de faire; **it would ~ the company to expand** cela permettrait à la société de s'agrandir; **4** (allocate) prévoir; **to ~ two days for the job** prévoir deux jours pour faire le travail; **5** [*referee*] accorder [*goal*]; [*insurer*] agréer [*claim*]; **6** (condone) tolérer [*rudeness, swearing*].
■ **allow for** tenir compte de.

allowance *n* **1** (gen) allocation *f*; (from employer) indemnité *f*; **2** (**tax**) **~** abattement *m* fiscal; **3** (spending money) (for child) argent *m* de poche; (for student) argent *m* (pour vivre); (from trust, guardian) rente *f*; **4 your baggage ~ is 40 kg** vous avez droit à 40 kg de bagages; **5 to make ~(s) for sth** tenir compte de qch; **to make ~(s) for sb** essayer de comprendre qn.

all right, **alright** I *adj* [*film, garment, place*] pas mal°; **is my hair ~?** ça va mes cheveux?; **are you ~?** ça va?; **I'm ~ thanks** ça va merci; **is it ~ if...?** est-ce que ça va si...?
II *adv* **1** (giving agreement) d'accord; **2** [*work*] comme il faut; [*see, hear*] bien.

all-round *adj* [*athlete*] complet/-ète; [*improvement*] général/-e.

all told *adv* en tout.

allusion *n* allusion *f* (**to** à).

ally I *n* allié/-e *m/f*.
II *v refl* **to ~ oneself with** s'allier avec.

almond *n* **1** (nut) amande *f*; **2** (also **~ tree**) amandier *m*.

almost *adv* **1** (practically) presque; **we're ~ there** nous sommes presque arrivés; **it's ~ dark** il fait presque nuit; **2 he ~ died/forgot** il a failli mourir/oublier.

alone I *adj* seul/-e; **all ~** tout seul/toute seule; **to leave ~** laisser [qn] seul/-e; (in peace) laisser [qn] tranquille; **leave that bike ~!** ne touche pas à ce vélo!
II *adv* **1** [*work, live, travel*] seul/-e; **2 for this reason ~** rien que pour cette raison.
IDIOMS **to go it ~**° faire cavalier seul.

along

■ **Note** When *along* is used as a preposition meaning *all along* it can usually be translated by *le long de*: *there were trees along the road* = il y avait des arbres le long de la route. For particular usages see the entry below.
– *along* is often used after verbs of movement. If the addition of *along* does not change the meaning of the verb, *along* will not be translated: *as he walked along* = tout en marchant.

I *adv* **to push sth ~** pousser qch; **to be running ~** courir; **I'll be ~ in a second** j'arrive tout de suite.
II *prep* **1** (all along) le long de; **there were chairs ~ the wall** il y avait des chaises contre le mur; **2 to walk ~ the beach** marcher sur la plage; **to look ~ the shelves** chercher dans les rayons; **halfway ~ the path** à mi-chemin.
III **along with** *phr* (accompanied by) accompagné/-e de; (at same time as) en même temps que.

alongside I *prep* **1** (all along) le long de; **2 to draw up ~ sb** [*vehicle*] s'arrêter à la hauteur de qn.
II *adv* à côté.

aloud *adv* [*read*] à haute voix; [*think*] tout haut.

alphabet *n* alphabet *m*.

alphabetically *adv* par ordre alphabétique.

alpine *adj* (also **Alpine**) alpin/-e.

Alps *pr n pl* **the ~** les Alpes *fpl*.

already *adv* déjà; **it's 10 o'clock ~** il est déjà 10 heures; **he's ~ left** il est déjà parti.

alright = **all right**.

Alsatian *n* (GB) (dog) berger *m* allemand.

also *adv* aussi.

alter I *vtr* **1** changer [*person*]; (radically) transformer [*person*]; changer [*opinion, rule, timetable*]; modifier [*amount, document*]; affecter [*value, climate*]; **2** retoucher [*dress, shirt*].
II *vi* changer.

alteration I *n* modification *f* (**to, in** de).
II **alterations** *n pl* (building work) travaux *mpl*.

alternate I *adj* **1** (successive) [*chapters, layers*] en alternance; **2** (every other) **on ~ days** un jour sur deux; **3** (US) (other) autre.
II *vtr* **to ~ sth and** or **with sth** alterner qch et qch.
III *vi* [*people*] se relayer; [*colours, patterns, seasons*] alterner (**with** avec).

alternately *adv* alternativement.

alternative I *n* (from two) alternative *f*, autre possibilité *f*; (from several) possibilité *f*; **to have no ~** ne pas avoir le choix.
II *adj* **1** [*date, flight, plan*] autre; [*accommodation, product*] de remplacement; [*solution*] de rechange; **2** (unconventional) alternatif/-ive.

alternatively *adv* sinon; **~, you can book by phone** vous avez aussi la possibilité de réserver par téléphone.

alternative medicine *n* médecines *fpl* parallèles or douces.

although *conj* bien que (+ *subjunctive*); **~ he is shy** bien qu'il soit timide.

altitude *n* altitude *f*.

alto *n* (voice) (of female) contralto *m*; (of male) haute-contre *f*.

altogether *adv* **1** (completely) complètement; **not ~ true** pas complètement vrai; **2** (in total) en tout; **how much is that ~?** ça fait combien en tout?

aluminium foil *n* papier *m* aluminium.

always *adv* toujours; **he's ~ complaining** il n'arrête pas de se plaindre.

am ▶ 434 *adv* (*abbr* = **ante meridiem**) **three ~** trois heures (du matin).

amateur I *n* amateur *m*.
II *adj* [*sportsperson, musician*] amateur; [*sport*] en amateur.

amaze *vtr* surprendre; (stronger) stupéfier.

amazed *adj* stupéfait/-e; **I'm ~ (that)** ça m'étonne que (+ *subjunctive*).

amazement *n* stupéfaction *f*.

amazing *adj* extraordinaire.

Amazon *pr n* Amazone *m*.

ambassador ▶ 626 *n* ambassadeur *m*.

ambiguous *adj* ambigu/ambiguë.

ambition *n* ambition *f* (**to do** de faire).

ambitious *adj* ambitieux/-ieuse.

ambulance *n* ambulance *f*.

ambush I *n* embuscade *f*.
II *vtr* tendre une embuscade à.

amenable *adj* **~ to** [*person*] sensible à [*reason, advice*].

amend *vtr* amender [*law*]; modifier [*document*].

amendment *n* (to law) amendement *m* (**to** à); (to contract) modification *f* (**to** à).

amends *n pl* **to make ~** se racheter; **to make ~ for** réparer [*damage*]; **to make ~ to sb** (financially) dédommager qn.

amenities *n pl* (of hotel) équipements *mpl*; (of house, sports club) installations *fpl*.

America ▶ 448 *pr n* Amérique *f*.

American ▶ 553 I *n* **1** (person) Américain/-e *m/f*; **2** (also **~ English**) américain *m*.
II *adj* américain/-e; [*embassy*] des États-Unis.

amiable *adj* aimable (**to** avec).

amiss I *adj* **there is something ~** il y a quelque chose qui ne va pas.
II *adv* **to take sth ~** prendre qch de travers.

ammunition *n* munitions *fpl*.

amnesty *n* amnistie *f*.

among, amongst *prep* **1** (amidst) parmi; **~ the crowd** parmi la foule; **to be ~ friends** être entre amis; **2** (one of) **~ the world's poorest countries** un des pays les plus pauvres du monde; **she was ~ those who survived** elle faisait partie des survivants; **to be ~ the first** être dans les premiers; **3** (between) entre.

amount *n* (of goods, food) quantité *f*; (of people, objects) nombre *m*; (of money) somme *f*; **a large ~ of** beaucoup de; **the full ~** le montant total.
■ **amount to 1** s'élever à [*total*]; **2** (be equivalent to) revenir à [*confession, betrayal*]; **it ~s to the same thing** cela revient au même.

amp *n* **1** (*abbr* = **ampere**) ampère *m*; **2**○ (*abbr* = **amplifier**) ampli○ *m*.

ample *adj* **1** [*provisions, resources*] largement suffisant/-e (**for** pour); **there's ~ room** il y a largement la place; **2** [*proportions, bust*] généreux/-euse.

amplifier *n* amplificateur *m*.

amputate *vtr* amputer; **to ~ sb's leg** amputer qn de la jambe.

amuse I *vtr* **1** (cause laughter) amuser; **to be ~d at** or **by** s'amuser de; **2** (entertain) [*game, story*] distraire; **3** (occupy) [*activity, hobby*] occuper.
II *v refl* **to ~ oneself 1** (entertain) se distraire; **2** (occupy) s'occuper.

amusement *n* **1** (mirth) amusement *m* (**at** face à); **2** (diversion) distraction *f*.

amusement arcade *n* (GB) salle *f* de jeux électroniques.

amusement park *n* parc *m* d'attractions.

amusing *adj* amusant/-e.

an ▶ **a²**.

anachronism *n* anachronisme *m*.

anaesthetic (GB), **anesthetic** (US) *n, adj* anesthésique (*m*).

analyse (GB), **analyze** (US) *vtr* analyser.

analysis *n* analyse *f*.

analytic(al) *adj* analytique.

anatomy *n* anatomie *f*.

ancestor *n* ancêtre *mf*.

anchor *n* ancre *f*; **to drop ~** jeter l'ancre.

anchovy *n* anchois *m*.

ancient *adj* (dating from BC) antique; (very old) ancien/-ienne; **~ Greek** grec ancien; **~ Greece** la Grèce antique; **~ monument** monument *m* historique.

and *conj* et; **cups ~ plates** des tasses et des assiettes; **he stood up ~ went out** il s'est levé et il est sorti; **come ~ see** viens voir;

two hundred ~ sixty-two deux cent soixante-deux; **faster ~ faster** de plus en plus vite.

Andorra ▶448| *pr n* Andorre *f*.

angel *n* ange *m*.

anger I *n* colère *f* (**at** devant; **towards** contre).
II *vtr* mettre [qn] en colère [*person*].

angle I *n* angle *m*.
II *vi* **1** (fish) pêcher (à la ligne); **2**○ **to ~ for sth** chercher à obtenir qch.

angrily *adv* [*react, speak*] avec colère.

angry *adj* [*person, expression*] furieux/-ieuse; [*scene, words*] de colère; **to be ~** (**at** or **with sb**) être en colère (contre qn); **to get ~** se fâcher; **to make sb ~** mettre qn en colère.

animal I *n* animal *m*, bête *f*.
II *adj* animal/-e.

animated *adj* animé/-e.

ankle ▶413| *n* cheville *f*.

ankle sock *n* socquette *f*.

annex I *n* (also **annexe** GB) annexe *f*.
II *vtr* annexer [*territory, land, country*] (**to** à).

annihilate *vtr* anéantir.

anniversary *n* anniversaire *m* (**of** de).

announce *vtr* annoncer (**that** que).

announcement *n* **1** (spoken) annonce *f*; **2** (written) avis *m*; (of birth, death) faire-part *m inv*.

announcer *n* (on TV) speaker/-erine *m/f*; **radio ~** présentateur/-trice *m/f* de radio.

annoy *vtr* [*person*] (by behaviour) agacer; (by opposing wishes) contrarier; [*noise*] gêner.

annoyance *n* agacement *m* (**at** devant), contrariété *f* (**at** à cause de).

annoyed *adj* contrarié/-e (**at, by** par); (stronger) agacé/-e, fâché/-e (**at, by** par); **~ with sb** fâché/-e contre qn.

annoying *adj* agaçant/-e (**to do** de faire).

annual I *n* **1** (book) album *m* (annuel); **2** (plant) plante *f* annuelle.
II *adj* annuel/-elle.

annually *adv* [*earn, produce*] par an; [*do, inspect*] tous les ans.

anonymous *adj* anonyme.

anorexia (nervosa) ▶533| *n* anorexie *f* mentale.

another

■ **Note** *Another* is translated by *un autre* or *une autre* according to the gender of the noun it refers to: *another book* = un autre livre; *another chair* = une autre chaise.
– Note that *en* is always used with *un/une autre* in French to represent a noun that is understood: *that cake was delicious, can I have another* (*one*)? = ce gâteau était délicieux, est-ce que je peux en prendre un autre? For more examples and particular usages, see the entry below.

I *det* **1** (an additional) un/-e autre, encore un/-e; **would you like ~ drink?** est-ce que tu veux un autre verre?; **I've broken ~ plate** j'ai encore cassé une assiette; **that will cost you ~ £5** cela vous coûtera 5 livres sterling de plus; **in ~ five weeks** dans cinq semaines; **2** (a different) un/-e autre; **~ time** une autre fois; **he has ~ job now** il a un nouveau travail maintenant.
II *pron* un/-e autre; **she had ~** elle en a pris un/-e autre; **one after ~** l'un/l'une après l'autre; **in one way or ~** d'une façon ou d'une autre.

answer I *n* (gen) réponse *f* (**to** à); (to problem, puzzle) solution *f* (**to** à); **there's no ~** (to door) il n'y a personne; (on phone) ça ne répond pas; **the right/wrong ~** la bonne/mauvaise réponse.
II *vtr* répondre à; **to ~ the door** aller or venir ouvrir la porte; **to ~ the phone** répondre au téléphone.
III *vi* **1** répondre; **to ~ to** répondre or correspondre à [*description*]; **2** (be accountable) **to ~ to sb** être responsable devant qn.
■ **answer back** répondre.
■ **answer for** répondre de [*action, person*]; **they have a lot to ~ for!** ils ont beaucoup de comptes à rendre!

answerable *adj* responsable (**to sb** devant qn; **for sth** de qch).

answering machine, **answerphone** *n* répondeur *m* (téléphonique).

ant *n* fourmi *f*.

antagonize *vtr* (annoy) contrarier; (stronger) éveiller l'hostilité de.

Antarctic I *n* **the ~** l'Antarctique *m*.
II *adj* antarctique.

antelope *n* antilope *f*.

antenna *n* antenne *f*.

anti I *prep* contre.
II **anti(-)** *pref* anti(-).

antibiotic *n* antibiotique *m*; **on ~s** sous antibiotiques.

anticipate *vtr* **1** (foresee) prévoir, s'attendre à [*problem, delay*]; **as ~d** comme prévu; **2** (guess in advance) anticiper [*needs, result*]; **3** (preempt) devancer [*person, act*].

anticipation *n* **1** (excitement) excitation *f*; (pleasure in advance) plaisir *m* anticipé; **2** (expectation) prévision *f* (**of** de).

anticlimax *n* déception *f*.

anticlockwise *adj, adv* (GB) dans le sens inverse des aiguilles d'une montre.

antidote *n* antidote *m* (**to, for** contre, à).

antihistamine *n* antihistaminique *m*.

antique I *n* (object) objet *m* ancien or d'époque; (furniture) meuble *m* ancien or d'époque.
II *adj* ancien/-ienne.

antique shop ▶626| *n* magasin *m* d'antiquités.

antiseptic *n, adj* antiseptique (*m*).

antisocial *adj* **1 ~ behaviour** comportement *m* incorrect; (criminal behaviour) comportement *m* délinquant; **2** (reclusive) sauvage.

antlers *n pl* bois *mpl* de cerf.

anxiety *n* **1** (worry) grandes inquiétudes *fpl* (**about** à propos de; **for** pour); **to be in a state of ~** être angoissé/-e; **2** (eagerness) désir *m* ardent (**to do** de faire); **3** (in psychology) anxiété *f*.

anxious *adj* **1** (worried) très inquiet/-iète

(**about** à propos de; **for** pour); **to be ~ about doing** s'inquiéter de faire; **2** [*moment, time*] angoissant; **3** (eager) très désireux/-euse (**to do** de faire).

anxiously *adv* **1** (worriedly) avec inquiétude; **2** (eagerly) avec impatience.

any

■ **Note** When *any* is used as a determiner in questions and conditional sentences it is translated by *du, de l', de la* or *des* according to the gender and number of the noun that follows: *is there any soap?* = y a-t-il du savon?; *is there any flour?* = y a-t-il de la farine?; *are there any questions?* = est- ce qu'il y a des questions?

– In negative sentences *any* is translated by *de* or *d'* (before a vowel or mute 'h'): *we don't have any money* = nous n'avons pas d'argent.

– When *any* is used as a pronoun in negative sentences and in questions it is translated by *en*: *we don't have any* = nous n'en avons pas; *have you got any?* = est-ce que vous en avez?

– For more examples and other uses see the entry below.

I *det* **1** (in questions, conditional sentences) du/de l'/de la/des; **is there ~ tea?** est-ce qu'il y a du thé?; **if you have ~ money** si vous avez de l'argent; **2** (with negative) de, d'; **I don't need ~ advice** je n'ai pas besoin de conseils; **3** (no matter which) n'importe quel/quelle, tout; **~ pen will do** n'importe quel stylo fera l'affaire; **you can have ~ cup you like** vous pouvez prendre n'importe quelle tasse; **I'm ready to help in ~ way I can** je suis prêt à faire tout ce que je peux pour aider; **come round and see me ~ time** passe me voir quand tu veux.

II *pron, quantif* **1** (in questions, conditional sentences) **have you got ~?** est-ce que vous en avez?; **have ~ of you got a car?** est-ce que l'un/-e d'entre vous a une voiture?; **2** (with negative) en; **he hasn't got ~** il n'en a pas; **there is hardly ~ left** il n'en reste presque pas; **she doesn't like ~ of them** (people) elle n'aime aucun d'entre eux/elles; (things) elle n'en aime aucun/-e; **3** (no matter which) n'importe lequel/laquelle; **'which colour would you like?'—'~'** 'quelle couleur veux-tu?'—'n'importe laquelle'; **~ of those pens** n'importe lequel de ces stylos; **~ of them could do it** n'importe qui d'entre eux/elles pourrait le faire.

III *adv* **have you got ~ more of these?** est-ce que vous en avez d'autres?; **do you want ~ more wine?** voulez-vous encore du vin?; **he doesn't live here ~ more** il n'habite plus ici.

anybody *pron* (also **anyone**) **1** (in questions, conditional sentences) quelqu'un; **is there ~ in the house?** est-ce qu'il y a quelqu'un dans la maison?; **if ~ asks, tell them I've gone out** si quelqu'un me cherche, dis que je suis sorti; **2** (with negative) personne; **there wasn't ~ in the house** il n'y avait personne dans la maison; **I didn't have ~ to talk to** il n'y avait personne avec qui j'aurais pu parler; **3** (no matter who) n'importe qui; **~ could do it** n'importe qui pourrait le faire; **~ who wants to, can go** tous ceux qui le veulent, peuvent y aller; **~ can make a mistake** ça arrive à tout le monde de faire une erreur; **~ would think you were deaf** c'est à croire que tu es sourd.

anyhow *adv* **1** = **anyway 1**; **2** (carelessly) n'importe comment.

anyone = **anybody**.

anything *pron* **1** (in questions, conditional sentences) quelque chose; **is there ~ to be done?** peut-on faire quelque chose?; **2** (with negative) rien; **she didn't say ~** elle n'a rien dit; **he didn't have ~ to do** il n'avait rien à faire; **don't believe ~ he says** ne crois pas un mot de ce qu'il dit; **3** (no matter what) tout; **~ is possible** tout est possible; **she'll eat ~** elle mange tout; **he was ~ but happy** il n'était pas du tout heureux.

anytime *adv* (also **any time**) n'importe quand; **~ after 2 pm** n'importe quand à partir de 14 heures; **~ you like** quand tu veux; **he could arrive ~ now** il pourrait arriver d'un moment à l'autre.

anyway *adv* **1** (in any case) (also **anyhow**) de toute façon; **2** (all the same) quand même; **I don't really like hats, but I'll try it on ~** je n'aime pas vraiment les chapeaux, mais je vais quand même l'essayer; **thanks ~** merci quand même; **3** (at any rate) en tout cas; **we can't go out, not yet ~** nous ne pouvons pas sortir, pas pour l'instant en tout cas; **4** (well) **'~, we arrived at the station...'** 'bref, nous sommes arrivés à la gare...'

anywhere *adv* **1** (in questions, conditional sentences) quelque part; **we're going to Spain, if ~** si on va quelque part, ce sera en Espagne; **2** (with negative) nulle part; **you can't go ~** tu ne peux aller nulle part; **there isn't ~ to sit** il n'y a pas de place pour s'asseoir; **you won't get ~ if you don't pass your exams** tu n'arriveras à rien si tu ne réussis pas tes examens; **crying isn't going to get you ~** ça ne t'avancera à rien de pleurer; **3** (no matter where) n'importe où; **~ you like** où tu veux; **~ in England** partout en Angleterre.

apart I *adj, adv* **1 trees planted 10 metres ~** des arbres plantés à 10 mètres d'intervalle; **2** (separated) séparé/-e; **we hate being ~** nous détestons être séparés; **they need to be kept ~** il faut les garder séparés; **3** (to one side) **he stood ~ (from the group)** il se tenait à l'écart (du groupe).

II apart from *phr* **1** (separate from) à l'écart de; **it stands ~ from the other houses** elle est à l'écart des autres maisons; **he lives ~ from his wife** il vit séparé de sa femme; **2** (leaving aside) en dehors de, à part; **~ from being illegal, it's also dangerous** (mis) à part que c'est illégal, c'est aussi dangereux.

apartheid *n* apartheid *m*.

apartment *n* appartement *m*.

apartment block *n* immeuble *m*.

apartment house *n* (US) résidence *f*.

apathetic *adj* (by nature) amorphe; (from illness, depression) apathique.

apex *n* sommet *m*.

APEX *n* (*abbr* = **Advance Purchase Excursion**) APEX *m*.

apologetic *adj* [*gesture, letter*] d'excuse; **to be ~ (about)** s'excuser (de).

apologize *vi* s'excuser (**to sb** auprès de qn; **for sth** de qch; **for doing** d'avoir fait).

apology *n* excuses *fpl* (**for sth** pour qch; **for doing** pour avoir fait); **to make an ~** s'excuser.

apostrophe *n* apostrophe *f*.

appal (GB), **appall** (US) *vtr* (shock) scandaliser; (horrify, dismay) horrifier.

appalling *adj* **1** [*crime, conditions*] épouvantable; **2** [*manners, joke, taste*] exécrable; [*noise, weather*] épouvantable.

apparatus *n* (gen) appareil *m*; (in gym) agrès *mpl*.

apparent *adj* **1** (seeming) [*contradiction, willingness*] apparent/-e; **2** (clear) évident/-e; **for no ~ reason** sans raison apparente.

apparently *adv* apparemment.

appeal I *n* **1** (gen, Law) appel *m* (**for** à; **on behalf of** en faveur de); **2** (attraction) charme *m*; (interest) intérêt *m*.
II *vi* **1** (Law) faire appel (**against** de); **2** (Sport) **to ~ to** demander l'arbitrage de [*referee*]; **to ~ against** contester [*decision*]; **3 to ~ for** lancer un appel à [*order, tolerance*]; faire appel à [*witnesses*]; **to ~ for help** demander de l'aide; **4** (attract) **to ~ to sb** [*idea*] tenter qn; [*person*] plaire à qn; [*place*] attirer qn.

appealing *adj* **1** (attractive) [*child*] attachant/-e; [*idea*] séduisant/-e; [*modesty*] charmant/-e; **2** [*look*] suppliant/-e.

appear *vi* **1** (become visible) apparaître; **2** (turn up) arriver; **3** (seem) **to ~ to be/to do** [*person*] avoir l'air d'être/de faire; **to ~ depressed** avoir l'air déprimé; **it ~s that** il semble que; **4** [*book, article, name*] paraître; **5 to ~ on stage** paraître en scène; **to ~ on TV** passer à la télévision; **6** (Law) **to ~ in court** comparaître devant le tribunal.

appearance *n* **1** (arrival) (of person, vehicle) arrivée *f*; (of development, invention) apparition *f*; **to put in an ~** faire une apparition; **2** (on TV, in play, film) passage *m*; **3** (look) (of person) apparence *f*; (of district, object) aspect *m*; **to judge** or **go by ~s** se fier aux apparences.

appendicitis ▶ **533** *n* appendicite *f*.

appendix *n* appendice *m*; **to have one's ~ removed** se faire opérer de l'appendicite.

appetite *n* appétit *m*.

applaud *vtr, vi* applaudir.

applause *n* applaudissements *mpl*; **there was a burst of ~** les applaudissements ont éclaté.

apple *n* pomme *f*.

applecore *n* trognon *m* de pomme.

apple tree *n* pommier *m*.

appliance *n* appareil *m*; **household ~** appareil électroménager.

applicant *n* (for job, membership) candidat/-e *m/f* (**for** à); (for passport, benefit, loan) demandeur/-euse *m/f* (**for** de); (for citizenship) postulant/-e *m/f* (**for** à).

application *n* **1** (for job) candidature *f* (**for** à); (for membership, passport, loan) demande *f* (**for** de); **2** (of ointment) application *f* (**to** à); **3** (of law, penalty, rule) application *f*.

application form *n* (gen) formulaire *m* de demande; (for job) formulaire *m* de candidature; (for membership) demande *f* d'inscription.

apply I *vtr* (gen) appliquer; exercer [*pressure*] (**to** sur).
II *vi* **1 to ~ (for)** faire une demande (de) [*passport, loan, visa, permit*]; poser sa candidature (à) [*job*]; **to ~ to** faire une demande d'inscription à [*college*]; **2** (be valid) [*definition, term*] s'appliquer (**to** à); [*ban, rule, penalty*] être en vigueur.
III *v refl* **to ~ oneself** s'appliquer.

appoint *vtr* nommer [*person*] (**to sth** à qch; **to do** pour faire; **as** comme); fixer [*date, place*].

appointment *n* **1** (meeting) rendez-vous *m* (**at** chez; **with** avec; **to do** pour faire); **business ~** rendez-vous *m* d'affaires; **to make an ~** prendre rendez-vous; **2** (to post) nomination *f*.

appraisal *n* évaluation *f*.

appreciate I *vtr* **1** apprécier [*help, effort*]; être sensible à [*favour*]; être reconnaissant/-e de [*kindness, sympathy*]; **I'd ~ it if you could reply soon** je vous serais reconnaissant de répondre sans tarder; **2** (realize) se rendre (bien) compte de, être conscient/-e de; **3** (enjoy) apprécier [*music, art, food*].
II *vi* [*object*] prendre de la valeur; [*value*] monter.

appreciation *n* **1** (gratitude) remerciement *m* (**for** pour); **2** (enjoyment) appréciation *f* (**of** de); **3** (increase) hausse *f* (**of, in** de).

appreciative *adj* **1** (grateful) reconnaissant/-e (**of** de); **2** (admiring) admiratif/-ive.

apprehensive *adj* inquiet/-iète; **to be ~ about sth/doing** appréhender qch/de faire.

apprentice *n* apprenti/-e *m/f* (**to** de).

apprenticeship *n* apprentissage *m*.

approach I *n* **1** (route of access) voie *f* d'accès; **2** (arrival) approche *f*; **3** (to problem) approche *f*; **4 to make ~es to sb** faire des démarches auprès de qn.
II *vtr* **1** (draw near to) s'approcher de [*person, place*]; (verge on) approcher de; **2** (deal with) aborder [*problem, subject*]; **3 to ~ sb (about sth)** s'adresser à qn (au sujet de qch); (more formally) faire des démarches auprès de qn (pour qch).
III *vi* [*person, car*] (s')approcher; [*event, season*] approcher.

approachable *adj* abordable, d'un abord facile.

appropriate I *adj* **1** [*behaviour, choice, place*] approprié/-e (**for** pour); [*dress, gift*] qui convient (*after n*) (**for** à); [*punishment*] juste (**for** à); [*name*] bien choisi/-e; **2** (relevant) [*authority*] compétent/-e.
II *vtr* s'approprier [*property, document*]; affecter [*funds, land*] (**for** à).

appropriately *adv* **1** [*behave, dress, speak*] avec à-propos; [*dress*] convenablement; **2** [*designed, chosen, sited*] judicieusement.

approval *n* approbation *f* (**of** de; **to do** pour faire); **on ~** à l'essai.

approve I *vtr* approuver [*product, plan*]; accepter [*person*].
II *vi* **to ~ of sb/sth** apprécier qn/qch; **he doesn't ~ of drinking** il est contre l'alcool.

approving *adj* approbateur/-trice.

approximate *adj* approximatif/-ive.

approximately *adv* **1** (about) environ; **at ~ four o'clock** vers quatre heures; **2** [*equal, correct*] à peu près.

apricot *n* (fruit) abricot *m*.

April ▶**456**| *n* avril *m*.

April Fools' Day *n* le premier avril.

apron *n* tablier *m*.

apt *adj* [*choice, description*] heureux/-euse; [*title, style*] approprié/-e (**to, for** à).

aptitude *n* aptitude *f*.

aquarium *n* aquarium *m*.

Aquarius *n* Verseau *m*.

aquatic *adj* (gen) aquatique; [*sport*] nautique.

aqueduct *n* aqueduc *m*.

Arab ▶**553**| I *n* (person) Arabe *mf*.
II *adj* arabe.

Arabic ▶**553**| I *n* (language) arabe *m*.
II *adj* arabe; [*lesson, teacher*] d'arabe.

arbitrary *adj* arbitraire.

arbitration *n* arbitrage *m*; **to go to ~** ≈ aller aux prud'hommes.

arcade *n* arcade *f*; **shopping ~** galerie *f* marchande.

arch I *n* arche *f*.
II *vtr* arquer; **to ~ one's back** [*person*] cambrer le dos; [*cat*] faire le dos rond.
III **arch(-)** *pref* par excellence; **~-enemy** ennemi/-e *m/f* juré/-e; **~-rival** grand rival.

archaeologist (GB), **archeologist** (US) *n* archéologue *mf*.

archaeology (GB), **archeology** (US) *n* archéologie *f*.

architect ▶**626**| *n* architecte *mf*.

architecture *n* architecture *f*.

archive *n* archive *f*.

Arctic I *n* **the ~** l'Arctique *m*.
II *adj* arctique.

ardent *adj* [*defence, opposition, lover*] passionné/-e; [*supporter*] fervent/-e.

area *n* **1** (region) région *f*; (of city) zone *f*; (district) quartier *m*; **in the London ~** dans la région de Londres; **residential ~** zone *f* résidentielle; **2** (in building) **dining ~** coin *m* salle-à-manger; **no-smoking ~** zone *f* non-fumeurs; **waiting ~** salle *f* d'attente; **3** (of knowledge) domaine *m*; (of business) secteur *m*; **4** (in geometry) aire *f*; (of land) superficie *f*.

area code *n* indicatif *m* de zone.

arena *n* arène *f*.

argue I *vtr* (debate) discuter (de), débattre (de); **to ~ that** (maintain) soutenir que.
II *vi* **1** (quarrel) se disputer (**with** avec; **about, over** sur, pour); **2** (debate) discuter (**about** de); **3** (put one's case) argumenter (**for** en faveur de; **against** contre).

argument *n* **1** (quarrel) dispute *f* (**about** à propos de); **to have an ~** se disputer; **2** (discussion) débat *m*, discussion *f* (**about** à propos de); **3** (case) argument *m* (**for** en faveur de; **against** contre).

argumentative *adj* ergoteur/-euse.

Aries *n* Bélier *m*.

arise *vi* **1** [*problem*] survenir; [*question*] se poser; **if the need ~s** si le besoin se fait sentir; **2** (be the result of) résulter (**from** de).

aristocrat *n* aristocrate *mf*.

arithmetic *n* arithmétique *f*.

arm ▶**413**| I *n* bras *m*; (of chair) accoudoir *m*; **~ in ~** bras dessus bras dessous; **to have sth over/under one's ~** avoir qch sur/sous le bras; **to fold one's ~s** croiser les bras.
II **arms** *n pl* (weapons) armes *fpl*.
III *vtr* (Mil) armer.
IDIOMS **to keep sb at ~'s length** tenir qn à distance.

armaments *n pl* armements *mpl*.

armband *n* (for swimmer) bracelet *m* de natation; (for mourner) crêpe *m* de deuil.

armchair *n* fauteuil *m*.

armed *adj* armé/-e (**with** de); [*raid, robbery*] à main armée.

armed forces, **armed services** *n pl* forces *fpl* armées.

armour (GB), **armor** (US) *n* armure *f*.

armoured (GB), **armored** (US) *adj* blindé/-e.

armour-plated (GB), **armor-plated** (US) *adj* [*vehicle*] blindé/-e; [*ship*] cuirassé/-e.

armpit *n* aisselle *f*.

army I *n* armée *f*.
II *adj* militaire.

aroma *n* arôme *m*.

around I *adv* **1** (approximately) environ, à peu près; **at ~ 3 pm** vers 15 heures; **2** (in the vicinity) **to be (somewhere) ~** être dans les parages; **are they ~?** est-ce qu'ils sont là?; **3** (in circulation) **CDs have been ~ for years** ça fait des années que les CD existent; **one of the most gifted musicians ~** un des musiciens les plus doués du moment; **4 all ~** tout autour; **the only garage for miles ~** le seul garage à des kilomètres à la ronde; **to ask sb (to come) ~** dire à qn de passer.
II *prep* **1** autour de [*fire, table*]; **the villages ~ Dublin** les villages des environs de Dublin; **clothes scattered ~ the room** des vêtements éparpillés partout dans la pièce; **(all) ~ the world** partout dans le monde; **to walk ~ the town** se promener dans la ville; **the people ~ here** les gens d'ici; **2** (at) vers; **~ midnight** vers minuit.

arouse *vtr* éveiller [*interest, suspicion*]; exciter [*anger, jealousy*]; **to be ~d** [*person*] être excité/-e.

arrange I *vtr* **1** disposer [*chairs, ornaments*]; arranger [*room, hair, clothes*]; arranger, disposer [*flowers*]; **2** (organize) organiser [*party, meeting, holiday*]; fixer [*date, appointment*]; **to ~ to do** s'arranger pour faire; **3** convenir de [*loan*].

II *vi* **to ~ for sth** prendre des dispositions pour qch; **to ~ for sb to do** prendre des dispositions pour que qn fasse.

arrangement *n* **1** (of objects, chairs) disposition *f*; (of flowers) composition *f*; **2** (agreement) entente *f*, accord *m*; **to come to an ~** s'arranger; **3** (preparations) **~s** préparatifs *mpl*; **to make ~s to do** s'arranger pour faire.

array *n* gamme *f*.

arrears *n pl* arriéré *m*; **I am in ~ with my payments** j'ai du retard dans mes paiements.

arrest I *n* arrestation *f*; **to be under ~** être en état d'arrestation.
II *vtr* arrêter.

arrival *n* arrivée *f*; **on sb's ~** à l'arrivée de qn.

arrival lounge *n* salon *m* d'arrivée.

arrivals board *n* tableau *m* d'arrivée.

arrival time *n* heure *f* d'arrivée.

arrive *vi* **1** arriver (**at** à; **from** de); **2 to ~ at** parvenir à [*decision, solution*].

arrogant *adj* arrogant/-e.

arrow *n* flèche *f*.

arson *n* incendie *m* criminel.

art *n* art *m*.

artefact *n* objet *m* (fabriqué).

artery *n* artère *f*.

art exhibition *n* (paintings) exposition *f* de tableaux; (sculpture) exposition *f* de sculpture.

art gallery *n* (museum) musée *m* d'art; (commercial) galerie *f* d'art.

arthritis ▶533| *n* arthrite *f*.

artichoke *n* artichaut *m*.

article *n* article *m* (**about, on** sur).

artificial *adj* artificiel/-ielle.

artificial respiration *n* respiration *f* artificielle.

artillery *n* artillerie *f*.

artisan *n* artisan *m*.

artist ▶626| *n* artiste *mf*.

artistic *adj* [*talent*] artistique; [*temperament, person*] artiste.

arts *n pl* **1** (culture) **the ~** les arts *mpl*; **2** (Univ) lettres *fpl*; **3 ~ and crafts** artisanat *m*.

art school *n* école *f* des beaux-arts.

art student *n* étudiant/-e *m/f* des beaux-arts.

as I *conj* **1** comme; **~ you know** comme vous le savez; **~ usual** comme d'habitude; **do ~ I say** fais ce que je te dis; **leave it ~ it is** laisse-le tel quel; **~ she was coming down the stairs** comme elle descendait l'escalier; **~ she grew older** au fur et à mesure qu'elle vieillissait; **~ a child, he...** (quand il était) enfant, il...; **2** (because, since) comme, puisque; **~ you were out, I left a note** comme or puisque tu étais sorti, j'ai laissé un petit mot; **3** (although) **strange ~ it may seem** aussi curieux que cela puisse paraître; **try ~ he might, he could not forget it** il avait beau essayer, il ne pouvait pas oublier; **4 the same...~** le/la même...que; **I've got a jacket the same ~ yours** j'ai la même veste que toi; **5 so ~ to do** pour faire, afin de faire.
II *prep* comme, en; **dressed ~ a sailor** habillé/-e en marin; **he works ~ a pilot** il travaille comme pilote; **a job ~ a teacher** un poste d'enseignant/-e; **to treat sb ~ an equal** traiter qn en égal.
III *adv* (in comparisons) **he is ~ intelligent ~ you** il est aussi intelligent que toi; **~ fast ~ you can** aussi vite que possible; **he's twice ~ strong ~ me** il est deux fois plus fort que moi; **I have ~ much** or **~ many ~ she has** j'en ai autant qu'elle; **~ much ~ possible** autant que possible; **~ little ~ possible** le moins possible; **~ soon ~ possible** dès que possible; **he has a house in Nice ~ well ~ an apartment in Paris** il a une maison à Nice ainsi qu'un appartement à Paris.
IV **as for** *phr* quant à, pour ce qui est de.
V **as from**, **as of** *phr* à partir de.
VI **as if** *phr* comme (si); **it looks ~ if we've lost** on dirait que nous avons perdu.
VII **as long as** *phr* du moment que (+ *indicative*), pourvu que (+ *subjunctive*).
VIII **as such** *phr* en tant que tel.

asbestos *n* amiante *m*.

ascend *vtr* gravir [*steps, hill*].

ascent *n* ascension *f*.

ascertain *vtr* établir (**that** que).

ash *n* **1** cendre *f*; **2** (also **~ tree**) frêne *m*.

ashamed *adj* honteux/-euse; **to be ~** avoir honte (**of** de; **to do** de faire; **that** que (+ *subjunctive*)).

ashen *adj* [*complexion*] terreux/-euse.

ashore *adv* **to go ~** débarquer; **washed ~** rejeté/-e sur le rivage.

ashtray *n* cendrier *m*.

Asia ▶448| *pr n* Asie *f*.

Asian I *n* (from Far East) Asiatique *mf*; (in UK) personne *f* originaire du sous-continent indien.
II *adj* asiatique.

aside I *n* **to say sth in an ~** dire qch en aparté.
II *adv* **to stand ~** s'écarter; **to put sth ~** (save) mettre qch de côté; (in shop) réserver qch; **to take sb ~** prendre qn à part.
III **aside from** *phr* à part.

ask I *vtr* **1** demander; **to ~ a question** poser une question; **to ~ sb sth** demander qch à qn; **to ~ sb to do** demander à qn de faire; **2** (invite) inviter [*person*] (**to** à); **to ~ sb to dinner** inviter qn à dîner.
II *vi* **1** (request) demander; **2** (make enquiries) se renseigner; **to ~ about sb** s'informer au sujet de qn.
III *v refl* **to ~ oneself** se demander.
■ **ask after** demander des nouvelles de [*person*].
■ **ask for**: ¶ **~ for [sth]** demander [*drink, money, help*]; ¶ **~ for [sb]** demander à voir; (on phone) demander à parler à.

askance *adv* **to look ~ at sb/sth** considérer qn/qch avec méfiance.

askew *adj*, *adv* de travers.

asleep *adj* **to be ~** dormir; **to fall ~** s'endormir; **to be sound** or **fast ~** dormir à poings fermés.

asparagus *n* asperge *f*.
aspect *n* **1** aspect *m*; **2** (of house) orientation *f*.
asphalt *n* bitume *m*.
aspic *n* aspic *m*.
aspiration *n* aspiration *f* (**to** à).
aspire *vi* aspirer (**to** à; **to do** à faire).
aspirin *n* aspirine® *f*.
ass *n* **1** (donkey) âne *m*; **2**○ (fool) idiot/-e *m/f*.
assassin *n* assassin *m*.
assassinate *vtr* assassiner.
assassination *n* assassinat *m*.
assault I *n* **1** (Law) agression *f* (**on** sur); **2** (Mil) assaut *m* (**on** de).
II *vtr* **1** (Law) agresser; **to be indecently ~ed** être victime d'une agression sexuelle; **2** (Mil) assaillir.
assemble I *vtr* **1** (gather) rassembler; **2** (construct) assembler; **easy to ~** facile à monter.
II *vi* [*passengers, marchers*] se rassembler; [*parliament, team, family*] se réunir.
assembly *n* **1** (gen) assemblée *f*; **2** (Sch) rassemblement *m*; **3** (of components, machines) assemblage *m*.
assembly line *n* chaîne *f* de montage.
assent I *n* assentiment *m* (**to** à).
II *vi* donner son assentiment (**to** à).
assert *vtr* **1** (state) affirmer (**that** que); **to ~ oneself** s'affirmer; **2** revendiquer [*right, claim*].
assertion *n* déclaration *f* (**that** selon laquelle).
assertive *adj* assuré/-e.
assess *vtr* **1** évaluer [*person, problem*]; estimer [*damage, value*]; **2** fixer [*tax*]; **3** (Sch) contrôler [*pupil*].
assessment *n* **1** (evaluation) appréciation *f* (**of** de); (of damage, value) estimation *f* (**of** de); **2** (for tax) imposition *f*; **3** (Sch) contrôle *m*.
asset *n* atout *m*; **~s** (private) avoir *m*; (of company) actif *m*.
assign *vtr* **1** assigner [*resources*] (**to** à); **2 to ~ a task to sb** confier une tâche à qn; **3** (attribute) attribuer (**to** à); **4** (appoint) nommer (**to** à).
assignment *n* mission *f*.
assimilate I *vtr* assimiler.
II *vi* s'assimiler (**into** dans).
assist I *vtr* **1** (help) aider; (in organization) assister (**to do, in doing** à faire); **2** (facilitate) faciliter [*development, process*].
II *vi* aider (**in doing** à faire); **to ~ in** prendre part à [*operation, rescue*].
assistance *n* aide *f* (**to** à); (more formal) assistance *f* (**to** à).
assistant ▶626 I *n* **1** (helper) assistant/-e *m/f*; (in hierarchy) adjoint/-e *m/f*; **2** (also **shop ~**) vendeur/-euse *m/f*; **3** (GB) (**foreign language ~** (in school) assistant/-e *m/f*; (in university) lecteur/-trice *m/f*.
II *adj* [*editor, manager*] adjoint/-e.
associate I *n* associé/-e *m/f*.
II *vtr* **1** associer [*idea, memory*] (**with** à); **2 to be ~d with** [*person*] faire partie de [*movement, group*]; être mêlé/-e à [*shady deal*].
III *vi* **to ~ with sb** fréquenter qn.
association *n* association *f*.

assorted *adj* [*objects, colours*] varié/-e; [*foodstuffs*] assorti/-e.
assortment *n* (of objects, colours) assortiment *m* (**of** de); (of people) mélange *m* (**of** de).
assume *vtr* **1** (suppose) supposer (**that** que); **2** prendre [*control, identity, office*]; assumer [*responsibility*]; affecter [*expression, indifference*]; **under an ~d name** sous un nom d'emprunt.
assumption *n* supposition *f*.
assurance *n* assurance *f*.
assure *vtr* assurer; **to ~ sb that** assurer à qn que.
asterisk *n* astérisque *m*.
asthma ▶533 *n* asthme *m*.
asthmatic *n, adj* asthmatique (*mf*).
astonish *vtr* surprendre, étonner.
astonished *adj* étonné/-e (**by, at** par; **to do** de faire).
astonishing *adj* étonnant/-e.
astonishment *n* étonnement *m*.
astound *vtr* stupéfier.
astounding *adj* incroyable.
astray *adv* **1 to go ~** (go missing) se perdre; **2 to lead sb ~** (confuse) induire qn en erreur; (corrupt) détourner qn du droit chemin.
astride I *adv* à califourchon.
II *prep* à califourchon sur.
astrologer, **astrologist** ▶626 *n* astrologue *mf*.
astrology *n* astrologie *f*.
astronaut ▶626 *n* astronaute *mf*.
astronomer ▶626 *n* astronome *mf*.
astronomic, **astronomical** *adj* astronomique.
astronomy *n* astronomie *f*.
astute *adj* astucieux/-ieuse.
asylum *n* asile *m*; **lunatic ~** asile de fous.
at *prep*

■ **Note** *at* is often translated by *à*: *at the airport* = à l'aéroport; *at midnight* = à minuit; *at the age of 50* = à l'âge de 50 ans.
– Remember that *à* + *le always* becomes *au* and *à* + *les always* becomes *aux* (*au bureau, aux bureaux*).
– When *at* means *at the house, shop*, etc *of*, it is translated by *chez*: *at Amanda's* = chez Amanda; *at the hairdresser's* = chez le coiffeur.
– For examples and other usages, see the entry below.
– *At* is used with many verbs, adjectives and nouns (*look at, good at, at last*) etc. For translations consult the appropropriate verb, adjective or noun entry.

---

1 à; **~ school** à l'école; **~ 4 o'clock** à quatre heures; **~ Easter** à Pâques; **~ night** la nuit; **~ the moment** en ce moment; **2** chez; **~ my house** chez moi; **~ home** à la maison, chez soi.
atheist *n, adj* athée (*mf*).
Athens ▶448 *pr n* Athènes.
athlete *n* athlète *mf*.
athlete's foot ▶533 *n* mycose *f*.

athletic *adj* athlétique.

athletics ▶504 *n* (GB) athlétisme *m*; (US) sports *mpl*.

Atlantic I *pr n* **the ~** l'Atlantique *m*.
II *adj* [*coast*] atlantique.

atlas *n* atlas *m*.

atmosphere *n* **1** (air) atmosphère *f*; **2** (mood) ambiance *f*; (bad) atmosphère *f*.

atom *n* atome *m*.

atom bomb *n* bombe *f* atomique.

atomic *adj* atomique, nucléaire.

atrocious *adj* atroce.

atrocity *n* atrocité *f*.

attach *vtr* attacher (**to** à).

attaché *n* attaché/-e *m/f*.

attaché case *n* attaché-case *m*.

attached *adj* **1** (fond) **to be ~ to** être attaché/-e à; **2** [*document*] ci-joint/-e.

attachment *n* **1** (affection) attachement *m*; **2** (device) accessoire *m*.

attack I *n* **1** (gen) attaque *f* (**on** contre); (criminal) agression *f* (**against, on** contre); (terrorist) attentat *m*; **2** (of illness) crise *f* (**of** de).
II *vtr* **1** (gen) attaquer; (criminally) agresser [*victim*]; **2** s'attaquer à [*task, problem*].

attacker *n* (gen) agresseur *m*; (Mil, Sport) attaquant/-e *m/f*.

attempt I *n* **1** tentative *f* (**to do** de faire); **to make an ~ to do** or **at doing** tenter de faire; **2 to make an ~ on sb's life** attenter à la vie de qn.
II *vtr* tenter (**to do** de faire); **~ed murder** tentative de meurtre.

attend I *vtr* assister à [*ceremony, meeting*]; aller à [*church, school*]; suivre [*class, course*].
II *vi* être présent/-e.
■ **attend to** s'occuper de [*person, problem*].

attendance *n* présence *f* (**at** à).

attendant ▶626 *n* (in cloakroom, museum, car park) gardien/-ienne *m/f*; (at petrol station) pompiste *mf*; (at pool) surveillant/-e *m/f*.

attention *n* **1** attention *f*; **to draw ~ to sth** attirer l'attention sur qch; **2** (Mil) **to stand to** or **at ~** être au garde-à-vous; **~!** garde-à-vous!

attentive *adj* (alert) attentif/-ive; (solicitous) attentionné/-e (**to** à).

attic *n* grenier *m*; **the toys are in the ~** les jouets sont au grenier.

attic room *n* mansarde *f*.

attitude *n* attitude *f* (**to, towards** (GB) à l'égard de).

attorney ▶626 *n* (US) avocat *m*.

attract *vtr* attirer.

attraction *n* **1** (favourable feature) attrait *m* (**of** de; **for** pour); **2** (entertainment, sight) attraction *f*; **3** (sexual) attirance *f* (**to** pour).

attractive *adj* [*person, offer*] séduisant/-e; [*child*] charmant/-e; [*place*] attrayant/-e.

attribute I *n* attribut *m*.
II *vtr* attribuer (**to** à).

aubergine *n* (GB) aubergine *f*.

auburn ▶438 *adj* auburn *inv*.

auction I *n* enchères *fpl*.
II *vtr* (also **~ off**) vendre [qch] aux enchères.

auctioneer ▶626 *n* commissaire-priseur *m*.

audacity *n* audace *f*.

audible *adj* audible.

audience *n* (in cinema, concert, theatre) public *m*, salle *f*; (of radio programme) auditeurs *mpl*; (of TV programme) téléspectateurs *mpl*.

audio *adj* audio *inv*.

audiovisual, **AV** *adj* audiovisuel/-elle.

audit I *n* audit *m*.
II *vtr* auditer, vérifier.

audition I *n* audition *f* (**for** pour).
II *vtr*, *vi* auditionner (**for** pour).

auditor ▶626 *n* **1** commissaire *m* aux comptes; **2** (US) (student) auditeur/-trice *m/f*.

auditorium *n* salle *f*.

augur *vi* **to ~ well** être de bon augure.

August ▶456 *n* août *m*.

aunt *n* tante *f*.

au pair *n* (jeune) fille *f* au pair.

aura *n* (of place) atmosphère *f*; (of person) aura *f*.

aural *adj* **1** (gen) auditif/-ive; **2** (Sch) [*comprehension, test*] oral/-e.

auspicious *adj* prometteur/-euse.

austere *adj* austère.

austerity *n* austérité *f*.

Australia ▶448 *pr n* Australie *f*.

Australian ▶553 I *n* Australien/-ienne *m/f*.
II *adj* australien/-ienne; [*embassy*] d'Australie.

Austria ▶448 *pr n* Autriche *f*.

Austrian ▶553 I *n* Autrichien/-ienne *m/f*.
II *adj* autrichien/-ienne; [*embassy*] d'Autriche.

authentic *adj* authentique.

author ▶626 *n* auteur *m*.

authoritarian *adj* autoritaire.

authoritative *adj* **1** (forceful) autoritaire; **2** (reliable) [*work*] qui fait autorité; [*source*] bien informé.

authority *n* **1** autorité *f*; **the authorities** les autorités; **2** (permission) autorisation *f*.

authorization *n* autorisation *f*.

authorize *vtr* autoriser (**to do** à faire).

autobiography *n* autobiographie *f*.

autograph I *n* autographe *m*.
II *vtr* dédicacer.

automatic I *n* **1** (washing machine) machine *f* à laver automatique; **2** (car) voiture *f* (à changement de vitesse) automatique; **3** (gun) automatique *m*.
II *adj* automatique.

automatically *adv* automatiquement.

automation *n* automatisation *f*.

automobile *n* automobile *f*.

autonomy *n* autonomie *f*.

autopsy *n* autopsie *f*.

autumn *n* automne *m*; **in ~** en automne.

auxiliary *n*, *adj* auxiliaire (*mf*).

availability *n* (of option, service) existence *f*; **subject to ~** (of holidays, rooms, theatre seats) dans la limite des places disponibles.

available *adj* disponible (**for** pour; **to** à).
avalanche *n* avalanche *f*.
avarice *n* cupidité *f*.
avenge *vtr* venger.
avenue *n* **1** (street, road) avenue *f*; **2** (path, driveway) allée *f*.
average I *n* moyenne *f* (**of** de); **on (the) ~** en moyenne; **above/below (the) ~** au-dessus de/au-dessous de la moyenne.
II *adj* moyen/-enne.
III *vtr* faire en moyenne.
averse *adj* opposé/-e (**to** à); **to be ~ to doing** répugner à faire.
aversion *n* aversion *f* (**to** pour).
avert *vtr* éviter; **to ~ one's eyes from sth** détourner les yeux de qch.
aviary *n* volière *f*.
avid *adj* [*collector, reader*] passionné/-e; **to be ~ for sth** être avide de qch.
avocado *n* (also **~ pear**) avocat *m*.
avoid *vtr* (gen) éviter; esquiver [*issue, question*]; **to ~ doing** éviter de faire.
await *vtr* attendre.
awake I *adj* (not yet asleep) éveillé/-e; (after sleeping) réveillé/-e; **wide ~** bien réveillé/-e; **the noise kept me ~** le bruit m'a empêché de dormir.
II *vtr* réveiller [*person*].
III *vi* [*person*] se réveiller.
award I *n* (prize) prix *m* (**for** de).
II *vtr* décerner [*prize*]; attribuer [*grant*]; accorder [*points, penalty*].
aware *adj* (conscious) conscient/-e (**of** de); (informed) au courant (**of** de).
awareness *n* conscience *f* (**of** de; **that** que).
away

■ **Note** *away* often appears after a verb in English to show that an action is continuous or intense. If *away* does not change the basic meaning of the verb only the verb is translated: *he was snoring away* = il ronflait.

I *adj* (Sport) [*goal, match, win*] à l'extérieur; **the ~ team** les visiteurs *mpl*.
II *adv* **1 to be ~** être absent/-e (**from** de); **to be ~ on business** être en voyage d'affaires; **to be ~ from home** ne pas être chez soi, être absent/-e de chez soi; **she's ~ in Paris** elle est à Paris; **to crawl ~** partir en rampant; **3 km ~** à 3 km; **London is two hours ~** Londres est à deux heures d'ici; **my birthday is two months ~** mon anniversaire est dans deux mois; **2** (Sport) [*play*] à l'extérieur.
awe *n* crainte *f* mêlée d'admiration; **to listen in ~** écouter impressionné/-e; **to be in ~ of sb** avoir peur de qn.
awe-inspiring *adj* impressionnant/-e.
awful *adj* **1** affreux/-euse, atroce; (in quality) exécrable; **2 I feel ~** (ill) je ne me sens pas bien du tout; (guilty) je culpabilise; **3**○ **an ~ lot (of)** énormément (de).
awfully *adv* extrêmement.
awkward *adj* **1** [*tool*] peu commode; [*shape, design*] difficile; **2** (clumsy) [*person, gesture*] maladroit/-e; **3** [*issue, choice*] difficile; **at an ~ time** au mauvais moment; **4** (embarrassing) [*question*] embarrassant/-e; [*situation*] délicat/-e; [*silence*] gêné/-e; **5** (uncooperative) [*person*] difficile (**about** à propos de).
awning *n* (on shop) banne *f*, auvent *m*; (on tent, house) auvent *m*; (on market stall) bâche *f*.
awry I *adj* de travers *inv*.
II *adv* **to go ~** mal tourner.
axe, **ax** (US) I *n* hache *f*.
II *vtr* virer○ [*employee*]; supprimer [*jobs*]; abandonner [*plan*].
axis *n* axe *m*.
axle *n* essieu *m*.

Bb

b, **B** *n* **1** (letter) b, B *m*; **2 B** (Mus) si *m*.

BA *n* (*abbr* = **Bachelor of Arts**) (degree) diplôme *m* universitaire de lettres.

baby I *n* bébé *m*.
II *adj* [*clothes, food*] pour bébés; [*brother, sister*] petit/-e (*before n*); **~ seal** bébé phoque.

babysit *vi* faire du babysitting.

babysitter *n* baby-sitter *mf*.

bachelor *n* célibataire *m*.

Bachelor of Arts *n* (person) licencié/-e *m/f* ès lettres.

back ▶ 413 I *n* **1** (of person, animal) dos *m*; **to turn one's ~ on sb/sth** tourner le dos à qn/qch; **behind sb's ~** dans le dos de qn; **2** (of page, cheque, hand, envelope, coat) dos *m*; (of vehicle, plane, building, head) arrière *m*; (of chair, sofa) dossier *m*; (of cupboard, drawer, fridge, bus) fond *m*; **the ones at the ~ couldn't see** ceux qui étaient derrière ne pouvaient pas voir; **the steps at the ~ of the building** l'escalier à l'arrière de l'immeuble; **at the ~ of the drawer** au fond du tiroir; **at the ~ of the plane/bus** à l'arrière de l'avion/au fond du bus; **in the back (of the car)** à l'arrière; **3** (Sport) arrière *m*; **left ~** arrière gauche.
II *adj* [*paw, wheel*] arrière; [*bedroom*] du fond; [*page*] dernier/-ière (*before n*); [*garden, gate*] de derrière.
III *adv* **1 to be ~** être de retour; **I'll be ~ in five minutes** je reviens dans cinq minutes; **to come ~** rentrer (**from** de); **to come ~ home** rentrer chez soi; **2 to give/put sth ~** rendre/remettre qch; **to phone ~** rappeler; **I'll write ~ (to him)** je lui répondrai; **3** [*look, jump, lean*] en arrière; **4 ~ in 1964/April** en 1964/avril; **5 to travel to London and ~** faire un aller-retour à Londres.
IV *vtr* **1** (support) soutenir [*candidate, bill*]; apporter son soutien à [*project*]; justifier [*claim*] (**with** à l'aide de); financer [*venture*]; **2 to ~ the car into the garage** rentrer la voiture au garage en marche arrière; **3** (bet on) parier sur [*favourite, winner*].
V **back and forth** *phr* **to go** or **travel ~ and forth** (commute) [*person, bus*] faire la navette (**between** entre); **to go** or **walk ~ and forth** faire des allées et venues (**between** entre); **to sway ~ and forth** se balancer.
■ **back away** reculer; **to ~ away from** s'éloigner de [*person*]; chercher à éviter [*confrontation*].
■ **back down** céder.
■ **back out**: ¶ **~ out 1** [*car, driver*] sortir en marche arrière; **2** [*person*] se désister; **to ~ out of** annuler [*deal*]; ¶ **~ [sth] out**: **to ~ the car out of the garage** faire sortir la voiture du garage en marche arrière.
■ **back up** confirmer [*claims, theory*]; soutenir [*person*]; (Comput) sauvegarder.

backache *n* **to have ~** avoir mal au dos.

backbone *n* colonne *f* vertébrale.

backdate *vtr* antidater [*cheque, letter*].

back door *n* (of car) portière *f* arrière; (of building) porte *f* de derrière.

backfire *vi* **1** [*scheme*] avoir l'effet inverse; **to ~ on sb** se retourner contre qn; **2** [*car*] pétarader.

backgammon ▶ 504 *n* jaquet *m*.

background I *n* **1** (of person) (social) milieu *m*; (family) origines *fpl*; (professional) formation *f*; **2** (of events, situation) contexte *m*; **against a ~ of violence** dans un climat de violence; **to remain in the ~** rester au second plan; **voices in the ~** des voix en bruit de fond; **3** (of painting, photo, scene) arrière-plan *m*; **in the ~** à l'arrière-plan.
II *adj* **1** [*information*] sur les origines de la situation; **~ reading** lectures *fpl* complémentaires; **2** [*music, lighting*] d'ambiance; [*noise*] de fond.

backhand *n* (Sport) revers *m*.

backing *n* **1** (support) soutien *m*; **2** (reverse layer) revêtement *m* intérieur.

backing vocals *n pl* chœurs *mpl*.

backlash *n* réaction *f* violente (**against** contre).

backlog *n* retard *m*; **I've got a huge ~ (of work)** j'ai plein de travail en retard.

backpack I *n* sac *m* à dos.
II *vi* **to go ~ing** partir en voyage avec son sac à dos.

back pay *n* rappel *m* de salaire.

back seat *n* siège *m* arrière; **to take a ~** (figurative) s'effacer.

backside○ *n* derrière *m*.

backstage *adv* dans les coulisses.

backstreet *n* petite rue *f*.

backstroke *n* dos *m* crawlé.

back to back *adv* **to stand ~** [*two people*] se mettre dos à dos.

back to front *adj, adv* à l'envers.

backtrack *vi* rebrousser chemin; (figurative) faire marche arrière.

backup *n* (gen) soutien *m*; (Mil) renforts *mpl*.

backward I *adj* **1** [*look, step*] en arrière; **2** [*nation*] arriéré/-e; **3** [*person*] arriéré/-e.
II *adv* (also **backwards**) **1** [*walk*] à reculons; [*lean, step, fall*] en arrière; **to move ~** reculer; **to walk ~ and forward** faire des allées et venues; **2** [*count*] à rebours; [*play*] à l'envers.

backwards = **backward II**.

backyard *n* **1** (GB) (courtyard) arrière-cour *f*; **2** (US) (back garden) jardin *m* de derrière.

bacon *n* bacon *m*, ≈ lard *m*; **~ and egg(s)** des œufs au bacon.

bacteria *n pl* bactéries *fpl*.

bad I *n* **the good and the ~** le bon et le mauvais; **there is good and ~ in everyone** il y a du bon et du mauvais dans chacun.

II *adj* **1** (gen) mauvais/-e (*before n*); [*joke*] stupide; [*language*] grossier/-ière; **to be ~ at** être mauvais/-e en [*subject*]; **not ~**○ pas mal○; **too ~**○! (sympathetic) pas de chance!; (hard luck) tant pis!; **it will look ~** cela fera mauvais effet; **to feel ~** avoir mauvaise conscience (**about** à propos de); **2** (serious) [*accident, injury, mistake*] grave; **a ~ cold** un gros rhume; **3 it's ~ for you** or **your health** c'est mauvais pour la santé; **4 to have a ~ back** souffrir du dos; **to have a ~ chest** être malade des poumons; **to be in a ~ way**○ aller très mal; **5** [*fruit*] pourri; **to go ~** pourrir.

badge *n* (gen) badge *m*; (official) insigne *m*.

badly *adv* **1** [*begin, behave, sleep*] mal; [*made, worded*] mal; **to go ~** [*exam, interview*] mal se passer; **to do ~** [*candidate, company*] obtenir de mauvais résultats; **to take sth ~** mal prendre qch; **2** [*suffer*] beaucoup; [*affect*] sérieusement; [*hurt, damaged*] gravement; **3 to want/need sth ~** avoir très envie de/grand besoin de qch.

badly off *adj* pauvre.

bad-mannered *adj* [*person*] mal élevé.

badminton ▶504 *n* badminton *m*.

bad-tempered *adj* (temporarily) irrité/-e; (habitually) irritable.

baffle *vtr* rendre [qn] perplexe, confondre.

bag I *n* sac *m* (**of** de).

II **bags** *n pl* bagages *mpl*; **to pack one's ~s** faire ses bagages; (figurative) faire ses valises.

IDIOMS **to have ~s under one's eyes** avoir des valises sous les yeux○.

baggage *n* bagages *mpl*.

baggage allowance *n* franchise *f* de bagages.

baggage reclaim *n* réception *f* des bagages.

baggy *adj* large, ample.

bagpipes ▶586 *n* cornemuse *f*.

bail *n* caution *f*; **to be (out) on ~** être libéré/-e sous caution.

■ **bail out**: **~ out** (of plane) sauter; ¶ **~ [sb] out** (gen) tirer [qn] d'affaire [*person*]; (Law) payer la caution pour [*person*].

bailiff *n* huissier *m*.

bait *n* appât *m*.

bake I *vtr* faire cuire [qch] au four [*dish, vegetable*]; faire [*bread, cake*].

II *vi* **1** (make bread) faire du pain; (make cakes) faire de la pâtisserie; **2** (cook) [*food*] cuire.

baked beans *n pl* haricots *mpl* blancs à la sauce tomate.

baked potato *n* pomme *f* de terre en robe des champs (au four).

baker ▶626 *n* boulanger/-ère *m/f*.

bakery ▶626 *n* boulangerie *f*.

balance I *n* **1** équilibre *m* (**between** entre); **to lose one's ~** perdre l'équilibre; **the right ~** le juste milieu; **2** (scales) balance *f*; **to hang in the ~** être en jeu; **3** (of account) solde *m*; **to pay the ~** verser le surplus.

II *vtr* **1** mettre [qch] en équilibre [*ball, plate*] (**on** sur); **2** (compensate for) (also **~ out**) compenser, équilibrer; **3** (counterbalance) contrebalancer [*weights*]; **4** (adjust) équilibrer [*diet, budget*]; **to ~ the books** dresser le bilan.

III *vi* **1** [*person*] se tenir en équilibre (**on** sur); [*object*] tenir en équilibre (**on** sur); **2** (also **~ out**) s'equilibrer; **3** [*books, figures*] être en équilibre.

IV **balanced** *pp adj* [*person, view, diet*] équilibré/-e; [*article, report*] objectif/-ive.

balance of payments *n* balance *f* des paiements.

balance of power *n* équilibre *m* des forces.

balance of trade *n* balance *f* du commerce extérieur.

balance sheet *n* bilan *m*.

balcony *n* **1** (in house, hotel) balcon *m*; **2** (in theatre) deuxième balcon *m*.

bald *adj* **1** [*man, head*] chauve; **2** [*tyre*] lisse.

ball I *n* **1** (gen) balle *f*; (in football, rugby) ballon *m*; (in billiards) bille *f*; **2** (of dough, clay) boule *f* (**of** de); (of wool, string) pelote *f* (**of** de); **3** (dance) bal *m*.

II **balls**◐ *n pl* **1** (testicles) couilles◐ *fpl*; **2** (rubbish) conneries *fpl*.

ballet *n* ballet *m*.

balloon *n* **1** ballon *m*; **2** (also **hot air ~**) montgolfière *f*.

ballot I *n* **1** scrutin *m*; **2** (also **~ paper**) bulletin *m* de vote.

II *vtr* consulter [qn] (par vote) (**on** sur).

ballot box *n* urne *f* (électorale).

ballpoint (pen) *n* stylo *m* (à) bille.

ballroom *n* salle *f* de danse.

Baltic *adj* **the ~ Sea** la mer *f* Baltique.

ban I *n* interdiction *f* (**on** de).

II *vtr* (gen) interdire; suspendre [*athlete*]; **to ~ sb from doing** interdire à qn de faire.

banana *n* banane *f*.

band *n* **1** (of people) groupe *m* (**of** de); (of musicians) (rock) groupe (de rock); (municipal) fanfare *f*; **jazz ~** orchestre *m* de jazz; **2** (strip) bande *f*; **3** (GB) (of age, income tax) tranche *f*; **4** (around arm) brassard *m*; (**hair**) **~** bandeau *m*.

■ **band together** se réunir (**to do** pour faire).

bandage I *n* bandage *m*.

II *vtr* bander [*head, limb, wound*].

bandit *n* bandit *m*.

bandwagon *n* IDIOMS **to jump** or **climb on the ~** prendre le train en marche.

bang I *n* **1** (of explosion) détonation *f*, boum *m*; (of door, window) claquement *m*; **2** (knock) coup *m*.

II○ *adv* **~ in the middle** en plein centre.

III *vtr* **1** taper sur [*drum, saucepan*]; **to ~ sth down on the table** poser bruyamment qch sur la table; **to ~ one's head** se cogner la tête (**on** contre); **to ~ one's fist on the table** taper du poing sur la table; **2** (slam) claquer [*door, window*].

IV *vi* [*door, shutter*] claquer.

bangle *n* bracelet *m*.

banish *vtr* bannir (**from** de).

banister, **bannister** (GB) *n* rampe *f* (d'escalier).

bank I *n* **1** banque *f*; **2** (of river, lake) rive *f*; (of major river) bord *m*; (of canal) berge *f*; **3** (mound) talus *m*; (of snow) congère *f*; (of flowers) massif *m*; (of fog, mist) banc *m*.
II *vi* **to ~ with the National** avoir un compte (bancaire) à la Nationale.
■ **bank on** compter sur [*person*] (**to do** pour faire); **to ~ on doing** escompter faire.

bank account *n* compte *m* bancaire.

bank card *n* carte *f* bancaire.

bank charges *n pl* frais *mpl* bancaires.

bank clerk ▶626| *n* employé/-e *m/f* de banque.

banker ▶626| *n* banquier/-ière *m/f*.

banker's draft *n* traite *f* bancaire.

banker's order *n* virement *m* bancaire.

bank holiday *n* (GB) jour *m* férié; (US) jour *m* de fermeture des banques.

banking *n* **1** (business) opérations *fpl* bancaires; **2** (profession) la banque.

banking hours *n pl* heures *fpl* d'ouverture des banques.

bank manager ▶626| *n* directeur/-trice *m/f* d'agence bancaire.

banknote *n* billet *m* de banque.

bankrupt *adj* [*person*] ruiné/-e; [*economy*] en faillite; **to go ~** faire faillite.

bankruptcy *n* faillite *f*.

bank statement *n* relevé *m* de compte.

banner *n* banderole *f*.

baptism *n* baptême *m*.

baptize *vtr* baptiser.

bar I *n* **1** (of metal, wood) barre *f*; (on cage, window) barreau *m*; **2** (pub) bar *m*; (counter) comptoir *m*; **3 ~ of soap** savonnette *f*; **~ of chocolate** tablette *f* de chocolat; **4** (Law) (profession) **the ~** le barreau; **5** (Sport) barre *f*; **6** (Mus) mesure *f*.
II *prep* sauf; **all ~ one** tous sauf un seul/une seule.
III *vtr* **1** barrer [*way, path*]; **to ~ sb's way** barrer le passage à qn; **2** (ban) exclure [*person*] (**from sth** de qch); **to ~ sb from doing** interdire à qn de faire.

barbaric *adj* barbare.

barbecue *n* barbecue *m*.

barbed wire, **barbwire** (US) *n* (fil *m* de fer) barbelé *m*.

barber ▶626| *n* coiffeur *m* (pour hommes).

Barcelona ▶448| *pr n* Barcelone.

bar chart *n* histogramme *m*.

bar code *n* code *m* à barres.

bare I *adj* (gen) nu/-e; [*cupboard, room*] vide; **with one's ~ hands** à mains nues; **the ~ minimum** le strict nécessaire.
II *vtr* **to ~ one's teeth** montrer les dents.

barefoot I *adj* **to be ~** être nu-pieds.
II *adv* [*run, walk*] pieds nus.

barely *adv* à peine.

bargain I *n* **1** (deal) marché *m* (**between** entre); **2** (good buy) affaire *f*.
II *vi* **1** (for deal) négocier (**with** avec); **2** (over price) marchander (**with** avec).
■ **bargain for**, **bargain on** s'attendre à.

barge I *n* péniche *f*; (for freight) chaland *m*.
II *vi* **to ~ past sb** passer devant qn en le bousculant.
■ **barge in** (enter noisily) faire irruption; (interrupt) interrompre brutalement.

bark I *n* **1** (of tree) écorce *f*; **2** (of dog) aboiement *m*.
II *vi* aboyer (**at sb/sth** après qn/qch).

barley *n* orge *f*.

barmaid ▶626| *n* serveuse *f* de bar.

barman ▶626| *n* barman *m*.

barn *n* (for crops) grange *f*; (for cattle) étable *f*.

baron *n* baron *m*.

barracks *n* caserne *f*.

barrage *n* (gen) barrage *m*; (Mil) tir *m* de barrage.

barrel *n* **1** (for beer, wine) tonneau *m*, fût *m*; (for oil) baril *m*; **2** (of gun) canon *m*.

barricade *n* barricade *f*.

barrier *n* barrière *f*.

barrier cream *n* crème *f* protectrice.

barring *prep* à moins de.

barrister ▶626| *n* (GB) avocat/-e *m/f*.

base I *n* (gen, Mil) base *f*; (of tree, lamp) pied *m*.
II *adj* ignoble.
III *vtr* fonder (**on** sur); **the film is ~d on a true story** le film est tiré d'une histoire vraie; **to be ~d in Paris** [*person, company*] être basé/-e à Paris.

baseball ▶504| *n* base-ball *m*.

basement *n* sous-sol *m*; **in the ~** au sous-sol.

bashful *adj* timide.

basic *adj* **1** (gen) essentiel/-ielle; [*problem, principle*] fondamental/-e; **2** (elementary) [*knowledge, skill*] élémentaire; [*wage, training*] de base.

basically *adv* fondamentalement.

basics *n pl* essentiel *m*; **to get down to ~** aborder l'essentiel.

basil *n* basilic *m*.

basin *n* **1** (bowl) bol *m*; **2** (in bathroom) lavabo *m*; (portable) cuvette *f*.

basis *n* base *f* (**for, of** de); **on a regular/temporary ~** régulièrement/à titre provisoire.

basket *n* panier *m*.

basketball ▶504| *n* (game) basket(-ball) *m*; (ball) ballon *m* de basket.

bass ▶586| *n* basse *f*.

bass drum *n* grosse caisse *f*.

bass guitar *n* basse *f*.

bastard *n* **1** (illegitimate child) bâtard/-e *m/f*; **2**◐ salaud◐ *m*.

baste *vtr* (Culin) arroser.

bat *n* **1** (in cricket, baseball) batte *f*; (in table tennis) raquette *f*; **2** (Zool) chauve-souris *f*.

batch *n* (of loaves) fournée *f*; (of goods) lot *m*.

bated *adj* **with ~ breath** en retenant son souffle.

bath I *n* bain *m*; (GB) (tub) baignoire *f*; **to have a ~** prendre un bain.
II **baths** *n pl* **1** (for swimming) piscine *f*; **2** (in spa) thermes *mpl*.
III *vtr* (GB) baigner.

bathe I *vtr* laver [*wound*] (**in** dans; **with** à).
II *vi* **1** (swim) se baigner; **2** (US) (take bath) prendre un bain; **3 to be ~d in** ruisseler de [*sweat*]; être inondé/-e de [*light*].

bathing *n* baignade *f*.

bathing cap *n* bonnet *m* de bain.

bathing costume *n* costume *m* de bain.

bathrobe *n* sortie *f* de bain.

bathroom *n* **1** salle *f* de bains; **2** (US) (public lavatory) toilettes *fpl*.

bathroom cabinet *n* armoire *f* de toilette.

bathroom scales *n pl* pèse-personne *m*.

bath towel *n* serviette *f* de bain.

bathtub *n* baignoire *f*.

baton *n* (GB) (policeman's) matraque *f*; (traffic policeman's) bâton *m*; (Mus) baguette *f*; (in relay race) témoin *m*.

batter I *n* pâte *f*.
II *vtr* battre.

battered *adj* **1** [*kettle, hat*] cabossé/-e; [*suitcase*] très abîmé/-e; **2** [*wife*] battu/-e.

battery *n* pile *f*; (in car) batterie *f*.

battle I *n* bataille *f*; (figurative) lutte *f*.
II *vi* (gen, Mil) combattre (**with sb** contre qn); **to ~ for sth/to do** lutter pour qch/pour faire.

battlefield *n* champ *m* de bataille.

battleship *n* cuirassé *m*.

bawdy *adj* [*song*] grivois/-e; [*person*] paillard/-e.

bawl *vi* (weep) brailler; (shout) hurler.

bay I *n* **1** (on coast) baie *f*; **2** (Bot) (also **~ tree**) laurier(-sauce) *m*; **3 loading/parking ~** aire *f* de chargement/stationnement.
II *vi* [*dog*] aboyer (**at** contre, après).
IDIOMS **to hold [sb/sth] at ~** tenir [qn/qch] à distance.

bay leaf *n* feuille *f* de laurier.

bayonet *n* baïonnette *f*.

BC (*abbr* = **Before Christ**) av. J.-C.

be

■ **Note** For translations of *there is, there are, here is* and *here are*, see the entries ***there*** and ***here***.
– This dictionary contains usage notes on topics such as clocktime, age, many of which include translations of particular uses of *to be*. For the index to these notes ▶ 784.

I *vi* **1** être; **she is French** elle est française; **we are late** nous sommes en retard; **he is a doctor/widower** il est médecin/veuf; **it is Monday** c'est lundi; **it's me!** c'est moi!; **~ good!** sois sage!; **2** (physical and mental states) avoir; **I am cold/hot** j'ai froid/chaud; **are you hungry/thirsty?** as-tu faim/soif?; **his hands were cold** il avait froid aux mains; **3** (weather) faire; **it is cold/windy** il fait froid/du vent; **it is 40°** il fait 40°; **4** (health) aller; **how are you?** (polite) comment allez-vous?; (more informally) comment vas-tu?; (very informally) ça va?; **how is your son?** comment va votre fils?; ▶ **well**[1], **fine**, **better**; **5** (visit) **I've never been to Sweden** je ne suis jamais allé en Suède; **have you ever been to Africa?** tu es déjà allé en Afrique?; **has the postman been?** est-ce que le facteur est passé?; **6** (age) avoir; **how old are you?** quel âge as-tu?; **I am 23** j'ai 23 ans; **7** (in mathematics) faire; **2 plus 2 is 4** 2 et 2 font 4; **8** (cost) coûter; **how much is it?** combien ça coûte?; **9** (phrases) **so ~ it** d'accord; **if I were you** à ta place.
II *v aux* **1** (in passives) être; **the doors have been repainted** les portes ont été repeintes, on a repeint les portes; **it is said that...** on dit que...; **2** (in continuous tenses) **we are going to London tomorrow** nous allons à Londres demain; **it is raining** il pleut; **he is reading** il lit, il est en train de lire; ▶ **for**, **since**; **3** (with infinite) devoir; **you are to do it at once** tu dois le faire tout de suite; **they are to ~ married** ils vont se marier; **it was to ~ expected** il fallait s'y attendre; **it was nowhere to ~ found** il était introuvable; **4** (in tag questions) **it's a lovely house, isn't it?** c'est une très belle maison, n'est-ce pas?; **they're not in the garden, are they?** ils ne sont pas dans le jardin, par hasard?; **today is Tuesday, isn't it?** c'est bien mardi aujourd'hui?; **5** (in short answers) **'you are not going out'—'yes I am!'** 'tu ne sors pas'—'si!'; **'are you English?'—'yes, I am'** 'vous êtes anglais?'—'oui', 'oui, je suis anglais'.

beach *n* plage *f*.

beach ball *n* ballon *m* de plage.

beacon *n* **1** (on runway) balise *f*; **2** (lighthouse) phare *m*; **3** (also **radio ~**) radiobalise *f*.

bead *n* **1** perle *f*; **(string of) ~s** collier *m*; **2** (of sweat, dew) goutte *f*.

beak *n* bec *m*.

beam I *n* **1** (of light, torch) rayon *m*; (of car lights, lighthouse) faisceau *m*; **2** (wooden) poutre *f*.
II *vtr* transmettre [*signal*].
III *vi* rayonner.

bean *n* haricot *m*.

bear I *n* ours *m*.
II *vtr* **1** (carry) porter; **to ~ a resemblance to** ressembler à; **to ~ no relation to** n'avoir aucun rapport avec; **to ~ sth in mind** tenir compte de qch; **2** (endure) supporter; **I can't ~ to watch** je ne veux pas voir ça; **3** (stand up to) résister à [*scrutiny, inspection*]; **4** (yield) donner [*fruit, crop*]; [*investment*] rapporter [*interest*].
III *vi* **1 to ~ left/right** [*person*] prendre à gauche/à droite; **2 to bring pressure to ~ on sb** exercer une pression sur qn.
■ **bear out** confirmer [*claim, story*]; appuyer [*person*].
■ **bear up** [*person*] tenir le coup; [*structure*] résister.

beard *n* barbe *f*.

bearer *n* (of news, gift, letter) porteur/-euse *m/f*; (of passport) titulaire *mf*.

bearing *n* **1** (of person) allure *f*; **2 to have no/little ~ on sth** n'avoir aucun rapport/avoir peu de rapport avec qch; **3 to take a compass ~** faire un relevé au compas.

bearings *n pl* **to get one's ~** se repérer.

beast *n* **1** (animal) bête *f*; **2**○ (person) brute *f*.

beat I *n* **1** (of drum, heart) battement *m*; **2** (rhythm) rythme *m*; **3** (of policeman) ronde *f*.
II *vtr* **1** battre; **to ~ sb with a stick** donner des coups de bâton à qn; **to ~ sb at tennis** battre qn au tennis; **to ~ time** (Mus) battre la mesure; **she beat me to it** elle a été plus rapide que moi; **2 it ~s walking** c'est mieux que marcher; **you can't ~ Italian shoes** rien ne vaut les chaussures italiennes.
III *vi* [*waves, rain*] battre (**against** contre); [*person*] cogner (**at, on** à); [*heart, drum, wings*] battre.
■ **beat back** repousser [*group, flames*].
■ **beat down** [*rain*] tomber à verse (**on** sur); [*sun*] taper (**on** sur).
■ **beat off** repousser [*attacker*].
■ **beat up** tabasser○ [*person*].

beating *n* **1** (punishment) raclée○ *f*, correction *f*; **2** (of drum, heart, wings) battement *m*.

beautiful *adj* beau/belle (*before n*); [*weather, shot*] superbe; **a ~ place** un bel endroit.

■ **Note** the irregular form *bel* of the adjective *beau, belle* is used before masculine nouns beginning with a vowel or a mute 'h'.

beautifully *adv* **1** [*play, write*] admirablement; **2** [*furnished*] magnifiquement; **~ dressed** habillé/-e avec beaucoup de goût.

beauty *n* beauté *f*.

beauty parlour (GB), **beauty parlor** (US) ▶ **626** *n* salon *m* de beauté.

beauty queen *n* reine *f* de beauté.

beauty salon ▶ **626** *n* salon *m* de beauté.

beauty spot *n* **1** (on skin) grain *m* de beauté; (fake) mouche *f*; **2** (place) beau site *m* or coin *m*.

beaver *n* castor *m*.

because I *conj* parce que.
II because of *phr* à cause de.

beckon I *vtr* faire signe à; **to ~ sb in** faire signe à qn d'entrer.
II *vi* faire signe (**to sb to do** à qn de faire).

become I *vi* devenir; **to ~ ill** tomber malade.
II *v impers* **what has ~ of your brother?** qu'est-ce que ton frère est devenu?

becoming *adj* [*behaviour*] convenable; [*garment, haircut*] seyant/-e.

bed *n* **1** lit *m*; **to go to ~** aller au lit; **2** (of flowers) parterre *m*; **3** (of sea) fond *m*; (of river) lit *m*.

bed and breakfast, B and B *n* chambre *f* avec petit déjeuner, ≈ chambre *f* d'hôte.

bedclothes *n pl* couvertures *fpl*.

bedridden *adj* alité/-e, cloué/-e au lit.

bedroom *n* chambre *f* (à coucher).

bedside *n* chevet *m*.

bedsit○, **bedsitter** *n* (GB) chambre *f* meublée.

bedspread *n* dessus *m* de lit.

bedtime *n* **it's ~** c'est l'heure d'aller se coucher.

bee *n* abeille *f*.

beech *n* hêtre *m*.

beef *n* bœuf *m*; **roast ~** rôti *m* de bœuf.

beefburger *n* hamburger *m*.

beehive *n* ruche *f*.

beeline *n* IDIOMS **to make a ~ for** se diriger tout droit vers.

beer *n* bière *f*.

bee sting *n* piqûre *f* d'abeille.

beet *n* betterave *f*.

beetle *n* scarabée *m*.

beetroot *n* (GB) betterave *f*.

before ▶ **406** **I** *prep* **1** avant; **the day ~ yesterday** avant-hier; **the day ~ the exam** la veille de l'examen; **2** (in front of) devant; **3** ▶ **434** (US) (in telling time) **ten ~ six** six heures moins dix.
II *adj* précédent/-e, d'avant; **the day ~** la veille; **the week ~** la semaine précédente.
III *adv* avant; **long ~** bien avant; **two months ~** deux mois auparavant; **have you been to India ~?** est-ce que tu es déjà allé en Inde?; **I've never seen him ~ in my life** c'est la première fois que je le vois.
IV *conj* (in time) **~ I go, I would like to say that** avant de partir, je voudrais dire que; **~ he goes, I must remind him that** avant qu'il parte, il faut que je lui rappelle que.

beforehand *adv* (ahead of time) à l'avance; (earlier) auparavant, avant.

beg I *vtr* demander (**from** à); **to ~ sb for sth** demander qch à qn; **I ~ your pardon** je vous demande pardon.
II *vi* [*person*] mendier (**from** à); [*dog*] faire le beau; **to ~ for help** demander de l'aide.

beggar *n* mendiant/-e *m/f*.

begin I *vtr* commencer [*journey, meeting, meal, game*] (**with** par, avec); provoquer [*debate, dispute*]; lancer [*campaign, trend*]; déclencher [*war*]; **to ~ doing** commencer à faire.
II *vi* commencer; **to ~ with sth** commencer par qch; **to ~ again** recommencer.
III to begin with *phr* (at first) au début, au départ; (firstly) d'abord, premièrement.

beginner *n* débutant/-e *m/f*.

beginning *n* début *m*, commencement *m*; **in** or **at the ~** au départ, au début; **to go back to the ~** reprendre au début.

beginnings *n pl* (of person, business) débuts *mpl*; (of movement) origines *fpl*.

behalf: **on ~ of** (GB), **in ~ of** (US) *phr* [*act, speak*] au nom de, pour; [*phone, write*] de la part de; [*negotiate*] pour le compte de.

behave I *vi* se comporter, se conduire (**towards** envers).
II *v refl* **to ~ oneself** bien se comporter; **~ yourself!** tiens-toi bien!

behaviour (GB), **behavior** (US) *n* (gen) comportement *m* (**towards** envers); (Sch) conduite *f*; **to be on one's best ~** bien se tenir.

behead *vtr* décapiter.

behind I○ *n* derrière○ *m*.
II *adj* **to be ~ with** avoir du retard dans [*work*]; **to be too far ~** avoir trop de retard.

before

As a preposition

⇨ I1

When *before* is used as a preposition, it is generally translated by ***avant:***

***before** the meeting*	= **avant** la réunion
*she left **before** me*	= elle est partie **avant** moi

As an adjective

When *before* is used as an adjective after a noun, it is translated by ***précédent/-e***, or, less formally, ***d'avant***:

*the time **before***	= la fois **précédente**
	= la fois **d'avant**
*the month **before***	= le mois **précédent**
	= le mois **d'avant**

the one before is translated by ***le précédent*** or ***la précédente***: ⇨ II

*no, I'm not talking about that meeting but **the one before***	= non, je ne parle pas de cette réunion-là mais de **la précédente**

As an adverb

- When *before* is used as an adverb meaning *beforehand*, it is translated by ***avant*** in statements about the present or future:

*you could have told me **before***	= tu aurais pu me le dire **avant**
*I'll try to talk to her **before***	= j'essaierai de lui en parler **avant**

- When *before* means *previously* in statements about the past, it is translated by ***auparavant***:

*I had met her two or three times **before***	= je l'avais rencontrée deux ou trois fois **auparavant**

- When *before* means *already*, it is translated by ***déjà***:

*I've met her **before***	= je l'ai **déjà** rencontrée
*you've asked me that question **before***	= tu m'as **déjà** posé cette question

- In negative sentences, *before* is often used in English simply to reinforce the negative. In such cases it is not translated at all:

*I'd never eaten snails **before***	= je n'avais jamais mangé d'escargots
*you've never told me that **before***	= tu ne m'as jamais dit ça

⇨ III

As a conjunction

- When used as a conjunction, ***before*** + *verb* is translated by ***avant de*** + *infinitive*, where the two verbs have the same subject:

***before** I cook dinner* or ***before** cooking dinner* *I'm going to phone my mother*	= **avant de** préparer le dîner je vais appeler ma mère
she put in her lenses ***before** she put on her make-up* or ***before** putting on her make-up*	= elle a mis ses lentilles **avant de** se maquiller

- When used as a conjunction, ***before*** + *verb* is translated by ***avant que*** + *subjunctive*, where the two verbs have different subjects:

*Tom wants to see her **before** she leaves*	= Tom veut la voir **avant qu**'elle parte
*I wanted to let you know **before** you make any plans*	= je voulais te prévenir **avant que** tu fasses des projets

⇨ IV

III *adv* [*follow on*] derrière; [*look, glance*] en arrière; **the car ~** la voiture de derrière.
IV *prep* **1** derrière; **~ my back** derrière le dos; (figurative) derrière mon dos; **~ the scenes** en coulisses; **2** (supporting) **to be (solidly) ~ sb** soutenir qn (à fond).

beige ▶ 438 *n, adj* beige (*m*).

Beijing ▶ 448 *pr n* Pékin, Bei-jing.

being *n* **1** (**human**) **~** être *m* (humain); **2 to come into ~** prendre naissance.

Beirut ▶ 448 *pr n* Beyrouth.

belch I *n* renvoi *m*, rot *m*.
II *vtr* (also **~ out**) vomir, cracher [*smoke, fire*].
III *vi* avoir un renvoi.

belfry *n* beffroi *m*, clocher *m*.

Belgian ▶ 553 **I** *n* Belge *mf*.
II *adj* belge; [*embassy*] de Belgique.

Belgium ▶ 448 *pr n* Belgique *f*.

belie *vtr* démentir.

belief *n* **1** (opinion) conviction *f* (**about** sur, à propos de); **2** (confidence) confiance *f*, foi *f* (**in** dans); **3** (religious faith) foi *f*.

believe I *vtr* croire; **I don't ~ you!** ce n'est pas vrai!
II *vi* **to ~ in** croire à [*promises, ghosts*]; croire en [*God*].

believer *n* (in God) croyant/-e *m/f*; (in progress, liberty) adepte *mf* (**in** de).

belittle *vtr* rabaisser.

bell *n* (in church) cloche *f*; (handbell) clochette *f*; (on toy, cat) grelot *m*; (on bicycle) sonnette *f*; **door ~** sonnette *f*.
IDIOMS **that name rings a ~** ce nom me dit quelque chose.

belligerent I *n* belligérant *m*.
II *adj* [*person*] agressif/-ive; [*country*] belligérant/-e.

bellow *vi* [*bull*] mugir (**with** de); [*person*] hurler.

bellows *n pl* soufflet *m*.

belly *n* ventre *m*.

belong *vi* **to ~ to** [*property*] appartenir à [*person*]; [*person*] faire partie de [*club, society, set*]; **where do these books ~?** où vont ces livres?

belongings *n pl* affaires *fpl*; **personal ~** effets *mpl* personnels.

beloved *n, adj* bien-aimé/-e (*m/f*).

below I *prep* au-dessous de; **~ freezing** au-dessous de zéro; **~ the surface** sous la surface.
II *adv* **the apartment ~** l'appartement du dessous; **the people (in the street) ~** les gens en bas (dans la rue); **the village ~** le village en contrebas; **100 metres ~** 100 mètres plus bas; **see ~** (on page) voir ci-dessous.

belt I *n* (gen) ceinture *f*; **2** (Tech) courroie *f*.
II° *vtr* (hit) flanquer une beigne à° [*person*].
IDIOMS **to tighten one's ~** se serrer la ceinture; **that was below the ~** c'était un coup bas.

bemused *adj* perplexe.

bench *n* **1** (gen) banc *m*; (workbench) établi *m*; **2** (Law) (also **Bench**) (judges collectively) magistrature *f* (assise); (judges hearing a case) Cour *f*.

bend I *n* (in road) tournant *m*, virage *m*; (in river) courbe *f*.
II *vtr* plier [*arm, leg*]; pencher [*head*]; tordre [*pipe, nail, wire*].
III *vi* **1** [*road, path*] tourner; [*branch*] ployer; **2** [*person*] se pencher; **to ~ forward** se pencher en avant.
■ **bend down, bend over** se pencher.

beneath I *prep* **1** sous; **~ the calm exterior** sous des apparences calmes; **2 it is ~ you to do** c'est indigne de toi de faire.
II *adv* en dessous; **the apartment ~** l'appartement en dessous.

benefactor *n* bienfaiteur *m*.

beneficial *adj* [*effect, influence*] bénéfique; [*change*] salutaire.

benefit I *n* **1** (advantage) avantage *m* (**from** de); **2** (financial aid) allocation *f*; **to be on ~(s)** (GB) toucher les allocations.
II *adj* [*concert, match*] de bienfaisance.
III *vtr* profiter à [*person*]; être avantageux/-euse pour [*group, nation*].
IV *vi* profiter; **to ~ from** tirer profit de; **to ~ from doing** gagner à faire.
IDIOMS **to give sb the ~ of the doubt** accorder à qn le bénéfice du doute.

benevolent *adj* bienveillant/-e.

benign *adj* **1** [*person, smile*] bienveillant/-e; **2** (Med) bénin/-igne.

bent *adj* **1** [*nail, wire, stick*] tordu/-e; [*person*] (stooped) courbé/-e; **2 to be ~ on doing** vouloir à tout prix faire .

bereaved *adj* endeuillé/-e, en deuil.

berry *n* baie *f*.

berserk *adj* **to go ~** être pris/-e de folie furieuse.

berth I *n* **1** (bunk) couchette *f*; **2** (at dock) mouillage *m*.
II *vtr* faire mouiller [*ship*].
III *vi* [*ship*] venir à quai.
IDIOMS **to give sb/sth a wide ~**° éviter qn/qch.

beset *adj* **a country ~ by strikes** un pays en proie aux grèves.

beside *prep* **1** (next to) à côté de; **~ the sea** au bord de la mer; **2** (in comparison with) par rapport à.
IDIOMS **to be ~ oneself (with anger)** être hors de soi; **to be ~ oneself (with joy)** être fou/folle de joie.

besides I *adv* **1** (moreover) d'ailleurs; **2** (in addition) en plus, aussi.
II *prep* en plus de.

besiege *vtr* (Mil) assiéger; (figurative) assaillir.

besotted *adj* follement épris/-e (**with** de).

best I *n* **the ~** le meilleur/la meilleure *m/f*; **the ~ of friends** les meilleurs amis/meilleures amies du monde; **at ~** au mieux; **to make the ~ of sth** s'accommoder de qch; **to do one's ~ to do** faire de son mieux or faire (tout) son possible pour faire; **all the ~!** (good luck) bonne chance!; (cheers) à ta santé!
II *adj* meilleur/-e; **the ~ book I've ever read**

le meilleur livre que j'aie jamais lu; **my ~ dress** ma plus belle robe.
III *adv* le mieux; **~ of all** mieux que tout.

best man *n* témoin *m*.

bestow *vtr* accorder [*honour*] (**on** à); conférer [*title*] (**on** à).

bestseller *n* bestseller *m*.

bet I *n* pari *m*; (in casino) mise *f*.
II *vtr* parier (**on** sur).
III *vi* parier (**on** sur); (in casino) miser.

betray *vtr* trahir.

betrayal *n* trahison *f*.

better

■ **Note** When *better* is used as an adjective, it is translated by *meilleur* or *mieux* depending on the context (see **II** below, and note that *meilleur* is the comparative form of *bon*, *mieux* the comparative form of *bien*).

I *n* **the ~ of the two** le meilleur/la meilleure or le/la mieux des deux; **so much the ~** tant mieux.
II *adj* meilleur/-e; mieux; **this wine is ~** ce vin est meilleur; **to get ~** [*situation, weather*] s'améliorer; [*ill person*] aller mieux; **things are getting ~** ça va mieux; **to be ~** [*patient, cold*] aller mieux; **to be a ~ swimmer than sb** nager mieux que qn; **to be ~ at** être meilleur/-e en [*subject, sport*]; **it's ~ than nothing** c'est mieux que rien; **the bigger/sooner the ~** le plus grand/vite possible; **the less said about that the ~** mieux vaut ne pas parler de ça.
III *adv* mieux; **you had ~ do, you'd ~ do** (advising) tu ferais mieux de faire; (warning) tu as intérêt à faire; **we'd ~ leave** on ferait mieux de partir.
IV *vtr* améliorer.
IDIOMS **for ~ (or) for worse** advienne que pourra; (in wedding vow) pour le meilleur et pour le pire; **to get the ~ of** triompher de [*opponent*]; **his curiosity got the ~ of him** sa curiosité a pris le dessus; **to go one ~** faire encore mieux (**than** que); **to think ~ of it** changer d'avis.

better off *adj* **1** (more wealthy) plus riche (**than** que); **2** (in better situation) mieux.

betting *n* paris *mpl*.

betting shop *n* (GB) bureau *m* de PMU.

between I *prep* **1** entre; **~ you and me, ~ ourselves** entre nous; **~ now and next year** d'ici l'année prochaine; **2 they drank the whole bottle ~ (the two of) them** ils ont bu toute la bouteille à eux deux.
II *adv* (also **in ~**) (in space) au milieu, entre les deux; (in time) entre-temps; **the two main roads and the streets (in) ~** les deux rues principales et les petites rues situées entre elles; **neither red nor orange, but somewhere in ~** ni rouge ni orange mais entre les deux.

beverage *n* boisson *f*, breuvage *m*.

beware I *excl* prenez garde!, attention!
II *vi* se méfier (**of** de); **~ of...** attention à...

bewildered *adj* [*person*] déconcerté/-e (**at, by** par); [*look*] perplexe.

bewildering *adj* déconcertant/-e.

bewitch *vtr* ensorceler.

beyond I *prep* **1** (in space and time) au-delà de; **2 ~ one's means** au-dessus de ses moyens; **~ all hope** au-delà de toute espérance; **~ one's control** hors de son contrôle; **he is ~ help** on ne peut rien faire pour lui; **it's ~ me** ça me dépasse; **3** (other than) en dehors de, à part.
II *adv* au-delà.
III *conj* à part (+ *infinitive*).
IDIOMS **to be in the back of ~** être au bout du monde.

bias I *n* **1** (prejudice) parti *m* pris; **2** (tendency) tendance *f*.
II *vtr* **to ~ sb against/in favour of** prévenir qn contre/en faveur de.

biased, **biassed** *adj* [*person*] partial/-e; [*report*] manquant d'objectivité; **to be ~** [*person*] avoir des partis pris; **to be ~ against** avoir un préjugé défavorable envers.

Bible *n* Bible *f*.

biblical *adj* biblique.

bibliography *n* bibliographie *f*.

bicentenary, **bicentennial** *n* bicentenaire *m*.

biceps *n* biceps *m*.

bicker *vi* se chamailler (**about** au sujet de).

bicycle I *n* bicyclette *f*, vélo○ *m*; **on a/by ~** à bicyclette.
II *adj* [*pump*] à bicyclette; [*bell, lamp*] de bicyclette; [*race*] cycliste.

bicycle clip *n* pince *f* à vélo.

bicycle lane *n* piste *f* cyclable.

bid I *n* **1** (at auction) enchère *f* (**for** sur; **of** de); **2** (for contract) soumission *f*; **3** (attempt) tentative *f* (**to do** pour faire).
II *vtr* **1** offrir [*money*] (**for** pour); **2** (say) **to ~ sb good morning** dire bonjour à qn.
III *vi* (at auction) enchérir (**for** sur); (for contract) soumissionner (**for** pour).

bidder *n* (at auction) enchérisseur/-euse *m/f*; **to go to the highest ~** être adjugé/-e au plus offrant/-e.

bidding *n* (at auction) enchères *fpl*.

bide *vi* IDIOMS **to ~ one's time** attendre le bon moment.

bifocals *n pl* verres *mpl* à double foyer.

big *adj* (gen) grand/-e (*before n*); (bulky, fat) gros/grosse (*before n*); [*meal*] copieux/-ieuse; **to get ~(ger)** (taller) grandir; (fatter) grossir; **a ~ book** (thick) un gros livre; (large-format) un grand livre; **his ~ brother** son grand frère, son frère aîné; **a ~ mistake** une grave erreur; **to be in ~ trouble** être dans le pétrin○; **to have ~ ideas, to think ~** voir grand.

bigamy *n* bigamie *f*.

big business *n* **1** les grandes entreprises *fpl*; **2 to be ~** rapporter gros.

big dipper *n* (GB) (at fair) montagnes *fpl* russes.

big game *n* gros gibier *m*.

bigheaded○ *adj* prétentieux/-ieuse.

bigmouth○ *n* **he's such a ~**○**!** il ne sait pas tenir sa langue!
bigoted *adj* intolérant/-e, sectaire.
big shot○ *n* gros bonnet○ *m*.
big toe *n* gros orteil *m*.
big top *n* (tent) grand chapiteau *m*.
bike *n* (cycle) vélo *m*; (motorbike) moto *f*.
biker○ *n* motard○ *m*.
bikini *n* bikini® *m*.
bilingual *adj* bilingue.
bill I *n* **1** (in restaurant) addition *f*; (for services, electricity) facture *f*; (from hotel, doctor, dentist) note *f*; **2** (Pol) projet *m* de loi; **3** (poster) affiche *f*; **4** (US) **dollar ~** billet *m* d'un dollar; **5** (beak) bec *m*.
II *vtr* **to ~ sb for sth** facturer qch à qn.
IDIOMS **to fit** or **fill the ~** faire l'affaire.
billboard *n* panneau *m* d'affichage.
billet *vtr* cantonner (**on, with** chez).
billiards **▶504** *n* billard *m*.
billion *n* (a thousand million) milliard *m*; (GB) (a million million) billion *m*.
billionaire *n* milliardaire *mf*.
billow *vi* [*clouds, smoke*] s'élever en tourbillons.
■ **billow out** [*skirt, sail*] se gonfler; [*steam*] s'élever.
billy goat *n* bouc *m*.
bin *n* (GB) (for rubbish) poubelle *f*.
bind *vtr* **1** (tie up) attacher (**to** à); **2 to be bound by** être tenu/-e par [*law, oath*]; **3** (also **~ together**) unir [*people, community*]; **4** relier [*book*].
binder *n* (for papers, lecture notes) classeur *m*.
binding I *n* reliure *f*.
II *adj* [*agreement, contract*] qui engage.
binge○ *n* **to go on a ~** faire la noce.
bingo **▶504** *n* bingo *m*.
bin liner *n* (GB) sac *m* poubelle.
binoculars *n pl* jumelles *fpl*.
biochemistry *n* biochimie *f*.
biodegradable *adj* biodégradable.
biography *n* biographie *f*.
biological *adj* biologique.
biology *n* biologie *f*.
birch *n* bouleau *m*.
bird *n* **1** (Zool) oiseau *m*; **2**○ (GB) (girl) nana○ *f*.
IDIOMS **to kill two ~s with one stone** faire d'une pierre deux coups.
bird of prey *n* oiseau *m* de proie.
bird's eye view *n* vue *f* d'ensemble.
birdsong *n* chant *m* des oiseaux.
bird-watching *n* **to go ~** observer les oiseaux.
biro® *n* (GB) stylo-bille *m*, bic®.
birth *n* naissance *f* (**of** de).
birth certificate *n* certificat *m* de naissance.
birth control *n* (in society) contrôle *m* des naissances; (by couple) contraception *f*.
birthday *n* anniversaire *m*; **Happy Birthday!** Bon or Joyeux Anniversaire!
birthday party *n* (for child) goûter *m* d'anniversaire; (for adult) soirée *f* d'anniversaire.
birthmark *n* tache *f* de naissance.
birthplace *n* lieu *m* de naissance.
birthrate *n* taux *m* de natalité.
biscuit *n* **1** (GB) biscuit *m*, petit gâteau *m*; **2** (US) pain *m* au lait.
bisexual *n, adj* bisexuel/-elle (*m*/*f*).
bishop *n* **1** évêque *m*; **2** (in chess) fou *m*.
bit I *n* **1** (gen) morceau *m* (**of** de); (of paper, string, land) bout *m* (**of** de); (of book, film) passage *m*; **2**○ **a ~ (of)** un peu (de); **a little ~** un petit peu; **3** (of horse) mors *m*.
II **a bit**○ *phr* un peu; **a ~ early** un peu trop tôt; **she isn't a ~ like me** elle ne me ressemble pas du tout.
IDIOMS **~ by ~** petit à petit; **~s and pieces** (fragments) morceaux *mpl*; (belongings) affaires *fpl*.
bitch *n* **1** (dog) chienne *f*; **2**○ (derogatory) garce○ *f*.
bite I *n* **1** morsure *f*; (from insect) piqûre *f*; **2** (mouthful) bouchée *f*; **to have a ~ to eat** manger un morceau.
II *vtr* [*animal, person*] mordre; [*insect*] piquer; **to ~ one's nails** se ronger les ongles.
III *vi* [*fish*] mordre.
biting *adj* **1** [*wind*] cinglant/-e; **2** [*comment*] mordant/-e.
bitter *adj* (gen) amer/-ère; [*wind*] glacial/-e; [*disappointment, truth*] cruel/-elle.
IDIOMS **to the ~ end** jusqu'au bout.
bitterly *adv* [*complain, speak*] amèrement; [*regret*] profondément; **it's ~ cold** il fait un froid terrible.
bitterness *n* amertume *f*.
bizarre *adj* bizarre.
black **▶438** I *n* **1** (colour) noir *m*; **2** (also **Black**) (person) Noir/-e *m*/*f*; **3 to be in the ~** être créditeur/-trice.
II *adj* **1** (gen) noir/-e; [*night*] obscur/-e; [*tea*] nature; **to turn ~** noircir; **2** (also **Black**) [*community, culture*] noir/-e.
■ **black out** [*person*] s'évanouir.
blackberry *n* mûre *f*.
blackbird *n* merle *m*.
blackboard *n* tableau *m* (noir).
blackcurrant *n* cassis *m*.
blacken *vtr* noircir.
black eye *n* œil *m* poché.
blackhead *n* point *m* noir.
black ice *n* verglas *m*.
blacklist I *n* liste *f* noire.
II *vtr* mettre [qn] à l'index.
blackmail I *n* chantage *m*.
II *vtr* faire chanter [*victim*].
black market *n* **on the ~** au marché noir.
blackout *n* **1** (power cut) panne *f* de courant; (in wartime) black-out *m*; **2** (faint) étourdissement *m*.
Black Sea *pr n* mer *f* Noire.
black sheep *n* brebis *f* galeuse.
blacksmith **▶626** *n* forgeron *m*.
bladder *n* vessie *f*.

blade *n* (of knife, sword, axe) lame *f*; (of fan, propeller, oar) pale *f*; (of grass) brin *m*.

blame I *n* responsabilité *f* (**for** de).
II *vtr* **I ~ you** c'est ta faute; **to ~ sb for sth** reprocher qch à qn; **to ~ sth on sb** tenir qn responsable de qch; **to be to ~ for sth** être responsable de qch.
III *v refl* **to ~ oneself for sth** se sentir responsable de qch.

blameless *adj* irréprochable.

blancmange *n* blanc-manger *m*.

bland *adj* [*food, flavour*] fade; [*person*] terne.

blank I *n* **1** (empty space) blanc *m*; **my mind's a ~** j'ai la tête vide; **2** (cartridge) cartouche *f* à blanc.
II *adj* **1** [*paper, page*] blanc/blanche; [*screen*] vide; [*cassette*] vierge; **2** [*expression*] ébahi/-e; **my mind went ~** j'ai eu un trou de mémoire.

blank cheque (GB), **blank check** (US) *n* chèque *m* en blanc; (figurative) carte *f* blanche.

blanket *n* **1** couverture *f*; **2** (of snow) couche *f*; (of cloud, fog) nappe *f*.

blasphemous *adj* [*person*] blasphémateur/-trice; [*statement*] blasphématoire.

blasphemy *n* blasphème *m*.

blast I *n* **1** (explosion) explosion *f*; **2** (of air) souffle *m*; **3 at full ~** [*play music*] à plein volume.
II *vtr* (blow up) faire sauter; **to ~ a hole in the wall** percer un mur à l'explosif.
■ **blast off** [*rocket*] décoller.

blast-off *n* lancement *m*.

blatant *adj* [*lie, disregard*] éhonté/-e; [*abuse*] flagrant/-e.

blatantly *adv* ouvertement; **to be ~ obvious** sauter aux yeux.

blaze I *n* (fire) incendie *m*; (in hearth) feu *m*, flambée *f*; **in a ~ of publicity** sous les feux des médias.
II *vtr* **to ~ a trail** faire œuvre de pionnier.
III *vi* (also **~ away**) **1** [*fire, house*] brûler; **2** [*lights*] briller.

blazer *n* blazer *m*.

bleach I *n* **1** (disinfectant) eau *f* de javel; **2** (for hair) décolorant *m*.
II *vtr* décolorer [*hair*]; blanchir [*linen*].

bleak *adj* [*landscape*] désolé/-e; [*weather*] maussade; [*outlook, future*] sombre.

bleary *adj* [*eyes*] bouffi/-e; **to be ~-eyed** avoir les yeux bouffis.

bleat *vi* [*sheep, goat*] bêler.

bleed I *vtr* **to ~ sb dry** saigner qn à blanc.
II *vi* saigner; **my finger's ~ing** j'ai le doigt qui saigne.

bleeper *n* (GB) bip *m*.

blemish *n* (gen) imperfection *f*; (on fruit) tache *f*; (pimple) bouton *m*.

blend I *n* mélange *m* (**of** de).
II *vtr* mélanger [*ingredients, colours, styles*].
III *vi* **to ~ (together)** [*colours, tastes, styles*] se fondre; **to ~ with** [*colours, tastes, sounds*] se marier à; [*smells*] se mêler à.
■ **blend in**: ¶ **~ in** s'harmoniser (**with** avec); ¶ **~ [sth] in** incorporer [*ingredient*].

blender *n* mixeur *m*, mixer *m*.

bless *vtr* bénir; **~ you!** (after sneeze) à vos souhaits!; **to be ~ed with** jouir de [*health, beauty*].

blessing *n* **1** bénédiction *f*; **2** (good thing) bienfait *m*; **a ~ in disguise** un bienfait caché.

blight *n* (on society) plaie *f* (**on** de); **urban ~** délabrement *m* urbain.

blind I *n* **1 the ~** les aveugles *mpl*; **2** (on window) store *m*.
II *adj* [*person*] aveugle; **to go ~** perdre la vue; **~ in one eye** borgne.
III *vtr* **1** [*injury, accident*] rendre aveugle; **2** [*sun, light*] éblouir; **3** [*pride, love*] aveugler.
IDIOMS **to turn a ~ eye** fermer les yeux (**to** sur).

blind alley *n* voie *f* sans issue.

blindfold I *n* bandeau *m*.
II *adj* (also **~ed**) aux yeux bandés.
III *adv* les yeux bandés.
IV *vtr* bander les yeux à [*person*]

blindly *adv* [*obey, follow*] aveuglément.

blindness *n* cécité *f*; (figurative) aveuglement *m*.

blind spot *n* **1** (in eye) point *m* aveugle; **2** (in car, on hill) angle *m* mort.

blink *vi* [*person*] cligner des yeux; [*light*] clignoter.

blinker *n* **1** (Aut) clignotant *m*; **2 ~s** œillères *fpl*.

blinkered *adj* [*attitude, approach*] borné/-e.

bliss *n* bonheur *m* parfait.

blissfully *adv* **~ happy** au comble du bonheur; **~ ignorant** dans la plus parfaite ignorance.

blister I *n* (on skin) ampoule *f*.
II *vi* [*skin, paint*] cloquer.

blithely *adv* (nonchalantly) avec insouciance; (cheerfully) allègrement.

blitz I *n* bombardement *m* aérien.
II *vtr* bombarder.

blizzard *n* tempête *f* de neige; (in Arctic regions) blizzard *m*.

bloated *adj* [*face, body*] bouffi/-e; [*stomach*] ballonné/-e.

blob *n* **1** (drop) grosse goutte *f*; **2** (shape) forme *f* floue.

block I *n* **1** (slab) bloc *m*; **2 ~ of flats** immeuble *m* (d'habitation); **office ~** immeuble de bureaux; **3** (of houses) pâté *m* de maisons; **4** (for butcher, executioner) billot *m*.
II *vtr* bloquer [*exit, road, ball*]; boucher [*drain, hole, artery, view*]; **to have a ~ed nose** avoir le nez bouché.

blockade I *n* blocus *m*.
II *vtr* bloquer, faire le blocus de [*port*].

blockage *n* obstruction *f*.

blockbuster○ *n* **1** (book) livre *m* à succès, bestseller *m*; **2** (film) superproduction *f*.

block capitals, **block letters** *n pl* **in ~** (on form) en caractères *mpl* or capitales *fpl* d'imprimerie.

blonde ▶ **438** I *n* blonde *f*.
II *adj* blond/-e.

blood *n* sang *m*.
IDIOMS **in cold ~** de sang-froid.

bloodcurdling *adj* à vous figer le sang dans les veines.

blood donor *n* donneur/-euse *m/f* de sang.

blood group *n* groupe *m* sanguin.

blood pressure *n* tension *f* artérielle; **high ~** hypertension *f*.

bloodshed *n* effusion *f* de sang.

bloodshot *adj* injecté/-e de sang.

blood sport *n* sport *m* sanguinaire.

bloodstained *adj* taché/-e de sang.

bloodstream *n* sang *m*.

blood test *n* analyse *f* de sang.

bloodthirsty *adj* sanguinaire.

bloody I *adj* **1** [*hand, body*] ensanglanté/-e; [*battle*] sanglant/-e; **2**○ (GB) sacré/-e (*before n*); **~ fool!** espèce d'idiot!
II◑ *adv* (GB) sacrément○.

bloom I *n* (flower) fleur *f*; **in ~** en fleur.
II *vi* **1** (be in flower) être fleuri/-e; (come into flower) fleurir; **2 to be ~ing with health** être resplendissant/-e de santé.

blossom I *n* (flower) fleur *f*; (flowers) fleurs *fpl*.
II *vi* fleurir; (figurative) s'épanouir.

blot I *n* (gen) tache *f*; (of ink) pâté *m*; (figurative) ombre *f*.
II *vtr* **1** (dry) sécher [qch] au buvard [*ink*]; **2** (stain) tacher.
■ **blot out** effacer [*memories*]; masquer [*view*].

blotch *n* (on skin) plaque *f* rouge; (of ink, colour) tache *f*.

blotchy *adj* [*complexion*] marbré/-e.

blotting paper *n* papier *m* buvard.

blouse *n* chemisier *m*.

blow I *n* coup *m*.
II *vtr* **1 the wind blew the door shut** un coup de vent a fermé la porte; **to be blown off course** [*ship*] être dévié/-e par le vent; **2** [*person*] faire [*bubble, smoke ring*]; souffler [*glass*]; **to ~ one's nose** se moucher; **to ~ one's whistle** donner un coup de sifflet; **3** [*explosion*] faire [*hole*] (**in** dans); **to be blown to pieces** or **bits by** être réduit/-e en poussière par; **4** faire sauter [*fuse*]; griller [*light bulb*].
III *vi* **1** [*wind*] souffler; [*person*] souffler (**into** dans; **on** sur); **2 to ~ in the wind** [*flag, clothes*] voler au vent; **3** [*fuse*] sauter; [*bulb*] griller; [*tyre*] éclater.
■ **blow down** [*wind*] faire tomber [*tree*].
■ **blow off**: ¶ **~ off** [*hat*] s'envoler; ¶ **~ [sth] off** [*wind*] emporter [*hat*]; [*explosion*] emporter [*roof*].
■ **blow out** souffler [*candle*]; éteindre [*flames*].
■ **blow over** [*storm*] s'apaiser; [*affair*] être oublié/-e.
■ **blow up**: ¶ **~ up** [*building*] sauter; [*bomb*] exploser; ¶ **~ [sb/sth] up 1** faire sauter [*building, person*]; faire exploser [*bomb*]; **2** gonfler [*tyre*]; **3** agrandir [*photograph*].

blow-dry I *n* brushing *m*.
II *vtr* **to ~ sb's hair** faire un brushing à qn.

blubber *n* graisse *f* de baleine.

bludgeon *vtr* **to ~ sb to death** tuer qn à coups de matraque.

blue ▶ 438 I *n* bleu *m*.
II *adj* **1** bleu/-e; **2**○ [*movie*] porno○; [*joke*] cochon/-onne○.
IDIOMS **to appear/happen out of the ~** apparaître/se passer à l'improviste.

bluebell *n* jacinthe *f* des bois.

blueberry *n* (US) myrtille *f*.

blue cheese *n* (fromage *m*) bleu *m*.

blue collar worker *n* ouvrier *m*, col *m* bleu.

blue jeans *n pl* jean *m*.

blueprint *n* bleu *m*; (figurative) projet *m* (**for** pour; **for doing** pour faire).

blues *n pl* **1** (Mus) **the ~** le blues *m*; **2**○ **to have the ~** avoir le cafard○.

bluff *vtr, vi* bluffer○.
IDIOMS **to call sb's ~** prendre qn au mot.

blunder I *n* bourde *f*.
II *vi* **1** (make mistake) faire une bourde; **2** (move clumsily) **to ~ into sth** se cogner à qch.

blunt I *adj* **1** [*knife, scissors*] émoussé/-e; [*pencil*] mal taillé/-e; [*instrument*] contondant/-e; **2** [*person, manner*] abrupt/-e; [*criticism*] direct/-e.
II *vtr* émousser [*knife*].

bluntly *adv* franchement.

blur I *n* image *f* floue.
II *vtr* brouiller.

blurb *n* (on book cover) texte *m* de présentation; (derogatory) baratin *m*.

blurred *adj* indistinct/-e; [*image, idea*] flou/-e; [*memory*] confus/-e; **to have ~ vision** avoir des troubles de la vue.

blurt *v* ■ **blurt out** laisser échapper [*truth, secret*].

blush *vi* rougir (**at** devant; **with** de).

blusher *n* fard *m* à joues.

blustery *adj* **~ wind** bourrasque *f*.

BO○ *n* (*abbr* = **body odour**) odeur *f* corporelle; **he's got ~** il sent mauvais.

boar *n* (also **wild ~**) sanglier *m*.

board I *n* **1** (plank) planche *f*; **bare ~s** plancher nu; **2** (committee) conseil *m*; **~ of directors** conseil d'administration; **3** (for chess, draughts) tableau *m*; **4** (in classroom) tableau *m* (noir); **5** (notice board) panneau *m* d'affichage; (to advertise) panneau *m*; **6** (Comput) plaquette *f*; **7** (accommodation) **full ~** pension *f* complète; **half ~** demi-pension *f*; **~ and lodging** le gîte et le couvert.
II *vtr* monter à bord de [*plane, ship*]; monter dans [*bus, train*]; [*pirates*] aborder [*vessel*].
III **on board** *phr* à bord.
IDIOMS **above ~** légal/-e; **across the ~** à tous les niveaux.
■ **board up** boucher [qch] avec des planches [*window*]; barricader [qch] avec des planches [*house*].

boarder *n* **1** (lodger) pensionnaire *m*; **2** (school pupil) interne *mf*.

board game *n* jeu *m* de société (à damier).

boarding card *n* carte *f* d'embarquement.

boarding school *n* école *f* privée avec internat.

boardroom *n* salle *f* du conseil.

boast I *n* vantardise *f*.
II *vtr* s'enorgueillir de.
III *vi* se vanter (**about** de).

boastful *adj* vantard/-e.

boat *n* (gen) bateau *m*; (sailing) voilier *m*; (rowing) barque *f*; (liner) paquebot *m*.
IDIOMS **to be in the same ~**○ être tous/toutes dans la même galère.

boater *n* (hat) canotier *m*.

boathouse *n* abri *m* à bateaux.

bob I *n* (haircut) coupe *f* au carré.
II *vi* (also **~ up and down**) [*boat, float*] danser.

bobsled, **bobsleigh** ▶ 504 *n* bobsleigh *m*.

bode *vi* **to ~ well/ill** être de bon/mauvais augure.

bodily *adj* [*function*] physiologique; [*fluid*] organique.

body *n* **1** (of person, animal) corps *m*; **2** (corpse) corps *m*, cadavre *m*; **3** (of car) carrosserie *f*; **4** (of water) étendue *f*; **5** (organization) organisme *m*; **6** (of wine) corps *m*; (of hair) volume *m*.

body-building *n* culturisme *m*.

bodyguard *n* garde *m* du corps.

bodywork *n* carrosserie *f*.

bog *n* **1** (marshy ground) marais *m*; **2** (also **peat ~**) tourbière *f*.
IDIOMS **to get ~ged down in sth** s'enliser dans qch.

boggle *vi* **the mind ~s!** c'est époustouflant!

bogus *adj* [*doctor, document*] faux/fausse (*before n*); [*claim*] bidon *inv*; [*company*] factice.

bohemian *adj* [*lifestyle*] de bohème; [*person*] bohème.

boil I *n* **1 to bring sth to the ~** porter qch à ébullition; **2** (on skin) furoncle *m*.
II *vtr* faire bouillir; **to ~ an egg** faire cuire un œuf.
III *vi* bouillir; **the kettle is ~ing** l'eau bout (dans la bouilloire); **to make sb's blood ~** faire sortir qn de ses gonds.
■ **boil down to** (figurative) se ramener à.
■ **boil over** déborder.

boiled egg *n* œuf *m* à la coque.

boiled potatoes *n pl* pommes *fpl* de terre à l'anglaise.

boiler *n* chaudière *f*.

boiler suit *n* (GB) bleu *m* de travail.

boiling *adj* [*liquid*] bouillant/-e; **it's ~**○**!** il fait une chaleur infernale!

boiling point *n* point *m* d'ébullition; (figurative) point *m* limite.

boisterous *adj* [*adult, game*] bruyant/-e; [*child*] turbulent/-e.

bold *adj* **1** (daring) [*person*] intrépide; [*attempt, plan*] audacieux/-ieuse; **2** (cheeky) [*person*] effronté/-e; **3** [*colour*] vif/vive; [*design*] voyant/-e; **~ print** caractères *mpl* gras.

bollard *n* balise *f*.

bolster I *n* traversin *m*.
II *vtr* (also **~ up**) soutenir.

bolt I *n* **1** (lock) verrou *m*; **2 ~ of lightning** coup *m* de foudre.
II *vtr* **1** (lock) verrouiller; **2** (also **~ down**) engloutir [*food*].
III *vi* [*horse*] s'emballer; [*person*] détaler○.
IV **bolt upright** *phr* droit/-e comme un i.
IDIOMS **a ~ out of the blue** un coup de tonnerre.

bomb I *n* bombe *f*.
II *vtr* bombarder [*town, house*].

bombard *vtr* bombarder (**with** de).

bomb disposal unit *n* équipe *f* de déminage *m*.

bomber *n* **1** (plane) bombardier *m*; **2** (terrorist) poseur/-euse *m/f* de bombes.

bomber jacket *n* blouson *m* d'aviateur.

bombing *n* bombardement *m*; (by terrorists) attentat *m* à la bombe.

bombshell *n* obus *m*; (figurative) bombe *f*.

bombsite *n* zone *f* touchée par une explosion.

bona fide *adj* [*attempt*] sincère; [*member*] vrai/-e (*before n*); [*contract*] de bonne foi.

bond I *n* **1** (link) liens *mpl* (**of** de; **between** entre); **2** (in finance) obligation *f*; **savings ~** bon *m* d'épargne.
II *vtr* (stick) faire adhérer.
III *vi* [*person*] s'attacher (**with** à).

bone I *n* os *m*; (of fish) arête *f*.
II *vtr* désosser [*joint, chicken*]; enlever les arêtes de [*fish*].
IDIOMS **~ of contention** sujet *m* de dispute; **to have a ~ to pick with sb** avoir un compte à régler avec qn.

bone dry *adj* complètement sec/sèche.

bone idle *adj* flemmard/-e.

bonfire *n* (of rubbish) feu *m* de jardin; (for celebration) feu *m* de joie.

bonnet *n* **1** (hat) bonnet *m*; **2** (GB Aut) capot *m*.

bonus *n* **1** (payment) prime *f*; **2** (advantage) avantage *m*.

bony *adj* [*person, body*] anguleux/-euse; [*finger, arm*] osseux/-euse.

boo I *n* huée *f*.
II *excl* (to give sb a fright) hou!; (to jeer) hou! hou!
III *vtr* huer [*actor, speaker*].
IV *vi* pousser des huées.

booby trap I *n* **1** mécanisme *m* piégé; **2** (practical joke) traquenard *m*.
II *vtr* piéger.

book I *n* **1** livre *m* (**about** sur; **of** de); **history ~** livre d'histoire; **2** (exercise book) cahier *m*; **3** (of cheques, tickets, stamps) carnet *m*; **~ of matches** pochette *f* d'allumettes.
II **books** *n pl* (accounts) livres *mpl* de comptes.
III *vtr* **1** réserver [*table, room, taxi, ticket*]; faire les réservations pour [*holiday*]; **to be fully ~ed** être complet/-ète; **2** [*policeman*] dresser un procès-verbal or un P.V.○ à [*motorist, offender*]; (US) (arrest) arrêter [*suspect*]; **3** [*referee*] donner un carton jaune à [*player*].
IV *vi* réserver.
IDIOMS **to be in sb's good ~s** être dans les

The Human Body

When it is clear who owns the part of the body mentioned, French tends to use the definite article, where English uses a possessive adjective:

*he raised **his** hand*	= il a levé **la** main
*she closed **her** eyes*	= elle a fermé **les** yeux
*she ran **her** hand over **my** forehead*	= elle m'a passé **la** main sur **le** front

For expressions such as *he hurt his foot* or *she brushed her teeth*, where the action involves more than the simple movement of a body part, use a reflexive verb in French:

*she **has broken** her leg*	= elle **s'est cassé** la jambe
*he **was rubbing** his hands*	= il **se frottait** les mains
*she **was holding** her head*	= elle **se tenait** la tête

Note also the following:

*she broke **his** leg*	= elle **lui** a cassé **la** jambe (*literally* she broke to him the leg)
*the stone split **his** lip*	= le caillou **lui** a fendu **la** lèvre (*literally* the stone split to him the lip)

Describing people

- ❑ For ways of saying how tall someone is or of stating someone's weight, ▶ 573, and of talking about the colour of hair and eyes, ▶ 438.

Here are some ways of describing people in French:

his hair is long	= il a les cheveux longs
he has long hair	= il a les cheveux longs
a boy with long hair	= un garçon aux cheveux longs
a long-haired boy	= un garçon aux cheveux longs
the boy with long hair	= le garçon aux cheveux longs
her eyes are blue	= elle a les yeux bleus
she has blue eyes	= elle a les yeux bleus
she is blue-eyed	= elle a les yeux bleus
the girl with blue eyes	= la fille aux yeux bleus
a blue-eyed girl	= une fille aux yeux bleus
his nose is red	= il a le nez rouge
he has a red nose	= il a le nez rouge
a man with a red nose	= un homme au nez rouge
a red-nosed man	= un homme au nez rouge

When referring to a temporary state, the following phrases are useful:

his leg is broken	= il a la jambe cassée
the man with the broken leg	= l'homme à la jambe cassée

but note

a man with a broken leg	= un homme avec une jambe cassée

- ❑ For other expressions with terms relating to parts of the body, ▶ 533.

petits papiers de qn○; **to be in sb's bad ~s** ne pas avoir la cote avec qn.

bookcase *n* bibliothèque *f*.

booking *n* (GB) réservation *f*.

booking office *n* (GB) bureau *m* de location.

bookkeeping *n* comptabilité *f*.

booklet *n* brochure *f*.

bookmaker ▶ 626 *n* bookmaker *m*.

bookseller ▶ 626 *n* libraire *mf*.

bookshelf *n* (single) étagère *f*; (in bookcase) rayon *m*.

bookshop, **book store** (US) ▶ 626 *n* librairie *f*.

book token *n* (GB) chèque-livre *m*.

boom I *n* **1** (of cannon, thunder) grondement *m*; (of drum) boum *m*; (of explosion) détonation *f*; **~!** badaboum!; **2** (Econ) boom *m*; (in prices, sales) explosion *f* (**in** de).
II *vi* **1** [*cannon, thunder*] gronder; [*voice*] retentir; **2** [*economy*] prospérer; [*exports, sales*] monter en flèche; **business is ~ing** les affaires vont bien.

boon *n* **1** (asset) aide *f* précieuse (**to** à); **2** (stroke of luck) aubaine *f* (**for** pour).

boost I *n* **to give sb/sth a ~** encourager qn/stimuler qch.
II *vtr* stimuler [*economy, sales*]; encourager [*investment*]; augmenter [*profit*]; **to ~ sb's confidence** redonner confiance à qn; **to ~ morale** remonter le moral.

booster *n* (Med) vaccin *m* de rappel.

boot *n* **1** botte *f*; (of climber, hiker) chaussure *f*; (for workman, soldier) brodequin *m*; **football ~** (GB) chaussure *f* de football; **2** (GB) (of car) coffre *m*.

booth *n* (in language lab) cabine *f*; (at fair) baraque *f*; **polling ~** isoloir *m*; **telephone ~** cabine *f* (téléphonique).

bootlace *n* lacet *m* (de chaussure).

border I *n* **1** (frontier) frontière *f*; **to cross the ~** passer la frontière; **2** (edge) bord *m*; **3** (flower bed) plate-bande *f*.
II *vtr* **1** [*road, land*] longer [*lake, forest*]; [*country*] border [*ocean*]; avoir une frontière commune avec [*country*]; **2** (surround) border.
■ **border on**: **~ on [sth] 1** [*country*] être limitrophe de; [*garden, land*] toucher; **2** (verge on) friser [*rudeness, madness*].

borderline *n* frontière *f*, limite *f* (**between** entre); **a ~ case** un cas limite.

bore I *n* **1** (person) raseur/-euse○ *m/f*; **2** (situation) **what a ~!** quelle barbe!; **3** (of gun) calibre *m*.
II *vtr* **1** ennuyer [*person*]; **2** (drill) percer [*hole*]; creuser [*well, tunnel*].

bored *adj* [*expression*] ennuyé/-e; **to be** or **get ~** s'ennuyer (**with** de).
IDIOMS **to be ~ stiff** or **~ to tears** s'ennuyer à mourir.

boredom *n* ennui *m*.

boring *adj* ennuyeux/-euse.

born *adj* né/-e; **to be ~** naître; **she was ~ in May** elle est née en mai.

borough *n* arrondissement *m* urbain.

borrow *vtr* emprunter (**from** à).

Bosnia ▶ 448 *pr n* Bosnie *f*.

bosom *n* poitrine *f*; **in the ~ of one's family** au sein de sa famille; **~ friend** ami/-e *m/f* intime.

boss○ *n* patron/-onne *m/f*, chef *m*.
■ **boss about**○, **boss around**○ mener [qn] par le bout du nez [*person*].

bossy○ *adj* autoritaire.

botanic(al) *adj* botanique; **~ gardens** jardin *m* botanique.

botany *n* botanique *f*.

botch○ *vtr* bâcler.

both I *det* **~ sides of the road** les deux côtés de la rue; **~ children came** les enfants sont venus tous les deux; **~ her parents** ses deux parents.
II *conj* **~ here and abroad** ici comme à l'étranger.
III *pron*, *quantif* (of things) les deux; (of people) tous les deux; **let's take ~ of them** prenons les deux; **~ of you are wrong** vous avez tort tous les deux.

bother I *n* **1** (inconvenience) ennui *m*, embêtement○ *m*; **without any ~** sans aucune difficulté; **2**○ (GB) (trouble) ennuis *mpl*; **to be in a spot of ~** avoir des ennuis.
II *vtr* **1** (worry) tracasser; **don't let it ~ you** ne te tracasse pas avec ça; **2** (disturb) déranger; **I'm sorry to ~ you** je suis désolé de vous déranger.
III *vi* **1** (take trouble) **please don't ~** s'il te plaît, ne te dérange pas; **don't ~ doing** ce n'est pas la peine de faire; **2** (worry) **it's not worth ~ing about** ça ne vaut pas la peine qu'on s'en occupe.

bottle I *n* (gen) bouteille *f*; (for perfume, medicine) flacon *m*; (for baby) biberon *m*.
II *vtr* **1** embouteiller [*milk, wine*]; **2** (GB) mettre [qch] en conserve [*fruit*].
III bottled *pp adj* [*beer, gas*] en bouteille; **~d water** eau *f* minérale.
■ **bottle up** étouffer [*anger, grief*].

bottle bank *n* réceptacle *m* à verre.

bottle feed *vtr* nourrir [qn] au biberon.

bottleneck *n* **1** (traffic jam) embouteillage *m*; **2** (narrow part of road) rétrécissement *m* de la chaussée.

bottle-opener *n* décapsuleur *m*.

bottom I *n* **1** (of hill, steps, wall) pied *m*; (of page, list) bas *m*; (of bag, bottle, hole, river, sea, garden) fond *m*; (of boat) carène *f*; (of vase, box) dessous *m*; (of league) dernière place *f*; **at the ~ of the pile** sous le tas; **to be ~ of the class** être dernier/-ière de la classe; **2** (buttocks) derrière○ *m*.
II *adj* [*layer, shelf*] du bas; [*sheet*] de dessous; [*bunk*] inférieur/-e; [*division, half*] dernier/-ière (*before n*).
IDIOMS **to get to the ~ of a matter** découvrir le fin fond d'une affaire.

boulder *n* rocher *m*.

bounce I *n* **1** (of ball) rebond *m*; **2** (of mattress, material) élasticité *f*; (of hair) souplesse *f*.
II *vtr* faire rebondir [*ball*].

III *vi* **1** [*ball, object*] rebondir (**off** sur; **over** au dessus de); **to ~ up and down on sth** [*person*] sauter sur qch; **2**○ [*cheque*] être sans provision.
■ **bounce back** (after illness) se remettre; (in career) faire un retour en force.

bouncer○ *n* videur *m*.

bound I **bounds** *n pl* limites *fpl*; **to be out of ~s** être interdit/-e d'accès.
II *adj* **1 to be ~ to do sth** aller sûrement faire qch; **it was ~ to happen** cela devait arriver; **2** (obliged) (by promise, rules, terms) tenu/-e (**by** par; **to do** de faire); **3 ~ for** [*person, bus, train*] en route pour; [*aeroplane*] à destination de.
III *vi* bondir; **to ~ into the room** entrer dans la pièce en coup de vent.

boundary *n* (gen) limite *f* (**between** entre); (of sports field) limites *fpl* du terrain.

bouquet *n* bouquet *m*.

bourgeois *adj* bourgeois/-e.

bout *n* **1** (of fever, malaria) accès *m*; (of insomnia) crise *f*; **drinking ~** soûlerie *f*; **2** (in boxing) combat *m*; **3** (period of activity) période *f*.

boutique ▶ 626 *n* boutique *f*.

bow[1] *n* **1** (weapon) arc *m*; **2** (for violin) archet *m*; **3** (knot) nœud *m*.

bow[2] I *n* **1** (movement) salut *m*; **to take a ~** saluer; **2** (of ship) avant *m*, proue *f*.
II *vtr* baisser [*head*]; courber [*branch*]; incliner [*tree*].
III *vi* **1** saluer; **to ~ to sb** saluer qn; **2 to ~ to pressure** céder à la pression.

bowel *n* intestin *m*; **the ~s of the earth** les entrailles *fpl* de la terre.

bowl I *n* (for food) bol *m*; (for salad) saladier *m*; (for soup) assiette *f* creuse; (for washing) cuvette *f*; (of lavatory) cuvette *f*.
II *vtr* lancer [*ball*].
III *vi* **1** lancer; **to ~ to sb** lancer la balle à qn; **2** (US) (go bowling) aller au bowling.
■ **bowl over 1** (knock down) renverser [*person*]; **2 to be ~ed over** (by news) être stupéfait/-e; (by beauty, generosity) être bouleversé/-e.

bowlegged *adj* [*person*] aux jambes arquées.

bowler *n* **1** (in cricket) lanceur *m*; **2** (also **~ hat**) chapeau *m* melon.

bowling ▶ 504 *n* (also **tenpin ~**) bowling *m*.

bowling alley *n* bowling *m*.

bowling green *n* terrain *m* de boules (sur gazon).

bowls ▶ 504 *n* jeu *m* de boules (sur gazon).

bow tie *n* nœud-papillon *m*.

box I *n* **1** (cardboard) boîte *f*; (crate) caisse *f*; **~ of matches** boîte d'allumettes; **2** (on page, form) case *f*; **3** (in theatre) loge *f*; (in stadium) tribune *f*; **4** (also **PO Box**) boîte *f* postale.
II *vtr* **1** (pack) mettre [qch] en caisse; **2 to ~ sb's ears** gifler qn.
III *vi* (Sport) boxer.

boxer ▶ 626 *n* **1** (fighter) boxeur *m*; **2** (dog) boxer *m*.

boxer shorts *n pl* caleçon *m* (court).

boxing ▶ 504 *n* boxe *f*.

Boxing Day *n* (GB) lendemain *m* de Noël.

box office *n* guichet *m*.

boy *n* garçon *m*.

boycott I *n* boycottage *m* (**against, of, on** de).
II *vtr* boycotter.

boyfriend *n* (petit) copain *m* or ami *m*.

bra *n* soutien-gorge *m*.

brace I *n* **1** (for teeth) appareil *m* dentaire; **2** (for broken limb) attelle *f*.
II **braces** *n pl* (GB) bretelles *fpl*.
III *vtr* [*person*] arc-bouter [*body, back*] (**against** contre).
IV *v refl* **to ~ oneself** (physically) s'arc-bouter; (mentally) se préparer (**for** à; **to do** à faire).

bracelet *n* bracelet *m*.

bracing *adj* vivifiant/-e, tonifiant/-e.

bracken *n* fougère *f*.

bracket I *n* **1** (round) parenthèse *f*; (square) crochet *m*; **in ~s** entre parenthèses or crochets; **2** (for shelf) équerre *f*; (for lamp) applique *f*; **3** (category) **age ~** tranche *f* d'âge.
II *vtr* **1** (put in brackets) (round) mettre [qch] entre parenthèses; (square) mettre [qch] entre crochets; **2** (also **~ together**) mettre [qn] dans le même groupe [*people*].

brag *vi* se vanter (**to** auprès de; **about** de).

braid *n* **1** (of hair) tresse *f*, natte *f*; **2** (trimming) galon *m*.

brain *n* cerveau *m*; **~s** cervelle *f*.

brainchild *n* grande idée *f*.

brain drain *n* fuite *f* des cerveaux.

brain surgery *n* neurochirurgie *f*.

brainwash *vtr* faire subir un lavage de cerveau à.

brainwave *n* idée *f* géniale, illumination *f*.

braise *vtr* braiser.

brake I *n* frein *m*.
II *vi* freiner.

bramble *n* **1** ronce *f*; **2** (GB) (berry) mûre *f*.

bran *n* son *m*.

branch *n* **1** (of tree) branche *f*; (of road, railway) embranchement *m*; **2** (of shop) succursale *f*; (of bank) agence *f*; (of company) filiale *f*.
■ **branch off** bifurquer.
■ **branch out** se diversifier.

brand I *n* marque *f*.
II *vtr* **1** marquer (au fer) [*animal*]; **2 to ~ sb as sth** désigner qn comme qch.

brandish *vtr* brandir.

brand name *n* marque *f* déposée.

brand-new *adj* tout neuf/toute neuve.

brandy *n* eau-de-vie *f*; (cognac) cognac *m*.

brash *adj* [*person, manner*] bravache.

brass *n* **1** (metal) laiton *m*, cuivre *m* jaune; **2** (Mus) (also **~ section**) cuivres *mpl*.

brass band *n* fanfare *f*.

bravado *n* bravade *f*.

brave I *n* (Indian) brave *m*.
II *adj* (gen) courageux/-euse; [*smile*] brave; **to put on a ~ face** faire bonne contenance.
III *vtr* braver.

bravely *adv* courageusement.
bravery *n* courage *m*, bravoure *f*.
brawl I *n* bagarre *f*.
II *vi* se bagarrer (**with** avec).
bray *vi* [*donkey*] braire; [*person*] brailler.
brazen *adj* éhonté/-e.
■ **brazen out**: **~ it out** payer d'audace.
Brazil ▶448 *pr n* Brésil *m*.
breach I *n* **1** (of rule) infraction *f* (**of** à); (of discipline, duty) manquement *m* (**of** à); (of copyright) violation *f*; **to be in ~ of** enfreindre [*law*]; violer [*agreement*]; **2** (gap) brèche *f*.
II *vtr* faire une brèche dans [*defence*].
breach of contract *n* rupture *f* de contrat.
breach of the peace *n* atteinte *f* à l'ordre public.
bread *n* pain *m*.
bread and butter *n* tartine *f* de pain beurré; (figurative) gagne-pain *m*.
breadbin *n* (GB) boîte *f* or huche *f* à pain.
breadboard *n* planche *f* à pain.
breadcrumbs *n pl* miettes *fpl* de pain; (Culin) chapelure *f*.
breadline *n* **to be on the ~** être au seuil de l'indigence.
bread roll *n* petit pain *m*.
breadth ▶573 *n* largeur *f*; (figurative) (of experience, knowledge) étendue *f*.
breadwinner *n* soutien *m* de famille.
break I *n* **1** (gap) (in wall) brèche *f*; (in row, line) espace *m*; (in circuit) rupture *f*; **2** (pause) (gen) pause *f*; (at school) récréation *f*; **to take a ~** faire une pause; **the Christmas ~** les vacances de Noël; **to have a ~ from work** arrêter de travailler; **a ~ with the past** une rupture avec le passé; **3** (also **commercial ~**) page *f* de publicité; **4 a lucky ~** un coup de veine○.
II *vtr* **1** (gen) casser; briser [*seal*]; rompre [*silence, monotony, spell*]; **to ~ one's leg** se casser la jambe; **2** enfreindre [*law*]; **to ~ one's promise** manquer à sa promesse; **3** dépasser [*speed limit*]; battre [*record*]; **4** [*branches*] freiner [*fall*]; [*hay*] amortir [*fall*]; **5** débourrer [*horse*]; **6** (in tennis) **to ~ sb's serve** faire le break; **7 to ~ the news to sb** apprendre la nouvelle à qn.
III *vi* **1** (gen) se casser; [*arm, bone, leg*] se fracturer; [*bag*] se déchirer; **to ~ in two** se casser en deux; **2** [*waves*] se briser; **3** [*good weather*] se gâter; [*heatwave*] cesser; **4** [*storm, scandal, story*] éclater; **5 to ~ with sb** rompre les relations avec qn; **to ~ with tradition** rompre avec la tradition; **6** [*boy's voice*] muer.
■ **break away 1** se détacher (**from** de); **2** (escape) échapper.
■ **break down**: ¶ **~ down 1** [*car, machine*] tomber en panne; **2** [*person*] s'effondrer, craquer○; **to ~ down in tears** fondre en larmes; ¶ **~ [sth] down 1** enfoncer [*door*]; (figurative) faire tomber [*barriers*]; vaincre [*resistance*]; **2** (analyse) ventiler [*cost, statistics*]; décomposer [*data, findings*] (**into** par).
■ **break even** rentrer dans ses frais.
■ **break free** s'échapper.
■ **break in**: ¶ **~ in 1** [*thief*] entrer (par effraction); [*police*] entrer de force; **2** (interrupt) interrompre; ¶ **~ [sth] in** débourrer [*horse*]; assouplir [*shoe*].
■ **break into 1** entrer dans [qch] (par effraction) [*building*]; forcer [*safe*]; **2** entamer [*new packet, savings*]; **3 to ~ into song/into a run** se mettre à chanter/courir.
■ **break off**: ¶ **~ off 1** [*end*] se casser; [*handle, piece*] se détacher; **2** [*speaker*] s'interrompre; ¶ **~ [sth] off 1** casser [*branch, piece*]; **2** rompre [*engagement*]; interrompre [*conversation*].
■ **break out 1** [*epidemic, fire*] se déclarer; [*fight, riot, storm*] éclater; **to ~ out in a rash** avoir une éruption de boutons; **2** [*prisoner*] s'échapper (**of** de).
■ **break up**: ¶ **~ up 1** [*couple*] se séparer; **2** [*crowd, cloud*] se disperser; [*meeting*] se terminer; **3** (GB Sch) **schools ~ up on Friday** les cours finissent vendredi; ¶ **~ [sth] up** démanteler [*drugs ring*]; séparer [*couple*]; désunir [*family*]; briser [*marriage*]; mettre fin à [*demonstration*].
breakdown *n* **1** (of vehicle, machine) panne *f*; **2** (of communications, negotiations) rupture *f*; (of discipline, order) effondrement *m*; **3 to have a (nervous) ~** faire une dépression (nerveuse); **4** (of figures, statistics) ventilation *f*.
breakfast *n* petit déjeuner *m*.
break-in *n* cambriolage *m*.
breakneck *adj* [*pace, speed*] fou/folle, insensé/-e.
breakthrough *n* (gen) percée *f*; (in negotiations, investigation) progrès *m*.
breakwater *n* brise-lames *m inv*.
breast *n* **1** (woman's) sein *m*; (chest) poitrine *f*; **2** (Culin) (of poultry) blanc *m*, filet *m*.
breast-feed *vtr*, *vi* allaiter.
breast stroke *n* brasse *f*.
breath *n* **1** souffle *m*; **out of ~** à bout de souffle; **to hold one's ~** retenir sa respiration; (figurative) retenir son souffle; **2** (from mouth) haleine *f*; (visible) respiration *f*; **to have bad ~** avoir (une) mauvaise haleine.
IDIOMS **to take sb's ~ away** couper le souffle à qn.
breathalyse (GB), **breathalyze** (US) *vtr* faire subir un alcootest à [*driver*].
Breathalyzer® *n* alcootest *m*.
breathe I *vtr* **1** respirer [*oxygen*]; **2** souffler [*germs*] (**on** sur); **3 don't ~ a word!** pas un mot!
II *vi* **1** [*person, animal*] respirer; **to ~ heavily** souffler fort, haleter; **2** [*wine*] s'aérer.
■ **breathe in**: ¶ **~ in** inspirer; ¶ **~ [sth] in** inhaler.
■ **breathe out**: ¶ **~ out** expirer; ¶ **~ out, ~ [sth] out** exhaler.
breathing *n* respiration *f*.
breathing space *n* **1** (respite) répit *m*; **2** (postponement) délai *m*.
breathless *adj* [*runner*] hors d'haleine; [*asthmatic*] haletant/-e.

breathtaking *adj* [*feat, skill*] stupéfiant/-e; [*scenery*] à vous couper le souffle.

breed I *n* race *f*.
II *vtr* élever [*animals*]; (figurative) engendrer.
III *vi* se reproduire.
IV **bred** *pp adj* **ill-/well-~** mal/bien élevé/-e.

breeding *n* **1** (of animals) reproduction *f*; **2** (good manners) bonnes manières *fpl*.

breeze I *n* brise *f*.
II *vi* **to ~ in/out** entrer/sortir d'un air dégagé; **to ~ through an exam** réussir un examen sans difficulté.

brevity *n* brièveté *f*.

brew I *vtr* brasser [*beer*]; préparer [*tea*]; **freshly ~ed coffee** du café fraîchement passé.
II *vi* **1** [*beer*] fermenter; [*tea*] infuser; **2** [*storm, crisis*] se préparer.

brewer ▶ 626 *n* brasseur *m*.

brewery *n* brasserie *f*.

bribe I *n* pot-de-vin *m*.
II *vtr* soudoyer [*police*]; suborner [*witness*]; acheter [*servant, voter*].

bribery *n* corruption *f*.

brick *n* brique *f*.

bricklayer ▶ 626 *n* maçon *m*.

bridal *adj* [*gown*] de mariée; [*car*] des mariés; [*suite*] nuptial/-e.

bride *n* (jeune) mariée *f*; **the ~ and groom** les (jeunes) mariés *mpl*.

bridegroom *n* jeune marié *m*.

bridesmaid *n* demoiselle *f* d'honneur.

bridge I *n* **1** pont *m* (**over** sur; **across** au-dessus de); (figurative) (link) rapprochement *m*; **2** (on ship) passerelle *f*; **3** (of nose) arête *f*; (of spectacles) arcade *f*; **4** (on guitar, violin) chevalet *m*; **5** (for teeth) bridge *m*; **6** ▶ 504 (Games) bridge *m*.
II *vtr* **1 to ~ a gap in [sth]** combler un vide dans [*conversation*]; combler un trou dans [*budget*]; **2** (span) enjamber [*two eras*].

bridle I *n* bride *f*.
II *vtr* brider.
III *vi* se cabrer (**at** contre; **with** sous l'effet de).

brief I *n* **1** (GB) (remit) attributions *fpl*; (role) tâche *f*; **2** (Law) dossier *m*.
II **briefs** *n pl* slip *m*.
III *adj* bref/brève; **in ~** en bref.
IV *vtr* (inform) informer (**on** de); (instruct) donner des instructions à (**on** sur).

briefcase *n* serviette *f*; (without handle) porte-documents *m inv*.

briefing *n* briefing *m* (**on** sur).

briefly *adv* **1** (gen) brièvement; [*look, pause*] un bref instant; **2** (in short) en bref.

brigade *n* brigade *f*.

bright *adj* **1** [*colour*] vif/vive; [*garment*] aux couleurs vives; [*sunshine*] éclatant/-e; [*room, day*] clair/-e; [*star, eye, metal*] brillant/-e; **2** (clever) intelligent/-e; **a ~ idea** une idée lumineuse; **3 to look on the ~ side** voir le bon côté des choses.

brighten *v* ■ **brighten up**: ¶ **~ up 1** [*person*] s'égayer (**at** à); [*face*] s'éclairer (**at** à); **2** [*weather*] s'éclaircir; ¶ **~ [sth] up** égayer [*room, decor*].

brightly *adv* **1** [*dressed*] de couleurs vives; **2** [*shine, burn*] d'un vif éclat.

brightness *n* **1** (of colour, light, smile) éclat *m*; **2** (of room) clarté *f*.

bright spark○ *n* (GB) petit/-e futé/-e○ *m/f*.

brilliance *n* éclat *m*.

brilliant *adj* **1** [*student, career, success*] brillant/-e; **2** (bright) éclatant/-e; **3** (GB)○ (fantastic) super○, génial/-e○; **to be ~ at sth** être doué/-e en qch.

brim *n* bord *m*.

brine *n* **1** (sea water) eau *f* de mer; **2** (for pickling) saumure *f*.

bring *vtr* **1** apporter [*present, object, message*]; amener [*person, animal, car*]; **to ~ sth with one** apporter qch; **to ~ sb/sth into the room** faire entrer qn/qch dans la pièce; **2** apporter [*happiness, rain, change, hope*]; **to ~ a smile to sb's face** faire sourire qn.
■ **bring about** provoquer [*change, disaster*]; entraîner [*success, defeat*].
■ **bring along** apporter [*object*]; amener, venir avec [*friend, partner*].
■ **bring back 1** rapporter [*souvenir*] (**from** de); **to ~ back memories** ranimer des souvenirs; **2** rétablir [*custom*]; restaurer [*monarchy*].
■ **bring down 1** renverser [*government*]; **2** réduire [*inflation, expenditure*]; faire baisser [*price, temperature*]; **3** (shoot down) abattre.
■ **bring forward** avancer [*date*].
■ **bring in** rapporter [*money, interest*]; introduire [*legislation, measure*]; rentrer [*harvest*]; faire appel à [*expert, army*].
■ **bring off** réussir [*feat*]; conclure [*deal*].
■ **bring on 1** provoquer [*attack, migraine*]; **2** faire entrer [*substitute player*].
■ **bring out 1** sortir [*edition, new model*]; **2** (highlight) faire ressortir [*flavour, meaning*].
■ **bring round 1** (revive) faire revenir [qn] à soi; **2** (convince) convaincre.
■ **bring up 1** aborder, parler de [*subject*]; **2** vomir, rendre [*food*]; **3** élever [*child*]; **well brought up** bien élevé/-e.

brink *n* bord *m*.

brisk *adj* **1** (efficient) [*manner, tone*] vif/vive; [*person*] efficace; **2** (energetic) [*trot*] rapide; **at a ~ pace** à vive allure; **3** [*business, trade*] florissant/-e; **business was ~** les affaires marchaient bien; **4** [*air*] vivifiant/-e; [*wind*] vif/vive.

bristle I *n* (gen) poil *m*; (on pig) soie *f*.
II *vi* **1** [*hairs*] se dresser; **2** [*person*] se hérisser (**at** à; **with** de).

Britain *pr n* (also **Great ~**) Grande-Bretagne *f*.

British ▶ 553 I *n pl* **the ~** les Britanniques *mpl*.
II *adj* britannique; **the ~ embassy** l'ambassade *f* de Grande-Bretagne.

British Isles *n pl* îles *fpl* Britanniques.

Briton *n* Britannique *mf*.

Brittany *pr n* Bretagne *f*.

brittle *adj* [*twig*] cassant/-e; [*nails, hair*] fragile.

broach *vtr* aborder [*subject*].
broad ▶573| *adj* **1** (wide) large; **to have ~ shoulders** être large d'épaules; **2** [*meaning*] large; [*outline*] général/-e; **3** [*accent*] fort/-e (*before n*); **in ~ daylight** en plein jour.
broad bean *n* fève *f*.
broadcast I *n* émission *f*.
II *vtr* diffuser [*programme*] (**to** à).
III *vi* [*station, channel*] émettre (**on** sur).
broaden I *vtr* étendre [*appeal, scope*]; élargir [*horizons, knowledge*]; **travel ~s the mind** les voyages ouvrent l'esprit.
II *vi* s'élargir.
broadminded *adj* [*person*] large d'esprit; [*attitude*] libéral/-e.
brocade *n* brocart *m*.
broccoli *n* (Bot) brocoli *m*; (Culin) brocolis *mpl*.
brochure *n* (booklet) brochure *f*; (leaflet) dépliant *m*; (for hotel) prospectus *m*.
broil *vtr* (US) faire griller [*meat*].
broke *adj* [*person*] fauché/-e○.
broken *adj* **1** (gen) cassé/-e; [*glass, window, line*] brisé/-e; [*radio, machine*] détraqué/-e; **2** [*man, woman*] brisé/-e; **3** [*French*] mauvais/-e (*before n*).
broken-hearted *adj* **to be ~** avoir le cœur brisé.
broken home *n* famille *f* désunie.
broken marriage *n* foyer *m* désuni.
broker ▶626| *n* courtier *m*.
bronchitis ▶533| *n* bronchite *f*.
bronze ▶438| *n* bronze *m*.
brooch *n* broche *f*.
brood I *n* (of birds) couvée *f*; (of mammals) nichée *f*.
II *vi* **1** (ponder) broyer du noir; **to ~ about** ressasser, ruminer [*problem*]; **2** [*bird*] couver.
brook *n* ruisseau *m*.
broom *n* balai *m*.
broth *n* bouillon *m*.
brothel *n* maison *f* close.
brother *n* frère *m*.
brother-in-law *n* beau-frère *m*.
brotherly *adj* fraternel/-elle.
brow *n* **1** (forehead) front *m*; (eyebrow) sourcil *m*; **2** (of hill) sommet *m*.
brown ▶438| I *n* (of object) marron *m*; (of hair, skin, eyes) brun *m*.
II *adj* **1** [*shoes, leaves, paint, eyes*] marron *inv*; [*hair*] châtain *inv*; **light/dark ~** marron clair/foncé; **2** (tanned) bronzé/-e; **to go ~** bronzer.
III *vtr* faire roussir [*sauce*]; faire dorer [*meat, onions*].
IV *vi* [*meat, potatoes*] dorer.
brown bread *n* pain *m* complet.
brown paper *n* papier *m* kraft.
brown rice *n* riz *m* complet.
brown sugar *n* sucre *m* brun, cassonade *f*.
browse *vi* **1** (in shop) regarder; **2** (graze) brouter.
■ **browse through** feuilleter [*book*].
bruise I *n* (on skin) bleu *m*, ecchymose *f* (**on** sur); (on fruit) tache *f* (**on** sur).
II *vtr* meurtrir [*person*]; taler, abîmer [*fruit*]; **to ~ one's arm** se faire un bleu sur le bras.
brunette *n* brune *f*.
brunt *n* **to bear the ~ of** être le plus touché/la plus touchée par [*disaster*]; subir tout le poids de [*anger*].
brush I *n* **1** (for hair, clothes, shoes) brosse *f*; (small, for sweeping up) balayette *f*; (broom) balai *m*; (for paint) pinceau *m*; **2 to have a ~ with death** frôler la mort; **to have a ~ with the law** avoir des démêlés avec la justice.
II *vtr* brosser [*carpet, clothes*]; **to ~ one's hair/teeth** se brosser les cheveux/les dents.
III *vi* **to ~ against** frôler; **to ~ past sb** frôler qn en passant.
■ **brush aside** repousser [*criticism, person*].
■ **brush up** (**on**) se remettre à [*subject*].
brushwood *n* (firewood) brindilles *fpl*; (brush) broussailles *fpl*.
brusque *adj* brusque (**with** avec).
Brussels ▶448| *pr n* Bruxelles.
Brussels sprout *n* chou *m* de Bruxelles.
brutal *adj* brutal/-e.
brutality *n* brutalité *f* (**of** de).
brute I *n* **1** (man) brute *f*; **2** (animal) bête *f*.
II *adj* [*strength*] simple (*before n*); **by ~ force** par la force.
bubble I *n* bulle *f* (**in** dans); **to blow ~s** faire des bulles.
II *vi* [*fizzy drink*] pétiller; [*boiling liquid*] bouillonner; **to ~ (over) with** déborder de [*enthusiasm, ideas*].
bubble bath *n* bain *m* moussant.
buck I *n* **1** (US)○ dollar *m*; **2** (male animal) mâle *m*.
II *vi* [*horse*] ruer.
IDIOMS **to pass the ~** refiler○ la responsabilité à quelqu'un d'autre.
bucket *n* seau *m* (**of** de).
buckle I *n* boucle *f*.
II *vtr* **1** attacher, boucler [*belt, shoe*]; **2** (damage) gondoler.
III *vi* **1** [*metal, surface*] se gondoler; [*wheel*] se voiler; **2** [*belt, shoe*] s'attacher, se boucler; **3** [*knees, legs*] céder.
bud I *n* (of leaf) bourgeon *m*; (of flower) bouton *m*.
II *vi* **1** (develop leaf buds) bourgeonner; (develop flower buds) boutonner; **2** [*flower, breast*] pointer.
Buddha *pr n* Bouddha *m*.
Buddhism *n* bouddhisme *m*.
budding *adj* [*athlete, champion*] en herbe; [*talent, career, romance*] naissant/-e.
buddy○ *n* copain *m*, pote○ *m*.
budge I *vtr* **1** (move) bouger; **2** (persuade) faire changer d'avis à.
II *vi* **1** (move) bouger (**from, off** de); **2** (give way) changer d'avis (**on** sur).
budgerigar *n* perruche *f*.
budget I *n* budget *m* (**for** pour).

II *vi* **to ~ for** budgétiser ses dépenses en fonction de [*increase, needs*].

buff *n* **1**○ (enthusiast) mordu/-e *m/f*; **2** (colour) chamois *m*.

buffalo *n* (GB) buffle *m*; (US) bison *m*.

buffer *n* tampon *m*.

buffet[1] *n* buffet *m*.

buffet[2] *vtr* [*wind*] ballotter [*ship*]; battre [*coast*].

buffoon *n* bouffon/-onne *m/f*.

bug I *n* **1**○ (insect) (gen) bestiole *f*; (bedbug) punaise *f*; **2**○ (also **stomach ~**) ennuis *mpl* gastriques; **3** (germ) microbe *m*; **4** (fault) (gen) défaut *m*; (Comput) bogue *f*, bug *m*; **5** (hidden microphone) micro *m* caché.
II *vtr* **1** poser des micros dans [*room, building*]; **the room is ~ged** il y a un micro (caché) dans la pièce; **2**○ (annoy) embêter○ [*person*].

buggy *n* **1** (GB) (pushchair) poussette *f*; **2** (US) (pram) landau *m*; **3** (carriage) boghei *m*.

bugle ▶ 586 *n* clairon *m*.

build I *n* (of person) carrure *f*.
II *vtr* (gen) construire; édifier [*church, monument*]; bâtir [*career, future*]; fonder [*empire*]; **to be well built** [*person*] être bien bâti/-e.
III *vi* construire; **to ~ on** tirer parti de [*popularity, success*].
■ **build up**: ¶ **~ up** [*gas, deposits*] s'accumuler; [*traffic*] s'intensifier; [*business, trade*] se développer; [*tension, excitement*] monter; ¶ **~ [sth] up** accumuler [*wealth*]; établir [*trust*]; constituer [*collection*]; créer [*business*]; établir [*picture, profile*]; se faire [*reputation*]; affermir [*muscles*]; **to ~ oneself up, to ~ up one's strength** prendre des forces.

builder ▶ 626 *n* (contractor) entrepreneur *m* en bâtiment; (worker) ouvrier/-ière *m/f* du bâtiment.

building *n* (gen) bâtiment *m*; (with offices, apartments) immeuble *m*; (palace, church) édifice *m*.

building site *n* chantier *m* (de construction).

building society *n* (GB) société *f* d'investissement et de crédit immobilier.

build-up *n* **1** (in traffic, pressure) intensification *f* (**of** de); (in weapons, stocks) accumulation *f* (**of** de); (in tension) accroissement *m* (**of** de); **2** (publicity) **the ~ to sth** les préparatifs de qch.

built-in *adj* [*wardrobe*] encastré/-e; (figurative) intégré/-e.

built-up *adj* [*region*] urbanisé/-e; **~ area** agglomération *f*.

bulb *n* **1** (electric) ampoule *f* (électrique); **2** (of plant) bulbe *m*.

Bulgaria ▶ 448 *n* Bulgarie *f*.

Bulgarian ▶ 553 **I** *n* **1** (person) Bulgare *mf*; **2** (language) bulgare *m*.
II *adj* bulgare.

bulge I *n* (in clothing, carpet) bosse *f*; (in pipe, tube) renflement *m*; (in tyre) hernie *f*; (in wall) bombement *m*; (in cheek) gonflement *m*.
II *vi* [*bag, pocket, cheeks*] être gonflé/-e; [*wallet*] être bourré/-e; [*surface*] se boursoufler; [*stomach*] ballonner; **his eyes were bulging** les yeux lui sortaient de la tête.

bulimia (nervosa) ▶ 533 *n* boulimie *f*.

bulk *n* **1** (of package, correspondence) volume *m*; (of building, vehicle) masse *f*; **the ~ of** la majeure partie de; **2 in ~** [*buy, sell*] en gros; [*transport*] en vrac.

bulky *adj* [*person*] corpulent/-e; [*package*] volumineux/-euse; [*book*] épais/-aisse.

bull *n* (ox) taureau *m*; (elephant, whale) mâle *m*.

bulldog *n* bouledogue *m*.

bulldozer *n* bulldozer *m*, bouteur *m*.

bullet *n* balle *f*.

bulletin *n* bulletin *m*; **news ~** bulletin d'informations.

bulletin board *n* (gen) tableau *m* d'affichage; (Comput) messagerie *f*.

bulletproof *adj* [*glass, vehicle, door*] blindé/-e.

bulletproof vest *n* gilet *m* pare-balles *inv*.

bullfight *n* corrida *f*.

bullfighter ▶ 626 *n* torero *m*.

bullfighting *n* (gen) corridas *fpl*; (art) tauromachie *f*.

bullion *n* lingots *mpl*.

bullock *n* bœuf *m*.

bullring *n* arène *f*.

bull's-eye *n* mille *m*.

bully I *n* (child) petite brute *f*; (adult) tyran *m*.
II *vtr* intimider; (stronger) tyranniser.

bum○ *n* **1** (GB) (buttocks) derrière *m*; **2** (US) (vagrant) clochard *m*.

bumblebee *n* bourdon *m*.

bumf○, **bumph**○ *n* (GB) paperasserie○ *f*.

bump I *n* **1** (lump) (on body) bosse *f* (**on** à); (on road) bosse *f* (**on, in** sur); **2** (jolt) secousse *f*; **3** (sound) bruit *m* sourd.
II *vtr* cogner (**against, on** contre); **to ~ one's head** se cogner la tête.
■ **bump into** rentrer dans [*person, object*]; (meet) tomber sur○ [*person*].

bumper I *n* pare-chocs *m*.
II *adj* [*crop, sales, year*] record (*after n*); [*edition*] exceptionnel/-elle.

bumper car *n* auto *f* tamponneuse.

bumpkin○ *n* (also **country ~**) péquenaud/-e○ *m/f*.

bumpy *adj* [*road*] accidenté/-e; [*wall*] irrégulier/-ière; [*landing*] agité/-e.

bun *n* **1** (cake) petit pain *m* sucré; **2** (hairstyle) chignon *m*.

bunch *n* (of flowers) bouquet *m*; (of vegetables) botte *f*; (of grapes) grappe *f*; (of bananas) régime *m*; (of keys) trousseau *m*; (of people) groupe *m*.

bundle *n* (of clothes) ballot *m*; (of papers, notes) liasse *f*; (of books) paquet *m*; (of straw) botte *f*; **~ of sticks** fagot *m* de bois; **~ of nerves** boule *f* de nerfs.

bungalow *n* pavillon *m* (sans étage).

bungle *vtr* rater○ [*attempt, burglary*].

bunion *n* oignon *m*.

bunk *n* **1** (on ship, train) couchette *f*; **2** (also **~ bed**) lits *mpl* superposés.

bunker *n* **1** (Mil) bunker *m*; **2** (in golf) bunker *m*; **3** (for coal) soute *f*.

bunny *n* **1** (also **~ rabbit**) (Jeannot) lapin *m*; **2** (also **~ girl**) hôtesse *f*.

bunting *n* guirlandes *fpl*.

buoy I *n* (gen) bouée *f*; (for marking) balise *f* (flottante).
II *vtr* (also **~ up**) **1** revigorer [*person, morale*]; **2** stimuler [*prices, economy*]; **3** (keep afloat) maintenir à flot.

buoyant *adj* **1** [*object*] qui flotte; **2** [*person*] vif/vive; [*mood, spirits*] enjoué/-e; [*step*] allègre; **3** [*market, prices*] ferme; [*economy*] en expansion.

burden I *n* fardeau *m* (**to sb** pour qn).
II *vtr* **1** (also **~ down**) encombrer (**with** de); **2** (figurative) (with work, taxes) accabler (**with** de); **I don't want to ~ you with my problems** je ne veux pas vous ennuyer avec mes problèmes.

bureau *n* **1** (office) bureau *m*; **2** (US) (government department) service *m*; **3** (GB) (desk) secrétaire *m*; **4** (US) (chest of drawers) commode *f*.

bureaucracy *n* bureaucratie *f*.

bureaucrat *n* bureaucrate *mf*.

bureaucratic *adj* bureaucratique.

burger *n* hamburger *m*.

burglar *n* cambrioleur/-euse *m/f*.

burglar alarm *n* sonnerie *f* d'alarme.

burglary *n* (gen) cambriolage *m*; (Law) vol *m* avec effraction.

burgle *vtr* cambrioler.

burgundy ▶438 I **Burgundy** *pr n* Bourgogne *f*.
II *n* **1** (also **Burgundy**) (wine) bourgogne *m*; **2** (colour) (couleur *f*) bordeaux *m*.

burial *n* enterrement *m*.

burly *adj* [*person*] solidement charpenté/-e.

burn I *n* brûlure *f*.
II *vtr* (gen) brûler; laisser brûler [*food*].
III *vi* brûler.
■ **burn down**: ¶ **~ down** [*house*] être détruit/-e par le feu; ¶ **~ [sth] down** réduire [qch] en cendres [*house*].
■ **burn up** brûler [*calories*]; dépenser [*energy*].

burning I *n* **there's a smell of ~** ça sent le brûlé.
II *adj* **1** (on fire) en flammes, en feu; (alight) [*candle, lamp, fire*] allumé/-e; **2** [*desire*] brûlant/-e; [*passion*] ardent/-e.

burnt-out *adj* [*building, car*] calciné/-e; [*person*] usé/-e (par le travail).

burp○ I *n* rot○ *m*, renvoi *m*.
II *vi* [*person*] roter○; [*baby*] faire son rot○.

burrow I *n* terrier *m*.
II *vi* [*animal*] creuser un terrier; **to ~ into/under sth** creuser dans/sous qch.

burst I *n* (of flame) jaillissement *m*; (of gunfire) rafale *f*; (of activity, enthusiasm) accès *m*; **a ~ of laughter** un éclat de rire; **a ~ of applause** un tonnerre d'applaudissements.
II *vtr* (gen) crever; rompre [*blood vessel*]; **to ~ its banks** [*river*] déborder.
III *vi* (gen) crever; [*pipe*] éclater; [*dam*] rompre; **to be ~ing with health/pride** déborder de santé/fierté.
■ **burst into** **1** faire irruption dans [*room*]; **2** **to ~ into flames** s'enflammer; **to ~ into tears** fondre en larmes.
■ **burst out**: **to ~ out laughing** éclater de rire; **to ~ out crying** fondre en larmes.
■ **burst through** rompre [*barricade*]; **to ~ through the door** entrer violemment.

bury *vtr* enterrer.

bus *n* autobus *m*, bus *m*; (long-distance) autocar *m*, car *m*; **by ~** en (auto)bus, par le bus; **on the ~** dans le bus.

bus conductor ▶626 *n* receveur *m* d'autobus.

bus driver ▶626 *n* conducteur/-trice *m/f* d'autobus.

bush *n* **1** buisson *m*; **2** (bushland) **the ~** la brousse *f*.
IDIOMS **don't beat about the ~** cessez de tourner autour du pot.

bushfire *n* feu *m* de brousse.

bushy *adj* [*hair, tail*] touffu/-e; [*beard*] épais/-aisse; [*eyebrows*] broussailleux/-euse.

business I *n* **1** (commerce) affaires *fpl*; **to go into ~** se lancer dans les affaires; **she's gone to Brussels on ~** elle est allée à Bruxelles en voyage d'affaires; **to mix ~ with pleasure** joindre l'utile à l'agréable; **he's in the insurance ~** il travaille dans les assurances; **2** (company, firm) affaire *f*, entreprise *f*; (shop) commerce *m*, boutique *f*; **small ~es** les petites entreprises; **3** **let's get down to ~** passons aux choses sérieuses; **to go about one's ~** vaquer à ses occupations; **4** (concern) **that's her ~** ça la regarde; **it's none of your ~!** ça ne te regarde pas!; **mind your own ~**○**!** occupe-toi de tes affaires○!
II *adj* [*address, letter, transaction*] commercial/-e; [*meeting*] d'affaires.
IDIOMS **she means ~!** elle ne plaisante pas!; **to work like nobody's ~**○ travailler d'arrache-pied.

business card *n* carte *f* de visite.

business class *n* (on plane) classe *f* affaires.

business hours *n pl* (in office) heures *fpl* de bureau; (of shop) heures *fpl* d'ouverture.

businesslike *adj* sérieux/-ieuse.

businessman ▶626 *n* homme *m* d'affaires.

business school *n* école *f* de commerce.

business studies *n pl* études *fpl* de commerce.

businesswoman *n* femme *f* d'affaires.

busker *n* (GB) musicien/-ienne *m/f* ambulant/-e.

bus lane *n* couloir *m* d'autobus.

bus pass *n* carte *f* de bus.

bus shelter *n* abribus® *m*.

bus station *n* gare *f* routière.

bus stop *n* arrêt *m* de bus.

bust I *n* **1** (breasts) poitrine *f*; **2** (statue) buste *m*.
II○ *adj* **1** (broken) fichu/-e○; **2** (bankrupt) **to go ~** faire faillite.

bustle I *n* (activity) affairement *m* (**of** de); **hustle and ~** grande animation *f*.
II *vi* [*person, crowd*] s'affairer; **to ~ in/out** entrer/sortir d'un air affairé.

bustling *adj* [*street, shop, town*] animé/-e.

busy I *adj* **1** [*person*] occupé/-e (**with** avec;

doing à faire); **2** [*shop*] où il y a beaucoup de monde; [*junction, airport*] où le trafic est intense; [*road*] très fréquenté/-e; [*street, town*] animé/-e; [*day, week*] chargé/-e; **3** (engaged) [*line*] occupé/-e.
II *v refl* **to ~ oneself doing** s'occuper à faire.

busybody○ *n* **he's a real ~** il se mêle de tout.

but I *conj* mais.
II *prep* sauf; **anybody ~ him** n'importe qui sauf lui; **nobody ~ me knows how to do it** il n'y a que moi qui sache le faire; **he's nothing ~ a coward** ce n'est qu'un lâche; **the last ~ one** l'avant-dernier.
III *adv* **one can't help ~ admire her** on ne peut pas s'empêcher de l'admirer.
IV **but for** *phr* **~ for you, I would have died** sans toi je serais mort; **he would have gone ~ for me** si je n'avais pas été là il serait parti.

butane *n* butane *m*.

butcher ▶626| I *n* boucher *m*; **~'s (shop)** boucherie *f*.
II *vtr* abattre [*animal*]; massacrer [*people*].

butler ▶626| *n* maître *m* d'hôtel, majordome *m*.

butt I *n* **1** (of rifle) crosse *f*; (of cigarette) mégot○ *m*; **2**○ (US) (buttocks) derrière○ *m*; **3 to be the ~ of sb's jokes** être la cible des blagues de qn.
II *vtr* [*person*] donner un coup de tête à; [*animal*] donner un coup de corne à.
■ **butt in** interrompre.

butter I *n* beurre *m*.
II *vtr* beurrer [*bread*].

buttercup *n* bouton d'or *m*.

butterfly *n* papillon *m*.
IDIOMS **to have butterflies (in one's stomach)** avoir le trac○.

butterfly stroke *n* brasse *f* papillon.

buttock *n* fesse *f*.

button I *n* **1** bouton *m*; **2** (US) (badge) badge *m*.
II *vi* [*dress*] se boutonner.
■ **button up** boutonner [*garment*].

buttonhole I *n* **1** (on garment) boutonnière *f*; **2** (GB) (flower) (fleur *f* de) boutonnière *f*.
II○ *vtr* accrocher○ [*person*].

buttress *n* **1** contrefort *m*; (figurative) soutien *m*; **2** (also **flying ~**) arc-boutant *m*.

buxom *adj* [*woman*] à la poitrine généreuse.

buy I *n* **a good ~** une bonne affaire.
II *vtr* acheter (**from sb** à qn); **to ~ sth from the supermarket/from the baker's** acheter qch au supermarché/chez le boulanger; **to ~ sb sth** acheter qch à qn; **to ~ some time** gagner du temps.
■ **buy off** acheter [*person, witness*].
■ **buy out** racheter la part de [*co-owner*].
■ **buy up** acheter systématiquement [*shares, property*].

buyer ▶626| *n* acheteur/-euse *m*/*f*.

buyout *n* rachat *m* d'entreprise.

buzz I *n* bourdonnement *m*.
II *vtr* **to ~ sb** appeler qn au bip, biper.
III *vi* [*bee, fly*] bourdonner; [*buzzer*] sonner.

buzzard *n* buse *f*.

buzzer *n* (gen) sonnerie *f*; (on pocket) bip *m*.

by I *prep* **1** (with passive verbs) par; **he was bitten ~ a snake** il a été mordu par un serpent; **2** (with present participle) en; **~ working extra hours** en faisant des heures supplémentaires; **to learn French ~ listening to the radio** apprendre le français en écoutant la radio; **to begin ~ doing** commencer par faire; **3** (by means of) par; **to pay ~ cheque** payer par chèque; **~ mistake/accident** par erreur/accident; **to travel to Rome ~ Venice** aller à Rome en passant par Venise; **to travel ~ bus/train** voyager en bus/train; **~ bicycle** à bicyclette, en vélo; **~ candlelight** [*dine*] aux chandelles; [*read*] à la bougie; **4** (from) à; **I could tell ~ the look on her face that** rien qu'à la regarder je savais que; **5** (near) à côté de, près de; **~ the window** à côté de la fenêtre; **~ the sea** au bord de la mer; **6** (showing authorship) de; **a film ~ Claude Chabrol** un film de Claude Chabrol; **who is it ~?** c'est de qui?; **7** (in time expressions) avant; **~ midnight** avant minuit; **~ this time next week** d'ici la semaine prochaine; **~ the time she had got downstairs he was gone** le temps qu'elle descende, il était parti; **he should be here ~ now** il devrait être déjà là; **8** (according to) selon; **to play ~ the rules** jouer selon les règles; **~ my watch** à ma montre; **9** (showing amount) de; **prices have risen ~ 20%** les prix ont augmenté de 20%; **he's taller than me ~ two centimetres** il fait deux centimètres de plus que moi; **10** (in measurements) sur; **20 metres ~ 10 metres** 20 mètres sur 10; **11** (showing rate, quantity) à; **paid ~ the hour** payé à l'heure; **12 little ~ little** peu à peu; **day ~ day** jour après jour; **one ~ one** un par un, une par une; **~ oneself** tout seul/toute seule; **to go** or **pass ~ sb/sth** passer devant qn/qch; **13** (in compass directions) quart; **south ~ south-west** sud quart sud-ouest.
II *adv* **1** (past) **to go ~** passer; **the people walking ~** les gens qui passent/passaient, les passants; **as time goes ~** avec le temps; **2** (near) près; **he lives close ~** il habite tout près; **3** (aside) **to put money ~** mettre de l'argent de côté.

bye○ *excl* (also **~-bye**) au revoir!

by(e)-election *n* (GB) élection *f* partielle.

bygone *adj* [*days, years, scene*] d'antan; **a ~ era** une époque révolue.
IDIOMS **to let ~s be ~s** enterrer le passé.

by(e)law *n* arrêté *m* municipal.

bypass I *n* **1** (road) rocade *f*; **2** (pipe, channel) by-pass *m inv*; **3** (in electricity) dérivation *f*; **4** (Med) (also **~ operation**) pontage *m*.
II *vtr* contourner [*town, city*].

by-product *n* dérivé *m*; (figurative) effet *m* secondaire.

bystander *n* spectateur/-trice *m*/*f*.

byte *n* (Comput) octet *m*.

Cc

c, **C** *n* **1** (letter) c, C *m*; **2 C** (Mus) do *m*.
cab *n* **1** (taxi) taxi *m*; **2** (for driver) cabine *f*.
cabbage *n* chou *m*.
cabin *n* **1** (hut) cabane *f*; (in holiday camp) chalet *m*; **2** (in boat, plane) cabine *f*.
cabin crew *n* personnel *m* de bord.
cabinet *n* **1** (cupboard) petit placard *m*; **display ~** vitrine *f*; **cocktail ~** meuble *m* bar; **2** (GB Pol) cabinet *m*.
cabinet minister *n* (GB) ministre *m*.
cable *n* câble *m*.
cable car *n* téléphérique *m*.
cable TV *n* télévision *f* par câble.
cab-rank, **cab stand** *n* station *f* de taxis.
cackle *vi* [*hen*] caqueter; [*person*] (talk) caqueter; (laugh) ricaner.
caddy *n* caddie *m*.
cadet *n* (Mil) élève *mf* officier.
café *n* **1** ≈ snack-bar *m*; **pavement ~**, **sidewalk ~** café *m*; **2** (US) bistro *m*.
cafeteria *n* (gen) cafétéria *f*; (Sch) cantine *f*; (Univ) restaurant *m* universitaire.
caffein(e) *n* caféine *f*; **~-free** décaféiné/-e.
cage I *n* cage *f*.
II *vtr* mettre [qch] en cage [*animal*]; **a ~d animal** un animal en cage.
cagoule *n* (GB) K-way® *m*.
cahoots○ *n pl* **to be in ~** être de mèche○ (**with** avec).
Cairo ▶ 448 *pr n* Le Caire.
cajole *vtr* cajoler.
cake *n* **1** (Culin) gâteau *m*; (sponge) génoise *f*; **2** (of soap, wax) pain *m*.
IDIOMS **it's a piece of ~**○ c'est du gâteau○.
cake shop *n* ≈ pâtisserie *f*.
calcium *n* calcium *m*.
calculate *vtr* **1** calculer [*cost, distance, price*]; **2** évaluer [*effect, probability*]; **3 to be ~d to do** avoir été conçu pour faire.
calculating *adj* [*manner, person*] calculateur/-trice.
calculation *n* calcul *m*.
calculator *n* calculatrice *f*, calculette *f*.
calendar *n* calendrier *m*.
calf *n* **1** (Zool) veau *m*; **2** (also **~skin**) vachette *f*; **3** (Anat) mollet *m*.
calibre (GB), **caliber** (US) *n* calibre *m*.
call I *n* **1** (also **phone ~**) appel *m* (téléphonique) (**from** de); **to make a ~** appeler, téléphoner; **2** (cry) (human) appel *m* (**for** à); (animal) cri *m*; **3** (summons) appel *m*; **4** (visit) visite *f*; **5** (demand) demande *f* (**for** de); **6 there's no ~ for sth** il n'y a pas de raison pour qch; **7** (Sport) décision *f*; **8 to be on ~** [*doctor*] être de garde; [*engineer*] être de service.
II *vtr* **1** (gen) appeler; **what is he ~ed?** comment sappelle-t-il?; **the boss ~ed me into his office** le chef m'a fait venir dans son bureau; **2** organiser [*strike*]; convoquer [*meeting*]; fixer [*election*]; **3** (waken) réveiller [*person*]; **4** (describe as) **to ~ sb stupid** traiter qn d'imbécile; **I wouldn't ~ it spacious** je ne dirais pas que c'est spacieux.
III *vi* **1** (gen) appeler; **who's ~ing?** qui est à l'appareil?; **2** (visit) passer; **to ~ at** passer chez [*person, shop*]; passer à [*bank, library*]; [*train*] s'arrêter à [*town, station*].
■ **call back**: ¶ **~ back** (on phone) rappeler; ¶ **~ [sb] back** rappeler [*person*].
■ **call for**: **~ for [sth] 1** (shout) appeler [*ambulance, doctor*]; **to ~ for help** appeler à l'aide; **2** (demand) réclamer; **3** (require) exiger [*treatment, skill*]; nécessiter [*change*].
■ **call in**: ¶ **~ in** (visit) passer; ¶ **~ [sb] in** faire entrer [*client, patient*]; faire appel à [*expert*].
■ **call off** abandonner [*investigation*]; annuler [*deal, wedding*]; rompre [*engagement*].
■ **call on 1** (visit) rendre visite à [*relative, friend*]; visiter [*patient, client*]; **2 to ~ on sb to do** demander à qn de faire.
■ **call out**: ¶ **~ out** appeler; (louder) crier; ¶ **~ [sb] out 1** appeler [*doctor, troops*]; **2** [*union*] lancer un ordre de grève à [*members*]; ¶ **~ [sth] out** appeler [*name, number*].
■ **call up**: ¶ **~ up** appeler; ¶ **~ [sb/sth] up 1** (on phone) appeler; **2** (Mil) appeler [qn] sous les drapeaux [*soldier*].
call box *n* (GB) cabine *f* téléphonique; (US) poste *m* téléphonique.
caller *n* **1** (on phone) personne *f* qui appelle; **2** (visitor) visiteur/-euse *m/f*.
callous *adj* inhumain/-e.
calm I *n* calme *m*; (in adversity) sang-froid *m*.
II *adj* calme; **keep ~!** du calme!
III *vtr* calmer.
■ **calm down**: ¶ **~ down** se calmer; ¶ **~ [sb/sth] down** calmer.
Calor gas® *n* (GB) butane *m*.
calorie *n* calorie *f*.
camcorder *n* caméscope® *m*.
camel ▶ 438 *n* chameau *m*.
camera *n* **1** (for photos) appareil *m* photo; **2** (for movies) caméra *f*.
cameraman ▶ 626 *n* cadreur *m*, cameraman *m*.
camisole *n* caraco *m*.
camouflage I *n* camouflage *m*.
II *vtr* camoufler (**with** avec).
camp I *n* camp *m*.
II *vi* camper; **to go ~ing** faire du camping.
campaign I *n* campagne *f*.
II *vi* faire campagne (**for** pour; **against** contre).
camp bed *n* lit *m* de camp.

camper *n* **1** (person) campeur/-euse *m/f*; **2** (also **~ van**) camping-car *m*.

campsite *n* terrain *m* de camping, camping *m*.

campus *n* campus *m*.

can[1] *modal aux* **1** (be able to) pouvoir; **~ you come?** est-ce que tu peux venir?, peux-tu venir?; **we will do all we ~** nous ferons tout ce que nous pouvons or tout notre possible; **2** (know how to) savoir; **she ~ swim** elle sait nager; **I can't drive** je ne sais pas conduire; **he ~ speak French** il parle français; **3** (permission, requests, offers, suggestions) pouvoir; **~ we park here?** est-ce que nous pouvons nous garer ici?; **you can't turn right** vous ne pouvez pas or vous n'avez pas le droit de tourner à droite; **~ you do me a favour?** peux-tu or est-ce que tu peux me rendre un service?; **4** (with verbs of perception) **~ they see us?** est-ce qu'ils nous voient?; **I can't feel a thing** je ne sens rien; **she can't understand English** elle ne comprend pas l'anglais; **5** (in expressions) **you can't be hungry!** tu ne peux pas avoir faim!; **you can't be serious!** tu veux rire!; **this can't be right** il doit y avoir une erreur; **~ you believe it!** tu te rends compte?; **what ~ she want from me?** qu'est-ce qu'elle peut bien me vouloir?

can[2] **I** *n* (of food) boîte *f*; (of drink) cannette *f*; (aerosol) bombe *f*; (for petrol) bidon *m*; (of paint) pot *m*.
II *vtr* mettre [qch] en conserve.

Canada ▶ 448 *pr n* Canada *m*.

Canadian ▶ 553 **I** *n* Canadien/-ienne *m/f*.
II *adj* canadien/-ienne; [*embassy*] du Canada.

canal *n* canal *m*.

canal boat, **canal barge** *n* péniche *f*.

Canaries *pr n pl* (also **Canary Islands**) **the ~** les Canaries *fpl*.

cancel *vtr* (gen) annuler; mettre une opposition à [*cheque*].

cancellation *n* annulation *f*.

cancer ▶ 533 *n* cancer *m*.

Cancer *n* Cancer *m*.

candid *adj* franc/franche.

candidate *n* candidat/-e *m/f*.

candle *n* bougie *f*; (in church) cierge *m*.

candlelight *n* lueur *f* de bougie.

candlestick *n* bougeoir *m*; (ornate) chandelier *m*.

candy *n* (US) (sweets) bonbons *mpl*; (sweet) bonbon *m*.

candyfloss *n* (GB) barbe *f* à papa.

cane *n* **1** (material) rotin *m*; **~ furniture** meubles en rotin; **2** (of sugar, bamboo) canne *f*; **3** (for walking) canne *f*; (for plant) tuteur *m*; (GB) (for punishment) badine *f*.

canine *n* canine *f*.

canned *adj* **1** [*food*] en boîte; **2**° [*laughter*] enregistré/-e.

cannibal *n* cannibale *mf*.

cannon *n* canon *m*.

canoe ▶ 504 **I** *n* (gen) canoë *m*; (dugout) pirogue *f*; (Sport) canoë-kayac *m*.
II *vi* faire du canoë.

canoeing ▶ 504 *n* **to go ~** faire du canoë-kayac.

can-opener *n* ouvre-boîtes *m inv*.

cantankerous *adj* acariâtre.

canteen *n* **1** (GB) (dining room) cantine *f*; **2** (Mil) (flask) bidon *m*; (mess tin) gamelle *f*; **3 a ~ of cutlery** une ménagère.

canter *vi* [*rider*] faire un petit galop; [*horse*] galoper.

canvas *n* toile *f*.

canvass *vtr* **1 to ~ voters** faire du démarchage électoral auprès des électeurs; **2 to ~ opinion on sth** sonder l'opinion au sujet de qch; **3** (for business) prospecter [*area*].

canyon *n* cañon *m*.

cap I *n* **1** casquette *f*; **baseball ~** casquette de baseball; **2** (of pen) capuchon *m*; (of bottle) capsule *f*; **3** (for tooth) couronne *f*.
II *vtr* **1** (limit) imposer une limite budgétaire à [*local authority*]; plafonner [*budget*]; **2** (cover) couronner (**with** de).
IDIOMS **to ~ it all** pour couronner le tout.

capability *n* **1** (capacity) capacité *f* (**to do** de faire); **2** (aptitude) aptitude *f*; **outside my capabilities** au-delà de mes compétences.

capable *adj* **1** (competent) compétent/-e; **2** (able) capable (**of** de).

capacity *n* **1** (of box, bottle) contenance *f*; (of building) capacité *f* d'accueil; **full to ~** comble; **2** (of factory) capacité *f* de production; **3** (role) **in my ~ as a doctor** en ma qualité de médecin; **4** (ability) **to have a ~ for** avoir des facilités pour [*learning, mathematics*]; **a ~ for doing** une aptitude à faire.

cape *n* **1** (cloak) cape *f*; **2** (on coast) cap *m*.

caper *n* **1** (Culin) câpre *f*; **2**° (scheme) combine *f*; **3**° (antic) pitrerie *f*.

Cape Town ▶ 448 *pr n* Le Cap.

capital I *n* **1** (letter) majuscule *f*; **2** (also **~ city**) capitale *f*; **3** (money) capital *m*.
II *adj* **1** [*letter*] majuscule; **~ A** A majuscule; **2** (Law) [*offence*] capital/-e.

capitalism *n* capitalisme *m*.

capitalist *n, adj* capitaliste (*m*).

capitalize *vi* **to ~ on** tirer parti de [*situation, advantage*].

capital punishment *n* peine *f* capitale.

Capricorn *n* Capricorne *m*.

capsize *vi* chavirer.

captain *n* capitaine *m*.
II *vtr* être le capitaine de [*team*]; commander [*ship, platoon*].

caption *n* légende *f*.

captivate *vtr* captiver, fasciner.

captive *n* captif/-ive *m/f*.

capture I *n* (of person, animal) capture *f*; (of stronghold) prise *f*.
II *vtr* **1** capturer [*person, animal*]; prendre [*stronghold*]; **2** saisir [*likeness*]; rendre [*feeling*].

car *n* **1** (Aut) voiture *f*; **2** (on train) wagon *m*; **restaurant ~** wagon-restaurant *m*.

caravan I *n* caravane *f*; (horse-drawn) roulotte *f*.
II *vi* **to go ~ning** (GB) faire du caravanage.

caravan site *n* camping *m* pour caravanes.
carbohydrate *n* hydrate *m* de carbone.
car bomb *n* bombe *f* dissimulée dans une voiture.
carbon *n* carbone *m*.
carbon copy *n* copie *f* carbone; (figurative) réplique *f* exacte.
carbon dioxide *n* dioxyde *m* de carbone.
carburettor (GB), **carburetor** (US) *n* carburateur *m*.
card *n* carte *f*.
IDIOMS **to play one's ~s right** bien jouer son jeu○.
cardboard *n* carton *m*.
cardboard box *n* (boîte *f* en) carton *m*.
card game *n* partie *f* de cartes.
cardiac *adj* cardiaque.
cardiac arrest *n* arrêt *m* du cœur.
cardphone *n* téléphone *m* à carte.
card trick *n* tour *m* de cartes.
care I *n* **1** (attention) attention *f*, soin *m*; **to take ~ to do** prendre soin de faire; **'take ~!'** (be careful) 'fais attention!'; (goodbye) 'à bientôt!'; **'handle with ~'** 'fragile'; **2** (looking after) (of person, animal) soins *mpl*; (of car, plant, clothes) entretien *m* (**of** de); **to take ~ of** (deal with) s'occuper de [*child, client, garden, details*]; (be careful with) prendre soin de [*machine, car*]; (keep in good condition) entretenir [*car, teeth*]; (look after) garder [*shop, watch*]; **to take ~ of oneself** (look after oneself) prendre soin de soi; (cope) se débrouiller tout seul/toute seule; (defend oneself) se défendre; **3** (Med) soins *mpl*; **4** (GB) **to be in ~** [*child*] être (placé/-e) en garde; **5** (worry) souci *m*.
II *vi* **1** (be concerned) **to ~ about** s'intéresser à [*art, environment*]; se soucier du bien-être de [*pupils, the elderly*]; **I don't ~!** ça m'est égal!; **she couldn't ~ less about**... elle se moque or se fiche○ complètement de...; **I'm past caring** je m'en moque; **2** (love) **to ~ about sb** aimer qn.
■ **care for**: ¶ **~ for [sth] 1** (like) aimer; **would you ~ for a drink?** voulez-vous boire quelque chose?; **2** (maintain) entretenir [*car, garden*]; prendre soin de [*skin, plant*]; ¶ **~ for [sb/sth]** s'occuper de [*child, animal*]; soigner [*patient*].
career *n* carrière *f*.
careers adviser, **careers officer** *n* conseiller/-ère *m/f* d'orientation.
carefree *adj* insouciant/-e.
careful *adj* [*person, driving*] prudent/-e; [*planning, preparation*] minutieux/-ieuse; [*research, examination*] méticuleux/-euse; **to be ~ to do** or **about doing** prendre soin de faire; **to be ~ with sth** faire attention à qch; **be ~!** (fais) attention!
carefully *adv* [*walk, open, handle*] prudemment; [*write*] soigneusement; [*listen, read, look*] attentivement.
careless *adj* [*person*] négligent/-e, imprudent/-e; [*work*] bâclé/-e; [*writing*] négligé/-e; [*driving*] négligent/-e; **~ mistake** faute d'étourderie; **it was ~ of me to do** ça a été de la négligence de ma part de faire.
carelessness *n* négligence *f*.
carer *n* aide *f* familiale.
caress *vtr* caresser.
caretaker ▶ 626 *n* concierge *mf*.
car ferry *n* ferry *m*.
cargo *n* chargement *m*.
cargo ship *n* cargo *m*.
car hire *n* location *f* de voitures.
Caribbean *n* **the ~ (sea)** la mer des Antilles or des Caraïbes.
caring *adj* **1** (loving) [*parent*] affectueux/-euse; **2** (compassionate) [*person, attitude*] compréhensif/-ive; [*society*] humain/-e.
carnage *n* carnage *m*.
carnation *n* œillet *m*.
carnival *n* **1** carnaval *m*; **2** (US) (funfair) fête *f* foraine.
carol *n* chant *m* de Noël.
carousel *n* **1** (merry-go-round) manège *m*; **2** (for luggage, slides) carrousel *m*.
car park *n* (GB) parc *m* de stationnement.
carpenter ▶ 626 *n* menuisier *m*.
carpentry *n* menuiserie *f*.
carpet *n* (fitted) moquette *f*; (loose) tapis *m*.
carpet sweeper *n* balai *m* mécanique.
car phone *n* téléphone *m* de voiture.
carriage *n* **1** (ceremonial) carrosse *m*; **2** (of train) wagon *m*, voiture *f*; **3** (of goods) transport *m*; **~ paid** port *m* payé; **4** (of typewriter) chariot *m*.
carrier *n* **1** (transport company) transporteur *m*; (airline) compagnie *f* aérienne; **2** (of disease) porteur/-euse *m/f*; **3** (GB) (also **~ bag**) sac *m* (en plastique).
carrot *n* carotte *f*.
carry I *vtr* **1** [*person*] porter; **to ~ sth in/out** apporter/emporter qch; **2** [*vehicle, pipe, vein*] transporter; [*tide, current*] emporter; **3** comporter [*warning*]; **4** comporter [*risk, responsibility*]; être passible de [*penalty*]; **5** [*bridge, road*] supporter [*load, traffic*]; **6** faire voter [*bill*]; **the motion was carried by 20 votes to 13** la motion l'a emporté par 20 votes contre 13; **7** (Med) être porteur/-euse de [*disease, virus*]; **8** (in mathematics) retenir; **9** (hold) porter [*head*].
II *vi* [*sound, voice*] porter.
IDIOMS **to get carried away**○ s'emballer○, se laisser emporter.
■ **carry forward** reporter [*balance, total*].
■ **carry off** (gen) emporter; remporter [*prize*]; **to ~ it off**○ réussir, y arriver.
■ **carry on**: ¶ **~ on 1** (continue) continuer (**doing** à faire); **2**○ (behave) se conduire; ¶ **~ on [sth]** maintenir [*tradition*]; poursuivre [*activity, discussion*].
■ **carry out** réaliser [*study*]; effectuer [*experiment, reform, attack, repairs*]; exécuter [*plan, orders*]; mener [*investigation, campaign*]; accomplir [*mission*]; remplir [*duties*]; mettre [qch] à exécution [*threat*]; tenir [*promise*].
carryall *n* (US) fourre-tout *m inv*.
carrycot *n* (GB) porte-bébé *m*.

carry-on○ *n* cirque *m*.

carryout *n* repas *m* à emporter.

carsick *adj* **to be ~** avoir le mal de la route.

cart I *n* charrette *f*.
II○ *vtr* (also **~ around**, **~ about**)○ trimballer○ [*bags*].

carton *n* (of juice, milk) carton *m*, brique *f*; (of yoghurt, cream) pot *m*; (of cigarettes) cartouche *f*; (US) (for house removals) carton *m*.

cartoon *n* **1** (film) dessin *m* animé; **2** (drawing) dessin *m* humoristique; (comic strip) bande *f* dessinée.

cartridge *n* (for pen, gun, video) cartouche *f*; (for camera) chargeur *m*.

cartwheel *n* **to do a ~** faire la roue.

carve I *vtr* **1** tailler, sculpter [*wood, stone, figure*] (**out of** dans); **2** graver [*letters, name*] (**onto** sur); **3** découper [*meat*].
II *vi* découper.
■ **carve out 1** se faire [*niche, name*]; se tailler [*reputation, market*]; **2** creuser [*gorge, channel*].

carving *n* sculpture *f*.

carving knife *n* couteau *m* à découper.

car wash *n* lavage *m* automatique.

case[1] **I** *n* **1** (gen) cas *m*; **in that ~** en ce cas, dans ce cas-là; **in 7 out of 10 ~s** 7 fois sur 10, dans 7 cas sur 10; **a ~ in point** un cas d'espèce, un exemple typique; **2** (Law) affaire *f*; procès *m*; **the ~ for the Crown** (GB), **the ~ for the State** (US) l'accusation *f*; **the ~ for the defence** la défense; **3** (argument) arguments *mpl*.
II in any case *phr* **1** (besides, anyway) de toute façon; **2** (at any rate) en tout cas.
III in case *phr* au cas où (+ *conditional*); **just in ~** au cas où.
IV in case of *phr* en cas de [*fire, accident*].

case[2] *n* **1** (suitcase) valise *f*; (crate, chest) caisse *f*; **2** (display cabinet) vitrine *f*; **3** (for spectacles, binoculars, weapon) étui *m*; (for camera, watch) boîtier *m*.

cash I *n* **1** (notes and coin) espèces *fpl*, argent *m* liquide; **to pay in ~** payer en espèces; **I haven't got any ~ on me** je n'ai pas d'argent liquide; **2** (money in general) argent *m*; **3** (payment) comptant *m*; **discount for ~** remise *f* pour paiement comptant.
II *vtr* encaisser [*cheque*].
■ **cash in**: ¶ **to ~ in on** tirer profit de, profiter de; ¶ **~ [sth] in** se faire rembourser, réaliser [*bond, policy*]; (US) encaisser [*check*].

cash-and-carry *n* libre-service *m* de vente en gros.

cash card *n* carte *f* de retrait.

cash desk *n* caisse *f*.

cash dispenser *n* (also **cashpoint**) distributeur *m* automatique de billets de banque, billetterie *f*.

cashew nut *n* cajou *m*.

cash flow *n* marge *f* brute d'auto-financement, MBA *f*.

cashier ▶ 626 *n* caissier/-ière *m/f*.

cashmere *n* (lainage *m* en) cachemire *m*.

cash on delivery, **COD** *n* envoi *m* contre remboursement.

cashpoint = **cash dispenser**.

cash register *n* caisse *f* enregistreuse.

casino *n* casino *m*.

cask *n* fût *m*, tonneau *m*.

casserole *n* **1** (container) daubière *f*, cocotte *f*; **2** (GB) (food) ragoût *m* cuit au four.

cassette *n* cassette *f*.

cassette deck *n* platine *f* à cassettes.

cassette player *n* lecteur *m* de cassettes.

cast I *n* **1** (list of actors) distribution *f*; (actors) acteurs *mpl*; **2** (Med) (also **plaster ~**) plâtre *m*; **3** (mould) moule *m*.
II *vtr* **1** jeter, lancer [*stone, fishing line*]; projeter [*shadow*]; **to ~ doubt on** émettre des doutes sur; **to ~ light on** éclairer; **to ~ a spell on** jeter un sort à; **2** jeter [*glance*] (**at** sur); **3** distribuer les rôles de [*play, film*]; **she was cast as Blanche** elle a joué Blanche; **4** couler [*plaster, metal*]; **5 to ~ one's vote** voter.

castaway *n* naufragé/-e *m/f*.

caste *n* caste *f*.

caster sugar *n* (GB) sucre *m* en poudre.

casting *n* distribution *f*.

casting vote *n* voix *f* prépondérante.

cast iron *n* fonte *f*; **a ~ alibi** un alibi en béton○.

castle *n* **1** château *m*; **2** (in chess) tour *f*.

cast-offs *n pl* vêtements *mpl* dont on n'a plus besoin, vieux vêtements.

castrate *vtr* castrer.

casual *adj* **1** (informal) [*clothes, person*] décontracté/-e; **2** [*acquaintance, relationship*] de passage; **~ sex** relations *fpl* sexuelles non suivies; **3** [*attitude, gesture, remark*] désinvolte; **4** [*glance*] superficiel/-ielle; **5** [*work*] (temporary) temporaire; (occasional) occasionnel/-elle.

casually *adv* **1** [*enquire, remark*] d'un air détaché; **2** [*dressed*] simplement.

casualty I *n* **1** (person) victime *f*; **2** (hospital ward) urgences *fpl*; **in ~** aux urgences.
II casualties *n pl* (soldiers) pertes *fpl*; (civilians) victimes *fpl*.

casual wear *n* vêtements *mpl* sport.

cat *n* (domestic) chat *m*; (female) chatte *f*; **the big ~s** les grands félins *mpl*.
IDIOMS **to let the ~ out of the bag** vendre la mèche; **to rain ~s and dogs** pleuvoir des cordes.

catalogue, **catalog** (US) *n* catalogue *m*.

catalyst *n* catalyseur *m*.

catapult *n* (hand-held) lance-pierres *m inv*.

catarrh *n* catarrhe *m*.

catastrophe *n* catastrophe *f*.

catch I *n* **1** (on purse, door) fermeture *f*; **2** (drawback) piège *m*; **3** (act of catching) prise *f*; **to play ~** jouer à la balle; **4** (in fishing) pêche *f*; (one fish) prise *f*.
II *vtr* **1** [*person*] attraper [*ball, fish, person*]; **to ~ hold of sth** attraper qch; **to ~ sb's attention** or **eye** attirer l'attention de qn; **to ~**

sight of sb/sth surprendre qn/qch; **2** (take by surprise) prendre, attraper; **to ~ sb doing** surprendre qn en train de faire; **we got caught in the rain** nous avons été surpris par la pluie; **3** prendre [*bus, plane*]; **4** (grasp) prendre [*hand, arm*]; agripper [*branch, rope*]; captiver, éveiller [*interest*]; **5** (hear) saisir○, comprendre; **6 to ~ one's fingers in** se prendre les doigts dans [*drawer, door*]; **to get one's shirt caught on** accrocher sa chemise à [*nail*]; **to get caught in** se prendre dans [*barbed wire, thorns*]; **7** attraper [*cold, disease, flu*]; **8 to ~ fire** prendre feu, s'enflammer.
III *vi* **1 to ~ on** [*shirt*] s'accrocher à [*nail*]; [*wheel*] frotter contre [*frame*]; **2** [*wood, fire*] prendre.
■ **catch on 1** (become popular) devenir populaire (**with** auprès de); **2** (understand) comprendre, saisir.
■ **catch out 1** (take by surprise) prendre [qn] de court; (doing something wrong) prendre [qn] sur le fait; **2** (trick) attraper, jouer un tour à.
■ **catch up**: ¶ **~ up** (in race) regagner du terrain; (in work) rattraper son retard; **to ~ up on** rattraper [*work, sleep*]; se remettre au courant de [*news*]; ¶ **~ [sb/sth] up** rattraper.
catching *adj* contagieux/-ieuse.
catchphrase *n* formule *f* favorite, rengaine *f*.
catchy *adj* [*tune*] entraînant/-e; [*slogan*] accrocheur/-euse.
categorical *adj* catégorique.
categorize *vtr* classer (**by** d'après).
category *n* catégorie *f*.
cater *vi* **1** [*caterer*] organiser des réceptions; **2 to ~ for** (GB) or **to** (US) accueillir [*children, guests*]; pourvoir à [*needs*]; [*programme*] s'adresser à [*audience*].
caterer ▶626| *n* traiteur *m*.
catering *n* (provision) approvisionnement *m*; (trade, industry, career) restauration *f*.
caterpillar *n* chenille *f*.
cathedral *n* cathédrale *f*.
Catholic *n*, *adj* catholique (*mf*).
Catseye® *n* (GB) plot *m* rétroréfléchissant.
cattle *n* bétail *m*.
catwalk *n* podium *m*.
cauliflower *n* chou-fleur *m*.
cause I *n* cause *f* (**of** de); **there is ~ for concern** il y a des raisons de s'inquiéter; **to have ~ to do** avoir des raisons de faire; **with good ~** à juste titre.
II *vtr* causer, occasionner [*damage, grief, problem*]; provoquer [*chaos, disease, controversy*]; entraîner [*suffering*]; amener [*confusion*]; **to ~ sb problems** causer des problèmes à qn; **to ~ trouble** créer des problèmes.
caustic *adj* caustique.
caution I *n* **1** (care) prudence *f*; **2** (wariness) circonspection *f*; **3** (warning) avertissement *m*.
II *vtr* **1** (warn) avertir (**that** que); **2** (Sport) donner un avertissement à [*player*].
IDIOMS **to throw** or **cast ~ to the wind(s)** oublier toute prudence.
cautious *adj* **1** (careful) prudent/-e; **2** (wary) [*person, reception, response*] réservé/-e; [*optimism*] prudent/-e.
cave *n* grotte *f*.
■ **cave in 1** [*tunnel, roof*] s'effondrer; **2** [*person*] céder.
caveman *n* homme *m* des cavernes.
caviar(e) *n* caviar *m*.
caving *n* spéléologie *f*; **to go ~** faire de la spéléologie.
cavity *n* cavité *f*.
cavort *vi* faire des cabrioles.
caw *vi* croasser.
cc *n* (*abbr* = **cubic centimetre**) cm^3.
CD *n* (*abbr* = **compact disc**) CD *m*.
CD player, **CD system** *n* platine *f* laser.
CD-ROM *n* disque *m* optique compact, CD-ROM *m*.
cease *vtr*, *vi* cesser.
cease-fire *n* cessez-le-feu *m inv*.
cedar *n* cèdre *m*.
ceiling *n* plafond *m*.
celebrate I *vtr* fêter; (more formally) célébrer.
II *vi* faire la fête.
celebrated *adj* célèbre (**for** pour).
celebration *n* **1** (celebrating) célébration *f*; **2** (party) fête *f*; **3** (public festivities) **~s** cérémonies *fpl*.
celebrity *n* célébrité *f*.
celery *n* céleri *m*.
celibate *adj* célibataire.
cell *n* cellule *f*.
cellar *n* cave *f*.
cello ▶586| *n* violoncelle *m*.
cellphone, **cellular phone** *n* radiotéléphone *m*.
Celsius *adj* Celsius *inv*.
Celt *n* Celte *mf*.
Celtic *adj* celtique, celte.
cement *n* ciment *m*.
cement mixer *n* bétonnière *f*.
cemetery *n* cimetière *m*.
censor I *n* censeur *mf*.
II *vtr* censurer.
censorship *n* censure *f* (**of** de).
census *n* recensement *m*.
cent ▶582| *n* cent *m*.
centenary *n* centenaire *m*.
center (US) = **centre**.
centigrade *adj* **in degrees ~** en degrés Celsius.
centimetre (GB), **centimeter** (US) ▶573| *n* centimètre *m*.
central *adj* **1** central/-e; **~ London** le centre de Londres; **2** (in the town centre) situé/-e en centre-ville; **3** (key) principal/-e.
central heating *n* chauffage *m* central.
centralize *vtr* centraliser.
central locking *n* verrouillage *m* central or centralisé.
centre (GB), **center** (US) I *n* centre *m*; **in the**

~ au centre; **town ~**, **city ~** centre-ville *m*; **the ~ of attention** le centre de l'attention; **the ~ of power** le siège du pouvoir; **shopping/sports ~** centre *m* commercial/sportif.
II *vtr, vi* centrer.
■ **centre around**, **centre on** [*activities, person*] se concentrer sur; [*people, industry*] se situer autour de [*town*]; [*life, thoughts*] être centré/-e sur [*person, work*].

centre-forward *n* (Sport) avant-centre *m*.

centre-half *n* (Sport) demi-centre *m*.

centrepiece (GB), **centerpiece** (US) *n* (of table) décoration *f* centrale; (of exhibition) clou *m*.

century ▶ 708 *n* siècle *m*; **in the 20th ~** au XXe siècle; **at the turn of the ~** au début du siècle.

ceramic *adj* en céramique.

ceramics *n* céramiques *fpl*.

cereal *n* céréale *f*.

ceremony *n* cérémonie *f*; **to stand on ~** faire des cérémonies.

certain *adj* **1** (sure) certain/-e, sûr/-e (**about, of** de); **I'm ~ (of it)** j'en suis certain or sûr; **absolutely ~** sûr et certain; **I'm ~ that I checked** je suis sûr d'avoir vérifié; **I'm ~ that he refused** je suis sûr qu'il a refusé; **2** (specific) [*amount, number, conditions*] certain/-e (*before n*); **~ people** certains *mpl*; **to a ~ extent** dans une certaine mesure.

certainly *adv* certainement.

certainty *n* certitude *f*.

certificate *n* (gen) certificat *m*; (of birth, death, marriage) acte *m*; **18-~ film** film interdit aux moins de 18 ans.

certified *adj* certifié/-e.

certified mail *n* (US) **to send by ~** envoyer en recommandé.

certified public accountant *n* (US) expert-comptable *m*.

certify *vtr* **1** (confirm) certifier; **2** (authenticate) authentifier.

cervical cancer *n* ▶ 533 cancer *m* du col de l'utérus.

cervical smear *n* frottis *m* vaginal.

CFC *n* (*abbr* = **chlorofluorocarbon**) CFC *m*.

chafe *vi* frotter (**on, against** sur).

chain I *n* **1** (metal links) chaîne *f*; **2** (on lavatory) chasse *f* (d'eau); **3** (on door) chaîne *f* de sûreté; **4** (of shops, hotels) chaîne *f* (**of** de); **5** (of events) série *f*; (of ideas) enchaînement *m*.
II *vtr* enchaîner [*person, animal*]; **to ~ a bicycle to sth** attacher une bicyclette à qch avec une chaîne.

chain reaction *n* réaction *f* en chaîne.

chain saw *n* tronçonneuse *f*.

chain-smoker *n* gros fumeur/grosse fumeuse *m/f*.

chain store *n* (single shop) magasin *m* faisant partie d'une chaîne; (retail group) magasin *m* à succursales multiples.

chair I *n* **1** chaise *f*; (armchair) fauteuil *m*; **2** (chairperson) président/-e *m/f*; **3** (Univ) chaire *f* (**of, in** de).
II *vtr* présider [*meeting*].

chair lift *n* télésiège *m*.

chairman ▶ 498 *n* président/-e *m/f*; **Mr Chairman** monsieur le Président; **Madam Chairman** madame la Présidente.

chairperson *n* président/-e *m/f*.

chalet *n* (mountain) chalet *m*; (in holiday camp) bungalow *m*.

chalk *n* craie *f*.

challenge I *n* **1** défi *m*; **to take up a ~** relever un défi; **2** (challenging task) challenge *m*; **to rise to the ~** relever le challenge.
II *vtr* **1** défier [*person*] (**to** à; **to do** de faire); **2** débattre [*ideas*]; contester [*statement, authority*].

challenging *adj* **1** [*work*] stimulant/-e; **2** [*lock*] provocateur/-trice.

chamber I *n* chambre *f*.
II **chambers** *n pl* (Law) cabinet *m*.

chambermaid ▶ 626 *n* femme *f* de chambre.

chamber music *n* musique *f* de chambre.

chameleon *n* caméléon *m*.

champagne *n, adj* champagne (*m*) *inv*.

champion *n* champion/-ionne *m/f*.

championship *n* championnat *m*.

chance I *n* **1** (opportunity) occasion *f*; **to have** or **get the ~ to do** avoir l'occasion de faire; **you've missed your ~** tu as laissé passer l'occasion; **2** (likelihood) chance *f*; **there is a ~ that she'll get a job in Paris** il y a des chances qu'elle trouve un travail à Paris; **she has a good ~** elle a de bonnes chances; **3** (luck) hasard *m*; **by ~** par hasard; **4** (risk) risque *m*; **to take a ~** prendre un risque; **5** (possibility) chance *f*; **not to stand a ~** n'avoir aucune chance; **by any ~** par hasard.
II *vtr* **to ~ doing** courir le risque de faire; **to ~ it** tenter sa chance.
IDIOMS **no ~**○! pas question○!

chancellor *n* chancelier *m*; (Univ) président *m*.

Chancellor of the Exchequer *n* (GB) Chancelier *m* de l'Échiquier.

chandelier *n* lustre *m*.

change I *n* **1** (gen) changement *m*; (adjustment) modification *f*; **the ~ in the schedule** la modification du programme; **~ of plan** changement de programme; **a ~ of clothes** des vêtements de rechange; **a ~ for the better** un changement en mieux; **that makes a nice ~** ça change agréablement; **she needs a ~** elle a besoin de se changer les idées; **to need a ~ of air** avoir besoin de changer d'air; **for a ~** pour changer; **2** (cash) monnaie *f*; **small ~** petite monnaie; **she gave me 10 francs ~** elle m'a rendu 10 francs; **have you got ~ for 50 francs?** pouvez-vous me changer un billet de 50 francs?
II *vtr* **1** (alter) changer; (in part) modifier; **to ~ sb/sth into** transformer qn/qch en; **to ~ one's mind** changer d'avis; **to ~ one's mind about doing** abandonner l'idée de faire; **to ~ colour** changer de couleur; **2** changer de [*clothes, name, car, job, TV channel*]; (in shop) échanger [*item*] (**for** pour); **to ~ places** (seats) changer de place (**with** avec); **3** changer [*bat-*

tery, tyre]; **to ~ a bed** changer les draps; **4** changer [*cheque, currency*] (**into, for** en).
III *vi* **1** [*situation, person*] changer; [*wind*] tourner; **the lights ~d from red to orange** les feux sont passés du rouge à l'orange; **2** (into different clothes) se changer; **to ~ into** passer [*garment*]; **to ~ out of** ôter, enlever [*garment*]; **3** (from bus, train) changer.
■ **change round** déplacer [*large objects*]; changer [qn/qch] de place [*workers, objects, words*].

changeable *adj* [*condition, weather*] changeant/-e; [*price*] variable.

changeover *n* passage *m* (**to** à).

changing *adj* [*colours, environment*] changeant/-e; [*attitude, world*] en évolution.

changing room *n* (at sports centre) vestiaire *m*; (US) (in shop) cabine *f* d'essayage.

channel I *n* **1** (TV station) chaîne *f*; (radio band) canal *m*; **2** (groove) rainure *f*; **3** (in sea, river) chenal *m*; **4 through the proper ~s** par la voie normale; **to go through official ~s** passer par la voie officielle.
II *vtr* canaliser (**to, into** dans).

Channel *pr n* **the (English) ~** la Manche.

channel ferry *n* ferry *m* trans-Manche.

Channel Islands *pr n pl* îles *fpl* Anglo-Normandes.

Channel Tunnel *pr n* tunnel *m* sous la Manche.

chant I *n* **1** (of crowd) chant *m* scandé; **2** (of devotees) mélopée *f*.
II *vi* [*crowd*] scander des slogans; [*choir, monks*] psalmodier.

chaos *n* (gen) pagaille○ *f*; (economic, cosmic) chaos *m*; **in a state of ~** [*house*] sens dessus dessous; [*country*] en plein chaos.

chaotic *adj* désordonné/-e.

chap I○ *n* (GB) type○ *m*.
II *vtr* gercer; **~ped lips** lèvres gercées.

chapel *n* chapelle *f*.

chaperone I *n* chaperon *m*.
II *vtr* chaperonner.

chaplain *n* aumônier *m*.

chapter *n* chapitre *m*; **in ~ 3** au chapitre 3.

character *n* **1** (gen) caractère *m*; **2** (in book, play, film) personnage *m* (**from** de); **3 a real ~** un sacré numéro○; **a local ~** une figure locale.

characteristic I *n* (gen) caractéristique *f*; (of person) trait *m* de caractère.
II *adj* caractéristique (**of** de).

characterize *vtr* **1** (depict) dépeindre (**as** comme); **2** (typify) caractériser; **to be ~d by** se caractériser par.

charade *n* comédie *f*.

charades *n pl* (game) charades *fpl*.

charcoal ▶ 438 I *n* **1** (fuel) charbon *m* de bois; **2** (for drawing) fusain *m*.
II *adj* (also **~ grey**) (gris) anthracite *inv*.

charge I *n* **1** (fee) frais *mpl*; **additional** or **extra ~** supplément *m*; **to reverse the ~s** (on phone) appeler en PCV; **2** (accusation) accusation *f* (**of** de); (Law) inculpation *f*; **murder ~** inculpation d'assassinat; **to press ~s against sth** engager des poursuites contre qch; **3** (attack) charge *f* (**against** contre); **4 to be in ~** (gen) être responsable (**of** de); (Mil) commander; **the person in ~** le/la responsable; **to take ~** prendre les choses en main; **5** (child) enfant *mf* dont on s'occupe; (pupil) élève *mf*; (patient) malade *mf*; **6** (explosive, electrical) charge *f*.
II *vtr* **1** prélever [*commission*]; percevoir [*interest*] (**on** sur); **to ~ sb for sth** faire payer qch à qn; **how much do you ~?** vous prenez combien?; **I ~ £20 an hour** je prends 20 livres de l'heure; **2 to ~ sth to** mettre qch sur [*account*]; **3** [*police*] inculper [*suspect*] (**with** de); **4** (rush at) charger [*enemy*]; [*bull*] foncer sur [*person*]; **5** charger [*battery*].
III *vi* **to ~ into/out of** se précipiter dans/de [*room*].

charge account *n* (US) compte-client *m*.

charge card *n* (credit card) carte *f* de crédit; (store card) carte *f* d'achat.

char-grilled *adj* [*steak*] grillé/-e au charbon de bois.

charisma *n* charisme *m*.

charismatic *adj* charismatique.

charitable *adj* charitable (**to** envers).

charity *n* **1** (virtue) charité *f*; **2** (organization) organisation *f* caritative; **to give to/collect money for ~** donner à/collecter des fonds pour des œuvres de bienfaisance.

charm *n* **1** charme *m*; **2 lucky ~** porte-bonheur *m inv*.

charming *adj* [*person, place*] charmant/-e; [*child, animal*] adorable.

charred *adj* carbonisé/-e.

chart I *n* **1** (graph) graphique *m*; **2** (table) tableau *m*; **3** (map) carte *f*; **4 the ~s** le hit-parade.
II *vtr* **1** (on map) tracer [*route*]; **2** enregistrer [*progress*].

charter I *n* charte *f*.
II *vtr* affréter [*plane*].

chartered accountant, **CA** ▶ 626 *n* (GB) ≈ expert-comptable *m*.

charter flight *n* (GB) vol *m* charter.

chase I *n* poursuite *f* (**after** de).
II *vtr* **1** pourchasser [*person, animal*]; **to ~ sb/sth up** or **down the street** courir après qn/qch dans la rue; **2** (also **~ after**) courir après [*woman, man, success*].
■ **chase away**, **chase off** chasser [*person, animal*].

chassis *n* châssis *m*.

chastity *n* chasteté *f*.

chat I *n* conversation *f*; **to have a ~** bavarder (**with** avec; **about** sur).
II *vi* bavarder (**with, to** avec).
■ **chat up**○ (GB) draguer○.

chat show *n* (GB) talk-show *m*.

chatter I *n* (of person) bavardage *m*; (of birds) gazouillis *m*.
II *vi* [*person*] bavarder; [*birds*] gazouiller; **her teeth were ~ing** elle claquait des dents.

chatty *adj* [*person*] ouvert/-e; [*letter*] vivant/-e.

chauffeur ▶626| I *n* chauffeur *m*; **a ~-driven car** une voiture avec chauffeur.
II *vtr* conduire.

chauvinist *n*, *adj* **1** (gen) chauvin/-e (*m/f*); **2** (also **male ~**) macho○ (*m*).

cheap *adj* **1** bon marché *inv*; **to be ~** être bon marché, ne pas coûter cher *inv*; **~er** moins cher/-ère; **2** (shoddy) de mauvaise qualité; **3** [*joke*] facile; [*trick*] sale (*before n*).

cheapen *vtr* rabaisser.

cheaply *adv* [*produce, sell*] à bas prix; **to eat ~** manger pour pas cher.

cheap rate *adj*, *adv* à tarif réduit.

cheat I *n* tricheur/-euse *m/f*.
II *vtr* tromper; **to feel ~ed** se sentir lésé/-e; **to ~ sb (out) of** dépouiller qn de.
III *vi* tricher (**in** à); **to ~ at cards** tricher aux cartes; **to ~ on sb** tromper qn.

check I *n* **1** (for quality, security) contrôle *m* (**on** sur); **2** (medical) examen *m*; **3** (restraint) frein *m* (**on** à); **4** (in chess) **~!** échec au roi!; **in ~** en échec; **5** (also **~ fabric**) tissu *m* à carreaux; (also **~ pattern**) carreaux *mpl*; **6** (US) (cheque) chèque *m*; **7** (US) (bill) addition *f*; **8** (US) (receipt) ticket *m*; **9** (US) (tick) croix *f*.
II *adj* [*shirt, skirt*] à carreaux.
III *vtr* **1** (gen) vérifier; contrôler [*ticket, area, work*]; prendre [*temperature*]; examiner [*watch, map, pocket*]; **2** (curb) contrôler [*prices, inflation*]; freiner [*growth*]; maîtriser [*emotions*].
IV *vi* **1** vérifier; **to ~ with sb** demander à qn; **to ~ for** dépister [*problems*]; chercher [*leaks, flaws*]; **2 to ~ into** arriver à [*hotel*].
■ **check in**: ¶ **~ in** (at airport) enregistrer; (at hotel) arriver (**at** à); ¶ **~ [sb/sth] in** enregistrer [*baggage, passengers*].
■ **check off** cocher [*items*].
■ **check out**: ¶ **~ out** (leave) partir; **to ~ out of** quitter [*hotel*]; ¶ **~ [sth] out** vérifier [*information*]; examiner [*package, building*]; se renseigner sur [*club, scheme*].
■ **check up on** faire une enquête sur [*person*]; vérifier [*story, details*].

checkbook *n* (US) carnet *m* de chèques, chéquier *m*.

checkered (US) = **chequered**.

checkers (US) = **chequers**.

check-in *n* enregistrement *m*.

checking account *n* (US) compte *m* courant.

checklist *n* liste *f* de contrôle.

checkmate *n* échec *m* et mat.

checkout *n* caisse *f*.

checkpoint *n* poste *m* de contrôle.

checkroom *n* (US) (cloakroom) vestiaire *m*; (for baggage) consigne *f*.

checkup *n* **1** (at doctor's) examen *m* médical, bilan *m* de santé; **2** (at dentist's) visite *f* de routine.

cheek *n* **1** (of face) joue *f*; **~ to ~** joue contre joue; **2** culot○ *m*; **what a ~!** quel culot!

cheekbone *n* pommette *f*.

cheeky *adj* [*person*] effronté/-e, insolent/-e; [*question*] impoli/-e; [*grin*] espiègle, coquin/-e.

cheer I *n* acclamation *f*; **to get a ~** être acclamé/-e.
II **cheers** *excl* **1** (toast) à la vôtre○!; (to close friend) à la tienne○!; **2**○ (GB) (thanks) merci!; **3**○ (GB) (goodbye) salut!
III *vtr*, *vi* applaudir.
■ **cheer up**: ¶ **~ up** reprendre courage; **~ up!** courage!; ¶ **~ [sb] up** remonter le moral à [*person*]; ¶ **~ [sth] up** égayer [*room*].

cheerful *adj* [*person, mood, music*] joyeux/-euse; [*tone*] enjoué/-e; [*colour*] gai/-e.

cheerleader *n* majorette *f*.

cheese *n* fromage *m*; **~ sandwich** sandwich *m* au fromage.

cheeseboard *n* (object) plateau *m* à fromage; (selection) plateau *m* de fromages.

cheetah *n* guépard *m*.

chef ▶626| *n* chef *m* cuisinier.

chemical I *n* produit *m* chimique.
II *adj* chimique.

chemist ▶626| *n* **1** (GB) pharmacien/-ienne *m/f*; **~'s (shop)** pharmacie *f*; **2** (scientist) chimiste *mf*.

chemistry *n* chimie *f*.

cheque (GB), **check** (US) *n* chèque *m*; **to make out** or **write a ~ for £20** faire un chèque de 20 livres sterling.

chequebook (GB), **checkbook** (US) *n* chéquier *m*, carnet *m* de chèques.

cheque card *n* (GB) carte *f* de garantie bancaire.

chequered (GB), **checkered** (US) *adj* **1** [*cloth*] à damiers; **2** [*career, history*] en dents de scie.

chequers (GB), **checkers** (US) ▶504| *n* jeu *m* de dames.

cherish *vtr* caresser [*hope*]; chérir [*memory, person*].

cherry ▶438| I *n* **1** (fruit) cerise *f*; **2** (also **~ tree**) cerisier *m*.
II *adj* (also **~-red**) rouge cerise *inv*.

chess ▶504| *n* échecs *mpl*; **a game of ~** une partie d'échecs.

chessboard *n* échiquier *m*.

chess set *n* jeu *m* d'échecs.

chest *n* **1** (of person) poitrine *f*; **~ measurement** tour *m* de poitrine; **2** (furniture) coffre *m*; **~ of drawers** commode *f*; **3** (crate) caisse *f*.
IDIOMS **to get something off one's chest**○ vider son sac○.

chestnut I *n* **1** (nut) marron *m*, châtaigne *f*; **2** (also **~ tree**) (horse) marronnier *m* (d'Inde); (sweet) châtaignier *m*.
II *adj* [*hair*] châtain; **a ~ horse** un (cheval) alezan.

chew *vtr* mâcher [*food, gum*]; mordiller [*pencil*]; ronger [*bone*].

chewing gum *n* chewing-gum *m*.

chick *n* (fledgling) oisillon *m*; (of fowl) poussin *m*.

chicken *n* **1** (fowl) poulet *m*, poule *f*; **2** (meat) poulet *m*; **3**○ (coward) poule *f* mouillée.

chicken pox ▶533| *n* varicelle *f*.

chicken wire *n* grillage *m* (à mailles fines).

chickpea *n* pois *m* chiche.
chicory *n* **1** (vegetable) endive *f*; **2** (in coffee) chicorée *f*.
chief I *n* chef *m*.
II *adj* **1** [*reason*] principal/-e; **2** [*editor*] en chef.
chief executive *n* directeur *m* général.
chiefly *adv* notamment, surtout.
Chief of Staff *n* (Mil) chef *m* d'état-major; (of White House) secrétaire *m* général.
chiffon *n* mousseline *f*.
chilblain *n* engelure *f*.
child *n* enfant *mf*; **when I was a ~** quand j'étais enfant.
childbirth *n* accouchement *m*.
childhood I *n* enfance *f*; **in (his) early ~** dans sa prime enfance.
II *adj* [*friend, memory*] d'enfance; [*illness*] infantile.
childish *adj* puéril/-e.
childlike *adj* enfantin/-e.
childminder ▶626 *n* (GB) nourrice *f*.
Chile ▶448 *pr n* Chili *m*.
chill I *n* **1** (coldness) fraîcheur *f*; **there is a ~ in the air** le fond de l'air est frais; **to send a ~ down sb's spine** donner des frissons à qn; **2** (illness) coup *m* de froid.
II *adj* **1** [*wind*] frais/fraîche; **2** [*reminder, words*] brutal.
III *vtr* **1** mettre [qch] à refroidir [*dessert, soup*]; rafraîchir [*wine*]; **2** (make cold) faire frissonner [*person*]; **to ~ sb's** or **the blood** glacer le sang à qn.
IV *vi* [*dessert*] refroidir; [*wine*] rafraîchir.
chilli, **chili** *n* **1** (also **~ pepper**) piment *m* rouge; **2** (also **~ powder**) chili *m*; **3** (also **~ con carne**) chili *m* con carne.
chilly *adj* froid; **it's ~** il fait froid.
chime *n* carillon *m*.
chimney *n* cheminée *f*.
chimpanzee *n* chimpanzé *m*.
chin *n* menton *m*.
china I *n* porcelaine *f*.
II *adj* [*cup, plate*] en porcelaine.
China ▶448 *pr n* Chine *f*.
Chinese ▶553 I *n* **1** (person) Chinois/-oise *m/f*; **2** (language) chinois *m*.
II *adj* chinois/-oise; [*embassy*] de Chine.
chink *n* **1** (in wall) fente *f*; (in curtain) entrebâillement *m*; **2** (sound) tintement *m*.
chip I *n* **1** (fragment) fragment *m* (**of** de); (of wood) copeau *m*; (of glass) éclat *m*; **2** (in wood, china) ébréchure *f*; **3** (microchip) puce *f* (électronique).
II **chips** *n pl* **1** (GB) (fried potatoes) frites *fpl*; **2** (US) (crisps) chips *fpl*.
III *vtr* ébrécher [*glass, plate*]; écailler [*paint*]; **to ~ a tooth** se casser une dent.
IDIOMS **to have a ~ on one's shoulder** être amer/-ère.
■ **chip in** (GB)○ (financially) donner un peu d'argent.
chipboard *n* aggloméré *m*.
chiropodist ▶626 *n* pédicure *mf*.
chiropractor ▶626 *n* chiropraticien/-ienne *m/f*, chiropracteur *m*.
chirp *vi* [*bird*] pépier.
chisel I *n* ciseau *m*.
II *vtr* ciseler.
chitchat○ *n* bavardage *m*.
chivalry *n* **1** chevalerie *f*; **2** (courtesy) galanterie *f*.
chive *n* ciboulette *f*.
chlorine *n* chlore *m*.
choc-ice *n* (GB) esquimau *m*.
chock-a-block *adj* plein à craquer.
chocolate I *n* chocolat *m*.
II *adj* [*sweets*] en chocolat; [*biscuit, cake, ice cream*] au chocolat.
choice *n* choix *m* (**between, of** entre); **to make a ~** faire un choix, choisir; **to be spoilt for ~** avoir l'embarras du choix; **out of** or **from ~** par choix.
choir *n* (of church, school) chorale *f*; (professional) chœur *m*.
choirboy *n* petit chanteur *m*, jeune choriste *m*.
choke I *n* (Aut) starter *m*.
II *vtr* **1** (throttle) étrangler [*person*]; **2** [*fumes, smoke*] étouffer.
III *vi* s'étouffer.
■ **choke back** étouffer [*cough, sob*]; **to ~ back one's tears** retenir ses larmes.
cholera ▶533 *n* choléra *m*.
cholesterol *n* cholestérol *m*.
choose I *vtr* **1** (select) choisir (**from** parmi); **2** (decide) décider (**to do** de faire).
II *vi* **1** (select) choisir (**between** entre); **2** (prefer) **to ~ to do** préférer faire.
choosy *adj* difficile (**about** en ce qui concerne).
chop I *n* (Culin) côtelette *f*; **pork ~** côtelette *f* de porc.
II *vtr* **1** (also **~ up**) couper [*wood*]; couper, émincer [*vegetable, meat*]; hacher [*parsley, onion*]; **to ~ sth finely** hacher qch; **2** réduire [*service, deficit*].
IDIOMS **to ~ and change** [*person*] changer d'avis comme de chemise.
■ **chop down** abattre [*tree*].
■ **chop off** couper [*branch, end*]; trancher [*head, hand, finger*].
chopping board *n* planche *f* à découper.
chopping knife *n* couteau *m* de cuisine.
choppy *adj* [*sea, water*] agité/-e.
chopstick *n* baguette *f* (chinoise).
chord *n* accord *m*.
chore *n* tâche *f*; **to do the ~s** faire le ménage.
chorus *n* **1** (singers) chœur *m*; **2** (piece of music) chœur *m*; **3** (refrain) refrain *m*.
Christ *pr n* le Christ, Jésus-Christ.
christen *vtr* baptiser.
christening *n* baptême *m*.
Christian I *n* chrétien/-ienne *m/f*.
II *adj* chrétien/-ienne; [*attitude*] charitable.
Christianity *n* christianisme *m*.
Christian name *n* nom *m* de baptême.
Christmas *n* **~ (day)** (jour *m* de) Noël; **at**

~ à Noël; **Merry ~!**, **Happy ~!** Joyeux Noël!

Christmas card *n* carte *f* de Noël.

Christmas eve *n* veille *f* de Noël.

Christmas tree *n* sapin *m* de Noël.

chrome *n* chrome *m*.

chronic *adj* **1** [*illness*] chronique; **2** [*liar*] invétéré/-e; [*problem, shortage*] chronique.

chronicle *n* chronique *f*.

chronological *adj* chronologique.

chubby *adj* [*child, finger*] potelé/-e; [*cheek*] rebondi/-e; [*face*] joufflu/-e; [*adult*] rondelet/-ette.

chuck *vtr* **1**○ (also **~ away**) balancer○, jeter; **2** larguer○ [*boyfriend, girlfriend*].

chuckle *vi* glousser; **to ~ at sth** rire de qch.

chuffed○ *adj* (GB) vachement○ content/-e (**about, at, with** de).

chum○ *n* copain/copine○ *m/f*, pote○ *m*.

chunk *n* **1** (of meat, fruit) morceau *m*; (of wood) tronçon *m*; (of bread) quignon *m*; **pineapple ~s** ananas *m* en morceaux; **2** (of population, text, day) partie *f* (**of** de).

church I *n* (Catholic, Anglican) église *f*; (Protestant) temple *m*.
II *adj* [*bell, choir, steeple*] d'église; [*fête*] paroissial; [*wedding*] religieux/-ieuse.

churchgoer *n* pratiquant/-e *m/f*.

churchyard *n* cimetière *m*.

churn I *n* **1** (for butter) baratte *f*; **2** (GB) (for milk) bidon *m*.
II *vtr* **to ~ butter** baratter.
■ **churn out** pondre [qch] en série [*novels*]; produire [qch] en série [*goods*].
■ **churn up** faire des remous dans [*water*].

chute *n* **1** (slide) toboggan *m*; **2** (for rubbish) vide-ordures *m inv*; **3** (for toboggan) piste *f* de toboggan.

cicada *n* cigale *f*.

cider *n* cidre *m*.

cigar *n* cigare *m*.

cigarette *n* cigarette *f*.

cinder *n* (glowing) braise *f*; (ash) cendre *f*.

Cinderella *pr n* Cendrillon.

cinecamera *n* caméra *f* (d'amateur).

cine film *n* pellicule *f* cinématographique.

cinema *n* cinéma *m*.

cinnamon ▶ 438 *n* cannelle *f*.

circle I *n* **1** (gen) cercle *m*; **to go round in ~s** tourner en rond; **to have ~s under one's eyes** avoir les yeux cernés; **2** (in theatre) balcon *m*; **in the ~** au balcon.
II *vtr* **1** [*plane*] tourner autour de [*airport*]; [*person, animal, vehicle*] faire le tour de [*building*]; tourner autour de [*person, animal*]; **2** (surround) encercler.
III *vi* tourner en rond (**around** autour de).

circuit *n* **1** (gen) circuit *m*; **2** (lap) tour *m*.

circular I *n* (newsletter) circulaire *f*; (advertisement) prospectus *m*.
II *adj* [*object*] rond; [*argument*] circulaire.

circulate I *vtr* faire circuler.
II *vi* **1** (gen) circuler; **2** (at party) **let's ~** on va aller faire connaissance.

circulation *n* **1** (gen) circulation *f*; **2** (of newspaper) tirage *m*.

circumcision *n* (of boy) circoncision *f*; (of girl) excision *f*.

circumference *n* circonférence *f*.

circumflex *n* accent *m* circonflexe.

circumstances *n pl* **1** circonstances *fpl*; **in** or **under the ~** dans ces circonstances; **under no ~** en aucun cas; **2** (financial position) situation *f*.

circus *n* cirque *m*.

CIS *pr n* (*abbr* = **Commonwealth of Independent States**) CEI *f*.

cistern *n* (of lavatory) réservoir *m* de chasse d'eau; (in loft or underground) citerne *f*.

citizen *n* **1** (of state) citoyen/-enne *m/f*; (when abroad) ressortissant/-e *m/f*; **2** (of town) habitant/-e *m/f*.

citizenship *n* nationalité *f*.

citrus fruit *n* agrume *m*.

city *n* (grande) ville *f*; **the City** (GB) la City.

city centre (GB), **city center** (US) *n* centre-ville *m*.

civic *adj* [*administration, official*] municipal/-e; [*pride, responsibility*] civique.

civic centre (GB), **civic center** (US) *n* centre *m* municipal (culturel et administratif).

civil *adj* **1** [*case, court, offence*] civil/-e; **2** (polite) courtois/-e.

civil engineering *n* génie *m* civil.

civilian *n* civil/-e *m/f*.

civilization *n* civilisation *f*.

civilized *adj* civilisé/-e.

civil law *n* droit *m* civil.

civil rights *n pl* droits *mpl* civils.

civil servant ▶ 626 *n* fonctionnaire *mf*.

civil service *n* fonction *f* publique.

civil war *n* guerre *f* civile.

claim I *n* **1** (demand) revendication *f*; **2** (in insurance) (against a person) réclamation *f*; (for fire, theft) demande *f* d'indemnisation; **3** (for welfare benefit) demande *f* d'allocation; **4** (assertion) affirmation *f*.
II *vtr* **1** (maintain) prétendre; **2** revendiquer [*money, property, responsibility, right*]; **3** faire une demande de [*benefit*]; faire une demande de remboursement de [*expenses*].
III *vi* **1 to ~ for damages** faire une demande pour dommages et intérêts; **2** (apply for benefit) faire une demande d'allocation.

claimant *n* **1** (for benefit, compensation) demandeur/-euse *m/f* (**to** à); **2** (to title, estate) prétendant/-e *m/f* (**to** à).

claim form *n* déclaration *f* de sinistre.

clairvoyant *n* voyant/-e *m/f*, extralucide *mf*.

clam *n* palourde *f*.
■ **clam up** ne plus piper mot (**on sb** à qn).

clammy *adj* moite.

clamour (GB), **clamor** (US) I *n* (shouting) clameur *f*.
II *vi* **1** (demand) **to ~ for sth** réclamer qch; **to**

~ for sb to do réclamer à qn de faire; **2** (rush, fight) se bousculer (**for** pour avoir; **to do** pour faire).

clamp I *n* **1** (on bench) valet *m*; **2** (also **wheel~**) sabot *m* de Denver.
II *vtr* **1** cramponner [*two parts*]; (at bench) fixer [qch] à l'aide d'un valet (**onto** à); **2** serrer [*jaw, teeth*]; **3** (also **wheel~**) mettre un sabot de Denver à [*car*].

clan *n* clan *m*.

clandestine *adj* clandestin/-e.

clang I *n* fracas *m*, bruit *m* métallique.
II *vi* [*gate*] claquer avec un son métallique; [*bell*] retentir.

clap I *n* **to give sb a ~** applaudir qn; **a ~ of thunder** un coup de tonnerre.
II *vtr* **to ~ one's hands** battre or taper des mains, frapper dans ses mains.
III *vi* applaudir.

clapping *n* applaudissements *mpl*.

claret ▶438| *n* **1** (wine) bordeaux *m* (rouge); **2** (colour) bordeaux *m*.

clarify *vtr* éclaircir, clarifier.

clarinet ▶586| *n* clarinette *f*.

clarity *n* clarté *f*.

clash I *n* **1** (confrontation) affrontement *m*; **2** (of cultures, interests, personalities) conflit *m*; **3 a ~ of cymbals** un coup de cymbales.
II *vtr* entrechoquer [*bin lids*]; frapper [*cymbals*].
III *vi* **1** (fight, disagree) s'affronter; **to ~ with sb** (fight) se heurter à qn; (disagree) se quereller avec qn (**on, over** au sujet de); **2** (be in conflict) [*interests, beliefs*] être incompatibles; **3** (coincide) [*meetings*] avoir lieu en même temps (**with** que); **4** [*colours*] jurer.

clasp *n* (on bracelet, bag, purse) fermoir *m*; (on belt) boucle *f*.

class I *n* (gen) classe *f*; (lesson) cours *m* (**in** de); **to be in a ~ of one's own** être hors catégorie; **to travel first/second ~** voyager en première/deuxième classe.
II *vtr* classer.

classic *n, adj* classique (*m*).

classical *adj* classique.

classics *n* lettres *fpl* classiques.

classification *n* **1** (category) classification *f*, catégorie *f*; **2** (categorization) classement *m*.

classified I *n* (also **~ ad**) petite annonce *f*.
II *adj* (secret) confidentiel/-ielle.

classify *vtr* **1** (file) classer; **2** (declare secret) classer [qch] confidentiel/-ielle.

classmate *n* camarade *mf* de classe.

classroom *n* salle *f* de classe.

class system *n* système *m* de classes.

clatter I *n* cliquetis *m*; (loud) fracas *m*.
II *vi* [*typewriter*] cliqueter; [*dishes*] s'entrechoquer.

clause *n* **1** (in grammar) proposition *f*; **2** (in contract, treaty) clause *f*; (in will, act of Parliament) disposition *f*.

claustrophobia *n* claustrophobie *f*.

claw *n* **1** (gen) griffe *f*; (of bird of prey) serre *f*; (of crab, lobster) pince *f*; **2** (on hammer) arrache-clou *m*, pied-de-biche *m*.

clay *n* argile *f*.

clean I *adj* **1** (gen) propre; [*air, water*] pur/-e; **my hands are ~** j'ai les mains propres; **~ and tidy** d'une propreté irréprochable; **a ~ sheet of paper** une feuille blanche; **2** [*joke*] anodin/-e; **3** [*reputation*] sans tache; [*record, licence*] vierge; **4** (Sport) [*tackle*] sans faute; [*hit*] précis/-e; **5** (neat) [*lines, profile*] pur/-e.
II *vtr* nettoyer; **to ~ one's teeth** se brosser les dents.
■ **clean out** nettoyer [qch] à fond [*cupboard, room*].
■ **clean up**: ¶ **~ up 1** tout nettoyer; **2** (wash oneself) se débarbouiller; ¶ **~ [sth] up** nettoyer.

cleaner ▶626| *n* **1** (woman) femme *f* de ménage; (man) agent *m* de nettoyage; **2** (detergent) produit *m* de nettoyage; **3** (shop) **cleaner's** pressing *m*.

cleaning *n* (domestic) ménage *m*; (commercial) nettoyage *m*, entretien *m*.

cleanliness *n* propreté *f*.

cleanse *vtr* nettoyer [*skin, wound*].

cleanser *n* **1** (for face) démaquillant *m*; **2** (household) produit *m* d'entretien.

clean-shaven *adj* **he's ~** il n'a ni barbe ni moustache.

clear I *adj* **1** (transparent) [*glass, liquid*] transparent/-e; [*blue*] limpide; [*lens, varnish*] incolore; [*honey*] liquide; **~ soup** consommé *m*; **2** (distinct) [*image, outline*] net/nette; [*sound, voice*] clair/-e; **3** (comprehensible) [*description, instruction*] clair/-e; **to make sth ~ to sb** faire comprendre qch à qn; **is that ~?** est-ce que c'est clair?; **4** (obvious) [*need, sign*] évident/-e; [*advantage*] net/nette (*before n*); [*majority*] large (*before n*); **it is ~ that** il est clair que; **5** (not confused) [*idea, memory*] clair/-e; [*plan*] précis/-e; **to keep a ~ head** garder les idées claires; **6** (empty) [*view*] dégagé/-e; [*table*] débarrassé/-e; [*space*] libre; **7** [*conscience*] tranquille; **8** [*skin*] net/nette; [*sky*] sans nuage; [*day, night*] clair/-e; **on a ~ day** par temps clair/-e.
II *adv* **to jump ~ of sth** éviter qch en sautant sur le côté; **to pull sb ~ of** extraire qn de [*wreckage*]; **to stay** or **steer ~ of** éviter [*town centre, troublemakers*].
III *vtr* **1** enlever [*rubbish, papers, mines*]; dégager [*snow*] (**from, off** de); **2** déboucher [*drains*]; débarrasser [*table, room*]; vider [*desk*]; évacuer [*area, building*]; effacer [*screen*]; défricher [*land*]; **to ~ one's throat** se racler la gorge; **to ~ a path through sth** se frayer un chemin à travers qch; **3** dissiper [*fog, smoke*]; disperser [*crowd*]; **4** s'acquitter de [*debt*]; **5** [*bank*] compenser [*cheque*]; **6** innocenter [*accused*] (**of** de); **to ~ one's name** blanchir son nom; **7** approuver [*request*]; **to ~ sth with sb** obtenir l'accord de qn pour qch; **8** franchir [*hurdle, wall*]; **9 to ~ customs** passer à la douane.
IV *vi* **1** [*liquid, sky*] s'éclaircir; **2** [*smoke, fog, cloud*] se dissiper; **3** [*air*] se purifier; **4** [*rash*] disparaître; **5** [*cheque*] être compensé/-e.
■ **clear away**: ¶ **~ away** débarrasser; ¶ **~**

[sth] away balayer [*leaves*]; enlever [*rubbish*]; ranger [*papers, toys*].
■ **clear up**: ¶ **~ up 1** (tidy up) faire du rangement; **2** [*weather*] s'éclaircir; [*infection*] disparaître; ¶ **~ [sth] up 1** ranger [*mess, room, toys*]; ramasser [*litter*]; **2** résoudre [*problem*]; dissiper [*misunderstanding*].

clearance *n* **1** (of rubbish) enlèvement *m*; **land ~** défrichement *m* du terrain; **2** (permission) autorisation *f*; **3** (also **~ sale**) liquidation *f*.

clear-cut *adj* [*plan, division*] précis/-e; [*difference*] net/nette (*before n*); [*problem, rule*] clair/-e.

clear-headed *adj* lucide.

clearing *n* (glade) clairière *f*.

clearly *adv* **1** [*speak, hear, think, write*] clairement; [*see*] bien; [*visible*] bien; [*labelled*] clairement; **2** (obviously) manifestement.

cleavage *n* décolleté *m*.

cleaver *n* fendoir *m*.

clef *n* clef *f*; **in the treble ~** en clef de fa.

cleft *adj* [*chin*] marqué/-e d'un sillon; [*palate*] fendu/-e.

clench *vtr* serrer.

clergy *n* clergé *m*.

clergyman *n* ecclésiastique *m*.

clerical *adj* **1** (of clergy) clérical/-e; **2** [*staff*] de bureau; **~ work** travail *m* de bureau.

clerk ▶626 *n* **1** (in office, bank) employé/-e *m/f*; **2** (GB) (to lawyer) ≈ clerc *m*; (in court) greffier/-ière *m/f*; **3** (US) (in hotel) réceptionniste *mf*; (in shop) vendeur/-euse *m/f*.

clever *adj* **1** (intelligent) intelligent/-e; **2** (ingenious) [*solution, gadget, person*] astucieux/-ieuse, futé/-e; **3** (skilful) habile, adroit/-e.

cliché *n* cliché *m*, lieu *m* commun.

click I *n* (of machine, lock) déclic *m*; (of fingers, heels, tongue) claquement *m*.
II *vtr* **to ~ one's fingers** faire claquer ses doigts; **to ~ one's heels** claquer des talons.
III *vi* [*camera, lock*] faire un déclic; [*door*] faire un petit bruit sec.

client *n* client/-e *m/f*.

clientele *n* clientèle *f*.

cliff *n* (by sea) falaise *f*; (inland) escarpement *m*.

climate *n* climat *m*.

climax *n* (of war, conflict) paroxysme *m*; (of plot, speech, play) point *m* culminant; (of career) apogée *m*.

climb I *n* (up hill) escalade *f*; (up tower) montée *f*; (up mountain) ascension *f*.
II *vtr* grimper [*hill*]; faire l'ascension de [*mountain*]; escalader [*lamppost, wall*]; grimper à [*ladder, tree*]; monter [*staircase*].
III *vi* **1** [*person*] grimper; **to ~ down** descendre [*rock face*]; **to ~ over** enjamber [*stile*]; passer par-dessus [*fence, wall*]; escalader [*debris, rocks*]; **to ~ up** grimper à [*ladder, tree*]; monter [*steps*]; **2** [*aircraft*] monter; **3** [*road*] monter; **4** (increase) monter.
■ **climb down** revenir sur sa décision.

climber *n* grimpeur/-euse *m/f*, alpiniste *mf*.

climbing ▶504 *n* escalade *f*.

clinch *vtr* **1 to ~ a deal** conclure une affaire; **2** décider de [*argument*].

cling *vi* **1 to ~ (on) to sb/sth** se cramponner à qn/qch; **to ~ together** se cramponner l'un à l'autre; **2** [*clothes*] coller (**to** à); **3** [*smell*] résister.

clingfilm *n* (GB) scellofrais® *m*.

clinic *n* centre *m* médical.

clinical *adj* **1** [*medicine*] clinique; [*approach*] objectif/-ive; **2** (unfeeling) froid/-e.

clink I *vtr* faire tinter [*glass, keys*]; **to ~ glasses with** trinquer avec.
II *vi* [*glass, keys*] tinter.

clip I *n* **1** (on earring) clip *m*; (for hair) barrette *f*; **2** (from film) extrait *m*.
II *vtr* **1** tailler [*hedge*]; couper [*nails, moustache*]; tondre [*dog, sheep*]; **2** accrocher [*microphone*] (**to** à); fixer [*brooch*] (**to** à).
IDIOMS **to ~ sb's wings** rogner les ailes à qn.

clipboard *n* (gen) porte-bloc *m inv* à pince; (Comput) presse-papiers *m inv*.

clip-ons *n pl* clips *mpl*.

clippers *n pl* (for nails) coupe-ongles *m inv*; (for hair, hedge) tondeuse *f*.

clipping *n* (from paper) coupure *f* de presse.

cloak I *n* cape *f*.
II *vtr* **1 ~ed in** enveloppé/-e dans [*darkness*]; enveloppé/-e de [*secrecy*]; **2** (disguise) masquer.

cloakroom *n* **1** (for coats) vestiaire *m*; **2** (GB) (lavatory) toilettes *fpl*.

clock ▶434 *n* (large) horloge *f*; (small) pendule *f*; (Sport) chronomètre *m*; **to put the ~s forward/back one hour** avancer/reculer les pendules d'une heure; **to work around the ~** travailler 24 heures sur 24.
■ **clock off** (GB) pointer (à la sortie).
■ **clock on** (GB) pointer.

clock radio *n* radio-réveil *m*.

clock tower *n* beffroi *m*.

clockwise *adj, adv* dans le sens des aiguilles d'une montre.

clockwork *adj* [*toy*] mécanique.
IDIOMS **to go like ~** aller comme sur des roulettes.

clog *n* sabot *m*.

cloister *n* cloître *m*.

clone *n* clone *m*.

close[1] **I** *adj* **1** (near) proche (**to** de), voisin/-e (**to** de); **2** [*relative, friend*] proche; [*resemblance*] frappant/-e; **3** [*contest, result*] serré/-e; **4** [*scrutiny*] minutieux/-ieuse; [*supervision*] étroit/-e; **to pay ~ attention to sth** faire une attention toute particulière à qch; **to keep a ~ watch** or **eye on sb/sth** surveiller étroitement qn/qch; **5** [*print, formation*] serré/-e; **6** [*weather*] lourd/-e; **it's ~** il fait lourd.
II *adv* **to live quite ~ (by)** habiter tout près; **to move sth ~r** approcher qch; **to follow ~ behind** suivre de près; **to hold sb ~** serrer qn; **~ together** serrés les uns contre les autres; **Christmas is ~** Noël approche.
III close to *phr* **1** (near) près de; **2** (on point of) au bord de [*tears, hysteria*]; **to be ~ to doing**

The Clock

What time is it?

what time is it? = quelle heure est-il?
could you tell me the time? = pouvez-vous me donner l'heure?
it's exactly four o'clock = il est exactement quatre heures

It is . . .	*Il est . . .*	*say . . .*
4 o'clock	4 heures	
	4 h	quatre heures
4 o'clock in the morning / 4 am	4 h 00	quatre heures du matin
4 o'clock in the afternoon / 4 pm	16 h 00	quatre heures de l'après-midi
		seize heures*
4.10 / ten past four	4 h 10	quatre heures dix
4.15	4 h 15	quatre heures quinze
a quarter past four	4 h 15	quatre heures et quart
4.20	4 h 20	quatre heures vingt
4.25	4 h 25	quatre heures vingt-cinq
4.30	4 h 30	quatre heures trente
half past four	4 h 30	quatre heures et demie†
4.35	4 h 35	quatre heures trente-cinq
twenty-five to five	4 h 35	cinq heures moins vingt-cinq
4.40	4 h 40	quatre heures quarante
twenty to five	4 h 40	cinq heures moins vingt
4.45 / a quarter to five	4 h 45	cinq heures moins le quart
4.50	4 h 50	quatre heures cinquante
ten to five	4 h 50	cinq heures moins dix
4.55	4 h 55	quatre heures cinquante-cinq
five to five	4 h 55	cinq heures moins cinq
5 o'clock	5 h	cinq heures
16.15	16 h 15	seize heures quinze
8 o'clock in the evening	8 h du soir	huit heures du soir
8 pm	20 h 00	vingt heures
12.00	12 h 00	douze heures
noon / 12 noon	12 h 00	midi
midnight / 12 midnight	24 h 00	minuit

* In timetables etc, the twenty-four hour clock is used, so that ***4 pm*** is ***seize heures***. In ordinary usage, one says ***quatre heures*** (***de l'après-midi***).

† ***Demi*** agrees when it follows its noun, but not when it comes before the noun to which it is hyphenated, eg ***quatre heures et demie*** but ***les demi-heures*** etc. Note that ***midi*** and ***minuit*** are masculine, so ***midi et demi*** and ***minuit et demi***.

When?

French never drops the word ***heures***: ***at five*** is ***à cinq heures*** and so on.

French always uses ***à***, whether or not English includes the word ***at***. The only exception is when there is another preposition present, as in ***vers cinq heures*** (*about five o'clock*), ***avant cinq heures*** (*before five o'clock*) etc:

***what** time did it happen?* = **à quelle** heure cela s'est-il passé?
***what** time will he come **at**?* = **à quelle** heure va-t-il venir?
*it happened **at** two o'clock* = c'est arrivé **à** deux heures
*he'll come **at** four* = il viendra **à** quatre heures
***at about** five* = **vers** cinq heures / **à** cinq heures **environ**
*it must be ready **by** ten* = il faut que ce soit prêt **avant** dix heures
*closed **from** 1 **to** 2 pm* = fermé **de** treize **à** quatorze heures
*every hour **on** the hour* = toutes les heures **à** l'heure juste

être sur le point de faire; **3** (almost) près de; **to come ~ to doing** faillir faire.
IV close by *phr* près de [*wall, bridge*]; **the ambulance is ~ by** l'ambulance n'est pas loin.
IDIOMS **it was a ~ call**○ or **shave**○ or **thing** je l'ai/tu l'as etc échappé belle.
close² **I** *n* fin *f*.
II *vtr* **1** fermer [*door, book*]; **2** fermer [*border, port*]; barrer [*road*]; interdire l'accès à [*area*]; **3** mettre fin à [*meeting*]; fermer [*account*]; **4 to ~ the gap** réduire l'écart; **5** conclure [*deal*].
III *vi* **1** [*airport, polls, shop*] fermer; [*door, container, eyes, mouth*] se fermer; **2** (cease to operate) fermer définitivement; **3** [*meeting, play*] prendre fin; **to ~ with** se terminer par [*song*]; **4** [*currency, index*] clôturer (**at** à); **5** [*gap*] se réduire.
IV closed *pp adj* fermé/-e; **behind ~d doors** à huis clos.
■ **close down**: ¶ **~ down** fermer définitivement; ¶ **~ [sth] down** fermer [qch] définitivement.
■ **close up**: ¶ **~ up 1** [*flower, wound*] se refermer; [*group*] se serrer; **2** [*shopkeeper*] fermer; ¶ **~ [sth] up 1** fermer [*shop*]; **2** boucher [*hole*].
closed-circuit television *n* télévision *f* en circuit fermé.
close-fitting *adj* [*garment*] ajusté/-e, près du corps.
close-knit *adj* [*family, group*] très uni/-e.
closely *adv* [*follow, watch*] de près; [*resemble*] beaucoup; **to be ~ related** [*people*] être proches parents.
closet **I** *n* (US) (cupboard) placard *m*; (for clothes) penderie *f*.
II *adj* [*alcoholic, fascist*] inavoué/-e.
close-up **I** *n* gros plan *m*; **in ~** en gros plan.
II close up *adv* (**from**) **~** de près.
closing **I** *n* fermeture *f*.
II *adj* [*minutes, words*] dernier/-ière (*before n*); [*scene, stage*] final/-e; [*speech*] de clôture.
closing date *n* date *f* limite (**for** de).
closing-down sale, **closing-out sale** (US) *n* liquidation *f*.
closing time *n* heure *f* de fermeture.
closure *n* fermeture *f*.
clot **I** *n* caillot *m*.
II *vtr, vi* coaguler, cailler.
cloth *n* **1** (fabric) tissu *m*; **2** (for polishing, dusting) chiffon *m*; (for floor) serpillière *f*; (for drying dishes) torchon *m*; (for table) nappe *f*.
clothes *n pl* vêtements *mpl*; **to put on/take off one's ~** s'habiller/se déshabiller.
clothes brush *n* brosse *f* à habits.
clotheshanger *n* cintre *m*.
clothes line *n* corde *f* à linge.
clothes peg *n* pince *f* à linge.
clothing *n* vêtements *mpl*; **an item** or **article of ~** un vêtement.
cloud **I** *n* nuage *m*; **to cast a ~ over sth** jeter une ombre sur qch.
II *vtr* **1** [*steam, breath*] embuer [*mirror*]; [*tears*] brouiller [*vision*]; **2** obscurcir [*judgment*]; brouiller [*memory*]; **to ~ the issue** brouiller les cartes.
IDIOMS **to be living in ~-cuckoo-land** croire au père Noël.
■ **cloud over** [*sky*] se couvrir (de nuages); [*face*] s'assombrir.
cloudy *adj* **1** [*weather*] couvert/-e; **2** [*liquid*] trouble.
clout *n* **1** (blow) claque *f*, coup *m*; **2** (influence) influence *f* (**with** auprès de, sur).
clove *n* **1** (spice) clou *m* de girofle; **2** (of garlic) gousse *f*.
clover *n* trèfle *m*.
clown *n* clown *m*.
■ **clown around** (GB) faire le clown or le pitre.
club ▶**504** *n* **1** (association) club *m*; **2**○ (nightclub) boîte *f* de nuit○; **3** (in cards) trèfle *m*; **4** (for golf) club *m*; **5** (weapon) massue *f*.
■ **club together** cotiser.
club car *n* (US) wagon-bar *m* de première classe.
club class *n* classe *f* club or affaires.
cluck *vi* [*hen*] glousser.
clue *n* indication *f* (**to, as to** quant à); (in police investigation) indice *m* (**to** quant à); (in crossword) définition *f*; **I haven't (got) a ~**○ je n'ai aucune idée.
clump *n* (of flowers, grass) touffe *f*; (of trees) massif *m*; (of earth) motte *f*.
clumsy *adj* [*person, attempt*] maladroit/-e; [*object*] grossier/-ière; [*animal*] pataud/-e; [*tool*] peu maniable; [*style*] lourd/-e.
cluster **I** *n* (of flowers, berries) grappe *f*; (of people, islands, trees) groupe *m*; (of houses) ensemble *m*; (of diamonds) entourage *m*; (of stars) amas *m*.
II *vi* [*people*] se rassembler (**around** autour de).
clutch **I** *n* (Aut) embrayage *m*.
II *vtr* tenir fermement.
■ **clutch at** tenter d'attraper [*branch, rail, person*]; saisir [*arm*].
clutch bag *n* pochette *f*.
clutches *n pl* **to fall into the ~ of** tomber sous les griffes or la patte○ de.
clutter **I** *n* désordre *m*.
II *vtr* (also **~ up**) encombrer.
c/o *prep* (*abbr* = **care of**) chez.
coach **I** *n* **1** (bus) (auto)car *m*; **2** (GB) (of train) wagon *m*; **3** (Sport) entraîneur/-euse *m/f*; **4** (for drama, voice) répétiteur/-trice *m/f*; **5** (horse-drawn) carrosse *m*.
II *vtr* **1** (Sport) entraîner [*team*]; **2** (teach) **to ~ sb** donner des leçons particulières à qn (**in** en).
coal *n* charbon *m*.
IDIOMS **to haul sb over the ~s**○ passer un savon à qn○.
coalfield *n* bassin *m* houiller.
coalition *n* coalition *f*.
coalmine *n* mine *f* de charbon.
coalminer ▶**626** *n* mineur *m*.
coarse *adj* **1** [*texture*] grossier/-ière; [*skin*] épais/-aisse; [*sand, salt*] gros/grosse (*before n*);

2 [*manners*] grossier/-ière; [*language, joke*] cru/-e.

coast I *n* côte *f*; **off the ~** près de la côte.
II *vi* [*car, bicycle*] descendre en roue libre.

coastal *adj* côtier/-ière.

coaster *n* (mat) dessous-de-verre *m inv*.

coastguard ▶626| *n* **1** (person) garde-côte *m*; **2** (organization) gendarmerie *f* maritime.

coastline *n* littoral *m*.

coat I *n* **1** (garment) manteau *m*; **2** (of dog, cat) pelage *m*; (of horse, leopard) robe *f*; **3** (layer) couche *f*.
II *vtr* **to ~ sth with** enduire qch de [*paint, adhesive*]; couvrir qch de [*dust, oil*]; enrober qch de [*breadcrumbs, chocolate, sauce*].

coat hanger *n* cintre *m*.

coat of arms *n* blason *m*, armoiries *fpl*.

coatrack *n* portemanteau *m*.

coax *vtr* cajoler; **to ~ sb into doing** persuader qn (gentiment) de faire.

cobbler ▶626| *n* cordonnier *m*.

cobblestones *n pl* pavés *mpl*.

cobweb *n* toile *f* d'araignée.

cocaine *n* cocaïne *f*.

cock I *n* **1** (rooster) coq *m*; **2** (male bird) (oiseau *m*) mâle *m*.
II *vtr* **1 to ~ an eyebrow** hausser les sourcils; **to ~ a leg** [*dog*] lever la patte; **to ~ an ear** dresser l'oreille; **2** (tilt) pencher; **3** (Mil) armer [*gun*].

cock-and-bull story *n* histoire *f* abracadabrante or à dormir debout.

cockatoo *n* cacatoès *m*.

cockerel *n* jeune coq *m*.

cockle *n* coque *f*.

cockpit *n* cockpit *m*, poste *m* de pilotage.

cockroach *n* cafard *m*.

cocktail *n* cocktail *m*.

cocktail bar *n* bar *m*.

cocky *adj* impudent/-e.

cocoa *n* cacao *m*; (drink) chocolat *m*.

coconut *n* noix *f* de coco.

cocoon *n* cocon *m*.

cod *n* morue *f*.

COD *n* (*abbr* = **cash on delivery**) envoi *m* contre remboursement.

code I *n* **1** (gen) code *m*; **2** (also **dialling ~**) indicatif *m*.
II *vtr* coder.

coerce *vtr* exercer des pressions sur; **to ~ sb into doing** contraindre qn à faire.

coexist *vi* coexister (**with** avec).

coffee *n* café *m*; **a black/white ~** un café (noir)/au lait.

coffee break *n* pause(-)café *f*.

coffee pot *n* cafetière *f*.

coffee table *n* table *f* basse.

coffin *n* cercueil *m*.

cog *n* (tooth) dent *f* d'engrenage; (wheel) pignon *m*.

cohabit *vi* cohabiter (**with** avec).

coherent *adj* cohérent/-e.

coil I *n* **1** (of rope, barbed wire) rouleau *m*; (of electric wire) bobine *f*; (of hair) boucle *f*; (of snake) anneau *m*; **2** (contraceptive) stérilet *m*.
II *vtr* (also **~ up**) enrouler [*hair, rope, wire*].
III *vi* s'enrouler (**round** autour de).

coin I *n* pièce *f* (de monnaie); **a pound ~** une pièce d'une livre.
II *vtr* forger [*term*].

coin box *n* (pay phone) cabine *f* (téléphonique) à pièces.

coincide *vi* coïncider (**with** avec).

coincidence *n* coïncidence *f*, hasard *m*; **it is a ~ that** c'est par coïncidence que; **by ~** par hasard.

coincidental *adj* fortuit/-e.

coke *n* **1** (fuel) coke *m*; **2**○ (cocaine) coke◑ *f*.

Coke® *n* coca *m*.

colander *n* passoire *f*.

cold I *n* **1** (chilliness) froid *m*; **to feel the ~** être sensible au froid, être frileux/-euse; **2** (Med) rhume *m*; **to have a ~** être enrhumé/-e, avoir un rhume.
II *adj* **1** (chilly) froid; **to be** or **feel ~** [*person*] avoir froid; **the room was ~** il faisait froid dans la pièce; **it's** or **the weather's ~** il fait froid; **to go ~** [*food, water*] se refroidir; **2** [*manner*] froid/-e; **to be ~ to** or **towards sb** être froid/-e avec qn.
IDIOMS **in ~ blood** de sang-froid; **to be out ~** être sans connaissance.

coldness *n* froideur *f*.

cold shoulder *n* **to give sb the ~** snober qn, battre froid à qn.

cold sore *n* bouton *m* de fièvre.

cold sweat *n* **to bring sb out in a ~** donner des sueurs froides à qn.

coleslaw, **slaw** (US) *n* salade *f* à base de chou cru.

colic *n* coliques *fpl*.

collaborate *vi* collaborer (**on, in** à; **with** avec).

collaborator *n* collaborateur/-trice *m/f*.

collapse I *n* **1** (of regime, economy) effondrement *m* (**of, in** de); **2** (of deal, talks) échec *m*; **3** (of company) faillite *f* (**of** de); **4** (of person) (physical) écroulement *m*; (mental) effondrement *m*; **5** (of building, bridge) effondrement *m*; (of tunnel, wall) écroulement *m*; **6** (Med) (of lung) collapsus *m*.
II *vi* **1** [*regime, economy*] s'effondrer; [*deal, talks*] échouer; **2** [*company*] faire faillite; **3** [*person*] s'écrouler; **4** [*building, bridge*] s'effondrer; [*tunnel, wall*] s'écrouler; [*chair*] s'affaisser (**under** sous); **5** (Med) [*lung*] se dégonfler; **6** (fold) [*bike, pushchair*] se plier.

collapsible *adj* pliant/-e.

collar *n* **1** (on garment) col *m*; **2** (for animal) collier *m*.
IDIOMS **to get hot under the ~** se mettre en rogne○.

collarbone *n* clavicule *f*.

colleague *n* collègue *mf*.

collect I *adv* (US) **to call sb ~** appeler qn en PCV.
II *vtr* **1** ramasser [*wood, litter, rubbish*]; rassembler [*information*]; recueillir [*signatures*]; **2** (as hobby) collectionner, faire collection de [*stamps, coins*]; **3** [*objects*] prendre, ramasser [*dust*]; **4** percevoir [*rent*]; encaisser [*fares, money*]; recouvrer [*debt*]; toucher [*pension*]; percevoir [*tax, fine*]; **5** faire la levée de [*mail, post*]; **6** (pick up) aller chercher [*person*]; récupérer [*keys, book*].
III *vi* **1** [*dust, leaves*] saccumuler; [*people*] se rassembler; **2 to ~ for charity** faire la quête pour des bonnes œuvres.

collection *n* **1** (of coins, records) collection *f*; (anthology) recueil *m*; **art ~** collection *f* (de tableaux); **2** (money) collecte *f* (**for** pour); (in church) quête *f*; **3** (of mail) levée *f*.

collective *adj* collectif/-ive.

collector *n* **1** (of coins, stamps) collectionneur/-euse *m/f*; **2** (of taxes) percepteur *m*; (of rent, debts) encaisseur *m*.

college *n* établissement *m* d'enseignement supérieur; (school, part of university) collège *m*; (US Univ) faculté *f*; **to go to ~, to be at** or **in** (US) **~** faire des études supérieures.

collide *vi* [*vehicle, plane*] entrer en collision (**with** avec).

collie *n* (dog) colley *m*.

colliery *n* houillère *f*.

collision *n* collision *f*.

colloquial *adj* familier/-ière.

colon *n* **1** (Anat) côlon *m*; **2** (punctuation) deux points *mpl*.

colonel *n* colonel *m*.

colonialist *n*, *adj* colonialiste (*mf*).

colonize *vtr* coloniser.

colony *n* colonie *f*.

colour (GB), **color** (US) **▶438** I *n* **1** couleur *f*; **what ~ is it?** de quelle couleur est-il/elle?; **to put ~ into sb's cheeks** redonner des couleurs à qn; **2** (dye) (for food) colorant *m*; (for hair) teinture *f*.
II *vtr* **1** (with paints, crayons) colorier; (with food dye) colorer; **2** (prejudice) fausser [*judgment*].
III *vi* [*person*] rougir.
IDIOMS **to be off ~** ne pas être en forme; **to show one's true ~s** se montrer sous son vrai jour.

colour blind *adj* daltonien/-ienne.

coloured (GB), **colored** (US) *adj* [*pen, paper, bead*] de couleur; [*picture*] en couleur; [*light, glass*] coloré/-e.

colour film *n* (for camera) pellicule *f* couleur.

colourful (GB), **colorful** (US) *adj* **1** [*dress, shirt*] aux couleurs vives; **2** [*story, life*] haut en couleur; [*character*] pittoresque.

colouring (GB), **coloring** (US) *n* **1** (of animal) couleurs *fpl*; (of person) teint *m*; **2** (for food) colorant *m*.

colour scheme *n* couleurs *fpl*, coloris *m*.

colour television *n* télévision *f* (en) couleur.

colt *n* poulain *m*.

column *n* **1** (pillar) colonne *f*; **2** (on page, list) colonne *f*; **3** (newspaper article) rubrique *f*; **sports ~** rubrique sportive.

columnist *n* journaliste *mf*.

coma *n* coma *m*; **in a ~** dans le coma.

comb I *n* peigne *m*.
II *vtr* **to ~ sb's hair** peigner qn; **to ~ one's hair** se peigner.

combat I *n* combat *m*.
II *vtr* lutter contre, combattre.

combination *n* combinaison *f*.

combine I *n* groupe *m*.
II *vtr* **1** combiner [*activities, colours, items*] (**with** avec); associer [*ideas, aims*] (**with** à); **to ~ forces** (merge) s'allier; (cooperate) collaborer; **2** (Culin) mélanger (**with** avec).
III *vi* **1** [*activities, colours, elements*] se combiner; **2** [*people, groups*] s'associer; [*firms*] fusionner.

combine harvester *n* moissonneuse-batteuse *f*.

come *vi* **1** [*person, day*] venir; [*bus, news, winter, war*] arriver; [*dustman, postman*] passer; **to ~ down** descendre [*stairs, street*]; **to ~ up** monter [*stairs, street*]; **to ~ into** entrer dans [*house, room*]; **when the time ~s** lorsque le moment sera venu; **(I'm) coming!** j'arrive!; **to ~ to sb for** venir demander [qch] à qn [*money, advice*]; **don't ~ any closer** ne vous approchez pas (plus); **to ~ as a shock/surprise** être un choc/une surprise; **2** (reach) **to ~ up/down to** [*water*] venir jusqu'à; [*dress, curtain*] arriver à; **3** (happen) **how ~?** comment ça se fait?; **to take things as they ~** prendre les choses comme elles viennent; **~ what may** advienne que pourra; **4** (begin) **to ~ to do** finir par faire; **5 to ~ from** [*person*] être originaire de, venir de [*city, country*]; [*word, legend*] venir de [*language, country*]; [*stamps, painting*] provenir de [*place*]; [*smell, sound*] venir de [*place*]; **6** (in order) **to ~ after** suivre, venir après; **to ~ before** (in time, list, queue) précéder; (in importance) passer avant; **to ~ first/last** (in race) arriver premier/dernier; **7 when it ~s to sth/to doing** lorsqu'il s'agit de qch/de faire; **8 to ~ true** se réaliser; **to ~ undone** se défaire.

■ **come across**: ¶ **~ across** [*meaning, message*] passer; [*feelings*] transparaître; **~ across as** donner l'impression d'être [*liar, expert*]; paraître [*honest*]; ¶ **~ across [sth]** tomber sur [*article*].

■ **come along 1** [*bus, person*] arriver; [*opportunity*] se présenter; **2** (hurry up) **~ along!** dépêche-toi!; **3** (attend) venir (**to** à); **4** (progress) [*pupil*] faire des progrès; [*book, work, project*] avancer; [*painting, tennis*] progresser.

■ **come apart 1** (accidentally) [*book, box*] se déchirer; [*toy, camera*] se casser; **2** (intentionally) [*components*] se séparer; [*machine*] se démonter.

■ **come around** (US) = **come round**.

■ **come away** partir.

■ **come back 1** (return) revenir (**from** de; **to** à); (to one's house) rentrer; **2** [*law, system*] être rétabli/-e; [*trend*] revenir à la mode.

■ **come down 1** [*person, lift, blind*] descendre; [*curtain*] tomber; **2** [*price, inflation,*

Colours

Not all English colour terms have a single exact equivalent in French: eg in some cases ***brown*** is ***marron***, in others ***brun***. If in doubt, look the word up in the dictionary.

Colour terms

what colour is it? = il / elle est **de quelle couleur**?
= (*more formally*)
de quelle couleur est-il / est-elle?
it's green = il est vert / elle est verte
to paint something green = peindre quelque chose en vert
dressed in green = habillé en vert
green suits her = le vert lui va bien

Most adjectives of colour agree with the noun they modify:

a blue coat / dress = un manteau **bleu** / une robe **bleue**

But some words that translate English adjectives are really nouns in French, and so don't show agreement:

brown shoes / eyes = des chaussures *fpl* / les yeux *mpl* **marron**
orange tablecloths = des nappes *fpl* **orange**

Shades of colour

Expressions like ***pale blue***, ***dark green*** or ***light yellow*** are also invariable in French and show no agreement:

*a **blue** / **pale blue** shirt* = une chemise **bleue** / **bleu pâle**
***green** / **dark green** blankets* = des couvertures *fpl* **vertes** / **vert foncé**

In the following examples, ***blue*** stands for most basic colour terms:

***pale** / **light** / **bright** blue* = bleu **pâle** / **clair** / **vif**

For colour terms with the ending ***-ish***, to show that something is approximately a certain colour, the French equivalent is ***-âtre***:

bluish = bleuâtre

Note that these words are often rather negative in French. It is better not to use them if you want to be complimentary. Use instead ***tirant sur le rouge*** / ***jaune*** etc.

English colour compounds consisting of a *noun* + *-coloured* are translated as follows:

*a **chocolate-coloured** skirt* = une jupe **couleur chocolat**

Colour verbs

to blacken / redden / whiten = noircir / rougir / blanchir

Other French colour terms that behave like this are: ***bleu*** (*bleuir*), ***jaune*** (*jaunir*), ***rose*** (*rosir*) and ***vert*** (*verdir*). It is always safe, however, to use ***devenir***, thus:

*to **turn** purple* = **devenir** violet

Describing people

Note the use of the definite article in the following:

*to have **blue eyes*** = avoir **les yeux bleus**

Note the use of ***à*** in the following:

*a girl **with** blue eyes* = une jeune fille **aux** yeux bleus

Note these nouns in French:

a fair-haired man / woman = un blond / une blonde
a dark-haired man / woman = un brun / une brune

temperature] baisser; [*cost*] diminuer; **3** [*snow, rain*] tomber; **4** [*ceiling, wall*] s'écrouler; [*hem*] se défaire; **5 to ~ down with** attraper [*flu*].

■ **come forward 1** (step forward) s'avancer; **2** (volunteer) se présenter.

■ **come in 1** (enter) entrer (**through** par); **2** [*tide*] monter; **3 to ~ in useful** être utile; **4 to ~ in for criticism** [*person*] être critiqué/-e; [*plan*] faire l'objet de nombreuses critiques.

■ **come into 1** hériter de [*money*]; entrer en possession de [*inheritance*]; **2 luck doesn't ~ into it** ce n'est pas une question de hasard.

■ **come off 1** [*button, handle*] se détacher; [*lid*] s'enlever; [*paint*] s'écailler; **2** [*ink*] s'effacer; [*stain*] partir; **3** [*plan, trick*] réussir.

■ **come on 1 ~ on!** allez!; **2** [*person, patient*] faire des progrès; [*bridge, novel*] avancer; [*plant*] pousser; **3** [*light*] s'allumer; [*heating, fan*] se mettre en route; **4** [*actor*] entrer en scène.

■ **come out 1** [*person, animal, vehicle*] sortir (**of** de); [*star*] apparaître; [*sun, moon*] se montrer; **2** (strike) faire la grève; **to ~ out on strike** faire la grève; **3** [*contact lens, tooth*] tomber; [*contents*] sortir; [*cork*] s'enlever; **4** [*water, smoke*] sortir (**through** par); **5** [*stain*] s'en aller, partir; **6** [*magazine, novel*] paraître; [*album, film, product*] sortir; **7** [*details, facts*] être révélé/-e; [*results*] être connu/-e; **8** [*photo, photocopy*] être réussi/-e; **9 to ~ out with** sortir [*excuse*]; raconter [*nonsense*]; **to ~ straight out with it** le dire franchement.

■ **come over**: **~ over** venir (**to do** faire); **what's ~ over you?** qu'est-ce qui te prend?

■ **come round** (GB), **come around** (US) **1** (regain consciousness) reprendre connaissance; **2** (visit) venir; **3** (change mind) changer d'avis.

■ **come through**: ¶ **~ through 1** (survive) s'en tirer; **2** [*heat, ink*] traverser; [*light*] passer; ¶ **~ through [sth]** se tirer de [*crisis*]; survivre à [*operation, ordeal*].

■ **come to**: ¶ **~ to** reprendre connaissance; ¶ **~ to [sth]** [*shopping*] revenir à; [*bill, total*] s'élever à; **that ~s to £40** cela fait 40 livres sterling; **it may not ~ to that** nous n'en arriverons peut-être pas là.

■ **come under 1 to ~ under threat** être menacé/-e; **2** (be classified under) être classé/-e dans le rayon [*reference, history*].

■ **come up 1** [*problem, issue*] être soulevé/-e; [*name*] être mentionné/-e; **2** [*opportunity*] se présenter; **something urgent has come up** j'ai quelque chose d'urgent à faire; **3** [*sun, moon*] sortir; [*daffodils*] sortir; **4** (Law) [*case*] passer au tribunal; **5 to ~ up against** se heurter à [*problem*]; **6 to ~ up with** trouver [*answer, idea*].

comeback *n* come-back *m*; **to make a ~** [*person*] faire un come-back; [*trend*] revenir à la mode.

comedian ▶**626** *n* (male) comique *m*.

comedienne ▶**626** *n* actrice *f* comique.

comedy *n* comédie *f*.

comet *n* comète *f*.

comfort I *n* **1** confort *m*; **to live in ~** vivre dans l'aisance; **home ~s** le confort du foyer; **2** (consolation) réconfort *m*, consolation *f*.

II *vtr* consoler; (stronger) réconforter.

comfortable *adj* **1** [*chair, clothes, journey*] confortable; [*temperature*] agréable; **2** [*person*] à l'aise.

comfortably *adv* (gen) confortablement; (easily) facilement, aisément; **to be ~ off** être à l'aise.

comforting *adj* réconfortant/-e.

comic I *n* **1** = **comedian**; **2** (magazine) bande *f* dessinée.

II *adj* comique.

comical *adj* cocasse, comique.

comic strip *n* bande *f* dessinée.

coming I *n* arrivée *f*; **~s and goings** allées et venues *fpl*.

II *adj* [*election, event*] prochain/-e (*before n*); [*months, weeks*] à venir.

comma *n* virgule *f*.

command I *n* **1** (order) ordre *m*; **2** (military control) commandement *m*; **to be in ~** commander; **3** (of language) maîtrise *f*; **to be in ~ of the situation** avoir la situation en main; **4** (Comput) commande *f*.

II *vtr* **1** ordonner à [*person*] (**to do** de faire); **2** inspirer [*affection, respect*]; **3** (Mil) commander [*regiment*].

commander *n* (gen) chef *m*; (Mil) commandant *m*.

commanding *adj* [*manner, voice*] impérieux/-ieuse; [*presence*] imposant/-e.

commando *n* commando *m*.

commemorate *vtr* commémorer.

commence *vtr*, *vi* commencer.

commend *vtr* louer (**on** pour).

comment I *n* **1** (public) commentaire *m* (**on** sur); (in conversation) remarque *f* (**on** sur); (written) annotation *f*; **2 to be a ~ on** en dire long sur.

II *vi* faire des commentaires (**on** sur).

commentary *n* commentaire *m* (**on** de).

commentator ▶**626** *n* (sports) commentateur/-trice *m/f*; (current affairs) journaliste *mf*.

commerce *n* commerce *m*.

commercial I *n* annonce *f* publicitaire.

II *adj* commercial/-e.

commiserate *vi* compatir (**with** avec; **about, over** à propos de).

commission I *n* **1** (fee) commission *f*; **2** (order) commande *f* (**for** de); **3** (committee) commission *f* (**on** sur).

II *vtr* **1** commander [*work*] (**from** à); **to ~ sb to do** charger qn de faire; **2** (Mil) **to be ~ed (as) an officer** être nommé/-e officier.

commissioner *n* **1** (gen) membre *m* d'une commission; **2** (GB) (in police) ≈ préfet *m* de police; **3** (in the EC) membre *m* de la Commission européenne.

commit *vtr* **1** commettre [*crime, error, sin*]; **to ~ suicide** se suicider; **2 to ~ oneself** s'engager (**to** à); **3** consacrer [*money, time*] (**to** à).

commitment *n* **1** (obligation) engagement *m* (**to do** à faire); **2** (sense of duty) attachement *m* (**to** à).

committee *n* comité *m*; (to investigate, report) commission *f*.
commodity *n* article *m*; (food) denrée *f*.
common I *n* terrain *m* communal.
II Commons *n pl* **the Commons** les Communes *fpl*.
III *adj* **1** (frequent) courant/-e, fréquent/-e; **in ~ use** d'un usage courant; **2** (shared) commun/-e (**to** à); **in ~** en commun; **it is ~ knowledge** c'est de notoriété publique; **3 the ~ people** le peuple; **a ~ criminal** un criminel ordinaire; **4** (low-class) commun/-e; **it looks/ sounds ~** ça fait commun.
commonly *adv* communément.
Common Market *n* Marché *m* commun.
commonplace *adj* (common) commun/-e; (trite) banal/-e.
common room *n* salle *f* de détente.
common sense *n* bon sens *m*, sens *m* commun.
Commonwealth *n* **the ~** le Commonwealth.
commotion *n* **1** (noise) vacarme *m*, brouhaha *m*; **2** (disturbance) émoi *m*, agitation *f*.
communal *adj* [*property, area, showers*] commun/-e; [*garden*] collectif/-ive; [*life*] communautaire.
commune *n* communauté *f*.
communicate I *vtr* communiquer [*ideas, feelings*] (**to** à); transmettre [*information*] (**to** à).
II *vi* communiquer.
communication *n* communication *f*.
communication cord *n* (GB) sonnette *f* d'alarme.
communications *n pl* (GB) communications *fpl*, liaison *f*.
communion *n* communion *f*.
communism *n* communisme *m*.
communist *n*, *adj* communiste (*mf*).
community *n* communauté *f*.
community centre (GB), **community center** (US) *n* maison *f* de quartier.
commute *vi* **to ~ between Oxford and London** faire le trajet entre Oxford et Londres tous les jours.
commuter *n* navetteur/-euse *m/f*, migrant/-e *m/f* journalier/-ière.
compact I *n* poudrier *m*.
II *adj* compact/-e.
compact disc *n* disque *m* compact.
companion *n* compagnon/compagne *m/f*.
companionship *n* compagnie *f*.
company *n* **1** (firm) société *f*; **airline ~** compagnie *f* aérienne; **2 theatre ~** troupe *f* de théâtre, compagnie *f* théâtrale; **3** (Mil) compagnie *f*; **4** (companionship) compagnie *f*; **to keep sb ~** tenir compagnie à qn; **5** (visitors) visiteurs *mpl*.
company car *n* voiture *f* de fonction.
company director **▶626** *n* directeur/-trice *m/f* général/-e.
company secretary **▶626** *n* secrétaire *mf* général/-e.
comparable *adj* comparable (**to, with** à).
comparative *adj* **1** (in grammar) comparatif/-ive; **2** (relative) relatif/-ive; **in ~ terms** en termes relatifs; **3** [*study*] comparatif/-ive.
comparatively *adv* relativement.
compare I *vtr* comparer (**with, to** avec, à); **~d with sb/sth** par rapport à qn/qch.
II *vi* être comparable (**with** à)
comparison *n* comparaison *f*; **in** or **by ~ with** par rapport à.
compartment *n* compartiment *m*.
compass *n* boussole *f*; (also **ship's ~**) compas *m*; **the points of the ~** les points *mpl* cardinaux.
compasses *n pl* (**a pair of**) **~** un compas.
compassion *n* compassion *f* (**for** pour).
compassionate *adj* compatissant/-e.
compatible *adj* compatible (**with** avec).
compel *vtr* contraindre (**to do** à faire), obliger (**to do** de faire).
compelling *adj* [*reason, argument*] convaincant/-e; [*speaker*] fascinant/-e.
compensate I *vtr* dédommager, indemniser.
II *vi* **to ~ for** compenser.
compensation *n* **1** (gen) compensation *f* (**for** de); **2** (financial) indemnisation *f*.
compete *vi* **1** (gen) rivaliser; **to ~ against** or **with** rivaliser avec (**for** pour obtenir); **2** (commercially) [*companies*] se faire concurrence; **to ~ with** faire concurrence à (**for** pour obtenir); **3** (Sport) être en compétition (**against, with** avec); **to ~ in** participer à [*Olympics, race*].
competence *n* **1** (ability) compétence *f*; **2** (skill) compétences *fpl*.
competent *adj* compétent/-e, capable.
competition *n* **1** (gen) concurrence *f*; **2** (contest) concours *m*; (race) compétition *f*; **3** (competitors) concurrence *f*.
competitive *adj* **1** [*person*] qui a l'esprit de compétition; [*environment*] compétitif/-ive; **2** [*price, product*] compétitif/-ive; **3** [*sport*] de compétition.
competitor *n* concurrent/-e *m/f*.
compile *vtr* **1** dresser [*list, catalogue*]; établir [*report*]; **2** (Comput) compiler.
complacent *adj* suffisant/-e; **to be ~ about** être trop confiant/-e de [*success, future*].
complain *vi* se plaindre (**to** à; **about** de; **of** de); (officially) se plaindre (**to** auprès de).
complaint *n* plainte *f*; (official) réclamation *f*; **there have been ~s about the noise** on s'est plaint du bruit; **to have grounds** or **cause for ~** avoir lieu de se plaindre.
complement I *n* complément *m*.
II *vtr* compléter.
complementary *adj* complémentaire (**to** de).
complete I *adj* **1** complet/-ète; **2** (finished) achevé/-e.
II *vtr* **1** (finish) terminer [*building, course, exercise*]; achever [*task, journey*]; **2** compléter [*collection, phrase*]; **3** remplir [*form*].
completely *adv* complètement.

completion *n* achèvement *m*.
complex I *n* complexe *m*; **sports ~** complexe sportif; **he's got a ~ about his weight** son poids le complexe.
II *adj* complexe.
complexion *n* teint *m*.
complexity *n* complexité *f*.
compliance *n* conformité (**with** à).
compliant *adj* conciliant/-e.
complicate *vtr* compliquer.
complicated *adj* compliqué/-e.
complication *n* **1** (problem) inconvénient *m*, problème *m*; **2** (Med) complication *f*.
compliment I *n* compliment *m*; **to pay sb a ~** faire un compliment à qn.
II *vtr* complimenter, faire des compliments à.
complimentary *adj* **1** [*remark*] flatteur/-euse; **2** (free) gratuit/-e.
compliments *n pl* compliments *mpl* (**to** à).
comply *vi* **to ~ with** se conformer à [*orders*]; respecter, observer [*rules*].
component *n* (gen) composante *f*; (in car, machine) pièce *f*; (electrical) composant *m*.
compose *vtr* **1** (gen) composer; **~d of** composé/-e de; **2 to ~ oneself** se ressaisir.
composed *adj* calme.
composer ▶ 626 *n* compositeur/-trice *m*/*f*.
composition *n* **1** (gen) composition *f*; **2** (essay) rédaction *f* (**about, on** sur).
compost *n* compost *m*.
composure *n* calme *m*.
compound I *n* **1** (enclosure) enceinte *f*; **2** (in chemistry) composé *m* (**of** de); **3** (word) mot *m* composé.
II *adj* **1** (gen) composé/-e; **2** (Med) [*fracture*] multiple.
comprehend *vtr* comprendre.
comprehension *n* compréhension *f*.
comprehensive I *n* (GB Sch) (also **~ school**) école *f* (publique) secondaire.
II *adj* [*report, list*] complet/-ète, détaillé/-e; [*knowledge*] étendu/-e; **~ insurance policy** assurance *f* tous risques.
compress I *n* compresse *f*.
II *vtr* comprimer.
comprise *vtr* comprendre; **to be ~d of** être composé/-e de.
compromise I *n* compromis *m*.
II *vtr* compromettre.
III *vi* transiger, arriver à un compromis; **to ~ on sth** trouver un compromis sur qch.
compulsive *adj* **1** (inveterate) invétéré/-e; (psychologically) compulsif/-ive; **2** (fascinating) fascinant/-e.
compulsory *adj* obligatoire.
computer *n* ordinateur *m*.
computer game *n* jeu *m* informatique.
computer graphics *n* infographie *f*.
computer hacker *n* pirate *m* informatique.
computerize *vtr* mettre [qch] sur ordinateur [*accounts*]; informatiser [*list*].
computer program *n* programme *m* informatique.
computer programmer ▶ 626 *n* programmeur/-euse *m*/*f*.
computer science *n* informatique *f*.
computing *n* informatique *f*.
comrade *n* camarade *mf*.
comradeship *n* camaraderie *f*.
con○ I *n* escroquerie *f*, arnaque◑ *f*.
II *vtr* tromper, rouler○, arnaquer◑.
conceal *vtr* dissimuler (**from** à).
concede I *vtr* concéder.
II *vi* céder.
conceit *n* suffisance *f*.
conceited *adj* [*person*] vaniteux/-euse; [*remark*] suffisant/-e.
conceive *vtr*, *vi* concevoir.
concentrate I *vtr* concentrer [*effort*]; employer [*resources*]; centrer [*attention*].
II *vi* **1** [*person*] se concentrer (**on** sur); **to ~ on doing** s'appliquer à faire; **2 to ~ on** [*film, journalist*] s'intéresser surtout à.
concentration *n* concentration *f* (**on** sur); **to lose one's ~** se déconcentrer.
concept *n* concept *m*.
concern I *n* **1** (worry) inquiétude *f* (**about** à propos de); **to cause ~** être inquiétant/-e; **2** (preoccupation) préoccupation *f*; **environmental ~s** des préoccupations écologiques; **3** (company) entreprise *f*; **a going ~** une affaire rentable.
II *vtr* **1** (worry) inquiéter; **2** (affect, interest) concerner, intéresser; **to whom it may ~** à qui de droit; (in letter) Monsieur; **as far as the pay is ~ed** en ce qui concerne le salaire; **3** (be about) [*book, programme*] traiter de; [*fax, letter*] concerner.
concerned *adj* **1** (anxious) inquiet/-ète (**about** à propos de); **to be ~ for sb** se faire du souci pour qn; **2** (involved) concerné/-e; **all (those) ~** toutes les personnes concernées.
concerning *prep* concernant.
concert *n* concert *m*.
concert hall *n* salle *f* de concert.
concertina I *n* concertina *m*.
II *vi* se plier en accordéon.
concerto *n* concerto *m*.
concession *n* **1** (compromise) concession *f* (**on** sur; **to** à); **2** (discount) réduction *f*.
conciliatory *adj* [*gesture, terms*] conciliant/-e; [*measures*] conciliatoire.
concise *adj* concis/-e.
conclude I *vtr* conclure.
II *vi* [*story, event*] se terminer (**with** par, sur); [*speaker*] conclure (**with** par).
conclusion *n* **1** (end) fin *f*; **2** (opinion, resolution) conclusion *f*.
conclusive *adj* concluant/-e.
concrete I *n* béton *m*.
II *adj* **1** [*block*] de béton; [*base*] en béton; **2** (real) concret/-ète.
concuss *vtr* **to be ~ed** être commotionné/-e.
concussion *n* commotion *f* cérébrale.

condemn *vtr* **1** (gen) condamner; **2** déclarer [qch] inhabitable [*building*].
condensation *n* (on walls) condensation *f*; (on windows) buée *f*.
condense I *vtr* condenser.
II *vi* se condenser.
condensed milk *n* lait *m* concentré sucré.
condescending *adj* condescendant/-e.
condition *n* **1** (gen) condition *f*; **on ~ that you come** à condition que tu viennes; **2** (state) état *m*, condition *f*; **to be in good/bad ~** [*house, car*] être en bon/mauvais état; **3** (disease) maladie *f*.
conditional *adj* conditionnel/-elle.
conditioner *n* après-shampooing *m*, démêlant *m*.
condolences *n pl* condoléances *fpl*.
condom *n* préservatif *m*.
condominium *n* (US) (also **~ unit**) appartement *m* (dans une copropriété).
condone *vtr* tolérer.
conducive *adj* **~ to** favorable à.
conduct I *n* conduite *f* (**towards** envers).
II *vtr* **1** mener [*business, campaign*]; **2** mener [*experiment, inquiry*]; célébrer [*ceremony*]; **3** (Mus) diriger [*orchestra*]; **4** conduire [*electricity, heat*].
conductor ▶626 *n* **1** (Mus) chef *m* d'orchestre; **2** (on bus) receveur *m*; (on train) chef *m* de train.
conductress ▶626 *n* receveuse *f*.
cone *n* **1** (shape) cône *m*; **2** (also **ice-cream ~**) cornet *m*; **3** (for traffic) balise *f*.
confectioner ▶626 *n* (of sweets) confiseur/-euse *m/f*; (of cakes) pâtissier-confiseur *m*; **~'s (shop)** pâtisserie-confiserie *f*.
confectionery *n* (sweets) confiserie *f*; (cakes) pâtisserie *f*.
confer I *vtr* conférer (**on** à).
II *vi* conférer (**about** de; **with** avec).
conference *n* (academic, business) conférence *f*; (political) congrès *m*.
confess I *vtr* **1** avouer (**that** que); **2** confesser [*sins*].
II *vi* avouer; **to ~ to a crime** avouer (avoir commis) un crime.
confession *n* **1** (gen, Law) aveu *m* (**of** de); **2** (in religion) confession *f*; **to go to ~** se confesser.
confetti *n* confettis *mpl*.
confide *vi* **to ~ in** se confier à [*person*].
confidence *n* **1** (faith) confiance *f* (**in** en); **to have (every) ~ in sb/sth** avoir (pleine) confiance en qn/qch; **2** (in politics) **vote of ~** vote *m* de confiance; **motion of no ~** motion *f* de censure; **3** (self-assurance) assurance *f*, confiance *f* en soi; **4 to tell sb sth in ~** dire qch à qn confidentiellement.
confidence trick *n* escroquerie *f*.
confident *adj* **1** (sure) sûr/-e, confiant/-e; **2** (self-assured) assuré/-e, sûr/-e de soi.
confidential *adj* confidentiel/-ielle.
confine *vtr* **1** confiner [*person*] (**in, to** dans); enfermer [*animal*] (**in** dans); **2** (limit) limiter (**to** à).
confined *adj* (gen) confiné/-e; [*space*] restreint/-e.
confinement *n* (in prison) détention *f*.
confirm *vtr* confirmer.
confirmation *n* confirmation *f*.
confiscate *vtr* confisquer (**from** à).
conflict I *n* conflit *m*.
II *vi* être en contradiction (**with** avec).
conflicting *adj* contradictoire.
conform I *vtr* conformer (**to** à).
II *vi* [*person*] se conformer (**with, to** à).
confront *vtr* affronter [*danger, enemy*]; faire face à [*problem*].
confrontation *n* affrontement *m*.
confuse *vtr* **1** (bewilder) troubler [*person*]; **2** (mistake) confondre (**with** avec); **3** (complicate) compliquer [*argument*]; **to ~ the issue** compliquer les choses.
confused *adj* [*person*] troublé/-e; [*account, thoughts, mind*] confus/-e; **to get ~** s'embrouiller.
confusing *adj* déroutant/-e, peu clair/-e.
confusion *n* confusion *f*.
congeal *vi* [*fat*] se figer; [*blood*] se coaguler.
congenial *adj* agréable.
congenital *adj* congénital/-e.
congested *adj* **1** [*road*] embouteillé/-e; [*district*] surpeuplé/-e; **2** [*lungs*] congestionné/-e.
congestion *n* **1 traffic ~** embouteillages *mpl*; **2** (of lungs) congestion *f*.
conglomerate *n* conglomérat *m*.
congratulate *vtr* féliciter (**on** de).
congratulations *n pl* félicitations *fpl*.
congregate *vi* se rassembler.
congregation *n* assemblée *f* des fidèles.
congress *n* congrès *m* (**on** sur).
Congress *n* (US) Congrès *m*.
congressman *n* (US) membre *m* du Congrès.
conifer *n* conifère *m*.
conjugal *adj* conjugal/-e.
conjunctivitis ▶533 *n* conjonctivite *f*.
conjure *vi* faire des tours de prestidigitation.
■ **conjure up** évoquer [*image*].
conjurer *n* prestidigitateur/-trice *m/f*.
con man *n* arnaqueur◑ *m*, escroc *m*.
connect *vtr* **1** raccorder [*end, hose*] (**to** à); accrocher [*coach*] (**to** à); **2** [*road, railway*] relier [*place, road*] (**to, with** à); **3** brancher [*appliance*] (**to** à); **4** raccorder [*phone, subscriber*].
connected *adj* **1** [*idea, event*] lié/-e (**to, with** à); **everything ~ with music** tout ce qui se rapporte à la musique; **2** (in family) apparenté/-e (**to** à).
connecting *adj* **1** [*flight*] de correspondance; **2** [*room*] attenant/-e.
connection *n* **1** (link) (between events) rapport *m*; (of person) lien *m* (**between** entre; **with** avec); **in ~ with** au sujet de, à propos de; **2** (contact) relation *f*; **to have useful ~s** avoir des relations; **3** (to mains) branchement *m*; **4** (to

telephone network) raccordement *m*; (to number) mise *f* en communication (**to** avec); **bad ~** mauvaise communication *f*; **5** (in travel) correspondance *f*.

connive *vi* **to ~ at** contribuer délibérément à; **to ~ (with sb) to do** être de connivence or de mèche○ (avec qn) pour faire.

connoisseur *n* connaisseur/-euse *m/f*.

connotation *n* connotation *f* (**of** de).

conquer *vtr* conquérir [*territory, people*]; vaincre [*enemy, unemployment*].

conqueror *n* conquérant/-e *m/f*.

conquest *n* conquête *f*.

conscience *n* conscience *f*; **they have no ~** ils n'ont aucun sens moral.

conscientious *adj* consciencieux/-ieuse.

conscious *adj* **1** (aware) conscient/-e (**of** de; **that** du fait que); **2** (deliberate) [*decision*] réfléchi/-e; [*effort*] consciencieux/-ieuse; **3** (awake) réveillé/-e.

consciousness *n* **to lose/regain ~** perdre/reprendre connaissance.

conscript *n* appelé *m*.

consecrate *vtr* consacrer.

consecutive *adj* consécutif/-ive.

consensus *n* consensus *m* (**among** au sein de; **about** quant à; **on** sur).

consent I *n* consentement *m*; **age of ~** âge *m* légal; **by common** or **mutual ~** d'un commun accord.
II *vi* consentir (**to** à); **to ~ to sb doing** consentir à ce que qn fasse.

consequence *n* **1** conséquence *f*; **as a ~ of** du fait de [*change, process*]; à la suite de [*event*]; **2** (importance) importance *f*.

consequently *adv* par conséquent.

conservation *n* **1** (of nature) protection *f* (**of** de); **energy ~** maîtrise *f* de l'énergie; **2** (of heritage) conservation *f*.

conservation area *n* zone *f* protégée.

conservative I *n* conservateur/-trice *m/f*.
II *adj* **1** [*party*] conservateur/-trice; **2** [*taste, style*] classique.

Conservative Party *n* (GB) parti *m* conservateur.

conservatory *n* **1** (for plants) jardin *m* d'hiver; **2** (academy) conservatoire *m*.

conserve I *n* confiture *f*.
II *vtr* **1** protéger [*forest*]; sauvegarder [*wildlife*]; conserver [*remains, ruins*]; **2** économiser [*resources*]; ménager [*energy*].

consider *vtr* **1** (give thought to) considérer [*options, facts*]; examiner [*evidence, problem*]; étudier [*offer*]; **2** (take into account) prendre [qch] en considération [*risk, cost*]; songer à [*person*]; faire attention à [*person's feelings*]; **3** (envisage) **to ~ doing** envisager de faire; **to ~ sb/sth as sth** penser à qn/qch comme qch; **4** (regard) **to ~ that** considérer or estimer que; **to ~ oneself (to be) a genius** se considérer comme un génie.

considerable *adj* considérable.

considerate *adj* [*person*] attentionné/-e; [*behaviour*] courtois/-e; **to be ~ towards sb** avoir des égards pour qn.

consideration *n* **1** considération *f* (**for** envers); **to give sth careful ~** réfléchir longuement à qch; **to take sth into ~** prendre qch en considération; **out of ~** par considération; **2** (fee) **for a ~** moyennant finance.

considering *prep, conj* étant donné, compte tenu de.

consign *vtr* expédier [*goods*] (**to** à).

consignment *n* (sending) expédition *f*; (goods) lot *m*, livraison *f*.

consist *vi* **to ~ of** se composer de; **to ~ in** résider dans; **to ~ in doing** consister à faire.

consistency *n* **1** (texture) consistance *f*; **2** (of view, policy) cohérence *f*.

consistent *adj* **1** [*growth, level, quality*] régulier/-ière; **2** [*attempts, demands*] répété/-e; **3** [*argument*] cohérent/-e; **~ with** en accord avec [*account, belief*].

consolation *n* consolation *f* (**to** pour).

console I *n* **1** (control panel) console *f*; **2** (for hi-fi) meuble *m* hi-fi; (for video) meuble *m* vidéo.
II *vtr* consoler (**for, on** de; **with** avec).

consolidate *vtr* **1** consolider [*position*]; **2** réunir [*resources*]; fusionner [*companies*].

consonant *n* consonne *f*.

consortium *n* consortium *m*.

conspicuous *adj* [*feature, sign*] visible; [*garment*] voyant/-e; **to be ~** se remarquer.

conspiracy *n* conspiration *f*.

conspire *vi* conspirer; **to ~ to do** [*people*] conspirer en vue de faire; [*events*] conspirer à faire.

constable *n* (GB) agent *m* de police.

constant *adj* [*problem, reminder, threat*] permanent/-e; [*care, temperature*] constant/-e; [*disputes, questions*] incessant/-e; [*attempts*] répété/-e; [*companion*] éternel/-elle.

constantly *adv* constamment.

constellation *n* constellation *f*.

constipated *adj* constipé/-e.

constipation ▶533 *n* constipation *f*.

constituency *n* (district) circonscription *f* électorale; (voters) électeurs *mpl*.

constitute *vtr* constituer.

constitution *n* constitution *f*.

constitutional *adj* constitutionnel/-elle.

constraint *n* contrainte *f*.

constrict *vtr* comprimer [*flow, blood vessel*]; gêner [*breathing, movement*].

construct *vtr* construire (**of** avec; **in** en).

construction *n* construction *f*.

constructive *adj* constructif/-ive.

consul *n* consul *m*.

consulate *n* consulat *m*.

consult I *vtr* consulter (**about** sur).
II *vi* s'entretenir (**about** sur; **with** avec).

consultancy *n* (also **~ firm**) cabinet-conseil *m*.

consultant ▶626 *n* **1** (expert) consultant/-e

m/f, conseiller/-ère *m/f* (**on, in** en); **2** (GB) (doctor) spécialiste *mf*.

consume *vtr* **1** (use up) consommer [*fuel, food, drink*]; **2 to be ~d by** or **with** être dévoré/-e par [*envy*]; brûler de [*desire*]; être rongé/-e par [*guilt*].

consumer *n* consommateur/-trice *m/f*; (of electricity, gas) abonné/-e *m/f*.

consumer goods *n pl* biens *mpl* de consommation.

consumer society *n* société *f* de consommation.

consummate *vtr* consommer [*marriage*].

consumption *n* consommation *f*.

contact I *n* **1** (gen) contact *m* (**between** entre; **with** avec); **to be in/make ~** être en/se mettre en contact; **2** (acquaintance) connaissance *f*; (professional) contact *m*.
II *vtr* contacter, se mettre en rapport avec.

contact lens *n* lentille *f* or verre *m* de contact.

contagious *adj* contagieux/-ieuse.

contain *vtr* **1** contenir [*amount, ingredients*]; contenir, comporter [*information, mistakes*]; **2** (curb) maîtriser [*blaze*]; enrayer [*epidemic*]; limiter [*costs, problem*]; retenir [*flood*].

container *n* (for food, liquids) récipient *m*; (for plants) bac *m*; (for waste, for transporting) conteneur *m*.

contaminate *vtr* contaminer.

contamination *n* contamination *f*.

contemplate *vtr* **1** (consider) envisager (**doing** de faire); **2** (look at) contempler.

contemporary I *n* contemporain/-e *m/f*.
II *adj* (present-day) contemporain/-e; (up-to-date) moderne; (of same period) de l'époque.

contempt *n* mépris *m* (**for** de); **to hold sb/sth in ~** mépriser qn/qch; **~ of court** (Law) outrage *m* à magistrat.

contemptible *adj* méprisable.

contemptuous *adj* méprisant/-e.

contend I *vtr* soutenir (**that** que).
II *vi* **1** (deal with) **to ~ with** affronter; **2** (compete) **to ~ with sb for sth** disputer qch à qn.

contender *n* **1** (in competition) concurrent/-e *m/f*; **2** (for post) candidat/-e *m/f* (**for** à).

content I *n* **1** (quantity) teneur *f*; **2** (of book, essay) fond *m*.
II *adj* satisfait/-e (**with** de).

contented *adj* [*person*] content/-e (**with** de); [*feeling*] de bien-être.

contention *n* **1** (opinion) assertion *f*; **2** (dispute) dispute *f*.

contentment *n* contentement *m*.

contents *n pl* (gen) contenu *m*; (of house, for insurance) biens *mpl* mobiliers; **list** or **table of ~** table *f* des matières.

contest I *n* **1** (competition) concours *m*; **2** (struggle) lutte *f*.
II *vtr* **1** contester [*decision, will*]; **2** (compete for) disputer [*match*].

contestant *n* (in competition, game) concurrent/-e *m/f*; (in fight) adversaire *mf*; (for job, in election) candidat/-e *m/f*.

context *n* contexte *m*.

continent *n* **1** continent *m*; **2 the Continent** (GB) l'Europe *f* continentale.

continental *adj* **1** continental/-e; **2** (GB) [*holiday*] en Europe continentale.

continental quilt *n* (GB) couette *f*.

contingency *n* imprévu *m*.

contingency plan *n* plan *m* de réserve.

continual *adj* continuel/-elle.

continually *adv* continuellement.

continuation *n* **1** (gen) continuation *f*; **2** (of story) suite *f*; (of route) prolongement *m*.

continue I *vtr* continuer.
II *vi* [*person*] continuer (**doing, to do** à or de faire); [*noise, debate, strike*] se poursuivre; **to ~ with** continuer, poursuivre [*task, treatment*].

continuous *adj* **1** [*growth, decline, noise*] continu/-e; [*care*] constant/-e; [*line*] ininterrompu/-e; **~ assessment** (GB) contrôle *m* continu; **2** [*tense*] progressif/-ive.

continuously *adv* (without a break) sans interruption; (repeatedly) continuellement.

contort *vtr* tordre.

contortion *n* contorsion *f*.

contour *n* **1** (outline) contour *m*; **2** (also **~ line**) courbe *f* hypsométrique or de niveau.

contraband *n* contrebande *f*.

contraception *n* contraception *f*.

contraceptive I *n* contraceptif *m*.
II *adj* contraceptif/-ive.

contract I *n* contrat *m*.
II *vtr* **1** (gen) contracter; **2 to be ~ed to do** être tenu/-e par contrat de faire.
III *vi* **1 to ~ to do** s'engager par contrat à faire; **2** [*muscle, wood*] se contracter.

contraction *n* contraction *f*.

contractor ▶ 626 *n* **1** (business) entrepreneur/-euse *m/f*; **2** (worker) contractuel/-elle *m/f*.

contradict *vtr, vi* contredire.

contradiction *n* contradiction *f*.

contradictory *adj* contradictoire (**to** à).

contraflow *n* (GB) circulation *f* à sens alterné.

contrary I *n* contraire *m*; **on the ~** (bien) au contraire; **unless you hear anything to the ~** sauf contrordre.
II *adj* **1** [*idea, view*] contraire; **2** [*person*] contrariant/-e.
III contrary to *phr* contrairement à.

contrast I *n* contraste *m*; **in ~ to sth, by ~ with sth** par contraste avec qch; **in ~ to sb** à la différence de qn; **by** or **in ~** par contre.
II *vtr* **to ~ X with Y** faire ressortir le contraste (qui existe) entre X et Y.
III *vi* contraster (**with** avec).

contribute I *vtr* **1** verser [*sum*] (**to** à); **to ~ £5m** contribuer pour 5 millions de livres; **2** (to gift, charity) donner (**to** à; **towards** pour); **3** apporter [*ideas*] (**to** à); écrire [*article*] (**to** pour).
II *vi* **1 to ~ to** or **towards** contribuer à [*change, decline*]; **2** (to community life, research)

participer (**to** à); (to programme, magazine) collaborer (**to** à); **3 to ~ to** cotiser à [*pension fund*]; **4** (to charity) donner (de l'argent) (**to** à).

contribution *n* **1** (to tax, pension, profits, cost) contribution *f* (**towards** à); **2** (to charity, campaign) don *m*; **to make a ~** faire un don (**to** à); **3 sb's ~ to** le rôle que qn a joué dans [*success, undertaking*]; ce que qn a apporté à [*science, sport*]; **4** (to programme) participation *f*; (to magazine) article *m*.

contributor *n* (to charity) donateur/-trice *m/f*; (in discussion) participant/-e *m/f*; (to magazine, book) collaborateur/-trice *m/f*.

contrive *vtr* (arrange) organiser; **to ~ to do** parvenir à faire.

contrived *adj* **1** [*incident, meeting*] non fortuit/-e; **2** [*plot*] tiré/-e par les cheveux; [*style, effect*] étudié/-e.

control I *n* **1** (gen) contrôle *m* (**of** de); (of operation, project) direction *f* (**of** de); (of life, emotion, self) maîtrise *f* (**of, over** de); **to be in ~ of** contrôler [*territory*]; diriger [*operation, organization*]; maîtriser [*problem*]; avoir le contrôle de [*ball, vehicle*] **to be in ~ (of oneself)** se maîtriser; **to bring** or **keep [sth] under ~** maîtriser; **to lose ~ (of sth)** perdre le contrôle (de qch); **2** (on vehicle, equipment) commande *f*; (on TV) bouton *m* de réglage; **to be at the ~s** être aux commandes.

II *vtr* **1** dominer [*organization, situation*]; contrôler [*territory*]; diriger [*traffic, project*]; être majoritaire dans [*company*]; **2** maîtriser [*person, animal, inflation, fire*]; endiguer [*epidemic*]; dominer [*emotion*]; retenir [*laughter*]; **to ~ oneself** se contrôler; **3** commander [*machine*]; manœuvrer [*boat, vehicle*]; piloter [*plane*]; contrôler [*ball*]; **4** régler [*speed, temperature*]; contrôler [*immigration, prices*].

control panel *n* (on plane) tableau *m* de bord; (on machine) tableau *m* de contrôle; (on TV) (panneau *m* de) commandes *fpl*.

control tower *n* tour *f* de contrôle.

controversial *adj* (gen) controversé/-e; (open to criticism) qui prête à controverse.

controversy *n* controverse *f*.

conundrum *n* énigme *f*.

convalesce *vi* se remettre.

convene *vtr* organiser [*meeting*]; convoquer [*group*].

convenience *n* avantage *m* (**of doing** de faire); (of device, food, shop) commodité *f*; **for (the sake of) ~** pour raisons de commodité; **at your ~** quand cela vous conviendra.

convenient *adj* **1** [*place, time*] commode; **to be ~ for sb** convenir à qn; **2** (useful, practical) pratique, commode; **3** [*shops*] situé/-e tout près; [*chair*] à portée de main.

convent *n* couvent *m*.

convention *n* **1** (gen) convention *f*; **2** (social norms) convenances *fpl*; conventions *fpl*.

conventional *adj* (gen) conventionnel/-elle; [*person*] conformiste; [*medicine*] traditionnel/-elle.

converge *vi* converger.

conversant *adj* **to be ~ with** être versé/-e dans.

conversation *n* conversation *f*.

converse *vi* converser (**with** avec; **in** en).

conversion *n* (of currency, measurement) conversion *f* (**from** de; **into** en); (of building) aménagement *m* (**to, into** en); (to new beliefs) conversion *f* (**from** de; **to** à); (in rugby) transformation *f*.

convert I *n* converti/-e *m/f* (**to** à).

II *vtr* **1** (change into sth else) transformer; (modify) adapter; **2** convertir [*currency, measurement*] (**from** de; **to, into** en); **3** aménager [*building, loft*] (**to, into** en); **4** (to new beliefs) convertir (**to** à; **from** de); **5** (in rugby) transformer [*try*].

III *vi* **1** [*sofa, device*] être convertible (**into** en); **2** [*person*] se convertir (**to** à; **from** de).

convertible *n* décapotable *f*.

convex *adj* convexe.

convey *vtr* **1** [*person*] transmettre [*information*] (**to** à); exprimer [*condolences, feeling, idea*] (**to** à); **2** [*words, images*] traduire [*mood, impression*]; **3** [*vehicle*] transporter; [*pipes*] amener.

conveyor belt *n* (in factory) transporteur *m* à bande or à courroie; (for luggage) tapis *m* roulant.

convict I *n* (imprisoned criminal) détenu/-e *m/f*; (deported criminal) bagnard *m*.

II *vtr* reconnaître or déclarer [qn] coupable (**of** de; **of doing** d'avoir fait).

conviction *n* **1** (Law) condamnation *f* (**for** pour); **2** (belief) conviction *f* (**that** que).

convince *vtr* convaincre [*person*] (**to do** de faire).

convincing *adj* [*account, evidence*] convaincant/-e; [*victory, lead*] indiscutable.

convoy *n* convoi *m*.

convulsion *n* convulsion *f*.

coo *vi* roucouler.

cook ▶ 626 I *n* cuisinier/-ière *m/f*.

II *vtr* faire cuire [*vegetables, pasta, eggs*]; préparer [*meal*] (**for** pour).

III *vi* [*person*] cuisiner, faire la cuisine; [*vegetable, meat, meal*] cuire.

cooker *n* (GB) cuisinière *f*.

cookery book *n* (GB) livre de cuisine.

cookie *n* gâteau *m* sec, biscuit *m*.

cooking *n* cuisine *f*.

cooking apple *n* pomme *f* à cuire.

cooking chocolate *n* chocolat *m* de couverture.

cool I *n* **1** (coldness) fraîcheur *f*; **2**○ (calm) sang-froid *m*; **to keep one's ~** (not get angry) ne pas s'énerver; (stay calm) garder son sang-froid; **to lose one's ~** (get angry) s'énerver; (panic) perdre son sang-froid.

II *adj* **1** [*day, drink, water, weather*] frais/fraîche; [*dress*] léger/-ère; [*colour*] froid/-e; **2** (calm) calme; **3** (unfriendly) froid/-e; **4** (casual) décontracté/-e, cool○; **5**○ (trendy) branché/-e○.

III *vtr* **1** refroidir [*soup*]; rafraîchir [*wine, room*]; **2** calmer [*anger, ardour*].

IV *vi* **1** (get colder) refroidir; **2** [*enthusiasm*] faiblir; [*friendship*] se dégrader.

■ **cool down** [*engine, water*] refroidir; [*person, situation*] se calmer.

cooperate *vi* coopérer (**with** avec; **in** à; **in doing** pour faire).

cooperation *n* coopération *f* (**on** à).

cooperative I *n* **1** (organization) coopérative *f*; **2** (US) (apartment house) immeuble *m* en copropriété.
II *adj* coopératif/-ive.

coordinate I *n* (on map, graph) coordonnée *f*.
II *vtr* coordonner (**with** avec).

coordinates *n pl* (clothes) ensemble *m*.

coordination *n* coordination *f*.

cope *vi* s'en sortir○, se débrouiller; **to ~ with** s'occuper de [*person, work*]; faire face à [*demand, disaster, problem*]; supporter [*death, depression, difficult person*].

Copenhagen ▶**448** *pr n* Copenhague.

copper ▶**438** *n* **1** (metal) cuivre *m*; **2**○ (GB) (coin) petite monnaie *f*; **3**○ (GB) (policeman) flic *m*; **4** (colour) couleur *f* cuivre.

copy I *n* **1** (gen) copie *f*; **2** (of book, newspaper, report) exemplaire *m*.
II *vtr* copier (**from** sur).
III *vi* copier.
■ **copy down**, **copy out** recopier [*quote, address*].

copyright *n* copyright *m*, droit *m* d'auteur.

coral *n* corail *m*.

cord I *n* cordon *m*.
II **cords**○ *n pl* (also **corduroys**) pantalon *m* en velours (côtelé).

cordial I *n* **1** (fruit drink) sirop *m* de fruits; **2** (US) (liqueur) liqueur *m*.
II *adj* cordial/-e (**to, with** avec).

cordless *adj* [*telephone, kettle*] sans fil.

cordon *n* cordon *m*.
■ **cordon off** boucler [*street, area*]; contenir [*crowd*].

corduroy *n* velours *m* côtelé.

core *n* **1** (of apple) trognon *m*; **2** (of problem) cœur *m*; **3 rotten to the ~** pourri/-e jusqu'à l'os; **English to the ~** anglais/-e jusqu'au bout des ongles; **4** (of nuclear reactor) cœur *m*; **5** (small group) noyau *m*; **hard ~** noyau dur.

Corfu *pr n* Corfou *f*.

cork *n* **1** (substance) liège *m*; **2** (object) bouchon *m*.

corkscrew *n* tire-bouchon *m*.

corn *n* **1** (GB) (wheat) blé *m*; **2** (US) (maize) maïs *m*; **3** (on foot) cor *m*.

cornea *n* cornée *f*.

corner I *n* **1** (gen) coin *m*; **the house on the ~** la maison qui fait l'angle; **at the ~ of the street** au coin de la rue; **to go round the ~** tourner au coin de la rue; **just around the ~** (nearby) tout près; (around the bend) juste après le coin; **out of the ~ of one's eye** du coin de l'œil; **2** (bend) virage *m*; **3** (in boxing) coin *m* (de repos); (in football, hockey) corner *m*.
II *vtr* **1** acculer [*animal, enemy*]; coincer○ [*person*]; **2** accaparer [*market*].
IDIOMS **in a tight ~** dans une impasse; **to cut ~s** (financially) faire des économies.

corner shop *n* petite épicerie *f*.

cornerstone *n* pierre *f* angulaire.

cornflour *n* farine *f* de maïs.

cornflower *n* bleuet *m*, barbeau *m*.

corn on the cob *n* maïs *m* en épi.

Cornwall *pr n* (comté *m* de) Cornouailles *f*.

corny○ *adj* [*joke*] (old) éculé/-e; (feeble) faiblard/-e○; [*film, story*] à la guimauve.

coronary *n* infarctus *m*.

coronation *n* couronnement *m*.

coroner *n* coroner *m*.

corporal *n* (gen) caporal *m*; (in artillery) brigadier *m*.

corporal punishment *n* châtiment *m* corporel.

corporate *adj* **1** [*accounts, funds*] appartenant/-e à une société; [*clients, employees*] d'une société (or de sociétés); **2** [*action*] commun/-e; [*decision*] collectif/-ive.

corporation *n* (grande) société *f*.

corps *n* corps *m*.

corpse *n* cadavre *m*.

correct I *adj* **1** [*amount, answer, decision*] correct/-e; [*figure, time*] exact/-e; **2** [*behaviour*] correct/-e, convenable.
II *vtr* corriger.

correction *n* correction *f*.

correspond *vi* **1** (match) concorder, correspondre (**with** à); **2** (be equivalent) être équivalent/-e (**to** à); **3** (exchange letters) correspondre (**with** avec; **about** au sujet de).

correspondence *n* correspondance *f*.

correspondence course *n* cours *m* par correspondance.

correspondent ▶**626** *n* **1** (journalist) journaliste *mf*; (abroad) correspondant/-e *m/f*; **2** (letter writer) correspondant/-e *m/f*.

corridor *n* **1** couloir *m*; **2** (of land) corridor *m*.

corroborate *vtr* corroborer.

corrode I *vtr* corroder.
II *vi* se corroder.

corrosion *n* corrosion *f*.

corrugated *adj* ondulé/-e.

corrugated iron *n* tôle *f* ondulée.

corrupt I *adj* corrompu/-e.
II *vtr* corrompre.

corruption *n* corruption *f*.

Corsica *pr n* Corse *f*.

cosh *n* (GB) matraque *f*.

cosmetic I *n* produit *m* de beauté.
II *adj* (figurative) superficiel/-ielle.

cosmetic surgery *n* chirurgie *f* esthétique.

cosmonaut ▶**626** *n* cosmonaute *mf*.

cosmopolitan *n, adj* cosmopolite (*mf*).

cost I *n* **1** (price) coût *m*, prix *m* (**of** de); (expense incurred) frais *mpl*; **at ~** au prix coûtant; **2** (figurative) prix *m*; **at all ~s** à tout prix; **he knows to his ~ that** il a appris à ses dépens que.
II *vtr* **1** coûter; **how much does it ~?** combien ça coûte?; **the TV will ~ £100 to repair** la réparation de la télé coûtera 100

livres; **2** (estimate price of) calculer le prix de revient de [*product*]; calculer le coût de [*project, work*].

cost-effective *adj* rentable.

costly *adv* coûteux/-euse.

cost of living *n* coût *m* de la vie.

cost price *n* (for producer) prix *m* de revient; (for consumer) prix *m* coûtant.

costume *n* **1** (clothes) costume *m*; **2** (GB) (also **swimming ~**) maillot *m* de bain.

costume jewellery (GB), **costume jewelry** (US) *n* bijoux *mpl* fantaisie.

cosy (GB), **cozy** (US) *adj* (comfortable) douillet/-ette; (intimate) intime; **it's ~ here** on est bien ici.

cot *n* **1** (GB) (for baby) lit *m* de bébé; **2** (US) (bed) lit *m* de camp.

cottage *n* maisonnette *f*; (thatched) chaumière *f*.

cottage cheese *n* fromage *m* blanc à gros grains.

cotton *n* **1** (plant, material) coton *m*; **2** (thread) fil *m* de coton.

cotton wool *n* ouate *f* (de coton).

couch *n* **1** (sofa) canapé *m*; **2** (doctor's) lit *m*; (psychoanalyst's) divan *m*.

cough **I** *n* toux *f*; **to have a ~** tousser.
II *vi* tousser.

cough mixture *n* (sirop *m*) antitussif *m*.

could *modal aux* **1** (be able to) pouvoir; **I couldn't move** je ne pouvais pas bouger; **she couldn't come yesterday** elle n'a pas pu venir hier; **2** (know how to) savoir; **he couldn't swim** il ne savait pas nager; **she ~ speak four languages** elle parlait quatre langues; **3** (permission, requests, suggestions) pouvoir; **we ~ only go out at weekends** nous ne pouvions sortir or nous n'avions le droit de sortir que le week-end; **~ I speak to Annie?** est-ce que je pourrais parler à Annie?; **~ you help me?** pourrais-tu m'aider?; **4** (with verbs of perception) **I couldn't see a thing** je n'y voyais rien; **they couldn't understand me** ils ne me comprenaient pas; **we ~ hear them laughing** on les entendait rire; **5 you ~ have died** tu aurais pu mourir; **they ~ have warned us** ils auraient pu nous prévenir; **I ~ be wrong** je me trompe peut-être; **if only I ~ start again** si seulement je pouvais tout recommencer.

council *n* conseil *m*; **the town ~** le conseil municipal; **the Council of Europe** le Conseil de l'Europe.

council house *n* habitation *f* à loyer modéré.

councillor, **councilor** (US) *n* conseiller/-ère *m/f*.

council tax *n* (GB) ≈ impôts *mpl* locaux.

counsel **I** *n* (lawyer) avocat/-e *m/f*.
II *vtr* conseiller [*person*] (**about, on** sur).

counsellor, **counselor** (US) ▶ 626 *n* conseiller/-ère *m/f*.

count **I** *n* **1** (numerical record) décompte *m*; (at election) dépouillement *m*; **at the last ~** au dernier décompte; **to keep (a) ~ of** tenir compte de; **to lose ~** ne plus savoir où on en est dans ses calculs; **to be out for the ~**○ être KO○; **2** (level) taux *m*; **cholesterol ~** taux de cholestérol; **3** (figure) chiffre *m*; **4** (Law) chef *m* d'accusation; **on three ~s** pour trois chefs d'accusation; **5** (nobleman) comte *m*.
II *vtr* **1** compter [*points, people, objects*]; énumérer [*reasons, causes*]; **~ing the children** en comptant les enfants; **not ~ing my sister** sans compter ma sœur; **2** (consider) **to ~ sb as sth** considérer qn comme qch.
III *vi* compter; **it's the thought that ~s** c'est l'intention qui compte.
■ **count against** jouer contre [*person*].
■ **count on** compter sur [*person, event*]; **don't ~ on it!** ne comptez pas dessus!
■ **count up** calculer [*cost, hours*]; compter [*money, boxes*].

countdown *n* compte *m* à rebours (**to** avant).

counter **I** *n* **1** (in shop, snack bar) comptoir *m*; (in bank, post office) guichet *m*; (in pub, bar) bar *m*; **2** (in game) jeton *m*.
II *vtr* répondre à [*threat*]; neutraliser [*effet*]; parer [*blow*]; enrayer [*inflation*].
III *vi* riposter (**with sth** par qch).
IV **counter to** *phr* (gen) contrairement à; [*be, go, run*] à l'encontre de.

counteract *vtr* contrebalancer [*influence*]; contrecarrer [*negative effects*].

counter-attack *n* contre-attaque *f* (**against** sur).

counter-clockwise *adj, adv* (US) dans le sens inverse des aiguilles d'une montre.

counterfeit **I** *adj* [*signature, note*] contrefait/-e; **~ money** fausse monnaie *f*.
II *vtr* contrefaire.

counterfoil *n* talon *m*, souche *f*.

counterpart *n* (of person) homologue *mf*; (of company, institution) équivalent *m*.

counter-productive *adj* contre-productif/-ive.

countersign *vtr* contresigner.

countess *n* comtesse *f*.

countless *adj* **~ letters** un nombre incalculable de lettres; **on ~ occasions** je ne sais combien de fois.

country ▶ 448 *n* **1** pays *m*; **developing/third world ~** pays en voie de développement/du tiers monde; **2** (countryside) campagne *f*; **in the ~** à la campagne; **open ~** rase campagne; **across ~** à travers la campagne.

country dancing *n* danse *f* folklorique.

country house *n* manoir *m*.

country music *n* country music *f*.

countryside *n* campagne *f*.

county *n* comté *m*.

county council *n* (GB) ≈ conseil *m* régional.

coup *n* **1** (also **~ d'état**) coup *m* d'État; **2 to pull off a ~** réussir un beau coup.

couple *n* **1** couple *m*; **2 a ~ (of)** (two) deux; (a few) deux ou trois; **a ~ of times** deux ou trois fois.

coupon *n* **1** (voucher) bon *m*; **petrol ~** (GB) bon d'essence; **2** (in ad) coupon *m*; **reply ~** coupon-réponse *m*.

courage *n* courage *m*.

Countries, Cities, and Continents

Countries and continents

Most countries and all continents are used with the definite article in French:

I like France / Canada = j'aime **la** France / **le** Canada

to visit the United States = visiter **les** États-Unis

A very few countries are not:

to visit Israel = visiter Israël

All the continent names are feminine in French. Most names of countries are feminine eg ***la France***, but some are masculine eg ***le Canada***.

Most names of countries are singular in French, but some are plural eg ***les États-Unis mpl***. Note the plural verb:

*the United States **is** a rich country* = les États-Unis **sont** un pays riche

In, to, and from somewhere

With continent names, feminine singular names of countries and masculine singular names of countries beginning with a vowel, for ***in*** and ***to*** use ***en***, and for ***from*** use ***de*** (or ***d'*** before a vowel or mute 'h'):

*to go **to** Europe / **to** France / **to** Iraq* = aller **en** Europe / **en** France / **en** Irak

*to come **from** France* = venir **de** France

With masculine countries beginning with a consonant, use ***au*** for ***in*** and ***to***, and ***du*** for ***from***. With plurals, use ***aux*** for ***in*** and ***to***, and ***des*** for ***from***:

*to live **in** Canada / **in** the United States* = vivre **au** Canada / **aux** États-Unis

*to come **from the** United States* = venir **des** États-Unis

Adjective uses: français *or* de France?

Taking the word ***French*** as an example, the translation ***français*** is usually safe.

Some nouns, however, occur more commonly with ***de France***:

*the Ambassador **of France***
*the **French** Ambassador* = l'ambassadeur **de France**

Towns and cities

For ***in*** and ***to*** with the name of a town, use ***à*** in French; if the French name includes the definite article, ***à*** will become ***au***, ***à la***, ***à l'*** or ***aux***.

*to live **in** Toulouse / **in** le Havre/ **in** la Rochelle* = vivre **à** Toulouse / **au** Havre/ **à la** Rochelle

Similarly, ***from*** is ***de***, becoming ***du***, ***de la***, ***de l'*** or ***des*** when it combines with the definite article in town names:

*to come **from** Toulouse / **from** le Havre / **from** les Arcs* = venir **de** Toulouse / **du** Havre / **des** Arcs

Most towns in French-speaking countries have a corresponding adjective and noun. The noun forms, spelt with a capital letter, mean *a person from X*:

*the inhabitants **of Bordeaux*** = les **Bordelais** *mpl*

The adjective forms, spelt with a small letter, are often used where in English the town name is used as an adjective:

***Paris** shops* = les magasins **parisiens**

However, some of these French words are fairly rare and it is always safe to say ***les habitants de X*** or, for the adjective, simply ***de X***:

*a **Bordeaux** accent* = l'accent **de Bordeaux**

courageous *adj* courageux/-euse.

courier ▶626 *n* **1** (also **travel ~**) accompagnateur/-trice *m/f*; **2** (for parcels, documents) coursier *m*; (for drugs) transporteur *m*.

course I *n* **1** (gen) cours *m* (**of** de); **in the ~ of** au cours de; **in the ~ of time** avec le temps; **in due ~** en temps utile; **~ of action** moyen *m* d'action, parti *m*; **2** (route) cours *m*; (of boat, plane) cap *m*; **to be on ~** [*boat, plane*] tenir le cap; **to go off ~** [*ship*] dévier de son cap; **to change ~** (gen) changer de direction; [*boat, plane*] changer de cap; **3** (classes) cours *m* (**in** en; **of** de); **4** (Med) **a ~ of treatment** un traitement; **5** (Sport) (in golf, athletics) parcours *m*; (in racing) cours *m*; **6** (part of meal) plat *m*; **the main ~** le plat principal; **five-~ meal** repas *m* de cinq plats.
II **of course** *phr* bien sûr, évidemment.

court I *n* **1** (Law) cour *f*, tribunal *m*; **to go to ~** aller devant les tribunaux (**over** pour); **to take sb to ~** poursuivre qn en justice; **2** (for tennis, squash) court *m*; (for basketball) terrain *m*; **3** (of sovereign) cour *f*; **4** (courtyard) cour *f*.
II *vtr* courtiser [*woman, voters*].

court case *n* procès *m*, affaire *f*.

courteous *adj* courtois/-e (**to** envers).

courtesy *n* courtoisie *f*.

courthouse *n* (Law) palais *m* de justice.

court-martial *vtr* faire passer [qn] en cour martiale.

courtroom *n* salle *f* d'audience.

courtyard *n* cour *f*.

cousin *n* cousin/-e *m/f*.

cove *n* (bay) avise *f*.

cover I *n* **1** (gen) couverture *f*; (for duvet, typewriter, cushion, furniture) housse *f*; (of record) pochette *f*; **2** (shelter) abri *m*; **to take ~** se mettre à l'abri; **under ~** à l'abri; **3** (for teacher, doctor) remplacement *m*; **4** (insurance) assurance *f* (**for** pour; **against** contre).
II *vtr* **1** (gen) couvrir (**with** avec); recouvrir [*cushion, sofa, surface, person, cake*] (**with** de); **2** (deal with) [*article, speaker*] traiter; [*journalist*] couvrir; **3** (insure) assurer, couvrir (**for, against** contre; **for doing** pour faire).
■ **cover for** remplacer [*employee*].
■ **cover up**: ¶ **to ~ up for** couvrir [*friend*]; ¶ **~ [sth] up** recouvrir [*object*]; dissimuler [*mistake, truth*]; étouffer [*scandal*].

coverage *n* (gen) couverture *f*; **newspaper ~** couverture par les journaux; **live ~** reportage *m* en direct.

cover charge *n* prix *m* de couvert.

covering *n* **1** (for wall, floor) revêtement *m*; **2** (layer of snow, moss) couche *f*.

covering letter *n* lettre *f* d'accompagnement.

covert *adj* [*operation*] secret/-ète; [*glance*] furtif/-ive; [*threat*] voilé/-e.

cover-up *n* opération *f* de camouflage.

cover version *n* version *f*.

covetous *adj* cupide.

cow *n* vache *f*.

coward *n* lâche *mf*.

cowardice *n* lâcheté *f*.

cowardly *adj* lâche.

cowboy ▶626 *n* **1** (US) cowboy *m*; **2** (incompetent worker) fumiste *m*.

cower *vi* se recroqueviller.

coy *adj* **1** [*smile, look*] de fausse modestie; **2** (reticent) réservé/-e (**about** à propos de).

cozy (US) = **cosy**.

crab *n* crabe *m*.

crack I *n* **1** (in rock) fissure *f*; (in varnish, ground) craquelure *f*; (in wall, cup, bone) fêlure *f*; **2** (in door) entrebâillement *m*; (in curtains) fente *f*; **3** (also **~ cocaine**) crack *m*; **4** (noise) craquement *m*; **5**○ (attempt) essai *m*, tentative *f*; **to have a ~ at doing** essayer de faire.
II *adj* [*player*] de première; [*troops, shot*] d'élite.
III *vtr* **1** fêler [*bone, wall, cup*]; **2** casser [*nut, egg*]; **to ~ a safe** fracturer un coffre-fort; **to ~ sth open** ouvrir qch; **to ~ one's head open** se fendre le crâne; **3** déchiffrer [*code*]; **4** faire claquer [*whip*]; faire craquer [*knuckles, joints*].
IV *vi* **1** [*bone, cup, wall, ice*] se fêler; [*varnish*] se craqueler; [*skin*] se crevasser; [*ground*] se fendre; **2** [*person*] craquer; **3** [*knuckles, twig*] craquer; [*whip*] claquer; **4** [*voice*] se casser.
■ **crack down** prendre des mesures énergiques, sévir (**on** contre).

cracker *n* **1** (biscuit) cracker *m*, biscuit *m* salé; **2** (for Christmas) diablotin *m*.

crackle I *n* crépitement *m*.
II *vi* [*fire, radio*] crépiter; [*hot fat*] grésiller.

cradle I *n* berceau *m*.
II *vtr* bercer [*baby*]; tenir [qch] délicatement [*object*].

craft *n* **1** (skill) métier *m*; **2** (craftwork) artisanat *m*; **arts and ~s** artisanat (d'art); **3** (boat) embarcation *f*.

craftsman *n* artisan *m*.

crafty *adj* astucieux/-ieuse.

crag *n* rocher *m* escarpé.

cram I *vtr* **to ~ sth into** enfoncer or fourrer○ qch dans [*bag, car*]; **~med full** plein à craquer.
II *vi* [*student*] bachoter (**for** pour).

cramp I *n* crampe *f*.
II *vtr* gêner.

cramped *adj* [*house, office*] exigu/-uë.

cranberry *n* canneberge *f*.

crane *n* grue *f*.

crank *n* **1**○ (freak) fanatique *mf*, fana○ *mf*; **2** (handle) manivelle *f*.

crash I *n* **1** (noise) fracas *m*; **2** (accident) accident *m*; **car ~** accident de voiture; **train ~** catastrophe *f* ferroviaire; **3** (of stock market) krach *m*.
II *vtr* **to ~ one's car** avoir un accident de voiture.
III *vi* **1** [*car, plane*] s'écraser; [*vehicles, planes*] se rentrer dedans, se percuter; **to ~ into sth** rentrer dans or percuter qch; **2** [*share prices*] s'effondrer.

crash course *n* cours *m* intensif.

crash diet *n* régime *m* d'amaigrissement intensif.

crash helmet *n* casque *m*.

crash landing *n* atterrissage *m* en catastrophe.

crate *n* (for bottles, china) caisse *f*; (for fruit, vegetables) cageot *m*.

crater *n* (of volcano) cratère *m*; (caused by explosion) entonnoir *m*.

cravat *n* foulard *m* (pour homme).

crave *vtr* (also **~ for**) avoir un besoin maladif de [*drug*]; avoir soif de [*affection*]; avoir envie de [*food*].

crawl I *n* **1** (in swimming) crawl *m*; **2 at a ~** au pas; **to go at a ~** [*vehicle*] rouler au pas.
II *vi* **1** [*insect, snake, person*] ramper; **2** [*baby*] marcher à quatre pattes; **3** [*vehicle*] rouler au pas; **4** [*time*] se traîner; **5 to be ~ing with** fourmiller de [*insects, tourists*]; **6**○ (flatter) faire du lèche-bottes○ (**to** à).

crayfish *n* **1** (freshwater) écrevisse *f*; **2** (spiny lobster) langouste *f*.

crayon *n* (wax) craie *f* grasse; (pencil) crayon *m* de couleur.

craze *n* vogue *f*; **to be the latest ~** faire fureur.

crazy○ *adj* (gen) fou/folle; [*idea*] insensé/-e; **~ about** fou/folle de [*person*]; passionné/-e de [*activity*].

crazy golf ▶504 *n* (GB) mini-golf *m*.

creak *vi* [*hinge*] grincer; [*floorboard*] craquer.

cream ▶438 I *n* crème *f*; **strawberries and ~** fraises à la crème.
II *adj* **1** (couleur) crème *inv*; **2** [*cake, bun*] à la crème.

cream cheese *n* fromage *m* à tartiner.

cream soda *n* soda *m* parfumé à la vanille.

crease I *n* (intentional) pli *m*; (accidental) faux pli *m*.
II *vtr* froisser [*paper, cloth*].
III *vi* [*cloth*] se froisser.

create *vtr* (gen) créer; provoquer [*interest*]; poser [*problem*]; faire [*good impression*].

creation *n* création *f*.

creative *adj* **1** [*person*] créatif/-ive; **2** [*process, imagination*] créateur/-trice.

creator *n* créateur/-trice *m/f* (**of** de).

creature *n* **1** (living being) créature *f*; **2** (animal) animal *m*.

crèche *n* (GB) (nursery) crèche *f*; (in shopping centre) halte-garderie *f*.

credentials *n pl* **1** (reputation) qualifications *fpl*; **2** (reference) pièce *f* d'identité.

credibility *n* crédibilité *f*.

credible *adj* crédible.

credit I *n* **1** (merit) mérite *m* (**for** de); **to get/take the ~** se voir attribuer/s'attribuer le mérite (**for** de); **to be a ~ to sb/sth** faire honneur à qn/qch; **2** (in business) crédit *m*; **to buy sth on ~** acheter qch à crédit; **to be in ~** être créditeur/-trice.
II *vtr* **1 to ~ sb with** attribuer à qn [*achievement*]; **2** créditer [*account*] (**with** de).

credit card *n* carte *f* de crédit.

creditor *n* créancier/-ière *m/f*.

credits *n pl* générique *m*.

creed *n* (religious persuasion) croyance *f*; (opinions) principes *mpl*, credo *m*.

creek *n* **1** (GB) crique *f*; **2** (US) (stream) ruisseau *m*.

creep *vi* **1 to ~ in/out** [*person*] entrer/sortir à pas de loup; **to ~ under sth** se glisser sous qch; **to ~ along** [*vehicle*] avancer lentement; [*insect, cat*] ramper; **2** [*plant*] grimper.

creeper *n* (in jungle) liane *f*; (climbing plant) plante *f* grimpante.

creepy○ *adj* qui donne la chair de poule.

cremate *vtr* incinérer.

cremation *n* **1** (ceremony) crémation *f*; **2** (practice) incinération *f*.

crematorium *n* (GB) crématorium *m*.

crepe, crêpe *n* crêpe *m*.

crescent *n* croissant *m*.

crescent moon *n* croissant *m* de (la) lune.

cress *n* cresson *m*.

crest *n* **1** (ridge) crête *f*; **2** (coat of arms) armoiries *fpl*.

Crete *pr n* Crète *f*.

crevice *n* fissure *f*.

crew *n* **1** (on ship, plane) équipage *m*; **2** (on film, radio) équipe *f*.

crewcut *n* coupe *f* (de cheveux) en brosse.

crew neck sweater *n* pull *m* ras du cou.

crib I *n* (cot) lit *m* d'enfant.
II *vi* copier (**from** sur).

crick *n* **a ~ in one's neck** un torticolis.

cricket ▶504 *n* **1** (insect) grillon *m*; **2** (game) cricket *m*.

crime *n* **1** (minor) délit *m*; (serious) crime *m* (**against** contre); **2** (phenomenon) criminalité *f*.

criminal *n, adj* criminel/-elle *m/f*.

criminal record *n* casier *m* judiciaire; **to have a/no ~** avoir un casier judiciaire chargé/vierge.

crimson ▶438 I *n* cramoisi *m*.
II *adj* pourpre.

cringe *vi* **1** (in fear) avoir un mouvement de recul; **2** (with embarrassment) avoir envie de rentrer sous terre.

cripple I *n* impotent/-e *m/f*.
II *vtr* **1** estropier; **~d for life** infirme à vie; **2** paralyser [*country, industry*].

crisis *n* crise *f* (**in** dans; **over** à cause de).

crisp *adj* [*biscuit*] croustillant/-e; [*fruit*] croquant/-e; [*garment*] frais/fraîche; [*banknote, snow*] craquant/-e; [*air*] vif/vive; [*manner*] brusque.

crisps *n pl* (also **potato ~**) chips *fpl*.

crisscross I *adj* [*pattern*] en croisillons.
II *vi* s'entrecroiser.

criterion *n* critère *m* (**for** de).

critic ▶626 *n* **1** (reviewer) critique *m*; **2** (opponent) détracteur/-trice *m/f*.

critical *adj* [*point, condition, remark*] critique;

[*stage*] crucial/-e; [*moment*] décisif/-ive; **to be ~ of sb/sth** critiquer qn/qch.

critically *adv* **1** [*examine*] d'un œil critique; **2** [*ill*] très gravement.

criticism *n* critique *f*.

criticize *vtr*, *vi* critiquer.

croak *vi* [*frog*] coasser.

Croatia ▶ **448** *pr n* Croatie *f*.

crochet *vtr* faire [qch] au crochet; **a ~(ed) sweater** un pull au crochet.

crockery *n* vaisselle *f*.

crocodile *n* crocodile *m*.

crony *n* (petit/-e) copain/copine *m/f*.

crook *n* **1** (person) escroc *m*; **2** (shepherd's) houlette *f*; **3** (of arm) creux *m*.
IDIOMS **by hook or by ~** coûte que coûte.

crooked *adj* **1** [*line*] brisé/-e; [*picture, teeth, beam*] de travers; **2**° (dishonest) malhonnête.

crop *n* **1** (produce) culture *f*; (harvest) récolte *f*; **2** (whip) cravache *f*.
■ **crop up** [*matter, problem*] surgir; [*name*] être mentionné/-e; [*opportunity*] se présenter.

cross I *n* **1** croix *f*; **to put a ~ against** cocher [*name, item*]; **2** (hybrid) croisement *m*.
II *adj* (angry) fâché/-e (**with** contre); **to get ~** se fâcher.
III *vtr* **1** (gen) traverser; franchir [*border, line*]; **it ~ed his mind that** il lui est venu à l'esprit or l'idée que; **to ~ one's legs** croiser les jambes; **2** (intersect) couper; **3** barrer [*cheque*].
IV *vi* se croiser.
■ **cross off, cross out** barrer, rayer [*name, item*].

cross-check *vtr*, *vi* revérifier.

cross-country ▶ **504** *n* **1** (running) cross *m*; **2** (skiing) ski *m* de fond.

cross-examine *vtr* (gen) interroger; (Law) faire subir un contre-interrogatoire à.

cross-eyed *adj* [*person*] atteint/-e de strabisme; **to be ~** loucher, avoir un strabisme.

crossfire *n* feux *mpl* croisés; **to get caught in the ~** être pris/-e entre deux feux.

crossing *n* **1** (journey) traversée *f*; **2** (on road) passage *m* clouté; (level crossing) passage *m* à niveau.

cross-legged *adv* [*sit*] en tailleur.

cross-purposes *n pl* **we are at ~** il y a un malentendu; (disagreement) nous sommes en désaccord.

cross-reference *n* renvoi *m* (**to** à).

crossroads *n* carrefour *m*.

cross-section *n* échantillon *m* (**of** de).

crossword *n* (also **~ puzzle**) mots *mpl* croisés.

crotch *n* **1** (of body) entrecuisse *m*; **2** (in trousers) entrejambe *m*.

crotchet *n* (GB) noire *f*.

crouch *vi* (also **~ down**) [*person*] s'accroupir; (to spring) [*animal*] se ramasser.

crow I *n* corbeau *m*.
II *vi* **1** (exult) exulter; **2** [*cock*] chanter.
IDIOMS **as the ~ flies** à vol d'oiseau.

crowbar *n* pince-monseigneur *f*.

crowd I *n* foule *f*; (watching sport, play) spectateurs *mpl*.
II *vtr* **1** entasser [*people, furniture*] (**into** dans); **2** encombrer [*room, house*] (**with** de).
III *vi* **to ~ into** s'entasser dans [*room, lift, vehicle*].

crowded *adj* **1** [*place*] plein/-e de monde; (jam-packed) bondé/-e; **to be ~ with** être plein/-e de; **2** [*schedule*] chargé/-e.

crown I *n* **1** (of monarch) couronne *f*; **2** (of hill) crête *f*; (of head) crâne *m*; **3** (on tooth) couronne *f*.
II *vtr* couronner.

crown jewels *n pl* joyaux *mpl* de la Couronne.

crown prince *n* prince *m* héritier.

crow's nest *n* nid *m* de pie.

crucial *adj* crucial/-e.

crucifix *n* crucifix *m*.

crude *adj* **1** [*method*] rudimentaire; [*estimate*] approximatif/-ive; **2** [*joke*] grossier/-ière; [*person*] vulgaire; **3** (unprocessed) brut/-e; **~ oil** pétrole *m* brut.

cruel *adj* cruel/-elle.

cruelty *n* cruauté *f* (**to** envers).

cruise I *n* croisière *f*; **to go on a ~** faire une croisière.
II *vtr* [*driver, taxi*] parcourir [*street, city*].
III *vi* [*ship*] croiser; [*plane*] voler.

cruiser *n* **1** (cabin cruiser) petit bateau *m* de croisière; **2** (Mil) croiseur *m*.

crumb *n* miette *f*.

crumble I *vtr* émietter [*bread*].
II *vi* **1** [*rock*] s'effriter; [*building*] se délabrer; **2** [*relationship, economy*] se désagréger; [*opposition*] s'effondrer.

crumple *vtr* froisser [*paper*]; **to ~ sth into a ball** rouler qch en boule.

crunch *vtr* croquer [*apple, biscuit*].
IDIOMS **when** or **if it comes to the ~** au moment crucial.

crunchy *adj* croquant/-e.

crusade *n* croisade *f*.

crush I *n* bousculade *f*.
II *vtr* **1** écraser [*can, fruit, person, vehicle*] (**against** contre); broyer [*arm, leg*]; piler [*ice*]; **2** écraser [*enemy, uprising*]; étouffer [*protest*]; **3** chiffonner [*garment, fabric*].

crust *n* (gen) croûte *f*; **the earth's ~** l'écorce *f* terrestre.

crutch *n* béquille *f*.

crux *n* **the ~ of the matter** le point crucial.

cry I *n* cri *m*.
II *vi* pleurer (**about** à cause de); **to ~ with laughter** rire aux larmes.
■ **cry out 1** (with pain, grief) pousser un cri or des cris; **2** (call) crier, s'écrier.

crypt *n* crypte *f*.

cryptic *adj* [*remark*] énigmatique; [*crossword*] crypté/-e.

crystal *n* cristal *m*.

crystal clear *adj* **1** [*water*] cristallin/-e; **2** (obvious) clair/-e comme de l'eau de roche.

cub *n* (Zool) petit *m*.
Cuba ▶448| *pr n* Cuba *f*.
cubby-hole○ *n* cagibi○ *m*.
cube I *n* (gen) cube *m*; **ice ~** glaçon *m*.
II *vtr* couper [qch] en cubes [*meat*].
cubic *adj* **1** cubique; **2** [*metre, centimetre*] cube.
cubicle *n* (in changing room) cabine *f*; (in public toilets) cabinet *m*.
cuckoo *n* coucou *m*.
cucumber *n* concombre *m*.
cuddle I *n* câlin *m*; **to give sb a ~** faire un câlin à qn.
II *vtr* câliner.
cuddly toy *n* (GB) peluche *f*.
cue *n* **1** (line) réplique *f*; (action) signal *m*; **2** (Sport) queue *f* de billard.
cuff *n* **1** poignet *m*; **2** (US) (on trousers) revers *m*.
IDIOMS **off the ~** au pied levé.
cuff link *n* bouton *m* de manchette.
cul-de-sac *n* impasse *f*, cul-de-sac *m*.
cull I *n* massacre *m*.
II *vtr* massacrer [*seals, whales*].
culminate *vtr* aboutir (**in** à).
culottes *n pl* jupe-culotte *f*.
culprit *n* coupable *mf*.
cult I *n* culte *m*; (contemporary religion) secte *f*.
II *adj* **a ~ film** un film-culte; **to be a ~ figure** faire l'objet d'un culte.
cultivate *vtr* cultiver.
cultural *adj* culturel/-elle.
cultural attaché ▶626| *n* attaché/-e *m/f* culturel/-elle.
culture *n* culture *f*.
cultured *adj* cultivé/-e.
culture shock *n* choc *m* culturel.
cumbersome *adj* encombrant/-e.
cumulative *adj* cumulatif/-ive.
cunning I *n* **1** (of person) ruse *f*; (nastier) fourberie *f*.
II *adj* **1** [*person*] rusé/-e; (nastier) fourbe; **2** [*trick*] habile; [*device*] astucieux/-ieuse.
cup I *n* **1** tasse *f*; **2** (trophy) coupe *f*.
II *vtr* **to ~ sth in one's hands** prendre qch dans le creux de ses mains.
cupboard *n* placard *m*.
curable *adj* guérissable.
curate *n* vicaire *m*.
curator ▶626| *n* conservateur/-trice *m/f*.
curb I *n* **1** restriction *f* (**on** à); **2** (US) (sidewalk) bord *m* du trottoir.
II *vtr* refréner [*desires*]; limiter [*powers*]; juguler [*spending*]; restreindre [*consumption*].
curdle *vi* [*milk*] se cailler; [*sauce*] tourner.
cure I *n* remède *m* (**for** à).
II *vtr* **1** (gen) guérir (**of** de); **2** (Culin) (dry) sécher; (salt) saler; (smoke) fumer.
cure-all *n* panacée *f* (**for** contre).
curfew *n* couvre-feu *m*; **ten o'clock ~** couvre-feu à partir de dix heures.
curio *n* curiosité *f*, objet *m* rare.
curiosity *n* curiosité *f* (**about** sur, au sujet de); **out of ~** par curiosité.
curious *adj* curieux/-ieuse.
curiously *adv* [*silent, detached*] étrangement; **~ enough** chose assez curieuse.
curl I *n* boucle *f*.
II *vtr* friser [*hair*].
III *vi* **1** [*hair*] friser; **2** (also **~ up**) [*paper*] (se) gondoler; [*edges, leaf*] se racornir.
■ **curl up** [*person*] se pelotonner; [*cat*] se mettre en rond; **to ~ up in bed** se blottir dans son lit.
curler *n* bigoudi *m*.
curly *adj* [*hair*] (tight curls) frisé/-e; (loose curls) bouclé/-e; [*tail, eyelashes*] recourbé/-e.
currant *n* raisin *m* de Corinthe.
currency ▶582| *n* monnaie *f*, devise *f*.
current I *n* courant *m*.
II *adj* [*leader, situation, policy*] actuel/-elle; [*year, research*] en cours.
current account *n* (GB) compte *m* courant.
current affairs *n* actualité *f*.
currently *adv* actuellement, en ce moment.
curriculum *n* programme *m*.
curriculum vitae *n* curriculum vitae *m*.
curry I *n* curry *m*; **chicken ~** curry de poulet.
II *vtr* **to ~ favour** chercher à se faire bien voir (**with sb** de qn).
curse I *n* **1** (scourge) fléau *m*; **2** (swearword) juron *m*; **3** (spell) malédiction *f*.
II *vtr* maudire.
III *vi* jurer (**at** après).
cursor *n* curseur *m*.
curt *adj* sec/sèche.
curtain *n* rideau *m*.
curtsey I *n* révérence *f*.
II *vi* faire la révérence (**to** à).
curve I *n* courbe *f*.
II *vi* [*line, wall*] s'incurver; [*road, railway*] faire une courbe.
cushion I *n* coussin *m*.
II *vtr* amortir.
custard *n* (GB) (creamy) ≈ crème *f* anglaise.
custodian ▶626| *n* (of collection) gardien/-ienne *m/f*; (in museum) conservateur/-trice *m/f*.
custody *n* **1** (detention) détention *f*; **to take sb into ~** arrêter qn; **2** (of child) garde *f*.
custom *n* **1** coutume *f*, usage *m*; **2** (customers) clientèle *f*.
customary *adj* habituel/-elle; (more formal) coutumier/-ière.
customer *n* client/-e *m/f*.
customize *vtr* fabriquer [qch] sur commande [*car*].
custom-made *adj* [*clothes*] fait/-e sur mesure.
customs *n* douane *f*; **to go through ~** passer à la douane.
customs hall *n* douane *f*.
customs officer, customs official ▶626| *n* douanier/-ière *m/f*.
cut I *n* **1** (incision) entaille *f*; (in surgery) incision *f*; **2** (wound) coupure *f*; **3** (hairstyle) coupe *f*; **4**○ (share) part *f*; **5** (reduction) réduction *f* (**in** de); **job ~s** suppression *f* d'emplois; **a ~ in salary** une baisse de salaire.

II *vtr* **1** (gen) couper; **to ~ oneself** se couper; **to ~ one's finger** se couper le doigt; **to have one's hair cut** se faire couper les cheveux; **2** tailler [*gem, suit, marble*]; [*locksmith*] faire [*key*]; **3** (edit) couper [*article, film*]; supprimer [*scene*]; **4** (reduce) réduire [*cost, inflation, list*] (**by** de); baisser [*price*]; **5 to ~ a tooth** percer une dent; **6** (record) faire, graver [*album*].

III *vi* **1** (with knife, scissors) couper; **to ~ into** entamer [*cake*]; couper [*fabric, paper*]; inciser [*flesh*]; **2 to ~ down a sidestreet** couper par une petite rue.

IDIOMS **to ~ sb dead** ignorer complètement qn.

■ **cut back**: ¶ **~ back** faire des économies; ¶ **~ [sth] back 1** (reduce) réduire (**to** à); **2** (prune) tailler.

■ **cut down**: ¶ **~ down** réduire sa consommation; **to ~ down on smoking** fumer moins; ¶ **~ [sth] down 1** (chop down) abattre; **2** (reduce) réduire.

■ **cut off 1** couper [*hair, piece, corner*]; enlever [*excess, crusts*]; amputer [*limb*]; **2** (disconnect) couper [*mains service*]; **3 to ~ off sb's allowance** couper les vivres à qn; **4 to ~ sb off** (on phone) couper qn; (interrupt) interrompre qn; **5 to feel ~ off** se sentir isolé/-e.

■ **cut out**: ¶ **~ out** [*engine, fan*] s'arrêter; ¶ **~ [sth] out 1** découper [*article, picture*] (**from** dans); **2**○ **~ it out!** ça suffit!

■ **cut short** abréger [*holiday, discussion*].

■ **cut up** couper.

cutback *n* réduction *f*.

cute○ *adj* **1** mignon/-onne; **2** (US) (clever) malin/-igne.

cutlery *n* couverts *mpl*.

cutlet *n* côtelette *f*.

cut-price (GB), **cut-rate** (US) *adj* à prix réduit.

cut-throat *adj* [*competition*] acharné/-e; **a ~ business** un milieu très dur.

cutting I *n* **1** (from newspaper) coupure *f* (**from** de); **2** (in film-making) montage *m*.

II *adj* [*tone*] cassant/-e; [*remark*] désobligeant/-e.

cutting edge *n* **to be at the ~ of** être à l'avant-garde de.

CV, **cv** *n* (*abbr* = **curriculum vitae**) cv, CV *m*.

cyanide *n* cyanure *m*.

cycle I *n* **1** cycle *m*; **2** (bicycle) vélo *m*.

II *vi* faire du vélo.

cycling ▶ 504 *n* cyclisme *m*.

cycling shorts *n pl* cuissard *m*.

cyclist *n* (gen) cycliste *mf*; (Sport) coureur/-euse *m/f* cycliste.

cygnet *n* jeune cygne *m*.

cylinder *n* **1** (in engine) cylindre *m*; **2** (of gas) bouteille *f*; **3** (GB) (also **hot water ~**) ballon *m* d'eau chaude.

cynic *n* cynique *mf*.

cynical *adj* cynique.

cynicism *n* cynisme *m*.

Cyprus ▶ 448 *pr n* Chypre *f*.

cyst *n* kyste *m*.

Czech ▶ 553 **I** *n* **1** (person) Tchèque *mf*; **2** (language) tchèque *m*.

II *adj* tchèque.

Czech Republic ▶ 448 *pr n* République *f* tchèque.

Dd

d, **D** *n* **1** (letter) d, D *m*; **2** D (Mus) ré *m*.

dab I *n* (of paint) touche *f*; (of butter) petit morceau *m*.
II *vtr* tamponner [*stain*] (**with** de); **to ~ one's eyes** se tamponner les yeux.

dabble *v* ■ **dabble in** faire [qch] en amateur [*painting, politics*].

dachshund *n* teckel *m*.

dad○, **Dad**○ *n* papa *m*; père *m*.

daddy○, **Daddy**○ *n* papa *m*.

daffodil *n* jonquille *f*.

dagger *n* poignard *m*.
IDIOMS **to look ~s at sb** fusiller qn du regard.

daily I *n* (newspaper) quotidien *m*.
II *adj* **1** [*visit, routine*] quotidien/-ienne; **on a ~ basis** tous les jours; **2** [*wage, rate*] journalier/-ière.
III *adv* quotidiennement; **twice ~** deux fois par jour.

dainty *adj* [*porcelain, handkerchief*] délicat/-e; [*shoe, hand, foot*] mignon/-onne.

dairy I *n* **1** (on farm) laiterie *f*; (shop) crémerie *f*; **2** (company) société *f* laitière.
II *adj* [*butter*] fermier/-ière; [*cow, farm, product, cream*] laitier/-ière.

daisy *n* (common) pâquerette *f*; (garden) marguerite *f*.
IDIOMS **to be as fresh as a ~** être frais/fraîche comme un gardon.

dam *n* barrage *m*.

damage I *n* **1** (gen) dégâts *mpl* (**to** causés à); **2** (Med) **brain ~** lésions *fpl* cérébrales; **3** (figurative) **to do ~ to** porter atteinte à; **the ~ is done** le mal est fait.
II *vtr* **1** endommager [*building*]; nuire à [*environment, health*]; **to ~ one's eyesight** s'abîmer les yeux; **2** porter atteinte à [*reputation*].

damages *n pl* (Law) dommages-interêts *mpl*.

damn○ **I** *n* **not to give a ~ about sb/sth** se ficher○ éperdument de qn/qch.
II *adj* (also **damned**) [*key, car*] fichu/-e○ (*before n*).
III *excl* merde○!, zut○!

damp I *n* humidité *f*.
II *adj* [*clothes, house*] humide; [*skin*] moite.

dampen *vtr* **1** humecter [*cloth*]; **2** refroidir [*enthusiasm*].

damson *n* prune *f* (de Damas).

dance I *n* (gen) danse *f*; (social occasion) soirée *f* dansante.
II *vi* **1** [*person*] danser (**with** avec); **2** [*eyes*] briller (**with** de).
■ **dance about**, **dance up and down** sautiller sur place.

dancer *n* danseur/-euse *m/f*.

dancing *n* danse *f*.

dandruff *n* pellicules *fpl*.

danger *n* danger *m* (**of** de; **to** pour); **to be in ~** être en danger; **to be in ~ of doing** risquer de faire.

dangerous *adj* dangereux/-euse (**for** pour; **to do** de faire).
IDIOMS **to be on ~ ground** avancer en terrain miné.

dangerously *adv* (gen) dangereusement; [*ill*] gravement; **to live ~** prendre des risques.

danger signal *n* signal *m* de danger.

dangle I *vtr* balancer [*puppet, keys*]; laisser pendre [*legs*].
II *vi* [*puppet, keys*] se balancer (**from** à); [*earrings*] pendiller; [*legs*] pendre.

Danish ▶ 553 **I** *n* (language) danois *m*.
II *adj* (gen) danois/-e; [*embassy*] du Danemark.

dare I *n* défi *m*.
II *modal aux* oser; **to ~ (to) do** oser faire; **I ~ say** c'est bien possible.
III *vtr* **to ~ sb to do** défier qn de faire; **I ~ you!** chiche que tu ne le fais pas○!

daredevil *n, adj* casse-cou (*mf*) *inv*.

daring *adj* **1** (courageous, novel) audacieux/-ieuse; **2** [*suggestion, dress*] osé/-e.

dark I *n* **in the ~** dans le noir or l'obscurité; **before ~** avant la (tombée de la) nuit; **after ~** après la tombée de la nuit.
II *adj* **1** [*room, alley, day, sky*] sombre; **it is getting ~** il commence à faire noir or nuit; **it's ~** il fait noir or nuit; **2** [*colour, suit*] sombre; **a ~ blue dress** une robe bleu foncé; **3** [*hair, complexion*] brun/-e; **4** [*secret, thought*] noir/-e (*before n*).
IDIOMS **to be in the ~** être dans le noir; **to leave sb in the ~** laisser qn dans l'ignorance; **to keep sb in the ~ about sth** cacher qch à qn.

darken I *vtr* **1** obscurcir [*sky, landscape*]; assombrir [*house*]; **2** foncer [*colour*].
II *vi* **1** [*sky, room*] s'obscurcir; **2** (in colour) foncer; [*skin*] brunir.

dark glasses *n pl* lunettes *fpl* noires.

darkness *n* obscurité *f*; **in ~** dans l'obscurité.

darkroom *n* chambre *f* noire.

dark-skinned *adj* basané/-e.

darling *n* **1** (**my**) **~** (to loved one) chéri/-e *m/f*; (to child) mon chou○; (to acquaintance) mon cher/ma chère *m/f*; **2** (kind, lovable person) amour *m*, ange *m*.

darn *vtr* repriser.

dart ▶ 504 *n* fléchette *f*; **to play ~s** jouer aux fléchettes.

dartboard *n* cible *f*.

dash I *n* **1** (rush) course *f* folle; **it was a mad ~** on a dû se presser; **2** (small amount) (of liquid) goutte *f*; (of powder) pincée *f*; (of colour) touche *f*; **3** (punctuation) tiret *m*.

II *vtr* **1 to ~ sb/sth against** projeter qn/qch contre [*rocks*]; **2** anéantir [*hopes*].
III *vi* se précipiter (**into** dans); **to ~ out of** sortir en courant de [*shop, room*].
■ **dash off**: ¶ **~ off** se sauver; ¶ **~ [sth] off** écrire [qch] en vitesse.

dashboard *n* tableau *m* de bord.

data *n pl* données *fpl*.

database *n* base *f* de données.

data processing *n* (procedure) traitement *m* des données; (career) informatique *f*; (department) service *m* informatique.

date ▶**456** I *n* **1** date *f*; **~ of birth** date de naissance; **what's the ~ today?** on est le combien aujourd'hui?; **at a later ~, at some future ~** plus tard; **2** (on coin) millésime *m*; **3** (meeting) rendez-vous *m*; **to have a lunch ~** être pris/-e à déjeuner; **4 who's your ~ for tonight?** avec qui sors-tu ce soir?; **5** (fruit) datte *f*.
II *vtr* **1** (gen) dater; **2** sortir avec [*person*].
III *vi* **to ~ from** or **back to** [*building*] dater de; [*problem, friendship*] remonter à.
IV **to date** *phr* à ce jour, jusqu'ici.

dated *adj* [*clothes, style*] démodé/-e; [*idea, custom*] dépassé/-e; [*language*] vieilli/-e; **the film seems ~ now** le film a mal vieilli.

daughter *n* fille *f*.

daughter-in-law *n* belle-fille *f*, bru *f*.

daunting *adj* [*task, prospect*] décourageant/-e; [*person*] intimidant/-e.

dawdle *vi* flâner, traînasser○.

dawn I *n* aube *f*; **at ~** à l'aube; **at the crack of ~** à l'aube.
II *vi* **1** [*day*] se lever; **2 it ~ed on me that** je me suis rendu compte que; **it suddenly ~ed on her why** elle a soudain compris pourquoi.

day ▶**708** *n* **1** jour *m*; **what ~ is it today?** quel jour sommes-nous aujourd'hui? **every ~** tous les jours; **every other ~** tous les deux jours; **from ~ to ~** [*live*] au jour le jour; [*change*] d'un jour à l'autre; **the ~ when** or **that** le jour où; **the ~ after** le lendemain; **the ~ before** la veille; **the ~ before yesterday** avant-hier; **the ~ after tomorrow** après-demain; **2** (with emphasis on duration) journée *f*; **all ~** toute la journée; **during the ~** pendant la journée; **3** (age, period) époque *f*; **in those ~s** à cette époque; **these ~s** ces temps-ci.
IDIOMS **those were the ~s** c'était le bon temps; **that'll be the ~!** je voudrais voir ça!; **to call it a ~** s'arrêter là; **to save the ~** sauver la situation.

daybreak *n* aube *f*.

daydream I *n* rêves *mpl*.
II *vi* rêvasser.

daylight *n* **1** (light) jour *m*, lumière *f* du jour; **it was still ~** il faisait encore jour; **2** (dawn) lever *m* du jour, point *m* du jour.

daytime *n* journée *f*.

day-to-day *adj* quotidien/-ienne.

day-trip *n* excursion *f* pour la journée.

daze *n* **in a ~** (from news) ahuri/-e; (from blow) étourdi/-e; (from drugs) hébété/-e.

dazed *adj* (by news) ahuri/-e; (by blow) étourdi/-e.

dazzle *vtr* éblouir; **to ~ sb with** éblouir qn par [*beauty, knowledge*].

dazzling *adj* éblouissant/-e.

dead I *n* **1 the ~** les morts *mpl*; **2 at ~ of night** en pleine nuit; **in the ~ of winter** en plein hiver.
II *adj* mort/-e; **the ~ man/woman** le mort/la morte; **a ~ body** un cadavre; **to drop (down) ~** tomber raide mort/-e; **the phone went ~** la ligne a été coupée.
III *adv* (GB) [*certain, straight*] absolument; **~ on time** pile○ à l'heure; **~ easy**○ simple comme bonjour○; **they were ~ lucky**○**!** ils ont eu du pot○!; **~ tired**○ crevé/-e○, claqué/-e○; **to be ~ set on doing** être tout à fait décidé/-e à faire; **to stop ~** s'arrêter net.

deaden *vtr* calmer [*pain*]; amortir [*blow*]; assourdir [*sound*].

dead end I *n* impasse *f*.
II **dead-end** *adj* [*job*] sans perspectives.

dead heat *n* (in athletics) arrivée *f* ex-aequo; (in horseracing) dead-heat *m inv*.

deadline *n* date *f* or heure *f* limite, délai *m*; **to meet a ~** respecter un délai.

deadlock *n* impasse *f*; **to reach (a) ~** aboutir à une impasse.

dead loss○ *n* **to be a ~** être nul/nulle○.

deadly I *adj* **1** [*poison, enemy*] mortel/-elle; **2 in ~ earnest** avec le plus grand sérieux.
II *adv* [*dull, boring*] terriblement.

deadpan *adj* [*humour*] pince-sans-rire *inv*.

deaf I *n* **the ~** les sourds *mpl*, les malentendants *mpl*.
II *adj* **1** sourd/-e; **to go ~** devenir sourd/-e; **2 to turn a ~ ear to** faire la sourde oreille à, rester sourd/-e à.

deaf aid *n* (GB) prothèse *f* auditive.

deaf and dumb, deaf without speech *adj* sourd-muet/sourde-muette.

deafening *adj* assourdissant/-e.

deal I *n* **1** (agreement) accord *m*; (in business) affaire *f*; (with friend) marché *m*; **it's a ~!** marché conclu!; **2 a great** or **good ~** beaucoup (**of** de).
II *vtr* **1** porter [*blow*] (**to** à); **2** distribuer [*cards*]; donner [*hand*].
III *vi* **to ~ in** être dans le commerce de [*commodity, shares*].
■ **deal with 1** s'occuper de [*problem, request*]; **2** traiter de [*topic*].

dealer ▶**626** *n* **1** (in business) marchand/-e *m/f*; (large-scale) négociant/-e *m/f*; **2** (on stock exchange) opérateur/-trice *m/f*; **3** (in drugs) revendeur/-euse *m/f* de drogue, dealer○ *m*; **4** (in cards) donneur/-euse *m/f*.

dealing I *n* vente *f*.
II **dealings** *n pl* relations *fpl* (**with** avec).

dear I *n* **(my) ~** mon chéri/ma chérie *m/f*; (more formal) mon cher/ma chère *m/f*.
II *adj* **1** (gen) cher/chère; **he's my ~est friend** c'est mon meilleur ami; **to hold sb/sth ~** être attaché/-e à qn/qch, chérir qn/qch;

Dates, Days, and Months

The days of the week

Note that the French uses lower-case letters for the names of days.
Write the names of days in full; do not abbreviate as in English (*Tues*, *Sat* and so on).

Monday	= lundi	*Friday*	= vendredi
Tuesday	= mardi	*Saturday*	= samedi
Wednesday	= mercredi	*Sunday*	= dimanche
Thursday	= jeudi		

lundi in the notes below stands for any day; they all work the same way.
Note the use of ***le*** for regular occurrences, and no article for single ones. (*Remember*: do not translate ***on***.)

on Monday	= lundi
on Mondays	= le lundi
what day is it?	= quel jour sommes-nous? / on est quel jour?
Monday afternoon	= lundi après-midi
last Monday night	= la nuit de lundi dernier (*if evening*) lundi dernier dans la soirée
early on Monday	= lundi matin de bonne heure
late on Monday	= lundi soir tard
last / next Monday	= lundi dernier / prochain
the Monday before last	= l'autre lundi
a month from Monday	= dans un mois lundi
from Monday on	= à partir de lundi

The months of the year

As with the days of the week, do not use capitals to spell the names of the months in French, and do not abbreviate as in English (*Jan*, *Feb* and so on).

January	= janvier	*May*	= mai	*September*	= septembre
February	= février	*June*	= juin	*October*	= octobre
March	= mars	*July*	= juillet	*November*	= novembre
April	= avril	*August*	= août	*December*	= décembre

May in the notes below stands for any month; they all work the same way.

in May	= en mai / au mois de mai
next May	= en mai prochain
last May	= l'année dernière en mai
in early / late May	= début / fin mai

Dates

French has only one generally accepted way of writing dates: ***le 10 mai*** (*say* ***le dix mai***).
If the day of the week is included, put it after the ***le***:

Monday, May 1st 1901	= le lundi 1er mai 1901
what's the date?	= quel jour sommes-nous?
it's the tenth of May	= nous sommes / on est le dix mai
in 1968	= en 1968
in the year 2000	= en l'an deux mille
in the seventeenth century	= au dix-septième siècle

	Write	***Say***
May 1	le 1er mai	le premier mai
May 2	le 2 mai	le deux mai
from 4th to 16th May	du 4 au 16 mai	du quatre au seize mai
May 6 1968	le 6 mai 1968	le six mai mille neuf cent soixante-huit
in the 1980s	dans les années 80	dans les années quatre-vingt
the 16th century	le XVIe siècle	le seizième siècle

2 (in letter) cher/chère; **Dear Sir/Madam** Monsieur, Madame; **Dear Sirs** Messieurs; **Dear Mr Jones** Cher Monsieur; **Dear Mr and Mrs Jones** Cher Monsieur, Chère Madame; **Dear Anne and Paul** Chers Anne et Paul.
III *excl* **oh ~!** (dismay, surprise) oh mon Dieu!; (less serious) aïe!, oh là là!

death *n* mort *f*; (more formally) décès *m*; **to drink/to work oneself to ~** se tuer en buvant/au travail.
IDIOMS **to be at ~'s door** être à l'article de la mort; **to frighten sb to ~** faire une peur bleue à qn○; **to be bored to ~**○ s'ennuyer à mourir; **I'm sick to ~**○ **of this!** j'en ai par-dessus la tête!

death penalty *n* peine *f* de mort.

death sentence *n* condamnation *f* à mort.

death toll *n* nombre *m* de morts.

debar *vtr* **to be ~red from doing** ne pas avoir le droit de faire.

debate *n* débat *m* (**on, about** sur); (informal discussion) discussion *f* (**about** à propos de); **to hold a ~ on** débattre de [*issue*].

debauchery *n* débauche *f*.

debit I *n* débit *m*.
II *vtr* débiter [*account*] (**with** de).

debrief *vtr* interroger; **to be ~ed** [*diplomat, agent*] rendre compte (oralement) d'une mission; [*defector, freed hostage*] être interrogé/-e.

debris *n* (of plane) débris *mpl*; (of building) décombres *mpl*; (rubbish) déchets *mpl*.

debt *n* dette *f* (**to** envers); **to get into ~** s'endetter.

debtor *n* débiteur/-trice *m/f*.

debug *vtr* déboguer [*computer*].

debut *n* débuts *mpl*.

decade *n* décennie *f*.

decadent *adj* décadent/-e.

decaffeinated *adj* décaféiné/-e.

decanter *n* (for wine, port) carafe *f* (à décanter); (for whisky) flacon *m* à whisky.

decay I *n* **1** (of vegetation, body) pourriture *f*; (of building) délabrement; **2 tooth ~** carie *f* dentaire; **3** (of society) décadence *f*.
II *vi* [*timber, vegetation*] pourrir; [*tooth*] se carier; [*building*] se détériorer.

deceased I *n* **the ~** le défunt/la défunte.
II *adj* décédé/-e, défunt/-e.

deceit *n* malhonnêteté *f*.

deceitful *adj* malhonnête.

deceive I *vtr* **1** tromper, duper [*friend*]; **to be ~d** être dupe; **2** tromper [*spouse, lover*].
II *v refl* **to ~ oneself** se faire des illusions.

December ▶456 *n* décembre *m*.

decency *n* **1** (good manners) politesse *f*; **2** (propriety) convenances *fpl*.

decent *adj* **1** [*family, man, woman*] comme il faut, bien○ *inv*; **it's ~ of him** c'est très gentil à lui; **2** (adequate) convenable; **3** (good) [*camera, education, result*] bon/bonne (*before n*); [*profit*] appréciable; **to make a ~ living** bien gagner sa vie; **4** [*behaviour, clothes, language*] décent/-e, correct/-e.

deception *n* duplicité *f*.

deceptive *adj* trompeur/-euse.

decide I *vtr* **1 to ~ to do** décider de faire; (after much hesitation) se décider à faire; **2** (settle) régler [*matter*]; décider de [*fate, outcome*].
II *vi* décider; **to ~ against** écarter [*plan, idea*]; **to ~ between** choisir, faire un choix entre [*applicants, books*].
■ **decide on 1** se décider pour [*hat, wallpaper*]; fixer [*date*]; **2** décider de [*course of action, size, budget*].

deciduous *adj* [*tree*] à feuilles caduques.

decimal *adj* [*system, currency*] décimal/-e; **~ point** virgule *f*.

decipher *vtr* déchiffrer.

decision *n* décision *f*; **to make** or **take a ~** prendre une décision.

decision-making *n* **to be good/bad at ~** savoir/ne pas savoir prendre des décisions.

decisive *adj* **1** [*manner, tone*] ferme; **2** [*battle, factor*] décisif/-ive; [*argument*] concluant/-e.

deck *n* **1** (on ship) pont *m*; **on ~** sur le pont; **below ~(s)** sur le pont inférieur; **2** (US) (terrace) terrasse *f*; **3 ~ of cards** jeu *m* de cartes.
IDIOMS **to clear the ~s** déblayer le terrain.

deckchair *n* chaise *f* longue.

declaration *n* déclaration *f*.

declare *vtr* **1** déclarer (**that** que); annoncer [*intention, support*]; **2** déclarer [*war*] (**on** à); proclamer [*independence*]; **3** déclarer [*income*].

decline I *n* **1** (waning) déclin *m* (**of** de); **to be in ~** être sur le déclin; **2** (drop) baisse *f* (**in, of** de); **to be on the** or **in ~** être en baisse.
II *vi* **1** (drop) [*demand, quality*] baisser (**by** de); [*support*] être en baisse; **2** (wane) être sur le déclin; **3** (refuse) refuser.

decode *vtr* décoder [*code, message, signal*].

decompose *vi* se décomposer.

decorate I *vtr* **1** décorer [*cake, tree*] (**with** de, avec); **2 to ~ a room** (paint) peindre une pièce; (paper) tapisser une pièce.
II *vi* faire des travaux de décoration.

decoration *n* décoration *f*.

decorator *n* peintre *m*, décorateur/-trice *m/f*.

decoy I *n* leurre *m*.
II *vtr* attirer [qn] dans un piège.

decrease I *n* diminution *f* (**in** de); (in price) baisse *f* (**in** de).
II *vi* [*population*] diminuer; [*price, popularity, rate*] baisser, diminuer.

decreasing *adj* décroissant/-e.

decree *n* **1** (order) décret *m*; **2** (judgment) jugement *m*, arrêt *m*.

decrepit *adj* [*building*] délabré/-e; [*horse, old person*] décrépit/-e.

dedicate *vtr* dédier [*book*] (**to** à); consacrer [*life*] (**to** à).

dedicated *adj* [*teacher, mother, fan*] dévoué/-e; [*worker*] zélé/-e.

dedication *n* **1** (devotion) dévouement *m* (**to** à);

~ to duty dévouement; **2** (in a book, on music programme) dédicace *f*.

deduce *vtr* déduire (**that** que).

deduct *vtr* prélever [*subscription, tax*] (**from** sur); déduire [*sum*] (**from** de).

deduction *n* **1** (from wages) retenue *f* (**from** sur); (of tax) prélèvement *m*; **2** (conclusion) déduction *f*, conclusion *f*.

deed *n* **1** (action) action *f*; **to do one's good ~ for the day** faire sa bonne action or sa B.A.○; **2** (for property) acte *m* de propriété.

deep ▶**573** I *adj* **1** (gen) profond/-e; [*snow*] épais/épaisse; **a ~-pile carpet** une moquette de haute laine; **how ~ is the lake?** quelle est la profondeur du lac?; **the lake is 13 m ~** le lac fait 13 m de profondeur; **2** (dark) [*colour*] intense; [*tan*] prononcé/-e; **~ blue eyes** des yeux d'un bleu profond; **3 to be ~ in thought** être plongé/-e dans ses pensées; **to be ~ in conversation** être en grande conversation.
II *adv* **1** [*dig, bury, cut*] profondément; **2 ~ down** or **inside she was frightened** dans son for intérieur elle avait peur.

deepen I *vtr* **1** creuser [*channel*]; **2** approfondir [*knowledge, understanding*].
II *vi* **1** [*concern, love*] augmenter; [*knowledge*] s'approfondir; [*crisis*] s'aggraver; [*mystery*] s'épaissir; [*silence*] se faire plus profond; **2** [*voice*] devenir plus grave; **3** [*colour*] foncer.

deep-freeze *n* congélateur *m*.

deep-fry *vtr* faire frire.

deeply *adv* profondément.

deep-rooted *adj* [*anxiety, prejudice*] profondément enraciné/-e.

deep-sea *adj* [*diver, diving*] sous-marin/-e; [*fisherman, fishing*] hauturier/-ière.

deer *n* (red) cerf *m*; (roe) chevreuil *m*; (fallow) daim *m*; (doe) biche *f*.

deface *vtr* abîmer [*wall*]; couvrir [qch] d'inscriptions, dégrader [*monument*].

default I *vi* ne pas régler ses échéances.
II **by default** *phr* par défaut; **to win by ~** gagner par forfait.

defeat I *n* défaite *f*; **to admit ~** [*team, troops*] concéder la défaite; [*person*] avouer son échec.
II *vtr* **1** vaincre [*enemy*]; battre [*team, opposition, candidate*]; **the government was ~ed** le gouvernement a été mis en échec; **2** rejeter [*bill, proposal*]; **3 it ~s me** ça me dépasse.

defeatist *n, adj* défaitiste (*mf*).

defect I *n* (flaw) défaut *m*; (minor) imperfection *f*; **a speech ~** un défaut d'élocution.
II *vi* faire défection; **to ~ to the West** passer à l'Ouest.

defective *adj* défectueux/-euse.

defence (GB), **defense** (US) *n* (gen, Law, Sport) défense *f*; **in her ~** à sa décharge.

defenceless (GB), **defenseless** (US) *adj* [*person, animal*] sans défense; [*town, country*] sans défenses.

defend *vtr* défendre [*fort, freedom, interests, title*]; justifier [*behaviour, decision*].

defendant *n* accusé/-e *m*/*f*.

defender *n* défenseur *m*.

defensive *adj* [*reaction, behaviour*] de défense; **to be (very) ~** être sur la défensive.

defer I *vtr* reporter [*meeting, decision*] (**until** à); remettre [qch] à plus tard [*departure*]; différer [*payment*].
II *vi* **to ~ to sb** s'incliner devant qn.

deference *n* déférence *f*; **in ~ to** par déférence pour.

defiance *n* attitude *f* de défi.

defiant *adj* [*person*] rebelle; [*behaviour*] provocant/-e.

deficiency *n* **1** (shortage) insuffisance *f* (**of, in** de); (of vitamins) carence *f* (**of** en); **2** (weakness) faiblesse *f*.

deficient *adj* déficient/-e (**in** en).

deficit *n* déficit *m*.

define *vtr* définir.

definite *adj* [*plan, amount*] précis/-e; [*feeling, improvement, increase*] net/nette; [*decision, agreement*] ferme; **a ~ answer** une réponse claire et nette; **nothing is ~ yet** rien n'est encore sûr; **to be ~** (sure) être certain/-e (**about** de); (unyielding) être formel/-elle (**about** sur).

definitely *adv* sans aucun doute; **he ~ said he wasn't coming** il a bien dit qu'il ne viendrait pas.

definition *n* définition *f*.

deflate *vtr* dégonfler.

deflect *vtr* **1** défléchir, dévier [*missile*]; **2** détourner [*blame, criticism, attention*].

deformed *adj* déformé/-e; (from birth) difforme.

defraud *vtr* escroquer [*client, employer*]; frauder [*tax office*].

defrost I *vtr* décongeler [*food*]; dégivrer [*refrigerator*].
II *vi* [*refrigerator*] dégivrer; [*food*] décongeler.

deft *adj* adroit/-e de ses mains, habile.

defunct *adj* défunt/-e.

defuse *vtr* désamorcer.

defy *vtr* **1** défier [*authority, person*]; **2 to ~ sb to do** mettre qn au défi de faire; **3** défier [*description*]; résister à [*efforts*].

degenerate I *adj* dégénéré/-e.
II *vi* dégénérer.

degrade *vtr* humilier [*person*].

degrading *adj* [*conditions, film*] dégradant/-e; [*job*] avilissant/-e; [*treatment*] humiliant/-e.

degree *n* **1** (measurement) degré *m*; **2** (from university) diplôme *m* universitaire; **first** or **bachelor's ~** ≈ licence *f*; **3 to such a ~ that** à tel point que; **to a ~, to some ~** dans une certaine mesure; **by ~s** petit à petit; **4** (US) **first ~ murder** homicide *m* volontaire avec préméditation.

dehydrated *adj* déshydraté/-e; [*milk*] en poudre; **to become ~** se déshydrater.

de-icer *n* dégivrant *m*.

deign *vtr* **to ~ to do** condescendre à faire, daigner faire.

deity *n* divinité *f*.

dejected *adj* découragé/-e.

delay I *n* (gen) retard *m* (**of** de; **to, on** sur);

a few minutes' ~ un délai de quelques minutes; **without (further) ~** sans (plus) tarder.
II *vtr* **1** différer [*decision, publication*]; **to ~ doing** attendre pour faire; **2** retarder [*train, arrival, post*].
delayed *adj* **to be ~** être retardé/-e.
delegate I *n* délégué/-e *m/f*.
II *vtr* déléguer [*responsibility, task*] (**to** à).
delegation *n* délégation *f*.
delete *vtr* supprimer (**from** de); (with pen) barrer; (on computer) effacer.
deliberate *adj* **1** (intentional) délibéré/-e; **it was ~** il/elle l'a fait etc exprès; **2** (measured) [*movement*] mesuré/-e.
deliberately *adv* [*do, say*] exprès; [*sarcastic, provocative*] délibérément.
delicacy *n* **1** (of object, situation) délicatesse *f*; (of mechanism) sensibilité *f*; **2** (food) (savoury) mets *m* raffiné; (sweet) friandise *f*.
delicate *adj* (gen) délicat/-e; [*features*] fin/-e.
delicatessen *n* **1** (shop) épicerie *f* fine; **2** (US) (eating-place) restaurant-traiteur *m*.
delicious *adj* délicieux/-ieuse.
delight I *n* joie *f*, plaisir *m*; **to take ~ in sth/in doing** prendre plaisir à qch/à faire.
II *vtr* ravir [*person*] (**with** par).
delighted *adj* ravi/-e (**at, by, with** de; **to do** de faire); **~ to meet you** enchanté/-e.
delightful *adj* charmant/-e.
delinquent *n, adj* délinquant/-e (*m/f*).
delirious *adj* **to be ~** délirer.
deliver I *vtr* **1** livrer [*goods, groceries*] (**to** à); distribuer [*mail*] (**to** à); remettre [*note*] (**to** à); **2** mettre au monde [*baby*]; délivrer [*baby animal*]; **3** faire [*speech*]; donner [*ultimatum*]; rendre [*verdict*].
II *vi* [*tradesman*] livrer; [*postman*] distribuer le courrier.
delivery *n* **1** (of goods, milk) livraison *f*; (of mail) distribution *f*; **on ~** à la livraison; **2** (of baby) accouchement *m*.
delude *vtr* tromper; **to ~ oneself** se faire des illusions.
deluge *n* déluge *m*.
delusion *n* illusion *f*.
demand I *n* **1** (gen) demande *f* (**for** de); **on ~** (gen) à la demande; [*payable*] à vue; **to be in ~** être très demandé/-e; **2** (pressure) exigence *f*.
II *vtr* **1** (request) demander [*reform*]; (forcefully) exiger [*ransom*]; réclamer [*inquiry*]; **2** (require) demander [*skill, time, patience*] (**of sb** de qn); (more imperatively) exiger.
demanding *adj* **1** [*person*] exigeant/-e; **2** [*work, course*] ardu/-e; [*schedule*] chargé/-e.
demented *adj* fou/folle.
demerara (sugar) *n* sucre *m* roux cristallisé.
demister *n* (GB) dispositif *m* antibuée.
demo○ *n* (protest) manif○ *f*.
democracy *n* démocratie *f*.
democrat *n* démocrate *mf*.
democratic *adj* démocratique.
demolish *vtr* démolir.
demolition *n* démolition *f*.
demon *n* démon *m*.
demonstrate I *vtr* **1** démontrer [*theory, truth*]; **2** manifester [*concern, support*]; montrer [*skill*]; **3** faire la démonstration de [*machine, product*]; **to ~ how to do** montrer comment faire.
II *vi* manifester (**for** en faveur de; **against** contre).
demonstration *n* **1** (march) manifestation *f* (**against** contre; **for** en faveur de); **2** (of machine, theory) démonstration *f*.
demonstrative *adj* démonstratif/-ive.
demonstrator *n* manifestant/-e *m/f*.
demoralize *vtr* démoraliser.
demote *vtr* rétrograder.
den *n* **1** (of lion) antre *m*; (of fox) tanière *f*; **2** (room) tanière *f*.
denial *n* (of accusation, rumour) démenti *m*; (of guilt, rights, freedom) négation *f*.
denim I *n* jean *m*; **~s** jean *m*.
II *adj* [*jacket, skirt*] en jean; **~ jeans** jean *m*.
Denmark ▶ 448 *pr n* Danemark *m*.
denounce *vtr* **1** (inform on, criticize) dénoncer; **2** (accuse) accuser.
dense *adj* dense.
density *n* densité *f*.
dent I *n* (in metal) bosse *f*.
II *vtr* cabosser [*car*].
dental *adj* dentaire.
dental floss *n* fil *m* dentaire.
dental surgeon ▶ 626 *n* chirurgien-dentiste *m*.
dental surgery *n* (GB) (premises) cabinet *m* dentaire.
dentist ▶ 626 *n* dentiste *mf*.
dentistry *n* médecine *f* dentaire.
dentures *n pl* dentier *m sg*.
deny *vtr* **1** démentir [*rumour*]; nier [*accusation*]; **to ~ doing** or **having done** nier avoir fait; **2 to ~ sb sth** refuser qch à qn.
deodorant *n* (personal) déodorant *m*; (for room) déodorisant *m*.
depart *vi* **1** partir (**from** de; **for** pour); **2** (deviate) **to ~ from** s'éloigner de.
department *n* **1** (of company) service *m*; **2** (governmental) ministère *m*; (administrative) service *m*; **social services ~** services sociaux; **3** (in store) rayon *m*; **toy ~** rayon jouets; **4** (in hospital) service *m*; **5** (in university) département *m*; **6** (in school) section *f*.
department store *n* grand magasin *m*.
departure *n* (of person, train) départ *m*; (from truth, regulation) entorse *f* (**from** à); (from policy, tradition) rupture *f* (**from** par rapport à).
departure gate *n* porte *f* de départ.
departures board *n* tableau *m* des départs.
depend *vi* **to ~ on** dépendre de, compter sur (**for** pour); **to ~ on sb/sth to do** compter sur qn/qch pour faire; **that ~s** cela dépend; **~ing on the season** suivant la saison.
dependable *adj* [*person*] digne de confiance; [*machine*] fiable.

dependant *n* personne *f* à charge.

dependence, dependance (US) *n* **1** (reliance) dépendance *f* (**on** vis-à-vis de); **2** (addiction) dépendance *f* (**on** à).

dependent *adj* [*relative*] à charge; **to be ~ (up)on** (gen) dépendre de; (financially) vivre à la charge de.

depict *vtr* (visually) représenter; (in writing) dépeindre (**as** comme).

deplete *vtr* réduire.

deplorable *adj* déplorable.

deploy *vtr* déployer.

deport *vtr* expulser (**to** vers).

depose *vtr* déposer.

deposit I *n* **1** (to bank account) dépôt *m*; **on ~** en dépôt; **2** (on house, hire purchase goods) versement *m* initial (**on** sur); (on holiday, goods) acompte *m*, arrhes *fpl* (**on** sur); **3** (against damage, breakages) caution *f*; **4** (on bottle) consigne *f*; **5** (of silt, mud) dépôt *m*; (of coal, mineral) gisement *m*.
II *vtr* déposer [*money*]; **to ~ sth with sb** confier qch à qn.

deposit account *n* (GB) compte *m* de dépôt.

depot *n* **1** (gen) dépôt *m*; **2** (US) (station) (bus) gare *f* routière; (rail) gare *f* ferroviaire.

depress *vtr* **1** déprimer [*person*]; **2** appuyer sur [*button*]; **3** faire baisser [*prices*]; affaiblir [*trading*].

depressed *adj* **1** [*person*] déprimé/-e; **2** [*region, industry*] en déclin.

depressing *adj* déprimant/-e.

depression *n* dépression *f*.

deprive *vtr* priver (**of** de).

deprived *adj* [*area, family*] démuni/-e; [*childhood*] malheureux/-euse.

depth ▶ 573 **I** *n* **1** (of hole, water) profondeur *f*; (of layer) épaisseur *f*; **to be out of one's ~** (in water) ne plus avoir pied; (in situation) être complètement perdu/-e; **2** (of colour, emotion) intensité *f*; (of crisis) gravité *f*; **3** (of knowledge) étendue *f*; (of analysis, novel) profondeur *f*; **to examine sth in ~** examiner qch en détail.
II depths *n pl* (of sea) profondeurs *fpl*; **in the ~s of winter** au plus profond de l'hiver; **to be in the ~s of despair** toucher le fond du désespoir.

deputize *vi* **to ~ for sb** remplacer qn.

deputy I *n* **1** (aide) adjoint/-e *m/f*; (replacement) remplaçant/-e *m/f*; **2** (politician) député *m*.
II *adj* adjoint/-e.

deputy chairman *n* vice-président *m*.

derail *vtr* faire dérailler.

deranged *adj* dérangé/-e.

derelict *adj* [*building*] délabré/-e.

derision *n* moqueries *fpl*.

derogatory *adj* désobligeant/-e (**about** envers); [*term*] péjoratif/-ive.

descend I *vtr* descendre [*steps, slope, path*].
II *vi* **1** [*person, plane*] descendre (**from** de); **2** [*rain, darkness, mist*] tomber (**on, over** sur); **3 to ~ on sb** débarquer○ chez qn; **4 to be ~ed from** descendre de.

descendant *n* descendant/-e *m/f* (**of** de).

descent *n* **1** descente *f* (**on, upon** sur); **2** (extraction) descendance *f*.

describe *vtr* décrire.

description *n* description *f* (**of** de); (for police) signalement *m* (**of** de).

descriptive *adj* descriptif/-ive.

desert I *n* désert *m*.
II *vtr* abandonner [*person*] (**for** pour); déserter [*cause*]; abandonner [*post*].
III *vi* [*soldier*] déserter.
IDIOMS **to get one's just ~s** avoir ce qu'on mérite.

desert boot *n* bottine *f* en croûte de cuir, clarks® *f inv*.

deserted *adj* désert/-e.

deserter *n* déserteur *m* (**from** de).

desert island *n* île *f* déserte.

deserve *vtr* mériter (**to do** de faire).

deserving *adj* [*winner*] méritant/-e; [*cause*] louable.

design I *n* **1** (development) (of object, appliance) conception *f*; (of building, room) agencement *m*; (of clothing) création *f*; **2** (drawing, plan) plan *m* (**for** de); **3** (art of designing) design *m*; (fashion) stylisme *m*; **4** (pattern) motif *m*; **a leaf ~** un motif de feuilles; **5** (subject of study) arts *mpl* appliqués.
II *vtr* **1** concevoir [*building, appliance*]; **to be ~ed for sth/to do** être conçu/-e pour qch/pour faire; **2** [*designer*] créer [*costume, garment*]; dessiner [*building, appliance*].

designate *vtr* **to ~ sb (as) sth** désigner qn (comme) qch; **to ~ sth (as) sth** classer qch (comme) qch; **to ~ sth for** destiner qch à.

designer ▶ 626 **I** *n* (gen) concepteur/-trice *m/f*; (of furniture, in fashion) créateur/-trice *m/f*; (of sets) décorateur/-trice *m/f*; **costume ~** costumier/-ière *m/f*.
II *adj* **~ clothes, ~ labels** vêtements *mpl* griffés; **~ label** griffe *f*.

desirable *adj* **1** [*outcome, solution*] souhaitable; [*area, position*] convoité/-e; [*job, gift*] séduisant/-e; **2** (sexually) désirable.

desire I *n* désir *m* (**for** de); **to have no ~ to do** n'avoir aucune envie de faire.
II *vtr* désirer; **it leaves a lot to be ~d** cela laisse beaucoup à désirer.

desk *n* **1** bureau *m*; **writing ~** secrétaire *m*; **2** (in classroom) (pupil's) table *f*; (teacher's) bureau *m*; **3 reception ~** réception *f*; **information ~** bureau *m* de renseignements; **cash ~** caisse *f*.

desktop *n* (also **~ computer**) ordinateur *m* de bureau.

desolate *adj* désolé/-e.

despair I *n* désespoir *m*; **in** or **out of ~** de désespoir.
II *vi* désespérer (**of** de; **of doing** de faire).

desperate *adj* [*person, plea, situation*] désespéré/-e; [*criminal*] prêt/-e à tout; **to be ~ for** avoir désespérément besoin de [*affection, help*]; attendre désespérément [*news*].

desperately *adv* **1** [*plead, look, fight*] désespérément; **to need sth ~** avoir très besoin de qch; **2** [*poor*] terriblement; [*ill*] très gravement.

desperation *n* désespoir *m*.

despicable *adj* méprisable.

despise *vtr* mépriser.

despite *prep* malgré.

despondent *adj* abattu/-e, découragé/-e.

dessert *n* dessert *m*.

dessertspoon *n* cuillère *f* à dessert.

dessert wine *n* vin *m* doux.

destination *n* destination *f*.

destined *adj* **1** destiné/-e (**for**, **to** à; **to do** à faire); **2** (bound for) **~ for Paris** à destination de Paris.

destiny *n* destin *m*, destinée *f*.

destitute *adj* sans ressources.

destroy *vtr* **1** détruire [*building, evidence*]; briser [*career, person*]; **2** (kill) abattre [*animal*]; détruire, anéantir [*population, enemy*].

destruction *n* destruction *f*.

destructive *adj* destructeur/-trice.

detach *vtr* détacher (**from** de).

detached *adj* détaché/-e.

detached house *n* maison *f* (individuelle).

detachment *n* détachement *m*.

detail I *n* détail *m*; **in (more) ~** (plus) en détail; **to go into ~s** entrer dans les détails; **to have an eye for ~** prêter attention aux détails.
II *vtr* exposer [qch] en détail [*plans*]; énumérer [*items*].

detain *vtr* **1** (delay) retenir; **2** (keep in custody) placer [qn] en détention.

detect *vtr* déceler [*error, traces*]; détecter [*crime, leak, sound*]; sentir [*mood*].

detection *n* (of disease, error) détection *f*; **crime ~** la lutte contre la criminalité; **to escape ~** [*criminal*] ne pas être découvert/-e; [*error*] ne pas être décelé/-e.

detective *n* ≈ inspecteur/-trice *m/f* (de police); **private ~** détective *m*.

detective story *n* roman *m* policier.

detention *n* **1** (confinement) détention *f*; **2** (in school) retenue *f*, colle° *f*.

deter *vtr* dissuader (**from doing** de faire).

detergent *n* détergent *m*.

deteriorate *vi* se détériorer.

determination *n* détermination *f*.

determine *vtr* déterminer; **to ~ how** établir comment.

determined *adj* [*person*] fermement décidé/-e (**to do** à faire); [*air*] résolu/-e.

deterrent *n* (gen) moyen *m* de dissuasion; (Mil) force *f* de dissuasion.

detest *vtr* détester (**doing** faire).

detonate *vtr* faire exploser [*bomb*].

detour *n* détour *m*.

detract *vi* **to ~ from** porter atteinte à [*success, value*]; nuire à [*image*]; diminuer [*pleasure*].

detrimental *adj* nuisible (**to** à).

deuce *n* (in tennis) **~!** égalité!

devaluation *n* (of currency) dévaluation *f*.

devastated *adj* [*land, region*] ravagé/-e; [*person*] anéanti/-e.

develop I *vtr* **1** attraper [*illness*]; prendre [*habit*]; présenter [*symptom*]; **2** élaborer [*plan*]; mettre au point [*technique*]; développer [*argument*]; **3** développer [*mind, business, market*]; **4** mettre en valeur [*land, site*]; aménager [*city centre*]; **5** (in photography) développer.
II *vi* **1** (evolve) [*child, society, country, plot*] se développer; [*skills*] s'améliorer; **to ~ into** devenir; **2** (come into being) [*friendship, difficulty*] naître; [*crack*] se former; [*illness*] se déclarer; **3** (progress, advance) [*friendship*] se développer; [*difficulty, illness*] s'aggraver; [*crack, fault*] s'accentuer; [*game, story*] se dérouler; **4** (in size) [*town, business*] se développer.

developing country *n* pays *m* en voie de développement.

development *n* **1** (gen) développement *m*; **2** (of product) mise *f* au point; (of housing, industry) création *f*; **3** (of land) mise *f* en valeur; (of site, city centre) aménagement *m*; **4** (innovation) progrès *m*; **major ~s** des découvertes *fpl* majeures (**in** dans le domaine de); **5** (event) changement *m*; **recent ~s in Europe** les derniers événements en Europe.

deviate *vi* **1** (from norm) s'écarter (**from** de); **2** (from course) dévier (**from** de).

device *n* **1** (household) appareil *m*; **2** (Tech) dispositif *m*; **3** (also **explosive ~**, **incendiary ~**) engin *m* explosif; **4** (means) moyen *m* (**for doing, to do** de or pour faire).
IDIOMS **to be left to one's own ~s** être laissé/-e à soi-même.

devil *n* **1** (also **Devil**) **the ~** le Diable; **2** (evil spirit) démon *m*.
IDIOMS **speak of the ~!** quand on parle du loup (on en voit la queue)°!

devious *adj* retors/-e.

devise *vtr* concevoir [*scheme, course*]; inventer [*product, machine*].

devoid *adj* **~ of** dépourvu/-e de.

devolution *n* **1** (of powers) transfert *m* (**from** de; **to** à); **2** (policy) régionalisation *f*.

devote *vtr* consacrer (**to** à; **to doing** à faire); **to ~ oneself** se consacrer (**to** à).

devoted *adj* [*person, animal*] dévoué/-e (**to** à); [*fan*] fervent/-e.

devotion *n* (to person, work) dévouement *m* (**to** à); (to cause) attachement *m* (**to** à); (to God) dévotion *f* (**to** à).

devour *vtr* dévorer.

devout *adj* [*Catholic, prayer*] fervent/-e; [*person*] pieux/pieuse.

dew *n* rosée *f*.

diabetic *n, adj* diabétique (*mf*).

diagnose *vtr* diagnostiquer.

diagnosis *n* diagnostic *m*.

diagonal I *n* diagonale *f*.
II *adj* diagonal/-e.

diagram *n* schéma *m*; (in mathematics) figure *f*.

dial I *n* cadran *m*.
II *vtr* faire, composer [*number*]; appeler

[*person*]; **to ~ 999** (for police, ambulance) ≈ appeler police secours; (for fire brigade) ≈ appeler les pompiers.

dialect *n* dialecte *m*.

dialling code *n* (GB) indicatif *m*.

dialling tone (GB), **dial tone** (US) *n* tonalité *f*.

dialogue *n* dialogue *m*.

diameter *n* diamètre *m*.

diamond ▶504 *n* **1** (gem) diamant *m*; **2** (shape) losange *m*; **3** (in cards) carreau *m*.

diaper *n* (US) couche *f* (de bébé).

diaphragm *n* diaphragme *m*.

diarrhoea (GB), **diarrhea** (US) *n* diarrhée *f*.

diary *n* **1** (for appointments) agenda *m*; **to put sth in one's ~** noter qch dans son agenda; **2** (journal) journal *m* intime.

dice I *n* (object) dé *m*; (game) dés *mpl*.
II *vtr* couper [qch] en cubes [*vegetable, meat*].

dictate I *vtr* **1** dicter [*letter*]; **2** imposer [*terms*] (**to** à); déterminer [*outcome*].
II *vi* **1 to ~ to one's secretary** dicter une lettre (or un texte) à sa secrétaire; **2 to ~ to sb** imposer sa volonté à qn.

dictation *n* dictée *f*.

dictator *n* dictateur *m*.

dictatorship *n* dictature *f*.

dictionary *n* dictionnaire *m*.

die *vi* mourir (**of, from** de); **to be dying** être mourant/-e, se mourir; **to be dying to do** mourir d'envie de faire; **to be dying for** avoir une envie folle de.
■ **die down** [*emotion, row*] s'apaiser; [*fighting*] s'achever; [*storm*] se calmer; [*laughter*] diminuer; [*applause*] se calmer.
■ **die out** [*species*] disparaître.

diesel *n* **1** (also **~ fuel, ~ oil**) gazole *m*; **2** (also **~ car**) diesel *m*.

diesel engine *n* (moteur *m*) diesel *m*.

diet *n* **1** (normal food) alimentation *f* (**of** à base de); **2** (slimming food) régime *m*; **to go on a ~** se mettre au régime.

differ *vi* **1** (be different) différer (**from** de; **in** par); **2** (disagree) différer (d'opinion) (**on** sur; **from sb** de qn).

difference *n* **1** différence *f* (**in, of** de); **to tell the ~ between** faire la différence entre; **it won't make any ~** ça ne changera rien; **it makes no ~ to me** cela m'est égal; **2** (disagreement) différend *m* (**over** à propos de; **with** avec); **a ~ of opinion** une divergence d'opinion.

different *adj* différent/-e (**from, to** (GB), **than** (US) de).

differentiate I *vtr* différencier (**from** de).
II *vi* **1** (tell the difference) faire la différence (**between** entre); **2** (show the difference) faire la distinction (**between** entre).

difficult *adj* difficile; **to find it ~ to do** avoir du mal à faire; **to be ~ to get on with** être difficile à vivre.

difficulty *n* difficulté *f*; **to have ~ (in) doing** avoir du mal à faire.

diffident *adj* [*person*] qui manque d'assurance; [*smile, gesture*] timide.

dig I *n* **1** (with elbow) coup *m* de coude (**in** dans); **2**○ (jibe) **to take a ~ at sb** lancer une pique○ à qn; **3** (in archaeology) fouilles *fpl*; **to go on a ~** aller faire des fouilles.
II **digs** *n pl* (GB) chambre *f* (meublée).
III *vtr* **1** creuser [*hole, tunnel, grave*] (**in** dans); **2** bêcher [*garden*]; fouiller [*site*]; **3** extraire [*coal*] (**out of** de).
IV *vi* [*miner*] creuser; [*archaeologist*] fouiller; [*gardener*] bêcher.
■ **dig up 1** déterrer [*body, treasure, scandal*]; arracher [*roots, weeds*]; excaver [*road*]; **2** bêcher [*garden*].

digest *vtr* digérer [*food*]; assimiler [*facts*].

digestion *n* digestion *f*.

digit *n* **1** (number) chiffre *m*; **2** (finger) doigt *m*; (toe) orteil *m*.

digital *adj* [*display, recording*] numérique; [*watch*] à affichage numérique.

dignified *adj* [*person*] digne; [*manner*] empreint/-e de dignité.

dignity *n* dignité *f*.

digress *vi* faire une digression; **to ~ from** s'écarter de.

dilapidated *adj* délabré/-e.

dilate I *vtr* dilater.
II *vi* se dilater.

dilemma *n* dilemme *m* (**about** à propos de); **to be in a ~** être pris/-e dans un dilemme.

diligent *adj* appliqué/-e.

dilute *vtr* diluer (**with** avec).

dim I *adj* **1** [*room*] sombre; **2** [*light*] faible; **to grow ~** baisser; **3** [*outline*] vague; **4** [*memory*] vague (*before n*); **5**○ (stupid) bouché/-e○.
II *vtr* baisser [*light, headlights*]; mettre [qch] en veilleuse [*lamp*].

dime *n* (US) (pièce *f* de) dix cents *mpl*.
IDIOMS **they're a ~ a dozen**○ on en trouve à la pelle○.

dimension *n* dimension *f*.

-dimensional *combining form* **three~** à trois dimensions.

dime store *n* (US) bazar *m*.

diminish *vtr, vi* diminuer.

dimple *n* fossette *f*.

din *n* vacarme *m*.

dine *vi* dîner.

diner *n* **1** (person) dîneur/-euse *m/f*; **2** (US) (restaurant) café-restaurant *m*.

dinghy *n* **1** (also **sailing ~**) dériveur *m*; **2** (inflatable) canot *m*.

dining car *n* wagon-restaurant *m*.

dining room *n* (in house) salle *f* à manger; (in hotel) salle *f* de restaurant.

dinner *n* **1** dîner *m*; **to go out to ~** dîner dehors; **to have ~** dîner; **2** (banquet) dîner *m* (**for** en l'honneur de).

dinner jacket, DJ *n* smoking *m*.

dinner party *n* dîner *m*.

dinnertime *n* heure *f* du dîner.

dinosaur *n* dinosaure *m*.

dip I *n* **1** (in ground, road) creux *m*; **2** (bathe) baignade *f*; **3** (in prices, rate, sales) (mouvement *m* de) baisse *f* (**in** dans); **4** (Culin) sauce *f*.
II *vtr* **1** tremper (**in, into** dans); **2** (GB Aut) baisser [*headlights*]; **~ped headlights** codes *mpl*.
III *vi* **1** [*bird, plane*] piquer; **2** [*land, road*] être en pente; **3 to ~ into** puiser dans [*savings*]; parcourir [*novel*].

diploma *n* diplôme *m* (**in** en).

diplomacy *n* diplomatie *f*.

diplomat ▶ 626 *n* diplomate *mf*.

diplomatic *adj* diplomatique; **to be ~** avoir du tact.

direct I *adj* (gen) direct/-e; [*person*] franc/franche.
II *adv* directement; **to fly ~** prendre un vol direct.
III *vtr* **1** (address, aim) adresser [*appeal, criticism*] (**at** à; **against** contre); cibler [*campaign*] (**at** sur); orienter [*effort, resource*] (**to, towards** vers); **2** (control) diriger [*company, project*]; régler [*traffic*]; **3** diriger [*attack, light*] (**at** vers); **4** réaliser [*film, programme*]; mettre [qch] en scène [*play*]; diriger [*actor, opera*]; **5** (show route) **to ~ sb to sth** indiquer le chemin de qch à qn.
IV *vi* (in cinema, radio, TV) faire de la réalisation; (in theatre) faire de la mise en scène.

direct debit *n* prélèvement *m* automatique.

direction I *n* direction *f*; **in the right/wrong ~** dans la bonne/mauvaise direction; **to go in the opposite ~** aller en sens inverse; **from all ~s** de tous les côtés.
II **directions** *n pl* **1** (for route) indications *fpl*; **to ask for ~s** demander son chemin (**from** à); **2** (for use) instructions *fpl* (**as to, about** sur); **~s for use** mode *m* d'emploi.

directly *adv* **1** [*connect, challenge, go*] directement; [*point*] droit; [*above*] juste; **2** (at once) **~ after** aussitôt après; **~ before** juste avant; **3** (very soon) d'ici peu; **4** (frankly) [*speak*] franchement.

director *n* **1** (of company) (sole) directeur/-trice *m/f*; (on board) administrateur/-trice *m/f*; **2** (of play, film) metteur *m* en scène; (of orchestra) chef *m* d'orchestre; (of choir) chef *m* des chœurs.

directory *n* **1** (also **telephone ~**) annuaire *m*; **2** (for business use) répertoire *m* d'adresses; **street ~** répertoire *m* des rues; **3** (Comput) répertoire *m*.

directory assistance *n* (US), **directory enquiries** *n pl* (GB) (service *m* des) renseignements *mpl*.

dirt *n* **1** (on clothing, in room) saleté *f*; (on body, cooker) crasse *f*; (in carpet, engine, filter) saletés *fpl*; **2** (soil) terre *f*; (mud) boue *f*.

dirty I *adj* **1** [*face, clothing, street*] sale; [*work*] salissant/-e; **to get ~** se salir; **to get sth ~** salir qch; **2** [*needle*] qui a déjà servi; [*wound*] infecté/-e; **3**○ [*book, joke*] cochon/-onne○; [*mind*] mal tourné/-e; **4**○ [*trick*] sale (*before n*).
II *vtr* salir.

IDIOMS **to give sb a ~ look**○ regarder qn d'un sale œil.

disability *n* infirmité *f*.

disable *vtr* **1** [*accident*] rendre [qn] infirme; **2** immobiliser [*machine*]; **3** (Comput) désactiver.

disabled *adj* handicapé/-e.

disadvantage *n* inconvénient *m*; **to be at a ~** être désavantagé/-e.

disadvantaged *adj* défavorisé/-e.

disagree *vi* **1** ne pas être d'accord (**with** avec; **on, about** sur); **we often ~** nous avons souvent des avis différents; **2** [*facts, accounts, result*] être en désaccord (**with** avec); **3 to ~ with sb** [*food*] ne pas réussir à qn.

disagreeable *adj* désagréable.

disagreement *n* **1** (difference of opinion) désaccord *m* (**about, on** sur); **2** (argument) différend *m* (**about, over** sur).

disallow *vtr* **1** (Sport) refuser [*goal*]; **2** (gen, Law) rejeter [*claim, decision*].

disappear *vi* disparaître.

disappearance *n* disparition *f* (**of** de).

disappoint *vtr* décevoir.

disappointed *adj* déçu/-e (**about, with sth** par qch).

disappointing *adj* décevant/-e.

disappointment *n* déception *f*; **to be a ~ to sb** décevoir qn.

disapproval *n* désapprobation *f* (**of** de).

disapprove *vi* **to ~ of** désapprouver [*person, lifestyle*]; être contre [*smoking*].

disarm *vtr, vi* désarmer.

disarmament *n* désarmement *m*.

disaster *n* catastrophe *f*; (long-term) désastre *m*.

disastrous *adj* désastreux/-euse.

disbelief *n* incrédulité *f*.

disc, disk (US) *n* **1** (gen, Mus) disque *m*; **2 identity ~** plaque *f* d'identité; **tax ~** vignette *f* (automobile).

discard *vtr* **1** (get rid of) se débarrasser de [*possessions*]; mettre [qch] au rebut [*furniture*]; **2** (drop) abandonner [*plan, policy*]; laisser tomber [*person*].

discerning *adj* perspicace.

discharge I *n* **1** (of patient) renvoi *m* au foyer; **2** (of gas, smoke) émission *f*; (of liquid) écoulement *m*; (of waste) déversement *m*; **3** (from eye, wound) sécrétions *fpl*.
II *vtr* **1** renvoyer [*patient*]; décharger [*accused*]; **to be ~d from hospital** être autorisé/-e à quitter l'hôpital; **to be ~d from the army** être libéré/-e de l'armée; **2** renvoyer [*employee*]; **3** émettre [*gas*]; déverser [*sewage*]; **4** (Med) **to ~ pus** suppurer.

discipline I *n* discipline *f*.
II *vtr* **1** (control) discipliner; **2** (punish) punir.

disclaim *vtr* nier.

disclose *vtr* révéler [*information*].

disclosure *n* révélation *f* (**of** de).

disco *n* discothèque *f*.

discomfort *n* **1** (physical) sensation *f* pénible; **2** (embarrassment) sentiment *m* de gêne.

disconcerting *adj* (worrying) troublant/-e; (unnerving) déconcertant/-e.
disconnect *vtr* débrancher [*pipe, fridge*]; couper [*telephone*]; décrocher [*carriage*].
discontent *n* mécontentement *m*.
discontinue *vtr* supprimer [*service*]; arrêter [*production*]; cesser [*visits*].
discount I *n* remise *f* (**on** sur); **to give sb a ~** faire une remise à qn.
II *vtr* écarter [*idea, possibility*]; ne pas tenir compte de [*advice, report*].
discourage *vtr* décourager.
discover *vtr* découvrir (**that** que).
discovery *n* découverte *f*.
discredit *vtr* discréditer [*person, organization*]; mettre en doute [*report, theory*].
discreet *adj* discret/-ète.
discrepancy *n* divergence *f*.
discretion *n* discrétion *f*; **to use one's ~** agir à sa discrétion.
discriminate *vi* **1** (act with bias) établir une discrimination (**against** envers; **in favour of** en faveur de); **2** (distinguish) **to ~ between** faire une or la distinction entre.
discrimination *n* discrimination *f*.
discus *n* disque *m*.
discuss *vtr* (talk about) discuter de; (in writing) examiner.
discussion *n* discussion *f*; (in public) débat *m*.
disdainful *adj* dédaigneux/-euse.
disease *n* maladie *f*.
disembark *vtr, vi* débarquer.
disenchanted *adj* désabusé/-e.
disengage *vtr* dégager (**from** de).
disfigure *vtr* défigurer.
disgrace I *n* honte *f*; **to be in ~** (officially) être en disgrâce.
II *vtr* déshonorer [*team, family*].
disgraceful *adj* scandaleux/-euse.
disguise I *n* déguisement *m*; **in ~** déguisé/-e.
II *vtr* déguiser [*person, voice*]; camoufler [*blemish*]; cacher [*emotion, fact*].
disgust I *n* (physical) dégoût *m*; (moral) écœurement *m* (**at** devant).
II *vtr* (physically) dégoûter; (morally) écœurer.
disgusting *adj* (physically) répugnant/-e; (morally) écœurant/-e.
dish *n* **1** plat *m*; **to do the ~es** faire la vaisselle; **2** (also **satellite ~**) antenne *f* parabolique.
■ **dish out** distribuer [*advice, compliments, money*]; servir [*food*].
dishcloth *n* (for washing) lavette *f*; (for drying) torchon *m* (à vaisselle).
dishevelled *adj* [*person*] débraillé/-e; [*hair*] décoiffé/-e; [*clothes*] en désordre.
dishonest *adj* malhonnête.
dishtowel *n* torchon *m*.
dishwasher *n* (machine) lave-vaisselle *m inv*; (person) plongeur/-euse *m/f*.
disillusioned *adj* désabusé/-e; **to be ~ with** perdre ses illusions sur.
disinfect *vtr* désinfecter.
disinfectant *n* désinfectant *m*.
disintegrate *vi* se désagréger.
disinterested *adj* impartial/-e.
disk *n* **1** (Comput) disque *m*; **2** (US) = **disc**.
disk drive (**unit**) *n* unité *f* de disques.
dislike I *n* aversion *f* (**for** pour); **to take a ~ to sb** prendre qn en aversion.
II *vtr* ne pas aimer (**doing** faire).
dislocate *vtr* **to ~ one's shoulder** se démettre l'épaule.
dislodge *vtr* déplacer [*rock, tile, obstacle*].
disloyal *adj* déloyal/-e (**to** envers).
dismal *adj* **1** [*place, sight*] lugubre; **2**° [*failure, attempt*] lamentable.
dismantle *vtr* **1** démonter [*construction*]; **2** démanteler [*organization*].
dismay *n* consternation *f* (**at** devant).
dismiss *vtr* **1** écarter [*idea, suggestion*]; exclure [*possibility*]; **2** chasser [*thought, worry*]; **3** licencier [*employee*]; démettre [qn] de ses fonctions [*director, official*]; **4** (end interview with) congédier [*person*]; (send out) [*teacher*] laisser sortir [*class*]; **5** (Law) **the case was ~ed** il y a eu non-lieu.
dismissal *n* (of employee) licenciement *m*; (of manager, minister) destitution *f*.
dismissive *adj* dédaigneux/-euse.
disobedient *adj* désobéissant/-e.
disobey I *vtr* désobéir à [*person*]; enfreindre [*law*].
II *vi* [*person*] désobéir.
disorder *n* **1** (lack of order) désordre *m*; **2** (disturbances) émeutes *fpl*; **3** (Med) (malfunction) troubles *mpl*; (disease) maladie *f*.
disorganized *adj* désorganisé/-e.
disorientate *vtr* désorienter.
disown *vtr* renier [*person*]; désavouer [*document*].
dispatch I *n* (report) dépêche *f*.
II *vtr* envoyer [*person*] (**to** à); expédier [*letter, parcel*] (**to** à).
dispel *vtr* dissiper [*doubt, fear, myth*].
dispensary *n* (GB) (in hospital) pharmacie *f*; (in chemist's) officine *f*.
dispense *vtr* **1** [*machine*] distribuer [*drinks, money*]; **2** [*chemist*] préparer [*medicine, prescription*]; **3** (exempt) dispenser (**from sth** de qch; **from doing** de faire).
■ **dispense with** **1** se passer de [*services, formalities*]; **2** abandonner [*policy*]; **3** (make unnecessary) rendre inutile.
dispenser *n* distributeur *m*.
disperse I *vtr* disperser [*crowd, fumes*].
II *vi* **1** [*crowd*] se disperser; **2** [*mist*] se dissiper.
displaced person *n* personne *f* déplacée.
display I *n* **1** (in shop) étalage *m*; (of furniture, vehicles) exposition *f*; **window ~** vitrine *f*; **to be on ~** être exposé/-e; **2** (demonstration) (of art, craft) démonstration *f*; (of dance, sport) exhibition *f*; **air ~** fête *f* aéronautique; **3** (of emotion)

démonstration *f*; (of strength) déploiement *m*; (of wealth) étalage *m*; **4** (Aut, Comput) écran *m*.
II *vtr* **1** (show, set out) afficher [*information, poster*]; exposer [*object*]; **2** (reveal) faire preuve de [*intelligence, interest, skill*]; révéler [*emotion, vice, virtue*]; **3** (flaunt) faire étalage de [*beauty, knowledge, wealth*]; exhiber [*legs, chest*].

displeased *adj* mécontent/-e (**with, at** de).

disposable *adj* **1** (throwaway) jetable; **2** (available) disponible.

disposal *n* **1** (of waste product) élimination *f*; **for ~** à jeter; **2** (of company, property) vente *f*; **3 to be at sb's ~** être à la disposition de qn.

dispose *v* ■ **dispose of 1** se débarrasser de [*body, rubbish*]; détruire [*evidence*]; désarmer [*bomb*]; **2** écouler [*stock*]; vendre [*car, shares*].

disproportionate *adj* disproportionné/-e (**to** par rapport à).

disprove *vtr* réfuter.

dispute I *n* **1** (quarrel) (between individuals) dispute *f*; (between groups) conflit *m* (**over, about** à propos de); **2** (controversy) controverse *f* (**over, about** sur).
II *vtr* **1** contester [*claim, figures*]; **2** se disputer [*property, title*].

disqualify *vtr* **1** (gen) exclure; **to ~ sb from doing** interdire à qn de faire; **2** (Sport) disqualifier; **3** (GB Aut) **to ~ sb from driving** retirer le permis de conduire à qn.

disregard I *n* (for problem, person) indifférence *f* (**for sth** à qch; **for sb** envers qn); (for danger, life, law) mépris *m* (**for** de).
II *vtr* **1** ne pas tenir compte de [*problem, evidence, remark*]; fermer les yeux sur [*fault*]; mépriser [*danger*]; **2** ne pas respecter [*law, instruction*].

disrepair *n* délabrement *m*; **to fall into ~** se délabrer.

disreputable *adj* [*person*] peu recommandable; [*place*] mal famé/-e.

disrespect *n* manque *m* de respect (**for** envers).

disrespectful *adj* [*person*] irrespectueux/-euse (**to, towards** envers).

disrupt *vtr* perturber [*traffic, trade, meeting*]; bouleverser [*lifestyle, schedule, routine*]; interrompre [*power supply*].

dissatisfaction *n* mécontentement *m*.

dissatisfied *adj* mécontent/-e (**with** de).

dissect *vtr* disséquer.

dissident *n, adj* dissident/-e (*m/f*).

dissolve I *vtr* **1** [*acid, water*] dissoudre [*solid, grease*]; **2** faire dissoudre [*tablet, powder*] (**in** dans); **3** dissoudre [*assembly, parliament, partnership*].
II *vi* **1** [*tablet*] se dissoudre (**in** dans; **into** en); **2** [*hope*] s'évanouir; [*outline, image*] disparaître; **3 to ~ into tears** fondre en larmes.

dissuade *vtr* dissuader (**from doing** de faire).

distance **▶573** *n* distance *f* (**between** entre; **from** de; **to** à); **to keep one's ~** garder ses distances (**from** avec); **in the ~** au loin; **it's within walking ~** on peut y aller à pied.

distant *adj* **1** (remote) éloigné/-e; **2** (faint) [*memory, prospect*] lointain/-e; **3** (cool) [*person*] distant/-e.

distaste *n* dégoût *m*.

distinct *adj* (gen) distinct/-e (**from** de); [*resemblance, preference, progress*] net/nette (*before n*); [*advantage*] indéniable.

distinction *n* **1** (gen) distinction *f*; **2** (Univ) mention *f* très bien.

distinctive *adj* caractéristique (**of** de).

distinguish *vtr* distinguer (**from** de); **to be ~ed by** se caractériser par.

distinguished *adj* **1** (elegant) distingué/-e; **2** (famous) éminent/-e.

distinguishing *adj* distinctif/-ive.

distort *vtr* déformer.

distract *vtr* distraire; **to ~ sb from doing** empêcher qn de faire.

distraction *n* **1** (from concentration) distraction *f*; **2** (diversion) diversion *f*.

distraught *adj* éperdu/-e.

distress I *n* **1** (emotional) désarroi *m*; **to cause sb ~** faire de la peine à qn; **2** (physical) souffrance *f*; **3** [*ship*] **in ~** en détresse.
II *vtr* faire de la peine à [*person*]; (stronger) bouleverser [*person*] (**to do** de faire).

distressing *adj* [*case, event, idea*] pénible; [*news*] navrant/-e; [*sight*] affligeant/-e.

distribute *vtr* **1** (share out) distribuer [*films, supplies, money*] (**to** à; **among** entre); **2** (spread out) répartir [*load, tax burden*].

distribution *n* distribution *f*.

distributor *n* distributeur *m* (**for sth** de qch).

district *n* (in country) région *f*; (in city) quartier *m*; (administrative) district *m*.

district attorney *n* (US) représentant *m* du ministère public.

disturb *vtr* **1** (interrupt) déranger [*person*]; troubler [*silence, sleep*]; **2** (upset) troubler [*person*]; (concern) inquiéter [*person*].

disturbance *n* **1** (interruption, inconvenience) dérangement *m*; **2** (riot) troubles *mpl*; (fight) altercation *f*.

disturbed *adj* **1** [*sleep*] agité/-e; **2** [*child*] perturbé/-e.

disturbing *adj* [*portrayal*] troublant/-e; [*book, film*] perturbant/-e; [*report, increase*] inquiétant/-e.

disused *adj* désaffecté/-e.

ditch I *n* fossé *m*.
II○ *vtr* laisser tomber [*friend*]; abandonner [*idea, vehicle*]; plaquer○ [*girlfriend, boyfriend*].

dither *vi* tergiverser (**about, over** sur).

ditto *adv* idem.

dive I *n* **1** (by swimmer) plongeon *m*; **2** (of plane, bird) piqué *m*.
II *vi* **1** [*person*] plonger (**off, from** de; **down to** jusqu'à); **2** (as hobby) faire de la plongée.

diver *n* plongeur/-euse *m/f*; (deep-sea) scaphandrier *m*.

diverge *vi* diverger; **to ~ from** s'écarter de.

diversion *n* **1** (distraction) diversion *f* (**from** à); **2** (of river, money) détournement *m*; **3** (of traffic) déviation *f*.

divert *vtr* **1** détourner [*water*]; dévier [*traffic*]; dérouter [*flight*] (**to** sur); détourner [*funds*] (**to** au profit de); **2** (distract) détourner.

divide I *vtr* **1** (also **~ up**) partager [*food, money, time, work*]; **2** (separate) séparer (**from** de); **3** (split) diviser [*friends, group*]; **4** (in mathematics) diviser (**by** par).
II *vi* [*road*] bifurquer; [*river, train*] se séparer en deux; [*group*] (into two) se séparer en deux; [*cell, organism*] se diviser.

dividend *n* dividende *m*.

diving *n* (from board) plongeon *m*; (under sea) plongée *f* sous-marine.

diving board *n* plongeoir *m*.

diving suit *n* scaphandre *m*.

division *n* (gen) division *f*.

divorce I *n* divorce *m*.
II *vtr* **to ~ sb** divorcer de or d'avec qn; **they're ~d** ils ont divorcé; **she's ~d** elle est divorcée.

DIY *n* (GB) (*abbr* = **do-it-yourself**) bricolage *m*.

dizzy *adj* [*height*] vertigineux/-euse; **to make sb ~** donner le vertige à qn; **to feel ~** avoir la tête qui tourne.

DJ *n* (*abbr* = **disc jockey**) DJ *mf*.

DNA *n* (*abbr* = **deoxyribonucleic acid**) ADN *m*.

do I *v aux* **don't ~ that!** ne fais pas ça!; **he said he'd tell her and he did** il a dit qu'il le lui dirait et il l'a fait; **so/neither does he** lui aussi/non plus; **'I love peaches'—'so ~ I'** 'j'adore les pêches'—'moi aussi'; **'who wrote it?'—'I did'** 'qui l'a écrit?'—'moi'; **'shall I tell him?'—'no don't'** 'est-ce que je le lui dis?'—'non'; **he lives in London, doesn't he?** il habite à Londres, n'est-ce pas?; **'he knows the President'—'does he?'** 'il connaît le Président'—'vraiment?'
II *vtr* **1** (gen) faire; **to ~ the cooking/one's homework** faire la cuisine/ses devoirs; **to ~ sth again** refaire qch; **to ~ sb's hair** coiffer qn; **to ~ one's teeth** se brosser les dents; **what have you done to your hair?** qu'est-ce que vous avez fait à vos cheveux?; **what has he done with the newspaper?** qu'est-ce qu'il a fait du journal?; **to ~ 60** [*car, driver*] faire du 60 à l'heure; **2**○ (cheat) **we've been done** on s'est fait avoir; **to ~ sb out of £5** refaire○ qn de 5 livres sterling.
III *vi* **1** (behave) faire; **~ as you're told** (by me) fais ce que je te dis; (by others) fais ce qu'on te dit; **2** (serve purpose) faire l'affaire; **that box will ~** cette boîte fera l'affaire; **3** (be acceptable) **this really won't ~!** [*situation, attitude*] ça ne peut pas continuer comme ça!; [*work*] c'est franchement mauvais!; **4** (be enough) [*amount of money*] suffire; **5** (get on) [*person*] s'en sortir; [*business*] marcher; **6** (in health) **mother and baby are both ~ing well** la mère et l'enfant se portent bien; **the patient is ~ing well** le malade est en bonne voie.
IDIOMS **how ~ you do** enchanté; **well done!** bravo!; **it doesn't ~ to be** ce n'est pas une bonne chose d'être; **it was all I could ~ not to laugh** je me suis retenu pour ne pas rire; **she does nothing but moan** elle ne fait que se plaindre.
■ **do away with** se débarrasser de.
■ **do up 1** (fasten) nouer [*laces*]; remonter [*zip*]; **~ up your buttons** boutonne-toi; **2** (wrap) faire [*parcel*]; **3** (renovate) restaurer [*house*].
■ **do with 1 what's it (got) to ~ with you?** en quoi est-ce que ça te regarde?; **it has nothing to ~ with you** cela ne vous concerne pas; **2** (tolerate) supporter; **3** (need) **I could ~ with a holiday** j'aurais bien besoin de partir en vacances; **4** (finish) **it's all over and done with** c'est bien fini.
■ **do without** se passer de [*person, advice*].

dock I *n* **1** (in port) dock *m*; (for repairing ship) cale *f*; **2** (US) (wharf) appontement *m*; **3** (GB Law) banc *m* des accusés.
II *vi* arriver au port.

dockworker ▶ 626 *n* docker *m*.

dockyard *n* chantier *m* naval.

doctor ▶ 626, ▶ 498 **I** *n* **1** (Med) médecin *m*, docteur *m*; **2** (Univ) docteur *m*.
II *vtr* frelater [*food, wine*]; falsifier [*figures*]; altérer [*document*].

document *n* document *m*.

documentary *n* documentaire *m* (**about, on** sur).

dodge I *n* ○(GB) (trick) combine○ *f*.
II *vtr* esquiver [*bullet, blow, question*].

dodgem (car) *n* (GB) auto *f* tamponneuse.

dog *n* **1** chien *m*; (female) chienne *f*; **2** (male fox, wolf) mâle *m*.
IDIOMS **to go to the ~s** [*company, country*] aller à vau-l'eau.

dog collar *n* **1** collier *m* de chien; **2** col *m* romain.

dog-eared *adj* écorné/-e.

dogged *adj* [*attempt*] obstiné/-e; [*person, refusal*] tenace; [*resistance*] opiniâtre.

doghouse *n* (US) niche *f* (à chien).
IDIOMS **to be in the ~** être tombé/-e en disgrâce.

dogmatic *adj* dogmatique (**about** sur).

dog paddle *n* nage *f* à la manière d'un chien.

dogsbody○ *n* (GB) bonne *f* à tout faire.

doh *n* (Mus) do *m*, ut *m*.

doing *n* **this is her ~** c'est son ouvrage; **it takes some ~!** ce n'est pas facile du tout!

dole○ *n* (GB) allocation *f* de chômage; **on the ~** au chômage.
■ **dole out**○ distribuer.

doll *n* poupée *f*.

dollar ▶ 582 *n* dollar *m*.

dollar bill *n* billet *m* d'un dollar.

dolphin *n* dauphin *m*.

domain *n* domaine *m* (**of** de).

dome *n* dôme *m*.

domestic *adj* **1** [*market, flight*] intérieur/-e; [*crisis, issue*] de politique intérieure; **2** [*life, harmony*] familial/-e; [*dispute*] conjugal/-e; [*violence*] dans la famille.

do

The French equivalent of the verb ***to do*** in *subject + to do + object* sentences is ***faire***:

*she's **doing** her homework* = elle **fait** ses devoirs

*what **has** he **done** with the newspaper?* = qu'est-ce qu'il **a fait** du journal?

Grammatical functions of *do*, auxiliary verb

In questions

In French there is no auxiliary verb in questions equivalent to ***do*** in English.

When the subject is a pronoun, use either of these structures: *verb + hyphen + subject* or, less formally, ***est-ce que*** *+ subject + verb*:

***do** you like Mozart?* = aimes-tu Mozart?
= **est-ce que** tu aimes Mozart?

When the subject is a noun, there are again two possibilities:

***did** your sister ring?* = **est-ce que** ta sœur a téléphoné?
= ta sœur a-t-elle téléphoné?

In negatives

Equally, auxiliaries are not used in negatives in French:

*I **don't** like Mozart* = je n'aime pas Mozart

In emphatic uses

There is no verbal equivalent for the use of ***do*** in such expressions as *I do like your dress*. In emphatic uses, French may use an intensifying adverb (***beaucoup***, ***vraiment***):

*I **do** like your dress* = j'aime **beaucoup** ta robe

*I **do** think you should go* = je crois **vraiment** que tu devrais y aller

When referring back to another verb

In this case the verb ***to do*** is not translated at all:

*I live in Oxford and so **does** Lily* = j'habite à Oxford et Lily aussi

*she gets paid more than I **do*** = elle est payée plus que moi

*'I don't like carrots' – 'Neither **do** I'* = 'je n'aime pas les carottes' – 'moi non plus'

In polite requests

In polite requests the phrase ***je vous en prie*** or ***je t'en prie*** is useful:

***do** sit down* = asseyez-vous, **je vous en prie**

In imperatives

In French there is no use of an auxiliary verb in imperatives:

***don't** shut the door* = ne ferme pas la porte

***do** be quiet!* = tais-toi!

In tag questions

With tag questions like ***doesn't he?*** or ***didn't it?***, there is a general tag question ***n'est-ce pas?*** which will work in many cases:

*you like fish, **don't you**?* = tu aimes le poisson, **n'est-ce pas**?

With positive tag questions ***par hasard*** can often be useful as a translation:

*Lola didn't phone, **did she**?* = Lola n'a pas téléphoné **par hasard**?

In short answers

Where the answer ***yes*** is used to contradict a negative question or statement, ***si*** is often employed:

*'Marion didn't say that' – '**yes she did**'* = 'Marion n'a pas dit ça' – '**si**'

In response to a standard enquiry, the tag will not be translated:

*'do you like strawberries?' – '**yes I do**'* = 'aimez-vous les fraises?' – '**oui**'

For more examples, see the entry **do** I.

domestic appliance *n* appareil *m* électroménager.
domesticate *vtr* domestiquer.
dominant *adj* dominant/-e.
dominate *vtr*, *vi* dominer.
domineering *adj* autoritaire.
domino ▶504 *n* domino *m*; **to play ~es** jouer aux dominos.
donate *vtr* faire don de (**to** à).
donation *n* don *m* (**of** de; **à** to).
done I *adj* [*food*] cuit/-e; **well ~** bien cuit/-e.
II *excl* (deal) marché conclu!
IDIOMS **it's not the ~ thing** ça ne se fait pas.
donkey *n* âne *m*.
donor *n* **1** (of organ) donneur/-euse *m/f*; **2** (of money) donateur/-trice *m/f*.
doodle *vi* gribouiller.
doom *n* (of person) perte *f*; (of country) catastrophe *f*.
doomed *adj* condamné/-e; **to be ~ to failure** être voué/-e à l'échec.
door *n* (in building) porte *f* (**to** de); (in car, train) porte *f*, portière *f*; **behind closed ~s** à huis clos.
doorbell *n* sonnette *f*.
doorman *n* portier *m*.
doormat *n* paillasson *m*.
doorstep *n* pas *m* de porte.
doorway *n* **1** (frame) embrasure *f*; **2** (entrance) porte *f*, entrée *f*.
dope I○ *n* **1** cannabis *m*; **2** (fool) imbécile○ *mf*.
II *vtr* (Sport) doper [*horse, athlete*]; (gen) droguer [*person*].
dope test *n* (Sport) contrôle *m* antidopage.
dormant *adj* **1** [*emotion, talent*] latent/-e; **2** [*volcano*] en repos.
dormitory *n* **1** (GB) dortoir *m*; **2** (US Univ) résidence *f*, foyer *m*.
dormouse *n* muscardin *m*.
dose *n* dose *f* (**of** de); **a ~ of flu** une bonne grippe.
IDIOMS **he's all right in small ~s** il est supportable à doses homéopathiques.
dot *n* (gen) point *m*; (on fabric) pois *m*.
IDIOMS **at ten on the ~** à dix heures pile.
dote *vi* **to ~ on sb/sth** adorer qn/qch.
dotted line *n* pointillé *m*.
double I *n* **1** (drink) double *m*; **2** (of person) sosie *m*; (in film, play) doublure *f*.
II **doubles** *n pl* double *m*; **mixed ~s** double mixte.
III *adj* double; **with a ~ 'n'** avec deux 'n'; **two ~ four (244)** deux cent quarante-quatre.
IV *adv* **1 ~ the amount** deux fois plus; **2 to see ~** voir double; **3** [*fold, bend*] en deux.
V *vtr* doubler [*amount, dose*]; multiplier [qch] par deux [*number*].
VI *vi* **1** [*sales, prices, salaries*] doubler; **2 to ~ for sb** (actor) doubler qn; **3 the sofa ~s as a bed** le canapé fait aussi lit.
IDIOMS **on** or **at the ~** au plus vite.
■ **double back** rebrousser chemin.
double act *n* duo *m*.
double-barrelled name *n* (GB) ≈ nom *m* à particule.
double bass ▶586 *n* contrebasse *f*.
double bed *n* lit *m* double, grand lit.
double-breasted *adj* [*jacket*] croisé/-e.
double-check *vtr* vérifier [qch] à nouveau.
double chin *n* double menton *m*.
double cream *n* (GB) ≈ crème *f* fraîche.
double-cross○ *vtr* doubler, trahir [*person*].
double-decker *n* (GB) (bus) autobus *m* à impériale or à deux étages; (sandwich) sandwich *m* double.
double door *n* porte *f* à deux battants.
double Dutch○ *n* baragouinage○ *m*.
double glazing *n* double vitrage *m*.
double room *n* chambre *f* pour deux personnes.
double standard *n* **to have ~s** faire deux poids deux mesures.
double vision *n* **to have ~** voir double.
doubt I *n* doute *m*; **there is no ~ (that)** il ne fait aucun doute que; **to have no ~ (that)** être certain/-e que; **to be in ~** [*person*] être dans le doute; [*outcome*] être incertain/-e; **if** or **when in ~** dans le doute; **without (a) ~** sans aucun doute.
II *vtr* douter de [*fact, ability, honesty, person*]; **I ~ it!** j'en doute!; **I ~ if he'll come** je doute qu'il vienne.
doubtful *adj* **1** (unsure) incertain/-e; **2** [*character, activity, taste*] douteux/-euse.
dough *n* (Culin) pâte *f*.
doughnut, **donut** (US) *n* beignet *m*.
douse, **dowse** *vtr* éteindre [*fire*]; tremper [*person*]; **to ~ sth with petrol** arroser qch d'essence.
dove *n* colombe *f*.
Dover ▶448 *pr n* Douvres.
dowdy *adj* [*person*] mal fagoté/-e; [*clothes*] sans chic.
down[1]

■ **Note** When used to indicate vague direction, *down* often has no explicit translation in French: *to go down to London* = aller à Londres; *down in Brighton* = à Brighton.
– For examples and further usages, see the entry below.

I *adv* **1 to go** or **come ~** descendre; **to fall ~** tomber; **to sit ~ on the floor** s'asseoir par terre; **to pull ~ a blind** baisser un store; **~ below** en bas; **the telephone lines are ~** les lignes téléphoniques sont coupées; **face ~** [*fall*] face contre terre; [*lie*] à plat ventre; (in water) le visage dans l'eau; **2** (lower) **profits are well ~ on last year's** les bénéfices sont nettement inférieurs à ceux de l'année dernière; **to get one's weight ~** maigrir; **I'm ~ to my last cigarette** il ne me reste plus qu'une cigarette; **3** Sport **to be two sets ~** [*tennis player*] perdre par deux sets; **4** (as deposit) **to pay £40 ~** payer 40 livres sterling comptant.
II *prep* **to go ~ the street** descendre la rue; **to run ~ the hill** descendre la colline en

courant; **to go ~ town** aller en ville; **they live ~ the road** ils habitent un peu plus loin dans la rue.
III *adj* **1**○ **to feel ~** être déprimé/-e; **2** [*escalator*] qui descend; **3** [*computer*] en panne.
IDIOMS **it's ~ to you to do it** c'est à toi de le faire; **~ with tyrants!** à bas les tyrans!

down² *n* duvet *m*.

down-and-out *n* clochard/-e *m/f*.

downfall *n* chute *f*; **drink proved to be his ~** c'est la boisson qui a causé sa perte.

downhearted *adj* abattu/-e.

downhill *adv* **to go ~** [*person, vehicle*] descendre; **he's going ~** (declining) il est sur le déclin.

downhill skiing *n* ski *m* de piste.

down payment *n* acompte *m*.

downpour *n* averse *f*.

downright I *adj* [*insult*] véritable (*before n*); [*refusal*] catégorique; [*liar*] fieffé/-e (*before n*).
II *adv* [*stupid, rude*] carrément.

downstairs I *adj* [*room*] en bas; (on ground-floor) du rez-de-chaussée; **the ~ flat** (GB) or **apartment** (US) l'appartement du rez-de-chaussée.
II *adv* en bas; **to go** or **come ~** descendre (l'escalier).

downstream *adj, adv* en aval (**of** de); **to go ~** descendre le courant.

down-to-earth *adj* pratique; **she's very ~** (practical) elle a les pieds sur terre; (unpretentious) elle est très simple.

downtown *adj* (US) [*store, hotel*] du centre ville.

down under○ *adv* en Australie.

downward I *adj* [*movement*] vers le bas; **~ trend** (Econ) tendance *f* à la baisse.
II *adv* = **downwards**.

downwards *adv* (also **downward**) [*look*] vers le bas; **to slope ~** descendre en pente (**to** vers).

doze *vi* somnoler.
■ **doze off** (momentarily) s'assoupir; (to sleep) s'endormir.

dozen ▶632 *n* **1** (twelve) douzaine *f*; **a ~ eggs** une douzaine d'œufs; **£1 a ~** une livre sterling la douzaine; **2** (several) **~s of** des dizaines de [*people, things, times*].

drab *adj* terne.

draft I *n* **1** (of letter, speech) brouillon *m*; (of novel, play) ébauche *f*; (of contract, law) avant-projet *m*; **2** (on bank) traite *f* (**on** sur); **3** (US) (conscription) service *m* militaire; **4** (US) = **draught**.
II *vtr* **1** faire le brouillon de [*letter, speech*]; rédiger [*contract, law*]; **2** (US) (conscript) incorporer (**into** dans); **3** (GB) (transfer) détacher (**to** auprès de; **from** de).
■ **draft in** (GB) faire venir, amener [*police, troops*].

draftsman (US) = **draughtsman**.

drag I *n* **1**○ **what a ~!** quelle barbe○!; **2** [*person*] **in ~** en travesti.
II *adj* **1** [*artist*] de spectacle de travestis; **2** [*racing*] de dragsters.
III *vtr* **1** (trail) traîner; (pull) tirer [*boat, sledge*]; **to ~ sth along the ground** traîner qch par terre; **to ~ one's feet** traîner les pieds; (figurative) faire preuve de mauvaise volonté (**on** quant à); **don't ~ my mother into this** ne mêle pas ma mère à ça; **2** draguer [*river, lake*].
IV *vi* **1** [*hours, days*] traîner; [*story, plot*] traîner en longueur; **2** (trail) **to ~ in** [*hem, belt*] traîner dans [*mud*]; **3 to ~ on** tirer une bouffée de [*cigarette*].
■ **drag on** traîner en longueur.

drain I *n* **1** (in street) canalisation *f*; (in building) canalisation *f* d'évacuation; (pipe) descente *f* d'eau; (ditch) fossé *m* d'écoulement; **2** (of people, skills, money) hémorragie *f*; **to be a ~ on sb's resources** épuiser les ressources de qn.
II *vtr* **1** drainer [*land*]; **2** épuiser [*resources*]; **3** vider [*glass*]; **4** (Culin) égoutter [*pasta, vegetables*].
III *vi* **1** [*liquid*] s'écouler (**out of, from** de; **into** dans); **2** [*dishes, food*] s'égoutter.

drainage *n* (of land) drainage *m*; (system) tout-à-l'égout *m inv*.

draining board *n* égouttoir *m*.

drainpipe *n* descente *f*.

drake *n* canard *m* (mâle).

drama *n* (genre) théâtre *m*; (acting, directing) art *m* dramatique; (play, dramatic event) drame *m*; **TV/radio ~** dramatique *f*; **to make a ~ out of sth** faire tout un drame de qch.

dramatic *adj* [*art, effect, event*] dramatique; [*change, landscape*] spectaculaire; [*entrance*] théâtral/-e.

dramatize *vtr* **1** (for stage) adapter [qch] à la scène; (for screen) adapter [qch] à l'écran; (for radio) adapter [qch] pour la radio; **2** (make dramatic) donner un caractère dramatique à; (excessively) dramatiser.

drape I *n* (US) rideau *m*.
II *vtr* draper (**in, with** de).

drastic *adj* [*policy, measure*] draconien/-ienne; [*reduction, remedy*] drastique; [*effect*] catastrophique; [*change*] radical/-e.

draught (GB), **draft** (US) *n* **1** (cold air) courant *m* d'air; **2 on ~** [*beer*] à la pression.

draughts ▶504 *n* (GB) jeu *m* de dames; **to play ~** jouer aux dames.

draughtsman (GB), **draftsman** (US) *n* dessinateur/-trice *m/f*.

draughty (GB), **drafty** (US) *adj* plein/-e de courants d'air.

draw I *n* **1** (in lottery) tirage *m* (au sort); **2** (Sport) match *m* nul; **it was a ~** (in race) ils sont arrivés ex aequo.
II *vtr* **1** faire [*picture, plan*]; dessiner [*person, object*]; tracer [*line*]; **2** (pull) [*animal, engine*] tirer; **3** tirer [*conclusion*] (**from** de); **4** (attract) attirer [*crowd*] (**to** vers); susciter [*reaction*]; **to ~ sb into** mêler qn à [*conversation*]; entraîner qn dans [*argument, battle*]; **5** retirer [*money*] (**from** de); tirer [*cheque*] (**on** sur); toucher [*wages, pension*]; **6** (in lottery) tirer [qch] au sort [*ticket*]; **7** sortir [*sword, knife*]; **to ~ a gun on sb** sortir un pistolet et le braquer sur qn.
III *vi* **1** (make picture) dessiner; **2 to ~ ahead**

(**of sb/sth**) (in race) gagner du terrain (sur qn/qch); (in contest, election) prendre de l'avance (sur qn/qch); **to ~ alongside** [*boat*] accoster; **to ~ near** [*time*] approcher; **to ~ level** se retrouver au même niveau; **3** (in match) faire match nul.
IDIOMS **to ~ the line** fixer des limites; **to ~ the line at doing** se refuser à faire.
■ **draw away** (move off) s'éloigner (**from** de); (move ahead) prendre de l'avance (**from** sur).
■ **draw in**: ¶ **~ in 1** [*days, nights*] raccourcir; **2** [*bus*] arriver; [*train*] entrer en gare; ¶ **~ [sth] in** rentrer [*stomach, claws*].
■ **draw out**: ¶ **~ out** [*train, bus*] partir; **the train drew out of the station** le train a quitté la gare; ¶ **~ [sth] out 1** (remove) tirer [*purse, knife*] (**of** de); retirer [*nail, cork*] (**of** de); **2** (withdraw) retirer [*money*]; **3** (prolong) faire durer; ¶ **~ [sb] out** faire sortir [qn] de sa coquille.
■ **draw up 1** établir [*contract*]; dresser, établir [*list, report*]; **2** approcher [*chair*] (**to** de).
drawback *n* inconvénient *m*.
drawer *n* tiroir *m*.
drawing *n* dessin *m*.
drawing board *n* planche *f* à dessin.
drawing pin *n* punaise *f*.
drawing room *n* salon *m*.
drawl *n* voix *f* traînante.
drawn *adj* **1 to look ~** avoir les traits tirés; **2** [*game, match*] nul/nulle.
dread *vtr* appréhender (**doing** de faire); (stronger) redouter (**doing** de faire).
dreadful *adj* épouvantable, affreux/-euse.
dreadfully *adv* [*disappointed*] terriblement; [*suffer*] affreusement; [*behave*] abominablement; **I'm ~ sorry** je suis navré.
dream I *n* rêve *m*.
II *adj* [*house, car, vacation*] de rêve.
III *vtr* rêver (**that** que).
IV *vi* rêver; **he dreamt about** or **of sth/doing** il a rêvé de qch/qu'il faisait; **I wouldn't ~ of selling the house** il ne me viendrait jamais à l'esprit de vendre la maison.
■ **dream up** concevoir [*idea*]; imaginer [*character, plot*].
dreamer *n* **1** (inattentive person) rêveur/-euse *m/f*; **2** (idealist) idéaliste *mf*.
dreary *adj* [*weather, landscape, life*] morne; [*person*] ennuyeux/-euse.
dredge *vtr* draguer [*river*].
dregs *n pl* (of wine) lie *f*; (of coffee) marc *m*.
drench *vtr* (in rain, sweat) tremper (**in** de).
dress I *n* **1** (garment) robe *f*; **2** (clothes) tenue *f*; **formal ~** tenue habillée.
II *vtr* **1** habiller [*person*]; **to get ~ed** s'habiller; **to be ~ed in** être vêtu/-e de; **2** assaisonner [*salad*]; préparer [*meat, fish*]; **3** panser [*wound*].
■ **dress up** (smartly) s'habiller; (in fancy dress) se déguiser (**as** en).
dress circle *n* premier balcon *m*.
dresser *n* **1 to be a stylish ~** s'habiller avec chic; **2** (for dishes) buffet *m*; **3** (US) (for clothes) commode-coiffeuse *f*.
dressing *n* **1** (Med) pansement *m*; **2** (sauce) assaisonnement *m*; **3** (US) (stuffing) farce *f*.
dressing gown *n* robe *f* de chambre.
dressing room *n* loge *f*.
dressing table *n* coiffeuse *f*.
dressmaker ▶ 626 *n* couturière *f*.
dress rehearsal *n* (répétition *f*) générale *f*.
dress sense *n* **to have ~** s'habiller avec goût.
dribble I *n* (of liquid) filet *m*; (of saliva) bave *f*.
II *vi* **1** [*liquid*] dégouliner (**on, onto** sur; **from** de); [*person*] baver; **2** (Sport) dribler.
dried *adj* [*fruit, herb*] sec/sèche; [*flower, vegetable*] séché/-e; [*milk, egg*] en poudre.
drier *n* séchoir *m*.
drift I *n* **1 the ~ of the current** le sens du courant; **2** (of snow) congère *f*; (of leaves) tas *m*; **3** (meaning) sens *m* (général).
II *vi* **1** [*boat*] dériver; [*balloon*] voler à la dérive; [*smoke, fog*] flotter; **2** [*snow*] former des congères *fpl*; [*leaves*] s'amonceler; **3 to ~ through life** errer sans but dans la vie.
■ **drift apart** [*friends*] se perdre de vue; [*lovers*] se détacher progressivement l'un de l'autre.
driftwood *n* bois *m* flotté.
drill I *n* **1** (for wood, masonry) perceuse *f*; (for oil) trépan *m*; (for mining) foreuse *f*; (for teeth) roulette *f*; **2** (Mil) exercice *m*; **3 fire ~** exercice *m* d'évacuation en cas d'incendie.
II *vtr* **1** percer [*hole, metal*]; passer la roulette à [*tooth*]; **2** (Mil) entraîner [*soldiers*].
III *vi* **1** (in wood, masonry) percer un trou (**into** dans); **to ~ for sth** faire des forages pour trouver qch; **2** (Mil) [*soldiers*] faire de l'exercice.
drink I *n* boisson *f*; **to have a ~** boire quelque chose; (alcoholic) prendre un verre.
II *vtr* boire (**from** dans).
III *vi* boire (**from** dans); **don't ~ and drive** ne conduisez pas si vous avez bu.
drink-driving *n* (GB) conduite *f* en état d'ivresse.
drinking water *n* eau *f* potable.
drip I *n* **1** (drop) goutte *f* (qui tombe); **2** (GB Med) **to be on a ~** être sous perfusion.
II *vi* **1** [*liquid*] tomber goutte à goutte; **to ~ from** or **off** dégouliner de; **2** [*tap, branches*] goutter; [*washing*] s'égoutter.
drive I *n* **1 to go for a ~** aller faire un tour (en voiture); **it's a 40 km ~** il y a 40 km de route; **2** (campaign) campagne *f* (**against** contre; **for, towards** pour; **to do** pour faire); **3** (motivation) dynamisme *m*; **4** (Comput) entraînement *m* de disques; **5** (Aut) transmission *f*; **6** (also **~way**) allée *f*; **7** (Sport) drive *m*.
II *vtr* **1** conduire [*vehicle, passenger*]; piloter [*racing car*]; **I ~ 15 km every day** je fais 15 km en voiture chaque jour; **to ~ sth into** rentrer qch dans [*garage, space*]; **2** (compel) pousser [*person*] (**to do** à faire); **3** (power, propel) actionner [*engine, pump*]; **4 to ~ a nail through sth** enfoncer un clou dans qch.
III *vi* conduire; **to ~ along** rouler; **to ~ to work** aller au travail en voiture; **to ~ into** entrer dans [*car park*]; rentrer dans [*tree*].

■ **drive back 1** repousser [*people, animals*]; **2** ramener [*passenger*].

driver *n* **1** conducteur/-trice *m/f*; **~s** (motorists) automobilistes *mfpl*; **2** (of taxi) chauffeur *m*.

driver's license *n* (US) permis *m* de conduire.

driving I *n* conduite *f*.
II *adj* [*rain*] battant/-e; [*wind, hail*] cinglant/-e.

driving force *n* (person) force *f* agissante (**behind** de); (money, ambition) moteur *m* (**behind** de).

driving instructor ▶ 626 *n* moniteur/-trice *m/f* d'auto-école.

driving lesson *n* leçon *f* de conduite.

driving licence *n* (GB) permis *m* de conduire.

driving test *n* examen *m* du permis de conduire; **to take/pass one's ~** passer/réussir son permis (de conduire).

drizzle I *n* bruine *f*.
II *vi* bruiner.

drone *n* **1** (of engine) ronronnement *m*; (of insects) bourdonnement *m*; **2** (Zool) faux bourdon *m*.

drool *vi* baver; **to ~ over sb/sth** s'extasier sur qn/qch.

droop *vi* [*eyelids, head, shoulders*] tomber; [*plant*] commencer à se faner.

drop I *n* **1** (of liquid) goutte *f*; **2** (decrease) baisse *f* (**in** de); **a 5% ~ in sth** une baisse de 5% de qch; **3** (fall) **there's a ~ of 100 m** il y a un dénivelé de 100 m; **a steep ~ on either side** une pente abrupte de chaque côté; **a sheer ~** un à-pic; **4** (delivery) (from aircraft) largage *m*.
II *vtr* **1** (by accident) laisser tomber; (on purpose) lâcher; **2** [*aircraft*] parachuter [*person, supplies*]; larguer [*bomb*]; **3** (also **~ off**) déposer [*person, object*]; **4** (lower) baisser [*eyes, voice, level, price*]; **5 to ~ a hint about sth** faire allusion à qch; **to ~ sb a line** envoyer un mot à qn; **6** laisser tomber [*friend, school subject*]; renoncer à [*habit, idea*].
III *vi* **1** (fall) [*object*] tomber; [*person*] (deliberately) se laisser tomber; (by accident) tomber; **the plane ~ped to an altitude of 1,000 m** l'avion est descendu à une altitude de 1000 m; **2 the cliff ~s into the sea** la falaise tombe dans la mer; **3** (decrease) baisser; **to ~ (from sth) to sth** tomber (de qch) à qch.
IDIOMS **a ~ in the ocean** une goutte d'eau dans la mer.
■ **drop in** passer; **to ~ in on sb** passer voir qn.
■ **drop off 1** (fall off) tomber; **2 ~ off (to sleep)** s'endormir; **3** (decrease) diminuer.
■ **drop out 1** (fall out) tomber (**of** de); **2** (from race) se désister; (from project) se retirer; (from school, university) abandonner ses études; (from society) se marginaliser.

dropout *n* marginal/-e *m/f*.

droppings *n pl* (of mouse, sheep) crottes *fpl*; (of horse) crottin *m*; (of bird) fiente *f*.

drop shot *n* (Sport) amorti *m*.

drought *n* sécheresse *f*.

drown I *vtr* **1** noyer [*person, animal*]; **2** (also **~ out**) couvrir [*sound*].
II *vi* se noyer.
IDIOMS **to ~ one's sorrows** noyer son chagrin dans l'alcool.

drowsy *adj* à moitié endormi/-e; **to feel ~** avoir envie de dormir.

drug I *n* **1** (Med) médicament *m*; **to be on ~s** prendre des médicaments; **2** (narcotic) drogue *f*; **to be on** or **to take ~s** (gen) se droguer; [*athlete*] se doper.
II *vtr* administrer des somnifères à [*person*].

drug abuse *n* consommation *f* de stupéfiants.

drug addict *n* toxicomane *mf*.

drugstore *n* (US) drugstore *m*.

drug test *n* (Sport) contrôle *m* antidopage.

drum I ▶ 586 *n* **1** (Mus) tambour *m*; **2** (barrel) bidon *m*; (larger) baril *m*.
II drums *n pl* batterie *f*; **to play ~s** jouer de la batterie.
III *vtr* **to ~ one's fingers** tambouriner des doigts (**on** sur); **to ~ sth into sb** enfoncer qch dans le crâne de qn○.
■ **drum up** trouver [*business*]; racoler [*customers*].

drummer ▶ 626, ▶ 586 *n* (in army) tambour *m*; (jazz or pop) batteur *m*; (classical) percussionniste *mf*.

drumstick *n* **1** (Mus) baguette *f* de tambour; **2** (of chicken, turkey) pilon *m*.

drunk I *n* (also **drunkard**) ivrogne *m*.
II *adj* ivre; **to get ~** s'enivrer (**on** de).

drunken *adj* [*person*] ivre; [*party*] bien arrosé/-e; [*sleep*] éthylique; [*state*] d'ivresse.

dry I *adj* **1** sec/sèche; **to keep sth ~** tenir qch au sec; **on ~ land** sur la terre ferme; **a ~ day** un jour sans pluie; **2** [*wit, person, remark*] pince-sans-rire *inv*; [*book*] aride.
II *vtr* faire sécher [*clothes, washing*]; sécher [*meat, produce*]; **to ~ the dishes** essuyer la vaisselle; **to ~ one's hands** se sécher les mains.
III *vi* [*clothes, washing*] sécher.
■ **dry out 1** [*cloth*] sécher; [*plant*] se dessécher; **2**○ [*alcoholic*] se faire désintoxiquer.
■ **dry up**: ¶ **~ up 1** [*river, well*] s'assécher; **2** (run out) se tarir; **3** (dry the dishes) essuyer la vaisselle; ¶ **~ [sth] up** essuyer [*dishes*].

dry-clean *vtr* **to have sth ~ed** faire nettoyer qch (chez le teinturier).

dry-cleaner's ▶ 626 *n* teinturerie *f*.

dryer *n* séchoir *m*.

DTP *n* (*abbr* = **desktop publishing**) PAO *f*.

dual *adj* double.

dual carriageway *n* (GB) route *f* à quatre voies.

dual nationality *n* double nationalité *f*.

dub *vtr* (into foreign language) doubler (**into** en); **~bed film** film doublé.

dubious *adj* [*reputation, answer*] douteux/-euse; [*claim*] suspect/-e.

duchess ▶ 498 *n* duchesse *f*.

duck I *n* canard *m*.
II *vtr* **1 to ~ one's head** baisser vivement la

tête; **2** (dodge) esquiver [*blow*]; **3** se dérober de [*responsibility*].
III *vi* baisser vivement la tête; [*boxer*] esquiver un coup; **to ~ behind** se cacher derrière.

duckling *n* caneton *m*.

duct *n* **1** (for air, water) conduit *m*; (for wiring) canalisation *f*; **2** (Anat, Med) conduit *m*.

dud○ *adj* [*banknote*] faux/fausse (*before n*); [*cheque*] en bois○; [*book, movie*] nul/nulle○.

due I *n* dû *m*; **I must give her her ~, she**... il faut lui rendre cette justice, elle...
II *adj* **1** (payable) **to be/fall ~** arriver/venir à échéance; **the rent is ~ on the 6th** le loyer doit être payé le 6; **the balance ~** le solde dû; **2** (owed) **the respect ~ to him** le respect auquel il a droit, le respect qu'on lui doit; **3 we are ~ (for) a wage increase soon** nos salaires doivent bientôt être augmentés; **4 after ~ consideration** après mûre réflexion; **in ~ course** (at the proper time) en temps voulu; (later) plus tard; **5 to be ~ to do** devoir faire; **to be ~ (in)** [*train, bus*] être attendu/-e; [*person*] devoir arriver.
III *adv* **to face ~ north** [*building*] être orienté/-e plein nord; **to go ~ south** aller droit vers le sud.
IV **due to** *phr* en raison de; **to be ~ to** [*delay, cancellation*] être dû/due à; **~ to unforeseen circumstances** pour des raisons indépendantes de notre volonté.

dues *n pl* (for membership) cotisation *f*; (for import, taxes) droits *mpl*.

duet *n* duo *m*.

duffel bag *n* sac *m* (de) marin.

duffel coat *n* duffle-coat *m*.

duke ▶ **498** *n* duc *m*.

dull I *adj* **1** [*person, book*] ennuyeux/-euse; [*life, journey*] monotone; [*appearance*] triste; [*weather*] maussade; **2** [*eye, colour, complexion*] terne.
II *vtr* ternir [*shine*]; émousser [*blade, pain*].

duly *adv* (in proper fashion) dûment; (as expected, as arranged) comme prévu.

dumb *adj* **1** muet/muette; **to be struck ~** rester muet/muette (**with** de); **2**○ (stupid) [*person*] bête; [*question, idea*] idiot/-e.

dumbfounded *adj* abasourdi/-e.

dummy I *n* **1** (model) mannequin *m*; **2** (GB) (for baby) tétine *f*.
II *adj* faux/fausse.

dump I *n* **1** (for rubbish) décharge *f* publique; **2** (Mil) **arms ~** dépôt *m* d'armes; **3**○ (town, village) trou○ *m*; (house) baraque○ *f* minable.
II *vtr* **1** jeter [*refuse*]; ensevelir [*nuclear waste*]; déverser [*sewage*]; **2**○ plaquer○ [*boyfriend*]; se débarasser de [*car*].
IDIOMS **to be down in the ~s**○ avoir le cafard○.

dumper (truck), **dump truck** *n* tombereau *m*.

dunce *n* cancre *m* (**at, in** en).

dune *n* dune *f*.

dung *n* (for manure) fumier *m*.

dungarees *n pl* (fashionwear) salopette *f*; (workwear) bleu *m* de travail.

Dunkirk ▶ **448** *pr n* Dunkerque.

duo *n* duo *m*.

duplicate I *n* (of document) double *m* (**of** de); (of painting, cassette) copie *f*.
II *adj* **1** [*cheque, receipt*] en duplicata; **a ~ key** un double de clé; **2** (in two parts) [*form, invoice*] en deux exemplaires.
III *vtr* **1** (copy) faire un double de [*document*]; copier [*painting, cassette*]; **2** (photocopy) photocopier.

durable *adj* [*material*] résistant/-e; [*equipment*] solide; [*friendship, tradition*] durable.

duration *n* durée *f*.

duress *n* **under ~** sous la contrainte.

during *prep* pendant, au cours de.

dusk *n* nuit *f* tombante, crépuscule *m*; **at ~** à la nuit tombante.

dust I *n* poussière *f*.
II *vtr* épousseter [*furniture*]; saupoudrer [*cake*] (**with** de, avec).

dustbin *n* (GB) poubelle *f*.

dust cover *n* (on book) jaquette *f*; (on furniture) housse *f* (de protection).

duster *n* chiffon *m* (à poussière).

dustman *n* (GB) éboueur *m*.

dustpan *n* pelle *f* (à poussière).

dusty *adj* poussiéreux/-euse.

Dutch ▶ **553** I *n* **1** (people) **the ~** les Néerlandais *mpl*; **2** (language) néerlandais *m*.
II *adj* (gen) néerlandais/-e; [*embassy*] des Pays-Bas.
IDIOMS **to go ~**○ payer chacun sa part; **to go ~ with sb**○ faire fifty-fifty avec qn○.

duty *n* **1** (obligation) devoir *m* (**to** envers); **in the course of ~** (Mil) en service; (gen) dans l'exercice de ses fonctions; **2** (task) fonction *f*; **to take up one's duties** prendre ses fonctions; **3** (work) service *m*; **to be on/off ~** (Mil, Med) être/ne pas être de service; (Sch) être/ne pas être de surveillance; **4** (tax) taxe *f*; **customs duties** droits *mpl* de douane.

duty-free *adj, adv* hors taxe(s).

duvet *n* (GB) couette *f*.

duvet cover *n* housse *f* de couette.

dwarf *n, adj* nain/naine (*m/f*).

dwell *v* ■ **dwell on** (talk about) s'étendre sur; (think about) s'attarder sur.

dwindle *vi* diminuer.

dye I *n* teinture *f*.
II *vtr* teindre; **to ~ sth red** teindre qch en rouge; **to ~ one's hair** se teindre les cheveux.

dying *adj* [*person, animal*] mourant/-e; [*art*] en voie de disparition.

dyke *n* **1** (on coast) digue *f*; (beside ditch) remblai *m*; **2** (GB) (ditch) fossé *m*.

dynamic *adj* dynamique.

dynamite *n* dynamite *f*.

dynamo *n* **1** dynamo *f*; **2**○ **he's a real ~** il déborde d'énergie.

dysentery ▶ **533** *n* dysenterie *f*.

dyslexic *n, adj* dyslexique (*mf*).

Ee

e, **E** *n* **1** (letter) e, E *m*; **2 E** (Mus) mi *m*.

each I *det* [*person, group, object*] chaque *inv*; **~ morning** chaque matin, tous les matins; **~ one** chacun/-e.

II *pron* chacun/-e *m/f*; **~ of you** chacun/-e de vous, chacun/-e d'entre vous; **oranges at 30p ~** des oranges à 30 pence (la) pièce.

each other *pron*

■ **Note** *each other* is very often translated by using a reflexive pronoun (*nous, vous, se, s'*).

(also **one another**) **they know ~** ils se connaissent; **to help ~** s'entraider; **kept apart from ~** séparés l'un de l'autre.

eager *adj* [*person, acceptance*] enthousiaste; [*face*] où se lit l'enthousiasme; [*student*] plein d'enthousiasme; **~ to do** (keen) désireux/-euse de faire; (impatient) pressé/-e de faire; **~ for sth** avide de qch; **to be ~ to please** chercher à faire plaisir.

eagle *n* aigle *m*.

ear ▶413 *n* **1** oreille *f*; **2** (of wheat, corn) épi *m*.

IDIOMS **to play it by ~** improviser.

earache *n* **to have ~** (GB) or **an ~** avoir une otite.

eardrum *n* tympan *m*.

earl *n* comte *m*.

early I *adj* **1** (one of the first) [*years, novels*] premier/-ière (*before n*); **~ man** les premiers hommes; **2** [*delivery*] rapide; [*vegetable, fruit*] précoce; **to have an ~ lunch/night** déjeuner/se coucher tôt; **in ~ childhood** dans la petite or première enfance; **at an ~ age** à un très jeune âge; **to be in one's ~ thirties** avoir entre 30 et 35 ans; **at the earliest** au plus tôt; **in the ~ spring** au début du printemps; **in the ~ afternoon** en début d'après-midi.

II *adv* **1** tôt; **to get up ~** se lever tôt or de bonne heure; **it's too ~** il est trop tôt; **as I said earlier** comme je l'ai déjà dit; **2** (sooner than expected) en avance; **I'm a bit ~** je suis un peu en avance.

earn *vtr* **1** [*person*] gagner [*money*]; [*investment*] rapporter [*interest*]; **to ~ a** or **one's living** gagner sa vie; **2 to ~ sb's respect** se faire respecter de qn.

earnest I *n* **in ~** [*speak*] sérieusement; [*begin*] vraiment, pour de bon.

II *adj* [*person*] sérieux/-ieuse; [*wish*] sincère.

earnings *n pl* (of person) salaire *m*, revenu *m* (**from** de); (of company) gains *mpl* (**from** de); (from shares) (taux *m* de) rendement *m*.

earphones *n pl* (over ears) casque *m*; (in ears) écouteurs *mpl*.

earring *n* boucle *f* d'oreille.

earth I *n* **1** terre *f*; **2**° **how/where/who on ~...?** comment/où/qui donc or diable°...?; **nothing on ~ would persuade me to come** je ne viendrais pour rien au monde.

II *vtr* (GB) mettre [qch] à la terre.

earthenware *n* faïence *f*.

earthquake *n* tremblement *m* de terre.

earth tremor *n* secousse *f* sismique.

earwig *n* perce-oreille *m*.

ease I *n* **1** (lack of difficulty) facilité *f*; **2 to feel/to be at ~** se sentir/être à l'aise; **to put sb's mind at ~** rassurer qn (**about** à propos de).

II *vtr* **1** atténuer [*pain, tension, pressure*]; réduire [*congestion*]; diminuer [*burden*]; **2** faciliter [*communication, transition*]; **3 to ~ sth into** introduire qch délicatement dans.

III *vi* [*tension, pain, pressure*] s'atténuer; [*rain*] diminuer.

■ **ease off** [*business*] ralentir; [*demand*] se réduire; [*traffic, rain*] diminuer; [*person*] relâcher son effort.

■ **ease up** [*tense person, storm*] se calmer; [*authorities*] relâcher la discipline; **to ~ up on sb/on sth** être moins sévère envers qn/pour qch.

easel *n* chevalet *m*.

easily *adv* facilement; **it's ~ the best** c'est de loin le meilleur; **she could ~ die** elle pourrait bien mourir.

east I *n* **1** (compass direction) est *m*; **2 the East** (Orient) l'Orient *m*; (part of country) l'Est *m*.

II *adj* (gen) est *inv*; [*wind*] d'est.

III *adv* [*move*] vers l'est; [*live, lie*] à l'est (**of** de).

Easter I *n* Pâques *m*; **at ~** à Pâques; **Happy ~** Joyeuses Pâques.

II *adj* [*Sunday, egg*] de Pâques.

eastern *adj* **1** [*coast*] est *inv*; [*town, accent*] de l'est; **Eastern Europe** l'Europe de l'Est; **~ France** l'est de la France; **2** (also **Eastern**) (oriental) oriental/-e.

easy I *adj* **1** [*job, question, life, victim*] facile; **it's ~ to do** c'est facile à faire; **it's ~ to make a mistake** il est facile de se tromper; **it isn't ~ to do** ce n'est pas facile à faire; **it isn't ~ to park** il n'est pas facile de se garer; **to make it** or **things easier** faciliter les choses (**for** pour); **2** (relaxed) [*smile, grace*] décontracté/-e; [*style*] plein/-e d'aisance; **at an ~ pace** d'un pas tranquille; **3**° **I'm ~** ça m'est égal.

II *adv* **1 to take it** or **things ~** ne pas s'en faire; **2**° **to go ~ on** or **with** y aller doucement avec.

easygoing *adj* [*person*] accommodant/-e; [*manner, attitude*] souple.

eat I *vtr* manger [*food*]; prendre [*meal*].

II *vi* manger.

■ **eat out** aller au restaurant.

eavesdrop *vi* écouter aux portes.

ebb I *n* reflux *m*.

II *vi* [*tide*] descendre; [*enthusiasm*] décliner.

ebony *n* **1** (wood) ébène *f*; **2** ▶ 438 (colour) noir *m* d'ébène.
EC *n* (*abbr* = **European Community**) CEE *f*.
eccentric *n, adj* excentrique (*mf*).
echo I *n* écho *m*.
II *vtr* **1** répercuter [*sound*]; **2** reprendre [*ideas, opinions*].
III *vi* retentir, résonner.
eclipse I *n* éclipse *f* (**of** de).
II *vtr* éclipser.
ecologist *n, adj* écologiste (*mf*).
ecology *n* écologie *f*.
economic *adj* (gen) économique; (profitable) rentable.
economical *adj* [*person*] économe; [*machine, method*] économique.
economics *n* (science) économie *f*; (subject of study) sciences *fpl* économiques; (financial aspects) aspects *mpl* économiques (**of** de).
economist ▶ 626 *n* économiste *mf*.
economize *vtr, vi* économiser.
economy *n* économie *f*.
ecstasy *n* **1** extase *f*; **2** (drug) ecstasy *m*.
ecu, **ECU** ▶ 582 *n* (*abbr* = **European Currency Unit**) écu *m*, ÉCU *m*.
Eden *pr n* Éden *m*, paradis *m* terrestre.
edge I *n* **1** (outer limit) bord *m*; (of wood, clearing) lisière *f*; **the film had us on the ~ of our seats** le film nous a tenus en haleine; **2** (of blade) tranchant *m*; **3** (of book, plank) tranche *f*; **4 to be on ~** [*person*] être énervé/-e.
II *vi* **to ~ forward** avancer doucement; **to ~ towards** s'approcher à petits pas de.
edgeways, **edgewise** *adv* [*move*] latéralement; [*lay, put*] sur le côté.
IDIOMS **I can't get a word in ~** je n'arrive pas à placer un mot.
edible *adj* comestible.
Edinburgh ▶ 448 *pr n* Édimbourg.
edit *vtr* **1** (in publishing) éditer; **2** (cut) couper [*text, version*]; **3** monter [*film, programme*].
edition *n* édition *f*.
editor ▶ 626 *n* (of newspaper) rédacteur/-trice *m/f* en chef (**of** de); (of book, manuscript) correcteur/-trice *m/f*; (of writer, works, anthology) éditeur/-trice *m/f*; (of film) monteur/-euse *m/f*.
editorial I *n* éditorial *m* (**on** sur).
II *adj* **1** (in journalism) de la rédaction, rédactionnel/-elle; **2** (in publishing) éditorial/-e.
educate *vtr* **1** [*teacher*] instruire; [*parent*] assurer l'instruction de; **to be ~d in Paris** faire ses études à Paris; **2** informer [*public*] (**about, in** sur).
educated *adj* [*person, classes*] instruit/-e; [*accent*] élégant/-e.
education *n* **1** éducation *f*, instruction *f*; **health ~** hygiène *f*; **2** (formal schooling) études *fpl*; **to have had a university** or **college ~** avoir fait des études supérieures; **3** (national system) enseignement *m*.
educational *adj* **1** [*establishment*] d'enseignement; **2** [*game, programme*] éducatif/-ive; [*talk*] instructif/-ive.
EEC *n* (*abbr* = **European Economic Community**) CEE *f*.
eel *n* anguille *f*.
eerie *adj* [*silence, place*] étrange et inquiétant/-e.
effect I *n* **1** effet *m* (**of** de; **on** sur); **to take ~** [*price increases*] prendre effet; [*pills, anaesthetic*] commencer à agir; **to come into ~** [*law, rate*] entrer en vigueur; **she dresses like that for ~** elle s'habille comme ça pour faire de l'effet; **2** (repercussions) répercussions *fpl* (**of** de; **on** sur).
II **effects** *n pl* effets *mpl*.
III *vtr* effectuer [*repair, sale, change*].
IV **in effect** *phr* en fait, en réalité.
effective *adj* efficace.
effectively *adv* **1** (efficiently) efficacement; **2** (in effect) en fait, en réalité.
effeminate *adj* efféminé/-e.
efficiency *n* (of person, method, organization) efficacité *f* (**in doing** à faire); (of machine) rendement *m*.
efficient *adj* **1** [*person, management*] efficace (**at doing** pour ce qui est de faire); **2** [*machine*] économique.
effort *n* effort *m*; **to make the ~** faire l'effort; **to spare no ~** ne pas ménager ses efforts; **to be worth the ~** en valoir la peine; **it is an ~ to do** il est pénible de faire.
eg (*abbr* = **exempli gratia**) par ex.
egg *n* œuf *m*.
■ **egg on** pousser [*person*].
eggcup *n* coquetier *m*.
eggplant *n* (US) aubergine *f*.
egg white *n* blanc *m* d'œuf.
egg yolk *n* jaune *m* d'œuf.
ego *n* **1** amour-propre *m*; **it boosted his ~** ça lui a redonné confiance en lui-même; **2** (in psychology) moi *m*, ego *m*.
egoism *n* égoïsme *m*.
egoist *n* égoïste *mf*.
egotist *n* égotiste *mf*.
Egypt ▶ 448 *pr n* Égypte *f*.
eiderdown *n* édredon *m*.
eight ▶ 389, 434 *n, pron, det* huit (*m*) *inv*.
eighteen ▶ 389, 434 *n, pron, det* dix-huit (*m*) *inv*.
eighteenth ▶ 456, 498 I *n* **1** (in order) dix-huitième *mf*; **2** (of month) dix-huit *m inv*; **3** (fraction) dix-huitième *m*.
II *adj, adv* dix-huitième.
eighth ▶ 456, 498 I *n* **1** (in order) huitième *mf*; **2** (of month) huit *m inv*; **3** (fraction) huitième *m*.
II *adj, adv* huitième.
eighties ▶ 389, 456 *n pl* **1** (era) **the ~** les années *fpl* quatre-vingt; **2** (age) **to be in one's ~** avoir entre quatre-vingts et quatre-vingt-dix ans.
eightieth *n, adj, adv* quatre-vingtième (*mf*).
eighty ▶ 389 *n, pron, det* quatre-vingts (*m*).
eighty-one *n, pron, det* quatre-vingt-un (*m*).
Éire ▶ 448 *pr n* Éire *f*, République *f* d'Irlande.
either I *pron, quantif* **1** (one or other) l'un/-e ou l'autre; **take ~ (of them)** prends l'un/-e ou

l'autre; **I don't like ~ (of them)** je n'aime ni l'un/-e ni l'autre; **'which book do you want?'—'~'** 'quel livre veux-tu?'—'n'importe'; **2** (both) **~ of the two is possible** les deux sont possibles.
II *det* **1** (one or the other) n'importe lequel/laquelle; **take ~ road** prenez n'importe laquelle des deux routes; **I can't see ~ child** je ne vois aucun des deux enfants; **2** (both) **in ~ case** dans un cas comme dans l'autre; **~ way, it will be difficult** de toute manière, ce sera difficile.
III *adv* non plus; **I can't do it ~** je ne peux pas le faire non plus.
IV *conj* **1** (as alternatives) **~...or...** soit...soit..., (ou)...ou...; **2** (in the negative) **I wouldn't believe ~ Patrick or Emily** je ne croirais ni Patrick ni Emily.
eject I *vtr* **1** [*machine, system*] rejeter [*waste*]; [*volcano*] cracher [*lava*]; **2** faire sortir [*cassette*]; **3** expulser [*troublemaker*].
II *vi* [*pilot*] s'éjecter.
eke *v* ■ **eke out** faire durer [*income, supplies*] (**by** à force de; **by doing** en faisant); **to ~ out a living** essayer de joindre les deux bouts.
elaborate I *adj* [*excuse*] compliqué/-e; [*network, plan*] complexe; [*design*] travaillé/-e; [*painting, sculpture*] ouvragé/-e.
II *vtr* élaborer [*theory*].
III *vi* entrer dans les détails; **to ~ on** s'étendre sur [*proposal*]; développer [*remark*].
elapse *vi* s'écouler.
elastic *n, adj* élastique (*m*).
elasticated *adj* élastique.
elastic band *n* élastique *m*.
elated *adj* transporté/-e de joie.
elbow *n* coude *m*.
elbowroom *n* (room to move) espace *m* vital; (figurative) marge *f* de manœuvre.
elder I *n* **1** (older person) aîné/-e *m/f*; (of tribe, group) ancien *m*; **2** (tree) sureau *m*.
II *adj* aîné/-e; **the ~ girl** l'aînée *f*, la fille aînée.
elderly I *n* **the ~** les personnes *fpl* âgées.
II *adj* [*person, population*] âgé/-e.
eldest I *n* aîné/-e *m/f*.
II *adj* aîné/-e; **the ~ child** l'aîné/-e.
elect *vtr* **1** (by vote) élire (**from, from among** parmi); **2** (choose) choisir (**to do** de faire).
election *n* élection *f*, scrutin *m*; **to win an ~** gagner aux élections.
electoral *adj* électoral/-e.
electorate *n* électorat *m*, électeurs *mpl*.
electric *adj* électrique.
electrical *adj* électrique.
electrician ▶626 *n* électricien/-ienne *m/f*.
electricity *n* électricité *f*; **to turn off/on the ~** couper/rétablir le courant (électrique).
electric shock *n* décharge *f* électrique.
electrify *vtr* **1** électrifier [*railway*]; **2** électriser [*audience*].
electrocute *vtr* électrocuter.
electronic *adj* électronique.
electronics *n* électronique *f*.
elegant *adj* [*person, clothes, gesture*] élégant/-e; [*manners*] distingué/-e; [*restaurant*] chic.
element *n* **1** élément *m*; **an ~ of luck** une part de chance; **2** (in heater, kettle) résistance *f*.
elementary *adj* **1** (basic) élémentaire; **2** [*school*] primaire; [*teacher*] de primaire.
elephant *n* éléphant *m*.
elevate *vtr* élever (**to** au rang de).
elevated *adj* [*language, rank, site*] élevé/-e; [*railway, canal*] surélevé/-e.
elevator *n* **1** (US) (lift) ascenseur *m*; **2** (hoist) élévateur *m*.
eleven ▶389, 434 *n, pron, det* onze (*m*) *inv*.
eleventh ▶456, 498 I *n* **1** (in order) onzième *mf*; **2** (of month) onze *m inv*; **3** (fraction) onzième *m*.
II *adj, adv* onzième.
elf *n* lutin *m*.
eligible *adj* **to be ~ for** avoir droit à [*allowance, benefit, membership*]; **to be ~ to do** être en droit de faire.
eliminate *vtr* (gen) éliminer; écarter [*suspect*].
elimination *n* élimination *f*; **by a process of ~** en procédant par élimination.
élite I *n* élite *f*.
II *adj* [*group, minority*] élitaire; [*restaurant, club*] réservé/-e à l'élite; [*squad*] d'élite.
elm *n* orme *m*.
elongated *adj* allongé/-e.
elope *vi* s'enfuir (**with** avec).
eloquent *adj* éloquent/-e.
else I *adv* d'autre; **somebody/nothing ~** quelqu'un/rien d'autre; **something ~** autre chose; **somewhere** or **someplace** (US) **~** ailleurs; **how ~ can we do it?** comment le faire autrement?; **what ~ would you like?** qu'est-ce que tu voudrais d'autre?
II **or else** *phr* sinon.
elsewhere *adv* ailleurs.
elusive *adj* [*person, animal, happiness*] insaisissable; [*prize, victory*] hors d'atteinte.
emaciated *adj* [*person, feature*] émacié/-e; [*limb, body*] décharné/-e; [*animal*] étique.
e-mail *n* (*abbr* = **electronic mail**) courrier *m* or messagerie *f* électronique.
emancipate *vtr* émanciper.
embalm *vtr* embaumer.
embankment *n* **1** (for railway, road) remblai *m*; **2** (by river) quai *m*, digue *f*.
embargo *n* embargo *m*.
embark *vi* **1** (on ship) s'embarquer (**for** pour); **2 to ~ on** entreprendre [*journey*]; se lancer dans [*career, process, project*].
embarrass *vtr* plonger [qn] dans l'embarras; **to be/to feel ~ed** être/se sentir gêné/-e.
embarrassing *adj* embarrassant/-e.
embarrassment *n* confusion *f*, gêne *f* (**about, at** devant); **to my ~** à ma grande confusion.
embassy *n* ambassade *f*.
embers *n pl* braises *fpl*.

embezzle *vtr* détourner [*funds*] (**from** de).
emblem *n* emblème *m*.
embrace I *n* étreinte *f*.
II *vtr* **1** (hug) étreindre; **2** (include) comprendre.
III *vi* s'étreindre.
embroider I *vtr* **1** broder (**with** de); **2** embellir [*story, truth*].
II *vi* broder, faire de la broderie.
embroidery *n* broderie *f*.
embryo *n* embryon *m*.
emerald *n* **1** (stone) émeraude *f*; **2** ▶438 (colour) émeraude *m*.
emerge *vi* **1** [*person, animal*] sortir (**from** de); **2** [*problem, result*] se faire jour; [*pattern*] se dégager; [*truth*] apparaître.
emergency I *n* (gen) cas *m* d'urgence; (Med) urgence *f*; **in an ~, in case of ~** en cas d'urgence; **it's an ~** c'est urgent.
II *adj* [*plan, repairs, call, stop*] d'urgence; [*brakes, vehicle*] de secours.
emergency exit *n* sortie *f* de secours.
emergency landing *n* atterrissage *m* d'urgence.
emergency services *n pl* (police) ≈ police *f* secours; (ambulance) service *m* d'aide médicale d'urgence; (fire brigade) (sapeurs-)pompiers *mpl*.
emigrant *n* (about to leave) émigrant/-e *m/f*; (settled elsewhere) émigré/-e *m/f*.
emigrate *vi* émigrer.
emission *n* émission *f* (**from** provenant de).
emit *vtr* émettre.
emotion *n* émotion *f*.
emotional *adj* [*problem*] émotif/-ive; [*reaction*] émotionnel/-elle; [*tie, response*] affectif/-ive; [*speech*] passionné/-e; **to feel ~** être ému/-e (**about** par); **she's rather ~** elle est assez émotive.
emperor *n* empereur *m*.
emphasis *n* accent *m*; **to lay** or **put the ~ on sth** mettre l'accent sur qch.
emphasize *vtr* mettre l'accent sur [*policy, need*]; mettre [qch] en valeur [*eyes*].
emphatic *adj* [*statement*] catégorique; [*voice, manner*] énergique; **to be ~ about** insister sur.
empire *n* empire *m*.
employ *vtr* **1** employer [*person, company*] (**as** en qualité de); **to be ~ed** avoir un emploi; **2** (use) utiliser [*machine, tool*]; employer [*tactics, technique*]; recourir à [*measures*].
employee *n* salarié/-e *m/f*.
employer *n* employeur/-euse *m/f*.
employment *n* travail *m*, emploi *m*.
employment agency *n* bureau *m* de recrutement.
empress *n* impératrice *f*.
empty I *adj* **1** [*street*] désert/-e; [*desk*] libre; [*container*] vide; [*page*] vierge; **2** [*promise, threat*] en l'air; [*gesture*] vide de sens; [*life*] vide.
II *vtr, vi* = **empty out**.
■ **empty out**: ¶ **~ out** [*building, container*] se vider; [*contents*] se répandre; ¶ **~ [sth] out** vider [*container, drawer*]; verser [*liquid*].
emulsion *n* émulsion *f*.
enable *vtr* **1 to ~ sb to do** permettre à qn de faire; **2** faciliter [*growth*]; favoriser [*learning*].
enamel *n* émail *m*.
enchant *vtr* enchanter.
enchanting *adj* enchanteur/-eresse.
encircle *vtr* [*troops, police*] encercler; [*fence, wall*] entourer; [*belt, bracelet*] enserrer.
enclose *vtr* **1** (gen) entourer (**with, by** de); (with fence, wall) clôturer (**with, by** avec); **2** (in letter) joindre (**with, in** à); **please find ~d a cheque for £10** veuillez trouver ci-joint un chèque de dix livres.
enclosure *n* **1** (for animals) enclos *m*; (for racehorses) paddock *m*; (for officials) enceinte *f*; **2** (fence) clôture *f*.
encompass *vtr* inclure, comprendre.
encore I *n* bis *m*; **to play an ~** jouer un bis.
II *excl* **~!** bis!
encounter I *n* (gen) rencontre *f* (**with** avec); (Mil) affrontement *m*.
II *vtr* rencontrer [*opponent, resistance, problem*]; essuyer [*setback*]; croiser [*person*].
encourage *vtr* **1** encourager (**to do** à faire); **2** stimuler [*investment*]; favoriser [*growth*].
encouragement *n* encouragement *m*.
encouraging *adj* encourageant/-e.
encroach *vi* **to ~ on** [*person*] empiéter sur; [*sea, vegetation*] gagner du terrain sur [*land*].
encyclop(a)edia *n* encyclopédie *f*.
end I *n* **1** (final part) fin *f*; **'The End'** 'Fin'; **to put an ~ to sth** mettre fin à qch; **to come to an ~** se terminer; **in the ~ I went home** finalement je suis rentré chez moi; **for days on ~** pendant des jours et des jours; **2** (extremity) bout *m*, extrémité *f*; **at the ~ of, on the ~ of** au bout de; **at the ~ of the garden** au fond du jardin; **the third from the ~** le/la troisième avant la fin; **to stand sth on (its) ~** mettre qch debout; **3** (aim) but *m*; **to this ~** dans ce but; **a means to an ~** un moyen d'arriver à ses fins; **4** (Sport) **to change ~s** changer de côté.
II *vtr* mettre fin à; **to ~ sth with** terminer qch par; **to ~ it all** en finir avec la vie.
III *vi* [*day, book*] se terminer (**in, with** par); [*contract, agreement*] expirer.
■ **end up** finir par devenir [*president*]; finir par être [*rich*]; **to ~ up doing** finir par faire.
endanger *vtr* mettre [qch] en danger [*health, life*]; compromettre [*career, prospects*].
endangered species *n* espèce *f* menacée.
endearing *adj* [*person, habit*] attachant/-e; [*smile*] engageant/-e.
endeavour, endeavor (US) **I** *n* tentative *f* (**to do** de faire).
II *vtr* **to ~ to do** (do one's best) faire tout son possible pour faire; (find a means) trouver un moyen de faire.
ending *n* fin *f*, dénouement *m*.
endive *n* (GB) chicorée *f*; (US) endive *f*.

endless *adj* [*patience, choice*] infini/-e; [*supply*] inépuisable; [*list, search, meeting*] interminable.

endorse *vtr* donner son aval à [*policy*]; appuyer [*decision*]; approuver [*product*]; endosser [*cheque*].

endow *vtr* doter (**with** de).

endurance *n* endurance *f*.

endure I *vtr* endurer [*hardship*]; supporter [*behaviour, person*]; subir [*attack, defeat*].
II *vi* durer.

enemy I *n* ennemi/-e *m/f*.
II *adj* [*forces, aircraft, territory*] ennemi/-e; [*agent*] de l'ennemi.

energetic *adj* énergique.

energy *n* énergie *f*.

enforce *vtr* appliquer [*rule, policy*]; faire respecter [*law, court order*].

engage I *vtr* **1 to be ~d in** se livrer à [*activity*]; **to ~ sb in conversation** engager la conversation avec qn; **2** passer [*gear*]; **to ~ the clutch** embrayer.
II *vi* **to ~ in** se livrer à [*activity*]; se lancer dans [*research*].

engaged *adj* **1 to be ~** être fiancé/-e (**to** à); **to get ~** se fiancer (**to** à); **2** [*WC, phone*] occupé/-e.

engaged tone *n* (GB) tonalité *f* 'occupé'.

engagement *n* **1** (appointment) rendez-vous *m inv*; **2** (before marriage) fiançailles *fpl*.

engagement ring *n* bague *f* de fiançailles.

engine *n* **1** (gen) moteur *m*; (in ship) machines *fpl*; **2** locomotive *f*; **steam ~** locomotive à vapeur.

engine driver ▶ 626 *n* mécanicien *m*.

engineer ▶ 626 I *n* (graduate) ingénieur *m*; (in factory) mécanicien *m* monteur; (repairer) technicien *m*; (on ship) mécanicien *m*.
II *vtr* **1** (plot) manigancer; **2** (build) construire.

engineering *n* ingénierie *f*; **civil ~** génie *m* civil.

England ▶ 448 *pr n* Angleterre *f*.

English ▶ 553 I *n* **1** (people) **the ~** les Anglais; **2** (language) anglais *m*.
II *adj* [*language, food*] anglais/-e; [*lesson, teacher*] d'anglais; [*ambassador, embassy*] d'Angleterre.

English Channel *n* **the ~** la Manche.

Englishman *n* Anglais *m*.

Englishwoman *n* Anglaise *f*.

engrave *vtr* graver.

engraving *n* gravure *f*.

engrossed *adj* **to be ~ in** être absorbé/-e par, être plongé/-e dans.

engulf *vtr* engloutir.

enhance *vtr* améliorer [*prospects, status*]; mettre [qch] en valeur [*appearance, qualities*].

enigma *n* énigme *f*.

enigmatic *adj* énigmatique.

enjoy I *vtr* **1** aimer (**doing** faire); **I didn't ~ the party** je ne me suis pas amusé à la soirée; **2** (have) jouir de [*good health, popularity*].
II *v refl* **to ~ oneself** s'amuser.

enjoyable *adj* agréable.

enjoyment *n* plaisir *m*.

enlarge I *vtr* agrandir.
II *vi* **1** [*pupil, pores*] se dilater; [*tonsils*] enfler; **2 to ~ on** s'étendre sur [*subject*]; développer [*idea*].

enlighten *vtr* éclairer (**on** sur).

enlightening *adj* instructif/-ive.

enlightenment *n* (edification) instruction *f*; (clarification) éclaircissement *m*; **the (Age of) Enlightenment** le Siècle des lumières.

enlist I *vtr* recruter; **to ~ sb's help** s'assurer l'aide de qn.
II *vi* s'enrôler, s'engager.

enmity *n* inimitié *f* (**towards** envers).

enormity *n* énormité *f*.

enormous *adj* (gen) énorme; [*effort*] prodigieux/-ieuse.

enough

■ **Note** When *enough* is used as a pronoun and if the sentence does not specify what it is enough of, the pronoun *en*, meaning *of it/of them*, must be added before the verb in French: *will there be enough?* = est-ce qu'il y en aura assez?

I *pron, quantif* assez; **have you had ~ to eat?** avez-vous assez mangé?; **more than ~** largement assez; **is that ~?** ça suffit?; **I've had ~ of him** j'en ai assez de lui.
II *adv* assez; **curiously ~,...** aussi bizarre que cela puisse paraître...
III *det* assez de; **have you got ~ chairs?** avez-vous assez de chaises?

enquire I *vtr* demander.
II *vi* se renseigner (**about** sur); **to ~ after sb** demander des nouvelles de qn.

enquiring *adj* [*look, voice*] interrogateur/-trice; [*mind*] curieux/-ieuse.

enquiry *n* demande *f* de renseignements; **to make enquiries** demander des renseignements (**about** sur); ▶ **inquiry**.

enrage *vtr* rendre [qn] furieux/-ieuse.

enrich *vtr* enrichir.

enrol, **enroll** (US) I *vtr* (gen) inscrire; (Mil) enrôler.
II *vi* (gen) s'inscrire (**in**, **on** à); (Mil) s'engager (**in** dans).

enrolment, **enrollment** (US) *n* (gen) inscription *f* (**in, on** à); (Mil) enrôlement *m*.

en suite *adj* attenant/-e.

ensure *vtr* garantir; **to ~ that...** s'assurer que...

entail *vtr* impliquer [*travel, work*]; entraîner [*expense*]; nécessiter [*effort*].

enter I *vtr* **1** entrer dans [*room, house, phase, period, profession, army*]; participer à [*race, competition*]; entrer à [*parliament*]; **to ~ sb's mind** or **head** venir à l'idée or à l'esprit de qn; **2** engager [*horse*] (**for** dans); présenter [*poem, picture*] (**for** à); **3** inscrire [*figure, fact*] (**in** dans); (in diary) noter [*appointment*] (**in** dans); (in computer) entrer [*data*].
II *vi* **1** (come in) entrer; **2 to ~ for** s'inscrire à [*exam*]; s'inscrire pour [*race*].

■ **enter into** entrer en [*conversation*]; entamer [*negotiations*]; passer [*contract*].
enterprise *n* **1** (gen) entreprise *f*; **2** (initiative) esprit *m* d'initiative.
enterprising *adj* [*person*] entreprenant/-e; [*plan*] audacieux/-ieuse.
entertain I *vtr* **1** (keep amused) divertir; (make laugh) amuser; (keep occupied) distraire, occuper; **2** (play host to) recevoir [*guests*]; **3** entretenir [*idea*]; nourrir [*doubt, ambition, illusion*].
II *vi* recevoir.
entertainer ▶626 *n* (comic) comique *mf*; (performer, raconteur) amuseur/-euse *m/f*.
entertaining I *adj* divertissant/-e.
II *n* **they do a lot of ~** ils reçoivent beaucoup.
entertainment *n* **1** divertissement *m*, distractions *fpl*; **2** (event) spectacle *m*.
enthusiasm *n* enthousiasme *m* (**for** pour).
enthusiast *n* (for sport, DIY) passionné/-e *m/f*; (for music, composer) fervent/-e *m/f*.
enthusiastic *adj* (gen) enthousiaste; [*discussion*] exalté/-e; [*worker, gardener*] passionné/-e.
entice *vtr* (with offer, charms, prospects) attirer; (with food, money) appâter.
entire *adj* entier/-ière; **the ~ family** toute la famille, la famille entière.
entirely *adv* [*destroy, escape*] entièrement; [*different, unnecessary*] complètement.
entirety *n* ensemble *m*, totalité *f*.
entitle *vtr* **to ~ sb to sth** donner droit à qch à qn; **to be ~d to sth** avoir droit à qch; **to be ~d to do** avoir le droit de faire.
entitlement *n* droit *m*.
entity *n* entité *f*.
entrance I *n* (gen) entrée *f*; **to gain ~ to** être admis/-e à or dans [*club, university*].
II *vtr* transporter, ravir.
entrance examination *n* (GB Sch, Univ) examen *m* d'entrée; (for civil service) concours *m* d'entrée.
entrance fee *n* droit *m* d'entrée.
entrance hall *n* (in house) vestibule *m*; (in public building) hall *m*.
entreat *vtr* implorer, supplier (**to do** de faire).
entreaty *n* prière *f*, supplication *f*.
entrepreneur *n* entrepreneur/-euse *m/f*.
entrust *vtr* confier; **to ~ sb with sth, to ~ sth to sb** confier qch à qn.
entry *n* **1** (gen) entrée *f*; **to gain ~ to** or **into** s'introduire dans [*building*]; accéder à [*computer file*]; **'no ~'** (on door) 'défense d'entrer'; (in one way street) 'sens interdit'; **2** (in diary) note *f*; (in ledger) écriture *f*; **3** (for competition) œuvre *f* présentée à un concours.
entry form *n* (for membership) fiche *f* d'inscription; (for competition) bulletin *m* de participation.
entry phone *n* interphone *m*.
envelope *n* enveloppe *f*.
envious *adj* envieux/-ieuse; **to be ~ of sb/sth** envier qn/qch.
environment *n* (physical, cultural) environnement *m*; (social) milieu *m*.
environmental *adj* [*conditions, changes*] du milieu; [*concern, issue*] lié/-e à l'environnement, écologique; [*protection, pollution*] de l'environnement.
environmentally *adv* **~ safe, ~ sound** qui ne nuit pas à l'environnement; **~ friendly product** produit qui respecte l'environnement.
envisage *vtr* (anticipate) prévoir (**doing** de faire); (visualize) envisager (**doing** de faire).
envoy *n* envoyé/-e *m/f*.
envy I *n* envie *f*; (long-term) jalousie *f*.
II *vtr* **to ~ sb sth** envier qch à qn.
enzyme *n* enzyme *f*.
epic I *n* (gen) épopée *f*; (film) film *m* à grand spectacle; (novel) roman-fleuve *m*.
II *adj* épique.
epidemic I *n* épidémie *f*.
II *adj* épidémique.
epileptic *n, adj* épileptique (*mf*).
episode *n* épisode *m*.
epitome *n* épitomé *m*; **the ~ of kindness** la bonté incarnée.
epitomize *vtr* personnifier, incarner.
epoch *n* époque *f*.
equal I *n* égal/-e *m/f*.
II *adj* **1** égal/-e (**to** à); **~ opportunities/rights** égalité *f* des chances/des droits; **2 to be ~ to** être à la hauteur de [*task*].
III *adv* [*finish*] à égalité.
IV *vtr* égaler.
equality *n* égalité *f*.
equally *adv* [*divide, share*] en parts égales; **~ difficult** tout aussi difficile; **~, we might say that...** de même, on pourrait dire que...
equate *vtr* (identify) assimiler (**with, to** à); (compare) comparer (**with, to** à).
equation *n* équation *f*.
equator *n* équateur *m*.
equilibrium *n* équilibre *m*.
equip *vtr* équiper (**for** pour; **with** de).
equipment *n* (gen) équipement *m*; (office, electrical, photographic) matériel *m*; **a piece** or **item of ~** un article.
equivalent I *n* équivalent *m*.
II *adj* équivalent/-e.
era *n* (in history, geology) ère *f*; (in politics, fashion) époque *f*.
eradicate *vtr* éliminer [*poverty, crime*]; éradiquer [*disease*].
erase *vtr* effacer.
eraser *n* (rubber) gomme *f*; (for blackboard) brosse *f* feutrée.
erect I *adj* [*posture*] droit/-e; [*tail, ears*] dressé/-e.
II *vtr* ériger [*building*]; monter [*scaffolding, tent, screen*].
erection *n* (gen) érection *f*; (of building) construction *f*; (edifice) édifice *m*.
ermine *n* hermine *f*.
erode *vtr* éroder [*rock, metal*]; saper [*confidence*].
erosion *n* érosion *f*.
erotic *adj* érotique.

err *vi* **1** (make mistake) faire erreur; **2 to ~ on the side of caution** pécher par excès de prudence.

errand *n* commission *f*, course *f*; **to run an ~ for sb** aller faire une commission pour qn.

erratic *adj* [*behaviour, person, driver*] imprévisible; [*moods*] changeant/-e.

error *n* (in spelling, grammar, typing) faute *f*; (in calculation, on computer) erreur *f*.

erupt *vi* **1** [*volcano*] entrer en éruption; **2** [*violence*] éclater.

eruption *n* (of volcano) éruption *f*; (of violence, anger) explosion *f*.

escalate *vi* [*conflict, violence*] s'intensifier; [*prices*] monter en flèche; [*unemployment*] augmenter rapidement.

escalator *n* escalier *m* mécanique, escalator® *m*.

escapade *n* frasque *f*.

escape I *n* fuite *f* (**from** de; **to** vers); **to have a narrow** or **lucky ~** l'échapper belle.
II *vtr* échapper à.
III *vi* **1** [*person*] s'enfuir, s'évader (**from** de); [*animal*] s'échapper (**from** de); (figurative) s'évader; **to ~ with one's life** s'en sortir vivant; **2** (leak) fuir.

escapism *n* évasion *f* (du réel).

escort I *n* **1** escorte *f*; **police ~** escorte de police; **2** (companion) compagnon/compagne *m/f*.
II *vtr* **1** escorter; **to ~ sb in/out** faire entrer/sortir qn sous escorte; **2** (to a function) accompagner; (home) raccompagner.

especially *adv* **1** (above all) surtout, en particulier; **him ~** lui en particulier; **~ as it's so hot** d'autant plus qu'il fait si chaud; **2** (on purpose) exprès, spécialement; **3** (unusually) particulièrement.

espresso *n* express *m inv*.

essay *n* **1** (Sch) rédaction *f* (**on, about** sur); (extended) dissertation *f* (**on** sur); **2** (literary) essai *m* (**on** sur).

essence *n* essence *f*.

essential I *n* **a car is not an ~** une voiture n'est pas indispensable; **the ~s** l'essentiel *m*.
II *adj* [*role, feature, element*] essentiel/-ielle; [*ingredient, reading*] indispensable; [*difference*] fondamental; **it is ~ that we agree** il est indispensable que nous soyons d'accord.

essentially *adv* essentiellement.

establish *vtr* (gen) établir; fonder [*company*].

establishment *n* **1** (gen) établissement *m*; **2** (shop, business) maison *f*; **3 the Establishment** l'ordre *m* établi.

estate *n* **1** (stately home and park) domaine *m*, propriété *f*; **2** = **housing estate**; **3** (assets) biens *mpl*; **4** (GB) (also **~ car**) break *m*.

estate agency *n* (GB) agence *f* immobilière.

estate agent *n* (GB) agent *m* immobilier.

esteem *n* estime *f*.

estimate I *n* **1** estimation *f*; **2** (quote for client) devis *m*.
II *vtr* évaluer [*value, size, distance*]; **to ~ that** estimer que.
III estimated *pp adj* [*cost, figure*] approximatif/-ive; **an ~d 300 people** environ 300 personnes.

estranged *adj* **~ from sb** séparé/-e de qn; **her ~ husband** son mari dont elle est séparée.

etc *adv* (*written abbr* = **et cetera**) etc.

etching *n* eau-forte *f*.

eternal *adj* [*life*] éternel/-elle; [*chatter, optimist*] perpétuel/-elle.

ethical *adj* moral/-e.

ethics *n* (code) moralité *f*; **professional ~** déontologie *f*.

ethnic *adj* ethnique.

etiquette *n* **1** (social) bienséance *f*, étiquette *f*; **2** (professional, diplomatic) protocole *m*.

eurocheque *n* Eurochèque *m*.

Euro-MP *n* député *m* européen.

Europe ▶ **448** *pr n* Europe *f*.

European I *n* Européen/-éenne *m/f*.
II *adj* européen/-éenne.

European Commission *n* Commission *f* européenne.

European Monetary System, **EMS** *n* système *m* monétaire européen, SME *m*.

European Union, **EU** *n* Union *f* européenne, UE *f*.

euthanasia *n* euthanasie *f*.

evacuate *vtr* évacuer.

evade *vtr* esquiver [*blow*]; éluder [*question, problem*].

evaluate *vtr* évaluer.

evaporate *vi* [*liquid*] s'évaporer.

evaporated milk *n* lait *m* condensé non sucré.

evasion *n* (of responsibility) dérobade *f* (**of** à); **tax ~** évasion *f* fiscale.

evasive *adj* [*answer*] évasif/-ive; [*look*] fuyant/-e.

eve *n* veille *f*; **on the ~ of** à la veille de.

even[1] **I** *adv* **1** (gen) même; **he didn't ~ try** il n'a même pas essayé; **don't tell anyone, not ~ Bob** ne dis rien à personne, pas même à Bob; **~ if/when** même si/quand; **2** (with comparative) encore; **~ colder** encore plus froid.
II even so *phr* quand même.
III even though *phr* bien que (+ *subjunctive*).

even[2] *adj* [*surface, voice, temper*] égal/-e; [*teeth, hemline*] régulier/-ière; [*temperature*] constant/-e; [*number*] pair/-e; **to get ~ with sb** rendre à qn la monnaie de sa pièce.

evening ▶ **434** *n* soir *m*; (with emphasis on duration) soirée *f*; **in the ~** le soir; **all ~** toute la soirée; **every ~** tous les soirs.

evening class *n* cours *m* du soir.

evening dress *n* (formal clothes) tenue *f* de soirée.

event *n* **1** événement *m*; **2** (eventuality) cas *m*; **in the ~ of a fire** en cas d'incendie; **in any ~** de toute façon; **3** (in athletics) épreuve *f*.

eventful *adj* mouvementé/-e.

eventually *adv* finalement; **to do sth ~** finir par faire qch.

ever I *adv* **1** jamais; **no-one will ~ forget** personne n'oubliera jamais; **hardly ~** rarement, presque jamais; **has he ~ lived abroad?** est-ce qu'il a déjà vécu à l'étranger?; **do you ~ make mistakes?** est-ce qu'il t'arrive de te tromper?; **he's happier than he's ~ been** il n'a jamais été aussi heureux; **more beautiful than ~** plus beau/belle que jamais; **2** (always) toujours; **as cheerful as ~** toujours aussi gai; **the same as ~** toujours le même; **they lived happily ~ after** ils vécurent toujours heureux.
II **ever since** *phr* depuis; **~ since we arrived** depuis notre arrivée.

evergreen *n* arbre *m* à feuilles persistantes.

every I *det* **1** (each) chaque; **~ time** chaque fois; **~ house in the street** toutes les maisons de la rue; **I've read ~ one of her books** j'ai lu tous ses livres; **2** (emphatic) **there is ~ chance that you'll have a place** il y a toutes les chances que tu aies une place; **to have ~ right to complain** avoir tous les droits de se plaindre; **3** (indicating frequency) **~ day** tous les jours; **~ Thursday** tous les jeudis; **once ~ few days** tous les deux ou trois jours.
II **every other** *phr* **~ other day** tous les deux jours; **~ other Sunday** un dimanche sur deux.
IDIOMS **~ now and then**, **~ so often** de temps en temps.

everybody *pron* (also **everyone**) tout le monde.

everyday *adj* [*life*] quotidien/-ienne; [*clothes*] de tous les jours; **in ~ use** d'usage courant.

everyone = **everybody**.

everything *pron* tout.

everywhere *adv* partout.

evict *vtr* expulser (**from** de).

evidence *n* **1** (proof) preuves *fpl* (**that** que; **of, for** de; **against** contre); **2** (testimony) témoignage *m* (**from** de); **to give ~** témoigner, déposer (**for sb** en faveur de qn; **against sb** contre qn); **3** (trace) trace *f* (**of** de).

evident *adj* manifeste.

evidently *adv* **1** (apparently) apparemment; **2** (patently) manifestement.

evil I *n* mal *m*.
II *adj* [*person, forces*] malfaisant/-e; [*act*] diabolique; [*spirit*] maléfique; [*smell*] nauséabond/-e.

evolution *n* évolution *f* (**from** à partir de).

ewe *n* brebis *f*.

ex- *pref* ex-, ancien/-ienne (*before n*).

exact *adj* exact/-e; **to be (more) ~** plus précisément.

exactly *adv* exactement.

exaggerate *vtr, vi* exagérer.

exaggeration *n* exagération *f*

exam *n* examen *m*.

examination *n* examen *m* (**in** de); **French ~** examen *m* de français; **to take/pass an ~** passer/réussir un examen; **to have an ~** (Med) passer un examen médical.

examine *vtr* examiner.

example *n* exemple *m*; **for ~** par exemple; **to set a good ~** donner l'exemple; **to make an ~ of sb** punir qn pour l'exemple.

excavate I *vtr* fouiller [*site*]; creuser [*tunnel*].
II *vi* faire des fouilles.

exceed *vtr* dépasser (**by** de).

excel *vi* exceller (**at, in** en; **at** or **in doing** à faire).

excellent *adj* excellent/-e.

except I *prep* sauf; **everybody ~ Lisa** tout le monde sauf Lisa, tout le monde à l'exception de or excepté Lisa; **who could have done it ~ him?** qui aurait pu le faire sinon lui?
II **except for** *phr* à part, à l'exception de.

exception *n* **1** exception *f* (**for** pour); **with the ~ of** à l'exception de; **2 to take ~ to** prendre [qch] comme une insulte.

exceptional *adj* exceptionnel/-elle.

excess I *n* excès *m* (**of** de).
II *adj* **~ weight** excès *m* de poids; **~ baggage** excédent *m* de bagages.

excessive *adj* excessif/-ive.

exchange I *n* **1** échange *m*; **in ~** en échange (**for** de); **2** (in banking) change *m*; **the ~ rate** le taux de change; **3** (also **telephone ~**) central *m* (téléphonique).
II *vtr* échanger (**for** contre; **with** avec).

Exchange Rate Mechanism, **ERM** *n* système *m* monétaire européen.

Exchequer *pr n* (GB) **the ~** l'Échiquier *m*, le ministère des finances.

excite *vtr* exciter.

excited *adj* (gen) excité/-e; [*voice, conversation*] animé/-e.

excitement *n* excitation *f*.

exciting *adj* passionnant/-e.

exclaim *vtr* s'exclamer.

exclamation mark, **exclamation point** (US) *n* point *m* d'exclamation.

exclude *vtr* exclure (**from** de).

excluding *prep* à l'exclusion de; **~ VAT** TVA non comprise.

exclusive I *n* (report) exclusivité *f*.
II *adj* **1** [*club*] fermé/-e; [*hotel*] de luxe; [*district*] huppé/-e; **2** [*story, rights*] exclusif/-ive; [*interview*] en exclusivité; **~ of meals** les repas non compris.

excruciating *adj* [*pain*] atroce.

excursion *n* (organized) excursion *f*.

excuse I *n* excuse *f* (**for sth** à qch; **for doing** pour faire; **to do** pour faire); **to make ~s** trouver des excuses; **an ~ to leave early** un bon prétexte pour partir tôt; **there's no ~ for such behaviour** ce genre de conduite est inexcusable.
II *vtr* **1** excuser [*person*] (**for doing** de faire, d'avoir fait); **~ me!** (apology) excusez-moi!, pardon!; (beginning an enquiry) excusez-moi; (pardon) pardon?; **2** (exempt) dispenser (**from sth** de qch; **from doing** de faire).

execute *vtr* exécuter.

execution *n* exécution *f*.

executioner *n* bourreau *m*.

executive I *n* **1** cadre *m*; **sales ~** cadre *m*

commercial; **2** (committee) exécutif *m*, comité *m* exécutif; **party ~** bureau *m* du parti.
II *adj* **1** [*post*] de cadre; **2** [*power*] exécutif/-ive.

exemplify *vtr* illustrer, exemplifier.

exempt I *adj* exempt/-e (**from** de).
II *vtr* exempter (**from** de).

exercise I *n* exercice *m*.
II *vtr* **1** exercer [*body*]; faire travailler [*limb, muscles*]; **2** faire preuve de [*control, restraint*]; exercer [*power, right*].
III *vi* faire de l'exercice.

exercise book *n* cahier *m*.

exert *vtr* exercer [*pressure, influence*] (**on** sur); **to ~ oneself** se fatiguer.

exhale *vi* [*person*] expirer.

exhaust I *n* **1** (also **~ pipe**) pot *m* d'échappement; **2** (also **~ fumes**) gaz *mpl* d'échappement.
II *vtr* épuiser; **~ed** épuisé/-e.

exhaustion *n* épuisement *m*.

exhibit I *n* **1** œuvre *f* exposée; **2** (US) (exhibition) exposition *f*.
II *vtr* exposer [*work of art*]; manifester [*preference, sign*].

exhibition *n* exposition *f*; **art ~** exposition; **to make an ~ of oneself** se donner en spectacle.

exhibition centre (GB), **exhibition center** (US) *n* palais *m* des expositions.

exhilarating *adj* [*game*] stimulant/-e; [*experience*] exaltant/-e; [*speed*] enivrant/-e.

exile I *n* **1** (person) exilé/-e *m/f*; **2** (expulsion) exil *m* (**from** de); **in ~** en exil.
II *vtr* exiler (**de** from).

exist *vi* exister.

existence *n* existence *f* (**of** de).

existing *adj* [*laws, order*] existant/-e; [*policy, management*] actuel/-elle.

exit I *n* sortie *f*; **'no ~'** 'interdit'.
II *vi* sortir.

exodus *n* exode *m*.

exotic *adj* exotique.

expand I *vtr* développer [*business, network, range*]; élargir [*horizon, knowledge*]; étendre [*empire*]; gonfler [*lungs*].
II *vi* [*business, sector, town*] se développer; [*economy*] être en expansion; [*metal*] se dilater.

expanse *n* étendue *f*.

expatriate *n, adj* expatrié/-e (*m/f*).

expect I *vtr* **1** s'attendre à [*event, victory, defeat, trouble*]; **to ~ the worst** s'attendre au pire; **to ~ sb to do** s'attendre à ce que qn fasse; **I ~ (that) I'll lose** je m'attends à perdre; **more than ~ed** plus que prévu; **2** s'attendre à [*sympathy, help*] (**from** de la part de); **3** attendre [*baby, guest*]; **4** (require) demander, attendre [*hard work*] (**from** de); **I ~ you to be punctual** je vous demande d'être ponctuel; **5** (GB) (suppose) **I ~ so** je pense que oui; **I ~ he's tired** il doit être fatigué.
II *vi* **1 to ~ to do** s'attendre à faire; **2** (require) **I ~ to see you there** je compte bien vous y voir; **3** (be pregnant) **to be ~ing** attendre un enfant.

expectant *adj* **1** [*look*] plein d'attente; **2** [*mother*] futur/-e (*before n*).

expectation *n* **1** (prediction) prévision *f*; **against all ~(s)** à l'encontre des prévisions générales; **2** (hope) aspiration *f*, attente *f*; **to live up to sb's ~s** répondre à l'attente de qn.

expedient *adj* **1** (appropriate) opportun/-e; **2** (advantageous) politique.

expedition *n* expédition *f*; **to go on an ~** partir en expédition.

expel *vtr* (gen) expulser; renvoyer [*pupil*].

expenditure *n* dépense *f*.

expense I *n* **1** (cost) frais *mpl*; (money spent) dépense *f*; **at one's own ~** à ses propres frais; **to go to great ~** dépenser beaucoup d'argent (**to do** pour faire); **to spare no ~** ne pas regarder à la dépense; **2 at the ~ of** au détriment de [*health, public, safety*]; **at sb's ~** [*laugh, joke*] aux dépens de qn.
II **expenses** *n pl* frais *mpl*.

expensive *adj* (gen) cher/chère; [*holiday, mistake*] coûteux/-euse; [*taste*] de luxe.

experience I *n* expérience *f*.
II *vtr* connaître [*loss, problem*]; éprouver [*emotion*].

experienced *adj* (gen) expérimenté/-e; [*eye*] entraîné/-e.

experiment I *n* expérience *f* (**in** en; **on** sur).
II *vi* expérimenter, faire des essais.

experimental *adj* expérimental/-e.

expert I *n* spécialiste *mf* (**in** en, de), expert *m* (**in** en).
II *adj* [*opinion, advice*] autorisé/-e; [*witness*] expert/-e; [*eye*] exercé/-e; **an ~ cook** un cordon bleu.

expertise *n* compétences *fpl*; (very specialized) expertise *f* (**in** dans le domaine de).

expire *vi* [*deadline, offer*] expirer; [*period*] arriver à terme; **my passport has ~d** mon passeport est périmé.

explain *vtr* expliquer (**that** que; **to** à).

explanation *n* explication *f* (**of** de; **for** à).

explicit *adj* explicite.

explode I *vtr* **1** faire exploser [*bomb*]; **2** pulvériser [*theory, rumour, myth*].
II *vi* (gen) exploser; [*boiler, building, ship*] sauter.

exploit I *n* exploit *m*.
II *vtr* exploiter.

exploitation *n* exploitation *f*.

explore I *vtr* explorer.
II *vi* **to go exploring** partir en exploration.

explorer *n* explorateur/-trice *m/f*.

explosion *n* explosion *f*.

explosive I *n* explosif *m*.
II *adj* [*device, force*] explosif/-ive; [*substance*] explosible.

export I *n* (process) exportation *f* (**of** de); (product) produit *m* d'exportation.
II *vtr, vi* exporter.

exporter *n* exportateur/-trice *m/f* (**of** de).

expose *vtr* **1** exposer (**to** à); **2** (make public) révéler [*identity*]; dénoncer [*person, scandal*];

3 to ~ oneself commettre un outrage à la pudeur.

exposure *n* **1** (of secret, crime) révélation *f*; **2** (to light, sun, radiation) exposition *f* (**to** à); **3 to die of ~** mourir de froid; **4** (also **~ time**) temps *m* de pose; **5** (picture) pose *f*.

express I *n* rapide *m*.
II *adj* [*letter, parcel*] exprès; [*delivery, train*] rapide.
III *adv* **to send sth ~** envoyer qch en exprès.
IV *vtr* exprimer; **to ~ oneself** s'exprimer.

expression *n* expression *f*.

expressive *adj* expressif/-ive.

exquisite *adj* exquis/-e.

extend I *vtr* **1** agrandir [*house*]; prolonger [*runway*]; élargir [*range*]; **2** prolonger [*visit, visa*]; **3** étendre [*arm, leg*]; tendre [*hand*].
II *vi* s'étendre (**as far as** jusqu'à; **from** de).

extension *n* **1** (on cable, table) rallonge *f*; (to house) addition *f*; **2** (phone) poste *m* supplémentaire; **~ (number)** (numéro *m* de) poste *m*; **3** (of deadline) délai *m* supplémentaire.

extension lead *n* rallonge *f*.

extensive *adj* **1** [*network*] vaste (*before n*); [*list*] long/longue (*before n*); [*tests*] approfondi/-e; [*changes*] important/-e; **2** [*damage, loss*] grave, considérable; [*burns*] grave.

extent *n* **1** (of area, problem, power) étendue *f*; (of damage) ampleur *f*; **2** (degree) mesure *f*; **to a certain/great ~** dans une certaine/large mesure.

exterior I *n* extérieur *m* (**of** de).
II *adj* extérieur/-e (**to** à).

exterminate *vtr* éliminer [*vermin*]; exterminer [*people, race*].

external *adj* (gen) extérieur/-e (**to** à); [*surface, injury, examiner*] externe.

extinct *adj* [*species*] disparu/-e; [*volcano*] éteint/-e; **to become ~** [*species, animal, plant*] disparaître.

extinguish *vtr* éteindre [*fire, cigarette*].

extinguisher *n* extincteur *m*.

extra I *n* **1** (feature) option *f*; **the sunroof is an ~** le toit ouvrant est en option; **2** (actor) figurant/-e *m/f*.
II *adj* supplémentaire; **an ~ £1,000** 1 000 livres de plus.
III *adv* **~ careful** encore plus prudent (que d'habitude); **you have to pay ~** il faut payer un supplément.

extract I *n* extrait *m* (**from** de).
II *vtr* **1** extraire (**from** de); **2** arracher [*promise*] (**from** à).

extraordinary *adj* extraordinaire.

extravagance *n* **1** (trait) prodigalité *f*; **2** (luxury) luxe *m*.

extravagant *adj* **1** [*person*] dépensier/-ière; [*way of life*] dispendieux/-ieuse; **to be ~ with sth** gaspiller qch; **2** (luxurious) luxueux/-euse.

extreme I *n* extrême *m*; **to go to ~s** pousser les choses à l'extrême.
II *adj* (gen) extrême; [*view, measure, reaction*] extrémiste.

extremely *adv* extrêmement.

extrovert *n, adj* extraverti/-e (*m/f*).

eye ▶413 I *n* **1** œil *m*; **with blue ~s** aux yeux bleus; **in front of** or **before your (very) ~s** sous vos yeux; **to keep an ~ on sb/sth** surveiller qn/qch; **to have one's ~ on** (watch) surveiller [*person*]; (want) avoir envie de [*house*]; viser [*job*]; **to catch sb's ~** attirer l'attention de qn; **as far as the ~ can see** à perte de vue; **to have an ~ for** avoir le sens de [*detail*]; **2** (of needle) chas *m*.
II *vtr* regarder.
IDIOMS **an ~ for an ~** œil pour œil; **to make ~s at sb** faire les yeux doux à qn; **to see ~ to ~ with sb (about sth)** partager le point de vue de qn (au sujet de qch).

eyeball *n* globe *m* oculaire.

eyebrow *n* sourcil *m*.

eyebrow pencil *n* crayon *m* à sourcils.

eye-catching *adj* [*design, poster*] attrayant/-e; [*advertisement, headline*] accrocheur/-euse.

eyedrops *n pl* gouttes *fpl* pour les yeux.

eyelash *n* cil *m*.

eyelid *n* paupière *f*.

eye liner *n* eye-liner *m*.

eye shadow *n* fard *m* à paupières.

eyesight *n* vue *f*.

eye test *n* examen *m* de la vue.

eyewitness *n* témoin *m* oculaire.

Ff

f, **F** *n* **1** (letter) f, F *m*; **2 F** (Mus) fa *m*.

fable *n* fable *f*.

fabric *n* **1** (cloth) tissu *m*; **2** (of building) structure *f*; **the ~ of society** le tissu social.

fabricate *vtr* **1** inventer [qch] de toutes pièces [*story, evidence*]; **2** fabriquer [*document*].

fabulous *adj* **1** fabuleux/-euse; **2**○ (wonderful) sensationnel/-elle○.

façade, **facade** *n* façade *f* (**of** de).

face I *n* **1** (of person) visage *m*, figure *f*; (of animal) face *f*; **to slam the door/laugh in sb's ~** claquer la porte/rire au nez de qn; **to pull** or **make a ~** faire une grimace; (in disgust) faire la grimace; **2 to lose ~** perdre la face; **to save ~** sauver la face; **3** (of clock, watch) cadran *m*; (of coin) côté *m*; (of planet) surface *f*; (of cliff, mountain) face *f*; (of playing card) face *f*; **~ up/down** à l'endroit/l'envers.

II *vtr* **1** (look towards) [*person*] faire face à; [*building, room*] donner sur; **to ~ south** [*person*] regarder au sud; [*building*] être orienté/-e au sud; **2** se trouver face à [*challenge, crisis*]; se trouver menacé/-e de [*defeat, redundancy*]; affronter [*rival, team*]; **to be ~d with** se trouver confronté/-e à [*problem, decision*]; **3** (acknowledge) **~ the facts, you're finished!** regarde la réalité en face, tu es fini!; **let's ~ it, nobody's perfect** admettons-le, personne n'est parfait; **4** (tolerate prospect) **I can't ~ doing** je n'ai pas le courage de faire; **he couldn't ~ the thought of eating** l'idée de manger lui était insupportable; **5** revêtir [*façade, wall*] (**with** de).

III in the face of *phr* **1** en dépit de [*difficulties*]; **2** face à, devant [*opposition, enemy, danger*]

IV face to face *adv* [*be seated*] face à face; **to come ~ to ~ with** se retrouver face à; **to talk to sb ~ to ~** parler à qn en personne.

■ **face up to** faire face à [*problem, responsibilities*].

face-lift *n* lifting *m*; **to have a ~** se faire faire un lifting; **to give [sth] a ~** rénover [*building*]; réaménager [*town centre*].

facet *n* facette *f*.

facetious *adj* [*remark*] facétieux/-ieuse; [*person*] farceur/-euse.

face value *n* (of coin) valeur *f* nominale; **to take [sth] at ~** prendre [qch] au pied de la lettre; **to take sb at ~** juger qn sur les apparences.

facilitate *vtr* faciliter [*progress, talks*]; favoriser [*development*].

facility I *n* **1** (building) complexe *m*, installation *f*; **2** (ease) facilité *f*; **3** (feature) fonction *f*.

II facilities *n pl* (equipment) équipement *m*; (infrastructure) infrastructure *f*; **facilities for the disabled** installations *fpl* pour les handicapés; **parking facilities** parking *m*.

facsimile *n* (gen) fac-similé *m*; (sculpture) reproduction *f*.

fact *n* fait *m*; **~s and figures** les faits et les chiffres; **to know for a ~ that** savoir de source sûre que; **due to the ~ that** étant donné que; **in ~**, **as a matter of ~** en fait; **to be based on ~** être fondé/-e sur des faits réels.

IDIOMS **to know the ~s of life** savoir comment les enfants viennent au monde; **the (hard) ~s of life** les réalités de la vie.

factor *n* facteur *m*; **common ~** point *m* commun; (in mathematics) facteur commun; **protection ~** indice *m* de protection.

factory *n* usine *f*.

fact sheet *n* bulletin *m* d'informations.

factual *adj* [*evidence*] factuel/-elle; [*account, description*] basé/-e sur les faits.

faculty *n* **1** (ability) faculté *f* (**for** de); **2** (GB Univ) faculté *f*; **3** (US Univ, Sch) (staff) corps *m* enseignant.

fad *n* **1** (craze) engouement *m* (**for** pour); **2** (whim) (petite) manie *f*.

fade I *vtr* décolorer.

II *vi* [*fabric*] se décolorer, se défraîchir; [*colour*] passer; [*lettering, smile, memory*] s'effacer; [*flowers*] se faner; [*image*] s'estomper; [*sound*] s'affaiblir; [*interest, excitement*] s'évanouir; [*hearing, light*] baisser.

■ **fade away** [*sound*] s'éteindre; [*sick person*] dépérir.

faeces, **feces** (US) *n pl* matières *fpl* fécales.

fail I *n* (in exam) échec *m*.

II *vtr* **1** échouer à [*exam, driving test*]; échouer en [*subject*]; coller○ [*candidate, pupil*]; **2** (omit) **to ~ to do** manquer de faire; **to ~ to mention that...** omettre de signaler que...; **3** (be unable) **to ~ to do** ne pas réussir à faire; **4** [*person*] laisser tomber [*friend*]; [*courage*] manquer à [*person*]; [*memory*] faire défaut à [*person*].

III *vi* **1** (not succeed) ne pas réussir; [*exam candidate, attempt, plan*] échouer; [*crop*] être mauvais/-e; **if all else ~s** en dernier recours; **2** [*eyesight, hearing, light*] baisser; [*health*] décliner; **3** [*brakes*] lâcher; [*power*] être coupé/-e; [*heart*] lâcher.

IV without fail *phr* [*arrive, do*] sans faute; [*happen*] à coup sûr.

failing I *n* défaut *m*.

II *prep* **~ that**, **~ this** sinon.

failure *n* **1** (lack of success) échec *m* (**in** à); **2** (person) raté/-e○ *m/f*; (venture or event) échec *m*; **3** (of engine, machine) panne *f*; **4** (Med) défaillance *f*; **5** (omission) **~ to comply with the rules** non-respect *m* de la réglementation; **~ to pay** non-paiement *m*.

faint I *adj* **1** [*smell, accent, breeze*] léger/-ère; [*sound, voice, protest*] faible; [*markings*] à peine

visible; [*recollection*] vague; **I haven't the ~est idea** je n'en ai pas la moindre idée; **2 to feel ~** se sentir mal, défaillir.
II *vi* s'évanouir (**from** sous l'effet de).

fair I *n* (funfair, market) foire *f*; (for charity) kermesse *f*; **trade ~** foire commerciale.
II *adj* **1** (just) [*arrangement, person, trial, wage*] équitable (**to** pour); [*comment, decision, point*] juste; **it's only ~ that she should be first** ce n'est que justice qu'elle soit la première; **it isn't ~** ce n'est pas juste; **2** (quite good) assez bon/bonne; **3 a ~ number of** un bon nombre de; **the house was a ~ size** la maison était de bonne taille; **4** [*weather*] beau/belle (*before n*); [*wind*] favorable; **5** [*hair*] blond/-e; [*complexion*] clair/-e; **6 with her own ~ hands** de ses blanches mains; **the ~ sex** le beau sexe.
III *adv* [*play*] franc jeu.
IDIOMS **to win ~ and square** remporter une victoire indiscutable.

fairground *n* champ *m* de foire.

fair-haired *adj* blond/-e.

fairly *adv* **1** (quite, rather) assez; [*sure*] pratiquement; **2** (justly) [*obtain, win*] honnêtement.

fair-minded *adj* impartial/-e.

fairness *n* **1** (of person) équité *f*; (of judgment) impartialité *f*; **in all ~** en toute justice; **2** (of complexion) blancheur *f*; (of hair) blondeur *f*.

fairy *n* fée *f*.

fairy story, **fairy tale** *n* conte *m* de fées.

faith *n* **1** (confidence) confiance *f*; **I have no ~ in her** elle ne m'inspire pas confiance; **in good ~** en toute bonne foi; **2** (belief) foi *f* (**in** en); **the Muslim ~** la foi musulmane.

faithful I *n* **the ~** les fidèles *mpl*.
II *adj* fidèle (**to** à).

faithfully *adv* fidèlement; **yours ~** (in letter) veuillez agréer, Monsieur/Madame, mes/nos salutations distinguées.

fake I *n* **1** (jewel, work of art, note) faux *m*; **2** (person) imposteur *m*.
II *adj* faux/fausse (*before n*).
III *vtr* contrefaire [*signature, document*]; falsifier [*results*]; feindre [*emotion, illness*].
IV *vi* faire semblant.

falcon *n* faucon *m*.

fall I *n* **1** (gen) chute *f* (**from** de); (in wrestling) tombé *m*; **2** (decrease) baisse *f* (**in** de); (more drastic) chute *f* (**in** de); **3** (in pitch) descente *f*; **4** (of government) chute *f*; (of monarchy) renversement *m*; **5** (US) (autumn) automne *m*.
II **falls** *n pl* chutes *fpl*.
III *vi* **1** (gen) tomber (**from, off, out of** de; **into** dans); **to ~ 10 metres** tomber de 10 mètres; **to ~ down** tomber dans [*hole, stairs*]; **to ~ on** or **to the floor** or **the ground** tomber par terre; **to ~ at sb's feet** se jeter aux pieds de qn; **to ~ from power** tomber; **2** [*quality, standard, level*] diminuer; [*temperature, price, production, number*] baisser (**by** de); **to ~ to/from** descendre à/de.
■ **fall apart 1** [*bike, table*] être délabré/-e; [*shoes*] être usé/-e; [*car, house*] tomber en ruine; **2** [*country*] se désagréger; [*person*] craquer○.
■ **fall back** reculer; (Mil) se replier.
■ **fall back on** avoir recours à [*savings, parents*].
■ **fall behind** prendre du retard; **to ~ behind with** (GB) or **in** (US) prendre du retard dans [*work, project*]; être en retard pour [*payments, rent*].
■ **fall down 1** [*person, poster*] tomber; [*tent, scaffolding*] s'effondrer; **2** (GB) [*argument, comparison*] faiblir.
■ **fall for**: ¶ **~ for [sth]** se laisser prendre à [*trick, story*]; ¶ **~ for [sb]** tomber amoureux/-euse de.
■ **fall in 1** [*walls, roof*] s'écrouler, s'effondrer; **2** [*soldiers*] former les rangs.
■ **fall off 1** [*person, hat, label*] tomber; **2** [*attendance, sales, output*] diminuer; [*quality*] baisser; [*support*] retomber.
■ **fall open** [*book*] tomber ouvert/-e; [*robe*] s'entrebâiller.
■ **fall out 1** tomber; **his hair is ~ing out** il perd ses cheveux; **2** (quarrel) se brouiller (**over** à propos de; **with** avec).
■ **fall over**: ¶ **~ over** [*person*] tomber (par terre); [*object*] se renverser; ¶ **~ over [sth]** trébucher sur [*object*].
■ **fall through** [*plans, deal*] échouer.

fallacy *n* erreur *f*.

fallible *adj* faillible.

false *adj* faux/fausse.

false alarm *n* fausse alerte *f*.

false bottom *n* (in bag, box) double fond *m*.

falsely *adv* **1** (wrongly) faussement; (mistakenly) à tort; **2** [*smile, laugh*] avec affectation.

false teeth *n pl* dentier *m sg*.

falsify *vtr* falsifier.

falsity *n* fausseté *f*.

falter *vi* **1** [*person, courage*] faiblir; **2** (when speaking) [*person*] bafouiller; [*voice*] trembloter; **3** (when walking) [*person*] chanceler; [*footstep*] hésiter.

fame *n* renommée *f* (**as** en tant que); **~ and fortune** la gloire et la fortune.

familiar *adj* familier/-ière (**to** à); **her face looked ~ to me** son visage m'était familier; **that name sounds ~** ce nom me dit quelque chose; **it's a ~ story** c'est un scénario connu; **to be ~ with sth** connaître qch.

familiarity *n* familiarité *f* (**with** avec).

familiarize I *vtr* **to ~ sb with** familiariser qn avec.
II *v refl* **to ~ oneself with** se familiariser avec [*system, work*]; s'habituer à [*person, place*].

family *n* famille *f*; **this must run in the ~** ça doit être de famille.

family name *n* nom *m* de famille.

family planning *n* planning *m* familial.

family tree *n* arbre *m* généalogique.

famine *n* famine *f*.

famous *adj* (gen) célèbre (**for** pour); [*school, university*] réputé/-e (**for** pour).

fan I *n* **1** (of jazz) mordu/-e○ *m/f*; (of star, actor) fan○ *mf*; (Sport) supporter *m*; **2** (for cooling) (mechanical) ventilateur *m*; (hand-held) éventail *m*.

II *vtr* attiser [*fire*]; **to ~ one's face** s'éventer le visage.
■ **fan out**: ¶ **~ out** [*police, troops*] se déployer (en éventail); ¶ **~ [sth] out** ouvrir [qch] en éventail [*cards, papers*].

fanatic *n* fanatique *mf*.

fan belt *n* courroie *f* de ventilateur.

fancy I *n* **1** (liking) **to take sb's ~** [*object*] faire envie à qn; **to take a ~ to sb** s'attacher à qn; (sexually) (GB) s'enticher de qn; **2** (whim) caprice *m*; **as the ~ takes me** comme ça me prend; **3** (fantasy) imagination *f*; **a flight of ~** une lubie.
II *adj* [*equipment*] sophistiqué/-e; [*food, hotel, restaurant*] de luxe; [*paper, box*] fantaisie *inv*; [*clothes*] chic.
III *vtr* **1**○ (want) avoir (bien) envie de [*food, drink, object*]; **what do you ~ for lunch?** qu'est-ce qui te plairait pour le déjeuner?; **2**○ (GB) **she fancies him** elle s'est entichée de lui; **3 ~ seeing you here**○**!** tiens donc, toi ici?; **4** (Sport) voir [qn/qch] gagnant [*athlete, horse*].

fancy dress *n* (GB) déguisement *m*; **in ~** déguisé/-e.

fancy dress party *n* bal *m* costumé.

fang *n* (of dog, wolf) croc *m*; (of snake) crochet *m* (à venin).

fantasize *vi* fantasmer (**about** sur); **to ~ about doing** rêver de faire.

fantastic *adj* **1**○ (wonderful) merveilleux/-euse, super○ *inv*; **2** (unrealistic) [*story*] invraisemblable; **3**○ (huge) [*profit*] fabuleux/-euse; [*speed, increase*] vertigineux/-euse; **4** (magical) fantastique.

fantasy *n* **1** (dream) rêve *m*; (in psychology) fantasme *m*; **2** (fiction) fantastique *m*.

far I *adv* **1** (in space) loin; **~ off, ~ away** au loin; **is it ~ to York?** est-ce que York est loin d'ici?; **how ~ is it to Leeds?** combien y a-t-il (de kilomètres) jusqu'à Leeds?; **how ~ is Glasgow from London?** Glasgow est à quelle distance de Londres?; **as ~ as** jusqu'à; **2** (in time) **as ~ back as 1965** déjà en 1965; **as ~ back as he can remember** d'aussi loin qu'il s'en souvienne; **the holidays are not ~ off** c'est bientôt les vacances; **3** (very much) bien; **~ better** bien mieux; **~ too fast** bien trop vite; **4 how ~ have they got?** où en sont-ils?; **as ~ as possible** autant que possible, dans la mesure du possible; **as ~ as we know** pour autant que nous le sachions; **as ~ as I am concerned** quant à moi; **5 to go too ~** aller trop loin; **to push sb too ~** pousser qn à bout.
II *adj* **1 the ~ north/south (of)** l'extrême nord/sud (de); **the ~ east/west (of)** tout à fait à l'est/l'ouest (de); **2** autre; **at the ~ end of the room** à l'autre bout de la pièce; **on the ~ side of the wall** de l'autre côté du mur; **3** (of party) **the ~ right/left** l'extrême droite/gauche.
III by far *phr* de loin.
IV far from *phr* loin de; **~ from satisfied** loin d'être satisfait/-e.
V so far *phr* **1** (up till now) jusqu'ici, jusqu'à présent; **so ~, so good** pour l'instant tout va bien; **2** (up to a point) **you can only trust him so ~** tu ne peux pas lui faire entièrement confiance.
IDIOMS **not to be ~ off** or **out** or **wrong** ne pas être loin du compte; **~ and wide** partout; **to be a ~ cry from** être bien loin de; **she will go ~** elle ira loin; **this wine won't go very ~** on ne va pas aller loin avec ce vin.

faraway *adj* lointain/-e.

farce *n* farce *f*.

fare *n* (on bus, underground) prix *m* du ticket; (on train, plane) prix du billet; **half/full ~** demi-/plein tarif *m*.

Far East *pr n* Extrême-Orient *m*.

farewell *n* adieu *m*.

far-fetched *adj* tiré/-e par les cheveux○.

farm I *n* ferme *f*.
II *vtr* cultiver, exploiter [*land*].

farmer ▶**626** *n* (gen) fermier *m*; (in official terminology) agriculteur *m*; (arable) cultivateur *m*; **pig ~** éleveur *m* de porcs.

farming *n* (profession) agriculture *f*; (of land) exploitation *f*; **sheep ~** élevage *m* de moutons.

farmyard *n* cour *f* de ferme.

far-off *adj* lointain/-e.

far-sighted *adj* **1** (prudent) [*person, policy*] prévoyant/-e; **2** (US) [*person*] presbyte.

farther *adj, adv* = **further I 1, 2; II, 2**.

farthest = **furthest**.

fascinate *vtr* (interest) passionner; (stronger) fasciner.

fascinating *adj* [*book, discussion*] passionnant/-e; [*person*] fascinant/-e.

fascination *n* passion *f* (**with, for** pour).

fascism *n* fascisme *m*.

fascist *n, adj* fasciste (*mf*).

fashion I *n* **1** mode *f* (**for** de); **in ~** à la mode; **to go out of ~** se démoder, passer de mode; **to be all the ~** faire fureur; **2** (manner) façon *f*, manière *f*; **after a ~** plus ou moins bien.
II *vtr* façonner [*clay, wood*] (**into** en); fabriquer [*object*] (**out of, from** de).

fashionable *adj* [*clothes*] à la mode (**among, with** parmi); [*resort, restaurant*] chic (**among, with** parmi).

fashion model ▶**626** *n* mannequin *m*.

fashion show *n* présentation *f* de collection.

fast I *n* jeûne *m*.
II *adj* **1** rapide; **to be a ~ reader/runner** lire/courir vite; **2** (ahead of time) **my watch is ~** ma montre avance; **you're five minutes ~** ta montre avance de cinq minutes.
III *adv* **1** vite, rapidement; **how ~ can you run?** est-ce que tu cours vite?; **2** [*hold*] ferme; [*stuck*] bel et bien; [*shut*] bien; **to be ~ asleep** dormir à poings fermés.

fasten I *vtr* **1** fermer [*lid, case*]; attacher [*belt, necklace*]; boutonner [*coat*]; **2** fixer [*notice, shelf*] (**to** à; **onto** sur); attacher [*lead, rope*] (**to** à).
II *vi* [*box*] se fermer; [*necklace, skirt*] s'attacher.

fastener *n* (gen) attache *f*; (hook) agrafe *f*; (clasp) fermoir *m*.

fast food *n* restauration *f* rapide.

fast food restaurant *n* fast-food *m*, restovite *m*.

fast-forward **I** *n* avance *f* rapide.
II *vtr* faire avancer rapidement [*tape*].

fast lane *n* voie *f* de dépassement.

fat **I** *n* **1** (in diet) matières *fpl* grasses; **animal ~s** graisses *fpl* animales; **2** (on meat) gras *m*; **3** (for cooking) matière *f* grasse; **4** (in body) graisse *f*.
II *adj* **1** [*person, animal, body, bottom*] gros/grosse (*before n*); **to get ~** grossir; **2** [*wallet*] rebondi/-e; [*envelope, file, magazine*] épais/épaisse; **3** [*profit, cheque*] gros/grosse (*before n*).

fatal *adj* [*accident, injury*] mortel/-elle (**to** pour); [*flaw, mistake*] fatal/-e; [*decision*] funeste; [*day, hour*] fatidique.

fatalist *n* fataliste *mf*.

fatality *n* (person killed) mort *m*.

fatally *adv* **1** [*wounded*] mortellement; **2** [*flawed*] irrémédiablement.

fate *n* sort *m*.

fateful *adj* [*decision*] fatal/-e; [*day*] fatidique.

father *n* père *m*.

Father Christmas *n* (GB) le père Noël.

father-in-law *n* beau-père *m*.

fatherly *adj* paternel/-elle.

fathom **I** *n* brasse *f* anglaise (= *1.83 m*).
II *vtr* (also **~ out** GB) comprendre.

fatigue *n* **1** (of person) épuisement *m*; **2 metal ~** fatigue *f* du métal; **3** (US Mil) corvée *f*.

fatten *vtr* (also **~ up**) engraisser [*animal*]; faire grossir [*person*].

fattening *adj* [*food, drink*] qui fait grossir.

fatty *adj* [*tissue, deposit*] graisseux/-euse; [*food, meat*] gras/grasse.

fatuous *adj* stupide.

faucet *n* (US) robinet *m*.

fault **I** *n* **1** (flaw) défaut *m* (**in** dans); **he's always finding ~** il trouve toujours quelque chose à redire; **2** (responsibility) faute *f*; **to be sb's ~** être (de) la faute de qn; **it's my own ~** c'est de ma faute; **3** (in tennis) **~!** faute!; **4** (in earth) faille *f*.
II *vtr* prendre [qn/qch] en défaut; **it cannot be ~ed** c'est irréprochable.

faulty *adj* [*wiring, machine*] défectueux/-euse.

fauna *n* faune *f*.

faux pas *n* impair *m*.

favour (GB), **favor** (US) **I** *n* **1** (kindness) service *m*; **to do sb a ~** rendre service à qn; **to return a** or **the ~** rendre la pareille; **2 to be in sb's ~** [*situation*] être avantageux/-euse pour qn; [*financial rates, wind*] être favorable à qn; **3 to win/lose ~ with sb** s'attirer/perdre les bonnes grâces de qn.
II *vtr* **1** (prefer) être pour [*method, solution*]; être partisan de [*political party*]; **2** (benefit) [*circumstances*] favoriser [*person*]; [*law*] privilégier [*person*].
III in favour of *phr* **1** (on the side of) en faveur de; **to be in ~ of sb/sth** être pour qn/qch; **2** (to the advantage of) **to work in sb's ~** avantager qn; **to decide in sb's ~** (Law) donner gain de cause à qn; **3** (out of preference for) [*reject*] au profit de.

favourable (GB), **favorable** (US) *adj* [*conditions, impression, reply*] favorable (**to** à); [*result, sign*] bon/bonne (*before n*).

favourite (GB), **favorite** (US) **I** *n* (gen) préféré/-e *m/f*; (Sport) favori/-ite *m/f*.
II *adj* préféré/-e, favori/-ite.

favouritism (GB), **favoritism** (US) *n* favoritisme *m*.

fawn **I** *n* (Zool) faon *m*.
II *vtr* **to ~ on sb** flagorner qn.

fax **I** *n* **1** (also **~ message**) télécopie *f*, fax *m*; **2** (also **~ machine**) télécopieur *m*, fax *m*.
II *vtr* télécopier, faxer [*document*]; envoyer une télécopie or un fax à [*person*].

fax number *n* numéro *m* de télécopie or de fax.

fear **I** *n* **1** (fright) peur *f*; **2** (apprehension) crainte *f* (**for** pour); **3** (possibility) **there's no ~ of him** or **his being late** il n'y a pas de danger qu'il soit en retard.
II *vtr* craindre; **to ~ the worst** craindre le pire, s'attendre au pire.
III *vi* **to ~ for sb/sth** craindre pour qn/qch.

feasible *adj* **1** [*project*] réalisable; **2** [*excuse, explanation*] plausible.

feast **I** *n* (meal) festin *m*; (religious) fête *f*.
II *vi* se régaler (**on** de).

feat *n* exploit *m*; **it was no mean ~** cela n'a pas été une mince affaire; **a ~ of engineering** une prouesse technologique.

feather *n* plume *f*.

feature **I** *n* **1** (distinctive characteristic) trait *m*, caractéristique *f*; **2** (aspect) aspect *m*, côté *m*; **3** (of face) trait *m*; **4** (of car, computer, product) accessoire *m*; **5** (report) (in paper) article *m* de fond (**on** sur); (on TV, radio) reportage *m* (**on** sur).
II *vtr* [*film, magazine*] présenter [*story, star*]; [*advert, poster*] représenter [*person*].
III *vi* **1** (figure) figurer; **2** [*performer*] jouer (**in** dans).

feature film *n* long métrage *m*.

February **▶ 456** *n* février *m*.

federal *adj* fédéral/-e.

federation *n* fédération *f*.

fed up○ *adj* **to be ~** en avoir marre○ (**of** de).

fee *n* **1** (for service) honoraires *mpl*; **school ~s** frais *mpl* de scolarité; **2** (for admission) droit *m* d'entrée; (for membership) cotisation *f*.

feeble *adj* (gen) faible; [*excuse*] peu convaincant/-e; [*joke, attempt*] médiocre.

feed **I** *n* (for animals) ration *f* de nourriture; (for baby) (breast) tétée *f*; (bottle) biberon *m*.
II *vtr* **1** nourrir [*animal, plant, person*] (**on** de); donner à manger à [*pet*]; ravitailler [*army*]; **2** (supply) alimenter [*machine*]; mettre des pièces dans [*meter*]; faire passer [*ball*] (**to** à); **to ~ sth into** mettre or introduire qch dans.

feedback *n* **1** (from people) remarques *fpl* (**on** sur; **from** de la part de); **2** (on hi-fi) réaction *f* parasite.

feel I *n* **1** (atmosphere) atmosphère *f*; **2** (sensation) sensation *f*; **3 to get the ~ of** se faire à [*controls, system*]; **to have a ~ for language** bien savoir manier la langue.
II *vtr* **1** éprouver [*affection, desire, pride*]; ressentir [*hostility, obligation, effects*]; **2** (believe) **to ~ (that)** estimer que; **3** sentir [*blow, draught, heat*]; ressentir [*ache, stiffness, effects*]; **4** (touch) tâter [*washing, cloth*]; palper [*patient, shoulder, parcel*]; **to ~ one's way** avancer à tâtons; (figurative) tâter le terrain; **5** avoir conscience de [*presence, tension*].
III *vi* **1** se sentir [*sad, happy, nervous, safe, ill, tired*]; être [*sure, surprised*]; avoir l'impression d'être [*trapped, betrayed*]; **to ~ afraid/ashamed** avoir peur/honte; **to ~ hot/thirsty** avoir chaud/soif; **to ~ as if** or **as though** avoir l'impression que; **she isn't ~ing herself today** elle n'est pas dans son assiette aujourd'hui○; **2** (seem) être [*cold, smooth*]; avoir l'air [*eerie*]; **it ~s odd** ça fait drôle; **it ~s like** (**a**) **Sunday** on se croirait un dimanche; **3** (want) **to ~ like sth** avoir envie de qch; **I ~ like a drink** je prendrais bien un verre; **4 to ~** (**around** or **about**) **in** fouiller dans [*bag, pocket, drawer*]; **to ~ along** tâtonner le long de [*edge, wall*].
■ **feel for**: ¶ **~ (around) for [sth]** chercher [qch] à tâtons; ¶ **~ for [sb]** plaindre.
■ **feel up to**: **~ up to (doing) sth** se sentir d'attaque○ or assez bien pour (faire) qch.

feeling *n* **1** (emotion) sentiment *m*; **to hurt sb's ~s** blesser qn; **2** (opinion, belief) sentiment *m*; **~s are running high** les esprits s'échauffent; **3** (sensitivity) sensibilité *f*; **to speak with great ~** parler avec beaucoup de passion; **4** (impression) impression *f*; **I had a ~ you'd say that** je sentais que tu allais dire ça; **I've got a bad ~ about this** j'ai le pressentiment que cela va mal se passer; **5** (physical sensation) sensation *f*; **a dizzy ~** une sensation de vertige.

feign *vtr* feindre [*innocence, surprise*]; simuler [*illness, sleep*].

fell I *n* montagne *f*.
II *vtr* abattre [*tree*]; assommer [*person*].
IDIOMS **in one ~ swoop** d'un seul coup.

fellow I *n* **1**○ (man) type○ *m*, homme *m*; **2** (of society, association) membre *m* (**of** de); **3** (GB) (lecturer) membre *m* (du corps enseignant) d'un collège universitaire; **4** (US) (researcher) universitaire *mf* titulaire d'une bourse de recherche.
II *adj* **her ~ teachers** ses collègues professeurs; **a ~ Englishman** un compatriote anglais.

fellowship *n* **1** (companionship) camaraderie *f*; **2** (association) association *f*.

felony *n* crime *m*.

felt *n* feutre *m*.

felt-tip (pen) *n* feutre *m*.

female I *n* **1** (Bot, Zool) femelle *f*; **2** (woman) femme *f*.
II *adj* **1** (Bot, Zool) femelle; **~ rabbit** lapine *f*; **2** [*population, role*] féminin/-e; [*voice*] de femme; **~ student** étudiante *f*; **3** [*plug, socket*] femelle.

feminine I *n* féminin *m*.
II *adj* féminin/-e.

feminist *n, adj* féministe (*mf*).

fence I *n* **1** clôture *f*; **2** (in showjumping) obstacle *m*; (in horseracing) haie *f*.
II *vtr* clôturer [*area, garden*].
IDIOMS **to sit on the ~** ne pas prendre position.

fencing ▶ **504** *n* escrime *f*.

fend *vi* **to ~ for oneself** se débrouiller (tout seul/toute seule).
■ **fend off** repousser [*attacker*]; parer [*blow*]; écarter [*question*].

fender *n* **1** (for fire) garde-cendre *m*; **2** (US Aut) aile *f*.

fennel *n* fenouil *m*.

fern *n* fougère *f*.

ferocious *adj* [*animal*] féroce; [*attack*] sauvage; [*heat*] accablant/-e.

ferret *n* furet *m*.

ferry I *n* (long-distance) ferry *m*; (over short distances) bac *m*.
II *vtr* transporter [*passenger, goods*].

fertile *adj* [*land, imagination*] fertile; [*human, animal, egg*] fécond/-e.

fertilize *vtr* fertiliser [*land*]; féconder [*animal, plant, egg*].

fertilizer *n* engrais *m*.

fervent *adj* [*admirer*] fervent/-e.

fester *vi* [*wound, sore*] suppurer.

festival *n* (gen) fête *f*; (arts event) festival *m*.

festivity *n* réjouissance *f*.

fetch *vtr* **1** aller chercher; **~!** (to dog) rapporte!; **2** [*goods*] rapporter; **to ~ a good price** rapporter un bon prix; **these vases can ~ up to £600** le prix de ces vases peut atteindre 600 livres.

fête *n* (church, village) kermesse *f* (paroissiale).

fetus (US) = **foetus**.

feud I *n* querelle *f*.
II *vi* se quereller.

feudal *adj* féodal/-e.

fever *n* fièvre *f*; **to have a ~** avoir de la fièvre; **gold ~** la fièvre de l'or.

feverish *adj* [*person, eyes*] fiévreux/-euse; [*dreams*] délirant/-e; [*excitement, activity*] fébrile.

few

■ **Note** When *a few* is used as a pronoun and if the sentence does not specify what it refers to, the pronoun *en* (= *of them*) must be added before the verb in French: *there were only a few* = il n'y en avait que quelques-uns/quelques-unes.

I *det* **1** (not many) peu de; **~ visitors/letters** peu de visiteurs/lettres; **2** (couple of) **every ~ days** tous les deux ou trois jours; **the first ~ weeks** les premières semaines.
II *pron, quantif* peu; **~ of us succeeded** peu d'entre nous ont réussi.
III **a few** *det, quantif, pron* **1** (as determiner, quantifier) quelques; **a ~ people** quelques personnes; **quite a ~ people** pas mal○ de gens, un bon nombre de personnes; **a ~ of the soldiers** quelques soldats; **a ~ of us** un

certain nombre d'entre nous; **2** (as pronoun) quelques-uns/quelques-unes; **I would like a ~ more** j'en voudrais quelques-uns/quelques-unes de plus; **I only need a ~** il ne m'en faut que quelques-uns/quelques-unes.
IDIOMS **they are ~ and far between** ils sont rarissimes.

fewer I *det* moins de; **~ and ~ pupils** de moins en moins d'élèves.
II *pron* moins; **~ than 50 people** moins de 50 personnes; **no ~ than** pas moins de.

fewest *det* le moins de.

fiancé *n* fiancé *m*.

fiancée *n* fiancée *f*.

fibre (GB), **fiber** (US) *n* **1** (gen) fibre *f*; **2** (in diet) fibres *fpl*.

fibreglass (GB), **fiberglass** (US) *n* fibres *fpl* de verre.

fickle *adj* [*lover, friend*] inconstant/-e; [*fate, public opinion*] changeant/-e; [*weather*] capricieux/-ieuse.

fiction *n* **1** (genre) le roman; **2** (invention) fiction *f*.

fictional *adj* [*character, event*] imaginaire.

fictitious *adj* **1** (false) [*name, address*] fictif/-ive; **2** (imaginary) imaginaire.

fiddle I○ *vtr* falsifier [*tax return, figures*].
II *vi* **1** (fidget) **to ~ with sth** tripoter qch; **2** (adjust) **to ~ with** tourner [*knobs, controls*].

fidelity *n* fidélité *f* (**of** de; **to** à).

fidget *vi* ne pas tenir en place.

field I *n* **1** (gen) champ *m* (**of** de); (sports ground) terrain *m*; **football ~** terrain de football; **2** (of knowledge) domaine *m* (**of** de).
II *adj* **1** [*hospital*] de campagne; **2** [*test, study*] sur le terrain; [*work*] de terrain.

field day *n* **1** (school trip) sortie *f* (éducative); **2** (US) (sports day) journée *f* sportive.
IDIOMS **to have a ~** (gen) s'amuser comme un fou/une folle; [*press, critics*] jubiler; (make money) [*shopkeepers*] faire d'excellentes affaires.

fierce *adj* [*animal, expression, person*] féroce; [*battle, storm*] violent/-e; [*competition*] acharné/-e; [*flames, heat*] intense.

fifteen ▶389, 434 *n, pron, det* quinze (*m*) *inv*.

fifteenth ▶456, 498 I *n* **1** (in order) quinzième *mf*; **2** (of month) quinze *m inv*; **3** (fraction) quinzième *m*.
II *adj, adv* quinzième.

fifth ▶456, 498 I *n* **1** (in order) cinquième *mf*; **2** (of month) cinq *m*; **3** (fraction) cinquième *m*.
II *adj, adv* cinquième.

fifties ▶389, 456 *n pl* **1** (era) **the ~** les années *fpl* cinquante; **2** (age) **to be in one's ~** avoir entre cinquante et soixante ans.

fiftieth *n, adj, adv* cinquantième (*mf*).

fifty ▶389, 434 *n, pron, det* cinquante (*m*) *inv*.

fifty-fifty I *adj* **to have a ~ chance** avoir une chance sur deux (**of doing** de faire).
II *adv* **to share sth ~** partager qch moitié-moitié; **to go ~** faire moitié-moitié.

fig *n* figue *f*.

fight I *n* **1** (gen) bagarre *f* (**between** entre; **over** pour); (Mil) bataille *f* (**between** entre; **for** pour); (in boxing) combat *m* (**between** entre); **2** (struggle) lutte *f* (**against** contre; **for** pour; **to do** pour faire); **3** (argument) dispute *f* (**over** au sujet de; **with** avec).
II *vtr* **1** se battre contre [*person*]; **2** lutter contre [*disease, opponent, emotion, proposal*]; combattre [*fire*]; mener [*campaign, war*] (**against** contre); **to ~ one's way through** se frayer un passage dans [*crowd*].
III *vi* **1** (gen, Mil) se battre; **2** (campaign) lutter; **3** (argue) se quereller (**over** à propos de).
■ **fight back**: ¶ **~ back** se défendre; ¶ **~ back [sth]** refréner [*tears, fear, anger*].

fighter *n* **1** (Sport) boxeur *m*; **2** (determined person) lutteur/-euse *m/f*; **3** (also **~ plane**) avion *m* de chasse.

fighting I *n* (gen) bagarre *f*; (Mil) combat *m*.
II *adj* **1** [*unit, force*] de combat; **2** [*talk*] agressif/-ive.

figment *n* **a ~ of your imagination** un produit de ton imagination.

figurative *adj* figuré/-e.

figure I *n* **1** chiffre *m*; **a four-~ number** un nombre de quatre chiffres; **in double ~s** à deux chiffres; **2** (person) personnage *m*; **well-known ~** personnalité *f* célèbre; **father ~** image *f* du père; **3** (body shape) ligne *f*; **to lose one's ~** prendre de l'embonpoint; **4** (diagram, shape) figure *f*.
II *vi* (appear) figurer (**in** dans).
■ **figure out** trouver [*answer, reason*]; **to ~ out who/why** arriver à comprendre qui/pourquoi.

figurehead *n* (symbolic leader) représentant/-e *m/f* nominal/-e; (of ship) figure *f* de proue.

figure of speech *n* figure *f* de rhétorique.

file I *n* **1** (for papers) (gen) dossier *m*; (cardboard) chemise *f*; **2** (record) dossier *m* (**on** sur); **3** (Comput) fichier *m*; **4** (tool) lime *f*; **5 in single ~** en file indienne.
II *vtr* **1** classer [*invoice, letter, record*] (**under** sous); **2** déposer [*application, complaint*] (**with** auprès de); **to ~ a lawsuit** (**against sb**) intenter or faire un procès (à qn); **3** limer [*wood, metal*]; **to ~ one's nails** se limer les ongles.
III *vi* **they ~d into/out of the classroom** ils sont entrés dans/sortis de la salle l'un après l'autre.

file cabinet (US), **filing cabinet** *n* classeur *m* à tiroirs.

fill I *vtr* **1** remplir [*container, page*] (**with** de); garnir [*cushion, pie, sandwich*] (**with** de); [*dentist*] plomber [*tooth, cavity*]; **2** [*crowd, sound*] remplir [*room, street*]; [*smoke, protesters*] envahir [*building, room*]; occuper [*time, day, hours*]; [*emotion, thought*] remplir [*mind, person*]; **3** boucher [*crack, hole, void*] (**with** avec); **4** répondre à [*need*]; **5** [*company, university*] pourvoir [*post, vacancy*]; **6** [*applicant*] occuper [*post, vacancy*]; **7** [*wind*] gonfler [*sail*].
II *vi* se remplir (**with** de).
■ **fill in**: **to ~ in for sb** remplacer qn; ¶ **~ [sth] in** remplir [*form*]; donner [*detail, name,*

date]; ¶ **~ [sb] in** mettre [qn] au courant (**on** de).

■ **fill out**: ¶ **~ out** [*person*] prendre du poids; [*face*] s'arrondir; ¶ **~ [sth] out** remplir [*form*]; faire [*prescription*].

■ **fill up**: ¶ **~ up** [*bath, theatre, bus*] se remplir (**with** de); ¶ **~ [sth] up** remplir [*kettle, box, room*] (**with** de).

fillet I *n* filet *m*; **~ steak** filet *m* de bœuf.
II *vtr* enlever les arêtes de, fileter [*fish*].

filling I *n* **1** (of sandwich, baked potato) garniture *f*; (for peppers, meat) farce *f*; **2** (for tooth) plombage *m*.
II *adj* [*food, dish*] bourratif/-ive○.

filling station *n* station-service *f*.

film I *n* **1** (movie) film *m*; **2** (for camera) pellicule *f*; **3** (layer) pellicule *f*.
II *vtr* filmer.
III *vi* tourner.

film star *n* vedette *f* de cinéma.

filter I *n* filtre *m*.
II *vtr* filtrer [*liquid, gas*]; faire passer [*coffee*].
III *vi* **to ~ into** [*light, sound, water*] pénétrer dans [*area*].

filth *n* **1** (dirt) crasse *f*; **2** (vulgarity) obscénités *fpl*; (swearing) grossièretés *fpl*.

filthy *adj* **1** (dirty) crasseux/-euse; (revolting) répugnant/-e; **2** [*language*] ordurier/-ière; [*mind*] mal tourné/-e; **3** (GB) [*look*] noir/-e.

fin *n* (of fish, seal) nageoire *f*; (of shark) aileron *m*.

final I *n* (Sport) finale *f*.
II *adj* **1** (last) dernier/-ière; **2** [*decision*] définitif/-ive; [*result*] final/-e.

finale *n* finale *f*.

finalist *n* finaliste *mf*.

finalize *vtr* conclure [*contract*]; arrêter [*plan, details*]; faire la dernière mise au point de [*article*]; fixer [*timetable, route*].

finally *adv* **1** (eventually) finalement, enfin; **2** (lastly) finalement, pour finir; **3** (definitively) définitivement.

finals *n pl* (GB Univ) examens *mpl* de fin d'études; (US Univ) examens *mpl* de fin de semestre.

finance I *n* **1** (gen) finance *f*; **2** (funds) fonds *mpl* (**for** pour; **from** auprès de).
II *vtr* financer [*project*].

finances *n pl* situation *f* financière.

financial *adj* financier/-ière.

find I *n* **1** (gen) découverte *f*; **2** (good buy) trouvaille *f*.
II *vtr* **1** trouver; **I can't ~ my keys** je ne trouve pas mes clés; **I couldn't ~ the time** je n'ai pas eu le temps; **2** (experience) éprouver [*pleasure, satisfaction*] (**in** dans); **3** (Law) **to ~ that** conclure que; **to ~ sb guilty** déclarer qn coupable.

■ **find out**: ¶ **~ out** se renseigner; **if he ever ~s out** si jamais il l'apprend; ¶ **~ [sth] out** découvrir [*fact, answer, name, cause, truth*]; ¶ **~ out who/why/where** trouver qui/pourquoi/où; ¶ **~ out about [sth] 1** (learn by chance) découvrir [*plan, affair, breakage*]; **2** (research) faire des recherches sur [*subject*].

findings *n pl* conclusions *fpl*.

fine I *n* (gen) amende *f*; (for traffic offence) contravention *f*.
II *adj* **1** (very good) excellent/-e; **2** (satisfactory) bon/bonne (*before n*); **that's ~** très bien; **'~, thanks'** 'très bien, merci'; **3** (nice) [*weather, day*] beau/belle (*before n*); **4** (delicate) fin/-e; **5** (subtle) [*adjustment, detail, distinction*] subtil/-e; **6** (refined) [*lady, clothes*] beau/belle (*before n*); **7** (commendable) [*person*] merveilleux/-euse.
III *adv* [*get along, come along, do*] très bien.
IV *vtr* (gen) condamner [qn] à une amende; (for traffic offence) donner une contravention à.

fine art *n* beaux-arts *mpl*.
IDIOMS **she's got cheating down to a ~** elle est passée maître dans l'art de tricher.

fine-tune *vtr* ajuster.

finger I *n* ▶ 413 doigt *m*.
II *vtr* toucher [*fruit, goods*]; tripoter○ [*necklace*].
IDIOMS **to keep one's ~s crossed** croiser les doigts (**for sb** pour qn).

finger-nail *n* ongle *m*.

fingerprint *n* empreinte *f* digitale.

fingertip *n* bout *m* du doigt.

finicky *adj* [*person*] difficile (**about** pour); [*job, task*] minutieux/-ieuse.

finish I *n* **1** (end) fin *f*; **2** (Sport) arrivée *f*; **3** (of wood, car) finition *f*; (of fabric, leather) apprêt *m*.
II *vtr* **1** finir, terminer [*chapter, sentence, task*]; terminer, achever [*building, novel*]; **to ~ doing** finir de faire; **2** (leave) finir [*work, school*]; **3** (consume) finir [*cigarette, drink, meal*]; **4** (put an end to) briser [*career*].
III *vi* (gen) finir; [*speaker*] finir de parler; [*conference, programme, term*] finir, se terminer; [*holidays*] se terminer.

■ **finish off** finir, terminer [*letter, meal, task*].

■ **finish up**: ¶ **~ up** finir; ¶ **~ [sth] up** finir [*milk, paint, cake*].

finishing line (GB), **finish line** (US) *n* ligne *f* d'arrivée.

finishing touch *n* **to put the ~(es) to sth** mettre la dernière main à qch.

finite *adj* (gen) fini/-e; [*resources*] limité/-e.

Finland ▶ 448 *pr n* Finlande *f*.

Finn ▶ 553 *n* Finlandais/-e *m*/*f*.

Finnish ▶ 553 I *n* (language) finnois *m*.
II *adj* **1** [*culture, food, politics*] finlandais/-e; [*ambassador, embassy*] de Finlande; **2** [*grammar*] finnois/-e; [*teacher, lesson*] de finnois.

fir *n* (also **~ tree**) sapin *m*.

fire I *n* **1** feu *m*; **to set ~ to sth** mettre le feu à qch; **to be on ~** être en feu; **to catch ~** prendre feu; **to sit by the ~** s'asseoir près du feu or au coin du feu; **2** (blaze) incendie *m*; **to start a ~** provoquer un incendie; **3 to open ~ on sb** ouvrir le feu sur qn.
II *excl* **1** (raising alarm) au feu!; **2** (Mil) feu!
III *vtr* **1** décharger [*gun, weapon*]; tirer [*shot*]; lancer [*arrow, missile*]; **to ~ questions at sb** bombarder qn de questions; **2** (dismiss) renvoyer, virer○ [*person*].
IV *vi* tirer (**at, on** sur).

fire alarm *n* alarme *f* incendie.

firearm *n* arme *f* à feu.
firebomb I *n* bombe *f* incendiaire.
II *vtr* incendier [*building*].
fire brigade *n* pompiers *mpl*.
fire engine *n* voiture *f* de pompiers.
fire escape *n* escalier *m* de secours.
fire exit *n* sortie *f* de secours.
fire extinguisher *n* extincteur *m*.
fireguard *n* pare-étincelles *m inv*.
fireman ▶626| *n* pompier *m*.
fireplace *n* cheminée *f*.
fireproof *adj* [*door, clothing*] ignifugé/-e.
fire station *n* caserne *f* de pompiers.
firewood *n* bois *m* à brûler.
firework *n* feu *m* d'artifice.
firing *n* (of guns) tir *m*.
firing squad *n* peloton *m* d'exécution.
firm I *n* entreprise *f*, société *f*.
II *adj* **1** [*mattress, fruit, handshake*] ferme; **2** [*basis, grasp*] solide; **3** [*offer, intention, refusal*] ferme; [*evidence*] concret/-ète; **4** [*person, leadership*] ferme (**with sb** avec qn).
III *adv* **to stand ~** tenir bon.
first ▶456|, 498| I *n* **1** (gen) premier/-ière *m/f* (**to do** à faire); **2** (of month) premier *m inv*; **the ~ of May** le premier mai; **3** (GB Univ) (also **~-class honours degree**) ≈ licence *f* avec mention très bien.
II *adj* premier/-ière (*before n*); **the ~ three pages** les trois premières pages; **at ~ glance** or **sight** à première vue; **I'll ring ~ thing in the morning** je vous appellerai en tout début de matinée.
III *adv* **1** [*arrive, leave*] le premier/la première; **women and children ~** les femmes et les enfants d'abord; **to come ~** [*contestant*] terminer premier/première (**in** à); [*career, family*] passer avant tout; **2** (to begin with) d'abord; **~ of all** tout d'abord; **3** (for the first time) pour la première fois; **I ~ met him in Paris** je l'ai rencontré pour la première fois à Paris.
IV **at first** *phr* au début.
IDIOMS **~ things ~** chaque chose en son temps.
first aid *n* **1** (treatment) premiers soins *mpl*; **2** (as skill) secourisme *m*.
first-aid kit *n* trousse *f* de secours.
first class *adj* **1** [*hotel, ticket*] de première (classe); **2** [*stamp, mail*] (au) tarif rapide; **3** (GB) [*degree*] avec mention très bien; **4** (excellent) excellent/-e.
first cousin *n* (male) cousin *m* germain; (female) cousine *f* germaine.
first floor *n* (GB) premier étage *m*; (US) rez-de-chaussée *m*.
first form *n* (GB Sch) (classe *f* de) sixième *f*.
first grade *n* (US Sch) cours *m* préparatoire.
firstly *adv* premièrement.
first name *n* prénom *m*.
first-rate *adj* excellent/-e.
fish I *n* poisson *m*.
II *vi* pêcher; **to ~ for trout** pêcher la truite; **to ~ for compliments** rechercher les compliments.
fish and chips *n* poisson *m* frit avec des frites.
fish and chip shop ▶626| *n* (GB) friterie *f*.
fishbowl *n* bocal *m* (à poissons).
fisherman ▶626| *n* pêcheur *m*.
fishing *n* pêche *f*; **to go ~** aller à la pêche.
fishing boat *n* bateau *m* de pêche.
fishing rod *n* canne *f* à pêche.
fish market *n* halle *f* aux poissons.
fishmonger ▶626| *n* (GB) poissonnier/-ière *m*, *f*; **~'s (shop)** poissonnerie *f*.
fishnet *adj* [*stockings*] à résille.
fish tank *n* aquarium *m*.
fishy *adj* **1** [*smell, taste*] de poisson; **2**○ (suspect) louche○.
fist *n* poing *m*.
fit I *n* **1** (Med) crise *f*, attaque *f*; **2** (of anger, passion, panic) accès *m*; **~ of coughing** quinte *f* de toux; **to have sb in ~s**○ donner le fou rire à qn; **3** (of garment) **to be a good ~** être à la bonne taille; **to be a tight ~** être juste.
II *adj* **1** [*person*] (in trim) en forme; (not ill) en bonne santé; **to get ~** retrouver la forme; **2 to be ~ for** (worthy of) être digne de [*person, hero, king*]; (capable of) être capable de faire [*job*]; **not ~ for human consumption** impropre à la consommation; **to see** or **think ~ to do** juger bon de faire; **to be in no ~ state to do** ne pas être en état de faire.
III *vtr* **1** [*garment*] être à la taille de; [*shoe*] être à la pointure de; [*key*] aller dans [*lock*]; aller dans [*envelope, space*]; **2 to ~ sth in** or **into** trouver de la place pour qch dans [*room, house, car*]; **3** (install) mettre [qch] en place [*lock, door, kitchen, shower*]; **4** correspondre à [*description, requirements*].
IV *vi* **1** [*garment*] être à ma/ta/sa taille, aller; [*shoes*] être à ma/ta/sa pointure, aller; [*key, lid, sheet*] aller; **2** [*toys, books*] tenir (**into** dans); **will the table ~ in that corner?** y a-t-il de la place pour la table dans ce coin?; **3 to ~ with** correspondre à [*story, facts*].
IDIOMS **in ~s and starts** par à-coups.
■ **fit in**: ¶ **~ in 1** [*key, object*] aller; **will you all ~ in?** (into car, room) est-ce qu'il y a de la place pour vous tous?; **2** (figurative) [*person*] s'intégrer (**with** à); **I'll ~ in with your plans** j'accorderai mes projets avec les vôtres; ¶ **~ [sb/sth] in** caser [*objects*]; caser [*game, meeting*]; trouver le temps pour voir [*patient, colleague*].
fitness *n* (physical) forme *f*.
fitted *adj* [*wardrobe*] encastré/-e; [*kitchen*] intégré/-e.
fitted carpet *n* moquette *f*.
fitting I *n* **1** (part) installation *f*; **2** (for clothes, hearing aid) essayage *m*.
II *adj* [*description*] adéquat/-e; [*memorial, testament*] qui convient.
fitting room *n* salon *m* d'essayage.
five ▶389|, 434| *n, pron, det* cinq (*m*) *inv*.
fix I *n* **to be in a ~**○ être dans le pétrin○.

II *vtr* **1** fixer [*date, venue, price, limit*]; déterminer [*position*]; **2** arranger [*meeting, visit*]; préparer [*drink, meal*]; **to ~ one's hair** se donner un coup de peigne; **how are we ~ed for time/money?** qu'est-ce qu'on a comme temps/argent°?; **3** (mend) réparer; **4** fixer [*handle, shelf*] (**on** sur; **to** à); **5** fixer [*attention*] (**on** sur); tourner [*thoughts*] (**on** vers); **6**° truquer [*contest, election*].
III fixed *pp adj* [*gaze, income, price*] fixe; [*expression*] figé/-e; [*menu*] à prix fixe.
■ **fix up** organiser [*holiday, meeting*]; décider de [*date*].

fixture *n* **1** installation *f*; **~s and fittings** équipements *mpl*; **2** (Sport) rencontre *f*.

fizzy *adj* gazeux/-euse.

flabby *adj* [*skin, muscle*] flasque; [*person*] aux chairs flasques.

flag I *n* drapeau *m*.
II *vi* [*interest*] faiblir; [*strength*] baisser; [*conversation*] languir; [*athlete*] flancher°.
■ **flag down** faire signe de s'arrêter à [*person*]; héler [*taxi*].

flagpole *n* mât *m*.

flagstone *n* dalle *f*.

flair *n* **1** (talent) don; **to have a ~ for** être doué/-e pour [*languages*]; **2** (style) classe *f*.

flake I *n* (of snow) flocon *m*.
II *vi* (also **~ off**) [*paint, varnish*] s'écailler; [*plaster, stone*] s'effriter; [*skin*] peler.

flamboyant *adj* [*person*] haut/-e en couleur; [*lifestyle*] exubérant/-e; [*colour, clothes*] voyant/-e; [*gesture*] extravagant/-e.

flame *n* flamme *f*; **in ~s** en flammes; **to go up in ~s** s'enflammer; **to burst into ~s** s'embraser.

flamingo *n* flamant *m* (rose).

flammable *adj* inflammable.

flan *n* (savoury) quiche *f*, tarte *f*; (sweet) tarte *f*.

flank I *n* flanc *m*.
II *vtr* **to be ~ed by** [*person*] être flanqué/-e par; [*place*] être bordé/-e par.

flannel *n* **1** (wool) flanelle *f*; (cotton) pilou *m*; **2** (GB) (also **face ~**) ≈ gant *m* de toilette.

flap I *n* **1** (on pocket, envelope, tent) rabat *m*; (on table) abattant *m*; **2** (of wings) battement *m*.
II *vtr* **the bird ~ped its wings** l'oiseau battait des ailes.
III *vi* [*wing*] battre; [*sail, flag*] claquer; [*clothes*] voleter.

flare I *n* **1** (on runway) balise *f* lumineuse; (distress signal) fusée *f* (de détresse); (Mil) (on target) fusée *f* éclairante; **2** (of match, lighter) lueur *f*.
II *vi* **1** [*firework, match*] jeter une brève lueur; **2** [*skirt*] s'évaser; [*nostrils*] se dilater.
■ **flare up 1** [*fire*] s'embraser; **2** [*violence*] éclater; [*person*] s'emporter; **3** [*illness*] réapparaître; [*pain*] se réveiller.

flares *n pl* pantalon *m* à pattes d'éléphant.

flash I *n* **1** (of torch, headlights) lueur *f* soudaine; (of jewels, metal) éclat *m*; **a ~ of lightning** un éclair; **2 in** or **like a ~** en un clin d'œil; **3** (on camera) flash *m*.
II *vtr* **1 to ~ one's headlights** (**at**) faire un appel de phares (à); **2** lancer [*look, smile*] (**at** à); **3** (transmit) faire apparaître [*message*]; **4**° (show) [*person*] montrer [qch] rapidement [*card, money*]; **5** (also **~ about**, **~ around**) exhiber [*credit card*]; étaler [*money*].
III *vi* [*light*] clignoter; [*eyes*] lancer des éclairs; **to ~ on and off** clignoter.
■ **flash by**, **flash past** [*person, bird*] passer comme un éclair; [*landscape*] défiler.

flashback *n* **1** (in film) flash-back *m* (**to** à); **2** (memory) souvenir *m*.

flashing *adj* [*light, sign*] clignotant/-e.

flash light *n* lampe *f* de poche.

flashy° *adj* [*car, dress, tie*] tape-à-l'œil *inv*; [*jewellery*] clinquant/-e.

flask *n* thermos® *f* or *m inv*; (**hip**) **~** flasque *f*.

flat I *n* **1** (GB) appartement *m*; **one-bedroom ~** deux pièces *m inv*; **2 the ~ of** le plat de [*hand, sword*].
II *adj* **1** (gen) plat/-e; [*nose, face*] aplati/-e; **2** [*tyre, ball*] dégonflé/-e; **to have a ~ tyre** avoir un pneu à plat; **3** [*refusal, denial*] catégorique; **4** [*fare, fee*] forfaitaire; [*charge, rate*] fixe; **5** [*beer*] éventé/-e; **6** (GB) [*car battery*] à plat; [*battery*] usé/-e; **7** (Mus) [*note*] bémol *inv*; [*voice, instrument*] faux/fausse.
III *adv* **1** [*lay, lie*] à plat; **~ on one's back** sur le dos; **2 in 10 minutes ~** en 10 minutes pile; **3** [*sing*] faux.
IDIOMS **to fall ~** [*joke*] tomber à plat; [*party*] tourner court; [*plan*] tomber à l'eau.

flatmate *n* (GB) colocataire *mf*.

flat out° *adv* [*drive*] à fond de train; [*work*] d'arrache-pied.

flatten I *vtr* **1** [*rain*] coucher [*crops, grass*]; abattre [*fence*]; [*bombing*] raser [*building*]; **2** (smooth out) aplanir [*surface*]; aplatir [*metal*]; **3** (crush) écraser [*fruit, object*].
II *v refl* **to ~ oneself** s'aplatir (**against** contre).

flatter *vtr* flatter (**on** sur).

flattering *adj* flatteur/-euse.

flattery *n* flatterie *f*.

flaunt *vtr* étaler [*wealth*]; faire étalage de [*charms, knowledge*].

flavour (GB), **flavor** (US) **I** *n* goût *m*; (subtler) saveur *f*; **full of ~** savoureux/-euse.
II *vtr* (gen) donner du goût à; (add specific taste) parfumer (**with** à).

flavouring (GB), **flavoring** (US) *n* (for sweet taste) parfum *m*; (for meat, fish) assaisonnement *m*.

flaw *n* défaut *m*.

flawed *adj* défectueux/-euse.

flea *n* puce *f*.

flea market *n* marché *m* aux puces.

fleck I *n* (of colour, light) tache *f*; (of foam) flocon *m*; (of blood, paint) petite tache *f*; (of dust) particule *f*.
II *vtr* **~ed with** [*fabric*] moucheté/-e de [*colour*].

fledg(e)ling *n* oisillon *m*.

flee *vtr*, *vi* fuir.

fleece *n* toison *f*; **~-lined** fourré/-e.

fleet *n* **1** (of ships) flotte *f*; (of small vessels) flottille *f*; **2** (of vehicles) (on road) convoi *m*.
fleeting *adj* [*memory, pleasure*] fugace; [*moment*] bref/brève (*before n*); [*glance*] rapide.
Flemish ▶553 **I** *n* **1 the ~** les Flamands *mpl*; **2** (language) flamand *m*.
II *adj* flamand/-e.
flesh *n* chair *f*.
fleshy *adj* charnu/-e.
flex I *n* (GB) fil *m*.
II *vtr* faire jouer [*muscle*]; fléchir [*limb*].
flexible *adj* **1** [*arrangement, plan*] flexible; **2** [*person*] souple (**about** en ce qui concerne).
flexitime *n* horaire *m* flexible or souple.
flick I *n* (with finger) chiquenaude *f*; (with whip, cloth) petit coup *m*.
II *vtr* **1** (with finger) donner une chiquenaude à; (with tail, cloth) donner un petit coup à; **he ~ed his ash on the floor** il a fait tomber sa cendre par terre; **2** appuyer sur [*switch*].
flicker *vi* [*fire, light*] vaciller, trembloter; [*image*] clignoter; [*eye, eyelid*] cligner.
■ **flick through** feuilleter [*book*].
flick knife *n* (GB) couteau *m* à cran d'arrêt.
flight *n* **1** (gen) vol *m* (**to** vers; **from** de); **we took the next ~ (out)** nous avons pris l'avion suivant; **2** (escape) fuite *f* (**from** devant); **to take ~** prendre la fuite; **3 a ~ of steps** une volée de marches; **six ~s (of stairs)** six étages; **4 a ~ of fancy** une invention.
flight attendant ▶626 *n* (male) steward *m*; (female) hôtesse *f* de l'air.
flimsy *adj* [*fabric*] léger/-ère; [*structure*] peu solide; [*excuse*] piètre (*before n*); [*evidence*] mince.
flinch *vi* tressaillir; **without ~ing** sans broncher; **to ~ from doing** hésiter à faire.
fling I *n* **1**○ (spree) bon temps *m*; **2**○ (affair) aventure *f*.
II *vtr* lancer.
■ **fling open** ouvrir [qch] brusquement [*door*]; ouvrir [qch] tout grand [*window*].
flint *n* **1** (rock) silex *m*; **2** (in lighter) pierre *f* à briquet.
flip I *n* (somersault) tour *m*.
II *vtr* **1** lancer [*coin*]; faire sauter [*pancake*]; **2** basculer [*switch*].
■ **flip through** feuilleter [*book*].
flip-flop *n* **1** (sandal) tong *f*; **2** (US) (about-face) volte-face *f inv*.
flippant *adj* [*remark, person*] désinvolte; [*tone, attitude*] cavalier/-ière.
flipper *n* **1** (Zool) nageoire *f*; **2** (for swimmer) palme *f*.
flirt I *n* flirteur/-euse *m/f*.
II *vi* flirter; **to ~ with** flirter avec [*person*]; jouer avec [*danger*]; caresser [*idea*].
flirtatious *adj* charmeur/-euse, dragueur/-euse○ (derogatory).
flit *vi* **1** (also **~ about**) [*bird, moth*] voleter; [*person*] aller d'un pas léger; **2 a look of panic ~ted across his face** une expression de panique lui traversa le visage.
float I *n* **1** (on net) flotteur *m*; (on line) bouchon *m*; **2** (GB) (swimmer's aid) planche *f*; (US) (life jacket) gilet *m* de sauvetage; **3** (carnival vehicle) char *m*.
II *vtr* **1** [*person*] faire flotter [*boat, logs*]; **2** émettre [*shares, loan*]; lancer [qch] en Bourse [*company*]; laisser flotter [*currency*].
III *vi* **1** flotter; **to ~ on one's back** [*swimmer*] faire la planche; **the boat was ~ing out to sea** le bateau voguait vers le large; **to ~ up into the air** s'envoler; **2** [*currency*] flotter.
floating *adj* **1** [*bridge*] flottant/-e; **2** [*population*] instable.
floating voter *n* électeur *m* indécis.
flock I *n* (of sheep, goats) troupeau *m*; (of birds) volée *f*.
II *vi* [*animals, people*] affluer (**around** autour de; **into** dans); **to ~ together** [*people*] s'assembler; [*animals*] se rassembler.
flog *vtr* (beat) flageller.
flood I *n* **1** inondation *f*; **2 a ~ of** un flot de [*people, memories*]; un déluge de [*letters, complaints*]; **to be in ~s of tears** verser des torrents de larmes.
II *vtr* **1** inonder [*area*]; faire déborder [*river*]; **2** [*light*] inonder; **3** inonder [*market*] (**with** de); **4** (Aut) noyer [*engine*].
III *vi* **1** [*river*] déborder; **2 to ~ into sth** [*light*] inonder qch; [*people*] envahir qch; **to ~ over sb** [*emotion*] envahir qn.
floodgate *n* vanne *f*.
floodlight I *n* projecteur *m*; **under ~s** (Sport) en nocturne.
II *vtr* illuminer [*building*]; éclairer [*stage*].
floor I *n* **1** (of room) (wooden) plancher *m*, parquet *m*; (stone) sol *m*; (of car, lift) plancher *m*; **dance ~** piste *f* de danse; **on the ~** par terre; **2** (of stock exchange) parquet *m*; (of debating chamber) auditoire *m*; (of factory) atelier *m*; **3** (storey) étage *m*; **on the first ~** (GB) au premier étage; (US) au rez-de-chaussée.
II *vtr* **1** terrasser [*attacker, boxer*]; **2** [*question*] décontenancer [*candidate*].
IDIOMS **to wipe the ~ with sb** battre qn à plates coutures.
floorboard *n* latte *f*, planche *f*.
floor cloth *n* serpillière *f*.
flop I○ *n* (failure) fiasco○ *m*.
II *vi* **1 to ~ (down)** s'effondrer; **2**○ [*play, film*] faire un four○; [*project, venture*] être un fiasco○.
floppy *adj* [*ears*] pendant/-e; [*hat*] à bords tombants.
floppy disk *n* disquette *f*.
flora *n* flore *f*.
floral *adj* [*design, fabric*] à fleurs; [*arrangement*] floral/-e.
Florida *pr n* Floride *f*.
florist ▶626 *n* (person) fleuriste *mf*; (shop) fleuriste *m*.
floss *n* fil *m* dentaire.
flotsam *n* **~ and jetsam** épaves *fpl*.
flounce I *n* (frill) volant *m*.

II *vi* **to ~ in/off** entrer/partir dans un mouvement d'indignation.

flounder *vi* **1** [*animal, person*] se débattre (**in** dans); **2** (falter) [*speaker*] bredouiller; [*economy*] stagner; [*career, company*] piétiner.

flour *n* farine *f*.

flourish I *n* **1** (gesture) geste *m* théâtral; **with a ~** [*do*] de façon théâtrale; **2** (in style) fioriture *f*.
II *vtr* brandir [*ticket, document*].
III *vi* prospérer.

flourishing *adj* [*garden, industry*] florissant/-e; [*business, town*] prospère.

flout *vtr* se moquer de [*convention, rules*].

flow I *n* **1** (of liquid) écoulement *m*; (of blood, electricity, water) circulation *f*; (of refugees, words) flot *m*; (of information) circulation *f*; **in full ~** [*speaker*] en plein discours; **traffic ~** circulation *f*; **2** (of tide) flux *m*.
II *vi* **1** [*liquid*] couler (**into** dans); **the river ~s into the sea** le fleuve se jette dans la mer; **2** [*conversation, words*] couler; [*wine, beer*] couler à flots; **3** [*blood, electricity*] circuler (**through, round** dans); **4** [*hair, dress*] flotter.

flowchart *n* organigramme *m*.

flower I *n* fleur *f*; **to be in ~** être en fleur.
II *vi* **1** [*flower, tree*] fleurir; **2** [*love, person*] s'épanouir.

flower bed *n* parterre *m* de fleurs.

flowering I *n* floraison *f* (**of** de).
II *adj* (producing blooms) à fleurs; (in bloom) en fleurs.

flower pot *n* pot *m* de fleurs.

flowery *adj* [*design*] à fleurs; [*language, speech*] fleuri/-e.

flu ▶ 533 *n* grippe *f*.

fluctuate *vi* fluctuer (**between** entre).

flue *n* (of chimney) conduit *m*; (of stove, boiler) tuyau *m*.

fluency *n* aisance *f*.

fluent *adj* **1 her French is ~** elle parle couramment français; **in ~ English** dans un anglais parfait; **2** [*speech*] éloquent/-e; [*style*] coulant/-e.

fluently *adv* couramment.

fluff I *n* (on clothes) peluche *f*; (on carpet) poussière *f*; (under furniture) mouton *m*, flocon *m* de poussière.
II *vtr* **1** (also **~ up**) hérisser [*feathers*]; faire bouffer [*hair*]; **2**○ rater [*cue, exam*].

fluffy *adj* **1** [*toy*] en peluche; [*hair*] bouffant/-e; **2** (light) [*mixture*] léger/-ère; [*egg white, rice*] moelleux/-euse.

fluid *n, adj* fluide (*m*).

fluid ounce *n* once *f* liquide (GB = *0.028 l*; US = *0.030 l*).

fluke *n* coup *m* de veine○; **by a (sheer) ~** (tout à fait) par hasard.

fluorescent *adj* fluorescent/-e.

fluoride *n* fluorure *m*.

flush I *n* **1** (blush) rougeur *f*; **2** (surge) **a ~ of** un élan de [*pleasure, pride*]; un accès de [*anger, shame*]; **3** (of toilet) chasse *f* d'eau.
II *vtr* **to ~ the toilet** tirer la chasse (d'eau); **to ~ sth down the toilet** faire partir qch dans les toilettes.
III *vi* **1** (redden) rougir (**with** de); **2 the toilet doesn't ~** la chasse d'eau ne fonctionne pas.
■ **flush out** débusquer [*sniper, spy*]; **to ~ sb/sth out of** faire sortir qn/qch de [*shelter*].

flushed *adj* **1** [*cheeks*] rouge (**with** de); **to be ~** avoir les joues rouges; **2 ~ with** rayonnant/-e de [*pride*].

fluster I *n* agitation *f*.
II *vtr* énerver; **to look ~ed** avoir l'air énervé.

flute ▶ 586 *n* flûte *f*.

flutter I *n* (of wings, lashes) battement *m*.
II *vtr* **1 the bird ~ed its wings** l'oiseau battait des ailes; **2** agiter [*fan, handkerchief*]; **to ~ one's eyelashes** battre des cils.
III *vi* **1 the bird's wings ~ed** l'oiseau battit des ailes; **2** [*flag*] flotter; [*clothes, curtains*] s'agiter; [*eyelids, lashes*] battre; **3** (also **~ down**) [*leaves*] tomber en voltigeant; **4** [*heart*] palpiter (**with** de); [*pulse*] battre faiblement.

flux *n* **in (a state of) ~** dans un état de perpétuel changement.

fly I *n* mouche *f*.
II **flies** *n pl* (of trousers) braguette *f*.
III *vtr* **1** piloter [*aircraft, balloon*]; faire voler [*kite*]; **2** (transport) emmener [qn] par avion [*person*]; **3** [*bird, aircraft*] parcourir [*distance*]; **4** [*ship*] arborer [*flag*].
IV *vi* **1** [*bird, insect, aircraft, kite*] voler; **to ~ over** or **across sth** survoler qch; **2** [*passenger*] voyager en avion, prendre l'avion; [*pilot*] piloter, voler; **to ~ from Rome to Athens** aller de Rome à Athènes en avion; **3** [*sparks, insults*] voler; **to ~ open** s'ouvrir brusquement; **to go ~ing**○ [*person*] faire un vol plané; [*object*] valdinguer○; **to ~ into a rage** se mettre en colère; **4** (also **~ past, ~ by**) [*time, holidays*] passer très vite, filer○; **5** [*flag, scarf, hair*] flotter; **to ~ in the wind** flotter au vent.
■ **fly away** s'envoler.

flying I *n* **to be afraid of ~** avoir peur de l'avion.
II *adj* **1** [*insect, machine*] volant/-e; [*object, broken glass*] qui vole; **to take a ~ leap** sauter avec élan; **2** [*visit*] éclair *inv*.
IDIOMS **with ~ colours** [*pass*] haut la main; **to get off to a ~ start** prendre un très bon départ.

flyover *n* **1** (GB) pont *m* routier; **2** (US) (aerial display) défilé *m* aérien.

fly spray *n* bombe *f* insecticide.

FM *n* (*abbr* = **frequency modulation**) FM *f*.

foal *n* poulain *m*.

foam I *n* **1** (on sea, from mouth) écume *f*; (on drinks) mousse *f*; **2** (chemical) mousse *f*; **3** (also **~ rubber**) mousse *f*.
II *vi* **1** (also **~ up**) [*beer*] mousser; [*sea*] se couvrir d'écume; **to ~ at the mouth** écumer; (figurative) écumer de rage; **2** [*horse*] suer.

foam bath *n* bain *m* moussant.

fob *n* (pocket) gousset *m*; (chain) chaîne *f*.
■ **fob off** se débarrasser de [*enquirer, customer*]; rejeter [*enquiry*].

focal point *n* **1** (in optics) foyer *m*; **2** (of village, building) point *m* de convergence (**of** de; **for** pour); **3** (main concern) point *m* central.

focus I *n* **1** (focal point) foyer *m*; **in ~** au point; **to go out of ~** [*device*] se dérégler; [*image*] devenir flou; **2** (device on lens) mise *f* au point; **3** (of attention, interest) centre *m*; **4** (emphasis) accent *m*.
II *vtr* **1** concentrer [*ray*] (**on** sur); fixer [*eyes*] (**on** sur); **2** mettre [qch] au point, régler [*lens, camera*].
III *vi* **to ~ on** [*photographer*] cadrer sur; [*eyes, attention*] se fixer sur; [*report*] se concentrer sur.

fodder *n* fourrage *m*.

foe *n* ennemi/-e *m/f*.

foetus, fetus (US) *n* fœtus *m*.

fog I *n* brouillard *m*.
II *vtr* (also **~ up**) [*steam*] embuer [*glass*]; [*light*] voiler [*film*].

foggy *adj* [*day, weather*] brumeux/-euse; **it's ~** il y a du brouillard.

foghorn *n* corne *f* de brume.

foible *n* petite manie *f*.

foil I *n* papier *m* d'aluminium; **silver ~** papier argenté.
II *vtr* contrecarrer [*person*]; déjouer [*attempt*].

foist *vtr* **to ~ sth on sb** repasser qch à qn.

fold I *n* **1** (in fabric, paper, skin) pli *m*; **2** (for sheep) parc *m*.
II *vtr* **1** plier [*paper, shirt, chair*]; replier [*wings*]; **2** croiser [*arms*]; joindre [*hands*].
III *vi* **1** [*chair*] se plier; **2** (fail) [*play*] quitter l'affiche; [*company*] fermer.
IDIOMS **to return to the ~** rentrer au bercail.
■ **fold back** rabattre [*shutters, sheet, sleeve*].
■ **fold in** incorporer [*sugar, flour*].
■ **fold up** plier [*newspaper, chair*].

folder *n* **1** (for papers) chemise *f*; **2** (for artwork) carton *m*.

folding *adj* [*bed, table, chair*] pliant/-e; [*door*] en accordéon.

foliage *n* feuillage *m*.

folk I *n* (people) gens *mpl*.
II *adj* **1** (traditional) [*tale, song*] folklorique; **2** (modern) [*music*] folk *inv*; **3** [*hero*] populaire.

folklore *n* folklore *m*.

follow I *vtr* (gen) suivre; poursuivre [*career*]; **~ed by** suivi/-e de.
II *vi* **1** suivre; **to ~ in sb's footsteps** suivre les traces de qn; **there's ice cream to ~** ensuite il y a de la glace; **the results were as ~s** les résultats ont été les suivants; **2** (understand) suivre; **I don't ~** je ne suis pas; **3 it ~s that** il s'ensuit que.
■ **follow through** mener [qch] à terme [*project*]; aller jusqu'au bout de [*idea*].
■ **follow up** donner suite à [*letter, threat, offer*] (**with** par); suivre [*story, lead*].

follower *n* **1** (of thinker, artist) disciple *m*; (of political leader) partisan/-e *m/f*; **2** (of team) supporter *m*.

following I *n* (of religion, cult) adeptes *mfpl*; (of party, political figure) partisans/-anes *mpl/fpl*; (of soap opera, show) public *m*; (of sports team) supporters *mpl*.
II *adj* suivant/-e.
III *prep* suite à, à la suite de.

folly *n* folie *f*.

fond *adj* **1** [*embrace, farewell*] affectueux/-euse; [*eyes, smile*] tendre; **~ memories** de très bons souvenirs; **2** [*wish, ambition*] cher/chère; **3 to be ~ of sb** aimer beaucoup qn; **to be ~ of sth** aimer qch.

fondle *vtr* caresser.

food *n* nourriture *f*, alimentation *f*; **frozen ~** aliments surgelés; **Chinese ~** la cuisine chinoise; **that's ~ for thought** ça donne à réfléchir.

food poisoning *n* intoxication *f* alimentaire.

food processor *n* robot *m* ménager.

foodstuff *n* denrée *f* alimentaire.

fool I *n* **1** idiot/-e *m/f* (**to do** de faire); **you stupid ~**○**!** espèce d'idiot/-e!; **to make sb look a ~** faire passer qn pour un/-e idiot/-e; **to act the ~** faire l'imbécile; **2** (jester) fou *m*.
II *vtr* tromper, duper.

foolhardy *adj* téméraire.

foolish *adj* **1** [*person*] bête (**to do** de faire); **2** [*grin, expression*] stupide; **to feel ~** se sentir ridicule; **3** [*decision, question, remark*] idiot/-e.

foolproof *adj* **1** [*method, plan*] infaillible; **2** [*machine*] d'utilisation très simple.

foot ▶413, 573 **I** *n* **1** (of person) pied *m*; (of animal) patte *f*; (of sock, chair) pied *m*; **on ~** à pied; **from head to ~** de la tête aux pieds; **to put one's ~ down** faire acte d'autorité; (Aut) accélérer; **2** (measurement) pied *m* (= *0.3048 m*); **3** (of mountain) pied *m* (**of** de); **at the ~ of** au pied de [*bed*]; à la fin de [*list, letter*]; en bas de [*page, stairs*].
II *vtr* **to ~ the bill** payer la facture (**for** de, pour).
IDIOMS **to be under sb's feet** être dans les jambes de qn; **rushed off one's feet** débordé/-e; **to put one's ~ in it**○ faire une gaffe; **to stand on one's own two feet** se débrouiller tout seul/toute seule.

footage *n* film *m*, pellicule *f*; **some ~ of** des images de.

foot and mouth (disease) *n* fièvre *f* aphteuse.

football ▶504 *n* **1** (game) (GB) football *m*; (US) football *m* américain; **2** (ball) ballon *m* de football.

footballer ▶626 *n* (GB) joueur/-euse *m/f* de football.

foot brake *n* (Aut) frein *m* (à pied).

footbridge *n* passerelle *f*.

foothold *n* prise *f* (de pied); **to gain a ~** [*company*] prendre pied; [*ideology*] s'imposer.

footlights *n pl* rampe *f*.

footloose *adj* libre comme l'air.

footnote *n* note *f* de bas de page.

footpath *n* (in countryside) sentier *m*; (in town) trottoir *m*.

footprint *n* empreinte *f* (de pied).

footstep *n* pas *m*.

footstool *n* repose-pied *m*.

footwear *n* chaussures *fpl*.

for ▶496 *prep* **1** (gen) pour; **~ sb** pour qn; **he cooked dinner ~ us** il nous a préparé à manger; **what's it ~?** c'est pour quoi faire?, ça sert à quoi?; **to go ~ a swim** aller nager; **that's ~ us to decide** c'est à nous de décider; **she's the person ~ the job** elle est la personne qu'il faut pour le travail; **the reason ~ doing** la raison pour laquelle on fait; **if it weren't ~ her**... sans elle...; **'~ sale'** 'à vendre'; **2** [*work, play*] pour; [*MP*] de; **the minister ~ education** le ministre de l'éducation; **3** (on behalf of) pour; **to be pleased ~ sb** être content/e pour qn; **say hello to him ~ me** dis-lui bonjour de ma part; **4** (in time expressions) **the best show I've seen ~ years** le meilleur spectacle que j'aie vu depuis des années; **we've been together ~ two years** ça fait deux ans que nous sommes ensemble; **she's off to Paris ~ the weekend** elle va à Paris pour le week-end; **to stay ~ a year** rester un an; **to be away ~ a year** être absent/-e pendant un an; **I was in Paris ~ two weeks** j'ai passé deux semaines à Paris; **the car won't be ready ~ another six weeks** la voiture ne sera pas prête avant six semaines; **it's time ~ bed** c'est l'heure d'aller au lit; **5** (indicating distance) pendant; **to drive ~ miles** rouler pendant des kilomètres; **the last shop ~ 30 miles** le dernier magasin avant 50 kilomètres; **6** (indicating cost, value) pour; **it was sold ~ £100** ça s'est vendu (pour) 100 livres sterling; **a cheque ~ £20** un chèque de 20 livres sterling; **7** (in favour of) **to be ~** être pour [*peace, divorce*]; **the argument ~ recycling** l'argument en faveur du recyclage; **8 T ~ Tom** T comme Tom; **what's the French ~ 'boot'?** comment dit-on 'boot' en français?; **9 ~ one thing... and ~ another**... premièrement... et deuxièmement...; **I, ~ one, agree with her** en tout cas moi, je suis d'accord avec elle.

forbid *vtr* défendre, interdire; **to ~ sb to do** défendre or interdire à qn de faire; **to ~ sb sth** défendre or interdire qch à qn; **God ~!** Dieu m'en/l'en etc garde!

forbidden *adj* [*subject, fruit*] défendu/-e; [*place*] interdit/-e; **smoking is ~** il est interdit de fumer.

forbidding *adj* [*building*] intimidant/-e; [*landscape*] inhospitalier/-ière; [*expression*] rébarbatif/-ive.

force I *n* force *f*; **by ~** par la force; **the police ~** la police; **a ~ 10 gale** un vent de force 10.
II **forces** *n pl* (also **armed ~s**) **the ~s** les forces *fpl* armées.
III *vtr* forcer (**to do** à faire).
IV **in force** *phr* **1** (in large numbers) en force; **2** [*law, prices, ban*] en vigueur.
■ **force on**: **~ [sth] on sb** imposer [qch] à qn, forcer qn à accepter [qch].

forced *adj* [*smile, landing*] forcé/-e; [*conversation*] peu naturel/-elle.

force-feed *vtr* gaver [*animal, bird*]; alimenter [qn] de force [*person*].

forceful *adj* [*person, behaviour*] énergique; [*attack, speech*] vigoureux/-euse.

ford I *n* gué *m*.
II *vtr* **to ~ a river** passer une rivière à gué.

fore *n* **to the ~** en vue, en avant; **to come to the ~** [*person, issue*] s'imposer à l'attention; [*quality*] ressortir.

forearm *n* avant-bras *m inv*.

foreboding *n* pressentiment *m*.

forecast I *n* **1** (also **weather ~**) météo° *f*, bulletin *m* météorologique; **2** (outlook) (gen) pronostics *mpl*; (Econ) prévisions *fpl*.
II *vtr* prévoir (**that** que).

forefinger *n* index *m*.

forefront *n* **at** or **in the ~ of** à la pointe de [*change, research, debate*]; au premier plan de [*campaign, struggle*].

foregone *adj* **it is a ~ conclusion** c'est couru d'avance.

foreground *n* premier plan *m*.

forehand *n* (Sport) coup *m* droit.

forehead *n* front *m*.

foreign *adj* **1** [*country, imports, policy*] étranger/-ère; [*market*] extérieur/-e; [*trade, travel*] à l'étranger; **2** (alien) [*concept*] étranger/-ère (**to** à).

foreign affairs *n pl* affaires *fpl* étrangères.

foreign body *n* corps *m* étranger.

foreigner *n* étranger/-ère *m/f*.

foreign exchange *n* devises *fpl*.

foreign minister, **foreign secretary** (GB) *n* ministre *m* des Affaires étrangères.

Foreign Office, **FO** *n* (GB) ministère *m* des Affaires étrangères.

foreman ▶626 *n* **1** (supervisor) contremaître *m*; **2** (Law) président *m* (d'un jury).

foremost I *adj* premier/-ière (*before n*), plus grand.
II *adv* **first and ~** avant tout.

forename *n* prénom *m*.

forensic evidence *n* résultats *mpl* des expertises médico-légales.

forensic science *n* médecine *f* légale.

forensic tests *n pl* expertises *fpl* médico-légales.

forerunner *n* (person) précurseur *m*; (institution, invention, model) ancêtre *m*.

foresee *vtr* prévoir.

foreseeable *adj* prévisible.

foresight *n* prévoyance *f* (**to do** de faire).

foreskin *n* prépuce *m*.

forest *n* forêt *f*.

forester *n* forestier/-ière *m/f*.

foretaste *n* avant-goût *m* (**of** de).

foretell *vtr* prédire.

forever *adv* pour toujours; **to go on ~** [*pain, noise, journey*] durer une éternité; **the desert seemed to go on ~** le désert semblait ne pas avoir de limites; **she is ~ complaining** elle est toujours en train de se plaindre.

foreword *n* avant-propos *m inv*.

forfeit I *n* gage *m*.

for

Some general uses

- ***for*** is generally translated by ***pour***:

***for** my sister*	= **pour** ma sœur
***for** me*	= **pour** moi

- When ***for*** is used as a preposition indicating purpose followed by a verb, it is translated by ***pour*** + *infinitive*:

***for** cleaning windows*	= **pour** nettoyer les vitres

- When ***for*** is used in the construction ***it is/was*** etc + *adjective* + ***for*** + *pronoun* + *infinitive*, the translation in French is as follows:

*it's impossible **for** me to stay*	= il m'est impossible de rester
*it was hard **for** him to understand that . . .*	= il lui était difficile de comprendre que . . .

For examples and particular usages, see the entry **for**.

In time expressions

- When ***for*** is used to express the time period of something that started in the past and is still going on, French uses *present tense* + ***depuis***:

*I have been waiting **for** three hours* (and I am still waiting)	= j'attends **depuis** trois heures
*we've been together **for** two years* (and we're still together)	= nous sommes ensemble **depuis** deux ans

- When ***for*** is used after a verb in the past perfect tense, French uses *imperfect* + ***depuis***:

*I had been waiting **for** two hours* (and was still waiting)	= j'attendais **depuis** deux heures

- When ***for*** is used in negative sentences with the present perfect tense to express the time that has elapsed since something has happened, French uses the same tense as English, *perfect* + ***depuis***:

*I haven't seen him **for** ten years* (and I still haven't seen him)	= je ne l'ai pas vu **depuis** dix ans

  In spoken French, there are two ways of expressing this:

  = ça fait dix ans que je ne l'ai pas vu
  = il y a dix ans que je ne l'ai pas vu

- When ***for*** is used in negative sentences after a verb in the past perfect tense, French uses *past perfect* + ***depuis***:

*I hadn't seen him **for** ten years*	= je ne l'avais pas vu **depuis** dix ans

- When ***for*** is used after the preterite to express the time period of something that happened in the past and is no longer going on, French uses *present perfect* + ***pendant***:

*last Sunday I gardened **for** two hours*	= dimanche dernier j'ai jardiné **pendant** deux heures

- When ***for*** is used after the present progressive or the future tense to express an anticipated time period in the future, French uses *present* or *future* + ***pour***:

*I'm going to Rome **for** six weeks*	= je vais à Rome **pour** six semaines
*I will go to Rome **for** six weeks*	= j'irai à Rome **pour** six semaines

- When the verb ***to be*** is used in the future with ***for*** to emphasize the period of time, French uses *future* + ***pendant***:

*I will be in Rome **for** six weeks*	= je serai à Rome **pendant** six semaines

II *vtr* perdre [*right, liberty*].

forge I *n* forge *f*.
II *vtr* **1** forger [*metal*]; **2** contrefaire [*banknotes, signature*]; **a ~d passport** un faux passeport; **3** forger [*alliance*]; établir [*identity, link*].
III *vi* **to ~ ahead** accélérer; **to ~ ahead with** aller de l'avant dans [*plan*].

forger *n* (of documents) faussaire *m*; (of artefacts) contrefacteur/-trice *m/f*; (of money) faux-monnayeur *m*.

forgery *n* contrefaçon *f*.

forget I *vtr* oublier (**that** que; **to do** de faire).
II *vi* oublier.
■ **forget about** oublier.

forgetful *adj* distrait/-e.

forget-me-not *n* myosotis *m*.

forgive *vtr* pardonner à [*person*]; pardonner [*act, remark*]; **to ~ sb sth** pardonner qch à qn; **to ~ sb for doing** pardonner à qn d'avoir fait.

fork I *n* **1** (for eating) fourchette *f*; **2** (tool) fourche *f*; **3** (in river, on bicycle) fourche *f*; (in railway) embranchement *m*; (in road) bifurcation *f*.
II *vi* (also **~ off**) bifurquer.
■ **fork out**○ casquer○ (**for** pour).

forked lightning *n* éclair *m* ramifié.

forklift truck *n* (GB) (also **forklift** US) chariot *m* élévateur à fourche.

form I *n* **1** (gen) forme *f*; **in the ~ of** sous forme de; **to be in good ~** être en bonne *or* pleine forme; **it is bad ~ (to do)** cela ne se fait pas (de faire); **as a matter of ~** pour la forme; **2** (document) formulaire *m*; **blank ~** formulaire vierge; **3** (GB Sch) classe *f*; **in the first ~** ≈ en sixième.
II *vtr* **1** former [*queue, circle, barrier*] (**from** avec); nouer [*friendship, relationship*]; **to ~ part of** faire partie de; **2** se faire [*impression, opinion*]; **3** former [*personality, tastes, ideas, attitudes*].
III *vi* se former.

formal *adj* **1** (official) [*agreement, complaint, invitation*] officiel/-ielle; **2** (not casual) [*language*] soutenu/-e; [*occasion*] solennel/-elle; [*manner*] cérémonieux/-ieuse; [*clothing*] habillé/-e; **3** [*training*] professionnel/-elle; [*qualification*] reconnu/-e.

formal dress *n* tenue *f* de soirée.

formality *n* **1** (legal or social convention) formalité *f*; **2** (of occasion, manner) solennité *f*; (of language) caractère *m* soutenu.

formally *adv* **1** (officially) officiellement; **2** (not casually) cérémonieusement.

format I *n* format *m*.
II *vtr* (Comput) formater.

formation *n* formation *f*.

former I *n* **the ~** (singular noun) celui-là/celle-là *m/f*; (plural noun) ceux-là/celles-là *mpl/fpl*.
II *adj* **1** [*era, life*] antérieur/-e; [*size, state*] initial/-e, original/-e; **he's a shadow of his ~ self** il n'est plus que l'ombre de lui-même; **2** [*leader, husband, champion*] ancien/-ienne (*before n*); **3** (first of two) premier/-ière (*before n*).

formerly *adv* autrefois.

formidable *adj* **1** (intimidating) redoutable; **2** (awe-inspiring) impressionnant/-e.

formula *n* **1** formule *f* (**for** de; **for doing** pour faire); **2** (US) lait *m* en poudre.

fort *n* fort *m*.

forte *n* **to be sb's ~** être le fort de qn.

forth *adv* **from this day ~** à partir d'aujourd'hui; **from that day ~** à dater de ce jour; ▶ **back, so.**

forthcoming *adj* **1** [*event, book*] prochain/-e (*before n*); **2 she wasn't very ~ about it** elle était peu disposée à en parler.

forthright *adj* direct/-e.

forties ▶ 389, 456 *n pl* **1** (era) **the ~** les années *fpl* quarante; **2** (age) **to be in one's ~** avoir entre quarante et cinquante ans.

fortieth *n, adj, adv* quarantième (*mf*).

fortified *adj* [*place*] fortifié/-e; **~ wine** vin *m* doux; **~ with vitamins** vitaminé/-e.

fortify *vtr* fortifier.

fortnight ▶ 708 *n* (GB) quinze jours *mpl*; **the first ~ in August** la première quinzaine d'août.

fortunate *adj* heureux/-euse.

fortunately *adv* heureusement.

fortune *n* **1** fortune *f*; **to make a ~** faire fortune; **2 to have the good ~ to do** avoir la chance or le bonheur de faire; **3 to tell sb's ~** dire la bonne aventure à qn.

fortune-teller *n* diseur/-euse *m/f* de bonne aventure.

forty ▶ 389, 434 *n, pron, det* quarante (*m*) *inv*.

forward I *n* (Sport) avant *m*.
II *adj* **1** (bold) effronté/-e; **2** (towards the front) [*movement*] en avant; **to be too far ~** [*seat*] être trop en avant; **3** (advanced) avancé/-e; **he's no further ~** il n'est pas plus avancé.
III *adv* (also **forwards**) **to step ~** faire un pas en avant; **to fall ~** tomber en avant; **to go** or **walk ~** avancer; **to move sth ~** avancer qch; **a way ~** une solution.
IV *vtr* **1** expédier [*goods*]; envoyer [*parcel*]; **2** (send on) faire suivre, réexpédier [*mail*].

forward planning *n* planification *f* à long terme.

forwards = **forward III**.

fossil *n* fossile *m*.

foster I *adj* [*child, parent*] adoptif/-ive.
II *vtr* **1** (encourage) encourager [*attitude*]; promouvoir [*activity*]; **2** prendre [qn] en placement [*child*].

foster family *n* famille *f* de placement.

foster home *n* foyer *m* de placement.

foul I *n* (Sport) faute *f* (**by** de; **on** sur).
II *adj* **1** [*smell, air*] fétide; [*taste*] infect/-e; **2** [*weather, day*] épouvantable; **to be in a ~ mood** être d'une humeur massacrante○; **to have a ~ temper** avoir un sale caractère; **3** [*language*] ordurier/-ière.
III *adv* **to taste ~** avoir un goût infect.
IV *vtr* **1** polluer [*environment*]; souiller [*pavement*]; **2** (Sport) commettre une faute contre [*player*].

Forms of Address

Only those forms of address in frequent use are included here; for letter formulae (openings and closings), see the *French correspondence* section.

Speaking to someone

Where English puts the surname after the title, French normally uses the title alone (note that in written conversations French does not use a capital letter for ***monsieur***, ***madame*** and ***mademoiselle***, unlike English ***Mr*** etc, nor for titles such as ***docteur***).

good morning, Mr Johnson	= bonjour, monsieur
good evening, Mrs Jones	= bonsoir, madame

The French ***monsieur*** and ***madame*** tend to be used more often than the English ***Mr X*** or ***Mrs Y***. Also, in English, people often say simply ***good morning*** or ***excuse me***; in the equivalent situation in French, they might say ***bonjour, monsieur*** or ***pardon, madame***. In both languages, other titles are also used:

hello, Dr. Brown	
hello, Doctor	= bonjour, docteur

In some cases where titles are not used in English, they are used in French, eg ***bonjour, Monsieur le directeur*** or ***bonjour, Madame la directrice*** to a head teacher, or ***bonjour, maître*** to a lawyer of either sex. Other titles, such as ***professeur*** (in the sense of ***professor***), are used much less than their English equivalents in direct address. Where in English one might say ***good morning, Professor***, in French one would probably say ***bonjour, monsieur*** or ***bonjour, madame***.

Titles of important positions are used in direct forms of address, preceded by ***Monsieur le*** or ***Madame la*** or ***Madame le***, as in:

yes, Chair	= oui, **Monsieur le** président
	= (*to a woman*) oui, **Madame la** présidente
yes, Minister	= oui, Monsieur le ministre
	= (*to a woman*) oui, **Madame le** ministre

Note the use of ***Madame le*** when the noun in question, like ***ministre*** here, or ***professeur*** and other titles, has no feminine form.

Speaking about someone

Mr Smith is here	= monsieur Smith est là
Mrs Jones phoned	= madame Jones a téléphoné
Miss Black has arrived	= mademoiselle Black est arrivée (*French has no equivalent of Ms.*)

When the title accompanies someone's name, the definite article must be used in French:

Dr Blake has arrived	= **le** docteur Blake est arrivé
Professor Jones spoke	= **le** professeur Jones a parlé

This is true of all titles:

Prince Charles	= **le** prince Charles
Princess Marie	= **la** princesse Marie

Note that with royal etc titles, only ***Ier*** is spoken as an ordinal number (***premier***) in French; unlike English, all the others are spoken as cardinal numbers (***deux***, ***trois***, and so on):

King Richard I	= le roi Richard **Ier** (*say* Richard **premier**)
Queen Elizabeth II	= la reine Elizabeth **II** (*say* Elizabeth **deux**)
Pope John XXIII	= le pape Jean **XXIII** (*say* Jean **vingt-trois**)

foul-mouthed *adj* grossier/-ière.
found *vtr* fonder (**on** sur).
foundation *n* **1** (founding) fondation *f*; **2 ~s** (of building) fondations *fpl*; **3** (also **~ cream**) fond *m* de teint.
founder *n* fondateur/-trice *m/f*.
foundry *n* fonderie *f*.
fountain *n* fontaine *f*.
fountain pen *n* stylo *m* (à encre).
four ▶ 389, 434 *n, pron, det* quatre (*m*) *inv*. IDIOMS **on all ~s** à quatre pattes.
four-letter word *n* mot *m* grossier.
four-star I *n* (GB) (also **~ petrol**) super(carburant) *m*.
II *adj* [*hotel, restaurant*] quatre étoiles.
fourteen ▶ 389, 434 *n, pron, det* quatorze (*m*) *inv*.
fourteenth ▶ 456, 498 **I** *n* **1** (in order) quatorzième *mf*; **2** (of month) quatorze *m inv*; **3** (fraction) quatorzième *m*.
II *adj, adv* quatorzième.
fourth ▶ 456, 498 **I** *n* **1** (in order) quatrième *mf*; **2** (of month) quatre *m inv*; **3** (fraction) quatrième *m*; **4** (also **~ gear**) (Aut) quatrième *f*.
II *adj, adv* quatrième.
fowl *n* volaille *f*.
fox *n* renard *m*.
fox hunting *n* chasse *f* au renard.
fraction *n* fraction *f* (**of** de).
fracture I *n* fracture *f*.
II *vtr* fracturer [*bone, rock*].
III *vi* [*bone*] se fracturer.
fragile *adj* fragile.
fragment *n* (of rock, manuscript) fragment *m*; (of glass, china) morceau *m*.
fragrance *n* parfum *m*.
fragrant *adj* odorant/-e.
frail *adj* [*person*] frêle; [*health, hope*] précaire.
frame I *n* **1** (of building, boat, roof) charpente *f*; (of car) châssis *m*; (of bicycle, racquet) cadre *m*; (of bed) sommier *m*; (of tent) armature *f*; **2** (of picture, window) cadre *m*; (of door) encadrement *m*; **3** (body) corps *m*.
II **frames** *n pl* (of spectacles) monture *f*.
III *vtr* **1** encadrer [*picture, face*]; **2** formuler [*question*].
frame of mind *n* état *m* d'esprit; **to be in the right/wrong ~ for doing** être/ne pas être d'humeur à faire.
framework *n* structure *f*; (figurative) cadre *m*.
franc ▶ 582 *n* franc *m*.
France ▶ 448 *pr n* France *f*.
franchise *n* **1** (right to vote) droit *m* de vote; **2** (commercial) franchise *f*.
frank *adj* franc/franche.
Frankfurt ▶ 448 *pr n* Francfort.
frankly *adv* franchement.
frantic *adj* **1** [*activity*] frénétique; **2** [*effort, search*] désespéré/-e; **to be ~ with worry** être fou/folle d'inquiétude.
fraternal *adj* fraternel/-elle.
fraternity *n* fraternité *f*.
fraud *n* fraude *f*.
fraudulent *adj* [*practice, use*] frauduleux/-euse; [*signature, cheque*] falsifié/-e; [*earnings*] illicite.
fray *vi* [*material, rope*] s'effilocher.
frayed *adj* [*nerves*] à bout; **tempers were ~** les gens s'énervaient.
freak I *n* **1** (strange person) original/-e *m/f*; **2** (at circus) phénomène *m*; **~ show** exhibition *f* de monstres; **3** (unusual occurrence) aberration *f*; **a ~ of nature** une bizarrerie de la nature; **4**° (enthusiast) mordu/-e° *m/f*, fana° *mf*.
II *adj* [*accident, storm*] exceptionnel/-elle.
■ **freak out**° (get angry) piquer une crise°; (go mad) flipper°.
freckle *n* tache *f* de rousseur.
free I *adj* **1** (gen) libre; **to be ~ to do** être libre de faire; **to set [sb/sth] ~** libérer [*person*]; rendre la liberté à [*animal*]; **2** (also **~ of charge**) gratuit/-e; **'admission ~'** 'entrée gratuite'; **3** être prodigue de [*advice*]; **to be very ~ with money** dépenser sans compter.
II *adv* **1** [*run, roam*] librement, en toute liberté; **to go ~** [*hostage*] être libéré/-e; [*criminal*] circuler en toute liberté; **2** (without paying) gratuitement.
III *vtr* **1** (gen) libérer; (from wreckage) dégager; **2** débloquer [*money, resources*].
IV **-free** *combining form* **smoke/sugar-~** sans fumée/sucre; **interest-~** sans intérêt.
V **for free** *phr* gratuitement.
IDIOMS **to have a ~ hand** avoir carte blanche (**in** pour); **to be a ~ agent** pouvoir agir à sa guise; **~ and easy** décontracté/-e.
freedom *n* liberté *f* (**to do** de faire); **~ of the press** liberté de la presse; **~ of information** libre accès *m* à l'information.
freefall *n* chute *f* libre.
Freefone® *n* (also **Freephone**®) numéro *m* d'appel gratuit.
free-for-all *n* mêlée *f* générale.
free gift *n* cadeau *m*.
free kick *n* coup *m* franc.
freelance I *n* (also **freelancer**) free-lance *mf*.
II *adv* [*work*] en free-lance.
freely *adv* (gen) librement; [*spend, give*] sans compter; [*admit*] volontiers.
Freephone® = **Freefone**®.
freepost *n* (GB) port *m* payé.
freestyle *n* (in swimming) nage *f* libre; (in skiing) figures *fpl* libres; (in wrestling) lutte *f* libre.
free trade *n* libre-échange *m*.
freeway *n* (US) autoroute *f*.
free will *n* libre arbitre *m*; **of one's (own) ~** de plein gré.
freeze I *n* **1** (in weather) gelées *fpl*; **2** (Econ) gel *m* (**on** de).
II *vtr* **1** congeler [*food*]; [*cold weather*] geler [*liquid, pipes*]; **2** (Econ) bloquer, geler [*prices, wages, assets*]; **3** (anaesthetize) insensibiliser [*gum, skin*].
III *vi* **1** [*water, pipes*] geler; [*food*] se congeler;

2 (feel cold) geler; **to be freezing to death** mourir de froid; **3** (not move) [*person, blood, smile*] se figer.
IV *v impers* geler.

freeze-dried *adj* lyophilisé.

freeze frame *n* arrêt *m* sur image.

freezer *n* congélateur *m*.

freezer compartment *n* freezer *m*.

freezing I *n* zéro *m*; **below ~** en-dessous de zéro.
II *adj* **I'm ~** je suis gelé; **it's ~ in here** on gèle ici.

freezing cold *adj* [*room, wind*] glacial/-e; [*water*] glacé/-e.

freight *n* **1** (goods) fret *m*, marchandises *fpl*; **2** (transport system) transport *m*; **3** (cost) (frais *mpl* de) port *m*.

freighter *n* **1** (ship) cargo *m*; **2** (plane) avion-cargo *m*.

French ▶553 **I** *n* **1** (people) **the ~** les Français *mpl*; **2** (language) français *m*.
II *adj* [*culture, food, politics*] français/-e; [*teacher, lesson*] de français; [*ambassador, embassy*] de France.

French fries *n pl* frites *fpl*.

Frenchman *n* Français *m*.

French toast *n* pain *m* perdu.

French window *n* porte-fenêtre *f*.

Frenchwoman *n* Française *f*.

frenetic *adj* [*activity*] frénétique; [*lifestyle*] trépidant/-e.

frenzied *adj* [*activity*] frénétique; [*attempt*] désespéré/-e.

frenzy *n* frénésie *f*, délire *m*.

frequency *n* fréquence *f* (**of** de).

frequent *adj* **1** (common) [*expression*] courant/-e; **2** (happening often) fréquent/-e; **to make ~ use of sth** se servir souvent or fréquemment de qch.

frequently *adv* souvent, fréquemment.

fresco *n* fresque *f*.

fresh *adj* **1** frais/fraîche; **to smell ~** avoir une odeur fraîche; **~ orange juice** jus d'orange pressée; **while it is still ~ in your mind** tant que tu l'as tout frais à l'esprit; **2** [*evidence, attempt*] nouveau/-elle (*before n*); [*linen*] propre; **to make a ~ start** prendre un nouveau départ; **3** [*approach, outlook*] (tout) nouveau/(toute) nouvelle (*before n*); **4 to feel** or **be ~** [*person*] être plein/-e d'entrain; **5**○ (cheeky) impertinent/-e; **to be ~ with sb** être un peu familier/-ière avec qn.

fresh air *n* air *m* frais; **to get some ~** prendre l'air, s'oxygéner.

freshen *v* ■ **freshen up** faire un brin de toilette.

fresh water *n* eau *f* douce.

fret *vi* **1** (be anxious) s'inquiéter (**over, about** pour, au sujet de); **2** (cry) pleurer.

Freudian slip *n* lapsus *m*.

friction *n* **1** (rubbing) frottement *m*; **2** (conflict) conflits *mpl* (**between** entre); **to cause ~** être cause de friction.

Friday ▶456 *n* vendredi *m*.

fridge *n* (GB) frigo○ *m*, réfrigérateur *m*.

fridge-freezer *n* réfrigérateur-congélateur *m*.

friend *n* ami/-e *m/f* (**of** de); **to make ~s** se faire des amis; **to make ~s with sb** devenir ami/-e *m/f* avec qn.

friendly I *adj* [*person, attitude, argument, match*] amical/-e, sympathique; [*animal*] affectueux/-euse; [*government, nation*] ami (*after n*); **to be ~ with sb** être ami/-e *m/f* avec qn.
II -friendly *combining form* **environment-~** qui ne nuit pas à l'environnement; **user-~** d'utilisation facile, convivial/-e.

friendship *n* amitié *f*.

fright *n* peur *f*; **to take ~** prendre peur, s'effrayer; **to give sb a ~** faire peur à qn, effrayer qn.

frighten *vtr* faire peur à, effrayer.

frightened *adj* **to be ~** avoir peur (**of** de; **to do** de faire).

frightening *adj* effrayant/-e.

frill *n* (on dress) volant *m*; (on shirt) jabot *m*.

fringe *n* **1** frange *f*; **on the ~s of society** en marge de la societé; **2** (in theatre) **the ~** théâtre *m* alternatif.

fringe benefits *n pl* avantages *mpl* sociaux or en nature.

frisk *vtr* fouiller [*person*].

fritter *n* beignet *m*.
■ **fritter away** gaspiller [*time, money*].

frivolous *adj* frivole.

frizzy *adj* [*hair*] crépu/-e.

frog *n* grenouille *f*.
IDIOMS **to have a ~ in one's throat** avoir un chat dans la gorge.

frogman *n* homme-grenouille *m*.

from *prep*

■ **Note** *from* is often translated by *de*: *from Rome* = de Rome; *from the sea* = de la mer.
– Remember that *de* + *le* always becomes *du* (*from the office* = du bureau), and *de* + *les* always becomes *des* (*from the United States* = des États-Unis).
– For examples and particular usages, see the entry below.

---

1 de; **where is he ~?** d'où est-il?, d'où vient-il?; **she comes ~ Oxford** elle vient d'Oxford; **paper ~ Denmark** du papier provenant du Danemark; **a flight ~ Nice** un vol en provenance de Nice; **a friend ~ Chicago** un ami (qui vient) de Chicago; **a colleague ~ Japan** un collègue japonais; **a man ~ the council** un homme qui travaille pour le conseil municipal; **a letter ~ Tim** une lettre (de la part) de Tim; **who is it ~?** c'est de la part de qui?; **alcohol can be made ~ a wide range of products** on peut faire de l'alcool à partir de produits très variés; **10 km ~ the sea** à 10 km de la mer; **15 years ~ now** dans 15 ans, d'ici 15 ans; **2 ~ ... to...** de ... à...; **the journey ~ A to B** le voyage de A à B; **the road ~ A to B** la route qui va de A à B; **open ~ 2 pm to 5 pm** ouvert de 14 à 17 heures; **~ June to August** du mois de juin au mois d'août; **to rise ~ 10**

to 17% passer de 10 à 17%; **~ start to finish** du début à la fin; **everything ~ paperclips to wigs** tout, des trombones aux perruques; **~ day to day** de jour en jour; **3** (starting from) à partir de; **~ today/May** à partir d'aujourd'hui/du mois de mai; **wine ~ £5 a bottle** du vin à partir de 5 livres la bouteille; **~ then on** dès lors; **~ the age of 8** depuis l'âge de 8 ans; **4** (based on) **~ a short story** d'après un conte; **to speak ~ experience** parler d'expérience; **5** (among) **to choose** or **pick ~** choisir parmi; **6** (in mathematics) **10 ~ 27 leaves 17** 27 moins 10 égale 17; **7** (because of) **I know her ~ work** je la connais car on travaille ensemble; **~ what I saw/he said** d'après ce que j'ai vu/ce qu'il a dit.

front I *n* **1** (of house) façade *f*; (of shop) devanture *f*; (of cupboard, box, sweater, building) devant *m*; (of book) couverture *f*; (of card, coin, banknote) recto *m*; (of car, boat) avant *m*; (of fabric) endroit *m*; **to button at the ~** se boutonner sur le devant; **on the ~ of the envelope** au recto de l'enveloppe; **2** (of train, queue) tête *f*; (of auditorium) premier rang *m*; **at the ~ of the line** en tête de la file; **to sit at the ~ of the class** s'asseoir au premier rang de la classe; **I'll sit in the ~** je vais m'asseoir devant; **at the ~ of the coach** à l'avant du car; **3** (GB) (promenade) front *m* de mer, bord *m* de mer; **on the sea ~** au bord de la mer; **4** (Mil) front *m*; **5** (in weather) front *m*; **6** (façade) façade *f*; **it's just a ~** ce n'est qu'une façade.
II *adj* [*entrance*] côté rue; [*garden, window*] de devant; [*bedroom*] qui donne sur la rue; [*wheel*] avant; [*seat*] (in cinema) au premier rang; (in vehicle) de devant; [*leg, paw, tooth*] de devant; [*page*] premier/-ière (*before n*); [*view*] de face.
III *vtr* **1**° être à la tête de [*band*]; **2** présenter [*TV show*].
IV *vi* **to ~ onto** (GB) or **on** (US) donner sur.
V in front *phr* [*walk*] devant; **the car in ~** la voiture de devant; **the people in ~** les gens qui sont devant; **to be in ~** (in race) être en tête; **I'm 30 points in ~** j'ai 30 points d'avance.
VI in front of *phr* devant.

front door *n* porte *f* d'entrée.

frontier *n* frontière *f*.

frost *n* gel *m*.

frostbite *n* gelures *fpl*.

frosty *adj* **1** [*morning*] glacial/-e; [*windscreen*] couvert/-e de givre; **it was a ~ night** il gelait cette nuit-là; **2** (unfriendly) glacial/-e.

froth *n* (on beer, champagne) mousse *f*; (on water) écume *f*; (around mouth) écume *f*.

frown *vi* froncer les sourcils; **to ~ at sb** regarder qn en fronçant les sourcils.
■ **frown on, frown upon** désapprouver, critiquer.

frozen *adj* **1** [*food*] congelé/-e; **2** [*lake, pipe, ground*] gelé/-e; **I'm ~** je suis gelé; **to be ~ stiff** être transi/-e de froid.

fruit *n* fruit *m*; **a piece of ~** un fruit.

fruit cake *n* cake *m*.

fruit juice *n* jus *m* de fruits.

fruit machine *n* machine *f* à sous.

fruit salad *n* salade *f* de fruits.

fruity *adj* [*wine, fragrance*] fruité/-e.

frustrate *vtr* frustrer [*person*]; réduire [qch] à néant [*effort*]; contrarier [*plan*]; entraver [*attempt*].

frustrated *adj* frustré/-e.

frustration *n* frustration *f* (**at, with** quant à).

fry I *vtr* faire frire.
II fried *pp adj* **fried fish** poisson *m* frit; **fried food** friture *f*; **fried eggs** œufs *mpl* au plat; **fried potatoes** pommes *fpl* de terre sautées.

frying pan *n* (GB) poêle *f* (à frire).

fuel I *n* (for heating) combustible *m*; (for car, plane) carburant *m*.
II *vtr* **1** alimenter [*engine*]; **2** ravitailler [*plane*]; **3** aggraver [*tension*]; attiser [*hatred*].

fuel tank *n* (of car) réservoir *m*.

fugitive *n* fugitif/-ive *m/f*, fuyard/-e *m/f*.

fulfil (GB), **fulfill** (US) *vtr* **1** réaliser [*ambition*]; répondre à [*desire, need*]; **to feel ~led** se sentir comblé/-e; **2** remplir [*duty, conditions, contract*].

fulfilment (GB), **fulfillment** (US) *n* **1** (satisfaction) épanouissement *m*; **2 the ~ of** la réalisation de [*ambition, need*].

full I *adj* **1** (gen) plein/-e (**of** de); [*hotel, flight, car park*] complet/-ète; [*theatre*] comble; **I'm ~ (up)** je n'en peux plus; **2** (busy) [*day, week*] chargé/-e, bien rempli/-e; **a very ~ life** une vie très remplie; **3** (complete) [*name, breakfast, story*] complet/-ète; [*price, control*] total/-e; [*responsibility*] entier/-ière; [*support*] inconditionnel/-elle; **4** [*member*] à part entière; **5** [*employment, bloom*] plein/-e (*before n*); **at ~ volume** à plein volume; **at ~ speed** à toute vitesse; **to get ~ marks** (GB) obtenir la note maximale; **6** (for emphasis) [*hour, kilo, month*] bon/bonne (*before n*); **7** (rounded) [*cheeks*] rond/-e; [*figure*] fort/-e; [*skirt, sleeve*] ample.
II *adv* **to know ~ well that** savoir fort bien que; **with the heating up ~** avec le chauffage à fond.
III in full *phr* [*pay*] intégralement; **to write sth in ~** écrire qch en toutes lettres.

full-blown *adj* **1** [*disease*] déclaré/-e; [*epidemic*] extensif/-ive; **2** [*crisis, war*] à grande échelle.

full board *n* (in hotel) pension *f* complète.

full-cream milk *n* (GB) lait *m* entier.

full-length *adj* [*coat, curtain*] long/longue; [*mirror*] en pied; **a ~ film** un long métrage.

full moon *n* pleine lune *f*.

full name *n* nom *m* et prénom *m*.

full price *adj, adv* au prix fort.

full-scale *adj* **1** [*drawing*] grandeur *f* nature; **2** [*investigation*] approfondi/-e; **3** [*alert*] général/-e; [*crisis*] généralisé/-e.

full-size(d) *adj* grand format *inv*.

full stop *n* (GB) point *m*.

full time I *n* (Sport) fin *m* du match.
II full-time *adj* **1** (Sport) [*score*] final/-e; **2** [*job, student*] à plein temps.
III *adv* [*study, work*] à plein temps.

fully *adv* **1** [*understand*] très bien; [*recover*] complètement; [*dressed*] entièrement; [*awake, developed*] complètement; **to be ~ qualified** avoir obtenu tous ses diplômes; **2** [*open*] à fond; **~ booked** complet/-ète.

fume *vi* **1** [*chemical, mixture*] fumer; **2**○ **to be fuming** être furibond/-e○.

fumes *n pl* émanations *fpl*; **petrol ~** (GB), **gas ~** (US) vapeurs *fpl* d'essence.

fun *n* plaisir *m*, amusement *m*; **to have ~** s'amuser (**doing** en faisant; **with** avec); **windsurfing is ~** c'est amusant de faire de la planche à voile; **for ~** pour s'amuser; **she is great ~ to be with** on s'amuse beaucoup avec elle.
IDIOMS **to make ~ of** or **poke ~ at sb/sth** se moquer de qn/qch.

function I *n* **1** (gen) fonction *f*; **2** (reception) réception *f*; (ceremony) cérémonie *f* (officielle).
II *vi* **1** (work properly) fonctionner; **2 to ~ as** [*object*] faire fonction de, servir de; [*person*] jouer le rôle de.

functional *adj* **1** (in working order) opérationnel/-elle; **2** [*furniture, design*] fonctionnel/-elle.

fund I *n* fonds *m*; **relief ~** caisse *f* de secours; **disaster ~** collecte *f* en faveur des sinistrés.
II funds *n pl* fonds *mpl*, capitaux *mpl*; **to be in ~s** avoir de l'argent.
III *vtr* financer [*company, project*].

fundamental *adj* [*issue*] fondamental/-e; [*error, importance*] capital/-e; [*concern*] principal/-e.

funding *n* financement *m*.

funeral *n* enterrement *m*, obsèques *fpl* (formal).

funeral home (US), **funeral parlour** *n* entreprise *f* de pompes funèbres.

fun fair *n* fête *f* foraine.

fungus *n* **1** (mushroom) champignon *m*; **2** (mould) moisissure *f*.

funnel *n* **1** (for liquids) entonnoir *m*; **2** (on ship) cheminée *f*.

funny *adj* (amusing) drôle, amusant/-e; (odd) bizarre; **to feel ~**○ se sentir tout/-e chose○.

fur I *n* (of animal) poils *mpl*; (for garment) fourrure *f*.
II *adj* [*collar, coat*] de fourrure.

furious *adj* **1** furieux/-ieuse (**with, at** contre); **he's ~ about it** cela l'a rendu furieux; **2** [*debate, struggle*] acharné/-e; [*storm*] déchaîné/-e; **at a ~ rate** à un rythme effréné.

furnace *n* (boiler) chaudière *f*; (in foundry) fourneau *m*; (for forging) four *m*.

furnish *vtr* meubler [*room, apartment*].

furnishings *n pl* ameublement *m*.

furniture *n* mobilier *m*, meubles *mpl*; **a piece of ~** un meuble.

furry *adj* [*toy*] en peluche; [*kitten*] au poil touffu.

further I *adv* **1** (gen) (also **farther**) plus loin (**than** que); **how much ~ is it?** c'est encore loin?; **~ back/forward** plus en arrière/en avant; **~ away** or **off** plus loin; **~ on** encore plus loin; **2** (in time) (also **farther**) **~ back than 1964** avant 1964; **we must look ~ ahead** nous devons regarder plus vers l'avenir; **3 I haven't read ~ than page twenty** je n'ai pas lu au-delà de la page vingt; **prices fell (even) ~** les prix ont baissé encore plus.
II *adj* **1** (additional) **a ~ 500 people** 500 personnes de plus; **~ changes** d'autres changements; **without ~ delay** sans plus attendre; **2** (also **farther**) [*side, end*] autre.
III *vtr* augmenter [*chances*]; faire avancer [*career, plan*]; servir [*cause*].

further education *n* (GB Univ) ≈ enseignement *m* professionnel.

furthest (also **farthest**) **I** *adj* le plus éloigné/la plus éloignée.
II *adv* (also **the ~**) le plus loin.

furtive *adj* [*glance, movement*] furtif/-ive; [*behaviour*] suspect/-e.

fury *n* fureur *f*; **to be in a ~** être en fureur.

fuse, **fuze** (US) **I** *n* fusible *m*; **to blow a ~** faire sauter un fusible; (get angry) piquer une crise○.
II *vtr* **1** (GB) **to ~ the lights** faire sauter les plombs; **2** (join) fondre [qch] ensemble [*metals*].

fuse box *n* boîte *f* à fusibles.

fuse wire *n* fusible *m*.

fuss I *n* **1** (agitation) remue-ménage *m inv*; **to make a ~** faire des histoires; **to make a ~ about sth** faire toute une histoire à propos de qch; **2 to kick up a ~ about sth**○ piquer une crise○ à propos de qch; **3** (attention) **to make a ~ of** être aux petits soins avec or pour [*person*]; caresser [*animal*].
II *vi* **1** (worry) se faire du souci (**about** pour); **2** (show attention) **to ~ over sb**○ être aux petits soins avec or pour qn.

fussy *adj* **to be ~ about one's food/about details** être maniaque sur la nourriture/sur les détails.

future I *n* **1** avenir *m*; **in the ~** dans l'avenir; **in ~** à l'avenir; **2** (also **~ tense**) futur *m*.
II *adj* [*generation, developments, investment, earnings*] futur/-e; [*prospects*] d'avenir; [*queen, king*] futur/-e (*before n*); **at some ~ date** à une date ultérieure.

fuze (US) = **fuse**.

fuzzy *adj* **1** [*hair, beard*] crépu/-e; **2** [*image*] flou/-e; [*idea, mind*] confus/-e.

Gg

g, G *n* **1** (letter) g, G *m*; **2 G** (Mus) sol *m*; **3 g** (*written abbr* = **gram**) g.

gadget *n* gadget *m*.

gag I *n* **1** (on mouth) bâillon *m*; **2**○ (joke) blague○ *f*.
II *vtr* bâillonner [*person*].
III *vi* avoir un haut-le-cœur.

gage (US) = **gauge**.

gain I *n* **1** (financial) gain *m*, profit *m*; **2** (increase) augmentation *f* (**in** de); **3** (advantage) gain *m*; (advances) progrès *m* (**in** de).
II *vtr* **1** (gen) gagner; acquérir [*experience*] (**from** de); obtenir [*advantage*] (**from** grâce à); **we have nothing to ~** nous n'avons rien à gagner; **2 to ~ speed** prendre de la vitesse or de l'élan; **to ~ weight** prendre du poids.
III *vi* **1** (increase) **to ~ in popularity** gagner en popularité; **to ~ in value** prendre de la valeur; **2** (profit) **she hasn't ~ed by it** cela ne lui a rien rapporté.
■ **gain on** rattraper [*person, vehicle*].

galaxy *n* galaxie *f*.

gale *n* vent *m* violent.

gallery *n* **1** (gen) galerie *f*; **2** (**art**) **~** musée *m* (d'art); **3** (in theatre) dernier balcon *m*.

Gallic *adj* (French) français/-e.

gallon *n* gallon *m* (GB = *4.546 l*; US = *3.785 l*).

gallop I *n* galop *m*.
II *vi* galoper.

gambit *n* **1** tactique *f*; **2** (in chess) gambit *m*.

gamble I *n* pari *m*; **it's a ~** c'est risqué.
II *vtr* **1** jouer [*money*]; **2** (figurative) miser (**on** sur).
III *vi* (at cards, on shares) jouer; (on horses) parier; (figurative) miser (**on** sur).

gambling *n* jeu *m* (d'argent).

game I *n* **1** jeu *m*; **to play a ~** jouer à un jeu; **to have a ~ of** faire une partie de; **2** (match) match *m* (**of** de); (in tennis) jeu *m*; **3** (Culin) gibier *m*.
II games *n pl* **1** (GB Sch) sport *m*; **2** (also **Games**) (sporting event) Jeux *mpl*.
IDIOMS **to give the ~ away** vendre la mèche.

game reserve *n* (for hunting) réserve *f* de chasse; (for protection) réserve *f* naturelle.

game show *n* jeu *m* télévisé.

gammon *n* jambon *m*.

gang *n* **1** (of criminals) gang *m*; (of youths, friends) bande *f*; **2** (of workmen, prisoners) équipe *f*.

gangster *n* gangster *m*.

gangway *n* **1** (to ship) passerelle *f*; **2** (GB) (in bus, cinema) allée *f*.

gap *n* **1** (gen) trou *m* (**in** dans); (between planks, curtains) interstice *m* (**in** entre); (between cars) espace *m* (**in** entre); (in cloud) trouée *f* (**in** dans); **2** (of time) intervalle *m*; (in conversation) silence *m*; **3** (discrepancy) écart *m* (**between** entre); **a 15-year age ~** une différence d'âge de 15 ans; **4** (in knowledge) lacune *f* (**in** dans); **5** (in market) créneau *m*.

gape *vi* **1** (stare) rester bouche bée; **to ~ at sb/sth** regarder qn/qch bouche bée; **2 to ~ open** [*chasm*] s'ouvrir tout grand; [*wound*] être béant/-e; [*garment*] bâiller.

gaping *adj* [*person*] bouche bée; [*wound, hole*] béant/-e.

garage *n* garage *m*.

garbage *n* **1** (US) (refuse) ordures *fpl*; **2** (nonsense) âneries *fpl*, bêtises *fpl*.

garbage can *n* (US) poubelle *f*.

garbage truck *n* (US) camion *m* des éboueurs.

garden I *n* jardin *m*.
II *vi* jardiner, faire du jardinage.

garden centre (GB), **garden center** (US) *n* jardinerie *f*.

gardener ▶ 626 *n* jardinier/-ière *m/f*.

gardening *n* jardinage *m*.

gargle *vi* se gargariser (**with** avec).

garish *adj* tape-à-l'œil *inv*.

garland *n* guirlande *f*.

garlic *n* ail *m*.

garment *n* vêtement *m*.

garnish I *n* garniture *f*.
II *vtr* garnir (**with** de).

garter *n* **1** (for stocking) jarretière *f*; (for socks) fixe-chaussette *m*; **2** (US) (suspender) jarretelle *f*.

gas I *n* **1** (fuel) gaz *m*; **2** (anaesthetic) anesthésie *f*; **3** (US) (petrol) essence *f*.
II *vtr* gazer.

gas cooker *n* cuisinière *f* à gaz.

gash I *n* entaille *f*.
II *vtr* entailler.

gasoline *n* (US) essence *f*.

gasp I *n* halètement *m*.
II *vi* **1** (for air) haleter; **2 to ~** (**in amazement**) avoir le souffle coupé (par la surprise).

gas pedal *n* (US) accélérateur *m*.

gas station *n* (US) station-service *f*.

gate *n* (of field, level crossing) barrière *f*; (in town, prison, airport, garden) porte *f*; (of courtyard, palace) portail *m*; **at the ~** à l'entrée.

gather I *n* (in garment) fronce *f*.
II *vtr* **1** cueillir [*fruit, flowers*]; ramasser [*fallen fruit, wood*]; recueillir [*information*]; rassembler [*courage, strength*]; **to ~ speed** prendre de la vitesse; **2 to ~ that**... déduire que...; **I ~ (that) he was there** d'après ce que j'ai compris il était là; **3** (in sewing) faire des fronces à.
III *vi* [*people, crowd*] se rassembler; [*family*] se réunir; [*clouds*] s'amonceler.

gathering *n* réunion *f*; **social/family ~** réunion entre amis/de famille.

Games and Sports

With or without the definite article?

French normally uses the definite article with names of games and sports:

football	= **le** football
bridge	= **le** bridge
chess	= **les** échecs *mpl*
to play football	= jouer **au** football
to play bridge	= jouer **au** bridge
to play chess	= jouer **aux** échecs
to like football	= aimer **le** football

But most compound nouns (eg ***saute-mouton***) work like this:

hide-and-seek	= cache-cache *m*
to play at hide-and-seek	= jouer à cache-cache
to like hide-and-seek	= aimer jouer à cache-cache

Names of other 'official' games and sports follow the same pattern as ***bridge*** in the following phrases:

to play bridge with X against Y	= jouer au bridge avec X contre Y
to beat sb at bridge	= battre qn au bridge
to win at bridge	= gagner au bridge
to lose at bridge	= perdre au bridge
she's good at bridge	= elle joue bien au bridge

Players and events

a bridge player	= un joueur de bridge

but

I'm not a bridge player	= je ne joue pas au bridge
he's a good bridge player	= il joue bien au bridge
a game of bridge	= une partie de bridge
a bridge champion	= un champion de bridge
the French bridge champion	= le champion de France de bridge
a bridge championship	= un championnat de bridge
the rules of bridge	= les règles du bridge

Playing cards

The names of the four suits work like ***clubs*** here:

clubs	= les trèfles *mpl*
to play a club	= jouer un trèfle
the eight of clubs	= le huit de trèfle
the ace of clubs	= l'as de trèfle
I've no clubs left	= je n'ai plus de trèfle
have you any clubs?	= as-tu du trèfle?
clubs are trumps	= l'atout est trèfle
to call two clubs	= demander deux trèfles

Other games vocabulary can be found in the dictionary at *game*, *trick* etc.

gauge, **gage** (US) **I** *n* **1** (of gun, screw) calibre *m*; (of metal, wire) épaisseur *f*; **2** (of railway) écartement *m* (des voies); **3** (measuring instrument) jauge *f*; **fuel ~** jauge d'essence.
II *vtr* **1** mesurer [*diameter*]; jauger [*distance, quantity*]; calibrer [*gun*]; **2** évaluer [*mood, reaction*].

gaunt *adj* décharné/-e.

gauze *n* (fabric) gaze *f*; (wire) grillage *m*.

gay I *n* homosexuel/-elle *m/f*, gay *mf*.
II *adj* **1** homosexuel/-elle; **2** (happy) gai/-e; [*laughter*] joyeux/-euse.

gaze I *n* regard *m*.
II *vi* **to ~ at sb/sth** regarder qn/qch; (in wonder) contempler qn/qch.

GCSE *n* (*abbr* = **General Certificate of Secondary Education**) certificat *m* d'études secondaires.

gear *n* **1** (equipment) matériel *m*; **2** (clothes) fringues○ *fpl*; **football ~** tenue *f* de football; **3** (Aut) vitesse *f*; **to be in third ~** être en troisième; **to put a car in ~** passer la vitesse; **you're not in ~** tu es au point mort.

gearbox *n* boîte *f* de vitesses.

gearstick (GB), **gearshift** (US) *n* levier *m* de vitesses.

gear wheel *n* pignon *m*.

gel I *n* gel *m*.
II *vi* **1** (Culin) prendre; **2** (figurative) prendre forme.

gem *n* (jewel) pierre *f* précieuse.

Gemini *n* Gémeaux *mpl*.

gender *n* **1** (of word) genre *m*; **2** (of person, animal) sexe *m*.

gene *n* gène *m*.

general I *n* général *m*.
II *adj* général/-e.
III in general *phr* (usually) en général; (overall) dans l'ensemble.

general election *n* élections *fpl* législatives.

generalization *n* généralisation *f* (**about** sur).

generalize *vtr*, *vi* généraliser (**about** à propos de).

general knowledge *n* culture *f* générale.

generally *adv* **1** (usually) en général, généralement; **~ speaking**... en règle générale...; **2** (overall) **the quality is ~ good** dans l'ensemble la qualité est bonne; **3** [*talk*] d'une manière générale.

general practitioner, **GP** ▶ 626 *n* (médecin *m*) généraliste *mf*.

general public *n* (grand) public *m*.

general-purpose *adj* à usages multiples.

general strike *n* grève *f* générale.

generate *vtr* produire [*power, heat, income, waste*]; créer [*employment*]; susciter [*interest, tension, ideas*]; entraîner [*profit, publicity*].

generation *n* **1** génération *f*; **the younger/older ~** la jeune/l'ancienne génération; **2** (of electricity, data) production *f*.

generator *n* (of electricity) générateur *m*; (in hospital, on farm) groupe *m* électrogène.

generosity *n* générosité *f*.

generous *adj* (gen) généreux/-euse; [*size*] grand/-e (*before n*); [*hem*] bon/bonne (*before n*).

genetics *n* génétique *f*.

Geneva ▶ 448 *pr n* Genève.

genial *adj* cordial/-e.

genitals *n pl* organes *mpl* génitaux.

genius *n* génie *m*.

gentle *adj* (gen) doux/douce; [*hint, reminder*] discret/-ète; [*pressure, touch, breeze*] léger/-ère; [*exercise*] modéré/-e.

gentleman *n* **1** (man) monsieur *m*; **2** (well-bred) gentleman *m*.

gently *adv* (gen) doucement; [*treat, cleanse*] avec douceur; [*cook*] à feu doux; [*speak*] gentiment; **to break the news ~** annoncer la nouvelle avec ménagement.

gents *n pl* (toilets) toilettes *fpl*; (on sign) 'Messieurs'.

genuine *adj* [*reason, motive*] vrai/-e (*before n*); [*work of art*] authentique; [*jewel, substance*] véritable; [*person, effort, interest*] sincère; [*buyer*] sérieux/-ieuse.

geography *n* géographie *f*.

geology *n* géologie *f*.

geometry *n* géométrie *f*.

geriatric *adj* [*hospital, ward*] gériatrique.

germ *n* **1** (microbe) microbe *m*; **2** (seed) germe *m*.

German ▶ 553 **I** *n* **1** (person) Allemand/-e *m/f*; **2** (language) allemand *m*.
II *adj* [*custom, food*] allemand/-e; [*ambassador, embassy*] d'Allemagne; [*teacher, course*] d'allemand.

German measles ▶ 533 *n* rubéole *f*.

Germany ▶ 448 *pr n* Allemagne *f*.

germinate I *vtr* faire germer.
II *vi* germer.

gesticulate *vi* gesticuler.

gesture I *n* geste *m* (**of** de).
II *vi* faire un geste; **to ~ at** or **towards sth** désigner qch d'un geste; **to ~ to sb** faire signe à qn.

get

■ **Note** This much-used verb has no multi-purpose equivalent in French and therefore is very often translated by choosing a synonym: *to get lunch* = *to prepare lunch* = préparer le déjeuner.
– When *get* is used to express the idea that a job is done not by you but by somebody else (*to get a room painted*), *faire* is used in French followed by an infinitive (*faire repeindre une pièce*).
– When *get* has the meaning of *become* and is followed by an adjective (*to get rich*), *devenir* is sometimes useful but check the appropriate entry (***rich***) as a single verb often suffices (*s'enrichir*).
– The phrasal verbs (*get around*, *get down*, *get on* etc) are listed separately at the end of the entry ***get***.
– For examples and further uses of *get* see the entry below .

I *vtr* **1** (receive) recevoir [*letter, grant*]; recevoir, percevoir [*salary, pension*]; capter [*channel*]; **2** (inherit) **to ~ sth from sb** hériter qch de qn [*article, money*]; tenir qch de qn [*trait*]; **3** (obtain) obtenir [*permission, divorce*]; trouver [*job*]; **4** (buy) acheter [*item, newspaper*] (**from** chez); avoir [*ticket*]; **to ~ sb sth, to ~ sth for sb** (as gift) acheter qch à qn; **5** (acquire) se faire [*reputation*]; **6** (achieve) obtenir [*grade*]; **7** (fetch) chercher [*person, help*]; **to ~ sb sth, to ~ sth for sb** aller chercher qch pour qn; **8** (move) **to ~ sb/sth downstairs** faire descendre qn/qch; **9** (help progress) **this is ~ting us nowhere** ça ne nous avance à rien; **where will that ~ you?** à quoi ça t'avancera?; **10** (deal with) **I'll ~ it** (of phone) je réponds; (of doorbell) j'y vais; **11** (prepare) préparer [*breakfast, lunch*]; **12** (take hold of) attraper [*person*] (**by** par); **13**○ (oblige to give) **to ~ sth out of sb** faire sortir qch à qn [*money*]; obtenir qch de qn [*truth*]; **14** (contract) attraper [*cold, disease*]; **he got measles from his sister** sa sœur lui a passé la rougeole; **15** (catch) prendre [*bus, train*]; **16** (have) **to have got** avoir [*object, money, friend*]; **I've got a headache** j'ai mal à la tête; **to ~ the idea that** se mettre dans la tête que; **17 to ~ a surprise** être surpris/-e; **to ~ a shock** avoir un choc; **to ~ a bang on the head** recevoir un coup sur la tête; **18** (as punishment) prendre [*five years*]; avoir [*fine*]; **19** (understand, hear) comprendre; **20**○ (annoy) **what ~s me is...** ce qui m'agace c'est que...; **21 to ~ to like sb** finir par apprécier qn; **how did you ~ to hear of...?** comment avez-vous entendu parler de...?; **we got to know them last year** on a fait leur connaissance l'année dernière; **22** (have opportunity) **to ~ to do** avoir l'occasion de faire, pouvoir faire; **23** (must) **to have got to do** devoir faire [*homework, chore*]; **it's got to be done** il faut le faire; **you've got to realize that...** il faut que tu te rendes compte que...; **24** (make) **to ~ sb to pay** faire payer qn; **to ~ sb to tell the truth** faire dire la vérité à qn; **25** (ask) **to ~ sb to wash the dishes** demander à qn de faire la vaisselle; **26 to ~ the car repaired** faire réparer la voiture; **to ~ one's hair cut** se faire couper les cheveux; **to ~ the car going** faire démarrer la voiture; **to ~ one's socks wet** mouiller ses chaussettes; **to ~ one's finger trapped** se coincer le doigt; **to ~ a dress made** se faire faire une robe.

II *vi* **1** (become) devenir [*suspicious, old*]; **it's ~ting late** il se fait tard; **2** (forming passive) **to ~ killed** se faire tuer; **to ~ hurt** être blessé/-e; **3** (become involved in) **to ~ into**○ se mettre à [*hobby*]; commencer dans [*profession*]; **to ~ into a fight** se battre; **4** (arrive) **to ~ there** arriver; **to ~ to the airport** arriver à l'aéroport; **how did you ~ here?** comment est-ce que tu es venu?; **where did you ~ to?** où est-ce que tu étais passé?; **5** (progress) **I'm ~ting nowhere with this essay** je n'avance pas dans cette dissertation; **now we're ~ting somewhere** il y a du progrès; **6** (put on) **to ~ into** mettre, enfiler○ [*pyjamas*].

■ **get about 1** (move) se déplacer; **2** (travel) voyager.

■ **get across 1** traverser [*river, road*]; **2** faire passer [*message*] (**to** à).

■ **get ahead** (make progress) progresser.

■ **get along 1 how are you ~ting along?** (in job, school) comment ça se passe?; **2** [*people*] bien s'entendre (**with** avec).

■ **get around**: ¶ **~ around 1** = **get about**; **2** (manage to do) **she'll ~ around to visiting us eventually** elle va bien finir par venir nous voir; **I haven't got around to it yet** je n'ai pas encore eu le temps de m'en occuper; ¶ **~ around [sth]** contourner [*problem, law*].

■ **get at**○ **1** (reach) atteindre [*object*]; découvrir [*truth*]; **2** (criticize) être après [*person*]; **3** (insinuate) **what are you ~ting at?** où est-ce que tu veux en venir?

■ **get away 1** (leave) partir; **2** (escape) s'échapper; **3 to ~ away with a crime** échapper à la justice; **you won't ~ away with it!** tu ne vas pas t'en tirer comme ça!

■ **get away from 1** quitter [*place*]; échapper à [*person*]; **2 there's no ~ting away from it** on ne peut pas le nier.

■ **get back**: ¶ **~ back 1** (return) rentrer; (after short time) revenir; **2** (move backwards) reculer; ¶ **~ back to [sth] 1** (return to) rentrer à [*house, city*]; revenir à [*office, point*]; **when we ~ back to London** à notre retour à Londres; **to ~ back to sleep** se rendormir; **to ~ back to normal** redevenir normal; **2** (return to earlier stage) revenir à [*main topic, former point*]; ¶ **~ back to [sb]** revenir à; **I'll ~ back to you** (on phone) je vous rappelle; ¶ **~ [sth] back** (regain) récupérer [*lost object*]; reprendre [*strength*]; **she got her money back** elle a été remboursée.

■ **get by 1** (pass) passer; **2** (survive) s'en sortir (**on, with** avec).

■ **get down**: ¶ **~ down 1** (descend) descendre (**from, out of** de); **2** (on floor) se coucher; (crouch) se baisser; **to ~ down on one's knees** s'agenouiller; **3 to ~ down to** se mettre à [*work*]; **to ~ down to doing** se mettre à faire; ¶ **~ down [sth]** descendre [*slope*]; ¶ **~ [sth] down** (from height) descendre; ¶ **~ [sb] down**○ (depress) déprimer.

■ **get in**: ¶ **~ in 1** (to building) entrer; (to vehicle) monter; **2** (return home) rentrer; **3** (arrive) arriver; **4** (penetrate) pénétrer; **5** [*party*] passer; [*candidate*] être élu/-e; **6** (Sch, Univ) [*applicant*] être admis/-e; ¶ **~ [sth] in 1** (buy) acheter; **2 I can't ~ the drawer in** je n'arrive pas à faire rentrer le tiroir.

■ **get into 1** (enter) entrer dans [*building*]; monter dans [*vehicle*]; **2** (as member) devenir membre de; (as student) être admis/-e à; **3** (squeeze into) rentrer dans [*garment, size*].

■ **get off**: ¶ **~ off 1** (from bus) descendre (**at** à); **2** (start on journey) partir; **3** (leave work) finir; **4**○ (escape punishment) s'en tirer (**with** avec); **5 to ~ off to a good start** prendre un bon départ; **to ~ off to sleep** s'endormir; ¶ **~ off [sth] 1** descendre de [*wall, bus*]; **2** s'écarter de [*subject*]; ¶ **~ [sth] off 1** (send off) envoyer [*letter*]; **2** (remove) enlever.

■ **get on**: ¶ **~ on 1** (climb aboard) monter; **2** (GB) (like each other) bien s'entendre; **3** (fare)

how did you ~ on? comment est-ce que ça s'est passé?; **how are you ~ting on?** comment est-ce que tu t'en sors?; **4** (GB) (approach) **he's ~ting on for 40** il approche des quarante ans; **it's ~ting on for midnight** il est presque minuit; ¶ **~ on [sth]** monter dans [*vehicle*]; ¶ **~ [sth] on** mettre [*garment, lid*]; monter [*tyre*].

■ **get on with**: **to ~ on with one's work** continuer à travailler; ¶ **~ on with [sb]** (GB) s'entendre avec [*person*].

■ **get out**: ¶ **~ out 1** (exit) sortir (**through, by** par); **~ out!** va-t'en!; **2** (alight) descendre; **3** [*prisoner*] être libéré/-e; **4** [*news*] être révélé/-e; ¶ **~ [sth] out 1** (take out) sortir (**of** de); **2** retirer [*cork*]; **3** enlever [*stain*]; **4** emprunter [*library book*].

■ **get out of 1** sortir de [*building*]; descendre de [*vehicle*]; être libéré/-e de [*prison*]; quitter [*profession*]; **2 to ~ out of doing** s'arranger pour ne pas faire; **I'll try to ~ out of it** j'essaierai de me libérer; **3** perdre [*habit*]; **4 what do you ~ out of your job?** qu'est-ce que ton travail t'apporte?; **what will you ~ out of it?** qu'est-ce que vous en retirerez?

■ **get over 1** traverser [*stream, bridge*]; passer au-dessus de [*wall*]; **2** se remettre de [*illness, shock*]; **I can't ~ over it** (amazed) je n'en reviens pas; **3** surmonter [*problem*]; **to ~ sth over with** en finir avec qch.

■ **get round** (GB): ¶ **~ round** = **get around**; ¶ **~ round**○ **[sb]** persuader [qn].

■ **get through**: ¶ **~ through 1** (squeeze through) passer; **2 to ~ through to sb** (on phone) avoir qn au téléphone; (make oneself understood) se faire comprendre; **3** [*news, supplies*] arriver; **4** [*examinee*] réussir; ¶ **~ through [sth] 1** terminer [*book*]; finir [*meal, task*]; réussir à [*exam*]; **2** (use) manger [*food*]; dépenser [*money*]; **3** endurer [*bad experience*].

■ **get together**: ¶ **~ together** se réunir (**about, over** pour discuter de); ¶ **~ [sb/sth] together** réunir [*people*]; former [*company*].

■ **get up**: ¶ **~ up 1** (from bed, chair) se lever (**from** de); **2** (on ledge, wall) monter; **3** [*storm*] se préparer; [*wind*] se lever; **4 what did you ~ up to?** (enjoyment) qu'est-ce que tu as fait de beau?; (mischief) qu'est-ce que tu as fabriqué○?; ¶ **~ up [sth] 1** arriver en haut de [*hill, ladder*]; **2** augmenter [*speed*].

get-together *n* réunion *f* (entre amis).

ghastly *adj* horrible.

ghost *n* fantôme *m*.

giant I *n* géant *m*.
II *adj* géant/-e.

giddy *adj* **1 to feel ~** avoir la tête qui tourne; **2** [*height, speed*] vertigineux/-euse.

gift *n* **1** (present) cadeau *m* (**to** à); **to give sb a ~** faire or offrir un cadeau à qn; **2** (donation) don *m*; **3** (talent) don *m*; **to have a ~ for doing** avoir le don de faire; **to have the ~ of the gab** avoir du bagou(t)○.

gifted *adj* doué/-e.

gift shop *n* magasin *m* de cadeaux.

gift token, **gift voucher** *n* (GB) chèque-cadeau *m*.

gift wrap *n* papier *m* cadeau.

gigantic *adj* gigantesque.

giggle I *n* petit rire *m*; **to get the ~s** attraper le fou rire.
II *vi* rire.

gimmick *n* (scheme) truc○ *m*; (object) gadget *m*.

gin *n* gin *m*; **~ and tonic** gin tonic *m*.

ginger *n* **1** (Bot, Culin) gingembre *m*; **2** (colour) roux *m*.

girl *n* **1** (child) fille *f*; (teenager) jeune fille *f*; **baby ~** petite fille *f*, bébé *m*; **little ~** petite fille *f*, fillette *f*; **2** (daughter) fille *f*.

girlfriend *n* (female friend) amie *f*; (sweetheart) (petite) amie *f*.

giro *n* (GB) (system) système *m* de virement bancaire; (cheque) mandat *m*.

gist *n* essentiel *m* (**of** de).

give I *n* élasticité *f*.
II *vtr* (gen) donner (**to** à); transmettre [*message*] (**to** à); transmettre, passer [*illness*] (**to** à); laisser [*seat*] (**to** à); accorder [*grant*] (**to** à); faire [*injection, massage*] (**to** à); faire [*speech*]; **to ~ sb sth** donner qch à qn; (politely, as a gift) offrir qch à qn; **to ~ sb pleasure** faire plaisir à qn; **~ him my best (wishes)** transmets-lui mes amitiés; **she gave him a drink** elle lui a donné à boire; **to ~ sb enough room** laisser suffisamment de place à qn.
III *vi* [*mattress, sofa*] s'affaisser; [*shelf, floorboard*] fléchir; [*branch*] ployer.
IDIOMS **~ or take an inch (or two)** à quelques centimètres près; **to ~ and take** faire des concessions; **to ~ as good as one gets** rendre coup pour coup; **to ~ it all one's got**○ (y) mettre le paquet.

■ **give away**: ¶ **~ [sth] away 1** donner [*item, sample*]; **2** révéler [*secret*]; **3** laisser échapper [*match, goal, advantage*] (**to** au bénéfice de); ¶ **~ [sb] away 1** (betray) [*expression, fingerprints*] trahir; [*person*] dénoncer (**to** à); **to ~ oneself away** se trahir; **2** (in marriage) conduire [qn] à l'autel.

■ **give back** rendre (**to** à).

■ **give in**: ¶ **~ in 1** (yield) céder (**to** à); **2** (stop trying) abandonner; **I ~ in—tell me!** je donne ma langue au chat○—dis-le-moi!; ¶ **~ [sth] in** rendre [*work*]; remettre [*ticket, key*].

■ **give off** émettre [*signal, radiation, light*]; dégager [*heat, fumes*].

■ **give out**: ¶ **~ out** [*strength*] s'épuiser; [*engine*] tomber en panne; ¶ **~ [sth] out 1** (distribute) distribuer (**to** à); **2** (emit) = **give off**.

■ **give up**: ¶ **~ up** abandonner; **to ~ up on** laisser tomber [*diet, crossword, pupil, patient*]; ne plus compter sur [*friend, partner*]; ¶ **~ up [sth] 1** renoncer à [*habit, title, claim*]; sacrifier [*free time*]; quitter [*job*]; **to ~ up smoking/drinking** cesser de fumer/de boire; **2** abandonner [*search, hope, struggle*]; renoncer à [*idea*]; **3** céder [*seat, territory*]; ¶ **~ [sb] up 1** (hand over) livrer (**to** à); **to ~ oneself up** se livrer (**to** à); **2** laisser tomber [*lover*].

■ **give way 1** (collapse) s'effondrer; [*fence, cable*] céder; **his legs gave way** ses jambes se sont dérobées sous lui; **2** (GB) (when driving) céder le passage (**to** à); **3** (yield) céder; **to ~ way to** faire place à.

given I *adj* **1** [*point, level, number*] donné/-e; [*volume, length*] déterminé/-e; **at any ~ moment** à n'importe quel moment; **2 to be ~ to sth/to doing** avoir tendance à qch/à faire; **I am not ~ to doing** je n'ai pas l'habitude de faire.
II *prep* **1** (in view of) **~ (the fact) that** étant donné que; **2** (with) avec [*training, proper care*].

given name *n* prénom *m*.

glad *adj* content/-e, heureux/-euse (**about** de; **that** que; **to do** de faire); **he was only too ~ to help me** il ne demandait qu'à m'aider.

gladly *adv* (willingly) volontiers; (with pleasure) avec plaisir.

glamorize *vtr* peindre [qn/qch] sous de belles couleurs.

glamorous *adj* [*person, image, look*] séduisant/-e; [*older person*] élégant/-e; [*dress*] splendide; [*occasion*] brillant/-e; [*job*] prestigieux/-ieuse.

glamour, **glamor** (US) *n* (of person) séduction *f*; (of job) prestige *m*; (of travel, cars) fascination *f*.

glance I *n* coup *m* d'œil.
II *vi* **to ~ at** jeter un coup d'œil à; **to ~ around the room** parcourir la pièce du regard.
■ **glance off** [*bullet, stone*] ricocher sur *or* contre.

glancing *adj* [*blow, kick*] oblique.

gland *n* glande *f*; **to have swollen ~s** avoir des ganglions.

glare I *n* **1** (angry look) regard *m* furieux; **2** (from lights) lumière *f* éblouissante.
II *vi* [*person*] lancer un regard furieux (**at** à).

glaring *adj* **1** [*mistake, injustice*] flagrant/-e; **2** [*light*] éblouissant/-e.

glass I *n* **1** verre *m*; **wine ~** verre à vin; **a ~ of wine** un verre de vin; **2** (mirror) miroir *m*.
II *adj* [*bottle, shelf*] en verre; [*door*] vitré/-e.
III **glasses** *n pl* lunettes *fpl*.

glassy-eyed *adj* (from drink, illness) aux yeux vitreux; (hostile) au regard glacial.

glaze I *n* **1** (on pottery) vernis *m*; **2** (Culin) nappage *m*; (icing) glaçage *m*.
II *vtr* **1** vernisser [*pottery*]; **2** (Culin) glacer.

gleam I *n* (of light) lueur *f*; (of sunshine) rayon *m*; (of gold, polished surface) reflet *m*.
II *vi* [*light*] luire; [*knife, leather, surface*] reluire; [*eyes*] briller.

gleaming *adj* **1** [*eyes, light*] brillant/-e; [*leather, surface*] reluisant/-e; **2** (clean) étincelant/-e (de propreté).

glide *vi* [*skater, boat*] glisser (**on, over** sur); (in air) planer.

glider *n* planeur *m*.

gliding ▶ 504 *n* vol *m* à voile.

glimpse I *n* **1** vision *f* fugitive (**of** de); **to catch a ~ of sth** entrevoir qch; **2** (insight) aperçu *m* (**of, at** de).
II *vtr* entrevoir.

glitter I *n* **1** (substance) paillettes *fpl*; **2** (sparkle) éclat *m*.
II *vi* scintiller.

gloat *vi* jubiler (**at, over** à l'idée de).

global *adj* **1** (world-wide) mondial/-e; **2** (comprehensive) global/-e.

global warming *n* réchauffement *m* de la planète.

globe *n* **1 the ~** le globe; **2** (model) globe *m* terrestre.

gloom *n* **1** (darkness) obscurité *f*; **2** (despondency) morosité *f* (**about, over** à propos de).

gloomy *adj* **1** (dark) sombre; **2** [*expression, person, voice*] lugubre; [*weather*] morose; [*news, outlook*] déprimant/-e.

glorious *adj* **1** [*view, weather*] magnifique; [*holiday*] merveilleux/-euse; **2** (illustrious) glorieux/-ieuse.

glory I *n* **1** (honour) gloire *f*; **2** (splendour) splendeur *f*.
II *vi* **to ~ in** être très fier/fière de.

gloss *n* **1** (shine) lustre *m*; **2** (paint) laque *f*.
■ **gloss over** (pass rapidly over) glisser sur; (hide) dissimuler.

glossy *adj* [*hair, material*] luisant/-e; [*photograph*] brillant/-e; [*brochure*] luxueux/-euse.

glove *n* gant *m*.

glow I *n* **1** (from fire) rougeoiement *m*; (of candle) lueur *f*; **2** (of complexion) éclat *m*.
II *vi* **1** [*metal, embers*] rougeoyer; [*lamp, cigarette*] luire; **2 to ~ with health** resplendir de santé; **to ~ with pride** rayonner de fierté.

glower *vi* lancer des regards noirs (**at** à).

glowing *adj* **1** [*ember*] rougeoyant/-e; [*face, cheeks*] (from exercise) rouge; (from pleasure) radieux/-ieuse; **2** [*account, terms*] élogieux/-ieuse.

glue I *n* colle *f*.
II *vtr* coller; **to ~ sth on** *or* **down** coller qch.
III **glued**○ *pp adj* **to be ~d to the TV** être collé/-e○ devant la télé; **to be ~d to the spot** être cloué/-e sur place.

glut *n* surabondance *f*, excès *m*.

glutton *n* glouton/-onne *m/f*.

glycerin(e) *n* glycérine *f*.

GMT *n* (*abbr* = **Greenwich Mean Time**) TU.

gnash *vtr* **to ~ one's teeth** grincer des dents.

gnaw I *vtr* ronger [*bone, wood*].
II *vi* **1 to ~ at** *or* **on sth** ronger qch; **2 to ~ at sb** [*hunger, remorse, pain*] tenailler qn.

go

■ **Note As an intransitive verb**

– *go* as a simple intransitive verb is translated by *aller*: *where are you going?* = où vas-tu?; *Sasha went to London last week* = Sasha est allé à Londres la semaine dernière.

– Note that *aller* conjugates with *être* in compound tenses. For the conjugation of *aller*, see the French verb tables.

– The verb *go* produces a great many phrasal verbs (*go up, go down, go out, go back* etc). Many of these are translated by a single verb in French (*monter, descendre, sortir, retourner* etc). The phrasal verbs are listed separately at the end of the entry *go*.

– As an auxiliary verb

– When *go* is used as an auxiliary to show intention, it is also translated by *aller*: *I'm going to buy a car* = je vais acheter une voiture; *I was going to talk to you about it* = j'allais t'en parler.

– For translations of *go* used with destinations, consult the Usage Note on ***Countries, Cities, and Continents*** ▶ 448.

– For examples and particular usages, see the entry below.

I *vi* **1** aller (**from** de; **to** à, en); **to ~ to Paris/to California** aller à Paris/en Californie; **to ~ to town/to the country** aller en ville/à la campagne; **they went home** ils sont rentrés chez eux; **to ~ on holiday** partir en vacances; **to ~ for a drink** aller prendre un verre; **~ and ask her** va lui demander; **to ~ to school/work** aller à l'école/au travail; **to ~ to the doctor's** aller chez le médecin; **let's ~, let's get ~ing** allons-y; **2** (leave) partir; **I'm ~ing** je m'en vais; **3** (become) **to ~ red** rougir; **to ~ white** blanchir; **to ~ mad** devenir fou/folle; **4 to ~ unnoticed** passer inaperçu/-e; **the question went unanswered** la question est restée sans réponse; **to ~ free** être libéré/-e; **5** (become impaired) **his memory is going** il perd la mémoire; **my voice is going** je n'ai plus de voix; **the battery is going** la pile est presque à plat; **6** (of time) passer, s'écouler; **7** (operate, function) [*vehicle, machine, clock*] marcher, fonctionner; **to get [sth] going** mettre [qch] en marche; **to keep going** [*business*] se maintenir; [*machine*] continuer à marcher; [*person*] continuer; **8** (belong, be placed) aller; **where do these plates ~?** où vont ces assiettes?; **it won't ~ into the box** ça ne rentre pas dans la boîte; **five into four won't ~** quatre n'est pas divisible par cinq; **9** (be about to) **to be going to do** aller faire; **it's going to snow** il va neiger; **10** (turn out) passer; **how did the party ~?** comment s'est passée la soirée?; **it went well/badly** ça s'est bien/mal passé; **11** (make sound, perform action or movement) (gen) faire; [*bell, alarm*] sonner; **she went like this with her fingers** elle a fait comme ça avec ses doigts; **12** (take one's turn) **you ~ next** c'est ton tour après, c'est à toi après; **you ~ first** après vous; **13** (match) **those two colours don't ~ together** ces deux couleurs ne vont pas ensemble.

II *vtr* faire [*distance, number of miles*].

III *n* **1** (GB) (turn) tour *m*; (try) essai *m*; **whose ~ is it?** à qui le tour?; (in game) à qui de jouer?; **2**○ (energy) **to be full of ~, to be all ~** être très dynamique.

IV to go *phr* **there are three days/pages to ~** il reste encore trois jours/pages.

IDIOMS **to make a ~ of sth** réussir qch; **she's always on the ~** elle n'arrête jamais; **in one ~** d'un seul coup; **it goes without saying that** il va sans dire que; **as the saying goes** comme dit le proverbe; **anything goes** tout est permis.

■ **go about** s'attaquer à [*task*]; **to ~ about one's business** vaquer à ses occupations.

■ **go ahead** [*event*] avoir lieu; **~ ahead!** vas-y!; **they are going ahead with the project** ils ont décidé de mettre le projet en route.

■ **go along** aller; **to make sth up as one goes along** inventer qch au fur et à mesure.

■ **go along with** être d'accord avec [*person, view*]; accepter [*plan*].

■ **go around 1** se promener, circuler; **they ~ around everywhere together** ils vont partout ensemble; **2** [*rumour*] courir.

■ **go away** partir; **~ away!** va-t-en!

■ **go back 1** (return) retourner; (turn back) rebrousser chemin; **to ~ back to sleep** se rendormir; **to ~ back to work** se remettre au travail; **2** (date back) remonter (**to** à); **3** (revert) revenir (**to** à).

■ **go back on** revenir sur [*promise, decision*].

■ **go by**: ¶ **~ by** [*person*] passer; **as time goes by** avec le temps; ¶ **~ by [sth] 1** juger d'après [*appearances*]; **2 to ~ by the rules** suivre le règlement.

■ **go down**: ¶ **~ down 1** (descend) (gen) descendre; [*sun*] se coucher; **to ~ down on one's knees** se mettre à genoux; **2 to ~ down well/badly** être bien/mal reçu/-e; **3** [*price, temperature, standard*] baisser; **4** [*swelling*] désenfler; [*tyre*] se dégonfler; **5** (Comput) tomber en panne; ¶ **~ down [sth]** descendre [*hill*].

■ **go for**: ¶ **~ for [sb/sth] 1**○ (be keen on) aimer; **2** (apply to) **the same goes for him!** c'est valable pour lui aussi!; ¶ **~ for [sb] 1** (attack) attaquer; **2 he has a lot going for him** il a beaucoup de choses pour lui; ¶ **~ for [sth] 1** essayer d'obtenir [*honour, victory*]; **she's going for the world record** elle vise le record mondial; **~ for it**○**!** vas-y, fonce○!; **2** (choose) choisir, prendre.

■ **go in 1** (enter) entrer; (go back in) rentrer; **2** [*troops*] attaquer; **3** [*sun*] se cacher.

■ **go in for 1** (be keen on) aimer; **2** s'inscrire à [*exam, competition*].

■ **go into 1** (enter) entrer dans [*building*]; se lancer dans [*business, profession*]; **2** (examine) étudier [*question*]; **3 a lot of work went into this project** beaucoup de travail a été investi dans ce projet.

■ **go off**: ¶ **~ off 1** [*bomb*] exploser; **2** [*alarm clock*] sonner; [*fire alarm*] se déclencher; **3** [*person*] partir, s'en aller; **4** (GB) [*milk, cream*] tourner; [*meat*] s'avarier; [*butter*] rancir; [*performer, athlete*] perdre sa forme; **5** [*lights, heating*] s'éteindre; **6** (happen, take place) **the concert went off very well** le concert s'est très bien passé; ¶ **~ off [sb/sth]** (GB) n'aimer plus.

■ **go on**: ¶ **~ on 1** (happen) se passer; **how long has this been going on?** depuis combien de temps est-ce que ça dure?; **2** (continue on one's way) poursuivre son chemin; **3** (continue) continuer; **the list goes on and on** la liste est infinie; **4** (of time) (elapse) **as time went on, they...** avec le temps, ils...; **as the evening went on** au fur et à mesure que la soirée avançait; **5 to ~ on about sth** ne pas arrêter de parler de qch; **6** (proceed) passer; **let's ~ on to the next item** passons au point suivant; **he went on to**

say that... puis il a dit que...; **7** [*heating, lights*] s'allumer; **8** [*actor*] entrer en scène; ¶ **~ on [sth]** se fonder sur [*evidence, information*]; **that's all we've got to ~ on** c'est tout ce que nous savons avec certitude.
■ **go on at** s'en prendre à [*person*].
■ **go out 1** (leave, depart) sortir; **to ~ out for a drink** aller prendre un verre; **2 to ~ out with sb** sortir avec qn; **3** [*tide*] descendre; **4** [*fire, light*] s'éteindre.
■ **go over**: ¶ **~ over** (cross over) aller (**to** vers); ¶ **~ over [sth] 1** passer [qch] en revue [*details, facts*]; vérifier [*accounts, figures*]; relire [*article*]; **2** (exceed) dépasser [*limit, sum*].
■ **go round** (GB): ¶ **~ round 1** [*wheel*] tourner; **2 to ~ round to see sb** aller voir qn; **3** [*rumour*] circuler; **4** (make detour) faire un détour; ¶ **~ round [sth]** faire le tour de [*shops, house, museum*].
■ **go through**: ¶ **~ through** [*law*] passer; [*business deal*] être conclu/-e; ¶ **~ through [sth] 1** endurer, subir [*experience*]; passer par [*stage, phase*]; **she's gone through a lot** elle a beaucoup souffert; **2** (check) examiner; **3** (search) fouiller [*belongings*]; **4** (perform) remplir [*formalities*]; **5** (use up) dépenser [*money*]; consommer [*food, drink*].
■ **go through with** réaliser [*plan*]; **I can't ~ through with it** je ne peux pas le faire.
■ **go under** couler.
■ **go up**: ¶ **~ up 1** (ascend) monter; **to ~ up to bed** monter se coucher; **2** [*price, temperature*] monter; [*figures*] augmenter; [*curtain*] se lever (**on** sur); ¶ **~ up [sth]** monter, gravir [*hill*].
■ **go without**: ¶ **~ without** s'en passer; ¶ **~ without [sth]** se passer de.

go-ahead○ *n* **to give sb the ~** donner le feu vert à qn; **to get the ~** recevoir le feu vert.

goal *n* but *m*.

goalkeeper *n* gardien *m* de but.

goalpost *n* poteau *m* de but.

goat *n* chèvre *f*.

gobble I *vtr* (also **~ down**, **~ up**) engloutir.
II *vi* [*turkey*] glouglouter.

go-between *n* intermédiaire *mf*.

god *n* dieu *m*; **God** Dieu *m*.

godchild *n* filleul/-e *m/f*.

goddaughter *n* filleule *f*.

goddess *n* déesse *f*.

godfather *n* parrain *m*.

godmother *n* marraine *f*.

godsend *n* aubaine *f*.

godson *n* filleul *m*.

goggles *n pl* lunettes *fpl*.

going I *n* **1** (departure) départ *m*; **2** (progress) **that's good ~!** c'est rapide!; **it was slow ~** (on journey) ça a été long; (at work) ça n'avançait pas vite; **to be heavy ~** [*book*] être difficile à lire; [*work, conversation*] être laborieux/-ieuse; **3 when the ~ gets tough** quand les choses vont mal; **she finds her new job hard ~** elle trouve que son nouveau travail est difficile; **they got out while the ~ was good** ils s'en sont tirés○ avant qu'il ne soit trop tard.
II *adj* **1** [*price*] actuel/-elle, en cours; **the ~ rate** le tarif en vigueur; **2 ~ concern** affaire *f* qui marche; **3 it's the best model ~** c'est le meilleur modèle sur le marché.

go-kart *n* kart *m*.

gold I *n* or *m*.
II *adj* [*jewellery, tooth*] en or; [*coin, ingot, ore, wire*] d'or.
IDIOMS **as good as ~** sage comme une image; **to be worth one's weight in ~** valoir son pesant d'or.

golden *adj* **1** (made of gold) en or, d'or; **2** (gold coloured) doré/-e, d'or; **~ hair** cheveux *mpl* blonds dorés; **3** [*age, days*] d'or; **a ~ opportunity** une occasion en or.

goldfish *n* poisson *m* rouge.

gold medal *n* médaille *f* d'or.

gold mine *n* mine *f* d'or.

gold-plated *adj* plaqué/-e or.

gold rush *n* ruée *f* vers l'or.

goldsmith ▶ 626 *n* orfèvre *m*.

golf ▶ 504 *n* golf *m*; **to play ~** faire du golf.

golf club *n* (place) club *m* de golf; (stick) crosse *f* de golf.

golf course *n* (terrain *m* de) golf *m*.

gone *adj* **1** (departed) parti/-e; (dead) disparu/-e; **2** (past) **it's ~ six o'clock** il est six heures passées.

gong *n* gong *m*.

good I *n* **1** (virtue) bien *m*; **~ and evil** le bien et le mal; **to be up to no ~**○ mijoter qch○; **to come to no ~** mal tourner; **2** (benefit) bien *m*; **it'll do you ~** ça te fera du bien; **it didn't do my migraine any ~** ça n'a pas arrangé ma migraine; **3** (use) **it's no ~ crying** ça ne sert à rien de pleurer; **what ~ would it do me?** à quoi cela me servirait-il?
II *adj* **1** (gen) bon/bonne (*before n*); **it's a ~ film** c'est un bon film; **it was a ~ party** c'était une soirée réussie; **the ~ weather** le beau temps; **she's a ~ swimmer** elle nage bien; **to be ~ at** être bon/bonne en [*Latin, physics*]; être bon/bonne à [*badminton, chess*]; **to be ~ with** savoir comment s'y prendre avec [*children, animals*]; aimer [*figures*]; **to have a ~ time** bien s'amuser; **it's ~ to see you again** je suis content de vous revoir; **I don't feel too ~** je ne me sens pas très bien; **the ~ thing is that**... ce qui est bien c'est que...; **to taste ~** avoir bon goût; **to smell ~** sentir bon; **we had a ~ laugh** on a bien ri; **to wait/walk for a ~ hour** attendre/marcher une bonne heure; **2** (well-behaved) [*child, dog*] sage; **be ~!** sois sage!; **3** (high quality) [*hotel*] bon/bonne (*before n*); [*coat, china*] beau/belle (*before n*); [*degree*] avec mention; **4** (kind) [*person*] gentil/-ille; (virtuous) [*man, life*] vertueux/-euse; **to do sb a ~ turn** rendre service à qn; **would you be ~ enough to do** auriez-vous la gentillesse de faire; **5** (beneficial) **to be ~ for** faire du bien à [*person, plant*]; être bon/bonne pour [*health, business, morale*]; **6** (fortunate) **it's a ~ job** or **thing (that)** heureu-

sement que; **it's a ~ job** or **thing too!** tant mieux!; ▶ **better**, **best**.

III *excl* (expressing pleasure, satisfaction) c'est bien!; (with relief) tant mieux!; (to encourage, approve) très bien!

IV as good as *phr* quasiment; **to be as ~ as new** être comme neuf/neuve.

V for good *phr* pour toujours.

IDIOMS **~ for you!** bravo!; **it's too ~ to be true** c'est trop beau pour être vrai.

good afternoon *phr* bonjour.

goodbye *phr* au revoir.

good evening *phr* bonsoir.

good-for-nothing *n* bon/bonne *m/f* à rien.

good-humoured (GB), **good-humored** (US) *adj* [*crowd, discussion*] détendu/-e; [*rivalry*] amical/-e; [*remark, smile*] plaisant/-e; **to be ~** [*person*] avoir bon caractère.

good-looking *adj* beau/belle (*before n*).

good morning *phr* bonjour.

good-natured *adj* [*person*] agréable; [*animal*] placide.

goodness I *n* **1** (quality, virtue) bonté *f*; **2** (nourishment) **to be full of ~** être plein/-e de bonnes choses.

II *excl* (also **~ gracious!**) mon Dieu!

IDIOMS **for ~' sake!** pour l'amour de Dieu!

goodnight *phr* bonne nuit.

goods *n pl* articles *mpl*, marchandise *f*.

goods train *n* (GB) train *m* de marchandises.

goodwill *n* **1** (kindness) bonne volonté *f*; **2** (of business) clientèle *f*.

goose *n* oie *f*.

gooseberry *n* groseille *f* à maquereau.

IDIOMS **to be a** or **play ~** tenir la chandelle.

goose pimples *n pl* chair *f* de poule.

gorge I *n* gorge *f*.

II *v refl* **to ~ oneself** se gaver (**on** de).

gorgeous *adj* **1**○ [*food, scenery*] formidable○; [*kitten, baby*] adorable; [*weather, day, person*] splendide; **2** (sumptuous) somptueux/-euse.

gorilla *n* gorille *m*.

gorse *n* ajoncs *mpl*.

gory *adj* sanglant/-e.

gosh○ *excl* ça alors○!

gospel *n* Évangile *m*.

gospel music *n* gospel *m*.

gossip I *n* **1** (malicious) commérages *mpl* (**about** sur); (not malicious) nouvelles *fpl* (**about** sur); **2** (person) commère *f*.

II *vi* bavarder; (more maliciously) faire des commérages (**about** sur).

gossip column *n* échos *mpl*.

got: **to have got** *phr* **1 to have ~** avoir; **2 I've ~ to go** il faut que j'y aille.

gourd *n* **1** (container) gourde *f*; **2** (fruit) calebasse *f*.

gout ▶ **533** *n* goutte *f*.

govern I *vtr* **1** gouverner [*country, state, city*]; administrer [*colony, province*]; **2** (control) régir [*use, conduct, treatment*]; **3** (determine) déterminer [*decision*]; régler [*flow, speed*].

II *vi* [*parliament, president*] gouverner.

governess *n* gouvernante *f*.

government *n* gouvernement *m*.

governmental *adj* gouvernemental/-e.

governor *n* (of state, colony, bank) gouverneur *m*; (of prison) directeur *m*; (of school) membre *m* du conseil d'établissement.

gown *n* (dress) robe *f*; (of judge, academic) toge *f*; (of surgeon) blouse *f*.

GP ▶ **626** *n* (*abbr* = **general practitioner**) (médecin *m*) généraliste *mf*.

grab I *vtr* empoigner [*money, object*]; saisir [*arm, person, opportunity*]; **to ~ hold of** se saisir de.

II *vi* **to ~ at** se jeter sur.

grace *n* **1** (gen) grâce *f*; **sb's saving ~** ce qui sauve qn; **2 to give sb two days' ~** accorder un délai de deux jours à qn; **3** (prayer) (before meal) bénédicité *m*; (after meal) grâces *fpl*.

IDIOMS **to be full of airs and ~s** prendre des airs.

graceful *adj* [*dancer, movement*] gracieux/-ieuse; [*person*] élégant/-e.

grade I *n* **1** (quality) qualité *f*; **high-/low-~** de qualité supérieure/inférieure; **2** (mark) note *f* (**in** en); **3** (rank) échelon *m*; **4** (US) (class) classe *f*.

II *vtr* (by quality) classer (**according to** selon); (by size) calibrer (**according to** selon).

grade school *n* (US) école *f* primaire.

gradient *n* pente *f*, inclinaison *f*.

gradual *adj* **1** [*change, increase*] progressif/-ive; **2** [*slope*] doux/douce.

gradually *adv* (slowly) peu à peu; (by degrees) progressivement.

graduate I *n* diplômé/-e *m/f*.

II *vi* **1** terminer ses études (**at** or **from** à); (US Sch) ≈ finir le lycée; **2** (progress) **to ~ (from sth) to** passer (de qch) à.

graduation *n* (also **~ ceremony**) (cérémonie *f* de) remise *f* des diplômes.

graffiti *n* graffiti *mpl*.

graffiti artist *n* tagger *m*.

graft I *n* greffe *f*; **skin ~** greffe de la peau.

II *vtr* greffer (**onto** sur).

grain *n* **1** (of rice, wheat, sand, salt) grain *m*; **2** (crops) céréales *fpl*; **3** (figurative) (of truth, comfort) brin *m*; **4** (in wood, stone) veines *fpl*; (in leather, paper, fabric) grain *m*.

IDIOMS **it goes against the ~** c'est contre tous mes/nos/leurs principes.

gram(me) ▶ **573** *n* gramme *m*.

grammar *n* grammaire *f*.

grammar school *n* (GB) ≈ lycée *m* (à recrutement sélectif).

grammatical *adj* **1** [*error*] de grammaire; **2** (correct) grammaticalement correct.

granary *n* grenier *m*.

granary bread *n* pain *m* aux céréales.

grand *adj* [*building, ceremony*] grandiose; **on a ~ scale** à très grande échelle; **the Grand Canyon** le Grand Cañon *m*; **to play the ~ lady** jouer à la grande dame.

grandchild *n* (girl) petite-fille *f*; (boy) petit-fils *m*; **his grandchildren** ses petits-enfants *mpl*.

granddaughter *n* petite-fille *f*.
grandeur *n* (of scenery) majesté *f*; (of building) caractère *m* grandiose.
grandfather *n* grand-père *m*.
grandfather clock *n* horloge *f* comtoise.
grandma○ *n* mémé○ *f*, mamy○ *f*, mamie○ *f*.
grandmother *n* grand-mère *f*.
grandpa○ *n* pépé○ *m*, papy○ *m*, papi○ *m*.
grandparents *n pl* grands-parents *mpl*.
grand piano ▶ 586 *n* piano *m* à queue.
grandson *n* petit-fils *m*.
grandstand *n* tribune *f*.
grand total *n* total *m*.
granite *n* granit(e) *m*.
granny○ *n* mémé○ *f*.
grant I *n* (gen) subvention *f*; (for study) bourse *f*.
II *vtr* **1** accorder [*permission*]; accéder à [*request*]; **2 to ~ sb [sth]** accorder [qch] à qn [*interview, leave, visa*]; concéder [qch] à qn [*citizenship*]; **3 to ~ that** reconnaître que.
IDIOMS **to take sth for ~ed** considérer qch comme allant de soi; **he takes his mother for ~ed** il croit que sa mère est à son service.
granulated *adj* [*sugar*] cristallisé/-e.
granule *n* (of sugar, salt) grain *m*; (of coffee) granulé *m*.
grape *n* grain *m* de raisin; **a bunch of ~s** une grappe de raisin.
grapefruit *n* pamplemousse *m*.
grapevine *n* (in vineyard) pied *m* de vigne; (in greenhouse, garden) vigne *f*.
IDIOMS **to hear sth on the ~** apprendre qch par le téléphone arabe.
graph *n* graphique *m*.
graphic *adj* **1** [*art, display, technique*] graphique; **2** [*account*] (pleasantly described) vivant/-e; (gory) cru/-e.
graphic design *n* graphisme *m*.
graphics *n pl* **1** (on screen) visualisation *f* graphique; **2 computer ~** infographie *f*; **3** (in film, TV) images *fpl*; (in book) illustrations *fpl*.
graph paper *n* papier *m* millimétré.
grasp I *n* **1** (hold, grip) prise *f*; **2** (understanding) maîtrise *f*.
II *vtr* **1** empoigner [*rope, hand*]; saisir [*opportunity*]; **2** (comprehend) saisir, comprendre.
III *vi* **to ~ at** tenter de saisir.
grasping *adj* cupide.
grass *n* herbe *f*; (lawn) pelouse *f*.
IDIOMS **the ~ is greener (on the other side of the fence)** on croit toujours que c'est mieux ailleurs.
grass court *n* court *m* en gazon.
grasshopper *n* sauterelle *f*.
grassroots I *n pl* **the ~** le peuple.
II *adj* [*movement*] populaire; [*support*] de base.
grate I *n* grille *f* de foyer.
II *vtr* râper [*carrot, cheese*].
III *vi* **1** [*metal object*] grincer (**on** sur); **2** (annoy) agacer; **that ~s** ça m'agace.
grateful *adj* reconnaissant/-e (**to** à; **for** de).
grater *n* râpe *f*.
gratify *vtr* faire plaisir à [*person*]; satisfaire [*desire*]; **to be gratified** être satisfait/-e.
grating I *n* (bars) grille *f*.
II *adj* [*noise*] grinçant/-e; [*voice*] désagréable.
gratitude *n* reconnaissance *f* (**to, towards** envers; **for** de).
gratuitous *adj* gratuit/-e.
grave I *n* tombe *f*.
II *adj* **1** [*illness*] grave; [*risk*] sérieux/-ieuse; [*danger*] grand/-e (*before n*); **2** (solemn) sérieux/-ieuse.
gravel *n* (coarse) graviers *mpl*; (fine) gravillons *mpl*.
gravestone *n* pierre *f* tombale.
graveyard *n* cimetière *m*.
gravitate *vi* **to ~ to(wards)** graviter vers.
gravity *n* **1** pesanteur *f*; **centre of ~** centre *m* de gravité; **2** (of situation) gravité *f*.
gravy *n* sauce *f* (au jus de rôti).
gravy boat *n* saucière *f*.
gray (US) = **grey**
graze I *n* écorchure *f*.
II *vtr* **1 to ~ one's knee** s'écorcher le genou (**on, against** sur); **2** (touch lightly) frôler.
III *vi* [*sheep*] brouter; [*cow*] paître.
grease I *n* graisse *f*.
II *vtr* graisser.
greasy *adj* [*hair, skin, food*] gras/grasse; [*overalls*] graisseux/-euse.
great *adj* **1** (gen) grand/-e (*before n*); [*number, increase*] important/-e; [*heat*] fort/-e (*before n*); **a ~ deal (of)** beaucoup (de); **with ~ difficulty** avec beaucoup de mal; **2**○ [*book, party, weather*] génial/-e○, formidable○; [*opportunity*] formidable○; **to feel ~** se sentir en pleine forme; **~!** génial!
Great Britain ▶ 448 *pr n* Grande-Bretagne *f*.
great grandchild *n* (girl) arrière-petite-fille *f*; (garçon) arrière-petit-fils *m*.
great grandfather *n* arrière-grand-père *m*.
great grandmother *n* arrière-grand-mère *f*.
great-great grandchild *n* (girl) arrière-arrière-petite-fille *f*; (boy) arrière-arrière-petit-fils *m*.
greatly *adv* [*admire, regret*] beaucoup, énormément; [*surprised, distressed*] très, extrêmement; [*improved, changed*] considérablement.
Greece ▶ 448 *pr n* Grèce *f*.
greed *n* **1** (for money, power) avidité *f* (**for** de); **2** (also **greediness**) (for food) gourmandise *f*.
greedy *adj* **1** (for food) gourmand/-e; (stronger) goulu/-e; [*look*] avide; **a ~ pig**○ un goinfre○; **2** (for money, power) avide (**for** de).
Greek ▶ 553 I *n* **1** (person) Grec/Grecque *m/f*; **2** (language) grec *m*.
II *adj* [*government, island*] grec/grecque; [*embassy*] de Grèce.
IDIOMS **it's all ~ to me** c'est du chinois pour moi.
green ▶ 438 I *n* **1** (colour) vert *m*; **2 village ~** terrain *m* communal; **3** (in bowling) boulingrin *m*; (in golf) green *m*; **4** (person) écologiste *mf*; **the Greens** les Verts.

II greens *n pl* (GB) légumes *mpl* verts.
III *adj* **1** (in colour) vert/-e; **2** [*countryside*] verdoyant/-e; **3**○ (naïve) naïf/naïve; **4** (inexperienced) novice; **5** [*policies, candidate, issues*] écologiste; [*product*] écologique.

green card *n* **1** (driving insurance) carte *f* verte (internationale); **2** (US) (residence and work permit) carte *f* de séjour.

greenery *n* verdure *f*.

greengrocer ▶626 *n* marchand *m* de fruits et légumes.

greenhouse *n* serre *f*.

greenhouse effect *n* effet *m* de serre.

greet *vtr* **1** (say hello to) saluer; **2 to be ~ed with** or **by** provoquer [*dismay, amusement*].

greeting I *n* salutation *f*.
II greetings *n pl* **Christmas ~s** vœux *mpl* de Noël; **Season's ~s** meilleurs vœux.

greetings card (GB), **greeting card** (US) *n* carte *f* de vœux.

grey (GB), **gray** (US) ▶438 **I** *n* gris *m*.
II *adj* **1** (in colour) gris/-e; **2** (grey-haired) **to go** or **turn ~** grisonner; **3** (dull) [*existence, day*] morne; [*person, town*] terne.

greyhound *n* lévrier *m*.

grid *n* **1** grille *f*; **2** (GB) (network) réseau *m*.

gridlock *n* embouteillage *m*, bouchon *m*.

grief *n* chagrin *m*.
IDIOMS **to come to ~** [*person*] (have an accident) avoir un accident; (fail) échouer; [*business*] péricliter; **good ~!** mon Dieu!

grievance *n* griefs *mpl* (**against** contre).

grieve *vi* **to ~ for** or **over** pleurer [*person*].

grievous bodily harm, GBH *n* (Law) coups *mpl* et blessures *fpl*.

grill I *n* gril *m*.
II *vtr* **1** faire griller [*meat, fish*]; **2**○ (interrogate) mettre [qn] sur la sellette○.

grille *n* (gen) grille *f*; (on car) calandre *f*.

grim *adj* **1** [*news, town, future*] sinistre; [*sight, conditions*] effroyable; [*reality*] dur/-e; **2** [*struggle*] acharné/-e; [*resolve*] terrible; **3** [*face*] grave.

grimace I *n* grimace *f* (**of** de).
II *vi* (involuntary) faire une grimace (**with, in** de); (pull a face) faire la grimace.

grime *n* (of city) saleté *f*; (on object, person) crasse *f*.

grimy *adj* [*city*] noir/-e; [*hands, window*] crasseux/-euse.

grin I *n* sourire *m*.
II *vi* sourire (**at** à; **with** de).

grind I○ *n* boulot○ *m* or travail *m* monotone.
II *vtr* moudre [*corn, coffee beans*]; écraser [*grain*]; hacher [*meat*]; **to ~ one's teeth** grincer des dents.
III *vi* [*machine*] grincer; **to ~ to a halt** [*machine*] s'arrêter; [*vehicle*] s'arrêter avec un grincement de freins; [*factory, production*] s'immobiliser.

grip I *n* **1** prise *f* (**on** sur); **2 to lose one's ~ on reality** perdre contact avec la réalité; **to come to ~s with sth** en venir aux prises avec qch; **get a ~ on yourself!** ressaisis-toi!; **3** (of tyre) adhérence *f*.
II *vtr* **1** (grab) agripper; (hold) serrer; **2** [*tyres*] adhérer à [*road*]; [*shoes*] accrocher à [*ground*]; **3** (captivate) captiver.

gripping *adj* captivant/-e.

grisly *adj* [*story, sight*] horrible; [*remains*] macabre.

gristle *n* cartilage *m*.

grit I *n* **1** (on lens) grains *mpl* de poussière; (sandy dirt) grains *mpl* de sable; **2** (GB) (for roads) sable *m*.
II *vtr* (GB) sabler [*road*].
IDIOMS **to ~ one's teeth** serrer les dents.

grizzly *n* (also **~ bear**) grizzli *m*.

groan I *n* (of pain, despair) gémissement *m*; (of disgust, protest) grognement *m*.
II *vi* (in pain) gémir; (in disgust, protest) grogner.

grocer ▶626 *n* (person) épicier/-ière *m/f*; **~'s (shop)** épicerie *f*.

groceries *n pl* provisions *fpl*.

grocery ▶626 *n* (also **~ shop** (GB), **~ store**) épicerie *f*.

groggy *adj* groggy; **to feel ~** avoir les jambes en coton○.

groin ▶413 *n* aine *f*.

groom I *n* **1** (bridegroom) **the ~** le jeune marié; **2** (for horse) palefrenier/-ière *m/f*.
II *vtr* **1** panser [*horse*]; **2 to ~ sb for** préparer qn [*exam, career*].

groove *n* (gen) rainure *f*; (on record) sillon *m*; (on screw) fente *f*.

grope I○ *vtr* (sexually) tripoter○.
II *vi* **to ~ for sth** chercher qch à tâtons.

gross I *n* grosse *f*.
II *adj* **1** [*income, profit*] brut/-e; **2** [*error, exaggeration*] grossier/-ière; [*abuse, inequality*] choquant/-e; [*injustice*] flagrant/-e; **3** [*behaviour*] vulgaire; [*language*] cru/-e; **4**○ (revolting) dégoûtant/-e; **5**○ (obese) obèse.
III *vtr* [*business, company*] faire un bénéfice brut de.

grotesque *n, adj* grotesque (*m*).

grotto *n* grotte *f*.

ground I *n* **1** sol *m*, terre *f*; **on the ~** par terre; **above ~** en surface; **below ~** sous terre; **2** (area, territory) terrain *m*; **a piece of ~** un terrain; **3** (sportsground) terrain *m*.
II grounds *n pl* **1** (garden) parc *m* (**of** de); **2** (reasons) **~s for sth** motifs *mpl* de qch; **~s for doing** motifs pour faire; **on the ~s that** en raison du fait que.
III *pp adj* [*coffee, pepper*] moulu/-e.
IV *vtr* **1** immobiliser [*aircraft*]; **2** [*ship*] **to be ~ed** s'échouer.
IDIOMS **to gain ~** gagner du terrain (**on, over** sur); **to hold one's ~** tenir bon; **to go to ~** se terrer; **that suits me down to the ~** ça me convient parfaitement.

ground floor *n* rez-de-chaussée *m inv*; **on the ~** au rez-de-chaussée.

grounding *n* bases *fpl* (**in** en, de).

groundwork *n* travail *m* préparatoire (**for** à).

group I *n* groupe *m*; **in ~s** en groupes.

II *vtr* grouper.
III *vi* **~ together** [*people*] se grouper.

grouse *n* tétras *m*.

grove *n* bosquet *m*; **lemon ~** verger *m* de citronniers.

grovel *vi* ramper (**to, before** devant).

grow I *vtr* **1** cultiver [*plant, crop*]; **2** laisser pousser [*beard, nails*]; **to ~ 5 cm** [*person*] grandir de 5 cm; [*plant*] pousser de 5 cm.
II *vi* **1** [*person*] grandir (**by** de); [*plant, hair*] pousser (**by** de); **2** [*population, tension*] augmenter (**by** de); [*company, economy*] se développer; [*opposition, support, problem*] devenir plus important; [*crisis*] s'aggraver; **3** devenir [*hotter, stronger*]; **to ~ old** vieillir; **to ~ impatient** s'impatienter; **I grew to like him** j'ai appris à l'aimer.
■ **grow apart** s'éloigner l'un de l'autre.
■ **grow on**: **it ~s on you** on finit par l'aimer; **he's ~ing on me** je commence à le trouver plus sympathique.
■ **grow out of 1 he's grown out of his suit** son costume est devenu trop petit pour lui; **2 he'll ~ out of it** (of habit) ça lui passera.
■ **grow up** (gen) grandir; (become mature) devenir adulte; **when I ~ up** quand je serai grand.

grower *n* (of fruit) producteur/-trice *m/f*; (of crops) cultivateur/-trice *m/f*.

growl I *n* grondement *m*.
II *vi* [*dog*] gronder.

grown-up I *n* adulte *mf*, grande personne *f*.
II *adj* adulte.

growth *n* **1** (gen) croissance *f* (**in, of** de); (of hair, nails) pousse *f*; (of economy) expansion *f* (**in, of** de); (in numbers, productivity) augmentation *f* (**in** de); **2** (tumour) grosseur *f*, tumeur *f*.

grudge I *n* **to bear sb a ~** en vouloir à qn.
II *vtr* **to ~ sb their success** en vouloir à qn de sa réussite; **to ~ doing** rechigner à faire.

gruelling, **grueling** (US) *adj* exténuant/-e.

gruesome *adj* horrible.

gruff *adj* bourru/-e.

grumble *vi* [*person*] ronchonner (**at sb** après qn; **to** auprès de); **to ~ about** se plaindre de.

grumpy *adj* grincheux/-euse.

grunt I *n* grognement *m*.
II *vi* grogner.

guarantee I *n* garantie *f*.
II *vtr* garantir.

guard I *n* **1** (for person) surveillant/-e *m/f*; (for place, object, at prison) gardien/-ienne *m/f*; (soldier) garde *m*; **2** (military duty) garde *f*, surveillance *f*; **to be on ~** être de garde; **3 to catch sb off ~** prendre qn au dépourvu; **4** (GB) (on train) chef *m* de train.
II *vtr* **1** (protect) surveiller [*place, object*]; protéger [*person*]; **2** surveiller [*hostage, prisoner*]; **3** garder [*secret*].

guard dog *n* chien *m* de garde.

guarded *adj* circonspect/-e (**about** à propos de).

guardian *n* **1** (gen) gardien/-ienne *m/f* (**of** de); **2** (of child) tuteur/-trice *m/f*.

guardian angel *n* ange *m* gardien.

Guernsey *pr n* Guernesey *f*.

guerrilla *n* guérillero *m*.

guerrilla war *n* guérilla *f*.

guess I *n* supposition *f*, conjecture *f*; **at a (rough) ~ I would say that**... au hasard je dirais que...; **it's anybody's ~!** les paris sont ouverts!
II *vtr* **1** deviner; **~ what!** tu sais quoi○!; **2** (suppose) supposer.
III *vi* deviner; **to keep sb ~ing** ne pas satisfaire la curiosité de qn.

guesswork *n* conjecture *f*.

guest *n* (in one's home) invité/-e *m/f*; (at hotel) client/-e *m/f*; **be my ~!** je vous en prie!

guesthouse *n* pension *f* de famille.

guest room *n* chambre *f* d'amis.

guidance *n* conseils *mpl* (**from** de).

guide I *n* **1** (person, book) guide *m* (**to** de); **2** (idea) indication *f*; **as a rough ~** à titre d'indication; **3** (also **Girl Guide**) guide *f*.
II *vtr* guider (**to** vers).

guide book *n* guide *m*.

guide dog *n* chien *m* d'aveugle.

guided tour *n* visite *f* guidée.

guideline *n* (rough guide) indication *f*; (in political context) directive *f*; (advice) conseils *mpl*.

guild *n* (medieval) guilde *f*; (modern) association *f*.

guillotine *n* **1** guillotine *f*; **2** (for paper) massicot *m*.

guilt *n* culpabilité *f*.

guilty *adj* coupable; **to feel ~** culpabiliser; **to feel ~ about** se sentir coupable vis-à-vis de.

guinea-pig *n* **1** (Zool) cochon *m* d'Inde; **2** (in experiment) cobaye *m*.

guitar ▶**586** *n* guitare *f*.

guitarist ▶**586**, **626** *n* guitariste *mf*.

gulch *n* (US) ravin *m*.

gulf *n* **1** golfe *m*; **the Gulf** la région *f* du Golfe; **2** (figurative) fossé *m* (**between** qui sépare).

gull *n* mouette *f*.

gullible *adj* crédule.

gully *n* ravin *m*.

gulp I *n* (of liquid) gorgée *f*; (of air) bouffée *f*, goulée *f*; (of food) bouchée *f*.
II *vtr* (also **~ down**) engloutir [*food, drink*].
III *vi* avoir la gorge serrée.

gum *n* **1** (in mouth) gencive *f*; **2** (also **chewing ~**) chewing-gum *m*; **3** (adhesive) colle *f*; (resin) gomme *f*.

gun *n* (weapon) arme *f* à feu; (revolver) revolver *m*; (rifle) fusil *m*; (cannon) canon *m*; **to fire a ~** tirer.
IDIOMS **to jump the ~** agir prématurément; **to stick to one's ~s**○ s'accrocher○.
■ **gun down** abattre, descendre.

gunfire *n* (from hand-held gun) coups *mpl* de feu; (from artillery) fusillade *f*.

gunman *n* homme *m* armé.

gunpoint *n* **to hold sb up at ~** tenir qn sous la menace d'une arme.

gunpowder *n* poudre *f*.

gunshot *n* coup *m* de feu.

gunshot wound *n* blessure *f* par balle.

gurgle I *n* (of water) gargouillement *m*; (of baby) gazouillis *m*.
II *vi* [*water*] gargouiller; [*baby*] gazouiller.

guru *n* gourou *m*.

gush *vi* jaillir.

gust *n* rafale *f*.

gusto *n* **with ~** avec enthousiasme.

gut I○ *n* bide○ *m*.
II *adj* [*feeling, reaction*] viscéral/-e, instinctif/-ive.
III *vtr* [*fire*] ravager [*building*].

guts○ *n pl* **1** (of human) tripes○ *fpl*; (of animal) entrailles *fpl*; **2** (courage) cran○ *m*.

gutter *n* (on roof) gouttière *f*; (in street) caniveau *m*.

gutter press *n* presse *f* à sensation.

guy○ *n* type○ *m*; **a good/bad ~** (in films) un bon/méchant.

guzzle○ *vtr* engloutir.

gym ▶ 504 *n* **1** (*abbr* = **gymnasium**) salle *f* de gym○, gymnase *m*; **2** (*abbr* = **gymnastics**) gym○ *f*.

gymnasium *n* gymnase *m*.

gymnast *n* gymnaste *mf*.

gymnastics ▶ 504 *n pl* gymnastique *f*.

gym shoe *n* tennis *f*.

gynaecologist (GB), **gynecologist** (US) ▶ 626 *n* gynécologue *mf*.

gypsy *n* (gen) bohémien/-ienne *m/f*; (Central European) tzigane *mf*; (Spanish) gitan/-e *m/f*.

Hh

h, **H** *n* h, H *m*.

habit *n* **1** habitude *f*; **to get into/out of the ~ of doing** prendre/perdre l'habitude de faire; **out of ~** par habitude; **2** (addiction) accoutumance *f*; **3** (of monk, nun) habit *m*.

habitat *n* habitat *m*.

habitual *adj* [*behaviour, reaction*] habituel/-elle; [*drinker, smoker, liar*] invétéré/-e.

hack **I** *n* ○(writer) écrivaillon *m*; (journalist) journaliste *m/f* qui fait la rubrique des chiens écrasés.
II *vtr* tailler dans [*bushes*] (**with** à coups de); **to ~ sb/sth to pieces** tailler qn/qch en pièces.
III *vi* **1 to ~ through sth** tailler dans qch; **2**○ (Comput) pirater○; **to ~ into** s'introduire dans [*system*].

hacker *n* (**computer**) **~** pirate *m* informatique.

hackles *n pl* (on dog) poils *mpl* du cou; **the dog's ~ began to rise** le chien se hérissait.

hackneyed *adj* [*joke*] éculé/-e; [*subject*] rebattu/-e; **~ phrase** cliché *m*.

haddock *n* églefin *m*.

haemophilia (GB), **hemophilia** (US) ▶ 533 *n* hémophilie *f*.

haemorrhage (GB), **hemorrhage** (US) **I** *n* hémorragie *f*.
II *vi* faire une hémorragie.

haemorrhoids (GB), **hemorrhoids** (US) *n pl* hémorroïdes *fpl*.

haggard *adj* [*appearance, person*] exténué/-e; [*face, expression*] défait/-e.

haggle *vi* marchander; **to ~ over sth** discuter du prix de qch.

Hague ▶ 448 *pr n* **The ~** La Haye.

hail **I** *n* grêle *f*.
II *vtr* **1** héler [*person, taxi, ship*]; **2** (praise) **to ~ sb as** acclamer qn comme; **to ~ sth as sth** saluer qch comme qch.
III *v impers* grêler.

hailstone *n* grêlon *m*.

hailstorm *n* averse *f* de grêle.

hair *n* **1** (on head) cheveux *mpl*; (on body) poils *mpl*; (of animal) poil *m*; **to have one's ~ done** se faire coiffer; **long-~ed** [*person*] aux cheveux longs; [*animal*] à poil long; **2** (individually) (on head) cheveu *m*; (on body) poil *m*.
IDIOMS **to split ~s** couper les cheveux en quatre.

hairband *n* bandeau *m*.

hairbrush *n* brosse *f* à cheveux.

haircut *n* coupe *f* (de cheveux).

hairdo○ *n* coiffure *f*.

hairdresser ▶ 626 *n* coiffeur/-euse *m/f*.

hairdrier *n* (hand-held) sèche-cheveux *m inv*; (hood) casque *m*.

hairgrip *n* (GB) pince *f* à cheveux.

hairpin bend *n* virage *m* en épingle à cheveux.

hair-raising *adj* [*adventure, tale*] à vous faire dresser les cheveux sur la tête.

hair remover *n* crème *f* dépilatoire.

hair-slide *n* (GB) barrette *f*.

hairspray *n* laque *f*.

hairstyle *n* coiffure *f*.

hairy *adj* (gen) poilu/-e.

halal *adj* [*meat*] hallal *inv*.

half ▶ 434 **I** *n* **1** moitié *f*; **to cut sth in ~** couper qch en deux; **2** (fraction) demi *m*; **four and a ~** quatre et demi; **3**○ (GB) (half pint) demi-pinte *f*.
II *adj* **~ an hour** une demi-heure; **a ~-litre**, **~ a litre** un demi-litre; **two and a ~ cups** deux tasses et demie.
III *pron* **1** la moitié *f*; **~ of the students** la moitié des étudiants; **2** (in time) demi/-e *m/f*; **an hour and a ~** une heure et demie; **~ past two** (GB) deux heures et demie.
IV *adv* à moitié; **to ~ close sth** fermer qch à moitié; **it's ~ the price** c'est moitié moins cher; **I ~ expected it** je m'y attendais plus ou moins.
IDIOMS **to go halves with sb** partager avec qn.

halfback *n* (Sport) demi *m*.

half day *n* demi-journée *f*.

half fare *n* demi-tarif *m*.

half-hearted *adj* peu enthousiaste.

half-heartedly *adv* sans conviction.

half hour ▶ 708 *n* demi-heure *f*; **on the ~** à la demie.

half-mast *n* **at ~** en berne.

half-moon *n* **1** demi-lune *f*; **2** (of fingernail) lunule *f*.

half price *adv, adj* à moitié prix.

half term *n* (GB Sch) vacances *fpl* de la mi-trimestre.

half-time *n* (Sport) mi-temps *f*; **at ~** à la mi-temps.

halfway *adv* **1** à mi-chemin (**between** entre; **to** de); **~ up** or **down** à mi-hauteur de [*stairs, tree*]; **~ down the page** à mi-page; **2** (in time) **~ through** au milieu.

hall *n* **1** (in house) entrée *f*; (in hotel, airport) hall *m*; (for public events) (grande) salle *f*; **2** (country house) manoir *m*.

hallelujah *excl* alléluia!

hallmark **I** *n* **1** (GB) (on metal) poinçon *m*; **2** (typical feature) caractéristique *f*.
II *vtr* poinçonner; **to be ~ed** porter un poinçon.

Halloween *n*: *la veille de la Toussaint*.

hallucinate *vi* avoir des hallucinations.

hallway *n* entrée *f*.

halo *n* **1** auréole *f*; **2** (in astronomy) halo *m*.
halt I *n* (stop) arrêt *m*; **to come to a ~** [*vehicle, troops*] s'arrêter; [*work*] être interrompu/-e; **to call a ~ to sth** mettre fin à qch.
II *vtr* arrêter.
III *vi* s'arrêter.
halve I *vtr* réduire [qch] de moitié [*number, rate*]; couper [qch] en deux [*carrot, cake*].
II *vi* [*number, rate, time*] diminuer de moitié.
ham *n* jambon *m*.
hamburger *n* **1** (burger) hamburger *m*; **2** (US) (ground beef) pâté *m* de viande.
hammer I *n* marteau *m*.
II *vtr* **1** marteler [*metal, table*]; **to ~ sth into** enfoncer qch dans [*wall, fence*]; **2 to ~ sth into sb** faire entrer qch dans la tête de qn; **to ~ home a message** bien faire comprendre un message; **3**○ (defeat) battre [qn] à plates coutures.
III *vi* (pound) tambouriner (**on**, **at** contre).
hamper I *n* panier *m* à pique-nique.
II *vtr* entraver [*movement, career, progress*].
hamster *n* hamster *m*.
hamstring *n* tendon *m* du jarret.
hand ▶413 I *n* **1** main *f*; **he had a pencil in his ~** il avait un crayon à la main; **to hold sb's ~** tenir qn par la main; **to make sth by ~** faire qch à la main; **the letter was delivered by ~** la lettre a été remise en mains propres; **to give sb a (helping) ~** donner un coup de main à qn; **to have sth to ~** avoir qch sous la main; **to be on ~** [*person*] être disponible; **to get out of ~** devenir incontrôlable; **to take sb/sth in ~** prendre qn/qch en main [*situation, person*]; **2** (cards) jeu *m*; **3** (worker) ouvrier/-ière *m/f*; (crew member) membre *m* de l'équipage; **4** (on clock, dial) aiguille *f*; **5 on the one ~..., on the other ~...** d'une part..., d'autre part...
II *vtr* **to ~ sth to sb** donner qch à qn.
III **hand in hand** *phr* [*run, walk*] la main dans la main; **to go ~ in ~** aller de pair (**with** avec).
IV **out of hand** *phr* [*reject*] d'emblée.
IDIOMS **to have one's ~s full** avoir assez à faire; **to try one's ~ at sth** s'essayer à; **to know sth like the back of one's ~** connaître qch comme sa poche.
■ **hand down** passer [*object, clothes*] (**to sb** à qn); transmettre [*property*].
■ **hand in** remettre [*form*] (**to** à); rendre [*homework, keys*].
■ **hand out** distribuer [*food, leaflets*].
■ **hand over**: ¶ **~ over to [sb]** passer l'antenne à [*reporter*]; passer la main à [*deputy, successor*]; ¶ **~ [sth] over** rendre [*weapon*]; céder [*business*]; remettre [*keys, money*]; ¶ **~ [sb] over** livrer [*prisoner*].
handbag *n* sac *m* à main.
hand baggage *n* bagages *mpl* à main.
handball ▶504 *n* (Sport) handball *m*.
handbook *n* manuel *m*; (technical) livret *m* technique.
handbrake *n* frein *m* à main.
handcuffs *n pl* menottes *fpl*.
handful *n* **1** (fistful) poignée *f*; **2** (of people) poignée *f*; (of buildings, objects) petit nombre *m*; **3**○ **to be a ~** être épuisant/-e.
handicap I *n* handicap *m*.
II *vtr* handicaper.
handicapped *adj* [*person*] handicapé/-e; **mentally/physically ~ children** des enfants handicapés mentaux/physiques.
handiwork *n* ouvrage *m*.
handkerchief *n* mouchoir *m*.
handle I *n* (on door, drawer, bag) poignée *f*; (on bucket, cup, basket) anse *f*; (on frying pan) queue *f*; (on saucepan, cutlery, hammer, spade) manche *m*; (on wheelbarrow, pump) bras *m*.
II *vtr* **1** manipuler [*explosives, food*]; manier [*gun*]; **'~ with care'** 'fragile'; **2** (manage) manier [*horse*]; manœuvrer [*car*]; **to know how to ~ children** savoir s'y prendre avec les enfants; **3** (deal with) faire face à [*crisis*]; supporter [*stress*]; [*department, lawyer*] s'occuper de [*enquiries, case*].
handlebars *n pl* guidon *m*.
hand luggage *n* bagages *mpl* à main.
handmade *adj* fait/-e à la main.
handout *n* **1** (charitable) don *m*; **2** (leaflet) prospectus *m*.
handpick *vtr* **1** cueillir [qch] à la main [*grapes*]; **2** trier [qn] sur le volet [*staff*].
handshake *n* poignée *f* de main.
handsome *adj* beau/belle (*before n*).
handstand *n* (Sport) équilibre *m*.
handwriting *n* écriture *f*.
handy *adj* [*book, skill*] utile; [*tool, pocket, size*] pratique; [*shop*] bien situé/-e; **to keep/have [sth] ~** garder/avoir [qch] sous la main [*keys, passport*].
handyman *n* bricoleur *m*.
hang I *n* **to get the ~ of sth**○ piger○ qch.
II *vtr* **1** (from hook, coat hanger) accrocher (**from** à; **by** par; **on** à); (from string, rope) suspendre (**from** à); (peg up) étendre [*washing*] (**on** sur); **2** poser [*wallpaper*]; **3** pendre [*criminal, victim*].
III *vi* **1** (on hook) être accroché/-e; (from height) être suspendu/-e; (on washing line) être étendu/-e; **2** [*arm, leg*] pendre; **3** [*curtain, garment*] tomber; **4** [*person*] être pendu/-e (**for** pour).
IV *v refl* **to ~ oneself** se pendre (**from** à).
■ **hang around**○ **1** (also **~ about**) (wait) attendre; (aimlessly) traîner; **2 to ~ around with sb** passer son temps avec qn.
■ **hang back** (in fear) rester derrière; (figurative) être réticent/-e.
■ **hang down** (gen) pendre; [*hem*] être défait/-e.
■ **hang on**: ¶ **~ on 1** (hold on) **to ~ on (to sth)** s'accrocher (à qch); **2**○ (wait) attendre; **3**○ (survive) tenir○; **~ on in there**○! tiens bon!; ¶ **~ on [sth]** (depend on) dépendre de.
■ **hang out**: ¶ **~ out** [*handkerchief, shirt*] pendre; ¶ **~ [sth] out** étendre [*washing*]; sortir [*flag*].
■ **hang up**: ¶ **~ up** (on phone) raccrocher; **to ~ up on sb** raccrocher au nez de qn; ¶ **~ [sth] up** (on hook) accrocher; (on hanger) suspendre; (on line) étendre.

hangar *n* hangar *m*.
hang-glider *n* deltaplane *m*.
hanging *n* **1** (of person) pendaison *f*; **2** (curtain) rideau *m*; (on wall) tenture *f*.
hangover *n* (from drink) gueule *f* de bois○.
hang-up○ *n* complexe *m*, problème *m*.
hanker *vi* **to ~ after** or **for sth** rêver de qch.
haphazard *adj* peu méthodique.
happen *vi* **1** (occur) arriver, se passer, se produire; **what's ~ing?** qu'est-ce qui se passe?; **to ~ again** se reproduire; **whatever ~s** quoi qu'il arrive; **2** (occur by chance) **if you ~ to see her, say hello** si par hasard tu la vois, salue-la de ma part; **as it ~ed, the weather that day was bad** il s'est trouvé qu'il faisait mauvais ce jour-là.
happily *adv* **1** (cheerfully) joyeusement; **a ~ married man** un mari heureux; **they all lived ~ ever after** ils vécurent heureux jusqu'à la fin de leurs jours; **2** (willingly) [*admit*] volontiers; **3** (luckily) heureusement.
happiness *n* bonheur *m*.
happy *adj* **1** heureux/-euse (**about** de; **that** que + *subjunctive*); **to be ~ with sth** être satisfait/-e de qch; **to keep a child ~** amuser un enfant; **to be ~ to do** être heureux/-euse de faire; **2** (in greetings) **Happy Birthday!** Bon anniversaire!; **Happy Christmas!** Joyeux Noël!; **Happy New Year!** Bonne année!
happy ending *n* heureux dénouement *m*.
happy medium *n* juste milieu *m*.
harangue *vtr* (about politics) haranguer; (moralize) sermonner.
harass *vtr* harceler.
harbour (GB), **harbor** (US) **I** *n* port *m*.
II *vtr* nourrir [*suspicion, illusion*]; receler [*criminal*].
hard I *adj* **1** (firm) dur/-e; **to go ~** durcir; **2** (difficult) [*problem, question, task*] dur/-e, difficile; [*choice, decision, life*] difficile; **it's ~ to do** c'est dur or difficile à faire; **to find it ~ to do** avoir du mal à faire; **it was ~ work** ça a été dur or difficile; **to be a ~ worker** être travailleur/-euse; **3** (severe) [*person, look, words*] dur/-e, sévère; [*blow*] dur/-e, terrible; [*winter*] rude; **to be ~ on sb** [*person*] être dur/-e envers qn; **~ luck!** pas de chance!; **no ~ feelings!** sans rancune!; **4** [*evidence, fact*] solide; **5** [*liquor*] fort/-e; [*drug*] dur/-e; **6** [*water*] dur/-e, calcaire.
II *adv* [*push, hit, cry*] fort; [*work*] dur; [*study, think*] sérieusement; [*look, listen*] attentivement; **to try ~** (mentally) faire beaucoup d'efforts; (physically) essayer de toutes ses forces.
hardback (book) *n* livre *m* relié.
hardboard *n* aggloméré *m*.
hard-boiled egg *n* œuf *m* dur.
hard court *n* court *m* en dur.
harden I *vtr* **1** (faire) durcir [*glue, wax*]; **2** endurcir [*person*] (**to** à); durcir [*attitude*]; **to ~ one's heart** s'endurcir (**to** à).
II *vi* **1** [*glue, wax, skin*] durcir; **2** [*voice, stance*] se durcir.
hardened *adj* [*criminal*] endurci/-e; [*drinker*] invétéré/-e.
hard hat *n* (helmet) casque *m*; (for riding) bombe *f*.
hard-hearted *adj* insensible.
hard labour (GB), **hard labor** (US) *n* travaux *mpl* forcés.
hardliner *n* jusqu'au-boutiste *mf*; (political) partisan/-e *m/f* de la ligne dure.
hardly *adv* **1** (barely) [*begin, know, see*] à peine; **~ had they set off when** à peine étaient-ils partis que; **2** (not really) **one can ~ expect that** on ne peut guère s'attendre à ce que; **it's ~ likely** c'est peu probable; **it's ~ surprising** ce n'est guère étonnant; **I can ~ believe it!** j'ai peine à le croire!; **3 ~ any/ever/anybody** presque pas/jamais/personne; **he ~ ever writes** il n'écrit presque jamais.
hardship *n* **1** (difficulty) détresse *f*; (poverty) privations *fpl*; **2** (ordeal) épreuve *f*.
hard up○ *adj* fauché/-e○.
hardware *n* **1** (gen) articles *mpl* de quincaillerie; **2** (Comput) matériel *m* (informatique); **3** (Mil) équipement *m*.
hardware shop, **hardware store** ▶626 *n* quincaillerie *f*.
hard-working *adj* travailleur/-euse.
hardy *adj* [*person*] robuste; [*plant*] résistant/-e.
hare *n* lièvre *m*.
haricot *n* (GB) (also **~ bean**) (dried) haricot *m* blanc; (fresh) haricot *m* vert.
harm I *n* mal *m*; **to do sb ~** faire du mal à qn; **to do ~ to sth** endommager qch; **out of ~'s way** en sûreté.
II *vtr* faire du mal à [*person*]; endommager [*crops, lungs*]; nuire à [*population*].
harmful *adj* [*chemical, ray*] nocif/-ive; [*behaviour, gossip*] nuisible (**to** pour).
harmless *adj* **1** [*chemical, virus*] inoffensif/-ive (**to** pour); [*growth*] bénin/bénigne; **2** [*person*] inoffensif/-ive; [*fun, joke*] innocent/-e
harmonica ▶586 *n* harmonica *m*.
harmonious *adj* harmonieux/-ieuse.
harmonize I *vtr* harmoniser.
II *vi* jouer en harmonie (**with** avec).
harmony *n* harmonie *f*.
harness I *n* harnais *m*.
II *vtr* **1** harnacher [*horse*]; **2** (attach) atteler [*animal*] (**to** à); **3** exploiter [*power, energy*].
harp ▶586 *n* harpe *f*.
harpoon *n* harpon *m*.
harrowing *adj* [*experience*] atroce; [*film, image*] déchirant/-e.
harsh *adj* **1** [*punishment, measures*] sévère; [*tone, regime, person*] dur/-e; [*conditions*] difficile; **2** [*light, colour*] cru/-e; [*sound*] rude, dur/-e à l'oreille.
harvest I *n* (of wheat, fruit) récolte *f*; (of grapes) vendange *f*.
II *vtr* moissonner [*corn*]; récolter [*vegetables*]; cueillir [*fruit*]; vendanger [*grapes*].
hassle○ **I** *n* complications *fpl*; **it was a real ~** c'était enquiquinant○.

II *vtr* talonner (**about** à propos de).

haste *n* hâte *f*; **to act in ~** agir à la hâte.

hasten I *vtr* accélérer [*destruction*]; précipiter [*departure, death, decline*].
II *vi* se hâter; **to ~ to do** s'empresser de faire.

hasty *adj* [*talks, marriage, departure*] précipité/-e; [*meal*] rapide; [*note*] écrit/-e à la hâte; [*decision*] inconsidéré/-e; [*conclusion*] hâtif/-ive.

hat *n* chapeau *m*.

hatch I *n* **1** (on aircraft) panneau *m* mobile; (in boat) écoutille *f*; (in car) portière *f*; **2** (also **serving ~**) passe-plats *m inv*.
II *vtr* **1** faire éclore [*eggs*]; **2** tramer [*plot, scheme*].
III *vi* [*chicks, fish eggs*] éclore.

hatchback *n* voiture *f* avec hayon.

hatchet *n* hachette *f*.

hate I *n* haine *f*.
II *vtr* **1** (dislike) détester; (violently) haïr; **2** (not enjoy) avoir horreur de [*sport, food*]; **to ~ doing** avoir horreur de faire; **3** (in apology) **to ~ to do** être désolé/-e de faire.

hatred *n* haine *f* (**of** de; **for** pour).

haughty *adj* [*person*] hautain/-e; [*manner*] altier/-ière.

haul I *n* **1** (taken by criminals) butin *m*; **2** (found by police, customs) saisie *f*; **arms ~** saisie d'armes; **3 it's a long ~** la route est longue; **4** (of fish) pêche *f*.
II *vtr* (drag) tirer.

haulage *n* **1** (transport) transport *m* routier; **2** (cost) frais *mpl* de transport.

haunch *n* hanche *f*.

haunt I *n* lieu *m* de prédilection.
II *vtr* hanter.

haunted *adj* [*house*] hanté/-e; [*face, look*] tourmenté/-e.

haunting *adj* (gen) lancinant/-e; [*memory*] obsédant/-e.

have ▶**520** I *vtr* (*uses not covered in note*) **1** (possess) avoir; **she has (got) a dog** elle a un chien; **I haven't (got) enough time** je n'ai pas assez de temps; **2** (with noun object) **to ~ a wash** se laver; **to ~ a sandwich** manger un sandwich; **to ~ a whisky** boire un whisky; **to ~ a cigarette** fumer une cigarette; **to ~ breakfast** prendre le petit déjeuner; **to ~ lunch** déjeuner; **I had some more cake** j'ai repris du gâteau; **3** (receive, get) recevoir [*letter*]; **I've had no news from him** je n'ai pas eu de nouvelles de lui; **to let sb ~ sth** donner qch à qn; **4** (hold) faire [*party*]; tenir [*meeting*]; organiser [*competition, exhibition*]; avoir [*conversation*]; **5** (exert, exhibit) avoir [*effect, influence*]; avoir [*courage, courtesy*] (**to do** de faire); **6** (spend) passer; **to ~ a nice day** passer une journée agréable; **to ~ a good time** bien s'amuser; **to ~ a hard time** traverser une période difficile; **to ~ a good holiday** (GB) or **vacation** (US) passer de bonnes vacances; **7** (also **~ got**) **to ~ sth to do** avoir qch à faire; **I've got letters to write** j'ai du courrier à faire; **I've got a lot of work to do** j'ai beaucoup de travail; **8** (suffer) avoir; **to ~ (the) flu/a heart attack** avoir la grippe/une crise cardiaque; **to ~ toothache** avoir mal aux dents; **he had his car stolen** il s'est fait voler sa voiture; **she has had her windows broken** on lui a cassé ses vitres; **9 to ~ the car fixed** faire réparer la voiture; **to ~ the house painted** faire peindre la maison; **to ~ one's hair cut** se faire couper les cheveux; **to ~ an injection** se faire faire une piqûre; **10** (cause to become) **she had them completely baffled** elle les a complètement déroutés; **I had it finished by 5 o'clock** je l'avais fini avant 5 heures; **11** (allow) tolérer; **I won't ~ this kind of behaviour!** je ne tolérerai pas ce comportement!; **12** (give birth to) [*woman*] avoir [*child*]; [*animal*] mettre bas, avoir [*young*].
II *modal aux* (must) **something has (got) to be done** il faut faire quelque chose; **you don't ~ to leave so early** tu n'as pas besoin de or tu n'es pas obligé de partir si tôt.
III *v aux* **1** avoir; (with movement and reflexive verbs) être; **she has lost her bag** elle a perdu son sac; **she has already left** elle est déjà partie; **he has hurt himself** il s'est blessé; **having finished his breakfast, he went out** après avoir fini son petit déjeuner, il est sorti; **2** (in tags, short answers) **you've seen the film, haven't you?** tu as vu le film, n'est-ce pas?; **you haven't seen the film, ~ you?** tu n'as pas vu le film?; **you haven't seen my bag, ~ you?** tu n'as pas vu mon sac, par hasard?; **'~ you seen him?'—'yes, I ~'** 'est-ce que tu l'as vu?'—'oui'; **'you've never met him'—'yes I ~!'** 'tu ne l'as jamais rencontré'—'mais si!'
IDIOMS **I've had it (up to here) with...**○ j'en ai marre de...○; **to ~ it in for sb**○ avoir qn dans le collimateur○; **she doesn't ~ it in her to do** elle est incapablede faire; **to ~ it out with sb** s'expliquer avec qn; **the ~s and the ~-nots** les riches et les pauvres.
■ **have on 1** porter [*coat, skirt*]; **he had (got) nothing on** il n'avait rien sur lui; **2 to ~ sth on** (be busy) avoir qch de prévu; **3 to ~ sb on**○ faire marcher qn○.

haven *n* **1** (safe place) refuge *m* (**for** pour); **2** (harbour) port *m*.

havoc *n* dévastation *f*; **to wreak ~** provoquer des dégâts; (figurative) tout mettre sens dessus dessous.

Hawaii *pr n* Hawaï *m*.

hawk *n* faucon *m*.

hawthorn *n* aubépine *f*.

hay *n* foin *m*.

hay fever ▶**533** *n* rhume *m* des foins.

haystack *n* meule *f* de foin.
IDIOMS **it is/was like looking for a needle in a ~** autant chercher une aiguille dans une botte de foin.

hazard I *n* risque *m* (**to** pour); **a health ~** un risque pour la santé.
II *vtr* hasarder [*opinion, guess*].

hazardous *adj* dangereux/-euse.

haze *n* (mist) brume *f*; (of smoke, dust) nuage *m*.

hazel I *n* noisetier *m*.
II ▶**438** *adj* [*eyes*] (couleur de) noisette *inv*.

have

As a transitive verb

◆ When ***have*** or ***have got*** is used as a transitive verb meaning ***possess***, it can generally be translated by ***avoir***:

I ***have*** *(got) a car*	= j'**ai** une voiture
she ***has (got)*** *a good memory*	= elle **a** une bonne mémoire
they ***have (got)*** *problems*	= ils **ont** des problèmes

For examples and particular usages see the entry **have**; see also the entry **got**.

◆ ***have*** is also used with certain noun objects where the whole expression is equivalent to a verb: *to have dinner* = to dine; *to have a try* = to try.
In such cases, the phrase is very often translated by the equivalent verb in French (*dîner*, *essayer*). For translations, consult the appropriate noun entry (*dinner*, *try*).

As an auxiliary verb

◆ When used as an auxiliary in present perfect, future perfect and past perfect tenses, ***have*** is normally translated by ***avoir***:

I ***have*** *seen*	= j'**ai** vu
I ***had*** *seen*	= j'**avais** vu

◆ However, some verbs in French, especially verbs of movement and change of state (*aller*, *venir*, *descendre*, *mourir*), always take ***être*** in these tenses:

he ***has*** *left*	= il **est** parti

In this case, remember the past participle agrees with the subject of the verb:

she ***has*** *gone*	= elle **est** allée
they ***had*** *come back*	= ils **étaient** revenus
we ***had*** *stayed at home*	= nous **étions** restés chez nous

If you are in doubt as to whether a verb conjugates with ***être*** or ***avoir***, consult the French entry, where verbs taking ***être*** will be indicated like this: (*+v être*).

◆ Reflexive verbs (*se lever*, *se coucher*) always conjugate with ***être***:

she ***has*** *fainted*	= elle s'**est** évanouie
he ***had*** *fallen asleep*	= il s'**était** endormi

In this case, the past participle agrees with the reflexive pronoun only when the pronoun is a direct object. Otherwise there is no agreement:

she ***has*** *hurt herself*	= elle s'est fait mal
*I****'ve*** *washed my hair*	= je me suis lavé les cheveux

to have (got) to

◆ ***to have (got) to*** meaning *must* is translated by either ***devoir*** or the impersonal construction ***il faut que*** + *subjunctive*:

I ***have to*** *leave now*	= **il faut que** je parte maintenant
	= je **dois** partir maintenant

◆ In negative sentences, ***not to have to*** is usually translated by ***ne pas être obligé de***:

you ***don't have to*** *go*	= tu **n'es pas obligé d**'y aller

Conditional

◆ ***had*** is used in English at the beginning of a clause to replace an expression with ***if***. Such expressions are generally translated by ***si*** + *past perfect tense*:

had I taken *the train, this would never have happened*	= **si j'avais pris** le train, cela ne serait jamais arrivé

❑ For ***have*** used with illnesses, see usage note **Illnesses, Aches, and Pains**, ▶ 533.

hazelnut *n* noisette *f.*

hazy *adj* [*weather, morning*] brumeux/-euse; [*sunshine*] voilé/-e; [*idea, memory*] vague (*before n*).

he *pron* il; (emphatic) lui; **~'s seen us** il nous a vus; **there ~ is** le voilà; **she lives in Oxford but ~ doesn't** elle habite Oxford mais lui non; **~'s a genius** c'est un génie; **~ and I** lui et moi.

head ▶413 I *n* **1** (gen) tête *f*; **from ~ to foot** or **toe** de la tête aux pieds; **to stand on one's ~** faire le poirier; **£10 a ~** or **per ~** 10 livres sterling par personne; **2** (of family, church) chef *m*; (of organization) responsable *mf*, directeur/-trice *m/f*; **~ of State** chef d'État.
II **heads** *n pl* (of coin) face *f*; **'~s or tails?'** 'pile ou face?'
III *adj* **1** [*injury*] à la tête; **2** (chief) [*cashier, cook, gardener*] en chef.
IV *vtr* **1** être en tête de [*list, queue*]; être à la tête de [*firm, team*]; mener [*expedition, inquiry*]; **2 ~ed writing paper** papier *m* à lettres à en-tête; **3** (steer) diriger [*vehicle*] (**towards** vers); **4** (Sport) **to ~ the ball** faire une tête.
V *vi* **where was the train ~ed** or **~ing?** où allait le train?; **to ~ home** rentrer; **he's ~ing this way!** il vient par ici!
IDIOMS **to go to sb's ~** monter à la tête de qn; **to keep/lose one's ~** garder/perdre son sang-froid; **off the top of one's ~** [*say, answer*] sans réfléchir.
■ **head for 1** se diriger vers [*place*]; **2** courir à [*defeat*]; courir vers [*trouble*].

headache ▶533 *n* mal *m* de tête; **to have a ~** avoir mal à la tête.

head cold ▶533 *n* rhume *m* de cerveau.

headdress *n* (of feathers) coiffure *f*; (of lace) coiffe *f*.

headfirst *adv* [*fall, plunge*] la tête la première; [*rush into*] tête baissée.

headlamp, **headlight** *n* (of car) phare *m*.

headline *n* (in paper) gros titre *m*; **to hit the ~s** faire la une○; **the front-page ~** la manchette; **the news ~s** les grands titres (de l'actualité).

headlong I *adj* **a ~ dash** une ruée.
II *adv* [*fall*] la tête la première; [*run*] à toute vitesse.

head office *n* siège *m* social.

head-on *adj* [*crash, collision*] de front.

headphones *n pl* casque *m*.

headquarters *n pl* (gen) siège *m* social; (Mil) quartier *m* général.

head rest *n* (gen) appui-tête *m*; (Aut) repose-tête *m inv*.

head start *n* **to have a ~** avoir une longueur d'avance (**over** sur).

headstone *n* pierre *f* tombale.

headstrong *adj* [*person*] têtu/-e; [*attitude*] obstiné/-e.

head teacher ▶626 *n* directeur/-trice *m/f*.

headway *n* **to make ~** avancer, faire des progrès.

heady *adj* [*wine, mixture*] capiteux/-euse; [*perfume*] entêtant/-e; [*experience*] grisant/-e.

heal I *vtr* guérir [*person, injury*].
II *vi* [*wound, cut*] se cicatriser; **the fracture has ~ed** l'os s'est ressoudé.

healer *n* guérisseur/-euse *m/f*.

healing I *n* guérison *f*.
II *adj* [*power*] curatif/-ive; [*effect*] salutaire; **the ~ process** le rétablissement.

health *n* santé *f*; **in good/bad ~** en bonne/mauvaise santé; **here's to your ~!** à votre santé!

health food *n* aliments *mpl* naturels, aliments *mpl* diététiques.

health insurance *n* assurance *f* maladie.

Health Service *n* **1** (GB) (for public) services *mpl* de santé; **2** (US Univ) infirmerie *f*.

healthy *adj* [*person, dog*] en bonne santé; [*livestock, plant, lifestyle, diet*] sain/-e; [*air*] salutaire; [*appetite*] robuste; [*economy*] sain/-e; [*profit*] excellent/-e.

heap I *n* **1** (pile) tas *m*; **2**○ **~s of** plein de.
II *vtr* **1** (pile) entasser; **2 to ~ sth on sb** couvrir qn de qch [*praise*]; accabler qn de qch [*scorn*].

heaped *adj* **a ~ spoonful** une bonne cuillerée.

hear I *vtr* **1** (gen) entendre; **to make oneself heard** se faire entendre; (figurative) faire entendre sa voix; **2** apprendre [*news, rumour*]; **3** (listen to) écouter [*lecture, broadcast*]; [*judge*] entendre [*case, evidence*].
II *vi* entendre; **to ~ about** entendre parler de.
IDIOMS **~! ~!** bravo!
■ **hear from** avoir des nouvelles de [*person*].
■ **hear of** entendre parler de; **I won't ~ of it!** il n'en est pas question!

hearing *n* **1** (sense) ouïe *f*, audition *f*; **his ~ is not very good** il n'a pas l'oreille très fine; **2** (before court) audience *f*.

hearing aid *n* prothèse *f* auditive.

hearing-impaired *adj* malentendant/-e.

hearsay *n* ouï-dire *m inv*, on-dit *m inv*.

hearse *n* corbillard *m*.

heart ▶504 *n* **1** (gen) cœur *m*; **by ~** [*learn, know*] par cœur; **to take sth to ~** prendre qch à cœur; **right in the ~ of London** en plein cœur de Londres; **the ~ of the matter** le fond du problème; **2** (in cards) **~(s)** cœur *m*.
IDIOMS **to have one's ~ set on sth** vouloir qch à tout prix; **to take/lose ~** prendre/perdre courage.

heartache *n* chagrin *m*.

heart attack *n* crise *f* cardiaque, infarctus *m*.

heartbeat *n* battement *m* de cœur.

heartbreaking *adj* [*sight, story*] navrant/-e; [*cry, appeal*] déchirant/-e.

heartbroken *adj* **to be ~** avoir le cœur brisé.

heart failure *n* arrêt *m* du cœur.

heartfelt *adj* sincère.

hearth *n* foyer *m*; **~ rug** petit tapis *m*.

heartless *adj* [*person*] sans cœur; [*attitude, treatment*] cruel/-elle.

heart-to-heart *n* **to have a ~ (with sb)** parler à cœur ouvert (avec qn).

hearty *adj* [*welcome, greeting*] cordial/-e; [*person*] jovial/-e; [*laugh*] franc/franche; [*appetite*] solide; [*approval*] chaleureux/-euse.

heat I *n* **1** chaleur *f*; **in this ~** par cette chaleur; **in the ~ of the moment** dans le feu de l'action; **2** (Sport) (round) épreuve *f* éliminatoire; (in athletics) série *f*; **3** (Zool) **to be on** or **in ~** être en chaleur.
II *vtr* chauffer [*house, pool*]; faire chauffer [*food, oven*].
■ **heat up** faire chauffer [*food*]; (reheat) faire réchauffer.

heated *adj* **1** [*water, pool*] chauffé/-e; **2** [*debate, argument*] animé/-e.

heater *n* appareil *m* de chauffage.

heathen *n, adj* (irreligious) païen/-ïenne (*m/f*); (uncivilized) barbare (*mf*).

heather *n* bruyère *f*.

heating *n* chauffage *m*.

heatwave *n* vague *f* de chaleur.

heave I *vtr* (lift) hisser; (pull) traîner péniblement; (throw) lancer (**at** sur); **to ~ a sigh** pousser un soupir.
II *vi* **1** [*sea, ground*] se soulever et s'abaisser; **2** (pull) tirer de toutes ses forces; **3** (retch) avoir un haut-le-cœur; (vomit) vomir.

heaven *n* ciel *m*, paradis *m*; **thank ~(s)!** Dieu soit loué!; **good ~s!** grands dieux!

heavenly *adj* **1** [*choir, body*] céleste; [*peace*] divin/-e; **2**○ (wonderful) divin/-e.

heavily *adv* **1** [*lean, fall*] lourdement; [*sleep, sigh*] profondément; [*breathe*] (noisily) bruyamment; (with difficulty) péniblement; **~ underlined** souligné/-e d'un gros trait; **2** [*rain*] très fort; [*snow, invest, smoke, drink, rely*] beaucoup; [*bleed*] abondamment; [*taxed, armed*] fortement.

heavy ▶573 *adj* (gen) lourd/-e; [*shoes, frame*] gros/grosse (*before n*); [*line, features*] épais/épaisse; [*blow, fighting*] violent/-e; [*rain, frost, perfume, accent*] fort/-e; [*snow*] abondant/-e; [*traffic*] dense; [*gunfire*] nourri/-e; [*bleeding*] abondant/-e; [*sentence, fine*] sévère; [*cold*] gros/grosse (*before n*); **with a ~ heart** le cœur gros; **to be a ~ sleeper** avoir le sommeil lourd; **to be a ~ drinker** boire beaucoup.

heavy-handed *adj* maladroit/-e.

heavy metal *n* hard rock *m*.

heavyweight *n* **1** (boxer) poids *m* lourd; **2**○ (figurative) grosse légume○ *f*.

Hebrew ▶553 I *n* **1** (person) Hébreu *m*; **2** (language) hébreu *m*.
II *adj* [*language*] hébraïque; [*person*] hébreu/hébraïque.

heckle I *vtr* interpeller.
II *vi* chahuter.

hectic *adj* [*activity*] intense; [*day, life, schedule*] mouvementé/-e.

hedge I *n* haie *f*.
II *vi* se dérober.
IDIOMS **to ~ one's bets** se couvrir.

hedgehog *n* hérisson *m*.

hedgerow *n* haie *f*.

heed I *n* **to take ~ of sb** tenir compte de ce que dit qn; **to take ~ of sth** tenir compte de qch.
II *vtr* tenir compte de [*warning, advice*].

heel *n* talon *m*.
IDIOMS **to fall head over ~s in love with sb** tomber éperdument amoureux de qn; **to be hot on sb's ~s** talonner qn.

hefty *adj* [*person*] costaud○; [*object*] pesant/-e; [*blow*] puissant/-e; [*sum*] considérable.

heifer *n* génisse *f*.

height ▶573 *n* **1** (of person) taille *f*; (of table, tower, tree) hauteur *f*; **2** (of plane) altitude *f*; **to be scared of ~s** avoir le vertige; **3** (peak) **at the ~ of the season** en pleine saison; **at the ~ of** au plus fort de [*storm, crisis*]; **the ~ of** le comble de [*luxury, stupidity, cheek*]; **to be the ~ of fashion** être le dernier cri.

heighten I *vtr* intensifier [*emotion*]; augmenter [*tension, suspense*]; accentuer [*effect*].
II *vi* [*tension*] monter.

heir *n* héritier/-ière *m/f* (**to** de).

heiress *n* héritière *f*.

heirloom *n* héritage *m*; **a family ~** un objet de famille.

helicopter *n* hélicoptère *m*.

hell *n* **1** enfer *m*; **to make sb's life ~** rendre la vie infernale à qn; **2**○ **a ~ of a shock** un choc terrible; **a ~ of a lot worse** nettement pire; **oh, what the ~!** tant pis!; **why/what the ~...?** pourquoi/que..., bon Dieu○?
IDIOMS **for the ~ of it**○ par plaisir; **to raise ~**○ faire une scène (**with sb** à qn).

hello *excl* **1** (greeting) bonjour!; (on the phone) allô!; **2** (in surprise) tiens!

helm *n* barre *f*; **at the ~** à la barre.

helmet *n* casque *m*.

help I *n* aide *f*; (in emergency) secours *m*; **with the ~ of** à l'aide de [*stick, knife*]; avec l'aide de [*person*]; **it's/she's a (great) ~** ça/elle aide beaucoup; **to cry for ~** appeler au secours.
II *excl* au secours!
III *vtr* **1** aider (**to do** à faire); (more urgently) secourir; **to ~ each other** s'entraider; **to ~ sb across** aider qn à traverser; **2** (serve) **to ~ sb to** servir [qch] à qn [*food, wine*]; **to ~ oneself** se servir; **3** (prevent) **I couldn't ~ laughing** je n'ai pas pu m'empêcher de rire; **it can't be ~ed!** on n'y peut rien!; **he can't ~ being stupid!** ce n'est pas de sa faute s'il est stupide!
IV *vi* aider; **he never ~s with the housework** il n'aide jamais à faire le ménage; **this map doesn't ~ much** cette carte n'est pas d'un grand secours.
■ **help out**: ¶ **~ out** aider, donner un coup de main○; ¶ **~ [sb] out** aider, donner un coup de main○ à; (financially) dépanner○.

helper *n* aide *mf*, assistant/-e *m/f*; (for handicapped person) aide *f* sociale.

helpful *adj* [*person*] serviable; [*advice, suggestion*] utile.

helping *n* portion *f*.
helpless *adj* **1** (powerless) [*person*] impuissant/-e; (because of infirmity, disability) impotent/-e; **2** (defenceless) [*person*] sans défense.
hem *n* ourlet *m*.
■ **hem in** cerner [*person*].
hemisphere *n* hémisphère *m*.
hemp *n* chanvre *m*.
hen *n* (chicken) poule *f*; (female bird) femelle *f*.
hence *adv* **1** (for this reason) (before noun) d'où; (before adjective) donc; **2** (from now) d'ici.
henchman *n* acolyte *m*.
hen-pecked *adj* **~ husband** mari *m* mené par le bout du nez.
hepatitis **▶533** *n* hépatite *f*.
her **▶524** **I** *pron* (direct object) la, l'; (indirect object) lui; **I saw ~** je l'ai vue; **he gave ~ the book** il lui a donné le livre.
II *det* son/sa/ses; **~ dog** son chien.
herald I *n* héraut *m*.
II *vtr* (also **~ in**) annoncer.
heraldry *n* héraldique *f*.
herb *n* herbe *f*; **mixed ~s** ≈ herbes de Provence.
herd I *n* troupeau *m*.
II *vtr* rassembler [*animals*]; **to ~ people into a room** conduire des gens dans une pièce.
IDIOMS **to follow the ~** être un mouton de Panurge.
here *adv*

■ **Note** When *here* is used to indicate the location of an object, a point etc close to the speaker, it is generally translated by *ici*: *come and sit here* = viens t'asseoir ici.
– When the location is not so clearly defined, *là* is the usual translation: *he's not here at the moment* = il n'est pas là pour l'instant.
– *voici* is used to translate *here is* and *here are* when the speaker is drawing attention to an object, a place, a person etc physically close to him or her.
– For examples and particular usages, see the entry below.

1 ici; **near ~** près d'ici; **come over ~** venez par ici; **~ and there** par endroits; **~ they are/she comes!** les/la voici!; **~ are my keys** voici mes clés; **~ you are** tiens, tenez; **2** (indicating presence, arrival) **she's not ~ right now** elle n'est pas là pour le moment; **~ we are at last** nous voilà enfin; **we get off ~** c'est là qu'on descend; **now that summer's ~** maintenant que c'est l'été; **~'s our chance** voilà notre chance.
IDIOMS **~'s to our success!** à notre succès!; **~'s to you!** à la tienne!
hereabout (US), **hereabouts** (GB) *adv* par ici.
hereafter I *n* **the ~** l'au-delà *m*.
II *adv* (Law) ci-après.
hereby *adv* par la présente.
hereditary *adj* héréditaire.
heresy *n* hérésie *f*.
heritage *n* patrimoine *m*.
hermit *n* ermite *m*.
hernia *n* hernie *f*.
hero *n* héros *m*.
heroic *adj* héroïque.
heroin *n* héroïne *f*.
heroine *n* héroïne *f*.
heroism *n* héroïsme *m*.
heron *n* héron *m*.
hero-worship I *n* culte *m* du héros, adulation *f*.
II *vtr* aduler.
herring *n* hareng *m*.
hers *pron*

■ **Note** In French, possessive pronouns reflect the gender and number of the noun they are standing for; *hers* is translated by *le sien*, *la sienne*, *les siens*, *les siennes*, according to what is being referred to.

my car is red but ~ is blue ma voiture est rouge mais la sienne est bleue; **the green pen is ~** le stylo vert est à elle; **which house is ~?** laquelle est sa maison?; **I'm a friend of ~** c'est une amie à moi; **it's not ~** ce n'est pas à elle.
herself *pron* **1** (reflexive) se, s'; **she's hurt ~** elle s'est blessée; **2** (after preposition) elle, elle-même; **for ~** pour elle, pour elle-même; **(all) by ~** toute seule; **3** (emphatic) elle-même; **she made it ~** elle l'a fait elle-même; **4 she's not ~ today** elle n'est pas dans son assiette aujourd'hui.
hesitant *adj* hésitant/-e; **to be ~ about doing** hésiter à faire.
hesitate *vi* hésiter (**over** sur; **to do** à faire).
hesitation *n* hésitation *f*.
heterosexual *n*, *adj* hétérosexuel/-elle (*m*/*f*).
hexagon *n* hexagone *m*.
hey○ *excl* (call for attention) hé!, eh!; (in protest) dis donc!
heyday *n* (gen) âge *m* d'or; (of person) beaux jours *mpl*.
HGV *n* (GB) (*abbr* = **heavy goods vehicle**) PL *m*, poids *m* lourd.
hi○ *excl* salut○!
hibernate *vi* hiberner.
hiccup, **hiccough** *n* **1** hoquet *m*; **to have (the) ~s** avoir le hoquet; **2** (setback) anicroche *f*.
hidden *adj* caché/-e.
hide I *n* (skin) peau *f*; (leather) cuir *m*.
II *vtr* cacher [*object, person*] (**from** à); dissimuler [*feeling*] (**from** à).
III *vi* se cacher.
hide and seek (GB), **hide-and-go-seek** (US) **▶504** *n* cache-cache *m inv*.
hideaway *n* retraite *f*.
hideous *adj* [*person, monster, object*] hideux/-euse; [*noise*] affreux/-euse.
hiding *n* **1 to go into ~** se cacher; **to come out of ~** sortir de sa cachette; **2** (beating) correction *f*.
hiding place *n* cachette *f*.

her

As a pronoun

◆ When used as a direct object pronoun, ***her*** is translated by ***la*** (***l'*** before a vowel or mute 'h'). Note that the object pronoun normally comes before the verb in French and that, in compound tenses like the perfect and past perfect, the past participle agrees with the pronoun:

*I know **her*** = je **la** connais
*I've already seen **her*** = je l'ai déjà vue
*I'll try to contact **her*** = je vais essayer de **la** contacter

In imperatives, the direct object pronoun is translated by ***la*** and comes after the verb:

*catch **her**!* = attrape-**la**!*

In negative commands, however, ***la*** comes before the verb:

*don't hit **her**!* = ne **la** frappe pas!

◆ When used as an indirect object pronoun, ***her*** is translated by ***lui***:

*I've given **her** the book* = je **lui** ai donné le livre
*I've given it to **her*** = je le **lui** ai donné
*I'm going to write to **her*** = je vais **lui** écrire

In imperatives, the indirect object pronoun is translated by ***lui*** and comes after the verb:

*phone **her*** = téléphone-**lui***
*give them to **her*** = donne-les-**lui***

In negative commands, however, ***lui*** comes before the verb:

*don't tell **her** the truth* = ne **lui** dis pas la vérité

After prepositions and after the verb ***to be***, the translation is ***elle***:

*he did it for **her*** = il l'a fait pour **elle**
*it's **her*** = c'est **elle**

* Note the hyphen(s).

As a determiner

◆ When translating ***her*** as a determiner (***her house*** etc), remember that in French determiners agree in gender and number with the noun that follows; ***her*** is translated by

son + *masculine singular noun*:

***her** dog* = **son** chien

sa + *feminine singular noun* beginning with a consonant:

***her** house* = **sa** maison

son + *feminine singular noun* beginning with a vowel or mute 'h':

***her** plate* = **son** assiette

ses + *plural noun*:

***her** children* = **ses** enfants

When ***her*** is stressed, ***à elle*** is added after the noun:

***her** house* = **sa** maison **à elle**
***her** books* = **ses** livres **à elle**

❑ For ***her*** used with parts of the body, see the usage note **The Human Body ▶ 413**.

hierarchy *n* hiérarchie *f*.

hieroglyph, **hieroglyphic** *n* hiéroglyphe *m*.

hi-fi *n* **1** (set of equipment) chaîne *f* hi-fi *inv*; **2** (*abbr* = **high fidelity**) hi-fi *f inv*.

high ▶573 I *n* **1 to reach a new ~** atteindre son niveau le plus élevé; **2**○ **to be on a ~** être en pleine euphorie.
II *adj* **1** (gen) haut/-e; **how ~ is the cliff?** quelle est la hauteur de la falaise?; **it is 50 m ~** ça fait 50 m de haut; **2** [*number, price, volume*] élevé/-e; [*wind*] violent/-e; [*hope*] grand/-e (*before n*); **at ~ speed** à grande vitesse; **to have a ~ temperature** avoir de la fièvre; **~ in** riche en [*fat, iron*]; **3** [*quality, standard, rank*] supérieur/-e; **friends in ~ places** des amis haut placés; **4** [*ideal, principle*] noble; **5** [*pitch, voice*] aigu/aiguë; [*note*] haut/-e; **6**○ (on drug) défoncé/-e○; (happy) ivre de joie.
III *adv* haut.

highbrow *n, adj* intellectuel/-elle (*m/f*).

high chair *n* chaise *f* de bébé.

high-class *adj* [*hotel, shop, car*] de luxe; [*goods*] de première qualité; [*area*] de grand standing.

high court *n* cour *f* suprême.

higher education *n* enseignement *m* supérieur.

high-handed *adj* despotique.

high heels *n pl* hauts talons *mpl*.

high jump ▶504 *n* (Sport) saut *m* en hauteur.

Highlands *pr n pl* Highlands *mpl*, Hautes-Terres *fpl* (d'Écosse).

highlight I *n* **1** (in hair) (natural) reflet *m*; (artificial) mèche *f*; **2** (of match, event) point *m* culminant; (of year, evening) point *m* fort.
II **highlights** *n pl* (on radio, TV) résumé *m*.
III *vtr* **1** (with pen) surligner; **2** (emphasize) mettre l'accent sur.

highly *adv* [*dangerous, intelligent*] extrêmement; **~ unlikely** fort peu probable; **to think ~ of sb** penser beaucoup de bien de qn.

highly-strung *adj* très tendu/-e.

Highness ▶498 *n* **His** or **Her** (**Royal**) **~** Son Altesse *f*.

high-pitched *adj* [*voice, sound*] aigu/aiguë.

high point *n* point *m* culminant.

high-powered *adj* [*car, engine*] de grande puissance; [*person*] dynamique; [*job*] de haute responsabilité.

high-ranking *adj* de haut rang.

high rise (**building**) *n* tour *f* (d'habitation).

high school *n* (US Sch) ≈ lycée *m*; (GB Sch) établissement *m* secondaire.

high-speed *adj* [*train*] à grande vitesse.

high street (GB) (also **High Street**) *n* (in town) rue *f* principale; (in village) grand-rue *f*.

high-tech *adj* [*industry*] de pointe; [*equipment, car*] ultramoderne.

high tide *n* marée *f* haute.

highway *n* (GB) route *f* nationale; (US) autoroute *f*.

Highway Code *n* (GB) Code *m* de la Route.

hijack *vtr* détourner [*plane*].

hijacker *n* (of plane) pirate *m* (de l'air); (of bus, truck) pirate *m* (de la route).

hijacking *n* détournement *m*.

hike I *n* randonnée *f*; **to go on a ~** faire une randonnée.
II *vtr* (also **~ up**) augmenter [*rate, price*].

hiker *n* randonneur/-euse *m/f*.

hiking ▶504 *n* randonnée *f*.

hilarious *adj* désopilant/-e, hilarant/-e.

hill *n* colline *f*; (hillside) coteau *m*; (incline) pente *f*, côte *f*.

hillside *n* **on the ~** à flanc de coteau.

hilltop *n* sommet *m* de colline.

hilly *adj* vallonné/-e.

him *pron* **1** (direct object) le, l'; (indirect object) lui; **I know ~** je le connais; **catch ~!** attrape-le!; **I gave ~ the book** je lui ai donné le livre; **phone ~!** téléphone-lui!; **2** (after preposition, to be) lui; **it's for ~** c'est pour lui; **it's ~** c'est lui.

Himalayas *pr n pl* **the ~** (les montagnes *fpl* de) l'Himalaya *m*.

himself *pron* **1** (reflexive) se, s'; **he's hurt ~** il s'est blessé; **2** (after preposition) lui, lui-même; **for ~** pour lui, pour lui-même; **(all) by ~** tout seul; **3** (emphatic) lui-même; **he made it ~** il l'a fait lui-même; **4 he's not ~ today** il n'est pas dans son assiette aujourd'hui.

hinder *vtr* entraver [*development, career*]; freiner [*progress, efforts*].

hind legs *n pl* pattes *fpl* de derrière.

hindsight *n* **with (the benefit of) ~** avec le recul, rétrospectivement.

Hindu I *n* Hindou/-e *m/f*.
II *adj* hindou/-e.

hinge I *n* charnière *f*; (lift-off) gond *m*.
II *vi* **to ~ on** dépendre de.

hint I *n* **1** (remark) allusion *f* (**about** à); **to drop ~s** faire des allusions; **2** (clue) indication *f*; (piece of advice) conseil *m*; **3** (of spice, accent) pointe *f*; (of colour) touche *f*; (of smile) ébauche *f*; (of irony) soupçon *m*.
II *vtr* **to ~ that** laisser entendre que (**to** à).
III *vi* faire des allusions; **to ~ at** faire allusion à.

hip I ▶413 *n* hanche *f*.
II *excl* **~ ~ hurrah!** hip hip hip hourra!

hippie, **hippy** *n, adj* hippie (*mf*).

hippopotamus, **hippo** *n* hippopotame *m*.

hire I *n* location *f*; **for ~** [*boat, skis*] à louer; [*taxi*] libre.
II *vtr* louer [*equipment, vehicle*]; engager [*person*].

hire purchase, **HP** *n* achat *m* à crédit; **on ~** à crédit.

his

■ **Note** In French determiners agree in gender and number with the noun that follows. So *his*, when used as a determiner, is translated by *son* + masculine singular noun (son chien), by *sa* + feminine singular noun (sa maison) BUT by *son* + feminine noun beginning with a vowel or mute 'h' (son assiette) and by *ses* + plural noun (ses enfants).

– When *his* is stressed, *à lui* is added after the noun: HIS *house* = sa maison à lui.
– For *his* used with parts of the body ▶ 413.
– In French possessive pronouns reflect the gender and number of the noun they are standing for. When used as a possessive pronoun, *his* is translated by *le sien*, *la sienne*, *les siens* or *les siennes* according to what is being referred to.

I *det* son/sa/ses.
II *pron* **all the drawings were good but ~ was the best** tous les dessins étaient bons mais le sien était le meilleur; **the blue car is ~** la voiture bleue est à lui; **it's not ~** ce n'est pas à lui; **which house is ~?** laquelle est sa maison?; **I'm a colleague of ~** je suis un/-e de ses collègues.

hiss I *n* sifflement *m*.
II *vi* [*person, steam, snake*] siffler; [*cat*] cracher; [*fat*] grésiller.

historian ▶ 626 *n* historien/-ienne *m/f*.

historic(al) *adj* historique.

history *n* **1** histoire *f*; **to make ~** entrer dans l'histoire; **2** (past experience) antécédents *mpl*; **to have a ~ of violence** avoir un passé violent.

hit I *n* **1** (blow, stroke) coup *m*; **2** (success) (play, film) succès *m*; (record) tube○ *m*; **to be a big ~** avoir un succès fou.
II *vtr* **1** (strike) frapper [*person, ball*]; **to ~ one's head on sth** se cogner la tête contre qch; **2** atteindre [*target, enemy*]; **3** (collide with) heurter [*wall*]; [*vehicle*] renverser [*person*]; **4** (affect adversely) affecter, toucher; **5** (reach) arriver à [*motorway*]; rencontrer [*traffic, bad weather*]; [*figures, weight*] atteindre [*level*].
IDIOMS **to ~ it off with sb** bien s'entendre avec qn.
■ **hit back**: ¶ **~ [sb] back** rendre un coup à; ¶ **~ [sth] back** renvoyer [*ball*].

hit-and-run *adj* [*accident*] où le chauffeur a pris la fuite.

hitch I *n* problème *m*, pépin○ *m*.
II *vtr* **1** attacher [*trailer*] (**to** à); **2**○ **to ~ a lift** faire du stop○.
III○ *vi* faire du stop○.

hitchhike *vi* faire du stop○; **to ~ to Paris** aller à Paris en stop○.

hitchhiker *n* auto-stoppeur/-euse *m/f*.

hit parade *m* palmarès *m*, hit-parade *m*.

HIV *n* (*abbr* = **human immunodeficiency virus**) (virus *m*) VIH *m*; **~ positive** séropositif/-ive.

hive *n* ruche *f*; **a ~ of activity** une vraie ruche.

hoard I *n* (of treasure) trésor *m*; (of provisions) provisions *fpl*; (of miser) magot○ *m*.
II *vtr* amasser [*objects, money, food*].

hoarding *n* (GB) **1** (billboard) panneau *m* publicitaire; **2** (fence) palissade *f*.

hoarse *adj* [*voice*] rauque; **to be ~** être enroué/-e.

hoax I *n* canular *m*.
II *adj* [*call, warning*] bidon○ *inv*.

hob *n* (on cooker) table *f* de cuisson.

hobble *vi* boitiller.

hobby *n* passe-temps *m inv*.

hockey ▶ 504 *n* (GB) hockey *m*; (US) hockey *m* sur glace; **~ stick** crosse *f* de hockey.

hoe I *n* houe *f*, binette *f*.
II *vtr* biner [*ground*]; sarcler [*flower beds*].

hog I *n* (US) (pig) porc *m*, verrat *m*.
II○ *vtr* monopoliser.
IDIOMS **to go the whole ~**○ (be extravagant) faire les choses en grand; (go to extremes) aller jusqu'au bout.

hoist *vtr* hisser [*flag, sail, heavy object*].

hold I *n* **1** (grasp) prise *f*; **to get ~ of** attraper [*rope, handle*]; **2 to get ~ of** se procurer [*book, ticket*]; découvrir [*information*]; **3 to get ~ of sb** (contact) joindre qn; (find) trouver qn; **4** (control) emprise *f* (**on, over** sur); **to have a ~ on** or **over sb** avoir de l'emprise sur qn; **to get a ~ of oneself** se reprendre; **5 to put a call on ~** mettre un appel en attente; **6** (in plane) soute *f*; (on boat) cale *f*.
II *vtr* **1** tenir; **to ~ sth in one's hand** tenir qch à la main [*brush, pencil*]; (enclosed) tenir qch dans la main [*coin, sweet*]; **to ~ sb (in one's arms)** serrer qn dans ses bras; **to ~ sth in place** maintenir qch en place; **2** organiser [*meeting, competition, reception*]; célébrer [*church service*]; mener [*inquiry*]; faire passer [*interview*]; **3** (contain) [*drawer, box, case*] contenir [*objects, possessions*]; **4** avoir [*opinion, belief*]; **5** (keep against will) détenir [*person*]; **to ~ sb hostage** garder qn en otage; **6** détenir, avoir [*power, record*]; être titulaire de [*degree*]; **7 to ~ sb's attention** retenir l'attention de qn; **to ~ sb responsible** tenir qn pour responsable; **8** (defend successfully) tenir [*territory, city*]; conserver [*title, seat*]; **to ~ one's own** bien se défendre; **9** (on phone) **can you ~ the line please?** ne quittez pas s'il vous plaît.
III *vi* **1** [*bridge, dam, rope*] tenir; **2** [*weather*] se maintenir; [*luck*] durer; **3** (on phone) patienter; **4 ~ still!** tiens-toi tranquille!
■ **hold against**: **to ~ sth against sb** reprocher qch à qn.
■ **hold back**: ¶ **~ back** se retenir (**from doing** de faire); ¶ **~ [sb/sth] back 1** contenir [*water, crowd, anger*]; retenir [*tears, person*]; **2** entraver [*development*].
■ **hold down 1** tenir, maîtriser [*person*]; **2** garder [*job*].
■ **hold on 1** (wait) attendre; **'~ on...'** (on phone) 'ne quittez pas...'; **2** (grip) s'accrocher; **'~ on (tight)!'** 'tiens-toi (bien)!'
■ **hold on to** s'agripper à [*branch, rope, person*]; (to prevent from falling) retenir [*person*]; serrer [*object, purse*].
■ **hold out**: ¶ **~ out** tenir bon; **to ~ out against** tenir bon devant [*threat, changes*]; ¶ **~ [sth] out** tendre [*hand*] (**to** à).
■ **hold to**: **~ sb to [sth]** faire tenir [qch] à qn [*promise*].
■ **hold up 1** soutenir [*shelf*]; tenir [*trousers*]; **2** (raise) lever; **to ~ one's hand up** lever la main; **3** (delay) retarder [*person, flight*]; ralentir [*production, traffic*]; **4** (rob) attaquer.

holdall *n* fourre-tout *m*, sac *m*.

holder *n* (of passport, degree, post, account) titulaire *mf*; (of ticket, record) détenteur/-trice *m/f*; (of title) tenant/-e *m/f*.

hold-up *n* **1** (delay) retard *m*; (on road) embouteillage *m*, bouchon *m*; **2** (robbery) hold-up *m*.

hole *n* **1** (gen) trou *m*; **2** (GB) (in tooth) cavité *f*; **3** (of fox, rabbit) terrier *m*.

holiday *n* **1** (GB) (vacation) vacances *fpl*; **to go on ~** partir en vacances; **2** (GB) (time off work) congé *m*; **3** (public, bank) jour *m* férié.

holidaymaker *n* (GB) vacancier/-ière *m/f*.

holiday resort *n* lieu *m* de villégiature.

Holland ▶ 448 *pr n* Hollande *f*, Pays-Bas *mpl*.

hollow I *n* creux *m*.
II *adj* [*object, cheeks*] creux/creuse; [*words*] faux/fausse, vain/-e; **a ~ laugh** un rire forcé; **to sound ~** sonner faux.

holly *n* houx *m*.

holocaust *n* holocauste *m*; **the Holocaust** l'Holocauste *m*.

hologram *n* hologramme *m*.

holster *n* étui *m* de revolver.

holy *adj* (gen) saint/-e; [*water*] bénit/-e.

Holy Bible *n* Sainte Bible *f*.

Holy Land *pr n* Terre *f* Sainte.

Holy Spirit *n* Saint-Esprit *m*.

homage *n* hommage *m*; **to pay ~ to** rendre hommage à.

home I *n* **1** (house) maison *f*; (country) pays *m* natal; **broken ~** foyer désuni; **to leave ~** quitter la maison; **2** (institution) maison *f*; **to put sb in a ~** mettre qn dans un établissement spécialisé; **3** (Sport) **to play at ~** jouer à domicile.
II *adj* **1** [*life*] de famille; [*comforts*] du foyer; **2** [*market, affairs*] intérieur/-e; [*news*] national/-e; **3** (Sport) [*match, win*] à domicile; [*team*] qui reçoit.
III *adv* **1** [*come, go*] (to house) à la maison, chez soi; (to country) dans son pays; **2 to bring sth ~ to sb** faire comprendre or voir qch à qn; **to strike ~** toucher juste.
IV at home *phr* **1** [*be, work, stay*] à la maison, chez soi; **2** (Sport) [*play*] à domicile; **3** (at ease) [*feel*] à l'aise (**with** avec); **make yourself at ~** fais comme chez toi.

home address *n* adresse *f* personnelle.

home cooking *n* bonne cuisine *f* familiale.

home help *n* (GB) aide *f* familiale.

homeland *n* pays *m* d'origine, patrie *f*.

homeless *n* **the ~** les sans-abri *mpl*.

homely *adj* **1** (GB) (cosy, welcoming) accueillant/-e; **2** (GB) (unpretentious) simple; **3** (US) (plain) [*person*] sans attraits.

homemade *adj* fait/-e maison, maison *inv*.

Home Office *n* ministère *m* de l'Intérieur.

homeopathic *adj* homéopathique.

home owner *n* propriétaire *mf*.

Home Secretary *n* Ministre *m* de l'Intérieur.

homesick *adj* **to be ~** (for country) avoir le mal du pays.

home town *n* ville *f* natale.

homeward *adv* **to travel ~(s)** rentrer; **to be ~ bound** être sur le chemin de retour.

homework *n* **1** (Sch) devoirs *mpl*; **2** (research) **to do some ~ on** faire quelques recherches au sujet de.

homicidal *adj* homicide.

homicide *n* **1** (murder) homicide *m*; **2** (person) meurtrier/-ière *m/f*.

homogenous *adj* homogène.

homosexual *n, adj* homosexuel/-elle (*m/f*).

honest *adj* [*answer, account*] sincère; [*person*] (truthful, trustworthy) honnête; (frank) franc/franche; **to be ~ with sb** être franc/franche avec qn; **to be ~, I don't care** à dire vrai, ça m'est égal.

honestly *adv* **1** (truthfully) honnêtement; **2** (really) vraiment; **3** (sincerely) franchement.

honesty *n* honnêteté *f*.

honey *n* **1** miel *m*; **2**○ (dear) chéri/-e *m/f*.

honeycomb *n* (in hive) rayon *m* de miel; (for sale) gâteau *m* de miel.

honeymoon *n* lune *f* de miel; **to go on ~** partir en voyage de noces.

honeysuckle *n* chèvrefeuille *m*.

Hong Kong ▶ 448 *pr n* Hongkong *m*.

honk *vtr* **to ~ one's horn** donner un coup de klaxon®.

honor (US) = **honour**.

honorable (US) = **honourable**.

honorary *adj* honoraire.

honour (GB), **honor** (US) **I** *n* **1** honneur *m*; **in ~ of** en l'honneur de; **2** (in titles) **Your Honour** Votre Honneur.
II *vtr* honorer [*person, cheque, contract*]; tenir [*promise, commitment*].

honourable (GB), **honorable** (US) *adj* (gen) honorable; [*person, intention*] honnête.

hood *n* **1** (of coat) capuchon *m*; (balaclava) cagoule *f*; **2** (on cooker) hotte *f*; **3** (GB) (on car, pram) capote *f*; **4** (US Aut) (bonnet) capot *m*; **5**○ (US) (gangster) truand *m*.

hoof *n* sabot *m*.

hook I *n* **1** (on wall, for picture) crochet *m*; **2** (on fishing line) hameçon *m*; **3** (fastener) agrafe *f*; **~s and eyes** agrafes *fpl*; **4 to take the phone off the ~** décrocher le téléphone; **5** (in boxing) crochet *m*; **left ~** crochet du gauche.
II *vtr* accrocher (**on, onto** à).
IDIOMS **to get sb off the ~** tirer qn d'affaire.

hooked *adj* **1** [*nose, beak*] crochu/-e; **2 to be ~ on** se camer○ à [*drugs*]; être mordu/-e○ de [*films, computer games*].

hooligan *n* vandale *m*, voyou *m*; **soccer ~** hooligan *m*.

hoop *n* (ring) cerceau *m*; (in croquet) arceau *m*.

hooray *excl* hourra!

hoot I *n* (of owl) (h)ululement *m*; (of car) coup *m* de klaxon®.
II *vtr* **to ~ one's horn** donner un coup de klaxon®.
III *vi* [*owl*] (h)ululer; [*car*] klaxonner; [*person, crowd*] (derisively) huer; **to ~ with laughter** éclater de rire.

hoover *vtr* (GB) **to ~ a room** passer l'aspirateur dans une pièce.

Hoover® *n* (GB) aspirateur *m*.

hop I *n* (of frog, rabbit, child) bond *m*; (of bird) sautillement *m*.
II **hops** *n pl* houblon *m*.
III *vi* [*person*] sauter; (on one leg) sauter à cloche-pied; [*bird*] sautiller; **to ~ into bed/off a bus** sauter dans son lit/d'un bus.

hope I *n* espoir *m* (**of** de); **to raise sb's ~s** faire naître l'espoir chez qn; **to give up ~** abandonner tout espoir; **to have no ~ of sth** n'avoir aucune chance de qch.
II *vtr* espérer (**that** que); **to ~ to do** espérer faire; **I (do) ~ so/not** j'espère (bien) que oui/que non.
III *vi* espérer; **to ~ for a reward** espérer avoir une récompense; **let's ~ for the best** espérons que tout se passera bien.

hopeful *adj* [*person, expression*] plein/-e d'espoir; [*attitude, mood*] optimiste; [*sign, situation*] encourageant/-e.

hopefully *adv* **1** (with luck) avec un peu de chance; **2** (with hope) [*say*] avec optimisme.

hopeless *adj* **1** [*attempt, case, struggle*] désespéré/-e; **it's ~!** inutile!; **2**○ (incompetent) nul/nulle○.

hopscotch ▶ **504** *n* marelle *f*.

horizon *n* horizon *m*; **on the ~** à l'horizon; (figurative) en vue.

horizontal *adj* horizontal/-e.

hormone *n* hormone *f*.

horn *n* **1** (of animal, snail) corne *f*; **2** ▶ **586** (Mus) cor *m*; **3** (of car) klaxon® *m*; (of ship) sirène *f*.

hornet *n* frelon *m*.

horoscope *n* horoscope *m*.

horrendous *adj* épouvantable.

horrible *adj* **1** (unpleasant) [*place, clothes, smell*] affreux/-euse; [*weather, food, person*] épouvantable; **to be ~ to sb** être méchant/-e avec qn; **2** (shocking) [*death, crime*] horrible.

horrid *adj* affreux/-euse.

horrific *adj* atroce.

horrify *vtr* horrifier.

horrifying *adj* [*experience, sight*] horrifiant/-e; [*behaviour*] effroyable.

horror *n* horreur *f* (**at** devant); **to have a ~ of sth/of doing** avoir horreur de qch/de faire.

horror film *n* film *m* d'épouvante.

horse *n* cheval *m*.
IDIOMS **from the ~'s mouth** de source sûre.
■ **horse about, horse around** chahuter.

horseback riding ▶ **504** *n* (US) équitation *f*.

horse chestnut *n* (tree) marronnier *m* (d'Inde); (fruit) marron *m* (d'Inde).

horsefly *n* taon *m*.

horsepower *n* puissance *f* (en chevaux).

horseracing *n* courses *fpl* de chevaux, courses *fpl* hippiques.

horseradish sauce *n* sauce *f* au raifort.

horseriding ▶ **504** *n* équitation *f*.

horseshoe *n* fer *m* à cheval.

horseshow *n* concours *m* hippique.

horticulture *n* horticulture *f*.

hose, hosepipe (GB) *n* (gen) tuyau *m*; (for garden) tuyau *m* d'arrosage; (**fire**) **~** lance *f* à incendie.

hospice *n* établissement *m* de soins palliatifs.

hospitable *adj* hospitalier/-ière (**to** envers).

hospital *n* hôpital *m*; **to be taken to ~** être hospitalisé/-e; **in ~** à l'hôpital.

hospitality *n* hospitalité *f*.

hospitalize *vtr* hospitaliser.

host I *n* **1** (gen) hôte *m*; **2** (on radio, TV) animateur/-trice *m/f*; **3** (multitude) foule *f* (**of** de).
II *vtr* organiser [*party*]; animer [*show*].

hostage *n* otage *m*; **to hold sb ~** garder qn en otage.

hostel *n* (for workers, refugees) foyer *m*; (**youth**) **~** auberge *f* de jeunesse.

hostess *n* hôtesse *f*.

hostile *adj* hostile (**to** à).

hostility *n* hostilité *f* (**towards** à l'égard de).

hot *adj* **1** (gen) chaud/-e; **it's ~ here** il fait chaud ici; **to be** or **feel ~** [*person*] avoir chaud; **to go ~ and cold** (with fever) être fiévreux/-euse; (with fear) avoir des sueurs froides; **2** (Culin) [*mustard, spice*] fort/-e; [*sauce, dish*] épicé/-e; **3 to be ~ on sb's trail** être sur les talons de qn.

hot air balloon *n* montgolfière *f*.

hot dog *n* hot dog *m*.

hotel *n* hôtel *m*.

hotelier, hotelkeeper ▶ **626** *n* (GB) hôtelier/-ière *m/f*.

hotplate *n* plaque *f* de cuisson.

hotshot *n* gros bonnet○ *m*.

hot spot○ *n* **1** (trouble spot) point *m* chaud; **2** (sunny country) pays *m* chaud.

hot-tempered *adj* colérique.

hot water bottle *n* bouillotte *f*.

hound I *n* chien *m* de chasse.
II *vtr* harceler, traquer [*person*].
■ **hound out** chasser (**of** de).

hour ▶ **434**, **708** *n* heure *f*; **£10 per ~** 10 livres sterling (de) l'heure; **to be paid by the ~** être payé/-e à l'heure; **60 km an hour** 60 km à l'heure; **in the early ~s** au petit matin.

hourly I *adj* horaire.
II *adv* [*arrive, phone*] toutes les heures.

house I *n* **1** (gen) maison *f*; **at my/his ~** chez moi/lui; **to go to sb's ~** aller chez qn; **on the ~** aux frais de la maison; **2** (in theatre) (audience) assistance *f*; (auditorium) salle *f*; (performance) séance *f*; **3** (music) house music *f*.
II *vtr* loger [*person*]; abriter [*collection*].

houseboat *n* péniche *f* aménagée.

household I *n* maison *f*; (in survey) ménage *m*; **head of the ~** chef *m* de famille.
II *adj* [*expenses*] du ménage; [*chore*] ménager/-ère.

household appliance *n* appareil *m* électroménager.

householder *n* **1** (occupier) occupant/-e *m/f*; **2** (owner) propriétaire *mf*.

housekeeper ▶ **626** *n* gouvernante *f*.

housekeeping *n* (money) argent *m* du ménage.

House of Commons *n* Chambre *f* des communes.

House of Lords *n* (GB) Chambre *f* des lords, Chambre *f* haute.

House of Representatives *n* (US) Chambre *f* des représentants.

houseplant *n* plante *f* d'intérieur.

house-proud *adj* fier/fière de son intérieur.

Houses of Parliament *n pl* (GB) Parlement *m* Britannique.

house-trained *adj* (GB) propre.

house-warming (party) *n* pendaison *f* de crémaillère.

housewife *n* femme *f* au foyer; ménagère *f*.

housework *n* travaux *mpl* ménagers; **to do the ~** faire le ménage.

housing *n* logements *mpl*.

housing estate *n* (GB) cité *f*.

hover *vi* [*eagle*] planer; [*helicopter*] faire du surplace; **to ~ around sb/sth** tourner autour de qn/qch.

hovercraft *n* aéroglisseur *m*.

how I *adv* **1** (gen) comment; **~ are you?** comment allez-vous?; **~'s your brother?** comment va ton frère?; **~ are things?** comment ça va?; **~ do you do!** enchanté!; **to know ~ to do** savoir faire; **2** (in number, quantity questions) **~ much is this?** combien ça coûte?; **~ much do you weigh?** combien pèses-tu?; **~ many people?** combien de personnes?; **~ many times** combien de fois; **~ long will it take?** combien de temps cela va-t-il prendre?; **~ tall are you?** combien mesures-tu?; **~ far is it?** c'est à quelle distance?; **~ old is she?** quel âge a-t-elle?; **~ soon can you get here?** dans combien de temps peux-tu être ici?; **4** (in exclamations) **~ wonderful/awful!** c'est fantastique/affreux!; **~ clever of you!** comme c'est intelligent de ta part!
II○ **how come** *phr* **~ come?** pourquoi?; **~ come you always get the best place?** comment ça se fait que tu aies toujours la meilleure place?

however I *conj* (nevertheless) toutefois, cependant.
II *adv* (no matter how) **~ hard I try, I can't** j'ai beau essayer, je n'y arrive pas; **~ difficult the task is** aussi difficile que soit la tâche; **~ small she may be** si petite soit-elle; **~ much it costs** quel qu'en soit le prix; **~ long it takes** quel que soit le temps que ça prendra; **~ you like** comme tu veux.

howl I *n* hurlement *m*.
II *vi* hurler.

HQ *n* (Mil) (*abbr* = **headquarters**) QG *m*.

hub *n* (of wheel) moyeu *m*; (figurative) centre *m*.

huddle *vi* **to ~ around** se presser autour de [*fire, radio*]; **to ~ together** se serrer les uns contre les autres.

hue *n* **1** (colour) couleur *f*, teinte *f*; **2 ~ and cry** tollé *m*.

huff○ I *n* **in a ~** vexé/-e.
II *vi* souffler.

hug I *n* étreinte *f*; **to give sb a ~** serrer qn dans ses bras.
II *vtr* **1** (embrace) serrer [qn] dans ses bras; **2 to ~ the coast/kerb** serrer la côte/le trottoir.

huge *adj* [*object, garden, city, country*] immense; [*person, animal*] gigantesque; [*appetite, success*] énorme; [*debts, sum*] gros/grosse (*before n*).

hull *n* (of ship, plane) coque *f*; (of tank) carcasse *f*.

hum I *n* (of insect, traffic, voices) bourdonnement *m*; (of machinery) ronronnement *m*.
II *vi* [*person*] fredonner; [*insect, aircraft*] bourdonner; [*machine*] ronronner.

human I *n* humain *m*.
II *adj* [*body, behaviour*] humain/-e; [*characteristic, rights*] de l'homme.

human being *n* être *m* humain.

humane *adj* [*person*] humain/-e; [*act*] d'humanité.

humanitarian *adj* humanitaire.

humanity *n* humanité *f*.

human nature *n* nature *f* humaine.

humble *adj* (gen) modeste; [*person*] humble.

humid *adj* [*climate*] humide; [*weather*] lourd/-e.

humiliate *vtr* humilier.

humiliating *adj* humiliant/-e.

humorous *adj* **1** [*story, book*] humoristique; **2** [*person, look*] plein/-e d'humour.

humour (GB), **humor** (US) I *n* **1** (wit) humour *m*; **a good sense of ~** le sens de l'humour; **2** (mood) humeur *f*; **to be in good/bad ~** être de bonne/mauvaise humeur.
II *vtr* amadouer [*person*].

hump *n* bosse *f*.

hunch I *n* intuition *f*.
II *vtr* **to ~ one's shoulders** rentrer les épaules.

hunched *adj* [*back, figure*] voûté/-e; [*shoulders*] rentré/-e.

hundred ▶389 I *n* cent *m*; **two ~** deux cents; **two ~ and one** deux cent un; **in nineteen ~** en mille neuf cents; **in nineteen ~ and three** en mille neuf cent trois; **~s of times** des centaines de fois.
II *pron, det* cent; **two ~ francs** deux cents francs; **two ~ and five francs** deux cent cinq francs; **about a ~ people** une centaine de personnes.

hundredth *n, adj, adv* centième (*mf*).

hundredweight ▶573 *n* (GB) = *50.80 kg*; (US) = *45.36 kg*.

Hungarian ▶553 I *n* **1** (person) Hongrois/-e *m/f*; **2** (language) hongrois *m*.
II *adj* hongrois/-e.

Hungary ▶448 *pr n* Hongrie *f*.

hunger *n* faim *f*.

hunger strike *n* grève *f* de la faim.

hungry *adj* **to be ~** avoir faim; **to make sb ~** donner faim à qn; **~ for** assoiffé/-e de [*success, power*].

hunk *n* **1** (of bread, cheese) gros morceau *m*; **2**○ (man) beau mec○ *m*.

hunt I *n* **1** (for animals) chasse *f* (**for** à); **2** (search) recherche *f* (**for** de).
II *vtr* rechercher [*person*]; chasser [*animal*].
III *vi* **1** (for prey) chasser; **2** (search) **to ~ for sth** chercher [qch] partout [*object, person*].

hunter *n* (person) chasseur/-euse *m/f*.

hunting *n* chasse *f* (**of** à); **to go ~** aller à la chasse.

hurdle ▶504 *n* **1** (Sport) haie *f*; **2** (obstacle) obstacle *m*.

hurl *vtr* **1** (throw) lancer (**at** sur); **2** (shout) **to ~ insults at sb** accabler qn d'injures.

hurrah, **hurray** *n*, *excl* hourra (*m*).

hurricane *n* ouragan *m*.

hurry I *n* hâte *f*, empressement *m*; **to be in a ~** être pressé/-e (**to do** de faire); **to leave in a ~** partir à la hâte.
II *vtr* terminer [qch] à la hâte [*meal, task*]; bousculer [*person*].
III *vi* se dépêcher (**over doing** de faire); **to ~ out** sortir précipitamment.
■ **hurry up** se dépêcher; **~ up!** dépêche-toi!

hurt I *adj* (gen) blessé/-e; **to feel ~** être peiné/-e.
II *vtr* **1** (injure) **to ~ oneself** se blesser, se faire mal; **to ~ one's back** se blesser or se faire mal au dos; **2** (cause pain to) faire mal à; **you're ~ing my arm** vous me faites mal au bras; **3** (emotionally) blesser; (offend) froisser; **to ~ sb's feelings** blesser quelqu'un.
III *vi* **1** (be painful) faire mal; **my throat ~s** j'ai mal à la gorge; **2** (emotionally) blesser.

hurtful *adj* blessant/-e.

hurtle *vi* **to ~ down sth** dévaler qch; **to ~ along a road** foncer sur une route.

husband *n* mari *m*; (on form) époux *m*.

hush I *n* silence *m*.
II *excl* chut!
■ **hush up**: ¶ **~ [sth] up** étouffer [*affair*]; ¶ **~ [sb] up** faire taire [*person*].

hustle I *n* **~ (and bustle)** (lively) effervescence *f*; (tiring) agitation *f*.
II *vtr* pousser, bousculer [*person*].

hut *n* (gen) cabane *f*; (dwelling) hutte *f*; (on beach) cabine *f* (de plage).

hutch *n* (for rabbits) clapier *m*.

hydrant *n* (also **fire ~**) bouche *f* d'incendie.

hydraulic *adj* hydraulique.

hydrofoil *n* **1** (craft) hydroptère *m*; **2** (foil) aile *f* portante.

hydrogen *n* hydrogène *m*.

hyena *n* hyène *f*.

hygiene *n* hygiène *f*.

hygienic *adj* hygiénique.

hymn *n* cantique *m*.

hype○ *n* battage *m* publicitaire.
■ **hype up** faire du battage pour [*film, star, book*]; gonfler [*story*].

hyperactive *adj* hyperactif/-ive.

hypermarket *n* (GB) hypermarché *m*.

hyperventilate *vi* être en hyperventilation.

hyphen *n* trait *m* d'union.

hypnosis *n* hypnose *f*.

hypnotist *n* hypnotiseur *m*.

hypnotize *vtr* hypnotiser.

hypocrisy *n* hypocrisie *f*.

hypocrite *n* hypocrite *mf*.

hypocritical *adj* hypocrite.

hypodermic *adj* hypodermique.

hypothermia *n* hypothermie *f*.

hysteria *n* hystérie *f*.

hysterical *adj* **1** [*person, behaviour*] hystérique; **2**○ (funny) délirant/-e.

hysterics *n* **1** (fit) crise *f* de nerfs; **to have ~** avoir une crise de nerfs; **2** (laughter) **to be in ~** rire aux larmes.

Ii

i, I[1] *n* i, I *m*.

I[2] *pron* je, j'; **I am called Frances** je m'appelle Frances; **I closed the door** j'ai fermé la porte; **he's a student but I'm not** il est étudiant mais moi pas; **he and I went to the cinema** lui et moi sommes allés au cinéma.

ice I *n* glace *f*; (on roads) verglas *m*; (in drink) glaçons *mpl*.
II *vtr* glacer [*cake*].
III iced *pp adj* [*water*] avec des glaçons; **~d tea** thé glacé.
■ **ice over** [*windscreen, river*] se couvrir de glace.

iceberg *n* iceberg *m*.

icebox *n* **1** (GB) (freezer compartment) freezer *m*; **2** (US) (fridge) réfrigérateur *m*.

ice cream *n* glace *f*.

ice-cube *n* glaçon *m*.

ice hockey ▶504 *n* hockey *m* sur glace.

Iceland ▶448 *pr n* Islande *f*.

Icelandic ▶553 **I** *n* (language) islandais.
II *adj* [*people, customs*] islandais/-e.

ice rink *n* patinoire *f*.

ice-skate ▶504 **I** *n* patin *m* à glace.
II *vi* faire du patin *m* à glace.

ice-skating ▶504 *n* patinage *m* sur glace.

icicle *n* stalactite *f* (de glace).

icing *n* glaçage *m*.

icing sugar *n* (GB) sucre *m* glace.

icon *n* icône *f*.

icy *adj* **1** [*road*] verglacé/-e; **2** [*wind*] glacial/-e; [*hands*] glacé/-e; **3** [*look, reception*] glacial/-e.

ID *n* pièce *f* d'identité.

ID card *n* carte *f* d'identité.

idea *n* idée *f* (**about, on** sur); **I have no ~** je n'ai aucune idée; **to have no ~ why/how** ne pas savoir pourquoi/comment; **I've an ~ that he might be lying** j'ai dans l'idée qu'il ment.

ideal I *n* idéal *m*.
II *adj* idéal/-e.

idealism *n* idéalisme *m*.

idealist *n* idéaliste *mf*.

idealistic *adj* idéaliste.

idealize *vtr* idéaliser.

identical *adj* identique (**to, with** à).

identical twin *n* vrai jumeau/vraie jumelle *m/f*.

identification *n* **1** identification *f* (**with** à); **2** (proof of identity) pièce *f* d'identité.

identify I *vtr* identifier (**as** comme étant; **to** à); (pick out) distinguer; **to ~ sb/sth with sb/sth** identifier qn/qch à qn/qch.
II *vi* **to ~ with** s'identifier à.

identity *n* identité *f*.

identity card *n* carte *f* d'identité.

identity parade *n* (GB) séance *f* d'identification.

ideological *adj* idéologique.

ideology *n* idéologie *f*.

idiom *n* **1** (phrase) idiome *m*; **2** (language) (of speakers) parler *m*; (of theatre, sport) langue *f*; (of music) style *m*.

idiomatic *adj* idiomatique.

idiosyncrasy *n* particularité *f*.

idiot *n* idiot/-e *m/f*.

idiotic *adj* bête.

idle I *adj* **1** (lazy) [*person*] paresseux/-euse; **2** [*boast, threat*] vain/-e; [*curiosity*] oiseux/-euse; [*chatter*] inutile; **3** (without occupation) [*person*] oisif/-ive; [*day, hour, moment*] de loisir; **4** [*dock, mine*] à l'arrêt; [*machine*] arrêté/-e.
II *vi* [*engine*] tourner au ralenti.
■ **idle away** passer [qch] à ne rien faire [*day, time*].

idol *n* idole *f*.

idolize *vtr* adorer [*friend, parent*]; idolâtrer [*star*].

idyllic *adj* idyllique.

ie (*abbr* = **that is**) c-à-d.

if I *conj* **1** si; **~ I won a lot of money, I would travel** si je gagnais beaucoup d'argent, je voyagerais; **~ I had known, I would have told you** si j'avais su, je te l'aurais dit; **~ I were you, I...** (moi) à ta place, je...; **~ not** sinon; **I wonder ~ they will come** je me demande s'ils vont venir; **do you mind ~ I smoke?** cela vous dérange si je fume?; **what ~ he died?** et s'il mourait?; **2** (although) bien que; **it's a good shop, ~ a little expensive** c'est un bon magasin, bien qu'un peu cher.
II if only *phr* **1** (I wish) si seulement; **~ only I had known!** si (seulement) j'avais su!; **2 ~ only because (of)** ne serait-ce qu'à cause de; **~ only for a moment** ne serait-ce que pour un instant.

igloo *n* igloo *m*, iglou *m*.

ignite I *vtr* faire exploser [*fuel*]; enflammer [*material*].
II *vi* [*petrol, gas*] s'enflammer; [*rubbish, timber*] prendre feu.

ignition *n* **1** (system) allumage *m*; **2** (also **~ switch**) contact *m*.

ignorance *n* ignorance *f*.

ignorant *adj* (of a subject) ignorant/-e; (uneducated) inculte; **to be ~ about** tout ignorer de [*subject*]; **to be ~ of** ignorer [*possibilities*].

ignore *vtr* ignorer [*person*]; ne pas relever [*mistake, remark*]; ne pas tenir compte de [*feeling, fact*]; ne pas suivre [*advice*]; se désintéresser complètement de [*problem*].

ill I *n* mal *m*; **to wish sb ~** souhaiter du mal à qn.

II *adj* malade; **I feel ~** je ne me sens pas bien; **to be taken ~**, **to fall ~** tomber malade.
III *adv* **he is ~ suited to the post** il n'est guère fait pour ce poste; **to speak ~ of sb** dire du mal de qn.

ill at ease *adj* gêné/-e, mal à l'aise.

illegal I *n* (US) immigrant/-e *m/f* clandestin/-e.
II *adj* (gen) illégal/-e; [*parking*] illicite; [*immigrant*] clandestin/-e; (Sport) irrégulier/-ière.

illegible *adj* illisible.

illegitimate *adj* illégitime.

illicit *adj* illicite.

illiterate *n, adj* analphabète (*mf*).

illness ▶ 533 *n* maladie *f*.

illogical *adj* illogique.

illuminate *vtr* éclairer.

illuminated *adj* [*sign*] lumineux/-euse.

illumination *n* (lighting) éclairage *m*.

illuminations *n pl* (GB) illuminations *fpl*.

illusion *n* illusion *f*; **to have no ~s about sth** ne pas se faire d'illusions sur qch; **to be** or **to labour under the ~ that** s'imaginer que.

illustrate *vtr* illustrer.

illustration *n* illustration *f*.

illustrator ▶ 626 *n* illustrateur/-trice *m/f*.

ill will *n* rancune *f*.

image *n* (gen) image *f*; (of company, personality) image *f* de marque; **he is the (spitting) ~ of you** c'est toi tout craché.

imagery *n* images *fpl*.

imaginary *adj* imaginaire.

imagination *n* imagination *f*.

imaginative *adj* [*person, performance*] plein d'imagination; [*mind*] imaginatif/-ive; [*solution, device*] ingénieux/-ieuse.

imagine *vtr* **1** (visualize, picture) (s')imaginer; **to ~ being rich/king** s'imaginer riche/roi; **you must have ~d it** ce doit être un effet de ton imagination; **2** (suppose) supposer, imaginer (**that** que).

imbalance *n* déséquilibre *m*.

imbecile *n, adj* imbécile (*mf*).

imitate *vtr* imiter.

imitation I *n* imitation *f*.
II *adj* [*snow*] artificiel/-ielle; **~ fur** imitation *f* fourrure; **~ jewel** faux bijou *m*; **~ leather** similicuir *m*.

immaculate *adj* [*dress, manners*] impeccable; [*performance*] parfait/-e.

immaterial *adj* **1** (unimportant) sans importance; **2** (intangible) immatériel/-ielle.

immature *adj* **1** [*plant*] qui n'est pas arrivé à maturité; **2** (childish) immature; **don't be so ~!** ne te conduis pas comme un enfant!

immediate *adj* **1** [*effect, reaction*] immédiat/-e; [*thought*] premier/-ière (*before n*); **2** [*concern, goal*] premier/-ière (*before n*); [*problem, crisis*] urgent/-e; **3** [*vicinity*] immédiat/-e; **his ~ family** ses proches; **in the ~ future** dans l'avenir proche.

immediately *adv* immédiatement; **~ after/before** juste avant/après.

immense *adj* immense.

immerse *vtr* plonger (**in** dans).

immigrant *n, adj* (recent) immigrant/-e (*m/f*); (established) immigré/-e (*m/f*).

immigration *n* immigration *f*.

imminent *adj* imminent/-e.

immobile *adj* immobile.

immobilize *vtr* paralyser [*traffic, organization*]; immobiliser [*engine, patient, limb*].

immoral *adj* immoral/-e.

immortal *n, adj* immortel/-elle (*m/f*).

immortality *n* immortalité *f*.

immune *adj* **1** (Med) [*person*] immunisé/-e (**to** contre); [*reaction, system*] immunitaire; **2** (oblivious) **~ to** insensible à; **3 to be ~ from** être à l'abri de [*attack, arrest*]; être exempté/-e de [*tax*].

immunity *n* immunité *f* (**to, against** contre).

immunize *vtr* immuniser.

impact *n* **1** (effect) impact *m* (**on** sur); **to make an ~** faire de l'effet; **2** (of hammer, vehicle) choc *m*; (of bomb, bullet) impact *m*; **on ~** au moment de l'impact.

impair *vtr* affecter [*performance*]; diminuer [*ability*]; affaiblir [*hearing, vision*]; détériorer [*health*].

impaired *adj* [*hearing, vision*] affaibli/-e; **his speech is ~** il a des problèmes d'élocution.

impart *vtr* **1** transmettre [*knowledge, enthusiasm*] (**to** à); communiquer [*information*] (**to** à); **2** donner [*atmosphere*].

impartial *adj* [*advice, judge*] impartial/-e; [*account*] objectif/-ive.

impassable *adj* [*obstacle*] infranchissable; [*road*] impraticable.

impassive *adj* impassible.

impatience *n* **1** (eagerness) impatience *f* (**to do** de faire); **2** (irritation) agacement *m* (**with** à l'égard de; **at** devant).

impatient *adj* **1** (eager) [*person*] impatient/-e; [*gesture, tone*] d'impatience; **to be ~ to do** être impatient/-e or avoir hâte de faire; **2** (irritable) agacé/-e (**at** par); **to be/get ~ with sb** s'impatienter contre qn.

impeccable *adj* [*behaviour*] irréprochable; [*appearance*] impeccable.

impede *vtr* entraver.

impenetrable *adj* impénétrable.

imperative I *n* impératif *m*.
II *adj* [*need*] urgent/-e; [*tone*] impérieux/-ieuse.

imperceptible *adj* imperceptible.

imperfect I *n* imparfait *m*.
II *adj* [*goods*] défectueux/-euse; [*logic, knowledge*] imparfait/-e; **the ~ tense** l'imparfait *m*.

imperial *adj* **1** (gen) impérial/-e; **2** (GB) [*measure*] conforme aux normes britanniques.

imperious *adj* impérieux/-ieuse.

impersonal *adj* impersonnel/-elle.

impersonate *vtr* (imitate) imiter; (pretend to be) se faire passer pour [*police officer*].

impersonator *n* imitateur/-trice *m/f*.

impertinent *adj* impertinent/-e (**to** envers).

Illnesses, Aches, and Pains

Where does it hurt?

where does it hurt? = où est-ce que ça vous fait mal?
his leg hurts = sa jambe lui fait mal

(Do not confuse ***faire mal à qn*** with ***faire du mal à qn***, which means *to harm sb.*)

he has a pain in his leg = il a mal à la jambe

Note that with ***avoir mal à*** French uses the definite article (*le, la, les,* or *l'*) with the part of the body, where English has a possessive, hence:

***his head** was aching* = il avait mal à **la tête**

Accidents

*she broke **her** leg* = elle s'est cassé **la** jambe
*they burned **their** hands* = ils se sont brûlé **les** mains

Chronic conditions

French often uses ***fragile*** (***weak***) to express a chronic condition:

*he has a **weak** heart* = il a le cœur **fragile**

Note that French uses the definite article here.

Being ill

French mostly uses the definite article with the name of an illness:

to have flu / measles = avoir **la** grippe / **la** rougeole

This applies to most infectious diseases. However, note the exceptions ending in ***-ite*** (eg ***une hépatite***, ***une bronchite***) below.

When the illness affects a specific part of the body, French uses the indefinite article:

to have cancer / pneumonia = avoir **un** cancer / **une** pneumonie
to have a stomach ulcer = avoir **un** ulcère à l'estomac

Most English words in ***-itis*** (French ***-ite***) work like this:

to have bronchitis / hepatitis = avoir **une** bronchite / **une** hépatite

When the illness is a generalized condition, French tends to use ***du***, ***de la*** or ***des***:

to have rheumatism = avoir **des** rhumatismes
to have asthma / arthritis = avoir **de l'**asthme / **de l'**arthrite

One exception here is:

to have hay fever = avoir le rhume des foins

When there is an adjective for such conditions, this is often preferred in French:

to have asthma / epilepsy = être asthmatique / épileptique

Falling ill

The above guidelines on the use of the definite and indefinite articles in French hold good for talking about the onset of illnesses.

French has no general equivalent of ***to get***. However, where English can use ***catch***, French can use ***attraper***:

*to **catch** malaria* = **attraper** la malaria
*to **catch** a cold / bronchitis* = **attraper** un rhume / une bronchite

For attacks of chronic illnesses, French uses ***faire une crise de***:

to have an** asthma / epileptic **attack = **faire une crise** d'asthme / d'épilepsie

Treatment

*to be treated **for** polio* = se faire soigner **contre** la polio
*to take sth **for** hay fever* = prendre qch **contre** le rhume des foins
*to be operated on **for** cancer* = être opéré **d'**un cancer
*to operate on sb **for** appendicitis* = opérer qn **de** l'appendicite

impervious *adj* (to charm, suffering) indifférent/-e (**to** à); (to demands) imperméable (**to** à).

impetuous *adj* [*person*] impétueux/-euse; [*action*] impulsif/-ive.

impetus *n* **1** impulsion *f* (**to** à); **2** (momentum) élan *m*; **to gain/lose ~** prendre/perdre de l'élan.

impinge *vi* **to ~ on** (restrict) empiéter sur; (affect) affecter.

implacable *adj* implacable.

implant I *n* implant *m*.
II *vtr* implanter (**in** dans).

implement I *n* (gen) instrument *m*; (tool) outil *m*; **farm ~s** outillage *m* agricole.
II *vtr* exécuter [*contract, decision, idea*]; mettre [qch] en application [*law*].

implicate *vtr* impliquer (**in** dans).

implication *n* **1** (possible consequence) implication *f*; **2** (suggestion) insinuation *f*.

implicit *adj* **1** (implied) implicite (**in** dans); **2** [*faith, trust*] absolu/-e.

imply *vtr* **1** [*person*] (insinuate) insinuer (**that** que); (make known) laisser entendre (**that** que); **2** (mean) [*argument*] impliquer; [*term, word*] laisser supposer (**that** que).

impolite *adj* impoli/-e (**to** envers).

import I *n* importation *f*.
II *vtr* importer (**from** de; **to** en).

importance *n* importance *f*.

important *adj* important/-e; **it is ~ that** il est important que (+ *subjunctive*); **his children are very ~ to him** ses enfants comptent beaucoup pour lui.

importer *n* importateur/-trice *m/f*.

impose I *vtr* imposer [*embargo, rule*] (**on sb** à qn; **on sth** sur qch); infliger [*sanction*] (**on** à); **to ~ a fine on sb** frapper qn d'une amende; **to ~ a tax on tobacco** imposer le tabac.
II *vi* s'imposer; **to ~ on sb's kindness** abuser de la bonté de qn.

imposing *adj* [*person*] imposant/-e; [*sight*] impressionnant/-e.

impossible I *n* **the ~** l'impossible *m*.
II *adj* impossible; **to make it ~ for sb to do** mettre qn dans l'impossibilité de faire.

impotent *adj* impuissant/-e.

impound *vtr* emmener [qch] à la fourrière [*vehicle*]; confisquer [*goods*].

impractical *adj* [*suggestion, idea*] peu réaliste; **to be ~** [*person*] manquer d'esprit pratique.

imprecise *adj* imprécis/-e.

impress I *vtr* **1** impressionner [*person*] (**with** par; **by doing** en faisant); **they were ~ed** ça leur a fait bonne impression; **2 to ~ sth (up)on sb** faire bien comprendre qch à qn.
II *vi* faire bonne impression.

impression *n* **1** (gen) impression *f*; **to be under** or **have the ~ that** avoir l'impression que; **to make a good/bad ~** faire bonne/mauvaise impression (**on** sur); **2** (imitation) imitation *f*; **to do ~s** faire des imitations.

impressionable *adj* influençable.

impressive *adj* (gen) impressionnant/-e; [*building, sight*] imposant/-e.

imprint I *n* empreinte *f*.
II *vtr* **1** (fix) graver (**on** dans); **2** (print) imprimer (**on** sur).

imprison *vtr* emprisonner.

improbable *adj* (unlikely to happen) improbable; (unlikely to be true) invraisemblable.

impromptu *adj* impromptu/-e.

improper *adj* (dishonest) irrégulier/-ière; (indecent) indécent/-e; (incorrect) impropre, abusif/-ive.

improve I *vtr* (gen) améliorer; augmenter [*chances*]; **to ~ one's mind** se cultiver (l'esprit).
II *vi* **1** s'améliorer; **2 to ~ on** améliorer [*score*]; renchérir sur [*offer*].

improvement *n* **1** amélioration *f* (**in, of, to** de); **the new edition is an ~ on the old one** la nouvelle édition est bien meilleure que l'ancienne; **2** (in house) aménagement *m*; **home ~s** aménagements *mpl* du domicile.

improvise I *vtr* improviser; **an ~d table** une table de fortune.
II *vi* improviser.

impudent *adj* insolent/-e, impudent/-e.

impulse *n* impulsion *f*; **to have a sudden ~ to do** avoir une envie soudaine de faire; **on (an) ~** sur un coup de tête.

impulsive *adj* (spontaneous) spontané/-e; (rash) impulsif/-ive.

impure *adj* impur/-e.

in

■ **Note** For translations of *in* with geographical place names (*in Europe*, *in Greece*, *in Rome*), see the usage note for ***Countries, Cities, and Continents*** ▶ 448.

I *prep* **1** (inside) dans; **~ the box** dans la boîte; **~ the newspaper** dans le journal; **~ the school/town** dans l'école/la ville; **~ school/town** à l'école/en ville; **~ the country(side)** à la campagne; **~ the photo** sur la photo; **chicken ~ a white wine sauce** du poulet à la sauce au vin blanc; **2** (showing occupation, activity) dans; **~ insurance** dans les assurances; **to be ~ politics** faire de la politique; **to be ~ the team** faire partie de l'équipe; **3** (present in) chez; **it's rare ~ cats** c'est rare chez les chats; **he hasn't got it ~ him to succeed** il n'est pas fait pour réussir; **4** (showing manner, medium) en; **~ Greek** en grec; **~ B flat** en si bémol; **~ a skirt** en jupe; **dressed ~ black** habillé/-e en noir; **~ pencil/ink** au crayon/à l'encre; **to speak ~ a whisper** chuchoter; **~ pairs** par deux; **~ a circle** en cercle; **~ the rain** sous la pluie; **5** (as regards) **rich ~ minerals** riche en minéraux; **deaf ~ one ear** sourd/-e d'une oreille; **10 cm ~ length** 10 cm de long; **6** (because of) dans; **~ his hurry** dans sa précipitation; **~ the confusion** dans la mêlée; **7** (with present participle) en; **~ accepting** en acceptant; **~ doing so** en faisant cela; **8** (with superlatives) de; **the tallest tower ~ the world** la plus grande tour du monde; **9** (in ratios) **a gradient of 1 ~ 4** une pente de 25%; **a tax of 20 pence ~ the pound** une taxe de 20 pence par livre sterling; **to have a one ~ five chance** avoir une chance sur cinq; **10** (with numbers) **she's ~ her twenties** elle a entre vingt et trente ans; **to cut sth ~ three** couper qch en trois; **the temperature was ~ the thirties** il faisait dans les trente degrés; **11** (during) **~ May** en mai; **~ 1963** en 1963; **~ summer** en été; **~ the night** pendant la nuit; **~ the morning(s)** le matin; **at four ~ the morning** à quatre heures du matin; **~ the twenties** dans les années 20; **12** (within) **~ ten minutes** en dix minutes; **I'll be back ~ half an hour** je serai de retour dans une demi-heure; **13** (for) depuis; **it hasn't rained ~ weeks** il n'a pas plu depuis des semaines.

II *adv* **1 to come ~** entrer; **to run ~** entrer en courant; **to ask** or **invite sb ~** faire entrer qn; **2** (at home) **to be ~** être là; **to stay ~** rester à la maison; **3** (arrived) **the train is ~** le train est en gare; **the ferry is ~** le ferry est à quai; **4 the tide is ~** c'est marée haute; **5** (Sport) **the ball is ~** la balle est bonne; **6** (in supply) **we don't have any ~** nous n'en avons pas en stock; **to get some beer ~** aller chercher de la bière.

III○ *adj* **to be ~**, **to be the ~ thing** être à la mode.

IV in and out *phr* **to come ~ and out** entrer et sortir; **to weave ~ and out of** se faufiler entre [*traffic, tables*].

IDIOMS **he's ~ for a shock/surprise** il va avoir un choc/être surpris.

inability *n* incapacité *f* (**to do** de faire).

inaccessible *adj* (out of reach) inaccessible; (hard to understand) peu accessible (**to** à).

inaccurate *adj* inexact/-e.

inadequate *adj* insuffisant/-e (**for** pour).

inadvisable *adj* inopportun/-e, à déconseiller.

inane *adj* [*person, conversation*] idiot/-e; [*programme*] débile○.

inanimate *adj* inanimé/-e.

inappropriate *adj* **1** [*behaviour*] inconvenant/-e, peu convenable; [*remark*] inopportun/-e; **2** [*advice, word*] qui n'est pas approprié.

inarticulate *adj* **1 to be ~** ne pas savoir s'exprimer; **2** [*mumble*] inarticulé/-e; [*speech*] inintelligible.

inasmuch: **inasmuch as** *phr* (insofar as) dans la mesure où; (seeing as) vu que.

inaudible *adj* inaudible.

inauguration *n* (of exhibition) inauguration *f*; (of president) investiture *f*.

in-between *adj* intermédiaire.

inbuilt *adj* intrinsèque.

incapable *adj* incapable (**of doing** de faire).

incapacitate *vtr* [*accident, illness*] immobiliser.

incense *n* encens *m*.

incensed *adj* outré/-e (**at** de; **by** par).

incentive *n* **1 to give sb the ~ to do** donner envie à qn de faire; **there is no ~ for people to save** rien n'incite les gens à faire des économies; **2** (also **cash ~**) prime *f*.

incessant *adj* incessant/-e.

incessantly *adv* sans cesse.

incest *n* inceste *m*.

incestuous *adj* incestueux/-euse.

inch ▶573 *n* **1** pouce *m* (= *2.54 cm*); **2 ~ by ~** petit à petit; **to come within an ~ of winning** passer à deux doigts de la victoire.

incident *n* incident *m*.

incidental *adj* [*detail, remark*] secondaire.

incidentally *adv* (by the way) à propos; (by chance) par la même occasion.

incinerate *vtr* incinérer.

incite *vtr* **to ~ violence** inciter à la violence; **to ~ sb to do** pousser or inciter qn à faire.

inclination *n* inclination *f*.

incline I *vtr* **1** incliner [*head*]; **2 to be ~d to do** avoir tendance à faire; **if you feel so ~d** si l'envie vous en prend.

II *vi* **1** (tend) **to ~ to** or **towards** tendre vers; **2** [*road, tower*] s'incliner.

include *vtr* inclure, comprendre; **all the ministers, Blanc ~d** tous les ministres, Blanc inclu; **breakfast is ~d in the price** le petit déjeuner est compris.

including *prep* (y) compris; **£50 ~ VAT** 50 livres sterling TVA comprise; **~ service** service compris; **~ July** y compris juillet; **not ~ July** sans compter juillet.

inclusive *adj* inclus/-e; [*price*] forfaitaire; **all-~** tout compris.

incoherent *adj* incohérent/-e.

income *n* revenus *mpl*, revenu *m*.

income tax *n* impôt *m* sur le revenu.

incomparable *adj* sans pareil/-eille.

incompatible *adj* incompatible.

incompetent *adj* [*doctor, government*] incompétent/-e; [*work, performance*] mauvais/-e (*before n*).

incomplete *adj* **1** [*work, building*] inachevé/-e; **2** [*set*] incomplet/-ète.

incomprehensible *adj* [*reason*] incompréhensible; [*speech*] inintelligible.

inconceivable *adj* inconcevable.

incongruous *adj* [*sight*] déconcertant/-e; [*appearance*] surprenant/-e.

inconsiderate *adj* [*person*] peu attentif/-ive à autrui; [*remark*] maladroit/-e; **to be ~ towards sb** manquer d'égards envers qn.

inconsistent *adj* [*work*] inégal/-e; [*behaviour*] changeant/-e; [*argument*] incohérent/-e; [*attitude*] inconsistant/-e; **to be ~ with** être en contradiction avec.

inconspicuous *adj* [*person*] qui passe inaperçu/-e; [*place, clothing*] discret/-ète.

inconvenience I *n* **1** (trouble) dérangement *m*; **to put sb to great ~** causer beaucoup de dérangement à qn; **2** (disadvantage) inconvénient *m*.

II *vtr* déranger.

inconvenient *adj* [*location, arrangement*] incommode; [*time*] inopportun/-e.

incorporate *vtr* **1** (make part of) incorporer (**into** dans); **2** (contain) comporter; **3 Smith and Brown Incorporated** Smith et Brown SA.
incorrect *adj* incorrect/-e (**to do** de faire).
incorrigible *adj* incorrigible.
increase I *n* **1** (in amount) augmentation *f* (**in, of** de); **a 5% ~** une augmentation de 5%; **2** (in degree) accroissement *m*; **to be on the ~** être en progression.
II *vtr* augmenter (**by** de; **to** jusqu'à).
III *vi* augmenter (**by** de); **to ~ in value** prendre de la valeur; **to ~ in size** s'agrandir.
increased *adj* [*demand, risk*] accru/-e.
increasing *adj* [*number*] croissant/-e.
increasingly *adv* de plus en plus.
incredible *adj* incroyable.
incredulous *adj* incrédule.
incriminating *adj* [*statement, document*] compromettant/-e; [*evidence*] incriminant/-e.
incubator *n* (for child) couveuse *f*; (for eggs, bacteria) incubateur *m*.
incur *vtr* contracter [*debts*]; subir [*loss*]; encourir [*expense, risk, wrath*].
incurable *adj* **1** [*disease*] incurable; **2** [*optimist, romantic*] incorrigible.
incursion *n* (gen) intrusion *f*; (Mil) incursion *f*.
indebted *adj* **to be ~ to sb** (under an obligation) être redevable à qn; (grateful) être reconnaissant/-e à qn.
indecent *adj* **1** (improper) indécent/-e; **2** (unreasonable) [*haste*] malséant/-e.
indecent assault *n* attentat *m* à la pudeur.
indecent exposure *n* outrage *m* public à la pudeur.
indecisive *adj* (gen) indécis/-e (**about** quant à); [*battle, election*] peu concluant/-e.
indeed *adv* **1** (certainly) en effet, effectivement; **yes ~!** bien sûr que oui!; **'~ you can'** 'bien sûr que oui'; **2** (in fact) en fait; **3** (for emphasis) vraiment; **that was praise ~** c'était vraiment un compliment; **thank you very much ~** merci mille fois.
indefinite *adj* **1** (vague) vague; **2** [*period, delay*] illimité/-e; [*number*] indéterminé/-e; **3 the ~ article** l'article *m* indéfini.
indefinitely *adv* [*continue, stay*] indéfiniment; [*postpone, ban*] pour une durée indéterminée.
indelible *adj* [*ink, mark*] indélébile; [*impression*] ineffaçable.
independence *n* indépendance *f*.
Independence Day *n* (US) fête *f* de l'Indépendance.
independent *adj* indépendant/-e (**of** de).
in-depth I *adj* [*analysis, study*] approfondi/-e; [*guide*] détaillé/-e.
II **in depth** *adv* [*examine, study*] en détail.
indescribable *adj* [*chaos, noise*] indescriptible; [*pleasure, beauty*] inexprimable.
indestructible *adj* indestructible.
index *n* **1** (of book) index *m inv*; **2** (catalogue) catalogue *m*; **card ~** fichier *m*; **3** (Econ) indice *m*.
index card *n* fiche *f*.
index finger *n* index *m inv*.
index-linked *adj* indexé/-e.
India ▶ 448 *pr n* Inde *f*.
Indian ▶ 553 I *n* **1** (from India) Indien/-ienne *m/f*; **2** (Native American) Indien/-ienne *m/f* d'Amérique.
II *adj* **1** (of India) indien/-ienne; **2** (Native American) indien/-ienne, amérindien/-ienne.
Indian Ocean *pr n* **the ~** l'océan *m* Indien.
Indian summer *n* été *m* de la Saint Martin.
indicate I *vtr* indiquer (**that** que; **with** de).
II *vi* [*driver*] mettre son clignotant; [*cyclist*] faire signe.
indication *n* indication *f*, indice *m*.
indicative I *n* (in grammar) indicatif *m*.
II *adj* **to be ~ of** montrer.
indicator *n* **1** (pointer) aiguille *f*; **2** (board) tableau *m*; **3** (on car) clignotant *m*.
indict *vtr* inculper.
indictment *n* **1** (Law) acte *m* d'accusation; **2** (criticism) mise *f* en accusation.
indifference *n* indifférence *f*.
indifferent *adj* **1** (uninterested) indifférent/-e (**to, as to** à); **2** (mediocre) médiocre.
indigenous *adj* indigène (**to** à).
indigestion *n* indigestion *f*; **to have ~** avoir des brûlures d'estomac.
indignant *adj* indigné/-e (**at** de; **about, over** par).
indigo ▶ 438 *n, adj* indigo (*m*) *inv*.
indirect *adj* indirect/-e.
indirectly *adv* indirectement.
indiscreet *adj* indiscret/-ète.
indiscriminate *adj* **1** (random) sans distinction; **2** [*person*] sans discernement.
indispensable *adj* indispensable.
indisputable *adj* [*champion*] indiscuté/-e; [*fact*] indiscutable.
indistinct *adj* [*sound, markings*] indistinct/-e; [*memory*] confus/-e; [*photograph*] flou/-e.
individual I *n* individu *m*.
II *adj* **1** [*effort, freedom, portion*] individuel/-elle; [*comfort, attitude*] personnel/-elle; [*tuition*] particulier/-ière; **2** (separate) **each ~ article** chaque article (individuellement); **3** (idiosyncratic) particulier/-ière.
individually *adv* (personally, in person) individuellement; (one at a time) séparément.
indoctrinate *vtr* endoctriner.
indoor *adj* [*pool, court*] couvert/-e; [*lavatory*] à l'intérieur; [*photography, shoes*] d'intérieur.
indoors *adv* à l'intérieur, dans la maison; **~ and outdoors** dedans et dehors; **to go ~** rentrer.
induce *vtr* **1** (persuade) persuader (**to do** de faire); (stronger) inciter (**to** à; **to do** à faire); **2** (bring about) provoquer.
indulge I *vtr* **1** céder à [*whim, desire*]; **2** gâter [*child*]; céder à [*adult*].
II *vi* **to ~ in** se livrer à [*speculation*]; se complaire dans [*nostalgia*]; se laisser tenter par [*food*].
III *v refl* **to ~ oneself** se faire plaisir.

indulgence *n* **1** (tolerance) indulgence *f* (**towards** envers; **for** pour); **2 ~ in food** gourmandise *f*; **it's my one ~** c'est mon péché mignon.
indulgent *adj* indulgent/-e (**to, towards** pour, envers).
industrial *adj* (gen) industriel/-ielle; [*accident*] du travail.
industrialize *vtr* industrialiser.
industrious *adj* diligent/-e.
industry *n* **1** industrie *f*; **the oil ~** l'industrie du pétrole; **2** (diligence) zèle *m* (au travail).
inedible *adj* [*meal*] immangeable; [*plants*] non comestible.
ineffective *adj* inefficace.
ineffectual *adj* [*person*] incapable; [*policy*] inefficace; [*attempt*] infructueux/-euse.
inefficiency *n* (lack of organization) manque *m* d'organisation; (incompetence) incompétence *f*; (of machine, method) inefficacité *f*.
inefficient *adj* (disorganized) mal organisé/-e; (incompetent) incompétent/-e; (not effective) inefficace.
ineligible *adj* **to be ~** (for job) ne pas remplir les conditions pour poser sa candidature (**for** à); (for election) être inéligible; (for pension, benefit) ne pas avoir droit (**for** à).
inequality *n* inégalité *f*.
inert *adj* inerte.
inertia *n* inertie *f*.
inevitable *adj* inévitable (**that** que + *subjunctive*).
inexcusable *adj* inexcusable (**that** que + *subjunctive*).
inexpensive *adj* pas cher/chère.
inexperienced *adj* inexpérimenté/-e.
inexplicable *adj* inexplicable.
infallible *adj* infaillible.
infamous *adj* [*person*] tristement célèbre; [*crime*] infâme.
infancy *n* **1** petite enfance *f*; **2** (figurative) débuts *mpl*; **in its ~** à ses débuts.
infant *n* (baby) bébé *m*; (child) petit enfant *m*.
infantry *n* infanterie *f*, fantassins *mpl*.
infant school *n* ≈ école *f* maternelle.
infatuated *adj* **to be ~ with** être entiché/-e de.
infatuation *n* engouement *m* (**with** pour).
infect *vtr* contaminer [*person, blood, food*]; infecter [*wound*].
infection *n* infection *f*.
infectious *adj* **1** [*disease*] infectieux/-ieuse; [*person*] contagieux/-ieuse; **2** [*laughter*] communicatif/-ive.
infer *vtr* déduire.
inferior I *n* inférieur/-e *m/f*.
II *adj* **1** [*goods, work*] de qualité inférieure; **2** [*position*] inférieur/-e; **to make sb feel ~** donner un sentiment d'infériorité à qn.
inferiority *n* infériorité *f* (**to** vis-à-vis de).
inferiority complex *n* complexe *m* d'infériorité.
inferno *n* brasier *m*.
infertile *adj* [*land*] infertile; [*person*] stérile.
infest *vtr* infester (**with** de).
infidelity *n* infidélité *f*.
infighting *n* conflits *mpl* internes.
infiltrate *vtr* infiltrer [*organization, group*].
infinite *adj* infini/-e.
infinitely *adv* infiniment.
infinitive *n* infinitif *m*; **in the ~** à l'infinitif.
infinity *n* infini *m*.
infirmary *n* **1** (hospital) hôpital *m*; **2** (in school, prison) infirmerie *f*.
inflamed *adj* (Med) enflammé/-e.
inflammable *adj* inflammable.
inflammation *n* inflammation *f*.
inflatable *adj* [*mattress, dinghy*] pneumatique; [*toy*] gonflable.
inflate *vtr* gonfler [*tyre, dinghy*].
inflation *n* inflation *f*.
inflexible *adj* **1** [*person, attitude*] inflexible; [*system*] rigide; **2** [*material*] rigide.
inflict *vtr* infliger [*pain, presence, defeat*] (**on** à); causer [*damage*] (**on** à).
influence I *n* influence *f*; **to be** or **have an ~ on** avoir une influence sur; **to drive while under the ~ of alcohol** conduire en état d'ébriété.
II *vtr* influencer [*person*] (**in** dans); influer sur [*decision, choice, result*]; **to be ~d by sb/sth** se laisser influencer par qn/qch.
influential *adj* influent/-e.
influenza ▶ 533 *n* grippe *f*.
influx *n* afflux *m*.
info○ *n* renseignements *mpl*, tuyaux○ *mpl*.
inform I *vtr* informer, avertir (**of, about** de; **that** du fait que); **to keep sb ~ed** tenir qn informé/-e or au courant (**of, as to** de).
II *vi* **to ~ on** or **against** dénoncer.
informal *adj* **1** [*person*] sans façons; [*manner, style*] simple; [*language*] familier/-ière; [*clothes*] de tous les jours; **2** [*visit*] privé/-e; [*invitation*] verbal/-e; [*discussion, interview*] informel/-elle.
information *n* **1** renseignements *mpl*, informations *fpl* (**on, about** sur); **a piece of ~** un renseignement, une information; **2** (US) (service *m* des) renseignements *mpl*.
information desk, **information office** *n* bureau *m* des renseignements.
information technology, **IT** *n* informatique *f*.
informative *adj* instructif/-ive.
informer *n* indicateur/-trice *m/f*.
infrared *adj* infrarouge.
infrastructure *n* infrastructure *f*.
infringe I *vtr* enfreindre [*rule*]; ne pas respecter [*rights*].
II *vi* **to ~ on** or **upon** empiéter sur [*rights*].
infringement *n* (of rule) infraction *f* (**of** à); (of rights) violation *f*.
infuriating *adj* exaspérant/-e.
ingenious *adj* ingénieux/-ieuse, astucieux/-ieuse.

ingenuity *n* ingéniosité *f*.

ingenuous *adj* ingénu/-e, candide.

ingot *n* lingot *m*.

ingrained *adj* [*dirt*] bien incrusté/-e; [*habit, hatred*] enraciné/-e.

ingratitude *n* ingratitude *f*.

ingredient *n* (Culin) ingrédient *m*; (figurative) élément *m* (**of** de).

inhabit *vtr* **1** habiter [*house, region, planet*]; **2** vivre dans [*fantasy world*].

inhabitant *n* habitant/-e *m*/*f*.

inhale I *vtr* aspirer, inhaler.
II *vi* (breathe in) inspirer; (smoke) avaler la fumée.

inhaler *n* inhalateur *m*.

inherent *adj* inhérent/-e (**to** à).

inherit *vtr* hériter de [*money, property, title*]; **to ~ sth from sb** hériter qch de qn.

inheritance *n* héritage *m*; **to come into an ~** faire un héritage.

inhibit *vtr* inhiber [*person, reaction*]; entraver [*activity, progress*].

inhibited *adj* inhibé/-e, refoulé/-e.

inhibition *n* inhibition *f*.

inhospitable *adj* inhospitalier/-ière.

inhuman *adj* inhumain/-e.

inhumanity *n* inhumanité *f* (**to** envers).

initial I *n* initiale *f*.
II *adj* initial/-e; **~ letter** initiale *f*.
III *vtr* parapher, parafer.

initially *adv* au départ.

initiate I *n* initié/-e *m*/*f*.
II *vtr* **1** mettre en œuvre [*project, reform*]; amorcer [*talks*]; entamer, engager [*proceedings*]; **2** (teach) **to ~ sb into** initier qn à.

initiative *n* initiative *f*; **on one's own ~** de son propre chef.

inject *vtr* injecter [*vaccine*] (**into** dans); **to ~ sb (with sth)** faire une injection or une piqûre (de qch) à qn.

injection *n* **1** (Med) piqûre *f*; **2** (Tech) injection *f*.

injure *vtr* **1** blesser [*person*]; **to ~ one's hand** se blesser la main; **2** nuire à, compromettre [*health, reputation*].

injured I *n* **the ~** les blessés *mpl*.
II *adj* **1** (gen) blessé/-e; **2** (Law) **the ~ party** la partie lésée.

injury *n* blessure *f*; **head injuries** blessures à la tête.

injury time *n* (Sport) arrêts *mpl* de jeu.

injustice *n* injustice *f*.

ink *n* encre *f*; **in ~** à l'encre.

inkling *n* petite idée *f*; **to have an ~ that** avoir idée que.

inland I *adj* intérieur/-e.
II *adv* [*travel, lie*] à l'intérieur des terres.

Inland Revenue *n* (GB) service *m* des impôts britannique.

in-laws *n pl* (parents) beaux-parents *mpl*; (other relatives) belle-famille *f*, parents *mpl* par alliance.

inmate *n* (of mental hospital) interné/-e *m*/*f*; (of prison) détenu/-e *m*/*f*.

inn *n* **1** (hotel) auberge *f*; **2** (pub) pub *m*.

inner *adj* intérieur/-e.

innermost *adj* **sb's ~ thoughts** les pensées les plus intimes de qn.

innocence *n* innocence *f*.

innocent *n, adj* innocent/-e (*m*/*f*).

innovation *n* innovation *f*.

innovative *adj* innovateur/-trice.

innuendo *n* (veiled slights) insinuations *fpl*; (sexual references) allusions *fpl* grivoises.

inoculation *n* vaccination *f*, inoculation *f*.

inoffensive *adj* inoffensif/-ive.

in-patient *n* malade *mf* hospitalisé/-e.

input *n* **1** (of money) apport *m*; (of energy) alimentation *f* (**of** en); **2** (contribution) contribution *f*; **3** (Comput) (data) données *fpl* d'entrée or à traiter.

inquest *n* enquête *f* (**on, into** sur).

inquire = **enquire**.

inquiry *n* enquête *f* (**into** sur); **murder ~** enquête criminelle; ▶ **enquiry**.

inquisitive *adj* curieux/-ieuse.

insane *adj* (gen) fou/folle; (Law) aliéné/-e.

insanity *n* (gen) folie *f*; (Law) aliénation *f* mentale.

insatiable *adj* insatiable.

inscription *n* inscription *f*.

insect *n* insecte *m*; **~ bite** piqûre *f* d'insecte.

insecticide *n, adj* insecticide (*m*).

insect repellent *n* insectifuge *m*, produit *m* anti-insecte.

insecure *adj* **1** [*person*] qui manque d'assurance; **2** [*job*] précaire; [*investment*] risqué/-e.

insensitive *adj* [*person*] (tactless) sans tact; (unfeeling) insensible (**to** à); [*remark*] indélicat/-e.

inseparable *adj* inséparable (**from** de).

insert *vtr* insérer (**in** dans).

inside I *n* intérieur *m*; **to overtake on the ~** (in Europe, US) doubler à droite; (in GB, Australia) doubler à gauche; **people on the ~** les gens qui sont dans la place.
II *prep* (also (US) **~ of**) **1** à l'intérieur de; **~ the box** à l'intérieur de or dans la boîte; **to be ~ (the house)** être à l'intérieur (de la maison); **2** (under) **~ (of) an hour** en moins d'une heure.
III *adj* **1** [*cover, pocket*] intérieur/-e; [*toilet*] à l'intérieur; **2** [*information*] de première main; **3 the ~ lane** (of road) (in Europe, US) la voie de droite; (in GB, Australia) la voie de gauche; (of athletics track) le couloir intérieur.
IV *adv* (indoors) à l'intérieur; (in a container) à l'intérieur, dedans; **she's ~** elle est à l'intérieur; **to look ~** regarder à l'intérieur or dedans; **to go** or **come ~** entrer; **to bring sth ~** rentrer [*chairs*].
V inside out *phr* à l'envers; **to turn sth ~ out** retourner qch; **to know sb/sth ~ out** connaître qn/qch à fond.

insides○ *n pl* (of human) intestin *m*, estomac *m*, boyaux○ *mpl*.

insight *n* **1** (glimpse, understanding) aperçu *m*, idée *f* (**into** de); **2** (intuition) perspicacité *f*, intuition *f*.
insignificant *adj* [*cost, difference*] négligeable; [*person, detail*] insignifiant/-e.
insincere *adj* peu sincère; **to be ~** manquer de sincérité.
insinuate *vtr* insinuer (**that** que).
insinuation *n* insinuation *f*.
insipid *adj* fade.
insist I *vtr* **1** (demand) insister (**that** pour que); **2** (maintain) affirmer (**that** que).
II *vi* insister; **to ~ on** exiger [*punctuality, silence*]; **to ~ on doing** vouloir à tout prix faire, tenir à faire.
insistent *adj* **to be ~** insister (**about** sur; **that** pour que + *subjunctive*).
insofar: **insofar as** *phr* **~ as** dans la mesure où.
insole *n* semelle *f* (intérieure).
insolent *adj* insolent/-e.
insomnia *n* insomnie *f*.
inspect *vtr* examiner [qch] de près [*document, product*]; contrôler, vérifier [*accounts*]; inspecter [*school, factory, pitch, wiring*]; contrôler [*passport, ticket, baggage*].
inspection *n* (gen) inspection *f*; (of ticket, passport) contrôle *m*; **on closer ~** en y regardant de plus près.
inspector *n* **1** (gen) inspecteur/-trice *m/f*; **2** (GB) **police ~** inspecteur *m* de police; **3** (GB) (on bus) contrôleur/-euse *m/f*.
inspiration *n* inspiration *f* (**for** pour).
inspire *vtr* inspirer; **to be ~d by sth** s'inspirer de qch.
instal(l) *vtr* **1** installer [*equipment*]; poser [*windows*]; **2 to ~ sb in office** installer qn.
installation *n* installation *f*.
instalment (GB), **installment** (US) *n* versement *m* partiel; **in ~s** en plusieurs versements.
instance *n* exemple *m*; **for ~** par exemple.
instant I *n* instant *m*; **come here this ~!** viens ici tout de suite!
II *adj* **1** [*access, effect, rapport, success*] immédiat/-e; [*solution*] instantané/-e; **2** [*coffee, soup*] instantané/-e.
instant camera *n* polaroïd® *m*.
instantly *adv* immédiatement.
instead I *adv* **we didn't go home—we went to the park ~** au lieu de rentrer nous sommes allés au parc; **let's take a taxi ~** prenons plutôt un taxi; **I was going to phone but wrote ~** j'allais téléphoner mais finalement j'ai écrit; **her son went ~** son fils y est allé à sa place.
II **instead of** *phr* **~ of sth/of doing** au lieu de qch/de faire; **use oil ~ of butter** utilisez de l'huile à la place du beurre; **~ of sb** à la place de qn.
instep *n* cou-de-pied *m*.
instigate *vtr* lancer [*attack*]; engager [*proceedings*].
instil (GB), **instill** (US) *vtr* inculquer [*attitude*] (**in** à); donner [*confidence*] (**in** à).
instinct *n* instinct *m* (**for** de).
instinctive *adj* instinctif/-ive.
institute I *n* institut *m*.
II *vtr* instituer.
institution *n* **1** (gen) institution *f*; **financial ~** organisme *m* financier; **2** (home, hospital) établissement *m* spécialisé.
instruct *vtr* **1 to ~ sb to do** donner l'ordre à qn de faire; **to be ~ed to do** recevoir l'ordre de faire; **2** (teach) instruire; **to ~ sb in** enseigner [qch] à qn [*subject*].
instruction *n* instruction *f*; **~s for use** mode *m* d'emploi.
instruction book *n* livret *m* de l'utilisateur.
instructor ▶626 *n* **1** (in sports, driving) moniteur/-trice *m/f* (**in** de); (military) instructeur *m*; **2** (US) professeur *m*.
instrument ▶586 *n* instrument *m*; **to play an ~** jouer d'un instrument.
instrument panel *n* tableau *m* de bord.
insulate *vtr* isoler [*roof, room, wire*].
insulation *n* isolation *f*.
insulin *n* insuline *f*.
insult I *n* insulte *f*.
II *vtr* insulter.
insurance *n* assurance *f* (**against** contre; **for** pour); **to take out ~ against sth** s'assurer contre qch.
insurance policy *n* (police *f* d')assurance *f*.
insure *vtr* assurer (**against** contre).
intact *adj* intact/-e.
intake *n* **1** (consumption) consommation *f*; **2** (Sch, Univ) (admissions) admissions *fpl*; **3 an ~ of breath** une inspiration *f*.
intangible *adj* insaisissable.
integral *adj* intégral/-e; [*part*] intégrant/-e; **~ to** intrinsèque à.
integrate I *vtr* **1** (incorporate, absorb) intégrer (**into** dans; **with** à); **2** (combine) combiner [*systems*].
II *vi* [*person*] s'intégrer (**with** à; **into** dans).
integration *n* intégration *f* (**with** à).
integrity *n* intégrité *f*.
intellect *n* **1** (mental capacity) intelligence *f*; **2** (person) esprit *m*.
intellectual *n, adj* intellectuel/-elle (*m/f*).
intelligence *n* **1** intelligence *f* (**to do** de faire); **2** (gen, Mil) (information) renseignements *mpl*; **3** (Mil) (secret service) services *mpl* de renseignements.
intelligent *adj* intelligent/-e.
intelligible *adj* intelligible (**to** à).
intend *vtr* vouloir; **to ~ to do, to ~ doing** avoir l'intention de faire; **to be ~ed for** être destiné/-e à [*person*]; être prévu/-e pour [*purpose*].
intense *adj* **1** (gen) intense; **2** [*person*] sérieux/-ieuse.
intensify I *vtr* intensifier.
II *vi* s'intensifier.

intensive *adj* intensif/-ive.

intensive care *n* **in ~** en réanimation.

intensive care unit *n* service *m* de soins intensifs.

intent *adj* [*person, expression*] absorbé/-e; **~ on doing** résolu/-e à faire.
IDIOMS **to all ~s and purposes** quasiment, en fait.

intention *n* intention *f* (**to do, of doing** de faire).

intentional *adj* intentionnel/-elle.

interact *vi* [*two factors, phenomena*] agir l'un sur l'autre; [*people*] communiquer; (Comput) dialoguer.

interactive *adj* interactif/-ive.

intercept *vtr* intercepter.

interchange I *n* **1** (road junction) échangeur *m*; **2** (exchange) échange *m*.
II *vtr* échanger.

interchangeable *adj* interchangeable.

intercom *n* interphone® *m*.

intercourse *n* rapports *mpl* (sexuels).

interest I *n* **1** (gen) intérêt *m* (**in** pour); **to hold sb's ~** retenir l'attention de qn; **it's in your (own) ~(s) to do** il est dans ton intérêt de faire; **to have sb's best ~s at heart** vouloir le bien de qn; **2** (hobby) centre *m* d'intérêt; **3** (on loan, from investment) intérêts *mpl* (**on** de).
II *vtr* intéresser (**in** à).

interested *adj* [*expression, onlooker*] intéressé/-e; **to be ~ in** s'intéresser à [*subject, activity*]; **I am ~ in doing** ça m'intéresse de faire.

interesting *adj* intéressant/-e.

interest rate *n* taux *m* d'intérêt.

interfere *vi* **1 to ~ in** se mêler de [*affairs*]; **she never ~s** elle ne se mêle jamais de ce qui ne la regarde pas; **2** (intervene) intervenir; **3 to ~ with** [*person*] toucher, traficoter○ [*machine*]; **4 to ~ with** [*activity*] empiéter sur [*family life*].

interference *n* (on radio) parasites *mpl*.

interfering *adj* [*person*] envahissant/-e.

interim I *n* **in the ~** entre-temps.
II *adj* [*arrangement, government*] provisoire; [*post, employee*] intérimaire.

interior I *n* **1** intérieur *m*; **2 Secretary/Department of the Interior** (US) ministre *m*/ministère *m* de l'Intérieur.
II *adj* intérieur/-e.

interior decorator ▶626 *n* décorateur/-trice *m/f*.

interlink *vtr* **to be ~ed** être lié/-e (**with** à).

interlock *vi* [*pipes*] s'emboîter; [*mechanisms*] s'enclencher; [*fingers*] s'entrelacer.

interlude *n* (interval) intervalle *m*; (during play, concert) entracte *m*.

intermediary *n, adj* intermédiaire (*mf*).

intermediate *adj* **1** (gen) intermédiaire; **2** (Sch) [*course*] de niveau moyen; [*level*] moyen/-enne.

intermission *n* entracte *m*.

intern I *n* (US) **1** (Med) interne *mf*; **2** (gen) stagiaire *mf*.
II *vtr* (Mil) interner.

internal *adj* **1** (gen) interne; **2** (within country) intérieur/-e.

international *adj* international/-e.

internationally *adv* [*known, respected*] dans le monde entier.

interpret I *vtr* interpréter (**as** comme).
II *vi* faire l'interprète.

interpreter *n* interprète *mf*.

interrogate *vtr* interroger.

interrogation *n* interrogatoire *m*.

interrogative *n* interrogatif *m*; **in the ~** à la forme interrogative.

interrupt *vtr, vi* interrompre.

interruption *n* interruption *f*.

intersect I *vtr* croiser.
II *vi* [*roads*] se croiser; **to ~ with** croiser.

intersection *n* intersection *f*.

interstate *n* (US) (also **~ highway**) autoroute *f* (inter-États).

interval *n* **1** intervalle *m*; **at regular ~s** à intervalles réguliers; **at four-hourly ~s** toutes les quatre heures; **at 100 metre ~s** à 100 mètres d'intervalle; **2** (GB) (in theatre) entracte *m*.

intervene *vi* intervenir (**on behalf of** en faveur de).

interview I *n* **1** (also **job ~**) entretien *m*; **2** (in newspaper) interview *f*.
II *vtr* **1** faire passer un entretien à [*candidate*]; **2** [*journalist*] interviewer [*celebrity*]; [*police*] interroger [*suspect*].

interviewer *n* **1** (for job) personne *f* faisant passer l'entretien; **2** (on radio, TV, in press) intervieweur/-euse *m/f*.

intestine *n* intestin *m*.

intimacy *n* intimité *f*.

intimate *adj* **1** (gen) intime; **to be on ~ terms with sb** être intime avec qn; **2** [*knowledge*] approfondi/-e.

intimidate *vtr* intimider.

intimidating *adj* [*behaviour, person*] intimidant/-e; [*obstacle, sight, size*] impressionnant/-e; [*prospect*] redoutable.

into *prep* **1** [*put, go, disappear*] dans [*place*]; **to run ~ a wall** rentrer dans un mur; **to bang ~ sb/sth** heurter qn/qch; **to go ~ town/~ the office** aller en ville/au bureau; **to get ~ a car** monter dans une voiture; **to get ~ bed** se mettre au lit; **2** [*transform*] en; **to change dollars ~ francs** changer des dollars en francs; **to translate sth ~ French** traduire qch en français; **3 to continue ~ the 18th century** continuer jusqu'au XVIIIe siècle; **well ~ the afternoon** jusque tard dans l'après-midi; **4**○ (keen on) **to be ~ sth** être fana○ de qch; **to be ~ drugs** se droguer; **5** (in division) **8 ~ 24 goes 3 times** or **is 3** 24 divisé par 8 égale 3.

intolerable *adj* intolérable, insupportable.

intolerance *n* intolérance *f* (**of, towards** vis-à-vis de; **to** à).

intolerant *adj* intolérant/-e (**of, towards** vis-à-vis de; **with** envers).
intoxicated *adj* ivre.
intoxicating *adj* [*drink*] alcoolisé/-e; [*effect, substance*] toxique.
intransitive *adj* intransitif/-ive.
intravenous *adj* intraveineux/-euse.
in-tray *n* corbeille *f* arrivée.
intrepid *adj* intrépide.
intricate *adj* [*mechanism, pattern, plot*] compliqué/-e; [*problem*] complexe.
intrigue I *n* intrigue *f*.
II *vtr* intriguer; **she was ~d by his story** son histoire l'intriguait.
intriguing *adj* [*person, smile*] fascinant/-e; [*story*] curieux/-ieuse, intéressant/-e.
introduce *vtr* **1** présenter [*person*] (**as** comme; **to** à); **may I ~ my son?** je vous présente mon fils; **to ~ sb to** initier qn à [*painting, drugs*]; **2** introduire [*law, reform, word, product, change*] (**in, into** dans); **3** (on TV, radio) présenter [*programme*].
introduction *n* **1** (of person) présentation *f*; **letter of ~** lettre de recommandation; **2** (of liquid, system, law) introduction *f* (**into** dans); **3** (to speech, book) introduction *f*.
introductory *adj* **1** [*speech, paragraph*] préliminaire; [*course*] d'initiation; **2** [*offer*] de lancement.
introvert *n* introverti/-e *m/f*.
intrude *vi* **1 to ~ in** s'immiscer dans [*affairs, conversation*]; **2 to ~ (on sb's privacy)** être importun/-e.
intruder *n* intrus/-e *m/f*.
intuition *n* intuition *f* (**about** concernant).
intuitive *adj* intuitif/-ive.
inundate *vtr* inonder [*land*]; submerger [*organization, market*].
invade *vtr* envahir.
invalid I *n* (sick person) malade *mf*; (disabled person) infirme *mf*.
II *adj* [*claim, passport*] pas valable; [*contract, marriage*] nul/nulle.
invaluable *adj* [*assistance, experience*] inestimable; [*person, service*] précieux/-ieuse.
invasion *n* invasion *f*; **~ of (sb's) privacy** atteinte *f* à la vie privée (de qn).
invent *vtr* inventer.
invention *n* invention *f*.
inventive *adj* inventif/-ive.
inventor *n* inventeur/-trice *m/f*.
inventory *n* **1** inventaire *m*; **2** (US) stock *m*.
inverted commas *n pl* (GB) guillemets *mpl*; **in ~** entre guillemets.
invest I *vtr* investir, placer [*money*]; consacrer [*time, energy*] (**in** à).
II *vi* **1** investir; **to ~ in shares** placer son argent en valeurs; **2** (buy) **to ~ in sth** s'acheter qch.
investigate *vtr* **1** enquêter sur [*crime, case*]; faire une enquête sur [*person*]; **2** (study) examiner [*possibility, report*].
investigation *n* **1** (inquiry) enquête *f* (**of, into** sur); **2** (of accounts, reports) vérification *f*.
investment *n* (financial) investissement *m*, placement *m*.
investor *n* investisseur/-euse *m/f* (**in** dans); (in shares) actionnaire *mf*.
invisible *adj* invisible.
invisible ink *n* encre *f* sympathique.
invitation *n* invitation *f*.
invitation card *n* carton *m* (d'invitation).
invite *vtr* inviter [*person*]; **to ~ sb for a drink** inviter qn à prendre un verre; **to ~ sb in** inviter qn à entrer; **to ~ sb over** or **round (to one's house)** inviter qn chez soi.
inviting *adj* [*room*] accueillant/-e; [*meal*] appétissant/-e; [*prospect*] alléchant/-e.
invoice I *n* facture *f*.
II *vtr* envoyer une facture à [*customer*]; **to ~ sb for sth** facturer qch à qn.
involve *vtr* **1** (entail) impliquer, nécessiter [*effort, travel*]; entraîner [*problems*]; **2** (cause to participate) faire participer [*person*] (**in** à); **to be ~d in** participer à, être engagé/-e dans [*business, project*]; être mêlé/-e à [*scandal, robbery*]; **3** (affect) concerner, impliquer [*person, animal, vehicle*]; **4** (engross) **to get ~d in** se laisser prendre par, se plonger dans [*film, book, work*]; **5 to get ~d with sb** avoir une liaison avec qn.
involved *adj* **1** (complicated) [*explanation*] compliqué/-e; **2** [*person, group*] (implicated) impliqué/-e; (affected) concerné/-e; **3** (necessary) [*effort*] à fournir; **because of the expense ~** à cause de la dépense que cela entraîne.
involvement *n* **1** (in activity, task) participation *f* (**in** à); (in enterprise, politics) engagement *m* (**in** dans); **2** (with group) liens *mpl*; (with person) relations *fpl*.
inward I *adj* [*satisfaction*] personnel/-elle; [*relief, calm*] intérieur/-e.
II *adv* (also **inwards**) [*open, move, grow*] vers l'intérieur.
inwards = **inward** II.
iodine *n* (element) iode *m*; (antiseptic) teinture *f* d'iode.
IOU *n* reconnaissance *f* de dette.
IQ *n* (*abbr* = **intelligence quotient**) QI *m*.
Iraq **▶ 448** *pr n* Iraq *m*.
irate *adj* furieux/-ieuse (**about** au sujet de).
Ireland **▶ 448** *pr n* Irlande *f*.
Irish **▶ 553** I *n* **1** (people) **the ~** les Irlandais *mpl*; **2** (language) irlandais *m*.
II *adj* irlandais/-e.
Irishman *n* Irlandais *m*.
Irish Republic **▶ 448** *n* République *f* d'Irlande.
Irish sea *n* mer *f* d'Irlande.
Irishwoman *n* Irlandaise *f*.
iron I *n* **1** (metal) fer *m*; **scrap ~** ferraille *f*; **2** (for clothes) fer *m* (à repasser).
II *vtr* repasser [*clothes*].
ironic(al) *adj* ironique.
ironing *n* repassage *m*.

it

Pronoun uses

◆ When *it* is used as a subject pronoun to stand for a specific object (or animal), *il* or *elle* is used in French according to the gender of the object referred to:

'where is the book / chair?'–	= 'où est le livre / la chaise?'–
'it's in the kitchen'	'**il** / **elle** est dans la cuisine'

However, if the object referred to is named in the same sentence, *it* is translated by *ce* (*c'* before a vowel):

it's a good film	= **c'**est un bon film

◆ When *it* is used as an object pronoun, it is translated by *le* or *la* (*l'* before a vowel or mute 'h') according to the gender of the object referred to:

*it's my book / my chair and I want **it***	= c'est mon livre / ma chaise et je **le** / **la** veux

Note that the object pronoun normally comes before the verb in French and that in tenses like the perfect and the past perfect, the past participle agrees with it:

*I liked his shirt, did you notice **it**?*	= sa chemise m'a plu, est-ce que tu **l'**as remarquée? *or* l'as-tu remarquée?

In imperatives the pronoun comes after the verb:

it's my book, give it to me	= c'est mon livre, donne-**le**-moi*

* Note the hyphens.

However, in negative commands, the pronoun comes before the verb:

*it's my book, don't give **it** to him!*	= c'est mon livre, ne **le** lui donne pas!

◆ When *it* is used after a preposition in English, the two words (*preposition* + *it*) are often translated by one word in French. If the preposition would normally be translated by *de* in French (*of*, *about*, *from* etc), the preposition + *it* = *en*:

*I've heard **about it***	= j'**en** ai entendu parler

If the preposition would normally be translated by *à* in French (*to*, *in*, *at* etc), the preposition + *it* = *y*:

*they went **to it***	= ils **y** sont allés

For translations of *it* following prepositions not normally translated by *de* or *à* (*above, under, over* etc), consult the entry for the preposition.

Impersonal uses of pronoun

◆ When *it* refers back to something that has already been mentioned, French will use either *ce* (*c'* before a vowel) + *être*:

*they like English because **it**'s easy to learn*	= ils aiment l'anglais parce que **c'**est facile à apprendre

or *ça* (*cela*) + *other French verbs*:

*'I'm sorry' – '**it** doesn't matter'*	= 'je suis désolé' – '**ça** ne fait rien'

◆ When *it* introduces an idea or information, French will use either *il* + *être*:

***it** is easy to learn English*	= **il** est facile d'apprendre l'anglais

or *ça* (*cela*) + *other French verbs*:

***it** upset me to see that . . .*	= **ça** m'a fait de la peine de voir que . . .

◆ When *it* is used in expressions like *it's raining, it will snow* etc, the translation will always be *il*: *il pleut*, *il va neiger*.
See the entry for the verb in question.

❑ For translations of *it's Friday, it's five o'clock* etc, consult the usage notes on **Dates, Days, and Months**, ▶ 456 and **The Clock**, ▶ 434.

For other uses, see the entry **it**.

ironing board *n* planche *f* à repasser.

ironmonger ▶626| *n* quincaillier/-ière *m/f*; **~'s (shop)** quincaillerie *f*.

irony *n* ironie *f*.

irrational *adj* [*behaviour*] irrationnel/-elle; [*fear, hostility*] sans fondement; **he's rather ~** il n'est pas très raisonnable.

irregular *adj* **1** irrégulier/-ière; **2** (US) [*merchandise*] de second choix.

irrelevant *adj* **1** [*remark*] hors de propos; [*fact*] qui n'est pas pertinent; [*question*] sans rapport avec le sujet; **2** (unimportant) **the money's ~** ce n'est pas l'argent qui compte.

irreligious *adj* irréligieux/-ieuse.

irreparable *adj* irréparable.

irreplaceable *adj* irremplaçable.

irrepressible *adj* [*high spirits*] irrépressible; [*person*] infatigable.

irresistible *adj* irrésistible.

irrespective: **irrespective of** *phr* sans tenir compte de [*age, class*]; sans distinction de [*race*].

irresponsible *adj* irresponsable.

irritable *adj* irritable.

irritate *vtr* irriter.

irritating *adj* irritant/-e.

Islam *n* Islam *m*.

Islamic *adj* islamique.

island *n* **1** île *f*; (small) îlot *m*; **2** (also **traffic ~**) refuge *m*.

islander *n* insulaire *mf*, habitant/-e *m/f* d'une île (or de l'île).

Isle of Man *pr n* île *f* de Man.

isolate *vtr* isoler (**from** de).

isolation *n* isolement *m*.

Israel ▶448| *pr n* Israël (*never with article*).

Israeli ▶553| **I** *n* Israélien/-ienne *m/f*.
II *adj* israélien/-ienne.

issue **I** *n* **1** problème *m*, question *f*; **to make an ~ (out) of** faire une histoire de; **at ~** en question; **2** (of stamps, shares) émission *f*; (of book) publication *f*; **3** (journal, magazine) numéro *m*; **back ~** vieux numéro *m*.
II *vtr* **1** (allocate) distribuer; **to ~ sb with sth** fournir qch à qn; **2** délivrer [*declaration*]; émettre [*order, warning*]; **3** émettre [*stamps, shares*]; publier [*book*].

it *pron* (in questions) **who is ~?** qui est-ce?, qui c'est°?; **~'s me** c'est moi; **where is ~?** (of object) où est-il/elle?; (of place) où est-ce?, où est-ce que c'est?, c'est où°?; **what is ~?** (of object, noise) qu'est-ce que c'est?, c'est quoi°?; (what's happening?) qu'est-ce qui se passe?; (what is the matter?) qu'est-ce qu'il y a?

IT *n* (*abbr* = **information technology**) informatique *f*.

Italian ▶553| **I** *n* **1** (person) Italien/-ienne *m/f*; **2** (language) italien *m*.
II *adj* (gen) italien/-ienne; [*embassy*] d'Italie.

italics *n pl* italique *m*; **in ~** en italique.

Italy ▶448| *pr n* Italie *f*.

itch **I** *n* démangeaison *f*.
II *vi* avoir des démangeaisons; **my back is ~ing** j'ai le dos qui me démange; **these socks make me ~** ces chaussettes me grattent.

itchy° *adj* **I feel ~ all over** ça me gratte partout.
IDIOMS **to have ~ feet**° avoir la bougeotte°.

item *n* **1** article *m*; **~s of clothing** vêtements *mpl*; **news ~** article *m*; **2** (on agenda) point *m*.

itinerary *n* itinéraire *m*.

its *det* son/sa/ses.

■ **Note** In French determiners agree in number and gender with the noun that follows. *its* is translated by *son + masculine noun*: *its nose* = son nez; by *sa + feminine noun*: *its tail* = sa queue; BUT by *son + feminine noun beginning with a vowel or mute 'h'*: *its ear* = son oreille; and by *ses + plural noun*: *its ears* = ses oreilles.

itself *pron* **1** (reflexive) se, s'; **the cat hurt ~** le chat s'est fait mal; **2** (emphatic) lui-même/elle-même; **the house ~ was pretty** la maison elle-même était jolie; **he was kindness ~** c'était la bonté même or personnifiée; **3** (after prepositions) **the heating comes on by ~** le chauffage se met en marche tout seul; **learning French is not difficult in ~** l'apprentissage du français n'est pas difficile en soi.

ivory *n, adj* ivoire (*m*).

ivy *n* lierre *m*.

j, J *n* j, J *m*.

jab I *n* **1** (GB) (vaccination) vaccin *m*; (injection) piqûre *f*; **2** (in boxing) direct *m*.
II *vtr* **to ~ sth into sth** planter qch dans qch.

jabber *vi* (chatter) jacasser; (in foreign language) baragouiner.

jack *n* **1** (for car) cric *m*; **2** (in cards) valet *m* (**of** de); **3** (in bowls) cochonnet *m*.
IDIOMS **to be a ~ of all trades** être un/-e touche-à-tout *inv*.

jackal *n* chacal *m*.

jackdaw *n* choucas *m*.

jacket *n* **1** (garment) veste *f*; (man's) veste *f*, veston *m*; **2** (also **dust ~**) jaquette *f*; **3** (US) (of record) pochette *f*.

jacket potato *n* pomme *f* de terre en robe des champs (au four).

jack-in-the-box *n* diable *m* à ressort.

jackknife *vi* [*lorry*] se mettre en portefeuille.

jackpot *n* **to hit the ~** (win prize) gagner le gros lot; (have great success) faire un tabac○.

jade *n* **1** (stone) jade *m*; **2** ▶ **438** (also **~ green**) vert *m* jade.

jaded *adj* **1** (exhausted) fatigué/-e; **2** (bored) [*person, palate*] blasé/-e.

jagged *adj* [*rock, cliff*] déchiqueté/-e; [*tooth, blade*] ébréché/-e; [*knife, saw*] dentelé/-e.

jail I *n* prison *f*.
II *vtr* mettre [qn] en prison.

jam I *n* **1** confiture *f*; **apricot ~** confiture d'abricots; **2** (of traffic) embouteillage *m*; **3** (in machine, system) blocage *m*; **4**○ (difficulty) pétrin○ *m*; **to be in a ~** être dans le pétrin○; **5** (also **~ session**) bœuf○ *m*, jam-session *f*.
II *vtr* **1 to ~ one's foot on the brake** freiner à bloc; **2** (wedge) coincer; **the key's ~med** la clé s'est coincée; **3** (block) enrayer [*mechanism*]; coincer [*lock, door, system*]; **4** (also **~ up**) (crowd) encombrer; **cars ~med (up) the roads** les routes étaient embouteillées; **5** (cause interference in) brouiller [*frequency*].
III *vi* **1** [*mechanism*] s'enrayer; [*lock, door*] se coincer; **2** (Mus) improviser.

Jamaica ▶ **448** *pr n* Jamaïque *f*.

jam-packed *adj* bondé/-e; **to be ~ with sth** être bourré/-e de qch.

jangle I *n* (of bells, pots) tintement *m*; (of keys) cliquetis *m*.
II *vi* [*bells*] tinter; [*bangles, keys*] cliqueter.

janitor *n* (US) gardien *m*.

January ▶ **456** *n* janvier *m*.

Japan ▶ **448** *pr n* Japon *m*.

Japanese ▶ **553** **I** *n* **1** (person) Japonais/-e *m*/*f*; **2** (language) japonais *m*.
II *adj* [*culture, food, politics*] japonais/-e; [*teacher, lesson*] de japonais; [*ambassador, embassy*] du Japon.

jar I *n* **1** pot *m*; (large) bocal *m*; (earthenware) jarre *f*; **2** (jolt) secousse *f*, choc *m*.
II *vtr* **1** ébranler, secouer; **to ~ one's shoulder** se cogner l'épaule; **2** (US) **to ~ sb into action** pousser qn à agir.
III *vi* **1** [*music, voice*] rendre un son discordant; **to ~ on sb's nerves** agacer qn; **2** (clash) [*colours*] jurer; [*note*] sonner faux.

jargon *n* jargon *m*.

jasmine *n* jasmin *m*.

jaundice ▶ **533** *n* jaunisse *f*.

javelin ▶ **504** *n* javelot *m*.

jaw ▶ **413** *n* mâchoire *f*.

jawbone *n* mâchoire *f*.

jawline *n* menton *m*.

jay *n* geai *m*.

jazz I *n* jazz *m*.
II *adj* [*musician, singer*] de jazz; **~ band** jazz-band *m*.
IDIOMS **and all that ~**○ et tout le bataclan○.
■ **jazz up**○ rajeunir [*dress*]; égayer [*room*].

jazzy *adj* **1** [*colour*] voyant/-e; [*pattern, dress*] bariolé/-e; **2** [*music*] jazzy *inv*.

jealous *adj* jaloux/-ouse (**of** de); **to make sb ~** rendre qn jaloux.

jealousy *n* jalousie *f*.

jeans *n pl* jean *m*; **a pair of ~** un jean.

jeer I *n* huée *f*.
II *vtr* huer.
III *vi* se moquer; **to ~ at sb** [*crowd*] huer qn; [*individual*] railler qn.

jeering *n* huées *fpl*.

jellied *adj* en aspic; **~ eels** anguilles *fpl* en gelée.

Jell-o® *n* (US) gelée *f* de fruits.

jelly *n* **1** (savoury) gelée *f*; (sweet) gelée *f* de fruits; **2** (jam) gelée *f*.

jellyfish *n* méduse *f*.

jeopardize *vtr* compromettre [*career, plans*]; mettre [qch] en péril [*lives, troops*].

jeopardy *n* **in ~** en péril, menacé/-e.

jerk I *n* (of vehicle) secousse *f*; (of muscle, limb) tressaillement *m*, (petit) mouvement *m* brusque; **with a ~ of his head** d'un brusque mouvement de la tête.
II *vtr* tirer brusquement [*object*].
III *vi* [*person, limb, muscle*] tressaillir.

jerky I *n* (US) (also **beef ~**) bœuf *m* séché.
II *adj* [*movement*] saccadé/-e; [*style, phrase*] haché/-e.

jersey *n* **1** (sweater) pull-over *m*; **2** (for sports) maillot *m*; **3** (fabric) jersey *m*.

Jersey *pr n* Jersey *f*.

Jerusalem ▶ **448** *pr n* Jérusalem.

jest I *n* plaisanterie *f*; **in ~** pour plaisanter.
II *vi* plaisanter.

jester *n* bouffon *m*.
Jesuit *n*, *adj* jésuite (*m*).
Jesus I *pr n* Jésus; **~ Christ** Jésus-Christ.
II◐ *excl* **~ (Christ)**! nom de Dieu○!
jet I *n* **1** (also **~ plane**) jet *m*, avion *m* à réaction; **2** (of water, flame) jet *m*; **3** (on hob) brûleur *m*; (of engine) gicleur *m*; **4** (stone) jais *m*.
II *vi* **to ~ off to** s'envoler pour.
jet black *adj* de jais *inv*.
jet engine *n* moteur *m* à réaction, réacteur *m*.
jetlag *n* décalage *m* horaire.
jetlagged *adj* **to be ~** souffrir du décalage horaire.
jet setter *n* **to be a ~** faire partie du jet-set.
jettison *vtr* (from ship) jeter [qch] par-dessus bord; (from plane) larguer.
jetty *n* (of stone) jetée *f*; (of wood) appontement *m*.
Jew *n* juif/juive *m/f*.
jewel *n* **1** (gem) pierre *f* précieuse; (piece of jewellery) bijou *m*; (in watch) rubis *m*; **2** (person) perle *f*; (town, object) joyau *m*.
jeweller (GB), **jeweler** (US) ▶626 *n* (person) bijoutier/-ière *m/f*; **~'s (shop)** bijouterie *f*.
jewellery (GB), **jewelry** (US) *n* (gen) bijoux *mpl*; (in shop, workshop) bijouterie *f*; **a piece of ~** un bijou.
Jewish *adj* juif/juive.
jib *n* **1** (sail) foc *m*; **2** (of crane) flèche *f*.
jibe *n* moquerie *f*.
jiffy *n* **in a ~** en un clin d'œil.
Jiffy bag® *n* enveloppe *f* matelassée.
jig *n* gigue *f*.
jiggle I *vtr* agiter.
II *vi* (also **~ about**, **~ around**) gigoter; (impatiently) se trémousser.
jigsaw *n* **1** (also **~ puzzle**) puzzle *m*; **2** (saw) scie *f* sauteuse.
jingle I *n* **1** (of bells) tintement *m*; (of keys) cliquetis *m*; **2** (verse) ritournelle *f*; (for advert) refrain *m* publicitaire, sonal *m*.
II *vi* [*keys, coins*] cliqueter.
jingoist *n*, *adj* chauvin/-e (*m/f*).
jinx *n* **1** (curse) sort *m*; **to put a ~ on** jeter un sort à; **there's a ~ on me** j'ai la poisse○; **2** (unlucky person, object) **it's a ~** ça porte la poisse.
jitters *n pl* **to have the ~** [*person, stock market*] être nerveux/-euse; [*actor*] avoir le trac.
job I *n* **1** (employment) emploi *m*; (post) poste *m*; **to get a ~** trouver un emploi; **a teaching ~** un poste d'enseignant; **what's her ~?** qu'est-ce qu'elle fait (comme travail)?; **2** (role) fonction *f*; **it's my ~ to do** c'est à moi de faire; **3** (duty) travail *m*; **she's only doing her ~** elle fait son travail; **4** (task) travail *m*; **to find a ~ for sb to do** trouver du travail pour qn; **5** (assignment) tâche *f*; **6 to make a good ~ of sth** faire du bon travail avec qch; **7**○ **quite a ~** toute une affaire○ (**to do, doing** de faire).
II *adj* [*advert, offer*] d'emploi; [*pages*] des emplois.
IDIOMS **that'll do the ~** ça fera l'affaire.
job centre *n* (GB) bureau *m* des services nationaux de l'emploi.
job-hunting *n* chasse *f* à l'emploi.
jobless *n* **the ~** les sans-emplois *mpl*.
jockey *n* jockey *m*.
jockey shorts *n pl* (US) slip *m* (d'homme).
jockstrap○ *n* suspensoir *m*.
jodhpurs *n pl* jodhpurs *mpl*.
jog I *n* **1** (with elbow) coup *m* de coude; **2 at a ~** au petit trot○; **3** (Sport) **to go for a ~** aller faire un jogging; **4** (US) (in road) coude *m*.
II *vtr* (with elbow) donner un coup de coude à; **to ~ sb's memory** rafraîchir la mémoire de qn.
III *vi* **to go ~ging** faire du jogging.
jogger *n* joggeur/-euse *m/f*.
jogging ▶504 *n* jogging *m*.
join I *n* raccord *m*.
II *vtr* **1** devenir membre de [*organization, team*]; adhérer à [*club*]; s'inscrire à [*library*]; entrer dans [*firm*]; s'engager dans [*army*]; **to ~ a union** se syndiquer; **2** se mettre dans [*queue*]; **3** (meet up with) rejoindre [*person*]; **may I ~ you?** (sit down) puis-je me joindre à vous?; **4** (connect) réunir, joindre [*ends, pieces*]; assembler [*parts*]; relier [*points, towns*] (**to** à); **5** [*road*] rejoindre [*motorway*]; [*river*] se jeter dans [*sea*].
III *vi* **1** (become member) (of party, club) adhérer; (of group, class) s'inscrire; **2** [*pieces*] se joindre; [*wires*] se raccorder; [*roads*] se rejoindre.
■ **join in**: ¶ **~ in** participer; ¶ **~ in [sth]** participer à [*talks, game*]; prendre part à [*strike, demonstration, bidding*]; **to ~ in the fun** se joindre à la fête.
■ **join up**: ¶ **~ up 1** (enlist) s'engager; **2** (meet up) [*people*] se retrouver; [*roads, tracks*] se rejoindre; ¶ **~ [sth] up** relier [*characters, dots*].
joiner ▶626 *n* menuisier/-ière *m/f*.
joint I *n* **1** (Anat) articulation *f*; **to be out of ~** [*shoulder*] être déboîté/-e; **2** (in carpentry) assemblage *m*; (in metalwork) joint *m*; **3** (of meat) rôti *m*; **4**○ (place) endroit *m*; (café) boui-boui○ *m*; **5**○ (cannabis) joint○ *m*.
II *adj* [*action*] collectif/-ive; [*programme, session*] mixte; [*measures, procedure*] commun/-e; [*winner*] ex aequo *inv*; [*talks*] multilatéral/-e.
joint account *n* compte *m* joint.
joint effort *n* collaboration *f*.
jointly *adv* conjointement; **to be ~ owned by** être la copropriété de.
joint venture *n* **1** (Econ) coentreprise *f*; **2** (gen) projet *m* en commun.
joke I *n* **1** plaisanterie *f*, blague○ *f* (**about** sur); **to tell a ~** raconter une blague; **to play a ~ on sb** jouer un tour à qn; **it's no ~ doing** ce n'est pas facile de faire; **2** (person) guignol *m*; (event, situation) farce *f*.
II *vi* plaisanter, blaguer○; **you must be joking!** tu veux rire!
joker *n* **1** (prankster) farceur/-euse *m/f*; **2** (in cards) joker *m*.
jolly I *adj* [*person*] enjoué/-e; [*tune*] joyeux/-euse.

II *vtr* **to ~ sb along** amadouer qn.
jolt I *n* **1** (jerk) secousse *f*; **2** (shock) choc *m*.
II *vtr* secouer [*passenger*].
III *vi* [*vehicle*] cahoter.
jostle *vi* se bousculer (**for** pour; **to do** pour faire).
jot *v* ■ **jot down** noter [*ideas, names*].
journal *n* **1** (diary) journal *m*; **2** (periodical) revue *f*; (newspaper) journal *m*.
journalism *n* journalisme *m*.
journalist *n* journaliste *mf*.
journey *n* (long) voyage *m*; (short or habitual) trajet *m*; **bus ~** trajet en bus; **to go on a ~** partir en voyage.
jowl *n* (jaw) mâchoire *f*; (fleshy fold) bajoue *f*.
joy *n* **1** (delight) joie *f* (**at** devant); **2** (pleasure) plaisir *m*; **the ~ of doing** le plaisir de faire.
IDIOMS **to be full of the ~s of spring** être en pleine forme.
joyrider *n* jeune chauffard *m* en voiture volée.
joyriding *n* rodéo *m* à la voiture volée.
joystick *n* (in plane) manche *m* à balai; (for video game) manette *f*.
jubilant *adj* [*person*] exultant/-e; [*crowd*] en liesse; [*expression, mood*] réjoui/-e.
jubilee *n* jubilé *m*.
Judaism *n* judaïsme *m*.
judge I *n* **1** ▶ **498** (in court) juge *m*; **2** (at competition) (gen) membre *m* du jury; (Sport) juge *m*; **3 to be a good ~ of character** savoir juger les gens.
II *vtr* **1** juger [*person*]; **2** faire partie du jury de [*show, competition*]; **3** estimer [*distance, age*]; prévoir [*outcome, reaction*]; **4** (consider) juger, estimer.
III *vi* juger; **judging by** or **from**... à en juger d'après...
judgment, **judgement** *n* jugement *m*.
judicial *adj* (gen) judiciaire; [*decision*] jurisprudentiel/-ielle.
judiciary *n* **1** (system of courts) système *m* judiciaire; **2** (judges) magistrature *f*.
judo ▶ **504** *n* judo *m*.
jug *n* **1** (GB) (earthenware) pichet *m*; (pot-bellied) cruche *f*; (glass) carafe *f*; (for cream, milk, water) pot *m*; **2** (US) (flagon) cruche *f*.
juggernaut *n* (GB) poids *m* lourd.
juggle *vi* jongler (**with** avec).
juggler *n* jongleur/-euse *m/f*.
jugular *n*, *adj* jugulaire (*f*).
juice *n* **1** (from fruit, meat) jus *m*; **fruit ~** jus de fruit; **2** (sap) suc *m*; **3 gastric ~s** sucs digestifs or gastriques.
juicy *adj* **1** [*fruit*] juteux/-euse; **2**○ [*story*] croustillant/-e.
jukebox *n* juke-box *m*.
July ▶ **456** *n* juillet *m*.
jumble *n* **1** (of papers, objects) tas *m*; (of ideas) fouillis *m*; (of words) fatras *m*; **2** (GB) (items for sale) bric-à-brac *m*, vieux objets *mpl*.
■ **jumble up** mélanger [*letters, shapes*].
jumble sale *n* (GB) vente *f* de charité.
jumbo *n* (also **~ jet**) gros-porteur *m*.
jump I *n* **1** (leap) saut *m*, bond *m*; **parachute ~** saut en parachute; **2** (in horse race) obstacle *m*; **3** (in price, wages) bond *m* (**in** dans).
II *vtr* **1** sauter [*obstacle, ditch*]; **2 to ~ the lights** griller○ le feu (rouge); **to ~ the queue** passer devant tout le monde; **3 to ~ ship** ne pas rejoindre son bâtiment.
III *vi* **1** (leap) sauter; **to ~ across** or **over sth** franchir qch d'un bond; **to ~ up and down** sautiller; (in anger) trépigner de colère; **2** (start in surprise) sursauter; **3** [*prices, rate*] monter en flèche; **4 to ~ at** sauter sur [*opportunity*]; accepter [qch] avec enthousiasme [*offer*].
■ **jump back** [*person*] faire un bond en arrière; [*lever*] lâcher brusquement.
■ **jump down** [*person*] sauter (**from** de).
■ **jump on**: ¶ **~ on [sth]** sauter dans [*bus, train*]; sauter sur [*bicycle, horse*]; ¶ **~ on [sb]** sauter sur qn.
■ **jump out** [*person*] sauter; **to ~ out of** sauter par [*window*]; sauter de [*bed, train*].
■ **jump up** [*person*] se lever d'un bond.
jumper *n* **1** (GB) (sweater) pull *m*, pull-over *m*; **2** (US) (pinafore) robe *f* chasuble.
jump-start *vtr* faire démarrer [qch] avec des câbles [*car*].
jump suit *n* combinaison *f*.
jumpy○ *adj* [*person*] nerveux/-euse; [*market*] instable.
junction *n* **1** (of two roads) carrefour *m*; (on motorway) échangeur *m*; **2** (of railway lines) nœud *m* ferroviaire; (station) gare *f* de jonction.
June ▶ **456** *n* juin *m*.
jungle *n* jungle *f*.
junior I *n* **1** (younger person) cadet/-ette *m/f*; **2** (low-ranking worker) subalterne *mf*; **3** (GB Sch) élève *mf* du primaire; **4** (US Univ) ≈ étudiant/-e *m/f* de premier cycle; (in high school) ≈ élève *mf* de première.
II *adj* **1** [*colleague, rank, position*] subalterne; **2** (Sport) [*race, team*] des cadets; [*player*] jeune; **3** (also **Junior**) **Mortimer ~** Mortimer fils or junior.
junior high school *n* (US) ≈ collège *m*.
junior minister *n* secrétaire *m* d'État.
junior school *n* (GB) école *f* (primaire).
junk *n* **1** (rubbish) camelote○ *f*; **2** (second-hand) bric-à-brac *m*; **3** (boat) jonque *f*.
junk food *n* nourriture *f* industrielle.
junk mail *n* prospectus *mpl*.
junk shop *n* boutique *f* de bric-à-brac.
junkyard *n* (for scrap) dépotoir *m*; (for old cars) cimetière *f* de voitures.
junta *n* junte *f*.
Jupiter *pr n* Jupiter *f*.
jurisdiction *n* **1** (gen) compétence *f* (**over** sur); **2** (Law) juridiction *f* (**over** sur).
juror *n* juré *m*.
jury *n* jury *m*.
jury box *n* banc *m* des jurés.
jury duty (US), **jury service** (GB) *n* **to do ~** faire partie d'un jury.
just[1] I *adv* **1 to have ~ done** venir (juste) de faire; **he had only ~ left** il venait tout juste

de partir; **2** (immediately) juste; **~ before/after** juste avant/après; **3** (slightly) **~ over/under 20 kg** un peu plus/moins de 20 kg; **4** (only, merely) juste; **~ for fun** juste pour rire; **~ two days ago** il y a juste deux jours; **he's ~ a child** ce n'est qu'un enfant; **5** (purposely) exprès; **he did it ~ to annoy us** il l'a fait exprès pour nous embêter; **6** (barely) tout juste; **~ on time** tout juste à l'heure; **he's ~ 20** il a tout juste 20 ans; **I (only) ~ caught the train** j'ai eu le train de justesse; **7** (simply) tout simplement; **~ tell the truth** dis la vérité, tout simplement; **she ~ won't listen** elle ne veut tout simplement pas écouter; **'~ a moment'** 'un instant'; **8** (exactly) exactement; **that's ~ what I want** c'est exactement ce que je veux; **it's ~ right** c'est parfait; **she looks ~ like her father** c'est son père tout craché○; **it's ~ like him to forget** c'est bien de lui d'oublier; **9** (possibly) **it might** or **could ~ be true** il se peut que ce soit vrai; **10** (at this or that very moment) **to be ~ doing** être en train de faire; **to be ~ about to do** être sur le point de faire; **he was ~ leaving** il partait; **11** (positively, totally) vraiment; **that's ~ wonderful** c'est vraiment merveilleux; **12** (in requests) **if you could ~ hold this box** si vous pouvez tenir cette boîte; **13** (equally) **~ as big as**... (tout) aussi grand que...; **14** (with imperative) donc; **~ you dare!** essaie donc voir!; **~ imagine!** imagine donc!

II just about *phr* presque; **~ about everything** à peu près tout; **I can ~ about see it** je peux tout juste le voir.

III just as *phr* **~ as he came** juste au moment où il est arrivé.

IV just now *phr* en ce moment; **I saw him ~ now** je viens juste de le voir.

just² *adj* [*person, decision*] juste; [*demand*] justifié/-e; [*claim, criticism*] légitime.

justice *n* **1** (fairness) justice *f*; **the portrait doesn't do her ~** le portrait ne l'avantage pas; **2** (the law) justice *f*; **to bring sb to ~** traduire qn en justice.

Justice Department *n* (US) ministère *m* de la justice.

Justice of the Peace *n* juge *m* de paix.

justifiable *adj* (that is justified) légitime; (that can be justified) justifiable.

justification *n* raison *f*; **to have some ~ for doing** avoir des raisons de faire.

justified *adj* justifié/-e; **to feel ~ in doing** se sentir en droit de faire.

justify *vtr* justifier.

jut *vi* (also **~ out**) [*cliffs*] avancer en saillie (**into** dans); [*balcony*] faire saillie (**over** sur).

juvenile *n* (gen) jeune *mf*; (Law) mineur/-e *m/f*.

juvenile delinquent *n* jeune délinquant/-e *m/f*.

juvenile offender *n* délinquant/-e *m/f* mineur/-e.

juxtapose *vtr* juxtaposer (**with** à).

Kk

k, K *n* k, K *m*.
kale *n* (also **curly ~**) chou *m* frisé.
kaleidoscope *n* kaléidoscope *m*.
kangaroo *n* kangourou *m*.
karaoke *n* karaoké *m*.
karate ▶ 504 *n* karaté *m*.
kayak *n* kayak *m*.
kebab *n* (also **shish ~**) chiche-kebab *m*.
kedgeree *n* (GB) pilaf *m* de poisson.
keel *n* quille *f*.
■ **keel over** [*boat*] chavirer; [*person*] s'écrouler; [*tree*] s'abattre.
keen *adj* **1** (eager) [*artist, footballer, supporter*] enthousiaste; [*student*] assidu/-e; **to be ~ on** tenir à [*plan, project*]; être chaud/-e○ pour [*idea*]; être passionné/-e de [*activity*]; **to be ~ on doing** or **to do** tenir à faire; **to be ~ on sb**○ en pincer○ pour qn; **2** [*appetite, interest*] vif/vive; [*eye, intelligence*] vif/vive; [*sight*] perçant/-e; [*hearing, sense of smell*] fin/-e; **3** [*competition*] intense.
keep I *n* **1** pension *f*; **to pay for one's ~** payer une pension; **2** (tower) donjon *m*.
II *vtr* **1** (retain) garder [*receipt, money, letter, seat*]; **to ~ sb/sth clean** garder qn/qch propre; **to ~ sth warm** garder qch au chaud; **to ~ sb warm** protéger qn du froid; **to ~ sb waiting** faire attendre qn; **to ~ sb talking** retenir qn; **to ~ an engine running** laisser un moteur en marche; **2** (detain) retenir; **I won't ~ you a minute** je n'en ai pas pour longtemps; **3** tenir [*shop*]; élever [*chickens*]; **4** (sustain) **to ~ [sth] going** entretenir [*conversation, fire*]; maintenir [*tradition*]; **I'll make you a sandwich to ~ you going** je te ferai un sandwich pour que tu tiennes le coup; **5** (store) mettre, ranger; **where do you ~ your cups?** où rangez-vous vos tasses?; **6** (support) faire vivre, entretenir [*family*]; **7** tenir [*accounts, diary*]; **8 to ~ sth from sb** taire or cacher qch à qn; **to ~ sth to oneself** garder qch pour soi; **9** (prevent) **to ~ sb from doing** empêcher qn de faire; **10** tenir [*promise*]; garder [*secret*]; se rendre à [*appointment*]; **11** (Mus) **to ~ time** battre la mesure.
III *vi* **1** (continue) **to ~ doing** continuer à or de faire, ne pas arrêter de faire; **to ~ going** [*person*] continuer; **2** (remain) **to ~ out of the rain** se protéger de la pluie; **to ~ warm** se protéger du froid; **to ~ calm** rester calme; **to ~ silent** garder le silence; **3** [*food*] se conserver, se garder; **4** [*news, business*] attendre; **5 'how are you ~ing?'** 'comment allez-vous?'; **she's ~ing well** elle va bien.
IV *v refl* **to ~ oneself to oneself** ne pas être sociable.
V for keeps *phr* pour de bon, pour toujours.
■ **keep back**: ¶ **~ back** ne pas s'approcher (**from** de); ¶ **~ [sb/sth] back 1** empêcher [qn] de s'approcher [*crowd*] (**from** de); [*dam*] retenir [*water*]; **2** (retain) garder [*money*]; conserver [*food*].
■ **keep off**: ¶ **~ off [sth] 1** ne pas marcher sur [*grass*]; **2** éviter [*alcohol*]; s'abstenir de parler de [*subject*]; ¶ **~ [sth] off** éloigner [*insects*]; **this plastic sheet will ~ the rain off** cette housse en plastique protège de la pluie.
■ **keep on**: ¶ **~ on doing** continuer à faire; **to ~ on about** ne pas arrêter de parler de; **to ~ on at sb** harceler qn (**to do** pour qu'il fasse); ¶ **~ [sb] on** garder.
■ **keep out**: ¶ **~ out of [sth] 1** ne pas entrer dans [*house*]; **'~ out!'** 'défense d'entrer'; **2** rester à l'abri de [*sun, danger*]; **3** ne pas se mêler de [*argument*]; **to ~ out of sb's way** (not hinder) ne pas gêner qn; (avoid seeing) éviter qn; ¶ **~ [sb/sth] out** ne pas laisser entrer [*person, animal*].
■ **keep to** ne pas s'écarter de [*road*]; respecter, s'en tenir à [*facts*]; respecter [*law, rules*].
■ **keep up**: ¶ **~ up** [*car, runner, person*] suivre; ¶ **~ [sth] up 1** tenir [*trousers*]; **2** continuer [*attack, studies*]; entretenir [*correspondence, friendship*]; maintenir [*membership, tradition, pace*]; ¶ **~ [sb] up** [*noise*] empêcher [qn] de dormir.
■ **keep up with 1** aller aussi vite que [*person*]; suivre [*class*]; [*wages*] suivre [*inflation*]; faire face à [*demand*]; **2** suivre [*fashion, developments*].
keeper *n* (curator) conservateur/-trice *m/f*; (guard) gardien/-ienne *m/f*.
keep fit *n* gymnastique *f* d'entretien.
keeping *n* **1** (custody) **in sb's ~** à la garde de qn; **to put sb/sth in sb's ~** confier qn/qch à qn; **2** (conformity) **in ~ with** conforme à [*law, tradition*]; **to be in ~ with** correspondre à [*image, character*]; s'harmoniser avec [*surroundings*].
keg *n* (for liquid) fût *m*; (for gunpowder) baril *m*.
kennel *n* **1** (GB) (for dog) niche *f*; **2** (establishment) chenil *m*.
kerb *n* (GB) bord *m* du trottoir.
kernel *n* (of nut, fruitstone) amande *f*.
kerosene, **kerosine** *n* **1** (US) (paraffin) pétrole *m* (lampant); **2** (fuel) kérosène *m*.
kestrel *n* (faucon *m*) crécerelle *f*.
kettle *n* bouilloire *f*; **to put the ~ on** mettre l'eau à chauffer.
kettledrum ▶ 586 *n* timbale *f*.
key I *n* **1** clé *f*; **a front-door ~** une clé de maison; **a set** or **bunch of ~s** un jeu de clés; **under lock and ~** sous clé; **radiator ~** clavette *f* à radiateur; **2** (on computer, piano) touche *f*; (on oboe, flute) clé *f*; **3** (vital clue) clé *f*, secret *m* (**to** de); **4** (on map) légende *f*; (to abbreviations, symbols) liste *f*; (for code) clé *f*; **5** (to test, riddle) solutions *fpl*; (Sch) corrigé *m*; **6** (Mus) ton

m, tonalité *f*; **to sing in/off ~** chanter juste/faux.
II *adj* [*figure, role*] clé; [*point*] capital/-e.
III *vtr* **1** (also **~ in**) saisir [*data*]; **2** (adapt) adapter (**to** à).
keyboard ▶586 *n* clavier *m*.
keyboards *n pl* synthétiseur *m*.
keyed-up *adj* (excited) excité/-e; (tense) tendu/-e.
keyhole *n* trou *m* de serrure.
key-ring *n* porte-clés *m inv*.
khaki *adj* kaki *inv*.
kibbutz *n* kibboutz *m*.
kick I *n* **1** (of person, horse) coup *m* de pied; (of donkey, cow) coup *m* de sabot; (of swimmer) battement *m* de pieds; (of footballer) tir *m*; **2**○ (thrill) **to get a ~ out of doing** prendre plaisir à faire; **3** (of firearm) recul *m*.
II *vtr* (once) [*person*] donner un coup de pied à [*person*]; donner un coup de pied dans [*door, ball, tin can*]; [*horse*] botter [*person*]; [*donkey, cow*] donner un coup de sabot à [*person*]; (repeatedly) [*person*] donner des coups de pied à [*person*]; donner des coups de pieds dans [*object*]; **to ~ sb on the leg** [*person, horse*] donner à qn un coup de pied à la jambe; [*donkey, cow*] donner à qn un coup de sabot dans la jambe.
III *vi* [*person*] (once) donner un coup de pied; (repeatedly) donner des coups de pied; [*swimmer*] faire des battements de pieds; [*cow*] ruer; [*horse*] botter.
IDIOMS **to ~ the habit**○ (of drug addiction) décrocher○; (of smoking) arrêter de fumer; **I could have ~ed myself** je me serais donné des claques○.
■ **kick around, kick about** donner des coups de pied dans, s'amuser avec [*ball*].
■ **kick off 1** (Sport) donner le coup d'envoi; **2**○ (start) commencer.
■ **kick out**: ¶ **~ out** [*animal*] ruer; ¶ **~ [sb] out**○ virer○.
kick-off *n* (Sport) coup *m* d'envoi.
kick-start I *n* (also **~-starter**) kick *m*.
II *vtr* **1** faire démarrer [qch] au pied [*motorbike*]; **2** relancer [*economy*].
kid I *n* **1**○ (child) enfant *mf*, gosse○ *mf*; (youth) gamin/-e○ *m/f*; **2** (young goat) chevreau/-ette *m/f*; **3** (goatskin) chevreau *m*.
II○ *vtr* charrier○ (**about** à propos de).
III○ *vi* rigoler○; **no ~ding!** sans blague○!
IV○ *v refl* **to ~ oneself** se faire des illusions.
kidnap *vtr* enlever.
kidnapper *n* ravisseur/-euse *m/f*.
kidney *n* **1** (Anat) rein *m*; **2** (Culin) rognon *m*.
kidney bean *n* haricot *m* rouge.
kidney machine *n* rein *m* artificiel; **to be on a ~** être sous dialyse.
kill I *n* mise *f* à mort.
II *vtr* **1** tuer [*person, animal*]; **they ~ed each other** ils se sont entre-tués; **even if it ~s me**○! même si je dois y laisser ma peau○!; **my feet are ~ing me**○ j'ai mal aux pieds; **2** mettre fin à, étouffer [*rumour*]; [*editor*] supprimer [*story*]; **3** faire disparaître [*pain*]; ôter [*appetite*]; **4** (spend) **to ~ time** tuer le temps (**by doing** en faisant).
III *vi* [*person, animal, drug*] tuer.
IV *v refl* **to ~ oneself** se suicider.
killer *n* (person) meurtrier *m*; (animal) tueur/-euse *m/f*; **heroin is a ~** l'héroïne tue.
killing *n* (of individual) meurtre *m* (**of** de); (of animal) mise *f* à mort (**of** de).
kiln *n* four *m*.
kilo ▶573 *n* kilo *m*.
kilobyte, KB *n* kilo-octet *m*, Ko *m*.
kilogram(me) ▶573 *n* kilogramme *m*.
kilometre (GB), **kilometer** (US) ▶573 *n* kilomètre *m*.
kilowatt *n* kilowatt *m*.
kind I *n* **1** (sort, type) sorte *f*, genre *m*, type *m*; **this ~ of person** ce genre de personne; **all ~s of people** toutes sortes de personnes; **what ~ of dog is it?** qu'est-ce que c'est comme chien?; **what ~ of person is she?** comment est-elle?, quel genre de personne est-ce?; **this is one of a ~** il/elle est unique en son genre; **2** (in vague descriptions) **a ~ of** une sorte de; **I heard a ~ of rattling noise** j'ai entendu comme un cliquetis; **3** (classified type) espèce *f*, genre *m*; **one's own ~** les gens de son espèce.
II *adj* [*person, gesture, words*] gentil/-ille; [*act*] bon/bonne (*before n*); **to be ~ to sb** être gentil/-ille avec qn; **to be ~ to animals** bien traiter les animaux; **that's very ~ of you** c'est très gentil or aimable de votre part; **would you be ~ enough to pass me the salt?** auriez-vous l'amabilité de me passer le sel?
III **in kind** *phr* [*pay*] en nature.
IV **kind of**○ *phr* **he's ~ of cute** il est plutôt mignon; **I ~ of like him** en fait, je l'aime bien; **'is it interesting?'—'~ of'** 'est-ce que c'est intéressant?'—'assez'.
kindergarten *n* jardin *m* d'enfants.
kind-hearted *adj* [*person*] de cœur.
kindle *vtr* **1** allumer [*fire*]; **2** attiser [*desire, passion*]; susciter [*interest*].
kindly I *adj* [*person*] gentil/-ille; [*smile*] bienveillant/-e.
II *adv* **1** (in a kind way) avec gentillesse; **to speak ~ of sb** dire du bien de qn; **2** (obligingly) gentiment; **would you ~ do/refrain from doing** auriez-vous l'amabilité de faire/de ne pas faire; **3** (favourably) **to take ~ to** apprécier.
kindness *n* gentillesse *f*, bonté *f*.
kindred spirit *n* âme *f* sœur.
kinetics *n* cinétique *f*.
king ▶498 *n* **1** (monarch) roi *m*; **King Charles** le roi Charles; **2** (in chess, cards) roi *m*; (in draughts, checkers) dame *f*.
kingdom *n* **1** (country) royaume *m*; **2** (Bot, Zool) règne *m*; **the animal ~** le règne animal.
kingfisher *n* martin-pêcheur *m*.
king-size(d) *adj* [*packet*] géant/-e; [*portion, garden*] énorme; **~ bed** grand lit *m*; **~ cigarettes** cigarettes *fpl* extra-longues.

kink *n* (in rope, tube) nœud *m*; **the hosepipe has a ~ in it** le tuyau d'arrosage est tordu.

kiosk *n* **1** (stand) kiosque *m*; **2** (GB) (phone box) cabine *f*.

kipper *n* (GB) hareng *m* fumé et salé, kipper *m*.

kiss I *n* baiser *m*; **to give sb a ~** embrasser qn, donner un baiser à qn.
II *vtr* embrasser, donner un baiser à [*person*]; **to ~ sb on** embrasser qn sur [*cheek, lips*]; **we ~ed each other** nous nous sommes embrassés.
III *vi* s'embrasser.

kiss of life *n* (GB) bouche-à-bouche *m inv*; **to give sb the ~** faire le bouche-à-bouche à qn.

kit *n* **1** (implements) trousse *f*; **2** (gear, clothes) affaires *fpl*; **football ~** affaires de football; **3** (for assembly) kit *m*; **4** (Mil) paquetage *m*.
■ **kit out** (GB) équiper (**with** de).

kitbag *n* (for sport) sac *m* de sport; (for travel) sac *m* de voyage; (Mil) sac *m* de soldat.

kitchen *n* cuisine *f*.

kitchen foil *n* papier *m* d'aluminium.

kitchen roll *n* essuie-tout *m inv*.

kitchen sink *n* évier *m*.

kite *n* cerf-volant *m*; **to fly a ~** faire voler un cerf-volant.

kitten *n* chaton *m*.

kitty *n* cagnotte *f*.

kiwi fruit *n* kiwi *m*.

kleptomaniac *n, adj* kleptomane (*mf*).

knack *n* **1** (dexterity) tour *m* de main (**of doing** pour faire); **to get the ~** attraper le tour de main; **to lose the ~** perdre la main; **2** (talent) don *m* (**for doing** de faire).

knapsack *n* sac *m* à dos.

knave *n* (in cards) valet *m*.

knead *vtr* pétrir [*dough*]; masser [*flesh*].

knee I ▶413 *n* genou *m*; **on (one's) hands and ~s** à quatre pattes.
II *vtr* donner un coup de genou à [*person*].
IDIOMS **to go weak at the ~s** avoir les jambes qui flageolent.

kneecap *n* rotule *f*.

knee-deep *adj* **the water was ~** l'eau arrivait aux genoux.

kneel *vi* (also **~ down**) se mettre à genoux; (in prayer) s'agenouiller; **to be ~ing** être à genoux.

knee-length *adj* [*skirt*] qui s'arrête au genou; [*boots*] haut/-e; [*socks*] long/longue.

knickers *n pl* (GB) petite culotte *f*.

knick-knack *n* bibelot *m*.

knife I *n* couteau *m*.
II *vtr* donner un coup de couteau à; **to be ~d** recevoir un coup de couteau.

knight I *n* (gen) chevalier *m*; (in chess) cavalier *m*.
II *vtr* (GB) anoblir [*person*] (**for** pour).

knighthood *n* titre *m* de chevalier.

knit I *vtr* tricoter [*sweater, hat*]; **~ted** en tricot.
II *vi* **1** tricoter; **2** [*broken bones*] se souder.

knitting *n* tricot *m*.

knob *n* **1** (of door) bouton *m*; (on bannister) boule *f*; **2** (control button) bouton *m*.

knobbly (GB), **knobby** (US) *adj* [*fingers*] noueux/-euse; [*knees*] saillant/-e.

knock I *n* **1** (blow) coup *m* (**on** sur; **with** de); **a ~ at the door** un coup à la porte; **~! ~!** toc! toc!; **2** (setback) coup *m*; **to take a ~** en prendre un coup.
II *vtr* **1** (strike) cogner [*object*]; **to ~ one's head on sth** se cogner la tête contre qch; **to ~ sb unconscious** assommer qn; **to ~ sth off** or **out of sth** faire tomber qch de qch; **2**○ (criticize) dénigrer.
III *vi* **1** [*branch, engine, object*] cogner (**on, against** contre); [*person*] frapper (**at, on** à); **2** (collide) **to ~ into** or **against sth** heurter qch.
■ **knock down 1** (deliberately) jeter [qn] à terre [*person*]; défoncer [*door*]; démolir [*building*]; (accidentally) renverser [*person, object*]; abattre [*fence*]; **2** [*buyer*] faire baisser [*price*]; [*seller*] baisser [*price*].
■ **knock off**: ¶ **~ off**○ arrêter de travailler; ¶ **~ [sb/sth] off, ~ off [sb/sth] 1** (cause to fall) faire tomber [*person, object*]; **2**○ (reduce) **to ~ £10 off the price of sth** réduire le prix de qch de 10 livres; **3**○ **~ it off!** ça suffit!
■ **knock out 1** casser [*tooth*]; **2** (make unconscious) [*person, blow*] assommer; [*drug*] endormir; [*boxer*] mettre [qn] au tapis [*opponent*]; **3** (Sport) éliminer [*opponent, team*].
■ **knock over** renverser [*person, object*].

knockabout *n* (Sport) échange *m* de balles.

knocker *n* heurtoir *m*.

knocking *n* (at door) coups *mpl*; (in engine) cognement *m*.

knock-kneed *adj* cagneux/-euse.

knock-on effect *n* implications *fpl*.

knock-out I *n* (in boxing) knock-out *m*.
II *adj* **1** (Sport) [*competition*] avec tours éliminatoires; **2**○ [*pills*] sédatif/-ive.

knot I *n* **1** nœud *m*; **to tie a ~** faire un nœud; **to tie sth in a ~** nouer qch; **2** (in wood) nœud *m*; **3** (group) petit groupe *m* (**of** de).
II *vtr* nouer (**together** ensemble).

know I *vtr* (gen) savoir; (be acquainted or familiar with) connaître [*place, person, way*]; **to ~ why/how** savoir pourquoi/comment; **to ~ how to do** savoir faire; **to ~ sb by sight** connaître qn de vue; **to get to ~ sb** faire connaissance avec qn; **he ~s all about it** il est au courant; **I knew it!** j'en étais sûr!
II *vi* savoir; **as you ~** comme vous le savez; **to ~ about** (have information) être au courant de [*event*]; (have skill) s'y connaître en [*computing, engines*]; **to ~ of** (from experience) connaître; (from information) avoir entendu parler de; **to let sb ~ of** or **about** tenir qn au courant de.
IDIOMS **to be in the ~**○ être bien informé/-e.

know-all○ *n* (GB) je-sais-tout *mf inv*.

know-how○ *n* savoir-faire *m inv*.

knowing *adj* [*look, smile*] entendu/-e.

knowledge *n* **1** (awareness) connaissance *f*; **to my ~** à ma connaissance; **without sb's ~** à l'insu de qn; **2** (factual wisdom) connaissances *fpl*; (of specific field) connaissance *f*; **technical ~** connaissances techniques.

knowledgeable *adj* [*person*] savant/-e; **to be ~ about** s'y connaître en [*subject*].

known *adj* [*authority, danger*] reconnu/-e; [*cure*] connu/-e.

knuckle *n* **1** (of person) jointure *f*, articulation *f*; **2** (Culin) (of lamb, mutton) manche *m* de gigot; (of pork, veal) jarret *m*.

■ **knuckle down**○ s'y mettre (sérieusement).

knuckle-duster *n* coup-de-poing *m* américain.

koala (bear) *n* koala *m*.

Koran *n* Coran *m*.

Korea ▶ 448 *pr n* Corée *f*.

kosher *adj* **1** [*food, restaurant*] casher; **2**○ (not illegal) **it's ~** c'est réglo○.

l, L *n* l, L *m*.
lab *n* labo○ *m*.
label I *n* **1** (on clothing, jar) étiquette *f*; **2** (also **record ~**) label *m*; **3** (Comput) label *m*.
II *vtr* **1** étiqueter [*clothing, jar*]; **2** classer, étiqueter (derogatory) [*person*] (**as** comme).
labor (US) = **labour**.
laboratory *n* laboratoire *m*.
laborer (US) = **labourer**.
labor union *n* (US) syndicat *m*.
labour (GB), **labor** (US) **I** *n* **1** (work) travail *m*; **2** (also **~ force**) main-d'œuvre *f*; **3** (Med) accouchement *m*; **to be in ~** être en train d'accoucher.
II *vi* travailler (dur) (**at** à; **on** sur; **to do** pour faire).
IDIOMS **to ~ the point** insister lourdement.
Labour I *n* (GB) parti *m* travailliste.
II *adj* travailliste.
labourer (GB), **laborer** (US) ▶626 *n* ouvrier/-ière *m/f* du bâtiment.
Labour Party *n* (GB) parti *m* travailliste.
lace I *n* **1** (fabric) dentelle *f*; **2** (on shoe, boot, dress) lacet *m*; (on tent) cordon *m*.
II *vtr* **1** lacer [*shoes*]; **2 to ~ a drink with sth** mettre qch dans une boisson.
lace-up (shoe) *n* chaussure *f* à lacet.
lack I *n* manque *m* (**of** de); **through ~ of** par manque de.
II *vtr* manquer de.
III *vi* **to be ~ing** manquer; **to be ~ing in** manquer de.
lacquer *n* **1** (for hair) laque *f*; **2** (varnish) laque *f*.
lad○ *n* (boy) garçon *m*.
ladder I *n* **1** (for climbing) échelle *f*; **2** (GB) (in stockings) échelle *f*, maille *f* filée.
II *vtr, vi* filer.
ladle *n* (Culin) louche *f*.
lady I *n* **1** (woman) dame *f*; **ladies and gentlemen** mesdames et messieurs; **a little old ~** une petite vieille; **she's a real ~** elle est très distinguée; **2** ▶498 (in titles) **Lady Churchill** Lady Churchill.
II ladies *n pl* toilettes *fpl*; (on sign) 'Dames'.
ladybird *n* coccinelle *f*.
ladylike *adj* [*behaviour*] distingué/-e.
lag I *n* (also **time ~**) décalage *m*.
II *vtr* calorifuger [*pipe, tank*]; isoler [*roof*].
■ **lag behind**: ¶ **~ behind** [*person, prices*] être à la traîne; ¶ **~ behind [sb/sth]** traîner derrière [*person*]; être en retard sur [*rival, product*].
lager *n* bière *f* blonde.
lagoon *n* lagune *f*.
laidback○ *adj* décontracté/-e.
laid up *adj* **to be ~** être alité/-e.
lake *n* lac *m*.
lamb *n* agneau *m*; **leg of ~** gigot *m* d'agneau.
lamb's wool *n* laine *f* d'agneau, lambswool *m*.
lame *adj* boiteux/-euse.
lament I *n* lamentation *f*.
II *vtr* se lamenter sur [*fate, misfortune*].
laminated *adj* [*plastic*] stratifié/-e; [*wood*] contreplaqué/-e; [*card*] plastifié/-e.
lamp *n* lampe *f*.
lamppost *n* réverbère *m*.
lampshade *n* abat-jour *m*.
lance *vtr* percer [*boil, abscess*].
land I *n* **1** (terrain, property) terrain *m*; (very large) terres *fpl*; **2** (farmland) terre *f*; **3** (country) pays *m*; **4** (not sea) terre *f*; **dry ~** terre ferme; **to reach ~** toucher terre; **by ~** par voie de terre.
II *vtr* **1** [*pilot*] poser [*aircraft*]; faire atterrir [*space capsule*]; **2** prendre [*fish*]; **3**○ décrocher○ [*job, contract, prize*]; **4**○ **to be ~ed with sb/sth** se retrouver avec qn/qch sur les bras.
III *vi* **1** [*aircraft, passenger*] atterrir; **2** [*ship*] accoster; **3** [*person, animal, object*] atterrir; [*ball*] toucher le sol; **most of the paint ~ed on me** presque toute la peinture m'est tombée dessus.
landing *n* **1** (at turn of stairs) palier *m*; (storey) étage *m*; **2** (from boat) (of people) débarquement *m*; (of cargo) déchargement *m*; **3** (by plane) atterrissage *m* (**on** sur).
landing card *n* carte *f* de débarquement.
landing gear *n* train *m* d'atterrissage.
landing strip *n* piste *f* d'atterrissage.
landlady *n* (owner) propriétaire *f*; (live-in) logeuse *f*; (of pub) patronne *f*.
landlord *n* (owner) propriétaire *m*; (live-in) logeur *m*; (of pub) patron *m*.
landmark *n* (for bearings) point *m* de repère; (major step) étape *f* importante.
land mine *n* mine *f* terrestre.
landowner *n* propriétaire *mf* foncier/-ière.
landscape *n* paysage *m*.
landslide *n* **1** glissement *m* de terrain; **2** (also **~ victory**) victoire *f* écrasante.
lane *n* **1** (in country) chemin *m*, petite route *f*; (in town) ruelle *f*; **2** (of road) voie *f*, file *f*; (air, sea) couloir *m*; (Sport) couloir *m*.
language *n* **1** (system in general) langage *m*; **2** (of a particular nation) langue *f*; **the French ~** la langue française; **3** (of a particular group, style) langage *m*; **legal ~** langage juridique; **bad** or **foul ~** langage grossier; **4** (Comput) langage *m*.
language laboratory, **language lab** *n* laboratoire *m* de langues.
lantern *n* lanterne *f*.
lap *n* **1** (of person) genoux *mpl*; **in one's ~** sur les genoux; **2** (Sport) (of track) tour *m* de piste; (of racecourse) tour *m* de circuit.

Languages and Nationalities

Languages

Note that names of languages in French are always written with a small letter, not a capital as in English; also, French almost always uses the definite article with languages, while English does not. In the examples below, the name of any language may be substituted for ***French*** and ***français***:

to learn French	= apprendre le français

However, the article is never used after ***en***:

*say it **in** French*	= dis-le **en** français
*to translate sth **into** French*	= traduire qch **en** français

and it may be omitted with ***parler***:

to speak French	= parler français / parler le français

but

the lecturer spoke in French	= le conférencier a parlé en français

When ***French*** means *in French* or *of the French*, it is translated by ***français***:

*the **French** language*	= la langue **française**
*a **French** word*	= un mot **français**

If you want to make it clear you mean *in French* and not *from France*, use ***en français***:

*a **French** book*	= un livre **en français**
*a **French** broadcast*	= une émission **en français**

When ***French*** means *relating to French* or *about French*, it is translated by ***de français***:

*a **French** class*	= un cours **de français**
*a **French** dictionary*	= un dictionnaire **de français**

but

*a **French-English** dictionary*	= un dictionnaire **français-anglais**

See the dictionary entry for **speaking** and **speaker** for expressions like *French-speaking* or *French speaker*. French has special words for some of these expressions:

English-speaking	= anglophone
a French speaker	= un / une francophone

Nationalities

Note again the different use of capital letters in English and French; adjectives never have capitals in French:

a French student	= un étudiant français / une étudiante française

Nouns have capitals in French when they mean a person of a specific nationality:

a Frenchman	= un Français
a Frenchwoman	= une Française
French people or *the French*	= les Français *mpl*

English sometimes has a special word for a person of a specific nationality; in French, the same word is almost always either an adjective (no capitals) or a noun (with capitals):

Danish	= danois
a Dane	= un Danois / une Danoise
the Danes	= les Danois *mpl*

Note the alternatives using either adjective (***il/elle est . . .*** etc) or noun (***c'est un/une, ce sont des . . .*** etc) in French:

***he is** French*	= **il est** français / **c'est un** Français

When the subject is a noun, the adjective construction is normally used in French:

*the teacher **is** French*	= le professeur **est** français

IDIOMS **in the ~ of luxury** dans le plus grand luxe.
■ **lap up 1** laper [*milk, water*]; **2** boire [qch] comme du petit lait [*compliment, flattery*].

lapel *n* revers *m*.

lapse I *n* **1** (slip) défaillance *f*; **a ~ in concentration** un relâchement de l'attention; **2** (interval) intervalle *m*, laps *m* de temps.
II *vi* **1** [*contract, membership*] expirer; [*insurance*] prendre fin; **2 to ~ into** se mettre à parler [*jargon, German*]; tomber dans [*coma*]; prendre [*bad habits*].

laptop *n* (also **~ computer**) portable *m*.

lard *n* saindoux *m*.

larder *n* garde-manger *m inv*.

large I *adj* **1** (gen) grand/-e (*before n*); [*appetite, piece, person, nose*] gros/grosse (*before n*); [*amount*] important/-e; [*crowd, family*] nombreux/-euse.
II **at large** *phr* **1** [*prisoner, criminal*] en liberté; **2** [*society, population*] en général, dans son ensemble.
IDIOMS **by and ~** en général.

lark *n* **1** (Zool) alouette *f*; **2**○ (fun) **for a ~** pour rigoler○.

laryngitis ▶ 533 *n* laryngite *f*.

larynx *n* larynx *m*.

lasagne *n* lasagnes *fpl*.

laser I *n* laser *m*.
II *adj* [*beam, disc*] laser *inv*; [*printer*] à laser.

lash I *n* **1** (eyelash) cil *m*; **2** (whipstroke) coup *m* de fouet.
II *vtr* fouetter [*person, animal*]; [*rain*] cingler [*windows*].
■ **lash out** [*person*] devenir violent/-e; **to ~ out at sb** (physically) frapper qn; (verbally) invectiver qn.

last I *pron* **the ~** le dernier/la dernière *m/f* (**to do** à faire); **the ~ but one** l'avant-dernier/-ière; **the night before ~** (evening) avant-hier soir; (night) la nuit d'avant-hier; **the week before ~** il y a deux semaines.
II *adj* dernier/-ière (*before n*); **~ week/year** la semaine/l'année dernière; **~ Christmas** à Noël l'an dernier; **over the ~ ten years** durant ces dix dernières années; **~ night** (evening) hier soir; (night-time) la nuit dernière.
III *adv* **1 to come in ~** [*runner, racing car*] arriver en dernier; **the girls left ~** les filles sont parties les dernières; **to leave sth till ~** s'occuper de qch en dernier (lieu); **~ of all** en dernier lieu; **2 she was ~ here in 1976** la dernière fois qu'elle est venue ici, c'était en 1976.
IV *vi* **1** durer; **it's too good to ~!** c'est trop beau pour que ça dure!; **he won't ~ long here** il ne tiendra pas longtemps ici; **2** [*fabric*] faire de l'usage; [*perishables*] se conserver.
V **at last** *adv* enfin.

lasting *adj* [*effect, impression*] durable; [*relationship*] sérieux/-ieuse.

lastly *adv* enfin, finalement.

last-minute *adj* de dernière minute.

last name *n* nom *m* de famille.

last rites *n pl* derniers sacrements *mpl*.

latch *n* (fastening) loquet *m*; (spring lock) serrure *f* (de sûreté).
■ **latch on to**○ s'accrocher à [*object, person*]; exploiter [*idea*].

late I *adj* **1** [*arrival*] tardif/-ive; **to be ~ (for sth)** être en retard (pour qch); **to make sb ~** retarder qn; **to be ~ with the rent** payer son loyer avec du retard; **dinner will be a bit ~** le dîner sera retardé; **2** [*hour, supper, date*] tardif/-ive; **to have a ~ night** (aller) se coucher tard; **to be in one's ~ fifties** approcher de la soixantaine; **in ~ January** (à la) fin janvier; **in the ~ 50s** à la fin des années 50; **3** (deceased) feu/-e.
II *adv* **1** [*arrive, start, finish*] en retard; **to be running ~** [*person*] être en retard; [*train, bus*] avoir du retard; **to start three months ~** commencer avec trois mois de retard; **2** [*get up, open, close*] tard; [*marry*] sur le tard; **~ last night/in the evening** tard hier soir/dans la soirée.

latecomer *n* retardataire *mf*.

lately *adv* ces derniers temps.

later I *adj* [*date*] ultérieur/-e; [*model, novel*] postérieur/-e.
II *adv* plus tard; **~ on** plus tard; **six months ~** six mois après; **to leave no ~ than 6 am** partir au plus tard à 6 heures; **see you ~!** à tout à l'heure!

latest I *adj* dernier/-ière (*before n*).
II **at the latest** *phr* au plus tard.

lathe *n* tour *m*.

lather *n* mousse *f*.

Latin ▶ 553 I *n* (language) latin *m*.
II *adj* latin/-e.

Latin America *pr n* Amérique *f* latine.

Latin American *adj* latino-américain/-e.

latitude *n* latitude *f*.

latter *n* **the ~** ce dernier/cette dernière *m/f*; ces derniers/ces dernières *mpl/fpl*.

Latvia ▶ 448 *pr n* Lettonie *f*.

laugh I *n* rire *m*; **to like a good ~** aimer bien rire; **to get a ~** faire rire; **for a ~**○ pour rigoler○.
II *vi* rire (**about, over** de); **to ~ at sb/sth** rire de qn/qch; **the children ~ed at the clown** le clown a fait rire les enfants; **he's afraid of being ~ed at** il a peur qu'on se moque de lui.
■ **laugh off** choisir de rire de [*criticism, insult*].

laughable *adj* ridicule.

laughing stock *n* risée *f*.

laughter *n* rires *mpl*.

launch I *n* **1** (for patrolling) vedette *f*; (for pleasure) bateau *m* de plaisance; **2** (of new boat, rocket) lancement *m*; (of lifeboat) mise *f* à l'eau; (of campaign, product) lancement *m*.
II *vtr* **1** mettre [qch] à l'eau [*dinghy, lifeboat*]; lancer [*new ship, missile, rocket*]; **2** (start) lancer [*campaign, career, product*]; ouvrir [*investigation*].

launch pad, launching pad *n* aire *f* de lancement.

launder *vtr* **1** laver [*clothes*]; **2** blanchir [*money*].
launderette (GB), **laundromat** (US) *n* laverie *f* automatique.
laundry *n* **1** (place) (commercial) blanchisserie *f*; (in hotel, house) laverie *f*; **2** (linen) linge *m*; **to do the ~** faire la lessive.
laurel *n* laurier *m*.
lava *n* lave *f*.
lavatory *n* toilettes *fpl*.
lavender ▶438 *n* lavande *f*.
lavish I *adj* [*party, lifestyle*] somptueux/-euse.
II *vtr* prodiguer [*money, affection*] (**on** à).
law *n* **1** (gen) loi *f*; **to obey/break the ~** respecter/enfreindre la loi; **to be against the ~** être interdit/-e; **by ~** conformément à la loi; **2** (Univ) droit *m*; **to study ~** faire son droit.
law-abiding *adj* respectueux/-euse des lois.
law and order *n* ordre *m* public.
law court *n* tribunal *m*.
lawful *adj* [*owner, strike*] légal/-e; [*conduct*] licite; [*wife, husband*] légitime.
lawn *n* pelouse *f*.
lawnmower *n* tondeuse *f* (à gazon).
law school *n* faculté *f* de droit.
lawsuit *n* procès *m*.
lawyer ▶626 *n* (who practises law) avocat/-e *m/f*; (expert in law) juriste *mf*.
lax *adj* relâché/-e.
laxative *n* laxatif *m*.
lay I *adj* **1** (non-specialist) **~ person** profane *mf*; **2** [*preacher, member*] laïque.
II *vtr* **1** (place) poser [*object, card*] (**in** dans; **on** sur); (spread out) étaler [*rug, newspaper*] (**on** sur); (arrange) disposer (**on** sur); **to ~ the table** (**for**) mettre la table (pour); **2** (prepare) préparer [*plan, trail*]; poser [*basis, foundation*]; tendre [*trap*]; **3** (Zool) pondre [*egg*].
III *vi* [*bird*] pondre.
■ **lay down 1** coucher [*baby, patient*]; étaler [*rug, cards*]; poser [*book, implement*]; déposer [*weapon*]; **2 to ~ down one's life for** sacrifier sa vie pour; **3** établir [*rule*]; poser [*condition*].
■ **lay off** (temporarily) mettre [qn] en chômage technique; (permanently) licencier.
■ **lay on** prévoir [*meal, transport*]; organiser [*trip*].
■ **lay out 1** disposer [*goods, food*]; étaler [*map, garment, fabric*]; **2** concevoir [*building, advert*]; mettre [qch] en page [*letter*]; monter [*page*].
layabout○ *n* fainéant/-e○ *m/f*.
lay-by *n* (GB) aire *f* de repos.
layer I *n* couche *f*.
II *vtr* **1** couper [qch] en dégradé [*hair*]; **2** disposer [qch] en couches [*cheese, potatoes*].
layman *n* profane *m*.
layout *n* (of page, book, computer screen) mise *f* en page; (of advert, article) présentation *f*; (of building) agencement *m*; (of town) plan *m*; (of garden) dessin *m*.
laze *vi* (also **~ about**, **~ around**) paresser.
laziness *n* paresse *f*.
lazy *adj* [*person*] paresseux/-euse; [*day, holiday*] paisible; [*movement, pace*] lent/-e.
lead[1] I *n* **1 to be in the ~** être en tête; **to go into the ~** passer en tête; **2** (initiative) **to take the ~** prendre l'initiative; **to follow sb's ~** suivre l'exemple de qn; **3** (clue) piste *f*; **4** (leading role) rôle *m* principal; **5** (wire) fil *m*; **6** (GB) (for dog) laisse *f*.
II *adj* [*guitarist*] premier/-ière (*before n*); [*role, singer*] principal/-e.
III *vtr* **1** (guide, escort) mener, conduire [*person*] (**to sth** à qch; **to sb** auprès de qn); **to ~ sb away** éloigner qn (**from** de); **2** (bring) [*path, sign*] mener (**to** à); **3** (cause) **to ~ sb to do** amener qn à faire; **4** mener [*army, team, attack, strike*]; diriger [*orchestra, research*]; **5** (conduct, have) mener [*active life*]; **to ~ a life of luxury** vivre dans le luxe.
IV *vi* **1 to ~ to** [*path*] mener à; [*door*] s'ouvrir sur; [*exit, trapdoor*] donner accès à; **2** (result in) **to ~ to** entraîner [*complication, discovery, accident*]; **3** [*runner, car, company*] être en tête; [*team, side*] mener; **to ~ by 15 seconds** avoir 15 secondes d'avance; **4** (in walk) aller devant; (in action, discussion) prendre l'initiative; (in dancing) conduire.
■ **lead up to 1** (precede) précéder [*event*]; **2** (build up to) amener [*topic*].
lead[2] *n* plomb *m*; (in pencil) mine *f*.
leader *n* **1** (of nation) chef *m* d'État, dirigeant/-e *m/f*; (of gang) chef *m*; (of party) leader *m*; (of trade union) secrétaire *mf*; (of strike, movement) meneur/-euse *m/f*; **2** (in competition) premier/-ière *m/f*; (horse) cheval *m* de tête; (in market, field) leader *m*.
leadership *n* dirigeants *mpl*, direction *f*; **under the ~ of** sous la direction de.
leadership qualities *n pl* qualités *fpl* de leader.
lead-free *adj* sans plomb.
leading *adj* **1** [*lawyer, politician*] éminent/-e, important/-e; [*company, bank*] important/-e; [*brand*] dominant/-e; **2** [*role*] (main) majeur/-e; (in theatre) principal/-e; **3** (Sport) [*driver, car*] en tête de course; [*team*] en tête du classement.
lead story *n* histoire *f* à la une○.
leaf *n* **1** (of plant) feuille *f*; **2** (of book) page *f*.
IDIOMS **to turn over a new ~** tourner la page.
■ **leaf through** feuilleter [*papers, book*].
leaflet *n* (gen) dépliant *m*; (advertising) prospectus *m*.
league *n* **1** (alliance) ligue *f*; **to be in ~ with sb** être de mèche○ avec qn; **2** (GB Sport) (competition) championnat *m*; (association) ligue *f*; **3 they're not in the same ~** ils ne sont pas comparables.
leak I *n* fuite *f*.
II *vtr* divulguer [*information, document*].
III *vi* **1** [*container, roof*] fuir; [*boat*] faire eau; **2** [*liquid, gas*] s'échapper (**from** de).
lean I *adj* **1** [*body, face*] mince; [*meat*] maigre; **2** [*year, times*] difficile.
II *vtr* appuyer (**against** contre).

III *vi* [*wall, building*] pencher; **to ~ against sth** [*bicycle, ladder*] être appuyé/-e contre qch; [*person*] s'appuyer à qch; (with back) s'adosser à qch; **to ~ out of the window** se pencher par la fenêtre.

■ **lean back** se pencher en arrière.

■ **lean forward** se pencher en avant.

■ **lean on**: ¶ **~ on [sth]** s'appuyer sur [*stick*]; s'accouder à [*windowsill*]; ¶ **~ on [sb]** **1** (as support) s'appuyer sur [*person*]; **2** (depend on) compter sur [*person*]; **3** (pressurize) faire pression sur [*person*].

leap I *n* **1** (jump) saut *m*, bond *m*; **2** (step in process) bond *m* (en avant); **3** (in price) bond *m* (**in** dans).

II *vi* **1** [*person, animal*] bondir, sauter; **to ~ to one's feet, to ~ up** se lever d'un bond; **to ~ across** or **over sth** franchir qch d'un bond; **2** [*heart*] bondir (**with** de); **3** (also **~ up**) [*price, profit*] grimper (**by** de).

leapfrog *n* saute-mouton *m*.

leap year *n* année *f* bissextile.

learn I *vtr* (gen) apprendre; acquérir [*skills*] (**from** de); **to ~ (how) to do** apprendre à faire; **to ~ that** apprendre que.

II *vi* apprendre; **to ~ about sth** apprendre qch; **to ~ from one's mistakes** tirer la leçon de ses erreurs.

learned *adj* [*person, book*] érudit/-e; [*journal*] spécialisé/-e; [*society*] savant/-e.

learner *n* apprenant/-e *m/f*.

learner driver *n* élève *mf* d'auto-école.

lease I *n* bail *m*.

II *vtr* louer [qch] à bail [*house*]; louer [*car*].

leaseholder *n* locataire *mf* à bail.

leash *n* laisse *f*.

least I *det* **the ~** le moins de; (in negative constructions) le or la moindre; **they have the ~ money** ce sont eux qui ont le moins d'argent; **I haven't the ~ idea** je n'en ai pas la moindre idée.

II *pron* **the ~** le moins; **we have the ~** c'est nous qui en avons le moins; **it was the ~ I could do!** c'est la moindre des choses!

III *adv* **1** (with adjective or noun) **the ~** le/la moins; (with plural noun) les moins; **the ~ wealthy families** les familles les moins riches; **2** (with verbs) le moins *inv*; **I like that one (the) ~** c'est celui-là que j'aime le moins; **nobody liked it, ~ of all John** personne ne l'aimait, John encore moins que les autres.

IV **at least** *phr* (at the minimum) au moins; (qualifying statement) du moins; **she's at ~ 40** elle a au moins 40 ans; **they could at ~ have phoned!** ils auraient au moins pu téléphoner!; **he's gone to bed—at ~ I think so** il est allé se coucher—du moins, je pense.

V **in the least** *phr* **not in the ~** pas du tout.

IDIOMS **last but not ~, last but by no means ~** enfin et surtout.

leather I *n* cuir *m*.

II *adj* [*garment, object*] de cuir, en cuir.

leave I *n* congé *m*; **three days' ~** trois jours de congé.

II *vtr* **1** (depart from) partir de [*house, station etc*]; (more permanently) quitter [*country, city etc*]; (go out of) sortir de [*room, building*]; **he left home early** il est parti tôt de chez lui; **to ~ school** quitter l'école; **2** (forget) oublier [*child, object*]; **3** quitter [*partner*]; **4** laisser [*instructions, tip*] (**for** pour; **with** à); **to ~ sb sth** laisser qch à qn; **to ~ sb/sth in sb's care** confier qn/qch à qn; **5** laisser [*food, drink, gap*]; **to ~ sth lying around** laisser traîner qch; **to ~ sth tidy** laisser qch en ordre; **6 to ~ sth to sb** laisser [qch] à qn [*job, task*]; **to ~ it (up) to sb to do** laisser à qn le soin de faire; **to ~ sb to it** laisser qn se débrouiller; **~ it to** or **with me** je m'en occupe; **7** [*oil, wine*] faire [*stain*]; [*cup, plate*] laisser [*stain, mark*]; **8** (postpone) laisser [*task, homework*]; **~ it till tomorrow** laisse ça pour demain; **9** (bequeath) léguer (**to sb** à qn).

III *vi* partir (**for** pour).

■ **leave behind 1** (go faster than) distancer [*person, competitor*]; **to be** or **get left behind** (physically) se faire distancer; (intellectually) ne pas suivre; (in business) [*country, company*] se laisser distancer; **2** [*traveller*] laisser [qch] derrière soi [*town, country*]; [*person*] quitter [*family, husband*]; en finir avec [*past*]; **3** (forget) oublier, laisser [*object, child, animal*].

■ **leave out 1** (accidentally) oublier [*word, ingredient, person*]; (deliberately) omettre [*name, fact*]; ne pas mettre [*ingredient, object*]; tenir [qn] à l'écart [*person*]; **to ~ sb out of** exclure qn de [*group*]; **2** (outdoors) laisser [qch] dehors.

Lebanon ▶ 448 *pr n* (**the**) **~** (le) Liban *m*.

lecherous *adj* lubrique.

lecture I *n* conférence *f* (**on** sur); (GB Univ) cours *m* magistral (**on** sur).

II *vtr* **1** (GB Univ) donner des cours à [*class*]; **2** (scold) faire la leçon à [*person*].

III *vi* **1** (gen) donner une conférence (**on** sur); **2** (GB Univ) **to ~ in sth** enseigner qch (à l'université).

lecturer ▶ 626 *n* **1** (speaker) conférencier/-ière *m/f*; **2** (GB Univ) enseignant/-e *m/f* (du supérieur); **3** (US Univ) ≈ chargé *m* de cours.

ledge *n* **1** (shelf) rebord *m*; **2** (on mountain) saillie *f* (rocheuse).

ledger *n* registre *m* de comptabilité, grand livre *m*.

leech *n* sangsue *f*.

leek *n* poireau *m*.

leer *vi* **to ~ at sb/sth** lorgner○ qn/qch.

left I *n* gauche *f*; **on the ~** sur la gauche; (politically) à gauche.

II *adj* **1** [*eye, hand, shoe*] gauche; **2** (remaining) **to be ~** rester; **there are/we have five minutes ~** il reste/il nous reste cinq minutes; **I've got one ~** il m'en reste un.

III *adv* [*go, look, turn*] à gauche.

left-hand *adj* [*side*] de gauche.

left-hand drive *n* voiture *f* avec la conduite à gauche.

left-handed *adj* gaucher/-ère.

left-luggage (office) *n* (GB) consigne *f*.

leftovers *n pl* restes *mpl*.

left wing I *n* **the ~** la gauche *f*.

II left-wing *adj* [*attitude*] de gauche; **they are very ~** ils sont très à gauche.

leg *n* **1** ▶413 (of person, horse) jambe *f*; (of other animal) patte *f*; **2** (of furniture) pied *m*; **3** (Culin) (of lamb) gigot *m*; (of poultry, pork, frog) cuisse *f*; **4** (of trousers) jambe *f*; **5** (of journey, race) étape *f*.
IDIOMS **to pull sb's ~** faire marcher qn.

legacy *n* **1** (Law) legs *m*; **2** (figurative) héritage *m*; (of war) séquelles *fpl*.

legal *adj* **1** [*document, system*] juridique; [*costs*] de justice; **to take ~ advice** consulter un avocat; **2** [*heir, right, separation*] légal/-e; [*owner, claim*] légitime.

legal action *n* **to take ~ against sb** intenter un procès à qn.

legal aid *n* aide *f* juridique.

legal holiday *n* (US) jour *m* férié.

legalize *vtr* légaliser.

legal tender *n* monnaie *f* légale.

legend *n* légende *f* (**of** de).

legendary *adj* légendaire.

leggings *n pl* (for baby) collant *m*; (for woman) caleçon *m*.

legible *adj* lisible.

legislation *n* législation *f*.

legitimate *adj* **1** (justifiable) [*action, question, request*] légitime; [*excuse*] valable; **2** (lawful) [*organization*] régulier/-ière; [*child, heir, owner*] légitime.

leisure I *n* loisirs *mpl*; **to do sth at (one's) ~** prendre son temps pour faire qch.
II *adj* [*centre, facilities*] de loisirs.

leisure time *n* loisirs *mpl*, temps *m* libre.

lemon *n* (fruit) citron *m*.

lemonade *n* (fizzy) limonade *f*; (still) citronnade *f*; (US) (fresh) citron *m* pressé.

lemon juice *n* jus *m* de citron; (GB) (drink) citron *m* pressé.

lemon tea *n* thé *m* au citron.

lemon tree *n* citronnier *m*.

lend *vtr* **1** (loan) prêter [*object, money*]; **to ~ sb sth, to ~ sth to sb** prêter qch à qn; **to ~ a hand** donner un coup de main; **2** (give) conférer [*quality, credibility*] (**to** à); prêter [*support*]; **to ~ weight to sth** donner du poids à qch.

length ▶573 **I** *n* **1** longueur *f*; **what ~ is the plank?** de quelle longueur est la planche?; **to be 50 cm in ~** faire 50 cm de long; **2** (of book, film, list) longueur *f*; (of event, prison sentence) durée *f*; **~ of time** temps *m*; **3** (of string, carpet, wood) morceau *m*; (of fabric) ≈ métrage *m*; (of pipe, track) tronçon *m*; **dress ~** hauteur *f* de robe; **4** (Sport) longueur *f*.
II at length *phr* longuement.
IDIOMS **to go to great ~s to do** se donner beaucoup de mal pour faire.

lengthen I *vtr* rallonger [*garment*] (**by** de, par); prolonger [*shelf, road*] (**by** de, par); prolonger [*stay*].
II *vi* [*queue, list*] s'allonger; [*days*] rallonger.

lengthy *adj* long/longue.

lenient *adj* [*person*] indulgent/-e (**with** pour); [*punishment*] léger/-ère.

lens *n* (in optical instruments) lentille *f*; (in spectacles) verre *m*; (in camera) objectif *m*; (contact) lentille *f*.

Lent *n* carême *m*.

lentil *n* lentille *f*.

Leo *pr n* Lion *m*.

leopard *n* léopard *m*.

leotard *n* justaucorps *m inv*.

leprosy *n* lèpre *f*.

lesbian *n* lesbienne *f*.

less I *det* moins de; **~ beer** moins de bière; **I have ~ money than him** j'ai moins d'argent que lui.
II *pron* moins; **I have ~ than you** j'en ai moins que toi; **~ than 10** moins de dix; **in ~ than three hours** en moins de trois heures; **even ~** encore moins.
III *adv* moins; **I read ~ these days** je lis moins à présent; **the more I see him, the ~ I like him** plus je le vois, moins je l'aime.
IV *prep* moins; **~ 15% discount** moins 15% de remise; **~ tax** avant impôts.
V less and less *phr* de moins en moins.

lessen *vtr* diminuer [*influence, feelings*]; réduire [*cost*]; atténuer [*impact, pain*].

lesser I *adj* moindre; **to a ~ extent** à un moindre degré.
II *adv* moins; **~ known** moins connu.

lesson *n* cours *m*, leçon *f*; **Spanish ~** cours d'espagnol; **driving ~** leçon de conduite; **I'm going to teach him a ~!** je vais lui donner une bonne leçon!

let[1]

■ **Note** When *let* is used with another verb to make a suggestion (*let's do it at once*), the first person plural of the appropriate verb can generally be used to express this in French: *faisons-le tout de suite*. (Note that the verb alone translates *let us do* and no pronoun appears in French.)
– In the spoken language, however, French speakers will use the much more colloquial *on + present tense* or *si on + imperfect tense*:
– *let's go!* = allons-y *or* on y va!; *let's go to the cinema tonight* = si on allait au cinéma ce soir?
– These translations can also be used for suggestions in the negative:
– *let's not take* or *don't let's take the bus—let's walk* = on ne prend pas le bus, on y va à pied *or* ne prenons pas le bus, allons-y à pied.
– When *let* is used to mean *allow*, it is generally translated by the verb *laisser*. For more examples and particular usages, see the entry below.

vtr **1** (in suggestions, commands) **~'s get out of here!** sortons d'ici!; **~'s not** or **don't ~'s** (GB) **talk about that!** n'en parlons pas!; **2** (allow) **to ~ sb do** laisser qn faire; **~ me explain** laisse-moi t'expliquer; **don't ~ it get you down** ne te laisse pas abattre; **she wanted to go but they wouldn't ~ her** elle voulait y aller mais ils ne l'ont pas laissée faire; **to ~ one's hair grow** se laisser pousser les cheveux.

■ **let down**: ¶ **~ [sb] down 1** (disappoint) laisser tomber [qn]; **to feel let down** être déçu/-e; **2** (embarrass) faire honte à [qn]; ¶ **~ [sth]**

down **1** (GB) dégonfler [*tyre*]; **2** rallonger [*garment*].

■ **let go**: ¶ **~ go** lâcher prise; **to ~ go of sb/sth** lâcher qn/qch; ¶ **~ [sb] go 1** relâcher [*prisoner*]; **2** lâcher [*person, arm*]; **3** licencier [*employee*]; **4 to ~ oneself go** se laisser aller; ¶ **~ [sth] go** lâcher [*rope, bar*].

■ **let in**: ¶ **~ [sth] in** [*roof, window*] laisser passer [*rain*]; [*shoes*] prendre [*water*]; [*curtains*] laisser passer [*light*]; ¶ **~ [sb] in 1** (show in) faire entrer; (admit) laisser entrer; **2 to ~ oneself in for** aller au devant de [*trouble*].

■ **let off**: ¶ **~ off [sth]** tirer [*fireworks*]; faire exploser [*bomb*]; faire partir [*gun*]; ¶ **~ [sb] off 1** (excuse) **to ~ sb off** dispenser qn de [*homework*]; **2** (leave unpunished) ne pas punir [*culprit*].

■ **let out**: ¶ **~ out** (US) [*school*] finir (**at** à); ¶ **~ out [sth] 1** laisser échapper [*cry*]; **to ~ out a roar** beugler; **2** (GB) (reveal) révéler (**that** que); ¶ **~ [sth] out 1** faire sortir [*animal*]; donner libre cours à [*anger*]; **2** élargir [*waistband*]; ¶ **~ [sb] out** laisser sortir [*prisoner*] (**of** de); faire sortir [*pupils, employees*] (**of** de).

■ **let up** [*rain, wind*] se calmer; [*pressure*] s'arrêter; [*heat*] diminuer.

let[2] *vtr* (also **~ out** GB) louer (**to** à); **'to ~'** 'à louer'.

letdown *n* déception *f*.

lethal *adj* [*substance, gas, dose*] mortel/-elle; [*weapon*] meurtrier/-ière.

letter *n* **1** lettre *f* (**to** pour; **from** de); **2** (of alphabet) lettre *f*.

letter box *n* boîte *f* à lettres.

letterhead *n* en-tête *m*.

lettuce *n* salade *f*, laitue *f*.

leuk(a)emia ▶ 533 *n* leucémie *f*.

level I *n* **1** (gen) niveau *m*; **to be on the same ~ as sb** être du même niveau que qn; **at street ~** au niveau de la rue; **2** (of unemployment, illiteracy) taux *m*; (of spending) montant *m*; (of satisfaction, anxiety) degré *m*; **3** (in hierarchy) échelon *m*.

II *adj* **1** [*shelf, floor*] droit/-e; [*table*] horizontal/-e; **2** [*ground, surface, land*] plat/-e; **3** (Culin) [*teaspoonful*] ras/-e; **4 to be ~** [*shoulders, windows*] être à la même hauteur; [*floor, building*] être au même niveau; **~ with the ground** au ras du sol; **5 to remain ~** [*figures*] rester stable.

III *adv* **to draw ~** arriver à la même hauteur (**with** que).

IV *vtr* **1** (destroy) raser [*village*]; **2** lancer [*accusation*] (**at** contre); adresser [*criticism*] (**at** à); braquer [*gun*] (**at** sur); **3** aplanir [*ground, surface*].

IDIOMS **to be ~-pegging** être à égalité; **to ~ with sb** être honnête avec qn.

■ **level off** [*prices, curve*] se stabiliser.

level crossing *n* passage *m* à niveau.

level-headed *adj* sensé/-e.

lever *n* (Aut, Tech) levier *m*; (small) manette *f*.

levy I *n* taxe *f*, impôt *m*.

II *vtr* prélever [*tax, duty*]; imposer [*fine*].

lewd *adj* [*joke, gesture, remark*] obscène; [*person*] lubrique.

lexicon *n* lexique *m*.

liability I *n* **1** (Law) responsabilité *f*; **2** (drawback) handicap *m*.

II liabilities *n pl* passif *m*, dettes *fpl*.

liable *adj* **1** (likely) **to be ~ to do** risquer de faire; **it's ~ to rain** il risque de pleuvoir, il se peut qu'il pleuve; **2** (legally subject) **to be ~ to** être passible de [*fine*]; **to be ~ for tax** [*person, company*] être imposable; [*goods*] être soumis/-e à l'impôt.

liaise *vi* travailler en liaison (**with** avec).

liaison *n* liaison *f*.

liar *n* menteur/-euse *m/f*.

libel I *n* diffamation *f*.

II *vtr* diffamer.

liberal I *n* libéral/-e *m/f*.

II *adj* **1** (politically) libéral/-e; **2** [*amount*] généreux/-euse; [*person*] prodigue (**with** de).

Liberal *n* libéral/-e *m/f*.

Liberal Democrat *n* (GB) libéral-démocrate *mf*.

liberate *vtr* libérer (**from** de).

liberation *n* libération *f* (**from** de); **women's ~** libération de la femme.

liberty *n* liberté *f*.

Libra *n* Balance *f*.

librarian ▶ 626 *n* bibliothécaire *mf*.

library *n* bibliothèque *f*; **public ~** bibliothèque municipale; **mobile ~** (GB) bibliobus *m*.

lice *n pl* poux *mpl*.

licence (GB), **license** (US) *n* **1** (for trading) licence *f*; **2** (to drive, fish) permis *m*; (for TV) redevance *f*; **to lose one's (driving) ~** se faire retirer son permis (de conduire); **3** (freedom) licence *f*.

licence number *n* (of car) numéro *m* minéralogique or d'immatriculation.

licence plate *n* plaque *f* minéralogique or d'immatriculation.

license I *n* (US) = **licence**.

II *vtr* **1** (authorize) autoriser (**to do** à faire); **2** faire immatriculer [*vehicle*].

licensed *adj* **1** [*restaurant*] qui a une licence de débit de boissons; **2** [*dealer, firm, taxi*] agréé/-e; [*pilot*] breveté/-e; [*vehicle*] en règle.

lick I *n* **1** coup *m* de langue; **2 a ~ of paint** un petit coup de peinture.

II *vtr* **1** lécher; **to ~ one's lips** se lécher les babines; **2**° écraser [*team, opponent*]; **to get ~ed** se faire écraser.

IDIOMS **to ~ one's wounds** panser ses blessures.

licorice (US) = **liquorice**.

lid *n* **1** (cover) couvercle *m*; **2** (eyelid) paupière *f*.

lie I *n* mensonge *m*; **to tell a ~** mentir.

II *vi* **1** (tell falsehood) mentir (**to sb** à qn; **about** à propos de); **he ~d about her** il a menti à son propos; **2** [*person, animal*] (action) s'allonger; (state) être allongé/-e; [*objects*] être couché/-e; **he was lying on the bed** il était allongé sur le lit; **to ~ on one's back** s'allonger sur le dos; **~ still** ne bougez pas; **here ~s John Brown** ci-gît John Brown; **3** (be situated) être; (remain) rester; **to ~ open** [*book*] être ouvert/-e; **that's where our future ~s** c'est là qu'est notre avenir; **to ~ before sb** [*life, career*] s'ouvrir devant qn; **what ~s ahead?** qu'est-ce qui nous attend?; **the house lay empty for years** la maison est restée vide pendant des années; **4** (can be found) résider; **their interests ~ elsewhere** leurs intérêts résident ailleurs; **to ~ in** [*cause, secret, talent*] résider dans; [*popularity, strength, fault*] venir de; **the responsibility ~s with them** ce sont eux qui sont responsables.

IDIOMS **to ~ low** garder un profil bas; **to take it lying down**○ se laisser faire.

■ **lie around** traîner; **to leave sth lying around** laisser traîner qch.

■ **lie down** (briefly) s'allonger; (for longer period) se coucher.

lie-in *n* **to have a ~** faire la grasse matinée.

life *n* **1** (gen) vie *f*; **that's ~!** c'est la vie!; **the first time in my ~** la première fois de ma vie; **a job for ~** un emploi à vie; **a friend for ~** un ami pour la vie; **for the rest of one's ~** pour le restant de ses jours; **full of ~** plein/-e de vie; **to come to ~** [*shy person*] sortir de sa réserve; [*fictional character*] prendre vie; [*party*] s'animer; **2** (of machine, product) durée *f*; **3** (Law) **to serve ~** être emprisonné/-e à vie; **to sentence sb to ~** condamner qn à perpétuité.

IDIOMS **to have the time of one's ~** s'amuser comme un fou/une folle.

lifebelt *n* bouée *f* de sauvetage.

lifeboat *n* canot *m* de sauvetage.

life drawing *n* dessin *m* d'après modèle.

lifeguard ▶ 626 *n* surveillant/-e *m/f* de baignade.

life imprisonment *n* réclusion *f* à perpétuité.

life insurance *n* assurance-vie *f*.

lifejacket *n* gilet *m* de sauvetage.

lifeless *adj* [*body, object*] inanimé/-e; [*performance*] peu vivant/-e; [*voice*] éteint/-e.

lifelike *adj* très ressemblant/-e.

lifeline *n* bouée *f* de sauvetage.

lifesaving *n* (gen) sauvetage *m*; (Med) secourisme *m*.

life-size *adj* grandeur nature *inv*.

life span *n* durée *f* de vie.

life story *n* vie *f*.

lifestyle *n* style *m* de vie.

life-support machine *n* **to be on a ~** être sous assistance respiratoire.

lifetime *n* vie *f*; **in her ~** de son vivant; **the chance of a ~** une chance unique; **to seem like a ~** sembler une éternité.

lift I *n* **1** (GB) (elevator) ascenseur *m*; (for goods) monte-charge *m inv*; **2** (ride) **she asked me for a ~** elle m'a demandé de la conduire; **can I give you a ~?** je peux te déposer quelque part?; **3**○ (boost) **to give sb a ~** remonter le moral à qn.

II *vtr* **1** (pick up) soulever [*object, person*]; **to ~ sth out of the box** sortir qch de la boîte; **2** (raise) lever [*arm, head*]; **3** (remove) lever [*ban, sanctions*]; **4** (boost) **to ~ sb's spirits** remonter le moral à qn; **5**○ (steal) piquer○ (**from** dans).

III *vi* [*bad mood, headache*] disparaître; [*fog*] se dissiper.

■ **lift off**: ¶ **~ off** [*rocket*] décoller; [*top, cover*] s'enlever; ¶ **~ [sth] off** enlever [*cover, lid*].

■ **lift up** soulever [*book, suitcase, lid*]; lever [*head, veil, eyes*]; relever [*jumper, coat*].

lift-off *n* lancement *m*.

ligament *n* ligament *m*.

light I *n* **1** (brightness) lumière *f*; **against the ~** à contre-jour; **2** (in building, machine) lumière *f*; (in street) réverbère *m*; (on ship) feu *m*; (on dashboard) voyant *m* (lumineux); **3** (Aut) (headlight) phare *m*; (rearlight) feu *m* arrière; (inside car) veilleuse *f*; **4** (flame) **to set ~ to** mettre le feu à; **have you got a ~?** tu as du feu?; **5** (aspect) jour *m*; **to see sth in a different ~** voir qch sous un jour différent; **6 to come to** or **be brought to ~** être découvert/-e.

II **lights** *n pl* (**traffic**) **~s** feu *m*, feux *mpl*; **the ~s are red** le feu est au rouge.

III *adj* **1** (bright) **to get** or **grow ~er** [*sky*] s'éclaircir; **while it's still ~** pendant qu'il fait encore jour; **2** [*colour, wood, skin*] clair/-e; **~ blue** bleu clair *inv*; **3** [*material, wind, clothing, meal*] léger/-ère; [*rain*] fin/-e; [*drinker*] modéré/-e; **to be a ~ sleeper** avoir le sommeil léger; **4** [*knock, footsteps*] léger/-ère; **5** [*work*] peu fatigant/-e; [*exercise*] léger/-ère; **6** [*music*] léger/-ère; **a bit of ~ relief** un peu de divertissement; **some ~ reading** quelque chose de facile à lire.

IV *vtr* **1** allumer [*oven, cigarette, fire*]; enflammer [*paper*]; craquer [*match*]; **2** [*torch, lamp*] éclairer.

■ **light up** [*lamp*] s'allumer; [*face*] s'éclairer; [*eyes*] briller de joie.

light bulb *n* ampoule *f*.

lighten I *vtr* éclaircir [*colour, hair, skin*]; détendre [*atmosphere*].

II *vi* [*sky, hair*] s'éclaircir; [*atmosphere*] se détendre.

light entertainment *n* variétés *fpl*.

lighter *n* (for smokers) briquet *m*; (for gas cooker) allume-gaz *m inv*.

light-hearted *adj* [*person*] enjoué/-e; [*book*] humoristique.

lighthouse *n* phare *m*.

lighting *n* éclairage *m*.

lightly *adv* **1** [*touch, kiss, season*] légèrement; **2** [*undertake, dismiss*] à la légère; **3 to get off ~** s'en tirer à bon compte.

lightning I *n* (in sky) éclairs *mpl*; (striking sth) foudre *f*; **a flash of ~** un éclair; **struck by ~** frappé/-e par la foudre.

II *adj* [*visit, raid*] éclair (*inv*).

light switch *n* interrupteur *m*.

lightweight *adj* [*garment*] léger/-ère; [*champion*] des poids légers.

light year *n* année-lumière *f*.

like[1] **I** *prep* **1** (gen) comme; **to be ~ sb/sth** être comme qn/qch; **to look ~** ressembler à; **big cities ~ London** les grandes villes comme Londres or telles que Londres; **you know what she's ~!** tu sais comment elle est!; **it was just ~ a fairytale!** on aurait dit un conte de fée!; **it looks ~ rain** on dirait qu'il va pleuvoir; **what's it ~?** c'est comment?; **what was the weather ~?** quel temps faisait-il?; **2** (typical of) **it's not ~ her to be late** ça ne lui ressemble pas or ce n'est pas son genre d'être en retard; **that's just ~ him!** c'est bien (de) lui!
II *conj* **1** (in the same way as) comme; **~ they used to** comme ils le faisaient autrefois; **2**○ (as if) comme si; **he acts ~ he owns the place** il se conduit comme s'il était chez lui.
III *n* **fires, floods and the ~** les incendies, les inondations et autres catastrophes de ce genre; **she won't speak to the ~s of us**○! elle refuse de parler à des gens comme nous!

like[2] *vtr* **1** aimer bien [*person*]; aimer (bien) [*artist, food, music, style*]; **to ~ doing** or **to do** aimer (bien) faire; **to ~ A best** préférer A; **how do you ~ living in London?** ça te plaît de vivre à Londres?; **she doesn't ~ to be kept waiting** elle n'aime pas qu'on la fasse attendre; **2** (wish) vouloir, aimer; **I would ~ a ticket** je voudrais un billet; **I would ~ to do** je voudrais or j'aimerais faire; **would you ~ to come to dinner?** voudriez-vous venir dîner?; **we'd ~ her to come** nous voudrions or aimerions qu'elle vienne; **if you ~** si tu veux; **you can do what you ~** tu peux faire ce que tu veux.

likeable *adj* [*person*] sympathique; [*novel, music*] agréable.

likelihood *n* probabilité *f*, chances *fpl*; **in all ~** selon toute probabilité.

likely *adj* **1** (probable) probable; [*explanation*] plausible; **prices are ~ to rise** les prix risquent d'augmenter; **it is** or **seems ~ that she'll come** il est probable qu'elle viendra; **it is hardly ~ that she'll come** il y a peu de chances qu'elle vienne; **a ~ story!** à d'autres○!; **2** (promising) [*candidate*] prometteur/-euse.

liken *vtr* comparer (**to** à).

likeness *n* **1** (similarity) ressemblance *f*; **family ~** air *m* de famille; **2** (picture) **to be a good ~** être ressemblant/-e.

likewise *adv* (similarly) également, de même; (also) aussi, de même.

liking *n* **to take a ~ to sb** se prendre d'affection pour qn; **to be to sb's ~** plaire à qn.

lilac ▶438 *n, adj* lilas (*m*) *inv*.

lily *n* lys *m inv*.

lily of the valley *n* muguet *m*.

limb *n* **1** (arm, leg) membre *m*; **2** (of tree) branche *f* (maîtresse).

limber *v* ■ **limber up** s'échauffer.

limbo *n* **1** (state) les limbes *mpl*; **to be in ~** être dans les limbes; **2** (dance) limbo *m*.

lime *n* **1** (calcium) chaux *f*; **2** (fruit) citron *m* vert; **3** (also **~ tree**) tilleul *m*.

lime green ▶438 *n, adj* citron (*m*) vert *inv*.

lime juice *n* jus *m* de citron vert.

limelight *n* vedette *f*; **to be in the ~** tenir la vedette.

limestone *n* calcaire *m*.

limit I *n* limite *f*; **within ~s** dans une certaine limite; **to push sb to the ~** pousser qn à bout.
II *vtr* limiter (**to** à).

limitation *n* **1** (restriction) restriction *f* (**on** à); **2** (shortcoming) limite *f*; **to know one's (own) ~s** connaître ses propres limites.

limited *adj* limité/-e.

limited company *n* (GB) société *f* anonyme.

limousine *n* limousine *f*.

limp I *n* **to have a ~** boiter.
II *adj* mou/molle.
III *vi* boiter; **to ~ in/away** entrer/s'éloigner en boitant.

line I *n* **1** (gen, Sport) ligne *f*; (shorter, thicker) trait *m*; (in drawing) trait *m*; **a straight ~** une ligne droite; **2** (of people, cars) file *f*; (of trees) rangée *f*; **to stand** or **wait in ~** faire la queue; **3** (on face) ride *f*; **4** (rope) corde *f*; (for fishing) ligne *f*; **to put the washing on the ~** étendre le linge; **5** (electric cable) ligne *f* (électrique); **6** (phone connection) ligne *f*; **at the other end of the ~** au bout du fil; **the ~ went dead** la ligne a été coupée; **7** (rail route) ligne *f* (**between** entre); (rails) voie *f*; **8** (shipping company, airline) compagnie *f*; **9** (in genealogy) lignée *f*; **10** (in prose) ligne *f*; (in poetry) vers *m*; **to learn one's ~s** [*actor*] apprendre son texte; **11 to fall into ~ with** s'aligner sur; **to bring sb into ~** ramener qn dans le rang; **to keep sb in ~** tenir qn en main; **12** (stance) **the official ~** la position officielle; **to take a firm ~ with sb** se montrer ferme avec qn; **13** (type of product) gamme *f*; **14** (Mil) **enemy ~s** lignes *fpl* ennemies.
II *vtr* doubler [*garment*] (**with** avec); tapisser [*shelf*] (**with** de); border [*route*].
III in line with *phr* en accord avec [*policy, trend*]; **to increase in ~ with** augmenter proportionnellement à.
■ **line up**: ¶ **~ up** (side by side) se mettre en rang; (one behind the other) se mettre en file; ¶ **~ [sth] up 1** (align) aligner (**with** sur); **2** sélectionner [*team*].

lined *adj* [*face*] ridé/-e; [*paper*] ligné/-e; [*curtains*] doublé/-e.

linen *n* **1** (fabric) lin *m*; **2** (household) linge *m* de maison; (underwear) linge *m* de corps.

linen basket *n* panier *m* à linge sale.

linen cupboard (GB), **linen closet** (US) *n* armoire *f* à linge.

line of fire *n* ligne *f* de tir.

liner *n* paquebot *m* de grande ligne.

linesman *n* (GB) (in tennis) juge *m* de ligne; (in football, hockey) juge *m* de touche.

line-up *n* (Sport) équipe *f*; (personnel, pop group) groupe *m*.

linger *vi* **1** [*person*] s'attarder; [*gaze*] s'attarder (**on** sur); **2** [*memory, smell*] persister; **3** [*doubt, suspicion*] subsister.

lingerie *n* lingerie *f*.

linguist *n* linguiste *mf*.

linguistic *adj* linguistique.

linguistics *n* linguistique *f*.

lining *n* doublure *f*.

link I *n* **1** (in chain) maillon *m*; **2** (connection by rail, road) liaison *f*; **3** (between facts, events) rapport *m* (**between** entre); (between people) lien *m* (**with** avec); **4** (tie) relation *f*, lien *m* (**with** avec; **between** entre); **5** (in TV, radio, computing) liaison *f*.

II *vtr* **1** [*road, cable*] relier [*places, objects*]; **to ~ A to B** or **A and B** relier A à B; **to ~ arms** [*people*] se donner le bras; **2 to ~ sth to** or **with** lier qch à [*inflation*]; établir un lien entre qch et [*fact, crime, illness*]; **3** connecter [*terminals*]; **4** (in TV, radio) établir une liaison entre [*places*] (**by** par).

■ **link up**: ¶ **~ up** [*firms*] s'associer; **to ~ up with** s'associer avec [*college, firm*]; ¶ **~ [sth] up** relier.

lino *n* lino *m*.

lint *n* tissu *m* ouaté.

lion *n* lion *m*.

lion cub *n* lionceau *m*.

lioness *n* lionne *f*.

lip *n* **1** lèvre *f*; **2** (of jug) bec *m*.

lip-read *vi* lire sur les lèvres de quelqu'un.

lipsalve *n* baume *m* pour les lèvres.

lipstick *n* rouge *m* à lèvres.

liqueur *n* liqueur *f*.

liquid *n, adj* liquide (*m*).

liquidate *vtr* liquider.

liquidation *n* liquidation *f*.

liquidizer *n* (GB Culin) mixeur *m*.

liquor *n* alcool *m*.

liquorice, **licorice** (US) *n* **1** (plant) réglisse *f*; **2** (substance) réglisse *m*.

liquor store *n* (US) magasin *m* de vins et spiritueux.

Lisbon ▶ **448** *pr n* Lisbonne.

lisp *n* zézaiement *m*; **to have a ~** zézayer.

list I *n* liste *f* (**of** de).

II *vtr* **1** (gen) faire la liste de [*objects, people*]; **to be ~ed in a directory** être repris/-e dans un répertoire; **2** (Comput) lister.

III *vi* [*vessel*] donner de la bande.

IV **listed** *pp adj* (GB) [*building*] classé/-e.

listen *vi* écouter; **to ~ to sb/sth** écouter qn/qch; **to ~ to reason** écouter la voix de la raison; **to ~ (out) for** guetter.

■ **listen in** écouter (par indiscrétion).

listener *n* **1 to be a good ~** savoir écouter; **2** (to radio) auditeur/-trice *m/f*.

listless *adj* [*person*] apathique.

literal *adj* **1** [*meaning*] littéral/-e; **2** [*translation*] mot à mot.

literally *adv* [*mean*] littéralement; [*translate*] mot à mot; **to take sth ~** prendre qch au pied de la lettre; (**quite**) **~** bel et bien.

literary *adj* littéraire.

literate *adj* **1** (able to read and write) **to be ~** savoir lire et écrire; **2** (cultured) [*person*] cultivé/-e.

literature *n* **1** littérature *f*; **a work of ~** une œuvre littéraire; **2** (pamphlets, brochures) documentation *f*.

lithe *adj* leste.

Lithuania ▶ **448** *pr n* Lituanie *f*.

litigation *n* litiges *mpl*.

litre, **liter** (US) *n* litre *m*.

litter I *n* **1** (rubbish) détritus *mpl*; (substantial) ordures *fpl*; (paper) papiers *mpl*; **2** (of young) portée *f*; **to have a ~** mettre bas; **3** (for pet tray) litière *f*.

II *vtr* **to be ~ed with** [*ground*] être jonché/-e de.

litter bin *n* poubelle *f*.

little

■ **Note** When *a little* is used as a pronoun and if the sentence does not specify what it refers to, the pronoun *en* (= *of it*) must be added before the verb: *I have a little left* = il m'en reste un peu.

I *adj* **1** (small) petit/-e (*before n*); **2** (not much) peu de; **~ chance** peu de chances; **very ~ damage** très peu de dégâts; **there's so ~ time** il y a si peu de temps.

II *pron* **a ~** un peu; **I only ate a ~** je n'en ai mangé qu'un peu; **he remembers very ~** il ne se souvient pas bien; **there's ~ I can do** je ne peux pas faire grand-chose; **to do as ~ as possible** en faire le moins possible; **~ or nothing** quasiment rien.

III *adv* **1** (not much) peu; **I go there very ~** j'y vais très peu; **the next results were ~ better** les résultats suivants étaient à peine meilleurs; **~ more than an hour ago** il y a à peine plus d'une heure; **2** (not at all) **~ did they know that** ils étaient bien loin de se douter que.

IV **a little** (**bit**) *phr* un peu; **a ~ (bit) anxious** un peu inquiet/-iète; **a ~ less/more** un peu moins/plus; **stay a ~ longer** reste encore un peu.

V **as little as** *phr* **for as ~ as 10 dollars a day** pour seulement 10 dollars par jour; **as ~ as £60** juste 60 livres sterling.

IDIOMS **~ by ~** petit à petit.

little finger *n* petit doigt *m*, auriculaire *m*.

IDIOMS **to wrap** or **twist sb around one's ~** mener qn par le bout du nez.

live[1] *vi* **1** (gen) vivre; **as long as I ~**... tant que je vivrai...; **to ~ to regret sth** en venir à regretter qch; **long ~ democracy!** vive la démocratie!; **to ~ on** or **off** vivre de [*fruit, charity*]; vivre sur [*wage*]; **2** (dwell) [*person*] vivre, habiter (**with** avec); [*animal*] vivre; **they ~ at number 7** ils habitent au numéro 7; **to ~ in** vivre dans, habiter [*house, apartment*]; **easy to ~ with** facile à vivre; **3** (put up with) **to ~ with** accepter [*situation*]; supporter [*decor*].

IDIOMS **to ~ it up**○ mener la grande vie.

■ **live in** [*maid*] être logé/-e et nourri/-e.

■ **live on** [*reputation, tradition*] se perpétuer.

■ **live up to** [*person*] répondre à [*expectations*]; être à la hauteur de [*reputation*].

live[2] I *adj* **1** (alive) vivant/-e; **2** [*broadcast*] en direct; [*performance*] sur scène; [*album*] enregistré/-e en public; **before a ~ audience** devant un public; **3** [*cable*] sous tension.
II *adv* [*appear, broadcast*] en direct.

livelihood *n* gagne-pain *m*.

lively *adj* **1** [*person*] plein/-e d'entrain; [*place, atmosphere, conversation*] animé/-e; **2** (fast) [*pace*] vif/vive; [*music, dance*] entraînant/-e.

liven *v* ■ **liven up**: ¶ **~ up** s'animer; ¶ **~ [sth] up** animer [*event*].

liver *n* foie *m*.

livestock *n* bétail *m*.

livid *adj* **1** (furious) furieux/-ieuse; **2** (in colour) [*face, scar*] livide.

living I *n* **1** vie *f*; **to work for a ~** travailler pour gagner sa vie; **what do you do for a ~?** qu'est-ce que vous faites dans la vie?; **2** (lifestyle) vie *f*; **easy ~** une vie facile.
II *adj* vivant/-e; **within ~ memory** de mémoire d'homme.

living conditions *n pl* conditions *fpl* de vie.

living room *n* salle *f* de séjour, salon *m*.

living standards *n pl* niveau *m* de vie.

lizard *n* lézard *m*.

llama *n* lama *m*.

load I *n* **1** (gen) charge *f*; (on vehicle, animal) chargement *m*; (on ship, plane) cargaison *f*; (figurative) fardeau *m*; **three (lorry-)~s of sand** trois camions de sable; **2**○ (a lot) **a (whole) ~ of people** des tas○ de gens; **that's a ~ of nonsense**○ c'est vraiment n'importe quoi○.
II **loads**○ *n pl* **~s of** (+ plural nouns) des tas○ de; **~s of times** plein de or des tas○ de fois; **we've got ~s of time** nous avons tout notre temps; **~s of work** un travail fou○.
III *vtr* **1** (gen) charger [*vehicle, gun*] (**with** de); mettre un film dans [*camera*]; **2** (Comput) charger [*program*]; **3 to ~ sb with** combler qn de [*presents, honours*].

loaded *adj* **1** [*tray, lorry, gun*] chargé/-e (**with** de); **2**○ (rich) bourré/-e de fric○; **3** [*question*] tendancieux/-ieuse.

loaf *n* pain *m*; **a ~ of bread** un pain.
■ **loaf about, loaf around** traînasser.

loafer *n* **1** (shoe) mocassin *m*; **2** (idler) flemmard/-e○ *m/f*.

loan I *n* (when borrowing) emprunt *m*; (when lending) prêt *m*; **to be on ~** être prêté/-e (**to** à).
II *vtr* (also **~ out**) prêter (**to** à).

loathe *vtr* détester (**doing** faire).

loathsome *adj* répugnant/-e.

lobby I *n* **1** (of hotel) hall *m*; (of theatre) lobby *m*; **2** (also **~ group**) lobby *m*.
II *vi* faire pression (**for** pour obtenir).

lobe *n* lobe *m*.

lobster *n* homard *m*.

local I *n* **1 the ~s** les gens *mpl* du coin; **2** (pub) pub *m* du coin.
II *adj* (gen) local/-e; [*library, shop*] du quartier; [*radio, news*] régional/-e.

locality *n* **1** (neighbourhood) voisinage *m*; **2** (place) endroit *m*.

localized *adj* localisé/-e.

locate *vtr* **1** (find) retrouver [*object*]; localiser [*fault*]; **2** (position) situer [*site*].

location *n* endroit *m*; **on ~** [*filmed*] en extérieur.

lock I *n* **1** (with key) serrure *f*; (with bolt) verrou *m*; **under ~ and key** sous clé; **2** (of hair) mèche *f*; **3** (on canal) écluse *f*; **4** (Comput) verrouillage *m*.
II *vtr* fermer [qch] à clé.
III *vi* **1** [*door, drawer*] fermer à clé; **2** [*steering wheel*] se bloquer.
■ **lock in** enfermer [*person*]; **to ~ oneself in** s'enfermer.
■ **lock out**: **~ sb out** enfermer qn dehors; **to ~ oneself out** s'enfermer dehors.
■ **lock together** [*components, pieces*] s'emboîter.
■ **lock up**: ¶ **~ up** fermer; ¶ **~ [sth] up** fermer [qch] à clé [*house*]; ¶ **~ [sb] up** enfermer [*hostage*]; mettre [qn] sous les verrous [*killer*].

locker *n* casier *m*, vestiaire *m*.

locker room *n* vestiaire *m*.

locket *n* médaillon *m*.

locksmith *n* serrurier *m*.

locomotive *n* locomotive *f*.

lodge I *n* (small house) pavillon *m*; (for gatekeeper) loge *f* (du gardien).
II *vtr* **to ~ an appeal** faire appel; **to ~ a complaint** porter plainte; **to ~ a protest** protester.
III *vi* **1** [*person*] loger (**with** chez); **2** [*bullet*] se loger; [*small object*] se coincer.

lodger *n* (room only) locataire *mf*; (with meals) pensionnaire *mf*.

lodgings *n pl* logement *m*.

loft *n* **1** (attic) grenier *m*; **2** (US) (apartment) loft *m*.

log I *n* **1** (of wood) rondin *m*; (for burning) bûche *f*; **2** (of ship) journal *m* de bord; (of plane) carnet *m* de vol.
II *vtr* **1** (record) noter; **2** (also **~ up**) avoir à son actif [*miles*].
IDIOMS **to sleep like a ~** dormir comme une souche.
■ **log in, log on** (Comput) ouvrir une session, se connecter.
■ **log off, log out** (Comput) clore une session, se déconnecter.

log cabin *n* cabane *f* en rondins.

log fire *n* feu *m* de bois.

loggerheads *n pl* **to be at ~** être en désaccord (**with** avec).

logic *n* logique *f*.

logical *adj* logique.

logo *n* logo *m*.

loin *n* (Culin) (GB) ≈ côtes *fpl* premières; (US) ≈ filet *m*.

loiter *vi* (idly) traîner; (pleasurably) flâner; (suspiciously) rôder.

loll *vi* [*person*] se prélasser; [*head*] tomber; [*tongue*] pendre.

lollipop *n* sucette *f*.

London ▶448 *pr n* Londres.

Londoner *n* Londonien/-ienne *m/f*.

lone *adj* solitaire.

loneliness *n* (of person) solitude *f*; (of place) isolement *m*.

lonely *adj* [*person*] seul/-e; [*life*] solitaire; [*place*] isolé/-e.

loner *n* solitaire *mf*.

lonesome *adj* (US) solitaire.

long ▶573 **I** *adj* (gen) long/longue; [*delay*] important/-e; [*grass*] haut/-e; **to be 20 minutes ~** durer 20 minutes; **to be 20 metres ~** avoir or faire 20 mètres de long; **to get ~er** [*days, list, queue*] s'allonger; [*grass, hair*] pousser; **she's been away a ~ time** elle est restée longtemps absente; **it's been a ~ time since**... ça fait longtemps que...; **to take a ~ time** [*person*] être lent/-e; [*task*] prendre longtemps; **a ~ way off** loin; **we've come a ~ way** nous avons fait beaucoup de chemin.

II *adv* **1** (a long time) longtemps; **I won't be ~** je n'en ai pas pour longtemps; **how ~ will you be?** tu en as pour combien de temps?; **how ~ did it take him?** il lui a fallu combien de temps?; **how ~ is the interval?** combien de temps dure l'entracte?; **I haven't got ~** je n'ai pas beaucoup de temps; **how ~ did it take him?** il lui a fallu combien de temps?; **~er than he thought** plus de temps qu'il ne pensait; **before ~** (in past) peu après; (in future) dans peu de temps; **not for ~** pas longtemps; **~ after** longtemps après; **not ~ after** peu après; **~ ago** il y a longtemps; **~ before** bien avant; **he's no ~er head** il n'est plus chef; **I can't stay any ~er** je ne peux pas rester plus longtemps; **2** (for a long time) depuis longtemps; **those days are ~ gone** ce temps-là n'est plus.

III *vi* **to ~ for sth** avoir très envie de qch; **to ~ to do** rêver de faire.

IV as long as *phr* (provided) du moment que (+ *indicative*), pourvu que (+ *subjunctive*).

IDIOMS **~ time no see**○! ça fait une paye○ qu'on ne s'est pas vus!; **so ~**○! salut!

long-distance *adj* [*runner*] de fond; [*telephone call*] (within the country) interurbain/-e; (abroad) international/-e; **~ lorry driver** (GB) routier *m*.

long-haul *adj* [*flight, aircraft*] long-courrier *inv*.

longing *n* **1** grand désir *m* (**for** de; **to do** de faire); **2** (nostalgia) nostalgie *f* (**for** de).

longitude *n* longitude *f*.

long jump ▶504 *n* (GB) saut *m* en longueur.

long-life *adj* [*milk*] longue conservation *inv*; [*battery*] longue durée *inv*.

long-range *adj* [*missile*] (à) longue portée; [*forecast*] à long terme.

long-sighted *adj* presbyte.

long-standing *adj* de longue date.

long-wave *n* grandes ondes *fpl*.

long-winded *adj* verbeux/-euse.

loo○ *n* (GB) vécés○ *mpl*, toilettes *fpl*.

look I *n* **1** (glance) coup *m* d'œil; **to have** or **take a ~ at sth** jeter un coup d'œil à or sur qch; **to have** or **take a good ~ at** regarder [qch] de près; **to have a ~ inside/behind sth** regarder à l'intérieur de/derrière qch; **to have a ~ round** faire un tour dans [*park, town*]; **2** (search) **to have a (good) ~** (bien) chercher; **3** (expression) regard *m*; **a ~ of sadness** un regard triste; **from the ~ on his face**... à son expression...; **4** (appearance) (of person) air *m*; (of building, scenery) aspect *m*.

II looks *n pl* **~s aren't everything** il n'y a pas que la beauté qui compte; **he's losing his ~s** il n'est pas aussi beau qu'autrefois.

III *vi* **1** regarder (**into** dans; **over** par-dessus); **to ~ away** détourner le regard or les yeux; **to ~ out of the window** regarder par la fenêtre; **2** (search) chercher, regarder; **3** (appear, seem) avoir l'air, paraître; **you ~ cold** tu as l'air d'avoir froid; **he ~s young for his age** il fait jeune pour son âge; **that makes you ~ younger** ça te rajeunit; **the picture will ~ good in the study** le tableau ira bien dans le bureau; **it doesn't ~ right** ça ne va pas; **things are ~ing good** les choses se présentent bien; **to ~ like sb/sth** ressembler à qn/qch; **what does the house ~ like?** comment est la maison?; **it ~s like rain** on dirait qu'il va pleuvoir.

IV *vtr* **1** (gaze, stare) regarder; **to ~ sb in the eye** regarder qn dans les yeux; **2** (appear) **to ~ one's age** faire son âge; **she's 40 but she doesn't ~ it** elle a 40 ans mais elle ne les fait pas; **to ~ one's best** être à son avantage.

■ **look after** soigner [*patient*]; garder [*child*]; s'occuper de [*customer, plant, finances, shop*]; surveiller [*class, luggage*]; entretenir [*car*].

■ **look around**: ¶ **~ around 1** (glance) regarder autour de soi; **2 to ~ around for sb/sth** chercher qn/qch; **3** (in town) faire un tour; ¶ **~ around [sth]** visiter [*church, town*].

■ **look at 1** regarder; (briefly) jeter un coup d'œil sur; **2** (examine) examiner [*patient*]; jeter un coup d'œil à [*car*]; étudier [*problem, options*]; **3** (see, view) voir [*life, situation*]; envisager [*problem*].

■ **look back 1** (turn around) se retourner (**at** pour regarder); **2 to ~ back on** se tourner sur [*past*]; repenser à [*experience*]; **~ing back on it** rétrospectivement.

■ **look down**: ¶ **~ down** (from a height) regarder en bas; ¶ **~ down on [sb/sth] 1** regarder [qch] d'en haut; **2** (condescendingly) mépriser.

■ **look for** chercher [*person, object*].

■ **look forward to** attendre [qch] avec impatience; **she's ~ing forward to going on holiday** elle a hâte de partir en vacances; **I ~ forward to hearing from you** (in letter) j'espère avoir bientôt de tes nouvelles; (formal) dans l'attente de votre réponse, je vous prie d'agréer mes sincères salutations.

■ **look into** examiner [*matter*]; enquêter sur [*death*].

■ **look on**: ¶ **~ on** (watch) regarder; (be

present) assister à; ¶ **~ on [sb/sth]** considérer [*person, event*] (**as** comme; **with** avec).

▪ **look onto** [*house*] donner sur [*street*].

▪ **look out**: ¶ **~ out** (take care) faire attention (**for** à); (be wary) se méfier (**for** de); **~ out!** attention!; ¶ **~ out for [sb/sth]** guetter [*person*]; être à l'affût de [*bargain, new talent*].

▪ **look round** (look behind) se retourner; (look about) regarder autour de soi; ¶ **~ round [sth]** visiter [*town*]; **to ~ round the shops** faire les magasins.

▪ **look through**: ¶ **~ through [sth] 1** parcourir [*report*]; feuilleter [*magazine*]; **2** fouiller dans [*belongings*]; ¶ **~ through [sb]** faire semblant de ne pas voir.

▪ **look to 1** (rely on) compter sur [qn/qch]; **2** (turn to) se tourner vers [*future, friends*].

▪ **look up**: ¶ **~ up** (raise eyes) lever les yeux (**from** de); (raise head) lever la tête; **things are ~ing up for us** les choses s'arrangent pour nous; ¶ **~ [sb/sth] up 1** chercher [*phone number, price*] (**in** dans); **2** passer voir [*acquaintance*]; ¶ **~ up to [sb]** admirer [*person*].

look-in *n* (GB) **to get a ~** avoir sa chance; **to give sb a ~** donner sa chance à qn.

look-out *n* **1 to be on the ~ for** rechercher [*stolen vehicle*]; être à l'affût de [*bargain, new talent*]; guetter [*visitor*]; **2** (place) poste *m* d'observation.

loom I *n* métier *m* à tisser.

II *vi* **1** (also **~ up**) surgir (**out of** de; **over** au-dessus de); **2** [*war, crisis*] menacer; [*exam, interview*] être imminent/-e; **to ~ large** [*issue*] peser lourd.

loop I *n* (gen, Comput) boucle *f*.

II *vtr* nouer.

III *vi* [*road, path*] faire une boucle.

loophole *n* lacune *f*.

loose *adj* **1** [*knot, screw*] desserré/-e; [*handle, tooth*] branlant/-e; [*button*] qui se découd; [*thread*] décousu/-e; **to hang ~** [*hair*] être dénoué/-e; **~ connection** faux contact; **2** (free) **to break ~** [*animal*] s'échapper (**from** de); **to cut sb ~** détacher qn; **to let ~** libérer [*animal, prisoner*]; **3** [*page*] détaché/-e; **~ change** petite monnaie; **4** [*jacket, trousers*] ample; [*collar*] lâche; **5** [*link, weave*] lâche; **6** [*translation, interpretation*] assez libre; [*wording*] imprécis/-e; [*connection, guideline*] vague; [*style*] relâché/-e; **7** [*morals*] dissolu/-e.

IDIOMS **to be at a ~ end** (GB), **to be at ~ ends** (US) ne pas trop savoir quoi faire.

loosely *adv* **1** [*hold, wind, wrap*] sans serrer; **his clothes hung ~ on him** il flottait dans ses vêtements; **2** [*connected, organized*] de façon souple; **3** [*translate, describe*] assez librement.

loosen *vtr* desserrer [*belt, strap, collar*]; dégager [*nail, post*]; relâcher [*grip, rope, control*]; dénouer [*hair*].

▪ **loosen up 1** (sport) s'échauffer; **2** (relax) se détendre.

loot I *n* butin *m*.

II *vtr* piller [*shops*].

lopsided *adj* [*object, smile*] de travers; [*argument, view*] irrationnel/-elle.

lord ▶ 498 *n* **1** (ruler) seigneur *m* (**of** de); **2** (peer) lord *m*; **the (House of) Lords** la Chambre des Lords; **my Lord** (to noble) Monsieur le comte/duc etc.

IDIOMS **to ~ it over sb**○ regarder qn de haut.

Lord *n* **1** (in prayers) Seigneur *m*; **2**○ (in exclamations) **good ~!** grand Dieu!

Lord Mayor ▶ 498 *n* lord-maire *m*.

lordship ▶ 498 *n* (also **Lordship**) **your/his ~** (of noble) Monsieur; (of judge) Monsieur le Juge.

lorry *n* (GB) camion *m*.

lorry driver ▶ 626 *n* (GB) routier *m*, chauffeur *m* de poids lourd.

lose I *vtr* **1** (gen) perdre; **to ~ one's way** se perdre; **to ~ interest in sth** se désintéresser de qch; **2** [*clock*] retarder de [*minutes, seconds*]; **3** (get rid of) semer○ [*pursuer*].

II *vi* **1** (gen) perdre; **2** [*clock*] retarder.

▪ **lose out** être perdant/-e.

loser *n* (gen, Sport) perdant/-e *m/f*.

loss *n* perte *f* (**of** de); **to be at a ~** (puzzled); être perplexe; (helpless) être perdu/-e.

lost *adj* **1** [*person, animal*] perdu/-e; **to get ~** [*person, animal*] se perdre; [*object*] s'égarer; **get ~**○! fiche le camp○!; **2** [*opportunity*] manqué/-e; [*cause*] perdu/-e; [*civilization*] disparu/-e; **to be ~ on sb** passer au-dessus de la tête de qn; **to be ~ for words** être interloqué/-e; **to be ~ in** être plongé/-e dans [*book, thought*].

lost and found *n* objets *mpl* trouvés.

lost property *n* (GB) objets *mpl* trouvés.

lot[1] **I** *pron* **1** (great deal) **a ~** beaucoup; **he spent a ~** il a beaucoup dépensé, il a dépensé beaucoup d'argent; **to mean a ~ to sb** avoir beaucoup d'importance pour qn; **2**○ **the ~** (le) tout.

II *quantif* **a ~ of money/time** beaucoup d'argent/de temps; **I see a ~ of him** je le vois beaucoup.

III lots○ *quantif, pron* **~s (and ~s) of** des tas○ de, beaucoup de; **~s of things** des tas○ de choses.

IV a lot *adv* beaucoup; **he's a ~ better/worse** il va beaucoup mieux/plus mal; **this happens quite a ~** cela arrive très souvent.

lot[2] *n* **1** (destiny) sort *m*; (quality of life) condition *f*; **2** (US) parcelle *f* (de terrain); **3** (at auction) lot *m*; **4 to draw ~s** tirer au sort; **5** (batch) fournée *f*.

lotion *n* lotion *f*.

lottery *n* loterie *f*.

loud I *adj* **1** [*music, voice*] fort/-e; [*noise, scream*] grand/-e (*before n*); [*comment, laugh*] bruyant/-e; [*applause*] vif/vive; **2** [*colour*] criard/-e; [*person, behaviour*] exubérant/-e.

II *adv* fort; **out ~** à voix haute.

loudly *adv* [*knock, talk*] bruyamment; [*scream*] fort; [*protest*] vivement.

loudspeaker *n* (for announcements) haut-parleur *m*; (for hi-fi) enceinte *f*.

lounge *n* **1** (in house, hotel) salon *m*; **2** (in airport) **departure ~** salle *f* d'embarquement; **3** (US) (also **cocktail ~**) bar *m*.

■ **lounge about**, **lounge around** paresser.

lousy *adj* minable○; **a ~ trick** un sale tour.

louvred (GB), **louvered** (US) *adj* [*doors*] à lamelles.

lovable *adj* [*person*] sympathique; [*child*] adorable.

love I *n* **1** amour *m*; **to be/fall in ~** être/tomber amoureux/-euse (**with** de); **to make ~** faire l'amour; **Andy sends his ~** Andy t'embrasse; **with ~ from Bob, ~ Bob** affectueusement, Bob; **2** (GB) (term of affection) mon chéri/ma chérie *m/f*; **3** (in tennis) zéro *m*.
II *vtr* aimer; **to ~ each other** s'aimer; **to ~ doing** or **to do** aimer beaucoup faire; **'I'd ~ to!'** 'avec plaisir!'
IDIOMS **~ at first sight** le coup de foudre.

love affair *n* liaison *f* (**with** avec; **between** entre).

love-life *n* vie *f* amoureuse.

lovely *adj* **1** (beautiful) [*colour, garden, woman*] beau/belle (*before n*), joli/-e (*before n*); **to look ~** [*child, dress*] être ravissant/-e; **2** (pleasant) [*letter, person*] charmant/-e; [*meal, smell*] délicieux/-ieuse; [*idea, surprise*] bon/bonne (*before n*); [*present, weather*] magnifique.

lover *n* **1** (male) amant *m*; (female) maîtresse *f*; **they are ~s** ils sont amants; **2** (person in love) amoureux/-euse *m/f*; **3** (enthusiast) amateur *m*; **jazz ~** amateur de jazz.

loving *adj* (gen) tendre; [*care*] affectueux/-euse.

low I *n* **1** (in weather) dépression *f*; **2 to be at** or **have hit an all-time ~** être au plus bas.
II *adj* **1** (gen) bas/basse; [*speed*] réduit/-e; [*number, rate*] faible (*before n*); [*battery*] presque à plat *inv*; **in a ~ voice** tout bas; **to be ~ on staff** manquer de personnel; **to be ~ in sugar** contenir peu de sucre; **2** [*mark, quality*] mauvais/-e (*before n*); **3** (depressed) déprimé/-e; **4** [*behaviour*] ignoble.
III *adv* **1** [*aim*] bas; [*bend*] très bas; [*fly*] à basse altitude; **2** (in importance) **it's very ~ (down) on the list** c'est tout à fait secondaire; **3** [*speak, sing*] bas; **to turn [sth] down ~** baisser [*heating, light*].
IV *vi* [*cow*] meugler.

low-budget *adj* à petit budget.

low-calorie *adj* [*diet*] hypocalorique; [*food*] à faible teneur en calories.

low-cut *adj* décolleté/-e.

lower I *adj* inférieur/-e.
II *vtr* **1** baisser [*barrier, curtain, flag*]; abaisser [*ceiling*]; **to ~ sb/sth** descendre qn/qch (**into** dans; **onto** sur); **2** (reduce) baisser [*prices, standards*]; réduire [*pressure, temperature*]; abaisser [*age limit*]; **to ~ one's voice** baisser la voix; **3** affaler [*sail*].
III *v refl* **to ~ oneself 1** s'abaisser; **2 to ~ oneself into** s'asseoir précautionneusement dans [*bath, armchair*].

lower class *n* **the ~(es)** la classe ouvrière.

low-fat *adj* [*diet*] sans matières grasses; [*cheese*] allégé/-e; [*milk*] écrémé/-e.

low-key *adj* [*approach*] discret/-ète; [*meeting, talks*] informel/-elle.

low-level *adj* [*bombing*] à basse altitude; [*talks*] informel/-elle; [*radiation*] faible.

low-lying *adj* à basse altitude.

low-paid *adj* [*job*] faiblement rémunéré/-e; [*worker*] peu rémunéré/-e.

low-quality *adj* de qualité inférieure.

low tide *n* marée *f* basse.

loyal *adj* [*friend*] loyal/-e (**to** envers); [*customer*] fidèle (**to** à).

loyalty *n* loyauté *f* (**to, towards** envers).

lozenge *n* pastille *f*.

LP *n* (disque *m*) 33 tours *m*.

L-plate *n* (GB Aut) plaque *f* d'élève conducteur débutant accompagné.

lubricant *n* lubrifiant *m*.

lucid *adj* **1** (clear) clair/-e; **2** (sane) [*person*] lucide; [*moment*] de lucidité.

luck *n* chance *f*; **good ~** chance *f*; **bad ~** malchance *f*; **to bring sb good/bad ~** porter bonheur/malheur à qn; **it's good ~** ça porte bonheur; **bad** or **hard ~!** pas de chance!; **good ~!** bonne chance!; **to be in/out of ~** avoir de la/ne pas avoir de chance.

luckily *adv* heureusement (**for** pour).

lucky *adj* **1** (fortunate) **to be ~** avoir de la chance; **2** [*charm, colour, number*] porte-bonheur *inv*; **it's my ~ day!** c'est mon jour de chance!

lucrative *adj* lucratif/-ive.

ludicrous *adj* grotesque.

luggage *n* bagages *mpl*.

luggage rack *n* porte-bagages *m inv*.

lukewarm *adj* tiède.

lull I *n* (in storm, fighting) accalmie *f*; (in conversation) pause *f*.
II *vtr* **to ~ sb to sleep** endormir qn en le berçant; **to ~ sb into thinking that...** faire croire à qn que...; **to be ~ed into a false sense of security** se laisser aller à un sentiment de sécurité trompeur.

lullaby *n* berceuse *f*.

lumber I *n* (US) bois *m* de construction.
II○ *vtr* (GB) **to get** or **be ~ed with sb/sth** se retrouver avec qn/qch sur les bras.
III *vi* (also **~ along**) avancer d'un pas lourd; [*vehicle*] avancer péniblement.

lumberjack ▶ **626** *n* bûcheron/-onne *m/f*.

luminous *adj* lumineux/-euse.

lump I *n* **1** (gen) morceau *m*; (of soil, clay) motte *f*; (in sauce) grumeau *m*; **2** (on body) (from knock) bosse *f* (**on** sur); **3** (tumour) grosseur *f* (**in, on** à).
II *vtr* **to ~ X and Y together** mettre X et Y dans le même panier○.
IDIOMS **to have a ~ in one's throat** avoir la gorge serrée.

lunar *adj* [*landscape*] lunaire; [*eclipse*] de lune; [*landing*] sur la lune.

lunatic *n* fou/folle *m/f*.

lunch *n* déjeuner *m*; **to have ~** déjeuner; **to take sb out for ~** emmener qn déjeuner au restaurant; **to close for ~** fermer le midi.

lunchbox *n* boîte *f* à sandwichs.

lunchbreak *n* pause-déjeuner *f*.

luncheon voucher, **LV** *n* ticket-repas *m*, ticket-restaurant® *m*.

lunch hour *n* heure *f* du déjeuner.

lunchtime *n* heure *f* du déjeuner.

lung *n* poumon *m*.

lunge *vi* bondir (**at** vers; **forward** en avant).

lurch *vi* [*person, vehicle*] tanguer; **to ~ forward** [*car*] faire un bond en avant.
IDIOMS **to leave sb in the ~** abandonner qn.

lure I *n* **1** (attraction) attrait *m* (**of** de); **2** (in hunting) leurre *m*.
II *vtr* attirer (**into** dans; **with** avec); **they ~d him out of his house** ils ont réussi à le faire sortir de chez lui par la ruse.

lurid *adj* **1** [*colour*] criard/-e; **2** [*detail, past*] épouvantable.

lurk *vi* **he was ~ing in the bushes** il était tapi dans les buissons; **to ~ in the garden** rôder dans le jardin.

luscious *adj* [*food*] succulent/-e; [*woman*] pulpeux/-euse.

lush *adj* [*vegetation*] luxuriant/-e; [*hotel, surroundings*] luxueux/-euse.

lust I *n* **1** désir *m*; (deadly sin) luxure *f*; **2** (for power, blood) soif *f* (**for** de).
II *vi* **to ~ for** or **after sb/sth** convoiter qn/qch.

Luxembourg ▶ 448 *pr n* Luxembourg *m*.

luxurious *adj* [*apartment, lifestyle*] de luxe (*never after v*); **his apartment is ~** son appartement est luxueux.

luxury I *n* luxe *m*.
II *adj* [*hotel, product, holiday*] de luxe.

lychee *n* litchi *m*.

lying *n* mensonges *mpl*.

lynch *vtr* lyncher.

lynch mob *n* lyncheurs *mpl*.

lyrical *adj* lyrique; **to wax ~ (about sth)** disserter avec lyrisme (sur qch).

lyrics *n pl* paroles *fpl*.

Mm

m, **M** *n* m, M *m*.
MA *n* (*abbr* = **Master of Arts**) diplôme *m* supérieur de lettres.
macabre *adj* macabre.
macaroni *n* macaronis *mpl*.
mace *n* **1** (spice) macis *m*; **2** (ceremonial staff) masse *f*.
machete *n* machette *f*.
machine *n* machine *f*; **sewing ~** machine à coudre; **by ~** à la machine.
machine gun *n* mitrailleuse *f*.
machinery *n* **1** (equipment) machines *fpl*; (working parts) mécanisme *m*, rouages *mpl*; **a piece of ~** une machine; **2** (figurative) dispositifs *mpl*.
mackerel *n* maquereau *m*.
mackintosh, **macintosh** *n* imperméable *m*.
mad *adj* **1** [*person*] fou/folle (**with** de); [*dog*] enragé/-e; [*idea, scheme*] insensé/-e; **to go ~** devenir fou/folle; **to drive sb ~** rendre qn fou; **2**○ (angry) furieux/-ieuse; **to be ~ at** or **with sb** être très en colère contre qn; **to go ~** se mettre dans une colère folle; **3**○ (enthusiastic) **~ about** or **on** fou/folle de○ [*person, hobby*]; **4** [*panic*] infernal/-e; **the audience went ~** le public s'est déchaîné.
IDIOMS **to work like ~** travailler comme un fou/une folle.
madam ▶498 *n* madame *f*; **Dear Madam** (in letter) Madame.
maddening *adj* [*person*] énervant/-e; [*delay, situation*] exaspérant/-e.
made *adj* **a ~ man** un homme qui a réussi; **he's got it ~**○ (sure to succeed) sa réussite est assurée; (has succeeded) il n'a plus à s'en faire.
Madeira *pr n* Madère.
made-to-measure *adj* [*garment*] fait/-e sur mesure.
made-up *adj* **1** (wearing make-up) maquillé/-e; **2** [*story*] fabriqué/-e.
madly *adv* **1** (frantically) frénétiquement; **2** [*jealous*] follement; **~ in love (with sb)** follement or éperdument amoureux (de qn).
madman○ *n* fou○ *m*, malade○ *m*.
madness *n* folie *f*; **it is ~ to do** c'est de la folie de faire.
Mafia *n* **the ~** la Mafia.
magazine *n* **1** revue *f*; (mainly photos) magazine *m*; **fashion ~** magazine de mode; **women's ~** journal *m* féminin; **2** (on radio, TV) magazine *m*; **3** (of gun, camera) magasin *m*.
maggot *n* (in fruit) ver *m*; (for fishing) asticot *m*.
magic I *n* magie *f*.
II *adj* magique.
magical *adj* magique.
magic carpet *n* tapis *m* volant.
magician *n* (wizard) magicien *m*; (entertainer) illusionniste *m*.
magistrate ▶626 *n* magistrat *m*.
magnanimous *adj* magnanime.
magnate *n* magnat *m*; **oil ~** magnat du pétrole.
magnesium *n* magnésium *m*.
magnet *n* aimant *m*; (figurative) pôle *m* d'attraction (**for** pour).
magnetic *adj* **1** [*rod*] aimanté/-e; [*field, force, storm*] magnétique; **2** [*appeal*] irrésistible; **to have a ~ personality** avoir du charisme.
magnetism *n* magnétisme *m*.
magnificent *adj* magnifique.
magnify *vtr* grossir.
magnifying glass *n* loupe *f*.
magnitude *n* ampleur *f* (**of** de).
magnolia ▶438 *n* **1** (also **~ tree**) magnolia *m*; **2** (colour) crème *m*.
magpie *n* pie *f*.
mahogany ▶438 *n* acajou *m*.
maid *n* (in house) bonne *f*; (in hotel) femme *f* de chambre.
maiden I *n* jeune fille *f*.
II *adj* [*flight, voyage, speech*] inaugural/-e.
maiden name *n* nom *m* de jeune fille.
mail I *n* **1** (postal service) poste *f*; **by ~** par la poste; **2** (letters) courrier *m*.
II *vtr* envoyer, expédier [*letter, parcel*] (**to** à).
mailbox *n* (for posting) boîte *f* aux lettres; (for delivery) boîte *f* à lettres.
mailman ▶626 *n* (US) facteur *m*.
mail order I *n* **to buy (by) ~** acheter par correspondance.
II *adj* [*business, goods*] de vente *f* par correspondance.
maim *vtr* estropier.
main I *n* **1** (pipe) canalisation *f*; **2 the ~s** (of electricity) secteur *m*; (of water, gas) le réseau de distribution; (of sewage) le réseau d'évacuation.
II *adj* principal/-e.
main course *n* plat *m* principal.
mainframe *n* (also **~ computer**) ordinateur *m* central.
mainland *n* territoire *m* continental; **on the ~** sur le continent.
mainly *adv* surtout, essentiellement.
main road *n* (in country) route *f* principale; (in town) grande rue *f*.
mainstream I *n* courant *m* dominant.
II *adj* **1** (conventional) traditionnel/-elle; **2 ~ jazz** jazz mainstream.
maintain *vtr* **1** (keep steady) maintenir; **2** subvenir aux besoins de [*family*]; entretenir [*army, house, property*]; **3** continuer à affirmer [*innocence*]; **to ~ that** soutenir que.
maintenance *n* **1** (upkeep) entretien *m* (**of** de); **2** (GB Law) (alimony) pension *f* alimentaire.

maisonette *n* duplex *m*.
maize *n* maïs *m*.
majestic *adj* majestueux/-euse.
majesty *n* **1** (grandeur) majesté *f*; **2 His/Her Majesty** sa Majesté.
major I *n* **1** (Mil) commandant *m*; **2** (US Univ) matière *f* principale; **3** (Mus) ton *m* majeur.
II *adj* **1** [*event*] important/-e; [*role*] majeur/-e; [*significance*] capital/-e; **a ~ operation, ~ surgery** une grosse opération; **2** (main) principal/-e; **3** (Mus) majeur/-e; **in a ~ key** en majeur.
III *vi* (US Univ) **to ~ in** se spécialiser en.
Majorca *pr n* Majorque *f*; **in ~** à Majorque.
majority *n* majorité *f* (**of** de); **to be in a** or **the ~** être en majorité.
make I *n* marque *f*.
II *vtr* **1** (gen) faire; **to ~ the bed** faire le lit; **to ~ a noise** faire du bruit; **to ~ a rule** établir une règle; **to ~ room/the time (for sth)** trouver de la place/du temps (pour qch); **to ~ friends/enemies** se faire des amis/des ennemis; **to ~ oneself understood** se faire comprendre; **it's made (out) of gold** c'est en or; **made in France** fabriqué en France; **he was made treasurer** on l'a fait trésorier; **to ~ a habit/an issue of sth** faire de qch une habitude/une affaire; **it's been made into a film** on en a fait or tiré un film; **three and three ~ six** trois et trois font six; **2** (with adjective) **to ~ sb happy/ill** rendre qn heureux/malade; **to ~ sb hungry** donner faim à qn; **to ~ sth better/bigger/worse** améliorer/agrandir/aggraver qch; **3** (with infinitive) **to ~ sb cry** faire pleurer qn; **I made her smile** je l'ai fait sourire; **to ~ sb pay the bill** faire payer l'addition à qn; **to ~ sb wait** faire attendre qn; **they made me do it** ils m'ont obligé or forcé; **it ~s her voice sound funny** ça lui donne une drôle de voix; **4** (earn) gagner [*salary*]; **to ~ a living** gagner sa vie; **to ~ a profit** réaliser des bénéfices; **to ~ a loss** subir des pertes; **5** (reach) arriver jusqu'à [*place, position*]; atteindre [*ranking, level*]; **we'll never ~ it** nous n'y arriverons jamais; **to ~ the front page** faire la une; **6** (estimate, say) **what time do you ~ it?** quelle heure as-tu?; **I ~ it five o'clock** il est cinq heures à ma montre; **let's ~ it five dollars** disons cinq dollars; **can we ~ it a bit later?** peut-on dire un peu plus tard?; **what do you ~ of it?** qu'en dis-tu?; **7** (cause success of) assurer la réussite de [*holiday, meal*]; **it really made my day** ça m'a rendu heureux pour la journée.
IDIOMS **to ~ it**○ (in career, life) y arriver; (to party, meeting) réussir à venir; **I can't ~ it** je ne peux pas venir.
■ **make do** faire avec; **to ~ do with** se contenter de qch.
■ **make for 1** (head for) se diriger vers; **2** (help create) permettre, assurer.
■ **make good**: ¶ **~ good** réussir; ¶ **~ good [sth] 1** réparer [*damage, omission*]; rattraper [*lost time*]; combler [*deficit*]; **2** tenir [*promise*].
■ **make out**: ¶ **~ out** affirmer, prétendre (**that** que); ¶ **~ [sb/sth] out 1** (see, distinguish) distinguer; **2** (claim) **to ~ sth out to be easy/difficult** prétendre que qch est facile/difficile; **3** (understand) comprendre (**if** si); **I can't ~ him out** je n'arrive pas à le comprendre; **4** (write out) faire, rédiger; **to ~ out a cheque to sb** faire un chèque à qn; **it is made out to X** il est à l'ordre de X.
■ **make up**: ¶ **~ up 1** (after quarrel) se réconcilier (**with** avec); **2 to ~ up for** rattraper [*lost time, lost sleep*]; compenser [*personal loss*]; ¶ **~ [sth] up 1** inventer [*story, excuse*]; **2** (prepare) faire [*parcel, garment, bed*]; préparer [*prescription*]; **3** (constitute) faire; **to be made up of** être fait/-e or composé/-e de; **4** (compensate for) rattraper [*loss, time*]; combler [*deficit*].
make-believe *n* fantaisie *f*.
maker *n* (of clothes, food, appliance) fabricant *m*; (of cars, aircraft) constructeur *m*.
makeshift *adj* improvisé/-e.
make-up *n* **1** maquillage *m*; **to put on one's ~** se maquiller; **2** (character) caractère *m*.
make-up remover *n* démaquillant *m*.
making *n* (of film, programme) réalisation *f*; (of product) fabrication *f*; (of clothes) confection *f*; **his problems are of his own ~** ses ennuis sont de sa faute; **a disaster is in the ~** une catastrophe se prépare.
IDIOMS **to have all the ~s of** avoir tout pour faire.
malaria **▶533** *n* paludisme *m*.
Malaysia **▶448** *pr n* Malaisie *f*.
male I *n* **1** (animal) mâle *m*; **2** (man) homme *m*.
II *adj* **1** [*plant, animal*] mâle; **2** [*population, role, trait*] masculin/-e; [*company*] des hommes; **a ~ voice** une voix d'homme; **~ student** étudiant *m*; **3** [*plug, socket*] mâle.
male chauvinist *n* phallocrate *m*.
malevolent *adj* malveillant/-e.
malfunction I *n* **1** (poor operation) mauvais fonctionnement *m*; **2** (breakdown) défaillance *f*.
II *vi* mal fonctionner.
malice *n* méchanceté *f* (**towards** à).
malicious *adj* [*comment, person*] malveillant/-e; [*act*] méchant/-e; [*lie*] calomnieux/-ieuse.
malign *vtr* calomnier.
malignant *adj* **1** [*look*] malveillant/-e; [*person*] malfaisant/-e; **2** (Med) malin/-igne.
mall *n* **1** (shopping arcade) (in town) galerie *f* marchande; (in suburbs) (US) centre *m* commercial; **2** (US) (street) rue *f* piétonne.
mallet *n* maillet *m*.
malpractice *n* **1** (gen, Law) malversations *fpl*; **2** (US Med) erreur *f* médicale.
malt *n* **1** (grain) malt *m*; **2** (whisky) whisky *m* pur malt; **3** (US) (malted milk) lait *m* malté.
Malta *pr n* Malte *f*.
mammal *n* mammifère *m*.
mammoth I *n* mammouth *m*.
II *adj* [*task*] gigantesque; [*organization*] géant/-e.
man I *n* **1** homme *m*; **an old ~** un vieillard; **~ to ~** d'homme à homme; **~ and wife**

mari et femme; **2** (mankind) l'humanité *f*; **3** (in chess) pièce *f*; (in draughts) pion *m*.
II *vtr* **1** tenir [*switchboard, desk*]; **2** armer [qch] en hommes [*ship*].
IDIOMS **every ~ for himself** chacun pour soi.

manage I *vtr* **1 to ~ to do** réussir à faire, se débrouiller○ pour faire; **2** diriger [*project, finances, organization*]; gérer [*business, shop, hotel, estate*]; gérer [*money, time*]; **3** (handle) savoir s'y prendre avec [*person, animal*]; manier [*tool, boat*].
II *vi* se débrouiller○.

manageable *adj* [*size, car*] maniable; [*problem*] maîtrisable; [*person, animal*] docile.

management *n* **1** (system, field) gestion *f*; **bad ~** mauvaise gestion; **2** (managers) direction *f*; **top ~** la haute direction.

manager *n* (of firm, bank) directeur/-trice *m/f*; (of shop) gérant/-e *m/f*; (of farm) exploitant/-e *m/f*; (of project) responsable *mf*, directeur/-trice *m/f*; (in show business) directeur/-trice *m/f* artistique; (Sport) manager *m*.

manageress *n* (of firm, bank) directrice *f*; (of shop, hotel) gérante *f*; (of project) responsable *f*, directrice *f*; (in show business) directrice *f* artistique.

managing director, MD *n* directeur/-trice *m/f* général/-e.

mandarin *n* **1** (fruit) mandarine *f*; (tree) mandarinier *m*; **2** (person) mandarin *m*.

mane *n* crinière *f*.

manger *n* mangeoire *f*.

mangle *vtr* mutiler [*body*]; broyer [*vehicle*].

mango *n* (fruit) mangue *f*.

mangrove *n* palétuvier *m*, manglier *m*.

mangy *adj* [*dog*] galeux/-euse.

manhandle *vtr* malmener, maltraiter.

manhole *n* regard *m*.

manhood *n* **1** âge *m* d'homme; **2** (masculinity) masculinité *f*.

mania *n* manie *f*.

maniac *n* **1**○ fou/folle *m/f*; **2** (in psychology) maniaque *mf*.

manic *adj* **1** (manic-depressive) maniaco-dépressif/-ive; (obsessive) obsessionnel/-elle; **2** (figurative) [*activity, behaviour*] frénétique.

manicure I *n* manucure *f*.
II *vtr* **to ~ one's nails** se faire les ongles.

manifest I *adj* manifeste, évident/-e.
II *vtr* manifester.

manifesto *n* manifeste *m*, programme *m*.

manipulate *vtr* manipuler.

manipulative *adj* manipulateur/-trice.

mankind *n* humanité *f*.

manly *adj* viril/-e.

man-made *adj* [*fibre, fabric*] synthétique; [*lake*] artificiel/-ielle; [*tools*] fait/-e à la main.

manner I *n* **1** (way, method) manière *f*, façon *f*; **in this ~** de cette manière or façon; **in a ~ of speaking** pour ainsi dire; **2** (way of behaving) attitude *f*; **she has an aggressive ~** elle a une attitude agressive; **3** (sort, kind) sorte *f*, genre *m* (**of** de).
II **manners** *n pl* **1** manières *fpl*; **to have good/bad ~s** avoir de bonnes/mauvaises manières; **it's bad ~s to do** il est mal élevé de faire; **2** (customs) mœurs *fpl*.

mannerism *n* (habit) particularité *f*; (quirk) manie *f*.

manoeuvre (GB), **maneuver** (US) I *n* manœuvre *f*.
II *vtr* **1** manœuvrer [*vehicle, object*]; **2** (figurative) manœuvrer [*person*]; faire dévier [*discussion*] (**to** vers).
III *vi* manœuvrer.

manor *n* (also **~ house**) manoir *m*.

manpower *n* main-d'œuvre *f*.

mansion *n* (in countryside) demeure *f*; (in town) hôtel *m* particulier.

manslaughter *n* homicide *m* involontaire.

mantelpiece *n* (manteau *m* de) cheminée *f*.

manual I *n* manuel *m*.
II *adj* [*labour, worker*] manuel/-elle; [*gearbox, typewriter*] mécanique.

manufacture I *n* (gen) fabrication *f*; (of clothes) confection *f*; (of cars) construction *f*.
II *vtr* (gen) fabriquer; construire [*cars*].

manufacturer *n* (gen) fabricant *m* (**of** de); (of cars) constructeur *m*.

manure *n* fumier *m*; **horse ~** crottin *m* de cheval.

manuscript *n* manuscrit *m*.

many I *det* beaucoup de, un grand nombre de; **~ people** beaucoup de gens, un grand nombre de personnes; **~ times** de nombreuses fois, bien des fois; **for ~ years** pendant de nombreuses années; **how ~ people/times?** combien de personnes/fois?; **too ~** trop de; **I have as ~ books as you (do)** j'ai autant de livres que toi; **so ~** tant de.
II *pron, quantif* beaucoup; **not ~** pas beaucoup; **too ~** trop; **how ~?** combien?; **as ~ as you like** autant que tu veux; **I didn't know there were so ~** je ne savais pas qu'il y en avait autant; **~ (of them) were killed** beaucoup d'entre eux ont été tués.

map *n* carte *f* (**of** de); (of town, underground) plan *m* (**of** de); **street ~** plan des rues.
■ **map out** élaborer, mettre [qch] au point [*plans, strategy*]; tracer [*future*].

maple *n* érable *m*.

mar *vtr* gâcher.

marathon I *n* marathon *m*.
II *adj* **1** (Sport) **~ runner** marathonien/-ienne *m/f*; **2** (massive) -marathon; **a ~ session** une séance-marathon.

marble *n* **1** (stone) marbre *m*; **2** (Games) bille *f*; **to play ~s** jouer aux billes.

march I *n* marche *f*.
II *vi* **1** (Mil) marcher au pas; **to ~ (for) 40 km** faire une marche de 40 km; **forward ~!** en avant, marche!; **2** (in protest) manifester (**against** contre; **for** pour); **3 to ~ along** (walk briskly) marcher d'un pas vif; **to ~ in** (angrily) entrer l'air furieux; **she ~ed up to his desk** elle s'est dirigée droit sur son bureau.

March ▶ 456 *n* mars *m*.

mare *n* (horse) jument *f*; (donkey) ânesse *f*.

margarine *n* margarine *f*.

margin *n* marge *f*; **by a narrow ~** de justesse, de peu.

marginal *adj* marginal/-e.

marigold *n* souci *m*.

marijuana *n* marijuana *f*.

marinade *vtr* (also **marinate**) faire mariner.

marine I *n* **1** (soldier) fusilier *m* marin; **the Marines** les marines *mpl*; **2** (navy) **the merchant ~** la marine marchande.
II *adj* [*mammal, biology*] marin/-e; [*explorer, life*] sous-marin/-e; [*insurance, law*] maritime.

marital *adj* conjugal/-e.

marital status *n* situation *f* de famille.

marjoram *n* marjolaine *f*.

mark I *n* **1** (gen) marque *f*; (stain) tache *f*; **2 as a ~ of** en signe de [*esteem, respect*]; **3** (Sch, Univ) note *f*; **4 the high-tide ~** le maximum de la marée haute; **at gas ~ 7** à thermostat 7; **5** (Sport) **on your ~s!** à vos marques!; **6** ▶ 582 (also **Deutschmark**) deutschmark *m*.
II *vtr* **1** (gen) marquer; (stain) tacher; **2** [*arrow, sign, label*] indiquer [*position, road*]; **3** (Sch, Univ) corriger; **to ~ sb absent** noter qn absent; **4** (Sport) marquer.
III *vi* **1** [*teacher*] faire des corrections; **2** (stain) se tacher; **3** (Sport) marquer.
IDIOMS **~ my words** crois-moi; **to ~ time** (Mil) marquer le pas; (figurative) (wait) attendre; (wait for right moment) attendre le bon moment.

marked *adj* **1** [*difference, increase, contrast*] marqué/-e, net/nette (*before n*); [*accent*] prononcé/-e; **2 he's a ~ man** on en veut à sa vie.

marker *n* **1** (pen) marqueur *m*; **2** (tag) repère *m*.

market I *n* **1** (gen, Econ) marché *m*; **2** (stock market) Bourse *f*.
II *vtr* **1** (sell) commercialiser, vendre; **2** (promote) lancer or mettre [qch] sur le marché.

market day *n* jour *m* du marché.

market gardening *n* culture *f* maraîchère.

marketing *n* **1** (field) marketing *m*, mercatique *f*; **2** (department) service *m* de marketing.

marketplace *n* place *f* du marché.

market research *n* étude *f* de marché.

market town *n* bourg *m*.

markings *n pl* (on animal) taches *fpl*; (on aircraft) marques *fpl*; **road ~** signalisation *f* horizontale.

marksman *n* tireur *m* d'élite.

marmalade *n* confiture *f* or marmelade *f* d'oranges.

maroon ▶ 438 I *n* bordeaux *m*.
II *vtr* **to be ~ed on an island** être bloqué/-e sur une île; **the ~ed sailors** les naufragés.

marquee *n* **1** (GB) (tent) grande tente *f*; (of circus) chapiteau *m*; **2** (US) (canopy) (grand) auvent *m*.

marriage *n* mariage *m* (**to** avec).

marriage certificate *n* extrait *m* d'acte de mariage.

married *adj* [*person*] marié/-e (**to** à); [*life*] conjugal/-e; **~ couple** couple *m*.

marrow *n* **1** (in bone) moelle *f*; **2** (GB) (vegetable) courge *f*; **baby ~** (GB) courgette *f*.

marrowbone *n* os *m* à moelle.

marry I *vtr* se marier avec, épouser [*fiancé(e)*]; [*priest*] marier [*couple*]; **to get married** se marier (**to** avec); **will you ~ me?** veux-tu m'épouser?
II *vi* se marier.

Mars *pr n* Mars *f*.

marsh *n* (also **marshland**) (terrain) marécage *m*; (region) marais *m*.

marshal I *n* **1** (Mil) maréchal *m*; **2** (at rally, ceremony) membre *m* du service d'ordre; **3** (US) (in fire service) capitaine *m* des pompiers.
II *vtr* rassembler.

martial *adj* [*art, law*] martial/-e; [*spirit*] guerrier/-ière.

martyr I *n* martyr/-e *m/f*.
II *vtr* martyriser.

martyrdom *n* martyre *m*.

marvel I *n* merveille *f*.
II *vi* s'étonner (**at** de), être émerveillé/-e (**at** par).

marvellous (GB), **marvelous** (US) *adj* merveilleux/-euse; **that's ~!** c'est formidable!

marzipan *n* pâte *f* d'amandes.

mascot *n* mascotte *f*; **lucky ~** porte-bonheur *m inv*.

masculine *adj* masculin/-e.

masculinity *n* masculinité *f*.

mash I *n* (for animals) pâtée *f*.
II *vtr* (also **~ up**) écraser.

mashed potatoes *n pl* purée *f* de pommes de terre.

mask I *n* masque *m*; (for eyes only) loup *m*.
II *vtr* masquer.

masking tape *n* ruban *m* adhésif.

masochist *n, adj* masochiste (*mf*).

mason ▶ 626 *n* **1** (in building) maçon *m*; **2 Mason** (also **Free~**) franc-maçon *m*.

masonry *n* maçonnerie *f*.

masquerade I *n* bal *m* masqué; (figurative) mascarade *f*.
II *vi* **to ~ as sb/sth** se faire passer pour qn/qch.

mass I *n* **1** masse *f* (**of** de); (of people) foule *f* (**of** de); (of details) quantité *f* (**of** de); **2** (in church) messe *f*.
II **masses** *n pl* **1 the ~es** les masses *fpl*; **2**○ (GB) **~es of work** beaucoup or plein○ de travail; **~es of people** des tas○ de gens.
III *adj* [*audience, movement, meeting, tourism*] de masse; [*exodus, protest, unemployment*] massif/-ive; **~ hysteria** hystérie *f* collective.
IV *vi* [*troops*] se regrouper; [*bees*] se masser; [*clouds*] s'amonceler.

massacre I *n* massacre *m*.
II *vtr* massacrer.

massage I *n* massage *m*.
II *vtr* masser.

massive *adj* (gen) énorme; [*increase, cut*] massif/-ive.

mass media *n* (mass) médias *mpl.*

mass production *n* fabrication *f* en série.

mast *n* (on ship, for flags) mât *m*; (for aerial) pylône *m.*

master I *n* **1** (gen) maître *m*; **2** (Sch) (primary) maître *m*, instituteur *m*; (secondary) professeur *m*; (GB Univ) (of college) principal *m*; **3** (also **~ copy**) original *m.*
II *adj* [*chef, craftsman*] maître (*before n*); [*spy*] professionnel/-elle.
III *vtr* **1** maîtriser [*subject*]; posséder [*art, skill*]; **2** dominer [*feelings*]; surmonter [*phobia*].

master key *n* passe-partout *m inv.*

masterly *adj* magistral/-e.

mastermind I *n* cerveau *m* (**of, behind** de).
II *vtr* organiser [*robbery, event*].

Master of Arts *n* diplôme *m* supérieur de lettres.

master of ceremonies *n* (in cabaret) animateur/-trice *m/f*; (at banquet) maître *m* des cérémonies.

Master of Science *n* diplôme *m* supérieur en sciences.

masterpiece *n* chef-d'œuvre *m.*

master plan *n* plan *m* d'ensemble.

master's (degree) *n* ≈ maîtrise (**in** de).

mastery *n* maîtrise *f* (**of** de).

mat I *n* **1** (on floor) (petit) tapis *m*; (for wiping feet) paillasson *m*; **2** (on table) dessous-de-plat *m inv*; **place ~** set *m* de table.
II *vi* [*hair*] s'emmêler; [*wool*] se feutrer; [*fibres*] s'enchevêtrer.

match I *n* **1** (Sport) match *m*; **2** (matchstick) allumette *f*; **3 to be a ~ for sb** être un adversaire à la mesure de qn; **to be no ~ for sb** être trop faible pour qn.
II *vtr* **1** (gen) correspondre à; [*colour, bag*] être assorti/-e à; **to ~ (up) the names to the photos** trouver les noms qui correspondent aux photos; **2** (equal) égaler [*record, achievements*].
III *vi* [*colours, clothes, curtains*] être assortis/-ies; [*components*] aller ensemble; **with gloves to ~** avec des gants assortis.

matchbox *n* boîte *f* d'allumettes.

match point *n* balle *f* de match.

matchstick *n* allumette *f.*

mate I *n* **1**○ (GB) (friend) copain○ *m*; (at work, school) camarade *mf*; **2** (Zool) (male) mâle *m*; (female) femelle *f*; **3** (assistant) aide *mf*; **4** (in navy) second *m.*
II *vtr* **1** accoupler [*animal*] (**with** à or avec); **2** (in chess) faire mat.
III *vi* [*animal*] s'accoupler (**with** à, avec).

material I *n* **1** (substance) (gen) matière *f*, substance *f*; (Tech) matériau *m*; **waste ~** déchets *mpl*; **2** (fabric) tissu *m*, étoffe *f*; **3** (written matter) documentation *f*; **teaching ~** matériel *m* pédagogique; **reading ~** lecture *f*; **4** (potential) étoffe *f*; **she is star ~** elle a l'étoffe d'une vedette.
II materials *n pl* (equipment) matériel *m*; **cleaning ~s** produits *mpl* d'entretien; **building ~s** matériaux de construction.
III *adj* matériel/-ielle.

materialistic *adj* matérialiste.

materialize *vi* **1** [*hope, offer, plan, threat*] se concrétiser; [*event, situation*] se réaliser; [*idea*] prendre forme; **2** (appear) [*person, object*] surgir; [*spirit*] se matérialiser.

maternal *adj* maternel/-elle (**towards** avec).

maternity *n* maternité *f.*

maternity ward *n* maternité *f.*

math○ *n* (US) math○ *fpl.*

mathematical *adj* mathématique.

mathematician ▶626 *n* mathématicien/-ienne *m/f.*

mathematics *n* mathématiques *fpl.*

maths○ *n* (GB) maths○ *fpl.*

matinée *n* matinée *f.*

mating season *n* saison *f* des amours.

matriculate *vi* [*student*] s'inscrire.

matrimony *n* mariage *m.*

matrix *n* matrice *f.*

matron *n* **1** (GB) (in hospital) infirmière *f* en chef; (in school) infirmière *f*; **2** (of nursing home) directrice *f*; **3** (US) (warder) gardienne *f.*

matt (GB), **matte** (US) *adj* [*paint*] mat/-e; [*photograph*] sur papier mat.

matter I *n* **1** (affair) affaire *f*; (requiring solution) problème *m*; (on agenda) point *m*; **it will be no easy ~** cela ne sera pas (une affaire) facile; **important ~s to discuss** des choses importantes à discuter; **private ~** affaire privée; **a ~ for the police** un problème qui relève de la police; **that's another ~** c'est une autre histoire; **the fact of the ~ is that** la vérité est que; **2** (question) question *f*; **a ~ of** une question de [*opinion, principle, taste*]; **a ~ of life and death** une question de vie ou de mort; **3** (trouble) **is anything the ~?** y a-t-il un problème?; **what's the ~?** qu'est-ce qu'il y a?; **what's the ~ with Louise?** qu'est-ce qu'elle a, Louise?; **there's something the ~ with my car** ma voiture a un problème; **4** (substance) matière *f*; **vegetable ~** matière végétale; **5 printed ~** imprimés *mpl*; **advertising ~** publicité *f*; **reading ~** lecture *f*; **subject ~** contenu *m*; **6** (Med) (pus) pus *m.*
II *vi* être important/-e; **it doesn't ~** ça ne fait rien; **it doesn't ~ whether he comes or not** peu importe qu'il vienne ou pas.
IDIOMS **as a ~ of course** automatiquement; **as a ~ of fact** en fait; **for that ~** d'ailleurs; **no ~ how late it is** peu importe l'heure; **no ~ what (happens)** quoi qu'il arrive; **and to make ~s worse** et pour ne rien arranger.

matter-of-fact *adj* [*voice, tone*] détaché/-e; [*person*] terre à terre.

mattress *n* matelas *m.*

mature I *adj* **1** [*plant, animal*] adulte; **2** [*person*] mûr/-e; [*attitude, reader*] adulte; **3** [*hard cheese*] fort/-e; [*soft cheese*] affiné/-e; [*whisky*] vieux/vieille.
II *vi* **1** (physically) [*person, animal*] devenir

adulte; **2** (psychologically) [*person*] mûrir; **3** [*wine*] vieillir; [*cheese*] s'affiner; **4** [*policy*] arriver à échéance.

maul *vtr* [*animal*] lacérer.

mauve ▶438 *n, adj* mauve (*m*).

maverick *n, adj* nonconformiste (*mf*).

maxim *n* maxime *f*.

maximum **I** *n* maximum *m*.
II *adj* maximum (*inv*).

may *modal aux* **1** (expressing possibility) **it ~ rain** il pleuvra peut-être, il se peut qu'il pleuve; **she ~ not have seen him** elle ne l'a peut-être pas vu; **'are you going to accept?'—'I ~'** 'tu vas accepter'—'peut-être'; **he ~ not come** il risque de ne pas venir; **be that as it ~** quoi qu'il en soi; **come what ~** advienne que pourra; **2** (expressing permission) **you ~ sit down** vous pouvez vous asseoir; **~ I come in?** puis-je entrer?; **3** (wish) **~ he rest in peace** qu'il repose en paix.

May ▶456 *n* mai *m*.

maybe *adv* peut-être; **~ they'll arrive early** peut-être qu'ils arriveront tôt.

mayday *n* (distress signal) mayday *m*.

May Day *n* premier mai *m*, fête *f* du travail.

mayhem *n* (chaos) désordre *m*; (violence) grabuge○ *m*.

mayor ▶498 *n* maire *m*.

mayoress ▶498 *n* (wife of mayor) femme *f* du maire; (lady mayor) mairesse *f*.

maze *n* (puzzle, in gardens) labyrinthe *m*; (of streets, corridors) dédale *m*.

MC *n* (*abbr* = **Master of Ceremonies**) (in cabaret) animateur/-trice *m/f*; (at banquet) maître *m* des cérémonies.

me *pron* **1** me, m'; **she knows ~** elle me connaît; **he loves ~** il m'aime; **2** (in imperatives, after prepositions and to be) moi; **give it to ~!** donne-le-moi!; **it's for ~** c'est pour moi; **it's ~** c'est moi.

meadow *n* **1** (field) pré *m*; **2** (also **~land**) prés *mpl*, prairies *fpl*; **3** (also **water ~**) prairie *f* inondable.

meagre (GB), **meager** (US) *adj* maigre (*before n*).

meal *n* **1** repas *m*; **to go out for a ~** aller (manger) au restaurant; **2** (from grain) farine *f*.

mean **I** *n* moyenne *f*.
II *adj* **1** [*person*] avare, radin/-e○; **he's ~ with money** il est près de ses sous; **2** (unkind, vicious) méchant/-e (**to** avec); **a ~ trick** un sale tour; **3** (average) [*weight, age*] moyen/-enne; **4 that's no ~ feat!** ce n'est pas un mince exploit!
III *vtr* **1** [*word, phrase, symbol*] signifier, vouloir dire; [*sign*] vouloir dire; **the name ~s nothing to me** ce nom ne me dit rien; **2** (intend) **to ~ to do** avoir l'intention de faire; **to be meant for sb** être destiné/-e à qn; **I didn't ~ to do it** je ne l'ai pas fait exprès; **she meant no offence** elle ne pensait pas à mal; **he doesn't ~ you any harm** il ne te veut aucun mal; **to ~ well** avoir de bonnes intentions; **he ~s what he says** (he is sincere) il est sérieux; (he is menacing) il ne plaisante pas; **without ~ing to** par inadvertance; **3** (entail) [*strike, law*] entraîner [*shortages, changes*]; **4** (intend to say) vouloir dire; **what do you ~ by that remark?** qu'est-ce que tu veux dire par là?; **I know what you ~** je comprends; **5 money ~s a lot to him** l'argent compte beaucoup pour lui; **your friendship ~s a lot to me** ton amitié est très importante pour moi; **6** (be destined) **to be meant to do** être destiné/-e à faire; **it was meant to be** or **happen** cela devait arriver; **they were meant for each other** ils étaient faits l'un pour l'autre; **7** (be supposed to be) **he's meant to be/to be doing** il est censé être/faire.

meander *vi* [*river, road*] serpenter.

meaning *n* (of word, remark, action, life) sens *m*; (of symbol, film, dream) signification *f*.

meaningful *adj* **1** (significant) [*word, statement, result*] significatif/-ive; **2** (profound) [*relationship, comment, lyrics*] sérieux/-ieuse; [*experience*] riche; **3** (eloquent) [*look, smile*] entendu/-e; [*gesture*] significatif/-ive.

meaningless *adj* **1** [*word, phrase*] dépourvu/-e de sens; **2** (pointless) [*act, sacrifice*] futile, vain/-e; [*violence*] insensé/-e.

means **I** *n* moyen *m* (**of doing** de faire); **a ~ of** un moyen de [*communication, transport*]; **by ~ of** au moyen de; **yes, by all ~** oui, certainement; **it is by no ~ certain** c'est loin d'être sûr.
II *n pl* moyens *mpl*, revenus *mpl*; **to live within one's ~** vivre selon ses moyens.

means test *n* enquête *f* sur les ressources.

meantime *adv* (**in the**) **~** pendant ce temps; **for the ~** pour le moment.

meanwhile *adv* **1** (during this time) pendant ce temps; **2** (until then) en attendant; **3** (since then) entre-temps.

measles ▶533 *n* rougeole *f*.

measure ▶573 **I** *n* **1** (gen) mesure *f*; **to take ~s** prendre des mesures; **weights and ~s** les poids et mesures *mpl*; **2** (measuring device) instrument *m* de mesure.
II *vtr* **1** mesurer; **to ~ four by five metres** mesurer quatre mètres sur cinq; **2** (compare) **to ~ sth against** comparer qch à.
IDIOMS **for good ~** pour faire bonne mesure.
■ **measure out** mesurer [*land, flour, liquid*]; doser [*medicine*].
■ **measure up** [*person*] avoir les qualités requises; **to ~ up to** être à la hauteur de [*expectations*]; soutenir la comparaison avec [*achievement*].

measurement ▶573 *n* **1** (of room, object) dimension *f*; **2** (of person) **to take sb's ~s** prendre les mensurations de qn; **chest ~** tour *m* de poitrine; **leg ~** longueur *f* de jambe.

measuring jug *n* verre *m* gradué.

meat *n* viande *f*; **crab ~** chair *f* de crabe.

meaty *adj* **1** [*flavour, smell*] de viande; **2** [*article, book*] substantiel/-ielle; **3** [*person, hand*] épais/-aisse.

Mecca ▶448 *pr n* La Mecque.

Length and Weight Measurements

Note that French has a comma where English has a decimal point:

1 in	= 2,54 cm (centimètres)	*1 yd*	= 91,44 cm
1 ft	= 30,48 cm	*1 ml*	= 1,61 km (kilomètres)

Length

	how long is the rope?	= quelle est la longueur de la corde?
	it's ten metres long	= elle fait dix mètres (de† long)
	it's three metres too short / long	= il est trop court / long de trois mètres

Height

People	*how tall is he?*	= combien mesure-t-il? combien est-ce qu'il mesure?
	he's six feet tall	= il fait / il mesure un mètre quatre-vingts
	Tom is taller / smaller than Jane	= Tom est plus grand / plus petit que Jane
Things	*how high is the tower?*	= quelle est la hauteur de la tour?
	it's 100 metres high	= elle fait cent mètres de† haut / de hauteur
	at a height of two metres	= à deux mètres de† hauteur
	A is higher / lower than B	= A est plus haut / moins haut que B

Distance

	what's the distance from Paris to Nice?	= quelle distance y a-t-il entre Paris et Nice?
	how far is it from Paris to Nice?	= combien y a-t-il de kilomètres de Paris à Nice?
	it's about 800 kilometres	= il y a environ 800 kilomètres
	at a distance of five kilometres	= à une distance de cinq kilomètres

Width / breadth

	how wide is it?	= combien fait-elle de† large?
	it's seven metres wide	= elle fait sept mètres de† large / de† largeur

Depth

	how deep is it?	= combien fait-elle de† profondeur?
	it's four metres deep	= elle fait quatre mètres de† profondeur
	at a depth of ten metres	= à une profondeur de dix mètres

Note the French construction with ***de***, coming after the noun it describes:

	an avenue four kilometres long	= une avenue **de** quatre kilomètres de† long
	a 100-metre-high tower	= une tour **de** 100 mètres de† haut
	a ten-kilometre walk	= une promenade **de** dix kilomètres
	a river 50 metres wide	= une rivière **de** 50 mètres de† largeur

Weight measurement

Again, note that French has a comma where English has a decimal point:

1 oz	= 28,35 g (grammes)	*1 st*	= 6,35 kg (kilos)
*1 lb**	= 453,60 g	*1 ton*	= 1 014,60 kg

* ***a pound*** is translated by ***une livre*** in French, but the French *livre* = 500 grams (half a kilo).

People	*how much does he weigh?*	= combien pèse-t-il?
	he weighs 10 st / 140 lbs	= il pèse 63 kg 500 (soixante-trois kilos et demi)
Things	*what does the parcel weigh?*	= combien pèse le colis?
	how heavy is it?	= quel poids fait-il?
	it weighs ten kilos	= il pèse dix kilos
	it was 2 kilos overweight	= il pesait deux kilos **de** trop
	A weighs more than B	= A pèse plus lourd que B
	a parcel 3 kilos in weight	= un colis de† trois kilos
	sold by the kilo	= vendu au kilo

† The use of ***de*** is obligatory in these constructions.

mechanic ▶626 *n* mécanicien/-ienne *m/f*.
mechanical *adj* mécanique.
mechanics *n pl* **1** (field) mécanique *f*; **2** (workings) mécanisme *m*.
mechanism *n* mécanisme *m* (**of** de).
mechanization *n* mécanisation *f*.
medal *n* médaille *f*; **gold ~** médaille d'or.
medallion *n* médaillon *m*.
medallist (GB), **medalist** (US) *n* médaillé/-e *m/f*; **gold ~** médaillé/-e *m/f* d'or.
meddle *vi* **to ~ in** se mêler de [*affairs*]; **to ~ with** toucher à [*property*].
media *n* **the ~** les médias *mpl*.
median (**strip**) *n* (US) terre-plein *m* central.
mediate I *vtr* négocier [*settlement, peace*].
II *vi* [*person*] arbitrer; **to ~ in/between** servir de médiateur dans/entre.
medical I *n* (in school, army, for job) visite *f* médicale; (private) examen *m* médical.
II *adj* médical/-e.
medicated *adj* (gen) médical/-e; [*shampoo*] traitant/-e.
medication *n* médicaments *mpl*.
medicinal *adj* [*property, use*] thérapeutique; [*herb*] médicinal/-e.
medicine *n* **1** (field) médecine *f*; **2** (drug) médicament *m* (**for** pour).
medicine cabinet, **medicine cupboard** *n* armoire *f* à pharmacie.
medicine man *n* sorcier *m* guérisseur.
medieval *adj* médiéval/-e.
mediocre *adj* médiocre.
mediocrity *n* **1** (state) médiocrité *f*; **2** (person) médiocre *mf*.
meditate *vtr*, *vi* méditer.
Mediterranean I *pr n* **1 the ~** (**sea**) la (mer) Méditerranée; **2** (region) **the ~** les pays méditerranéens.
II *adj* méditerranéen/-éenne.
medium I *n* **1** (means) moyen *m*; **2 to find** or **strike a happy ~** trouver le juste milieu; **3** (spiritualist) médium *m*.
II *adj* moyen/-enne.
medium-dry *adj* [*drink*] demi-sec.
medium-rare *adj* [*meat*] à point.
medium-sized *adj* de taille moyenne.
medley *n* **1** (Mus) pot-pourri *m* (**of** de); **2** (mixture) mélange *m*.
meek *adj* docile.
meet I *n* **1** (Sport) rencontre *f* (sportive); **track ~** (US) rencontre *f* d'athlétisme; **2** (GB) (in hunting) rendez-vous *m* de chasseurs.
II *vtr* **1** rencontrer [*person, team, enemy*]; **2** (make acquaintance of) faire la connaissance de [*person*]; **have you met each other?** vous vous connaissez?; **3** (await) attendre; (fetch) chercher; **she went to ~ them** elle est allée les attendre or chercher; **to ~ sb off** (GB) or **at** (US) **the plane** attendre qn à l'aéroport; **4** répondre à, satisfaire à [*criteria, standards, needs*]; payer [*bills, costs*]; couvrir [*debts*]; faire face à [*obligations, commitments*]; remplir [*conditions*]; **5** se montrer à la hauteur de [*challenge*].
III *vi* **1** [*people, teams*] se rencontrer; [*committee, parliament*] se réunir; **to ~ again** [*people*] se revoir; **2** (by appointment) [*people*] se retrouver; **3** (make acquaintance) [*people*] se connaître; **4** [*lips, roads*] se rencontrer; **their eyes met** leurs regards se croisèrent.
IDIOMS **to make ends ~** joindre les deux bouts.
■ **meet up**○ se retrouver; **to ~ up with**○ retrouver [*friend*].
■ **meet with**: ¶ **~ with** [**sb**] rencontrer [*person, delegation*]; ¶ **~ with** [**sth**] rencontrer [*opposition, success, suspicion*]; être accueilli/-e avec [*approval*]; subir [*failure*].
meeting *n* **1** (official) réunion *f*; **in a ~** en réunion; **2** (informal) recontre *f*; **3** (GB Sport) **athletics ~** rencontre *f* d'athlétisme; **race ~** réunion *f* de courses.
meeting-place *n* (lieu *m* de) rendez-vous *m*.
meeting point *n* point *m* de rencontre.
megabyte, MB *n* mégaoctet *m*, Mo *m*.
megalomaniac *n*, *adj* mégalomane (*mf*).
megaphone *n* porte-voix *m inv*.
melancholy I *n* mélancolie *f*.
II *adj* [*person*] mélancolique; [*music, occasion*] triste.
mellow I *adj* **1** [*wine*] moelleux/-euse; [*flavour*] suave; [*tone*] mélodieux/-ieuse; **2** [*person*] détendu/-e; [*atmosphere*] serein/-e.
II *vtr* [*experience*] assagir [*person*].
III *vi* [*person, behaviour*] s'assagir.
melodrama *n* mélodrame *m*.
melodramatic *adj* mélodramatique.
melody *n* mélodie *f*.
melon *n* melon *m*.
melt I *vtr* **1** faire fondre [*snow, plastic, butter*]; **2** attendrir [*heart*].
II *vi* **1** fondre; **to ~ in your mouth** fondre dans la bouche; **2 to ~ into** se fondre dans [*crowd*].
meltdown *n* fusion *f* du cœur d'un réacteur.
melting point *n* point *m* de fusion.
member *n* **1** membre *m*; **to be a ~ of** faire partie de [*group*]; être membre de [*club, committee*]; **~ of staff** (gen) employé/-e *m/f*; (Sch, Univ) enseignant/-e *m/f*; **~ of the public** (in street) passant/-e *m/f*; (in theatre, cinema) spectateur/-trice *m/f*; **2** (also **Member**) (of parliament) député *m*; **3** (limb) membre *m*.
Member of Congress, MC *n* (US) membre *m* du Congrès.
Member of Parliament, MP ▶498 *n* (GB) député *m* (**for** de).
Member of the European Parliament, MEP *n* (GB) député *m* au Parlement européen.
membership *n* **1** (of club, organization) adhésion *f* (**of** à); **2** (fee) cotisation *f*; **3** (members) membres *mpl*.
membrane *n* membrane *f*.
memento *n* souvenir *m* (**of** de).
memo *n* note *f* de service.
memoirs *n pl* mémoires *mpl*.

memorable *adj* [*event*] mémorable; [*person, quality*] inoubliable.

memorial I *n* mémorial *m* (**to** à).
II *adj* commémoratif/-ive.

memorize *vtr* apprendre [qch] par cœur.

memory *n* **1** mémoire *f*; **from ~** de mémoire; **to have a good ~ for faces** être physionomiste; **in (loving) ~ of** à la mémoire de; **2** (recollection) souvenir *m*; **childhood memories** souvenirs d'enfance.

menace I *n* menace *f*.
II *vtr* menacer (**with** de, avec).

menacing *adj* menaçant/-e.

mend I *n* **to be on the ~** [*person*] être en voie de guérison; [*economy*] reprendre.
II *vtr* réparer [*object, road*]; (stitch) raccommoder; (darn) repriser; (add patch) rapiécer; **that won't ~ matters** ça n'arrangera pas les choses.
III *vi* [*injury*] guérir; [*person*] se rétablir.
IDIOMS **to ~ one's ways** s'amender.

menial *adj* [*job*] subalterne; [*attitude*] servile; **~ tasks** basses besognes.

menopause *n* ménopause *f*.

men's room *n* (US) toilettes *fpl* pour hommes.

menstruation *n* menstruation *f*.

menswear *n* prêt-à-porter *m* pour hommes.

mental *adj* (gen) mental/-e; [*ability, effort, energy*] intellectuel/-elle; [*hospital, institution*] psychiatrique.

mentality *n* mentalité *f*.

mentally *adv* **1 ~ handicapped** handicapé/-e mental; **the ~ ill** les malades mentaux; **2 ~ exhausted** surmené/-e intellectuellement.

mentholated *adj* au menthol.

mention I *n* mention *f* (**of** de); **it got a ~ on the radio** on en a parlé à la radio.
II *vtr* **1** faire mention de [*person, topic, fact*]; **please don't ~ my name** ne mentionnez pas mon nom; **to ~ sb/sth to sb** parler de qn/qch à qn; **not to ~** sans parler de; **without ~ing any names** sans nommer personne; **don't ~ it!** je vous en prie!, je t'en prie!; **2** (acknowledge) citer [*name*].

menu *n* menu *m*.

MEP *n* (GB) (*abbr* = **Member of the European Parliament**) député *m* au Parlement européen.

mercenary I *n* mercenaire *mf*.
II *adj* [*person*] intéressé/-e.

merchandise *n* marchandises *fpl*.

merchant *n* (selling in bulk) négociant *m*; (selling small quantities) marchand *m*.

merchant bank *n* (GB) banque *f* d'affaires.

merchant navy (GB), **merchant marine** (US) *n* marine *f* marchande.

merciful *adj* **1** [*person*] clément/-e (**to, towards** envers); [*act*] charitable; **2** [*occurrence*] heureux/-euse; **a ~ release** une délivrance.

merciless *adj* [*ruler, criticism*] impitoyable (**to, towards** envers); [*heat*] implacable.

mercury I *n* mercure *m*.
II **Mercury** *pr n* Mercure *f*.

mercy *n* clémence *f*; **to have ~ on sb** avoir pitié de qn; **to beg for ~** demander grâce; **at the ~ of** à la merci de.

mere *adj* **1** [*coincidence, nonsense*] pur/-e (*before n*); [*formality*] simple (*before n*); **he's a ~ child** ce n'est qu'un enfant; **the beach is a ~ 2 km from here** la plage n'est qu'à 2 km d'ici; **2** (very) [*idea*] simple (*before n*); **the ~ sight of her makes me nervous** rien que de la voir, ça rend nerveux.

merely *adv* simplement, seulement.

merge I *vtr* **1 to ~ sth with** fusionner qch avec [*company, group*]; **2** mélanger [*colours, designs*].
II *vi* **1** (also **~ together**) [*companies, departments*] fusionner (**with** avec; [*roads, rivers*] se rejoindre; **2** [*colours, sounds*] se confondre.

merger *n* fusion *f*.

meringue *n* meringue *f*.

merit I *n* mérite *m*.
II *vtr* mériter.

mermaid *n* sirène *f*.

merrily *adv* **1** (happily) joyeusement; **2** (unconcernedly) avec insouciance.

merry *adj* **1** (happy) joyeux/-euse, gai/-e; **Merry Christmas!** joyeux Noël!; **2**○ (tipsy) éméché/-e.

merry-go-round *n* manège *m*.

mesh I *n* **1** (netting) (of string) filet *m*; (of metal) grillage *m*; **2** (net) mailles *fpl*.
II *vi* (Tech) [*cogs*] s'engrener; **to ~ with** s'emboîter dans.

mesmerize I *vtr* hypnotiser.
II **mesmerized** *pp adj* fasciné/-e, médusé/-e.

mess I *n* **1** désordre *m*; **what a ~!** quel désordre!, quelle pagaille○!; **to make a ~** [*person*] mettre du désordre; **this report is a ~!** ce rapport est fait n'importe comment!; **to make a ~ on the carpet** salir la moquette; **to make a ~ of the job** massacrer○ le travail; **2** (Mil) cantine *f*.
II○ *vi* **1 to ~ with** toucher à [*drugs*]; **2 don't ~ with him** évite-le; **don't ~ with me** ne me cherche pas.
■ **mess about**○, **mess around**○: ¶ **~ around** faire l'imbécile; ¶ **~ [sb] around**○ traiter qn par-dessus la jambe○, prendre qn pour un imbécile.
■ **mess up**○: ¶ **~ up** (US) faire l'imbécile; ¶ **~ [sth] up 1** semer la pagaille dans [*papers*]; mettre du désordre dans [*kitchen*]; **2** (ruin) louper○ [*exam*]; gâcher [*chances, life*]; ¶ **~ [sb] up** [*drugs, alcohol*] détruire; [*experience*] faire perdre les pédales○ à qn.

message *n* message *m* (**about** au sujet de).

messenger *n* messager/-ère *m/f*; (for hotel, company) garçon *m* de courses, coursier/-ière *m/f*.

messy *adj* **1** [*house*] en désordre; [*appearance*] négligé/-e; [*handwriting*] peu soigné/-e; **2** [*work, job*] salissant/-e; **he's a ~ eater** il mange comme un cochon; **3** [*lawsuit*] compliqué/-e; **a ~ business** une sale affaire.

metal I *n* métal *m*.
II *adj* en métal.

metallic *adj* [*substance*] métallique; [*paint, finish*] métallisé/-e; [*taste*] de métal.
metaphor *n* métaphore *f*.
mete *v* ■ **mete out** infliger [*punishment*]; rendre [*justice*].
meteor *n* météore *m*.
meteorite *n* météorite *f*.
meter I *n* **1** compteur *m*; **gas ~** compteur de gaz; **2** (also **parking ~**) parcmètre *m*; **3** (US) = **metre**.
II *vtr* mesurer la consommation de [*electricity, gas*].
method *n* **1** (of teaching, contraception, training) méthode *f* (**for doing** pour faire); (of payment, treatment, production) mode *m* (**of** de); **2** (orderliness) méthode *f*.
methodical *adj* méthodique.
Methodist *n*, *adj* méthodiste (*mf*).
methylated spirit(s) *n* alcool *m* à brûler.
meticulous *adj* méticuleux/-euse.
metre (GB), **meter** (US) ▶**573** *n* mètre *m*.
metric *adj* métrique.
metropolitan *adj* **1** [*area, population*] urbain/-e; **~ New York** l'agglomération de New York; **2 ~ France** la France métropolitaine.
mettle *n* courage *m*; **to be on one's ~** être sur la sellette; **to put sb on his ~** amener qn à montrer de quoi il est capable.
Mexico ▶**448** *pr n* Mexique *m*.
miaow I *n* miaou *m*.
II *vi* miauler.
microbe *n* microbe *m*.
microchip *n* puce *f*, circuit *m* intégré.
microcosm *n* microcosme *m*.
microfilm *n* microfilm *m*.
microlighting ▶**504** *n* ULM *m*, ultra léger *m* motorisé.
microphone *n* microphone *m*.
microscope *n* microscope *m*.
microwave I *n* **~ (oven)** four *m* à micro-ondes.
II *vtr* passer [qch] au four à micro-ondes.
mid- *pref* **in the ~20th century** au milieu du vingtième siècle; **~afternoon** milieu *m* de l'après-midi; **(in) ~May** (à la) mi-mai; **he's in his ~forties** il a environ quarante-cinq ans.
midair I *adj* [*collision*] en plein vol.
II **in midair** *phr* (in mid-flight) en plein vol; (in the air) en l'air.
midday ▶**434** *n* midi *m*.
middle I *n* **1** milieu *m*; **in the ~ of** au milieu de; **in the ~ of May** à la mi-mai; **to be in the ~ of doing** être en train de faire; **to split [sth] down the ~** partager [qch] en deux [*bill, work*]; diviser [qch] en deux [*group, opinion*]; **in the ~ of nowhere** en pleine brousse○; **2** (waist) taille *f*.
II *adj* [*door, shelf*] du milieu; [*size, difficulty*] moyen/-enne; **there must be a ~ way** il doit y avoir une solution intermédiaire.
middle-aged *adj* [*person*] d'âge mûr; [*outlook, view*] vieux jeu *inv*.
Middle Ages *n pl* **the ~** le Moyen Âge.
middle class I *n* classe *f* moyenne.
II **middle-class** *adj* [*person*] de la classe moyenne; [*attitude, view*] bourgeois/-e.
Middle East *pr n* Moyen-Orient *m*.
middleman *n* intermédiaire *m*.
middleweight *n* poids *m* moyen.
middling *adj* moyen/-enne; **fair to ~** pas trop mal.
midfield *n* milieu *m* du terrain.
midge *n* moucheron *m*.
midget *n* nain/-e *m/f*.
midnight ▶**434** *n* minuit *m*.
midst *n* **in the ~ of** au beau milieu de; **in the ~ of change/war** en plein changement/pleine guerre; **in our ~** parmi nous.
midsummer *n* milieu *m* de l'été.
Midsummer('s) Day *n* la Saint-Jean.
midtown *n* (US) centre-ville *m*.
midway I *n* (US) attractions *fpl* foraines.
II *adj* [*post, position*] de mi-course; [*stage, point*] de mi-parcours.
III *adv* **~ between/along** à mi-chemin entre/le long de; **~ through** au milieu de.
midweek I *adj* de milieu de semaine.
II *adv* en milieu de semaine.
midwife ▶**626** *n* sage-femme *f*; **male ~** homme *m* sage-femme.
midwinter *n* milieu *m* de l'hiver.
might[1] *modal aux* **1 'will you come?'—'I ~'** 'tu viendras?'—'peut-être'; **she ~ not have heard the news** elle n'a peut-être pas entendu la nouvelle; **I ~ lose my job** je risque de perdre mon travail; **2 you ~ have been killed!** tu aurais pu te faire tuer!; **I ~ have known!** j'aurais dû m'en douter!; **3 I thought it ~ rain** j'ai pensé qu'il risquait de pleuvoir; **I thought you ~ say that** je m'attendais à ce que tu dises ça; **4 ~ I make a suggestion?** puis-je me permettre de faire une suggestion?
might[2] *n* **1** (power) puissance *f*; **2** (physical strength) force *f*; **with all his ~** de toutes ses forces.
mighty *adj* puissant/-e.
migrant I *n* (person) migrant/-e *m/f*; (bird) oiseau *m* migrateur; (animal) animal *m* migrateur.
II *adj* [*labour*] saisonnier/-ière; [*bird, animal*] migrateur/-trice.
migrate *vi* **1** [*person*] émigrer; **2** [*bird, animal*] migrer.
mike○ *n* micro○ *m*.
mild *adj* **1** [*surprise*] léger/-ère; [*interest, irritation*] modéré/-e; **2** [*weather, winter*] doux/douce; [*climate*] tempéré/-e; **3** [*beer, taste, tobacco*] léger/-ère; [*cheese*] doux/douce; [*curry*] peu épicé/-e; **4** [*soap, detergent*] doux/douce; **5** [*infection*] bénin/-igne; [*attack, sedative*] léger/-ère; **6** [*person, voice*] doux/douce.
mildew *n* moisissure *f*.
mile ▶**573**, **632** *n* **1** mile *m* (= *1,609 m*); **it's 50 ~s away** ≈ c'est à 80 kilomètres d'ici; **2 to walk for ~s** marcher pendant des kilomètres; **it's ~s away!** c'est au bout du monde; **to be ~s away** (daydreaming) être complètement

might[1]

◆ ***might***, when it means that something is possible, is translated using the adverb ***peut-être*** with the appropriate verb:

*it **might** be true* = c'est **peut-être** vrai

*she **might** be right* = elle a **peut-être** raison

*they **might** not or **might**n't go* = **peut-être** qu'ils n'iront pas

*she **might** have got lost* = elle s'est **peut-être** perdue

*they **might** have to go away* = il va **peut-être** falloir qu'ils partent ⇨ **1**

Sometimes it is possible to translate ***might*** by using the construction ***risquer de*** + *infinitive,* in contexts where the speaker views the outcome as undesirable:

*you **might** miss the plane if you leave later* = tu **risques de** rater l'avion si tu pars plus tard

*they **might** lose a lot of money* = ils **risquent de** perdre beaucoup d'argent

◆ ***might***, when it refers to something which could have happened (but didn't), is usually translated by the past conditional of the verb *pouvoir* in French:

it might have been serious = ça **aurait pu** être grave

more might have been done to improve standards = on **aurait pu** faire plus pour améliorer le niveau

he was thinking about what might have been = il pensait à ce qui **aurait pu** se passer

It can also express annoyance:

you might have warned me! = tu aurais pu me prévenir!

they might at least have apologized = ils **auraient** au moins **pu** s'excuser

I might have guessed = j'**aurais dû** m'en douter ⇨ **2**

◆ ***might***, when it occurs in indirect statements, indicates possibility and *conditional* + ***peut-être*** is useful as a translation:

he said you might be hurt = il a dit que tu serais peut-être blessé

I thought you might like to see the film = j'ai pensé que tu aimerais peut-être voir le film

they said they might go into town = ils ont dit qu'ils iraient peut-être en ville ⇨ **3**

◆ ***might*** can be used to make polite suggestions and French often uses the conditional of the verb:

it might be better to wait = ce serait peut-être mieux d'attendre

it might be a good idea to phone her = ce serait peut-être une bonne idée de lui téléphoner

you might try making some more enquiries = vous devriez essayer d'obtenir plus d'informations ⇨ **4**

ailleurs; **~s from anywhere** loin de tout; **to stand out a ~** sauter aux yeux.

mileage *n* **1** nombre *m* de miles; **2** (done by car) kilométrage *m*; **3** (miles per gallon) consommation *f*.

milestone *n* borne *f* (milliaire); (figurative) étape *f* importante.

militant I *n* agitateur/-trice *m/f*.
II *adj* militant/-e.

military I *n* **the ~** (army) l'armée *f*; (soldiers) les militaires *mpl*.
II *adj* militaire.

military service *n* service *m* militaire.

milk I *n* lait *m*; **powdered ~** lait en poudre; **full cream ~** lait entier; **skimmed ~** lait écrémé.
II *vtr* **1** traire [*cow*]; **2** (exploit) exploiter [*situation, system*]; **to ~ sb dry** saigner qn à blanc.

milk chocolate *n* chocolat *m* au lait.

milkman ▶626| *n* laitier *m*.

milky *adj* **1** [*drink*] au lait; **2** [*skin, liquid, colour*] laiteux/-euse.

Milky Way *pr n* Voie *f* lactée.

mill I *n* **1** moulin *m*; **water/pepper ~** moulin à eau/à poivre; **2** (factory) fabrique *f*; **steel ~** aciérie *f*.
II *vtr* moudre [*flour, pepper*].

millennium *n* millénaire *m*.

milligram(me) ▶573| *n* milligramme *m*.

millimetre (GB), **millimeter** (US) ▶573| *n* millimètre *m*.

million I *n* million *m*; **~s of** des millions de.
II *adj* **a ~ people/pounds** un million de personnes/de livres.

millionaire *n* millionnaire *mf*.

milometer *n* (GB) ≈ compteur *m* kilométrique.

mime I *n* mime *m*; **~ show** pantomime *f*.
II *vtr, vi* mimer.

mime artist ▶626| *n* mime *mf*.

mimic I *n* imitateur/-trice *m/f*.
II *vtr* imiter.

mince I *n* (GB) viande *f* hachée; **beef ~** bœuf *m* haché.
II *vtr* hacher [*meat*].

mind I *n* **1** esprit *m*; **peace of ~** tranquillité d'esprit; **it's all in the ~** c'est tout dans la tête○; **to cross sb's ~** venir à l'esprit de qn; **to have something on one's ~** être préoccupé/-e; **to set sb's ~ at rest** rassurer qn; **nothing could be further from my ~** loin de moi cette pensée; **to take sb's ~ off sth** distraire qn de qch; **my ~'s a blank** j'ai un trou de mémoire; **I can't get him out of my ~** je n'arrive pas à l'oublier; **are you out of your ~○?** tu es fou/folle○?; **2** (brain) intelligence *f*; **with the ~ of a two-year-old** avec l'intelligence d'un enfant de deux ans; **3** (opinion) avis *m*; **to my ~** à mon avis; **to make up one's ~ about/to do** se décider à propos de/à faire; **to change one's ~ about sth** changer d'avis sur qch; **to keep an open ~ about sth** réserver son jugement sur qch; **to know one's own ~** avoir des idées bien à soi; **to speak one's ~** dire ce qu'on a à dire.
II *vtr* **1** surveiller [*manners, language*]; faire attention à [*hazard*]; **2 I don't ~** ça m'est égal, ça ne me dérange pas; **I don't ~ the cold** le froid ne me dérange pas; **I don't ~ cats, but I prefer dogs** je n'ai rien contre les chats, mais je préfère les chiens; **will they ~ us being late?** est-ce qu'ils seront fâchés si nous sommes en retard?; **would you ~ keeping my seat for me?** est-ce que ça vous ennuierait de garder ma place?; **I wouldn't ~ a glass of wine** je prendrais volontiers un verre de vin; **if you don't ~** si cela ne vous fait rien; **never ~** (don't worry) ne t'en fais pas; (it doesn't matter) peu importe; **he can't afford an apartment, never ~ a big house** il ne peut pas se permettre un appartement encore moins une grande maison; **3** s'occuper de [*animal, children*]; tenir [*shop*].
III **in mind** *phr* **I have something in ~ for this evening** j'ai une idée pour ce soir; **to bear sth in ~** (remember) ne pas oublier qch; (take into account) prendre qch en compte.
IDIOMS **to read sb's ~** lire dans les pensées de qn; **to see sth in one's ~'s eye** imaginer qch; **to have a ~ of one's own** savoir ce qu'on veut.

mindless *adj* [*person, programme*] bête; [*work*] abrutissant/-e; [*vandalism*] gratuit/-e; [*task*] machinal/-e.

mine[1] *pron*

■ **Note** In French, possessive pronouns reflect the gender and number of the noun they are standing for. So *mine* is translated by *le mien, la mienne, les miens, les miennes*, according to what is being referred to.

his car is red but ~ is blue sa voiture est rouge mais la mienne est bleue; **which (glass) is ~?** lequel (de ces verres) est le mien or est à moi?; **his children are older than ~** ses enfants sont plus âgés que les miens; **the blue car is ~** la voiture bleue est à moi; **she's a friend of ~** c'est une amie à moi; **it's not ~** ce n'est pas à moi.

mine[2] I *n* mine *f*.
II *vtr* **1** extraire [*gems, mineral*]; exploiter [*area*]; **2** (Mil) miner [*area*].

minefield *n* champ *m* de mines; (figurative) terrain *m* miné.

miner ▶626| *n* mineur *m*.

mineral I *n* (substance, class) minéral *m*; (for extraction) minerai *m*.
II *adj* minéral/-e; **~ ore** minerai *m*.

mineral water *n* eau *f* minérale.

mingle *vi* **1 to ~ with** se mêler à [*crowd, guests*]; **2** [*sounds*] se confondre (**with** à); [*smells, feelings*] se mêler (**with** à).

miniature I *n* miniature *f*.
II *adj* (gen) miniature; [*dog, horse*] nain/-e.

minicab *n* (GB) taxi *m* (non agréé).

minimum I *n* minimum *m* (**of** de).
II *adj* minimum, minimal/-e.

mining I *n* exploitation *f* minière.
II *adj* [*industry, town*] minier/-ière; [*accident*] de mine.

mini-skirt *n* mini-jupe *f*.

minister I *n* **1** (GB) ministre *m*; **~ of** or **for Defence, Defence ~** ministre de la Défense; **2** (clergyman) ministre *m* du culte.
II *vi* **to ~ to** donner des soins à [*person*]; **to ~ to sb's needs** pourvoir aux besoins de qn.

minister of state *n* (GB) ministre *m* délégué.

ministry *n* (GB) ministère *m*.

mink *n* vison *m*.

minor I *n* (Law) mineur/-e *m/f*.
II *adj* (gen, Mus) mineur/-e; [*injury, burn*] léger/-ère; **~ road** route secondaire.

minority *n* minorité *f* (**of** de).

minstrel *n* ménestrel *m*.

mint I *n* **1** (herb) menthe *f*; **2** (sweet) bonbon *m* à la menthe; **3** (for coins) hôtel *m* des Monnaies.
II *adj* **in ~ condition** à l'état neuf.
III *vtr* **1** frapper [*coin*]; **2** forger [*word, expression*].

minuet *n* menuet *m*.

minus I *n* **1** (in mathematics) moins *m*; **2** (drawback) inconvénient *m*.
II *adj* [*symbol, button*] moins; [*number, quantity, value*] négatif/-ive; **~ sign** signe moins.
III *prep* **1** moins; **what is 20 ~ 8?** combien font 20 moins 8?; **it is ~ 15 (degrees)** il fait moins 15 (degrés); **2** (without) sans.

minuscule *adj* minuscule.

minute[1] **▶434|, 708|** I *n* minute *f*; **five ~s past ten** dix heures cinq; **it's five ~s' walk away** c'est à cinq minutes à pied; **the ~ I heard the news** dès que j'ai appris la nouvelle; **any ~ now** d'une minute à l'autre; **at the last ~** à la dernière minute.
II **minutes** *n pl* compte-rendu *m*.

minute[2] *adj* [*particle*] minuscule; [*quantity*] infime; [*risk, variation*] minime.

minute hand *n* aiguille *f* des minutes.

miracle *n* miracle *m*; **to work** or **perform ~s** faire des miracles.

miraculous *adj* **1** [*escape, recovery*] miraculeux/-euse; **2** [*speed, strength*] prodigieux/-ieuse.

mirror I *n* **1** (gen) miroir *m*, glace *f*; (Aut) rétroviseur *m*; **2** (figurative) reflet *m*.
II *vtr* refléter; **to be ~ed in** se refléter dans.

mirth *n* (laughter) hilarité *f*; (joy) joie *f*.

misapprehension *n* malentendu *m*, erreur *f*; **to be (labouring) under a ~** se tromper.

misappropriate *vtr* détourner [*funds*].

misbehave *vi* [*child*] se tenir mal; [*adult*] se conduire mal.

miscalculation *n* erreur *f* de calcul; (figurative) mauvais calcul *m*.

miscarriage *n* **1** (Med) fausse couche *f*; **to have a ~** faire une fausse couche; **2** (Law) **a ~ of justice** une grave erreur judiciaire.

miscellaneous *adj* divers/-e.

mischief *n* espièglerie *f*; **to get into** or **make ~** faire des bêtises; **he's up to ~** il prépare quelque chose; **to be full of ~** être espiègle; **it keeps them out of ~** ça les occupe.

mischievous *adj* [*child, comedy, humour*] espiègle; [*smile, eyes*] malicieux/-ieuse.

misconception *n* idée *f* fausse.

misdemeanour, **misdemeanor** (US) *n* délit *m*.

miser *n* avare *mf*.

miserable *adj* **1** [*person, event, expression*] malheureux/-euse; [*thoughts*] noir/-e; [*weather*] sale (*before n*); **to feel ~** avoir le cafard; **2** [*amount*] misérable; [*wage, life*] de misère; [*attempt, failure, performance*] lamentable.

miserly *adj* [*person*] avare; [*amount*] maigre.

misery *n* **1** (unhappiness) souffrance *f*; (gloom) abattement *m*; **to make sb's life a ~** faire de la vie de qn un enfer; **2** (misfortune) **the miseries of unemployment** le chômage et son cortège de misères; **3**○ (GB) (child) pleurnicheur/-euse *m/f*; (adult) rabat-joie *m inv*.

misfire *vi* **1** [*gun, rocket*] faire long feu; [*engine*] avoir des ratés; **2** [*plan, joke*] tomber à plat.

misfit *n* marginal/-e *m/f*.

misfortune *n* (unfortunate event) malheur *m*; (bad luck) malchance *f*.

misgiving *n* crainte *f*; **to have ~s about sth** avoir des craintes quant à qch; **to have ~s about sb** avoir des doutes au sujet de qn.

misguided *adj* [*strategy, attempt*] peu judicieux/-ieuse; [*person*] malavisé/-e.

mishandle *vtr* **1** mal conduire [*operation, meeting*]; mal s'y prendre avec [*person*]; **2** (roughly) manier [qch] sans précaution [*object*]; malmener [*person, animal*].

mishap *n* incident *m*.

mishear *vtr* mal entendre.

misinform *vtr* mal renseigner.

misinterpret *vtr* mal interpréter.

misjudge *vtr* mal évaluer [*speed, distance*]; mal calculer [*shot*]; mal juger [*person*].

mislay *vtr* égarer.

mislead *vtr* (deliberately) tromper; (unintentionally) induire [qn] en erreur.

misleading *adj* [*impression, title, information*] trompeur/-euse; [*claim, statement, advertising*] mensonger/-ère.

mismanage *vtr* mal diriger [*firm, project*]; mal gérer [*finances*].

misplace *vtr* égarer.

misprint *n* coquille *f*, faute *f* typographique.

mispronounce *vtr* mal prononcer.

misrepresent *vtr* présenter [qn] sous un faux jour [*person*]; déformer [*views, facts*].

miss I *n* **1** (in game) coup *m* manqué or raté; **2 to give [sth] a ~**○ ne pas aller à [*film, lecture*]; se passer de [*dish, drink, meal*].
II *vtr* **1** manquer [*target*]; **2** rater [*bus, plane, event, meeting*]; laisser passer [*chance*]; **I ~ed the train by five minutes** j'ai raté le train de cinq minutes; **3** ne pas saisir [*joke, remark*]; **4** sauter [*line, class*]; manquer [*school*]; **5** (avoid) échapper à [*death, injury*]; éviter [*traffic, bad weather, rush hour*]; **he just ~ed being caught** il a failli être pris; **6 I ~ you** tu me manques; **he ~ed Paris** Paris lui manquait; **I'll ~ coming to the office** le bureau va me manquer.

III *vi* **1** (Games, Sport, Mil) rater son coup; **~ed!** raté!; **2** [*engine*] avoir des ratés.
■ **miss out**: ¶ **~ out** être lésé/-e; ¶ **~ out on** [**sth**] laisser passer, louper○; ¶ **~** [**sb/sth**] **out** sauter [*line, verse*]; omettre [*fact, point, person*].

Miss ▶ 498 *n* Mademoiselle *f*; (written abbreviation) Mlle.

misshapen *adj* [*leg*] difforme; [*object*] déformé/-e.

missile *n* **1** (Mil) missile *m*; **2** (rock, bottle) projectile *m*.

missing *adj* **to be ~** manquer; **to go ~** [*person, object*] disparaître; **the ~ jewels/child** les bijoux disparus/l'enfant disparu; **there are two books ~** il manque deux livres.

mission *n* mission *f*.

missionary ▶ 626 *n* missionnaire *mf*.

mist *n* brume *f*.
■ **mist over, mist up** [*lens, window*] s'embuer.

mistake I *n* (gen) erreur *f*; (in text, spelling, typing) faute *f*; **to make a ~** se tromper; **by ~** par erreur.
II *vtr* **1 to ~ sth for sth else** prendre qch pour qch d'autre; **to ~ sb for sb else** confondre qn avec qn d'autre; **2** mal interpréter [*meaning*].

mistaken *adj* **1 to be ~** avoir tort; **he was ~ in thinking it was over** il avait tort de croire que c'était fini; **2** [*enthusiasm, generosity*] mal placé/-e.

mistletoe *n* gui *m*.

mistranslation *n* erreur *f* de traduction.

mistreat *vtr* maltraiter.

mistress *n* maîtresse *f*.

mistrust I *n* méfiance *f* (**of** à l'égard de).
II *vtr* se méfier de.

misty *adj* [*conditions, morning*] brumeux/-euse; [*lens, window*] embué/-e; [*photo*] flou/-e.

misunderstand *vtr* mal comprendre; (completely) ne pas comprendre.

misunderstanding *n* malentendu *m*.

misuse I *n* (of equipment) mauvais usage *m*; (of word) usage *m* impropre; (of power, authority) abus *m*.
II *vtr* faire mauvais usage de [*equipment*]; mal employer [*word, resources*]; abuser de [*authority*].

mitigate *vtr* atténuer [*effects, distress, sentence*]; réduire [*risks*]; minimiser [*loss*].

mitre (GB), **miter** (US) *n* mitre *f*.

mitten *n* moufle *f*.

mix I *n* **1** (gen) mélange *m*; **2** (Mus) mixage *m*, mix *m*.
II *vtr* **1** (gen) mélanger (**with** avec; **and** à); **2** préparer [*drink*]; malaxer [*cement, paste*]; **3** (Mus) mixer.
III *vi* **1** (also **~ together**) se mélanger (**with** avec, à); **2** (socialize) être sociable; **to ~ with** fréquenter.
■ **mix up 1** (confuse) confondre; **to get two things/people ~ed up** confondre deux choses/personnes; **2** (jumble up) mélanger, mêler [*papers, photos*]; **3 to get ~ed up in** se trouver mêlé/-e à.

mixed *adj* **1** [*collection, programme, diet*] varié/-e; [*nuts, sweets*] assorti/-e; [*salad*] composé/-e; [*group, community*] (socially, in age) mélangé/-e; (racially) d'origines diverses; **of ~ blood** de sang mêlé; **2** (for both sexes) mixte; **3** [*reaction, feelings, reception*] mitigé/-e.

mixer *n* **1** (Culin) batteur *m* électrique; **2** (drink) boisson *f* nonalcoolisée.

mixture *n* mélange *m* (**of** de).

mix-up *n* confusion *f* (**over** sur).

moan I *n* **1** (noise) gémissement *m*; **2**○ (complaint) plainte *f* (**about** au sujet de).
II *vi* **1** (groan) gémir (**with** de); **2**○ (complain) râler○ (**about** contre).

moat *n* douve *f*.

mob I *n* foule *f* (**of** de).
II *vtr* assaillir [*person*]; envahir [*place*].

mobile I *n* mobile *m*.
II *adj* **1** [*object, population*] mobile; [*canteen*] ambulant/-e; **2 to be ~** (able to walk) pouvoir marcher; (able to travel) pouvoir se déplacer.

mobile phone *n* téléphone *m* sans fil.

mocha *n* **1** (coffee) moka *m*; **2** (flavour) arôme *m* de café et de chocolat.

mock I *n* (GB Sch) examen *m* blanc.
II *adj* **1** [*suede, ivory*] faux/fausse (*before n*); **~ leather** similicuir *m*; **2** (feigned) simulé/-e; **in ~ terror** en feignant la terreur.
III *vtr* se moquer de [*person, efforts, beliefs*].
IV *vi* [*person*] se moquer.

mockery *n* moquerie *f*.

mod con *n* (GB) confort *m* (moderne).

mode *n* mode *m*.

model I *n* **1** (of car, appliance, garment) modèle *m*; **2** (person) (artist's) modèle *m*; (fashion) mannequin *m*; **3** (scale model) maquette *f*; **4** (perfect example) modèle *m* (**of** de).
II *adj* **1** [*railway, soldier, village*] miniature; [*aeroplane, boat, car*] modèle réduit; **2** [*husband, student, prison*] modèle.
III *vtr* **1** modeler [*clay, wax*]; **2** [*fashion model*] présenter [*garment*].
IV *vi* **1** [*artist's model*] poser; **2** [*fashion model*] travailler comme mannequin.

moderate I *adj* **1** (not extreme) modéré/-e (**in** dans); **2** [*success, income*] moyen/-enne.
II *vtr* modérer.
III *vi* se modérer.

moderation *n* modération *f* (**in** dans); **in ~** avec modération.

modern *adj* moderne; **the ~ world** le monde contemporain.

modernize *vtr* moderniser.

modern languages *n pl* langues *fpl* vivantes.

modest *adj* **1** modeste (**about** au sujet de); **2** [*gift, aim*] modeste; [*sum, salary*] modique.

modesty *n* modestie *f*.

modify *vtr* modifier.

mogul *n* magnat *m*.

Mohammed, **Mahomet** *pr n* Mahomet.

moist *adj* [*soil*] humide; [*cake*] moelleux/-euse; [*hands*] moite; [*skin*] bien hydraté/-e.
moisten *vtr* humecter.
moisture *n* humidité *f*.
moisturizer *n* (lotion) lait *m* hydratant; (cream) crème *f* hydratante.
molar *n*, *adj* molaire (*f*).
mold (US) = **mould**.
mole *n* **1** (Zool) taupe *f*; **2** (on skin) grain *m* de beauté.
molecule *n* molécule *f*.
molest *vtr* agresser [qn] sexuellement.
mollycoddle *vtr* dorloter.
molt (US) = **moult**.
molten *adj* en fusion.
moment *n* **1** (instant) instant *m*; **in a ~** dans un instant; **at any ~** à tout instant; **2** (point in time) moment *m*; **at the ~** en ce moment; **at the right ~** au bon moment.
momentarily *adv* **1** (for an instant) momentanément; **2** (US) (very soon) dans un instant; (at any moment) d'un moment à l'autre.
momentary *adj* passager/-ère.
momentous *adj* capital/-e.
momentum *n* (gen) élan *m*; (in physics) vitesse *f*.
monarchy *n* monarchie *f*.
monastery *n* monastère *m*.
Monday ▶456 *n* lundi *m*.
money ▶582 *n* argent *m*; **to make ~** [*person*] gagner de l'argent; [*business, project*] rapporter de l'argent.
IDIOMS **to get one's ~'s worth, to get a good run for one's ~** en avoir pour son argent; **your ~ or your life!** la bourse ou la vie!
money belt *n* ceinture *f* porte-monnaie.
moneybox *n* tirelire *f*.
money order, MO *n* mandat *m* postal.
mongrel *n* (chien *m*) bâtard *m*.
monitor I *n* (Comput, Med) moniteur *m*.
II *vtr* **1** surveiller [*results, patient, breathing*]; **2** être à l'écoute de [*broadcast*].
monk *n* moine *m*.
monkey *n* **1** (Zool) singe *m*; **2**○ (rascal) galopin○ *m*.
monochrome *adj* [*film*] en noir et blanc; [*colour scheme*] monochrome.
monogamy *n* monogamie *f*.
monologue, monolog (US) *n* monologue *m*.
monopolize *vtr* **1** détenir le monopole de [*market, supply*]; **2** (figurative) monopoliser.
monopoly *n* monopole *m*.
monotonous *adj* monotone.
monotony *n* monotonie *f*.
monsoon *n* mousson *f*.
monster *n* monstre *m*.
monstrous *adj* **1** (ugly) monstrueux/-euse; [*building*] hideux/-euse; **2** (huge) énorme.
month ▶708 *n* mois *m*; **in two ~s, in two ~s' time** dans deux mois; **every other ~** tous les deux mois; **in the ~ of June** au mois de juin.
monthly I *n* (journal) mensuel *m*.
II *adj* mensuel/-elle; **~ instalment** mensualité *f*.
III *adv* [*pay, earn*] au mois; [*happen, visit, publish*] tous les mois.
Montreal ▶448 *pr n* Montréal.
monument *n* monument *m*.
moo *vi* meugler.
mood *n* **1** (humour) humeur *f*; **in a good/bad ~** de bonne/mauvaise humeur; **to be in the ~ for doing** avoir envie de faire; **to be in no ~ for doing** ne pas être d'humeur à faire; **2** (bad temper) saute *f* d'humeur; **to be in a ~** être de mauvaise humeur.
moody *adj* **1** (unpredictable) d'humeur changeante, lunatique; **2** (sulky) de mauvaise humeur.
moon *n* lune *f*.
IDIOMS **to be over the ~** être aux anges; **once in a blue ~** tous les trente-six du mois○; **the man in the ~** le visage de la Lune.
moonlight I *n* clair *m* de lune.
II *vi* travailler au noir.
moonlit *adj* éclairé/-e par la lune; **a ~ night** une nuit de lune.
moor I *n* lande *f*.
II *vtr* amarrer [*boat*].
III *vi* [*boat*] mouiller.
moorings *n pl* amarres *fpl*.
moorland *n* lande *f*.
moose *n* (Canadian) orignal *m*; (European) élan *m*.
mop I *n* **1** (of cotton) balai *m* à franges; (of sponge) balai *m* éponge; **2 ~ of hair** crinière○ *f*.
II *vtr* **1** laver [qch] à grande eau [*floor*]; **2 to ~ one's face/brow** s'éponger le visage/le front.
■ **mop up** éponger [*milk, wine*].
mope *vi* se morfondre.
■ **mope about, mope around** traîner (comme une âme en peine).
moped *n* vélomoteur *m*.
moral I *n* morale *f*.
II morals *n pl* moralité *f*.
III *adj* moral/-e.
morale *n* moral *m*.
morality *n* moralité *f*.
morbid *adj* morbide.
more I *adv* **1** (comparative) plus (**than** que); **~ expensive** plus cher/chère; **~ easily** plus facilement; **2** (to a greater extent) plus, davantage; **you must rest ~** il faut que tu te reposes davantage; **he is all the ~ angry because** il est d'autant plus en colère que; **3** (longer) **I don't work there any ~** je n'y travaille plus; **4** (again) **once ~** une fois de plus, encore une fois; **5** (else) **nothing ~** rien de plus; **something ~** autre chose.
II *det* plus de; **I have ~ money than him** j'ai plus d'argent que lui; **some ~ books** quelques livres de plus; **there's no ~ bread** il

Currencies and Money

French money

write	say
25 c	vingt-cinq centimes
1 F	un franc
1,50 F†	un franc cinquante
	un franc cinquante centimes
2 F	deux francs
2,75 F†	deux francs soixante-quinze
20 F	vingt francs
100 F	cent francs
1 000 F	mille francs
1 000 000 F	un million de francs

† French uses a comma to separate units (***2,75 F***), where English normally has a full stop or period (***£5.50***).

British money

write	say
1p	un penny
25p	vingt-cinq pence
50p	cinquante pence
£1	une livre
£1.50	une livre cinquante
	une livre cinquante pence
£2.00	deux livres

American money

write	say
12c	douze cents
$1	un dollar
$1.50	un dollar cinquante
	un dollar cinquante cents

a dollar bill = un billet d'un dollar
a dollar coin = une pièce d'un dollar

How much?

how much is it / does it cost? = combien est-ce que cela coûte?
it's / it costs 15 francs = cela coûte 15 francs
it costs 100 francs a metre = cela coûte 100 francs le mètre

Note the use of ***à*** in French to introduce the amount that something costs:

a five-franc stamp = un timbre **à** cinq francs
a £10 meal = un repas **à** 10 livres

and the use of ***de*** to introduce the amount that something consists of:

a £500 cheque = un chèque **de** 500 livres
a ten-franc coin = une pièce **de** dix francs
a 50-centime piece = une pièce **de** cinquante centimes
a five-pound note = un billet **de** cinq livres

Handling money

500 francs in cash = 500 francs en liquide
there are 6 francs to the dollar = le dollar vaut 6 francs

n'y a plus de pain; **have some ~ beer!** reprenez de la bière!
III *pron*, *quantif* **1** (larger amount or number) plus; **it costs ~** il/elle coûte plus cher (**than** que); **he eats ~ than you** il mange plus que toi; **2** (additional amount) davantage; (additional number) plus; **I need ~ of them** il m'en faut plus; **I need ~ of it** il m'en faut davantage.
IV more and more *phr* de plus en plus; **~ and ~ work** de plus en plus de travail.
V more or less *phr* plus ou moins.
VI more than *phr* **1** (greater amount or number) plus de; **~ than 20 people** plus de 20 personnes; **~ than half** plus de la moitié; **~ than enough** plus qu'assez; **2** (extremely) **~ than generous** plus que généreux.

moreover *adv* de plus, qui plus est.

morning ▶ **434** **I** *n* matin *m*; (with emphasis on duration) matinée *f*; **in the ~** le matin; **on Monday ~s** le lundi matin; (**on**) **Monday ~** lundi matin; **later this ~** plus tard dans la matinée; **yesterday/tomorrow ~** hier/demain matin.
II *excl* (**good**) **~!** bonjour!

Morocco ▶ **448** *pr n* Maroc *m*.

Morse (**code**) *n* morse *m*; **in ~** en morse.

morsel *n* morceau *m*.

mortal *n*, *adj* mortel/-elle (*m*/*f*).

mortality *n* mortalité *f*.

mortgage *n* emprunt-logement *m* (**on** pour).

mortuary *n* morgue *f*.

mosaic *n* mosaïque *f*.

Moscow ▶ **448** *pr n* Moscou.

Moslem = **Muslim**.

mosque *n* mosquée *f*.

mosquito *n* moustique *m*.

mosquito repellent *n* anti-moustique *m*.

moss *n* mousse *f*.

most

■ **Note** When used to form the superlative of adjectives, *most* is translated by *le plus* or *la plus* depending on the gender of the noun and by *les plus* with plural noun: *the most beautiful woman in the room* = la plus belle femme de la pièce; *the most expensive hotel in Paris* = l'hôtel le plus cher de Paris; *the most difficult problems* = les problèmes les plus difficiles. For examples and further uses, see the entry below.

I *det* **1** (the majority of) la plupart de; **~ people** la plupart des gens; **2** (in superlatives) le plus de; **she got the ~ votes** c'est elle qui a obtenu le plus de voix.
II *pron* **1** (the greatest number) la plupart (**of** de); (the largest part) la plus grande partie (**of** de); **~ of the time** la plupart du temps; **~ of us** la plupart d'entre nous; **for ~ of the day** pendant la plus grande partie de la journée; **~ of the bread** presque tout le pain; **2** (all) **the ~ you can expect is...** tout ce que tu peux espérer c'est...; **3** (in superlatives) le plus; **John has got the ~** c'est John qui en a le plus.
III *adv* **1** (in superlatives) **the ~ beautiful château in France** le plus beau château de France; **~ easily** le plus facilement; **2** (very) très, extrêmement; **~ encouraging** très or extrêmement encourageant; **~ probably** très vraisemblablement; **3** (more than all the rest) le plus; **what annoyed him ~** (**of all**) **was** ce qui l'ennuyait le plus c'était que.
IV at (**the**) **most** *phr* au maximum, au plus.
V for the most part *phr* (most of them) pour la plupart; (most of the time) la plupart du temps; (chiefly) surtout, essentiellement.
VI most of all *phr* par-dessus tout.
IDIOMS **to make the ~ of** tirer le meilleur parti de [*situation, resources, abilities*]; profiter de [*opportunity, good weather*].

mostly *adv* **1** (chiefly) surtout, essentiellement; (most of them) pour la plupart; **2** (most of the time) la plupart du temps.

MOT *n* (GB) (also **~ test**) contrôle *m* technique des véhicules.

moth *n* papillon *m* de nuit; (in clothes) mite *f*.

mother I *n* mère *f*.
II *vtr* (coddle) dorloter.

motherhood *n* maternité *f*.

mother-in-law *n* belle-mère *f*.

motherly *adj* maternel/-elle.

mother-of-pearl *n* nacre *f*.

Mother's Day *n* fête *f* des Mères.

motion I *n* **1** mouvement *m*; **to set [sth] in ~** mettre [qch] en marche [*machine*]; mettre [qch] en route [*plan*]; déclencher [*chain of events*]; **2** (proposal) motion *f*.
II *vi* **to ~ to sb** (**to do**) faire signe à qn (de faire).

motionless *adj* immobile.

motivate *vtr* motiver [*person*].

motivated *adj* **1** [*person, pupil*] motivé/-e; **2 politically/racially ~** [*act*] politique/raciste.

motivation *n* motivation *f*.

motive *n* (gen) motif *m* (**for, behind** de); (for crime) mobile *m* (**for** de).

motley *adj* [*crowd, gathering*] bigarré/-e; [*collection*] hétéroclite.

motor I *n* moteur *m*.
II *adj* **1** [*vehicle*] automobile; [*show*] de l'automobile; **2** [*mower*] à moteur.

motorbike *n* moto *f*.

motorboat *n* canot *m* automobile.

motorcycle *n* motocyclette *f*.

motorcyclist *n* motocycliste *mf*.

motor home *n* auto-caravane *f*.

motorist *n* automobiliste *mf*.

motor racing ▶ **504** *n* course *f* automobile.

motorway *n* (GB) autoroute *f*.

mottled *adj* [*skin, paper*] marbré/-e; [*hands*] tacheté/-e.

motto *n* devise *f*.

mould (GB), **mold** (US) **I** *n* **1** (Culin, figurative) moule *m*; **2** (fungi) moisissure *f*.
II *vtr* modeler [*plastic, clay, shape*]; façonner [*character, opinions*] (**into** pour en faire).

mouldy (GB), **moldy** (US) *adj* moisi/-e; **to go ~** moisir.

moult (GB), **molt** (US) *vi* [*cat, dog*] perdre ses poils; [*bird*] muer.

mound *n* **1** (hillock) tertre *m*; **2** (heap) monceau *m* (**of** de).

mount I *vtr* **1** monter sur [*platform, horse*]; **2** monter [*jewel, picture, exhibit*]; **3** organiser [*demonstration*].
II *vi* **1** [*person, staircase*] monter (**to** jusqu'à); **2** [*number, toll*] augmenter; [*concern*] grandir; **3** (on horse) se mettre en selle.

mountain *n* montagne *f*.

mountain bike *n* vélo *m* tout-terrain, VTT *m*.

mountaineer ▶ 626 *n* alpiniste *mf*.

mountaineering ▶ 504 *n* alpinisme *m*.

mountainous *adj* montagneux/-euse.

mourn I *vtr* pleurer [*person, death*].
II *vi* [*person*] porter le deuil; **to ~ for sb/sth** pleurer qn/qch.

mourning *n* deuil *m*.

mouse *n* souris *f*.

moustache, **mustache** (US) *n* moustache *f*.

mouth I *n* **1** (of human, horse) bouche *f*; (of other animal) gueule *f*; **2** (of cave, tunnel) entrée *f*; (of river) embouchure *f*; (of volcano) bouche *f*.
II *vtr* articuler silencieusement.
IDIOMS **by word of ~** de bouche à oreille.

mouthful *n* (of food) bouchée *f*; (of liquid) gorgée *f*.

mouth organ ▶ 586 *n* harmonica *m*.

mouthwash *n* eau *f* dentifrice.

mouth-watering *adj* appétissant/-e.

move I *n* **1** (movement) mouvement *m*; (gesture) geste *m*; **2** (of residence) déménagement *m*; (of company) transfert *m*; **3** (in game) coup *m*; **it's your ~** c'est ton tour; **4** (step, act) manœuvre *f*; **a good/bad ~** une bonne/mauvaise idée; **to make the first ~** faire le premier pas.
II *vtr* **1** déplacer [*game piece, cursor, car, furniture*]; transporter [*patient, army*]; **to ~ sth (out of the way)** enlever qch; **2** [*person*] bouger [*limb, head*]; [*wind, mechanism*] faire bouger [*leaf, wheel*]; **3** (relocate) muter [*staff*]; transférer [*office*]; **to ~ house** déménager; **4** (affect) émouvoir; **to be deeply ~d** être très ému/-e.
III *vi* **1** (stir) bouger; [*lips*] remuer; **2** (travel) [*vehicle*] rouler; [*person*] avancer; [*procession, army*] être en marche; **to ~ back** reculer; **to ~ forward** s'avancer; **to ~ away** s'éloigner; **3** (change home, location) déménager; **to ~ to the countryside/to Japan** s'installer à la campagne/au Japon; **4** (change job) être muté/-e; **5** (act) agir.
IDIOMS **to get a ~ on**○ se dépêcher.
■ **move about**, **move around** [*person*] (fidget) remuer; (move home) déménager.
■ **move along**: ¶ **~ along** (stop loitering) circuler; (proceed) avancer; (squeeze up) se pousser; ¶ **~ [sb/sth] along** faire circuler [*onlookers, crowd*].
■ **move away** s'éloigner; (move house) déménager.
■ **move in 1** (to house) emménager; **to ~ in with** s'installer avec [*friend, lover*]; **2** (advance, attack) s'avancer (**on** sur).
■ **move on** [*person, traveller*] se mettre en route; [*vehicle*] repartir; **to ~ on to** passer à [*next item*].
■ **move out** (of house) déménager; **to ~ out of** quitter.
■ **move over** se pousser.
■ **move up 1** (make room) se pousser; **2** (be promoted) être promu/-e.

movement *n* mouvement *m*; (of hand, arm) geste *m*.

movie I *n* film *m*.
II **movies** *n pl* **the ~s** le cinéma.

movie star *n* vedette *f* de cinéma.

movie theater *n* (US) cinéma *m*.

moving *adj* **1** [*vehicle*] en marche; [*parts, target*] mobile; [*staircase, walkway*] roulant/-e; **2** [*scene, speech*] émouvant/-e.

mow *vtr* tondre [*grass, lawn*].

mower *n* tondeuse *f* à gazon.

MP *n* (GB) (*abbr* = **Member of Parliament**) député *m* (**for** de).

Mr ▶ 498 *n* M., Monsieur.

Mrs ▶ 498 *n* Mme, Madame.

Ms ▶ 498 *n* ≈ Mme.

MSc *n* (*abbr* = **Master of Science**) diplôme *m* supérieur en sciences.

much I *adv* beaucoup; **~ more/less** beaucoup plus/moins; **~ smaller** beaucoup plus petit; **I don't read ~** je ne lis pas beaucoup; **we'd ~ rather stay here** nous préférerions de beaucoup rester ici; **does it hurt ~?** est-ce que ça fait très mal?; **we don't go out ~** nous ne sortons pas beaucoup or souvent; **it's ~ the same** c'est à peu près pareil (**as** que); **too ~** trop; **very ~** beaucoup; **thank you very ~** merci beaucoup; **so ~** tellement; **as ~** autant (**as** que); **they hated each other as ~ as ever** ils se détestaient toujours autant.
II *pron* beaucoup; **do you have ~ left?** est-ce qu'il vous en reste beaucoup?; **we didn't eat ~** nous n'avons pas mangé grand-chose; **I don't see ~ of them now** je ne les vois plus beaucoup maintenant; **so ~** tellement, tant; **we'd eaten so ~ that** nous avions tellement mangé que; **too ~** trop; **it costs too ~** c'est trop cher; **twice as ~** deux fois plus; **as ~ as possible** autant que possible; **how ~?** combien?; **it's not** or **nothing ~** ce n'est pas grand-chose; **he's not ~ to look at** il n'est pas très beau.
III *det* beaucoup de; **I haven't got ~ time** je n'ai pas beaucoup de temps; **she didn't speak ~ English** elle ne connaissait que quelques mots d'anglais; **too ~ money** trop d'argent; **don't use so ~ salt** ne mets pas tant de sel; **we paid twice as ~** nous avons payé deux fois plus; **how ~ time have we got left?** combien de temps nous reste-t-il?
IV **much as** *phr* bien que (+ *subjunctive*).
V **so much as** *phr* **without so ~ as an apology** sans même s'excuser; **if you so ~ as move** si tu fais le moindre mouvement.

mud *n* boue *f*.

muddle *n* **1** (mess) pagaille○; **2** (mix-up) malentendu *m* (**over** à propos de); **3 to get into a ~** [*person*] s'embrouiller.

■ **muddle up**: ¶ **~ [sth] up** (disorder) semer la pagaille○ dans; ¶ **~ [sb] up** embrouiller les idées de; **to get [sth] ~d up** s'embrouiller dans [*dates, names*].

muddled *adj* confus/-e.

muddy *adj* [*hand*] couvert/-e de boue; [*shoe, garment*] crotté/-e; [*road, water*] boueux/-euse; [*green, yellow*] terne.

mudguard *n* garde-boue *m inv*.

muffle *vtr* assourdir [*bell, drum*].

mug I *n* **1** grande tasse *f*; **2** (GB) (fool) poire○ *f*; **it's a ~'s game** c'est un attrape-nigaud.
II *vtr* agresser; **to be ~ged** se faire agresser.

mugger *n* agresseur *m*.

muggy *adj* [*room, day*] étouffant/-e; [*weather*] lourd/-e.

Muhammad *pr n* Mahomet.

mule *n* mulet *m*, mule *f*.
IDIOMS **as stubborn as a ~** têtu/-e comme une mule.

mull *v* ■ **mull over** retourner [qch] dans sa tête.

mulled wine *n* vin *m* chaud.

multinational *adj* multinational/-e.

multiple *n, adj* multiple (*m*).

multiple sclerosis, **MS** ▶**533** *n* sclérose *f* en plaques.

multiply I *vtr* multiplier (**by** par).
II *vi* se multiplier.

multipurpose *adj* [*tool, gadget*] à usages multiples; [*area, organization*] polyvalent/-e.

multistorey *adj* (GB) [*car park*] à niveaux multiples; [*building*] à étages.

multitude *n* multitude *f*.

mum○, **Mum**○ *n* (GB) maman *f*.
IDIOMS **to keep ~** ne pas piper mot.

mumble *vtr, vi* marmonner.

mumbo jumbo○ *n* charabia○ *m*.

mummy *n* **1**○ (also **Mummy**) maman *f*; **2** (embalmed body) momie *f*.

mumps ▶**533** *n* oreillons *mpl*.

munch *vtr* [*person*] mâcher; [*animal*] mâchonner.

mundane *adj* terre-à-terre, quelconque.

municipal *adj* municipal/-e.

mural *n* (wall painting) peinture *f* murale; (in cave) peinture *f* rupestre.

murder *n* meurtre *m*.
II *vtr* assassiner.
IDIOMS **to get away with ~** exercer ses talents en toute impunité.

murderer *n* assassin *m*, meurtrier *m*.

murderess *n* meurtrière *f*.

murderous *adj* [*look*] assassin/-e; [*deeds, thoughts*] meurtrier/-ière.

murky *adj* **1** [*light, water, colour*] glauque; **2** [*past*] trouble.

murmur I *n* murmure *m* (**of** de).
II *vtr, vi* murmurer.

muscle *n* muscle *m*.
■ **muscle in**○ s'imposer (**on** dans).

muscular *adj* [*disease, tissue*] musculaire; [*person, body, limbs*] musclé/-e.

museum *n* musée *m*.

mushroom ▶**438** *n* **1** (Bot, Culin) champignon *m*; **2** (colour) beige *m* rosé.

music *n* musique *f*.

musical I *n* comédie *f* musicale.
II *adj* **1** [*person*] musicien/-ienne; **2** [*voice, laughter*] mélodieux/-ieuse; [*score*] musical/-e.

musical instrument ▶**586** *n* instrument *m* de musique.

musician ▶**626** *n* musicien/-ienne *m/f*.

musk *n* musc *m*.

Muslim (also **Moslem**) I *n* Musulman/-e *m/f*.
II *adj* musulman/-e.

mussel *n* moule *f*.

must I *modal aux* **1** (expressing obligation) **I ~ go** je dois partir, il faut que je parte; **he ~ sit the exam in June** il faut qu'il passe l'examen au mois de juin; **you ~ check your rear-view mirror first** il faut regarder dans le rétroviseur d'abord; **I ~ say I was impressed** je dois dire que j'ai été impressionné; **we mustn't tell anyone** il ne faut en parler à personne, nous ne devons en parler à personne; **2** (making deductions) **they ~ really detest each other** ils doivent vraiment se détester; **it ~ be pleasant living there** ça doit être agréable de vivre là-bas; **he ~ have been surprised** il a dû être surpris.
II *n* **it's a ~** c'est indispensable; **this film is a ~** ce film est à voir or à ne pas rater; **a visit to the Louvre is a ~** une visite au Louvre s'impose.

mustache (US) = **moustache**.

mustard *n* moutarde *f*.

muster *vtr* (also **~ up**) rassembler [*troops*]; rallier [*support*]; trouver [*energy, enthusiasm*].
IDIOMS **to pass ~** être acceptable.

musty *adj* **to smell ~** sentir le moisi or le renfermé.

mute *adj* muet/-ette.

mutilate *vtr* mutiler.

mutiny *n* mutinerie *f*.

mutter *vtr, vi* marmonner.

mutton *n* mouton *m*.

mutual *adj* **1** (reciprocal) réciproque; **the feeling is ~** c'est réciproque; **2** [*friend, interests*] commun; [*consent*] mutuel/-elle; **by ~ agreement** d'un commun accord.

my

■ **Note** In French, determiners agree in gender and number with the noun that follows. So *my* is translated by *mon* + masculine singular noun (mon chien), *ma* + feminine singular noun (ma maison) BUT by *mon* + feminine noun beginning with a vowel or mute 'h' (mon assiette) and by *mes* + plural noun (mes enfants).
– When *my* is stressed, *à moi* is added after the noun: MY *house* = ma maison à moi.
– For *my* used with parts of the body, see the Usage Note ▶**413**.

I *det* mon/ma/mes.

Musical Instruments

Playing an instrument

Note the use of ***de*** with ***jouer***:

to play the piano	= jouer **du** piano
to play the violin	= jouer **du** violon
to play the clarinet	= jouer **de la** clarinette
to play the flute	= jouer **de la** flûte

but

to learn the piano	= apprendre **le** piano
to learn the guitar	= apprendre **la** guitare

Players

English ***-ist*** is often French ***-iste***; the gender reflects the sex of the player:

a violinist	= un violoniste / une violoniste
a pianist	= un pianiste / une pianiste
a flautist	= un flûtiste / une flûtiste
a cellist	= un violoncelliste / une violoncelliste

A phrase with ***joueur*** / ***joueuse de X*** is usually safe:

a piccolo player	= un joueur de piccolo / une joueuse de piccolo
a horn player	= un joueur de cor / une joueuse de cor

But note the French when these words are used with *good* and *bad* like this:

he's a good pianist	= il joue bien du piano
he's not a good pianist	= il ne joue pas bien du piano
he's a bad pianist	= il joue mal du piano

As in English, the name of the instrument is often used to refer to its player:

she's a first violin	= elle est premier violon

Music

a piano piece	= un morceau pour piano
a piano arrangement	= un arrangement pour piano
a piano sonata	= une sonate pour piano
a concerto for piano and orchestra	= un concerto pour piano et orchestre
the piano part	= la partie pour piano
a piano trio	= un trio pour piano

Use with another noun

de is usually correct:

to take piano lessons	= prendre des leçons **de** piano
a violin maker	= un fabricant **de** violons
a violin solo	= un solo **de** violon
a piano teacher	= un professeur **de** piano
a piano tuner	= un accordeur **de** pianos

but note the ***à*** here:

a violin case	= un étui **à** violon

II *excl* **~ ~**! ça alors!

myself *pron* **1** (reflexive) me, m'; **I've hurt ~** je me suis fait mal; **2** (emphatic) moi-même; **I saw it ~** je l'ai vu moi-même; **(all) by ~** tout seul/toute seule; **3** (after prepositions) moi, moi-même; **I feel proud of ~** je suis fier de moi; **4** (expressions) **I'm not much of a dog-lover ~** personnellement je n'aime pas trop les chiens; **I'm not ~ today** je ne suis pas dans mon assiette aujourd'hui.

mysterious *adj* mystérieux/-ieuse.

mystery *n* **1** mystère *m*; **2** (book) roman *m* policier.

mystify *vtr* laisser [qn] perplexe.

myth *n* mythe *m*.

mythology *n* mythologie *f*.

Nn

n, **N** *n* n, N *m*.

nag *vtr* enquiquiner○ (**about** au sujet de).

nagging *adj* **1** **his ~ wife** sa mégère de femme; **2** [*pain, doubt*] tenace.

nail I *n* **1** (on finger, toe) ongle *m*; **2** (Tech) clou *m*.
II *vtr* clouer.
■ **nail down**: ¶ **~ [sth] down** clouer; ¶ **~ [sb] down** coincer○ [*person*].

nailbrush *n* brosse *f* à ongles.

nail file *n* lime *f* à ongles.

nail varnish *n* vernis *m* à ongles.

nail varnish remover *n* dissolvant *m*.

naïve *adj* naïf/naïve.

naked *adj* nu/-e.

name I *n* **1** (gen) nom *m*; (of book, film) titre *m*; **first ~** prénom *m*; **my ~ is Louis** je m'appelle Louis; **2** (reputation) réputation *f*; **3** (insult) **to call sb ~s** injurier qn.
II *vtr* **1** (call) appeler [*person, area*]; baptiser [*boat*]; **they ~d her after** (GB) or **for** (US) **her mother** ils l'ont appelée comme sa mère; **a boy ~d Pascal** un garçon nommé Pascal; **2** (cite) citer; **~ three American States** citez trois États américains; **3** révéler [*sources*]; révéler l'identité de [*suspect*]; **to ~ ~s** donner des noms; **4** (state) indiquer [*place, time*]; fixer [*price, terms*].

namely *adv* à savoir.

namesake *n* homonyme *m*.

nanny *n* (GB) bonne *f* d'enfants.

nanny goat *n* chèvre *f*.

nap I *n* petit somme *m*; **afternoon ~** sieste *f*.
II *vi* sommeiller.

nape *n* nuque *f*; **the ~ of the neck** la nuque.

napkin *n* serviette *f* (de table).

nappy *n* (GB) couche *f* (de bébé).

narcotic I *n* (soporific) narcotique *m*; (illegal drug) stupéfiant *m*.
II *adj* narcotique.

narration *n* récit *m*, narration *f*.

narrative I *n* (account) récit *m*; (storytelling) narration *f*.
II *adj* [*prose, poem*] narratif/-ive; [*skill, talent*] de conteur.

narrator *n* narrateur/-trice *m*/*f*.

narrow ▶573 I *adj* (gen) étroit/-e; [*views*] étriqué/-e; [*majority, margin*] faible (*before n*); **to have a ~ lead** avoir une légère avance; **to have a ~ escape** l'échapper belle.
II *vtr* **1** (limit) limiter (**to** à); **to ~ the gap** réduire l'écart; **2** rétrécir [*road, path, arteries*]; **to ~ one's eyes** plisser les yeux.
III *vi* (gen) se rétrécir; [*gap, margin*] se réduire (**to** à).
■ **narrow down** réduire [*numbers, list, choice*] (**to** à); limiter [*investigation, research*] (**to** à).

narrowly *adv* (barely) de justesse.

narrow-minded *adj* borné/-e.

nasal *adj* [*vowel*] nasal/-e; [*accent, voice*] nasillard/-e.

nasty *adj* **1** [*person, expression, remark*] méchant/-e; [*experience, surprise, feeling, task*] désagréable; [*habit, smell, taste*] mauvais/-e (*before n*); [*trick*] sale (*before n*); [*cut, bruise*] vilain/-e (*before n*); [*accident*] grave; **2** (ugly) affreux/-euse.

nation *n* nation *f*; (people) peuple *m*.

national I *n* ressortissant/-e *m*/*f*.
II *adj* national/-e; **the ~ press** (GB) les grands quotidiens *mpl*.

national anthem *n* hymne *m* national.

National Health Service, **NHS** *n* (GB) services *mpl* de santé britanniques, ≈ Sécurité *f* Sociale.

National Insurance, **NI** *n* (GB) securité *f* sociale britannique.

nationalism *n* nationalisme *m*.

nationality *n* nationalité *f*.

nationalize *vtr* nationaliser [*industry*].

nationwide I *adj* [*appeal, coverage, strike*] sur l'ensemble du territoire; [*campaign*] national/-e; [*survey, poll*] à l'échelle nationale.
II *adv* dans tout le pays.

native I *n* autochtone *mf*; **to be a ~ of** être originaire de.
II *adj* **1** [*land*] natal/-e; [*tongue*] maternel/-elle; **~ German speaker** personne *f* de langue maternelle allemande; **2** [*flora, fauna, peoples*] indigène.

Native American *n*, *adj* amérindien/-ienne (*m*/*f*).

Nativity *n* nativité *f*.

NATO *n* (*abbr* = **North Atlantic Treaty Organization**) OTAN *f*.

natural *adj* **1** (gen) naturel/-elle; **2** [*gift, talent*] inné/-e; [*artist, storyteller*] né/-e; **3** (unaffected) simple, naturel/-elle.

naturalize *vtr* naturaliser [*person*]; **to be ~d** se faire naturaliser.

naturally *adv* **1** (obviously, of course) naturellement; **2** (by nature) de nature; **politeness comes ~ to him** il est d'un naturel poli; **3** [*behave, smile, speak*] avec naturel.

nature *n* nature *f*; **let ~ take its course** laissez faire la nature; **it's not in her ~ to be aggressive** elle n'est pas agressive de nature; **it is in the ~ of things** il est dans l'ordre des choses.

nature reserve *n* réserve *f* naturelle.

naughty *adj* **1** (disobedient) vilain/-e; **2** (rude) [*joke, picture, story*] coquin/-e.

nausea *n* nausée *f*.

nauseating *adj* écœurant/-e.

nauseous *adj* [*taste, smell*] écœurant/-e; **to feel ~** avoir la nausée.

nautical *adj* nautique.

naval *adj* [*battle, forces, base*] naval/-e; [*officer, recruit, uniform, affairs*] de la marine.

nave *n* nef *f*.

navel *n* nombril *m*.

navigate I *vtr* **1** parcourir [*seas*]; **2** piloter [*plane*]; gouverner [*ship*].
II *vi* (in vessel, plane) naviguer; (in rally) faire le copilote; (on journey) tenir la carte.

navigation *n* navigation *f*.

navigator *n* (in vessel, plane) navigateur/-trice *m/f*; (in car) copilote *mf*.

navy I *n* **1** (fleet) flotte *f*; (fighting force) marine *f*; **2** (also **~ blue**) bleu *m* marine.
II ▶438 *adj* (also **~ blue**) bleu marine *inv*.

Nazi *n, adj* nazi/-e (*m/f*).

near I *adv* **1** (close) près; **to live quite ~** habiter tout près; **to move ~er** s'approcher davantage (**to** de); **to bring sth ~er** approcher qch; **2** (nearly) **as ~ perfect as it could be** aussi proche de la perfection que possible; **nowhere ~ finished** loin d'être fini.
II *prep* **1** près de; **~ here** près d'ici; **~ the beginning of the article** presque au début de l'article; **he's no ~er (making) a decision** il n'est pas plus décidé; **2** (in time) **~er the time** quand la date approchera; **it's getting ~ Christmas** Noël approche.
III *adj* proche; **in the ~ future** dans un avenir proche; **the ~est shops** les magasins les plus proches.
IV *vtr* approcher de; **to ~ completion** toucher à sa fin.
V **near enough** *phr* à peu près.
VI **near to** *phr* **1** (in space) près de; **~er to** plus près de; **2** (on point of) au bord de [*tears, collapse*]; **3 to come ~ to doing** faillir faire.

nearby I *adj* [*person*] qui se trouve/trouvait etc à proximité; [*town, village*] d'à côté.
II *adv* tout près; [*park, stand, wait*] à proximité.

nearly *adv* presque; **I very ~ gave up** j'ai bien failli abandonner; **not ~ as talented as** loin d'être aussi doué que.

near-sighted *adj* myope.

neat I *adj* **1** [*person*] (in habits) ordonné/-e; (in appearance) soigné/-e; [*room, house, desk*] bien rangé/-e; [*garden, handwriting*] soigné/-e; **2** [*explanation, solution*] habile; **3** [*figure*] bien fait/-e; [*features*] régulier/-ière; **4** [*alcohol, spirits*] sans eau.
II *adv* [*drink whisky*] sec, sans eau.

neatly *adv* **1** (tidily) [*dress, fold, arrange*] avec soin; [*write*] proprement; **2** (perfectly) [*illustrate, summarize*] parfaitement; [*link*] habilement.

necessarily *adv* (definitely) forcément; (of necessity) nécessairement; **not ~** pas forcément.

necessary *adj* (gen) nécessaire; [*qualification*] requis/-e; **if ~, as ~** si besoin est; **it is ~ for him to do** il faut qu'il fasse.

necessitate *vtr* nécessiter.

necessity *n* **1** (need) nécessité *f*; **from ~** par nécessité; **the ~ for** le besoin de; **2** (essential item) **to be an absolute ~** être indispensable.

neck *n* ▶413 **1** (of person) cou *m*; (of horse, donkey) encolure *f*; **2** (collar) col *m*; (neckline) encolure *f*; **3** (of bottle, vase, womb) col *m*.
IDIOMS **to be ~ and ~** être à égalité; **to stick one's ~ out**° prendre des risques.

necklace *n* collier *m*.

neckline *n* encolure *f*.

necktie *n* (US) cravate *f*.

nectar *n* nectar *m*.

nectarine *n* nectarine *f*, brugnon *m*.

need I *modal aux* **you needn't finish it today** tu n'es pas obligé de le finir aujourd'hui; **~ he reply?** est-ce qu'il faut qu'il réponde?, est-ce qu'il doit répondre?; **I needn't have hurried** ce n'était pas la peine de me dépêcher, ce n'était pas la peine que je me dépêche.
II *vtr* **1** (require) **to ~ sth/to do** avoir besoin de qch/de faire; **more money is ~ed** nous avons besoin de plus d'argent; **everything you ~** tout ce qu'il vous faut; **everything you ~ to know about computers** tout ce que vous devez savoir sur les ordinateurs; **2** (have to) **you'll ~ to work hard** il va falloir que tu travailles dur; **he didn't ~ to ask permission** il n'était pas obligé de demander la permission; **something ~ed to be done** il fallait faire quelque chose.
III *n* **1** (necessity) nécessité *f* (**for** de); **I can't see the ~ for it** je n'en vois pas la nécessité; **to feel the ~ to do** éprouver le besoin de faire; **there's no ~ to wait** inutile d'attendre; **there's no ~ to worry** ce n'est pas la peine de s'inquiéter; **there's no ~, I've done it** inutile, c'est fait; **if ~ be** s'il le faut, si nécessaire; **2** (want, requirement) besoin *m* (**for** de); **to be in ~ of sth** avoir besoin de qch; **3** (poverty) **to be in ~** être dans le besoin.

needle I *n* aiguille *f*.
II *vtr* harceler.
IDIOMS **to have pins and ~s** avoir des fourmis.

needless *adj* [*anxiety, suffering*] inutile; [*intrusion, intervention*] inopportun/-e.

needlework *n* couture *f*.

needy *adj* [*person*] nécessiteux/-euse; [*sector, area*] sans ressources.

negative I *n* **1** (of photo) négatif *m*; **2** (in grammar) négation *f*; **in the ~** à la forme négative.
II *adj* (gen) négatif/-ive; [*effect, influence*] néfaste.

neglect I *n* **1** (of person) négligence *f*; (of building, garden) manque *m* d'entretien; (of health, appearance) manque *m* de soin; **2** (lack of interest) indifférence *f* (**of** à l'égard de).
II *vtr* **1** ne pas s'occuper de [*person, dog, plant*]; ne pas entretenir [*garden, house*]; négliger [*health, friend, work*]; **2** (fail) **to ~ to do** négliger de faire.

neglected *adj* (gen) négligé/-e; [*garden, building*] mal entretenu/-e; **to feel ~** se sentir délaissé/-e.

negligence *n* négligence *f*.

negligent *adj* [*person, procedure*] négligent/-e; [*air, manner*] nonchalant/-e.

negligible *adj* négligeable.

negotiate I *vtr* **1** (in business, diplomacy) négocier; **2** négocier [*bend*]; franchir [*obstacle*].
II *vi* négocier (**with** avec; **for** pour obtenir).

negotiation *n* négociation *f*; **to be under ~** être en cours de négociations.

neigh *vi* hennir.

neighbour (GB), **neighbor** (US) *n* voisin/-e *m/f*.

neighbourhood (GB), **neighborhood** (US) *n* **1** (district) quartier *m*; **2** (vicinity) **in the ~** dans le voisinage.

neighbouring (GB), **neighboring** (US) *adj* voisin/-e.

neither I *conj* **I have ~ the time nor the money** je n'ai ni le temps ni l'argent; **~ tea, nor milk** ni (le) thé, ni (le) lait; **'I can't sleep'—'~ can I'** 'je n'arrive pas à dormir'—'moi non plus'.
II *det* aucun/-e des deux; **~ book is suitable** aucun des deux livres ne convient; **~ girl replied** aucune des deux filles n'a répondu.
III *pron, quantif* ni l'un/-e ni l'autre *m/f*; **~ of them came** ni l'un ni l'autre n'est venu.

neon I *n* néon *m*.
II *adj* [*light, sign*] au néon; [*atom*] de néon.

nephew *n* neveu *m*.

Neptune *pr n* (planet) Neptune *f*.

nerve I *n* **1** (Anat) nerf *m*; (Bot) nervure *f*; **2** (courage) courage *m*; **to lose one's ~** perdre son courage; **3**○ (cheek) culot○*m*; **you've got a ~!** tu as un sacré culot○!
II **nerves** *n pl* (gen) nerfs *mpl*; (stage fright) trac○ *m*; **to get on sb's ~s** taper sur les nerfs de qn.

nerve (w)racking *adj* angoissant/-e.

nervous *adj* **1** [*person*] (fearful) timide; (anxious) angoissé/-e; (highly strung) nerveux/-euse; [*smile, laugh, habit*] nerveux/-euse; **to be ~ about doing** avoir peur de faire; **to feel ~** (apprehensive) être angoissé/-e; (before performance) avoir le trac○; (afraid) avoir peur; (ill at ease) se sentir mal à l'aise; **2** (Anat, Med) nerveux/-euse.

nervous breakdown *n* dépression *f* nerveuse.

nest I *n* **1** (of bird, animal) nid *m*; **2 ~ of tables** tables *fpl* gigognes.
II *vi* [*bird*] faire son nid.

nest egg *n* magot○ *m*.

nestle *vi* **1** [*person, animal*] se blottir (**against** contre; **under** sous); **2** [*village, house*] être niché/-e.

net I *n* (gen) filet *m*; (in football) filets *mpl*.
II *adj* (also **nett**) (gen) net/nette; [*loss*] sec/sèche.
III *vtr* **1** prendre [qch] au filet [*fish*]; **2** (financially) [*person*] faire un bénéfice de; [*sale, export, deal*] rapporter.

net curtain *n* voilage *m*.

Netherlands ▶448 *pr n* **the ~** les Pays-Bas *mpl*, la Hollande.

netting *n* (of rope) filet *m*; (of metal, plastic) grillage *m*; (fabric) voile *m*.

nettle *n* (also **stinging ~**) ortie *f*.

network *n* réseau *m* (**of** de).

network television *n* (US) chaîne *f* nationale.

neurosis *n* névrose *f*.

neurotic *adj* névrosé/-e.

neuter I *n* neutre *m*.
II *adj* neutre.
III *vtr* châtrer [*animal*].

neutral I *n* (Aut) **in/into ~** au point mort.
II *adj* neutre (**about** en ce qui concerne).

neutrality *n* neutralité *f*.

neutralize *vtr* neutraliser.

never *adv* **1** (not ever) **I ~ go to London** je ne vais jamais à Londres; **she ~ says anything** elle ne dit jamais rien; **it's now or ~** c'est le moment ou jamais; **~ again** plus jamais; **~ lie to me again!** ne me mens plus jamais!; **2** (emphatic negative) **he ~ said a word** il n'a rien dit; **I ~ knew that** je ne le savais pas; **he ~ so much as apologized** il ne s'est même pas excusé.

nevertheless *adv* **1** (all the same) quand même; **2** (nonetheless) pourtant, néanmoins.

new *adj* nouveau/-elle (*before n*); (brand new) neuf/neuve; **I bought a ~ computer** (to replace old one) j'ai acheté un nouvel ordinateur; (a brand new model) j'ai acheté un ordinateur neuf; **as good as ~** comme neuf; **to be ~ to** ne pas être habitué/-e à [*job, way of life*]; **we're ~ to the area** nous sommes nouveaux venus dans la région.

newborn *adj* nouveau-né/-née.

newcomer *n* (in place, job, club) nouveau venu/nouvelle venue *m/f*; (in sport, theatre, cinema) nouveau/-elle *m/f*.

newfound *adj* tout nouveau/toute nouvelle.

newly *adv* [*arrived, built, formed, qualified*] nouvellement; [*washed*] fraîchement.

newlyweds *n pl* jeunes mariés *mpl*.

news *n* **1** nouvelle(s) *f(pl)*; **a piece of ~** une nouvelle; (in newspaper) une information; **have you heard the ~?** tu connais la nouvelle?; **2** (on radio, TV) **the ~** les informations *fpl*, le journal *m*.

news agency *n* agence *f* de presse.

newsagent's *n* (GB) magasin *m* de journaux.

news bulletin (GB), **newscast** (US) *n* bulletin *m* d'information.

newscaster ▶626 *n* présentateur/-trice *m/f* des informations.

newsdealer ▶626 *n* (US) marchand *m* de journaux.

news headlines *n pl* (on TV) titres *mpl* de l'actualité.

newsletter *n* bulletin *m*.

newspaper *n* journal *m*.

newsreader ▶626 *n* (GB) présentateur/-trice *m/f* des informations.

newsreel *n* actualités *fpl*.

newsstand *n* kiosque *m* à journaux.

New Year *n* le nouvel an *m*; **to see in the ~** fêter la Saint-Sylvestre; **Happy ~!** bonne année!

New Year's day (GB), **New Year's** (US) *n* le jour *m* de l'an.

New Year's Eve *n* la Saint-Sylvestre.

New Zealand ▶448 *pr n* Nouvelle-Zélande *f*.

next

■ **Note** When *next* is used as an adjective, it is generally translated by *prochain* when referring to something which is still to come or happen and by *suivant* when it generally means *following*: *I'll be 40 next year* = j'aurai 40 ans l'année prochaine; *the next year, he went to Spain* = l'année suivante il est allé en Espagne.
– For examples and further usages see the entry below.

I *pron* **from one minute to the ~** d'un instant à l'autre; **the week after ~** dans deux semaines.
II *adj* **1** prochain/-e, suivant/-e; **get the ~ train** prenez le prochain train; **he got on the ~ train** il a pris le train suivant; **'~!'** 'au suivant!'; **'you're ~'** 'c'est à vous'; **the ~ size (up)** la taille au-dessus; **~ Thursday** jeudi prochain; **he's due to arrive in the ~ 10 minutes** il devrait arriver d'ici 10 minutes; **this time ~ week** dans une semaine; **the ~ day** le lendemain; **2** [*room, street*] voisin/-e; [*building, house*] voisin/-e, d'à côté.
III *adv* **1** (afterwards) ensuite, après; **what happened ~?** que s'est-il passé ensuite?; **2** (on a future occasion) **when I ~ go there** la prochaine fois que j'irai; **2** (in order) **the ~ tallest is Patrick** ensuite c'est Patrick qui est le plus grand
IV next to *phr* **1** (almost) presque; **~ to impossible** presque impossible; **to get sth for ~ to nothing** avoir qch pour quasiment rien; **in ~ to no time it was over** en un rien de temps c'était fini; **2** (beside, close to) à côté de; **two seats ~ to each other** deux sièges l'un à côté de l'autre; **to wear silk ~ to the skin** porter de la soie à même la peau.

next door I *adj* (also **next-door**) d'à côté.
II *adv* [*live, move in*] à côté.

next of kin *n* **to be sb's ~** être le parent le plus proche de qn.

nib *n* plume *f*.

nibble *vi* [*animal*] mordiller; [*person*] grignoter.

nice *adj* **1** [*drive, holiday, place*] agréable; [*house, picture, outfit, weather*] beau/belle (*before n*); **did you have a ~ time?** tu t'es bien amusé?; **~ to have met you** ravi d'avoir fait votre connaissance; **have a ~ day!** bonne journée!; **you look very ~** tu es très chic; **2** (tasty) bon/bonne (*before n*); **to taste ~** avoir bon goût; **3** [*person*] sympathique; **to be ~ to sb** être gentil/-ille avec qn; **4** [*neighbourhood, school*] comme il faut *inv*; **it is not ~ to tell lies** ce n'est pas bien de mentir.

nice-looking *adj* beau/belle (*before n*).

nicely *adv* **1** (kindly) gentiment; **2** (attractively) agréablement; **3** (politely) poliment; **4** (satisfactorily) bien; **that'll do ~** cela fera l'affaire.

niche *n* (recess) niche *f*; (figurative) place *f*.

nick I *n* encoche *f* (**in** dans).
II *vtr* **1** (cut) faire une entaille dans; **2**○ (GB) (steal) piquer○; (arrest) pincer○.

nickel *n* **1** (US) pièce *f* de cinq cents; **2** (metal) nickel *m*.

nickname I *n* surnom *m*.
II *vtr* surnommer.

nicotine *n* nicotine *f*.

niece *n* nièce *f*.

night ▶708 *n* nuit *f*; (before going to bed) soir *m*; **at ~** la nuit; **all ~ long** toute la nuit; **late at ~** tard le soir; **he arrived last ~** il est arrivé hier soir; **I slept badly last ~** j'ai mal dormi cette nuit or la nuit dernière; **the ~ before last** avant-hier soir; **on Tuesday ~s** le mardi soir; **to get an early ~** se coucher tôt; **a ~ at the opera** une soirée à l'opéra.

nightclub *n* boîte *f* de nuit○.

nightdress *n* chemise *f* de nuit.

nightingale *n* rossignol *m*.

nightlife *n* vie *f* nocturne.

nightmare *n* cauchemar *m*; **to have a ~** faire un cauchemar.

night school *n* cours *mpl* du soir.

night shelter *n* asile *m* de nuit.

nightshirt *n* chemise *f* de nuit (d'homme).

night-time *n* nuit *f*; **at ~** la nuit.

night watchman ▶626 *n* veilleur *m* de nuit.

nil *n* (gen) néant *m*; (Sport) zéro *m*.

Nile *pr n* Nil *m*.

nimble *adj* [*person*] agile; [*fingers*] habile.

nine ▶389, 434 *n, pron, det* neuf (*m*) *inv*.

nineteen ▶389, 434 *n, pron, det* dix-neuf (*m*) *inv*.

nineteenth ▶456, 498 **I** *n* **1** (in order) dix-neuvième *mf*; **2** (of month) dix-neuf *m inv*; **3** (fraction) dix-neuvième *m*.
II *adj, adv* dix-neuvième.

nineties ▶389, 456 *n pl* **1** (era) **the ~** les années *fpl* quatre-vingt-dix; **2** (age) **to be in one's ~** avoir entre quatre-vingt-dix et cent ans.

ninetieth *n, adj, adv* quatre-vingt-dixième (*mf*).

nine-to-five *adj* [*job, routine*] de bureau.

ninety ▶389 *n, pron, det* quatre-vingt-dix (*m*) *inv*.

ninth ▶456, 498 **I** *n* **1** (in order) neuvième *mf*; **2** (of month) neuf *m inv*; **3** (fraction) neuvième *m*.
II *adj, adv* neuvième.

nip I *n* (pinch) pincement *m*; (bite) morsure *f*; **there's a ~ in the air** il fait frisquet○.
II *vtr* (pinch) pincer; (bite) donner un petit coup de dent à; (playfully) mordiller.

III *vi* (bite) mordre; (playfully) mordiller.
nipple *n* mamelon *m*.
nit *n* (egg) lente *f*; (larva) larve *f* de pou.
nit-pick *vi* chercher la petite bête○, pinailler○.
nitrogen *n* azote *m*.
nitty-gritty○ *n* **to get down to the ~** passer aux choses sérieuses.
no I *particle* non; **~ thanks** non merci.
II *det* **1** (none, not any) aucun/-e; **to have ~ money** ne pas avoir d'argent; **she has ~ talent** elle n'a aucun talent; **of ~ interest** sans intérêt; **2** (prohibiting) **~ smoking** défense de fumer; **~ parking** stationnement interdit; **~ talking!** silence!; **3** (for emphasis) **he's ~ expert** ce n'est certes pas un expert; **this is ~ time to cry** ce n'est pas le moment de pleurer; **4** (hardly any) **in ~ time** en un rien de temps.
III *adv* **it's ~ further/easier** ce n'est pas plus loin/facile; **I ~ longer work there** je n'y travaille plus; **~ later than Wednesday** pas plus tard que mercredi.
no., **No.** (*written abbr* = **number**) n°.
nobility *n* noblesse *f*.
noble *n, adj* noble (*m*).
nobody I *pron* (also **no-one**) personne; **~ saw her** personne ne l'a vue; **there was ~ in the car** il n'y avait personne dans la voiture; **I heard ~** je n'ai entendu personne; **~ but me** personne sauf moi.
II *n* **to be a ~** être insignifiant/-e.
nocturnal *adj* nocturne.
nod I *n* **she gave him a ~** elle lui a fait un signe de (la) tête; (as greeting) elle l'a salué d'un signe de tête; (indicating assent) elle a fait oui de la tête.
II *vtr* **to ~ one's head** faire un signe de tête; (to indicate assent) hocher la tête.
III *vi* faire un signe de tête (**to** à); (in assent) faire oui de la tête.
noise *n* bruit *m*; (shouting) tapage *m*; **to make a ~** faire du bruit.
noisy *adj* [*person, place*] bruyant/-e; [*meeting, protest*] tumultueux/-euse.
nomad *n* nomade *mf*.
nominal *adj* (gen) nominal/-e; [*fee, sum*] minime; [*fine*] symbolique.
nominate *vtr* **1** (propose) proposer; **to ~ sb for a prize** sélectionner qn pour un prix; **2** (appoint) nommer (**to sth** à qch); **to ~ sb (as) chairman** nommer qn président.
nominative *n, adj* nominatif (*m*).
nonalcoholic *adj* non alcoolisé/-e.
nonchalant *adj* nonchalant/-e.
noncommittal *adj* évasif/-ive.
nonconformist *adj* non conformiste.
nondescript *adj* [*person, clothes*] insignifiant/-e; [*building*] quelconque.
none *pron* **1** (not any) aucun/-e *m/f*; **~ of us/them** aucun de nous/d'entre eux; **~ of the wine was French** il n'y avait aucun vin français; **~ of the milk had been drunk** on n'avait pas touché au lait; **~ of the bread was fresh** tout le pain était rassis; **we have ~** nous n'en avons pas; **there's ~ left** il n'y en a plus; **~ of it was true** il n'y avait rien de vrai; **2** (nobody) personne; **~ but him** personne sauf lui.
nonentity *n* (person) personne *f* insignifiante.
nonetheless *adv* pourtant, néanmoins.
nonexistent *adj* inexistant/-e.
nonfiction *n* œuvres *fpl* non fictionnelles.
nonresident *n* non-résident/-e *m/f*.
nonsense *n* (foolishness) absurdités *fpl*; **to talk/write ~** dire/écrire n'importe quoi; **~!** balivernes! *fpl*; **I won't stand for this ~** j'en ai assez de ces bêtises.
nonsmoker *n* non-fumeur/-euse *m/f*.
nonstick *adj* antiadhésif/-ive.
nonstop I *adj* [*journey*] sans arrêt; [*train, flight*] direct/-e; [*noise*] incessant/-e.
II *adv* [*work, talk, drive, argue*] sans arrêt; [*fly*] sans escale.
noodles *n pl* nouilles *fpl*.
nook *n* coin *m*; **every ~ and cranny** tous les coins et recoins.
noon *n* midi *m*; **at 12 ~** à midi.
no-one = **nobody** I.
noose *n* (loop) nœud *m* coulant; (for hanging) corde *f*.
nor *conj* **~ do I** moi non plus; **~ can he** lui non plus; **he was not a cruel man, ~ a mean one** il n'était ni cruel, ni méchant; **she hasn't written, ~ has she telephoned** elle n'a pas écrit, et elle n'a pas téléphoné non plus.
norm *n* norme *f* (**for** pour; **to do** de faire).
normal I *n* normale *f*; **above/below ~** au-dessus/en dessous de la norme.
II *adj* (gen) normal/-e; [*place, time*] habituel/-elle.
normality *n* normalité *f*.
normally *adv* normalement.
Normandy *pr n* Normandie *f*.
north I *n* **1** (compass direction) nord *m*; **2** (part of world, country) **the North** le Nord.
II *adj* (gen) nord *inv*; [*wind*] du nord; **in ~ London** dans le nord de Londres.
III *adv* [*move*] vers le nord; [*lie, live*] au nord (**of** de).
North Africa ▶448 *pr n* Afrique *f* du Nord.
North America ▶448 *pr n* Amérique *f* du Nord.
northeast I *n* nord-est *m*.
II *adj* [*coast, side*] nord-est *inv*; [*wind*] de nord-est.
III *adv* [*move*] vers le nord-est; [*lie, live*] au nord-est.
northern *adj* [*coast*] nord *inv*; [*town, accent*] du nord; [*hemisphere*] Nord *inv*; **~ England** le nord de l'Angleterre.
Northern Ireland ▶448 *pr n* Irlande *f* du Nord.
North Pole *pr n* pôle *m* Nord.
North Sea *pr n* **the ~** la mer du Nord.
northwest I *n* nord-ouest *m*.
II *adj* [*coast*] nord-ouest *inv*; [*wind*] de nord-ouest.

III *adv* [*move*] vers le nord-ouest; [*lie, live*] au nord-ouest.

Norway ▶448 *pr n* Norvège *f*.

Norwegian ▶553 I *n* **1** (person) Norvégien/-ienne *m/f*; **2** (language) norvégien *m*.
II *adj* norvégien/-ienne.

nose ▶413 *n* nez *m*.
IDIOMS **to look down one's ~ at sb/sth** prendre qn/qch de haut; **to turn one's ~ up at sth** faire le dégoûté/la dégoûtée devant qch; **to poke** or **stick one's ~ into sth**○ fourrer○ son nez dans qch.
■ **nose about**, **nose around** fouiner (**in** dans).

nosebleed *n* saignement *m* de nez.

nose-dive *n* piqué *m*; **to go into a ~** [*plane*] faire un piqué; (figurative) chuter.

nostalgia *n* nostalgie *f*.

nostalgic *adj* nostalgique.

nostril *n* (of person) narine *f*; (of horse) naseau *m*.

nosy○ *adj* fouineur/-euse○.

not ▶594 I *adv* ne...pas; **she isn't at home** elle n'est pas chez elle; **we won't need a car** nous n'aurons pas besoin d'une voiture; **hasn't he seen it?** il ne l'a pas vu alors?; **I hope ~** j'espère que non; **certainly ~** sûrement pas; **~ only** or **just** non seulement; **whether it rains or ~** qu'il pleuve ou non; **why ~?** pourquoi pas?; **~ everyone likes it** ça ne plaît pas à tout le monde; **it's ~ every day that** ce n'est pas tous les jours que; **~ a sound was heard** on n'entendait pas un bruit.
II **not at all** *phr* (in no way) pas du tout; (responding to thanks) de rien.
III **not that** *phr* **~ that I know of** pas (autant) que je sache; **if she refuses, ~ that she will**... si elle refuse, je ne dis pas qu'elle le fera...

notable *adj* [*person*] remarquable; [*event, success, difference*] notable.

notably *adv* (in particular) notamment; (markedly) remarquablement.

notch I *n* entaille *f*.
II *vtr* encocher [*stick*].
■ **notch up**○ remporter [*point, prize*].

note I *n* **1** (gen) note *f*; (short letter) mot *m*; **to take ~ of** prendre note de; **2** (Mus) (sound, symbol) note *f*; (piano key) touche *f*; **3** (**bank**) **~** billet *m*.
II *vtr* noter.
III **of note** *phr* [*person*] éminent/-e, réputé/-e; [*development*] digne d'intérêt.
IDIOMS **to compare ~s** échanger ses impressions (**with** avec).
■ **note down** noter.

notebook *n* carnet *m*.

noted *adj* [*intellectual, criminal*] célèbre; **to be ~ for** être réputé/-e pour.

notepad *n* bloc-notes *m*.

notepaper *n* papier *m* à lettres.

noteworthy *adj* remarquable.

nothing

■ **Note** When *nothing* is used alone as a reply to a question in English, it is translated by *rien*: *'what are you doing?'—'nothing'* = 'que fais-tu?'—'rien'.
– *nothing* as a pronoun, when it is the subject of a verb, is translated by *rien ne* (+ verb or, in compound tenses, + auxiliary verb): *nothing changes* = rien ne change; *nothing has changed* = rien n'a changé.
– *nothing* as a pronoun, when it is the object of a verb, is translated by *ne...rien*; *ne* comes before the verb, and before the auxiliary in compound tenses, and *rien* comes after the verb or auxiliary: *I see nothing* = je ne vois rien; *I saw nothing* = je n'ai rien vu.
– When *ne rien* is used with an infinitive, the two words are not separated: *I prefer to say nothing* = je préfère ne rien dire.
– For more examples and particular usages, see the entry below.

I *pron* **I knew ~ about it** je n'en savais rien; **we can do ~ (about it)** nous n'y pouvons rien; **~ much** pas grand-chose; **~ else** rien d'autre; **I had ~ to do with it!** je n'y étais pour rien!; **it's ~ to do with us** ça ne nous regarde pas; **to stop at ~** ne reculer devant rien (**to do** pour faire); **he means ~ to me** il n'est rien pour moi; **the names meant ~ to him** les noms ne lui disaient rien; **for ~** (for free) gratuitement; (pointlessly) pour rien.
II *adv* **it is ~ like as difficult as** c'est loin d'être aussi difficile que; **she is** or **looks ~ like her sister** elle ne ressemble pas du tout à sa sœur.
III **nothing but** *phr* **he's ~ but a coward** ce n'est qu'un lâche; **they've done ~ but moan**○ ils n'ont fait que râler○; **it's caused me ~ but trouble** ça ne m'a valu que des ennuis.

notice I *n* **1** (written sign) pancarte *f*; (advertisement) annonce *f*; (announcing birth, marriage, death) avis *m*; **2** (attention) attention *f*; **to take ~** faire attention (**of** à); **to take no ~ (of)** ne pas faire attention (à); **3** (notification) préavis *m*; **one month's ~** un mois de préavis; **until further ~** jusqu'à nouvel ordre; **at short ~** à la dernière minute; **to give in one's ~** donner sa démission.
II *vtr* remarquer [*absence, mark*]; **to get oneself ~d** se faire remarquer.

noticeable *adj* visible.

noticeboard *n* panneau *m* d'affichage.

notify *vtr* notifier; **to ~ sb of** aviser qn de [*result, incident*]; avertir qn de [*intention*]; informer qn de [*birth, death*].

notion *n* **1** (idea) idée *f*; **2** (understanding) notion *f*.

notorious *adj* [*criminal, organization*] notoire; [*district*] mal famé/-e; [*case*] tristement célèbre.

notwithstanding I *adv* néanmoins.
II *prep* (in spite of) en dépit de; (excepted) exception faite de.

nought *n* zéro *m*.

noun *n* nom *m*, substantif *m*.

nourish *vtr* nourrir (**with** avec; **on** de).

nourishment *n* nourriture *f*.

novel I *n* roman *m*.

not

Used without a verb

When ***not*** is used without a verb before an adjective, a noun, an adverb, a verb or a pronoun it is translated by ***pas***:

not *at all*	= **pas** du tout
not *bad*	= **pas** mal
it's a cat ***not*** *a dog*	= c'est un chat **pas** un chien
they're children ***not*** *adults*	= ce sont des enfants **pas** des adultes
you should walk, ***not*** *run*	= il faut marcher, **pas** courir
she should apologise, ***not*** *me*	= c'est elle qui devrait s'excuser, **pas** moi

Used with a verb

- When ***not*** is used to form the negative of a verb, the translation is ***ne . . . pas*** (***n'*** before a vowel or mute 'h'): ***ne*** comes before the verb or the auxiliary, and ***pas*** comes after the verb or auxiliary:

it's ***not*** *a cat*	= ce **n'**est **pas** un chat
*he does**n't** like oranges*	= il **n'**aime **pas** les oranges
*I have**n't** seen him*	= je **ne** l'ai **pas** vu
*she has**n't** arrived yet*	= elle **n'**est **pas** encore arrivée
they will ***not*** *agree to the reforms*	= ils **n'**accepteront **pas** les réformes
*she wo**n't** come by car*	= elle **ne** viendra **pas** en voiture
*it would**n't** matter*	= ce **ne** serait **pas** grave

- When used with a verb in the infinitive, ***ne*** and ***pas*** are placed together before the verb:

he decided ***not*** *to go*	= il a décidé de **ne pas** y aller
you were wrong ***not*** *to tell her*	= tu as eu tort de **ne pas** le lui dire
it's difficult ***not*** *to take things to heart*	= il est difficile de **ne pas** prendre les choses à cœur

Used in question tags

When ***not*** is used in question tags, the whole tag can usually be translated by the French ***n'est-ce pas***:

she bought it, ***didn't she****?*	= elle l'a acheté, **n'est-ce pas**?
you were there too, ***weren't you****?*	= tu y étais aussi, **n'est-ce pas**?
they're living in Germany, ***aren't they****?*	= ils habitent en Allemagne, **n'est-ce pas**?
he likes fish, ***doesn't he****?*	= il aime le poisson, **n'est-ce pas**?
he's got a lot of money, ***hasn't he****?*	= il a beaucoup d'argent, **n'est-ce pas**?
you'll come too, ***won't you****?*	= vous viendrez vous aussi, **n'est-ce pas**?
she's English, ***isn't she****?*	= elle est anglaise, **n'est-ce pas**?
we should let them know, ***shouldn't we****?*	= nous devrions les prévenir, **n'est-ce pas**?

For examples and particular usages, see the entry **not**.

II *adj* original/-e.

novelist ▶626| *n* romancier/-ière *m/f*.

novelty *n* nouveauté *f* (**of doing** de faire).

November ▶456| *n* novembre *m*.

novice *n* débutant/-e *m/f*; (in religious order) novice *mf*.

now I *conj* ~ (**that**) maintenant que.

II *adv* **1** maintenant; **do it ~** fais-le maintenant; **right ~** tout de suite; **any time ~** d'un moment à l'autre; (**every**) **~ and then** or **again** de temps en temps; **2** (with preposition) **you should have phoned him before ~** tu aurais dû lui téléphoner avant; **before** or **until ~** jusqu'à présent; **he should be finished by ~** il devrait avoir déjà fini; **between ~ and next Friday** d'ici vendredi prochain; **between ~ and then** d'ici là; **from ~ on(wards)** dorénavant; **3** (in the past) **it was ~ 4 pm** il était alors 16 heures; **by ~ it was too late** à ce moment-là, il était trop tard; **4 ~ there's a man I can trust!** ah! voilà un homme en qui on peut avoir confiance!; **careful ~!** attention!; **~ then, let's get back to work** bon, reprenons le travail.

nowadays *adv* (these days) de nos jours; (now) actuellement.

nowhere I *adv* nulle part; **I've got ~ else to go** je n'ai nulle part où aller; **there's ~ to sit down** il n'y a pas d'endroit pour s'asseoir; **all this talk is getting us ~** tout ce bavardage ne nous avance à rien; **flattery will get you ~!** tu n'arriveras à rien en me flattant.

II **nowhere near** *phr* loin de; **~ near sufficient** loin d'être suffisant/-e.

nozzle *n* (of hose, pipe) ajutage *m*; (of hoover) suceur *m*; (for icing) douille *f*.

nuance *n* nuance *f*.

nuclear *adj* nucléaire.

nuclear bomb *n* bombe *f* atomique.

nuclear energy, **nuclear power** *n* énergie *f* nucléaire or atomique.

nuclear power station *n* centrale *f* nucléaire.

nucleus *n* noyau *m*.

nude I *n* nu/-e *m/f*; **in the ~** nu/-e.

II *adj* [*person*] nu/-e.

nudge *vtr* (push) pousser du coude; (accidentally) heurter; (brush against) frôler.

nudist *n*, *adj* nudiste (*mf*).

nugget *n* pépite *f*.

nuisance *n* (gen) embêtement *m*; (Law) nuisance *f*; **what a ~!** que c'est agaçant!

null *adj* (Law) **~ and void** nul et non avenu.

numb I *adj* **1** (from cold) engourdi/-e (**with** par); (from anaesthetic) insensible; **to go ~** s'engourdir; **2** (figurative) hébété/-e (**with** par).

II *vtr* [*cold*] engourdir; (Med) insensibiliser; **to ~ the pain** endormir la douleur.

number I *n* **1** (gen) nombre *m*; (written figure) chiffre *m*; **a three-figure ~** un nombre à trois chiffres; **a ~ of** un certain nombre de; **2** (of bus, house, page, telephone) numéro *m*; **a wrong ~** un faux numéro; **3** (by performer) (act) numéro *m*; (song) chanson *f*.

II *vtr* **1** (allocate number to) numéroter; **2** (amount to, include) compter.

IDIOMS **his days are ~ed** ses jours sont comptés.

numberplate *n* (GB) plaque *f* minéralogique or d'immatriculation.

numeral *n* chiffre *m*.

numerical *adj* numérique.

numerous *adj* nombreux/-euse.

nun *n* religieuse *f*, bonne sœur *f*.

nurse ▶626| I *n* **1** (Med) infirmier/-ière *m/f*; **male ~** infirmier *m*; **2** = **nursemaid**.

II *vtr* **1** soigner [*person, cold*]; **2** allaiter [*baby*]; **3** nourrir [*grievance, hope*].

nursemaid *n* nurse *f*, bonne *f* d'enfants.

nursery *n* **1** (also **day ~**) crèche *f*; (in hotel, shop) garderie *f*; **2** (room) chambre *f* d'enfants; **3** (for plants) pépinière *f*.

nursery rhyme *n* comptine *f*.

nursery school *n* école *f* maternelle.

nursing ▶626| *n* profession *f* d'infirmier/-ière.

nursing home *n* **1** (old people's) maison *f* de retraite; (convalescent) maison *f* de repos; **2** (GB) (maternity) clinique *f* obstétrique.

nurture *vtr* **1** élever [*child*]; soigner [*plant*]; **2** nourrir [*hope, feeling, talent*].

nut *n* **1** (walnut) noix *f*; (hazel) noisette *f*; (almond) amande *f*; (peanut) cacahuète *f*; **2** (Tech) écrou *m*.

nutcracker *n* casse-noisettes *m inv*.

nutmeg *n* noix *f* de muscade.

nutrition *n* (process) nutrition *f*, alimentation *f*; (science) diététique *f*.

nutritious *adj* nourrissant/-e.

nutshell *n* **1** coquille *f* de noix or noisette; **2** (figurative) **in a ~** en un mot.

nuzzle *vtr* frotter son nez contre.

■ **nuzzle up**: **to ~ up against** or **to sb** se blottir contre qn.

nylon *n* nylon® *m*.

nymph *n* nymphe *f*.

Oo

o, **O** *n* **1** (letter) o, O *m*; **2 O** (spoken number) zéro.
oaf *n* (clumsy) balourd/-e *m/f*; (loutish) mufle *m*.
oak I *n* chêne *m*.
II *adj* de or en chêne.
oar *n* rame *f*.
oasis *n* (in desert) oasis *f*; (figurative) havre *m*.
oath *n* **1** serment *m*; **under ~**, **on ~** (GB) sous serment; **2** (swearword) juron *m*.
oatmeal *n* **1** (cereal) farine *f* d'avoine; **2** (US) (porridge) bouillie *f* d'avoine.
oats *n pl* avoine *f*.
obedience *n* obéissance *f* (**to** à).
obedient *adj* obéissant/-e.
obese *adj* obèse.
obey I *vtr* obéir à [*person, instinct*]; se conformer à [*instructions, law*].
II *vi* [*person*] obéir.
obituary *n* (also **~ notice**) nécrologie *f*.
object I *n* **1** (item) objet *m*; **2** (goal) but *m* (**of** de); **3** (focus) **to be the ~ of** être l'objet de; **4** (in grammar) complément *m* d'objet.
II *vtr* objecter (**that** que).
III *vi* soulever des objections; **to ~ to** protester contre [*attitude, comment*]; **to ~ to doing** se refuser à faire; **I ~ to their behaviour** je trouve leur comportement inadmissible.
objection *n* objection *f* (**to** à; **from** de la part de); **I've no ~(s)** je n'y vois pas d'inconvénient.
objectionable *adj* [*remark*] désobligeant/-e; [*behaviour, language*] choquant/-e; [*person*] insupportable.
objective I *n* objectif *m*.
II *adj* objectif/-ive, impartial/-e.
obligation *n* **1** (duty) devoir *m* (**towards, to** envers); **to be under (an) ~ to do** être obligé/-e de faire; **2** (commitment) obligation *f* (**to** envers; **to do** de faire); **3** (debt) dette *f*.
obligatory *adj* obligatoire (**to do** de faire).
oblige *vtr* **1** (compel) obliger (**to do** à faire); **2** (be helpful) rendre service à; **3 to be ~d to sb** être reconnaissant/-e à qn (**for** de).
obliging *adj* serviable.
obliterate *vtr* effacer [*trace, word, memory*]; anéantir [*landmark, city*].
oblivion *n* oubli *m*.
oblivious *adj* (unaware) inconscient/-e; **to be ~ of** or **to** ne pas être conscient/-e de.
oblong I *n* rectangle *m*.
II *adj* oblong/oblongue, rectangulaire.
obnoxious *adj* odieux/-ieuse, exécrable.
obscene *adj* obscène.
obscure I *adj* obscur/-e; (indistinct) vague.
II *vtr* obscurcir [*truth*]; cacher [*view*]; **to ~ the issue** embrouiller la question.
observant *adj* observateur/-trice.
observation *n* observation *f* (**of** de); **to keep sb/sth under ~** surveiller qn/qch.
observe *vtr* **1** (see, notice) observer (**that** que); **2** [*doctor, police*] surveiller; **3** (remark) faire observer (**that** que); **4** observer [*law, custom*].
observer *n* observateur/-trice *m/f* (**of** de).
obsess *vtr* obséder.
obsession *n* obsession *f*.
obsessive *adj* [*person*] maniaque; [*neurosis*] obsessionnel/-elle; [*thought*] obsédant/-e.
obsolete *adj* [*technology*] dépassé/-e; [*custom, idea*] démodé/-e; [*word*] désuet/-ète.
obstacle *n* obstacle *m*; **to be an ~** faire obstacle (**to** à).
obstacle race *n* course *f* d'obstacles.
obstinate *adj* [*person*] têtu/-e (**about** en ce qui concerne); [*behaviour, silence, effort*] obstiné/-e; [*resistance*] acharné/-e.
obstruct *vtr* cacher [*view*]; bloquer [*road*]; gêner [*traffic, person, progress*]; faire obstruction à [*player*]; entraver le cours de [*justice*].
obstruction *n* **1** (to traffic, progress) obstacle *m*; (in pipe) bouchon *m*; **2** (in sport) obstruction *f*.
obtain *vtr* obtenir.
obtrusive *adj* [*noise*] gênant/-e; [*person, behaviour*] importun/-e.
obtuse *adj* [*person*] obtus/-e; [*remark*] stupide.
obvious I *n* **to state the ~** enfoncer les portes ouvertes.
II *adj* évident/-e (**to** pour).
obviously I *adv* manifestement; **she ~ needs help** il est évident qu'elle a besoin d'aide; **he's ~ lying** il est clair qu'il ment.
II *excl* bien sûr!, évidemment!
occasion *n* occasion *f*; **on one ~** une fois; **to rise to the ~** se montrer à la hauteur des circonstances; **on special ~s** dans les grandes occasions.
occasional *adj* [*event*] qui a lieu de temps en temps; **the ~ letter** une lettre de temps en temps.
occasionally *adv* de temps à autre; **very ~** très rarement.
occupant *n* **1** (of building, bed) occupant/-e *m/f*; **2** (of vehicle) passager/-ère *m/f*.
occupation *n* **1** (Mil) occupation *f* (**de** of); **2** (trade) métier *m*; (profession) profession *f*; **3** (activity) occupation *f*.
occupational hazard *n* **it's an ~** ça fait partie des risques du métier.
occupier *n* occupant/-e *m/f*.
occupy *vtr* occuper; **to keep oneself occupied** s'occuper (**by doing** en faisant).
occur *vi* **1** (happen) se produire; **2** (be present) se trouver; **3 the idea ~red to me that...** l'idée

m'est venue à l'esprit que...; **it didn't ~ to me** ça ne m'est pas venu à l'idée.

occurrence *n* **1** (event) fait *m*; **to be a rare ~** se produire rarement; **2** (instance) occurrence *f*; **3** (of disease, phenomenon) cas *m*.

ocean *n* océan *m*.

o'clock ▶434 *adv* **at one ~** à une heure; **it's two ~** il est deux heures.

octagon *n* octogone *m*.

octave *n* octave *f*.

October ▶456 *n* octobre *m*.

octopus *n* **1** (Zool) pieuvre *f*; **2** (Culin) poulpe *m*.

odd I *adj* **1** (strange, unusual) [*person, object, occurrence*] bizarre; **2** [*socks, gloves*] dépareillés; **3** (miscellaneous) **some ~ bits of cloth** quelques bouts de tissu; **4** [*number*] impair/-e; **5 to be the ~ one out** [*person, animal, plant*] être l'exception *f*; [*drawing, word*] être l'intrus *m*; (when selecting team) [*person*] être sans partenaire.

II **-odd** *combining form* **sixty-~ people/years** une soixantaine de personnes/d'années.

oddity *n* (odd thing) bizarrerie *f*; (person) excentrique *mf*.

odd job *n* (for money) petit boulot *m*; **~s** (in house, garden) petits travaux *mpl*.

odd-job man *n* homme *m* à tout faire.

odds *n pl* **1** (in betting) cote *f* (**on** sur); **2** (chance, likelihood) chances *fpl*; **the ~ are against his winning** il y a peu de chances qu'il gagne; **to win against the ~** gagner contre toute attente.

IDIOMS **at ~** (in dispute) être en conflit; (inconsistent) en contradiction (**with** avec).

odds and ends *n pl* (GB) bricoles○ *fpl*.

odour (GB), **odor** (US) *n* odeur *f*.

of *prep*

■ **Note** In almost all its uses, the preposition *of* is translated by *de*. For exceptions, see the entry below.
– Remember that *de* + *le* always becomes *du* and that *de* + *les* always becomes *des*.
– When *of it* or *of them* are used for something already referred to, they are translated by *en*: *there's a lot of it* = il y en a beaucoup; *there are several of them* = il y en a plusieurs.
– Note, however, the following expressions used when referring to people: *there are six of them* = ils sont six; *there were several of them* = ils étaient plusieurs.
– See also the usage note on ***dates*** ▶456.

1 (in most uses) de; **the leg ~ the table** le pied de la table; **2** (made of) en; **a ring (made) ~ gold** une bague en or; **3 a friend ~ mine** un ami à moi; **that's kind ~ you** c'est très gentil de votre part or à vous; **some ~ us/them** quelques-uns d'entre nous/d'entre eux.

off I *adv* **1** (leaving) **to be ~** partir, s'en aller; **it's time you were ~** il est temps que tu partes; **I'm ~** je m'en vais; **2** (at a distance) **to be 30 metres ~** être à 30 mètres; **some way ~** assez loin; **3** (ahead in time) **Easter is a month ~** Pâques est dans un mois; **the exam is still several months ~** l'examen n'aura pas lieu avant plusieurs mois.

II *adj* **1** (free) **Tuesday's my day ~** je ne travaille pas le mardi; **to have the morning ~** avoir la matinée libre; **2** (turned off) **to be ~** [*water, gas*] être coupé/-e; [*tap*] être fermé/-e; [*light, TV*] être éteint/-e; **3** (cancelled) [*match, party*] annulé/-e; **4** (removed) **the lid is ~** il n'y a pas de couvercle; **with her make-up ~** sans maquillage; **25% ~** 25% de remise; **5**○ (bad) **to be ~** [*food*] être avarié/-e; [*milk*] avoir tourné/-e.

III *prep* **1** (also **just ~**) juste à côté de [*kitchen*]; **~ the west coast** au large de la côte ouest; **just ~ the path** tout près du sentier; **2 it is ~ the point** là n'est pas la question; **3**○ **to be ~ one's food** ne pas avoir d'appétit.

IDIOMS **to feel a bit ~**○**(-colour)** (GB) ne pas être dans son assiette○; **to have an ~ day** ne pas être dans un de ses bons jours.

off-centre (GB), **off-center** (US) *adj* décentré/-e.

off-chance *n* **just on the ~** au cas où.

offence (GB), **offense** (US) *n* **1** (crime) délit *m*; **2** (insult) **to cause ~ to sb** offenser qn; **to take ~ (at)** s'offenser (de); **3** (Mil) offensive *f*.

offend I *vtr* offenser [*person*].

II *vi* commettre une infraction (**against** à).

offender *n* **1** (Law) délinquant/-e *m/f*; **2** (culprit) coupable *mf*.

offensive I *n* (Mil, Sport) offensive *f*.

II *adj* [*remark*] injurieux/-ieuse (**to** pour); [*behaviour*] insultant/-e; [*language*] grossier/-ière.

offer I *n* **1** offre *f* (**to do** de faire); **job ~** offre d'emploi; **2** (of goods) **to be on special ~** être en promotion.

II *vtr* (gen) offrir; donner [*advice, explanation, information*]; émettre [*opinion*]; proposer [*service*]; **to ~ sb sth** offrir qch à qn; **to ~ to do** se proposer pour faire.

III *vi* se proposer.

offering *n* (gift) cadeau *m*; (sacrifice) offrande *f*.

offhand I *adj* désinvolte.

II *adv* **~, I don't know** comme ça au pied levé je ne sais pas.

office *n* **1** (place) bureau *m*; **2** (position) fonction *f*, charge *f*; **public ~** fonctions *fpl* officielles; **to hold ~** [*president, mayor*] être en fonction; [*political party*] être au pouvoir.

office block, **office building** *n* (GB) immeuble *m* de bureaux.

officer *n* **1** (in army, navy) officier *m*; **2** (also **police ~**) policier *m*.

office worker ▶626 *n* employé/-e *m/f* de bureau.

official I *n* fonctionnaire *mf*; (of party, union) officiel/-ielle *m/f*; (at town hall) employé/-e *m/f*.

II *adj* officiel/-ielle.

offing *n* **in the ~** en perspective.

off-licence *n* (GB) magasin *m* de vins et de spiritueux.

off-limits *adj* interdit/-e.

off-peak *adj* [*electricity*] au tarif de nuit; [*travel*] en période creuse; [*call*] au tarif réduit.

off-putting *adj* (GB) [*manner*] peu engageant/-e; **it was very ~** c'était déroutant.
off-season *adj* [*cruise, holiday*] hors saison.
offset *vtr* compenser (**by** par); **to ~ sth against sth** mettre qch et qch en balance.
offshore *adj* [*waters*] du large; [*fishing*] au large; [*oil rig*] offshore *inv*.
offside I *n* (GB) côté *m* conducteur.
II *adj* **1** (GB) [*lane*] (in France) de gauche; (in UK) de droite; **2** (Sport) hors jeu *inv*.
offspring *n* progéniture *f*.
offstage *adj, adv* dans les coulisses.
off-the-cuff *adj* [*remark, speech*] impromptu/-e.
off-the-peg *adj* [*garment*] de prêt-à-porter.
off-white *adj* blanc cassé *inv*.
often *adv* souvent; **as ~ as not, more ~ than not** le plus souvent; **how ~ do you meet?** vous vous voyez tous les combien?; **once too ~** une fois de trop; **every so ~** de temps en temps.
oh *excl* oh!; **~ dear!** oh là là!; **~ (really)?** ah bon?
oil I *n* (gen) huile *f*; (petroleum) pétrole *m*; **crude ~** pétrole brut; **engine ~** huile de moteur; **heating ~** fioul *m*.
II *vtr* huiler.
oilcloth *n* toile *f* cirée.
oil field *n* champ *m* pétrolifère.
oil painting *n* peinture *f* à l'huile.
oil rig *n* (offshore) plate-forme *f* pétrolière offshore; (on land) tour *f* de forage.
oilskins *n pl* (GB) ciré *m*.
oil slick *n* marée *f* noire.
oil well *n* puits *m* de pétrole.
oily *adj* [*cloth, food, hair*] gras/grasse; [*dressing, substance*] huileux/-euse.
ointment *n* pommade *f*.
okay, OK○ I *n* **to give sb/sth the ~** donner le feu vert à qn/qch.
II *adj* **it's ~ by me** ça ne me dérange pas; **is it ~ if...?** est-ce que ça va si...?; **he's ~** (nice) il est sympa○; **to feel ~** aller bien; **I'm ~** ça va; **'how was the match?'—'~'** 'comment as-tu trouvé le match?'—'pas mal'.
III *adv* [*cope, work out*] (assez) bien.
IV *particle* **1** (giving agreement) d'accord; **2** (introducing topic) bien.
old ▶389 *adj* **1** [*person*] vieux/vieille (*before n*), âgé/-e; [*object, tradition, song*] vieux/vieille (*before n*); **an ~ man** un vieil homme, un vieillard; **an ~ woman** une vieille femme, une vieille; **to get ~** vieillir; **how ~ are you?** quel âge as-tu?; **I'm ten years ~** j'ai dix ans; **a six-year-~ boy** un garçon (âgé) de six ans; **my ~er brother** mon frère aîné; **I'm the ~est** c'est moi l'aîné/-e; **2** (former, previous) [*address, school, job, system*] ancien/-ienne (*before n*); **in the ~ days** autrefois.

■ **Note** The irregular form *vieil* of the adjective vieux/vieille is used before masculine nouns beginning with a vowel or a mute 'h'.

old age *n* vieillesse *f*.
old-age pensioner, OAP *n* (GB) retraité/-e *m/f*.
old-fashioned *adj* [*person, ways*] vieux jeu *inv*; [*idea, attitude, garment, machine*] démodé/-e.
old people's home *n* maison *f* de retraite.
old wives' tale *n* conte *m* de bonne femme.
olive I *n* **1** (fruit) olive *f*; **2** (also **~ tree**) olivier *m*.
II *adj* [*dress, eyes*] vert olive *inv*; [*complexion*] olivâtre.
olive green ▶438 *n, adj* vert (*m*) olive *inv*.
olive oil *n* huile *f* d'olive.
Olympics *n pl* (also **Olympic Games**) jeux *mpl* Olympiques.
ombudsman *n* médiateur *m*.
omelette *n* omelette *f*.
omen *n* présage *m*.
ominous *adj* [*cloud*] menaçant/-e; [*news*] inquiétant/-e; [*sign*] de mauvais augure.
omission *n* omission *f*.
omit *vtr* omettre (**from** de; **to do** de faire).
omnipotent *adj* omnipotent/-e.
omnipresent *adj* omniprésent/-e.
on I *prep* **1** (position) sur [*table, coast, motorway*]; **~ the beach** sur la plage; **~ top of the piano** sur le piano; **~ the floor** par terre; **there's a stain ~ it** il y a une tache dessus; **to live ~ Park Avenue** habiter Park Avenue; **a studio flat ~ Avenue Montaigne** un studio Avenue Montaigne; **the paintings ~ the wall** les tableaux qui sont au mur; **I've got no small change ~ me** je n'ai pas de monnaie sur moi; **to have a smile ~ one's face** sourire; **to hang sth ~ a nail** accrocher qch à un clou; **~ a string** au bout d'une ficelle; **2** (about, on the subject of) sur; **~ Africa** sur l'Afrique; **3 to be ~** faire partie de [*team*]; être membre de [*committee*]; **4** (in expressions of time) **~ 22 February** le 22 février; **~ Friday** vendredi; **~ Saturdays** le samedi; **~ my birthday** le jour de mon anniversaire; **~ sunny days** quand il fait beau; **5** (immediately after) **~ his arrival** à son arrivée; **~ hearing the truth she...** quand elle a appris la vérité, elle...; **6** (taking) **to be ~ steroids** prendre des stéroïdes; **to be ~ drugs** se droguer; **7** (powered by) **to run ~ batteries** fonctionner sur piles; **to run ~ electricity** marcher à l'électricité; **8** (indicating a medium) **~ TV** à la télé; **~ the news** aux informations; **~ video** en vidéo; **~ drums** à la batterie; **9** (earning) **to be ~ £20,000 a year** gagner 20 000 livres sterling par an; **to be ~ a low income** avoir un bas salaire; **10** (paid for by) **it's ~ me** je t'invite; **11** (indicating transport) **to travel ~ the bus** voyager en bus; **~ the plane** dans l'avion; **to be ~ one's bike** être à vélo; **to leave ~ the first train** prendre le premier train.
II *adj* **1 while the meeting is ~** pendant la réunion; **I've got a lot ~** je suis très occupé; **the news is ~ in 10 minutes** les informations sont dans 10 minutes; **what's ~?** (on TV) qu'est-ce qu'il y a à la télé?; (at the cinema, theatre) qu'est-ce qu'on joue?; **there's nothing**

~ il n'y a rien de bien; **2 to be ~** [*TV, oven, light*] être allumé/-e; [*dishwasher, radio*] marcher; [*tap*] être ouvert/-e; **the power is ~** il y a du courant; **3 to be ~** [*lid*] être mis/-e.
III *adv* **1 to have nothing ~** être nu/-e; **to have make-up ~** être maquillé/-e; **with slippers ~** en pantoufles; **2 from that day ~** à partir de ce jour-là; **20 years ~** 20 ans plus tard; **to walk ~** continuer à marcher; **to go to Paris then ~ to Marseilles** aller à Paris et de là à Marseille; **a little further ~** un peu plus loin.
IV **on and off** *phr* de temps en temps.
V **on and on** *phr* **to go ~ and ~** [*speaker*] parler pendant des heures; [*speech*] durer des heures; **to go ~ and ~ about** ne pas arrêter de parler de.
IDIOMS **it's just** or **simply not ~** (GB) (out of the question) c'est hors de question; (not the done thing) ça ne se fait pas; (unacceptable) c'est inadmissible.

once I *n* **just this ~** pour cette fois; **for ~** pour une fois.
II *adv* **1** (one time) une fois; **~ and for all** une (bonne) fois pour toutes; **~ too often** une fois de trop; **~ a day** une fois par jour; **2** (formerly) autrefois; **~ upon a time there was a king** il était une fois un roi.
III *conj* une fois que, dès que.
IV **at once** *phr* **1** (immediately) tout de suite; **all at ~** tout d'un coup; **2** (simultaneously) à la fois.

oncoming *adj* [*car, vehicle*] venant en sens inverse.

one ▶ 389, 434 I *det* **1** (single) un/une; **~ car** une voiture; **~ dog** un chien; **to raise ~ hand** lever la main; **2** (unique, sole) seul/-e (*before n*); **my ~ vice** mon seul vice; **my ~ and only tie** ma seule et unique cravate; **the ~ and only Edith Piaf** l'incomparable Edith Piaf; **3** (same) même; **at ~ and the same time** en même temps.
II *pron* **1** (indefinite) un/une *m/f*; **can you lend me ~?** tu peux m'en prêter un/une?; **~ of them** (person) l'un d'eux/l'une d'elles; (thing) l'un/l'une *m/f*; **2** (impersonal) (as subject) on; (as object) vous; **~ never knows** on ne sait jamais; **3** (demonstrative) **the grey ~** le gris/la grise; **this ~** celui-ci/celle-ci; **which ~?** lequel/laquelle?; **that's the ~** c'est celui-là/celle-là; **he's/she's the ~ who** c'est lui/elle qui; **5 ~-fifty** (in sterling) une livre cinquante.
III *n* (number) un *m*; (referring to feminine) une *f*; **~ o'clock** une heure; **in ~s and twos** par petits groupes.
IV **one by one** *phr* un par un/une par une.
IDIOMS **to be ~ up on sb**○ avoir un avantage sur qn; **to go ~ better than sb** faire mieux que qn; **I for ~ think that** pour ma part je crois que.

one another *pron*

■ **Note** *one another* is very often translated by using a reflexive pronoun (*nous, vous, se, s'*).

(also **each other**) **they love ~** ils s'aiment; **to help ~** s'entraider; **to worry about ~** s'inquiéter l'un pour l'autre; **kept apart from ~** séparés l'un de l'autre.

one-off *adj* (GB) [*experiment*] unique; [*event, payment*] exceptionnel/-elle.

one-parent family *n* famille *f* monoparentale.

one-piece *adj* **~ swimsuit** maillot *m* de bain une pièce.

one's *det* son/sa/ses; **~ books/friends** ses livres/amis; **to wash ~ hands** se laver les mains; **to do ~ best** faire de son mieux.

oneself *pron* **1** (reflexive) se, s'; **to wash/cut ~** se laver/couper; **2** (for emphasis) soi-même; **3** (after prepositions) soi; **sure of ~** sûr/-e de soi; **(all) by ~** tout seul/toute seule.

one-sided *adj* [*account*] partial/-e; [*contest*] inégal/-e; [*deal*] inéquitable.

one-to-one *adj* [*talk*] en tête à tête; **~ meeting** tête-à-tête *m inv*; **~ tuition** cours *mpl* particuliers.

one-way *adj* **1** [*traffic*] à sens unique; **~ street** sens *m* unique; **2 ~ ticket** aller *m* simple.

ongoing *adj* [*process*] continu/-e; [*battle, story*] continuel/-elle.

onion *n* oignon *m*.

onlooker *n* spectateur/-trice *m/f*.

only I *conj* mais, seulement; **I'd go ~ I'm too old** j'irais bien mais je suis trop vieux.
II *adj* seul/-e; **~ child** enfant unique.
III *adv* **1** (exclusively) **~ in Italy can one...** il n'y a qu'en Italie que l'on peut...; **~ time will tell** seul l'avenir nous le dira; **'men ~'** 'réservé aux hommes'; **2** (in expressions of time) **~ yesterday** pas plus tard qu'hier; **it seems like ~ yesterday** j'ai l'impression que c'était hier; **3** (merely) **you ~ had to ask** tu n'avais qu'à demander; **it's ~ fair** ce n'est que justice; **he ~ grazed his knees** il s'est juste égratigné les genoux; **~ half the money** juste la moitié de l'argent.
IV **only just** *phr* **1** (very recently) **to have ~ just done** venir juste de faire; **2** (barely) **~ just wide enough** juste assez large; **~ just** (narrowly) de justesse.
V **only too** *phr* **~ too well** trop bien; **~ too pleased** trop content/-e.

onset *n* début *m* (**of** de).

onslaught *n* attaque *f* (**on** contre).

on the spot *adv* [*decide*] sur-le-champ; [*killed*] sur le coup; **to be ~** être sur place.

onto *prep* (also **on to**) sur.
IDIOMS **to be ~ something**○ être sur une piste.

onus *n* obligation *f*; **the ~ is on sb to do** il incombe à qn de faire.

onward I *adj* **~ flight** correspondance *f* (**to** à destination de).
II *adv* = **onwards**.

onwards *adv* (also **onward**) **to carry ~** continuer; **from now ~** à partir d'aujourd'hui; **from that day ~** à dater de ce jour.

ooze I *vtr* **the wound ~d blood** du sang suintait de la blessure.

II *vi* **to ~ with** [*person*] rayonner de [*charm, sexuality*].

opal *n* opale *f*.

opaque *adj* opaque.

open I *n* **in the ~** (outside) dehors, en plein air; **to bring sth out into the ~** mettre qch au grand jour.

II *adj* **1** (gen) ouvert/-e; **to be half ~** [*door*] être entrouvert/-e; **the ~ air** le plein air; **in ~ country** en rase campagne; **on ~ ground** sur un terrain découvert; **the ~ road** la grand-route; **the ~ sea** la haute mer; **2** (not covered) [*car, carriage*] découvert/-e, décapoté/-e; **3 ~ to** exposé/-e à [*air, wind, elements*]; **~ to attack** exposé/-e à l'attaque; **to lay oneself ~ to criticism** s'exposer (ouvertement) à la critique; **4** [*access, competition*] ouvert/-e à tous; [*meeting*] public/-ique; **5** (candid) [*person*] franc/franche (**about** à propos de); **6** (blatant) [*hostility, contempt*] non dissimulé/-e; **7 to leave the date ~** laisser la date en suspens; **to keep an ~ mind** réserver son jugement.

III *vtr* (gen) ouvrir; entamer [*discussions*].

IV *vi* **1** [*door, flower, curtain*] s'ouvrir; **to ~ onto sth** [*door, window*] donner sur qch; **2** [*shop, bar*] ouvrir; [*meeting, play*] commencer (**with** par); **3** [*film*] sortir (sur les écrans).

■ **open up**: ¶ **~ up 1** [*shop, branch*] ouvrir; **2** [*gap*] se creuser; **3** (figurative) [*person*] se confier; ¶ **~ [sth] up** ouvrir.

open-air *adj* [*pool, stage*] en plein air.

opener *n* (for bottles) décapsuleur *m*; (for cans) ouvre-boîte *m*.

opening I *n* **1** (start) début *m*; **2** (of exhibition, shop) ouverture *f*; (of play, film) première *f*; **3** (gap) trouée *f*; **4** (opportunity) occasion *f* (**to do** de faire); (in market) débouché *m* (**for** pour); (for job) poste *m*.

II *adj* [*scene, move*] premier/-ière (*before n*); [*remarks*] préliminaire; [*ceremony*] d'inauguration.

opening hours *n pl* heures *fpl* d'ouverture.

open-minded *adj* **to be ~** avoir l'esprit ouvert.

open-plan *adj* [*office*] paysagé/-e.

opera *n* opéra *m*.

opera glasses *n* jumelles *fpl* de théâtre.

opera house *n* opéra *m*.

operate ▶533 I *vtr* **1** faire marcher [*appliance, vehicle*]; **2** pratiquer [*policy, system*]; **3** (manage) gérer.

II *vi* **1** (do business) opérer; **2** (function) marcher; **3** (run) [*service*] fonctionner; **4** (Med) opérer; **to ~ on** opérer [*person*]; **to ~ on sb's leg** opérer qn à la jambe.

operating room (US), **operating theatre** (GB) *n* salle *f* d'opération.

operation *n* **1** (gen, Med) opération *f*; **to have a heart ~** se faire opérer du cœur; **2 to be in ~** [*plan*] être en vigueur; [*machine*] fonctionner; [*oil rig, mine*] être en exploitation.

operative I *n* (worker) employé/-e *m/f*.

II *adj* en vigueur.

operator ▶626 *n* **1** (on telephone) standardiste *mf*; **2** (of radio, computer) opérateur *m*; **3 he's a smooth ~** il sait s'y prendre.

opinion *n* opinion *f* (**about** de), avis *m* (**about, on** sur); **to have a high/low ~ of sb/sth** avoir une bonne/mauvaise opinion de qn/qch; **in my ~** à mon avis.

opinionated *adj* **to be ~** avoir des avis sur tout.

opinion poll *n* sondage *m* d'opinion.

opponent *n* (in contest) adversaire *mf*; (of regime) opposant/-e *m/f* (**of** à).

opportunity *n* occasion *f* (**for** de); **to take the ~ to do** profiter de l'occasion pour faire.

oppose I *vtr* s'opposer à [*plan, bill*]; **to be ~d to sth/to doing** être contre qch/contre l'idée de faire.

II **opposing** *pres p adj* [*party, team*] adverse; [*view, style*] opposé/-e.

III **as opposed to** *phr* par opposition à.

opposite I *n* contraire *m* (**to, of** de).

II *adj* (gen) opposé/-e; [*building*] d'en face; [*page*] ci-contre; [*effect*] inverse; **at ~ ends of** aux deux bouts de [*table, street*].

III *adv* en face; **directly ~** juste en face.

IV *prep* en face de [*building, park, person*].

opposite number *n* (gen) homologue *m*; (Sport) adversaire *mf*.

opposition *n* opposition *f* (**to** à); **the Opposition** (in politics) l'opposition *f*.

oppress *vtr* opprimer [*people, nation*].

oppressive *adj* **1** [*law*] oppressif/-ive; **2** [*heat, atmosphere*] oppressant/-e.

opt *vi* **to ~ for sth** opter pour qch; **to ~ to do** choisir de faire.

■ **opt out** décider de ne pas participer (**of** à).

optical *adj* optique.

optical illusion *n* illusion *f* d'optique.

optician ▶626 *n* (selling glasses) opticien/-ienne *m/f*; (eye specialist) (GB) optométriste *mf*.

optimism *n* optimisme *m*.

optimist *n* optimiste *mf*.

optimistic *adj* optimiste (**about** quant à).

option *n* option *f* (**to do** de faire); **to have the ~ of doing** pouvoir choisir de faire; **I didn't have much ~** je n'avais guère le choix.

optional *adj* facultatif/-ive; **~ extras** accessoires *mpl* en option.

or *conj* **1** (gen) ou; **black ~ white?** noir ou blanc?; **either here ~ at Dave's** soit ici soit chez Dave; **whether he likes it ~ not** que cela lui plaise ou non; **in a week ~ so** dans huit jours environ; **~ should I say** ou bien devrais-je dire; **2** (linking alternatives in the negative) **I can't come today ~ tomorrow** je ne peux venir ni aujourd'hui ni demain; **without food ~ lodgings** sans nourriture ni abri; **3** (otherwise) sinon, autrement.

oral I *n* oral *m*.

II *adj* [*examination, communication, contraceptive*] oral/-e; [*medicine*] par voie orale.

orange ▶438 I *n* **1** (fruit) orange *f*; **2** (colour) orange *m*.

II *adj* orange *inv*.

orange juice *n* jus *m* d'orange.

orbit I *n* orbite *f*.

II *vtr* décrire une orbite autour de [*sun, planet*].

orchard *n* verger *m*.

orchestra *n* orchestre *m*.

orchid *n* orchidée *f*.

ordeal *n* épreuve *f*.

order I *n* **1** (gen) ordre *m*; **in alphabetical ~** dans l'ordre alphabétique; **to restore ~** rétablir l'ordre; **2** (command) ordre *m* (**to do** de faire); **to be under ~s to do** avoir (l')ordre de faire; **3** (in shop, restaurant) commande *f*; **4** (operational state) **in working ~** en état de marche; **to be out of ~** [*phone line*] être en dérangement; [*lift, machine*] être en panne; **5** (all right) **in ~** [*documents*] en règle; **that remark was way out of ~** cette remarque était tout à fait déplacée; **6** (also **religious ~**) ordre *m*.
II *vtr* **1** (command) ordonner; **to ~ sb to do** ordonner à qn de faire; **2** commander [*goods, meal*]; réserver [*taxi*] (**for** pour).
III *vi* [*diner, customer*] commander.
IV **in order that** *phr* (with the same subject) afin de (+ *infinitive*), pour (+ *infinitive*); (when subject of verb changes) afin que (+ *subjunctive*), pour que (+ *subjunctive*).
V **in order to** *phr* pour, afin de.
■ **order about**, **order around**: **to ~ people around** donner des ordres.

order form *n* bon *m* or bulletin *m* de commande.

orderly I *n* (medical) aide-soignant/-e *m/f*.
II *adj* [*queue*] ordonné/-e; [*pattern, row*] régulier/-ière; [*mind, system*] méthodique; [*crowd, demonstration*] calme.

ordinary I *n* **to be out of the ~** sortir de l'ordinaire.
II *adj* **1** (normal) [*family, life, person*] ordinaire; [*clothes*] de tous les jours; **2** (average) [*consumer, family*] moyen/-enne; **3** (uninspiring) quelconque (derogatory).

ore *n* minerai *m*; **iron ~** minerai de fer.

organ ▶ 586 *n* **1** (gen) organe *m*; **2** (Mus) orgue *m*.

organic *adj* [*substance, development*] organique; [*produce, farming*] biologique.

organism *n* organisme *m*.

organization *n* **1** (group) organisation *f*; (government) organisme *m*; (voluntary) association *f*; **2** (arrangement) organisation *f* (**of** de).

organize *vtr* organiser [*event, time, life*]; ranger [*books, papers*].

organizer *n* organisateur/-trice *m/f* (**of** de).

orgy *n* orgie *f*.

orient I *n* **the Orient** l'Orient *m*.
II *vtr* (also **orientate**) orienter (**towards** vers).

oriental *adj* (gen) oriental/-e; [*appearance, eyes*] d'Oriental; [*carpet*] d'Orient.

orienteering ▶ 504 *n* course *f* d'orientation.

origin *n* origine *f*.

original I *n* original *m*.
II *adj* **1** (gen) original/-e; **2** (initial) [*inhabitant, owner*] premier/-ière (*before n*); [*question, site*] originel/-elle.

originality *n* originalité *f*.

originally *adv* **1** (initially) au départ; **2** (in the first place) à l'origine.

originate *vi* [*custom, style, tradition*] voir le jour; [*fire*] se déclarer; **to ~ from** [*goods*] provenir de.

ornament *n* **1** (trinket) bibelot *m*; **2** (ornamentation) ornement *m*.

ornamental *adj* [*plant*] ornemental/-e; [*lake*] d'agrément; [*motif*] décoratif/-ive.

ornate *adj* richement orné/-e.

ornithology *n* ornithologie *f*.

orphan *n* orphelin/-e *m/f*.

orphanage *n* orphelinat *m*.

orthodox *adj* orthodoxe.

orthopaedic (GB), **orthopedic** (US) *adj* orthopédique.

ostentatious *adj* ostentatoire.

osteopath ▶ 626 *n* ostéopathe *mf*.

ostracize *vtr* ostraciser.

ostrich *n* autruche *f*.

other I *adj* autre; **the ~ one** l'autre; **the ~ 25** les 25 autres; **~ people** les autres; **he was going the ~ way** il allait dans la direction opposée; **the ~ day** l'autre jour; **every ~ year** tous les deux ans; **every ~ Saturday** un samedi sur deux.
II *pron* **the ~s** les autres; **~s** (as subject) d'autres; (as object) les autres; **one after the ~** l'un après l'autre; **someone or ~** quelqu'un; **some book or ~** un livre, je ne sais plus lequel; **somehow or ~** d'une manière ou d'une autre.
III **other than** *phr* **~ than that** à part ça; **nobody knows ~ than you** tu es le seul à le savoir.

otherwise I *adv* autrement; **no woman, married or ~** aucune femme, mariée ou non.
II *conj* sinon; **it's quite safe, ~ I wouldn't do it** ce n'est pas dangereux du tout, sinon je ne le ferais pas.

otter *n* loutre *f*.

ouch *excl* aïe!

ought *modal aux* **I ~ to do/to have done** je devrais/j'aurais dû faire; **that ~ to fix it** ça devrait arranger les choses; **oughtn't we to ask?** ne croyez-vous pas que nous devrions demander?; **we ~ to say something** nous devrions dire quelque chose; **someone ~ to have accompanied her** quelqu'un aurait dû l'accompagner.

ounce ▶ 573 *n* once *f* (*= 28.35 g*).

our *det* notre/nos.

■ **Note** In French, determiners agree in gender and number with the noun that follows. So *our* is translated by *notre* + masculine or feminine singular noun (notre chien, notre maison) and *nos* + plural noun (nos enfants).
– When *our* is stressed, *à nous* is added after the noun: OUR house = notre maison à nous.
– For *our* used with parts of the body ▶ 413.

ours *pron*

■ **Note** In French, possessive pronouns reflect the number and gender of the noun they are standing for. Thus *ours* is translated by *le nôtre*, *la nôtre* or *les nôtres* according to what is being referred to.

their children are older than ~ leurs enfants sont plus âgés que les nôtres; **which tickets are ~?** lesquels de ces billets sont les nôtres or à nous?; **a friend of ~** un ami à nous; **the blue car is ~** la voiture bleue est à nous; **it's not ~** ce n'est pas à nous.

ourselves *pron* **1** (reflexive) nous; **we've hurt ~** nous nous sommes fait mal; **2** (emphatic) nous-mêmes; **we did it ~** nous l'avons fait nous-mêmes; **3** (after prepositions) **for ~** pour nous, pour nous-mêmes; **(all) by ~** tout seuls/toutes seules.

out

■ **Note** When *out* is used as an adverb meaning *outside*, it often adds little to the sense of the phrase: *they're out in the garden = they're in the garden*. In such cases *out* will not usually be translated: *ils sont dans le jardin*.

I *adv* **1** (outside) dehors; **to stay ~ in the rain** rester (dehors) sous la pluie; **~ there** dehors; **2 to go** or **walk ~** sortir; **I couldn't find my way ~** je ne trouvais pas la sortie; **when the tide is ~** à marée basse; **further ~** plus loin; **to invite sb ~ to dinner** inviter qn au restaurant; **3** (absent) **to be ~** être sorti/-e; **4 to be ~** [*book, exam results*] être publié/-e; **5 to be ~** [*sun, moon, stars*] briller; **6 to be ~** [*fire, light*] être éteint/-e; **7** (Sport) **to be ~** [*player*] être éliminé/-e; **'~!'** (of ball) 'out!'; **8** (over) **before the week is ~** avant la fin de la semaine; **9**○ **to be ~ to do** être bien décidé/-e à faire; **he's just ~ for what he can get** c'est l'intérêt qui le guide.

II **out of** *phr* **1 to go** or **walk** or **come ~ of** sortir de; **to jump ~ of the window** sauter par la fenêtre; **to take sth ~ of one's bag** prendre qch dans son sac; **2** (expressing ratio) sur; **two ~ of every three** deux sur trois; **3** hors de [*reach, sight*]; en dehors de [*city*]; à l'abri de [*sun*]; **4 to be (right) ~ of** ne plus avoir de [*item*].

IDIOMS **to be ~ of it**○ être dans les vapes○.

outback *n* **the ~** la brousse (australienne).

outbreak *n* (of war) début *m*; (of violence, spots) éruption *f*; (of disease) déclaration *f*.

outbuilding *n* dépendance *f*.

outburst *n* accès *m*.

outcast *n* exclu/-e *m/f*.

outcome *n* résultat *m*.

outcry *n* tollé *m* (**about, against** contre).

outdated *adj* [*idea, practice, theory*] dépassé/-e; [*clothing*] démodé/-e.

outdo *vtr* surpasser.

outdoor *adj* [*life, activity, sport*] de plein air; [*restaurant*] en plein air.

outdoors *adv* [*sit, work, play*] dehors; [*live*] en plein air; [*sleep*] à la belle étoile; **to go ~** sortir.

outer *adj* **1** (outside) extérieur/-e; **2** [*limit*] extrême.

outer space *n* espace *m* (extra-atmosphérique).

outfit *n* tenue *f*.

outgoing *adj* **1** (sociable) ouvert/-e et sociable; **2** [*government*] sortant/-e.

outgoings *n pl* (GB) sorties *fpl* (de fonds).

outgrow *vtr* **1** (grow too big for) devenir trop grand pour; **2** (grow too old for) se lasser de [qch] avec le temps; **he'll ~ it** ça lui passera.

outlast *vtr* durer plus longtemps que.

outlaw I *n* hors-la-loi *m inv*.

II *vtr* déclarer illégal/-e [*practice, organization*].

outlay *n* dépenses *fpl* (**on** en).

outlet *n* **1** (for gas, air, water) tuyau *m* de sortie; **2 retail ~** point *m* de vente; **3** (for emotion, talent) exutoire *m*; **4** (US) (socket) prise *f* de courant.

outline I *n* **1** (silhouette) contour *m*; **2** (of plan, policy) grandes lignes *fpl*; (of essay) plan *m*.

II *vtr* exposer brièvement [*aims, plan, reasons*].

outlive *vtr* survivre à [*person*].

outlook *n* **1** (attitude) vue *f*; **2** (prospects) perspectives *fpl*.

outnumber *vtr* être plus nombreux/-euses que.

out-of-date *adj* [*ticket, passport*] périmé/-e; [*concept*] dépassé/-e.

outpatient *n* malade *mf* externe.

outpost *n* avant-poste *m*.

output *n* (yield) rendement *m*; (of factory) production *f*.

outrage I *n* **1** (anger) indignation *f* (**at** devant); **2** (atrocity) atrocité *f*; **3** (scandal) scandale *m*.

II *vtr* scandaliser [*public*].

outrageous *adj* scandaleux/-euse; [*remark*] outrancier/-ière.

outright I *adj* [*control, majority*] absolu/-e; [*ban*] catégorique; [*victory, winner*] incontesté/-e.

II *adv* (gen) catégoriquement; [*killed*] sur le coup.

outside I *n* **1** extérieur *m*; **on the ~** à l'extérieur; **2** (maximum) **at the ~** au maximum.

II *adj* extérieur/-e; **~ lane** (in GB) voie *f* de droite; (in US, Europe) voie *f* de gauche; (on athletics track) couloir *m* extérieur; **an ~ chance** une faible chance.

III *adv* dehors.

IV *prep* (also **~ of**) **1** en dehors de [*city*]; de l'autre côté de [*boundary*]; à l'extérieur de [*building*]; **2** (in front of) devant [*house, shop*].

outsider *n* **1** (in community) étranger/-ère *m/f*; **2** (Sport) outsider *m*.

outsize *adj* [*clothes*] grande taille.

outskirts *n pl* périphérie *f*.

outspoken *adj* **to be ~** parler sans détour.

outstanding *adj* **1** (praiseworthy) remarquable; **2** (striking) frappant/-e; **3** [*bill*] impayé/-e; [*work*] inachevé/-e; **~ debts** créances *fpl* à recouvrer.

outstretched *adj* [*hand, arm*] tendu/-e; [*wings*] déployé/-e.

outward I *adj* [*appearance, sign*] extérieur/-e; [*calm*] apparent/-e; **~ journey** aller *m*.

II *adv* (also **outwards**) vers l'extérieur.

outwardly *adv* (apparently) en apparence.

outwards = **outward II**.

outweigh *vtr* l'emporter sur.
outwit *vtr* être plus futé/-e que [*person*].
oval *n*, *adj* ovale (*m*).
ovary *n* ovaire *m*.
ovation *n* ovation *f*; **to give sb a standing ~** se lever pour ovationner qn.
oven *n* four *m*.
over

■ **Note** *over* is often used with another preposition in English (*to*, *in*, *on*) without altering the meaning. In this case *over* is usually not translated in French: *to be over in France* = être en France; *to swim over to sb* = nager vers qn.

I *prep* **1** par-dessus; **he jumped ~ it** il a sauté par-dessus; **to wear a sweater ~ one's shirt** porter un pull par-dessus sa chemise; **a bridge ~ the Thames** un pont sur la Tamise; **2** (across) **it's just ~ the road** c'est juste de l'autre côté de la rue; **~ here/there** par ici/là; **come ~ here!** viens (par) ici!; **3** (above) au-dessus de; **they live ~ the shop** ils habitent au-dessus de la boutique; **children ~ six** les enfants de plus de six ans; **temperatures ~ 40°** des températures supérieures à or au-dessus de 40°; **4** (in the course of) **~ the weekend** pendant le week-end; **~ the last few days** au cours de ces derniers jours; **~ the years** avec le temps; **~ Christmas** à Noël; **5 to be ~** s'être remis/-e de [*illness, operation*]; **to be ~ the worst** avoir passé le pire; **6** (by means of) **~ the phone** par téléphone; **~ the radio** à la radio; **7** (everywhere) **all ~ the house** partout dans la maison.
II *adj*, *adv* **1** (finished) **to be ~** [*term, meeting*] être terminé/-e; [*war*] être fini/-e; **2** (more) **children of six and ~** les enfants de plus de six ans; **3 to invite** or **ask sb ~** inviter qn; **we had them ~ on Sunday** ils sont venus dimanche; **4** (on radio, TV) **~ to you** à vous; **now ~ to our Paris studios** nous passons l'antenne à nos studios de Paris; **5** (showing repetition) **five times ~** cinq fois de suite; **to start all ~ again** recommencer à zéro; **I had to do it ~** (US) j'ai dû recommencer; **I've told you ~ and ~ (again)**... je t'ai dit je ne sais combien de fois...
overact *vi* en faire trop.
overall I *n* (GB) (coat-type) blouse *f*; (child's) tablier *m*.
II **overalls** *n pl* (GB) combinaison *f*; (US) salopette *f*.
III *adj* [*cost*] global/-e; [*improvement*] général/-e; [*effect*] d'ensemble; [*majority*] absolu/-e.
IV *adv* **1** (in total) en tout; **2** (in general) dans l'ensemble.
overawe *vtr* intimider.
overboard *adv* par-dessus bord, à l'eau.
overbook *vtr*, *vi* surréserver.
overcast *adj* [*sky*] couvert/-e.
overcharge *vtr* faire payer trop cher à.
overcoat *n* pardessus *m*.
overcome I *vtr* battre [*opponent*]; vaincre [*enemy*]; surmonter [*dislike, fear*]; **to be ~ with despair** succomber au désespoir.
II *vi* triompher.
overcook *vtr* trop cuire.
overcrowded *adj* [*train, room*] bondé/-e; [*city*] surpeuplé/-e; [*class*] surchargé/-e.
overdo *vtr* **to ~ it** (when describing) exagérer; (when performing) forcer la note○; (when working) en faire trop○.
overdose *n* surdose *f*.
overdraft *n* découvert *m*.
overdrawn *adj* à découvert.
overdue *adj* [*baby, work*] en retard (**by** de); [*bill*] impayé/-e; **this measure is long ~** cette mesure aurait dû être prise il y a longtemps.
overeat *vi* manger à l'excès.
overestimate *vtr* surestimer.
overflow I *vtr* [*river*] inonder [*banks*].
II *vi* déborder (**into** dans; **with** de).
overhaul I *n* (of machine) révision *f*; (of system) restructuration *f*.
II *vtr* réviser [*car, machine*]; restructurer [*system*].
overhead I *adj* [*cable, railway*] aérien/-ienne.
II *adv* **1** (in sky) dans le ciel; **2** (above sb's head) au-dessus de ma/sa etc tête.
overhead projector *n* rétroprojecteur *m*.
overheads *n pl* frais *mpl* généraux.
overhear *vtr* entendre par hasard.
overindulge *vi* faire des excès.
overland I *adj* [*route*] terrestre; [*journey*] par route.
II *adv* par route.
overlap *vi* se chevaucher.
overload *vtr* surcharger (**with** de).
overlook *vtr* **1** [*building, window*] donner sur; **2** (miss) ne pas voir [*detail, error*]; **to ~ the fact that** négliger le fait que; **3** (ignore) ignorer [*effect, need*].
overnight I *adj* **1** [*journey, train*] de nuit; [*stop*] pour une nuit; **2** [*success*] immédiat/-e.
II *adv* **1 to stay ~** passer la nuit; **2** [*change, disappear, transform*] du jour au lendemain.
overpopulated *adj* surpeuplé/-e.
overpower *vtr* **1** maîtriser [*thief*]; vaincre [*army*]; **2** [*smell, smoke*] accabler.
overpowering *adj* [*person*] intimidant/-e; [*desire, urge*] irrésistible; [*heat*] accablant/-e; [*smell*] irrespirable.
overrated *adj* [*person, work*] surfait/-e.
overreact *vi* réagir de façon excessive.
overrule *vtr* **to be ~d** [*decision*] être annulé/-e.
overrun *vtr* **1** (invade) envahir [*country, site*]; **2** (exceed) dépasser [*time, budget*].
overseas I *adj* **1** [*student, investor*] étranger/-ère; **2** [*trade, market*] extérieur/-e.
II *adv* à l'étranger.
oversight *n* erreur *f*; **due to an ~** par inadvertance.
oversleep *vi* se réveiller trop tard.
overstep *vtr* dépasser [*bounds*]; **to ~ the mark** aller trop loin.
overt *adj* évident/-e, manifeste.

overtake *vtr, vi* dépasser.
overthrow *vtr* renverser [*government, system*].
overtime I *n* heures *fpl* supplémentaires.
II *adv* **to work ~** [*person*] faire des heures supplémentaires.
overtone *n* sous-entendu *m*, connotation *f*.
overture *n* ouverture *f*.
overturn I *vtr* **1** renverser [*car, chair*]; faire chavirer [*boat*]; **2** faire annuler [*decision, sentence*].
II *vi* [*car, chair*] se renverser; [*boat*] chavirer.
overweight *adj* **1** [*person*] trop gros/grosse; **2** [*suitcase*] être trop lourd/-e.
overwhelm I *vtr* **1** [*wave, avalanche*] submerger; [*enemy*] écraser; **2** [*shame, grief*] accabler.
II **overwhelmed** *pp adj* (with letters, offers, kindness) submergé/-e (**with, by** de); (with shame, work) accablé/-e (**with, by** de); (by sight, experience) ébloui/-e (**by** par).
overwhelming *adj* [*defeat, victory, majority*] écrasant/-e; [*desire*] irrésistible; [*heat, sorrow*] accablant/-e; [*support*] massif/-ive.
overwork *vi* se surmener.
owe *vtr* devoir; **to ~ sth to sb** devoir qch à qn.
owing I *adj* à payer, dû/-e.
II **owing to** *phr* en raison de.
owl *n* hibou *m*; (with tufted ears) chouette *f*.
own I *adj* propre; **her ~ car** sa propre voiture.
II *pron* **my ~** le mien, la mienne; **his/her ~** le sien, la sienne; **he has a room of his ~** il a sa propre chambre or une chambre à lui; **a house of our (very) ~** une maison (bien) à nous.
III *vtr* avoir [*car, house, dog*]; **she ~s three shops** elle est propriétaire de trois magasins; **who ~s that house?** à qui est cette maison?
IDIOMS **to get one's ~ back** se venger (**on sb** de qn); **on one's ~** tout seul/toute seule.
■ **own up** avouer.
owner *n* propriétaire *mf*; **car ~** automobiliste *mf*; **home ~** propriétaire *mf*.
ownership *n* propriété *f*; (of land) possession *f*.
ox *n* bœuf *m*.
oxygen *n* oxygène *m*.
oyster *n* huître *f*.
ozone *n* ozone *m*.
ozone layer *n* couche *f* d'ozone.

Pp

p, **P** *n* p, P *m*.
PA ▶626 *n* (*abbr* = **personal assistant**) secrétaire *mf* de direction.
pace I *n* (step) pas *m*; (rate) rythme *m*; (speed) vitesse *f*; **at a fast/slow ~** vite/lentement; **at walking ~** au pas.
II *vi* **to ~ up and down** faire les cent pas; **to ~ up and down** arpenter [*cage, room*].
pacemaker *n* **1** (Med) stimulateur *m* cardiaque; **2** (athlete) lièvre *m*.
Pacific *pr n* **the ~** le Pacifique; **the ~ Ocean** l'océan Pacifique.
pacifist *n, adj* pacifiste (*mf*).
pacify *vtr* apaiser [*person*]; pacifier [*country*].
pack I *n* **1** (US) (box) paquet *m*; (large box) boîte *f*; (bag) sachet *m*; **2** (group) bande *f*; (of hounds) meute *f*; **a ~ of lies** un tissu de mensonges; **3** (in rugby) pack *m*; **4** (of cards) jeu *m* de cartes; **5** (backpack) sac *m* à dos.
II *vtr* **1** (in suitcase) mettre [qch] dans une valise [*clothes*]; (in box, crate) emballer [*ornaments, books*]; **2** emballer [*box, crate*]; **to ~ one's suitcase** faire sa valise; **3** [*crowd*] remplir complètement [*church, theatre*]; **4** tasser [*snow, earth*].
III *vi* **1** [*person*] faire ses valises; **2 to ~ into** [*crowd*] s'entasser dans [*place*].
■ **pack up**: ¶ **~ up 1** [*person*] faire ses valises; **2**○ (break down) [*TV, machine*] se détraquer○; [*car*] tomber en panne; ¶ **~ [sth] up, ~ up [sth]** (in boxes, crates) emballer.
package I *n* **1** (parcel) paquet *m*, colis *m*; **2** (of proposals, measures, aid) ensemble *m* (**of** de); **3** (Comput) progiciel *m*.
II *vtr* conditionner, emballer.
package deal *n* offre *f* globale.
package holiday (GB), **package tour** *n* voyage *m* organisé.
packaging *n* conditionnement *m*.
packed *adj* comble; **~ with** plein/-e de.
packed lunch *n* panier-repas *m*.
packet *n* (gen) paquet *m*; (sachet) sachet *m*.
packing *n* **1** (packaging) emballage *m*; **2 to do one's ~** faire ses valises.
pact *n* pacte *m*.
pad I *n* **1** (of paper) bloc *m*; **2** (for leg) jambière *f*; **3** (of paw) coussinet *m*; (of finger) pulpe *f*; **4** (also **launch ~**) rampe *f* de lancement.
II *vtr* rembourrer [*chair, shoulders, jacket*] (**with** avec); capitonner [*walls*].
III *vi* **to ~ along/around** avancer/aller et venir à pas feutrés.
■ **pad out** étoffer, délayer [*essay, speech*].
padding *n* (stuffing) rembourrage *m*.
paddle I *n* **1** (oar) pagaie *f*; **2 to go for a ~** faire trempette *f*.
II *vi* **1** (row) pagayer; **2** (wade) patauger; **3** [*duck, swan*] barboter.
paddling pool *n* (public) pataugeoire *f*; (inflatable) piscine *f* gonflable.
padlock I *n* (on door) cadenas *m*; (for bicycle) antivol *m*.
II *vtr* cadenasser [*door, gate*]; mettre un antivol à [*bicycle*].
paediatrician (GB), **pediatrician** (US) ▶626 *n* pédiatre *mf*.
pagan *n, adj* païen/païenne (*m/f*).
page I *n* **1** (in book) page *f*; **on ~ two** à la page deux; **2** (attendant) groom *m*; (US) coursier *m*.
II *vtr* (on pager) rechercher; (over loudspeaker) faire appeler.
pageant *n* (play) reconstitution *f* historique; (carnival) fête *f* à thème historique.
pageboy *n* (at wedding) garçon *m* d'honneur.
pager *n* récepteur *m* d'appel.
paid *adj* [*work, job*] rémunéré/-e; [*holiday*] payé/-e; **~ assassin** tueur *m* à gages.
pain I *n* **1** douleur *f*; **to be in ~** souffrir; **period ~s** règles *fpl* douloureuses; **2**○ (annoying person, thing) **he's/it's a ~** il est/c'est enquiquinant○; **he's a ~ in the neck**○ il est casse-pieds○.
II **pains** *n pl* **to be at ~s to do** prendre grand soin de faire; **to take great ~s over** or **with sth** se donner beaucoup de mal pour qch.
painful *adj* douloureux/-euse; [*lesson, memory*] pénible.
painkiller *n* analgésique *m*.
painless *adj* **1** (pain-free) indolore; **2** (trouble-free) sans peine.
painstaking *adj* minutieux/-ieuse.
paint I *n* peinture *f*.
II **paints** *n pl* couleurs *fpl*.
III *vtr* **1** (gen) peindre; peindre le portrait de [*person*]; **to ~ one's nails** se vernir les ongles; **2** (depict) dépeindre.
IV *vi* peindre.
paintbox *n* boîte *f* de couleurs.
paintbrush *n* pinceau *m*.
painter ▶626 *n* peintre *m*.
painting *n* **1** (activity, art form) peinture *f*; **2** (work of art) tableau *m*; (unframed) toile *f*; (of person) portrait *m*; **3** (decorating) peintures *fpl*.
pair *n* **1** (gen) paire *f*; **to be one of a ~** faire partie d'une paire; **in ~s** [*work*] en groupes de deux;**a ~ of scissors** une paire de ciseaux; **a ~ of trousers** un pantalon; **2** (couple) couple *m*.
■ **pair up** [*dancers, lovers*] former un couple; [*competitors*] faire équipe.
paisley *n* tissu *m* à motifs cachemire.
pajamas (US) = **pyjamas**.
Pakistan ▶448 *pr n* Pakistan *m*.
Pakistani ▶553 I *n* Pakistanais/-e *m/f*.

II *adj* pakistanais/-e.

palace *n* palais *m*.

palatable *n* [*food*] savoureux/-euse; [*solution, idea*] acceptable.

palate *n* palais *m*.

pale I *adj* (gen) pâle; [*light, dawn*] blafard/-e; **to turn** or **go ~** pâlir.
II *vi* pâlir; **to ~ into insignificance** devenir dérisoire.

Palestine ▶448 *pr n* Palestine *f*.

Palestinian ▶553 I *n* Palestinien/-ienne *m/f*.
II *adj* palestinien/-ienne.

palette *n* palette *f*.

pallet *n* (for loading) palette *f*.

pallid *adj* [*skin, light*] blafard/-e.

palm *n* **1** paume *f*; **in the ~ of one's hand** dans le creux de la main; **he read my ~** il m'a lu les lignes de la main; **2** (also **~ tree**) palmier *m*; **3** (also **~ leaf**) palme *f*.
■ **palm off**○: **to ~ sth off** faire passer qch (**as** pour); **to ~ sth off on sb, to ~ sb off with sth** refiler○ qch à qn.

Palm Sunday *n* dimanche *m* des Rameaux.

palpable *adj* [*fear, tension*] palpable; [*lie, error, nonsense*] manifeste.

palpitate *vi* palpiter (**with** de).

paltry *adj* [*sum*] dérisoire; [*excuse*] piètre (*before n*).

pamper *vtr* choyer [*person, pet*].

pamphlet *n* brochure *f*; (political) tract *m*.

pan I *n* (saucepan) casserole *f*.
II *vtr* **1**○ (criticize) éreinter; **2** (in photography) faire un panoramique de.

pancake *n* crêpe *f*.

pancake day *n* mardi *m* gras.

pandemonium *n* tohu-bohu *m*.

pander *vi* **to ~ to** céder aux exigences de [*person*]; flatter [*whim*].

pane *n* vitre *f*, carreau *m*; **a ~ of glass** une vitre, un carreau.

panel *n* **1** (of experts, judges) commission *f*; (on discussion programme) invités *mpl*; (on quiz show) jury *m*; **2** (section of wall) panneau *m*; **3** (of instruments, switches) tableau *m*.

pang *n* **1** (emotional) serrement *m* de cœur; **a ~ of jealousy** une pointe de jalousie; **2 ~s of hunger** crampes *fpl* d'estomac.

panhandler○ *n* (US) mendiant/-e *m/f*.

panic I *n* panique *f*, affolement *m*.
II *vtr* affoler [*person, animal*]; semer la panique dans [*crowd*].
III *vi* s'affoler.

panic-stricken *adj* pris/-e de panique.

panorama *n* panorama *m*.

pansy *n* pensée *f*.

pant *vi* haleter.

panther *n* **1** (leopard) panthère *f*; **2** (US) (puma) puma *m*.

pantomime *n* (GB) spectacle *m* pour enfants.

pantry *n* garde-manger *m inv*.

pants *n pl* **1** (US) (trousers) pantalon *m*; **2** (GB) (underwear) slip *m*.

panty hose *n* (US) collant *m*.

panty-liner *n* protège-slip *m*.

paper I *n* **1** (for writing, drawing) papier *m*; **a piece of ~** (scrap) un bout de papier; (clean sheet) une feuille (de papier); (for wrapping) un morceau de papier; **writing/tissue ~** papier à lettres/de soie; **2** (also **wall~**) papier *m* peint; **3** (newspaper) journal *m*; **4** article *m* (**on** sur); (lecture) communication *f* (**on** sur); **5** (exam) épreuve *f* (**on** de).
II **papers** *n pl* (documents) papiers *mpl*.
III *adj* [*bag, hat, handkerchief, napkin*] en papier; [*plate, cup*] en carton.
IV *vtr* tapisser [*room, wall*].

paperback *n* livre *m* de poche.

paperclip *n* trombone *m*.

paper knife *n* coupe-papier *m inv*.

paper shop *n* marchand *m* de journaux.

paper towel *n* essuie-tout *m inv*.

paperweight *n* presse-papier *m inv*.

paperwork *n* (administration) travail *m* administratif; (documentation) documents *mpl*.

par *n* **1 to be on a ~ with** [*performance*] être comparable à; [*person*] être l'égal/-e de; **to be up to ~** être à la hauteur; **to be below** or **under ~** [*performance*] être en dessous de la moyenne; [*person*] ne pas se sentir en forme; **2** (in golf) par *m*.

parachute I *n* parachute *m*.
II *vi* descendre en parachute.

parachute drop *n* parachutage *m*.

parachute jump *n* saut *m* en parachute.

parachuting ▶504 *n* parachutisme *m*.

parade I *n* **1** (procession) parade *f*; **2** (Mil) défilé *m*.
II *vtr* (display) faire étalage de.
III *vi* défiler (**through** dans); **to ~ up and down** [*soldier, model*] défiler; [*child*] parader.

parade ground *n* champ *m* de manœuvres.

paradise *n* paradis *m*; **in ~** au paradis.

paradox *n* paradoxe *m*.

paradoxical *adj* paradoxal/-e.

paraffin *n* **1** (GB) (fuel) pétrole *m*; **2** (also **~ wax**) paraffine *f*.

paragliding ▶504 *n* parapente *m*.

paragon *n* modèle *m* (**of** de).

paragraph *n* paragraphe *m*.

parallel I *n* **1** (gen) parallèle *m*; **2** (in mathematics) parallèle *f*.
II *adj* **1** (gen) parallèle (**to, with** à); **2** (similar) analogue (**to, with** à).
III *adv* **~ to, ~ with** parallèlement à.

paralyse (GB), **paralyze** (US) *vtr* paralyser.

paralysis *n* paralysie *f*.

paramedic ▶626 *n* auxiliaire *mf* médical/-e.

parameter *n* paramètre *m*.

paramount *adj* **to be ~, to be of ~ importance** être d'une importance capitale.

paranoid *adj* (Med) paranoïde; (gen) paranoïaque (**about** au sujet de).

paraphernalia *n* attirail *m*.

paraphrase *vtr* paraphraser.

parasite *n* parasite *m*.

paratrooper *n* parachutiste *m*.

parcel *n* paquet *m*, colis *m*.
IDIOMS **to be part and ~ of** faire partie intégrante de.

parcel bomb *n* colis *m* piégé.

parched *adj* **1** (dry) desséché/-e; **2** (thirsty) **to be ~** mourir de soif.

parchment *n* (document) parchemin *m*; (paper) papier-parchemin *m*.

pardon I *n* **1** (gen) pardon *m*; **2** (Law) (also **free ~**) grâce *f*.
II *excl* (what?) pardon?; (sorry!) pardon!
III *vtr* **1** (gen) pardonner; **~ me!** pardon!; **2** (Law) grâcier [*criminal*].

parent *n* parent *m*.

parental *adj* des parents, parental/-e.

parent company *n* maison *f* mère.

parenthood *n* (fatherhood) paternité *f*; (motherhood) maternité *f*.

Paris ▶ 448 *pr n* Paris.

parish *n* **1** paroisse *f*; **2** (GB) (administrative) commune *f*.

Parisian I *n* Parisien/-ienne *m/f*.
II *adj* parisien/-ienne.

park I *n* **1** (public garden) jardin *m* public, parc *m*; **2** (estate) parc *m*.
II *vtr* garer [*car*].
III *vi* [*driver*] se garer.

parking *n* stationnement *m*; **'No ~'** 'stationnement interdit'.

parking lot *n* (US) parking *m*.

parking meter *n* parcmètre *m*.

parking place, **parking space** *n* place *f*.

parking ticket *n* (fine) contravention *f*, PV○ *m*.

parliament *n* parlement *m*.

parliamentary *adj* parlementaire.

parlour †(GB), **parlor** (US) *n* petit salon *m*.

parody I *n* parodie *f*.
II *vtr* parodier [*person, style*].

parole *n* liberté *f* conditionnelle; **on ~** en liberté conditionnelle.

parrot *n* perroquet *m*.

parry *vtr* **1** (Sport) parer; **2** éluder [*question*].

parsley *n* persil *m*.

parsnip *n* panais *m*.

part I *n* **1** (of whole) partie *f*; (of country) région *f*; **to be (a) ~ of** faire partie de; **that's the best/hardest ~** c'est ça le meilleur/le plus dur; **for the most ~** dans l'ensemble; **2** (Tech) (component) pièce *f*; **spare ~s** pièces détachées; **3** (of serial) épisode *m*; **4** (role) rôle *m* (**in** dans); **to take ~** participer (**in** à); **5** (actor's role) rôle *m* (**of** de); **6** (measure) mesure *f*; **7** (behalf) **on the ~ of** de la part de; **for my ~** pour ma part; **8** (US) (in hair) raie *f*.
II *adv* en partie; **~ French, ~ Chinese** moitié français, moitié Chinois.
III *vtr* séparer [*two people*]; écarter [*legs*]; entrouvrir [*lips, curtains*]; **to ~ one's hair** se faire une raie.
IV *vi* **1** (split up) se séparer; **to ~ from sb** quitter qn; **2** [*crowd, clouds*] s'ouvrir.
■ **part with** se séparer de [*object*]; **to ~ with money** débourser.

part exchange *n* (GB) reprise *f*; **to take sth in ~** reprendre qch.

partial *adj* **1** (not complete) partiel/-ielle; **2** (biased) partial/-e; **3** (fond) **to be ~ to** avoir un faible pour.

participant *n* participant/-e *m/f* (**in** à).

participate *vi* participer (**in** à).

participle *n* participe *m*.

particle *n* particule *f*.

particular I *adj* **1** (gen) particulier/-ière; **for no ~ reason** sans raison particulière; **2** (fussy) méticuleux/-euse; **to be ~ about** être exigeant/-e sur [*cleanliness, punctuality*]; prendre grand soin de [*appearance*]; être difficile pour [*food*].
II **in particular** *phr* en particulier.

particularly *adv* **1** (in particular) en particulier; **2** (especially) spécialement.

particulars *n pl* (information) détails *mpl*; (name, address) coordonnées *fpl*.

parting *n* **1** séparation *f*; **2** (GB) (in hair) raie *f*.

partisan *n* (gen, Mil) partisan *m*.

partition I *n* **1** (in room, house) cloison *f*; **2** (of country) partition *f*.
II *vtr* **1** cloisonner [*area, room*]; **2** diviser [*country*].

partly *adv* en partie.

partner *n* **1** (professional) associé/-e *m/f* (**in** dans); **2** (economic, political, sporting) partenaire *m*; **3** (married) époux/-se *m/f*; (unmarried) partenaire *mf*.

partnership *n* association *f*; **to go into ~ with** s'associer à.

part-time *adj*, *adv* à temps partiel.

party *n* **1** (social event) fête *f*; (in evening) soirée *f*; (formal) réception *f*; **to have a ~** faire une fête; **birthday ~** (fête d')anniversaire *m*; **children's ~** goûter *m* d'enfants; **2** (group) groupe *m*; (Mil) détachement *m*; **rescue ~** équipe *f* de secouristes; **3** (in politics) parti *m*; **4** (Law) partie *f*.

party line *n* **1 the ~** la ligne du parti; **2** (phone line) ligne *f* commune.

pass I *n* **1** (permit) laisser-passer *m inv*; (for journalists) coupe-file *m inv*; **travel ~** carte *f* d'abonnement; **2** (Sch, Univ) (in exam) moyenne *f* (**in** en); **to get a ~** être reçu/-e; **3** (Sport) (in ball games) passe *f*; (in fencing) botte *f*; **4** (in mountains) col *m*.
II *vtr* **1** (gen) passer [*plate, ball, time*]; **2** passer [*checkpoint, customs*]; passer devant [*building, area*]; dépasser [*vehicle, level, expectation*]; **to ~ sb in the street** croiser qn dans la rue; **3** [*person*] réussir [*test, exam*]; [*car, machine*] passer [qch] (avec succès) [*test*]; **4** adopter [*bill, motion*]; **5** admettre [*candidate*]; **6** prononcer [*sentence*].
III *vi* (gen) passer; (in exam) réussir.
IDIOMS **to make a ~ at sb** faire du plat○ à qn.

■ **pass around**, **pass round** faire circuler [*document, photos*]; faire passer [*food, plates*].
■ **pass away** décéder.
■ **pass by** [*procession*] défiler; [*person*] passer.
■ **pass down** transmettre (**from** de; **to** à).
■ **pass off** faire passer [*person, incident*] (**as** pour).
■ **pass on** transmettre [*condolences, message*]; passer [*clothes, cold*] (**to** à).
■ **pass out** (faint) perdre connaissance; (fall drunk) tomber ivre mort.
■ **pass through** traverser.

passable *adj* **1** [*standard, quality*] passable; [*knowledge, performance*] assez bon/bonne; **2** [*road*] praticable; [*river*] franchissable.

passage *n* **1** (gen) passage; **2** (also **~way**) (indoors) corridor *m*; **3** (journey) traversée *f*.

passenger *n* (in car, plane, ship) passager/-ère *m/f*; (in train, bus, on underground) voyageur/-euse *m/f*.

passerby *n* passant/-e *m/f*.

passing *adj* **1** [*motorist, policeman*] qui passe/qui passait; **2** [*whim*] passager/-ère; **3** [*reference*] en passant *inv*; **4** [*resemblance*] vague (*before n*).

passion *n* passion *f*.

passionate *adj* passionné/-e.

passive I *n* **the ~** le passif, la voix passive.
II *adj* passif/-ive.

Passover *n* Pâque *f* juive.

passport *n* passeport *m*.

password *n* mot *m* de passe.

past

■ **Note** For a full set of translations for *past* used in clocktime, consult the Usage Note ▶ 434.

I *n* passé *m*; **in the ~** dans le passé.
II *adj* **1** (preceding) [*weeks, months*] dernier/-ière (*before n*); **in the ~ two years** dans les deux dernières années; **during the ~ few days** ces derniers jours; **2** (former) [*times, problems, experience*] passé/-e; [*president*] ancien/-ienne (*before n*); [*government*] précédent/-e; **in times ~** autrefois, jadis; **3 summer is ~** l'été est fini; **that's all ~** c'est du passé.
III *prep* **1 to walk** or **go ~ sb/sth** passer devant qn/qch; **to drive ~ sth** passer devant qch (en voiture); **2** (in time) **it's ~ 6** il est 6 heures passées; **twenty ~ two** deux heures vingt; **half ~ two** deux heures et demie; **he is ~ 70** il a 70 ans passés; **3** (beyond) après; **~ the church** après l'église; **to be ~ caring** ne plus s'en faire.
IV *adv* **to go** or **walk ~** passer.
IDIOMS **to be ~ it**○ avoir passé l'âge; **to be ~ its best** [*food*] être un peu avancé/-e; [*wine*] être un peu éventé/-e; **I wouldn't put it ~ him** (**to do**) ça ne m'étonnerait pas de lui (qu'il fasse).

pasta *n* pâtes *fpl* (alimentaires).

paste I *n* **1** (glue) colle *f*; **2** (mixture) pâte *f*; **3** (Culin) (fish, meat) pâté *m*; (vegetable) purée *f*.
II *vtr* coller (**onto** sur; **into** dans; **together** ensemble).

pastel I *n* pastel *m*.
II *adj* [*colour, pink, shade*] pastel *inv*.

pasteurize *vtr* pasteuriser.

pastime *n* passe-temps *m inv*.

pastor ▶ 626 *n* pasteur *m*.

pastrami *n* bœuf *m* fumé.

pastry *n* **1** (mixture) pâte *f*; **2** (cake) pâtisserie *f*.

past tense *n* passé *m*.

pasture *n* pré *m*, pâturage *m*.

pat I *n* **1** (gentle tap) petite tape *f*; **2** (of butter) noix *f*.
II *vtr* tapoter [*hand*]; caresser [*dog*].
IDIOMS **to have sth off** (GB) or **down ~** connaître qch par cœur.

patch I *n* **1** (in clothes) pièce *f*; (on tyre) rustine® *f*; (on eye) bandeau *m*; **2** (of snow, ice) plaque *f*; (of damp, rust, sunlight) tache *f*; (of fog) nappe *f*; (of blue sky) coin *m*; **3** (area of ground) zone *f*; (for planting) carré *m*; **a ~ of grass** un coin d'herbe; **4**○ (GB) (territory) territoire *m*; **5**○ (period) période *f*.
II *vtr* rapiécer [*hole, trousers*]; réparer [*tyre*].

paté *n* pâté *m*; **salmon ~** terrine *f* de saumon.

patent I *n* brevet *m* (**for, on** pour).
II *adj* (obvious) manifeste.
III *vtr* faire breveter.

patent leather *n* (cuir *m*) verni *m*.

paternal *adj* paternel/-elle.

path *n* **1** (track) (also **~way**) chemin *m*; (narrower) sentier *m*; (in garden) allée *f*; **2** (course) (of projectile, vehicle, sun) trajectoire *f*; (of river) cours *m*; (of hurricane) itinéraire *m*; **3** (option) voie *f*.

pathetic *adj* **1** (moving) pathétique; **2** (inadequate) misérable; **3**○ (awful) lamentable.

pathological *adj* [*fear, hatred*] pathologique; [*jealousy*] maladif/ive.

pathology *n* pathologie *f*.

patience ▶ 504 *n* **1** patience *f* (**with** avec); **2** (card game) réussite *f*.

patient I *n* patient/-e *m/f*.
II *adj* patient (**with** avec).

patiently *adv* avec patience, patiemment.

patio *n* **1** (terrace) terrasse *f*; **2** (courtyard) patio *m*.

patriotic *adj* [*mood, song*] patriotique; [*person*] patriote.

patrol I *n* patrouille *f*.
II *vtr, vi* patrouiller.

patrol boat, **patrol vessel** *n* patrouilleur *m*.

patrol car *n* voiture *f* de police.

patron *n* **1** (of artist) mécène *m*; (of person) protecteur/-trice *m/f*; (of charity) bienfaiteur/-trice *m/f*; **2** (client) client/-e *m/f* (**of** de).

patronize *vtr* **1** traiter [qn] avec condescendance [*person*]; **2** fréquenter [*restaurant, cinema*].

patronizing *adj* condescendant/-e.

patron saint *n* saint/-e *m/f* patron/-onne.

patter I *n* **1** (of rain) crépitement *m*; **~ of footsteps** bruit *m* de pas rapides et légers; **2** (talk) baratin *m*.
II *vi* [*child, mouse*] trottiner; [*rain*] crépiter.

pattern *n* **1** (design) dessin *m*, motif *m*; **2** (of behaviour) mode *m*; **weather ~s** tendances *fpl* climatiques; **3** (in dressmaking) patron *m*; (in knitting) modèle *m*; **4** (model, example) modèle *m*.

patterned *adj* [*fabric*] à motifs.

pauper *n* indigent/-e *m/f*.

pause I *n* **1** (silence) silence *m*; **2** (break) pause *f*; **3** (stoppage) interruption *f*.
II *vi* **1** (stop speaking) marquer une pause; **2** (stop) s'arrêter; **to ~ in** interrompre [*activity*]; **to ~ for thought** faire une pause pour réfléchir; **3** (hesitate) hésiter.

pave *vtr* paver (**with** de); **to ~ the way for sb/sth** ouvrir la voie à qn/qch.

pavement *n* **1** (GB) (footpath) trottoir *m*; **2** (US) (roadway) chaussée *f*.

pavilion *n* pavillon *m*.

paving slab, **paving stone** *n* dalle *f*.

paw I *n* patte *f*.
II *vtr* **to ~ the ground** [*horse*] piaffer; [*bull*] frapper le sol du sabot.

pawn I *n* pion *m*.
II *vtr* mettre [qch] au mont-de-piété.

pawnbroker ▶626 *n* prêteur/-euse *m/f* sur gages.

pawnshop *n* mont-de-piété *m*.

pay I *n* salaire *m*.
II *vtr* **1** payer (**for** pour); **to ~ cash** payer comptant; **to ~ sth into** verser qch sur [*account*]; **all expenses paid** tous frais payés; **2** [*account*] rapporter [*interest*]; **3** (give) **to ~ attention to** faire attention à; **to ~ a tribute to sb** rendre hommage à qn; **to ~ sb a compliment** faire des compliments à qn; **to ~ sb a visit** rendre visite à qn; **4** (benefit) **it would ~ him to do** il y gagnerait à faire; **it doesn't ~ to do** cela ne sert à rien de faire.
IV *vi* **1** [*person*] payer; **to ~ for sth** payer qch; **you have to ~ to get in** l'entrée est payante; **to ~ one's own way** payer sa part; **the work doesn't ~ very well** le travail est mal payé; **2** [*business*] rapporter; [*activity*] payer; **to ~ for itself** [*business, purchase*] s'amortir.
■ **pay back** rembourser [*person, money*].
■ **pay in** (GB) déposer [*cheque, sum*].
■ **pay off**: ¶ **~ off** être payant/-e; ¶ **~ [sb] off 1** (dismiss) congédier [*worker*]; **2** (bribe) acheter le silence de [*person*]; ¶ **~ [sth] off** rembourser [*debt*].
■ **pay up**○ payer.

payable *adj* **1** (gen) payable; **2 to make a cheque ~ to** faire un chèque à l'ordre de.

pay cheque (GB), **pay check** (US) *n* chèque *m* de paie.

payday *n* jour *m* de paie.

payee *n* bénéficiaire *mf*.

payment *n* (gen) paiement *m*; (in settlement) règlement *m*; (into account, of instalments) versement *m*; **monthly ~** mensualité.

pay phone *n* téléphone *m* public.

payslip *n* bulletin *m* de salaire.

pc, **PC** *n* (*abbr* = **personal computer**) ordinateur *m* (personnel), PC *m*.

PE *n* (*abbr* = **physical education**) éducation *f* physique.

pea *n* pois *m*.

peace *n* paix *f*; **to keep the ~** (between countries, individuals) maintenir la paix; (in town) [*police*] maintenir l'ordre public; **I need a bit of ~ and quiet** j'ai besoin d'un peu de calme; **to find ~ of mind** trouver la paix.

peaceful *adj* **1** (tranquil) paisible; **2** (without conflict) pacifique.

peacefully *adv* **1** [*sleep*] paisiblement; **2** (without violence) pacifiquement.

peacetime *n* temps *m* de paix.

peach *n* pêche *f*.

peacock *n* paon *m*.

peak I *n* **1** (of mountain) pic *m* (**of** de); **2** (of cap) visière *f*; **3** (of inflation, demand, price) maximum *m* (**in** dans; **of** de); (on a graph) sommet *m*; **4** (of career, empire) apogée *m* (**of** de); (of fitness, form) meilleur *m* (**of** de); **in the ~ of condition** en excellente santé; **to be past its** or **one's ~** avoir fait son temps.
II *adj* [*figure, level, price*] maximum; [*fitness*] meilleur/-e.
III *vi* culminer (**at** à).

peaked *adj* **1** [*cap, hat*] à visière; [*roof*] pointu/-e; **2** (US) pâlot/-otte.

peak period *n* période *f* de pointe.

peak rate *n* (for phone calls) tarif *m* rouge.

peak time *n* (on TV) heures *fpl* de grande écoute; (for switchboard, traffic) heures *fpl* de pointe.

peaky○ *adj* pâlot/-otte.

peal *n* (of bells) carillonnement *m*; (of thunder) grondement *m*; **~s of laughter** éclats *mpl* de rire.

peanut *n* (nut) cacahuète *f*; (plant) arachide *f*.

pear *n* poire *f*.

pearl ▶438 I *n* perle *f*.
II *adj* [*necklace, brooch*] de perles; [*button*] en nacre.

pear tree *n* poirier *m*.

peasant *n* paysan/-anne *m/f*.

peat *n* tourbe *f*.

pebble *n* caillou *m*; (on beach) galet *m*.

pecan *n* noix *f* de pecan.

peck I *n* **1** (from bird) coup *m* de bec; **2**○ **to give sb a ~ (on the cheek)** faire une bise à qn.
II *vtr* [*bird*] picorer [*food*]; donner un coup de bec à [*person, animal*].
III *vi* **1** [*bird*] **to ~ at** picorer [*food*]; **2**○ **to ~ at one's food** [*person*] chipoter.

pecking order *n* ordre *m* hiérarchique.

pectorals *n pl* (also **pecs**○) pectoraux *mpl*.

peculiar *adj* **1** (odd) bizarre; **2 to be ~ to** être particulier/-ière à or propre à.

peculiarity *n* **1** (feature) particularité *f*; **2** (strangeness) bizarrerie *f*.

pedal I *n* pédale *f*.
II *vi* pédaler.

pedal bin *n* (GB) poubelle *f* à pédale.

pedal boat *n* pédalo® *m*.

pedantic *adj* pédant/-e.

peddle *vtr* colporter [*wares, ideas*]; **to ~ drugs** revendre de la drogue.

pedestal *n* socle *m*, piédestal *m*; **to put sb on a ~** mettre qn sur un piédestal.

pedestrian *n* piéton *m*.

pedestrian crossing *n* passage *m* pour piétons, passage *m* clouté.

pedestrian precinct *n* (GB) zone *f* piétonne.

pediatrician (US) = **paediatrician**.

pedigree I *n* **1** (of animal) pedigree *m*; (of person) ascendance *f*; **2** (purebred animal) animal *m* avec pedigree.
II *adj* [*animal*] de pure race.

pee° *n* pipi° *m*; **to have a ~** faire pipi°.

peek *n* **to have a ~ at** jeter un coup d'œil furtif à.

peel I *n* (gen) peau *f*; (of citrus fruit) écorce *f*; (of onion) pelure *f*; (peelings) épluchures *fpl*.
II *vtr* éplucher [*vegetable, fruit*]; décortiquer [*prawn*]; écorcer [*stick*].
III *vi* [*skin*] peler; [*fruit, vegetable*] s'éplucher.
■ **peel off**: ¶ **~ off** [*label*] se détacher; [*paint*] s'écailler; [*paper*] se décoller; ¶ **~ [sth] off** enlever [*clothing, label*].

peelings *n pl* épluchures *fpl*.

peep I *n* **to have a ~ at sth** jeter un coup d'œil à qch; (furtively) regarder qch à la dérobée.
II *vi* **1** jeter un coup d'œil (**over** par-dessus; **through** par); **to ~ at sb/sth** jeter un coup d'œil à qn/qch; (furtively) regarder qn/qch furtivement; **2** [*chick*] pépier.

peephole *n* (in fence) trou *m*; (in door) judas *m*.

peer I *n* **1** (equal) (in status) pair *m*; (in profession) collègue *m/f*; **2** (contemporary) (adult) personne *f* de la même génération; (child) enfant *mf* du même âge; **3** (GB) (also **~ of the realm**) pair *m*.
II *vi* **to ~ at** scruter, regarder attentivement.

peer group *n* **1** (of same status) pairs *mpl*; **2** (contemporaries) (adults) personnes *fpl* de la même génération; (children) enfants *mpl* du même âge.

peg *n* **1** (hook) patère *f*; **2** (GB) (also **clothes ~**) pince *f* à linge; **3** (of tent) piquet *m*; **4** (in carpentry) cheville *f*.

pejorative *adj* péjoratif/-ive.

Peking ▶ **448** *pr n* Pékin.

pelican *n* pélican *m*.

pellet *n* **1** (of paper, wax, mud) boulette *f*; **2** (of shot) plomb *m*.

pelmet *n* cantonnière *f*.

pelt I *n* (fur) fourrure *f*; (hide) peau *f*.
II *vtr* bombarder (**with sth** de qch).
III *vi* **1** (also **~ down**) [*rain*] tomber à verse; **2** (run) **to ~ along** courir à toutes jambes.

pelvis ▶ **413** *n* bassin *m*, pelvis *m*.

pen *n* **1** (for writing) stylo *m*; **2** (for animals) parc *m*, enclos *m*.

penal *n* [*law, code, system*] pénal/-e; [*colony, institution*] pénitentiaire.

penalize *vtr* pénaliser.

penalty *n* **1** (punishment) peine *f*, pénalité *f*; (fine) amende *f*; **2** (figurative) prix *m* (**for** de); **3** (in soccer) penalty *m*; (in rugby) pénalité *f*.

pence (GB) ▶ **penny**.

pencil *n* crayon *m*; **in ~** au crayon.

pencil sharpener *n* taille-crayon *m*.

pendant *n* (on necklace) pendentif *m*.

pending I *adj* **1** [*case*] en instance; [*matter*] en souffrance; **2** (imminent) imminent/-e.
II *prep* en attendant.

pendulum *n* pendule *m*, balancier *m*.

penetrate *vtr* pénétrer; percer [*cloud, silence, defences*]; traverser [*wall*]; [*spy*] infiltrer [*organization*].

penetrating *adj* [*cold, eyes, question*] pénétrant/-e; [*sound, voice*] perçant/-e.

pen friend *n* correspondant/-e *m/f*.

penguin *n* pingouin *m*, manchot *m*.

penicillin *n* pénicilline *f*.

peninsula *n* péninsule *f*.

penis *n* pénis *m*.

penitent *n, adj* pénitent/-e (*m/f*).

penitentiary *n* (US) prison *f*.

penknife *n* canif *m*.

pennant *n* **1** (flag) fanion *m*; (on boat) flamme *f*; **2** (US Sport) championnat *m*.

penny *n* **1** (GB) penny *m*; **a five pence** or **five p piece** une pièce de cinq pence; **a 25p stamp** un timbre-poste à 25 pence; **2** (US) cent *m*.
IDIOMS **the ~ dropped**° ça a fait tilt°; **not to have a ~ to one's name** être sans le sou.

pension *n* (from state) pension *f*; (from employer) retraite *f*.

pensioner *n* retraité/-e *m/f*.

pentagon *n* **1** pentagone *m*; **2 the Pentagon** (US) le Pentagone *m*.

Pentecost *n* Pentecôte *f*.

penthouse *n* appartement *m* de grand standing.

pent-up *adj* [*energy, frustration*] contenu/-e; [*feelings*] réprimé/-e.

penultimate *adj* avant-dernier/-ière.

people I *n* (nation) peuple *m*.
II *n pl* **1** (in general) gens *mpl*; (specified or counted) personnes *fpl*; **old ~** les personnes âgées; **they're nice ~** ce sont des gens sympathiques; **there were a lot of ~** il y avait beaucoup de monde; **other ~'s property** le bien des autres; **2** (of a town) habitants *mpl*; (of a country) peuple *m*; **3** (citizens) **the ~** le peuple.

■ **Note** *gens* is masculine plural and never countable. When counting people, you must use *personnes* rather than *gens*: *three people* = trois personnes.
– When used with *gens*, some adjectives such as *vieux*, *bon*, *mauvais*, *petit*, *vilain* placed before *gens* take the feminine form: *les vieilles gens*.

---

pep *v* ■ **pep up** remettre [qn] d'aplomb [*person*]; animer [*party, team*].

pepper *n* **1** (spice) poivre *m*; **2** (vegetable) poivron *m*.

peppercorn *n* grain *m* de poivre.

pepper mill *n* moulin *m* à poivre.

peppermint *n* **1** (sweet) pastille *f* de menthe; **2** (plant) menthe *f* poivrée.

pepper pot, **pepper shaker** *n* poivrier *m*.
pep talk○ *n* laïus○ *m* d'encouragement.
per *prep* par; **~ annum** par an; **~ head** par tête or personne; **80 km ~ hour** 80 km à l'heure; **£5 ~ hour** 5 livres (de) l'heure; **as ~ your instructions** conformément à vos instructions.
per capita *adj*, *adv* par personne.
perceive *vtr* percevoir.
per cent *n*, *adv* pour cent (*m*).
percentage *n* pourcentage *m*.
perceptible *adj* perceptible (**to** à).
perception *n* **1** (by senses) perception *f*; **2** (view) **my ~ of him** l'idée que je me fais de lui; **3** (insight) perspicacité *f*.
perceptive *adj* [*person*] perspicace; [*analysis*] fin/-e; [*article*] intelligent/-e.
perch I *n* **1** (gen) perchoir *m*; **2** (fish) perche *f*.
II *vi* se percher (**on** sur).
percolator *n* cafetière *f* à pression.
percussion *n* (Mus) percussions *fpl*.
perennial *adj* **1** perpétuel/-elle; **2** [*plant*] vivace.
perfect I *n* parfait *m*; **in the ~** au parfait.
II *adj* (gen) parfait/-e (**for** pour); [*moment, name, place, partner, solution*] idéal/-e (**for** pour); [*hostess*] exemplaire.
III *vtr* perfectionner.
perfection *n* perfection *f* (**of** de).
perfectionist *n*, *adj* perfectionniste (*mf*).
perfectly *adv* **1** (totally) [*clear, happy*] tout à fait; **2** (very well) [*fit, illustrate*] parfaitement.
perforate *vtr* perforer.
perform I *vtr* **1** exécuter [*task*]; accomplir [*duties*]; procéder à [*operation*]; **2** jouer [*play*]; chanter [*song*]; exécuter [*dance, trick*]; **3** célébrer [*ceremony*].
II *vi* **1** [*actor, musician*] jouer; **2 to ~ well/badly** [*team*] bien/mal jouer; [*interviewee*] faire bonne/mauvaise impression; [*exam candidate, company*] avoir de bons/de mauvais résultats.
performance *n* **1** (rendition) interprétation *f* (**of** de); **2** (concert, show, play) représentation *f* (**of** de); **to put on a ~ of Hamlet** donner une représentation d'Hamlet; **3** (of team, sportsman) performance *f* (**in** à); **4** (of duties) exercice *m* (**of** de); (of task) exécution *f* (**of** de); **5** (of car, engine) performances *fpl*.
performer *n* artiste *mf*.
perfume I *n* parfum *m*.
II *vtr* parfumer.
perhaps *adv* peut-être; **~ she's forgotten** elle a peut-être oublié.
peril *n* péril *m*, danger *m*.
perimeter *n* périmètre *m*.
period I *n* **1** (gen) période *f*; (era) époque *f*; **2** (US) (full stop) point *m*; **3** (menstruation) règles *fpl*; **4** (Sch) (lesson) cours *m*, leçon *f*.
II *adj* (of a certain era) [*costume, furniture*] d'époque.
periodical *n*, *adj* périodique (*m*).
peripheral *adj* [*vision, suburb*] périphérique; [*issue, investment*] annexe.
periscope *n* périscope *m*.
perish *vi* **1** (die) périr (**from** de); **2** [*food*] se gâter; [*rubber*] se détériorer.
perishables *n pl* denrées *fpl* périssables.
perjure *v refl* **to ~ oneself** faire un faux témoignage.
perjury *n* faux témoignage *m*.
perk○ *n* avantage *m*.
■ **perk up** [*person*] se ragaillardir; [*business, life, plant*] reprendre.
perky *adj* guilleret/-ette.
perm *n* permanente *f*; **to have a ~** se faire faire une permanente.
permanent I *n* (US) permanente *f*.
II *adj* permanent/-e.
permanently *adv* [*happy, tired*] en permanence; [*employed, disabled*] de façon permanente; [*close, emigrate, settle*] définitivement.
permeate *vtr* **1** [*liquid, gas*] s'infiltrer dans; [*odour*] pénétrer dans; **2** [*ideas*] imprégner.
permissible *adj* [*level, conduct*] admissible; [*error*] acceptable.
permission *n* permission *f*; (official) autorisation *f*; **to get ~ to do** obtenir la permission or l'autorisation de faire.
permissive *adj* permissif/-ive.
permit I *n* **1** permis *m*; **work ~** permis *m* de travail: **2** (US Aut) permis *m* (de conduire).
II *vtr* permettre; **to ~ sb to do** permettre à qn de faire; **smoking is not ~ted** il est interdit de fumer.
III *vi* permettre.
perpendicular *adj* perpendiculaire.
perpetrator *n* auteur *m* (**of** de).
perpetual *adj* [*meetings, longing, turmoil*] perpétuel/-elle; [*darkness, stench*] permanent/-e.
perpetuate *vtr* perpétuer.
perplexed *adj* perplexe.
persecute *vtr* persécuter.
persecution *n* persécution *f*.
perseverance *n* persévérance *f*.
persevere *vi* persévérer (**with, at** dans).
persist *vi* persister (**in** dans; **in doing** à faire).
persistent *adj* **1** (persevering) persévérant/-e; (obstinate) obstiné/-e (**in** dans); **2** [*rain, denial*] persistant/-e; [*enquiries, noise, pressure*] continuel/-elle; [*illness, fears, idea*] tenace.
person *n* personne *f*; **in ~** en personne; **to have sth about one's ~** avoir qch sur soi.
personable *adj* [*person*] qui présente bien.
personal I *n* (US) petite annonce *f* personnelle.
II *adj* [*opinion, life, call, matter*] personnel/-elle; [*safety, choice, income, insurance*] individuel/-elle; [*service*] personnalisé/-e; **to make a ~ appearance** venir en personne (**at** à).
personal column *n* petites annonces *fpl* personnelles.
personality *n* personnalité *f*.
personally *adv* personnellement.
personal organizer *n* ≈ agenda *m*.
personal property *n* biens *mpl* personnels.

personnel *n* **1** (staff, troops) personnel *m*; **2** (department) service *m* du personnel.

perspective *n* perspective *f*; **to keep things in ~** garder un sens de la mesure; **to put things into ~** relativiser les choses.

perspex® *n* plexiglas® *m*.

perspiration *n* **1** (sweat) sueur *f*; **2** (sweating) transpiration *f*.

perspire *vi* transpirer.

persuade *vtr* **1** (influence) persuader; **to ~ sb to do** persuader qn de faire; **2** (convince) convaincre (**of** de; **that** que).

persuasion *n* **1** (persuading) persuasion *f*; **2** (religion) confession *f*; **3** (political views) conviction *f*.

persuasive *adj* [*person*] persuasif/-ive; [*argument, evidence*] convaincant/-e.

pert *adj* [*person, manner*] espiègle; [*hat, nose*] coquin/-e.

pertinent *adj* pertinent/-e.

perturb *vtr* perturber.

pervade *vtr* imprégner.

perverse *adj* **1** (twisted) [*person*] retors/-e; [*desire*] pervers/-e; **2** (contrary) [*refusal, attempt, attitude*] illogique; **to take a ~ pleasure in doing** prendre un malin plaisir à faire.

perversion *n* **1** (deviation) perversion *f*; **2** (of facts, justice) travestissement *m*.

pervert I *n* pervers/-e *m/f*.
II *vtr* **1** (corrupt) corrompre; **2** (misrepresent) travestir [*truth*]; dénaturer [*meaning*]; **to ~ the course of justice** entraver l'action de la justice.

pessimist *n* pessimiste *mf*.

pessimistic *adj* pessimiste.

pest *n* **1** (animal) animal *m* nuisible; (insect) insecte *m* nuisible; **2**○ (person) enquiquineur/-euse○ *m/f*.

pester *vtr* harceler.

pet I *n* **1** (animal) animal *m* de compagnie; **2** (favourite) chouchou/chouchoute○ *m/f*.
II *adj* **1** (favourite) favori/-ite; **2 ~ dog** chien.
III *vtr* caresser [*animal*].
IV *vi* [*people*] échanger des caresses.

petal *n* pétale *m*.

peter *v* ■ **peter out** [*conversation*] tarir; [*supplies*] s'épuiser.

pet food *n* aliments *mpl* pour chiens et chats.

pet hate (GB) *n* bête *f* noire.

petition I *n* pétition *f*.
II *vtr* adresser une pétition à [*person, body*].
III *vi* **to ~ for divorce** demander le divorce.

petrified *adj* pétrifié/-e.

petrol (GB) *n* essence *f*; **to fill up with ~** faire le plein (d'essence).

petroleum *n* pétrole *m*.

petrol station *n* (GB) station *f* d'essence.

pet shop (GB), **pet store** (US) *n* animalerie *f*.

petticoat *n* (full slip) combinaison *m*; (half slip) jupon *m*.

petty *adj* [*person, squabble*] mesquin/-e; [*detail*] insignifiant/-e.

petty cash *n* petite caisse *f*.

petty officer *n* ≈ maître *m*.

pew *n* banc *m* (d'église).

pewter *n* étain *m*.

pharmaceutical *adj* pharmaceutique.

pharmacist ▶ **626** *n* pharmacien/-ienne *m/f*.

pharmacy ▶ **626** *n* pharmacie *f*.

phase I *n* phase *f*; **it's just a ~ (he's/they're going through)** ça lui/leur passera.
II *vtr* échelonner (**over** sur).
■ **phase in** introduire [qch] progressivement.
■ **phase out** supprimer [qch] peu à peu.

PhD *n* (*abbr* = **Doctor of Philosophy**) doctorat *m*.

pheasant *n* faisan/-e *m/f*.

phenomenal *adj* phénoménal/-e.

phenomenon *n* phénomène *m*.

phew *excl* (in relief) ouf!; (when too hot) pff!

philanthropist *n* philanthrope *mf*.

philistine *n* béotien/-ienne *m/f*.

philosopher ▶ **626** *n* philosophe *mf*.

philosophic(al) *adj* **1** [*knowledge, question*] philosophique; **2** (calm, stoical) philosophe (**about** à propos de).

philosophy *n* philosophie *f*.

phobia *n* phobie *f*.

phone I *n* téléphone *m*; **to be on the ~** (be talking) être au téléphone (**to sb** avec qn); (be subscriber) avoir le téléphone.
II *vtr* (also **~ up**) passer un coup de fil à○, téléphoner à, appeler.
III *vi* (also **~ up**) téléphoner; **to ~ for a taxi** appeler un taxi.

phone book *n* annuaire *m* (téléphonique).

phone booth, phone box (GB) *n* cabine *f* téléphonique.

phone call *n* coup *m* de fil○; (more formal) communication *f* (téléphonique).

phone card *n* (GB) télécarte *f*.

phone number *n* numéro *m* de téléphone.

phoney○ I *n* **1** (affected person) poseur/-euse *m/f*; **2** (impostor) charlatan *m*.
II *adj* [*address, accent*] faux/fausse (*before n*); [*company, excuse*] bidon○ *inv*; [*emotion*] simulé/-e.

photo = **photograph** I.

photo album *n* album *m* de photos.

photo booth *n* photomaton® *m*.

photocopier *n* photocopieuse *f*.

photocopy I *n* photocopie *f*.
II *vtr* photocopier.

photogenic *adj* photogénique.

photograph I *n* (also **photo**) photo *f*; **in the ~** sur la photo; **to take a ~ of sb/sth** prendre qn/qch en photo.
II *vtr* photographier, prendre [qn/qch] en photo.

photographer ▶ **626** *n* photographe *mf*.

photography *n* photographie *f*.

phrase I *n* expression *f*.
II *vtr* formuler [*question, speech*].

phrasebook *n* manuel *m* de conversation.

physical I○ *n* (check-up) bilan *m* de santé.
II *adj* physique.

physically handicapped *adj* **to be ~** être handicapé/-e *m/f* physique.

physicist ▶ 626 *n* physicien/-ienne *m/f*.

physics *n* physique *f*.

physiotherapy *n* kinésithérapie *f*.

physique *n* physique *m*.

pianist ▶ 586, 626 *n* pianiste *mf*.

piano ▶ 586 *n* piano *m*.

pick I *n* **1** (tool) pioche *f*, pic *m*; (of climber) piolet *m*; **2** (choice) choix *m*; **to have one's ~ of** avoir le choix parmi; **take your ~** choisis; **3 the ~ of the bunch** (singular) le meilleur/la meilleure du lot.
II *vtr* **1** (choose) choisir (**from** parmi); (in sport) sélectionner [*player*] (**from** parmi); **to ~ a fight** chercher à se bagarrer○ (**with** avec); (quarrel) chercher querelle (**with** à); **2 to ~ one's way through** avancer avec précaution parmi [*rubble, litter*]; **3** cueillir [*fruit, flowers*]; **4** gratter [*spot, scab*]; enlever qch de; **to ~ one's teeth/nose** se curer les dents/le nez.
III *vi* choisir.
■ **pick at 1** [*person*] manger [qch] du bout des dents [*food*]; gratter [*spot, scab*]; **2** [*bird*] picorer [*crumbs*].
■ **pick on** harceler, s'en prendre à [*person*].
■ **pick out 1** (select) choisir; (single out) repérer; **2** distinguer [*landmark*]; reconnaître [*person in photo*]; repérer [*person in crowd*].
■ **pick up**: ¶ **~ up** [*business*] reprendre; [*weather, health*] s'améliorer; [*ill person*] se rétablir; ¶ **~ [sb/sth] up 1** (lift up) ramasser [*object, litter, toys*]; relever [*person*]; **to ~ up the receiver** décrocher le téléphone; **to ~ oneself up** se relever; **2** prendre [*passenger, cargo*]; passer prendre [*ticket, keys*]; prendre, acheter [*milk, paper*]; **could you ~ me up?** est-ce que tu peux venir me chercher?; **3** apprendre [*language*]; prendre [*habit, accent*]; développer [*skill*]; **you'll soon ~ it up** tu t'y mettras vite; **4** trouver [*trail, scent*]; [*radar*] détecter la présence de [*aircraft, person, object*]; [*radio receiver*] capter [*signal*]; **5** gagner [*point*]; acquérir [*reputation*]; **to ~ up speed** prendre de la vitesse; **6** (resume) reprendre [*conversation, career*]; **7** ramasser [*partner, prostitute*].

pickaxe (GB), **pickax** (US) *n* pioche *f*.

picket I *n* piquet *m* (de grève).
II *vtr* installer un piquet de grève aux portes de [*factory*].

pickle I *n* **1** (preserves) conserves *fpl* au vinaigre; **2** (gherkin) cornichon *m*.
II *vtr* (in vinegar) conserver [qch] dans du vinaigre.
IDIOMS **to be in a ~** être dans le pétrin○.

pick-me-up *n* remontant *m*.

pickpocket *n* voleur *m* à la tire.

pickup truck *n* (GB) pick-up *m inv*.

picnic *n* pique-nique *m*.

picture I *n* **1** (painting) peinture *f*, tableau *m*; (drawing) dessin *m*; (in book) illustration *f*; (in mind) image *f*; **2** (description) description *f*; **3** (snapshot) photo *f*, photographie *f*; **4 I get the ~** je vois; **to put sb in the ~** mettre qn au courant; **5** (film) film *m*; **6** (on TV screen) image *f*.
II *vtr* s'imaginer.

picturesque *adj* pittoresque.

pie *n* tourte *f*; **meat ~** tourte à la viande.

piece *n* **1** (gen) morceau *m*; (of string, ribbon) bout *m*; **a ~ of furniture** un meuble; **a ~ of luggage** une valise; **a ~ of advice** un conseil; **a ~ of information** un renseignement; **a ~ of luck** un coup de chance; **£20 a~** 20 livres pièce; **to fall to ~s** [*object*] tomber en morceaux; [*argument*] s'effondrer; **to go to ~s** (from shock) s'effondrer; (emotionally) craquer○; (in interview) paniquer complètement; **2** (of jigsaw, machine, model) pièce *f*; **to take sth to ~s** démonter qch; **3** (article) article *m* (**on** sur); **4** (coin) **a 50p ~** une pièce de 50 pence; **5** (in chess) pièce *f*.
IDIOMS **to give sb a ~ of one's mind** dire ses quatre vérités à qn.

piecemeal I *adj* (random) fragmentaire; (at different times) irrégulier/-ière.
II *adv* petit à petit.

pier *n* (at seaside) jetée *f* (sur pilotis); (landing stage) embarcadère *f*.

pierce *vtr* (make hole in) percer; (penetrate) transpercer.

piercing *adj* [*scream, eyes*] perçant/-e; [*light*] intense; [*wind*] glacial/-e, pénétrant/-e.

pig *n* **1** (animal) porc *m*, cochon *m*; **2**○ [*person*] (greedy) goinfre○ *m*; (dirty) cochon/-onne○ *m/f*; (nasty) sale type○ *m*.
■ **pig out**○ se goinfrer○, s'empiffrer○ (**on** de).

pigeon *n* pigeon *m*.

pigeonhole (GB) I *n* casier *m*.
II *vtr* étiqueter, cataloguer.

pigeon-toed *adj* **to be ~** marcher les pieds en dedans.

piggyback (ride) *n* **to give sb a ~** porter qn sur son dos or sur ses épaules.

piggy bank *n* tirelire *f*.

pigheaded *adj* entêté/-e, obstiné/-e.

pigment *n* pigment *m*.

pigpen (US) = **pigsty**.

pigskin *n* peau *f* de porc.

pigsty, **pigpen** (US) *n* porcherie *f*.

pigtail *n* natte *f*.

pike *n* (fish) brochet *m*.

pile I *n* **1** (heap) tas *m* (**of** de); (stack) pile *f* (**of** de); **in a ~** en tas or en pile; **2** (of fabric, carpet) poil *m*; **3**○ **~s of** des tas○ de [*books, letters*]; **~s of money** plein d'argent○.
II **piles** ▶ 533 *n pl* hémorroïdes *fpl*.
III *vtr* entasser (**on** sur; **into** dans).
■ **pile up** [*debts, problems, work*] s'accumuler.

pileup *n* carambolage *m*.

pilfer I *vtr* dérober (**from** dans).
II *vi* commettre des larcins.

pilgrim *n* pèlerin *m* (**to** de).

pilgrimage *n* pèlerinage *m*.

pill *n* **1** (gen) comprimé *m*, cachet *m*; **2** (contraceptive) **the ~** la pilule.

pillar *n* pilier *m*.
pillar box *n* (GB) boîte *f* aux lettres.
pillion I *n* (also **~ seat**) siège *m* de passager.
II *adv* **to ride ~** monter en croupe.
pillow *n* oreiller *m*.
pillowcase *n* taie *f* d'oreiller.
pilot ▶626 I *n* pilote *m*.
II *vtr* piloter.
III *adj* pilote.
pilot light *n* veilleuse *f*; (electric) voyant *m* lumineux.
pilot scheme *n* projet-pilote *m*.
pimple *n* bouton *m*.
pin I *n* **1** (for cloth, paper) épingle *f*; **2 three-~ plug** prise *f* à trois fiches; **3** (for wood, metal) goujon *m*; **4** (Med) broche *f*; **5** (brooch) barrette *f*.
II *vtr* **1** épingler [*dress, hem, curtain*] (**to** à); **2** (trap) **to ~ sb to** coincer qn contre [*wall, floor*]; **3**○ **to ~ [sth] on sb** mettre [qch] sur le dos de qn [*theft*].
■ **pin down**: ¶ **~ [sb] down 1** (physically) immobiliser (**to** à); **2** (figurative) coincer; **to ~ sb down to a definite date** arriver à fixer une date ferme avec qn; ¶ **~ [sth] down** identifier [*concept, feeling*].
■ **pin up** accrocher [*poster, notice*] (**on** à).
PIN (number) *n* (*abbr* = **personal identification number**) code *m* confidentiel (pour carte bancaire).
pinafore *n* **1** (apron) tablier *m*; **2** (dress) robe-chasuble *f*.
pinball ▶504 *n* flipper *m*.
pincers *n pl* tenailles *fpl*.
pinch I *n* **1** pincement *m*; **to give sb a ~** pincer qn; **2** (of salt, spice) pincée *f*.
II *vtr* **1** (on arm, leg) pincer; **2** [*shoe*] serrer; **3**○ (steal) faucher○ (**from** à).
III *vi* [*shoe*] serrer.
IDIOMS **to feel the ~** avoir de la peine à joindre les deux bouts.
pine I *n* pin *m*.
II *adj* [*furniture*] en pin.
III *vi* [*person*] languir (**for** après); [*animal*] s'ennuyer (**for** de).
pineapple *n* ananas *m*.
pinecone *n* pomme *f* de pin.
ping-pong® ▶504 *n* ping-pong® *m*.
pink ▶438 I *n* **1** (colour) rose *m*; **2** (flower) œillet *m* mignardise.
II *adj* rose; **to go** or **turn ~** rosir; (blush) rougir (**with** de).
pinnacle *n* **1** (on building) pinacle *m*; **2** (of rock) cime *f* (**of** de); **3** (figurative) apogée *m* (**of** de).
pinpoint *vtr* indiquer [*problem, causes, location, site*]; déterminer [*time*].
pinstripe(d) *adj* [*fabric, suit*] à fines rayures.
pint *n* pinte *f* (GB = *0.57 l*, US = *0.47 l*); **a ~ of milk** ≈ un demi-litre de lait; **a ~ (of beer)** un demi.
pioneer I *n* pionnier *m* (**of, in** de).
II *vtr* **to ~ the use of** être le premier/la première à utiliser.
pip *n* **1** (seed) pépin *m*; **2** (on radio) top *m*.
IDIOMS **to be ~ped at** or **to the post** se faire souffler la victoire.
pipe ▶586 I *n* **1** (for gas, water) tuyau *m*; (underground) conduite *f*; **2** (smoker's) pipe *f*.
II **pipes** *n pl* (Mus) cornemuse *f*.
III *vtr* **water is ~d across/to** l'eau est acheminée par canalisation à travers/jusqu'à.
■ **pipe down**○ faire moins de bruit.
pipe-dream *n* chimère *f*.
pipeline *n* oléoduc *m*; **to be in the ~** être prévu/-e.
piping hot *adj* fumant/-e.
pique *n* dépit *m*; **a fit of ~** un accès de dépit.
pirate I *n* pirate *m*.
II *adj* [*video, tape, radio*] pirate (*after n*); [*ship*] de pirates.
III *vtr* pirater [*tape, video, software*].
pirouette *n* pirouette *f*.
Pisa ▶448 *pr n* Pise.
Pisces *n* Poissons *mpl*.
pistol *n* pistolet *m*.
pit I *n* **1** (in ground, in garage) fosse *f*; **gravel ~** carrière *f* de gravier; **2** (mine) mine *f*; **3** (in theatre) parterre *m*; **orchestra ~** fosse *f* d'orchestre; **4** (US) (in fruit) noyau *m*.
II *vtr* **to ~ sb against** opposer qn à [*opponent*]; **to ~ one's wits against sb** se mesurer à qn.
IDIOMS **it's the ~s**○! c'est l'horreur!
pitch I *n* **1** (sportsground) terrain *m*; **football ~** terrain de foot(ball); **2** (of note, voice) hauteur *f*; (in music) ton *m*; ; **3** (highest point) comble *m*; **4** (sales talk) boniment *m*; **5** (for street trader) emplacement *m*.
II *vtr* **1** (throw) jeter (**into** dans); (Sport) lancer; **2** adapter [*campaign, speech*] (**at** à); **3** [*singer*] trouver [*note*]; **4** planter [*tent*]; **to ~ camp** établir un camp.
III *vi* **1** [*boat*] tanguer; **2** (US) (in baseball) lancer (la balle).
■ **pitch in**○ (eat) attaquer○; (help) donner un coup de main○.
pitcher *n* **1** (jug) cruche *f*; **2** (US Sport) lanceur *m*.
pitchfork *n* fourche *f*.
pitfall *n* écueil *m* (**of** de).
pith *n* **1** (of fruit) peau *f* blanche; **2** (of plant) moelle *f*.
pitiful *adj* [*cry, sight*] pitoyable; [*state*] lamentable; [*amount*] ridicule.
pitiless *adj* impitoyable.
pittance *n* **to live on/earn a ~** vivre avec/gagner trois fois rien.
pity I *n* **1** (compassion) pitié *f* (**for** pour); **out of ~** par pitié; **to take ~ on sb** avoir pitié de qn; **2** (shame) dommage *m*; **what a ~!** quel dommage!
II *vtr* plaindre.
pivot I *vtr* faire pivoter [*lever*]; orienter [*lamp*].
II *vi* **1** [*lamp, device*] pivoter (**on** sur); **2** (figurative) [*outcome, success*] reposer (**on** sur).
pizza *n* pizza *f*.
placard *n* (at protest march) pancarte *f*; (on wall) affiche *f*.

place I *n* **1** (location, position) endroit *m*; **in ~s** [*hilly, damaged, worn*] par endroits; **~ of birth/work** lieu *m* de naissance/travail; **~ of residence** domicile *m*; **to be in the right ~ at the right time** être là où il faut quand il le faut; **to lose/find one's ~** (in book) perdre/retrouver sa page; (in paragraph, speech) perdre/retrouver le fil; **all over the ~** (everywhere) partout; **2** (home) **at Isabelle's ~** chez Isabelle; **your ~ or mine?** chez toi ou chez moi?; **3** (on bus, at table, in queue) place *f*; **4** (on team, with firm, on course) place *f* (**on** dans, **as** comme); **5** (in competition, race) place *f*; **to finish in first ~** terminer premier/-ière or à la première place; **in the first ~** (firstly, when listing) premièrement; (most importantly, most notably) tout d'abord, pour commencer; **6** (correct position) **everything is in its ~** tout est bien à sa place; **to hold sth in ~** maintenir qch en place; **in ~** [*law, system, scheme*] en place; **to put sb in his/her ~** remettre qn à sa place; **7** (personal level or position) **it's not my ~ to do** ce n'est pas à moi de faire; **in his ~** à sa place; **8** (moment) moment *m*; **in ~s** [*funny, boring, silly*] par moments.
II *vtr* **1** (gen) placer; **2** passer [*order*]; **to place a bet** parier (**on** sur); **3** (in competition, exam) classer; **4** (identify) situer [*person*]; reconnaître [*accent*].
III **out of place** *phr* déplacé/-e; **to look out of ~** [*building, person*] détonner.

place-name *n* nom *m* de lieu.

placid *adj* placide.

plagiarize *vtr, vi* plagier.

plague I *n* **1** (bubonic) peste *f*; **2** (epidemic) épidémie *f*; **3** (of ants, locusts) invasion *f*; **4** (figurative) plaie *f*.
II *vtr* **1 to be ~d by** être en proie à [*doubts, difficulties*]; **2** (harass) harceler.

plaice *n* plie *f*, carrelet *m*.

plaid *adj* écossais/-e.

plain I *n* plaine *f*.
II *adj* **1** (simple) simple; **2** (of one colour) uni/-e; [*envelope*] sans inscription; **a ~ blue dress** une robe toute bleue; **3** [*woman*] quelconque; **4** (obvious) évident/-e, clair/-e; **it's ~ to see** ça saute aux yeux; **5** [*common sense*] simple (*before n*); [*ignorance*] pur/-e et simple (*after n*); **6** [*yoghurt, rice*] nature *inv*.

plain chocolate *n* choclat *m* à croquer.

plain clothes *adj* [*policeman*] en civil.

plainly *adv* **1** (obviously) manifestement; **2** [*see, remember*] clairement; **3** [*speak*] franchement; **4** [*dress, eat*] simplement; [*furnished*] sobrement.

plait *n* natte *f*.

plan I *n* (gen) plan *m*; (definite aim) projet *m* (**for** de; **to do** pour faire); **to go according to ~** se passer comme prévu.
II *vtr* **1** (prepare, organize) planifier [*future*]; organiser, préparer [*timetable, meeting, expedition*]; organiser [*day*]; faire un plan de [*career*]; faire le plan de [*essay, book*]; préméditer [*crime*]; **2** (intend, propose) projeter [*visit, trip*]; **to ~ to do** projeter de faire; **3** (design) concevoir.
IV *vi* prévoir; **to ~ for sth** prévoir qch; **to ~ on doing** compter faire.
■ **plan ahead** (vaguely) faire des projets; (look, think ahead) prévoir.

plane *n* **1** (aircraft) avion *m*; **2** (in geometry) plan *m*; **3** (tool) rabot *m*; **4** (also **~ tree**) platane *m*.

planet *n* planète *f*.

plank *n* planche *f*.

planning *n* **1** (of industry, economy, work) planification *f*; (of holiday, party) organisation *f*; **2** (in town) urbanisme *m*; (out of town) aménagement *m* du territoire.

planning permission *n* permis *m* de construire.

plant I *n* **1** (Bot) plante *f*; **2** (factory) usine *f*.
II *vtr* **1** planter [*seed, bulb, tree*]; **2** placer [*bomb, spy*]; **to ~ drugs on sb** cacher de la drogue sur qn pour l'incriminer.
III *v refl* **to ~ oneself between/in front of** se planter entre/devant.

plantation *n* plantation *f*.

plaque *n* **1** (on wall, monument) plaque *f*; **2** (on teeth) plaque *f* dentaire.

plaster I *n* **1** (gen) plâtre *m*; **2** (GB) (also **sticking ~**) sparadrap *m*.
II *vtr* **1** faire les plâtres de [*house*]; **2** (cover) couvrir (**with** de).

plasterer ▶626 *n* plâtrier *m*.

plastic I *n* plastique *m*.
II *adj* [*bag, toys, container*] en plastique.

plastic surgery *n* chirurgie *f* plastique.

plate *n* **1** (dish) (for eating) assiette *f*; (for serving) plat *m*; **2** (sheet of metal) plaque *f*, tôle *f*; **3** (numberplate) plaque *f* minéralogique; **4** (illustration) planche *f*; **5** (in dentistry) dentier *m*; **6** (in earth's crust) plaque *f*.

plate glass *n* verre *m* à vitre.

platform *n* **1** (for performance) estrade *f*; (at public meeting) tribune *f*; **2** (in scaffolding) plateforme *f*; **3** (in politics) plate-forme *f* électorale; **4** (at station) quai *m*.

platinum *n* platine *m*.

platonic *adj* platonique.

platoon *n* (of soldiers, police, firemen) section *f*; (in cavalry) peloton *m*.

platter *n* (dish) plat *m*.

plausible *adj* plausible, vraisemblable.

play ▶504, 586 I *n* **1** (in theatre) pièce *f* (**about** sur); **2** (recreation) jeu *m*; **3** (Sport) (game) partie *f*; **out of ~/in ~** [*ball*] hors jeu/en jeu; **4** (movement, interaction) jeu *m*; **to come into ~** entrer en jeu; **a ~ on words** un jeu de mots.
II *vtr* **1** jouer à [*game, cards*]; jouer [*card*]; **to ~ hide and seek** jouer à cache-cache; **to ~ a joke on sb** jouer un tour à qn; **2** jouer de [*instrument*]; jouer [*tune, symphony, chord*]; jouer à [*venue*]; **3** (in theatre) interpréter, jouer [*role*]; **4** mettre [*tape, video, CD*].
III *vi* jouer.
IDIOMS **to ~ for time** essayer de gagner du temps.
■ **play along**: **to ~ along with sb** entrer dans le jeu de qn.
■ **play down** minimiser [*effects, disaster*].

■ **play up**○ [*computer, person*] faire des siennes○.
play-acting *n* comédie *f*, simagrées *fpl*.
playboy *n* playboy *m*.
player *n* (in sport, music) joueur/-euse *m/f*; (actor) comédien/-ienne *m/f*; **tennis ~** joueur/-euse *m/f* de tennis.
playful *adj* [*remark*] taquin/-e; [*child, kitten*] joueur/-euse.
playground *n* cour *f* de récréation.
playhouse *n* théâtre *m*.
play-off *n* (GB) prolongation *f*; (US) match *m* crucial.
playroom *n* salle *f* de jeux.
playschool *n* ≈ halte-garderie *f*.
playtime *n* récréation *f*.
playwright *n* auteur *m* dramatique.
plaza *n* **1** (square) place *f*; **shopping ~** centre *m* commercial; **2** (US) péage *m*.
plc, PLC *n* (GB) (*abbr* = **public limited company**) SA.
plea *n* **1** (gen) appel *m* (**for** à); (for money, food) demande *f* (**for** de); **2** (Law) **to enter a ~ of guilty/not guilty** plaider coupable/non coupable.
plead I *vtr* plaider.
II *vi* **1 to ~ with sb** supplier qn; **2** (Law) plaider.
pleasant *adj* agréable.
please I *adv* s'il vous plaît; (informally) s'il te plaît; **'may I?'—'~ do'** 'je peux?'—'oui, je vous en prie'.
II *vtr* faire plaisir à [*person*]; **she is hard to ~** elle est difficile (à contenter).
III *vi* plaire; **do as you ~** fais comme il te plaira, fais comme tu veux.
pleased *adj* content/-e (**that** que + *subjunctive*; **about, at** de; **with** de); **to look ~ with oneself** avoir l'air content de soi; **I am ~ to announce that...** j'ai le plaisir d'annoncer que...; **~ to meet you** enchanté.
pleasing *adj* [*appearance, colour, voice*] agréable; [*manner, personality*] avenant/-e; [*effect, result*] heureux/-euse.
pleasure *n* plaisir *m* (**of** de; **of doing** de faire); **for ~** par plaisir; **my ~** (replying to request for help) avec plaisir; (replying to thanks) je vous en prie.
pleat *n* pli *m*.
pleated *adj* [*skirt*] plissé/-e; [*trousers*] à plis (*after n*).
pledge I *n* **1** (promise) promesse *f*; **2** (money promised to charity) promesse *f* de don.
II *vtr* promettre [*allegiance, aid, support*] (**to** à); **to ~ one's word** donner sa parole.
plentiful *adj* abondant/-e.
plenty *quantif, pron* **~ of** beaucoup de; **~ to do** beaucoup à faire.
pliable *adj* [*twig, plastic*] flexible; [*person*] malléable.
pliers *n pl* pinces *fpl*; **a pair of ~s** des pinces.
plight *n* **1** (dilemma) situation *f* désespérée; **2** (suffering) détresse *f*.
plimsoll *n* (GB) chaussure *f* de tennis.
plod *v* ■ **plod along** [*walk*] avancer d'un pas lent.
■ **plod away** [*work*] travailler ferme, bosser○.
plodder *n* bûcheur/-euse○ *m/f*.
plonk○ I *n* (wine) vin *m* ordinaire, pinard◑ *m*.
II *vtr* (also **~ down**) planter [*plate, bottle, box*] (**on** sur).
plot I *n* **1** (conspiracy) complot *m*; **2** (of novel, film, play) intrigue *f*; **3 ~ of land** parcelle *f* de terre; **a vegetable ~** un carré de légumes; **4** (building site) terrain *m* à bâtir.
II *vtr* **1** (plan) comploter [*murder, attack, return*]; fomenter [*revolution*]; **2** (chart) relever [qch] sur une carte [*course*]; **3** (on graph) tracer [qch] point par point [*curve, graph*].
III *vi* conspirer (**against** contre).
plough (GB), **plow** (US) I *n* charrue *f*.
II *vtr* **1** labourer [*land, field*]; creuser [*furrow*]; **2** (invest) **to ~ money into** investir beaucoup d'argent dans [*project, company*].
■ **plough through** avancer péniblement dans [*mud, snow*]; ramer○ sur [*book*].
ploy *n* stratagème *m* (**to do** pour faire).
pluck I *n* courage *m*, cran○ *m*.
II *vtr* **1** cueillir [*flower, fruit*]; **2** plumer [*chicken*]; **3** (in music) pincer [*strings*]; pincer les cordes de [*guitar*]; **4 to ~ one's eyebrows** s'épiler les sourcils.
IDIOMS **to ~ up one's courage** prendre son courage à deux mains.
plucky *adj* courageux/-euse.
plug I *n* **1** (on appliance) prise *f* (de courant); **2** (in bath, sink) bonde *f*; **3** (also **spark ~**) bougie *f*; **4** (in advertising) pub○, publicité *f* (**for** pour).
II *vtr* **1** boucher [*hole*] (**with** avec); **2**○ (promote) faire de la publicité pour [*book, show, product*]; **3 to ~ sth into** brancher qch à.
■ **plug in**: ¶ **~ in** se brancher; ¶ **~ [sth] in** brancher [*appliance*].
plughole *n* (GB) bonde *f*.
plum ▶ 438 I *n* prune *f*.
II *adj* **1** (colour) prune *inv*; **2**○ **to get a ~ job** décrocher un boulot en or○.
plumb I *adv* **1**○ (US) [*crazy*] complètement; **2**○ **~ in the middle** en plein milieu.
II *vtr* sonder [*depths*]; **to ~ the depths of** toucher le fond de [*despair, misery*].
plumber *n* plombier *m*.
plumbing *n* plomberie *f*.
plummet *vi* chuter, dégringoler○.
plump *adj* [*person, arm, leg*] potelé/-e; [*cheek, face*] rond/-e, plein/-e.
plunge I *vtr* plonger (**into** dans).
II *vi* [*road, cliff, waterfall*] plonger; [*bird, plane*] piquer; [*person*] (dive) plonger; (fall) tomber (**from** de); [*rate, value*] chuter.
IDIOMS **to take the ~** se jeter à l'eau.
plunger *n* ventouse *f*.
plural I *n* pluriel *m*; **in the ~** au pluriel.
II *adj* [*noun, adjective*] au pluriel; [*form, ending*] du pluriel.
plus I *n* avantage *m*.
II *adj* **the ~ side** le côté positif; **50 ~** plus

de 50; **the 65-~ age group** les personnes qui ont 65 ans et plus.
III *prep* plus; **15 ~ 12** 15 plus 12.
IV *conj* et; **bedroom ~ bathroom** chambre et salle de bains.

plus-fours *n pl* culotte *f* de golf.

plus sign *n* signe *m* plus.

Pluto *pr n* (planet) Pluton *f*.

ply I *vtr* **1** vendre [*wares*]; **to ~ one's trade** exercer son métier; **2 to ~ sb with food/drink** ne cesser de remplir l'assiette/le verre de qn.
II *vi* [*boat, bus*] faire la navette (**between** entre).

plywood *n* contreplaqué *m*.

pm ▶ 434 *adv* (*abbr* = **post meridiem**) **two ~** deux heures de l'après-midi; **nine ~** neuf heures du soir.

pneumatic drill *n* marteau *m* piqueur.

pneumonia ▶ 533 *n* pneumonie *f*.

poach I *vtr* **1** chasser [qch] illégalement [*game*]; **2** (Culin) faire pocher.
II *vi* braconner.

poacher *n* braconnier *m*.

PO Box *n* boîte *f* postale.

pocket I *n* **1** (in garment) poche *f*; **2** (in billiards) bourse *f*.
II *adj* [*diary, dictionary, edition*] de poche.
III *vtr* empocher.

pocketbook *n* (US) (wallet) portefeuille *m*; (handbag) sac *m* à main.

pocketknife *n* couteau *m* de poche.

pocket money *n* argent *m* de poche.

podium *n* (for speaker, conductor) estrade *f*; (for winner) podium *m*.

poem *n* poème *m*.

poet *n* poète *m*.

poetic *adj* poétique.

poetry *n* poésie *f*; **to write/read ~** écrire/lire des poèmes.

poignant *adj* poignant/-e.

point I *n* **1** (of knife, needle, pencil) pointe *f*; **2** (location, position on scale) point *m*; (less specific) endroit *m*; **3** (extent, degree) point *m*; **up to a ~** jusqu'à un certain point; **4** (moment) (precise) moment *m*; (stage) stade *m*; **to be on the ~ of doing** être sur le point de faire; **at this ~ in her career** à ce stade(-là) de sa carrière; **at some ~ in the future** plus tard; **at one ~** à un moment donné; **5** (question, idea) point *m*; **to make the ~ that** faire remarquer que; **you've made your ~** vous vous êtes exprimé; **to make a ~ of doing** (as matter of pride) mettre un point d'honneur à faire; (do deliberately) faire exprès; **6** (central idea) point *m* essentiel; **to come straight to the ~** aller droit au fait; **to keep** or **stick to the ~** rester dans le sujet; **to miss the ~** ne pas comprendre; **that's beside the ~** là n'est pas la question; **to get the ~** comprendre; **that's not the ~** il ne s'agit pas de cela; **7** (purpose) objet *m*; **what's the ~ of doing...?** à quoi bon faire...?; **there's no ~ in doing** ça ne sert à rien de faire; **I don't see the ~ of doing** je ne vois pas l'intérêt de faire; **8** (feature, characteristic) point *m*, côté *m*; **her strong ~** son point fort; **9** (in scoring) point *m*; **match ~** (in tennis) balle *f* de match; **10** (decimal point) virgule *f*; **11** (headland) pointe *f*.
II *vtr* **1** (aim, direct) **to ~ sth at sb** braquer qch sur qn [*camera, gun*]; **to ~ one's finger at sb** montrer qn du doigt; **2** (show) **to ~ the way to** indiquer la direction de; **3** (in ballet, gym) **to ~ one's toes** faire des pointes.
III *vi* **1** (indicate) indiquer or montrer (du doigt); **to ~ at sb/sth** montrer qn/qch du doigt; **2** [*signpost, arrow, compass*] indiquer; **to be ~ing at sb** [*gun, camera*] être braqué/-e sur qn.
■ **point out** montrer [*place, person*] (**to** à); faire remarquer [*fact, discrepancy*].

point-blank *adv* **1** [*shoot*] à bout portant; **2** [*refuse, deny*] catégoriquement.

pointed *adj* **1** [*hat, stick, chin*] pointu/-e; **2** [*remark*] qui vise quelqu'un.

pointless *adj* [*request, activity*] absurde; **it's ~ to do/for me to do** ça ne sert à rien de faire/que je fasse.

point of view *n* point *m* de vue.

poise *n* **1** (confidence) assurance *f*; **2** (physical elegance) aisance *f*.

poised *adj* **1** (self-possessed) plein/-e d'assurance; **2** (elegant) plein/-e d'aisance; **3** (on the point of) **to be ~ to do** être sur le point de faire.

poison I *n* poison *m*.
II *vtr* empoisonner [*person, environment, relationship*]; [*fumes*] intoxiquer [*person*].

poisoning *n* empoisonnement *m*.

poisonous *adj* **1** [*chemicals, gas*] toxique; [*mushroom, berry*] vénéneux/-euse; [*snake, insect, bite*] venimeux/-euse; **2** [*rumour, propaganda*] pernicieux/-ieuse.

poke *vtr* **1** (jab, prod) pousser [qn] du bout du doigt [*person*]; donner un coup dans [*pile, substance*]; tisonner [*fire*]; **2** (push, put) **to ~ sth into** enfoncer qch dans [*hole, pot*]; **to ~ one's head out of the window** passer la tête par la fenêtre.
■ **poke around**, **poke about** farfouiller (**in** dans).

poker *n* **1** (for fire) tisonnier *m*; **2** ▶ 504 (cardgame) poker *m*.
IDIOMS **(as) stiff as a ~** raide comme la justice.

poker-faced *adj* [*person*] impassible.

Poland ▶ 448 *pr n* Pologne *f*.

polar *adj* polaire.

pole *n* **1** (stick) perche *f*; (for tent, flag) mât *m*; (for skiing) bâton *m*; **2** (of earth's axis) pôle *m*.

Pole ▶ 553 *n* Polonais/-e *m/f*.

pole star *n* étoile *f* polaire.

pole vault *n* saut *m* à la perche.

police I *n* **1** (police force) **the ~** la police; **2** (policemen) policiers *mpl*.
II *vtr* maintenir l'ordre dans [*area*].

police constable, **PC** *n* agent *m* de police.

Police Department, **PD** *n* (US) services *mpl* de police (d'une ville).

police force *n* police *f*.

policeman *n* agent *m* de police.

police officer *n* policier *m*.

police station *n* poste *m* de police; (larger) commissariat *m*.

policewoman *n* femme *f* policier.

policy *n* **1** (plan, rule) politique *f* (**on** sur); **2** (in insurance) (cover) contrat *m*; (document) police *f*.

polio ▶533 *n* poliomyélite *f*.

polish I *n* **1** (for wood, floor) cire *f*; (for shoes) cirage *m*; (for brass, silver) pâte *f* à polir; (for car) lustre *m*; **2** (shiny surface) éclat *m*; **3** (of manner, performance) élégance *f*.

II *vtr* **1** cirer [*shoes, furniture*]; astiquer [*leather, car, glass, brass*]; polir [*stone*]; **2** (refine) soigner [*performance, image*]; affiner [*style*].

■ **polish off**○ expédier○ [*food, job*].

Polish ▶553 **I** *n* (language) polonais *m*.

II *adj* polonais/-e.

polished *adj* **1** [*surface, wood*] poli/-e; [*floor, shoes*] ciré/-e; **2** [*manner*] raffiné/-e; **3** [*performance*] (bien) rodé/-e.

polite *adj* poli/-e (**to** avec).

politeness *n* politesse *f*.

political *adj* politique.

politician ▶626 *n* homme/femme *m/f* politique.

politics *n* **1** (gen) politique *f*; **2** (subject) sciences *fpl* politiques; **3** (views) opinions *fpl* politiques.

poll I *n* **1** (vote casting) scrutin *m*, vote *m*; (election) élections *fpl*; **to go to the ~s** se rendre aux urnes; **2** (survey) sondage *m* (**on** sur).

II *vtr* **1** obtenir [*votes*]; **2** (canvass) interroger [*group*].

pollen *n* pollen *m*.

polling booth *n* isoloir *m*.

polling day *n* jour *m* des élections.

polling station *n* bureau *m* de vote.

poll tax *n* (GB) ≈ impôts *mpl* locaux.

pollute *vtr* polluer.

pollution *n* pollution *f*.

polo ▶504 *n* polo *m*.

polo neck *n* (GB) col *m* roulé.

poltergeist *n* esprit *m* frappeur.

poly I○ *n* (GB) *abbr* = **polytechnic**.

II poly+ *pref* poly-.

polystyrene *n* polystyrène *m*.

polytechnic *n* (GB) (also **poly**) établissement *m* d'enseignement supérieur.

polythene *n* (GB) polyéthylène *m*.

pomegranate *n* grenade *f*.

pompom, **pompon** *n* pompon *m*.

pompous *adj* [*person*] plein/-e de suffisance; [*air, speech, style*] pompeux/-euse.

pond *n* (large) étang *m*; (smaller) mare *f*; (in garden) bassin *m*.

ponder *vi* réfléchir (**on** à); (more deeply) méditer (**on** sur).

pontiff *n* pontife *m*.

pontoon *n* **1** (pier) ponton *m*; **2** ▶504 (GB Games) vingt-et-un *m*.

pony *n* poney *m*.

ponytail *n* queue *f* de cheval.

poodle *n* caniche *m*.

pool I *n* **1** (pond) étang *m*; (artificial) bassin *m*; **2** (also **swimming ~**) piscine *f*; **3** (of water, light) flaque *f*; **a ~ of blood** une mare de sang; **4** (kitty) cagnotte *f*; (in cards) mises *fpl*; **5** (of money, resources) pool *m*; (of ideas, experience) réservoir *m*; **6** (billiards) billard *m* américain.

II pools *n pl* (GB) (also **football ~s**) ≈ loto *m* sportif.

III *vtr* mettre [qch] en commun.

poor *adj* **1** [*person, country*] pauvre (**in** en); **2** [*quality, work, planning, weather, visibility*] mauvais/-e (*before n*); [*attendance*] faible; **3** (deserving pity) pauvre (*before n*); **~ you!** mon/ma pauvre!; **4** [*attempt, excuse*] piètre (*before n*).

poorly *adv* **1** [*live, dress, dressed*] pauvrement; **2** [*written, lit, paid*] mal.

pop I *n* **1** (sound) pan *m*; **to go ~** faire pan; **2**○ (drink) soda *m*; **3** (music) musique *f* pop.

II *adj* [*concert, group, music, song*] pop; [*record, singer*] de pop.

III *vtr* **1** faire éclater [*balloon, bubble*]; **2** faire sauter [*cork*]; **3**○ **to ~ sth in(to)** mettre qch dans [*oven, cupboard, mouth*].

IV *vi* **1** [*balloon*] éclater; [*cork, buttons*] sauter; **2** [*ears*] se déboucher brusquement; **her eyes were ~ping out of her head** les yeux lui sortaient de la tête; **3**○ (GB) **to ~ into town/the bank** faire un saut○ en ville/à la banque.

■ **pop in**○ (GB) passer.

■ **pop out** (GB) sortir.

pope *n* pape *m*; **Pope Paul VI** le Pape Paul VI.

poplar *n* peuplier *m*.

poppy *n* pavot *m*; **wild ~** coquelicot *m*.

pop sock *n* mi-bas *m*.

popular *adj* **1** [*actor, politician*] populaire (**with, among** parmi); [*hobby, sport*] répandu/-e (**with, among** chez); [*food, dish*] prisé/-e (**with, among** par); [*product, resort, colour, design*] en vogue (**with, among** chez); **John is very ~** John a beaucoup d'amis; **2** (of or for the people) [*music, movement, press*] populaire; [*entertainment*] grand public *inv*; [*science, history*] de vulgarisation.

popularity *n* popularité *f* (**of** de; **with** auprès de).

population *n* population *f*.

porcelain *n* porcelaine *f*.

porch *n* **1** (of house, church) porche *m*; **2** (US) (veranda) véranda *f*.

porcupine *n* porc-épic *m*.

pore *n* pore *m*.

■ **pore over** être plongé/-e dans [*book*]; étudier soigneusement [*map*].

pork *n* (viande *f* de) porc *m*.

pornography *n* pornographie *f*.

porpoise *n* marsouin *m*.

port *n* **1** (harbour) port *m*; **in ~** au port; **~ of**

call escale *f*; (figurative) arrêt *m*; **2** (drink) porto *m*.

portable *adj* portable.

porter ▶626 *n* **1** (in station, airport, hotel) porteur *m*; (in hospital) brancardier *m*; **2** (GB) (doorman) (of hotel) portier *m*; (of apartment block) gardien/-ienne *m/f*; **3** (US) (steward) employé *m* des wagons-lits.

portfolio *n* **1** (case) porte-documents *m inv*; (for drawings) carton *m* (à dessins); **2** (sample) portfolio *m*; **3** (in politics, finance) portefeuille *m*.

porthole *n* hublot *m*.

portion *n* **1** (of house, machine, document, country) partie *f* (**of** de); **2** (share) (of money, blame) part *f* (**of** de); **3** (at meal) portion *f*.

portrait *n* portrait *m*.

portray *vtr* **1** (depict) décrire [*place, era, event*]; présenter [*person, situation*]; **2** [*actor*] interpréter [*character*]; **3** [*artist*] peindre [*person*]; [*picture, artist*] représenter [*scene*].

Portugal ▶448 *pr n* Portugal *m*.

Portuguese ▶553 **I** *n* **1** (person) Portugais/-e *m/f*; **2** (language) portugais *m*.
II *adj* portugais/-e.

pose I *vtr* poser [*problem*] (**for** pour); présenter [*challenge*] (**to** à); représenter [*threat, risk*] (**to** pour); soulever [*question*] (**about** de).
II *vi* **1** [*artist's model*] poser; [*performer*] prendre des poses; **2 to ~ as** se faire passer pour; **3** (posture) frimer°.

poser° *n* **1** (person) frimeur/-euse° *m/f*; **2** (puzzle) colle° *f*.

posh° *adj* [*person*] huppé/-e°; [*house, area, clothes, car*] chic; [*voice*] distingué/-e.

position I *n* **1** (gen) position *f*; **to be in ~** (in place) être en place; (ready) être prêt/-e; **2** (situation, state) situation *f*; **to be in a ~ to do** être en mesure de faire; **3** (Sport) poste *m*; **what ~ does he play?** quel est son poste?; **4** (job) poste *m*.
II *vtr* poster [*policemen, soldiers*]; disposer [*object*].

positive *adj* **1** (affirmative) [*answer, reaction, result*] positif/-ive; **2** (optimistic) [*message, person, feeling, tone*] positif/-ive; **3** (constructive) [*contribution, effect, progress*] positif/-ive; [*advantage, good*] réel/réelle (*before n*); **4** (sure) [*identification, proof*] formel/-elle; [*fact*] indéniable; **to be ~** être sûr/-e (**about** de; **that** que); **5** (forceful) [*action*] catégorique; **6** (in mathematics, science) positif/-ive; **7** (extreme) [*pleasure*] pur/-e (*before n*); [*disgrace, outrage, genius*] véritable (*before n*).

possess *vtr* **1** posséder [*property, weapon, proof, charm*]; avoir [*power, advantage*]; (illegally) détenir [*arms, drugs*]; **2** (take control of) [*anger, fury*] s'emparer de [*person*]; [*devil*] posséder [*person*]; **what ~ed you to do that?** qu'est-ce qui t'a pris de faire ça?

possession I *n* **1** (gen) possession *f*; **2** (Law) (illegal) détention *f* (**of** de).
II possessions *n pl* biens *mpl*.

possessive I *n* (in grammar) possessif *m*.
II *adj* possessif/-ive (**towards** à l'égard de; **with** avec).

possibility *n* **1** (chance, prospect) possibilité *f*; **2** (eventuality) éventualité *f*.

possible *adj* possible; **he did as much as ~** il a fait tout son possible; **as far as ~** dans la mesure du possible; **as quickly as ~** le plus vite possible; **as soon as ~** dès que possible.

possibly *adv* **1** (maybe) peut-être; **2** (for emphasis) **how could they ~ understand?** comment donc pourraient-ils comprendre?; **we can't ~ afford it** nous n'en avons absolument pas les moyens.

post I *n* **1** (job) poste *m* (**as, of** de); **to hold a ~** occuper un poste; **2** (GB) (postal system) poste *f*; (letters) courrier *m*; (delivery) distribution *f*; **by return of ~** par retour du courrier; **it was lost in the ~** cela s'est égaré dans le courrier; **3** (Mil) poste *m*; **4** (pole) poteau *m*.
II post- *pref* post-; **in ~-1992 Europe** dans l'Europe d'après 1992.
III *vtr* **1** (GB) (send by post) poster, expédier [qch] (par la poste); (put in letterbox) mettre [qch] à la poste; **2** (stick up) afficher [*notice, poster*]; annoncer [*details, results*]; **3** (gen, Mil) (send abroad) affecter (**to** à); **4** (station) poster [*guard, sentry*].

postage *n* affranchissement *m*; **including ~ and packing** frais *mpl* d'expédition inclus; **~ free** franc de port.

postal *adj* [*charges, district*] postal/-e; [*application*] par la poste.

postal order, PO *n* (GB) mandat *m* (**for** de).

postbox *n* (GB) boîte *f* aux lettres.

postcard *n* carte *f* postale.

post code *n* (GB) code *m* postal.

postdate *vtr* postdater.

poster *n* (for information) affiche *f*; (decorative) poster *m*.

posterity *n* postérité *f*.

poster paint *n* gouache *f*.

postgraduate I *n* ≈ étudiant/-e *m/f* de troisième cycle.
II *adj* ≈ de troisième cycle.

posthumous *adj* posthume.

postman ▶626 *n* facteur *m*.

postmark *n* cachet *m* de la poste.

post-mortem *n* autopsie *f*.

post-natal *adj* post-natal.

post office, PO *n* poste *f*.

postpone *vtr* reporter, remettre (**until** à; **for** de).

postscript *n* (in letter) post-scriptum *m inv* (**to** à); (to book) postface *f* (**to** à).

posture I *n* **1** (pose) posture *f*; (figurative) (stance) position *f*; **2** (bearing) maintien *m*; **to have good/bad ~** se tenir bien/mal.
II *vi* poser, prendre des poses.

postwar *adj* d'après-guerre.

pot I *n* **1** (container) pot *m*; **2** (teapot) théière *f*; (coffee pot) cafetière *f* ; **3 ~s and pans** casseroles *fpl*; **4** (piece of pottery) poterie *f*.
II *vtr* **1** mettre [qch] en pot [*jam*]; **2** (in billiards) blouser [*ball*]; **3** mettre [qch] en pot [*plant*].
III potted *pp adj* **1** [*plant*] en pot; **2** [*biography, history*] bref/brève (*before n*).

IDIOMS **to go to ~**○ (person) se laisser aller; (situation) aller à vau-l'eau; **to take ~ luck** (for meal) (GB) manger à la fortune du pot; (gen) prendre ce que l'on trouve.

potassium *n* potassium *m*.

potato *n* pomme *f* de terre.

potato chips (US), **potato crisps** (GB) *n pl* chips *fpl*.

pot belly *n* bedaine *f*.

potent *adj* **1** [*symbol, drug*] puissant/-e; [*drink*] fort/-e; **2** (sexually) viril.

potential I *n* potentiel *m* (**as** en tant que; **for** de); **the ~ to do** les qualités *fpl* nécessaires pour faire; **to fulfil one's ~** montrer de quoi on est capable.
II *adj* [*buyer, danger, energy, market, victim*] potentiel/-ielle; [*champion, rival*] en puissance; [*investor*] éventuel/-elle.

pothole *n* fondrière *f*, nid *m* de poule.

potholing ▶ 504 *n* (GB) spéléologie *f*.

pot plant *n* plante *f* d'appartement.

potter ▶ 626 *n* potier *m*.
■ **potter about**, **potter around** (GB) (do odd jobs) bricoler○; (go about daily chores) suivre son petit train-train○.

pottery *n* poterie *f*.

potty○ I *n* pot *m* (d'enfant).
II *adj* (GB) [*person*] dingue○; [*idea*] farfelu/-e○; **to be ~ about** être toqué/-e○ de.

pouch *n* **1** (bag) petit sac *m*; (for tobacco) blague *f* (à tabac); (for ammunition) étui *m* (à munitions); **2** (of marsupials) poche *f* ventrale.

poultry *n* (birds) volailles *fpl*; (meat) volaille *f*.

pounce *vi* bondir; **to ~ on** [*animal*] bondir sur [*prey, object*]; [*person*] se jeter sur [*victim*].

pound I *n* **1** ▶ 573 (weight measurement) livre *f* (= *453.6 g*); **two ~s of apples** ≈ un kilo de pommes; **2** ▶ 582 (unit of currency) livre *f*; **3** (for dogs, cars) fourrière *f*.
II *vtr* **1** (Culin) piler [*spices, grain*]; aplatir [*meat*]; **2** [*waves*] battre [*shore*]; **3** [*artillery*] pilonner [*city*].
III *vi* **1 to ~ on** marteler [*door, wall*]; **2** [*heart*] battre; **3 to ~ up/down the stairs** monter/descendre l'escalier d'un pas lourd; **4 my head is ~ing** j'ai l'impression que ma tête va éclater.

pour I *vtr* **1** verser [*liquid*]; couler [*cement, metal, wax*]; **2** (also **~ out**) servir [*drink*]; **3 to ~ money into** investir des sommes énormes dans.
II *vi* **1** [*liquid*] couler (à flots); **to ~ into** [*water, liquid*] couler dans; [*smoke, fumes*] se répandre dans; [*light*] inonder [*room*]; **tears ~ed down her face** les larmes ruisselaient sur son visage; **2 to ~ into** [*people*] affluer dans; **to ~ out of** [*people, cars*] sortir en grand nombre de.
III *v impers* **it's ~ing (with rain)** il pleut à verse.
■ **pour away** vider.
■ **pour in** [*people*] affluer; [*letters, money*] pleuvoir; [*water*] entrer à flots.
■ **pour out**: ¶ **~ out** [*liquid, smoke, crowd*] se déverser; [*people*] sortir en grand nombre; ¶ **~ [sth] out 1** verser, servir [*coffee, wine*]; **2** rejeter [*fumes, sewage*]; **to ~ out one's troubles** or **heart to sb** s'épancher auprès de qn.

pout *vi* faire la moue.

poverty *n* pauvreté *f*; (more severe) misère *f*.

poverty-stricken *adj* dans la misère.

powder I *n* poudre *f*.
II *vtr* **to ~ one's face** se poudrer le visage.

powdered *adj* [*egg, milk, coffee*] en poudre.

powdery *adj* [*snow*] poudreux/-euse; [*stone*] friable.

power I *n* **1** (control) pouvoir *m*; **to be in/come to ~** être/accéder au pouvoir; **to be in sb's ~** être à la merci de qn; **2** (influence) influence *f* (**over** sur); **3** (capability) pouvoir *m*; **to do everything in one's ~** faire tout ce qui est en son pouvoir (**to do** pour faire); **4** (also **~s**) (authority) attributions *fpl*; **5** (physical force) (of person, explosion) force *f*; (of storm) violence *f*; **6** (Tech) énergie *f*; (current) courant *m*; **to switch on the ~** mettre le courant; **7** (of vehicle, plane) puissance *f*; **to be running at full/half ~** fonctionner à plein/mi-régime; **8** (in mathematics) **6 to the ~ of 3** 6 puissance 3; **9** (country) puissance *f*.
II *adj* [*drill, cable*] électrique; [*steering, brakes*] assisté.
III *vtr* faire marcher [*engine*]; propulser [*plane, boat*].
IDIOMS **to do sb a ~ of good** faire à qn un bien fou; **the ~s that be** les autorités.

powerboat *n* hors-bord *m inv*.

power cut *n* coupure *f* de courant.

powerful *adj* [*person, engine, computer*] puissant/-e; [*smell, emotion, voice, government*] fort/-e; [*argument*] solide.

powerless *adj* impuissant/-e (**against** face à); **to be ~ to do** ne pas pouvoir faire.

power line *n* ligne *f* à haute tension.

power plant (US), **power station** *n* centrale *f* (électrique)

PR *n* **1** (*abbr* = **public relations**) relations *fpl* publiques; **2** *abbr* = **proportional representation**.

practical I *n* (exam) épreuve *f* pratique; (lesson) travaux *mpl* pratiques.
II *adj* **1** (gen) pratique; **2** [*plan*] réalisable.

practicality *n* **1** (of person) esprit *m* pratique; (of equipment) facilité *f* d'utilisation; **2** (of scheme, idea, project) aspect *m* pratique.

practical joke *n* farce *f*.

practically *adv* **1** (almost) pratiquement; **2** (in practical way) d'une manière pratique.

practice I *n* **1** (exercises) exercices *mpl*; (experience) entraînement *m*; **to have had ~ in** or **at sth/in** or **at doing sth** avoir déjà fait qch; **to be out of ~** être rouillé/-e○; **2** (for sport) entraînement *m*; (for music, drama) répétition *f*; **3** (procedure) pratique *f*, usage *m*; **it's standard ~ to do** il est d'usage de faire; **business ~** usage en affaires; **4** (habit) habitude *f*; **5** (custom) coutume *f*; **6** (business of doctor, lawyer)

cabinet *m*; **7** (not theory) pratique *f*; **in ~** en pratique.
II *adj* [*game, match*] d'essai; [*flight*] d'entraînement.
III *vtr*, *vi* (US) = **practise**.
IDIOMS **~ makes perfect** c'est en forgeant qu'on devient forgeron (Proverb).

practise (GB), **practice** (US) **I** *vtr* **1** travailler [*song, speech, French*]; s'exercer à [*movement, shot*]; répéter [*play*]; **to ~ the piano** travailler le piano; **to ~ doing** or **how to do** s'entraîner à faire; **2** (use) pratiquer [*restraint, kindness*]; utiliser [*method*]; **3** exercer [*profession*]; **4** (observe) pratiquer [*custom, religion*].
II *vi* **1** (at instrument) s'exercer; (for sports) s'entraîner; (for play, concert) répéter; **2** (work) exercer; **to ~ as** exercer la profession de [*doctor, lawyer*].

pragmatic *adj* pragmatique.

prairie *n* plaine *f* (herbeuse).

praise I *n* éloges *mpl*, louanges *fpl*.
II *vtr* **1** faire l'éloge de [*person, book*] (**as** en tant que); **2** louer [*God*] (**for** pour).

praiseworthy *adj* digne d'éloges.

pram *n* (GB) landau *m*.

prance *vi* [*horse*] caracoler; [*person*] sautiller.

prattle *vi* bavarder; [*children*] babiller; **to ~ on about sth** parler de qch à n'en plus finir.

prawn *n* crevette *f* rose, bouquet *m*.

pray *vi* prier (**for** pour).

prayer *n* prière *f*; **to say one's ~s** faire sa prière.

preach I *vtr* prêcher (**to** à).
II *vi* prêcher (**to** à); (figurative) sermonner.
IDIOMS **to practise what one ~es** prêcher d'exemple.

preacher *n* prédicateur *m*; (clergyman) pasteur *m*.

precarious *adj* précaire.

precaution *n* précaution *f* (**against** contre).

precautionary *adj* préventif/-ive.

precede *vtr* précéder.

precedence *n* **1** (in importance) priorité *f* (**over** sur); **2** (in rank) préséance *f* (**over** sur).

precedent *n* précédent *m*; **to set a ~** créer un précédent.

preceding *adj* précédent/-e.

precinct *n* **1** (GB) (also **shopping ~**) quartier *m* commerçant; **2** (GB) (also **pedestrian ~**) zone *f* piétonne; **3** (US) (administrative district) circonscription *f*.

precious *adj* **1** (valuable) précieux/-ieuse; **2** (held dear) [*person*] cher/chère (**to** à); **3** (affected) précieux/-ieuse, affecté/-e.

precipice *n* précipice *m*.

precise *adj* **1** (exact) précis/-e; **2** [*person, mind*] méticuleux/-euse.

precisely *adv* **1** (exactly) exactement, précisément; **at ten o'clock ~** à dix heures précises; **2** (accurately) [*describe, record*] avec précision.

precision *n* précision *f*.

preclude *vtr* exclure [*possibility*]; empêcher [*action*].

precocious *adj* précoce.

preconceived *adj* préconçu/-e.

precondition *n* condition *f* requise.

precursor *n* (person) précurseur *m*; (sign) signe *m* avant-coureur.

predator *n* prédateur *m*.

predecessor *n* prédécesseur *m*.

predicament *n* situation *f* difficile.

predict *vtr* prédire.

predictable *adj* prévisible.

prediction *n* prédiction *f* (**that** selon laquelle).

predispose *vtr* prédisposer.

predominant *adj* prédominant/-e.

predominantly *adv* principalement.

pre-eminent *adj* éminent/-e.

pre-empt *vtr* **1** anticiper [*question, decision, move*]; devancer [*person*]; **2** (thwart) contrecarrer [*action, plan*].

pre-emptive *adj* préventif/-ive.

preen *v refl* **to ~ oneself** [*bird*] se lisser les plumes; [*person*] se pomponner.

prefab *n* (bâtiment *m*) préfabriqué *m*.

preface *n* (to book) préface *f*; (to speech) préambule *m*.

prefect *n* (GB Sch) élève *m/f* chargé/-e de la surveillance.

prefer *vtr* **1** (like better) préférer, aimer mieux; **I ~ painting to drawing** je préfère la peinture au dessin; **to ~ it if** aimer mieux que (+ *subjunctive*); **2** (Law) **to ~ charges** [*police*] déférer [qn] au parquet.

preferable *adj* préférable (**to** à).

preferably *adv* de préférence.

preference *n* préférence *f* (**for** pour).

preferential *adj* préférentiel/-ielle.

prefix *n* préfixe *m*.

pregnancy *n* (gen) grossesse *f*; (Zool) gestation *f*.

pregnant *adj* (gen) enceinte; (Zool) pleine.

preheat *vtr* préchauffer [*oven*].

prehistoric *adj* préhistorique.

prejudice I *n* préjugé *m*; **racial/political ~** préjugés raciaux/en matière de politique.
II *vtr* **1** (bias) influencer; **to ~ sb against/in favour of** prévenir qn contre/en faveur de; **2** porter préjudice à [*claim, case*]; léser [*person*]; compromettre [*chances*].

prejudiced *adj* [*person*] plein/-e de préjugés; [*account*] partial/-e; [*opinion*] préconçu/-e.

preliminary I *n* **1** (gen) **as a ~ to** en prélude à; **2** (Sport) épreuve *f* éliminatoire.
II preliminaries *n pl* préliminaires *mpl* (**to** à).
III *adj* préliminaire.

prelude *n* prélude *m* (**to** à).

premature *adj* [*baby, action*] prématuré/-e; [*ejaculation, menopause*] précoce.

premeditate *vtr* préméditer.

premier I *n* premier ministre *m*.
II *adj* premier/-ière (*before n*).

première I *n* première *f*.
II *vtr* donner [qch] en première [*film, play*].

premises *n pl* locaux *mpl*; **on the ~** sur place; **off the ~** à l'extérieur; **to leave the ~** quitter les lieux.
premium *n* **1** (extra payment) supplément *m*; **2** (on stock exchange) prime *f* d'émission; **3** (in insurance) prime *f* (d'assurance); **4 to be at a ~** valoir de l'or; **to set a (high) ~ on sth** mettre qch au (tout) premier plan.
premium bond (GB) *n* obligation *f* à lots.
premonition *n* prémonition *f*.
prenatal *adj* prénatal/-e.
preoccupation *n* préoccupation *f*.
preoccupied *adj* préoccupé/-e.
prepaid *adj* payé/-e d'avance; **~ envelope** enveloppe *f* affranchie pour la réponse.
preparation *n* préparation *f*; **~s** préparatifs *mpl*; **in ~ for sth** en vue de qch.
preparatory *adj* [*training, course, drawing*] préparatoire; [*meeting, report, investigations*] préliminaire.
preparatory school *n* **1** (GB) école *f* primaire privée; **2** (US) lycée *m* privé.
prepare I *vtr* préparer; **to ~ to do** se préparer à faire; **to ~ sb for** préparer qn à.
II *vi* **to ~ for** se préparer à [*trip, talks, exam, war*]; se préparer pour [*party, ceremony, game*]; **to ~ oneself** se préparer.
prepared *adj* **1** (willing) **to be ~ to do** être prêt/-e à faire; **2** (ready) **to be ~ for** être prêt/-e pour [*event*]; **to come ~** venir bien préparé/-e; **to be ~ for the worst** s'attendre au pire.
preposition *n* préposition *f*.
preposterous *adj* grotesque.
prerequisite *n* **1** (gen) préalable *m* (**of** de; **for** à); **2** (US Univ) unité *f* de valeur.
prerogative *n* (official) prérogative *f*; (personal) droit *m*.
preschool I *n* (US) école *f* maternelle.
II *adj* préscolaire.
prescribe *vtr* **1** (Med, figurative) prescrire (**for sb** à qn; **for sth** pour qch); **2** imposer [*rule*].
prescription *n* ordonnance *f*.
presence *n* présence *f*.
presence of mind *n* présence *f* d'esprit.
present I *n* **1** (gift) cadeau *m*; **to give sb a ~** offrir un cadeau à qn; **2 the ~** le présent; **for the ~** pour le moment, pour l'instant; **3** (also **~ tense**) présent *m*.
II *adj* **1** (attending) présent/-e; **to be ~ at** assister à; **2** (current) actuel/-elle; **up to the ~ day** jusqu'à ce jour.
III *vtr* **1** (gen) présenter; offrir [*chance, opportunity*]; **to be ~ed with a choice** se trouver face à un choix; **2** remettre [*prize, certificate*] (**to** à).
IV *v refl* **to ~ oneself** se présenter; **to ~ itself** [*opportunity, thought*] se présenter.
V at present *phr* (at this moment) en ce moment; (nowadays) actuellement.
presentable *adj* présentable.
presentation *n* **1** (gen) présentation *f*; **2** (talk) exposé *m*; **3** (of gift, award) remise *f* (**of** de); **4** (portrayal) représentation *f*.
presenter ▶ 626 *n* présentateur/-trice *m/f*.
presently *adv* (currently) à présent; (soon, in future) bientôt.
present perfect *n* passé *m* composé.
preservation *n* (of building, wildlife, peace) préservation *f* (**of** de); (of food) conservation *f* (**of** de); (of life) protection *f* (**of** de).
preservative *n* (for food) agent *m* de conservation; (for wood) revêtement *m* (protecteur).
preserve I *n* **1** (Culin) (jam) confiture *f*; (pickle) conserve *f*; **2** (territory) chasse *f* gardée (**of** de).
II *vtr* **1** (save) préserver [*land, building, tradition*] (**for** pour); entretenir [*wood, leather, painting*]; **2** (maintain) préserver [*peace, standards, rights*]; maintenir [*order*]; garder [*humour, dignity, health*]; **3** conserver [*food*].
preset *vtr* régler (à l'avance) [*timer, cooker*]; programmer [*video*].
presidency *n* présidence *f*.
president ▶ 498 *n* **1** président/-e *m/f*; **to run for ~** être candidat/-e à la présidence; **2** (US) (managing director) président-directeur *m* général.
presidential *adj* présidentiel/-ielle.
press I *n* **1 the ~, the Press** la presse *f*; **to get a good/bad ~** avoir bonne/mauvaise presse; **2** (also **printing ~**) presse *f*; **3** (device for flattening) presse *f*.
II *vtr* **1** (push) appuyer sur; **to ~ sth in** enfoncer qch; **to ~ one's nose against sth** coller son nez contre qch; **2** (squeeze) presser [*fruit, flower*]; serrer [*arm, hand, person*]; **3** (iron) repasser [*clothes*]; **4** (urge) faire pression sur [*person*]; mettre [qch] en avant [*issue*]; **to ~ sb to do** presser qn de faire; **to ~ a point** insister.
III *vi* **1 to ~ (down)** appuyer; **2** [*crowd, person*] se presser (**forward** vers l'avant).
IV *v refl* **to ~ oneself against** se plaquer contre [*wall*]; se presser contre [*person*].
■ **press for** faire pression pour obtenir [*change, release*]; **to be ~ed for** ne pas avoir beaucoup de [*time, cash*].
■ **press on** continuer; **to ~ on with** faire avancer [*reform, plan*].
press conference *n* conférence *f* de presse.
pressing *adj* **1** (urgent) urgent/-e; **2** [*invitation*] pressant/-e.
press release *n* communiqué *m* de presse.
press-stud *n* (GB) (bouton-)pression *m*.
press-up *n* pompe○ *f*.
pressure *n* **1** (gen) pression *f*; **to put ~ on sb** faire pression sur qn; **to do sth under ~** faire qch sous la contrainte; **2** (of traffic, tourists) flux *m*.
pressure cooker *n* cocotte-minute® *f*.
pressure group *n* groupe *m* de pression.
pressurize *vtr* **1** pressuriser [*cabin, suit, gas*]; **2** faire pression sur [*person*]; **he was ~d into going** on a fait pression sur lui pour qu'il y aille.
prestige *n* prestige *m*.
prestigious *adj* prestigieux/-ieuse.
presumably *adv* sans doute.
presume *vtr* **1** (suppose) supposer, présumer; **2** (dare) **to ~ to do** se permettre de faire.

presumptuous *adj* présomptueux/-euse, arrogant/-e.

presuppose *vtr* présupposer (**that** que).

pretence (GB), **pretense** (US) *n* faux-semblant *m*; **to make a ~ of sth** feindre qch; **to make a ~ of doing** faire semblant de faire.

pretend I *vtr* **to ~ that** faire comme si; **to ~ to do** faire semblant de faire.
II *vi* faire semblant.

pretension *n* prétention *f*.

pretentious *adj* prétentieux/-ieuse.

preterite *n* prétérit.

pretext *n* prétexte *m*.

pretty I *adj* joli/-e; **it was not a ~ sight** ce n'était pas beau à voir.
II° *adv* (very) vraiment; (fairly) assez; **~ good** pas mal du tout.

prevail *vi* **1** (win) prévaloir (**against** contre; **2** (be common) prédominer.
■ **prevail upon** persuader [*person*].

prevailing *adj* [*attitude, style*] qui prévaut; [*rate*] en vigueur; [*wind*] dominant/-e.

prevalent *adj* **1** (widespread) répandu/-e; **2** (ruling) qui prévaut.

prevent *vtr* prévenir [*fire, illness, violence*]; éviter [*conflict, disaster, damage*]; faire obstacle à [*marriage*]; **to ~ sb from doing** empêcher qn de faire.

prevention *n* prévention *f*; **crime ~** lutte *f* contre la délinquance.

preventive *adj* préventif/-ive.

preview *n* (of film, play) avant-première *f*.

previous *adj* précédent/-e; (further back in time) antérieur/-e.

previously *adv* (before) auparavant, avant; (already) déjà.

prewar *adj* d'avant-guerre *inv*.

prey *n* proie *f*.
■ **prey on 1** (hunt) chasser; **2** (worry) **to ~ on sb's mind** préoccuper qn.

price I *n* **1** (cost) prix *m*; **to go up in ~** augmenter; **to pay a high ~ for sth** payer qch cher; **at any ~** à tout prix; **2** (value) valeur *f*; **to put a ~ on** évaluer [*object, antique*].
II *vtr* fixer le prix de (**at** à).

priceless *adj* **1** (extremely valuable) inestimable; **2°** (amusing) impayable°.

price list *n* (in shop, catalogue) liste *f* des prix; (in bar, restaurant) tarif *m*.

price tag *n* (label) étiquette *f*.

prick I *n* (of needle) piqûre *f*.
II *vtr* piquer; **to ~ one's finger** se piquer le doigt.
III *vi* piquer.
■ **prick up**: **to ~ up one's ears** [*person*] dresser l'oreille; **the dog ~ed up its ears** le chien a dressé les oreilles.

prickle I *n* (of hedgehog, plant) piquant *m*.
II *vi* [*hairs*] se hérisser (**with** de).

prickly *adj* **1** [*bush, leaf*] épineux/-euse; [*animal*] armé/-e de piquants; [*thorn*] piquant/-e; **2** (itchy) qui gratte; **3°** (touchy) irritable (**about** à propos de).

pride I *n* **1** fierté *f*; **to take ~ in** être fier/fière de [*ability, achievement*]; soigner [*appearance, work*]; **to be sb's ~ and joy** être la (grande) fierté de qn; **2** (self-respect) amour-propre *m*; (excessive) orgueil *m*; **3** (of lions) troupe *f*.
II *v refl* **to ~ oneself on sth/on doing** être fier/fière de qch/de faire.
IDIOMS **to have ~ of place** occuper la place d'honneur.

priest *n* prêtre *m*; **parish ~** curé *m*.

priesthood *n* (calling) prêtrise *f*; **to enter the ~** entrer dans les ordres.

prig *n* bégueule *mf*.

prim *adj* (also **~ and proper**) [*person, manner, appearance*] guindé/-e; [*expression*] pincé/-e; [*voice*] affecté/-e; [*clothing*] très convenable.

primarily *adv* (chiefly) essentiellement; (originally) à l'origine.

primary I *n* (US) (also **~ election**) primaire *f*.
II *adj* **1** (main) principal/-e; [*sense, meaning, stage*] premier/-ière; **of ~ importance** de première importance; **2** (Sch) [*teaching, education*] primaire; **3** [*industry, products*] de base.

primary colour (GB), **primary color** (US) *n* couleur *f* primaire.

primary school *n* école *f* primaire.

primary (school) teacher ▶ 626 *n* (GB) instituteur/-trice *m/f*.

primate *n* **1** (mammal) primate *m*; **2** (archbishop) primat *m* (**of** de).

prime I *n* **in one's ~** (professionally) à son apogée; (physically) dans la fleur de l'âge; **in its ~** à son apogée; **to be past its ~** avoir connu des jours meilleurs.
II *adj* **1** (chief) principal/-e; [*importance*] primordial/-e; **2** (good quality) [*site*] de premier ordre; [*meat, cuts*] de premier choix; **of ~ quality** de première qualité; **3** (classic) [*example*] excellent/-e (before n).
III *vtr* **1** (brief) préparer; **to ~ sb about** mettre qn au courant de; **to ~ sb to say** souffler à qn de dire; **2** (Mil, Tech) amorcer.

prime minister, **PM** ▶ 498 *n* Premier ministre *m*.

prime number *n* nombre *m* premier.

prime time *n* heures *fpl* de grande écoute *m*.

primeval *adj* primitif/-ive.

primitive I *n* primitif *m*.
II *adj* primitif/-ive.

primrose *n* primevère *f* (jaune).

prince ▶ 498 *n* prince *m*.

princess ▶ 498 *n* princesse *f*.

principal I *n* ▶ 498 (of senior school) proviseur *m*; (of junior school, college) directeur/-trice *m/f*.
II *adj* principal/-e.

principle *n* principe *m*; **in ~** en principe; **on ~** par principe.

print I *n* **1** (typeface) caractères *mpl*; **the small** or **fine ~** les détails; **in ~** disponible en librairie; **out of ~** épuisé/-e; **2** (etching)

estampe *f*; (engraving) gravure *f*; **3** (of photo) épreuve *f*; **4** (of finger, hand, foot) empreinte *f*; (of tyre) trace *f*; **5** (fabric) tissu *m* imprimé.
II *vtr* **1** imprimer [*book, banknote, pattern, design*]; **2** (publish) publier; **3** faire développer [*photos*]; **4** (write) écrire [qch] en script.
■ **print off** tirer [*copies*].
■ **print out** imprimer.

printer *n* (person, firm) imprimeur *m*; (machine) imprimante *f*.

prior I *adj* **1** (previous) préalable; **~ notice** préavis *m*; **2** (more important) prioritaire.
II **prior to** *phr* avant.

priority *n* priorité *f*.

priory *n* prieuré *m*.

prise *v* ■ **prise apart** séparer [*layers, people*].
■ **prise off** enlever [qch] en forçant [*lid*].
■ **prise open** ouvrir [qch] en forçant [*door*].

prism *n* prisme *m*.

prison *n* prison *f*; **to put sb in ~** emprisonner qn.

prison camp *n* camp *m* de prisonniers.

prisoner *n* prisonnier/-ière *m/f*; (in jail) détenu/-e *m/f*.

prison sentence *n* peine *f* de prison.

privacy *n* **1** (private life) vie *f* privée; **to invade sb's ~** s'immiscer dans la vie privée de qn; **2** (solitude) intimité *f* (**of** de).

private I *n* simple soldat *m*.
II *adj* **1** [*property, vehicle, meeting, life*] privé/-e; [*letter, phone call*] personnel/-elle; [*sale*] de particulier à particulier; [*place*] tranquille; **room with ~ bath** chambre avec salle de bains particulière; **a ~ joke** une plaisanterie pour initiés; **2** [*sector, education, school, hospital*] privé/-e; [*accommodation, lesson*] particulier/-ière.
III **in private** *phr* en privé.

privately *adv* **1** (in private) en privé; **2** (in private) dans le privé; **~-owned** privé/-e.

privatize *vtr* privatiser.

privilege *n* privilège *m*.

privileged *adj* [*minority, life*] privilégié/-e; [*information*] confidentiel/-ielle.

prize I *n* **1** (award) prix *m*; (in lottery) lot *m*; **first ~** premier prix; (in lottery) gros lot; **2** (valued object) trésor *m*; (reward for effort) récompense *f*.
II *adj* **1** [*vegetable, bull*] primé/-e; [*pupil*] hors-pair *inv*; **2** [*possession*] précieux/-ieuse; **3** [*idiot, example*] parfait/-e (*before n*).

prize-giving *n* remise *f* des prix.

prize money *n* argent *m* du prix.

prizewinner *n* (in lottery) gagnant/-e *m/f*; (of award) lauréat/-e *m/f*.

pro I *n* **1**○ (professional) pro○ *mf*; **2** (advantage) **the ~s and cons** le pour et le contre; **the ~s and cons of sth** les avantages et les inconvénients de qch.
II○ *prep* (in favour of) pour.

probability *n* (of desirable event) chances *fpl*; (of unwelcome event) risques *mpl*.

probable *adj* probable.

probably *adv* probablement.

probation *n* **1** (for adult) sursis *m* avec mise à l'épreuve; (for juvenile) mise *f* en liberté surveillée; **2** (trial period) période *f* d'essai.

probe I *n* **1** (investigation) enquête *f*; **2** (instrument) sonde *f*.
II *vtr* (Med, Tech) sonder (**with** avec).

problem I *n* problème *m*.
II *adj* [*child*] difficile; [*family*] à problèmes.

problematic(al) *adj* problématique.

problem page *n* courrier *m* du cœur.

procedure *n* procédure *f*.

proceed *vi* **1** (set about) procéder; (continue) poursuivre; **to ~ with** poursuivre; **2** (be in progress) [*project, work*] avancer; [*interview, talks, trial*] se poursuivre; **3** [*person, road*] continuer; [*vehicle*] avancer.

proceedings *n pl* **1** (meeting) réunion *f*; (ceremony) cérémonie *f*; (discussion) débats *mpl*; **2** (Law) poursuites *fpl*.

proceeds *n pl* (of sale) produit *m*; (of event) recette *f*.

process I *n* **1** (gen) processus *m* (**of** de); **to be in the ~ of doing** être en train de faire; **in the ~** en même temps; **2** (method) procédé *m*.
II *vtr* **1** traiter [*applications, data*]; **2** traiter [*raw materials, chemical, waste*]; **3** développer [*film*]; **4** (Culin) (mix) mixer; (chop) hacher.

processing *n* traitement *m*; **the food ~ industry** l'industrie alimentaire.

procession *n* (of demonstration, carnival) défilé *m*; (formal) cortège *m*; (religious) procession *f*.

proclaim *vtr* proclamer (**that** que).

proclamation *n* proclamation *f*.

procrastinate *vi* atermoyer.

procure *vtr* procurer; **to ~ sth for sb** procurer qch à qn; **to ~ sth for oneself** se procurer qch.

prod I *n* **1** (poke) petit coup *m*; **2**○ (reminder) **to give sb a ~** secouer○ qn.
II *vtr* (also **~ at**) (with foot, instrument, stick) donner des petits coups à; (with finger) toucher.

prodigy *n* prodige *m*.

produce I *n* produits *mpl*.
II *vtr* **1** (cause) produire [*result, effect*]; provoquer [*reaction, change*]; **2** [*region, farmer, company*] produire (**from** à partir de); [*worker, machine*] fabriquer; **3** (generate) produire [*heat, sound, energy*]; rapporter [*profits*]; **4** (present) produire [*passport, report*]; fournir [*evidence, argument, example*]; **to ~ sth from** sortir qch de [*pocket, bag*]; **5** produire [*show, film*]; (GB) mettre [qch] en scène [*play*]; **6** (put together) préparer [*meal*]; mettre au point [*timetable, package, solution*]; éditer [*brochure, guide*].

producer ▶ 626 *n* **1** (of produce) producteur *m*; (of machinery, goods) fabricant *m*; **2** (of film) producteur/-trice *m/f*; (GB) (of play) metteur *m* en scène.

product *n* produit *m*.

production *n* **1** (of crop, foodstuffs, metal) production *f* (**of** de); (of machinery, furniture, cars) fabrication (**of** de); **2** (output) production *f*; **3** (of film, opera) production *f* (**of** de); (of play) mise *f* en scène (**of** de).

production line *n* chaîne *f* de fabrication.

productive *adj* [*factory, land, day*] productif/-ive; [*system, method, use*] efficace; [*discussion*] fructueux/-euse.

productivity *n* productivité *f*.

profane *adj* **1** (blasphemous) impie; **2** (secular) profane.

profession ▶626 *n* profession *f*.

professional I *n* professionnel/-elle *m/f*.
II *adj* professionnel/-elle.

professor ▶498 *n* **1** (Univ) (chair holder) professeur *m* d'Université; **2** (US Univ) (teacher) professeur *m*.

proficiency *n* (practical) compétence *f* (**in, at** en); (academic) niveau *m* (**in** en).

proficient *adj* compétent/-e.

profile *n* (of face) profil *m*; (of body) silhouette *f*; **in ~** de profil; **to have/maintain a high ~** occuper/rester sur le devant de la scène.

profit I *n* **1** bénéfice *m*, profit *m*; **gross/net ~** bénéfice brut/net; **2** (figurative) profit *m*.
II *vtr* profiter à [*person, group*].
III *vi* **to ~ by** or **from sth** tirer profit de qch.

profitable *adj* rentable; (figurative) fructueux/-euse.

profound *adj* profond/-e.

profusely *adv* [*sweat, bleed*] abondamment; **to apologize ~** se confondre en excuses.

prognosis *n* **1** (Med) pronostic *m* (**on, about** sur); **2** (prediction) pronostics *mpl*.

program I *n* **1** (Comput) programme *m*; **2** (US) (on radio, TV) émission *f*.
II *vtr, vi* programmer (**to do** pour faire).

programme (GB), **program** (US) I *n* **1** (broadcast) émission *f* (**about** sur); **2** (schedule) programme *m*; **3** (for play, opera) programme *m*.
II *vtr* programmer [*machine*] (**to do** pour faire).

programmer ▶626 *n* programmeur/-euse *m/f*.

progress I *n* **1** (advances) progrès *m*; **to make ~** [*person*] faire des progrès; **2** (of person, inquiry) progression *f*; (of talks, disease, career) évolution *f*; **to be in ~** [*discussions, exam*] être en cours.
II *vi* progresser.

progression *n* **1** (evolution) évolution *f*; **2** (improvement) progression *f*; **3** (series) suite *f*.

progressive *adj* **1** (gen) progressif/-ive; **2** (forward-looking) [*person, policy*] progressiste; [*school*] parallèle.

prohibit *vtr* interdire; **to ~ sb from doing** interdire à qn de faire.

prohibition *n* interdiction *f* (**on, against** de).

project I *n* **1** (scheme) projet *m* (**to do** pour faire); **2** (Sch) dossier *m* (**on** sur); (Univ) mémoire *m* (**on** sur); **research ~** programme *m* de recherches; **3** (US) (state housing) (large) ≈ cité *f* HLM; (small) ≈ lotissement *m* HLM.
II *vtr* **1** envoyer [*missile*]; faire porter [*voice*]; **2** projeter [*guilt, anxiety*] (**onto** sur); **3** (estimate) prévoir; **4** projeter [*image, slides*].

projecting *adj* saillant/-e.

projector *n* projecteur *m*.

proliferate *vi* proliférer.

prolific *adj* (gen) prolifique; [*decade*] fécond/-e; [*growth*] rapide.

prologue *n* prologue *m* (**to** de).

prolong *vtr* prolonger.

promenade *n* (path) promenade *f*; (by sea) front *m* de mer.

prominent *adj* **1** [*figure, campaigner*] très en vue; [*artist*] éminent/-e; **to play a ~ part in sth** jouer un rôle de premier plan dans qch; **2** [*place, feature*] proéminent/-e; [*ridge, cheekbone*] saillant/-e; [*eye*] exorbité/-e.

promiscuous *adj* [*person*] aux mœurs légères.

promise I *n* promesse *f*; **to break one's ~** manquer à sa promesse; **she shows great ~** elle promet beaucoup.
II *vtr* **to ~ to do** promettre de faire; **to ~ sb sth** promettre qch à qn.
III *vi* promettre; **do you ~?** c'est promis?

promising *adj* [*situation, result, future*] prometteur/-euse; [*artist, candidate*] qui promet.

promote *vtr* **1** (in rank) promouvoir (**to** à); **2** (advertise) faire de la publicité pour; (market) promouvoir; **3** (encourage) promouvoir; **4** (GB) (in football) **to be ~d from the fourth to the third division** passer de quatrième en troisième division.

promotion *n* promotion *f*.

prompt I *adj* rapide; **to be ~ to do** être prompt/-e à faire.
II *vtr* **1** provoquer [*reaction, decision*]; susciter [*concern, comment*]; **to ~ sb to do** inciter qn à faire; **2** (remind) souffler à [*actor*].

prompter *n* **1** (in theatre) souffleur/-euse *m/f*; **2** (US) (teleprompter) téléprompteur *m*.

promptly *adv* **1** (immediately) immédiatement; **2** (without delay) rapidement; **3** (punctually) à l'heure; **~ at six o'clock** à six heures précises.

prone *adj* **1 to be ~ to** être sujet/-ette à [*colds*]; être enclin/-e à [*depression*]; **2 to lie ~** être allongé/-e face contre terre.

pronoun *n* pronom *m*.

pronounce *vtr* prononcer.
■ **pronounce on** se prononcer sur [*case, matter*].

pronounced *adj* [*accent, tendency*] prononcé/-e; [*change, increase*] marqué/-e.

pronunciation *n* prononciation *f*.

proof *n* **1** (evidence) preuve *f*; **~ of identity** pièce *f* d'identité; **2** (in printing, photography) épreuve *f*; **3** (of alcohol) **to be 70% ~** ≈ titrer 40° d'alcool.

proofread *vtr* corriger les épreuves de.

prop I *n* étai *m*.
II **props** *n pl* accessoires *mpl*.
III *vtr* **1** (also **~ up**) étayer; **2 to ~ sb/sth against sth** appuyer qn/qch contre qch.

propaganda *n* propagande *f*.

propagate *vi* se propager.

propel *vtr* propulser.

propeller *n* hélice *f*.

proper *adj* **1** (right) [*term, spelling*] correct/-e; [*order, tool, response*] bon/bonne (*before n*);

Shops, Trades, and Professions

Shops

In English you can say *at the baker's* or *at the baker's shop*; in French the construction with ***chez*** (*at the house* or *premises of*. . .) is common but you can also use the name of the particular shop:

at *the baker's*	= **à** la boulangerie
	= **chez** le boulanger
I'm going ***to*** *the grocer's*	= je vais **à** l'épicerie
	= je vais **chez** l'épicier
I bought it ***at*** *the fishmonger's*	= je l'ai acheté **à** la poissonnerie
	= je l'ai acheté **chez** le poissonnier
go to the chemist's	= va **à** la pharmacie
	= va **chez** le pharmacien
to work ***in*** *a butcher's*	= travailler **dans** une boucherie

chez is also used with the names of professions:

at / ***to*** *the doctor's*	= **chez** le médecin
at / ***to*** *the lawyer's*	= **chez** le notaire
at / ***to*** *the dentist's*	= **chez** le dentiste

Note that there are specific names for the place of work of some professions:

the lawyer's ***office***	= l'**étude** *f* du notaire
the doctor's ***surgery*** (GB) / ***office*** (US)	= le **cabinet** du médecin

cabinet is also used for architects and dentists. If in doubt, check in the dictionary.

People

Talking of someone's profession, we could say *he is a dentist*. In French this would be either *il est dentiste* or *c'est un dentiste*. Only when the sentence begins with ***c'est*** can the indefinite article (*un* or *une*) be used:

Paul is a dentist	= Paul est dentiste
she's a geography teacher	= elle est professeur de géographie
	= c'est un professeur de géographie

With adjectives, only the ***c'est*** construction is possible:

she is a good dentist	= c'est une bonne dentiste

In the plural, if the construction begins with ***ce sont*** then you need to use ***des*** (or ***de*** before an adjective):

they are mechanics	= ils sont mécaniciens
	= ce sont **des** mécaniciens
they are good mechanics	= ce sont **de** bons mécaniciens

Trades and professions

what does he do?	= qu'est-ce qu'il fait?
what's your job?	= qu'est-ce que vous faites dans la vie?
I'm a teacher	= je suis professeur
to work as a dentist	= travailler comme dentiste
to work for an electrician	= travailler pour un électricien
he wants to be a baker	= il veut devenir boulanger

[*clothing*] qu'il faut; **everything is in the ~ place** tout est à sa place; **2** (adequate) [*recognition, facilities*] convenable; [*education, training*] bon/bonne (*before n*); [*care*] requis/-e; **3** (respectable) [*person*] correct/-e; [*upbringing*] convenable; **4** (real, full) [*doctor, holiday, job*] vrai/-e (*before n*); **5** (actual) **in the village ~** dans le village même.

properly *adv* **1** (correctly) correctement; **2** (fully) complètement; **I didn't have time to thank you ~** je n'ai pas eu le temps de vous remercier; **3** (adequately) convenablement.

proper name, **proper noun** *n* nom *m* propre.

property *n* **1** (belongings) propriété *f*, biens *mpl*; **2** (real estate) biens *mpl* immobiliers; **3** (house) propriété *f*; **4** (characteristic) propriété *f*.

property owner *n* propriétaire *mf*.

prophecy *n* prophétie *f*.

prophet *n* prophète *m*.

proportion I *n* **1** (of group, population) proportion *f* (**of** de); (of income, profit, work) part *f* (**of** de); **2** (ratio) proportion *f*; **3** (harmony) **out of/in ~** hors de/en proportion; **4** (perspective) **to get sth out of all ~** faire tout un drame de qch; **to be out of all ~** être tout à fait disproportionné/-e (**to** par rapport à).
II **proportions** *n pl* dimensions *fpl*.

proportional *adj* proportionnel/-elle.

proportional representation, **PR** *n* représentation *f* proportionnelle.

proposal *n* **1** (suggestion) proposition *f*; **2** (of marriage) demande *f* en mariage.

propose I *vtr* proposer [*course of action, solution*]; présenter [*motion*].
II *vi* faire sa demande en mariage (**to** à).

proposition I *n* **1** (suggestion) proposition *f*; **2** (assertion) assertion *f*.
II *vtr* faire une proposition à [*person*].

proprietor *n* propriétaire *mf* (**of** de).

propriety *n* **1** (politeness) correction *f*; **2** (morality) décence *f*.

proscribe *vtr* proscrire.

prose *n* **1** prose *f*; **2** (GB) (translation) thème *m*.

prosecute I *vtr* poursuivre [qn] en justice.
II *vi* engager des poursuites.

prosecution *n* (Law) **1** (accusation) poursuites *fpl* (judiciaires); **2 the ~** le/les plaignant/-s; (state, Crown) le ministère public.

prosecutor *n* (Law) procureur *m*.

prospect I *n* **1** (hope) espoir *m*, chance *f*; **2** (outlook) perspective *f*.
II **prospects** *n pl* perspectives *fpl*.

prospective *adj* [*buyer, candidate*] potentiel/-ielle; [*husband, wife*] futur/-e (*before n*).

prospectus *n* brochure *f*.

prosperity *n* prospérité *f*.

prosperous *adj* prospère.

prostate *n* (also **~ gland**) prostate *f*.

prostitute I *n* prostituée *f*; **male ~** prostitué *m*.
II *vtr* prostituer [*person, talent*].

prostrate *adj* **to lie ~** être allongé/-e de tout son long; **~ with grief** accablé/-e de chagrin.

protagonist *n* protagoniste *mf*.

protect *vtr* (gen) protéger (**against** contre; **from** de, contre); défendre [*consumer, interests*] (**against** contre).

protection *n* protection *f*.

protection factor *n* indice *m* de protection.

protective *adj* protecteur/-trice.

protein *n* protéine *f*.

protest I *n* **1** protestation *f*; **in ~** en signe de protestation; **2** (demonstration) manifestation *f*.
II *vtr* **1 to ~ that** protester que; **to ~ one's innocence** protester de son innocence; **2** (US) (complain about) protester contre (**to** auprès de).
III *vi* **1** (complain) protester; **2** (demonstrate) manifester (**against** contre).

Protestant *n*, *adj* protestant/-e (*m/f*).

protester *n* manifestant/-e *m/f*.

protocol *n* protocole *m*.

prototype *n* prototype *m* (**of** de).

protrude *vi* (gen) dépasser; [*teeth*] avancer.

protruding *adj* [*rock*] en saillie; [*eyes*] globuleux/-euse; [*ears*] décollé/-e; [*ribs*] saillant/-e; [*chin*] en avant.

proud *adj* **1** fier/fière (**of** de); [*owner*] heureux/-euse (*before n*); **2** [*day, moment*] grand/-e (*before n*).

prove I *vtr* prouver; (by demonstration) démontrer; **to ~ a point** montrer qu'on a raison.
II *vi* **to ~ to be** s'avérer être.
III *v refl* **to ~ oneself** faire ses preuves; **to ~ oneself (to be)** se révéler.

proverb *n* proverbe *m*.

provide *vtr* **1** (supply) fournir [*opportunity, evidence, jobs, meals*] (**for** à); apporter [*answer, support*] (**for** à); assurer [*service, access, training, shelter*] (**for** à); **2** [*clause, law*] prévoir (**that** que).
■ **provide for 1** envisager [*eventuality, expenses*]; **2** subvenir aux besoins de [*family*].

provided, **providing** *conj* (also **~ that**) à condition que (+ *subjunctive*).

province *n* province *f*; **in the ~s** en province.

provincial *adj* **1** [*newspaper, town*] de province; [*life*] provincial/-e; **2** (narrow) provincial/-e.

provision I *n* **1** (of goods, equipment) fourniture *f* (**of** de; **to** à); (of service) prestation *f*; **~ of food/supplies** approvisionnement *m* (**to** de); **2** (for future) dispositions *fpl*; **3** (in agreement) clause *f*; (in bill, act) disposition *f*.
II **provisions** *n pl* (supplies) provisions *fpl*.

provisional *adj* provisoire.

provocative *adj* **1** [*dress, remark*] provocant/-e; **2** [*book*] qui fait réfléchir.

provoke *vtr* **1** (annoy) provoquer; **2** (cause) susciter [*anger, complaints*]; provoquer [*laughter, reaction*].

prow *n* proue *f*.

prowess *n* **1** (skill) prouesses *fpl*; **2** (bravery) vaillance *f*.

prowl I *vtr* **to ~ the streets** rôder dans les rues.
II *vi* [*animal, person*] rôder.

proximity *n* proximité *f*.

proxy *n* **1** (person) mandataire *mf*; **2 by ~** par procuration.

prudent *adj* prudent/-e.

prudish *adj* pudibond/-e, prude.

prune I *n* (Culin) pruneau *m*.
II *vtr* (cut back) tailler; (thin out) élaguer.

pry *vi* **to ~ into** mettre son nez dans.

PS *n* (*abbr* = **postscriptum**) PS *m*.

psalm *n* psaume *m*.

pseudonym *n* pseudonyme *m*.

psychiatric *adj* psychiatrique.

psychiatrist ▶ 626 *n* psychiatre *mf*.

psychiatry *n* psychiatrie *f*.

psychic *n* médium *m*, voyant/-e *m/f*.

psychoanalysis *n* psychanalyse *f*.

psychological *adj* psychologique.

psychologist ▶ 626 *n* psychologue *mf*.

psychology *n* psychologie *f*.

psychopath *n* psychopathe *mf*.

PTO (*abbr* = **please turn over**) TSVP.

pub *n* (GB) pub *m*.

puberty *n* puberté *f*.

public I *n* **the ~** le public.
II *adj* (gen) public/-ique; [*library, amenity*] municipal/-e; [*duty, spirit*] civique; **to be in the ~ eye** occuper le devant de la scène.
III **in public** *phr* en public.

public address (system) *n* (système *m* de) sonorisation *f*.

public assistance *n* (US) aide *f* sociale.

publication *n* publication *f*.

public convenience *n* (GB) toilettes *fpl*.

public holiday *n* (GB) jour *m* férié.

publicity *n* publicité *f*; **to attract ~** attirer l'attention des médias.

publicity stunt *n* coup *m* publicitaire.

publicize *vtr* **1** attirer l'attention du public sur [*issue, problem*]; **2** rendre [qch] public [*information, facts*]; **3** faire de la publicité pour [*show*].

publicly *adv* publiquement.

public opinion *n* opinion *f* publique.

public prosecutor *n* procureur *m* général.

public relations, PR *n* relations *fpl* publiques.

public school *n* (GB) école *f* privée; (US) école *f* publique.

public transport *n* transports *mpl* en commun.

publish *vtr* publier [*book, letter, guide*]; éditer [*newspaper, magazine*].

publisher ▶ 626 *n* (person) éditeur/-trice *m/f*; (also **publishing house**) maison *f* d'édition.

publishing *n* édition *f*.

pudding *n* **1** (GB) (dessert course) dessert *m*; **2** (cooked dish) pudding *m*; **3** (GB) (sausage) **black/white ~** boudin *m* noir/blanc.

puddle *n* flaque *f*.

puff I *n* (of air, smoke, steam) bouffée *f*; (of breath) souffle *m*.
II *vtr* tirer sur [*pipe*].
III *vi* **1 to ~ at** tirer des bouffées de [*cigarette, pipe*]; **2** (pant) souffler.
■ **puff out 1** gonfler [*cheeks*]; [*bird*] hérisser [*feathers*]; **2 to ~ out smoke** lancer des bouffées de fumée.
■ **puff up**: ¶ **~ up** [*feathers*] se hérisser; [*eye*] devenir bouffi/-e; [*rice*] gonfler; ¶ **~ [sth] up** hérisser [*feathers, fur*]; **~ed up with pride** rempli/-e d'orgueil.

puff pastry *n* pâte *f* feuilletée.

puffy *adj* bouffi/-e.

pull I *n* **1** (tug) coup *m*; **to give sth a ~** tirer sur qch; **2** (attraction) force *f*; (figurative) attrait *m* (**of** de); **3**○ (influence) influence *f* (**over, with** sur).
II *vtr* **1** (gen) tirer; tirer sur [*cord, rope*]; **to ~ sb/sth through** faire passer qn/qch par [*hole, window*]; **to ~ sth out of** tirer qch de [*pocket, drawer*]; **to ~ sb out of** retirer qn de [*wreckage*]; sortir qn de [*river*]; **2**○ sortir [*gun, knife*]; **to ~ a gun on sb** menacer qn avec un pistolet; **3** appuyer sur [*trigger*]; **4** se faire une élongation à [*muscle*]; **5 to ~ a face** faire la grimace.
III *vi* tirer (**at, on** sur).
■ **pull apart 1** (dismantle) démonter; **2** (destroy) [*child*] mettre en pièces; [*animal*] déchiqueter.
■ **pull away**: ¶ **~ away** [*car*] démarrer; ¶ **~ [sb/sth] away** éloigner [*person*]; retirer [*hand*]; **to ~ sb/sth away from** écarter qn/qch de [*window, wall*].
■ **pull back 1** [*troops*] se retirer (**from** de); **2** [*car, person*] reculer.
■ **pull down** démolir [*building*]; baisser [*blind, trousers*].
■ **pull in** [*car, bus, driver*] s'arrêter.
■ **pull off 1** ôter [*coat, sweater*]; enlever [*shoes, lid, sticker*]; **2** conclure [*deal*]; réaliser [*feat*].
■ **pull out**: ¶ **~ out 1** [*car, truck*] déboîter; **to ~ out of sth** quitter qch [*station, drive*]; **2** [*troops, participants*] se retirer (**of** de); ¶ **~ [sth] out 1** extraire [*tooth*]; enlever [*splinter*]; arracher [*weeds*]; **2** (from pocket) sortir.
■ **pull over**: ¶ **~ over** [*motorist, car*] s'arrêter (sur le côté); ¶ **~ [sb/sth] over** [*police*] forcer [qn/qch] à se ranger sur le côté.
■ **pull through** [*accident victim*] s'en tirer.
■ **pull together**: ¶ **~ together** faire un effort; ¶ **~ oneself together** se ressaisir.
■ **pull up**: ¶ **~ up** s'arrêter; ¶ **~ up [sth], ~ [sth] up 1** (uproot) arracher; **2** lever [*anchor*]; remonter [*trousers, socks*]; prendre [*chair*]; ¶ **~ [sb] up 1** (lift) hisser; **2** (reprimand) réprimander; **3** arrêter [*driver*].

pulley *n* poulie *f*.

pullover *n* pull-over *m*.

pulp I *n* (soft centre) pulpe *f*; (crushed mass) pâte *f*.
II *vtr* écraser [*fruit, vegetable*]; réduire [qch] en pâte [*wood, cloth*]; mettre [qch] au pilon [*newspapers, books*].

pulp fiction *n* littérature *f* de gare.

pulpit *n* chaire *f*.

pulse *n* pouls *m*.

pulse rate *n* pouls *m*.

pulverize *vtr* pulvériser.

pump I *n* **1** (for air) pompe *f*; **bicycle ~** pompe à vélo; **2** (plimsoll) chaussure *f* de sport; (GB) (flat shoe) ballerine *f*; (US) (shoe with heel) chaussure *f* à talon.
II *vtr* **1** pomper [*air, gas, water*] (**out of** de); **2**○ (question) cuisiner○ [*person*]; **3** (Med) **to ~ sb's stomach** faire un lavage d'estomac à qn.
III *vi* [*heat*] battre violemment.
■ **pump up** gonfler [*tyre, air bed*].

pumpkin *n* citrouille *f*.

pun *n* jeu *m* de mots, calembour *m*.

punch I *n* **1** (blow) coup *m* de poing; **2** (of style, performance) énergie *f*; **3** (drink) punch *m*.
II *vtr* **1** donner un coup de poing à [*person*]; **to ~ sb in the face** donner un coup de poing dans la figure de qn; **2** perforer [*cards, tape*]; (manually) poinçonner [*ticket*].

Punch-and-Judy show *n* ≈ (spectacle *m* de) guignol *m*.

punchbag *n* (GB) sac *m* de sable.

punch line *n* chute *f*.

punctual *adj* ponctuel/-elle.

punctually *adv* [*start, arrive, leave*] à l'heure.

punctuation *n* ponctuation *f*.

punctuation mark *n* signe *m* de ponctuation.

puncture I *n* crevaison *f*; **we had a ~ on the way** on a crevé en chemin.
II *vtr* crever [*tyre, balloon, air bed*]; **to ~ a lung** se perforer un poumon.

puncture (repair) kit *n* boîte *f* de rustines®.

pungent *adj* [*flavour*] relevé/-e; [*smell*] fort/-e; [*gas, smoke*] âcre.

punish *vtr* punir.

punishment *n* punition *f*; (stronger) châtiment *m*.

punk I *n* **1** (music) punk *m*; **2** (punk rocker) punk *mf*; **3**○ (US) voyou *m*.
II *adj* punk *inv*.

punnet *n* (GB) barquette *f*.

punt *n* **1** (boat) barque *f* (à fond plat); **2** (Irish pound) livre *f* irlandaise.

puny *adj* [*person, body*] chétif/-ive.

pup *n* **1** (also **puppy**) chiot *m*; **2** (seal, otter) petit *m*.

pupil *n* **1** (Sch) élève *mf*; **2** (in eye) pupille *f*.

puppet *n* marionnette *f*.

purchase I *n* achat *m*.
II *vtr* acheter.

pure *adj* pur/-e.

puree *n* purée *f*.

purely *adv* purement.

purge I *n* purge *f*.
II *vtr* purger [*party, system*] (**of** de); expier [*sin*].

purify *vtr* (gen) purifier; épurer [*water, chemical*].

purist *n, adj* puriste (*mf*).

purity *n* pureté *f*.

purple ▶438 I *n* violet *m*.
II *adj* (bluish) violet/-ette; (reddish) pourpre.

purpose I *n* **1** (aim) but *m*; **for the ~ of doing** dans le but de faire; **2** (also **strength of ~**) résolution *f*.
II **on ~** *phr* exprès.

purposely *adv* exprès, intentionnellement.

purr I *n* (of cat, engine) ronronnement *m*.
II *vi* [*cat, engine*] ronronner.

purse *n* (for money) porte-monnaie *m inv*; (US) (handbag) sac *m* à main.
IDIOMS **to hold the ~-strings** tenir les cordons de la bourse.

purser ▶626 *n* commissaire *m* de bord.

pursue *vtr* **1** (chase) poursuivre; **2** poursuivre [*aim, ambition, studies*]; mener [*policy*]; se livrer à [*occupation, interest*]; **to ~ a career** faire carrière (**in** dans).

pursuer *n* poursuivant/-e *m/f*.

pursuit *n* **1** poursuite *f*; **in ~ of** à la poursuite de; **in hot ~** à vos/ses etc trousses; **2** (hobby) passe-temps *m inv*; **artistic ~s** activités *fpl* artistiques.

push I *n* poussée *f*; **to give sb/sth a ~** pousser qn/qch.
II *vtr* **1** pousser [*person, car, pram*]; appuyer sur [*button, switch*]; **to ~ sb/sth away** repousser qn/qch; **she ~ed him down the stairs** elle l'a poussé dans l'escalier; **to ~ sb aside** écarter qn; **to ~ sb too far** pousser qn à bout; **2**○ (promote) promouvoir [*policy, theory*]; **3**○ (sell) vendre [*drugs*].
III *vi* pousser; **to ~ past sb** bousculer qn.
IDIOMS **at a ~**○ (GB) s'il le faut; **to ~ one's luck** aller un peu trop loin.
■ **push around**○ (bully) bousculer [*person*].
■ **push for** faire pression en faveur de [*reform*].
■ **push in**: ¶ **~ in** resquiller; ¶ **~ [sth] in** enfoncer [*button, door, window*].
■ **push over**: ¶ **~ over**○! pousse-toi!; ¶ **~ [sb/sth] over** renverser [*person, table, car*].
■ **push through** faire voter [*bill, legislation*]; faire passer [*deal*].

push-button *adj* [*telephone*] à touches.

pushchair *n* (GB) poussette *f*.

pusher *n* ○(also **drug ~**) revendeur/-euse *m/f* de drogue.

push-up *n* (Sport) pompe○ *f*.

put *vtr* **1** (place) mettre [*object, person*] (**in** dans; **on** sur); **to ~ sth through** glisser qch dans [*letterbox*]; **to ~ sb through** envoyer qn à [*university*]; faire passer qn par [*ordeal*]; faire passer [qch] à qn [*test*]; **to ~ one's hand to** porter la main à [*mouth*]; **2** (devote, invest) **to ~ money/energy into sth** investir de l'argent/son énergie dans qch; **to ~ a lot into** s'engager à fond pour [*work, project*]; sacrifier beaucoup à [*marriage*]; **3 to ~ money towards** donner de l'argent pour [*gift*]; **~ it towards some new clothes** sers-t'en pour acheter des vêtements; **to ~ tax on sth** taxer qch; **4** (express) **to ~ it bluntly** pour parler franchement; **let me ~ it another way** laissez-moi m'exprimer différemment.

IDIOMS **I wouldn't ~ it past him!** ça ne m'étonnerait pas de lui!

■ **put across** communiquer [*idea, case*].

■ **put away 1** (tidy away) ranger; **2** (save) mettre [qch] de côté; **3**○ avaler [*food*]; descendre○ [*drink*].

■ **put back 1** (return) remettre; **to ~ sth back where it belongs** remettre qch à sa place; **2** remettre [*meeting*] (**to** à; **until** jusqu'à); repousser [*date*]; **3** retarder [*clock, watch*].

■ **put down**: ¶ **~ [sth] down 1** poser [*object*]; **2** réprimer [*rebellion*]; **3** (write down) mettre (par écrit); **4 to ~ sth down to** mettre qch sur le compte de; **to ~ sth down to the fact that** imputer qch au fait que; **5** (by injection) piquer [*animal*]; **6 to ~ down a deposit** verser des arrhes; **to ~ £50 down on sth** verser 50 livres d'arrhes sur qch; ¶ **~ [sb] down 1** déposer [*passenger*]; **2**○ (humiliate) rabaisser.

■ **put forward 1** (propose) avancer [*theory, name*]; soumettre [*plan*]; présenter la candidature de [*person*]; **2** (in time) avancer [*meeting, date, clock*] (**by** de; **to** à).

■ **put in**: ¶ **~ in 1** [*ship*] faire escale (**at** à; **to** dans); **2 to ~ in for** postuler pour [*job, promotion, rise*]; demander [*transfer*]; ¶ **~ [sth] in 1** installer [*heating, units*]; **2** (make) faire [*request, claim*]; **to ~ in an appearance** faire une apparition; **3** passer [*time*]; **4** (insert) mettre.

■ **put off**: ¶ **~ [sth] off 1** (delay, defer) remettre [qch] (à plus tard); **2** (turn off) éteindre [*light, radio*]; ¶ **~ [sb] off 1** décommander [*guest*]; dissuader [*person*]; **to be easily put off** se décourager facilement; **2** (repel) [*appearance, smell*] dégoûter; [*manner, person*] déconcerter.

■ **put on 1** mettre [*garment, make-up*]; **2** allumer [*light, heating*]; mettre [*record, music*]; **to ~ the kettle on** mettre de l'eau à chauffer; **3** prendre [*weight, kilo*]; **4** (produce) monter [*play, exhibition*]; **5** (adopt) prendre [*accent, expression*]; **he's ~ting it on** il fait semblant.

■ **put out 1** (extend) tendre [*hand*]; **to ~ out one's tongue** tirer la langue; **2** éteindre [*fire, cigarette*]; **3** sortir [*bin, garbage*]; faire sortir [*cat*]; **4** diffuser [*warning, statement*]; **5** mettre [*food, towels*]; **6** (dislocate) se démettre [*shoulder*]; **7** (inconvenience) déranger [*person*]; (annoy) contrarier [*person*].

■ **put through 1** (implement) faire passer [*bill, reform*]; **2** passer [*caller*] (**to** à).

■ **put together 1** (assemble) assembler [*pieces, parts*]; **to ~ sth back together** reconstituer qch; **2** (place together) mettre ensemble; **3** établir [*list*]; faire [*film, programme*]; **4** construire [*argument*].

■ **put up**: ¶ **~ up [sth]** opposer [*resistance*]; **to ~ up a fight** combattre; ¶ **~ [sth] up 1** hisser [*flag, sail*]; relever [*hair*]; **to ~ up one's hand** lever la main; **2** mettre [*sign, plaque*]; afficher [*list*]; **3** dresser [*fence, tent*]; **4** augmenter [*rent, prices, tax*]; faire monter [*temperature*]; **5** (provide) fournir [*money*]; ¶ **~ [sb] up 1** (lodge) héberger; **2 to ~ sb up to sth** pousser qn à qch.

■ **put up with** supporter [*person, situation*].

put-down *n* remarque *f* humiliante.

putty *n* mastic *m*.

puzzle I *n* **1** (mystery) mystère *m*; **2** (Games) casse-tête *m inv*.

II *vtr* déconcerter.

puzzle book *n* livre *m* de jeux.

puzzled *adj* perplexe.

PVC *n* (*abbr* = **polyvinyl chloride**) PVC *m*.

pygmy *n* pygmée *mf*.

pyjamas (GB), **pajamas** (US) *n pl* pyjama *m* **a pair of ~** un pyjama.

pylon *n* pylône *m*.

pyramid *n* pyramide *f*.

python *n* python *m*.

Qq

q, **Q** *n* q, Q *m*.

quack I *n* **1** (of duck) coin-coin *m inv*; **2**○ (GB) (doctor) toubib○ *m*; **3** (impostor) charlatan *m*.
II *vi* cancaner.

quadrangle *n* **1** (shape) quadrilatère *m*; **2** (courtyard) cour *f* carrée.

quadruple I *n*, *adj* quadruple (*m*).
II *vtr*, *vi* quadrupler.

quadruplet *n* quadruplé/-e *m*/*f*.

quagmire *n* bourbier *m*.

quail I *n* caille *f*; **~'s egg** œuf *m* de caille.
II *vi* trembler.

quaint *adj* **1** (pretty) pittoresque; **2** (old-world) au charme vieillot; **3** (odd) bizarre.

quake *vi* trembler.

qualification *n* **1** (diploma, degree) diplôme *m* (**in** en); (experience, skills) qualification *f*; **2** (restriction) restriction *f*; **without ~** sans réserves.

qualified *adj* **1** (for job) (having diploma) diplômé/-e; (having experience, skills) qualifié/-e; **2** (competent) (having authority) qualifié/-e (**to do** pour faire); (having knowledge) compétent/-e (**to do** pour faire); **3** (modified) nuancé/-e, mitigé/-e.

qualify I *vtr* **1** (modify) nuancer [*approval, opinion*]; préciser [*statement, remark*]; **2** (entitle) **to ~ sb to do** donner à qn le droit de faire.
II *vi* **1** (get diploma, degree) obtenir son diplôme (**as** de, en); **2** (be eligible) remplir les conditions (requises); **to ~ for** avoir droit à [*membership, legal aid*]; **to ~ to do** avoir le droit de faire; **3** (Sport) se qualifier.

quality I *n* qualité *f*.
II *adj* de qualité.

qualm *n* scrupule *m*.

quandary *n* embarras *m*; (serious) dilemme *m*.

quantify *vtr* quantifier.

quantity ▶632 *n* quantité *f*; **in ~** en grande quantité.

quantity surveyor ▶626 *n* métreur *m*.

quantum leap *n* saut *m* quantique; (figurative) bond *m* prodigieux.

quarantine I *n* quarantaine *f*; **in ~** en quarantaine.
II *vtr* mettre [qn/qch] en quarantaine.

quarrel I *n* dispute *f* (**between** entre; **over** au sujet de); **to have a ~** se disputer.
II *vi* **1** (argue) se disputer; **2** (sever relations) se brouiller; **3 to ~ with** contester [*claim, idea*]; se plaindre de [*price, verdict*].

quarrelsome *adj* [*person*] querelleur/-euse; [*remark*] agressif/-ive.

quarry I *n* **1** (in ground) carrière *f*; **2** (prey) proie *f*; (in hunting) gibier *m*.
II *vtr* extraire [*stone*].

quart *n* (GB) = *1.136 l*, (US) = *0.946 l*.

quarter ▶434, 573, 582 I *n* **1** (one fourth) quart *m*; **in ~ of an hour** dans un quart d'heure; **2** (three months) trimestre *m*; **3** (district) quartier *m*.
II **quarters** *n pl* (Mil) quartiers *mpl*; (gen) logement *m*.
III *pron* **1** (25%) quart *m*; **only a ~ passed** seul le quart a réussi; **2** (in time phrases) **at (a) ~ to 11** (GB), **at a ~ of 11** (US) à onze heures moins le quart; **an hour and a ~** une heure et quart.
IV *adj* **a ~ century** un quart de siècle.
V *adv* **a ~ full** au quart plein; **~ the price** quatre fois moins cher.
VI *vtr* couper [qch] en quatre [*cake, apple*].
VII **at close quarters** *phr* de près.

quarterfinal *n* quart *m* de finale.

quarterly I *adj* trimestriel/-ielle.
II *adv* tous les trois mois.

quartermaster *n* (in army) intendant *m*; (in navy) maître *m* de timonerie.

quartet *n* quatuor *m*; **jazz ~** quartette *m*.

quartz *n* quartz *m*.

quash *vtr* rejeter [*proposal*]; réprimer [*rebellion*].

quasi(-) *pref* quasi (+ *adj*), quasi- (+ *n*).

quaver I *n* **1** (GB Mus) croche *f*; **2** (trembling) tremblement *m* (**in** dans).
II *vi* trembloter.

quay *n* quai *m*; **on the ~** sur le quai.

quayside *n* quai *m*.

queasiness *n* nausée *f*.

queasy *adj* **to be** or **feel ~** avoir mal au cœur.

Quebec ▶448 *pr n* Québec *m*; **in ~** (city) à Québec; (province) au Québec.

queen ▶498 *n* **1** (gen) reine *f*; **2** (in cards) dame *f*.

queen bee *n* reine *f* des abeilles.

queen mother *n* Reine mère *f*.

Queen's Counsel, **QC** *n* (GB Law) avocat *m* éminent.

queer *adj* **1** (strange) étrange, bizarre; **2** (suspicious) louche, suspect.

quell *vtr* étouffer [*anger, anxiety, revolt*].

quench *vtr* étancher [*thirst*]; étouffer [*desire*].

querulous *adj* grincheux/-euse.

query I *n* question *f* (**about** au sujet de); **a ~ from sb** une question venant de qn.
II *vtr* mettre en doute; **to ~ whether** demander si.

quest *n* quête *f*; **the ~ for sb/sth** la recherche de qn/qch.

question I *n* **1** (gen) question *f* (**about** sur); **to ask sb a ~** poser une question à qn; **it's a ~ of doing** il s'agit de faire; **that's another ~** c'est une autre affaire; **there was never any ~ of you paying** il n'a jamais été question que tu paies; **the person in ~** la personne en

Quantities

Note the use of ***en*** (*of it* or *of them*) in the following examples. This word must be included when the thing you are talking about is not expressed. However, ***en*** is not needed when the commodity is specified (*there is a lot of butter = il y a beaucoup de beurre*):

how much is there?	= combien y **en** a-t-il?
there's a lot	= il y **en** a beaucoup
there's not much	= il n'y **en** a pas beaucoup
there's two kilos	= il y **en** a deux kilos
how much sugar have you?	= combien de sucre as-tu?
I've got a lot	= j'en ai beaucoup
I haven't got (very) much	= je n'**en** ai pas beaucoup
I've got two kilos	= j'**en** ai deux kilos
how many are there?	= combien y **en** a-t-il?
there are a lot	= il y **en** a beaucoup
there aren't many	= il n'y **en** a pas beaucoup
there are twenty	= il y **en** a vingt
how many apples have you?	= combien de pommes as-tu? tu as combien de pommes?
I've got a lot	= j'**en** ai beaucoup
I haven't got many	= je n'**en** ai pas beaucoup
I've got twenty	= j'**en** ai vingt
Tim has got more than Tom	= Tim **en** a plus que Tom
Tim has got more money than Tom	= Tim a plus d'argent que Tom
much more than	= beaucoup plus que
a little more than	= un peu plus que
Tim has got more apples than Tom	= Tim a plus de pommes que Tom
many more apples than Tom	= beaucoup plus de pommes que Tom
a few more apples than Tom	= quelques pommes de plus que Tom
a few more people than yesterday	= quelques personnes de plus qu'hier
Tom has got less than Tim	= Tom **en** a moins que Tim
Tom has got less money than Tim	= Tom a moins d'argent que Tim
much less than	= beaucoup moins que
a little less than	= un peu moins que
Tom has got fewer than Tim	= Tom **en** a moins que Tim
Tom has got fewer apples than Tim	= Tom a moins de pommes que Tim
many fewer than	= beaucoup moins que

Relative quantities

how many are there to the kilo?	= combien y **en** a-t-il au kilo?
there are ten to the kilo	= il y **en** a dix au kilo
how many do you get for ten francs?	= combien peut-on **en** avoir pour dix francs?
you get five for ten francs	= il y **en** a cinq pour dix francs
how much does it cost a litre?	= combien coûte le litre?
it costs £5 a litre	= ça coûte cinq livres le litre
how much do apples cost a kilo?	= combien coûte le kilo de pommes?
apples cost ten francs a kilo	= les pommes coûtent dix francs le kilo
how many glasses do you get to the bottle?	= combien y a-t-il de verres par bouteille?
you get six glasses to the bottle	= il y a six verres par bouteille

question; **it's out of the ~ for him to leave** il est hors de question qu'il parte; **2** (doubt) doute *m*; **to call sth into ~** mettre qch en doute; **it's open to ~** cela se discute.
II *vtr* **1** (interrogate) questionner [*suspect, politician*]; **2** (cast doubt upon) mettre en doute [*tactics, methods*].

questionable *adj* **1** (debatable) discutable; **2** (dubious) douteux/-euse.

questioner *n* interrogateur/-trice *m/f*.

question mark *n* point *m* d'interrogation.

questionnaire *n* questionnaire *m* (**on** sur).

queue I *n* (GB) (of people) queue *f*, file *f* (d'attente); (of vehicles) file *f*; **to stand in a ~** faire la queue; **to join the ~** [*person*] se mettre à la queue; [*car*] se mettre dans la file; **to jump the ~**○ passer avant son tour.
II *vi* (also **~ up**) [*people*] faire la queue (**for** pour); [*taxis*] attendre en ligne.

quibble *vi* chicaner (**about, over** sur).

quick I *n* **to bite one's nails to the ~** se ronger les ongles jusqu'au sang.
II *adj* **1** (speedy) [*pace, reply, profit, meal*] rapide; [*storm, shower*] bref/brève (*before n*); **to have a ~ coffee** prendre un café en vitesse; **to have a ~ wash** faire une toilette rapide; **she's a ~ worker** elle travaille vite; **the ~est way to do** le meilleur moyen de faire; **to make a ~ recovery** se rétablir vite; **be ~ (about it)!** dépêche-toi!; **2** (clever) [*child, student*] vif/vive d'esprit; **3** (prompt) [*reaction*] vif/vive; **to be a ~ learner** apprendre vite.
III *adv* **~!** vite!; **~ as a flash** avec la rapidité de l'éclair.
IDIOMS **to cut** or **sting sb to the ~** piquer qn au vif.

quicken I *vtr* accélérer [*pace*]; stimuler [*interest*].
II *vi* [*pace*] s'accélérer; [*anger*] s'intensifier.

quicklime *n* chaux *f* vive.

quickly *adv* (rapidly) vite, rapidement; (without delay) sans tarder; **(come) ~!** (viens) vite!

quick march *n* (Mil) ≈ pas *m* cadencé.

quicksand *n* sables *mpl* mouvants; (figurative) bourbier *m*.

quicksilver *n* mercure *m*.

quick-tempered *adj* coléreux/-euse.

quick time *n* (US) marche *f* rapide.

quiet I *n* **1** (silence) silence *m*; **2** (peace) tranquillité *f*; **3**○ (secret) **on the ~** discrètement.
II *adj* **1** (silent) [*church, person, room*] silencieux/-ieuse; **to keep ~** garder le silence; **to go ~** se taire; **to keep sb ~** faire taire [*dog, child*]; **be ~** (stop talking) tais-toi; (make no noise) ne fais pas de bruit; **2** (not noisy) [*voice*] bas/basse; [*engine*] silencieux/-ieuse; [*music*] doux/douce; **in a ~ voice** à voix basse; **to keep the children ~** [*activity*] tenir les enfants tranquilles; **3** (discreet) discret/-ète; **to have a ~ word with sb** prendre qn à part pour lui parler; **4** (calm) [*village, holiday, night, life*] tranquille; **5** [*meal*] intime; [*wedding*] célébré/-e dans l'intimité; **6** (secret) **to keep [sth] ~** ne pas divulguer [*plans*]; garder [qch] secret/-ète [*engagement*].

quieten *vtr* **1** (calm) calmer [*person, animal*]; **2** (silence) faire taire [*critics, children*].
■ **quieten down**: ¶ **~ down 1** (become calm) [*person, activity*] se calmer; **2** (fall silent) se taire; ¶ **~ [sb/sth] down 1** (calm) calmer; **2** (silence) faire taire.

quietly *adv* **1** (not noisily) [*move*] sans bruit; [*cough, speak*] doucement; **2** (silently) [*play, read, sit*] en silence; **3** (calmly) calmement.

quietness *n* **1** (silence) silence *m*; **2** (of voice) faiblesse *f*; **3** (of place) tranquillité *f*.

quiff *n* (GB) (on forehead) toupet *m*; (on top of head) houppe *f*.

quill *n* **1** (feather) penne *f*; (stem of feather) tuyau *m* de plume; **2** (on porcupine) piquant *m*; **3** (also **~ pen**) plume *f* d'oie.

quilt I *n* **1** (GB) (duvet) couette *f*; **2** (bed cover) dessus *m* de lit.
II *vtr* matelasser.

quinine *n* quinine *f*.

quintuplet *n* quintuplé/-e *m/f*.

quip I *n* trait *m* d'esprit.
II *vi* plaisanter.

quirk *n* (of person) excentricité *f*; (of fate, nature) caprice *m*.

quit I *vtr* démissionner de [*job*]; quitter [*place, person, profession*].
II *vi* **1** (give up) arrêter (**doing** de faire); **2** (resign) démissionner.

quite *adv* **1** (completely) [*new, ready, understand*] tout à fait; [*alone, empty, exhausted*] complètement; [*impossible*] totalement; [*extraordinary*] vraiment; **I ~ agree** je suis tout à fait d'accord; **you're ~ right** vous avez entièrement raison; **it's ~ all right** c'est sans importance; **are you ~ sure?** en êtes-vous certain?; **~ clearly** [*see*] très clairement; **2** (exactly) **not ~** pas exactement; **I don't ~ know** je ne sais pas du tout; **3** (rather) [*big, easily, often*] assez; **it's ~ small** ce n'est pas très grand; **it's ~ warm today** il fait bon aujourd'hui; **it's ~ likely that** il est très probable que; **I ~ like Chinese food** j'aime assez la cuisine chinoise; **~ a few** un bon nombre de [*people, examples*]; **~ a lot of money** pas mal d'argent; **I've thought about it ~ a bit** j'y ai pas mal réfléchi; **4** (as intensifier) **~ simply** tout simplement; **~ a difference** une différence considérable; **that will be ~ a change for you** ce sera un grand changement pour toi; **she's ~ a woman!** quelle femme!; **5** (expressing agreement) **~ (so)** c'est sûr.

quits○ *adj* **to be ~** être quitte (**with sb** envers qn).

quiver I *n* **1** tremblement *m*; **2** (for arrows) carquois *m*.
II *vi* [*voice, lip, animal*] trembler (**with** de); [*leaves*] frémir; [*flame*] vaciller.

quiz I *n* **1** (game) jeu *m* de questions-réponses, quiz *m*; (written, in magazine) questionnaire *m* (**about** sur); **2** (US Sch) interrogation *f*.
II *vtr* questionner (**about** au sujet de).

quiz game, **quiz show** *n* jeu *m* de questions-réponses.

quizzical *adj* interrogateur/-trice.

quota *n* **1** (prescribed number, amount) quota *m* (**of, for** de); **2** (share) part *f* (**of** de); (officially allocated) quote-part *f*.

quotation *n* **1** (quote) citation *f*; **2** (estimate) devis *m*.

quotation marks *n pl* (also **quotes**) guillemets *mpl*; **in ~** entre guillemets.

quote I *n* **1** (quotation) citation *f* (**from** de); **2** (statement to journalist) déclaration *f*; **3** (estimate) devis *m*.

II quotes *n pl* = **quotation marks**.

III *vtr* **1** citer [*person, passage, proverb*]; rapporter [*words*]; rappeler [*reference number*]; **she was ~d as saying that**... elle aurait dit que...; **2** (state) indiquer [*price, figure*]; **they ~d us £200** dans leur devis, ils ont demandé £200; **3** (on stock exchange) coter [*share, price*] (**at** à); **4** (in betting) **to be ~d 6 to 1** être coté/-e entre 6 et 1.

IV *vi* (from text, author) faire des citations; **to ~ from Keats** citer Keats.

Rr

r, R *n* r, R *m*.
rabbi ▶626 *n* rabbin *m*.
rabbit *n* lapin *m*.
rabid *adj* **1** (with rabies) enragé/-e; **2** (fanatical) fanatique.
rabies ▶533 *n* rage *f*.
race I *n* **1** (gen, Sport) course *f*; **to have a ~** faire la course; **2** (ethnic group) race *f*.
II *vtr* faire la course avec [*person, car, horse*] (**to** jusqu'à).
III *vi* **1** (gen, Sport) courir; **to ~ in/away** entrer/partir en courant; **2** (hurry) se dépêcher (**to do** de faire); **3** [*heart*] battre précipitamment; [*engine*] s'emballer.
racehorse *n* cheval *m* de course.
racer *n* (bike) vélo *m* de course.
racetrack *n* (for horses) champ *m* de courses; (for cars) circuit *m*; (for dogs, cycles) piste *f*.
racial *adj* racial/-e.
racing *n* courses *fpl*.
racing car *n* voiture *f* de course.
racing driver *n* coureur/-euse *m/f* automobile.
racist *n, adj* raciste (*mf*).
rack I *n* **1** (for plates) égouttoir *m*; (for clothes) portant *m*; (for bottles) casier *m*; **2** = **roof rack**; **3** (torture) chevalet *m*.
II *vtr* **~ed with** torturé/-e par [*guilt*].
IDIOMS **to ~ one's brains** se creuser la cervelle○.
racket *n* **1** (Sport) (also **racquet**) raquette *f*; **2**○ (noise) vacarme *m*; **3** (swindle) escroquerie *f*.
racquetball ▶504 *n* (US) ≈ squash *m*.
racy *adj* **1** (lively) plein/-e de verve; **2** (risqué) osé/-e.
radar *n* radar *m*.
radiant *adj* radieux/-ieuse.
radiate *vtr* **1** rayonner de [*happiness*]; déborder de [*confidence*]; **2** émettre [*heat*].
radiation *n* (medical, nuclear) radiation *f*; (rays) radiations *fpl*.
radiator *n* radiateur *m*.
radical *n, adj* radical/-e (*m/f*).
radio I *n* radio *f*; **on the ~** à la radio.
II *adj* [*signal*] radio *inv*; [*programme*] de radio.
III *vtr* **to ~ sth (to sb)** communiquer qch par radio (à qn).
IV *vi* **to ~ for help** appeler au secours par radio.
radioactive *adj* radioactif/-ive.
radio alarm *n* radio-réveil *m*.
radio announcer *n* speaker/-erine *m/f*.
radio cassette (recorder) *n* radiocassette *f*.
radiology *n* radiologie *f*.
radio station *n* (channel) station *f* de radio; (installation) station *f* émettrice.
radiotherapy *n* radiothérapie *f*.
radish *n* radis *m*.
radius *n* rayon *m*.
raffle *n* tombola *f*.
raft *n* radeau *m*.
rafter *n* chevron *m*.
rag *n* **1** (cloth) chiffon *m*; **2**○ (newspaper) torchon○ *m*.
rage I *n* **1** rage *f*, colère *f*; **to fly into a ~** entrer dans une colère noire; **2**○ **to be (all) the ~** faire fureur.
II *vi* **1** [*storm, battle*] faire rage; **2** [*person*] tempêter (**at, against** contre).
ragged *adj* **1** [*garment*] en loques; [*cuff, collar*] effiloché/-e; [*person*] dépenaillé/-e; **2** [*outline*] déchiqueté/-e.
raging *adj* **1** [*passion, argument*] violent/-e; [*thirst, pain*] atroce; **a ~ toothache** une rage de dents; **2** [*blizzard, sea*] déchaîné/-e.
rags *n pl* loques *fpl*; **in ~** en haillons.
raid I *n* raid *m* (**on** sur); (on bank) hold-up *m* (**on** de); (by police, customs) rafle *f* (**on** dans).
II *vtr* [*military*] faire un raid sur; [*police*] faire une rafle dans; [*criminals*] attaquer [*bank*].
raider *n* **1** (thief) pillard *m*; **2** (also **corporate ~**) raider *m*.
rail *n* **1** (on balcony) balustrade *f*; (on tower) garde-fou *m*; (handrail) rampe *f*; **2** (for curtains) tringle *f*; **3** (for train) rail *m*; **by ~** par chemin de fer.
railing *n* (also **~s**) grille *f*.
railroad *n* (US) **1** (network) chemin *m* de fer; **2** (also **~ track**) voie *f* ferrée.
railroad car *n* (US) wagon *m*.
railway *n* (GB) **1** (network) chemin *m* de fer; **2** (also **~ line**) ligne *f* de chemin de fer; **3** (also **~ track**) voie *f* ferrée.
railway carriage *n* (GB) wagon *m*.
railway station *n* (GB) gare *f*.
rain I *n* pluie *f*; **in the ~** sous la pluie.
II *v impers* pleuvoir; **it's ~ing (hard)** il pleut (à verse).
rainbow *n* arc-en-ciel *m*.
raincoat *n* imperméable *m*.
raindrop *n* goutte *f* de pluie,
rainfall *n* niveau *m* de précipitations.
rain forest *n* forêt *f* tropicale.
rainy *adj* [*afternoon, climate*] pluvieux/-ieuse.
rainy season *n* saison *f* des pluies.
raise I *n* (US) (pay rise) augmentation *f*.
II *vtr* **1** (lift) lever [*baton, barrier, curtain*]; hisser [*flag*]; soulever [*lid*]; renflouer [*sunken ship*]; **to ~ one's hand/head** lever la main/tête; **2** (increase) augmenter [*price, offer, salary*] (**from** de; **to** à); élever [*standard*]; reculer [*age limit*]; **to ~ one's voice** (to be heard) parler plus fort; (in anger) hausser le ton; **to ~ the bidding** (in gambling) monter la mise; (at auction) monter l'enchère; **3** (cause) faire naître [*fears*];

soulever [*dust*]; **4** (mention) soulever [*issue, objection*]; **5** (bring up) élever [*child, family*]; **6** (breed) élever [*livestock*]; **7** (find) trouver [*capital*]; **8** (collect) lever [*tax*]; [*person*] collecter [*money*]; **9** (end) lever [*ban*]; **10** (give) **to ~ the alarm** donner l'alarme.

raised *adj* [*platform, jetty*] surélevé/-e; **~ voices** des éclats de voix.

raisin *n* raisin *m* sec.

rake I *n* râteau *m*.
II *vtr* ratisser [*grass, leaves*].

rally I *n* **1** (meeting) rassemblement *m*; **2** (race) rallye *m*; **3** (in tennis) échange *m*.
II *vtr* rassembler [*support, troops*].
III *vi* **1** [*people*] se rallier (**to** à); **2** (recover) [*patient*] se rétablir.

ram I *n* bélier *m*.
II *vtr* **1** (crash into) rentrer dans, heurter; **2** (push) enfoncer.

RAM *n* (Comput) (*abbr* = **random access memory**) RAM *f*.

ramble *n* randonnée *f*, balade *f*.
■ **ramble on** discourir (**about** sur).

rambler *n* randonneur/-euse *m/f*.

rambling *adj* **1** [*house*] plein/-e de coins et de recoins; **2** [*talk, article*] décousu/-e.

ramp *n* rampe *f*; (GB) (to slow traffic) ralentisseur *m*; (up to plane) passerelle *f*; (US) (slip road) bretelle *f*.

rampage *n* **to be** or **go on the ~** tout saccager.

rampant *adj* [*crime, disease*] endémique.

rampart *n* rempart *m*.

ramshackle *adj* délabré/-e.

ranch *n* ranch *m*.

rancid *adj* rance; **to go ~** rancir.

random *adj* (fait/-e) au hasard.

range I *n* **1** (of prices, products) gamme *f*; (of activities) éventail *m*, choix *m*; (of radar, weapon) portée *f* (**of** de); **2** (US) (prairie) prairie *f*; **3** (of mountains) chaîne *f*; **4** (stove) (wood) fourneau *m*; **5** (also **shooting ~**) champ *m* de tir.
II *vi* **1** (vary) varier (**between** entre); **2** (cover) **to ~ over sth** couvrir qch.

ranger *n* garde-forestier *m*.

rank I *n* **1** (gen) rang *m*; (in military, police) grade *m*; **to break ~s** [*soldiers*] rompre les rangs; **to close ~s** serrer les rangs; **2 taxi ~** station de taxis.
II *adj* **1** [*outsider, beginner*] complet/-ète; **2** [*odour*] fétide.
III *vtr* classer (**among** parmi).
IV *vi* se classer (**among** parmi).

rank and file *n* **the ~** la base *f*.

rankle *vi* **it still ~s** je ne l'ai pas encore digéré○.

ransack *vtr* fouiller [*drawer*] (**for** pour trouver); mettre [qch] à sac [*house*].

ransom *n* rançon *f*; **to hold sb to** (GB) or **for** (US) **~** garder qn en otage.

rant *vi* déclamer; **to ~ and rave** tempêter.

rap I *n* **1** (tap) coup *m* sec; **2** (music) rap *m*.
II *vtr* frapper sur [*table, door*].

rape I *n* **1** (attack) viol *m*; **2** (plant) colza *m*.
II *vtr* violer.

rapid *adj* rapide.

rapidly *adv* rapidement.

rapids *n pl* rapides *mpl*.

rapist *n* violeur *m*.

rapture *n* ravissement *m*; **to go into ~s about sth** s'extasier sur qch.

rapturous *adj* [*delight*] extasié/-e; [*applause*] frénétique.

rare *adj* **1** (uncommon) rare; **2** [*steak*] saignant -e.

rarely *adv* rarement.

rarity *n* **1 to be a ~** [*occurrence*] être rare [*plant*] être une plante rare; [*collector's item*] être une pièce rare; **2** (rareness) rareté *f*.

rascal *n* coquin/-e *m/f*.

rash I *n* **1** (on skin) rougeurs *fpl*; **2** (figurative) vague *f* (**of** de).
II *adj* irréfléchi/-e.

rasher *n* tranche *f*.

raspberry *n* framboise *f*.

rasping *adj* [*voice, sound*] râpeux/-euse.

rat *n* rat *m*.

rate I *n* **1** (speed) rythme *m*; **at this ~** (figurative) à ce train-là; **2** (level) taux *m*; **the interest ~** le taux d'intérêt; **3** (charge, fee) tarif *m*; **4** (in foreign exchange) cours *m*.
II **rates** *n pl* (GB) impôts *mpl* locaux; **business ~s** ≈ taxe *f* professionnelle.
III *vtr* **1** (classify) **to ~ sb as sth** considérer qn comme qch; **to ~ sb among** classer qn parmi; **2** estimer [*honesty, friendship, person*].
IDIOMS **at any ~** en tout cas.

rather *adv* **1** plutôt (**than** que); **I ~ like him** je le trouve plutôt sympathique; **it's ~ like an apple** ça ressemble un peu à une pomme; **2** (preferably) **I would** (**much**) **~ do** je préférerais (de loin) faire (**than do** que faire); **I'd ~ not** j'aimerais mieux pas.

ratify *vtr* ratifier.

rating *n* cote *f*.

ratings *n pl* indice *m* d'écoute, audimat® *m*.

ratio *n* proportion *f*, rapport *m*.

ration I *n* ration *f*.
II *vtr* rationner [*food*] (**to** à); limiter la ration de [*person*] (**to** à).

rational *adj* [*approach, argument*] rationnel -elle; [*person*] sensé/-e.

rationale *n* **1** (reasons) raisons *fpl* (**for** pour **for doing** de faire); **2** (logic) logique *f* (**behind** de).

rationalize *vtr* **1** (justify) justifier; **2** (GB (streamline) rationaliser.

rat race *n* foire *f* d'empoigne.

rattle I *n* **1** (of bottles, cutlery, chains) cliquetis *m* (of window, engine) vibrations *fpl*; **2** (baby's hochet *m*.
II *vtr* [*wind*] faire vibrer [*window*]; [*person*] s'acharner sur [*handle*].
III *vi* [*bottles, cutlery, chains*] s'entrechoquer [*window*] vibrer.

rattlesnake *n* serpent *m* à sonnette, crotale *m*.

raucous *adj* [*laugh*] éraillé/-e; [*person*] bruyant/-e.
ravage *vtr* ravager.
rave I○ *n* (GB) (party) bringue○ *f* (branchée○).
II○ *adj* [*review*] dithyrambique.
III *vi* (enthusiastically) parler avec enthousiasme (**about** de); (when fevered) délirer.
ravenous *adj* [*animal*] vorace; **to be ~** avoir une faim de loup.
ravine *n* ravin *m*.
raving *adj* (fanatical) enragé/-e; **a ~ lunatic** un fou furieux/une folle furieuse.
ravishing *adj* ravissant/-e.
raw *adj* **1** [*food*] cru/-e; [*rubber, sugar, data*] brut/-e; [*sewage*] non traité/-e; **2** (without skin) [*patch*] à vif; **3** (cold) [*weather*] froid/-e et humide; **4** (inexperienced) inexpérimenté/-e.
IDIOMS **to get a ~ deal**○ être défavorisé/-e.
raw material *n* matière *f* première.
ray *n* rayon *m*; **a ~ of** une lueur de [*hope*].
raze *vtr* raser.
razor *n* rasoir *m*.
razor blade *n* lame *f* de rasoir.
re[1] *n* (Mus) ré *m*.
re[2] *prep* (*abbr* = **with reference to**) (about) au sujet de; (in letterhead) 'objet'.
reach I *n* portée *f*; **out of ~** hors de portée; **within (arm's) ~** à portée de (la) main; **within easy ~** [*place*] tout près.
II *vtr* **1** atteindre [*place, person, object, switch*]; [*sound, news, letter*] parvenir à [*person, place*]; **2** (come to) arriver à [*decision, understanding*]; **to ~ a verdict** (Law) rendre un verdict; **3** toucher [*audience, market*].
III *vi* **1 to ~ up/down** lever/baisser le bras; **to ~ out** tendre le bras; **2** (extend) **to ~ (up/down) to** arriver jusqu'à.
reaches *n pl* **the upper/lower ~** (of river) la partie supérieure/inférieure.
react *vi* réagir (**to** à; **against** contre).
reaction *n* réaction *f*.
reactionary *n*, *adj* réactionnaire (*mf*).
reactor *n* réacteur *m*.
read I *vtr* **1** (gen) lire; **to ~ sb's mind** lire dans les pensées de qn; **2** (at university) faire des études de [*history, French*]; **3** relever [*meter*].
II *vi* lire (**to sb** à qn).
■ **read out** lire [qch] à haute voix.
reader *n* lecteur/-trice *m/f*.
readily *adv* **1** (willingly) sans hésiter; **2** (easily) facilement.
reading *n* **1** lecture *f*; **2** (on meter) relevé *m* (**on** de); (on instrument) indication *f* (**on** de); **3** (interpretation) interprétation *f* (**of** de).
reading glasses *n pl* lunettes *fpl* (pour lire).
readjust I *vtr* régler [qch] de nouveau.
II *vi* [*person*] se réadapter (**to** à).
ready *adj* **1** (prepared) prêt/-e (**for** pour; **to do** à faire); **to get ~** se préparer; **to get sth ~** préparer qch; **~, steady, go** à vos marques, prêts, partez!; **2** (willing) prêt/-e (**to do** à faire).
ready-made *adj* [*clothes*] de confection; [*excuse*] tout/-e fait/-e.
ready-to-wear *adj* [*garment*] prêt-à-porter.
real *adj* **1** (not imaginary) véritable, réel/réelle; **in ~ life** dans la réalité; **2** (genuine) [*diamond, flower, leather*] vrai/-e (*before n*), authentique; **3** (proper) [*holiday, rest*] véritable, vrai/-e (*before n*); **4** (for emphasis) [*charmer, pleasure*] vrai/-e (*before n*).
real estate *n* **1** (property) biens *mpl* immobiliers; **2** (US) (profession) immobilier *m*.
realism *n* réalisme *m*.
realistic *adj* réaliste.
reality *n* réalité *f* (**of** de).
realization *n* prise *f* de conscience.
realize *vtr* **1** se rendre compte de; **to ~ that** se rendre compte que; **to make sb ~ sth** faire comprendre qch à qn; **2** réaliser [*idea, dream, goal*]; **to ~ one's potential** développer ses capacités.
really I *adv* **1** (gen) vraiment; **2** (in actual fact) en fait, réellement; **~?** (expressing disbelief) c'est vrai?
II *excl* (also **well ~**) franchement!
reap *vtr* **1** moissonner [*corn*]; **2** récolter [*benefits*].
reappear *vi* reparaître.
reapply *vi* reposer sa candidature (**for** à).
rear I *n* **1** (of building, car, room) arrière *m*; (of procession, train) queue *f*; **2** (of person) derrière○ *m*.
II *adj* **1** [*door, garden*] de derrière; **2** (of car) [*light, seat, wheel*] arrière *inv*.
III *vtr* élever [*child, animals*]; cultiver [*plants*].
IV *vi* (also **~ up**) [*horse*] se cabrer.
rearrange *vtr* réaménager [*room*]; modifier [*plans*]; changer [*appointment*].
rear-view mirror *n* rétroviseur *m*.
reason I *n* **1** (cause) raison *f* (**for, behind** de); **for no (good) ~** sans raison valable; **to have ~ to do** avoir des raisons de faire; **the ~ why...** la raison pour laquelle...; **I'll tell you the ~ why** je vais te or vous dire pourquoi; **to have every ~ to do** avoir tout lieu de faire; **with good ~** à juste titre; **2** (common sense) raison *f*; **to listen to** or **see ~** entendre raison; **it stands to ~ that** il va sans dire que; **within ~** dans la limite du raisonnable.
II *vi* **to ~ with sb** raisonner qn.
reasonable *adj* **1** (sensible) raisonnable; **2** (moderately good) convenable.
reasonably *adv* **1** (sensibly) raisonnablement; **2** (rather) assez.
reasoning *n* raisonnement *m*.
reassess *vtr* réexaminer, reconsidérer.
reassurance *n* **1** (comfort) réconfort *m*; **2** (guarantee) garantie *f*.
reassure *vtr* rassurer [*person*] (**about** sur).
reassuring *adj* rassurant/-e.
rebate *n* remboursement *m*.
rebel I *n* rebelle *mf*.
II *vi* se rebeller.
rebellion *n* rébellion *f*, révolte *f*.
rebellious *adj* rebelle, insoumis/-e.
rebuff I *n* rebuffade *f*.

II *vtr* rabrouer [*person*]; repousser [*advances*].
rebuild *vtr* reconstruire.
rebuke I *n* réprimande *f*.
II *vtr* réprimander (**for** pour).
rebut *vtr* réfuter.
recall I *n* (memory) mémoire *f*.
II *vtr* **1** (remember) se souvenir de; **2** (summon back) rappeler.
recapitulate *vtr*, *vi* récapituler.
recede *vi* (gen) s'éloigner; [*hope, memory*] s'estomper.
receding *adj* [*chin*] fuyant/-e; **he has a ~ hairline** son front se dégarnit.
receipt I *n* **1** reçu *m*, récépissé *m* (**for** pour); (from till) ticket *m* de caisse; **2** (act of receiving) réception *f*.
II **receipts** *n pl* (takings) recette *f* (**from** de).
receive *vtr* **1** (gen) recevoir; receler [*stolen goods*]; **2** (greet) accueillir, recevoir [*visitor, proposal, play*] (**with** avec); **to be well ~d** être bien reçu/-e.
receiver *n* **1** (telephone) combiné *m*; **2** (radio or TV) (poste *m*) récepteur *m*.
receivership *n* (GB) **to go into ~** être placé/-e sous administration judiciaire.
recent *adj* [*event, change, arrival, film*] récent/-e; [*acquaintance, development*] nouveau/-elle (*before n*); **in ~ years** au cours des dernières années.
recently *adv* récemment; **until ~** jusqu'à ces derniers temps.
reception *n* **1** (also **~ desk**) réception *f*; **2** (gathering) réception *f* (**for sb** en l'honneur de qn; **for sth** à l'occasion de qch); **3** (welcome) accueil *m* (**for** de).
receptionist ▶ 626 *n* réceptionniste *mf*.
receptive *adj* réceptif/-ive (**to** à).
recess *n* **1** (in parliament) (holiday) vacances *fpl*; **2** (US) (break) (in school) récréation *f*; (during meeting) pause *f*; **3** (alcove) alcôve *f*, recoin *m*.
recession *n* récession *f*.
recharge *vtr* recharger.
recipe *n* recette *f* (**for** de).
recipient *n* (of letter) destinataire *mf*; (of benefits, aid, cheque) bénéficiaire *mf*; (of prize, award) lauréat/-e *m/f*.
reciprocal *adj* réciproque.
reciprocate I *vtr* retourner [*compliment*]; payer [qch] de retour [*love*]; rendre [*affection*].
II *vi* rendre la pareille.
recital *n* récital *m*.
recite *vtr*, *vi* réciter.
reckless *adj* imprudent/-e.
reckon *vtr* **1** (judge) considérer (**that** que); **2**° (think) **to ~ (that)** croire que; **3** calculer [*amount*].
■ **reckon on**°: ¶ **~ on [sb/sth]** compter sur; ¶ **~ on doing** compter faire.
■ **reckon with** compter avec.
reckoning *n* (estimation) estimation *f*; (accurate calculation) calculs *mpl*.
reclaim *vtr* **1** reconquérir [*coastal land*]; assécher [*marsh*]; défricher [*forest*]; récupérer [*glass, metal*]; **2** récupérer [*deposit, money*].
recline *vi* [*person*] s'allonger; [*seat*] s'incliner.
reclining *adj* **1** [*figure*] allongé/-e; **2** [*seat*] inclinable; [*chair*] réglable.
recluse *n* reclus/-e *m/f*.
recognition *n* reconnaissance *f*; **in ~ of** en reconnaissance de.
recognizable *adj* reconnaissable.
recognize *vtr* reconnaître (**by** à).
recoil *vi* reculer (**from** devant).
recollect I *vtr* se souvenir de, se rappeler.
II *vi* se souvenir.
recollection *n* souvenir *m*.
recommend *vtr* **1** (commend) recommander **2** (advise) conseiller, recommander.
reconcile *vtr* **1** réconcilier [*people*]; **2** concilier [*attitudes, views*]; **3 to become ~d to sth** se résigner à qch.
reconnaissance *n* reconnaissance *f*.
reconnoitre (GB), **reconnoiter** (US) I *vtr* reconnaître.
II *vi* faire une reconnaissance.
reconsider I *vtr* réexaminer.
II *vi* réfléchir.
reconstruction *n* **1** (of building) reconstruction *f*; **2** (of crime) reconstitution *f*.
record I *n* **1** (of events) compte-rendu *m*; (of official proceedings) procès-verbal *m*; **to keep a ~ of sth** noter qch; **to say sth off the ~** dire qch en privé; **to set the ~ straight** mettre les choses au clair; **2** (data) **~s** (historical, public) archives *fpl*; (personal, administrative) dossier *m*; **3** (history) (of individual) passé *m*; (of organization, group) réputation *f*; **4** (also **criminal ~**) casier *m* judiciaire; **5** (Mus) disque *m*; **6** (of athlete) record *m* (**for, in** de).
II *adj* **1** [*company, label*] de disques; **2** [*sales, time*] record (*after n*); **to be at a ~ high/low** être à son niveau le plus haut/bas.
III *vtr* **1** (note) noter [*detail, idea, opinion*]; **2** (on disc, tape) enregistrer; **3** [*instrument*] enregistrer [*temperature, rainfall*].
recorded delivery *n* (GB) **to send sth ~** envoyer qch en recommandé.
recorder *n* (Mus) flûte *f* à bec.
record-holder *n* recordman/recordwoman *m/f*.
recording *n* enregistrement *m*.
record player *n* tourne-disque *m*.
recourse *n* recours *m* (**to** à).
recover I *vtr* **1** retrouver, récupérer [*money, vehicle*]; récupérer [*territory*]; (from water) repêcher, retrouver [*body, wreck*]; **to ~ one's strength** reprendre des forces; **2** (recoup) réparer, compenser [*losses*].
II *vi* **1** (from illness) se remettre (**from** de); (from defeat) se ressaisir (**from** après); **2** [*economy*] se redresser.
recovery *n* **1** (getting better) rétablissement *m*, guérison *f*; **2** (of economy, company, market) reprise *f*; **3** (getting back) (of vehicle) rapatriement *m*; (of money) récupération *f*.
recreate *vtr* recréer.

recreation *n* **1** (leisure) loisirs *mpl*; **2** (playtime) récréation *f*.
recrimination *n* récrimination *f*.
recruit I *n* recrue *f*.
II *vtr* recruter (**from** dans).
recruitment *n* recrutement *m*.
rectangle *n* rectangle *m*.
rectangular *adj* rectangulaire.
rectify *vtr* rectifier.
rector *n* pasteur *m*.
recuperate *vi* se rétablir (**from** de), récupérer.
recur *vi* [*event, error*] se reproduire; [*illness*] réapparaître; [*theme*] revenir.
recurrent *adj* récurrent/-e.
recycle *vtr* recycler [*paper, waste*].
red ▶438 I *n* **1** (colour) rouge *m*; **in ~** en rouge; **2 to be in the ~** [*person, account*] être à découvert; [*company*] être en déficit.
II *adj* rouge (**with** de); [*hair*] roux/rousse; **to go** or **turn ~** rougir.
red alert *n* alerte *f* rouge.
Red Cross *n* Croix-Rouge *f*.
redden *vtr, vi* rougir.
redecorate *vtr* repeindre et retapisser, refaire.
redeem *vtr* **1** retirer [*pawned goods*]; rembourser [*debt*]; **2** racheter [*sinner*]; **her one ~ing feature is**... ce qui la rachète, c'est...
redeploy *vtr* redéployer [*troops*]; réaffecter [*staff*].
redevelop *vtr* réaménager [*site, town*].
redhead *n* roux/rousse *m/f*.
red herring *n* faux problème *m*.
red-hot *adj* [*metal, coal*] chauffé/-e au rouge.
redial I *vtr* refaire [*number*].
II *vi* recomposer le numéro.
redirect *vtr* canaliser [*resources*]; dévier [*traffic*]; réexpédier [*mail*].
rediscover *vtr* redécouvrir.
redo *vtr* refaire.
redress *vtr* **to ~ the balance** rétablir l'équilibre.
red tape *n* paperasserie *f*.
reduce *vtr* **1** réduire [*inflation, number, pressure, sentence*] (**by** de); baisser [*prices, temperature*]; **to ~ speed** ralentir; **to ~ sb to tears** faire pleurer qn; **to be ~d to begging** en être réduit/-e à la mendicité; **2** (in cooking) faire réduire [*sauce, stock*].
reduction *n* **1** (in inflation, pressure, number) réduction *f* (**in** de); (of weight, size) diminution *f* (**in** de); **2** (discount) réduction *f*, rabais *m*.
redundancy *n* **1** (unemployment) chômage *m*; **2** (dismissal) licenciement *m*.
redundant *adj* **1** (GB) (dismissed) licencié/-e; (out of work) au chômage; **to be made ~** être licencié/-e; **2** (not needed) superflu/-e.
reed *n* **1** (plant) roseau *m*; **2** (Mus) anche *f*.
reef *n* récif *m*, écueil *m*.
reek *vi* **to ~ (of sth)** puer (qch).
reel I *n* bobine *f*; (for fishing) moulinet *m*.
II *vi* (sway) [*person*] tituber; **the blow sent him ~ing** le coup l'a projeté en arrière.
■ **reel off** débiter [*list, names*].
refectory *n* réfectoire *m*.
refer I *vtr* renvoyer [*task, problem*] (**to** à); **to ~ sb to** [*person*] envoyer qn à [*department*].
II *vi* **1** (allude to) **to ~ to** parler de, faire allusion à [*person, topic, event*]; **2** (relate, apply) **to ~ to** [*number, date, term*] se rapporter à; **3** (consult) **to ~ to** consulter [*notes, article*].
referee I *n* **1** arbitre *m*; **2** (GB) (giving job reference) personne *f* pouvant fournir des références.
II *vtr, vi* arbitrer.
reference I *n* **1** (allusion) référence *f* (**to** à), allusion *f* (**to** à); **2** (consultation) **without ~ to sb/sth** sans consulter qn/qch; **for future ~** pour information; **3** (in book, letter) référence *f*; **4** (testimonial) références *fpl*.
II **with reference to** *phr* **with ~ to your letter** suite à votre lettre.
reference book *n* ouvrage *m* de référence.
reference number *n* numéro *m* de référence.
referendum *n* référendum *m*.
refill I *n* (for ballpoint, lighter, perfume) recharge *f*.
II *vtr* recharger [*pen, lighter*]; remplir [qch] à nouveau [*glass, bottle*].
refine *vtr* **1** raffiner [*oil, sugar*]; **2** (improve) peaufiner [*theory*].
refined *adj* raffiné/-e.
refinement *n* (elegance) raffinement *m*.
refinery *n* raffinerie *f*.
reflect I *vtr* **1** refléter [*image*]; **to be ~ed in sth** se refléter dans qch; **2** renvoyer, réfléchir [*light, heat*]; **3** (think) se dire.
II *vi* **1** (think) réfléchir (**on, upon** à); **2 to ~ well/badly on sb** faire honneur/du tort à qn.
reflection *n* **1** (image) reflet *m* (**of** de), image *f* (**of** de); **2** (thought) réflexion *f*; **on ~** à la réflexion.
reflector *n* (on vehicle) catadioptre *m*.
reflex I *n* réflexe *m*.
II *adj* réflexe; **a ~ action** un réflexe.
reflexive verb *n* verbe *m* pronominal réfléchi.
reform I *n* réforme *f*.
II *vtr* réformer.
reformation *n* réforme *f*; **the Reformation** la Réforme.
refrain I *n* refrain *m*.
II *vi* se retenir; **to ~ from doing** s'abstenir de faire.
refresh *vtr* [*bath, drink*] rafraîchir; [*rest*] reposer.
refreshing *adj* [*drink, shower*] rafraîchissant/-e; [*rest*] réparateur/-trice.
refreshments *n pl* (drinks) rafraîchissements *mpl*; **light ~** repas *m* léger.
refrigerate *vtr* frigorifier.
refrigerator *n* réfrigérateur *m*, frigidaire® *m*.
refuel *vi* se ravitailler en carburant.
refuge *n* **1** (shelter, protection) refuge *m* (**from** contre); **to take ~ from** s'abriter de [*storm*]; **2** (hostel) foyer *m*.

refugee *n* réfugié/-e *m/f*.
refund I *n* remboursement *m*.
II *vtr* rembourser.
refurbish *vtr* rénover.
refusal *n* refus *m* (**to do** de faire); (to application) réponse *f* négative.
refuse[1] I *vtr* refuser (**to do** de faire).
II *vi* refuser.
refuse[2] *n* (GB) (household) ordures *fpl*; (industrial) déchets *mpl*; (garden) déchets *mpl* de jardinage.
refuse collector ▶626 *n* (GB) éboueur *m*.
refute *vtr* réfuter.
regain *vtr* retrouver [*health, strength, sight, composure*]; reconquérir [*power, seat*]; reprendre [*lead, control*]; **to ~ consciousness** reprendre connaissance.
regal *adj* royal/-e.
regale *vtr* régaler (**with** de).
regalia *n pl* insignes *mpl*.
regard I *n* **1** (consideration) égard *m*; **out of ~ for** par égard pour; **2** (esteem) estime *f* (**for** pour); **to hold sb/sth in high ~** avoir beaucoup d'estime pour qn/qch; **3 with** or **in ~ to** en ce qui concerne; **in this ~** à cet égard.
II *vtr* considérer (**as** comme).
regarding *prep* concernant.
regardless I *prep* **~ of** sans tenir compte de.
II *adv* malgré tout.
regards *n pl* amitiés *fpl*; **give them my ~** transmettez-leur mes amitiés.
regatta *n* régate *f*.
regent *n* régent/-e *m/f*.
reggae *n* reggae *m*.
regime, régime *n* régime *m*.
regiment *n* régiment *m*.
region *n* région *f*; **(somewhere) in the ~ of £300** environ 300 livres sterling.
regional *adj* régional/-e.
register I *n* registre *m*; (at school) cahier *m* des absences.
II *vtr* **1** déclarer [*birth, death*]; faire immatriculer [*vehicle*]; faire enregistrer [*luggage, company*]; déposer [*trademark, complaint*]; **2** [*instrument*] indiquer [*speed, temperature*]; [*person*] exprimer [*anger, disapproval*]; **3** envoyer [qch] en recommandé [*letter*].
III *vi* (for course, school, to vote) s'inscrire; (at hotel) se présenter.
registered *adj* **1** [*voter*] inscrit/-e; [*vehicle, student*] immatriculé/-e; [*charity*] ≈ agréé/-e; **2** [*letter*] recommandé/-e; **by ~ post** en recommandé.
registered trademark *n* marque *m* déposée.
registrar ▶626 *n* **1** (GB gen) officier *m* d'état civil; (medical) adjoint *m*; **2** (academic) responsable *mf* du bureau de la scolarité.
registration *n* (of person) inscription *f*; (of trademark, patent) dépôt *m*; (of birth, death, marriage) déclaration *f*.
registration number *n* numéro *m* d'immatriculation.
registry office *n* (GB) bureau *m* de l'état civil.
regret I *n* regret *m* (**about** à propos de); **to have no ~s about doing** ne pas regrette d'avoir fait.
II *vtr* regretter (**that** que + *subjunctive*); **to ~ doing** regretter d'avoir fait; **I ~ to inforr you that** j'ai le regret de vous informer que.
regretfully *adv* à regret.
regrettable *adj* regrettable (**that** que *subjunctive*).
regular I *n* **1** (client, visitor) habitué/-e *m/f*; **2** (US) (petrol) ordinaire *m*.
II *adj* **1** (gen) régulier/-ière; **to take ~ exercise** faire de l'exercice régulièrement; **2** (usual) [*activity, customer, visitor*] habituel/-elle [*viewer, listener*] fidèle; **3** [*army, soldier*] de métier.
regularity *n* régularité *f*.
regularly *adv* régulièrement.
regulate *vtr* **1** (gen, Econ) réguler; **2** (adjus régler [*mechanism*].
regulation I *n* **1** (gen) règlement *m*; (for safety fire) consigne *f*; **under the (new) ~s** selon l (nouvelle) réglementation; **against the ~** contraire au règlement or aux normes; **2** (controlling) réglementation *f*.
II *adj* [*width, length, uniform*] réglementaire.
regurgitate *vtr* régurgiter; (figurative) ressortir
rehabilitate *vtr* réinsérer [*handicappe person, ex-prisoner*]; réhabiliter [*addict, area*].
rehearsal *n* répétition *f* (**of** de).
rehearse I *vtr* répéter [*scene*]; préparer [*speech excuse*].
II *vi* répéter (**for** pour).
reheat *vtr* réchauffer.
reign I *n* règne *m*.
II *vi* régner (**over** sur).
reimburse *vtr* rembourser.
rein *n* rêne *f*.
reincarnation *n* réincarnation *f*.
reindeer *n* renne *m*.
reinforce *vtr* renforcer.
reinforced concrete *n* béton *m* armé.
reinforcement *n* (support) renfort *m*; **~** (Mil) renforts.
reject I *n* marchandise *f* de deuxième choix.
II *vtr* rejeter [*advice, application, persor transplant*]; refuser [*candidate, manuscript*]; démentir [*claim, suggestion*].
rejection *n* (gen) rejet *m*; (of candidate, manuscript) refus *m*.
rejoice *vi* se réjouir (**at, over** de).
rejuvenate *vtr* rajeunir.
rekindle *vtr* ranimer.
relapse I *n* rechute *f*.
II *vi* (Med) rechuter; (gen) **to ~ into** retombe dans.
relate I *vtr* **1** (connect) faire le rapprochemen entre; **2** raconter [*story*] (**to** à).
II *vi* **to ~ to** (have connection) se rapporter à (communicate) s'entendre avec.
related *adj* **1** [*person*] apparenté/-e (**by through** par; **to** à); **2** (connected) [*area, idea incident*] lié/-e (**to** à); **drug-~** lié/-e à la drogue.

relation I *n* **1** (relative) parent/-e *m/f*; **my ~s** ma famille; **2** (connection) rapport *m*.
II **relations** *n pl* (dealings) relations *fpl* (**with** avec).

relationship *n* **1** (between people) relations *fpl*; (with colleagues) rapports *mpl*; **2** (connection) rapport *m* (**to, with** avec).

relative I *n* parent/-e *m/f*; **my ~s** ma famille.
II *adj* **1** (gen) relatif/-ive; **2** (respective) respectif/-ive.

relatively *adv* relativement; **~ speaking** toutes proportions gardées.

relax I *vtr* décontracter [*muscle*]; assouplir [*restrictions, discipline*]; détendre [*body*]; relâcher [*efforts, grip, concentration*].
II *vi* **1** [*person*] se détendre; **2** [*grip*] se relâcher; [*jaw, muscle*] se décontracter.

relaxation *n* **1** (of person) détente *f*; **2** (of restrictions, discipline) assouplissement *m* (**in** de).

relaxed *adj* détendu/-e, décontracté/-e.

relaxing *adj* [*atmosphere, activity*] délassant/-e; [*vacation*] reposant/-e.

relay I *n* **1** (of workers) équipe *f* (de relais); **2** (also **~ race**) course *f* de relais.
II *vtr* transmettre [*message*] (**to** à).

release I *n* **1** (liberation) libération *f*; **2** (relief) soulagement *m*; **3** (for press) communiqué *m*; **4** (of film) sortie *f*; **5** (film, video, record) (also **new ~**) nouveauté *f*.
II *vtr* **1** libérer [*prisoner*]; dégager [*accident victim*]; relâcher [*animal*]; **to ~ sb from** dégager qn de [*promise*]; **2** faire jouer [*catch, clasp*]; déclencher [*shutter*]; desserrer [*handbrake*]; larguer [*bomb*]; **3** (let go) lâcher [*object, arm, hand*]; **4** faire sortir [*film, record*].

relegate *vtr* **1** reléguer [*person, object*] (**to** à); **2** (GB Sport) reléguer (**to** en).

relent *vi* céder.

relentless *adj* [*pressure*] implacable; [*noise, activity*] incessant/-e; [*attack*] acharné/-e.

relevant *adj* **1** [*issue, facts, point*] pertinent/-e; [*information*] utile; **to be ~ to** avoir rapport à; **2** (appropriate) [*chapter*] , correspondant/-e; [*period*] en question.

reliable *adj* [*friend, witness*] digne de confiance, fiable; [*employee, firm*] sérieux/-ieuse; [*car, memory, account*] fiable; [*information, source*] sûr/-e.

reliant *adj* **to be ~ on** être dépendant/-e de.

relic *n* relique *f*.

relief *n* **1** (from pain, distress) soulagement *m*; **2** (aid) aide *f*, secours *m*; **3** (in sculpture, geography) relief *m*.

relieve *vtr* **1** soulager [*pain, suffering, tension*]; dissiper [*boredom*]; remédier à [*poverty, famine*]; **to be ~d** être soulagé/-e; **2 to ~ sb of** débarrasser qn de [*coat, bag*]; soulager qn de [*burden*]; **3** (help) secourir [*troops, population*]; **4** relever [*worker, sentry*].

religion *n* religion *f*.

religious *adj* (gen) religieux/-ieuse; [*person*] croyant/-e; [*war*] de religion.

relinquish *vtr* renoncer à [*claim, right*] (**to** en faveur de); céder [*task, power*] (**to** à).

relish I *n* **1 with ~** [*eat, drink*] avec un plaisir évident; **2** (Culin) condiment *m*.
II *vtr* savourer [*food*]; se réjouir de [*prospect*].

reluctance *n* réticence *f* (**to do** à faire).

reluctant *adj* [*person*] peu enthousiaste; **to be ~ to do** être peu disposé/-e à faire.

reluctantly *adv* à contrecœur.

rely *vi* **1** (be dependent) **to ~ on** dépendre de [*person, aid, industry*]; reposer sur [*method, technology, exports*]; **2** (count) **to ~ on sb/sth** compter sur qn/qch (**to do** pour faire).

remain *vi* rester; **to ~ silent** garder le silence.

remainder *n* reste *m* (**of** de).

remains *n pl* restes *mpl*.

remand I *n* **on ~** (in custody) en détention provisoire; (on bail) en liberté sous caution.
II *vtr* **to be ~ed in custody** être placé/-e en détention provisoire.

remark I *n* remarque *f*.
II *vtr* **1** (comment) faire remarquer (**that** que; **to** à); **2** (notice) remarquer (**that** que).

remarkable *adj* remarquable.

remarry *vi* se remarier.

remedial *adj* (Sch) [*class*] de rattrapage.

remedy I *n* remède *m* (**for** à, contre).
II *vtr* remédier à.

remember I *vtr* **1** (recall) se souvenir de, se rappeler [*fact, name, place, event*]; se souvenir de [*person*]; **to ~ doing** se rappeler avoir fait, se souvenir d'avoir fait; **2** (not forget) **to ~ to do** penser à faire, ne pas oublier de faire.
II *vi* se souvenir.

remind *vtr* rappeler; **to ~ sb of sb/sth** rappeler qn/qch à qn; **to ~ sb to do** rappeler à qn de faire.

reminder *n* rappel *m* (**of** de; **that** du fait que).

reminisce *vi* évoquer ses souvenirs (**about** de).

reminiscent *adj* **to be ~ of sb/sth** faire penser à qn/qch.

remiss *adj* négligent/-e.

remission *n* **1** (of sentence, debt) remise *f*; **2** (Med) rémission *f*.

remit *n* attributions *fpl*.

remnant *n* (gen) reste *m*; (of building, past) vestige *m*; (of fabric) coupon *m*.

remorse *n* remords *m* (**for** de).

remote *adj* **1** [*area, village*] isolé/-e; [*ancestor, country*] éloigné/-e; **2** (aloof) [*person*] distant/-e; **3** (slight) [*chance*] vague, infime.

remote control *n* télécommande *f*.

removal *n* **1** (of furniture, parcel, rubbish) enlèvement *m*; (Med) ablation *f*; **stain ~** détachage *m*; **2** (change of home) déménagement *m* (**from** de; **to** à).

remove *vtr* **1** (gen, Med) enlever (**from** de); enlever, ôter [*clothes, shoes*]; supprimer [*threat*]; chasser [*doubt*]; **cousin once ~d** cousin au deuxième degré; **2 to ~ sb from office** démettre qn de ses fonctions.

remuneration *n* rémunération *f*.

Renaissance *n* **the ~** la Renaissance.

render *vtr* rendre.
rendezvous I *n* rendez-vous *m inv*.
II *vi* **to ~ with sb** rejoindre qn.
renegade *n* renégat/-e *m/f*.
renew I *vtr* (gen) renouveler; renouer [*acquaintance*]; raviver [*courage*]; faire prolonger [*library book*].
renewal *n* (of contract, passport) renouvellement *m*; (of hostilities) reprise *f*; (of interest) regain *m*.
renewed *adj* [*interest, optimism*] accru/-e; [*attack, call*] renouvelé/-e.
renounce *vtr* (gen) renoncer à; renier [*faith, friend*].
renovate *vtr* rénover [*building*].
renowned *adj* célèbre (**for** pour).
rent I *n* loyer *m*; **for ~** à louer.
II *vtr* louer.
rental *n* (of car, premises, equipment) location *f*; (of phone line) abonnement *m*.
reopen *vtr*, *vi* rouvrir.
reorganize *vtr* réorganiser.
rep ▶ 626 *n* représentant/-e *m/f* (de commerce).
repair I *n* réparation *f*; **to be (damaged) beyond ~** ne pas être réparable; **to be in good/bad ~** être en bon/mauvais état.
II *vtr* réparer.
repairman *n* réparateur *m*.
repatriate *vtr* rapatrier.
repay *vtr* rembourser [*person, sum*]; rendre [*hospitality, favour*].
repayment *n* remboursement *m* (**on** de).
repeal I *n* abrogation *f* (**of** de).
II *vtr* abroger.
repeat I *n* (gen) répétition *f*; (on radio, TV) rediffusion *f*; (Mus) reprise *f*.
II *vtr* (gen) répéter; (Sch) redoubler [*year*]; rediffuser [*programme*].
repeatedly *adv* plusieurs fois, à plusieurs reprises.
repel *vtr* repousser.
repellent *adj* repoussant/-e.
repent *vi* se repentir.
repercussion *n* répercussion *f*.
repertoire *n* répertoire *m*.
repetition *n* répétition *f*.
repetitive *adj* répétitif/-ive.
replace *vtr* **1** (put back) remettre [*lid, cork*]; remettre [qch] à sa place [*book, ornament*]; **2** (provide replacement for) remplacer (**with** par).
replacement *n* **1** (person) remplaçant/-e *m/f* (**for** de); **2** (act) remplacement *m*; **3** (spare part) pièce *f* de rechange.
replay I *n* (Sport) match *m* rejoué.
II *vtr* rejouer.
replenish *vtr* reconstituer [*stocks*].
replica *n* réplique *f*, copie *f* (**of** de).
reply I *n* réponse *f*.
II *vtr*, *vi* répondre.
report I *n* **1** (written account) rapport *m* (**on** sur); (verbal account, minutes) compte-rendu *m*; (in media) communiqué *m*; (longer) reportage *m*; **2** (GB Sch) (also **school ~**) bulletin *m* scolaire; (US Sch) (review) critique *f*.
II *vtr* **1** signaler [*fact, event, theft, accident*]; **to ~ sth to sb** transmettre qch à qn [*result, decision, news*]; **2** (make complaint about) signaler [*person*]; se plaindre de [*noise*].
III *vi* **1 to ~ on** faire un compte-rendu sur [*talks, progress*]; [*reporter*] faire un reportage sur [*events*]; [*committee, group*] faire son rapport sur; **2** (present oneself) se présenter; **to ~ for duty** prendre son service; **3 to ~ to** être sous les ordres (directs) de [*manager, superior*].
report card *n* (US) bulletin *m* scolaire.
reporter ▶ 626 *n* journaliste *mf*, reporter *mf*.
repose *n* repos *m*; **in ~** au repos.
repossess *vtr* [*bank*] saisir [*house*]; [*creditor*] reprendre possession de [*property*].
reprehensible *adj* répréhensible.
represent *vtr* **1** (gen) représenter; **2** (present) présenter [*person, event*] (**as** comme).
representation *n* **1** représentation *f* (**of** de; **by** par); **2 to make ~s to sb** faire des démarches *fpl* auprès de qn.
representative I ▶ 626 *n* **1** représentant/-e *m/f*; **2** (US) (politician) député *m*.
II *adj* représentatif/-ive (**of** de), typique (**of** de).
repress *vtr* réprimer [*reaction, smile*]; refouler [*feelings*].
reprieve I *n* **1** (Law) remise *f* de peine; **2** (delay) sursis *m*; **3** (respite) répit *m*.
II *vtr* accorder une remise de peine à [*prisoner*].
reprimand I *n* réprimande *f*.
II *vtr* réprimander.
reprisal *n* représailles *fpl*.
reproach I *n* reproche *m*; **beyond ~** irréprochable.
II *vtr* reprocher à [*person*]; **to ~ sb with** or **for sth** reprocher qch à qn.
reproduce I *vtr* reproduire.
II *vi* se reproduire.
reproduction *n* reproduction *f*.
reproductive *adj* reproducteur/-trice.
reproof *n* réprimande *f*.
reprove *vtr* réprimander (**for doing** de faire).
reptile *n* reptile *m*.
republic *n* république *f*.
republican I *n* républicain/-e *m/f*; **Republican** (US) Républicain/-e *m/f*.
II *adj* (also **Republican**) républicain/-e.
repudiate *vtr* rejeter.
repugnant *adj* répugnant/-e.
repulse *vtr* repousser.
repulsion *n* répulsion *f*.
repulsive *adj* repoussant/-e.
reputable *adj* de bonne réputation.
reputation *n* réputation *f* (**as** de).
repute *n* **of ~** réputé/-e.
reputed *adj* (gen) réputé/-e; (Law) putatif/-ive; **he is ~ to be very rich** à ce que l'on dit il serait très riche.
request I *n* **1** demande *f* (**for** de; **to** à), requête

f (**for** de; **to** à); **on ~** sur demande; **2** (on radio) dédicace *f*.
II *vtr* demander (**from** à); **to ~ sb to do** demander à qn de faire.

require *vtr* **1** (need) avoir besoin de; **2** (necessitate) [*job, situation*] exiger [*funds, qualifications*]; **to be ~d to do** être tenu/-e de faire.

requirement *n* **1** (need) besoin *m*; **2** (condition) condition *f*; **3** (obligation) obligation *f* (**to do** de faire); **4** (US Univ) matière *f* obligatoire.

requisite *adj* exigé/-e, requis/-e.

requisition *vtr* réquisitionner.

reschedule *vtr* (change time) changer l'heure de; (change date) changer la date de.

rescue I *n* **1** (aid) secours *m*; **to come/go to sb's ~** venir/aller au secours de qn; **to come to the ~** venir à la rescousse; **2** (operation) sauvetage *m* (**of** de).
II *vtr* **1** (save) sauver; **2** (aid) porter secours à; **3** (release) libérer.

rescue worker *n* secouriste *mf*.

research I *n* recherche *f* (**into, on** sur).
II *vtr* faire des recherches sur [*topic*]; préparer [*book, article*].

research and development, **R&D** *n* recherche-développement *f*, recherche *f* et développement *m*.

researcher ▶626 *n* chercheur/-euse *m/f*; (in TV) documentaliste *mf*.

resemblance *n* ressemblance *f* (**between** entre; **to** avec).

resemble *vtr* ressembler à; **to ~ each other** se ressembler.

resent *vtr* en vouloir à [*person*] (**for doing** d'avoir fait); ne pas aimer [*tone*].

resentful *adj* plein/-e de ressentiment (**of sb** envers qn).

resentment *n* ressentiment *m*.

reservation *n* **1** (doubt) réserve *f*; **without ~** sans réserve; **to have ~s about sth** avoir des doutes sur qch; **2** (booking) réservation *f*; **3** (US) (**Indian**) **~** réserve *f* (indienne).

reserve I *n* **1** (stock) réserve *f*; **to keep sth in ~** tenir qch en réserve; **2** (reticence) réserve *f*; **3** (Mil) **the ~(s)** la réserve; **4** (Sport) remplaçant/-e *m/f*; **5** réserve *f*; **wildlife ~** réserve naturelle.
II *vtr* réserver.

reserved *adj* réservé/-e.

reservoir *n* réservoir *m*.

reset *vtr* régler [*machine*]; remettre [qch] à l'heure [*clock*].

reshuffle *n* remaniement *m*.

reside *vi* résider, habiter (**with** avec).

residence *n* résidence *f*.

residence permit *n* permis *m* de séjour.

resident I *n* (gen) résident/-e *m/f*; (of street) riverain/-e *m/f*; (of guest house) pensionnaire *mf*.
II *adj* [*population*] local/-e; [*staff, tutor*] à demeure.

residential *adj* [*area*] résidentiel/-ielle; [*staff*] à demeure; [*course*] en internat; **to be in ~ care** être pris en charge par une institution.

residue *n* résidu *m* (**of** de).

resign I *vtr* démissionner de [*post, job*].
II *vi* démissionner (**as** du poste de; **from** de).
III *v refl* **to ~ oneself** se résigner (**to** à).

resignation *n* **1** (from post) démission *f* (**from** de; **as** du poste de); **2** (patience) résignation *f*.

resigned *adj* résigné/-e (**to** à).

resilient *adj* (morally) déterminé/-e; (physically) résistant/-e.

resin *n* résine *f*.

resist I *vtr* résister à.
II *vi* résister.

resistance *n* résistance *f* (**to** à).

Resistance *n* **the ~** la Résistance.

resistant *adj* **1** **heat-~** résistant/-e à la chaleur; **water-~** imperméable; **2** (opposed) **~ to** réfractaire à.

resit *vtr* (GB) repasser [*exam, test*].

resolute *adj* [*person*] résolu/-e.

resolution *n* résolution *f*; **to make a ~ to do** prendre la résolution de faire.

resolve I *n* détermination *f*.
II *vtr* **1** (gen) résoudre; **2** (decide) **to ~ that** décider que; **to ~ to do** résoudre de faire.

resonant *adj* [*voice*] sonore.

resort I *n* **1** recours *m*; **as a last ~** en dernier recours; **2** **seaside ~** station *f* balnéaire; **ski ~** station *f* de ski.
II *vi* **to ~ to** recourir à.

resound *vi* **1** [*noise*] retentir (**through** dans); **2** [*place*] retentir (**with** de).

resounding *adj* [*cheers*] retentissant/-e; [*success*] éclatant/-e.

resource *n* ressource *f*.

resourceful *adj* plein/-e de ressources, débrouillard/-e○.

respect I *n* **1** (gen) respect *m*; **out of ~** par respect (**for** pour); **with** (**all due**) **~** sauf votre respect; **with ~ to** par rapport à; **2** (aspect) égard *m*; **in many ~s** à bien des égards.
II **respects** *n pl* respects *mpl*; **to pay one's ~s to sb** présenter ses respects à qn.
III *vtr* respecter.

respectable *adj* **1** [*person, family*] respectable; **2** (adequate) [*amount*] respectable; [*performance*] honorable.

respectful *adj* respectueux/-euse.

respective *adj* respectif/-ive.

respiration *n* respiration *f*.

respirator *n* respirateur *m*.

respiratory *adj* respiratoire.

respite *n* répit *m* (**from** dans).

respond *vi* **1** (answer) répondre (**to** à; **with** par); **2** (react) réagir (**to** à).

response *n* **1** (answer) réponse *f* (**to** à); **in ~ to** en réponse à; **2** (reaction) réaction *f* (**to** à; **from** de).

responsibility *n* responsabilité *f* (**for** de); **to take ~ for sth** prendre la responsabilité de qch.

responsible *adj* **1** (to blame) responsable (**for** de); **2** (in charge) **~ for doing** chargé/-e de faire; **3** (trustworthy) responsable; **4** [*job*] à responsabilités.

responsive *adj* réceptif/-ive.

rest I *n* **1** (remainder) **the ~** le reste (**of** de); **for the ~ of my life** pour le restant de mes jours; **2** (other people) **the ~** (**of them**) les autres; **3** (repose) repos *m*; (break) pause *f*; **to have a ~** se reposer.
II *vtr* **1** (lean) **to ~ sth on** appuyer qch sur; **2** reposer [*legs*]; ne pas utiliser [*injured limb*].
III *vi* **1** se reposer; **to ~ easy** être tranquille; **to let the matter ~** en rester là; **2** (be supported) **to ~ on** reposer sur; **3 to ~ on** [*decision*] reposer sur [*assumption*].

restaurant *n* restaurant *m*.

restaurant car *n* (GB) wagon-restaurant *m*.

restless *adj* [*person*] nerveux/-euse; [*patient, sleep*] agité/-e.

restoration *n* restauration *f*.

restore *vtr* **1** restituer [*property*] (**to** à); **2** rétablir [*health, peace, monarchy*]; rendre [*faculty*]; **to ~ sb to power** ramener qn au pouvoir; **3** (repair) restaurer.

restrain I *vtr* retenir [*person*]; contenir [*crowd*]; maîtriser [*animal*].
II *v refl* **to ~ oneself** se retenir.

restrained *adj* [*manner*] calme; [*reaction*] modéré/-e; [*person*] posé/-e.

restraint *n* **1** (moderation) modération *f*; **2** (restriction) restriction *f*; **wage ~** contrôle *m* des salaires; **3** (constraint) contrainte *f*.

restrict *vtr* limiter [*activity, choice, growth*] (**to** à); restreindre [*freedom*]; réserver [*access, membership*] (**to** à).

restriction *n* limitation *f*.

re-string *vtr* changer les cordes de [*guitar*]; recorder [*racket*]; renfiler [*necklace*].

rest room *n* (US) toilettes *fpl*.

result I *n* résultat *m* (**of** de); **as a ~ of** à la suite de; **as a ~** en conséquence.
II *vi* résulter; **to ~ in** avoir pour résultat.

resume *vtr, vi* reprendre.

résumé *n* **1** (summary) résumé *m*; **2** (US) (CV) curriculum vitae *m inv*.

resumption *n* reprise *f* (**of** de).

resurface I *vtr* refaire (la surface de) [*road*].
II *vi* [*submarine*] faire surface; [*person*] refaire surface.

resurrect *vtr* ressusciter.

resurrection *n* résurrection *f*; **the Resurrection** la Résurrection.

resuscitate *vtr* (Med) réanimer.

resuscitation *n* réanimation *f*.

retail I *n* vente *f* au détail.
II *adv* au détail.
III *vi* **to ~ at** se vendre au détail à.

retailer *n* détaillant *m*.

retail price *n* prix *m* de détail.

retain *vtr* garder [*control, identity*]; conserver [*heat, title*]; retenir [*water, fact*].

retaliate *vi* réagir.

retaliation *n* représailles *fpl* (**for** de).

retarded *adj* retardé/-e.

retch *vi* avoir des haut-le-cœur.

rethink *n* **to have a ~** y repenser.

reticent *adj* réticent/-e; **to be ~ about sth** être discret/-ète sur qch.

retina *n* rétine *f*.

retinue *n* escorte *f*.

retire *vi* **1** (from work) prendre sa retraite; **2** (withdraw) se retirer (**from** de).

retired *adj* retraité/-e.

retirement *n* retraite *f*.

retiring *adj* (shy) réservé/-e.

retort I *n* riposte *f*.
II *vtr* rétorquer (**that** que).

retrace *vtr* **to ~ one's steps** revenir sur ses pas.

retract I *vtr* rétracter [*statement, claws*]; escamoter [*landing gear*].
II *vi* [*landing gear*] s'escamoter.

retrain I *vtr* recycler [*staff*].
II *vi* [*person*] se recycler.

retreat I *n* retraite *f*.
II *vi* [*person*] se retirer (**into** dans; **from** de); [*army*] se replier (**to** sur); [*flood water*] reculer; **to ~ into a dream world** se réfugier dans un monde imaginaire.

retrial *n* nouveau procès *m*.

retrieve *vtr* récupérer [*object*]; redresser [*situation*]; extraire [*data*].

retrograde *adj* rétrograde.

retrospect: **in retrospect** *phr* rétrospectivement.

retrospective I *n* (also **~ exhibition** or **~ show**) rétrospective *f*.
II *adj* **1** (gen) rétrospectif/-ive; **2** (Law) rétroactif/-ive.

return I *n* **1** (gen) retour *m* (**to** à; **from** de; **of** de); **by ~ of post** par retour du courrier; **2** (on investment) rendement *m* (**on** de).
II *vtr* **1** (give back) rendre; (pay back) rembourser; **to ~ sb's call** rappeler qn; **2** (bring back) rapporter (**to** à); **3** (put back) remettre; **4** (send back) renvoyer; **'~ to sender'** 'retour à l'expéditeur'; **5** (reciprocate) répondre à [*love*]; **6** (Mil) riposter à [*fire*]; **7** (Law) prononcer [*verdict*]; **8** rapporter [*profit*].
III *vi* **1** (come back) revenir (**from** de); retourner (**to** à); (get back from abroad) rentrer (**from** de); (get back home) rentrer chez soi; **2** (resume) **to ~ to** reprendre [*activity*]; **to ~ to power** revenir au pouvoir; **3** (recur) [*symptom, doubt*] réapparaître.
IV **in return** *phr* en échange (**for** de).
IDIOMS **many happy ~s!** bon anniversaire!

return ticket *n* billet *m* aller-retour.

return trip *n* retour *m*.

reunification *n* réunification *f*.

reunion *n* réunion *f*.

reunite *vtr* réunir [*family*]; réunifier [*party*].

rev○ *vtr* monter le régime de [*engine*].

revalue *vtr* réévaluer.

revamp *vtr* rajeunir [*image*]; réorganiser [*company*]; retaper○ [*building*].

reveal *vtr* (gen) révéler; dévoiler [*truth, plan*]; **to ~ sth to sb** révéler qch à qn.

revealing *adj* **1** [*remark*] révélateur/-trice; **2** [*blouse*] décolleté/-e.

revel *vi* **to ~ in sth/in doing** se délecter de qch/à faire.

revelation *n* révélation *f*.

revenge I *n* vengeance *f*; **to get one's ~** se venger (**for** de; **on** sur).
II *v refl* **to ~ oneself** se venger.

revenue *n* revenus *mpl*.

reverberate *vi* résonner (**with** de; **through** dans, par); (figurative) se propager.

revere *vtr* révérer.

reverence *n* profond respect *m*.

Reverend ▶498 *n* **1** (Protestant) pasteur *m*; **2** (as title) **the ~ Jones** le révérend Jones; **~ Mother** Révérende Mère.

reverent *adj* [*hush*] religieux/-ieuse; [*expression*] de respect.

reverie *n* rêverie *f*.

reversal *n* (of policy, roles) renversement *m*; (of order, trend) inversion *f*; (of fortune) revers *m*.

reverse I *n* **1** (opposite) **the ~** le contraire; **2** (back) **the ~** (of coin) le revers; (of banknote) le verso; (of fabric) l'envers *m*; **3** (Aut) (also **~ gear**) marche *f* arrière.
II *adj* **1** [*effect*] contraire; **in ~ order** [*answer question*] en commençant par le dernier; [*list*] en commençant par la fin; **2** (Aut) **~ gear** marche *f* arrière.
III *vtr* inverser [*trend, process*]; renverser [*roles*]; faire rouler [qch] en marche arrière [*car*]; **to ~ the charges** appeler en PCV.
IV *vi* [*driver*] faire marche arrière.
V in reverse *phr* en sens inverse.

reverse charge call *n* appel *m* en PCV.

reversible *adj* réversible.

revert *vi* **to ~ to** reprendre [*habit, name*]; redevenir [*wilderness*].

review I *n* **1** (reconsideration) révision *f* (**of** de); (report) rapport *m* (**of** sur); **2** (of book, film) critique *f* (**of** de); **3** (magazine) revue *f*; **4** (Mil) revue *f*; **5** (US Sch, Univ) révision *f*.
II *vtr* **1** reconsidérer [*situation*]; réviser [*attitude, policy*]; passer [qch] en revue [*troops*]; **2** faire la critique de [*book, film*]; **3** (US Sch, Univ) réviser.

reviewer *n* critique *m*.

revise I *vtr* **1** (alter) réviser, modifier [*estimate, figures*]; **2** (GB) (for exam) réviser [*subject*]; **3** (correct) revoir, réviser [*text*].
II *vi* (GB) [*student*] réviser.

revision *n* révision *f*.

revitalize *vtr* revitaliser.

revival *n* (of economy) reprise *f*; (of interest) regain *m*; (of custom, language) renouveau *m*.

revive I *vtr* **1** ranimer [*person*]; **2** raviver [*custom*]; ranimer [*interest, hopes*]; relancer [*movement, fashion*]; revigorer [*economy*].
II *vi* **1** [*person*] reprendre connaissance; **2** [*economy*] reprendre.

revoke *vtr* révoquer [*will*]; annuler [*decision*].

revolt I *n* révolte *f* (**against** contre).
II *vtr* dégoûter, révolter.
III *vi* se révolter (**against** contre).

revolting *adj* **1** (physically) répugnant/-e; (morally) révoltant/-e; **2**° [*food*] infect/-e; [*person*] affreux/-euse.

revolution *n* **1** révolution *f* (**in** dans); **2** (Aut, Tech) tour *m*.

revolutionary *n, adj* révolutionnaire (*mf*).

revolutionize *vtr* révolutionner.

revolve *vi* **1** (turn) tourner (**around** autour de); **2 to ~ around** (be focused on) être axé/-e sur.

revolving *adj* [*chair*] pivotant/-e; [*stage*] tournant/-e; **~ door** porte *f* à tambour *m*.

revue *n* revue *f*.

revulsion *n* dégoût *m*.

reward I *n* récompense *f*; **a £50 ~** 50 livres sterling de récompense.
II *vtr* récompenser (**for** de, pour).

rewarding *adj* [*experience*] enrichissant/-e; [*job*] gratifiant/-e.

rewind *vtr* rembobiner [*tape, film*].

rewire *vtr* refaire l'installation électrique de [*building*].

reword *vtr* reformuler.

rewrite *vtr* ré(é)crire [*story, history*].

rhapsody *n* rhapsodie *f*.

rhetoric *n* rhétorique *f*.

rhetorical *adj* rhétorique.

rheumatism ▶533 *n* rhumatisme *m*.

Rhine *pr n* Rhin *m*.

rhinoceros *n* rhinocéros *m*.

rhubarb *n* rhubarbe *f*.

rhyme I *n* **1** (gen) rime *f*; **2** (poem) vers *mpl*; (children's) comptine *f*.
II *vi* rimer (**with** avec).

rhythm *n* rythme *m*.

rhythmic(al) *adj* rythmique.

rib *n* **1** (Anat, Culin) côte *f*; **2** (in umbrella) baleine *f*; (in plane, building) nervure *f*.

ribbon *n* ruban *m*.

rib cage *n* cage *f* thoracique.

rice *n* riz *m*.

rich I *n* **the ~** les riches *mpl*.
II *adj* riche; **to grow** or **get ~** s'enrichir; **to make sb ~** enrichir qn.

riches *n pl* richesses *fpl*.

richness *n* richesse *f*.

rickety *adj* branlant/-e.

rickshaw *n* pousse-pousse *m inv*.

ricochet *vi* ricocher (**off** sur).

rid I *vtr* **to ~ sb/sth of** débarrasser qn/qch de.
II *pp adj* **to get ~ of** se débarrasser de [*old car, guests*]; éliminer [*poverty*].

riddance *n* IDIOMS **good ~ (to bad rubbish)**! bon débarras°!

riddle I *n* **1** (puzzle) devinette *f*; **2** (mystery) énigme *f*.
II *vtr* **to be ~d with** être criblé/-e de [*bullets*]; être rongé/-e par [*disease, guilt*].

ride I *n* **1** (in vehicle, on bike) trajet *m* (**in, on** en, à); (for pleasure) tour *m*, promenade *f*; **to go for a ~** aller faire un tour; **to give sb a ~** (US)

emmener qn (en voiture); **2** (on horse) promenade *f* à cheval.
II *vtr* **1** rouler à [*bike*]; **to ~ a horse** monter à cheval; **can you ~ a bike?** sais-tu faire du vélo?; **2** (US) prendre [*bus, subway*]; parcourir [*range*]; **3** chevaucher [*wave*].
III *vi* (go horse-riding) faire du cheval; **to ~ in** or **on** prendre [*bus*].
IDIOMS **to take sb for a ~**○ rouler qn○.
■ **ride out** surmonter [*crisis*]; survivre à [*recession*]; **to ~ out the storm** surmonter la crise.
■ **ride up 1** [*rider*] s'approcher (**to** de); **2** [*skirt*] remonter.

rider *n* **1** (on horse) cavalier/-ière *m/f*; (on motorbike) motocycliste *mf*; (on bike) cycliste *mf*; **2** (to document) annexe *f*.

ridge *n* **1** (along mountain top) arête *f*, crête *f*; **2** (on rock, metal surface) strie *f*; (in ploughed land) crête *f*; **3** (on roof) faîte *m*, faîtage *m*.

ridicule I *n* ridicule *m*.
II *vtr* tourner [qn/qch] en ridicule.

ridiculous *adj* ridicule.

riding ▶ 504 *n* équitation *f*; **to go ~** faire de l'équitation.

riding school *n* centre *m* équestre.

rife *adj* **to be ~** être répandu/-e.

riffraff *n* populace *f*.

rifle I *n* (firearm) fusil *m*.
II *vtr* vider [*wallet, safe*].
■ **rifle through** fouiller dans.

rift *n* **1** (disagreement) désaccord *m*; (permanent) rupture *f*; **2** (in rock) fissure *f*; (in clouds) trouée *f*.

rig I *n* (for oil) (on land) tour *f* de forage; (offshore) plate-forme *f* pétrolière offshore.
II *vtr* truquer [*election, result*].
■ **rig up** installer [*equipment*]; improviser [*clothes line, shelter*].

rigging *n* **1** (on ship) gréement *m*; **2** (of election, competition, result) truquage *m*.

right I *n* **1** (side, direction) droite *f*; **on** or **to your ~** à votre droite; **2** (in politics) (also **Right**) **the ~** la droite; **3** (morally) bien *m*; **~ and wrong** le bien et le mal; **4** (just claim) droit *m*; **to have a ~ to sth** avoir droit à qch; **civil ~s** droits civils.
II *adj* **1** (not left) droit/-e, de droite; **2** (morally) bien; (fair) juste; **it is only ~ and proper** ce n'est que justice; **to do the ~ thing** faire ce qu'il faut; **3** (correct) [*choice, direction, size, answer*] bon/bonne (*before n*); [*word*] juste; [*time*] exact/-e; **to be ~** [*person*] avoir raison; [*answer*] être juste; **4** (suitable) qui convient; **the ~ person for the job** la personne qu'il faut pour le poste; **to be in the ~ place at the ~ time** être là où il faut au bon moment; **5** (in good order) **the engine isn't quite ~** le moteur ne fonctionne pas très bien; **I don't feel quite ~ these days** je ne me sens pas très bien ces jours-ci; **6 to put** or **set ~** corriger [*mistake*]; réparer [*injustice*]; arranger [*situation*]; réparer [*machine*]; **7** [*angle*] droit/-e; **at ~ angles to** à angle droit avec, perpendiculaire à.
IV *adv* **1** (not left) à droite; **to turn/look ~** tourner/regarder à droite; **2** (directly) droit, directement; **it's ~ in front of you** c'est droit or juste devant toi; **I'll be ~ back** je reviens tout de suite; **3** (exactly) **~ in the middle of the room** en plein milieu de la pièce; **~ now** (immediately) tout de suite; (US) (at this point in time) en ce moment; **4** (correctly) juste, comme il faut; **you're not doing it ~** tu ne fais pas ça comme il faut; **to guess ~** deviner juste; **5** (completely) tout; **go ~ back to the beginning** revenez tout au début; **~ at the bottom** tout au fond; **to turn the central heating ~ up** mettre le chauffage central à fond; **6** (very well) bon; **~, let's have a look** bon, voyons ça.
V *vtr* redresser.
IDIOMS **by ~s** normalement, en principe.

right angle *n* angle *m* droit.

right away *adv* tout de suite.

righteous *adj* vertueux/-euse.

rightful *adj* légitime.

right-hand *adj* du côté droit; **on the ~ side** sur la droite.

right-hand drive *n* conduite *f* à droite.

right-handed *adv* [*person*] droitier/-ière; [*blow*] du droit.

right-hand man *n* bras *m* droit.

rightly *adv* **1** (accurately) correctement; **2** (justifiably) à juste titre; **~ or wrongly** à tort ou à raison; **3** (with certainty) au juste; **I don't ~ know** je ne sais pas au juste.

right of way *n* **1** (Aut) priorité *f*; **2** (over land) droit *m* de passage; **'no ~'** 'entrée *f* interdite'.

right wing I *n* **the ~** la droite.
II **right-wing** *adj* [*attitude*] de droite; **they are very ~** ils sont très à droite.

rigid *adj* [*rules, person, material*] rigide; [*controls, timetable*] strict/-e.

rigorous *adj* rigoureux/-euse.

rigour (GB), **rigor** (US) *n* rigueur *f*.

rim *n* bord *m*; (on wheel) jante *f*.

rind *n* **1** (on cheese) croûte *f*; (on bacon) couenne *f*; **2** (on fruit) peau *f*.

ring I *n* **1** anneau *m*; (with stone) bague *f*; **a diamond ~** une bague de diamants; **a wedding ~** une alliance; **2** (circle) cercle *m*; **to have ~s under one's eyes** avoir les yeux cernés; **3** (at door) coup *m* de sonnette; (of phone) sonnerie *f*; **4** (in circus) piste *f*; (in boxing) ring *m*; **5** (of smugglers, spies) réseau *m*; **6** (on cooker) (electric) plaque *f*; (gas) brûleur *m*.
II *vtr* **1** sonner [*church bells*]; **to ~ the doorbell** or **bell** sonner; **2** (GB) (also **~ up**) appeler.
III *vi* **1** [*bell, phone, person*] sonner; **the doorbell rang** on a sonné à la porte; **2** [*footsteps, laughter*] résonner; **to ~ true** sonner vrai; **3** (GB) (phone) téléphoner; **to ~ for** appeler [*taxi*].
■ **ring off** (GB) raccrocher.
■ **ring out** [*voice, cry*] retentir; [*bells*] sonner.

ring binder *n* classeur *m* à anneaux.

ringing *n* **1** (of bell, alarm) sonnerie *f*; **2** (in ears) bourdonnement *m*.

ringleader *n* meneur/-euse *m/f*.

ringlet *n* anglaise *f*.

ringroad *n* (GB) périphérique *m*.

rinse I *n* rinçage *m*.
II *vtr* rincer; (wash) laver.

riot I *n* **1** émeute *f*, révolte *f*; **prison ~** mutinerie *f*; **2 a ~ of** une profusion de [*colours*].
II *vi* [*crowd, demonstrators*] se soulever; [*prisoners*] se mutiner.
IDIOMS **to run ~** [*crowd*] se déchaîner; [*imagination*] se débrider; [*plant*] proliférer.

rioter *n* émeutier/-ière *m/f*; (in prison) mutin *m*.

rioting *n* émeutes *fpl*, bagarres *fpl*.

riot police *n* forces *fpl* antiémeutes.

rip I *vtr* déchirer; **to ~ sth out** arracher qch.
II *vi* [*fabric*] se déchirer.

RIP *abbr* qu'il/elle repose en paix.

ripe *adj* [*fruit*] mûr/-e; [*cheese*] fait/-e.

ripen I *vtr* mûrir [*fruit*]; affiner [*cheese*].
II *vi* [*fruit*] mûrir; [*cheese*] se faire.

ripple I *n* ondulation *f*.
II *vi* **1** [*water*] se rider; (making noise) clapoter; **2** [*hair, corn*] onduler; [*muscles*] saillir.

rise I *n* **1** (increase) augmentation *f* (**in** de); (in prices, pressure) hausse *f* (**in** de); (in temperature) élévation *f* (**in** de); **2** (of person) ascension *f*; (of empire) essor *m*; **3** (slope) montée *f*.
II *vi* **1** [*water, tension*] monter; [*price, temperature*] augmenter; [*voice*] devenir plus fort; [*hopes*] grandir; **2** (get up) [*person*] se lever; (after falling) se relever; **to ~ from the dead** ressusciter; **to ~ to the occasion** se montrer à la hauteur; **3** [*road*] monter; [*cliff*] s'élever; **4** [*sun, moon*] se lever; **5** [*dough*] lever.
IDIOMS **to give ~ to** donner lieu à [*rumours*]; causer [*problem*].

rising I *n* soulèvement *m*.
II *adj* (gen) en hausse; [*tension*] grandissant/-e; [*sun, moon*] levant/-e.

risk I *n* risque *m*; **to run a ~** courir un risque; **to take ~s** prendre des risques; **at ~** menacé/-e.
II *vtr* risquer; **to ~ doing** courir le risque de faire.

risky *adj* [*decision, undertaking*] risqué/-e; [*share, investment*] à risques.

risqué *adj* osé/-e.

rite *n* rite *m*.

ritual I *n* rituel *m*, rites *mpl*.
II *adj* rituel/-elle.

rival I *n* (person) rival/-e *m/f*; (company) concurrent/-e *m/f*.
II *adj* [*team, business*] rival/-e; [*claim*] opposé/-e.
III *vtr* rivaliser avec (**in** de).

rivalry *n* rivalité *f* (**between** entre).

river *n* (flowing into sea) fleuve *m*; (tributary) rivière *f*.

riverbank *n* berge *f*; **along the ~** le long de la rivière.

riverside I *n* berges *fpl*.
II *adj* [*pub*] au bord de la rivière.

rivet I *n* rivet *m*.
II *vtr* **1** (Tech) riveter; **2 to be ~ed by** être captivé/-e par; **to be ~ed to the spot** être cloué/-e sur place.

riveting *adj* fascinant/-e.

Riviera *n* **the Italian ~** la Riviera; **the French ~** la Côte d'Azur.

road *n* **1** route *f*; **the ~ to Leeds** la route de Leeds; **2** (street) rue *f*; **3** (figurative) voie *f* (**to** de); **to be on the right ~** être sur la bonne voie.

roadblock *n* barrage *m* routier.

roadside *n* bord *m* de la route.

roadsign *n* panneau *m* de signalisation.

roadworks *n pl* travaux *mpl* (routiers).

roam *vtr* parcourir [*countryside*]; faire le tour de [*shops*]; traîner dans [*streets*].
■ **roam around** [*person*] vadrouiller○.

roar I *n* (of lion) rugissement *m*; (of person) hurlement *m*; (of engine) vrombissement *m*; (of traffic) grondement *m*; **a ~ of laughter** un éclat de rire.
II *vi* [*lion*] rugir; [*person*] hurler; [*sea, wind*] mugir; [*fire*] ronfler; [*engine*] vrombir.

roaring *adj* **1** [*engine, traffic*] grondant/-e; **a ~ fire** une belle flambée; **2** [*success*] fou/folle.

roast I *n* (Culin) rôti *m*; (US) barbecue *m*.
II *adj* [*meat, potatoes*] rôti/-e; **~ beef** rôti *m* de bœuf, rosbif *m*.
III *vtr* rôtir [*meat, potatoes*]; (faire) griller [*chestnuts*]; torréfier [*coffee beans*].

rob *vtr* voler [*person*]; dévaliser [*bank, train*]; **to ~ sb of sth** voler qch à qn; (figurative) priver qn de qch.

robber *n* voleur/-euse *m/f*.

robbery *n* vol *m*.

robe *n* robe *f*.

robin *n* (also **~ redbreast**) rouge-gorge *m*.

robot *n* robot *m*.

robust *adj* robuste.

rock I *n* **1** (substance) roche *f*; **solid ~** roche dure; **2** (boulder) rocher *m*; **3** (also **~ music**) rock *m*.
II *vtr* **1** balancer [*cradle*]; bercer [*baby, boat*]; **2** [*tremor*] secouer [*town*]; [*scandal*] ébranler [*government*].
III *vi* [*person*] se balancer; **to ~ back and forth** se balancer d'avant en arrière.
IDIOMS **on the ~s** [*drink*] avec des glaçons; **to be on the ~s** [*marriage*] aller à vau-l'eau.

rock and roll *n* (also **rock'n'roll**) rock and roll *m*.

rock bottom *n* **to hit ~** toucher le fond.

rock climbing ▶ 504 *n* varappe *f*.

rockery *n* (GB) rocaille *f*.

rocket I *n* **1** (gen, Mil) fusée *f*; **2** (salad) roquette *f*.
II *vi* [*price, profit*] monter en flèche.

rocking chair *n* fauteuil *m* à bascule.

rocking horse *n* cheval *m* à bascule.

rocky *adj* **1** [*beach, path, road*] rocailleux/-euse; [*coast*] rocheux/-euse; **2** [*relationship, period*] difficile; [*business*] précaire.

Rocky Mountains *pr n pl* (also **Rockies**) **the ~** les montagnes *fpl* Rocheuses.

rod *n* **1** (gen, Tech) tige *f*; **curtain/stair ~** tringle à rideaux/de marche; **2** (for punishment) baguette *f*; **3** (for fishing) canne *f* à pêche.

rodent *n* rongeur *m*.

roe *n* œufs *mpl* (de poisson).

roe deer *n* (male) chevreuil *m*; (female) chevrette *f*.

rogue *n* **1** (rascal) coquin *m*; **2** (animal) solitaire *m*.

role *n* rôle *m* (**of** de); **title ~** rôle-titre *m*.

roll I *n* **1** (of paper, cloth) rouleau *m*; (of banknotes) liasse *f*; (of flesh) bourrelet *m*; **a ~ of film** une pellicule; **2** (bread) petit pain *m*; **cheese ~** sandwich *m* au fromage; **3** (of dice) lancer *m*; **4** (register) liste *f*; **to call the ~** faire l'appel.
II *vtr* **1** (gen) rouler; faire rouler [*dice*]; **to ~ sth into a ball** faire une boulette de [*paper*]; faire une boule de [*clay, dough*]; **2** étirer [*dough*].
III *vi* **1** [*person, animal*] rouler (**onto** sur); [*car, plane*] faire un tonneau; [*ship*] tanguer; **2** [*thunder*] gronder; [*drum*] rouler; **3** [*camera, press*] tourner.
■ **roll about** (GB), **roll around** [*animal, person*] se rouler; [*marbles, tins*] rouler.
■ **roll down** baisser [*blind, sleeve*].
■ **roll over** se retourner.
■ **roll up** enrouler [*rug, poster*]; **to ~ up one's sleeves** retrousser ses manches.

roller *n* **1** (gen) rouleau *m*; **2** (curler) bigoudi *m*.

roller blind *n* store *m*.

roller coaster *n* montagnes *fpl* russes.

roller-skate *n* patin *m* à roulettes.

roller-skating **▶504|** *n* patinage *m* à roulettes; **to go ~** faire du patin à roulettes.

rolling pin *n* rouleau *m* à pâtisserie.

rollneck *n* col *m* roulé.

Roman I *n* Romain/-e *m/f*.
II *adj* romain/-e.

Roman Catholic *n*, *adj* catholique (*mf*).

romance *n* **1** (of era, place) charme *m*; (of travel) côté *m* romantique; **2** (love affair) histoire *f* d'amour; (love) amour *m*; **3** (novel) roman *m* d'amour; (film) film *m* d'amour.

Romania **▶448|** *pr n* Roumanie *f*.

Romanian **▶553|** **I** *n* **1** (person) Roumain/-e *m/f*; **2** (language) roumain *m*.
II *adj* roumain/-e.

romantic I *n* romantique *mf*.
II *adj* **1** [*setting, story, person*] romantique; **2** [*attachment*] sentimental/-e; **3** [*novel, film*] d'amour.

romanticize *vtr* idéaliser.

Romany *n* Tzigane *mf*, Romani *mf*.

romp I *n* ébats *mpl*.
II *vi* s'ébattre.

rompers *n pl* (also **romper suit**) barboteuse *f*.

roof *n* **1** (on building) toit *m*; **2** (Anat) **the ~ of the mouth** la voûte du palais.

roof rack *n* galerie *f*.

rooftop *n* toit *m*.

rook *n* **1** (bird) (corbeau *m*) freux *m*; **2** (in chess) tour *f*.

room I *n* **1** pièce *f*; (bedroom) chambre *f*; (for working) bureau *m*; (for meetings, teaching, operating) salle *f*; **2** (space) place *f*; **to make ~** faire de la place.
II *vi* (US) loger (**with** chez).

room service *n* service *m* de chambre.

room temperature *n* température *f* ambiante; **at ~** [*wine*] chambré/-e.

roomy *adj* [*car, house*] spacieux/-ieuse; [*garment*] ample; [*bag, cupboard*] grand/-e (*before n*).

roost I *n* perchoir *m*.
II *vi* (in trees) percher (pour la nuit); (in attic) se nicher.
IDIOMS **to rule the ~** faire la loi.

rooster *n* coq *m*.

root I *n* **1** racine *f*; **to take ~** [*plant*] prendre racine; [*idea, value*] s'établir; [*industry*] s'implanter; **2** (of problem) fond *m*; (of evil) origine *f*.
II *vtr* **to be ~ed in** être ancré/-e dans; **deeply-~ed** bien enraciné/-e; **~ed to the spot** figé/-e sur place.
■ **root around**, **root about** fouiller (**in** dans).
■ **root out** traquer [*corruption*]; déloger [*person*].

rope I *n* (gen, Sport) corde *f*; (of pearls) rang *m*.
II *vtr* attacher [*victim, animal*] (**to** à); encorder [*climber*].
IDIOMS **to know the ~s** connaître les ficelles°.

rope ladder *n* échelle *f* de corde.

rosary *n* (prayer) rosaire *m*; (beads) chapelet *m*.

rose *n* rose *f*.

rosebud *n* bouton *m* de rose.

rose bush *n* rosier *m*.

rosemary *n* romarin *m*.

rose-tinted *adj* IDIOMS **to see the world through ~ spectacles** voir la vie en rose.

rosette *n* (for winner) cocarde *f*.

roster *n* (also **duty ~**) tableau *m* de service.

rostrum *n* estrade *f*.

rosy *adj* [*cheek, light*] rose; **to paint a ~ picture** peindre un tableau favorable.

rot I *n* pourriture *f*.
II *vtr* pourrir.
III *vi* (also **~ away**) pourrir.

rota *n* (GB) tableau *m* de service.

rotary *adj* rotatif/-ive.

rotate I *vtr* faire tourner [*blade*].
II *vi* [*blade, handle, wings*] tourner.

rotation *n* rotation *f*.

rote *n* **by ~** par cœur.

rotten *adj* **1** [*produce*] pourri/-e; [*teeth*] gâté/-e; [*smell*] de pourriture; **2** (corrupt) pourri/-e°; **3**° (bad) [*weather*] pourri/-e; [*cook, driver*] exécrable.

rouble **▶582|** *n* rouble *m*.

rough I *adj* **1** [*material*] rêche; [*hand, skin, surface, rock*] rugueux/-euse; [*terrain*] cahoteux/-euse; **2** [*person, behaviour, sport*] brutal/-e, violent/-e; [*landing*] brutal/-e; [*area*] dur/-e; **3** [*description, map*] sommaire; [*figure, idea, estimate*] approximatif/-ive; **4** (difficult) dur, difficile; **a ~ time** une période difficile; **5** (crude)

grossier/-ière; **6** (harsh) [*voice, taste, wine*] âpre; **7** (stormy) [*sea, crossing*] agité/-e.
II *adv* **to sleep ~** dormir à la dure.
IDIOMS **to ~ it** vivre à la dure.

roughage *n* fibres *fpl*.

rough-and-ready *adj* [*person, manner*] fruste; [*conditions*] rudimentaire; [*method, system*] sommaire.

roughen *vtr* rendre [qch] rêche or rugueux.

roughly *adv* **1** [*calculate*] grossièrement; **~ speaking** en gros; **~ 10%** à peu près 10%; **2** [*treat, hit*] brutalement; **3** [*make*] grossièrement.

rough paper *n* feuille *f* de brouillon.

roulette *n* roulette *f*.

round I *adv* (GB) **1 all ~** tout autour; **whisky all ~!** du whisky pour tout le monde!; **to go all the way ~** faire tout le tour; **to go ~ and ~** tourner en rond; **2** (to place, home) **to go ~ to sb's house** passer chez qn; **to ask sb ~** dire à qn de passer à la maison; **to invite sb ~ for lunch** inviter qn à déjeuner (chez soi); **3 all year ~** toute l'année; **this time ~** cette fois-ci.
II *prep* (GB) **1** autour de [*table*]; **to sit ~ the fire** s'asseoir au coin du feu; **2 to go ~ the corner** tourner au coin de la rue; **just ~ the corner** tout près; **to go ~ an obstacle** contourner un obstacle; **3 her sister took us ~ Oxford** sa sœur nous a fait visiter Oxford; **to go ~ the shops** faire les magasins.
III *n* **1** (of competition) manche *f*; (of golf, cards) partie *f*; (in boxing) round *m*; (in showjumping) parcours *m*; (in election) tour *m*; (of talks) série *f*; **a ~ of drinks** une tournée; **a ~ of ammunition** une cartouche; **a ~ of applause** une salve d'applaudissements; **a ~ of toast** un toast; **2 to do one's ~s** [*postman, milkman*] faire sa tournée; [*doctor*] visiter ses malades; [*guard*] faire sa ronde; **to go** or **do the ~s** [*rumour, flu*] circuler; **3** (shape) rondelle *f*.
IV *adj* **1** rond/-e; **in ~ figures, that's £100** si on arrondit, ça fait 100 livres sterling; **a ~ dozen** une douzaine exactement; **2 to have ~ shoulders** avoir le dos voûté; .
V *vtr* contourner [*headland*]; **to ~ the corner** tourner au coin; **to ~ a bend** prendre un virage.
VI **round about** *phr* **1** (approximately) à peu près, environ; **2** (vicinity) **the people ~ about** les gens des environs.
■ **round off 1** finir [*meal, evening*] (**with** par); conclure [*speech*]; **2** arrondir [*corner, figure*].
■ **round on** (GB): **~ on [sb]** attaquer violemment; **she ~ed on me** elle m'est tombée dessus○.
■ **round up 1** regrouper [*people*]; rassembler [*livestock*]; **2** arrondir [qch] au chiffre supérieur [*figure*].

roundabout I *n* (GB) (in fairground) manège *m*; (in playground) tourniquet *m*; (for traffic) rond-point *m*.
II *adj* **to come by a ~ way** faire un détour; **by ~ means** par des moyens détournés; **a ~ way of saying** une façon détournée de dire.

rounders *n* (GB) ≈ baseball *m*.

round trip *n* aller-retour *m*.

roundup *n* **1** (herding) rassemblement *m* (**of** de); **2** (by police) rafle *f*.

rouse *vtr* réveiller [*person*]; susciter [*anger, interest*].

rousing *adj* [*speech*] galvanisant/-e; [*music*] exaltant/-e.

rout I *n* déroute *f*, défaite *f*.
II *vtr* (Mil) mettre en déroute; (figurative) battre à plates coutures.

route I *n* chemin *m*, itinéraire *m*; (in shipping) route *f*; (in aviation) ligne *f*; (figurative) (to power) voie *f* (**to** de); **bus ~** ligne d'autobus.
II *vtr* expédier, acheminer [*goods*].

routine I *n* **1** routine *f*; **2** (act) numéro *m*.
II *adj* **1** [*enquiry, matter*] de routine; **2** (uninspiring) routinier/-ière.

row[1] ▶ 504 I *n* **1** (of people, plants, stitches) rang *m* (**of** de); (of houses, seats, books) rangée *f* (**of** de); **2** (succession) **six times in a ~** six fois de suite; **the third week in a ~** la troisième semaine d'affilée.
II *vtr* **to ~ a boat up the river** remonter la rivière à la rame.
III *vi* (gen) ramer; (Sport) faire de l'aviron; **to ~ across** traverser [qch] à la rame [*lake*].

row[2] I *n* **1** (quarrel) dispute *f* (**about** à propos de); (public) querelle *f*; **to have a ~ with** se disputer avec; **2** (noise) tapage *m*.
II *vi* se disputer (**with** avec; **about, over** à propos de).

rowboat *n* (US) bateau *m* à rames.

rowdy *adj* (noisy) tapageur/-euse; (in class) chahuteur/-euse.

rowing ▶ 504 *n* aviron *m*.

rowing boat *n* (GB) bateau *m* à rames.

royal *adj* royal/-e.

royal blue ▶ 438 *n, adj* bleu (*m*) roi *inv*.

Royal Highness ▶ 498 *n* **His ~** Son Altesse *f* royale; **Your ~** Votre Altesse *f*.

royalty *n* **1** (persons) membres *mpl* d'une famille royale; **2** (to author, musician) droits *mpl* d'auteur; (on patent) royalties *fpl*.

rub I *n* **1** (massage) friction *f*; **2** (polish) coup *m* de chiffon.
II *vtr* se frotter [*chin, eyes*]; frotter [*stain, surface*]; frictionner [*sb's back*]; **to ~ sth into the skin** faire pénétrer qch dans la peau.
III *vi* frotter.
IDIOMS **to ~ sb up the wrong way** prendre qn à rebrousse-poil○.
■ **rub out** (erase) effacer.

rubber I *n* **1** (substance) caoutchouc *m*; **2** (GB) (eraser) gomme *f*.
II *adj* de or en caoutchouc.

rubber band *n* élastique *m*.

rubber plant *n* caoutchouc *m*.

rubber stamp *n* tampon *m*.

rubber tree *n* hévéa *m*.

rubbish I *n* **1** (refuse) déchets *mpl*; (domestic) ordures *fpl*; (on site) gravats *mpl*; **2** (inferior goods) camelote○ *f*; **this book is ~**○! ce livre est nul○!; **3** (nonsense) bêtises *fpl*.
II *vtr* (GB) descendre [qn/qch] en flammes.

rubbish bin *n* (GB) poubelle *f*.
rubbish heap *n* tas *m* d'ordures.
rubble *n* (after explosion) décombres *mpl*; (on site) gravats *mpl*.
ruby ▶438 I *n* **1** (gem) rubis *m*; **2** (also **~ red**) rouge *m* rubis.
II *adj* **1** [*liquid, lips*] vermeil/-eille; **~ wedding** noces *fpl* de vermeil; **2** [*bracelet, necklace*] de rubis.
rucksack *n* sac *m* à dos.
rudder *n* (on boat) gouvernail *m*; (on plane) gouverne *f*.
ruddy *adj* [*cheeks*] coloré/-e.
rude *adj* **1** (impolite) [*comment*] impoli/-e; [*person*] mal élevé/-e; **to be ~ to sb** être impoli/-e envers qn; **2** (indecent) [*joke*] grossier/-ière; **a ~ word** un gros mot.
rudimentary *adj* rudimentaire.
rudiments *n pl* rudiments *mpl* (**of** de).
rueful *adj* [*smile, thought*] triste.
ruff *n* (of lace) fraise *f*; (of fur, feathers) collier *m*.
ruffle I *n* (at sleeve) manchette *f*; (at neck) ruche *f*; (on shirt front) jabot *m*.
II *vtr* **1** ébouriffer [*hair, fur*]; hérisser [*feathers*]; rider [*water*]; **2** (disconcert) énerver; (upset) froisser.
rug *n* **1** tapis *m*; (by bed) descente *f* de lit; **2** (GB) (blanket) couverture *f*.
rugby ▶504 *n* rugby *m*.
rugged *adj* **1** [*landscape*] accidenté/-e; [*coastline*] déchiqueté/-e; **2** [*man, features*] rude.
ruin I *n* ruine *f*.
II *vtr* **1** ruiner [*economy, career*]; **to ~ one's eyesight** s'abîmer la vue; **2** gâcher [*holiday, meal*]; abîmer [*clothes*].
IDIOMS **to go to rack and ~** se délabrer.
rule I *n* **1** (of game, language) règle *f*; (of school, organization) règlement *m*; **against the ~s** contraire aux règles or au règlement (**to do** de faire); **~s and regulations** réglementation *f*; **as a ~** généralement; **2** (authority) domination *f*, gouvernement *m*; **3** (for measuring) règle *f*.
II *vtr* **1** [*ruler, law*] gouverner; [*monarch*] régner sur; [*party*] diriger; [*army*] commander; **2** [*factor*] dicter [*strategy*]; **to be ~d by** [*person*] être mené/-e par [*passions, spouse*]; **3** (draw) faire, tirer [*line*]; **4** [*court, umpire*] **to ~ that** décréter que.
III *vi* **1** [*monarch, anarchy*] régner; **2** [*court, umpire*] statuer.
■ **rule out** **1** exclure [*possibility, candidate*] (**of** de); **to ~ out doing** exclure de faire; **2** interdire [*activity*].
ruler *n* **1** (leader) dirigeant/-e *m/f*; **2** (measure) règle *f*.
ruling I *n* décision *f*.
II *adj* **1** (in power) dirigeant/-e; **2** (dominant) dominant/-e.
rum *n* rhum *m*.
rumble I *n* (of thunder, artillery, trucks) grondement *m*; (of stomach) gargouillement *m*.
II *vi* [*thunder, artillery*] gronder; [*stomach*] gargouiller.
ruminate *vi* **1** (think) **to ~ on** or **about** ruminer sur; **2** (Zool) ruminer.
rummage *vi* fouiller (**through** dans).
rummy ▶504 *n* rami *m*.
rumour (GB), **rumor** (US) *n* rumeur *f*, bruit *m*.
rumoured (GB), **rumored** (US) *adj* **it is ~ that** il paraît que, on dit que.
rump *n* **1** (also **~ steak**) rumsteck *m*; **2** (of animal) croupe *f*.
rumple *vtr* ébouriffer [*hair*]; froisser [*clothes, sheets, papers*].
run I *n* **1** course *f*; **a two-mile ~** une course de deux miles; **to go for a ~** aller courir; **to break into a ~** se mettre à courir; **2** (flight) **on the ~** en fuite; **to make a ~ for it** fuir, s'enfuir; **3** (series) (of successes, failures) série *f*; (in printing) tirage *m*; **to have a ~ of luck** être en veine; **4** (trip, route) trajet *m*; **5** (in cricket, baseball) point *m*; **6** (for rabbit, chickens) enclos *m*; **7** (in tights) échelle *f*; **8** (for skiing) piste *f*; **9** (in cards) suite *f*.
II *vtr* **1** courir [*distance, marathon*]; **to ~ a race** faire une course; **2** (drive) **to ~ sb to the station** conduire qn à la gare; **3** (pass, move) **to ~ one's hand over** passer la main sur; **to ~ one's eye(s) over** parcourir rapidement; **4** (manage) diriger; **a well-/badly-run organization** une organisation bien/mal dirigée; **5** (operate) faire fonctionner [*machine*]; faire tourner [*motor*]; exécuter [*program*]; entretenir [*car*]; **to ~ tests on** effectuer des tests sur; **6** (organize, offer) organiser [*competition, course*]; mettre [qch] en place [*bus service*]; **7** faire couler [*bath*]; ouvrir [*tap*]; **8** (enter) faire courir [*horse*]; présenter [*candidate*].
III *vi* **1** [*person, animal*] courir; **to ~ across/down sth** traverser/descendre qch en courant; **to ~ for the bus** courir pour attraper le bus; **to come ~ning** accourir (**towards** vers); **2** (flee) fuir, s'enfuir; **to ~ for one's life** s'enfuir pour sauver sa peau○; **3**○ (rush off) filer○; **4** (function) [*machine*] marcher; **to leave the engine ~ning** laisser tourner le moteur; **5** (continue, last) [*contract, lease*] être valide; **6** [*play, musical*] tenir l'affiche (**for** pendant); **7** (pass) **to ~ past/through** [*road, frontier, path*] passer/traverser; **to ~ (from) east to west** aller d'est en ouest; **8** (move) [*sledge*] glisser; [*curtain*] coulisser; **9** [*bus, train*] circuler; **10** (flow) couler; **tears ran down his face** les larmes coulaient sur son visage; **my nose is ~ning** j'ai le nez qui coule; **11** [*dye, garment*] déteindre; [*make-up*] couler; **12** (as candidate) se présenter; **to ~ for president** être candidat/-e à la présidence.
IDIOMS **in the long ~** à long terme; **in the short ~** à brève échéance.
■ **run about**, **run around** courir.
■ **run away**: ¶ **~ away** s'enfuir; **to ~ away from home** [*child*] faire une fugue; ¶ **~ away with [sb/sth]** **1** (flee) partir avec; **2** rafler○ [*prize, title*].
■ **run down**: ¶ **~ down** [*battery*] se décharger; [*watch*] retarder; ¶ **~ [sb/sth] down** **1** (in vehicle) renverser; **2** réduire [*production, defences*]; user [*battery*]; **3** (disparage) dénigrer.

■ **run into 1** heurter, rentrer dans° [*car, wall*]; **2** (encounter) rencontrer [*person, difficulty*]; **3** (amount to) s'élever à [*hundreds, millions*].
■ **run off** partir en courant.
■ **run out**: ¶ **~ out 1** [*supplies, oil*] s'épuiser; **time is ~ning out** le temps manque; **2** [*pen, machine*] être vide; **3** [*contract, passport*] expirer; ¶ **~ out of** ne plus avoir de [*petrol, time, money, ideas*]; **to be ~ning out of** n'avoir presque plus de [*petrol, time, money, ideas*].
■ **run over** (in vehicle) (injure) renverser; (kill) écraser.
■ **run through** parcourir [*list, article*]; répéter [*scene, speech*].
■ **run up** accumuler [*debt*].
■ **run up against** se heurter à [*difficulty*].

runaway *adj* [*teenager*] fugueur/-euse; [*slave*] fugitif/-ive; [*horse*] emballé/-e.

rundown *n* récapitulatif *m* (**on** de).

run-down *adj* **1** (exhausted) fatigué/-e, à plat°; **2** (shabby) décrépit/-e.

rung *n* **1** (of ladder) barreau *m*; **2** (in hierarchy) échelon *m*.

runner *n* **1** (person, animal) coureur *m*; **2** (horse) partant/-e *m/f*; **3** (messenger) estafette *f*; **4** (for door, seat) glissière *f*; (for drawer) coulisseau *m*; (on sled) patin *m*; **5** (on stairs) chemin *m* d'escalier.

runner bean *n* (GB) haricot *m* d'Espagne.

runner up *n* second/-e *m/f* (**to** après).

running ▶504 **I** *n* **1** (sport, exercise) course *f* à pied; **2** (management) direction *f* (**of** de).
II *adj* **1** [*water*] courant/-e; [*tap*] ouvert/-e; **2** **five days ~** cinq jours de suite.
IDIOMS **to be in/out of the ~** être/ne plus être dans la course (**for** pour).

runny *adj* [*jam, sauce*] liquide; [*butter*] fondu/-e; [*omelette*] baveux/-euse; **to have a ~ nose** avoir le nez qui coule.

run-of-the-mill *adj* ordinaire, banal/-e.

runt *n* **1** (of litter) le plus faible *m* de la portée; **2** (weakling) avorton *m*.

run-up *n* **1** (Sport) course *f* d'élan; **2 the ~ to** la dernière ligne droite avant.

runway *n* piste *f* d'aviation.

rupee ▶582 *n* roupie *f*.

rupture *n* rupture *f*.

rural *adj* (country) rural/-e; (pastoral) champêtre.

ruse *n* stratagème *m*.

rush I *n* **1** (surge) ruée *f* (**to do** pour faire); **to make a ~ for sth** [*crowd*] se ruer vers qch; [*individual*] se précipiter vers qch; **2** (hurry) **to be in a ~** être pressé/-e (**to do** de faire); **to leave in a ~** partir en vitesse; **3** (of liquid, adrenalin) montée *f*; (of air) bouffée *f*; **4** (plant) jonc *m*.
II *vtr* **1 to ~ sth to** envoyer qch d'urgence à; **to be ~ed to the hospital** être emmené/-e d'urgence à l'hôpital; **2** expédier [*task, speech*]; **3** (hurry) bousculer [*person*]; **4** (charge at) sauter sur [*person*]; prendre d'assaut [*building*].
III *vi* [*person*] (hurry) se dépêcher (**to do** de faire); (rush forward) se précipiter (**to do** pour faire); **to ~ out of the room** se précipiter hors de la pièce; **to ~ down the stairs/past** descendre l'escalier/passer à toute vitesse.
■ **rush into**: ¶ **to ~ into marriage/a purchase** se marier/acheter sans prendre le temps de réfléchir; ¶ **~ [sb] into doing** bousculer [qn] pour qu'il/elle fasse.
■ **rush through**: ¶ **~ through [sth]** expédier [*task*]; ¶ **~ [sth] through** adopter en vitesse [*legislation*]; traiter en priorité [*order, application*].

rush hour *n* heures *fpl* de pointe.

rusk *n* biscuit *m* pour bébés.

russet *adj* roussâtre.

Russia ▶448 *pr n* Russie *f*.

Russian ▶553 **I** *n* **1** (person) Russe *mf*; **2** (language) russe *m*.
II *adj* [*culture, food, politics*] russe; [*teacher, lesson*] de russe; [*embassy*] de Russie.

rust I *n* rouille *f*.
II *vtr* rouiller [*metal*].
III *vi* [*metal*] se rouiller.

rustic *adj* rustique.

rustle I *n* (of paper, dry leaves) froissement *m*; (of leaves, silk) bruissement *m*.
II *vtr* froisser [*papers*].

rusty *adj* rouillé/-e.

rut *n* **1** (in ground) ornière *f*; **2** (routine) **be in a ~** être enlisé/-e dans la routine; **3** (Zool) **the ~** le rut.

ruthless *adj* impitoyable (**in** dans).

RV *n* (US) (*abbr* = **recreational vehicle**) camping-car *m*, autocaravane *f*.

rye *n* **1** (cereal) seigle *m*; **2** (US) (also **~ whiskey**) whisky *m* à base de seigle.

rye bread *n* pain *m* de seigle.

Ss

s, S *n* s, S *m*.
sabbath *n* (also **Sabbath**) (Jewish) sabbat *m*; (Christian) jour *m* du seigneur.
sabotage I *n* sabotage *m*.
II *vtr* saboter.
saboteur *n* saboteur/-euse *m/f*.
sabre, **saber** (US) *n* sabre *m*.
sachet *n* sachet *m*.
sack I *n* **1** sac *m*; **2 to get the ~**○ se faire mettre à la porte○.
II *vtr* **1**○ mettre [qn] à la porte○ [*employee*]; **2** mettre [qch] à sac [*town*].
sacrament *n* sacrement *m*.
sacred *adj* sacré/-e (**to** pour).
sacrifice I *n* sacrifice *m* (**to** à; **of** de).
II *vtr* **1** (gen) sacrifier (**to** à); **2** (to the gods) offrir [qch] en sacrifice (**to** à).
sacrilege *n* sacrilège *m*.
sacrosanct *adj* sacro-saint/-e.
sad *adj* triste (**that** que + *subjunctive*); **it makes me ~** cela me rend triste.
sadden *vtr* attrister.
saddle I *n* selle *f*.
II *vtr* **1** seller [*horse*]; **2 to ~ sb with** mettre [qch] sur les bras de qn [*responsibility, task*].
saddle bag *n* sacoche *f*.
sadist *n* sadique *mf*.
sadistic *adj* sadique.
sadness *n* tristesse *f*.
sae *n*: *abbr* = **stamped addressed envelope**.
safari *n* safari *m*.
safe I *n* coffre-fort *m*.
II *adj* **1** (after ordeal, risk) [*person*] sain et sauf/saine et sauve; [*object*] intact/-e; **~ and sound** sain et sauf/saine et sauve; **2** (free from threat, harm) **to be ~** [*person*] être en sécurité; [*document, valuables*] être en lieu sûr; [*company, job, reputation*] ne pas être menacé/-e; **is the bike ~ here?** est-ce qu'on peut laisser le vélo ici sans risque?; **have a ~ journey!** bon voyage!; **3** (risk-free) [*toy, level, method*] sans danger; [*place, vehicle*] sûr/-e; [*structure, building*] solide; **it's not ~** c'est dangereux; **4** (prudent) [*investment*] sûr/-e; [*choice*] prudent/-e; **5** (reliable) **to be in ~ hands** être en bonnes mains.
IDIOMS **better ~ than sorry!** mieux vaut prévenir que guérir!; **just to be on the ~ side** simplement par précaution.
safe bet *n* **it's a ~** c'est quelque chose de sûr.
safe-deposit box *n* coffre *m* (à la banque).
safeguard I *n* garantie *f* (**for** pour; **against** contre).
II *vtr* protéger (**against, from** contre).
safekeeping *n* **in sb's ~** à la garde de qn.
safely *adv* **1** [*come back*] (of person) sans encombre; (of parcel, goods) sans dommage; (of plane) [*land, take off*] sans problème; **I arrived ~** je suis bien arrivé; **2 we can ~ assume that**... nous pouvons être certains que...; **3** [*locked, hidden*] bien.
safety *n* sécurité *f*; **in ~** en (toute) sécurité; **to reach ~** parvenir en lieu sûr.
safety belt *n* ceinture *f* de sécurité.
safety net *n* filet *m* (de protection); (figurative) filet *m* de sécurité.
safety pin *n* épingle *f* de sûreté.
sag *vi* **1** [*beam, mattress*] s'affaisser; [*tent, rope*] ne pas être bien tendu/-e; **2** [*breasts*] pendre; [*flesh*] être flasque.
sage *n* **1** (herb) sauge *f*; **2** (wise person) sage *m*.
Sagittarius *n* Sagittaire *m*.
Sahara *pr n* Sahara *m*; **the ~ desert** le désert du Sahara.
sail I *n* **1** (of boat) voile *f*; **to set sail** prendre la mer; **a ship in full ~** un navire toutes voiles dehors; **2** (of windmill) aile *f*.
II *vtr* **1** piloter [*ship, yacht*]; **2** traverser [qch] en bateau [*ocean, channel*].
III *vi* **1** [*person*] voyager en bateau; **to ~ around the world** faire le tour du monde en bateau; **2** [*ship*] **to ~ across** traverser [*ocean*]; **the boat ~s at 10 am** le bateau part à 10 h; **3** (as hobby) **to go ~ing** faire de la voile.
■ **sail through** gagner [qch] facilement [*match*]; **to ~ through an exam** réussir un examen les doigts dans le nez○.
sailboat *n* (US) bateau *m* à voiles.
sailing ▶504 *n* voile *f*.
sailing boat *n* bateau *m* à voiles.
sailing ship *n* voilier *m*.
sailor *n* marin *m*.
saint *n* saint/-e *m/f*; **Saint Mark** saint Marc.
sake *n* **1 for the ~ of clarity** pour la clarté; **for the ~ of argument** à titre d'exemple; **to kill for the ~ of killing** tuer pour le plaisir de tuer; **for old times' ~** en souvenir du bon vieux temps; **2** (benefit) **for the ~ of sb, for sb's ~** par égard pour qn; **for God's/heaven's ~!** pour l'amour de Dieu/du ciel!
salad *n* salade *f*; **ham ~** salade au jambon.
salad dressing *n* sauce *f* pour salade.
salami *n* saucisson *m* sec.
salary *n* salaire *m*.
sale *n* **1** (gen) vente *f* (**of** de; **to** à); **for sale** à vendre; **on ~** (GB) en vente; **2** (at cut prices) solde *f*; **the sales** les soldes; **in the ~(s)** (GB), **on ~** (US) en solde.
sales assistant ▶626 *n* (GB) vendeur/-euse *m/f*.
salesman ▶626 *n* (rep) représentant *m*; (in shop) vendeur *m*.

sales rep, **sales representative** ▶626| *n* représentant/-e *m/f*.

saleswoman ▶626| *n* (rep) représentante *f*; (in shop) vendeuse *f*.

saliva *n* salive *f*.

salivate *vi* saliver.

sallow *adj* cireux/-euse.

salmon *n* saumon *m*

salmonella *n* salmonelle *f*.

salon *n* salon *m*.

saloon *n* **1** (GB) (also **~ car**) berline *f*; **2** (US) saloon *m*, bar *m*; **3** (on boat) salon *m*.

salt I *n* sel *m*.
II *vtr* saler [*meat, fish, road, path*].

saltcellar *n* salière *f*.

salty *adj* [*water, food, flavour*] salé/-e.

salute I *n* salut *m*.
II *vtr, vi* saluer.

salvage I *n* **1** (rescue) sauvetage *m* (**of** de); **2** (goods rescued) biens *mpl* récupérés.
II *vtr* **1** sauver [*cargo, materials, belongings*] (**from** de); effectuer le sauvetage de [*ship*]; **2** sauver [*marriage, reputation, game*]; **3** (for recycling) récupérer [*metal, paper*].

salvation *n* salut *m*.

Salvation Army *n* Armée *f* du Salut.

salve I *n* baume *m*.
II *vtr* **to ~ one's conscience** soulager sa conscience.

Samaritan *n* **the Good ~** le bon Samaritain; **the ~s** les Samaritains *mpl*.

same I *adj* même (**as** que); **to be the ~** être le/la même; **to look the ~** être pareil/-eille; **to be the ~ as sth** être comme qch; **it amounts** or **comes to the ~ thing** cela revient au même; **it's all the ~ to me** ça m'est complètement égal; **if it's all the ~ to you** si ça ne te fait rien; **at the ~ time** en même temps; **to remain** or **stay the ~** ne pas changer.
II the same *pron* la même chose (**as** que); **I'll have the ~** je prendrai la même chose; **to do the ~ as sb** faire comme qn; **the ~ to you!** (in greeting) à toi aussi, à toi de même!; (of insult) toi-même○!
III the same *adv* [*act, dress*] de la même façon; **to feel the ~ as sb** penser comme qn.
IDIOMS **all the ~..., just the ~,...** tout de même,...; **thanks all the ~** merci quand même.

sample I *n* **1** (of product, fabric) échantillon *m*; **2** (for analysis) prélèvement *m*.
II *vtr* **1** (taste) goûter (à) [*food, wine*]; **2** (test) essayer [*products*]; sonder [*opinion, market*].

sanatorium (GB), **sanitarium** (US) *n* sanatorium *m*.

sanctimonious *adj* supérieur/-e.

sanction I *n* sanction *f*; **to impose ~s** prendre des sanctions.
II *vtr* (permit) autoriser; (approve) sanctionner.

sanctity *n* sainteté *f*.

sanctuary *n* **1** (safe place) refuge *m*; **2** (holy place) sanctuaire *m*; **3** (for wildlife) réserve *f*; (for mistreated pets) refuge *m*.

sand I *n* sable *m*.
II *vtr* **1** (also **~ down**) poncer [*floor*]; frotter [qch] au papier de verre [*woodwork*]; **2** sabler [*icy road*].

sandal *n* sandale *f*.

sand castle *n* château *m* de sable.

sand dune *n* dune *f*.

sandpaper I *n* papier *m* de verre.
II *vtr* poncer.

sandpit *n* (quarry) sablière *f*; (for children) bac *m* à sable.

sandstone *n* grès *m*.

sandwich I *n* sandwich *m*; **cucumber ~** sandwich au concombre.
II *vtr* **to be ~ed between** [*car, building, person*] être pris/-e en sandwich entre.

sandy *adj* **1** [*beach*] de sable; [*path, soil*] sablonneux/-euse; **2** [*hair*] blond roux *inv*; [*colour*] sable *inv* (*after n*).

sane *adj* **1** [*person*] sain/-e d'esprit; **2** [*policy, judgment*] sensé/-e.

sanitarium (US) = **sanatorium**.

sanitary *adj* **1** [*engineer, installations*] sanitaire; **2** (hygienic) hygiénique; (clean) propre.

sanitary towel (GB), **sanitary napkin** (US) *n* serviette *f* hygiénique or périodique.

sanity *n* équilibre *m* mental.

Santa (**Claus**) *pr n* le père Noël.

sap I *n* sève *f*.
II *vtr* saper [*strength, courage, confidence*].

sapling *n* jeune arbre *m*.

sapphire ▶438| *n* **1** (stone) saphir *m*; **2** (colour) bleu *m* saphir.

sarcasm *n* sarcasme *m*.

sarcastic *adj* sarcastique.

sardine *n* sardine *f*.

Sardinia *pr n* Sardaigne *f*.

sardonic *adj* [*laugh, look*] sardonique; [*person, remark*] acerbe.

sash *n* (round waist) large ceinture *f*; (ceremonial) écharpe *f*.

Satan *pr n* Satan.

satanic *adj* [*rites*] satanique; [*pride, smile*] démoniaque.

satchel *n* cartable *m* (à bandoulière).

satellite *n* satellite *m*.

satellite dish *n* antenne *f* parabolique.

satellite TV *n* télévision *f* par satellite.

satin I *n* satin *m*.
II *adj* [*garment, shoe*] de satin; **with a ~ finish** satiné/-e.

satire *n* satire *f* (**on** sur).

satiric(al) *adj* satirique.

satirize *vtr* faire la satire de.

satisfaction *n* satisfaction *f*.

satisfactory *adj* satisfaisant/-e.

satisfied *adj* **1** (pleased) satisfait/-e (**with, about** de); **2** (convinced) convaincu/-e (**by** par; **that** que).

satisfy *vtr* **1** satisfaire [*person, need, desires, curiosity*]; assouvir [*hunger*]; **2** (persuade) convaincre [*person, public opinion*] (**that** que);

3 (meet) satisfaire à [*demand, requirements, conditions*].

satisfying *adj* **1** [*meal*] substantiel/-ielle; **2** [*job*] qui apporte de la satisfaction; **3** [*result, progress*] satisfaisant/-e.

saturate *vtr* saturer (**with** de).

saturated *adj* (wet) [*person, clothes*] trempé/-e; [*ground*] détrempé/-e.

Saturday ▶ 456 *n* samedi *m*.

Saturn *pr n* (planet) Saturne *f*.

sauce *n* sauce *f*.

saucepan *n* casserole *f*.

saucer *n* soucoupe *f*.

Saudi Arabia ▶ 448 *pr n* Arabie *f* saoudite.

sauna *n* sauna *m*.

saunter *vi* (also **~ along**) marcher d'un pas nonchalant; **to ~ off** s'éloigner d'un pas nonchalant.

sausage *n* saucisse *f*.

savage I *n* sauvage *mf*.
II *adj* (gen) féroce; [*blow, beating*] violent/-e; [*attack*] sauvage; [*criticism*] virulent/-e.
III *vtr* [*dog*] attaquer [qn/qch] sauvagement; [*lion*] déchiqueter.

save I *n* (Sport) arrêt *m* de but.
II *vtr* **1** (rescue) sauver (**from** de); **to ~ sb's life** sauver la vie à qn; **2** (put by, keep) mettre [qch] de côté [*money, food*] (**to do** pour faire); garder [*goods, documents*] (**for** pour); sauvegarder [*data, file*]; **to have money ~d** avoir de l'argent de côté; **to ~ sth for sb, to ~ sb sth** garder qch pour qn; **3** (economize on) économiser [*money*] (**by doing** en faisant); gagner [*time, space*] (**by doing** en faisant); **to ~ one's energy** ménager ses forces; **you'll ~ money** vous ferez des économies; **to ~ sb/sth (from) having to do** éviter à qn/qch de faire; **4** (Sport) arrêter.
III *vi* **1** (put money by) = **save up**; **2** (economize) économiser, faire des économies; **to ~ on** faire des économies de [*energy, paper*].
■ **save up** faire des économies; **to ~ up for** mettre de l'argent de côté pour s'acheter [*car, house*]; mettre de l'argent de côté pour s'offrir [*holiday*].

saving grace *n* bon côté *m*; **it's his ~** c'est ce qui le sauve.

savings *n pl* économies *fpl*.

savings account *n* (GB) compte *m* d'épargne; (US) compte *m* rémunéré.

saviour (GB), **savior** (US) *n* sauveur *m*.

savour (GB), **savor** (US) I *n* saveur *f*.
II *vtr* savourer.

savoury (GB), **savory** (US) *adj* (not sweet) salé/-e; (appetizing) appétissant/-e.

saw I *n* scie *f*.
II *vtr* scier; **to ~ through/down/off** scier.

sawdust *n* sciure *f* (de bois).

sawn-off shotgun *n* (GB) fusil *m* à canon scié.

saxophone ▶ 586 *n* saxophone *m*.

say I *n* **to have one's ~** dire ce qu'on a à dire (**on** sur); **to have a ~/no ~ in sth** avoir/ne pas avoir son mot à dire sur qch; **to have no ~ in the matter** ne pas avoir voix au chapitre.
II *vtr* **1** (gen) dire (**to** à); **'hello,' he said** 'bonjour,' dit-il; **to ~ (that)** dire que; **they ~ she's very rich, she is said to be very rich** on dit qu'elle est très riche; **to ~ sth about sb/sth** dire qch au sujet de qn/qch; **to ~ sth to oneself** se dire qch; **let's ~ no more about it** n'en parlons plus; **it goes without ~ing that** il va sans dire que; **that is to ~** c'est-à-dire; **let's ~ there are 20** mettons or supposons qu'il y en ait 20; **how high would you ~ it is?** à ton avis, quelle en est la hauteur?; **I'd ~ she was about 25** je lui donnerais environ 25 ans; **2** [*sign, clock, dial, gauge*] indiquer.
III *vi* **stop when I ~** arrête quand je te le dirai; **he wouldn't ~** il n'a pas voulu le dire.
IDIOMS **it ~s a lot for sb/sth** c'est tout à l'honneur de qn/qch; **there's a lot to be said for that method** cette méthode est très intéressante à bien des égards; **when all is said and done** tout compte fait, en fin de compte.

saying *n* dicton *m*.

scab *n* croûte *f*.

scaffolding *n* échafaudage *m*.

scald *vtr* ébouillanter.

scale I *n* **1** (gen) échelle *f*; **pay ~, salary ~** échelle des salaires; **on a ~ of 1 to 10** sur une échelle allant de 1 à 10; **2** (extent) (of disaster, success, violence) étendue *f* (**of** de); (of defeat, recession, task) ampleur *f* (**of** de); (of activity, operation) envergure *f* (**of** de); **3** (on ruler, gauge) graduation *f*; **4** (for weighing) balance *f*; **5** (Mus) gamme *f*; **6** (on fish, insect) écaille *f*.
II **scales** *n pl* balance *f*.
III *vtr* **1** escalader [*wall, mountain*]; **2** écailler [*fish*].

scale drawing *n* dessin *m* à l'échelle.

scale model *n* maquette *f* à l'échelle.

scallop, scollop *n* coquille *f* Saint-Jacques.

scalp I *n* cuir *m* chevelu.
II *vtr* scalper.

scamper *vi* **to ~ about** or **around** [*child, dog*] gambader; [*mouse*] trottiner.

scan *vtr* **1** lire rapidement [*page, newspaper*]; **2** (examine) scruter [*face, horizon*]; **3** [*beam of light, radar*] balayer; **4** (Med) faire un scanner de [*organ*].

scandal *n* scandale *m*.

scandalize *vtr* scandaliser.

scandalous *adj* scandaleux/-euse.

Scandinavia *pr n* Scandinavie *f*.

scanty *adj* [*meal, supply*] maigre (*before n*); [*information*] sommaire; [*knowledge*] rudimentaire; [*swimsuit*] minuscule.

scapegoat *n* bouc *m* émissaire (**for** de).

scar I *n* cicatrice *f*; (on face from knife) balafre *f*.
II *vtr* marquer; (on face with knife) balafrer; **to ~ sb for life** laisser à qn une cicatrice permanente; (figurative) marquer qn pour la vie.

scarce *adj* rare; **to become ~** se faire rare.

scarcely *adv* à peine; **~ anybody believes it** presque personne ne le croit.

scare I *n* **1** peur *f*; **to give sb a ~** faire peur

à qn; **2** (alert) alerte *f*; **bomb ~** alerte à la bombe.
II *vtr* faire peur à.
■ **scare away**, **scare off** faire fuir [*animal, attacker*]; (figurative) dissuader.
scarecrow *n* épouvantail *m*.
scared *adj* [*animal, person*] effrayé/-e; [*look*] apeuré/-e; **to be** or **feel ~** avoir peur; **to be ~ stiff**° avoir une peur bleue°.
scarf *n* (long) écharpe *f*; (square) foulard *m*.
scarlet ▶438 *n, adj* écarlate (*f*).
scarlet fever ▶533 *n* scarlatine *f*.
scathing *adj* [*remark, tone, wit*] cinglant/-e; [*criticism*] virulent/-e.
scatter I *vtr* **1** (also **~ around**, **~ about**) répandre [*seeds, earth*]; éparpiller [*books, papers, clothes*]; **2** disperser [*crowd, herd*].
II *vi* [*people, animals, birds*] se disperser.
scatter-brained *adj* [*person*] étourdi/-e; [*idea*] farfelu/-e°.
scattered *adj* [*houses, trees, population, clouds*] épars/-e; [*books, litter*] éparpillé/-e; [*support, resistance*] clairsemé/-e.
scavenge *vi* **to ~ for food** [*bird, animal*] chercher de la nourriture.
scavenger *n* **1** (animal) charognard *m*; **2** (person) (for food) faiseur *m* de poubelles; (for objects) récupérateur *m*.
scenario *n* (gen) cas *m* de figure; (of film, play) scénario *m*.
scene *n* **1** (gen) scène *f*; **behind the ~s** dans les coulisses *fpl*; **you need a change of ~** tu as besoin de changer de décor; **2** (of crime, accident) lieu *m*; **at** or **on the ~** sur les lieux; **3** (image, sight) image *f*; **4** (view) vue *f*.
scenery *n* **1** (landscape) paysage *m*; **2** (in theatre) décors *mpl*.
scent I *n* **1** (smell) odeur *f*; **2** (perfume) parfum *m*; **3** (of animal) fumet *m*; (in hunting) piste *f*.
II *vtr* **1** flairer [*prey, animal*]; **2** pressentir [*danger, trouble*]; **3** (perfume) parfumer [*air*].
sceptic (GB), **skeptic** (US) *n* sceptique *mf*.
sceptical (GB), **skeptical** (US) *adj* sceptique.
scepticism (GB), **skepticism** (US) *n* scepticisme *m*.
schedule I *n* **1** (of work, events) programme *m*; (timetable) horaire *m*; **to be ahead of/behind ~** être en avance/en retard; **to arrive on/ahead of ~** [*bus, train, plane*] arriver à l'heure/en avance; **2** (list) liste *f*.
II *vtr* (plan) prévoir; (arrange) programmer.
scheduled flight *n* vol *m* régulier.
scheme I *n* **1** projet *m*, plan *m* (**to do, for doing** pour faire); **pension ~** régime *m* de retraite; **2** (plot) combine *f* (**to do** pour faire).
II *vi* comploter.
scholar *n* érudit/-e *m/f*.
scholarship *n* bourse *f* (**to** pour).
school I *n* **1** école *f*; **at ~** à l'école; **2** (US) (university) université *f*; **3** (of fish) banc *m*.
II *adj* [*holiday, outing, uniform, year*] scolaire.
schoolboy *n* (pupil) élève *m*; (primary) écolier *m*; (secondary) collégien *m*.
schoolchild *n* écolier/-ière *m/f*.
schoolgirl *n* (pupil) élève *f*; (primary) écolière *f*; (secondary) collégienne *f*.
school-leaver *n* (GB) jeune *mf* ayant fini sa scolarité.
school report (GB), **school report card** (US) *n* bulletin *m* scolaire.
schoolteacher ▶626 *n* enseignant/-e *m/f*; (primary) instituteur/-trice *m/f*; (secondary) professeur *m*.
schoolwork *n* travail *m* de classe.
science *n* science *f*; **to study ~** étudier les sciences.
science fiction *n* science-fiction *f*.
scientific *adj* scientifique.
scientist ▶626 *n* scientifique *mf*.
scissors *n pl* ciseaux *mpl*.
scoff I° *vtr* (GB) (eat) engloutir°, bouffer°.
II *vi* se moquer (**at** de).
scold *vtr* gronder (**for doing** pour avoir fait).
scoop I *n* **1** (for measuring) mesure *f*; **2** (of ice cream) boule *f*; **3** (in journalism) exclusivité *f*.
II° *vtr* décrocher° [*prize, sum of money, story*].
scooter *n* **1** (child's) trottinette *f*; **2** (motorized) scooter *m*.
scope *n* **1** (opportunity) possibilité *f* (**for** de); **2** (of inquiry, report, book) portée *f*; (of plan) envergure *f*; **3** (of person) compétences *fpl*.
scorch I *n* (also **~ mark**) légère brûlure *f*.
II *vtr* [*fire*] brûler; [*sun*] dessécher [*grass, trees*]; griller [*lawn*]; [*iron*] roussir [*fabric*].
score I *n* **1** (Sport) score *m*; (in cards) marque *f*; **to keep (the) ~** marquer les points; (in cards) tenir la marque; **2** (in exam, test) note *f*, résultat *m*; **3** (Mus) (written music) partition *f*; (for film) musique *f* (de film); **4** (twenty) **a ~** vingt *m*, une vingtaine *f*; **5 on this** or **that ~** à ce sujet.
II *vtr* **1** marquer [*goal, point*]; remporter [*victory, success*]; **to ~ 9 out of 10** avoir 9 sur 10; **2** (cut) entailler.
III *vi* (gain point) marquer un point; (obtain goal) marquer un but.
IDIOMS **to settle a ~** régler ses comptes.
scoreboard *n* tableau *m* d'affichage.
scorn *n* mépris *m* (**for** pour).
scornful *adj* méprisant/-e.
Scorpio *n* Scorpion *m*.
Scot ▶553 *n* Écossais/-e *m/f*.
Scotch I *n* (also **~ whisky**) whisky *m*, scotch *m*.
II *adj* écossais/-e.
Scotch tape® *n* (US) scotch® *m*.
Scotland ▶448 *pr n* Écosse *f*.
Scottish ▶553 *adj* écossais/-e.
scour *vtr* **1** (scrub) récurer; **2** (search) parcourir [*area, list*] (**for** à la recherche de).
scourge *n* fléau *m*.
scout *n* **1** (also **boy ~**) scout *m*; **2** (Mil) éclaireur *m*; **3** (also **talent ~**) découvreur/-euse *m/f* de nouveaux talents.
■ **scout around** explorer; **to ~ around for sth** rechercher qch.
scowl I *n* air *m* renfrogné.

II *vi* prendre un air renfrogné.

scramble I *n* **1** (rush) course *f* (**for** pour; **to do** pour faire); **2** (climb) escalade *f*.
II *vtr* brouiller [*signal*].
III *vi* **1 to ~ up** escalader; **to ~ down** dégringoler.

scrambled egg *n* (also **~s** *pl*) œufs *mpl* brouillés.

scrap I *n* **1** (of paper, cloth) petit morceau *m*; (of news, information) fragment *m*; **2** (old iron) ferraille *f*.
II scraps *n pl* (of food) restes *mpl*; (from butcher's) déchets *mpl*.
III *vtr* **1**○ abandonner [*idea, plan, system*]; **2** détruire [*aircraft, equipment*].

scrapbook *n* album *m*.

scrap dealer *n* ferrailleur *m*.

scrape I *n* **to get into a ~**○ s'attirer des ennuis.
II *vtr* **1** (clean) gratter [*vegetables, shoes*]; **2** érafler [*car, paintwork, furniture*]; **to ~ one's knees** s'écorcher les genoux.
III *vi* **to ~ against sth** (rub) frotter contre qch; (scratch) érafler qch.
■ **scrape by** (financially) s'en sortir à peine; (in situation) s'en tirer de justesse.
■ **scrape through**: ¶ **~ through** s'en tirer de justesse; ¶ **~ through sth** réussir de justesse à qch [*exam, test*].

scrap iron, **scrap metal** *n* ferraille *f*.

scrap paper *n* papier *m* brouillon.

scrap yard *n* chantier *m* de ferraille, casse *f*.

scratch I *n* **1** (on skin) égratignure *f*; (from a claw, fingernail) griffure *f*; **2** (on metal, furniture) éraflure *f*; (on record, glass) rayure *f*; **3** (sound) grattement *m*; **4**○ **he/his work is not up to ~** il/son travail n'est pas à la hauteur; **5 to start from ~** partir de zéro.
II *vtr* **1 to ~ one's initials on sth** graver ses initiales sur qch; **2** [*cat, person*] griffer [*person*]; [*thorns, rose bush*] égratigner [*person*]; érafler [*car, wood*]; rayer [*record*]; [*cat*] se faire les griffes sur [*furniture*]; [*person*] **to ~ sb's eyes out** arracher les yeux à quelqu'un; **3 to ~ sb's back** gratter le dos de qn.
III *vi* se gratter.

scrawl I *n* gribouillage *m*.
II *vtr, vi* gribouiller.

scrawny *adj* [*person, animal*] décharné/-e.

scream I *n* (of person, animal) cri *m* (perçant); (stronger) hurlement *m*; (of brakes) grincement *m*; (of tyres) crissement *m*.
II *vtr* crier.
III *vi* crier; (stronger) hurler.

screech I *n* (of person, animal) cri *m* strident; (of tyres) crissement *m*.
II *vi* [*person, animal*] pousser un cri strident; [*tyres*] crisser.

screen I *n* **1** (on TV, VDU, at cinema) écran *m*; **2** (furniture) paravent *m*; **3** (US) (in door) grille *f*.
II *vtr* **1** (at cinema) projeter; (on TV) diffuser; **2** (conceal) cacher; (protect) protéger (**from** de); **3** (test) examiner le cas de [*applicants, candidates*]; contrôler [*baggage*]; **to ~ sb for cancer** faire passer à qn des tests de dépistage du cancer.

screenplay *n* scénario *m*.

screw I *n* vis *f*.
II *vtr* visser (**into** dans; **onto** sur).
■ **screw up 1** froisser [*piece of paper, material*]; **to ~ up one's eyes** plisser les yeux; **to ~ up one's face** faire la grimace; **2**○ faire foirer○ [*plan, task*].

screwdriver *n* **1** (tool) tournevis *m*; **2** (cocktail) vodka-orange *f*.

scribble *vtr, vi* griffonner, gribouiller.

scrimp *vi* économiser; **to ~ and save** se priver de tout.

script *n* **1** (for film, radio, TV) script *m*; (for play) texte *m*; **2** (GB Sch, Univ) copie *f* (d'examen).

scripture *n* (also **Holy Scripture**, **Holy Scriptures**) (Christian) Écritures *fpl*; (other) textes *mpl* sacrés.

scriptwriter ▶626 *n* scénariste *mf*.

scroll *n* rouleau *m*.

scrub I *n* **1** (clean) **to give sth a (good) ~** (bien) nettoyer qch; **2** (Bot) broussailles *fpl*.
II *vtr* frotter [*back, clothes*]; récurer [*pan, floor*]; nettoyer [*vegetable*]; **to ~ one's nails** se brosser les ongles.
■ **scrub up** [*doctor*] se stériliser les mains.

scrubbing brush, **scrub brush** (US) *n* brosse *f* de ménage.

scruff *n* **by the ~ of the neck** par la peau du cou.

scruffy *adj* [*clothes, person*] dépenaillé/-e; [*flat, town*] délabré/-e.

scrum, **scrummage** *n* (in rugby) mêlée *f*.

scruple *n* scrupule *m* (**about** vis-à-vis de).

scrupulous *adj* scrupuleux/-euse.

scrutinize *vtr* scruter [*face, motives*]; examiner [qch] minutieusement [*document, plan*]; vérifier [*accounts, votes*].

scrutiny *n* examen *m*.

scuba diving ▶504 *n* plongée *f* sous-marine.

scuff I *n* (also **~ mark**) (on floor, furniture) rayure *f*; (on leather) éraflure *f*.
II *vtr* érafler [*shoes*]; rayer [*floor, furniture*].

scuffle *n* bagarre *f*.

sculpt *vtr, vi* sculpter.

sculptor ▶626 *n* sculpteur *m*.

sculpture *n* sculpture *f*.

scum *n* **1** (on pond) écume *f*; **2** (on liquid) mousse *f*; **3 they're the ~ of the earth** c'est de la racaille.

scuttle I *vtr* **1** saborder [*ship*]; **2** faire échouer [*talks, project*].
II *vi* **to ~ away** or **off** filer.

scythe *n* faux *f inv*.

sea I *n* mer *f*; **beside** or **by the ~** au bord de la mer; **the open ~** le large; **by ~** [*travel*] en bateau; [*send*] par bateau.
II *adj* [*air, breeze*] marin/-e; [*bird, water*] de mer; [*crossing, voyage*] par mer; [*battle*] naval/-e; [*power*] maritime.

seafood *n* fruits *mpl* de mer.

seagull *n* mouette *f*.

sea horse *n* hippocampe *m*.
seal I *n* **1** (Zool) phoque *m*; **2** (stamp) sceau *m*; **3** (on container) plomb *m*; (on package, letter) cachet *m*; (on door) scellés *mpl*.
II *vtr* **1** cacheter [*document*]; **2** fermer, cacheter [*envelope*]; **3** fermer [qch] hermétiquement [*jar, tin*]; rendre [qch] étanche [*window frame*]; **4** sceller [*alliance, friendship*] (**with** par); **to ~ sb's fate** décider du sort de qn.
■ **seal off** isoler [*ward*]; boucler [*area, building*]; barrer [*street*].
sea lion *n* lion *m* de mer.
seam *n* (of garment) couture *f*.
seaplane *n* hydravion *m*.
search I *n* **1** (for person, object) recherches *fpl* (**for sb/sth** pour retrouver qn/qch); **in ~ of** à la recherche de; **2** (of place) fouille *f* (**of** de); **3** (Comput) recherche *f*.
II *vtr* **1** fouiller [*area, building*]; fouiller dans [*cupboard, drawer, memory*]; **2** examiner (attentivement) [*map, records*].
III *vi* **1** chercher; **to ~ for** or **after sb/sth** chercher qn/qch; **to ~ through** fouiller dans [*cupboard, bag*]; examiner [*records, file*]; **2** (Comput) **to ~ for** rechercher [*data, file*].
searching *adj* [*look, question*] pénétrant/-e.
searchlight *n* projecteur *m*.
search party *n* équipe *f* de secours.
search warrant *n* mandat *m* de perquisition.
sea salt *n* sel *m* de mer.
seashell *n* coquillage *m*.
seashore *n* (part of coast) littoral *m*; (beach) plage *f*.
seasick *adj* **to feel ~** avoir le mal de mer.
seaside I *n* **the ~** le bord de la mer.
II *adj* [*hotel*] en bord de mer; [*town*] maritime; **~ resort** station *f* balnéaire.
season I *n* saison *f*; **strawberries are in/out of ~** c'est/ce n'est pas la saison des fraises; **the holiday ~** la période des vacances; **Season's greetings!** Joyeuses fêtes!
II *vtr* (with spices) relever; (with condiments) assaisonner.
seasonal *adj* [*work, change*] saisonnier/-ière; [*fruit, produce*] de saison.
seasoning *n* assaisonnement *m*.
season ticket *n* (for travel) carte *f* d'abonnement; (for theatre, matches) abonnement *m*.
seat I *n* **1** (chair) siège *m*; (bench-type) banquette *f*; **2** (place) place *f*; **take** or **have a ~** asseyez-vous; **to book a ~** réserver une place; **3** (of trousers) fond *m*.
II *vtr* **1** placer [*person*]; **2 the car ~s five** c'est une voiture à cinq places; **the table ~s six** c'est une table de six couverts.
seatbelt *n* ceinture *f* (de sécurité).
-seater *combining form* **a two~** (plane) un avion *m* à deux places; (car) un coupé; (sofa) un (canapé) deux places.
seating *n* places *fpl* assises; **I'll organize the ~** je placerai les gens.
sea urchin *n* oursin *m*.
seaweed *n* algue *f* marine.
secateurs *n pl* (GB) sécateur *m*.
secluded *adj* retiré/-e.
seclusion *n* isolement *m* (**from** à l'écart de).
second ▶**434**, **456**, **498** **I** *n* **1** (in order) deuxième *mf*, second/-e *m/f*; **2** (unit of time) seconde *f*; (instant) instant *m*; **3** (of month) deux *m inv*; **4** (Aut) (also **~ gear**) deuxième *f*, seconde *f*; **5** (defective article) article *m* qui a un défaut; **6** (also **~-class honours degree**) (GB Univ) ≈ licence *f* avec mention bien.
II *adj* deuxième, second/-e; **to have a ~ helping (of sth)** reprendre (de qch); **to have a ~ chance to do sth** avoir une nouvelle chance de faire.
III *adv* **1** (in second place) deuxième; **to come** or **finish ~** arriver deuxième; **the ~ biggest building** le deuxième bâtiment de par sa grandeur; **2** (also **secondly**) deuxièmement.
IV *vtr* (in debate) appuyer [*proposal*].
IDIOMS **to be ~ nature** être automatique; **to be ~ to none** être sans pareil; **on ~ thoughts** à la réflexion; **to have ~ thoughts** avoir quelques hésitations or doutes.
secondary *adj* secondaire.
secondary school *n* ≈ école *f* secondaire.
second class I second-class *adj* **1** [*post, stamp*] au tarif lent; **2** [*carriage, ticket*] de deuxième classe; **3** (second-rate) de qualité inférieure.
II *adv* [*travel*] en deuxième classe; [*send*] au tarif lent.
second hand I *n* (on watch, clock) trotteuse *f*.
II second-hand *adj* [*clothes, car*] d'occasion; [*news, information*] de seconde main.
III *adv* [*buy*] d'occasion; [*find out, hear*] indirectement.
secondly *adv* deuxièmement.
second-rate *adj* de second ordre.
secrecy *n* secret *m*.
secret I *n* secret *m*; **to tell sb a ~** confier un secret à qn.
II *adj* secret/-ète.
III in secret *phr* en secret.
secretary ▶**626** *n* **1** (assistant) secrétaire *mf* (**to sb** de qn); **2 Foreign Secretary** (GB), **Secretary of State** (US) ministre *m* des Affaires étrangères.
secretive *adj* [*person, organization*] secret/-ète; **to be ~ about sth** faire un mystère de qch.
sect *n* secte *f*.
section *n* **1** (of train, aircraft, town, book) partie *f*; (of pipe, tunnel, road) tronçon *m*; (of object, kit) élément *m*; (of fruit) quartier *m*; (of population) tranche *f*; **2** (of company, department) service *m*; (of library, shop) rayon *m*; **3** (of act, bill, report) article *m*; (of newspaper) rubrique *f*.
sector *n* secteur *m*.
secular *adj* [*politics, society, education*] laïque; [*belief, music*] profane.
secure I *adj* **1** [*job, marriage, income*] stable; [*basis, base*] solide; **2** [*hiding place*] sûr/-e; **3** [*padlock, knot*] solide; [*structure, ladder*] stable; [*rope*] bien attaché/-e; [*door, window*] bien fermé/-e; **4 to feel ~** se sentir en sécurité.
II *vtr* **1** obtenir [*promise, release, right,*

victory]; **2** bien attacher [*rope*]; bien fermer [*door, window*]; stabiliser [*ladder*]; **3** protéger [*house*]; assurer [*position, future*]; **4** garantir [*loan, debt*] (**against, on** sur).

securities *n pl* titres *mpl*.

security *n* **1** sécurité *f*; **job ~** sécurité de l'emploi; **national ~** sûreté *f* de l'État; **2** (guarantee) garantie *f* (**on** sur).

security guard ▶626 *n* garde *m* sécurité, vigile *m*.

sedate I *adj* [*person*] posé/-e; [*lifestyle, pace*] tranquille.
II *vtr* mettre [qn] sous calmants [*patient*].

sedation *n* sédation *f*; **under ~** sous calmants.

sedative *n* sédatif *m*, calmant *m*.

seduce *vtr* séduire.

seductive *adj* [*person*] séduisant/-e; [*smile*] aguicheur/-euse.

see I *vtr* **1** voir; **can you ~ him?** est-ce que tu le vois?; **I can't ~ him** je ne le vois pas; **to ~ the sights** faire du tourisme; **~ you next week!** à la semaine prochaine!; **to ~ sb as** considérer qn comme [*friend, hero*]; **it remains to be seen whether** or **if** reste à voir si; **2** (make sure) **to ~ (to it) that** veiller à ce que (+ *subjunctive*); **~ (to it) that the children are in bed by nine** veillez à ce que les enfants soient couchés à neuf heures; **3** (accompany) **to ~ sb to the station** accompagner qn à la gare; **to ~ sb home** raccompagner qn chez lui/elle.
II *vi* voir; **I can't ~** je ne vois rien; **I'll go and ~** je vais voir; **we'll just have to wait and ~** il ne nous reste plus qu'à attendre; **let's ~, let me ~** voyons (un peu).
■ **see off**: **to ~ sb off** dire au revoir à qn.
■ **see out**: **to ~ sb out** raccompagner qn à la porte.
■ **see through**: ¶ **~ through [sth]** déceler [*deception, lie*]; ¶ **~ through [sb]** percer [qn] à jour; ¶ **~ [sth] through** mener [qch] à bonne fin.
■ **see to** s'occuper de [*arrangements*].

seed *n* **1** (gen) graine *f*; (fruit pip) pépin *m*; (for sowing) semences *fpl*; **to go to ~** [*plant*] monter en graine; [*person*] se ramollir; [*organization, country*] être en déclin; **2** (Sport) tête *f* de série.

seedling *n* plant *m*.

seedy *adj* [*person*] louche; [*area, club*] mal famé/-e.

seek *vtr* **1** chercher [*agreement, refuge, solution*]; demander [*advice, help, permission*]; **2** [*police, employer*] rechercher [*person*].
■ **seek out** aller chercher, dénicher.

seem *vi* sembler; **it ~s that** il semble que (+ *subjunctive*); **it ~s to me that** il me semble que (+ *indicative*); **he ~s happy/disappointed** il a l'air heureux/déçu; **it ~s odd (to me)** ça (me) parait bizarre; **he ~s to be looking for someone** on dirait qu'il cherche quelqu'un.

seep *vi* suinter; **to ~ away** s'écouler; **to ~ through sth** [*water, gas*] s'infiltrer à travers qch; [*light*] filtrer à travers qch.

seesaw *n* tapecul *m*.

seethe *vi* **1 to ~ with rage** bouillir de colère; **he was seething** il était furibond; **2** (teem) grouiller; **the streets were seething with tourists** les rues grouillaient de touristes.

see-through *adj* transparent/-e.

segment *n* segment *m*; (of orange) quartier *m*.

segregate *vtr* **1** (separate) séparer (**from** de); **2** (isolate) isoler (**from** de).

segregation *n* ségrégation *f* (**from** de).

seize *vtr* **1** saisir; **to ~ hold of** se saisir de [*person*]; s'emparer de [*object*]; **2** s'emparer de [*territory, prisoner, power*]; prendre [*control*].
■ **seize up** [*engine*] se gripper; [*limb*] se bloquer.

seizure *n* **1** (of territory, power) prise *f*; (of arms, drugs, property) saisie *f*; **2** (Med) attaque *f*.

seldom *adv* rarement.

select I *adj* [*group*] privilégié/-e; [*hotel*] chic, sélect/-e; [*area*] chic, cossu/-e.
II *vtr* sélectionner (**from, from among** parmi).

selection *n* sélection *f*.

self *n* moi *m*; **he's back to his old ~ again** il est redevenu lui-même.

self-addressed envelope, **SAE** *n* enveloppe *f* à mon/votre etc adresse.

self-assured *adj* plein/-e d'assurance.

self-centred (GB), **self-centered** (US) *adj* égocentrique.

self-confidence *n* assurance *f*.

self-confident *adj* [*person*] sûr/-e de soi; [*attitude*] plein/-e d'assurance.

self-conscious *adj* **1** (shy) timide; **to be ~ about sth/about doing** être gêné/-e par qch/de faire; **2** [*style*] conscient/-e.

self-control *n* sang-froid *m*.

self-defence (GB), **self-defense** (US) *n* (gen) autodéfense *f*; (Law) légitime défense *f*.

self-destructive *adj* autodestructeur/-trice.

self-disciplined *adj* autodiscipliné/-e.

self-effacing *adj* effacé/-e.

self-employed *adj* indépendant/-e; **to be ~** travailler à son compte.

self-esteem *n* amour-propre *m*.

self-evident *adj* évident/-e.

self-explanatory *adj* explicite.

self-important *adj* suffisant/-e.

self-indulgent *adj* complaisant/-e.

self-interested *adj* intéressé/-e.

selfish *adj* égoïste (**to do** de faire).

selfishness *n* égoïsme *m*.

self-pity *n* apitoiement *m* sur soi-même.

self-portrait *n* autoportrait *m*.

self-raising flour (GB), **self-rising flour** (US) *n* farine *f* à gâteau.

self-reliant *adj* autosuffisant/-e.

self-respect *n* respect *m* de soi.

self-respecting *adj* [*teacher, journalist, comedian*] qui se respecte.

self-righteous *adj* satisfait/-e de soi-même.

self-rule *n* autonomie *f*.

self-sacrifice *n* abnégation *f*.
self-satisfied *adj* satisfait/-e de soi-même.
self-service I *n* libre-service *m*.
II *adj* [*cafeteria*] en libre-service.
self-sufficient *adj* autosuffisant/-e.
self-taught *adj* autodidacte.
sell I *vtr* **1** vendre; **to ~ sth to sb, to ~ sb sth** vendre qch à qn; **to ~ sth for £5** vendre qch 5 livres sterling; **2** (promote sale of) faire vendre; **3** faire accepter [*idea, image, policy, party*].
II *vi* **1** [*person, shop, dealer*] vendre (**to sb** à qn); **2** [*goods, product, house, book*] se vendre.
■ **sell out 1** [*merchandise*] se vendre; **we've sold out of tickets** tous les billets ont été vendus; **we've sold out** nous avons tout vendu; **the play has sold out** la pièce affiche complet; **2**○ (betray one's principles) retourner sa veste○.
sell-by date *n* date *f* limite de vente.
selling I *n* vente *f*.
II *adj* [*price*] de vente.
Sellotape® I *n* scotch® *m*.
II **sellotape** *vtr* scotcher.
semen *n* sperme *m*.
semester *n* (US) semestre *m*.
semiautomatic *n, adj* semi-automatique (*m*).
semibreve *n* (GB Mus) ronde *f*.
semicircle *n* demi-cercle *m*.
semicolon *n* point-virgule *m*.
semiconscious *adj* à peine conscient/-e.
semidarkness *n* pénombre *f*, demi-jour *m*.
semi-detached (house) *n* maison *f* jumelée.
semifinal *n* demi-finale *f*.
semifinalist *n* demi-finaliste *mf*.
seminar *n* séminaire *m* (**on** sur).
semi-skimmed *adj* [*milk*] demi-écrémé/-e.
senate *n* sénat *m*.
senator ▶ 498 *n* sénateur *m* (**for** de).
send *vtr* **1** envoyer; **to ~ sth to sb, to ~ sb sth** envoyer qch à qn; **to ~ sb home** (from school, work) renvoyer qn chez lui/elle; **to ~ sb to prison** mettre qn en prison; **~ her my love!** embrasse-la de ma part; **~ them my regards** transmettez-leur mes amitiés; **2 to ~ shivers down sb's spine** donner froid dans le dos à qn; **to ~ sb to sleep** endormir qn; **it sent him into fits of laughter** ça l'a fait éclater de rire.
IDIOMS **to ~ sb packing**○ envoyer balader qn○.
■ **send away**: ¶ **~ away for [sth]** commander [qch] par correspondance; ¶ **~ [sb/sth] away** faire partir; ¶ **to ~ an appliance away to be mended** envoyer un appareil chez le fabricant pour le faire réparer.
■ **send for** appeler [*doctor, plumber*]; demander [*reinforcements*].
■ **send in** envoyer [*letter, form, troops*]; faire entrer [*visitor*]; **to ~ in one's application** poser sa candidature.
■ **send off**: ¶ **~ off for [sth]** commander [qch] par correspondance; ¶ **~ [sth] off** envoyer, expédier [*letter*]; ¶ **~ [sb] off** (Sport) expulser.
■ **send on** expédier [qch] à l'avance [*baggage*]; faire suivre [*letter, parcel*].
■ **send out 1** émettre [*light, heat*]; **2** faire sortir [*pupil*].
■ **send up**○ (GB) (parody) parodier.
sender *n* expéditeur/-trice *m/f*.
send-off *n* adieux *mpl*.
send-up○ *n* (GB) parodie *f*.
senile *adj* sénile.
senior I *n* **1** (gen) aîné/-e *m/f*; **to be sb's ~** être plus âgé/-e que qn; **2** (GB Sch) élève *mf* dans les grandes classes; (US Sch) élève *mf* de terminale.
II *adj* **1** (older) [*person*] plus âgé/-e; **2** [*civil servant*] haut/-e (*before n*); [*partner*] principal/-e; [*officer, job, post*] supérieur/-e.
senior citizen *n* personne *f* du troisième âge.
senior high school *n* (US Sch) ≈ lycée *m*.
seniority *n* (in years) âge *m*; (in rank) statut *m* supérieur; (in years of service) ancienneté *f*.
sensation *n* sensation *f*; **to cause** or **create a ~** faire sensation.
sensational *adj* sensationnel/-elle.
sensationalist *adj* [*headline, story, writer*] à sensation.
sense I *n* **1** (faculty, ability) sens *m*; **a ~ of humour/direction** le sens de l'humour/de l'orientation; **~ of hearing** ouïe *f*; **~ of sight** vue *f*; **~ of smell** odorat *m*; **~ of taste** goût *m*; **~ of touch** toucher *m*; **to lose all ~ of time** perdre toute notion du temps; **2** (feeling) **a ~ of identity** un sentiment d'identité; **a ~ of purpose** le sentiment d'avoir un but; **3 (common) ~** bon sens *m*; **to have the ~ to do** avoir le bon sens de faire; **4** (meaning) sens *m*; (reason) **there's no ~ in doing** cela ne sert à rien de faire; **to make ~ of sth** comprendre qch; **I can't make ~ of this article** je ne comprends rien à cet article; **to make ~** [*sentence, film*] avoir un sens.
II **senses** *n pl* **to come to one's senses** revenir à la raison.
III *vtr* **1** deviner (**that** que); **to ~ danger** sentir un danger; **2** [*machine*] détecter.
IDIOMS **to see ~** entendre raison; **to talk ~** dire des choses sensées.
senseless *adj* **1** [*violence*] gratuit/-e; [*discussion*] absurde; [*act, waste*] insensé/-e; **2 to knock sb ~** faire perdre connaissance à qn.
sensible *adj* [*person, attitude*] raisonnable; [*decision, solution*] judicieux/-ieuse; [*garment*] pratique; [*diet*] intelligent/-e.
sensitive *adj* **1** (gen) sensible (**to** à); **2** [*person*] (easily hurt) sensible, susceptible (**to** à); **3** [*situation*] délicat/-e; [*issue*] difficile; [*information*] confidentiel/-ielle.
sensitivity *n* sensibilité *f* (**to** à).
sensual *adj* sensuel/-elle.
sentence I *n* **1** (Law) peine *f*; **to serve a ~** purger une peine; **2** (in grammar) phrase *f*.
II *vtr* condamner (**to** à; **to do** à faire; **for** pour).

sentiment *n* **1** (feeling) sentiment *m* (**for** pour; **towards** envers); **2** (opinion) opinion *f*

sentimental *adj* sentimental/-e.

sentry *n* sentinelle *f*.

separate I *adj* **1** (independent, apart) [*piece, section*] à part; **she has a ~ room** elle a une chambre à part; **the flat is ~ from the rest of the house** l'appartement est indépendant du reste de la maison; **keep the knives ~** rangez les couteaux séparément; **keep the knives ~ from the forks** séparez les couteaux des fourchettes; **2** (different) [*sections, problems*] différent/-e; [*organizations, agreements*] distinct/-e; **they have ~ rooms** ils ont chacun leur chambre; **they asked for ~ bills** (in restaurant) ils ont demandé chacun leur addition.
II *vtr* **1** séparer (**from** de); **2** (sort out) répartir [*people*]; trier [*objects, produce*].
III *vi* se séparer (**from** de).

separately *adv* séparément.

separates *n pl* (garments) coordonnés *mpl*.

separation *n* séparation *f* (**from** de).

September ▶ 456 *n* septembre *m*.

septic *adj* infecté/-e; **to go** or **turn ~** s'infecter.

septic tank *n* fosse *f* septique.

sequel *n* suite *f* (**to** à).

sequence *n* **1** (series) série *f*; **2** (order) ordre *m*; **in ~** dans l'ordre; **3** (in film) séquence *f*.

Serbia ▶ 448 *pr n* Serbie *f*.

serene *adj* serein/-e.

sergeant *n* **1** (GB Mil) sergent *m*; **2** (US Mil) caporal-chef *m*; **3** (in police) ≈ brigadier *m*.

serial *n* feuilleton *m*; **TV ~** feuilleton télévisé.

serialize *vtr* adapter [qch] en feuilleton.

serial killer *n* auteur *m* d'une série de meurtres.

serial number *n* numéro *m* de série.

series *n* série *f*; **a drama ~** une série de fiction.

serious *adj* [*person, expression, discussion, offer*] sérieux/-ieuse; [*accident, crime, crisis, problem*] grave; [*literature, actor*] de qualité; [*attempt, concern*] réel/réelle; **to be ~ about sth** prendre qch au sérieux; **to be ~ about doing** avoir vraiment l'intention de faire.

seriously *adv* **1** [*speak, think*] sérieusement; **to take sb/sth ~** prendre qn/qch au sérieux; **2** [*ill, injured*] gravement; [*underestimate*] vraiment.

seriousness *n* **1** (of person, film, study) sérieux *m*; (of tone, occasion, reply) gravité *f*; **in all ~** sérieusement; **2** (of illness, problem, situation) gravité *f*.

sermon *n* sermon *m*.

serrated *adj* dentelé/-e; **~ knife** couteau-scie *m*.

serum *n* sérum *m*.

servant *n* ▶ 626 domestique *mf*.

serve I *n* (Sport) service *m*.
II *vtr* **1** servir [*country, cause, public*]; travailler au service de [*employer, family*]; **2** servir [*customer, guest, meal, dish*]; **to ~ sb with sth** servir qch à qn; **3** (provide facility) [*power station, reservoir*] alimenter; [*public transport, library, hospital*] desservir; **4** (satisfy) servir [*interests*]; satisfaire [*needs*]; **5 to ~ a purpose** être utile; **to ~ the** or **sb's purpose** faire l'affaire; **6** purger [*prison sentence*]; **7** (Law) délivrer [*injunction*] (**on sb** à qn); **to ~ a summons on sb** citer qn à comparaître; **8** (Sport) servir.
III *vi* **1** (in shop) servir; (at table) faire le service; **2 to ~ on** être membre de [*committee, jury*]; **3 to ~ as sth** servir de qch; **4** (Mil) servir (**as** comme; **under** sous); **5** (Sport) servir (**for** pour); **Bruno to ~** au service, Bruno.
IDIOMS **it ~s you right!** ça t'apprendra!

service I *n* **1** (gen) service *m*; (**accident and**) **emergency ~** service des urgences; **'out of ~'** (on machine) 'en panne'; **2** (overhaul) révision *f*; **3** (ceremony) office *m*; **Sunday ~** office du dimanche; **marriage ~** cérémonie *f* nuptiale.
II **services** *n pl* **1** (also **~ area**) aire *m* de services; **2** (Mil) **the Services** les armées.
III *vtr* faire la révision de [*vehicle*]; entretenir [*machine, boiler*]; **to have one's car ~d** faire réviser sa voiture.

service charge *n* **1** (in restaurant) service *m*; **what is the ~?** le service est de combien?; **2** (in banking) frais *mpl* de gestion de compte.

service station *n* station-service *f*.

serving *n* portion *f*.

serving dish *n* plat *m* (de service).

serving spoon *n* cuillère *f* de service.

session *n* **1** (gen) séance *f*; **2** (of parliament) session *f*; **3** (US Sch) (term) trimestre *m*; (period of lessons) cours *mpl*.

set I *n* **1** (of keys, tools) jeu *m*; (of golf clubs, chairs) série *f*; (of cutlery) service *m*; (of rules, instructions, tests) série *f*; **a new ~ of clothes** des vêtements neufs; **they're sold in ~s of 10** ils sont vendus par lots de 10; **a ~ of fingerprints** des empreintes digitales; **a ~ of traffic lights** des feux *mpl* (de signalisation); **a chess ~** un jeu d'échecs; **a ~ of false teeth** un dentier; **2** (Sport) (in tennis) set *m*; **3 TV** or **television ~** poste *m* de télévision; **4** (scenery) (for play) décor *m*; (for film) plateau *m*; **5** (GB Sch) groupe *m*; **6** (hair-do) mise *f* en plis.
II *adj* **1** [*pattern, procedure, rule, task*] bien déterminé/-e; [*time, price*] fixe; [*menu*] à prix fixe; **~ phrase** expression *f* consacrée; **to be ~ in one's ways** avoir ses habitudes; **2** [*expression, smile*] figé/-e; **3** (Sch, Univ) [*text*] au programme; **4** (ready) prêt/-e (**for** pour; **to do** à faire); **5 to be (dead) ~ against sth/doing** être tout à fait contre qch/l'idée de faire; **to be ~ on doing** tenir absolument à faire; **6** [*jam, jelly, honey*] épais/épaisse; [*cement*] dur/-e; [*yoghurt*] ferme.
III *vtr* **1** (place) placer [*object*] (**on** sur); monter [*gem*] (**in** dans); **a house ~ among the trees** une maison située au milieu des arbres; **to ~ the record straight** mettre les choses au point; **his eyes are ~ very close together** ses yeux sont très rapprochés; **2** mettre [*table*]; tendre [*trap*]; **3** fixer [*date, deadline, price, target*]; lancer [*fashion, trend*]; donner [*tone*]; établir [*precedent, record*]; **to ~ a good/bad ex-**

ample to sb montrer le bon/mauvais exemple à qn; **to ~ one's sights on** viser; **4** mettre [qch] à l'heure [*clock*]; mettre [*alarm clock, burglar alarm*]; **5** (start) **to ~ sth going** mettre qch en marche [*machine*]; **to ~ sb laughing/thinking** faire rire/réfléchir qn; **6** donner [*homework, essay*]; **to ~ an exam** préparer les sujets d'examen; **7** (in fiction, film) situer; **the film is ~ in Munich** le film se passe à Munich; **8 to ~ sth to music** mettre qch en musique; **9** (Med) immobiliser [*broken bone*]; **10 to have one's hair ~** se faire faire une mise en plis.

IV *vi* **1** [*sun*] se coucher; **2** [*jam, concrete*] prendre; [*glue*] sécher; **3** (Med) [*fracture*] se ressouder.

■ **set about** se mettre à [*work*]; **to ~ about (the job** or **task of) doing** commencer à faire.

■ **set apart** distinguer (**from** de).

■ **set aside** réserver [*area, room, time*] (**for** pour); mettre [qch] de côté [*money, stock*].

■ **set in** [*infection*] se déclarer; [*winter*] arriver; [*depression*] s'installer; **the rain has ~ in for the afternoon** la pluie va durer toute l'après-midi.

■ **set off**: ¶ **~off** partir (**for** pour); **to ~ off on a journey** partir en voyage; ¶ **~ [sth] off 1** faire partir [*firework*]; faire exploser [*bomb*]; déclencher [*riot, panic, alarm*]; **2** (enhance) mettre [qch] en valeur [*garment*]; **3 to ~ sth off against profits/debts** déduire qch des bénéfices/des dettes; ¶ **~ [sb] off** faire pleurer [*baby*]; **she laughed and that ~ me off** elle a ri et ça m'a fait rire à mon tour.

■ **set on**: ¶ **~ on [sb]** attaquer qn; ¶ **~ [sth] on sb** lâcher [qch] contre qn [*dog*].

■ **set out**: ¶ **~ out** se mettre en route (**for** pour; **to do** pour faire); **to ~ out to do** [*person*] entreprendre de faire; ¶ **~ [sth] out 1** disposer [*goods, chairs, food*]; préparer [*board game*]; **2** présenter [*ideas, proposals*]; formuler [*objections, terms*].

■ **set up**: ¶ **to ~ up on one's own** s'établir à son compte; **to ~ up in business** monter une affaire; ¶ **~ [sth] up 1** monter [*stand, stall*]; assembler [*equipment, easel*]; ériger [*roadblock*]; **to ~ up home** s'installer; **2** préparer [*experiment*]; (Sport) préparer [*goal, try*]; **3** créer [*business, company*]; implanter [*factory*]; former [*support group, charity*]; constituer [*committee*]; **4** organiser [*meeting*]; mettre [qch] en place [*procedures*]; ¶ **~ [sb] up 1 she ~ her son up (in business) as a gardener** elle a aidé son fils à s'installer comme jardinier; **2 that deal has ~ her up for life** grâce à ce contrat elle n'aura plus à se soucier de rien; **3**° (GB) [*police*] tendre un piège à [*criminal*]; [*friend*] monter un coup contre [*person*].

setback *n* revers *m* (**for** pour).

settee *n* canapé *m*.

setting *n* **1** (location) cadre *m*; **2** (in jewellery) monture *f*; **3** (position on dial) position *f* (de réglage).

settle I *vtr* **1** installer [*person, animal*]; **2** calmer [*stomach, nerves*]; **3** régler [*matter, business, dispute*]; mettre fin à [*conflict, strike*]; régler, résoudre [*problem*]; décider [*match*]; **that's ~d** voilà qui est réglé; **4** fixer [*arrangements, price*]; **5 to ~ one's affairs** mettre de l'ordre dans ses affaires; **6** régler [*bill, debt, claim*].

II *vi* **1** [*dust*] se déposer; [*bird, insect*] se poser; **2** (in new home) s'installer; **3** [*contents, ground*] se tasser; **4** [*weather*] se mettre au beau fixe; **5** (Law) régler; **to ~ out of court** parvenir à un règlement à l'amiable.

■ **settle down 1** (get comfortable) s'installer (**on** sur; **in** dans); **2** (calm down) [*person*] se calmer; **3** (marry) se ranger.

■ **settle for**: **~ for sth** se contenter de qch.

■ **settle in 1** (move in) s'installer; **2** (become acclimatized) s'adapter.

■ **settle up** (pay) payer.

settlement *n* **1** (agreement) accord *m*; **2** (Law) règlement *m*; **3** (dwellings) village *m*; (colonial) territoire *m*.

seven ▶ 389, 434 *n, pron, det* sept (*m*) *inv*.

seventeen ▶ 389, 434 *n, pron, det* dix-sept (*m*) *inv*.

seventeenth ▶ 456, 498 **I** *n* **1** (in order) dix-septième *mf*; **2** (of month) dix-sept *m inv*; **3** (fraction) dix-septième *m*.

II *adj, adv* dix-septième.

seventh ▶ 456, 498 **I** *n* **1** (in order) septième *mf*; **2** (of month) sept *m inv*; **3** (fraction) septième *m*.

II *adj, adv* septième.

seventies ▶ 389, 456 *n pl* **1** (era) **the ~** les années *fpl* soixante-dix; **2** (age) **to be in one's ~** avoir plus de soixante-dix ans.

seventieth *n, adj, adv* soixante-dixième (*mf*).

seventy ▶ 389 *n, pron, det* soixante-dix (*m*) *inv*.

sever *vtr* **1** sectionner [*limb, artery*]; couper [*rope, branch*]; **2** rompre [*link, relations*]; couper [*communications*].

several I *quantif* **~ of you/us** plusieurs d'entre vous/d'entre nous.

II *det* plusieurs; **~ books** plusieurs livres.

severe *adj* **1** [*problem, damage, shortage, injury, depression, shock*] grave; [*weather, cold, winter*] rigoureux/-euse; **2** (harsh) sévère (**with sb** avec qn); **3** [*haircut, clothes*] austère.

severity *n* (of problem, illness) gravité *f*; (of punishment, treatment) sévérité *f*; (of climate) rigueur *f*.

sew I *vtr* coudre.

II *vi* coudre, faire de la couture.

■ **sew up** recoudre [*hole, tear*]; faire [*seam*]; (re)coudre [*wound*].

sewage *n* eaux *fpl* usées.

sewer *n* égout *m*.

sewing *n* (activity) couture *f*; (piece of work) ouvrage *m*.

sewing machine *n* machine *f* à coudre.

sex I *n* **1** (gender) sexe *m*; **the opposite ~** le sexe opposé; **2** (intercourse) (one act) rapport *m* sexuel; (repeated) rapports *mpl* sexuels.

II *adj* sexuel/-elle.

sexist *n, adj* sexiste (*mf*).

sexual *adj* sexuel/-elle.
sexuality *n* sexualité *f*.
sexy○ *adj* [*person, clothing*] sexy○ *inv*; [*book*] érotique.
shabby *adj* [*person*] habillé/-e de façon miteuse; [*room, furnishings, clothing*] miteux/-euse; [*treatment*] mesquin/-e.
shack *n* cabane *f*.
shade I *n* **1** (shadow) ombre *f*; **in the ~** à l'ombre (**of** de); **2** (of colour) ton *m*; **3** (also **lamp ~**) abat-jour *m inv*; **4** (US) (also **window ~**) store *m*.
II *vtr* donner de l'ombre à; **to ~ one's eyes (with one's hand)** s'abriter les yeux de la main.
IDIOMS **to put sb in the ~** éclipser qn; **to put sth in the ~** surpasser or surclasser qch.
shadow I *n* ombre *f*; **to have ~s under one's eyes** avoir les yeux cernés.
II *vtr* filer [*person*].
shadow cabinet *n* (GB) cabinet *m* fantôme.
shady *adj* **1** [*place*] ombragé/-e; **2** [*deal, businessman*] véreux/-euse.
shaft *n* **1** (of tool) manche *m*; (of arrow) tige *f*; (in machine) axe *m*; **2** (passage, vent) puits *m*; **3 ~ of light** rai *m*; **~ of lightning** éclair *m*.
shaggy *adj* [*hair, beard, eyebrows*] en broussailles; [*animal*] poilu/-e.
shake I *n* **1 to give sb/sth a ~** secouer qn/qch; **2** (also **milk-~**) milk-shake *m*.
II *vtr* **1** (gen) secouer; **to ~ one's head** (in dismay) hocher la tête; (to say no) faire non de la tête; **to ~ hands with sb, to ~ sb's hand** serrer la main de qn, donner une poignée de main à qn; **2** ébranler [*confidence, faith, resolve*]; [*event, disaster*] secouer [*person*].
III *vi* **1** trembler; **to ~ with** trembler de [*fear, cold, emotion*]; se tordre de [*laughter*]; **2** (shake hands) **'let's ~ on it!'** 'serrons-nous la main!'
■ **shake off** se débarrasser de [*cold, depression, habit, person*]; se défaire de [*feeling*].
■ **shake up 1** agiter [*bottle, mixture*]; **2** [*experience, news*] secouer [*person*].
shaken *adj* (shocked) choqué/-e.
shaky *adj* **1** [*chair, ladder*] branlant/-e; **I feel a bit ~** je me sens un peu flageolant; **2** [*relationship, position*] instable; [*evidence, argument*] peu solide; [*knowledge, memory*] peu sûr/-e; [*regime*] chancelant/-e; **my French is a bit ~** mon français est un peu hésitant.
shall *modal aux* **1** (in future tense) **I ~** or **I'll see you tomorrow** je vous verrai demain; **we ~ not** or **shan't have a reply before Friday** nous n'aurons pas de réponse avant vendredi; **2** (in suggestions) **~ I set the table?** est-ce que je mets la table?; **~ we go to the cinema tonight?** et si on allait au cinéma ce soir?; **let's buy some peaches, ~ we?** et si on achetait des pêches?
shallot *n* **1** (GB) échalote *f*; **2** (US) cive *f*.
shallow ▶573 *adj* [*container, water, grave*] peu profond/-e; [*breathing, character, response*] superficiel/-ielle.
shallows *n pl* bas-fonds *mpl*.

sham I *n* **1** (person) imposteur *m*; **2 it's (all) a ~** c'est de la comédie.
II *adj* [*event*] prétendu/-e (*before n*); [*object, building, idea*] factice; [*activity, emotion*] feint/-e.
III *vi* faire semblant.
shambles○ *n* pagaille○ *f*.
shame I *n* **1** (gen) honte *f*; **2 it's a (real) shame** c'est (vraiment) dommage; **it was a ~ (that) she lost** c'est dommage qu'elle ait perdu.
II *vtr* **1** (embarrass) faire honte à; **2** (disgrace) déshonorer (**by doing** en faisant).
shameful *adj* honteux/-euse.
shameless *adj* [*person*] éhonté/-e; [*attitude*] effronté/-e; [*negligence*] scandaleux/-euse.
shampoo I *n* shampooing *m*.
II *vtr* faire un shampooing à; **to ~ one's hair** se faire un shampooing.
shamrock *n* trèfle *m*.
shandy, shandygaff (US) *n* panaché *m*.
shape I *n* **1** forme *f*; **a square ~** une forme carrée; **what ~ is the room?** quelle forme a la pièce?; **to take ~** prendre forme; **to be in/out of ~** [*person*] être/ne pas être en forme; **to get in ~** se mettre en forme; **to knock sth into ~** mettre qch au point [*project, idea, essay*].
II *vtr* **1** modeler [*clay*]; sculpter [*wood*]; **2** [*person, event*] déterminer [*future, idea*]; modeler [*character*].
-shaped *combining form* **star-/V-~** en forme d'étoile/de V.
shapeless *adj* sans forme, informe.
shapely *adj* [*woman*] bien fait/-e; [*ankle*] fin/-e; [*leg*] bien galbé/-e.
share I *n* **1** part *f* (**of** de); **to pay one's (fair) ~** payer sa part; **2** (in stock market) action *f*.
II *vtr* partager (**with** avec); **we ~ an interest in animals** nous aimons tous les deux les animaux.
III *vi* **to ~ in** prendre part à.
■ **share out** (amongst selves) partager [*food*]; (amongst others) répartir [*food*] (**among, between** entre).
shareholder *n* actionnaire *mf*.
shark *n* requin *m*.
sharp I *adj* **1** [*razor*] tranchant/-e; [*edge*] coupant/-e; [*blade, scissors, knife*] bien aiguisé/-e; **2** [*tooth, fingernail, end, needle*] pointu/-e; [*pencil*] bien taillé/-e; [*features*] anguleux/-euse; **3** [*angle*] aigu/aiguë; [*bend*] brusque; [*drop, incline*] fort/-e; [*fall, rise*] brusque, brutal/-e; **4** [*taste, smell*] âcre; [*fruit*] acide; **5** [*pain, cold*] vif/vive; [*cry*] aigu/aiguë; [*blow*] sévère; [*frost*] intense; **6** [*tongue*] acéré/-e; [*tone*] acerbe; **7** [*person, mind*] vif/vive; [*eyesight*] perçant/-e; **8** [*businessman*] malin/-igne; **~ operator** filou *m*; **9** [*image*] net/nette; [*contrast*] prononcé/-e; **10** (Mus) [*note*] dièse *inv*; (too high) aigu/aiguë.
II *adv* **1** [*stop*] net; **to turn ~ left** tourner brusquement vers la gauche; **2**○ **at 9 o'clock ~** à neuf heures pile○; **3** (Mus) [*sing, play*] trop haut.
sharpen *vtr* aiguiser, affûter [*blade, scissors*]; tailler [*pencil*].

sharpener *n* taille-crayon *m*.
sharply *adv* **1** [*turn, rise, fall*] brusquement, brutalement; **2** [*speak*] d'un ton brusque.
shatter I *vtr* fracasser [*window, glass*]; rompre [*peace, silence*]; briser [*hope*]; démolir [*nerves*].
II *vi* [*window, glass*] voler en éclats.
shattered *adj* **1** [*dream*] brisé/-e; [*life, confidence*] anéanti/-e; **2** [*person*] (devastated) effondré/-e; (tired)○ crevé/-e○, épuisé/-e.
shave I *n* **to have a ~** se raser.
II *vtr* [*barber*] raser [*person*]; **to ~ one's beard off** se raser la barbe; **to ~ one's legs** se raser les jambes.
III *vi* se raser.
IDIOMS **that was a close ~!** je l'ai/il l'a etc échappé belle!
shaver *n* (also **electric ~**) rasoir *m* électrique.
shaving I *n* **1** (action) rasage *m*; **2 ~s** (of wood, metal) copeaux *mpl*.
II *adj* [*cream, foam*] à raser.
shaving brush *n* blaireau *m*.
shaving mirror *n* petit miroir *m*.
shawl *n* châle *m*.
she *pron* elle; **~'s not at home** elle n'est pas chez elle; **here ~ is** la voici; **there ~ is** la voilà; **~'s a beautiful woman** c'est une belle femme.
shear *vtr* tondre [*grass, sheep*].
shears *n pl* **1** (for garden) cisaille *f*; **2** (for sheep) tondeuse *f*.
shed I *n* (in garden) remise *f*, abri *m*; (at factory site, port) hangar *m*.
II *vtr* **1** verser [*tears*]; perdre [*leaves, weight, antlers*]; [*lorry*] déverser [*load*]; verser [*blood*]; **to ~ skin** muer; **2** répandre [*light, happiness*].
sheep *n* mouton *m*; (ewe) brebis *f*; **black ~** brebis *f* galeuse.
sheep dog *n* chien *m* de berger.
sheepish *adj* penaud/-e.
sheepskin *n* peau *f* de mouton.
sheer *adj* **1** [*boredom, hypocrisy, stupidity*] pur/-e (*before n*); **2** [*cliff*] à pic; **3** [*fabric*] léger/-ère, fin/-e; [*stockings*] extra-fin/-e.
sheet *n* **1** (of paper, stamps) feuille *f*; (of metal, glass) plaque *f*; **2** (for bed) drap *m*; **dust ~** housse *f*; **3 fact ~** bulletin *m* d'informations; **4** (of ice) couche *f*; (of flame) rideau *m*.
sheet lightning *n* éclair *m* en nappe.
sheik *n* cheik *m*.
shelf *n* **1** étagère *f*; (in oven) plaque *f*; (in shop, fridge) rayon *m*; **(a set of) shelves** une étagère; **2** (in rock, ice) corniche *f*.
shell I *n* **1** (of egg, nut, snail) coquille *f*; (of crab, tortoise, shrimp) carapace *f*; **sea ~** coquillage *m*; **to come out of one's ~** sortir de sa coquille; **2** (bomb) obus *m*; (cartridge) cartouche *f*; **3** (of building) carcasse *f*.
II *vtr* **1** (Mil) pilonner [*town, installation*]; **2** (Culin) écosser [*peas*]; décortiquer [*prawn, nut*].
shellfish *n pl* **1** (Zool) crustacés *mpl*; (mussels, oysters) coquillages *mpl*; **2** (Culin) fruits *mpl* de mer.
shelter I *n* **1** abri *m*; **to take ~ from** s'abriter de [*weather*]; **2** (for homeless) refuge *m* (**for** pour); (for refugee) asile *m*.
II *vtr* **1** (against weather) abriter (**from, against** de); (from truth) protéger (**from** de); **2** donner refuge or asile à [*refugee, criminal*].
III *vi* se mettre à l'abri; **to ~ from the storm** s'abriter de l'orage.
shepherd ▶ 626 *n* berger *m*.
sheriff ▶ 626 *n* shérif *m*.
sherry *n* xérès *m*, sherry *m*.
shield I *n* **1** (Mil) bouclier *m*; **2** (on machine) écran *m* de protection; (around gun) pare-balles *m inv*; **3** (US) (policeman's badge) insigne *m*.
II *vtr* protéger; **to ~ one's eyes** se protéger les yeux.
shift I *n* **1** (change) changement *m* (**in** de), modification *f* (**in** de); **2** (at work) période *f* de travail; (group of workers) équipe *f*; **to work an eight-hour ~** faire les trois-huit.
II *vtr* **1** déplacer [*furniture, vehicle*]; bouger, remuer [*arm*]; changer [*theatre scenery*]; **2** faire partir, enlever [*stain, dirt*]; **3** rejeter [*blame, responsibility*] (**onto** sur); **to ~ attention away from a problem** détourner l'attention d'un problème; **4** (US Aut) **to ~ gear** changer de vitesse.
III *vi* (also **~ about**) [*load*] bouger; **to ~ from one foot to the other** se dandiner d'un pied sur l'autre.
shiftless *adj* paresseux/-euse, apathique.
shift work *n* travail *m* posté.
shifty *adj* louche, sournois/-e.
shimmer *vi* **1** [*jewels, water*] scintiller; [*silk*] chatoyer; **2** (in heat) [*landscape*] vibrer.
shin, shinbone *n* tibia *m*.
shine I *n* lustre *m*.
II *vtr* **1** braquer [*headlights, spotlight, torch*] (**on** sur); **2** faire reluire [*silver*]; cirer [*shoes*].
III *vi* **1** [*hair, light, sun*] briller; [*brass, floor*] reluire; **the light is shining in my eyes** j'ai la lumière dans les yeux; **2** [*eyes*] briller (**with** de); [*face*] rayonner (**with** de); **3** (excel) briller; **to ~ at** être brillant en [*science, languages*].
IDIOMS **to take a ~ to sb**○ s'enticher○ de qn.
shingle I *n* **1** (on beach) galets *mpl*; **2** (on roof) bardeau *m*.
II shingles ▶ 533 *n pl* (Med) zona *m*.
shining *adj* **1** [*hair, metal, eyes*] brillant/-e; **2** [*face*] radieux/-ieuse; **3** [*example*] parfait/-e (*before n*).
shiny *adj* **1** [*metal, surface, hair*] brillant/-e; **2** [*shoes, wood*] bien ciré/-e.
ship I *n* navire *m*; (smaller) bateau *m*; **passenger ~** paquebot *m*.
II *vtr* transporter [qch] par mer.
shipment *n* cargaison *f*.
ship owner *n* armateur *m*.
shipping *n* navigation *f*, trafic *m* maritime.
shipwreck I *n* (event) naufrage *m*; (ship) épave *f*.
II *vtr* **to be ~ed** faire naufrage; **a ~ed sailor** un marin naufragé.
shirk *vtr* esquiver [*task, duty*]; fuir [*responsibility*].

shirt *n* (man's) chemise *f*; (woman's) chemisier *m*; (for sport) maillot *m*.
shirt-sleeve *n* manche *f* de chemise; **in one's ~s** en manches de chemise.
shit◑ *excl* merde◑!
shiver I *n* frisson *m*; **to give sb the ~s** donner froid dans le dos à qn.
II *vi* (with cold) grelotter (**with** de); (with fear) frémir (**with** de); (with disgust) frissonner (**with** de).
shoal *n* (of fish) banc *m*.
shock I *n* **1** choc *m*; **to get** or **have a ~** avoir un choc; **to give sb a ~** faire un choc à qn; **to be in ~** être en état de choc; **2** (electrical) décharge *f*; **to get a ~** prendre une décharge; **3** (of collision) choc *m*; (of explosion) souffle *m*; **4 a ~ of red hair** une tignasse rousse.
II *vtr* (distress) consterner; (scandalize) choquer.
shock absorber *n* amortisseur *m*.
shocking *adj* [*sight*] consternant/-e; [*news*] choquant/-e.
shoddy *adj* [*product*] de mauvaise qualité; [*work*] mal fait/-e.
shoe I *n* chaussure *f*; (for horse) fer *m*.
II *vtr* ferrer [*horse*].
shoelace *n* lacet *m* de chaussure.
shoe polish *n* cirage *m*.
shoe shop ▶ 626 *n* magasin *m* de chaussures.
shoe size *n* pointure *f*.
shoestring *n* (US) lacet *m* de chaussure.
shoo *vtr* (also **~ away**) chasser.
shoot I *n* (Bot) pousse *f*.
II *vtr* **1** tirer [*bullet, arrow*] (**at** sur); lancer [*missile*] (**at** sur); **2** tirer sur [*person, animal*]; (kill) abattre [*person, animal*]; **she shot him in the leg** elle lui a tiré dans la jambe; **to ~ sb dead** abattre qn; **to ~ oneself** se tirer une balle; **3 to ~ questions at sb** bombarder qn de questions; **4** (film) tourner [*film, scene*]; prendre [qch] (en photo) [*subject*]; **5** mettre [*bolt*]; **6 to ~ the rapids** franchir les rapides; **7** (US) jouer à [*pool*].
III *vi* **1** tirer (**at** sur); **2 to ~ forward** s'élancer à toute vitesse; **the car shot past** la voiture est passée en trombe; **3** (Sport) tirer, shooter.
■ **shoot down** abattre, descendre○ [*plane, pilot*].
■ **shoot up** [*flames, spray*] jaillir; [*prices, profits*] monter en flèche.
shooting I *n* **1** (killing) meurtre *m* (par arme à feu); **2** (shots) coups *mpl* de feu, fusillade *f*.
II *adj* [*pain*] lancinant/-e.
shooting range *n* stand *m* de tir.
shooting star *n* étoile *f* filante.
shop I *n* **1** magasin *m*; (small, fashionable) boutique *f*; **to go to the ~s** aller faire les courses; **2** (US) (in department store) rayon *m*; **3** (workshop) atelier *m*.
II *vi* **to go ~ping** aller faire des courses; (browse) aller faire les magasins.
IDIOMS **to talk ~** parler boutique.
shop assistant ▶ 626 *n* (GB) vendeur/-euse *m*/*f*.
shopkeeper ▶ 626 *n* commerçant/-e *m*/*f*.
shoplifter *n* voleur/-euse *m*/*f* à l'étalage.
shopping *n* courses *fpl*.
shopping bag *n* sac *m* à provisions.
shopping centre (GB), **shopping mall** (US) *n* centre *m* commercial.
shop-soiled *adj* [*garment*] sali/-e.
shop window *n* vitrine *f*.
shore *n* (of sea) côte *f*, rivage *m*; (of lake) rive *f*; **on ~** à terre.
short ▶ 573 **I** *n* **1** (drink) alcool *m* fort; **2** (film) court métrage *m*.
II **shorts** *n pl* short *m*; (underwear) caleçon *m*.
III *adj* **1** [*stay, memory, period*] court/-e (*before n*); [*course*] de courte durée; [*conversation, speech, chapter*] bref/brève (*before n*); [*walk*] petit/-e (*before n*); **the days are getting ~er** les jours diminuent or raccourcissent; **2** [*hair, dress, distance, stick*] court/-e (*before n*); **3** [*person*] petit/-e (*before n*); **4 to be in ~ supply** être difficile à trouver; **time is getting ~** le temps presse; **5** (lacking) **he is ~ of sth** il lui manque qch; **to be ~ on** [*person*] manquer de [*talent, tact*]; **to run ~ of** manquer de [*clothes, money, food*]; **6 Tom is ~ for Thomas** Tom est le diminutif de Thomas; **7** (abrupt) **to be ~ with sb** être brusque avec qn; **8** [*pastry*] brisé/-e.
IV *adv* [*stop*] net; **to stop ~ of doing** se retenir pour ne pas faire.
V **in short** *phr* bref.
VI **short of** *phr* **~ of doing** à moins de faire.
shortage *n* pénurie *f*, manque *m* (**of** de).
shortbread, **shortcake** *n* sablé *m*.
short-change *vtr* ne pas rendre toute sa monnaie à.
short circuit I *n* court-circuit *m*.
II **short-circuit** *vtr* court-circuiter.
III **short-circuit** *vi* faire court-circuit.
shortcomings *n pl* points *mpl* faibles.
shortcut *n* raccourci *m*.
shorten I *vtr* abréger [*visit, life*]; raccourcir [*garment, talk*]; réduire [*time, list*].
II *vi* [*days*] diminuer.
shortfall *n* (in budget, accounts) déficit *m*; (in earnings, exports) manque *m*.
shorthand *n* sténographie *f*, sténo○ *f*.
shorthand-typist ▶ 626 *n* sténo-dactylo *f*.
shortlist I *n* liste *f* des candidats sélectionnés.
II *vtr* sélectionner [*applicant*] (**for** pour).
short-lived *adj* **to be ~** ne pas durer longtemps.
shortly *adv* **1** [*return*] bientôt; [*be published*] prochainement; **2 ~ after(wards)/before** peu (de temps) après/avant; **3** (crossly) sèchement.
shortsighted *adj* **1** myope; **2** (figurative) [*person*] peu clairvoyant/-e; [*policy, decision*] à courte vue.
short-staffed *adj* **to be ~** manquer de personnel.
short story *n* nouvelle *f*.
short term I *n* **in the ~** dans l'immédiat.
II **short-term** *adj* à court terme.

shortwave *n* ondes *fpl* courtes.

shot I *n* **1** (from gun) coup *m* (de feu); **2** (Sport) (in tennis, golf, cricket) coup *m*; (in football) tir *m*; **3** (snapshot) photo *f* (**of** de); **4** (in film-making) plan *m* (**of** de); **action ~** scène *f* d'action; **5** (injection) piqûre *f* (**of** de); **6 to have a ~ at doing** essayer de faire; **7** (person) **a good ~** un bon tireur.
II *adj* [*silk*] changeant/-e.

shotgun *n* fusil *m*.

shot put *n* (Sport) lancer *m* de poids.

should ▶666 *modal aux* **1 ~ I call the doctor?** est-ce que je devrais faire venir le médecin?; **why shouldn't I do it?** pourquoi est-ce que je ne le ferais pas?; **2 it shouldn't be difficult** ça ne devrait pas être difficile; **she ~ have been here hours ago** elle aurait dû arriver il y a plusieurs heures déjà; **3 I ~ think she's about 40** à mon avis, elle doit avoir à peu près 40 ans; **4 ~ you require any further information, please contact...** si vous souhaitez plus de renseignements, adressez-vous à...; **5 I ~ think so!** je l'espère!; **I ~ think not!** j'espère bien que non!; **how ~ I know?** comment veux-tu que je le sache?; **flowers? you shouldn't have!** des fleurs? il ne fallait pas!

shoulder I ▶413 *n* épaule *f*.
II *vtr* se charger de [*burden, expense, task*]; endosser [*responsibility*].
IDIOMS **to rub ~s with sb** côtoyer qn.

shoulder blade ▶413 *n* omoplate *f*.

shoulder pad *n* épaulette *f*.

shout I *n* cri *m* (**of** de).
II *vtr* crier; (stronger) hurler.
III *vi* crier; **to ~ at sb** crier après qn; **he was ~ing to me** il me criait quelque chose.
■ **shout out** pousser un cri.

shouting *n* cris *mpl*.

shove○ I *n* **to give sb/sth a ~** pousser qn/qch.
II *vtr* **1** (push) pousser (**against** contre); **to ~ sth into sth** fourrer qch dans qch; **2** (jostle) bousculer [*person*].
III *vi* pousser.

shovel I *n* pelle *f*.
II *vtr* enlever [qch] à la pelle [*leaves, snow*] (**off** de).

show I *n* **1** spectacle *m*; (in cinema) séance *f*; (on radio, TV) émission *f*; (of slides) projection *f*; **2** (exhibition) exposition *f*; (of cars, boats) salon *m*; (of fashion) défilé *m*; **flower/dog ~** exposition florale/canine; **3** (of feelings) semblant *m* (**of** de); (of strength) démonstration *f* (**of** de); (of wealth) étalage *m* (**of** de); **he made a ~ of concern** il a affiché sa sollicitude; **to be just for ~** être de l'esbroufe○.
II *vtr* **1** montrer [*person, object, photo, feelings*] (**to** à); présenter [*ticket*] (**to** à); [*TV channel, cinema*] passer [*film*]; [*garment*] laisser voir [*underclothes, stain*]; indiquer [*time, direction*]; **to ~ sb sth** montrer qch à qn; **that carpet ~s the dirt** cette moquette est salissante; **2** (exhibit) présenter [*animal*]; exposer [*flower, vegetables*]; **3** (prove) démontrer [*truth, guilt*]; **4 to ~ sb to their seat** placer qn; **to ~ sb to their room** accompagner qn à sa chambre; **to ~ sb to the door** reconduire qn.
III *vi* **1** [*stain, label*] se voir; [*emotion*] se voir; (in eyes) se lire; **2** [*film*] passer.
IDIOMS **to have nothing to ~ for sth** ne rien avoir tiré de qch.
■ **show in**: **~** [**sb**] **in** faire entrer.
■ **show off**: ¶ **~ off**○ faire le fier/la fière; ¶ **~** [**sb/sth**] **off** faire admirer [*skill*]; exhiber [*baby, car*].
■ **show out**: **~** [**sb**] **out** accompagner [qn] à la porte.
■ **show round**: **~** [**sb**] **round** faire visiter.
■ **show up**: ¶ **~ up**○(arrive) se montrer○; ¶ **~ up** [**sth**] révéler [*fault, mark*]; ¶ **~** [**sb**] **up** faire honte à [*person*].

show business *n* industrie *f* du spectacle.

showdown *n* confrontation *f*.

shower I *n* **1** douche *f*; **to have a ~** prendre une douche; **2** (of rain) averse *f*.
II *vtr* **1 to ~ sb with sth** couvrir qn de [*gifts, compliments, praise*].
III *vi* [*person*] prendre une douche.

showjumping *n* saut *m* d'obstacles.

shrapnel *n* éclats *mpl* d'obus.

shred I *n* **1** (of paper, fabric) lambeau *m*; **2** (of evidence, truth) parcelle *f*.
II *vtr* déchiqueter [*paper*]; râper [*vegetables*].

shrewd *adj* [*person*] habile; [*move, investment*] astucieux/-ieuse.

shriek I *n* **1** (of pain, fear) cri *m* perçant, hurlement *m*; (of delight) cri *m*; **~s of laughter** éclats *mpl* de rire; **2** (of bird) cri *m*.
II *vi* crier, hurler (**in, with** de).

shrill *adj* [*voice, cry, laugh*] perçant/-e; [*whistle, tone*] strident/-e.

shrimp *n* crevette *f* grise.

shrine *n* **1** (place) lieu *m* de pèlerinage; **2** (building) chapelle *f*; **3** (tomb) tombeau *m*.

shrink I *vtr* faire rétrécir [*fabric*]; contracter [*wood*].
II *vi* **1** [*fabric*] rétrécir; [*timber*] se contracter; [*dough, meat*] réduire; [*sales*] être en recul; [*resources*] s'amenuiser; [*old person, body*] se tasser; **2 to ~ from** se dérober devant [*conflict, responsibility*]; **to ~ from doing** hésiter à faire.

shrivel I *vtr* [*sun, heat*] flétrir [*skin*]; dessécher [*plant, leaf*].
II *vi* (also **~ up**) [*fruit, vegetable*] se ratatiner; [*skin*] se flétrir; [*plant, meat*] se dessécher.

shroud I *n* linceul *m*.
II *vtr* envelopper (**in** dans).

Shrove Tuesday *n* mardi *m* gras.

shrub *n* arbuste *m*.

shrubbery *n* massif *m* d'arbustes.

shrug I *n* haussement *m* d'épaules.
II *vtr* **to ~ one's shoulders** hausser les épaules.
■ **shrug off** ignorer [*problem, rumour*].

shudder I *n* **1** (of person) frisson *m* (**of** de); **2** (of vehicle) secousse *f*.
II *vi* **1** [*person*] frissonner (**with** de); **2** [*vehicle*]

should

◆ ***should***, when it implies an *obligation* (= ***ought to***), is translated by the present conditional of ***devoir***:

*she **should** learn to drive*	= elle **devrait** apprendre à conduire
*we **should** leave now*	= nous **devrions** partir maintenant
shouldn't *you be at school?*	= est-ce que tu ne **devrais** pas être à l'école?
*he **shouldn't** smoke so much*	= il ne **devrait** pas tant fumer
*I **should** explain that she's shortsighted*	= je **devrais** peut-être expliquer qu'elle est myope

To translate ***should have*** (= ***ought to have***), use the past conditional of ***devoir***:

*we **should have** had a party*	= nous **aurions dû** faire une fête
*you **should have** told me before*	= tu **aurais dû** me le dire avant
*you **shouldn't** have said that*	= tu n'**aurais** pas **dû** dire ça ⇨ **1**

◆ ***should*** can also mean that something is *probable*: use the present conditional of ***devoir***:

*dinner **should** be ready soon*	= le dîner **devrait** être bientôt prêt
*it **should**n't be difficult to convince her*	= ça ne **devrait** pas être trop difficile de la convaincre
*we **should** be there by six o'clock*	= nous **devrions** arriver vers six heures

The past tense ***should have*** (***done/said*** etc) is translated by the past conditional of ***devoir*** and implies that what was *probable* did not occur:

*the letter **should have** arrived yesterday*	= la lettre **aurait dû** arriver hier
*the ticket **should**n't have cost so much*	= le billet n'**aurait** pas **dû** coûter si cher
should*n't they have consulted you first?*	= est-ce qu'ils n'**auraient** pas **dû** te consulter avant? ⇨ **2**

◆ ***should***, as a more formal version of ***would***, is translated by the conditional of the appropriate verb:

*I **should like** to go to Paris*	= j'**aimerais** aller à Paris
*I **shouldn't be** surprised*	= cela ne m'**étonnerait** pas
*I **should have thought** he'd be delighted*	= j'**aurais pensé** qu'il serait ravi ⇨ **3**

◆ In formal uses, ***should*** can refer to a future possibility, and the structure ***si*** + *present tense* is often used:

should *the opportunity arise*	= **si** l'occasion se présente
if *you **should** change your mind, don't hesitate to contact me*	= **si** vous changez d'avis, n'hésitez pas à me contacter
should *you be interested, I should be happy to provide further details*	= **si** vous désirez obtenir des renseignements supplémentaires, je reste à votre disposition ⇨ **4**

For translations of some idiomatic expressions using ***should***, see the entry **should**. ⇨ **5**

to ~ to a halt avoir quelques soubresauts et s'arrêter.

shuffle *vtr* **1** battre [*cards*]; **2** brasser [*papers*]; **3 to ~ one's feet** traîner les pieds.

shun *vtr* fuir [*people, publicity, temptation*]; dédaigner [*work*].

shunt I *vtr* aiguiller [*wagon, engine*] (**into** sur). II *vi* [*train*] changer de voie.

shut I *adj* fermé/-e; **her eyes were ~** elle avait les yeux fermés; **to slam the door ~** claquer la porte (pour bien la fermer); **to keep one's mouth**○ **~** se taire.
II *vtr* fermer.
III *vi* **1** [*door, book, box, mouth*] se fermer; **2** [*office, factory*] fermer.
■ **shut down**: ¶ **~ down** [*business*] fermer; [*machinery*] s'arrêter; ¶ **~ [sth] down** fermer [*business*]; arrêter [*machinery*].
■ **shut out 1** laisser [qn/qch] dehors [*animal, person*]; éliminer [*noise*]; **to be ~ out** être à la porte; **2** empêcher [qch] d'entrer [*light*].
■ **shut up**: ¶ **~ up**○ se taire (**about** au sujet de); ¶ **~ [sb] up 1**○ (silence) faire taire [*person*]; **2** (confine) enfermer [*person, animal*] (**in** dans); **3** fermer [*house*].

shutter *n* **1** (wooden, metal) volet *m*; (on shop front) store *m*; **2** (on camera) obturateur *m*.

shuttle I *n* **1** navette *f*; **2** (also **~cock**) volant *m*.
II *vtr* transporter [*passengers*].

shy I *adj* [*person*] timide (**with, of** avec); [*animal*] farouche (**with, of** avec).
II *vi* [*horse*] faire un écart (**at** devant).

Sicily *pr n* Sicile *f*.

sick *adj* **1** (ill) malade; **worried ~** malade d'inquiétude; **2** (nauseous) **to be ~** vomir; **to feel ~** avoir mal au cœur; **3** [*joke, mind*] malsain/-e; **4** (disgusted) écœuré/-e, dégoûté/-e; **5**○ **to be ~ of sb/sth** en avoir assez or marre○ de qn/qch.

sick bay *n* infirmerie *f*.

sicken I *vtr* (disgust) écœurer.
II *vi* **to be ~ing for sth** couver qch.

sick leave *n* congé *m* de maladie.

sickly *adj* **1** [*person, plant*] chétif/-ive; **2** [*smell, taste*] écœurant/-e; [*colour*] fadasse; **~ sweet** douceâtre.

sickness *n* **1** (illness) maladie *f*; **2** (nausea) nausée *f*; **bouts of ~** vomissements *mpl*.

sickpay *n* indemnité *f* de maladie.

sickroom *n* infirmerie *f*.

side I *n* **1** (gen) côté *m*; (of animal's body, hill) flanc *m*; (of lake, road) bord *m*; **on one's/its ~** sur le côté; **~ by ~** côte à côte; **at** or **by the ~ of** au bord de [*lake, road*]; à côté de [*building*]; **2 to take ~s** prendre position; **to change ~s** changer de camp; **3** (Sport) (team) équipe *f*.
II *adj* [*door, window, entrance, view*] latéral/-e.
III **on the side** *phr* **with salad on the ~** avec de la salade; **to work on the ~** (in addition) travailler à côté; (illegally) travailler au noir.
■ **side with** se mettre du côté de [*person*].

sideboard *n* buffet *m*.

sideboards (GB), **sideburns** *n pl* pattes *fpl*.

side effect *n* (of drug) effet *m* secondaire; (of action) répercussion *f*.

sideline *n* **1 as a ~** comme à-côté; **2** (Sport) ligne *f* de touche; **on the ~s** sur la touche.

sidelong *adj* [*look*] oblique.

side plate *n* petite assiette *f*.

side saddle *adv* en amazone.

side show *n* attraction *f*.

sidestep *vtr* éviter [*opponent*]; éluder [*issue*].

side street *n* petite rue *f*.

side stroke *n* brasse *f* indienne.

sidetrack *vtr* fourvoyer [*person*]; **to get ~ed** se fourvoyer.

sidewalk *n* (US) trottoir *m*.

sideways I *adj* [*look, glance*] de travers.
II *adv* [*move*] latéralement; [*look at*] de travers.

siding *n* voie *f* de garage.

siege *n* siège *m*; **to lay ~ to sth** assiéger qch.

siesta *n* sieste *f*; **to have a ~** faire la sieste.

sieve I *n* (for draining) passoire *f*; (for sifting) tamis *m*.
II *vtr* tamiser [*flour*].

sift *vtr* **1** tamiser, passer [qch] au tamis [*flour*]; **2** passer [qch] au crible [*information*].
■ **sift through** trier [*applications*]; fouiller (dans) [*ashes*].

sigh I *n* soupir *m*.
II *vi* soupirer, pousser un soupir; **to ~ with relief** pousser un soupir de soulagement.

sight I *n* **1** vue *f*; **at first ~** à première vue; **to catch ~ of sb/sth** apercevoir qn/qch; **to lose ~ of sb/sth** perdre qn/qch de vue; **I can't stand the ~ of him!** je ne peux pas le voir○ (en peinture)!; **to be in ~** [*land, border*] être en vue; [*peace, freedom*] être proche; **to be out of ~** être caché/-e; **don't let her out of your ~!** ne la quitte pas des yeux!; **2** (scene) spectacle *m*; **it was not a pretty ~!** ce n'était pas beau à voir!
II **sights** *n pl* **1** attractions *fpl* touristiques (**of** de); **to see the ~s** faire du tourisme; **2** (on rifle, telescope) viseur *m*; **3 to set one's ~s on sth** viser qch.

sightseeing *n* tourisme *m*; **to go ~** faire du tourisme.

sightseer *n* touriste *mf*.

sign I *n* **1** (gen) signe *m*; **the pound ~** le symbole de la livre sterling; **2** (road sign) panneau *m* (**for** pour); (smaller) pancarte *f*; (outside shop) enseigne *f*.
II *vtr*, *vi* signer.
■ **sign on 1** (GB) (for benefit) pointer au chômage; **2** (for course) s'inscrire (**for** à, dans).
■ **sign up 1** (in forces) s'engager; **2** (for course) s'inscrire (**for** à, dans).

signal I *n* signal *m* (**for** de).
II *vtr* **to ~ (to sb) that** faire signe (à qn) que.
III *vi* **1** (gesture) faire des signes; **2** (in car) mettre son clignotant.

signature *n* signature *f*.

significance *n* **1** (importance) importance *f*; **2** (meaning) signification *f*.

significant *adj* [*amount, impact*] considérable; [*event, role*] important/-e; [*name*] significatif/-ive.
signify *vtr* indiquer.
sign language *n* code *m* or langage *m* gestuel.
signpost *n* panneau *m* indicateur.
silence I *n* silence *m*; **in ~** en silence.
II *vtr* faire taire.
silencer *n* silencieux *m*.
silent *adj* **1** silencieux/-ieuse; **to be ~** se taire; **2** [*disapproval, prayer*] muet/muette; **3** [*film*] muet/muette.
silhouette *n* silhouette *f*.
silicon chip *n* puce *f* électronique.
silk *n* soie *f*.
silky *adj* soyeux/-euse.
silly I *adj* [*person*] idiot/-e; [*question, game*] stupide; [*behaviour, clothes*] ridicule.
II *adv* **to drink oneself ~** s'abrutir d'alcool; **to bore sb ~** assommer qn.
silo *n* silo *m*.
silt *n* limon *m*, vase *f*.
silver ▶ **438** I *n* **1** (metal, colour) argent *m*; **2** (silverware) argenterie *f*; **3** (medal) médaille *f* d'argent.
II *adj* [*ring, coin*] en argent.
silver birch *n* bouleau *m* argenté.
silver foil *n* (GB) papier *m* d'aluminium.
silverware *n* argenterie *f*.
similar *adj* similaire, analogue; **~ to** analogue à, comparable à.
similarity *n* ressemblance *f* (**to, with** avec).
similarly *adv* de la même façon.
simmer *vi* **1** [*soup*] cuire à feu doux, mijoter; [*water*] frémir; **2** [*person*] bouillonner (**with** de); [*revolt, violence*] couver.
simple *adj* **1** (gen) simple; [*dress, style*] sobre; **2** (dimwitted) simplet/-ette○, simple d'esprit.
simplicity *n* simplicité *f*.
simplify *vtr* simplifier.
simplistic *adj* simpliste.
simultaneous *adj* simultané/-e.
sin I *n* péché *m*, crime *m*.
II *vi* pécher (**against** contre).
since I *prep* depuis; **I haven't seen him ~ then** je ne l'ai pas vu depuis; **I haven't been feeling well ~ Monday** je ne me sens pas bien depuis lundi.
II *conj* **1** (from the time when) depuis que; **~ he's been away** depuis qu' il est absent; **ever ~ I married him** depuis que nous nous sommes mariés, depuis notre mariage; **I've known him ~ I was 12** je le connais depuis que j'ai 12 ans or depuis l'âge de 12 ans; **it's 10 years ~ we last met** cela fait 10 ans que nous ne nous sommes pas revus; **2** (because) comme; **~ you're so clever, do it yourself!** puisque tu es tellement malin, fais-le toi-même!
III *adv* **she has ~ qualified** depuis elle a obtenu son diplôme; **I haven't phoned her ~** je ne lui ai pas téléphoné depuis.
sincere *adj* sincère.
sincerely *adv* sincèrement; **Yours ~, Sincerely yours** (US) Veuillez agréer Monsieur/Madame, l'expression de mes sentiments les meilleurs.
sincerity *n* sincérité *f*.
sinew *n* tendon *m*.
sing I *vtr* chanter; **to ~ sb's praises** chanter les louanges de qn.
II *vi* chanter.
Singapore ▶ **448** *pr n* Singapour *f*.
singe *vtr* brûler [qch] légèrement [*hair, clothing*]; (with iron) roussir [*clothes*].
singer ▶ **626** *n* chanteur/-euse *m/f*.
singing *n* chant *m*.
single I *n* **1** (also **~ ticket**) aller *m* simple; **2** (also **~ room**) chambre *f* pour une personne; **3** (record) 45 tours *m*.
II *adj* **1** (sole) seul/-e (*before n*); **2** (for one) [*sheet, bed, person*] pour une personne; **3** (unmarried) célibataire; **4 every ~ day** tous les jours sans exception; **every ~ one of those people** chacune de ces personnes.
■ **single out** choisir [*person*].
single cream *n* ≈ crème *f* fraîche liquide.
single file *adv* en file indienne.
single-handed(ly) *adv* tout seul/toute seule.
single market *n* marché *m* unique.
single-minded *adj* tenace, résolu/-e.
single mother *n* mère *f* qui élève ses enfants seule.
single-parent *adj* [*family*] monoparental/-e.
singles *n pl* (Sport) **the women's/men's ~** le simple dames/messieurs.
singlet *n* (GB) **1** (Sport) maillot *m*; **2** (vest) maillot *m* de corps.
singular I *n* singulier *m*.
II *adj* singulier/-ière.
sinister *adj* sinistre.
sink I *n* (in kitchen) évier *m*; (in bathroom) lavabo *m*.
II *vtr* **1** couler [*ship*]; **2** forer [*oil well, shaft*] creuser [*foundations*]; enfoncer [*post, pillar*] (**into** dans); **the dog sank its teeth into my arm** le chien a planté ses crocs dans mon bras.
III *vi* **1** [*ship, object, person*] couler; **2** [*sun*] baisser; [*cake*] redescendre; **to ~ to the floor** s'effondrer; **to ~ into a chair** s'affaler dans un fauteuil; **to ~ into a deep sleep** sombrer dans un profond sommeil; **3** [*building, wall*] s'effondrer; **to ~ into** s'enfoncer dans [*mud*] sombrer dans [*anarchy, obscurity*].
■ **sink in** [*news*] faire son chemin.
sinus *n* sinus *m inv*.
sip I *n* petite gorgée *f*.
II *vtr* boire [qch] à petites gorgées.
siphon I *n* siphon *m*.
II *vtr* (also **~ off**) siphonner [*petrol, water*].
sir ▶ **498** *n* **1** Monsieur; **Dear Sir** Monsieur **2** (GB) (in titles) **Sir James** Sir James.
siren *n* sirène *f*.
sirloin *n* aloyau *m*.
sister *n* **1** (gen) sœur *f*; **2** (GB) (nurse) infirmière *f* chef.
sister-in-law *n* belle-sœur *f*.

since

As a preposition

◆ *since* is used in English to indicate the point when an event that is still going on started. To express this, French uses *present* + ***depuis***:

*I've been waiting **since** Saturday*	= j'attends **depuis** samedi
*I've lived in Rome **since** 1988*	= je vis à Rome **depuis** 1988
*he's been in France **since** March*	= il est en France **depuis** le mois de mars

◆ When ***since*** places the event further back in the past, French uses *imperfect* + ***depuis***:

*I had been waiting **since** 9 o'clock*	= j'attendais **depuis** 9 heures
*she had been a teacher **since** 1965*	= elle était professeur **depuis** 1965
*they had been living there **since** 1960*	= ils habitaient là **depuis** 1960

◆ In negative sentences, ***since*** is again translated by ***depuis***, but the tenses used are generally the same in both languages:

*I haven't seen him **since** Monday*	= je ne l'ai pas vu **depuis** lundi
*we haven't heard from them **since** June*	= nous n'avons pas eu de leurs nouvelles depuis le mois de juin
*I hadn't seen him **since** 1978*	= je ne l'avais pas vu **depuis** 1978
*he hadn't been back to Poland **since** the end of the war*	= il n'était pas retourné en Pologne **depuis** la fin de la guerre ⇨ **I**

As a conjunction

◆ When ***since*** is used as a conjunction in time expressions, it is usually translated by ***depuis que*** and the tenses used are the same as those used with the preposition ***depuis***:

***since** she's been living in Oxford*	= **depuis qu**'elle habite à Oxford
***since** I'd been in Paris*	= **depuis que** j'étais à Paris
***since** we've been working here*	= **depuis que** nous travaillons ici ⇨ **II 1**

◆ Note that in time expressions with ***since***, where English uses a verb (*arrive* = arriver; *leave* = partir; *die* = mourir etc), French native speakers will generally prefer to use the corresponding noun (*arrival* = arrivée; *departure* = départ; *death* = mort etc):

*I haven't seen him **since he left***	= je ne l'ai pas vu **depuis son départ**
*she's been living in Nice **since she got married***	= elle habite à Nice **depuis son mariage**
*we've known each other **since we were 12 years old***	= nous nous connaissons **depuis l'âge de 12 ans**

◆ When ***since*** is used as a conjunction to mean *because* it is translated by ***comme***:

***since** it was raining, we stayed at home*	= **comme** il pleuvait, nous sommes restés à la maison
***since** I haven't got her address, I can't write to her*	= **comme** je n'ai pas son adresse, je ne peux pas lui écrire ⇨ **II 2**

As an adverb

◆ When ***since*** is used as an adverb, it is translated by ***depuis***:

*he hasn't been seen **since***	= on ne l'a pas vu **depuis**
*we've kept in touch ever **since***	= nous sommes restés en contact **depuis** ⇨ **III**

sit I *vtr* (GB) se présenter à, passer [*exam*].
II *vi* **1** s'asseoir (**at** à; **in** dans; **on** sur); **to be sitting** être assis/-e; **to ~ still** se tenir tranquille; **2** [*committee, court*] siéger; **3 to ~ on** faire partie de [*committee, jury*]; **4** [*hen*] **to ~ on** couver [*eggs*].
■ **sit about**, **sit around** rester assis à ne rien faire.
■ **sit down** s'asseoir (**at** à; **in** dans; **on** sur).
■ **sit in** [*observer*] assister (**on** à).
■ **sit up** se redresser; **to be ~ing up** être assis/-e; **~ up straight!** tiens-toi droit!

sitcom○ *n* sitcom *m*.

site *n* **1** (also **building ~**) (before building) terrain *m*; (during building) chantier *m*; **2** (for tent) emplacement *m*; **caravan ~** (GB) terrain *m* de caravaning; **3** (archaeological) site *m*.

sitting *n* **1** (session) séance *f*; **2** (in canteen) service *m*.

sitting room *n* salon *m*.

sitting target *n* cible *f* facile.

situate *vtr* situer; **to be ~d** être situé/-e, se trouver.

situation *n* situation *f*.

sit-ups *n pl* abdominaux *mpl*.

six ▶389, 434 *n, pron, det* six (*m*) *inv*.

sixteen ▶389, 434 *n, pron, det* seize (*m*) *inv*.

sixteenth ▶456, 498 I *n* **1** (in order) seizième *mf*; **2** (of month) seize *m inv*; **3** (fraction) seizième *m*.
II *adj, adv* seizième.

sixth ▶456, 498 I *n* **1** (in order) sixième *mf*; **2** (of month) six *m inv*; **3** (fraction) sixième *m*.
II *adj, adv* sixième.

sixth form (GB Sch) *n* (lower) ≈ classes *fpl* de première; (upper) ≈ classes *fpl* de terminale.

sixth sense *n* sixième sens *m*.

sixties ▶389, 456 *n pl* **1 the ~** les années *fpl* soixante; **2 to be in one's ~** avoir entre soixante et soixante-dix ans.

sixtieth *n, adj, adv* soixantième (*mf*).

sixty ▶389 *n, pron, det* soixante (*m*) *inv*.

size *n* (of person, paper, clothes) taille *f*; (of container, room, building, region) grandeur *f*; (of apple, egg, book, parcel) grosseur *f*; (of carpet, bed, machine) dimensions *fpl*; (of population, audience) importance *f*; (of class, company) effectif *m*; (of shoes, gloves) pointure *f*.
IDIOMS **to cut sb down to ~** remettre qn à sa place, rabattre le caquet à qn○.
■ **size up** se faire une opinion de [*person*]; évaluer [*situation*]; mesurer [*problem*].

sizeable *adj* [*amount*] assez important/-e; [*house, field, town*] assez grand/-e.

sizzle *vi* grésiller.

skate I *n* **1** (ice) patin *m* à glace; (roller) patin *m* à roulettes; **2** (fish) raie *f*.
II *vi* patiner (**on, along** sur).

skateboard *n* skateboard *m*, planche *f* à roulettes.

skater *n* patineur/-euse *m/f*.

skating ▶504 *n* patinage *m*.

skating rink *n* (ice) patinoire *f*; (roller-skating) piste *f* de patins à roulettes.

skeleton *n* squelette *m*.

skeleton key *n* passe-partout *m inv*.

skeptic (US) = **sceptic**.

skeptical (US) = **sceptical**.

skepticism (US) = **scepticism**.

sketch I *n* **1** (drawing, draft) esquisse *f*; (hasty outline) croquis *m*; **rough ~** ébauche *f*; **2** (comic scene) sketch *m*.
II *vtr* faire une esquisse de; (hastily) faire un croquis de.

sketchbook *n* carnet *m* à croquis.

sketchpad *n* bloc *m* à dessin.

skewer I *n* (for kebab) brochette *f*; (for joint) broche *f*.
II *vtr* embrocher.

ski I *n* ski *m*.
II *vi* faire du ski; **to ~ down a slope** descendre une pente à skis.

skid I *n* dérapage *m*.
II *vi* déraper (**on** sur).

skier *n* skieur/-ieuse *m/f*.

skiing ▶504 *n* ski *m*; **to go ~** faire du ski.

skilful (GB), **skillful** (US) *adj* habile, adroit/-e.

ski lift *n* remontée *f* mécanique.

skill I *n* **1** (intellectual) habileté *f*, adresse *f*; (physical) dextérité *f*; **2** (special ability) (acquired) compétence *f*, capacités *fpl*; (practical) technique *f*.
II **skills** *n pl* (training) connaissances *fpl*.

skilled *adj* **1** (trained) [*labour, work*] qualifié/-e **2** (talented) consommé/-e.

skim I *vtr* **1** (remove cream) écrémer; (remove scum) écumer; **2** [*plane, bird*] raser, frôler [*surface, treetops*]; **3 to ~ stones** faire des ricochets avec des cailloux.
II *vi* **to ~ through** parcourir [*book, article*] **to ~ over** passer rapidement sur [*event, facts*].

skim(med) milk *n* lait *m* écrémé.

skimp *vi* **to ~ on** lésiner sur.

skimpy *adj* [*garment*] minuscule; [*portion allowance, income*] maigre (*before n*).

skin I *n* peau *f*; (of onion) pelure *f*.
II *vtr* **1** dépecer [*animal*]; **2 to ~ one's knee** s'écorcher le genou.
IDIOMS **to have a thick ~** être insensible; **to be** or **get soaked to the ~** être trempé/-e jusqu'aux os○; **by the ~ of one's teeth** de justesse.

skin diving ▶504 *n* plongée *f* sous-marine.

skinny○ *adj* maigre.

skintight *adj* moulant/-e.

skip I *n* **1** (jump) petit bond *m*; **2** (GB) (container) benne *f*.
II *vtr* sauter [*page, lunch, school*].
III *vi* **1** (once) bondir; (several times) sautiller **2** (with rope) sauter à la corde.

ski pants *n* fuseau *m* (de ski).

skipper *n* (of ship) capitaine *m*; (of fishing boat) patron *m*; (of yacht) skipper *m*.

skipping rope *n* corde *f* à sauter.

skirt I *n* jupe *f*.
II *vtr* **1** contourner [*wood, village, city*]; **2** esquiver [*problem*].

skirting board *n* plinthe *f*.

ski slope *n* piste *f*.

skittle ▶504 I *n* quille *f*.
II **skittles** *n pl* (jeu *m* de) quilles *fpl*.

skulk *vi* rôder; **to ~ out/off** sortir/s'éloigner furtivement.

skull *n* crâne *m*.

skunk *n* moufette *f*.

sky *n* ciel *m*.

skylight *n* fenêtre *f* à tabatière.

skyscraper *n* gratte-ciel *m inv*.

slab *n* (of stone, wood, concrete) dalle *f*; (of meat, cheese, cake) pavé *m*; (of chocolate) tablette *f*.

slack I *n* (in rope, cable) mou *m*.
II *adj* **1** [*worker*] peu consciencieux/-ieuse; [*work*] peu soigné/-e; **2** [*period*] creux/creuse (*after n*); [*demand, sales*] faible; **3** [*cable, rope, body*] détendu/-e.
III *vi* [*worker*] se relâcher dans son travail.

slacken I *vtr* **1** donner du mou à [*rope*]; lâcher [*reins*]; **2** réduire [*pace*].
II *vi* **1** [*rope*] se relâcher; **2** [*activity, pace, speed, business*] ralentir.

slalom ▶504 *n* slalom *m*.

slam I *vtr* [*person*] claquer [*door*]; [*wind*] faire claquer [*door*]; **to ~ the door in sb's face** claquer la porte au nez de qn; **to ~ the ball into the net** renvoyer brutalement la balle dans le filet.
II *vi* [*door*] claquer (**against** contre); **to ~ shut** se refermer en claquant.

slander *n* (gen) calomnie *f* (**on** sur); (Law) diffamation *f* orale.

slang *n* argot *m*.

slant I *n* **1** (perspective) point *m* de vue (**on** sur); **2** (bias) tendance *f*; **3** (slope) pente *f*.
II *vi* [*floor, ground*] être en pente; [*handwriting*] pencher (**to** vers).

slanting *adj* [*roof*] en pente; **~ eyes** yeux *mpl* bridés.

slap I *n* tape *f* (**on** sur); (stronger) claque *f* (**on** sur); **a ~ in the face** une gifle.
II *vtr* donner une tape à [*person, animal*]; **to ~ sb in the face** gifler qn.

slap bang○ *adv* **he ran ~ into the wall** il s'est cogné en plein dans le mur en courant; **~ in the middle (of)** au beau milieu (de).

slapdash○ *adj* [*person*] brouillon/-onne○; **in a ~ way** à la va-vite.

slash I *n* **1** (wound) balafre *f* (**on** à); **2** (in fabric, seat, tyre) lacération *f*; (in painting) entaille *f*; (in skirt) fente *f*; **3** (in printing) barre *f* oblique.
II *vtr* **1** balafrer [*cheek*]; faire une balafre à [*person*]; couper [*throat*]; [*knife*] entailler [*face*]; **to ~ one's wrists** se tailler les veines; **2** taillader [*painting, fabric, tyres*]; trancher [*cord*]; **3** (reduce) réduire [qch] (considérablement) [*amount, spending*]; sacrifier [*prices*].

slat *n* (of shutter, blind) lamelle *f*; (of bench, bed) lame *f*.

slate I *n* ardoise *f*.
II *vtr* **1** couvrir [qch] d'ardoises [*roof*]; **2**○ (GB) (criticize) taper sur○ (**for** pour).
IDIOMS **to wipe the ~ clean** faire table rase.

slaughter I *n* **1** (in butchery) abattage *m*; **2** (massacre) massacre *m*, boucherie○ *f*.
II *vtr* **1** abattre [*animal*]; **2** massacrer [*people*]; **3**○ (defeat) écraser.

slaughterhouse *n* abattoir *m*.

Slav I *n* Slave *mf*.
II *adj* slave.

slave I *n* esclave *mf*.
II *vi* (also **~ away**) travailler comme un forçat, trimer○.

slaver *vi* [*person, animal*] baver.

slavery *n* esclavage *m*.

slaw (US) = **coleslaw**.

slay *vtr* faire périr [*enemy*]; pourfendre [*dragon*].

sleazy○ *adj* [*club, area, character*] louche; [*story, aspect*] scabreux/-euse; [*café, hotel*] borgne.

sled, sledge (GB) I *n* luge *f*; (sleigh) traîneau *m*.
II *vi* faire de la luge.

sledgehammer *n* masse *f*.

sleek *adj* **1** [*hair*] lisse et brillant/-e; [*animal*] au poil lisse et brillant; **2** [*shape*] élégant/-e; [*figure*] mince et harmonieux/-ieuse.

sleep I *n* sommeil *m*; **to go to ~** s'endormir; **to go back to ~** se rendormir; **to send** or **put sb to ~** endormir qn; **to have a ~** dormir; **my leg has gone to ~**○ j'ai la jambe engourdie; **to put an animal to ~** faire piquer un animal.
II *vi* dormir; **to ~ at a friend's house** coucher chez un ami.
IDIOMS **to ~ like a log** or **top** dormir comme une souche or un loir.
■ **sleep in 1** (US) (lie in) faire la grasse matinée; **2** (live in) être logé/-e sur place.
■ **sleep on**: **to ~ on a decision** attendre le lendemain pour prendre une décision.

sleeping bag *n* sac *m* de couchage.

sleeping car *n* voiture-lit *f*, wagon-lit *m*.

sleeping pill *n* somnifère *m*.

sleepwalk *vi* marcher en dormant, être somnambule.

sleepy *adj* [*voice, village*] endormi/-e, somnolent/-e; **to feel** or **be ~** avoir envie de dormir, avoir sommeil; **to make sb ~** [*fresh air*] donner envie de dormir à qn; [*wine*] endormir qn, assoupir qn.

sleet *n* neige *f* fondue.

sleeve *n* **1** (of garment) manche *f*; **2** (of record) pochette *f*; **3** (Tech) (inner) chemise *f*; (outer) gaine *f*.
IDIOMS **to have something up one's ~** avoir quelque chose en réserve.

sleeveless *adj* sans manches.

sleigh *n* traîneau *m*.

sleight of hand *n* **1** (dexterity) dextérité *f*; **2** (trick) tour *m* de passe-passe.

slender *adj* **1** [*person*] mince; [*waist*] fin/-e; **2** [*income, means*] modeste, maigre (*before n*).

sleuth *n* limier *m*, détective *m*.

slew *vi* [*vehicle*] déraper; [*mast*] pivoter.

slice I *n* **1** (of bread, meat) tranche *f*; (of cheese)

morceau *m*; (of pie, tart) part *m*; (of lemon, cucumber, sausage) rondelle *f*; **2** (of profits) part *f*; (of territory, population) partie *f*; **3** (utensil) spatule *f*.
II *vtr* **1** couper [qch] (en tranches) [*loaf, roast*]; couper [qch] en rondelles [*lemon, cucumber*]; **2** fendre [*air*]; **3** (Sport) slicer, couper [*ball*].
III *vi* **to ~ through** fendre [*water, air*]; trancher [*timber, rope, meat*].

sliced bread *n* pain *m* en tranches.

slick I *n* (also **oil ~**) (on water) nappe *f* de pétrole; (on shore) marée *f* noire.
II *adj* **1** [*production*] habile; [*operation*] mené/-e rondement; **2** (superficial) qui a un éclat plutôt superficiel; **3** [*person*] roublard/-e○; [*answer*] astucieux/-ieuse; [*excuse*] facile; **4** (US) (slippery) [*road, surface*] glissant/-e; [*hair*] lissé/-e.

slide I *n* **1** (in playground) toboggan *m*; **2** (photographic) diapositive *f*; **3** (microscope plate) lame *f* porte-objet; **4** (GB) (also **hair ~**) barrette *f*; **5** (decline) baisse *f* (**in** de).
II *vtr* faire glisser.
III *vi* **1** [*car, person*] glisser, partir en glissade (**into** dans; **on** sur); **to ~ in and out** [*drawer*] coulisser; **2** [*prices, shares*] baisser.

slide rule (GB), **slide ruler** (US) *n* règle *f* à calcul.

sliding *adj* [*door*] coulissant/-e; [*roof*] ouvrant/-e.

sliding scale *n* échelle *f* mobile.

slight I *n* affront *m* (**on** à; **from** de la part de).
II *adj* **1** (gen) léger/-ère (*before n*); [*risk, danger*] faible (*before n*); [*pause, hesitation*] petit (*before n*); **not to have the ~est difficulty** ne pas avoir la moindre difficulté; **2** (in build) mince.
III *vtr* **1** (offend) humilier [*person*]; **2** (US) (underestimate) sous-estimer.

slightly *adv* [*fall, change*] légèrement; [*different, more, less*] un peu.

slim I *adj* [*person, figure*] mince; [*ankle, leg*] fin/-e, mince; [*watch, calculator*] plat/-e.
II *vi* (GB) maigrir; **I'm ~ming** je fais un régime amaigrissant.

slime *n* dépôt *m* gluant or visqueux; (of slug, snail) bave *f*.

sling I *n* **1** (Med) écharpe *f*; **2** (for carrying baby) porte-bébé *m*; (for carrying load) élingue *f*.
II *vtr* lancer [*object, insult*] (**at** à).

slip I *n* **1** (error) erreur *f*; **~ of the tongue** lapsus *m*; **2** (receipt) reçu *m*; (for salary) bulletin *m*; **~ of paper** bout *m* de papier; **3** (stumble) faux pas *m*; **4** (petticoat) (full) combinaison *f*; (half) jupon *m*.
II *vtr* **1** (gen) glisser (**into** dans); **she ~ped the shirt over her head** (put on) elle a enfilé sa chemise; (take off) elle a retiré sa chemise; **2** [*dog*] se dégager de [*leash*]; [*boat*] filer [*moorings*]; **it had ~ped my mind (that)** j'avais complètement oublié (que); **to let ~ a remark** laisser échapper une remarque; **3** (Med) **to ~ a disc** se déplacer une vertèbre.
III *vi* **1 to ~ into** passer [*dress, costume*]; tomber dans [*coma*]; **2 to ~ into/out of** se glisser dans/hors de [*room, building*]; **3** [*person, vehicle*] glisser (**on** sur; **off** de); [*knife, razor, pen*] glisser, déraper; **to ~ through sb's fingers** [*money, opportunity*] filer entre les doigts de qn; **4** (Aut) [*clutch*] patiner.

slipknot *n* nœud *m* coulant.

slip-on (shoe) *n* mocassin *m*.

slipped disc *n* hernie *f* discale.

slipper *n* pantoufle *f*.

slippery *adj* glissant/-e.

slip road *n* bretelle *f* d'accès.

slipshod *adj* [*person*] négligent/-e; [*appearance, work*] négligé/-e, peu soigné/-e.

slip-up○ *n* bourde○ *f*.

slit I *n* fente *f* (**in** dans).
II *adj* [*eyes*] bridé/-e; [*skirt*] fendu/-e.
III *vtr* (on purpose) faire une fente dans; (by accident) déchirer; **to ~ sb's throat** égorger qn; **to ~ one's wrists** s'ouvrir les veines.

slither *vi* glisser.

sliver *n* (of glass) éclat *m*; (of food) mince tranche *f*.

slog○ *vi* (also **~ away**) travailler dur, bosser○.

slop I *vtr* renverser [*liquid*].
II *vi* (also **~ over**) [*liquid*] déborder.

slope I *n* pente *f*.
II *vi* être en pente (**towards** vers); [*writing*] pencher (**to** vers).

sloppy *adj* **1**○ [*appearance*] débraillé/-e; [*work*] peu soigné/-e; **2**○ (over-emotional) sentimental/-e.

slot I *n* **1** (for coin, ticket) fente *f*; (for letters) ouverture *f*; (groove) rainure *f*; **2** (in timetable, schedule) créneau *m*.
II *vtr* **to ~ sth into a machine** insérer qch dans une machine.
III *vi* **to ~ into sth** [*coin, piece*] s'insérer dans; **to ~ into place** or **position** s'encastrer.

sloth *n* (Zool) paresseux *m*.

slot machine *n* (Games) machine *f* à sous; (vending machine) distributeur *m* automatique.

slouch *vi* être avachi/-e.

Slovakia ▶ 448 *pr n* Slovaquie *f*.

Slovenia ▶ 448 *pr n* Slovénie *f*.

slovenly *adj* négligé/-e.

slow I *adj* **1** (gen) lent/-e; ; **2** [*business, market*] stagnant/-e; **3** (dull-witted) lent/-e (d'esprit); **4 to be ~** [*clock, watch*] retarder; **to be 10 minutes ~** retarder de 10 minutes.
II *adv* lentement.
III *vtr, vi* (also **~ down**) ralentir.

slowly *adv* lentement.

slow motion *n* ralenti *m*; **in ~** au ralenti.

sludge *n* **1** (also **sewage ~**) eaux *fpl* usées; **2** (mud) vase *f*.

slug *n* limace *f*.

sluggish *adj* **1** [*person, animal*] léthargique; [*circulation*] lent/-e; **2** [*market, trade*] qui stagne.

sluice *n* **1** (also **~ gate**) vanne *f*; **2** (also **~way**) canal *m*.

slum *n* **1** (area) quartier *m* pauvre; **2** (dwelling) taudis *m*.

slumber I *n* sommeil *m*.
II *vi* sommeiller.

slump I *n* (in trade, prices) effondrement *m* (**in** de).
II *vi* **1** [*demand, trade, price*] chuter (**from** de; **to** à; **by** de); [*economy, market*] s'effondrer; [*popularity*] être en forte baisse; **2** [*person, body*] s'affaler○.

slur I *n* **1** (in speech) marmonnement *m*; **2** (Mus) liaison *f*; **3** (aspersion) calomnie *f*.
II *vi* avoir du mal à articuler.

slush *n* neige *f* fondue.

sly *adj* [*person, animal*] rusé/-e; [*remark, smile*] entendu/-e.
IDIOMS **on the ~** en douce○, en cachette.

smack I *n* claque *f*; (on face) gifle *f*.
II *vtr* (on face) gifler [*person*]; taper [*object*] (**on** sur; **against** contre); **she ~ed him on the bottom** elle lui a donné une tape sur les fesses.
III *vi* **to ~ of** sentir.

small I *n* **the ~ of the back** le creux du dos.
II *adj* **1** (gen) petit/-e (*before n*); [*quantity, amount*] faible (*before n*); **2 to feel ~** être dans ses petits souliers○; **to make sb feel** or **look ~** humilier qn.
III *adv* [*write*] petit.

small ad *n* (GB) petite annonce *f*.

small talk *n* banalités *fpl*; **to make ~** faire la conversation.

smart I *adj* **1** (elegant) [*person, clothes*] élégant/-e; [*restaurant, hotel, street*] chic; **2** (clever) malin/-e; **3** [*blow*] vif/vive; [*rebuke*] cinglant/-e; **to walk at a ~ pace** marcher à vive allure; **4** (Comput) intelligent/-e.
II *vi* [*cut, cheeks*] brûler; **his eyes were ~ing from the smoke** la fumée lui brûlait les yeux.

smarten *v* ■ **smarten up** embellir [*room*]; **to ~ oneself up** se faire beau.

smash I *n* **1**○ (also **~-up**) (accident) collision *f*; **2**○ (also **~ hit**) tube○ *m*; **3** (in tennis) smash *m*; **4** (sound) fracas *m*.
II *vtr* **1** briser [*glass, door, car*]; (more violently) fracasser; **2** démanteler [*drugs ring, gang*]; **3** (Sport) **to ~ the ball** faire un smash.
III *vi* se briser, se fracasser.

smashing○ *adj* (GB) formidable○.

smattering *n* notions *fpl* (**of** de); **to have a ~ of Russian** avoir quelques connaissances en russe.

smear I *n* **1** (spot) tache *f*; (streak) traînée *f*; **2** (defamation) propos *m* diffamatoire; **3** (Med) (also **~ test**) frottis *m*.
II *vtr* **1** faire des taches sur [*glass, window*]; **her face was ~ed with jam** elle avait le visage barbouillé de confiture; **2** (spread) étaler [*butter, paint*]; appliquer [*lotion*] (**on** sur).
III *vi* [*ink, paint*] s'étaler; [*lipstick, make-up*] couler.

smell I *n* **1** odeur *f*; **2** (sense) odorat *m*.
II *vtr* [*person*] sentir; [*animal*] renifler, sentir; **I can ~ burning** ça sent le brûlé.
III *vi* sentir; **that ~s nice/horrible** ça sent bon/très mauvais; **to ~ of sth** sentir qch.

smelling salts *n pl* sels *mpl*.

smelly *adj* malodorant/-e, qui sent mauvais.

smile I *n* sourire *m*.
II *vi* sourire (**at sb** à qn).

smirk I *n* (self-satisfied) petit sourire *m* satisfait; (knowing) sourire *m* en coin.
II *vi* (in a self-satisfied way) avoir un petit sourire satisfait; (knowingly) avoir un sourire en coin.

smithereens *n pl* **in ~** en mille morceaux; **to smash sth to ~** faire voler qch en éclats.

smock *n* blouse *f*, sarrau *m*.

smog *n* smog *m*.

smoke I *n* fumée *f*.
II *vtr* fumer.
III *vi* fumer.

smoked *adj* fumé/e.

smoker *n* fumeur/-euse *m/f*.

smoke screen *n* (Mil) écran *m* de fumée; (figurative) diversion *f*.

smoking I *n* **~ and drinking** le tabac et l'alcool; **to give up ~** arrêter de fumer; **'no ~'** 'défense de fumer'.
II *adj* [*compartment, section*] fumeurs (*after n*).

smoky *adj* [*room*] enfumé/-e; [*cheese, bacon*] fumé/-e.

smooth I *adj* **1** [*stone, sea, surface, skin, fabric*] lisse; [*curve, breathing*] régulier/-ière; [*sauce*] homogène; [*crossing, flight*] sans heurts; [*movement*] aisé/-e; **2** [*taste, wine, whisky*] moelleux/-euse; **3** (suave) [*person*] mielleux/-euse; [*manners, appearance*] onctueux/-euse; **to be a ~ talker** être enjôleur/-euse.
II *vtr* **1** (flatten out) lisser; (get creases out) défroisser; **2** faciliter [*transition, path*].

smother *vtr* étouffer.

smoulder (GB), **smolder** (US) *vi* **1** [*cigarette, fire*] se consumer; **2** [*hatred, jealousy*] couver; **to ~ with** être consumé/-e de.

smudge I *n* trace *f*.
II *vtr* étaler [*make-up, print, ink, paint*]; faire des traces sur [*paper, paintwork*].
III *vi* [*make-up, print, ink, paint*] s'étaler.

smug *adj* suffisant/-e.

smuggle *vtr* faire du trafic de [*arms, drugs*]; faire passer [qch] en contrebande [*watches, alcohol, cigarettes*]; **to ~ sb/sth in** faire entrer qn/qch clandestinement.

smuggler *n* contrebandier/-ière *m/f*; **drug/arms ~** passeur/-euse *m/f* de drogue/d'armes.

smuggling *n* contrebande *f*; **drug/arms ~** trafic *m* de drogue/d'armes.

smutty *adj* **1** (crude) grivois/-e; **2** (dirty) [*face*] noir/-e; [*mark*] noirâtre.

snack *n* **1** (small meal) repas *m* léger; (instead of meal) casse-croûte *m inv*; **2** (crisps, peanuts) **~s** amuse-gueule *m inv*.

snag *n* **1** (hitch) inconvénient *m* (**in** de); **2** (tear) accroc *m* (**in** à).

snail *n* escargot *m*.

snake *n* serpent *m*.

snap **▶504** **I** *n* **1** (of branch) craquement *m*; (of fingers, elastic) claquement *m*; **2**○ (photograph) photo *f*; **3** (Games) ≈ bataille *f*.
II *adj* [*decision, judgment, vote*] rapide.
III *vtr* **1** faire claquer [*fingers, jaws, elastic*]; **2** (break) (faire) casser net; **3** (say crossly) dire [qch] hargneusement.

IV *vi* **1** (break) se casser; **2** (speak sharply) parler hargneusement.
■ **snap at 1** (speak sharply) parler sèchement à; **2** [*dog*] essayer de mordre.
■ **snap up** sauter sur [*bargain*].

snapshot *n* photo *f*.

snare I *n* piège *m*.
II *vtr* prendre [qn/qch] au piège.

snarl *vi* [*animal*] gronder férocement; [*person*] grogner.

snatch I *n* **1** (of conversation) bribe *f*; (of tune) quelques notes *fpl*; **2** (theft) vol *m*.
II *vtr* **1** (grab) attraper [*book, key*]; **to ~ sth from sb** arracher qch à qn; **2**° (steal) voler [*handbag*] (**from** à).

sneak *vi* **to ~ in/out** entrer/sortir furtivement; **to ~ up on sb/sth** s'approcher sans bruit de qn/qch.

sneaker *n* (US) basket *f*, (chaussure *f* de) tennis *f*.

sneaky *adj* sournois/-e.

sneer I *n* sourire *m* méprisant.
II *vi* sourire avec mépris.

sneeze I *n* éternuement *m*.
II *vi* éternuer.

snide *adj* sournois/-e.

sniff I *n* reniflement *m*.
II *vtr* [*dog*] flairer; [*person*] sentir [*food*]; inhaler [*glue, cocaine*].
III *vi* renifler.

snigger I *n* ricanement *m*.
II *vi* ricaner.

snip *vtr* découper (à petits coups de ciseaux) [*fabric, paper*]; tailler [*hedge*].
■ **snip off** couper.

sniper *n* tireur *m* embusqué.

snippet *n* (of conversation, information) bribes *f*; (of text, fabric, music) fragment *m*.

snivel *vi* pleurnicher.

snob *n* snob *mf*.

snobbery *n* snobisme *m*.

snobbish *adj* snob.

snooker ▶ **504** I *n* (game) snooker *m*.
II *vtr* **1** (Sport, figurative) coincer [*player, person*]; **2** (US) (deceive) avoir° [*person*].

snoop° I *n* fouineur/-euse *m/f*.
II *vi* fouiner, fureter.

snooze° I *n* petit somme *m*.
II *vi* sommeiller.

snore I *n* ronflement *m*.
II *vi* ronfler.

snorkel *n* tuba *m*.

snorkelling ▶ **504** *n* plongée *f* avec tuba.

snort *vi* [*person, pig*] grogner; [*horse, bull*] s'ébrouer.

snout *n* museau *m*; (of pig) groin *m*.

snow I *n* neige *f*.
II *v impers* neiger; **it's ~ing** il neige.

snowball I *n* boule *f* de neige.
II *vi* faire boule de neige.

snowdrift *n* congère *f*.

snowdrop *n* perce-neige *m inv*.

snowflake *n* flocon *m* de neige.

snowman *n* bonhomme *m* de neige.

snow plough (GB), **snow plow** (US) *n* chasse-neige *m inv*.

snow shoe *n* raquette *f*.

snub I *n* rebuffade *f*.
II *vtr* rembarrer.

snub-nosed *adj* au nez retroussé.

snuff *n* tabac *m* à priser.

snug *adj* [*bed, room*] douillet/-ette; [*coat*] chaud/-e.

snuggle *vi* se blottir.

so I *adv* **1** (to such an extent) si, tellement; **~ happy/quickly** si or tellement heureux/vite; **~ much noise/many things** tant de bruit/de choses; **2** (in such a way) **~ arranged/worded that** organisé/rédigé d'une telle façon que; **and ~ on and ~ forth** et ainsi de suite; **~ be it!** soit!; **3** (thus) ainsi; (therefore) donc; **~ that's the reason** voilà donc pourquoi; **~ you're going are you?** alors tu y vas?; **4** (true) **is that ~?** c'est vrai?; **if (that's) ~** si c'est vrai; **5** (also) aussi; **~ is she** elle aussi; **~ do I** moi aussi; **6**° (thereabouts) environ; **20 or ~** environ 20; **7** (other uses) **I think/don't think ~** je crois/ne crois pas; **I'm afraid ~** j'ai bien peur que oui or si; **~ it would appear** c'est ce qu'il semble; **~ to speak** si je puis dire; **I told you ~** je te l'avais bien dit; **~ I see** je le vois bien; **who says ~?** qui dit ça?; **only more ~** mais encore plus; **he dived and as he did ~**... il a plongé et en le faisant... **'it's broken'—'~ it is'** 'c'est cassé'—'je le vois bien!'; **~ (what)?** et alors?
II **so (that)** *phr* (in order that) pour que (+ *subjunctive*).
III **so as** *phr* pour; **~ as to attract attention** pour attirer l'attention.
IV **so much** *phr* (see also **I 1**) tellement; **she worries ~ much** elle s'inquiète tellement; **she taught me ~ much** elle m'a tant appris; **thank you ~ much** merci beaucoup.
IDIOMS **~ much the better** tant mieux; **~ ~** comme ci comme ça.

soak I *vtr* **1** [*rain*] tremper [*person, clothes*]; **2** [*person*] faire tremper [*clothes, foods*].
II *vi* **1** [*clothes, foods*] tremper; **2** [*liquid*] **to ~ into** être absorbé/-e par; **to ~ through** traverser.

soaked *adj* trempé/-e; **to be ~ through** or **~ to the skin** être trempé/-e jusqu'aux os.

soap *n* savon *m*; **a bar of ~** un savon.

soap opera *n* feuilleton *m*.

soap powder *n* lessive *f* (en poudre).

soar *vi* **1** [*ball*] filer; [*bird, plane*] prendre son essor; ; **2** (glide) planer; **3** [*price, temperature, costs*] monter en flèche; [*hopes*] grandir considérablement; **4** [*tower, cliffs*] se dresser.

sob I *n* sanglot *m*.
II *vi* sangloter.

sober I *adj* **1 I'm ~** (not drunk) je n'ai pas bu d'alcool; (in protest) je ne suis pas ivre; **2** (no longer drunk) dessoûlé/-e; **3** (serious) [*person*] sérieux/-ieuse; [*mood*] grave; **4** [*colour, suit*] sobre.
II *vtr* [*news, reprimand*] calmer.

■ **sober up** dessoûler.

soccer ▶504| *n* football *m*.

sociable *adj* [*person*] sociable; [*evening*] agréable.

social *adj* **1** (gen) social/-e; **2** [*call, visit*] amical/-e.

socialism *n* socialisme *m*.

socialist *n, adj* (also **Socialist**) socialiste (*mf*).

socialite *n* mondain/-e *m/f*.

socialize *vi* rencontrer des gens; **to ~ with sb** fréquenter qn.

social life *n* (of person) vie *f* sociale; (of town) vie *f* culturelle.

social security *n* aide *f* sociale; **to be on ~** recevoir l'aide sociale.

Social Services *n pl* (GB) services *mpl* sociaux.

social worker ▶626| *n* travailleur/-euse *m/f* social/-e.

society *n* **1** (gen) société *f*; **2** (club) société *f*; (for social contact) association *f*; **3** (also **high ~**) haute société *f*.

sociology *n* sociologie *f*.

sock *n* chaussette *f*.

socket *n* **1** (for plug) prise *f* (de courant); (for bulb) douille *f*; **2** (of joint) cavité *f* articulaire; (of eye) orbite *f*.

soda *n* **1** (chemical) soude *f*; **2** (also **washing ~**) soude *f* ménagère; **3** (also **~ water**) eau *f* de seltz; **whisky and ~** whisky *m* soda; **4** (also **~ pop**) (US) soda *m*.

sofa *n* canapé *m*.

sofa bed *n* canapé-lit *m*.

soft *adj* **1** (gen) doux/douce; [*ground*] meuble; [*bed, cushion*] moelleux/-euse; [*brush, hair*] souple; [*dough, butter*] mou/molle; [*impact, touch*] léger/-ère; [*eyes, heart*] tendre; [*fold*] souple; **2** (lenient) [*parent, teacher*] (trop) indulgent/-e.

soft drink *n* boisson *f* non alcoolisée.

soften **I** *vtr* **1** adoucir [*skin, water, light, outline*]; ramollir [*butter*]; **2** atténuer [*blow, shock, pain*].

II *vi* **1** [*light, outline, music, colour*] s'adoucir; [*skin*] devenir plus doux; [*substance*] se ramollir; **2** [*person*] s'assouplir (**towards sb** vis-à-vis de qn).

■ **soften up**: ¶ **~ up** amollir; ¶ **~ [sb] up** affaiblir [*enemy, opponent*]; attendrir [*customer*].

softly *adv* [*speak, touch, blow*] doucement; [*fall*] en douceur.

soft spot○ *n* **to have a ~ for sb** avoir un faible○ pour qn.

soft-top *n* décapotable *f*.

soft touch○ *n* poire○ *f*.

soft toy *n* peluche *f*.

software *n* logiciel *m*.

soggy *adj* [*ground*] détrempé/-e; [*food*] ramolli/-e.

soil **I** *n* sol *m*, terre *f*.

II *vtr* salir.

soiled *adj* **1** (dirty) sali/-e; **2** (also **shop-~**) vendu/-e avec défaut.

solace **I** *n* (feeling of comfort) consolation *f*; (source of comfort) réconfort *m*.

II *vtr* consoler (**for** de).

solar *adj* solaire.

solder *vtr, vi* souder (**onto, to** à).

soldier ▶626| *n* soldat *m*.

sole **I** *n* **1** (fish) sole *f*; **2** (of foot) plante *f*; (of shoe, sock) semelle *f*.

II *adj* **1** (single) seul/-e (*before n*), unique (*before n*); **2** [*agent, right*] exclusif/-ive; [*trader*] indépendant.

solemn *adj* [*occasion, person, voice*] solennel/-elle; [*duty, warning*] formel/-elle.

solicit **I** *vtr* solliciter [*information, help, money, votes*]; rechercher [*business, investment, orders*].

II *vi* [*prostitute*] racoler.

solicitor ▶626| *n* (GB) (for documents, oaths) ≈ notaire *m*; (for court and police work) ≈ avocat/-e *m/f*.

solid **I** *n* solide *m*.

II *adj* **1** (gen) solide; **to go** or **become ~** se solidifier; **2** [*gold, marble*] massif/-ive; **the gate was made of ~ steel** le portail était tout en acier; **cut through ~ rock** taillé dans la roche; **3** [*crowd*] compact/-e; [*line*] continu/-e; **five ~ days, five days ~** cinq jours entiers; **4** [*advice, worker*] sérieux/-ieuse; [*investment*] sûr/-e.

IV *adv* [*freeze*] complètement; **to be packed ~** [*hall*] être bondé/-e; **the play is booked ~** la pièce affiche complet.

solidarity *n* solidarité *f*.

solidify **I** *vtr* solidifier.

II *vi* [*liquid*] se solidifier; [*honey, oil*] se figer.

solitary *adj* **1** (unaccompanied) [*occupation, walker*] solitaire; **2** (lonely) [*person*] très seul/-e; [*farm, village*] isolé/-e; **3** (single) seul/-e.

solitary confinement *n* isolement *m* cellulaire.

solo **I** *n* solo *m*.

II *adj, adv* en solo.

soloist *n* soliste *mf*.

solstice *n* solstice *m*.

soluble *adj* soluble.

solution *n* solution *f*.

solve *vtr* résoudre [*equation, problem*]; élucider [*crime*]; trouver la solution de [*mystery*]; trouver la solution à [*clue, crossword*]; trouver une solution à [*crisis, poverty, unemployment*].

solvent **I** *n* solvant *m*.

II *adj* (in funds) solvable.

sombre (GB), **somber** (US) *adj* sombre.

some

■ **Note** When *some* is used to mean an unspecified amount of something, it is translated by *du, de l'* (before a vowel or mute 'h'), *de la* or *des* according to the gender and number of the noun that follows: *I'd like some bread* = je voudrais du pain; *have some water* = prenez de l'eau; *we've bought some beer* = nous avons acheté de la bière; *they've bought some peaches* = ils ont acheté des pêches.

– But note that when a plural noun is preceded by

an adjective in French, *some* is translated by *de* alone: *some pretty dresses* = de jolies robes.
– When *some* is used as a pronoun, it is translated by *en* which is placed before the verb in French: *would you like some?* = est-ce que vous en voulez?; *I've got some* = j'en ai.
– For further examples, see the entry below.

I *det* **1** (an unspecified amount or number) du/de l'/de la/des; **~ old socks** de vieilles chaussettes; **~ red socks** des chaussettes rouges; **I need ~ help** j'ai besoin d'aide; **2** (certain) certain/-e (*before n*); **~ people say that** certaines personnes disent que; **to ~ extent** dans une certaine mesure; **3** (a considerable amount or number) **his suggestion was greeted with ~ hostility** sa suggestion a été accueillie avec hostilité; **it will take ~ doing** ça ne va pas être facile à faire; **we stayed there for ~ time** nous sommes restés là assez longtemps; **4** (a little, a slight) **the meeting did have ~ effect** la réunion a eu un certain effet; **you must have ~ idea where the house is** tu dois avoir une idée de l'endroit où se trouve la maison; **5** (an unknown) **he's doing ~ course** il suit des cours; **a car of ~ sort, ~ sort of car** une voiture quelconque.
II *pron, quantif* **1** (an unspecified amount or number) en; **he took ~ of it/of them** il en a pris un peu/quelques-uns; **(do) have ~!** servez-vous!; **2** (certain ones) certain/-e; **~ (of them) are blue** certains sont bleus; **~ (of them) arrived early** certains d'entre eux sont arrivés tôt.
III *adv* **1** (approximately) environ; **~ 20 people** environ 20 personnes; **2**° (US) un peu.

somebody *pron* (also **someone**) quelqu'un; **~ famous** quelqu'un de célèbre.

somehow *adv* **1** (also **~ or other**) (of future action) d'une manière ou d'une autre; (of past action) je ne sais comment; **we'll get there ~** on y arrivera d'une manière ou d'une autre; **we managed it ~** nous avons réussi je ne sais comment; **2** (for some reason) **~ it doesn't seem very important** en fait, ça ne semble pas très important.

someone = **somebody**.

somersault I *n* (of gymnast) roulade *f*; (of child) galipette *f*; (accidental) culbute *f*.
II *vi* [*gymnast*] faire une roulade; [*vehicle*] faire un tonneau.

something I *pron* quelque chose; **~ interesting** quelque chose d'intéressant; **~ to do** quelque chose à faire; **there's ~ wrong** il y a un problème; **~ or other** quelque chose; **in nineteen-sixty-~** en mille neuf cent soixante et quelques; **she's gone shopping or ~** elle est allée faire les courses ou quelque chose comme ça.
II **something of** *phr* **she is ~ of an expert on**... elle est assez experte en...; **it was ~ of a surprise** c'était assez étonnant.

sometime *adv* **we'll have to do it ~** il va falloir qu'on le fasse un jour ou l'autre; **I'll tell you about it ~** je te raconterai ça un de ces jours; **I'll phone you ~ next week** je te téléphonerai dans le courant de la semaine prochaine.

sometimes *adv* parfois, quelquefois.

somewhat *adv* (with adjective) plutôt; (with verb, adverb) un peu.

somewhere *adv* (some place) quelque part; **~ hot** un endroit chaud; **~ or other** je ne sais où; **~ between 50 and 100 people** entre 50 et 100 personnes.

son *n* fils *m*.

sonata *n* sonate *f*.

song *n* chanson *f*; (of bird) chant *m*.

sonic *adj* sonore.

sonic boom *n* bang *m*.

son-in-law *n* gendre *m*.

sonnet *n* sonnet *m*.

soon *adv* **1** (in a short time) bientôt; **see you ~!** à bientôt!; **2** (quickly) vite; **3** (early) tôt; **the ~er the better** le plus tôt sera le mieux; **as ~ as possible** dès que possible; **as ~ as you can** dès que tu pourras; **as ~ as he has finished** dès qu'il aura fini; **~er or later** tôt ou tard; **4** (not long) **~ afterwards** peu après; **no ~er had I finished than**... j'avais à peine fini que...

soot *n* suie *f*.

soothe *vtr* calmer [*pain, nerves, person*]; apaiser [*sunburn*].

soothing *adj* [*music, voice*] apaisant/-e; [*cream, effect*] calmant/-e; [*words*] rassurant/-e.

sophisticated *adj* **1** [*person*] (cultured) raffiné/-e; (affected) sophistiqué/-e; (elegant) chic; [*restaurant*] chic; **2** [*taste*] raffiné/-e; [*civilization*] évolué/-e; **3** [*equipment, technology*] sophistiqué/-e.

soporific *adj* soporifique.

soprano *n* (person) soprano *mf*; (voice, instrument) soprano *m*.

sorcerer *n* sorcier *m*.

sordid *adj* sordide.

sore I *n* plaie *f*.
II *adj* **1** [*eyes, gums*] irrité/-e; [*muscle, arm, foot*] endolori/-e; **to have a ~ throat** avoir mal à la gorge; **2** [*subject, point*] délicat/-e.

sorrow *n* chagrin *m*.

sorrowful *adj* [*look*] affligé/-e; [*voice*] triste.

sorry I *adj* **1** désolé/-e; **I'm terribly ~** je suis vraiment désolé, je suis navré; **I'm ~ I'm late** je suis désolé d'être en retard; **to be ~ about sth** s'excuser de qch; **to say ~** s'excuser; **to be ~ to do** regretter de faire; **2** (pitying) **to be** or **feel ~ for sb** plaindre qn; **to feel ~ for oneself** s'apitoyer sur soi-même; **3** [*state, sight, business*] triste; [*person*] minable.
II *excl* **1** (apologizing) pardon!, désolé!; **2** (pardon) **~?** pardon?

sort I *n* sorte *f*, genre *m*; **books, records—that ~ of thing** des livres, des disques, ce genre de choses; **I'm not that ~ of person** ce n'est pas mon genre; **some ~ of computer** une sorte d'ordinateur.
II *vtr* classer [*data, files, stamps*]; trier [*letters, apples, potatoes*]; **to ~ books into piles** ranger des livres en piles.

III **of sorts**, **of a sort** *phr* **a duck of ~s** or **of a ~** une sorte de canard; **progress of ~s** un semblant de progrès.
IV○ **sort of** *phr* **~ of cute** plutôt mignon/-onne; **I ~ of understand** je comprends plus ou moins; **~ of blue-green** dans les bleu-vert; **it just ~ of happened** c'est arrivé comme ça.
IDIOMS **to be** or **feel out of ~s** (ill) ne pas être dans son assiette; (grumpy) être de mauvais poil○; **it takes all ~s (to make a world)** il faut de tout pour faire un monde.
■ **sort out 1** régler [*problem, matter*]; **2** s'occuper de [*details, arrangements*]; **I'll ~ it out** je m'en occuperai; **3** ranger [*cupboard, desk*]; classer [*files, documents*]; mettre de l'ordre dans [*finances, affairs*]; clarifier [*ideas*]; **4** trier [*photos, clothes*].

SOS *n* SOS *m*.

so-so○ I *adj* moyen/-enne.
II *adv* comme ci comme ça○.

soul *n* **1** (gen) âme *f*; **2** (also **~ music**) soul *m*.

sound I *n* **1** (gen) son *m*; (noise) bruit *m* (**of** de); **to turn the ~ up/down** augmenter/baisser le volume; **the ~ of voices** un bruit de voix; **a grating** or **rasping ~** un grincement; **without a ~** sans bruit; **2** (figurative) **by the ~ of it, we're in for a rough crossing** d'après ce qu'on a dit, la traversée va être mauvaise; **3** (Med) sonde *f*; **4** (strait) détroit *m*.
II *adj* **1** [*heart, constitution*] solide; [*health*] bon/bonne (*before n*); **to be of ~ mind** être sain/-e d'esprit; **2** [*basis, argument*] solide; [*judgment*] sain/-e; [*advice, investment*] bon/bonne (*before n*), sûr/-e.
III *vtr* faire retentir [*siren, foghorn*]; **to ~ one's horn** klaxonner; **to ~ the alarm** sonner l'alarme.
IV *vi* **1** (seem) sembler; **it ~s as if he's really in trouble** il semble qu'il ait vraiment des ennuis; **it ~s like it might be dangerous** ça a l'air dangereux; **to ~ boring** paraître ennuyeux; **it ~s like a flute** on dirait une flûte; **2** [*alarm, buzzer, bugle*] sonner.
V *adv* **to be ~ asleep** dormir à poings fermés.
■ **sound out** sonder, interroger [*person*].

sound barrier *n* mur *m* du son.

sound effect *n* effet *m* sonore.

soundproof *adj* insonorisé/-e.

soundtrack *n* (of film) bande *f* sonore; (on record) bande *f* originale.

soup *n* soupe *f*, potage *m*.

soupspoon *n* cuillère *f* à soupe.

sour I *adj* **1** aigre; **to go ~** [*milk*] tourner; **2** (bad-tempered) revêche.
II *vtr* gâter [*relations, atmosphere*].

source *n* source *f*; **at ~** à la source; **~ of** source *f* de [*anxiety, resentment, satisfaction*]; cause *f* de [*problem, error, infection, pollution*].

sourdough *n* (US) levain *m*.

south I *n* **1** (compass direction) sud *m*; **2** (part of world, country) **the South** le Sud.
II *adj* (gen) sud *inv*; [*wind*] du sud; **in ~ London** dans le sud de Londres.
III *adv* [*move*] vers le sud; [*lie, live*] au sud (**of** de).

South Africa ▶448 *pr n* Afrique *f* du Sud.

South America ▶448 *pr n* Amérique *f* du Sud.

southeast I *n* sud-est *m*.
II *adj* [*coast, side*] sud-est *inv*; [*wind*] de sud-est.
III *adv* [*move*] vers le sud-est; [*lie, live*] au sud-est.

southern *adj* [*coast*] sud *inv*; [*town, accent*] du sud; [*hemisphere*] Sud *inv*; **~ England** le sud de l'Angleterre.

South Pole *pr n* pôle *m* Sud.

southwest I *n* sud-ouest *m*.
II *adj* [*coast*] sud-ouest *inv*; [*wind*] de sud-ouest.
III *adv* [*move*] vers le sud-ouest; [*lie, live*] au sud-ouest.

souvenir *n* souvenir *m*.

sovereign I *n* **1** (monarch) souverain/-e *m/f*; **2** (coin) souverain *m*.
II *adj* souverain/-e (*after n*).

Soviet Union *pr n* Union *f* soviétique.

sow[1] *n* truie *f*.

sow[2] *vtr* **1** semer [*seeds, corn*]; **2** ensemencer [*field, garden*] (**with** de); **3** (figurative) semer.

soya *n* soja *m*.

soya sauce, **soy sauce** *n* sauce *f* soja.

spa *n* **1** (town) station *f* thermale; **2** (US) (health club) club *m* de remise en forme.

space I *n* **1** (also **outer ~**) espace *m*; **2** (room) place *f*, espace *m*; **3** (gap) espace *m* (**between** entre); (on form) case *f*; **4** (interval of time) intervalle *m*; **in the ~ of five minutes** en l'espace de cinq minutes; **5** (area of land) espace *m*; **open ~s** espaces libres.
II *adj* [*programme, rocket*] spatial/-e.
III *vtr* espacer.
■ **space out** espacer [*words, objects*]; échelonner [*payments*].

spaceship *n* vaisseau *m* spatial.

space station *n* station *f* orbitale.

spacesuit *n* combinaison *f* spatiale.

spacious *adj* spacieux/-ieuse.

spade ▶504 *n* **1** (implement) bêche *f*, pelle *f*; **2** (in cards) pique *m*.

Spain ▶448 *pr n* Espagne *f*.

span I *n* **1** (of time) durée *f*; **2** (of bridge) travée *f*; (**wing**)**~** envergure *f*.
II *vtr* **1** [*bridge, arch*] enjamber; **2** (figurative) s'étendre sur.

Spaniard ▶553 *n* Espagnol/-e *m/f*.

spaniel *n* épagneul *m*.

Spanish ▶553 I *n* **1** (people) **the ~** les Espagnols *mpl*; **2** (language) espagnol *m*.
II *adj* (gen) espagnol/-e; [*teacher, lesson*] d'espagnol; [*embassy*] d'Espagne.

spank *vtr* donner une fessée à.

spanner *n* (GB) clé *f* (de serrage).

spar *vi* [*boxers*] échanger des coups.

spare I *n* (part) pièce *f* de rechange; (wheel) roue *f* de secours.
II *adj* **1** [*cash*] restant/-e; [*seat*] disponible; [*copy*] en plus; **I've got a ~ ticket** j'ai un

ticket en trop; **a ~ moment** un moment de libre; **2** [*part*] de rechange; [*wheel*] de secours; **3** [*person, build*] élancé/-e.
III *vtr* **1 to have sth to ~** avoir qch de disponible; **to catch the train with five minutes to ~** prendre le train avec cinq minutes d'avance; **can you ~ a minute?** as-tu un moment?; **2** (treat leniently) épargner; **to ~ sb sth** épargner qch à qn; **3** (manage without) se passer de [*person*].
IDIOMS **to ~ no effort** faire tout son possible.

spare part *n* pièce *f* de rechange.

spare time *n* loisirs *mpl*.

sparingly *adv* [*use, add*] en petite quantité.

spark I *n* étincelle *f*.
II *vtr* (also **~ off**) provoquer [*reaction, panic*]; être à l'origine de [*friendship, affair*].

sparkle I *n* scintillement *m*; (in eye) éclair *m*.
II *vi* [*flame, light*] étinceler; [*jewel, frost, metal, water*] scintiller; [*eyes*] briller; [*drink*] pétiller.

sparkler *n* cierge *m* magique.

sparkling *adj* **1** [*eyes*] brillant/-e; **2** [*wit*] plein/-e de brio; **3** [*drink*] pétillant/-e.

sparrow *n* moineau *m*.

sparse *adj* clairsemé/-e.

spasm *n* (of pain) spasme *m* (**of** de); (of panic, rage) accès *m* (**of** de).

spate *n* **1 in full ~** (GB) (river) en pleine crue; (person) en plein discours; **2 a ~ of** une série de [*incidents*].

spatula *n* spatule *f*.

speak I *vtr* **1** parler [*language*]; **can you ~ English?** parlez-vous (l')anglais?; **2** dire [*truth*]; prononcer [*word, name*]; **to ~ one's mind** dire ce qu'on pense.
II *vi* parler (**to, with** à; **about, of** de); **who's ~ing?** (on phone) qui est à l'appareil?; **(this is) Eileen ~ing** c'est Eileen; **generally ~ing** en règle générale; **roughly ~ing** en gros; **strictly ~ing** à proprement parler.
■ **speak up 1** (louder) parler plus fort; **2** (dare to speak) intervenir.

speaker *n* **1** (person talking) personne *f* qui parle; (public speaker) orateur/-trice *m/f*; **2 a French ~** un/-e francophone; **a Russian ~** un/-e russophone; **3** (on stereo system) haut-parleur *m*.

spear *n* lance *f*.

spearmint *n* menthe *f* verte.

special *adj* (gen) spécial/-e; [*case, reason, treatment*] particulier/-ière; [*friend*] très cher/chère.

special effect *n* effet *m* spécial.

specialist ▶ 626 *n* spécialiste *mf* (**in** de).

speciality (GB), **specialty** (US) *n* spécialité *f*.

specialize *vi* se spécialiser.

specially *adv* **1** (specifically) spécialement; **I made it ~ for you** je l'ai fait exprès pour toi; **2** (particularly) particulièrement; [*like, enjoy*] surtout.

species *n* espèce *f*.

specific *adj* précis/-e.

specifically *adv* **1** (specially) spécialement; **2** (explicitly) explicitement; **3** (in particular) en particulier.

specify *vtr* stipuler; [*person*] préciser.

specimen *n* (of rock, urine, handwriting) échantillon *m*; (of blood, tissue) prélèvement; (of species, plant) spécimen *m*.

speck *n* (of dust, soot) grain *m*; (of dirt, mud, blood) petite tache *f*; (of light) point *m*.

spectacle I *n* spectacle *m*.
II spectacles *n pl* lunettes *fpl*.

spectacular *adj* spectaculaire.

spectator *n* spectateur/-trice *m/f*.

spectre (GB), **specter** (US) *n* spectre *m*.

spectrum *n* **1** (of colours) spectre *m*; **2** (range) gamme *f*.

speculate I *vtr* **to ~ that** supposer que.
II *vi* spéculer (**on** sur; **about** à propos de).

speculation *n* **1** (conjecture) spéculations *fpl*; **2** (financial) spéculation *f* (**in** sur).

speech *n* **1** discours *m* (**on** sur; **about** à propos de); **to give a ~** faire un discours; **2** (faculty) parole *f*; **3** (language) langage *m*.

speech impediment *n* défaut *m* d'élocution.

speechless *adj* muet/-ette (**with** de).

speed I *n* **1** vitesse *f*; (of response, reaction) rapidité *f*; **at top ~** à toute vitesse; **2**° (drug) amphétamines *fpl*.
II *vtr* hâter [*process, recovery*].
III *vi* **1 to ~ along** [*driver, car*] rouler à toute allure; **to ~ away** s'eloigner à toute allure; **2** (drive too fast) conduire trop vite.
■ **speed up**: ¶ **~ up** [*walker*] aller plus vite; [*athlete, driver, car*] accélérer; [*worker*] travailler plus vite; ¶ **~ [sth] up** accélérer.

speedboat *n* hors-bord *m*.

speeding *n* excès *m* de vitesse.

speed limit *n* limitation *f* de vitesse.

speedometer *n* compteur *m* (de vitesse).

spell I *n* **1** (period) moment *m*, période *f*; **sunny ~** éclaircie *f*; **2** (magic words) formule *f* magique; **to be under a ~** être envoûté/-e; **to cast** or **put a ~ on sb** jeter un sort à qn; **to be under sb's ~** être sous le charme de qn.
II *vtr* **1** écrire [*word*]; **2** signifier [*danger, disaster*].
III *vi* **he can't/can ~** il a une mauvaise/bonne orthographe.
■ **spell out 1** épeler [*word*]; **2** (explain) expliquer [qch] clairement.

spellbound *adj* envoûté/-e (**by** par).

spelling *n* orthographe *f*.

spend I *vtr* **1** dépenser [*money, salary*] (**on** en); **2** passer [*time*] (**doing** à faire).
II *vi* dépenser.

spendthrift *adj* [*person*] dépensier/-ière.

sperm *n* sperme *m*.

spew *vtr* vomir.

sphere *n* **1** (shape) sphère *f*; **2** (field) domaine *m* (**of** de); **~ of influence** sphère *f* d'influence.

spherical *adj* sphérique.

spice *n* (Culin) épice *f*; (figurative) piment *m*.

spick-and-span *adj* impeccable.

spicy *adj* **1** [*food*] épicé/-e; **2** [*detail*] croustillant/-e.

spider *n* araignée *f*.

spiderweb *n* (US) toile *f* d'araignée.

spike I *n* pointe *f*.
II○ *vtr* corser [*drink*] (**with** de).

spiky *adj* [*hair*] en brosse *inv*; [*branch*] piquant/-e; [*object*] acéré/-e.

spill I *vtr* renverser [*drink*] (**on, over** sur).
II *vi* se répandre (**onto** sur; **into** dans).

spin I *n* **1** (of wheel) tour *m*; (of dancer, skate) pirouette *f*; **2 to go into a ~** [*plane*] descendre en vrille; **3 to go for a ~** (in car) aller faire un tour.
II *vtr* **1** lancer [*top*]; faire tourner [*globe, wheel*]; **2** filer [*wool, thread*]; **3** [*spider*] tisser [*web*].
III *vi* tourner; [*weathercock, top*] tournoyer; [*dancer*] pirouetter; **my head is ~ning** j'ai la tête qui tourne.
■ **spin out** prolonger [*visit*]; faire traîner [qch] en longueur [*speech*]; faire durer [*work, money*].
■ **spin round**: ¶ **~ round** [*person*] se retourner rapidement; [*dancer, skater*] pirouetter; [*car*] faire un tête-à-queue; ¶ **~ [sb/sth] round** faire tourner [*wheel*].

spinach *n* (Culin) épinards *mpl*.

spinal cord *n* moelle *f* épinière.

spindly *adj* grêle.

spin-drier, **spin dryer** *n* essoreuse *f*.

spine *n* **1** (Anat) colonne *f* vertébrale; **2** (on hedgehog, cactus) piquant *m*; **3** (of book) dos *m*.

spineless *adj* mou/molle.

spin-off *n* **1** (incidental benefit) retombée *f* favorable; **2** (by-product) sous-produit *m*.

spinster *n* célibataire *f*; (derogatory) vieille fille *f*.

spiral I *n* spirale *f*.
II *adj* [*structure*] en spirale.
III *vi* [*prices, costs*] monter en flèche.

spiral staircase *n* escalier *m* en colimaçon.

spire *n* flèche *f*.

spirit I *n* **1** (gen) esprit *m*; **2** (courage, determination) courage *m*.
II **spirits** *n pl* **1** (alcohol) spiritueux *mpl*; **2 to be in good ~s** être de bonne humeur; **to be in high ~s** être d'excellente humeur; **to keep one's ~s up** garder le moral.

spirited *adj* [*horse, debate, reply*] fougueux/-euse; [*attack, defence*] vif/vive.

spiritual I *n* spiritual *m*.
II *adj* spirituel/-elle.

spit I *n* **1** (saliva) salive *f*; **2** (Culin) broche *f*.
II *vtr* [*person*] cracher; [*pan*] projeter [*oil*].
III *vi* [*cat, person*] cracher (**at, on** sur); [*oil, sausage*] grésiller; [*logs, fire*] crépiter.
IV *v impers* **it's ~ting** (**with rain**) il bruine.
IDIOMS **to be the ~ting image of sb** être le portrait tout craché de qn.

spite I *n* rancune *f*.
II *vtr* faire du mal à; (less strong) embêter.
III **in spite of** *phr* malgré; **in ~ of the fact that** bien que.

spiteful *adj* [*person*] rancunier/-ière; [*remark*] méchant/-e.

splash I *n* **1** (sound) plouf *m*; **2** (of mud) tache *f*; (of water, oil) éclaboussure *f*; (of colour) touche *f*; (of tonic, soda) goutte *f*.
II *vtr* éclabousser; **to ~ water on to one's face** s'asperger le visage d'eau.
III *vi* faire des éclaboussures.
■ **splash out**○ faire des folies; **to ~ out on sth** faire la folie de s'offrir qch.

splay *vtr* écarter [*feet, fingers*].

spleen *n* (Anat) rate *f*.

splendid *adj* splendide; [*idea, holiday, performance*] merveilleux/-euse.

splendour (GB), **splendor** (US) *n* splendeur *f*.

splice *vtr* coller [*tape, film*]; épisser [*ends of rope*].

splint *n* (for injury) attelle *f*.

splinter I *n* éclat *m*.
II *vi* [*glass, windscreen*] se briser; [*wood*] se fendre; [*alliance*] se scinder.

splinter group *n* groupe *m* dissident.

split I *n* **1** (in fabric) déchirure *f*; (in rock, wood) fissure *f*; **2** (in party, alliance) scission *f* (**in** de).
II **splits** *n pl* **to do the ~s** faire le grand écart.
III *adj* [*fabric*] déchiré/-e; [*seam*] défait/-e; [*log, lip*] fendu/-e.
IV *vtr* **1** fendre [*log, rock*] (**in, into** en); déchirer [*garment*]; **2** diviser [*party*]; **3** (share) partager (**between** entre).
V *vi* **1** [*wood, log, rock*] se fendre (**in , into** en); [*fabric, garment*] se déchirer; **2** [*party*] se diviser.
■ **split up**: ¶ **~ up** [*couple, band*] se séparer; ¶ **~ [sth] up** diviser (**into** en).

split second *n* fraction *f* de seconde.

spoil I *vtr* **1** (mar) gâcher [*event, view, game*]; gâter [*place, taste, effect*]; **to ~ sth for sb** gâcher qch à qn; **2** (ruin) abîmer [*garment, crops*]; **3** (pamper) gâter [*child, pet*].
II *vi* [*product, foodstuff*] s'abîmer.

spoiled, **spoilt** (GB) *adj* [*child, dog*] gâté/-e; **a ~ brat**○ un gamin pourri○.

spoils *n pl* (of war) butin *m* (**of** de).

spoilsport○ *n* **to be a ~** être un rabat-joie.

spoke *n* rayon *m*.

spokesman *n* porte-parole *m inv*.

spokeswoman *n* porte-parole *m inv*.

sponge I *n* **1** éponge *f*; **2** (also **~ cake**) génoise *f*.
II *vtr* éponger [*material, stain, face*].
III○ *vi* **to ~ off** or **on** vivre sur le dos de [*family, state*].

sponsor I *n* **1** (advertiser, backer) sponsor *m*; **2** (patron) mécène *m*.
II *vtr* sponsoriser [*event, team*]; financer [*student*]; parrainer [*child*].

sponsorship *n* sponsorat *m*.

spontaneous *adj* spontané/-e.

spontaneously *adv* spontanément.

spoof○ *n* (parody) parodie *f* (**on** de).

spooky○ *adj* [*house, atmosphere*] sinistre; [*story*] qui fait froid dans le dos.

spool *n* bobine *f*.

spoon *n* cuillère *f*; (teaspoon) petite cuillère *f*.

spoonful *n* cuillerée *f*, cuillère *f*.

sporadic *adj* sporadique.

sport ▶504 *n* **1** sport *m*; **2 he's a good ~** (good loser) il est beau joueur.

sporting *adj* **1** [*fixture, event*] sportif/-ive; **2** (fair, generous) généreux/-euse; **to have a ~ chance of doing** avoir de bonnes chances de faire.

sports car *n* voiture *f* de sport.

sports club *n* club *m* sportif.

sports ground *n* (large) stade *m*; (in school, club) terrain *m* de sports.

sports jacket *n* (GB) veste *f* en tweed.

sportsman *n* sportif *m*.

sportswoman *n* sportive *f*.

spot I *n* **1** (on animal) tache *f*; (on fabric) pois *m*; (on dice, domino) point *m*; **2** (stain) tache *f*; **3** (pimple) bouton *m*; **4** (place) endroit *m*; **on the ~** sur place; **to decide on the ~** décider sur-le-champ; **5**○ (small amount) **a ~ of** un peu de; **6**○ **to be in a (tight) ~** être dans une situation embêtante.
II *vtr* **1** apercevoir [*person*]; repérer [*difference, mistake*]; **2** (stain) tacher.

spot check *n* contrôle *m* surprise.

spotless *adj* impeccable.

spotlight *n* (in theatre, film set) projecteur *m*; (in home) spot *m*.

spout I *n* (of kettle, teapot) bec *m* verseur.
II *vtr* **1** (spurt) faire jaillir [*water*]; **2** (recite) débiter [*poetry, statistics*].
III *vi* [*liquid*] jaillir (**from, out of** de).

sprain I *n* entorse *f*.
II *vtr* **to ~ one's ankle** se faire une entorse à la cheville; (less severely) se fouler la cheville.

sprawl I *n* (of suburbs, buildings) étendue *f*.
II *vi* s'étaler.

spray I *n* **1** (seawater) embruns *mpl*; (other) nuages *mpl* de (fines) gouttelettes; **2** (container) (for perfume) vaporisateur *m*; (can) bombe *f*; (for inhalant, throat, nose) pulvérisateur *m*; **3** (of flowers) (bunch) gerbe *f*; (single branch) rameau *m*.
II *vtr* **1** vaporiser [*liquid*]; asperger [*person*] (**with** de); **to ~ sth onto sth** (onto fire) projeter qch sur qch [*foam, water*]; (onto surface, flowers) vaporiser qch sur qch [*paint, water*].

spread I *n* **1** (of disease, drugs) propagation *f*; (of news, information) diffusion *f*; **2** (Culin) pâte *f* à tartiner.
II *vtr* **1** (unfold) étaler, étendre [*cloth, newspaper, map*] (**on, over** sur); [*bird*] déployer [*wings*]; **2** étaler [*butter, jam, glue*] (**on, over** sur); **3** (distribute) disperser [*troops*]; répartir [*workload, responsibility*]; **4** (also **~ out**) étaler, échelonner [*payments, meetings*] (**over** sur); **5** propager [*disease, fire*]; semer [*confusion, panic*]; faire circuler [*rumour, story*].
III *vi* **1** [*butter, jam, glue*] s'étaler; **2** [*forest, drought*] s'étendre (**over** sur); [*disease, fear, fire*] se propager; [*rumour, story*] circuler; [*stain, damp*] s'étaler.
■ **spread out**: ¶ **~ out** [*group*] se disperser (**over** sur); [*wings, tail*] se déployer; ¶ **~ [sth] out** étaler, étendre [*cloth, map, rug*] (**on, over** sur).

spread-eagled *adj* bras et jambes écartés.

spreadsheet *n* tableur *m*.

spree *n* **to go on a ~** (drinking) faire la bringue○; **to go on a shopping ~** aller faire des folies dans les magasins.

sprig *n* (of holly) petite branche *f*; (of parsley) brin *m*.

sprightly *adj* alerte, gaillard.

spring I *n* **1** (season) printemps *m*; **in ~** au printemps; **2** (of wire) ressort *m*; **3** (leap) bond *m*; **4** (water source) source *f*.
II *vtr* **1** déclencher [*trap, lock*]; **2 to ~ a leak** [*tank, barrel*] commencer à fuir; **3 to ~ [sth] on sb** annoncer [qch] de but en blanc à qn [*news, plan*].
III *vi* **1** (jump) bondir (**onto** sur); **2** (originate) **to ~ from** venir de.
■ **spring up** [*new building*] apparaître.

spring-clean *vtr* nettoyer [qch] de fond en comble [*house*].

springtime *n* printemps *m*.

springy *adj* [*mattress, seat*] élastique.

sprinkle *vtr* **to ~ sth with** saupoudrer qch de [*salt, sugar*]; parsemer qch de [*herbs*]; **to ~ sth with water** humecter qch.

sprinkler *n* **1** (for lawn) arroseur *m*; **2** (to extinguish fires) diffuseur *m*.

sprint I *n* (race) sprint *m*, course *f* de vitesse.
II *vi* (in athletics) sprinter; (to catch bus) courir (à toute vitesse).

sprout I *n* (also **Brussels ~**) chou *m* de Bruxelles.
II *vi* [*seed, shoot*] germer; [*grass, weeds*] pousser.

spruce I *n* (also **~ tree**) épicéa *m*.
II *adj* [*person*] soigné/-e; [*house, garden*] bien tenu/-e.
■ **spruce up** astiquer [*house*]; nettoyer [*garden*]; **to ~ oneself up** se faire beau/belle.

spry *adj* alerte, leste.

spun *adj* [*glass, gold, sugar*] filé/-e.

spur I *n* **1** (for horse) éperon *m*; (figurative) aiguillon *m*; **2** (of rock) contrefort *m*.
II *vtr* (also **~ on**) éperonner [*horse*]; aiguillonner [*person*]; **to ~ sb to do** inciter qn à faire.
IDIOMS **on the ~ of the moment** sur une impulsion.

spurn *vtr* refuser [qch] (avec mépris).

spurt I *n* **1** (gush) (of water, oil, blood) giclée *f*; (of flame) jaillissement *m*; **2** (of activity) regain *m*; (of energy) sursaut *m*; (in growth) poussée *f*; **to put on a ~** [*runner, cyclist*] pousser une pointe de vitesse.
II *vi* (also **~ out**) jaillir (**from, out of** de).

spy I *n* espion/-ionne *m/f*.
II *vtr* remarquer, discerner [*figure, object*].
III *vi* **to ~ on sb/sth** espionner qn/qch.

spying *n* espionnage *m*.

squabble *vi* se disputer, se chamailler○.

squad *n* (Mil) escouade *f*; (Sport) sélection *f*.

squad car *n* voiture *f* de police.

squadron *n* escadron *m*.

squalid *adj* sordide.

squall *n* (wind) bourrasque *f*, rafale *f* (**of** de); (at sea) grain *m*.

squalor *n* (filth) saleté *f* repoussante; (wretchedness) misère *f* (noire).

squander *vtr* gaspiller.

square I *n* **1** (shape) carré *m*; **2** (in town) place *f*; **3** (in game, crossword) case *f*; (of glass, linoleum) carreau *m*; **4**° (person) ringard/-e° *m/f*.
II *adj* **1** (in shape) carré/-e; **four ~ metres** quatre mètres carrés; **2** (quits) **to be ~** [*people*] être quitte.
III *vtr* **1 to ~ one's shoulders** redresser les épaules; **2** (settle) régler [*account, debt*].
IDIOMS **to go back to ~ one** retourner à la case départ.
■ **square up** (settle accounts) régler ses comptes.

squash I *n* **1** ▶**504** (Sport) squash *m*; **2** (drink) sirop *m*; **3** (vegetable) courge *f*.
II *vtr* écraser.

squat I *adj* [*person, structure, object*] trapu/-e.
II *vi* **1** (crouch) s'accroupir; **2 to ~ in** squatter [*building*].

squawk *vi* [*hen*] pousser des gloussements; [*duck, parrot*] pousser des cris rauques.

squeak I *n* (of door, wheel, chalk) grincement *m*; (of mouse, soft toy) couinement *m*; (of furniture, shoes) craquement *m*.
II *vi* [*door, wheel, chalk*] grincer; [*mouse, soft toy*] couiner; [*shoes, furniture*] craquer (**on** sur).

squeaky *adj* [*voice*] aigu/aiguë; [*gate, hinge, wheel*] grinçant.

squeal *vi* [*person, animal*] pousser des cris aigus.

squeamish *adj* impressionnable, sensible.

squeeze I *n* **1** (on credit, finances) resserrement *m* (**on** de); **2**° (crush) **it will be a tight ~** ce sera un peu juste.
II *vtr* **1** presser [*lemon, bottle, tube*]; serrer [*arm, hand*]; appuyer sur [*trigger*]; percer [*spot*]; **to ~ water out of** essorer, tordre [*cloth*]; **2** (figurative) réussir à obtenir [*money*] (**out of** de); **to ~ the truth out of sb** arracher la vérité à qn; **3** (fit) **to ~ sth into sth** entasser qch dans qch.

squelch *vi* [*water, mud*] glouglouter; **to ~ along** avancer en pataugeant.

squid *n* calmar *m*, encornet *m*.

squiggle *n* gribouillis *m*.

squint I *n* strabisme *m*; **to have a ~** loucher.
II *vi* **1** (look) plisser les yeux; **2** (have eye condition) loucher.

squire *n* ≈ châtelain *m*.

squirm *vi* (wriggle) se tortiller; [*person*] (in pain) se tordre; (with embarrassment) être très mal à l'aise.

squirrel *n* écureuil *m*.

squirt I *vtr* faire gicler [*liquid*].
II *vi* [*liquid*] jaillir (**from, out of** de).

stab I *n* **1** (act) coup *m* de couteau; **a ~ in the back** (figurative) un coup en traître; **2** (of pain) élancement *m* (**of** de).
II *vtr* poignarder [*person*].

stabilize I *vtr* stabiliser.
II *vi* se stabiliser.

stable I *n* écurie *f*; **riding ~s** manège *m*.
II *adj* **1** (steady) stable; **2** (psychologically) équilibré/-e.

stack I *n* (pile) pile *f*; (of hay, straw) meule *f*.
II *vtr* **1** (also **~ up**) (pile) empiler; **2** (fill) remplir [*shelves*]; **3** mettre [qch] en attente [*planes, calls*].

stadium *n* stade *m*.

staff *n* (of company) personnel *m*; (of a school, college) personnel *m* enseignant.

stag *n* cerf *m*.

stage I *n* **1** (phase) (of illness, career, life) stade *m* (**of, in** de); (of project, process, plan) phase *f* (**of, in** de); (of journey, negotiations) étape *f* (**of, in** de); **2** (raised platform) estrade *f*; (in theatre) scène *f*.
II *vtr* **1** (organize) organiser [*event, rebellion, strike*]; **2** (fake) simuler [*quarrel, scene*]; **3** (in theatre) monter [*play*].

stagecoach *n* diligence *f*.

stage fright *n* trac *m*.

stagger I *vtr* **1** (astonish) stupéfier, abasourdir; **2** échelonner [*holidays, payments*].
II *vi* (from weakness) chanceler; (drunkenly) tituber.

stagnant *adj* stagnant/-e.

stagnate *vi* stagner.

stag night, **stag party** *n* soirée *f* pour enterrer une vie de garçon.

staid *adj* guindé/-e.

stain I *n* **1** (mark) tache *f*; **2** (dye) teinture *f*.
II *vtr* **1** (soil) tacher [*clothes, carpet, table*]; **2** teindre [*wood*].

stained glass *n* verre *m* coloré.

stained glass window *n* vitrail *m*.

stainless steel *n* acier *m* inoxydable.

stain remover *n* détachant *m*.

stair I *n* (step) marche *f* (d'escalier).
II **stairs** *n pl* **the ~s** l'escalier; **to fall down the ~s** tomber dans l'escalier.

staircase, **stairway** *n* escalier *m*.

stake I *n* **1** (amount risked) enjeu *m*; **to be at ~** être en jeu; **2** (investment) participation *f* (**in** dans); **3** (post) pieu *m*.
II *vtr* miser [*money, property*]; risquer [*reputation*].

stale *adj* [*bread, cake*] rassis/-e; [*beer*] éventé/-e; [*smell*] de renfermé; [*ideas*] éculé/-e.

stalemate *n* **1** (in chess) pat *m*; **2** (deadlock) impasse *f*.

stalk I *n* (on plant, flower) tige *f*; (of leaf, apple) queue *f*; (of mushroom) pied *m*.
II *vtr* [*hunter, murderer*] traquer [*prey, victim*]; [*animal*] chasser [*prey*].

stall I *n* **1** (at market, fair) stand *m*; **2** (in stable) stalle *f*.
II **stalls** *n pl* (GB) orchestre *m*.
III *vtr* caler [*engine, car*].
IV *vi* **1** [*car*] caler; **2** (play for time) temporiser.

stallion *n* étalon *m*.

stalwart *adj* loyal/-e.

stamina *n* résistance *f*, endurance *f*.

stammer I *n* bégaiement *m*.

II *vi* bégayer.

stamp I *n* **1** (for envelope) timbre *m*; **2** (on passport, document) cachet *m*; **3** (marker) (rubber) tampon *m*; (metal) cachet *m*.
II *vtr* **1** apposer [qch] au tampon [*date, name*] (**on** sur); tamponner [*ticket, book*]; viser [*document, passport*]; **2 to ~ one's foot** (in anger) taper du pied.
III *vi* [*horse*] piaffer; **to ~ on** écraser (du pied) [*toy, foot*]; piétiner [*soil, ground*].

stamp-collecting *n* philatélie *f*.

stamped addressed envelope, **sae** *n* enveloppe *f* timbrée à votre/son etc adresse.

stampede I *n* débandade *f*.
II *vi* s'enfuir (pris d'affolement).

stance *n* position *f*.

stand I *n* **1** (support, frame) support *m*; (for coats) portemanteau *m*; **2** (stall) (in market) éventaire *m*; (kiosk) kiosque *m*; (at exhibition, trade fair) stand *m*; **3** (in stadium) tribunes *fpl*; **4** (witness box) barre *f*; **5** (stance) **to take a ~ on sth** prendre position sur qch; **6** (**to make**) **a last ~** (livrer) une dernière bataille.
II *vtr* **1** (place) mettre [*person, object*] (**against** contre; **in** dans; **on** sur); **2** (bear) supporter [*cold, weight*]; tolérer [*nonsense, bad behaviour*]; **I can't ~ him** je ne peux pas le supporter or le sentir; **I can't ~ this town** je déteste cette ville; **I can't ~ doing** je déteste faire; **3**○ **to ~ sb a drink** payer un verre à qn; **4 to ~ trial** passer en jugement.
III *vi* **1** (also **~ up**) se lever; **2** (be upright) [*person*] se tenir debout; [*object*] tenir debout; **to remain ~ing** rester debout; **3** [*building, village*] se trouver, être; **4** (step) **to ~ on** marcher sur [*insect, foot*]; **5** (be) **as things ~**... étant donné l'état actuel des choses...; **the total ~s at 300** le total est de 300; **to ~ in sb's way** (figurative) faire obstacle à qn; **6** (remain valid) [*offer, agreement*] rester valable; **7** (be a candidate) se présenter (**as** comme); **to ~ for election** se présenter aux élections.
■ **stand back** [*person, crowd*] reculer (**from** de); (figurative) prendre du recul (**from** par rapport à).
■ **stand by**: ¶ **~ by** [*doctor, army*] être prêt/-e à intervenir; ¶ **~ by** [**sb/sth**] soutenir [*person*]; s'en tenir à [*principles, decision*].
■ **stand for 1** (represent) représenter; [*initials*] vouloir dire; **2** (tolerate) tolérer.
■ **stand in**: **to ~ in for sb** remplacer qn.
■ **stand out** [*person*] sortir de l'ordinaire; [*work, ability*] être remarquable.
■ **stand up**: ¶ **~ up 1** (rise) se lever; **2** (stay upright) se tenir debout; **3** [*theory, story*] tenir debout; **4 to ~ up to** tenir tête à [*person*]; **5 to ~ up for** défendre [*person, rights*]; ¶ **~** [**sth**] **up** redresser [*object*]; ¶ **~** [**sb**] **up**○ poser un lapin à○.

standard I *n* **1** (level) niveau *m*; **not to be up to ~** ne pas avoir le niveau requis; **2** (official specification) norme *f* (**for** de); **3** (banner) étendard *m*.
II *adj* [*size, rate, pay*] standard *inv*; [*procedure*] habituel/-elle; [*image*] traditionnel/-elle; **it's ~ practice** c'est l'usage.

standardize *vtr* normaliser, standardiser.

standard lamp *n* (GB) lampadaire *m*.

standard of living *n* niveau *m* de vie.

standby *n* (person) remplaçant/-e *m/f*; **to be on ~** [*army, emergency services*] être prêt/-e à intervenir; (for airline ticket) être en stand-by.

stand-in *n* remplaçant/-e *m/f*.

standing I *n* **1** (reputation) réputation *f*, rang *m* (**among** parmi; **with** chez); **2** (length of time) **of long ~** de longue date.
II *adj* **1** [*army, committee, force*] actif/-ive; **2** [*invitation*] permanent/-e.

standing order *n* virement *m* automatique.

stand-off *n* (US) impasse *f*.

standpoint *n* point *m* de vue.

standstill *n* **to be at a ~** [*traffic*] être à l'arrêt; [*factory, port*] être au point mort; [*work*] être arrêté/e; [*talks*] être arrivé/-e à une impasse; **to come to a ~** [*person, car*] s'arrêter.

staple I *n* **1** (for paper) agrafe *f*; **2** (basic food) aliment *m* de base.
II *adj* [*product, food, diet*] de base.
III *vtr* agrafer (**to** à; **onto** sur).

stapler *n* agrafeuse *f*.

star I *n* **1** (in sky) étoile *f*; **2** (celebrity) vedette *f*, star *f*; **3** (asterisk) astérisque *m*; **4 a three-~ hotel** un hôtel (à) trois étoiles.
II *vi* [*actor*] jouer le rôle principal (**in** dans).

starch *n* **1** (carbohydrate) féculents *mpl*; **2** (for clothes) amidon *m*.

stardom *n* célébrité *f*; **to rise to ~** devenir une vedette.

stare I *n* regard *m* fixe.
II *vi* **to ~ at sb/sth** regarder fixement qn/qch.

starfish *n* étoile *f* de mer.

stark *adj* [*landscape*] désolé/-e; [*room, decor*] nu/-e; **in ~ contrast to** en opposition totale avec.
IDIOMS **~ naked** tout/-e nu/-e.

starry *adj* [*night, sky*] étoilé/-e.

starry-eyed *adj* ébloui/-e (**about** par).

start I *n* **1** (beginning) début *m*; **2** (in sport) (advantage) avantage *m*; (in time, distance) avance *f*; (departure line) ligne *f* de départ; **3** (movement) **with a ~** en sursaut.
II *vtr* **1** (begin) commencer; entamer [*bottle, packet*]; **to ~ doing** commencer à faire; **2** (cause, initiate) déclencher [*quarrel, war*]; lancer [*fashion, rumour*]; **3** faire démarrer [*car*]; mettre [qch] en marche [*machine*].
III *vi* **1** (begin) commencer (**by doing** par faire); **to ~ again** recommencer; **2** [*car, engine, machine*] démarrer; **3** (depart) partir; **4** (jump nervously) sursauter (**in** de).
IV **to start with** *phr* **1** (firstly) d'abord, premièrement; **2** (at first) au début.
■ **start off**: ¶ **~ off 1** (set off) [*train, bus*] démarrer; [*person*] partir; **2** (begin) [*person*] commencer; [*business, employee*] débuter (**as** comme; **in** dans); ¶ **~** [**sth**] **off 1** commencer [*visit, talk*] (**with** par); **2** mettre [qch] en marche [*machine*].

■ **start out** (on journey) partir.
■ **start over** (US) recommencer (à zéro).
■ **start up**: ¶ **~ up** [*engine*] démarrer; ¶ **~** [**sth**] **up** faire démarrer [*car*]; ouvrir [*shop*]; créer [*business*].

starter *n* **1** (of race) starter *m*; **2** (on menu) hors-d'œuvre *m inv*.

startle *vtr* **1** (take aback) surprendre; **2** (alarm) effrayer.

startling *adj* saisissant/-e.

starvation *n* famine *f*; **to die of ~** mourir de faim.

starve I *vtr* affamer; (figurative) priver (**of** de).
II *vi* mourir de faim.

state I *n* **1** état *m*; **he's not in a fit ~ to drive** il n'est pas en état de conduire; **2** (government, nation) (also **State**) État *m*.
II **States** *n pl* **the States** les États-Unis *mpl*.
III *adj* **1** [*school, sector*] public/-ique; [*enterprise, pension*] d'État; [*subsidy*] de l'État; **2** [*occasion*] d'apparat; [*visit*] officiel/-ielle.
IV *vtr* **1** (declare) exposer [*fact, opinion*]; indiquer [*age, income*]; **to ~ that** [*person*] déclarer que; **2** (specify) spécifier [*amount, time, terms*]; exprimer [*preference*].
IDIOMS **to be in a ~** être dans tous ses états.

State Department *n* (US) ministère *m* des Affaires étrangères.

stately *adj* imposant/-e.

stately home *n* (GB) château *m*.

statement *n* **1** déclaration *f*; (official) communiqué *m*; **2** (also **bank ~**) relevé *m* de compte.

statesman *n* homme *m* d'État.

static I *n* **1** (also **~ electricity**) électricité *f* statique; **2** (interference) parasites *mpl*.
II *adj* **1** (stationary) [*image*] fixe; [*traffic*] bloqué; **2** (stable) [*population, prices*] stationnaire.

station I *n* **1** (also **railway ~** GB) gare *f*; **2** (radio, TV) station *f*; **3** (also **police ~**) commissariat *m*; (small) poste *m* de police.
II *vtr* poster [*officer, guard*]; stationner [*troops*].

stationary *adj* immobile, à l'arrêt.

stationer ▶ 626 *n* (also **~'s**) papeterie *f*.

stationery *n* fournitures *fpl* de bureau; (writing paper) papier *m* à lettres.

station wagon *n* (US) break *m*.

statistic *n* statistique *f*.

statistical *adj* statistique.

statue *n* statue *f*.

stature *n* **1** (height) taille *f*; **2** (status) envergure *f*.

status *n* **1** (position) position *f*; **2** (prestige) prestige *m*; **3** (legal, professional) statut *m* (**as** de); **financial ~** situation *f* financière.

status quo *n* statu quo *m*.

status symbol *n* signe *m* de prestige.

statute *n* texte *m* de loi; **by ~** par la loi.

staunch *adj* [*supporter, defence*] loyal/-e; [*Catholic, communist*] fervent/-e.

stave *n* (Mus) portée *f*.
■ **stave off** tromper [*hunger, fatigue*]; écarter [*threat*].

stay I *n* **1** (visit) séjour *m*; **2 ~ of execution** sursis *m*.
II *vi* **1** (remain) rester; **to ~ for lunch** rester (à) déjeuner; **2** (have accommodation) loger; **to ~ in a hotel/with a friend** loger à l'hôtel/chez un ami; **to ~ overnight** passer la nuit; **3** (visit) passer quelques jours (**with** chez).
■ **stay in** rester à la maison.
■ **stay out**: **to ~ out late/all night** rentrer tard/ne pas rentrer de la nuit; **to ~ out of trouble** éviter les ennuis.
■ **stay up 1** (waiting for sb) veiller; **2** (as habit) se coucher tard; **3** (not fall down) tenir.

staying-power *n* endurance *f*.

steadfast *adj* tenace.

steadily *adv* **1** (gradually) progressivement; **2** [*work, rain*] sans interruption.

steady I *adj* **1** (continual) [*stream, increase*] constant/-e; [*rain*] incessant/-e; [*breathing, progress*] régulier/-ière; **2** (stable) stable; **to hold** [**sth**] **~** bien tenir [*ladder*]; **3** [*voice, hand*] ferme; [*gaze*] calme; **4** (reliable) [*job*] stable; [*relationship*] durable.
II *vtr* **to ~ one's nerves** se calmer les nerfs.

steak *n* (of beef) steak *m*; (of fish) darne *f*.

steal I *vtr* voler (**from sb** à qn).
II *vi* **1** (thieve) voler; **2** (creep) **to ~ into/out of a room** entrer/quitter une pièce subrepticement.

stealing *n* vol *m*.

stealthy *adj* [*step, glance*] furtif/-ive.

steam I *n* vapeur *f*.
II *vtr* faire cuire [qch] à la vapeur [*vegetables*].
III *vi* fumer, dégager de la vapeur.
IDIOMS **to run out of ~** s'essouffler; **to let off ~** décompresser.
■ **steam up** [*window, glasses*] s'embuer.

steam engine *n* locomotive *f* à vapeur.

steamer *n* (boat) (bateau *m* à) vapeur *m*.

steamroller *n* rouleau *m* compresseur.

steel I *n* acier *m*.
II *v refl* **to ~ oneself** s'armer de courage.

steelworks, **steelyard** *n* installations *fpl* sidérurgiques.

steep I *adj* **1** [*slope, stairs*] raide; [*street, path*] escarpé/-e; [*roof*] en pente raide; **2** (sharp) [*rise, fall*] fort/-e (*before n*); **3**○ [*price*] exorbitant/-e.
II *vtr* **to ~ sth in** faire tremper qch dans.

steeple *n* (tower) clocher *m*; (spire) flèche *f*.

steer I *n* (animal) bouvillon *m*.
II *vtr* **1** piloter [*ship, car*]; **2** (guide) diriger [*person*].
III *vi* (in car) piloter; (in boat) gouverner.
IDIOMS **to ~ clear of sb/sth** se tenir à l'écart de qn/qch.

steering wheel *n* volant *m*.

stem I *n* **1** (of flower, leaf) tige *f*; (of fruit) queue *f*; **2** (of glass) pied *m*.
II *vtr* arrêter [*flow*]; enrayer [*advance, tide*].
III *vi* **to ~ from** provenir de.

stencil I *n* pochoir *m*.
II *vtr* décorer [qch] au pochoir [*fabric, surface*].

stenography *n* (US) sténographie *f*.

step I *n* **1** (pace) pas *m*; **2** (measure) mesure *f*; **to**

take ~s prendre des mesures; **3** (stage) étape *f* (**in** dans); **4** (stair) marche *f*; **~s** (small ladder) escabeau *m*.
II *vi* marcher (**in** dans; **on** sur); **to ~ into** entrer dans [*lift*]; monter dans [*dinghy*]; **to ~ off** descendre de [*pavement*]; **to ~ over** enjamber [*fence*].
IDIOMS **one ~ at a time** chaque chose en son temps.
■ **step down** se retirer; (as electoral candidate) se désister.
■ **step in** intervenir (**and do** pour faire).
■ **step up** accroître [*production*]; intensifier [*campaign*].

stepbrother *n* demi-frère *m*.

step-by-step I *adj* [*guide*] complet/-ète.
II **step by step** *adv* [*explain*] étape par étape.

stepdaughter *n* belle-fille *f*.

stepfather *n* beau-père *m*.

stepladder *n* escabeau *m*.

stepmother *n* belle-mère *f*.

stepping stone *n* pierre *f* de gué; (figurative) tremplin *m*.

stepsister *n* demi-sœur *f*.

stepson *n* beau-fils *m*.

stereo *n* **1** (sound) stéréo *f*; **in ~** en stéréo; **2** (also **~ system**) chaîne *f* stéréo; **personal ~** baladeur *m*.

stereotype *n* stéréotype *m*.

sterile *adj* stérile.

sterilize *vtr* stériliser.

sterling ▶**582** *n* livre *f* sterling *inv*.

stern I *n* (of ship) poupe *f*.
II *adj* sévère.

steroid *n* stéroïde *m*.

stew I *n* ragoût *m*.
II *vtr* cuire [qch] en ragoût [*meat*]; faire cuire [*fruit*]; **~ed apples** compote *f* de pommes.

steward ▶**626** *n* (on plane, ship) steward *m*; (of club) intendant/-e *m/f*; (at races) organisateur *m*.

stewardess ▶**626** *n* (on plane) hôtesse *f* (de l'air).

stick I *n* **1** (of wood, chalk, dynamite) bâton *m*; **2** (also **walking ~**) canne *f*; **3** (in hockey) crosse *f*.
II *vtr* **1 to ~ sth into sth** planter qch dans qch; **2**○ (put) mettre; **3** (fix in place) coller [*poster, stamp*] (**on** sur; **to** à).
III *vi* **1 the thorn stuck in my finger** l'épine m'est restée dans le doigt; **2** [*stamp, glue*] coller; **to ~ to the pan** [*sauce, rice*] attacher○; **3** [*drawer, door, lift*] se coincer; **4** (remain) rester; **to ~ in sb's mind** rester gravé dans la mémoire de qn.
■ **stick out**: ¶ **~ out** [*nail, sharp object*] dépasser (**of** de); **his ears ~ out** il a les oreilles décollées; ¶ **~ [sth] out**: **to ~ out one's hand/foot** tendre la main/le pied; **to ~ one's tongue out** tirer la langue.
■ **stick to 1** (keep to) s'en tenir à [*facts, point*]; maintenir [*story, version*]; **2** (follow) suivre [*river, road*].
■ **stick together 1** [*pages*] se coller; **2**○ (be loyal) être solidaires; **3**○ (not separate) rester ensemble.
■ **stick up** (project) se dresser; **to ~ up for sb** défendre qn.

sticker *n* autocollant *m*.

sticking plaster *n* pansement *m* adhésif, sparadrap *m*.

sticky *n* **1** [*floor, fingers*] poisseux/-euse; [*label*] adhésif/-ive; **2** (sweaty) [*hand, palm*] moite.

stiff I *adj* **1** raide; (after sport, sleeping badly) courbaturé/-e; **~ neck** torticolis *m*; **to have ~ legs** (after sport) avoir des courbatures dans les jambes; **2** [*lever, handle*] dur/-e à manier; **3** [*manner, style*] compassé/-e; **4** (tough) [*sentence*] sévère; [*exam, climb*] difficile; [*competition*] rude; **5** (high) [*charge, fine*] élevé/-e; **6 a ~ drink** un remontant.
II○ *adv* **to bore sb ~** ennuyer qn à mourir; **to be scared ~** avoir une peur bleue.

stiffen I *vtr* renforcer [*card*]; empeser [*fabric*].
II *vi* **1** [*person*] se raidir; **2** [*egg white*] devenir ferme; [*mixture*] prendre de la consistance.

stifle *vtr* étouffer.

stigma *n* stigmate *m*.

stile *n* échalier *m*.

still[1] *adv* **1** encore, toujours; **he's ~ as crazy as ever!** il est toujours aussi fou!; **they're ~ in town** ils sont encore en ville; **2** (referring to the future) encore; **I have four exams ~ to go** j'ai encore quatre examens à passer; **3** (nevertheless) quand même; **4** (with comparatives) encore; **better/worse ~** encore mieux/pire.

still[2] I *n* **1** (for making alcohol) alambic *m*; **2** (photograph) photo *f* de plateau.
II *adj* **1** (motionless) [*air, water*] calme; [*hand, person*] immobile; **2** (peaceful) [*countryside, streets*] tranquille; **3** [*drink*] non gazeux/-euse.
III *adv* [*lie, stay*] immobile; **to sit ~** se tenir tranquille; **to stand ~** ne pas bouger.

still life *n* nature *f* morte.

stilted *adj* guindé/-e.

stimulate *vtr* stimuler.

stimulating *adj* stimulant/-e.

stimulus *n* **1** (physical) stimulus *m*; **2** (boost) impulsion *f*; **3** (incentive) stimulant *m*.

sting I *n* **1** (part of insect) aiguillon *m*; **2** (result of being stung) piqûre *f*.
II *vtr* **1** [*insect*] piquer; **2** [*wind*] cingler.
III *vi* (gen) piquer; [*cut*] cuire.

stingy *adj* radin/-e○.

stink I *n* (mauvaise) odeur *f*.
II *vi* puer.

stint I *n* **to do a three-year ~** travailler trois ans.
II *vi* **to ~ on** lésiner sur [*drink, presents*].

stipulate *vtr* stipuler (**that** que).

stir I *n* **to cause (quite) a ~** faire sensation.
II *vtr* **1** remuer [*liquid, sauce*]; mélanger [*paint, powder*]; **to ~ sth into sth** incorporer qch à qch; **2** [*breeze*] agiter [*leaves, papers*].
III *vi* **1** [*leaves, papers*] trembler; [*curtains*] remuer; **2** (budge) bouger.
■ **stir up** provoquer [*trouble*]; attiser [*hatred, unrest*]; exciter [*crowd*].

stir-fry I *n* sauté *m*.
II *vtr* faire sauter [*beef, vegetable*].
stirring *adj* [*story*] passionnant/-e; [*music, speech*] enthousiasmant/-e.
stirrup *n* étrier *m*.
stitch I *n* **1** (in sewing, embroidery) point *m*; (in knitting, crochet) maille *f*; **2** (in wound) point *m* de suture; **3** (pain) point *m* de côté.
II *vtr* coudre (**to, onto** à); recoudre [*wound*].
stoat *n* hermine *f*.
stock I *n* **1** (supply) stock *m*; **we're out of ~** nous n'en avons plus; **2** (descent) souche *f*, origine *f*; **3** (Culin) bouillon *m*; **4** (livestock) bétail *m*.
II **stocks** *n pl* **1** (GB) (in finance) valeurs *fpl*, titres *mpl*; **~s and shares** valeurs *fpl* mobilières; **2** (US) actions *fpl*; **3 the ~s** le pilori.
III *adj* [*size*] courant/-e; [*answer*] classique; [*character*] stéréotypé/-e.
IV *vtr* **1** (sell) avoir, vendre; **2** remplir [*fridge*]; garnir [*shelves*]; approvisionner [*shop*].
IDIOMS **to take ~** faire le point (**of** sur).
■ **stock up** s'approvisionner (**with, on** en).
stockbroker ▶ 626 *n* agent *m* de change.
stock exchange *n* **the ~** la Bourse.
Stockholm ▶ 448 *pr n* Stockholm.
stocking *n* bas *m*.
stock market *n* **1** (stock exchange) Bourse *f* (des valeurs); **2** (prices, trading activity) marché *m* (des valeurs).
stockpile *vtr* stocker [*weapons*]; faire des stocks de [*food, goods*].
stock room *n* magasin *m*.
stocktaking *n* inventaire *m*.
stocky *adj* trapu/-e.
stodgy *adj* [*food*] bourratif/-ive.
stoical *adj* stoïque.
stoke *vtr* (also **~ up**) alimenter [*fire, furnace*].
stolid *adj* [*person, character*] flegmatique.
stomach I *n* estomac *m*; (belly) ventre *m*.
II *vtr* supporter [*person, attitude*].
stomach ache *n* **to have (a) ~** avoir mal au ventre.
stone ▶ 573 I *n* **1** pierre *f*; (pebble) caillou *m*; **2** (in fruit) noyau *m*; **3** (GB) (weight) = *6.35 kg*.
II *vtr* dénoyauter [*peach*].
Stone Age *n* âge *m* de pierre.
stone mason ▶ 626 *n* tailleur *m* de pierre.
stony *adj* **1** (rocky) pierreux/-euse; **2** [*look, silence*] glacial/-e.
stool *n* tabouret *m*.
stoop I *n* **to have a ~** avoir le dos voûté.
II *vi* être voûté/-e; (bend down) se baisser; **to ~ so low as to do** s'abaisser jusqu'à faire.
stop I *n* **1** (gen) arrêt *m*; **to come to a ~** [*vehicle, work, progress*] s'arrêter; **to put a ~ to** mettre fin à; **2** (in telegram) stop *m*.
II *vtr* **1** (cease) arrêter; (temporarily) interrompre [*activity*]; **to ~ doing** arrêter de faire; **2** (prevent) empêcher; **to ~ sb (from) doing** empêcher qn de faire; **3** supprimer [*allowance*]; **to ~ a cheque** faire opposition à un chèque; **4** (plug) boucher [*gap, hole, bottle*].
III *vi* s'arrêter.
IV *v refl* **to ~ oneself** se retenir.
■ **stop off** (on journey) faire un arrêt.
stopgap *n* bouche-trou *m*.
stopover *n* escale *f*.
stoppage *n* (strike) arrêt *m* de travail.
stopper *n* (for flask, jar) bouchon *m*.
stopwatch *n* chronomètre *m*.
storage I *n* (of food, fuel) stockage *m* (**of** de); **to be in ~** [*furniture*] être au garde-meuble.
II *adj* [*space*] de rangement.
storage heater *n* radiateur *m* électrique à accumulation.
store I *n* **1** ▶ 626 (shop) magasin *m*; (smaller) boutique *f*; **2** (supply) provision *f*; **3** (place) (for food, fuel) réserve *f*; (for furniture) garde-meuble *m*; **4 what does the future have in ~ for us?** qu'est-ce que l'avenir nous réserve?
II *vtr* **1** conserver [*food, information*]; ranger [*furniture*]; **2** (Comput) mémoriser [*data*].
storekeeper ▶ 626 *n* (US) commerçant/-e *m/f*.
storeroom *n* (in house, school, office) réserve *f*; (in factory, shop) magasin *m*.
storey (GB), **story** (US) *n* étage *m*; **on the third ~** (GB) au troisième étage; (US) au quatrième étage.
stork *n* cigogne *f*.
storm I *n* tempête *f*; (thunderstorm) orage *m*.
II *vtr* prendre [qch] d'assaut [*citadel, prison*].
III *vi* **he ~ed off in a temper** il est parti furibond.
stormy *adj* orageux/-euse.
story *n* **1** (gen) histoire *f* (**about, of** de); **a true ~** une histoire vécue; **a ghost ~** une histoire de fantômes; **2** (in newspaper) article *m* (**on, about** sur); **3** (rumour) rumeur *f* (**about** sur); **the ~ goes that** on raconte que; **4** (US) (floor) étage *m*.
storybook *n* livre *m* de contes.
stout *adj* **1** (fat) corpulent/-e; **2** (strong) [*wall*] épais/-aisse.
stove *n* **1** (cooker) cuisinière *f*; **2** (heater) poêle *m*.
stow *vtr* ranger [*baggage*].
stowaway *n* passager/-ère *m/f* clandestin/-e.
straddle *vtr* enfourcher [*horse, bike*]; s'asseoir à califourchon sur [*chair*].
straggle *vi* **1** [*houses, villages*] être disséminé/-e le long de; **2** (dawdle) traîner.
straggler *n* traînard/-e *m/f*.
straggly *adj* [*beard*] clairsemé/-e; [*hair*] mou/molle.
straight I *adj* **1** [*line, nose, road*] droit/-e; [*hair*] raide; **in a ~ line** en ligne droite; **2** (level, upright) bien droit/-e; **the picture isn't ~** le tableau est de travers; **3** (tidy, in order) en ordre; **4** (clear) **to get sth ~** comprendre qch; **to set the record ~** mettre les choses au clair; **5** (honest, direct) [*person*] honnête, droit/-e; [*answer, question*] clair/-e; **to be ~ with sb** jouer franc-jeu avec qn; **6** [*choice*] simple; **7** [*spirits, drink*] sec, sans eau; **8** [*actor, role*] sérieux/-ieuse.
II *adv* **1** droit; **stand up ~!** tenez-vous droit!;

to go/keep ~ ahead aller/continuer tout droit; **to look ~ ahead** regarder droit devant soi; **2** (without delay) directement; **to go ~ back to Paris** rentrer directement à Paris; **3** (frankly) tout net; **I'll tell you ~**○ je vous le dirai tout net; **~ out** carrément; **4** (neat) [*drink*] sec, sans eau.
IDIOMS **to keep a ~ face** garder son sérieux.

straightaway *adv* tout de suite.

straighten *vtr* tendre [*arm, leg*]; redresser [*picture, teeth*]; ajuster [*tie, hat*]; défriser [*hair*].
■ **straighten out**: **to ~ things out** (resolve) arranger les choses.
■ **straighten up**: ¶ **~ up** [*person*] se redresser; ¶ **~ [sth] up** (tidy) ranger [*objects, room*].

straightforward *adj* [*answer, person*] franc/franche; [*account*] simple.

straight-laced *adj* collet-monté *inv*.

strain I *n* **1** (force) effort *m* (**on** sur); **2** (pressure) (on person) stress *m*; (in relations) tension *f*; **3** (of virus, bacteria) souche *f*.
II *vtr* **1 to ~ one's eyes** (to see) plisser les yeux; **to ~ one's ears** tendre l'oreille; **2** (try) mettre [qch] à rude épreuve [*patience*]; **3** (injure) **to ~ a muscle** se froisser un muscle; **to ~ one's eyes** se fatiguer les yeux; **to ~ one's back** se faire un tour de reins; **4** (sieve) passer [*sauce*]; égoutter [*vegetables, pasta, rice*].
IV *vi* **to ~ at** tirer sur [*leash, rope*].

strainer *n* passoire *f*.

strait *n* détroit *m*.
IDIOMS **to be in dire ~s** être aux abois.

straitjacket *n* camisole *f* de force.

strand I *n* (gen) fil *m*; (of hair) mèche *f*.
II *vtr* **to be ~ed** rester en rade○; **to leave sb ~ed** laisser qn en rade○.

strange *adj* **1** (unfamiliar) inconnu/-e; **a ~ man** un inconnu; **2** (odd) bizarre; **it is ~ (that)** il est bizarre que (+ *subjunctive*).

strangely *adj* [*behave, react*] d'une façon étrange; [*quiet, empty*] étrangement; **~ enough,...** chose étrange,...

stranger *n* (from elsewhere) étranger/-ère *m/f*; (unknown person) inconnu/-e *m/f*.

strangle *vtr* étrangler.

strap I *n* (on shoe) bride *f*; (on case, harness) courroie *f*; (on watch) bracelet *m*; (on handbag) bandoulière *f*; (on dress, bra) bretelle *f*.
II *vtr* attacher (**to** à).

stratagem *n* stratagème *m*.

strategic *adj* stratégique.

strategy *n* stratégie *f*.

straw *n* paille *f*.
IDIOMS **to clutch at ~s** se raccrocher à n'importe quoi; **the last ~** la goutte qui fait déborder le vase.

strawberry I *n* fraise *f*; **strawberries and cream** fraises à la crème.
II *adj* [*tart*] aux fraises; [*ice cream*] à la fraise; [*jam*] de fraises.

stray I *n* (dog) chien *m* errant; (cat) chat *m* vagabond.
II *adj* [*dog*] errant/-e; [*cat*] vagabond/-e; [*bullet*] perdu/-e; [*tourist*] isolé/-e.
III *vi* **1** (wander) s'égarer; **to ~ from the road** s'écarter de la route; **2** [*eyes, mind*] errer.

streak I *n* **1** (in character) côté *m*; **2** (period) **a winning/losing ~** une bonne/mauvaise passe; **3** (of paint) traînée *f*; **~ of lightning** éclair *m*; **4** (in hair) mèche *f*.
II *vtr* **1** strier [*sea, sky*]; **2 to get one's hair ~ed** se faire faire des mèches.
III *vi* **to ~ past** passer comme une flèche.

streaky bacon *n* (GB) bacon *m* entrelardé.

stream I *n* **1** (brook) ruisseau *m*; **2 a ~ of** un flot de [*traffic, questions*]; **a ~ of abuse** un torrent d'insultes.
II *vi* **1** (flow) ruisseler; **sunlight was ~ing into the room** le soleil entrait à flots dans la pièce; **people ~ed out of the theatre** un flot de gens sortait du théâtre; **2** [*banners, hair*] **to ~ in the wind** flotter au vent; **3** [*eyes, nose*] couler.

streamer *n* (of paper) banderole *f*.

streamlined *adj* **1** [*cooker, furniture*] aux lignes modernes; [*hull, body*] caréné/-e; **2** [*production, system*] simplifié/-e.

street *n* rue *f*; **in** or **on the ~** dans la rue.

streetlamp *n* (old gas-lamp) réverbère *m*; (modern) lampadaire *m*.

street market *n* marché *m* en plein air.

street plan *n* indicateur *m* des rues.

strength *n* (of wind, person, government, bond, argument) force *f*; (of lens, magnet, voice, army) puissance *f*; (of structure, equipment) solidité *f*; (of material) résistance *f*; (of feeling) intensité *f*.

strengthen *vtr* renforcer [*building, argument, love, position*]; consolider [*bond, links*]; affirmer [*power, role*]; fortifier [*muscles*]; raffermir [*dollar*].

strenuous *adj* [*exercise*] énergique; [*activity, job*] ardu/-e.

stress I *n* **1** (nervous) tension *f*, stress *m*; **mental ~** tension nerveuse; **to be under ~** être stressé/-e; **2** (emphasis) accent *m* (**on** sur); **to lay ~ on** insister sur [*fact, problem*]; **3** (in physics) effort *m*; **4** (in pronouncing) accent *m*.
II *vtr* mettre l'accent sur, insister sur; **to ~ the importance of sth** souligner l'importance *f* de qch; **to ~ (that)** souligner que.

stressed *adj* **1** (also **~ out**) stressé/-e; **2** [*syllable*] accentué/-e.

stressful *adj* stressant/-e.

stretch I *n* **1** (of road, track) tronçon *m*; (of coastline, river) partie *f*; **2** (of water, countryside) étendue *f*; **3** (period) période *f*; **to work for 12 hours at a ~** travailler 12 heures d'affilée.
II *adj* [*cover, fabric, waist*] extensible.
III *vtr* **1** (extend) tendre [*rope, net*]; étirer [*arms, legs*]; **to ~ one's legs** (figurative) se dégourdir les jambes; **2** étirer [*elastic*]; élargir [*shoe*]; **3** déformer [*truth*]; **4** utiliser [qch] au maximum [*budget, resources*].
IV *vi* **1** [*person*] s'étirer; **2** [*road, track*] s'étaler (**for, over** sur); [*beach, moor*] s'étendre (**for** sur); **3** [*elastic*] s'étendre; [*shoe*] s'élargir.
■ **stretch out**: ¶ **~ out** s'étendre; ¶ **~**

[sth] out tendre [*hand, foot*] (**towards** vers); étendre [*arm, leg*]; étaler [*nets, sheet*].

stretcher *n* brancard *m*.

strew *vtr* éparpiller [*litter, paper*] (**on** sur); **~n with** jonché/-e de.

stricken *adj* **1** [*face*] affligé/-e; [*area*] sinistré/-e; **~ by** frappé/-e de [*illness*]; pris/-e de [*fear*]; accablé/-e de [*guilt*]; **2** [*plane, ship*] en détresse.

strict *adj* [*person*] strict/-e (**about** sur); [*view*] rigide; [*silence*] absolu/-e; [*Methodist, Catholic*] de stricte observance.

strictly *adv* **1** [*treat*] avec sévérité; **2** [*confidential, prohibited*] strictement; **~ speaking** à proprement parler.

stride I *n* enjambée *f*.
II *vi* **to ~ out/in** sortir/entrer à grands pas; **to ~ across sth** enjamber qch.
IDIOMS **to take sth in one's ~** prendre qch calmement.

strife *n* conflits *mpl*.

strike I *n* **1** grève *f*; **on ~** en grève; **2** (attack) attaque *f*.
II *vtr* **1** (hit) frapper [*person, vessel*]; heurter [*rock, tree, pedestrian*]; **he struck his head on the table** il s'est cogné la tête contre la table; **to be struck by lightning** être frappé/-e par la foudre; **2** (afflict) frapper [*area, people*]; **3** [*idea, thought*] venir à l'esprit de [*person*]; [*resemblance*] frapper; **to ~ sb as odd** paraître étrange à qn; **4**○ tomber sur○ [*oil, gold*]; **5** conclure [*deal, bargain*]; **to ~ a balance** trouver le juste milieu (**between** entre); **6** frotter [*match*]; **7** [*clock*] sonner.
III *vi* **1** (gen) frapper; **2** [*workers*] faire (la) grève.
■ **strike down** terrasser [*person*].
■ **strike out**: ¶ **~ out** (hit out) frapper; **to ~ out at** attaquer [*adversary*]; s'en prendre à [*critics*]; ¶ **~ [sth] out** rayer.
■ **strike up** [*orchestra*] commencer à jouer; **to ~ up a conversation with** engager la conversation avec; **to ~ up a friendship with** se lier d'amitié avec.

strikebreaker *n* briseur/-euse *m/f* de grève.

strikebreaking *n* retour *m* au travail.

striker *n* **1** (person on strike) gréviste *mf*; **2** (in football) attaquant/-e *m/f*.

striking *adj* [*person*] (good-looking) beau/belle (*before n*); [*design, contrast*] frappant/-e.

string I *n* **1** (twine) ficelle *f*; **a piece of ~** un bout de ficelle; **2** (on bow, racket) corde *f*; (on puppet) fil *m*; **3** (series) **a ~ of** un défilé de [*visitors*]; une succession de [*successes, awards*]; **4** (set) **~ of pearls** collier *m* de perles.
II **strings** *n pl* (Mus) **the ~s** les cordes *fpl*.
III *vtr* enfiler [*beads, pearls*] (**on** sur).
IDIOMS **to pull ~s**○ faire jouer le piston○.
■ **string along**○ (GB): ¶ **~ along** suivre; ¶ **~ [sb] along** mener qn en bateau○.
■ **string together** aligner [*words*].

string bean *n* haricot *m* à écosser.

stringed instrument ▶586 *n* instrument *m* à cordes.

stringent *adj* rigoureux/-euse.

strip I *n* bande *f* (**of** de).
II *vtr* **1** déshabiller [*person*]; vider [*house, room*]; défaire [*bed*]; **to ~ sb of** dépouiller qn de [*belongings, rights*]; **2** (remove paint from) décaper; **3** (dismantle) démonter.
III *vi* se déshabiller.

strip cartoon *n* bande *f* dessinée.

stripe *n* **1** (on fabric, wallpaper) rayure *f*; **2** (on animal) (isolated) rayure *f*; (one of many) zébrure *f*.

striped *adj* rayé/-e.

strip lighting *n* éclairage *m* au néon *m*.

strive *vi* s'efforcer (**to do** de faire).

stroke I *n* **1** (gen) coup *m*; **at a single ~** d'un seul coup; **a ~ of luck** un coup de chance; **a ~ of genius** un trait de génie; **2** (in swimming) mouvement *m* des bras; (particular style) nage *f*; **3** (of pen) trait *m*; (of brush) touche *f*; **4** (Med) congestion *f* cérébrale.
II *vtr* caresser.

stroll I *n* promenade *f*, tour *m*.
II *vi* se promener; (aimlessly) flâner.

stroller *n* (US) (pushchair) poussette *f*.

strong *adj* **1** (powerful) [*arm, person, current, wind*] fort/-e; [*army, swimmer, country*] puissant/-e; **2** [*heart, fabric, table*] solide; [*candidate, argument*] de poids; **3** [*tea, medicine, glue*] fort/-e; [*coffee*] serré/-e; **4** [*smell, taste*] fort/-e; **5** [*desire, feeling*] profond/-e; **6** [*chance, possibility*] fort/-e (*before n*).
IDIOMS **to be still going ~** [*person*] se porter toujours très bien; [*relationship*] aller toujours bien; **it's not my ~ point** ce n'est pas mon fort.

strongbox *n* coffre-fort *m*.

stronghold *n* forteresse *f*; (figurative) fief *m*.

strongly *adv* **1** [*oppose, advise*] vivement; [*protest, deny*] énergiquement; [*suspect*] fortement; [*believe*] fermement; **I feel ~ about this** c'est quelque chose qui me tient à cœur; **2** (solidly) solidement.

strongroom *n* chambre *f* forte.

strong-willed *adj* obstiné/-e.

structure I *n* **1** (organization) structure *f*; **2** (building) construction *f*.
II *vtr* structurer [*argument, essay, novel*]; organiser [*day, life*].

struggle I *n* (gen) lutte *f*; (scuffle) rixe *f*.
II *vi* **1** (put up a fight) se débattre (**to do** pour faire); (tussle, scuffle) se battre; **2** (try hard) lutter (**to do** pour faire; **for** pour).

strum *vtr* (carelessly) gratter [*guitar, tune*]; (gently) jouer doucement de [*guitar*].

strut I *n* montant *m*.
II *vi* (also **~ about**, **~ around**) se pavaner.

stub I *n* (of pencil) bout *m*; (of cheque, ticket) talon *m*; (of cigarette) mégot *m*.
II *vtr* **to ~ one's toe** se cogner l'orteil.
■ **stub out** écraser [*cigarette*].

stubble *n* **1** (straw) chaume *m*; **2** (beard) barbe *f* de plusieurs jours.

stubborn *adj* [*person, animal*] entêté/-e; [*behaviour*] obstiné/-e; [*refusal*] opiniâtre; [*stain*] rebelle.

stuck *adj* **1** (jammed, trapped) coincé/-e; **to get ~ in** rester coincé/-e dans [*lift*]; s'enliser dans [*mud*]; **2 to be ~ for an answer** ne pas savoir quoi répondre.

stuck-up° *adj* bêcheur/-euse°.

stud *n* **1** (on jacket) clou *m*; (on door) clou *m* à grosse tête; (on boot) crampon *m*; **2** (stallion) étalon *m*; (horse farm) haras *m*; **3** (earring) clou *m* d'oreilles.

student *n* étudiant/-e *m/f*.

student ID card *n* carte *f* d'étudiant.

student nurse *n* élève *mf* infirmier/-ière.

student teacher *n* enseignant/-e *m/f* stagiaire.

studio *n* (gen) studio *m*; (of painter) atelier *m*.

studious *adj* studieux/-ieuse.

study I *n* **1** étude *f* (**of, on** de); **2** (room) bureau *m*.
II *vtr* étudier.
III *vi* faire ses études.

stuff I *n* (things) choses *fpl*, trucs° *mpl*; (personal belongings) affaires *fpl*; (rubbish, junk) bazar° *m*; (substance) truc° *m*.
II *vtr* **1** rembourrer [*cushion*] (**with** de); bourrer [*suitcase, room*] (**with** de); **2** (shove) fourrer° (**in, into** dans); **3** (Culin) farcir [*turkey, chicken*]; **4** empailler [*dead animal, bird*].

stuffed *adj* [*turkey, chicken*] farci/-e; [*toy animal*] en peluche; [*bird, fox*] empaillé/-e.

stuffing *n* **1** (Culin) farce *f*; **2** (of furniture, pillow) rembourrage *m*.

stuffy *adj* **1** (airless) étouffant/-e; **2** (staid) guindé/-e.

stumble *vi* **1** (trip) trébucher (**against** contre; **on, over** sur); **2** (in speech) hésiter.
■ **stumble across** tomber par hasard sur [*rare find*].

stumbling block *n* obstacle *m*.

stump I *n* (of tree) souche *f*; (of candle, pencil, cigar) bout *m*; (of tooth) chicot *m*; (part of limb, tail) moignon *m*.
II° *vtr* **to be ~ed by sth** être en peine d'expliquer qch; **I'm ~ed!** (in quiz) je sèche°!; (nonplussed) aucune idée!

stun *vtr* **1** (daze) assommer; **2** (amaze) stupéfier.

stunned *adj* **1** (dazed) assommé/-e; **2** (amazed) [*person*] stupéfait/-e; [*silence*] figé/-e.

stunning *adj* (beautiful) sensationnel/-elle.

stunt I *n* **1** (for attention) coup *m* organisé, truc° *m*; **2** (in film) cascade *f*.
II *vtr* empêcher [*development*]; nuire à [*plant growth*].

stunted *adj* rabougri/-e.

stupefying *adj* stupéfiant/-e.

stupid *adj* bête, stupide; **I've done something ~** j'ai fait une bêtise.

stupidity *n* bêtise *f*.

stupor *n* stupeur *f*; **in a drunken ~** hébété/-e par l'alcool.

sturdy *adj* robuste, solide.

stutter *vtr, vi* bégayer.

St Valentine's Day *n* la Saint-Valentin.

sty *n* **1** (for pigs) porcherie *f*; **2** (also **stye**) orgelet *m*.

style I *n* **1** (manner) style *m*; **2** (elegance) classe *f*; **to do things in ~** faire les choses en grand **3** (design) (of car, clothing) modèle *m*; (of house type *m*; **4** (fashion) mode *f*.
II *vtr* couper [*hair*].

stylish *adj* [*car, coat, person*] élégant/-e; [*resort restaurant*] chic.

stylist ▶ 626 *n* **1** (hairdresser) coiffeur/-euse *m, f*; **2** (designer) concepteur/-trice *m/f*.

stylus *n* pointe *f* de lecture.

suave *adj* [*person*] mielleux/-euse.

subconscious I *n* **the ~** le subconscient.
II *adj* inconscient/-e.

subcontinent *n* sous-continent *m*.

subcontract *vtr* sous-traiter (**out to** à).

subdivide *vtr* subdiviser.

subdue *vtr* soumettre [*people, nation*].

subdued *adj* [*person*] silencieux/-ieuse; [*excitement*] contenu/-e; [*lighting*] tamisé/-e.

subject I *n* **1** (topic) sujet *m*; **to change the ~** parler d'autre chose; **2** (at school, college) matière *f*; (for research, study) sujet *m*; **3 to be the ~ of an inquiry** faire l'objet d'une enquête; **4** (citizen) sujet/-ette *m/f*.
II *adj* **1** (liable) **to be ~ to** être sujet/-ette à [*flooding, fits*]; être passible de [*tax*]; **2** (dependent) **to be ~ to** dépendre de [*approval*]; être soumis/-e à [*law*].
III *vtr* **to ~ sb to sth** faire subir qch à qn.

subjective *adj* subjectif/-ive.

subjugate *vtr* subjuguer [*country, people*].

subjunctive *n* subjonctif *m*.

sublet *vtr, vi* sous-louer.

sublime *adj* [*beauty, genius*] sublime; [*indifference*] suprême.

subliminal *adj* subliminal/-e.

submarine *n* sous-marin *m*.

submerge *vtr* [*sea, flood*] submerger; [*person*] immerger (**in** dans).

submission *n* soumission *f* (**to** à).

submissive *adj* [*person*] soumis/-e; [*behaviour*] docile.

submit I *vtr* soumettre [*report, plan, script*] (**to** à); présenter [*bill, application*].
II *vi* se soumettre; **to ~ to** subir [*indignity, injustice*]; céder à [*will, demand*].

subnormal *adj* [*person*] arriéré/-e.

subordinate *n, adj* subalterne (*mf*).

subpoena *vtr* assigner [qn] à comparaître.

subscribe *vi* **1 to ~ to** partager [*view, values*]; **2 to ~ to** être abonné/-e à [*magazine*].

subscriber *n* abonné/-e *m/f* (**to** de).

subscription *n* abonnement *m* (**to** à).

subsequent *adj* (in past) ultérieur/-e; (in future) à venir.

subsequently *adv* par la suite.

subservient *adj* servile (**to** envers).

subside *vi* **1** [*storm, wind, noise*] s'apaiser; [*emotion*] se calmer; [*fever, excitement*] retomber; **2** [*building, land*] s'affaisser.

subsidiary I *n* (also **~ company**) filiale *f*.
II *adj* secondaire (**to** par rapport à).

subsidize *vtr* subventionner.
subsidy *n* subvention *f* (**to, for** à).
subsist *vi* subsister.
subsistence *n* subsistance *f*.
substance *n* **1** (gen) substance *f*; **2** (of argument, talks) essentiel *m*; (of claim, accusation) fondement *m*.
substandard *adj* de qualité inférieure.
substantial *adj* **1** (considerable) considérable; [*sum, quantity*] important/-e; [*meal*] substantiel/-ielle; **2** (solid) [*proof, lock*] solide.
substitute **I** *n* **1** (person) remplaçant/-e *m/f*; **2** (product, substance) succédané *m*.
II *vtr* substituer (**for** à).
subtitle *n* sous-titre *m*.
subtle *adj* (gen) subtil/-e; [*change*] imperceptible; [*hint*] voilé/-e; [*lighting*] tamisé/-e.
subtlety *n* subtilité *f*.
subtotal *n* sous-total *m*.
subtract *vtr* soustraire (**from** de).
subtraction *n* soustraction *f*.
suburb **I** *n* banlieue *f*; **inner ~** faubourg *m*.
II suburbs *n pl* **the ~s** la banlieue.
suburban *adj* [*street, shop, train*] de banlieue; (US) [*shopping mall*] à l'extérieur de la ville.
suburbia *n* banlieue *f*.
subversive **I** *n* élément *m* subversif.
II *adj* subversif/-ive.
subway *n* **1** (GB) (for pedestrians) passage *m* souterrain; **2** (US) (underground railway) métro *m*.
succeed **I** *vtr* succéder à [*person*].
II *vi* réussir; **to ~ in doing** réussir à faire.
succeeding *adj* qui suit, suivant/-e.
success *n* succès *m*, réussite *f*; **to be a ~** [*party*] être réussi/-e; [*film, person*] avoir du succès.
successful *adj* [*attempt, operation*] réussi/-e; [*plan, campaign*] couronné/-e de succès; [*film, book, writer*] (profitable) à succès; (well regarded) apprécié/-e; [*businessman*] prospère; [*career*] brillant/-e; **to be ~** réussir (**in doing** à faire).
successfully *adv* avec succès.
succession *n* **1** (sequence) série *f* (**of** de); **in ~** de suite; **in close ~** coup sur coup; **2** (inheriting) succession *f* (**to** à).
successive *adj* successif/-ive; [*day, week*] consécutif/-ive.
successor *n* successeur *m*.
succinct *adj* succinct/-e.
succulent *adj* succulent/-e.
succumb *vi* succomber (**to** à).
such **I** *det* tel/telle; (similar) pareil/-eille; **~ a situation** une telle situation; **in ~ a situation** dans une situation pareille; **some ~ remark** quelque chose comme ça; **there's no ~ thing** ça n'existe pas; **you'll do no ~ thing!** il n'en est pas question!; **in ~ a way that** d'une telle façon que; **~ money as I have** le peu d'argent or tout l'argent que j'ai.
II *adv* (with adjectives) si, tellement; (with nouns) tel/telle; **in ~ a persuasive way** d'une façon si convaincante; **~ a nice boy!** un garçon si gentil!; **~ good quality** une telle qualité; **I hadn't seen ~ a good film for years** je n'avais pas vu un aussi bon film depuis des années; **~ a lot of problems** tant de problèmes; **there were (ever○) ~ a lot of people** il y avait beaucoup de monde.
III such as *phr* comme, tel/telle que; **a house ~ as this** une maison comme celle-ci; **a person ~ as her** une personne comme elle; **have you ~ a thing as a screwdriver?** auriez-vous un tournevis par hasard?
such and such *det* tel/telle; **on ~ a topic** sur tel ou tel sujet.
suck **I** *vtr* sucer [*thumb, fruit, lollipop, pencil*]; (drink in) aspirer [*liquid, air*].
II *vi* **to ~ at** sucer; **to ~ on** tirer sur [*pipe*].
■ **suck up**: ¶ **~ up○** faire de la lèche○; **to ~ up to sb** cirer les pompes à qn○; ¶ **~ [sth] up** pomper [*liquid*]; aspirer [*dirt*].
sucker *n* **1○** (dupe) bonne poire○ *f*; **2** (on plant) surgeon *m*; **3** (pad) ventouse *f*.
suction *n* succion *f*.
sudden *adj* (gen) soudain/-e; [*movement*] brusque; **all of a ~** tout à coup.
suddenly *adv* [*die, grow pale*] subitement; [*happen*] tout à coup.
suds *n pl* (also **soap ~**) (foam) mousse *f* (de savon); (soapy water) eau *f* savonneuse.
sue **I** *vtr* intenter un procès à; **to ~ sb for divorce** demander le divorce à qn; **to ~ sb for damages** réclamer à qn des dommages-intérêts.
II *vi* intenter un procès.
suede **I** *n* daim *m*.
II *adj* [*shoe, glove*] en daim.
suffer **I** *vtr* subir [*loss, consequences, defeat*]; **to ~ a heart attack** avoir une crise cardiaque.
II *vi* **1** souffrir; **to ~ from** souffrir de [*rheumatism, heat*]; avoir [*headache, blood pressure, cold*]; **to ~ from depression** être dépressif/-ive; **2** (do badly) [*company, profits*] souffrir; [*health, quality, work*] s'en ressentir.
suffering **I** *n* souffrances *fpl* (**of** de).
II *adj* souffrant/-e.
sufficient *adj* suffisamment de, assez de; **to be ~** suffire.
sufficiently *adv* suffisamment, assez.
suffocate **I** *vtr* [*smoke, fumes*] asphyxier; [*person, anger*] étouffer.
II *vi* **1** (by smoke, fumes) être asphyxié/-e; (by pillow) être étouffé/-e; **2** (figurative) suffoquer.
suffocating *adj* [*smoke*] asphyxiant/-e; [*atmosphere, heat*] étouffant/-e.
suffrage *n* (right) droit *m* de vote; (system) suffrage *m*.
sugar *n* sucre *m*; **brown ~** sucre *m* roux.
sugar beet *n* betterave *f* à sucre.
sugar cane *n* canne *f* à sucre.
sugar lump *n* morceau *m* de sucre.
suggest *vtr* suggérer; **they ~ed that I (should) leave** ils m'ont suggéré de partir.
suggestion *n* **1** (gen) suggestion *f*; **at sb's ~** sur le conseil de qn; **2** (hint) soupçon *m* (**of** de); (of smile) pointe *f*.

suggestive *adj* suggestif/-ive.

suicidal *adj* suicidaire.

suicide *n* (action) suicide *m*; (person) suicidé/-e *m/f*; **to commit ~** se suicider.

suit I *n* **1** (man's) costume *m*; (woman's) tailleur *m*; **a ~ of armour** une armure (complète); **2** (lawsuit) procès *m*; **3** (in cards) couleur *f*.
II *vtr* **1** [*colour, outfit*] aller à [*person*]; **2** [*date, climate, arrangement*] convenir à.
III *vi* convenir.
IV *v refl* **to ~ oneself** faire comme on veut.

suitable *adj* [*accommodation, clothing, employment*] adéquat/-e; [*candidate*] apte; [*gift, gesture*] approprié/-e; [*moment*] opportun/-e; **to be ~ for** convenir à [*person*]; bien se prêter à [*climate, activity, occasion*].

suitably *adv* convenablement.

suitcase *n* valise *f*.

suite *n* **1** (gen) suite *f*; **2** (furniture) mobilier *m*.

suited *adj* **to be ~ to** [*place, clothes*] être commode pour; [*game, style*] convenir à; [*person*] être fait/-e pour.

sulk *vi* bouder (**about, over** à cause de).

sulky *adj* boudeur/-euse; **to look ~** faire la tête.

sullen *adj* [*person, expression*] renfrogné/-e; [*day, sky, mood*] maussade.

sulphur (GB), **sulfur** (US) *n* soufre *m*.

sulphuric acid *n* acide *m* sulfurique.

sultana *n* (Culin) raisin *m* de Smyrne.

sultry *adj* **1** [*day*] étouffant/-e; [*weather*] lourd/-e; **2** [*look, smile*] sensuel/-elle.

sum *n* **1** (of money) somme *f*; **2** (calculation) calcul *m*.
■ **sum up**: ¶ **~ up** récapituler; ¶ **~ up [sth]** résumer.

summarize *vtr* résumer [*book, problem*]; récapituler [*argument, speech*].

summary *n* résumé *m*.

summer I *n* été *m*; **in ~** en été.
II *adj* [*evening, resort, clothes*] d'été.

summer camp *n* (US) colonie *f* de vacances.

summer holiday (GB), **summer vacation** (US) *n* (gen) vacances *fpl* (d'été); (Sch, Univ) grandes vacances *fpl*.

summerhouse *n* pavillon *m* (de jardin).

summertime *n* été *m*.

summit *n* sommet *m*.

summon *vtr* **1** (gen) faire venir; **2** (Law) citer.
■ **summon up** rassembler [*energy, strength*] (**to do** pour faire).

summons I *n* **1** (Law) citation *f*; **2** (gen) injonction *f* (**from** de; **to** à).
II *vtr* citer (**to** à; **to do** à faire; **for** pour).

sumptuous *adj* somptueux/-euse.

sun *n* soleil *m*; **in the ~** au soleil.

sunbathe *vi* se faire bronzer.

sunbed *n* (lounger) chaise *f* longue; (with sunlamp) lit *m* solaire.

sun block *n* crème *f* écran total.

sunburn *n* coup *m* de soleil.

sunburned, **sunburnt** *adj* (burnt) brûlé/-e par le soleil; (tanned) (GB) bronzé/-e; **to get ~** attraper un coup de soleil.

Sunday ▶456 *pr n* dimanche *m*.

Sunday best *n* (**dressed**) **in one's ~** endimanché/-e.

sundial *n* cadran *m* solaire.

sundress *n* robe *f* bain de soleil.

sundries *n pl* articles *mpl* divers.

sundry *adj* divers/-e; (**to**) **all and ~** (à) tout le monde.

sunflower *n* tournesol *m*.

sunglasses *n pl* lunettes *fpl* de soleil.

sun hat *n* chapeau *m* de soleil.

sunken *adj* **1** [*treasure, wreck*] immergé/-e; **2** [*cheek*] creux/creuse; [*eye*] cave; **3** [*bath*] encastré/-e; [*garden*] en contrebas.

sunlight *n* lumière *f* du soleil.

sunny *adj* **1** ensoleillé/-e; **it's going to be ~** il va faire (du) soleil; **2** [*child, temperament*] enjoué/-e.

sunrise *n* lever *m* du soleil.

sunroof *n* toit *m* ouvrant.

sunset *n* coucher *m* du soleil.

sunshade *n* parasol *m*.

sunshine *n* soleil *m*.

sunstroke *n* insolation *f*.

suntan *n* bronzage *m*; **to get a ~** bronzer.

suntan lotion *n* lotion *f* solaire.

suntanned *adj* bronzé/-e.

suntan oil *n* huile *f* solaire.

super○ *adj, excl* formidable.

superb *adj* superbe.

supercilious *adj* dédaigneux/-euse.

superficial *adj* superficiel/-ielle.

superfluous *adj* superflu/-e.

superimpose *vtr* superposer (**on** à).

superintendent *n* **1** (supervisor) responsable *mf*; **2** (also **police ~**) ≈ commissaire *m* de police; **3** (US) (for apartments) concierge *mf*; **4** (US) (also **school ~**) inspecteur/-trice *m/f*.

superior I *n* supérieur/-e *m/f*.
II *adj* **1** supérieur/-e (**to** à; **in** en); [*product*] de qualité supérieure; **2** (condescending) condescendant/-e.

superiority *n* supériorité *f*.

superlative I *n* superlatif *m*.
II *adj* [*performance, service*] superbe.

supermarket *n* supermarché *m*.

supernatural I *n* surnaturel *m*.
II *adj* surnaturel/-elle.

superpower *n* superpuissance *f*.

supersonic *adj* supersonique.

superstition *n* superstition *f*.

superstitious *adj* superstitieux/-ieuse.

supervise *vtr* superviser [*activity, staff*]; surveiller [*child, patient*].

supervision *n* **1** (of staff, work) supervision *f*; **2** (of child, patient) surveillance *f*.

supervisor ▶626 *n* **1** (for staff) responsable *m*; **2** (GB) (for thesis) directeur/-trice *m/f* de thèse; **3** (US Sch) directeur/-trice *m/f* d'études.

supper *n* (evening meal) dîner *m*; (late snack) collation *f* (du soir); (after a show) souper *m*; **the Last Supper** la Cène *f*.

supple *adj* souple.

supplement I *n* **1** (fee) supplément *m*; **2** (to diet, income) complément *m* (**to** à); **3** (in newspaper) supplément *m*.
II *vtr* compléter [*diet, resources, training*] (**with** de); augmenter [*income, staff*] (**with** de).

supplementary *adj* supplémentaire.

supplier *n* fournisseur *m* (**of, to** de).

supply I *n* **1** (stock) réserves *fpl*; **in short ~** difficile à obtenir; **to get in a ~ of sth** s'approvisionner en qch; **2** (source) (of fuel, gas, oxygen) alimentation *f*; (of food) approvisionnement *m*; (of equipment) fourniture *f*.
II supplies *n pl* **1** (equipment) réserves *fpl*; **food supplies** ravitaillement *m*; **2** (for office) fournitures *fpl*.
III *vtr* (provide) fournir (**to, for** à); approvisionner [*factory, company*] (**with** en); (with fuel, food) ravitailler [*town, area*] (**with** en).

supply and demand *n* l'offre *f* et la demande.

support I *n* **1** (moral, financial, political) soutien *m*, appui *m*; **to give sb/sth (one's) ~** apporter son soutien à qn/qch; **means of ~** (financial) moyens *mpl* de subsistance; **2** (physical, for weight) support *m*; **3** (person) soutien *m*; **to be a ~ to sb** aider qn.
II *vtr* **1** (morally, financially) soutenir [*person, cause, organization, currency*]; donner à [*charity*]; **2** (physically) supporter [*weight*]; soutenir [*person*]; **3** confirmer [*argument, theory*]; **4** (maintain) [*breadwinner, farm*] subvenir aux besoins de.

supporter *n* (gen) partisan *m*; (Sport) supporter *m*; (of political party) sympathisant/-e *m/f*.

suppose *vtr* **1** (assume) supposer (**that** que); **I ~ so/not** je suppose que oui/non; **2** (think) **to ~ (that)** penser or croire que.

supposed *adj* **to be ~ to do/be** être censé/-e faire/être; **it's ~ to be a good hotel** il paraît que c'est un bon hôtel.

supposing *conj* **~ (that) he says no?** et s'il dit non?; **~ your income is X** supposons que ton revenu soit de X.

suppress *vtr* supprimer [*evidence, information*]; réprimer [*smile, urge, rebellion*]; étouffer [*scandal, yawn*]; dissimuler [*truth*].

supreme *adj* suprême.

sure I *adj* (gen) sûr/-e (**about, of** de); **I'm not ~ when he's coming** je ne sais pas trop quand il viendra; **we'll be there tomorrow for ~!** on y sera demain sans faute!; **nobody knows for ~** personne ne (le) sait au juste; **to make ~ that** (ascertain) s'assurer que; (ensure) faire en sorte que; **he's ~ to fail** il va sûrement échouer; **to be ~ of oneself** être sûr/-e de soi.
II *adv* **'~!'** (of course) 'bien sûr!'; **~ enough** effectivement.

sure-footed *adj* agile.

surely *adv* sûrement, certainement.

surf I *n* (waves) vagues *fpl* (déferlantes); (foam) écume *f*.
II ▶ 504 *vi* faire du surf.

surface I *n* **1** surface *f*; **on the ~** (of liquid) à la surface; (of solid) sur la surface; **2** (of solid, cube) côté *m*; **3** (worktop) plan *m* de travail.
II *vi* **1** [*person, object*] remonter à la surface; [*submarine*] faire surface; **2** [*problem*] se manifester.

surface area *n* superficie *f*.

surfboard *n* planche *f* de surf.

surfing ▶ 504 *n* surf *m*.

surge I *n* **1** (of water, blood, energy) montée *f* (**of** de); (of anger, desire) accès *m* (**of** de); **2** (in prices, unemployment) hausse *f* (**in** de); (in demand) accroissement *m* (**in** de).
II *vi* **1** [*water, waves*] déferler; [*blood, energy, emotion*] monter; **to ~ forward** [*crowd*] s'élancer en avant; **2** [*prices, demand*] monter en flèche.

surgeon ▶ 626 *n* chirurgien *m*.

surgery *n* **1** (operation) chirurgie *f*; **to have ~** se faire opérer; **2** (GB Med) (premises) cabinet *m*.

surgical *adj* [*instrument*] chirurgical/-e; [*boot, stocking*] orthopédique.

surgical spirit *n* alcool *m* (à 90 degrés).

surly *adj* revêche.

surname *n* nom *m* de famille.

surplus I *n* surplus *m*; (in business) excédent *m*.
II *adj* (gen) en trop; (in business) excédentaire.

surprise I *n* surprise *f*; **to take sb by ~** (gen) prendre qn au dépourvu; (Mil) surprendre qn.
II *vtr* **1** surprendre, étonner; **it ~d them that no-one came** ils ont été surpris que personne ne vienne; **2** surprendre [*intruder*]; attaquer [qch] par surprise [*garrison*].

surprised *adj* étonné/-e; **I'm not ~** ça ne m'étonne pas.

surprising *adj* étonnant/-e, surprenant/-e.

surprisingly *adv* [*well, quickly*] étonnamment; **~ frank** d'une franchise étonnante.

surreal *adj* surréaliste.

surrealist *n*, *adj* surréaliste (*mf*).

surrender I *n* **1** (of army) capitulation *f* (**to** devant); (of soldier, town) reddition *f* (**to** à); **2** (of territory, rights) abandon *m* (**to** à); (of weapons, document) remise *f* (**to** à).
II *vtr* **1** livrer [*town*] (**to** à); céder [*weapons*] (**to** à); **2** racheter [*insurance policy*]; rendre [*passport*] (**to** à).
III *vi* [*army, soldier*] se rendre (**to** à); [*country*] capituler (**to** devant).

surrogate I *n* substitut *m* (**for** de).
II *adj* de substitution.

surrogate mother *n* mère *f* porteuse.

surround *vtr* (gen) entourer; [*police*] encercler [*building*]; cerner [*person*].

surrounding *adj* environnant/-e; **the ~ area** les environs *mpl*.

surroundings *n pl* cadre *m*; (of town) environs *mpl*; **natural ~** milieu *m* naturel.

surveillance *n* surveillance *f*.

survey I *n* **1** (of trends, prices) enquête *f* (**of** sur); (by questioning people) sondage *m*; (study) étude *f* (**of** de); **2** (GB) (of house) expertise *f* (**on** de); **3** (of land) étude *f* topographique; (map) levé *m* topographique.
II *vtr* **1** faire une étude de [*market, trends*]; **2** (GB) faire une expertise de [*house*]; **3** faire l'étude topographique de [*area*]; **4** contempler [*scene, landscape*].

surveyor ▶626 *n* **1** (GB) (in housebuying) expert *m* (en immobilier); **2** (for map-making) topographe *mf*.

survival *n* (of person, animal) survie *f* (**of** de); (of custom, belief) survivance *f* (**of** de).

survive I *vtr* **1** survivre à [*winter, heart attack*]; réchapper de [*accident*]; surmonter [*crisis*]; **2** survivre à [*person*].
II *vi* survivre; **to ~ on sth** vivre de qch.

survivor *n* **1** (of accident, attack) rescapé/-e *m/f*; **2** (Law) survivant/-e *m/f*.

susceptible *adj* sensible (**to** à).

suspect I *n* suspect/-e *m/f*.
II *adj* suspect/-e.
III *vtr* **1** (believe) soupçonner [*murder, plot*]; **to ~ that** penser que; **2** (doubt) douter de [*truth, motives*]; **3** (have under suspicion) soupçonner [*person*].

suspend *vtr* **1** (gen) suspendre; **2** exclure [qn] temporairement [*pupil*] (**from** de).

suspender belt *n* (GB) porte-jarretelles *m inv*.

suspenders *n pl* **1** (GB) (for stockings) jarretelles *fpl*; **2** (US) (braces) bretelles *fpl*.

suspense *n* (in film, novel) suspense *m*; **to leave sb in ~** laisser qn dans l'expectative.

suspension *n* **1** (gen, Aut) suspension *f*; **2** (of pupil) exclusion *f* temporaire.

suspicion *n* méfiance *f* (**of** de); **to arouse ~** éveiller des soupçons; **to have ~s about sb/sth** avoir des doutes *mpl* sur qn/qch.

suspicious *adj* **1** (wary) méfiant/-e; **to be ~ of sth** se méfier de qch; **2** [*person, object*] suspect/-e; [*behaviour, activity*] louche.

sustain *vtr* **1** (maintain) maintenir [*interest, success*]; **2** (Mus) soutenir [*note*]; **3** (support) soutenir; (physically) donner des forces à; **to ~ life** rendre la vie possible; **4** recevoir [*injury, burn*]; éprouver [*loss*].

sustenance *n* nourriture *f*.

swab *n* (Med) tampon *m*.

swagger *vi* **1** (walk) se pavaner; **2** (boast) fanfaronner.

swallow I *n* **1** (bird) hirondelle *f*; **2** (gulp) gorgée *f*.
II *vtr* **1** (eat) avaler; **2** ravaler [*pride*]; **3**○ (believe) avaler○.
III *vi* avaler; (nervously) avaler sa salive.

swamp I *n* marais *m*, marécage *m*.
II *vtr* inonder.

swan *n* cygne *m*.

swap○ I *n* échange *m*.
II *vtr* échanger; **to ~ sth for sth** échanger qch contre qch; **to ~ places** changer de place.

swarm I *n* (of bees) essaim *m*; (of flies) nuée *f*.
II *vi* [*bees*] essaimer; **to be ~ing with** grouiller de [*people, maggots*].

swarthy *adj* basané/-e.

swastika *n* svastika *m*.

swat *vtr* écraser [*fly, wasp*] (**with** avec).

sway I *n* **to hold ~** avoir une grande influence; **to hold ~ over** dominer.
II *vtr* **1** (influence) influencer; **2** (rock) osciller.
III *vi* [*tree, bridge*] osciller; [*person*] chanceler; (to music) se balancer.

swear I *vtr* jurer (**to do** de faire); **to ~ sb to secrecy** faire jurer le secret à qn.
II *vi* **1** (curse) jurer; **2** (attest) **to ~ to having done** jurer avoir fait.

swearword *n* juron *m*, gros mot *m*.

sweat I *n* sueur *f*; **to break out into a ~** se mettre à suer; **to be in a cold ~ about sth** avoir des sueurs froides à l'idée de qch.
II **sweats** *n pl* (US) survêtement *m*.
III *vi* [*person, horse*] transpirer, suer; [*hands, feet, cheese*] transpirer.

sweater *n* pull *m*.

sweat pants *n pl* (US) pantalon *m* de survêtement.

sweatshirt *n* sweatshirt *m*.

sweaty *adj* [*person*] en sueur; [*hand, palm*] moite.

swede *n* (GB) rutabaga *m*.

Swede ▶553 *n* Suédois/-e *m/f*.

Sweden ▶448 *pr n* Suède *f*.

Swedish ▶553 I *n* (language) suédois *m*.
II *adj* suédois/-e.

sweep I *n* **1 to give sth a ~** donner un coup de balai à qch; **2** (movement) **with a ~ of his arm** d'un grand geste du bras; **3** (of land, woods) étendue *f*; **4** (also **chimney ~**) ramoneur *m*.
II *vtr* **1** balayer [*floor, path*]; ramoner [*chimney*]; **2** (push) **to ~ sth off the table** faire tomber qch de la table (d'un grand geste de la main); **to ~ sb off his/her feet** (figurative) faire perdre la tête à qn; **3** [*beam, searchlight*] balayer.
III *vi* **1** (clean) balayer; **2 to ~ in/out** (majestically) entrer/sortir majestueusement.
■ **sweep aside** écarter [*person, objection*].
■ **sweep up** balayer.

sweeping *adj* **1** [*change, review*] radical/-e; **2 ~ generalization** généralisation *f* à l'emporte-pièce.

sweet I *n* (GB) **1** (candy) bonbon *m*; **2** (dessert) dessert *m*.
II *adj* **1** (gen) doux/douce; [*food, tea, taste*] sucré/-e; **to have a ~ tooth** aimer les sucreries; **2** (kind) [*person*] gentil/-ille; **3** (cute) [*baby, cottage*] mignon/-onne.
III *adv* **to taste ~** avoir un goût sucré; **to smell ~** sentir bon.

sweet-and-sour *adj* aigre-doux/-douce.

sweetcorn *n* maïs *m*.

sweeten *vtr* **1** (Culin) sucrer (**with** avec); **2** rendre [qch] plus tentant [*offer*].
■ **sweeten up** amadouer [*person*].

sweetener *n* **1** (in food) édulcorant *m*; **2**○ (bribe) incitation *f*; (illegal) pot-de-vin○ *m*.

sweetheart *n* (boyfriend) petit ami *m*; (girlfriend) petite amie *f*.

sweetly *adv* [*say, smile*] gentiment.

swell I *n* (of waves, sea) houle *f*.
II *vtr* gonfler [*crowd, funds*]; grossir [*river*].
III *vi* [*balloon, tyre, stomach*] se gonfler; [*wood*] gonfler; [*ankle, gland*] enfler; [*river*] grossir; [*crowd*] s'accroître.

swelling *n* (on limb, skin) enflure *f*; (on head) bosse *f*.

sweltering○ *adj* torride.

swerve *vi* faire un écart; **to ~ off the road** sortir de la route.

swift I *n* martinet *m*.
II *adj* rapide, prompt/-e.

swill *n* pâtée *f* (des porcs).

swim I *n* baignade *f*; **to go for a ~** (in sea, river) aller se baigner; (in pool) aller à la piscine.
II *vtr* nager [*distance, stroke*].
III *vi* **1** nager; **to ~ across sth** traverser qch à la nage; **2 to be ~ming in** baigner dans [*sauce, oil*]; **3** [*scene, room*] tourner.

swimmer *n* nageur/-euse *m/f*.

swimming ▶ 504 *n* natation *f*.

swimming costume *n* (GB) maillot *m* de bain.

swimming pool *n* piscine *f*.

swimming trunks *n pl* slip *m* de bain.

swimsuit *n* maillot *m* de bain.

swindle I *n* escroquerie *f*.
II *vtr* escroquer; **to ~ sb out of sth** escroquer qch à qn.

swindler *n* escroc *m*.

swing I *n* **1** (of pendulum, needle) oscillation *f*; (of hips, body) balancement *m*; **2** (in public opinion) revirement *m* (**in** de); (in prices, economy) fluctuation *f* (**in** de); (in mood) saute *f* (**in** de); **3** (in playground) balançoire *f*.
II *vtr* (to and fro) balancer; **to ~ sb round and round** faire tournoyer qn.
III *vi* **1** (to and fro) se balancer; [*pendulum*] osciller; **2 to ~ open** s'ouvrir; **the car swung into the drive** la voiture s'est engagée dans l'allée; **to ~ around** [*person*] se retourner (brusquement); **3** (change) **to ~ from optimism to despair** passer de l'optimisme au désespoir; **the party swung towards the left** le parti a basculé vers la gauche.
IDIOMS **to get into the ~ of things**○ se mettre dans le bain○; **to be in full ~** battre son plein○.

swing door (GB), **swinging door** (US) *n* porte *f* battante.

swirl *vi* tourbillonner.

Swiss ▶ 553 **I** *n* Suisse *mf*.
II *adj* suisse; [*embassy*] de Suisse.

switch I *n* **1** (change) changement *m* (**in** de); **2** (for light) interrupteur *m*; (on radio, appliance) bouton *m*.
II *vtr* **1** reporter [*attention*] (**to** sur); **to ~ flights** changer de vol; **2** intervertir [*objects, roles*]; **I've ~ed the furniture round** j'ai changé la disposition des meubles.
III *vi* changer.
■ **switch off** éteindre [*appliance, light, engine*]; couper [*supply*].
■ **switch on** allumer [*appliance, light, engine*].
■ **switch over** (on TV) changer de chaîne.

switchboard *n* standard *m*.

switchboard operator ▶ 626 *n* standardiste *mf*.

Switzerland ▶ 448 *pr n* Suisse *f*.

swivel *vtr* faire pivoter [*chair, camera*]; tourner [*head, body*].
■ **swivel round** pivoter.

swivel chair, swivel seat *n* fauteuil *m* tournant, chaise *f* tournante.

swollen *adj* [*ankle, gland*] enflé/-e; [*eyes*] gonflé/-e; [*river*] en crue.

swoop *vi* **1** [*bird, bat, plane*] plonger; **to ~ down** descendre en piqué; **to ~ down on** fondre sur; **2** [*police, raider*] faire une descente.

sword *n* épée *f*.

swordfish *n* espadon *m*.

sworn *adj* **1** [*statement*] fait/-e sous serment; **2** [*enemy*] juré/-e; [*ally*] pour la vie.

swot○ **I** *n* bûcheur/-euse○ *m/f*.
II *vi* bûcher○.

sycamore *n* (also **~ tree**) sycomore *m*.

syllable *n* syllabe *f*.

syllabus *n* programme *m*.

symbol *n* symbole *m* (**of, for** de).

symbolic *adj* symbolique (**of** de).

symbolism *n* symbolisme *m*.

symbolize *vtr* symboliser (**by** par).

symmetric(al) *adj* symétrique.

sympathetic *adj* (compassionate) compatissant/-e (**to, towards** envers); (understanding) compréhensif/-ive; (kindly) gentil/-ille; (well disposed) bien disposé/-e (**to, towards** à l'égard de).

sympathize *vi* **1** témoigner de la sympathie (**with** à); **I ~ with you in your grief** je compatis à votre douleur; **2** (support) **to ~ with** souscrire à [*aims, views*].

sympathy *n* **1** (compassion) compassion *f*; **2** (solidarity) solidarité *f*.

symphony *n* symphonie *f*.

symphony orchestra *n* orchestre *m* symphonique.

symptom *n* symptôme *m*.

synchronize *vtr* synchroniser.

syndicate *n* (gen) syndicat *m*; (of companies) consortium *m*.

syndrome *n* syndrome *m*.

synonymous *adj* synonyme (**with** de).

synopsis *n* (of play) synopsis *m*; (of book) résumé *m*.

syntax *n* syntaxe *f*.

synthesis *n* synthèse *f*.

synthesizer *n* synthétiseur *m*.

synthetic *adj* synthétique.

syringe I *n* seringue *f*.
II *vtr* **to have one's ears ~d** se faire déboucher les oreilles (avec une seringue).

syrup *n* sirop *m*.

system *n* système *m* (**for doing, to do** pour faire); **road ~** réseau *m* routier; **reproductive ~** appareil *m* reproducteur.

systematic *adj* **1** (efficient) méthodique; **2** (deliberate) systématique

systems analyst ▶626 *n* analyste *mf* (de) systèmes.

Tt

t, T *n* t, T *m*.
tab *n* **1** (loop) attache *f*; **2** (on can) languette *f*; **3** (label) étiquette *f*.
tabby (cat) *n* chat/chatte *m/f* tigré/-e.
table I *n* **1** table *f*; **to set the ~** mettre le couvert; **2** (list) table *f*, tableau *m*.
II *vtr* **1** (GB) (present) présenter; **2** (US) (postpone) ajourner.
tablecloth *n* nappe *f*.
table mat *n* (under plate) set *m* de table; (under serving-dish) dessous-de-plat *m inv*.
tablespoon *n* **1** (object) cuillère *f* de service; **2** (also **~ful**) cuillerée *f* à soupe.
tablet *n* comprimé *m* (**for** pour).
table tennis *n* tennis *m* de table, ping-pong® *m*.
tabloid *n* tabloïde *m*.
taboo *n*, *adj* tabou (*m*).
tacit *adj* tacite.
tack I *n* **1** (nail) clou *m*; **2** (US) (drawing pin) punaise *f*; **3** (Naut) bordée *f*; **4** (tactic) tactique *f*.
II *vtr* **1** (nail) **to ~ sth to** clouer qch à; **2** (in sewing) bâtir.
III *vi* [*sailor*] faire une bordée; [*yacht*] louvoyer.
tackle I *n* **1** (in soccer, hockey) tacle *m*; (in rugby, American football) plaquage *m*; **2** (for fishing) articles *mpl* de pêche; **3** (on ship) gréement *m*; (for lifting) palan *m*.
II *vtr* **1** s'attaquer à [*task, problem*]; **2** (confront) **to ~ sb about** parler à qn de; **3** (in soccer, hockey) tacler; (in rugby, American football) plaquer.
tact *n* tact *m*.
tactful *adj* [*person, letter*] plein/-e de tact; [*enquiry*] discret/-ète.
tactical *adj* tactique; **~ voting** vote *m* utile.
tactics *n pl* tactique *f*.
tactless *adj* [*person, question, suggestion*] indélicat/-e; **to be ~** [*person, remark*] manquer de tact.
tadpole *n* têtard *m*.
tag *n* (label) étiquette *f*; (on cat, dog) plaque *f*; (on file) onglet *m*.
■ **tag along** suivre.
tail *n* queue *f*.
■ **tail off 1** [*figures, demand*] diminuer; **2** [*voice*] s'éteindre.
tailgate *n* hayon *m*.
tailor ▶626 **I** *n* tailleur *m*.
II *vtr* **to ~ sth to** adapter qch à [*needs, person*].
tailor-made *adj* [*garment*] fait/-e sur mesure; (figurative) conçu/-e spécialement.
tails *n pl* **1** (tailcoat) habit *m*; **2** (of coin) pile *f*; **heads or ~?** pile ou face?
tainted *adj* [*food*] avarié/-e; [*water, air*] pollué/-e (**with** par); [*reputation*] entaché/-e.

take I *n* (in film-making) prise *f* (de vues); (Mus) enregistrement *m*.
II *vtr* **1** (gen) prendre; **he took the book off the shelf** il a pris le livre sur l'étagère; **she took a chocolate from the box** elle a pris un chocolat dans la boîte; **he took a pen out of his pocket** il a sorti un stylo de sa poche; **to ~ an exam** passer un examen; **to ~ a shower** prendre une douche; **to ~ sb/sth seriously** prendre qn/qch au sérieux; **2** (carry with one) emporter, prendre [*object*]; (carry to a place) emporter, porter [*object*]; **to ~ sb sth, to ~ sth to sb** apporter qch à qn; **he took his umbrella with him** il a emporté son parapluie; **to ~ a letter to the post office** porter une lettre à la poste; **to ~ the car to the garage** emmener la voiture au garage; **to ~ sth upstairs/downstairs** monter/descendre qch; **3** (accompany, lead) emmener [*person*]; **to ~ sb to** [*bus*] emmener qn à [*place*]; [*road*] conduire or mener qn à [*place*]; **I'll ~ you to your room** je vais vous conduire à votre chambre; **he took her home** il l'a raccompagnée; **to ~ a dog/a child for a walk** promener un chien/emmener un enfant faire une promenade; **4** (accept) [*person*] accepter [*job, bribe*]; [*shop*] accepter [*credit card, cheque*]; [*person*] supporter [*pain, criticism*]; **she can't ~ a joke** elle ne comprend pas la plaisanterie; **I can't ~ any more!** je n'en peux plus!; **5** ▶708 (require) demander, exiger [*patience, skill, courage*]; **it ~s patience to do** il faut de la patience pour faire; **it ~s three hours to get there** il faut trois heures pour y aller; **it won't ~ long** ça ne prendra pas longtemps; **it took her ten minutes to repair it** elle a mis dix minutes pour le réparer; **to have what it ~s** avoir tout ce qu'il faut (**to do** pour faire); **6** (assume) **I ~ it that** je suppose que; **7** (hold) [*hall, bus*] pouvoir contenir [*50 people*]; [*tank, container*] avoir une capacité de [*quantity*]; **8** (wear) **what size do you ~?** (in clothes) quelle taille faites-vous?; (in shoes) quelle pointure faites-vous?; **I ~ a size 10** (in clothes) je m'habille en 36; **I ~ a size 5** (in shoes) je chausse du 38; **9** (subtract) soustraire [*number, quantity*] (**from** de).
III *vi* [*drug*] faire effet; [*dye, plant*] prendre.
IDIOMS **that's my last offer, ~ it or leave it!** c'est ma dernière proposition, c'est à prendre ou à laisser!; **to ~ a lot out of sb** fatiguer beaucoup qn.
■ **take aback** interloquer; **to be ~n aback** rester interloqué/-e.
■ **take after** tenir de [*person*].
■ **take apart** démonter [*car, machine*].
■ **take away 1** (carry away) emporter; **2** (remove) enlever [*object*]; emmener [*person*]; **3** (subtract) soustraire [*number*]; **that doesn't ~ anything away from his achievement** ça n'enlève rien à ce qu'il a accompli.

■ **take back** **1** (to shop) rapporter [*goods*]; **2** retirer [*statement, words*]; **3** (accompany) ramener [*person*]; **4** (accept again) reprendre.
■ **take down** **1** enlever [*picture, curtains*]; démonter [*tent, scaffolding*]; **2** noter [*name, details*].
■ **take hold** [*disease, epidemic*] s'installer; [*idea, ideology*] se répandre; **to ~ hold of** prendre [*object, hand*].
■ **take in** **1** (deceive) tromper; **I wasn't taken in by him** je ne me suis pas laissé prendre à son jeu; **2** recueillir [*refugee*]; prendre [*lodger*]; **3** (understand) saisir, comprendre [*situation*]; **4** (observe) noter [*detail*]; **5** (encompass) inclure; **6** (absorb) absorber [*nutrients, oxygen*]; **7** [*boat*] prendre [*water*]; **8** (in sewing) reprendre [*garment*].
■ **take off**: ¶ **~ off** **1** [*plane*] décoller; **2** [*idea, fashion*] prendre; ¶ **~ [sth] off**: **1 to ~ £10 off (the price)** réduire le prix de 10 livres sterling; **2 to ~ two days off** prendre deux jours de congé; ¶ **~ off [sth]** enlever [*clothing, shoes, lid*]; ¶ **~ [sb] off**○ (imitate) imiter [*person*].
■ **take on** **1** (employ) embaucher [*staff, worker*]; **2** jouer contre [*team, player*]; (fight) se battre contre [*person*]; **3** (accept) prendre [*responsibilities, work*].
■ **take out**: ¶ **~ [sth] out** **1** sortir [*object*] (**from, of** de); extraire [*tooth*]; enlever [*appendix*]; retirer [*money*]; **2 to ~ [sth] out on sb** passer [qch] sur qn [*anger, frustration*]; **to ~ it out on sb** s'en prendre à qn; ¶ **~ [sb] out** sortir avec [*person*]; **to ~ sb out to dinner** emmener qn dîner.
■ **take over**: ¶ **~ over** **1** [*army, faction*] prendre le pouvoir; **2** (be successor) [*person*] prendre la suite; **to ~ over from** remplacer [*predecessor*]; ¶ **~ over [sth]** prendre le contrôle de [*town, region*]; reprendre [*business*].
■ **take part** prendre part; **to ~ part in** participer à.
■ **take place** avoir lieu.
■ **take to** **1** se prendre de sympathie pour [*person*]; **2** (begin) **to ~ to doing** se mettre à faire; **3** (go) se réfugier dans [*forest, hills*]; **to ~ to the streets** descendre dans la rue.
■ **take up**: ¶ **to ~ up with** s'attacher à [*person, group*]; ¶ **~ up [sth]** **1** (lift) enlever [*carpet, pavement*]; **2** (start) se mettre à [*golf, guitar*]; prendre [*job*]; **to ~ up one's duties** entrer dans ses fonctions; **3** (continue) reprendre [*story, cry, refrain*]; **4** (accept) accepter [*offer, invitation*]; relever [*challenge*]; **5 to ~ sth up with sb** soulever [qch] avec qn [*matter*]; **6** (occupy) prendre [*space, time, energy*]; **7** prendre [*position, stance*]; **8** (shorten) raccourcir [*skirt, curtains*]; ¶ **~ sb up on** **1** reprendre qn sur [*point, assertion*]; **2 to ~ sb up on an offer** accepter l'offre de qn.

take-away *n* (GB) **1** (meal) repas *m* à emporter; **2** (restaurant) restaurant *m* qui fait des plats à emporter.

taken *adj* **1 to be ~** [*seat, room*] être occupé/-e; **2** (impressed) **to be ~ with** être emballé/-e○ par [*idea, person*].

take-off *n* **1** (by plane) décollage *m*; **2**○ (imitation) imitation *f* (**of** de).

take-out *adj* (US) [*food*] à emporter.

takeover *n* (of company) rachat *m*; (of political power) prise *f* de pouvoir.

taker *n* preneur/-euse *m/f*.

takings *n pl* recette *f*.

talc, **talcum (powder)** *n* talc *m*.

tale *n* (story) histoire *f*; (fantasy story) conte *m*; (narrative, account) récit *m*.

talent *n* talent *m*.

talented *adj* doué/-e, talentueux/-euse.

talisman *n* talisman *m*.

talk **I** *n* **1** (talking, gossip) propos *mpl*; **they are the ~ of the town** on ne parle que d'eux; **2** (conversation) conversation *f*, discussion *f*; **3** (speech) exposé *m* (**about, on** sur); (more informal) causerie *f*.
II talks *n pl* négociations *fpl*; (political) pourparlers *mpl*; **peace ~** pourparlers de paix.
III *vtr* parler; **to ~ business** parler affaires; **to ~ nonsense** raconter n'importe quoi; **to ~ sb into/out of doing** persuader/dissuader qn de faire; **he ~ed his way out of it** il s'en est tiré grâce à son bagout○.
IV *vi* parler; (gossip) bavarder; **to ~ to oneself** parler tout seul/toute seule.

talkative *adj* bavard/-e.

talking **I** *n* **I'll do the ~** c'est moi qui parlerai; **'no ~!'** 'silence!'
II *adj* [*bird, doll*] qui parle.

tall ▶ 573 *adj* [*person*] grand/-e; [*building, tree, chimney*] haut/-e; **he's six feet ~** ≈ il mesure un mètre quatre-vingts; **to grow ~er** grandir.

tally **I** *n* compte *m*.
II *vi* concorder.

tambourine ▶ 586 *n* tambourin *m*.

tame **I** *adj* **1** [*animal*] apprivoisé/-e; **2** [*story, party*] sage; [*reform*] timide.
II *vtr* **1** apprivoiser [*bird, wild animal*]; dompter [*lion, tiger*]; **2** soumettre [*person*].

tamper *vi* **to ~ with** tripoter [*machinery, lock*]; trafiquer [*accounts, evidence*].

tan ▶ 438 **I** *n* **1** (also **sun~**) bronzage *m*; **2** (colour) fauve *m*.
II *adj* fauve.
III *vtr* **1** bronzer [*skin*]; **2** tanner [*animal hide*].
IV *vi* [*skin, person*] bronzer.

tandem *n* tandem *m*; **in ~** en tandem.

tang *n* (taste) goût *m* acidulé; (smell) odeur *f* piquante.

tangent *n* tangente *f*; **to go off on a ~** partir dans une digression.

tangerine ▶ 438 *n* tangerine *f*.

tangible *adj* tangible.

tangle **I** *n* (of hair, string, wires) enchevêtrement *m*; (of clothes, sheets) fouillis *m*.
II *vi* [*hair, string, cable*] s'emmêler.

tank *n* **1** (gen, Aut) réservoir *m*; (for oil) cuve *f*; (for water) citerne *f*; (for fish) aquarium *m*; **2** (Mil) char *m* (de combat).

tankard *n* chope *f*.

tanker *n* **1** (ship) navire-citerne *m*; **oil ~** pétrolier *m*; **2** (lorry) camion-citerne *m*.
tanned *adj* (also **sun~**) bronzé/-e.
tantalizing *adj* [*suggestion*] tentant/-e; [*possibility*] séduisant/-e; [*glimpse*] excitant/-e.
tantamount *adj* **to be ~ to** équivaloir à, être équivalent/-e à.
tantrum *n* crise *f* de colère; **to throw a ~** piquer une crise°.
tap I *n* **1** (for water, gas) robinet *m*; **2** (blow) petit coup *m*.
II *vtr* **1** (knock) taper (doucement); (repeatedly) tapoter; **2** mettre [qch] sur écoute [*telephone*]; **3** inciser [*rubber tree*]; exploiter [*resources*].
tap dance *n* (also **~ dancing**) claquettes *fpl*.
tape I *n* **1** bande *f* (magnétique); (cassette) cassette *f*; (video) cassette *f* vidéo; (recording) enregistrement *m*; **2** (also **adhesive ~**) scotch® *m*.
II *vtr* **1** (record) enregistrer; **2** (stick) **to ~ sth to** coller qch à [*surface, door*].
tape deck *n* platine *f* cassette.
tape measure *n* mètre *m* ruban.
taper *vi* [*sleeve, trouser leg*] se resserrer; [*column, spire*] s'effiler.
tape recorder *n* magnétophone *m*.
tapestry *n* tapisserie *f*.
tapeworm *n* ver *m* solitaire, ténia *m*.
tar *n* goudron *m*; (on roads) bitume *m*..
target I *n* **1** (in archery, shooting) cible *f*; (Mil) objectif *f*; **2** (butt) cible *f*; **to be the ~ of abuse** être insulté/-e; **3** (goal) objectif *m*.
II *vtr* **1** diriger [*weapon, missile*]; prendre [qch] pour cible [*city, site*]; **2** (in marketing) viser [*group, sector*].
tariff *n* **1** (price list) tarif *m*; **2** (customs duty) droit *m* de douane.
tarmac *n* **1** (also **Tarmac**®) macadam *m*; **2** (GB) (of airfield) piste *f*.
tarnish I *vtr* ternir.
II *vi* se ternir.
tarpaulin *n* (material) toile *f* de bâche; (sheet) bâche *f*.
tarragon *n* estragon *m*.
tart *n* (small) tartelette *f*; (GB) (large) tarte *f*.
tartan *adj* écossais/-e.
task *n* tâche *f*; **a hard ~** une lourde tâche.
tassel *n* gland *m*.
taste I *n* **1** (gen) goût *m*; **that's a matter of ~** ça dépend des goûts; **to be in bad ~** être de mauvais goût; **2** (brief experience) expérience *f*; (foretaste) avant-goût *m*.
II *vtr* **1** (try) goûter [*food, drink*]; **2 I can ~ the brandy in this coffee** je sens le (goût du) cognac dans ce café; **3** (experience) goûter à [*freedom, success*].
III *vi* **to ~ sweet** avoir un goût sucré; **to ~ horrible** avoir mauvais goût; **to ~ like sth** avoir le goût de qch; **to ~ of** avoir un goût de.
taste bud *n* papille *f* gustative.
tasteful *adj* de bon goût.
tasteless *adj* **1** [*remark, joke*] de mauvais goût; **2** [*food, drink*] insipide.
tasty *adj* [*food*] succulent/-e.
tatters *n pl* **to be in ~** [*clothing*] être en lambeaux; [*career, reputation*] être en ruines.
tattoo I *n* tatouage *m*.
II *vtr* tatouer (**on** sur).
taunt *vtr* railler [*person*].
Taurus *n* Taureau *m*.
taut *adj* tendu/-e.
tax I *n* (on goods, services, property) taxe *f*; (on income, profits) impôt *m*.
II *vtr* **1** imposer [*earnings, person*]; taxer [*luxury goods*]; **2** mettre [qch] à l'épreuve [*patience*].
taxation *n* **1** (imposition of taxes) imposition *f*; **2** (revenue from taxes) impôts *mpl*.
tax collector *n* percepteur *m*.
tax disc *n* vignette *f* (automobile).
tax evasion *n* fraude *f* fiscale.
tax-free *adj* exempt/-e d'impôt.
taxi *n* taxi *m*; **by ~** en taxi.
taxing *adj* épuisant/-e.
taxi rank (GB), **taxi stand** *n* station *f* de taxis.
taxpayer *n* contribuable *mf*.
TB ▶533 *n* (*abbr* = **tuberculosis**) tuberculose *f*.
tea *n* **1** (drink) thé *m*; **2** (GB) (afternoon meal) thé *m*; (for children) goûter *m*; (evening meal) dîner *m*.
tea bag *n* sachet *m* de thé.
teach I *vtr* enseigner à [*children, adults*]; enseigner [*subject*]; **to ~ sb** enseigner [qch] à qn [*academic subject*]; apprendre [qch] à qn [*practical skill*]; **to ~ school** (US) être instituteur/-trice; **to ~ sb a lesson** [*person*] donner une bonne leçon à qn; [*experience*] servir de leçon à qn.
II *vi* enseigner.
teacher ▶626 *n* (in general) enseignant/-e *m/f*; (secondary) professeur *m*; (primary) instituteur/-trice *m/f*; (special needs) éducateur/-trice *m/f*.
teaching *n* enseignement *m*.
teacup *n* tasse *f* à thé.
teak *n* teck *m*.
team *n* équipe *f*.
teamwork *n* collaboration *f*.
teapot *n* théière *f*.
tear[1] **I** *n* (gen) accroc *m*; (Med) déchirure *f*.
II *vtr* déchirer [*garment, paper*]; **to ~ sth out of** arracher qch de [*book, notepad*].
III *vi* **1** (rip) se déchirer; **2** (rush) **to ~ out/off** sortir/partir en trombe.
■ **tear apart 1** mettre [qch] en pièces [*prey*]; déchirer [*country*]; **2** (separate) séparer; **3**° (criticize) descendre [qn] en flammes.
■ **tear off** (carefully) détacher; (violently) arracher.
■ **tear open** ouvrir [qch] en le/la déchirant.
■ **tear out** détacher [*coupon, cheque*]; arracher [*page*].
■ **tear up** déchirer [*letter, document*].
tear[2] *n* larme *f*; **to burst into ~s** fondre en larmes.

tearful *adj* [*person, face*] en larmes; [*voice*] larmoyant/-e.

tear gas *n* gaz *m* lacrymogène.

tease *vtr* taquiner [*person*] (**about** à propos de); tourmenter [*animal*].

teaspoon *n* petite cuillère *f*, cuillère *f* à café.

teaspoonful *n* cuillerée *f* à café.

teat *n* **1** (of cow, goat, ewe) trayon *m*; **2** (GB) (on baby's bottle) tétine *f*.

teatime *n* l'heure *f* du thé.

tea towel *n* (GB) torchon *m* (à vaisselle).

technical *adj* technique.

technical college *n* institut *m* d'enseignement technique.

technicality *n* **1** (technical detail) détail *m* technique (**of** de); **2** (minor detail) point *m* de détail; **3** (technical nature) technicité *f*.

technically *adv* **1** (strictly speaking) théoriquement; **2** (technologically) techniquement.

technician ▶ 626 *n* technicien/-ienne *m/f*.

technique *n* technique *f*.

technological *adj* technologique.

technology *n* technologie *f*; **information ~** informatique *f*.

teddy *n* (also **~ bear**) ours *m* en peluche.

tedious *adj* ennuyeux/-euse.

teem *vi* **to be ~ing with** grouiller de [*people*].

teenage *adj* [*son, daughter*] qui est adolescent/-e; [*singer, player*] jeune (*before n*); [*fashion*] des adolescents.

teenager *n* jeune *mf*, adolescent/-e *m/f*.

teens *n pl* adolescence *f*; **to be in one's ~** être adolescent/-e.

tee-shirt *n* tee-shirt, T-shirt *m*.

teeter *vi* vaciller.

teethe *vi* faire ses dents.

teething troubles *n pl* difficultés *fpl* initiales.

teetotaller (GB), **teetotaler** (US) *n* personne *f* qui ne boit jamais d'alcool.

TEFL *n* (*abbr* = **Teaching of English as a Foreign Language**) enseignement *m* de l'anglais langue étrangère.

telecommunications *n pl* télécommunications *fpl*.

telegram *n* télégramme *m*.

telegraph I *n* télégraphe *m*.
II *vtr* télégraphier.

telegraph pole *n* poteau *m* télégraphique.

telepathy *n* télépathie *f*.

telephone I *n* téléphone *m*; **to be on the ~** (connected) avoir le téléphone; (talking) être au téléphone.
II *vtr* téléphoner à [*person*]; téléphoner [*instructions*]; **to ~ France** appeler la France.
III *vi* appeler, téléphoner.

telephone booth, **telephone box** (GB) *n* cabine *f* téléphonique.

telephone call *n* appel *m* téléphonique.

telephone directory *n* annuaire *m* (du téléphone).

telephone number *n* numéro *m* de téléphone.

telephonist ▶ 626 *n* (GB) standardiste *mf*.

telephoto lens *n* téléobjectif *m*.

telescope *n* télescope *m*.

teletext *n* télétexte *m*.

televise *vtr* téléviser.

television *n* **1** (medium) télévision *f*; **on ~** à la télévision; **2** (set) téléviseur *m*.

television set *n* téléviseur *m*, poste *m* de télévision.

telex ▶ 626 **I** *n* télex *m*.
II *vtr* télexer.

tell I *vtr* **1** (gen) dire; raconter [*joke, story*]; prédire [*future*]; **to ~ sb about sth** parler de qch à qn; **to ~ sb to do** dire à qn de faire; **to ~ sb how to do/what to do** expliquer à qn comment faire/ce qu'il faut faire; **to ~ the time** [*clock*] indiquer or marquer l'heure; [*person*] lire l'heure; **can you ~ me the time please?** peux-tu me dire l'heure (qu'il est), s'il te plaît?; **I was told that** on m'a dit que; **I told you so!** je te l'avais bien dit!; **2** (deduce) **you can ~ (that) he's lying** on voit bien qu'il ment; **I can ~ (that) he's disappointed** je sais qu'il est déçu; **3** (distinguish) distinguer; **can you ~ the difference?** est-ce que vous voyez la différence?; **how can you ~ them apart?** comment peut-on les distinguer l'un de l'autre?
II *vi* **1** (reveal secret) **don't ~!** ne le répète pas!; **2** (know) savoir; **as far as I can ~** pour autant que je sache; **how can you ~?** comment le sais-tu?; **3** (show effect) **her age is beginning to ~** elle commence à faire son âge.
■ **tell off** réprimander [*person*].
■ **tell on 1** dénoncer [*person*] (**to** à); **2 the strain is beginning to ~ on him** on commence à voir sur lui les effets de la fatigue.

telling *adj* [*remark, omission*] révélateur/-trice.

tell-tale I *n* rapporteur/-euse *m/f*.
II *adj* [*sign*] révélateur/-trice.

temp° (GB) **I** *n* intérimaire *mf*.
II *vi* travailler comme intérimaire.

temper I *n* **1** (mood) humeur *f*; **to be in a good/bad ~** être de bonne/mauvaise humeur; **2 to be in a ~** être en colère; **to lose one's ~** se mettre en colère (**with** contre); **3** (nature) caractère *m*.
II *vtr* **1** (moderate) tempérer; **2** tremper [*steel*].

temperament *n* **1** (nature) tempérament *m*; **2** (excitability) humeur *f*.

temperamental *adj* (volatile) capricieux/-ieuse.

temperate *adj* [*climate, zone*] tempéré/-e; [*person, habit*] modéré/-e.

temperature *n* température *f*; **to have a ~** avoir de la température or de la fièvre.

tempest *n* tempête *f*.

tempestuous *adj* turbulent/-e.

temple *n* **1** (building) temple *m*; **2** (Anat) tempe *f*.

temporarily *adv* (for a limited time) temporairement; (provisionally) provisoirement.

temporary *adj* [*job, contract*] temporaire;

[*manager, secretary*] intérimaire; [*arrangement, accommodation*] provisoire.

tempt *vtr* tenter; **to be ~ed to do** être tenté/-e de faire.

temptation *n* tentation *f*.

tempting *adj* [*offer*] alléchant/-e; [*food, smell*] appétissant/-e; [*idea*] tentant/-e.

ten ▶389, 434 *n, pron, det* dix (*m*) *inv*.

tenacious *adj* tenace.

tenancy *n* location *f*.

tenant *n* locataire *mf*.

tend I *vtr* soigner [*patient*]; entretenir [*garden*]; s'occuper de [*stall, store*].
II *vi* **to ~ to do** avoir tendance à faire.

tendency *n* tendance *f* (**to do** à faire).

tender I *n* soumission.
II *adj* **1** [*meat*] tendre; **2** [*kiss, love, smile*] tendre; **3** [*bruise, skin*] sensible.
III présenter [*apology, fare*]; donner [*resignation*].

tendon *n* tendon *m*.

tendril *n* vrille *f*.

tenement *n* immeuble *m* ancien.

tennis ▶504 *n* tennis *m*.

tennis court *n* court *m* de tennis, tennis *m* *inv*.

tenor *n* (Mus) ténor *m*.

tenpin bowling (GB), **tenpins** (US) ▶504 *n* bowling *m* (à dix quilles).

tense I *n* temps *m*; **the present ~** le présent; **in the past ~** au passé.
II *adj* [*person, atmosphere, conversation*] tendu/-e; [*moment*] de tension; **to make sb ~** rendre qn nerveux.
III *vtr* tendre [*muscle*]; raidir [*body*].
■ **tense up** [*person*] se crisper.

tension *n* **1** (gen, Tech) tension *f*; **2** (suspense) suspense *m*.

tent *n* tente *f*.

tentacle *n* tentacule *m*.

tentative *adj* [*smile, suggestion*] timide; [*conclusion, offer*] provisoire.

tenth ▶456, 498 **I** *n* **1** (in order) dixième *mf*; **2** (of month) dix *m inv*; **3** (fraction) dixième *m*.
II *adj, adv* dixième.

tenuous *adj* [*link*] ténu/-e; [*distinction, theory*] mince.

term I *n* **1** (period of time) (gen) période *f*, terme *m*; (Sch, Univ) trimestre *m*; **autumn/spring/summer ~** (Sch, Univ) premier/deuxième/troisième trimestre; **2** (word, phrase) terme *m*.
II **terms** *n pl* **1** (conditions) termes *mpl*; (of financial arrangement) conditions *fpl* de paiement; **2 to come to ~s with** assumer [*identity, past, disability*]; accepter [*death, defeat, failure*]; affronter [*issue*]; **3** (relations) termes *mpl*; **to be on good ~s with** être en bons termes avec.
III *vtr* appeler, nommer.
IV **in terms of** *phr* du point de vue de, sur le plan de.

terminal I *n* **1** (at station) terminus *m*; (in airport) aérogare *f*; **ferry ~** gare *f* maritime; **2** (Comput) terminal *m*; **3** (for electricity) borne *f*.
II *adj* [*stage*] terminal/-e; [*illness*] (incurable) incurable; (at final stage) en phase terminale.

terminate I *vtr* mettre fin à [*meeting, phase, relationship*]; résilier [*contract*]; annuler [*agreement*].
II *vi* se terminer.

terminology *n* terminologie *f*.

terminus *n* (GB) terminus *m*.

terrace I *n* **1** (patio) terrasse *f*; **2** (row of houses) alignement *m* de maisons.
II **terraces** *n pl* (GB) (in stadium) gradins *mpl*.

terracotta ▶438 *n* **1** (earthenware) terre *f* cuite; **2** (colour) ocre brun *m*.

terrain *n* terrain *m*.

terrible *adj* **1** [*pain, noise, sight*] épouvantable; [*accident, fight*] terrible; [*mistake*] grave; **2**○ [*food, weather*] affreux/-euse.

terribly *adv* **1** (very) [*pleased, obvious*] très; [*clever*] extrêmement; **I'm ~ sorry** je suis navré; **2** (badly) [*suffer*] horriblement; [*sing, drive*] affreusement mal.

terrific *adj* **1** (huge) [*amount*] énorme; [*noise*] épouvantable; [*speed*] fou/folle; [*accident, shock*] terrible; **2**○ (wonderful) formidable.

terrified *adj* terrifié/-e; **to be ~ of** avoir une peur folle de.

terrify *vtr* terrifier.

terrifying *adj* (frightening) terrifiant/-e; (alarming) effroyable.

territorial *adj* territorial/-e.

territory *n* territoire *m*; (figurative) domaine *m*.

terror *n* terreur *f*.

terrorism *n* terrorisme *m*.

terrorist *n* terroriste *mf*.

terrorize *vtr* terroriser.

terry *n* (also **~ towelling** GB, **~ cloth** US) tissu *m* éponge.

terse *adj* [*style*] succinct/-e; [*person, statement*] laconique.

test I *n* **1** (gen) test *m*; (Sch, Univ) (written) contrôle *m*; (oral) épreuve *f* orale; **to put sb/sth to the ~** mettre qn/qch à l'épreuve; **2** (of equipment, machine, new model) essai *m*; **3** (Med) (of blood, urine) analyse *f*; (of organ) examen *m*; (to detect virus, cancer) test *m* de dépistage; **to have a blood ~** se faire faire une analyse de sang; **4** (Aut) (also **driving ~**) examen *m* du permis de conduire.
II *vtr* **1** (gen) évaluer [*intelligence, efficiency*]; (Sch) (in classroom) interroger (**on** en); (at exam time) contrôler; **2** (new model, product) essayer; (Med) analyser [*blood, sample*]; expérimenter [*new drug*]; **to have one's eyes ~ed** se faire faire un examen des yeux; **3** mettre [qch] à l'épreuve [*strength, patience*].

testament *n* **1** (proof) témoignage *m*; **to be a ~ to sth** témoigner de qch; **2 the Old/the New Testament** l'Ancien/le Nouveau Testament.

testicle *n* testicule *m*.

testify I *vtr* témoigner (**that** que).
II *vi* témoigner; **to ~ to** témoigner de.

testimony *n* témoignage *m*, déposition *f*.

that

As a determiner

In French, determiners agree in gender and number with the noun that follows; ***that*** is translated by ***ce*** + *masculine singular noun* (***ce monsieur***), ***cet*** + *masculine singular noun beginning with a vowel or mute 'h'* (***cet homme***) and ***cette*** + *feminine singular noun* (***cette femme***). The plural form ***those*** is translated by ***ces*** (*ces livres, ces histoires*).

Note, however, that the above translations are also used for the English ***this*** (plural ***these***). So when it is necessary to insist on ***that*** as opposed to another or others of the same sort, the adverbial tag ***-là*** is added to the noun:

*I prefer **that** version*	= je préfère **cette** version-**là**

As a pronoun

- In French, pronouns reflect the gender and number of the noun they are standing for. So ***that*** (meaning *that one*) is translated by ***celui-là*** for a masculine noun, ***celle-là*** for a feminine noun and ***those*** (meaning *those ones*) is translated by ***ceux-là*** for a masculine noun and ***celles-là*** for a feminine noun:

*all the dresses are nice but I like **that** best*	= toutes les robes sont jolies mais je préfère **celle-là**

- When used as a relative pronoun, ***that*** is translated by ***qui*** when it is the subject of the verb and by ***que*** when it is the object:

*the man **that** stole the car*	= l'homme **qui** a volé la voiture
*the film **that** I saw*	= le film **que** j'ai vu

Remember that in the present perfect and past perfect tenses, the past participle agrees in gender and number with the noun that ***que*** is referring back to:

*the girl **that** I met*	= la fille **que** j'ai rencontrée
*the apples **that** I bought*	= les pommes **que** j'ai achetées

- When ***that*** is used as a relative pronoun with a preposition, it is translated by ***lequel*** when standing for a masculine singular noun, by ***laquelle*** when standing for a feminine singular noun, by ***lesquels*** when standing for a masculine plural noun, and by ***lesquelles*** when standing for a feminine plural noun:

*the chair **that** I was sitting on*	= la chaise sur **laquelle** j'étais assis
*the children **that** I bought the books for*	= les enfants pour **lesquels** j'ai acheté les livres

If the preposition would normally be translated by ***à*** in French (***to***, ***at*** etc), the translation of the whole (*preposition + relative pronoun*) will be ***auquel***, ***à laquelle***, ***auxquels***, ***auxquelles***:

*the girls **that** I was talking **to***	= les filles **auxquelles** je parlais

If the preposition used would normally be translated by ***de*** in French (***of***, ***from*** etc), the translation of the whole (*preposition + relative pronoun*) will be ***dont*** in all cases:

*the people **that** I've talked **about***	= les personnes **dont** j'ai parlé

As a conjunction

When used as a conjunction, ***that*** can almost always be translated by ***que*** (***qu'*** before a vowel or mute 'h'):

*she said **that** she would do it*	= elle a dit **qu'**elle le ferait

In certain verbal constructions, ***que*** is followed by a subjunctive. For more information, consult the appropriate verb entry. For particular usages see the entry **that**.

test tube *n* éprouvette *f*.

tetanus ▶533| *n* tétanos *m*.

tether *vtr* attacher (**to** à).
IDIOMS **to be at the end of one's ~** être au bout du rouleau○.

text *n* texte *m*.

textbook *n* manuel *m* (**about, on** sur).

textile *n* textile *m*.

texture *n* texture *f*.

Thames *pr n* **the** (**river**) **~** la Tamise.

than I *prep* **1** (in comparisons) que; **he's taller ~ me** il est plus grand que moi; **he has more ~ me** il en a plus que moi; **2** (expressing quantity, degree, value) de; **more/less ~ 100** plus/moins de 100; **more ~ half** plus de la moitié; **temperatures lower ~ 30 degrees** des températures de moins de 30 degrés.
II *conj* **1** (in comparisons) que; **he's older ~ I am** il est plus âgé que moi; **it took us longer ~ we expected** ça nous a pris plus de temps que prévu; **2** (expressing preferences) **I'd sooner** or **rather go to Rome ~ go to Venice** je préférerais aller à Rome que d'aller à Venise, j'aimerais mieux aller à Rome qu'à Venise; **3** (when) **hardly** or **no sooner had he left ~ the phone rang** à peine était-il parti que le téléphone a sonné; **4** (US) **to be different ~ sth** être différent/-e de qch.

thank *vtr* remercier [*person*]; **~ God!** Dieu merci!

thankful *adj* (grateful) reconnaissant/-e; (relieved) soulagé/-e.

thankfully *adv* **1** (luckily) heureusement; **2** (with relief) avec soulagement; (with gratitude) avec gratitude.

thankless *adj* [*task, person*] ingrat/-e.

thanks I *n pl* remerciements *mpl*; **with ~** avec mes/nos remerciements.
II○ *adv* merci; **~ a lot** merci beaucoup; **no ~** non merci.
III **thanks to** *phr* grâce à.

Thanksgiving (**Day**) *n* (US) jour *m* d'Action de Grâces.

thank you I *n* (also **thank-you**, **thankyou**) merci *m*; **to say ~ to sb** dire merci à qn.
II *adj* [*letter, gift*] de remerciement.
III *adv* merci; **~ for coming** merci d'être venu; **~ very much** merci beaucoup.

that I *det* ce/cet/cette/ces; **~ chair** cette chaise; **those chairs** ces chaises; **at ~ moment** à ce moment-là; **at ~ time** à cette époque-là; **you can't do it ~ way** tu ne peux pas le faire comme ça; **he went ~ way** il est allé par là; **~ lazy son of yours** ton paresseux de fils.
II *dem pron* **1** (that one) celui-/celle-/ceux-/celles-là; **2** (that thing, that person) **what's ~?** qu'est-ce que c'est que ça?; **who's ~?** qui est-ce?; (on phone) qui est à l'appareil?; **is ~ Françoise?** c'est Françoise?; **who told you ~?** qui t'a dit ça?; **~'s how he did it** c'est comme ça qu'il l'a fait; **what did he mean by ~?** qu'est-ce qu'il entendait par là?; **~'s the kitchen** ça, c'est la cuisine.
III *rel pron* (as subject) qui; (as object) que; **the house ~ they live in** la maison dans laquelle ils vivent; **the day ~ she arrived** le jour où elle est arrivée.
IV *conj* que; **he said ~ he had finished** il a dit qu'il avait fini.
V *adv* **it's about ~ thick** c'est à peu près épais comme ça; **I can't do ~ much work in one day** je ne peux pas faire autant de travail dans une journée; **he can't swim ~ far** il ne peut pas nager aussi loin.
IDIOMS **~ is** (**to say**)... c'est-à-dire...; **~'s it!** (that's right) c'est ça!; (that's enough) ça suffit!; **I don't want to see you again and ~'s ~!** je ne veux pas te revoir point final!

thatched cottage *n* chaumière *f*.

thatched roof *n* toit *m* de chaume.

thaw I *n* dégel *m*.
II *vtr* faire fondre [*ice, snow*]; décongeler [*frozen food*].
III *vi* **1** [*snow*] fondre; [*ground, frozen food*] dégeler; **2** (figurative) se détendre.

the ▶702| *det* le/la/l'/les; **two chapters of ~ book** deux chapitres du livre; **I met them at ~ supermarket** je les ai rencontrés au supermarché; **~ French** les Français; **~ wounded** les blessés; **she buys only ~ best** elle n'achète que ce qu'il y a de mieux; **~ more I learn ~ less I understand** plus j'apprends moins je comprends; **~ longer he waits ~ harder it will be** plus il attendra plus ce sera difficile; **~ sooner ~ better** le plus tôt sera le mieux; **~ fastest train** le train le plus rapide; **~ prettiest house in the village** la plus jolie maison du village; **THE book of the year** le meilleur livre de l'année; **do you mean THE Charlie Parker?** tu veux dire le célèbre Charlie Parker?

theatre, theater (US) *n* **1** théâtre *m*; **to go to the ~** aller au théâtre; **2** (US) (cinema) cinéma *m*.

theatrical *adj* théâtral/-e; [*group*] de théâtre.

theft *n* vol *m* (**of** de).

their *det* leur/leurs.

■ **Note** In French, determiners agree in gender and number with the noun that follows. So *their* is translated by *leur* + masculine or feminine singular noun (*leur chien*, *leur maison*) and by *leurs* + plural noun (*leurs enfants*).
– When *their* is stressed, *à eux* is added after the noun: THEIR house = leur maison à eux.
– For *their* used with parts of the body ▶413|.

---

theirs *pron*

■ **Note** In French, possessive pronouns reflect the gender and number of the noun they are standing for; *theirs* is translated by *le leur*, *la leur*, *les leurs*, according to what is being referred to.

---

my car is red but ~ is blue ma voiture est rouge mais la leur est bleue; **my children are older than ~** mes enfants sont plus âgés que les leurs; **which house is ~?** c'est laquelle leur maison?; **the money wasn't ~ to give away** ils or elles n'avaient pas à donner cet argent.

the

◆ In French the definite article, like determiners, agrees in gender and number with the noun that follows; so ***the*** is translated as follows:

le or **l'** + masculine singular noun	**le** chien, **l'**ami
la or **l'** + feminine singular noun	**la** chaise, **l'**amie
les + masculine plural noun	**les** hommes, **les** avions
les + feminine plural noun	**les** femmes, **les** autos

◆ When ***the*** is used after a preposition in English, the two words (*preposition* + ***the***) are often translated by one word in French. If the preposition would normally be translated by ***de*** in French (***of***, ***about***, ***from*** etc), the *preposition* + ***the*** is translated according to the number and gender of the noun:

de + **le** or **l'** + masculine singular noun	**du** chien, **de l'**ami
de + **la** or **l'** + feminine singular noun	**de la** chaise, **de l'**amie
de + **les** + masculine plural noun	**des** hommes, **des** avions
de + **les** + feminine plural noun	**des** femmes, **des** autos

If the preposition would usually be translated by ***à*** (***at***, ***to*** etc) the *preposition* + ***the*** is translated according to the number and gender of the noun:

à + **le** or **l'** + masculine singular noun	**au** chien, **à l'**ami
à + **la** or **l'** + feminine singular noun	**à la** chaise, **à l'**amie
à + **les** + masculine plural noun	**aux** hommes, **aux** avions
à + **les** + feminine plural noun	**aux** femmes, **aux** autos

◆ Other than this, there are few problems in translating ***the*** into French. The following cases are, however, worth remembering as not following exactly the pattern of the English:

the *good*, ***the*** *poor*, ***the*** *unemployed etc*	= **les** bons, **les** pauvres, **les** chômeurs etc
Charles ***the*** *First*, *Elizabeth* ***the*** *Second etc*	= Charles Ier (Premier), Elizabeth II (Deux) etc
she's ***<u>the</u>*** *violinist of the century*	= c'est **la plus grande** violoniste du siècle
the *Tudors*, ***the*** *Batemans*, ***the*** *Kennedys etc*	= **les** Tudor, **les** Bateman, **les** Kennedy etc.
<u>the</u> *sporting event of the year*	= **le grand** événement sportif de l'année
it's ***<u>the</u>*** *film to see*	= c'est **le** film à voir

❑ This dictionary contains usage notes on such topics as *days of the week*, *illnesses*, *the human body*, and *musical instruments*, many of which use ***the***; for the index to these notes see **▶ 784**.

For other particular usages, see the entry **the**.

them ▶ 704 *pron* **both of ~** tous/toutes les deux; **both of ~ work in London** ils/elles travaillent à Londres tous/toutes les deux; **some of ~** quelques-uns d'entre eux/quelques-unes d'entre elles.

theme *n* thème *m*.

theme park *n* parc *m* de loisirs (à thème).

theme song, **theme tune** *n* (of film) musique *f*; (of radio, TV programme) indicatif *m*.

themselves *pron*

■ **Note** When used as a reflexive pronoun, direct and indirect, *themselves* is translated by *se* (or *s'* before a vowel or mute 'h').
– When used for emphasis, the translation is *eux-mêmes* in the masculine and *elles-mêmes* in the feminine: *they did it themselves* = ils l'ont fait eux-mêmes or elles l'ont fait elles-mêmes.
– After a preposition, the translation is *eux* or *elles* or *eux-mêmes* or *elles-mêmes*: *they bought the painting for themselves* = (*masculine or mixed gender*) ils ont acheté le tableau pour eux *or* pour eux-mêmes; (*feminine gender*) elles ont acheté le tableau pour elles *or* pour elles-mêmes.

1 (reflexive) se, s'; **they washed ~** ils se sont lavés; **2** (emphatic) eux-mêmes/elles-mêmes; **3** (after preposition) eux/elles, eux-mêmes/elles-mêmes; **(all) by ~** tout seuls/toutes seules.

then *adv* **1** (at that time) alors, à ce moment-là; (implying more distant past) en ce temps-là; **I was working in Oxford ~** je travaillais alors à Oxford; **since ~** depuis; **2** (afterwards, next) puis, ensuite; **3** (in that case, so) alors; **4** (therefore) donc; **5** (in addition, besides) puis, aussi.

thence *adv* de là.

theology *n* théologie *f*.

theorem *n* théorème *m*.

theoretical *adj* théorique.

theoretically *adv* théoriquement; **~ speaking** en théorie.

theory *n* théorie *f*; **in ~** en théorie.

therapeutic *adj* thérapeutique.

therapist *n* thérapeute *mf*.

therapy *n* thérapie *f*.

there

■ **Note** *there* is generally translated by *là* after prepositions (*near there* = près de là) and when emphasizing the location of an object/a point etc visible to the speaker: *put them there* = mettez-les là.
– *voilà* is used to draw attention to a visible place/object/person: *there's my watch* = voilà ma montre, whereas *il y a* is used for generalizations: *there's a village nearby* = il y a un village tout près.
– *there*, when unstressed with verbs such as *aller* and *être*, is translated by *y*: *we went there last year* = nous y sommes allés l'année dernière, but not where emphasis is made: *it was there that we went last year* = c'est là que nous sommes allés l'année dernière.
– For examples of the above and further uses, see the entry below.

I *pron* **~ is/are** il y a; **~ isn't any room** il n'y a pas de place; **~ are many reasons** il y a beaucoup de raisons; **~ are two** il y en a deux; **~ is some left** il en reste; **~ seems to be** il semble y avoir.
II *adv* **1** là; **up to ~, down to ~** jusque là; **put it in ~** mettez-le là-dedans; **stand ~** mettez-vous là; **go over ~** va là-bas; **will she be ~ now?** est-ce qu'elle y est maintenant?; **2** (to draw attention) (to person, activity) voilà; **~ you are** (seeing somebody arrive) vous voilà; (giving object) tenez, voilà; (that's done) et voilà; **~'s a bus coming** voilà un bus; **that paragraph ~** ce paragraphe.
III *excl* **~ ~!** allez! allez!; **~, I told you!** voilà, je te l'avais bien dit!; **~, you've woken the baby!** c'est malin, tu as réveillé le bébé!
IV there again *phr* (on the other hand) d'un autre côté.

thereabouts (GB), **thereabout** (US) *adv* **1** (in the vicinity) par là; **2** (roughly) **100 dollars or ~** 100 dollars environ.

thereby *conj* ainsi.

therefore *adv* donc, par conséquent.

thermal *adj* thermique; [*spring*] thermal/-e; [*garment*] en thermolactyl®.

thermometer *n* thermomètre *m*.

Thermos® *n* (also **~ flask**) bouteille *f* thermos®.

thermostat *n* thermostat *m*.

thesaurus *n* dictionnaire *m* analogique.

these ▶ **this**.

thesis *n* **1** (Univ) (doctoral) thèse *f*; (master's) mémoire *m*; **2** (theory) thèse *f*.

they *pron*

■ **Note** *they* is translated by *ils* (masculine) or *elles* (feminine). For a group of people or things of mixed gender, *ils* is always used. The emphatic form is *eux* (masculine) or *elles* (feminine).

~ have already gone (masculine or mixed) ils sont déjà partis; (feminine) elles sont déjà parties; **here ~ are!** les voici!; **there ~ are!** les voilà!

thick I *adj* **1** (gen) épais/épaisse; [*forest, vegetation, fog*] dense, épais/épaisse; **to be 6 cm ~** faire 6 cm d'épaisseur; **2**° (stupid) bête.
II *adv* **don't spread the butter on too ~** ne mets pas trop de beurre; **the snow lay ~ on the ground** il y avait une épaisse couche de neige sur le sol.
IDIOMS **to be in the ~ of** être au beau milieu de.

thicken I *vtr* épaissir.
II *vi* s'épaissir; [*voice*] s'enrouer.

thicket *n* fourré *m*.

thickness *n* épaisseur *f*.

thickset *adj* trapu/-e.

thick-skinned *adj* insensible.

thief *n* voleur/-euse *m/f*.

thieve *vtr, vi* voler.

thigh *n* cuisse *f*.

thimble *n* dé *m* à coudre.

thin I *adj* **1** [*nose, lips, wall*] mince; [*line, stripe, wire, paper*] fin/-e; [*slice, layer*] fin/-e, mince; [*fabric, mist*] léger/-ère; **2** [*mixture*] liquide;

them

◆ When used as a direct object pronoun, referring to people, animals or things, ***them*** is translated by ***les***:

I know ***them*** = je **les** connais
I don't know ***them*** = je ne **les** connais pas
do I know ***them****?* = est-ce que je **les** connais?

◆ Note that the object pronoun normally comes before the verb in French and that, in compound tenses like the present perfect and past perfect, the past participle agrees in gender and number with the direct object pronoun:

he's seen ***them*** = il **les** a vu**s**
(***them*** being masculine or of mixed gender)
= il **les** a vu**es**
(***them*** being all feminine gender)
he hasn't seen ***them*** = il ne **les** a pas vu**s**
= il ne **les** a pas vu**es**
has he seen ***them****?* = est-ce qu'il **les** a vu**s**?
= est-ce qu'il **les** a vu**es**?

◆ In imperatives, the direct object pronoun is translated by ***les*** and comes after the verb:

catch ***them!*** = attrape-**les**!*
take ***them!*** = prenez-**les**!*

But in negative commands, ***les*** comes before the verb:

don't take ***them!*** = ne **les** prenez pas!
don't hit ***them!*** = ne **les** frappe pas!

◆ When used as an indirect object pronoun, ***them*** is translated by ***leur***:

I gave it ***to them*** = je le **leur** ai donné
I didn't give it ***to them*** = je ne le **leur** ai pas donné
did I give it ***to them****?* = est-ce que je le **leur** ai donné?

◆ In imperatives, the indirect object pronoun is translated by ***leur*** and comes after the verb:

write ***to them!*** = écris-**leur**!*
say it ***to them!*** = dis-le-**leur**!*

But in negative commands, ***leur*** comes before the verb:

don't show it ***to them!*** = ne le **leur** montre pas!

◆ After prepositions and the verb ***to be***, the translation is ***eux*** for masculine or mixed gender and ***elles*** for feminine gender:

he did it ***for them*** = il l'a fait **pour eux**
(***them*** being masculine or of mixed gender)
= il l'a fait pour **elles**
(***them*** being all feminine gender)
it's ***them*** = ce sont **eux**
ce sont **elles**

* Note the hyphen(s).

❑ For particular usages see the entry **them**.

[*soup, sauce*] clair/-e; **3** [*person, body*] maigre; **to get ~** maigrir; **4 to wear ~** [*joke, excuse*] être usé/-e.
II *vtr* diluer [*paint*]; allonger [*sauce, soup*].
III *vi* (also **~ out**) [*crowd*] se disperser; [*hair*] se clairsemer.

thing I *n* **1** (object) chose *f*, truc○ *m*; (action, task, event) chose *f*; **the best ~ (to do) would be to go and see her** le mieux serait d'aller la voir; **I couldn't hear a ~ (that) he said** je n'ai rien entendu de ce qu'il a dit; **the ~ is, (that)**... ce qu'il y a, c'est que...; **the only ~ is,**... la seule chose, c'est que...; **2** (person, animal) **she's a pretty little ~** c'est une jolie petite fille; **you lucky ~○!** veinard/-e○!
II **things** *n pl* **1** (personal belongings, equipment) affaires *fpl*; **2** (situation, circumstances, matters) les choses *fpl*; **how are ~s with you?** comment ça va?; **all ~s considered** tout compte fait.
IDIOMS **for one ~... (and) for another ~...** premièrement... et deuxièmement...; **I must be seeing ~s!** je dois avoir des visions!

think I *vtr* **1** (believe) croire, penser; **I ~ so** je crois; **I don't ~ so** je ne crois pas; **what do you ~ it will cost?** combien ça va coûter à ton avis?; **2** (imagine) imaginer, croire; **3** (have opinion) **to ~ a lot/not much of** penser/ne pas penser beaucoup de bien de; **what do you ~ of him?** que penses-tu de lui?
II *vi* **1** penser; (carefully) réfléchir; **to ~ about** or **of sb/sth** penser à qn/qch; **I'll have to ~ about it** il faudra que j'y réfléchisse; **to ~ hard** bien réfléchir; **to be ~ing of doing** envisager de faire; **to ~ about doing** penser à faire; **2** (consider) **to ~ of sb as** considérer qn comme; **3** (remember) **to ~ of** se rappeler.
■ **think ahead** bien réfléchir (à l'avance).
■ **think back** se reporter en arrière (**to** à).
■ **think through** bien réfléchir à [*proposal, action*]; faire le tour de [*problem, question*].

thinner *n* diluant *m*.

third ▶456|, 498| I *n* **1** (in order) troisième *mf*; **2** (of month) trois *m inv*; **3** (fraction) tiers *m*; **4** (also **~-class honours degree**) (GB Univ) ≈ licence *f* avec mention passable; **5** (also **~ gear**) (Aut) troisième *f*.
II *adj* troisième.
III *adv* **1** [*come, finish*] troisième; **2** (also **thirdly**) troisièmement.

third-class *adj* de troisième classe.

third party *n* tiers *m*.

Third World *n* tiers-monde *m*.

thirst *n* soif *f* (**for** de).

thirsty *adj* assoiffé/-e; **to be ~** avoir soif; **to make sb ~** donner soif à qn.

thirteen ▶389|, 434| *n, pron, det* treize (*m*) *inv*.

thirteenth ▶456|, 498| I *n* **1** (in order) treizième *mf*; **2** (of month) treize *m inv*; **3** (fraction) treizième *m*.
II *adj, adv* treizième.

thirties ▶389|, 456| *n pl* **1** (era) **the ~** les années *fpl* trente; **2** (age) **to be in one's ~** avoir entre trente et quarante ans.

thirtieth ▶456| I *n* **1** (in order) trentième *mf*; **2** (of month) trente *m inv*; **3** (fraction) trentième *m*.
II *adj, adv* trentième.

thirty ▶389|, 434| *n, pron, det* trente (*m*) *inv*.

thirty-first ▶456| I *n* (of month) trente et un *m*.
II *adj* trente et unième.

this

■ **Note As a determiner**
– In French, determiners agree in gender and number with the noun that follows; *this* is translated by *ce* + masculine singular noun (*ce monsieur*) BUT by *cet* + masculine singular noun beginning with a vowel or mute 'h' (*cet arbre, cet homme*) and by *cette* + feminine singular noun (*cette femme*). The plural form *these* is translated by *ces* (*ces livres, ces histoires*).
– Note, however, that the above translations are also used for the English *that* (plural *those*). So when it is necessary to insist on *this* as opposed to another or others of the same sort, the adverbial tag *-ci* (*this one here*) is added to the noun: *I prefer* THIS *version* = je préfère cette version-ci.
– **As a pronoun** (*meaning this one*)
– In French, pronouns reflect the gender and number of the noun they are standing for. So *this* (meaning *this one*) is translated by *celui-ci* for a masculine noun, *celle-ci* for a feminine noun; *those* (meaning *those ones*) is translated by *ceux-ci* for a masculine plural noun, *celles-ci* for a feminine plural noun: *of all the dresses this is the prettiest one* = de toutes les robes celle-ci est la plus jolie.
– This dictionary contains usage notes on such topics as ***time units*** and ***dates***. For the index to these notes ▶784|.
– For other uses of *this*, see the entry below.

I *det* **~ paper** ce papier; **~ lamp** cette lampe; **do it ~ way not that way** fais-le comme ça et pas comme ça.
II *pron* **what's ~?** qu'est-ce que c'est?; **who's ~?** qui est-ce?; (on telephone) qui est à l'appareil?; **whose is ~?** à qui appartient ceci?; **~ is the dining room** voici la salle à manger; **~ is my sister Moira** (introduction) voici ma sœur Moira; (on photo) c'est ma sœur, Moira; **~ is not the right one** ce n'est pas le bon; **who did ~?** qui a fait ça?; **~ is what happens when** voilà ce qui se passe quand.
III *adv* **it's ~ big** c'est grand comme ça.
IDIOMS **to talk about ~ and that** parler de tout et de rien.

thistle *n* chardon *m*.

thong *n* **1** (on whip) lanière *f*; **2** (on shoe, garment) lacet *m*.

thorn *n* épine *f*.

thorough *adj* **1** (detailed) [*analysis, knowledge*] approfondi/-e; [*search, work*] minutieux/-ieuse; **2** (meticulous) minutieux/-ieuse.

thoroughbred I *n* pur-sang *m*.
II *adj* de pure race.

thoroughfare *n* rue *f*; **'no ~'** 'passage interdit'.

thoroughly *adv* **1** (meticulously) [*clean, examine, read*] à fond; [*check, search*] minutieusement; **2** (completely) [*clean, reliable, dangerous*] tout à fait; [*agree*] parfaitement; [*recommend*] chaleureusement.

those ▶ **that**.

though I *conj* bien que (+ *subjunctive*); **a foolish ~ courageous act** un acte stupide quoique courageux.
II *adv* quand même, pourtant; **it's very expensive, ~** c'est très cher, pourtant.

thought *n* **1** (idea) idée *f*, pensée *f*; **2** (reflection) pensée *f*; **deep in ~** plongé dans ses pensées; **3** (consideration) considération *f*; **to give ~ to sth** considérer qch.

thoughtful *adj* **1** (reflective) pensif/-ive; **2** (considerate) [*person, gesture*] prévenant/-e; [*letter*] gentil/-ille.

thoughtless *adj* irréfléchi/-e.

thought-out *adj* **well/badly ~** bien/mal conçu/-e.

thought-provoking *adj* qui fait réfléchir.

thousand *n, pron, det* mille *m inv*; **a ~ and two** mille deux; **about a ~** un millier; **four ~ pounds** quatre mille livres; **~s of** des milliers de.

thousandth *n, adj, adv* millième (*mf*).

thrash *vtr* **1** (whip) rouer [qn] de coups; **2**○ (Mil, Sport) écraser.
■ **thrash about, thrash around** se débattre.
■ **thrash out** venir à bout de [*problem*]; réussir à élaborer [*plan*].

thrashing *n* raclée *f*.

thread I *n* **1** (for sewing) fil *m*; **2** (of screw) filetage *m*; **3** (of story, argument) fil *m*.
II *vtr* enfiler [*bead, needle*].

threadbare *adj* usé/-e jusqu'à la corde.

threat *n* menace *f* (**to** pour).

threaten I *vtr* menacer; **to ~ to do** [*person*] menacer de faire; [*event, thing*] risquer de faire; **to be ~ed with extinction** risquer de disparaître.
II *vi* menacer.

three ▶ 389, 434 *n, pron, det* trois (*m*) *inv*.

three-dimensional *adj* en trois dimensions.

threefold I *adj* triple.
II *adv* triplement; **to increase ~** tripler.

three-piece suit *n* (costume *m*) trois-pièces *m inv*.

three-piece suite *n* salon *m* trois pièces.

thresh *vtr* battre.

threshold *n* seuil *m*.

thrift *n* économie *f*.

thrifty *adj* [*person*] économe (**in** dans).

thrill I *n* **1** (sensation) frisson *m*; **2** (pleasure) plaisir *m*.
II *vtr* transporter [qn] de joie.
III *vi* frissonner (**at, to** à).

thrilled *adj* ravi/-e; **~ed with** enchanté/-e de.

thriller *n* thriller *m*.

thrilling *adj* [*adventure, match, story*] palpitant/-e; [*concert, moment, sensation*] exaltant/-e.

thrive *vi* [*person*] se porter bien; [*plant*] pousser bien; [*business, community*] prospérer.

throat *n* gorge *f*; **to have a sore ~** avoir mal à la gorge.

throb *vi* **1** [*heart, pulse*] battre; **my head is ~bing** ça me lance dans la tête; **2** [*motor*] vibrer; [*music, building*] résonner.

throne *n* trône *m*.

throng I *n* foule *f* (**of** de).
II *vtr* envahir [*street, town*].

through I *prep* **1** (from one side to the other) à travers; **the nail went right ~ the wall** le clou a traversé le mur; **2** (via, by way of) **to go ~ the town centre** passer par le centre-ville; **to look ~** regarder avec [*telescope*]; regarder par [*hole, window*]; **it was ~ her that I got this job** c'est par son intermédiaire que j'ai eu ce travail; **3** (past) **to go ~** brûler [*red light*]; **to get** or **go ~** passer à travers [*barricade*]; passer [*customs*]; **she's been ~ a lot** elle en a vu des vertes et des pas mures○; **4** (because of) **~ carelessness** par négligence; **~ illness** pour cause de maladie; **5** (until the end of) **all** or **right ~ the day** toute la journée; **6** (up to and including) jusqu'à; **from Friday ~ to Sunday** de vendredi jusqu'à dimanche.
II *adj* **1** [*train, ticket, route*] direct/-e; [*freight*] à forfait; **'no ~ road'** 'voie sans issue'; **2** (successful) **to be ~ to the next round** être sélectionné/-e pour le deuxième tour; **3**○ (finished) fini/-e; **are you ~ with the paper?** as-tu fini de lire le journal?
III *adv* **the water went ~** l'eau est passée à travers; **to let sb ~** laisser passer qn; **to read sth right ~** lire qch jusqu'au bout.
IV **through and through** *phr* **English ~ and ~** anglais jusqu'au bout des ongles.

throughout I *prep* **1** (all over) **~ France** dans toute la France; **~ the world** dans le monde entier; **2** (for the duration of) tout au long de; **~ his life** toute sa vie; **~ history** à travers l'histoire.
II *adv* (in every part) partout; (the whole time) tout le temps.

throughway *n* (US) voie *f* rapide or express.

throw I *n* (in football) touche *f*; (of javelin) lancer *m*; (in judo, wrestling) jeté *m*; (of dice) coup *m*.
II *vtr* **1** (with careful aim) lancer; (downwards) jeter; (with violence) projeter; **to ~ sth at sb** lancer qch à qn; **to ~ a six** (in dice) faire un six; **2** [*horse*] désarçonner [*rider*]; **3** lancer [*punch*]; jeter [*glance*]; projeter [*light, shadow*] (**on** sur); **4** (disconcert) désarçonner; **5 to ~ a party** faire une fête○; **6** (in pottery) tourner.
III *vi* lancer.
■ **throw away** jeter [*paper, old clothes*]; gâcher [*chance, life*].
■ **throw back** rejeter [*fish*]; relancer [*ball*].
■ **throw out 1** jeter [*rubbish*]; expulser [*person*] (**of** de); **2** rejeter [*application, decision*].
■ **throw up**: ¶ **~ up**○ vomir; ¶ **~ [sth] up 1** lever [*arms, hands*]; lancer [*ball*]; **2**○ (abandon) laisser tomber [*job*].

throwback *n* survivance *f* (**to** de).

thrush *n* (Zool) grive *f*.

thrust I *n* **1** (gen, Mil, Tech) poussée *f*; **sword ~** coup *m* d'épée; **2** (of argument) portée *f*.
II *vtr* **to ~ sth towards** or **at sb** mettre brusquement qch sous le nez de qn; **to ~ sth into sth** enfoncer qch dans qch.

thud I *n* bruit *m* sourd.
II *vi* faire un bruit sourd.

thug *n* voyou *m*.

thumb I *n* pouce *m*.
II *vtr* **1** (also **~ through**) feuilleter [*book, magazine*]; **2**○ **to ~ a lift** faire du stop○.
IDIOMS **to be under sb's ~** être sous la domination de qn.

thumbtack *n* punaise *f*.

thump I *n* **1** (blow) (grand) coup *m*; **2** (sound) bruit *m* sourd.
II *vtr* taper sur; **he ~ed me** il m'a tapé dessus.
III *vi* [*heart*] battre violemment; [*music, rhythm*] résonner.

thunder I *n* **1** tonnerre *m*; **a peal of ~** un roulement de tonnerre; **2** (of hooves) fracas *m*; (of applause) tonnerre *m*.
II *v impers* tonner.

thunderbolt *n* foudre *f*.

thunderstorm *n* orage *m*.

thunderstruck *adj* abasourdi/-e.

Thursday ▶ 456 *pr n* jeudi *m*.

thus *adv* ainsi; **~ far** jusqu'à présent.

thwart *vtr* contrarier [*plan*]; contrecarrer les desseins de [*person*].

thyme *n* thym *m*.

thyroid *n* (also **~ gland**) thyroïde *f*.

tiara *n* (woman's) diadème *m*; (Pope's) tiare *f*.

tick I *n* **1** (of clock) tic-tac *m*; **2** (mark) coche *f*; **3** (Zool) tique *f*.
II *vtr* cocher [*box, name, answer*].
III *vi* [*bomb, clock, watch*] faire tic-tac.
■ **tick off** cocher [*name, item*].

ticket *n* **1** (for plane, train, cinema, exhibition) billet *m* (**for** pour); (for bus, underground, cloakroom, left-luggage) ticket *m*; (for library) carte *f*; (label) étiquette *f*; **2**○ (Aut) (for fine) PV○ *m*; **3** (US) (of political party) liste *f* (électorale).

ticket office *n* (office) bureau *m* de vente (des billets); (booth) guichet *m*.

tickle I *n* chatouillement *m*.
II *vtr* **1** [*person, feather*] chatouiller; [*wool, garment*] gratter; **2**○ (gratify) chatouiller [*palate, vanity*]; **3** (amuse) amuser.
III *vi* chatouiller.

tidal wave *n* raz-de-marée *m inv*.

tide *n* marée *f*; (figurative) (of emotion) vague *f*; (of events) cours *m*.

tidy I *adj* **1** [*house, room, desk*] bien rangé/-e; [*garden, work, appearance*] soigné/-e; [*habits, person*] ordonné/-e; [*hair*] bien coiffé/-e; **2**○ [*amount*] beau/belle (*before n*).
II *vtr, vi* = **tidy up**.
■ **tidy up**: ¶ **~ up** faire du rangement; **to ~ up after** ranger derrière [*person*]; ¶ **~ up [sth]** ranger [*house, room, objects*]; arranger [*appearance, hair*].

tie I *n* **1** (piece of clothing) cravate *f*; **2** (bond) lien *m*; **3** (constraint) contrainte *f*; **4** (draw) match *m* nul.
II *vtr* **1** attacher [*label, animal*] (**to** à); ligoter [*hands*]; ficeler [*parcel*] (**with** avec); nouer [*scarf, cravate*]; attacher [*laces*]; **to ~ a knot in sth** faire un nœud à qch; **2** (link) associer (**to** à); **3 to be ~d to** être rivé/-e à [*job*]; être cloué/-e○ à [*house*].
III *vi* **1** (fasten) s'attacher; **2** (draw) (in match) faire match nul; (in race) être ex aequo; (in vote) obtenir le même nombre de voix.
■ **tie back** nouer [qch] derrière [*hair*].
■ **tie in with** concorder avec [*fact, event*].
■ **tie up 1** ligoter [*prisoner*]; ficeler [*parcel*]; attacher [*animal*]; **2** (freeze) immobiliser [*capital*]; **3 to be ~d up** (busy) être pris/-e.

tie break(er) *n* (in tennis) tie-break *m*; (in quiz) question *f* subsidiaire.

tier *n* (of cake, sandwich) étage *m*; (of system) niveau *m*; (of seating) gradin *m*.

tiger *n* tigre *m*.

tight I *adj* **1** [*grip*] ferme; [*knot*] serré/-e; [*rope, voice*] tendu/-e; **2** [*space*] étroit/-e; [*clothing*] serré/-e; (closefitting) [*jacket, shirt*] ajusté/-e; **my shoes are too ~** mes chaussures me serrent; **3** (strict) [*security, deadline*] strict/-e; [*budget, credit, schedule*] serré/-e.
II *adv* [*hold, grip*] fermement; **hold ~!** cramponne-toi!; **sit ~!** ne bouge pas!

tighten I *vtr* serrer [*lid, screw*]; resserrer [*grip*]; renforcer [*security, restrictions*].
II *vi* [*lips*] se serrer; [*muscle*] se contracter.

tight-fisted○ *adj* radin/-e○.

tight-fitting *adj* ajusté/-e.

tightly *adv* [*grasp, hold*] fermement; [*embrace*] bien fort; [*fastened*] bien.

tightrope *n* corde *f* raide.

tightrope walker *n* funambule *mf*.

tights *n pl* (GB) collant *m*.

tile I *n* (for roof) tuile *f*; (for floor, wall) carreau *m*.
II *vtr* poser des tuiles sur [*roof*]; carreler [*floor, wall*].

till[1] = **until**.

till[2] *n* caisse *f*.

tiller *n* barre *f*.

tilt I *vtr* pencher [*table, sunshade*]; incliner [*head*]; rabattre [*hat, cap*].
II *vi* (slant) pencher.

timber *n* (for building) bois *m* (de construction); (trees) arbres *mpl*; (beam) poutre *f*.

time ▶ 434, 708 I *n* **1** temps *m*; **as ~ goes/went by** avec le temps; **you've got plenty of ~** tu as tout ton temps; **a long ~** longtemps; **a long ~ ago** il y a longtemps; **in five days' ~** dans cinq jours; **2** (hour of the day, night) heure *f*; **what ~ is it?, what's the ~?** quelle heure est-il?; **10 am French ~** 10 heures, heure française; **this ~ last week** il y a exactement huit jours; **on ~** à l'heure; **the train ~s** les horaires *mpl* des trains; **it's ~ for bed** c'est l'heure d'aller au lit; **it's ~ we started** il est temps de commencer; **about ~ too!** ce n'est pas trop tôt!; **in ~ for Christmas** à temps pour Noël; **3** (era, epoch) époque *f*; **at the ~** à l'époque; **in former ~s** autrefois; **it's just like old ~s** c'est comme au bon vieux temps; **4** (moment) moment *m*; **at ~s** par moments; **at the right ~** au bon moment; **this is no ~ for jokes** ce n'est pas le moment de plaisanter; **at all ~s** à tout moment; **any ~**

Talking about Time

❑ For time by the clock, ▶ **434**; for days of the week, months and dates, ▶ **456**.

How long?

Note the various ways of translating ***take*** into French:

how long does it take? = combien de temps faut-il?
it took me a week = cela m'a pris / il m'a fallu une semaine
it'll take at least a year = il faudra au moins un an / une bonne année
it'll only take a moment = c'est l'affaire de quelques instants

Use ***dans*** for ***in*** when something is seen as happening in the future:

*I'll be there **in** an hour* = je serai là **dans** une heure
***in** three weeks' time* = **dans** trois semaines

Use ***en*** for ***in*** when expressing the time something took or will take:

*he did it **in** an hour* = il l'a fait **en** une heure

The commonest translation of ***for*** in the 'how long' sense is ***pendant***:

*I worked in the factory **for** a year* = j'ai travaillé à l'usine **pendant** un an

But use ***pour*** to translate ***for*** when the length of time is seen as being still to come:

*we're here **for** a month* = nous sommes là **pour** un mois

And use ***depuis*** to translate ***for*** when the action began in the past and is still going on:

*she has been here **for** a week* = elle est ici **depuis** une semaine
*I haven't seen her **for** years* = je ne l'ai pas vue **depuis** des années

Note the use of ***de*** when expressing how long something lasted or will last:

an eight-hour day = une journée **de** huit heures

When?

when did it happen? = quand est-ce que c'est arrivé?
a month ago = il y a un mois
a week ago yesterday = il y a eu huit jours hier
when will you see him? = quand est-ce que tu le verras?
in a few days = dans quelques jours

(See above, the phrases with ***in*** translated by ***dans***.)

a month from tomorrow = dans un mois demain

How often?

how often does it happen? = cela arrive tous les combien?
every year = tous les ans
five times a day = cinq fois par jour
once every three months = une fois tous les trois mois

How much an hour (etc)?

*how much do you get **an** hour?* = combien gagnez-vous **de l'**heure?
*to be paid $20 **an** hour* = être payé 20 dollars **de l'**heure
*to be paid **by the** hour* = être payé **à l'**heure
*how much do you get **a** week / **a** month?* = combien gagnez-vous **par** semaine / **par** mois?
*$3,000 **a** month* = 3 000 dollars **par** mois

Forms in -ée: an / année, matin / matinée etc.

The *-ée* forms are often used to express a rather vague amount of time passing or spent in something, and so tend to give a subjective slant to what is being said, as in:

a long day / evening / year = une longue journée / soirée / année
a whole day = toute une journée / une journée entière

When an exact number is specified, the shorter forms are generally used, as in:

it lasted six days = cela a duré six jours

now d'un moment à l'autre; **by the ~ I finished the letter the post had gone** le temps de finir ma lettre et le courrier était parti; **some ~ next month** dans le courant du mois prochain; **for the ~ being** pour le moment; **5** (occasion) fois *f*; **nine ~s out of ten** neuf fois sur dix; **three ~s a month** trois fois par mois; **three at a ~** trois à la fois; **from ~ to ~** de temps en temps; **6** (experience) **to have a hard ~ doing** avoir du mal à faire; **he's having a hard ~** il traverse une période difficile; **we had a good ~** on s'est bien amusés; **7** (Mus) mesure *f*; **8 ten ~s longer/stronger** dix fois plus long/plus fort; **eight ~s as much** huit fois autant/-e; **9** (in mathematics) fois.
II *vtr* **1** (schedule) prévoir [*holiday, visit, attack*]; fixer [*appointment, meeting*]; **2** (judge) calculer [*blow, shot*]; **3** chronométrer [*athlete, cyclist*].

time bomb *n* bombe *f* à retardement.

time-consuming *adj* qui prend du temps.

time difference *n* décalage *m* horaire.

timeless *adj* éternel/-elle.

time-limit *n* **1** (deadline) date *f* limite; **2** (maximum duration) durée *f* maximum.

timely *adj* opportun/-e.

time off *n* (leave) congé *m*; (free time) temps *m* libre.

timer *n* (on light) minuterie *f*; (for cooking) minuteur *m*.

timespan *n* durée *f*.

timetable *n* (Sch) emploi *m* du temps; (for plans, negotiations) calendrier *m*; (for buses, trains) horaire *m*.

timid *adj* timide; [*animal*] craintif/-ive.

timing *n* **1** (gen) **the ~ of the announcement was unfortunate** le moment choisi pour la déclaration était inopportun; **2** (Aut) réglage *m* de l'allumage; **3** (Mus) sens *m* du rythme.

tin *n* **1** (metal) étain *m*; **2** (GB) (can) boîte *f* (de conserve); **3** (for biscuits, cake) boîte *f*; (for paint) pot *m*; (for baking) moule *m*; (for roasting) plat *m* (à rôtir).

tin can *n* boîte *f* en fer-blanc.

tin foil *n* papier *m* (d')aluminium.

tinge I *n* nuance *f*.
II *vtr* teinter (**with** de).

tingle I *n* (physical) picotement *m*; (psychological) frisson *m*.
II *vi* (physically) picoter; (psychologically) frissonner.

tinker *vi* **to ~ with** bricoler [*car*]; faire des retouches à [*document*].

tinkle I *n* tintement *m*.
II *vi* tinter.

tin opener *n* (GB) ouvre-boîtes *m inv*.

tinsel *n* guirlandes *fpl*.

tint *n* (trace) nuance *f*; (pale colour) teinte *f*; (hair colour) shampooing *m* colorant.

tinted *adj* [*glass, spectacles*] fumé/-e; [*hair*] teint/-e.

tiny *adj* tout/-e petit/-e.

tip I *n* **1** (of stick, sword, pen, shoe, spire) pointe *f*; (of branch, leaf, shoot, tail, feather) extrémité *f*; (of finger, nose, tongue) bout *m*; **2** (gratuity) pourboire *m*; **3** (practical hint) truc° *m*, conseil *m*; (in betting) tuyau° *m*.
II *vtr* **1** (tilt) incliner; (pour) verser; (dump) déverser [*waste, rubbish*]; **2** (predict) **to ~ sb/sth to win** prédire que qn/qch va gagner; **3** donner un pourboire à [*waiter, driver*].
III *vi* (tilt) s'incliner.
■ **tip over** faire basculer [*chair*]; renverser [*bucket, pile*].

tiptoe I *n* **on ~** sur la pointe des pieds.
II *vi* marcher sur la pointe des pieds.

tire I *n* (US) pneu *m*.
II *vtr* fatiguer.
III *vi* **1** (get tired) se fatiguer; **2** (get bored) **to ~ of** se lasser de.
■ **tire out** épuiser [*person*]; **to be ~d out** être éreinté/-e.

tired *adj* **1** (weary) [*person, face, legs*] fatigué/-e; [*voice*] las/lasse; **2** (bored) **to be ~ of sth/of doing** en avoir assez de qch/de faire; **to grow ~ of sth/of doing** se lasser de qch/de faire.

tiredness *n* fatigue *f*.

tireless *adj* [*person*] inlassable, infatigable; [*efforts*] constant/-e.

tiresome *adj* [*person, habit*] agaçant/-e; [*problem, duty*] fastidieux/-ieuse.

tiring *adj* fatigant/-e (**to do** de faire).

tissue *n* **1** (handkerchief) mouchoir *m* en papier; **2** (also **~ paper**) papier *m* de soie; **3** (Anat, Bot) tissu *m*.

tit *n* (Zool) mésange *f*.
IDIOMS **~ for tat** un prêté pour un rendu.

titbit *n* (GB) (of food) gâterie *f*; (of gossip) cancan° *m*.

title I *n* titre *m*.
II **titles** *n pl* (in film) générique *m*.
III *vtr* intituler [*book, play*].

titter I *n* ricanement *m*.
II *vi* ricaner.

to ▶434 I *infinitive particle* **1** (expressing purpose) pour; **to do sth ~ impress one's friends** faire qch pour impressionner ses amis; **2** (linking consecutive acts) **he looked up ~ see...** en levant les yeux, il a vu...; **3** (after superlatives) à; **the youngest ~ do** le or la plus jeune à faire; **4** (avoiding repetition of verb) **'did you go?'—'no I promised not ~'** 'tu y es allé?'—'non j'avais promis de ne pas le faire'; **'are you staying? '—'I want ~ but...'** 'tu restes?'—'j'aimerais bien mais...'; **5** (following impersonal verb) **it is difficult ~ do** il est difficile de faire; **it's difficult ~ understand** c'est difficile à comprendre
II *prep* **1** (in direction of) à [*shops, school*]; (with purpose of visiting) chez [*doctor's*]; (towards) vers; **she's gone ~ Mary's** elle est partie chez Mary; **~ Paris** à Paris; **~ Spain** en Espagne; **~ town** en ville; **the road ~ the village** la route qui mène au village; **turned ~ the wall** tourné vers le mur; **2** (up to) jusqu'à; **~ the end/this day** jusqu'à la fin/ce jour; **3** (in telling time) **ten (minutes) ~ three** trois heures moins dix; **it's five ~** il est moins cinq; **4** (introducing direct or indirect object) [*give, offer*]

to

❑ This dictionary contains usage notes and appendices on such topics as *The Clock, Length and Weight Measurements, Games and Sports* etc. Many of these use the preposition ***to***. For the index to these notes ▶ **784**.

As a preposition

◆ When ***to*** is used as a preposition with verbs of movement (*go, travel* etc), it is often translated by ***à*** (*à Paris, à Londres*), but remember to use ***en*** with feminine countries (*en France*) and ***au*** with masculine countries (*au Portugal*) ▶ **448**.

Remember when using ***à*** in French that ***à*** + *le* always becomes ***au***:

***to the** office* = **au** bureau

and ***à*** + *les* always becomes ***aux***:

***to the** shops* = **aux** magasins

◆ When ***to*** is used as a preposition with verbs such as *speak, give, say* etc, it is usually translated by ***à***:

*give the book **to** Jane*	= donne le livre **à** Jane
*I'll speak **to** the headmistress*	= je vais parler **à** la directrice
*she said it **to** my father*	= elle l'a dit **à** mon père
*show it **to** the policeman*	= montre-le **à** l'agent
*I pointed it out **to** the stewardess*	= je l'ai signalé **à** l'hôtesse
*give the ball **to** the little boy*	= donne le ballon **au*** petit garçon
*we gave it **to** the children*	= nous l'avons donné **aux*** enfants

* Remember that ***à*** + *le* = ***au*** and ***à*** + *les* = **aux**

◆ When ***to*** is used as a preposition with personal pronouns (*me, you, him, her, us, them*), the two words (*preposition* + *pronoun*) are translated by ***me/te/lui/lui/nous/vous/leur***:

*she gave it **to them***	= elle le **leur** a donné
*I'll say it **to her***	= je vais le **lui** dire

As part of an infinitive

◆ When ***to*** forms the infinitive of a verb taken alone, it needs no translation:

***to** go* = aller

However, when ***to*** is used as part of an infinitive giving the meaning ***in order to***, it is translated by ***pour***:

*he's gone into town **to buy** a shirt*	= il est parti en ville **pour acheter** une chemise

◆ ***to*** is also used as part of an infinitive after certain adjectives: ***easy to read*** etc. Here ***to*** is usually translated by ***à***:

*her writing is easy **to** read* = son écriture est facile **à** lire

However, when the infinitive has an object, ***to*** is usually translated by ***de***:

*it's easy **to** lose one's way* = il est facile **de** perdre son chemin

❑ To find out more about this point, see the note at ***it*** ▶ **542**.

◆ ***to*** is also used as part of an infinitive after certain verbs: *she told me **to** wash my hands, I'll help him **to** tidy the room* etc. Here the translation, usually either ***à*** or ***de***, depends on the verb used in French. To find the correct translation, consult the appropriate verb entry: **tell**, **help** etc. For all other uses, see the entry **to**.

à; **give the book ~ Sophie** donne le livre à Sophie; **be nice ~ your brother** sois gentil avec ton frère; **~ me it's just a minor problem** pour moi ce n'est qu'un problème mineur; **5** (in toasts, dedications) à; **~ prosperity** à la prospérité; **~ our dear son** (on tombstone) à notre cher fils; **6** (in accordance with) **is it ~ your taste?** c'est à ton goût?; **to dance ~ the music** danser sur la musique; **7** (in relationships, comparisons) **to win by three goals ~ two** gagner par trois buts à deux; **next door ~ the school** à côté de l'école; **8** (showing accuracy) **three weeks ~ the day** trois semaines jour pour jour; **~ scale** à l'échelle; **9** (showing reason) **to invite sb ~ dinner** inviter qn à dîner; **~ this end** à cette fin; **10** (belonging to) de; **the key ~ the safe** la clé du coffre; **a room ~ myself** une chambre pour moi tout seul; **personal assistant ~ the director** assistant du directeur; **11** [*tied*] à; [*pinned*] à [*noticeboard*]; sur [*lapel, dress*]; **12** (showing reaction) à; **~ his surprise/dismay** à sa grande surprise/consternation.

toad *n* crapaud *m*.

toadstool *n* champignon *m* vénéneux.

to and fro *adv* [*swing*] d'avant en arrière; **to go ~** [*person*] aller et venir.

toast I *n* **1** (bread) toast *m*; **a slice of ~** un toast; **2** (drink) toast *m*; **to drink a ~** lever son verre.
II *vtr* **1** faire griller [*bread*]; **2** porter un toast à [*person, success*].

toaster *n* grille-pain *m inv*.

tobacco *n* tabac *m*.

toboggan *n* luge *f*, toboggan *m*.

today ▶456 I *n* aujourd'hui *m*; **~ is Monday** (aujourd'hui) nous sommes lundi.
II *adv* aujourd'hui; (nowadays) de nos jours; **~ week** dans une semaine aujourd'hui; **a week ago ~** il y a une semaine aujourd'hui; **later ~** plus tard dans la journée.

toddler *n* trés jeune enfant *m*.

toe ▶413 *n* **1** (Anat) orteil *m*; **big/little ~** gros/petit orteil; **2** (of sock, shoe) bout *m*.
IDIOMS **to ~ the line** marcher droit; **from top to ~** de la tête aux pieds.

toffee *n* caramel *m* (au beurre).

together I *adv* **1** ensemble; **to get back ~ again** se remettre ensemble; **to be close ~** être rapprochés/-es; **she's cleverer than all the rest of them put ~** elle est plus intelligente que tous les autres réunis; **they belong ~** (objects) ils vont ensemble; (people) ils sont faits l'un pour l'autre; **the talks brought the two sides closer ~** les négociations ont rapproché les deux parties; **2** (at the same time) à la fois.
II **together with** *phr* (as well as) ainsi que; (in the company of) avec.
IDIOMS **to get one's act ~** s'organiser.

togetherness *n* (in team, friendship) camaraderie *f*; (in family, couple) intimité *f*.

toil I *n* labeur *m*.
II *vi* **1** (also **toil away**) (work) peiner; **2** (struggle) **to ~ up the hill** monter péniblement la côte.

toilet *n* toilettes *fpl*; **public ~(s)** toilettes publiques.

toilet bag *n* trousse *f* de toilette.

toilet paper, **toilet tissue** *n* papier *m* hygiénique.

toilet roll *n* (roll) rouleau *m* de papier toilette; (tissue) papier *m* toilette.

token I *n* **1** (for machine, phone) jeton *m*; **2** (voucher) bon *m*; **book/record ~** chèque-cadeau *m* pour livre/pour disque; **3** témoignage *m*; **as a ~ of** en signe de.
II *adj* symbolique; **to make a ~ gesture** faire un geste pour la forme.

tolerable *adj* (bearable) tolérable; (adequate) acceptable.

tolerance *n* (gen, Med) tolérance *f*.

tolerant *adj* tolérant/-e.

tolerate *vtr* (permit) tolérer; (put up with) supporter.

toll I *n* **1 death ~** nombre *m* de victimes (**from** de); **2** (levy) (on road, bridge) péage *m*; **3** (of bell) son *m*; (for funeral) glas *m*.
II *vtr, vi* sonner.

toll call *n* (US) communication *f* interurbaine.

tomato *n* tomate *f*.

tomato sauce *n* sauce *f* tomate.

tomb *n* tombeau *m*.

tomboy *n* garçon *m* manqué.

tombstone *n* pierre *f* tombale.

tomcat *n* matou *m*.

tomorrow ▶456 I *n* demain *m*; **I'll do it by ~** je le ferai d'ici demain.
II *adv* demain; **see you ~!** à demain!; **~ week** demain en huit; **a week ago ~** il y aura une semaine demain.

tomorrow afternoon *n, adv* demain après-midi.

tomorrow evening *n, adv* demain soir.

tomorrow morning *n, adv* demain matin.

ton ▶573 *n* **1** (in weight) (GB) (also **gross ~** or **long ~**) tonne *f* britannique (= *1,016 kg*); (US) (also **net ~** or **short ~**) tonne *f* américaine (= *907 kg*); **metric ~** tonne *f*; **2**° (a lot) **~s of** des tas de° [*food, paper, bands*].

tone I *n* **1** (gen) ton *m*; **his ~ of voice** son ton; **to set the ~** donner le ton à (**for** à); **2** (Mus) timbre *m*; (on phone) tonalité *f*; **3** (of muscle) tonus *m*.
II *vtr* (also **~ up**) tonifier [*body, muscles*].
III *vi* (also **~in**) (blend) [*colours*] s'harmoniser.
■ **tone down** atténuer [*colours, criticism*]; adoucir le ton de [*letter, statement*].

tone-deaf *adj* **to be ~** ne pas avoir l'oreille musicale.

tongs *n pl* (for coal) pincettes *fpl*; (in laboratory, for sugar) pince *f*.

tongue *n* **1** (gen) langue *f*; **to stick one's ~ out at sb** tirer la langue à qn; **to lose one's ~** (figurative) avaler sa langue; **2** (on shoe) languette *f*.
IDIOMS **I have his name on the tip of my ~** j'ai son nom sur le bout de la langue; **a slip of the ~** un lapsus.

tongue-in-cheek *adj, adv* au deuxième degré.

tongue-tied *adj* muet/-ette.

tongue-twister *n* phrase *f* difficile à dire.

tonic *n* **1** (also **~ water**) eau *f* tonique; **a gin and ~** un gin tonic; **2** (Med) remontant *m*.

tonight I *n* ce soir.
II *adv* (this evening) ce soir; (after bedtime) cette nuit.

tonne ▶573 *n* tonne *f*.

tonsil *n* amygdale *f*; **to have one's ~s out** se faire opérer des amygdales.

tonsillitis ▶533 *n* amygdalite *f*.

too *adv* **1** (also) aussi; **have you been to India ~?** (like me) est-ce que toi aussi tu es allé en Inde?; (as well as other countries) est-ce que tu es allé en Inde aussi?; **2** (excessively) trop; **~ big** trop grand/-e; **~ many/~ few people** trop de/trop peu de gens; **I ate ~ much** j'ai trop mangé; **you're ~ kind!** vous êtes trop aimable!; **I'm not ~ sure about that** je n'en suis pas si sûr.

tool *n* outil *m*.

toolbox *n* boîte *f* à outils.

tool kit *n* trousse *f* à outils.

tooth *n* dent *f*.

toothache *n* mal *m* de dents; **to have ~** (GB) or **a ~** avoir mal aux dents.

toothbrush *n* brosse *f* à dents.

toothpaste *n* dentifrice *m*.

toothpick *n* cure-dents *m inv*.

top I *n* **1** (of page, ladder, stairs, wall) haut *m*; (of list) tête *f*; (of mountain, hill) sommet *m*; (of garden, field) (autre) bout *m*; (of vegetable) fane *f*; (of box, cake) dessus *m*; (surface) surface *f*; **at the ~ of** en haut de [*page, stairs, street, scale*]; au sommet de [*hill*]; en tête de [*list*]; **at the ~ of the building** au dernier étage de l'immeuble; **at the ~ of the table** à la place d'honneur; **to be at the ~ of the agenda** être une priorité; **2** (highest position) **to aim for the ~** viser haut; **to get to** or **make it to the ~** réussir; **to be ~ of the class** être le premier/la première de la classe; **to be ~ of the bill** être la tête d'affiche; **3** (cap, lid) (of pen) capuchon *m*; (of bottle) bouchon *m*; (with serrated edge) capsule *f*; (of paint-tin, saucepan) couvercle *m*; **4** (item of clothing) haut *m*; **5** (toy) toupie *f*.
II *adj* **1** (highest) [*step, storey*] dernier/-ière (*before n*); [*bunk*] de haut; [*button, shelf*] du haut; [*layer, lip*] supérieur/-e; [*speed*] maximum; [*concern, priority*] majeur/-e; **in the ~ left-hand corner** en haut à gauche; **to get ~ marks** (Sch) avoir dix sur dix or vingt sur vingt; **2** (furthest away) [*field, house*] du bout; **3** (leading) [*adviser, politician*] de haut niveau; [*job*] élevé/-e; [*wine, restaurant*] haut/-e de gamme.
III *vtr* **1** être en tête de [*charts, polls*]; **2** (exceed) dépasser [*sum, figure*]; **3** (finish off) compléter (**with** par); (Culin) recouvrir [*cake*].
IV on top of *phr* **1** (on) sur [*cupboard, fridge, layer*]; **2** (in addition to) en plus de [*salary, workload*].
IDIOMS **on ~ of all this, to ~ it all** par-dessus le marché○; **from ~ to bottom** de fond en comble; **to be over the ~, to be OTT**○ [*behaviour, reaction*] être exagéré/-e; **to feel on ~ of the world** être aux anges; **to shout at the ~ of one's voice** crier à tue-tête.
■ **top up** remplir (à nouveau) [*tank, glass*].

topaz *n* topaze *f*.

top hat *n* haut-de-forme *m*.

top-heavy *adj* lourd/-e du haut.

topic *n* (of conversation, conference) sujet *m*; (of essay, research) thème *m*.

topical *adj* d'actualité.

topless *adj* [*model*] aux seins nus.

top-level *adj* [*talks, negotiations*] au plus haut niveau.

top management *n* (haute) direction *f*.

topple I *vtr* renverser.
II *vi* (sway) [*vase, pile of books*] vaciller; (fall) (also **~ over**) [*vase, person*] basculer; [*pile of books*] s'effondrer.

top-ranking *adj* important/-e.

top secret *adj* ultrasecret/-ète.

topsy-turvy○ *adj, adv* sens dessus dessous.

torch *n* **1** (GB) (flashlight) lampe *f* de poche; **2** (burning) flambeau *m*, torche *f*.

torment I *n* supplice *m*.
II *vtr* tourmenter.

tormentor *n* persécuteur/-trice *m/f*.

torn *adj* déchiré/-e.

tornado *n* tornade *f*.

torpedo *n* torpille *f*.

torrent *n* torrent *m*; (figurative) flot *m*.

torrential *adj* torrentiel/-ielle.

torrid *adj* torride.

torso *n* torse *m*.

tortoise *n* tortue *f*.

tortuous *adj* tortueux/-euse.

torture I *n* torture *f*; (figurative) supplice *m*.
II *vtr* torturer; (figurative) tourmenter.

Tory *n* (GB) Tory *mf*, conservateur/-trice *m/f*.

toss I *n* **1** (throw) jet *m*; **a ~ of the head** un mouvement brusque de la tête; **2 to decide sth on the ~ of a coin** décider qch à pile ou face.
II *vtr* **1** (throw) lancer [*ball, stick, dice*]; faire sauter [*pancake*]; tourner [*salad*]; **to ~ a coin** jouer à pile ou face; **2** [*animal*] secouer [*head, mane*]; **to ~ one's head** [*person*] rejeter la tête en arrière; **3** [*horse*] désarçonner [*rider*]; **4** [*wind*] agiter [*branches, leaves*].
III *vi* **1** [*person*] se retourner; **I ~ed and turned all night** je me suis tourné et retourné toute la nuit; **2** (flip a coin) tirer à pile ou face; **to ~ for first turn** tirer le premier tour à pile ou face.

tot *n* **1**○ (toddler) tout/-e petit/-e enfant *m/f*; **2** (GB) (of whisky, rum) petite dose *f*.

total I *n* total *m*; **in ~** au total.
II *adj* **1** [*cost, amount, profit*] total/-e; **2** (complete) [*effect*] global/-e; [*disaster, eclipse*] total/-e; [*ignorance*] complet/-ète.
III *vtr* **1** (add up) additionner [*figures*]; **2** [*bill*] se monter à [*sum*].

totalitarian *n, adj* totalitaire (*mf*).

totally *adv* [*blind, deaf*] complètement; [*unacceptable, convinced*] totalement; [*agree, change, new, different*] entièrement.

totem *n* (pole) totem *m*; (symbol) symbole *m*.

totter *vi* [*person, regime, government*] chanceler; [*drunk person*] tituber; [*baby*] trébucher; [*pile of books, building*] chanceler.

touch I *n* **1** contact *m* (physique); **the ~ of her hand** le contact de sa main; **2** (sense) toucher *m*; **3** (style, skill) (of artist, writer) touche *f*; (of musician) toucher *m*; **to lose one's ~** perdre la main; **that's a clever ~!** ça, c'est génial!; **4** (little) **a ~** un petit peu; **5** (communication) **to get/stay in ~ with** se mettre/rester en contact avec; **he's out of ~ with reality** il est déconnecté de la réalité; **6** (Sport) touche *f*.
II *vtr* **1** toucher; (interfere with) toucher à; **to ~ sb on the shoulder** toucher l'épaule de qn; **I never ~ alcohol** je ne prends jamais d'alcool; **2** (affect) toucher; (adversely) affecter; (as matter of concern) concerner; **we were most ~ed** nous avons été très touchés.
III *vi* se toucher.
IDIOMS **to be a soft ~**○ être un pigeon○; **it's ~ and go whether he'll make it through the night** il risque fort de ne pas passer la nuit.
■ **touch down 1** [*plane*] atterrir; **2** (Sport) (in rugby) marquer un essai.
■ **touch (up)on** effleurer [*topic*].

touchdown *n* **1** (by plane) atterrissage *m*; **2** (Sport) essai *m*.

touched *adj* **1** (emotionally) touché/-e; **2**○ (mad) dérangé/-e○.

touching *adj* touchant/-e.

touch-type *vi* taper au toucher.

touchy *adj* susceptible (**about** sur la question de).

tough I *adj* **1** [*businessman*] coriace; [*criminal*] endurci/-e; [*policy, measure, law*] sévère; [*opposition, competition*] rude; **a ~ guy** un dur○; **2** (difficult) difficile; **3** (robust) [*person, animal*] robuste; [*plant, material*] résistant/-e; **4** [*meat*] coriace; **5** (rough) [*area, school*] dur/-e.
II○ *excl* tant pis pour toi!

toughen *vtr* **1** renforcer [*leather, plastic*]; tremper [*glass, steel*]; durcir [*skin*]; **2** (also **~ up**) endurcir [*person*]; renforcer [*law*].

toupee *n* postiche *m*.

tour I *n* **1** (of country) circuit *m*; (of city) tour *m*; (of building) visite *f*; (trip in bus) excursion *f*; **2** (by team, band, theatre company) tournée *f*.
II *vtr* **1** visiter [*building, country, gallery*]; **2** [*band, team*] être en tournée en [*country*]; [*theatre production*] tourner en [*country*].
III *vi* [*orchestra, play, team*] être en tournée.

touring *n* **1** (by tourist) tourisme *m*; **2** (by team, theatre company, band) tournée *f*.

tourism *n* tourisme *m*.

tourist *n* touriste *mf*.

tourist class *n* (on flight) classe *f* touriste.

tourist (information) office *n* (in town) syndicat *m* d'initiative; (national organization) office *m* du tourisme.

tournament *n* tournoi *m*.

tousle *vtr* ébouriffer [*hair*].

tousled *adj* [*hair*] ébouriffé/-e; [*person, appearance*] débraillé/-e.

tout *n* **1** (GB) (selling tickets) revendeur *m* de billets au marché noir; **2** (soliciting custom) racoleur/-euse○ *m/f* (derogatory); **3** (racing) vendeur *m* de tuyaux.

tow I *n* (Aut) **to be on ~** être en remorque.
II *vtr* remorquer, tracter [*trailer, caravan*].

toward(s) *prep*

■ **Note** When *towards* is used to talk about direction or position, it is generally translated by *vers*: *she ran toward(s) him* = elle a couru vers lui.
– When *toward(s)* is used to mean *in relation to*, it is translated by *envers*: *his attitude toward(s) his parents* = son attitude envers ses parents. For further examples, see the entry below.

1 vers; **~ the east** vers l'est; **he was standing with his back ~ me** il me tournait le dos; **~ evening** vers le soir; **~ the end of** vers la fin de [*month, life*]; **2** envers; **to be friendly/hostile ~ sb** se montrer cordial/hostile envers qn; **3** (as contribution) **the money will go ~ a new car** l'argent servira à payer une nouvelle voiture.

towel *n* serviette *f* (de toilette).

tower I *n* tour *f*.
II *vi* **to ~ above** or **over** dominer.
IDIOMS **to be a ~ of strength** être solide comme un roc.

tower block *n* (GB) tour *f* (d'habitation).

town *n* ville *f*; **to go into ~** aller en ville.
IDIOMS **to go to ~ on** ne pas lésiner sur [*decor, catering*]; exploiter [qch] à fond [*story, scandal*]; **he's the talk of the ~** on ne parle que de lui.

town centre (GB), **town center** (US) *n* centre-ville *m*.

town council *n* (GB) conseil *m* municipal.

town hall *n* mairie *f*.

town house *n* petite maison *f* en centre ville; (mansion) hôtel *m* particulier.

town planning *n* (GB) urbanisme *m*.

township *n* commune *f*; (in South Africa) township *m*.

towpath *n* chemin *m* de halage.

tow truck *n* dépanneuse *f*.

toxic *adj* toxique.

toxin *n* toxine *f*.

toy I *n* jouet *m*.
II *vi* **to ~ with** jouer avec [*object, feelings*]; caresser [*idea*]; **to ~ with one's food** chipoter.

toyshop *n* magasin *m* de jouets.

trace I *n* trace *f*.
II *vtr* **1** (locate) retrouver [*person, weapon, car*]; dépister [*fault*]; déterminer [*cause*]; **the call was ~d to a London number** on a pu établir que le coup de téléphone venait d'un numéro à Londres; **2** (also **~ back**) faire remonter [*origins, ancestry*] (**to** à); **3** (draw) tracer; (copy) décalquer [*map, outline*].

tracing paper *n* papier-calque *m*.

track I *n* **1** (print) (of animal, person, vehicle) traces *fpl*; **2** (course, trajectory) (of person) trace *f*; (of missile, aircraft, storm) trajectoire *f*; **to keep ~ of** [*person*] se tenir au courant de [*developments, events*]; suivre le fil de [*conversation*]; [*police*] suivre les mouvements de [*criminal*]; **to lose ~ of** perdre de vue [*friend*]; perdre la trace de [*document, aircraft, suspect*]; perdre le fil de [*conversation*]; **to lose ~ of (the) time** perdre la notion du temps; **3** (path, road) sentier *m*, chemin *m*; (Sport) piste *f*; **4** (railtrack) voie *f* ferrée; (US) (platform) quai *m*; **to leave the ~(s)** [*train*] dérailler; **5** (on record, tape, CD) morceau *m*; **6** (of tank, tractor) chenille *f*; **7** (US Sch) (stream) groupe *m* de niveau.
II *vtr* suivre la trace de [*person, animal*]; suivre la trajectoire de [*rocket, plane*].
■ **track down** retrouver [*person, object*].

track record *n* **to have a good ~** avoir de bons antécédents.

track shoe *n* chaussure *f* de course à pointes.

tracksuit *n* survêtement *m*.

tract *n* **1** (of land) étendue *f*; **2** (pamphlet) pamphlet *m*.

tractor *n* tracteur *m*.

trade I *n* **1** (activity) commerce *m*; **to do a good ~** faire de bonnes affaires; **2** (sector of industry) industrie *f*; **3** (profession) (manual) métier *m*; (intellectual) profession *f*; **by ~** de métier.
II *vtr* échanger (**for** contre).
III *vi* faire du commerce.
■ **trade in**: **he ~d in his old car for a new one** on lui a repris sa vieille voiture et il en a acheté une nouvelle.

trade fair *n* salon *m*.

trademark *n* marque *f* déposée.

trader *n* **1** (shopkeeper, stallholder) commerçant/-e *m/f*; **2** (at stock exchange) opérateur/-trice *m/f* (en Bourse).

tradesman's entrance *n* entrée *f* de service.

Trades Union Congress, TUC *n* (GB) Confédération *f* des syndicats (britanniques).

trade union *n* syndicat *m*.

trade union member *n* syndiqué/-e *m/f*.

trading *n* **1** (business) commerce *m*; **2** (at stock exchange) transactions *fpl* (boursières).

tradition *n* tradition *f*.

traditional *adj* traditionnel/-elle.

traffic I *n* **1** (on road) circulation *f*; (air, sea, rail) trafic *m*; **2** (in drugs, arms, slaves, goods) trafic *m* (**in** de).
II *vi* **to ~ in** faire du trafic de [*drugs, arms, stolen goods*].

traffic jam *n* embouteillage *m*.

trafficker *n* trafiquant/-e *m/f* (**in** de).

traffic lights *n pl* feux *mpl* (de signalisation).

traffic warden ▶ 626 *n* (GB) contractuel/-elle *m/f*.

tragedy *n* tragédie *f*.

tragic *adj* tragique.

trail I *n* **1** (path) chemin *m*, piste *f*; **2** (of blood, dust, slime) traînée *f*, trace *f*; **3** (trace) trace *f*, piste *f*.
II *vtr* **1** (follow) [*animal, person*] suivre la piste de; [*car*] suivre; **2** (drag) traîner.
III *vi* **1** [*skirt, scarf*] traîner; [*plant*] pendre; **2** (shuffle) **to ~ in/out** entrer/sortir en traînant les pieds; **3** (lag) traîner; **our team were ~ing by 3 goals to 1** notre équipe avait un retard de 2 buts.

trailer *n* **1** (vehicle, boat) remorque *f*; **2** (US) (caravan) caravane *f*; **3** (for film) bande-annonce *f*.

trailer park *n* (US) terrain *m* de caravaning.

train I *n* **1** (means of transport) train *m*; (underground) rame *f*; **a ~ to Paris** un train pour Paris; **to go to Paris by ~** aller à Paris en train; **2** (succession) (of events) série *f*; **my ~ of thought** le fil de mes pensées; **3** (procession) (of animals, vehicles, people) file *f*; (of mourners) cortège *m*; **4** (of dress) traîne *f*.
II *vtr* **1** former [*staff, worker, musician*]; entraîner [*athlete, player*]; dresser [*circus animal, dog*]; **2** (aim) braquer [*gun, binoculars*] (**on** sur).
III *vi* **1** (for profession) être formé/-e, étudier; **he's ~ing to be/he ~ed as a doctor** il suit/il a reçu une formation de docteur; **2** (Sport) s'entraîner.

trained *adj* [*staff*] qualifié/-e; [*professional*] diplômé/-e; [*voice, eye, ear*] exercé/-e; [*singer, actor*] professionnel/-elle; [*animal*] dressé/-e.

trainee *n* stagiaire *mf*.

trainer *n* **1** (of athlete, horse) entraîneur/-euse *m/f*; (of circus animal, dogs) dresseur/-euse *m/f*; **2** (GB) (shoe) (high) basket *f*; (low) tennis *m*.

training *n* **1** (gen) formation *f*; (less specialized) apprentissage *m*; **2** (Mil, Sport) entraînement *m*.

training college *n* (GB) école *f* professionnelle; (for teachers) centre *m* de formation pédagogique.

trait *n* trait *m*.

traitor *n* traître/traîtresse *m/f* (**to** à).

tram *n* (GB) tramway *m*.

tramp *n* (rural) vagabond *m*; (urban) clochard/-e *m/f*.

trample *vtr* piétiner.

trampoline *n* trampoline *m*.

trance *n* transe *f*; (figurative) état *m* second; **to go into a ~** entrer en transe.

tranquil *adj* tranquille.

tranquillizer, tranquilizer (US) *n* tranquillisant *m*.

transaction *n* transaction *f*.

transatlantic *adj* [*crossing, flight*] transatlantique; [*accent*] d'outre-atlantique *inv*.

transcript *n* **1** (copy) transcription *f*; **2** (US Sch) duplicata *m* de livret scolaire.

transfer I *n* **1** (gen) transfert *m*; (of property, debt) cession *f*; (of funds) virement *m*; (of employee) mutation *f*; **2** (GB) (on skin, china, paper) décalcomanie *f*; (on T-shirt) transfert *m*.
II *vtr* **1** transférer [*data, baggage*]; virer [*money*]; céder [*property, power*]; reporter [*allegiance, support*]; **I'm ~ring you to reception**

je vous passe la réception; **2** (relocate) transférer [*office, prisoner, player*]; muter [*employee*].
III *vi* **1** [*player, passenger*] être transféré/-e; [*employee*] être muté/-e; **2** [*traveller*] changer d'avion.

transferred charge call *n* appel *m* en PCV.

transform *vtr* transformer.

transformation *n* transformation *f*.

transformer *n* transformateur *m*.

transfusion *n* transfusion *f*.

transient *adj* [*phase*] transitoire; [*emotion, beauty*] éphémère; [*population*] de passage.

transistor *n* transistor *m*.

transit *n* transit *m*; **in ~** en transit.

transition *n* transition *f*.

transitive *adj* transitif/-ive.

translate I *vtr* traduire.
II *vi* **1** [*person*] traduire; **2** [*word, phrase, text*] se traduire.

translation *n* (profession) traduction *f*; (school exercise) version *f*.

translator *n* traducteur/-trice *m/f*.

transmission *n* transmission *f*.

transmit I *vtr* transmettre.
II *vi* émettre.

transmitter *n* (in radio, TV) émetteur *m*; (in telecommunications) capsule *f* microphonique.

transparency *n* (slide) diapositive *f*; (for overhead projector) transparent *m*.

transparent *adj* transparent/-e.

transplant I *n* (operation) transplantation *f*; (organ, tissue transplanted) transplant *m*.
II *vtr* transplanter.

transport I *n* (also **transportation** US) transport *m*; **air/road ~** transport aérien/par route; **to travel by public ~** utiliser les transports en commun.
II *vtr* transporter.

transportation *n* transport *m*.

transsexual *n, adj* transsexuel/-elle (*m/f*).

transvestite *n* travesti/-e *m/f*.

trap I *n* **1** (snare) piège *m*; **2** (vehicle) cabriolet *m*.
II *vtr* **1** (snare) prendre [qn/qch] au piège; **2** (catch) coincer [*person, finger*]; retenir [*heat*].

trapdoor *n* trappe *f*.

trash *n* **1** (US) (refuse) (in streets) déchets *mpl*; (from household) ordures *fpl*; **2** (low-grade goods) camelote○ *f*; **3** (nonsense) âneries *fpl*; **the film is (absolute) ~** le film est (complètement) nul○.

trashcan *n* (US) poubelle *f*.

trauma *n* traumatisme *m*.

traumatic *adj* (psychologically) traumatisant/-e; (Med) traumatique.

traumatize *vtr* traumatiser.

travel I *n* voyages *mpl*; **foreign ~** voyages à l'étranger.
II *vtr* parcourir [*country, road, distance*].
III *vi* **1** (journey) voyager; **he ~s widely** il voyage beaucoup; **to ~ abroad/to Brazil** aller à l'étranger/au Brésil; **2** (move) [*person, object, plane, boat*] aller; [*car, train*] aller, rouler; [*light, sound*] se propager; **to ~ back in time** remonter le temps; **3 to ~ well** [*cheese, wine*] supporter le transport.

travel agency *n* agence *f* de voyages.

travel agent ▶ 626 *n* agent *m* de voyages.

travel insurance *n* assurance *f* voyage.

traveller (GB), **traveler** (US) *n* **1** (voyager) voyageur/-euse *m/f*; **2** (GB) (gypsy) nomade *mf*.

traveller's cheque (GB), **traveler's check** (US) *n* chèque-voyage *m*.

travelling (GB), **traveling** (US) **I** *n* (touring) voyages *mpl*; (on single occasion) voyage *m*; **to go ~** partir en voyage; **the job involves ~** le poste exige des déplacements.
II *adj* **1** [*actor, company, circus*] itinérant/-e; **2** [*companion, rug*] de voyage; [*conditions*] (on road) de route; **3** [*allowance, expenses*] de déplacement.

travel-sick *adj* **to be** or **get ~** souffrir du mal des transports.

trawler *n* chalutier *m*.

tray *n* plateau *m*.

treacherous *adj* traître/traîtresse.

treachery *n* traîtrise *f*.

treacle *n* (GB) (black) mélasse *f*; (golden syrup) mélasse *f* raffinée.

tread I *n* (of tyre) (pattern) sculptures *fpl*; (outer surface) chape *f*.
II *vtr* fouler [*street, path, area*]; **to ~ water** nager sur place.
III *vi* marcher; **to ~ on** (walk) marcher sur; (squash) piétiner; **to ~ carefully** être prudent/-e.

treason *n* trahison *f*; **high ~** haute trahison.

treasure I *n* trésor *m*.
II *vtr* **1** (cherish) chérir [*person, gift*]; **2** (prize) tenir beaucoup à [*friendship*].

treasurer *n* **1** (on committee) trésorier/-ière *m/f*; **2** (US) (in company) directeur *m* financier.

Treasury *n* (also **~ Department**) ministère *m* des finances.

treat I *n* (pleasure) (petit) plaisir *m*; (food) gâterie *f*; **I took them to the museum as a ~** je les ai emmenés au musée pour leur faire plaisir; **it's my ~**○ c'est moi qui paie.
II *vtr* **1** (gen, Med) traiter; **to ~ sb well/badly** bien traiter/maltraiter qn; **to ~ sb/sth with care** prendre soin de qn/qch; **they ~ the house like a hotel** ils prennent la maison pour un hôtel; **2** (pay for) **to ~ sb to sth** payer or offrir qch à qn; **to ~ oneself to** s'offrir [*holiday, hairdo*].

treatment *n* traitement *m*.

treaty *n* traité *m*.

treble I *adj* triple.
II *vtr, vi* tripler.

tree *n* arbre *m*; **an apple/a cherry ~** un pommier/un cerisier.

tree stump *n* souche *f*.

treetop *n* cime *f* (d'un arbre).

tree trunk *n* tronc *m* d'arbre.

trek I *n* (long journey) randonnée *f*; (laborious) randonnée *f* pénible.

II *vi* **to ~ across** traverser péniblement [*desert*]; **to go ~king** faire de la randonnée pédestre.

tremble *vi* trembler.

tremendous *adj* [*effort, improvement, amount*] énorme; [*pleasure*] immense; [*storm, explosion*] violent/-e; [*success*] fou/folle○.

tremor *n* **1** (in voice) tremblement *m*; **2** (in earthquake) secousse *f*.

trench *n* tranchée *f*.

trench coat *n* imperméable *m*, trench-coat *m*.

trend *n* **1** (tendency) tendance *f*; **2** (fashion) mode *f*; **to set a new ~** lancer une nouvelle mode.

trendy○ *adj* branché/-e○.

trespass *vi* s'introduire illégalement; **'no ~ing'** 'défense d'entrer'.

trespasser *n* intrus/-e *m/f*.

trial I *n* **1** (Law) procès *m*; **to go on ~**, **to stand ~** passer en jugement; **2** (test) (of machine, vehicle) essai *m*; (of drug, new product) test *m*; **on ~** à l'essai; **by ~ and error** [*learn*] par l'expérience; [*proceed*] par tâtonnements; **3** (Sport) épreuve *f*; **4** (trouble) épreuve *f*; (less strong) difficulté *f*.
II *adj* [*period, separation*] d'essai; **on a ~ basis** à titre expérimental.

trial run *n* essai *m*; **to take a car for a ~** essayer une voiture.

triangle *n* triangle *m*.

tribe *n* tribu *f*.

tributary *n* affluent *m*.

tribute *n* hommage *m*; **to pay ~ to** rendre hommage à; **floral ~** (spray) gerbe *f*; (wreath) couronne *f*.

trick I *n* **1** (to deceive) tour *m*, combine *f*; **to play a ~ on sb** jouer un tour à qn; **a ~ of the light** un effet de lumière; **2** (by magician, conjurer, dog) tour *m*; **to do a ~** faire un tour; **3** (knack, secret) astuce *f*; **4** (in cards) pli *m*; **to take** or **win a ~** faire un pli.
II *adj* [*photo, shot*] truqué/-e.
III *vtr* duper, rouler○; **to ~ sb into doing sth** amener qn à faire qch par la ruse.
IDIOMS **the ~s of the trade** les ficelles du métier; **that'll do the ~** ça fera l'affaire.

trickle I *n* (of liquid) filet *m*; (of powder, sand) écoulement *m*; (of investment, orders) petite quantité *f*; (of people) petit nombre *m*.
II *vi* **to ~ down** dégouliner le long de [*pane, wall*]; **to ~ into** [*liquid*] s'écouler dans [*container*]; [*people*] s'infiltrer dans [*country, organization*].

trick question *n* question *f* piège.

tricky *adj* **1** [*decision, task*] difficile; [*problem*] épineux/-euse; [*situation*] délicat/-e; **2** (wily) malin/-igne.

tricycle *n* (cycle) tricycle *m*.

trifle I *n* **1** (GB Culin) ≈ diplomate *m*; **2** (triviality) bagatelle *f*.
II *vi* **to ~ with** jouer avec [*feelings, affections*]; **to ~ with sb** traiter qn à la légère.

trifling *adj* [*sum, cost, detail*] insignifiant/-e.

trigger *n* **1** (on gun) gâchette *f*; **2** (on machine) manette *f*.
■ **trigger off** déclencher.

trilogy *n* trilogie *f*.

trim I *n* **1** (of hair) coupe *f* d'entretien; **2** (good condition) **to keep oneself in ~** se maintenir en bonne forme physique.
II *adj* [*garden*] soigné/-e; [*boat, house*] bien tenu/-e; [*figure*] svelte; [*waist*] fin/-e.
III *vtr* **1** (cut) couper [*hair, grass, material*]; tailler [*beard, hedge*]; **2** (reduce) réduire (**by** de); **3** (Culin) dégraisser [*meat*]; **4** (decorate) décorer [*tree, furniture*]; border [*dress, handkerchief*].

trimming *n* (on clothing) garniture *f*; **~s** (Culin) (with dish) accompagnements *mpl* traditionnels.

trinket *n* babiole *f*.

trio *n* trio *m* (**of** de).

trip I *n* (abroad) voyage *m*; (excursion) excursion *f*; **business ~** voyage d'affaires.
II *vtr* (also **~ over, ~ up**) faire trébucher; (with foot) faire un croche-pied à.
III *vi* **1** (also **~ over, ~ up**) (stumble) trébucher, faire un faux pas; **to ~ on** or **over** trébucher sur [*step, rock*]; se prendre les pieds dans [*scarf, rope*]; **2** (walk lightly) **to ~ along** [*child*] gambader; [*adult*] marcher d'un pas léger.

triple *adj* triple.

triplet *n* (child) triplé/-e *m/f*.

triplicate: **in ~** *phr* en trois exemplaires.

tripod *n* trépied *m*.

triumph I *n* triomphe *m*.
II *vi* triompher (**over** de).

triumphant *adj* [*person, team*] triomphant/-e; [*return, success*] triomphal/-e.

trivia *n pl* futilités *fpl*.

trivial *adj* [*matter, scale, film*] insignifiant/-e; [*error, offence*] léger/-ère (*before n*); [*conversation, argument, person*] futile.

trolley *n* **1** (GB) (for food, drinks, luggage, shopping) chariot *m*; **2** (US) tramway *m*.

trolley bus *n* trolleybus *m*.

trolley car *n* tramway *m*, tram *m*.

troop *n* troupe *f*.

trooper *n* **1** (Mil) homme *m* de troupe; **2** (US) (policeman) policier *m*.

trophy *n* trophée *m*.

tropic *n* tropique *m*; **in the ~s** sous les tropiques.

tropical *adj* tropical/-e.

trot I *n* trot *m*; **at a ~** au trot.
II *vi* [*animal, rider*] trotter; [*person*] courir, trotter○; [*child*] trottiner.
IDIOMS **on the ~**○ (one after the other) coup sur coup; (continuously) d'affilée.

trouble I *n* **1** (problems) problèmes *mpl*; (personal) ennuis *mpl*; (difficulties) difficultés *fpl*; **to be in** or **get into ~** [*person*] avoir des ennuis; [*company*] avoir des difficultés; **to get sb into ~** créer des ennuis à qn; **back ~** mal *m* de dos; **what's the ~?** qu'est-ce qui ne va pas?; **to have ~ doing** avoir du mal à faire; **to get sb out of ~** tirer qn d'affaire; **2** (effort, inconvenience) peine *f*; **it's not worth the ~** cela n'en vaut pas la peine; **to take the ~ to do, to go to the ~ of doing** se donner la peine de

faire; **to save sb the ~ of doing** épargner à qn la peine de faire; **to go to a lot of ~** se donner beaucoup de mal.
II **troubles** *n pl* soucis *mpl*; **money ~s** problèmes *mpl* d'argent.
III *vtr* **1** (disturb, inconvenience) déranger [*person*]; **may** or **could I ~ you to do?** puis-je vous demander de faire?; **2** (bother) **to be ~d by** être incommodé/-e par [*cough, pain*]; **3** (worry) tracasser [*person*]; **don't let that ~ you** ne te tracasse pas pour cela.

troubled *adj* [*person, expression*] soucieux/-ieuse; [*mind*] inquiet/-iète; [*sleep, times, area*] agité/-e.

troublemaker *n* fauteur/-trice *m/f* de troubles.

troublesome *adj* [*person*] ennuyeux/-euse; [*problem*] gênant/-e; [*cough, pain*] désagréable.

trough *n* **1** (for drinking) abreuvoir *m*; (for animal feed) auge *f*; **2** (between waves, hills, on graph) creux *m*; **3** (in weather) zone *f* dépressionnaire.

trousers *n pl* pantalon *m*; **short ~** culotte *f* courte.

trout *n* truite *f*.

trowel *n* **1** (for cement) truelle *f*; **2** (for gardening) déplantoir *m*.

truant *n* **to play ~** faire l'école buissonnière.

truce *n* trêve *f*.

truck *n* **1** (lorry) camion *m*; **2** (rail wagon) wagon *m* de marchandises.

truck driver, **trucker**○ ▶626| *n* routier *m*.

trudge *vi* marcher d'un pas lourd; **to ~ through the snow** marcher péniblement dans la neige.

true I *adj* **1** (based on fact, not a lie) [*news, fact, story*] vrai/-e; (from real life) [*story*] vécu/-e; **2** (real, genuine) vrai/-e (*before n*); [*identity, age*] véritable (*before n*); **to come ~** se réaliser; **3** (heartfelt, sincere) [*feeling, understanding*] sincère; **~ love** le véritable amour; **4** (accurate) [*copy*] conforme; [*assessment*] correct, juste; **5** (faithful, loyal) fidèle; (**to** à); **6** (Mus) [*note, instrument*] juste.
II *adv* [*aim, fire*] juste.

truffle *n* truffe *f*.

truly *adv* **1** (gen) vraiment; **well and ~** bel et bien; **2** (in letter) **yours ~** je vous prie d'agréer l'expression de mes sentiments distingués (formal).

trump *n* atout *m*.

trumpet ▶586| *n* **1** (instrument, player) trompette *f*; **2** (elephant call) barrissement *m*.
IDIOMS **to blow one's own ~** vanter ses propres mérites.

trumpeter ▶586|, 626| *n* trompettiste *mf*.

truncheon *n* matraque *f*.

trunk I *n* **1** (of tree, body) tronc *m*; **2** (of elephant) trompe *f*; **3** (for travel) malle *f*; **4** (US) (car boot) coffre *m*.

trunks *n pl* slip *msg* de bain.

truss *n* (Med) bandage *m* herniaire.
■ **truss up** brider, trousser [*chicken*]; ligoter [*person*].

trust I *n* **1** (faith) confiance *f*; **to put one's ~ in** se fier à; **2** (Law) (arrangement) fidéicommis *m*; (property involved) propriété *f* fiduciaire.
II *vtr* **1** (believe) se fier à [*person, judgment*]; **2** (rely on) faire confiance à; **3** (entrust) **to ~ sb with sth** confier qch à qn.
III *vi* **to ~ in** faire confiance à [*person*]; croire en [*God, fortune*]; **to ~ to luck** se fier au hasard.

trust company *n* société *f* fiduciaire.

trustee *n* **1** (who administers property in trust) fiduciaire *m*; **2** (of company) administrateur/-trice *m/f* (**of** de).

trust fund *n* fonds *m* en fidéicommis.

trusting *adj* [*person*] qui fait facilement confiance aux gens.

trustworthy *adj* [*staff, firm*] sérieux/-ieuse; [*friend, lover*] digne de confiance.

truth *n* (real facts) **the ~** la vérité; **there is some ~ in it** il y a du vrai dans cela.

truthful *adj* [*person*] honnête; [*account, version*] vrai/-e.

try I *n* **1** (attempt) essai *m*; **to have a ~** essayer (**at doing** de faire); **2** (Sport) essai *m*.
II *vtr* **1** (attempt) essayer de répondre à [*exam question*]; **to ~ doing** or **to do** essayer de faire; **to ~ hard to do** faire de gros efforts pour faire; **to ~ one's best to do** faire tout son possible pour faire; **2** (test out) essayer [*tool, product, method, activity*]; prendre [qn] à l'essai [*person*]; [*thief*] essayer d'ouvrir [*door, window*]; tourner [*door knob*]; **to ~ one's hand at sth** s'essayer à qch; **3** (taste) goûter [*food*]; **4** (consult) demander à [*person*]; consulter [*book*]; **~ the library** demandez à la bibliothèque; **5** (subject to stress) **to ~ sb's patience** pousser qn à bout; **6** (Law) juger [*case, criminal*].
III *vi* essayer; **to ~ again** (to perform task) recommencer; (to see somebody) repasser; (to phone) rappeler; **to ~ for** essayer d'obtenir [*loan, university place*]; essayer de battre [*world record*]; essayer d'avoir [*baby*]; **keep ~ing!** essaie encore!
■ **try on** essayer [*hat, dress*].

trying *adj* [*person*] pénible; [*experience*] éprouvant/-e.

T-shirt *n* T-shirt *m*.

tub *n* **1** (for flowers, water) bac *m*; (of ice cream, pâté) pot *m*; **2** (US) (bath) baignoire *f*.

tubby○ *adj* grassouillet/-ette○.

tube *n* **1** (cylinder, container) tube *m*; **2**○ (GB) **the ~** le métro (londonien); **3**○ (US) (TV) télé○ *f*; **4** (in TV set) tube *m* cathodique; **5** (in tyre) chambre *f* à air.

tuberculosis ▶533| *n* tuberculose *f*.

tuck I *n* (in sewing) pli *m*.
II *vtr* (put) glisser; **to ~ one's shirt into one's trousers** rentrer sa chemise dans son pantalon; mettre.
■ **tuck away** (put away) ranger; (hide) cacher; **the house was ~ed away in the wood** la maison se cachait or était cachée dans le bois.
■ **tuck in** rentrer [*garment, shirt*]; border [*bedclothes, person*].

Tuesday ▶456| *pr n* mardi *m*.

tuft *n* touffe *f*.

tug I *n* **1** (pull) secousse *f*; **to give sth a ~** tirer sur qch; **2** (also **tug boat**) remorqueur *m*.
II *vtr* (pull) tirer.
III *vi* **to ~ at** or **on** tirer sur [*rope, hair*].

tug-of-war *n* (Sport) gagne-terrain *m*.

tuition *n* cours *mpl*.

tulip *n* tulipe *f*.

tumble I *n* **1** (fall) chute *f*; **to take a ~** [*person*] faire une chute; **2** (of clown, acrobat) culbute *f*.
II *vi* **1** (fall) [*person, object*] tomber (**off, out of** de); **2** [*price, share, currency*] chuter; **3** (Sport) [*clown, acrobat, child*] faire des culbutes.

tumbler *n* verre *m* droit.

tumour (GB), **tumor** (US) *n* tumeur *f*.

tumult *n* **1** (noise) tumulte *m*; **2** (disorder) agitation *f*.

tuna *n* (also **~ fish**) thon *m*.

tune I *n* air *m*; **to be in/out of ~** [*instrument*] être/ne pas être en accord; **to sing in/out of ~** chanter juste/faux.
II *vtr* accorder [*musical instrument*]; régler [*engine, radio, TV*].
■ **tune in**: ¶ **~ in** mettre la radio; **to ~ in to** se mettre à l'écoute de [*programme*]; régler sur [*channel*]; ¶ **~ [sth] in** régler (**to** sur).

tunic *n* (for gym) tunique *f*; (for nurse, schoolgirl) blouse *f*; (for soldier) vareuse *f*.

tuning fork *n* diapason *m*.

tunnel I *n* tunnel *m*.
II *vtr, vi* creuser.

turbine *n* turbine *f*.

turbo *n* (engine) turbo *m*; (car) turbo *f*.

turbocharged *adj* turbo *inv*.

turbot *n* turbot *m*.

turbulent *adj* **1** [*water*] agité/-e; **2** [*times, situation*] agité/-e; [*career, history*] mouvementé/-e; [*passions, character, faction*] turbulent/-e.

tureen *n* soupière *f*.

turf I *n* (grass) gazon *m*; (peat) tourbe *f*.
II *vtr* gazonner [*lawn, patch, pitch*].

Turk ▶ 553 *n* Turc/Turque *m/f*.

turkey *n* **1** (bird) dinde *f*; **2**○ (US) (flop) bide○ *m*; (bad film) navet○ *m*.

Turkey ▶ 448 *pr n* Turquie *f*.

Turkish ▶ 553 **I** *n* (language) turc *m*.
II *adj* turc/turque.

turmoil *n* désarroi *m*.

turn I *n* **1** (in games, sequence) tour *m*; **whose ~ is it?** c'est à qui le tour?; **to be sb's ~ to do** être le tour de qn de faire; **to take ~s at sleeping**, **to take it in ~s to sleep** dormir à tour de rôle; **by ~s** tour à tour; **to speak out of ~** commettre un impair; **2** (circular movement) tour *m*; **to give sth a ~** tourner qch; **to do a ~** [*dancer*] faire un tour; **3** (in vehicle) virage *m*; **to make** or **do a left/right ~** tourner à gauche/à droite; **4** (bend, side road) tournant *m*, virage *m*; **take the next right ~**, **take the next ~ on the right** prenez la prochaine (rue) à droite; **5** (change, development) tournure *f*; **to take a ~ for the better** [*things, events, situation*] prendre une meilleure tournure; **to take a ~ for the worse** [*situation*] se dégrader; [*health*] s'aggraver; **6**○ (GB) (attack) crise *f*; **a dizzy ~** un vertige; **it gave me quite a ~**, **it gave me a nasty ~** ça m'a fait un coup○; **7** (act) numéro *m*.
II *vtr* **1** (rotate) [*person*] tourner [*wheel, handle*]; serrer [*screw*]; [*mechanism*] faire tourner [*cog, wheel*]; **2** (turn over, reverse) retourner [*mattress, soil, steak, collar*]; tourner [*page*]; **it ~s my stomach** ça me soulève le cœur; **3** (change direction of) tourner [*chair, head, face, car*]; **4** (focus direction of) **to ~ [sth] on sb** braquer [qch] sur qn [*gun, hose, torch*]; **5** (transform) **to ~ sth white/black** blanchir/noircir qch; **to ~ sth opaque** rendre qch opaque; **to ~ sth into** transformer qch en [*office, car park, desert*]; **to ~ a book into a film** adapter un livre pour le cinéma; **to ~ sb into** [*magician*] changer qn en [*frog*]; [*experience*] faire de qn [*extrovert, maniac*]; **6** (deflect) détourner [*person, conversation*] (**towards** vers; **from** de); **7**○ (pass the age of) **he has ~ed 50** il a 50 ans passés; **she has just ~ed 30** elle vient d'avoir 30 ans; **8** (on lathe) tourner [*wood, piece*].
III *vi* **1** (change direction) [*person, car, plane, road*] tourner; [*ship*] virer; **to ~ down** or **into** tourner dans [*street, alley*]; **to ~ towards** tourner en direction de [*village, mountains*]; **2** (reverse direction) [*person, vehicle*] faire demi-tour; [*tide*] changer; [*luck*] tourner; **3** (revolve) [*key, wheel, planet*] tourner; [*person*] se tourner; **4** (hinge) **to ~ on** [*argument*] tourner autour de [*point, issue*]; [*outcome*] dépendre de [*factor*]; **5** (spin round angrily) **to ~ on sb** [*dog*] attaquer qn; [*person*] se retourner contre qn; **6** (resort to) **to ~ to** se tourner vers [*person, religion*]; **to ~ to drink/drugs** se mettre à boire/se droguer; **I don't know where to ~** je ne sais plus où donner de la tête○; **7** (change) **to ~ into** [*person, tadpole*] se transformer en [*frog*]; [*sofa*] se transformer en [*bed*]; [*situation, evening*] tourner à [*farce, disaster*]; **to ~ to** [*substance*] se changer en [*ice, gold*]; [*fear, surprise*] faire place à [*horror, relief*]; **8** (become by transformation) devenir [*pale, cloudy, green*]; **to ~ white/black/red** blanchir/noircir/rougir; **the weather is ~ing cold/warm** le temps se rafraîchit/se réchauffe; **9**○ (become) devenir [*Conservative, Communist*]; **businessman ~ed politician** ex-homme d'affaires devenu homme politique; **10** (go sour) [*milk*] tourner; **11** [*trees, leaves*] jaunir.
IV in turn *phr* [*answer, speak*] à tour de rôle; **she spoke to each of us in ~** elle nous a parlé chacun à notre tour.
IDIOMS **to do sb a good ~** rendre un service à qn.
■ **turn against**: ¶ **~ against [sb/sth]** se retourner contre; ¶ **~ [sb] against** retourner [qn] contre.
■ **turn around**: ¶ **~ around 1** (to face other way) [*person*] se retourner; [*bus, vehicle*] faire demi-tour; **2** (revolve, rotate) [*object, windmill, dancer*] tourner; ¶ **~ [sth] around** tourner [qch] dans l'autre sens [*object*].
■ **turn aside** se détourner (**from** de).

■ **turn away**: ¶ **~ away** se détourner; ¶ **~ [sb] away** refuser [*spectator, applicant*]; ne pas laisser entrer [*salesman, caller*].
■ **turn back**: ¶ **~ back 1** (on foot) rebrousser chemin; (in vehicle) faire demi-tour; **there's no ~ing back** il n'est pas question de revenir en arrière; **2** (in book) revenir; ¶ **~ [sth] back** reculer [*dial, clock*]; ¶ **~ [sb] back** refouler [*people, vehicles*].
■ **turn down 1** (reduce) baisser [*volume, radio, gas*]; **2** (fold over) rabattre [*sheet, collar*]; retourner [*corner of page*]; **3** (refuse) refuser [*person, request*]; rejeter [*offer, suggestion*].
■ **turn off**: ¶ **~ off 1** [*driver, walker*] tourner; **2** [*motor, fan*] s'arrêter; ¶ **~ [sth] off 1** éteindre [*light, oven, TV, radio*]; fermer [*tap*]; couper [*water, gas, engine*]; **2** (leave) quitter [*road*]; ¶ **~ [sb] off**○ rebuter.
■ **turn on 1** allumer [*light, oven, TV, radio, gas*]; ouvrir [*tap*]; **2**○ exciter [*person*].
■ **turn out**: ¶ **~ out 1** (be eventually) **to ~ out well/badly** bien/mal se terminer; **it depends how things ~ out** cela dépend de la façon dont les choses vont tourner; **to ~ out to be wrong/easy** se révéler faux/facile; **it ~s out that they know each other already** il se trouve qu'ils se connaissent déjà; **2** (come out) [*crowd, people*] venir; ¶ **~ [sth] out 1** (turn off) éteindre [*light*]; **2** (empty) vider [*pocket, bag*]; (Culin) démouler [*mousse*]; **3** (produce) fabriquer [*goods*]; former [*scientists, graduates*]; ¶ **~ [sb] out** (evict) mettre [qn] à la porte.
■ **turn over**: ¶ **~ over 1** (roll over) [*person, vehicle*] se retourner; **2** (turn page) tourner la page; **3** [*engine*] se mettre en marche; ¶ **~ [sb/sth] over 1** (turn) tourner [*page, paper*]; retourner [*card, object, mattress, soil, patient*]; **2** (hand over) remettre [*object, money, find, papers*]; livrer [*person*] (**to** à); remettre la succession de [*company*].
■ **turn round** (GB) = **turn around**.
■ **turn up**: ¶ **~ up 1** (arrive, show up) arriver, se pointer○; **don't worry—it will ~ up** ne t'inquiète pas—tu finiras par le retrouver; **2** (present itself) [*opportunity, job*] se présenter; **3** (point up) [*corner, edge*] être relevé/-e; ¶ **~ [sth] up 1** (increase, intensify) augmenter [*heating, volume, gas*]; mettre [qch] plus fort [*TV, radio, music*]; **2** (point up) relever [*collar*].

turning *n* (GB) (in road) virage *m*.
turning point *n* tournant *m* (**in, of** de).
turnip *n* navet *m*.
turnout *n* (to vote, strike, demonstrate) taux *m* de participation; **there was a magnificent ~ for the parade** beaucoup de gens sont venus voir le défilé.
turnover *n* **1** (of company) chiffre *m* d'affaires; **2** (of stock) rotation *f*; (of staff) taux *m* de renouvellement.
turnpike *n* (tollgate) barrière *f* de péage; (US) (toll expressway) autoroute *f* à péage.
turnstile *n* (gate) tourniquet *m*; (to count number of visitors) compteur *m* pour entrées.
turntable *n* (on record player) platine *f*.
turnup *n* (GB) (of trousers) revers *m*.
turpentine, **turps**○ *n* térébenthine *f*.
turret *n* tourelle *f*.
turtle *n* (GB) tortue *f* marine; (US) tortue *f*.
turtle dove *n* tourterelle *f*.
turtleneck (sweater) *n* pull-over *m* à col cheminée.
tusk *n* défense *f*.
tussle *n* empoignade *f* (**for** pour).
tutor ▶626 *n* **1** (private teacher) professeur *m* particulier; **2** (GB Univ) chargé/-e *m/f* de travaux dirigés; **3** (US Univ) assistant/-e *m/f*.
tutorial *n* (Univ) (group) classe *f* de travaux dirigés; (private) cours *m* privé.
tuxedo *n* (US) smoking *m*.
TV○ *n* (*abbr* = **television**) télé○ *f*.
twang *n* (of string, wire) vibration *f*; (of tone) ton *m* nasillard.
tweak *vtr* tordre [*ear, nose*]; tirer [*hair, moustache*].
tweezers *n pl* pincettes *fpl*; (for eyebrows) pince *f* à épiler.
twelfth ▶456, 498 **I** *n* **1** (in order) douzième *mf*; **2** (of month) douze *m inv*; **3** (fraction) douzième *m*.
II *adj, adv* douzième.
twelve ▶389, 434 *n, pron, det* douze (*m*) *inv*.
twenties ▶389, 456 *n pl* **1** (era) **the ~** les années *fpl* vingt; **2** (age) **to be in one's ~** avoir entre vingt et trente ans.
twentieth ▶456 **I** *n* **1** (in order) vingtième *mf*; **2** (of month) vingt *m*; **3** (fraction) vingtième *m*.
II *adj, adv* vingtième.
twenty ▶389, 434 *n, pron, det* vingt (*m*) *inv*.
twice *adv* deux fois; **~ a day** or **daily** deux fois par jour; **she's ~ his age** elle a le double de son âge; **~ as much**, **~ as many** deux fois plus.
twiddle *vtr* tripoter; **to ~ one's thumbs** se tourner les pouces.
twig *n* brindille *f*.
twilight *n* crépuscule *m*.
twilight zone *n* zone *f* d'ombre.
twin I *n* jumeau/-elle *m/f*.
II *adj* **1** [*brother, sister*] jumeau/-elle; **2** [*masts, propellers*] jumeaux/-elles (*after n*); [*speakers*] jumelés.
III *vtr* jumeler [*town*] (**with** avec).
twine *n* ficelle *f*.
twinge *n* (of pain) élancement *m*; (of conscience, doubt) accès *m*; (of jealousy) pointe *f*.
twinkle *vi* [*light, star, jewel*] scintiller; [*eyes*] pétiller.
twin town *n* ville *f* jumelle.
twirl I *n* tournoiement *m*.
II *vtr* faire tournoyer [*baton, partner*]; entortiller [*ribbon, vine*].
III *vi* [*dancer*] tournoyer; **to ~ round** (turn round) se retourner brusquement.
twist I *n* **1** (in rope, cord, wool) tortillon *m*; (in road) zigzag *m*; (in river) coude *m*; **2** (in play, story) coup *m* de théâtre; (in events) rebondissement *m*; **3** (small amount) (of yarn, thread, hair) torsade *f*; **a ~ of lemon** une tranche de citron.
II *vtr* **1** (turn) tourner [*knob, handle*]; (open) dé-

visser [*cap, lid*]; (close) visser [*cap, lid*]; **he ~ed around in his chair** il s'est retourné dans son fauteuil; **2** (wind) enrouler; **to ~ threads together** torsader des fils; **3** (bend, distort) tordre [*metal, rod, branch*]; déformer [*words, facts, meaning*]; **his face was ~ed with pain** son visage était tordu de douleur; **4** (injure) **to ~ one's ankle/wrist** se tordre le bras/le poignet; **to ~ one's neck** attraper un torticolis.
III *vi* **1** [*person*] **to ~ round** (turn round) se retourner; **2** [*rope, flex, coil*] s'entortiller; **to ~ and turn** [*road, path*] serpenter.

twit○ *n* idiot/-e *m/f*.

twitch I *n* **1** (tic) tic *m*; **2** (spasm) soubresaut *m*.
II *vtr* tirer sur [qch] d'un coup sec [*fabric, curtain*].
III *vi* [*person*] avoir des tics; [*mouth*] trembler; [*eye*] cligner nerveusement; [*limb, muscle*] tressauter.

twitchy *adj* agité/-e.

two ▶389|, 434| *n, det, pron* deux (*m*) *inv*; **in ~s and threes** par deux ou trois, deux ou trois à la fois; **to break sth in ~** casser qch en deux.
IDIOMS **to be in ~ minds about doing** hésiter à faire; **to put ~ and ~ together** faire le rapprochement.

two-faced *adj* hypocrite, fourbe.

twofold I *adj* double.
II *adv* doublement; **to increase ~** doubler.

two-piece *n* (also **~ suit**) (woman's) tailleur *m*; (man's) costume *m* (deux-pièces).

two-seater *n* (car) voiture *f* à deux places; (plane) avion *m* à deux places.

two-time○ *vtr* être infidèle envers, tromper [*partner*].

two-way *adj* [*street*] à double sens; [*traffic*] dans les deux sens; [*communication, exchange*] bilatéral/-e.

two-way mirror *n* glace *f* sans tain.

two-way radio *n* émetteur-récepteur *m*.

tycoon *n* magnat *m*.

type I *n* **1** (variety, kind) type *m*, genre *m* (**of** de); **2** (in printing) caractères *mpl*.
II *vtr* taper (à la machine) [*word, letter*]; **a ~d letter** une lettre dactylographiée.
III *vi* taper (à la machine).

typecast *vtr* cataloguer [*person*].

typewriter *n* machine *f* à écrire.

typhoon *n* typhon *m*.

typical *adj* [*case, example, day, village*] typique; [*generosity, compassion*] caractéristique; **it's ~ of him to be late** cela ne m'étonne pas de lui qu'il soit en retard.

typically *adv* [*react, behave*] (of person) comme à mon/ton etc habitude; **~ English** [*place, behaviour*] typiquement anglais; **she's ~ English** c'est l'Anglaise type.

typing *n* dactylo *f*.

typist *n* dactylo *mf*.

typographic(al) *adj* typographique.

typography *n* typographie *f*.

tyrannize *vtr* tyranniser.

tyranny *n* tyrannie *f* (**over** sur).

tyrant *n* tyran *m*.

tyre (GB), **tire** (US) *n* pneu *m*; **spare ~** (for car) pneu *m* de rechange; (fat) bourrelet *m*.

Uu

u, **U** *n* u, U *m*.
udder *n* pis *m*.
UFO *n* (*abbr* = **unidentified flying object**) ovni *m inv*.
ugly *adj* **1** [*person, building*] laid/-e; **2** [*situation*] dangereux/-euse.
UK ▶448 *pr n* (*abbr* = **United Kingdom**) Royaume-Uni *m*.
ulcer *n* ulcère *m*.
ulterior *adj* **without any ~ motive** sans arrière-pensée.
ultimate I *n* **the ~ in** le nec plus ultra de [*comfort, luxury*].
II *adj* [*result, destination*] final/-e; [*sacrifice*] ultime (*before n*).
ultimately *adv* en fin de compte, au bout du compte.
ultimatum *n* ultimatum *m*.
ultramarine *n, adj* outremer (*m*) *inv*.
ultrasound *n* ultrasons *mpl*.
ultraviolet *adj* ultraviolet/-ette.
umbilical cord *n* cordon *m* ombilical.
umbrella *n* parapluie *m*.
umpire *n* arbitre *m*.
UN *n* (*abbr* = **United Nations**) **the ~** l'ONU *f*.
unable *adj* **to be ~ to do** (lacking means or opportunity) ne pas pouvoir faire; (lacking knowledge or skill) ne pas savoir faire; (incapable, not qualified) être incapable de faire.
unacceptable *adj* [*proposal*] inacceptable; [*behaviour*] inadmissible.
unaccompanied *adj* **1** [*child, baggage*] non accompagné/-e; [*man, woman*] seul/-e; **2** (Mus) sans accompagnement.
unaccustomed *adj* **to be ~ to sth/to doing** ne pas avoir l'habitude de qch/de faire.
unaffected *adj* **1 to be ~** ne pas être affecté/-e (**by** par); **2** (natural) tout simple.
unafraid *adj* [*person*] sans peur.
unaided *adv* [*stand, sit, walk*] sans aide.
unambiguous *adj* sans équivoque.
unanimous *adj* unanime.
unanimously *adv* [*agree, condemn*] unanimement; [*vote*] à l'unanimité.
unannounced *adv* [*arrive, call*] sans prévenir.
unanswered *adj* [*letter, question*] resté/-e sans réponse.
unappetizing *adj* peu appétissant/-e.
unappreciative *adj* [*person, audience*] ingrat/-e.
unapproachable *adj* inaccessible.
unarmed *adj* [*person*] non armé/-e; [*combat*] sans armes.
unashamedly *adv* ouvertement.
unasked *adv* [*come, attend*] sans être invité/-e; **to do sth ~** faire qch spontanément.
unassuming *adj* modeste.
unattached *adj* **1** [*part, element*] détaché/-e; **2** (single) [*person*] célibataire.
unattainable *adj* inaccessible.
unattractive *adj* [*person*] peu attirant/-e; [*proposition*] peu intéressant/-e (**to** pour).
unavailable *adj* **to be ~** [*person*] ne pas être disponible.
unavoidable *adj* inévitable.
unaware *adj* **1** (not informed) **to be ~ that** ignorer que; **2** (not conscious) **to be ~ of sth** ne pas être conscient/-e de qch.
unawares *adv* **to catch** or **take sb ~** prendre qn au dépourvu.
unbearable *adj* insupportable.
unbeatable *adj* imbattable.
unbelievable *adj* incroyable.
unbending *adj* inflexible.
unbias(s)ed *adj* impartial/-e.
unblock *vtr* déboucher [*pipe, sink*].
unbreakable *adj* incassable.
unbroken *adj* **1** [*sequence, silence, view*] ininterrompu/-e; **2** [*pottery*] intact/-e.
unbuckle *vtr* déboucler [*belt*]; défaire la boucle de [*shoe*].
unbutton *vtr* déboutonner.
uncalled-for *adj* [*remark*] déplacé/-e.
uncanny *adj* [*resemblance*] étrange; [*accuracy*] étonnant/-e; [*silence*] troublant/-e.
uncaring *adj* [*world*] indifférent/-e.
uncertain I *adj* **1** (unsure) incertain/-e; **to be ~ about** ne pas être certain/-e de; **2** (changeable) [*temper*] instable; [*weather*] variable.
II in no ~ terms *phr* [*state*] en termes on ne peut plus clairs.
uncertainty *n* incertitude *f*.
unchanged *adj* inchangé/-e.
uncharitable *adj* peu charitable .
unchecked *adv* de manière incontrôlée.
uncivilized *adj* **1** (inhumane) [*treatment, conditions*] inhumain/-e; **2** (uncouth, rude) grossier/-ière; **3** (barbarous) [*people, nation*] non civilisé/-e.
uncle *n* oncle *m*.
unclear *adj* **1** [*motive, reason*] peu clair/-e; **it is ~ how/whether**... on ne sait pas très bien comment/si...; **2** [*instructions, voice*] pas clair/-e; [*answer*] peu clair/-e; [*handwriting*] difficile à lire.
uncomfortable *adj* **1** [*shoes, garment, seat*] inconfortable; [*journey, heat*] pénible; **you look ~ in that chair** tu n'as pas l'air à l'aise dans ce fauteuil; **2** [*feeling, silence, situation*] pé-

nible; **to make sb (feel) ~** mettre qn mal à l'aise.

uncommon *adj* rare.

uncommunicative *adj* peu communicatif/-ive.

uncompromising *adj* intransigeant/-e.

unconcerned *adj* (uninterested) indifférent/-e (**with** à); (not caring) insouciant/-e; (untroubled) imperturbable.

unconditional *adj* [*obedience, support, love*] inconditionnel/-elle; [*offer, surrender*] sans condition.

unconscious I *n* **the ~** l'inconscient *m*.
II *adj* **1** (insensible) sans connaissance; **to knock sb ~** assommer qn; **2** (unaware) **to be ~ of sth** ne pas être conscient/-e de qch; **3** [*bias, hostility*] inconscient/-e.

unconstitutional *adj* inconstitutionnel/-elle.

uncontested *adj* [*leader, fact*] incontesté/-e; [*seat*] non disputé/-e.

uncontrollable *adj* [*emotion*] incontrôlable; [*tears*] qu'on ne peut retenir.

uncontrollably *adv* [*laugh, sob*] sans pouvoir se contrôler.

unconventional *adj* peu conventionnel/-elle.

unconvincing *adj* peu convaincant/-e.

uncooked *adj* non cuit/-e.

uncooperative *adj* peu coopératif/-ive.

uncoordinated *adj* [*efforts, service*] désordonné/-e; **to be ~** [*person*] manquer de coordination.

uncouth *adj* [*person*] grossier/-ière; [*accent*] peu raffiné/-e.

uncover *vtr* dévoiler [*scandal*]; découvrir [*evidence, body*].

uncritical *adj* peu critique.

unctuous *adj* onctueux/-euse, mielleux/-euse.

uncut *adj* **1** [*film, version*] intégral/-e; **2** [*gem*] non taillé/-e.

undamaged *adj* [*crops*] non endommagé/-e; [*building, reputation*] intact/-e.

undecided *adj* [*person*] indécis/-e; [*outcome*] incertain/-e.

undemanding *adj* [*task*] peu fatigant/-e; [*person*] peu exigeant/-e.

undemocratic *adj* antidémocratique.

undeniable *adj* indéniable.

under I *prep* **1** sous; **~ the bed** sous le lit; **~ it** en dessous; **it's ~ there** c'est là-dessous; **~ letter D** sous la lettre D; **2** (less than) **~ £10** moins de 10 livres sterling; **children ~ five** les enfants de moins de cinq ans or au-dessous de cinq ans; **a number ~ ten** un nombre inférieur à dix; **temperatures ~ 10°C** des températures inférieures à or au-dessous de 10°C; **3** (according to) **~ the law** selon la loi; **4** (subordinate to) sous; **I have 50 people ~ me** j'ai 50 employés sous mes ordres.
II *adv* **1** [*crawl, sit, hide*] en dessous; **to go ~** [*diver, swimmer*] disparaître sous l'eau; **2** (less) moins; **£10 and ~** 10 livres sterling et moins; **children of six and ~** des enfants de six ans et au-dessous; **3** (anaesthetized) **to put sb ~** endormir qn.

underage *adj* **~ drinking** la consommation d'alcool par les mineurs; **to be ~** être mineur/-e.

undercarriage *n* train *m* d'atterrissage.

underclothes *n pl* sous-vêtements *mpl*.

undercoat *n* couche *f* de fond.

undercooked *adj* pas assez cuit/-e; **the meat is ~** la viande n'est pas assez cuite.

undercover *adj* [*activity, group*] clandestin/-e; [*agent*] secret/-ète.

undercurrent *n* (in water) courant *m* profond; (in sea) courant *m* sous-marin; (figurative) courant *m* sous-jacent.

underdeveloped *adj* [*country*] sous-développé/-e; [*negative*] pas assez développé/-e.

underdog *n* (in society) opprimé/-e *m/f*; (in game, contest) perdant/-e *m/f*.

underdone *adj* [*food*] pas assez cuit/-e; [*steak*] (GB) saignant/-e.

underestimate *vtr* sous-estimer.

underexpose *vtr* sous-exposer.

underfed *adj* sous-alimenté/-e.

underfoot *adv* sous les pieds; **the ground was wet ~** le sol était humide.

undergo *vtr* subir [*change, test, operation*]; suivre [*treatment, training*]; **to ~ surgery** subir une intervention chirurgicale.

undergraduate *n* étudiant/-e *m/f*.

underground I *n* **1** (GB) (subway) métro *m*; **on the ~** dans le métro; **2 the ~** (political) la clandestinité; (artistic) l'underground *m*.
II *adj* **1** (below ground) souterrain/-e; **2** (secret) clandestin/-e; **3** (artistic) underground *inv*.
III *adv* **1** (below ground) sous terre; **2** (secretly) **to go ~** passer dans la clandestinité.

undergrowth *n* sous-bois *m*.

underhand *adj* (also **underhanded** US) [*person, method*] sournois/-e; **~ dealings** magouilles○ *fpl*.

underline *vtr* souligner.

underling *n* subordonné/-e *m/f*.

underlying *adj* [*problem*] sous-jacent/-e.

undermine *vtr* saper [*foundations, authority, efforts*]; ébranler [*confidence, position*].

underneath I *n* dessous *m*.
II *adv* dessous, en dessous.
III *prep* sous, au-dessous de; **from ~ a pile of books** de dessous une pile de livres.

undernourished *adj* sous-alimenté/-e.

underpants *n pl* slip *m*; **a pair of ~** un slip.

underpass *n* (for traffic) voie *f* inférieure; (for pedestrians) passage *m* souterrain.

underpay *vtr* sous-payer [*employee*].

underprivileged *adj* défavorisé/-e.

underrate *vtr* sous-estimer.

under-secretary *n* (also **~ of state**) (GB) sous-secrétaire *mf* d'État.

undershirt *n* (US) maillot *m* de corps.

understaffed *adj* **to be ~** manquer de personnel.

understand I *vtr* **1** (gen) comprendre; **to make oneself understood** se faire comprendre; **2** (believe) **to ~ that** croire que.
II *vi* comprendre (**about** à propos de).

understandable *adj* compréhensible; **it's ~** ça se comprend.

understandably *adv* naturellement.

understanding I *n* **1** (grasp of subject, issue) compréhension *f*; **2** (arrangement) entente *f* (**about** sur; **between** entre); **3** (sympathy) compréhension *f*; **4** (powers of reason) entendement *m*.
II *adj* [*tone*] bienveillant/-e; [*person*] compréhensif/-ive.

understatement *n* litote *f*.

understudy *n* doublure *f* (**to** de).

undertake *vtr* **1** entreprendre [*search, study, trip*]; se charger de [*mission, offensive*]; **2 to ~ to do** s'engager à faire.

undertaker *n* (person) entrepreneur *m* de pompes funèbres; (company) entreprise *f* de pompes funèbres.

undertaking *n* **1** (venture) entreprise *f*; **2** (promise) garantie *f*.

under-the-counter *adj* [*goods, trade*] illicite; [*payment*] sous le manteau.

undertone *n* **1** (low voice) voix *f* basse; **2** (hint) nuance *f*.

undervalue *vtr* **1** (financially) sous-évaluer; **2** sous-estimer [*person, quality*].

underwater I *adj* [*cable, exploration*] sous-marin/-e; [*lighting*] sous l'eau.
II *adv* sous l'eau.

underway *adj* **to get ~** [*vehicle*] se mettre en route; [*season*] commencer.

underwear *n* sous-vêtements *mpl*.

underweight *adj* trop maigre.

underworld *n* milieu *m*, pègre *f*.

undesirable *adj* [*aspect, habit, result*] indésirable; [*influence*] néfaste; [*friend*] peu recommandable.

undetected *adv* [*break in, listen*] sans être aperçu/-e; **to go ~** [*person*] rester inaperçu/-e; [*cancer*] rester non décelé/-e; [*crime*] rester non découvert/-e.

undeterred *adj* **to be ~ by sb/sth** ne pas se laisser démonter par qn/qch.

undeveloped *adj* [*person, organ, idea*] non développé/-e; [*land*] inexploité/-e; [*country*] sous-développé/-e.

undignified *adj* indigne.

undisciplined *adj* indiscipliné/-e.

undiscriminating *adj* sans discernement.

undisguised *adj* non déguisé/-e.

undisputed *adj* incontesté/-e.

undisturbed *adj* [*sleep*] paisible, tranquille; **to leave sb/sth ~** ne pas déranger qn/qch.

undivided *adj* **to give sb one's ~ attention** accorder à qn toute son attention.

undo *vtr* **1** défaire [*button, lock*]; ouvrir [*parcel*]; **2** annuler [*good, effort*].

undone *adj* défait/-e; **to come ~** [*parcel, button*] se défaire.

undoubtedly *adv* indubitablement.

undress I *vtr* déshabiller.
II *vi* se déshabiller.

undue *adj* excessif/-ive.

unduly *adv* [*optimistic, surprised*] excessivement; [*neglect, worry*] outre mesure.

unearthly *adj* [*light, landscape*] surnaturel/-elle; [*cry, silence*] étrange; **at an ~ hour** à une heure indue.

uneasily *adv* **1** (anxiously) avec inquiétude; **2** (uncomfortably) avec gêne.

uneasy *adj* **1** [*person*] inquiet/-iète (**about, at** au sujet de); [*conscience*] pas tranquille; **2** [*compromise*] difficile; [*peace*] boiteux/-euse; [*silence*] gêné/-e; **3** [*sleep*] agité/-e.

uneducated *adj* **1** [*person*] sans instruction; **2** [*person, speech*] inculte; [*accent, tastes*] commun/-e.

unemotional *adj* [*person*] impassible; [*account, reunion*] froid/-e.

unemployed I *n* **the ~** les chômeurs *mpl*.
II *adj* au chômage, sans emploi.

unemployment *n* chômage *m*.

unemployment benefit (GB), **unemployment compensation** (US) *n* allocations *fpl* de chômage.

unenthusiastic *adj* peu enthousiaste.

unequal *adj* [*amounts, contest, pay*] inégal/-e.

unequivocal *adj* [*person, declaration*] explicite; [*answer, support*] sans équivoque.

unethical *adj* (gen) contraire à la morale; (Med) contraire à la déontologie.

uneven *adj* [*hem, teeth*] irrégulier/-ière; [*contest, surface*] inégal/-e.

uneventful *adj* [*day, life, career*] ordinaire; [*journey, period*] sans histoires.

unexciting *adj* sans intérêt.

unexpected *adj* [*arrival, success*] imprévu/-e; [*ally, outcome*] inattendu/-e; [*death*] inopiné/-e.

unexpectedly *adv* [*happen*] à l'improviste; [*large, small, fast*] étonnamment.

unexplored *adj* inexploré/-e.

unfailing *adj* [*support*] fidèle; [*optimism*] à toute épreuve; [*efforts*] constant/-e.

unfair *adj* injuste (**to, on** envers; **to do** de faire); [*play, tactics*] irrégulier/-ière; [*trading*] frauduleux/-euse.

unfair dismissal *n* licenciement *m* abusif.

unfairness *n* injustice *f*.

unfaithful *adj* infidèle (**to** à).

unfamiliar *adj* **1** [*face, name, place*] inconnu/-e (**to** à); [*concept, feeling, situation*] inhabituel/-elle (**to** à); **2 to be ~ with sth** ne pas connaître qch.

unfashionable *adj* qui n'est pas à la mode.

unfasten *vtr* défaire [*clothing, button*]; ouvrir [*bag*].

unfavourable *adj* défavorable.

unfinished *adj* [*work*] inachevé/-e; **to have ~ business** avoir des choses à régler.

unfit *adj* **1** (out of condition) qui n'est pas en forme; **2** [*housing*] inadéquat/-e; [*pitch, road*] impraticable (**for** à); **~ for human consumption** impropre à la consommation humaine.

unflattering *adj* peu flatteur/-euse.

unfold I *vtr* déplier [*paper, map, deck, chair*]; déployer [*wings*]; décroiser [*arms*].
II *vi* **1** [*leaf*] s'ouvrir; **2** [*scene*] se dérouler; [*mystery*] se dévoiler.

unforgettable *adj* inoubliable.

unforgivable *adj* impardonnable.

unforgiving *adj* impitoyable.

unfortunate *adj* **1** (pitiable) malheureux/-euse; **2** (regrettable) [*incident, choice*] malencontreux/-euse; [*remark*] fâcheux/-euse; **3** (unlucky) malchanceux/-euse.

unfortunately *adv* malheureusement.

unfounded *adj* sans fondement.

unfriendly *adj* [*person, attitude, reception*] peu amical/-e; [*place*] inhospitalier/-ière.

unfulfilled *adj* [*ambition*] non réalisé/-e; [*desire, need*] inassouvi/-e; **to feel ~** se sentir insatisfait/-e.

unfurnished *adj* non meublé/-e.

ungracious *adj* désobligeant/-e (**of** de la part de).

ungrammatical *adj* incorrect/-e.

ungrateful *adj* ingrat/-e (**of** de la part de; **towards** envers).

unhappily *adv* **1** (miserably) d'un air malheureux; **2** (unfortunately) malheureusement; **3** (inappropriately) malencontreusement.

unhappiness *n* **1** (misery) tristesse *f*; **2** (dissatisfaction) mécontentement *m*.

unhappy *adj* **1** [*person, childhood, situation*] malheureux/-euse; [*face, occasion*] triste; **2** (dissatisfied) mécontent/-e; **to be ~ with sth** ne pas être satisfait/-e de qch; **3** (concerned) inquiet/-iète.

unharmed *adj* [*person*] indemne; [*object*] intact/-e.

unhealthy *adj* **1** [*person*] maladif/-ive; [*diet*] malsain/-e; [*conditions*] insalubre; **2** (unwholesome) malsain/-e.

unheard-of *adj* **1** (shocking) inouï/-e; **2** [*price*] record; [*actor*] inconnu/-e.

unheeded *adj* **to go ~** [*warning, plea*] rester vain/-e.

unhelpful *adj* [*employee*] peu serviable; [*attitude*] peu obligeant/-e.

unhindered *adj* **~ by** sans être entravé/-e par [*rules*]; sans être encombré/-e par [*luggage*].

unhurried *adj* [*person*] posé/-e; [*pace, meal*] tranquille.

unhygienic *adj* [*conditions*] insalubre; [*way, method*] peu hygiénique.

uniform I *n* uniforme *m*.
II *adj* identique; [*temperature*] constant/-e.

unify *vtr* unifier.

unilateral *adj* unilatéral/-e.

unimaginative *adj* [*style*] sans originalité; **to be ~** manquer d'imagination.

unimportant *adj* sans importance.

uninhabitable *adj* inhabitable.

uninhabited *adj* inhabité/-e.

uninhibited *adj* [*person*] sans complexes (**about** en ce qui concerne).

uninitiated *n* **the ~** les profanes.

uninjured *adj* indemne.

unintelligible *adj* incompréhensible.

unintentional *adj* involontaire.

uninterested *adj* indifférent/-e (**in** à).

uninteresting *adj* sans intérêt.

uninvited *adj* [*attentions*] non sollicité/-e; [*remark*] gratuit/-e; **~ guest** intrus/-e *m/f*.

uninviting *adj* [*place*] rébarbatif/-ive; [*food*] peu appétissant/-e.

union *n* **1** (also **trade ~**) syndicat *m*; **2** (uniting) union *f*; (marriage) union *f*, mariage *m*.

Unionist *n*, *adj* unioniste (*mf*).

unique *adj* **1** (sole) unique; **to be ~ to** être particulier/-ière à; **2** (remarkable) unique, exceptionnel/-elle.

unit *n* **1** (gen) unité *f*; **2** (group) groupe *m*; (in army, police) unité *f*; **3** (department) (gen, Med) service *m*; **4** (piece of furniture) élément *m*.

unite I *vtr* unir (**with** à).
II *vi* s'unir (**with** à).

united *adj* [*group, front*] uni/-e (**in** dans); [*effort*] conjoint/-e.

United Kingdom ▶ **448** *pr n* Royaume-Uni *m*.

United Nations (**Organization**) *n* (Organisation *f* des) Nations *fpl* unies.

United States (**of America**) ▶ **448** *pr n* États-Unis *mpl* (d'Amérique).

unity *n* unité *f*.

universal *adj* [*acclaim, reaction*] général/-e; [*education*] pour tous; [*principle, truth*] universel/-elle.

universally *adv* [*believed*] par tous, universellement; [*known, loved*] de tous.

universe *n* univers *m*.

university *n* université *f*.

unjust *adj* injuste (**to** envers).

unjustified *adj* injustifié/-e.

unkempt *adj* [*appearance*] négligé/-e; [*hair*] ébouriffé/-e; [*beard*] peu soigné/-e.

unkind *adj* [*person, thought, act*] pas très gentil/-ille; [*remark*] désobligeant/-e; **to be ~ to sb** (by deed) ne pas être gentil avec qn; (verbally) être méchant/-e avec qn.

unknown I *n* **1 the ~** l'inconnu *m*; **2** (person) inconnu/-e *m/f*.
II *adj* inconnu/-e

unlace *vtr* délacer.

unlawful *adj* [*activity*] illégal/-e; [*detention*] arbitraire; **~ killing** meurtre *m*.

unleaded petrol (GB), **unleaded gasoline** (US) *n* essence *f* sans plomb.

unleavened *adj* sans levain.

unless *conj* à moins que (+ *subjunctive*), à moins de (+ *infinitive*); **he won't come ~ you invite him** il ne viendra pas à moins que tu (ne) l'invites; **she can't take the job ~ she finds a nanny** elle ne peut pas accepter le poste à moins de trouver une nourrice.

unlike *prep* **1** (in contrast to) contrairement à, à la différence de; **~ me, he**... contrairement à moi, il...; **2** (different from) différent/-e de; **3** (uncharacteristic of) **it's ~ her (to be so rude)** ça ne lui ressemble pas (d'être aussi impolie).

unlikely *adj* **1** (unexpected) improbable, peu probable; **it is ~ that** il est peu probable que (+ *subjunctive*); **2** [*partner, choice, situation*] inattendu/-e; **3** [*story*] invraisemblable.

unlimited *adj* illimité/-e; [*access*] libre (*before n*).

unlined *adj* **1** [*garment, curtain*] sans doublure; **2** [*paper*] non réglé.

unload I *vtr* **1** décharger [*goods, vessel, gun, camera*]; **2** (get rid of) se décharger de [*feelings*] (**on(to)** sur); se débarrasser de [*goods*].
II *vi* [*truck, ship*] décharger.

unlock *vtr* ouvrir [*door*]; **to be ~ed** ne pas être fermé/-e à clé.

unluckily *adv* malheureusement (**for** pour).

unlucky *adj* **1** [*person*] malchanceux/-euse; [*event*] malencontreux/-euse; [*day*] de malchance; **2** [*number, colour*] néfaste, maléfique; **it's ~ to do** ça porte malheur de faire.

unmade *adj* [*bed*] défait/-e.

unmanageable *adj* [*child, dog*] difficile; [*system*] ingérable; [*hair*] rebelle.

unmarried *adj* célibataire.

unmistakable *adj* **1** (recognizable) caractéristique (**of** de); **2** (unambiguous) sans ambiguïté; **3** (marked) net/nette.

unmoved *adj* (unconcerned) indifférent/-e (**by** à); (emotionally) insensible (**by** à).

unnatural *adj* **1** (odd) anormal/-e; **it is ~ that** ce n'est pas normal que (+ *subjunctive*); **2** [*style, laugh*] affecté/-e; **3** [*silence, colour*] insolite.

unnecessarily *adv* inutilement.

unnecessary *adj* **1** (not needed) inutile; **it is ~ to do** il est inutile de faire; **it is ~ for you to do** il est inutile que tu fasses; **2** (uncalled for) déplacé/-e.

unnerve *vtr* décontenancer, rendre [qn] nerveux/-euse.

unnoticed *adj* inaperçu/-e.

unobstructed *adj* [*view, exit, road*] dégagé/-e.

unobtrusive *adj* [*person*] effacé/-e; [*site, object, noise*] discret/-ète.

unoccupied *adj* [*house, shop*] inoccupé/-e; [*seat*] libre.

unofficial *adj* [*figure*] officieux/-ieuse; [*candidate*] indépendant/-e; [*strike*] sauvage.

unorthodox *adj* peu orthodoxe.

unpack *vtr* défaire [*suitcase*]; déballer [*belongings*].

unpaid *adj* [*bill, tax*] impayé/-e; [*debt*] non acquitté/-e; [*work*] non rémunéré/-e; **~ leave** congé *m* sans solde.

unparalleled *adj* **1** [*strength, luxury*] sans égal; [*success*] hors pair; **2** (unprecedented) sans précédent.

unpasteurized *adj* [*milk*] cru/-e; [*cheese*] au lait cru.

unplanned *adj* [*stoppage, increase*] imprévu/-e; [*pregnancy, baby*] non prévu/-e.

unpleasant *adj* désagréable.

unpleasantness *n* **1** (of odour, experience, remark) caractère *m* désagréable; **2** (bad feeling) dissensions *fpl* (**between** entre).

unplug *vtr* débrancher [*appliance*]; déboucher [*sink*].

unpopular *adj* impopulaire.

unprecedented *adj* sans précédent.

unpredictable *adj* [*event*] imprévisible; [*weather*] incertain/-e; **he's ~** on ne sait jamais à quoi s'attendre avec lui.

unprepared *adj* **1** [*person*] pas préparé/-e (**for** pour); **2** [*speech*] improvisé/-e; [*translation*] non préparé/-e.

unprepossessing *adj* peu avenant/-e.

unpretentious *adj* sans prétention.

unproductive *adj* improductif/-ive.

unprofessional *adj* peu professionnel/-elle.

unprofitable *adj* non rentable.

unqualified *adj* **1** [*person*] non qualifié/-e; **2** [*support, respect*] inconditionnel/-elle; [*success*] grand/-e (*before n*).

unquestionable *adj* incontestable.

unravel I *vtr* défaire [*knitting*]; démêler [*thread, mystery*].
II *vi* [*knitting*] se défaire; [*mystery, thread*] se démêler; [*plot*] se dénouer.

unreal *adj* **1** (not real) irréel/-éelle; **2**° (unbelievable) incroyable.

unrealistic *adj* irréaliste, peu réaliste.

unreasonable *adj* **1** [*behaviour, expectation*] qui n'est pas raisonnable; **he's being very ~ about it** il n'est vraiment pas raisonnable; **2** [*price, demand*] excessif/-ive.

unrecognizable *adj* méconnaissable.

unrelated *adj* **1** (not connected) sans rapport (**to** avec); **2** (as family) **to be ~** ne pas avoir de lien de parenté.

unrelenting *adj* [*heat, stare, person*] implacable; [*pursuit, zeal*] acharné/-e.

unreliable *adj* [*evidence*] douteux/-euse; [*method, employee*] peu sûr/-e; [*equipment*] peu fiable; **she's very ~** on ne peut pas compter sur elle.

unrepentant *adj* impénitent/-e.

unrequited *adj* [*love*] sans retour.

unresolved *adj* irrésolu/-e.

unrest *n* **1** (dissatisfaction) malaise *m*; **2** (agitation) troubles *mpl*.

unrestricted *adj* [*access*] libre (*before n*); [*power*] illimité/-e.

unrewarding *adj* (unfulfilling) peu gratifiant/-e; (thankless) ingrat/-e.

unrivalled *adj* sans égal.

unroll *vtr* dérouler.

unruffled *adj* **1** (calm) imperturbable; **2** [*hair*] lisse.

unruly *adj* indiscipliné/-e.

unsafe *adj* **1** [*environment*] malsain/-e; [*drinking water*] non potable; [*goods, working condi-*

tions] dangereux/-euse; **2** (threatened) **to feel ~** ne pas se sentir en sécurité.

unsaid *adj* **to leave sth ~** passer qch sous silence.

unsatisfactory *adj* insatisfaisant/-e.

unsatisfied *adj* [*person*] insatisfait/-e; [*need*] inassouvi/-e.

unsatisfying *adj* peu satisfaisant/-e.

unsavoury (GB), **unsavory** (US) *adj* [*individual*] louche, répugnant/-e.

unscheduled *adj* [*appearance, speech*] surprise (*after n*); [*flight*] supplémentaire; [*stop*] qui n'a pas été prévu.

unscrew *vtr* dévisser.

unscrupulous *adj* [*person*] sans scrupules; [*tactic*] peu scrupuleux/-euse.

unseat *vtr* désarçonner [*rider*].

unseen *adv* [*escape, slip away*] sans être vu/-e.

unselfconscious *adj* **1** (natural) naturel/-elle; **2** (uninhibited) sans complexes.

unselfish *adj* [*person*] qui pense aux autres; [*act*] désintéressé/-e.

unsettled *adj* **1** [*weather, climate*] instable; [*person*] perturbé/-e; **2** [*account*] impayé/-e.

unsettling *adj* [*question, experience*] troublant/-e; [*work of art*] dérangeant/-e.

unshaken *adj* [*person*] imperturbable (**by** devant); [*belief*] inébranlable.

unskilled *adj* [*worker, labour*] non qualifié/-e; [*job, work*] qui n'exige pas de qualification professionnelle.

unsociable *adj* peu sociable.

unsocial *adj* **to work ~ hours** travailler en dehors des heures normales.

unsolicited *adj* non sollicité/-e.

unsophisticated *adj* [*person*] sans façons; [*mind*] simple; [*analysis*] simpliste.

unspeakable *adj* **1** (dreadful) [*pain, sorrow*] inexprimable; [*act*] innommable; **2** (inexpressible) (joy) indescriptible.

unspoiled, **unspoilt** *adj* [*landscape, town*] préservé/-e intact.

unspoken *adj* **1** (secret) inexprimé/-e; **2** (implicit) tacite.

unstable *adj* instable.

unsteady *adj* [*steps, legs, voice*] chancelant/-e; [*ladder*] instable; [*hand*] tremblant/-e; **to be ~ on one's feet** marcher de façon mal assurée.

unstoppable *adj* [*force, momentum*] irrésistible; [*athlete, leader*] imbattable.

unstuck *adj* **to come ~** [*stamp*] se décoller; [*person*] connaître un échec.

unsuccessful *adj* **1** [*attempt, campaign*] infructueux/-euse; [*novel, film*] sans succès; [*effort, search*] vain/-e; **to be ~** [*attempt*] échouer; **2** [*candidate*] (for job) malchanceux/-euse; (in election) malheureux/-euse; [*business person*] malchanceux/-euse; [*artist*] inconnu/-e; **to be ~ in doing** ne pas réussir à faire.

unsuccessfully *adv* [*try*] en vain; [*challenge, bid*] sans succès.

unsuitable *adj* [*location, clothing, accommodation, time*] inapproprié/-e; [*moment*] inopportun/-e; **to be ~** ne pas convenir (**for sb** à qn); **to be ~ for a job** ne pas convenir pour un travail.

unsure *adj* peu sûr/-e (**of** de); **to be ~ about how/why/where** ne pas savoir très bien comment/pourquoi/où; **to be ~ of oneself** manquer de confiance en soi.

unsweetened *adj* sans sucre, non sucré/-e.

unsympathetic *adj* **1** (uncaring) [*person, attitude, tone*] peu compatissant/-e; **2** (unattractive) [*person, character*] antipathique.

untenable *adj* [*position*] intenable; [*claim, argument*] indéfendable.

unthinkable *adj* impensable.

untidy *adj* [*person*] (in habits) désordonné/-e; (in appearance) peu soigné/-e; [*habits, clothes*] négligé/-e; [*room*] en désordre.

untie *vtr* défaire, dénouer [*knot, rope, laces*]; défaire [*parcel*]; délier [*hands, hostage*].

until (also **till**)

■ **Note** When used as a preposition in positive sentences, *until* is translated by *jusqu'à*: *they're staying until Monday* = ils restent jusqu'à lundi.
– Remember that *jusqu'à + le* becomes *jusqu'au* and *jusqu'à + les* becomes *jusqu'aux*: *until the right moment* = jusqu'au bon moment; *until the exams* = jusqu'aux examens.
– In negative sentences, *not until* is translated by *ne...pas avant*: *I can't see you until Friday* = je ne peux pas vous voir avant vendredi.
– When used as a conjunction in positive sentences, *until* is translated by *jusqu'à ce que + subjunctive*: *we'll stay here until Maya comes back* = nous resterons ici jusqu'à ce que Maya revienne.
– In negative sentences where the two verbs have different subjects, *not until* is translated by *ne...pas avant que + subjunctive*: *we won't leave until Maya comes back* = nous ne partirons pas avant que Maya revienne.
– In negative sentences where the two verbs have the same subject, *not until* is translated by *pas avant de + infinitive*: *we won't leave until we've seen Claire* = nous ne partirons pas avant d'avoir vu Claire.
– For more examples and particular usages, see the entry below.

I *prep* jusqu'à; (after negative verb) avant; **~ Tuesday** jusqu'à mardi; **~ the sixties** jusqu'aux années soixante; **~ now** jusqu'à présent; **~ then** jusqu'à ce moment-là, jusque-là; **(up) ~ 1901** jusqu'en or jusqu'à 1901; **valid (up) ~ April 1998** valable jusqu'en avril 1998; **to work from Monday ~ Saturday** travailler du lundi au samedi.

II *conj* jusqu'à ce que (+ *subjunctive*); (in negative constructions) avant que (+ *subjunctive*), avant de (+ *infinitive*); **we'll stay ~ a solution is reached** nous resterons jusqu'à ce que nous trouvions une solution; **let's watch TV ~ he's ready** regardons la télévision en attendant qu'il soit prêt; **I'll wait ~ I get back** j'attendrai d'être rentré (**before doing** pour faire); **she waited ~ they were alone** elle a attendu qu'ils soient seuls.

untimely *adj* [*arrival, announcement*] inopportun/-e; [*death*] prématuré/-e.

untranslatable *adj* intraduisible (**into** en).

untroubled *adj* [*face, life*] paisible; **to be ~** (by news) ne pas être troublé/-e (**by** par).

untrue *adj* faux/fausse.

unused[1] *adj* **to be ~ to sth/to doing** ne pas être habitué/-e à qch/à faire.

unused[2] *adj* [*machine, building*] inutilisé/-e; [*stamp*] neuf/neuve.

unusual *adj* [*colour, animal, flower*] peu commun/-e; [*feature, occurrence, skill*] peu commun/-e, inhabituel/-elle; [*dish, dress, person*] original/-e; **it is ~ to find/see** il est rare de trouver/voir; **there's nothing ~ about it** cela n'a rien d'extraordinaire.

unusually *adv* exceptionnellement.

unwanted *adj* [*goods, produce*] superflu/-e; [*pet*] abandonné/-e; [*visitor*] indésirable; [*child*] non souhaité/-e; **to feel ~** se sentir de trop.

unwarranted *adj* injustifié/-e.

unwelcome *adj* [*visitor, interruption*] importun/-e; [*news*] fâcheux/-euse.

unwell *adj* souffrant/-e; **he is feeling ~** il ne se sent pas très bien.

unwilling *adj* [*attention, departure*] forcé/-e; **he is ~ to do it** il n'est pas disposé à le faire; (stronger) il ne veut pas le faire.

unwind I *vtr* dérouler [*cable, bandage, scarf*].
II *vi* **1** [*tape, cable, scarf*] se dérouler; **2** (relax) se relaxer.

unwise *adj* [*choice, loan, decision*] peu judicieux/-ieuse; [*person*] imprudent/-e.

unwisely *adv* imprudemment.

unworthy *adj* indigne (**of** de).

unwrap *vtr* déballer [*parcel*].

unwritten *adj* [*rule, agreement*] tacite.

up I *adj* **1** (out of bed) **she's ~** elle est levée; **we were ~ very late last night** nous nous sommes couchés très tard hier soir; **they were ~ all night** ils ont veillé toute la nuit; **I was still ~ at 2 am** j'étais toujours debout à 2 heures du matin; **2** (higher in amount, level) **sales are ~ (by 10%)** les ventes ont augmenté (de 10%); **numbers of students are ~** le nombre d'étudiants est en hausse; **3**○ (wrong) **what's ~?** qu'est-ce qui se passe?; **what's ~ with him?** qu'est-ce qu'il a?; **4** (erected, affixed) **the notice is ~ on the board** l'annonce est affichée sur le panneau; **is the tent ~?** est-ce que la tente est déjà montée?; **he had his hand ~ for five minutes** il a gardé la main levée pendant cinq minutes; **5** (open) **the blinds were ~** les stores étaient levés; **when the lever is ~ the machine is off** si le levier est vers le haut la machine est arrêtée; **6** (finished) **'time's ~!'** 'c'est l'heure!'; **when the four days were ~** à la fin des quatre jours; **7** (facing upwards) **'this side ~'** 'haut'; **she was floating face ~** elle flottait sur le dos; **8** (pinned up) **her hair was ~** elle avait les cheveux relevés.
II *adv* **1 ~ here/there** là-haut; **~ on the wardrobe** sur l'armoire; **~ in the tree/the clouds** dans l'arbre/les nuages; **~ in London** à Londres; **~ to/in Scotland** en Écosse; **~ North** au Nord; **four floors ~ from here** quatre étages au-dessus; **on the second shelf ~** sur la deuxième étagère en partant du bas; **2** (ahead) d'avance; **to be four points ~ (on sb)** avoir quatre points d'avance (sur qn); **3** (upwards) **T-shirts from £2 ~** des T-shirts à partir de deux livres.
III *prep* **~ the tree** dans l'arbre; **the library is ~ the stairs** la bibliothèque se trouve en haut de l'escalier; **he ran ~ the stairs** il a monté l'escalier en courant; **he lives just ~ the road** il habite juste à côté; **to walk/drive ~ the road** remonter la rue; **he put it ~ his sleeve** il l'a mis dans sa manche.
IV up above *phr* au-dessus; **~ above sth** au-dessus de qch.
V up against *phr* contre [*wall*]; **to come ~ against** rencontrer [*opposition*].
VI up and about *phr* debout; **to be ~ and about again** être de nouveau sur pied.
VII up and down *phr* **1** (to and fro) **to walk ~ and down** aller et venir, faire les cent pas; **2** (throughout) **~ and down the country** dans tout le pays.
VIII up to *phr* **1** (to particular level) jusqu'à; **~ to here/there** jusqu'ici/jusque là; **2** (as many as) jusqu'à, près de; **~ to 20 people/50 dollars** jusqu'à 20 personnes/50 dollars; **3** (until) jusqu'à; **~ to 1964** jusqu'en 1964; **~ to 10.30 pm** jusqu'à 22 h 30; **~ to now** jusqu'à maintenant; **4 I'm not ~ to it** (not capable) je n'en suis pas capable; (not well enough) je n'en ai pas la force; (can't face it) je n'en ai pas le courage; **5 it's ~ to him to do** c'est à lui de faire; **it's ~ to you!** c'est à toi de décider!; **6** (doing) **what is he ~ to?** qu'est-ce qu'il fait?; **they're ~ to something** ils mijotent○ quelque chose.
IDIOMS **to be one ~ on sb** faire mieux que qn; **to be (well) ~ on** s'y connaître en [*art, history*]; être au courant de [*news*]; **the ~s and downs** les hauts et les bas (**of** de)

upbringing *n* éducation *f*.

update *vtr* **1** (revise) mettre or remettre [qch] à jour [*database, information*]; actualiser [*price, value*]; **2** (modernize) moderniser; **3** (inform) mettre [qn] au courant (**on** de).

upgrade *vtr* **1** (modernize) moderniser; (improve) améliorer; **2** promouvoir [*employee*].

upheaval *n* **1** (disturbance) bouleversement *m*; **2** (instability) (political, emotional) bouleversements *mpl*; (physical) remue-ménage *m inv*.

uphill I *adj* **1** [*road*] qui monte; **~ slope** côte *f*, montée *f*; **2** [*task*] difficile.
II *adv* **to go/walk ~** monter.

uphold *vtr* soutenir [*right*]; faire respecter [*law*]; confirmer [*decision*].

upholstery *n* **1** (covering) revêtement *m*; **2** (stuffing) rembourrage *m*.

upkeep *n* **1** (of property) entretien *m* (**of** de); **2** (cost) frais *mpl* d'entretien.

uplifting *adj* tonique.

upmarket *adj* [*car, hotel*] haut de gamme; [*area*] riche.

upon *prep* **1** (on) sur; **2** (linking two nouns) **thousands ~ thousands of people** des milliers et des milliers de personnes.

upper I *n* (of shoe) empeigne *f*.
II *adj* **1** [*shelf, cupboard*] du haut; [*floor, deck, lip*] supérieur/-e; [*teeth*] du haut; **2** (in rank, scale) supérieur/-e; **3 the ~ limit** la limite maximale (**on** de).
IDIOMS **to have/get the ~ hand** avoir/prendre le dessus.

upper case *adj* **~ letters** (lettres *fpl*) majuscules *fpl*.

upper class *n* (*pl* **~es**) **the ~, the ~es** l'aristocratie *f* et la haute bourgeoisie.

uppermost *adj* **1** (highest) [*branch*] le plus haut/la plus haute; (in rank) [*echelon*] le plus élevé/la plus élevée; **2 to be ~ in sb's mind** être au premier plan des préoccupations de qn.

upright I *adj* **1** (physically) droit/-e; **to stay ~** [*person*] rester debout; **2** (morally) droit/-e.
II *adv* **to stand ~** se tenir droit; **to sit ~** (action) se redresser.

uprising *n* soulèvement *m* (**against** contre).

uproar *n* (noise) tumulte *m*; (protest) protestations *fpl*.

uproot *vtr* déraciner.

upset I *n* **1** (surprise, setback) revers *m*; **2** (upheaval) bouleversement *m*; **3** (distress) peine *f*; **4 to have a stomach ~** avoir un problème d'estomac.
II *adj* **to be** or **feel ~** (distressed) être très affecté/-e; (annoyed) être contrarié/-e; **to get ~** (angry) se fâcher (**about** pour); (distressed) se tracasser (**about** pour).
III *vtr* **1** (distress) [*sight, news*] bouleverser; [*person*] faire de la peine à; **2** (annoy) contrarier; **3** bouleverser [*plan*]; déjouer [*calculations*]; **4** (destabilize) rompre [*balance*]; **5** (Med) rendre [qn] malade [*person*]; perturber [*digestion*].

upside down I *adj* à l'envers.
II *adv* à l'envers; **to turn the house ~** mettre la maison sens dessus dessous.

upstage *vtr* éclipser.

upstairs I *n* haut *m*.
II *adj* [*room*] du haut; **an ~ bedroom** une chambre à l'étage.
III *adv* en haut; **to go ~** monter (l'escalier).

upstart *n, adj* arriviste (*mf*).

upstream *adv* [*travel*] vers l'amont; **~ from here** en amont d'ici.

uptight○ *adj* **1** (tense) tendu/-e; **2** (inhibited) coincé/-e○.

up-to-date *adj* **1** [*music, clothes*] à la mode; [*equipment*] moderne; **2** [*records, timetable*] à jour; [*information*] récent/-e; **3** (informed) [*person*] au courant (**with** de).

upward I *adj* [*push, movement*] vers le haut; [*path, road*] qui monte; [*trend*] à la hausse.
II *adv* (also **upwards**) [*look, point*] vers le haut; **to go** or **move ~** monter; **from £10 ~** à partir de 10 livres sterling.

upwards = **upward II**.

uranium *n* uranium *m*.

Uranus *pr n* Uranus *f*.

urban *adj* urbain/-e.

urchin *n* gamin *m*.

Urdu ▶ **553** *n* urdu *m*.

urge I *n* forte envie *f*, désir *m* (**to do** de faire).
II *vtr* conseiller vivement, préconiser [*caution, restraint, resistance*]; **to ~ sb to do** conseiller vivement à qn de faire; (stronger) pousser qn à faire.

urgency *n* (of situation, appeal, request) urgence *f*; (of voice, tone) insistance *f*; **a matter of ~** une affaire urgente.

urgent *adj* **1** (pressing) [*case, need*] urgent/-e, pressant/-e; [*message, demand*] urgent/-e; [*meeting, measures*] d'urgence; **2** [*request, tone*] insistant/-e.

urgently *adv* [*request*] d'urgence; [*plead*] instamment.

urinal *n* (place) urinoir *m*; (fixture) urinal *m*.

urinate *vi* uriner.

urine *n* urine *f*.

urn *n* urne *f*.

us *pron* nous; **she knows ~** elle nous connaît; **both of ~** tous/toutes les deux; **every single one of ~** chacun/-e d'entre nous; **some of ~** quelques-uns/-unes d'entre nous; **she's one of ~** elle est des nôtres.

US *pr n* (*abbr* = **United States**) USA *mpl*.

USA *pr n* (*abbr* = **United States of America**) USA *mpl*.

use I *n* **1** (act of using) (of substance, object, machine) emploi *m*, utilisation *f* (**of** de); (of word, expression) emploi *m*, usage *m* (**of** de); **for the ~ of** à l'usage de [*customer, staff*]; **for my own ~** pour mon usage personnel; **to make ~ of sth** utiliser qch; **to put sth to good ~** tirer parti de qch; **while the machine is in ~** lorsque la machine est en service or en fonctionnement; **to have the ~ of** avoir l'usage de [*house, car, kitchen*]; avoir la jouissance de [*garden*]; **to lose the ~ of one's legs** perdre l'usage de ses jambes; **2** (way of using) (of resource, object, material) utilisation *f*; (of term) emploi *m*; **to have no further ~ for sb/sth** ne plus avoir besoin de qn/qch; **3** (usefulness) **to be of ~** être utile (**to** à); **to be (of) no ~** [*object*] ne servir à rien; [*person*] n'être bon/bonne à rien; **what's the ~ of crying?** à quoi bon pleurer?; **it's no ~ (he won't listen)** c'est inutile (il n'écoutera pas).
II *vtr* **1** se servir de, utiliser [*object, car, room, money*]; employer [*method, word*]; profiter de, saisir [*opportunity*]; faire jouer [*influence*]; avoir recours à [*blackmail*]; utiliser [*knowledge, talent*]; **to ~ sb/sth as** se servir de qn/qch comme; **to ~ sth to do** se servir de qch pour faire; **2** (consume) consommer [*fuel, food*]; utiliser [*water, leftovers*]; **3** (exploit) se servir de [*person*].
III used *pp adj* [*car*] d'occasion; [*envelope*] qui a déjà servi.
■ **use up** finir [*food*]; dépenser [*money*]; épuiser [*supplies*].

used

■ **Note** To translate *used to do*, use the imperfect tense in French: *he used to live in York* = il habitait York.
– To emphasize a contrast between past and present, you can use *avant*: *I used to love sport* = avant, j'adorais le sport.

I *modal aux* **I ~ to read a lot** je lisais beaucoup; **she ~ to smoke, didn't she?** elle fumait avant, non?; **she doesn't smoke now, but she ~ to** elle ne fume plus maintenant, mais elle fumait avant; **there ~ to be a pub here** il y avait un pub ici (dans le temps).
II *adj* **to be ~ to sth** avoir l'habitude de qch, être habitué/-e à qch; **to get ~ to** s'habituer à; **I'm not ~ to it** je n'ai pas l'habitude; **you'll get ~ to it** tu t'y habitueras.

useful *adj* utile.

useless *adj* **1** (not helpful) inutile; **2** (not able to be used) inutilisable; **3**° (incompetent) incapable, nul/nulle°.

user *n* (of public service) usager *m*; (of product, machine) utilisateur/-trice *m/f*.

user-friendly *adj* (Comput) convivial/-e; (gen) facile à utiliser.

usher *vtr* conduire, escorter; **to ~ sb in/out** faire entrer/sortir qn.

usherette ▶ **626** *n* ouvreuse *f*.

USSR *pr n* (*abbr* = **Union of Soviet Socialist Republics**) URSS *f*.

usual *adj* (gen) habituel/-elle; [*word, term*] usuel/-elle; **it is ~ for sb to do** c'est normal pour qn de faire; **it is ~ to do** il est d'usage de faire; **as ~** comme d'habitude; **more/less than ~** plus/moins que d'habitude.

usually *adv* d'habitude, normalement.

utensil *n* ustensile *m*.

uterus *n* utérus *m*.

utility I *n* **1** (usefulness) utilité *f*; **2** (also **public ~**) (service) service *m* public.
II **utilities** *n pl* (US) factures *fpl*.

utmost I *n* **to do** or **try one's ~ to do** faire tout son possible pour faire; **to the ~ of one's abilities** au maximum de ses capacités.
II *adj* [*caution, ease, secrecy*] le plus grand/la plus grande (*before n*); [*limit*] extrême; **it is of the ~ importance that** il est extrêmement important que (+ *subjunctive*).

utter I *adj* [*disaster, boredom, despair*] total/-e; [*honesty, sincerity*] absolu/-e; [*fool, stranger*] parfait/-e (*before n*).
II *vtr* prononcer [*word, curse*]; pousser [*cry*]; émettre [*sound*].

utterly *adv* complètement; [*condemn*] avec vigueur.

U-turn *n* demi-tour *m*; (figurative) volte-face *f inv*.

UV *adj* (*abbr* = **ultraviolet**) [*light, ray, radiation*] ultraviolet/-ette.

Vv

v, **V** *n* **1** (letter) v, V *m*; **2 v** (*abbr* = **versus**) contre.

vacancy *n* **1** (room) **'vacancies'** 'chambres libres'; **'no vacancies'** 'complet'; **2** (unfilled job) poste *m* à pourvoir, poste *m* vacant.

vacant *adj* **1** [*flat, room, seat*] libre, disponible; [*office, land*] inoccupé/-e; **2** [*job, post*] vacant/-e, à pourvoir; **3** [*look, stare*] absent/-e; [*expression*] vide.

vacate *vtr* quitter [*house, premises, job*].

vacation *n* vacances *fpl*; **on ~** en vacances.

vacationer *n* (US) vacancier/-ière *m*/*f*.

vaccinate *vtr* vacciner (**against** contre).

vaccination *n* vaccination *f* (**against** contre).

vaccine *n* vaccin *m* (**against** contre).

vacillate *vi* hésiter.

vacuum I *n* **1** (gen) vide *m*; **2** (also **~ cleaner**) aspirateur *m*.
II *vtr* passer [qch] à l'aspirateur [*carpet*]; passer l'aspirateur dans [*room*].

vagrant *n, adj* vagabond/-e (*m*/*f*).

vague *adj* **1** (gen) vague; **to be ~ about** rester vague sur or évasif/-ive au sujet de [*plans, past*]; **2** (distracted) [*person, expression*] distrait/-e.

vaguely *adv* **1** (gen) vaguement; **2** (distractedly) [*smile, gaze*] d'un air distrait or vague.

vain I *adj* **1** (conceited) vaniteux/-euse, vain/-e (*after n*); **2** (futile) [*attempt, promise, hope*] vain/-e (*before n*).
II in vain *phr* en vain.

valentine card *n* carte *f* de la Saint-Valentin.

valet ▶ 626 *n* **1** (employee) valet *m* de chambre; **2** (US) (rack) valet *m* de nuit.

valiant *adj* [*soldier*] vaillant/-e; [*attempt*] courageux/-euse.

valid *adj* **1** [*passport, licence*] valide; [*ticket, offer*] valable (**for** pour); **2** [*argument, excuse*] valable; [*complaint*] fondé/-e; [*point, comment*] pertinent/-e.

valley *n* vallée *f*; (small) vallon *m*.

valour (GB), **valor** (US) *n* bravoure *f*.

valuable *adj* **1** [*object, asset*] de valeur; **to be ~** avoir de la valeur; **a very ~ ring** une bague de grande valeur; **2** [*advice, information, lesson, member*] précieux/-ieuse.

valuables *n pl* objets *mpl* de valeur.

valuation *n* (of house, land, company) évaluation *f*; (of antique, art) expertise *f*; **to have a ~ done on sth** faire évaluer qch.

value I *n* valeur *f*; **novelty ~** caractère nouveau; **to be good ~** avoir un bon rapport qualité-prix; **to get ~ for money** en avoir pour son argent.
II *vtr* **1** évaluer [*house, asset, company*] (**at** à); expertiser [*antique, jewel, painting*]; **2** (appreciate) apprécier [*person, friendship, opinion, help*]; tenir à [*independence, life*].

valve *n* **1** (in machine, engine) soupape *f*; (on tyre, football) valve *f*; **2** (Anat) valvule *f*.

van *n* **1** (small, for deliveries) fourgonnette *f*, camionnette *f*; (larger, for removals) fourgon *m*; **2** (US) (camper) auto-caravane *f*, camping-car *m*.

vandal *n* vandale *mf*.

vandalism *n* vandalisme *m*.

vandalize *vtr* vandaliser.

vanguard *n* avant-garde *f*; **in the ~** à l'avant-garde.

vanilla *n* vanille *f*.

vanish *vi* disparaître (**from** de); **to ~ into thin air** se volatiliser.

vanity *n* vanité *f*.

vantage point *n* point *m* de vue, position *f* élevée.

vaporizer *n* vaporisateur *m*.

vapour (GB), **vapor** (US) *n* vapeur *f*.

vapour trail *n* traînée *f* de condensation, traînée *f* d'avion.

variable *n, adj* variable (*f*).

variance *n* **to be at ~ with** ne pas concorder avec [*evidence, facts*].

variant *n* variante *f* (**of** de; **on** par rapport à).

variation *n* **1** (change) variation *f*, différence *f* (**in, of** de); **2** (new version) variante *f* (**of** de); (in music) variation *f* (**on** sur).

varied *adj* varié/-e.

variety *n* **1** (diversity, range) variété *f* (**in, of** de); **for a ~ of reasons** pour diverses raisons; **a ~ of sizes/colours** un grand choix de tailles/de coloris; **2** (type) type *m*; (of plant) variété *f*.

variety show *n* spectacle de variétés.

various *adj* **1** (different) différents/-es (*before n*); **2** (several) divers/-es.

varnish I *n* vernis *m*.
II *vtr* vernir [*woodwork*]; **to ~ one's nails** se vernir les ongles.

vary I *vtr* varier [*menu, programme*]; faire varier [*temperature*]; changer de [*method, pace, route*].
II *vi* varier (**with, according to** selon); **it varies from one town to another** cela varie d'une ville à l'autre.

varying *adj* variable.

vase *n* vase *m*; **flower ~** vase à fleurs.

vast *adj* **1** [*amount, sum, improvement, difference*] énorme; **the ~ majority** la très grande majorité; **2** [*room, area, plain*] vaste (*before n*), immense.

vat *n* cuve *f*; **beer/wine ~** cuve à bière/vin.

VAT *n* (GB) (*abbr* = **value-added tax**) TVA *f*, taxe *f* à la valeur ajoutée.

Vatican *pr n* Vatican *m*; **~ City** cité *f* du Vatican.

vault I *n* **1** (roof) voûte *f*; **2** (also **~s**) (of house, for wine) cave *f*; (of bank) chambre *f* forte; (for safe-deposit boxes) salle *f* des coffres.
II *vtr* sauter par-dessus [*fence, bar*].
III *vi* sauter (**over** par-dessus).

VCR *n* (*abbr* = **video cassette recorder**) magnétoscope *m*.

VD ▶533 *n* (*abbr* = **venereal disease**) MST *f*.

VDU *n* (*abbr* = **visual display unit**) écran *m* de visualisation.

veal *n* veau *m*.

veer *vi* [*ship*] virer; (also **~ off**) [*person, road*] tourner; **to ~ off course** dévier de sa route.

vegan *n, adj* végétalien/-ienne (*m/f*).

vegetable I *n* légume *m*.
II *adj* [*soup, patch*] de légumes; [*fat, oil*] végétal/-e; **~ garden** potager *m*.

vegetarian *n, adj* végétarien/-ienne (*m/f*).

vegetate *vi* végéter.

vegetation *n* végétation *f*.

vehement *adj* véhément/-e.

vehicle *n* véhicule *m*.

veil I *n* (gen, figurative) voile *m*; (on hat) voilette *f*.
II *vtr* [*mist, cloud*] voiler.

vein *n* (blood vessel) veine *f*; (on insect wing, leaf) nervure *f*; (in cheese) veinure *f*; (of ore) veine *f*.

velocity *n* vélocité *f*.

velour(s) *n* velours *m*.

velvet *n* velours *m*; **crushed ~** velours frappé.

velvety *adj* velouté/-e.

vending machine *n* distributeur *m* automatique.

vendor ▶626 *n* **1** (in street, kiosk) marchand/-e *m/f*; **2** (as opposed to buyer) vendeur/-euse *m/f*.

veneer *n* placage *m*; (figurative) vernis *m*.

venereal disease ▶533 *n* maladie *f* vénérienne.

venetian blind *n* store *m* vénitien.

vengeance *n* vengeance *f*; **with a ~** de plus belle.

Venice ▶448 *pr n* Venise.

venison *n* (viande *f* de) chevreuil *m*.

venom *n* venim *m*.

venomous *adj* venimeux/-euse.

vent I *n* (outlet for gas, pressure) bouche *f*, conduit *m*; **air ~** bouche d'aération; **to give ~ to** décharger [*anger, feelings*].
II *vtr* décharger [*anger, frustration*] (**on** sur).

ventilate *vtr* aérer [*room*].

ventilator *n* (for patient) respirateur *m* artificiel.

ventriloquist ▶626 *n* ventriloque *mf*.

venture I *n* **1** (undertaking) aventure *f*, entreprise *f*; **a commercial ~** une entreprise commerciale; **2** (experiment) essai *m*.
II *vtr* hasarder [*opinion, suggestion*]; **to ~ to do** se risquer à faire.
III *vi* **to ~ into** s'aventurer dans [*place, street, city*]; **to ~ out(doors)** s'aventurer dehors.

venue *n* lieu *m*.

Venus *pr n* Vénus *f*.

verb *n* verbe *m*.

verbal *adj* verbal/-e.

verbatim I *adj* [*report, account*] textuel/-elle.
II *adv* [*describe, record*] mot pour mot.

verbose *adj* verbeux/-euse.

verdict *n* **1** (Law) verdict *m*; **a ~ of guilty/not guilty** un verdict positif/négatif; **2** (figurative) (opinion) verdict *m*; **well, what's the ~**°**?** eh bien, qu'est-ce que tu en penses?

verge *n* **1** (GB) (by road) accotement *m*, bas-côté *m*; **2** (brink) **on the ~ of** au bord de [*tears*]; au seuil de [*adolescence, death*]; **on the ~ of doing** sur le point de faire.
■ **verge on** friser [*panic, stupidity, contempt*].

verification *n* vérification *f*.

verify *vtr* vérifier.

vermicelli *n* vermicelles *mpl*.

vermilion ▶438 *n, adj* vermillon (*m*) *inv*.

vermin *n* **1** (rodents) animaux *mpl* nuisibles; **2** (lice, insects) vermine *f*.

verruca *n* verrue *f* plantaire.

versatile *adj* **1** [*person*] plein/-e de ressources, aux talents divers (*after n*); [*mind*] souple; **2** [*vehicle*] polyvalent/-e; [*equipment*] à usages multiples.

verse *n* **1** (poems) poésie *f*; **2** (form) vers *mpl*; **in ~** en vers; **3** (part of poem) strophe *f*; (of song) couplet *m*.

version *n* version *f* (**of** de).

versus *prep* contre.

vertebra *n* vertèbre *f*.

vertebrate *n* vertébré *m*.

vertical *adj* vertical/-e; **a ~ drop** un à-pic.

vertigo *n* vertige *m*; **to get ~** avoir le vertige.

verve *n* brio *m*, verve *f*.

very I *adj* **1** (actual) même (*after n*); **this ~ second** immédiatement; **2** (ideal) **the ~ person I need** exactement la personne qu'il me faut; **3** (ultimate) tout/-e; **from the ~ beginning** depuis le tout début; **at the ~ front** tout devant; **on the ~ edge** à l'extrême bord; **4** (mere) [*mention, thought, word*] seul/-e (*before n*); **the ~ idea!** quelle idée!
II *adv* **1** (extremely) très; **I'm ~ sorry** je suis vraiment désolé; **~ well** très bien; **that's all ~ well but who's going to pay for it?** c'est bien beau, tout ça, mais qui va payer?; **~ much** beaucoup; **I didn't eat ~ much** je n'ai pas mangé grand-chose; **2** (absolutely) **the ~ best/worst thing** de loin la meilleure/pire chose; **at the ~ latest** au plus tard; **at the ~ least** tout au moins; **the ~ next day** le lendemain même; **a car of your ~ own** ta propre voiture.

vessel *n* **1** (ship) vaisseau *m*; **2** (Anat) **blood ~** vaisseau sanguin; **3** (container) vase *m*.

vest *n* **1** (underwear) maillot *m* de corps; **2** (for sport, fashion) débardeur *m*; **3** (US) (waistcoat) gilet *m*.

vested interest *n* **to have a ~** être personnellement intéressé/-e (**in** dans).

vestige *n* vestige *m*.

vet I *n* **1** ▶626 (*abbr* = **veterinary surgeon**) vétérinaire *mf*; **2**○ (US Mil) ancien combattant *m*, vétéran *m*.
II *vtr* mener une enquête approfondie sur [*person*]; passer [qch] en revue [*plan*]; approuver [*publication*].

veteran I *n* vétéran *m*.
II *adj* [*sportsman, politician*] chevronné/-e.

veterinarian ▶626 *n* (US) vétérinaire *mf*.

veterinary surgeon ▶626 *n* vétérinaire *mf*.

veto I *n* **1** (practice) veto *m*; **2** (right) droit *m* de veto (**over, on** sur).
II *vtr* mettre or opposer son veto à.

vex *vtr* (annoy) contrarier; (worry) tracasser.

vexed *adj* **1** (annoyed) mécontent/-e (**with** de); **2** [*question, issue*] épineux/-euse.

VHF *n* (*abbr* = **very high frequency**) VHF.

via *prep* **1** (by way of) (on ticket, timetable) via; (other contexts) en passant par; **we came ~ Paris** nous sommes venus en passant par Paris; **2** (by means of) par.

viable *adj* [*company, government, farm*] viable; [*project, idea, plan*] réalisable, valable.

viaduct *n* viaduc *m*.

vibrant *adj* [*person, place, personality*] plein/-e de vie; [*colour*] éclatant/-e.

vibrate *vi* vibrer (**with** de).

vibration *n* vibration *f*.

vicar *n* pasteur *m*.

vicarage *n* presbytère *m*.

vicarious *adj* [*pleasure*] indirect/-e.

vice *n* **1** vice *m*; (amusing weakness) faiblesse *f*; **2** (also **vise** US) (tool) étau *m*.

vice-captain *n* capitaine *m* en second.

vice-chancellor ▶626 *n* président/-e *m/f* d'Université.

vice-president *n* vice-président/-e *m/f*.

vice squad *n* brigade *f* des mœurs.

vicinity *n* voisinage *m*; **in the (immediate) ~ of Oxford** à proximité (immédiate) d'Oxford.

vicious *adj* [*animal*] malfaisant/-e; [*speech, attack*] brutal/-e; [*rumour, person, lie*] malveillant/-e.

vicious circle *n* cercle *m* vicieux.

victim *n* victime *f*.

victimize *vtr* persécuter.

victor *n* vainqueur *m*.

Victorian *adj* victorien/-ienne.

victorious *adj* victorieux/-ieuse (**over** sur).

victory *n* victoire *f*.

video I *n* **1** (also **~ recorder**) magnétoscope *m*; **2** (also **~ cassette**) cassette *f* vidéo; **on ~** en vidéo; **3** (also **~ film**) vidéo *f*.
II *adj* vidéo (*inv*).
III *vtr* **1** (from TV) enregistrer [qch]; **2** (on camcorder) filmer [qch] en vidéo.

video camera *n* caméra *f* vidéo.

video shop (GB), **video store** (US) ▶626 *n* vidéoclub *m*.

videotape *n* bande *f* vidéo.

vie *vi* rivaliser (**with** avec; **for** pour; **to do** pour faire).

Vienna ▶448 *pr n* Vienne.

view I *n* **1** (gen) vue *f*; **in (full) ~ of sb** devant qn or sous les yeux de qn; **to disappear from ~** disparaître; **2** (personal opinion, attitude) avis *m*, opinion *f*; **point of ~** point *m* de vue; **in his ~** à son avis.
II *vtr* **1** (consider) considérer; (envisage) envisager; **2** (look at) voir [*scene, building, collection, exhibition*]; visiter [*house, castle*]; regarder [*programme*].
III **in view of** *phr* (considering) vu, étant donné.
IV **with a view to** *phr* **with a ~ to doing** en vue de faire, afin de faire.

viewer *n* **1** (of TV) téléspectateur/-trice *m/f*; **2** (of property) visiteur/-euse *m/f*; **3** (on camera) visionneuse *f*.

viewfinder *n* viseur *m*.

viewpoint *n* (all contexts) point *m* de vue.

vigil *n* (gen) veille *f*; (by sickbed) veillée *f*; (by demonstrators) manifestation *f* silencieuse.

vigilant *adj* vigilant/-e.

vigilante *n* membre *m* d'un groupe d'autodéfense.

vigorous *adj* vigoureux/-euse.

vigour (GB), **vigor** (US) *n* vigueur *f*.

vile *adj* [*smell*] infect/-e; [*weather*] abominable; [*place, colour*] horrible; [*mood*] exécrable.

villa *n* (in town) pavillon *m*; (in country, for holiday) villa *f*.

village *n* village *m*.

village green *n* terrain *m* communal.

village hall *n* salle *f* des fêtes.

villager *n* villageois/-e *m/f*.

villain *n* (in book, film) méchant *m*; (child) coquin/-e *m/f*; (criminal) bandit *m*.

vindicate *vtr* justifier.

vindictive *adj* vindicatif/-ive.

vindictiveness *n* esprit *m* de vengeance.

vine *n* **1** (grapevine) vigne *f*; **2** (climbing plant) plante *f* grimpante.

vinegar *n* vinaigre *m*.

vineyard *n* vignoble *m*.

vintage I *n* (wine) millésime *m*.
II *adj* **1** [*wine, champagne*] millésimé/-e; [*port*] vieux/vieille; **2** [*comedy*] classique.

vintage car *n* voiture *f* d'époque.

vinyl I *n* vinyle *m*.
II *adj* en vinyle; [*paint*] vinylique.

viola ▶586 *n* (violon *m*) alto *m*.

violate *vtr* **1** violer [*law, agreement, rights*]; **2** profaner [*sacred place*]; troubler [*peace*].

violation *n* violation *f*; **traffic ~** infraction *f* au code de la route.

violence *n* violence *f*.

violent *adj* **1** [*crime, behaviour, film, storm,*

emotion] violent/-e; **2** [*contrast*] brutal/-e; **3** [*colour*] criard/-e.

violet ▶438 I *n* **1** (flower) violette *f*; **2** (colour) violet *m*.
II *adj* violet/-ette.

violin ▶586 *n* violon *m*.

violinist ▶626 *n* violoniste *mf*.

VIP (*abbr* = **very important person**) I *n* personnalité *f* (en vue).
II *adj* [*area, lounge*] réservé/-e aux personnalités; **~ guest** hôte *mf* de marque; **to give sb (the) ~ treatment** recevoir qn en hôte de marque.

viper *n* vipère *f*.

virgin *n, adj* vierge (*f*).

Virgo *n* Vierge *f*.

virile *adj* viril/-e.

virtual *adj* **1** (gen) quasi-total/-e; **he was a ~ prisoner** il était pratiquement prisonnier; **2** (Comput) virtuel/-elle.

virtually *adv* pratiquement, presque; **it's ~ impossible** c'est quasiment○ impossible.

virtual reality *n* réalité *f* virtuelle.

virtue I *n* **1** (goodness) vertu *f*; **2** (advantage) avantage *m*.
II **by virtue of** *phr* en raison de.

virtuoso *n* virtuose *mf* (**of** de).

virtuous *adj* vertueux/-euse.

virus ▶533 *n* virus *m*.

visa *n* visa *m*; **tourist ~** visa de touriste.

vis-à-vis *prep* (in relation to) par rapport à; (concerning) en ce qui concerne.

visibility *n* visibilité *f*.

visible *adj* **1** (able to be seen) visible; **clearly ~** bien visible; **2** (concrete) [*improvement, sign*] évident/-e.

visibly *adv* [*moved, shocked*] manifestement.

vision *n* **1** (idea, mental picture, hallucination) vision *f*; **2** (ability to see) vue *f*; **3** (foresight) sagacité *f*.

visionary *n, adj* visionnaire (*mf*).

visit I *n* (gen) visite *f*; (stay) séjour *m*; **a state ~** une visite officielle; **to pay a ~ to sb, to pay sb a ~** aller voir qn; (more formal) rendre visite à qn.
II *vtr* **1 to ~ Paris** (see) visiter Paris; (stay) faire un séjour à Paris, aller passer quelques jours à Paris; **to ~ sb** (call) aller voir qn; (more formal) rendre visite à qn; (stay with) aller (passer quelques jours) chez qn; **2** (US) **to ~ with sb** aller voir qn.

visiting card *n* (US) carte *f* de visite.

visiting hours *n pl* heures *fpl* de visite.

visitor *n* **1** (caller) invité/-e *m/f*; **2** (tourist) visiteur/-euse *m/f*.

visitors' book *n* (in exhibition) livre *m* d'or; (in hotel) registre *m*.

visor *n* visière *f*.

vista *n* panorama *m*; (figurative) perspective *f*.

visual *adj* visuel/-elle.

visual aid *n* support *m* visuel.

visual arts *n pl* arts *mpl* plastiques.

visualize *vtr* **1** (picture) s'imaginer; **2** (envisage) envisager.

vital *adj* **1** (essential) (gen) primordial/-e; [*match, point, support, factor*] décisif/-ive; [*service, help*] indispensable; [*treatment, organ, force*] vital/-e; **of ~ importance** d'une importance capitale; **2** [*person*] plein/-e de vie.

vitality *n* vitalité *f*.

vitally *adv* [*important*] extrêmement; [*needed*] absolument.

vital statistics *n* (of woman) mensurations *fpl*.

vitamin *n* vitamine *f*.

viva I *n* oral *m*.
II *excl* vive!

vivacious *adj* plein/-e de vivacité.

vivid *adj* **1** (bright) [*colour, light*] vif/vive; **2** (graphic) [*imagination*] vif/vive; [*memory, picture*] (très) net/nette; [*dream, impression, description*] frappant/-e.

vividly *adv* [*describe, illustrate*] de façon très vivante; [*remember, recall*] très bien.

vivisection *n* vivisection *f*.

vixen *n* **1** (fox) renarde *f*; **2** (woman) mégère *f*.

viz *adv* (*abbr* = **videlicet**) à savoir.

V-neck *n* **1** (neck) encolure *f* en V; **2** (sweater) pull *m* en V.

vocabulary *n* vocabulaire *m*.

vocal *adj* **1** (concerning speech) vocal/-e; **2** (vociferous) [*person*] qui se fait entendre.

vocals *n pl* chant *m*; **to do the backing ~** faire les chœurs.

vocation *n* vocation *f*.

vocational *adj* professionnel/-elle.

vociferous *adj* [*person, protest*] véhément/-e.

vogue *n* vogue *f* (**for** de).

voice I *n* voix *f*; **in a loud ~** à haute voix; **in a low ~** à voix basse; **in a cross ~** d'une voix irritée; **to have lost one's ~** (when ill) être aphone; **at the top of one's ~** à tue-tête.
II *vtr* exprimer [*concern, grievance*].

voice-over *n* voix-off *f*.

void I *n* vide *m*; **to fill the ~** combler le vide.
II *adj* **1** (Law) [*contract, agreement*] nul/nulle; [*cheque*] annulé/-e; **2** (empty) vide; **~ of** dépourvu/-e de.

volatile *adj* [*situation*] explosif/-ive; [*person*] lunatique; [*market, exchange rate*] instable.

volcano *n* volcan *m*.

volley I *n* **1** (in tennis) volée *f*; **2** (of gunfire) salve *f* (**of** de); **3** (series) **a ~ of** un feu roulant de [*questions*]; une bordée de [*insults, oaths*].
II *vtr* (in tennis) prendre [qch] de volée [*ball*].
III *vi* (in tennis) jouer à la volée.

volleyball ▶504 *n* volley(-ball) *m*.

volt *n* volt *m*.

voltage *n* tension *f*.

volume *n* **1** (gen) volume *m* (**of** de); (of container) capacité *f*; **2** (book) volume *m*; (part of set) tome *m*.

voluntarily *adv* de plein gré, volontairement.

voluntary *adj* **1** (gen) volontaire; **2** (unpaid) bénévole.

volunteer I *n* **1** (offering to do sth) volontaire *mf*; **2** (unpaid worker) bénévole *mf*.
II *vtr* **1** (offer) offrir; **to ~ to do** offrir de faire, se porter volontaire pour faire; **2** fournir [qch] spontanément [*information*].
III *vi* **1** se porter volontaire (**for** pour); **2** (as soldier) s'engager comme volontaire.

voluptuous *adj* voluptueux/-euse.

vomit I *n* vomi *m*.
II *vtr*, *vi* vomir.

voodoo *n* vaudou *m*.

voracious *adj* vorace.

vortex *n* tourbillon *m*.

vote I *n* **1** (gen) vote *m*; **2** (franchise) **the ~** le droit de vote.
II *vtr* **1** (gen) voter; **to ~ sb into/out of office** élire/ne pas réélire qn; **2**° (propose) proposer.
III *vi* voter (**on** sur; **for sb** pour qn; **against** contre); **let's ~ on it** mettons-le aux voix; **to ~ to strike** voter la grève.

vote of confidence *n* vote *m* de confiance (**in** en).

vote of thanks *n* discours *m* de remerciement.

voter *n* électeur/-trice *m/f*.

voting *n* scrutin *m*.

vouch *v* ■ **vouch for 1** (informally) répondre de [*person*]; témoigner de [*fact*]; **2** (officially) se porter garant de.

voucher *n* bon *m*.

vow I *n* (religious) vœu *m*; (of honour) serment *m*; **marriage** or **wedding ~s** promesses *fpl* du mariage.
II *vtr* faire vœu de [*love, revenge, allegiance*]; **to ~ to do** jurer de faire.

vowel *n* voyelle *f*.

voyage *n* voyage *m*.

V-sign *n* **1** (victory sign) V *m* de la victoire; **2** (GB) (offensive gesture) geste *m* obscène.

vulgar *adj* **1** (tasteless) [*furniture, clothes*] de mauvais goût; [*taste*] douteux/-euse; [*person*] vulgaire; **2** (rude) grossier/-ière.

vulnerable *adj* vulnérable (**to** à).

vulture *n* vautour *m*.

Ww

w, **W** *n* w, W *m*.
wad *n* **1** (of banknotes, paper) liasse *f* (**of** de); **2** (of cotton wool, padding) boule *f* (**of** de).
waddle *vi* [*duck, person*] se dandiner.
wade *vi* **1** (in water) **to ~ into the water** entrer dans l'eau; **to ~ ashore** marcher dans l'eau jusqu'au rivage; **to ~ across** traverser à gué; **2 he was wading through 'War and Peace'** il lisait 'Guerre et Paix', mais ça avançait lentement.
waders *n pl* cuissardes *fpl*.
wafer *n* (Culin) gaufrette *f*.
wafer-thin *adj* [*slice*] ultrafin/-e.
waffle I *n* **1** (Culin) gaufre *f*; **2**○ (empty words) verbiage *m*.
II○ *vi* (also **~ on**) (speaking) bavasser○; (writing) faire du remplissage.
waft *vi* **to ~ towards** flotter vers; **to ~ up** monter.
wag I *vtr* remuer [*tail*].
II *vi* [*tail*] remuer, frétiller; **tongues will ~** ça va faire jaser.
wage I *n* (also **~s** *pl*) salaire *m*.
II *vtr* mener [*campaign*]; **to ~ (a) war against sb/sth** faire la guerre contre qn/qch.
wage earner *n* **1** (person earning a wage) salarié/-e *m/f* (hebdomadaire); **2** (breadwinner) soutien *m* de famille.
wage packet *n* **1** (envelope) enveloppe *f* de paie; **2** (money) paie *f*.
wager *n* pari *m*; **to make** or **lay a ~** parier, faire un pari.
waggon (GB), **wagon** *n* **1** (horse-drawn) chariot *m*; **2** (GB) (on rail) wagon *m* (de marchandises).
IDIOMS **to be on the ~**○ être au régime sec.
wail I *n* (of person) gémissement *m*; (of siren) hurlement *m*; (of musical instrument) son *m* plaintif.
II *vi* [*person, wind*] gémir; [*siren*] hurler; [*music*] pleurer.
waist *n* taille *f*.
waistband *n* ceinture *f*.
waistcoat *n* (GB) gilet *m*.
waistline *n* taille *f*.
wait I *n* attente *f*; **an hour's ~** une heure d'attente.
II *vtr* **1** attendre [*one's turn*]; **2** (US) **to ~ table** servir à table.
III *vi* attendre; **to keep sb ~ing** faire attendre qn; **to ~ for sb/sth** attendre qn/qch; **to ~ for sb/sth to do** attendre que qn/qch fasse; **to ~ to do** attendre de faire; **I can't ~ to do** j'ai hâte de faire; (stronger) je meurs d'impatience de faire; **you'll have to ~ and see** attends et tu verras.
IDIOMS **to lie in ~ for sb** guetter qn.
■ **wait around**, **wait about** (GB) attendre.
■ **wait behind** attendre un peu; **to ~ behind for sb** attendre qn.
■ **wait on** servir [*person*]; **to ~ on sb hand and foot** être aux petits soins pour qn.
■ **wait up 1** (stay awake) veiller; **to ~ up for sb** veiller jusqu'au retour de qn; **2** (US) **~ up!** attends!
waiter ▶**626** *n* serveur *m*; **'~!'** 'monsieur!'
waiting game *n* **to play a ~** attendre son heure; (in politics) faire de l'attentisme.
waiting list *n* liste *f* d'attente.
waiting room *n* salle *f* d'attente.
waitress ▶**626** *n* serveuse *f*; **'~!'** 'madame!', 'mademoiselle!'
waive *vtr* déroger à [*rule*]; renoncer à [*claim, right*]; supprimer [*fee*].
wake I *vtr* réveiller; **to ~ sb from a dream** tirer qn d'un rêve.
II *vi* se réveiller.
■ **wake up**: ¶ **~ up** se réveiller; **~ up!** réveille-toi!; (to reality) ouvre les yeux!; ¶ **~ [sb] up** réveiller.
wake-up call *n* réveil *m* téléphoné.
Wales *pr n* pays *m* de Galles.
walk I *n* **1** promenade *f*; (shorter) tour *m*; (hike) randonnée *f*; **it's about ten minutes' ~** c'est à environ dix minutes à pied; **to go for a ~** (aller) faire une promenade; **2** (gait) démarche *f*; **3** (pace) pas *m*; **4** (path) allée *f*; **5** (Sport) épreuve *f* de marche.
II *vtr* **1** faire [qch] à pied [*distance, path, road*]; **2** conduire [*horse*]; promener [*dog*]; **to ~ sb home** raccompagner qn chez lui/elle.
III *vi* (in general) marcher; (for pleasure) se promener; (not run) aller au pas; (not ride or drive) aller à pied; **it's not very far, let's ~** ce n'est pas très loin, allons-y à pied; **he ~ed up/down the road** il a remonté/descendu la rue (à pied).

■ **Note** *à pied* is often omitted with movement verbs if we already know that the person is on foot. If it is surprising or ambiguous, *à pied* should be included.

■ **walk around**: ¶ **~ around** se promener; (aimlessly) traîner; ¶ **~ around [sth]** (to and fro) faire un tour dans; (make circuit of) faire le tour de.
■ **walk away 1** s'éloigner (**from** de); **2** (refuse to face) **to ~ away from** se désintéresser de [*problem*]; **3** (survive unscathed) sortir indemne (**from** de); **4** (win easily) **to ~ away with** gagner [qch] haut la main [*game, tournament*]; remporter [qch] haut la main [*election*]; décrocher [*prize, honour*].
■ **walk back** revenir sur ses pas (**to** jusqu'à); **we ~ed back (home)** nous sommes rentrés à pied.
■ **walk in** entrer; **I'd just ~ed in when** je venais à peine d'entrer quand.

■ **walk into**: **~ into [sth] 1** (enter) entrer dans; **2** tomber dans [*trap*]; se fourrer dans [*tricky situation*]; **3** (bump into) rentrer dans [*door, person*].
■ **walk off**: ¶ **~ off 1** partir brusquement; **2**○ **to ~ off with sth** (innocently) partir avec qch; (as theft) filer○ avec qch; ¶ **~ [sth] off** se promener pour faire passer [*hangover, large meal*].
■ **walk out 1** sortir (**of** de); **2** (desert) partir; **to ~ out on** laisser tomber○ [*lover*]; rompre [*contract, undertaking*]; **3** (as protest) partir en signe de protestation; (on strike) se mettre en grève.
■ **walk over**: ¶ **~ over** s'approcher (**to** de); ¶ **~ over [sb]**○ **1** (defeat) battre [qn] à plates coutures; **2** (humiliate) marcher sur les pieds de.
■ **walk round**: ¶ **~ round** faire le tour; ¶ **~ round [sth]** (round edge of) faire le tour de; (visit) visiter [*town*].
■ **walk through**: traverser [*house, forest*]; passer [*door*]; parcourir [*streets*]; marcher dans [*snow, mud, grass*].
■ **walk up**: **to ~ up to** s'approcher de.

walkie-talkie *n* talkie-walkie *m*.

walking *n* (for pleasure) promenades *fpl* à pied; (for exercise) marche *f* à pied.

walking boots *n pl* chaussures *fpl* de marche.

walking distance *n* **to be within ~** être à quelques minutes de marche (**of** de).

walking stick *n* canne *f*.

walkman® *n* walkman® *m*, baladeur *m*.

walkout *n* (strike) grève *f* surprise.

walkover *n* victoire *f* facile (**for** pour).

walkway *n* allée *f*.

wall *n* **1** (construction) mur *m*; **2** (of cave, tunnel) paroi *f*; **3** (Anat) paroi *f*.

wall chart *n* affiche *f*.

walled *adj* [*city*] fortifié/-e; [*garden*] clos/-e.

wallet *n* (for notes) portefeuille *m*; (for documents) porte-documents *m inv*.

wallflower *n* giroflée *f* jaune.
IDIOMS **to be a ~** faire tapisserie.

wallow *vi* **to ~ in** se vautrer dans [*mud, luxury*]; se complaire dans [*self-pity, nostalgia*].

wallpaper I *n* papier *m* peint.
II *vtr* tapisser [*room*].

walnut *n* **1** (nut) noix *f*; **2** (tree, wood) noyer *m*.

walrus *n* morse *m*.

waltz I *n* valse *f*.
II *vi* danser la valse (**with** avec).

wand *n* baguette *f*.

wander I *vtr* parcourir; **to ~ the streets** traîner dans la rue.
II *vi* **1** (walk, stroll) se promener; **to ~ around town** se balader en ville; **2** (stray) errer; **to ~ away** or **off** s'éloigner (**from** de); **3** [*eyes, hands*] errer (**over** sur); [*attention*] se relâcher; **her mind is ~ing** elle divague.
■ **wander about**, **wander around** (stroll) se balader; (when lost) errer.

wane *vi* [*moon*] décroître; [*enthusiasm, popularity*] diminuer.

wangle○ **I** *n* combine○ *f*.
II *vtr* soutirer [*money, promise*]; se débrouiller pour avoir [*leave*]; **to ~ sth for sb** se débrouiller pour faire avoir qch à qn.

want I *n* **1** (need) besoin *m*; **2** (lack) défaut *m*; **for ~ of** à défaut or faute de; **it's not for ~ of trying** ce n'est pas faute d'avoir essayé.
II *vtr* **1** (desire) vouloir; **I ~** (as general statement) je veux; (would like) je voudrais; (am seeking) je souhaite; **I don't ~ to** je n'en ai pas envie; (flat refusal) je ne veux pas; **to ~ to do** vouloir faire; **to ~ sb to do** vouloir que qn fasse; **2**○ (need) avoir besoin de; **3** (require presence of) demander; **if anyone ~s me** si quelqu'un me demande; **you're ~ed on the phone** on vous demande au téléphone; **to be ~ed by the police** être recherché/-e par la police.
III *vi* **to ~ for** manquer de.

wanting *adj* **to be ~** faire défaut; **to be ~ in** manquer de; **to be found ~** s'avérer décevant/-e.

wanton *adj* [*cruelty, damage, waste*] gratuit/-e; [*disregard*] délibéré/-e.

war *n* guerre *f*; **in the ~** à la guerre; **to wage ~ on** faire la guerre contre; (figurative) mener une lutte contre.

ward *n* **1** (in hospital) (unit) service *m*; (room) unité *f*; (separate building) pavillon *m*; **maternity ~** service de maternité; **hospital ~** salle *f* d'hôpital; **2** (electoral) circonscription *f* électorale; **3** (also **~ of court**) (Law) pupille *m*.
■ **ward off** chasser [*evil, predator*]; faire taire [*accusations, criticism*]; écarter [*attack, threat*]; éviter [*disaster*].

warden ▶626 *n* (of institution, college) directeur/-trice *m/f*; (of park, estate) gardien/-ienne *m/f*.

warder *n* (GB) gardien/-ienne *m/f*.

wardrobe *n* **1** (furniture) armoire *f*; **2** (set of clothes) garde-robe *f*; (for theatre) costumes *mpl*.

warehouse *n* entrepôt *m*.

wares *n pl* marchandise *f*, marchandises *fpl*.

warfare *n* guerre *f*.

warhead *n* ogive *f*.

warlike *adj* [*people*] guerrier/-ière; [*mood, words*] belliqueux/-euse.

warm I *adj* **1** [*place, food, temperature, water, day, clothing*] chaud/-e; **to be ~** [*person*] avoir chaud; **it's ~** il fait bon or chaud; **2** (affectionate) [*person, atmosphere, welcome*] chaleureux/-euse; [*admiration, support*] enthousiaste; **3** [*colour*] chaud/-e.
II *vtr* chauffer [*plate, food, water*]; réchauffer [*implement, bed*]; **to ~ oneself** se réchauffer; **to ~ one's hands** se réchauffer les mains.
III *vi* [*food, liquid, object*] chauffer.
■ **warm to, warm towards** se prendre de sympathie pour [*person*]; se faire à [*idea*]; prendre goût à [*task*].
■ **warm up**: ¶ **~ up 1** [*person, room, house*] se réchauffer; [*food, liquid, engine*] chauffer; **2** (become lively) s'animer; **3** [*athlete*] s'échauffer; [*singer*] s'échauffer la voix; [*orchestra, musi-*

cian] se préparer; ¶ **~ [sth] up** réchauffer [*room, bed, person*]; faire réchauffer [*food*].

warm-hearted *adj* chaleureux/-euse.

warmly *adv* [*smile, thank, recommend*] chaleureusement; [*speak, praise*] avec enthousiasme.

warmth *n* chaleur *f*.

warm-up *n* échauffement *m*.

warn I *vtr* avertir, prévenir; **to ~ sb about** or **against sth** mettre qn en garde contre qch; **to ~ sb to do** conseiller or dire à qn de faire; **to ~ sb not to do** déconseiller à qn de faire.
II *vi* **to ~ of sth** annoncer qch.

warning *n* avertissement *m*; (by an authority) avis *m*; (by light, siren) alerte *f*; **to give sb ~** avertir qn (**of** de); **advance ~** préavis *m*; **health ~** mise en garde; **flood ~** avis de crue.

warning light *n* voyant *m* lumineux.

warning shot *n* coup *m* de semonce.

warning sign *n* (on road) panneau *m* d'avertissement; (of illness, stress) signe *m* annonciateur.

warp I *vtr* **1** déformer [*metal, wood, record*]; **2** pervertir [*mind, personality*].
II *vi* se déformer.

warped *adj* **1** [*metal, wood, record*] déformé/-e; **2** [*mind, humour*] tordu/-e; [*personality, sexuality*] perverti/-e; [*account, view*] faussé/-e.

warrant I *n* (Law) mandat *m*.
II *vtr* justifier [*action, measure*].

warranty *n* garantie *f*.

warren *n* **1** (rabbits') garenne *f*; **2** (building, maze of streets) labyrinthe *m*.

warring *adj* en conflit.

Warsaw ▶ 448 *pr n* Varsovie.

warship *n* navire *m* de guerre.

wart *n* verrue *f*.

wartime *n* **in ~** en temps de guerre.

war-torn *adj* déchiré/-e par la guerre.

wary *adj* **1** (cautious) prudent/-e; **to be ~** montrer de la circonspection (**of** vis-à-vis de); **to be ~ of doing** hésiter à faire; **2** (distrustful) méfiant/-e; **to be ~** se méfier (**of** de).

wash I *n* **1** (clean) **to have a ~** se laver; **to give [sth] a ~** laver [*window, floor*]; nettoyer [*object*]; lessiver [*paintwork, walls*]; **to give [sb] a ~** débarbouiller [*child*]; **2** (laundry process) lavage *m*; **weekly ~** lessive *f* hebdomadaire; **in the ~** (about to be cleaned) au sale; (being cleaned) au lavage; **3** (from boat) remous *m*.
II *vtr* laver [*person, clothes, floor*]; nettoyer [*object, wound*]; lessiver [*paintwork, surface*]; **to get ~ed** se laver; **to ~ one's hands/face** se laver les mains/le visage; **to ~ the dishes** faire la vaisselle.
III *vi* **1** [*person*] se laver, faire sa toilette; [*animal*] faire sa toilette; **2** (do laundry) faire la lessive.
■ **wash away** emporter [*structure, debris, person*].
■ **wash up**: ¶ **~ up 1** (GB) (do dishes) faire la vaisselle; **2** (US) (clean oneself) faire un brin de toilette°; ¶ **~ [sth] up 1** (clean) laver [*plate*]; nettoyer [*pan*]; **2** [*tide*] rejeter [*debris*].

washable *adj* lavable.

washbasin *n* lavabo *m*.

washbowl *n* (US) lavabo *m*.

washcloth *n* (US) lavette *f*.

washed-out *adj* **1** (faded) délavé/-e; **2** (tired) épuisé/-e, lessivé/-e°.

washer *n* (Tech) (as seal) joint *m*.

washer-dryer *n* lave-linge/sèche-linge *m inv*.

washing *n* (laundry) (to be cleaned) linge *m* sale; (when clean) linge *m*; **to do the ~** faire la lessive.

washing line *n* corde *f* à linge.

washing machine *n* machine *f* à laver.

washing powder *n* (GB) lessive *f* (en poudre).

washing-up *n* (GB) vaisselle *f*.

washing-up liquid *n* (GB) liquide *m* (à) vaisselle.

washout *n* **1**° (project, system) fiasco *m*; **2**° (person) nullité° *f*; **3** (game, camp) fiasco *m* dû à la pluie.

washroom *n* toilettes *fpl*.

wash-stand *n* (US) lavabo *m*.

wasp *n* guêpe *f*.

waspish *adj* acerbe.

wastage *n* **1** (of money, resources, talent) gaspillage *m*; (of heat, energy) déperdition *f*; **2** (also **natural ~**) élimination *f* naturelle.

waste I *n* **1** (of food, money, energy) gaspillage *m* (**of** de); (of time) perte *f* (**of** de); **a ~ of effort** un effort inutile; **that car is such a ~ of money!** cette voiture, c'est vraiment de l'argent jeté par les fenêtres!; **to let sth go to ~** gaspiller qch; **2** (detritus) (also **wastes** US) déchets *mpl* (**from** de).
II **wastes** *n pl* **1** (wilderness) étendues *fpl* sauvages; **2** (US) = **waste I 2**.
III *adj* **1** [*heat, energy*] gaspillé/-e; [*water*] usé/-e; **~ materials** déchets *mpl*; **2** [*land*] inculte; **3 to lay ~ to** dévaster.
IV *vtr* **1** (squander) gaspiller [*food, resources, energy, money, talents*]; perdre [*time, opportunity*]; user [*strength*]; **2** (make thinner) décharner; (make weaker) atrophier.

wastebasket *n* corbeille *f* à papier.

wastebin *n* (GB) (for paper) corbeille *f* à papier; (for rubbish) poubelle *f*.

wasted *adj* **1** [*effort, life, vote*] inutile; [*energy, years*] gaspillé/-e; **2** (fleshless) [*body, limb*] décharné/-e; (weak) [*body, limb*] atrophié/-e.

waste disposal *n* traitement *m* des déchets.

waste disposal unit *n* (GB) broyeur *m* d'ordures.

wasteful *adj* [*product, machine*] qui consomme beaucoup; [*method, process*] peu économique; [*person*] gaspilleur/-euse.

wasteland *n* (urban) terrain *m* vague; (rural) terre *f* à l'abandon.

wastepaper *n* papier *m* or papiers *mpl* à jeter.

wastepaper basket, **wastepaper bin** (GB) *n* corbeille *f* à papier.

waste pipe *n* tuyau *m* de vidange.

wasting *adj* [*disease*] débilitant/-e.

watch I *n* **1** (timepiece) montre *f*; **2** (surveillance) surveillance *f* (**on** sur); **to keep ~** monter la garde; **to keep (a) ~ on sb/sth** surveiller qn/qch.
II *vtr* **1** (look at) regarder; (observe) observer; **2** (monitor) suivre [*career, development*]; surveiller [*situation*]; **3** (keep under surveillance) surveiller [*person, movements*]; **4** (pay attention to) faire attention à [*obstacle, dangerous object, money*]; surveiller [*language, manners, weight*]; **to ~ one's step** (figurative) faire attention; **5** (look after) garder [*person, property*].
IV *vi* regarder (**from** de).
■ **watch for** guetter [*person, chance*]; surveiller l'apparition de [*symptom*].
■ **watch out** (be careful) faire attention (**for** à); (keep watch) guetter; **~ out!** attention!
■ **watch over** veiller sur [*person*]; veiller à [*interests, rights, welfare*].
watchband *n* (US) bracelet *m* de montre.
watchdog *n* **1** (dog) chien *m* de garde; **2** (organization) organisme *m* de surveillance.
watchmaker ▶ 626 *n* horloger/-ère *m/f*.
watchman ▶ 626 *n* (guard) gardien *m*.
watch strap *n* bracelet *m* de montre.
water I *n* eau *f*.
II *vtr* arroser [*lawn, plant*]; irriguer [*crop, field*]; abreuver [*livestock*].
III *vi* **the smell of cooking makes my mouth ~** l'odeur de cuisine me fait venir l'eau à la bouche; **the smoke made her eyes ~** la fumée l'a fait pleurer.
■ **water down 1** couper [qch] d'eau [*beer, wine*]; diluer [*syrup*]; **2** atténuer [*effect, plans, policy*]; édulcorer [*description, story*].
water bed *n* matelas *m* d'eau.
water bird *n* oiseau *m* aquatique.
water bottle *n* (for cyclist) bidon *m*.
water cannon *n* canon *m* à eau.
watercolour (GB), **watercolor** (US) *n* (paint) peinture *f* pour aquarelle; (painting) aquarelle *f*.
watercress *n* cresson *m* (de fontaine).
waterfall *n* cascade *f*.
water filter *n* filtre *m* à eau.
waterfront *n* (on harbour) front *m* de mer; (by lakeside, riverside) bord *m* de l'eau.
water-heater *n* chauffe-eau *m inv*.
watering can *n* arrosoir *m*.
water jump *n* rivière *f*.
water level *n* niveau *m* d'eau.
water lily *n* nénuphar *m*.
waterlogged *adj* [*ground, pitch*] détrempé/-e.
water main *n* canalisation *f* d'eau.
watermark *n* (of sea) laisse *f*; (of river) ligne *f* des hautes eaux; (on paper) filigrane *m*.
watermelon *n* pastèque *f*.
waterproof *adj* [*coat*] imperméable; [*make-up*] résistant/-e à l'eau.
waterproofs *n pl* vêtements *mpl* imperméables.
water-resistant *adj* qui résiste à l'eau.
water-ski I *n* ski *m* nautique.
II *vi* faire du ski nautique.
water-skiing ▶ 504 *n* ski *m* nautique.
water slide *n* toboggan *m* de piscine.
water sport *n* sport *m* nautique.
water supply *n* (in an area) approvisionnement *m* en eau; (to a building) alimentation *f* en eau.
watertight *adj* **1** [*container, seal*] étanche; **2** [*argument, case*] incontestable; [*alibi*] irréfutable.
water tower *n* château *m* d'eau.
water trough *n* abreuvoir *m*.
waterway *n* voie *f* navigable.
water wings *n pl* bracelets *mpl* de natation.
watery *adj* **1** [*sauce, paint*] trop liquide; [*coffee*] trop léger/-ère; **2** [*colour, smile*] pâle.
watt *n* watt *m*.
wave I *n* **1** (of hand) signe *m* (de la main); **2** (of water) vague *f*; **to make ~s** [*wind*] faire des vagues; (cause a stir) faire du bruit; (cause trouble) créer des histoires°; **3** (outbreak, surge) vague *f* (**of** de); **4** (of light, radio) onde *f*; **5** (in hair) cran *m*.
II *vtr* **1** agiter [*flag, ticket, banknote*]; brandir [*umbrella, stick, gun*]; **2 to ~ goodbye to sb** faire au revoir de la main à qn.
III *vi* **1** (with hand) **to ~ to** or **at sb** saluer qn de la main; **2** [*branches*] être agité/-e par le vent; [*corn*] ondoyer; [*flag*] flotter au vent.
wave band *n* bande *f* de fréquence.
wavelength *n* (on radio) longueur *f* d'onde.
IDIOMS **to be on the same ~ as sb** être sur la même longueur d'onde que qn.
waver *vi* **1** (weaken) [*person*] vaciller; [*courage, love*] faiblir; [*voice*] trembler; **2** (hesitate) hésiter (**between** entre; **over** sur).
wavy *adj* [*hair, line*] ondulé/-e.
wax I *n* (for candle, seal) cire *f*; (for skis) fart *m*; (in ear) cérumen *m*.
II *vtr* **1** cirer [*floor*]; lustrer [*car*]; farter [*ski*]; **2** (depilate) épiler [qch] à la cire [*legs*].
III *vi* [*moon*] croître.
wax paper *n* papier *m* paraffin.
waxwork *n* personnage *m* en cire.
waxworks *n* musée *m* de cire.
waxy *adj* cireux/-euse.
way I *n* **1** (route, road) chemin *m* (**from** de; **to** à); **the quickest ~ to town** le chemin le plus court pour aller en ville; **to ask the ~ to the station** demander le chemin pour aller à la gare; **there is no ~ around the problem** il n'y a pas moyen de contourner le problème; **on the ~ back** sur le chemin du retour; **on the ~ back from the meeting** en revenant de la réunion; **the ~ in** l'entrée (**to** de); **the ~ out** la sortie (**of** de); **a ~ out of our difficulties** un moyen de nous sortir de nos difficultés; **the ~ up** la montée; **on the ~** en route; **to be out of sb's ~** [*place*] ne pas être sur le chemin de qn; **don't go out of your ~ to do** ne te donne pas de mal pour faire; **out of the ~** (isolated) isolé/-e; (unusual) extraordinaire; **by ~ of** (via) en passant par; **to make one's ~ towards** se diriger vers; **to make one's ~ along** avancer le long de; **to make one's**

own ~ there y aller par ses propres moyens; **2** (direction) direction *f*, sens *m*; **which ~ did he go?** dans quelle direction est-il parti?; **he went that ~** il est parti par là; **come this ~** suivez-moi, venez par ici; **'this ~ up'** 'haut'; **to look the other ~** (to see) regarder de l'autre côté; (to avoid seeing unpleasant thing) détourner les yeux; (to ignore wrongdoing) fermer les yeux; **the other ~ up** dans l'autre sens; **the right ~ up** dans le bon sens; **the wrong ~ up** à l'envers; **to turn sth the other ~ around** retourner qch; **I didn't ask her, it was the other ~ around** ce n'est pas moi qui le lui ai demandé, c'est l'inverse; **the wrong/right ~ around** dans le mauvais/bon sens; **3** (space in front, projected route) passage *m*; **to be in sb's ~** empêcher qn de passer; **to be in the ~** gêner le passage; **to get out of the ~** s'écarter (du chemin); **to get out of sb's ~** laisser passer qn; **to keep out of the ~** rester à l'écart; **to keep out of sb's ~** éviter qn; **to make ~** s'écarter; **to make ~ for sb/sth** faire place à qn/qch; **4** (distance) distance *f*; **it's a long ~** c'est loin (**to** jusqu'à); **to go all the ~ to China** aller jusqu'en Chine; **5** (manner) façon *f*, manière *f*; **do it this/that ~** fais-le comme ceci/cela; **to do another ~** faire autrement; **the French ~** à la française; **to write sth the right/wrong ~** écrire qch bien/mal; **try to see it my ~** mets-toi à ma place; **in his/her/its own ~** à sa façon; **to have a ~ with words** savoir manier les mots; **to have a ~ with children** savoir s'y prendre avec les enfants; **a ~ of doing** (method) une façon or manière de faire; (means) un moyen de faire; **I like the ~ he dresses** j'aime la façon dont il s'habille; **either ~, she's wrong** de toute façon, elle a tort; **one ~ or another** d'une façon ou d'une autre; **I don't care one ~ or the other** ça m'est égal; **you can't have it both ~s** on ne peut pas avoir le beurre et l'argent du beurre; **no ~**○! pas question○!; **6** (respect, aspect) sens *m*; **in a ~ it's sad** en un sens c'est triste; **in a ~ that's true** dans une certaine mesure c'est vrai; **in many ~s** à bien des égards; **in some ~s** à certains égards; **in no ~, not in any ~** aucunement; **7** (custom, manner) coutume *f*, manière *f*; **that's the modern ~** c'est ce qui se fait de nos jours; **I know all her little ~s** je connais toutes ses petites habitudes; **that's just his ~** il est comme ça; **it's the ~ of the world** c'est la vie; **8** (will, desire) **to get one's ~, to have one's own ~** faire à son idée; **she likes (to have) her own ~** elle aime n'en faire qu'à sa tête; **if I had my ~** si cela ne tenait qu'à moi; **have it your (own) ~** comme tu voudras.
II *adv* **we went ~ over budget** le budget a été largement dépassé; **to be ~ out** (in guess, estimate) être loin du compte; **that's ~ out of order** je trouve ça un peu fort.
III by the way *phr* en passant; **by the ~,...** à propos,...; **what time is it, by the ~?** quelle heure est-il, au fait?

waylay *vtr* [*attacker*] attaquer; [*beggar, friend*] arrêter, harponner○.

waymark *n* balise *f*.

wayside *n* IDIOMS **to fall by the ~** (stray morally) quitter le droit chemin; (fail, not stay the course) abandonner en cours de route; (be cancelled, fall through) tomber à l'eau.

we *pron* nous.

■ Note In standard French, *we* is translated by *nous* but in informal French, *on* is frequently used: *we're going to the cinema* = nous allons au cinéma *or more informally* on va au cinéma.
– *on* is also used in correct French to refer to a large, vaguely defined group: *we shouldn't lie to our children* = on ne devrait pas mentir à ses enfants.

~ saw her yesterday nous l'avons vue hier; **~ left at six** nous sommes partis à six heures; (informal) on est partis○ à six heures; **~ Scots like the sun** nous autres Écossais, nous aimons le soleil; **WE didn't say that** nous, nous n'avons pas dit cela; (informal) nous, on n'a pas dit ça○; **~ all make mistakes** tout le monde peut se tromper.

weak *adj* **1** [*person, animal, muscle, limb*] faible; [*health, ankle, heart, nerves*] fragile; [*stomach*] délicat/-e; [*intellect*] médiocre; [*chin*] fuyant/-e; **to be ~ with** or **from hunger** être affaibli/-e par la faim; **to grow** or **become ~(er)** [*person*] s'affaiblir; [*pulse, heartbeat*] faiblir; **2** [*beam, support*] peu solide; [*structure*] fragile; **3** (lacking authority, strength) [*government, team, pupil, president*] faible; [*parent, teacher*] (not firm) qui manque de fermeté; (poor) piètre (*before n*); [*plot*] mince; [*actor, protest, excuse, argument*] peu convaincant/-e; **~ link** or **spot** point *m* faible; **4** (faint) [*light, current, concentration, sound*] faible; [*tea, coffee*] léger/-ère; **5** [*economy, dollar*] faible (**against** par rapport à).

weaken I *vtr* **1** (through illness, damage) affaiblir [*person, heart, structure*]; diminuer [*resistance*]; rendre [qch] moins solide [*joint, bank, wall*]; **2** (undermine) nuire à l'autorité de [*government, president*]; affaiblir [*team, company, authority, defence*]; amoindrir [*argument, power*]; nuire à [*morale*]; **3** (dilute) diluer.
II *vi* **1** (physically) s'affaiblir; **2** [*government, resolve*] fléchir; [*support, alliance*] se relâcher; **3** (Econ) [*economy, currency*] être en baisse.

weakling *n* (physically) gringalet *m*; (morally) mauviette *f*.

weakness *n* **1** (weak point) point *m* faible; **2** (liking) faible *m* (**for** pour); **3** (physical, moral) faiblesse *f*; **4** (lack of authority) faiblesse *f*; (of evidence, position) fragilité *f*; **5** (of light, current, sound) faiblesse *f*; (of tea, solution) légèreté *f*; **6** (of economy, currency) faiblesse *f*.

weak-willed *adj* **to be ~** manquer de fermeté.

wealth *n* **1** (possessions) fortune *f*; **2** (state) richesse *f*; **3** (large amount) **a ~ of** une mine de [*information*]; une profusion de [*detail*]; énormément de [*experience, talent*].

wealthy *adj* riche.

wean *vtr* sevrer [*baby*]; **to ~ sb away from** or **off sth** détourner qn de qch.

weapon *n* arme *f*.

weaponry *n* matériel *m* de guerre.

wear I *n* **1** (clothing) **children's/sports ~** vêtements *mpl* pour enfants/de sport; **2** (use) **for everyday ~** de tous les jours; **for summer ~** pour l'été; **3** (damage) usure *f* (**on** de); **~ and tear** usure *f*; **to be the worse for ~** (drunk) être ivre; (tired) être épuisé/-e.
II *vtr* **1** (be dressed in) porter; **to ~ blue** s'habiller en bleu; **to ~ one's hair long/short** avoir les cheveux longs/courts; **2** (put on, use) mettre; **I haven't got a thing to ~** je n'ai rien à me mettre; **to ~ make-up** se maquiller; **3** (display) **he wore a puzzled frown** il fronçait les sourcils d'un air perplexe; **4** (damage by use) user; **to ~ a hole in** trouer [*garment, sheet*].
III *vi* [*carpet, shoes*] s'user; **my patience is ~ing thin** je commence à être à bout de patience.
■ **wear away** [*inscription*] s'effacer; [*tread, cliff, façade*] s'user.
■ **wear down**: ¶ **~ down** s'user; **to be worn down** être usé/-e; ¶ **~ [sth] down** user [*steps*]; saper [*resistance, resolve*]; ¶ **~ [sb] down** épuiser.
■ **wear off 1** [*drug, effect*] se dissiper; [*sensation*] passer; **2** (come off) s'effacer.
■ **wear out**: ¶ **~ out** s'user; ¶ **~ [sth] out** user; ¶ **~ [sb] out** épuiser.
■ **wear through** [*elbow, trousers*] se trouer; [*sole, metal, fabric*] se percer.

weariness *n* lassitude *f*.

weary I *adj* [*person, smile, sigh, voice*] las/lasse; [*eyes, limbs, mind*] fatigué/-e; **to grow ~** se lasser (**of** de; **of doing** de faire).
II *vi* se lasser (**of** de; **of doing** de faire).

weasel *n* **1** (Zool) belette *f*; **2** (sly person) sournois/-e *m/f*.

weather I *n* temps *m*; **what's the ~ like?** quel temps fait-il?; **the ~ here is hot** il fait chaud ici; **in hot/cold ~** quand il fait chaud/froid; **~ permitting** si le temps le permet; **in all ~s** par tous les temps.
II *vtr* survivre à [*crisis, upheaval*]; **to ~ the storm** (figurative) surmonter la crise.
IDIOMS **to be under the ~** ne pas se sentir bien.

weatherbeaten *adj* [*face*] hâlé/-e; [*rocks, landscape*] battu/-e par les vents.

weathercock *n* girouette *f*.

weather forecast *n* bulletin *m* météorologique.

weather forecaster ▶**626** *n* (on TV) présentateur/-trice *m/f* de la météo; (specialist) météorologue *mf*, météorologiste *mf*.

weatherproof *adj* [*garment, shoe*] imperméable; [*shelter, door*] étanche.

weave I *vtr* **1** tisser [*rug, fabric*]; **2** tresser [*cane, basket, wreath*].
II *vi* **to ~ in and out** se faufiler (**of** entre); **to ~ towards sth** (drunk) s'approcher en titubant de qch.

weaving *n* tissage *m*.

web *n* **1** (also **spider's ~**) toile *f* (d'araignée); **2** (network) **a ~ of** un réseau de [*ropes, lines*]; **a ~ of lies** un tissu de mensonges.

webbing *n* (material) sangles *fpl*.

web foot *n* patte *f* palmée.

wed *n* **the newly ~s** les jeunes mariés *mpl*.

wedding *n* mariage *m*; **a church ~** u[n] mariage religieux.

wedding anniversary *n* anniversaire *m* d[e] mariage.

wedding day *n* jour *m* des noces.

wedding dress, **wedding gown** *n* robe de mariée.

wedding reception *n* repas *m* de mariage.

wedding ring *n* alliance *f*.

wedge I *n* **1** (to insert in rock, wood) coin *m*; (t[o] hold sth in position) cale *f*; (in rock climbing) pito[n] *m*; **2** (of cake, pie, cheese) morceau *m*.
II *vtr* **1 to ~ sth in place** caler qch; **to ~ [a] door open** caler une porte pour la teni[r] ouverte; **2** (jam) **to ~ sth into** enfoncer qc[h] dans; **to be ~d between** être coincé/-e entre.
IDIOMS **that's the thin end of the ~** c'est l[e] commencement de la fin.

Wednesday ▶**456** *n* mercredi *m*.

wee○ *vi* (GB) faire pipi.

weed I *n* mauvaise herbe *f*; (in water) herbes *fp[l]* aquatiques.
II *vtr, vi* désherber.

weedkiller *n* désherbant *m*, herbicide *m*.

weedy○ *adj* [*person, build*] malingre; [*character, personality*] faible.

week ▶**708** *n* semaine *f*; **last/next ~** l[a] semaine dernière/prochaine; **this ~** cett[e] semaine; **the ~ before last** il y a deu[x] semaines; **the ~ after next** dans deu[x] semaines; **every other ~** tous les quinz[e] jours; **twice a ~** deux fois par semaine; **~ i[n] ~ out** toutes les semaines; **a ~ today/o[n] Monday** (GB), **today/Monday ~** aujourd'hu[i] lundi en huit; **a ~ yesterday** (GB), **a ~ fron[m] yesterday** (US) il y a eu huit jours or un[e] semaine hier; **in three ~s' time** dans troi[s] semaines; **the working** or **work** (US) **~** l[a] semaine de travail.

weekday *n* jour *m* de (la) semaine; **on ~s** e[n] semaine.

weekend *n* week-end *m*; **at the ~** (GB), **o[n] the ~** (US) pendant le week-end; **at ~s** (GB), **on ~s** (US) le week-end.

weekend bag *n* petit sac *m* de voyage.

weekend cottage *n* résidence *f* secondaire.

weekly I *n* (newspaper) journal *m* hebdoma[daire]; (magazine) (revue *f*) hebdomadaire *m*.
II *adj* hebdomadaire; **on a ~ basis** à l[a] semaine.
III *adv* [*pay*] à la semaine; [*meet, visit*] une foi[s] par semaine.

weep *vi* **1** (cry) pleurer (**over** sur); **2** (ooze[)] suinter.

weepy *adj* [*mood, film*] larmoyant/-e; **to fee[l] ~** avoir envie de pleurer.

weigh ▶**573** I *vtr* **1** (on scales) peser; **to ~ 10 kilos** peser 10 kilos; **how much** or **what d[o] you ~?** combien pèses-tu?; **to ~ oneself** s[e] peser; **2** (assess) évaluer [*arguments, advantages, options*]; peser [*consequences, risks, words*].

II *vi* **to ~ on sb** peser sur qn; **to ~ on sb's mind** préoccuper qn.
■ **weigh down**: ¶ **~ down on [sb/sth]** peser sur; ¶ **~ [sb/sth] down** surcharger [*vehicle, boat*]; faire plier [*branches*]; [*responsibility, debt*] accabler; **to be ~ed down with** crouler sous le poids de [*luggage*]; être accablé/-e de [*worry, guilt*].
■ **weigh in** [*boxer, wrestler*] se faire peser; [*jockey*] aller au pesage.
■ **weigh out** peser [*ingredients, quantity*].
■ **weigh up** évaluer [*prospects, situation*]; juger [*person*]; mettre [qch] en balance [*options, benefits, risks*].

weighing machine *n* (for people) balance *f*; (for luggage, freight) bascule *f*.

weight I *n* poids *m*; **to put on/lose ~** prendre/perdre du poids.
II *vtr* lester [*net, arrow*].
IDIOMS **not to carry much ~** ne pas peser lourd (**with** pour); **to be a ~ off one's mind** être un grand soulagement; **to pull one's ~** faire sa part de travail; **to throw one's ~ about** or **around** faire l'important/-e *m/f*.

weightlessness *n* (in space) apesanteur *f*.

weight-lifter *n* haltérophile *m*.

weight-lifting ▶504 *n* haltérophilie *f*.

weight training ▶504 *n* musculation *f* (en salle).

weighty *adj* **1** (serious) de grand poids; **2** (heavy) lourd/-e.

weir *n* barrage *m*.

weird *adj* (strange) bizarre; (eerie) mystérieux/-ieuse.

welcome I *n* accueil *m*; **to give sb a warm ~** faire un accueil chaleureux à qn.
II *adj* **1** bienvenu/-e; **to be ~** être le bienvenu/la bienvenue *m/f*; **to make sb ~** (on arrival) réserver un bon accueil à qn; **2 'thanks'—'you're ~'** 'merci'—'de rien'.
III *excl* (to respected guest) soyez le bienvenu/la bienvenue *m/f* chez nous!; (greeting friend) entre donc!; **~ back!**, **~ home!** je suis content que tu sois de retour!
IV *vtr* accueillir [*person*]; se réjouir de [*news, decision, change*]; être heureux/-euse de recevoir [*contribution*]; accueillir favorablement [*initiative, move*].

welcoming *adj* [*atmosphere, person*] accueillant/-e; [*ceremony, committee*] d'accueil.

weld *vtr* (also **~ together**) souder; **to ~ sth on** or **to** souder qch à.

welfare I *n* **1** (well-being) bien-être *m inv*; (interest) intérêt *m*; **2** (state assistance) assistance *f* sociale; (money) aide *f* sociale.
II *adj* [*system*] de protection sociale; (US) [*meal*] gratuit/-e.

welfare benefit *n* prestation *f* sociale.

welfare services *n* services *mpl* sociaux.

well[1] I *adj* bien; **to feel ~** se sentir bien; **are you ~?** vous allez bien?, tu vas bien?; **she's not ~ enough to travel** elle n'est pas en état de voyager; **to get ~** se rétablir; **that's all very ~, but** tout ça c'est bien beau, mais; **it would be just as ~ to check** il vaudrait mieux vérifier; **it would be as ~ for you not to get involved** tu ferais mieux de ne pas t'en mêler; **the flight was delayed, which was just as ~** le vol a été retardé, ce qui n'était pas plus mal.
II *adv* bien; **to do ~ at school** être bon/bonne élève; **mother and baby are both doing ~** la mère et l'enfant se portent bien; **the operation went ~** l'opération s'est bien passée; **~ done!** bravo!; **you may ~ be right** il se pourrait bien que tu aies raison; **we may as ~ go home** on ferait aussi bien de rentrer; **it was ~ worth waiting for** ça valait vraiment la peine d'attendre; **to wish sb ~** souhaiter beaucoup de chance à qn.
III *excl* **1** (expressing astonishment) eh bien!; (expressing indignation, disgust) ça alors!; (expressing disappointment) tant pis!; (qualifying statement) enfin; **~, you may be right** après tout, tu as peut-être raison; **~, that's too bad** c'est vraiment dommage; **~ then, what's the problem?** alors, quel est le problème?; **very ~ then** très bien.
IV **as well** *phr* aussi.
V **as well as** *phr* aussi bien que; **they have a house in the country as ~ as an apartment in Paris** ils ont à la fois une maison à la campagne et un appartement à Paris.
IDIOMS **to be ~ in with sb**○ être bien avec qn○; **to be ~ up in sth** s'y connaître en qch; **to leave ~ alone** (GB) or **~ enough alone** (US) ne pas s'en mêler.

well[2] *n* (sunk in ground) puits *m*; (pool) source *f*.

well-balanced *adj* équilibré/-e.

well-behaved *adj* [*child*] sage; [*dog*] bien dressé/-e.

well-being *n* bien-être *m inv*.

well-disposed *adj* **to be ~ towards** être bien disposé/-e envers [*person*]; être favcrable à [*regime, idea, policy*].

well done *adj* [*steak*] bien cuit/-e; [*task*] bien fait/-e.

well-educated *adj* (having a good education) instruit/-e; (cultured) cultivé/-e.

well-informed *adj* bien informé/-e (**about** sur); **he's very ~** il est très au courant de l'actualité.

wellington (boot) *n* (GB) botte *f* de caoutchouc.

well-kept *adj* [*house, garden, village*] bien entretenu/-e.

well-known *adj* [*person, place*] célèbre; **to be ~ to sb** être connu/-e de qn; **it is ~ that, it is a ~ fact that** il est bien connu que.

well-liked *adj* très apprécié/-e.

well-made *adj* bien fait/-e.

well-meaning *adj* [*person*] bien intentionné/-e; [*advice*] qui part d'une bonne intention.

well-meant *adj* **his offer was ~** sa proposition partait d'une bonne intention.

well-off I *n* **the ~** les gens *mpl* aisés; **the less ~** les plus défavorisés *mpl*.
II *adj* (wealthy) aisé/-e; **to be ~ for** avoir beaucoup de [*space, provisions*].

well-read *adj* cultivé/-e.

well-respected *adj* très respecté/-e.

well-rounded *adj* [*education, programme*] complet/-ète; [*individual*] qui a reçu une éducation complète.

well-thought-out *adj* bien élaboré/-e.

well-to-do *adj* aisé/-e.

well-wisher *n* personne *f* qui veut témoigner sa sympathie.

well-worn *adj* [*carpet, garment*] élimé/-e; [*steps*] usé/-e; [*joke*] rebattu/-e.

Welsh ▶553 I *n* **1** (people) **the ~** les Gallois *mpl*; **2** (language) gallois *m*.
II *adj* gallois/-e.

welt *n* (on skin) marque *f* (de coup).

welterweight *n* poids *m* welter.

west I *n* **1** (compass direction) ouest *m*; **2 the West** l'Occident *m*, l'Ouest *m*; (part of country) l'Ouest *m*; (political entity) l'Occident *m*.
II *adj* (gen) ouest *inv*; [*wind*] d'ouest.
III *adv* [*move*] vers l'ouest; [*lie, live*] à l'ouest (**of** de).

western I *n* (film) western *m*.
II *adj* **1** [*coast*] ouest *inv*; [*town, accent*] de l'ouest; **~ France** l'ouest de la France; **2** (Pol) occidental/-e.

westerner *n* Occidental/-e *m/f*.

westernize *vtr* occidentaliser; **to become ~d** s'occidentaliser.

west-facing *adj* exposé/-e à l'ouest.

West Indian ▶553 I *n* Antillais/-e *m/f*.
II *adj* antillais/-e.

West Indies ▶448 *pr n pl* Antilles *fpl*.

wet I *adj* **1** (damp) [*hair, clothes, grass, surface*] mouillé/-e; **to get ~** se faire mouiller; **to get one's feet ~** se mouiller les pieds; **to get the floor ~** tremper le sol; **~ through** trempé/-e; **2** (freshly applied) [*cement, varnish*] humide; **'~ paint'** 'peinture fraîche'; **3** (rainy) [*weather, day, night*] pluvieux/-ieuse; [*season*] des pluies; **when it's ~** quand il pleut; **4** (GB) [*person*] qui manque de caractère.
II *vtr* **1** mouiller [*floor, object, clothes*]; **2 to ~ one's pants/the bed** [*adult*] mouiller sa culotte/le lit; [*child*] faire pipi dans sa culotte/dans son lit.

wet blanket○ *n* rabat-joie *mf inv*.

wet suit *n* combinaison *f* de plongée.

whack I *n* (blow) (grand) coup *m*.
II *excl* paf!
III *vtr* **1** (hit) battre [*person, animal*]; frapper [*ball*]; **2**○ (GB) (defeat) piler○.

whacky○ *adj* [*person*] dingue○; [*sense of humour*] farfelu/-e○.

whale I *n* **1** (Zool) baleine *f*; **2**○ **to have a ~ of a time** s'amuser comme un fou.
II○ *vtr* (US) (thrash) donner une raclée○ à.

wharf *n* quai *m*.

what I *pron* **with ~?** avec quoi?; **and ~ else?** et quoi d'autre?; **~ for?** (why) pourquoi?; (about what) à propos de quoi? **~'s the matter?** qu'est-ce qu'il y a?; **~'s her telephone number?** quel est son numéro de téléphone?; **~'s that button for?** à quoi sert ce bouton?; **~'s it like?** comment c'est?; **do ~ you want** fais ce que tu veux; **take ~ you need** prend ce dont tu as besoin; **~ I need is** ce dont j'ai besoin c'est; **and ~'s more** et en plus; **and ~'s worse** et en plus; **he did ~?** il a fait quoi?; **George ~?** George comment?
II *det* **do you know ~ train he took?** est-ce que tu sais quel train il a pris?; **~ a nice dress/car!** quelle belle robe/voiture!; **~ a strange thing to do!** quelle drôle d'idée!; **~ use is that?** à quoi ça sert?; **~ money he earns he spends** tout ce qu'il gagne, il le dépense; **~ few friends she had** les quelques amis qu'elle avait.
III **what about** *phr* **1** (to draw attention) **~ about the children?** et les enfants (alors)?; **2** (to make suggestion) **~ about a meal out?** et si on dînait au restaurant?; **~ about Tuesday?** qu'est-ce que tu dirais de mardi?
IV **what if** *phr* et si; **~ if I bring the dessert?** et si j'apportais le dessert?
V *excl* quoi!, comment!
IDIOMS **~ with one thing and another** avec ceci et cela.

what-d'yer-call-it○ *n* machin○ *m*.

whatever I *pron* **1** (that which) (as subject) ce qui; (as object) ce que; **to do ~ one can** faire ce qu'on peut; **2** (anything that) (as subject) tout ce qui; (as object) tout ce que; **do ~ you like** fais tout ce que tu veux; **~ you say** (as you like) tout ce qui vous plaira; **3** (no matter what) quoi que (+ *subjunctive*); **~ happens** quoi qu'il arrive; **~ she says, ignore it** quoi qu'elle dise n'en tiens pas compte; **~ it costs it doesn't matter** quel que soit le prix, ça n'a pas d'importance; **4** (what on earth) (as subject) qu'est-ce qui; (as object) qu'est-ce que; **~'s that?** qu'est-ce c'est que ça?
II *det* **1** (any) **they eat ~ food they can get** ils mangent tout ce qu'ils trouvent à manger; **2** (no matter what) **~ their arguments** quels que soient leurs arguments; **~ the reason** quelle que soit la raison; **for ~ reason** pour je ne sais quelle raison.
III *adv* (also **whatsoever**) **to have no idea ~** ne pas avoir la moindre idée; **'any petrol?'—'none ~'** 'il y a de l'essence?'—'pas du tout'.

what's-her-name○ *n* Machin○ *m*.

what's-his-name○ *n* Machin○ *m*.

wheat *n* blé *m*.

wheat germ *n* germe *m* de blé.

wheatmeal *n* farine *f* complète.

wheedle *vtr* **to ~ sth out of sb** soutirer qch à qn par la cajolerie.

wheel I *n* **1** (on vehicle) roue *f*; (on trolley, piece of furniture) roulette *f*; **2** (for steering) (in vehicle) volant *m*; (on boat) roue *f* (de gouvernail); **to be at** or **behind the ~** être au volant; **3** (in watch, mechanism, machine) rouage *m*; **4** (for pottery) tour *m*.
II *vtr* pousser [*bicycle, barrow*]; **they ~ed me into the operating theatre** ils m'ont emmené dans la salle d'opération sur un chariot.
III *vi* (also **~ round**) [*person, regiment*] faire demi-tour; [*car, motorbike*] braquer fortement; [*ship*] virer de bord.

what

As a pronoun

In questions

◆ When used in questions as an object pronoun, ***what*** is translated by ***qu'est-ce que*** (***qu'est-ce qu'*** in front of a vowel or mute 'h'):

***what** is he doing?*	= **qu'est-ce qu**'il fait?
***what** did you say?*	= **qu'est-ce que** tu as dit?
***what** are we going to do?*	= **qu'est-ce que** nous allons faire?

◆ Alternatively, you can use ***que*** (***qu'*** before a vowel or mute 'h'), but note that, after ***que***, the order of subject and verb is reversed and a hyphen is inserted between them if the subject is a pronoun:

***what** is he doing?*	= **que** fait-il?
***what** did you say?*	= **qu'**as-tu dit?
***what** are we going to do?*	= **qu'**allons-nous faire?

◆ When used in questions as a subject pronoun, ***what*** is translated by ***qu'est-ce qui***:

***what** is happening?*	= **qu'est-ce qui** se passe?
***what** happened?*	= **qu'est-ce qui** s'est passé?
***what** is going to happen?*	= **qu'est-ce qui** va se passer?

Again, if you use ***que***, the order of subject and verb is reversed, the subject becomes ***il*** and a hyphen is inserted between them:

***what** is happening?*	= **que** se passe-t-il?*
***what** happened?*	= **que** s'est-il passé?
***what** is going to happen?*	= **que** va-t-il se passer?

* In this case, an additional -***t***- is required for the liaison between the two vowels to be made.

To introduce a clause

◆ When used to introduce a clause as the object of the verb, ***what*** is translated by ***ce que*** (***ce qu'*** before a vowel or mute 'h'):

*I don't know **what** he wants*	= je ne sais pas **ce qu'**il veut
*did they have **what** you wanted?*	= est-ce qu'ils avaient **ce que** tu voulais?
***what** he said was that . . .*	= **ce qu'**il a dit c'est que . . .

◆ When ***what*** is the subject of the verb, it is translated by ***ce qui***:

*tell me **what** happened*	= raconte-moi **ce qui** s'est passé
*I want to know **what**'s happening*	= je veux savoir **ce qui** se passe
***what** matters is that . . .*	= **ce qui** compte, c'est que . . .

With prepositions

What, when it is used with a preposition in English, is translated by ***quoi***. In French, however, the preposition always comes before ***quoi***:

***what** are you thinking about?*	= à **quoi** penses-tu?
*I don't know **what** he is talking about*	= je ne sais pas de **quoi** il parle

As a determiner

When ***what*** is used as a determiner, it is translated by ***quel***, ***quelle***, ***quels*** or ***quelles***, according to the gender and number of the noun that follows:

***what** train did you catch?*	= **quel** train as-tu pris?
***what** time is it?*	= **quelle** heure est-il?
***what** books do you like?*	= **quels** livres aimes-tu?
***what** colours do you like?*	= **quelles** couleurs aimes-tu?

❑ For further usages, see the entry **what**.

IDIOMS **to ~ and deal** magouiller○.

wheelbarrow *n* brouette *f*.

wheelchair *n* fauteuil *m* roulant.

wheelclamp *n* (Aut) sabot *m* de Denver.

wheeler dealer○ *n* magouilleur/-euse○ *m/f*.

wheeze *vi* avoir la respiration sifflante.

when

■ **Note** *When* in questions is usually translated by *quand*.
– Note that there are three ways of asking questions using *quand*: *when did she leave?* = quand est-ce qu'elle est partie?, elle est partie quand?, quand est-elle partie?
– When talking about future time, *quand* will be used with the future tense of the verb: *tell him when you see him* = dis-lui quand tu le verras.

I *adv* **1** (in questions) quand; **~ are we leaving?** quand est-ce qu'on part?; **~ is the concert?** c'est quand le concert?; **I wonder ~ the film starts** je me demande à quelle heure commence le film; **say ~** dis-moi stop; **2** (whenever) quand; **he's only happy ~ he's moaning** il n'est content que quand il rouspète; **~ I eat ice cream, I feel ill** quand or chaque fois que je mange de la glace, j'ai mal au cœur.
II *rel pron* où; **the week ~ it all happened** la semaine où tout cela s'est produit; **there are times ~ it's too stressful** il y a des moments où c'est trop stressant.
III *conj* **1** (expressing time) quand; **~ he was at school** quand il était à l'école, lorsqu'il était à l'école; **~ I am 18** quand j'aurai 18 ans; **~ he arrives, I'll let you know** quand il arrivera or dès qu'il arrivera, je te le dirai; **2** (expressing contrast) alors que; **why buy their products ~ ours are cheaper?** pourquoi acheter leurs produits alors que les nôtres sont moins chers?
IV *pron* quand; **until/since ~?** jusqu'à/depuis quand?; **1982, that's ~ I was born** 1982, c'est l'année où je suis né; **that's ~ I found out** c'est à ce moment-là que j'ai su.

whenever *adv* **1** (no matter when) **~ you want** quand tu veux; **I'll come ~ it is convenient** je viendrai quand cela vous arrangera; **2** (every time that) chaque fois que; **~ I see a black cat, I make a wish** chaque fois que je vois un chat noir, je fais un vœu.

where

■ **Note** *where* in questions is usually translated by *où*: *where are the plates?* = où sont les assiettes?; *I don't know where the plates are* = je ne sais pas où sont les assiettes; *do you know where he is?* = est-ce que tu sais où il est?; *do you know where Paul is?* = est-ce que tu sais où est Paul?
– Note that *où + est-ce que* does not require a change in word order: *where did you see her?* = où est-ce que tu l'as vue?

I *adv* où; **~ is my coat?** où est mon manteau?; **~ do you work?** où est-ce que vous travaillez; **ask him ~ he went** demande-lui où il est allé; **do you know ~ she's going?** est-ce tu sais où elle va?; **sit ~ you like** asseyez-vous où vous voulez; **it's cold ~ we live** il fait froid là où nous habitons; **~ necessary** si nécessaire; **~ possible** dans la mesure du possible.
II *pron* **from ~?** d'où?; **that's ~ I fell** c'est là que je suis tombé; **that is ~ he is mistaken** c'est là qu'il se trompe.

whereas *conj* **she likes dogs ~ I prefer cats** elle aime les chiens mais moi je préfère les chats; **he chose to stay quiet ~ I would have complained** il a choisi de ne rien dire alors que moi je me serais sûrement plaint.

whereby *conj* **a system ~ all staff will carry identification** un système qui prévoit que tous les membres du personnel auront une carte.

wherever *adv* **1** (in questions) **~ has he got to?** où est-ce qu'il a bien pu passer?; **2** (anywhere) **~ she goes I'll go** où qu'elle aille, j'irai; **~ you want** où tu veux; **we'll meet ~'s convenient for you** nous nous retrouverons là où ça t'arrange; **3** (whenever) **~ necessary** quand c'est nécessaire; **~ possible** dans la mesure du possible.

whet *vtr* **to ~ the appetite** stimuler l'appétit; **the book ~ted his appetite for travel** les livres lui donnèrent envie de voyager.

whether *conj*

■ **Note** When *whether* is used to mean *if*, it is translated by *si*: *I wonder whether she got my letter* = je me demande si elle a reçu ma lettre.
– In *whether...or not* sentences, *whether* is translated by *que* and the verb that follows is in the subjunctive.

1 (when outcome is uncertain) si; **I wasn't sure ~ to answer or not** je ne savais pas s'il fallait répondre; **can you check ~ it's cooked?** est-ce que tu peux vérifier si c'est cuit?; **2** (no matter if) **you're coming ~ you like it or not!** tu viendras que cela te plaise ou non!; **~ you have children or not, this book should interest you** que vous ayez des enfants ou non, ce livre devrait vous intéresser.

whew *excl* (in relief) ouf!; (in hot weather) pff!; (in surprise) hein!

which I *pron* **show her ~ you mean** montre-lui celui/celle etc dont tu parles; **I don't mind ~** ça m'est égal; **can you tell ~ is ~?** peux-tu les distinguer?; **the contract ~ he's spoken about** le contrat dont il a parlé; **~ reminds me**... ce qui me fait penser que...
II *det* **~ books?** quels livres?; **she asked me ~ coach was leaving first** elle m'a demandé lequel des cars allait partir le premier; **~ one of the children**...? lequel or laquelle des enfants...?; **you may wish to join, in ~ case**... vous voulez peut-être vous inscrire, auquel cas...

whichever I *pron* **1** (the one that) (as subject) celui *m* qui, celle *f* qui; (as object) celui *m* que, celle *f* que; **'which restaurant?'—'~ is nearest'** 'quel restaurant?'—'celui qui est le plus proche'; **come at 2 or 2.30, ~ suits you best** viens à 14 h ou 14 h 30, comme cela te convient le mieux; **2** (no matter which one) (as subject) quel *m* que soit celui qui, quelle *f* que soit celle qui; (as object) quel *m* que soit celui que, quelle *f* que soit celle que; **'do you want**

which

As a pronoun

In questions

◆ When ***which*** (meaning *which one* or *which ones*) is used as a pronoun in questions, it is translated by ***lequel***, ***laquelle***, ***lesquels*** or ***lesquelles***, according to the gender and number of the noun it is standing for:

there are three peaches, ***which*** *do you want?*	= il y a trois pêches, **laquelle** veux-tu?

◆ When ***which*** is followed by a superlative adjective, then the translation is ***quel***, ***quelle***, ***quels*** or ***quelles***, according to the gender and number of the noun it is standing for:

(of the apples) ***which*** *is the biggest?*	= **quelle** est la plus grosse?
(of the books) ***which*** *are the cheapest?*	= **quels** sont les moins chers?

In relative clauses

◆ When used as a relative pronoun, ***which*** is translated by ***qui*** when it is the subject of the verb, and by ***que*** when it is the object:

the book ***which*** *is on the table*	= le livre **qui** est sur la table
the book ***which*** *Tina is reading*	= le livre **que** lit Tina

Note the different word order of subject and verb; this is the case where the subject is a noun but not where the subject is a pronoun:

the book ***which*** *I am reading*	= le livre **que** je lis

Remember that in the present perfect and past perfect tenses, the past participle agrees in gender and number with the noun ***que*** is referring back to:

the books ***which*** *I gave you*	= les livres **que** je t'ai donnés
the dresses ***which*** *she bought yesterday*	= les robes **qu'**elle a achetées hier

◆ When ***which*** is used as a relative pronoun with a preposition, it is translated by ***lequel***, ***laquelle***, ***lesquels*** or ***lesquelles*** according to the gender and number of the noun it is standing for:

the road ***by which*** *we came*	= la route **par laquelle** nous sommes venus
the crates ***behind which*** *he hid*	= les caisses **derrière lesquelles** il s'est caché

If the preposition would normally be translated by ***à*** in French (***to***, ***at*** etc), the *preposition* + ***which*** is translated by ***auquel***, ***à laquelle***, ***auxquels*** or ***auxquelles***:

the addresses ***to which*** *we sent letters*	= les adresses **auxquelles** nous avons envoyé des lettres

With prepositions normally translated by ***de*** in French (***of***, ***from*** etc), the translation of *preposition* + ***which*** becomes ***dont*** in all cases:

a blue book, the title ***of which*** *I've forgotten*	= un livre bleu **dont** j'ai oublié le titre

As a determiner

When ***which*** is used as a determiner in questions, it is translated by ***quel***, ***quelle***, ***quels*** or ***quelles*** according to the gender and number of the noun that follows:

which *car is yours?*	= **quelle** voiture est la vôtre?
which *dress did she buy?*	= **quelle** robe a-t-elle achetée?*
which *books did he borrow?*	= **quels** livres a-t-il empruntés?*

Note that, in the second and third examples, the object precedes the verb so that the past participle agrees in gender and number with the object.

* In these cases, an additional *-t-* is required for the liaison between the two vowels to be made.

For particular usages see the entry **which**.

the big piece or the small piece?'—'~' 'est-ce que tu veux le gros ou le petit morceau?'—'n'importe'.
II *det* **1** (the one that) **let's go to ~ station is nearest** allons à la gare la plus proche; **2** (no matter which) **I'll be happy ~ horse wins** quel que soit le cheval qui gagne je serai content.

while I *conj* (also **whilst**) **1** (during the time that) pendant que; **he made a sandwich ~ I phoned** il s'est fait un sandwich pendant que je téléphonais; **~ in Spain, I visited Madrid** pendant que j'étais en Espagne, j'ai visité Madrid; **I fell asleep ~ watching TV** je me suis endormi en regardant la télé; **close the door ~ you're at it** ferme la porte pendant que tu y es; **2** (although) bien que (+ *subjunctive*), quoique (+ *subjunctive*); **3** (whereas) alors que, tandis que; **she likes dogs ~ I prefer cats** elle aime les chiens mais moi je préfère les chats.
II *n* **a ~ ago** il y a quelque temps; **a ~ later** quelque temps plus tard; **for a good ~** pendant longtemps; **a short ~ ago** il y a peu de temps; **it will take a ~** cela va prendre un certain temps; **after a (short) ~** au bout d'un moment; **once in a ~** de temps en temps.
■ **while away** tuer [*time*] (**doing, by doing** en faisant).

whilst = **while** I.

whim *n* caprice *m*; **on a ~** sur un coup de tête.

whimper I *n* gémissement *m* (**of** de).
II *vi* **1** [*person, animal*] gémir; **2** (whinge) [*person*] pleurnicher.

whimsical *adj* [*person*] fantasque; [*play, tale, manner, idea*] saugrenu/-e.

whine *vi* (complain) se plaindre (**about** de); (snivel) pleurnicher; [*dog*] gémir.

whinge○ *vi* râler.

whinny *vi* [*horse*] hennir doucement.

whip I *n* **1** (for punishment) fouet *m*; (for horse) cravache *f*; **2** (Culin) mousse *f*.
II *vtr* **1** (beat) fouetter; **2** (Culin) fouetter [*cream*]; battre [qch] en neige [*egg whites*]; **3**○ **to ~ sth out** sortir qch brusquement; (remove quickly) **he ~ped the plates off the table** il a prestement retiré les assiettes de la table; **I ~ped the key out of his hand** je lui ai arraché la clé des mains; **to ~ the crowd up into a frenzy** mettre la foule en délire.

whiplash injury *n* (Med) coup *m* du lapin.

whip-round○ *n* (GB) collecte *f*.

whirl I *n* **1** (of activity, excitement) tourbillon *m* (**of** de); **2** (spiral motif) spirale *f*.
II *vi* [*dancer*] tournoyer; [*blade, propeller*] tourner; [*snowflakes, dust, thoughts*] tourbillonner.
IDIOMS **to give sth a ~**○ essayer qch.
■ **whirl round** [*person*] se retourner brusquement; [*blade, clock hand*] tourner brusquement.

whirlpool *n* tourbillon *m*.

whirlwind *n* tourbillon *m*.

whirr *vi* [*motor*] vrombir; [*camera, fan*] tourner; [*insect*] bourdonner; [*wings*] bruire.

whisk I *n* (also **egg ~**) (manual) fouet *m*; (electric) batteur *m*.
II *vtr* **1** (Culin) battre; **2** (transport quickly) **he was ~ed off to meet the president** on l'a emmené sur le champ rencontrer le président; **she was ~ed off to hospital** elle a été emmenée d'urgence à l'hôpital.

whisker I *n* (of animal) poil *m* de moustache.
II **whiskers** *n pl* (of animal) moustaches *fpl*; (of man) (beard) barbe *f*; (moustache) moustache *f*.

whisper I *n* chuchotement *m*; **to speak in a ~** or **in ~s** parler à voix basse.
II *vtr* chuchoter (**to** à); **to ~ sth to sb** chuchoter qch à qn; **'she's asleep', he ~ed** 'elle dort', dit-il en chuchotant.
III *vi* chuchoter; **to ~ to sb** parler à voix basse à qn.

whistle I *n* **1** (object) sifflet *m*; **to blow the** or **one's ~** donner un coup de sifflet; **2** (sound) (through mouth) sifflement *m*; (by referee) coup *m* de sifflet; (of bird, train) sifflement *m*.
II *vtr* siffler; (casually) siffloter.
III *vi* siffler; **to ~ at sb/sth** siffler qn/qch; **to ~ for** siffler [*dog*].

white ▶438 I *n* **1** (gen) blanc *m*; **2** (also **White**) (Caucasian) Blanc/Blanche *m/f*; **3** (in chess, draughts) blancs *mpl*.
II *adj* **1** blanc/blanche; **bright ~ teeth** dents d'un blanc éclatant; **to go** or **turn ~** devenir blanc, blanchir; **to paint sth ~** peindre qch en blanc; **2** [*race, child, skin*] blanc/blanche; [*area*] habité/-e par des Blancs; [*culture, prejudice*] des Blancs; **a ~ man/woman** un Blanc/une Blanche; **3** (pale) pâle (**with** de); **to go** or **turn ~** pâlir (**with** de).

whitebait *n* (raw) blanchaille *f*; (fried) petite friture *f*.

white coffee *n* (at home) café *m* au lait; (in café) (café *m*) crème *m*.

white-collar *adj* [*job, work*] d'employé de bureau; [*staff*] de bureau; **~ worker** col *m* blanc, employé/-e *m/f* de bureau.

white elephant *n* **1** (item, knicknack) bibelot *m*; **2** (public project) réalisation *f* coûteuse et peu rentable.

white horses *n pl* (waves) moutons *mpl*.

White House *n* **the ~** la Maison Blanche.

white lie *n* pieux mensonge *m*.

whitener *n* **1** (for clothes) agent *m* blanchissant; **2** (for shoes) produit *m* pour blanchir; **3** (for coffee, tea) succédané *m* de lait en poudre.

whiteness *n* blancheur *f*.

white spirit *n* white-spirit *m*.

whitewash I *n* **1** (for walls) lait *m* de chaux; **2** (figurative) (cover-up) mise *f* en scène.
II *vtr* **1** blanchir [qch] à la chaux [*wall*]; **2** (also **~ over**) blanchir [*facts*].

white water *n* eau *f* vive.

white wedding *n* mariage *m* en blanc.

Whitsun *n* (also **Whitsuntide**) Pentecôte *f*.

Whit Sunday *n* Pentecôte *f*.

whittle *vtr* tailler [qch] au couteau; **to ~ sth away** or **down** réduire qch (**to** à).

whizz-kid○ *n* jeune prodige *m*.

who *pron*

■ **Note** Note that there are three ways of asking questions using *qui* as the object of the verb: *who did he call?* = qui est-ce qu'il a appelé?, qui a-t-il appelé?, il a appelé qui?

1 (in questions) (as subject) qui (est-ce qui); (as object) qui (est-ce que); (after prepositions) qui; **~ knows the answer?** qui connaît la réponse?; **~'s going to be there?** qui sera là?; **~ did you invite?** qui est-ce que tu as invité?, qui as-tu invité?; **~ was she with?** avec qui était-elle?; **~ did you buy it for?** pour qui l'as-tu acheté?; **~ did you get it from?** qui te l'a donné?; **2** (relative) (as subject) qui; (as object) que; (after prepositions) qui; **his friend, ~ lives in Paris** son ami, qui habite Paris; **his friend ~ he sees once a week** l'ami qu'il voit une fois par semaine; **3** (whoever) **bring ~ you like** tu peux amener qui tu veux; **~ do you think you are?** tu te prends pour qui?

whodun(n)it *n* polar○ *m*, roman *m* policier.

whoever *pron* **1** (the one that) **~ wins the election** celui ou celle qui gagnera les élections; **2** (anyone that) (as subject) quiconque; (as object) qui; **~ saw the accident should contact us** quiconque a assisté à l'accident devrait nous contacter; **invite ~ you like** invite qui tu veux; **3** (no matter who) **~ you are** qui que vous soyez.

whole **I** *n* **1** (total unit) tout *m*; **as a ~** (not in separate parts) en entier; (overall) dans l'ensemble; **2** (all) **the ~ of** tout/-e; **the ~ of the weekend/August** tout le week-end/mois d'août; **the ~ of London is talking about it** tout Londres en parle; **nearly the ~ of Berlin was destroyed** Berlin a été presque entièrement détruit.
II *adj* **1** (entire) tout/-e, entier/-ière; (more emphatic) tout entier/-ière; **a ~ hour** une heure entière; **a ~ day** toute une journée; **for three ~ weeks** pendant trois semaines entières; **his ~ life** toute sa vie, sa vie entière; **the ~ truth** toute la vérité; **the most beautiful city in the ~ world** la plus belle ville du monde; **2** (emphatic use) **a ~ new way of life** un mode de vie complètement différent; **that's the ~ point of the exercise** c'est tout l'intérêt de l'exercice; **3** (intact) intact/-e.
III *adv* [*swallow, cook*] tout entier.
IV **on the whole** *phr* dans l'ensemble.

wholefood *n* (GB) produits *mpl* biologiques.

wholehearted *adj* [*approval, support*] sans réserve; **to be in ~ agreement with** être en accord total avec.

wholeheartedly *adv* sans réserve.

wholemeal *adj* (also **wholewheat**) complet/-ète.

whole milk *n* lait *m* entier.

wholesale **I** *adj* **1** [*business*] de gros; **2** (large-scale) [*destruction*] total/-e; [*acceptance, rejection*] en bloc; [*attack*] sur tous les fronts.
II *adv* **1** [*buy, sell*] en gros; **2** [*accept, reject*] en bloc.

wholesaler *n* grossiste *mf*, marchand/-e *m/f* en gros.

wholesome *adj* **1** (healthy) sain/-e; **2** (decent) [*person, appearance*] bien propre; [*entertainment*] innocent/-e.

wholewheat = **wholemeal**.

wholly *adv* entièrement, tout à fait.

whom *pron* **1** (in questions) qui (est-ce que); (after prepositions) qui; **~ did she meet?** qui a-t-elle rencontré?, qui est-ce qu'elle a rencontré?; **to ~ are you referring?** à qui est-ce que vous faites allusion?; **2** (relative) que; (after prepositions) qui; **the person to ~/of ~ I spoke** la personne à qui/dont j'ai parlé.

whooping cough ▶533 *n* coqueluche *f*.

whorl *n* (of cream, chocolate) spirale *f*; (on fingerprint) volute *f*; (shell pattern) spire *f*; (of petals) verticille *m*.

whose **I** *pron* **1** (in questions) à qui; **~ is this?** à qui est ceci?; **2** (relative) dont; **the boy ~ dog was killed** le garçon dont le chien a été tué; **the man ~ daughter he was married to** l'homme dont il avait épousé la fille.
II *det* **~ pen is that?** à qui est ce stylo?; **do you know ~ car was stolen?** est-ce que tu sais à qui appartenait la voiture volée?; **~ coat did you take?** tu as pris le manteau de qui?

why

■ **Note** Note that there are three ways of asking questions using *why*:
– *why did you go?* = pourquoi est-ce que tu y es allé?, pourquoi y es-tu allé?, tu y es allé pourquoi?

I *adv* **1** (in questions) pourquoi; **~ do you ask?** pourquoi est-ce que tu me poses la question?, pourquoi me poses-tu la question?; **~ bother?** pourquoi se tracasser?; **~ the delay?** pourquoi ce retard?; **~ not?** pourquoi pas?; **'tell them'—'~ should I?'** 'dis-le-leur'—'et pourquoi (est-ce que je devrais le faire)?'; **2** (making suggestions) pourquoi; **~ don't we go away for the weekend?** pourquoi ne pas partir quelque part pour le week-end?; **~ don't I invite them for dinner?** et si je les invitais à manger?
II *conj* pour ça; **that is ~ they came** c'est pour ça qu'ils sont venus; **I need to know the reason ~** j'ai besoin de savoir pourquoi.

wick *n* mèche *f*.

wicked *adj* **1** (evil) [*person*] méchant/-e; [*heart, deed*] cruel/-elle; [*plot*] pernicieux/-ieuse; [*intention*] mauvais/-e (*before n*); **2** [*grin, humour*] malicieux/-ieuse; [*thoughts*] pervers/-e; **3** (vicious) [*wind*] méchant/-e; [*weapon*] redoutable; **to have a ~ tongue** être mauvaise langue.

wicker **I** *n* (also **wickerwork**) osier *m*.
II *adj* [*basket, furniture*] en osier.

wide ▶573 **I** *adj* **1** (broad) [*river, opening, mouth*] large; [*margin*] grand/-e; **how ~ is your garden?** quelle est la largeur de votre jardin?; **it's 30 cm ~** il fait 30 cm de large; **the river is 1 km across at its ~st** le fleuve fait or atteint 1 km à son point le plus large; **her eyes were ~ with fear** ses yeux étaient agrandis par la peur; **2** (immense) [*ocean, desert, expanse*] vaste (*before n*); **3** (extensive) [*variety, choice*] grand/-e (*before n*); **a ~ range of**

opinions une grande variété d'opinions; **a ~ range of products** une vaste gamme de produits; **4** (Sport) [*ball, shot*] perdu/-e.
II *adv* **to open one's eyes ~** ouvrir grand les yeux; **to open the door/window ~** ouvrir la porte/la fenêtre en grand; **his eyes are (set) ~ apart** il a les yeux très écartés; **his legs were ~ apart** il avait les jambes écartées; **to be ~ of the mark** [*ball, dart*] être à côté; [*guess*] être loin de la vérité.

wide-angle lens *n* objectif *m* à grand angle.

wide awake *adj* complètement éveillé/-e.

wide-eyed *adj* **1** (with surprise, fear) **he was ~** il ouvrait de grands yeux; **~ with fear/surprise** les yeux écarquillés de peur/surprise; **she stared/listened ~** elle regardait/écoutait les yeux écarquillés; **2** (naïve) [*person, innocence*] ingénu/-e.

widely *adv* **1** (commonly) [*accepted, used*] largement; **this product is now ~ available** on trouve maintenant ce produit partout; **2** [*spaced, planted*] à de grands intervalles; [*travel, differ, vary*] beaucoup.

widely-read *adj* [*student*] qui a beaucoup lu; [*author*] très lu/-e.

widen I *vtr* élargir [*road, gap*]; étendre [*powers*]; **this has ~ed their lead in the opinion polls** ceci a renforcé leur position dominante dans les sondages.
II *vi* s'élargir.

wide open *adj* **1** [*door, window, eyes, mouth*] grand/-e ouvert/-e; **2 the race is ~** l'issue de la course est indécise.

wide-ranging *adj* [*reforms*] de grande envergure; [*interests*] très variés.

wide screen *n* grand écran *m*.

widespread *adj* [*epidemic*] généralisé/-e; [*devastation*] étendu/-e; [*belief*] très répandu/-e.

widow I *n* veuve *f*.
II *vtr* **to be ~ed** devenir veuf/veuve *m/f*.

widower *n* veuf *m*.

width ▶573 *n* **1** largeur *f*; **it is 30 metres in ~** il fait or mesure 30 mètres de large; **2** (of fabric) lé *m*.

wield *vtr* **1** brandir [*weapon, tool*]; **2** exercer [*power*] (**over** sur).

wife *n* femme *f*; (more formally) épouse *f*; **the baker's/farmer's ~** la boulangère/la fermière.

wig *n* (whole head) perruque *f*; (partial) postiche *m*.

wiggle○ I *n* **a ~ of the hips** un roulement des hanches.
II *vtr* faire bouger [*tooth, wedged object*]; **to ~ one's hips** rouler les hanches; **to ~ one's fingers/toes** remuer les doigts/orteils.
III *vi* [*snake, worm*] se tortiller.

wild I *n* **in the ~** [*conditions, life*] en liberté; **to grow in the ~** pousser à l'état sauvage; **the call of the ~** l'appel de la nature.
II *adj* **1** [*animal, plant*] sauvage; **the pony is still quite ~** le poney est encore assez farouche; **2** [*landscape*] sauvage; **3** [*wind*] violent/-e; [*sea*] agité/-e; **it was a ~ night** c'était une nuit de tempête; **4** [*party, laughter, person*] fou/folle; [*imagination*] délirant/-e; [*applause*] déchaîné/-e; **to go ~** se déchaîner; **5**○ (furious) furieux/-ieuse; **he'll go** or **be ~!** ça va le mettre hors de lui!; **6**○ (enthusiastic) **to be ~ about** être un/une fana○ de; **I'm not ~ about him/it** il/ça ne m'emballe○ pas; **7** (outlandish) [*idea, plan*] fou/folle; [*claim, promise, accusation*] extravagant/-e; [*story*] farfelu/-e○.
III *adv* **1** [*grow*] à l'état sauvage; **the garden had run ~** le jardin était devenu une vraie jungle; **those children are allowed to run ~!** on permet à ces enfants de faire n'importe quoi!; **to let one's imagination run ~** laisser libre cours à son imagination.

wild boar *n* sanglier *m*.

wilderness *n* étendue *f* sauvage et désolée.

wild-eyed *adj* au regard égaré.

wildfire *n* **to spread like ~** se répandre comme une traînée de poudre.

wild flower *n* fleur *f* des champs, fleur *f* sauvage.

wild-goose chase *n* **it turned out to be a ~** ça n'a abouti à rien; **to lead sb on a ~** mettre qn sur une mauvaise piste.

wildlife *n* (animals) faune *f*; (animals and plants) faune *f* et flore *f*.

wildlife park, **wildlife reserve**, **wildlife sanctuary** *n* réserve *f* naturelle.

wildly *adv* **1** [*invest, spend, talk*] de façon insensée; [*fire, shoot*] au hasard; **to hit out/run ~** envoyer des coups/courir dans tous les sens; **2** [*wave, gesture*] de manière très agitée; [*applaud*] à tout rompre; **to fluctuate ~** subir des fluctuations violentes; **to beat ~** [*heart*] battre à tout rompre; **3** [*enthusiastic, optimistic*] extrêmement.

wilds *n pl* **to live in the ~ of Arizona** habiter au fin fond de l'Arizona.

Wild West *n* Far West *m*.

wilful (GB), **willful** (US) *adj* **1** [*person, behaviour*] volontaire; **2** [*damage, disobedience*] délibéré/-e.

wilfully (GB), **willfully** (US) *adv* **1** (in headstrong way) obstinément; **2** (deliberately) délibérément.

will[1] I *modal aux* **1** (expressing the future) **I'll see you tomorrow** je te verrai demain; **it won't rain** il ne pleuvra pas; **~ there be many people?** est-ce qu'il y aura beaucoup de monde?; **they'll come tomorrow** ils vont venir demain; **what ~ you do now?** qu'est-ce que tu vas faire maintenant?; **2** (expressing willingness or intention) **~ you help me?** est-ce que tu m'aideras?; **we won't stay too long** nous ne resterons pas trop longtemps; **he won't cooperate** il ne veut pas coopérer; **3** (in requests, commands) **~ you pass the salt please?** est-ce que tu peux me passer le sel s'il te plaît; **~ you please be quiet!** est-ce que tu vas te taire?; **wait a minute, ~ you!** attends un peu!; **4** (in invitations) **~ you have some tea?** est-ce que vous voulez du thé?; **won't you join us for dinner?** est-ce que tu veux dîner avec nous?; **what ~ you have to drink?** qu'est-ce que tu prends?; **5** (in assumptions) **he'll be about 30 now** il doit avoir 30 ans maintenant; **you'll be**

tired, I expect tu dois être fatigué je suppose; **6** (indicating sth predictable or customary) **they ~ ask for a deposit** ils demandent une caution; **these things ~ happen** ce sont des choses qui arrivent; **you ~ keep contradicting her!** il faut toujours que tu la contredises!; **7** (in short answers and tag questions) **you'll come again, won't you?** tu reviendras, n'est-ce pas?; **you won't forget, ~ you?** tu n'oublieras pas, n'est-ce pas?; **that'll be cheaper, won't it?** ça sera moins cher, non?; **'they won't be ready'—'yes, they ~'** 'ils ne seront pas prêts'—'(bien sûr que) si'; **'~ you call me?'—'yes, I ~'** 'est-ce que tu me téléphoneras?'—'bien sûr que oui'; **'she'll be furious'—'no, she won't!'** 'elle sera furieuse'—'bien sûr que non!'; **'I'll do it'—'no you won't!'** 'je le ferai'—'il n'en est pas question!'

II *vtr* **1** (urge mentally) **to ~ sb to do** supplier mentalement qn de faire; **to ~ sb to live** prier pour que qn vive; **2** (wish, desire) vouloir; **3** (Law) léguer (**to** à).

will² **I** *n* **1** volonté *f* (**to do** de faire); **to have a ~ of one's own** n'en faire qu'à sa tête; **against my ~** contre mon gré; **to do with a ~** faire de bon cœur; **to lose the ~ to live** ne plus avoir envie de vivre; **2** (Law) testament *m*; **to leave sb sth in one's ~** léguer qch à qn.

II at will *phr* [*select, take*] à volonté; **they can wander about at ~** ils peuvent se promener comme ils veulent.

willing *adj* **1** (prepared) **to be ~ to do** être prêt/-e à faire; **2** (eager) [*pupil, helper*] de bonne volonté; [*slave*] consentant/-e; [*recruit, victim*] volontaire; **to show ~** faire preuve de bonne volonté.

willingly *adv* [*accept, help*] volontiers; [*work*] avec bonne volonté.

willow *n* (also **~ tree**) saule *m*.

will power *n* volonté *f* (**to do** de faire).

willy-nilly *adv* **1** (regardless of choice) bon gré mal gré; **2** (haphazardly) au hasard.

wilt *vi* **1** [*plant, flower*] se faner; **2** [*person*] (from heat, fatigue) se sentir faible; (at daunting prospect) perdre courage.

win **I** *n* victoire *f* (**over** sur).

II *vtr* **1** gagner [*match, bet, battle, money*]; remporter [*election*]; **2** (acquire) obtenir [*delay, reprieve*]; gagner [*friendship, heart*]; s'attirer [*sympathy*]; s'acquérir [*support*] (**of** de); **to ~ sb's love/respect** se faire aimer/respecter de qn.

III *vi* gagner; **to ~ against sb** l'emporter sur qn.

■ **win over, win round** convaincre [*person*].

wince **I** *n* grimace *f*.

II *vi* grimacer, faire une grimace.

winch **I** *n* treuil *m*.

II *vtr* **to ~ sth down/up** descendre/hisser qch au treuil.

wind¹ **I** *n* **1** vent *m*; **the ~ is blowing** il y a du vent; **which way is the ~ blowing?** d'où vient le vent?; **2** (breath) **to knock the ~ out of sb** couper le souffle à qn; **to get one's ~** reprendre souffle; **3** (flatulence) vents *mpl*; **to break ~** lâcher un vent.

II *vtr* **1** (make breathless) [*blow, punch*] couper la respiration à; [*climb*] essouffler; **2** faire faire son rot à [*baby*].

wind² **I** *vtr* **1** (coil up) enrouler [*hair, rope, wire*] (**on, onto** sur; **round** autour de); **2** (also **~ up**) remonter [*clock, toy*]; **3** donner un tour de [*handle*]; **4 to ~ its way** [*procession, road, river*] serpenter.

II *vi* [*road, river*] serpenter (**along** le long de); [*stairs*] tourner.

■ **wind down**: ¶ **~ down 1** [*organization*] réduire ses activités; [*activity, production*] toucher à sa fin; [*person*] se détendre; **2** [*clockwork*] être sur le point de s'arrêter; ¶ **~ [sth] down 1** baisser [*car window*]; **2** mettre fin à [*activity, organization*].

■ **wind up**: ¶ **~ up 1** (finish) [*event*] se terminer (**with** par); [*speaker*] conclure; **2**○ (end up) finir, se retrouver; ¶ **~ [sth] up 1** liquider [*business*]; mettre fin à [*debate, meeting, project*]; **2** remonter [*clock, car window*]; ¶ **~ [sb] up 1** (tease) faire marcher [*person*]; **2** (make tense) énerver.

windfall *n* fruit *m* tombé par terre; (figurative) aubaine *f*.

winding *adj* [*road, river*] sinueux/-euse; [*stairs*] en spirale.

wind instrument ▶586| *n* instrument *m* à vent.

windmill *n* moulin *m* à vent.

window *n* **1** (of house) fenêtre *f*; (of shop, public building) vitrine *f*; (of vehicle) (gen) vitre *f*; (of plane) hublot *m*; (stained glass) vitrail *m*; **to look out of** or **through the ~** regarder par la fenêtre; **2** (for service at bank or post office) guichet *m*.

window box *n* jardinière *f*.

window cleaner ▶626| *n* laveur/-euse *m/f* de carreaux.

window display *n* vitrine *f*.

window ledge *n* appui *m* de fenêtre.

windowpane *n* carreau *m*.

window seat *n* **1** (in room) banquette *f*; **2** (in plane, bus, train) place *f* côté vitre.

window-shopping *n* **to go ~** faire du lèche-vitrines○ *m inv*.

windowsill *n* rebord *m* de fenêtre.

windpipe *n* trachée-artère *f*.

windscreen (GB), **windshield** (US) *n* pare-brise *m inv*.

windscreen wiper *n* (GB) essuie-glace *m inv*.

windshield (US) = **windscreen**.

windsurf ▶504| *vi* faire de la planche à voile.

windsurfer *n* (person) véliplanchiste *mf*; (board) planche *f* à voile.

windswept *adj* venteux/-euse.

windy *adj* [*place*] venteux/-euse; [*day*] de vent; **it was very ~** il faisait beaucoup de vent.

wine ▶438| *n* **1** (drink) vin *m*; **2** (colour) lie-de-vin *m*.

wine bar *n* bar *m* à vin.

wine box *n* ≈ cubitainer® *m*.

wine cellar *n* cave *f*.

wine glass *n* verre *m* à vin.

wine grower *n* viticulteur/-trice *m/f*.

wine list *n* carte *f* des vins.

wine rack *n* casier *m* à bouteilles.

wine tasting *n* dégustation *f* de vins.

wine vinegar *n* vinaigre *m* de vin.

wine waiter ▶ 626 *n* sommelier/-ière *m/f*.

wing I *n* aile *f*.
II **wings** *n pl* (in theatre) **the ~s** les coulisses *fpl*; **to be waiting in the ~s** (figurative) attendre son heure.

wink I *n* clin *m* d'œil; **we didn't get a ~ of sleep all night** nous n'avons pas fermé l'œil de la nuit.
II *vi* cligner de l'œil; **to ~ at sb** faire un clin d'œil à qn.

winner *n* **1** (victor) gagnant/-e *m/f*; **2** (success) **to be a ~** [*film, book, song*] avoir un gros succès.

winning *adj* **1** (victorious) gagnant/-e; **2** [*smile*] engageant/-e; **to have ~ ways** avoir du charme.

winnings *n pl* gains *mpl*.

winter I *n* hiver *m*; **in ~** en hiver.
II *adj* [*sports, clothes, weather*] d'hiver.
III *vi* passer l'hiver.

wintertime *n* hiver *m*.

wipe I *n* **1 to give sth a ~** (clean, dust) donner un coup de chiffon à qch; (dry) essuyer qch; **2** (for face, baby) lingette *f*.
II *vtr* essuyer [*table, glass*] (**on** sur; **with** avec); **to ~ one's hands/feet** s'essuyer les mains/les pieds; **to ~ one's nose** se moucher; **to ~ a baby's bottom** essuyer (les fesses d')un bébé; **to ~ the dishes** essuyer la vaisselle.
■ **wipe away** essuyer [*tears, sweat*]; faire partir [*dirt, mark*].
■ **wipe out 1** nettoyer [*container, cupboard*]; **2** annuler [*inflation*]; anéantir [*species, enemy, population*].
■ **wipe up**: ¶ **~ up** essuyer la vaisselle; ¶ **~ [sth] up** essuyer.

wire I *n* **1** fil *m*; **electric/telephone ~** fil électrique/téléphonique; **2** (US) (telegram) télégramme *m*.
II *vtr* **1 to ~ a house** installer l'électricité dans une maison; **to ~ a plug/a lamp** connecter une prise/une lampe; **2** (telegraph) télégraphier à [*person*]; télégraphier [*money*].

wiring *n* (in house) installation *f* électrique; (in appliance) circuit *m* (électrique).

wiry *adj* **1** [*person, body*] mince et nerveux/-euse; **2** [*hair*] rêche.

wisdom *n* sagesse *f*.

wisdom tooth *n* dent *f* de sagesse.

wise I *adj* [*person, words, precaution, saying*] sage; [*choice, investment*] judicieux/-ieuse; [*smile, nod*] avisé/-e; **a ~ man** un sage; **a ~ move** une décision judicieuse; **to be none the ~r** (understand no better) ne pas être plus avancé/-e; (not realize) ne s'apercevoir de rien.
II **-wise** *combining form* **1** (direction) dans le sens de; **length-~** dans le sens de la longueur; **2** (with regard to) pour ce qui est de; **work-~** pour ce qui est du travail.

wise guy○ *n* gros malin○ *m*.

wisely *adv* judicieusement.

wish I *n* **1** (request) souhait *m* (**for** de); **to make a ~** faire un vœu; **her ~ came true** son souhait s'est réalisé; **2** (desire) désir *m* (**for** de; **to do** de faire); **to go against sb's ~es** aller contre la volonté de qn.
II **wishes** *n pl* vœux *mpl*; **good** or **best ~es** meilleurs vœux; (ending letter) bien amicalement; **best ~es on your birthday** meilleurs vœux pour votre anniversaire; **please give him my best ~es** je vous prie de lui faire toutes mes amitiés.
III *vtr* **1** (expressing longing) **I ~ he were here/had been here** si seulement il était ici/avait été ici; **he ~ed he had written** il regrettait de ne pas avoir écrit; **2** (express congratulations, greetings) souhaiter; **I ~ you good luck/a happy birthday** je vous souhaite bonne chance/un bon anniversaire; **I ~ him well** je souhaite que tout aille bien pour lui; **3** (want) souhaiter, désirer.
IV *vi* **1** (desire) vouloir; **just as you ~** comme vous voudrez; **2** (make a wish) faire un vœu.

wishful thinking *n* **that's ~** c'est prendre ses désirs pour des réalités.

wisp *n* (of hair) mèche *f*; (of straw) brin *m*; (of smoke, cloud) volute *f*.

wispy *adj* [*hair, beard*] fin/-e; [*cloud, smoke*] léger/-ère.

wisteria *n* glycine *f*.

wistful *adj* (sad) mélancolique; (nostalgic) nostalgique.

wit I *n* **1** (sense of humour) esprit *m*; **2** (witty person) personne *f* spirituelle.
II **to wit** *phr* à savoir.

witch *n* sorcière *f*.

witchcraft *n* sorcellerie *f*.

witch doctor *n* shaman *m*.

with *prep*

■ **Note** This dictionary contains Usage Notes on such topics as the human body which use the preposition *with*. For the index to these Notes ▶ 784.

1 (gen) avec; **a meeting ~ sb** une réunion avec qn; **to hit sb ~ sth** frapper qn avec qch; **~ difficulty/pleasure** avec difficulté/plaisir; **to be patient ~ sb** être patient/-e avec qn; **delighted ~ sth** ravi/-e de qch; **to travel ~ sb** voyager avec qn; **to live ~ sb** (in one's own house) vivre avec qn; (in their house) vivre chez qn; **I'll be ~ you in a second** je suis à vous dans un instant; **take your umbrella ~ you** emporte ton parapluie; **bring the books back ~ you** rapporte les livres; **2** (in descriptions) à; avec; de; **a girl ~ black hair** une fille aux cheveux noirs; **the boy ~ the broken leg** le garçon à la jambe cassée; **a boy ~ a broken leg** un garçon avec une jambe cassée; **a TV ~ remote control** une télévision avec télécommande; **furnished ~ antiques** meublé/-e avec des meubles anciens; **covered ~ mud**

couvert/-e de boue; **to lie ~ one's eyes closed** être allongé/-e les yeux fermés; **to stand ~ one's arms folded** se tenir les bras croisés; **filled ~ sth** rempli/-e de qch; **3** (according to) **to increase ~ time** augmenter avec le temps; **to vary ~ the temperature** varier selon la température; **4** (owning, bringing) **passengers ~ tickets** les passagers munis de billets; **people ~ qualifications** les gens qualifiés; **somebody ~ your experience** quelqu'un qui a ton expérience; **have you got the report ~ you?** est-ce que tu as (amené) le rapport?; **5** (as regards) **how are things ~ you?** comment ça va?; **what's up ~ you?** qu'est-ce que tu as?; **what do you want ~ another car?** qu'est-ce que tu veux faire d'une deuxième voiture?; **6** (because of) **sick ~ worry** malade d'inquiétude; **he can see better ~ his glasses on** il voit mieux avec ses lunettes; **I can't do it ~ you watching** je ne peux pas le faire si tu me regardes; **7** (suffering from) **people ~ Aids/leukemia** les personnes atteintes du sida/de leucémie; **to be ill ~ flu** avoir la grippe; **8** (employed by, customer of) **a reporter ~ the Gazette** un journaliste de la Gazette; **he's ~ the UN** il travaille pour l'ONU; **I'm ~ Chemco** je travaille chez Chemco; **we're ~ the National Bank** nous sommes à la National Bank; **9** (in the same direction as) **to sail ~ the wind** naviguer dans le sens du vent; **to drift ~ the tide** dériver avec le courant.

withdraw I *vtr* retirer [*hand, money, application, permission, troops*]; renoncer à, retirer [*claim*]; rétracter [*accusation, statement*].
II *vi* **1** (gen) se retirer (**from** de); **2** (psychologically) se replier sur soi-même.

withdrawal *n* **1** (of money, troops) retrait *m* (**of, from** de); **2** (psychological reaction) repli *m* sur soi; **3** (of drug addict) état *m* de manque.

withdrawal symptoms *n pl* symptômes *mpl* de manque; **to be suffering from ~** être en état de manque.

withdrawn *adj* [*person*] renfermé/-e, replié/-e sur soi-même.

wither I *vtr* flétrir.
II *vi* se flétrir.

withering *adj* [*look*] plein/-e de mépris; [*contempt, comment*] cinglant/-e.

withhold *vtr* différer [*payment*]; retenir [*tax, grant, rent*]; refuser [*consent, permission*]; ne pas divulguer [*information*].

within I *prep* **1** (inside) **~ the city walls** dans l'enceinte de la ville; **~ the party** au sein du parti; **it's a play ~ a play** c'est une pièce dans la pièce; **2** (in expressions of time) **I'll do it ~ the hour** je le ferai en moins d'une heure; **15 burglaries ~ a month** 15 cambriolages en (moins d')un mois; **they died ~ a week of each other** ils sont morts à une semaine d'intervalle; **3** (not more than) **to be ~ several metres of sth** être à quelques mètres seulement de qch; **it's accurate to ~ a millimetre** c'est exact au millimètre près; **4 to live ~ one's income** vivre selon ses moyens.
II *adv* à l'intérieur; **from ~** de l'intérieur.

without I *prep* sans; **~ a key** sans clé; **~ any money** sans argent; **she left ~ it** elle est partie sans; **they left ~ me** ils sont partis sans moi; **~ looking** sans regarder; **it goes ~ saying** cela va de soi.
II *adv* à l'extérieur; **from ~** de l'extérieur.

withstand *vtr* résister à.

witness I *n* **1** (gen, Law) (person) témoin *m*; **she was a ~ to the accident** elle a été témoin de l'accident; **~ for the prosecution/the defence** témoin à charge/à décharge; **2** (testimony) témoignage *m*; **to be** or **bear ~ to sth** témoigner de qch.
II *vtr* **1** (see) être témoin de, assister à [*incident, attack*]; **2** servir de témoin lors de la signature de [*will, treaty*]; être témoin à [*marriage*].

witness box (GB), **witness stand** (US) *n* barre *f* des témoins.

wits *n pl* (intelligence) intelligence *f*; (presence of mind) présence *f* d'esprit; **to collect** or **gather one's ~** rassembler ses esprits; **to frighten sb out of their ~** faire une peur épouvantable à qn; **to live by one's ~** vivre d'expédients; **a battle of ~** une joute verbale.
IDIOMS **to be at one's ~ end** ne plus savoir quoi faire.

witticism *n* bon mot *m*.

witty *adj* spirituel/-elle.

wizard *n* **1** (magician) magicien *m*; **2** (expert) **to be a ~ at chess/computing** être un as○ aux échecs/en informatique.

wizened *adj* ratatiné/-e.

wobble *vi* [*table, chair*] branler; [*pile of books, plates*] osciller; [*jelly*] trembloter; [*person*] (on bicycle) osciller; (on ladder, tightrope) chanceler.

wobbly *adj* [*table, chair*] bancal/-e; [*tooth*] branlant/-e.

woe *n* malheur *m*; **a tale of ~** une histoire pathétique.

wolf *n* loup *m*; **she-~** louve *f*.
IDIOMS **to cry ~** crier au loup.

wolf-whistle I *n* sifflement *m*.
II *vi* siffler.

woman *n* femme *f*; **a ~ Prime Minister** une femme premier ministre; **he's always criticizing women drivers** il est toujours en train de critiquer les femmes au volant.

woman friend *n* amie *f*.

womanizer *n* coureur *m* (de jupons○).

womb *n* (Anat) uterus *m*.

wonder I *n* **1** (miracle) merveille *f*; **to do** or **work ~s** faire des merveilles (**for** pour; **with** avec); **(it's) no ~ that he's late** (ce n'est) pas étonnant qu'il soit en retard; **2** (amazement) émerveillement *m*.
II *vtr* (ask oneself) se demander; **I ~ how/why/whether** je me demande comment/pourquoi/si; (as polite request) **I ~ if you could help me?** pourriez-vous m'aider?; **it makes you ~** cela donne à penser; **it makes you ~ why** c'est à se demander pourquoi.
III *vi* **1** (think) **to ~ about sth/about doing sth** penser à qch/à faire qch; **2** (be surprised) **to ~ at sth** s'étonner de qch; (admiringly) s'émerveiller de qch.

wonderful *adj* [*book, film, meal, experience, holiday*] merveilleux/-euse; [*musician, teacher*] excellent/-e.

wonderfully *adv* [*funny, exciting, clever*] très; [*work, cope, drive*] admirablement.

wont *adj* **to be ~ to do** avoir coutume de faire; **as is his/their ~** comme à son/leur habitude.

woo *vtr* courtiser.

wood I *n* bois *m*.
II **woods** *n pl* bois *mpl*.
III *adj* [*fire, smoke*] de bois; **~ floor** plancher *m*.
IDIOMS **touch ~!** (GB), **knock on ~!** (US) touchons du bois!; **we are not out of the ~ yet** on n'est pas encore sorti de l'auberge.

wooden *adj* **1** [*furniture, object, house*] en bois; [*leg, spoon*] de bois; **2** [*expression*] figé/-e.

woodland *n* bois *m*.

woodpecker *n* pic *m*.

wood pigeon *n* pigeon *m* ramier.

woodwind *n pl* bois *mpl*.

woodwork *n* **1** (carpentry) menuiserie *f*; **2** (doors, windows) boiseries *fpl*.

woodworm *n* ver *m* du bois.

wool *n* laine *f*; **pure (new) ~** pure laine (vierge).
IDIOMS **to pull the ~ over sb's eyes** duper qn.

woollen (GB), **woolen** (US) I *n* (garment) lainage *m*.
II *adj* [*garment*] de laine.

woolly (GB), **wooly** (US) I° *n* lainage *m*.
II *adj* **1** [*garment*] de laine; [*animal coat, hair*] laineux/-euse; [*cloud*] cotonneux/-euse; **2** [*thinking*] flou/-e.

word I *n* **1** mot *m*; **to have the last ~** avoir le dernier mot; **I couldn't get a ~ in** je n'ai pas pu placer un mot; **in other ~s** en d'autres termes; **a ~ of warning** un avertissement; **a ~ of advice** un conseil; **too sad for ~s** trop triste; **I believed every ~ he said** je croyais tout ce qu'il me disait; **I mean every ~ of it** je pense ce que je dis; **a man of few ~s** un homme peu loquace; **not a ~ to anybody** pas un mot à qui que ce soit; **I don't believe a ~ of it** je n'en crois pas un mot; **2** (information) nouvelles *fpl* (**about** concernant); **there is no ~ of the missing climbers** on est sans nouvelles des alpinistes disparus; **~ got out that**... la nouvelle a transpiré que...; **to bring/send ~ that** annoncer/faire savoir que; **3** (promise, affirmation) parole *f*; **he gave me his ~** il m'a donné sa parole; **to keep/break one's ~** tenir/ne pas tenir parole; **to take sb's ~ for it** croire qn sur parole; **take my ~ for it!** crois-moi!; **4** (rumour) **~ has it that he's a millionaire** on dit qu'il est millionnaire; **~ got around that**... le bruit a couru que...; **5** (command) ordre *m*; **to give the ~ to do** donner l'ordre de faire.
II **words** *n pl* (of play) texte *m*; (of song) paroles *fpl*.
III *vtr* formuler [*reply, letter, statement*].
IDIOMS **my ~!** (in surprise) ma parole!; **right from the ~ go** dès le départ; **to have a ~ with sb about sth** parler à qn à propos de qch; **to have ~s with sb** s'accrocher avec qn; **to put in a good ~ for sb** glisser un mot en faveur de qn.

word for word *adv* [*copy, translate*] mot à mot; [*repeat*] mot pour mot.

wording *n* formulation *f*.

word-of-mouth I *adj* verbal.
II **by word of mouth** *phr* verbalement.

word processing, **WP** *n* traitement *m* de texte.

word processor *n* machine *f* à traitement de texte.

work I *n* **1** (physical or mental activity) travail *m* (**on** sur); **it was hard ~ doing** ça a été dur de faire; **to be hard at ~** travailler dur; **it's thirsty ~** ça donne soif; **2** (occupation) travail *m*; **to be in ~** avoir du travail or un emploi; **place of ~** lieu *m* de travail; **to be off ~** (on vacation) être en congé; **to be off ~ with flu** être en arrêt de travail parce qu'on a la grippe; **to be out of ~** être au chômage; **3** (place of employment) **to go to ~** aller au travail; **4** (building, construction) travaux *mpl* (**on** sur); **5** (essay, report) travail *m*; (artwork, novel, sculpture) œuvre *f* (**by** de); (study) ouvrage *m* (**by** de; **on** sur); (research) recherches *fpl* (**on** sur); **a ~ of reference** un ouvrage de référence; **a ~ of fiction** une œuvre de fiction; **the ~s of Racine** l'œuvre *m* de Racine; **this attack is the ~ of professionals** l'attaque est l'œuvre de professionnels.
II **works** *n pl* **1** (factory) usine *f*; **2** (building work) travaux *mpl*; **3**° (everything) **the (full** or **whole) ~s** toute la panoplie°.
III *vtr* **1** (drive) **to ~ sb hard** surmener qn; **2** (labour) **to ~ days/nights** travailler de jour/de nuit; **to ~ a 40 hour week** faire la semaine de 40 heures; **he ~ed his way through college** il a travaillé pour payer ses études; **3** (operate) se servir de [*computer, machine*]; **4** (exploit commercially) exploiter [*mine, seam*]; **5** (bring about) **to ~ wonders** or **miracles** faire des merveilles; **6** (use to one's advantage) **to ~ the system** exploiter le système; **7** (fashion) travailler [*clay, metal*]; **8** (manoeuvre) **to ~ sth into** introduire qch dans [*slot, hole*]; **to ~ a lever up and down** actionner un levier; **9** (exercise) faire travailler [*muscles*]; **10** (move) **to ~ one's way through** se frayer un passage à travers [*crowd*]; **to ~ one's way along** avancer le long de [*ledge, windowsill*]; **to ~ one's hands free** se libérer les mains; **it ~ed its way loose, it ~ed itself loose** cela s'est desserré peu à peu.
IV *vi* **1** (do a job) travailler (**doing** à faire); **to ~ for a living** gagner sa vie; **2** (strive) lutter (**against** contre; **for** pour; **to do** pour faire); **to ~ towards** aller vers [*solution*]; s'acheminer vers [*compromise*]; négocier [*agreement*]; **3** (function) fonctionner; **to ~ on electricity** marcher or fonctionner à l'électricité; **the washing machine isn't ~ing** la machine à laver est en panne; **4** (act, operate) **it doesn't** or **things don't ~ like that** ça ne marche pas comme ça; **to**

~ in sb's favour tourner à l'avantage de qn; **to ~ against sb** jouer en la défaveur de qn; **5** (be successful) [*treatment*] avoir de l'effet; [*detergent, drug*] agir (**against** contre; **on** sur); [*plan*] réussir; [*argument, theory*] tenir debout; **flattery won't ~ with me** la flatterie ne marche pas avec moi; **6** [*face, features*] se contracter.

IDIOMS **to ~ one's way up** gravir tous les échelons; **to ~ one's way up the company** faire son chemin dans l'entreprise.

■ **work off 1** (remove) retirer [*lid*]; **2** (repay) travailler pour rembourser [*loan, debt*]; **3** (get rid of) se débarrasser de [*excess weight*]; dépenser [*excess energy*]; passer [*anger, frustration*].

■ **work on**: ¶ **~ on** continuer à travailler; ¶ **~ on [sb]** travailler○ [*person*]; ¶ **~ on [sth]** travailler à [*book, report*]; travailler sur [*project*]; s'occuper de [*case, problem*]; chercher [*cure, solution*]; examiner [*idea, theory*].

■ **work out**: ¶ **~ out 1** (exercise) s'entraîner; **2** (go according to plan) marcher; **3** (add up) **to ~ out at** (GB) or **to** (US) s'élever à; ¶ **~ [sth] out 1** (calculate) calculer [*amount*]; **2** (solve) trouver [*answer, reason, culprit*]; résoudre [*problem*]; comprendre [*clue*]; **3** (devise) concevoir [*plan, scheme*]; trouver [*route*]; ¶ **~ [sb] out** comprendre [*person*].

■ **work up**: ¶ **~ up [sth]** développer [*interest*]; accroître [*support*]; **to ~ up the courage to do** trouver le courage de faire; **to ~ up some enthusiasm for** s'enthousiasmer pour; **to ~ up an appetite** s'ouvrir l'appétit; ¶ **~ up to [sth]** se préparer à [*confrontation, announcement*]; ¶ **~ [sb] up 1** (excite) exciter [*child, crowd*]; **2** (annoy) **to get ~ed up, to ~ oneself up** s'énerver.

workable *adj* **1** [*idea, plan, suggestion*] réalisable; [*system*] pratique; [*arrangement, compromise*] possible; **2** [*land, mine*] exploitable; [*cement*] maniable.

worker *n* (in manual job) ouvrier/-ière *m/f*; (in white-collar job) employé/-e *m/f*.

workforce *n* (in industry) main-d'œuvre *f*; (in service sector) effectifs *mpl*.

working *adj* **1** [*parent, woman*] qui travaille; [*conditions, environment, methods*] de travail; [*population, life*] actif/-ive; [*breakfast, lunch, day*] de travail; **during ~ hours** (in office) pendant les heures de bureau; (in shop) pendant les heures d'ouverture; **2** (provisional) [*document*] de travail; [*definition, title*] provisoire; **3** (functional) [*model*] qui fonctionne; [*farm, mine*] en exploitation; **in full ~ order** en parfait état de marche.

working class I *n* classe *f* ouvrière; **the ~es** les classes *fpl* laborieuses.
II **working-class** *adj* [*area, background, family, life*] ouvrier/-ière; [*culture, London*] prolétarien/-ienne; [*person*] de la classe ouvrière.

workings *n pl* rouages *mpl*.

workload *n* charge *f* de travail.

workman *n* ouvrier *m*.

workmanship *n* **a carpenter famous for sound ~** un menuisier connu pour la qualité de son travail; **furniture of the finest ~** des meubles d'une belle facture; **a piece of poor** or **shoddy ~** du travail mal fait or bâclé.

work of art *n* œuvre *f* d'art.

work permit *n* permis *m* de travail.

workplace *n* lieu *m* de travail.

workshop *n* atelier *m*.

worktop *n* plan *m* de travail.

work-to-rule *n* grève *f* du zèle.

world I *n* monde *m*; **throughout the ~** dans le monde entier; **to go round the ~** faire le tour du monde; **the biggest in the ~** le plus grand du monde; **more than anything in the ~** plus que tout au monde; **to go up in the ~** faire du chemin; **to go down in the ~** déchoir; **the Eastern/Western ~** les pays de l'Est/occidentaux; **the ancient ~** l'antiquité; **he lives in a ~ of his own** il vit dans un monde à part.
II *adj* [*events, market, leader, politics, rights, scale*] mondial; [*record, tour, championship*] du monde; [*cruise*] autour du monde.

IDIOMS **to be on top of the ~** être aux anges; **to get the best of both ~s** gagner sur les deux tableaux; **a man/woman of the ~** un homme/une femme d'expérience; **out of this ~** extraordinaire; **there's a ~ of difference** il y a une différence énorme; **it did him the** or **a ~ of good** ça lui a fait énormément de bien; **to think the ~ of sb** penser le plus grand bien de qn; **what/where/who in the ~?** que/où/qui etc diable?; **~s apart** diamétralement opposé.

world-class *adj* de niveau mondial.

World Cup *n* Coupe *f* du Monde.

World Fair *n* Exposition *f* universelle.

world-famous *adj* mondialement connu/-e.

world leader *n* **1** (politician) chef *m* d'État; **2** (athlete) meilleur/-e *m/f* du monde; (company) leader *m* mondial.

worldly *adj* **1** (not spiritual) matériel/-ielle; **2** (experienced) [*person*] avisé/-e, qui a de l'expérience.

worldly-wise *adj* avisé/-e, qui a de l'expérience.

world power *n* puissance *f* mondiale.

world war *n* guerre *f* mondiale; **the First/Second World War** la Première/Seconde Guerre mondiale.

world-wide I *adj* mondial/-e.
II *adv* dans le monde entier.

worm *n* ver *m*.

worn *adj* [*carpet, clothing, shoe, tyre*] usé/-e; [*stone*] abîmé/-e; [*tread*] lisse.

worn-out *adj* **1** [*carpet, brake*] complètement usé/-e; **2** [*person*] épuisé/-e.

worried *adj* [*person, face*] inquiet/-iète; **to be ~ about sb/sth** se faire du souci or s'inquiéter pour qn/qch; **I'm ~ (that) he might get lost** j'ai peur qu'il ne se perde.

worrier *n* anxieux/-ieuse *m/f*.

worry I *n* **1** (anxiety) soucis *mpl* (**about, over** à

propos de); **2** (problem) souci *m* (**about, over** au sujet de).
II *vtr* **1** (concern) inquiéter; **I ~ that he won't come** j'ai peur qu'il ne vienne pas; **it worried him that he couldn't find the keys** ça l'a inquiété de ne pas trouver les clés; **2** (bother) ennuyer; **would it ~ you if I opened the window?** est-ce que ça vous ennuierait que j'ouvre la fenêtre?; **3** [*dog*] harceler [*sheep*].
III *vi* (be anxious) s'inquiéter; **to ~ about** or **over sb/sth** s'inquiéter or se faire du souci pour qn/qch; **don't ~!** ne t'inquiète pas!; **there's nothing to ~ about** il n'y a pas lieu de s'inquiéter.
IV *v refl* **to ~ oneself** s'inquiéter, se faire de souci (**about sb** au sujet de qn; **about sth** à propos de qch); **to ~ oneself sick over sth** se ronger les sangs○ au sujet de qch.
■ **worry at** [*dog*] mordiller, jouer avec [*toy*]; [*person*] retourner [qch] dans tous les sens [*problem*].

worry beads *n pl* chapelet *m* antistress.

worrying *adj* inquiétant/-e.

worse I *adj* pire (**than** que); **to get ~** [*pressure, noise*] augmenter; [*conditions, weather*] empirer; [*illness, conflict*] s'aggraver; **he's getting ~** (in health) il va plus mal; **the cough is getting ~** la toux empire; **to feel ~** (more ill) se sentir plus malade; (more unhappy) aller moins bien; **and what is ~** et le pire, c'est que; **and to make matters ~, he lied** et pour ne rien arranger, il a menti.
II *n* **there is ~ to come** ce n'est pas encore le pire; **to change for the ~** empirer.
III *adv* [*play, sing*] moins bien (**than** que); **to behave ~** se conduire plus mal; **she could do ~ than follow his example** ce ne serait pas si mal si elle suivait son exemple.

worsen I *vtr* aggraver [*situation, problem*].
II *vi* [*condition, health, weather, situation*] se détériorer; [*problem, crisis, shortage, flooding*] s'aggraver.

worse off *adj* **1** (less wealthy) **to be ~** avoir moins d'argent (**than** que); **I'm £10 a week ~** j'ai dix livres de moins par semaine; **2** (in a worse situation) **to be ~** être dans une situation pire.

worship I *n* **1** (religious devotion) culte *m*; **sun/ancestor ~** culte du soleil/des ancêtres; **place of ~** lieu *m* de culte; **2** (veneration) vénération *f*.
II Worship ▶ 498 *pr n* (GB) **Your Worship** (to judge) Monsieur le juge; (to mayor) Monsieur le maire.
III *vtr* **1** (venerate) vénérer [*God, Buddha*]; (give praise) rendre hommage à; **2** adorer, avoir un culte pour [*person*]; avoir le culte de [*money, success*].
IV *vi* pratiquer sa religion.

worshipper *n* fidèle *mf*.

worst I *n* **1** (most difficult, unpleasant) **the ~** le/la pire *m/f*; **if the ~ came to the ~** (in serious circumstances) dans le pire des cas; (involving fatality) si le pire devait arriver; **2** (most negative trait) **to bring out the ~ in sb** mettre à jour ce qu'il y a de plus mauvais chez qn; **3** (of the lowest standard, quality) **the ~** le plus mauvais/la plus mauvaise *m/f*; **he's one of the ~** c'est un des plus mauvais; **to be the ~ at French** être le plus mauvais en français.
II *adj* **1** (most unsatisfactory, unpleasant) pire, plus mauvais/-e; **the ~ book I've ever read** le plus mauvais livre que j'aie jamais lu; **the ~ thing about the film is...** ce qu'il y a de pire dans le film c'est...; **2** (most serious) plus grave; **one of the ~ recessions** une des crises les plus graves.
III *adv* **the children suffer (the) ~** ce sont les enfants qui souffrent le plus; **they were (the) ~ hit by the strike** ce sont eux qui ont été les plus touchés par la grève; **~ of all,...** le pire de tout, c'est que...

worth I *n* **1** (quantity) **five pounds' ~ of sth** pour cinq livres de qch; **thousands of pounds' ~ of damage** des milliers de livres de dégâts; **a week's ~ of supplies** une semaine de provisions; **to get one's money's ~** en avoir pour son argent; **2** (value) valeur *f*; **of great ~** de grande valeur; **of no ~** sans valeur.
II *adj* **1** (of financial value) **to be ~ sth** valoir qch; **how much is it ~?** combien cela vaut-il?; **the pound was ~ 10 francs then** à l'époque, la livre valait 10 francs; **2** (of abstract value) **to be ~ sth** valoir qch; **to be ~ it** (en) valoir la peine; **the book isn't ~ reading** le livre ne vaut pas la peine d'être lu; **that's ~ knowing** cela est bon à savoir; **those little pleasures that make life ~ living** ces petits plaisirs qui rendent la vie agréable.
IDIOMS **for all one is ~** de toutes ses forces; **for what it's ~** pour ce que cela vaut; **to be ~ sb's while** valoir le coup.

worthless *adj* sans valeur; **he's ~** c'est un bon à rien.

worthwhile *adj* [*discussion, undertaking, visit*] qui en vaut la peine; [*career, project*] intéressant/-e; **to be ~ doing** valoir la peine de faire.

worthy *adj* **1** (deserving) **to be ~ of sth** mériter qch, être digne de qch; **~ of note** digne d'intérêt; **to be ~ of doing** [*person*] être digne de faire; **2** (admirable) [*cause*] noble; [*citizen, friend*] digne.

would *modal aux* **1** (expressing the conditional) **it ~ be nice if everyone were there, wouldn't it?** ce serait bien si tout le monde était là, n'est ce pas?; **if he had more money, he'd buy a car** s'il avait plus d'argent il achèterait une voiture; **we ~ have missed the train if we had left later** si nous étions partis plus tard nous aurions raté le train; **we wouldn't have succeeded without him** nous n'aurions pas réussi sans lui; **2** (in indirect statements or questions) **we thought he'd forget** nous pensions qu'il oublierait; **did she say she ~ be coming?** est-ce qu'elle a dit qu'elle viendrait?; **wish he ~ be quiet!** il ne pourrait pas se taire!; **3** (expressing willingness to act) **she wouldn't listen to me** elle ne voulait pas m'écouter; **he wouldn't do a thing to help us** il n'a rien voulu faire pour nous aider; **they asked me to leave but I wouldn't** ils m'ont demandé de partir mais j'ai refusé; **of course you ~ contradict him!** bien sûr il a fallu que tu le contredises!; **4** (in requests) **~ you give her the message?** est-ce que vous voulez bien lui transmettre le message?; **switch off the radio, ~ you?** éteins la radio, tu veux bien?; **~ you excuse me for a moment?** excusez-moi un instant; **5** (expressing one's wishes) **~ you like something to eat?** désirez-vous or voulez-vous manger quelque chose?; **I ~ like a beer** je voudrais une bière; **we ~ like to stay another night** nous aimerions rester une nuit de plus; **she'd have liked to stay here** elle aurait aimé rester ici; **I wouldn't mind another slice of cake** je prendrais bien un autre morceau de gâteau; **6** (offering advice) **if I were you, I wouldn't say anything** à ta place, je ne dirais rien; **it ~ be better to write** il vaudrait mieux écrire; **it ~ be a good idea to wait** ce serait une bonne idée d'attendre; **you ~ do well to check the timetable** tu ferais bien de vérifier l'horaire; **7** (in assumptions) **I ~ have been 12** je devais avoir 12 ans; **it ~ have been about midday** il devait être à peu près midi; **8** (used to) **she ~ talk for hours** elle parlait pendant des heures.

would-be *adj* **1** (desirous of being) **~ emigrants/investors** personnes or ceux qui désirent émigrer/investir; **2** (so-called) **~ intellectuals** les soi-disant intellectuels; **3** (having intended to be) **the ~ thieves were arrested** les voleurs ont été arrêtés avant qu'ils aient pu passer à l'acte.

wound I *n* **1** (injury) blessure *f*; (cut) plaie *f*; **bullet ~** blessure par balle; **knife ~** coup *m* de couteau; **a ~ to** or **in the head** une blessure à la tête; **2** (figurative) blessure *f*.
II *vtr* blesser.
IDIOMS **to lick one's ~s** panser ses blessures; **to rub salt into the ~** remuer le couteau dans la plaie.

wounded I *n* **the ~** les blessés/-es *m/f*.
II *adj* blessé/-e; **~ in the arm** blessé au bras.

wrangle I *n* querelle *f*.
II *vi* se quereller (**over, about** sur, à propos de; **with** avec).

wrap I *n* (shawl) châle *m*; (stole) étole *f*.
II *vtr* (in paper) emballer (**in** dans); (in blanket, garment) envelopper (**in** dans); **to be ~ped in** être emmitouflé/-e dans [*blanket*]; être enveloppé/-e dans [*newspaper*]; être enveloppé/-e de [*mystery*]
IDIOMS **to keep sth/to be under ~s** garder qch/être secret/-ète.
■ **wrap up**: ¶ **~ up** se couvrir; **~ up well** or **warm!** couvre-toi bien!; ¶ **~ [sth] up 1** faire [*parcel*]; envelopper [*gift, purchase*]; emballer [*rubbish*]; **2 to be ~ped up in** ne s'occuper que de [*person, child*]; être absorbé/-e dans [*activity, work*]; **they are completely ~ped up in each other** ils ne vivent que l'un pour l'autre; **3** dissimuler [*meaning, facts, ideas*] (**in** derrière).

wrap-around *adj* [*window, windscreen*] panoramique; [*skirt*] portefeuille.

wrap-over *adj* [*skirt*] portefeuille; [*dress*] croisé/-e.

wrapper *n* (of sweet) papier *m*.

wrapping *n* emballage *m*.

wrapping paper *n* (brown) papier *m* d'emballage; (decorative) papier *m* cadeau.

wreak *vtr* assouvir [*revenge*] (**on** sur); **to ~ havoc** or **damage** infliger des dégâts; **to ~ havoc** or **damage on sth** dévaster qch.

wreath *n* couronne *f*; **to lay a ~** déposer une gerbe.

wreck I *n* **1** (car, plane) (crashed) épave *f*; (burnt out) carcasse *f*; **2** (sunken ship) épave *f*; **3** (person) épave *f*.
II *vtr* **1** [*explosion, fire, vandals*] dévaster [*building, machinery*]; [*person, driver, impact*] détruire [*vehicle*]; **2** ruiner [*career, chances, health, life, marriage*]; gâcher [*holiday, weekend*].

wreckage *n* **1** (of plane, car, ship) épave *f*; (of building) décombres *mpl*; **2** (of hopes, plans) naufrage *m*.

wrecked *adj* **1** [*car, plane*] accidenté/-e; [*ship*] naufragé/-e; [*building*] démoli/-e; **2** [*life, career, marriage*] ruiné/-e.

wren *n* roitelet *m*.

wrench I *n* **1** (tool) tourne-à-gauche *m inv*; **2** (emotional upheaval) déchirement *m*.
II *vtr* tirer violemment sur [*handle*]; **to ~ one's ankle/knee** se tordre la cheville/le genou; **to ~ sth from sb** arracher qch à qn; **to ~ sth away from sth** arracher qch de qch.

wrestle I *vtr* **to ~ sb for sth** lutter contre qn pour qch; **to ~ sb to the ground** terrasser qn.
II *vi* **1** (Sport) faire du catch; **2** (struggle) **to ~ with** se débattre avec [*person, problem, homework, conscience*]; se battre avec [*controls, zip, suitcase*]; lutter contre [*temptation*].

wrestler *n* catcheur/-euse *m/f*.

wrestling ▶ **504** *n* catch *m*.

wretched *adj* [*person*] infortuné/-e; [*existence, appearance, conditions*] misérable; [*weather*] affreux/-euse; [*accommodation*] minable; [*amount*] dérisoire.

wriggle I *vtr* **to ~ one's toes/fingers** remuer les orteils/doigts; **to ~ one's way out of sth** se sortir de qch.
II *vi* [*person*] s'agiter, gigoter; [*snake, worm*] se tortiller; [*fish*] frétiller; **to ~ out of** se défiler devant [*duty, task*].

wring *vtr* **1** (also **~ out**) essorer [*clothes, cloth*]; **2** (extract) arracher [*confession, money*] (**from, out of** à); **3** (twist) **to ~ sb's/sth's neck** tordre le cou à qn/qch; **to ~ one's hands** se tordre les mains; (figurative) se lamenter.

wrinkle I *n* (on skin) ride *f*; (in fabric) pli *m*.
II *vtr* **1** rider [*skin*]; **to ~ one's nose** faire la grimace (**at** devant); **2** froisser [*fabric*].
III *vi* [*skin*] se rider; [*fabric*] se froisser; [*wallpaper*] gondoler.

wrist ▶ **413** *n* poignet *m*.

wristwatch *n* montre-bracelet *f*.

writ *n* assignation *f* (**for** pour); **to issue** or **serve a ~ against sb, to serve sb with a ~** assigner qn en justice.

write I *vtr* **1** écrire [*letter, poem, novel*] (**to** à); composer [*song, symphony*]; rédiger [*business letter, article, report, prescription*]; faire [*cheque*]; écrire [*software, program*]; élaborer [*legislation*]; **he wrote me a cheque for £100** il m'a fait un chèque de 100 livres sterling; **I wrote home** j'ai écrit à ma famille; **2** (US) écrire à [*person*].
II *vi* écrire (**to sb** à qn).
■ **write back** répondre (**to** à).
■ **write down** noter [*details, name*]; mettre [qch] par écrit [*ideas, suggestions*]; consigner [qch] par écrit [*information, findings*].
■ **write off**: ¶ **~ off** écrire une lettre (**to** à); **to ~ off for** écrire pour demander; ¶ **~ [sb/ sth] off 1** (wreck) bousiller complètement○ [*car*]; **2** (in bookkeeping) passer [qch] aux pertes et profits [*bad debt, loss*]; amortir [*capital*]; **3** (end) annuler [*debt, project, operation*].
■ **write out 1** (put down on paper) écrire; **2** (copy) copier.

write-off *n* **1** (US) (in taxation) somme *f* déductible de la déclaration des revenus; **2** (wreck) épave *f*.

writer ▶ **626** *n* (author) (professional) écrivain *m*; (nonprofessional) auteur *m*.

writer's block *n* l'angoisse *f* de la page blanche.

write-up *n* **1** (review) critique *f*; **2** (account) rapport *m* (**of** sur).

writhe *vi* (also **~ about**, **~ around**) se tortiller; **to ~ in agony** se tordre de douleur.

writing *n* **1** (activity) **~ is her life** écrire, c'est sa vie; **2** (handwriting) écriture *f*; **his ~ is poor/good** il écrit mal/bien; **3** (words and letters) écriture *f*; **to put sth in ~** mettre qch par écrit; **4** (literature) littérature *f*.

writing pad *n* bloc *m* de papier à lettres.

writing paper *n* papier *m* à lettres.

writing table *n* bureau *m*.

written *adj* [*reply, guarantee, proof*] écrit/-e; **he failed the ~ paper** il a échoué à l'écrit; **~ evidence** or **proof** (Law) preuves *fpl* écrites; **the ~ word** l'écriture.

wrong I *n* **1** (evil) mal *m*; **2** (injustice) tort *m*; **to right a ~** réparer un tort.
II *adj* **1** (incorrect) faux/fausse (*before n*); (ill-chosen) mauvais/-e (*before n*); **he took the ~ key** il a pris la mauvaise clé; **it's the ~ glue for the purpose** ce n'est pas la colle qu'il faut; **to go the ~ way** se tromper de chemin; **I dialled the ~ number** je me suis trompé de numéro, j'ai fait un faux or mauvais numéro; **you've got the ~ number** vous faites erreur; **2** (reprehensible, unjust) **it is ~ to cheat** c'est mal de tricher; **she hasn't done anything ~** elle n'a rien fait de mal; **it was ~ of me to do** je n'aurais pas dû faire; **it is ~ that** c'est injuste que; **there's nothing ~ with** or **in sth** il n'y a pas de mal à qch; **(so) what's ~ with that?** où est le mal?; **3** (mistaken) **to be ~** [*person*] avoir tort, se tromper; **to be ~ about** se tromper sur; **she was ~ about him** elle s'est trompée sur son compte; **to prove sb ~** donner tort à qn; **4** (not as it should be) **there is something (badly) ~** il y a quelque chose qui ne va pas (du tout); **there's something ~ with this computer** il y a un problème avec cet ordinateur; **the wording is all ~** la formulation ne va pas du tout; **what's ~ with your arm?** qu'est-ce que tu as au bras?; **what's ~ with you?** (to person suffering) qu'est-ce que tu as?; (to person behaving oddly) qu'est-ce qui t'arrive?; **your clock is ~** votre pendule n'est pas à l'heure.
III *adv* **to get [sth] ~** se tromper de [*date, time, details*]; se tromper dans qch [*calculations*]; **I think you've got it ~** je pense que tu te trompes; **to go ~** [*person*] se tromper; [*machine*] ne plus marcher.
IV *vtr* faire du tort à [*person, family*].
IDIOMS **to be in the ~** être dans mon/ton etc tort; **to get on the ~ side of sb** se faire mal voir de qn; **to go down the ~ way** [*food, drink*] passer de travers.

wrongdoer *n* malfaiteur *m*.

wrongfoot *vtr* (Sport) prendre [qn] à contre-pied; (figurative) prendre [qn] au dépourvu.

wrongly *adv* mal; **he concluded, ~, that...** il a conclu, à tort, que...; **rightly or ~** à tort ou à raison.

wrought *adj* [*silver, gold*] travaillé/-e.

wrought iron *n* fer *m* forgé.

wry *adj* [*smile, look, humour*] narquois/-e; **to have a ~ sense of humour** être pince-sans-rire.

x, **X** *n* **1** (letter) x, X *m*; **2** (standing for number, name) **for x people** pour x personnes; **Ms X** Mme X; **X marks the spot** l'endroit est marqué d'une croix; **3** (kisses ending letter) grosses bises.

X-certificate *adj* [*film*] interdit/-e aux moins de 18 ans.

xenophobia *n* xénophobie *f*.

xerox® *vtr* photocopier.

Xmas *n* Noël *m*.

X-rated *adj* [*film, video*] interdit/-e aux moins de 18 ans.

X-ray I *n* **1** (ray) rayon *m* X; **2** (photo) radiographie *f*, radio○ *f*; **to have an ~** se faire radiographier; **to give sb an ~** faire une radiographie à qn.
II *vtr* radiographier.

Yy

y, **Y** *n* y, Y *m*.

yacht *n* yacht *m*.

yachting ▶504| *n* yachting *m*; **to go ~** faire du yachting.

yachtsman *n* yachtman *m*.

yahoo I *n* abruti/-e° *m*.
II *excl* hourra!

yak *n* yack *m*.

Yale lock® *n* serrure *f* de sûreté.

yank I *n* coup *m* sec; **to give sth a ~** tirer qch d'un coup sec.
II *vtr* tirer [*person, rope*].
■ **yank out** arracher.

Yank *n* yankee *mf*.

Yankee *n* yankee *m*.

yap I *n* jappement *m*.
II *vi* [*dog*] japper (**at** après).

yapping I *n* jappements *mpl*.
II *adj* [*dog*] jappeur/-euse.

yard *n* **1** ▶573| yard *m* (= *0.9144 m*); **2** (of house, farm, prison, hospital) cour *f*; **3** (US) (garden) jardin *m*; **4** (for storage) dépôt *m*; (for construction) chantier *m*; **builder's ~** dépôt *m* de matériaux de construction.

yardarm *n* bout *m* de vergue.

yardstick *n* (figurative) critères *mpl*.

yarn *n* **1** (fibre) fibre *f* textile; (wool) laine *f*; **2** (tale) histoire *f*; **to spin a ~** raconter des histoires.

yashmak *n* voile *m* islamique.

yawn I *n* bâillement *m*; **to give a ~** bâiller
II *vi* **1** [*person*] bâiller; **2** [*abyss, chasm*] béer.

yeah° *particle* ouais°, oui; **oh ~?** vraiment?

year ▶708| I *n* **1** (period of time) an *m*; (with emphasis on duration) année *f*; **in the ~ 1789/2000** en 1789/l'an 2000; **two ~s ago** il y a deux ans; **all (the) ~ round** toute l'année; **every ~** tous les ans; **over the ~s** au cours des ans or des années; **the ~ before last** il y a deux ans; **every ~** tous les ans; **they have been living in Paris for ~s** ils habitent Paris depuis des années; **for the first time in ~s** pour la première fois depuis des années; **it's a ~ since I heard from him** je n'ai plus de ses nouvelles depuis un an; **they lived in Paris for ~s** ils ont habité Paris pendant des années; **to earn £30,000 a ~** gagner 30 000 livres sterling par an; **2** (indicating age) **to be 19 ~s old** or **19 ~s of age** avoir 19 ans; **a two-~-old child** un enfant de deux ans; **3** (pupil) **first/second-~** ≈ élève *mf* de sixième/cinquième.
II **years**° *n pl* (a long time) **that would take ~s!** ça prendrait une éternité!; **it's ~s since we last met!** ça fait un siècle qu'on ne s'est pas vus!
IDIOMS **this job has put ~s on me!** ce travail m'a vieilli de 10 ans!

yearbook *n* **1** (directory) annuaire *m*; **2** (US) album *m* de promotion.

yearlong *adj* [*stay, course, absence*] d'un an, d'une année.

yearly I *adj* [*visit, account, income*] annuel/-elle.
II *adv* annuellement.

yearn *vi* **1 to ~ for** désirer (avoir) [*child*]; aspirer à [*freedom, unity*]; attendre [*season, event*]; **to ~ to do** avoir très envie de faire; **2** (miss) **she ~s for her son** son fils lui manque terriblement.

yearning I *n* désir *m* ardent (**for** de; **to do** de faire).
II **yearnings** *n pl* aspirations *fpl*.
II *adj* [*expression*] plein/-e de désir.

yeast *n* levure *f*.

yell I *n* (shout) cri *m*; (of rage, pain) hurlement *m*.
II *vtr* crier [*warning*]; (louder) hurler [*insults*].
III *vi* crier; **to ~ at sb** crier après qn.

yelling *n* cris *mpl*.

yellow ▶438| I *n* jaune *m*.
II *adj* **1** (in colour) jaune; **to go** or **turn ~** jaunir; **2**° (cowardly) trouillard/-e°.
III *vi* jaunir.

yellow-belly° *n* trouillard/-e° *m/f*.

yellow card *n* (Sport) carton *m* jaune.

yellowish ▶438| *adj* tirant sur le jaune; (unpleasantly) jaunâtre.

Yellow Pages® *n pl* pages *fpl* jaunes.

yelp I *n* glapissement *m*.
II *vi* glapir.

yen *n* **1** ▶582| (currency) yen *m*; **2**° (craving) **to have a ~ for sth/to do** avoir grande envie de qch/de faire.

yeoman *n* (also **~ farmer**) franc tenancier *m*.

yeoman of the guard *n* (GB) membre *m* de la garde royale.

yep°, **yup**° *particle* (US) ouais°, oui.

yes *particle* oui; (in reply to negative question) si.

■ **Note** *yes* is translated by *oui*, except when used in reply to a negative question in which case the translation is *si* or, more emphatically, *mais si*: *'did you see him?'—'yes (I did)'* = 'est-ce que tu l'as vu?'—'oui (je l'ai vu)'; *'you're not hungry, are you?'—'yes I am'* = 'tu n'as pas faim?'—'si (j'ai faim)'.
– Note that there are no direct equivalents in French for tag questions and short replies such as *yes I did, yes I am*.
– For some suggestions on how to translate these, see the note at ***do***.

---

yes-man° *n* lèche-bottes *m inv*.

yesterday ▶456| I *n* hier *m*; **~'s newspaper** le journal d'hier; **~ was a sad day for all of us** la journée d'hier a été triste pour nous tous; **~ was the fifth of April** hier nous

you

◆ In English ***you*** is used to address everybody, whereas French has two forms: ***tu*** and ***vous***. The usual word to use when you are speaking to anyone you do not know very well is ***vous***. This is sometimes called the polite form:

*would **you** like some coffee?*	= voulez-**vous** du café?
*can I help **you**?*	= est-ce que je peux **vous** aider?
*what can I do for **you**?*	= qu'est-ce que je peux faire pour **vous**?

The more informal pronoun ***tu*** is used between close friends and family members, within groups of children and young people, by adults when talking to children and always when talking to animals; ***tu*** is the subject form, the direct and indirect object form is ***te*** (***t'*** before a vowel or mute 'h') and the form for emphatic use or use after a preposition is ***toi***:

*would **you** like some coffee?*	= veux-**tu** du café?
*can I help **you**?*	= est-ce que je peux **t'**aider?
*there's a letter for **you***	= il y a une lettre pour **toi**

As a general rule, when talking to a French person use ***vous***, wait to see how they address you and follow suit. It is safer to wait for the French person to suggest using ***tu***. The suggestion will usually be phrased as *on se tutoie?* or *on peut se tutoyer?*

Note that ***tu*** is only a singular pronoun and ***vous*** is its plural form.

Remember that in French the object and indirect object pronouns are always placed before the verb:

*she knows **you***	= elle **vous** connaît = elle **te** connaît
*I'll give **you** my address*	= je **vous** donnerai mon adresse je **te** donnerai mon adresse

◆ In compound tenses like the present perfect and the past perfect, the past participle agrees in number and gender with the direct object:

*I saw **you** on Saturday*	
(to one male: polite form)	= je **vous** ai vu samedi
(to one female: polite form)	= je **vous** ai vu**e** samedi
(to one male: informal form)	= je **t'**ai vu samedi
(to one female: informal form)	= je **t'**ai vu**e** samedi
(to two or more people, male or mixed)	= je **vous** ai vu**s** samedi
(to two or more females)	= je **vous** ai vu**es** samedi

When ***you*** is used impersonally as the more informal form of ***one***, it is translated by ***on*** for the subject form and by ***vous*** or ***te*** for the object form, depending on whether the comment is being made amongst friends or in a more formal context:

***you** can do as **you** like here*	= **on** peut faire ce qu'**on** veut ici
***you** could easily lose your bag here*	= **on** pourrait facilement perdre son sac ici
*these mushrooms can make **you** ill*	= ces champignons peuvent **vous** rendre malade = ces champignons peuvent **te** rendre malade

For a guide to the correct verb forms with **vous**, **tu** and **on**, consult the verb in the French-English part of the dictionary and check the number in square brackets, which will refer you to the French verb tables at the back of the dictionary.

For particular usages, see the entry for **you**.

étions le cinq avril; **the day before ~** avant-hier.
II *adv* hier; **only ~** pas plus tard qu'hier; **all day ~** toute la journée d'hier.

yesterday afternoon *n, adv* hier après-midi.

yesterday evening *n, adv* hier soir.

yesterday morning *n, adv* hier matin.

yesteryear *n* temps *m* jadis; **the fashions of ~** la mode d'antan or du temps jadis.

yet I *conj* pourtant.
II *adv* **1** (up till now, so far) encore; (in questions) déjà; (with superlatives) jusqu'ici; **it's not ready ~** ce n'est pas encore prêt; **has he arrived ~?** est-il (déjà) arrivé?; **not ~** pas encore, pas pour l'instant; **it's the best ~** jusqu'ici, c'est le meilleur; **2** (also **just ~**) tout de suite, encore; **don't start ~** ne commence pas tout de suite; **3** (still) encore; **they may ~ come** ils pourraient encore arriver; **he'll finish it ~** il va le finir; **he won't come for hours ~** il ne viendra pas avant quelques heures; **4** (even, still) encore; **~ more cars** encore plus de voitures; **~ another attack** encore une autre attaque; **~ again** encore une fois.

yew *n* (also **~ tree**) if *m*.

Y-fronts *n pl* (GB) slip *m* ouvert.

YHA *n* (GB) (*abbr* = **Youth Hostels Association**) association *f* des auberges de jeunesse.

yield I *n* rendement *m*.
II *vtr* **1** (produce) produire; **2** (provide) donner, fournir [*result, meaning*]; fournir [*clue*]; **3** (surrender) céder (**to** à); **to ~ ground** (figurative) céder du terrain.
III *vi* **1** (to person, temptation, pressure, threats) céder (**to** à); **2** (under weight, physical pressure) céder (**under** sous); **3** (be superseded) **to ~ to** [*technology, phenomenon*] céder le pas à; **4** (US) (driving) céder le passage.

yob○, **yobbo**○ *n* (GB) loubard○ *m*, voyou *m*.

yodel *vi* jodler, iodler.

yoga *n* yoga *m*.

yoghurt *n* yaourt *m*, yoghourt *m*.

yo-heave-ho *excl* oh! hisse!

yoke I *n* joug *m*.
II *vtr* (also **~ up**) atteler.

yokel *n* péquenaud/-e○ *m/f*, plouc○ *mf*.

yolk *n* jaune *m* (d'œuf).

you ▶759 *pron* **1** (addressing sb) YOU **would never do that** (polite) vous, vous ne feriez jamais cela; (informal) toi, tu ne ferais jamais ça; **~ English** vous autres Anglais; **~ idiot**○! espèce d'imbécile○!; **~ two can stay** vous deux, vous pouvez rester; **2** (as indefinite pronoun) (subject) on; (object, indirect object) vous, te; **~ never know!** on ne sait jamais!; **it makes ~ sleepy** ça fait dormir.

you-know-what○ *pron* vous-savez-quoi, tu-sais-quoi.

you-know-who○ *pron* qui-vous-savez, qui-tu-sais.

young I *n* **1** (young people) **the ~** les jeunes *mpl*, la jeunesse *f*; **2** (animal's offspring) petits *mpl*.
II *adj* (not very old) jeune; **to be ~ at heart** avoir l'esprit jeune; **she is ten years ~er than him** elle a dix ans de moins que lui; **I feel ten years ~er** j'ai l'impression d'avoir rajeuni de dix ans; **~ lady** jeune femme *f*; **~ people** jeunes gens *mpl*; **~ person** jeune *m*; **the ~er generation** la jeune génération; **her ~er brother** son frère cadet; **I'm not as ~ as I used to be** je n'ai plus 20 ans.

young blood *n* sang *m* neuf.

youngish *adj* assez jeune.

young-looking *adj* **to be ~** faire (très) jeune.

young offender *n* délinquant/-e *m/f*.

young professional *n* jeune salarié/-e *m/f*.

youngster *n* **1** (young person) jeune *m*; **2** (child) enfant *mf*.

your *det* votre/vos; (more informally) ton/ta/tes.

yours *pron*

■ **Note** For a full note on the use of the *vous* and *tu* forms in French, see the boxed note for the entry ***you***.
– In French, possessive pronouns reflect the gender and number of the noun they are standing for. When *yours* is referring to only one person, it is translated by *le vôtre*, *la vôtre*, *les vôtres* or, more informally, *le tien*, *la tienne*, *les tiens*, *les tiennes*. When *yours* is referring to more than one person, it is translated by *le vôtre*, *la vôtre*, *les vôtres*.

my car is red but ~ is blue ma voiture est rouge mais la vôtre or la tienne est bleue; **her children are older than ~** ses enfants sont plus âgés que les vôtres or les tiens; **which house is ~?** votre or ta maison c'est laquelle? **he's a colleague of ~** c'est un de vos or tes collègues; **it's not ~** ce n'est pas à vous or à toi; **the money wasn't ~ to give away** vous n'aviez pas à donner cet argent.

yourself *pron*

■ **Note** For a full note on the use of the *vous* and *tu* forms in French, see the entry ***you***.
– When used as a reflexive pronoun, direct [or] indirect, *yourself* is translated by *vous* or familiarly *te* (or *t'* before a vowel or mute 'h'): *you've hurt yourself* = vous vous êtes fait mal *or* tu t'es fait mal.
– In imperatives, the translation is *vous* or *toi*: *help yourself* = servez-vous *or* sers-toi. (Note the hyphens).
– When used for emphasis, the translation is *vous-même* or *toi-même*: *you yourself don't know* = vous ne savez pas vous-même *or* tu ne sais pas toi-même.

1 (reflexive) vous, te, t'; **have you hurt ~?** est-ce que tu t'es fait mal?; **2** (in imperatives) vous, toi; **3** (emphatic) vous-même, toi-même; **you ~ said that...** vous avez dit vous-même que..., tu as dit toi-même que...; **4** (after prepositions) vous, vous-même, toi, toi-même; **5** (expressions) (**all**) **by ~** tout seul/toute seule; **you're not ~ today** tu n'as pas l'air dans ton assiette aujourd'hui.

your

❑ For a full note on the use of the *vous* and *tu* forms in French, see the note on *you* ▶ 759.

◆ In French, determiners agree in gender and number with the noun that follows:

***your* + masculine singular noun** (chien *m*, ami *m*)

(to one person: polite form) (to two or more people)	**votre** chien, **votre** ami
(to one person: informal form)	**ton** chien, **ton** ami

***your* + feminine singular noun** (pomme *f*, orange *f*)

(to one person: polite form) (to two or more people)	**votre** pomme, **votre** orange
(to one person: informal form)	**ta** pomme, **ton*** orange

* Note that *ton* is used with a feminine noun beginning with a vowel or mute 'h'.

***your* + plural noun**

(to one person: polite form) (to two or more people)	**vos** chiens, **vos** amis, **vos** pommes, **vos** oranges
(to one person: informal form)	**tes** chiens, **tes** amis, **tes** pommes, **tes** oranges

When *your* is stressed, *à vous* or *à toi* is added after the noun:

(to one person: polite form) **your** house = **votre** maison **à vous**
(to two or more people)

(to one person: informal form) **your** house = **ta** maison **à toi**

(to one person: polite form) **your** parents = **vos** parents à **vous**
(to two or more people)

(to one person: informal form) **your** parents = **tes** parents à **toi**

◆ When used impersonally to mean *one's*, *your* is translated by *son*, *sa* or *ses*, when *you* is translated by *on*:

*you pay **your** bills at the end of the week* = on paie **ses** factures à la fin de la semaine

*you buy **your** tickets at the door* = on prend **ses** billets à l'entrée

*you get good value for **your** money* = on en a pour **son** argent

The translation after an impersonal verb in French is *son*, *sa*, *ses*:

*you have to buy **your** tickets at the door* = il faut prendre **ses** billets à l'entrée

*you should always look after **your** health* = il faut prendre soin de **sa** santé

Note, however, the following:

*smoking is bad for **your** health* = le tabac est mauvais pour **la** santé

*sweets are bad for **your** teeth* = les bonbons sont mauvais pour **les** dents

***your** average student* = **l'**étudiant moyen

❑ For *your* used with *parts of the body*, see the usage note on **The Human Body** ▶ 413.

yourselves *pron*

■ **Note**
– When used as a reflexive pronoun, direct and indirect, *yourselves* is translated by *vous: help yourselves* = servez-vous.
– When used for emphasis, the translation is *vous-mêmes: do it yourselves* = faites-le vous-mêmes.

1 (reflexive) vous; **help ~** servez-vous; **2** (emphatic) vous-mêmes; **3** (after prepositions) vous, vous-mêmes; **all by ~** tous seuls/toutes seules.

youth *n* **1** (young man) jeune homme *m*; **a gang of ~s** une bande de jeunes gens; **2** (period, state of being young) jeunesse *f*; **because of his ~** à cause de son jeune âge; **3** (young people) jeunes *mpl*.

youth club *n* centre *m* de jeunes.

youthful *adj* **1** (young) jeune; **2** (typical of youth) **his ~ looks** son air jeune.

youth hostel *n* auberge *f* de jeunesse.

youth hostelling *n* logement *m* en auberge de jeunesse.

youth work *n* travail *m* social auprès des jeunes.

youth worker ▶ 626 *n* éducateur/-trice *m/f*.

yowl *vi* [*person, dog*] hurler; [*cat*] miauler; [*baby*] brailler.

yoyo *n* yo-yo *m*.

yuck○ *excl* (GB) berk○!

yucky○ *adj* (GB) dégoûtant/-e.

Yule log *n* bûche *f* de Noël.

yummy○ **I** *adj* délicieux/-ieuse.
II *excl* miam-miam○.

yuppie *n* **I** jeune cadre *m* dynamique.
II *adj* [*image, style, fashion*] de jeune cadre dynamique.

Zz

z, Z *n* z, Z *m*.
zany *adj* loufoque○.
zap○ **I** *excl* paf!
II *vtr* **1** (destroy) détruire [*town*]; tuer [*person, animal*]; **2** (fire at) tirer sur [*person*]; **3** (delete from computer screen) supprimer.
III *vi* **to ~ into town/a shop** faire un saut○ en ville/dans un magasin; **to ~ from channel to channel** zapper○.
zapper○ *n* (TV remote control) télécommande *f*.
zeal *n* **1** (fanaticism) zèle *m*; (religious) ferveur *f*; **2** (enthusiasm) ardeur *f*, zèle *m*.
zealot *n* fanatique *mf*.
zebra *n* zèbre *m*.
zebra crossing *n* (GB) passage *m* (protégé) pour piétons.
zenith *n* (figurative) apogée *m*.
zero I *n* zéro *m*.
II *adj* [*altitude, growth, inflation, voltage*] zéro *inv*; [*confidence, interest, involvement, development*] nul/nulle; **sub-~ temperatures** des températures en dessous de zéro.
■ **zero in**: **to ~ in on [sth]** (Mil) viser [*target*]; (figurative) cerner [*problem*]; foncer droit sur [*person*]; repérer [*place*].
zero hour *n* heure *f* H.
zest *n* (enthusiasm) entrain *m*; **his ~ for life** sa joie de vivre.
zigzag I *n* zigzag *m*.
II *adj* [*design, pattern*] à zigzags; [*route, road*] en zigzag.
III *vi* [*person, vehicle, road*] zigzaguer; [*river, path*] serpenter; **to ~ up/down** monter/descendre en zigzag.
zilch○ *n* que dalle◑.
zing○ *n* (energy) entrain *m*.
zip I *n* **1** (also **~ fastener, zipper** US) fermeture *f* à glissière, fermeture *f* éclair®; **to do up/undo a ~** tirer/défaire une fermeture à glissière; **2**○ (energy) tonus *m*; **3** (US) (also **~ code**) code *m* postal.
II *vtr* **to ~ sth open/shut** ouvrir/fermer qch en tirant la fermeture à glissière.
III○ *vi* **to ~ along, to ~ past** filer à toute allure; **to ~ past sb/sth** dépasser qn/qch à toute allure.
■ **zip through**○: **to ~ through a book** lire un livre en diagonale○.
■ **zip up**: ¶ **~ up** [*garment, bag*] se fermer par une fermeture à glissière; ¶ **~ [sb/sth] up** remonter la fermeture à glissière de qn/qch.
zipper (US) = **zip I 1**.
zodiac *n* zodiaque *m*.
zombie *n* zombi(e) *m*; (figurative) abruti/-e○ *m/f*.
zone I *n* zone *f*.
II *vtr* (divide) diviser [qch] en zones.
zonked○ *adj* (also **zonked out**) (tired) crevé/-e○.
zoo *n* zoo *m*.
zoo keeper ▶626 *n* gardien/-ienne *m/f* de zoo.
zoologist ▶626 *n* zoologue *mf*, zoologiste *mf*.
zoology *n* zoologie *f*.
zoom I *n* (also **~ lens**) zoom *m*.
II *vi* **1**○ (move quickly) **to ~ past** passer en trombe; **to ~ around** passer à toute vitesse dans; **he's ~ed off to Paris** il a foncé○ à Paris; **2**○ (rocket) [*prices, profits*] monter en flèche.
zucchini *n* (US) courgette *f*.

French verbs

Standard verb endings

		-er	-ir	-r, -re
		INDICATIVE Present		
Singular	**1**	-e	-is	-s *or* -e
	2	-es	-is	-s *or* -es
	3	-e	-it	-t *or* -e
Plural	**1**	-ons	-(iss)ons	-ons
	2	-ez	-(iss)ez	-ez
	3	-ent	-(iss)ent	-ent
		INDICATIVE Imperfect		
Singular	**1**	-ais	-(iss)ais	-ais
	2	-ais	-(iss)ais	-ais
	3	-ait	-(iss)ait	-ait
Plural	**1**	-ions	-(iss)ions	-ions
	2	-iez	-(iss)iez	-iez
	3	-aient	-(iss)aient	-aient
		INDICATIVE Past historic		
Singular	**1**	-ai	-is	-s
	2	-as	-is	-s
	3	-a	-it	-t
Plural	**1**	-âmes	-îmes	-mes
	2	-âtes	-îtes	-tes
	3	-èrent	-irent	-rent
		INDICATIVE Future		
Singular	**1**	-erai	-rai	-rai
	2	-eras	-ras	-ras
	3	-era	-ra	-ra
Plural	**1**	-erons	-rons	-rons
	2	-erez	-rez	-rez
	3	-eront	-ront	-ront
		INFINITIVE		
Present		-er	-ir	-r *or* -re

		-er	-ir	-r, -re
		SUBJUNCTIVE Present		
Singular	**1**	-e	-(iss)e	-e
	2	-es	-(iss)es	-es
	3	-e	-(iss)e	-e
Plural	**1**	-ions	-(iss)ions	-ions
	2	-iez	-(iss)iez	-iez
	3	-ent	-(iss)ent	-ent
		SUBJUNCTIVE Imperfect		
Singular	**1**	-asse	-sse	-sse
	2	-asses	-sses	-sses
	3	-ât	-ît	-ît *or* -ût
Plural	**1**	-assions	-ssions	-ssions
	2	-assiez	-ssiez	-ssiez
	3	-assent	-issent	-ssent
		IMPERATIVE Present		
Singular				
	3	-e	-s	-s
Plural	**1**	-ons	-(iss)ons	-ons
	2	-ez	-(iss)ez	-ez
		CONDITIONAL Present		
Singular	**1**	-erais	-rais	-rais
	2	-erais	-rais	-rais
	3	-erait	-rait	-rait
Plural	**1**	-erions	-rions	-rions
	2	-eriez	-riez	-riez
	3	-eraient	-raient	-raient
		PARTICIPLE		
Present		-ant	-(iss)ant	-ant
Past		-é	-i	-i *or* -u

1 aimer

INDICATIVE

Present

j'	aim**e**
tu	aim**es**
il	aim**e**
nous	aim**ons**
vous	aim**ez**
ils	aim**ent**

Imperfect

j'	aim**ais**
tu	aim**ais**
il	aim**ait**
nous	aim**ions**
vous	aim**iez**
ils	aim**aient**

Past historic

j'	aim**ai**
tu	aim**as**
il	aim**a**
nous	aim**âmes**
vous	aim**âtes**
ils	aim**èrent**

Future

j'	aim**erai**
tu	aim**eras**
il	aim**era**
nous	aim**erons**
vous	aim**erez**
ils	aim**eront**

Perfect

j'	ai	aim**é**
tu	as	aim**é**
il	a	aim**é**
nous	avons	aim**é**
vous	avez	aim**é**
ils	ont	aim**é**

Pluperfect

j'	avais	aim**é**
tu	avais	aim**é**
il	avait	aim**é**
nous	avions	aim**é**
vous	aviez	aim**é**
ils	avaient	aim**é**

IMPERATIVE

Present	aim**e**	
	aim**ons**	
	aim**ez**	
Past	aie	aim**é**
	ayons	aim**é**
	ayez	aim**é**

SUBJUNCTIVE

Present

(que) j'	aim**e**
(que) tu	aim**es**
(qu')il	aim**e**
(que) nous	aim**ions**
(que) vous	aim**iez**
(qu')ils	aim**ent**

Perfect

(que) j'	aie	aim**é**
(que) tu	aies	aim**é**
(qu')il	ait	aim**é**
(que) nous	ayons	aim**é**
(que) vous	ayez	aim**é**
(qu')ils	aient	aim**é**

Pluperfect

(que) j'	eusse	aim**é**
(que) tu	eusses	aim**é**
(qu')il	eût	aim**é**
(que) nous	eussions	aim**é**
(que) vous	eussiez	aim**é**
(qu')ils	eussent	aim**é**

CONDITIONAL

Present

j'	aim**erais**
tu	aim**erais**
il	aim**erait**
nous	aim**erions**
vous	aim**eriez**
ils	aim**eraient**

Past I

j'	aurais	aim**é**
tu	aurais	aim**é**
il	aurait	aim**é**
nous	aurions	aim**é**
vous	auriez	aim**é**
ils	auraient	aim**é**

PARTICIPLE

Present	aim**ant**
Past	aim**é, -e**
	ayant aim**é**

INFINITIVE

Present	aim**er**
Past	avoir aim**é**

2 plier

INDICATIVE

Present

je	pli**e**
tu	pli**es**
il	pli**e**
nous	pli**ons**
vous	pli**ez**
ils	pli**ent**

Imperfect

je	pli**ais**
tu	pli**ais**
il	pli**ait**
nous	pli**ions**
vous	pli**iez**
ils	pli**aient**

Past historic

je	pli**ai**
tu	pli**as**
il	pli**a**
nous	pli**âmes**
vous	pli**âtes**
ils	pli**èrent**

Future

je	pli**erai**
tu	pli**eras**
il	pli**era**
nous	pli**erons**
vous	pli**erez**
ils	pli**eront**

Perfect

j'	ai	pli**é**
tu	as	pli**é**
il	a	pli**é**
nous	avons	pli**é**
vous	avez	pli**é**
ils	ont	pli**é**

Pluperfect

j'	avais	pli**é**
tu	avais	pli**é**
il	avait	pli**é**
nous	avions	pli**é**
vous	aviez	pli**é**
ils	avaient	pli**é**

IMPERATIVE

Present	pli**e**	
	pli**ons**	
	pli**ez**	
Past	aie	pli**é**
	ayons	pli**é**
	ayez	pli**é**

SUBJUNCTIVE

Present

(que) je	pli**e**
(que) tu	pli**es**
(qu')il	pli**e**
(que) nous	pli**ions**
(que) vous	pli**iez**
(qu')ils	pli**ent**

Perfect

(que) j'	aie	pli**é**
(que) tu	aies	pli**é**
(qu')il	ait	pli**é**
(que) nous	ayons	pli**é**
(que) vous	ayez	pli**é**
(qu')ils	aient	pli**é**

Pluperfect

(que) j'	eusse	pli**é**
(que) tu	eusses	pli**é**
(qu')il	eût	pli**é**
(que) nous	eussions	pli**é**
(que) vous	eussiez	pli**é**
(qu')ils	eussent	pli**é**

CONDITIONAL

Present

je	pli**erais**
tu	pli**erais**
il	pli**erait**
nous	pli**erions**
vous	pli**eriez**
ils	pli**eraient**

Past I

j'	aurais	pli**é**
tu	aurais	pli**é**
il	aurait	pli**é**
nous	aurions	pli**é**
vous	auriez	pli**é**
ils	auraient	pli**é**

PARTICIPLE

Present	pli**ant**
Past	pli**é, -e**
	ayant pli**é**

INFINITIVE

Present	pli**er**
Past	avoir pli**é**

3 finir

INDICATIVE

Present

je	fin**is**
tu	fin**is**
il	fin**it**
nous	fin**issons**
vous	fin**issez**
ils	fin**issent**

Imperfect

je	fin**issais**
tu	fin**issais**
il	fin**issait**
nous	fin**issions**
vous	fin**issiez**
ils	fin**issaient**

Past historic

je	fin**is**
tu	fin**is**
il	fin**it**
nous	fin**îmes**
vous	fin**îtes**
ils	fin**irent**

Future

je	fin**irai**
tu	fin**iras**
il	fin**ira**
nous	fin**irons**
vous	fin**irez**
ils	fin**iront**

Perfect

j'	ai	fin**i**
tu	as	fin**i**
il	a	fin**i**
nous	avons	fin**i**
vous	avez	fin**i**
ils	ont	fin**i**

Pluperfect

j'	avais	fin**i**
tu	avais	fin**i**
il	avait	fin**i**
nous	avions	fin**i**
vous	aviez	fin**i**
ils	avaient	fin**i**

IMPERATIVE

Present	fin**is**	
	fin**issons**	
	fin**issez**	
Past	aie	fin**i**
	ayons	fin**i**
	ayez	fin**i**

SUBJUNCTIVE

Present

(que) je	fin**isse**
(que) tu	fin**isses**
(qu')il	fin**isse**
(que) nous	fin**issions**
(que) vous	fin**issiez**
(qu')ils	fin**issent**

Perfect

(que) j'	aie	fin**i**
(que) tu	aies	fin**i**
(qu')il	ait	fin**i**
(que) nous	ayons	fin**i**
(que) vous	ayez	fin**i**
(qu')ils	aient	fin**i**

Pluperfect

(que) j'	eusse	fin**i**
(que) tu	eusses	fin**i**
(qu')il	eût	fin**i**
(que) nous	eussions	fin**i**
(que) vous	eussiez	fin**i**
(qu')ils	eussent	fin**i**

CONDITIONAL

Present

je	fin**irais**
tu	fin**irais**
il	fin**irait**
nous	fin**irions**
vous	fin**iriez**
ils	fin**iraient**

Past I

j'	aurais	fin**i**
tu	aurais	fin**i**
il	aurait	fin**i**
nous	aurions	fin**i**
vous	auriez	fin**i**
ils	auraient	fin**i**

PARTICIPLE

Present	fin**issant**
Past	fin**i, -e**
	ayant fin**i**

INFINITIVE

Present	fin**ir**
Past	avoir fin**i**

4 offrir

INDICATIVE

Present

j'	offr**e**
tu	offr**es**
il	offr**e**
nous	offr**ons**
vous	offr**ez**
ils	offr**ent**

Imperfect

j'	offr**ais**
tu	offr**ais**
il	offr**ait**
nous	offr**ions**
vous	offr**iez**
ils	offr**aient**

Past historic

j'	offr**is**
tu	offr**is**
il	offr**it**
nous	offr**îmes**
vous	offr**îtes**
ils	offr**irent**

Future

j'	offr**irai**
tu	offr**iras**
il	offr**ira**
nous	offr**irons**
vous	offr**irez**
ils	offr**iront**

Perfect

j'	ai	offert
tu	as	offert
il	a	offert
nous	avons	offert
vous	avez	offert
ils	ont	offert

Pluperfect

j'	avais	offert
tu	avais	offert
il	avait	offert
nous	avions	offert
vous	aviez	offert
ils	avaient	offert

IMPERATIVE

Present	offr**e**	
	offr**ons**	
	offr**ez**	
Past	aie	offert
	ayons	offert
	ayez	offert

SUBJUNCTIVE

Present

(que) j'	offr**e**
(que) tu	offr**es**
(qu')il	offr**e**
(que) nous	offr**ions**
(que) vous	offr**iez**
(qu')ils	offr**ent**

Perfect

(que) j'	aie	offert
(que) tu	aies	offert
(qu')il	ait	offert
(que) nous	ayons	offert
(que) vous	ayez	offert
(qu')ils	aient	offert

Pluperfect

(que) j'	eusse	offert
(que) tu	eusses	offert
(qu')il	eût	offert
(que) nous	eussions	offert
(que) vous	eussiez	offert
(qu')ils	eussent	offert

CONDITIONAL

Present

j'	offr**irais**
tu	offr**irais**
il	offr**irait**
nous	offr**irions**
vous	offr**iriez**
ils	offr**iraient**

Past I

j'	aurais	offert
tu	aurais	offert
il	aurait	offert
nous	aurions	offert
vous	auriez	offert
ils	auraient	offert

PARTICIPLE

Present	offr**ant**
Past	offert, -e
	ayant offert

INFINITIVE

Present	offr**ir**
Past	avoir offert

5 recevoir

INDICATIVE

Present

je	reç**ois**
tu	reç**ois**
il	reç**oit**
nous	rec**evons**
vous	rec**evez**
ils	reç**oivent**

Imperfect

je	rec**evais**
tu	rec**evais**
il	rec**evait**
nous	rec**evions**
vous	rec**eviez**
ils	rec**evaient**

Past historic

je	reç**us**
tu	reç**us**
il	reç**ut**
nous	reç**ûmes**
vous	reç**ûtes**
ils	reç**urent**

Future

je	rec**evrai**
tu	rec**evras**
il	rec**evra**
nous	rec**evrons**
vous	rec**evrez**
ils	rec**evront**

Perfect

j'	ai	reç**u**
tu	as	reç**u**
il	a	reç**u**
nous	avons	reç**u**
vous	avez	reç**u**
ils	ont	reç**u**

Pluperfect

j'	avais	reç**u**
tu	avais	reç**u**
il	avait	reç**u**
nous	avions	reç**u**
vous	aviez	reç**u**
ils	avaient	reç**u**

IMPERATIVE

Present	reç**ois**	
	rec**evons**	
	rec**evez**	
Past	aie	reç**u**
	ayons	reç**u**
	ayez	reç**u**

SUBJUNCTIVE

Present

(que) je	reç**oive**
(que) tu	reç**oives**
(qu')il	reç**oive**
(que) nous	rec**evions**
(que) vous	rec**eviez**
(qu')ils	reç**oivent**

Perfect

(que) j'	aie	reç**u**
(que) tu	aies	reç**u**
(qu')il	ait	reç**u**
(que) nous	ayons	reç**u**
(que) vous	ayez	reç**u**
(qu')ils	aient	reç**u**

Pluperfect

(que) j'	eusse	reç**u**
(que) tu	eusses	reç**u**
(qu')il	eût	reç**u**
(que) nous	eussions	reç**u**
(que) vous	eussiez	reç**u**
(qu')ils	eussent	reç**u**

CONDITIONAL

Present

je	rec**evrais**
tu	rec**evrais**
il	rec**evrait**
nous	rec**evrions**
vous	rec**evriez**
ils	rec**evraient**

Past I

j'	aurais	reç**u**
tu	aurais	reç**u**
il	aurait	reç**u**
nous	aurions	reç**u**
vous	auriez	reç**u**
ils	auraient	reç**u**

PARTICIPLE

Present	rec**evant**
Past	reç**u, -e**
	ayant reç**u**

INFINITIVE

Present	rec**evoir**
Past	avoir reç**u**

6 rendre

INDICATIVE

Present

je	rend**s**
tu	rend**s**
il	rend
nous	rend**ons**
vous	rend**ez**
ils	rend**ent**

Imperfect

je	rend**ais**
tu	rend**ais**
il	rend**ait**
nous	rend**ions**
vous	rend**iez**
ils	rend**aient**

Past historic

je	rend**is**
tu	rend**is**
il	rend**it**
nous	rend**îmes**
vous	rend**îtes**
ils	rend**irent**

Future

je	rend**rai**
tu	rend**ras**
il	rend**ra**
nous	rend**rons**
vous	rend**rez**
ils	rend**ront**

Perfect

j'	ai	rend**u**
tu	as	rend**u**
il	a	rend**u**
nous	avons	rend**u**
vous	avez	rend**u**
ils	ont	rend**u**

Pluperfect

j'	avais	rend**u**
tu	avais	rend**u**
il	avait	rend**u**
nous	avions	rend**u**
vous	aviez	rend**u**
ils	avaient	rend**u**

IMPERATIVE

Present	rend**s**	
	rend**ons**	
	rend**ez**	
Past	aie	rend**u**
	ayons	rend**u**
	ayez	rend**u**

SUBJUNCTIVE

Present

(que) je	rend**e**
(que) tu	rend**es**
(qu')il	rend**e**
(que) nous	rend**ions**
(que) vous	rend**iez**
(qu')ils	rend**ent**

Perfect

(que) j'	aie	rend**u**
(que) tu	aies	rend**u**
(qu')il	ait	rend**u**
(que) nous	ayons	rend**u**
(que) vous	ayez	rend**u**
(qu')ils	aient	rend**u**

Pluperfect

(que) j'	eusse	rend**u**
(que) tu	eusses	rend**u**
(qu')il	eût	rend**u**
(que) nous	eussions	rend**u**
(que) vous	eussiez	rend**u**
(qu')ils	eussent	rend**u**

CONDITIONAL

Present

je	rend**rais**
tu	rend**rais**
il	rend**rait**
nous	rend**rions**
vous	rend**riez**
ils	rend**raient**

Past I

j'	aurais	rend**u**
tu	aurais	rend**u**
il	aurait	rend**u**
nous	aurions	rend**u**
vous	auriez	rend**u**
ils	auraient	rend**u**

PARTICIPLE

Present	rend**ant**
Past	rend**u, -e**
	ayant rend**u**

INFINITIVE

Present	rend**re**
Past	avoir rend**u**

7 être

INDICATIVE

Present

je	suis
tu	es
il	est
nous	sommes
vous	êtes
ils	sont

Imperfect

j'	étais
tu	étais
il	était
nous	étions
vous	étiez
ils	étaient

Past historic

je	fus
tu	fus
il	fut
nous	fûmes
vous	fûtes
ils	furent

Future

je	serai
tu	seras
il	sera
nous	serons
vous	serez
ils	seront

Perfect

j'	ai	été
tu	as	été
il	a	été
nous	avons	été
vous	avez	été
ils	ont	été

Pluperfect

j'	avais	été
tu	avais	été
il	avait	été
nous	avions	été
vous	aviez	été
ils	avaient	été

IMPERATIVE

Present sois
soyons
soyez

Past aie été
ayons été
ayez été

SUBJUNCTIVE

Present

(que) je	sois
(que) tu	sois
(qu')il	soit
(que) nous	soyons
(que) vous	soyez
(qu')ils	soient

Perfect

(que) j'	aie	été
(que) tu	aies	été
(qu')il	ait	été
(que) nous	ayons	été
(que) vous	ayez	été
(qu')ils	aient	été

Pluperfect

(que) j'	eusse	été
(que) tu	eusses	été
(qu')il	eût	été
(que) nous	eussions	été
(que) vous	eussiez	été
(qu')ils	eussent	été

CONDITIONAL

Present

je	serais
tu	serais
il	serait
nous	serions
vous	seriez
ils	seraient

Past I

j'	aurais	été
tu	aurais	été
il	aurait	été
nous	aurions	été
vous	auriez	été
ils	auraient	été

PARTICIPLE

Present étant

Past été (invariable)
ayant été

INFINITIVE

Present être

Past avoir été

8 avoir

INDICATIVE

Present

j'	ai
tu	as
il	a
nous	avons
vous	avez
ils	ont

Imperfect

j'	avais
tu	avais
il	avait
nous	avions
vous	aviez
ils	avaient

Past historic

j'	eus
tu	eus
il	eut
nous	eûmes
vous	eûtes
ils	eurent

Future

j'	aurai
tu	auras
il	aura
nous	aurons
vous	aurez
ils	auront

Perfect

j'	ai	eu
tu	as	eu
il	a	eu
nous	avons	eu
vous	avez	eu
ils	ont	eu

Pluperfect

j'	avais	eu
tu	avais	eu
il	avait	eu
nous	avions	eu
vous	aviez	eu
ils	avaient	eu

IMPERATIVE

Present aie
ayons
ayez

Past aie eu
ayons eu
ayez eu

SUBJUNCTIVE

Present

(que) j'	aie
(que) tu	aies
(qu')il	ait
(que) nous	ayons
(que) vous	ayez
(qu')ils	aient

Perfect

(que) j'	aie	eu
(que) tu	aies	eu
(qu')il	ait	eu
(que) nous	ayons	eu
(que) vous	ayez	eu
(qu')ils	aient	eu

Pluperfect

(que) j'	eusse	eu
(que) tu	eusses	eu
(qu')il	eût	eu
(que) nous	eussions	eu
(que) vous	eussiez	eu
(qu')ils	eussent	eu

CONDITIONAL

Present

j'	aurais
tu	aurais
il	aurait
nous	aurions
vous	auriez
ils	auraient

Past I

j'	aurais	eu
tu	aurais	eu
il	aurait	eu
nous	aurions	eu
vous	auriez	eu
ils	auraient	eu

PARTICIPLE

Present ayant

Past eu, -e
ayant eu

INFINITIVE

Present avoir

Past avoir eu

9 aller

INDICATIVE

Present	
je	vais
tu	vas
il	va
nous	allons
vous	allez
ils	vont

Imperfect	
j'	all**ais**
tu	all**ais**
il	all**ait**
nous	all**ions**
vous	all**iez**
ils	all**aient**

Past historic	
j'	all**ai**
tu	all**as**
il	all**a**
nous	all**âmes**
vous	all**âtes**
ils	all**èrent**

Future	
j'	**irai**
tu	**iras**
il	**ira**
nous	**irons**
vous	**irez**
ils	**iront**

Perfect		
je	suis	**allé**
tu	es	**allé**
il	est	**allé**
nous	sommes	**allés**
vous	êtes	**allés**
ils	sont	**allés**

Pluperfect		
j'	étais	**allé**
tu	étais	**allé**
il	était	**allé**
nous	étions	**allés**
vous	étiez	**allés**
ils	étaient	**allés**

IMPERATIVE

Present		
	va	
	allons	
	allez	
Past	sois	**allé**
	soyons	**allés**
	soyez	**allés**

SUBJUNCTIVE

Present	
(que) j'	aill**e**
(que) tu	aill**es**
(qu')il	aill**e**
(que) nous	all**ions**
(que) vous	all**iez**
(qu')ils	aill**ent**

Perfect		
(que) je	sois	**allé**
(que) tu	sois	**allé**
(qu')il	soit	**allé**
(que) nous	soyons	**allés**
(que) vous	soyez	**allés**
(qu')ils	soient	**allés**

Pluperfect		
(que) je	fusse	**allé**
(que) tu	fusses	**allé**
(qu')il	fût	**allé**
(que) nous	fussions	**allés**
(que) vous	fussiez	**allés**
(qu')ils	fussent	**allés**

CONDITIONAL

Present	
j'	**irais**
tu	**irais**
il	**irait**
nous	**irions**
vous	**iriez**
ils	**iraient**

Past I		
je	serais	**allé**
tu	serais	**allé**
il	serait	**allé**
nous	serions	**allés**
vous	seriez	**allés**
ils	seraient	**allés**

PARTICIPLE

Present	all**ant**
Past	**allé, -e** étant **allé**

INFINITIVE

Present	all**er**
Past	être **allé**

10 faire

INDICATIVE

Present	
je	fais
tu	fais
il	fait
nous	faisons
vous	faites
ils	font

Imperfect	
je	fais**ais**
tu	fais**ais**
il	fais**ait**
nous	fais**ions**
vous	fais**iez**
ils	fais**aient**

Past historic	
je	fis
tu	fis
il	fit
nous	fîmes
vous	fîtes
ils	firent

Future	
je	fer**ai**
tu	fer**as**
il	fer**a**
nous	fer**ons**
vous	fer**ez**
ils	fer**ont**

Perfect		
j'	ai	fait
tu	as	fait
il	a	fait
nous	avons	fait
vous	avez	fait
ils	ont	fait

Pluperfect		
j'	avais	fait
tu	avais	fait
il	avait	fait
nous	avions	fait
vous	aviez	fait
ils	avaient	fait

IMPERATIVE

Present		
	fais	
	faisons	
	faites	
Past	aie	fait
	ayons	fait
	ayez	fait

SUBJUNCTIVE

Present	
(que) je	fass**e**
(que) tu	fass**es**
(qu')il	fass**e**
(que) nous	fass**ions**
(que) vous	fass**iez**
(qu')ils	fass**ent**

Perfect		
(que) j'	aie	fait
(que) tu	aies	fait
(qu')il	ait	fait
(que) nous	ayons	fait
(que) vous	ayez	fait
(qu')ils	aient	fait

Pluperfect		
(que) j'	eusse	fait
(que) tu	eusses	fait
(qu')il	eût	fait
(que) nous	eussions	fait
(que) vous	eussiez	fait
(qu')ils	eussent	fait

CONDITIONAL

Present	
je	fer**ais**
tu	fer**ais**
il	fer**ait**
nous	fer**ions**
vous	fer**iez**
ils	fer**aient**

Past I		
j'	aurais	fait
tu	aurais	fait
il	aurait	fait
nous	aurions	fait
vous	auriez	fait
ils	auraient	fait

PARTICIPLE

Present	faisant
Past	fait, -e ayant fait

INFINITIVE

Present	faire
Past	avoir fait

INFINITIVE	Rules	INDICATIVE Present	Imperfect	Past Historic	Future
11 créer	*always* é	je crée, -es, -e, -ent nous créons, -ez	je créais …	je créai …	je créerai …
12 placer	c	je place, -es, -e, -ez, -ent	nous placions, -iez	ils placèrent	je placerai …
	ç *before* a *and* o	nous plaçons	je plaçais, -ais, -ait, -aient	je plaçai, -as, -a, -âmes, -âtes	
13 manger	g	je mange, -es, -e, -ez, -ent	nous mangions, -iez	ils mangèrent	je mangerai …
	ge *before* a *and* o	nous mangeons	je mangeais, -eais, -eait, -eaient	je mangeai, -as, -a, -âmes, -âtes	
14 céder	è *before silent final syllable*	je cède, -es, -e, -ent			
	é	nous cédons, -ez	je cédais …	je cédai …	je céderai …
15 assiéger	è *before silent final syllable*	j'assiège, -es, -e, -ent			
	ge *before* a *and* o	nous assiégeons	j'assiégeais, -eais, -eait, -eaient	j'assiégeai	
	é *before silent syllable*				j'assiégerai …
16 lever	è *before silent syllable*	je lève, -es, -e, -ent			je lèverai …
	e	nous levons, -ez	je levais …	je levai …	
17 geler	è *before silent syllable*	je gèle, -es, -e, -ent			je gèlerai …
	e	nous gelons, -ez	je gelais …	je gelai …	
18 acheter	è *before silent syllable*	j'achète, -es, -e, -ent			j'achèterai …
	e	nous achetons, -ez	j'achetais …	j'achetai …	
19 appeler	ll *before mute* e	j'appelle, -es, -e, -ent			j'appellerai …
	l	nous appelons, -ez	j'appelais …	j'appelai …	
20 jeter	tt *before mute* e	je jette, -es, -e, -ent			je jetterai …
	t	nous jetons, -ez	je jetais …	je jetai …	
21 payer	i *before mute* e	je paie, -es, -e, -ent			je paierai …
	or y	je paye, -es, -e, -ent nous payons, -ez	je payais …	je payai …	je payerai …

CONDITIONAL	SUBJUNCTIVE	IMPERATIVE	PARTICIPLE		
Present	Present		Present	Past	
je créerais ...	que je crée ...	crée créons, -ez	créant	créé, -e	11
je placerais ...	que je place ...	place, -ez plaçons	plaçant	placé, -e	12
je mangerais ...	que je mange ...	mange, -ez mangeons	mangeant	mangé, -e	13
je céderais ...	que je cède, -es, -e, -ent que nous cédions, -iez	cède cédons, -ez	cédant	cédé, -e	14
j'assiégerais ...	que j'assiège ... que nous assiégions , -iez	assiège assiégeons	assiégeant	assiégé, -e	15
je lèverais ...	que je lève, -es, -e, -ent que nous levions, -iez	lève levons, -ez	levant	levé, -e	16
je gèlerais ...	que je gèle, -es, -e, -ent que nous gelions, -iez	gèle gelons, -ez	gelant	gelé, -e	17
j'achèterais ...	que j'achète, -es, -e, -ent que nous achetions, -iez	achète achetons, -ez	achetant	acheté, -e	18
j'appellerais ...	que j'appelle, -es, -e, -ent que nous appelions, -iez	appelle appelons, -ez	appelant	appelé, -e	19
je jetterais ...	que je jette, -es, -e, -ent que nous jetions, -iez	jette jetons, -ez	jetant	jeté, -e	20
je paierais ... je payerais ...	que je paie, -es, -e, -ent que je paye, -es, -e, -ent que nous payions, -iez	paie paye payons, -ez	payant	payé, -e	21

INFINITIVE	Rules	INDICATIVE			
		Present	Imperfect	Past Historic	Future
22 essuyer	i *before mute* e	j'essuie, -es, -e, -ent			j'essuierai …
	y	nous essuyons, -ez	j'essuyais …	j'essuyai …	
23 employer	i *before mute* e	j'emploie, -es, -e, -ent			j'emploierai …
	y	nous employons, -ez	j'employais …	j'employai …	
24 envoyer	i *before mute* e	j'envoie, -es, -e, -ent			
	y	nous envoyons, -ez	j'envoyais …	j'envoyai …	
	err				j'enverrai …
25 haïr	i	je hais, -s, -t			
	ï	ns haïssons, -ez, -ent	je haïssais …	je haïs … (haïmes, haïtes)	je haïrai …
26 courir		je cours …	je courais …	je courus …	je courrai …
27 cueillir		je cueille, -es, -e, nous cueillons …	je cueillais …	je cueillis …	je cueillerai …
28 assaillir		j'assaille, -es, -e, nous assaillons, -ez, -ent	j'assaillais …	j'assaillis …	j'assaillirai …
29 fuir	i *before consonants and* e	je fuis, -s, -t, -ent		je fuis …	je fuirai …
	y *before* a, ez, i, o	nous fuyons, -ez	je fuyais …		
30 partir	*without* t	je pars …			
	with t	il part …	je partais …	je partis …	je partirai …
31 bouillir	ou	je bous, s, t			
	ouill	nous bouillons …	je bouillais …	je bouillis …	je bouillirai …
32 couvrir		je couvre, -es, -e, nous couvrons …	je couvrais …	je couvris …	je couvrirai …
33 vêtir		je vêts …	je vêtais …	je vêtis …	je vêtirai …
34 mourir	eur	je meurs, -s, -t, -ent			
	our	nous mourons, -ez	je mourais …	je mourus …	je mourrai …
35 acquérir	quier	j'acquiers, -s, -t, -ièrent			
	quer	nous acquérons -ez	j'acquérais …		j'acquerrai …
	qu			j'acquis …	

CONDITIONAL	SUBJUNCTIVE	IMPERATIVE	PARTICIPLE		
Present	Present		Present	Past	
j'essuierais …	que j'essuie, -es, -e, -ent que nous essuyions, -iez	essuie essuyons, -ez	essuyant	essuyé, e	22
j'emploierais …	que j'emploie, -es, -e, -ent que nous employions, -iez	emploie employons, -ez	employant	employé, -e	23
j'enverrais …	que j'envoie, -es, -e, -ent que nous envoyions, -iez	envoie envoyons, -ez	envoyant	envoyé, -e	24
je haïrais …	que je haïsse, qu'il haïsse	hais haïssons, haïssez	haïssant	haï, -e	25
je courrais …	que je coure …	cours, courons, -ez	courant	couru, -e	26
je cueillerais …	que je cueille …	cueille cuillons, -ez	cueillant	cueilli, -e	27
j'assaillirais …	que j'assaille …	assaille assaillons, -ez	assaillant	assailli, -e	28
je fuirais …	que je fuie, -es, -e, -ent que nous fuyions, -iez	fuis fuyons, -ez	fuyant	fui, -e	29
je partirais …	que je parte …	pars partons, -ez	partant	parti, -e	30
je bouillirais …	que je bouille …	bous bouillons, -ez	bouillant	bouilli, -e	31
e couvrirais …	que je couvre, -es, -e, que nous couvrions …	couvre couvrons, -ez	couvrant	couvert, -e	32
e vêtirais …	que je vête …	vêts vêtons, vêtez	vêtant	vêtu, -e	33
e mourrais …	que je meure …	meurs mourons, -ez	mourant	mort, -e	34
acquerrais …	que j'acquière, -es, -e, -ent que nous acquérions, -iez	acquiers acquérons, -ez	acquérant	acquis, -e	35

INFINITIVE	Rules	INDICATIVE Present	Imperfect	Past Historic	Future
36 venir	i	je viens, -s, -t, -nent		je vins ... ils vinrent	je viendrai ...
	e	nous venons, -ez	je venais ...		
37 gésir	*Defective*	je gis, tu gis, il gît, nous gisons, -ez, -ent	je gisais ...		
38 ouïr	*Archaic*	j'ois ... nous oyons ...	j'oyais ...	j'ouïs ...	j'ouïrai ...
39 pleuvoir		il pleut	il pleuvait	il plut	il pleuvra
		ils pleuvent	ils pleuvaient	ils plurent	ils pleuvront
40 pourvoir	i	je pourvois, -s, -t, -ent			je pourvoirai ...
	y	nous pourvoyons, -ez	je pourvoyais ...		
	u			je pourvus ...	
41 asseoir	ie	j'assieds, -ds, -d			j'assiérai ...
	ey	nous asseyons, -ez, -ent	j'asseyais ...		
	i			j'assis ...	
asseoir (oi/oy *replace* ie/ey)	oi	j'assois, -s, -t, -ent			j'assoirai ...
	oy	nous assoyons, -ez	j'assoyais ...		
42 prévoir	oi	je prévois, -s, -t, -ent			je prévoirai ...
	oy	nous prévoyons, -ez	je prévoyais ...		
	i/u			je prévis ...	
43 mouvoir	eu	je meus, -s, -t, -vent			
	ou	nous mouvons, -ez	je mouvais ...		je mouvrai ...
	u			je mus, -s, -t, -(û)mes, -(û)tes, -rent	
44 devoir	û *in the past participle masc. sing.*	je dois, -s, -t -vent nous devons, -ez	je devais ...	je dus ...	je devrai ...
45 valoir	au, aille	je vaux, -x, -t			je vaudrai ...
	al	nous valons, -ez, -ent	je valais ...	je valus ...	
prévaloir					

CONDITIONAL	SUBJUNCTIVE	IMPERATIVE	PARTICIPLE		
Present	Present		Present	Past	
je viendrais …	que je vienne, -es, -e, -ent	viens			36
	que nous venions, -iez	venons, -ez	venant	venu, -e	
			gisant		37
j'ouïrais …	que j'oie …	ois		ouï, -e	38
	que nous oyions …	oyons, -ez	oyant		
il pleuvrait	qu'il pleuve		pleuvant	plu	39
ils pleuvraient	qu'ils pleuvent				
je pourvoirais …	que je pourvoie, -es, -e, -ent	pourvois			40
	que nous pourvoyions, -iez	pourvoyons, -ez	pourvoyant		
				pourvu, -e	
j'assiérais …		assieds			41
	que j'asseye …	asseyons, -ez	asséyant		
	que nous asseyions …				
				assis, -e	
j'assoirais …	que j'assoie, -es, -e, -ent	assois			
	que nous assoyions, -iez	assoyons, -ez	assoyant		
je prévoirais …	que je prévoie, -es, -e, -ent	prévois			42
	que ns prévoyions, -iez	prévoyons, -ez	prévoyant		
				prévu, -e	
	que je meuve, -es, -e, -ent	meus			43
je mouvrais …	que nous mouvions, -iez	mouvons, -ez	mouvant		
				mû, mue	
	que je doive, -es, -e, -ent	dois		dû, due	44
je devrais …	que nous devions, -iez	devons, -ez	devant		
je vaudrais …	que je vaille, -es, -e, -ent	vaux			45
	que nous valions, -iez	valons, -ez	valant	valu, -e	
	que je prévale, -es, -e				

INFINITIVE	Rules	INDICATIVE			
		Present	Imperfect	Past Historic	Future
46 voir	oi	je vois, -s, -t, -ent			
	oy	nous voyons, -ez	je voyais ...		
	i/e/u			je vis ...	je verrai ...
47 savoir	5 forms	je sais, -s, -t, nous savons, -ez, -ent	je savais ...	je sus ...	je saurai ...
48 vouloir	veu/veuil	je veux, -x, -t, veulent			
	voul/voudr	nous voulons, -ez	je voulais ...	je voulus ...	je voudrai ...
49 pouvoir	eu/u(i)	je peux, -x, -t, peuvent		je pus ...	
	ouv/our	nous pouvons, -ez	je pouvais ...		je pourrai ...
50 falloir	*Impersonal*	il faut	il fallait	il fallut	il faudra
51 déchoir	choir *and* échoir *are defective*	je déchois, -s, -t, -ent nous déchoyons, -ez	je déchoyais ...	je déchus ...	je décherrai ...
52 prendre	prend	je prends, -ds, -d			je prendrai ...
	pren	nous prenons, -ez ils prennent	je prenais ...		
	pri(s)			je pris ...	
53 rompre		je romps, -ps, -pt, nous rompons ...	je rompais ...	je rompis ...	je romprai ...
54 craindre	ain/aind	je crains, -s, -t			je craindrai ...
	aign	nous craignons, -ez, -ent	je craignais ...	je craignis ...	
55 peindre	ein	je peins, -s, -t			je peindrai ...
	eign	nous peignons, -ez, -ent	je peignais ...	je peignis ...	
56 joindre	oin/oind	je joins, -s, -t			je joindrai ...
	oign	nous joignons, -ez, -ent	je joignais ...	je joignis ...	
57 vaincre	ainc	je vaincs, -cs, -c			je vaincrai ...
	ainqu	nous vainquons, -ez, -ent	je vainquais ...	je vainquis ...	
58 traire	i	je trais, -s, -t, -ent		(*obsolete*)	je trairai ...
	y	nous trayons, -ez	je trayais ...		

CONDITIONAL	SUBJUNCTIVE	IMPERATIVE	PARTICIPLE		
Present	**Present**		**Present**	**Past**	
	que je voie, -es, -e, -ent	vois			**46**
	que nous voyions, -iez	voyons, -ez	voyant		
je verrais …				vu, -e	
je saurais …	que je sache …	sache, -ons, -ez	sachant	su, -e	**47**
	que je veuille, -es, -e, -ent	veux (veuille)			**48**
je voudrais …	que nous voulions, -iez	voulons, -ez (veuillez)	voulant	voulu, -e	
	que je puisse …	(*obsolete*)		pu	**49**
je pourrais …			pouvant		
il faudrait	qu'il faille	(*no form*)	(*obsolete*)	fallu	**50**
	que je déchoie, -es, -e, -ent	déchois	(*no form* *but* échéant)		**51**
je décherrais …	que nous déchoyions, -iez	déchoyons, -ez		déchu, -e	
je prendrais …		prends			**52**
	que je prenne …	prenons, -ez	prenant		
				pris, -e	
je romprais …	que je rompe …	romps -pons, -pez	rompant	rompu, -e	**53**
e craindrais …		crains		craint, -e	**54**
	que je craigne …	craignons, -ez	craignant		
e peindrais …		peins		peint, -e	**55**
	que je peigne …	peignons, -ez	peignant		
e joindrais …		joins		joint, -e	**56**
	que je joigne …	joignons, -ez	joignant		
e vaincrais …		vaincs		vaincu, -e	**57**
	que je vainque …	vainquons, -ez	vainquant		
e trairais …	que je traie, -es, -e, -ent	trais		trait, -e	**58**
	que nous trayions,	trayons, -ez	trayant		

INFINITIVE	Rules	INDICATIVE Present	Imperfect	Past Historic	Future
59 plaire	ai	je plais, tu plais, il plaît (*but* il tait) nous plaisons ...	je plaisais ...		je plairai ...
	u			je plus ...	
60 mettre	met	je mets, nous mettons	je mettais ...		je mettrai ...
	mis			je mis ...	
61 battre	t	je bats, -ts, -t			
	tt	nous battons ...	je battais ...	je battis ...	je battrai ...
62 suivre	ui	je suis, -s, -t			
	uiv	nous suivons ...	je suivais ...	je suivis ...	je suivrai ...
63 vivre	vi/viv	je vis, -s, -t, nous vivons ...	je vivais ...		je vivrai ...
	véc			je vécus ...	
64 suffire		je suffis, -s, -t, nous suffisons ...	je suffisais ...	je suffis ...	je suffirai ...
65 médire		je médis, -s, -t, nous médisons, vous médisez (*but* vous dites, redites)	je médisais ...	je médis ...	je médirai ...
66 lire	i	je lis, -s, -t			je lirai ...
	is	nous lisons, -ez, -ent	je lisais ...		
	u			je lus ...	
67 écrire	i	j'écris, -s, -t			j'écrirai ...
	iv	nous écrivons, -ez, -ent	j'écrivais ...	j'écrivis ...	
68 rire		je ris, -s, -t, nous rions ...	je riais ... nous riions, -iez	je ris ... nous rîmes ...	je rirai ...
69 conduire		je conduis ...	je conduisais ...	je conduisis...	je conduirai ...
70 boire	oi	je bois, -s, -t, -vent			je boirai ...
	u(v)	nous buvons, -ez	je buvais ...	je bus ...	
71 croire	oi	je crois, -s, -t, ils croient			je croirai ...
	oy	nous croyons, -ez	je croyais ...		
	u			je crus ...	

CONDITIONAL	SUBJUNCTIVE	IMPERATIVE	PARTICIPLE		
Present	Present		Present	Past	
je plairais …	que je plaise …	plais plaisons, -ez	plaisant	plu	59
je mettrais …	que je mette …	mets mettons, -ez	mettant	mis, -e	60
je battrais …	que je batte …	bats battons, -ez	battant	battu, -e	61
je suivrais …	que je suive …	suis suivons, -ez	suivant	suivi, -e	62
je vivrais …	que je vive …	vis vivons, -ez	vivant	vécu, -e	63
je suffirais …	que je suffise …	suffis suffisons, -ez	suffisant	suffi (*but* confit, déconfit, frit, circoncis)	64
je médirais …	que je médise … que nous médisions, -iez	médis médisons médisez (*but* dites, redites)	médisant	médit	65
je lirais …	que je lise …	lis lisons, -ez	lisant	lu, -e	66
j'écrirais …	que j'écrive …	écris écrivons, -ez	écrivant	écrit, -e	67
je rirais …	que je rie … que nous riions, -iez	ris, rions, riez	riant	ri	68
je conduirais …	que je conduise …	conduis conduisons, -ez	conduisant	conduit, -e (*but* lui, nui)	69
je boirais …	que je boive, -es, -e, -ent que nous buvions, -iez	bois buvons, -ez	buvant	bu, -e	70
je croirais …	que je croie …	crois croyons, -ez	croyant	cru, -e	71

INFINITIVE	Rules	INDICATIVE			
		Present	**Imperfect**	**Past Historic**	**Future**
72 croître	oî	je crois, -s, -t			je croîtrai ...
	oiss	nous croissons, -ez, -ent	je croissais ...		
	û			je crûs ...	
73 connaître	je connais, -s,	-ssons, -ssez, -ssent	je connaissais ...	je connus ...	
	î *before* t	il connaît			je connaîtrai ..
74 naître	î *before* t	je nais, nais, naît			je naîtrai ...
	naisse	nous naissons, -ez, -ent	je naissais ...		
	naqu			je naquis ...	
75 résoudre	ou/oudr	je résous, -s, -t		(absoudre *and* dissoudre *have no past historic*)	je résoudrai.
	ol/olv	nous résolvons, -ez, -ent	je résolvais ...		
	olu			je résolus ...	
76 coudre	oud	je couds, -ds, -d			je coudrai ...
	ous	nous cousons, -ez, -ent	je cousais ...	je cousis ...	
77 moudre	moud	je mouds, -ds, -d			je moudrai ...
	moul	nous moulons, -ez, -ent	je moulais ...	je moulus ...	
78 conclure		je conclus, -s, -t, nous concluons, -ez, -ent	je concluais ...	je conclus ...	je conclurai .
79 clore	*Defective*	je clos, -os, -ôt ils closent	(*obsolete*)	(*obsolete*)	je clorai ...
80 maudire		je maudis, -s, -t nous maudissons, -ez, -ent	je maudissais ...	je maudis ...	je maudirai ..

CONDITIONAL	SUBJUNCTIVE	IMPERATIVE	PARTICIPLE		
Present	**Present**		**Present**	**Past**	
je croîtrais...	que je croisse ...	croîs croissons, -ez	croissant	crû, crue (*but* accru, -e)	**72**
je connaîtrais ...	que je connaisse ...	connais, -ssons, -ssez	connaissant	connu, -e	**73**
je naîtrais ...	que je naisse ...	nais naissons, -ez	naissant	né, -e	**74**
je résoudrais ...	que je résolve ...	résous résolvons, -ez	résolvant	(absous, -oute; dissous, -oute) résolu, -e	**75**
je coudrais ...	que je couse ...	couds cousons, -ez	cousant	cousu, -e	**76**
je moudrais ...	que je moule ...	mouds moulons, -ez	moulant	moulu, -e	**77**
je conclurais ...	que je conclue ...	conclus concluons, -ez	concluant	conclu, -e (*but* inclus, -e)	**78**
je clorais ...	que je close ...	clos	closant	clos, -e	**79**
je maudirais ...	que je maudisse qu'il maudisse	maudis -ssons, -ssez	maudissant	maudit, -e	**80**

Numbers

Cardinal numbers in French

0	zéro*	80	quatre-vingts‡§
1	un†	81	quatre-vingt-un¶
2	deux	82	quatre-vingt-deux
3	trois	90	quatre-vingt-dix‡
4	quatre	91	quatre-vingt-onze
5	cinq	92	quatre-vingt-douze
6	six	99	quatre-vingt-dix-neuf
7	sept	100	cent
8	huit	101	cent un†
9	neuf	102	cent deux
10	dix	110	cent dix
11	onze	187	cent quatre-vingt-sept
12	douze	200	deux cents
13	treize	250	deux cent◊ cinquante
14	quatorze	1 000	∞mille
15	quinze	1 001	mille un†
16	seize	1 002	mille deux
17	dix-sept	1 020	mille vingt
18	dix-huit	1 200	mille** deux cents
19	dix-neuf	2 000	deux mille††
20	vingt	1 0000	dix mille
21	vingt et un	100 000	cent mille
22	vingt-deux	100 200	cent deux mille
30	trente	1 000 000	un million‡‡
40	quarante	1 264 932	un million deux cent
50	cinquante		soixante-quatre mille
60	soixante		neuf cent trente-deux
70	soixante-dix‡	1 000 000 000	un milliard‡‡
71	soixante et onze	1 000 000 000 000	un billion‡‡

* In English *0* may be called *nought*, *zero* or even nothing; French is always *zéro*: ***a nought*** = ***un zéro***.

† ***one*** is ***une*** in French when it agrees with a feminine noun, so *un crayon* but *une table*, *une des tables*, *vingt et une tables*, etc.

‡ (70) Also ***septante*** in Belgium and Switzerland. (80) Also ***octante*** in Switzerland and Canada, ***huitante*** in Switzerland. (90) Also ***nonante*** in Belgium and Switzerland.

§ Note that when *80* is used as a page number it has no *s*: ***page eighty*** = ***page quatre-vingt***.

¶ ***vingt*** has no *s* when it is in the middle of a number. The only exception to this rule is when *quatre-vingts* is followed by *millions*, *milliards* or *billions*, eg ***quatre-vingts millions***, ***quatre-vingts billions*** etc.

◊ ***cent*** does not take an *s* when it is in the middle of a number. The only exception to this rule is when it is followed by *millions*, *milliards* or *billions*, eg ***trois cents millions***, ***six cents billions*** etc. It has a normal plural when it modifies other nouns: ***200 inhabitants*** = ***deux cents habitants***.

∞ Where English would have a comma, French has simply a space. A full stop (period) can be used, e.g. ***1.000***. As in English,there is no separation in dates between thousands and hundreds: ***in 1995*** = ***en 1995***.

** In dates, the spelling ***mil*** is preferred to ***mille***, i.e. ***en 1200*** = ***en mil deux cents***. However, when the year is a round number of thousands, the spelling is always ***mille***, so ***en l'an mille***, ***en l'an deux mille*** etc.

†† ***mille*** is invariable; it never takes an *s*.

‡‡ The French words ***million***, ***milliard*** and ***billion*** are nouns, and when written out in full they take ***de*** before another noun, eg ***a million inhabitants*** = ***un million d'habitants***. However, when written in figures, ***1,000,000 inhabitants*** = ***1 000 000 habitants***, but is still spoken as *un million d'habitants*. When *million* etc. is part of a complex number, *de* is not used before the nouns, eg ***6,000,210 people*** = ***six millions deux cent dix personnes***.

Use of en

Note the use of ***en*** in the following examples:

there are six	= il y en a six
I've got a hundred	= j'en ai cent

en must be used when the thing you are talking about is not expressed (the French says literally *there of them are six*, *I of them have a hundred* etc.). However, ***en*** is not needed when the object is specified:

there are six apples = il y a six pommes

Approximate numbers

When you want to say *about* ... , remember the French ending ***-aine***:

about ten	= une dizaine
about ten books	= une dizaine de livres
about fifteen	= une quinzaine
about fifteen people	= une quinzaine de personnes

Similarly ***une trentaine***, ***une quarantaine***, ***une cinquantaine***, ***une soixantaine*** and ***une centaine*** (and ***une douzaine*** means ***a dozen***). For other numbers, use ***environ*** (***about***):

about thirty-five	= environ trente-cinq
about four thousand pages	= environ quatre mille pages

Note the use of ***centaines*** and ***milliers*** to express approximate quantities:

hundreds of books	= des centaines de livres
thousands of books	= des milliers de livres
I've got thousands	= j'en ai des milliers

Phrases

numbers up to ten	= les nombres jusqu'à dix
to count up to ten	= compter jusqu'à dix
almost ten	= presque dix
less than ten	= moins de dix
more than ten	= plus de dix
all ten of them	= tous les dix
all ten boys	= les dix garçons

Note the French word order:

my last ten pounds	= mes dix dernières livres
the next twelve weeks	= les douze prochaines semaines
the other two	= les deux autres
the last four	= les quatre derniers

Calculations in French

$10 + 3 = 13$	dix et trois font *or* égalent treize
$10 - 3 = 7$	trois ôté de dix il reste sept *or* dix moins trois égalent sept
$10 \times 3 = 30$	dix fois trois égalent trente
$30 : 3 = 10$	($30 \div 3 = 10$) trente divisé par trois égalent dix

Note how the French division sign differs from the English.

5^2	cinq au carré
5^3	cinq puissance trois
5^{100}	cinq puissance cent
$\sqrt{12}$	racine carrée de douze
$\sqrt{25} = 5$	racine carrée de vingt-cinq égalent cinq
$B > A$	B est plus grand que A
$A < B$	A est plus petit que B

Decimals in French

Note that French uses a comma where English has a decimal point.

	say
0,25	zéro virgule vingt-cinq
0,05	zéro virgule zéro cinq
0,75	zéro virgule soixante-quinze
3,45	trois virgule quarante-cinq
8,195	huit virgule cent quatre-vingt-quinze
9,1567	neuf virgule quinze cent soixante-sept *or* neuf virgule mille cinq cent soixante-sept
9,3456	neuf virgule trois mille quatre cent cinquante-six

Percentages in French

	say
25%	vingt-cinq pour cent
50%	cinquante pour cent
100%	cent pour cent
200%	deux cents pour cent
365%	trois cent soixante-cinq pour cent
4,25%	quatre virgule vingt-cinq pour cent

Fractions in French

	say
$\frac{1}{2}$	un demi*
$\frac{1}{3}$	un tiers
$\frac{1}{4}$	un quart
$\frac{1}{5}$	un cinquième
$\frac{1}{6}$	un sixième
$\frac{1}{7}$	un septième
$\frac{1}{8}$	un huitième
$\frac{1}{9}$	un neuvième
$\frac{1}{10}$	un dixième
$\frac{1}{11}$	un onzième
$\frac{1}{12}$	un douzième (*etc*)
$\frac{2}{3}$	deux tiers†
$\frac{2}{5}$	deux cinquièmes
$\frac{2}{10}$	deux dixièmes (*etc*)
$\frac{3}{4}$	trois quarts
$\frac{3}{5}$	trois cinquièmes
$\frac{3}{10}$	trois dixièmes (*etc*)
$1\frac{1}{2}$	un et demi
$1\frac{1}{3}$	un (et) un tiers
$1\frac{1}{4}$	un et quart
$1\frac{1}{5}$	un (et) un cinquième
$1\frac{1}{6}$	un (et) un sixième
$1\frac{1}{7}$	un (et) un septième (*etc*)
$5\frac{2}{3}$	cinq (et) deux tiers
$5\frac{3}{4}$	cinq (et) trois quarts
$5\frac{4}{5}$	cinq (et) quatre cinquièmes

45/100ths of a second = quarante-cinq centièmes de seconde

Ordinal numbers in French§

1st	1er‡	premier (*fem.* première)
2nd	2^{e}	second *or* deuxième
3rd	3^{e}	troisième
4th	4^{e}	quatrième
5th	5^{e}	cinquième
6th	6^{e}	sixième
7th	7^{e}	septième
8th	8^{e}	huitième
9th	9^{e}	neuvième
10th	10^{e}	dixième
11th	11^{e}	onzième
12th	12^{e}	douzième
13th	13^{e}	treizième
14th	14^{e}	quatorzième
15th	15^{e}	quinzième
16th	16^{e}	seizième
17th	17^{e}	dix-septième
18th	18^{e}	dix-huitième
19th	19^{e}	dix-neuvième
20th	20^{e}	vingtième
21st	21^{e}	vingt et unième
22nd	22^{e}	vingt-deuxième
23rd	23^{e}	vingt-troisième
24th	24^{e}	vingt-quatrième
25th	25^{e}	vingt-cinquième
30th	30^{e}	trentième
31st	31^{e}	trente et unième
40th	40^{e}	quarantième
50th	50^{e}	cinquantième
60th	60^{e}	soixantième
70th	70^{e}	soixante-dixième¶
71st	71^{e}	soixante et onzième
72nd	72^{e}	soixante-douzième
73rd	73^{e}	soixante-treizième
74th	74^{e}	soixante-quartorzième
75th	75^{e}	soixante-quinzième
79th	79^{e}	soixante-dix-neuvième
80th	80^{e}	quatre-vingtième¶
81st	81^{e}	quatre-vingt-unième
90th	90^{e}	quatre-vingt-dixième¶
91st	91^{e}	quatre-vingt-onzième
99th	99^{e}	quatre-vingt-dix-neuvième
100th	100^{e}	centième
101st	101^{e}	cent et unième
102nd	102^{e}	cent-deuxième
196th	196^{e}	cent quatre-vingt-seizième
200th	200^{e}	deux centième
300th	300^{e}	trois centième
400th	400^{e}	quatre centième
1,000th	$1\ 000^{e}$	millième
2,000th	$2\ 000^{e}$	deux millième
1,000,000th	$1\ 000\ 000^{e}$	millionième

Like English, French makes nouns by adding the definite article:

the first	= le premier (*or* la première, *or* les premiers *m pl* *or* les premières *f pl*)
the second	= le second (*or* la seconde *etc*)
the first three	= les trois premiers *or* les trois premières

Note the French word order in:

the third richest country in the world	= le troisième pays le plus riche du monde

* Note that *half*, when not a fraction, is translated by the noun ***moitié*** or the adjective ***demi***; see the dictionary entry.

† Note the use of ***les*** and ***d'entre*** when these fractions are used about a group of people or things: ***two-thirds of them = les deux tiers d'entre eux***.

‡ This is the masculine form; the feminine is ***1re*** and the plural ***1ers*** (*m*) or ***1res*** (*f*). All the other abbreviations of ordinal numbers are invariable.

§ All the ordinal numbers in French behave like ordinary adjectives and take normal plural endings where appropriate.

¶ (70e) Also ***septantième*** in Belgium and Switzerland. (80e) Also ***octantième*** in Switzerland and Canada, and ***huitantième*** in Switzerland. (90e) Also ***nonantième*** in Belgium and Switzerland.

Index of lexical and grammar notes

Lexical notes

Grammar notes